The Grants Register 2020

The Grants Register 2020

The Complete Guide to Postgraduate Funding Worldwide

Thirty-Eighth Edition

Palgrave Macmillan
Macmillan Publishers Ltd.

ISBN 978-1-349-95942-6   ISBN 978-1-349-95943-3 (eBook)
ISBN 978-1-349-95944-0 (print and electronic bundle)
https://doi.org/10.1057/978-1-349-95943-3

The Palgrave imprint is published by Springer Nature.
The registered company is Macmillan Publishers Ltd. London.

Preface

The thirty-eighth edition of *The Grants Register* provides a detailed, accurate and comprehensive survey of awards intended for students at or above the postgraduate level, or those who require further professional or advanced vocational training.

Student numbers around the world continue to grow rapidly, and overseas study is now the first choice for many of these students. *The Grants Register* provides comprehensive, up-to-date information about the availability of, and eligibility for, non-refundable postgraduate and professional awards worldwide.

We remain grateful to the institutions which have supplied information for inclusion in this edition, and would also like to thank the International Association of Universities for continued permission to use their subject index within our Subject and Eligibility Guide to Awards.

The Grants Register database is updated continually in order to ensure that the information provided is the most current available. **Therefore, if your details have changed or you would like to be included for the first time, please contact the Senior Editor, at the address below.** If you wish to obtain further information relating to specific application procedures, please contact the relevant grant-awarding institution, rather than the publisher.

The Grants Register
Palgrave Macmillan
The Macmillan Campus
4 Crinan St
London
N1 9XW
United Kingdom
Tel: 144 (0)207 843 4634
Fax: 144 (0)207 843 4650
Email: Grants.Register@spi-global.com

Ruth Lefèvre
Senior Editor

For ease of use, *The Grants Register 2020* is divided into four sections:

- The Grants Register
- Subject and Eligibility Guide to Awards
- Index of Awards
- Index of Awarding Organisations

The Grants Register

Information in this section is supplied directly by the awarding organisations. Entries are arranged alphabetically by name of organisation, and awards are listed alphabetically within the awarding organisation. This section includes details on subject area, eligibility, purpose, type, numbers offered, frequency, value, length of study, study establishment, country of study, and application procedure. Full contact details appear with each awarding organisation and also appended to individual awards where additional addresses are given.

A

Aarhus University

Nordre Ringgade 1, DNK-8000 Aarhus C, Denmark

Tel: (45) 8715 0000, (45) 30 31478610
Website: www.au.dk

Established in 1928, Aarhus University has since developed into a major Danish university with a strong international reputation across the entire research spectrum.

Aarhus University Scholarships

Subjects: Arts, Business and Social Sciences, Science and Technology, and Health
Purpose: Aarhus University Scholarships are available for highly qualified non-European Union/EEA/Swiss applicants to pursue 2-year master's degree programmes
Value: A monthly scholarship for a maximum of 1 year and 11 months
Country of Study: Denmark
Application Procedure: All applications for Master's degree programmes at Aarhus University must be submitted online through the digital application portal
Closing Date: 15 March
Additional Information: The scholarships are awarded on the basis of the following criteria: 1. Students may apply for any English-taught Master's degree programme at Aarhus University. 2. The scholarships generally include a full tuition waiver and generally, but not always, including a monthly scholarship for a maximum of 1 year and 11 months for the duration of the degree programme. 3. The general admission requirements and application procedures and deadlines at Aarhus University apply. Prior to applying for admission,

applicants are kindly asked to make themselves acquainted with the specific admission requirements for the Master's degree programmes they wish to apply for

For further information contact:

Email: ELKLIT@ps.au.dk

Aaron Siskind Foundation

C/o School of Visual Arts, MFA Photography, 209 East 23rd Street, New York, NY 10010, United States of America

Tel: (1) 212 592 2363
Fax: (1) 212 592 2366
Email: info@aaronsiskind.org
Website: www.aaronsiskind.org

The Foundation works to preserve and protect Aaron Siskind's artistic legacy, and foster knowledge of and appreciation of his art.

Individual Photographer

Purpose: To stimulate excellence and the promise of future achievement in the photographic field
Eligibility: Open to citizens or permanent residents of the United States of America. Applications sent from outside the United States of America will not be accepted
Level of Study: Postgraduate
Type: Fellowship or Grant

Subject and Eligibility Guide to Awards

Awards can be located through the Subject and Eligibility Guide to Awards. This section allows the user to find an award within a specific subject area. *The Grants Register* uses a list of subjects endorsed by the International Association of Universities (IAU), the information centre on higher education, located at UNESCO, Paris. It is further subdivided into eligibility by nationality. Thereafter, awards are listed alphabetically within their designated category, along with a page reference where full details of the award can be found.

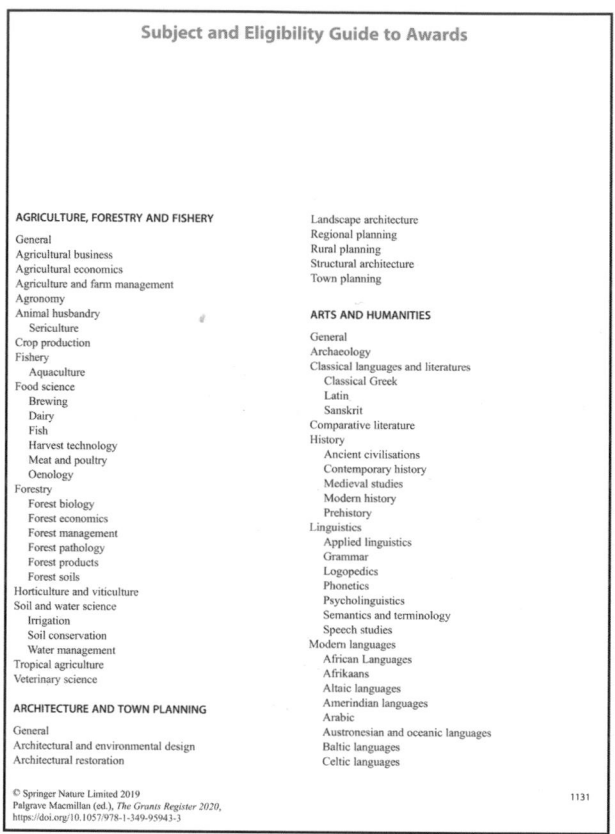

Subject and Eligibility Guide to Awards

AGRICULTURE, FORESTRY AND FISHERY

General
Agricultural business
Agricultural economics
Agriculture and farm management
Agronomy
Animal husbandry
   Sericulture
Crop production
Fishery
   Aquaculture
Food science
   Brewing
   Dairy
   Fish
   Harvest technology
   Meat and poultry
   Oenology
Forestry
   Forest biology
   Forest economics
   Forest management
   Forest pathology
   Forest products
   Forest soils
Horticulture and viticulture
Soil and water science
   Irrigation
   Soil conservation
   Water management
Tropical agriculture
Veterinary science

ARCHITECTURE AND TOWN PLANNING

General
Architectural and environmental design
Architectural restoration
Landscape architecture
Regional planning
Rural planning
Structural architecture
Town planning

ARTS AND HUMANITIES

General
Archaeology
Classical languages and literatures
   Classical Greek
   Latin
   Sanskrit
Comparative literature
History
   Ancient civilisations
   Contemporary history
   Medieval studies
   Modern history
   Prehistory
Linguistics
   Applied linguistics
   Grammar
   Logopedics
   Phonetics
   Psycholinguistics
   Semantics and terminology
   Speech studies
Modern languages
   African Languages
   Afrikaans
   Altaic languages
   Amerindian languages
   Arabic
   Austronesian and oceanic languages
   Baltic languages
   Celtic languages

© Springer Nature Limited 2019
Palgrave Macmillan (ed.), *The Grants Register 2020*,
https://doi.org/10.1057/978-1-349-95943-3

1131

Index of Awards

All awards are indexed alphabetically with a page reference.

Index of Awarding Organisations

A complete list of all awarding organisations, with country name and page reference.

List of Contents

A

Aarhus University

Nordre Ringgade 1, DNK-8000 Aarhus C, Denmark

Tel: (45) 8715 0000, (45) 30 31478610
Website: www.au.dk

Established in 1928, Aarhus University has since developed into a major Danish university with a strong international reputation across the entire research spectrum.

Aarhus University Scholarships

Subjects: Arts, Business and Social Sciences, Science and Technology, and Health
Purpose: Aarhus University Scholarships are available for highly qualified non-European Union/EEA/Swiss applicants to pursue 2-year master's degree programmes
Value: A monthly scholarship for a maximum of 1 year and 11 months
Country of Study: Denmark
Application Procedure: All applications for Master's degree programmes at Aarhus University must be submitted online through the digital application portal
Closing Date: 15 March
Additional Information: The scholarships are awarded on the basis of the following criteria: 1. Students may apply for any English-taught Master's degree programme at Aarhus University. 2. The scholarships generally include a full tuition waiver and generally, but not always, including a monthly scholarship for a maximum of 1 year and 11 months for the duration of the degree programme. 3. The general admission requirements and application procedures and deadlines at Aarhus University apply. Prior to applying for admission, applicants are kindly asked to make themselves acquainted with the specific admission requirements for the Master's degree programmes they wish to apply for

For further information contact:

Email: ELKLIT@ps.au.dk

Aaron Siskind Foundation

C/o School of Visual Arts, MFA Photography, 209 East 23rd Street, New York, NY 10010, United States of America

Tel: (1) 212 592 2363
Fax: (1) 212 592 2366
Email: info@aaronsiskind.org
Website: www.aaronsiskind.org

The Foundation works to preserve and protect Aaron Siskind's artistic legacy, and foster knowledge of and appreciation of his art.

Individual Photographer

Purpose: To stimulate excellence and the promise of future achievement in the photographic field
Eligibility: Open to citizens or permanent residents of the United States of America. Applications sent from outside the United States of America will not be accepted
Level of Study: Postgraduate
Type: Fellowship or Grant

© Springer Nature Limited 2019
Palgrave Macmillan (ed.), *The Grants Register 2020*,
https://doi.org/10.1057/978-1-349-95943-3

Value: US$10,000 each
Frequency: Annual
Country of Study: Any country
Application Procedure: Applications must be submitted through the Slideroom application portal at www.slideroom.com
Closing Date: 18 May
Funding: Private

For further information contact:

Email: info@aaronsiskind.org

Abbey Harris Mural Fund

43 Carson Road, SE21 8HT, London, United Kingdom

Tel: (44) 20 8761 7980
Email: administrator@abbey.org.uk
Website: www.abbey.org.uk
Contact: Ms Jane Reid, Administrator

The Abbey Harris Mural Fund supports the creation of murals in public places in the United Kingdom.

Abbey Harris Mural Fund

Subjects: Mural painting
Purpose: To provide grants to artists who have been commissioned to create murals in public places or in charitable institutions in the United Kingdom
Eligibility: Awards are for painters and the work must be carried out in the United Kingdom. There are other restrictions
Level of Study: Unrestricted
Type: Grant
Value: Approx. £3,000
Frequency: Annual
Country of Study: United Kingdom
No. of awards offered: 6
Application Procedure: Applicants must send for an application form, enclosing a stamped addressed envelope. Application forms can also be requested by email
Closing Date: Applications are accepted at any time. Decisions may be made at twice-yearly meetings of the Trustees in May and November
Funding: Private
Contributor: E A Abbey Memorial Trust Fund for Mural Painting in Great Britain and E Vincent Harris Fund for Mural Decoration
No. of awards given last year: 2
No. of applicants last year: 6

For further information contact:

Email: contact@abbey.org.uk

Abdul Aziz Al Ghurair Foundation For Education

The Abdul Aziz Al Ghurair Refugee Education Fund

Purpose: The Abdul Aziz Al Ghurair Refugee Education Fund invites proposals for programs that explore and identify new solutions to long-standing challenges in refugee education that can improve impact at scale. The Abdul Aziz Al Ghurair Refugee Education Fund aims to equip young refugees with a pathway to sustainable livelihoods
Eligibility: 1. Organisations must have experience in at least one successful program with refugees (Syrian and/or Palestinian). 2. be able to demonstrate proof of concept and potential for scale; be a non-profit organisation; be registered in either Jordan and/or Lebanon or have programmes or partners based there. Other eligibility terms for this fundings are listed below. Able to demonstrate proof of concept, that the program or pilot has had significant impact and has potential to be scaled to benefit larger number of refugee youth in Jordan and/or Lebanon. 1. Be a non-profit organization, including educational institutions. The Fund will consider forprofit companies on an exceptional basis and with clear rationale. 2. Be a registered organization in either Jordan and/or Lebanon where the activities would take place or have programs or partners based in either Lebanon and/or Jordan
Level of Study: Professional development, Foundation programme
Type: Funding support
Frequency: Annual
Country of Study: Jordan
Application Procedure: Application form details are entitled on the below link. Kindly check the following files. www.alghurairfoundation.org/sites/default/files/The%20Abdul %20Aziz%20Al%20Ghurair%20Refugee%20Education%20 Fund%20Grant%20Guidelines%20February%202019.pdf
Closing Date: 19 March
Funding: Private

For further information contact:

Abdulla Al Ghurair Foundation for Education, P.O.Box 6999, Dubai, UAE

Email: info@alghurairfoundation.org

Abdus Salam International Centre for Theoretical Physics (ICTP)

Strada Costiera 11, ITA-34151 Trieste, Italy

Tel: (39) 40 224 0111
Fax: (39) 40 224 163
Email: sci_info@ictp.it
Website: www.ictp.it
Contact: May Ann Williams, Public Information Officer

The Abdus Salam International Centre for Theoretical Physics (ICTP) is an institution for research and high-level training in physics and mathematics, mainly for scientists from developing countries. It also maintains a network of associate members and federated institutes.

Abdus Salam ICTP Fellowships

Subjects: Physics and mathematics
Purpose: To enable qualified applicants to pursue research in the fields of condensed matter physics, mathematics and high-energy physics
Eligibility: Open to qualified applicants of any nationality who have a PhD in physics or mathematics
Level of Study: Postdoctorate
Type: Fellowship
Value: Monthly stipend and round-trip expenses where applicable, and allowances according to the length of the visit
Length of Study: Up to 1 year
Frequency: Dependent on funds available
Study Establishment: ICTP
Country of Study: Italy
Application Procedure: Applicants must visit the ICTP website
Closing Date: 31 January
Funding: Government
Contributor: The Italian government, IAEA and UNESCO

For further information contact:

Email: calligar@ictp.it

Abilene Christian University

College of Business Administration, MBA Program Graduate School Office, PO Box 29140, Abilene, TX 79699, United States of America

Tel: (1) 915 674 2466
Fax: (1) 915 674 6717
Email: mbainfo@web.acu.edu
Contact: MBA Admissions Officer

Abilene Christian University National Merit Finalist or Semifinalist Scholarship

Purpose: Abilene Christian University offers a variety of levels of academic scholarships to incoming first-time freshmen (students entering ACU with fewer than 12 hours, excluding dual credit, AP and IB) based on academic achievements, class rank, and standardized test scores
Eligibility: To be eligible for this award, 1. National Merit Finalists and Semifinalist are required to list ACU as first choice with the National Merit Corporation. 2. Recipients must also participate in the Honors College by completing four honors courses within your first year. Students must complete an Honors College application as soon as he/she is awarded a scholarship
Level of Study: Postgraduate
Type: Scholarship
Value: US$32,020
Frequency: Annual
Country of Study: Any country
Application Procedure: To apply, students must apply for admission to Abilene Christian University (ACU) and provide their National Merit Certificate to the admissions office. For further information, check the below link. www.acu.edu/parents.html
Closing Date: 1 February
Funding: Private

For further information contact:

1600 Campus Ct, Abilene, TX 79601, United States of America

Tel: (1) 800 460 6228
Email: info@admissions.acu.edu

Abilene Christian University Valedictorian/ Salutatorian Scholarship

Purpose: Abilene Christian University offers a variety of levels of academic scholarships to incoming first-time freshmen (students entering ACU with fewer than 12 hours, excluding dual credit, AP and IB) based on academic achievements
Eligibility: Submit your official high school transcript to receive this one-year scholarship. For further information,

refer the website link. www.acu.edu/admissions-aid/under graduate/financial-aid/scholarships.html
Level of Study: Postgraduate
Type: Scholarship
Value: US$1,000
Frequency: Annual
Country of Study: Any country
Closing Date: 1 June
Funding: Private

For further information contact:

1600 Campus Court, Abilene, TX 79699, United States of America

Tel: (1) 800 460 6228
Email: info@admissions.acu.edu

Society for Immunotherapy of Cancer Scholarship

Purpose: The School of Information Technology and Computing awards scholarships in varying amounts to a select number of incoming freshmen and transfer students each year
Eligibility: Scholarship applicants must declare a major in Computer Science, Computer Science/Math Teaching or Digital Entertainment Technology (DET)
Level of Study: Graduate
Type: Scholarship
Frequency: Annual
Country of Study: Any country
Application Procedure: Application has to be processed through physical mailing address. apply.acu.edu/register/?id=3f5eee06-eddd-41c3-9d36-2dffb4f8400b
Funding: Private

For further information contact:

Email: info@admissions.acu.edu

Abraham Lincoln High School

Abraham Lincoln High School Alumni Association

Purpose: The purpose of the ALHS Alumni Association Scholarship Program is to make available scholarships to Lincoln High School students who are graduating and going onto college or continuing education
Eligibility: 1. ALHS Alumni will award scholarships. 2. ALHS graduating seniors seeking to further his/her education by obtaining a higher degree such as AA, BA, BS, or Certificated from a Trade, Vocational School or Military Academy. 3. Applications shall be completed by the applicant together with the official transcript, recommendation(s) by faculty/staff member(s), school activities records and a personal statement by the applicant of his/her goals. 4. Applicants will be evaluated and judged on the following factors. a. Their scholastic record. b. Their activity and other evidence of leadership and character. c. Recommendations of faculty and/or staff. d. A personal statement by applicant of his/her goals must be attached together with official transcripts, school activities records and personal statement by the applicant. 5. Results of the competition will be announced in April. Judging will be done by the ALHS Alumni Association Scholarship Committee. The committee looks forward to honoring the recipients in person at the Annual Wall of Fame/Scholarship Dinner. If the recipient is unable to attend the Scholarship Dinner a family member should attend to accept the scholarship on their behalf
Level of Study: Postgraduate
Type: Funding support
Frequency: Annual
Country of Study: Any country
Closing Date: 15 March
Funding: Private

For further information contact:

2162 24th Avenue San Francisco, CA 94116, United States of America

Tel: (1) 415 759 2700
Email: scholarships@lincolnalumni.com

Academia Resource Management (ARM)

535 East 4500 South, Suite D-120, Salt Lake City, UT 84107, United States of America

Tel: (1) 801 273 8911
Fax: (1) 801 277 5632
Email: info@armanagement.org
Website: www.awu.org

Academia Resource Management (ARM) is committed to the advancement of scientific knowledge and enrichment of the academic experience. Its mission is to identify and facilitate mutually beneficial research and training endeavours among academic institutions, government agencies and private industry.

Academia Resource Management Postgraduate Fellowship

Subjects: Physical sciences and mathematics, engineering/technology, earth science, meteorology/atmospheric science, chemical engineering, civil engineering, electrical engineering/electronics, mechanical, engineering, nuclear science, applied sciences and computer science/data processing
Purpose: To fund postgraduate research and technology at co-operating facilities
Level of Study: Postgraduate
Type: Fellowship
Value: Varies
Frequency: Annual
Country of Study: United States of America
Application Procedure: Applicants need to submit their application form, transcripts and reference letters
Funding: Foundation
Contributor: Academia Resource Management

For further information contact:

Email: info@armanagement.org

Academy of Marketing Science Foundation

424 Santa Teresa Street Stanford University, Stanford, CA 94305-4015, United States of America

Tel: (1) 650 723 3054
Email: ams.sba@miami.edu
Website: www.ams-web.org
Contact: Ms Rania Hegazi, Fellowship Administrator

Under the direction of Dr Harold W Berkman, the Academy of Marketing Science may be considered a full service scholarly professional organisation. The AMS established the Academy of Marketing Science Foundation to provide awards to marketing students, primarily at the graduate level. It is also the intention of the Foundation to provide awards for both the advancement of the teaching of marketing and for research in marketing.

Mary Kay Doctoral Dissertation Award

Subjects: Areas related to the discipline of marketing, ie. buyer behaviour, channels of distribution, advertising and promotion

Purpose: To recognise and reward a research contribution to the discipline of marketing
Eligibility: Open to individuals of any nationality
Level of Study: Doctorate
Value: US$500 cash prize and a waiver of the conference registration fee
Frequency: Annual
Country of Study: Any country
No. of awards offered: AMS members who participate
Closing Date: 1 December
No. of applicants last year: AMS members who participate
Additional Information: The Academy of Marketing Science (AMS) does not fund scholarships or grants towards studies. Awards and cash prizes are presented at the AMS Annual Conference to Academy members that participated in various paper competitions

Academy of Medical Sciences

41 Portland Place, W1B 1QH, London, United Kingdom

Email: newton-advanced@acmedsci.ac.uk
Website: www.acmedsci.ac.uk

Finding the brightest and best, celebrating their achievements and harnessing their expertise for the benefit of wider society is central to our role as a National Academy.

Daniel Turnberg Travel Fellowships

Purpose: This scheme aims to build research links and developing ongoing scientific collaborations between the United Kingdom and the Middle East. Daniel Turnberg Travel Fellowships give chance to undertake short-term visits to learn research techniques
Eligibility: These travel fellowships provide an opportunity for biomedical researchers from the Middle East to visit a research institution of their choice in the United Kingdom, and for those from the United Kingdom to visit a research institution of their choice in the Middle East. They are open to medical and non-medical graduates who can show a commitment to a career in research. Applicants will typically, but not necessarily, be at post-doctoral level
Level of Study: Research
Type: Fellowship
Value: Each fellowship will receive an average of €750 for cost of airfares and €3,500 per fellowship
Frequency: Annual
Country of Study: United Kingdom

Application Procedure: Applications will need to be submitted online using the Academy's electronic Grants and Awards management system Flexi-Grant®. Please download the guidance notes from the right hand side of this page to assist you in your application. If you have any queries after referring to the guidance notes. For further details, contact turnberg.fellowships@acmedsci.ac.uk
Closing Date: January (every year)
Funding: Private
Additional Information: You could use the below link for scholarship application. acmedsci.ac.uk/grants-and-schemes/grant-schemes/daniel-turnberg-travel-fellowship

For further information contact:

The Academy of Medical Sciences, 41 Portland Place, W1B 1QH, London, United Kingdom

Email: turnberg.fellowships@acmedsci.ac.uk

Global Challenges Research Fund Networking Grants

Purpose: These grants provide opportunities for researchers, drawn from a wide spectrum of disciplines and backgrounds. It helps to develop new collaborations and improve interactions between United Kingdom researchers and those in developing countries
Eligibility: The GCRF Networking Grants will be delivered as part of the Joint Academies Resilient Futures programme. Your application will be reviewed by Fellows across all of the partnership Academies and experts from developing or Low and Middle Income Countries (LMICs), and you will not need to attend an interview
Level of Study: Research
Type: Grant
Value: Awards provide Upto £25,000 over a year
Frequency: Annual
Country of Study: Any country
Application Procedure: 1. There will be two further rounds of the grant scheme, Round 4 and Round 5. Round 4 is currently open for applications and Round 5 will be open in Summer. 2. Applications are invited from researchers affiliated to institutions in DAC-listed countries in collaboration with researchers within eligible United Kingdom higher education institutions (HEIs). 3. You will need to apply for the programme using the Academy's online grant management system: Flexi-Grant. Grants cannot be used to pay for salary costs or to employ research assistants, PhD students or post-doctoral staff
Closing Date: 21 March
Funding: Private

For further information contact:

Email: gcrfnetworking@acmedsci.ac.uk

Newton Advanced Fellowships

Subjects: Any research area in the humanities and social sciences
Purpose: Mid-career postdoctoral career-development fellowship. Available for overseas researchers from specific countries in collaboration with a researcher at a United Kingdom institution
Eligibility: This scheme is currently open for applicants from Brazil, Mexico and South Africa. Applicants must have a PhD or equivalent research experience and hold a contract in an eligible university or research institute (in the partner countries), which must span the duration of the project. Applicants should have no more than 15 years postdoctoral experience. Collaborations should focus on a single project involving the overseas-based scientist ('the Applicant') and United Kingdom-based scientist (the Co-applicant). For more details on eligibility please check at www.acmedsci.ac.uk/snip/uploads/54c10a3af0414.pdf
Level of Study: Postdoctorate
Type: Fellowship
Value: Dependent on country
Length of Study: 2-years
Frequency: Annual
Country of Study: United Kingdom
Application Procedure: Applications can only be submitted online using the Royal Society's electronic Grant. Application and Processing (e-GAP) system. Please download Newton Advanced Fellowship Scheme notes for guidance on applying. To find out more information about the application process and to apply please follow the link royalsociety.org/grants/schemes/newton-advanced-fellowships
Closing Date: March
Funding: Government
Contributor: The Academy of Medical Sciences, in partnership with the Royal Society and the British Academy
Additional Information: We are working to include additional countries in future calls

For further information contact:

Email: newton-advanced@acmedsci.ac.uk

Newton International Fellowships

Subjects: Any research area in the humanities and social sciences

Purpose: Early-career postdoctoral fellowship opportunity for overseas (non-United Kingdom) researchers to spend 2 years, full-time researching at a United Kingdom institution
Eligibility: Applicants must have a PhD or equivalent research experience and hold a contract in an eligible university or research institute (in the partner countries), which must span the duration of the project. Applicants should have no more than 15 years postdoctoral experience. Collaborations should focus on a single project involving the overseas-based scientist ('the Applicant') and United Kingdom-based scientist ('the Co-applicant'). For more details on eligibility please see the detailed guidance (www.acmedsci.ac.uk/snip/uploads/54c10a3af0414.pdf). Note that partner countries have specific eligibility requirements so please do check the guidance carefully
Level of Study: Postdoctorate
Type: Fellowship
Value: £66,000 for the award holder and £33,000 for the host institution
Length of Study: 2 years
Frequency: Annual
Application Procedure: Applications can only be submitted online using the Royal Society's electronic Grant Application and Processing (e-GAP) system. Please download Newton Advanced Fellowship Scheme notes for guidance on applying. To find out more information about the application process and to apply please follow the link royalsociety.org/grants/schemes/newton-advanced-fellowships
Closing Date: February
Funding: Government

For further information contact:

Email: newton-international@acmedsci.ac.uk

Academy of Sciences of the Czech Republic

UNESCO-ROSTE Course Institute of Microbiology Videnská 1083, CS-142 20 Prague, Czech Republic

Tel:	(42) 2 4752 379
Fax:	(42) 2 4752 384
Email:	nerud@biomed.cas.cz
Website:	www.biomed.cas.cz
Contact:	Mr F Nerud, Director of Course

The Institute of Microbiology is one of the major biological institutes of the Academy of Sciences. Main areas of research at the Institute include biogenesis and biotechnology of natural compounds, cell and molecular microbiology, ecology, immunology, gnotobiology and autotrophic micro-organisms.

United Nations Educational, Scientific and Cultural Organization-ROSTE Long-term Postgraduate Training Course

Subjects: Microbiology, biochemistry, biophysics, molecular biology, biotechnology, genetics and ecology
Purpose: To enable young scientists to obtain a more profound education and prepare for a research career
Eligibility: Open to young scientists from European countries and a limited number of students from other regions who hold an MSc, PhD or equivalent degree, and who have two-three years of practical experience in their field. Candidates should be no more than 35 years of age and should possess a good knowledge of English
Level of Study: Postgraduate
Type: Grant
Value: KČ 5,000 plus accommodation
Length of Study: 11 months
Frequency: Annual
Study Establishment: Insitute of Microbiology of the Academy of Sciences of the Czech Republic
Country of Study: Czech Republic
No. of awards offered: 12
Application Procedure: Applicants must write for details
Closing Date: 31 March
Funding: Government
Contributor: The Academy of Sciences of the Czech Republic
No. of awards given last year: 6
No. of applicants last year: 12
Additional Information: The course is given in co-operation with the Czech Commission for UNESCO and sponsored by the Academy of Sciences of the Czech Republic

Acadia University

Room 214 Horton Hall, 18 University Avenue, Wolfville, NS B4P 2R6, Canada

Tel:	(1) 902 585 1914
Fax:	(1) 902 585 1096
Email:	theresa.starratt@acadiau.ca
Website:	www.acadiau.ca
Contact:	Ms Theresa Starratt, Graduate Studies Officer-Research and Graduate Studies

Acadia University is an institution that is committed to providing a liberal education based on the highest standards. The University houses a scholarly community that aims to ensure a broadening life experience for students, faculty and staff.

Acadia Graduate Scholarship / Acadia Graduate Teaching Assistantships

Subjects: English, political science, sociology, biology, chemistry, computer science, geology, psychology, education and recreation management, mathematics, applied geomatics and statistics, social and political thought. The specific duties will be established by agreement at the beginning of each academic year with the applicant's department/school coordinator

Purpose: To financially support students

Eligibility: Open to registered full-time graduate students at Acadia University. In order to be eligible for an award, students must have a GPA of not less than 3.0 in their major field in each of their last 2 years of undergraduate study

Level of Study: Postgraduate

Type: Award

Value: Canadian Dollars. Value can vary

Length of Study: 1–2 years

Frequency: Annual

Study Establishment: The Division of Research and Graduate Studies at Acadia University

Country of Study: Canada

Application Procedure: Applicants must write for details. In almost all cases, to be automatically considered for funding, applicants need to apply by 1 February of each year

Closing Date: When all spots have been filled

Funding: Private

Additional Information: Recipients of an Acadia Graduate Teaching Assistantship should expect to undertake certain duties during the academic year (up to 10 hours per week and a maximum of 120 hours per semester) as a condition of tenure

For further information contact:

Tel: (1) 902 585 1914
Email: theresa.starratt@acadiau.ca
Contact: Ms Theresa Starratt, Graduate Studies Officer

University of Geneva Excellence Masters Fellowships

Purpose: The Faculty of Science of the University of Geneva, in collaboration with several sponsors, has established an Excellence Fellowship Program to support outstanding and highly motivated candidates who intend to pursue a Master of Science in any of the disciplines covered by the Faculty

Eligibility: Regardless of your home university, whether you have passed or are doing a brilliant bachelor degree, and that you are one of the best in your year, this program is for you! You must meet the admission criteria of the Master of your choice and be selected on the basis of the application file for an Excellence Fellowship

Level of Study: Postgraduate

Type: Fellowship

Value: CHF 10,000 to CHF 15,000 per year

Frequency: Annual

Country of Study: Any country

Closing Date: 15 March

Funding: Private

Victoria Hardship Fund Equity Grants for International Students in New Zealand

Subjects: Scholarships are available to study the subject offered by the university

Purpose: These grants are to encourage students who are facing financial hardship to continue in their studies at Victoria University. The Grants are intended to assist with ongoing costs related to study. They are not intended for tuition fees

Eligibility: Scholarships are open to all students who are studying at Victoria University of Wellington including domestic, international, undergraduate, postgraduate, part-time and full-time students. The Victoria University has a tradition of fostering strong global links in teaching and research and program of national significance and international quality. Applicants must be enrolled in the trimester they are applying for e.g. students who apply for round 1 must be enrolled in trimester 1 of the same year. The grants will be awarded on the basis of financial need and satisfactory academic commitment and progress. Factors taken into consideration when assessing financial need could include - high course costs, high transport costs, medical conditions or disability preventing part-time work, family to support, any other relevant circumstances

Level of Study: Graduate

Type: Grant

Value: Scholarship upto NZ$2,000 will be provided

Frequency: Annual

Country of Study: Any country

Application Procedure: Application can be processed through online mode with the below link. www.victoria.ac.nz

Closing Date: 18 February

Funding: Private

For further information contact:

Victoria University of Wellington, PO Box 600, Wellington 6140, New Zealand

Tel: (64) 4 463 5557
Email: info@victoria.ac.nz

Action Cancer

1 Marlborough Park, Belfast, Co Antrim BT9 6XS, Northern Ireland

Tel: (44) 28 9080 3363
Fax: (44) 28 9080 3356
Email: info@actioncancer.org
Website: www.actioncancer.org
Contact: Mr Caroline Hughes, Research and Evaluation Officer

Action Cancer is a Northern Ireland cancer charity that relies entirely on voluntary donations. Founded in 1973, it offers awareness and health promotion, free early-detection clinics for men and women concerned about cancer and a support service for cancer patients and their families. Action Cancer also provides funding for research at local universities.

Action Cancer Project Grant

Subjects: Cancer-related projects
Purpose: To help researchers in Northern Ireland carry out significant cancer-related projects by contributing to salaries, the purchase of materials and equipments and to other appropriate costs
Eligibility: Researchers must be working in Northern Ireland
Level of Study: Postdoctorate
Type: Project grant
Value: Up to £45,000 per year for up to 3 years
Length of Study: 3 years
Frequency: Every 2 years
Country of Study: United Kingdom
Application Procedure: Awards are advertised in the local press in March. Applicants must submit a form, based on which a decision is taken by the Action Cancer Scientific and Research Committee, which also takes advice from external reviewers

Closing Date: Early May
Funding: Private
Contributor: Voluntary donations

For further information contact:

Email: grants@solvingkidscancer.org

Action Medical Research

Vincent House, North Parade, West Sussex RH12 2DP, Horsham, United Kingdom

Tel: (44) 14 0321 0406
Fax: (44) 14 0321 0541
Email: applications@action.org.uk
Website: www.action.org.uk

Action Medical Research is dedicated to preventing and treating disease and disability by funding vital medical research in United Kingdom-based hospitals and universities. The remit focuses on child health with an emphasis on clinical research or research at the clinical/basic interface. Research applications are judged by rigorous peer review.

Action Medical Research Project Grants

Subjects: A broad spectrum of research with the objective of preventing and treating disease and disability and alleviating physical disability. The remit focuses on child health to include problems affecting pregnancy, childbirth, babies, children and adolescents
Purpose: To support one precisely formulated line of research
Eligibility: Open to researchers based in the United Kingdom. Grants are not awarded to other charities or for higher education
Level of Study: Unrestricted
Type: Grant
Value: Varies
Length of Study: Up to 3 years, assessed annually
Frequency: Dependent on funds available
Study Establishment: Hospitals, universities and recognised research establishments in the United Kingdom
Country of Study: United Kingdom
No. of awards offered: 124 outline applications

Application Procedure: Applicants must submit a one-page outline of the project before an application form can be issued. Full details and outline proposals are available on the website
Closing Date: 20 November
Funding: Private, Trusts, Individuals
Contributor: Voluntary income
No. of awards given last year: 15
No. of applicants last year: 124 outline applications
Additional Information: 72 full applications invited, 69 received and assessed by Scientific Advisory Panel

For further information contact:

Email: applications@action.org.uk

Action Medical Research Training Fellowship

Subjects: A broad spectrum of research with the objective of preventing and treating disease and disability and alleviating physical disability. The remit focuses on child health to include problems affecting pregnancy, childbirth, babies, children and adolescents. We welcome applications from clinicians, bioengineers, research nurses and allied health professionals
Purpose: To enable the training of medical and bioengineering graduates in research techniques and methodology in areas of interest to Action Medical Research
Eligibility: Open to medical and non-medical graduates. Although it is not limited to United Kingdom citizens, those who do not hold United Kingdom citizenship must be able to show that they have all the required statutory documentation, e.g. work permits, to cover the period of the fellowship. Preference will be given to candidates resident in the United Kingdom. No grants are made purely for higher education. Although applicants are strongly encouraged to independently register for a Ph-D. Further guidelines are available on the organisations website
Level of Study: Doctorate, Postdoctorate, Postgraduate
Type: Fellowship
Value: Upper limit is £2,50,000
Length of Study: Up to 3 years
Frequency: Dependent on funds available
Study Establishment: A hospital, university department or recognised research institute in the United Kingdom
Country of Study: United Kingdom
No. of awards offered: 18
Application Procedure: Applicants must submit a one-page outline of the project before an application form can be issued. Full details and outline proposal forms are available on the website
Funding: Private, Individuals

Contributor: Voluntary income
No. of awards given last year: 1
No. of applicants last year: 18
Additional Information: 12 full applications invited, 10 received and assessed by scientific Advisory Panel

For further information contact:

Email: applications@action.org.uk

Adelphi University

1 South Avenue, PO BOX 701, Garden City, NY 11530-0701, United States of America

Tel: (1) 516 877 3412/3080
Fax: (1) 516 877 3424
Email: ucinfo@adelphi.edu
Website: www.adelphi.edu/

Adelphi University is the oldest institution of higher education for liberal arts and sciences on Long Island.

Adelphi University Full-Time Transfer Merit Award

Purpose: Adelphi University has made a substantial commitment to make the cost of attending the University more affordable through its institutional scholarship and grant programs
Eligibility: Eligible students will receive a letter of notification from the Scholarship Committee. After filing the FAFSA, a financial assistance summary detailing all financial aid will be mailed to the student
Type: Award
Value: Up to US$11,000 depending upon the individual's academic profile
Frequency: Annual
Country of Study: Any country
Application Procedure: A student must first file an admissions application and is encouraged to file the FAFSA as soon as possible after 1 January, but no later than 15 February to ensure maximum eligibility for other sources of financial aid
Closing Date: Check with website

For further information contact:

Tel: (1) 516 877 3080
Email: admissions@adelphi.edu
Contact: Adelphi University Office of Student Financial Services

Advance Africa

Baxter International Foundation Grants

Purpose: The Baxter International Foundation offers grants to NGOs working to provide accessibility and affordability of healthcare services to disadvantaged communities around the world

Eligibility: NGOs need to understand Foundation priorities, besides following the application procedures carefully while submitting the proposal. Although proposals are accepted round the year, there are quarterly deadlines

Level of Study: Graduate

Type: Grant

Frequency: Annual

Country of Study: Any country

Application Procedure: Submit the proposal through physical communication on the below address

Closing Date: Not specified

Funding: Private

For further information contact:

The Baxter International Foundation, One Baxter Parkway - DF2-2E, Deerfield, IL 60015, United States of America

Tel: (1) 847 948 4605

Email: fdninfo@baxter.com

Maypole Fund Grants for Women

Subjects: Maypole money is donated by women for women to use, and the group that runs the fund is all women. The money is invested so as to produce an income each year to distribute as grants

Purpose: Grants from the Maypole Fund have contributed to a wide range of activities

Eligibility: 1. Young women's groups/individuals. 2. Activities or projects not yet started. 3. Women who do not have access to other sources of funding or whose projects find it difficult to attract funding from elsewhere. 4. Imaginative/creative activities. 5. Individual and small women's groups over larger established women's groups

Level of Study: Postgraduate

Type: Funding support

Value: £750

Frequency: Annual

Country of Study: Any country

Application Procedure: Interested applicants can download the application forms via given website. The Maypole Fund is seeking applications from women only for projects and activities for any of the following: 1. Anti-militarism. 2. Action against the arms trade. 3. Action against nuclear weapons and weapons systems. Creating a culture of peace and non-violence and the prevention of conflict and war

Closing Date: 31 January

Funding: Private

Additional Information: www.maypolefund.org/the-grant/

Rudolf Steiner Foundation Seed Fund

Purpose: It helps in Providing Small Grants to Organizations. The Rudolf Steiner Foundation (RSF) is inviting applicants for its Seed Fund to provide small grants to organizations that offer innovative solutions to challenges in the areas of social finance, food and agriculture, education and the arts, or ecological stewardship

Eligibility: 1. Alignment with RSF's mission and focus areas. 2. Non-profit status: The RSF Seed Fund accepts proposals from organizations that are any of the following: 501(c)(3) tax-exempt per the IRS Fiscally sponsored with 501(c)(3) tax-exempt status per the IRS. 3. Schools or universities. 4. Non-governmental entities, Indian tribes or tribal non-profit organizations, and territorial, tribal, or unit of local government entities

Level of Study: Postgraduate

Type: Award

Value: provides grants between US$500 and US$3,500

Frequency: Annual

Country of Study: United States of America

Application Procedure: Apply online. 1. Interested applicants can apply online via given website. 2. Eligible Country: United States. For more information and grant application details, see; application details, see; RSF Seed Fund - Providing Small Grants to Organizations

Closing Date: March

Funding: Private

For further information contact:

Email: mark.herrera@rsfsocialfinance.org

African Forest Forum (AFF)

The African Forest Forum, United Nations Avenue, P.O. Box 30677, Nairobi, KE 00100, Kenya

Tel: (254) 207 224 000

Fax: (254) 207 224 001

Email: exec.sec@afforum.org

Website: www.afforum.org/

The African Forest Forum is an association of individuals with a commitment to the sustainable management, wise use and conservation of Africa's forest and tree resources for the socio-economic well-being of its peoples and for the stability and improvement of its environment.

African Forest Forum (AFF) Research Fellowships

Purpose: The African Forest Forum (AFF) is a pan-African non-governmental organization with its headquarters in Nairobi, Kenya. It is an association of individuals who share the quest for and commitment to the sustainable management, use and conservation of the forest and tree resources of Africa for the socio-economic wellbeing of its people and for the stability and improvement of its environment

Eligibility: Applicants must meet the general eligibility criteria as well as the specific eligibility criteria. Applications that do not meet eligibility criteria will not receive further evaluation. Should have a Master's or Bachelor's degree plus two or more years of professional experience related to forestry, natural resource management, development studies, climate change and environmental studies. Please refer to the website for more information

Level of Study: Postgraduate

Value: Each fellow will receive up to US$10,000 for research and US$2,000 to cover cost of travel, subsistence, and accommodation while in the field including supervision

Country of Study: Africa

Application Procedure: Check website for more details

Closing Date: 31 May

Funding: Trusts

For further information contact:

Email: exec.sec@afforum.org

African Mathematics Millennium Scientific Initiative

School of Mathematics, University of Nairobi, PO Box 30197, Nairobi, GPO 00100, Kenya

Tel: (254) 20 445 0934
Email: ammsi@uonbi.ac.ke
Website: www.ammsi.org
Contact: Professor Wandera Ogana, AMMSI Programme Director

The African Mathematics Millennium Science Initiative (AMMSI) is a distributed network of mathematics research,

training and promotion throughout sub-Saharan Africa. It has five regional offices located in Botswana, Cameroon, Kenya, Nigeria and Senegal. It is a project established by the Millennium Science Initiative (MSI), administered by the Science Initiative Group (SIG). The primary goal of the MSI is to create and nurture world-class science and scientific talent in the developing world by strengthening S&T capacity through integrated programmes of research and training, planned and driven by local scientists in the field of mathematics.

Research/Visiting Scientist Fellowships

Subjects: Mathematics

Purpose: To encourage research and postgraduate teaching in mathematics

Eligibility: Candidates should undertake research and postgraduate teaching in mathematics at any university in sub-Saharan Africa, should be a staff member at a university and hold at least a Master's degree, and should obtain an official invitation from the host institution

Level of Study: Postgraduate

Type: Fellowships

Value: US$5,000

Length of Study: 1–12 months

Application Procedure: Application forms should be filled and submitted online. In exceptional circumstances, hard copy application forms may be obtained from the nearest AMMSI Regional Coordinator whose contact details can be found in the website

Closing Date: 15 September

For further information contact:

Tel: (254) 20 235 8569/20 445 0934
Fax: (254) 20 445 0934
Email: progoffice@ammsi.org, ammsi@uonbi.ac.ke
Contact: Wandera Ogana, AMMSI Programme Director

African Wildlife Foundation (AWF)

PO Box 48177, Nairobi, Kenya

Tel: (254) 2 710 367
Fax: (254) 2 710 372
Email: awfnrb@awfke.org
Website: www.awf.org

The African Wildlife Foundation (AWF) has been working with the people of Africa to protect their environment since

1961. Most of AWF's staff are based in Africa, working with park managers and communities to safeguard wildlife and wilderness areas. AWF helps African nations design long-term strategies for conserving their magnificent natural treasures for all the world to enjoy.

African Institute for Mathematical Sciences Postdoctoral Fellowship in Data Science

Subjects: Mathematics and data science
Purpose: African Institute for Mathematical Sciences (AIMS) is a pan-African network of centers of excellence for Postgraduate education, research and outreach in mathematical sciences
Eligibility: Applicants should be SADC member state, and applicant should be proficient in English language with good communication skills. A relevant doctorate of high standing and developing research capability which will lead to good publications. Candidates should have a ability to tutor postgraduate students successfully work as part of an interdisciplinary team
Level of Study: Graduate
Type: Fellowship
Value: ZAR200–ZAR240k per annul, tax-free, subject to qualification and experience. Other benefits include the provision of a laptop, coverage of all cost associated with the use of HPC resource
Frequency: Annual
Country of Study: Any country
Closing Date: February
Funding: Private

For further information contact:

Email: joan@aims.ac.za

After School Africa

AfterCollege STEM Inclusion Scholarship

Purpose: AfterCollege has been connecting students and recent grads with employers hiring for internships and entry-level positions since it was founded in a dorm room in 1999
Eligibility: To be eligible for this scholarship, you must be applying with this condition. 1. Minimum 3.0 GPA. 2. Applicant must be from a group underrepresented in their field of study. 3. Underrepresented groups may be defined by: gender, race, ethnic background, disability, sexual orientation, age, socio-economic status, nationality, and other non-visible differences. 4. Quarterly deadlines: 3/31; 6/30; 9/30; 12/31.

5. Winners notified 30 days after scholarship deadline.
6. After College profiles are used as criteria to select recipients
Level of Study: Graduate
Type: Scholarship
Value: US$500
Frequency: Annual
Country of Study: Any country
Application Procedure: In order to process the scholarship application, check the website. www.aftercollege.com/company/aftercollege-inc/10/scholarship/220/?source=ur-sch-stem
Closing Date: 31 March
Funding: Private

For further information contact:

AfterCollege 98 Battery Street, Suite 502 San Francisco, CA, United States of America

Email: scholarships@aftercollege.com

Zhengzhou University President Scholarships

Purpose: The scholarship aims to sponsor international postgraduate students to pursue their degree, especially the doctor degree, in Zhengzhou University
Eligibility: This scholarship is eligible for International Candidates. 1. Non-Chinese citizen, physically healthy, without crime record. 2. Abide by the laws and regulations of the People's Republic of China as well as regulations of ZZU. 3. Good learning attitude and academic performance. 4. Requirements for applicant's degree and age
Level of Study: Postgraduate
Type: Scholarship
Value: Partial tuition fee
Length of Study: 3–4 years
Frequency: Annual
Country of Study: China
Application Procedure: Applicants must fill in an application form and submit the following supporting documents: 1. Original or notarized copies of highest degree (applicants must additionally submit study certificate or employment certificate issued by the applicants' schools if the applicants are students or employed). Documents in neither Chinese nor English must be attached with a notarized Chinese or English translations. 2. Applicants for master programs must provide original or notarized copies of bachelor study transcripts, and doctoral programs bachelor and master study transcripts. Documents in neither Chinese nor English must be attached with a notarized Chinese or English translations. 3. Applicants for master programs must provide study plans of 800 words, and for doctoral programs must provide research proposal of 2,000 words written in Chinese or

English. 4. Applicants for master and doctoral programs must provide two letters of recommendation from associate professors or professors respectively written in Chinese or English. 5. Applicants for programs of art must submit other documents as in the requirements of ZZU; Officially test results of Chinese or English language. 6. Original or notarized copies of Foreigner Physical Examination Form and blood test reports, filled in Chinese or English. 7. Original or notarized copies of certificates of no criminal record. Documents in neither Chinese nor English must be attached with a notarized Chinese or English translations

Closing Date: 30 June
Funding: Private

For further information contact:

No.100 Science Avenue, Zhengzhou, Henan Province, People's Republic of China

Tel: (86) 371 67780102
Email: zhaochun@zzu.edu.cn

Agency for Science, Technology and Research (A*STAR)

1 Fusionopolis Way, #20-10 Connexis North Tower, 138632, Singapore

Tel: (65) 6826 6111
Fax: (65) 6777 1711
Email: contact@a-star.edu.sg
Website: www.a-star.edu.sg/astar

A*STAR comprises of the Biomedical Research Council (BMRC), the Science and Engineering Research Council (SERC), Exploit Technologies Private Ltd (ETPL), the A*STAR Graduate Academy (AGA) and the Corporate Planning and Administration Division (CPAD). Both BMRC and SERC promote, support and oversee the public sector R&D research activities in Singapore.

Singapore International Graduate Award (SINGA)

Purpose: The Singapore International Graduate Award (SINGA) is a collaboration between the Agency for Science, Technology & Research (A*STAR), the Nanyang Technological University (NTU) and the National University of Singapore (NUS). PhD training will be carried out in English at chosen lab at A*STAR Research Institutes, NTU or NUS

Eligibility: Open to all international students; graduates with a passion for research and excellent academic results; good skills in written and spoken English; good reports from academic referees

Type: Award
Value: The stipend amount is S$24,000 annually, to be increased to S$30,000 after passing Qualifying Examination. Full support for tuition fees for 4 years of PhD studies. One-time S$1,000 Settling-in Allowance; one-time Airfare Grant of S$1,500

Country of Study: Singapore
Application Procedure: The mode of application is online. For detailed information, please visit: www.singa.a-star.edu.sg/howtoapply.php

Closing Date: 1 June
Additional Information: For detailed information, please visit www.singa.a-star.edu.sg/

Agilent Technology and American Association of Critical Care Nurses

3000 Minuteman Road MS210, Andover, MA 01810, United States of America

Tel: (1) 978 659 4748
Contact: Ms Joan Hodges, Learning Products Manager

Agilent Technology Critical Care Nursing Research Grant

Subjects: Nursing
Purpose: To support research in critical care nursing. Preferred topics will address information technology requirements of patient management in critical care
Eligibility: AACN members may apply (current registered nurse members only). Research must be undertaken in the United States of America
Level of Study: Postgraduate
Type: Other
Value: US$37,000
Length of Study: 1 year
Frequency: Annual
Study Establishment: Hospital
Country of Study: United States of America
No. of awards offered: 22
Application Procedure: Applicants must write to the Agilent Technology address for applications
No. of awards given last year: 1
No. of applicants last year: 22

Additional Information: Questions about suitability of research topics should be addressed to the AACN Research Department

For further information contact:

Tel: (1) 800 394 5995
Email: research@aacn.org

Agricultural History Society

MSU History Department, PO Box H, Mississippi State, MS 39762, United States of America

Tel: (1) 501 569 8782/662 268 2247
Fax: (1) 501 569 3059
Email: CSTROM@Rollins.edu
Website: www.aghistorysociety.org
Contact: Claire Strom, Editor, Agricultural History

The Agricultural History Society recognizes the roles of agriculture and agri-business in shaping the political, economic, social and historical profiles of different countries worldwide. Since 1927, the Society's publication, *Agricultural History*, has been the international journal for the field and publishes innovative research on agricultural and rural history.

Agriculture Awareness Grants

Subjects: College & Career Readiness, Instruction
Purpose: Suitable projects will promote an understanding of the food and fiber system in the state and the nation through the infusion of agricultural concepts into Pre K – 12th grade level curricula
Eligibility: 1. Funding will be available to nonprofit organizations within the state of Maine or serving students within the state of Maine. 2. $60K is earmarked for grants in 5 categories
Level of Study: Postgraduate
Type: Grant
Value: US$1,000
Frequency: Annual
Country of Study: Any country
Closing Date: 9 August
Funding: Private

For further information contact:

GrantsAlert P.O. Box 706 Newton, Catawba, NC 28658, United States of America

Email: maitca@maine.gov

Henry A Wallace Award

Subjects: The term "agricultural history" has always been interpreted broadly, and the Society encourages research and publishes articles from all countries and in all periods of history. Initially affiliated with the American Historical Association, the Agricultural History Society is the third oldest, discipline-based professional organization in the United States
Purpose: Presented to the author of the best book on any aspect of agricultural history outside the United States. The book must be based on substantial primary research and should represent new scholarly interpretation or reinterpretation of agricultural history scholarship
Level of Study: Unrestricted
Type: Award
Value: US$500
Frequency: Annual
Country of Study: Any country
Application Procedure: Applicants must send four copies of the book of the editor. Books may be nominated by their authors, the publisher, a member of the award committee, or a member of the society
Closing Date: 31 December
No. of awards given last year: 1
Additional Information: Available upon request to the Society

For further information contact:

Email: mikegaul@iastate.edu

Air-Conditioning, Heating, and Refrigeration Institute

Air-Conditioning, Heating, and Refrigeration Institute MSc Scholarship

Purpose: The AHRI MSc Scholarship, sponsored by University College London (UCL), is a singular award for the United Kingdom academic year. The scholarship is administered via AHRI and is for applicants whose academic background and interests are aligned with the programmes of research at AHRI

Eligibility: 1. Must be permanently based in South Africa at the time of application. 2. Must hold a valid passport at the time of application. 3. Must have an Honours degree equivalent to a Bachelor (Honours) degree with Second Class Division 1 Honours or 70% in an appropriate subject. 4. The successful applicant must be in London to start their chosen course in September

Level of Study: Postdoctorate

Type: Scholarship

Frequency: Annual

Country of Study: Any country

Closing Date: 29 March

Funding: Foundation

For further information contact:

Nelson R. Mandela School of Medicine, 3rd Floor, K-RITH Tower Building, 719 Umbilo Road, Durban, South Africa

Tel: (27) 31 260 4991
Email: info@ahri.org

Air Force Office of Scientific Research (AFOSR)

AFOSR/PIE, 4015 Wilson Boulevard Room 713, Arlington, VA 22203-1954, United States of America

Tel: (1) 703 696 7319
Fax: (1) 703 696 7364
Email: info@afosr.af.mil
Website: www.afosr.af.mil
Contact: Dr Koto White, Chief External Programmes & Resources Interface

The Air Force Office of Scientific Research's (AFOSR) mission is to sponsor and sustain basic research, transfer and transition research results and support Air Force goals of control and maximum utilisation of air and space.

United States Air Force Academy/National Research Council Summer Faculty Research Program (SFFP)

Subjects: Science, engineering or mathematics

Purpose: To provide research opportunities for qualified faculty members of United States colleges and universities at Air Force research facilities within the continental United States

Eligibility: Applicants must be United States citizens or permanent residents, faculty members of accredited United States of America colleges, universities or technical institutions, and have at least two years of teaching or research experience

Level of Study: Professional development

Value: Assistant professors receive US$1,250, associate professors receive US$1,450, and full professors receive US$1,650 per week

Length of Study: 8–12 weeks

Frequency: Annual

Study Establishment: An Air Force facility

Country of Study: United States of America

Application Procedure: Applicants must contact the National Research Council on (1) 202 334 2760

Closing Date: 1 November

Funding: Government

Additional Information: Please see the website www.national-academies.org/rap for details

Alabama A and M University

School of Business Administration, Office of the Dean of Graduate Studies & Extended Studies, PO Box 998, Normal, AL 35762, United States of America

Tel: (1) 256 851 5266
Fax: (1) 256 851 3641
Email: nmurrell@aamu.edu
Contact: MBA Admissions Officer

Alabama Student Assistance Program

Purpose: The Alabama Student Grant Program is a state student assistance program designed to provide financial assistance to residents of the State of Alabama for undergraduate study

Eligibility: To be eligible for an Alabama Student Grant Program award the student must: (1) Have obtained a certificate of graduation from a secondary school or the recognized equivalence of such graduation. (2) Be classified as an undergraduate student. (3) Be an Alabama resident as defined in Alabama Student Grant Program Act 90. (4) Be a citizen of the United States or in the process of becoming a citizen of the United States. (5) Be enrolled as a full-time or half-time student in an eligible program in an approved institution. (6)Applicants must have obtained a certificate of graduation from a secondary school or the recognized equivalence of such graduation. (7)be an Alabama resident as defined in Alabama Stud and Grant Program Act 90; be a citizen of the

United States or in the process of becoming a citizen of the United States
Level of Study: Postgraduate
Type: Programme grant
Value: US$300–US$2,500
Frequency: Annual
Country of Study: Any country
Closing Date: Varies
Funding: Private

For further information contact:

Scholarship Committee, 100 N. Union Street P.O. Box 302000, Montgomery, AL 36104, United States of America

Tel: (1) 334 242 2273
Email: Cheryl.Newton@ache.alabama.gov

Alberta Innovates Health Solutions

Suite 1500, Bell Tower, 10104-103 Avenue, Edmonton, AB T5J 4A7, Canada

Tel: (1) 780 423 5727
Fax: (1) 780 429 3509
Email: pamela.valentine@albertainnovates.ca
Website: www.albertainnovates.ca; www.ahfmr.ab.ca
Contact: Dr Pamela Valentine, Interim Vice-President

Alberta Innovates Health Solutions supports a community of researchers who generate knowledge that improves the health and quality of life of Albertans and people throughout the world. The long-term commitment is to fund basic patient and health research based on international standards of excellence and carried out by new and established investigators and researchers in training.

Alberta Heritage Foundation for Medical Research Part-Time Studentship

Subjects: Medical research
Purpose: To enable full-time degree students to continue research training on a part-time basis
Eligibility: Candidates must normally have been accepted into, or be currently engaged in, a full-time graduate program at an Alberta-based university in a health-related discipline leading to a Master's or doctoral degree
Level of Study: Doctorate, Graduate
Type: Studentship
Value: Pro-rated on full-time studentship stipend and dependent on the amount of time spent in research
Length of Study: 3 years, maximum
Frequency: Annual
Study Establishment: A university in Alberta
Country of Study: Canada
No. of awards offered: 1
Application Procedure: Applicants must complete an application form
Closing Date: 1 October
Funding: Government
No. of awards given last year: 1
No. of applicants last year: 1

For further information contact:

Email: grants.health@albertainnovates.ca

Alberta Innovates - Health Solutions Postgraduate Fellowships

Subjects: Medical research
Purpose: To provide opportunities for individuals to pursue postgraduate health-related research at an Alberta University
Eligibility: Open to candidates with a PhD, MD, DDS, DVM or DPharm degree. Normally, support will not be provided beyond 5 years after receipt of the PhD degree, or beyond 8 years after receipt of the MD, DDS, DVM or DPharm degrees
Level of Study: Postdoctorate
Type: Fellowship
Value: C$5,000 research allowance plus a stipend of $50,000
Length of Study: 1 year, with a possibility of renewal for a maximum of 3 years of support
Frequency: Annual
Study Establishment: Usually at a university in Alberta
Country of Study: Canada
No. of awards offered: 156
Application Procedure: Applicants must complete an application form. Candidates must submit, in full, the original application to the AIHS office by the deadline
Closing Date: 1 October
Funding: Government
No. of awards given last year: 39
No. of applicants last year: 156
Additional Information: Please contact at grants.health@albertainnovates.ca

For further information contact:

Email: Kathy.Morrison@albertainnovates.ca

Graduate Studentships

Subjects: Medical research
Purpose: To provide opportunities for support for individuals undertaking health-related research areas in pursuit of a Master's or PhD
Eligibility: Applicants must be currently enrolled in a graduate program at an Alberta University undertaking health-related research training leading to thesis-based graduate degree
Level of Study: Doctorate, Graduate
Type: Studentship
Value: C$30,000 stipend and a research and career development allowance of C$2,000 per year for up to 4 years (maximum of 2 years support towards a Master
Length of Study: 1 year with the possibility of renewal for a maximum of 5 years of support; 2 years maximum at the masters level
Frequency: Annual
Study Establishment: A university in Alberta
Country of Study: Canada
No. of awards offered: 200
Application Procedure: Candidates must submit, in full, the original application to the AIHS offices by the deadlines
Closing Date: 1 April
Funding: Government
No. of awards given last year: 49
No. of applicants last year: 200
Additional Information: Please contact at grants.health@albertainnovates.ca

For further information contact:

Email: health@albertainnovates.ca

Alexander von Humboldt Foundation

Jean-Paul-Str. 12, DEU-53173 Bonn, Germany

Tel: (49) 228 833 455
Fax: (49) 228 833 441
Email: regine.laroche@avh.de
Website: www.humboldt-foundation.de
Contact: Ms Regine Laroche

The Alexander von Humboldt Foundation is a non-profit foundation established by the Federal Republic of Germany for the promotion of international research co-operation. It enables highly qualified scientists and scholars not resident in Germany to spend extended periods of research in Germany and promotes the ensuing academic contacts. The Humboldt Foundation promotes an active world-wide network of researchers.

500 Humboldt Research Fellowships for International Applicants in Germany

Subjects: Applicants choose their own research projects and their host in Germany and prepare their research plan independently. Details of the research project and the time schedule must be agreed upon with the prospective host in advance
Purpose: Up to 500 Humboldt Research Fellowships are available for experienced researchers to carry out a long-term research project (6-18 months) at a research institution in Germany. Scientists and scholars of all nationalities and disciplines may apply
Eligibility: Scientists and scholars of all nationalities may apply for these Humboldt Research Fellowships
Type: Research
Value: See the website
Study Establishment: Applicants choose their own research projects and their host in Germany and prepare their research plan independently. Details of the research project and the time schedule must be agreed upon with the prospective host in advance
Country of Study: Germany
Application Procedure: Applications should be submitted by post
Closing Date: Applications may be sent at any time
Additional Information: For more information please visit the website scholarship-positions.com/humboldt-research-fellowships-experienced-researchers-germany-2015/2014/08/30/. The complete application should be submitted to the Humboldt Foundation at least four to seven months ahead of the prospective selection date. The selection committee meets three times a year, in March, July and November

Anneliese Maier Research Award

Subjects: Humanities, social science, cultural science, law, and economics
Purpose: To promote research collaboration between outstanding researchers from abroad and specialist colleagues in Germany, contributing towards the further internationalisation of the humanities and social sciences in Germany
Eligibility: Researchers from abroad who already number among the established leaders in their subject as well as researchers who are not yet so advanced in their scientific careers but who are already internationally established researchers
Level of Study: Research

Type: Prize
Value: €2,500,000 for annually
Frequency: Annual
Study Establishment: Universities and Research Institutions
Country of Study: Germany
Application Procedure: Nominations may be submitted by established academics in Germany. Direct applications are not accepted
Closing Date: 30 April
Funding: Government

For further information contact:

Email: info@avh.de

Humboldt Research Fellowships

Subjects: Humaniaties, social science and law
Purpose: To enable highly qualified young scholars from countries strongly influenced by Islamic culture to carry out research projects of their own choice in Germany
Eligibility: Open to applicants who have a Doctorate or comparable academic degree, with a good proven knowledge of German or English and who are not above 40 years of age
Level of Study: Research, Foundation programme
Type: Fellowships
Value: Covers long-term research costs
Frequency: Annual
Country of Study: Germany
Application Procedure: Applicants need to send their applications directly to the Selection Department at the Foundation. The applicant must also submit proof of independent research work, documented by academic publications in recognized journals
Funding: Foundation
Contributor: Humboldt Foundation
Additional Information: The applicants need to choose their own research projects and their own German hosts

For further information contact:

Email: info@avh.de

Humboldt Research Fellowships for Experienced Researchers

Subjects: All subjects
Purpose: To enable researchers from abroad to carry out long-term research project of their own choice in cooperation with an academic host at a research institution in Germany

Eligibility: This programme targets outstanding academics who completed their doctorates less than 12 years ago and whose work demonstrates an independent academic profile. Typically, applicants should be working at least at the level of an assistant professor or junior research group leader, or as an independent researcher in a comparable position
Level of Study: Postdoctorate
Type: Fellowship
Value: €3,150 per month (includes a mobility lump sum and a contribution towards health and liability insurance as well as additional benefits)
Length of Study: 6–18 months; The fellowship is flexible and may be divided into as many as three stays in Germany within three years
Frequency: Annual
Study Establishment: Universities or research institutions
Country of Study: Germany
Application Procedure: Information regarding the application procedure is available at the website
Closing Date: Applications are accepted at any time
Funding: Government
Additional Information: Applications should be sent directly to the Foundation or through diplomatic or consular offices of the federal Republic of Germany in the candidates respective countries

For further information contact:

Email: hgs-grants@hu-berlin.de

Alexander von Humboldt Foundation United States of America

Alexander von Humboldt Foundation, 1012, 14th Street NW, Suite 1015, Washington, DC 20005, United States of America

Tel: (1) 202 783 1907
Fax: (1) 202 783 1908
Email: info@americanfriends-of-avh.org
Website: www.humboldt-foundation.de
Contact: The Grants Management Officer

The Alexander von Humboldt Foundation is a non-profit foundation established by the Federal Republic of Germany for the promotion of international cooperation in research. It enables highly qualified scholars not resident in Germany to spend extended periods of research in Germany and promotes the ensuring academic contacts. The Humboldt Foundation supports an active world-wide network of scholars; since 1953 it has sponsored over 20,000 scholars from 131 countries.

Alexander von Humboldt 'Bundeskanzler' Scholarships

Subjects: Unrestricted, but a background in the humanities, social sciences, law or economics is preferred
Purpose: To enable highly qualified young Americans in academia, business or politics to gain a substantial insight into German political, economic, social and cultural life in the course of an extended, self-structured stay
Eligibility: Candidates with demonstrated leadership qualities and excellence in their field should be nominated by United States university presidents. Nominees must be United States citizens and no more than 35 years of age
Level of Study: Research
Type: Scholarship
Value: Varies
Length of Study: 1 year
Frequency: Annual
Study Establishment: German universities or research institutions
Country of Study: Germany
Application Procedure: Applicants must write to the Alexander Von Humboldt Foundation, email: humboldt@umail.umd.edu or refer to the DAAD website for details and application material

For further information contact:

Alexander von Humboldt Foundation, US Liaison, 1055 Thomas Jefferson Street NW, Suite 2030, Washington, DC 20007, United States of America

Tel:	(1) 202 296 2990
Fax:	(1) 202 833 8514
Email:	humboldt@umail.edu
Contact:	Grants Management Officer

Alexander von Humboldt Research Fellowship Program

Subjects: All subjects
Purpose: To enable highly qualified scholars and scientists to carry out research projects of their own design in Germany
Eligibility: Open to highly qualified Scholars and scientists of any nationality, who hold a PhD and are not yet 35 years of age
Level of Study: Postdoctorate, Research
Type: Fellowship
Value: Varies
Frequency: Annual
Study Establishment: German universities or research institutions
Country of Study: Germany

Application Procedure: Applicants must write for details
Closing Date: Applications may be submitted at any time
Additional Information: Applications should be received at the Foundation in Bonn at least five months prior to the meeting at which they are reviewed. The panel meets in March, June or July and November

Contemporary German Literature Grant

Subjects: Research in contemporary German literature
Purpose: To aid faculty planning to work in the field
Eligibility: Open to suitably qualified Scholars of any nationality
Level of Study: Postgraduate
Type: Grant
Value: US$3,000
Length of Study: 3 months
Frequency: Annual
Study Establishment: The Max Cade Center for Contemporary German Literature at Washington University in St Louis
Country of Study: United States of America
Application Procedure: Applicants must write for details
Closing Date: 1 March
Additional Information: The Center is administered by the German Department in conjunction with the Olin Library at Washington University. Further information is available from the website

For further information contact:

Washington University in St. Louis, Campus Box 1104, One Brookings Drive, St. Louis, MO 63130-4899, United States of America

Tel:	(1) 314 935 4784
Fax:	(1) 314 935 7255
Email:	jahrbuch@artsci.wustl.edu
Contact:	Professor Paul Michael Lutzeler

Deutscher Akademischer Austauschdienst Graduate Scholarship for Research in Germany

Subjects: Any subject other than dentistry, medicine, pharmacy and veterinary medicine
Purpose: To support highly qualified graduate students, PhD candidates and postdoctoral researchers to undertake research in Germany
Eligibility: Applicants must have a well-defined project that makes a stay in Germany essential
Level of Study: Doctorate, Postdoctorate, Postgraduate
Type: Scholarship

Value: €795–975 per month
Length of Study: 1–10 months
Study Establishment: A university or research institute in Germany
Country of Study: Germany
Application Procedure: Applicants must download application forms and guidelines from the website
Closing Date: 1 November
Funding: Private

For further information contact:

Email: daadny@daad.org

Deutscher Akademischer Austauschdienst-American Institute for Contemporary German Studies Grant

Subjects: Postwar Germany
Eligibility: Open to PhD candidates, recent PhDs and junior faculty members
Level of Study: Doctorate, Postdoctorate
Type: Fellowship
Value: Funds for Summer residency
Frequency: Annual
Study Establishment: The American Institute for Contemporary German Studies (AICGS)
Country of Study: United States of America
Application Procedure: Applicants must write for details
Closing Date: 15 April

For further information contact:

AICGS, 1400 16th Street, Suite 420, Washington, DC 20036-2217, United States of America

Tel: (1) 202 332 9312
Fax: (1) 202 265 9531
Email: info@aicgs.org

Leo Baeck Institute-DAAD Grants

Subjects: The social, communal and intellectual history of German-speaking Jewry
Purpose: To assist students in their research
Eligibility: Open to American doctoral students and recent PhDs
Level of Study: Doctorate, Postdoctorate
Type: Fellowship
Value: Varies
Frequency: Annual
Study Establishment: The Leo Baeck Institute

Country of Study: United States of America or Germany
Application Procedure: Applicants must write for details
Closing Date: 1 November
Additional Information: Further information is available from the website

For further information contact:

The Leo Baeck Institute, 129 East 73rd Street, New York, NY, 10021, United States of America

Tel: (1) 212 744 6400
Fax: (1) 212 988 1305
Email: lbi1@lbi.com

National Science Foundation (National Science Foundation)-DAAD Grants for the Natural, Engineering and Social Sciences

Subjects: Natural, engineering and social sciences
Purpose: To provide support for scholars and scientists who wish to carry out joint research projects with colleagues at German universities and Fachhochschulen
Eligibility: For Scholars and scientists at United States universities as well as university affiliated research institutes
Type: Grant
Value: Support for travel and living expenses
Study Establishment: Universities and Fachhochschulen
Country of Study: Germany
Application Procedure: Applicants must visit the NSF website for further information
Closing Date: 15 June

For further information contact:

National Science Foundation, 4201 Wilson Boulevard, Arlington, VA 22203, United States of America

Tel: (1) 703 292 8705
Fax: (1) 703 292 9177
Email: info@daad-iran.org
Contact: Dr Mark A Suskin

Alfred L and Constance C Wolf Aviation Fund

2060 State Highway 595, Gavilan Community, Lindrith, NM 87029, United States of America

Tel: (1) 575 774 0029
Email: mail@wolf-aviation.org

Website: www.wolf-aviation.org
Contact: Rol Murrow, Executive Director

The Wolf Aviation Fund was established in the wills of Alfred L. and Constance C. Wolf. The Wolf Foundation hopes to help people and projects that benefit general aviation by identifying talented, worthy individuals - often working in collaboration with others - and worthwhile projects and providing them support.

Wolf Aviation Fund Grants Program

Subjects: Aviation
Purpose: To promote and support the advancement of personal air transportation by seeking and funding the most promising individuals and worthy projects which advance the field of general aviation
Level of Study: Postgraduate
Type: Grant
Value: Grants range in size from a few hundred dollars to a maximum of five thousand dollars
Frequency: Annual
Country of Study: Any country
Application Procedure: For more details please visit the website
Closing Date: 15 December
Additional Information: In preparing proposals, the foundation strongly encourages applicants to browse the Resources section and learn how to find out what kinds of grants might be available from any source and to learn in general how to properly prepare grant requests

For further information contact:

Email: mail@wolf-aviation.org

Alfred Toepfer Foundation

Georgsplatz 10, DEU-20099 Hamburg, Germany

Tel: (49) 4033 4020
Fax: (49) 4033 5860
Email: mail@toepfer-fvs.de
Website: www.toepfer-fvs.de

Alfred Toepfer Natural Heritage Scholarships

Subjects: Humanities, social sciences
Purpose: To provide scholarships for doctoral candidates from the humanities and the social sciences who are in the final stages of research on European issues
Eligibility: Candidates should be no older than 30 years and should be from Central and Eastern Europe: Albania, Armenia, Azerbaijan, Belarus, Bosnia-Herzegovina, Bulgaria, Croatia, Czech Republic, Estonia, Georgia, Hungary, Kosovo, Latvia, Lithuania, Macedonia, Moldavia, Poland, Romania, Russia, Slovakia, Slovenia, Ukraine. Applicants should have a good knowledge of German. Elaborated guidelines are available on the official website. www.europarc.org/wp-content/uploads/2019/02/Alfred-Toepfer-Scholarships_Guidelines2019.pdf
Level of Study: Doctorate
Type: Scholarship
Value: €3,000
Length of Study: Up to 1 year
Frequency: Annual
Country of Study: Germany
Application Procedure: Applications have to be submitted online. 1. Online application form– that includes your Curriculum vitae, your motivation letter, the proposed programme of your study visit, and contact details of protected areas you want to visit (download a pdf of the online application form). 2. Proof of employment
Closing Date: 4 May
Contributor: Alfred Toepfer Foundation
Additional Information: Available on www.toepfer-fvs.de

For further information contact:

Email: ericke@toepfer-fvs.de
Contact: Hèléne Ericke, Scholarship Programme Administrator

Max Brauer Award

Purpose: To honour personalities and institutions in the City of Hamburg for their services to the city's cultural, scientific, or intellectual life and for extraordinary impulses for the preservation of its architecture and architectural monuments, its city and landscape and renewal of the city, as well as its tradition and its customs
Type: Award
Value: €20,000
Frequency: Annual
Contributor: Alfred Toepfer Foundation in association with European school
Additional Information: The selection of the Preisträgerin and/or the winner is decided by the Kuratorium Max Brauer award

For further information contact:

Tel:	(49) 4033 402 16
Email:	luthe@toepfer-fvs.de
Contact:	Ricarda Luthe

Alzheimer's Australia

1 Frewin Place, Scullin, ACT 2614, Australia

Tel:	(61) 2 6254 4233
Fax:	(61) 2 6278 7225
Email:	secretariat@alzheimers.org.au, nat. admin@alzheimers.org.au
Website:	www.fightdementia.org.au
Contact:	Dr Mary Gray, Manager AADRF

Alzheimer's Australia Dementia Research Foundation (AADRF) was established as the research arm of Alzheimer's Australia to provide funds and disseminate into Alzheimer's disease and other forms of dementia. AADRF provides annual research grants and a key priority is to support emerging researchers and to encourage the next generation of dementia researchers.

Association of American Railroads Janssen Cilag Dementia Research Grant

Subjects: Behavioural and cognitive sciences, biological sciences or medical and health sciences
Purpose: To support research into Alzheimer's disease and other types of dementia
Eligibility: Open to citizens of Australia or permanent residents
Level of Study: Postgraduate, Research
Type: Scholarship
Value: Maximum A$20,000
Length of Study: 1 year
Frequency: Annual
Country of Study: Australia
Application Procedure: Check website for further details
Closing Date: 4 June
Contributor: Janssen Cilag Pty Ltd

For further information contact:

Alzheimer's Australia Research Ltd, PO Box 4019, Scullin, ACT 2614, Australia

Tel:	(61) 2 6254 4233
Email:	aar@alzheimers.org.au
Contact:	Anna Cohn

Association of American Railroads Rosemary Foundation Travel Project Grant-Dementia Research

Subjects: Behavioural and cognitive sciences, biological sciences, medical and health sciences or general science
Purpose: For undertaking research that is not fully available in Australia and is relevant to the advancement of understanding dementia
Eligibility: Open to citizens of Australia or permanent residents who have a degree in a discipline relevant to the field of dementia and be associated with an institute of higher learning
Level of Study: Postgraduate, Research
Type: Scholarship
Value: A$10,000
Length of Study: 6 weeks to 3 months
Frequency: Annual
Application Procedure: Check website for further details
Closing Date: 4 June
Additional Information: The applicant must undertake to return to a position in Australia for at least 1 year after the completion of the travel

For further information contact:

Email:	aar@alzheimers.org.au
Contact:	Anna Cohn

Hunter Postgraduate Scholarship

Subjects: Health sciences
Purpose: To support research in an area relevant to understanding the causes of Alzheimer's disease
Eligibility: Open to current or prospective students who are Australian citizens or permanent residents
Level of Study: Doctorate, Research
Type: Scholarship
Value: A$23,000 per year
Length of Study: 3 years
Frequency: Annual
Application Procedure: Check website for further details. Applications will be open from 1 September
Closing Date: 1 October

For further information contact:

Tel:	(61) 2 6254 7233
Email:	aar@alzheimers.org.au
Contact:	Anna Cohn

Rosemary Foundation Travel Grant

Subjects: Dementia-related fields

Purpose: To enable an Australian researcher to travel overseas in order to learn new techniques and/or network with international dementia research teams
Eligibility: Open to citizens of Australia or permanent residents and New Zealand citizens residing permanently in Australia
Level of Study: Doctorate, Postdoctorate, Postgraduate, Research
Type: Grant
Value: A$15,000
Length of Study: 1 month
Country of Study: Any country
No. of awards offered: 5
Application Procedure: Please check the website for details
Closing Date: Mid-April
Funding: Foundation
Contributor: The Rosemary Foundation for Memory Support Inc
No. of awards given last year: 1
No. of applicants last year: 5

For further information contact:

Email: Admin@RosaMary.org

Alzheimer's Drug Discovery Foundation (ADDF)

57 W 57th Street, Suit 904, New York, NY 10019, United States of America

Tel: (1) 212 901 8000
Fax: (1) 212 901 8010
Email: nthakker@alzdiscovery.org
Website: www.alzdiscovery.org
Contact: Mr Niyati Thakker, Grants Associate

The ADDF is an affiliated public charity of the Institute for the Study of Aging (ISOA), a private foundation founded by the Estè Lauder family in 1998.

Alzheimers Drug Discovery Foundation Grants Program

Subjects: Early identification, prevention and treatment of Alzheimer's disease and cognitive decline
Purpose: To promote the research and development of technology and therapies to identify, treat and prevent cognitive decline, Alzheimer's disease and related dementias
Eligibility: There are no eligibility restrictions
Level of Study: Unrestricted

Type: Grant
Value: Negotiable
Length of Study: 1–3 years
Frequency: Dependent on funds available
Study Establishment: A non-profit public foundation
Country of Study: Any country
Application Procedure: Candidates must submit a letter of intent through our online submission system at www.alzdiscovery.org
Closing Date: Letters of intent are accepted at any time. There are quarterly deadlines for full proposals
Funding: Government, Private, Foundation, Individuals
No. of awards given last year: 29
Additional Information: In addition to funding research activities, the foundation sponsors and/or co-sponsors conferences, scientific and medical workshops to advance knowledge on issues related to Alzheimer's disease and cognitive vitality

For further information contact:

Contact: Niyati Thakker, Grants Associate

America–Israel Cultural Foundation (AICF)

1140 Broadway, Suite #304, New York, NY 10001, United States of America

Tel: (1) 212 557 1600
Fax: (1) 212 557 1611
Email: info@aicf.co.il
Website: www.aicf.org
Contact: Mr David Homan, Executive Director

The America–Israel Cultural Foundation (AICF) has been promoting and supporting the arts in Israel for over 60 years. Through its Sharett Scholarship Program, the AICF grants hundreds of study scholarships each year to Israeli students of the arts, music, dance, visual arts, film, television and theatre, mainly for studies in Israel. The AICF also provides short-term fellowships to artists and art teachers and financially supports various projects in art schools, workshops, master classes, etc.

AICF Sharett Scholarship Program

Subjects: Performing arts, visual arts, design, film or television
Purpose: To respond to Israel's ever-evolving artistic life and the needs of her artists and institutions

Eligibility: Open to Israeli citizens only
Level of Study: Unrestricted
Type: Scholarship
Value: US$750–2,000
Length of Study: Varies
Frequency: Annual
Country of Study: Any country
No. of awards offered: 2,300
Application Procedure: Applicants must complete and submit an application form with recommendations and pre-required repertoire. Application forms are available from 1 February of each year
Closing Date: End of February
Funding: Private
Contributor: America—Israel Cultural Foundation
No. of awards given last year: 1,110
No. of applicants last year: 2,300
Additional Information: The programme is revised on an annual basis. For more detailed information, please contact the Foundation after 1 February

For further information contact:

Email: info@aicf.co.il

America-Norway Heritage Fund

Norwegian Information Service in the US, 825 Third Avenue 38th Floor, New York, NY 10022-7584, United States of America

Tel: (1) 212 421 7333
Fax: (1) 212 421 7333
Email: norcons@interport.net
Website: www.norway.org
Contact: Grants Management Officer

Norwegian Emigration Fund

Subjects: Emigration history and relations between the United States and Norway
Purpose: To award scholarships to Americans for advanced or specialised studies in Norway of subjects dealing with emigration history and relations between the United States and Norway
Eligibility: Open to citizens and residents of the United States. The fund may also give grants to institutions in the United States whose activities are primarily centred on the subjects mentioned
Level of Study: Graduate, Professional development

Type: Grant
Value: The individual grants last year were between NOK 5,000 and NOK 20,000
Country of Study: Norway
Application Procedure: Applicants must send applications to Nordmanns-Forbundet in envelopes that are clearly marked with 'Emigration Fund'
Closing Date: 15 February
Additional Information: Please see the website www.folkehogskole.no/undersider/engminnefond.html

For further information contact:

Nordmanns-Forbundet Råhusgtgata 23 B, N-0158056, Norway

Tel: (47) 2 335 7170
Fax: (47) 2 335 7175
Email: norseman@online.no

American Academy of Neurology (AAN)

IAC Foreign Scholarship Award Subcommittee, 1080 Montreal Avenue, St Paul, MN 55116, United States of America

Tel: (1) 612 695 1940
Fax: (1) 612 695 2791
Email: kjames@aan.com
Website: www.aan.com
Contact: Ms Kathleen James

A. B. Baker Award for Lifetime Achievement in Neurologic Education

Subjects: Neurology
Purpose: To provide funding for training in neuropharmacology
Eligibility: Nominee should exhibit lifetime career achievements in the field of neurologic education, with an emphasis on national accomplishments. Nominee should exhibit leadership, creativity, and scholarship. Nominee's neurological education activities should include significant current or past work in the AAN. Nominations should be inclusive in regards to gender and under-represented groups. Posthumous nominations will not be accepted
Level of Study: Postgraduate
Type: Other
Value: The Award will consist of a minimum commitment of two years
Frequency: Annual

Country of Study: Any country
Closing Date: 31 December
Funding: Private

For further information contact:

Tel: (1) 612 623 8115
Fax: (1) 612 623 3504
Email: bmcdonald@aan.com
Contact: Ms Kathleen James

American Academy of Pediatrics (AAP)

Division of Member Sections, 141 Northwest Point Boulevard, Elk Grove Village, IL 60007, United States of America

Tel: (1) 847 952 4926
Fax: (1) 847 434 8000
Email: membership@aap.org
Website: www.aap.org
Contact: Division Co-ordinator

The American Academy of Pediatrics (AAP) is an organisation of 55,000 primary care paediatricians, paediatric medical subspecialists and paediatric surgical specialists dedicated to the health, safety and well being of infants, children, adolescents and young adults.

American Academy of Pediatrics Resident Research Grants

Subjects: Paediatrics
Purpose: To enhance the development of research skills among physicians in paediatric training. Pediatric residents have an opportunity to initiate and completeprojects related to their professional interests through the AAP Resident Research Grant program
Eligibility: Open to paediatric residents in a training programme and have a definite commitment for another year of residency in a programme accredited by the Residency Review Committee for Paediatrics. Applicants must be United States or Canadian citizens or permanent residents. International medical graduates are eligible
Type: Research grant
Value: Up to US$2,000

Length of Study: Up to 2 years
Frequency: Annual
Country of Study: Any country
Application Procedure: Applications are sent automatically to AAP Residents and programme directors every year. Non members should write for details
Funding: Private

American Alpine Club (AAC)

710 Tenth Street, Suite 100, Golden, CO 80401, United States of America

Tel: (1) 303 384 0110
Fax: (1) 303 384 0111
Email: getinfo@americanalpineclub.org
Website: www.americanalpineclub.org
Contact: Janet Miller, Grants Administrator

The American Alpine Club (AAC) is a national non-profit organization that has represented mountaineers and rock climbers for almost a century. AAC has been the only national climbers' organization devoted to the exploration and scientific study of high mountain elevations and polar regions of the world, and the promotion and dissemination of knowledge about the mountains and mountaineering through its meetings, publications and libraries. It is also dedicated to the conservation and preservation of mountain regions and other climbing areas and the representation of the interests and concerns of the American climbing community.

American Alpine Club Research Grants

Subjects: Scientific research focusing on mountain and polar areas
Purpose: To recognize a specific contribution to scientific endeavour germane to mountain regions and alpine research projects
Eligibility: There are no restrictions on eligibility, but grants will not be awarded for academic tuition. Applications are considered in terms of their scientific or technical quality and the purposes for which the funds and the AAC are established
Level of Study: Postgraduate
Type: Research grant
Value: US$200–1,000
Frequency: Annual
Country of Study: Any country

Application Procedure: Applicants must call or write for application forms, which are also available from the website

Closing Date: 15 November

Funding: Private

Contributor: The Arthur K. Gilkey Memorial Research Fund, the R.L.Putnam Research Fund, and the Bedayn Research Fund

Additional Information: A report must be submitted upon completion of the project

For further information contact:

Email: grants@americanalpineclub.org

American Association for Cancer Research (AACR)

615 Chestnut Street, 17th Floor, Philadelphia, PA 19106-4404, United States of America

Tel: (1) 215 440 9300
Fax: (1) 215 440 9313
Email: aacr@aacr.org
Website: www.aacr.org
Contact: Ms Sheri Ozard, Program Co-ordinator

The American Association for Cancer Research (AACR) is a scientific society of over 17,000 laboratory and clinical cancer researchers. It was founded in 1907 to facilitate communication and dissemination of knowledge among scientists and others dedicated to the cancer problem, and to foster research in cancer and related biomedical sciences. It is also dedicated to encouraging the presentation and discussion of new and important observations in the field, fostering public education, science education and training, and advancing the understanding of cancer aetiology, prevention, diagnosis and treatment throughout the world.

American Association for Cancer Research Anna D. Barker Basic Cancer Research Fellowship

Subjects: This fellowship provides a one-year grant of US$50,000 to support the salary and benefits of the fellow while working on a mentored basic cancer research project. A partial amount of funds may be designated for non-personnel expenses, such as research/laboratory supplies, equipment, publication charges for manuscripts that pertain directly to the funded project, and other research expenses

Purpose: The AACR Anna D. Barker Basic Cancer Research Fellowship encourages and supports postdoctoral or clinical research fellows to establish a successful career path in cancer research. The research proposed for funding may be in any area of basic cancer research

Eligibility: Applicants must have a doctoral degree (including PhD, MD, DO, DC, ND, DDS, DVM, ScD, DNS, PharmD, or equivalent) in a related field and not currently be a candidate for a further doctoral degree. applicants must: 1. Hold a mentored research position with the title of postdoctoral fellow, clinical research fellow, or the equivalent. i. If eligibility is based on a future position, the position must be confirmed at the time of application and CANNOT be contingent upon receiving this grant. ii. If the future position is at a different institution than the applicant's current institution, the applicant must contact AACR's Scientific Review and Grants Administration Department (AACR's SRGA) at 28Tgrants@aacr.org 28T before submitting their application for information on additional verification materials/signatures that may be required. 2. Have completed their most recent doctoral degree within the past three years (i.e., degree cannot have been conferred before 1 July; the formal date of receipt of doctoral degree is the date the degree was conferred, as indicated on their diploma and/or transcript). i. Applicants with a medical degree must have completed their most recent doctoral degree or medical residency - whichever date is later - within the past three years. 3. Work under the auspices of a mentor at an academic, medical, or research institution anywhere in the world (There are no citizenship or geographic requirements. However, by submitting a Letter of Intent for this grant, an applicant applying from an institution located in a country in which they are not a citizen or a permanent resident assures that the visa status will provide sufficient time to complete the project and grant term at the institution from which they applied)

Level of Study: Postdoctorate

Type: Fellowship or Grant

Value: US$50,000

Length of Study: 1 year

Frequency: Dependent on funds available

Country of Study: Any country

Application Procedure: Please visit funding page for details at www.aacr.org/FUNDING/PAGES/DEFAULT.ASPX

Closing Date: Fall

Funding: Private, Foundation

Contributor: AACR

No. of awards given last year: 2

For further information contact:

Email: grants@aacr.org
Contact: Kyle Wolfe, Program Associate

American Association for Cancer Research Career Development Awards

Subjects: Colorectal cancer research
Purpose: To support cancer research by junior faculty
Eligibility: Applicants must have a doctoral degree (including PhD, MD, DO, DC, ND, DDS, DVM, ScD, DNS, PharmD, or equivalent doctoral degree, or a combined clinical and research doctoral degree) in a related field and not currently be a candidate for a further doctoral or professional degree
Level of Study: Postdoctorate, Research
Type: Award
Value: US$50,000 per year
Length of Study: 2 years
Frequency: Annual
Study Establishment: Universities or research institutions
Country of Study: Any country
No. of awards offered: 75
Application Procedure: Candidates must be nominated by a member of AACR and must be an AACR member or apply for membership by the time the application is submitted. Associate members may not be nominators. The online application is available at the AACR website. Please see the website for further details regarding eligibility at www.aacr.org/Uploads/DocumentRepository/Grants/2012_FCC_CDA_PG.rev.pdf
Closing Date: 1 February
Funding: Private
Contributor: The Cancer Research and Prevention Foundation, the Susan G Komen Breast Cancer Foundation, Genentech Inc., the Pancreatic Cancer Action Network
No. of awards given last year: 6
No. of applicants last year: 75

For further information contact:

Tel: (1) 215 446 7191
Fax: (1) 215 440 9372
Email: grants@aacr.org
Contact: Hanna Hopfinger, Program Associate

American Association for Cancer Research Gertrude B. Elion Cancer Research Award

Subjects: The award provides a one-year grant of US$75,000 for expenses related to the research project, which may include salary and benefits of the grant recipient, postdoctoral or clinical research fellows, graduate students (including tuition costs), and research assistants; research/laboratory supplies; equipment; travel; publication charges for manuscripts that pertain directly to the funded project; and other research expenses. The research proposed for funding must focus on research in cancer etiology, diagnosis, treatment, or prevention and may be basic, translational, or clinical in nature
Purpose: The AACR Gertrude B. Elion Cancer Research Award represents a joint effort to encourage and support tenure-eligible junior faculty
Eligibility: Applicants must have a doctoral degree (including PhD, MD, DO, DC, ND, DDS, DVM, ScD, DNS, PharmD, or equivalent) in a related field and not currently be a candidate for a further doctoral degree. At the start of the grant term on 1 July, applicants must: 1. Hold a tenure-eligible appointment (or equivalent, if institution does not follow a tenure system) at the rank of assistant professor (Appointments such as research assistant professor, adjunct assistant professor, assistant professor research track, visiting professor, or instructor are not eligible. Applicants cannot be tenured or under consideration for a tenured academic position at the time of the application. Applicants that have progressed to associate professor appointments are also not eligible). i. If eligibility is based on a future position, the position must be confirmed at the time of application, and CANNOT be contingent upon receiving this grant. ii. If the future position is at a different institution than the applicant's current institution, the applicant must contact AACR's Scientific Review and Grants Administration Department (AACR's SRGA) at grants@aacr.org before submitting their application for information on additional verification materials/signatures that may be required. 2. Have completed their most recent doctoral degree within the past 11 years (i.e., degree cannot have been conferred before 1 July; the formal date of receipt of doctoral degree is the date the degree was conferred, as indicated on their diploma and/or transcript). i. Applicants with a medical degree must have completed their most recent doctoral degree or medical residency (or equivalent) - whichever date is later - within the past 11 years. 3. Work at an academic, medical, or research institution anywhere in the world. (There are no citizenship or geographic requirements. However, by submitting an application for this grant, an applicant applying from an institution located in a country in which they are not a citizen or a permanent resident assures that the visa status will provide sufficient time to complete the project and grant term at the institution from which they applied)
Level of Study: Postdoctorate, Research
Type: Grant
Value: US$75,000
Length of Study: 1 year
Frequency: Annual
Study Establishment: Universities or research institutions
Country of Study: Any country
Closing Date: Late Summer or Fall
Funding: Private
Contributor: GlaxoSmithKline
No. of awards given last year: 1

For further information contact:

Email: grants@aacr.org
Contact: Kyle Wolfe, Program Associate

American Association for Cancer Research NextGen Grants for Transformative Cancer Research

Subjects: The grants provide US$4,50,000 over three years for expenses related to the research project, which may include salary and benefits of the grant recipient, postdoctoral or clinical research fellows, graduate students (including tuition costs), and research assistants, research/laboratory supplies, equipment, travel applicable to the research project, publication charges for manuscripts that pertain directly to the funded project, other research expenses, and indirect costs

Purpose: The AACR NextGen Grants for Transformative Cancer Research represent the AACR's flagship funding initiative to stimulate highly innovative research from young investigators. This grant mechanism is intended to promote and support creative, paradigm-shifting cancer research that may not be funded through conventional channels. It is expected that these grants will catalyze significant scientific discoveries and help talented young investigators gain scientific independence

Eligibility: Applicants must have a doctoral degree (including PhD, MD, DO, DC, ND, DDS, DVM, ScD, DNS, PharmD, or equivalent) in a related field and not currently be a candidate for a further doctoral degree. At the start of the grant term on 1 July, applicants must: 1. Hold a tenure-eligible appointment (or equivalent, if institution does not follow a tenure system) at the rank of assistant professor (appointments such as research assistant professor, adjunct assistant professor, assistant professor research track, visiting professor, or instructor are not eligible. Applicants that have progressed to associate professor appointments are also not eligible). i. If eligibility is based on a future position, the position must be confirmed at the time of submission, and CANNOT be contingent upon receiving this grant. ii. If the future position is at a different institution than the applicant's current institution, the applicant must contact AACR's Scientific Review and Grants Administration. Department (AACR's SRGA) at grants@aacr.org before submitting their Letter of Intent for information on additional verification materials/signatures that may be required. 2. Have held a tenure-eligible assistant professor appointment for no more than three years (i.e., cannot have held a tenure-eligible appointment prior to 1 July). 3. Work at an academic, medical, or research institution anywhere in the world (there are no citizenship or geographic requirements. However, by submitting a Letter of Intent for this grant, an applicant applying

from an institution located in a country in which they are not a citizen or a permanent resident assures that their visa status will provide sufficient time to complete the project and grant term at the institution from which they applied)

Level of Study: Postdoctorate
Type: Grant
Value: US$4,50,000
Length of Study: 3 years
Frequency: Dependent on funds available
Country of Study: Any country
Application Procedure: Please visit our funding page for details: www.aacr.org/FUNDING/PAGES/DEFAULT.ASPX
Closing Date: Fall
Funding: Private, Foundation
Contributor: AACR
No. of awards given last year: 2

For further information contact:

Email: grants@aacr.org
Contact: Kyle Wolfe, Program Associate

American Association for Cancer Research-AstraZeneca Stimulating Therapeutic Advancements through Research Training (START) Grants

Subjects: Each fellowship provides a three-year grant of US$2,25,000 to support the salary and benefits of the fellow while working on a mentored cancer research project. Applicants must plan to spend one year on site at an AstraZeneca facility. One of a number of AstraZeneca's locations are possible, at the discretion of AstraZeneca. The year at AstraZeneca will be determined on a case-by-case basis, and will be at a time agreed upon by the fellow, the academic supervisor, the AstraZeneca mentor, and AstraZeneca. The research proposed for funding must have direct applicability to cancer with a specific focus on DNA Damage Response (DDR) pathways and may be basic, translational, or clinical in nature. Any proposals that address topics unrelated to DNA Damage Response pathways in cancer will NOT be accepted

Purpose: Dramatic advances made in recent years towards precision medicine initiatives, biomarker and novel target identification, and high-throughput examination of genomic data, have resulted in a trove of valuable data that can inform the development of new therapeutics to combat cancer. However, to effectively harness this wealth of information and advance the discovery and development of new therapies for cancer patients, enhanced collaboration between academia and industry will be needed. The AACR-AstraZeneca

Stimulating Therapeutic Advancements through Research Training (START) Grants represent an exciting new initiative to encourage and support such collaboration. This novel model, which will provide support to postdoctoral or clinical research fellows, combines research experiences in both an academic and industry setting, following a research timeline that will be of greatest benefit to the proposed work. The training provided through this grant program will be invaluable to young investigators, by allowing fellows to attain a comprehensive research experience that will make them highly desirable to potential employers in either academic research or the pharmaceutical industry. Likewise, academic research centers and industry will benefit from the introduction of such dual-trained individuals into the field

Eligibility: APPLICANT ELIGIBILITY CRITERIA Applicants must have a doctoral degree (including PhD, MD, DO, DC, ND, DDS, DVM, ScD, DNS, PharmD, or equivalent) in a related field and not currently be a candidate for a further doctoral degree. At the start of the grant term on 1 July, applicants must: 1. Hold a full-time, mentored research position with the title of postdoctoral fellow, clinical research fellow, or the equivalent; this position must have been held for at least one, but not more than three, years. i. If eligibility is based on a future position, the position must be confirmed at the time of application, and CANNOT be contingent upon receiving this grant. ii. If the future position is at a different institution than the applicant's current institution, the applicant must contact AACR's Scientific Review and Grants AdministrationDepartment (AACR's SRGA) at grants@aacr.org before submitting their application forinformation on additional verification materials/signatures that may be required. 2. Have completed their most recent doctoral degree within the past one to three years (i.e., degree cannot have been conferred before 1 July; the formal date of receipt ofdoctoral degree is the date the degree was conferred, as indicated on their diploma and/ortranscript). i. Applicants with a medical degree must have completed their most recent doctoraldegree or medical residency - whichever date is later - within the past three years. 3. Work under the auspices of a mentor at an academic, medical, or research institution in the United States of America (there are no citizenship requirements. However, by submitting an application for this grant, the applicant who is not a United States citizen or a permanent resident assures that the visa status will provide sufficient time to complete the project and grant term)

Level of Study: Postdoctorate
Type: Fellowship or Grant
Value: US$225,000
Length of Study: 3 years
Frequency: Dependent on funds available
Country of Study: United States of America

Application Procedure: Please visit funding page for details at www.aacr.org/FUNDING/PAGES/DEFAULT.ASPX
Closing Date: Fall
Funding: Private
Contributor: AstraZeneca
No. of awards given last year: 2

For further information contact:

Email: grants@aacr.org
Contact: Kyle Wolfe, Program Associate

QuadW Foundation-AACR Fellowship for Clinical/Translational Sarcoma Research

Subjects: The fellowship provides a one-year grant of US$55,000 to support the salary and benefits of the fellow while working on a mentored sarcoma research project. A partial amount of funds may be designated for non-personnel expenses, such as research/laboratory supplies, equipment, publication charges for manuscripts that pertain directly to the funded project, and other research expenses

Purpose: The QuadW Foundation-AACR Fellowship for Clinical/Translational Sarcoma Research represents a joint effort to encourage and support a postdoctoral or clinical research fellow to conduct translational or clinical sarcoma research and to establish a successful career path in this field

Eligibility: Applicants must have a doctoral degree (including PhD, MD, DO, DC, ND, DDS, DVM, ScD, DNS, PharmD, or equivalent) in a related field and not currently be a candidate for a further doctoral degree. At the start of the grant term on 1 July, applicants must: 1. Hold a mentored research position with the title of postdoctoral fellow, clinical research fellow, or the equivalent. i. If eligibility is based on a future position, the position must be confirmed at the time of application and CANNOT be contingent upon receiving this grant. ii. If the future position is at a different institution than the applicant's current institution, the applicant must contact AACR's Scientific Review and Grants Administration Department (AACR's SRGA) at grants@aacr.org before submitting their application for information on additional verification materials/signatures that may be required. 2. Have completed their most recent doctoral degree within the past five years (i.e., degree cannot have been conferred before 1 July; the formal date of receipt of doctoral degree is the date the degree was conferred, as indicated on your diploma and/or transcript). i. Applicants with a medical degree must have completed their most recent doctoral degree or medical residency - whichever date is later - within the past five years. 3. Work under the auspices of a mentor at an academic, medical, or research institution anywhere in the world. (There are no citizenship or geographic requirements. However, by submitting an application for this grant, an applicant applying from an institution located in a country in which they are not a citizen or a permanent resident assures that the visa status will provide sufficient time to complete the project and grant term at the institution from which they applied)

Level of Study: Postdoctorate
Type: Fellowship or Grant
Value: US$55,000
Length of Study: 1 year
Frequency: Dependent on funds available
Country of Study: Any country
Application Procedure: Please visit our funding page for details www.aacr.org/FUNDING/PAGES/DEFAULT.ASPX
Closing Date: Fall
Funding: Private, Foundation
Contributor: QuadW Foundation
No. of awards given last year: 1

For further information contact:

Email: grants@aacr.org
Contact: Kyle Wolfe, Program Associate

American Association for the History of Nursing (AAHN)

PO Box 175, Lanoka Harbor, NJ 08734, United States of America

Tel: (1) 609 693 7250
Fax: (1) 609 693 1037
Email: aahn@aahn.org
Website: www.aahn.org
Contact: Executive Secretary

The American Association for the History of Nursing (AAHN) is a professional organization accessible to everyone interested in the history of nursing. Originally founded in 1978 as a historical methodology group, the Association was briefly named the International History of Nursing Society. The Association's purpose is to foster the importance of history in understanding the present and guiding the future of nursing.

H 15 GRANT

Purpose: The H-15 Grant is awarded to faculty members or independent researchers for proposals outlining a historical research study
Eligibility: Applicants must be AAHN members and hold the doctorate
Level of Study: Doctorate
Type: Award/Grant
Value: US$3,000
Frequency: Annual
Country of Study: Any country
Application Procedure: A copy of the proposal should be sent by email to grants@aahn.org. Only word or pdf documents will be accepted. The application should not exceed 6 pages double-spaced, excluding references, curriculum vitae and writing sample. The outline below specifies the information which should be included in your application. The form and length of your application should be adapted to the research that you propose to do
Closing Date: 1 April
Funding: Private
No. of awards given last year: 1

For further information contact:

Email: aahn@aahn.org

H 31 Pre-Doctoral Grant

Subjects: Proposals will focus on a significant question in the history of nursing
Purpose: This grant is designed to encourage and support graduate training and historical research at the Masters and Doctoral levels. The grant will be US$2,000
Eligibility: Eligibility Criteria; 1. Proposals will focus on a significant question in the history of nursing. 2. The student will be enrolled in an accredited masters program or doctoral program. 3. The student will be a member of AAHN. 4. The research advisor will be doctorally prepared with scholarly activity in the field of nursing history and prior experience in guidance of research training
Level of Study: Doctorate
Type: Award/Grant
Value: US$2,000
Frequency: Annual
Country of Study: Any country
Application Procedure: Application: Form 1. Title Page. 2. Narrative (four [4] double-spaced pages, maximum). Include the following: 1. Central thesis or questions of the

study. 2. Explanation of your approach to the study, identifying pertinent secondary sources and primary sources critical to the project. 3. Any additional relevant facilities and resources. 4. Significance of the study. Attachments 1. Applicant's curriculum vitae, including education and any research publications and presentations relevant to the proposed project. 2. Letter of support from advisor. 3. Budget: Outline and itemize the budget detailing the ways you will use the award and briefly justify each item. For example: travel, purchase of equipment, copying. A copy of the proposal should be sent by email to grants@aahn.org. Only word or pdf documents will be accepted

Closing Date: 1 April
Funding: Private

For further information contact:

Email: aahn@aahn.org

H-21

Subjects: Proposals for a new historical research study in the history of nursing
Purpose: The Eleanor Crowder Bjoring Research (H-21) Grant is awarded to senior scholars (faculty members or independent researchers) for proposals outlining a new historical research study. The grant provides US$3,000 in funding. For faculty members affiliated with an academic institution, indirect costs for Facilities and Administration (F & A) of 8% are also available. Applicants must be AAHN members, hold a research doctorate, and be the author of a published book in the field of history that is based on original research. It is expected that the research and new materials produced by the grant recipient will help ensure the growth of scholarly work focused on the history of nursing
Eligibility: 1. Proposals for a new historical research study in the history of nursing. 2. The scholar will be a faculty member or independent researcher who holds a research doctorate. 3. The scholar will be the author of a published book in the field of history based on original research
Level of Study: Doctorate
Type: Award/Grant
Value: US$3,000
Frequency: Annual
Country of Study: Any country
Application Procedure: A copy of the proposal should be sent by email to grants@aahn.org. Only word or pdf documents will be accepted. The application should not exceed 6 pages double-spaced, excluding references, curriculum vitae and writing sample. The outline below specifies the

information which should be included in your application. The form and length of your application should be adapted to the research that you propose to do
Closing Date: 1 April
Funding: Private

For further information contact:

Email: aahn@aahn.org

American Association for Women Radiologists (AAWR)

1891 Preston White Drive, Reston, VA 20191, United States of America

Tel:	(1) 713 965 0566
Fax:	(1) 713 960 0488
Email:	admin@aawr.org
Website:	www.aawr.org

The Association was founded in 1981 to provide a forum for issues unique to women in radiology, radiation oncology and related professions; sponsor programs that promote opportunities for women; and facilitate networking among members and other professionals.

Alice Ettinger Distinguished Achievement Award

Subjects: Radiology
Purpose: To recognize long-term contribution to radiology and to the American Association for Women Radiologists
Eligibility: Open to AAWR members only
Level of Study: Unrestricted
Type: Award
Value: Plaque
Frequency: Annual
Country of Study: Any country
Application Procedure: Candidates must submit a current curriculum vitae and letters of support
Closing Date: 30 June
Contributor: Membership dues

For further information contact:

Email: admin@aawr.org

Lucy Frank Squire Distinguished Resident Award in Diagnostic Radiology

Subjects: Radiology
Purpose: To honor a resident diagnostic radiologist on the basis of outstanding contributions to clinical care, teaching, research and/or public service
Eligibility: Open to candidates in the field of diagnostic radiology who are members of the AAWR as of 1 January of the year of the award
Level of Study: Unrestricted
Type: Award
Value: Plaque
Frequency: Annual
Country of Study: Any country
Application Procedure: Candidates must submit an application including a curriculum vitae, a letter of nomination and a letter of concurrence
Closing Date: 30 June
Contributor: Membership dues
Additional Information: Nominees will be evaluated on the basis of outstanding contributions in clinical care, teaching, research, or public service

For further information contact:

Email: info@aawr.org

American Association of Critical-Care Nurses (AACN)

101 Columbia, Aliso Viejo, CA 92656-4109, United States of America

Tel: (1) 800 899 2226
Fax: (1) 949 362 2020
Email: info@aacn.org
Website: www.aacn.org
Contact: Research Department

The American Association of Critical-Care Nurses (AACN) is the world's largest nursing speciality organization with approx. 68,000 members worldwide. The AACN is committed to providing the highest quality resources to maximize nurses' contributions to caring and improving the healthcare of critically ill patients and their families.

Agilent Technologies - AACN Critical-Care Nursing Research Grant

Subjects: Preferred topics will address the information technology requirements of patient management in critical care
Purpose: To fund research for study conducted by a critical care nurse
Eligibility: Principal investigators must be nurses holding current AACN membership. Investigators who have received funding from the AACN are ineligible to receive additional funding during the lifetime of their original award. They may apply for a new award when their original award obligations have been met
Level of Study: Research
Type: Grant
Value: US$35,000, providing US$33,000 for the research study and US$2,000 for travel expenses associated with presentations of the study findings
Country of Study: Any country
Application Procedure: Applicants must submit a completed application form and supporting materials. Details and forms are available directly from the organisation or from the website
Closing Date: 1 September
Contributor: Hewlett-Packard, Inc

American Nurses Foundation Research Grant Program

Subjects: Clinical research
Purpose: To encourage the research career development of nurses
Eligibility: Principal investigators must be nurses holding current AACN membership. Investigators who have received funding from the AACN are ineligible to receive additional funding during the lifetime of their original award. They may apply for a new award when their original award obligations have been met
Level of Study: Research
Type: Research grant
Value: Up to US$5,000 is awarded by the American Nurses Foundation
Application Procedure: Applicants must obtain information and application forms from the American Nurses Foundation, and should see the website for further details
Closing Date: 1 May
Contributor: The AACN

For further information contact:

The American Nurses Foundation, 600 Maryland Avenue SW, Suite 100W, Washington DC 20024, United States of America

Tel: (1) 202 651 7298
Email: anf@ana.org

American Association of Family and Consumer Sciences (AAFCS)

400 N. Columbus Street, Suite 202, Alexandria, VA 22314-2752, United States of America

Tel: (1) 703 706 4600
Fax: (1) 703 706 4663
Email: cislamd@aafcs.org
Website: www.aafcs.org
Contact: Ms Amy Campbell, Grants Management Officer

Founded in 1909 as the American Home Economics Association, the American Association of Family and Consumer Sciences (AAFCS) is an organisation of members dedicated to improving the quality of individual and family life through programs that educate, influence public policy, disseminate information and publish research findings. Representing nearly 16,000 professionals in the family and consumer sciences, AAFCS members include elementary, secondary and post secondary educators and administrators, co-operative extension agents and other professionals in government, business and non-profit sectors.

American Association of Family and Consumer Sciences National Fellowships in Family and Consumer Sciences

Subjects: Family and consumer sciences
Purpose: To support a student pursuing study in family and consumer sciences at the graduate level
Eligibility: Applicants must be current members of the AAFCS
Level of Study: Doctorate, Graduate, Postgraduate
Type: Fellowship
Value: US$3,000–5,000
Frequency: Annual
Country of Study: United States of America
Application Procedure: Applicants must apply using official AAFCS application forms. Seven copies of the completed application must be submitted. All requests for fellowship application materials must be accompanied by a fee of US$25 (non refundable)

Closing Date: 31 December
Additional Information: awards@aafcs.org

American Association of Family and Consumer Sciences New Achievers Award

Subjects: Family and consumer sciences
Purpose: The programme was developed to recognise emerging professionals who have exhibited the potential for making significant contributions in or through family and consumer sciences
Eligibility: Any living family and consumer sciences professional who is 35 years of age or younger or who has a least three years service in the field, but no more than eight years of service to the field, and is an active member of AAFCS is eligible for consideration by a nominating group
Type: Award
Value: A desk plaque and commemorative pin
Frequency: Annual
Country of Study: Any country
Application Procedure: One nomination will be accepted from each nominating group. Eligible nominating groups include the AAFCS affiliates, sections and divisions, the Higher Education Unit, and the Past president Unit
Closing Date: Postmark deadline for submission of nominations is 15 January

Jewell L Taylor Fellowship

Subjects: Family and consumer sciences
Purpose: To support a student pursuing a degree in family and consumer sciences
Eligibility: Open only to United States citizens
Level of Study: Postgraduate
Type: Fellowship
Value: US$5,000
Frequency: Annual
Country of Study: United States of America
Application Procedure: Application must be made using official AAFCS application forms. Seven (7) copies of the completed application must be submitted. There is an application fee of US$15 for AAFCS members, US$30 for non members
Closing Date: 31 December
Funding: Private

Ruth O Brian Project Grant

Subjects: Home economics
Eligibility: Open to suitably qualified individuals of any nationality
Level of Study: Graduate, Postgraduate

Type: Project grant
Value: Up to US$5,000
Country of Study: Any country
Application Procedure: Applicants must write for details
Closing Date: 14 January

For further information contact:

Email: robrien@gc.cuny.edu

American Association of Law Libraries (AALL)

105 W. Adams Street, Suite 3300, Chicago, IL 60603, United States of America

Tel: (1) 312 939 4764
Fax: (1) 312 431 1097
Email: scholarships@aall.org
Website: www.aallnet.org

The American Association of Law Libraries (AALL) was founded in 1906 to promote and enhance the value of law libraries to legal and public communities, to foster the profession of law librarianship and to provide leadership in the field of legal information. Today, the AALL represents law librarians and related professionals who are affiliated with a wide range of institutions including law firms, law schools, corporate legal departments and courts, and local, state and federal government agencies.

American Association of Law Libraries James F Connolly LexisNexis Academic and Library Solutions Scholarship

Subjects: Law librarianship
Eligibility: Awarded to library school graduates with law library experience who are presently attending an accredited law school with the intention of pursuing a career as a law librarian. Preference will be given to individuals who have demonstrated an interest in government documents
Level of Study: Graduate
Type: Scholarship
Value: Up to US$3,000 for tuition and school-related expenses
Frequency: Annual
Study Establishment: ABA-accredited Law Schools
Country of Study: Any country

Application Procedure: Applicants must write for details or download an application form from the website
Closing Date: 1 April

For further information contact:

53 West Jackson Boulevard, Suite 940, United States of America

Email: scholarships@csulb.edu

American Association of Law Libraries LexisNexis/John R Johnson Memorial Scholarship Endowment

Subjects: Law librarianship
Eligibility: Candidates who apply for AALL educational scholarships, types I–IV, become automatically eligible to receive the LexisNexis/John R Johnson Memorial Scholarship
Level of Study: Graduate
Type: Scholarship
Value: Up to US$2,000 for tuition and school-related expenses
Frequency: Annual
Study Establishment: ALA-accredited library schools or ABA-Accredited Law Schools
Country of Study: Any country
Application Procedure: Applicants must write for details or download an application form from the website
Closing Date: 1 April

For further information contact:

Email: scholarships@aall.org

American Association of Law Libraries Scholarship (Type II)

Subjects: Law
Purpose: Candidates should apply for more than one scholarship when appropriate
Eligibility: Open to library school graduates working towards a degree in an accredited law school who have no more than 36 semester credit hours remaining before qualifying for the law degree, who have law library experience and who have the intention of pursuing a career as a law librarian. Preference is given to members of the AALL
Level of Study: Graduate
Value: Up to US$2,000 for tuition and school-related expenses
Frequency: Annual
Study Establishment: ABA-accredited law schools

Country of Study: Any country
Application Procedure: Applicants must write for details or download an application form from the website
Closing Date: 1 April

For further information contact:

Email: scholarships@aall.org

American Association of Neurological Surgeons (AANS)

5550 Meadowbrook Drive, Rolling Meadows, IL 60008-3852, United States of America

Tel:	(1) 847 378 0500
Fax:	(1) 847 378 0600
Email:	info@aans.org
Website:	www.aans.org
Contact:	Julie Qattrocchi, Development Coordinator

Founded in 1931 as the Harvey Cushing Society, the American Association of Neurological Surgeons (AANS) is a scientific and educational association with more than 6,500 members worldwide. The AANS is dedicated to advancing the specialty of neurological surgery in order to provide the highest quality of neurosurgical care to the public. All active members of the AANS are certified by the American Board of Neurological Surgery, The Royal College of Physicians and Surgeons (Neurosurgery) of Canada or the Mexican Council of Neurological Surgery, AC. Neurological surgery is the medical specialty concerned with the prevention, diagnosis, treatment and rehabilitation of disorders that affect the entire nervous system including the spinal column, spinal cord, brain and peripheral nerves.

Neurosurgery Research and Education Foundation Research Fellowship

Subjects: Any field of neurosurgery
Purpose: To provide training for neurosurgeons who are preparing for academic careers as clinician investigators
Eligibility: Open to MDs who have been accepted into, or who are in, an approved residency training programme in neurological surgery in North America
Level of Study: Postdoctorate
Type: Fellowship
Value: US$40,000 for a 1-year fellowship
Length of Study: 1–2 years

Frequency: Annual
Country of Study: Other
No. of awards offered: 25
Application Procedure: Applicants must send a completed application, sponsor statement, programme director comments and letters of recommendation. Responses to questions 1–9, a curriculum vitae and photographic images must also be submitted. Applications are available at the website www.aans.org
Closing Date: 31 October
Funding: Private
Contributor: Corporations and membership
No. of awards given last year: 5
No. of applicants last year: 25
Additional Information: Notification of awards will be made by 28 February. After notification of the award, the applicant must indicate acceptance, in writing, no later than 1 April. If unwilling to accept the award by that date, funds will be awarded to the first runner-up. A report of findings and accounting of funds will be expected at the halfway point and upon completion of the fellowship. Normally, no more than one award per year will be made to any one institution. Individuals who accept a grant from another source, NIH or private, for the same research project will become ineligible for the award. A budget must be prepared by the applicant and the sponsor indicating how the grant funds will be expended. It is the policy of the NREF to fund only direct costs involved with the research awards. This means no fringe benefits, publication costs or travel expenses. The signature representing the applicant's institution's financial officer on page four should be that of their chief financial officer or grants and contracts manager. The award will be made payable to the institution and disbursed by it according to its institutional policy

For further information contact:

Email: nref@aans.org

Neurosurgery Research and Education Foundation Young Clinician Investigator Award

Subjects: Any field of neurosurgery
Purpose: To fund pilot studies that provide preliminary data used to strengthen applications for more permanent funding from other sources
Eligibility: Candidates must be neurosurgeons who are full-time faculty in teaching institutions in North America and in the early years of their careers
Level of Study: Postdoctorate
Type: Award
Value: 1-year research project grant of US$40,000

Length of Study: 1 year
Frequency: Annual
No. of awards offered: 20
Application Procedure: Candidates must send a completed application, sponsor statement, programme director comments and letters of recommendation. Responses to questions 1–9, a curriculum vitae and photographic images must also be submitted. Applications are available at the website www. aans.org
Closing Date: 31 October
Funding: Private
Contributor: Corporations and membership
No. of awards given last year: 3
No. of applicants last year: 20
Additional Information: Notification of awards will be made by 28 February. After notification of the award, the applicant must indicate acceptance, in writing, no later than 1 April. If unwilling to accept the award by that date, funds will be awarded to the first runner-up. A summary report and an accounting of funds will be expected upon completion of the award. Normally, no more than one award per year will be made to any one institution. Individuals who accept a grant from another source, NIH or private, for the same research project will become ineligible for the award. The award is for those budget items necessary to pursue proper research. It may be used entirely, or in part, for stipend. A budget must be prepared by the applicant and sponsor indicating how the award funds will be expended. It is the policy of the NREF to fund only direct costs involved with the research awards. This means no fringe benefits, publication costs or travel expenses

For further information contact:

Email: NREF@aans.org

William P Van Wagenen Fellowship

Subjects: Any field of neurosurgery
Purpose: To fund quality research in which the plan for a period abroad has been designed
Eligibility: All senior neurological residents in approved neurosurgery residency programs
Level of Study: Postdoctorate
Type: Travelling fellowship
Value: US$120,000 stipend for living and travel expenses to a foreign country for a period of 12 months. A family travel and living allowance of US$6,000 is available if spouse and/or children are accompanying the Fellow. In addition, US$15,000 of research support is available to the University, hospital or laboratory, which has agreed to sponsor the Van Wagenen Fellow. If needed, US$5,000 is available for medical insurance

Length of Study: 6–12 months
Frequency: Annual
Country of Study: Country of study must be different than the country of residence
No. of awards offered: 6
Application Procedure: Application should be submitted with letters of reference, including one from the applicant's Program Director. A letter from the proposed sponsor and documentation of intent to pursue an academic career, while not required, will strengthen the application
Closing Date: 1 October
Funding: Private
Contributor: William P Van Wagenen
No. of awards given last year: 1
No. of applicants last year: 6
Additional Information: By 31 December, the Chairman of the Van Wagenen Selection Committee will notify the winning applicant, who will be expected to implement the fellowship within 6 months following notification. A formal announcement of the award will be made at the Annual Meeting of the AANS. Applications and additional information regarding the William P Van Wagenen Fellowship can be located at www.aans.org

For further information contact:

Tel: (1) 847 378 0500
Email: nref@aans.org

American Association of University Women Educational Foundation

1111 16 Street North West, Washington, DC 20036, United States of America

Tel: (1) 202 785 7700
Fax: (1) 202 463 7169
Email: fellowships@aauw.org
Website: www.aauw.org
Contact: Gloria Blackwell, Director of Fellowship

The AAUW Educational Foundation is composed of three corporations. These are the Association, a 150,000 member organization with more than 1,500 branches nationwide that lobbies and advocates for education and equity; the AAUW Educational Foundation, which funds pioneering research on girls and education, community action projects, and fellowships and grants for outstanding women around the globe; and the AAUW Legal Advocacy Fund, which provides funds and a support system for women seeking judicial redress for sexual discrimination in higher education.

American Association of University Women Career Development Grants

Purpose: To support women who hold a bachelor's degree and are preparing to advance their careers, change careers, or re-enter the work force
Eligibility: Primary consideration is given to women of color and women pursuing their first advanced degree or credentials in nontraditional fields
Level of Study: Graduate, Postgraduate
Type: Grant
Value: US$2,000–12,000 (Funds are available for tuition, fees, books, supplies, local transportation, and dependent care.)
Length of Study: 1 year
Frequency: Annual
Closing Date: 15 December
No. of awards given last year: 47
Additional Information: Materials sent to the Washington, DC office will be disqualified and will not be reviewed

For further information contact:

ACT, Inc., 101 ACT Dr., Iowa City, IA 52243, United States of America

Tel: (1) 319 337 1716 ext. 60
Email: aauw@act.org

American Association of University Women Case Support Travel Grants

Subjects: All subjects
Purpose: To enable Legal Advocacy Fund-supported plaintiffs, their lawyers, and related experts to speak at state meetings or conventions about LAF-supported cases, sex discrimination issues in the workplace and higher education, and the work of LAF
Eligibility: Please see website for conditions
Level of Study: Postgraduate, Research
Type: Grant
Value: The grant covers the speaker's travel, lodging, and meal expenses
Frequency: Annual
Application Procedure: Apply online
Closing Date: 15 October
Additional Information: Please note that materials sent to the Washington, DC office will be disqualified and will not be reviewed

For further information contact:

Fax: (1) 202 463 7169
Email: laf@aauw.org

American Association of University Women Community Action Grants

Subjects: All subjects
Purpose: To provide seed money to individual women, local community-based non-profit organizations, AAUW branches and AAUW state organizations for innovative programmes or non-degree research projects that engage girls in mathematics, science and technology
Eligibility: Applicants must be women who are citizens or permanent residents of the United States of America. Special consideration will be given to AAUW members and AAUW branch and state applicants who seek partners for collaborative projects. Collaborators can include local schools or school districts, businesses and other community-based organizations. 2-year grants are restricted to projects focused on girls' achievement in mathematics, science or technology. Projects must involve community and school collaboration. The fund supports planning and coalition-building activities during the 1st year and implementation and evaluation the following year
Type: Grant
Value: US$2,000–7,000 (1-year grant); US$5,000–10,000 (2-year grant)
Length of Study: 1 or 2 years
Frequency: Annual
Application Procedure: Applicants must write for an application form, which is also available from the website
Closing Date: 15 January
Funding: Private
Additional Information: Please note that materials sent to the Washington, DC office will be disqualified and will not be reviewed. Two types of grant are available: 1-year grants are for short-term projects. Topic areas are unrestricted but should have a clearly defined educational activity; 2-year grants are for longer term programmes and are restricted to projects focused on K-12 girls achievement in mathematics, science and/or technology. Funds support planning activities and coalition-building during the 1st year and implementation and evaluation the following year

For further information contact:

Tel: (1) 319 337 1716 ext. 60
Email: aauw@act.org

American Association of University Women Eleanor Roosevelt Fund Award

Subjects: Equity and education
Purpose: To remove barriers to women's and girls' participation in education; to promote the value of diversity and cross-cultural communication; and to develop greater understanding of the ways women learn, think, work, and play
Eligibility: To be eligible for the award, projects or activities must take place within the United States and recipients or organizational representatives must reside in the United States at the time the award is given. AAUA programs are not eligible for this award
Level of Study: Professional development
Type: Award
Value: US$5,000 plus travel expenses to attend the AAUW National Convention
Frequency: Every 2 years
Application Procedure: Please see the website for details
Closing Date: 1 August
Funding: Private, Individuals
No. of awards given last year: 1

For further information contact:

Tel: (1) 202 728 3300
Email: fellowships@aauw.org

American Association of University Women International Fellowships

Subjects: All subjects
Purpose: To support full-time study or research to women who are not United States citizen or permanent residents
Eligibility: Open to women who are not citizens of the United States of America or permanent residents, who hold a United States of America Bachelor's degree or equivalent. Applicants must be planning to return to their home country upon completion of degree and/or research. English proficiency is required
Level of Study: Doctorate, Postdoctorate, Postgraduate, Professional development, MBA
Type: Fellowship
Value: US$18,000 (Master's/First Professional Degree Fellowship); US$20,000 (Doctoral Fellowship); US$30,000 (Postdoctoral Fellowship)
Length of Study: 1 year
Frequency: Annual
Study Establishment: Any accredited institution
Country of Study: United States of America
No. of awards offered: 1,194
Application Procedure: Applicants must complete an application for each year applying. Applications must be obtained from the customer service centre or the AAUW website between 1 August and 15 December. Three letters of recommendation, transcripts and a minimum score of 550 on the Test of English as a Foreign Language (213 computer-based) are also required. Order for brochure at www.act.org/aauw/brochurerequest.html
Closing Date: 1 December
Funding: Foundation
No. of awards given last year: 36
No. of applicants last year: 1,194
Additional Information: Please note that materials sent to the Washington, DC office will be disqualified and will not be reviewed

For further information contact:

Tel: (1) 319 337 1716 ext. 60
Email: aauw@act.org

American Association of University Women Selected Professions Fellowships

Subjects: Architecture, computer/information sciences, engineering, mathematics/statistics, business administration, law and medicine
Purpose: To support women who intend to pursue a full-time course of study at accredited institutions during the fellowship year in one of the designated degree programs where women's participation has been low
Eligibility: Women candidates who intend to pursue a full-time course of study at accredited United States institutions during the fellowship year in one of the designated degree programs where women's participation traditionally has been low (see list below). Applicants must be United States citizens or permanent residents. Please check the website for further details of eligibility
Level of Study: Doctorate, Postdoctorate, Postgraduate
Type: Fellowships
Value: US$5,000–18,000
Length of Study: 1 year
Frequency: Annual
Study Establishment: Any accredited institution
Application Procedure: Check website for details
Closing Date: 10 January
Additional Information: Materials sent to the Washington, DC office will be disqualified and will not be reviewed

For further information contact:

C/O ACT, Inc., P.O. Box 4030, United States of America

Tel: (1) 319 337 1716 ext. 60
Email: aauw@act.org

American Australian Association (AAA)

50 Broadway, Suite 2003, New York, NY 10004, United States of America

Tel: (1) 212 338 6860
Fax: (1) 212 338 6864
Email: information@aaanyc.org
Website: www.americanaustralian.org
Contact: Diane Sinclair, Director of Education

The American Australian Association (AAA), founded in 1948, is the largest non-profit organization in the United States devoted to relations between the United States, Australia and New Zealand, with operations throughout the tri-state and the New England regions. Its goal is to encourage stronger ties across the Pacific, particularly in the private sector.

Sir Keith Murdoch Fellowships

Subjects: Engineering, medicine, mining, life sciences (particularly in the fields of oceanography/marine sciences and stem cell research)
Purpose: To facilitate intellectual interchange between Australia and the United States and create a channel for ongoing collaborative research
Level of Study: Graduate, Postdoctorate
Type: Fellowships
Value: Up to US$3,20,000
Frequency: Annual
Study Establishment: Harvard Medical, John Hopkins, MIT, Stanford Business School and Cold Spring Harbor Laboratory
Country of Study: United States of America
Closing Date: 31 October
Contributor: American Australian Association

For further information contact:

Email: jhelum.bagchi@aaanyc.org

American Cancer Society (ACS)

1599 Clifton Road North East, Atlanta, GA 30329-4251, United States of America

Email: fellows@uicc.org
Website: fellows.uicc.org
Contact: Ms Brita Baker, Head of Fellowships Department

The American Cancer Society (ACS) is the largest non government fund holder of cancer research in the United States. ACS has devoted more than US$2 billion to cancer research.

American Cancer Society International Fellowships for Beginning Investigators

Subjects: Epidemiology, prevention, detection, causation, diagnosis, treatment, psycho-oncology
Purpose: To foster a bi-directional flow of knowledge, experience, expertise, and innovation to and from the United States of America. To enable beginning investigators and clinicians, who are in the early stages of their careers, to carry out basic or clinical research projects and to develop, acquire and apply advanced research procedures and techniques
Eligibility: Eligible candidates should hold assistant professorships or similar positions at their home institutes and have a minimum of two and a maximum of 10 years of postdoctoral experience after obtaining their MD or PhD degrees or equivalents. Awards are conditional on the return of the Fellow to the home institute at the end of the Fellowship and on the availability of appropriate facilities and resources to develop the newly acquired skills. No extensions are permitted. Candidates who are already physically present at the proposed host institution whilst their applications are under consideration are not eligible
Level of Study: Postdoctorate
Type: Fellowship
Value: An average value of US$36,000 for travel and stipend support
Length of Study: 1 year
Frequency: Annual
Country of Study: United States of America
No. of awards offered: 23
Application Procedure: Applicants must obtain an application form from the Fellowships department
Closing Date: 1 November
No. of awards given last year: 9
No. of applicants last year: 23
Additional Information: No allowances are made for accompanying dependants

For further information contact:

International Union Against Cancer, 3 rue Conseil-Général, CH-1205 Genève, Switzerland

Tel:	(1) 22 809 1840
Fax:	(1) 22 809 1081
Email:	fellows@uicc.ch
Contact:	Grants Management Officer

American Chemical Society (ACS)

1155 16th Street, NW, Washington, DC 20036, United States of America

Tel:	(1) 202 872 4600
Fax:	(1) 202 776 8008
Email:	help@acs.org; awards@acs.org
Website:	portal.acs.org

The American Chemical Society is a self-governed individual membership organization that consists of more than 160,000 members at all degree levels and in all fields of chemistry. The organization provides a broad range of opportunities for peer interaction and career development, regardless of professional or scientific interests. The program and activities conducted by ACS today are the products of a tradition of excellence in meeting member needs that dates from the Society's founding in 1876.

Alfred Burger Award in Medicinal Chemistry

Subjects: Medicinal chemistry
Purpose: To acknowledge outstanding contributions to research in medicinal chemistry
Eligibility: The award will be granted for outstanding contributions in the field of medicinal chemistry regardless of race, gender, age, religion, ethnicity, nationality, sexual orientation, gender expression, gender identity, presence of disabilities and educational background
Level of Study: Postgraduate
Type: Award
Value: The award consists of US$5,000 and a certificate. Up to US$2,500 for travel expenses to the meeting at which the award will be presented will be reimbursed
Application Procedure: A completed nomination form available on the website www.chemistry.org must be sent as an email attachment

Closing Date: 1 November
Contributor: Glaxo Smith Kline

For further information contact:

Tel:	(1) 202 872 4575
Fax:	(1) 202 776 8008
Email:	awards@acs.org

American Chemical Society Ahmed Zewail Award in Ultrafast Science and Technology

Subjects: Physics, chemistry, biology, or related fields
Purpose: To recognize outstanding and creative contributions to fundamental discoveries or inventions in ultrafast science and technology
Eligibility: The award will be for outstanding and creative contributions by a nominee to fundamental discoveries or inventions in ultrafast science and technology in the areas of physics, chemistry, biology, or related fields. Please see the website for further details regarding eligibility
Level of Study: Postgraduate
Type: Award
Value: The award will consist of US$5,000 and a certificate. Up to US$2,500 for travel expenses to the meeting at which the award will be presented will be reimbursed
Frequency: Annual
Application Procedure: See website for details
Closing Date: 1 November
Funding: Trusts
Contributor: Ahmed Zewail Endowment Fund

For further information contact:

Tel:	(1) 202 872 4575
Fax:	(1) 202 776 8008
Email:	awards@acs.org

American Chemical Society Award for Creative Advances in Environmental Science and Technology

Subjects: Environmental science and technology
Purpose: To encourage creativity in research and technology
Eligibility: The award will be granted regardless of race, gender, age, religion, ethnicity, nationality, sexual orientation, gender expression, gender identity, presence of disabilities and educational background
Level of Study: Postgraduate
Type: Award

Value: The award consists of US$5,000 and a certificate. Up to US$2,500 for travel expenses to the meeting at which the award will be presented will be reimbursed
Frequency: Annual
Application Procedure: See the website for more details
Closing Date: 1 November
Contributor: ACS Division of Environmental Chemistry
Additional Information: Air Products and Chemicals, Inc

For further information contact:

Tel: (1) 202 872 4575
Fax: (1) 202 776 8008
Email: awards@acs.org

American Chemical Society Award for Creative Research and Applications of Iodine Chemistry

Subjects: Chemistry
Purpose: To support, promote, and motivate global research of iodine chemistry and develop its use and knowledge through applications
Eligibility: A nominee must have performed outstanding and creative research related to iodine chemistry or its applications. Please see the website for further details regarding eligibility
Level of Study: Postgraduate
Type: Award
Value: The award consists of US$10,000 and a certificate. Up to US$1,000 for travel expenses to the meeting at which the award will be presented will be reimbursed. The award is presented biennially in odd-numbered years
Application Procedure: A completed nomination form and curriculum vitae must be sent
Closing Date: 1 November
Contributor: Sociedad Quimica y Minera de chile S.A. (SQM S.A.)

For further information contact:

Tel: (1) 202 872 4575
Fax: (1) 202 776 8008
Email: awards@acs.org

American Chemical Society Award for Creative Work in Synthetic Organic Chemistry

Subjects: Organic chemistry
Purpose: To recognize and encourage creative work in synthetic organic chemistry
Eligibility: A nominee must have accomplished outstanding creative work in synthetic organic chemistry that has been published. Please see website for further details regarding eligibility
Level of Study: Postgraduate
Type: Award
Value: The award consists of US$5,000 and a certificate. Up to US$1,000 for travel expenses to the meeting at which the award will be presented will be reimbursed
Frequency: Annual
Application Procedure: See the website for more details
Closing Date: 1 November
Contributor: The Aldrich Chemical Company, Inc

For further information contact:

Tel: (1) 202 872 4575
Fax: (1) 202 776 8008
Email: awards@acs.org

American Chemical Society Award for Encouraging Disadvantaged Students into Careers in the Chemical Sciences

Subjects: Chemistry
Purpose: To recognize significant accomplishments by individuals in stimulating students, underrepresented in the profession, to elect careers in the chemical sciences and engineering
Eligibility: Nominees for the award may come from any professional setting: academia, industry, government or other independent facility. Please see the website for further details regarding eligibility
Level of Study: Postgraduate
Type: Award
Value: The award consists of US$5,000 and a certificate. A grant of US$10,000 will be made to an academic institution, designated by the recipient, to strengthen its activities in meeting the objectives of the award. Up to US$1,500 for travel expenses to the meeting at which the award will be presented will be reimbursed
Frequency: Annual
Country of Study: United States of America
Application Procedure: Completed nomination and optional support forms must be submitted to the awards office
Closing Date: 1 November
Contributor: The Camille and Henry Dreyfus Foundation, Inc

For further information contact:

Tel: (1) 202 872 4575
Fax: (1) 202 776 8008
Email: awards@acs.org

American Chemical Society Award for Encouraging Women into Careers in the Chemical Sciences

Subjects: Chemistry

Purpose: To recognize individuals who have significantly stimulated the interests of women in chemistry

Eligibility: Open to candidates of all nationalities. Nominees for the award may come from any professional setting: academia, industry, government, or other independent facility

Level of Study: Professional development

Type: Award

Value: The award consists of US$5,000 and a certificate. A grant of US$10,000 will be made to an academic institution, designated by the recipient, to strengthen its activities in meeting the objectives of the award. Up to US$1,500 for travel expenses to the meeting at which the award will be presented will be reimbursed

Frequency: Annual

Application Procedure: For more details visit the website

Closing Date: 1 November

Contributor: The Camille and Henry Dreyfus Foundation, Inc

For further information contact:

Tel: (1) 202 872 4575
Fax: (1) 202 776 8008
Email: awards@acs.org

American Chemical Society Award in Chromatography

Subjects: Chemistry

Purpose: To recognize outstanding contributions to the fields of chromatography

Eligibility: A nominee must have made an outstanding contribution to the fields of chromatography with particular consideration given to developments of new methods. Please see the website for further details regarding eligibility

Level of Study: Postgraduate

Type: Award

Value: The award consists of US$5,000 and a certificate. Up to US$2,500 for travel expenses to the meeting at which the award will be presented will be reimbursed

Frequency: Annual

Application Procedure: See the website for more details

Closing Date: 1 November

Contributor: SUPELCO, Inc

For further information contact:

The Awards Office, American Chemical Society, 1155 16th Street, NW, Washington, DC 20036-4801, United States of America

Tel: (1) 202 872 4575
Fax: (1) 202 776 8008
Email: awards@acs.org

American Chemical Society Award in Colloid Chemistry

Subjects: Chemistry

Purpose: To recognize and encourage outstanding scientific contributions to colloid chemistry

Eligibility: The nominee must have made outstanding scientific contributions to colloid chemistry. The award will be granted regardless of race, gender, age, religion, ethnicity, nationality, sexual orientation, gender expression, gender identity, presence of disabilities, and educational background

Level of Study: Postgraduate

Type: Award

Value: The award consists of US$5,000 and a certificate. Up to US$2,500 for travel expenses to the meeting at which the award will be presented will be reimbursed

Frequency: Annual

Application Procedure: Completed nomination and optional support forms must be submitted

Closing Date: 1 November

Contributor: Colgate-Palmolive Company

For further information contact:

Tel: (1) 202 872 4575
Fax: (1) 202 776 8008
Email: awards@acs.org

American Chemical Society National Awards

Subjects: Chemical sciences

Purpose: To recognize premier chemical professionals in extraordinary ways

Level of Study: Postgraduate

Type: Grant

Length of Study: 2 years

Frequency: Annual

Country of Study: Any country

Application Procedure: See website for details

Closing Date: Please see the website

Additional Information: Inquiries concerning awards should be directed to the office of the National Awards office awards@acs.org

For further information contact:

Email: awards@acs.org

American Chemical Society Priestley Medal

Subjects: Chemistry
Purpose: To recognize distinguished services to chemistry
Eligibility: Open to applicants of any nationality who may or may not be members of the Society
Level of Study: Doctorate
Type: Award
Value: A gold medallion, a presentation box and a certificate
Frequency: Annual
Application Procedure: Applicants must send their nominations to the ACS Board of Directors
Closing Date: 1 November
Funding: Trusts
Contributor: The American Chemical Society

For further information contact:

Email: awards@acs.org

American Chemical Society Roger Adams Award in Organic Chemistry

Subjects: Organic chemistry
Purpose: To recognize and encourage outstanding contributions to research in organic chemistry
Eligibility: The award will be granted regardless of race, gender, age, religion, ethnicity, nationality, sexual orientation, gender expression, gender identity, presence of disabilities and educational background
Type: Award
Value: The award consists of a medallion and a replica, a certificate and US$25,000
Application Procedure: A completed nomination form must be sent as an email attachment. See the website www.chemis try.org for further details
Closing Date: 1 November
Contributor: Organic Reactions, Inc. and Organic Synthesis, Inc

For further information contact:

Tel: (1) 202 872 4575
Fax: (1) 202 776 8008
Email: awards@acs.org

American Chemical Society Stanley C. Israel Regional Award for Advancing Diversity in the Chemical Sciences

Subjects: Chemical sciences
Purpose: To recognize individuals who have advanced diversity in the chemical sciences and significantly stimulated or fostered activities that promote inclusiveness within the region
Eligibility: Nominees may come from academia, industry, government, or independent entities, and may also be organizations, including ACS Local Sections and Divisions. The nominee must have created and fostered ongoing programs or activities that result in increased numbers of persons from diverse and underrepresented minority groups, persons with disabilities, or women who participate in the chemical enterprise
Level of Study: Postgraduate
Type: Award
Value: The award consists of a medal and a US$1,000 grant to support and further the activities for which the award was made. The award also will include funding to cover the recipient's travel expenses to the ACS regional meeting at which the award will be presented
Frequency: Annual
Application Procedure: See website for details
Closing Date: 1 August
Contributor: ACS Committee on Minority Affairs
Additional Information: First deadline is for Middle Atlantic (MARM), Central (CERM), and Northwest (NORM) and second deadline is for Midwest (MWRM), Northeast (NERM), Southeastern (SERMACS), Southwest (SWRM), and Rocky Mountain (RMRM)

For further information contact:

Fax: (1) 202 776 8003
Email: Diversity@acs.org

Arthur C. Cope Scholar Awards

Subjects: Organic chemistry
Purpose: To recognize outstanding achievement in the field of organic chemistry
Eligibility: The award will be granted regardless of race, gender, religion, ethnicity, nationality, sexual orientation, gender expression, gender identity, presence of disabilities and educational background. Please see the website for further details regarding eligibility
Level of Study: Postgraduate
Type: Award
Value: The award consists of US$5,000, a certificate, and a US$40,000 unrestricted research grant to be assigned by the

recipient to any university or nonprofit institution. Up to US$2,500 for travel expenses to the fall national meeting will be reimbursed
Frequency: Annual
Application Procedure: See the website
Closing Date: 1 November
Contributor: The Arthur C. Cope Fund

For further information contact:

Tel: (1) 202 872 4575
Fax: (1) 202 776 8008
Email: awards@acs.org

Award in Chemical Instrumentation

Subjects: All subjects
Purpose: Conceptualization and development of unique instrumentation that has made a significant impact on the field. Demonstration of innovative use of instrumentation in chemical measurement. Stimulation of other researchers to use instrumentation in chemical measurement. Authorship of research papers or books that have had an influential role in the use of chemical instrumentation
Eligibility: Eligibility is not restricted to members of the Division of Analytical Chemistry. Nominees for the J. Calvin Giddings Award for Excellence in Education must, however, must have demonstrated excellence in teaching through at least five years at the time the award is presented
Level of Study: Postgraduate
Type: Grant
Frequency: Annual
Country of Study: Any country
Application Procedure: Apply online
Funding: Trusts

For further information contact:

Email: miquela@sciencemanagers.com

Award in Spectrochemical Analysis

Subjects: All subjects
Purpose: Development of novel and important instrumentation. Elucidation of fundamental events or processes important to the field. Authorship of important research papers and/or books that have had an influential role in the development of the field. role in the use of chemical instrumentation
Eligibility: Eligibility is not restricted to members of the Division of Analytical Chemistry. Nominees for the J. Calvin Giddings Award for Excellence in Education must,

however, must have demonstrated excellence in teaching through at least five years at the time the award is presented
Level of Study: Postgraduate
Type: Award
Value: US$2,500
Length of Study: 1 year
Frequency: Annual
Country of Study: Any country
Application Procedure: Apply online
Funding: Trusts

For further information contact:

Email: miquela@sciencemanagers.com

Ernest Guenther Award in the Chemistry of Natural Products

Subjects: Organic chemistry
Purpose: To recognize and encourage outstanding achievements in analysis, structure elucidation and chemical synthesis of natural products
Eligibility: Open to all applicants
Type: Grant
Value: US$6,000, a medallion and a certificate. Up to US$2,500 for travel expenses to the meeting at which the award will be presented will be reimbursed
Frequency: Annual
Application Procedure: A completed nomination form and optional support forms must be mailed to awards@acs.org
Closing Date: 1 November
Contributor: Givaudan
No. of awards given last year: 1

For further information contact:

Tel: (1) 202 872 4575
Fax: (1) 202 776 8008
Email: awards@acs.org

F. Albert Cotton Award in Synthetic Inorganic Chemistry

Subjects: Inorganic chemistry
Purpose: To recognize distinguished work in synthetic inorganic chemistry
Eligibility: The award recognizes outstanding synthetic accomplishment in the field of inorganic chemistry. The award will be granted regardless of race, gender, age, religion, ethnicity, nationality, sexual orientation, gender expression, gender identity, presence of disabilities and educational background
Level of Study: Postgraduate

Type: Award
Value: US$5,000 and a certificate. Up to US$2,500 for travel expenses to the meeting at which the award will be presented will be reimbursed
Frequency: Annual
Application Procedure: A completed application form to be submitted as an email attachment to awards@acs.org
Closing Date: 1 November
Funding: Private
Contributor: F. Albert Cotton Endowment Fund
No. of awards given last year: 1

For further information contact:

Tel: (1) 202 872 4575
Fax: (1) 202 776 8008
Email: awards@acs.org

Frederic Stanley Kipping Award in Silicon Chemistry

Subjects: Chemistry
Purpose: To recognize distinguished contributions to the field of silicon chemistry
Eligibility: Open to all candidates who have contributed to the field of silicon chemistry. There are no limits on age or on nationality. A nominee must have made distinguished contributions in the field of silicon chemistry during the 10 years preceding the current nomination
Level of Study: Postgraduate
Type: Award
Value: US$5,000 and a certificate. Up to US$2,500 for travel expenses will be reimbursed to the spring national meeting at which the award will be presented and to the United States based Silicon Symposium to deliver an award address
Application Procedure: A completed nomination form to be mailed to awards@acs.org
Closing Date: 1 November
Funding: Corporation
Contributor: Dow Corning Corporation

For further information contact:

Tel: (1) 202 872 4575
Fax: (1) 202 776 8008
Email: awards@acs.org

Glenn T. Seaborg Award for Nuclear Chemistry

Subjects: Chemistry
Purpose: To recognize and encourage research in nuclear and radiochemistry or their applications

Eligibility: Nominee must have made outstanding contributions to nuclear or radiochemistry or to their applications. The award will be granted regardless of race, gender, age, religion, ethnicity, nationality, sexual orientation, gender expression, gender identity, presence of disabilities and educational background
Level of Study: Postgraduate
Type: Award
Value: US$5,000 and a certificate. Up to US$2,500 for expenses to the meeting at which the award will be presented will be reimbursed
Frequency: Annual
Application Procedure: See the website
Closing Date: 1 November
Contributor: ACS Division of Nuclear Chemistry and Technology
No. of awards given last year: 1

For further information contact:

Tel: (1) 202 8721 4575
Fax: (1) 202 776 8008
Email: awards@acs.org

Ipatieff Prize

Subjects: Chemistry
Purpose: To recognize outstanding chemical experimental work in the field of catalysis
Eligibility: 3Open to candidates who should not have passed his or her 40th birthday on 3 April of the year in which the award is presented, and must have done outstanding chemical experimental work in the field of catalysis or high pressure. Special weight will be given to independence of thought and originality. The award may be made for investigations carried out in any country and without consideration of nationality
Level of Study: Postgraduate
Type: Prize
Value: The award will consist of the income from a trust fund and a certificate. The financial value of the prize may vary, but it is expected that it will be approximately US$5,000 and that it will be awarded every three years. Travel expenses related to conferment of the award will be reimbursed
Frequency: Every 3 years
Country of Study: Any country
Application Procedure: Contact the awards office
Closing Date: 1 November
Contributor: Ipatieff Trust Fund
Additional Information: Preference will be given to American chemists

For further information contact:

Tel: (1) 202 872 4575
Email: awards@acs.org

Irving Langmuir Award in Chemical Physics

Subjects: Chemistry and physics
Purpose: To encourage research in chemistry and physics
Eligibility: A candidate must have made an outstanding contribution to chemical physics or physical chemistry within the 10 years preceding the year in which the award is made. The award will be granted without restriction, except that the recipient must be a resident of the United States and the monetary prize must be used in the United States or its possessions
Level of Study: Postgraduate
Type: Award
Value: US$10,000 and a certificate. Up to US$2,500 for travel expenses to the meeting at which the award will be presented will be reimbursed
Frequency: Every 2 years
Country of Study: United States of America
Application Procedure: Contact the Awards office
Closing Date: 1 November
Funding: Foundation
Contributor: GE Global Research and The American Chemical Society Division of Physical Chemistry

For further information contact:

Tel: (1) 202 872 4575
Email: awards@acs.org

James Bryant Conant Award in High School Chemistry Teaching

Subjects: Teaching
Purpose: To recognize outstanding teachers of high school chemistry in the United States
Eligibility: Open to candidates who are actively engaged in the teaching of chemistry in high school. The nominee must be actively engaged in the teaching of chemistry in a high school (grades 9–12). Please see the website for further details regarding eligibility
Level of Study: Postgraduate
Type: Award
Value: US$5,000 and a certificate. Up to US$2,500 for travel expenses to the meeting at which the award will be presented will be reimbursed
Frequency: Annual
Country of Study: United States of America

Application Procedure: A completed nomination form must be submitted as an email attachment
Closing Date: 1 November
Contributor: The Thermo Fisher Scientific, Inc
No. of awards given last year: 1
Additional Information: A certificate will also be provided to the recipient's institution for display

For further information contact:

Tel: (1) 202 872 4575
Email: awards@acs.org

Peter Debye Award in Physical Chemistry

Subjects: Physical chemistry
Purpose: To encourage and reward outstanding research in physical chemistry
Eligibility: Open to all candidates without regard to age or nationality. Please see the website for further details regarding eligibility
Level of Study: Postgraduate
Type: Award
Value: US$5,000 and a certificate. Up to US$2,500 for travel expenses to the meeting at which the award will be presented will be reimbursed
Frequency: Annual
Application Procedure: A completed nominations form to be sent as an email attachment to awards@acs.org
Closing Date: 1 November
Contributor: E.I. du Pont de Nemours and Company
No. of awards given last year: 1

For further information contact:

Tel: (1) 202 872 4575
Email: awards@acs.org

Pfizer Graduate Travel Awards in Analytical Chemistry

Subjects: Analytical chemistry
Purpose: To provide funds for students to travel to an ACS National meeting and present the results of their research
Eligibility: Open to candidates who are United States citizens and permanent residents
Level of Study: Postgraduate
Type: Award
Value: US$1,000
Frequency: Annual
Study Establishment: Open to candidates who are United States citizens and permanent residents

Application Procedure: A completed application form, which may be downloaded from the website, must be sent
Closing Date: 21 October
Contributor: The Division of Analytical Chemistry of the ACS

For further information contact:

Department of Chemistry, The College of Wooster, Wooster, OH 44691, United States of America

Tel: (1) 202 872 4575
Email: awards@acs.org

American Congress on Surveying and Mapping (ACSM)

6, Montgomery Village Avenue, Suite 403, Gaithersburg, MD 20879, United States of America

Tel: (1) 240 632 9716 ext. 109
Fax: (1) 240 632 1321
Email: ilse.genovese@acsm.net
Website: www.acsm.net

The ACSM is a nonprofit association dedicated to serving the public interest and advancing the profession of surveying and mapping.

American College of Sports Medicine Fellows Scholarship

Subjects: Any ACSM disciplines
Purpose: To encourage, recognize and support exceptional surveying and mapping students
Eligibility: Open to students with a junior or higher degree and enrolled in four-year degree programs in surveying or in closely related programs such as geomatics or surveying engineering
Level of Study: Graduate, Postgraduate
Type: Scholarship
Value: US$2,000
Length of Study: 4 years
Frequency: Annual
Country of Study: Any country
Application Procedure: Applicants must submit a completed application form along with proof of membership in ACSM, a complete statement indicating educational objectives, future plans of study or research, professional

activities and financial need, three letters of recommendation and a complete original official transcript
Closing Date: 17 February
Funding: Corporation
Additional Information: Prior scholarship winners are eligible to apply in succeeding years providing all appropriate criteria are satisfied

For further information contact:

Email: ilse.genovese@acsm.net

American Council of Learned Societies (ACLS)

633 3rd Avenue, 8th Floor between 40th & 41st Streets, New York, NY 10017-6795, United States of America

Tel: (1) 212 697 1505
Fax: (1) 212 949 8058
Email: sfisher@acls.org
Website: www.acls.org

The American Council of Learned Societies (ACLS) is a private non-profit federation of 68 national scholarly organizations. The mission of the ACLS, as set forth in its Constitution is the advancement of humanistic studies in all fields of learning in the humanities and the social sciences and the maintenance and strengthening of relations among the national societies devoted to such studies.

American Council of Learned Societies Humanities Program in Belarus, Russia and Ukraine

Subjects: History, archeology, literature, linguistics, film studies, art history
Purpose: To sustain individuals doing exemplary work, so as to assure continued future leadership in the humanities
Eligibility: Applicants should be involved in studies related to performing arts, ethnographic and cultural studies, gender studies, philosophy or religious studies. ACLS organizes annual regional meetings for advisers and grant recipients
Level of Study: Research
Type: Grant
Value: Varies
Frequency: Annual
Country of Study: Any country

Application Procedure: Application forms can be obtained by writing to hp@acls.org. Please see the website for further details at www.acls.org/programs/hp/

Closing Date: 18 November

Funding: Foundation

Additional Information: In 2007, with the help of the Carnegie Corporation of New York and the American Council of Learned Societies, the International Association for the Humanities (IAH) was founded as an independent association of humanities scholars primarily in Belarus, Russia and Ukraine to help represent the post-Soviet region in the international scholarly community. IAH organizes a competition for short-term grants in the humanities. For further details and current competition application form, see the IAH website

For further information contact:

Email: hp@acls.org

American Council of Learned Societies/New York Public Library (NYPL) Fellowships

Subjects: Arts, humanities or social sciences

Purpose: To explore the rich and diverse collections of the NYPL Humanities and Social Sciences Library

Eligibility: Applicants must be citizens or permanent residents of the United States of America as of the application deadline date, and hold a PhD degree. However, an established Scholar who can demonstrate the equivalent of a PhD in publications and professional experience may also qualify. Applicants will be asked to identify specific resources and benefits to be gained from affiliation with the Center. Scholars currently enrolled for any degree are not eligible

Level of Study: Postdoctorate

Type: Fellowship

Value: Up to US$50,000 for full professor and equivalent, US$40,000 for associate professor and equivalent and US$30,000 for assistant professor and equivalent

Length of Study: 6–12 months

Application Procedure: Applications must be made to the ACLS Fellowship Program. Note that applications must also be made to the competition for residential fellowships administered separately by the NYPL Center for Scholars and Writers

Closing Date: Please consult the organization

Additional Information: More information about the NYPL is available at www.nypl.org. It is possible that an application may have any one of the following outcomes: a fellowship awarded solely by the NYPL Center for Scholars and Writers, an ACLS Fellowship awarded solely by the ACLS or a joint NYPL/ACLS Residential Fellowship awarded by both organizations together

For further information contact:

Center for Scholars & Writers, The New York Public Library Humanities & Social Sciences Library, Fifth Avenue & 42nd Street, New York, NY, United States of America

Email: csw@nypl.org

Andrew W. Mellon Foundation/ACLS Early Career Fellowships Program Dissertation Completion Fellowships

Subjects: Humanities and related social sciences

Purpose: To assist graduates in the last year of their PhD dissertation writing

Eligibility: Open to a PhD candidate in a humanities or social science department in an American University. Applicant should not be in the degree programme for more than 6 years and the successful candidates cannot hold this fellowship after the 7th year

Level of Study: Doctorate

Type: Fellowships

Value: US$25,000, plus funds for research costs of up to US$3,000 and for university fees of up to US$5,000

Length of Study: 1 year

Frequency: Annual

Country of Study: United States of America

Application Procedure: Applicants can apply online (ofa. acls.org). Please see the website for further information www. acls.org/programs/dcf/

Closing Date: 9 November

Contributor: The Andrew W. Mellon Foundation

For further information contact:

Email: grants@acls.org

American Council on Education (ACE)

One Dupont Circle North West, Suite 800, Washington, DC 20036-1193, United States of America

Tel: (1) 202 939 9420
Fax: (1) 202 785 8056
Email: fellows@ace.nche.edu
Website: www.acenet.edu
Contact: Awards Committee

The American Council on Education (ACE), founded in 1918, is the nation's umbrella higher education association. ACE is dedicated to the belief that equal educational opportunity and a strong higher education system are essential cornerstones of a democratic society. ACE is a forum for the discussion of major issues related to higher education and its potential to contribute to the quality of American life. ACE maintains both a domestic and an international agenda and seeks to advance the interests and goals of higher and adult education in a changing environment by providing leadership and advocacy on important issues representing the views of the higher and adult education community to policy makers, and offering services to its members.

American Council on Education Fellows Program

Subjects: Administration, leadership and governance of higher education and management of colleges and universities
Purpose: To strengthen leadership in American higher education by identifying and preparing individuals who have shown promise for responsible positions in higher education administration
Eligibility: Open to senior members of college faculty or mid-level staff with a minimum of five years teaching or administrative experience who show evidence of potential for senior level administration. English is the language of instruction
Level of Study: Professional development
Type: Fellowship
Value: The nominating institution supports the salaries and benefits. The host institution supports the seminar and travel costs of the ACE Fellows and the Council provides support for programmatic costs
Length of Study: 1 academic year
Frequency: Annual
Study Establishment: A host college or university
Country of Study: Any country
Application Procedure: Applicants must be nominated by the president or vice president of a college or university. Applications must be submitted with a nomination form, along with four confidential letters of reference
Additional Information: ACE Fellows work with a mentor, normally a president or other senior officer, at policy and practical levels. The fellowship experience is supplemented with national and regional seminars and meetings. Contact could be established only through webform

For further information contact:

Email: ACELeadership@acenet.edu

American Council on Rural Special Education (ACRES)

West Virginia University, 509 Allen Hall, PO Box 6122, Morgantown, WV 26506-6122, United States of America

Tel: (1) 304 293 3450
Fax: (1) 435 797 3572
Email: acres-sped@mail.wvu.edu
Website: acres-sped.org
Contact: David Forbush, Headquarters Co-ordinator

Alliance for Clinical Research Excellence and Safety Teacher Scholarship Award

Subjects: Special education in the areas of the handicapped, those with specific learning disabilities and the socially disadvantaged
Purpose: To give a rural teacher an opportunity to pursue education and training not otherwise affordable within his or her district
Eligibility: To be eligible for an ACRES teacher scholarship award, an individual must be: currently or recently employed by a rural school district as a certified teacher in regular or special education; working with students with disabilities or with regular education students and "retooling" for work in a special education setting; pursuing a goal of increasing skills in special education or "retooling" from a regular education to a special education career; and a citizen of the United States
Level of Study: Graduate
Type: Scholarship
Value: Up to US$1,000
Length of Study: 1 year
Frequency: Annual
Country of Study: United States of America
Application Procedure: Applications must consist of: a completed application form; an essay describing the opportunities and challenges of rural special education, the reason why funds are needed for the training, the plans for using the scholarship award for further education or training, and how the information gained from the education or training will be shared with other educators in rural schools; and two letters of recommendation from persons in a position to judge capabilities as a rural special educator; at least one reference must be from an individual actively involved in rural special education
Closing Date: 15 February
Funding: Private
Additional Information: The award will be announced at the March ACRES conference

For further information contact:

Tel: (1) 304 293 4384
Email: acres-sped@mail.wvu.edu

American Diabetes Association (ADA)

1701 North Beauregard Street, Alexandria, VA 22311, United States of America

Tel: (1) 703 549 1500, ext. 2362
Fax: (1) 703 549 1715
Email: grantquestions@diabetes.org
Website: professional.diabetes.org/grants

The American Diabetes Association (ADA) is the nation's leading non-profit health organization providing diabetes research information and advocacy. The mission of the organization is to prevent and cure diabetes, and to improve the lives of all people affected by diabetes. To fulfil this mission, the ADA funds research, publishes scientific findings and provides information and other services to people with diabetes, their families, healthcare professionals and the public.

Lions Clubs International Foundation Clinical Research Grant Program

Subjects: New treatment regimens, epidemiology and translation research in the area of diabetic retinopathy
Purpose: To support clinical or applied research
Eligibility: Open to holders of an MD or PhD degree, or, in the case of other health professions, an appropriate health or science related degree. The applicant must hold a faculty level appointment or its equivalent at a research institution. The programme is intended for any investigator with or without NIH or other significant support
Level of Study: Postdoctorate
Type: Research grant
Value: Up to US$1,00,000 per year. The grants carry no commitment for overhead costs or tuition. The funds may be used for equipment, supplies, salary support or a combination of the three. The funds may not be used for the principal investigator
Length of Study: 3 years
Frequency: Annual
Country of Study: Any country
Closing Date: 1 July

Additional Information: This programme is part of the Lions Sightfirst Diabetic Retinopathy Research Program, funded by the Lions Club International Foundation

For further information contact:

Email: lcif@lionsclubs.org

Lions Clubs International Foundation Equipment Grant Program

Subjects: Clinical research in diabetic retinopathy
Purpose: To enable investigators to purchase equipment in order to conduct clinical research projects
Eligibility: Open to holders of an MD or PhD degree, or, in the case of other health professions, an appropriate health- or science-related degree. The applicant must hold a faculty-level appointment at a research institution
Level of Study: Research
Type: Grant
Value: US$25,000 for the purchase of equipment. One payment is made in July
Frequency: Annual
Country of Study: Any country
Application Procedure: Applicants must submit a detailed justification of the need to purchase the equipment and an explanation of its intended use. All applications must be submitted online via the website
Closing Date: 15 January
Additional Information: This programme is part of the Lions Sightfirst Diabetic Retinopathy Research Program, funded by the Lions Club International Foundation

For further information contact:

Email: lcif@lionsclubs.org

Lions Clubs International Foundation Training Grant Program

Subjects: Diabetic retinopathy
Purpose: To enable foreign investigators to visit American research institutions and receive training in clinical research and the implementation of public health programmes, eg. screening or epidemiology. The programme also aims to enable United States of America investigators to visit foreign institutions, particularly institutions in developing countries, to conduct training programmes in clinical research and implement public health programmes

Eligibility: Open to citizens of the United States of America who have an MD or a PhD degree, or, in the case of other health professions, an appropriate health- or science-related degree, and hold a faculty-level appointment at a United States of America research institution. The programme is also open to citizens of other countries who have an MD or a PhD degree

Level of Study: Research

Value: Up to US$40,000 per year

Length of Study: 2 years

Frequency: Annual

Study Establishment: An approved institution

Country of Study: Any country

Application Procedure: All applications must be submitted online via the website

Closing Date: 15 January

Additional Information: This programme is part of the Lions Sightfirst Diabetic Retinopathy Research Program, funded by the Lions Club International Foundation

For further information contact:

Email: LCIFHumanitarianPrograms@lionsclubs.org

American Federation for Aging Research (AFAR)

55 West 39th Street, 16th Floor, New York, NY 10018, United States of America

Tel: (1) 212 703 9977
Fax: (1) 212 997 0330
Email: grants@afar.org or info@afar.org
Website: www.afar.org
Contact: Director, Grant Programs

The American Federation for Aging Research (AFAR) is a leading non-profit organization supporting biomedical aging research. Since its founding in 1981, AFAR has provided approximately US$124 million to more than 2,600 new investigators and students conducting cutting-edge biomedical research on the aging process and age-related diseases. The important work AFAR supports leads to a better understanding of the aging process and to improvements in the health of all Americans as they age.

American Federation for Aging Research Research Grants for Junior Faculty

Subjects: Biomedical and clinical topics. Basic mechanisms of aging

Purpose: To help junior faculty to carry out research that will serve as the basis for longer term research efforts

Eligibility: Open to junior faculty with an MD or PhD degree

Level of Study: Postdoctorate, Research

Type: Research grant

Value: US$1,00,000

Length of Study: 1–2 years

Frequency: Annual

Country of Study: United States of America

Application Procedure: Applicants must complete and return the application by the annual deadline. These are available from the website

Closing Date: 15 December

Funding: Private, Foundation

Contributor: AFAR

Additional Information: Exceptions to the ten year rule may be requested for unusual circumstances by emailing an NIH-style biosketch to AFAR at grants@afar.org at least one week prior to the deadline date

For further information contact:

Email: grants@afar.org, info@afar.org

American Federation for Aging Research/Pfizer Research Grants in Metabolic Control and Late Life Diseases

Subjects: Metabolic control and aging

Purpose: To address specific areas of research that focus on the aging process and age related diseases

Eligibility: Applicants must be United States citizens or permanent residents

Level of Study: Research

Type: Grant

Value: US$60,000

Length of Study: 1–2 years

Frequency: Annual

Country of Study: United States of America

Application Procedure: Applicants must complete and return the application by the annual deadline. These are available from the website

Closing Date: 14 December

Funding: Private

Contributor: Pfizer Pharmaceuticals, Inc

Additional Information: Projects may involve basic, clinical or epidemiological research

For further information contact:

Email: grants@afar.org, info@afar.org

Glenn/American Federation for Aging Research Scholarships for Research in the Biology of Aging

Subjects: Biomedical research
Purpose: To attract potential scientists to aging research and provide students with the opportunity to conduct a research project
Eligibility: Open to students completing MD or PhD degrees
Level of Study: Doctorate, Research
Type: Scholarship
Value: US$6,000
Length of Study: 3 months
Frequency: Annual
Country of Study: Any country
Application Procedure: Applicants should submit one original and four copies of the application and of all supporting materials, including academic transcripts from all institutions attended, Graduate Record Examination and/or MCAT scores, and a biographical sketch and endorsing letter of the designated mentor. In addition, one letter of reference is also required
Closing Date: 26 February
Funding: Private
Contributor: The Glenn Foundation for Medical Research

For further information contact:

Email: info@afar.org

Merck/American Federation for Aging Research Junior investigator award in geriatric clinical pharmacology

Subjects: Geriatrics
Purpose: To help develop a cadre of physicians with a command of the emerging field of geriatric clinical pharmacology
Eligibility: Open to candidates who are board certified or eligible in a primary specialty having completed postdoctoral or fellowship training
Level of Study: Research
Type: Award
Value: US$60,000
Length of Study: 2 years
Frequency: Annual
Country of Study: Any country
Application Procedure: Applications must be submitted by an institution on behalf of the candidate. See the AFAR website for details
Funding: Foundation
Contributor: Merck Company Foundation

For further information contact:

Email: grants@afar.org

Royal Photographic Society/American Federation for Aging Research Medical Student Geriatric Scholars Program

Subjects: Geriatrics
Purpose: To encourage medical students, particularly budding researchers, to consider a career in academic geriatrics
Eligibility: Applicants must be citizens of the United States of America or permanent residents and have completed at least 1 year of medical school by the start date of the award
Level of Study: Doctorate
Type: Scholarship
Value: US$4,000
Length of Study: 8 weeks
Frequency: Annual
Country of Study: United States of America
Application Procedure: Applicants must complete and return the application by the annual deadline. Applications are available from the website
Closing Date: 6 February
Funding: Private
Contributor: Anonymous donor

For further information contact:

Email: info@afar.org

The Paul Beeson Career Development Awards in Aging Research for the Island of Ireland

Subjects: Aging-related research
Purpose: To encourage and assist the development of future leaders in the field of aging, deepen the commitment of research institutions to academic research in aging, and to expand medical research on aging
Level of Study: Research
Type: Award
Value: €339,390/£228,000
Length of Study: 3 years
Country of Study: Ireland
Application Procedure: All candidates must submit applications endorsed by the Dean of School of Medicine (or equivalent). Scholars will be required to submit a brief annual narrative report on the progress of their research and career plans
Closing Date: 22 January
Funding: Private

For further information contact:

Email: beeson@afar.org

American Foundation for Suicide Prevention (AFSP)

120 Wall Street, 29th Floor, New York, NY 10005, United States of America

Tel:	(1) 212 363 3500
Fax:	(1) 212 363 6237
Email:	grantsmanager@afsp.org
Website:	www.afsp.org
Contact:	Carl Niedzielski, Grants Manager

The American Foundation for Suicide Prevention (AFSP) is the only national non-profit organization exclusively dedicated to understanding and preventing suicide through research and education, and to reaching out to people with mood disorders and those affected by suicide.

American Foundation for Suicide Prevention Distinguished Investigator Awards

Subjects: The clinical, biological or psychosocial aspects of suicide

Purpose: Awarded to investigators at the level of associate professor or higher with a proven history of research in the area of suicide

Level of Study: Research

Type: Grant

Value: Up to US$1,25,000 over 2 years

Length of Study: 1–2 years

Frequency: Annual

Country of Study: Worldwide

No. of awards offered: 14

Application Procedure: Application information at afsp.org/grants. Apply online at afsp.org/grants

Closing Date: 15 November

Funding: Private

No. of applicants last year: 14

Additional Information: Decisions regarding awards are made in May and funding begins in October

For further information contact:

Email: cfr@unc.edu

Blue Sky Focus Grant

Subjects: Supports an innovative, impactful study in an area of suicide research that will achieve significant goals. This mechanism is intended for studies that, by their very nature, are clearly beyond the scope of our Innovation Grants. Innovative projects in new areas of investigation with potentially high impact for the understanding and prevention of suicide. Open to all fields of inquiry

Purpose: Focus grants are targeted, innovative and potentially high impact studies that seek to inform and even transform suicide prevention efforts

Eligibility: Investigators from all academic disciplines are eligible to apply, and both basic science and applied research projects will be considered, provided that the proposed study has an essential focus on suicide or suicide prevention. Grant applications are not accepted from for-profit organizations, or from federal or state government agencies. Applications from the Veterans Administration are eligible

Level of Study: Research

Type: Research grant

Value: They are awarded in the amount of US$5,00,000 per year for a maximum of three years

Length of Study: 3 years

Frequency: Annual

Country of Study: Any country

No. of awards offered: 4

Application Procedure: Applicants must submit a Letter of Intent by email to JHarkavyFriedman@afsp.org. If Letter of Intent is approved for application, applicants are instructed to apply at afsp.org/our-work/research/apply-for-a-grant/

Closing Date: 6 December

Funding: Private

No. of awards given last year: 1

No. of applicants last year: 4

For further information contact:

Email: grantsmanager@afsp.org

Distinguished Investigator Grant

Subjects: Investigators at the level of associate professor or higher with an established record of research and publication on suicide

Purpose: We welcome innovative studies relevant to understanding and preventing suicide. Applications are open to biological, psychological, and sociological approaches, and we encourage multidisciplinary research. These are investigator initiated grants

Eligibility: Investigators from all academic disciplines are eligible to apply, and both basic science and applied research projects will be considered, provided that the proposed study has an essential focus on suicide or suicide prevention. Grant applications are not accepted from for-profit organizations, or from federal or state government agencies. Applications from the Veterans Administration are eligible

Level of Study: Research
Type: Grant
Value: Up to US$1,25,000 over 2 Years
Length of Study: 2 years
Frequency: Annual
Country of Study: Any country
No. of awards offered: 9
Application Procedure: Applicants are instructed to apply afsp.org/our-work/research/apply-for-a-grant/
Closing Date: 14 November
Funding: Private
No. of awards given last year: 3
No. of applicants last year: 9

For further information contact:

Email: grantsmanager@afsp.org

Linked Standard Research Grant

Subjects: Investigators at any level performing research involving two or more institutions with each institution making a unique and significant research contribution
Purpose: We welcome innovative studies relevant to understanding and preventing suicide. Applications are open to biological, psychological, and sociological approaches, and we encourage multidisciplinary research. These are investigator initiated grants
Eligibility: Investigators from all academic disciplines are eligible to apply, and both basic science and applied research projects will be considered, provided that the proposed study has an essential focus on suicide or suicide prevention. Grant applications are not accepted from for-profit organizations, or from federal or state government agencies. Applications from the Veterans Administration are eligible
Level of Study: Research
Type: Grant
Value: Up to US$3,00,000 over 2 Years
Length of Study: 2 years
Frequency: Annual
Country of Study: Any country
No. of awards offered: 13
Application Procedure: Applicants must submit a Letter of Intent by email to JHarkavyFriedman@afsp.org. If Letter of Intent is approved for application, applicants are instructed to apply at afsp.org/our-work/research/apply-for-a-grant/
Closing Date: 14 November
Funding: Private

No. of awards given last year: 2
No. of applicants last year: 13

For further information contact:

Email: grantsmanager@afsp.org

Pilot Research Grant

Subjects: Investigators at any level. Provides seed money for innovative new projects with potential impact; typically more feasibility than hypothesis-driven studies
Purpose: We welcome innovative studies relevant to understanding and preventing suicide. Applications are open to biological, psychological, and sociological approaches, and we encourage multidisciplinary research. These are investigator initiated grants
Eligibility: Investigators from all academic disciplines are eligible to apply, and both basic science and applied research projects will be considered, provided that the proposed study has an essential focus on suicide or suicide prevention. Grant applications are not accepted from for-profit organizations, or from federal or state government agencies. Applications from the Veterans Administration are eligible
Level of Study: Research
Type: Grant
Value: Up to US$30,000 over 1–2 Years
Length of Study: 1–2 years
Frequency: Annual
Country of Study: Any country
No. of awards offered: 32
Application Procedure: Applicants are instructed to apply afsp.org/our-work/research/apply-for-a-grant/
Closing Date: 14 November
Funding: Private
No. of awards given last year: 3
No. of applicants last year: 32

For further information contact:

Email: grantsmanager@afsp.org

Postdoctoral Fellowship

Subjects: Investigators who have received a doctoral degree within the preceding six years, and have not had more than three years of fellowship support. Fellows receive a stipend of US$48,000 per year, with an institutional allowance of US$8,000 per year
Purpose: We welcome innovative studies relevant to understanding and preventing suicide. Applications are open to biological, psychological, and sociological approaches, and

we encourage multidisciplinary research. These are investigator initiated grants

Eligibility: Investigators from all academic disciplines are eligible to apply, and both basic science and applied research projects will be considered, provided that the proposed study has an essential focus on suicide or suicide prevention. New grantees must begin their studies within 6 months of the approved start date. Failure to begin the study within this time frame may result in withdrawal of the grant award

Level of Study: Postdoctorate, Research

Type: Grant

Value: Up to US$1,12,000 over 2 years

Length of Study: 2 years

Frequency: Annual

Country of Study: Any country

No. of awards offered: 9

Application Procedure: Applicants are instructed to apply afsp.org/our-work/research/apply-for-a-grant/

Closing Date: 14 November

Funding: Private

No. of awards given last year: 1

No. of applicants last year: 9

For further information contact:

Email: grantsmanager@afsp.org

Reaching 20% by 2025

Subjects: The American Foundation for Suicide Prevention has set a bold goal to reduce our nation's suicide rate 20% by the year 2025, and we seek the development of interventions that will save the greatest amount of lives. Universal, selective or indicated interventions that target suicide prevention in healthcare systems, emergency departments, corrections settings, or among the gun owning community, that, if implemented on a large scale, would reduce the annual United States suicide rate

Purpose: Focus grants are targeted, innovative and potentially high impact studies that seek to inform and even transform suicide prevention efforts

Eligibility: Investigators from all academic disciplines are eligible to apply, and both basic science and applied research projects will be considered, provided that the proposed study has an essential focus on suicide or suicide prevention. Grant applications are not accepted from for-profit organizations, or from federal or state government agencies. Applications from the Veterans Administration are eligible

Level of Study: Research

Type: Grant

Value: They are awarded in the amount of US$5,00,000 per year for a maximum of three years

Length of Study: 3 years

Frequency: Annual

Country of Study: Any country

Application Procedure: Applicants must submit a Letter of Intent by email to JHarkavyFriedman@afsp.org. If Letter of Intent is approved for application, applicants are instructed to apply at afsp.org/our-work/research/apply-for-a-grant/

Closing Date: 6 December

Funding: Private

For further information contact:

Email: grantsmanager@afsp.org

Short-Term Risk Focus Grant

Subjects: Supports innovative, potentially high-yield solutions that focus on short-term risk for suicide. The development of identification and/or intervention strategies for short-term suicide risk that can be readily implemented in clinical settings

Purpose: Focus grants are targeted, innovative and potentially high impact studies that seek to inform and even transform suicide prevention efforts

Eligibility: Investigators from all academic disciplines are eligible to apply, and both basic science and applied research projects will be considered, provided that the proposed study has an essential focus on suicide or suicide prevention. Grant applications are not accepted from for-profit organizations, or from federal or state government agencies. Applications from the Veterans Administration are eligible

Level of Study: Research

Type: Grant

Value: They are awarded in the amount of US$5,00,000 per year for a maximum of three years

Length of Study: 3 years

Frequency: Annual

Country of Study: Any country

No. of awards offered: 1

Application Procedure: Applicants must submit a Letter of Intent by email to JHarkavyFriedman@afsp.org. If Letter of Intent is approved for application, applicants are instructed to apply at afsp.org/our-work/research/apply-for-a-grant/

Closing Date: 6 December

Funding: Private

No. of awards given last year: 1

No. of applicants last year: 1

For further information contact:

Email: grantsmanager@afsp.org

Standard Research Grant

Subjects: Investigators at any level

Purpose: We welcome innovative studies relevant to understanding and preventing suicide. Applications are open to biological, psychological, and sociological approaches, and we encourage multidisciplinary research. These are investigator initiated grants

Eligibility: Investigators from all academic disciplines are eligible to apply, and both basic science and applied research projects will be considered, provided that the proposed study has an essential focus on suicide or suicide prevention. Grant applications are not accepted from for-profit organizations, or from federal or state government agencies. Applications from the Veterans Administration are eligible

Level of Study: Research

Type: Grant

Value: Up to US$1,00,000 over 2 Years

Length of Study: 2 years

Frequency: Annual

Country of Study: Any country

No. of awards offered: 70

Application Procedure: Applicants are instructed to apply afsp.org/our-work/research/apply-for-a-grant/

Closing Date: 14 November

Funding: Private

No. of awards given last year: 10

No. of applicants last year: 70

For further information contact:

Email: grantsmanager@afsp.org

American Foundation for Urologic Disease, Inc. (AFUD)

Research Program Division, 300 West Pratt Street Suite 401, Baltimore, MD 21202 2463, United States of America

Tel: (1) 410 689 3990
Fax: (1) 800 825 7866
Website: www.auanet.org/
Contact: Grants Management Officer

The mission of the American Foundation for Urologic Disease (AFUD) is the prevention and cure of urologic diseases through the expansion of medical research and the education of the public and health care professionals concerning urologic diseases.

National Institute of Diabetes and Digestive and Kidney Diseases (NIDDK)/ AFUD Intramural Urology Research Training Program

Subjects: Metabolic disease, molecular and cellular biology, cell biochemistry and biology, biochemistry and diabetes

Purpose: Provides an opportunity for selected individuals to complete a research project under the direction of a Senior Investigator in the Intramural Programme of NIDDK

Eligibility: Open to physicians who have recently completed a urology residency. Applicants must have less than five years postdoctoral experience (clinical residency training is not counted as postdoctoral research)

Level of Study: Postdoctorate

Type: Fellowship

Value: US$45,000–52,000 per year depending on experience

Length of Study: 2 years, possible extension for a further year

Study Establishment: Participating NIDDK laboratories

Country of Study: United States of America

Application Procedure: Applicants must submit a cover letter, curriculum vitae and three letters of recommendation. Further information available from NIDDK or the American Foundation for Urologic Disease

Closing Date: Accepted at any time

Additional Information: Further information available on request

For further information contact:

Division of Kidney, Urology & Hematology, National Institute of Diabetes, Digestive & Kidney Diseases, Natcher Building Room 6AS13D, Bethesda, MD 20892-6600, United States of America

Tel: (1) 301 594 7717
Fax: (1) 301 480 3510
Email: nybergl@ep.niddk.nih.gov
Contact: Dr Leroy M Nyberg, Director, Urology Programme

American Geophysical Union (AGU)

2000 Florida Avenue, N.W., Washington, DC 20009, United States of America

Tel:	(1) 202 462 6900
Fax:	(1) 202 328 0566
Email:	service@agu.org
Website:	www.agu.org
Contact:	Director, Outreach and Research Support

The American Geophysical Union (AGU) is an international scientific society with more than 45,000 members, primarily research scientists, dedicated to advancing the understanding of Earth and space and making the results of the AGU's research available to the public.

Fred. L. Scarf Award

Subjects: Solar-planetary science
Purpose: To award outstanding dissertation research that contributes directly to solar-planetary science
Eligibility: Open to all candidates with a PhD (or equivalent) degree
Level of Study: Doctorate
Value: US$1,000, a complimentary ticket for the SPA dinner, and a certificate
Frequency: Annual
Application Procedure: Nominations to be sent to outreach administrator at AGU
Closing Date: 15 April
Contributor: The Space Physics and Aeronomy section of AGU
Additional Information: Awardee will have the opportunity to deliver an invited paper on the dissertation topic at appropriate SPA session at the upcoming AGU Fall Meeting

For further information contact:

Tel:	(1) 202 777 7502
Email:	leadership@agu.org, mgl.scarf.award@nrl.navy.mil, dwilliams@agu.org

Mineral and Rock Physics Graduate Research Award

Subjects: Mineral and rock physics
Purpose: To recognize outstanding contributions by young scientists

Eligibility: Open to students who have completed their PhD
Level of Study: Doctorate
Type: Award
Value: US$500, a certificate and Announcement in Eos. Recognition at the AGU Fall Meeting during the award presentation year
Frequency: Annual
Application Procedure: A letter of nomination along with a curriculum vitae, two supporting letters and 3 reprints or preprints of the nominee's work should be sent
Closing Date: 15 April
Contributor: Mineral and Rock Physics community at AGU
No. of awards given last year: 2

For further information contact:

Department of Geology and Environmental Geoscience, Northern Illinois University, Davis Hall 312, Normal Road, DeKalb, IL 60115, United States of America

Email:	hwatson@niu.edu
Contact:	Dr Heather C. Watson, Assistant Professor

American Gynecological Club

American Gynecological Club / Gynaecological Visiting Society Fellowship

Purpose: Through generous funding from the American Gynecological Club and the Gynaecological Visiting Society of Great Britain, the RCOG can offer up to £1,200 to an individual to visit and gain knowledge from a specific centre offering new techniques of clinical management within O&G
Eligibility: 1. Travel must take place within 12 months of the award being made. 2. The award may only be used for the purpose outlined in your original application. 3. A detailed report (maximum 1,000 words), including pictures if necessary, must be submitted to the RCOG Awards Administrator within eight weeks after the elective
Level of Study: Postdoctorate
Type: Fellowship
Value: £1,200
Length of Study: 1 year
Frequency: Annual
Country of Study: Any country
Closing Date: 31 May
Funding: Foundation

For further information contact:

Email: awards@rcog.org.uk

American Head and Neck Society (AHNS)

AHNS, 11300 W. Olympic Boulevard, Suite 600, Los Angeles, CA 90064, United States of America

Tel: (1) 310 437 0559
Fax: (1) 310 437 0585
Email: admin@ahns.info
Website: www.headandneckcancer.org
Contact: Joyce Hasper, Research Grants Enquiries

The purpose of the American Head and Neck Society (AHNS) is to promote and advance the knowledge of prevention, diagnosis, treatment and rehabilitation of neoplasms and other diseases of the head and neck.

American Academy of Otolaryngology - Head and Neck Surgery Translational Innovator Award

Purpose: The purpose of this award is to support contemporary basic or clinical research focused on neoplastic disease by full time academic head and neck surgeons; to promote novel translational research preferably with biomarker ideas

Eligibility: Candidates for this award must be: 1. Otolaryngologist—Head and Neck surgeons, who are active members of the AAO-HNS. OR: Surgeons who are in head and neck fellowships, or have completed a head and neck surgery fellowship and are active or candidate members of the AHNS. PLEASE NOTE: Medical oncologists and radiation oncologists are not eligible to apply for this award. 2. Citizens of the United States, noncitizen nationals, or have been lawfully admitted for permanent residency at the time of application. 3. Full-time academic surgeons in faculty positions at the rank of instructor or assistant professor. 4. Hold a Doctor of Medicine (MD) degree or equivalent (DO, MBBS) from an accredited institution. 5. Have demonstrated the capacity or potential for a highly productive independent research career with an emphasis in head and neck surgical oncology

Level of Study: Graduate
Type: Award
Frequency: Annual
Country of Study: Any country
Closing Date: 1 January
Funding: Private

For further information contact:

AHNS, 11300 W. Olympic Blvd, Suite 600, Los Angeles, CA 90064, United States of America

Email: betty@ahns.info

American Head and Neck Society Endocrine Research Grant

Purpose: Open to medical students focusing in otolaryngology, otolaryngology residents, PhDs or faculty members in otolaryngology departments
Level of Study: Graduate
Type: Research grant
Value: Upto US$10,000 are available per year
Frequency: Annual
Country of Study: Any country
Closing Date: 15 March
Funding: Private

For further information contact:

Tel: (1) 310 437 0559
Email: betty@ahns.info

American Head and Neck Society Pilot Research Grant

Subjects: Diseases of the head and neck
Purpose: To support students who wish to try a pilot project in head- and neck-related research
Eligibility: Open to residents and fellows in the junior faculty
Level of Study: Doctorate, Postgraduate
Type: Award
Value: US$10,000
Length of Study: 1 year
Frequency: Annual
Study Establishment: A university in the United States of America
Country of Study: United States of America
Closing Date: 15 December
Funding: Private

For further information contact:

Email: betty@ahns.info

American Head and Neck Society Surgeon Scientist Career Development Award (with AAOHNS)

Subjects: Cancer and other diseases of the head and neck

Purpose: To support research in the pathogenesis, pathophysiology, diagnosis, prevention or treatment of head and neck neoplastic disease

Eligibility: Open to surgeons beginning a clinician-scientist career

Level of Study: Postdoctorate

Type: Award

Value: US$35,000 per year (non-renewable)

Length of Study: 2 years

Frequency: Annual

Study Establishment: A university in the United States of America

Country of Study: United States of America

Application Procedure: The grants are reviewed through the Academy CORE (combined otolaryngologic research evaluation) process

Closing Date: 16 January

Funding: Private

Additional Information: Applicants are requested to submit their LOI early to gain advanced access to the full application. Forms are available through American Academy of Otolaryngology CORE

For further information contact:

Email: pcsupport@altum.com

American Head and Neck Society Young Investigator Award (with AAOHNS)

Subjects: Cancer and other diseases of the head and neck

Purpose: To support research in neoplastic disease of the head and neck

Eligibility: Candidate must be a member of AHNS

Level of Study: Doctorate

Type: Award

Value: US$20,000 per year

Length of Study: Up to 2 years

Frequency: Annual

Study Establishment: A university in the United States of America

Country of Study: United States of America

Application Procedure: The grants are reviewed through the Academy CORE (combined otolaryngologic research evaluation) process

Closing Date: 15 January

Funding: Private

Additional Information: Submit your LOI early to gain advanced access to the full application. Forms are available through American Academy of Otolaryngology CORE

For further information contact:

Email: admin@ahns.info

American Head and Neck Society-American Cyronics Society Career Development Award

Subjects: Diseases of the head and neck

Purpose: To facilitate research in connection with career development

Eligibility: Applicants must be a member or candidate member of ACS and AHNS. Applicants must be within 5 years of completion of training, and be full-time faculty member

Level of Study: Postgraduate

Type: Award

Value: US$40,000 per year (non-renewable)

Length of Study: 2 years

Frequency: Annual

Study Establishment: A university in the United States of America

Country of Study: United States of America

Funding: Private

Additional Information: Please check website for more details

American Indian Science and Engineering Society

1630 30th Street Suite 301, Boulder, CO 80301-1014, United States of America

Tel: (1) 303 939 0023
Fax: (1) 303 939 8150
Email: ascholar@spot.colorado.edu
Contact: Ms Sonya Todacheene

Naval Sea Systems Command (NAVSEA) and Strategic Systems Programs Scholarship

Purpose: This scholarship is open to United States college freshmen who are American Indian, Alaskan Native, or Native Hawaiian and enrolled at a minority-serving institution (as designated by the United States Department of Education) that is ABET-accredited

Eligibility: Students must be pursuing a Navy-relevant Science, Technology, Engineering or Mathematics (STEM) degree and have a grade point average of 3.0 or higher

Level of Study: Graduate

Type: Scholarship

Value: US$10,000

Frequency: Annual
Country of Study: Any country
Application Procedure: Apply online: www.unigo.com/match/register?redirecturl=https%3a%2f%2fwww.unigo.com%2fscholarships%2fby-type%2fneed-based-scholarships%2fnaval-sea-systems-command-navsea-and-strategic-systems-programs-scholarship%2f1005894
Closing Date: 31 March
Funding: Foundation

For further information contact:

203 N. La Salle St. Suite 1675, Chicago, IL 60601, United States of America

Email: scholarships@swe.org

American Institute for Economic Research (AIER)

250 Division St, PO Box 1000, Great Barrington, MA 01230, United States of America

Tel: (1) 888 528 1216
Fax: (1) 413 528 0103
Email: info@aier.org; fellowships@aier.org
Website: www.aier.org

The American Institute for Economic Research (AIER), founded in 1933, is an independent scientific educational organization. The Institute conducts scientific enquiry into general economics with a focus on monetary issues. Attention is also given to business cycle analysis and forecasting as well as monetary economics.

American Institute for Economic Research Summer Fellowship

Subjects: Scientific procedures of enquiry, monetary economics, business cycle analysis and forecasting
Purpose: To further the development of economic scientists
Eligibility: Open to graduating seniors who are entering doctoral programmes in economics, or those enrolled in doctoral programmes in economics for no longer than 2 years. The programme is not designed for those enrolling into business school
Level of Study: Postgraduate
Type: Fellowship

Value: US$500 weekly stipend plus room and full board
Length of Study: 8 weeks
Frequency: Annual
Study Establishment: AIER
Country of Study: United States of America
No. of awards offered: 47
Application Procedure: A current resume; a writing sample; a statement explaining why you would like to be a student fellow at AIER and whether you qualify to reside on campus; an official transcript directly from your school or university; two letters of recommendation from teachers, college professors, or employers should be sent either by electronic or United States mail to the American Institute for Economic Research. Please state "Summer Fellowship Practicum" in the subject line
Closing Date: 23 March
Funding: Private
No. of awards given last year: 17
No. of applicants last year: 47
Additional Information: AIER does not sponsor visa applications for foreign nationals. However, foreign nationals are welcome to apply if they are enrolled in a United States degree granting institution, have CPT or OPT, or have employment authorization in the United States

For further information contact:

Summer Fellowship Program Coordinator, American Institute for Economic Research, PO Box 1000, United States of America

Fax: (1) 413 528 0103
Email: internships@aier.org

American Institute for Sri Lankan Studies (AISLS)

155 Pine Street, Belmont, MA 02478, United States of America

Email: rogersjohnd@aol.com
Website: www.aisls.org
Contact: John Rogers

The American Institute for Sri Lankan Studies (AISLS) was established in 1995, to foster excellence in American research and teaching on Sri Lanka, and to promote the exchange of scholars and scholarly information between the United States and Sri Lanka. The Institute serves as the professional association for United States-based scholars and other professionals who are interested in Sri Lanka.

Fellowship Program

Subjects: All social science and humanities fields, and topics in related fields such as environmental studies and law that contribute to the understanding of aspects of the society, history or culture of Sri Lanka
Purpose: Supports from 2 to 6 months research in Sri Lanka on topics in the social sciences, humanities, and related fields
Eligibility: Applicants must be United States citizens and hold a PhD or equivalent at the time they plan to begin research
Level of Study: Postdoctorate
Type: Fellowship
Value: per diem of US$3,700 per month, plus airfare
Length of Study: 2 to 6 months
Frequency: Annual
Country of Study: Asia
Application Procedure: Submit a pdf file with the information asked for in the application instructions available at www.aisls.org
Closing Date: 1 December
Funding: Government
Contributor: Bureau of Economic and Cultural Affairs, United States State Department
No. of awards given last year: 2

For further information contact:

Email: rogersjohnd@aol.com

American Institute of Bangladesh Studies (AIBS)

B 488 Medical Sciences Center, 1300 University Ave, Madison, WI 53706, United States of America

Tel: (1) 608 265 1471
Fax: (1) 608 265 3302
Email: info@aibs.net
Website: www.aibs.net
Contact: Laura Hammond, Administrative Program Manager

The American Institute of Bangladesh Studies (AIBS) is a consortium of United States universities and colleges involved in research on Bangladesh. It strives to improve the scholarly understanding of Bangladesh culture and society in the United States and to promote educational exchange between the two countries.

American Institute of Bangladesh Studies Junior Fellowship

Subjects: AIBS Junior Fellowship
Purpose: To improve the scholarly understanding of Bangladesh culture and society in the United States
Eligibility: Open to an individual member of AIBS; currently in the ABD phase of your PhD program; is in the data collection and writing stage of the dissertation, and must be United States citizen
Level of Study: Research
Type: Fellowship
Value: Fellowships will be equivalent to US$1,150 per month, plus economy Round-Trip Air Transportation (up to US$2,500) via the most direct route
Length of Study: 2–12 months
Frequency: Annual
Country of Study: Bangladesh
Application Procedure: Applicants can access our online application form at www.aibs.net
Closing Date: 15 September
Funding: Government
Contributor: United States Department of State Bureau of Educational and Cultural Affairs through the Council of American Overseas Research Centers
Additional Information: Please check AIBS website (www.aibs.net) for more information

For further information contact:

Email: info@aibs.net

American Institute of Bangladesh Studies Pre-Dissertation Fellowships

Purpose: The American Institute of Bangladesh Studies offers short-term grants to graduate students pursuing studies of Bangladesh funded by the United States Department of State Bureau of Educational and Cultural Affairs through the Council of American Overseas Research Centers
Eligibility: All applicants must be enrolled/employed at a United States academic institution and a United States citizen. Open to an individual member of AIBS and must have

completed at least 1 year of graduate study in a recognized PhD granting institution and enrolled in a graduate program but not yet at the dissertation research or writing stage

Level of Study: Research

Type: Fellowship

Value: The award is for US$3,000 plus economy round trip transportation (up to US$2,500) via the most direct route

Frequency: Annual

Country of Study: Bangladesh

No. of awards offered: Varies

Application Procedure: Applicants can access the online application at www.aibs.net

Closing Date: 15 September

Funding: Government

Contributor: United States Department of State Bureau of Educational and Cultural Affairs through the council of American Overseas Research Centres

No. of awards given last year: Varies

No. of applicants last year: Varies

Additional Information: Please check ABIS website (www.aibs.net) for more information

For further information contact:

Email: info@aibs.net

American Institute of Bangladesh Studies Senior Fellowship

Subjects: Area and cultural studies

Purpose: To improve the scholarly understanding of Bangladesh culture and society in the United States

Eligibility: Open to citizens of the United States. Senior Fellowships are available to applicants who have obtained a PhD and have a well-developed research agenda relevant to Bangladesh

Level of Study: Doctorate, Postdoctorate, Predoctorate, Research

Type: Fellowship

Value: US$1,400 per month plus research and dependent

Length of Study: 2–12 months

Frequency: Annual

Country of Study: Bangladesh

No. of awards offered: Varies

Application Procedure: Applicants can access our online application form at www.aibs.net

Closing Date: 15 September

Funding: Government

Contributor: United States department of State Bureau of Educational and Cultural Affairs through the council of American overseas research centres

No. of awards given last year: Varies

No. of applicants last year: Varies

Additional Information: Please check AIBS website for additional information (www.aibs.net)

For further information contact:

Email: info@aibs.net

American Institute of Bangladesh Studies Travel Grants

Subjects: All subjects

Purpose: AIBS can provide funding for conference travel for the presentation of papers or organization of panels that include topics relevant to Bangladesh Studies at scholarly conferences

Eligibility: Must be a United States citizen travelling within the United States

Level of Study: Graduate

Type: Travel grant

Value: Up to US$600 for travel to conferences within the United States. International travel grants have been suspended until further notice due to budgetary constraints

Frequency: Annual

Country of Study: Bangladesh

Application Procedure: Please fill out online application at www.aibs.net. or contact aibs@southasia.wisc.edu for more information

Closing Date: Any time as needed

Funding: Government

Additional Information: Please check the AIBS website for more information

For further information contact:

Email: info@aibs.net

American Institute of Certified Public Accountants (AICPA)

1211 Avenue of the Americas, New York, NY 10036-8775, United States of America

Tel: (1) 212 596 6200
Fax: (1) 212 596 6213
Email: service@aicpa.org
Website: www.aicpa.org

The American Institute of Certified Public Accountants (AICPA) is a national, professional organization for all Certified Public Accountants. Its mission is to provide members with the resources, information and leadership that enable them to provide valuable services in the highest professional manner to benefit the public as well as employers and clients. In fulfilling its mission, the AICPA works with state CPA organizations and gives priority to those areas where public reliance on CPA skills is most significant.

American Institute of Certified Public Accountants Fellowship for Minority Doctoral students

Subjects: Accounting
Purpose: To encourage practising CPAs to consider a career change to academe
Eligibility: 1. Open to United States citizens who hold a valid CPA certificate, and have at least five years of professional accounting experience. 2. Candidates must be accepted into or be in the process of applying to a doctoral programme in accounting at a college or university whose business administration programmes are accredited by the AACSB. 3. Applicants should have the intention to pursue an academic career in accounting in the United States. All applicants are expected to exhibit fluency in English appropriate to teaching
Level of Study: Doctorate
Type: Fellowship
Value: US$5,000 per year
Length of Study: A maximum of 3 years
Frequency: Annual
Study Establishment: A college or university whose business administration programs are accredited by the AACSB - the International Association for Management Education
Country of Study: United States of America
Application Procedure: An official academic transcript is required, in addition to references from three individuals, and the completion of an application form. Application procedure is as follows: 1. A completed application form. 2. An official academic transcript from each institution from which you have received a degree. 3. Confidential references from two individuals. 4. Visit ThisWayToCPA.com for more application requirements
Closing Date: 15 May

For further information contact:

Email: academics@aicpa.org

American Library Association (ALA)

50 E. Huron Street, Chicago, IL 60611, United States of America

Tel: (1) 800 545 2433 ext. 4274
Fax: (1) 312 440 9374
Email: ala@ala.org
Website: www.ala.org
Contact: Ms Melissa Jacobsen, Manager, Prof. Dev

Each year the American Library Association (ALA) and its member units sponsor awards to honour distinguished service and foster professional growth.

American Library Association Carroll Preston Baber Research Grant

Subjects: Library service
Purpose: To encourage innovative research that could lead to an improvement in library services to any specified group or groups of people. The project should aim to answer a question that is of vital importance to the library community and the researchers should plan to provide documentation of the results of their work
Eligibility: Any ALA member may apply. The Jury would welcome projects that involve both a practicing librarian and a researcher
Level of Study: Unrestricted
Type: Research grant
Value: Up to US$3,000
Length of Study: Up to 18 months
Frequency: Annual
Country of Study: Any country
No. of awards offered: 5
Application Procedure: Applicants must submit an application including a research proposal
Closing Date: 12 February
Funding: Private
Contributor: Eric R Baber
No. of awards given last year: 1
No. of applicants last year: 5
Additional Information: The project should aim to answer a question that is of vital importance to the library community and the researchers should plan to provide documentation of the results of their work. The jury would welcome proposals that involve innovative uses of technology and proposals that involve co-operation between libraries and other agencies, or between librarians and persons in other disciplines

For further information contact:

Tel: (1) 312 280 4273
Email: krosa@ala.org
Contact: Kathy Rosa, Director, Library & Research center

American Library Association John Phillip Immroth Memorial Award

Subjects: Intellectual freedom
Purpose: To recognize a notable contribution to intellectual freedom fuelled by personal courage
Eligibility: Open to intellectual freedom fighters. Individuals, a group of individuals or an organization are eligible for the award
Level of Study: Unrestricted
Type: Award
Value: US$500 plus a citation
Frequency: Annual
Country of Study: Any country
Application Procedure: Applicants must submit a detailed statement explaining why the nominator believes that the nominee should receive the award. Nominations should be submitted to IFRT Staff Liaison at the ALA
Closing Date: 17 February
Funding: Private
Contributor: Intellectual Freedom Round Table (IFRT) of the American Library Association

For further information contact:

Tel: (1) 312 280 4220/800 545 2433, ext. 4220
Fax: (1) 312 280 4227
Email: bcampbell@ala.org
Contact: Bryan Campbell

American Library Association Loleta D. Fyan Grant

Subjects: Library service
Purpose: To facilitate the development and improvement of public libraries and the services they provide
Eligibility: Applicants can include but are not limited to local, regional or state libraries, associations or organizations including units of the ALA, library schools or individuals
Level of Study: Unrestricted
Type: Research grant
Value: Up to US$5,000
Frequency: Annual
Country of Study: Any country
No. of awards offered: 10

Application Procedure: Applicants must submit an application form in addition to a proposal and budget to the ALA Staff Liaison. Please do not fax or mail
Closing Date: 21 December
Funding: Private
No. of awards given last year: 1
No. of applicants last year: 10
Additional Information: The project must result in the development and improvement of public libraries and the services they provide, have the potential for broader impact and application beyond meeting a specific local need, should be designed to effect changes in public library services that are innovative and responsive to the future and should be capable of completion within one year

For further information contact:

American Library Association, United States of America

Tel: (1) 312 280 3217
Email: cbourdon@ala.org
Contact: Cathleen Bourdon, Associate Executive Director, Communications & Member Relations

American Library Association Miriam L Hornback Scholarship

Subjects: Library science
Purpose: To assist an individual pursuing a Master's degree
Eligibility: Open to ALA or library support staff who are pursuing a Master's degree in library science and who are citizens of the United States of America or Canada
Level of Study: Postgraduate
Type: Scholarship
Value: US$3,000
Frequency: Annual
Application Procedure: Applicants must write for details
Closing Date: 1 March
No. of awards given last year: 2

For further information contact:

Email: klredd@ala.org
Contact: Kimberly L. Redd, Program Officer

American Library Association Shirley Olofson Memorial Awards

Subjects: Library science
Purpose: To allow individuals to attend ALA conferences
Eligibility: Open to members of the ALA who are also current or potential members of the New Members Round Table.

Applicants should not have attended any more than five conferences
Level of Study: Unrestricted
Type: Award
Value: US$1,000
Frequency: Annual
Country of Study: Any country
Application Procedure: Applicants must write for details. Fill out the application online
Closing Date: 10 December
Contributor: The New Members Round Table (NMRT) and the Shirley Olofson Memorial Award Committee

For further information contact:

Email: ala@ala.org

American Library Association W. David Rozkuszka Scholarship

Subjects: Library science
Purpose: To provide financial assistance to an individual who is currently working with government documents in a library
Eligibility: Open to applicants currently completing a Master's programme in library science
Level of Study: Postgraduate
Type: Scholarship
Value: US$3,000
Frequency: Annual
Country of Study: Any country
Application Procedure: Applicants must write for details
Closing Date: 31 December

For further information contact:

PO Box 515, United States of America

Tel: (1) 541 992 5461
Email: asevetson@hotmail.com
Contact: Andrea Sevetson

American Library Association YALSA/Baker and Taylor Conference Grant

Subjects: Library science
Purpose: To allow young adult librarians who work directly with young adults in either a public library or a school library to attend the Annual Conference of the ALA
Eligibility: Open to members of the Young Adult Library Services Association with between 1 and 10 years of library experience who have never attended an ALA Annual Conference

Level of Study: Professional development
Type: Grant
Value: US$1,000 each
Frequency: Annual
Country of Study: Any country
Application Procedure: Applicants must submit applications to the Young Adult Library Services Association, ALA, by email to Nichole Gilbert at ngilbert@ala.org. Attachments must be named the applicants last name, underscore, the name of the grant, e.g., Gilbert_BakerTaylor
Closing Date: 1 December

For further information contact:

50 E. Huron St. Chicago, IL 60611, United States of America

Tel: (1) 800 545 2433
Email: YALSA@ala.org

Dixie Electric Membership Corporation New Leaders Travel Grant

Subjects: Library science
Purpose: To enhance professional development and improve the expertise of public librarians new to the field by making possible their attendance at major PLA professional development activities
Eligibility: Open to qualified public librarians, MLS, PLA member
Level of Study: Professional development
Type: Travel grant
Value: Plaque and travel grant of up to US$1,500 per awardee
Frequency: Annual
Country of Study: Any country
Application Procedure: Visit website www.pla.org
Closing Date: 1 December
Funding: Corporation
No. of awards given last year: 4

For further information contact:

Email: jkloeppel@ala.org
Contact: Julianna Kloeppel

Spectrum Initiative Scholarship Program

Subjects: Library and information studies
Purpose: To encourage admission to an ALA recognized Master's degree programme by the four largest underrepresented minority groups
Eligibility: Open to citizens of the United States of America or Canada only, from one of the largest underrepresented

groups. These are African American or African Canadian, Asian or Pacific Islander, Latino or Hispanic and native people of the United States of America or Canada

Level of Study: Postgraduate
Type: Scholarship
Value: US$5,000
Frequency: Annual
Country of Study: United States of America or Canada
Application Procedure: Applicants must request details via fax or visit the website
Closing Date: 1 March
Additional Information: Applications accepted from mid-October to 1 March each year

For further information contact:

Tel: (1) 800 545 2433 ext 5048
Email: spectrum@ala.org

American Lung Association

1301 Pennsylvania Ave., NW, Suite 800, Washington, DC 20004, United States of America

Tel: (1) 202 785 3355
Fax: (1) 202 452 1805
Email: info@lungusa.org
Website: www.lungusa.org
Contact: Ms Evita Mendoza

The American Lung Association is the oldest voluntary health organization in the United States, with a National Office and constituent and affiliate associations around the country. Founded in 1904 to fight tuberculosis, the American Lung Association today fights lung disease in all its forms, with special emphasis on asthma, tobacco control and environmental health.

Lung Health (LH) Research Dissertation Grants

Subjects: Psychosocial, behavioral, health services, health policy, epidemiological, biostatistical and educational matters related to lung disease
Purpose: To provide financial assistance for Doctoral research training for dissertation research on issues relevant to lung disease
Eligibility: Open to citizens or permanent residents of the United States
Level of Study: Doctorate
Type: Research grant
Value: US$21,000 per year

Length of Study: 1–2 years
Frequency: Annual
Country of Study: United States of America
Closing Date: 20 October
Funding: Government, Corporation, Foundation
Contributor: American Lung Association
Additional Information: Up to US$16,000 of the award may be used for a student stipend. Funds may not be used for tuition. The award will terminate at the time the awardee is granted a doctoral degree

For further information contact:

Research and Program Services, American Lung Association, 14 Wall Street, 8th Floor, United States of America

Email: info@lungusa.org

American Mathematical Society

201 Charles Street, Providence, RI 02904-2294, United States of America

Tel: (1) 401 455 4000
Fax: (1) 401 331 3842
Website: www.ams.org

The AMS, founded in 1888 to further the interests of mathematical research and scholarship, serves the national and international community through its publications, meetings, advocacy and other programs, which promote mathematical research, its communication and uses, encourage and promote the transmission of mathematical understanding and skills, support mathematical education at all levels, advance the status of the profession of mathematics, encouraging and facilitating full participation of all individuals, foster an awareness and appreciation of mathematics and its connections to other disciplines and everyday life.

American Meteorological Society Centennial Fellowships in Mathematics

Subjects: Mathematics
Purpose: To help mathematicians do in their careers in research
Eligibility: The primary selection criterion for the Centennial Fellowship is the excellence of the candidate's research. Preference will be given to candidates who have not had extensive fellowship support in the past. Recipients may not hold the

Centennial Fellowship concurrently with other major research award such as a Sloan fellowship, NSF Postdoctoral fellowship, or career award. Under normal circumstances, the fellowship cannot be deferred. The students of North America can apply for these scholarships. For detailed information, visit website

Level of Study: Research
Type: Fellowship
Value: The stipend for fellowships awarded was US$89,000, with an additional expense allowance of US$8,900
Country of Study: Any country
Application Procedure: The mode of applying is by post
Closing Date: June
Additional Information: Scholarship can be taken at North America

For further information contact:

Email: development@ams.org

American Meteorological Society (AMS)

45 Beacon Street, Boston, MA 02108-3693, United States of America

Tel: (1) 617 227 2425
Fax: (1) 617 742 8718
Email: amsinfo@ametsoc.org
Website: www.ametsoc.org

The American Meteorological Society (AMS) promotes the development and dissemination of information and education on the atmospheric and related oceanic and hydrologic sciences and the advancement of their professional applications. Founded in 1919, AMS has a membership of more than 11,000 professionals, professors, students and weather enthusiasts.

American Meteorological Society Graduate Fellowships

Subjects: Atmospheric and related oceanic and hydrologic sciences
Purpose: To attract promising young scientists to prepare for careers in the atmospheric and related oceanic and hydrologic fields
Eligibility: Applicants must be United States citizens or hold permanent resident status entering their first year of graduate school and provide evidence of acceptance as a full-time student at an accredited United States institution at the time

of the award. Applicants must have a minimum grade point average of 3.25 on a 4.0-point scale
Level of Study: Graduate
Type: Fellowship
Value: US$25,000 to each recipient for a 9-month period
Length of Study: 9 months
Frequency: Annual
Country of Study: United States of America
Application Procedure: Application form should be completed and written references, official transcripts, and GRE score reports, may be sent under separate cover. Applications and written references can be sent via email to dFernandez@ametsoc.org. Also refer to website www.ametsoc.org
Closing Date: 13 January
Funding: Government, Corporation, Foundation
Contributor: Industry leaders and government agencies
No. of awards given last year: 13
Additional Information: The evaluation of applicants will be based on applicant's performance as an undergraduate student, including academic records, recommendations and GRE scores. Please see the website for further details www.ametsoc.org/amsstudentinfo/scholfeldocs/

For further information contact:

Email: dfernandez@ametsoc.org

American Museum of Natural History (AMNH)

Central Park West, 79th Street, New York, NY 10024-5192, United States of America

Tel: (1) 212 769 5100
Fax: (1) 212 769 5427
Email: yna@amnh.org
Website: www.amnh.org
Contact: Ms Maria Dixon, Office of Grants & Fellowships

For 125 years, the American Museum of Natural History (AMNH) has been one of the world's pre-eminent science and research institutions, renowned for its collections and exhibitions that illuminate millions of years of the Earth's evolution.

American Museum of Natural History Collection Study Grants

Subjects: Any of the fields covered by the scientific collections at the Museum such as zoology, anthropology, mineral science and astrophysics

Eligibility: Open to predoctoral and recent postdoctoral investigators. The award is not available to investigators residing within daily commuting distance of the Museum
Level of Study: Postdoctorate, Predoctorate
Type: Grant
Value: Up to US$1,500 to support travel and subsistence while visiting the Museum
Frequency: Twice a year
Study Establishment: The Museum
Country of Study: United States of America
Application Procedure: Applicants must contact the appropriate Museum department to discuss the feasibility of the project and obtain written approval from the Chairman. A special application form is required and should be requested by name from the Office of Grants and Fellowships. A final report is also required. Application forms can be obtained from the website
Closing Date: 1 November
Additional Information: Mammalogy, herpetology and ichthyology have one deadline date of 1 November. All other departments can submit 1 May and 1 November. Ornithology applications can be submitted two months prior to the visit and has no deadline date

For further information contact:

Email: careers@amnh.org

American Nuclear Society (ANS)

555 North Kensington Avenue, La Grange Park, IL 60526, United States of America

Tel: (1) 708 352 6611
Fax: (1) 708 352 0499
Email: outreach@ans.org
Website: www.ans.org
Contact: Scholarship Programme

The American Nuclear Society (ANS) is a non-profit, international, scientific and educational organization. It was established by a group of individuals who recognized the need to unify the professional activities within the diverse fields of nuclear science and technology.

American Nuclear Society Mishima Award

Subjects: Materials science and technology
Purpose: To recognize outstanding contributions in research

Eligibility: Open to candidates who may or may not be members of ANS
Level of Study: Postgraduate
Type: Award
Value: An engraved plaque and a monetary award
Frequency: Annual
Country of Study: Any country
Application Procedure: Eight sets of the nomination form and supporting materials must be submitted
Closing Date: 1 March

For further information contact:

Email: honors@ans.org

American Nuclear Society Utility Achievement Award

Subjects: Nuclear science
Purpose: To recognize professional excellence and leadership
Eligibility: Open to members of ANS
Level of Study: Postgraduate
Type: Award
Value: An engraved plaque that is presented in August each year in conjunction with the ANS
Frequency: Annual
Country of Study: Any country
Application Procedure: Nominations must be sent before the deadline
Closing Date: 30 April

For further information contact:

Center for Energy Research 460 EBU II, United States of America

Email: meetings@ans.org
Contact: Professor Farrokh Najmabadi

Ely M. Gelbard Graduate Scholarship

Purpose: Dr. Ely M. Gelbard obtained his PhD in physics from the University of Chicago. During World War II, he served in the United States Army Air Corps as a radar technician
Eligibility: na
Level of Study: Graduate, Postgraduate
Type: Scholarship
Value: US$3,500/each
Frequency: Annual
Country of Study: Any country

Application Procedure: A selection committee will be established by the Mathematics and Computation Division
Closing Date: 1 February
Funding: Private
Contributor: Mathematics and Computation Division (MCD)
Additional Information: For further information, check the below link. www.ans.org/honors/scholarships/gelbard/

For further information contact:

American Nuclear Society, 555 North Kensington Avenue, La Grange Park, IL 60526, United States of America

Tel: (1) 800 323 3044
Email: nuclear@illinois.edu

Henry DeWolf Smyth Nuclear Statesman Award

Subjects: Nuclear energy
Purpose: To recognize outstanding and statesmanlike contributions to many aspects of nuclear energy activities
Eligibility: Open to candidates of any nationality
Level of Study: Postgraduate
Type: Award
Value: An engraved medal
Country of Study: Any country
Application Procedure: Nomination to be sent, see the website for further information
Closing Date: 28 February
Contributor: ANS and Nuclear Energy Institute

For further information contact:

Email: honors@ans.org

John R. Lamarsh Scholarship

Subjects: Nuclear science and technology
Eligibility: United States and non-United States applicants must be ANS student members enrolled in and attending an accredited institution in the United States. Academic accomplishments must be confirmed by transcript
Value: US$2,000
Frequency: Annual
Study Establishment: An accredited institution
Country of Study: United States of America
Application Procedure: Applications are available online at www.ans.org/honors/scholarships

Closing Date: 1 February
No. of awards given last year: 1

For further information contact:

Email: outreach@ans.org

Landis Public Communication and Education Award

Subjects: Nuclear technology
Purpose: To award outstanding efforts in furthering public education
Eligibility: Open to both members and non-members of ANS
Level of Study: Postgraduate
Type: Award
Value: US$1,000 and an engraved plaque
Frequency: Annual
Country of Study: Any country
Application Procedure: Eight sets of the completed application form and supporting documents must be sent
Closing Date: 1 August
Contributor: The Landis Public Communication and Education Award

For further information contact:

Email: honors@ans.org

Landis Young Member Engineering Achievement Award

Subjects: Engineering
Purpose: To recognize outstanding achievement in the field of engineering
Eligibility: Open to candidates who are members of ANS below the age of 40 years
Level of Study: Postgraduate
Type: Award
Value: An engraved plaque and US$2,000
Frequency: Annual
Country of Study: Any country
Application Procedure: Eight sets of the completed application form and supporting documents to be submitted
Closing Date: 1 March

For further information contact:

Email: honors@ans.org

Mark Mills Award

Subjects: Nuclear physics particularly the advancement of science and engineering related to the atomic nucleus

Purpose: To recognise the important contributions of the late Mark Mills to the field. Established in 1958, it is awarded to the author who submits the best original technical paper

Eligibility: Applicants must have been registered in a graduate degree programme in a recognised Institute of Higher Education for one year prior to the award, and a certification of this fact must be made by the faculty advisor on the nomination form. Thus, this competition is open to a graduate student completing the work on which his or her paper is based from a minimum of four months prior to the award to a maximum of 16 months prior to the award. The paper should demonstrate originality and ingenuity and should be in a form suitable for publication. A thesis is not acceptable. A paper already published or submitted for publication is eligible if nominated by the faculty adviser. A paper jointly authored is eligible if the candidate has the primary responsibility

Level of Study: Graduate

Type: Award

Value: An engraved plaque and US$500

Country of Study: Any country

Application Procedure: Applicants must be nominated by the student faculty adviser. Multiple nominees by one nominator, nomination of past recipients of the award, and multiple year nominations of the same paper are prohibited. Forms are available from the ANS headquarters

Closing Date: 1 June

Additional Information: Awards are presented at the ANS Winter Meeting

Mary Jane Oestmann Professional Women

Subjects: Nuclear science and engineering

Purpose: To recognize outstanding personal dedication by a women

Eligibility: Open to female candidates who need not be members of ANS but should be affiliated with the nuclear community in some manner

Type: Award

Country of Study: Any country

Application Procedure: Eight sets of the nomination form and supporting documents be submitted

Closing Date: 1 July

For further information contact:

Email: honors@ans.org

Operations and Power Division Scholarship Award

Subjects: Nuclear science and technology

Eligibility: United States and non-United States applicants must be ANS student members enrolled in and attending an accredited institution in the United States. Academic accomplishments must be confirmed by transcript. The OPD Scholarship is intended for an undergraduate or graduate student. Applicants: must be enrolled in a course of study leading to a degree in nuclear science or engineering at an accredited institution in the United States; must have completed a minimum of two complete academic years in a four-year nuclear science or engineering program; must be United States citizens or possess a permanent resident visa; must have intentions of working in the nuclear power industry

Value: US$2,500

Frequency: Annual

Study Establishment: An accredited institution

Country of Study: United States of America

Application Procedure: Applications are available online at www.ans.org/honors/scholarships

Closing Date: 1 February

For further information contact:

Email: honors@ans.org

Samuel Glasstone Award

Subjects: The primary purpose of such a report is to share the activities of each student section with the others, helping all the student sections to expand and improve their programs

Purpose: This award was established in 1969 by ANS when Dr. Samuel Glasstone contributed funds to the Society to be used specifically for an annual award to the outstanding Student Section of ANS. These reports will be used to evaluate the student sections for the secondary purpose of selecting the Samuel J. Glasstone Award recipient

Eligibility: This award recognizes ANS student sections that have accomplished notable achievements in public service and the advancement of nuclear science and engineering

Level of Study: Postgraduate

Type: Award

Frequency: Annual

Country of Study: Any country

Closing Date: 1 May
Funding: Private

For further information contact:

Honors and Awards American Nuclear Society 555 N. Kensington Avenue La Grange Park, IL 60526-5535, United States of America

Email: ssc@ans.org

Verne R Dapp Memorial Scholarship

Subjects: Nuclear science or nuclear engineering
Eligibility: Open to citizens of the United States of America or holders of a permanent resident visa who are full-time graduate students enrolled in a programme leading to an advanced degree
Level of Study: Graduate
Type: Scholarship
Value: US$3,000
Frequency: Varies
Study Establishment: An accredited institution
Country of Study: United States of America
Application Procedure: Applicants must submit a request for an application form that includes the name of the university the candidate will be attending, the year the candidate will be in during the Autumn of the award, the major course of study and a stamped addressed envelope. Completed applications must include a grade transcript and three confidential reference forms. Candidates must be sponsored by an ANS section, division, student branch, committee, member or organization member. Applications are available online at www.ans.org/honors/scholarships
Closing Date: 1 February

For further information contact:

Email: outreach@ans.org

American Numismatic Society (ANS)

75 Varick Street, floor 11, New York, NY 10013, United States of America

Tel: (1) 212 571 4470
Fax: (1) 212 571 4479
Email: wartenberg@numismatics.org
Website: www.numismatics.org
Contact: Dr Ute Wartenberg Kagan, Executive Director

The mission of the American Numismatic Society (ANS) is to be the preeminent national institution advancing the study and appreciation of coins, medals and related objects of all cultures as historical and artistic documents. It aims to do this by maintaining the foremost numismatic collection and library, supporting scholarly research and publications, and sponsoring educational and interpretative programmes for diverse audiences.

Grants for ANS Summer Seminar in Numismatics

Subjects: Numismatics
Purpose: To provide a selected number of graduate students with a deeper understanding of the contribution that this subject makes to other fields
Eligibility: Open to applicants who have had at least one year's graduate study at a university in the United States of America or Canada and who are students of classical studies, history, near eastern studies or other humanistic fields
Level of Study: Postgraduate
Type: Grant
Value: US$4,000
Length of Study: 9 weeks during the Summer
Frequency: Annual
Study Establishment: Museum of the American Numismatic Society
Country of Study: United States of America
No. of awards offered: 21
Application Procedure: Applicants must write well in advance for details of the application process
Closing Date: 15 February
Funding: Private
No. of awards given last year: 12
No. of applicants last year: 21
Additional Information: One or two students from overseas are usually accepted to the seminar but will not receive a grant

For further information contact:

Email: vanAlfen@numismatics.org

American Orchid Society

Fairchild Tropical Botanic Garden, 10901 Old Cutler Road, Coral Gables, FL 33156, United States of America

Tel: (1) 305 740 2010
Fax: (1) 305 740 2011
Email: theaos@aos.org

Website: www.aos.org
Contact: Ms Pamela S Giust, Awards Registrar

Grants for Orchid Research

Subjects: Orchid research
Purpose: To advance scientific study of orchids in every respect and to assist in the publication of scholarly and popular scientific literature on orchids
Eligibility: There are no eligibility restrictions
Level of Study: Postgraduate
Type: Grant
Value: US$500–12,000
Length of Study: Up to 3 years
Frequency: Annual
Country of Study: Any country
Application Procedure: Applicants must write for guidelines
Closing Date: 1 January

For further information contact:

Tel: (1) 561 404 2000
Email: theaos@aos.org
Contact: Executive Director

American Ornithologists' Union (AOU)

MRC-116 National Museum of Natural History Smithsonian Institution, Washington, DC 20560-0116, United States of America

Tel: (1) 202 357 2051
Fax: (1) 202 633 8084
Email: aou@nmnh.si.edu
Website: www.aou.org
Contact: Secretary

The American Ornithologists' Union (AOU) is the oldest and largest organisation in the New World devoted to the scientific study of birds. The organisation's primary function is the publication and dissemination of ornithology research results.

Marcia Brady Tucker Travel Award

Subjects: Ornithology
Purpose: To assist student AOU members planning to give a paper to attend the annual meeting

Eligibility: Open to students in a relevant discipline. Applicants must be student members of the organisation and planning to present a paper or poster at the annual meeting
Level of Study: Unrestricted
Type: Travel grant
Value: Travel expenses. Maximum expense of US$1,000 will be given
Frequency: Annual
Country of Study: Any country
Application Procedure: Applicants must submit eight copies of an expanded abstract of the presentation or poster they plan to present at the meeting, a curriculum vitae and anticipated transportation costs to the Student Awards Committee
Closing Date: Three months prior to the meeting
Funding: Private

For further information contact:

American Ornithologists' Union, Archbold Biological Station, P.O. Box 2057, Lake Placid, FL 33862, United States of America

Email: aou@nmnh.si.edu
Contact: Reed Bowman, Associate Research Biologist

American Otological Society (AOS)

3096 Riverdale Road, The Villages, FL 32162, United States of America

Tel: (1) 352 751 0932
Fax: (1) 352 751 0696
Email: segossard@aol.com
Website: www.americanotologicalsociety.org
Contact: Ms Shirley Gossard, Administrator

The AOS is a society focused upon 'aural' medicine. The society's mission is to advance and promote medical and surgical otology, encouraging research in the related disciplines.

American Otological Society Research Training Fellowships

Subjects: All aspects of otosclerosis, Ménièe's disease and related disorders
Purpose: To support research

Eligibility: Open to physicians, residents and medical students in the United States of America and Canada
Level of Study: Postgraduate
Type: Fellowship
Value: Up to US$40,000 depending on position and institutional norms (US$35,000 for stipend, US$5,000 for supplies)
Length of Study: 1–2 years
Frequency: Annual
Country of Study: United States of America or Canada
No. of awards offered: 1
Closing Date: 31 January
Contributor: American Otological Society, Inc
No. of awards given last year: 1
No. of applicants last year: 1
Additional Information: The organization requires institutional documentation that facilities and faculty are appropriate for the requested research

For further information contact:

Research Fund of the American Otological Society, Inc., Johns Hopkins University, School of Medicine, Department of Otolaryngology-Head & Neck Surgery, 601 N. Caroline Street, JHOC 6210, United States of America

Tel:	(1) 410 955 7381
Fax:	(1) 410 955 0035
Email:	jcarey@jhmi.edu
Contact:	John P. Carey, MD, Executive Secretary

American Philosophical Association (APA)

University of Delaware, 31 Amstel Avenue, Newark, DE 19716, United States of America

Tel:	(1) 212 366 5260
Fax:	(1) 302 831 8690
Email:	anna@amc.net
Website:	www.apa.udel.edu/apa
Contact:	Dr Anna Smith, Manager of Grantmaking Programs

The American Philosophical Association (APA) was founded in 1,900 to promote the exchange of ideas among philosophers, to encourage creative and scholarly activity in philosophy, to facilitate the professional work and teaching of philosophers and to represent philosophy as a discipline.

Frank Chapman Sharp Memorial Prize

Subjects: The philosophy of war and peace
Purpose: To recognise unpublished work in philosophy
Eligibility: Authors must be members of the APA. Undergraduate entrants must be philosophy majors (or something close); graduate students must be enrolled in, or on leave from, a graduate program in philosophy. Manuscripts should be between 7,500 and 75,000 words (between 30 and 300 double-spaced typed pages)
Level of Study: Postgraduate
Type: Prize
Value: US$1,500
Country of Study: Any country
No. of awards offered: 8
Application Procedure: Applicants must write for details or visit the website
Closing Date: 15 March
Funding: Private
No. of awards given last year: 1
No. of applicants last year: 8

For further information contact:

Email: prizes@apaonline.org

American Physiological Society (APS)

9650 Rockville Pike, Bethesda, MD 20814-3991, United States of America

Tel:	(1) 301 634 7164
Fax:	(1) 301 634 7241
Email:	webmaster@the-aps.org
Website:	www.the-aps.org
Contact:	Ms Linda Jean Dresser, Executive Assistant

The American Physiological Society (APS) is a non-profit scientific society devoted to fostering education, scientific research and the dissemination of information in the physiological sciences. The Society strives to play a role in the progress of science and the advancement of knowledge.

American Physiological Society Minority Travel Fellowship Awards

Subjects: Biology and physiology
Purpose: To increase the participation of predoctoral and postdoctoral minority students in the physiological sciences

Eligibility: Open to advanced predoctoral and postdoctoral students. Students in the APS Porter Physiology Development programme are also eligible. Minority faculty members at MBRS and MARC eligible institutions may also submit applications
Level of Study: Postdoctorate, Predoctorate
Type: Travel grant
Value: Funds for travel to attend either the Experimental Biology meeting or one of the APS conferences
Length of Study: The duration of the conference or meeting
Country of Study: United States of America
Application Procedure: Applicants must contact the Education Office of the APS for further details
Closing Date: 15 January
Contributor: NIDDK and NIGMS

For further information contact:

Email: education@the-aps.org
Contact: Dr Marsha Matyas

American Psychological Association Minority Fellowship Program (APA/MFP)

Minority Fellowships Program (MFP), 750 First Street, N.E., Washington, DC 20002 4242, United States of America

Tel: (1) 800 374 2721, 202 336 5500
Fax: (1) 202 336 6012
Email: mfp@apa.org
Website: www.apa.org/pi/mfp
Contact: Administrative Assistant

The American Psychological Association's (APA) Minority Fellowship Program (MFP) is an innovative, comprehensive and coordinated training and career development program that promotes psychological and behavioural outcomes of ethnic minority communities. MFP is committed to increasing the number of ethnic minority professionals in the field and enhancing our understanding of the life experiences of ethnic minority communities.

Dissertation Research Grants

Purpose: Grants designed to support oncology nursing research for PhD dissertation
Eligibility: 1. Funding preference is given to projects that addresses the ONS Research Priorities and/or the ONS Research Agenda. 2. Membership in ONS is not required for eligibility
Type: Grants, work-study (not just grants)
Value: Upto US$5,000 each
Country of Study: Any country
Closing Date: 1 July

American Public Power Association (APPA)

2551 Crystal Drive, Suite 1000, Arlington, VA 22202, United States of America

Tel: (1) 202 467 2942
Fax: (1) 202 495 7460
Email: DEED@PublicPower.org
Website: www.PublicPower.org/DEED
Contact: Ms Michele Suddleson, DEED Program Manager

The American Public Power Association (APPA), based in Washington, D.C., is the service organization for the nation's more than 2,000 community-owned electric utilities. Collectively, these utilities serve more than 47 million Americans. Its purpose is to advance the public policy interests of its members and their consumers, and provide member services to ensure adequate, reliable electricity at a reasonable price with the proper protection of the environment.

Demonstration of Energy & Efficiency Developments (DEED) - Technical Design Project

Subjects: The scholarship supports energy-focused research projects, senior technical design projects, and students studying in technical programs and majors in short supply and high demand by the utility industry
Purpose: Provides funding to support the students working on a technical project of interest to electric utilities
Eligibility: This scholarship targets full-time college juniors and seniors, and graduate students attending a college/university or vocational school in the United States Students must be majoring in a field that could lead to a career in the public power industry. Applicants must obtain a DEED member utility to sponsor their application. An official transcript must be received by the application deadline
Level of Study: Doctorate, Graduate
Type: Scholarship

Value: US$5,000 plus up to US$3,000 in travel funds to share project results at APPA's Engineering & Operations Technical Conference
Frequency: Annual
Country of Study: United States of America
Application Procedure: If you wish to apply for a scholarship please DEED@publicpower.org and provide your name, address, telephone number, email address, scholarship you wish to apply for, and expected date of graduation. All required materials (application, official transcript, and signature pages) must be submitted by the application deadline
Closing Date: 15 October
Funding: Private

For further information contact:

Tel: (1) 202 467 2960
Email: DEED@publcipower.org

American Research Institute in Turkey (ARIT)

University of Pennsylvania Museum, 3260 South Street, Philadelphia, PA 19104-6324, United States of America

Tel: (1) 215 898 3474
Fax: (1) 215 898 0657
Email: leinwand@sas.upenn.edu
Website: ccat.sas.upenn.edu/ARIT
Contact: Nancy Leinwand, Executive Director

The American Research Institute in Turkey's (ARIT) aim is to support U.S based scholarly research in all fields of the humanities and social sciences in Turkey through administering fellowship programmes at the doctoral and postdoctoral level and through maintaining research centres in Ankara and Istanbul.

Fellowships for Intensive Advanced Turkish Language Study in Istanbul, Turkey

Subjects: Turkish language
Purpose: To provide full travel and fellowship to students and scholars for participation in the summer program in advanced Turkish language at Bogazici University in Istanbul
Eligibility: Applicant must be a citizen, national or permanent resident of the United States

Level of Study: Graduate, Postdoctorate, Postgraduate, Predoctorate
Type: Fellowship
Value: Fellowship includes round-trip airfare to Istanbul, application and tuition fees, and a maintenance stipend
Length of Study: 8 weeks
Frequency: Annual
Study Establishment: Bogazici University
Country of Study: Turkey
No. of awards offered: 65
Application Procedure: Application forms and procedure are available at the ARIT website ccat.sas.upenn.edu/ARIT. Nancy Leinwand at ARIT leinwand@sas.upenn.edu, or aritfellowship@georgtown.edu
Closing Date: 1 November
Funding: Government
Contributor: United States Department of Education, Fulbright-Hays Group Projects Abroad Programme
No. of awards given last year: 17
No. of applicants last year: 65

For further information contact:

Summer Program in Turkish Language and Culture, Bogaziçi University, Turkey

Tel: (90) 212 257 5039
Fax: (90) 212 265 7131
Email: aritfellowship@georgtown.edu
Contact: Erika H Gilson, The Language Center

National Endowment for the Humanities American Research Institute in Turkey-National Endowment for the Humanities Fellowships for Research in Turkey

Subjects: All subjects of the humanities and interdisciplinary approaches to social sciences, prehistory, history, art, archaeology, language and literature
Purpose: To support research on ancient, medieval or modern times
Eligibility: Open to scholars who have completed their formal training by the application deadline and plan to carry out research in Turkey may apply. They may be United States citizens or 3-year residents of the United States. Please consult ARIT headquarters on questions of eligibility. Advanced scholars also may apply for ARIT Fellowships in the Humanities and Social Sciences
Level of Study: Postdoctorate, Postgraduate, Professional development, Research
Type: Fellowship
Value: US$16,800–50,400
Length of Study: 4–12 months

Frequency: Annual
Study Establishment: Either of ARIT's two research establishments in Ankara or Istanbul
Country of Study: Turkey
No. of awards offered: 16
Application Procedure: Applicants must submit an application form, project statement and references
Closing Date: 1 November
Funding: Government
Contributor: National Endowment for the Humanities (NEH)
No. of awards given last year: 3
No. of applicants last year: 16
Additional Information: The hostel, research and study facilities are available at ARIT's branch centers in Istanbul and Ankara

For further information contact:

Tel: (90) 215 898 3474
Fax: (90) 215 898 0657
Email: leinwand@sas.upenn.edu
Contact: Nancy Leinwand, Executive Director

American School of Classical Studies at Athens (ASCSA)

6-8 Charlton Street, Princeton, NJ 08540-5232, United States of America

Tel: (1) 609 683 0800
Fax: (1) 609 924 0578
Email: ascsa@ascsa.org
Website: www.ascsa.edu.gr
Contact: Ms Mary E Darlington, Executive Associate

Established in 1881, the American School of Classical Studies at Athens (ASCSA) offers both graduate students and scholars the opportunity to study Greek civilization, first hand, in Greece. The ASCSA supports and encourages the teaching of the archaeology, art, history, language and literature of Greece from early times to the present.

American School of Classical Studies at Athens Advanced Fellowships

Subjects: Classical art history, history of architecture and study of pottery
Eligibility: Open to students that plan to return to or stay at the school. Applicants must pursue independent research and

have completed 1 year of Regular or Associate Membership at the school. All applicants must be enrolled. in a North American institution
Level of Study: Postgraduate, Predoctorate
Type: Fellowship
Value: A stipend of US$11,500 plus room, board, and waiver of School fees are available to students who have completed the Regular Program or 1 year as a Student Associate Member and plan to return to the School to pursue independent research, usually for their PhD
Length of Study: 1 academic year
Frequency: Annual
Study Establishment: ASCSA
Country of Study: Greece
No. of awards offered: 13
Application Procedure: Applicants must complete online applications. For guidelines and application visit www.ascsa.org
Closing Date: 19 February
Funding: Private
No. of applicants last year: 13
Additional Information: The fellowships include: the Edward Capps, the Doreen C Spitzer and the Eugene Vanderpool Fellowships (subject unrestricted); the Samuel H. Kress Fellowships in art and architecture in antiquity; the Gorham P Stevens Fellowship in the history of architecture; and the Homer A and Dorothy B Thompson Fellowship in the study of pottery. Ione Mylonas Shear in Mycenaean Archaeology or Athenian architecture.

For further information contact:

Email: ascsa@ascsa.org

American School of Classical Studies at Athens Fellowships

Subjects: Classical philology and archaeology, post-classical Greek studies or a related field
Eligibility: Open to graduate and well-qualified undergraduate students preparing for an advanced degree in Classical Studies or a related field. Applicants must be enrolled in a North American Institution
Level of Study: Graduate, Predoctorate
Type: Fellowship
Value: US$11,500 stipend plus fees, room and partial board
Length of Study: 1 academic year
Frequency: Annual
Study Establishment: ASCSA
Country of Study: Greece
No. of awards offered: 21
Application Procedure: Applicants must complete online applications. For guidelines and application visit www.ascsa.edu.gr

Closing Date: 15 January
Funding: Private
No. of awards given last year: 12
No. of applicants last year: 21

For further information contact:

Email: Ascsa_info@ascsa.edu.gr

American School of Classical Studies at Athens Research Fellowship in Environmental Studies

Subjects: Earth sciences, geological sciences and archaeological sciences
Purpose: To support research on studies from archaeological contexts in Greece
Eligibility: Doctoral candidates working on their dissertation and postdoctoral scholars with well-defined projects that can be completed during the academic year of the fellowship
Level of Study: Doctorate, Graduate, Postdoctorate, Postgraduate, Predoctorate
Type: Fellowship
Value: US$15,500–27,000 stipend depending on seniority and experience
Length of Study: 1 academic year
Frequency: Annual
Study Establishment: The Malcolm H Wiener Research Laboratory for Archaeological Science, ASCSA
Country of Study: Greece
No. of awards offered: 8
Application Procedure: Applicants must complete online applications. For guidelines and application visit www.ascsa.edu.gr
Closing Date: 15 January
Funding: Private
No. of awards given last year: 1
No. of applicants last year: 8

For further information contact:

Email: ascsa@ascsa.org

American School of Classical Studies at Athens Research Fellowship in Faunal Studies

Subjects: Biological sciences, life sciences and archaeological sciences
Purpose: To study faunal remains from archaeological contexts in Greece
Eligibility: Doctoral candidates working on their dissertation and postdoctoral scholars with well-defined projects that can be completed during the academic year of the fellowship. There is no citizenship requirement

Level of Study: Doctorate, Graduate, Postdoctorate, Postgraduate, Predoctorate
Type: Fellowship
Value: US$15,500–27,000 stipend depending on seniority and experience
Length of Study: 1 academic year
Frequency: Annual
Study Establishment: The Malcolm H Wiener Research Laboratory for Archaeological Science, ASCSA
Country of Study: Greece
No. of awards offered: 8
Application Procedure: Applicants must complete online applications. For guidelines and application visit www.ascsa.edu.gr
Closing Date: 15 January
Funding: Private
No. of awards given last year: 1
No. of applicants last year: 8

For further information contact:

Email: ascsa@ascsa.org

American School of Classical Studies at Athens Research Fellowship in Geoarchaeology

Subjects: Earth sciences, geological sciences and archaeological sciences
Purpose: To support research on a geoarchaeological topic in Greece
Eligibility: Doctoral candidates working on their dissertation and postdoctoral scholars with well-defined projects that can be completed during the academic year of the fellowship. There is no citizenship requirement
Level of Study: Doctorate, Graduate, Postdoctorate, Postgraduate, Predoctorate
Type: Fellowship
Value: US$15,500–27,000 stipend depending on seniority and experience
Length of Study: 1 academic year
Frequency: Annual
Study Establishment: The Malcolm H Wiener Research Laboratory for Archaeological Science, ASCSA
Country of Study: Greece
No. of awards offered: 8
Application Procedure: Applicants must complete online applications. For guidelines and application visit www.ascsa.edu.gr
Closing Date: 15 January
Funding: Private
No. of awards given last year: 1
No. of applicants last year: 8

For further information contact:

Email: ascsa@ascsa.org

American School of Classical Studies at Athens Summer Sessions

Subjects: Travel throughout Greece. The major archaeological sites and museum collections in North and Central Greece, the Peloponnesos and Crete
Purpose: The two 6-week sessions are designed for those who wish to become acquainted with Greece and its antiquities, and to improve their understanding of the relationship between the monuments, landscape, and climate of the country and its history, literature and culture
Eligibility: Enrolment is open to graduate and advanced undergraduate students and to high school and college instructors of classics and related subjects
Level of Study: Graduate, Postdoctorate, Postgraduate, Professional development
Type: Scholarship
Length of Study: 6 weeks
Frequency: Annual
Study Establishment: ASCSA
Country of Study: Greece
No. of awards offered: 83
Application Procedure: Applicants must submit a completed application form, transcripts and letters of recommendation. Applications should be made to the Committee on the Summer Sessions. ascsa.submittable.com/submit/115817/ascsa-summer-session-application
Closing Date: 15 January
Funding: Private
No. of awards given last year: 13
No. of applicants last year: 83

For further information contact:

Email: ssapplication@ascsa.org

Cotsen Traveling Fellowship for Research in Greece

Subjects: Post-classical studies in late antiquity, Byzantine studies, post-Byzantine studies, and modern Greek studies
Purpose: The Gennadius Library offers the Cotsen Traveling Fellowship, a short-term grant awarded each year to scholars and graduate students pursuing research topics that require the use of the Gennadeion collections
Eligibility: Postdoctoral scholars worldwide, applicants must show a need to perform research at the Gennadius Library

Level of Study: Doctorate, Graduate, Postdoctorate, Postgraduate
Type: Fellowship
Value: US$2,000
Length of Study: 1–2 months
Frequency: Annual
Study Establishment: The Gennadius Library of the American School of Classical Studies at Athens
Country of Study: United States of America
No. of awards offered: 12
Application Procedure: Applicants must complete online application. Visit www.ascsa.edu.gr/apply/fellowships-and-grants for guidelines and application
Closing Date: 15 January
Funding: Individuals
Contributor: Overseers of the Gennadius Library
No. of awards given last year: 1
No. of applicants last year: 12

For further information contact:

6-8 Charlton Street, Canada

Email: application@ascsa.org
Contact: Dr Alicia Dissinger

Cotsen Travelling Fellowship

Subjects: The grant was established by the Overseers of the Gennadius Library to honor Lloyd E. Cotsen, Chairman emeritus of the Overseers and benefactor of the Library
Purpose: The Gennadius Library offers the Cotsen Traveling Fellowship, a short-term grant awarded each year to scholars and graduate students pursuing research topics that require the use of the Gennadeion collections
Eligibility: 1. Senior scholars and graduate students of any nationality. 2. School fees are waived for a maximum of two months
Level of Study: Postgraduate
Type: Fellowship
Value: US$2,000
Frequency: Annual
Country of Study: Any country
Application Procedure: 1. Submit "Associate Membership with Fellowship" application online. 2. The application should include a curriculum vitae, a letter (up to 750 words) describing the project and its relation to the Gennadius Library collections, proposed dates, a brief budget (not more than one page), and two letters of recommendation
Closing Date: 15 January
Funding: Private

For further information contact:

ASCSA 54 Souidias Street GRC-106 76, Athens, Greece

Harry Bikakis Fellowship

Subjects: Ancient Greek law
Purpose: Graduate students at North American institutions or Greek graduate students whose research subject is ancient Greek law and who need to work at ASCSA libraries; or Greek graduate students working on excavations conducted by or affiliated with the ASCSA
Eligibility: Graduate students at North American institutions or Greek graduate students whose research subject is ancient Greek law and who need to work at ASCSA libraries; or Greek graduate students working on excavations conducted by or affiliated with the ASCSA
Level of Study: Graduate
Type: One fellowship
Value: US$1,875
Length of Study: can be determined by fellow
Frequency: Annual
Study Establishment: ASCSA
Country of Study: Greece
Application Procedure: Submit "Associate Membership with Fellowship" Application online. For more information about the application, visit the ASCSA web site at: www.ascsa.edu.gr/index.php/admission-membership/Graduate-and-Post-Doctoral. The application will include an outline of the proposed project, and two letters of reference
Closing Date: 15 January
Funding: Individuals
Contributor: Lloyd E. Cotsen, Chairman emeritus of the Overseers of the Gennadius Library

Jacob Hirsch Fellowship

Subjects: Pre-classical, classical or post-classical archaeology
Purpose: To support individuals completing a project that requires a lengthy residence in Greece
Eligibility: Open to graduate students of American or Israeli institutions who are writing a dissertation and to recent PhD graduates completing a project in Greece graduate students, citizens of Israel, at such as a dissertation in archaeology for publication. Applications will be judged on the basis of appropriate credentials including referees. Candidates must also meet all eligibility requirements for Associate Membership
Level of Study: Postdoctorate, Postgraduate, Predoctorate
Type: Fellowship
Value: US$11,500 stipend plus room, board and waiver of school fees

Length of Study: 1 academic year, non-renewable
Frequency: Annual
Study Establishment: ASCSA
Country of Study: Greece
No. of awards offered: 11
Application Procedure: Applicants must complete online applications. For guidelines and application visit www.ascsa.edu.gr
Closing Date: 15 January
Funding: Private
No. of awards given last year: 1
No. of applicants last year: 11

Malcolm H. Wiener Laboratory for Archaeological Science Senior Fellowship

Purpose: To conduct research at the Malcolm H. Wiener Laboratory for Archaeological Science pertaining to the ancient Greek world and adjacent areas through the application of interdisciplinary methods in the archaeological sciences. Laboratory facilities are especially well-equipped to support the study of human skeletal biology, archaeobiological remains (faunal and botanical), environmental studies, and geoarchaeology (particularly studies in human-landscape interactions and the study of site formation processes)
Eligibility: Open to recent PhDs (at least 5 years) previous to application. Research projects utilizing other archaeological scientific approaches are also eligible for consideration, depending on the; strength of the questions asked and the suitability of the plan for access to other equipment or resources available elsewhere in Greece
Level of Study: Postdoctorate
Type: Fellowship
Value: Stipend of US$15,000 (5-month term); stipend of US$30,000 (10-month term)
Length of Study: 5–10 months with the next term beginning early September. It is expected that the applicant will maintain a physical presence at the Wiener Laboratory during the academic year (1 September to 1 June)
Frequency: Annual
Country of Study: Greece
Application Procedure: Applicants must complete online application. For guidelines and application, visit www.asca.edu.gr/index.php/wiener-laboratory/senior-instructions. Email at application@ascsa.org
Closing Date: 15 January
Funding: Private

For further information contact:

Email: director@ascsa.edu.gr

Malcolm H. Wiener Laboratory Postdoctoral Fellowship

Subjects: Biological, life, archaeological, Earth, geological and environmental sciences
Eligibility: Postdoctoral scholars worldwide
Level of Study: Postdoctorate
Type: Fellowship
Value: US$35,000 per year
Length of Study: 3 years
Frequency: Every 3 years
Study Establishment: Malcom H. Wiener Laboratory for Archaeological Science at the American School of Classical Studies at Athens (ASCSA)
Country of Study: Greece
No. of awards offered: 8
Application Procedure: Applicants must complete online application. For guidelines and application visit www.ascsa.edu.gr
Closing Date: 15 January
No. of awards given last year: 1
No. of applicants last year: 8

For further information contact:

Email: ascsa@ascsa.org

Malcom H. Wiener Laboratory for Archaeological Science Research Associate Appointments

Subjects: Ancient Greek world and adjacent areas through the application of interdisciplinary methods in the archaeological sciences. Laboratory facilities are especially well equipped to support the study of human skeletal biology, archaeobiological remains (faunal and botanical), environmental studies, and geoarchaeology (particularly studies in human-landscape interactions and the study of site formation processes). Research projects utilizing other archaeological scientific approaches are also eligible for consideration
Purpose: To conduct short-term focused research at the Malcolm H. Wiener Laboratory for Archaeological Science of the American School of Classical Studies at Athens as part of a program of research that addresses substantive problems pertaining to the ancient Greek world and adjacent areas through the application of interdisciplinary methods in the archaeological sciences. Laboratory facilities are especially well equipped to support the study of human skeletal biology, archaeobiological remains (faunal and botanical), environmental studies, and geoarchaeology (particularly studies in human-landscape interactions and the study of site formation processes). Research projects utilizing other archaeological scientific approaches are also eligible for

consideration, depending on the strength of the questions asked and the suitability of the plan for access to other equipment or resources available elsewhere in Greece
Eligibility: Individuals actively enrolled in a graduate program and individuals with a Masters or Doctorate in a relevant discipline. Applicants are welcome from any college or university worldwide. Independent scholars are also welcome to apply
Level of Study: Doctorate, Graduate, Postdoctorate, Postgraduate
Type: One fellowship
Value: up to US$7,000
Length of Study: Variable up to nine (9) months
Frequency: Annual
Study Establishment: ASCSA
Country of Study: Greece
No. of awards offered: 14
Application Procedure: Link to Research Associate application instructions at: www.ascsa.edu.gr/index.php/wiener-laboratory/research-associate-appointment 1. Cover sheet naming the applicant, current research interests, and title and brief summary of the proposed research project 2. Project Description (max. 2 pages, double-spaced) including: objectives and expected significance, background and relation to present state of knowledge, research description, and timeframe 3. Results of prior Wiener Laboratory Research 4-7. References cited; Budget; Facilities, equipment, and other resources; Permits 8. Curriculum vitae following requested format. (No transcripts are required.) 9. One letter of reference from a scholar in the field 10. Expected contributions to and impact on the Wiener Laboratory and the ASCSA community
Closing Date: 15 January
Funding: Private
Contributor: ASCSA
No. of awards given last year: 1
No. of applicants last year: 14

Open Scholarship for Summer Sessions

Purpose: To attend ASCSA Summer Session
Level of Study: Postgraduate, Predoctorate, Professional development
Type: Scholarship
Value: US$5,000
Length of Study: 6 weeks
Study Establishment: American School of Classical Studies at Athens (ASCSA)
Country of Study: Greece
No. of awards offered: 65
Application Procedure: Applicants must complete online application. For guidelines and application visit www.ascsa.edu.gr

Closing Date: 15 January
No. of awards given last year: 5
No. of applicants last year: 65

For further information contact:

Email: ssapplication@ascsa.org

Samuel H Kress Joint Athens-Jerusalem Fellowship

Subjects: Ancient or post classical art history, architecture and archaeology
Purpose: To enable students to conduct research in Greece and Israel in the same academic year and to promote better understanding of interrelationships between the cultures, languages, literature and history of the Aegean and the Near East
Eligibility: Open to any nationality but applicants must be at a college or university in the United States of America or Canada
Level of Study: Doctorate, Postgraduate, Predoctorate
Type: Fellowship
Value: A stipend of US$7,600 plus room and partial board at each of the two institutions
Length of Study: 1 academic year
Frequency: Annual
Study Establishment: The ASCSA and the W F Albright Institute of Archaeological Research in Jerusalem
Country of Study: Other
No. of awards offered: 5
Application Procedure: Applicants must write for details or visit the website
Closing Date: 25 October
Funding: Private
No. of awards given last year: 1
No. of applicants last year: 5
Additional Information: Further information can be found on the website

For further information contact:

Albright Instituteco Department of Religious Studies, John Carroll University, 20,700 North Park Boulevard, University Heights, OH 44118, United States of America

Tel: (1) 216 397 4705
Fax: (1) 216 397 4478
Email: spencer@jcu.edu
Contact: Professor John Spencer

Wiener Laboratory Predoctoral Fellowship

Subjects: Biological, life, archaeological, Earth, geological and environmental sciences
Eligibility: PhD candidates from college or university worldwide
Level of Study: Predoctorate
Type: Fellowship
Value: up to US$20,000
Length of Study: 2 academic years
Study Establishment: Malcolm H. Wiener Laboratory for Archaeological Science at the American School of Classical Studies
Country of Study: Greece
Application Procedure: Applicants must complete online application. For guidelines and application visit www.ascsa.edu.gr
Closing Date: Check website

Wiener Laboratory Research Associate Appointment

Subjects: Biological, life, archaeological, Earth, geological and environmental sciences
Purpose: To conduct short-term focused research at the Malcolm H. Wiener Laboratory for Archaeological Science of the American School of Classical Studies at Athens as part of a program of research that addresses substantive problems pertaining to the ancient Greek world
Eligibility: PhD candidates and postdoctoral candidates worldwide
Level of Study: Postdoctorate, Predoctorate
Type: Research grant
Value: Up to US$7,000
Length of Study: Up to 9 months
Frequency: Annual
Study Establishment: Malcolm H. Wiener Laboratory for Archaelogical Science at the American School of Classical Studies at Athens
Country of Study: Greece
No. of awards offered: 5
Application Procedure: Applicants must complete online application. For guidelines and application visit www.ascsa.edu.gr
Closing Date: 15 January
No. of awards given last year: 3
No. of applicants last year: 5

For further information contact:

Email: TKarkanas@ascsa.edu.gr

American Schools of Oriental Research (ASOR)

656 Beacon Street, 5th Floor, Boston, MA 02215 2010, United States of America

Tel: (1) 617 353 6570
Fax: (1) 617 353 6575
Email: asor@bu.edu
Website: www.asor.org
Contact: Britta Abeln, Office Coordinator

The American Schools of Oriental Research's (ASOR) mission is to initiate, encourage and support research into, and public understanding of the people and cultures of the near East from the earliest times by fostering original research, archaeological excavations and explorations, by encouraging scholarship in the basic languages, cultural histories and traditions of the near Eastern world.

Albright Institute of Archaeological Research (AIAR) Annual Professorship

Subjects: Near Eastern archaeology, geography, history and biblical studies
Purpose: To support studies in Near Eastern archaeology, geography, history and biblical studies
Eligibility: Open to qualified applicants of any nationality. Citizens of the United States of America are eligible for the entire award. Non-United States of America citizens may apply but, by United States of America law, are only eligible for non-governmental funds
Level of Study: Postdoctorate
Type: Professorship
Value: A stipend of US$30,000. This consists of US$14,200 plus US$15,800 for room and half board for appointee and spouse at the Institute. The entire award is available via USIA for an appointee who is an citizen of the United States of America. Non-governmental funds for non United States of America citizens total US$15,000
Length of Study: 10 months
Frequency: Annual
Study Establishment: The W F Albright Institute of Archaeological Research (AIAR) in Jerusalem
Country of Study: Israel
No. of awards offered: 5
Application Procedure: Applicants must write for details
Closing Date: 15 October
No. of awards given last year: 1

No. of applicants last year: 5
Additional Information: The professorship period should be continuous, without frequent trips outside the country. Residence at the Institute is required

For further information contact:

Email: spencer@jcu.edu
Contact: Dr John R Spencer

American Schools of Oriental Research Mesopotamian Fellowship

Subjects: Social sciences, history, archaeology in Middle East studies
Purpose: To financially support field research in ancient Mesopotamian civilization carried out in Middle East
Eligibility: Open to applicants affiliated with an institution that is a corporate member of ASOR or who have an individual membership. See website for further details
Level of Study: Research
Type: Fellowship
Value: Amount of US$7,500 for one three-to-six month period of research
Length of Study: 3–12 months
Frequency: Annual
Application Procedure: Applicants need to submit cover sheet (with contact information, ASOR membership information, title of project, and brief abstract) and a short proposal. Applicants currently in graduate degree programs should provide three recommendations
Closing Date: 1 November
Additional Information: This fellowship is primarily intended to support field/research projects on ancient Mesopotamian civilization carried out in the Middle East, but other research projects such as museum or archival research related to Mesopotamian studies may also be considered

For further information contact:

Tel: (1) 617 353 6570
Email: asor@bu.edu

American Schools of Oriental Research W.F. Albright Institute of Archaeological Research/National Endowment of the Humanities Fellowships

Subjects: Archaeology, history, religion/theology, art history, literature/english/writing, social sciences, anthropology, geography, near and Middle East studies

Purpose: To financially support scholars holding a PhD or equivalent degree with a research project

Eligibility: Open to citizens of the United States or alien residents residing in the United States for the last 3 years. Please see the website for further details regarding eligibility   www.neh.gov/divisions/research/fellowship/alb right-institute-archaeological-research-jerusalem

Level of Study: Doctorate

Type: Fellowships

Value: Up to US$50,400 for 12 months and US$18,900 for 4.5 months. Stipend varies with the duration of the fellowship

Length of Study: 4–12 months

Frequency: Annual

Country of Study: United States of America

Application Procedure: A completed application form must be sent

Closing Date: 1 October

Contributor: National Endowment of the Humanities

Additional Information: Residence at the Institute in Jerusalem is preferred

For further information contact:

Albright Fellowship Committee, Department of Art and Art History, Providence College, Providence, RI 02918, United States of America

Tel: (1) 401 865 1789
Fax: (1) 401 865 2410
Email: jbranham@providence.edu
Contact: Professor Joan R. Branham, Chair

Andrew W Mellon Foundation Fellowships

Subjects: Humanities

Purpose: To support Eastern European scholars

Eligibility: Open to Bulgarian, Czech, Hungarian, Polish, Romanian and Slovak scholars who have obtained a doctorate by the time the fellowship is awarded. Candidates should not be permanently resident outside the six countries concerned

Level of Study: Postdoctorate

Type: Fellowship

Value: US$34,500 in total

Length of Study: 3 months

Frequency: Annual

Study Establishment: AIAR, Jerusalem

Country of Study: Israel

No. of awards offered: 15

Application Procedure: Applicants must write for details

Closing Date: 2 April

No. of awards given last year: 3

No. of applicants last year: 15

Additional Information: Fellows are expected to reside at the AIAR if room is available. The 3-month periods are 1 September – 30 November, 1 December – 29 February and 1 March – 31 May. The research period should be continuous without frequent trips outside the country

For further information contact:

Email: spencer@jcu.edu
Contact: Dr John R Spencer

Council of American Overseas Research Centers (CAORC) Fellowships for Advanced Multi-Country Research

Subjects: Multi-country research in the fields of humanities, social sciences and related natural sciences in countries in the Near and Middle East and South Asia

Eligibility: Open to doctoral candidates applying as individuals or in teams and established scholars with United States of the America citizenship

Level of Study: Doctorate

Type: Fellowship

Value: Up to US$6,000 plus an additional US$3,000 for travel

Frequency: Annual

Study Establishment: The W F Albright Institute of Archaeological Research in Jerusalem

Country of Study: Other

Application Procedure: Applicants must write for details

Closing Date: 31 December

Additional Information: Preference will be given to candidates examining comparative or cross-regional questions requiring research in two or more countries

For further information contact:

CAORC, Smithsonian Institution, 1c 3123 MRC 705, United States of America

Email: siwp01.ic.bwack@ic.si.edu
Contact: Grants Management Officer

Samuel H Kress Joint Athens-Jerusalem Fellowship

Subjects: Art history, architecture, archaeology and classical studies

Purpose: To support a joint fellowship for research

Eligibility: Open to predoctoral students who are United States citizens, or North American citizens studying at United States universities

Level of Study: Predoctorate
Type: Fellowship
Value: US$15,000. The stipend is US$7,600 and the remainder covers room and board at the two institutions
Length of Study: 10 months comprised of 5 months in Athens and 5 months in Jerusalem
Frequency: Annual
Study Establishment: The American School of Classical Studies in Athens and the W F Albright Institute of Archaeological Research in Jerusalem
Country of Study: Other
No. of awards offered: 4
Application Procedure: Applicants must write for details and an application form
Closing Date: 25 October
No. of awards given last year: 1
No. of applicants last year: 4
Additional Information: Residence at the Albright Institute is required. The research period should be continuous without frequent trips outside Greece and Israel

For further information contact:

Email: spencer@jcu.edu
Contact: Dr John Spencer

W. F. Albright Institute of Archaeological Research/National Endowment for the Humanities Fellowship

Subjects: Archaeology, anthropology, geography, ancient history, philology, epigraphy, Biblical studies, Islamic studies, religion, art history, literature, philosophy or related disciplines
Eligibility: Open to scholars in Near Eastern studies holding a PhD, who are citizens of the United States of America or alien residents residing in the country for the last 3 years. Research projects must have a clear humanities focus
Level of Study: Postdoctorate
Type: Fellowship
Value: US$40,000 for 1 year. A total of US$60,000 is to be available for 1.5 awards
Length of Study: 4 months–1 year
Frequency: Annual
Study Establishment: The W F Albright Institute of Archaeological Research in Jerusalem
Country of Study: Israel
No. of awards offered: 8
Application Procedure: Applicants must write for details
Closing Date: 17 October
Funding: Government
No. of awards given last year: 2
No. of applicants last year: 8

Additional Information: The research period should be continuous, without frequent trips outside the country. Residence at the Institute is preferred

For further information contact:

Department of Religious Studies, John Carroll University, 20,700 North Park Boulevard, United States of America

Email: spencer@jcu.edu
Contact: Dr John R Spencer

American Society for Engineering Education (ASEE)

1818 North Street NW, Suite 600, Washington, DC 20036 2479, United States of America

Tel: (1) 202 331 3500/3525/202 649 3834
Fax: (1) 202 265 8504
Email: sttp@asee.org
Website: www.asee.org
Contact: Mr Michael More, Projects Department

The American Society for Engineering Education (ASEE) is committed to furthering education in engineering and engineering technology by promoting excellence in instruction, research, public service and practice, exercising worldwide leadership, fostering the technological education of society and providing quality products and services to members.

American Society for Engineering Education Air Force Summer Faculty Fellowship Program

Subjects: Air Force research
Purpose: To enhance the research interests and capabilities of faculty and also to elevate the awareness in the United States academic community of Air Force research
Eligibility: Open to citizens or permanent residents of the United States and must hold a full-time appointment at a college or university located in the United States, preferably with a minimum of 2 years experience
Level of Study: Postgraduate, Research
Type: Fellowship
Value: A weekly stipend of up to US$1,650
Length of Study: 1 year
Frequency: Annual
Country of Study: United States of America

For further information contact:

Email: sttp@asee.org

American Society for Engineering Education Helen T Carr Fellowship Program

Subjects: Engineering

Purpose: To increase the number of engineering professors for the historically Black engineering colleges by providing financial aid for doctoral study in engineering

Eligibility: Open to African American faculty members, graduate students and other African Americans who have completed at least the equivalent of 1 academic year of full-time engineering graduate study. Candidates must be sponsored by the Dean of one of the historically Black engineering colleges at which they later intend to teach

Level of Study: Doctorate

Value: Up to US$10,000

Length of Study: 1 year, renewable as funding allows

Frequency: Annual

Country of Study: United States of America

Application Procedure: Applicants must first submit a letter to the Dean of a historically Black engineering college asking to be sponsored. Transcripts of undergraduate and graduate course credits and at least three references testifying to intellectual capacity and educational attainments, which give promise of satisfactory performance in advanced study, must then be submitted to the ASEE. A covering letter from the sponsoring Dean is required, and a single copy of each of these documents is to be sent to the committee through its secretary at ASEE headquarters

Closing Date: 15 May

Funding: Government, Commercial, Private

Contributor: The Allied-Signal Foundation, the AMOCO Foundation, AT&T-Bell Laboratories, EI Dupont De Numours & Co., the Exxon Education Foundation, the General Electric Foundation, the IBM Corporation, the Mobil Oil Corporation, NASA, RCA and the Union Carbide

For further information contact:

Email: a.hicks@asee.org
Contact: Artis Hicks

National Defense Science and Engineering Graduate Fellowship Program

Subjects: Aeronautical/astronautical engineering, biosciences, chemical engineering, chemistry, civil engineering, cognitive, neural and behavioral science, computer/computational sciences, electrical engineering, geosciences, materials science and engineering, mathematics, mechanical engineering, naval architecture and ocean engineering, oceanography, physics

Purpose: To increase the number of United States citizens and nationals trained in science and engineering disciplines of military importance

Eligibility: Must be a United States citizen or national. Applicants must be at or near beginning of graduate studies in one of the above-named fields. Applicants must be either enrolled in their final year of undergraduate studies or have completed no more than the equivalent of 2 year's of full-time graduate study in the field in which they are applying. Exceptional circumstances may qualify other applicants as being at the early stages of their graduate studies

Level of Study: Doctorate

Type: Fellowship

Value: US$34,000 annual stipend. Full tuition and required fees. Medical insurance coverage offered through the institution, up to a total value of US$1,000 per year

Length of Study: 3 years

Frequency: Annual

Country of Study: United States of America

No. of awards offered: 2,000

Application Procedure: Apply online at www.asee.org/ndseg

Closing Date: 18 December

Funding: Government

Contributor: United States Department of Defense

No. of awards given last year: 200

No. of applicants last year: 2,000

For further information contact:

Email: ndseg@asee.org
Contact: Rachel Kline

Naval Research Laboratory Post Doctoral Fellowship Program

Subjects: Computer science, artificial intelligence, plasma physics, acoustics, radar, fluid dynamics, chemistry, materials, science and many more specialist fields

Purpose: To increase the involvement of creative and highly trained scientists to scientific and technical areas of interest and relevance to the United States Navy

Eligibility: United States citizens and permanent residents

Level of Study: Doctorate, Postdoctorate

Type: Fellowship

Value: Up to a maximum of US$79,720

Length of Study: 1 year, renewable for a 2nd and 3rd year

Frequency: Annual

Study Establishment: Naval Research Laboratory

Country of Study: United States of America

Application Procedure: Apply online at www.asee.org/nrl or www.asee.org/fellowships/nrl/apply.cfm

Closing Date: Applications are accepted and processed on an on-going basis

Funding: Government

Contributor: United States Navy

No. of awards given last year: 35

Additional Information: A group health insurance program is provided for participants (paid for by the fellowship) and optional for dependents (paid for by participant)

For further information contact:

Email: postdocs@asee.org

Office of Naval Research Summer Faculty Research Program

Subjects: Science technology, engineering and mathematics

Purpose: To allow university faculty members to collaborate with the Navy Scientist on issues of mutual interest

Eligibility: United States citizen or permanent resident, must hold teaching or research appointment at United States college or university

Level of Study: Postdoctorate

Type: Fellowship

Value: US$1,400–1,900 (US$1,400 per week at the Summer Faculty Fellow level, US$1,650 per week at the Senior Summer Faculty Fellow level, and US$1,900 per week at the Distinguished Summer Faculty Fellow level)

Length of Study: 10 weeks

Frequency: Annual

Country of Study: United States of America

No. of awards offered: 544

Application Procedure: Apply online at www.asee.org/summer

Closing Date: 6 December

Funding: Government

No. of awards given last year: 73

No. of applicants last year: 544

Additional Information: There are three levels of appointment: Summer Faculty Fellow, Senior Summer Faculty Fellow, and Distinguished Summer Faculty Fellow. Each fellow will be reimbursed for expenses incurred on an optional pre-program visit to the sponsoring laboratory and one round-trip encompassing travel to the sponsoring laboratory at the beginning of the program and travel back to their home residence at the end of the program

For further information contact:

Email: onrsummer@asee.org
Contact: Artis Hicks

American Society for Microbiology (ASM)

1752 N Street North West, Washington, DC 20036-2904, United States of America

Tel: (1) 202 737 3600
Email: awards@asmusa.org
Website: www.asm.org/awards
Contact: Ms Leah Gibbons, Program Assistant

The American Society for Microbiology (ASM) is the oldest and largest single life science membership organization in the world. With 43,000 members throughout the world. The ASM represents all disciplines of microbiological specialization including microbiology education. The ASM's mission is to promote research and research training in the microbiological sciences and to assist communication between scientists, policymakers and the public to improve health, the environment and economic well-being.

American Society for Microbiology Microbe Minority Travel Awards

Purpose: The ASM Undergraduate Research Fellowship provides students an opportunity to conduct research and attend ASM Microbe to present their research results. Faculty have an opportunity to mentor students and receive stipend and travel support for their students to conduct research. It generally awards a limited number of travel awards to supports recipients and traval to ASM Microbe

Eligibility: To qualify for consideration the applicant must be: 1. A current ASM member at the time of ASM Microbe. 2. From one of the targeted groups. 3. Faculty from a Minority Serving Institution (MSI), such as Historically Black Colleges and Universities (HBCU), Hispanic Serving Institutions (HSI), and Tribal Colleges and Universities (TCU). Faculty from community colleges. 4. URM Faculty regardless of institutional type. 5. URM Postdoctoral Scholars. 6. URM Graduate Students

Level of Study: Graduate

Type: Travel award

Value: US$1,000 per awardee

Frequency: Annual

Country of Study: United States of America, Canada or Mexico

Application Procedure: The program requires a joint application from the student and the faculty research mentor, both parts must be completed by the deadline. The student's portion of the application includes: 1. ASM member number. 2. Letter of recommendation. 3. Personal statement

Closing Date: 15 January

Funding: Private

Additional Information: Each awardee will be offered up to US$1,000 to defray expenses associated with travel to the ASM Microbe

For further information contact:

Email: services@asm.org

American Society for Photogrammetry & Remote Sensing (ASPRS)

The Imaging and Geospatial Information Society 5410 Grosvenor Lane, Suite 210, Bethesda, MD 20814 2160, United States of America

Tel: (1) 301 493 0290
Fax: (1) 301 493 0208
Email: asprs@asprs.org; scholarships@asprs.org
Website: www.asprs.org

The American Society for Photogrammetry and Remote Sensing (ASPRS) was founded in 1934. It is a scientific association serving over 7,000 professional members around the world whose mission is to advance knowledge and improve understanding of mapping sciences to promote the responsible applications of photogrammetry, remote sensing, geographic information systems and supporting technologies.

American Society for Photogrammetry and Remote Sensing Robert N. Colwell Memorial Fellowship

Subjects: Remote sensing and geospatial information technologies

Purpose: To encourage and commend college/university students or postdoctoral researchers who display exceptional interest, desire, ability and aptitude in the specified field and who have a special interest in developing practical uses of these technologies

Eligibility: Open to student enrolled or intending to enrol in a college or university in the United States or Canada, or a recently graduated postdoctoral researcher who is pursuing a programme of study aimed at starting a professional career

Level of Study: Doctorate, Postgraduate

Type: Fellowship

Value: The award consists of a certificate and a check in the amount of US$6,500 and a one-year student or associate membership (new or renewal) in ASPRS

Frequency: Annual

Country of Study: United States of America or Canada

Application Procedure: Applicants must include a listing of courses, transcripts, listing of internship, 3 letters of recommendation and statement of purpose along with a completed application form

Closing Date: 18 October

Contributor: ASPRS Foundation

Additional Information: Please see the website for further details www.asprs.org/Awards-and-Scholarships/Robert-N-Colwell-Memorial-Fellowship.html

For further information contact:

Email: scholarships@asprs.org

American Society for Quality (ASQ)

600 North Plankinton Avenue, Milwaukee, WI 53203, United States of America

Tel: (1) 414 272 8575
Fax: (1) 414 272 1734
Email: help@asq.org
Website: www.asq.org

The American Society for Quality (ASQ) is the world's leading authority on quality. With more than 100,000 individual and organizational members, this professional association advances learning, quality improvement and knowledge exchange to improve business results and to create better workplaces and communities worldwide.

Ellis R. Ott Scholarship for Applied Statistics and Quality Management

Subjects: Statistics

Purpose: To encourage students to pursue a career in a field related to statistics and/or quality management

Eligibility: Open to candidates who are planning to enroll or are enrolled in a Master's degree or; higher level programme in the United States or Canada

Level of Study: Doctorate, Graduate, Postgraduate

Type: Scholarships

Value: US$5,000
Length of Study: 1 year
Frequency: Annual
Country of Study: United States of America
Application Procedure: Applicants can download the application form from the website. The completed application form along with curriculum vitae, academic transcripts and two letters of recommendation are to be submitted
Closing Date: 1 April
Funding: Foundation

For further information contact:

55 Buckskin Path, United States of America

Tel:	(1) 774 413 5268
Email:	lynne.hare@comcast.net
Contact:	Dr Lynne B Hare

American Society of Composers, Authors and Publishers Foundation

One Lincoln Plaza, New York, NY 10023 7142, United States of America

Tel:	(1) 212 621 6219
Fax:	(1) 212 595 3342
Email:	info@ascapfoundation.com
Website:	www.ascapfoundation.org
Contact:	Michael Spudic

The American Society of Composers, Authors and Publishers (ASCAP) is a membership association of over 260,000 composers, songwriters, lyricists and music publishers. It is dedicated to nurturing the music talent of tomorrow, preserving the legacy of the past and sustaining the creative incentive for today's creators through a variety of educational, professional and humanitarian programmes and activities which serve the entire music community. ASCAP's function is to protect the rights of its members by licensing and paying royalties for the public performances of their copyrighted works.

American Society of Composers, Authors and Publishers Foundation Morton Gould Young Composer Awards

Subjects: Music composition
Purpose: To encourage talented young composers by providing recognition, appreciation and monetary awards

Eligibility: Open to United States citizens or permanent residents who have not reached their 30th birthday by 1 January in the year of competition. Original concert music of any style will be considered. However, works which have previously earned awards or prizes in any other national competition are ineligible. Arrangements are also ineligible. Open to all composers of Original Concert Music (classical)
Level of Study: Unrestricted
Type: Award
Value: The winning composers share over US$40,000 in ASCAP Foundation Awards
Frequency: Annual
Application Procedure: Applicants must complete an application form and other materials. For more information write to organization
Closing Date: 1 February
Funding: Private, Foundation
Contributor: The ASCAP Foundation's Jack and Amy Norworth Memorial Fund, the Leo Kaplan Fund and the Frank & Lydia Bergen Foundation
No. of awards given last year: 39
Additional Information: Each year the top award winner receives an additional cash prize, The ASCAP Foundation Leo Kaplan Award

For further information contact:

c/o ASCAP, United States of America

Email:	concertmusic@ascap.com
Contact:	Cia Toscanini

American Society of Interior Designers (ASID) Educational Foundation, Inc.

608 Massachusetts Avenue North East, Washington, DC 20002, United States of America

Tel:	(1) 202 546 3480
Fax:	(1) 202 546 3480
Email:	education@asid.org
Website:	www.asidfoundation.org
Contact:	Education Department

The American Society of Interior Designers (ASID) Educational Foundation represents the interests of more than 30,500 members including interior design practitioners, students and industry and retail partners. ASID's mission is to be the definitive resource for professional education and knowledge sharing, advocacy of interior designers' right to practice and expansion of interior design markets.

The ASID Educational Foundation/Irene Winifred Eno Grant

Country of Study: Any country

For further information contact:

Email: schung@asid.org

American Society of Mechanical Engineers (ASME International)

Two Park Avenue, New York, NY 10016 5990, United States of America

Tel: (1) 800 843 2763
Fax: (1) 212 591 7143, 212 591 7856
Email: CustomerCare@asme.org
Website: www.asme.org/education/enged/aid
Contact: Theresa Oluwanifise, Coordinator Educational
                Operations

Founded in 1880 as the American Society of Mechanical Engineers (ASME International), today ASME International is a non-profit educational and technical organization serving a worldwide membership.

Elisabeth M and Winchell M Parsons Scholarship

Subjects: Mechanical engineering
Purpose: To assist ASME student members working towards a doctoral degree
Eligibility: Selection is based on academic performance, character, need and ASME participation. Applicants must be citizens of the United States of America and be enrolled in a United States school in an ABET-accredited mechanical engineering department. No student may receive more than one auxiliary scholarship or loan in the same academic year
Level of Study: Doctorate
Type: Award
Value: US$2,000
Frequency: Annual
Country of Study: United States of America
No. of awards offered: 5

Application Procedure: Application forms are available from the website
Closing Date: 15 March
No. of awards given last year: 3
No. of applicants last year: 5

For further information contact:

5025 Iroquois Avenue, United States of America

Tel: (1) 562 920 3653
Email: cindipool@gmail.com
Contact: Cynthia Pool

Marjorie Roy Rothermel Scholarship

Subjects: Mechanical engineering
Purpose: To assist students working towards a Master's degree
Eligibility: Selection is based on academic performance, character, need and ASME participation. Applicants must be citizens of the United States of America and must be enrolled in a United States school in an ABET-accredited mechanical engineering department. No student may receive more than one auxiliary scholarship or loan in the same academic year
Level of Study: Graduate
Type: Scholarship
Value: US$3,000
Frequency: Annual
Country of Study: United States of America
Application Procedure: Application forms are available from the website
Closing Date: 1 March

For further information contact:

332 Valencia Street, United States of America

Tel: (1) 850 932 3698
Email: eprocha340@aol.com
Contact: Mrs Otto Prochaska

American Society of Nephrology (ASN)

1510 H Street, NW, Suite 800, Washington, DC 20005, United States of America

Tel: (1) 202 640 4660
Fax: (1) 202 637 9793
Email: email@asn-online.org

Website: www.asn-online.org
Contact: Grants Co-ordinator

The American Society of Nephrology (ASN) was founded in 1967 as a non-profit corporation to enhance and assist the study and practice of nephrology, to provide a forum for the promulgation of research and to meet the professional and continuing education needs of its members.

Carl W Gottschalk Research Scholar Grant

Subjects: Nephrology
Purpose: To provide funding for young faculty to foster evolution to an independent research career and a successful application a National Institutes of Health (NIH) R01 grant or equivalent
Eligibility: Applicants must an active member of the ASN and hold an MD or PhD or equivalent degree. At the time of submission the applicant's membership must be current and their dues paid. Appointment to full-time faculty must be conformed in writing by the department chair
Level of Study: Postdoctorate, Postgraduate
Type: Grant
Value: US$100,000
Length of Study: 2 years
Frequency: Annual
Country of Study: United States of America
Application Procedure: Online application
Closing Date: 28 January
Funding: Foundation
Contributor: ASN Foundation for Kidney Research
Additional Information: Please visit the website for further details

For further information contact:

Tel: (1) 202 640 4660
Email: grants@asn-online.org
Contact: Mr

American University in Cairo (AUC)

PO Box 2511, 113 Kasr EI Aini Street, Cairo 11511, Egypt

Tel: (20) 20 2 2794 2964
Fax: (20) 20 2 2795 7565
Email: ocm@aucegypt.edu, aucegypt@aucegypt.edu, ouc@aucegypt.edu
Website: www.aucegypt.edu/Pages/default.aspx
Contact: Mrs Sawsan Mardini, Director of Graduate Students Services

The American University in Cairo (AUC) provides quality higher and continuing education for students from Egypt and the surrounding region. The University is an independent, non-profit, apolitical, non-sectarian and equal opportunity institution. English is the primary language of instruction. The University is accredited in the United States of America by the Commission of Higher Education of the Middle States Association of Colleges and Schools.

African Graduate Fellowships

Subjects: Art and humanities, business administration and management, engineering, mass communication and information, mathematics and computer science, social and behavioural sciences
Purpose: The African Graduate Fellowship is a competitive fellowship program for bright, highly motivated African students interested in pursuing a master's degree at AUC
Eligibility: Non-Egyptian African nationals; Open to all disciplines of graduate studies; For new graduate degree-seeking students; full admission to one of the graduate programs in AUC, satisfying AUC graduate full admissions requirements. 1. Submit an International TOEFL iBT exam score or academic IELTS exam score as per the cut-off scores for AUC graduate admissions. 2. For continuing students; to retain the fellowship, the recipient must maintain a GPA of 3.2. 3. Financial need
Level of Study: Graduate
Type: Fellowship
Value: A waiver of tuition fee; student services and activities fees; a monthly stipend of LE 600 for 10 months
Length of Study: One semester and may be renewed for a maximum period of 2 years. The fellowship may cover a summer session
Frequency: Annual
Country of Study: Any country except India
No. of awards offered: 123
Application Procedure: There are two steps which needs to be followed to process the application. To Apply Step 1: Check how to apply and submit the online application Step 2: Submit the online fellowship application Application link is mentioned as follows:
Closing Date: 15 February
No. of awards given last year: 18
No. of applicants last year: 123
Additional Information: For further information, refer the below link. ssb.aucegypt.edu:4444/PROD/twbkwbis.P_GenMenu?name=homepage

For further information contact:

Email: grad@aucegypt.edu

American University of Beirut

American University of Beirut, 3 Dag Hammarskjold Plaza, 8th Floor, New York, NY 10017-2303, United States of America

Tel: (1) 212 583 7600
Website: www.aub.edu.lb/main/about/Pages/index.aspx

AUB currently offers more than 120 programs leading to the bachelor's, master's, MD, and PhD degrees. The language of instruction is English (except for courses in the Arabic Department and other language courses).

American University of Beirut Mediterranean Scholarships

Subjects: The Faculty of Health Sciences (FHS) at the American University of Beirut (AUB), Lebanon is offering 10 scholarships for graduate education in public health. The scholarships will be open for the following degrees at AUB: Master of Public Health and Master of Science in Epidemiology
Purpose: To strengthen capacity in implementation research on the neglected tropical diseases as well as malaria and tuberculosis. The American University of Beirut (AUB) is delighted to offer a number of scholarships for students from low- and middle-income countries
Eligibility: To be eligible, all candidates are expected to have good academic record in undergraduate education (and graduate education where relevant) in any discipline (health sciences, social sciences, nutrition, medicine, nursing, pharmacy, dentistry sciences or related discipline) and hold a bachelor's degree from AUB, or an equivalent degree from another recognized institution. Please note, all candidates must be a national of and resident in a low- or middle-income country of the Eastern Mediterranean region
Level of Study: Postgraduate
Value: The scholarships cover travel, tuition and living expenses for the duration of the program. English language training at AUB prior to enrolment is also covered for some students who need it
Country of Study: Any country
Application Procedure: The application should be made through the online system at: graduateadmissions.aub.edu.lb/
Closing Date: 1 April
Funding: Trusts
Additional Information: Place of Study – American University of Beirut (AUB), Lebanon

For further information contact:
Email: GPHP@aub.edu.lb

American Water Works Association (AWWA)

6666 West Quincy Avenue, Denver, CO 80235, United States of America

Tel: (1) 303 794 7711
Fax: (1) 303 347 0804
Email: lmoody@awwa.org
Website: www.awwa.org
Contact: Administrative Assistant

The American Water Works Association (AWWA) is an international non-profit scientific and educational society dedicated to the improvement of drinking water quality and supply. The Association has more than 57,000 members who represent the full spectrum of the drinking water community, e.g. treatment plant operators and managers, scientists, environmentalists, manufacturers, academics, regulators and others who have a genuine interest in water supply and public health.

American Water Works Association Abel Wolman Fellowship

Subjects: Water supply and treatment
Purpose: To encourage and support promising students from countries with AWWA sections to pursue advanced training and research
Eligibility: Open to candidates who anticipate completing the requirements for their PhD degree within 2 years of the award. Applicants must be citizens of a country that has an AWWA section, i.e. the United States of America, Canada or Mexico. Applicants will be considered without regard to colour, gender, race, creed or country of origin
Level of Study: Doctorate
Type: Fellowship
Value: Up to US$20,000
Length of Study: Initially 1 year, renewable for 1 further year on submission of evidence of satisfactory progress and approval by a review committee
Frequency: Annual
Country of Study: United States of America, Canada or Mexico

Application Procedure: Applicants must submit an official application form, official transcripts of all university education, official copies of Graduate Record Examination scores, three letters of recommendation, a proposed curriculum of study and brief plans of dissertation research study

Closing Date: 15 January

Funding: Private

For further information contact:

Email: swheeler@awwa.org

American Woman's Society of Certified Public Accountants

AWSCPA Administrative Offices, 136 South Keowee Street, Dayton, OH 45402, United States of America

Tel: (1) 937 222 1872
Fax: (1) 937 222 5794
Email: info@awscpa.org
Website: www.awscpa.org

The American Woman's Society of CPA provides annual scholarships to women working towards an accounting degree as well as to those working towards their Certified Public Accountant License.

Call for Nominations for Urdang Medal and Kremers Award

Subjects: History of Science, Medicine, and Technology
Purpose: The George Urdang Medal is awarded for an original and scholarly publication, or series of publications, pertaining primarily to historical or historico-social aspects of pharmacy. The Medal may also be awarded for popular works intended to achieve more widespread appreciation for, and better understanding of, pharmacy and its past among members of the pharmaceutical profession, allied professions, or the public. The Urdang Medal was established in 1952 in honor of Professor George Urdang, one of AIHP's founders and a renowned scholar of the history of pharmacy
Eligibility: 1. The Urdang Medal is awarded without restriction as to citizenship of the author or place of publication. Evaluation is based on competence of research and skill of

interpretation and presentation. 2. The nominee's age, total number of publications or previous honors is not given primary consideration
Level of Study: Professional development
Type: Award
Frequency: Annual
Country of Study: Any country
Application Procedure: In order to apply for the nominations for this award, kindly access the below link for the application form and procedures to be followed. networks. h-net.org/node/9782/discussions/3798798/call-nominations-2019-urdang-medal-and-kremers-award
Closing Date: 30 April
Funding: Private

For further information contact:

H-Net: Humanities & Social Sciences Online Old Horticulture 141H 506 East Circle Drive, East Lansing, MI 48824, United States of America

Tel: (1) 517 432 5134
Email: aihp@aihp.org

American-Scandinavian Foundation (ASF)

58 Park Avenue at 38th Street, New York, NY 10016, United States of America

Tel: (1) 212 779 3587
Fax: (1) 212 249 3444
Email: grants@amscan.org
Website: www.amscan.org
Contact: Director of Fellowships and Grants

The ASF is a publicity supported, non-profit organization that promotes international understanding through educational and cultural exchange between the United States and the Nordic countries.

Awards for American Universities and Colleges to host Norwegian lecturers

Subjects: The competition is open to all American colleges and universities. The award is appropriate not just for Scandinavian studies departments, but for any department or interdisciplinary program with an interest in incorporating a Scandinavian focus into its course offerings

Purpose: The American-Scandinavian Foundation (ASF) invites United States colleges and universities to apply for funding to host a visiting lecturer from Norway. The awards are for appointments of one semester, and should fall within an academic year

Eligibility: TERMS OF AWARD; 1. US$20,000 teaching/research stipend. 2. 5,000 travel stipend for lecture appearances outside home institution. Lectureships should be in the area of contemporary studies with an emphasis on one of five areas: 1. Public Policy. 2. Conflict Resolution. 3. Environmental Studies. 4. Multiculturalism. 5. Healthcare. CONDITIONS OF AWARD; 1. The lecturer must be a Norwegian citizen, and a scholar or expert in a field appropriate to the host department or program. 2. The ASF encourages consideration of the practitioner as well as the academic as a lectureship candidate. RESPONSIBILITIES OF THE HOST INSTITUTION; 1. The institution is responsible for selecting the lecturer it wishes to host. The ASF cannot assist in establishing contacts. 2. All pre-appointment communication with the lecturer, and arrangements for teaching, public presentations and housing during the lectureship appointment are the responsibility of the host institution. The host institution would be expected to provide support complementing the US$20,000 stipend. Additional support may be in the form of: 1. Subsidized faculty housing. 2. International Travel and insurance expenses. 3. Office and computer use. 4. Additional stipend support. RESPONSIBILITIES OF THE LECTURER; 1. The selected lecturer is expected to teach one course (undergraduate or graduate level) and perform modest public activities (lectures, etc.) for which s/he will receive US$20,000. 2. The selected lecturer is expected to accept invitations to visit other academic institutions or conferences (including the NorTANA conference, the Swedish Teachers' conference, and the SASS conference) for which s/he will have US$5,000 available in travel funds

Level of Study: Unrestricted

Type: Lectureship/Prize

Value: US$25,000

Length of Study: One semester

Frequency: Annual

Country of Study: United States of America

Application Procedure: Complete online application - www.amscan.org/fellowships-grants/visiting-lectureships/

Closing Date: 15 February

Funding: Private

No. of awards given last year: 1

For further information contact:

Email: grants@amscan.org

Grants for Public Projects

Purpose: Through its public project grants, ASF funds a wide variety of programs that bring American and Scandinavian culture, art and thought to public audiences. The American-Scandinavian Foundation promotes the cultures of the Nordic countries in the United States and American culture in the Nordic countries by encouraging programs that will enhance public appreciation of culture, art, and thought

Eligibility: Must be a non-profit organization and the project must be open to the public. ASF's funding priority has traditionally been to underwrite public programming and defined events. Awards are given to non-profit organizations only. Proof of an organization's non-profit status (as a 501(c)(3) in the United States or equivalent in Scandinavia) is required. ASF does NOT support: 1. Capital expenses. 2. Institutional overhead and other administrative fees. 3. Underwriting book, periodical or website publication. 4. Production of commercial CDs or cassettes. 5. Conference participation or conference registration for individuals. However, general conference expenses such as costs for special invitees/speakers can be supported. 6. Participation in studio residencies other than those with which ASF already has an ongoing affiliation. 7. Retroactive funding. Projects cannot begin before the decision announcement date. 8. The maximum award amount is US$5,000; however, average grants range between US$1,000 to US$2,000. ASF will only accept one application per organization per competition cycle and will grant only one award per organization per fiscal year in any one grant category

Level of Study: Unrestricted

Type: Project grant

Value: up to US$5,000

Length of Study: varies

Frequency: Twice a year

Country of Study: Scandinavian countries

Application Procedure: Complete online application - www.amscan.org/fellowships-and-grants/public-project-proposal-guidelines/

Closing Date: 15 February

Funding: Private

For further information contact:

Email: grants@amscan.org

Translation Competition

Subjects: The annual ASF translation competition is awarded for the most outstanding translations of poetry, fiction, drama or literary prose written by a Scandinavian author born after 1900. Submission Information Entry deadline: 1 June5 The Nadia

Christensen Prize includes a US$2,500 award, publication of an excerpt in Scandinavian Review, and a commemorative bronze medallion. The Leif and Inger Sjöberg Award, given to an individual whose literature translations from a Nordic language have not previously been published, includes a US$2,000 award, publication of an excerpt in Scandinavian Review, and a commemorative bronze medallion

Purpose: ASF Translation Competition is an international competition for literary translations into English from any Nordic language and genre. Our annual competition recognizes outstanding translations of Scandinavian literature authored by a Scandinavian writer born after 1900

Eligibility: 1. The prizes are for outstanding English translations of poetry, fiction, drama or literary prose originally written in a Nordic language. 2. If prose, manuscripts must be no longer than 50 pages; if poetry, 25 (Do not exceed these limits). Manuscripts must be typed and double-spaced with numbered pages. 3. Translations must be from the writing of one author, although not necessarily from a single work. Please include a one-paragraph description about the author. 4. An entry must consist of: One copy of the translation, including a title page and a table of contents for the proposed book of which the manuscript submitted is a part. One copy of the work(s) in the original language; please send the relevant pages. A CV containing all contact information, including email address, for the translator; and; A letter or other document signed by the author, the author's agent or the author's estate granting permission for the translation to be entered in this competition and published in Scandinavian Review. 5. Translator's names may not appear on any page of their manuscripts, including the title page. 6. The translation submitted in the competition may not have been previously published in the English language by the submission deadline. (If the translation being submitted to this competition is also under consideration by a publisher, you must inform us of the expected publication date.); 7. Translators may submit one entry only and may not submit the same entry in more than two competitions. 8. The Translation Prize cannot be won more than three times by the same translator

Level of Study: Unrestricted
Type: Translation prize
Value: US$2,000–US$2,500
Frequency: Annual
Country of Study: Any country
Application Procedure: Complete online application - www.amscan.org/fellowships-grants/translation-competition/
Closing Date: 15 June
Funding: Private
No. of awards given last year: 2

For further information contact:

Email: grants@amscan.org

Analytics India

University of Sydney: Data Science Scholarships

Purpose: The University of Sydney, one of Australia's premier university is offering scholarships for international students for intake to high performing candidates
Eligibility: 1. Applicants must be a graduate of a quantitative degree program. A quantitative program includes Data Science, Computer Science, Mathematics, Statistics, Engineering, Physics, Economics and more. 2. Applicants must have achieved a minimum distinction average (equivalent to 75 at the University of Sydney) in their UG studies
Level of Study: Postgraduate
Type: Scholarship
Frequency: Annual
Study Establishment: University of Sydney
Country of Study: Australia
Closing Date: 30 April
Funding: Private

For further information contact:

#280, 2nd floor, 5th Main, 15 A cross, Sector 6, HSR layout Bengaluru, Karnataka 560102, India

Email: info@analyticsindiamag.com

Anglo-Austrian Music Society

Richard Tauber Prize for Singers, 158 Rosendale Road, SE21 8LG, London, United Kingdom

Tel: (44) 20 8761 0444
Fax: (44) 20 8766 6151
Email: info@aams.org.uk
Website: www.aams.org.uk
Contact: Jane Avery, Secretary

The Anglo-Austrian Music Society promotes lectures and concerts and is closely associated with its parent organization, the Anglo-Austrian Society, which was founded in 1944 to promote friendship and understanding between the people of the United Kingdom and Austria through personal contacts, educational programmes and cultural exchanges. AAMS awards the Richard Tauber prize for singers.

Wigmore Hall/Independent Opera International Song Competition

Subjects: The Competition is open to singers and pianists of all nationalities and celebrates the art of the Lied. Cash prizes and performance opportunities are available to the winner. Entrants must be under 33 at the start date of each Competition
Purpose: Wigmore Hall is responsible for the biennial International Song Competition
Eligibility: The Competition attracts singers and pianists of the highest calibre aged 33 or under, keen to pursue performing careers at the highest level
Level of Study: Graduate, Postgraduate, Undergraduate
Type: Competition
Value: It provides valuable opportunities for feedback from Jury members drawn from vocal artists of global stature; provides opportunities for participants to meet their peers from other countries and to exchange ideas on performance, technique and repertoire; and provides a vital public platform from which young singers and pianists can break into the world of professional performance at the highest level
Length of Study: n/a
Frequency: Every 2 years
Study Establishment: n/a
Country of Study: Any country
No. of awards offered: 150 plus
Application Procedure: Application form and recording (MP3 or WAV files only) of prescribed repertoire plus application fee
Closing Date: 15 March
Funding: Private
Contributor: Independent Opera
No. of awards given last year: 6
No. of applicants last year: 150 plus
Additional Information: Please check at www.wigmore-hall.org.uk/song-competition for more information and details of how to apply

For further information contact:

Wigmore Hall/Independent Opera International Song Competition, Wigmore Hall, 36 Wigmore Street, United Kingdom

Tel: (44) 20 7258 8244
Email: songcompetition@wigmore-hall.org.uk
Contact: Ruth Wheal, General Manager, Competitions

Anglo-Danish Society

43 Maresfield Gardens, NW3 5TF, London, United Kingdom

Tel: (44) 1728 638 345

Email: scholarships@anglo-danishsociety.org.uk
Website: www.anglo-danishsociety.org.uk
Contact: Mrs Margit Staehr, Administrator

The Anglo-Danish Society exists to promote closer understanding between the United Kingdom and Denmark by arranging lectures, outings, social gatherings and other events of interest for its members and their guests. The society administers scholarship funds which help Danish students visit the United Kingdom or British students visit Denmark, for the purpose of advanced or postgraduate studies.

Denmark Liberation Scholarships

Subjects: Anglo Danish cultural and scientific interests
Purpose: To promote Anglo Danish relations
Eligibility: Open to graduates of British nationality only
Level of Study: Doctorate, Postdoctorate, Postgraduate, Professional development
Type: Scholarship
Value: One major award of UK £9,000 and others at UK £6,000 each
Length of Study: A minimum of 6 months
Frequency: Annual
Study Establishment: A Danish university or other approved institution
Country of Study: Denmark
No. of awards offered: 12
Application Procedure: Applicants must complete an application form, available from the Secretary between 1 October and 31 December. Applicants should include a stamped addressed envelope or international reply coupons
Closing Date: 12 January
Funding: Private
No. of awards given last year: 4
No. of applicants last year: 12

Anglo-Norse Society

Norwegian Embassy 25, Belgrave Square, SW1X 8QD, London, United Kingdom

Tel: (44) 208 452 4843
Email: Secretariat@anglo-norse.org.uk
Website: www.anglo-norse.org.uk/

The Anglo-Norse Society in London is a registered charity for the purpose of promoting better understanding between

Britain and Norway through learning about each other's country and way of life.

The Anglo-Norse Dame Gillian Brown Postgraduate Scholarship

Subjects: The scholarship may be used to contribute towards the cost of study and research in the fields of Norwegian literature, history, music or cultural studies
Purpose: To help towards the cost for a British student to undertake 1 year of postgraduate study in Norway in the fields of the humanities or social sciences
Eligibility: Any person holding a British passport and normally resident in the United Kingdom
Level of Study: Postgraduate
Type: Scholarship
Value: £2,000
Length of Study: Up to a year
Frequency: Annual
Study Establishment: University or equivalent, dependent on the nature of the research
Country of Study: Norway
No. of awards offered: 1
Application Procedure: Students wishing to apply should request an application form which will ask for details of their degree results and the project for which they intend to use the scholarship, plus a letter of acceptance from the institution where they wish to pursue their research
Closing Date: 31 March
Contributor: A bequest from Dame Gillian Brown and interest on capital built up by the Society
No. of awards given last year: 1
No. of applicants last year: 1
Additional Information: The Anglo-Norse Society also offers two annual grants of up to £500 each that may be used for travel or research related to Norway

For further information contact:

The Secretary, The Anglo-Norse Society, 25 Belgrave Square SW1X 8QD, London, United Kingdom

Email: scholarships@anglo-norse.org.uk

Appraisal Institute Education Trust

200 W. Madison, Suite 1500, Chicago, IL 60606, United States of America

Tel: (1) 312 335 4133
Fax: (1) 312 335 4134

Email: educationtrust@appraisalinstitute.org
Website: www.aiedtrust.org

The Appraisal Institute is an international membership association of professional real estate appraisers, with more than 21,000 members and 99 chapters throughout the United States of America, Canada and abroad. Its mission is to support and advance its members as the choice for real estate solutions and uphold professional credentials, standards of professional practice and ethics consistent with the public good.

Appraisal Institute Education Trust Minorities and Women Education Scholarship

Subjects: Real estate appraisal or related fields
Purpose: The Minority and Women Educational Scholarship is geared towards college students working towards a degree in real estate appraisal or a related field. The scholarship is to help offset the cost of tuition
Eligibility: Applicant must be a member of a racial, ethnic or gender group underrepresented in the appraisal profession and full- or part-time student enroled-in real estate related courses at a degree-granting college/university or junior college/university. Individuals must have proof a cumulative grade point average of no less than 2.5 on 4.0 scale and have demonstrated financial need. Scholarship award must be used in the same calendar year as awarded by the committee
Level of Study: Graduate, Postgraduate
Type: Scholarship
Value: US$1,000 per person
Frequency: Annual
Country of Study: United States of America
Application Procedure: An official student transcript for all college work completed to date. A 500-word written essay stating why applicant should be awarded the scholarship. Two letters of recommendation from previous employers and/or college professors. An attestation that the scholarship will be applied toward tuition/books expense as stated in the application. Optional: Applicants are asked to include a head and shoulders photograph as scholarship recipients may be profiled in Appraisal Institute newsletter/news releases
Closing Date: 15 April
Funding: Private
Additional Information: Applicants must visit the website www.aiedtrust.org for further information

For further information contact:

Email: educationtrust@appraisalinstitute.org

Arc of the United States

1825 K Street, NW, Suite 1200, Washington, DC 20006, United States of America

Tel:	(1) 800 433 5255
Fax:	(1) 202 534 3731
Email:	info@thearc.org
Website:	www.thearc.org

The Arc of the United States advocates for the rights and full participation of all children and adults with intellectual and developmental disabilities. Together with our network of members and affiliation chapters, we improve systems of supports and services, connect families, inspire communities and influence public policy.

Arc of the United States Research Grant

Subjects: Social and preventative medicine
Purpose: To support research leading towards prevention, amelioration or cure of mental retardation
Eligibility: Open to United States nationals only
Level of Study: Unrestricted
Type: Research grant
Value: Various amounts up to US$25,000
Length of Study: 1 year, with the option of extension
Frequency: Annual
Country of Study: United States of America
No. of awards offered: 25
Application Procedure: Applicants must submit project authorisation form, budget form, project summary, maximum of 15 double-spaced pages for narrative, and letters of support
Closing Date: 1 April
Funding: Private
No. of awards given last year: 1
No. of applicants last year: 25

For further information contact:

Department of Research & Program Services, The Arc PO Box 1047, United States of America

Tel:	(1) 817 261 6003
Email:	mwehmeye@metronet.com

Archaeological Institute of America

Anna C. & Oliver C. Colburn Fellowships

Purpose: To support studies undertaken at the American School of Classical Studies at Athens, Greece for no more than a year
Eligibility: For members of the AIA at the time of application and until the end of the fellowship term. Applicant must be a citizen or permanent resident of the United States or Canada, must be at the pre-doctoral stage or have recently received a PhD (within five years of the date of the application)
Level of Study: Graduate
Type: Fellowship
Value: US$5,500
Frequency: Annual
Country of Study: United States of America or Canada
Application Procedure: Apply online: www.archaeological. org/grants/form/1307
Closing Date: 15 January
Funding: Foundation

For further information contact:

Email: fellowships@archaeological.org

Arctic Institute of North America (AINA)

The University of Calgary, 2500 University Drive North West, ES-1040, Calgary, AB T2N 1N4, Canada

Tel:	(1) 403 220 7515
Fax:	(1) 403 282 4609
Email:	arctic@ucalgary.ca
Website:	www.arctic.ucalgary.ca
Contact:	Executive Director

Created in 1945, the Arctic Institute of North America (AINA) is a non-profit membership organization and a multidisciplinary research institute for the University of Calgary.

Arctic Institute of North America Grants-in-Aid

Subjects: Preference is given to natural sciences, social sciences, anthropology and economics
Purpose: To support young investigators and provide funding to augment their research

Eligibility: Proposed projects can include field, library or office intensive investigations
Level of Study: Postgraduate
Type: Grant
Value: Up to C$1,000 which can be used for travel, supplies, equipment and services but not salary or wages
Length of Study: Varies
Frequency: Annual
Country of Study: United States of America
Application Procedure: Applicants must submit proposals which must not exceed four double spaced pages. A title, introduction, objectives, methodology, anticipated results, period of performance and proposed use of the AINA award should be clearly stated. The total estimated budget for the project should be provided on a separate page and should clearly identify other anticipated and committed sources and amounts of funding
Closing Date: 1 February
Additional Information: A report to the committee will be required within one year following the award. Any report or publication resulting from the investigation should include acknowledgement of the AINA Grant-in-Aid programme. One copy of all publications should be sent to ASTIS at the AINA Calgary office for inclusion in the ASTIS database and AINA library

For further information contact:

Email: majohnson@alaska.edu
Contact: Mark Johnson

Aristotle University of Thessaloniki

University Campus, GRC 541 24, Thessaloniki, Greece

Tel: (30) 2310 99 4168, 99 6771
Fax: (30) 2310 99 5112
Email: dps@auth.gr
Website: www.auth.gr/services/admin/studies_
               department.en.php3
Contact: Studies Department

Summer Intensive Course in modern Greek Language Scholarship

Subjects: 4/weeks, 20h/week intensive summer course of modern Greek language classes, plus cultural program Each year mid August to mid September 3 levels (beginners, intermediate, advance) following the common European framework of reference for languages
Purpose: Diffusion of Greek language & culture
Eligibility: nationals of any country; priority given to students of Greek (language, history, art, etc.)
Level of Study: Unrestricted
Type: Studentship
Value: tuition fee waiver (324 Euros)
Length of Study: 4 weeks
Frequency: Annual
Study Establishment: Aristotle University of Thessaloniki, School of Modern Greek Language
Country of Study: Greece
No. of awards offered: 72
Application Procedure: Application form and supporting documents to be sent to the Aristotle University Department of Studies by 28th February
Closing Date: 28 February
Funding: Government
No. of awards given last year: 11
No. of applicants last year: 72
Additional Information: While the application process, documents and deadline are standard each year, the type and number of awards are subject to change based on funds available and Senate's decision

For further information contact:

Aristotle University of Thessaloniki, Department of Studies, University Campus, 541 24 Thessaloniki Hellas, Greece

Email: dps@auth.gr

Arizona Community Foundation

George F. Wellik Scholarship

Purpose: This scholarship is available for high school seniors Wickenburg, Arizona. Applicants must demonstrate financial need and must have a grade point average of 2.5 or higher
Eligibility: 1. Must be a United States citizen or legal permanent resident. 2. Must have a grade point average of 2.5 or higher. 3. Must reside in Wickenburg, Arizona. 4. This award is for United States students
Level of Study: Graduate
Type: Scholarship
Value: US$5,000
Frequency: Annual
Country of Study: United States of America

Application Procedure: Applications for the George F. Wellik Scholarship are available on the Arizona Community Foundation website. To apply, the applicant must register with the foundation. In addition to a completed application, the applicant must also submit the following: two letters of recommendation, one from his/her guidance counselor and one from a high school academic teacher, attesting to his/her academic strengths and determination to succeed at the university; a high school transcript through the seventh semester; a 500- to 700-word essay addressing the topic listed on the application; typed personal statements; verification of SAT and/or ACT test scores; and a Free Application for Federal Student Aid form(FAFSA). The FAFSA is available online at www.fafsa.ed.gov, at high school guidance offices, and at college financial aid offices. All application materials must be submitted online by the deadline date

Closing Date: 8 April

Funding: Foundation

For further information contact:

2201 E. Camelback Road, Suite 202 Phoenix, AZ 85016, United States of America

Tel: (1) 800 222 8221
Email: scholarships@swe.org

Arizona State University College of Business

PO Box 874906, Tempe, AZ 85287-4906, United States of America

Tel: (1) 602 965 3332
Fax: (1) 602 965 8569
Email: asu.mba@asu.edu
Website: www.cob.asu.edu/mba
Contact: MBA Admissions Officer

Madbury Road Design Success Award Scholarship

Subjects: Designers and Architects
Purpose: Madbury Road is offering a US$1,000 scholarship in support designers and architects of the future
Eligibility: This is an award that is only available for students currently enrolled at a university or college
Level of Study: Professional development
Type: Scholarship
Value: US$1,000
Frequency: Annual
Country of Study: Any country

Application Procedure: The video should not be longer than two minutes. To enter, all you have to do is upload the video on YouTube and use Madbury Road Design Success Award Scholarship as the title. It is also necessary for you to put a link to this scholarship page within the description portion on YouTube. Once you have done all of the above steps, you can email us at scholarship@madburyroad.com providing us a link to your video and the following information: Your full name, telephone number and mailing address. The name of the college or university that you currently attend or will be attending. Proof that you have, either been accepted, or are currently attending the college or university that you specified. The area that you study

Closing Date: 31 March

Funding: Private

For further information contact:

Email: scholarship@madburyroad.com

The Ship Smart Annual Scholarship

Purpose: Ship Smart leads the industry in moving small amounts of high value goods and small shipments of household goods, electronics and artwork
Eligibility: Applications will be accepted on a rolling basis. Submit your essay or article to: scholarships@shipsmart.com including your full name, contact information, and school you will be attending. The winners will also be notified via email
Level of Study: Graduate
Type: Scholarship
Frequency: Annual
Country of Study: United States of America
Application Procedure: To apply for the scholarship write a 1,000 word original essay or article, that may not have been posted anywhere on the internet, about an article related to our website. Some topics could be anything related to: 1. Shipping Furniture. 2. Small Moves. 3. Shipping Antiques. 4. Shipping Artwork. 5. Shipping Electronics. 6. Packing and Shipping

Closing Date: 12 April

Funding: Private

For further information contact:

Email: scholarships@shipsmart.com

Armenian International Women's Association

Armenian International Women

Purpose: AIWA annually awards scholarships in honor of Ethel Jaffarian Duffett, Agnes Missirian, Lucy Kasparian Aharonian

Eligibility: 1. Female of Armenian Descent. 2. Financial Need. 3. Full-Time Student. 4. Accredited University/College. 5. Junior, Senior, or Graduate Student. 6. 3.2 Minimum GPA. 7. Certified Copy of University/College Transcripts. 8. Two Letters of Recommendation, one from an academic instructor/advisor, one from a community representative. 9. Small (Passport Size) Photograph
Level of Study: Graduate
Type: Scholarship
Frequency: Annual
Country of Study: Any country
Closing Date: 19 April
Funding: Private

For further information contact:

Armenian International Women's Association, Inc. 65 Main St., #3A Watertown, MA 02472, United States of America

Email: scholarships@aiwainternational.org

Arthritis Research United Kingdom

Copeman House, St Mary's Court, St Mary's Gate, S41 7TD, Chesterfield, United Kingdom

Tel: (44) 12 4655 8033
Fax: (44) 12 4655 8007
Email: info@arc.org.uk
Website: www.arc.org.uk
Contact: Mr Michael Patnick, Head of Research &
                   Education Funding

The Arthritis Research Campaign (arc) is the fourth largest medical research charity in the United Kingdom, and the only charity in the country dedicated to finding the cause of and cure for arthritis, relying entirely upon voluntary donations to sustain its wide-ranging research and educational programmes.

Clinical Research Fellowships

Subjects: Arthritis and related musculoskeletal diseases
Purpose: Aim to provide an opportunity for training in clinical and/or laboratory research techniques in a project that demonstrates clear relevance to the aims of Arthritis Research United Kingdom in a centre of excellence in the United Kingdom
Eligibility: Open to medical graduates (including orthopaedic surgeons), usually during speciality training, who are expected to register for a higher degree, usually a PhD

Level of Study: Doctorate, Professional development, Research
Type: Fellowship
Value: Salaries will be according to age and experience on the appropriate clinical salary scale. Applications may also be made for reasonable running costs although tuition fees will not generally be provided
Length of Study: 3 years
Frequency: Annual
Study Establishment: A university, hospital or recognized research institute
Country of Study: United Kingdom
No. of awards offered: 17
Application Procedure: Applications for funding are available via an online system accessible from the website
Closing Date: January
Funding: Private
Contributor: Voluntary charitable contributions
No. of awards given last year: 2
No. of applicants last year: 17

For further information contact:
Email: cdftdr@who.int

Arthritis Society

393 University Avenue, Suite 1700, Toronto, ON M5G 1E6, Canada

Tel: (1) 416 979 7228
Fax: (1) 416 979 8366
Email: scara@arthritis.ca/info@on.arthritis.ca
Website: www.arthritis.ca
Contact: Ms Julie Wysocki, Manager, Research and career
                   Development Program

The Arthritis Society is Canada's principal charity devoted solely to funding and promoting arthritis research and care

Artist Trust

1835, 12th Ave, Seattle, WA 98122, United States of America

Tel: (1) 2 064 678 734
Fax: (1) 2 064 679 633
Email: info@artisttrust.org
Website: www.artisttrust.org
Contact: Zach Frimmel, Programs Assistant

Artist Trust is a non-profit organization whose sole mission is to support and encourage individual artists working in all disciplines in order to enhance community life throughout Washington state.

Grants for Artist Projects (GAP)

Subjects: Art
Purpose: GAP awards provide support for artist-generated projects, which can include (but are not limited to) the development, completion or presentation of new work
Eligibility: Applicants must be a practicing artist, 18 years of age or older by application deadline date, a generative artist, and a resident of Washington State at the time of application and when the award is granted. Applicants may not be a graduate or undergraduate matriculated student enrolled in any degree program
Level of Study: Unrestricted
Type: Grant
Value: Up to US$1,400
Frequency: Annual
Country of Study: United States of America
No. of awards offered: 698
Application Procedure: Complete application form, submit work samples, work sample description, resume and WA state ID
Closing Date: February
Funding: Government, Commercial, Private, Corporation, Foundation, Individuals
No. of awards given last year: 58
No. of applicants last year: 698

For further information contact:

1835 12th Avenue, Seattle, WA 98122-2437, United States of America

Tel: (1) 206 467 8734
Fax: (1) 206 467 9633
Email: heatherjoy@srtisttrust.org
Contact: Heather Helbach-Olds, Director of Information Services

Irving and Yvonne Twining Humber Award for Lifetime Artistic Achievement

Subjects: Visual arts
Purpose: To reward a female visual artist over the age of 60 from Washington State
Eligibility: Artists must be nominated. Nominees must be female, over the age of 60, a Washington State resident and a visual artist who has been practicing for 25 years or more

Level of Study: Postgraduate, Unrestricted
Type: Award
Value: US$10,000
Frequency: Annual
Country of Study: Any country
No. of awards offered: Approx. 50
Application Procedure: Nomination forms are available by mail or online
Closing Date: 15 December
Funding: Government, Commercial, Private, Corporation, Foundation, Individuals
Contributor: Mrs Twining Humber
No. of awards given last year: 1
No. of applicants last year: Approx. 50

Arts Council of Ireland

70 Merrion Square, Dublin 2, Ireland

Tel: (353) 1 661 1840
Fax: (353) 1 676 1320
Email: info@artscouncil.ie
Website: www.artscouncil.ie
Contact: Ms Tara Byrne, Artists' Support Executive

The Arts Council, the development agency for the arts in Ireland, exists to promote and support the arts. Its core functions are to support the creation and dissemination of the work of Irish artists in all disciplines, and to promote public access to, and participation in, the contemporary arts. The Council expresses its support to the artist in a variety of ways, through grant aid to organisations, events and production companies, and more explicitly through award schemes where the primary relationship is between the artist and the Council. Their principal strategies are improving the professional formation, practice and career development of artists, directing funding towards excellence and innovation in the promotion of the arts and supporting artists working through Irish in indigenous arts to achieve their full potential and increase audiences.

Arts Council of Ireland Artist-in-the-Community Scheme

Subjects: The arts
Purpose: To enable artists and community groups to work together on projects
Eligibility: Open to artists of Irish birth or residence and community groups. The artist must have evidence of having

produced a body of work of recognised quality and significance, or in the case of individuals with less experience, demonstrable potential. They need to be able to show evidence of artistic developmental needs, evidence of financial need, including availability of other funding and a likelihood that an award will reach the desired effect. Applicants must be practising artists or arts workers but need not necessarily earn income from their arts practice. They must identify themselves and be recognised by their peers as practising artists

Level of Study: Professional development

Type: Grant

Length of Study: Varies

Country of Study: Ireland

Application Procedure: Applicants must contact CAFE for application information. Applications will be considered not eligible and returned if the eligibility criteria is not met, if all the support material specified is not included, if funding is requested for activities that have already occurred or will be completed before the closing date and also if the application or supporting documentation is late

Closing Date: Please contact CAFE or The Arts Council

Contributor: CAFE

For further information contact:

CAFE 10-11 Earl Street South, Ireland

Email: cafe@connect.ie

Arts Council of Ireland Frameworks Animation Scheme

Subjects: Animation

Purpose: To add to the range and scope of Irish animation and encourage new and established animation, which makes use of the medium and is primarily aimed at an adult audience

Eligibility: The artist must be an Irish national or permanent resident and have evidence of having produced a body of work of recognised quality and significance, or in the case of individuals with less experience, demonstrable potential. They need to be able to show evidence of artistic developmental needs, evidence of financial need, including availability of other funding and a likelihood that an award will reach the desired effect. Applicants must be practising artists or arts workers but need not necessarily earn income from their arts practice. They must identify themselves and be recognised by their peers as practising artists

Value: Approx. €25,000–32,000 to fund up to six animated shorts

Country of Study: Ireland

Application Procedure: Applicants must send completed applications to Bord Scannán na hÉireann. Applications will be considered not eligible and returned if the eligibility criteria is not met, if all the support material specified is not included, if funding is requested for activities that have already occurred or will be completed before the closing date and also if the application or supporting documentation is late

Closing Date: Please contact Bord Scannán na hÉireann or The Arts Council

Contributor: The scheme is co-funded by RTÉ, Bord Scannán na hÉireann and The Arts Council

Additional Information: Information can be obtained from both the Arts Council and the Bord Scannán na hÉireann

For further information contact:

Bord Scannán na hÉireann/The Irish Film Board, Rockfort House, St Augustine Street, Ireland

Tel: (353) 9 156 1398

Fax: (353) 9 156 1405

Email: info@filmboard.ie

Arts Council of Wales

Museum Place, Wales, CF10 3NX, Cardiff, United Kingdom

Tel: (44) 29 2037 6500

Fax: (44) 29 2022 1447

Email: info@artswales.org.uk

Website: www.artswales.org.uk

Contact: Angela Blackburn

The Arts Council of Wales is the national organization with specific responsibility for the funding and development of the arts in Wales. Most of its funds come from the National Assembly for Wales, but it also distributes National Lottery funds to the arts in Wales.

Artists at Work

Purpose: To support businesses and artists to benefit from sharing their workplaces

Eligibility: Available for businesses that are interested in exploring the potential of creative collaboration and hosting an artist in residence and for artists keen to develop their practice through working in industry

Type: Grant

Value: Up to £6,000

For further information contact:

11-12 Mount Stuart Square, United Kingdom

Tel: (44) 29 2048 9543
Email: info@cywaithcymru.org
Contact: The AiR Administrator

Arts Council of Wales Artform Development Scheme

Subjects: Fine art
Purpose: To support new talent and ideas in a range of activities eg. platforms of work in process or exploratory productions in mixed art-forms
Type: Grant
Value: UK £2,000–10,000
Country of Study: Wales
Application Procedure: Applicants must submit a completed application. These can be submitted at any time but early notice is needed for major projects. Applicants must contact Performing Arts at the Artform Development Division in Cardiff
Closing Date: March

For further information contact:

Email: acw@wilsonarts.com

Arts Council of Wales Awards for Career Development of Individual Visual Artists and Craftspeople

Subjects: Visual arts and crafts
Purpose: Financial assistance for travel, research, the acquisition of new skills and collaboration which extends professional horizons
Eligibility: For individual professional visual artists and craftspeople at all stages of career development and whose work shows originality and excellence. For those who live and work in Wales for at least nine months of the year
Level of Study: Professional development
Type: Grant
Country of Study: Wales
Application Procedure: Applicants must contact Visual Arts and Craft, Artform Development Division, Cardiff office
Closing Date: Please contact the Arts Council
Additional Information: Smaller awards of up to £500 are also available to emerging visual artists to help establish a studio, research contacts and potential markets

For further information contact:

Email: acw@wilsonarts.com

Arts Council of Wales Awards for Individual Visual Artists and Craftspeople

Subjects: Art and crafts
Purpose: To assist with research and developing skills to undertake a specific project or in developing new work in particular by releasing them from their normal commitments
Eligibility: For visual artists and individual craftspeople permanently living in Wales
Level of Study: Professional development
Type: Bursary
Frequency: Twice a year
Country of Study: Wales
Application Procedure: Applicants must contact Visual Arts and Craft, Artform Development Division, Cardiff office
Closing Date: Please contact the Arts Council

For further information contact:

Email: acw@wilsonarts.com

Arts Council of Wales Barclays Stage Partners

Subjects: Drama
Purpose: To enable the production and tour of a new theatrical production in Wales
Type: Grant
Value: Up to £53,000
Country of Study: Wales
Application Procedure: Applicants must contact the Arts Council for guidelines
Closing Date: Please contact the Arts Council
Funding: Commercial

For further information contact:

Email: acw@wilsonarts.com

Arts Council of Wales Community Touring Night Out

Subjects: Performing arts
Purpose: To support community-based organizations throughout Wales with access to suitable premises, who wish to promote occasional professional performing arts events for their locality

Eligibility: Eligibility for promoters of events is restricted to community organizations within Wales. Schools and colleges may participate if offering a service to the wider community that is beyond this normal educational role. Eligibility for performers governed by this ability to provide a professional service at an affordable price regardless of nationality and location

Type: Fees to performers

Value: Variable

Country of Study: Wales

No. of awards offered: 206

Application Procedure: Applications may be submitted at any time to the Community Touring unit in Cardiff and must come from the local promoters of the event. The single-page application form is obtainable from the unit by post or may be found on the website at www.nightout.org.uk

Closing Date: 6 weeks before the proposed event

Funding: Government

Contributor: 51% from National Assembly of Wales, 49% box office supported by local authority guarantees

No. of awards given last year: 392

No. of applicants last year: 206

Additional Information: Community-based organizations dedicated to the arts who wish to plan more than five events in a year or more than 6 months ahead should seek advice from their local ACW office or the Community Touring Manager. This scheme assists community organizations by making professional performances available at a fraction of their real price. It covers all aspects of the performing arts

For further information contact:

Community Touring Manager, Community Touring Unit, Arts Council of Wales, Museum Place, United Kingdom

Email: acw@wilsonarts.com

Arts Council of Wales Music Projects Grants

Subjects: Music production

Purpose: To help with either CD production of works by Welsh composers or books and journals concerned with Welsh music

Type: Grant

Country of Study: Any country

Application Procedure: Applications are invited from publishers and recording companies and should be sent to Performing Arts, Artform Development Division, Cardiff office

Closing Date: Please contact the Arts Council

For further information contact:

Email: acw@wilsonarts.com

Arts Council of Wales Performing Arts Projects

Subjects: Performing arts

Purpose: To enable production by professional artists based in Wales working with a presenting organisation

Eligibility: Partnerships are a particular feature of this scheme and the involvement of a venue or presenter is essential. Applications may come from groups of artists, arts organisations or presenters

Type: Grant

Value: Grants range from £5,000–40,000. Quality, innovation and potential to enrich programming for the public will be priorities

Country of Study: Any country

Application Procedure: Applications should be sent to Performing Arts, Artform Development Division in Cardiff

Closing Date: 1 February

Additional Information: Venue commissions of artists may be one form of application

For further information contact:

Email: acw@wilsonarts.com

Arts Council of Wales Pilot Training Grants Scheme

Subjects: Information technology, finance, marketing, management and vocational skills

Purpose: Provides grants to arts organisations and owner managers in Wales for members of staff to attend or deliver training in IT, finance, marketing, management and other vocational skills

Level of Study: Professional development

Type: Grant

Value: The maximum grant awarded will be UK £5,000 and the scheme will provide a maximum of 45% of the total cost of attending or delivering training

Country of Study: Wales

Application Procedure: Applications must be submitted to Access Development Division, Cardiff Office

Closing Date: Please contact the Arts Council

Additional Information: Training supported by this scheme must be completed and a monitoring report form submitted to ACW

For further information contact:

Email: acw@wilsonarts.com

Community Dance Wales Grants

Subjects: Arts

Purpose: To promote professional interest in community dance in Wales
Level of Study: Professional development
Type: Grant
Value: £25,342
Frequency: Annual
Country of Study: United Kingdom
Funding: Government

For further information contact:

Tel:	(44) 1495 224425
Fax:	(44) 1495 226457
Email:	roonem@caerphilly.gov.uk
Contact:	Ms Margaret Rooney

Cultural Enterprise Service Grant

Subjects: Arts
Purpose: To provide financial assistance in the purchase of equipment, software and consultancy
Level of Study: Professional development
Type: Grant
Value: UK £10,000
Frequency: Annual
Country of Study: United Kingdom
Application Procedure: See the website
Funding: Government
Contributor: The Arts Council of Wales

For further information contact:

Tel:	(44) 29 2034 3205
Fax:	(44) 29 2034 5436
Email:	stephan@cultural-enterprise.com
Contact:	Mr Stephan Caddict

Good Ideas-Artist Led Projects

Purpose: To fulfil the needs of artists by providing funding for projects that develop their artistic practice and to help alleviate the associated administration
Eligibility: Open to artists who have project initiatives that involve community collaboration and that demonstrate innovative thinking and artistic practice
Type: Grant
Value: £6,000

For further information contact:

Email:	info@cywaithcymru.org
Contact:	The AiR Administrator

International Opportunities Funding

Subjects: Arts
Purpose: To encourage professional arts practitioners and presenters
Type: Funding support
Closing Date: Last Friday of every month

For further information contact:

Wales Arts International, 28 Park place, United Kingdom

Tel:	(44) 29 20393037
Fax:	(44) 29 20398779
Email:	Nikki.Morgan@wai.org.uk, info@wai.org.uk
Contact:	Nicola Morgan

Vital Knowledge-Artists' Mentoring Scheme

Subjects: Residency projects
Purpose: To encourage new applicants to gain experience and mentoring in all aspects of residency work
Eligibility: Open to candidates who would benefit from working alongside an artist in residence on one of the Cywaith Cymru
Type: Grant
Value: £500

For further information contact:

Tel:	(44) 29 2048 9543
Email:	info@cywaithcymru.org
Contact:	The AiR Administrator

Wales One World Film Festival Grant

Subjects: Arts
Purpose: To present audiences with the best in world cinema through the Festival
Level of Study: Professional development
Type: Grant
Value: UK £24,936
Length of Study: 2 years
Frequency: Annual
Country of Study: United Kingdom
Application Procedure: See the website
Funding: Government
Contributor: The Media Agency for Wales and the Arts Council of Wales

For further information contact:

Tel:	(44) 1239 615066
Fax:	(44) 1239 615066

Email: sa3657@eclipse.co.uk
Contact: Mr David Gillam

Welsh Independent Dance Grant

Subjects: Arts
Purpose: To develop a successful dance sector in Wales
Level of Study: Professional development
Type: Grant
Length of Study: UK £71,296
Frequency: Annual
Country of Study: United Kingdom
Application Procedure: See the website
Funding: Government
Contributor: The Arts Council of Wales

For further information contact:

Tel: (44) 29 2038 7314
Fax: (44) 29 2038 7314
Email: welshindance@btconnect.com
Contact: Ms Kate Long

Arts International

251 Park Avenue South, 5th Floor, New York, NY 10010-7302, United States of America

Tel: (1) 212 674 9744
Fax: (1) 212 674 9092
Email: info@artsinternational.org
Website: www.artsinternational.org
Contact: Mr Adam Bernstein, Director, Advised Funds & Regranting Programs

Arts International is an independent, non-profit, contemporary arts organization dedicated to global, cultural interchange. It carries out its work through developing global networks and partnerships, information services and grantmaking opportunities.

Croatian Arts and Cultural Exchange Croatia

Subjects: Croatian Art
Purpose: FACE Croatia is designed to encourage tax deductible (for United States tax payers) donor advised contributions from private and public sources including individuals, private foundations, corporations and public sector donors. FACE

Croatia maintains an active database of information on Croatian artists, arts and culture
Eligibility: FACE Croatia has two funding categories: Croatian Arts and Culture Projects, and United States/Croatian Cultural Exchange. 1. Croatian Arts and Culture Projects Grants. Any Croatian organization that qualifies as a charity under Croatian law is eligible (museums, galleries, theaters, etc.). 2. Croatian based non-governmental organizations (NGO's) engaged in arts and culture activity in Croatia are eligible to apply. 3. The program is open to any arts discipline and/or cultural activity. 4. Individual artists may not make direct application to the program and must be sponsored by an eligible organization
Level of Study: Unrestricted
Type: Arts discipline or cultural activity
Value: Variable
Length of Study: Variable
Study Establishment: As approved. Typically museum, art gallery, theatre
Country of Study: United States of America and Croatia
Application Procedure: Proposals must include a narrative and budget, an organizational narrative and budget, evidence of non-profit status, and three letters of recommendation from professionals in the field
Closing Date: There is no deadline. Project proposals may be submitted at any time and will be reviewed by an advisory committee on a quarterly basis
Funding: Private
Contributor: Heathcote Art Foundation

For further information contact:

CEC ArtsLink, 291 Broadway, 14th Floor, New York, NY 10007, United States of America

Email: al@cecartslink.org

Arts NSW

Level 5, 323 Castlereagh Street, Sydney, NSW 2000, Australia

Tel: (61) 1800 358 594
Fax: (61) 292 284 722
Email: arts.funding@arts.nsw.gov.au
Website: www.arts.nsw.gov.au

Arts NSW is part of the NSW Department of the Arts, Sport and Recreation. Arts NSW advises the Minister for the Arts on all aspects of the arts and cultural activity. Arts NSW works closely with the state's 8 major cultural institutions, providing policy advice to Government on their operations. The institutions manage significant cultural heritage collections and provide services and programmes throughout the state and beyond.

Asialink Residency Program

Subjects: Arts management, literature, performing arts, and visual arts/crafts
Purpose: To promote cultural understanding, information exchange and artistic endeavour between Australia and Asian countries
Eligibility: Open to Australian citizens or permanent residents who have at least 3 years professional experience in their field
Level of Study: Unrestricted
Type: Grant
Value: A travel grant of $6,000–12,000 is provided to each resident to assist with residency-related expenses including air-fares, accommodation, language lessons, living expenses, materials and production costs. The amount awarded is reflective of the residency period
Length of Study: 3 months
Application Procedure: Check website for further details
Closing Date: 1 March
Contributor: Arts NSW, in association with the Asialink Centre

For further information contact:

Arts Program, The Asialink Centre, The University of Melbourne, Sidney Myer Asia Centre, Australia

Tel: (61) 3 8344 4800
Fax: (61) 3 9347 1768
Email: arts@asialink.unimelb.edu.au

David Paul Landa Memorial Scholarships for Pianists

Subjects: Music
Eligibility: Open to the Australian citizens currently residing in New South Wales or holding residence visas who have been residents of New South Wales for two consecutive years
Level of Study: Unrestricted
Type: Scholarship
Value: A$25,000
Frequency: Every 2 years
Application Procedure: Applicants must forward the completed application form (and one copy of it), two copies of all written supporting material, single copies of other supporting material, the completed EFT authorization form and, if applicable, two copies of the completed RCTI to Program Support
Additional Information: Previous recipients of Arts NSW's fellowships and scholarships are ineligible to apply for the same award twice

For further information contact:

David Paul Landa Memorial Scholarship for Pianists, Musica Viva Australia, PO Box 1687, Australia

Tel: (61) 2 8394 6666
Fax: (61) 2 9698 3878
Email: musicaviva@mva.org.au
Contact: The Administrator

New South Wales Indigenous History Fellowship

Subjects: History
Purpose: To assist a person living in New South Wales to research and produce a work on a subject of historical interest relating to New South Wales from an Indigenous point of view
Eligibility: Open to the candidates who may be independent historians, or historians working in conjunction with indigenous communities
Level of Study: Unrestricted
Type: Fellowship
Value: A$20,000
Length of Study: 2 years
Frequency: Every 2 years
Application Procedure: Applicants must submit form with details of the proposal and their qualifications and experience details. Check website for further details
Closing Date: Please check the website
Additional Information: The fellowship will be administered by the History Council of New South Wales

For further information contact:

History Council of New South Wales Inc., PO Box R1737, Royal Exchange, Australia

Tel: (61) 2 9252 8715
Fax: (61) 2 9252 8716
Email: office@historycouncilnsw.org.au
Contact: The Executive Officer

New South Wales Premier's History Awards

Subjects: History
Purpose: To establish values and standards in historical research and publication and promote the excellence in the interpretation of history
Eligibility: Open only to the citizens of Australia
Level of Study: Unrestricted
Type: Award
Value: A$15,000 each for 5 categories
Frequency: Annual
Application Procedure: Check website for further details

Closing Date: Please check the website

Additional Information: Nominees may enter a published book or ebook in only one of the following categories: Australian History Prize; General History Prize; New South Wales Community and Regional History Prize; Young People's History Prize. Nominees may enter a non-print media work such as a film, television, or radio program, a DVD or website in one or both of the following categories (if appropriate): Young People's History Prize; Multimedia History Prize. (Note: If entering into both categories, only one nomination form needs to be completed.) All works must have been first published, produced, performed or made publicly available between 1 April and 31 March

For further information contact:

Literature and History Program Staff, Australia

Tel: (61) 2 9228 5533/1800 358 594
Email: arts.funding@communities.nsw.gov.au

Philip Parsons Young Playwright's Award

Subjects: Theatre and language
Purpose: To honor a playwright living in NSW for an original and compelling theatrical voice
Eligibility: Writers must be under 35 years of age, based in NSW, and have had a play produced between 1 June and 31 May either in Australia or abroad. Shortlisted writers will be asked to submit a treatment of up to five pages for a proposed new work
Level of Study: Unrestricted
Type: Scholarship
Value: A$12,500
Frequency: Annual
Application Procedure: Check website for further details
Closing Date: October
Additional Information: Please check website for more details

For further information contact:

Tel: (61) 2 8399 2190
Email: tahni@belvoir.com.au
Contact: Downstairs Theatre Director

Western Sydney Artists

Subjects: Music and literature
Purpose: To support the creative development of new work or professional development by Western Sydney artists
Eligibility: Open to professional artists working in music or literature who are the residents of, or whose practice is located primarily in, Western Sydney
Level of Study: Unrestricted
Type: Fellowship

Value: A$5,000–25,000
Country of Study: Any country
Application Procedure: Check website for further details
Closing Date: 14 September

For further information contact:

Email: mail@create.nsw.gov.au

Artwork Archive

Aaron Siskind Foundation - Individual Photographer's Fellowship

Subjects: Work must be based on the idea of still-based photography, but can include digital imagery, installations, documentary projects, and photo-generated print media
Purpose: The Aaron Siskind Foundation is offering a limited number of Individual Photographer's Fellowship grants of up to US$15,000 each, for artists working in photography and photo-based art
Eligibility: Work must be based on the idea of still-based photography, but can include digital imagery, installations, documentary projects, and photo-generated print media. Doctoral candidates considered on a case-by-case basis. 1. Applicants must be at least 21 years of age. Students enrolled in a college degree program are not eligible to apply. 2. Previous IPF recipients are not currently being considered for new awards
Level of Study: Postgraduate
Type: Fellowship
Value: Up to US$10,000
Frequency: Annual
Country of Study: Any country
Closing Date: 31 May
Funding: Private

For further information contact:

Aaron Siskind Foundation, c/o School of Visual Arts, MFA Photo Dept. 209 East 23rd Street, New York, NY 10010, United States of America

Email: grant@aaronsiskind.org

Ashinaga

Ashinaga Scholarships

Purpose: Ashinaga is sponsoring scholarships to Bereaved Undergraduate Africans to Study in Japan, United States of America and the United Kingdom, Applicants are able to participate in the two Ashinaga preparatory programs before attending university

Eligibility: 1. Applicants should have a citizenship in any one of the countries listed below and pursued high school are eligible. 2. Applicants who have lost one or both parents (can submit an official document proving). 3. Applicants are able to participate in the two Ashinaga preparatory programs before attending university. 4. Students are willing to contribute to society in Africa after graduating from university and have no dependents who could interfere with academic progress and be in good condition of health and capable of studying abroad

Level of Study: Graduate

Type: Scholarship

Frequency: Annual

Country of Study: Any country

Application Procedure: Documents which have to be submitted for the scholarship are 1. A recent Passport Size photo. 2. Essays. 3. Birth Certificate. 4. Death Certificate of one or both the parents. 5. Academic school transcripts from last two years. GCES/Baccalaureate if you have already received it. Applicants who are registering application in online can visit ashinaga.typeform.com/to/cSwSkj. Applicants who are submitting documents by post can send application form along with documents to following address

Closing Date: August

Funding: Private

Additional Information: Citizens of the following Sub-Saharan African countries: a). English speaking: Uganda, Rwanda, Kenya, Ethiopia, Tanzania, Ghana, Namibia, Zimbabwe, Zambia, Malawi, Sudan, Botswana, South Africa, Lesotho, Swaziland, Mauritius, Somalia, Nigeria, The Gambia, Cape Verde, Mozambique, Guinea Bissau, Angola. b). French-speaking: Côte d'Ivoire, Senegal, Benin, Burundi, Gabon, Mali, Burkina Faso, Mauritania, DR Congo, Republic of Congo, Djibouti, Cameroon, Togo, Madagascar, Comoros

For further information contact:

1-6-8 Hirakawa-cho, Chiyoda-Ku, Tokyo 102-8639, Japan

Email: admissions.en@ashinaga.org

Ashley Family Foundation

6 Trull Farm Buildings, Trull, GL8 8SQ, Tetbury, United Kingdom

Tel: (44) 3030 401 005
Email: info@ashleyfamilyfoundation.org.uk
Website: www.ashleyfamilyfoundation.org.uk
Contact: The Administrator

The Ashley Family Foundation (formerly The Laura Ashley Foundation) is a United Kingdom registered charity, founded by Sir Bernard Ashley and his wife Laura Ashley following the success of the Laura Ashley brand.

Ashley Family Foundation MA Photography Scholarship

Subjects: MA photography

Eligibility: To be eligible for the Ashley Family Foundation MA Photography Scholarship students must be: ordinarily resident in the United Kingdom; and considered Home status. Accepted on the full-time MA Photography course at London College of Communication, commencing January. A graduate, having already gained a first or 2:1 in a Bachelor's degree from a Higher Education institution, or an HE accredited Further Education institution able to demonstrate substantial equivalent and applicable experience

Type: Scholarship

Value: £12,000 and will cover tuition fees and a contribution towards maintenance

Frequency: Annual

Study Establishment: London College of Communication

Country of Study: United Kingdom

Closing Date: 7 November

For further information contact:

Scholarships & Bursaries, SFS, University of the Arts London, 272 High Holborn, London, United Kingdom

Email: funding@arts.ac.uk

Asian Cultural Council (ACC)

6 West 48th Street, 12th floor, New York, NY 10036-1802, United States of America

Tel: (1) 212 843 0403
Fax: (1) 212 843 0343
Email: acc@accny.org
Website: www.asianculturalcouncil.org
Contact: Miho Walsh, Executive Director

The Asian Cultural Council (ACC) is a foundation that supports cultural exchange in the visual and performing arts between the United States and the countries of Asia. The emphasis of the ACC's programme is on providing individual fellowships to artists, scholars and specialists from Asia undertaking research, study and creative work in the United States. Grants are also made to United States citizens pursuing similar work in Asia.

Asian Cultural Council Humanities Fellowship Program

Subjects: Archaeology, conservation, museology and the theory, history and criticism of architecture, art, dance, film, music, photography and theater

Purpose: To assist American scholars, graduate students and specialists in the humanities to undertake research, training and study in Asia

Eligibility: Open to Asian individuals who are seeking grant assistance to conduct research, study, receive specialized training, undertake observation tours or pursue creative activity in the United States in the visual and performing arts. Americans seeking aid to undertake activities in Asia are also eligible to apply

Level of Study: Graduate, Postdoctorate, Postgraduate, Predoctorate, Professional development, Research, Unrestricted

Type: Fellowship or Grant

Value: Varies

Length of Study: 1–9 months

Frequency: Annual

Country of Study: United States of America or other countries if appropriate

No. of awards offered: 49 (Humanities Program only)

Application Procedure: Applicants should send a brief description of the activity for which assistance is being sought to the Council

Closing Date: 16 November

Funding: Government, Private, Foundation, Individuals

Contributor: The JDR 3rd Fund and the Andrew W. Mellon Foundation

No. of awards given last year: 11 (Humanities Program only)

No. of applicants last year: 49 (Humanities Program only)

Additional Information: The programme also supports American and Asian scholars participating in international conferences, exhibitions, visiting professorships and similar projects. Please see the website for further details www.asianculturalcouncil.org.hk/en/app/information_and_deadline

For further information contact:

Email: acc@accny.org

Asian Institute of Technology

58 Moo 9 - Paholyothin Highway, Nueng, Pathum Thani 12120, Thailand

Contact: Asian Institute of Technology

The Asian Institute of Technology promotes technological change and sustainable development in the Asian-Pacific region through higher education, research and outreach.

Kings Scholarship at Asian Institute of Technology

Subjects: Scholarship is awarded to study the subjects offered by the university

Purpose: The aim of the scholarship is to provide financial help to Thai and other Asian countries students

Eligibility: Thai national or other nationalities in the Asian region. Graduated in related fields from an accredited institution. Have a high proficiency in English as required by AIT. Applicants in Thailand can also take the AIT English Test administered by the AIT Language Center. Have a good education record in a 4-year undergraduate program: (a) From universities with QS Ranking within 1,000 or better with cGPA 3.0 and above (or equivalent) or (b) From other universities with cGPA 3.5 and above (or equivalent)

Value: Each scholarship award covers tuition fees, accommodation, and a bursary for living expenses in AIT's residential campus, for the entire period of the 22-month master degree program

Study Establishment: Scholarship is awarded to study the subjects offered by the university

Country of Study: Thailand

Application Procedure: The mode of applying is online

Closing Date: 31 March

Additional Information: For more details please browse the website scholarship-positions.com/kings-scholarship/2017/11/23/

For further information contact:

Email: rtg@ait.ac.th

Associated General Contractors of America (AGC)

2300 Wilson Boulevard, Suite 300, Arlington, VA 22201, United States of America

Tel: (1) 548 3118, 800 242 1767
Fax: (1) 548 3119
Email: info@agc.org
Website: www.agc.org

The Associated General Contractors of America (AGC), the voice of the construction industry, is an organization of qualified construction contractors and industry-related companies dedicated to skill, integrity and responsibility. Operating in partnership with its chapters, the association provides a full range of services satisfying the needs and concerns of its members, thereby improving the quality of construction and protecting the public interest.

Associated General Contractors of America The Saul Horowitz, Jr. Memorial Graduate Award

Subjects: Construction or civil engineering
Purpose: To provide financial assistance to students who wish to pursue higher studies
Eligibility: Open to applicants enroled or planning to enroll, in a Master's or Doctoral level construction or civil engineering programme as a full-time student
Level of Study: Doctorate, Postgraduate
Type: Scholarship
Value: US$7,500. Paid in 2 installments of US$3,750
Length of Study: Up to 5 years
Frequency: Annual
Country of Study: United States of America
Application Procedure: Applications will only be accepted online. Apply online at scholarship.agc.org. Applicants must send an email to foundation@agc.org
Closing Date: 3 November

For further information contact:

Email: info@agc.org

Association for Canadian Studies in the United States

1317 F Street NW Suite 920, Washington, DC 20004-1151, United States of America

Tel: (1) 202 393 2580
Fax: (1) 202 393 2582
Email: info@acsus.org
Website: www.acsus.org
Contact: Publication Award Committee

Distinguished Dissertation Award

Subjects: Canadian Studies; Comparative studies including Canada
Purpose: To recognize the best dissertation successfully defended in the two years prior to the Biennial conference that deals substantially or wholly with some aspect of Canada or Canadian Studies

Eligibility: Doctoral dissertations written at Universities in the United States within the two years before the Biennial conference at which the award will be made
Level of Study: Doctorate
Type: Cash prize
Value: US$500 and expenses to attend the Biennial conference
Frequency: Every 2 years
Country of Study: United States of America
No. of awards offered: 2
Application Procedure: The nomination must be accompanied by two letters of support, one from the student's dissertation advisor and one from a second referee. The advisor and referee need not be members of ACSUS. Supporting Materials. Each nomination should be accompanied by a copy of the dissertation, a dissertation abstract not to exceed 500 words (typed, double-spaced), and a one-page resume of the nominee. The successful nominee's dissertation should represent original work that makes a significant contribution to the nominee's discipline and to the study of Canada. The dissertation must contain at least 50% content on Canada; the topic may, however, be comparative in nature. The dissertation will be judged on substantive and methodological quality, originality of thought, and clarity
Closing Date: 1 August
Funding: Individuals
Contributor: Membership dues and royalties coming to the Association for Canadian Studies in the United States
No. of awards given last year: 1
No. of applicants last year: 2

For further information contact:

ACSUS Executive Director, 520 Park Hall, North Campus, University at Buffalo-SUNY, United States of America

Tel: (1) 716 645 8440
Fax: (1) 716 645 2166
Email: info@acsus.org
Contact: Dr Munroe Eagles

Donner Medal in Canadian Studies

Purpose: The Donner Medal in Canadian Studies is presented biennially by The Association for Canadian Studies in the United States (ACSUS) for distinguished achievement, scholarship and program innovation in the area of Canadian Studies in the United States
Eligibility: The recipient is selected by a committee of members of the Association after nominations have been publicly solicited. Nominees can include a person in any field who has made a significant contribution to Canadian studies in the United States during a reasonable period of residence in the United States, even if no longer a resident. Current officers of

ACSUS are ineligible for consideration. The primary criterion for selection is contribution to Canadian studies in the United States. The recipient shall have been active in and made contributions in at least one of the following categories: teaching, scholarship, administration, public affairs

Level of Study: Doctorate
Type: Honorific
Value: N/A
Frequency: Every 2 years
Country of Study: United States of America
No. of awards offered: 1
Closing Date: 1 August
Funding: Government, Foundation, Individuals
Contributor: Individual membership dues and royalties from publications; some government grants; Donner Foundation
No. of awards given last year: 1
No. of applicants last year: 1

For further information contact:

Tel:	(1) 716 645 8440
Fax:	(1) 716 645 2166
Email:	info@acsus.org
Contact:	Dr Munroe Eagles

Association for Spina Bifida and Hydrocephalus (ASBAH)

ASBAH House, 42 Park Road, Peterborough, PE1 2UQ, Cambridgeshire, United Kingdom

Tel:	(44) 1733 555 988, 0845 450 7755
Fax:	(44) 1733 421 395
Email:	info@asbah.org
Website:	www.mencap.org.uk
Contact:	Rylance

The Association for Spina Bifida and Hydrocephalus (ASBAH) is a voluntary organization that works for people with spina bifida and hydrocephalus. The charity lobbies for improvements in legislation and provides advisory and support services to clients and their families or carers, in addition to supplying information to professionals and sponsoring medical, social and educational research.

Association for Spina Bifida and Hydrocephalus Research Grant

Subjects: Medical sciences, natural sciences, education and teacher training, recreation, welfare and protective services

Purpose: To support research in an area directly related to spina bifida and/or hydrocephalus, and to explore ways of improving the quality of life for people with these conditions through medical, scientific, educational and social research
Eligibility: Applicants must be resident in the United Kingdom
Level of Study: Postgraduate
Value: Varies
Length of Study: Varies
Frequency: Dependent on funds available
Study Establishment: Varies
Country of Study: United Kingdom
No. of awards offered: 1
Application Procedure: Applicants must make an initial enquiry to the Chief Executive. If the proposed research is considered to be interesting, the applicant will be asked to complete an application form. Applications must be submitted on time to the committees, which meet in February and September to October
Closing Date: 1 August
Funding: Private, Trusts, Individuals
Contributor: Charitable donations
No. of awards given last year: 1
No. of applicants last year: 1
Additional Information: Award subjects: biology and life sciences; economics; medicine and surgery; social sciences; teacher training and education; theology and religious studies

For further information contact:

Email:	info@asbah.org

Association of American Geographers (AAG)

1710 16th Street NW, Washington, DC 20009-3198, United States of America

Tel:	(1) 202 234 1450
Fax:	(1) 202 234 2744
Email:	cmannozzi@aag.org, gaia@aag.org
Website:	www.aag.org
Contact:	Dr Patricia Solis, Director of Outreach and Strategic Initiatives

The Association of American Geographers (AAG) is a non-profit organization founded in 1904 to advance professional studies in geography and to encourage the application of geographic research in business, education and government. The AAG was amalgamated with the American Society of Professional Geographers (ASPG).

Association of American Geographers NSF International Geographical Union Conference Travel Grants

Subjects: Geography

Purpose: To provide Travel Grants to the IGU conference

Eligibility: All scientists employed by United States agencies, firms and academic institutions may apply for support. All grantees must: be citizens or hold permanent residency in the United States of America, be registered for the main international congress or main regional conference even if their presentations are scheduled for a symposium or study group, and travel via a United States carrier in accordance with United States government regulations

Level of Study: Professional development

Type: Grant

Value: US$1,250 each to junior scholars, including graduate students and US$1,000 each to senior scholars

Frequency: Annual

Country of Study: As applicable

Application Procedure: Applications must be submitted digitally using the online application form provided in website

Closing Date: 31 May (applications received after this may be accepted as alternates)

Contributor: National Science Foundation

Additional Information: Please see the website for further details www.aag.org/cs/grantsawards/igutravel

For further information contact:

Email: psolis@aag.org

Visiting Geographical Scientist Program

Subjects: Geography

Purpose: To stimulate interest in geography

Eligibility: To qualify for the program, at least one-half of the institutions hosting a visiting scientist during the academic year must have active chapters of Gamma Theta Upsilon (an active chapter is one that has reported initiates in the past 2 years)

Level of Study: Professional development

Type: Grant

Value: US$100 per institutional visit to each visiting scientist and will reimburse the visitor up to US$600 for travel costs to and from the area of the institutions visited

Frequency: Annual

Study Establishment: Institution with an active chapter of Gamma Theta Upsilon

Country of Study: United States of America

Application Procedure: Applicants must write to Oscar Laron, VGSP Coordinator, at the main organization address at olarson@aag.org

Closing Date: Please check website

Contributor: Gamma Theta Upsilon (GTU), the International Geographical Honor Society

Additional Information: The VGSP requires one scientist to visit two or more institutions over a one to three-day period. Please see the website for further details www.aag.org/cs/vgsp

Association of Anaesthetists of Great Britain and Ireland

9 Bedford Square, WC1B 3RA, London, United Kingdom

Tel: (44) 20 7631 1650
Fax: (44) 20 7631 4352
Email: 100567.3364@compuserve.com
Website: www.ncl.ac.uk/2nanaes/aagbi.html
Contact: Honorary Secretary

The Association of Anaesthetists of Great Britain and Ireland encourages its members to participate in research to increase knowledge, to improve standards of anaesthesia and to enhance the standing of the speciality. It also aims to enable members to travel to centres of excellence throughout the world to increase their expertise in clinical work, teaching or research so that there may be benefit to members, trainees and patients at home.

Baxter Travelling Fellowships, Research Grants, Travel Grants

Subjects: Anaesthesia or related fields - research or education

Eligibility: Open to members in any category of the Association

Level of Study: Unrestricted

Value: Up to £2,500 (Baxter Travelling Fellowship), up to £5,000 (Research Grants), up to £500 (Travel Grants)

Length of Study: Unspecified duration

Country of Study: Other

Application Procedure: Application form is required

Additional Information: There are also special Travel Grants to Third World Countries. Travel Grants are not awarded for attendance at a meeting of a learned society, but may be considered for extensions of such a journey. They may be given for study or for assistance in undertaking an approved teaching tour. Recipients of Travel Fellowships are expected to prepare a report

For further information contact:

Email: Education_Grants@baxter.com

Association of Clinical Pathologists

189 Dyke Road, East Sussex BN3 1TL, Hove, United Kingdom

Tel:	(44) 1273 775 700
Fax:	(44) 1273 773 303
Email:	info@pathologists.org.uk
Website:	www.pathologists.org.uk
Contact:	Administrative Assistant

The Association of Clinical Pathologists promotes the practice of clinical pathology by running postgraduate education courses and national scientific meetings and has a membership of 2,000 worldwide.

Student Research Fund

Subjects: Research projects within laboratory medicine (undergraduate) or to support students undertaking BSc/BMED Sci
Purpose: To encourage undergraduates to undertake some research within laboratory medicine, to raise the profile of laboratory medicine within the minds of undergraduates and to aid in recruitment of young graduates
Level of Study: Graduate
Type: Scholarship
Value: Up to £150 per week for a maximum of six weeks (Funding of a small project), £5,000 maximum (Financial sponsorship to help support living expenses during their extra undergraduate year), up to £1,000 (Funding for the cost of consumables). See the website for details: www.pathol ogists.org.uk/awards/studentresearchfund
Frequency: Annual
Country of Study: Any country
No. of awards offered: 5
Application Procedure: Applicants should complete the relevant application form, including a brief statement of not more than 400 words outlining their interest in laboratory medicine, and include a full curriculum vitae. Applications should include details of the work to be undertaken as part of the project or during the BSc and be supported in writing by the project supervisor, or by the Head of Department in which the student will be placed
Closing Date: 12 April
Contributor: Association of Clinical Pathologists
No. of awards given last year: 3
No. of applicants last year: 5
Additional Information: Please return completed form by post to ACP Postgraduate Education Secretary, and also by email to rachel@pathologists.org.uk

For further information contact:

Email: rachel@pathologists.org.uk

Association of Flight Attendants

Association of Flight Attendants Annual Scholarship

Purpose: This award is for United States high school seniors who are dependents of an Association of Flight Attendants member. Students must rank in the top 15% of their class, and must have or expect to have excellent SAT and ACT scores
Eligibility: 1. Must be a graduating high school senior at time of application. 2. Must be a United States citizen. 3. Must be ranked in the top 15% of his/her high school class. 4. Must be the dependent of an Association of Flight Attendants member. 5. Must have, or expect to have, excellent SAT or ACT scores. 6. This award is for United States students
Level of Study: Graduate
Type: Scholarship
Value: US$5,000
Frequency: Annual
Country of Study: United States of America
Application Procedure: Apply online: cdn.afacwa.org/docs/afa/afa-scholarship-application.pdf. Applications are available on the Association of Flight Attendants (AFA) website or from any AFA Union office. In addition to a completed application, the student must submit the following: three letters of reference from people who are not related to him/her (only one reference may be from a teacher, school administrator, or guidance counselor); transcripts that show all grades earned and SAT scores (if applicable); and a 300-word essay describing why the student believes he/she deserves the scholarship. The application and all supporting materials must be mailed to the address provided, postmarked by the deadline date
Closing Date: 10 April
Funding: Foundation

For further information contact:

Email: scholarships@swe.org

Association of Management Development Institutions in South Asia (AMDISA)

University of Hyderabad Campus, Central University, Post Office Gachibowli, Hyderabad, Telangana 500 046, India

Tel:	(91) 40 64545226, 40 64543774
Fax:	(91) 40 23013346
Email:	amdisa@amdisa.org
Website:	www.amdisa.org
Contact:	Executive Director

Association of Management Development Institutions in South Asia (AMDISA) was established in 1988, with the initiative of leading management development institutions in the SAARC region. It is the only association that networks management development centres across 8 nations and promotes partnership between business schools, business leaders and policy administrators for enhancing the quality and effectiveness of management education in South Asia.

Association of Management Development Institutions in South Asia Doctoral Fellowships

Subjects: Social sciences
Purpose: To contribute to the development of South Asian academic perspectives, networks and communities in management and related areas
Eligibility: Open to citizens of any South Asian Commonwealth member country who are registered PhD scholars in a recognized university and are not more than 40 years of age
Level of Study: Doctorate
Type: Fellowship
Value: UK £1,500–4,500
Country of Study: Commonwealth countries
Application Procedure: Applications must have the applicant's name and contact co-ordinates, proof of registration as PhD scholar, curriculum vitae with list of publications and confidential recommendation letters
Closing Date: 31 December

For further information contact:

Email:	arifwaqif@amdisa.org
Contact:	Professor Arif A Waqif, Chairman Regional Doctoral and Postdoctoral Fellowship Committee

Association of Management Development Institutions in South Asia Postdoctoral Fellowship

Subjects: Management and/or related social sciences
Purpose: To provide financial and academic-institutional assistance to PhD scholars and younger academics
Eligibility: Open to citizens of South Asian Commonwealth member country, not older than 50 years, who hold a PhD degree in management or related disciplines and are employed as a full-time teacher/researcher

Level of Study: Postdoctorate
Type: Fellowship
Value: £1,500–4,500
Frequency: Annual
Application Procedure: The application must contain proof of registration as PhD scholar, a curriculum vitae with list of publications
Closing Date: 30 April

For further information contact:

Email:	arifwaqif@amdisa.org
Contact:	Professor Arif A Waqif, Chairman Regional Doctoral and Postdoctoral Fellowship Committee

Association of periOperative Registered Nurses Foundation

2170 South Parker Road, Suite 300, Denver, CO 80231, United States of America

Tel:	(1) 800 755 2676
Email:	ibendzsa@aorn.org
Website:	www.aorn.org
Contact:	Ms Ingrid Bendzsa, Executive assistant

The AORN Foundation is a charitable and educational foundation created in 1992 by the Association of Perioperative Registered Nurses. Its mission is to secure resources and administer assets that provide support for the aim of preparing a new generation of surgical nurses.

Association of periOperative Registered Nurses Scholarship Program

Subjects: Nursing or complementary medicine
Purpose: To provide scholarships to registered nurses who are interested in and committed to preoperative nursing to pursue a doctoral degree
Eligibility: Applicant must have been a member of AORN for 1 year and have a current licence to practice nursing
Level of Study: Doctorate
Type: Scholarship
Frequency: Annual
Study Establishment: Suitable accredited institution
Country of Study: United States of America

Application Procedure: Applicants must check the detailed guidelines on the website or obtain a copy from the Foundation's offices

Closing Date: 1 May

For further information contact:

Email: ibendzsa@aorn.org

Association of Surgeons of Great Britain and Ireland

Association of Surgeons of Great Britain and Ireland, 35-43 Lincoln's Inn Fields, WC2A 3PE, London, United Kingdom

Tel:	(44) 20 7973 0300
Fax:	(44) 20 7430 9235
Email:	admin@asgbi.org.uk
Website:	www.asgbi.org.uk

The founding objectives of the Association of Surgeons of Great Britain and Ireland, in 1920, were the advancement of the science and art of surgery and the promotion of friendship among surgeons. As other surgical specialities developed, the Association came to represent general surgery, encompassing breast, colorectal, endocrine, laparoscopic, transplant, upper gastrointestinal and vascular surgery.

Moynihan Travelling Fellowship

Subjects: General surgery
Purpose: To enable specialist registrars or consultants to broaden their education, and to present and discuss their contribution to British or Irish surgery overseas
Eligibility: Open to either specialist registrars approaching the end of their higher surgical training or consultants in general surgery within 5 years of appointment after the closing date for applications. Candidates must be nationals of and residents of the United Kingdom or the Republic of Ireland, but need not be Fellows or affiliate Fellows of the Association. They may be engaged in general surgery or a sub-speciality thereof
Level of Study: Postdoctorate
Type: Fellowship
Value: Up to £1,000
Frequency: Annual
Country of Study: Any country
No. of awards offered: 6

Application Procedure: Applicants must submit 12 copies of an application, which must include a full curriculum vitae giving details of past and present appointments and publications, a detailed account of the proposed programme of travel, costs involved and the object to be achieved. Applications must be addressed to the Honorary Secretary at the Association of Surgeons. For further details contact Bhavnita Borkhatria at bhavnita@asgbi.org.uk

Closing Date: 28 September
Funding: Private
Contributor: Charitable association funds
No. of awards given last year: 1
No. of applicants last year: 6
Additional Information: Shortlisted candidates will be interviewed by the Scientific Committee of the Association, which will pay particular attention to the originality, scope and feasibility of the proposed itinerary. The successful candidate will be expected to act as an ambassador for British and Irish surgery and should therefore be fully acquainted with the aims and objectives of the Association of Surgeons and its role in surgery. After the completion of the fellowship, the successful candidate will be asked to address the Association at its annual general meeting and to provide a written report for inclusion in the Executive Newsletter. A critical appraisal of the centres visited should form the basis of the report. Please see the website for further details www.asgbi.org.uk/en/awards_fellowships/moynihan_travelling_fellowship.cfm

For further information contact:

Email: vicki@asgbi.org.uk

Association of Universities and Colleges of Canada (AUCC)

1710-350 Albert Street, Ottawa, ON K1R 1B1, Canada

Tel:	(1) 613 563 1236
Fax:	(1) 613 563 9745
Email:	info@aucc.ca
Website:	www.aucc.ca
Contact:	Mr Paul Davidson, President and CEO

The AUCC is a non-profit, non-governmental association that represents Canadian universities at home and abroad. The Association's mandate is to foster and promote the interests of higher education in the firm belief that strong universities are vital to the prosperity and wellbeing of Canada.

Department of National Defence Postdoctoral Fellowships in Military History

Subjects: History with special relevance to the Canadian armed forces. Studies may relate to any aspect of military history or related fields, including operations, policy, technology, and the economic and social dimensions of armed forces national security

Eligibility: Open to Canadian citizens or permanent residents who hold or will hold, prior to closing date of competition, a PhD degree or equivalent level of knowledge or experience in the field considered adequate by the Selection Committee

Level of Study: Postgraduate

Type: One fellowship

Value: C$24,000. Research expenses of up to C$1,500 may also be considered

Frequency: Annual

Study Establishment: for 1 year

Country of Study: Other

Closing Date: 1 February

Additional Information: Fellows may not concurrently hold any other awards whose cumulative value exceeds two thirds of the value of the fellowship accepted under this program. Upon completion of the fellowship, a manuscript resulting from research done should be submitted to AUCC

For further information contact:

Tel: (1) 613 563 1236
Fax: (1) 613 563 9745
Email: awards@aucc.ca
Contact: Canadian Awards Programme

Aston University

Aston University, Aston Triangle, B4 7ET, Birmingham, United Kingdom

Tel: (44) 121 204 3000
Fax: (44) 121 204 3696
Email: a.levey@aston.ac.uk
Website: www.aston.ac.uk
Contact: Alison Levey, Academic Registrar

Aston University is a long-established research – Centre for Executive Development (CED) university. It is Known for its world-class teaching quality, strong links to industry, government & commerce, and its friendly and safe campus environment. Aston University is consistently featured in the top 30 universities in the country.

Aston Dean

Purpose: To encourage students to pursue a PhD programme on a full-time basis

Eligibility: Scholarships are open to Home/European Union and Overseas applicants

Level of Study: Doctorate

Type: Scholarship

Value: £17,000 stipend and full fee waives

Length of Study: 3 years

Frequency: Annual

Country of Study: Any country

Application Procedure: Complete the online application form for entry to the programme: www.aston.ac.uk/study/postgraduate/apply/. Provide all relevant documentation

Closing Date: August

No. of awards given last year: 7

For further information contact:

Tel: (44) 121 204 3000
Email: a.levey@aston.ac.uk

Ferguson Scholarships

Subjects: MSc Cognitive Neuroscience MSc Drug Delivery MSc Pharmaceutical Sciences MSc Pharmacokinetics MSc Stem Cells & Regenerative Medicine

Purpose: The School of Life & Health Sciences is offering 9 scholarships of £15,000 to students from Africa and South America

Eligibility: Hold a conditional or unconditional offer for one of the above courses. 1. Be a national from an African or South American country. 2. Hold a 2:1 degree or equivalent in a relevant subject for the course you are applying for. 3. Be a self-funded student. 4. Provide a strong personal statement when submitting your course application

Level of Study: Postgraduate (MSc)

Type: Scholarship

Value: £15,000

Frequency: As available

Study Establishment: Aston University

Country of Study: United Kingdom

Application Procedure: Submit an application for your chosen course via our online application form before the scholarship deadline

Closing Date: 31 March

Funding: Trusts

Contributor: Allan and Nesta Ferguson Charitable Trust

For further information contact:

Email: a.levey@aston.ac.uk

Global Excellence Scholarship

Purpose: Scholarships of up to £5,000 for well-qualified international students wishing to study at Aston
Level of Study: Graduate, Postgraduate
Type: Scholarship
Value: £3,000–£5,000
Length of Study: n/a
Frequency: As available
Study Establishment: Aston University
Country of Study: United Kingdom
Closing Date: 21 June
Funding: International office

For further information contact:

Email: a.levey@aston.ac.uk

Master of Business Administration Global Ambassador Scholarship

Subjects: Master of Business Administration (MBA)
Purpose: We are launching an MBA Global Ambassador Network, and to celebrate this we are offering a tuition fee discount of up to 50% as part of the MBA Global Ambassador Scholarship. MBA Global Ambassadors will be part of a network of alumni who can inspire and inform others about the Aston MBA. The MBA Global Ambassador Scholarship offers well-qualified applicants a tuition fee discount of up to 50%
Eligibility: MBA Global Ambassador Scholarship recipients will be awarded on merit to well-qualified applicants applying to study the MBA programme starting in January
Level of Study: MBA
Type: Scholarship
Value: 50% reduction in tuition fee
Length of Study: 1 year
Frequency: As available
Study Establishment: Aston Business School
Country of Study: United Kingdom
Funding: International office
Contributor: Aston University

For further information contact:

Aston Business School, Aston University, United Kingdom

Email: a.levey@aston.ac.uk

Postgraduate Scholarships (ABS)

Purpose: To assist students with tuition fees
Eligibility: There are different eligibility criteria for each MSc scholarship. Please check website for complete and clear information
Level of Study: Postgraduate, MBA
Value: £1,000–5,000
Frequency: Annual
Study Establishment: Aston University
Country of Study: United Kingdom
Application Procedure: In order to be eligible to apply for a scholarship, candidates must hold an offer of a place. Notification of awards will be made at the end of July
Closing Date: Please contact the university
Funding: International office
Additional Information: There are many MSc scholarships as well as Aston award scholarships

For further information contact:

Email: apply@aston.ac.uk

School of Languages & Social Studies PhD Bursaries

Subjects: The school of languages and social sciences invites applications in any of the research areas covered by the school. LSS is a multi-disciplinary research-focused school which brings together researchers in the areas of languages (French, German, Spanish), politics and international relations, sociology and policy, and English language. Further information on the school's research areas can be found at www.aston.ac.uk/lss/research/research-degrees/lss-phd-studentships-2016/
Purpose: Financial support for PhD study
Level of Study: Doctorate
Value: Combination of fees only and fees plus maintenance offered
Length of Study: 3 years, full-time
Frequency: Annual
Study Establishment: Aston University
Country of Study: United Kingdom
No. of awards offered: 9
Application Procedure: Please visit www.aston.ac.uk/study/postgraduate/apply/
Closing Date: 29 February
No. of awards given last year: 4
No. of applicants last year: 9
Additional Information: Open to all nationals of any country; however, the bursaries only cover the HOME/European Union fees rate. Therefore those classified as overseas must pay the difference between the HOME and overseas fees rates

For further information contact:

Email: apply@aston.ac.uk

School of Life and Health Sciences Postgraduate Masters Scholarships – Commonwealth Shared Scholarship Scheme

Subjects: MSc molecular toxicology and MSc psychology of health and illness
Purpose: These scholarships are for students from developing Commonwealth countries who would not otherwise be able to study in the United Kingdom
Eligibility: Applicants must hold an offer for MSc in molecular toxicology or MSc in psychology of health and illness; must hold an undergraduate Bachelor's degree at either First/Upper Second class or equivalent (work experience cannot be accepted as an alternative); must be a national of an eligible Commonwealth country and permanently living in that country; must have the minimum English language requirement for the programme as no funding will be given for pre-sessional language programmes; must not have studied for 1 year or more in a developed country previously; must not be employed by a national government or an organisation owned or part-owned by the government (parastatal organisation) – higher education institutions are exempted from this restriction
Level of Study: Postgraduate
Type: Scholarship
Value: These are fully funded scholarships and include living stipend
Frequency: Annual
Study Establishment: Aston University
No. of awards offered: 16
Application Procedure: Application form is available on the website
Closing Date: 1 May
No. of awards given last year: 2
No. of applicants last year: 16

For further information contact:

School of Life and Health Sciences, Aston University, Aston Triangle, United Kingdom

Email: c.m.hoban@aston.ac.uk
Contact: Postgraduate Admissions

Vice-Chancellor's International Scholarship

Subjects: Postgraduate Taught Masters degree
Purpose: For international students applying to study a foundation, undergraduate or postgraduate Taught Masters at Aston University

Eligibility: International students from any country outside of the European Union can apply. This scholarship is available for applicants applying to all foundation, undergraduate and postgraduate programmes (except the MBChB in Medicine)
Level of Study: Postgraduate
Type: One scholarship
Value: £7,000
Frequency: As available
Study Establishment: Aston University
Country of Study: United Kingdom
Application Procedure: Online application form: www2.aston.ac.uk/scholarships/home-and-eu-scholarships/Vice-chancellors-international-scholarship/index
Closing Date: 21 June
Funding: International office

For further information contact:

Email: a.levey@aston.ac.uk

Ataxia United Kingdom

Lincoln House, Kennington Park, 1-3 Brixton Road, SW9 6DE, London, United Kingdom

Tel:	(44) 20 7582 1444
Fax:	(44) 20 7582 9444
Email:	research@ataxia.org.uk
Website:	www.ataxia.org.uk
Contact:	Mrs Julie Greenfield, Research Projects Manager

Ataxia United Kingdom is the leading charity in the United Kingdom working with and for people with ataxia. It will support research projects and related activities in order to enhance scientific understanding of ataxia, develop and evaluate therapeutic and supportive strategies and encourage wider involvement with ataxia research.

Ataxia United Kingdom PhD Studentship

Subjects: Any aspect of both inherited and sporadic progressive ataxias including Friedreich's ataxia and other cerebellar ataxias
Purpose: To further research into causes of and treatments for progressive ataxias
Eligibility: Proposals are accepted from academic institutions, private sector research companies and suitably qualified individuals. There are no restrictions on age, nationality or residency
Level of Study: Postgraduate

Type: Studentship
Value: Varies
Length of Study: Varies
Frequency: Annual, if funds are available
Country of Study: Any country
No. of awards offered: 3
Application Procedure: Applicants must complete an application form available from Ataxia United Kingdom Research Projects Manager at research@ataxia.org.uk, or online at ataxia.org.uk
Closing Date: Varies, refer to website for details
Funding: Commercial, Private, Trusts, Individuals
No. of applicants last year: 3
Additional Information: There are a number of priority areas of research and these can be obtained from the Research Projects Manager

For further information contact:

Tel: (44) 20 7582 1444
Email: research@ataxia.org.uk
Contact: Dr Julie Greenfield, Research Projects Manager

Ataxia United Kingdom Research Grant

Subjects: Any aspect of both inherited and sporadic progressive ataxias including Friedreich's ataxia and other cerebellar ataxias
Purpose: To further research into causes of and treatments for progressive ataxias
Eligibility: Proposals are accepted from academic institutions, private sector research companies and suitably qualified individuals. There are no restrictions on age, nationality or residency
Level of Study: Unrestricted
Type: Project grant
Value: Varies
Length of Study: Varies
Frequency: Dependent on funds available
Country of Study: Any country
No. of awards offered: 16
Application Procedure: Applicants must complete an application form available from Ataxia's Research Projects Manager at research@ataxia.org.uk, or online at ataxia.org.uk
Closing Date: Refer to the website for details
Funding: Commercial, Private, Trusts, Individuals
No. of awards given last year: 1
No. of applicants last year: 16
Additional Information: There are a number of priority areas of research and these can be obtained from the Research Projects Manager

For further information contact:

Tel: (44) 20 7582 1444
Email: research@ataxia.org.uk
Contact: Dr Julie Greenfield, Research Projects Manager

Ataxia United Kingdom Travel Grant

Subjects: Any aspect of both inherited and sporadic progressive ataxias including Friedreich's ataxia and other cerebellar ataxias
Purpose: To enable researchers to present their ataxia research at national and international conferences
Eligibility: Proposals are accepted from academic institutions, private sector research companies and suitably qualified individuals. There are no restrictions on age, nationality or residency, although preference will be given to events which could potentially benefit patients and researchers in the United Kingdom or Europe
Level of Study: Unrestricted
Type: Travel grant
Value: Dependent on the conference
Length of Study: Varies
Frequency: Dependent on funds available
Country of Study: Any country
Application Procedure: Applicants must complete an application form available from Ataxia's Research Projects Manager at research@ataxia.org.uk, or online at ataxia.org.uk
Closing Date: Contact Research Projects Manager for precise dates
Funding: Commercial, Private, Trusts, Individuals
Additional Information: There are a number of priority areas of research and these can be obtained from the Research Projects Manager

For further information contact:

Tel: (44) 20 7582 1444
Email: research@ataxia.org.uk
Contact: Dr Julie Greenfield, Research Projects Manager

Athens State University

300 North Beaty Street, Athens, AL 35611, United States of America

Website: www.athens.edu
Contact: Ms Helen Marks, Secretary, Financial Aid

Athens State University Phi Theta Kappa Transfer Scholarship

Purpose: This scholarship is in the form of a tuition waiver only and will not pay in combination with any other ASU institutional scholarship

Eligibility: 1. Must be a new entering student with a minimum of 36 transfer credit hours and plan to enroll immediately in Athens State University in Alabama after completion of coursework at the two-year college level. 2. Students must not have more than six hours of coursework attempted at ASU by the end of the spring term of application year

Level of Study: Graduate

Type: Scholarship

Frequency: Annual

Country of Study: United States of America

Application Procedure: 1. Applications are available online at the Athens State University (ASU) website. 2. The student must submit a complete ASU application form, official transcripts from all prior colleges, two letters of recommendation from faculty members at transfer institutions, a letter verifying membership in Phi Theta Kappa from an adviser at transfer institution, and an essay outlining why the student feels he/she is deserving of the scholarship. 3. The student must submit his/her application to Student Financial Services before 4:30 p.m. EST by the deadline date

Closing Date: 31 March

Funding: Private

For further information contact:

Email: sarah.mcabee@athens.edu

Contact: Sarah McAbee, Director

Auckland Medical Research Foundation

Box 7151, Auckland, New Zealand

Tel: (64) 9 307 2886

Contact: Secretary

Auckland Medical Research Foundation Travel Grant

Subjects: Medicine

Purpose: To allow staff engaged in or associated with research projects to travel for a specific purpose

Eligibility: Open normally, but not exclusively, to staff associated with the Auckland Area Health Board, the School of Medicine in the University of Auckland, or to recipients of other grants from the Foundation. There are no requirements as to age, sex or citizenship

Level of Study: Postgraduate

Type: Varies

Value: Varies

Study Establishment: as approved

Country of Study: Any country

For further information contact:

Email: amrf@medicalresearch.org.nz

Contact: Secretary

Auckland University of Technology University of Technology

55 Wellesley Street, Auckland 1010, New Zealand

Contact: Auckland University of Technology

Auckland University of Technology (AUT) is a university in New Zealand, formed on 1 January when a former technical college (originally established in 1895) was granted university status. It has five faculties across three campuses in Auckland: City, North, and South campuses, and an additional three specialist locations: AUT Millennium, Warkworth Radio Astronomical Observatory and AUT Centre for Refugee Education.

Access & Rural Women New Zealand Scholarship

Purpose: This is a scholarship for a health worker who wishes to further his/her studies in the health and/or disability fields, with a particular focus on the provision of services to the rural sector

Type: Scholarship

Value: $3,000

Length of Study: 1 year

Country of Study: Any country

Application Procedure: For application procedure, please visit website www.aut.ac.nz/study/fees-and-scholarships/scholarships-and-awards-at-aut/scholarships-database/detailpage?detailCode=802935&sessionID=27587614&sourceIP=&X_FORWARDED_FOR=

Closing Date: 1 July

Additional Information: For guidelines, application forms and more information about this award contact: Rural Women New Zealand, PO Box 12-021 Wellington, New Zealand; Email: enquiries@ruralwomen.org.nz

For further information contact:

Email: enquiries@ruralwomen.org.nz

Auckland University of Technology and Cyclone Computers Laptop and Tablet Scholarship

Purpose: The primary objectives of this award are to enhance the student learning experience and to increase study options for undergraduate and postgraduate students through the laptop scholarship programme
Type: Scholarship
Value: HP Elitebook or HP Elite X2 1012 G2or AUT Optn A Macbook (A&D only)or devices of similar specification
Country of Study: Any country
Closing Date: 1 July
Additional Information: For guidelines, application forms and more information about this award contact: Auckland University of Technology, Phone: +64 9 921 9837, Email: scholars@aut.ac.nz

For further information contact:

Email: scholars@aut.ac.nz

Auckland University of Technology Master of Human Rights Scholarship

Purpose: The purpose of this scholarship is to encourage and stimulate full-time students into the Master Human Rights, AUT will offer two AUT Master of Human Rights Scholarships to applicants wishing to enroll full-time into this Masters programme
Eligibility: 1. Bachelor's degree with a minimum of a B grade average or higher in papers at level 7 or equivalent
Type: Scholarship
Length of Study: 1 year full-time
Frequency: Annual
Country of Study: Any country
Closing Date: 1 October

For further information contact:

Tel: (1) 64 9 921 9999
Email: contact@studyspy.ac.nz

Auckland University of Technology Post Graduate Scholarships

Purpose: Auckland University of Technology offers AUT Postgraduate Scholarships - Equity (Maori and Pacific) to Maori and Pacific students for postgraduate study at AUT. UT Postgraduate Scholarship (coursework) is available to full-time students undertaking study at Level 8 or above (New Zealand Qualifications Framework) who have demonstrated the potential to achieve highly
Eligibility: Applicants must complete the online application available through the AUT Scholarships Database www.aut.ac.nz/scholarships. Applications will be open from 5 April
Level of Study: Postgraduate
Type: Scholarship
Value: Domestic full fees for 120pts
Length of Study: The scholarship is normally awarded for 12 months of full time study only
Frequency: Annual
Country of Study: New Zealand
Application Procedure: Application is through the AUT online scholarship portal accessed from the link above. Applications will open in October of the year preceding study for Semester 1 study or May for study in Semester 2. The following documentation must be received on or before the closing date. A one-page personal statement outlining the applicant's academic goals and career aspirations stating why they believe they merit the scholarship and provide an outline of their Maori or Pacific cultural involvement. The personal statement should also attach an outline of recent leadership positions or responsibilities held within the University or community. A copy of the applicant's transcript will be added to the application by the Scholarships Office once grades have been finalized
Closing Date: 15 June
Additional Information: For guidelines, application forms and more information about this award contact: Auckland University of Technology; Phone: +64 9 921 9837; Email: scholars@aut.ac.nz

Auckland University of Technology Vice Chancellor Doctoral Scholarship

Purpose: Auckland University of Technology (AUT) awards scholarships to high achieving candidates applying to an approved doctoral programme at AUT
Type: Scholarship
Value: Tuition fees (at the domestic rate) plus the compulsory student services fee; and an annual stipend of NZ$25,000 per annum

Length of Study: The scholarship is tenable for up to 3 years
Country of Study: New Zealand
Application Procedure: Applicants must meet the normal admission criteria for the doctoral programme. www.aut.ac.nz/study-at-aut/entry-requirements/postgraduate-and-graduate-admission-requirements
Closing Date: 15 October

For further information contact:

Email: scholars@aut.ac.nz

Awarua Trust Scholarship

Purpose: To provide financial support to people in their pursuit of excellence
Value: Up to NZ$2,000 (or more by approval)
Length of Study: One year
Country of Study: Any country
Closing Date: 30 June
Contributor: The Awarua Trust
Additional Information: For guidelines, application forms and more information about this award contact: Gavin Haddon, (CA) trustee, The Awarua Trust, PO Box 388, Email: info@awaruatrust.org.nz

For further information contact:

Email: info@awaruatrust.org.nz

Betty Loughhead Soroptimist Scholarship Trust

Purpose: This scholarship provides financial support to women over the age of 25 who are studying to gain a further qualification to advance a careers in business, the professions, the arts
Value: NZ$3,000–$5,000 (per award)
Country of Study: Any country
Closing Date: 31 August
Additional Information: For guidelines, application forms and more information about this award contact: Hayley Denoual, Secretary, The Betty Loughhead Soroptimist Scholarship Trust, BLSST Secretary Sarnia, 52 Raukawa Street Strathmore Park, New Zealand; Phone: 04 388 2115; Email: retary@blsst.co.nz

For further information contact:

Email: secretary@blsst.co.nz

Business, Economics & Law Postgraduate Academic Excellence Scholarship

Purpose: The purpose of the Business, Economics and Law Postgraduate Academic Excellence Scholarship is to encourage students with an excellent academic record to undertake postgraduate research in the Faculty of Business and Law
Eligibility: Applicants for this scholarship must complete an AUT Application for Enrolment (AFE) for the Bachelor of Business (Honours), the Master of Laws, the Master of Business or the Master of Philosophy
Type: Scholarship
Value: Tuition fees (up to 120 pts) and student levies
Country of Study: New Zealand
Application Procedure: Application for this scholarship is via our AUT online scholarship application portal
Closing Date: 1 June
Additional Information: For guidelines, application forms and more information about this award contact: Auckland University of Technology; Phone: +64 9 921 9837; Email: scholars@aut.ac.nz

For further information contact:

Email: scholars@aut.ac.nz

Colab PhD/MPhil Fees Scholarship

Type: Scholarship
Value: Full fees-PHD Domestic equivalent fees - MPhil
Length of Study: Up to 3 years for a PhD programme but will be reviewed annually
Country of Study: New Zealand
Closing Date: 14 December
Additional Information: For guidelines, application forms and more information about this award contact: Auckland University of Technology, Phone: +64 9 921 9837, Email: scholars@aut.ac.nz

For further information contact:

Email: scholars@aut.ac.nz

Discrete Cosine Transform Mâori and Pacific Mature Student Doctoral Scholarship

Purpose: This scholarship is intended to provide support for Doctoral study completion, to Mâori and Pacific Island students who choose to undertake Doctoral studies later in life and who are making good progress towards PhD studies
Eligibility: All students nominated for this scholarship must be:
1. Of Maori and/or Pacific Island descent, and be NZ Citizens or

permanent residents (Note: Pacific Island descent relates to one of the following Pacific countries, Cook Islands, Fiji, Kiribati, Nauru, Niue) Nominated by their PhD supervisor. Able to present a solid case for the scholarship to be awarded to them

Type: Scholarship
Value: An annual NZ$25,000 stipend, tuition fees
Length of Study: 2 years
Country of Study: New Zealand
Closing Date: 1 December
Additional Information: For guidelines, application forms and more information about this award contact: Auckland University of Technology, Phone: +64 9 921 9837, Email: scholars@aut.ac.nz

For further information contact:

Email: scholars@aut.ac.nz

Doctoral Fee Scholarships (Art & Design)

Purpose: The Doctoral Fee Scholarship (Art & Design) is offered to PhD candidates to nurture and support the research culture of the School of Art & Design
Value: Tuition fee + learner services levy
Length of Study: The tenure of this scholarship is for up to 4 years
Country of Study: Any country
Application Procedure: For application procedure, please visit website www.aut.ac.nz/study/fees-and-scholarships/scholarships-and-awards-at-aut/scholarships-database/detail page?detailCode=501191&sessionID=27587614&source IP=&X_FORWARDED_FOR=
Closing Date: 1 June
Additional Information: For guidelines, application forms and more information about this award contact: Auckland University of Technology; Phone: +64 9 921 9837; Email: scholars@aut.ac.nz

For further information contact:

Email: cde-enquiries@lists.bath.ac.uk

Fulbright New Zealand General Graduate Awards

Purpose: Fulbright New Zealand General Graduate Awards are for promising New Zealand graduate students to undertake postgraduate study or research at United States institutions in any field
Type: Award
Value: Up to US$31,000 plus travel expenses and insurance
Length of Study: 1 year
Country of Study: Any country

Application Procedure: For online application, please visit website apply.embark.com/student/fulbright/international/20/
Closing Date: 1 August
Additional Information: For guidelines, application forms and more information about this award contact: Shauna Mendez, Programme Manager, Fulbright New Zealand, PO Box 3465, New Zealand; Phone: +64 4 494 1500; Email: shauna@fulbright.org.nz

For further information contact:

Email: pip@fulbright.org.nz

Kate Edger Educational Charitable Trust - Expenses / Class Materials Awards

Purpose: The main purpose of these awards is to assist women, who are studying undergraduate or post graduate degree or diploma courses which incur high materials' expenditure, with payment of essential costs
Type: Grant
Value: NZ$300–$1,000 each
Length of Study: Each Expenses/Class Materials
Frequency: Annual
Country of Study: New Zealand
Application Procedure: Application forms for these awards are available from: www.academicdresshire.co.nz/Academic+Awards+Available/Postgraduate+Awards.html; enquiries to: awards@kateedgertrust.org.nz
Closing Date: 18 March
Additional Information: For guidelines, application forms and more information about this award contact: Kate Edger Educational Charitable Trust, Private Bag 93208 Parnell, Email: enquiries@kateedgertrust.org.nz

For further information contact:

Kate Edger Educational Charitable Trust, Private Bag 93208, Parnell, New Zealand

Email: awards@kateedgertrust.org.nz
Contact: Ms Katrina, Ford

Master of Arts Scholarship in Applied Language Studies or Professional Language Studies

Purpose: The purpose of this scholarship is to encourage and support postgraduate study in the area of Language Teaching or Applied Language Study AUT's language and culture programmes focus on language in its widest sense
Eligibility: Applicants must: 1. Be new students enrolling full-time into the Master of Professional Language Studies

(Language Teaching) or the Master of Arts in Applied Language Studies. Applicants who have not applied for admission to the master's programme should commence this process as well. Information about these programmes is available from www.aut.ac.nz/study-at-aut/study-areas/language-culture/postgraduate-study/. 2. Have demonstrated academic excellence in past tertiary study

Type: Scholarship

Value: NZ$8,000 towards fees

Length of Study: One year of full-time study only

Country of Study: New Zealand

Application Procedure: Information about these programmes is available from www.aut.ac.nz/study-at-aut/study-areas/language-culture/postgraduate-study/

Closing Date: 14 November

Additional Information: For guidelines, application forms and more information about this award contact: Auckland University of Technology, Phone: +64 9 921 9837

For further information contact:

Auckland University of Technology, United States of America

Tel: (1) 64 9 921 9837
Email: scholars@aut.ac.nz

Master of Cultural & Creative Practice Scholarships (Art & Design)

Purpose: The scholarship is offered to support postgraduate students and engender a creative led practice culture within the School of Art & Design in the of Cultural and Creative Practice (MCCP) programme

Type: Scholarship

Value: Tuition fees + Learner services levy for the MCCP programme of study

Length of Study: The tenure of this scholarship is for up to three semesters of full-time study in the Master of Cultural & Creative Practice programme of study (180 points)

Country of Study: New Zealand

Application Procedure: For details, please visit website www.aut.ac.nz/study/fees-and-scholarships/scholarships-and-awards-at-aut/scholarships-database/detailpage?detailCode=501192&sessionID=27587614&sourceIP=&X_FORWARDED_FOR=

Closing Date: 1 June

Additional Information: For guidelines, application forms and more information about this award contact: Auckland University of Technology; Phone: +64 9 921 9837; Email: scholars@aut.ac.nz

For further information contact:

Email: scholars@aut.ac.nz

Master of Professional Language Studies (Language Teaching) Scholarships

Purpose: The purpose of this scholarship is to encourage and support postgraduate study in the area of language teaching. The scholarship is open to domestic students only

Type: Scholarship

Value: Full fees and student levies up to 120 points of study

Length of Study: The scholarship is available for 3 consecutive semesters only (18 months) of full time or part time study

Country of Study: Any country

Application Procedure: Applications are available from www.aut.ac.nz/study-at-aut/study-areas/language-culture/postgraduate-study/master-of-professional-language-studies—language-teaching

Closing Date: 6 July

For further information contact:

Email: cdsouza@aut.ac.nz

Ministry of Primary Industries/National Institute of Water and Atmospheric Research Masters Scholarships in Quantitative Fisheries Science

Purpose: To attract high performing New Zealand students into quantitative marine science; to encourage postgraduate students to contribute to priority research areas identified by the New Zealand Government; to train students at the postgraduate level by sharing and using the combined expertise of university academics, MPI and practising NIWA scientists; and to facilitate the professional development of postgraduate students by exposure to an applied commercial research environment

Country of Study: Any country

Application Procedure: Application has to be processed using the link www.victoria.ac.nz/study/student-finance/scholarships

Closing Date: 20 September

For further information contact:

Email: scholarships-office@vuw.ac.nz

Peace and Disarmament Education Trust (PADET)

Purpose: The purpose of PADET is to advance education and promote international peace, arms control and disarmament. PADET funds not-for-profit projects and scholarship topics that support these objectives

Type: Scholarship

Value: Scholarships are awarded in two categories, depending on the individual
Length of Study: One year for a master
Country of Study: Any country
Closing Date: 4 July
Additional Information: For guidelines, application forms and more information about this award contact: Trust Advisor, Department of Internal Affairs, PO Box 805, Phone: 0800 824 824; Email: community.matters@dia.govt.nz

For further information contact:

Email: webmaster@dia.govt.nz

Resource Management Law Association of New Zealand Masters Scholarship

Purpose: To encourage graduate students studying law, planning, engineering, geography, science, landscape architecture, urban planning and resource management, to focus their research theses or dissertations on topics related to the application of resource management in New Zealand
Eligibility: The scholarship is open to any graduate student in a University (New Zealand or Overseas) registered for a Masters (including an undergraduate Honours degree involving advanced levels of research and study at Masters degree level)
Value: NZ$5,000 per year
Length of Study: Any scholarship will be tenable for 1 year only
Country of Study: Any country
Application Procedure: To apply for an RMLA scholarship, simply download the RMLA Scholarship 1. Application and post it to RMLA so it arrives before before 01 August. Selection will be based on relevance of the proposed thesis or dissertation topic to advancing. 2. Excellence in resource management policy and process. i. Resource management processes which are legally sound, effective and efficient and which produce high quality environmental outcomes
Closing Date: 1 August
Funding: Private
Additional Information: For guidelines, application forms and more information about this award contact: Karol Helmink, Executive Officer, Resource Management Law Association, RMLA Scholarship Selection Committee RMLA PO Box 89187 Torbay; Email: karol.helmink@rmla.org.nz

For further information contact:

Email: Karol.helmink@rmla.org.nz

The AUT Queen Elizabeth II Diamond Jubilee Doctoral Scholarship

Purpose: To develop an internationally aware, skilled future leader and establish enduring education and professional linkages. The Queen Elizabeth II Diamond Jubilee AUT Doctoral Scholarship marks the 60th anniversary of the accession of Her Majesty The Queen to the throne and will be awarded annually
Type: Scholarship
Value: $25,000 annual stipend tuition fees and student services levies
Country of Study: New Zealand
Closing Date: 15 October
Additional Information: For guidelines, application forms and more information about this award contact: Auckland University of Technology, Phone: +64 9 921 9837, Email: scholars@aut.ac.nz

For further information contact:

Auckland University of Technology, 55 Wellesley St E, Auckland 1010, New Zealand

Tel: (64) 9 921 9837
Email: srichard@nsf.gov, scholars@aut.ac.nz

The Capstone Editing Conference Travel Grant for Postgraduate Research Students

Purpose: The purpose of attending the conference should be to assist with the student's research or professional development. The student does not necessarily have to be presenting a paper or poster at the conference to be eligible to apply for the grant, though it is preferred
Eligibility: For eligibility, please visit website www.aut.ac.nz/study/fees-and-scholarships/scholarships-and-awards-at-aut/scholarships-database/detailpage?detailCode=804076&sessionID=27587614&sourceIP=&X_FORWARDED_FOR=
Type: Grant
Value: Up to A$3,000
Country of Study: Any country
Closing Date: 1 June
Additional Information: For guidelines, application forms and more information about this award contact: Lisa Lines, Director and Head Editor, Capstone Editing, Tower A Level 5, 7 London Circuit Australia; Phone: 1800 224 468; Email: lisa.lines@capstoneediting.com.au

For further information contact:

Email: scholarships@capstoneediting.com.au

The Capstone Editing Early Career Academic Research Grant for Women

Purpose: In offering this grant, Capstone Editing acknowledges the greater difficulties faced by female academics in developing and continuing their careers and seeks to ameliorate this situation with practical, financial support
Eligibility: Eligible to only women
Value: Up to NZ$5,000
Country of Study: New Zealand
Closing Date: 30 May

For further information contact:

Email: info@capstoneediting.com.au

Todd Foundation Postgraduate Scholarship in Energy Research

Purpose: The purpose of the Todd Foundation Postgraduate Scholarship in Energy Research is to support students undertaking doctoral research in the field of energy, research which may have wide relevance and add value to New Zealand. This scholarship recognises the work of Sir Bryan Todd
Level of Study: Graduate
Value: NZ$25,000 per year/plus one-off NZ$3,000
Length of Study: Up to 3 years
Country of Study: Any country
Closing Date: 1 September
Funding: Private
Additional Information: For guidelines, application forms and more information about this award contact: Scholarships, Universities New Zealand – Te Pôkai Tara, PO Box 11915, Wellington 6142; Phone: +64 4 381 8510; Email: scholarships@universitiesnz.ac.nz

For further information contact:

Email: scholarships@universitiesnz.ac.nz

Toloa Scholarships for Pacific STEM Scholars

Purpose: These scholarships are designed to motivate, celebrate and inspire Pacific people to study STEM courses and enter a career in STEM
Type: Scholarship
Value: NZ$25,000 each
Length of Study: Three years
Country of Study: New Zealand
Application Procedure: For application, visit website www.mpp.govt.nz/toloa-application-form-2018/
Closing Date: 15 November

Additional Information: For guidelines, application forms and more information about this award contact: Ofania Ikiua, Ministry for Pacific Peoples, PO Box 833, New Zealand, Phone: 04 473 4493, Email: contact@mpp.govt.nz

For further information contact:

Email: contact@mpp.govt.nz

Zonta Club of South Auckland Area Study Award

Purpose: To assist in women's education
Value: Up to NZ$5,000
Application Procedure: For further information and an application form see the website: www.zontasouthauckland.org.nz
Closing Date: 17 August

For further information contact:

Email: southauckland@zonta.org.nz

Zonta International Amelia Earhart Fellowships

Purpose: The Amelia Earhart Fellowship is awarded annually to women pursuing PhD/doctoral degrees in aerospace-related sciences and aerospace-related engineering
Type: Fellowship
Value: NZ$10,000
Length of Study: 1 year
Country of Study: New Zealand
Application Procedure: For application form, please visit website www.aut.ac.nz/study/fees-and-scholarships/scholarships-and-awards-at-aut/scholarships-database/detailpage?detailCode=100341&sessionID=26783186&sourceIP=&X_FORWARDED_FOR=
Closing Date: 15 November
Additional Information: For guidelines, application forms and more information about this award contact: Zonta International Foundation, 1211 West 22nd Street Suite 900 Oak Brook, United States, Phone: +1 630-928-1400, Email: programs@zonta.org

For further information contact:

Email: zifoundation@zonta.org

Australia Council for the Arts

372 Elizabeth Street, PO Box 788, Strawberry Hills, Surry Hills, NSW 2012, Australia

Tel: (61) 2 9215 9000
Fax: (61) 2 9215 9111
Email: mail@australiacouncil.gov.au
Website: www.australiacouncil.gov.au

The Australia Council for the Arts is the Australian Government's arts funding and advisory body. Each year, the council delivers more than $160 million in funding for arts organisations and individual artists across the country. Individuals, groups and organisations can apply to the Australia Council for funding. Individuals must be Australian citizens or have permanent resident status in Australia. All amounts are in Australian dollars.

Aboriginal and Torres Strait Islander Arts Fellowship

Subjects: Craft art, literature, performing arts, new media
Purpose: These grants provide financial support for two years to Aboriginal and Torres Strait Islander artists to enable them to undertake a major creative project or program in their artform
Eligibility: Open to practicing Aboriginal and Torres Strait Islander artists who are able to demonstrate at least 10 years experience as a practicing professional artist
Level of Study: Postgraduate
Type: Fellowship
Value: A$100,000 up to two years for dance, emerging artforms and experimental practices
Length of Study: 2 years
Frequency: Annual
Country of Study: Australia
Application Procedure: Apply online. For further details mail to atsia@australiacouncil.gov.au
Closing Date: 19 November
Funding: Government

For further information contact:

Email: stephanie.lord@sa.gov.au

Aboriginal and Torres Strait Islander Arts Key Organisations Triennial

Purpose: To support a limited number of Aboriginal and Torres Strait Islander arts organisations to advance Aboriginal and Torres Strait Islander arts in Australia
Eligibility: Open to Aboriginal and Torres Strait Islander arts organisations only and must be outstanding organisations with a substantial record of achievement in their field
Frequency: Annual
Country of Study: Any country

Application Procedure: Application forms should include evidence of eligibility and the required support materials. Check website for further details
Closing Date: 15 July

For further information contact:

Email: stephanie.lord@sa.gov.au

Aboriginal and Torres Strait Islander Arts Presentation and Promotion

Purpose: Presentation and Promotion grants support projects that promote Aboriginal and Torres Strait Islander artists and their work regionally, nationally and internationally through publications, recordings, performances, exhibitions and international export
Eligibility: Open to Aboriginal and Torres Strait Islander artists and community organisations and Aboriginal and Torres Strait Islander and non-indigenous arts organisations (including publishers)
Type: Grant
Value: Up to a maximum of A$10,000 for CD/DVD recording projects involving writing, recording, production, manufacture, distribution and promotion
Frequency: Annual
Country of Study: Any country
Application Procedure: Apply online. Please mail to atsia@australiacouncil.gov.au for further information
Closing Date: 18 November
Additional Information: Overseas applicants for international projects must provide written evidence of co-funding from the host country or organisation. All applicants are encouraged to seek further funding support for the project from other sources

For further information contact:

Email: vichealth@vichealth.vic.gov.au

Aboriginal and Torres Strait Islander Arts Program

Purpose: To provide support towards the cost of an organisation wishing to employ an Aboriginal and Torres Strait Islander artworker or artist to organise, develop and initiate a programme or arts activities in their community or region
Eligibility: Open to Aboriginal and Torres Strait Islander arts organisations only
Length of Study: 1 year
Frequency: Annual
Country of Study: Any country

Application Procedure: Applications should include evidence of eligibility and required support materials. Check website for further details
Closing Date: 15 July

For further information contact:

Email: stephanie.lord@sa.gov.au

Aboriginal and Torres Strait Islander Arts Skills and Arts Development

Purpose: These grants support Aboriginal and Torres Strait Islander artists, groups, organisations and accredited non-Indigenous organisations to develop their ideas and skills such as: mentorship programs, arts workshops, professional development programs, conferences, seminars or planning and development programs
Eligibility: Applicants should be Aboriginal and Torres Strait Islander individuals, organisations or groups
Type: Grant
Value: Varies
Country of Study: Any country
Application Procedure: Apply online
Closing Date: 19 November
Additional Information: Applicants are encouraged to seek funding from a number of sources. Please mail to atsia@australiacouncil.gov.au for further information

For further information contact:

Email: stephanie.lord@sa.gov.au

Aboriginal and Torres Strait Islander New Work Grant

Subjects: Theatre production, writing and music
Purpose: These grants support Aboriginal and Torres Strait Islander artists, groups, organisations and accredited non-Indigenous organisations to create new work with an expected public outcome
Eligibility: Open to Aboriginal and Torres Strait Islander artists who demonstrate artistic merit and innovation
Level of Study: Professional development
Type: Grant
Value: Varies
Length of Study: Up to 12 months
Frequency: Annual
Country of Study: Australia
Application Procedure: Apply online. For further information mail to atsia@australiacouncil.gov.au

Closing Date: 19 November
Funding: Government
Additional Information: All applicants are encouraged to seek further funding support for the project from other sources

For further information contact:

Email: mail@australiacouncil.gov.au

Community Cultural Development Category A

Purpose: To develop significant project ideas and/or extension of effective partnerships that enable future projects to take place
Eligibility: Open to individuals, groups and organisations and who have discussed their proposal with Community Partnerships staff
Type: Grant
Value: Up to A$5,000 per grant
Frequency: Annual
Country of Study: Any country
Application Procedure: Applications should include required support materials. Check website for further details
Closing Date: 1 November

Community Cultural Development Category B

Purpose: To support off community arts and culture projects which may have a public outcome and must involve a range of partners
Eligibility: Open to individuals, groups and organisations
Type: Grant
Value: Up to A$20,000
Frequency: Annual
Country of Study: Any country
Application Procedure: Applications should include required support materials. Check website for further details
Closing Date: 1 July

Community Cultural Development Category C

Purpose: To support one-off community arts and culture projects which have a public outcome and involve cross-sectoral partners
Eligibility: Open to individuals, groups and organisations who meet the general eligibility requirements
Value: A$20,000–35,000
Frequency: Annual
Country of Study: Any country
Application Procedure: Applications should include required support materials. Check website for further details
Closing Date: 1 July

Community Cultural Development Presentation and Promotion

Purpose: To support project that promote the value of community cultural development practice. This includes projects that create opportunities for practitioners to explore new ways of presenting the outcomes of existing best-practice models to new audiences

Eligibility: Open to individuals and organisations who meet the general eligibility requirements

Type: Grant

Frequency: Annual

Country of Study: Any country

Application Procedure: Applications should include required support materials. Check website for further details

Closing Date: 1 August

For further information contact:

Email: arts.office@nt.gov.au

Community Partnerships - Projects

Subjects: Geographic, demographic, and social contexts

Purpose: These grants provide funding for individuals, groups and organisations to develop and implement community arts and cultural development projects with a range of partners. These projects may or may not have a public outcome. Consideration of an evaluation strategy is recommended

Eligibility: Open to individuals, groups and organisations

Type: Grant

Value: Up to A$20,000

Length of Study: Varies

Frequency: Annual

Application Procedure: Apply online

Closing Date: 5 September

Additional Information: Please mail to cp@australiacouncil.gov.au for further information

For further information contact:

Tel: (61) 2 9215 9034
Email: cp@australiacouncil.gov.au
Contact: Community Partnerships

Dance New Work Creative Development

Subjects: Dance

Purpose: To support the creation of new dance works

Eligibility: Open to individuals, groups, and organisations who meet the general eligibility requirements

Level of Study: Professional development

Type: Grant

Value: Varies

Length of Study: Varies

Application Procedure: Applications should include required support materials. Apply online. Check website for further details or contact Program Officer

Closing Date: 10 February

Additional Information: These are Projects Creative Development and Projects Presentation

For further information contact:

Tel: (61) 2 9215 9179
Email: e.johnson@australiacouncil.gov.au
Contact: Emma Johnson, Program Officer, Dance

Dance New Work Presentation

Subjects: Dance

Purpose: To support public performance of a new work and any stages leading up to the production

Eligibility: Open to individuals who meet the general eligibility requirements. This can include final stage creative development and presentation/s and remounts of dance works. Applicants must provide information about presentation partner/s or presentation arrangements. Arrangements can include self presentation

Value: Varies

Application Procedure: Applications should include required support materials. Apply online. Check website for further details and contact Program Officer

Closing Date: 15 August

For further information contact:

Tel: (61) 2 9215 9179
Email: e.johnson@australiacouncil.gov.au
Contact: Emma Johnson, Program Officer, Dance

Festivals Australia

Purpose: These grants support regional, remote and community festivals to present quality arts projects which have not been presented before, and would not be possible without financial support

Eligibility: In order to apply you must be, or must apply through, a registered legal entity (with an ABN) or an incorporated organisation, which is able to produce an annual audited financial statement. Check website for complete details

Type: Grant

Application Procedure: Apply online

Closing Date: 29 August
Additional Information: Please mail to artsdevelopmen t@australiacouncil.gov.au for further information. Potential applicants are encouraged to discuss their application. For information and any questions relating to this grants program

For further information contact:

Tel: (61) 2 9215 9176
Email: T.Kita@australiacouncil.gov.au
Contact: Tara Kita, Program Officer, Market Development

International Market Development Program

Subjects: Music
Purpose: International Pathways aims to assist with strategic international artistic and market development activities for Australian music and musicians
Eligibility: Applicants must have a commercially available CD, and touring experience
Level of Study: Professional development
Type: Grant
Value: A$2,500–20,000
Length of Study: A maximum of 3 years
Frequency: Annual
Country of Study: Australia
Application Procedure: Contact the department
Funding: Government

For further information contact:

Tel: (61) 2 9215 9115
Email: music@ozco.gov.au
Contact: Andy Ratzen

Literature Program

Subjects: Literature
Purpose: These grants provide funding to established Australian organisations that support Australia's literary infrastructure
Eligibility: Open to Australian organisations which meet the eligibility requirements and provide the necessary support materials
Value: Covers production, program and/or operational costs
Length of Study: 1 year
Frequency: Annual
Application Procedure: Apply Online. Check website for further details. Applicant must provide evidence of his eligibility and all required support material by the application closing date. For further details contact the Program

For further information contact:

Tel: (61) 2 9215 9057
Email: l.byrne@australiacouncil.gov.au
Contact: Lucy Byrne, Program Officer, Literature

Music Presentation and Promotion

Subjects: Music
Purpose: To support one-off projects that present, publish, distribute and/or market quality music of any style within Australia
Eligibility: Open to individuals, performing groups/ensembles/bands and organisations which meet the eligibility requirements and provide the necessary support materials
Value: Up to A$30,000 and associated expenses
Length of Study: Varies
Application Procedure: Application form should include the required supporting materials. Apply online. Check website for further details. For further details contact the Program Officer
Closing Date: 12 November

For further information contact:

Tel: (61) 2 9215 9108
Email: p.keogh@australiacouncil.gov.au
Contact: Peter Keogh, Program Officer, Music

Music Program

Subjects: Music
Purpose: Supports organisations with a track record of achievement in presentation, service delivery, skills development or other relevant areas
Eligibility: Open to organisations which meet the eligibility requirements and provide the necessary support materials
Value: Up to A$50,000
Length of Study: 1 year
Frequency: Annual

For further information contact:

Tel: (61) 2 9215 9301
Email: m.collett@australiacouncil.gov.au
Contact: Morwenna Collett, Program Manager, Music

Music Skills and Development

Subjects: Music
Purpose: To support skills development for professional artists and arts workers

Eligibility: Open to individuals and organisations which meet the eligibility requirements and provide the necessary support materials
Type: Grant
Value: Up to A$10,000
Frequency: Every 2 years
Application Procedure: Apply online
Closing Date: 25 March
Additional Information: There are two subcategories: individuals and groups (established and emerging), and organisations (legally constituted). Please mail to music@australiacouncil.gov.au for further information

For further information contact:

Tel: (61) 2 9215 9108
Email: p.keogh@australiacouncil.gov.au
Contact: Peter Keogh, Program Officer

OZCO Community Cultural Development Fellowship

Subjects: Community-based arts
Purpose: To enhance the capacity of artists and artsworkers to provide leadership in the field
Eligibility: Applicants should have a solid record of achievement in community arts and culture, including community cultural development
Level of Study: Postgraduate, Professional development
Type: Fellowship
Value: A$40,000
Length of Study: 2 years
Frequency: Annual
Country of Study: Australia
Application Procedure: Contact the department
Closing Date: 15 April
Funding: Government

For further information contact:

Tel: (61) 2 9215 9029
Email: ccd@ozco.gov.au

OZCO Community Culture Development Grant Residency

Subjects: Arts
Purpose: To afford an artist or arts worker the opportunity to take time out of project-based work and focus on professional development, reflection or individual arts practice
Eligibility: Artists applying require a driver's licence
Level of Study: Professional development

Type: Grant
Value: A$14,000 and an A$1,000 materials allowance
Frequency: Annual
Study Establishment: Hastings Council and Camden Haven Community College Inc
Country of Study: Australia
Application Procedure: Contact the department
Closing Date: 1 August
Funding: Government

For further information contact:

Tel: (61) 2 9215 9034
Email: m.martin@ozco.gov.au

OZCO Dance Fellowship

Subjects: Dance
Purpose: This grant is designed to support an established dance artist to undertake creative or professional development
Eligibility: This category is only open to individuals who are practising artists or arts workers. Applicant must meet the general eligibility requirements
Level of Study: Postdoctorate, Professional development
Type: Fellowship
Value: A$50,000 per year
Length of Study: 2 years
Frequency: Annual
Country of Study: Australia
Application Procedure: Applicants are encouraged to apply online for this category
Closing Date: 31 July
Funding: Government
Additional Information: Please contact to dance@australiacouncil.gov.au for further information

For further information contact:

Tel: (61) 2 9215 9164
Email: a.burnett@australiacouncil.gov.au
Contact: Adrian Burnett, Program Manager, Dance

OZCO Dance Grant Initiative: Take Your Partner

Subjects: Dance and movement arts
Purpose: To support young and emerging dance artists and art workers to forge a new relationship or build on an existing one through a specific project
Level of Study: Professional development
Type: Grant
Value: A$15,000

Frequency: Annual
Country of Study: Australia
Application Procedure: Contact the department
Closing Date: May–June
Funding: Government

For further information contact:

Tel: (61) 2 9215 9179
Email: s.woo@ozco.gov.au
Contact: Sandi Woo

OZCO Literature Fellowships

Subjects: Fiction, literary non-fiction (defined by the Literature Board as autobiography, biography, essays, histories criticism or other analytical prose); children's and young adult literature; poetry; and creative writing for performance or new media
Purpose: To support excellence in Australian literature
Eligibility: Applications will only be accepted from individuals who have had a minimum of major works published or performed and have achieved substantial critical recognition
Level of Study: Postgraduate, Professional development
Type: Fellowship
Value: A$100,000 over two years (paid in three instalments)
Length of Study: 2 years
Frequency: Annual
Country of Study: Australia
Application Procedure: Applicants are encouraged to apply online for this category. Duly filled application along with relevant supporting material, curriculum vitae, and one copy of two published books or performed plays in the genre of the project should be provided. For further details contact the Program Manager
Closing Date: 15 May
Funding: Government

For further information contact:

Tel: (61) 2 9215 9057
Email: literature@ozco.gov.au;
               j.simpson@australiacouncil.gov.au
Contact: Joanne Simpson, Program Officer, Literature

OZCO Literature Grants Initiative: Write in Your Face

Subjects: Writing in zines, e-zines, comics, multimedia, multi-art forms, websites, live performance and spoken word
Purpose: To support young writers using language in innovative ways

Eligibility: Applicant must be aged 30 years or under
Level of Study: Professional development
Type: Grant
Value: Up to A$5,000
Frequency: Annual
Country of Study: Australia
Application Procedure: Contact the department. Apply online
Closing Date: 9 December

For further information contact:

Tel: (61) 29215 9058
Email: j.jones@ozco.gov.au
Contact: J. Jones

OZCO Music Fellowship

Subjects: Music
Purpose: These two-year fellowship support outstanding, established music artists to produce new work and/or undertake professional development
Eligibility: This category is open to individuals who meet the general eligibility requirements. Fellowship recipients may not apply for a Project Fellowship where the start date of the Project Fellowship is less than five years after the end date of their Fellowship
Level of Study: Postdoctorate, Professional development
Type: Fellowship
Value: A$100,000 ($50,000 per year for two years)
Length of Study: 2 years
Frequency: Annual
Country of Study: Australia
Application Procedure: Applicants are encouraged to apply online for this category
Closing Date: 31 July
Funding: Government
Additional Information: Fellowship recipients may apply for funding from other categories during the term of the Fellowship, with the exception of the project Fellowships initiative. Fellowships are granted only once in an artist's lifetime

For further information contact:

Tel: (61) 2 9215 9115
Email: music@australiacouncil.gov.au
Contact: Andy Rantzen, Program Officer, Music

OZCO Music Project Fellowship

Subjects: Music
Purpose: These grants support mid-career and established artists to develop significant creative and/or developmental projects over a period of up to 12 months

Eligibility: Music artists working in music theatre and indigenous music artists are particularly encouraged to apply
Level of Study: Postgraduate, Professional development
Type: Fellowship
Value: A$30,000
Length of Study: 1 year
Frequency: Annual
Country of Study: Australia
Application Procedure: Apply online
Closing Date: 31 July
Funding: Government
Additional Information: Please mail to music@austra liacouncil.gov.au for further information.

For further information contact:

Tel: (61) 2 9215 9108
Email: music@ozco.gov.au; p.keogh@australiacouncil. gov.au
Contact: Peter Keogh, Program Officer, Music

OZCO New Media Residency

Subjects: New Media Arts
Purpose: To support hybrid and new media study abroad
Level of Study: Postdoctorate, Postgraduate
Type: Fellowship
Length of Study: 1 year
Frequency: Annual
Study Establishment: Banff Centre for the Arts
Country of Study: Canada
Application Procedure: Apply online
Closing Date: 1 November
Funding: Government

For further information contact:

Email: nma@ozco.gov.au

OZCO Theatre Fellowship

Subjects: Theatre studies
Purpose: To financially support an individuals professional development
Eligibility: It is for artists with a record of outstanding achievement. Applicant must meet the general eligibility requirements and any specific eligibility requirements provided for this grant. In addition, applicant must be able to demonstrate at least 10 years' professional theatre experience

Level of Study: Postgraduate, Professional development
Type: Fellowship
Value: A$45,000 per year over two years
Length of Study: 2 years
Frequency: Annual
Country of Study: Australia
Application Procedure: It is strongly recommended that you discuss your application with staff before applying. Applicants are encouraged to apply online for this category. Duly filled application along with relevant supporting material should be sent. For further details contact the Program Manager
Closing Date: 5 November
Funding: Government

For further information contact:

Tel: (61) 2 9215 9040
Email: theatre@ozco.gov.au; w.stanton@australiacouncil.gov.au
Contact: Willa Stanton, Program Officer, Theatre

OZCO Visual Arts Fellowship

Subjects: Visual arts
Purpose: To provide financial support to visual artists, craftspeople and specialist visual arts and craft writers of outstanding achievement to enable them to create new work and further develop their practice
Eligibility: This category is open to individual artists. Applications will be selected that best demonstrate: outstanding professional achievement; the artistic merit of the activities proposed for the fellowship period
Level of Study: Postgraduate
Type: Fellowship
Value: A$120,000 over two years (in three instalments)
Length of Study: Up to 2 years
Frequency: Annual
Country of Study: Australia
Application Procedure: Applicants are encouraged to apply online for this category. Duly filled application along with relevant supporting material should be sent. For further details contact the Program Manager
Closing Date: 16 April
Funding: Government
Additional Information: Fellowships are granted only once in an artist's lifetime

For further information contact:

Tel: (61) 2 9215 9020
Email: vac@ozco.gov.au; s.saxon@australiacouncil.gov.au
Contact: Sandy Saxon, Program Officer, Visual Arts

Playing Australia: Regional Performing Arts Touring Fund

Purpose: These grants assist the touring of professionally produced performing arts across Australia, including regional and remote areas, where there is a demonstrated public demand and tours are otherwise not commercially viable ·
Eligibility: This category is open to organisations only
Type: Grant
Value: Varies
Application Procedure: Apply online. You are encouraged to apply online for this grants program. To begin an online application, use the 'Apply online' button in the right-hand column. Please select 'Market Development' when prompted to choose a board
Closing Date: 1 December
Additional Information: Please mail to artsdevelopment@australiacouncil.gov.au for further information.

For further information contact:

Tel: (61) 2 9215 9176
Email: T.Kita@australiacouncil.gov.au
Contact: Tara Kita, Program Officer, Market Development

Projects – Creative Development

Purpose: These grants provide support for the research and creative development of new dance works
Eligibility: To be eligible, you must meet the general eligibility requirements and the specific eligibility requirements given below. This category is open to individuals, groups and organisations. Dance Key Organisations are not eligible to apply to this category
Type: Grant
Application Procedure: You are encouraged to apply online for this grant. To begin an online application, use the 'Apply online' button in the right-hand column. Please select 'Dance' when prompted to choose a board for your application. For other ways to apply, please see How to apply in Your application
Closing Date: 16 August
Additional Information: Please mail to dance@australiacouncil.gov.au for further information

For further information contact:

Tel: (61) 2 9215 9179
Email: k.morcombe@australiacouncil.gov.au
Contact: Kiri Morcombe, Program Officer, Dance

Projects – Presentation

Subjects: Dance
Purpose: The purpose of this grant is to provide support for dance works with a presentation outcome. This can include final stage creative development and presentation/s and remounts of dance works
Eligibility: To be eligible, you must meet the general eligibility requirements and the specific eligibility requirements given at the website. This category is open to individuals, groups and organisations. Key Organisations are not eligible to apply to this category
Type: Grant
Value: Up to A$50,000
Application Procedure: You are encouraged to apply online for this grant. To begin an online application, use the 'Apply online' button in the right-hand column. Please select 'Dance' when prompted to choose a board for your application. For other ways to apply, please see How to apply in Your application
Closing Date: 15 August
Additional Information: Please mail to dance@australiacouncil.gov.au for further information

For further information contact:

Tel: (61) 2 9215 9179
Email: k.morcombe@australiacouncil.gov.au
Contact: Kiri Morcombe, Program Officer, Dance

The Dreaming Award

Purpose: This award supports a young artist aged 18–26 years to create a major body of work through mentoring and partnerships, either nationally or internationally
Eligibility: To be eligible you must be: an individual practicing Aboriginal and/or Torres Strait Islander artist aged 18-26 years
Type: Award
Value: A$20,000
Country of Study: Any country
Application Procedure: Apply online
Closing Date: 19 November
Additional Information: Please mail to atsia@australiacouncil.gov.au for further information

For further information contact:

Email: a.welch@australiacouncil.gov.au

The Red Ochre Award

Purpose: The Aboriginal and the Torres Strait Islander Arts Board established The Red Ochre Award in 1993 to pay tribute to an Aboriginal or Torres Strait Islander artist who, throughout their lifetime, has made outstanding contributions to the recognition of Aboriginal and Torres Strait Islander arts, both nationally and internationally

Eligibility: Nominations will be accepted from arts and community organisations and individuals. Nominations may only be made for living artists and individuals cannot nominate themselves. This award is not project based and, therefore is not given to assist any particular project, program or intended activity

Type: Award

Value: A$50,000

Country of Study: Any country

Application Procedure: Apply online. Contact organisation for details

Closing Date: 19 November

Additional Information: Please mail to atsia@australiacouncil.gov.au for further information

For further information contact:

Tel: (61) 2 9215 9067
Email: atsiamail@australiacouncil.gov.au
Contact: Frank Trotman-Golden, Program Officer

Visions of Australia: Regional Exhibition Touring Fund

Purpose: Visions of Australia supports the development and touring of major public exhibitions of Australian cultural material throughout Australia, particularly into regional and remote areas

Eligibility: To be eligible, you must meet the general eligibility requirements and the specific eligibility requirements given at the website. This category is open to organisations only

Type: Funding support

Value: No maximum grant amount

Application Procedure: You are encouraged to apply online for this grant. To begin an online application, use the 'Apply online' button (www.australiacouncil.gov.au/grants/2013/visions-of-australia). Please select 'Market Development' when prompted to choose a board for your application. For other ways to apply, please see How to apply in Your application

Closing Date: 1 December

Additional Information: Please mail to artsdevelopment@australiacouncil.gov.au for further information. Potential applicants are encouraged to discuss their application. For information and any questions relating to this grants program, please contact Tata Kita

For further information contact:

Tel: (61) 2 9215 9176
Email: t.kita@australiacouncil.gov.au
Contact: Tara Kita, Program Officer, Market Development

Visual Arts New Work

Subjects: Visual arts

Purpose: To support the creation of new work by emerging and established craftspeople, designers, new media artists, visual artists, and arts writers

Eligibility: Open to individuals and groups that meet the eligibility requirements and provide the necessary support materials

Value: A$10,000 for emerging and $20,000 for established craftspeople, designers, new media artists, visual artists and arts writers

Frequency: Annual

Application Procedure: Applications should include the required support materials. Apply online. Check website for further details. For further details contact the Program Officer

Closing Date: 16 April

Contributor: National Association for the Visual Arts (NAVA)

For further information contact:

Tel: (61) 2 9215 9020
Email: s.saxon@australiacouncil.gov.au
Contact: Sandy Saxon, Program Officer, Visual Arts

Visual Arts Presentation and Promotion

Subjects: Contemporary Australian craft, design, media and visual arts

Purpose: To assist arts organisations to present and promote contemporary Australian craft, design, new media art and visual arts, to audiences in Australia and overseas

Eligibility: Open to organisations that meet the eligibility requirements and provide the necessary support materials

Frequency: Annual

Application Procedure: Applications should include the required support materials and apply online

Closing Date: 20 August

For further information contact:

Tel: (61) 2 9215 9131
Email: v.lloyd@australiacouncil.gov.au
Contact: Vanessa Lloyd, Program Officer, Visual Arts Board

Visual Arts Skills and Arts Development

Subjects: Visual arts

Purpose: To enable professional development opportunities for craftspeople, designers, media artists, visual artists, arts writers and curators

Eligibility: Open to individuals and groups which meet the eligibility requirements and provide the necessary support materials

Type: Grant
Value: Supports artists to undertake professional development activities in Australia or overseas. A\$10,000 for Barcelona, Helsinki, Liverpool, London, New York, Paris, Rome or Tokyo; A\$25,000 for New York; A\$35,000 for Berlin residencies
Length of Study: More than 1 year (General). 3-month residency in Barcelona, Helsinki, Liverpool, London, New York, Paris, Rome or Tokyo; 6-month residency in New York; 12-month residency in Berlin
Frequency: Annual
Application Procedure: Apply online
Closing Date: 20 August
Additional Information: Please mail to visualarts@australiacouncil.gov.au for further information

For further information contact:

Tel: (61) 2 9215 9336
Email: r.petersen@australiacouncil.gov.au
Contact: Romany Petersen, Program Officer, Visual Arts

Australian Academy of Science

PO Box 783, Canberra, ACT 2601, Australia

Tel: (61) 2 6247 3966
Fax: (61) 2 6257 4620
Email: io@science.org.au
Website: www.science.org.au/internat
Contact: International Programmes Officer

The Australian Academy of Science is an independent, non-profit organisation with a membership of 300 Fellows elected for making distinguished contributions in the area of natural sciences and their applications. The objectives of the Academy are to promote science and science education through a range of activities.

Max Day Environmental Science Fellowship Award

Subjects: Applicants must demonstrate a multi-disciplinary approach to their research work and conduct their research in one or more of the biological sciences relating to one or more of the following disciplines: Conservation of Australia's flora and fauna, Ecologically sustainable resource use, Environmental protection and Ecosystem services (either provisioning services, or habitat and supporting services)

Purpose: The Australian Academy of Science is inviting applications Max Day Environmental Science Fellowship Award. These fellowships are available to assist early stage PhD students or early career researchers with their research
Eligibility: Citizens of Australia are eligible to apply
Type: Research
Value: The Max Day Environmental Science Fellowship Award is an annual award of up to A\$20,000 per awardee to assist early stage PhD students or early career researchers with their research. It provides funding support toward the costs of travel, courses or research expenses. Grants are GST exclusive
Study Establishment: Applicants must demonstrate a multi-disciplinary approach to their research work and conduct their research in one or more of the biological sciences relating to one or more of the following disciplines: Conservation of Australia's flora and fauna, Ecologically sustainable resource use, Environmental protection and Ecosystem services (either provisioning services, or habitat and supporting services)
Country of Study: Australia
Application Procedure: Applications must be sent via email
Closing Date: 1 June
Additional Information: For more details please visit the website scholarship-positions.com/max-day-environmental-science-fellowship-award-australia/2018/02/22/

For further information contact:

Email: awards@science.org.au

Prostate Cancer Research Centre - NSW

Purpose: The objectives of the grant are: 1. to safeguard a prostate cancer biobank and databank through providing support for infrastructure and its maintenance for a period of up to six months. 2. establish a sustainability plan for future funding for the Australian Prostate Cancer Research Centre – NSW, Garvan Institute of Medical Research
Eligibility: The Australian Prostate Cancer Research Centre (APCRC) – NSW is the eligible organisation to apply for this Grant Opportunity
Level of Study: Postgraduate, Research
Type: Grant
Frequency: Annual
Country of Study: Any country
Closing Date: 21 January
Funding: Government

For further information contact:

Email: Grant.ATM@health.gov.au

Australian Academy of the Humanities (AAH)

3 Liversidge Street Acton, Canberra, ACT 2601, Australia

Tel:	(61) 6125 9860
Fax:	(61) 6248 6287
Email:	enquiries@humanities.org.au
Website:	www.humanities.org.au
Contact:	Administration Officer

The Australian Academy of the Humanities (AAH) was established under Royal Charter in 1969 for the advancement of the scholarship, interest in and understanding of the humanities. Humanities disciplines include, but are not limited to, history, classics, English, European languages and cultures, Asian studies, philosophy, the arts, linguistics, prehistory and archaeology and cultural and communications studies.

Australian Academy of the Humanities Visiting Scholar Programmes

Subjects: Arts and humanities
Purpose: To encourage scholarly contact with scholars from both Russia/the former USSR and Indonesia/South—East Asia and to assist scholars from those countries to obtain access to research materials held in Australia
Eligibility: Applicants must be identified as being appropriate representatives at Australia-based conferences
Level of Study: Doctorate, Postdoctorate
Type: Award
Value: A$7,000 (for 2 scholars from Russia and the Former USSR) and A$4,000 (for 2 scholars from Indonesia and South—East Asia)
Frequency: Annual
Country of Study: Australia
No. of awards offered: 7
Application Procedure: Applicant (Australian host scholar) must send the Secretariat a brief explanation of the reason for the visit, a copy of the visiting scholar's curriculum vitae and a list of their most significant publications (in English), a provisional itinerary listing speaking engagements, potential contact with Australian scholars and research institutions to be visited and a provisional budget for the expenditure of the funds
Closing Date: 31 July
Funding: Government
No. of awards given last year: 2
No. of applicants last year: 7

Additional Information: Eligible to nationals of: Russia and SE Asia

For further information contact:

Tel:	(61) 2 6125 8950
Email:	grants@humanities.org.au
Contact:	Jorge Salavert

The British Special Joint Project Funding Scheme

Subjects: All subjects
Eligibility: The principal applicant on the Australian side should be normally a resident of Australia. Other scholars associated with the project will normally be expected to be of postdoctoral status
Level of Study: Postdoctorate
Type: Award
Value: Up to £8,000 (if 1 award is given) or up to £4,000 per project (if 2 awards are given)
Length of Study: Up to 1 year
Frequency: Annual
Country of Study: United Kingdom and Australia
No. of awards offered: 22
Application Procedure: Applicants from both sides must submit applications to the appropriate Academy. Australian scholars should apply through either the AAH or ASSA, depending on the nature of their project. Australian partners should consult the AAH or ASSA for application procedures. Equivalent information must be included on all application forms. All applications for Academy grants are considered in the light of referees comments
No. of awards given last year: 2
No. of applicants last year: 22

For further information contact:

Tel:	(61) 2 6125 8950
Email:	grants@humanities.org.au
Contact:	Jorge Salavert

Australian Bio Security-CRC (AB-CRC)

Building 76 Molecular Biosciences The University of Queensland, St Lucia, QLD 4072, Australia

Tel:	(61) 3346 8866
Fax:	(61) 3346 8862
Email:	corinna.lange@abcrc.org.au
Website:	www.abcrc.org.au
Contact:	Mrs Corinna Lange, Communications Manager

The mission of the ABCRC is to protect Australia's public health, livestock, wildlife and economic resources through research and education that strengthens the national capability to detect, diagnose, identify, monitor, assess, predict and to respond to emerging infectious disease threats.

AB-CRC Honours Scholarships

Subjects: Biosecurity and emerging infectious diseases
Purpose: To encourage students of high academic ability to take the first step in their career path as a researcher. To build research capacity in high priority areas related to biosecurity
Eligibility: Scholarships will be awarded preferentially to Australian residents and students from the Asia-Pacific region
Level of Study: Postgraduate
Type: Scholarship
Value: A$5,000 per year (full-time) or A$2,500 per year (part-time)
Length of Study: 1 or 2 years for a part-time scholarship
Frequency: Annual
Study Establishment: AB-CRC participating university
Country of Study: Australia
Application Procedure: Contact the scholarships Administrator officer
Closing Date: 31 October

For further information contact:

Tel: (61) 8 9266 1634
Email: debra.gendle@abcrc.org.au
Contact: Debra Gendle

AB-CRC Professional Development Scholarships

Subjects: Bio Security and emerging infectious diseases
Purpose: To enhance linkages with research projects of relevance to the AB-CRC. To expand our capability to support the training of specialists. To provide students with access to the AB-CRC network and enhanced learning opportunities
Eligibility: PhD students enroled at AB-CRC partner organizations
Level of Study: Professional development
Type: Scholarship
Value: A$2,000 per year
Length of Study: Varies
Frequency: Annual
Study Establishment: AB-CRC participating university
Country of Study: Australia

Application Procedure: Students must submit a Professional Development Plan. Contact the Scholarships Administration officer
Closing Date: 16 November
Additional Information: Candidates will be required to sign a confidentially agreement. Funding awarded in a Professional Development Scholarship will be on a sliding scale depending upon the student's enrolment date

For further information contact:

Email: debra.gendle@abcrc.org.uk
Contact: Debra Gendle

Australian Catholic University (ACU)

Brisbane Campus (McAuley at Banyo), PO Box 456, Virginia, QLD 4014, Australia

Tel: (61) 2 9739 2305, 7 3623 7100
Fax: (61) 7 3623 7249
Email: studentcentre@mcauley.acu.edu.au
Website: www.acu.edu.au

Australian Catholic University (ACU) is a public university funded by the Australian Government and is open to students and staff of all beliefs. It has established a reputation for quality and innovative teaching and specialist tertiary education in health, education, business and informatics, arts, social sciences and theology.

Adolescent Health and Performance Scholarship

Subjects: Exercise science
Purpose: To attract a highly motivated postgraduate student who is interested in serially tracking the musculoskeletal health and performance of elite adolescent female athletes
Eligibility: Open to citizens or permanent residents of Australia between the ages of 22 and 30 to study in Australia. The candidate must have achieved First Class Honours or equivalent and have studied at or be currently studying at Australian Catholic University
Level of Study: Graduate
Type: Scholarship
Value: A$25,627 per year
Length of Study: 3 years
Study Establishment: Australian Catholic University
Country of Study: Australia

Application Procedure: Candidates must apply directly to the Australian Catholic University

Additional Information: It is required that the study starts no earlier than 15 September and no later than 15 October

For further information contact:

Email: robina.bamforth@acu.edu.au
Contact: Ms Robina Bamforth, Manager

Co-op Bookshop Scholarship

Eligibility: Open to students from rural or regional areas enroled in any course at any campus at Australian Catholic University who are Australian citizens or permanent residents

Type: Scholarship

Value: One scholarship valued at A$2,500 is available each year, paid as a Co-op Bookshop Book Voucher

Length of Study: 2 years

Frequency: Annual

Country of Study: Any country

Closing Date: Early March

Council of Catholic School Parents (NSW) Indigenous Postgraduate Scholarship (IES)

Subjects: Education

Purpose: To encourage involvement of parents and the community in education

Eligibility: Open to Indigenous students enroled in a postgraduate course within the faculty of education at the Strathfield campus, and have a particular focus, interest, or understanding of the importance of parent and community involvement in education

Type: Scholarship

Value: A$1,000 and a certificate

Frequency: Annual

Study Establishment: Strathfield campus

Country of Study: Australia

Application Procedure: Candidates can obtain further information from Yalbalinga Indigenous Unit, Strathfield campus. Online applications only

Closing Date: 18 March

Contributor: Council of Catholic School Parents (NSW)

Additional Information: Please check further information from Yalbalinga Indigenous Unit, Strathfield campus OR www.acu.edu.au/scholarships

For further information contact:

Email: futurestudents@acu.edu.au

International Postgraduate Research Scholarships (IPRS)

Purpose: To financially assist student to undertake full time postgraduate study who are otherwise unable to take up studies due to personal reasons (excluding employment)

Eligibility: Only international students are eligible for IPRS

Level of Study: Research

Type: Scholarship

Value: Full tuition fees (as approved by Common wealth Govt)

Length of Study: 2–3 years

Frequency: Annual

Study Establishment: Australian Catholic University (ACU)

Country of Study: Australia

Application Procedure: Application forms and further information on scholarships may be obtained by accessing the research services web site www.acu.edu.au/research

Closing Date: 31 October

For further information contact:

Email: Res.Cand@patrick.acu.edu.au

Pratt Foundation Bursary (IES)

Subjects: All subjects

Purpose: To make available a bursary to a suitably qualified Aboriginal and Torres Strait Islander student undertaking postgraduate study at ACU

Eligibility: Open to suitably qualified Aboriginal and Torres Strait Islander student undertaking postgraduate study at ACU National

Level of Study: Graduate

Type: Bursary

Value: A$2,500

Frequency: Annual

Study Establishment: Australian Catholic University (ACU)

Country of Study: Australia

Application Procedure: Candidates can obtain further information from Weemala Indigenous Unit, Brisbane campus. Online applications only

Closing Date: 18 March

Funding: Foundation

Contributor: The Pratt Foundation

For further information contact:

Email: futurestudents@acu.edu.au

Victorian International Research Scholarships

Purpose: The Victorian International Research Scholarship (VIRS) is offered in partnership between the Victorian Government and Victorian Universities. The Scholarship supports high-calibre international PhD scholars to undertake research in Victoria

Eligibility: Open to an international student; who accepted into a doctoral programme at ACU; intend to complete the majority of work related to the doctorate in Victoria; not have completed a degree equivalent to an Australian doctorate; willingness to act as an ambassador for the (VIRS) program

Level of Study: Doctorate

Type: Scholarship

Value: A$90,000 over 3 years

Length of Study: Successful applicants will receive a scholarship of A$90,000 for the duration of their PhD

Frequency: Every 3 years

Country of Study: Any country

Application Procedure: Applicants must be a citizen of a country other than Australia

Closing Date: Please check website

Additional Information: For further information, visit Study Melbourne, or email your application (MS Word document, 2.8 MB) to VIC.cand@acu.edu.au. Please note that you will also be asked to submit an application for candidature at ACU

Australian Centre for Blood Diseases (ACBD)

6th Floor, Burnet Tower, 89 Commercial Road, Melbourne, VIC 3004, Australia

Tel: (61) 3 990 30122
Fax: (61) 3 990 30228
Email: acbd@med.monash.edu.au
Website: www.acbd.monash.org

The Australian Centre for Blood Diseases (ACBD) brings together the skills and facilities of separate yet complementary organizations to enhance understanding of blood and its diseases. Its aim is to provide excellence in the diagnosis and treatment of blood conditions as well as play a leading role in the advancement of knowledge in this increasingly important area of medicine.

Firkin PhD Scholarship

Subjects: Cardiovascular disciplines

Purpose: To undertake a PhD programme at the ACBD or affiliated institutes comprising AMREP

Eligibility: Open to students interested in pursuing doctorate studies in cardiovascular disciplines, and who have the appropriate graduate qualifications

Level of Study: Graduate

Type: Scholarships

Value: A$22,500 per year

Length of Study: 3 years

Frequency: Annual

Application Procedure: For further information, please contact Dr Robert Medcalf

Closing Date: See website for exact details

For further information contact:

Australian Centre for Blood Diseases, Monash University, 6th Floor, Burnet Building, AMREP, Commercial Road, Australia

Email: Robert.Medcalf@med.monash.edu.au
Contact: Dr Robert Medcalf, Associate Professor

Australian Department of Science

PO Box 65, Belconnen, ACT 2616, Australia

Contact: Grants & Fellowships Branch

Disability, Mental Health and Carers: National Disability Conference Initiative

Purpose: The Australian Government is inviting applications in an open process to apply to deliver services under the Disability, Mental Health and Carer: National Disability Conference Initiative in

Eligibility: To be eligible, applicants to the National Disability Conference Initiative (NDCI) must be one of the following entity types: 1. Indigenous Corporation. 2. Company. 3. Incorporated Association. 4. Cooperative. Applications from consortia are acceptable, as long as you have a lead applicant who is solely accountable to the Commonwealth for the delivery of grant activities

Level of Study: Graduate

Type: Grant
Value: A maximum of A\$10,000 (GST exclusive) per conference is available for this grant opportunity
Frequency: Annual
Country of Study: Any country
Application Procedure: For further information on this grants, visit the website. www.communitygrants.gov.au/grants/disability-mental-health-and-carers-conference
Closing Date: 20 February
Funding: Government

For further information contact:

Email: support@communitygrants.gov.au

Australian Federation of University Women (AFUW)

School of Education, University of Ballarat, PO Box 663, Ballarat, VIC 3353, Australia

Tel: (61) 9557 2556
Email: AFGW.Fellowships@gmail.com
Website: www.afuw.org.au
Contact: Dr Jacqueline Wilson, AFUW Vic Membership Secretary

Australian Federation of University Women (AFUW) Victoria was formed in 1922 as part of the international network of women Graduates for the benefit of women and society. AFUW Victoria is a member association of AFUW and serves a number of benefits both at personal and societal level in providing women with opportunities.

Australian Federation of University Women - Western Australian -Foundation Bursary

Subjects: Any subject. No specific criteria
Eligibility: Candidate should be women and must be a graduate members of the Australian Federation of University Women
Level of Study: Postdoctorate
Type: Bursary
Value: A\$2,500
Frequency: Annual
Country of Study: Any country
Funding: Private

For further information contact:

Bursary Office, AFUW (WA), Inc., PO Box 48, Nedlands, WT 6009, Australia

Email: afuwwa@afuw.org.au

Study in Australia - Northern Territory Scholarships

Subjects: The scholarships recognise student's academic merit, leadership and community engagement
Purpose: This scholarship is provided to talented students from all over the world to study in Australia's Northern Territory. The scholarships recognize student's academic merit, leadership and community engagement
Eligibility: Applicants must: 1. have a demonstrated record of academic excellence, community engagement and leadership. 2. meet the Northern Territory education provider's academic and English entry requirement. 3. have applied and obtained an offer of admission to a Northern Territory education provider for study in the Northern Territory. i. Alana Kaye College. ii. Australian Careers College. iii. BCA National Training Group. iv. Charles Darwin University. v. Darwin High School. vi. International College of Advanced Education. vii. International House Darwin. viii. Navitas English Darwin. ix. Navitas Professional. x. The Essington International School Darwin. 4. reside in the Northern Territory. 5. not already be studying in the Northern Territory, or with a Northern Territory education provider. 6. not hold any other scholarship
Level of Study: Graduate
Type: Scholarship
Value: The scholarships are worth school (\$10 000), English language (\$5,000), vocational education and training (\$7,500), Professional Year Program (\$2,500) and higher education
Frequency: Annual
Country of Study: Australia
Application Procedure: For the complete information on the application methods, use the below link. studynt.nt.gov.au/file/923
Closing Date: 31 January
Funding: Private

For further information contact:

Email: StudyNT.nt.gov.au

Women's Leadership and Development Program (WLDP) - Women's Economic Security Grant Guidelines

Subjects: 1. The WLDP - Women's Economic Security Grant Guidelines contain information specifically for Women's Economic Security grants. 2. Improving women's economic security across their lifetimes. 3. Improving women's financial literacy skills. 4. Improving women's health (including mental health) (as an obstacle to economic security). 5. Addressing the economic consequences of violence. 6. Reducing women's homelessness

Purpose: The grant opportunity is to provide funding for one-off or small-scale projects that contribute towards achieving Women's Economic Security on a national scale within Australia

Eligibility: 1. A Company incorporated in Australia. 2. A Company incorporated by guarantee. 3. An Incorporated trustee on behalf of a trust. 4. A Publicly funded research organisation as defined in the Glossary. 5. An Aboriginal and/or Torres Strait Islander Corporation registered under the Corporations

Level of Study: Foundation programme

Type: Grant

Frequency: Annual

Country of Study: Any country

Closing Date: 25 January

Funding: Foundation

For further information contact:

Tel: (61) 2 6271 6074
Email: WLDP17-18@pmc.gov.au

Australian Government Research Training Scholarships

Flinders University is a public university in Adelaide, South Australia. The university is ranked within the world's top 400 institutions in the Academic Ranking of World Universities. Flinders University offers more than 160 undergraduate and postgraduate courses, as well as higher degree research supervision across all disciplines. Flinders University is renowned for world-class research and innovation that is relevant, of high quality, and has real impact.

Australian Biological Resources Study (ABRS) National Taxonomy Research Grant Program

Purpose: The Australian Biological Resources Study (ABRS) provides research grants to Postdoctoral Fellows and established researchers to undertake research relevant to the taxonomy and systematics of the Australian biota

Eligibility: 1. All Research grants have a co-funding requirement. That is, applicants must have obtained a commitment for the applicable amount of co-funding for their application to be considered. 2. The ABRS will place no restrictions on the source of this contribution, but applicants will need to be aware of the rules of other granting agencies, which may limit how funds contributed by them may be used

Level of Study: Doctorate, Postdoctorate

Type: Research grant

Value: Research Grants of A$10,000, A$35,000, A$70,000 or A$90,000 per annum (excluding GST) are available, as well as a A$90,000 per annum (excluding GST) Postdoctoral Fellowship grant

Frequency: Every 3 years

Country of Study: Any country

Closing Date: 22 November

Funding: Private

Additional Information: There are some funding agreement being meant for this funding scheme. All grant recipients who receive funding from the ABRS under the current and upcoming round, are subject to the terms and conditions set out in the ABRS Grant Funding Agreement. The Department of the Environment and Energy has developed standard funding agreements for grants. Applicants who are successful in receiving funding under the ABRS NTRGP are subject to the conditions set out in the following funding agreement templates. For further information towards the template, kindly visit our website. www.environment.gov.au/science/abrs/grants/research-grants

For further information contact:

Business and Grants Manager Australian Biological Resources Study Department of the Environment and Energy GPO Box 787, Canberra ACT 2601, Australia

Email: abrs.grants@environment.gov.au

Australian Security Intelligence Organisation Scheme

Purpose: It provides legal financial assistance for a person summoned by the Australian Security Intelligence Organisation (ASIO) to appear before a prescribed authority for questioning

Eligibility: At a minimum, you must: be a non-tax-exempt company, Australian University, Cooperative Research Centre (CRC) or Publicly Funded Research Agency (PRFA) have ownership, access to, or the beneficial use of any intellectual property necessary to carry out the projects under the JSF Program be able to match the value of funding dollar for dollar (co-contribution required) not be one of the companies engaged on the development of the Joint Strike Fighter (JSF)

Level of Study: Graduate

Type: Other

Value: complete value of the award is A$3,316,000.00

Frequency: Annual

Country of Study: Any country

Closing Date: 7 September

Funding: Government

For further information contact:

Tel: (61) 3 9268 7974

Email: FinassGeneral@ag.gov.au

Expensive Commonwealth Criminal Cases Fund (ECCCF)

Purpose: The Australian Government is inviting legal aid commissions to apply for reimbursement under the Expensive Commonwealth Criminal Cases Fund. This program, open to legal aid commissions, ensures that legal aid commissions have sufficient resources to provide a legal defence for people charged with serious Commonwealth criminal offences who cannot afford private legal representation

Eligibility: 1. Only legal aid commissions can apply for reimbursement under the ECCCF. 2. A legal aid commission is a statutory body established pursuant to legislation in the relevant state or territory to provide legal aid services

Level of Study: Graduate

Type: Funding support

Frequency: Annual

Country of Study: Any country

Closing Date: 30 August

Funding: Private

For further information contact:

Email: support@communitygrants.gov.au

National Disability Insurance Scheme Jobs and Market Fund Round 1

Purpose: The National Disability Insurance Scheme (NDIS) is a significant social and economic policy reform representing one of the largest job creation opportunities in Australia. Achieving choice and control for participants requires a well-functioning market of NDIS providers, from which empowered NDIS participants are able to choose quality services that meet their needs

Eligibility: To be eligible you must be one of the following entity types: 1. Indigenous Corporation. 2. Company. 3. Local Government. 4. Cooperative. 5. Incorporated Association. 6. Sole Trader. 7. Statutory Entity. 8. Partnership. 9. Trustee on behalf of a Trust

Level of Study: Graduate

Type: Scholarships

Frequency: Annual

Country of Study: Any country

Closing Date: 17 January

Funding: Government

Additional Information: This grant round is being administered by the Community Grants Hub, on behalf of the Department of Social Services

For further information contact:

Email: support@communitygrants.gov.au

Volunteer Grants

Purpose: The Volunteer Grants program aims to support the efforts of Australia's Volunteers. They provide small amounts of money that organisations can use to help their volunteers. The grants form part of the Government's work to support the volunteers who help disadvantaged Australian communities and encourage inclusion of vulnerable people in community life

Eligibility: Eligible applicants must be Australian not-for-profit organisations or community groups; whose volunteers' work supports families and/or communities in Australia

Level of Study: Graduate

Type: Grants and studentships

Value: A$5,000

Frequency: Annual

Country of Study: United Kingdom

Closing Date: 18 September

Funding: Private

For further information contact:

Email: support@communitygrants.gov.au

Australian Institute of Aboriginal and Torres Strait Islander Studies (AIATSIS)

GPO Box 553, Canberra, ACT 2601, Australia

Tel: (61) 2 6246 1157

Fax: (61) 2 6261 4285

Email: grants@aiatsis.gov.au
Website: www.aiatsis.gov.au
Contact: Mr Peter Veth, Research Administration Team

The Australian Institute of Aboriginal and Torres Strait Islander Studies (AIATSIS) is a federally funded organization devoted to Aboriginal and Torres Strait Islander research. Its principal function is to promote Australian Aboriginal and Torres Strait Islander studies. A staff of 90, directed by the Principal, engages in a range of services through the Research Programme, the Research Grants Programme, the archives and production team and the library.

Australian Institute of Aboriginal and Torres Strait Islander Studies Conference Call for papers

Subjects: Health, human biology, social anthropology, linguistics, ethnomusicology, material culture, rock art, prehistory, ethnobotany, psychology, education and aboriginal history including oral history, native title and indigenous land use agreements, indigenous knowledge systems
Purpose: To promote research into Aboriginal and Torres Strait Islander studies. AIATSIS welcomes a variety of presentation and workshop formats (ranging from 30 mins to 1.5 hours) including:
Eligibility: Open to nationals of any country
Level of Study: Unrestricted
Type: Grant
Value: No pre-determined value
Length of Study: Up to 1 year
Frequency: Annual
Country of Study: Australia
No. of awards offered: 101
Application Procedure: Applicants must complete an application form, available from the website
Closing Date: 18 January
Funding: Government
Contributor: The Australian Federal Government
No. of awards given last year: 31
No. of applicants last year: 101
Additional Information: Permission to conduct research projects must be obtained from the appropriate Aboriginal or Torres Strait Island community or organization

For further information contact:

Email: research@aiatsis.gov.au

Australian Institute of Nuclear Science and Engineering (AINSE)

Private Mail Bag 1, Menai, NSW 2234, Australia

Tel: (61) 2 9717 3376
Fax: (61) 2 9717 9268
Email: ainse@ansto.gov.au
Website: www.ansto.gov.au
Contact: Dr Dennis Mather, Scientific Secretary

Established in 1958, the Australian Institute of Nuclear Science and Engineering (AINSE) is a consortium of Australian universities and the University of Auckland, New Zealand, in partnership with the Australian Nuclear Science and Technology Organization (ANSTO). Its aims are to assist research and training in nuclear science and engineering, and to make the facilities of the Lucas Heights Research Laboratories available to research staff and students from member institutions.

Australian Institute of Nuclear Science and Engineering Awards

Subjects: Nuclear science and engineering
Purpose: Postgraduate Research Awards (PGRAs) are offered by AINSE Limited (the Australian Institute of Nuclear Science and Engineering) for suitably qualified persons wishing to undertake studies in AINSE's fields of interest for a higher degree at an AINSE member university
Eligibility: Open to member organizations of AINSE that are undertaking projects in an appropriate field
Level of Study: Unrestricted
Type: Grant
Value: Supplement stipend of A$7,500 per annum and a generous travel and accommodation allowance to enable students to work at ANSTO facilities
Length of Study: 1 year
Frequency: Annual
Study Establishment: Lucas Heights Science and Technology Centre
Country of Study: Australia
No. of awards offered: 232
Application Procedure: Applicants must contact the Scientific Secretary, AINSE or Research Office at member universities
Closing Date: 15 April
Funding: Government
No. of awards given last year: 179
No. of applicants last year: 232

For further information contact:

AINSE Ltd, Locked Bag 2001, Kirrawee DC, NSW 2232, Australia

Tel: (61) 2 9717 3436
Email: ainse@ainse.edu.au

Australian National University (ANU)

Fees and Scholarships Office, Building X-005, Canberra, ACT 2601, Australia

Tel: (61) 2 6125 5111
Fax: (61) 2 6125 7535
Email: research.scholarships@anu.edu.au
Website: www.anu.edu.au

The Australian National University (ANU) was founded by the Australian Government in 1946 as Australia's only completely research-orientated university. It comprises of seven colleges and many research schools.

Australian National University Doctoral Fellowships

Subjects: All subjects
Purpose: To help Doctoral students pursue research and dissertation writing
Eligibility: Open to candidates who have obtained their graduate degree from a university located in the United States
Level of Study: Doctorate
Type: Fellowships
Value: A$1,600 per month, one round-trip economy class airfare and some funding for research
Length of Study: 3–9 months
Frequency: Annual
Study Establishment: Australian National University
Country of Study: Australia
Application Procedure: Applicants can download the application form from the website. The completed application form can be sent by post or electronically
Closing Date: 30 January
Additional Information: Fellows accompanied by their family and staying for 6 months or more at the ANU will be entitled to family support of up to A$5,000, depending on the number of family members and other circumstances

For further information contact:

Email: hr.rspas@anu.edu.au

Australian National University Excellence Scholarship Program

Purpose: To study full-time in postgraduate program at the Australian National University
Value: $5,000 in the first 12 months of study at ANU followed by 10% discount of tuition fees for years of study thereafter
Country of Study: Australia
Closing Date: 30 May

For further information contact:

Email: coursework.scholarships@anu.edu.au

Australian National University-Study Canberra India Scholarship for Postgraduate and Undergraduates in Australia

Subjects: Scholarships are awarded in any of the subjects offered by the university
Purpose: The objective of the award is to provide support for living costs to successful applicants who have achieved at an excellent level in their final years of schooling or university studies
Eligibility: Indian citizens are eligible to apply for this scholarship programme. Applicants whose first language is not English are usually required to provide evidence of proficiency in English at the higher level required by the University
Type: Postgraduate scholarships
Value: The Scholarship will be valued at A$10,000. The first instalment of A$2,500 will be paid to the student upon them enrolling in the first semester of their chosen undergraduate or postgraduate coursework program. The remaining funds will be paid after the census date of the first semester that the student is enrolled
Study Establishment: Scholarships are awarded in any of the subjects offered by the university
Country of Study: Australia
Application Procedure: The mode of application is online
Closing Date: 15 January
Additional Information: For more details please visit the website scholarship-positions.com/anu-study-canberra-india-scholarship-postgraduate-undergraduates-australia/2017/12/18/

For further information contact:

Email: international.recruitment@anu.edu.au

College of Engineering and Computer Science: College Postgraduate International Award

Eligibility: The Scholarships are offered on the basis of offer of a place in the Master Degree by Coursework programs offered by the College of Engineering and Computer Science and other criteria as set out from time to time by the Program Authority. Eligible students will be automatically considered for the Scholarship on academic merit. The Scholarship is offered on the condition that the recipient is admitted to and continues to pursue a full-time postgraduate program of study at this University and in a program offered by the College of Engineering and Computer Science

Type: Award

Value: Stipend is A\$5,000, payable in two equal instalments of \$2,500 at the beginning of each semester for one year. Scholars are required to meet all costs associated with their studies including travel, accommodation, books and incidental expenses. The scholar is responsible for paying International Tuition fees for the duration of the program

Frequency: Annual

Additional Information: A scholar may not hold concurrently another scholarship awarded by the University or another University College. A scholar must obtain permission from the College Coursework Scholarships Committee to hold any other scholarship or award concurrently with a College of Engineering and Computer Science Postgraduate Scholarship

For further information contact:

Tel: (61) 2 6125 0677
Email: student.services@cecs.anu.edu.au
Contact: Professor Chris Johnson

College of Engineering and Computer Science: College Postgraduate International Honours Award

Type: Award

Value: Stipend is A\$5,000, payable in two equal instalments of A\$2,500 at the beginning of each semester for one year

Frequency: Annual

Additional Information: The Scholarships are offered on the basis of offer of a place in the Master Degree by Coursework programs offered by the College of Engineering and Computer Science and other criteria as set out from time to time by the Program Authority

For further information contact:

Associate Dean (Education), ANU College of Engineering and Computer Science, Australia

Tel: (61) 2 6125 0677
Email: student.services@cecs.anu.edu.au
Contact: Professor Chris Johnson

Full Tuition International Relations Scholarships

Subjects: International relations covers more than most people realize. In the farthest reaches of space where lonely unmanned probes crawl through the void, they do so under the auspices of something known as the Treaty on Principles Governing the Activities of States in the Exploration and Use of Outer Space, including the Moon and Other Celestial Bodies

Eligibility: Scholarships are available for all students. There is no restriction or nationality criteria

Value: This scholarship will pay full tuition fees

Length of Study: Up to 4 full time semesters (24 months)

Country of Study: Australia

Closing Date: 31 October

For further information contact:

Email: info@InternationalRelationsEDU.org

National Security College Entry Scholarship for Aboriginal and Torres Strait Islander Students

Subjects: Any degrees offered by the ANU National Security College

Eligibility: The Scholarship shall be available to an applicant who is of Australian Aboriginal and/or Torres Strait Islander descent; has completed a Bachelors degree; has been offered admission to the Graduate Certificate in National Security Policy or Master of National Security Policy; is not the recipient of a College sponsored place

Type: Scholarship

Value: The Scholarship covers the full domestic tuition fee for up to 24 units of College core courses. The Scholarship does not cover any necessary admissions and deposit fees, the payment of reading and study materials, living expenses, accommodation or any other costs associated with studying

Country of Study: Any country

Application Procedure: Please print and complete application form, availabe at website

Closing Date: 20 July

Additional Information: The Scholarship is available in the first two semesters of study only. Please write to national.

security.college@anu.edu.au and check at nsc.anu.edu.au/grad_studies.php for more information

For further information contact:

Email: Crawford.degrees@anu.edu.au

Research School of Accounting India Merit Scholarships

Subjects: Accounting
Eligibility: Students from India are eligible to apply
Value: The award will cover 50% of the awardees ANU International Student Fees per semester, for the standard full time duration of the degree in which the student is enrolled in
Country of Study: Australia
Application Procedure: Applications are called for with a closing date as set by the ANU CBE Scholarships Office. The application is submitted on the prescribed electronic form and supporting documentation forwarded to CBE by email
Closing Date: 18 May
Additional Information: Please visit scholarship-positions.com/research-school-of-accounting-india-merit-scholarships-australia/2018/03/31/ for further information

For further information contact:

Email: scholarships.cbe@anu.edu.au

Tim and Margaret Bourke PhD Scholarships

Subjects: Scholarships are awarded in the field of Pure (Theoretical) Mathematics
Purpose: To support an ANU PhD student working in the area of pure (theoretical) mathematics, the advancement of women in the field of mathematics, and the teaching of mathematics at the Australian National University
Eligibility: A domestic or international student Enrolled or enrolling full-time in a program of study for the degree of Doctor of Philosophy at the Australian National University
Type: Scholarship
Value: A$5,000 per annum
Country of Study: Australia
Closing Date: 31 May
Additional Information: For further details, please visit www.scholarshipsupdates.com/australian-national-university-tim-and-margaret-bourke-phd-scholarships-2018/

For further information contact:

Email: msi.hdr.sa@anu.edu.au

Yuill Scholarship

Subjects: Law
Purpose: to Support the International Court of Justice Traineeship Program
Eligibility: The scholarship applicant must be: a final year student in a Bachelor of Laws program in the ANU College of Law; or a final year student in a Juris Doctor program in the ANU College of Law; or enrolled in a Master of Laws program in the ANU College of Law; or a recent graduate of the Bachelor of Laws, Juris Doctor or Master of Laws program from the ANU College of Law. The Bachelor of Laws program may be undertaken as a single or a combined degree
Type: Scholarship
Value: A$25,000
Frequency: Annual
Country of Study: Any country
Closing Date: As advised on ANU College of Law website
Additional Information: The scholarship will apply for the duration of the traineeship (9 months in total). Application process and criteria is set out in the Conditions of Award. Applications can be sent electronically or in hard copy. Electronic applications can be sent to karen.heuer@anu.edu.au. Hard copy applications should be mailed to Office of the Dean of Law, ANU College of Law

For further information contact:

Email: scholarships.law@anu.edu.au

Australian Research Council (ARC)

Level 2, 11 Lancaster Place, Canberra Airport, Canberra, ACT 2609, Australia

Tel:	(61) 2 6287 6600
Fax:	(61) 2 6287 6601
Email:	ncgp@arc.gov.au
Website:	www.arc.gov.au
Contact:	Dr Laura Dan, Chief Program Officer

The Australian Research Council (ARC) is a statutory authority within the Australian Government's Innovation, Industry, Science and Research portfolio. The ARC advises the Government on research matters, manages the National Competitive Grants Program, a significant component of Australia's investment in research and development, and has responsibility for the Excellence in Research for Australia initiative.

Australia-India Strategic Research Fund (AISRF)

Purpose: The aim of Australia- India Strategic Research Fund is to 1. increase the uptake of leading science and technology by supporting collaboration between Australian and Indian researchers in strategically focused, leading-edge scientific research and technology projects. 2. strengthen strategic alliances between Australian and Indian researchers

Eligibility: To be eligible you must: 1. have an Australian Business Number (ABN) and be one of the following entities. 2. a company, incorporated in Australia. 3. an incorporated not for profit organisation. We can only accept applications: that have a primary Indian partner that has submitted, or is in the process of submitting, a corresponding application to India's Department of Science and Technology (DST) or the Department of Biotechnology (DBT)

Level of Study: Graduate

Type: Funding support

Frequency: Annual

Country of Study: Any country

Closing Date: 23 January

Funding: Government

For further information contact:

Email: enquiries@industry.gov.au

Australian Sports Commission (ASC)

Australian Sports Commission, Leverrier Street, Bruce ACT 2617, PO Box 176, Belconnen, ACT 2616, Australia

Tel: (61) 2 6214 1111
Fax: (61) 2 6251 2680, 2 6214 1836
Email: recruitment@ausport.gov.au
Website: www.ausport.gov.au

The Australian Sports Commission (ASC) is responsible for implementing the Australian Government's national sports policy, which is based on a sports philosophy of excellence and participation. It promotes an effective national sports system that offers improved participation in quality sports activities by all Australians and helps the talented and motivated to reach their potential excellence in sports performance. Its work is guided by the Australian Government's national sports policy, Building Australian Communities through Sport (BACTS).

Biomechanics Postgraduate Scholarship (General Sports)

Subjects: Sports

Purpose: To provide an opportunity for graduates with degrees with a major emphasis in biomechanics to have experience in the application of biomechanics to enhance elite sports performance

Eligibility: Applicants must have tertiary qualification in science, human movement, mathematics or a related area, should have an interest and/or understanding of research principles and some knowledge of biomechanical systems and equipment

Level of Study: Graduate

Type: Scholarship

Value: A$21,434 per year

Length of Study: 48 weeks

Application Procedure: Applicants must submit a covering letter, a statement of experience and curriculum vitae along with the application form

Closing Date: 29 September

For further information contact:

Tel: (61) 2 6214 1659
Email: recruitment@ausport.gov.au
Contact: Dale Barnes

Indigenous Sporting Excellence Scholarships

Subjects: Sports

Purpose: To give indigenous sportspeople the opportunity to improve their sporting performance at an elite level

Eligibility: Applicants must be over 12 years of age, representing their state in national competition or Australia internationally within sport or the school sport system, a coach with level 1 or level 2 accreditation, a sports trainer with level 1 accreditation, a sports official with accreditation, competing in a sport that is recognized by the Australian Sports Commission

Type: Scholarship

Value: A$500

Country of Study: Any country

Application Procedure: Check website for further details

Closing Date: 31 May

Additional Information: Athletes, coaches, sports trainers and officials who receive this scholarship are also eligible to apply for the Elite Indigenous Travel and Accommodation Assistance Program if they are selected for a state representative team attending national championships or an Australian team competing internationally

For further information contact:

Email: school.sport.victoria@edumail.vic.gov.au

Performance Analysis Scholarship

Subjects: Sports
Purpose: To provide performance analysis services to AIS sport programmes through coaches as directed and as required work on projects relating to enhancement of knowledge and coach education
Eligibility: Applicants must have a tertiary qualification in computer science, software engineering, information technology, human movement or a related area and an interest and/or understanding of research principles
Type: Scholarship
Value: A$21,434 per year
Length of Study: 48 weeks
Application Procedure: Applicants must write a covering letter referencing the position title, prepare a thorough (but concise) statement that focuses on the relevant experience, curriculum vitae that summarize the qualifications including contact details for two referees and can be submitted by email
Closing Date: 29 September

For further information contact:

Tel: (61) 2 6214 1659
Email: recruitment@ausport.gov.au
Contact: Dale Barnes

PhD Scholarship Programs

Subjects: Physiology
Eligibility: Open to candidates who are keen to have a scholar carrying out innovative research specific to their needs
Level of Study: Doctorate
Type: Scholarship
Value: A$21,000 per year, with a further A$3,000 per year set aside to cover routine expenses
Country of Study: Australia
Application Procedure: For application details, please visit the website, www.ausport.gov.au/jobs/index.asp
Funding: Government
Contributor: Australian Institute of Sports Medicine
Additional Information: Interested applicants need to visit the site regularly to watch for vacancies

For further information contact:

Email: john.williamsr@ausport.gov.au
Contact: John Williams

Postgraduate Scholarship Program–Physiology (Quality Control)

Subjects: Physiology
Purpose: To provide opportunity for a graduate whose primary role will be to assist in the area of quality control under the direction of the laboratory manager
Eligibility: Applicants must have a tertiary qualification in science or a related area, an interest and/or understanding of research principles and an experience in an administrative role and good computing skills
Level of Study: Graduate
Type: Scholarship
Value: A$21,434 per year
Length of Study: 54 weeks
Application Procedure: Applicants must submit a covering letter, a statement of experience and curriculum vitae along with the application form
Closing Date: 29 September
Contributor: Australian Sports Commission
Additional Information: Terms and conditions are subject to change. Always confirm details with scholarship provider before applying

For further information contact:

Tel: (61) 2 6214 1564
Email: recruitment@ausport.gov.au
Contact: Marilyn Dickson, Manager

Postgraduate Scholarship–Biomechanics (Swimming)

Subjects: Sports
Purpose: To provide the opportunity for graduates of degrees with major emphasis in biomechanics and to have experience in the application of biomechanics to enhance elite sports performance
Eligibility: Applicants must have a degree in biomechanics or human movement sciences, an interest and/or understanding of research principles, experience in biomechanics services and knowledge of and experience in a competitive swimming environment
Level of Study: Graduate
Type: Scholarship
Value: A$21,434 per year
Length of Study: 48 weeks
Application Procedure: Applicants must submit a covering letter, a statement of experience and curriculum vitae along with the application form
Closing Date: 29 September

For further information contact:

Tel: (61) 2 6214 1732
Email: recruitment@ausport.gov.au
Contact: Clare Jones

Postgraduate Scholarship–Physiology (Biochemistry/Haematology)

Subjects: Physiology
Purpose: To provide an opportunity for a graduate whose primary role will be to assist in the area of biochemistry and haematology under the direction of the biochemistry/haematology manager
Eligibility: Applicants must have a degree in medical laboratory science or biological sciences and an interest and/or understanding of research principles, good computer skills
Level of Study: Postgraduate
Type: Scholarship
Value: A$21,434 per year
Length of Study: 50 weeks
Application Procedure: Applicants must write a covering letter referencing the position title, prepare a thorough (but concise) statement that focuses on the relevant experience, curriculum vitae that summarize the qualifications including contact details for two referees and can be submitted by email
Closing Date: 29 September

For further information contact:

Tel: (61) 2 6214 1700
Email: recruitment@ausport.gov.au
Contact: Graeme Allbon

Sport Leadership Grants for Women Program

Subjects: Sports
Purpose: To provide women with an opportunity to undertake sport leadership training
Eligibility: Applicants must be indigenous women, women in disability sport, women from culturally and linguistically diverse backgrounds and women in general sport leadership
Type: Grant
Value: Up to A$5,000 for individuals and up to A$10,000 for incorporated organizations
Application Procedure: Check website for further details
Closing Date: 29 April
Funding: Government

For further information contact:

Tel: (61) 2 6214 7994
Email: leadershipgrants@ausport.gov.au

Sports Medicine Fellowship Program

Subjects: Sports medicine
Eligibility: Open to Australasian College of Sports Physicians (ACSP) trainees
Level of Study: Postgraduate
Frequency: Annual
Study Establishment: Australian Institute of Sports Science
Country of Study: Australia
Application Procedure: For application details, please visit the website, www.ausport.gov.au/jobs/sssmpostgrad.asp
Funding: Government

For further information contact:

Tel: (61) 2 6214 1578
Email: jill.flanagan@ausport.gov.au
Contact: Mrs Jill Flanagan

Sports Physiology Postgraduate Scholarship–Fatigue and Recovery

Subjects: Physiology
Purpose: To offer an Honours graduate in science or a related field the opportunity to complete a scholarship in physiology (fatigue and recovery)
Eligibility: Applicants must have an Honours Degree in science or a related area, basic skills in conducting routine physiological testing procedures, good computing skills, outstanding organizational skills and a high level of initiative
Level of Study: Graduate
Type: Scholarship
Value: A$19,890 per year
Length of Study: 1 year
Application Procedure: Applicants must submit a covering letter, a statement of experience and curriculum vitae along with the application form
Closing Date: 6 April

For further information contact:

Tel: (61) 2 6214 1589
Email: Recruitment@ausport.gov.au
Contact: Shona Halson

Austrian Academy of Sciences

Institute of Limnology, Mondseestrasse 9, AUT-5310, Mondsee, Austria

Tel: (43) 623 240 79
Fax: (43) 623 235 78
Email: ipgl.mondsee@oeaw.ac.at
Website: www.ipgl.at
Contact: Mr Regina Brandstätter, IPGL Officer

The Institute of Limnology of the Austrian Academy of Sciences performs ecological research on inland waters. The overall research goal is to understand the structure, function and dynamics of freshwater ecosystems. Although the Institute primarily conducts basic research, aspects of applied research are also considered. The Institute at Mondsee, located close to Salzburg, was established in 1981 and has a staff of 26, including 13 scientists. Currently, the Institute's main fields of research are tropic interactions and food-web structures in lakes.

Austrian Academy of Sciences, 4-months Trimester at Egerton University, Kenya

Subjects: Lake ecology, stream and river ecology, wetlands for waterquality, fisheries and aquaculture
Purpose: Postgraduate training of water experts of African countries: Ethiopia, Uganda, Kenya, Burundi, Tansania, Rwanda, Cape Verde, Burkina Faso, Senegal
Eligibility: Principal requirement for admission is a BSc degree or equivalent qualification in a relevant subject from a recognized university (e.g. BSc in botany, zoology, chemistry, agriculture, environmental science, aquaculture and fisheries, water resource management, environmental economics or engineering, etc.). Priority countries: Eastern Africa: Ethiopia, Uganda, Kenya, Burundi, Tanzania, Rwanda, Western Africa: Cape Verde, Burkina Faso, Senegal. Southern Africa: Mozambique
Type: Fellowship
Value: €450 monthly, to cover food, personal needs plus free tuition, health insurance, study material, equipment for lab work, field work and travelling expenses
Length of Study: 4 months
Frequency: Annual
Study Establishment: Egerton University, Kenya
Country of Study: Any country
No. of awards offered: 2 qualified
Application Procedure: Application forms are provided by Egerton University and IPGL Office within the Institute for Limnology of the Austrian Academy of Sciences
Closing Date: 30 November
Funding: Government
Contributor: The Austrian Development Cooperation
No. of awards given last year: 2
No. of applicants last year: 2 qualified

Additional Information: No provisions are made for dependants. Country of study is Kenya

For further information contact:

Egerton University, PO Box 536, Austria

Email: info@egerton.ac.ke

Austrian Academy of Sciences, MSc Course in Limnology and Wetland Ecosystems

Subjects: Aquatic systems, Environmental Sciences
Purpose: To understand the structure and functioning of aquatic and wetland ecosystems for the conservation of biodiversity and sustainable management of natural resources. To acquire skills for interacting with stakeholders, managers and policy makers in the development of best practices
Eligibility: Open to candidates from developing countries who are maximum 35 years of age, have a good working knowledge of English and have an academic degree in science, agriculture or veterinary medicine from a university or any other recognized Institute of Higher Education. Applicants should have 3 years practical experience in at least one special subject in their field of professional training. All applications are considered on their individual merits
Level of Study: Postgraduate
Type: Scholarship
Value: US$1,350 paid monthly to cover food, lodging and personal needs plus free tuition, health insurance, study material and equipment for laboratory work, field work and travelling expenses
Length of Study: 18 months
Frequency: Annual
Study Establishment: Institute for Limnology, Mondsee; Institute UNESCO-IHE, Delft, The Netherlands; Egerton University, Kenya; Czech Academy of Sciences, Trebon, Czech Republic; Austrian Universities and Federal Institutes in Austria
No. of awards offered: 90
Application Procedure: Applicants must obtain application forms from the website. Filled application forms can be sent to Institute for Limnology of the Austrian Academy of Sciences
Closing Date: End of January
Funding: Government
Contributor: The Austrian Development Co-operation
No. of awards given last year: 4
No. of applicants last year: 90
Additional Information: No provisions are made for dependants. It is strongly advised that dependants do not accompany

fellows due to frequent moves during the course. Fellows must also provide their own transportation to and from Austria

For further information contact:

IPGL-Course, Institute for Limnology of the Austrian Academy of Sciences, Mondseestrasse 9, AUT-5310, Mondsee, Austria

Tel:	(43) 6232 4079
Fax:	(43) 6232 3578
Email:	ipgl.mondsee@oeaw.ac.at

Austrian Academy of Sciences, Short Course—Tropical Limnology

Subjects: Tropical limnology
Purpose: To assist students studying the special characteristics of tropical river and lake ecosystems, its interactions with activities, processes in the watershed and relevant ecosystem services
Eligibility: Open to candidates from East African countries who have a good working knowledge of English and have an academic degree either in science, agriculture or veterinary medicine from a university or other recognised Institute of Higher Education. Applicants should have practical experience within at least one special subject in their field of professional training
Level of Study: Postgraduate
Type: Scholarship
Value: US$21 paid per day including accommodation, full board and US$2,500 d.s.a. plus free tuition, health insurance, study material and equipment for laboratory work, field work and travelling expenses
Length of Study: 3 weeks
Frequency: Annual
Study Establishment: Egerton University, Kenya, Sagana Fish Farm, Kenya
No. of awards offered: 75
Application Procedure: Application forms are also available from the website
Closing Date: 30 July
Funding: Government
Contributor: The Austrian Development Co-operation
No. of awards given last year: 10
No. of applicants last year: 75
Additional Information: No provisions are made for dependants. It is strongly advised that dependants do not accompany Fellows due to frequent moves during the course. Fellows must also arrange their own transportation to and from Kenya

For further information contact:

Dept. of Zoology, Egerton University, Austria

Email:	mathookoj@yahoo.com
Contact:	Professor J Mathooko

Austrian Exchange Service

Agency for International Co-operation in Education & Research Bureau for Academic Mobility Alserstrasse 4/1/15/7, AUT-1090, Vienna, Austria

Tel:	(43) 142 772 8188
Fax:	(43) 142 779 281
Email:	bamo@oead.ac.at
Website:	www.oead.ac.at
Contact:	Dr Lydia Skarits, Head of Office

Austrian Academic Exchange Service Unilateral Scholarship Programs

Subjects: Natural scientific, technical, social and economic studies or medicine
Purpose: To enable postgraduates from developing countries to undertake professional training
Eligibility: Applicants must be postgraduates of natural scientific, technical, social and economic studies or medical doctors wishing to conduct professional training in Austria
Level of Study: Postgraduate, Professional development
Type: Scholarship
Value: Monthly scholarship payment, plus a possible additional payment for housing, as well as cover for accident and health insurance. After four months a start payment is granted. Under certain conditions there is the possibility of the coverage of travel costs
Country of Study: Austria
Application Procedure: Applicants can obtain information from the website or contact the Austrian Exchange Service

For further information contact:

Tel:	(43) 142 772 8180
Fax:	(43) 142 772 8195
Email:	vbs@oead.ac.at

Austrian Federal Ministry for Science and Research

Embassy of Austria, 12 Talbot Street, Forrest, ACT 2603, Australia

Tel: (61) 2 6295 1533
Fax: (61) 6 6239 6751
Contact: Grants Management Officer

Australia-India Strategic Research Fund (AISRF)

Subjects: 1. Increase the uptake of leading science and technology by supporting collaboration between Australian and Indian researchers in strategically focused, leading-edge scientific research and technology projects. 2. strengthen strategic alliances between Australian and Indian researchers, and facilitate Australia's and India's access to the global science and technology system
Purpose: Australia-India Collaborative Research Projects are funded by the Australia-India Strategic Research Fund (AISRF)
Eligibility: 1. A company, incorporated in Australia. 2. An incorporated not for profit organisation. 3. A publicly funded research organisation (PFRO) as defined in appendix A. 4. A Cooperative Research Centre. 5. An other Australian incorporated entity. 6. That have a primary Indian partner that has submitted, or is in the process of submitting, a corresponding application to India's Department of Science and Technology (DST) or the Department of Biotechnology (DBT)
Level of Study: Research
Type: Research grant
Value: AU$4,000,000.00
Frequency: Every 3 years
Country of Study: Any country
Application Procedure: Apply online
Closing Date: 23 January
Funding: Government
Additional Information: Business.gov.au provides information and advice to customers via a range of channels including phone (13 28 46), email and web chat. Contact us for assistance. Refer website www.business.gov.au/aisrf

For further information contact:

Email: enquiries@industry.gov.au

Australian Prostate Centre - Victoria

Subjects: The Grant Opportunity contributes to the achievement of the Department of Health's Portfolio Budget Outcome 1 – Health System Policy, Design and Innovation; Program 1.1: Health Policy Research and Analysis
Purpose: The purpose of the grant is to support prostate cancer research through the safeguarding of rare tissue and bioinformatics assets at the Australian Prostate Centre (Victoria)

Eligibility: The Australian Prostate Centre Victoria is the eligible organisation to apply for this Grant Opportunity
Level of Study: Research
Type: Grant
Value: A$600,000.00
Frequency: Annual
Country of Study: Australia
Closing Date: 21 January
Funding: Government

For further information contact:

Email: grant.atm@health.gov.au

Small and Medium Enterprises (SME) Export Hubs

Subjects: This grant opportunity complements existing initiatives, such as those delivered through the Australian Export Finance Corporation - Efic, the Australian Trade and Investment Commission - Austrade, the Entrepreneurs' Programme, and the Industry Growth Centres Initiative
Purpose: The Small and Medium Enterprises (SME) grant opportunity will support SME Export Hubs in the development of local, regional and Indigenous brands through business collaborations in the identified areas of competitive strength
Eligibility: 1. Incorporated association. 2. Company limited by guarantee. 3. Non-distributing co-operative. 4. Indigenous not for profit corporation. 5. Not-for-profit incorporated trustee on behalf of a trust. 6. Australian local government agency or body. 7. Australian state/territory government agency or body. 8. Regional Development Australia (RDA) committee
Level of Study: Professional development
Type: Grant
Value: A$18,800,000.00
Frequency: Annual
Country of Study: Any country
Closing Date: 21 January
Funding: Government
Additional Information: Business.gov.au provides information and advice to customers via a range of channels including phone (13 28 46), email and web chat. Contact us for assistance

For further information contact:

Email: enquiries@industry.gov.au

Austrian Science Fund (FWF)

Haus der Forschung, Sensengasse 1, AUT 1090, Vienna, Austria

Tel: (43) 1 505 67 40
Fax: (43) 1 505 67 39
Email: office@fwf.ac.at
Website: www.fwf.ac.at

The Austrian Science Fund (FWF) is Austria's central body for the promotion of basic research. It is equally committed to all branches of science and in all its activities it is guided solely by the standards of the international scientific community. Its mission is the promotion of high-quality basic research, education and training through research and scientific culture and knowledge transfer.

Elise Richter Program

Subjects: All subjects
Purpose: To provide support for outstanding female scientists and researchers, improve the career prospects for women in Austrian research facilities, and provide very generous support during the postdoc phase for women at the start of their scientific careers or on its resumption following maternity leave
Eligibility: The candidate should possess appropriate post-doctoral experience, international scientific publications, and preparatory work related to the proposed research project
Level of Study: Postdoctorate
Type: Research
Value: Personnel costs €69,810 (Senior Postdoc) Project specific costs up to €15,000 per year as outlined in the proposal (therefore €2,000 per year can be used for coaching purposes)
Length of Study: 12–48 months
Application Procedure: Please check website
Closing Date: Please check the website

For further information contact:

Tel: (43) 1 505 67 40 ext. 8503
Email: susanne.menschik@fwf.ac.at
Contact: Susanne Menschik

European Young Investigator Award

Subjects: All subjects
Purpose: To enable young scientists all over the world to work in European research institution for 5 years
Eligibility: Open to applicants who possess between 2 and a maximum of 8 years of postdoctoral experience
Level of Study: Postdoctorate
Type: Award

Value: The total value of an award will normally be no less than €750,000 over 5 years and shall not exceed a maximum of €1,250,000
Length of Study: 5 years
Application Procedure: Applicants should submit their application in English and the decision will be taken by EURYI–Jury on the basis of an international peer-review process. For further information, contact Bettina E. Bauer at bauer@fwf.ac.at, Tel. +43 1 505 6740, ext. 58
Closing Date: Please check the website
Contributor: EUROHORCS in co-operation with the European Science Foundation (ESF)
Additional Information: The European Research Council's recently launched Starting Investigator Research Grant Scheme shares many characteristics with EURYI, as well as a much larger scale in terms of the number of awards. The EuroHORCs have accordingly decided to indefinitely postpone future calls of EURYI. For more information, please contact euryi@esf.org

For further information contact:

Tel: (43) 1 505 6740 ext 8701
Email: reinhard.belocky@fwf.ac.at
Contact: Reinhard Belocky

Skin Treatment and Research Trust Program

Subjects: All subjects
Purpose: To provide highly promising young researchers of any discipline with the means to plan their research work on a long-term basis and with sufficient financial security
Eligibility: Open to applicants who possess at least 2 and at most 10 years of postdoctoral experience at the time of application. In addition it is desirable that candidates have completed a research stay abroad of at least 1 year
Level of Study: Postdoctorate
Value: Minimum €800,000 up to maximum €1,200,000
Length of Study: 6 years, with an interim review after 3 years
Closing Date: 18 September
Funding: Government
Contributor: Federal Ministry for Science and Research (BMWF)
Additional Information: Where additional funding applications are submitted to other FWF Programmes, those applications must differ substantially from the planned START project in terms of research questions and objectives. Applications which include work already proposed for a START project and are excessively similar to the START project will not be considered by the FWF Board. The sole exception to this rule is the Elise Richter Programme, where an application

which is substantially similar in content as long as the programme-specific guidelines are observed

For further information contact:

Tel: (43) 1 505 6740 ext 8605
Email: mario.mandl@fwf.ac.at
Contact: Mario Mandl

Translational Brainpower

Subjects: All subjects
Purpose: To support the integration of highly qualified scientists and researchers from abroad into research projects at the interface between basic and applied research in Austria
Eligibility: Open to candidates who possess high scientific quality at international level
Level of Study: Research
Value: According to the project; costs for the international partner (salary, max. €9,460 per month; travel costs, travel and subsistence costs)
Length of Study: Maximum 9 months
Application Procedure: Submit application to: FWF Der Wissenschaftsfonds, Haus der Forschung, Sensengasse 1, 1090 Wien
Closing Date: 22 March

For further information contact:

Tel: (43) 1 505 6740 ext. 8602
Email: milojka.gindl@fwf.ac.at
Contact: Milojka Gindl

Wittgenstein Award

Subjects: All subjects
Purpose: To provide highly qualified researchers of any discipline with a maximum of freedom and flexibility in carrying out their research work
Eligibility: The candidate should possess international recognition in the field and be employed in an Austrian research organization and should be aged 55 or under at the time of nomination
Level of Study: Professional development, Research
Type: Research
Value: Up to €1,500,000 per award
Length of Study: 5 years
Frequency: Annual
Closing Date: September
Funding: Government
Contributor: Federal Minister for Science
No. of awards given last year: 1 or 2

For further information contact:

Tel: (43) 1 505 6740 ext 8605
Email: mario.mandl@fwf.ac.at
Contact: Mario Mandl

Austro-American Association of Boston

Austro-American Association of Boston, Inc. c/o Traude Schieber-Acker, President 67 Bridle Path, Sudbury, MA 01776, United States of America

Tel: (1) 978 579 2191
Email: thansen@wellesley.edu
Website: www.austria-boston.org/

Membership of the Austro-American Association of Boston is open toany individual interested in any aspect of Austrian history, economy, culture, politics and tourism. The association conducts meetings and get togethers focusing on events and experiences related to Austria.

A-AA Austrian Studies Scholarship Award

Purpose: Project areas may include history, literature, art, architecture, folk customs, music and contemporary life
Eligibility: All undergraduate and graduate students at New England colleges and Universities are eligible to apply
Level of Study: Graduate
Type: Award
Value: US$1,500
Application Procedure: There is no application form. Applicants should submit the following information: a detailed project proposal, including the reason for selecting it; curriculum vitae; and two confidential letters of support from faculty members who know the applicant well and can comment on the feasibility of the project
Closing Date: 1 March
Additional Information: Please feel free to email any or submissions or inquiries to the co-chair of the scholarship committee, Dr Johann Nittmann at Johann.Nittmann@cavium.com

For further information contact:

Department of German, Wellesley College

Tel: (1) 781 283 2255
Email: thansen@wellesley.edu
Contact: Professor Thomas Hansen

Austro-American Association of Boston Stipend

Subjects: Austrian cultural studies, history, folklore, literature, music, fine and applied arts and film
Purpose: To promote the understanding and dissemination of Austrian culture
Eligibility: Junior faculty members and students enroled in a college in New England
Level of Study: Unrestricted
Type: Stipendiary
Value: US$1,500
Study Establishment: Any in New England
Country of Study: United States of America
No. of awards offered: 1
Application Procedure: Applicants must submit a detailed description of the project including the reasons for selecting it, a curriculum vitae and two letters of recommendation from faculty members who know the applicant well and can comment on the feasibility of the project
Closing Date: 1 April

Funding: Private
Contributor: Association members
No. of applicants last year: 1
Additional Information: The award is limited to individuals living or studying in New England. Projects funded in the past have included the preparation of musical or dramatic performances, the facilitation of appropriate publications and research trips to Austria. Culture is defined to include the humanities and the arts. The recipient may be asked to present the results of the project at an event of the Austro-American Association. The award may not be used to pay tuition fees at a college or university in New England

For further information contact:

Wellesley College, United States of America

Email: thansen@wellesley.edu
Contact: Professor Thomas Hansen, Department of German

B

Bath Spa University

Newton St Loe, BA2 9BN, Bath, United Kingdom

Website: www.bathspa.ac.uk

Bath Spa University's vision is to be a leading educational institution in creativity, culture and enterprise. Through innovative teaching and research, the University will provide a high quality student experience. Based in a world heritage city and connected to a network of international partners, Bath Spa University will ensure that its graduates are socially engaged global citizens.

International Partner Scholarship

Purpose: Bath Spa University's International Partner Scholarships celebrate our strong partnerships with leading universities across the world
Eligibility: Open to postgraduate taught Master's applicants from Bath Spa University partner institutions. Applications are welcome from international students who have completed undergraduate or postgraduate education at a partner institution; achieved high academic results; can demonstrate experience in university, community and society activities; can show future aspirations to become involved in university life at Bath Spa University; plus show ideas on how Bath Spa University can work with its partner institutions towards promoting global citizenship. For a list of partner institutions go to www.bathspa.ac.uk/international-students/international-partners-2
Type: Scholarship
Value: £3,000
Frequency: Annual
Application Procedure: Applications are made through the international scholarship application form. Applicants must

hold an offer of admission for a Bath Spa University postgraduate taught degree programme that is full-time and taught on-campus, be a graduate of a Bath Spa University partner institution, and complete the International Scholarship Application Form
Closing Date: June (for September/October entry)
Additional Information: For further information, please check at www.bathspa.ac.uk/international-students/scholarships/international-partner-scholarship

For further information contact:

Email: international@bathspa.ac.uk
Contact: International Relations team

Invertimos en el talento de los colombianos (ICETEX) Artistas Jovenes Scholarships

Subjects: Bath Spa University's programmes across art, design, film, writing, music and performance. Check complete details on the website
Purpose: ICETEX's Artistas Jovenes Talentos programme is a unique programme that supports young Colombian artists and designers, filmmakers, performers and musicians, writers and poets. As the leading United Kingdom university for partner of ICETEX, and the top United Kingdom creative university, the ICETEX Artistas Jovenes Talentos is a perfect fit for applicants to Bath Spa University's programmes across art, design, film, writing, music and performance
Eligibility: Applications are open for candidates who meet the requirements of ICETEX application process. Full details of eligibility are available on the ICETEX website
Level of Study: Graduate, Postgraduate
Type: Scholarship
Application Procedure: (i) Eligible candidates must first have an offer of admission for the chosen programme, If you meet the entry criteria for the chosen course you will be sent

© Springer Nature Limited 2019
Palgrave Macmillan (ed.), *The Grants Register 2020*,
https://doi.org/10.1057/978-1-349-95943-3

a conditional offer of admission by email. You must meet all the academic conditions of offer, including submission of certificates and transcripts, translated copies, English Language requirement, passport copy, references. (ii) Once you have received an offer letter to the chosen programme of study you then complete the ICETEX Artistas Jovenes Talentos process

Closing Date: April as per instructions of ICETEX

Additional Information: Bath Spa University can provide individual help and advice on your application and has a dedicated office in Colombia

For further information contact:

BSU Colombia, Colombia

Tel: (57) 1 300 3710
Email: BSUColombia@bathspa.ac.uk
Website: www.bathspa.ac.uk

Invertimos en el Talento de los Colombianos (ICETEX) Scholarships

Subjects: Eligible programmes are a range of Masters programmes in four schools of study. Details on this are available on the website

Purpose: The University of Salford is pleased to work with ICETEX to offer funding opportunities for Colombian students to study in the United Kingdom

Eligibility: Applications are open for candidates who meet the requirements of ICETEX application process. Full details of eligibility are available on the ICETEX website at www.icetex.gov.co/dnnpro5/es-co/becas/becasenelexterior/becasvigentes.aspx

Type: Scholarship

Value: 50% tuition fee

Frequency: Annual

Country of Study: Any country

Application Procedure: Applicants must apply for the programme of study and then the scholarship via ICETEX. Applicants must also submit a completed Bath Spa University International Scholarship Application form and include the ICETEX reference number. Further application details are given in the website

Closing Date: 10 May

Funding: Private

Additional Information: Applications will be reviewed on submission of the relevant documentation to ICETEX and the Bath Spa University Application Form. The applications are reviewed within two weeks after the deadline by the University Committee. For further information, refer the website link below. beta.salford.ac.uk/international/icetex-scholarships-colombia

Latin America – Creative and Culture Scholarships

Subjects: Any masters subject offered by the university

Purpose: Bath Spa University is the United Kingdom's leading university for creativity, culture and enterprise. To celebrate this excellence, and to support Bath Spa University's work in Latin America

Eligibility: Applicants must be nationals from Latin America who have applied for and hold an offer for any of the eligible programmes, have high academic results and can demonstrate a commitment to creativity, culture and enterprise in Latin America

Level of Study: Graduate, Postgraduate

Type: Scholarship

Value: £3,000; Fees coverage: 100% coverage. This scholarship covers the value of $1 \times 100\%$; $2 \times £3,000$

Application Procedure: Applicants must hold an offer of admission for an eligible programme that is full-time and taught on-campus, and complete the International Scholarship Application Form

Closing Date: For September/October entry, the application date is 15 June, 5pm GMT

Additional Information: Applications are reviewed on submission of the International Scholarship Application Form. Particular attention is given to the scholarship essay. The applications are reviewed in the month after the deadline by the University Committee

For further information contact:

Tel: (44) 1225 875777
Email: international@bathspa.ac.uk

Postgraduate Overseas Scholarship

Subjects: Any masters subject offered by the university

Eligibility: Open to applicants who have met the required entry qualification and been offered a place (conditional or unconditional) on a postgraduate taught Masters' programme. It is awarded on the basis of academic merit

Type: Scholarship

Value: £1,000

Application Procedure: Eligibility for the Overseas Scholarship is judged on the basis of the application to the chosen programme of study. There is no need to submit a separate application form. If you are selected for a Postgraduate Overseas Scholarship you will receive a confirmation letter at the time of your offer of admission

Closing Date: There is no deadline

For further information contact:

Tel: (44) 1225 875 777
Email: international@bathspa.ac.uk

Vice Chancellor's International Scholarship

Purpose: The Bath Spa University Vice Chancellor's International Scholarship celebrates our commitment to internationalization and excellence in creativity, culture and enterprise

Eligibility: Applications are welcome from international students who have achieved high academic results and can demonstrate a commitment to creativity, culture and enterprise

Level of Study: Graduate, Postgraduate

Type: Scholarship

Value: £5,000

Application Procedure: Applicants must hold an offer of admission for a Bath Spa University postgraduate taught Master's degree programme that is full-time and taught on-campus, and complete the International Scholarship Application Form. Please complete all the details, including your name, contact details, student number and qualifications. Applications with missing details will be automatically rejected

Closing Date: 31 January/30 June (annual)

Additional Information: Please check details at www. bathspa.ac.uk/international-students/scholarships/vice-chancellors-international-scholarship

For further information contact:

Tel: (44) 1225 875 777

Email: international@bathspa.ac.uk

Contact: International Relations team

Bayer AG

Werk Leverkusen, DEU 51368 Leverkusen, Germany

Tel: (49) 214 3026672

Email: gisela.dambach.gd@bayer-ag.de

Website: www.aspirin.com

Contact: Gisela Dambach, International Aspirin Award

Bayer Foundation Scholarships

Purpose: Bayer Foundation supports students aspiring to study in Germany with five fellowship programmes in biology, medical science, agricultural science, non-academic professions, and chemistry

Eligibility: The project to be supported must be innovative and international. 1. Scholarships are granted to students and young professionals (up to 2 years after graduation) German student wishing to realize a study or research project abroad or Foreign students pursuing a project in Germany. 2. An innovative project plan. All applicants should have a high level of commitment, dedication and an innovative project plan. Scholarships are granted to students and young professionals (up to two years after graduation) from Germany wishing to realize a study or research project abroad or to foreign students/young professionals pursuing a project in Germany

Level of Study: Graduate

Type: Research grant

Value: Approximately €6,400 per year up to 2 years after graduation

Frequency: Annual

Country of Study: Any country

Application Procedure: The Bayer Science & Education Foundation supports students and young professionals that would like to study or work outside of their home country with the Bayer Foundation Fellowship Program, which consists of five scholarships. All applicants should have a high level of commitment, dedication and an innovative project plan. Scholarships are granted to students and young professionals (up to two years after graduation) from Germany wishing to realize a study or research project abroad or to foreign students/young professionals pursuing a project in Germany

Closing Date: 18 July or 1 June (Yearly deadlines in alternate)

Funding: Private

For further information contact:

Email: info@global-opportunities.net

Bayreuth International Graduate School of African Studies (BIGSAS)

University of Bayreuth, DEU -95440 Bayreuth, Germany

Email: bigsas@uni-bayreuth.de

Contact: BIGSAS

The University of Bayreuth is a hub of international and interdisciplinary research. African Studies have been a priority at the University of Bayreuth since its foundation in 1975. The Bayreuth International Graduate School of African Studies (BIGSAS) brings together African and European academic networks and fosters partnership.

Bayreuth International Graduate School of African Studies Sandwich Scholarship Programme

Subjects: African Studies
Eligibility: Applicants must have a very good Master's Degree in one of the disciplines represented at the Graduate School. Applications may be sent in German, English or French; the working language of BIGSAS is English
Level of Study: Doctorate
Type: Programme grant
Value: €1,200 monthly
Length of Study: 3 years
Frequency: Annual
Study Establishment: The Bayreuth International Graduate School of African Studies
Country of Study: Germany
Application Procedure: For more information on your online application please refer to: www.bigsas.uni-bayreuth.de/en/phd_programme/application/index.html
Closing Date: 28 February
Contributor: German Research Foundation of the Excellence Initiative of the German Federal and State Governments

For further information contact:

Email: bigsas-application@uni-bayreuth.de

Beinecke Scholarship Program

Box 125, Fogelsville, PA 18051-0125, United States of America

Tel: (1) 610 395 5560
Email: BeineckeScholarship@earthlink.net
Website: www.beineckescholarship.org
Contact: Dr Thomas L. Parkinson, Program director

The Beinecke Scholarship Program, established in 1970, seeks to encourage and enable highly motivated students to take the fullest advantage of graduate opportunities available to them and be courageous in the selection of graduate study programmes.

Beinecke Scholarship

Subjects: Liberal arts mathematics and natural sciences
Purpose: To encourage and enable highly motivated students to pursue opportunities available to them
Eligibility: Open to United States citizens or United States national from American Samoa or the commonwealth of Northern Mariana Islands with superior standards of intellectual ability, scholastic achievement and personal
Level of Study: Postgraduate
Type: Scholarship
Value: US$34,000
Length of Study: 1–5 years
Study Establishment: Any accredited university
Application Procedure: Request and submit a completed application form a curriculum vitae, a personal statement of 1,000 words and three letters of recommendation from faculty members
Closing Date: 1 March
Funding: Corporation
Contributor: The Sperry Fund

For further information contact:

Email: scholarships@learning.berkeley.edu

Beit Trust (Zimbabwe, Zambia and Malawi)

PO Box CH 76, Chisipite, Harare, Zimbabwe

Tel: (263) 4 496132
Fax: (263) 4 494046
Email: beitrust@africaonline.co.zw
Website: www.beittrust.org.uk

Beit Trust Postgraduate Scholarships

Subjects: All subjects
Purpose: To support postgraduate study or research
Eligibility: Open to persons under 30 years of age or 35 years for medical doctors, who are university graduates domiciled in Zambia, Zimbabwe or Malawi. Applicants must be nationals of those countries
Level of Study: Postgraduate
Type: Scholarship
Value: Fees and costs of tuition and related academic expenses are paid by the Trust direct to the universities. Payment of a personal allowance, index linked in accordance with guidance from an independent authority covering maintenance support. Other allowances are paid for arrival, a laptop and printing of a thesis, and return home. Economy Class air passages are provided by the Trust for the initial journey to the place of study, and for the return at the end of the course
Length of Study: A maximum of 3 years depending on course sought
Frequency: Annual

Study Establishment: Approved universities and other institutions in South Africa, Britain and Ireland
No. of awards offered: 400
Application Procedure: Applicants must complete an application form
Closing Date: 31 August
Funding: Private
No. of awards given last year: 8
No. of applicants last year: 400
Additional Information: Zambian applicants should contact the BEIT Trust United Kingdom office. Zimbabwe and Malawi applicants should contact the Zimbabwe office

For further information contact:

The BEIT Trust, BEIT House, Grove Road, Woking, GU21 5JB, Surrey, United Kingdom

Tel: (44) 1483 772 575
Fax: (44) 1483 725 833
Email: enquiries@beittrust.org.uk

Belgian American Educational Foundation (B.A.E.F.)

195 Church Street, New Haven, NH, BEL United States of America

Email: Emile.Boulpaep@Yale.edu
Website: www.baef.us
Contact: BELGIAN AMERICAN EDUCATIONAL FOUNDATION, INC

Belgian American Educational Foundation (B.A.E.F.)

Purpose: For fellowships for advanced study or research
Eligibility: Applicants must be citizens or permanent residents of the United States. Knowledge of Dutch, or French, or German is optional
Type: Fellowship
Value: US$27,000 for Master
Length of Study: 1 year
Frequency: Annual
Country of Study: Any country
Application Procedure: Application forms can be downloaded from the B.A.E.F. website at: www.baef.us
Closing Date: 31 October
Additional Information: For additional information contact the Foundation at the above address or email: Emile. Boulpaep@Yale.edu

For further information contact:

Email: mail@baef.be

Fellowships for study of research in Belgium

Subjects: All fields
Purpose: Fellowships for advanced study or research during the academic year, at a Belgian university or institution of higher learning. The fellowships provide outright non-renewable grants carrying a stipend of US$28,000 for Master's or PhD students US$32,000 for Post-doctoral Fellows
Eligibility: Applicants must be citizens or permanent residents of the United States. Applicants must 1. Either at the time of application be registered in a PhD or equivalent degree program in the United States. 2. Or while holding the BAEF fellowship register in a graduate program (Master's or PhD) in Belgium. 3. Or hold a Master's, PhD, or equivalent degree. Post-doctoral applicants should by 1 July have no more than 2 years since obtaining their PhD degree
Level of Study: Doctorate, Graduate, Postdoctorate, Postgraduate, Predoctorate, Professional development, Research, MBA, Postgraduate (MSc)
Type: A variable number of fellowships
Value: US$28,000 to US$32,000
Length of Study: 1 year
Frequency: Annual
Country of Study: Belgium
No. of awards offered: 40
Application Procedure: Application forms can be downloaded from the BAEF website at: www.baef.us. In addition to a completed application form, applicants must furnish undergraduate and graduate transcripts, a brief autobiographical statement, a statement of purpose, and 3 letters of recommendation. Completed applications for the fellowships must be submitted as electronic documents in pdf format attached to an email sent no later than October 31 to emile. boulpaep@yale.edu
Closing Date: 31 October
Funding: Foundation
Contributor: Foundation Endowment
No. of awards given last year: 10
No. of applicants last year: 40

For further information contact:

Belgian American Educational Foundation, Inc., 195 Church Street, New Haven, CT 06510, United States of America

Email: emile.boulpaep@yale.edu
Contact: Professor Emile Boulpaep, President

Belgian Flemish University, VLIR-UOS

Website: www.vliruos.be/6323.aspx

VLIR-UOS Training and Masters Scholarships

Purpose: VLIR-UOS awards scholarships to students from 31 eligible countries in Africa, Asia and Latin-America, to follow an English-taught training or master programme at a Flemish university or university college in Belgium

Eligibility: VLIR-UOS gives priority to candidates who are employed in academic institutions, research institutes, governments, social economy or NGO's, or aim a career in one of these sectors

Level of Study: Postgraduate

Type: Scholarship

Value: VLIR-UOS only provides full scholarships for the total duration of the training or Master

Frequency: Annual

Country of Study: Belgium

Application Procedure: To apply for a training or Master programme, visit the website of the training or Master programme of your interest. www.vliruos.be/en/scholarships/6

Closing Date: Varies

Contributor: Flemish university

Additional Information: For more information, please visit official scholarship website: www.vliruos.be/6323.aspx

For further information contact:

Email: scholarships@vliruos.be

Belgian Technical Cooperation agency (BTC), Ghent University

BTC - Belgian Development Agency, Rue Haute, 147, BEL 1000, Brussels, Belgium

Tel: (32) 2 505 37 00
Fax: (32) 2 502 98 62
Website: www.belspo.be/belspo/index_nl.stm

The Belgian Technical Cooperation agency (BTC) is the administrator and coordinator for scholarships awarded by the Belgian Directorate-General for Development Cooperation (DGDC). The BTC itself does not award grants. The BTC's Scholarship Unit implements the scholarship files,

welcomes the students and provides them with guidance for the duration of their academic training and stay in Belgium.

Belgian Technical Cooperation Scholarships

Purpose: To finance postgraduate courses

Level of Study: Doctorate

Type: Scholarship

Value: Doctorate scholarships: covers registration fees, travel expenses and insurances

Country of Study: Belgium

Application Procedure: Candidates interested in a scholarship should send their application form directly to the Attaché for Development Cooperation or to the Embassy of Belgium in the partner country

Closing Date: Please check the website

Contributor: Belgian Directorate-General

For further information contact:

Email: development.cooperation@vub.ac.be

Berkeley Graduate Division

Robert E. Thunen Memorial Scholarships

Purpose: These scholarships are for students who wish to study any and all fields of lighting (such as architectural, commercial, residential, airport, navigational, theatrical or television, agricultural, and vision)

Eligibility: They arrange for at least three letters of recommendation, at least one of which shall be from someone involved with lighting professionally or academically. The Thunen Scholars for each year will be announced in mid-May of each year

Level of Study: Graduate

Type: Scholarship

Value: US$2,500

Frequency: Annual

Country of Study: Any country

Application Procedure: Applications and letters of recommendation should be submitted before 1 April of each year

Closing Date: 1 April of each year

Funding: Private

For further information contact:

Thunen Scholarship Committee, IES San Francisco Section, Mary-Jane Lawless, 1201 Park Ave Ste 100, Emeryville, CA 94608, United States of America

Email: mlaw@silvermanlight.com

Berlin Graduate School Muslim Cultures and Societies

Altensteinstrasse 48, DEU 14195, Berlin, Germany

Tel: (49) 30 838 53417
Fax: (49) 30 838 53244
Email: office@bgsmcs.fu-berlin.de
Website: www.fu-berlin.de/en/

Zentrum Moderner Orient and Berlin Graduate School of Muslim Cultures and Societies Visiting Research Fellowship

Purpose: We are interested in attracting outstanding researchers who are engaged in research projects that are relevant to the respective research profiles at ZMO and BGSMCS
Eligibility: The call is open for senior researchers and recent postdocs in the humanities and the social sciences. Applications by candidates from Africa, Asia and the Middle East are particularly encouraged
Level of Study: Postgraduate
Value: Successful applicants will receive a monthly stipend (€2,500, covering all expenses including travel and accommodation), and a period of stay that should normally last up to 3 months
Country of Study: Germany
Closing Date: 31 November
Funding: Trusts

For further information contact:

Tel: (49) 30 838 53417
Email: office@bgsmcs.fu-berlin.de

Berlin Mathematical School

TU Berlin, Sekr. MA 2-2, Strasse des 17. Juni 136, DEU 10623, Berlin, Germany

Tel: (49) 30-314-78611
Email: office@math-berlin.de
Contact: Berlin Mathematical School

The Berlin Mathematical School (BMS) is a joint graduate school of the mathematics departments of the three major Berlin universities, TU Berlin, FU Berlin, and HU Berlin.

BMS invite excellent mathematics students from Berlin, Germany, Europe and all over the world to join BMS – and to make good use of the ample opportunities offered by the rich and diverse mathematics teaching and research environment.

Dirichlet International Postdoctoral Fellowship at Berlin Mathematical School in Germany

Subjects: Fellowship is awarded to young mathematicians who want to pursue their own research in one of the eight research fields of mathematics offered by the Berlin Mathematical School
Purpose: The Berlin Mathematical School (BMS) is currently accepting applications for Dirichlet Postdoc Fellowship starting. This three-year position is open to promising young mathematicians who will have completed their PhD degree by 30 September and want to pursue their own research in one of the eight research fields of mathematics offered by the Berlin Mathematical School
Eligibility: International applicants are eligible to apply for this fellowship. For more details, please check the website
Type: Postdoctoral fellowship
Value: The competitive full-year salary includes health insurance
Frequency: Annual
Study Establishment: Fellowship is awarded to young mathematicians who want to pursue their own research in one of the eight research fields of mathematics offered by the Berlin Mathematical School
Country of Study: Germany
Application Procedure: In order to access the application form, you first have to register: Go to Registration. Then please submit your application via the online submission form. You are permitted to submit only one application. Please note that you will be asked to input the name and email address of three referees during the online application process. Please have the following PDF documents ready for upload during this process: Letter of Application 1. Curriculum Vitae. 2. University Certificates. 3. Research Statement. 4. List of Publications
Closing Date: 1 March
Additional Information: For more details, please browse the below website. scholarship-positions.com/dirichlet-international-postdoctoral-fellowship-berlin-mathematical-school-germany

For further information contact:

Email: postdoc@math-berlin.de

Beta Phi Mu Headquarters

PO Box 42139, Phildadelphia, PA 19101, United States of America

Tel:	(1) 267 361 5018
Fax:	(1) 215 895 2494
Email:	headquarters@betaphimu.org
Website:	www.betaphimu.org
Contact:	Isabel Gray, Program Director

Beta Phi Mu is a library and information studies honor society, founded in 1948, with over 35,000 graduates of the ALA-initiated accredited professional programmes. Beta Phi Mu was founded at the University of Illinois by a group of leading librarians and library educators. Aware of the notable achievements of honour societies in other professions, they believed that such a society would have much to offer librarianship and library education.

American Library Association Beta Phi Mu Award

Purpose: The Beta Phi Mu Award is given in recognition of the achievement of a library school faculty member or another individual for distinguished service to education for librarianship
Type: Award
Value: US$1,000 and a citation of achievement
Frequency: Annual
Country of Study: Any country
Application Procedure: Guidelines and application available on the American Library Association website: www.ala.org/awardsgrants/awards/43/apply. The Beta Phi Mu Award is given in recognition of the achievement of a library school faculty member or another individual for distinguished service to education for librarianship. This annual award consists of US$1,000 and a Citation of Achievement
Closing Date: 1 December
Funding: Trusts
Contributor: Beta Phi Mu International Library Science Honorary Society
No. of awards given last year: 1

For further information contact:

American Library Association 50 East Huron Street, Chicago, IL 60611 2795, United States of America

Tel:	(1) 312 944 6780
Fax:	(1) 312 440 9374
Email:	ala@ala.org

Bibliographical Society of America (BSA)

PO Box 1537, Lenox Hill Station, New York, NY 10021, United States of America

Tel:	(1) 212 452 2710
Fax:	(1) 212 452 2710
Email:	bsa@bibsocamer.org
Website:	www.bibsocamer.org
Contact:	Ms Michele Randall, Executive Director

The Bibliographical Society of America (BSA) invites applications for its annual short-term fellowships, which supports bibliographical inquiry as well as research in the history of the book trades and in publishing history.

Bibilography Society of America -Harry Ransom Center Pforzheimer Fellowship in Bibliography

Subjects: The bibliographical study of early modern books and manuscripts, 1455-1700, held in the Ransom Center's Pforzheimer Library and in related collections of early printed books and manuscripts, including the Pforzheimer Gutenberg Bible
Purpose: Supports the bibliographical study of early modern books and manuscripts, 1455-1700, held in the Ransom Center's Pforzheimer Library and in related collections of early printed books and manuscripts, including the Pforzheimer Gutenberg Bible
Eligibility: Supports the bibliographical study of early modern books and manuscripts, 1455-1700, held in the Ransom Center's Pforzheimer Library and in related collections of early printed books and manuscripts, including the Pforzheimer Gutenberg Bible
Level of Study: Unrestricted
Type: Fellowship
Value: US$3,000
Frequency: Annual
Country of Study: Any country
Application Procedure: For more info please visit www.hrc.utexas.edu/research/fellowships/bsa/. Applications are due 1 November of each year. Applications should include the following components: Application form Project proposal of no more than 1,000 words Applicant's curriculum vitae Two signed letters of recommendation on official letterhead submitted independently by referees. The two letters of recommendation must be signed and submitted independently by referees (in PDF or MS Word format) via the BSA Fellowship recommendation submission form. No other documentation will be considered by the committee. The fellowship

committee will match proposed projects to suitable fellow-ships, and the awards will be announced at the annual meeting of the Society in January of each year. All fellowships require a project report within one year of receipt of the award, and copies of any publications resulting from the project are to be sent to the BSA. Links to the new Fellowship Application form will be available by 1 August. The application package and two supporting letters of recommendation must be received by 1 November. We regret that we cannot consider late or incomplete applications. Applicants are advised to request recommendation letters well in advance. For more information, please contact Hope Mayo, Chair of the Fellow-ship Committee at bsafellowships@bibsocamer.org

Closing Date: 1 November
Funding: Private
Contributor: BSA-Harry Ransom Center Pforzheimer
Additional Information: www.hrc.utexas.edu/research/fellowships/bsa/. Links to the new Fellowship Application form will be available by 1 August. The application package and two supporting letters of recommendation must be received by 1 November. We regret that we cannot consider late or incomplete applications. Applicants are advised to request recommendation letters well in advance. For more information, please contact Hope Mayo, Chair of the Fellow-ship Committee at bsafellowships@bibsocamer.org

For further information contact:

Email: bsa@bibsocamer.org
Contact: Erin Schreiner, Executive Director

Justin G. Schiller Prize

Subjects: Pre-20th-Century Children's Books
Purpose: The Schiller Prize for Bibliographical Work on pre-twentieth century Children's Books is intended to encourage scholarship in the bibliography of historical chil-dren's books
Eligibility: Works put into nomination, which must be in English, may concentrate on any children's book printed before the year 1901 in any country or any language. Sub-missions should involve research into bibliography and printing history broadly conceived and should focus on the physical book as historical evidence for studying topics such as the history of book production, publication, distribution, collecting, or reading. Studies of the printing, publishing, and allied trades, as these relate to children's books, are also welcome. Eligible scholarship may take the form of a published book or article, a master's thesis or doctoral dissertation that has been defended and approved, or research results distributed in another manner, such as on a website or a CD-ROM. Eligible scholarship must have been published, approved, or posted between 1 January and

1 October. Nominations, with copies of the monographs or links to articles and websites, must be completed by 15 November
Level of Study: Unrestricted
Type: Prize
Value: US$3,000
Frequency: Every 3 years
Study Establishment: pre-twentieth century children's books
Country of Study: Any country
Application Procedure: Applications must contain the fol-lowing items: a letter of intent addressed to the "Schiller Prize Committee," a one-page curriculum vitae, any documentation regarding the approval of a thesis or a dissertation or confirming the date of a publication, if required. A hard copy of a published monograph or essay placed into nomina-tion is encouraged, but a PDF is acceptable. If a copy is not submitted, a complete citation of the work must be included with the application. Authors of web-based or online resources should provide the URL for the full-text or submit a PDF. Web-based resources require free access to the website and instructions regarding its use, along with a statement regarding plans for maintaining ongoing access
Closing Date: 15 November
Funding: Individuals
Contributor: Endowed by Justin G. Schiller
Additional Information: Please also send an additional applications to this email - aimmel@Princeton.EDU

For further information contact:

Department of Rare Books and Special Collections, Princeton University Library, 1 Washington Road, Princeton, NJ 08544-2098, United States of America

Tel: (1) 609 258 1470
Email: bsa@bibsocamer.org
Contact: Andrea Immel, Curator, Cotsen Children's Library, Schiller Prize Coordinator

St. Louis Mercantile Library Prize

Subjects: Submissions for the Mercantile Library Prize should concentrate on some aspect of American history and culture in territories that now comprise the United States, or on literature by American authors, or literature intended for publication in territories that now comprise the United States. They should involve research in bibliography and printing history broadly conceived and focus on the book (the physical object) as his-torical evidence for studying topics such as the history of book production, publication, distribution, collecting, or reading. Studies of the printing, publishing, and allied trades, as these relate to American history and literature, are also welcome

Purpose: Encourage scholarship in the bibliography of American history and literature

Eligibility: Submissions for the Mercantile Library Prize should concentrate on some aspect of American history and culture in territories that now comprise the United States, or on literature by American authors, or literature intended for publication in territories that now comprise the United States. They should involve research in bibliography and printing history broadly conceived and focus on the book (the physical object) as historical evidence for studying topics such as the history of book production, publication, distribution, collecting, or reading. Studies of the printing, publishing, and allied trades, as these relate to American history and literature, are also welcome. Submissions may take the form of a published book or article, a master's thesis or doctoral dissertation defended and approved, or research results distributed in another manner, such as the website or CD-ROM. Submissions must have been published or, if a dissertation or thesis, approved the year of the deadline or in the three previous calendar years. If a publication has an incorrect nominal date disqualifying it for submission but an actual date of publication within the prize period, it may be nominated with a letter by the publisher or editor testifying to the actual date of publication. Unpublished dissertations and theses must be accompanied by a letter from the director attesting their approval. Scholars are eligible to apply for the Prize without regard to membership in the Bibliographical Society of America or any other society, and without regard to citizenship or academic affiliation, degree, or rank. The Prize will be awarded to the author of a particular work of scholarship without regard to the author's prolonged or repeated contributions to the field. Applications are encouraged from young or junior scholars who have not as yet published extensively. Applicants may nominate themselves or be nominated by others

Level of Study: Doctorate

Type: Prize

Value: US$2,000

Frequency: Every 3 years

Study Establishment: bibliography of American history and literature

Country of Study: United States of America

Application Procedure: Please send the following as separate PDF or Word (.doc or .docx) files to mercantile. prize@bibsocamer.org. Mailed print copies of these documents will not be accepted. To assure consideration, applications must be received by 1 November. A letter of intent addressed to the "Mercantile Prize Committee," a one-page curriculum vitae, and, if required, any documentation regarding the approval of a thesis or a dissertation, or confirming the date of a publication. Web-based nominations must include a URL, and free access to the website and instructions regarding its use must be offered, along with a statement regarding plans for maintaining and/or archiving the website. This information should be included in the letter of intent (#1 above). Please also secure delivery of four (4) print copies or four (4) CD-ROMs of the nominated work to: Erin Schreiner Executive Director, Bibliographical Society of America 67 West Street, Suite 401 #C17 Brooklyn, NY 11222 If for any reason the cost of securing review copies is prohibitive to submitting a nomination, please contact Erin Schreiner, BSA Executive Director, by email at bsa@bibsocamer.org. Other questions regarding the award should be addressed to the Mercantile Library Prize Coordinator: John N. Hoover John Neal Hoover Endowed Mercantile Library Executive Directorship St. Louis Mercantile Library Association jhoover@umsl.edu

Closing Date: 1 November

Funding: Private

Contributor: St. Louis Mercantile Library at the University of Missouri, St. Louis

Additional Information: If for any reason the cost of securing review copies is prohibitive to submitting a nomination, please contact Erin Schreiner, BSA Executive Director, by email at bsa@bibsocamer.org. Other questions regarding the award should be addressed to the Mercantile Library Prize Coordinator: John N. Hoover John Neal Hoover Endowed Mercantile Library Executive Directorship St. Louis Mercantile Library Association jhoover@umsl.edu

For further information contact:

Email: bsa@bibsocamer.org

Contact: Ms Erin Schreiner, Executive Director, The Bibliographical Society

The Bibilographic Society of America -Rare Book School Fellowship

Subjects: To provide funds tuition for one course for one first-year attendee each year at the University of Virginia's Rare Book School, with an additional grant for travel or housing expenses

Purpose: To provide funds tuition for one course for one first-year attendee each year at the University of Virginia's Rare Book School, with an additional grant for travel or housing expenses

Eligibility: Awarded to students and professionals working on a bibliographical project that intersects with and could be informed by RBS course content; Preference given to applicants early in their careers

Level of Study: Unrestricted

Type: Scholarship

Value: Tuition for 1 course and US$500 toward travel

Length of Study: 1 year

Frequency: Annual

Country of Study: United States of America

Application Procedure: Please visit this webpage for more info on the scholarship rarebookschool.org/admissions-awards/faqs/. Applications are due 1 November of each year. Applications should include the following components: Application form Project proposal of no more than 1,000 words Applicant's curriculum vitae Two signed letters of recommendation on official letterhead submitted independently by referees. The two letters of recommendation must be signed and submitted independently by referees (in PDF or MS Word format) via the BSA Fellowship recommendation submission form. No other documentation will be considered by the committee. Please visit the website to download the form. The fellowship committee will match proposed projects to suitable fellowships, and the awards will be announced at the annual meeting of the Society in January of each year. All fellowships require a project report within one year of receipt of the award, and copies of any publications resulting from the project are to be sent to the BSA. Links to the new Fellowship Application form will be available by 1 August. The application package and two supporting letters of recommendation must be received by 1 November. We regret that we cannot consider late or incomplete applications. Applicants are advised to request recommendation letters well in advance. For more information, please contact Hope Mayo, Chair of the Fellowship Committee at bsafellowships@bibsocamer.org

Closing Date: 1 November

Funding: Private

Contributor: Rare Book School University of Virgina

Additional Information: Links to the new Fellowship Application form will be available by 1 August. The application package and two supporting letters of recommendation must be received by 1 November. We regret that we cannot consider late or incomplete applications. Applicants are advised to request recommendation letters well in advance. For more information, please contact Hope Mayo, Chair of the Fellowship Committee at bsafellowships@bibsocamer.org

For further information contact:

Email: bsa@bibsocamer.org
Contact: Erin Schreiner, Executive Director

The Bibilographic Society of America Short-term Fellowships

Subjects: Bibliographical research that focuses on the physical aspects of books or manuscripts as historical evidence. Books and manuscripts in any field and of any period are eligible for consideration

Purpose: These fellowships support bibliographical research that focuses on the physical aspects of books or manuscripts as historical evidence. Books and manuscripts in any field and of any period are eligible for consideration. Projects may include studying the history of book or manuscript production, publication, distribution, collecting, or reading. Projects to establish a text are also eligible

Eligibility: These fellowships support bibliographical research that focuses on the physical aspects of books or manuscripts as historical evidence. Books and manuscripts in any field and of any period are eligible for consideration. Projects may include studying the history of book or manuscript production, publication, distribution, collecting, or reading. Projects to establish a text are also eligible

Level of Study: Unrestricted

Type: Fellowship

Value: US$3,000

Frequency: Varies

Study Establishment: Bibliographical research that focuses on the physical aspects of books or manuscripts as historical evidence

Country of Study: Any country

Application Procedure: Applications are due 1 November of each year. Applications should include the following components: Application form Project proposal of no more than 1,000 words Applicant's curriculum vitae Two signed letters of recommendation on official letterhead submitted independently by referees. The two letters of recommendation must be signed and submitted independently by referees (in PDF or MS Word format) via the BSA Fellowship recommendation submission form. No other documentation will be considered by the committee. The fellowship committee will match proposed projects to suitable fellowships, and the awards will be announced at the annual meeting of the Society in January of each year. All fellowships require a project report within one year of receipt of the award, and copies of any publications resulting from the project are to be sent to the BSA. Links to the new Fellowship Application form will be available by 1 August. The application package and two supporting letters of recommendation must be received by 1 November. We regret that we cannot consider late or incomplete applications. Applicants are advised to request recommendation letters well in advance. For more information, please contact Hope Mayo, Chair of the Fellowship Committee at bsafellowships@bibsocamer.org

Closing Date: 1 November

Funding: Foundation

Contributor: The BSA

Additional Information: For more information, please contact Hope Mayo, Chair of the Fellowship Committee at bsafellowships@bibsocamer.org. Links to the new Fellowship Application form will be available by 1 August

For further information contact:

Email: bsa@bibsocamer.org
Contact: Erin Schriener, Executive Director

The Bibliographical Society of America-American Society for Eighteenth-Century Studies Fellowship for Bibliographical Studies in the Eighteenth Century

Subjects: Eighteenth-Century Studies
Purpose: Recipients must be a member of the American Society for Eighteenth-Century Studies at the time of the award
Eligibility: Recipients must be a member of the American Society for Eighteenth-Century Studies at the time of the award
Type: Fellowship
Value: US$3,000
Frequency: Annual
Country of Study: Any country
Application Procedure: Applications are due 1 November of each year. Applications should include the following components: Application form Project proposal of no more than 1,000 words Applicant's curriculum vitae Two signed letters of recommendation on official letterhead submitted independently by referees. The two letters of recommendation must be signed and submitted independently by referees (in PDF or MS Word format) via the BSA Fellowship recommendation submission form. No other documentation will be considered by the committee. Please visit the website to download the form. The fellowship committee will match proposed projects to suitable fellowships, and the awards will be announced at the annual meeting of the Society in January of each year. All fellowships require a project report within one year of receipt of the award, and copies of any publications resulting from the project are to be sent to the BSA. Links to the new Fellowship Application form will be available by 1 August. The application package and two supporting letters of recommendation must be received by 1 November. We regret that we cannot consider late or incomplete applications. Applicants are advised to request recommendation letters well in advance. For more information, please contact Hope Mayo, Chair of the Fellowship Committee at bsafellowships@bibsocamer.org
Closing Date: 1 November
Funding: Private
Contributor: American Society for Eighteenth-Century Studies
Additional Information: Links to the new Fellowship Application form will be available by 1 August. The application package and two supporting letters of recommendation must be received by 1 November. We regret that we cannot consider late or incomplete applications. Applicants are advised to request recommendation letters well in advance. For more information, please contact Hope Mayo, Chair of the Fellowship Committee at bsafellowships@bibsocamer.org

For further information contact:

Email: bsa@bibsocamer.org
Contact: Erin Schreiner, Executive Director

The Bibliographical Society of America-Pine Tree Foundation Fellowship in Culinary Bibliography

Subjects: The bibliographical study of printed and manuscript cookbooks (once commonly known as receipt books); medical recipe books that also contain culinary recipes; other types of books, manuscript, and printed material that include a substantial body of culinary recipes; treatises on and studies of gastronomy; or memoirs, diary accounts, or descriptions of food and cooking. Projects may cover any period or country
Purpose: Supports the bibliographical study of printed and manuscript cookbooks (once commonly known as receipt books); medical recipe books that also contain culinary recipes; other types of books, manuscript, and printed material that include a substantial body of culinary recipes; treatises on and studies of gastronomy; or memoirs, diary accounts, or descriptions of food and cooking. Projects may cover any period or country
Eligibility: Supports the bibliographical study of printed and manuscript cookbooks (once commonly known as receipt books); medical recipe books that also contain culinary recipes; other types of books, manuscript, and printed material that include a substantial body of culinary recipes; treatises on and studies of gastronomy; or memoirs, diary accounts, or descriptions of food and cooking. Projects may cover any period or country
Level of Study: Unrestricted
Type: Fellowship
Value: US$3,000
Frequency: Annual
Country of Study: Any country
Application Procedure: Applications are due 1 November of each year. Applications should include the following components: Application form Project proposal of no more than 1,000 words Applicant's curriculum vitae Two signed letters of recommendation on official letterhead submitted independently by referees. The two letters of recommendation must be signed and submitted independently by referees (in PDF or MS Word format) via the BSA Fellowship recommendation submission form. No other documentation will be considered

by the committee. The fellowship committee will match proposed projects to suitable fellowships, and the awards will be announced at the annual meeting of the Society in January of each year. All fellowships require a project report within one year of receipt of the award, and copies of any publications resulting from the project are to be sent to the BSA. Links to the new Fellowship Application form will be available by 1 August. The application package and two supporting letters of recommendation must be received by 1 November. We regret that we cannot consider late or incomplete applications. Applicants are advised to request recommendation letters well in advance. For more information, please contact Hope Mayo, Chair of the Fellowship Committee at bsafellowships@bibsocamer.org

Closing Date: 1 November

Funding: Foundation

Contributor: BSA-Pine Tree Foundation

Additional Information: Links to the new Fellowship Application form will be available by 1 August. The application package and two supporting letters of recommendation must be received by 1 November. We regret that we cannot consider late or incomplete applications. Applicants are advised to request recommendation letters well in advance. For more information, please contact Hope Mayo, Chair of the Fellowship Committee at bsafellowships@bibsocamer.org

For further information contact:

Email: bsa@bibsocamer.org
Contact: Erin Schreiner, Executive Director

The Bibliographical Society of America-Pine Tree Foundation Fellowship in Hispanic Bibliography

Subjects: The bibliographical study of printed and manuscript items 1) in the Spanish language produced during any period and in any country; or 2) in any language provided they were produced in Spain, or in its overseas dominions during the time of Spanish sovereignty; or 3) the bibliographical study of book and manuscript collections in Spain, or in its overseas dominions during the time of Spanish sovereignty; or 4) the bibliographical study of Spanish-language book and manuscript collections during any period and in any country

Purpose: Supports the bibliographical study of printed and manuscript items 1) in the Spanish language produced during any period and in any country; or 2) in any language provided they were produced in Spain, or in its overseas dominions during the time of Spanish sovereignty; or 3) the bibliographical study of book and manuscript collections in Spain, or in its overseas dominions during the time of Spanish sovereignty; or 4) the bibliographical study of Spanish-language

book and manuscript collections during any period and in any country

Eligibility: Supports the bibliographical study of printed and manuscript items 1) in the Spanish language produced during any period and in any country; or 2) in any language provided they were produced in Spain, or in its overseas dominions during the time of Spanish sovereignty; or 3) the bibliographical study of book and manuscript collections in Spain, or in its overseas dominions during the time of Spanish sovereignty; or 4) the bibliographical study of Spanish-language book and manuscript collections during any period and in any country

Level of Study: Unrestricted

Type: Fellowship

Value: US$3,000

Frequency: Annual

Country of Study: Any country

Application Procedure: Applications are due 1 November of each year. Applications should include the following components: Application form Project proposal of no more than 1,000 words Applicant's curriculum vitae Two signed letters of recommendation on official letterhead submitted independently by referees. The two letters of recommendation must be signed and submitted independently by referees (in PDF or MS Word format) via the BSA Fellowship recommendation submission form. No other documentation will be considered by the committee. Please visit the website to download the form. The fellowship committee will match proposed projects to suitable fellowships, and the awards will be announced at the annual meeting of the Society in January of each year. All fellowships require a project report within one year of receipt of the award, and copies of any publications resulting from the project are to be sent to the BSA. Links to the new Fellowship Application form will be available by 1 August. The application package and two supporting letters of recommendation must be received by 1 November. We regret that we cannot consider late or incomplete applications. Applicants are advised to request recommendation letters well in advance. For more information, please contact Hope Mayo, Chair of the Fellowship Committee at bsafellowships@bibsocamer.org

Closing Date: 1 November

Funding: Foundation

Contributor: BSA- Pine Tree Foundation

Additional Information: Links to the new Fellowship Application form will be available by 1 August. The application package and two supporting letters of recommendation must be received by 1 November. We regret that we cannot consider late or incomplete applications. Applicants are advised to request recommendation letters well in advance. For more information, please contact Hope Mayo, Chair of the Fellowship Committee at bsafellowships@bibsocamer.org

For further information contact:

Email: bsa@bibsocamer.org
Contact: Erin Schreiner, Executive Director

The Bibliographical Society of America-St. Louis Mercantile Library Fellowship

Subjects: Research in North American bibliography, including studies in the North American book trade, production and distribution of North American Books, North American book illustration and design, North American collecting and connoisseurship, and North American bibliographical history in general

Purpose: Supports research in North American bibliography, including studies in the North American book trade, production and distribution of North American Books, North American book illustration and design, North American collecting and connoisseurship, and North American bibliographical history in general. Non-traditional and innovative projects will be especially welcome and encouraged

Eligibility: Supports research in North American bibliography, including studies in the North American book trade, production and distribution of North American Books, North American book illustration and design, North American collecting and connoisseurship, and North American bibliographical history in general. Non-traditional and innovative projects will be especially welcome and encouraged

Level of Study: Unrestricted

Type: Fellowship

Value: US$3,000

Frequency: Annual

Country of Study: Any country

Application Procedure: Applications are due 1 November of each year. Applications should include the following components: Application form Project proposal of no more than 1,000 words Applicant's curriculum vitae Two signed letters of recommendation on official letterhead submitted independently by referees. The two letters of recommendation must be signed and submitted independently by referees (in PDF or MS Word format) via the BSA Fellowship recommendation submission form. No other documentation will be considered by the committee. Please visit the website to download the form. The fellowship committee will match proposed projects to suitable fellowships, and the awards will be announced at the annual meeting of the Society in January of each year. All fellowships require a project report within one year of receipt of the award, and copies of any publications resulting from the project are to be sent to the BSA. Links to the new Fellowship Application form will be available by 1 August. The application package and two supporting letters of recommendation must be received by 1 November. We regret that we cannot consider late or incomplete applications.

Applicants are advised to request recommendation letters well in advance. For more information, please contact Hope Mayo, Chair of the Fellowship Committee at bsafellowships@bibsocamer.org

Closing Date: 1 November

Funding: Private

Contributor: St. Louis Mercantile Library

Additional Information: Links to the new Fellowship Application form will be available by 1 August. The application package and two supporting letters of recommendation must be received by 1 November. We regret that we cannot consider late or incomplete applications. Applicants are advised to request recommendation letters well in advance. For more information, please contact Hope Mayo, Chair of the Fellowship Committee at bsafellowships@bibsocamer.org

For further information contact:

Email: bsa@bibsocamer.org
Contact: Erin Schreiner, Executive Director

The Charles J. Tanenbaum Fellowship in Cartographical Bibliography

Subjects: All aspects of the history, presentation, printing, design, distribution and reception of cartographical documents from Renaissance times to the present, with a special emphasis on eighteenth-century cartography

Purpose: Supports projects dealing with all aspects of the history, presentation, printing, design, distribution and reception of cartographical documents from Renaissance times to the present, with a special emphasis on eighteenth-century cartography

Eligibility: Supports projects dealing with all aspects of the history, presentation, printing, design, distribution and reception of cartographical documents from Renaissance times to the present, with a special emphasis on eighteenth-century cartography

Level of Study: Unrestricted

Type: Fellowship

Value: US$3,000

Frequency: Annual

Country of Study: Any country

Application Procedure: Applications are due 1 November of each year. Applications should include the following components: Application form Project proposal of no more than 1,000 words Applicant's curriculum vitae Two signed letters of recommendation on official letterhead submitted independently by referees. The two letters of recommendation must be signed and submitted independently by referees (in PDF or MS Word format) via the BSA Fellowship recommendation submission form. No other documentation will be considered by the committee. The fellowship committee will match proposed projects to suitable fellowships, and the awards will be announced at the annual meeting of the Society in January of each year. All fellowships require a project report within one year of receipt of the award, and copies of any publications resulting from the project are to be sent to the BSA. Links to the new Fellowship Application form will be available by 1 August. The application package and two supporting letters of recommendation must be received by 1 November. We regret that we cannot consider late or incomplete applications. Applicants are advised to request recommendation letters well in advance. For more information, please contact Hope Mayo, Chair of the Fellowship Committee at bsafellowships@bibsocamer.org

Closing Date: 1 November
Funding: Foundation
Contributor: Pine Tree Foundation of New York
Additional Information: Links to the new Fellowship Application form will be available by 1 August. The application package and two supporting letters of recommendation must be received by 1 November. We cannot consider late or incomplete applications. Applicants are advised to request recommendation letters well in advance. For more information, please contact Hope Mayo, Chair of the Fellowship Committee at bsafellowships@bibsocamer.org

For further information contact:

Email: bsa@bibsocamer.org
Contact: Erin Schreiner, Executive Director

The Fredson Bowers Award

Subjects: Support bibliographical research between BSA and BSA United Kingdom
Purpose: Support bibliographical research between BSA and BSA United Kingdom
Eligibility: Study of bibliographical materials in Americas or the United Kingdom
Level of Study: Unrestricted
Type: Bursary
Value: £1,500
Frequency: Annual
Country of Study: United Kingdom or United States of America
Application Procedure: Applications are due 1 November of each year. Applications should include the following components: United Kingdom entries should follow application instructions located at this website www. bibsoc.org.uk/fellowships/application-procedure. Procedure

for United States residents 1. Application form. 2. Project proposal of no more than 1,000 words. 3. Applicant's curriculum vitae. 4. Two signed letters of recommendation on official letterhead submitted independently by referees. The two letters of recommendation must be signed and submitted independently by referees (in PDF or MS Word format) via the BSA Fellowship recommendation submission form. No other documentation will be considered by the committee. 5. The fellowship committee will match proposed projects to suitable fellowships, and the awards will be announced at the annual meeting of the Society in January of each year. All fellowships require a project report within one year of receipt of the award, and copies of any publications resulting from the project are to be sent to the BSA. Links to the new Fellowship Application form will be available by 1 August. The application package and two supporting letters of recommendation must be received by 1 November. We regret that we cannot consider late or incomplete applications. Applicants are advised to request recommendation letters well in advance. For more information, please contact Hope Mayo, Chair of the Fellowship Committee at bsafellowships@bibsocamer.org

Closing Date: 1 November
Funding: Private
Contributor: Bibliographical Society of America and Bibliographical Society of the United Kingdom
Additional Information: United Kingdom entries should follow application instructions located at this website www. bibsoc.org.uk/fellowships/application-procedure. Links to the new Fellowship Application form will be available by 1 August. The application package and two supporting letters of recommendation must be received by 1 November. We regret that we cannot consider late or incomplete applications. Applicants are advised to request recommendation letters well in advance. For more information, please contact Hope Mayo, Chair of the Fellowship Committee at bsafellowships@bibsocamer.org

For further information contact:

Email: bsa@bibsocamer.org
Contact: Erin Schreiner, Executive Director

The Katharine F. Pantzer Senior Fellowship in the British Book Trades

Subjects: Bibliographical inquiry into the history of the book trades and publishing history in Britain during the hand-press period, as well as studies of authorship, reading and collecting based on the examination of British books published in that period, with a special emphasis on descriptive bibliography

Purpose: The Katharine F. Pantzer Senior Fellowship in the British Book Trades research by a senior scholar engaged in bibliographical inquiry into the history of the book trades and publishing history in Britain during the hand-press period, as well as studies of authorship, reading and collecting based on the examination of British books published in that period, with a special emphasis on descriptive bibliography

Eligibility: Supports research by a senior scholar engaged in bibliographical inquiry into the history of the book trades and publishing history in Britain during the hand-press period, as well as studies of authorship, reading and collecting based on the examination of British books published in that period, with a special emphasis on descriptive bibliography

Type: Fellowship

Value: US$6,000

Frequency: Varies

Study Establishment: Bibliographical research of the British Book Trades

Country of Study: Any country

Application Procedure: Applications are due 1 November of each year. Applications should include the following components: Application form Project proposal of no more than 1,000 words Applicant's curriculum vitae Two signed letters of recommendation on official letterhead submitted independently by referees. The two letters of recommendation must be signed and submitted independently by referees (in PDF or MS Word format) via the BSA Fellowship recommendation submission form. No other documentation will be considered by the committee. - Please visit the website to download the form. The fellowship committee will match proposed projects to suitable fellowships, and the awards will be announced at the annual meeting of the Society in January of each year. All fellowships require a project report within one year of receipt of the award, and copies of any publications resulting from the project are to be sent to the BSA. Links to the new Fellowship Application form will be available by 1 August. The application package and two supporting letters of recommendation must be received by 1 November. We regret that we cannot consider late or incomplete applications. Applicants are advised to request recommendation letters well in advance. For more information, please contact Hope Mayo, Chair of the Fellowship Committee at bsafellowships@bibsocamer.org

Closing Date: 1 November

Funding: Individuals

Contributor: Katherine Panzer

Additional Information: Links to the new Fellowship Application form will be available by 1 August. The application package and two supporting letters of recommendation must be received by 1 November. We regret that we cannot consider late or incomplete applications. Applicants are advised to request recommendation letters well in advance. For more information, please contact Hope Mayo,

Chair of the Fellowship Committee at bsafellowships@bibsocamer.org

For further information contact:

Email: bsa@bibsocamer.org
Contact: Erin Schreiner, Executive Director

The Katharine Pantzer Junior Fellowship in the British Book Trades

Subjects: The history of the book trades and publishing history in Britain during the hand-press period, as well as studies of authorship, reading and collecting based on the examination of British books published in that period, with a special emphasis on descriptive bibliography

Purpose: Supports bibliographical inquiry into the history of the book trades and publishing history in Britain during the hand-press period, as well as studies of authorship, reading and collecting based on the examination of British books published in that period, with a special emphasis on descriptive bibliography

Eligibility: Supports bibliographical inquiry into the history of the book trades and publishing history in Britain during the hand-press period, as well as studies of authorship, reading and collecting based on the examination of British books published in that period, with a special emphasis on descriptive bibliography

Level of Study: Unrestricted

Type: Fellowship

Value: US$3,000

Frequency: Annual

Country of Study: Any country

Application Procedure: Applications are due 1 November of each year. Applications should include the following components: Application form Project proposal of no more than 1,000 words Applicant's curriculum vitae Two signed letters of recommendation on official letterhead submitted independently by referees. The two letters of recommendation must be signed and submitted independently by referees (in PDF or MS Word format) via the BSA Fellowship recommendation submission form. No other documentation will be considered by the committee. Please visit the website to download the form. The fellowship committee will match proposed projects to suitable fellowships, and the awards will be announced at the annual meeting of the Society in January of each year. All fellowships require a project report within one year of receipt of the award, and copies of any publications resulting from the project are to be sent to the BSA. Links to the new Fellowship Application form will be available by 1 August. The application package and two supporting letters of recommendation must be received by 1 November. We regret that we cannot consider late or incomplete applications. Applicants are advised to request recommendation letters well in advance. For more information, please contact Hope Mayo, Chair of the Fellowship Committee at bsafellowships@bibsocamer.org

Closing Date: 1 November
Funding: Individuals
Contributor: Katherine Panzer
Additional Information: Links to the new Fellowship Application form will be available by 1 August. The application package and two supporting letters of recommendation must be received by 1 November. We regret that we cannot consider late or incomplete applications. Applicants are advised to request recommendation letters well in advance. For more information, please contact Hope Mayo, Chair of the Fellowship Committee at bsafellowships@bibsocamer.org

For further information contact:

Email: bsa@bibsocamer.org
Contact: Erin Schreiner, Executive Director

The Reese Fellowship for American Bibliography and the History of the Book in the Americas

Subjects: Explores the history of print culture in the Western Hemisphere
Purpose: The fellowship may be awarded to any scholar, whether academic or independent, whose project explores the history of print culture in the Western Hemisphere
Eligibility: The fellowship may be awarded to any scholar, whether academic or independent, whose project explores the history of print culture in the Western Hemisphere
Level of Study: Unrestricted
Type: Fellowship
Value: US$3,000
Frequency: Annual
Country of Study: Any country
Application Procedure: Applications are due 1 November of each year. Applications should include the following components: Application form Project proposal of no more than 1,000 words Applicant's curriculum vitae Two signed letters of recommendation on official letterhead submitted independently by referees. The two letters of recommendation must be signed and submitted independently by referees (in PDF or MS Word format) via the BSA Fellowship recommendation submission form. No other documentation will be considered by the committee. The fellowship committee will match proposed projects to suitable fellowships, and the awards will be announced at the annual meeting of the Society in January of each year.

All fellowships require a project report within one year of receipt of the award, and copies of any publications resulting from the project are to be sent to the BSA. Links to the new Fellowship Application form will be available by 1 August. The application package and two supporting letters of recommendation must be received by 1 November. We regret that we cannot consider late or incomplete applications. Applicants are advised to request recommendation letters well in advance. For more information, please contact Hope Mayo, Chair of the Fellowship Committee at bsafellowships@bibsocamer.org

Closing Date: 1 November
Funding: Corporation
Contributor: William Reese Company
Additional Information: Links to the new Fellowship Application form will be available by 01 August. The application package and two supporting letters of recommendation must be received by 1 November. We regret that we cannot consider late or incomplete applications. Applicants are advised to request recommendation letters well in advance. For more information, please contact Hope Mayo, Chair of the Fellowship Committee at bsafellowships@bibsocamer.org

For further information contact:

Email: bsa@bibsocamer.org
Contact: Erin Schreiner, Executive Director

Bielefeld University

Bielefeld Graduate School in History and Sociology, Postfach 10 01 31, DEU 33501 Bielefeld, Germany

Tel: (49) 521 106 6526
Email: bghs@uni-bielefeld.de
Website: www.uni-bielefeld.de/bghs

Bielefeld Graduate School in History and Sociology Start-up Doctoral Scholarships

Subjects: History, sociology, anthropology or political science
Purpose: The Bielefeld Graduate School in History and Sociology is inviting applications for six scholarships for international prospective doctoral researchers starting in 1 April
Eligibility: Applicants should hold a Master's degree or equivalent in sociology, history, political science, social anthropology or gender studies; applications from related

disciplines are welcome. The university strongly encourages women to apply. Graduates from abroad who wish to pursue a doctoral degree in history, sociology, anthropology or political science may apply for a start-up scholarship. We welcome applications from predoctoral researchers. Applicants should speak either German or English fluently

Level of Study: Doctorate, Postgraduate
Type: Scholarship
Value: A stipend of €1,200 per month. This amount will be supplemented by an allowance for children if applicable. Upon application, travel costs can also be covered by the Graduate School
Length of Study: 4 months
Frequency: Annual
Study Establishment: University of Bielefeld
Country of Study: Germany
Application Procedure: Applications should be submitted online (www.uni-bielefeld.de/(en)/bghs/bewerbung/startup/start-up.html). Please submit the following documents: covering letter (400 words max.); curriculum vitae (1,000 words max.); summary of your MA thesis (600 words max.); project description (800 words max.); letter of recommendation from your supervisor/advisor at your university (if preferred, your supervisor/advisor can send the letter directly to the BGHS: application-bghs@uni-bielefeld.de; university and college transcripts (Master's certificate or a statement from your examination office that you have successfully completed your Master's studies. All your grades, including the grade for your Master's thesis, must be displayed in this statement.)
Closing Date: October
Contributor: University of Bielefeld
Additional Information: Please check details at www.uni-bielefeld.de/(en)/bghs/bewerbung/startup/

Bilkent University

Faculty of Business Administration, MBA Programme, Office of the Dean, Ankara 06800, Turkey

Tel:	(90) 312 290 1596
Fax:	(90) 312 266 4958
Email:	fba@bilkent.edu.tr
Website:	www.bilkent.edu.tr
Contact:	MBA Admissions Officer

Bilkent University is a non-profit research university. Courses are conducted in English. The University has more than 11,000 students and an international teaching staff of 1,000.

Bilkent Industrial Engineering Fellowship

Subjects: Industrial Engineering and Operations Research
Level of Study: Doctorate

For further information contact:

Bilkent University Department of Industrial Engineering, Main Campus Engineering Building Floor 3, Bilkent, 06800 Ankara, Turkey

Tel:	(90) 312 290 1262
Fax:	(90) 312 266 4054
Email:	barbaros@bilkent.edu.tr
Contact:	Dr Barbaros Tansel, Department of Chairman

Bilkent International Relations Fellowship

Subjects: International relations theory, strategic studies, comparative foreign politics, and/or area studies
Purpose: To develop skills in international political analysis
Eligibility: Candidates are selected on the basis of past academic achievement and references
Level of Study: Doctorate
Type: Fellowship
Value: A monthly stipend and a tuition waiver
Frequency: Annual
Study Establishment: Bilkent University
Country of Study: Turkey
Application Procedure: Contact the Department of International Relations

For further information contact:

Tel:	(90) 312 266 4195
Fax:	(90) 312 266 4326
Email:	ir@bilkent.edu.tr
Contact:	Dr Ali Karaosmano

Bilkent Mathematics Fellowship

Subjects: Pure mathematics
Eligibility: Preference is given to research proposals focused on non-linear differential equations and general relativity
Level of Study: Doctorate, Postdoctorate
Type: Fellowship
Value: A monthly stipend and a tuition fee waiver
Frequency: Annual
Study Establishment: Bilkent University
Country of Study: Turkey
Application Procedure: Contact the department

For further information contact:

Tel:	(90) 312 266 4377
Fax:	(90) 312 266 4579
Email:	kocatepe@fen.bilkent.edu.tr
Contact:	Dr Metharet Kocatepe

Bilkent MIAPP Fellowship

Subjects: Politics, economics and international law
Purpose: To fund International and European affairs and executives who, understand and can dcal with the increasing complex problems of a rapidly changing world
Level of Study: Doctorate, Postdoctorate
Type: Fellowship
Value: A monthly stipend and a tuition fee waiver
Length of Study: 2 year
Frequency: Annual
Study Establishment: Bilkent University
Country of Study: Turkey
Application Procedure: Contact the Department

For further information contact:

Tel:	(90) 312 2901 249
Fax:	(90) 312 266 4960
Email:	muge@bilkent.edu.tr
Contact:	Dr Ali Karaosman

Bilkent Political Science Fellowship

Subjects: Political science
Purpose: To provide a sophisticated conceptual framework and the analytical skills to specialize in a particular aspect of Turkish or comparative politics
Eligibility: Applicants are required to have an MA degree in Political Science, Public Administrator or International Relations
Level of Study: Doctorate
Type: Fellowship
Value: A monthly stipend and a tuition fee waiver
Frequency: Annual
Study Establishment: Bilkent University
Country of Study: Turkey
Application Procedure: Contact the department

For further information contact:

Tel:	(90) 312 290 1931
Fax:	(90) 312 290 2792
Email:	cindoglu@bilkent.edu.tr
Contact:	Dr Dilek Cindo

Bilkent Turkish Literature Fellowship

Subjects: Turkish literature
Purpose: To enhance the standards of Turkish literary studies and universalize the field
Eligibility: Candidates will be required to take written and/or oral exams to prove their competence in Turkish, Ottoman and English
Level of Study: Doctorate
Type: Fellowship
Value: A monthly stipend and a tuition fee waiver
Length of Study: 3 years
Frequency: Annual
Study Establishment: Bilkent University
Country of Study: Turkey
Application Procedure: Contact the department

For further information contact:

Tel:	(90) 312 290 2711
Fax:	(90) 312 266 4059
Email:	turkedeb@bilkent.edu.tr
Contact:	Professor Talat S. Halman

Biola University

c/o The Financial Aid Office, 13800 Biola Avenue, La Mirada, CA 90639, United States of America

Tel:	(1) 562 903 4742
Fax:	(1) 562 906 4541
Email:	finaid@biola.edu
Website:	www.biola.edu
Contact:	Financial Aid Officer

Church Matching Scholarship

Purpose: Biola-funded match to church sponsorship
Eligibility: 1. Student must be enrolled in a traditional degree program. 2. ELP students once during first two semesters. 3. Student must be enrolled at least half-time. 4. Demonstrated need based on FAFSA information
Level of Study: Graduate
Type: Grant
Value: Up to US$750
Length of Study: 1 year
Frequency: Annual
Country of Study: Any country
Application Procedure: 1. Submit Church Matching Scholarship Application for appropriate aid year, and attach a church

sponsorship check made out to Biola University by the scholarship deadline. 2. Confirmed financial aid file by the scholarship deadline, which includes a completed FAFSA (online) and all requested forms, international students exempt

Closing Date: 1 October and 1 March are the deadlines (check website)

Funding: Private

Additional Information: For further information, visit the website at: offices.biola.edu/finaid/grad/talbot/scholarships/

For further information contact:

13800 Biola Ave. La Mirada, CA 90639, United States of America

Tel: (1) 562 903 6000
Email: business@biola.edu

Biotechnology and Biological Sciences Research Council (BBSRC)

Polaris House, North Star Avenue, Wiltshire SN2 1UH, Swindon, United Kingdom

Tel: (44) 1793 413 200
Fax: (44) 1793 413 201
Email: postdoc.fellowships@bbsrc.ac.uk
Website: www.bbsrc.ac.uk

BBSRC is the United Kingdom's principal funder of basic and strategic biological research. It is a non-departmental public body, one of the seven Research Councils supported through the Science and Innovation Group of the Department for Innovation, Universities and Skills (DIUS). It supports research and research training in universities and research centres throughout the United Kingdom, including BBSRC-sponsored institutes, and promotes knowledge transfer from research to applications in business, industry and policy, and public engagement in the biosciences. It funds research in some exciting areas including genomics, stem cell biology, and bionanotechnology.

David Phillips Fellowships

Subjects: All subjects

Purpose: To support outstanding early-career scientists who wish to establish themselves as independent researchers

Eligibility: Applicants should not exceed 10 years in active postgraduate research studies and postdoctoral research employment. Applicants should have no less than 3 years of active postdoctoral research experience

Level of Study: Postdoctorate

Type: Fellowship

Value: Personal salary and a significant research support grant to support the costs of the research

Length of Study: 5 years

Application Procedure: Submit a proposal electronically via the Joint Electronic Submissions (Je-S) system from July with the mandatory attachments mentioned at www.bbsrc.ac.uk/funding/fellowships/david-phillips.aspx

Closing Date: 21 October

Additional Information: Fellowships are awarded under full economic costing (fEC). Further queries, please contact Postgraduate Training and Research Career Development Branch. Important: applicants should ensure proposals are submitted to their host institution's Je-S submitter/approval pool well in advance (a minimum of 5 working days) of the published deadline

For further information contact:

Email: postdoc.fellowships@bbsrc.ac.uk

Institute Career Path Fellowships

Subjects: Animal biology

Eligibility: Open to candidates who have a minimum of 3 years and no more than 10 years of active postdoctoral research experience

Level of Study: Doctorate, Postdoctorate

For further information contact:

Email: fiona.tomley@bbsrc.ac.uk or bruce. whitelaw@bbsrc.ac.uk

Institute Development Fellowships

Subjects: Mathematics

Purpose: To enable BBSRC scientists to spend a period of collaborative work at another research organization and to provide a mechanism for the influx of new ideas and new skills in strategically important areas to enhance the quality of science in BBSRC sponsored institutes

Eligibility: Open to all BBSRC scientists at Band 5 and above on an open-ended contract, who have worked for a minimum of 5 years in their current or similar post

Level of Study: Research

Type: Fellowships

Value: To cover the costs associated with the proposed research development activities

Length of Study: 6–12 months
Application Procedure: All applications must be submitted online
Closing Date: 14 November
Additional Information: Further queries, please contact Postgraduate Training and Research Career Development Branch

For further information contact:

Email: postdoc.fellowships@bbsrc.ac.uk

Professorial Fellowships

Subjects: All subjects
Purpose: To support world-class scientists with a proven track record of developing new and innovative directions of research and who have the potential to use a fellowship to open up dramatic and novel lines of work
Eligibility: Open to scientists who are already recognized at an international level as outstanding researchers with exceptional research and interpretative achievements
Type: Fellowships
Value: Grant to cover the costs of the research programme
Length of Study: 5 years
Application Procedure: Check website for further details
Closing Date: 14 November
Additional Information: Further queries, please contact Postgraduate Training and Research Career Development Branch

For further information contact:

Email: postdoc.fellowships@bbsrc.ac.uk

Research Development Fellowships

Subjects: All subjects
Purpose: To support scientists wishing to undertake new directions in their research. Applicants seeking to develop interdisciplinary dimensions by integrating new techniques or methodologies into their research are particularly encouraged
Eligibility: Open to scientists who are full-time members of academic staff of a United Kingdom university who have worked for a minimum of 5 years in their current or similar post
Type: Fellowship
Value: To cover the costs associated with the proposed research development activities
Length of Study: 1–3 years
Application Procedure: Applications must be submitted online

Closing Date: 14 November
Additional Information: Further queries, please contact Postgraduate Training and Research Career Development Branch

For further information contact:

Email: postdoc.fellowships@bbsrc.ac.uk

Birbeck University of London

Bonnart Trust PhD Scholarship

Subjects: Diversity and Belonging or Minorities and Social Justice
Purpose: The purpose of The Bonnart Trust is to 'establish and maintain scholarships at universities in the United Kingdom for research at the postgraduate level into the nature of racial, religious and cultural intolerance with a view to finding a means to combat it'
Eligibility: Candidates will normally possess at least an upper second class undergraduate honours degree or equivalent and a master's degree or equivalent
Type: Scholarship and award
Frequency: Every 3 years
Country of Study: Any country
Application Procedure: For further information, check the following website. www.bbk.ac.uk/sshp/research/funding-for-research-students
Closing Date: 1 February
Funding: Private
Additional Information: Interviews for this grant will be held late March/early April

For further information contact:

School of Social Sciences, History and Philosophy, Birkbeck, University of London, 26 Russell Square London, United Kingdom

Email: studentships@bbk.ac.uk

Birkbeck, University of London

Malet Street, Bloomsbury WC1E 7HX, United Kingdom
Birkbeck, University of London, is a public research university located in Bloomsbury, London, United Kingdom, and a constituent college of the federal University of London

Birkbeck International Merit Scholarships

Subjects: Birkbeck International Merit Scholarships are provided by the Birkbeck, University of London. The applicants with excellent academic achievements receive this scholarship

Eligibility: Birkbeck is offering a number of merit scholarships to suitably qualified students from Japan, Russia, South Korea, Turkey, Latin America, South-East Asia (ASEAN) and Taiwan. Accepted International Student by the University; Excellent Academic and Leadership Achievements

Type: Scholarship

Value: Scholarship amount: £2,500–£5,000

Country of Study: United Kingdom

Application Procedure: 1. Initially, you will have to apply to Birkbeck, University of London. 2. Once you have received an offer from Birkbeck, you must email them an essay of no more than 500 words. The essay should detail why you are the ideal candidate to receive the International Merit Scholarship. Recipients will be chosen based on a combination of academic merit and financial need

Closing Date: 1 June

For further information contact:

Email: international-office@bbk.ac.uk

Blakemore Foundation

1201 3rd Avenue, Suite 4900, Seattle, WA 98101 3099, United States of America

Tel: (1) 206 359 8778
Fax: (1) 206 359 9778
Email: blakemorefoundation@gmail.com
Website: www.blakemorefoundation.org
Contact: Eugene H. Lee, Trustee

Blakemore Freeman Fellowships for Advanced Asian Language Study

Subjects: Blakemore Freeman Fellowships are awarded for one academic year of full-time, intensive language study of Chinese, Japanese, Korean, Thai, Vietnamese, Indonesian, Khmer or Burmese at the advanced level in approved language programs in East or Southeast Asia. Superior candidates pursuing careers in fields such as academia, STEM (science, technology, engineering, math), international business, accounting, law, medicine, journalism, architecture, teaching, social or NGO work, and government service are encouraged to apply

Purpose: To permit American citizens or permanent residents of the United States to raise their language skills in Chinese, Japanese, Korean, Thai, Vietnamese, Indonesian, Khmer or Burmese to professional working proficiency

Eligibility: Pursuing a professional, business, technical or academic career that involves the regular use of Chinese, Japanese, Korean, Thai, Vietnamese, Indonesian, Khmer or Burmese. 1. By the start of the grant, have (at minimum) a college undergraduate degree. 2. Be at or near an advanced level in the language. By the start of the grant, applicants must have completed (at minimum) the equivalent of the third year of languages classes at the college level, either through classes taken in the United States or through a combination of study at the college level in the United States and intensive language study abroad programs. 3. Be able to devote oneself exclusively to full-time intensive language study during the term of the grant; grants are not made for part-time study or research. 4. Be a citizen or permanent resident of the United States of America

Type: A variable number of grants

Value: Full tuition at approved language schools in East & SE Asia plus stipend for travel, study & living expenses

Length of Study: 9–10 months

Frequency: Annual

Study Establishment: See website for list of approved language programs

Country of Study: Other

No. of awards offered: 139

Application Procedure: To apply for a Blakemore Freeman Fellowship the applicant must complete an application form on our application portal at blakemorefoundation.communityforce.com. Information needed to complete application. 1. a list of all classes/training taken in the chosen language of study. 2. a list of any academic and professional honors applicant has have been awarded. 3. a copy in PDF format of the applicant's curriculum vitae or resume. 4. a personal essay, three to four pages in length, double-spaced, in PDF format, detailing applicant's career path and goals, discussing academic, professional or business background, prior study of the language and involvement with the Asian country, and how the language will be used to achieve career objectives. 5. Names and email addresses of two academic or professional contacts to submit letters of recommendation on applicant's behalf. 6. Official transcripts from all college-level institutions from a degree has been received or applicants is currently attending

Closing Date: 30 December

Funding: Foundation, Trusts

Contributor: Blakemore Foundation; The Freeman Foundation

No. of awards given last year: 14
No. of applicants last year: 139
Additional Information: Email address above is incorrect: The new email for the Foundation is contactus@blakemorefoundation.org. Application must be completed on-line at: blakemorefoundation.communityforce.com

Bond University

School of Business, c/o International Office, Gold Coast QLD 4229, Australia

Tel:	(61) 7 5595 1706
Fax:	(61) 7 5595 4062
Email:	international@bond.edu.au
Contact:	MBA Admissions Officer

Bond University United Kingdom Excellence Scholarship in Australia

Purpose: Bond University is now accepting applications from citizens of the United Kingdom for the United Kingdom Excellence Scholarship. Bond University aims to help identify future leaders and realize their full potential by providing access to an exceptional educational experience
Eligibility: To be considered applicants must: High achieving citizens of the United Kingdom who are currently residing outside of Australia are encouraged to apply; Applicants must have received an offer to study at Bond prior to applying. People studying in English as part of packaged offers at the Bond University College are still eligible to apply; Keep excellent academic qualifications; Students have already received a proposal from Bond University to start a bachelor or postgraduate degree; Examples of high academic achievement may include students with high achieving A Level or IB results; High achieving academic students applying for the undergraduate study who are not currently completing an Australian High School equivalent in the United Kingdom are also eligible to apply
Level of Study: Postgraduate
Type: Scholarship
Value: 50% tuition remission
Frequency: Annual
Country of Study: Australia, the United Kingdom, Europe or the United States of America
Application Procedure: To apply, students must complete the Bond University Online Application Form to receive their program offer before applying for this scholarship. 1. Once an offer has been received, students must download and complete the United Kingdom Excellence Scholarship Application Form through the given link: Application Form. 2. Applicants must submit their complete application to international@bond.edu.au by the relevant application closing date. 3. Recipients of the United Kingdom Excellence Scholarship are awarded 25% tuition waivers for their chosen program. 4. Scholarships are not available for some programs, visit bond.edu.au/scholarships/UK for full details. These scholarships are awarded on the basis of academic excellence and are a testament to Bond University's commitment to quality and outstanding international students
Closing Date: 24 May
Funding: Private
Contributor: Bond University
Additional Information: Applications close on 24 May for students commencing in September semester

For further information contact:

14 University Drive, Robina, QLD 4226, Australia

Email:	international@bond.edu.au

Boren Awards

Boren Scholarship

Purpose: Boren Scholars represent a vital pool of highly motivated individuals who wish to work in the federal national security arena. In exchange for funding, Boren Scholars commit to working in the federal government for at least one year after graduation
Eligibility: 1. A United States citizen at the time of application. 2. A high school graduate, or have earned a GED. 3. Matriculated in an undergraduate degree program located within the United States accredited by an accrediting body recognized by the United States Department of Education. Boren Scholars must remain matriculated in their undergraduate programs for the duration of the scholarship and may not graduate until the scholarship is complete. 4. Applying to a study abroad program that meets home institution standards in a country outside of Western Europe, Canada, Australia, or New Zealand. Boren Scholarships are not for study in the United States
Level of Study: Graduate
Type: Scholarship
Value: US$8,000 for a summer program, US$10,000 for a semester and US$20,000 for 6–12 months

Frequency: Annual
Country of Study: United States of America
Closing Date: 7 February
Funding: Private

For further information contact:

1400 K Street, NW 7TH floor, Washington DC 20005, United States of America

Email: boren@iie.org

Botswana Insurance Holdings Limited Trust

PO Box 336, Gaborone, BW, Botswana

Tel: (267) 3707400
Fax: (267) 3973705
Email: webmaster@bihl.co.bw
Website: www.bihl.co.bw/

BIHL Group is a leading financial services group, originally established in 1975. BIHL has been listed on the Botswana Stock Exchange and is the holding company for three subsidiaries and holds a stake in two associate companies.

Botswana Insurance Holdings Limited Trust Thomas Tlou Scholarship for Master Programme

Purpose: The BIHL Trust Thomas Tlou Scholarship aims to benefit talented young Batswana with aspirations to pursue postgraduate studies in any discipline aimed at contributing to Botswana's socio-economic development
Eligibility: The scholarship is open to all citizens of Botswana who wish to pursue a master's programme in any discipline at a local reputable and recognized institution of higher learning on Botswana. The intended recipients must be aged between 18–35
Level of Study: Postgraduate
Type: Scholarship
Value: The Trust will spend a total of P 4,50,000
Country of Study: Any country
Application Procedure: Citizens of Botswana can apply for this scholarship
Closing Date: 30 June

For further information contact:

BIHL Group, Plot 66458, Block A, 3rd Floor, Fairgrounds Office Park, Gaborone, Botswana

Tel: (267) 3707400
Fax: (267) 3973705
Email: tkeepetsoe@bihl.co.bw

Bournemouth University

Fern Barrow, Poole, Dorset, BH12 5BB, Poole, United Kingdom

Tel: (44) 1202 524111
Fax: (44) 1202 962736
Email: enquiries@bournemouth.ac.uk
Website: www.bournemouth.ac.uk
Contact: Ms Karen Ward, Research Administrator

If you choose BU, you'll be learning from top academics in a community of academic excellence, with excellent industry links, accredited courses and placement opportunities, preparing you for professional practice. With a range of scholarships available, there's never been a better time to take charge of your own future with BU.

Bournemouth University Dean

Subjects: Any full-time taught postgraduate course delivered by the School of Health & Social Care
Eligibility: You will need to have a minimum of an upper second-class honours degree (2i). You cannot be in receipt of any other BU scholarship
Type: Scholarship
Frequency: Annual
Study Establishment: Bournemouth University
Country of Study: Any country
Application Procedure: Apply via online application form available on the BU website
Closing Date: 31 May
Contributor: Bournemouth University

Bournemouth University Dean's Scholarship – The Media School

Subjects: Any full-time taught postgraduate course delivered by The Media School
Eligibility: You will need to have a minimum of an upper second-class honours degree (2i), or overseas equivalent
Level of Study: Graduate, Postgraduate
Value: 50% tuition fee reduction
Country of Study: Any country
Closing Date: 31 July

For further information contact:

Email: enquiries@bournemouth.ac.uk

Bournemouth University Music Scholarships

Purpose: The scholarship supports young people with academic ability, leadership potential and a commitment to their community to achieve their full academic and leadership potential
Eligibility: Any United Kingdom or European Union applicants (for fee purposes) applying for a full-time undergraduate or postgraduate course
Type: Scholarship
Value: £600
Frequency: Annual
Study Establishment: Bournemouth University
Country of Study: United Kingdom
No. of awards offered: 15
Application Procedure: Apply via online form available on the BU website. As part of your application, you will need to source two references. Referees can include your Director of Music, music teacher, instrumental/vocal coach, ensemble conductor etc, or any other person qualified to write about your musical abilities. They need to complete and submit the online reference form. Scholarships will be awarded for the first year of study and may be continued for subsequent years of study providing you continue to meet the criteria
Closing Date: 31 August
Contributor: Bournemouth University
No. of applicants last year: 15

For further information contact:

Email: enquiries@bournemouth.ac.uk

Bournemouth University Vice-Chancellor's Scholarship – Most Promising Postgraduate Applicant

Eligibility: Any United Kingdom or European Union student who has completed an undergraduate degree at BU and who is applying for postgraduate study at BU
Level of Study: Graduate, Postgraduate
Country of Study: Any country

Reham al-Farra International Scholarship in Journalism

Subjects: Journalism
Purpose: The Reham Al-Farra Memorial Journalism Fellowship is a unique opportunity for young journalists from developing countries and countries with economies in transition to cover the United Nations

Eligibility: The Reham al-Farra International Scholarship in Journalism is offered to an international applicant for MA Multimedia Journalism. You must be classed as an overseas student for fees purposes. You cannot be in receipt of any other BU scholarships
Type: Scholarship
Value: £3,000
Frequency: Annual
Study Establishment: Bournemouth University
Country of Study: Any country
Application Procedure: Apply via online form available on the BU website
Closing Date: 31 May
Funding: Private
Contributor: Bournemouth University

The Business School Dean's Scholarship

Subjects: Any full-time taught Master's degree delivery by The Business School
Eligibility: You must be an applicant for a full-time taught Master's degree delivered by The Business School. Applicants will be considered based upon: 1. Academic achievement. 2. Work or voluntary experience relevant to the programme for which they have applied. 3. Any additional skills, experience or extra-curricular activities that will add value and indicate that they will make a significant contribution to the cohort on the programme or the Business School
Level of Study: Graduate, Postgraduate
Type: Scholarship
Value: up to £12,500
Frequency: Annual
Country of Study: Any country
Application Procedure: In order to apply for the scholarship, the following steps needs to be followed. To secure the scholarship award applicants must confirm acceptance of the award by the date stated on the scholarship offer email. Failure to confirm acceptance of the scholarship by this date may result in the applicant's right to the scholarship being removed and the scholarship being awarded to another applicant
Closing Date: 31 May

Bradford Chamber of Commerce and Industry

Devere House, Vicar Lane, Little Germany, Yorkshire BD1 5AH, Bradford, United Kingdom

Tel: (44) 1274 772 777
Fax: (44) 1274 771 081
Email: info@bradfordchamber.co.uk

Website: www.bradfordchamber.co.uk
Contact: Julie Snook, Financial Controller

The Bradford Chamber of Commerce and Industry represents member companies in the Bradford and district area. It works with local partners to develop the economic health of the district and has a major voice within the British Chamber of Commerce movement in order to promote the needs of local business on a national basis.

John Speak Trust Scholarships

Subjects: Modern languages
Purpose: To promote British trade abroad by assisting people in perfecting their basic knowledge of a foreign language
Eligibility: Open to British nationals intending to follow a career connected with the export trade in the United Kingdom. Applicants must be over 18 years of age with a sound, basic knowledge of at least one language
Level of Study: Professional development
Type: Scholarship
Value: Contribution towards living expenses and an amount towards the cost of travel
Length of Study: Between 3 months and 1 full academic year abroad depending on the circumstances and each candidate
Frequency: Annual
Study Establishment: A recognized college or university
Country of Study: Any country
No. of awards offered: 14
Application Procedure: Applicants must complete an application form and undertake an interview
Closing Date: 28 February, 31 May or 31 October
Funding: Private
No. of awards given last year: 10
No. of applicants last year: 14

Brain Research Institute

Florey Institute of Neuroscience and Mental Health, Melbourne Brain Centre - Austin campus, 245 Burgundy Street, Heidelberg, Victoria, VIC 3084, Australia

Tel: (61) 3 9035 7000
Fax: (61) 3 9496 4071
Email: BRI@brain.org.au
Website: www.brain.org.au/

The Brain Research Institute (BRI) was established at Austin Health, Melbourne, Australia in 1996. It supports collaboration between specialities in order to develop a better understanding of how a healthy or diseased brain functions. It is an affiliated institution of The University of Melbourne, an administering institution of the National Health & Medical Research Council and a member of Research Australia.

Brain Research Institute PhD Scholarships

Subjects: Engineering and technology information, computing and communication sciences, medical and health sciences or physical sciences
Purpose: To encourage competitive research in understanding the structure and function of the human brain
Eligibility: Open to candidates who have obtained Honours 1 or equivalent, or Honours 2a or equivalent
Level of Study: Doctorate
Type: Scholarship
Value: Varies
Length of Study: 3 years
Frequency: Annual
Country of Study: Australia
Application Procedure: Applicants must send a curriculum vitae, academic transcripts, expression of interest for area of research and details of two academic referees
Closing Date: Please check website

For further information contact:

Email: scholarships@brain.org.au
Contact: Karen van Nugteren, Scholarships Officer

BrightFocus Foundation

22512 Gateway Center Drive, Clarksburg, MD 20871, United States of America

Tel: (1) 800 437 2423
Fax: (1) 301 258 9454
Email: info@brightfocus.org
Website: www.brightfocus.org/
Contact: Dr Kara Summers, Grants Coordinator

BrightFocus Foundation (formerly American Health Assistance Foundation [AHAF]) is a non-profit charitable organization that funds research and public education on age related and degenerative diseases including: Alzheimer's disease, macular degeneration, glaucoma.

American Health Assistance Foundation Macular Degeneration Research

Subjects: Ophthalmology, biomedicine, biochemistry, biophysics, genetics, molecular biology and pharmacology
Purpose: To enable basic research on the causes of, or the treatment for, macular degeneration
Eligibility: The principal investigator must hold a tenure track or tenured position and the rank of assistant professor or higher
Level of Study: Research
Type: Grant
Value: maximum US$60,000 per year, payable over 2 years (total value US$120,000)
Length of Study: 2 year
Frequency: Annual
Study Establishment: Non-profit institutions and organizations
Country of Study: Any country
No. of awards offered: 81
Application Procedure: Applicants must complete an application form. The current application form should be requested for each year or can be downloaded from the website
Closing Date: July
Funding: Private
No. of awards given last year: 16
No. of applicants last year: 81

For further information contact:

Email:	researchgrants@brightfocus.org

British & Foreign School Society

Maybrook House, Godstone Road, Caterham, CR3 6RE, Surrey, United Kingdom

Tel:	(44) 1883 331 177
Website:	www.bfss.org.uk
Contact:	Mr J Kidd ACIB, Director

Global Professorships

Purpose: The aim of the programme is to enable world-class internationally-recognised established scholars to further their individual research goals while strengthening the United Kingdom research base and advancing the research goals and strategies
Eligibility: Applications must be submitted online using the British Academy's grants application system, Flexi-Grant.

Be a world-class internationally-recognised mid-career to senior researchers who are currently employed outside the United Kingdom, on a permanent contract (which may be part-time or full-time) or, if temporary, would normally be on a contract that will not end during the course of the grant unless expressly agreed with the Academy prior to the application being submitted that such an application would be considered eligible, in any field of the humanities or the social sciences. Hold a doctoral degree (or have equivalent research experience). Be available to take up an unpaid leave of absence, a long-term secondment or employment at an eligible United Kingdom host institution. Eligible institutions include but are not limited to the British International Research Institutes
Level of Study: Graduate, Postgraduate, Professional development, Research, Unrestricted
Type: Position (Employment)
Value: The British Academy will provide funding of up to £187,500 per annum, and up to £750,000 over four years
Length of Study: For a period of 4 years
Frequency: Every 3 years
Country of Study: United Kingdom
Application Procedure: 1. Applications must be submitted online using the British Academy's grants application system, Flexi-Grant. 2. Application, reference, supporting statement and United Kingdom host institution application approval deadline: 17.00 (United Kingdom time) on Wednesday, 6 March. 3. Applicants will be nominated based on the application rate and evaluation
Closing Date: 6 March
Funding: Government
Additional Information: All eligible proposals submitted in response to this funding call will be assessed by relevant British Academy peer reviewers and then considered by a final selection panel

For further information contact:

Email:	internationalgrants@thebritishacademy.ac.uk

British Academy

10-11 Carlton House Terrace, SW1Y 5AH, London, United Kingdom

Tel:	(44) 20 7969 5200
Fax:	(44) 20 7969 5300
Email:	chiefexec@britac.ac.uk, kene@britac.ac.uk
Website:	www.britac.ac.uk
Contact:	Dr Ken Emond, Head of Research Awards

The British Academy is the premier national learned society in the United Kingdom devoted to the promotion of advanced research and scholarship in the humanities and social sciences.

Browning Fund Grants

Subjects: Early modern British history
Purpose: To promote historical studies in the field of British history in the early modern period with particular reference to the 17th century
Eligibility: Applicants must be of postdoctoral status and ordinarily resident in the United Kingdom
Level of Study: Postdoctorate
Type: Research grant
Value: Up to £10,000
Length of Study: Up to 2 years
Frequency: Annual
Country of Study: Any country
No. of awards offered: Part of a larger scheme
Application Procedure: Application must be made to the BA/Leverhulme Small Research Grants Scheme via the BA's online e-GAP system at egap.britac.ac.uk
Closing Date: Please check the website
Funding: Private
No. of awards given last year: 1
No. of applicants last year: Part of a larger scheme
Additional Information: www.britac.ac.uk

For further information contact:

Email: bfi@brownfoundation.org

Early Childhood Development Funding

Purpose: This programme is intended as the foundation for a wider research programme in subsequent years and thus aims to support a new generation of interlinked research and policy intervention that focuses on what works at scale in different contexts whilst building, and working with, local capacity to deliver effective research and change
Eligibility: 1. The Early Childhood Development Programme is open to researchers based at United Kingdom and overseas institutions. The main applicant must be based at a university or research institute and be of postdoctoral or above equivalent status. 2. The applicant must either be in a permanent position at the institution or have a fixed-term position for the duration of the award
Level of Study: Graduate
Type: Funding support

Frequency: Varies
Country of Study: Any country
Closing Date: 21 June
Funding: Private

For further information contact:

10-11 Carlton House Terrace, SW1Y 5AH, London, United Kingdom

Email: ECD@britac.ac.uk

Honor Frost Foundation Grants

Subjects: Maritime archaeology and maritime cultural heritage
Purpose: To provide support for research maritime archaeology and maritime cultural heritage
Level of Study: Postdoctorate
Type: Research grant
Value: Up to £10,000
Length of Study: Up to 2 years
Frequency: Annual
No. of awards offered: Part of a larger scheme
Application Procedure: Applications must be submitted via e-GAP2, the Academy's electronic grant application system, by applying for a BA/Leverhulme Small Research Grant
Closing Date: Please check the website
Funding: Private
Contributor: Honor Frost Foundation
No. of awards given last year: 2
No. of applicants last year: Part of a larger scheme

For further information contact:

Email: rebeccagould@honorfrostfoundation.org,
             gailcaddy@honorfrostfoundation.org

Newton Mobility Grants

Purpose: The aim of the Newton Mobility Grants is to: - Strengthen research capacity of the partner countries - by facilitating training and skill transfer from the United Kingdom to partner countries. - Support excellent research - by linking the best researchers in the United Kingdom with the best researchers in partner countries and providing support for collaborative research
Eligibility: 1. Both a United Kingdom-based applicant and an overseas-based applicant are required for this scheme. 2. Both applicants must have a PhD or equivalent research experience

and hold a permanent or fixed-term contract in an eligible university or research institute, which must span the duration of the project. 3. Collaborations should focus on a single jointly defined research project involving (or lead by) the two applicants

Type: Grant
Frequency: Annual
Country of Study: United Kingdom
Application Procedure: Kindly check the website www.thebritishacademy.ac.uk/newton-mobility-grants
Closing Date: 5 September
Funding: Private

For further information contact:

10-11 Carlton House Terrace, SW1Y 5AH, London, United Kingdom

Tel: (44) 20 7969 5200
Email: newtonfund@thebritishacademy.ac.uk

Sir Ernest Cassel Educational Trust Grants

Subjects: Humanities and social sciences
Purpose: To enable early career researchers to travel overseas as part of a winter project supported under the BA/Leverhulme Small Research Grants Scheme
Eligibility: Applicants must be of postdoctoral status and ordinarily resident in the United Kingdom, and must be early career (within 5 years of the award or the doctorate)
Level of Study: Postdoctorate
Type: Research grant
Value: Normally not more than £1,000
Length of Study: Up to 2 years
Frequency: Annual
Country of Study: Any country
No. of awards offered: Part of a larger scheme
Application Procedure: Application must be made to the BA/Leverhulme small research Grants online e-GAP system at egap.britac.ac.uk
Closing Date: July
Funding: Private
Contributor: Sir Ernest Cassel Trust
No. of awards given last year: 11
No. of applicants last year: Part of a larger scheme

For further information contact:

Email: casseltrust@btinternet.com

British Association for American Studies (BAAS)

American Studies, School of Humanities, Keele University, ST5 5BG, Staffordshire, United Kingdom

Tel: (44) 1782 732000
Email: jo.gill@baas.ac.uk
Website: www.baas.ac.uk
Contact: Dr Sue Currell, BAAS Chair

The British Association for American Studies (BAAS), established in 1955, promotes research and teaching in all aspects of American studies. The Association organizes annual conferences and specialist regional meetings for students, teachers and researchers. The publications produced are The Journal of American Studies with Cambridge University Press, BAAS Paperbacks with Edinburgh University Press and British Records Relating to America in Microform with Microform Publishing.

British Association for American Studies Postgraduate and Early Career Short-Term Travel Awards

Purpose: To foster talent among the American Studies community in the United Kingdom. Fund travel to the United States of America for short-term research projects
Eligibility: Open to residents in the United Kingdom. Preference is given to young postgraduates and to members of BAAS. Successful candidates are required to provide a brief report of their research trip for publication in American Studies in Britain, and they are requested to acknowledge the assistance of BAAS in any other publication that results from research carried out during the tenure of the award
Level of Study: Doctorate, Postdoctorate, Postgraduate, Professional development
Type: Award
Value: UK£1,000
Frequency: Annual
Country of Study: United Kingdom or Australia
No. of awards offered: Classified
Application Procedure: Applicants must complete an application form
Closing Date: 10 December
Funding: Foundation
Contributor: American Embassy

No. of awards given last year: 6
No. of applicants last year: Classified
Additional Information: Successful candidates must write a report and acknowledge BAAS assistance in any related publication. Please contact at awards@baas.ac.uk

For further information contact:

Email: awards@baas.ac.uk

British Association for Canadian Studies (BACS)

UCL Institute of the Americas 51 Gordon Square, WC1H 0PN, London, United Kingdom

Tel: (44) 20 3108 9711
Fax: (44) 20 7117 1875
Email: bacs@canadian-studies.org
Website: www.canadian-studies.net
Contact: Dr Tony McCulloch, President

In response to the growing academic interest in Canada, the British Association for Canadian Studies (BACS) was established in 1975. Its aim is to foster teaching and research on Canada and Canadian issues by locating study resources in Britain, facilitating travel and exchange schemes for professorial staff and ensuring that the expertise of Canadian scholars who visit the United Kingdom is put to effective use. Principal activities include the publication of The British Journal of Canadian Studies and the BACS Newsletter, and the organization of the Association's annual multidisciplinary conference, which attracts scholars from Canada and Europe as well as from the United Kingdom.

Ontario Bicentennial Award

Subjects: Canadian area and cultural studies
Purpose: To fund travel to Ontario to research topics concerned with that province in history or political science
Eligibility: Graduate students will normally only be considered in the final stages of their doctoral research, priority will be given to BACS members
Level of Study: Doctorate
Type: Travel grant
Value: £500 approximately
Length of Study: Short visit

Frequency: Dependent on funds available
Study Establishment: University or library
Country of Study: Canada
No. of awards offered: 2
Application Procedure: Application form, plus supporting letter, curriculum vitae, and the names of two referees must be submitted
Closing Date: 1 May
No. of awards given last year: 1
No. of applicants last year: 2
Additional Information: Administered by BACS on behalf of the Foundation for Canadian Studies in the United Kingdom

British Association for Japanese Studies

c/o Mrs Lynn Baird, BAJS Secretariat, University of Essex, Wivenhoe Park, Essex C04 3SQ, Colchester, United Kingdom

Tel: (44) 7580 178 960
Email: bajs@bajs.org.uk
Website: www.bajs.org.uk

The Association was formed in 1974, with the 'aim to encourage Japanese studies in the United Kingdom, in particular by stimulating teaching and research'. With this in mind, the Association's first Conference was convened in Cambridge at Easter 1975, and since then the BAJS Conference has been an annual event.

British Association for Japanese Studies Postgraduate Studentships

Eligibility: The studentships are open to postgraduate or prospective postgraduate students of all nationalities. Applicants must have been accepted onto a full-time or part-time course at a United Kingdom university at the time application. Their dissertation (or proposed dissertation) must be in the field of Japanese studies. For PhD students in particular, it will normally be expected that they will be using Japanese language materials in their research. They must use the award either to contribute towards their fees, maintenance, or extended fieldwork. Applicants must be a member of BAJS at the time of application
Type: Studentship
Value: Up to 5 individual scholarships of £4,000 will be granted for use in given academic year. No awards of less than £4,000 will be made
Country of Study: United Kingdom

Application Procedure: Application for BAJS Postgraduate Studentships is via the online application form. For detailed information, please visit www.bajs.org.uk/funding/bajs_ studentship/

Closing Date: 15 May

Additional Information: Applicants will not be eligible to receive an award if they accept full scholarships from the AHRC, ESRC, or any other funding body (United Kingdom or overseas). Successful applicants will be expected to acknowledge the support of BAJS in their dissertations, presentations, and any subsequent publications; they will also be expected to submit a 500-word report on how they used the studentship to BAJS council by the end of November. Unsuccessful applicants will be considered for the BAJS Toshiba International Foundation studentship, provided they are eligible

For further information contact:

Email: h.spurling@southampton.ac.uk

British Association of Plastic Reconstructive and Aesthetic Surgeons (BAPRAS)

The Royal College of Surgeons, 35-43 Lincoln's Inn Fields, WC2A 3PE, London, United Kingdom

Tel: (44) 20 7831 5161
Fax: (44) 20 7831 4041
Email: secretariat@bapras.org.uk
Website: www.bapras.org.uk
Contact: Ms Angela Rausch, Administrator

Founded in 1946 as British Association of Plastic Surgeons. The objective of the association is to relieve sickness and to protect and preserve public health by the promotion and development of Plastic Surgery. A name change to British Association of Plastic Reconstructive and Aesthetic Surgeons (BAPRAS).

British Association of Plastic Reconstructive and Aesthetic Surgeons European Travelling Scholarships

Purpose: To enable Specialist Registrars from United Kingdom to visit any plastic surgical centre in Europe

Eligibility: Specialist Registrars (4–6) enrolled on a recognised training programme with the Specialist Advisory Committee in plastic surgery are eligible to apply. Preference will be given to trainees travelling abroad without other financial awards and those applying for funding prior travel. Candidates seeking funds to travel abroad in paid jobs are less preferred

Type: Scholarship

Value: Maximum value of one award is £5,000

Frequency: Annual

Study Establishment: Plastic Surgery Units

Country of Study: European Union

No. of awards offered: 1

Application Procedure: Applicants should complete an application form, submit a proposed itinerary that should be detailed and give costs and the reasons for particular visits and a curriculum vitae (maximum length of two pages) to the Chairman of the Education and Research Sub-Committee, BAPRAS

Closing Date: 10 December

No. of awards given last year: 1

No. of applicants last year: 1

For further information contact:

Email: bursaries@bapras.org.uk

Travelling Bursaries for Presentation at Overseas Meetings

Purpose: To cover the expenses for overseas travel by a consultant or trainee to present papers at international meetings

Eligibility: Applicants must submit an application form to the Chairman of the Education and Research Sub-Committee, BAPRAS

Type: Travel award

Value: £600

Frequency: Annual

Study Establishment: Various

Country of Study: Any country

No. of awards offered: 9

Application Procedure: Applicants must submit application form, abstract of paper to be presented and letter of acceptance to BAPRAS secretariat

Closing Date: 10 December

Contributor: BAPRAS

No. of awards given last year: 5

No. of applicants last year: 9

For further information contact:

Email: bursaries@bapras.org.uk

British Broadcasting Corporation Writersroom

1st Floor, Grafton House, 379-381 Euston Road, NW1 3AU, London, United Kingdom

Email: writersroom@bbc.co.uk
Website: www.bbc.co.uk/writersroom/opportunity

BBC Writersroom identifies and champions new writing talent and diversity across BBC Drama, Entertainment and Children's programmes. Writersroom is constantly on the lookout for writers of any age and experience who show real potential for the BBC. It invests in new writing projects nationwide and builds creative partnerships, including work with theatres, writer's organizations and film agencies across the country.

Alfred Bradley Bursary Award

Subjects: Drama
Purpose: The aim of the Award is to encourage new radio drama writing in the North of United Kingdom
Eligibility: Open to people who live in the North of United Kingdom and who have not had a previous network radio drama commission
Level of Study: Professional development
Type: Bursary
Value: Up to £5,000, writing bursary and the chance of a Radio 4 drama commission to Northern writers new to radio, and a 12 month mentorship with a Radio Drama producer
Frequency: Every 2 years
Country of Study: United Kingdom
Application Procedure: Applicants must send completed afternoon play scripts for consideration. Details published on www.bbc.co.uk/writersroom
Closing Date: 9 November
Funding: Private, Corporation
Contributor: BBC
Additional Information: There is a change of focus for each award, e.g. previous years have targeted comedy, drama, verse drama, etc. In 2004, the brief was for a play suitable for the afternoon play slot

For further information contact:

Email: admin@nawe.co.uk

British Council

Bridgewater House, 58 Whitworth Street, M1 6BB, Manchester, United Kingdom

Tel: (44) 161 957 7755
Fax: (44) 161 957 7762
Email: general.enquiries@britishcouncil.org
Website: www.britishcouncil.org

The British Council is the United Kingdom's public diplomacy and cultural organization working in more than 100 countries, in arts, education, governance and science. The British Council promotes the diversity and creativity of British society and culture. The Foreign and Commonwealth Office provides The British Council with the core grant-in-aid.

Commonwealth Scholarships

Purpose: For students from the developed Commonwealth to study in the United Kingdom
Eligibility: Please check at www.britishcouncil.org/india-scholarships-commonwealth-scholarships.htm for eligibility criteria
Level of Study: Doctorate
Type: Scholarship
Value: Student visas for the United Kingdom will be arranged gratis by the British Council
Application Procedure: See British Council website
Closing Date: 22 February
Funding: Government

For further information contact:

Department of Higher Education, External Scholarship Division, ES.4 Section, West Block-1, Wing-6, 2nd Floor, R.K. Puram, New Delhi 110066, India

Tel: (91) 11 26172491/26172492
Email: delhi.scholarship@in.britishcouncil.org

Marshall Scholarships

Subjects: All subjects
Purpose: To finance young Americans of high ability to study for a degree in the United Kingdom
Eligibility: Open to United States citizens who graduated with a first degree from an accredited 4-year university or

college in the United States by the start of the scholarship tenure; graduated with a cumulative GPA of at least 3.7 (A-); have formulated a feasible program of study to culminate in a second degree within 2 years

Type: Scholarship

Value: University fees, cost of living expenses, annual book grant, thesis grant, research and daily travel grants, fares to and from the United States and, where applicable, a contribution towards the support of a dependent spouse

Frequency: Annual

Country of Study: United Kingdom

Closing Date: October

Funding: Government

Contributor: British Council

No. of awards given last year: 40

For further information contact:

11766 Wilshire Boulevard, Suite 1200, Los Angeles, CA 90025 6538, United States of America

Tel: (310) 996 3028
Email: Losangeles@marshallscholarship.org
Contact: Alison Snyder, British Consulate-General

The Goa Education Trust (GET) Scholarships

Subjects: Media management, architecture, computing and design, TV documentary, music therapy, architectural conservation and human rights, communication systems and signal processing and innovation technology and the law

Purpose: To provide opportunities for dynamic young men and women of Goan origin who have demonstrated academic excellence and extra-curricular achievements to study or train in the United Kingdom

Eligibility: Open to Indian nationals, domiciled and resident in Goa or born of Goan parents, who are not more than 30 years of age at the time of applying for the scholarship and have an excellent academic track record. Candidates must have confirmed admission for any technical/vocational/academic course of study in the United Kingdom for up to 1 year

Level of Study: Postgraduate

Type: Scholarship

Value: Scholarships will fund young Indians to pursue a Masters in the United Kingdom and will cover part or full tuition fees not exceeding £15,000

Length of Study: 1 year

Frequency: Annual

Country of Study: United Kingdom

Application Procedure: A completed application form must be sent by post

Closing Date: 10 May

For further information contact:

British Council Division, British Deputy High Commission, 901, 9th Floor, Tower1, One Indiabulls Centre, 841, Senapati Bapat Marg, Elphinstone Road (West), Mumbai 400 013, India

Tel: (91) 22 67486748
Email: mumbai.enquiry@in.britishcouncil.org
Contact: GET Scholarships

British Dental Association

64 Wimpole Street, W1G 8YS, London, United Kingdom

Tel: (44) 20 7935 0875
Fax: (44) 20 7487 5232
Email: enquiries@bda.org
Website: www.bda.org
Contact: Miss Sarah Leithead, Marketing Executive

The British Dental Association (BDA) is the national professional association for dentists. With over 20,000 members, the Association strives to enhance the science, art and ethics of dentistry, improve the nation's oral health and promote the interests of its members.

British Dental Association/Dentsply Student Support Fund

Subjects: Dentistry, maxillo-facial surgery

Purpose: To give financial assistance to students who are in severe financial hardship. Only open to 4th- and 5th-year BDS students or postgraduates

Eligibility: Open to BDA members only. All applicants must be registered students at a United Kingdom Dental School

Level of Study: Graduate, Postgraduate

Type: Scholarship/Hardship fund

Value: Varies

Frequency: Annual

Country of Study: United Kingdom

No. of awards offered: 30

Application Procedure: Applicants must complete and submit application forms, accompanied by an academic

reference or supporting letter. Application forms can be found in the student section of the BDA website
Closing Date: 4 January and 1 July
Funding: Commercial
Contributor: Dentsply United Kingdom Ltd
No. of awards given last year: 7
No. of applicants last year: 30
Additional Information: For BDS/Dental Students only

For further information contact:

Email: SSF@contacts.bham.ac.uk

British Dietetic Association

The British Dietetic Association, 5th floor, Charles House, 148/9 Great Charles Street Queensway, B3 3HT, Birmingham, United Kingdom

Tel: (44) 1 2120 0802
Fax: (44) 1 2120 8081
Email: info@bda.uk.com
Website: www.bda.uk.com
Contact: Mr Nula Marnell, Assistant to the Chief Executive

The British Dietetic Association (BDA) is the professional body for dietitians in the United Kingdom and provides grants for research into human nutrition and dietetic practice that advances the profession.

Pace Award

Subjects: Nutrition, dietetics, education programme
Purpose: For the development or implementation of a nutrition education programme for staff addressing the problem of undernutrition
Eligibility: Applicants should be full members of the BDA and resident in the United Kingdom or Eire
Level of Study: Research
Type: Grant
Value: UK£500 to fund the development of the project and UK£300 worth of pace learning units for staff to use
Country of Study: Any country
Application Procedure: To apply, dietitians are to submit an outline of the proposed education programme that includes: which staff is targeted, subject area and level of the programme, which format will be taken, how the learner will be

assessed, what effect it will have on nutritional care and how it will raise the profile of nutrition in your organization, potential benefits to employers and estimated cost of development and implementation. Four copies of the application are to be submitted
Closing Date: 28 January
Funding: Commercial
Additional Information: Applications should not exceed 1,000 words

For further information contact:

Email: financial.aid@ohio.edu

British Ecological Society (BES)

Charles Darwin House, 12 Roger Street, WC1N 2JU, London, United Kingdom

Tel: (44) 20 7685 2500
Fax: (44) 20 7685 2501
Email: grants@britishecologicalsociety.org
Website: www.britishecologicalsociety.org

As a learned society and registered charity, the British Ecological Society (BES) is an independent organization receiving little outside funding. The aims of the Society are to promote the science of ecology through research, publications and conferences and to use the findings of such research to educate the public and to influence policy decisions that involve ecological matters. The BES is an active and thriving organization with something to offer anyone with an interest in ecology. Academic journals, teaching resources, meetings for scientists and policy makers, career advice and grants for ecologists are just a few of the societies areas of activity.

Outreach Grant

Subjects: Ecology. The Society defines ecology as the scientific study of the distribution, abundance and dynamics of organisms, their interactions with other organisms and their physical environment. It is therefore essential that applications promote and engage the public with the science of ecology. Grants will not be awarded for purely nature conservation purposes or any activity that does not promote the science of ecology
Purpose: To promote ecological science to a wide audience

Eligibility: Awards are open to individuals and organizations to organize public engagement events in ecology. This includes, but is not limited to, members of the BES, researchers, schools, museums, libraries and community groups. Applications will not be considered for: staff salaries; Purchase of apparatus, including computers, cameras etc., unless these are integral to the application. Applications from museums and schools are welcome but projects must involve significant outreach beyond schools. Projects aimed solely at delivering curriculum to school children will not be considered

Type: Project grant
Value: Up to £1,000
Frequency: Annual
Country of Study: Any country
No. of awards offered: 113
Application Procedure: Applicants must complete an online application form through the BES website at www.britisheco logicalsociety.org/grants-awards/outreach-grants
Closing Date: 10 March and 15 September
Contributor: British Ecological Society
No. of awards given last year: 11
No. of applicants last year: 113
Additional Information: Published papers and reports to other organizations should include an acknowledgement of the support from the BES. Other conditions may apply

For further information contact:

Email: outreach@physoc.org

British Federation of Women Graduates (BFWG)

4 Mandeville Courtyard, 142 Battersea Park Road, SW11 4NB, London, United Kingdom

Tel: (44) 20 7498 8037
Fax: (44) 20 7498 5213
Email: awards@bfwg.org.uk
Website: www.bfwg.org.uk

The British Federation of Women Graduates (BFWG) provides opportunities to women in education and public life. BFWG works as part of an international organization to improve the lives of women and girls, fosters local, national and international friendship and offers scholarships for third year doctorate research.

American Association of University Women/ International Federation of University Women International Fellowships

Subjects: All subjects
Purpose: To assist study or research that demonstrates a continued interest in the advancement of women
Eligibility: Open to female members of the British Federation of Women Graduates (BFWG) or another national federation or association (NFA) of the International Federation of University Women (IFUW), who are not United States citizens, with acceptance by an institution in America at which the applicant proposes to undertake her work
Level of Study: Graduate, Postdoctorate, Postgraduate, Predoctorate, Research
Type: Fellowships
Value: Master's/first professional degree: US$18,000; Doctoral: US$20,000; Postdoctoral: US$30,000. These fellowships do not cover travel costs
Length of Study: 1 year
Frequency: Annual
Study Establishment: An Institute of Higher Education
Country of Study: United States of America
Application Procedure: Application material can be downloaded from AAUW's website
Closing Date: 1 December of the year preceding the competition
Funding: Private
Contributor: AAUW members
Additional Information: A list of NFA's can be found on IFUW's website (www.ifuw.org). Applicants studying in Great Britain (United Kingdom, Scotland or Wales) must be members of BFWG. See BFWG website or for paper membership application forms write to the BFWG contact address enclosing a C5 self addressed stamped envelope. A money order of US$20 must accompany all applications

For further information contact:

AAUW Educational Foundation, International Fellowships, PO Box 4030, Iowa City, IA 52243 4030, United States of America

Email: aauw@act.org

French Association of University Women (AFFDU) Grants

Subjects: All subjects
Purpose: To assist those at doctoral or postdoctoral levels whose studies or research take place in France

Eligibility: Open to female members of the British Federation of Women Graduates (BFWG) or another national federation or association (NFA) of the International Federation of University Women (IFUW), who know the language of the country in which they plan to study

Level of Study: Doctorate, Postdoctorate, Postgraduate, Research

Type: Grant

Value: Euros 1,000–1,500, should preferably cover a study or research project involving travelling to or outside of France

Length of Study: Up to 12 months

Frequency: Annual

Study Establishment: An Institute of Higher Education

Country of Study: France

Application Procedure: Applicants should be undergraduate or postgraduate students, should have applied for admission to the University for a full-time scheme and have satisfied the entry requirements

Closing Date: 30 April

Funding: Private

Contributor: AFFDU members

Additional Information: A list of NFA's can be found on IFUW's website (www.ifuw.org). Applicants studying in Great Britain (United Kingdom, Scotland or Wales) must be members of BFWG. See BFWG's website or for paper membership details write to BFWG, enclosing a C5 self- addressed stamped envelope

For further information contact:

AFFDU, Reid Hall, 4 rue de Chevreuse, F-75006, Paris, France

Email: affdu@club-internet.fr

French Association of University Women (AFFDU) Monique Fouet Grant

Subjects: Political sciences

Purpose: To support a women postgraduate studying Political Science

Eligibility: Open to female members of the British Federation of Women Graduates (BFWG) or another National Federation of Association (NFA) of the International Federation of University Women (IFUW), who wish to undertake research on the AFFDU project site in Nabasdju Civol. Candidates must speak French

Level of Study: Postgraduate, Research

Type: Grant

Value: From €1,000–1,500. The award does not cover travel costs

Length of Study: Up to 1 year

Frequency: Annual

Study Establishment: A university or institution of university status

Country of Study: Any country

Application Procedure: Application materials can be downloaded from AFFDU's website or obtained via email

Closing Date: Mid-March of the year preceding the competition

Funding: Private

Contributor: AFFDU members

Additional Information: A list of NFA's can be found on IFUW's website (www.ifuw.org). Applicants studying in Great Britain (United Kingdom, Scotland or Wales) must be members of BFWG. See BFWG's website or for paper membership details write to BFWG, enclosing a C5 self-addressed stamped envelope

For further information contact:

AFFDU, Reid Hall, 4 rue de Chevreuse, F-75006, Paris, France

Email: affdu@club-internet.fr

British Federation of Women Graduates Scholarships

Subjects: Research in any discipline

Purpose: To assist final-year PhD research students

Eligibility: Academic excellence as evidenced by a proven ability to carry out independent research is the chief criterion. Open to female students, regardless of nationality, whose studies take place in Great Britain. Research students should be entering into their final year of formal study towards a PhD degree. Taught Master's degrees do not count as research, although MPhil research students would need to be upgraded to a PhD during the close of the competition or thereabouts

Level of Study: Doctorate, Predoctorate, Research

Type: Scholarship

Value: The amounts offered in awards range upwards from £1,000 with the average award being around £3,000 and the maximum being £6,000

Length of Study: Student must be in her third year (or part time equivalent) at the time of giving out the awards (October each year)

Frequency: Annual

Study Establishment: A university or institution of university status in Britain

Country of Study: Great Britain

No. of awards offered: 235

Application Procedure: Application materials can be downloaded from BFWG's website or www.bfwg.org.uk and look under 'Scholarships'
Closing Date: 18 March
Funding: Private
Contributor: BFWG members
No. of awards given last year: 7
No. of applicants last year: 235
Additional Information: Recipients must submit a written report within 6 months of being awarded their PhD

For further information contact:

Email: awards@bfwg.org.uk

NKA Ellen Gleditsch Scholarship

Subjects: All subjects
Purpose: To assist independent research or advanced studies by women at the post-graduate or doctoral level
Eligibility: Open to female members of the British Federation of Women Graduates (BFWG) or another national federation or association (NFA) of the International Federation of University Women (IFUW) with acceptance by a Norwegian institution at which the applicant proposes to undertake her work and proof of adequate health insurance
Level of Study: Doctorate, Postgraduate, Research
Type: Scholarship
Value: Norwegian krone 40,000. The scholarship does not cover travel costs
Length of Study: 3–4 months
Frequency: Every 3 years
Study Establishment: A university or institution of university status
Country of Study: Norway
Application Procedure: Applicants studying in Great Britain must apply through BFWG. Application material and membership details can be downloaded from their website or for paper copies write to BFWG, 4 Mandeville Courtyard, 142 Battersea Park Road, London SW11 4NB enclosing a C5 self-addressed stamped envelope
Closing Date: Late March in the year preceding the competition for applicants studying in Great Britain. September 1st for applicants applying direct to Norway
Funding: Private
Contributor: NKA members
Additional Information: If studying outside Great Britain, candidates should check the list of NFAs on IFUW's website (www.ifuw.org) or contact EGS or via their website. BFWG will interview those short-listed in June then write a letter of recommendation to NKA

For further information contact:

EGS, PO Box 251, Bergen N-5000, Norway

Email: elisabeth.haavet@hi.uib.no

British Heart Foundation (BHF)

14 Fitzhardinge Street, W1H 6DH, London, United Kingdom

Tel: (44) 20 7935 0185
Fax: (44) 20 7486 5820
Email: internet@bhf.org.uk
Website: www.bhf.org.uk
Contact: Ms Valerie Mason, Research Funds Manager

The British Heart Foundation (BHF) exists to encourage research into the causes, diagnosis, prevention and advances of cardiovascular disease, to inform doctors throughout the country of advances in the diagnosis, cure and treatment of heart diseases, and to improve facilities for the treatment of heart patients where the National Health Service is unable to help.

British Heart Foundation-Daphne Jackson Fellowships

Subjects: The Daphne Jackson Trust offers support during the application process, and the fellowship includes mentoring and retraining, giving awardees the confidence and skills they need to successfully return to a research career
Purpose: To provide an opportunity for basic scientists to return to cardiovascular research at an established research institution in the United Kingdom after a career break of two years or more
Eligibility: Your eligibility and suitability are initially assessed using the information submitted to us in the CV and personal statement forms. If you do fit our eligibility criteria, one of our Fellowship Advisors will arrange an informal telephone interview with you to talk through your CV, your career break, your desire to retrain, your field of interest and assess your future employment prospects
Type: Fellowship
Length of Study: Up to three years
Frequency: Annual
Country of Study: Any country
Application Procedure: 1. Applicants will need to approach and agree a plan of work with a potential academic sponsor as part of the application process. We are particularly interested in

supporting applicants working in interdisciplinary research, but applicants working in single disciplines will be considered equally. 2. The Elizabeth Blackwell Institute will half-sponsor the Fellowship and the remaining funding will be secured by the Daphne Jackson Trust from an additional sponsor

Closing Date: 18 February

Funding: Private

Additional Information: The fellowship will be part-time for a fixed term of up to three years

For further information contact:

The Daphne Jackson Trust, Department of Physics, University of Surrey, Guildford, GU2 7XH, Surrey, United Kingdom

Email: djmft@surrey.ac.uk

Career Re-entry Research Fellowships

Purpose: To provide an opportunity to re-establish a career in cardiovascular science in an established research institution in the United Kingdom, after a break of more than one year

Eligibility: 1. Successful post-doc returning after a career break of one or more years. 2. The candidate must have the support of a named senior investigator who will guarantee access to space and resources and provide scientific guidance for the duration of their fellowship. This individual should be named on the application form as a 'Supervisor' and provide an appropriate letter of support as part of the application. 3. The fellowship may be taken up on a part-time employment basis, where appropriate, following discussion and agreement with us and the employing institution. For more information read about our Flexible working policies

Level of Study: Postdoctorate

Type: Fellowship

Frequency: Varies

Country of Study: United Kingdom

Application Procedure: Application link for the grants are as follows: gms.bhf.org.uk/Pages/Default.aspx?ReturnUrl=% 252f_layouts%252fAuthenticate.aspx%253fSource%253d% 252f&Source=%252f (nine months will be taken to decide on the grants approval)

Funding: Private

Additional Information: For further information, visit the website www.bhf.org.uk

For further information contact:

British Heart Foundation, Lyndon Place, 2096 Coventry Road, Sheldon, B26 3YU, Birmingham, United Kingdom

Email: research@bhf.org.uk

Clinical Research Leave Fellowships

Purpose: To provide an opportunity for talented NHS staff to undertake dedicated PAs in research in a recognised United Kingdom centre of excellence in cardiovascular medicine

Eligibility: Awards may include: 1. Reimbursement of reasonable costs to cover relinquished PAs. 2. Research consumables directly attributable to the project

Level of Study: Graduate

Type: Fellowship

Frequency: Annual

Country of Study: Any country

Application Procedure: Candidates may be interviewed and a decision on this will be reached by the Fellowships Committee (four meetings a year) after it has considered external peer review reports

Funding: Private

For further information contact:

180, Hampstead Road, NW1 7AW, London, United Kingdom

Tel: (44) 300 330 3322
Email: research@bhf.org.uk

Clinical Study Grants

Purpose: To provide an opportunity for talented NHS staff to undertake dedicated PAs in research in a recognised United Kingdom centre of excellence in cardiovascular medicine

Eligibility: 1. The principal investigator will be a senior researcher working in an established research institution in the United Kingdom. She/he must have a strong track record of grant support, usually from us, and an internationally recognised research profile. 2. Any multicentre interventional clinical trial, while remaining under the scientific control of the principal investigator, should usually be managed by a United Kingdom CRC-registered Clinical Trials Unit (CTU) and should usually include a member of the CTU as a co-applicant or principal investigator unless there are clearly justified reasons for not doing so

Level of Study: Graduate

Type: Fellowship or Grant

Length of Study: Usually up to 5 years, with regular progress reports, initially annual reports

Frequency: Every 5 years

Country of Study: Any country

Application Procedure: Once a preliminary application is approved you should submit a full application: 1. Read the information in How to apply. 2. Read about the SoECAT form. 3. Also read: Costing a clinical study. Excess treatment costs. Costing a clinical research imaging scan.

Clinical Trials Units. Clinical Study Guidelines. Patient and public involvement. 4. Log onto the online application form. Application has to be completed through online procedurals
Funding: Private

For further information contact:

180 Hampstead Road, NW1 7AW, London, United Kingdom

Tel: (44) 300 330 3311
Email: research@bhf.org.uk

Immediate Postdoctoral Basic Science Research Fellowships

Purpose: To provide an opportunity for the most promising newly qualified postdoctoral researchers to make an early start in developing their independent cardiovascular research careers in an established institution in the United Kingdom
Eligibility: Candidates should be in the final year of their PhD studies or have no more than two years of postdoctoral research experience from the date of the PhD viva. Candidates must be able to show, by publications or otherwise, evidence of exceptional research ability. The fellowship should not be held in the institution where the PhD was carried out. Residency requirements do not apply
Level of Study: Postgraduate
Type: Fellowship
Country of Study: Any country
Funding: Private

For further information contact:

Email: research@bhf.org.uk

Intermediate Clinical Research Fellowships

Purpose: To provide a career opportunity in an established research institution in the United Kingdom for individuals with an established research record who intend to become leaders in academic medical research
Eligibility: Successful PhD (or MD) plus NTN and at least two years completed specialist training, but usually no more than two years after CCT. NTN will be exchanged for NTN (A) on appointment, and the individual may progress to consultant level during the fellowship
Level of Study: Graduate
Type: Fellowships, operating grants
Value: Housing allowance of £3,000 will be provided
Frequency: Annual
Country of Study: Any country

Application Procedure: 1. Read the information in How to apply. 2. Read our commitment to Improving Support for Clinical Academics. If you are applying for funding for a clinical study, also read: 1. Costing a clinical study. 2. Costing a clinical research imaging scan. 3. Clinical Trials Units. 4. Clinical Study Guidelines. 5. Log onto the online application form. Complete all the sections of the online application form following the instructions in the GMS User Guide. The online application must be completed by the applicant. Short-listed candidates may be interviewed
Funding: Government

For further information contact:

Research Funds Department, British Heart Foundation, Greater London House, 180 Hampstead Road, NW1 7AW, London, United Kingdom

Email: research@bhf.org.uk

New Horizon Grants

Purpose: To encourage scientists from outside traditional cardiovascular biology to engage in cardiovascular research and bring novel expertise to the field, and to develop new technologies, models or methodologies
Eligibility: 1. The principal investigator will be a senior researcher working in an established research institution in the United Kingdom. He/she must have a strong track record of project grant support and an internationally recognised research profile. 2. The principal investigator or co-applicant (s) should include researcher(s) with a strong track record of relevant cardiovascular research. 3. The principal investigator or co-applicant(s) should include researcher(s) from outside traditional cardiovascular biology, who do not have extensive existing collaborations with cardiovascular researchers
Level of Study: Graduate
Type: Grant
Value: Up to £300,000 and up to three years
Frequency: Every 3 years
Country of Study: Any country
Application Procedure: Kindly check the website for further information. www.bhf.org.uk/for-professionals/information-for-researchers/what-we-fund/new-horizon-grants
Funding: Private
Additional Information: You will be asked to attach a single PDF document to your online application form containing the following information: 1. For resubmissions, include an unedited copy of the original feedback followed by a detailed response, limited to 3 sides of A4, explaining how the revised application has changed from the original submission. 2. Abstract of the proposed investigation in 200 words or

less. 3. Background to the project and pilot data. 4. Original hypothesis. 5. Experimental details and design of proposed investigation. 6. Power calculations. 7. Expected value of results. 8. List of references relevant to the proposed project

For further information contact:

180 Hampstead Road, NW1 7AW, London, United Kingdom

Tel: (44) 300 330 3322
Email: research@bhf.org.uk

Non-Clinical PhD Studentships

Purpose: To allow talented students to complete a PhD in cardiovascular science in an established research institution in the United Kingdom
Eligibility: The application must be made by an established investigator who will be the supervisor and may be for a named or unnamed student. The primary supervisor must devote a minimum of 10% of their time to supervising the student and a second supervisor should also be included. Extra scrutiny will be given to applications from institutions in receipt of a BHF Research Excellence award or from supervisors named on a BHF 4 year PhD Scheme. These applications will require additional justification and should be for named students only. The BHF does not provide 'top-up' funding for existing PhD studentships supported by other grant giving organisations, which are incompletely funded
Level of Study: Graduate, Postgraduate
Type: Studentship and scholarship
Frequency: Every 3 years
Country of Study: Any country
Application Procedure: Apply through online mode post registration on the below link. gms.bhf.org.uk/Pages/Default.aspx?ReturnUrl=%252f_layouts%252fAuthenticate.aspx%253fSource%253d%252f&Source=%252f. For further info, check website
Funding: Private

For further information contact:

Email: heretohelp@bhf.org.uk

Research Training Fellowships for Nurses and Allied Health Professionals

Purpose: To provide a foundation in research training in an established research institution in the United Kingdom for nurses and allied health professionals, leading to the award of a PhD

Eligibility: The named student should usually hold a good quality Masters degree or equivalent. 1. Students who have started a PhD (or equivalent) may be eligible to apply for a Research Training Fellowship, but the application must be received within 6 months of having registered for their PhD. In these circumstances, the proposed start date for the Research Training Fellowship should also be no more than 12 months (or full-time equivalent) from the date of registration for the degree. 2. If the fellowship is taken up on a full-time research basis, we recognise that part of the time (ideally no more than 20% though sometimes more if it can be argued that the research directly involves their patients) may be spent on patient care. 3. The fellowship may be taken up on a part-time employment basis, where appropriate, following discussion and agreement with us and the employing institution. For more information, read about our Flexible working policies
Level of Study: Postgraduate
Type: Fellowship
Value: It includes salary, tuition fee at standard home students rate(set by research institute)
Country of Study: Any country
Application Procedure: Check through the website link. www.bhf.org.uk/for-professionals/information-for-researchers/what-we-fund/research-training-fellowships-for-nurses-and-allied-health-professionals
Closing Date: 26 April
Funding: Foundation

For further information contact:

Email: research@bhf.org.uk

Travel Fellowships

Purpose: To enable a postdoctoral researcher to undertake a visit to a distinguished laboratory abroad, either for a short period of up to six months to acquire specialist knowledge or expertise, or for a longer period to carry out a research project that can not be done in United Kingdom
Eligibility: Usually more than three years postdoctoral experience, but applicants with less postdoctoral experience are also eligible to apply. Applicant must hold a post in the United Kingdom and a guaranteed post to return to after the fellowship
Level of Study: Postdoctorate
Type: Fellowship
Frequency: Annual
Country of Study: Any country
Application Procedure: 1. Read the information in How to apply. 2. Log onto the online application form. 3. Complete all the sections of the online application form following the

instructions in the GMS User Guide. 4. Ensure the named Supervisor in the application form is your United Kingdom Supervisor
Funding: Private

For further information contact:

Email: research@bhf.org.uk

British Institute at Ankara (BIAA)

10 Carlton House Terrace, SW1Y 5AH, London, United Kingdom

Tel:	(44) 20 7969 5204
Fax:	(44) 20 7969 5401
Email:	biaa@britac.ac.uk
Website:	www.biaa.ac.uk
Contact:	Claire McCafferty, London Administrator

BIAA aims to support, promote, facilitate, and publish British research focused on Turkey and the Black Sea littoral in all academic disciplines within the arts, humanities, and social sciences and to maintain a centre of excellence in Ankara focused on the archaeology and related subjects of Turkey.

British Institute at Ankara Research Scholarship

Subjects: Turkey and Black Sea littoral in any disciplines of the arts, humanities, and social sciences
Purpose: To conduct their own research at doctoral level
Eligibility: Open to candidates who hold a Master's degree and have a demonstrable connection to United Kingdom academia
Level of Study: Postgraduate, Research
Type: Research scholarship
Value: £800 per month and the cost of one return flight between the United Kingdom and Turkey
Length of Study: 9 months
Frequency: Annual
Country of Study: Turkey
Application Procedure: Deadline for applications is mid-September. Check website for further details
Closing Date: Deadline for applications is mid-September. Check website for further details

For further information contact:

British Institute at Ankara, Ankara, Turkey

Tel:	(44) 20 7969 5204
Fax:	(44) 20 7969 5401
Email:	biaa@britac.ac.uk
Contact:	Claire McCafferty

Martin Harrison Memorial Fellowship

Subjects: Archaeology
Purpose: To assist junior Turkish archaeologists, who are not able to take advantage of travelling, working in any area of the archaeology of Anatolia from Prehistory to the Ottoman period, to visit the United Kingdom, especially Oxford, in connection with their research work
Eligibility: Open to Turkish citizens residing in Turkey who have completed at least 2 years of postgraduate research and at most held a doctorate for 5 years, working in any area of the archaeology of Anatolia (from the Prehistoric to the Ottoman period)
Level of Study: Doctorate, Postgraduate, Research
Type: Short-term fellowship
Value: £1,500 and travel expenses from and to Turkey
Length of Study: 6–13 weeks
Frequency: Annual
Study Establishment: University of Oxford
Country of Study: United Kingdom
Application Procedure: Completed applications, including a curriculum vitae, should be sent to the Turkey address
Closing Date: 31 March
Funding: Foundation
Contributor: Martin Harrison Fund for living expenses and British Institute at Ankara (BlAA) for travel
Additional Information: The selection will be made on the basis of the applicant's academic record, coherent research proposal, ability to benefit from libraries and scholars in Oxford, and a working knowledge of spoken and written English

For further information contact:

The British Institute at Ankara, 24 Tahran Caddesi, Kavaklidere, Ankara TR 06700, Turkey

Tel:	(90) 312 427 5487
Fax:	(90) 312 428 0159
Email:	ggirdivan@biaatr.org

British Institute in Eastern Africa

British Institute in Eastern Africa, Laikipia Road, Kileleshwa, Nairobi, PO Box 30710 – 00100 GPO, Kenya

Tel: (254) 20 815 5186
Fax: (254) 20 7969 5401
Email: office@biea.ac.uk
Website: www.biea.ac.uk
Contact: Dr David Anderson, Director

The British Institute in Eastern Africa (BIEA) exists to promote research in the humanities and social sciences. BIEA is based in Nairobi, but supports work across Eastern Africa, and is one of the schools and institutes supported by the British Academy.

British Institute in Eastern Africa Minor Grants

Subjects: Humanities and social sciences
Purpose: To assist with the costs of research projects in Eastern Africa
Eligibility: Open to applicants from United Kingdom and Eastern Africa
Level of Study: Postgraduate
Type: Grant
Value: Up to UK£1,000
Study Establishment: The British Institute in Eastern Africa
No. of awards offered: 45
Application Procedure: Application forms can be downloaded from the BIEA website
Closing Date: 31 January
Funding: Government
Contributor: British Academy
No. of awards given last year: 22
No. of applicants last year: 45
Additional Information: Applicants must contact the Director for further information on relevant topics likely to receive support. Those awarded grants will be required to keep the Institute regularly informed of the progress of their research, to provide a preliminary statement of accounts within 18 months of the award dates and to provide the Institute with copies of all relevant publications. They are encouraged to discuss with the Director the possibility of publishing their results in the Institute's journal, Azania. Results for the Minor Grants Award may be expected within 2 months of either 30 May or 30 November. Those awarded grants are required to become members of the BIEA

For further information contact:

Email: pjlane@insightkenya.com

British Medical Association (BMA)

BMA Research Grants, BMA House, Tavistock Square, WC1H 9JP, London, United Kingdom

Tel: (44) 20 7383 6341
Fax: (44) 20 7383 6341
Email: info.sciencegrants@bma.org.uk
Website: www.bma.org.uk

The BMA is a voluntary professional association with over two-thirds of practising United Kingdom doctors in membership and an independent trade union dedicated to protecting individual members and the collective interests of doctors.

Helen H Lawson Research Grant

Subjects: Research into rehabilitation in stroke care
Purpose: To promote research into novel technologies and IT to assist in patient care, primary care or public health
Eligibility: Open to registered medical practitioners in the United Kingdom who are BMA members
Level of Study: Research
Type: Research grant
Value: UK£50,000
Length of Study: 3 years
Frequency: Annual
Country of Study: United Kingdom
No. of awards offered: 10
Application Procedure: Applicants must complete an online application form. Applications that do not comply with all of the above terms and conditions will be rejected without exception
Closing Date: 15 March at 17.00
Funding: Trusts
No. of awards given last year: 1
No. of applicants last year: 10
Additional Information: Please check at bma.org.uk/developing-your-career/portfolio-career/research-grants/research-grants-details/research-grants-roscoe for further information

For further information contact:

Email: info.sciencegrants@bma.org.uk

Josephine Lansdell Research Grant

Subjects: Research in the field of heart disease
Purpose: To assist and support research into the field of heart diseases
Eligibility: Open to registered medical practitioners in the United Kingdom who are BMA members
Level of Study: Research
Type: Research grant
Value: UK£50,000
Length of Study: 3 years
Frequency: Annual
Country of Study: Any country
No. of awards offered: 10
Application Procedure: Applicants must complete an online application form. Applicants are required to upload (PDF format) two references during the online application process. Please note each reference MUST bear the electronic (scanned) signature of the referee. For joint applications, each applicant requires two referees (these can be the same for both applicants)
Closing Date: 15 March at 17.00
Funding: Trusts
No. of awards given last year: 1
No. of applicants last year: 10
Additional Information: Please check at bma.org.uk/developing-your-career/portfolio-career/research-grants/research-grants-details/research-grants-lansdell for more information

For further information contact:

Email: researchgrants@bma.org.uk

Vera Down Research Grant

Subjects: Research into neurological disorders
Purpose: To assist and support research
Eligibility: Open to registered medical practitioners in the United Kingdom who are BMA members
Level of Study: Research
Type: Research grant
Value: UK£55,000
Length of Study: 3 years
Frequency: Annual
Country of Study: United Kingdom
No. of awards offered: 10
Application Procedure: Applicants must complete an online application form
Closing Date: 15 March

Funding: Trusts
No. of awards given last year: 1
No. of applicants last year: 10
Additional Information: Please check at bma.org.uk/developing-your-career/portfolio-career/research-grants/research-grants-details/research-grants-down for more information

For further information contact:

Email: info.sciencegrants@bma.org.uk

British School at Athens

52 Souedias Street, Athens GRC 10676, Athens, Greece

Tel:	(30) 211 102 2800
Fax:	(30) 211 102 2803
Email:	admin@bsa.ac.uk
Website:	www.bsa.gla.ac.uk
Contact:	Dr Chryssanthi Papadopoulou, Assistant Director

The British School at Athens promotes research into the archaeology, architecture, art, history, language, literature, religion and topography of Greece in ancient, medieval and modern times. It consists of the Library, Fitch Laboratory for Archaeological Science, Archive, Museum, hostel and a second base at Knossos for research and fieldwork.

Hector and Elizabeth Catling Bursary

Subjects: Greek studies including the archaeology, art, history, language, literature, religion, ethnography, anthropology or geography of any period and all branches of archaeological science
Purpose: To assist travel, maintenance costs and for the purchase of scientific equipments. Its aim is to encourage excellence in archaeological drawing, including the preparation of finished drawings for publication
Eligibility: Open to researchers of British, Irish or Commonwealth nationality
Level of Study: Doctorate, Postdoctorate, Postgraduate, Research
Type: Bursary
Value: £500 per bursary to assist with travel and maintenance costs incurred in fieldwork, to pay for the use of scientific or

other specialized equipment in or outside the laboratory in Greece or elsewhere and to buy necessary supplies

Frequency: Annual

Study Establishment: The British School at Athens

Country of Study: Any country

Application Procedure: 1. Applicants must submit a curriculum vitae and state concisely the nature of the intended work, a breakdown of budget, the amount requested from the Fund and how this will be spent. 2. Applications should include two sealed letters of reference. Bursary holders must submit a short report to the Committee upon completion of the project

Closing Date: 19 April

Funding: Private

Additional Information: The bursary is not intended for publication costs, and cannot be awarded to an excavation or field survey team

For further information contact:

Email: school.administrator@bsa.ac.uk

The Elizabeth Catling Memorial Fund for Archaeological Draughtsmanship

Purpose: To encourage excellence in archaeological drawing, including the preparation of finished drawings for publication. It is hoped that awards will help individuals to improve their standards of draughtsmanship and also enable the preparation of a larger number of drawings, of higher quality, than might otherwise have been possible

Eligibility: Individual applicants must show that drawings are an essential part of their research. Furthermore, although not a precondition, it is hoped that they may be draughtsmen themselves. Applications from project directors, who may also apply during the course of a field campaign, are limited to unexpected expenses that are not provided for in the project's budget, such as extra maintenance costs to enable a draughtsman to draw unforeseen material and finds

Level of Study: Predoctorate

Type: Funding support

Value: £200

Frequency: Annual

Application Procedure: Candidates should submit letters of application to the School's London office by post in four copies or by email. Letters should not be longer than two pages and should include a statement of the purposes of the application and a budget and timetable for the proposed work, together with the name and address of a referee whom the awarding panel(s) may consult. Applications may be made for but are not limited to, grants towards the maintenance costs of

longer stays at museums and other study centres so as to achieve work that would not otherwise have been attempted. Recipients of awards must have been admitted as Students of the School for the appropriate Session before receiving their grants, and must submit a short report on the use of the grant to the London office

Closing Date: 1 April

Additional Information: The Fund does not support printing expenses, or site drawings such as plans and sections, or computer graphics

For further information contact:

British School at Athens, Senate House, Malet Street, WC1E 7HU, London, United Kingdom

Email: bsa@sas.ac.uk

The John Morrison Memorial Fund for Hellenic Maritime Studies

Purpose: To further research into all branches of Hellenic maritime studies of any period

Type: Funding support

Value: £500

Frequency: Annual

Application Procedure: Candidates should submit letters of application to the School's London office by post in four copies or by email. Letters should not be longer than two pages and should include a statement of the purposes of the application and a budget and timetable for the proposed work, together with the name and address of a referee whom the awarding panel(s) may consult. Applications may be made for but are not limited to, grants towards the maintenance costs of longer stays at museums and other study centres so as to achieve work that would not otherwise have been attempted. Recipients of awards must have been admitted as Students of the School for the appropriate Session before receiving their grants, and must submit a short report on the use of the grant to the London office

Closing Date: 1 April

Additional Information: Grants may also be available from the Fund for buying maritime books and journals for the School's Library

For further information contact:

British School at Athens, Senate House, Malet Street, WC1E 7HU, London, United Kingdom

Email: bsa@sas.ac.uk

The Richard Bradford McConnell Fund for Landscape Studies

Subjects: All disciplines of the arts, humanities and sciences (or any combination of them)
Purpose: To assist research in the interaction of place and people in Greece and Cyprus at any period(s)
Type: Funding support
Value: £400
Frequency: Annual
Application Procedure: Candidates should submit letters of application to the School's London office by post in four copies or by email. Letters should not be longer than two pages and should include a statement of the purposes of the application and a budget and timetable for the proposed work, together with the name and address of a referee whom the awarding panel(s) may consult. Applications may be made for but are not limited to, grants towards the maintenance costs of longer stays at museums and other study centres so as to achieve work that would not otherwise have been attempted. Recipients of awards must have been admitted as Students of the School for the appropriate Session before receiving their grants, and must submit a short report on the use of the grant to the London office
Closing Date: 1 April
Contributor: Richard Bradford Trust

For further information contact:

British School at Athens, Senate House, Malet Street, WC1E 7HU, London, United Kingdom

Email: bsa@sas.ac.uk

To support research in the prehistory of the Aegean and its connections with the East Mediterranean

Purpose: To support research in the prehistory of the Aegean and its connections with the East Mediterranean
Eligibility: Preference may be given to younger Students
Type: Funding support
Value: £500 are available for the expenses (including, but not limited to, attending conferences to present papers, photography, and travel to museums and sites)
Application Procedure: Candidates should submit letters of application to the School's London office by post in four copies or by email. Letters should not be longer than two pages and should include a statement of the purposes of the application and a budget and timetable for the proposed work, together with the name and address of a referee whom the

awarding panel(s) may consult. Applications may be made for but are not limited to, grants towards the maintenance costs of longer stays at museums and other study centres so as to achieve work that would not otherwise have been attempted. Recipients of awards must have been admitted as Students of the School for the appropriate Session before receiving their grants, and must submit a short report on the use of the grant to the London office
Closing Date: 1 April
Additional Information: Check website for more details

For further information contact:

British School at Athens, Senate House, Malet Street, WC1E 7HU, London, United Kingdom

Email: bsa@sas.ac.uk

Visiting Fellowships

Purpose: Visiting Fellowships at the British School at Athens are offered for 2-3 months for research in any branch of the arts or social sciences related to Greece. The Fellowship is non-stipendiary, but accommodation and airfare are provided
Eligibility: The Fellow is required to submit a report covering their research and their time at the School to the School's Council
Level of Study: Postgraduate
Type: Fellowship
Frequency: Annual
Country of Study: Any country
Application Procedure: The School Administrator, school. administrator@bsa.ac.uk by Friday 19 April. Further information about the School can be found at www.bsa.ac.uk. Applicants should submit a covering letter, a Curriculum Vitae and a statement of their proposed programme of research in Greece
Closing Date: 19 April
Funding: Private

For further information contact:

The British School at Athens, 52 Souedias Street, GRC10676 Athens, Greece

Tel: (30) 211 102 2800
Fax: (30) 211 102 2803
Email: school.administrator@bsa.ac.uk,
admin@bsa.ac.uk

British School at Rome (BSR)

The BSR at the British Academy, 10 Carlton House Terrace, SW1Y 5AH, London, United Kingdom

Tel: (44) 20 7969 5202
Fax: (44) 20 7969 5401
Email: bsr@britac.ac.uk
Website: www.bsr.ac.uk
Contact: Natalie Arrowsmith, Communications Manager

The British School at Rome (BSR) is an interdisciplinary research centre for the humanities, visual arts and architecture. Each year, the School offers a range of awards in its principal fields of interest. These interests are further promoted by lectures, conferences, publications, exhibitions, archaeological research and an excellent reference library.

Abbey Scholarship in Painting

Subjects: Painting
Purpose: To give exceptionally promising early career painters the opportunity to work in Rome
Eligibility: Open to citizens of the United Kingdom and United States and to those of any other nationality provided that they have been resident in either country for at least five years
Level of Study: Doctorate, Graduate, Postdoctorate, Postgraduate
Type: Scholarship
Value: UK£700 per month plus board and lodging. one annual nine month residency for an early career artist, with a monthly stipend of £800
Length of Study: 9 months
Frequency: Annual
Study Establishment: The British School at Rome
Country of Study: Italy
Application Procedure: Applicants must complete an application form and pay an application fee
Closing Date: September
Funding: Private
Contributor: The Abbey Council
No. of awards given last year: 1
Additional Information: Check website for more details

For further information contact:

Abbey Awards, 1 St Lukes Court, 136 Falcon Road, SW11 2LP, London, United Kingdom

Email: contact@abbey.org.uk
Contact: The Administrator

Giles Worsley Travel Fellowship

Subjects: Architecture and architectural history
Purpose: To enable an architect or architectural historian to spend 3 months in Rome studying an architectural topic of his choice
Eligibility: Open to those who are of British nationality or who have been living and studying in Britain for at least the last 3 years
Level of Study: Postdoctorate, Postgraduate, Professional development
Type: Fellowship
Value: Approx. £700 per month plus full board and lodging at the British School at Rome
Length of Study: 3 months
Frequency: Annual
Study Establishment: The British School at Rome
Country of Study: Italy
Application Procedure: Applicants must submit a curriculum vitae, a statement indicating the subject of their proposal and arrange for two references to be sent
Closing Date: January/February
Funding: Private
No. of awards given last year: 1

For further information contact:

Email: bsr@britac.ac.uk

Paul Mellon Centre Rome Fellowship

Subjects: The Grand Tour and Anglo-Italian cultural and artistic relations
Purpose: To assist research on grand tour subjects or on Anglo-Italian cultural and artistic relations
Eligibility: Open to established scholars in the United Kingdom, United States or elsewhere. Applicants should be fluent in Italian
Level of Study: Doctorate, Graduate, Postdoctorate, Postgraduate, Professional development, Research
Type: Fellowship
Value: Full board at the British School at Rome. For independent scholars, the fellowship offers a stipend of UK£6,000 plus travel to and from Rome. For scholars in full-time university employment, the fellowship offers an honorarium of UK£2,000, travel to and from Rome and a sum of UK£6,000 towards replacement teaching costs for a term at the Fellow's home institution
Length of Study: 3 months
Frequency: Annual
Study Establishment: The British School at Rome
Country of Study: Italy

Application Procedure: Applicants must contact the Paul Mellon Centre for Studies in British Art for details
Closing Date: January
Funding: Private
Contributor: The Paul Mellon Centre for Studies in British Art
No. of awards given last year: 1
Additional Information: Please check website for more details

For further information contact:

The Paul Mellon Centre for Studies in British Art, 16 Bedford Square, WC1B 3JA, London, United Kingdom

Email: grants@paul-mellon-centre.ac.uk
Contact: The Grants Administrator

British Society for Antimicrobial Chemotherapy

British Society for Antimicrobial Chemotherapy, Griffin House, 53 Regent Place, B1 3NJ, Birmingham, United Kingdom

Tel: (44) 121 236 1988
Fax: (44) 121 212 9822
Email: tguise @bsac.org.uk
Website: www.bsac.org.uk
Contact: Ms Tracey Guise, Executive Director

BSAC is an inter-professional organization with 40 years of experience and achievement in antibiotic education, research and leadership. It is dedicated to saving lives through appropriate use and development of antibiotics now and in the future.

British Society for Antimicrobial Chemotherapy Overseas Scholarship

Subjects: Antimicrobial chemotherapy
Purpose: Overseas Scholarships are to enable workers from other countries the opportunity to work in United Kingdom Departments for up to 6 months
Level of Study: Postgraduate, Professional development
Type: Scholarship
Value: £1,000 per calendar month for up to 6 months. The host institution will receive a consumables grant of £200 per calendar month for the duration of the scholarship. The Society will reimburse the cost of return air fares and travel via the most economical route. Candidates will be asked to seek approval of travel costs in advance

Length of Study: 6 months
Frequency: Annual
Country of Study: United Kingdom
Application Procedure: Successful applicants are required to submit a 500-word written report to the Secretary of the Grants Committee on completion of their project, and to forward details of any publications arising from the work undertaken. Applications for Overseas Scholarships should be made to the Society's HQ using the form provided on the BSAC website
Closing Date: 1 December
Funding: Foundation
Additional Information: Excludes applicants from United Kingdom

For further information contact:

Email: tguise@bsac.org.uk

British Society for Middle Eastern Studies

Institute for Middle Eastern & Islamic Studies, Durham University, Al-Qasimi Building, Elvet Hill Road, DH1 3TU, Durham, United Kingdom

Tel: (44) 191 33 45179
Fax: (44) 191 33 45661
Email: a.l.haysey@durham.ac.uk
Website: www.brismes.ac.uk/

Master's Scholarship

Subjects: All subjects
Purpose: BRISMES offers an annual Master's scholarship for taught Master's study at a United Kingdom institution. The Master's programme can be in any discipline but should include a majority component specifically relating to the Middle East
Eligibility: Preference will be given to candidates resident in the European Union, and to institutions who are members of BRISMES
Level of Study: Doctorate
Type: Scholarship
Value: £1,200
Frequency: Annual
Country of Study: United Kingdom
Application Procedure: Applications should be forwarded by the Director of the Master's programme concerned, to the BRISMES Administrative Office, and should include: a supporting statement from the course Director not

exceeding 500 words; the programme syllabus; a statement by the candidate not exceeding 500 words; the candidate's curriculum vitae and transcript of previous academic results; two academic references. Applications should be sent to Institute for Middle Eastern & Islamic Studies

Closing Date: 31 March
Funding: Foundation
Additional Information: Please check website for more details

For further information contact:

Email: a.l.haysey@dur.ac.uk

The Abdullah Al-Mubarak Al-Sabah Foundation BRISMES Scholarships

Purpose: The purpose of the scholarships is to encourage more people to pursue postgraduate studies in disciplines related to the Middle East in British universities
Eligibility: To qualify you must be a paid-up member of BRISMES (student membership suffices) but the time you apply
Level of Study: Postgraduate
Type: Scholarship
Value: £2,000
Length of Study: 1 academic year
Frequency: Annual
Country of Study: United Kingdom
Application Procedure: Submit an application of 600–1,000 words, by email to the BRISMES research committee This should include a sketch of the overall research topic, and a description of the purpose for which the grant would be used. Also you must obtain a brief supporting statement from a supervisor. Applications should be sent to Institute for Middle Eastern & Islamic Studies
Closing Date: 31 March
Funding: Foundation

For further information contact:

Email: a.l.haysey@dur.ac.uk

British Veterinary Association

7 Mansfield Street, W1G 9NQ, London, United Kingdom

Tel: (44) 20 7636 6541
Fax: (44) 20 7908 6349
Email: bvahq@bva.co.uk
Website: www.bva.co.uk

The British Veterinary Association's chief interests are the standards of animal health and veterinary surgeons' working practices. The organization's main functions are the development of policy in areas affecting the profession, protecting and promoting the profession in matters propounded by government and other external bodies and the provision of services to members.

Harry Steele-Bodger Memorial Travelling Scholarship

Subjects: Veterinary science and agriculture
Purpose: To further the aims and aspirations of the late Harry Steele-Bodger
Eligibility: Open to graduates of veterinary schools in the United Kingdom or the Republic of Ireland who have been qualified for not more than 3 years, and to penultimate or final-year students at those schools
Level of Study: Graduate, Postgraduate
Type: Scholarship
Value: Approx. UK£1,100
Frequency: Annual
Study Establishment: A veterinary or agricultural research institute or some other course of study approved by the governing committee
Country of Study: United Kingdom
No. of awards offered: 5
Application Procedure: Applications can be submitted online www.bva.co.uk/Membership-and-benefits/Students/Travel-grants-for-students/
Closing Date: 3 May
Funding: Private
No. of awards given last year: 1
No. of applicants last year: 5
Additional Information: Please check at www.bva.co.uk/Membership-and-benefits/Students/Travel-grants-for-students/#HSBscholarship for further details

For further information contact:

BVA, 7 Mansfield Street, London, United Kingdom

Tel: (44) 20 7636 6541
Email: helenac@bva.co.uk
Contact: Ms Helena Cotton

Broadcast Education Association

613 Kane Street, Mount Pleasant, MI 48858, United States of America

Tel: (1) 989 773 9370
Email: orlik1pb@cmich.edu
Website: www.beaweb.org
Contact: Dr Peter Orlik, Scholarship Chair

Abe Voron Award

Subjects: Junior, senior and graduate students pursuing a career in radio
Purpose: For students preparing for a career in radio at a BEA member institution
Eligibility: Student must be a full-time junior, senior, or graduate level individual studying at a BEA member institution toward a career in radio
Level of Study: Graduate, Undergraduate
Type: Scholarship
Value: US$3,000
Length of Study: One full academic year
Frequency: Annual
Country of Study: Any country
No. of awards offered: 26
Application Procedure: See and fill out application found on the BEA website www.beaweb.org
Closing Date: October
Funding: Private
Contributor: Abe Voron Committee
No. of awards given last year: 3
No. of applicants last year: 26

John Bayliss Award

Subjects: Junior, senior or graduate student support for study toward a career in radio
Purpose: For full-time study at a BEA member institution leading to a career in radio
Eligibility: full-time undergraduate or graduate student at a BEA member institution, preparing for a radio career
Level of Study: Graduate, Undergraduate
Type: Scholarship
Value: US$2,500
Length of Study: Full-time for one academic year
Frequency: Annual
Country of Study: Any country
No. of awards offered: 26
Application Procedure: See and fill out application found at BEA website www.beaweb.org
Closing Date: 12 October
Funding: Private
Contributor: John Bayliss Foundation
No. of awards given last year: 1
No. of applicants last year: 26

Library of American Broadcasting Foundation Award

Subjects: Graduate study emphasizing broadcast history at a BEA member institution
Purpose: Support for a graduate student focusing on the study of broadcast history
Eligibility: graduate student focusing on broadcast history
Level of Study: Graduate
Type: Scholarship
Value: US$3,000
Length of Study: One full academic year
Frequency: Annual
Country of Study: Any country
No. of awards offered: 5
Application Procedure: see and fill out application found on BEA website www.beaweb.org
Closing Date: 12 October
Funding: Foundation
Contributor: Library of American Broadcasting Foundation
No. of awards given last year: 1
No. of applicants last year: 5

Peter B. Orlik Scholarship

Subjects: For full-time study in the current academic year at a BEA member school. For juniors, seniors, or graduate students
Purpose: Study by juniors, seniors or graduate students at a BEA member institution
Eligibility: Any junior, senior or graduate student at a BEA member institution
Level of Study: Graduate, Undergraduate
Type: Scholarship
Value: US$3,000
Length of Study: One full academic year
Frequency: Annual
Country of Study: Any country
No. of awards offered: 45
Application Procedure: See BEA website www.beaweb.org for application
Closing Date: 12 October
Funding: Private
Contributor: Broadcast Education Association
No. of awards given last year: 1
No. of applicants last year: 45

Richard Eaton Award

Subjects: For full-time study at a BEA member institution
Purpose: Given for study of electronic media by juniors, seniors, and graduate students

Eligibility: Junior, senior or graduate student at a BEA member institution
Level of Study: Graduate, Undergraduate
Type: Scholarship
Value: US$2,500
Length of Study: 1 academic year – full-time
Frequency: Annual
Country of Study: Any country
No. of awards offered: 45
Application Procedure: See and complete application on BEA website www.beaweb.org
Closing Date: 12 October
Funding: Private
Contributor: Richard Eaton Foundation
No. of awards given last year: 1
No. of applicants last year: 45

Vincent T. Wasilewski Award

Subjects: For full-time graduate study in the upcoming year academic year
Purpose: For graduate study of electronic media at a BEA member institution
Eligibility: Any full-time graduate student at a BEA member institution
Level of Study: Graduate
Type: Scholarship
Value: $4,000
Length of Study: One academic year
Frequency: Annual
Country of Study: Any country
No. of awards offered: 20
Application Procedure: See and complete application found at BEA website www.beaweb.org
Closing Date: 12 October
Funding: Private
Contributor: Patrick Communications
No. of awards given last year: 1
No. of applicants last year: 20

Brunel University

Kingston Lane, Middlesex UB8 3PH, Uxbridge, United Kingdom

Tel: (44) 1895 274000
Fax: (44) 1895 232806
Email: admissions@brunel.ac.uk
Website: www.brunel.ac.uk
Contact: Professor Adrian Woods, Dean of the Graduate School

Brunel Santander International Scholarship

Purpose: Brunel University London is pleased to offer a prestigious package of scholarships for International students. The scholarship scheme is for self-funded students only and is based on academic achievement. We will award scholarships to applicants who most closely meet or exceed the criteria for the award
Eligibility: 1. Must be classed as Overseas for fees purposes and be self-funded (not sponsored). 2. Applicants who are unsure of their fee status should note Brunel uses the information they have provided in their application form to assess fee status against regulations set by the United Kingdom government. For information on these regulations please visit the independent organisation United Kingdom CISA's website. 3. Must have an offer to study on a postgraduate taught or postgraduate research programme starting in September. 4. Must complete the relevant Scholarship application by the published deadlines. 5. Must have firmly accepted their course offer by the scholarship deadline date
Level of Study: Postgraduate
Type: Scholarship
Value: £3,000
Length of Study: 1 year
Frequency: Annual
Country of Study: Any country
Closing Date: 30 April
Funding: International office

For further information contact:

Email: scholarships@brunel.ac.uk

Budapest International Music Competition

Philharmonia Budapest, Alkotmany u.31 1/2, HUN-1054, Budapest, Hungary

Tel: (36) 1 266 1459, 302 4961
Fax: (36) 1 302 4962
Email: liszkay.maria@hu.inter.net
Contact: Ms Maria Liszkay, Secretary

The Budapest Music Competition has been held since 1933. Competitions in different categories alternate annually.

International Carl Flesch Violin Competition

Subjects: Music
Purpose: To promote European violinists

Eligibility: Competitors should possess at least 2 years of musical study in Europe and should be born on or after 1 January, 1980

Type: Competition

Value: €4,000 net (first prize), €3,000 net (second prize) and €2,000 net (third prize)

Country of Study: Hungary

Application Procedure: Application forms should contain brief curriculum vitae, certificate of musical qualification, letter of recommendation from a prominent musical personality, two recent photographs and a copy receipt about the transfer of the entry fee. For competitors outside Europe, a certificate of their European studies is required

Closing Date: 1 February

Funding: Private

Contributor: Philharmonia Budapest Concert Agency and Ms. Fejes Music Foundation

Additional Information: Special prizes will be offered to the winners

For further information contact:

Tel:	(36) 1 266 1459, 302 4961
Fax:	(36) 1 302 4962
Email:	liszkay.maria@hu.inter.net
Contact:	Mária Liszkay, Manager

Bupa Foundation

Bupa House, 15-19 Bloomsbury Way, WC1A 2BA, London, United Kingdom

Tel:	(44) 20 7656 2591
Fax:	(44) 20 7656 2708
Email:	Bupafoundation@Bupa.com
Website:	www.bupafoundation.co.uk
Contact:	Lee Saunders, Registrar

The Bupa Foundation is an independent medical research charity that funds medical research to prevent, relieve and cure sickness and ill health.

Bupa Foundation Annual Specialist Grant

Subjects: The subject of study may change each year

Eligibility: The competition is open to those based in the United Kingdom, Australia, Denmark, Hong Kong, New Zealand, Saudi Arabia, Spain and Thailand. Entries must be compliant with the local health and safety legislation if applicable. The Foundation will seek peer reviews from the home country of each shortlisted entry. Researchers and health professionals working for public or private organisations may apply for Bupa Foundation specialist grants for United Kingdom-based projects.

For further information contact:

Tel:	(36) 20 7656 2591
Email:	bupafoundation@bupa.com
Contact:	Mrs Lee Saunders, Registrar

Bupa Foundation Medical Research Grant for Health at Work

Subjects: To encourage promotion of good health by not only making people aware of healthy behaviour but also by motivating them to practice it

Purpose: To support research into the feasibility and potential value of workplace conditions for health promotion and active management of employee health

Eligibility: Open to health professionals and health researchers

Level of Study: Doctorate, Postdoctorate, Postgraduate, Research

Value: Restricted by project need only

Length of Study: A maximum of 3 years

Country of Study: United Kingdom

Application Procedure: For all queries contact Lee Saunders, the Foundation's Registrar

Funding: Foundation

For further information contact:

Email:	bupafoundation@bupa.com
Contact:	Mrs Lee Saunders

Bupa Foundation Medical Research Grant for Information and Communication

Subjects: Health information and communication

Purpose: To support research designed to enhance partnership between health professionals and public/patients

Eligibility: Open to health professional and health researchers

Level of Study: Doctorate, Postdoctorate, Postgraduate, Research

Value: Restricted by project needs only

Length of Study: Maximum of 3 years

Country of Study: United Kingdom

Application Procedure: For all queries contact Lee Saunders, the Foundation's Registrar

Funding: Foundation

For further information contact:

Email:	bupafoundation@bupa.com
Contact:	Mrs Lee Saunders

C

Camargo Foundation

1, Avenue Jermini, 13260 Cassis, France

Tel:	(33) 4 4201 1311
Email:	apply@camargofoundation.org
Website:	www.camargofoundation.org
Contact:	Cynthia A. Gehrig, President

The Camargo Foundation is a residential center offering programming in the humanities and the arts.

The Camargo Core Program

Subjects: The Camargo Foundation welcomes applications from all countries and nationalities. Three main categories are available, and several subcategories for artists' applications. 1. Scholars should be connected to the Arts and Humanities working on French and Francophone cultures, or cross-cultural studies that engage the cultures and influences of the Mediterranean region. 2. Thinkers include accomplished professionals and practitioners in cultural and creative fields (such as curators, journalists, critics, urban planners, independent scholars, etc.) who are professionally engaged in critical thought. We are interested in work attuned to the theoretical "arena", the arts, and society. 3. Artists, in all disciplines, should be the primary creators of a new work/project and should have achieved a track record of publications/performances/exhibitions, credits, awards and/or grants. We are interested in artists who have a fully developed, mature artistic voice. Applicants may include artists who are engaged in critical thought and research-oriented projects. When applying, artists will have to choose among the following subcategories: Visual Artists / Choreographers and Performance Artists / Writers and Playwrights / Film, Video and Digital Artists / Composers and Sound Artists / Multidisciplinary Artists

Purpose: The Camargo Foundation, located in Cassis, France, and founded by artist and philanthropist Jerome Hill, is a residential center offering programming in the Arts and Humanities. It offers time and space in a contemplative environment to think, create, and connect. The Foundation encourages the visionary work of artists, scholars, and thinkers in the Arts and Humanities. The Camargo Core Program is the historical and flagship program of the Camargo Foundation. Each year an international call is launched through which 18 fellows (9 artists and 9 scholars/thinkers) are selected. The Camargo Core Program offers time and space in a contemplative environment to think, create, and connect. By supporting groundbreaking research and experimentation, it contributes to the visionary work of artists, scholars and thinkers in the Arts and Humanities. By encouraging multidisciplinary and interdisciplinary approaches, it intends to foster connections between research and creation

Eligibility: Scholars should be connected to the Arts and Humanities working on French and Francophone cultures, or cross-cultural studies that engage the cultures and influences of the Mediterranean region. To be eligible for a fellowship in the "Scholars" category, applicants are expected either to hold a PhD and a record of post-doctoral scholarship, or to be PhD candidates completing the final stages of research for, or writing of, their dissertation

Level of Study: Doctorate, Postdoctorate, Postgraduate, Professional development, Research, Foundation programme

Type: Residential fellowships

Value: A stipend of 250 USD per week is available, as is funding for basic transportation to and from Cassis for the Fellow for the residency. In the case of air travel, basic coach class booked far in advance is covered

Frequency: Annual

Country of Study: France

No. of awards offered: 1038

Application Procedure: The call for applications for the Camargo Core Program for the upcoming years will be open

© Springer Nature Limited 2019
Palgrave Macmillan (ed.), *The Grants Register 2020*,
https://doi.org/10.1057/978-1-349-95943-3

in summer years. More information will be available on www. camargofoundation.org

Closing Date: Fall

Funding: Government, Private, Foundation, Trusts, Individuals

No. of awards given last year: 18

No. of applicants last year: 1038

Additional Information: More information is available on camargofoundation.org/programs/camargo-core-program/

Canada Council for the Arts

150 Elgin St., PO Box 1047, Ottawa, ON K1P 5V8, Canada

Tel: (1) 800 263 5588 or 613 566 4414
Fax: (1) 613 566 4390
Email: info@canadacouncil.ca
Website: www.canadacouncil.ca
Contact: Martin, Program Officer

The Canada Council for the Arts is a national agency that provides grants and services to professional Canadian artists and art organizations in dance, media arts, music, theatre, writing and publishing, inter-arts and the visual arts.

John G. Diefenbaker Award

Purpose: The John G. Diefenbaker Award is funded by an endowment given to the Canada Council for the Arts by the Government of Canada. The endowment, announced by Prime Minister Brian Mulroney during his visit to Germany in the spring of 1991, honours the memory of former Prime Minister John G. Diefenbaker. The award is given annually, and it enables a distinguished German scholar to do research in Canada, which may include brief periods in the United States. The spirit of the award is to encourage exchange between scholarly communities in Canada and Germany

Eligibility: Candidates may not apply for this award: they must be nominated by a department within a host university or research institute in Canada. This award is open to German scholars who have demonstrated outstanding ability, especially through a substantial publication record over several years. The award is offered in support of research in any of the disciplines of the social sciences and humanities. Candidates must be German citizens with a contractual or working relationship with an academic institution in Germany. They must have a sound working knowledge of at least one of Canada's two official languages

Value: Up to $95,000

Country of Study: Any country

Application Procedure: Check website for more details

Closing Date: 1 November

For further information contact:

Email: luiza.pereira@canadacouncil.ca

John Hobday Awards in Arts Management

Purpose: Established through a donation of $1,000,000 from The Samuel and Saidye Bronfman Family Foundation to the Canada Council for the Arts, the awards recognize outstanding established and mid-career arts managers in Canadian professional arts organizations. Arts managers from any artistic discipline supported by the Canada Council may apply for the awards, which are intended for professional development, mentoring and related purposes

Eligibility: Applicants should be a Canadian citizen or have permanent resident status, as defined by Citizenship and Immigration Canada. You do not need to be living in Canada when you apply. Applicants should have a minimum of 10 years' experience (not necessarily continuous years) as a professional arts manager

Level of Study: Postgraduate

Type: Cash prize

Value: Two awards of $10,000 each may be given annually

Frequency: Annual

Country of Study: Canada

Closing Date: 30 September

For further information contact:

Email: sarah.brown@canadacouncil.ca

Killam Research Fellowships

Subjects: Humanities, social sciences, natural sciences, health sciences, engineering and studies linking any of the disciplines within these broad fields

Purpose: To support Canadian scholars of exceptional ability engaged in advanced research projects

Eligibility: Open to Canadian citizens or permanent residents of Canada. Killam Research Fellowships are aimed at established scholars who have demonstrated outstanding ability through substantial publications in their fields over a period of several years. Killam Research Fellows are expected to continue contributing to the Canadian research community after they have completed their fellowship project

Level of Study: Postgraduate

Type: Fellowship

Value: C$70,000 per year, paid to the university or research institution which employs the fellow
Length of Study: 2 years
Frequency: Annual
Country of Study: Any country
Application Procedure: There are no hard copy application forms: applicants must submit their requests through the Canada Council's online application system at killam.canadacouncil.ca
Closing Date: 15 May
Funding: Private
Contributor: Killam Trust
Additional Information: Please check at canadacouncil.ca/en/council/grants/find-a-grant for further information

For further information contact:

Email: killam.canadacouncil.ca

Musical Instrument Bank

Subjects: Musical Instrument Bank
Purpose: Every 3 years, talented Canadian classical musicians compete for the chance to borrow legendary instruments from the Canada Council's Musical Instrument Bank (MIB). The competition is intense and is decided by a jury of professional musicians and peers. Musicians who win the competition are often invited to perform with their instruments on some of the world's most celebrated stages. The MIB includes over 20 magnificent instruments worth a total of over $41,000,000. These violins, cellos and bows, created by such master craftsmen as Stradivari, Gagliano and Pressenda, have been donated or lent to the MIB since it was created in 1985
Eligibility: Applicants to some grant programs are eligible and will be considered for prizes and apply to the Council
Level of Study: Doctorate
Value: Visit the website instrumentbank.canadacouncil.ca/ to learn about the instruments
Country of Study: Canada
Closing Date: 1 April

For further information contact:

Tel: (1) 403 244 3074

Prix de Rome in Architecture for Emerging Practitioners

Purpose: The Canada Council for the Arts Prix de Rome in Architecture for Emerging Practitioners is awarded to a recent graduate of a Canadian school of architecture who demonstrates exceptional potential in contemporary architectural design
Eligibility: Applicants must be a Canadian citizen or have Permanent Resident status, as defined by Citizenship and Immigration Canada
Value: The prize is $34,000, to contribute towards the costs of the proposed program of work and related travels, and of the proposed public presentation
Country of Study: Any country
Closing Date: 1 October
Additional Information: Should have received a professional Bachelor or Master degree from a Canadian school of architecture that is certified by the Canadian Architectural Certification Board within 14 months prior to the deadline for submitting applications

For further information contact:

Email: sarah.brown@canadacouncil.ca

Canadian Association of Broadcasters (CAB)

770-45 O'Connor St., Ottawa, ON K1P 1A4, Canada

Tel: (1) 613 233 4035
Fax: (1) 613 233 6961
Email: cab@cab-acr.ca
Website: www.cab-acr.ca
Contact: Vanessa Dawson, Special Events and Projects Co-ordinator

The Canadian Association of Broadcasters (CAB) is the collective voice of Canada's private radio and television stations and speciality services. The CAB develops industry-wide strategic plans, works to improve the financial health of the industry, and promotes private broadcasting's role as Canada's leading programmer and local service provider.

Horatio Alger Association Canadian Scholarships

Purpose: Horatio Alger Association Canadian Scholarships are funded through the generosity of the Association's Members
Eligibility: You only have to submit one application to receive consideration for all of our scholarship programs for which you are eligible
Level of Study: Graduate
Type: Scholarship
Frequency: Annual

Country of Study: Canada
Closing Date: 25 October
Funding: Private

For further information contact:

Email: scholarships@horatioalger.org

Canadian Blood Services (CBS)

1800 Alta Vista Drive, Ottawa, ON K1G 4J5, Canada

Tel: (1) 613 739 2300
Fax: (1) 613 731 1411
Email: onematch@blood.ca
Website: www.bloodservices.ca

Canadian Blood Services (CBS) is a non-profit, charitable organization whose sole mission is to manage the blood system for Canadians. CBS collects approx. 900,000 units of blood annually and processes it into components and products that are administered to thousands of patients each year.

Canadian Blood Services Graduate Fellowship Program

Subjects: Blood transfusion science focusing on aspects of the collection and preparation of blood from volunteer donors as well as on the biological materials derived from blood or their substitutes obtained through biotechnology. Research may encompass a broad variety of disciplines including, but not restricted to, epidemiology, surveillance, social sciences, blood banking, immunohaematology, haematology, infectious diseases, immunology, genetics, protein chemistry, molecular and cell biology, clinical medicine, laboratory sciences, virology, bioengineering, process engineering or biotechnology
Purpose: To attract and support young investigators to initiate or continue training in the field of blood or blood products research
Eligibility: Open to graduate students who are undertaking full-time research training leading to a PhD degree. Students registering solely for a Master's degree will not be considered and only those demonstrating acceptance into a PhD programme will receive continued support. Candidates must have completed sufficient academic work to be admitted in good standing to a graduate school by the time the award is to take effect, or be already engaged in a PhD

programme. Applicants possessing a medical degree but not licensed to practice medicine in Canada are eligible to apply for this award providing they meet the above criteria
Level of Study: Graduate
Type: Fellowship
Value: C$21,000 per year plus a yearly research and travel allowance of C$1,000 per year
Length of Study: Up to 4 years. The initial term is for 2 years, with the option for a 2-year renewal. Renewals must be requested in the form of a complete new application
Country of Study: Canada
No. of awards offered: 15
Application Procedure: Candidates are required to submit a completed application form (GFP-01) that is available either from the website, from or the main address
Closing Date: 15 November
Funding: Government
No. of awards given last year: 7
No. of applicants last year: 15
Additional Information: Please check at www.blood.ca/en/research/funding-programs for further details

For further information contact:

Program Assistant, R&D, Canadian Blood Services, 1800 Alta Vista Drive, Canada

Tel: (1) 613 739 2230
Fax: (1) 613 739 2201
Email: elaine.konecny@blood.ca
Contact: Elaine Konecny

Canadian Breast Cancer Research Alliance (CBCRA)

375 University Avenue, 6th Floor, Toronto, ON M5G 2JS, Canada

Tel: (1) 416 596 6598
Fax: (1) 416 596 1714
Email: pmacgregor@cbcra.ca
Website: www.breast.cancer.ca
Contact: Dr Pascale Macgregor, Research Program Director

Established in 1993, the Canadian Breast Cancer Research Alliance (CBCRA) is Canada's primary funder of breast cancer study. As a unique partnership of groups from the public, private and non-profit sectors, CBCRA is committed to reducing the incidence of breast cancer, increasing survival and enhancing the lives of those affected by the disease.

Canadian Federation of University Women Bourse Georgette Lemoyne

Country of Study: Any country

For further information contact:

Email: fellowships@cfuw.org

Canadian Bureau for International Education (CBIE)

220 Laurier West, Suite 1550, Ottawa, ON K1P 5Z9, Canada

Tel: (1) 613 237 4820
Fax: (1) 613 237 1073
Email: scholarships-bourses@cbie.ca
Website: www.cbie.ca

The Canadian Bureau for International Education (CBIE) is a national non-profit association comprising educational institutions, organizations and individuals dedicated to internal education and intercultural training. CBIE's mission is to promote the free movement of learners and trainees across national borders.

Canada-Asia-Pacific Awards

Subjects: International research
Purpose: To assist scholars in higher education institutions in Asia Pacific Region to undertake short-term research
Eligibility: Open to students from the Asia-Pacific region
Level of Study: Postgraduate
Type: Award
Value: C$5,000–10,000
Frequency: Annual
Country of Study: Canada
Application Procedure: A completed application form must be submitted
Closing Date: 30 September
Funding: Government

For further information contact:

Email: charles.labrecque@asiapacific.ca

Canada-Brazil Awards - Joint Research Projects

Purpose: The Canada-Brazil Awards - Joint Research Projects support exchanges of PhD students in the context of team based bilateral research projects. The projects must engage in collaborative research in key academic areas of bilateral cooperation leading to an eventual publication or collaborative research in line with the objectives of the Canada-Brazil Framework Agreement for Cooperation on Science, Technology and Innovation. Applicants must clearly explain the advantages of the partnership for both countries
Eligibility: This competition is open to research teams from Canadian and Brazilian universities. The coordination of the project will be the responsibility of both the Canadian and Brazilian Project Leads and the teams will consist of PhD students from both institutions. Canadian and Brazilian Project Members: Must be citizens or permanent residents of the country of their institution; Must be doctoral students - Master's students and post-doctoral researchers will not be considered; Must be enrolled full-time at a post-secondary institution in their country of origin and paying the tuition fees required by that institution for the full duration of the exchange; Must be proficient in the language of instruction at the Canadian institution (English or French). Students already participating in an exchange program in Canada or in Brazil are not eligible
Level of Study: Research
Value: $9,700 for Canadian PhD students; for values for Brazilian students see: external link
Length of Study: 2 years
Country of Study: Any country
Closing Date: 3 July
Funding: Government
Contributor: Government of Canada, Foreign Affairs, Trade and Development Canada (DFATD)

For further information contact:

Email: admin-scholarships-bourses@cbie.ca

Canada-CARICOM Faculty Leadership Program

Purpose: To support international collaboration between Canadian post-secondary institutions and institutions in the CARICOM, through professional development opportunities for faculty and staff
Eligibility: This competition is open to research teams from Canadian and Brazilian universities. The coordination of the project will be the responsibility of both the Canadian and Brazilian Project Leads and the teams will consist of graduate project members from Canadian institutions and PhD project members from Brazilian institutions

Value: C$2,700 for faculty members for 2 to 3 weeks of course work or research as part of their professional development; C$2,700 for international directors, managers or administrators for 2 to 3 weeks of course work, or for a practicum in the area of internationalization of post-secondary institutions or student mobility as part of their professional development; or C$9,700 for faculty members for 5 to 6 months of study or research at the graduate level
Country of Study: Any country
Closing Date: 25 April
Contributor: Global Affairs Canada: the Department of Foreign Affairs, Trade and Development (DFATD)
Additional Information: Further information is available on the International Scholarships Canada Application Tool Help webpages. If institutions experience difficulty filling out or submitting the form, they should send an email to admin-scholarships-bourses@cbie.ca

For further information contact:

Email: admin-scholarships-bourses@cbie.ca

Canada-CARICOM Leadership Scholarships Program

Purpose: The Canada-CARICOM Leadership Scholarships are facilitated through institutional collaborations and student exchange agreements between Canadian institutions and institutions in the CARICOM
Eligibility: Candidates must be citizens of one of the following eligible CARICOM countries: Anguilla, Antigua and Barbuda, Bahamas, Barbados, Belize, Bermuda, British Virgin Islands, Cayman Islands, Dominica, Grenada, Guyana, Haiti, Jamaica, Montserrat, Saint Kitts and Nevis, Saint Lucia, Saint Vincent and the Grenadines, Suriname, Trinidad and Tobago, Turks and Caicos
Value: C$7,200 for college, undergraduate or graduate (Master's and PhD) students for a minimum of 4 months or 1 academic term of study or research; $9,700 CAN for graduate students (Master's and PhD) for a period of 5 or 6 months of study or research; or C$14,700 for undergraduate and college students for a period of 8 months of study or research
Country of Study: Any country
Closing Date: 25 April
Additional Information: If institutions experience difficulty filling out or submitting the form, they should send an email to admin-scholarships-bourses@cbie.ca. Further information is available on the International Scholarships Canada Application Tool Help webpages

For further information contact:

Email: scholarships-bourses@cbie.ca

Canada-Chile Leadership Exchange Scholarship

Purpose: The Canada-Chile Leadership Exchange Scholarship program provides students and researchers from Chile with short-term exchange opportunities for study or research, in Canada, at the college, undergraduate and graduate levels
Eligibility: 1. Must be citizens of Chile. Must be enrolled full-time at a post-secondary institution in Chile and paying any tuition fees regulated by that institution for the full duration of the exchange. 2. People from Canadian institution can apply for this scholarship
Value: C$7,200 for college, undergraduate or graduate students (Master
Country of Study: Any country
Application Procedure: Selected candidates are encouraged to: ensure that they fulfill the requirements of the Canadian institution including academic requirements and language proficiency; submit their visa application as early as possible and follow the procedures of Immigration, Refugees and Citizenship Canada as outlined by the Canadian institution (generally a study permit is required for course work and a work permit is required for research); initiate the process for the transfer of credits to their home institution as soon as their Canadian courses have been identified; and contact alumni of the program through their home institution for advice and a local perspective on the scholarship experience
Closing Date: 21 March
Additional Information: If institutions experience difficulty filling out or submitting the form, they should send an email to admin-scholarships-bourses@cbie.ca. Further information is available on the International Scholarships Canada Application Tool Help webpages

For further information contact:

Email: scholarships-bourses@cbie.ca

Canadian Prime Minister's Awards for Publishing (CPMA)

Subjects: Area and cultural studies
Purpose: To increase the amount of published material related to Canada available in Japanese
Eligibility: Open to Japanese publishers who are likely to increase the knowledge and understanding of contemporary Canada

Level of Study: Postgraduate
Type: Scholarship
Frequency: Annual
Application Procedure: Further information available on the website
Closing Date: 15 November
Funding: Government

For further information contact:

Academic Relations (CPMA), Public Affairs, Embassy of Canada, 7-3-38 Akasaka, Minato-Ku, Japan

Tel: (81) 3 5412 6298
Fax: (81) 3 5412 6249
Email: tokyo.lib-bib@international.gc.ca

Emerging Leaders in the Americas Program (ELAP)

Purpose: The Emerging Leaders in the Americas Program (ELAP) scholarships provide students and researchers from Latin America and the Caribbean with short-term exchange opportunities for study or research, in Canada, at the college, undergraduate and graduate levels
Eligibility: Candidates who have obtained Canadian citizenship or who have applied for permanent residency in Canada are not eligible; candidates who have already participating in an exchange scholarship program funded by the Government of Canada are not eligible; candidates who have already enrolled in a degree or diploma program at a Canadian university or college are not eligible; and the candidates must be enrolled full-time at a post-secondary institution in an eligible country and paying any tuition fees regulated by that institution for the full duration of the exchange
Level of Study: Postgraduate
Type: Scholarship
Value: C$7,200 for college, undergraduate or graduate students (Master)
Length of Study: 4 months to 1 academic year (master's and PhD)/ 5 to 6 months of study of research
Country of Study: Canada
Application Procedure: If institutions experience difficulty filling out or submitting the form, they should send an email to admin-scholarships-bourses@cbie.ca. Further information is available on the International Scholarships Canada Application Tool Help (www.scholarships-bourses. gc.ca/scholarships-bourses/app/help-aide.aspx?lang=eng) webpages
Closing Date: 25 April
Contributor: Government of Canada

Additional Information: As part of the Emerging Leaders in the Americas Program, selected graduate-level recipients will be invited to participate in a study tour focused on Canadian democratic governance and civil society or other key priority areas

For further information contact:

Email: admin-scholarships-bourses@cbie.ca

International Council for Canadian Studies Graduate Student Scholarships

Subjects: Social sciences and humanities
Purpose: To provide access to crucial scholarly information and resources in Canada in support of a thesis/dissertation
Eligibility: Open to students at the thesis or dissertation stage in the field of social sciences or humanities
Type: Scholarship
Value: C$3,500
Frequency: Annual
Study Establishment: Any accredited Canadian University
Country of Study: Canada
Application Procedure: A completed application form and all supporting materials should be submitted to the Canadian Studies Associations
Closing Date: 31 December

For further information contact:

Tel: (1) 613 789 7834 ext. 242
Email: csppec@iccs-ciec.ca
Contact: Canadian Studies Programs coordinator

Organization of American States (OAS) Fellowships Programs

Subjects: Human development
Purpose: To fund education of Canadian residents and nationals in other American nations
Eligibility: Open to Canadian residents and nationals
Level of Study: Doctorate, Graduate, MBA
Type: Fellowship
Value: US$30,000 per academic year, which includes a round-trip economy-class airfare ticket; tuition fees and mandatory expenses for the academic program, a fixed monthly allowance, medical insurance, and a fixed annual book allowance
Length of Study: 1–2 years
Frequency: Annual

Country of Study: Any country
Application Procedure: A completed application form must be submitted on time. Please refer website for more information
Closing Date: 7 March
Funding: Government
Additional Information: Please check at www.cbie-bcei.ca/what-we-do/student-portal/scholarships/ for further details

For further information contact:

Email: scholarships@oas.org

Canadian Cancer Society Research Institute (CCSRI)

Suite 300, 55 St. Clair Avenue W, Toronto, ON M4V 2Y7, Canada

Tel: (1) 416 961 7223
Fax: (1) 416 961 4189
Email: research@cancer.ca
Website: www.cancer.ca/research

The Canadian Cancer Society (CCS) is the largest non-government funder of cancer research in Canada. The CCS provides support for research and related programmes undertaken at Canadian universities, hospitals and other research institutions.

Union for International Cancer Control American Cancer Society International Fellowships for Beginning Investigators (ACSBI)

Subjects: Basic, transitional or clinical research projects in the areas of epidemiology, prevention, cause, detection, diagnosis, treatment and psycho-oncology
Purpose: To provide funding for research that fosters a bi-directional flow of knowledge, experience, expertise and innovation to and from the United States of America
Eligibility: Candidates should be in the early stages of their career. Applications that are geared to the development of cancer control measures in developing central and east European countries are particularly encouraged
Level of Study: Postdoctorate, Professional development, Research
Type: Research grant
Value: Approx. US$35,000
Length of Study: 1 year

Frequency: Annual
Country of Study: Any country
Application Procedure: Applicants must write for details or refer to the website
Closing Date: 1 October
Funding: Private
Contributor: American Cancer Society
Additional Information: Results are available in April of the following year. Further information is available on the website

For further information contact:

UICC Fellowships Department 3 rue du Conseil-General, Geneva, Switzerland

Tel: (41) 22 809 1811
Fax: (41) 22 809 1810
Email: fellows@uicc.ch
Contact: UICC Fellowships Department

Union for International Cancer Control International Oncology Nursing Fellowships (IDNF)

Subjects: Cancer research
Purpose: The NCIC financially supports the International Union Against Cancer (UICC) which administers a number of fellowships to qualified professionals
Eligibility: English speaking nurses who are actively engaged in the management of cancer patients and who come from the developing and East European countries
Level of Study: Professional development
Type: Fellowship
Value: US$2,800
Length of Study: 1–3 months
Frequency: Annual
Application Procedure: Applicants must request information
Closing Date: 1 November
Additional Information: Further information available on request or from the website

For further information contact:

UICC Fellowships Department, 3 Rue de Conseil-Général, Geneva, Switzerland

Tel: (41) 22 809 1811
Fax: (41) 22 809 1810
Email: fellows@uicc.org

Canadian Crafts Council

345 Lakeshore Road West, Oakville, ON L6K 1G3, Canada

Tel: (1) 905 845 5357
Fax: (1) 905 845 8210
Email: kingfish@spectranet.ca
Contact: Ms Jan Waldorf

Saidye Bronfman Award

Subjects: Any discipline within the crafts
Purpose: To recognise excellence in the crafts. The award is made to a craftsperson judged to be an outstanding practitioner in their field, shown by their output over a working life, and their current level of achievement
Eligibility: Open to Canadian citizens, or individuals who have had landed immigrant status for at least three years. The nominee must have made a significant contribution to the development of crafts in Canada over a significant period of time, usually more than ten years
Level of Study: Postgraduate
Type: Award
Value: C$25,000
Frequency: Annual
Country of Study: Any country
Application Procedure: Nominations are made through CCC member associations across Canada. Award recipients are selected by a committee of leading Canadian craftspersons, including the current President of the Canadian Crafts Council, a past recipient of the Award, a nominee of the Bronfman Foundation, a gallery or museum director, and a member of the CCC Board. Members are selected to represent all major disciplines and geographic areas of Canada
Closing Date: 15 June

For further information contact:

Tel: (1) 613 566 4414
Email: jennifer.cherniack@canadacouncil.ca

Canadian Embassy (United States of America)

501 Pennsylvania Ave. N.W., Washington, DC 20001-2114, United States of America

Tel: (1) 202 682 1740
Fax: (1) 202 682 7726

Email: enqserv@dfait-maeci.gc.ca
Website: www.canadianembassy.org

Canadian Embassy (United States of America) Research Grant Program

Subjects: Business and economic issues, Canadian values and culture, communications, environment, national and international security or natural resources, e.g. energy, fisheries, forestry and trade
Purpose: To assist individual scholars or a group of scholars in writing an article length manuscript of publishable quality and reporting their findings in scholarly publications
Eligibility: Open to full-time faculty members at accredited 4-year United States colleges and universities, as well as scholars at American research and policy planning institutes who undertake significant research projects concerning Canada, Canada and the United States, or Canada and North America. Recent PhD recipients who are citizens or permanent residents of the United States are also eligible to apply
Level of Study: Postgraduate
Type: Programme grant
Value: Up to US$15,000; applicants whose project focuses on the priority topics listed above and who can demonstrate matching funds from others sources may request funding up to US$20,000
Frequency: Annual
Study Establishment: An accredited 4-year college or university
Country of Study: United States of America
Application Procedure: Applicants must provide 6 copies of the following in this order: the completed application form, a concise proposal of 4-8 pages which will identify all members of the research team, if a team project, and specify each member's affiliation and role in the study, identify the key issues or the main theoretical problem, describe and justify the appropriate methodology, present a general schedule of research activities, indicate clearly both the nature and scope of the projects contribution to the advancement of Canadian Studies, include a detailed budget including all other funding sources and a description of anticipated expenditures. A curriculum vitae, and the names and addresses of two scholars from whom the applicants will solicit recommendations should also be included. Application forms are available on request
Closing Date: 1 November
Funding: Government
Additional Information: The Research Grant Program promotes research in the social sciences and humanities with a view to contributing to a better knowledge and

understanding of Canada and its relationship with the United States or other countries of the world

For further information contact:

Tel: (1) 202 682 7717
Email: daniel.abele@dfait-maeci.gc.ca
Contact: Dan Abele, Academic Relations Officer

Canadian Embassy Faculty Enrichment Program

Subjects: Priority topics include bilateral trade and economics, Canada - United States border issues, cultural policy and values, environment, natural resources, energy issues and security co-operation, projects that examine Canadian politics, economics, culture and society as well as Canada's role in international affairs

Purpose: To provide faculty members with the opportunity to develop or redevelop courses with substantial Canadian content that will be offered as part of their regular teaching load, or as a special offering to select audiences in continuing or distance education

Eligibility: Open to full-time, tenured or tenure track faculty members at accredited 4-year United States colleges and universities. Candidates should be able to demonstrate that they are already teaching, or will be authorized to teach, courses with substantial Canadian content (33% or more). Team teaching applications are welcome. Applicants are ineligible to receive the same grant in 2 consecutive years or to receive two individual category Canadian Studies grants in the same grant period

Type: Programme

Value: Funding up to US$6,000; applicants may request an additional US$5,000 specifically to support student travel to Canada

Frequency: Annual

Country of Study: United States of America

Application Procedure: Applicants must contact the organization for an application form

Closing Date: 1 December

Additional Information: The Embassy especially encourages the use of new Internet technology to enhance existing courses, including the creation of instructional websites, interactive technologies and distance learning links to Canadian Universities

For further information contact:

Tel: (1) 202 682 7717
Email: daniel.abele@dfait-maeci.gc.ca
Contact: Dan Abele, Academic Relations Officer

Canadian Embassy Graduate Student Fellowship Program

Subjects: Business and economic issues, Canadian values and culture, communications, environment, national and international security or natural resources, e.g. energy, fisheries, forestry and trade

Purpose: To assist graduate students in conducting part of their doctoral research in Canada to acquire a better knowledge and understanding of Canada or its relationship with the United States and other countries of the world

Eligibility: Open to full-time doctoral students at accredited 4-year colleges and universities in the United States or Canada whose dissertations are related in substantial part to the study of Canada, Canada and the United States or Canada and North America. Candidates must be citizens or permanent residents of the United States and should have completed all doctoral requirements except the dissertation when they apply for a grant

Level of Study: Graduate

Type: Fellowship

Value: Fellowships carrying stipends of up to $850 per month for up to 9 months

Length of Study: 9 months

Frequency: Annual

Study Establishment: An accredited 4-year college or university

Country of Study: Other

Application Procedure: Applicants must provide six copies of the following in the order listed: the completed application form, a concise letter of three to four pages which will explain clearly the present status of the candidate's doctoral studies, describe the candidate's study plans in Canada, list Canadian contacts such as Scholars, research institutes, academic institutions or libraries, state clearly the exact number of months for which financial support is needed, provide a complete and detailed budget, indicate what other funding sources are available, give the names and addresses of two referees, one of which must be the dissertation advisor, contain the dissertation prospectus which must identify the key issues or the main theoretical problem, justify the methodology and indicate clearly the nature of the dissertation's contribution to the advancement of Canadian Studies. An unofficial transcript of grades, a curriculum vitae and proof of United States citizenship or permanent residency must also be included. Application forms are available on request

Closing Date: October

Funding: Government

Additional Information: The Graduate Student Fellowship Program promotes research in the social sciences and humanities with a view to contributing to a better knowledge and understanding of Canada and its relationship with the United States or other countries of the world

For further information contact:

Tel: (1) 202 682 7727
Email: daniel.abele@dfait-maeci.gc.ca
Contact: Dan Abele, Academic Relations Officer

Outreach Grant

Subjects: Teacher training
Purpose: To encourage training and resource development
Eligibility: Open to all K-12 teacher who teach about Canada or Canada–United States relations
Level of Study: Professional development
Type: Grant
Value: Up to US$14,000
Frequency: Annual
Country of Study: United States of America
Application Procedure: Contact the academic relations officer
Closing Date: 30 June
Funding: Government
Contributor: Foreign Affairs Canada

For further information contact:

Email: outreach@physoc.org

Canadian Federation of University Women (CFUW)

331 Cooper Street, Suite 502, Ottawa, ON K2P 0G5, Canada

Tel: (1) 613 234 8252 ext. 104
Fax: (1) 613 234 8221
Email: cfuwfls@rogers.com; fellowships@cfuw.org
Website: www.cfuw.org
Contact: Betty A Dunlop, CFUW Fellowships Program Manager

Found in 1919, the Canadian Federation of University Women (CFUW) is a voluntary, non-partisan, non-profit, self-funded bilingual organization of 9,000 women university graduates. CFUW members are active in public affairs, working to raise the social, economic, and legal status of women as well as to improve education, the environment, peace, justice and human rights.

Dr. A. Vibert Douglas Fellowship

Purpose: The Fellowship is for a PhD thesis/project which focuses on advancing gender equality. The project must be led by women. The Fellowship is for a PhD thesis/project which focuses on advancing gender equality
Eligibility: If an applicant does not belong to an NFA of the GWI or to an organization that belongs to the IAW but meets the other criteria for the Fellowship they must make a $10 donation that will be split between those two organizations
Level of Study: Postgraduate
Type: Fellowship
Value: $8,000
Frequency: Annual
Country of Study: Any country
Application Procedure: Those who are interested in this fellowship will need to pay a $60 application fee
Closing Date: 3 December
Funding: Private
Additional Information: For more information, visit fcfdu. fluidreview.com/

Canadian Foundation for the Study of Infant Deaths

Suite 308, 586 Eglinton Avenue East, Toronto, ON M4P 1P2, Canada

Tel: (1) 416 488 3260
Fax: (1) 416 488 3864
Email: sidsinfo@sidscanada.org
Website: www.sidscanada.org
Contact: Ravit Lasman, Executive Director

The Canadian Foundation for the Study of Infant Deaths is a federally incorporated charitable organization that was set up in 1973 to respond to the needs of families experiencing sudden and unexpected infant death. It is the only organization in Canada solely dedicated to finding the causes of Sudden Infant Death Syndrome, its effect on families and the education of the public.

Cypress-Fairbanks Independent School District/ CIHR Doctoral and Postdoctoral Research Awards

For further information contact:

The Canadian Institutes of Health Research, 440 Laurier Ave. 9th fl., Locator 4209A, Canada

Tel: (1) 613 954 1964
Fax: (1) 613 941 1800
Email: srobertson@cihr.ca
Contact: Sytephanie Robertson, Coordinator, Programs Branch

Canadian Institute for Advanced Legal Studies

PO Box 43538, Leaside Post Office, 1601 Bayview Avenue, Toronto, ON M4G 4G8, Canada

Tel: (1) 416 429 3292
Fax: (1) 416 429 9805
Email: info@canadian-institute.com
Website: www.canadian-institute.com
Contact: Mr Randall J. Hofley, Vice-President

The Canadian Institute for Advanced Legal Studies conducts legal seminars for judges and lawyers in Cambridge, United Kingdom and Strasbourg, France.

French Language Scholarship

Subjects: Law
Purpose: For graduate studies in law toward a second cycle or third cycle diploma (the equivalent of a Master's or Doctoral degree from a Canadian university), at a European university for a program of study that is conducted principally in the French language, to a person who has, in the four years before the candidate will commence the proposed studies been awarded a bachelor's degree in law from a Canadian university
Eligibility: An applicant must be accepted into a French-language European university for graduate studies in law in order to receive this Scholarship, although such acceptance need not be confirmed at the time of the application for the Scholarship or at the time that the Institute provides the candidate with notice that he or she has been selected to receive the Scholarship
Level of Study: Postgraduate
Type: Scholarship
Value: Full tuition fees payable by the recipient to a French-language European university and includes an allowance to cover a portion of living expenses and reasonable travel expenses to and from the European university, subject to any other awards received by the successful candidate. The Canadian Institute for Advanced Legal Studies shall determine each year the maximum amount of the scholarship, up to

an amount of $20,000 for the academic year, and in so doing will take into account the tuition fees as well as the anticipated living expenses and travel expenses of the successful candidate
Length of Study: 1 year
Frequency: Annual
Study Establishment: French Language European University
Country of Study: Europe, Germany
Application Procedure: Applications must include: Curriculum vitae; 1. A personal statement indicating why the applicant wishes to undertake graduate studies in law and why the applicant is suited to undertake such studies, as well as an undertaking that the proposed program study is conducted principally in the French language. 2. A copy of transcripts for undergraduate and graduate studies, for studies in law or for a Bar Admission Course, as applicable. 3. A maximum of three letters of reference. 4. A statement of tuition fees and anticipated living and travel expenses
Closing Date: 31 December
Funding: Trusts
Contributor: Canadian Institute for Advanced Legal Studies

For further information contact:

Contact: Ms Lynn Morrison, Executive Secretary

The Right Honorable Paul Martin Sr. Scholarship

Subjects: Law
Purpose: To study for an LLM at the University of Cambridge
Eligibility: Open to graduates who have been awarded a law degree from a 3- or 4-year program at a faculty of law in a Canadian university in the 4 years before the candidate will commence his or her studies at the University of Cambridge (supported by The Right Honourable Paul Martin Sr. Scholarship). An applicant must be accepted into the University of Cambridge and a college of the University of Cambridge for graduate studies in law in order to receive this scholarship, although such acceptance need not be confirmed at the time of the application for the scholarship nor at the time that the Institute provides the candidate with notice that he or she has been selected to receive the scholarship
Level of Study: Postgraduate
Type: Scholarship
Value: C$23,000
Length of Study: 1 year
Frequency: Annual
Study Establishment: The University of Cambridge
Country of Study: United Kingdom
No. of awards offered: 25
Application Procedure: Applications must include curriculum vitae; a personal statement indicating why the applicant

wishes to undertake graduate studies in law at the University of Cambridge and why the applicant is suited to undertake such studies; a copy of transcripts for undergraduate and graduate studies, for studies in law and for a Bar Admissions Course, as applicable; and a maximum of three letters of references

Closing Date: 31 December
Funding: Private
No. of awards given last year: 2
No. of applicants last year: 25
Additional Information: The scholarship may be held with another small award as approved by the Institute. Please check at www.canadian-institute.com/english/index.html for further details

For further information contact:

Canadian Institute for Advanced Legal Studies, 1601 Bayview Avenue, Canada

Tel: (1) 416 429 3292
Fax: (1) 416 429 9805
Email: info@canadian-institute.com
Contact: Anne Thomas, Vice President

Canadian Institutes of Health Research

Canadian Institutes of Health Research; 160 Elgin Street, 9th Floor; Address Locator 4809A; Ottawa, ON K1A 0W9, Canada

The Canadian Institutes of Health Research (CIHR) is Canada's federal funding agency for health research. Composed of 13 Institutes, we collaborate with partners and researchers to support the discoveries and innovations that improve our health and strengthen our health care system.

Banting Postdoctoral Fellowships

Subjects: Health research, natural sciences and/or engineering, social sciences and/or humanities
Eligibility: Open to Canadian citizen, permanent resident of Canada, foreign citizens
Level of Study: Postdoctorate
Type: Award
Value: $70,000 per year (taxable)
Length of Study: 2 years
Country of Study: Canada
Closing Date: End of April

Additional Information: For more details, visit website banting.fellowships-bourses.gc.ca/en/app-dem_guide.html

For further information contact:

Email: banting@cihr-irsc.gc.ca

Canadian Institutes of Health Research Gold Leaf Prizes

Subjects: Health research
Eligibility: Open to Canadian citizen, permanent resident of Canada, foreign citizens
Type: Grant
Value: $1,00,000
Length of Study: 2 years
Frequency: Every 2 years
Country of Study: Canada
Additional Information: For more details, please visit the Contact Centre: support@cihr-irsc.gc.ca

For further information contact:

Email: support@cihr-irsc.gc.ca

Foundation Grant Program

Subjects: Health research, natural sciences and/or engineering, social sciences and/or humanities
Purpose: Foundation grants are designed to support research leaders at any career stage to build and conduct programmes of health research across CIHR's mandate
Eligibility: Open to Canadian citizen, permanent resident of Canada, foreign citizens
Type: Grant
Value: Proportionate to the requirements of the research proposed and vary depending on the research field, research approach, and scope of programme activities
Length of Study: 5 to 7 years
Country of Study: Canada
Application Procedure: Please refer website www.cihr-irsc.gc.ca for application procedures
Closing Date: 14 March
Additional Information: For more details, please visit the Contact Centre: support@cihr-irsc.gc.ca

For further information contact:

Email: nbf@aabb.org

Project Grant Program

Subjects: Health research, natural sciences and/or engineering, social sciences and/or humanities
Purpose: Project grants are designed to support researchers at any career stage to build and conduct health-related research and knowledge translation projects across CIHR's mandate
Eligibility: Open to Canadian citizen, permanent resident of Canada, foreign citizens
Type: Grant
Country of Study: Canada
Closing Date: 15 May
Additional Information: For more details, please contact the Contact Centre: support@cihr-irsc.gc.ca

For further information contact:

Email: support@cihr-irsc.gc.ca

Vanier Canada Graduate Scholarships

Subjects: Health research, natural sciences and/or engineering, social sciences and/or humanities
Purpose: To strengthen Canada's ability to attract and retain world-class doctoral students and establish Canada as a global centre of excellence in research and higher learning
Eligibility: Open to Canadian citizen, permanent resident of Canada, foreign citizens
Level of Study: Doctorate
Type: Award
Value: $50,000 per year
Length of Study: 3 years
Country of Study: Canada
Closing Date: November

For further information contact:

Email: vanier@cihr-irsc.gc.ca

Canadian Library Association (CLA)

1150 Morrison Drive, Suite 400, Ottawa, ON K2H 8S9, Canada

Tel: (1) 613 232 9625
Fax: (1) 613 563 9895
Email: info@cla.ca
Website: www.cla.ca
Contact: Valoree McKay, Executive Director

The Canadian Library Association works to maintain a tradition of commitment to excellence in library education

and to advance continuing research in the field of library and information science.

Canadian Library Association Library Research and Development Grants

Subjects: Library and information sciences
Purpose: To support members of the Canadian Library Association for theoretical and applied research in the related fields. To encourage and support research undertaken by practitionares in the field of library and information services. To promote research in the field of library and information services by and/or about Canadians
Eligibility: Open to personal members of the Canadian Library Association
Level of Study: Postgraduate
Type: Grant
Value: C$1,000
Frequency: Annual
Country of Study: Canada
Application Procedure: Applicants must submit grant applications via emails and MS word document in either French or English containing contact details, description of the research project, duration of the project, detailed assessment of costs and statement of other grants/awards received. Proposals should be submitted via email
Closing Date: February (Check with website)
Additional Information: Please check at www.cla.ca/AM/Template.cfm?Section=Grants&Template=/CM/HTMLDisplay.cfm&ContentID=12526 for further details

For further information contact:

c/o Canadian Library Association, 1150 Morrison Drive, Suite 400, Canada

Tel: (1) 613 232 9625 ext 322
Fax: (1) 613 563 9895
Email: info@cla.ca
Contact: CLA Research & Development Grant

Canadian National Institute for the Blind (CNIB)

1929 Bayview Avenue, East York, Toronto, ON M4G 0A1, Canada

Tel: (1) 1800 563 2642, 1 416 486 2500
Fax: (1) 416 480 7700
Email: info@cnib.ca
Website: www.cnib.ca
Contact: Mr John M Rafferty, President and CEO

CNIB is a nationwide, community-based, registered charity committed to public education, research and the vision health of all Canadians. CNIB provides the services and support necessary to enjoy a good quality of life while living with vision loss. Founded in 1918, CNIB reaches out to communities across the country, offering access to rehabilitation training, innovative consumer products and peer support programs as well as one of the world's largest libraries for people with a print disability. CNIB supports research to advance knowledge in the field of vision health. Our research program funds projects that focus on ways to cure, treat and prevent eye disease, and improve the quality of life for people with vision loss.

Canadian National Institute for the Blind Baker Applied Research Fund

Subjects: Research focused on the social, educational, and cultural needs of Canadians who are blind or visually impaired

Purpose: To promote non-medical applied research that will enhance the life of the blind or visually impaired

Eligibility: Open to residents of Canada enrolled in graduate study in Canada, and includes a co-applicant who is either a supervisor or mentor with an academic appointment in Canada, or a supervisory position at a healthcare facility. Refer to the website for complete details

Level of Study: Research

Value: Up to C$40,000 plus travel and publications costs up to $2,000

Length of Study: One year

Frequency: Annual

Country of Study: Canada

Funding: Private

For further information contact:

Tel: (1) 416 486 2500 ext. 7622
Fax: (1) 416 480 7059
Email: shampa.bose@cnib.ca
Contact: Shampa Bose, Executive Assistant and Research Coordinator

Canadian National Institute for the Blind Baker Fellowship Fund

Subjects: Ophthalmology and optometry

Purpose: CNIB's Baker Fellowships are awarded annually for post-graduate training in ophthalmic subspecialties

Eligibility: Open to Canadians for research or study in Canada, or abroad if returning to practice in Canada, with priority given to university teaching

Level of Study: Postgraduate, Professional development, Research

Value: Up to C$40,000

Length of Study: 1–2 years

Frequency: Annual

Country of Study: Any country

Funding: Private

For further information contact:

Tel: (1) 416 486 2500 ext. 7622
Fax: (1) 416 480 7059
Email: shampa.bose@cnib.ca
Contact: Shampa Bose, Executive Assistant and Research Coordinator

Canadian National Institute for the Blind Baker New Researcher Fund

Purpose: To provide one-year grants to encourage new investigations that may lead to the prevention of vision loss. It is intended to benefit new investigators (within 5 years after an academic faculty appointment) by giving them experience and results which can assist them in further grant applications and pilot investigations

Eligibility: Applicants must be residents of Canada and research must be conducted primarily in Canada

Level of Study: Postdoctorate, Professional development, Research

Value: Up to C$35,000

Length of Study: 1 year

Frequency: Annual

Country of Study: Canada

Funding: Private

For further information contact:

Tel: (1) 416 486 2500 ext. 7622
Fax: (1) 416 480 7059
Email: shampa.bose@cnib.ca
Contact: Shampa Bose, Executive Assistant and Research Coordinator

Canadian National Institute for the Blind Winston Gordon Award

Subjects: Product Development assistive technology for the blind or are partially sighted

Purpose: The award is presented to an individual or group who has made significant technological advances benefiting people with vision loss

Eligibility: The significant advances in, or application of, technology must have occurred within 10 years of nomination.

The device or application must have a documented benefit to people who are blind or visually impaired. The award may be presented to an individual, group, or organization, including corporations and academic institutions

Type: Award
Value: The award consists of a cash prize of up to C$10,000
Country of Study: Any country
Application Procedure: To submit a nomination, please write a letter to the Winston Gordon Committee nominating the individual or group for its products or services, and explaining how the nominee meets or surpasses the eligibility criteria and matches the goals of the award
Closing Date: 16 January
Funding: Private

For further information contact:

Winston Gordon Award Committee, CNIB, 1929 Bayview Avenue, Canada

Fax: (1) 416 480 7000
Email: shampa.bose@cnib.ca
Contact: Shampa Bose, Grants and Awards Coordinator

Gretzky Scholarship Foundation for the Blind Youth of Canada

Subjects: The Gretzky family continue a tradition of assisting the blind youth of Canada to pursue their academic and lifelong dreams
Purpose: To provide scholarships to eligible blind and visually impaired students planning to study at the post-secondary level
Eligibility: All applicants must be blind or visually impaired, a graduate from secondary school entering their first year of post-secondary education, and a Canadian citizen. Candidates must be blind or living with vision loss. A secondary school graduate entering their first year of post-secondary education. A Canadian citizen or have held landed immigrant status for one year prior to date of application. Academic excellence, service to the community, financial need, superior leadership
Type: Scholarship
Value: C$3,000–5,000 each
Frequency: Annual
Country of Study: Canada
Application Procedure: All documents requested in the application form must be included with your application. Please send application and documents to Kim Kohler
Closing Date: 31 May
Funding: Private
No. of awards given last year: 23

For further information contact:

955256 Canning Road, R.R. 2, Paris, France

Tel: (33) 519 458 8665
Fax: (33) 519 458 8609
Email: Kim.Kohler@cnib.ca
Contact: Kim Kohler, Walter and Wayne Gretzky Scholarship Foundation

Ross Purse Doctoral Fellowship

Subjects: The fellowship will be awarded for research in social sciences, engineering and other fields of study that are immediately relevant to the field of vision loss
Purpose: To encourage and support theoretical and practical research and studies at the postgraduate or doctoral level in the field of vision loss in Canada
Eligibility: Applications will be considered from persons studying at a Canadian University or college, or at a foreign University, where a commitment to work in the field of vision loss in Canada for at least 2 years can be demonstrated
Level of Study: Doctorate, Postgraduate
Type: Fellowship
Value: Up to C$12,500 to be paid in three equal installments
Length of Study: 2 years
Frequency: Annual
Country of Study: Any country
Application Procedure: Please send completed applications to Research Coordinator
Closing Date: 2 April
Funding: Private

For further information contact:

CNIB, 1929 Bayview Avenue, Canada

Tel: (1) 416 486 2500 ext. 7622
Fax: (1) 416 480 7000
Email: shampa.bose@cnib.ca
Contact: Shampa Bose, Research Coordinator, Grants, Awards & Scholarship Program

The E. (Ben) & Mary Hochhausen Access Technology Research Award

Subjects: Research awards may be applied to: research projects, study at centers of excellence in Archnology, fellowships, development of prototypes and development costs of bringing important new products to market
Purpose: To encourage research in the field of access technology for people living with vision loss

Eligibility: Applications are accepted from any country in the world
Level of Study: Research
Type: Research award
Value: Up to C$10,000
Country of Study: International
Application Procedure: Please check at www.cnib.ca/en/research/funding/hochhausen/ for more information
Closing Date: 30 September
Funding: Private
No. of awards given last year: 1

For further information contact:

Email: shampa.bose@cnib.ca
Contact: Trustees, The Hochhausen Fund

Canadian Political Science Association

1 Stewart Street, Suite 205, University of Ottawa, Ottawa, ON K1N 6H7, Canada

Tel: (1) 613 562 1202
Fax: (1) 613 241 0019
Email: pip@csse.ca
Contact: Grants Management Officer

The Canadian Political Science Association was founded in 1913 with the aim of encouraging and developing political science and its relationship with other disciplines. To this end the Association holds conferences, meetings and exhibitions, gives grants, scholarships and fellowships and publishes journals, newspapers, books and monographs relating to political science.

Canadian Parliamentary Internship Programme

Subjects: Canadian parliamentary government
Purpose: To give university graduates an opportunity to supplement their theoretical knowledge of Parliament with practical experience of the day to day work of the Members of Parliament and to provide back bench Members with highly qualified assistants
Eligibility: Open to Canadian university graduates
Level of Study: Postgraduate
Type: Scholarship
Value: An estimated stipend of C$16,500, plus travel subsidies
Length of Study: 10 months

Frequency: Annual, if funds are available
Study Establishment: The Canadian Parliament
Country of Study: Canada
Application Procedure: Applicants must submit the original and four copies of the completed application form, transcripts, letters of reference (two academic, one employer), and US$10 administrative fee cheque
Closing Date: Last Friday in January
Funding: Private
Contributor: The Social Sciences and Humanities Research council of Canada, Bank of Montreal, Canadian Airlines International, Canadian Bankers Association, Canadian Cable Television Association, The Canadian Life and Health Association, The Co-operators
Additional Information: Interns will be assigned specific responsibilities with Members of the House of Commons and will be required to attend seminars and prepare a paper analysing an aspect of parliamentary government in Canada

For further information contact:

The Parliamentary Internship Programme, Room 1200, La Promenade Building, 151 Sparks Street, House of Commons, United Kingdom

Tel: (44) 613 995 0764
Fax: (44) 613 995 5357
Email: cartwj@parl.gc.ca

Ontario Legislature Internship Programme

Subjects: Political science and government
Purpose: To provide university graduates with the opportunity to supplement their theoretical knowledge of the Legislature and its processes with practical experience of the day to day work of the members, and to provide back bench members with highly qualified assistants
Eligibility: Open to Canadian citizens only
Level of Study: Postgraduate
Type: Internship
Value: C$16,000
Length of Study: 10 months
Frequency: Dependent on funds available
Country of Study: Canada
No. of awards offered: 97
Application Procedure: Applicants must complete an application form, available on request from the Program Officer
Closing Date: End of January
Funding: Government, Commercial, Private
No. of awards given last year: 8
No. of applicants last year: 97

For further information contact:

Department of Political Science, University of Waterloo, Canada

Tel:	(1) 519 888 4567 ext. 5682
Fax:	(1) 519 746 5622
Email:	olip@watarts.uwaterloo.ca
Contact:	Dr Robert Williams, Director

Canadian Society for Chemical Technology

Chemical Institute of Canada, 222 Queen street, Suite 400, Ottawa, ON K1P 5V9, Canada

Tel:	(1) 613 232 6252 ext 223, 1 888 542 2242
Fax:	(1) 613 232 5862
Email:	awards@cheminst.ca, gthirlwall@cheminst.ca
Website:	www.cheminst.ca/about/cic/csct
Contact:	Gale Thirlwall, Awards Manager

The Canadian Society for Chemical Technology is the national technical association of chemical and biochemical technicians and technologists with members across Canada who work in industry, government or academia. The purpose of the Society is the advancement of chemical technology, the maintenance and improvement of practitioners and educators and the continual evaluation of chemical technology in Canada. The Society hopes to maintain a dialogue with educators, government and industry, to assist in the technology content of the education process of technologists, to attract qualified people into the professions and the Society, to develop and maintain high standards and enhance the usefulness of chemical technology to both the industry and the public.

Canadian National Committee/IUPAC Travel Awards

Subjects: Chemistry, chemical engineering
Purpose: Helps young Canadian scientists and engineers who are within 10 years of gaining their PhD present a paper at an IUPAC-sponsored conference
Eligibility: Evidence of an independent research programme. High quality publication record. Ability to attract research funding
Level of Study: Postdoctorate
Value: Up to $2,500, paid in arrears after travel-expense receipts and a 150-word report on the conference have been received by the Secretary

Country of Study: Any country
Application Procedure: Curriculum vitae, 2 letters of reference, name and location of conference amount ($) needed
Closing Date: 17 October
Funding: Private
Contributor: Gendron Fund and CNC/IUPAC company associates
No. of awards given last year: 4

For further information contact:

Steacie Institute for Molecular Sciences, NRC, 100 Sussex Dr, Canada

Tel:	(1) 613 949 9675
Email:	Shan.Zou@nrc-cnrc.gc.ca
Contact:	Dr Shan Zou, Measurement Science and Standards

Canadian Society for Chemistry (CSC)

222 Queen Street, Suite 400, Ottawa, ON KIP 5V9, Canada

Tel:	(1) 613 232 6252 ext 223
Fax:	(1) 613 232 5862
Email:	awards@cheminst.ca, gthirlwall@cheminst.ca
Website:	www.cheminst.ca/about/cic/csc
Contact:	Gale Thirlwall, Awards Manager

The Canadian Society for Chemistry (CSC), one of three constituent societies of The Chemical Institute of Canada, is the national scientific and educational society of chemists. The purpose of the CSC is to promote the practice and application of chemistry in Canada.

Award for Research Excellence in Materials Chemistry

Subjects: Chemistry
Purpose: To recognize outstanding contribution to materials chemistry while working in Canada
Eligibility: Candidates must be within 15 years of their first independent appointment
Level of Study: Research
Type: Fellowship
Value: Up to $1,000 travel costs for award tour, framed scroll
Frequency: Annual
Application Procedure: Please check website for details
Closing Date: 2 July (check with website)
Funding: Private

Additional Information: Please check at www.cheminst.ca/awards/csc-awards for further details

For further information contact:

Email: awards@cheminst.ca, gthirlwall@cheminst.ca
Contact: Gale Thirlwall Awards Manager

Canadian Space agency

John H. Chapman Space Centre 6767 Route de l';Aéroport Saint-Hubert, Quebec J3Y 8Y9, Canada

Tel: (1) 450 926 4800
Fax: (1) 450 926 4352
Email: dave.kendall@space.gc.ca
Website: www.asc-csa.gc.ca
Contact: David Kendall, Director General, Space Science

The Canadian Space Agency (CSA) was established in 1989 by the Canadian Space Agency Act. The agency operates like a government department

Canadian Space Agency Supplements Postgraduate Scholarships

Subjects: Space science
Purpose: To foster advanced studies in space science by offering a supplement to the regular National Science and Engineering Research Council (NSERC) postgraduate scholarships
Eligibility: Open to graduate and permanent resident and citizen of Canada engaged in Masters or Doctoral studies in the natural sciences or engineering, or intend to pursue such studies in the following year, is successful in obtaining a NSERC postgraduate scholarship (PGS) or a Canada graduate scholarships (CGS-Master's)
Level of Study: Postgraduate
Type: Scholarship
Value: $7,500 per year for one year for masters students and up to two years for doctoral students
Length of Study: 2 years
Frequency: Annual
Country of Study: Canada
Application Procedure: Candidates should apply to the NSERC postgraduate scholarship or Canada graduate scholarship programs by completing Form 200. After reviewing the forms, notification of award will be sent to the selected applicants
Closing Date: 1 May (check with website)

Funding: Government
Contributor: National Science and Engineering Research Council
Additional Information: A candidate who is in receipt of a scholarship from federal sources other than NSERC will not be eligible for this supplement. Please check at www.asc-csa.gc.ca/eng/resources/gc/research.asp#recipients-2 for further details

For further information contact:

Email: sc-gc.centre.expertise@asc-csa.gc.ca

Cancer Council N.S.W

153 Dowling Street, Woolloomooloo, NSW 2011, Kings Cross, PO Box 572, NSW 1340, Australia

Tel: (61) 2 9334 1900
Fax: (61) 2 9326 9328
Email: rong@nswcc.org.au
Website: www.cancercouncil.com.au

The Cancer Council NSW is one of the leading cancer charity organizations in New South Wales. Its mission is to defeat cancer and is working to build a cancer-smart community. In building a cancer-smart community, the Council undertakes high-quality research and is an advocate on cancer issues, providing information and services to the public and raising funds for cancer programmes

The Cancer Council NSW Research Project Grants

Subjects: All aspects of cancer that elucidate its origin, cause and control at a fundamental and applied level. Grants are open to all research disciplines relevant to cancer including behavioural, biomedical, clinical, epidemiological, psychosocial and health services
Purpose: To provide flexible support for cancer researchers
Eligibility: Open to researchers working in NSW institutions
Level of Study: Unrestricted
Type: Project grant
Value: Generally a maximum of A$150,000 per year
Length of Study: Up to 3 years
Frequency: Annual
Study Establishment: An approved institution in New South Wales
Country of Study: Australia

No. of awards offered: 106
Application Procedure: Applicants must complete an application form, available on request or from the website. Applications are submitted through the researcher's institution to NHMRC. Applicants must also complete a supplementary question form and a consumer review form
Closing Date: 18 March (check with website)
Funding: Private
Contributor: Community fund-raising
No. of applicants last year: 106
Additional Information: Further information is available from either the NHMRC Liaison Officer (National Cancer Research Grants Secretariat) or from Cancer Council NSW. Please check at www.cancercouncil.com.au/1221/research/research-funding-and-governance/funding-opportunities/new-grants/ for further details

For further information contact:

NHMRC, GPO Box 9848, Australia

Tel: (61) 3 9635 5028
Email: CancerCouncilGrants@cancervic.org.au
Contact: Miss Josie Italia

Cancer Council South Australia

202 Greenhill Road, Eastwood, SA 5063, Australia

Tel: (61) 8291 4111
Fax: (61) 8291 4122
Email: cc@cancersa.org.au
Website: www.cancersa.org.au

The Cancer Council South Australia is a community-based charity independent of government control that has developed since 1928 with the support of South Australians. The Foundation's mission is to pursue the eradication of cancer through research and education on the prevention and early detection of cancer, thus enhancing the quality of life for people living with cancer.

PhD Scholarships

Subjects: Cancer research
Purpose: To support cancer researchers in South Australia through the provision of research and senior research fellowships
Eligibility: Applicant must be a student judged to be the best applicant from University of Adelaide, Flinders University or University of South Australia, who is commencing PhD studies. The applicant must not be currently enroled in a PhD, must be eligible for the Research Training Scheme and must not have been previously enroled for a Research Degree. Students are eligible to apply for the scholarship if they are enroled in the Faculty or Division of Health Sciences at their institution and if their PhD topic is in an area of cancer research
Level of Study: Postgraduate
Type: Scholarship
Value: Equivalent to the value of the stipend for an APA award
Length of Study: 3 years
Frequency: Annual
Country of Study: Australia
Application Procedure: Applicants must contact the relevant Scholarships Offices of The University of Adelaide, University of South Australia and Flinders University for further information and closing dates
Closing Date: See the website

For further information contact:

Tel: (61) 8 8291 4297
Email: npolglase@cancersa.org.au
Contact: Nicole Polglase, Executive Assistant Research and Development

Cancer Immunotherapy

National Cancer Institute Immunotherapy Fellowship

Purpose: This program allows the fellow to have exposure to multiple clinical immunotherapeutic approaches and key opinion leaders in the field of clinical immunotherapy. It helps to work with internationally recognized experts in immunotherapy
Eligibility: 1. Able to relocate to Bethesda, MD, for the duration of the fellowship. 2. Trained in Medical Oncology, Hematology, Pediatric Oncology, Radiation Oncology, or Surgical Oncology. 3. Interest in learning about immunotherapy. 4. Preference is given to those with an academic interest. 5. Open to United States and Non-United States trained physicians (the latter requires ECFMG certification)
Level of Study: Research
Type: Fellowships
Value: It is based on applicable laws, regulations, and policies
Frequency: Annual
Country of Study: Any country
Application Procedure: For further information, refer the below web link. www.sitcancer.org/funding/fellowships/2019/nci-immunotherapy-fellowship

Closing Date: 17 December
Funding: Private

For further information contact:

555 East Wells Street, Suite 1100, Milwaukee, WI 53202-3823, United States of America

Email: development@sitcancer.org

Society for Immunotherapy of Cancer-Amgen Cancer Immunotherapy in Hematologic Malignancies Fellowship Award

Purpose: This cancer immunotherapy fellowship award aims to provide support for an individual who has a vested interest in furthering the research and translation of immunotherapeutic approaches for treating patients with hematologic malignancies
Eligibility: Candidature must follow the below eligibility to obtain the fellowship award. 1. Current SITC member. 2. Hold an MD or combined MD/PhD degree. 3. Currently hold a position at a leading academic cancer center as a postdoctoral fellow, resident, research scientist or comparable position. 4. Be within postdoctoral or postgraduate training, or no more than four years from completing such training. 5. Commit 75% of workday to research supported by the fellowship
Level of Study: Professional development
Type: Award/Grant
Value: US$1,00,000
Frequency: Annual
Country of Study: Any country
Application Procedure: The people will obtain the following benefits along with the award amount, omce they are eligible for the fellowship award. 1. Complimentary registration and travel for SITC's 34th Annual Meeting. 2. Recognition during the Award Ceremony at SITC's 34th Annual Meeting
Closing Date: 20 December
Funding: Private

For further information contact:

Tel: (1) 414 271 2456

Cancer Research Fund of the Damon Runyon-Walter Winchell Foundation

Fellowship Department, 131 East 36th Street, New York, NY 10016, United States of America

Tel: (1) 212 532 3888
Fax: (1) 212 779 2236
Email: drwwfellow@aol.com
Contact: Ms Clare M Cahill, Assistant to the Director

Cancer Research Fund of the Damon Runyon-Walter Winchell Foundation Research Fellowships for Physician Scientists

Subjects: All theoretical and experimental research that is relevant to the study of cancer and the search for cancer causes, mechanisms, therapies and preventions
Purpose: To augment the training of a physician scientist who has demonstrated the motivation and potential to conduct original research under the supervision of a sponsor, thus, equipping the Fellow to become an independent investigator
Eligibility: Applicants must have completed at least one of the following degrees or its equivalent: MD, PhD, DDS, DVM, and have completed their residencies or clinical fellowship training within three years prior to the Scientific Advisory Committee meeting at which their applications are to be considered
Level of Study: Postdoctorate
Type: Fellowship
Value: US$46,500 stipend for the first year, US$47,500 for the second year and US$49,000 for the third year. In addition, US$2,000 expenses is awarded annually
Length of Study: 3 years, renewable annually
Frequency: 3 times each year
Study Establishment: An approved institution under a sponsor
Country of Study: Other
No. of awards offered: 700
Application Procedure: Application form must be completed
Closing Date: 15 March, 15 August and 15 December
No. of awards given last year: 45
No. of applicants last year: 700

Cancer Research Institute

681 Fifth Avenue, New York, NY 10022-2707, United States of America

Email: info@cancerresearch.org
Website: www.cancerresearch.org
Contact: Grants Enquiries

Cancer Research Institute Irvington Postdoctoral Fellowship Program

Subjects: The Institute seeks hypothesis-driven, mechanistic studies in both immunology and tumor immunology. The applicant and sponsor should make every effort to demonstrate the potential of the proposed studies to directly impact our understanding of the immune system's role in cancer

Purpose: The CRI Irvington Postdoctoral Fellowship Program supports qualified young scientists at leading universities and research centers around the world who wish to receive training in fundamental immunology or cancer immunology

Eligibility: Applicants for the CRI Irvington Postdoctoral Fellowship Program must be working in areas directly related to immunology or cancer immunology. An eligible project must fall into the broad field of immunology with relevance to solving the cancer problem. Applicants must have a doctoral degree by the date of award activation and must conduct their proposed research under a sponsor who holds a formal appointment at the host institution. Applicants with 5 or more years of relevant postdoctoral experience are not eligible, with the exception of M.D. applicants, who should not include years of residency in this calculation. Only in exceptional circumstances will applicants who have already spent 3 or more years in a sponsor's laboratory by the start date of fellowship be considered for a fellowship award. The fellowship can be performed in the United States or abroad, but must take place at a non-profit institution. There are no citizenship restrictions. Only one fellow per sponsor may apply per application round, and faculty sponsors may not have more than three CRI-supported fellows at any time

Level of Study: Doctorate, Postdoctorate

Type: Fellowships

Value: US$1,75,500

Length of Study: 3 years

Frequency: Twice a year

Country of Study: Any country

No. of awards offered: 400

Application Procedure: The application deadlines are April 1 and October 1; when those dates fall on the weekend, applications are due the following Monday. Applications are due by 5 p.m. Eastern Time on these dates. Applicants are notified of fellowship committee decisions within approximately 10–12 weeks of the application deadline. Fellowships can be activated three months after the application deadline but no later than one year following the deadline. Awards activate on the first of the month

Closing Date: 1 April

Funding: Private, Individuals

No. of awards given last year: 35

No. of applicants last year: 400

For further information contact:

29 Broadway, 4th fl, United States of America

Tel: (1) 212-688-7515
Email: grants@cancerresearch.org
Contact: Mr Ryan Godfrey, Grants Administrator

Clinical and Laboratory Integration Program

Subjects: e development of new and effective cancer treatment requires the translation of basic laboratory discoveries into novel therapies that can be tested in patients. This area of translational research-where laboratory findings move into clinical testing, and where questions from clinical studies are brought back into the lab-is critical to bringing new and better immunotherapies to patients

Purpose: The Cancer Research Institute funds research aimed at furthering the development of immunological approaches to the diagnosis, treatment, and prevention of cancer. The Institute's mission is to bring effective immune system-based therapies to cancer patients sooner. To this end, CRI offers its Clinic and Laboratory Integration Program (CLIP) Grants to qualified scientists who are working to explore clinically relevant questions aimed at improving the effectiveness of cancer immunotherapies. The program supports pre-clinical and translational research that can be directly applied to optimizing cancer immunotherapy in the clinic

Type: Grant

Country of Study: Africa

For further information contact:

Email: grants@cancerresearch.org

Lloyd J. Old STAR Program

Subjects: Rooted in CRI's exceptional track record of identifying and supporting people who have had a major impact on the cancer immunology enterprise, these new grants will not be tied to a specific research project, but rather would support outstanding researchers based on the quality and promise of their overall work

Purpose: The Lloyd J. Old STAR Program provides grants of US$1.25 million over 5 years to mid-career scientists. This long-term funding will not be tied to a specific research project, but rather will aim to provide a degree of flexibility and freedom for investigators to explore out-of-the-box and disruptive avenues of research. Candidates selected for this award are expected to be future "stars" in the field of cancer immunology: Scientists TAking Risks

Eligibility: Mid-career scientists: tenure-track assistant professors (minimum 3 years) and associate professors (maximum 3 years)

Level of Study: Research

Type: Grant

Value: US$1,250,000

Length of Study: 5 years

Frequency: Annual

Country of Study: Any country

Application Procedure: The deadline for the receipt of applications is 1 March. Candidates will be notified in early May whether or not they have been invited to the Cancer Research Institute in New York City for an interview. All invited applicants must be available for an in-person interview with members of CRI's Scientific Advisory Council. The earliest an award can activate is 1 July. Awards must activate on the first of the month

Closing Date: 1 March

Funding: Private, Foundation, Individuals

Technology Impact Award

Subjects: The most competitive applicants will address areas where technological innovation stands to benefit the field and cancer patients most, and that will ultimately lead to effective next-generation personalized cancer immunotherapies. These technologies may include but are not limited to: 1. New bioinformatics methods or technologies that speed collection and analysis of large sets of patient-derived biological data. 2. Computer simulations for modeling biological systems and responses to immunotherapy. 3. Tools and methods that improve profiling of tumors to inform therapeutic strategies. 4. Real-time visualizations of molecular and cellular activity to improve tracking of responses to immunotherapy. 5. In vitro tissue culture systems that recapitulate the interactions between primary tumor cells and the immune system

Purpose: The Cancer Research Institute Technology Impact Award provides seed funding of up to US$200,000 to be used over 12–24 months to address the gap between technology development and clinical application of cancer immunotherapies. These grants aim to encourage collaboration between technology developers and clinical cancer immunologists and to generate the proof-of-principle of a novel platform technology in bioinformatics, ex vivo or in silico modeling systems, immunological or tumor profiling instrumentation, methods, reagents and assays, or other relevant technologies that can enable clinician scientists to generate deeper insights into the mechanisms of action of effective or ineffective cancer immunotherapies

Eligibility: Applicants must hold a faculty appointment as a tenure-track assistant professor (or higher rank) at the time of award activation. The grant will be awarded to a scientist who describes an extraordinarily novel, yet practical research plan that is creative and technically sophisticated. Joint submissions from collaborators will also be considered. (The collaborators will share the award.) Each collaborator must meet the eligibility criteria

Level of Study: Research

Type: Grant

Frequency: Annual

Country of Study: Any country

No. of awards offered: 100

Application Procedure: Letters of Intent describing the research plan will be submitted electronically by November 15. Selected applicants will be invited to submit a full research proposal with a submission deadline of March 15. Award winners will be announced on or around June 30. Successful applicants will have their project reviewed at 12 and 24 months

Closing Date: 15 November

Funding: Private, Corporation, Foundation, Trusts, Individuals

No. of awards given last year: 5

No. of applicants last year: 100

For further information contact:

Email: grants@cancerresearch.org

Contact: Ryan Godfrey, Grants Administrator

Cancer Research United Kingdom

London Research Institute, PO Box 123, Lincoln's Inn Fields, WC2A 3PX, London, United Kingdom

Tel: (44) 20 7269 3609

Fax: (44) 20 7269 3585

Website: www.cancerresearch.org

Contact: Mrs Yvonne Harman, Graduate Programme Administrator

Cancer Research United Kingdom London Research Institute is part of CR-United Kingdom, which is a registered United Kingdom charity dedicated to saving lives through research into the causes, prevention, treatment and cure of cancer.

Cancer Research United Kingdom LRI Graduate Studentships

Subjects: All areas of cancer research

Purpose: To enable research training

Eligibility: Open to candidates who have normally been resident in the United Kingdom for more than 3 years and have obtained, or are about to obtain, a First or Upper Second Class (Honours) Degree in science. Applicants must also be aged 25 years or younger. Non-residents are not excluded from consideration

Level of Study: Doctorate

Type: Studentship

Value: Approx. United Kingdom £13,701–14,821 per year, depending on location

Length of Study: 3 years

Frequency: Annual

Study Establishment: Cancer Research United Kingdom LRI laboratories
Country of Study: United Kingdom
Application Procedure: Applicants must refer to the advertisements that list procedure information.

For further information contact:

Email: eric.eve@hmc.ox.ac.uk

Cancer Research United Kingdom Manchester Institute

The University of Manchester, Wilmslow Road, M20 4BX, Manchester, United Kingdom

Tel: (44) 16 1446 3156
Fax: (44) 16 1446 3109
Email: enquiries@cruk.manchester.ac.uk
Website: www.cruk.manchester.ac.uk

The CRUK Manchester Institute is a leading cancer research institute within The University of Manchester that is core-funded by CRUK. Research spans the whole spectrum of cancer research, from the molecular and cellular basis of cancer, to translational research and the development of therapeutics. It houses 14 diverse research groups.

4-Year Studentship

Subjects: Molecular and cellular basis of cancer and translational cancer research
Purpose: To support study towards a PhD
Eligibility: Open to candidates who have obtained a First or Second Class (Honours) Bachelor of Science Degree. International First or 2.1 degree equivalent in biological science, medicine, or related subject
Level of Study: Doctorate, Postgraduate
Type: Studentship
Value: UK£19,000 as stipend per year, university fees and bench fees
Length of Study: 4 years
Frequency: Annual
Study Establishment: The University of Manchester
Country of Study: United Kingdom
No. of awards offered: 343
Application Procedure: Please visit www.cruk.manchester.ac.uk for details and download application form
Closing Date: Refer to the website
Funding: Private

Contributor: Cancer Research United Kingdom
No. of awards given last year: 5
No. of applicants last year: 343
Additional Information: All positions are advertised on the website. Self-funded students are accepted subject to qualifications and 3-year fu.nding. Please use application form, available at website

For further information contact:

Oglesby Building, 555 Wilmslow Rd, M20 4G, Manchester, United Kingdom

Email: pgt@cruk.manchester.ac.uk
Contact: Postgraduate Tutor

Canon Collins Trust

22 The Ivories, 6 Northampton Street, N1 2HY, London, United Kingdom

Tel: (44) 20 7354 1462
Fax: (44) 20 7359 4875
Email: info@canoncollins.org.uk,
                victoria@canoncollins.org.uk
Website: www.canoncollins.org.uk
Contact: Victoria Reed, Scholarships Officer

We believe that southern Africa's development depends on strong leadership in key fields. Our scholars are outstanding academics and professionals who are dedicated to the development of their countries. We seek to invest in those who share our commitment to social justice and who can demonstrate their intention to return to their home countries after their study.

Canon Collins Scholarship for Distance Learning Master of Laws (LLM)

Subjects: Canon Collins Trust invites applications for scholarships for the Master of Laws (LLM) by distance learning of the University of London. These scholarships are made possible by the generosity of University of London International Programmes which shall waive full tuition and examination entry fees for four scholarship recipients
Purpose: This scholarship allows the individual to study for the Postgraduate certificate, Post graduate diploma and Master of laws
Eligibility: Applicants for this scholarship must be a national of South Africa, Malawi, Zimbabwe or Zambia, normally resident in one of these four countries

Frequency: Annual
Country of Study: United Kingdom
Application Procedure: Check website for more details
Closing Date: 11 January
Funding: Trusts

Canterbury Christ Church, University College, Graduate School

North Holmes Road, CT1 1QU, Canterbury, United Kingdom

Tel:	(44) 1227 767 700
Fax:	(44) 1227 782 900
Email:	research@cant.ac.uk
Website:	www.cant.ac.uk
Contact:	Miss Ashleigh Stuart, Research Secretary

L.B. Wood Travelling Scholarship

Subjects: All subjects
Purpose: This scholarship is available to all graduates from any university in New Zealand, from any faculty providing that the application for the scholarship is made within three years from the date of graduation. The scholarship is offered as a supplement to some other postgraduate scholarships held for the purpose of study in Great Britain
Eligibility: Applicants must be graduates of a New Zealand university. No distinction is made; regarding subject, disciple or faculty
Level of Study: Postgraduate
Type: Scholarship
Value: $3,000
Length of Study: 3 year
Frequency: Annual
Country of Study: Any country
Application Procedure: Apply online
Closing Date: 1 March
Funding: Foundation

For further information contact:

Email: scholarships-cf@universitiesnz.ac.nz

Lawson Robinson Hawke's Bay A&P Scholarship

Subjects: All subjects
Purpose: The Lawson Robinson Hawke's Bay A&P Scholarship aims to recognise outstanding academic and leadership qualities in a student currently enrolled in a full time land based programme. Applicants should have a familial association with Hawke's Bay
Eligibility: New Zealand Citizen or Permanent Resident Students
Level of Study: Postgraduate
Type: Scholarship
Value: $3,000
Length of Study: 1 year
Frequency: Varies
Country of Study: Any country
Application Procedure: Apply online
Closing Date: 28 February
Funding: Foundation

For further information contact:

Email: awards@showgroundshb.co.nz

Canterbury Historical Association

History Department, University of Canterbury, Private Bag 4800, Christchurch 8140, New Zealand

Tel:	(64) 3 364 2555
Fax:	(64) 3 364 2003
Email:	david.monger@canterbury.ac.nz
Website:	www.hums.canterbury.ac.nz/hist/
Contact:	Mrs Lynn McClelland, Director of Student Services and Communications

The Canterbury Historical Association (founded 1922, but in recess between 1940 and 1953) aims to foster public interest in all fields of history by holding meetings for the discussion of historical issues, and to promote historical research and writing through its administration of the J M Sherrard Award in New Zealand local and regional history.

Anne Reid Memorial Trust Scholarship

Subjects: All subjects
Purpose: The scholarship commemorates Anne Reid of Blenheim/Christchurch/Singapore/Auckland who studied and taught at the University of Canterbury and The National University of Singapore. The purpose of this scholarship is to assist a graduate student from either the University of Canterbury or the University of Auckland overseas in an environment that encourages the completion of a course or work in progress, or the undertaking of further training in a recognised institution

Level of Study: Postgraduate
Type: Scholarship
Value: $20,000
Length of Study: 1 year
Frequency: Annual
Country of Study: New Zealand
Application Procedure: Apply online
Closing Date: 30 April
Funding: Trusts

For further information contact:

Email: scholarships-cf@universitiesnz.ac.nz

BayTrust Bruce Cronin Scholarship

Subjects: All subjects
Purpose: This scholarship has been established to recognise his service to the people of the Bay of Plenty
Eligibility: Applicants will be eligible if they were born in, or attended school in, or have whakapapa back to the area
Level of Study: Postgraduate
Type: Scholarship
Value: $5,000
Length of Study: 1 year
Frequency: Annual
Country of Study: New Zealand
Application Procedure: Apply online universitiesnz. communityforce.com/
Closing Date: 1 February
Funding: Foundation

For further information contact:

73 Spring Street, Tauranga 3141, New Zealand

Email: info@baytrust.org.nz

Canterbury Scholarship

Subjects: All subjects
Purpose: These scholarships, tenable for study towards the degree of Doctor of Philosophy at the University of Canterbury, were established to recognise students of the highest calibre undertaking PhD research at the university
Level of Study: Postgraduate
Type: Scholarship
Value: $21,000
Length of Study: 3 year
Frequency: Annual
Country of Study: New Zealand
Application Procedure: Apply online

Closing Date: 15 May
Funding: Trusts

For further information contact:

Email: scholarships-cf@universitiesnz.ac.nz

Clifford Wallace Collins Memorial Trust Scholarship

Subjects: All subjects
Purpose: The trust fund was established in 1980 to provide an annual award to support graduates of the University of Canterbury undertaking a course of study in Librarianship at a New Zealand university, and to commemorate the contribution made to the University and its library by Clifford Wallace Collins (1909–1979). Applications, addressing the selection criteria, must be made by letter to the Information Studies Programme Director of Victoria University of Wellington by 15 April
Eligibility: The trust fund was established in 1980 to provide an annual award to support graduates of the University of Canterbury undertaking a course of study in Librarianship at a New Zealand university, and to commemorate the contribution made to the University and its library by Clifford Wallace Collins (1909–1979). Mr Collins was Librarian to Canterbury University College and the University of Canterbury from 1934 to 1971
Level of Study: Postgraduate
Type: Scholarship
Value: $750
Length of Study: 1 year
Frequency: Annual
Country of Study: New Zealand
Application Procedure: Apply online
Closing Date: 15 April
Funding: Trusts

For further information contact:

Email: scholarships-cf@universitiesnz.ac.nz

Marian D'Eve Memorial Scholarship

Purpose: This scholarship supports students studying, researching, or developing, resources for early-childhood special-needs education at the University of Canterbury. The scholarship was established in 2009 in memory of Marian D'Eve, an early-childhood education specialist and author of a handbook for teachers
Level of Study: Postgraduate

Type: Scholarship
Value: $2,000
Length of Study: 1 year
Frequency: Annual
Country of Study: Any country
Application Procedure: Apply online
Closing Date: 31 March
Funding: Foundation

For further information contact:

Email: scholarships-cf@universitiesnz.ac.nz

Roger Helm Scholarship in Pure Mathematics

Subjects: All subjects
Purpose: The scholarship supports students for study towards a research master's degree or a PhD degree in Pure Mathematics at the University of Canterbury. It was established in 2018 from a bequest by Roger Helm (1947-2015)
Eligibility: At the time of application, applicants must be enrolled in either a programme for a PhD degree in Pure Mathematics, or in Part II of a master's degree in Pure Mathematics. Applications are not accepted from candidates who already hold a research doctoral degree. Applications are not accepted from previous holders of the scholarship
Level of Study: Postgraduate
Type: Scholarship
Value: $5,000
Length of Study: 1 year
Frequency: Annual
Country of Study: New Zealand
Application Procedure: Apply online
Closing Date: 15 May
Funding: Trusts

For further information contact:

Email: scholarships-cf@universitiesnz.ac.nz

Susan Barnes Memorial Scholarship

Purpose: The scholarship supports students with a vision impairment in undertaking study at the University of Canterbury. It was established in 2016 by the Lighthouse Vision Trust
Level of Study: Postgraduate
Type: Scholarship
Value: $10,000
Length of Study: 1 year

Frequency: Annual
Country of Study: New Zealand
Application Procedure: Apply online
Closing Date: 31 March
Funding: Foundation

For further information contact:

Email: scholarships-cf@universitiesnz.ac.nz

The Auckland Medical Aid Trust Scholarship

Purpose: This scholarship was established in 2004 and is financed by the Auckland Medical Aid Trust to encourage research into social issues concerning being and becoming human, and provides funds for a doctoral candidate at a New Zealand university
Eligibility: An applicant will be registered as a candidate or will be in the process of registering; as a candidate for a doctoral degree at a New Zealand university. (No award will be made to a candidate who has not successfully completed; registration for a doctoral degree.)
Level of Study: Postdoctorate
Type: Scholarship
Value: $25,000
Length of Study: 3 year
Frequency: Annual
Country of Study: New Zealand
Closing Date: 1 October
Funding: Foundation

For further information contact:

Email: scholarships-cf@universitiesnz.ac.nz

Three Nations Conference Award

Purpose: This award assists Maori or Pasifika students, or students who are indigenous to states or territories of Australia, whose financial circumstances would otherwise preclude them from undertaking postgraduate study in the Department of Sociology and Anthropology at the University of Canterbury
Eligibility: Anthropology;Sociology
Level of Study: Postgraduate
Type: Award
Value: $1,000
Frequency: Annual
Country of Study: Any country
Application Procedure: Apply online
Closing Date: 31 March
Funding: Foundation

For further information contact:

Email: scholarships-cf@universitiesnz.ac.nz

University of Canterbury Mathematics and Statistics Scholarship

Purpose: These scholarships recognise and support high-achieving 200-, 300-, and 400-level students majoring in Mathematics, Statistics, Computational and Applied Mathematical Sciences, Data Science, Applied Data Science or Financial Engineering. The scholarships will be awarded in three categories, with the value of each category ($1,000, $2,500, $5,000) reflecting the recipients' levels of achievement. Up to 45 scholarships will be available annually

Eligibility: Applied Data Science; Computational and Applied Mathematics; Data Science; Financial Engineering; Mathematics; Statistics

Level of Study: Postgraduate

Type: Scholarship

Value: $5,000 (Category A awards) $2,500 (Category B awards) $1,000 (Category C awards)

Frequency: Annual

Country of Study: Any country

Application Procedure: Apply online

Closing Date: 31 March

Funding: Foundation

For further information contact:

Email: scholarships@canterbury.ac.nz

Cardiff University

Deri House, 2-4 Park Grove, Wales, CF10 3PA, Cardiff, United Kingdom

Tel: (44) 29 2087 0084
Fax: (44) 29 2087 0085
Email: graduate@cardiff.ac.uk
Website: www.cardiff.ac.uk/postgraduate

Cardiff University is recognized in independent government assessments as one of the UK's leading teaching and research universities. Founded by Royal Charter in 1883, the University today combines impressive modern facilities and a dynamic approach to teaching and research with its proud heritage of service and achievement. Having gained national and international standing, Cardiff University's vision is to be recognized as a world-class university and to achieve the associated benefits for its students, staff and all other stakeholders.

Cardiff Institute of Tissue Engineering and Repair (CITER) – EPSRC Studentship

Subjects: Tissue engineering

Purpose: To support study on the MSc in Tissue Engineering at CITER

Eligibility: Applicants must be graduates in a biomedical/veterinary or other science subject or an engineering or clinical discipline from medicine or dentistry. United Kingdom or European Union students who have been resident in the United Kingdom for at least 3 years can apply. Other European Union participants may receive a fees only award

Level of Study: Postgraduate

Type: Studentship

Value: Fees and stipend at the current EPSRC rate

Length of Study: 1 year

Application Procedure: Check website for further details

Closing Date: 30 June

For further information contact:

Tel: (1) 29 2087 0129
Email: HatchS@cardiff.ac.uk
Contact: Mrs Sarah Hatch

Cardiff School of Chemistry – Master's Bursaries

Subjects: Molecular Modelling

Purpose: To support study for the MSc in Molecular Modelling

Eligibility: Applicants must possess a 2:2 Honours Degree or equivalent in chemistry or a related discipline (e.g. physics, engineering, pharmacy, biosciences)

Level of Study: Postgraduate

Type: Bursary

Value: Cost of tuition fees at the United Kingdom/European Union rate

Length of Study: 1 year

Country of Study: United Kingdom

Application Procedure: Applicants must submit an application including two references for postgraduate study. Application forms can be downloaded from the website

Closing Date: 31 August

For further information contact:

The Postgraduate Admissions Office, The Registry, Cardiff University, 30-36 Newport Road, United Kingdom

Tel: (44) 29 2087 4950
Email: platts@cardifff.ac.uk
Contact: Dr Jamie Platts

Cardiff School of Chemistry – MSc Studentships in Computing in the Physical Sciences

Subjects: Computer science, mathematics
Purpose: To support study on a new MSc programme in Computing in the Physical Sciences
Eligibility: Applicants must be United Kingdom-resident European Union citizens. A minimum qualification of a 2ii degree or equivalent in a relevant scientific discipline is required
Level of Study: Postgraduate
Type: Studentship
Length of Study: 1 year
Application Procedure: Applicants must submit an application for postgraduate study along with two references
Closing Date: 31 August
Contributor: Schools of Computer Science and Mathematics

For further information contact:

Email: platts@cardiff.ac.uk
Contact: Dr Jamie Platts

Cardiff School of City and Regional Planning – Master's Bursaries

Subjects: Transport and planning
Purpose: To support study on the MSc in Transport and Planning
Eligibility: Applicants must have been offered and will have accepted a place on the MSc in Transport and Planning and must then be nominated for an award by the School. They must have a relevant honours degree at 2i or higher and they must be United Kingdom/European Union students intending to practice in the United Kingdom
Level of Study: Postgraduate
Type: Bursary
Value: Full United Kingdom/European Union fees and a maintenance stipend of £1,000 (by The Rees Jeffreys Road Fund Bursary) and £5,000 (by The Brian Largs Bursary Fund)

Length of Study: 1 year
Application Procedure: Check website for further details
Closing Date: 30 June
Contributor: The Rees Jeffreys Road Fund Bursary, The Brian Largs Bursary Fund

For further information contact:

Tel: (44) 29 2087 5294
Email: Yewlett@cardiff.ac.uk
Contact: Mr Chris Yewlett

Cardiff School of Mathematics – PhD Studentships

Subjects: Mathematics
Eligibility: Applicants must hold a Master's Degree or a First Class Bachelor's Degree in an appropriate subject. The studentships are available to United Kingdom and European Union students
Level of Study: Postgraduate
Type: Studentship
Value: Tuition fees at the United Kingdom/European Union level plus an annual stipend of £12,500 (for those United Kingdom and European Union students normally resident in the United Kingdom) and fees only (for European Union students not normally resident in the United Kingdom)
Length of Study: 3 years
Country of Study: United Kingdom
Application Procedure: Applicants must submit an application for postgraduate study which can be downloaded from the website
Closing Date: 30 April

For further information contact:

Cardiff School of Mathematics, United Kingdom

Tel: (44) 29 2087 5552
Email: MarlettaM@cardiff.ac.uk
Contact: Professor M Marletta, Director of Postgraduate Studies

Cardiff School of Medicine – PhD Studentships

Subjects: Medicine
Eligibility: Applicants must be United Kingdom/European Union students. They must possess a First or at least Upper Second Class Honours in a subject of relevance to the project (preferably biological science)
Level of Study: Postgraduate

Type: Studentship
Value: Fees support at the United Kingdom/European Union level along with a maintenance stipend at the Research Council level (£12,600)
Length of Study: 3 years
Application Procedure: Applicants must send a covering letter and an up-to-date curriculum vitae, including a breakdown of Year 2/Year 3 university grades, along with references
Closing Date: 30 June
Contributor: School and Research Council Funds

For further information contact:

Institute of Medical Genetics, Cardiff University, Heath Park, United Kingdom

Tel:	(44) 29 2074 2652
Fax:	(44) 29 2074 6551
Email:	CheadleJP@cardiff.ac.uk
Contact:	Professor Jeremy Cheadle

Cardiff School of Medicine – PhD Studentships (Department of Surgery)

Subjects: Medicine and surgery
Eligibility: Applicants must be United Kingdom/European Union students and must possess (or be expected to obtain) a First or at least Upper Second Class Honours in a subject of relevance to the project
Level of Study: Postgraduate
Type: Studentship
Value: Fees support at the United Kingdom/European Union level plus £12,600
Length of Study: 3 years
Application Procedure: Applicants must send a covering letter and an up-to-date curriculum vitae along with references
Closing Date: 30 June

For further information contact:

Department of Surgery, Cardiff School of Medicine, Cardiff University, Heath Park, United Kingdom

Tel:	(44) 29 2074 2895/2896
Fax:	(44) 29 2076 1623
Email:	JiangW@cardiff.ac.uk
Contact:	Professor Wen G Jiang, MB, BCh, MD, Professor of Surgery and Tumour Biology, Head, Metastasis & Angiogenesis Research Group

Cardiff School of Music – PhD Studentships

Subjects: Music
Eligibility: Applicants must have a good Honours Degree in Music (or be expecting to obtain one in the present year) and a Master's Degree is desirable. They should be United Kingdom/European Union citizens or have been resident in the United Kingdom/European Union for at least 3 years prior to starting their PhD
Level of Study: Postgraduate
Type: Studentship
Value: One full studentship covering United Kingdom/European Union tuition fees and a maintenance stipend at the AHRC level (£12,300) and another, United Kingdom/European Union fees-only studentship
Length of Study: 3 years
Application Procedure: Applicants must complete and submit an application for postgraduate study. Application forms can be downloaded from the website
Closing Date: 30 June

For further information contact:

School of Music, Cardiff University, 31 Corbett Road, United Kingdom

Tel:	(44) 29 2087 4816
Fax:	(44) 29 2087 4379
Email:	music-pg@cardiff.ac.uk
Contact:	Dr Ken Gloag, The Postgraduate Administrator

Cardiff School of Optometry and Vision Sciences – PhD Studentship

Subjects: Optometry
Purpose: To adopt a completely new approach to understanding the relationship between retinal structure and visual function in AMD
Eligibility: Applicants must possess a United Kingdom higher education Degree at First or Upper Second Class Honours or equivalent in a relevant discipline (optometry would be most suitable)
Level of Study: Postgraduate
Type: Studentship
Value: £12,600
Length of Study: 3 years
Application Procedure: Applicants must complete and submit a standard Cardiff University application form along with a curriculum vitae and covering letter. Application forms can be downloaded from the website
Closing Date: 1 November

Additional Information: The studentship is available to United Kingdom, European Union and overseas students, but will only cover tuition fees at the European Union/United Kingdom level

For further information contact:

Email: BinnsAM@cardiff.ac.uk
Contact: Dr Alison Binns

Cardiff University MSc/Diploma in Housing Studentship

Subjects: Housing
Purpose: To fund a postgraduate course in housing
Eligibility: Studentships are available to United Kingdom applicants with a First or Upper Second Class (Honours) Degree only
Level of Study: Postgraduate
Type: Studentship
Value: University fees and maintenance grant
Length of Study: 2 years
Frequency: Annual
Study Establishment: Cardiff University
Country of Study: United Kingdom
Application Procedure: Applicants must contact the School of City and Regional Planning
Closing Date: Around June

For further information contact:

Cardiff School of City and Regional Planning, Glamorgan Building, King Edward VII Avenue, CF10 3WA, Cardiff, United Kingdom

Tel: (44) 29 2087 6092
Email: cardpd@cardiff.ac.uk
Contact: Pauline Card

Cardiff University PhD Music Studentship

Subjects: Music
Purpose: To fund doctoral study in music
Eligibility: Applicants should have a good Honours degree in Music, be a United Kingdom or European Union citizen or have been a resident for at least 3 years for reasons other than education
Level of Study: Doctorate
Type: Studentship
Value: Tuition fees and maintenance

Length of Study: 3 years
Frequency: Annual
Study Establishment: Cardiff University
Country of Study: United Kingdom
Application Procedure: Applicants must contact the School of Music. They will need to have received an offer of a place to study before they can apply for financial support
Closing Date: Around June

For further information contact:

School of Music, 31 Corbett Road, CF10 3EB, Cardiff, United Kingdom

Tel: (44) 29 2087 4816
Fax: (44) 29 2087 4379
Email: music-pg@cardiff.ac.uk

Cardiff University PhD Social Sciences Studentship

Subjects: Social theory, environment and public policy, sociology of science and expertise, economic and social change, health, welfare and risk, lifelong learning, work and labour markets, young people, education and disadvantage, educational policy and schooling, human development and learning, crime risk and governance
Purpose: To fund PhD study in social sciences
Eligibility: Only United Kingdom and European Union students with a First or Upper Second Class (Honours) Degree can apply for a PhD studentship
Level of Study: Doctorate
Length of Study: 3 years
Frequency: Annual
Study Establishment: Cardiff University
Country of Study: United Kingdom
Application Procedure: Applicants must contact the School of Social Sciences. They will need to have received an offer of a place before they can apply for financial support
Closing Date: Around June

For further information contact:

School of Social Sciences, Glamorgan Building, King Edward VII Avenue, CF10 3WT, Cardiff, United Kingdom

Fax: (44) 29 2087 4436
Email: renton@cardiff.ac.uk
Contact: Elizabeth Renton

Cardiff University PhD Studentship in European Studies

Subjects: The literatures, cultures, societies, politics and policies of Europe
Purpose: To support students working towards a thesis in European Studies
Eligibility: All students accepted by the School of European Studies to study for a postgraduate research degree are automatically considered
Level of Study: Doctorate
Type: Studentship
Value: Full tuition fee plus stipend
Frequency: Annual
Study Establishment: Cardiff University
Country of Study: Wales
Application Procedure: Applicants must check the application guidelines available on the postgraduate webpages
Closing Date: 30 June

For further information contact:

Email: business-phd@cardiff.ac.uk

Economic & Social Research Council (1+3) Sociology Studentship

Subjects: Sociology and social policy
Purpose: To fund postgraduate training
Eligibility: Applicants must have a First or Upper Second Class (Honours) Degree
Level of Study: Postgraduate
Type: Studentship
Length of Study: 1 year for MSc and 3 years for PhD
Frequency: Annual
Study Establishment: Cardiff University
Country of Study: United Kingdom
Application Procedure: Applicants must contact the School of Social Sciences
Closing Date: Around June

Engineering and Physical Sciences Research Council Studentships for Biophotonics

Subjects: Biophotonics
Purpose: To support study on the new MSc in Biophotonics
Eligibility: Applicants must be excellent candidates. Funding is available to United Kingdom and European Union students only
Level of Study: Postgraduate
Type: Studentship

Value: Fully funded studentships include a maintenance stipend
Length of Study: 1 year
Application Procedure: Applicants can apply via the standard Cardiff University postgraduate application form, which can be downloaded from the website
Closing Date: 31 July
Contributor: Cardiff School of Biosciences and Cardiff School of Physics and Astronomy

For further information contact:

Tel: (44) 29 2087 0172
Email: mscbiophotonics@cardiff.ac.uk
Contact: Dr Wolfgang Langbein

Fully-Funded PhD Studentship in Sustainable Place-Making

Eligibility: Residency: full awards (fees plus maintenance stipend) are open to United Kingdom nationals and European Union students without further restrictions. Academic criteria: successful applicants are likely to have a very good first degree (a first or upper second class BA or BSc Honours or equivalent), and an appropriate Masters degree in a relevant subject (e.g. social sciences; environmental studies; sustainable development; environmental psychology; sociology of technology/environment; human geography), with an average mark of at least 65)
Level of Study: Postgraduate, Research
Type: Studentship
Value: Full United Kingdom/European Union tuition fees, as well as a doctoral stipend matching United Kingdom Research Council National minimum (£13,863 per year for current year, updated each year)
Length of Study: 3 years
Country of Study: United Kingdom
Application Procedure: (1) Submit a complete application form for admission to doctoral study in the School of Social Sciences, submitted to the Academic Registry via the online admissions portal (www.cardiff.ac.uk/regis/general/applyonline/index.html). Please specify the School of Social Sciences - Research Degree - Doctor of Philosophy (social sciences) with a start date of January. (2) Submit the following documentation to Parkinva@cardiff.ac.uk with a letter of application, stating your reasons for wishing to pursue PhD study; a full research proposal for the PhD study (maximum 1,000 words, excluding references); a curriculum vitae; official transcripts of previous higher education qualifications; two academic references
Closing Date: 17 November

Additional Information: Cardiff University reserves the right to close applications early should sufficient applications be received

For further information contact:

Tel: (44) 29 2087 0855
Email: parkinva@cardiff.ac.uk
Contact: Victoria Parkin

International Engineering MSc Studentship

Subjects: Civil engineering, water engineering, structural engineering, geoenvironmental engineering
Purpose: To fund postgraduate study in areas of engineering
Eligibility: First or Upper Second Class (Honours) Degree
Level of Study: Postgraduate
Type: Studentship
Value: UK£1,500
Length of Study: 1 year
Frequency: Annual
Study Establishment: Cardiff University
Country of Study: United Kingdom
Application Procedure: Applicants must contact the School of Engineering
Closing Date: Around June
Additional Information: There is no need to apply seperately for scholarships as eligible applicants will be considered on the basis of their application forms

For further information contact:

Admission Office, Cardiff School of Engineering, Cardiff University, Cardiff CF24 0YZ, Cardiff, United Kingdom

Tel: (44) 29 2087 4656
Email: engineering-pg@cardiff.ac.uk

Morgan E. Williams MRes Scholarship in Helminthology

Subjects: Scholarship is awarded for research project in helminth parasitology as part of the Masters of Research in Bio sciences at Cardiff School of Bio sciences
Eligibility: English language proficiency is required. Applicants must have a undergraduate degree at level 2:2 (or higher) in a relevant biological, bio medical or bio-molecular science subject. For detailed information, please visit the website
Level of Study: Postgraduate
Type: Scholarship
Value: There is one scholarship offering a reduction of £2,500 off the tuition fees for MRes Biosciences

Country of Study: United Kingdom
Application Procedure: Applicants should submit a curriculum vitae and Covering Letter to Rachel Patterson, PatersonRJ@cardiff.ac.uk
Closing Date: May
Contributor: Cardiff School of Bio sciences
Additional Information: Scholarship is offered for 1 year

For further information contact:

Email: BIOSI-MRes@cardiff.ac.uk

PhD Studentship in Organisms and Environment at Cardiff University

Subjects: Organisms and environment (fungal ecology)
Eligibility: Residency: full awards (fees plus maintenance stipend) are open to United Kingdom nationals and European Union students who can satisfy United Kingdom residency requirements. To be eligible for the full award, European Union nationals must have been in the United Kingdom for at least 3 years prior to the start of the course for which they are seeking funding, including for the purposes of full-time education. European Union nationals who do not meet the above residency requirement are eligible for a fees only award, provided that they have been ordinarily resident in the European Union for at least 3 years prior to the start of their proposed programme of study. Academic criteria: applicants for a studentship must have obtained, or be about to obtain, a 2.1 degree or higher in microbiology, ecology, biology or other relevant discipline. If you have a 2.2 degree, but have also obtained a Masters qualification, you are also eligible. If you do not have these qualifications but you have substantial relevant postgraduate experience please contact the department holding the studentship to find out if your relevant experience is sufficient
Level of Study: Doctorate, Postgraduate, Research
Type: Studentship
Value: This studentship consists of full United Kingdom/European Union tuition fees, as well as a Doctoral Stipend matching United Kingdom Research Council National Minimum
Length of Study: 3.5 years
Frequency: Annual
Country of Study: United Kingdom
Application Procedure: To apply, please email your curriculum vitae, 2 references and relevant academic qualifications along with a covering letter to Professor Lynne Boddy at BoddyL@cf.ac.uk
Closing Date: 15 January
Additional Information: Internal interviews will be conducted before the January 30th. Shortlisted candidates will then go on to an institutional interview which will take place between February 9th and 20th. Cardiff University

reserves the right to close applications early should sufficient applications be received

For further information contact:

Email: BoddyL@cf.ac.uk
Contact: Professor Lynne Boddy

Postgraduate History and Archaeology Studentship

Subjects: History and archaeology
Purpose: To fund postgraduate training in history and archaeology
Eligibility: First or Upper Second Class (Honours) Degree. Those from the United Kingdom should apply for an award from the Arts and Humanities Research Board (AHRB)
Level of Study: Doctorate, Postgraduate
Type: Studentship
Value: Tuition fees and maintenance grant
Length of Study: 1 year for Masters, 3 years for PhD
Frequency: Annual
Study Establishment: Cardiff University
Country of Study: United Kingdom
Application Procedure: Applicants must submit an application form, which includes a research proposal and the names of two referees
Closing Date: 1 June

For further information contact:

Cardiff School of History and Archaeology, Humanities Building, Colum Drive, CF10 3EU, Cardiff, United Kingdom

Tel: (44) 29 2087 4258
Email: hisaroffice@cardiff.ac.uk
Contact: The School Secretary

The Beacon Scholarship

Subjects: The Beacon Scholarship is a leadership development programme that nurtures 'change-makers'. We find young people with leadership potential who have financial need; provide them with access to the highest quality education
Purpose: The scholarship is awarded to students from Kenya, Tanzania, and Uganda looking to study a 3-4 year undergraduate course (excluding medicine)
Eligibility: To be eligible for this scheme, candidates must be able to demonstrate: 1. their normal residence is in Kenya,

Tanzania or Uganda. 2. leadership capabilities: i. academic excellence. ii. achievement in sport, music or drama. iii. social influence and communication. iv. citizenship. 3. a capacity to study independently overseas. 4. financial need for study, ie annual gross household income not exceeding £80k (US$100k). 5. that they are aged 18-21. 6. a commitment to return to their home country within one month of degree completion
Level of Study: Postgraduate
Type: Scholarship
Value: Tuition and maintenance fees
Frequency: Annual
Country of Study: Any country
Closing Date: 26 April
Funding: Private

For further information contact:

The Beacon Scholarship Sandells House Cliftons Lane Reigate, RH2 9RA, Surrey, United Kingdom

Email: delhi@studyin-uk.com

Ursula Henriques Scholarships

Subjects: Scholarships are awarded to study the subjects offered by the university
Purpose: Scholarships are available for pursuing postgraduate taught and postgraduate research programme
Eligibility: For eligibility details, please visit website scholarship-positions.com/ursula-henriques-scholarships-uk-eu-international-students/
Value: Cardiff University received a gift of £100,000 from Professor Henriques (1914–2008), a former member of staff in the Department of History and Welsh History, University College Cardiff
Frequency: Annual
Country of Study: Any country
Application Procedure: The application form can be obtained by email. Completed forms should be returned electronically to the School Postgraduate Office
Closing Date: 18 May
Contributor: Cardiff University
Additional Information: For more details, please visit website www.cardiff.ac.uk/study/postgraduate/funding/view/Ursula-Henriques-Scholarship

For further information contact:

Email: share-pg@cardiff.ac.uk

Carnegie Corporation of New York

437 Madison Avenue, New York, NY 10022, United States of America

Tel: (1) 212 371 3200
Fax: (1) 212 754 4073
Website: www.carnegie.org

Andrew Carnegie envisioned Carnegie Corporation as a foundation that would promote the advancement and diffusion of knowledge and understanding. In keeping with this mandate, our work incorporates an affirmation of our historic role as an education foundation but also honors Andrew Carnegie's passion for international peace and the health of our democracy.

Next Gen Fellowship Program for Sub-Saharan African Countries

Subjects: The fellowships support dissertations and research on peace, security and development topics
Purpose: This fellowship is available for pursuing PhD research level
Eligibility: All applicants must be citizens of and reside in a sub-Saharan African country while holding a current faculty position at an accredited college or university in Ghana, Nigeria, South Africa, Tanzania, or Uganda. Applicants for any of the funding opportunities offered through this program must have a master's degree and be working toward completion of the doctoral degree. The program seeks to promote diversity and encourages women to apply. To be eligible for the US$15,000 dissertation research fellowship, applicants must have an approved dissertation proposal but will not yet have undertaken research of 9 months or more. For detailed information, please visit website
Level of Study: Doctorate
Type: Fellowship
Value: The doctoral dissertation proposal fellowship supports short-term research costs of up to US$3,000 to develop a doctoral dissertation proposal. The doctoral dissertation completion fellowship supports a 1-year leave from teaching responsibilities and a stipend up to US$15,000 to permit the completion of a dissertation that advances research on peace, security, and development topics. The doctoral dissertation research fellowship supports 9–12 months of dissertation research costs of up to US$15,000 on a topic related to peace, security, and development
Length of Study: About 9–12 months
Country of Study: Africa

Application Procedure: The mode of applying is online. All applications must be submitted using the online application portal
Closing Date: 13 November
Additional Information: Citizens of and reside in a sub-Saharan African country while holding a current faculty position at an accredited college or university in Ghana, Nigeria, South Africa, Tanzania, or Uganda can apply for this PhD fellowship

For further information contact:

Email: nextgenafrica@ssrc.org

Carnegie Trust

Carnegie PhD Scholarships

Purpose: Candidates must have, or be on track to achieve, a first class Honours undergraduate degree from a Scottish institution of higher education
Eligibility: 1. You already hold, or are on track to graduate with a First Class Honours degree from one of the eligible host organisations in Scotland. 2. This undergraduate degree is in a subject related to the academic field of your proposed doctoral research. 3. You have been accepted on a doctoral programme at one of the eligible host organisations. 4. This doctoral programme will start in the coming academic year
Level of Study: Graduate
Type: Scholarship
Length of Study: 3 year
Frequency: Annual
Country of Study: Any country
Closing Date: 28 February
Funding: Foundation

St Andrews Society of New York Scholarships

Subjects: A university in the United States within a radius of 250 miles from New York City, or within the area of Washington DC
Purpose: The Carnegie Trust for the Universities of Scotland administers this scholarship programme for students in the United Kingdom who wish to apply for graduate study in the United States. Successful candidates are expected to be the highest caliber, both academically and in their wider personal interests
Eligibility: 1. Candidates must be Scottish by birth or descent, and have up-do-date knowledge of Scotland, Scottish current affairs and of the Scottish tradition generally. The Society expects its scholars to be good ambassadors for Scotland. 2. Either graduates of a Scottish university, Glasgow School

of Art, Royal Conservatoire of Scotland, or of Oxford or Cambridge, who have completed their first degree course (so as to be qualified to graduate) not earlier than previous year. 3. Students of a Scottish university, Glasgow School of Art, Royal Conservatoire of Scotland, or of Oxford or Cambridge, who expect to complete their first degree course (so as to be qualified to graduate) in current year. 4. Preference is given to candidates who have no previous, or limited, experience of the United States and for whom a period of study in that country may provide a life-changing experience

Level of Study: Postgraduate
Type: Scholarship
Value: US$35,000
Length of Study: 1 year
Frequency: Annual
Country of Study: Any country
Closing Date: 15 March
Funding: Private

For further information contact:

Saint Andrew's Society of the State of New York, 150 East 55th Street, 3rd Floor New York, NY 10022, United States of America

Tel: (1) 212 223 4248
Email: office@standrewsny.org

Casino Mucho

Casinomucho Research Scholarship (CSR)

Subjects: We are proud to offer financial aid to future and current college students majoring in Business, Digital Marketing, Finance, Mathematics, Management, and others preparing for a career in gaming industry
Purpose: This research scholarship help to give the grant to shape up and change the face of online gambling industry within the next few years
Eligibility: 1. Full time student at college/university (preferred Marketing, Business or Communication courses). 2. No entry limit per contestant. 3. Casinomucho.com employees immediate families are not eligible. 4. 3,000–5,000 words essay on one of the given topic in Microsoft Word format with correct grammar, heading and punctuation. 5. The article must be plagiarism free
Level of Study: Postgraduate
Type: Scholarship
Value: £500
Frequency: Annual
Country of Study: United Kingdom
Application Procedure: 1. Students must submit their applications to scholarship [at] muchoent.com. 2. Applications

should include: full name, date of birth, name or degree course, essay in Word format
Closing Date: 31 March
Funding: Private

For further information contact:

Email: scholarship@muchoent.com

Catholic University of Louvain

1, Place de l'Université, BEL -1348 Louvain-la-Neuve, Belgium

Tel: (32) 10 472 111
Fax: (32) 10 472 999
Website: www.uclouvain.be

Hoover Fellowships for International Scholars

Eligibility: Candidates must be scholars from outside Belgium, who hold a doctorate or possess equivalent qualifications and are active in the field of economic or social ethics broadly conceived. Candidates for a full fellowship must have no professional income from other sources in the period concerned. Proficiency in either English or French is required, and at least a passive knowledge in both is desirable
Type: Fellowship
Value: One full Hoover fellowship of €2,000 per month (plus social security contributions) for a duration of 3 months. Several honorary Hoover fellowships for a duration of 1 to 6 months with a contribution to housing and travelling costs of up to €500 per month
Frequency: Annual
Study Establishment: UCL
Country of Study: Belgium
Application Procedure: Applications must reach Thérèse Davio by email (therese.davio@uclouvain.be) by the deadline
Closing Date: 28 February
Contributor: UCL
Additional Information: For more information, please visit www.uclouvain.be/398682.html

CEC Artslink

291 Broadway, 12th Floor, NY 10007, United States of America

Tel: (1) 212 643 1985
Fax: (1) 212 643 1996
Email: info@cecartslink.org
Website: www.cecartslink.org

CEC Artslink is an international arts service organization. Our programmes encourage and support exchange of artists and cultural managers between the United States and Central Europe, Russia, and Eurasia. We believe that the arts are a society's most deliberate and complex means of communication.

ArtsLink Independent Projects

Subjects: Performing, design, media, literary and visual arts
Purpose: To provide funding to artists and arts managers who propose to undertake projects in the United States in collaboration with a United States non-profit arts organization
Eligibility: Candidates must be citizens of, and reside in, an eligible countries Albania, Armenia, Azerbaijan, Belarus, Bosnia and Herzegovina, Bulgaria, Croatia, Czech Republic, Estonia, Georgia, Hungary, Kazakhstan, Kosovo, Kyrgyzstan, Latvia, Lithuania, Macedonia, Moldova, Mongolia, Montenegro, Poland, Romania, Russia, Serbia, Slovak Republic, Slovenia, Tajikistan, Turkmenistan, Ukraine and Uzbekistan. There are no age limitations. Arts managers must be affiliated with an organization in the non-commercial sector
Type: Fellowship
Value: US$5,000
Length of Study: 1 year
Frequency: Annual
Country of Study: United States of America
Application Procedure: Complete online application form
Closing Date: December
Funding: Private, Trusts
No. of awards given last year: 5
Additional Information: Please check at www.cecartslink.org/grants/independent_projects/ for further details

For further information contact:

CEC ArtsLink, 435 Hudson Street, 8th Floor, United States of America

Email: al@cecartslink.org

ArtsLink Projects

Subjects: Performing Arts, visual and media arts
Purpose: To support United States artists, curators, presenters, and non-profit arts organizations undertaking projects in Eastern and Central Europe, Russia, Central Asia and the Caucasus
Eligibility: Open to citizens of eligible countries: Albania, Armenia, Azerbaijan, Belarus, Bosnia and Herzegovina, Bulgaria, Croatia, Czech Republic, Estonia, Georgia, Hungary, Kazakhstan, Kosovo, Kyrgyzstan, Latvia, Lithuania, Macedonia, Moldova, Mongolia, Montenegro, Poland, Romania, Russia, Serbia, Slovak Republic, Slovenia, Tajikistan, Turkmenistan, Ukraine and Uzbekistan
Level of Study: Postgraduate
Type: Fellowship
Value: Up to US$10,000
Length of Study: 1 year
Frequency: Annual
Application Procedure: Complete online application form
Closing Date: 15 January (Performing arts and literature application) and 15 January (Visual and media arts application)
Funding: Private, Trusts
No. of awards given last year: 10
Additional Information: Please check at www.cecartslink.org/grants/artslink_projects/ for further details

For further information contact:

Tel: (44) 212 643 1985
Email: al@cecartslink.org

ArtsLink Residencies

Subjects: Literature, Performing arts, Visual and Media Arts
Purpose: To create opportunities for artists and communities across the United States to share artistic practices with artists and arts managers from abroad and engage in dialogue that advances understanding across cultures
Eligibility: Applicants must be the citizens of, and reside in, eligible countries: Albania, Armenia, Azerbaijan, Belarus, Bosnia and Herzegovina, Bulgaria, Croatia, Czech Republic, Estonia, Georgia, Hungary, Kazakhstan, Kosovo, Kyrgyzstan, Latvia, Lithuania, Macedonia, Moldova, Mongolia, Montenegro, Poland, Romania, Russia, Serbia, Slovak Republic, Slovenia, Tajikistan, Turkmenistan, Ukraine and Uzbekistan
Level of Study: Postgraduate
Type: Fellowship
Value: offers artists and arts managers from eligible overseas countries a 5-week residency at an established, non-profit arts organization in the United States
Length of Study: 5 weeks
Frequency: Annual
Country of Study: United States of America
Application Procedure: Complete online application form
Closing Date: 15 October
Funding: Private, Trusts

Contributor: ArtsLink Residencies are funded through public and private sources including CEC ArtsLink, the National Endowment for the Arts, the Trust for Mutual Understanding, the Ohio Arts Council, the Kettering Fund and the Milton and Sally Avery Arts Foundation with additional support from the Polish Cultural Institute and the Romanian Cultural Institute
No. of awards given last year: 16
Additional Information: Please check at www.cecartslink. org/grants/artslink_residencies/ for further details

For further information contact:

Email: al@cecartslink.org

Center for Creative Photography (CCP)

The University of Arizona, 1030 North Olive Road, Tucson, AZ 210103, United States of America

Tel: (1) 520 621 7970
Fax: (1) 520 621 9444
Email: info@ccp.library.arizona.edu
Website: www.creativephotography.org/

The Center for Creative Photography (CCP) is an archive and research centre located on the University of Arizona campus.

Center for Creative Photography Ansel Adams Research Fellowship

Subjects: Curating/Research
Purpose: To promote and support research on the Center's photograph, archive and library collections
Eligibility: Open to researchers from any discipline who are engaged in studies that require an extended period of research in the collections of the Center
Level of Study: Research
Type: Fellowship
Value: Awards up to US$5,000 to promote new knowledge about photography and the history of photography
Length of Study: 2–4 weeks
Frequency: Annual
Country of Study: United States of America
Application Procedure: Applicants must send a cover letter along with 5 copies each of a curriculum vitae and a statement detailing the applicant's research interests
Closing Date: 16 January

Additional Information: Please check at www.creativephotography.org/study-research/fellowships-internships for further details

For further information contact:

Center for Creative Photography, 1030 N. Olive Road, United States of America

Fax: (1) 520 621 9444
Email: cass@ccp.library.arizona.edu
Contact: Cass Fey, Curator of Education

Center for Defense Information (CDI)

1100 G Street NW, Suite 500, Washington, DC 20005-3806, United States of America

Tel: (1) 202 347 1122
Fax: (1) 202 347 1116
Email: info@cdi.org
Website: www.cdi.org
Contact: Joe Newman, Director of Communications

The Center for Defense Information (CDI) provides responsible, non-partisan research and analysis on the social, economic, environmental, political and military components of national and global security, and aims to educate the public and inform policy makers about these issues. The organization is staffed by retired senior government officials and knowledgeable researchers and is directed by Dr Bruce G Blair.

Center for Defense Information Internship

Subjects: Weapons proliferation, military spending, military policy, diplomacy and foreign affairs
Purpose: To support the work of CDI's senior staff while gaining exposure to research, issues and communications related to national security and foreign policy
Eligibility: There are no eligibility restrictions. Paid internships are available for nationals of the United States and legal immigrants
Level of Study: Unrestricted
Type: Internship
Value: US$1,000 per month
Length of Study: 3–5 months
Study Establishment: CDI

Country of Study: Any country
No. of awards offered: 200
Application Procedure: Applicants must submit a curriculum vitae, covering letter, brief writing sample, transcript and two letters of recommendation
Closing Date: 1 July for the Autumn, 15 October for the Spring and 1 March for the Summer
Funding: Private
No. of awards given last year: 12
No. of applicants last year: 200

For further information contact:

Center for Defense Information, 1779 Massachusetts Avenue, N.W., United States of America

Fax: (1) 202 462 4559
Email: internships@cdi.org
Contact: Internship Coordinator

Central Queensland University

Building 5 Bruce Highway, Rockhampton, QLD 4702, Australia

Tel: (61) 7 4930 9000
Fax: (61) 7 4923 2100
Email: research-enquiries@cqu.edu.au
Website: www.cqu.edu.au

The Central Queensland University (CQU) is committed to excellence in research and innovation with a particular emphasis on issues that affect the region. CQU achieves relevance in its research goals through linkages with industry, business, government and the community and through collaboration with national and international researchers and research networks. CQU provides a range of exciting and relevant research opportunities for Masters and PhD candidates and is committed to excellence and quality in the research training experience of its candidates.

CQUniversity Indigenous Australian Postgraduate Research Award

Subjects: Any subject
Eligibility: The applicant should be an Australian citizen and must be a Aborginal or Torres Strait Islander
Level of Study: Postgraduate, Research
Type: Scholarship

Value: A$19,616 maximum 1 year
Frequency: Annual
Study Establishment: Central Queensland University
Country of Study: Australia
Application Procedure: For information on application procedure, check the website
Closing Date: 31 October
Funding: Government
Additional Information: This scholarship is paid fortnightly for the period of 2 years (Masters) or 3 years (PhD). Open for applications from June 30th

For further information contact:

Office of Research, Building 351, Central Queensland University, Australia

Tel: (61) 7 4923 2607
Fax: (61) 7 4923 2600
Email: research-enquiries@cqu.edu.au
Contact: Kerrie Hand, Executive Officer

CQUniversity Womens Equal Opportunity Research Award

Subjects: Any subject
Purpose: To enable a woman to undertake full-time postgraduate research towards a PhD or Master's degree after having experienced a break in study
Eligibility: Open only to female candiates who are citizens or permanent residents of Australia and New Zealand
Level of Study: Doctorate, Postgraduate
Type: Research award
Value: A$19,616 (maximum per year)
Frequency: Annual
Study Establishment: Central Queensland University
Country of Study: Australia
Application Procedure: Check website for further details
Closing Date: 31 October
Funding: Government
Additional Information: This scholarship is paid fortnightly for the period of 2 years (Masters) or 3 years (PhD). Open for applications from July 1st

CQUniversity/Industry Collaborative Grants Scheme

Subjects: Any subject
Purpose: To encourage active research collaboration between the university and eligible industry partners

Eligibility: Open for candidates who are full-time members of staff (either individuals or teams) and are able to demonstrate through their track record that they have the capability to successfully complete the proposed project
Type: Grant
Value: Up to A$10,000 is tenable for 1 year, commencing 1 January and ending 31 December
Length of Study: 12 months
Study Establishment: Central Queensland University
Country of Study: Australia
Application Procedure: Applications must be submitted on the current application form, in the required format with the required number of copies. One original application, and one identical copy must be submitted in hard copy, and one copy must be submitted electronically, either as a word or pdf document
Closing Date: 11 August

For further information contact:

Bldg 351, Rockhampton (City) Campus, Australia

Tel:	(61) 4923 2601
Fax:	(61) 4923 2600
Email:	l.walker@cqu.edu.au
Contact:	Leslie Walker, Grants and Industry Liaison Officer

Merit Grants Scheme

Subjects: Any subject
Purpose: To provide opportunities for individuals or groups with well established or developing track records in research to initiate high quality research projects
Eligibility: Members of the full-time staff of the University with a proven research record 'relative to opportunity' are eligible to compete for Merit Research Grants. Candidates must not be absent for a period exceeding eight weeks during the proposed period of grant. A researcher may be in receipt of only one Merit Grant at any one time
Type: Grant
Value: A$10,000–30,000
Length of Study: 1 year
Study Establishment: Central Queensland University
Country of Study: Australia
Application Procedure: Applications must be submitted on the current application form, in the required format, and with the required number of copies
Funding: Government
Additional Information: A researcher may be in receipt of only one Merit Grant at any one time

Research Administration Assistants Postdoctoral Award

Subjects: Any subject
Purpose: To provide for the university's intellectual environment by facilitating mentoring, team building, and career development in areas of current or future research strength
Eligibility: The applicant must remain based on a Central Queensland University campus (excluding international campuses) for the duration of the award
Level of Study: Postdoctorate
Type: Award
Value: On-costs of 28% will be paid in addition to salary
Frequency: Annual
Study Establishment: Central Queensland University
Country of Study: Australia
Application Procedure: Applications must be submitted on the current application form, in the required format, and with the required number of copies
Funding: Government
Additional Information: Applicants may seek funding for 1, 2, or 3 years

Seed Grants Scheme

Subjects: Any subject
Purpose: To provide seed funding to encourage new research-trained staff to undertake a funded research project
Eligibility: Open to newly trained researchers, who are currently within the first 5 years of academic or other research-related performance allowing uninterrupted, stable research development following completion of their postgraduate research training
Level of Study: Research
Type: Grant
Value: Up to A$10,000
Length of Study: 1 year
Study Establishment: Central Queensland University
Country of Study: Australia
Application Procedure: Applications must be submitted on the current application form, in the required format, and with the required number of copies
Closing Date: 11 August
Funding: Government

Centre de Recherches et dInvestigations Epidermiques et Sensorielles

20 rue Victor Noir, Neuilly-sur-Seine 92200, France

Tel:	(33) 146 434 900
Fax:	(33) 146 434 600
Email:	contact@ceries.com
Website:	www.ceries.com

CERIES (Centre de Recherches et d'Investigations Epidermiques et Sensorielles or Centre for Epidermal and Sensory Research and Investigation) is the healthy skin research centre of Chanel.

Centre de Recherches et d'Investigations Epidermiques et Sensorielles Research Award

Subjects: The biology and physiology of healthy skin and/or its reactions to environmental factors
Purpose: To honour a scientific researcher for a fundamental or clinical research project in the field of healthy skin
Eligibility: There are no eligibility restrictions
Level of Study: Research
Value: €40,000
Length of Study: 1 year
Frequency: Annual
Country of Study: Any country
No. of awards offered: 26
Application Procedure: Applicants must consult the website
Closing Date: 1 June
Funding: Private
Contributor: Chanel
No. of awards given last year: 1
No. of applicants last year: 26

For further information contact:

| Email: | chanelrt.award@ruderfinnasia.com |
| Contact: | Claire BERNIN-JUNG / Marie-Hélène LAIR |

Centre De Science Humaines (CSH)

2 Aurangzeb Road, New Delhi 110011, India

Tel:	(91) 11 30410070
Fax:	(91) 11 30410079
Email:	direction@csh-delhi.com
Website:	www.csh-delhi.com

The Centre de Sciences Humaines (CSH), created in 1989, is a research centre funded by the French Ministry of Foreign Affairs. It conducts research programmes and organizes seminars and lectures in the field of social sciences on contemporary India and South Asia.

Centre de Sciences Humaines Post-Doctoral Fellowship

Subjects: Urban studies
Purpose: To question the status of India as an emerging power in the international scene
Eligibility: Open to candidates who hold a PhD in economics/economic geography/urban studies and are prefereable below 35 years of age
Level of Study: Postdoctorate
Type: Fellowship
Value: Indian Rupees 20,000–25,000 per month
Length of Study: 1 year
Frequency: Annual
Country of Study: India
Application Procedure: Applicants must send their curriculum vitae, 2 academic references letters, a synopsis of the PhD theses and a comprehensive research proposal
Closing Date: 31 January

For further information contact:

| Email: | veronique.dupont@csh-delhi.com |
| Contact: | Director |

Centre for Clinical Research Excellence

Centre for Clinical Research Excellence - Infection and Bioethics in Haematological Malignancies, Level 3, ICPMR, Westmead Hospital, Institute Road, Westmead, Australia

Tel:	(61) 9845 6255
Fax:	(61) 9893 8659
Email:	cjordens@med.usyd.edu.au
Website:	www.ccre-ibhm.org.au

The Centre for Clinical Research Excellence (CCRE) is multi-centre research collaboration with a special focus on bioethics, consisting of four research sites affiliated with the University of Sydney, including the Western Clinical School at Westmead Hospital, The Children's Hospital Westmead, the National Centre for Immunization Research, and the Centre for Values, Ethics and the Law in Medicine (VELIM). The research collaboration will develop surveillance methods and interventions to improve infection-related outcomes in malignant haematology and bone marrow transplantation, with interdisciplinary bioethics research underpinning all major themes.

Postgraduate Scholarships for Interdisciplinary Bioethics Research

Subjects: Bioethics
Purpose: To develop surveillance methods and interventions to improve infection-related outcomes in malignant haematology and bone marrow transplantation, with interdisciplinary bioethics research underpinning all major themes
Eligibility: Open to Australian citizens or permanent resident meeting the standard criteria for NHMRC scholarships, including full-time enrollment and status, as well as the criteria for admission to postgraduate study in the faculty of medicine or faculty of science at the University of Sydney
Level of Study: Graduate
Type: Scholarship
Country of Study: Australia
Application Procedure: Check website for further details

For further information contact:

Tel: (61) 434 07 07 88
Email: cjordens@med.usyd.edu.au
Contact: Dr Chris Jordens, Clinical Research Fellow

Centre for Environment Planning and Technology University

Kasturbhai Lalbhai Campus, University Road, Vasant Vihar, Navrangpura, Ahmedabad, Gujarat 380009, India

Contact: CEPT University

Centre for Environmental Planning and Technology University, formerly the Centre for Environmental Planning and Technology, is an academic institution located near university area in Ahmedabad, India offering postgraduate programmes in areas of the natural and developed environment of human society and related disciplines.

Full-Tuition Fees Waiver for MPhil/PhD Students

Subjects: Architecture
Purpose: Scholarships are available for pursuing MPhil/PhD programme

Eligibility: Students from India are eligible to apply
Type: Grant
Value: The university offers full tuition fees waiver to MPhil/PhD students for their entire term of registration in the program. The university also offers a scholarship (Rs. 36,700 per month-subject to change) for the first six months (mandatory) of the coursework against teaching assignments (15–20 hours/week) as allocated by the respective faculty
Country of Study: India
Application Procedure: Go to the Centre for Environmental Planning and Technology(CEPT) website Click on the 'Admissions' button (on the header menu) at the top of the page. This will open a page with all the programs offered at CEPT University. Click on the program you wish to apply. This will open the tab with 'About' 'FAQ' & 'How to Apply'. Click on the 'How to Apply' button and you will be redirected to a page containing eligibility criteria, program details and the link to the admissions portal. For further information, kindly check the following link. cept.ac.in/2/37/faculty-of-architecture/479/fees-scholarship
Closing Date: 30 April
Additional Information: For detailed information, check with the below link. scholarship-positions.com/full-tuition-fees-waiver-mphil-phd-students-cept-university-india/

For further information contact:

Harvard Square, Mifflin Pl, Cambridge, MA 02138, United States of America

Centre for Groundwater Studies (CGS)

GPO Box 2100, Adelaide, SA 5001, Australia

Tel: (61) 8 8201 5632
Fax: (61) 8 8201 5635
Email: cgs@groundwater.com.au
Website: www.groundwater.com.au

Centre for Groundwater Studies (CGS) is an international leader in water and environmental research and education.

Chinese Government Scholarship Water and Environmental Research Scholarships

Subjects: Soil, geophysics, microbiology, hydrogeology, plant ecology, water chemistry and water science
Purpose: To assist students with research projects in the specified areas

Eligibility: Open to Australian citizens and permanent residents who have a background in science, mathematics or engineering
Level of Study: Postgraduate
Type: Scholarship
Value: A$22,231
Length of Study: 1 year
Frequency: Annual
Country of Study: Australia
Closing Date: September
Additional Information: For additional information see the website

For further information contact:

Email: impt@scholars4dev.com

Chandigarh University

NH-95 Chandigarh-Ludhiana Highway, Mohali, Punjab 140413, India

Contact: Chandigarh University

A renowned university in India is offering scholarships for brilliant but less privileged students across the globe who have the interest in studying in India.

Chandigarh University Scholarships in India

Subjects: Scholarships are awarded to study the subjects offered by the university
Purpose: Chandigarh University offers undergraduate and post-graduate and doctorate courses in various disciplines including Engineering, Management, Computing, Education, Animation and Multimedia, Tourism, Pharma Sciences, Bio-technology, Architecture, Commerce and Legal Studies
Eligibility: Students outside India, Nepal and Bhutan can apply for these scholarships.Not Required but all academic documents are to be sent to micheal.africa-at-cumail.in for eligibility checking. Not required but the applicant must be able to read, write and understand the English Language
Study Establishment: Scholarships are awarded to study the subjects offered by the university
Country of Study: India
Application Procedure: Interested students can contact Mr. Michael on micheal.africa-at-cumail.in The micheal.africa@cumail.in is the official email ID we are using now in terms of scholarship admission and enquiries

Closing Date: Last Week Of July
Additional Information: For more details please contact the website scholarship-positions.com/chandigarh-university-scholarships-india/

For further information contact:

Email: micheal.africa@cumail.in

Charles Babbage Institute (CBI)

211 Andersen Library, University of Minnesota, 222 21st Avenue South, Minneapolis, MN 55455, United States of America

Tel: (1) 612 624 5050
Fax: (1) 612 625 8054
Email: cbi@umn.edu
Website: www.cbi.umn.edu

The Charles Babbage Institute (CBI) is a research centre dedicated to promoting the study of the history of computing, its impact on society and preserving relevant documentation. CBI fosters research and writing in the history of computing by providing fellowship support, archival resources and information to scholars, computer scientists and the general public.

Adelle and Erwin Tomash Fellowship in the History of Information Processing

Subjects: The history of computing and information processing
Purpose: To advance the professional development of historians in the field
Eligibility: Open to graduate students whose dissertations deal with a historical aspect of information processing. Priority will be given to students who have completed all requirements for the doctoral degree except the research and writing of the dissertation
Level of Study: Doctorate
Type: Fellowship
Value: US$14,000
Length of Study: 1 year
Frequency: Annual
Country of Study: Any country
Application Procedure: Applicants must send their curriculum vitae, a five page statement and justification of the research problem, and a discussion of methods, research materials and evidence of faculty support for the project. Applicants should also arrange for three letters of reference

and certified transcripts of graduate school credits to be sent directly to the Institute

Closing Date: 15 January
Funding: Private
Additional Information: Please check at www.cbi.umn.edu/research/tfellowship.html for further details

For further information contact:

Charles Babbage Institute University of Minnesota 103 Walter Library 117 Pleasant Street, SE, United States of America

Tel: (1) 624 5050
Fax: (1) 625 8054
Email: nels0307@umn.edu
Contact: R. Arvid Nelsen, CBI Archivist

Charles Darwin University (CDU)

Charles Darwin University Ellengowan Drive, Casuarina, NT 0811, Australia

Tel: (61) 8 8946 6666
Fax: (61) 8 8946 6642
Email: scholarships@cdu.edu.au
Website: www.cdu.edu.au

The Charles Darwin University (CDU) offers programmes from certificate level to PhD, incorporating the full range of vocational education courses. CDU has a distinctive research profile, reflecting the priorities appropriate to its location. It is a participating member of several CRCs.

Nanyang Technological University MBA Programme

Length of Study: 1 year, 18 months or 4 years
Application Procedure: Applicants must submit, with their application form, three recent passport sized photographs, official copies of degrees and professional qualifications, two references in sealed envelopes, evidence of finance, TOEFL and IELTS scores (overseas applicants only)
Closing Date: Please contact the organisation

For further information contact:

Tel: (61) 8 8946 6447
Fax: (61) 8 8946 6777
Email: busgrad@business.ntu.edu.au
Contact: Ms Margaret Landrigan, Executive Officer

Charles Sturt University (CSU)

Charles Sturt University Boorooma Street, Locked Bag 588, Wagga Wagga, NSW 2678, Australia

Tel: (61) 2 6338 6077
Fax: (61) 2 6338 6001
Email: inquiry@csu.edu.au, research@csu.edu.au
Website: www.csu.edu.au

CSU is one of the leading Australian universities for graduate employment and largest provider in distance education. Utilizing our expertise in distance education, CSU provides educational opportunities to students around the world. Around 36,000 students undertake their choice of study with CSU on one of our campuses, from home, their workplace or anywhere around the globe.

Australian Postgraduate Awards

Subjects: All subjects
Purpose: To financially support postgraduate students of exceptional research promise in Master or Doctoral programs at Charles Sturt University
Eligibility: Awards will only be available to those who are Australian citizens and New Zealand citizens; have been granted permanent resident status by October 31st; have lived in Australia continuously for at least 12 months prior to October 31st; have completed at least 4 years of tertiary education studies at a high level of achievement; have obtained First Class Honours or equivalent results; will undertake a Master's (Honours) or Doctoral degree; are enroling as full-time students or, in exceptional circumstances, be granted approval by CSU for a part-time award; have had their enrolment into the proposed higher degree programme accepted by CSU
Level of Study: Postgraduate, Research
Type: Award
Value: $32,500 per year
Length of Study: 2-3 years
Frequency: Annual
Study Establishment: Charles Sturt University
Country of Study: Australia
Application Procedure: Applicants must submit an application form
Closing Date: 31 October
Funding: Government
Additional Information: Please check at www.csu.edu.au/research/support/research-students/my-hdr/getting-started/scholarship-opportunities/main-round for further details

For further information contact:

Email: rgs@latrobe.edu.au

Biology of Annual Ryegrass Scholarship

Subjects: Agricultural, veterinary and environmental sciences, or biological sciences
Purpose: To characterize annual ryegrass in Australian winter cropping areas
Eligibility: Open only for the citizens of Australia or permanent residents those who have a background in agriculture, biology, or plant science and achieved Honours 2a or equivalent
Level of Study: Graduate
Value: A$24,616 (maximum per year) paid fortnightly for the period of 3 years
Country of Study: Australia

For further information contact:

Charles Sturt University, Wagga Wagga, Australia

Tel: (61) 2 69 33 2862
Email: jpratley@csu.edu.au
Contact: Professor Jim Pratley

Charles Sturt University Postgraduate Research Studentships (CSUPRS)

Subjects: All subjects
Purpose: To support high quality research students in Masters or Doctoral programs at Charles Sturt University
Eligibility: Open to the candidates who hold or expect to hold, at least a Bachelor degree with upper second class honours or a qualification deemed equivalent from CSU
Level of Study: Graduate, Research
Type: Studentship
Value: $22,500 stipend plus allowances
Frequency: Annual
Application Procedure: Scholarship application form can be downloaded from the website. Send in the filled application to the center with original referee report and five copies of their report
Closing Date: 30 October
Additional Information: Offers of scholarships cannot be made to candidates until their enrolment as Research Higher Degree students has been approved by the Board of Graduate Studies. Please check at www.csu.edu.au/research/support/research-students/my-hdr/getting-started/scholarship-opportunities/main-round for further details

For further information contact:

Postgraduate Scholarships, Center for Research & Graduate Training, Charles Sturt University, Locked Bag 588, Australia

Tel: (61) 2 6933 4162
Email: pgscholars@csu.edu.au

Evidence-Based Approach to Improve Insulin Sensitivity in Horses, Using Dietary Ingredients

Subjects: Agricultural, veterinary and environmental sciences, or science
Eligibility: Open only for the citizens of Australia or permanent residents those who have achieved Honours 1 (Semester 1)
Level of Study: Graduate
Value: A$19,231 (maximum per year) paid fortnightly for the period of 3 years and to be used for living expenses
Country of Study: Australia

For further information contact:

Locked Bag 588, Australia

Tel: (61) 2 6933 4242
Email: gnoble@csu.edu.au
Contact: Dr Glenys Noble

Charlie Trotter Culinary Education Foundation

40 E. Chicago Avenue, Suite 418, Chicago, IL 60611, United States of America

Tel: (1) 312 600 9724
Fax: (1) 773 248 6088
Email: info@charlietrotters.com
Website: www.charlietrotters.com/about/foundation.asp

Charlie Trotter's is regarded as one of the finest restaurants in the world, dedicated to excellence in the culinary arts. It has been instrumental in establishing new standards for fine dining. Its main goal is to educate and expose the youth to the great culinary arts in as many ways as possible. The Charlie Trotter Culinary Education Foundation, a non-profit organization, has been established to promote culinary arts among youth. The foundation is involved in awarding scholarships to students who are seeking careers in the culinary arts and working with Chicago-area youth to promote the enthusiastic quest for education as well as an interest in the cooking and food.

Charlie Trotter's Culinary Education Foundation Culinary Study Scholarship

Subjects: Cooking
Eligibility: Open to an Illinois resident at the time of application
Level of Study: Professional development
Type: Scholarship
Value: US$5,000 cash scholarship for a pre-enroled student
Length of Study: 1 year
Frequency: Annual
Country of Study: United States of America
Application Procedure: Check website for further details
Closing Date: 1 March
Funding: Private, Foundation
Contributor: Charlie Trotter's
Additional Information: Please check website for more details

For further information contact:

The Culinary Trust Scholarship Program P.O. Box 273, United States of America

Tel: (1) 646 224 6989
Email: cholarships@theculinarytrust.com
Contact: Amy Blackburn, Director of Administration

Chiang Ching Kuo Foundation for International Scholarly Exchange

13F, 65 Tun Hwa South Road, Section 2, Taiwan 106-ROC, China

Tel: (886) 2 2704 5333
Fax: (886) 2 2701 6762
Email: cckf@ms1.hinet.net
Website: www.cckf.org

The Chiang Ching Kuo Foundation for International Scholarly Exchange is a non-profit organization headquartered in Taipei, the capital of the Republic of China. The Foundation was established in 1989 in honour of the late President Chiang Ching kuo. The main objective of the Foundation is to promote the study of Chinese culture and society, broadly defined.

Chiang Ching Kuo Foundation Doctoral Fellowships

Subjects: Chinese studies in the field of humanities and social sciences

Purpose: To financially support Doctoral candidates while writing their dissertations
Eligibility: Open to applicants who have completed all other requirements for their PhD degree except the dissertation. Candidates must not be employed or receive grants from other sources
Level of Study: Doctorate
Type: Fellowships
Value: Up to US$15,000
Length of Study: 1 year
Frequency: Annual
Application Procedure: Applicants need to submit a 1 page summary of the proposed project, budget, curriculum vitae and detailed description of the proposed project along with the application form. Application forms are available online
Closing Date: 15 October
Funding: Commercial, Private

For further information contact:

Email: cckf@ms1.hinet.net

Chiang Ching Kuo Foundation for International Scholarly Exchange Eminent Scholar Lectureship

Subjects: All subjects
Purpose: To sponsor eminent foreign scholars to come to Taiwan to take up lectureships or positions as visiting scholars
Eligibility: Open to eminent scholars invited by universities or academic institutions of Taiwan
Type: Lectureship/Prize
Value: New Taiwan $2,000,000
Length of Study: 1 year
Frequency: Annual
Study Establishment: Universities or academic institutions in Taiwan
Country of Study: Taiwan
Application Procedure: Applicants must use the application forms provided by the Foundation. The application must be sent by registered mail to the Secretariat. Electronic version of all application materials must be enclosed on diskette or sent as email attachment to cckf@ms1.hinet.net with heading 'Application Materials from (Name)' in the header of the message. Applications are accepted from June 1st
Closing Date: 15 October
Funding: Foundation
Additional Information: Project directors who are currently receiving Foundation aid are ineligible to apply. Project directors may not submit more than one application

For further information contact:

Email: cckf@ms1.hinet.net

Chiang Ching Kuo Foundation for International Scholarly Exchange Publication Subsidies

Subjects: Academic works, periodicals, and journals
Purpose: To assist in the final stages of publishing academic works
Eligibility: Open to scholars in the final stages of publishing academic works. Applications from scholars affiliated with institutions in Taiwan must involve cooperation with one or more scholars from other countries. Applicants for publication subsidies must be affiliated with a university or other academic institution
Type: Grant
Value: Ranges between New Taiwan $5,000 and $10,000. Publication Subsidy Grants may only be used to cover editing, indexing, and other relevant publication costs. Translation and research-related expenses may not be included
Application Procedure: Applicants must use the application forms provided directly from the Foundation Secretariat. Three copies of the application and supporting documents must be submitted by registered mail to the Secretariat. In addition, electronic version of all application materials must be enclosed on diskette or sent as email attachment to cckf@ms1.hinet.net with heading 'Application Materials from (Name)' in the header of the message
Closing Date: 15 September and 15 January
Funding: Trusts
Additional Information: Please check the website for more details

For further information contact:

The Chiang Ching-kuo Foundation for International Scholarly Exchange, 8361 B Greensboro Dr, China

Email: cckfnao@aol.com

Doctoral Fellowships

Subjects: Chinese studies in humanities and social sciences
Purpose: Supporting doctoral candidates for completing their dissertation in the last stage of their doctoral programs
Eligibility: Applicants should have completed all other requirements for their PhD degree. Applicants should be enroled in an accredited university in the United States, Canada, Mexico, and Central and Southern America
Level of Study: Doctorate
Type: Fellowship
Value: US$18,000
Length of Study: 1 year
Frequency: Annual
No. of awards offered: 104

Closing Date: 15 October
Funding: Foundation
No. of awards given last year: 28
No. of applicants last year: 104

Junior Scholar Grants

Purpose: The Foundation provides grants for time off for research and writing to postdoctoral and assistant professors without tenure who are affiliated with an accredited American university and who have taught for no more than 6 years since receiving PhD degree
Eligibility: Junior Scholar Grants is only available for applicants who are affiliated with an American university
Type: Grant
Value: Up to $30,000
Frequency: Annual
No. of awards offered: 80
Closing Date: 15 October
Funding: Foundation
No. of awards given last year: 20
No. of applicants last year: 80

Scholar Grants

Subjects: Chinese studies in humanities and social sciences
Purpose: To help replace half of the salary of faculty on sabbatical, or for time off for research and writing
Eligibility: Tenure faculty, including full professors and associate professor, in the accredited universities in the United States, Canada, Mexico, and Central and Southern America are eligible to apply for scholar grants
Type: Grant
Value: $40,000 or $35,000
Frequency: Annual
No. of awards offered: 42
Closing Date: 15 October
No. of awards given last year: 12
No. of applicants last year: 42

Chicago Tribune

435 North Michigan Avenue, Chicago, IL 60611, United States of America

Tel: (1) 312 222 3232
Fax: (1) 312 222 3751
Email: jwoelffer@tribune.com
Website: www.chicagotribune.com

The Chicago Tribune is the Midwest's leading newspaper. The Chicago Tribune Literary Awards are part of a continued dedication to readers, writers and ideas.

Nelson Algren Awards

Subjects: Short fiction
Purpose: To award writers of short fiction
Eligibility: Each entrant must be at least 18 years old and a legal resident of the Contest Area (above) as of the date of entry
Level of Study: Unrestricted
Type: Award
Value: US$3,500 (1 Grand Prize); US$1,000 (4 Finalist Prizes); and US$500 (5 Runnerup Prizes)
Frequency: Annual
Country of Study: Any country
Application Procedure: Visit algren.submittable.com (the "Contest Page"), complete an entry form with the following required information: (a) name, (b) telephone number, (c) email address, (d) the title and word count of your submission, and submit it along with your short story (a "Story") (together with the entry form referred as an "Entry") that otherwise meets all Submission Requirements below. Entries will not be accepted through any other method
Closing Date: 31 January
Funding: Corporation
Additional Information: Please contact to Chicago Tribune for latest updates. Please check at articles.chicagotribune.com/2013-11-26/news/chi-2013-nelson-algren-award-official-rules-20120906_1_grand-prize-enter-or-win-chicago-tribune-company-llc for further details

For further information contact:

Chicago Tribune, Nelson Algren Awards, 435 N. Michigan Avenue, TT200, United States of America

Email: printersrow@tribune.com

Chilean International Cooperation Agency

Chile: Nelson Mandela Scholarships

Purpose: The Chilean International Cooperation Agency (AGCI) is offering scholarships for accredited Spanish-taught Master's program at Chilean higher education institutions. The scholarships are offered to professionals who are citizens of South Africa, Mozambique and Angola

Eligibility: 1. Experience in the subjects they choose to pursue Master's studies in unconditional acceptance offer at a Chilean higher education institution. 2. 4-year university degree. 3. If employed already, you will need a letter of support, indicating that you will be released for the duration of your studies
Level of Study: Postgraduate
Type: Scholarship
Value: US$500
Length of Study: 4 year
Frequency: Annual
Country of Study: South Africa
Application Procedure: Apply online: www.agci.gob.cl
Closing Date: 31 October
Funding: Foundation

For further information contact:

Email: becasmandela@gmail.com

China Scholarship Council

Level 13, Building A3 No.9 Chegongzhuang Avenue, Beijing 100044, China

Tel:	(86) 660 93900
Fax:	(86) 664 3198
Email:	webmaster@csc.edu.cn
Website:	www.csc.edu.cn

The China Scholarship council (CSC) is a non-profit institution, which is affiliated with the ministry of education. The main objective of the CSC is to develop the educational, scientific and technological, and cultural exchanges and economic and trade cooperation between China and other countries.

K C Wong Postgraduate Scholarship Programme

Subjects: All subjects
Purpose: To support students who intend to study further at King's College London
Eligibility: Open to applicants who are citizens and permanent residents of People's Republic of china
Type: Scholarship
Value: Tuition fees at the international rate plus an annual stipend of £8,400
Length of Study: 3 years
Frequency: Annual

Study Establishment: King's College London
Country of Study: United Kingdom
Application Procedure: A completed application form, which is available online, must be sent
Closing Date: 1 February
Funding: Government
Contributor: K C Wong Education Foundation

For further information contact:

Research & Graduate School Support Section King's College London, United Kingdom

Tel: (44) 20 7848 3376
Fax: (44) 20 7848 3328
Email: graduateschool@kcl.ac.uk

Chinese American Medical Society (CAMS)

41 Elizabeth Street, Suite 600, New York, NY 10013, United States of America

Tel: (1) 212 334 4760
Fax: (1) 646 304 6373
Email: jlove@camsociety.org
Website: www.camsociety.org
Contact: Dr H H Wang, Executive Director

The Chinese American Medical Society (CAMS) is a non-profit, charitable, educational and scientific society that aims to promote the scientific association of medical professionals of Chinese descent. It also aims to advance medical knowledge and scientific research with emphasis on aspects unique to the Chinese and to promote the health status of Chinese Americans. The Society makes scholarships available to medical dental students and provides summer fellowships for students conducting research in health problems related to the Chinese

Chinese American Medical Society Scholarship Program

Purpose: In the early 1970's the Chinese American Medical Society went to considerable lengths to provide scholarships to outstanding medical students in need of financial assistance
Eligibility: 1. You must currently be in your first, second, or third year of medical or dental school in the United States of America when applying for this scholarship. 2. Students that have just been accepted into medical school or dental school at the time of application are not eligible to apply for this year's scholarship
Level of Study: Graduate, Postgraduate
Type: Programme grant
Value: US$5,000
Frequency: Annual
Country of Study: Any country
Application Procedure: The submission has to be made to the email address scholarship@camsociety.org Email is the preferred method of submission for applications. The committee asks that all applications and supporting materials be sent as a single PDF file and emailed to scholarship@camsociety.org
Closing Date: 30 April
Funding: Private

For further information contact:

Scholarship Committee, 265 Canal Street, Suite 515, New York, NY 10013, United States of America

Email: jlove@camsociety.org

Chinook Regional Career Transitions for Youth

Room B310, 1701 - 5 Avenue South, Lethbridge, AB T1J 0W4, Canada

Tel: (1) 403 328 3996
Fax: (1) 403 320 2365
Email: mvennard@pallisersd.ab.ca
Website: www.careersteps.ca

The Chinook regional career transitions for youth aims to improve the school-to-work transitions for students, promoting lifelong learning and coordinating and implementing career development activities and programming for youth.

Robin Rousseau Memorial Mountain Achievement Scholarship

Subjects: Mountain leadership and safety
Purpose: To bring about awareness of ways to improve safety in the mountains

Eligibility: Applicants must be Alberta residents and active in the mountain community; and plan to study in any recognized Mountain Leadership and Safety program
Level of Study: Professional development
Type: Scholarship
Value: Course fee
Frequency: Annual
Application Procedure: A completed application form must be sent
Closing Date: 30 January (check with website)

For further information contact:

Alberta Scholarship Programs Box 28000 Stn Main, Canada

Tel: (1) 780 427 8640
Fax: (1) 780 427 1288
Email: scholarships@gov.ab.ca

Toyota Earth Day Scholarship Program

Subjects: Environmental community service
Purpose: To encourage community service
Eligibility: Open to students who have achieved academic excellence and distinguished themselves in environmental community service and extracurricular and volunteer activities
Level of Study: Professional development
Type: Scholarship
Value: C$5,000
Frequency: Annual
Application Procedure: Application form available online
Closing Date: 15 February

For further information contact:

Toyota Earth Day Scholarship Program, III Peter Street, Suite 503, Canada

Email: scholarship@earthday.ca

Choirs Ontario

Choirs Ontario A-1422 Bayview Avenue, Toronto, ON M4G 3A7, Canada

Tel: (1) 416 923 1144
Fax: (1) 416 929 0415
Email: info@choirsontario.org

Website: www.choirsontario.org
Contact: Melva Graham

Choirs Ontario is an arts service organization dedicated to the promotion of choral activities and standards of excellence. Established in 1971 as the Ontario Choral Federation, Choirs Ontario provides services to choirs, conductors, choristers, composers, administrators and educators as well as anyone who enjoys listening to the sound of choral music. Choirs Ontario operates with the financial assistance of the Ministry of Culture, the Ontario Arts Council, the Trillium Foundation, the Toronto Arts Council and numerous foundations, corporations and individual donors.

Ruth Watson Henderson Choral Composition Competition

Subjects: Choral music, particularly composition
Purpose: To award new choral composition
Eligibility: Candidates must be Canadian citizens or landed immigrants who are permanent residents of Ontario
Level of Study: Postgraduate
Type: Prize
Value: C$1,000
Country of Study: Any country
Application Procedure: Further information available on the website
Closing Date: There are various deadlines
Funding: Private

For further information contact:

Email: info@choirsontario.org

Clara Haskil Competition

Case Postale 234, 31 rue du Conseil, CH-1800 Vevey, Switzerland

Tel: (41) 21 922 6704
Fax: (41) 21 922 6734
Email: info@clara-haskil.ch
Website: www.regart.ch/clara-haskil
Contact: Mr Patrick Peikert, Director

The Clara Haskil Competition exists to recognize and help a young pianist whose approach to piano interpretation is of the same spirit that constantly inspired Clara Haskil, and that she illustrated so perfectly.

Clara Haskil International Piano Competition

Subjects: Piano and music
Purpose: To recognize and financially help a young pianist
Eligibility: Open to pianists of any nationality and either sex who are no more than 27 years of age
Level of Study: Postgraduate
Type: Prize
Value: Swiss Franc 25,000
Frequency: Every 2 years
Country of Study: Any country
No. of awards offered: Approx. 150
Application Procedure: Applicants must pay an entry fee of Swiss Franc 200
Closing Date: Check the website
Funding: Corporation, Trusts, International office
Contributor: Fondation Nestlé pour l'Art
No. of awards given last year: 2
No. of applicants last year: Approx. 150
Additional Information: The competition is usually held during the last weeks of August or the beginning of September

For further information contact:

International Piano Competition, Concours Clara Haskil, Switzerland

Tel: (41) 21 922 67 04
Fax: (41) 21 922 67 34
Email: info@clara-haskil.ch

Clare Hall Cambridge

Clare Hall Research Fellowships in the Arts and Social Sciences

Purpose: Research Fellowships are primarily intended to provide opportunities for scholars at an early stage of their academic careers to establish and pursue their research in a supportive academic environment
Eligibility: 1. During their tenure, Research Fellows have no college teaching duties other than to pursue their research. They are however members of the College Governing Body and may serve on other College committees. 2. Successful

candidates are expected to be graduate students who have recently completed or who are about to complete their PhD. 3. There is no restriction on age, sex or previous standing, except that candidates may not already have held a Research Fellowship at a college of either the University of Oxford or the University of Cambridge, and some preference may be given to candidates who are at a fairly early stage of their research career. 4. Research Fellows are required to live in Cambridge during Full Term, but leave may be granted to work away if necessary. Small grants for research expenses may be made available on application to the Senior Tutor
Level of Study: Research
Type: Fellowship
Frequency: Annual
Country of Study: Any country
Application Procedure: 1. Applications will be examined by experts in the fields concerned and by the Fellowship Committee. 2. The final choice, however, will be made by the Governing Body, and the research proposal should, therefore, be written to convey to the non-specialist something of the interest and importance of the topic. 3. Short-listed candidates will be asked to submit written work for consideration, and the final round of candidates will be called for interview
Closing Date: 14 February
Funding: Private

For further information contact:

Clare Hall, Herschel Road, CB3 9AL, Cambridge, United Kingdom

Email: college.registrar@clarehall.cam.ac.uk

Claude Leon Foundation

P.O. Box 30538, Tokai 7966, South Africa

Tel: (27) 21 787 0418
Fax: (27) 86 614 5915
Email: postdocadmin@leonfoundation.co.za
Website: www.leonfoundation.co.za

The Claude Leon Foundation is a South African Charitable Trust. resulting from a Bequest by Claude Leon (1884-1972), A prominent Johannesburg businessman. CLF funds a postdoctoral fellowship programme, now in it's 18th Year - It's goal is the building of research capacity in the faculties of Science, Engineering and Medical Sciences at

South African Universities via awards to both South African and foreign postdoctoral scientists.

Claude Leon Foundation Postdoctoral Fellowship

Subjects: Natural sciences, mathematics, engineering and medical sciences
Purpose: To fund postdoctoral research
Eligibility: Open to South African and foreign nationals. Preference will be given to candidates who have received their doctoral degrees in the last 5 years, and to those who are currently underrepresented in South African tertiary institutions
Level of Study: Postdoctorate
Value: South African Rand 235,000 PA for a 2-year fellowship plus travel grant up to a maximum of South African Rand 45,000 to present a paper on poster at an international conference during the 2nd year of fellowship
Length of Study: 2 years on renewal after the first year
Frequency: Annual
Study Establishment: South African universities and some institutions. See: www.leonfoundation.co.za/postdoctoral-links.htm
Country of Study: South Africa
No. of awards offered: 400
Application Procedure: Applications are not accepted directly from candidates. They must have been offered a postdoctoral position at a tertiary institution. The application should then be sent to the foundation by the institution not by the candidate
Closing Date: 31 May
Contributor: The Claude Leon Foundation, South Africa
No. of awards given last year: 58
No. of applicants last year: 400
Additional Information: Applications should be sent to the foundation by the institution at which the candidate has secured a postdoctoral position, not by the candidate

For further information contact:

Email: billfrankel@kayacomm.com

Coimbra Group

Coimbra Group Scholarship Programme for Young Professors and Researchers from Latin American Universities

Purpose: It aims to increase cooperation amongst its members by enhancing special academic and cultural ties, and creating channels of information and exchange

Eligibility: To be a national of and currently resident in a Latin American country. Candidates already living and/or studying in Europe will not be considered. 1. To hold a university degree or equivalent. 2. To be linked as a professor or researcher to a Latin American University recognised as such by the authorities of the country. 3. To use the Coimbra Group Office electronic application process. Only one application per candidate will be accepted. 4. To submit online an Acceptance Letter/email from the tutor/partner with whom the work programme will be undertaken in the host institution. This document is mandatory. 5. To be born on or after 1 January 1979. 6. Previously selected candidates can apply for a second grant, but they will not be prioritised
Level of Study: Graduate
Type: Scholarship
Frequency: Annual
Country of Study: Any country
Application Procedure: Kindly check the website for further information. www.coimbra-group.eu/wp-content/uploads/CALL-LA-2019-brochure-1.pdf
Closing Date: 31 March
Funding: Private
Additional Information: The Coimbra Group Office will contact all candidates and inform them about the result of their application by the end of May

For further information contact:

Egmontstraat, 11, rue d'Egmont, BEL 1000 Brussels, Belgium

Tel: (32) 2 513 83 32
Email: Moleiro@coimbra-group.eu

Coimbra Group Scholarship Programme for Young Researchers from the European Neighbourhood

Purpose: The main aim of this scholarship programme is to enable scholars to undertake research in which they are engaged in their home institution and to help them to establish academic and research contacts
Eligibility: Applicants must fulfil all the following criteria: 1. Be Born On Or After 1 January 1984. 2. Be nationals of and current residents in one Of the above-listed countries. 3. Be Current Academic Staff Members Of A University Or An Equivalent Higher Education institution located in one of the above-listed countries and be of postdoctoral or equivalent status, although some institutions may offer opportunities to doctoral student
Level of Study: Graduate

Type: Programme grant
Frequency: Annual
Country of Study: Any country
Application Procedure: 1. Candidates may apply for one university only. Multiple applications will not be considered valid. 2. Only the universities listed in the table below are taking part in the current edition of the Coimbra Group Scholarship Programme. 3. Applicants will be able to fill in the on-line registration until 31 March midnight (Brussels time) on the Coimbra Group website: www.coimbra-group. eu/activities/scholarships
Closing Date: 31 March
Funding: Private

For further information contact:

Email: quici@coimbra-group.eu
Contact: Ms Anna Quici

Coimbra Group Short Stay Scholarship Programme for young researchers

Subjects: The Coimbra Group, which was set up in 1987, is an association of 39 European universities
Purpose: It aims to increase cooperation amongst its members by enhancing special academic and cultural ties, and creating channels of information and exchange
Eligibility: Applicants should be: 1. Born on or after 1 January 1974. 2. Nationals of and current residents in a country in Sub-Saharan Africa. 3. Current staff members of a university or an equivalent higher education institution in Sub-Saharan Africa. 4. Of doctoral/postdoctoral or equivalent status. Eligible countries are all African countries except Algeria, Egypt, Libya, Morocco, and Tunisia (applicants from these countries are eligible under the Scholarship Programme for Young Researchers from the European Neighbourhood
Level of Study: Graduate
Type: Scholarship
Frequency: Annual
Country of Study: Any country
Application Procedure: Online application form is available in the following link. There are two steps of application procedure to be followed. www.coimbra-group.eu/activities/scholarships
Closing Date: 31 March
Funding: Private

For further information contact:

Email: info@coimbra-group.eu

Collegeville Institute for Ecumenical and Cultural Research

14027 Fruit Farm Road, Box 2000, Collegeville, MN 56321, United States of America

Tel:	(1) 320 363 3366
Fax:	(1) 320 363 3313
Email:	staff@collegevilleinstitute.org
Website:	www.collegevilleinstitute.org
Contact:	Donald Ottenhoff, Executive Director

The Institute for Ecumenical and Cultural Research seeks to discern the meaning of Christian identity and unity in a religiously and culturally diverse nation and world and to communicate that meaning for the mission of the church and the renewal of human community. The Institute is committed to research, study, prayer, reflection and dialogue, in a place shaped by the Benedictine tradition of worship and work.

Bishop Thomas Hoyt Jr Fellowship

Subjects: Ecumenical and cultural research
Purpose: To provide the Institute's residency fee to a North American person of colour writing a doctoral dissertation, in order to help the churches to increase the number of persons of colour working in ecumenical and cultural research
Eligibility: Open to a North American, Canadian or Mexican person of colour writing a doctoral dissertation within the general area of the Institute's concern
Level of Study: Postgraduate
Type: Fellowship
Value: US$5,000 per year
Length of Study: 1 academic year
Frequency: Annual
Study Establishment: The Institute
Country of Study: United States of America
No. of awards offered: 1
Application Procedure: Applicants must apply in the usual way to the Resident Scholars Programme (see separate listing). If invited by the admissions committee to be a Resident Scholar, the person will then be eligible for consideration for the Hoyt Fellowship
Closing Date: 1 November and 1 February
Funding: Private
No. of awards given last year: 1
No. of applicants last year: 1

For further information contact:

Tel: (44) 320 363 3367
Email: dottenhoff@collegevilleinstitute.org
Contact: Donald B Ottenhoff, Director

Columbia College of Missouri

Columbia College of Missouri Boone County Endowed Award

Purpose: This award is for Missouri high school seniors who are residents of Boone County and planning to attend Columbia College

Eligibility: Must be a graduating high school senior. Must be a resident of Boone County, MO. 1. Must be a United States citizen or permanent resident. 2. Must demonstrate community service/volunteer work. 3. Must enroll as a full-time student. 4. Must have a cumulative grade point average of 3.1 or higher. 5. Must have an ACT score of 22 or higher or the equivalent SAT score

Level of Study: Graduate
Type: Award
Value: US$1,000
Frequency: Annual
Country of Study: United States of America
Application Procedure: The scholarship is made possible through the support of more than 200 area businesses. Recipients of the award will be chosen by committee in April and will be notified appropriately. Application details are available in the form of pdf. www.ccis.edu/offices/financialaid/booneendowed/boonecountyendowedscholarshipday.pdf. Download the smae and apply physically or online
Closing Date: 31 March
Funding: Private
No. of awards given last year: 5

For further information contact:

1001 Rogers St., Columbia, MO 65216, United States of America

Tel: (1) 573 875 7506
Email: admissions@ccis.edu

Columbia GSAS

Foreign Language and Area Studies Fellowship

Purpose: Administered by the Title VI National Resource Centers at the University of Pennsylvania, the Foreign Language and Area Studies (FLAS) Fellowships program funding to Graduate and Undergraduate Students studying modern foreign languages and related area studies

Eligibility: Students receiving Academic Year Fellowships must be enrolled in full-time study for the duration of the FLAS award and must take one language course and one related area or international studies course each semester. 1. Fellows must be United States Citizens or permanent residents. 2. Academic Year Fellows must be admitted to or enrolled in undergraduate, graduate, or professional programs at the University of Pennsylvania. FLAS awards may be used in some cases for students participating in official overseas language programs and in very limited cases for dissertators

Level of Study: Postgraduate
Type: Fellowship
Frequency: Annual
Country of Study: Any country
Application Procedure: You will need to create a free online Interfolio account and complete the application in that system. In addition to entering information into the account, you will need to upload: 1. A personal statement regarding your planned use of the FLAS fellowship. This is a one-page, single-spaced, essay describing why this language study is essential to realizing your study and career goals. 2. Your curriculum vitae. 3. Unofficial higher education transcript (s) of your most recent academic work, whether at the University of Pennsylvania or another university or college, in digital format. Transcripts may be verified during the review process. 4. Two letters of recommendation (you will request them through the system). When you ask the faculty members for a recommendation, tell them that all letters of recommendation must specifically address how a FLAS would contribute to your current program of study or would be integrated with it
Closing Date: 15 February
Funding: Private

For further information contact:

Email: molliel@sas.upenn.edu

Graduate School of Arts and Sciences International Travel Fellowships

Purpose: Travel Fellowships provide funding for international travel (outside of the United States) that is necessary for the completion of the dissertation. Travel Fellowship funds may not be used for research in residence at Columbia

Eligibility: GSAS International Travel Fellowships are open to PhD students in Arts and Sciences programs who will have completed all of the requirements for the PhD degree

Level of Study: Graduate
Type: Fellowships, operating grants
Frequency: Annual
Country of Study: Any country
Application Procedure: Applications must include the following items: 1. Completed GSAS online application form. 2. An up-to-date GSAS transcript (official PDF transcript from the Registrar's office). Note: The GSAS Fellowship application does not accept encrypted files for upload. Official Columbia transcript PDFs are encrypted; you may order a paper copy through SSOL or print the official transcript PDF you receive from Parchment, then scan and upload it. 3. A curriculum vitae (three pages maximum). 4. A statement of your language preparation for research abroad, specifying the language(s) needed to carry out your research and your proficiency in each (one page maximum). 5. A project proposal of no more than 1,500 words, which should include a justification of your need to travel and a specific discussion of your research plans during the fellowship period. Please do not submit a copy of the departmental dissertation prospectus. Proposals will be read by an inter-departmental faculty committee and should emphasize the potential of your research to make a contribution to the particular field and to scholarship in general. 6. A timetable for completion of research and writing (two pages maximum). Please be as specific as possible. Applicants can apply for only one of the following terms: academic year (fall and spring). 7. Two letters of recommendation. GSAS prefers that recommenders submit their letters of recommendation electronically to expedite processing. 8. A budget proposal
Closing Date: 26 February
Funding: Private
Additional Information: The terms of the GSAS Travel Fellowship prohibit grantees from holding teaching assignments or any other position concurrently

For further information contact:

109 Low Memorial Library, MC 4306, 535 West 116th Street, New York, NY 10027, United States of America

Email: gsas-admissions@columbia.edu

Columbia University

405 Low Library, MC 4335, 535 West 116th Street, New York, NY 10027, United States of America

Tel: (1) 212 854 3830
Fax: (1) 212 854 0274
Email: support@ei.columbia.edu
Website: www.earth.columbia.edu

The Earth Institute at Columbia University brings together talent from throughout the University to address complex issues facing the planet and its inhabitants, with particular focus on sustainable development and the needs of the world's poor.

Benjamin A. Gilman International Scholarship Program

Subjects: The Gilman Program provides grants for undergraduate United States citizens of limited financial means to study and intern abroad, thereby gaining skills critical to our national security and economic prosperity
Purpose: The United States Department of State's Benjamin A. Gilman International Scholarship is a grant program that enables students of limited financial means to study or intern abroad, thereby gaining skills critical to our national security and economic competitiveness
Eligibility: Gilman Scholarships are open to undergraduates in good academic standing at accredited United States colleges and universities who are United States citizens and who meet the following criteria: 1. They are receiving a federal Pell Grant or can provide proof that they will be receiving a Pell Grant at the time of application of during their term of study abroad. 2. They are applying to or have been accepted into a study abroad program eligible for credit at their home institution. 3. They are studying abroad for at least four consecutive weeks in one country. 4. They are studying abroad in any country except a country on the United States Department of State's current Travel Warning list
Level of Study: Postgraduate
Type: Scholarship
Value: Awards of up to US$5,000 for semester or academic year program
Frequency: Annual
Country of Study: Any country
Closing Date: 5 March
Funding: Private

For further information contact:

Gilman Scholarship Program, Institute of International Education, 1800 West Loop South, Suite 250, Houston, TX 77027, United States of America

Tel: (1) 212 853 2375
Fax: (1) 212 854 2797
Email: ugrad-urf@columbia.edu

Knight-Bagehot Fellowships in Economics and Business Journalism at Columbia University

Subjects: Economics and business journalism. journalism. columbia.edu/kb

Purpose: To improve the quality of economics and business journalism through instruction to mid career journalists. jour nalism.columbia.edu/kb

Eligibility: Open to professional journalists globally; journal ism.columbia.edu/kb

Level of Study: Graduate, Postgraduate, MBA

Type: Fellowship

Value: An approximately US$60,000 stipend to cover living expenses, plus tuition for the full academic year at Columbia University

Length of Study: 1 academic year

Frequency: Annual

Study Establishment: School of Journalism, Columbia University

Country of Study: United States of America

No. of awards offered: 100

Application Procedure: Applicants must submit a completed application form, two 1,000 word essays, three letters of reference, and five work samples. journalism.columbia.edu/kb

Closing Date: 31 January

Funding: Corporation, Foundation, Trusts

Contributor: Knight Foundation

No. of awards given last year: 10

No. of applicants last year: 100

Additional Information: journalism.columbia.edu/kb

For further information contact:

Graduate School of Journalism, Columbia University, United States of America

Tel:	(1) 212 854 2711
Fax:	(1) 212 854 7837
Email:	raju.narisetti@columbia.edu
Contact:	Director

Marie Tharp Visiting Fellowships

Subjects: Geosciences, social sciences, engineering and environmental health sciences

Purpose: To provide an opportunity for women scientists to conduct research at one of the related departments within the Earth Institute

Eligibility: Open to women candidates who have obtained their PhD and are citizens of the United States

Level of Study: Doctorate, Research

Type: Fellowships

Value: US$25,000

Length of Study: 3 months

Frequency: Annual

Country of Study: United States of America

Application Procedure: Applicants must submit a 3-page proposal, a curriculum vitae, a proposed budget and complete contact information of 3 references

Closing Date: Check website

Additional Information: All application materials may be submitted by mail or by email

For further information contact:

ADVANCE at The Earth Institute at Columbia University Lamont-Doherty Earth Observatory of Columbia University, United States of America

Email:	kdutt@ldeo.columbia.edu
Contact:	Kuheli Dutt

Commonwealth Eye Health Consortium

International Centre for Eye Health, London School of Hygiene & Tropical Medicine, Keppel Street, WC1E 7HT, London, United Kingdom

Tel:	(44) 20 7636 8636
Email:	press@lshtm.ac.uk
Website:	cehc.lshtm.ac.uk
Contact:	Commonwealth Eye Health Consortium

The Commonwealth Eye Health Consortium is a group of expert organizations working together to deliver a five-year programme of fellowships, research, and technology to strengthen eye health systems across the Commonwealth.

CEHC Masters Scholarships in Public Health for Eye Care

Subjects: Scholarships are awarded to undertake MSc in Public Health for Eye Care

Purpose: The Masters in Public Health for Eye Care at the London School of Hygiene & Tropical Medicine is a well-established course that aims to train leaders in the prevention of blindness and to strengthen research and academic capacity for eye care programmes and training facilities, particularly in low- and middle-income countries

Eligibility: See the website. Entrance Requirement : 1. Come from low or middle-income Commonwealth countries that are less represented in the alumni body of the MSc Public health for eye care. 2. Work in regions where there are severe constraints in human resources for eye health work in regions where there are no / limited training opportunities in PHEC / community eye health. 3. Demonstrate previous involvement/ commitment to community eye health activities or VISION2020 programmes Present a clear career plan in public health for eye care, which they will realistically. 4. Be able to follow on completion of the MSc. 5. Have experience in public health for eye care based research and/or training in eye care. 6. Fulfill the United Kingdom Border Agency English Language Requirement by passing the LSHTM English language requirement by 11 May

Value: Several scholarships are awarded each year. Each scholarship covers the following:All course feesTwo return flightsDissertation project fundLiving costsAccommodation with food at the International Students House in Central London. Find out more about the International Students House

Study Establishment: Scholarships are awarded to undertake MSc in Public Health for Eye Care

Country of Study: United Kingdom

Application Procedure: Apply to the London School of Hygiene & Tropical Medicine for a place on the course: if you have applied and been accepted to the academic year you must request to "be reconsidered" for the academic year. Please contact the LSHTM Registry to be asked to "be reconsidered" Once you have received an offer from the London School of Hygiene & Tropical Medicine here: CEHC; MSc Scholarships Application

Closing Date: 11 May

Additional Information: For more details please browse the website scholarship-positions.com/cehc-masters-scholarships-in-public-health-eye-care-uk/

For further information contact:

Email: Romulo.Fabunan@Lshtm.ac.uk

Commonwealth Fund

1 East 75th Street, NY 10021, United States of America

Tel: (1) 212 606 3800
Fax: (1) 212 606 3500
Email: grants@cmwf.org
Website: www.cmwf.org

The Commonwealth Fund of New York is a philanthropic foundation established in 1918. The Fund supports independent research on health and social issues and makes grants to improve healthcare practice and policy.

Australian-American Health Policy Fellowship

Subjects: Health policy issues in Australia and the United States of America, and shared lessons of both policies

Purpose: To enable Fellows to gain an in-depth understanding of the Australian health care system and policy process, recent reforms, and models for best practice, thus enhancing their ability to make innovative contributions to policymaking in the United States, to improve the theory and practice of health policy in Australia and the United States by stimulating the cross-fertilization of ideas and experience and to encourage ongoing health policy collaboration and exchange between Australia and the United States by creating a network of international health policy experts

Eligibility: Open to accomplished, mid-career health policy researchers and practitioners including academics, physicians, decision makers in managed care and other private organizations, federal and state health officials and journalists

Level of Study: Research

Type: Fellowship

Value: For a full 10-month stay in Australia, the fellowship awards up to A$87,000 which includes a living allowance, relocation expenses, research related travel and conferences, etc. There is also a family supplement available (e.g. up to $26,000 for a partner and two children). Round trip airfares to Australia are also covered

Length of Study: Up to 10 months

Frequency: Annual

Study Establishment: Suitable establishment in Australia

Country of Study: Australia

Application Procedure: Please go to www.commonwealthfund.org/grants-and-fellowships/fellowships/australian-american-health-policy-fellowship/application-form to know complete procedure to apply for this program

Closing Date: 2 October

Funding: Government

Additional Information: In Australia: Director; International Strategies Branch Portfolio Strategies Division Department of Health and Ageing MDP 85 GPO Box 9848 Canberra ACT 2601; Tel: 011 61 2 6289 4593; Fax: 011 61 2 6289 7087. Australian-American Health Policy Fellowships is the successor of the Packer Policy Fellowship Program, which ran from 2003 to 2009. Email at packerpolicyfellowship@health.gov.au

For further information contact:

Email: ro@cmwf.org
Contact: Robin Osborn, Vice President and Director

Harkness Fellowships in Health Care Policy

Subjects: Health care policy
Purpose: To build a network of policy orientated health care researchers whose multinational experience and outlook stimulate innovative policies and practices in the United States and other industrialised countries
Eligibility: Open to Australian, British, and New Zealand citizens. Applicants must be at postgraduate level or have equivalent experience
Level of Study: Postgraduate
Type: Fellowship
Value: Up to US$75,000
Length of Study: 4 months–1 year
Frequency: Annual
Study Establishment: A host institution which is normally, but not exclusively, of an intellectual kind, such as a university graduate school, a research institute or a 'think tank'
Country of Study: United States of America
Application Procedure: Applicants must write for details
Closing Date: 1 October

For further information contact:

Harkness Fellowship in Health Care, Associate Professor & Directo, Center for Health Economics Research & Evaluation, University of Sydney, Mallett Street Campus, 88 Mallett Street Level 6 Building F Camperdown, United States of America

Tel:	(61) 2 9351 0900
Fax:	(61) 2 9351 0930
Email:	mail@chere.usyd.edu.au
Contact:	Dr Jane Hall, Policy Representative

Harkness Fellowships in Healthcare Policy and Practice

Subjects: Healthcare policy and health services research
Purpose: To encourage the professional development of promising healthcare policy researchers and practitioners who will contribute to innovation in healthcare policy and practice in the United States of America and their home countries
Eligibility: Open to individuals who have completed a Master's degree or PhD in health services or health policy research. Applicants must also have shown significant promise as a policy-orientated researcher or practitioner, e.g. physicians or health service managers, journalists and government officials, with a strong interest in policy issues. Candidates should also be at the research Fellow to senior lecturer level, if academically based; be in their late 20s to early 40s, and have been nominated by their department chair or the director of their institution
Level of Study: Postgraduate, Professional development, Research
Type: Fellowship
Value: US$130,000, which covers roundtripairfare to the United States, a living allowance, funds for project-related travel, research, conferences, travel to attend
Length of Study: Up to 1 year. A minimum of 6 months must be spent in the United States of America
Frequency: Annual
Study Establishment: An academic or other research policy institution
Country of Study: United States of America
Application Procedure: Applicants must complete a formal application available online at the website www.cmwf.org/fellowships Applicants must be submitted via email
Closing Date: 6 September (for Australia and New Zealand) and 14 November (Canada, France, Germany, Netherlands, Norway, Sweden and United Kingdom)
Funding: Private
Contributor: The Commonwealth Fund

For further information contact:

Email: mail@chere.usyd.edu.au

The Commonwealth Fund Mongan Fellowship in Minority Health Policy

Subjects: Health policy, public health and management, with special programme activities on minority health issues
Purpose: To create physician-leaders who will pursue careers in minority health policy
Eligibility: Open to physicians who are citizens of the United States of America and who have completed their residency. Additional experience beyond residency is preferred. Applicants must demonstrate an awareness of, or interest and experience in dealing, with the health needs of minority populations, strong evidence of past leadership experience, as related to community efforts and health policy and the intention to pursue a career in public health practice, policy, or academia
Level of Study: Graduate, Postgraduate, Professional development, Research
Type: Fellowship
Value: US$60,000 stipend, full tuition, health insurance, books, travel, and related program expenses, including financial assistance for a practicum project
Length of Study: 1 year
Frequency: Annual
Study Establishment: Harvard Medical School
Country of Study: United States of America

Application Procedure: Applications available online at the website: www.cmwf.org/fellowships
Closing Date: 15 December
Funding: Foundation

For further information contact:

Minority Faculty Development Program, Harvard Medical School, 164 Longwood Avenue, 2nd Floor, United States of America

Tel: (1) 617 432 2922
Email: mfdp_cfhuf@hms.harvard.edu
Contact: JOAN Y. REEDE, Director, CFHUF

Commonwealth Scholarship and Fellowship Plan

Commonwealth Scholarship Commission in the United Kingdom, c/o Association of Commonwealth Universities, John Foster House, 36 Gordon Square, London, WC1H 0PF, United Kingdom
The Plan was drawn up at the first Commonwealth Education Conference held in Oxford in 1959. It is a system of awards for men and women from all Commonwealth countries to study in countries other than their own. One of its guiding principles is that it be based on mutual co-operation

Commonwealth Shared Scholarship Scheme at United Kingdom Universities

Purpose: Commonwealth Shared Scholarships are for candidates from least developed and lower middle income Commonwealth countries, for full-time Master's study on selected courses, jointly supported by United Kingdom universities. The scholarships do not cover undergraduate courses, PhD study, or any pre-sessional English language teaching
Eligibility: 1. Be a citizen of or have been granted refugee status by an eligible Commonwealth country, or be a British Protected Person. 2. Be permanently resident in a developing Commonwealth country. 3. Be available to start your academic studies in the United Kingdom by the start of the United Kingdom academic year in September/October. 4. By October, hold a first degree of at least upper second class (2:1) standard, or a second class degree and a relevant postgraduate qualification (usually a Master's degree). 5. Not have studied or worked for one (academic) year or more in

a developed country. 6. Be unable to afford to study in the United Kingdom without this scholarship
Level of Study: Postdoctorate
Type: Scholarship
Value: £1,330
Length of Study: 1 year
Frequency: Annual
Country of Study: Any country
Application Procedure: Apply online
Closing Date: 14 March
Funding: Foundation

For further information contact:

Woburn House, 20-24 Tavistock Square, WC1H 9HF, London, United Kingdom

Commonwealth Scholarship Commission in the United Kingdom

c/o The Association of Commonwealth Universities, Woburn House, 20;24 Tavistock Square, WC1H 9HF, London, United Kingdom

Tel: (44) 20 7380 6700
Fax: (44) 20 7387 2655
Email: info@cscuk.org.uk
Website: www.dfid.gov.uk/cscuk
Contact: Ms Natasha Lokhun, Communications Officer

The Commonwealth Scholarship Commission (CSC) in the United Kingdom is responsible for managing Britain's contribution to the Commonwealth Scholarship and Fellowship Plan (CSFP). The CSC makes available seven types of award and supports around 700 awards in total annually.

Association of Commonwealth Universities Titular Fellowships

Subjects: All subjects, but preference is given to those fields that are needed in developing countries
Purpose: To enable the universities of the commonwealth to develop the human resources of their institutions and countries through the interchanging of people, knowledge, skills and technologies. Not intended for degree courses, or for immediately postdoctoral programmes

Eligibility: Applicants must be on the staff of member universities under the ACU, the Commonwealth interuniversity organization or working in industry, commerce or public service in a Commonwealth country. Applicant must be within 28–50 years of age
Level of Study: Professional development
Type: Scholarship
Value: UK£5,000 for travel, board, insurance and fees where the approved programme includes a training programme
Length of Study: 6 months
Frequency: Annual
Study Establishment: ACU member university or in industry, commerce or public sector
Country of Study: Commonwealth countries
No. of awards offered: 50
Application Procedure: Candidates must be nominated by executive heads of ACU member universities or by the chief executive officer of a Commonwealth interuniversity organization. Full application details on ACU website
Closing Date: 30 April
Contributor: ACU
No. of awards given last year: 8
No. of applicants last year: 50

For further information contact:

Email: acuawards@acu.ac.uk
Contact: Patrice Ajai-Ajagbe

Community Foundation for Calderdale

Office 158, Dean Clough, Yorkshire HX3 5AX, Halifax, United Kingdom

Tel: (44) 1422 349 700
Fax: (44) 1422 350 017
Email: enquiries@ccfound.co.uk
Website: www.ccfund.co.uk
Contact: Mr Mohammad Aslam, Director of the Board, Grants

W.D. Farr Endowment Fund Grants

Purpose: The Greeley Rotary W. D. Farr Endowment Fund at the Community Foundation Serving Greeley and Weld County welcomes applications and considers grant requests from $500 to $2,500 for the benefit of the youth of Greeley,

Colorado. The W.D. Farr Endowment Fund supports programs in the Greeley area that enhance
Level of Study: Graduate
Type: Grant
Value: US$500 to US$2500
Frequency: Annual
Country of Study: Any country
Application Procedure: Attachment Checklist requires following information to process further proposal. 1. Cover letter. 2. Project budget sheet. 3. Board of Directors list
Closing Date: 31 January
Funding: Private

For further information contact:

2425 35th Avenue, Suite 201, Greeley, CO 80634, United States of America

Email: info@cfsgwc.org

Concordia University

1455 De Maisonneuve Blvd. W., Montréal, QC H3G 1M8, Canada

Tel: (1) 514 848 2424
Fax: (1) 514 848 2812
Website: www.concordia.ca
Contact: Ms Patricia Verret, Graduate Awards Manager

Concordia University is the result of the 1974 merger between Sir George Williams University and Loyola College. The University incorporates superior teaching methods with an interdisciplinary approach to learning and is dedicated to offering the best possible scholarship to the student body and to promoting research beneficial to society

Bank of Montréal Pauline Varnier Fellowship

Subjects: Business and commerce
Purpose: To support graduate students to acquire higher degree in the fields of business and commerce
Eligibility: Open to women with 2 years of cumulative business experience who are entering full-time studies in the MBA program at the John Molson School of Business. Candidates must be Canadian citizens or permanent residents
Level of Study: MBA

Type: Fellowship
Value: C$10,000 per year
Length of Study: 2 years
Frequency: Annual
Study Establishment: Concordia University
Country of Study: Canada
Application Procedure: Applicants must submit a completed application form, three letters of recommendation and official transcripts of all university studies by the closing date
Closing Date: 1 February
Funding: Private
No. of awards given last year: 1
Additional Information: Academic merit is the prime consideration in the granting of the awards

For further information contact:

M.B.A. Program, Faculty of Commerce and Administration, Concordia University, 1455 de Maisonneuve Blvd. W., Canada

Tel:	(1) 848 2424 ext 2717
Email:	gradprograms@jmsb.concordia.ca
Contact:	Graduate Program Director

Congressional Black Caucas Foundation

Congressional Black Caucus Foundation Spouses Visual Arts Scholarship

Purpose: This award is for students with majors in the visual arts including, but not limited to, architecture, ceramics, drawing, fashion, graphic design, illustration, interior design, painting, photography, sketching, video production and other decorative arts
Eligibility: 1. Must be a full-time student. 2. Must be planning to pursue a degree in a field that will lead to a career in the visual arts. The visual arts include architecture, ceramics, drawing, fashion, graphic design, illustration, interior design, painting, photography, sketching, video production and other visual arts. Must have minimum GPA of 2.5 on a 4.0 scale. This award is for United States students
Level of Study: Postgraduate
Type: Scholarship
Value: US$3,000
Frequency: Annual
Country of Study: United States of America
Application Procedure: 1. The online application is available on the Congressional Black Caucus Foundations (CBC) website. During the online application process, the applicant must upload and/or complete the following forms. 2. A personal statement essay from the student (500–1,000 words) that addresses all four (4) of the topics listed on the application in one cohesive essay. 3. Two (2) letters of recommendation (Email addresses will be requested of each recommender for electronic submission of the letter. Hard copy letters will not be accepted.)
Closing Date: 31 March
Funding: Private
Additional Information: Late applications and materials will not be accepted

For further information contact:

1720 Massachusetts Avenue NW, Washington, Columbia 20036, United States of America

Tel:	(1) 202 263 2800
Email:	scholarships@cbcfinc.org

Conseil Européen pour la Recherche Nucléaire European Organization for Nuclear Research

CH-1211, Geneva 23, Switzerland

Tel:	(41) 22 76 784 84
Fax:	(41) 22 767 8710
Email:	recruitment.service@cern.ch
Website:	www.cern.ch

CERN European Laboratory for Particle Physics is the world's leading laboratory in its field, that being the study of the smallest constituents of matter and of the forces that hold them together. The laboratory's tools are its particle accelerators and detectors, which are among the largest and most complex scientific instruments ever built

Conseil Européen pour la Recherche Nucléaire Summer Student Programme

Subjects: Physics, computing and engineering
Purpose: To awaken the interest of undergraduates in CERN's activities by offering them hands-on experience during their long summer vacation
Eligibility: Open to all interested students who have completed at least 3 years of full-time studies at university level
Value: Travel allowance and a daily stipend
Length of Study: 8–13 weeks
Study Establishment: CERN
Country of Study: Switzerland

Application Procedure: A completed application and curriculum vitae along with 2 references must be submitted to CERN

Closing Date: 20 January (check with website)

Additional Information: Please check at home.web.cern.ch/students-educators/summer-student-programme for further details

For further information contact:

Email: jkrich@umich.edu

Conseil Européen pour la Recherche Nucléaire-Japan Fellowship Programme

Subjects: LHC data analysis and physics

Purpose: To support young researchers who are interested in LHC data analysis and physics studies

Eligibility: Applicants should be nationals or permanent residents of Japan and have a doctorate for applicants in experimental or phenomenological physics and/or accelerator science. Candidates who are currently preparing a PhD are eligible to apply. However, they are expected to have obtained their PhD by the time they take up their appointment at CERN

Level of Study: Doctorate

Type: Fellowship

Value: Covers travel expense and insurance coverage

Length of Study: Up to 3 years

Frequency: Annual

Application Procedure: A completed electronic application form along with a curriculum vitae should be submitted

Closing Date: 1 December

Contributor: CERN

Additional Information: Please check at jobs.web.cern.ch/job/10941 for further details

For further information contact:

Email: recruitment.science@cern.ch

Marie Curie Fellowships for Early Stage Training at CERN

Subjects: Scientific training

Purpose: To offer structured scientific and/or technological training and to encourage participants to take up long-term research careers

Eligibility: Open to researchers in the first 4 years of their research activity. Persons who have obtained a doctorate are ineligible

Study Establishment: CERN

Application Procedure: Candidates should register and apply for the Marie Curie Fellowship programme using the CERN e-recruitment system

Contributor: European Comission

For further information contact:

Email: recruitment.service@cern.ch

Conservation Leadership Programme

Conservation Leadership Programme, Birdlife International, Wellbrook Court, Girton Road, Cambridgeshire CB3 0NA, Cambridge, United Kingdom

Tel: (44) 12 2327 7318
Fax: (44) 12 2327 7200
Email: clp@birdlife.org
Website: www.conservationleadershipprogramme.org
Contact: The Programme Manager

Since 1985, the Conservation Leadership Programme has supported and encouraged international conservation projects that address global conservation priorities at a local level. This is achieved through a comprehensive system of advice, training and awards. The programme is managed through a partnership between BP, FFI, CI, WCS and Birdlife International.

Future Conservationist Awards

Subjects: Biodiversity conservation

Purpose: To develop leadership capacity amongst emerging conservationists to address the most pressing conservation issues of our time

Eligibility: The project must address a globally recognized conservation priority, involve people, have host government approval, be run by teams of at least three people, be student-led, have over 50% students registered, last for less than 1 year and take place in Africa, Asia Pacific, Middle East, Eastern Europe, Latin America or the Caribbean

Level of Study: Doctorate, Graduate, Postgraduate

Type: Award

Value: Up to $12,500

Length of Study: Projects should be less than 1 year in length

Frequency: Annual

Country of Study: This is a global programme

No. of awards offered: 360

Application Procedure: Application forms are available from the website. Applications should be made electronically
Closing Date: Please check website
Funding: Private
Contributor: BP, BirdLife International, Conservation International, WildLife Conservation Society, and Fauna and Flora International
No. of awards given last year: 29
No. of applicants last year: 360
Additional Information: Please be sure to check at www.conservationleadershipprogramme.org/FutureConservationist Award.asp often for updated information

For further information contact:

Email: clp@birdlife.org

Conservation Trust

National Geographic Society, 1145 17th Street NW, Washington, DC 20036-4688, United States of America

Email: conservationtrust@ngs.org
Website: www.nationalgeographic.com/conservation

The objective of the Conservation Trust is to support conservation activities around the world as they fit within the mission of the National Geographic Society. The trust will fund projects that contribute significantly to the preservation and sustainable use of the Earth's biological, cultural, and historical resources.

National Geographic Conservation Trust Grant

Subjects: Conservation
Purpose: To support cutting programmes that contribute to the preservation and sustainable use of the Earth's resources
Eligibility: Applicants must provide a record of prior research or conservation action. Researchers planning work in foreign countries should include at least one local collaboration as part of their research teams. Grants recipients are excepted to provide the National Geographic Society with rights of first refusal for popular publication of their findings
Level of Study: Research
Type: Research grant
Value: US$15,000–20,000
Frequency: Annual

Application Procedure: Apply online at www.nationalgeographic.com/explorers/grants-programs/conservation-trust-application
Closing Date: Please check website
Funding: Trusts
Contributor: National Geographic Society

For further information contact:

Conservation Trust, National Geographic Society, 1145 17th Street NW, United States of America

Email: conservationtrust@ngs.org

Consortium for Advanced Research Training in Africa (CARTA)

Consortium for Advanced Research Training in Africa (CARTA), Nairobi, KE, Kenya

Tel: (254) 20 4001000
Email: carta@aphrc.org
Website: www.cartafrica.org/

CARTA's mission is to promote the health and development of African populations through high-quality research on policy-relevant priority issues. The initiative will foster the emergence of vibrant and viable multidisciplinary research hubs of locally-trained internationally recognized scholars.

Consortium for Advanced Research Training in Africa PhD Fellowships

Subjects: The Consortium for Advanced Research Training in Africa (CARTA) is an initiative of nine African universities, four African research institutes, and select northern partners. The multi-disciplinary CARTA program is open to staff of participating institutions who are interested in conducting their PhD research on topics relevant to the broad fields of public and population health
Purpose: CARTA offers an innovative model for doctoral training in sub-Saharan Africa to strengthen the capacity of participating institutions to conduct and lead internationally-competitive research
Eligibility: A Masters degree in a relevant field, Prior admission into a PhD program is not required for application but awards are contingent on such admission being obtained at one of the participating African universities, Male applicants

must be under the age of 40 years and female applicants under the age 45 years
Level of Study: Postgraduate
Type: Fellowship
Value: Fellowships cover tuition fees, medical insurance and other university fees in special circumstances only
Length of Study: The fellowship runs for a maximum of 4 years
Country of Study: Africa
Closing Date: Check the website
Funding: International office
Additional Information: Please check website for more details

For further information contact:

Email: carta@aphrc.org

Consortium for Applied Research on International Migration

PO Box 616, NLD, MD 6200, Maastricht, Netherlands

Email: secretariaat-carim@maaastrichtuniversity.nl

CARIM is one of the top institutes for translational cardiovascular research in Europe. It is among the world leaders in the fields of research into vascular and thrombotic disorders and atrial fibrillation as well as translational heart failure research. It has also made important international contributions to molecular imaging in the cardiovascular field.

Consortium for Applied Research on International Migration Postdoctoral Talent Fellowship

Subjects: The "CARIM - Postdoctoral Talent Fellowship" has been designed to support talented CARIM PhD students in realising an ambitious, innovative and international one-year research project as a postdoc. The "CARIM - Postdoctoral Talent Fellowship" is intended for recently graduated CARIM PhD students
Purpose: Purpose is to provide recently promoted top CARIM talent a chance to gain experience abroad and return to CARIM to perform excellent research
Eligibility: For eligibility details, please visit the website www.scholarshipsupdates.com/carim-postdoctoral-talent-fellowship-for-international-students-to-study-abroad/

Value: The fellowship amounts to € 53,011gross which is meant for a period of 12 months. Bench fees are not included in this fellowship. The fellowship includes one return flight to the host institute (based on economy fare)
Country of Study: Any country
Application Procedure: There will be one call a year, and the deadline for the "CARIM - Postdoctoral Talent Fellowship" is the 13th of May, 00.00 hours. To apply for the "CARIM - Postdoctoral Talent Fellowship", the applicants from within (or connected to) CARIM are invited to submit an application (by mail) to the CARIM office (secretariaat-carim-at-maastrichtuniversity.nl)
Closing Date: 13 of May every year

For further information contact:

Email: secretariaat-carim@maastrichtuniversity.nl

Cooperative Research Centre for Water Quality and Treatment (CRCWQT)

Australia Water Quality Centre, Private Mail Bag 3, Salisbury, SA 5108, Australia

Tel: (61) 8 8259 0326
Fax: (61) 8 8259 0228
Email: dennis.steffensen@sawater.com.au
Website: www.waterquality.crc.org.au
Contact: Professor Dennis Mulcahy, Training Leader

The Cooperative Research Centre for Water Quality and Treatment (CRCWQT) provides a national strategic research capacity for the Australian water industry and focuses on issues relating to water quality management and health risk reduction.

Cooperative Research Center for Water Quality and Treatment Young Water Scientist of the Year Scholarship

Subjects: Agriculture and natural resources, environmental studies and sciences
Purpose: To provide support to PhD students for research done within the Water Forum CRC
Eligibility: Open to candidates who are in the final year of their PhD
Level of Study: Doctorate
Type: Scholarship

Value: A$2,500
Length of Study: 1 year
Frequency: Annual
Country of Study: Australia

For further information contact:

Email: detr@wmo.int

Copenhagen Business School

Solbjerg Plads 3, DNK 2000 Frederiksberg, Denmark

Tel: (45) 3815 3815
Email: cbs@cbs.dk
Website: www.cbs.dk

Copenhagen Business School PhD Scholarship on IT Management

Subjects: Information technology management
Eligibility: To be considered, the candidate should have a basic training at the Masters level (similar to the 3 + 2 Bologna process). An educational background in the social sciences is necessary. The applicant must have successfully completed the Masters degree before commencing PhD at CBS. The applicants must be fluent in English
Level of Study: Doctorate, Research
Type: Scholarship
Value: The scholarships are fully salaried positions, according to the national Danish collective agreement. The scholarship includes the tuition fees, office space, travel grants, plus a salary, currently starting with per month approx. DKK 23,770 (approx. €3,160) up to DKK 28,964 (approx. €3,860) depending on seniority, plus a pension contribution totalling 17.1% of 85% of the base salary
Length of Study: 3 years
Country of Study: Denmark
Application Procedure: Application must be sent via the electronic recruitment system. The application must include a 5-page project description. This research proposal should contain a presentation of an original research question, a description of the initial theoretical framework and methodology, a presentation of the suggested empirical material as well as a work plan. In addition to the research proposal, the application must include copies of a Master's degree certificate or other certificates of a corresponding level, brief curriculum vitae, a list of papers and publications, and one copy of a selected written work (e.g. Master's thesis)
Closing Date: 28 February

Contributor: Copenhagen Business School
Additional Information: The scholarship requires the student to spend a minimum of 12 months of their PhD programme in a research institution in China. Countries of study are Denmark and China

For further information contact:

Email: dsi.msc@cbs.dk

Core

3 St Andrew's Place, NW1 4LB, London, United Kingdom

Tel: (44) 20 7486 0341
Fax: (44) 20 7487 3734
Email: info@corecharity.org.uk
Website: www.corecharity.org.uk
Contact: Alice Kington, Finance and Research Manager

Core, the Digestive Disorders Foundation, supports research into the cause, prevention and treatment of digestive disorders, including digestive cancers, ulcers, irritable bowel syndrome, inflammatory bowel disease, diverticulitis, liver disease and pancreatitis. Core also provides information for the public that explains the symptoms and treatment of these and other common digestive conditions.

Core Fellowships and Grants

Subjects: Gastroenterology, such as basic or applied clinical research into normal and abnormal aspects of the gastrointestinal tract, liver and pancreas, and the prevention of and treatment for digestive disorders
Purpose: To provide funding for gastroenterological research
Eligibility: Open to applicants resident within the United Kingdom. Fellowship projects must contain an element of basic science training
Level of Study: Doctorate, Postdoctorate, Postgraduate, Research
Type: Fellowship or Grant
Value: UK£50,000 per year salary and £10,000 per year consumables (Research Fellowships); £50,000 total (Development Grants)
Length of Study: 1–3 years
Frequency: Dependent on funds available
Study Establishment: Recognized and established research centres
Country of Study: United Kingdom
No. of awards offered: Varies

Application Procedure: Applicants must complete an application form for consideration in a research competition. Details are available from the website

Closing Date: Varies

Funding: Commercial, Private, Foundation, Trusts, Individuals

Contributor: Charitable donations

No. of awards given last year: 4

No. of applicants last year: Varies

Additional Information: Conditions are advertised on the core website www.corecharity.org.uk. Research grants are awarded for specific projects in the same field of interest

For further information contact:

Email: IAS_applications@ceu.edu

Council for British Archaeology (CBA)

St. Mary's House, 66 Bootham, Y030 7BZ, York, United Kingdom

Tel:	(44) 19 0467 1417
Fax:	(44) 19 0467 1384
Email:	info@britarch.ac.uk
Website:	www.britarch.ac.uk
Contact:	The Finance Director

The Council for British Archaeology (CBA) has been campaigning for the better care of Britain's archaeology for over 50 years. It works to improve awareness and enjoyment of archaeology for the benefit of all. The Council is the leading point of contact for information about the United Kingdom's historic environment.

Catholic Biblical Association Grant for Publication

Subjects: British archaeology

Purpose: To finance archaeological publications that contribute significantly to research on problems of national or special regional significance

Eligibility: Open to the general public, except those already in receipt of a direct government grant

Level of Study: Unrestricted

Type: Grant

Value: Usually no more than UK £1,000 but on average UK £400

Frequency: 3 times each year

Country of Study: United Kingdom

Application Procedure: Applicants must request an application form

Closing Date: 1 April, 1 July or 1 December

Additional Information: No grant will be made for the publication of records or of publications based exclusively on records, or for the publication of excavation reports where the excavation has been financed by government agencies. Grants will not normally be given to finance reports other than final excavation reports

For further information contact:

Email: cba-office@cua.edu

Council of American Overseas Research Centers (CAORC)

PO Box 37012, MRC 178, Washington, DC 20013 7012, United States of America

Tel:	(1) 202 633 1599
Fax:	(1) 202 786 2430
Email:	fellowships@caorc.org
Website:	www.caorc.org

Council of American Overseas Research Centers (CAORC) serve as a base for virtually every American scholar undertaking research in the host countries. The members have centres in many locations across the world.

Council of American Overseas Research Centers Andrew W. Mellon East-Central European Research Fellows

Subjects: Humanities and allied social sciences

Purpose: To help scholars in the humanities and allied social sciences to carry out research at institutes of advanced study in other countries

Eligibility: Open to candidates who have obtained a PhD and are nationals of Bulgaria, Czech, Estonia, Hungary, Latvia, Lithuania, Poland, Romania or Slovakia

Level of Study: Research

Type: Fellowships

Value: Varies

Length of Study: Short-term residencies
Frequency: Annual
Country of Study: Any country

For further information contact:

Email: fellowships@caorc.org

Council of American Overseas Research Centers Multi-Country Research Fellowship Program for Advanced Multi-Country Research

Subjects: Humanities, social sciences or allied natural sciences
Purpose: To advance higher learning and scholarly research and to conduct research of regional or trans-regional significance
Eligibility: Applicants must have obtained a PhD or be established postdoctoral scholars. The candidate should be a citizen of the United States. Preference will be given to Candidates examining comparative and/or cross-regional research
Level of Study: Doctorate, Postdoctorate, Research
Type: Fellowships
Value: Up to US$10,500
Frequency: Annual
Country of Study: Any country
No. of awards offered: 120
Application Procedure: The application can be downloaded from the website. To obtain hard copy of the application, please contact CAORC
Closing Date: January
Contributor: United States State Department
No. of awards given last year: 9
No. of applicants last year: 120
Additional Information: Scholars must carry out research in at least one of the countries that host overseas research centres. Please check website for further information

For further information contact:

Email: fellowships@caorc.org

Council of American Overseas Research Centers NEH RESEARCH FELLOWSHIPS

Purpose: The National Endowment for the Humanities (NEH) Senior Research Fellowship supports advanced research in the humanities. Fellowship awards are for four consecutive months

Eligibility: 1. Applicants must be United States citizens or foreign nationals who have resided in the United States for three years prior to the application deadline. 2. Applicants must be postdoctoral scholars. 3. Funding is not available for research conducted in the United States. 4. It is not required that you be affiliated with a United States academic institution to apply
Level of Study: Graduate
Type: Fellowship
Value: US$4,200
Frequency: Annual
Country of Study: Any country
Closing Date: 24 January
Funding: Foundation

For further information contact:

Email: fellowships@caorc.org

Council of Independent Colleges

One Dupont Circle, N.W, Suite 320, Washington, DC 20036-1142, United States of America

Tel: (1) 202 466 7230
Email: visitingfellows@cic.nche.edu
Website: www.cic.org/projects_services/visitingfellows.asp
Contact: Michelle Friedman, Program Manager

Woodrow Wilson Visiting Fellows

Subjects: All subjects
Purpose: To encourage the flow of ideas between the academic and non-academic sectors of society
Level of Study: Postgraduate
Type: Fellowships
Value: US$5,000
Length of Study: 1 year
Frequency: Annual
Application Procedure: Contact the Foundation
Funding: Private
Contributor: Lilly Endowment

For further information contact:

Visiting Fellows Program, United States of America

Tel: (1) 609 452 7007 ext. 181
Email: sanford@woodrow.org
Contact: Beverly Sanford, Director

Council of Supply Chain Management Professionals (CSCMP)

333 East Butterfield Road, Suite 140, Lombard, IL 60148, United States of America

Tel: (1) 630 574 0985
Fax: (1) 630 574 0989
Email: membership@cscmp.org
Website: www.cscmp.org
Contact: Kathleen Hedland, Director Education and Roundtable Services

The Council of Supply Chain Management Professionals (CSCMP) is a non-profit organization of business personnel who are interested in improving their logistics management skills. CSCMP works in co-operation with private industry and various organizations to further the understanding and development of the logistics concept. This is accomplished through a continuing programme of organized activities, research and meetings designed to develop the theory and understanding of the logistics process, promote the art and science of managing logistics systems, and foster professional dialogue and development within the profession.

Council of Supply Chain Management Professionals Distinguished Service Award

Subjects: Supply chain management and logistics
Purpose: To provide honor to an individual for achievement in supply chain management
Eligibility: All individuals who have made contributions to the field of supply chain management are eligible for the DSA. This includes practitioners with responsibilities in a functional area of supply chain management, consultants and educators-anyone who has made a significant contribution to the advancement of supply chain management. Please check at cscmp.org/career/awards/distinguished-service-award-process for more detailed information
Type: Award
Frequency: Annual
Application Procedure: Nominations must be accompanied by a fully completed nomination form and should be emailed to Sue Paulson
Closing Date: 30 April

For further information contact:

Tel: (1) 630 645 3469
Email: spaulson@cscmp.org
Contact: Sue Paulson

Council of Supply Chain Management Professionals Doctoral Dissertation Award

Subjects: Any supply chain function
Purpose: To encourage research leading to advancement of the theory and practice to supply chain management
Eligibility: Open to all candidates whose doctoral dissertation demonstrates signified originality and contributes to the logistics knowledge base. See cscmp.org/downloads/public/education/awards/dda-guidelines.pdf for details
Level of Study: Postdoctorate
Type: Award
Value: US$5,000
Frequency: Annual
Closing Date: May

For further information contact:

Email: kmcinerney@cscmp.org
Contact: Kathy McInerney, Education and Research Assistant

Supply Chain Innovation Award

Subjects: Supply chain
Purpose: CSCMP's Research Strategies Committee (RSC) and Supply Chain Brain established the Supply Chain Innovation Award in 2005 to highlight and recognize the top players in the supply chain industry when it comes to innovative programs, projects and collaboration
Eligibility: The submitting company must be a CSCMP member. In addition, each member of your team must be registered for the annual conference by August 1st. All travel, accommodations, and related expenses are the responsibilities of the finalist teams
Type: Scholarship
Frequency: Annual
Application Procedure: While the finalist teams present their case studies, the panel of judges evaluates the session as it happens live in front of the audience of conference attendees
Closing Date: Check website
Funding: Private
Contributor: CSCMP's Research Strategies Committee (RSC) and Supply Chain Brain
Additional Information: Please check complete guidelines at cscmp.org/career/awards/supply-chain-innovation-award-competition-guidelines

For further information contact:

Tel: (1) 630 645 3454
Email: cscmpresearch@cscmp.org
Contact: Heather Wood, CSCMP Education Services Coordinator

Council on Foreign Relations (CFR)

The Harold Pratt House, 58 East 68th Street, New York, NY 10065, United States of America

Tel:	(1) 212 434 9400
Fax:	(1) 212 434 9800
Email:	fellowships@cfr.org
Website:	www.cfr.org
Contact:	Janine Hill, Director, Fellowship Affairs and Studies

The Council on Foreign Relations (CFR) is dedicated to increasing America's understanding of the world and contributing ideas to United States foreign policy. The Council accomplishes this mainly by promoting constructive debates and discussions, clarifying world issues and publishing Foreign Affairs, the leading journal on global issues.

Council on Foreign Relations International Affairs Fellowship in Japan

Subjects: International relations
Purpose: To cultivate the United State's understanding of Japan and to strengthen communication between emerging leaders of the two nations
Eligibility: Open to citizens of the United States aged 27–45 who have not had prior substantial experience in Japan. Fellows will be drawn from academia, government institutions, the business community and the media. The programme does not fund pre- or postdoctoral scholarly research, work towards a degree or the completion of projects on which substantial progress has been made prior to the fellowship period. Knowledge of the Japanese language is not a requirement
Level of Study: Professional development
Type: Fellowship
Value: Living expenses in Japan plus international transportation, health and travel insurance and necessary research expenses
Length of Study: 3-12 months
Frequency: Annual
Country of Study: Japan
No. of awards offered: 6
Application Procedure: Application is primarily by invitation, on the recommendation of individuals in academic, government and other institutions who have occasion to know candidates particularly well suited for the experience offered by this fellowship. Others who inquire directly and who meet preliminary requirements may also be invited to

apply without formal nomination. Those invited to apply will be forwarded application materials
Closing Date: Between 1 July and 31 October
Funding: Private
Contributor: Hitachi Limited
No. of awards given last year: 3
No. of applicants last year: 6
Additional Information: While the Fellow is not required to produce a book, article or report, it is hoped that some written output will result. Please check at www.cfr.org/thinktank/fellowships/iaf_japan.html for more information

For further information contact:

Fellowship Affairs, Council on Foreign Relations, 58 East 68th Street, United States of America

Tel:	(1) 212 434 9489
Fax:	(1) 212 434 9870
Email:	fellowships@cfr.org

Council on Library and Information Resources (CLIR)

1707 L Street, NW Suite 650, Washington, DC 20036, United States of America

Tel:	(1) 202 939 4750/4751
Fax:	(1) 202 939 4765
Email:	abishop@clir.org
Website:	www.clir.org
Contact:	Alice Bishop, Senior Program Officer

CLIR is an independent, nonprofit organization that forges strategies to enhance research, teaching, and learning in collaboration with libraries, cultural institutions, and communities of higher learning.

Council on Library and Information Resources Postdoctoral Fellowship

Subjects: The program offers recent PhDs in the sciences, social sciences, and humanities opportunities to develop as scholars, scientists, and teachers while learning about modern librarianship, instructional technologies, research data management, data curation, digital humanities, e-publishing, archives, and/or collection development
Purpose: The CLIR Postdoctoral Fellowship Program offers recent PhD graduates the chance to develop research tools,

resources, and services while exploring new career opportunities. CLIR Postdoctoral Fellows work on projects that forge and strengthen connections among library collections, educational technologies, and current research. Host institutions benefit from fellows' field-specific expertise by gaining insights into their collections' potential uses and users, scholarly information behaviors, and current teaching and learning practices

Eligibility: Applicants must have received a PhD in a discipline no more than five years before applying; if a PhD has not yet been received, all work toward the degree (including dissertation defense and final dissertation editing) must be completed before starting the fellowship. Applicants can be citizens of any country but MUST be legally permitted to work in the United States and/or Canada
Level of Study: Postdoctorate
Type: Postdoctoral fellowship
Value: Varies by host institution
Length of Study: 2 years
Frequency: Annual
Country of Study: United States of America & Canada
No. of awards offered: 115
Application Procedure: Complete an online application www.clir.org/fellowships/postdoc/applicants/
Closing Date: 10 January
Funding: Private, Foundation
Contributor: Alfred P. Sloan Foundation, Andrew W. Mellon Foundation, individual host institutions
No. of awards given last year: 15
No. of applicants last year: 115

For further information contact:

Email: abishop@clir.org
Contact: Alice Bishop

Cranfield University

School of Applied Sciences, Bedfordshire, MK43 OAL, Bedfordshire, United Kingdom

Tel: (44) 1234 754086
Fax: (44) 1234 754109
Email: info@cranfield.ac.uk
Website: www.cranfield.ac.uk/sas
Contact: Vicky Mason, Online Marketing Manager

The School of Applied Sciences is recognized globally for its multidisciplinary approach to teaching and research in the key areas of manufacturing, materials, and environmental science and technology. Our focus is on fundamental research and its application, together with teaching, to meet the needs of industry and society.

Cranfield Global Manufacturing Leadership Masters Scholarship

Type: Scholarship
Value: Tuition fee plus £1,000 cash
Country of Study: United Kingdom
Application Procedure: A number of Cranfield's full-time Manufacturing programme MSc courses are applicable to the Global Manufacturing Leadership (GML) Scholarships, please see the course list above. Applicants should submit a normal Cranfield application through the online application system. The online application forms part of the evaluation of academic achievement. Note the 6-digit online application number
Closing Date: 17 March
Funding: Private

For further information contact:

Email: gmlscholarship@cranfield.ac.uk

Cranfield Merit Scholarship in Leadership and Management

Eligibility: Sub-Saharan African countries are eligible
Type: Scholarship
Value: £4,000 for tuition fees
Country of Study: United Kingdom
Application Procedure: For application details, send an email to studysom@cranfield.ac.uk
Closing Date: 25 May

For further information contact:

Email: studysom@cranfield.ac.uk

Cranfield Sub-Saharan Africa Merit Scholarship

Subjects: Science, engineering, technology, and management
Purpose: To commence full-time study in one of the eligible master courses for the current academic year
Type: Scholarship
Value: £4,000 for tuition fees
Frequency: Annual

Country of Study: Any country
Closing Date: 25 May

For further information contact:

Email: studysom@cranfield.ac.uk

Global Manufacturing Leadership Masters Scholarships

Purpose: The scholarships aim to contribute to the education of young professionals with the capabilities required to lead Manufacturing into the future
Eligibility: Applicants can be from any country. Please note Erasmus funded students are not eligible for this scholarship
Type: Scholarship
Value: The scholarship pays for the Cranfield Manufacturing Masters tuition fee and a £1000 cash maintenance grant
Country of Study: Any country
Application Procedure: Applicants can be from any country. Please note Erasmus funded students are not eligible for this scholarship
Closing Date: 17 March

For further information contact:

Email: gmlscholarship@cranfield.ac.uk

The Diamond Education Grant

Purpose: Its purpose is to provide grants to assist women to update their skills after employment breaks or to acquire new skills to improve their opportunities for employment and promotion
Type: Grant
Value: Small grants towards tuition fees and other study costs
Frequency: Annual
Country of Study: Any country
Application Procedure: Apply online at the Diamond Education Grant website
Closing Date: 15 April
Contributor: Soroptimist International

For further information contact:

Soroptimist International Great Britain & Ireland (SIGBI) Ltd, 2nd Floor, Beckwith House, 1-3 Wellington Road North, SK4 1AF, Stockport, United Kingdom

Tel: (44) 161 480 7686
Email: hq@sigbi.org

The Lorch Foundation MSc Student Bursary

Subjects: Available to students wishing to study full-time MSc Water and Wastewater Engineering or MSc Water Management
Purpose: To assist postgraduate study
Eligibility: Applicants should be United Kingdom citizens and possess a minimum 2:1 United Kingdom Honours degree in Engineering or Physical Sciences or related discipline, and have been offered a place on the 1-year full-time MSc in Water and Wastewater Engineering or Water and Wastewater Technology
Level of Study: Postgraduate
Type: Bursary
Value: UK£5,000 plus tuition fees
Length of Study: 1 year
Frequency: Annual
Study Establishment: Cranfield University, School of Applied Sciences
Country of Study: United Kingdom
Application Procedure: Applicants must apply directly to the university
Closing Date: 31 July
Funding: Foundation
Contributor: The Lorch Foundation
No. of awards given last year: 1
Additional Information: The bursary is provided by the Lorch Foundation, a charitable institution founded to support and promote education and research in the field of water purification and related sciences for the benefit of mankind. The successful applicant will undertake thesis research on processes of water purification and industrial effluent recycling as part of the MSc programme

For further information contact:

Email: appliedsciences@cranfield.ac.uk

Water MSc Scholarship for Students from Malawi and Vietnam

Purpose: The aim of the scholarship is to recruit students across all of our areas of academic specialisms with expertise in a wide range of disciplines to pursue MSc programme
Eligibility: The scholarship is open to students from Malawi and Vietnam
Value: The Cranfield Water Scholarship provides funding of £6,000 towards tuition fees
Country of Study: Any country
Closing Date: 25 May

For further information contact:

Email: studywater@cranfield.ac.uk

Women as Cyber Leaders Scholarship

Subjects: Science, engineering, technology and management
Purpose: For female students wishing to develop a career in Cyber
Type: Postgraduate scholarships
Value: £6,500 toward tuition fees
Country of Study: United Kingdom
Application Procedure: For eligibility and application details, please visit website www.cranfield.ac.uk/funding/funding-opportunities/women-as-cyber-leaders-scholarship
Closing Date: 30 June
Contributor: Cranfield Defence and Security

For further information contact:

Email: cdsadmissionsoffice@cranfield.ac.uk

Crohn's and Colitis Foundation of America

386 Park Avenue South, 17th Floor, NY 10016, United States of America

Tel: (1) 800 932 2423
Fax: (1) 212 779 4098
Email: info@ccfa.org
Website: www.ccfa.org/

Crohn's & Coltis Foundation Career Development Award

Purpose: To stimulate and encourage innovative research that is likely to increase our understanding of the aetiology, pathogenesis, therapy and preventive of Crohn's Disease and Ulcerative Clotis (IBD)
Eligibility: Candidates should hold an MD, must have 5 years of experience (with 2 years of research relevant to IBD)
Level of Study: Postdoctorate, Research
Type: Fellowship
Value: Not to exceed US$90,000 per year
Length of Study: 1–3 years
Frequency: Annual
Study Establishment: Approved research institute
Country of Study: United States of America
Application Procedure: See details at this link: www.crohnscolitisfoundation.org/sites/default/files/2019-06/CDA Guidelines2019.pdf
Closing Date: 14 January and 1 July
Funding: Corporation, Foundation, Individuals

For further information contact:

Crohn's & Colitis foundation of America, 386 park avenue south, 17th floor, United States of America

Tel: (1) 212-685-3440 / 800-932-2423
Email: info@icfa.org

Crohn's & Coltis Foundation Research Fellowship Awards

Subjects: Crohn's Disease and Ulcerative Clotis (IBD)
Level of Study: Predoctorate, Research
Funding: Corporation, Foundation, Individuals

Crohn's & Coltis Foundation Senior Research Award

Subjects: Crohn's Disease and Ulcerative Clotis (IBD)
Purpose: To stimulate and encourage innovative research that is likely to increase our understanding of the aetiology, pathogenesis, therapy and preventive of Crohnapos;s Disease and Ulcerative Clotis (IBD)
Eligibility: Applicants should be researchs who hold an MD, PhD or equivalent
Level of Study: Predoctorate, Research
Type: Research award
Value: Up to US$1,00,000 direct cost per year plus indirect cost of 15% of direct cost (or US$15,000, whichever is less)
Length of Study: Up to 2 years
Frequency: Annual
Study Establishment: Approved research institute
Country of Study: United States of America
Application Procedure: All completed applications must include one CD ROM or disk in PDF or word format, one master and four copies collected in order per check list. The complete application must be complied and saved as a single document
Closing Date: 14 January and 1 July
Funding: Corporation, Foundation, Individuals

Croucher Foundation

Suite 501, Nine Queen's Road Central, Hong Kong

Tel: (852) 2 736 6337
Fax: (852) 2 730 0742
Email: cfadmin@croucher.org.hk
Website: www.croucher.org.hk
Contact: Ms Elaine Sit, Administrative Officer

Founded to promote education, learning and research in the areas of natural sciences, technology and medicine, the Croucher Foundation operates a scholarship and fellowship scheme for individual applicants who are permanent residents of Hong Kong wishing to pursue doctoral or postdoctoral research overseas. The Foundation otherwise makes grants to institutions only.

Croucher Foundation PhD Scholarships and Postdoctoral Fellowships

Subjects: Natural Sciences, Technology and Medicine
Purpose: Our goal is to identify and support a group of talented Hong Kong students and early-career researchers who, through a process of intensive education and exposure to prominent academics in their respective fields, will develop independent and critical abilities and form enduring collaborative partnerships, to enable them to become next generation of leaders of science, technology and medicine in Hong Kong. Eligibility under the following programmes is restricted to permanent Hong Kong residents
Eligibility: 1. Fellows must be full-time research workers. 2. All applicants must disclose offers of financial support received, or likely to be received, from other sources. Applicants and Fellowship holders must keep the Foundation informed of the progress of applications for support from other sources. Croucher Fellowships are on occasion, and at the discretion of the Foundation as an exception, allowed to be held concurrently with other minor awards. 3. The Foundation occasionally gives approval for Fellows to be remunerated for a limited amount of teaching or research responsibilities but such Fellows must seek approval in advance from the Foundation which may in its absolute discretion modify the terms of the Fellowship
Level of Study: Doctorate, Postdoctorate
Type: Scholarships and fellowships
Value: an annual maintenance allowance has been set to USD48,240 per annum. one economy class single air fare and a one-off arrival allowance of USD1,000
Length of Study: for 3 years PhD studies up to the third year of relevant programme
Frequency: Annual
Country of Study: Any country
Closing Date: 15 November
Funding: Foundation
Additional Information: For further inquiries, check the website croucher.org.hk/funding/study_awards/postdoctoral_fellowships

For further information contact:

Croucher Foundation, Suite 501, Nine Queen's Road Central, Hong Kong

Email: cfadmin@croucher.org.hk

Culinary Trust

PO Box 5485, Portland, OR 10013, United States of America

Tel: (1) 97228-5485
Email: scholarships@theculinarytrust.org
Website: www.theculinarytrust.org/

The Culinary Trust has been the philanthropic partner to over 4,000 members of the International Association of Culinary Professionals (IACP) for over 20 years. The Trust solicits, manages and distributes funds for educational and charitable programmes related to the culinary industry in many areas.

L'Academie de Cuisine Culinary Arts Scholarship

Subjects: Culinary arts
Purpose: To financially prospective students prospective students for the Culinary Arts Program each year
Eligibility: Open to a student pre-enroled for the 12 months, Culinary Arts or Pastry Arts Certificate Program
Type: Scholarship
Value: US$5,000
Length of Study: 1 year
Application Procedure: Check the website for further details
Closing Date: December
Additional Information: Scholarship is valid for enrollment during July or October only

For further information contact:

Tel: (1) 646 224 6989
Email: scholarships@theculinarytrust.org
Contact: Amy Blackburn, Director of Administration for The Culinary Trust

The Julia Child Endowment Fund Scholarship

Subjects: Culinary arts
Purpose: To support a career professional to conduct independent study and research in France, as it relates to French food, wine, history, culture and traditions. This programme also

encourages, enables and assists aspiring students and career professionals to advance their knowledge of the culinary arts
Eligibility: Open to applicants who have 2 years of food service experience
Level of Study: Professional development
Type: Scholarship
Value: US$5,000
Frequency: Annual
Country of Study: France
Application Procedure: Applicants are required to include a three-page project proposal, an itemized budget detailing the use of this award, a tentative travel schedule with dates and locations, and provide a current curriculum vitae to qualify for this scholarship
Closing Date: 15 December
Funding: Trusts
Additional Information: Please check website for more details

For further information contact:

Email: foodwine@bu.edu

Zwilling, J.A. Henckels Culinary Arts Scholarship

Subjects: Culinary arts
Purpose: To provide financial assistance to students from designated states who are interested in pursuing a degree in the culinary arts
Eligibility: Open to any pre-enroled student, currently enroled student or career professional toward any culinary arts degree or certificate program at any nationally accredited culinary school
Level of Study: Postgraduate
Type: Scholarship
Value: US$5,000
Application Procedure: Check the website for further details
Closing Date: 15 December
Contributor: Zwilling, J.A. Henckels Trust

For further information contact:

Email: scholarships@theculinarytrust.org

Cultural Vistas

440 Park Avenue South, 2nd Floor (between 29th and 30th Streets), NY 10016, United States of America

Tel: (1) 212 497 3500
Fax: (1) 212 497 3535
Email: info@culturalvistas.org
Website: www.culturalvistas.org/

CDS International, Inc. is a non-profit organization that administers work exchange programmes. CDS International's goal is to further the international exchange of knowledge and technological skills, and to contribute to the development of a pool of highly trained and interculturally experienced business, academic and government leaders.

Robert Bosch Foundation Fellowship Program

Subjects: Business administration, journalism, law, public policy and closely related fields
Purpose: To support young Americans the opportunity to complete a high-level professional development program in Germany
Eligibility: Candidates for the Robert Bosch Foundation Fellowship Program must meet the following requirements: United States citizen; 23–34 years old at the application deadline; at least 2 years of relevant work experience; graduate degree or equivalent training in business administration, journalism, law, public policy, international relations or a closely related field; evidence of outstanding professional performance and community involvement; no German language skills are required at time of application; however, the willingness and commitment to participate in language training based on the results of an evaluation at the selection meeting is essential; most Bosch fellows are required to complete 4 months of private tutoring in the United States (up to 8 hours per week) and 3 months of intensive language training in Berlin prior to the start of the program. All language training is funded by Robert Bosch Stiftung
Level of Study: Graduate, Unrestricted
Type: Fellowship
Value: €2,000 per month stipend. See www.cdsintl.org/fellowshipsabroad/bosch.php for more details
Length of Study: 9 months
Frequency: Annual
Application Procedure: Application form and supporting documents
Closing Date: 15 October
Funding: Private

For further information contact:

Email: bosch@culturalvistas.org

Curtin University

Kent Street, Bentley, Perth, WA 6102, Australia

Contact: Curtin University

Curtin University is an Australian public research university based in Bentley and Perth, Western Australia. The university is named after the 14th Prime Minister of Australia, John Curtin, and is the largest university in Western Australia, with over 58,000 students (as of 2016).

Association of Firearm and Tool Mark Examiners Scholarship

Purpose: The scholarships listed here are offered to Curtin students by external organisations and individuals (Scholarship Providers) that are not affiliated with Curtin University. Curtin University cannot vouch for the accuracy of the information provided by these scholarship providers. All enquiries should be directed to the relevant scholarship provider

Eligibility: Scholarship is available for pursuing undergraduate and postgraduate degree program

Level of Study: Postgraduate

Type: Scholarship

Value: US$2,000

Length of Study: 3 year

Frequency: Annual

Country of Study: Any country

Closing Date: 1 April

Funding: International office

For further information contact:

Email: AFTEScholarship@gmail.com

Three-year Fully Funded PhD Scholarship in Public Health

Subjects: Scholarship is awarded to conduct health services research that focuses on health systems and implementation science at the School of Public Health

Purpose: Curtin University is offering three-year fully-funded PhD scholarship in Public Health. The scholarship is awarded to conduct health services research that focuses on health systems and implementation science at the School of Public Health

Eligibility: International students can apply for these scholarships. If English is not your first language then you will need to show that your English language skills are at a high enough level to succeed in your studies

Value: The successful candidate will receive a stipend of A$27,082 per annum

Study Establishment: Scholarship is awarded to conduct health services research that focuses on health systems and implementation science at the School of Public Health

Country of Study: Australia

Application Procedure: The mode of applying is online

Closing Date: 9 April

Additional Information: For more details please visit our website scholarship-positions.com/three-year-fully-funded-phd-scholarship-public-health-australia/2018/02/27/

For further information contact:

Email: lynda.bergey@curtin.edu.au

Curtin University of Technology

Office of Research and Development, GPO Box U1987, Perth, Western Australia 6845, Australia

Tel: (61) 8 9266 9266

Fax: (61) 8 9266 3131

Email: research_scholarships@curtin.edu.au

Website: www.curtin.edu.au/

Curtin University of Technology is a world class, internationally focused, culturally diverse institution. They foster tolerance and encourage the development of the individual. Their programmes centre around the provision of knowledge and skills to meet industry and workplace standards. A combination of first rate resources, staff and technology makes Curtin a forerunner in tertiary education both within Australia and internationally.

American Planning Association(I) - Innovation, Competition and Economic Performance

Subjects: Computing/Information Technology (IT) and Economics/Finance

Purpose: To encourage students to undertake a Higher Degree by Research within the the Centre for Research in Applied Economics (CRAE)

Eligibility: Candidates must be Australian citizens or permanent residents or New Zealand citizens, should hold or are expected to hold a First Class Honours Degree or its equivalent and must meet Curtin University of Technology's requirements for admission to a PhD

Level of Study: Graduate

Type: Competition

Value: A$25,118 per year

Length of Study: 3 years with the possibility of an extension of up to 6 months

Application Procedure: Candidates must forward the completed application for admission to a higher degree by research to the Centre for Research into Applied Economics (CRAE)

Closing Date: 31 March

For further information contact:

Tel: (1) 61 8 9266 2035
Email: H.Bloch@exchange.curtin.edu.au
Contact: Professor Harry Bloch

Australian Biological Resources Study Postgraduate Scholarship

Subjects: Agricultural science
Purpose: To foster research training compatible with ABRS and national research priorities
Eligibility: Applicants must be Australian citizens or permanent residents, must hold a First or Upper Second Class Honours or equivalent degree in an appropriate discipline and be enroled as a full-time student in a PhD degree at an Australian institution
Level of Study: Graduate
Type: Scholarship
Value: A$22,500
Country of Study: Australia
Application Procedure: Applicants must submit the application to ABRS through the host institution. The application form will then be submitted to the ABRS Advisory Committee for consideration and assessment using the selection criteria. The individual selected as most worthy of funding will be awarded the scholarship
Closing Date: 26 October

For further information contact:

Australian Biological Resources Study, GPO Box 787, Australia

Tel: (61) 2 6250 9554
Fax: (61) 2 6250 9555
Email: abrs.grants@environment.gov.au
Contact: Business Manager

Curtin Business School Doctoral Scholarship

Subjects: Economics/finance, human resources, legal studies/politics, management/administration, marketing/public relations
Purpose: To enable doctoral (PhD, DBA) students to study at the Curtin Business School

Eligibility: Applicants must have completed at least 4 years of tertiary education studies at a high level of achievement and have First/Upper Second Class Honours or equivalent results. See scholarships.curtin.edu.au/scholarship.cfm?id=52 for more details
Level of Study: Postgraduate
Type: Scholarship
Value: $25,000
Length of Study: Up to 3 years
Frequency: Annual
Country of Study: Any country
Application Procedure: Applicants can download the application form and obtain further information from the website
Closing Date: 31 December

For further information contact:

Tel: (1) 8 9266 4301
Email: GRS.CurrentStudents@curtin.edu.au
Contact: Ms Jo Boycott, Research Student Coordinator

Curtin University Postgraduate Scholarship (CUPS)

Subjects: All subjects
Purpose: To assist with general living costs
Eligibility: Applicants must be Australian or New Zealand citizens or Australian permanent residents and must have completed 4 years of higher education studies at a high level of achievement and must hold, or are expected to obtain, First Class Honours or equivalent results; be enroled in or accepted to enrol in a Higher Degree by Research as a full-time student in the previous year in which the award is to be given
Level of Study: Graduate, Postgraduate
Type: Scholarship
Value: Varies, an annual living allowance of $23,728 was given last year. This stipend is indexed annually and is tax-free unless taken on a part-time basis
Length of Study: 2 years for a Master by Research and 3 years, with a possible extension of up to 6 months, for a Doctoral degree
Application Procedure: Check website for further details
Closing Date: 31 October

For further information contact:

Tel: (1) 8 9266 4906
Fax: (1) 8 9266 3793
Email: research_scholarships@curtin.edu.au
Contact: Manager, Scholarships

Establishing the Source of Gas in Australia's Offshore Petroleum Basins Scholarship

Subjects: Chemistry, geochemistry, geology
Purpose: To develop an isotopic method to analyse gases in fluid inclusions and to establish the source of gas in Australia's offshore petroleum basins
Eligibility: Applicants must have First Class Honours or equivalent science degree, preferably in chemistry/geology/geochemistry. Interests in analytical organic chemistry, laboratory skills in trace analysis, wet chemical methods, GC/GCMS or GC-IRMS instrumentation and awareness of stable isotopic concepts is desirable
Level of Study: Postgraduate
Type: Scholarship
Value: At least $20,000 per year
Application Procedure: Check website for further details
Closing Date: 31 December
Contributor: The Stable Isotope and Molecular Biogeochemistry Research Group, Geoscience Australia, GFZ

For further information contact:

Stable Isotope and Molecular Biogeochemistry Group, Centre for Applied Organic Geochemistry, Department of Applied Chemistry, Curtin University of Technology, GPO Box U1987, Australia

Tel:	(61) 8 9266 2474
Fax:	(61) 8 9266 2300
Email:	K.grice@curtin.edu.au
Contact:	Professor Kliti Grice

French-Australian Cotutelle

Subjects: All subjects
Purpose: To support the development of the double doctoral degree Cotutelle' between Australia and France
Eligibility: Applicants must be PhD students (of any nationality) enroled in a Cotutelle project between a French and an Australian university; should not have benefited from the French Embassy Cotutelle grant in previous years and should be registered with FEAST-France
Level of Study: Postgraduate
Type: Grant
Value: $2,500
Application Procedure: Applicants must provide the French Embassy with the completed application form and a copy of the Cotutelle convention
Closing Date: 8 December

For further information contact:

Email:	Stephane.GRIVELET@diplomatie.gouv.fr
Contact:	Mr Stephane GRIVELET

Hunter Postgraduate Scholarship

Subjects: Alzheimer's disease
Purpose: To support a PhD student undertaking research in an area relevant to understanding the causes of Alzheimer's disease
Eligibility: Candidates must be PhD students undertaking research in an area relevant to understanding the causes of Alzheimer's disease
Level of Study: Postgraduate
Type: Scholarship
Value: Up to $5,000 towards fees subject to funds available
Length of Study: 1 years
Application Procedure: Check website for further details
Closing Date: 31 October

For further information contact:

Tel:	(1) 2 6254 7233
Email:	aar@alzheimers.org.au
Contact:	Anna Conn

Masters Scholarship in Scotland

Subjects: Accounting, mathematical and financial analysis, built and natural environment, computing/electronic, engineering, media/communication, people, society, language and culture, visual arts/design
Purpose: The Scottish International Scholarship Programme is targeted at graduates in science, technology and the creative industries, and aims to create lasting connections between Scotland and industry leaders and entrepreneurs across the world
Eligibility: Open to Australian citizens who are presently studing science and technology
Level of Study: Postgraduate
Value: The Scotland Scholarship covers the tuition fee, airfare and a stipend for a taught masters course of up to 12 months duration at any Scottish Institution
Length of Study: Varies
Frequency: Annual
Study Establishment: Any Scottish institution
Country of Study: Scotland
Application Procedure: For more information including application forms please visit: www.gla.ac.uk/

For further information contact:

Email: scholarships@glasgow.ac

Scots Australian Council Scholarships

Subjects: Humanities
Purpose: To develop lasting links between young Scots and Australians by offering outstanding graduates and young professionals the opportunity to study at a Scottish university
Eligibility: Applicants must be Australian citizens or Australian permanent residents or New Zealand citizens or on permanent Humanitarian Visa. They must be indigenous or Torres Strait Islander students or students with a disability or students from rural or regional areas or mature students or sole parents or current students or prospective students
Level of Study: Postgraduate
Type: Scholarship
Value: £12,000
Application Procedure: Check website for further details
Closing Date: 14 January
Contributor: Scottish universities, Scottish business and industry, British Foreign and Commonwealth Office

For further information contact:

The Scots Australian Council, 19 Dean Terrace, Australia

Email: scholarships@scotsoz.org
Contact: The Secretary

Sediment and Asphaltite Transport by Canyon Upwelling - Top Up Scholarship

Subjects: Chemistry, geochemistry and geology
Purpose: To investigate the role of upwelling currents in transporting material across the continental slope of the Morum Sub-Basin, southern Australia using an integrated geological, oceanographic, and organic geochemical approach
Eligibility: Applicants must be Australian and New Zealand residents, First Class Honours or equivalent science degree holders, preferably in chemistry/geology/geochemistry. Interests in analytical organic chemistry, laboratory skills in trace analysis, wet chemical methods, GC/GCMS or GC-IRMS instrumentation; awareness of stable isotopic concepts is desirable
Level of Study: Graduate

Type: Scholarship
Value: See the organization website
Application Procedure: Applicants must forward their interests, curriculum vitae and names of two referees to Stable Isotope and Molecular Biogeochemistry Group, Centre for Applied Organic Geochemistry, Department of Applied Chemistry
Closing Date: See the organization website
Contributor: The Stable Isotope and Molecular Biogeochemistry Research Group, Adelaide University, a petroleum industry partner

The General Sir John Monash Awards

Subjects: All subjects
Purpose: To enable them to undertake postgraduate study abroad at the world's best Universities, appropriate to their field of study
Eligibility: Applicants must be Australian citizens who have graduated from an Australian University with outstanding levels of academic achievement
Level of Study: Graduate
Type: Award
Value: A$60,000 per year
Length of Study: 3 years
Frequency: Annual
Application Procedure: Check website for further details
Closing Date: Mid-August

For further information contact:

The General Sir John Monash Foundation, Level 1, Bennelong House, 9 Queen Street, Australia

Tel: (61) 613 9620 2428
Email: peter.binks@monashawards.org
Contact: Dr Peter Binks, Chief Executive Officer

Water Corporation Scholarship in Biosolids Research

Subjects: Agriscience and environmental science
Purpose: To investigate the potential impacts to soil and plants following the agricultural land application of alum-dosed wastewater sludge
Eligibility: Applicants must be Australian Citizens, Australian permanent residents or must hold an Australian permanent Humanitarian Visa. They must hold a relevant degree from a recognized University in the preferred fields of Agriculture, Environmental Science or the equivalent and demonstrate a high level in their Honours project or equivalent

Level of Study: Graduate, Postgraduate
Type: Scholarship
Value: $23,400 per year
Length of Study: 3 years for a doctoral program and 2 years for a masters program
Application Procedure: Check website for further details
Closing Date: 31 October

For further information contact:

Email: D.Pritchard@curtin.edu.au
Contact: Dr Deborah Pritchard

D

Daiwa Anglo-Japanese Foundation

Daiwa Foundation Japan House 13-14 Cornwall Terrace, NW1 4QP, London, United Kingdom

Tel:	(44) 20 7486 4348
Fax:	(44) 20 7486 2914
Email:	grants@dajf.org.uk
Website:	www.dajf.org.uk
Contact:	Grants & Scholarships Office

The Daiwa Anglo-Japanese Foundation aims to enhance the United Kingdom and Japan's understanding of each other's people and culture, enable British and Japanese students and academics to further their education through exchanges and co-operation and make grants available to individuals and organisations to promote links between the United Kingdom and Japan at all levels.

Daiwa Foundation Awards

Subjects: Daiwa Foundation Awards can cover projects in academic, professional, arts, cultural and educational fields. Awards seek to encourage the development and sustainability of United Kingdom-Japan partnerships between such organisations as museums and art galleries, theatres and performing arts groups, schools and universities, and grassroots and professional bodies. Any project which involves a significant level of collaboration between British and Japanese partners can be considered
Purpose: Awards of £7,000–£15,000 are available for collaborative projects that enable British and Japanese partners to work together in the context of an institutional relationship. In order to fund as many applications as we possibly can, given our limited budget, we typically award an average of £7,000 to successful Award applications. Our funding rarely covers an application's budget in full, but is meant to be a "contribution" to the proposed project
Eligibility: Daiwa Foundation Awards cannot be used for: any project that does not involve both a British and a Japanese partner general appeals capital expenditure (eg, building refurbishment, equipment acquisition, etc) school, college or university fees research or study by an individual school/college/university student salary costs or professional fees commissions for works of art retrospective grants replacement of statutory funding commercial activities
Type: Award/Grant
Value: Between £7,000 and £15,000
Frequency: Twice a year
Country of Study: Japan
Application Procedure: Online: dajf.org.uk/grants-awards-prizes/daiwa-foundation-awards
Closing Date: 31 March and 30 September
Funding: Foundation

For further information contact:

Email: grants@dajf.org.uk

Daiwa Foundation Small Grants

Subjects: Daiwa Foundation Small Grants can cover all fields of activity linking the United Kingdom and Japan, including educational and grassroots exchanges, research travel, the organisation of conferences, exhibitions, and other projects and events that fulfil this broad objective. New initiatives are especially encouraged
Purpose: Grants of £2,000–£7,000 are available to individuals, societies, associations or other bodies in the United Kingdom or Japan to promote and support interaction between the two countries
Eligibility: Those applying from the United Kingdom must be United Kingdom residents
Type: Grant

© Springer Nature Limited 2019
Palgrave Macmillan (ed.), *The Grants Register 2020*,
https://doi.org/10.1057/978-1-349-95943-3

Frequency: Twice a year
Country of Study: Japan
Application Procedure: United Kingdom-based applicants can apply online. Applications from Japan should be posted to the Tokyo Office. dajf.org.uk/grants-awards-prizes/daiwa-foundation-small-grants
Closing Date: 31 March and 30 September every year
Funding: Foundation
Additional Information: Daiwa Foundation Small Grants cannot be used for: general appeals capital expenditure (eg, building refurbishment, equipment acquisition, etc) consumables (eg, stationery, scientific supplies, etc) school, college or university fees research or study by an individual school/college/university student salary costs or professional fees commissions for works of art retrospective grants replacement of statutory funding commercial activities

For further information contact:

Email: grants@dajf.org.uk

Daiwa Scholarships

Subjects: The aim is to study Japanese in Japan and then undertake a 6-month work placement in one's field of expertise
Purpose: The Daiwa Scholarship is a unique 19-month programme of language study, work placement and homestay in Japan, following a month of Japanese language tuition in the United Kingdom. Daiwa Scholarships offer young and talented United Kingdom citizens with strong leadership potential, the opportunity to acquire Japanese language skills, and to access expertise and knowledge relevant to their career goals. No previous experience of Japan or Japanese is necessary. Daiwa Scholarships are provided by the Foundation to encourage better understanding between both countries
Eligibility: Candidates for the Daiwa Scholarships must be: 1. British citizens. 2. aged between 21 and 35 years of age by the time of departure. Candidates should be: 1. graduates or due to graduate by the time of departure. 2. equipped with a strong degree in any subject* or with a strong record of achievement in their field. 3. in possession of clear career objectives and a commitment to furthering United Kingdom-Japan links. *Graduates in Japanese language studies are not eligible to apply for Daiwa Scholarships but may wish to apply for support through the Daiwa Scholarships in Japanese Studies or the Foundation's grant schemes. Preference will normally be given to candidates no older than 30
Type: Scholarship/Bursary
Value: ¥ 2,60,000 per month

Length of Study: Japanese for 1 year followed by a 6-month work placement
Frequency: Annual
Country of Study: Japan
No. of awards offered: 155
Application Procedure: Online: dajf.org.uk/scholarships/daiwa-scholarship/application-procedure
Closing Date: first Thursday in December
Funding: Foundation
No. of awards given last year: 7
No. of applicants last year: 155

For further information contact:

Email: grants@dajf.org.uk

Daiwa Scholarships in Japanese Studies

Subjects: Candidates for the Daiwa Scholarships in Japanese Studies must be: United Kingdom citizens who hold or are completing a degree in Japanese Studies, defined as a course focussing primarily on the study of Japan, and containing a substantial Japanese language component. Applicants who hold (or are completing) combined honours courses where Japanese Studies accounts for at least 50% of the course are also eligible to apply. The Scholarship would be to cover a further course of study related to Japanese Studies. enrolled* or enrolling in a further course of study related to Japanese Studies in either Japan or the United Kingdom. *Please note that Scholarships will not be granted in arrears. Strong Japanese language ability will be a key selection criterion. Scholarships will not be awarded to former recipients of Daiwa Scholarships or to the same individual more than once
Purpose: The Daiwa Scholarships in Japanese Studies, a postgraduate programme to support the study of Japanese Studies in either Japan or the United Kingdom. The Daiwa Anglo-Japanese Foundation gratefully acknowledges additional support for this programme from Daiwa Securities Group Inc. The intention is to support six individuals in any given year, of whom at least three must study full-time at a university in Japan
Eligibility: Candidates for the Daiwa Scholarships in Japanese Studies must be: United Kingdom citizens who hold or are completing a degree in Japanese Studies, defined as a course focussing primarily on the study of Japan, and containing a substantial Japanese language component. Applicants who hold (or are completing) combined honours courses where Japanese Studies accounts for at least 50% of the course are also eligible to apply. The Scholarship would be to cover a further course of study related to Japanese Studies. enrolled* or enrolling in a further course of study related to Japanese Studies in either Japan or the United Kingdom. *Please note that Scholarships will not

be granted in arrears. Strong Japanese language ability will be a key selection criterion. Scholarships will not be awarded to former recipients of Daiwa Scholarships or to the same individual more than once

Level of Study: Doctorate, Postdoctorate, Postgraduate, Postgraduate (MSc)

Type: Bursary and scholarship

Value: We cover the tuition fee and award maintenance of £1,000 in the United Kingdom or ¥ 2,60,000 in Japan

Length of Study: Dependent on programme

Frequency: Annual

Country of Study: Japan

No. of awards offered: 15

Application Procedure: Online application dajf.org.uk/scholarships/japanese-studies/application_procedure

Closing Date: Last Thursday in January

Funding: Foundation

No. of awards given last year: 4

No. of applicants last year: 15

Additional Information: For study in the United Kingdom or Japan

For further information contact:

Email: grants@dajf.org.uk

Dalai Lama Foundation

The Dalai Lama Foundation, 18579 Burke Ave N, Shoreline, WA 98133, United States of America

Email: scholarship@dalailamatrust.org
Contact: Scholarship Committee

The Dalai Lama Foundation was founded in 2009 by His Holiness the XIVth Dalai Lama. The Foundation was established to support the advancement and welfare of the Tibetan people, the culture and heritage of the ancient civilization of Tibet, and the promotion of the deep rooted values associated with its culture and people.

The Dalai Lama Foundation Graduate Scholarship Program

Purpose: The purpose of the scholarship program is to further the human capital development of Tibetan people by encouraging the pursuit of excellence among Tibetan students in a graduate field of study that has relevance and potential to contribute to the welfare of humanity and the Tibetan people in particular

Eligibility: Applicants must have already been enrolled in or be accepted to a full-time graduate degree program at a university in Australia, Europe or the Americas 1. Applicants must show proof of Tibetan heritage and continuity of Dhanglang Chatrel (Green Book) contribution. 2. Applicants are solely and directly responsible for obtaining the necessary visas to attend the university of their choice. 3. Eligible candidates must be pursuing graduate studies, whether at the master's or PhD level, or at a professional school. 4. All graduate programs should be at least one year or multi-year, full-time courses, offered by reputable and accredited universities

Level of Study: Doctorate, Postgraduate

Type: Scholarship

Value: US$10,000

Frequency: Annual

Country of Study: Any country

Application Procedure: For details, visit www.dalailamatrust.org/scholarship/127-scholarship

Closing Date: 30 April

Funding: Foundation

Additional Information: For further information, please contact: scholarship@dalailamatrust.org

For further information contact:

Email: scholarship@dalailamatrust.org

Davies Charitable Foundation

245 Alwington Place, Kingston, ON K7L 4P9, Canada

Tel: (1) 613 546 4000
Fax: (1) 613 546 9130
Email: daviesfoundation@cogeco.ca
Website: www.daviesfoundation.ca

The Davies Charitable Foundation is a registered, non-profit, charitable organization founded by Michael R.L. Davies, former owner and publisher of the Kingston Whig Standard. The purpose of the Foundation is to support individuals and organizations within the local district in the areas of the arts, education, health and sports. Since its inception the Davies Charitable Foundation has donated over $7,500,000 to over 400 individuals and institutions.

The Davies Charitable Foundation Fellowship

Subjects: All subjects
Purpose: To support a native of the Kingston, Ontario, area at the peak of academic excellence

Eligibility: Open to candidates born in the Kingston area or have resided in the area for at least 5 years prior to their 20th birthday and must have been accepted into a postdoctoral or fellowship position at the university of their choice
Level of Study: Postdoctorate
Type: Fellowship
Value: C$10,000
Length of Study: 1 year
Frequency: Annual
Country of Study: Canada
Application Procedure: Application form can be downloaded from the website
Closing Date: 19 October and 30 October
Funding: Foundation
Contributor: Davies Charitable Foundation

For further information contact:

The Davies Charitable Foundation, 245, Alwington Place, Canada

Tel: (1) 613 546 4000
Email: daviesfoundation@cogeco.ca

De Montfort University

The Gateway, Leicestershire, LE1 9BH, Leicester, United Kingdom

Tel: (44) 116 255 1551
Fax: (44) 1162 577 533
Email: enquiry@dmu.ac.uk
Website: www.dmu.ac.uk
Contact: The Registrar

De Montfort University is a dynamic organization, formed from a diverse range of specialist institutions. Its long history of excellent teaching, learning and research is founded in the technical and trade education of the late 19th century. Today, the university has two campuses in Leicester, and special arrangements with more than 60 universities and colleges in 40 countries. It has approximately 20,000 students and 2,500 staff.

De Montfort University Awards to Women for Final Year Doctoral Research

Subjects: All subjects
Purpose: To help women graduates with their living expenses (not fees) while registered for study or research at an approved institution of higher education in Great Britain

Eligibility: Open to students who are studying or intend to study in Great Britain at a postgraduate or postdoctoral level, there is no upper age limit to apply
Level of Study: Postdoctorate, Postgraduate
Type: Award/Grant
Value: Up to UK £2,500
Frequency: Annual
Country of Study: United Kingdom
Funding: Foundation

For further information contact:

BFWG Charitable Foundation, 28 Great James Street, United Kingdom

Tel: (44) 20 7404 6447
Fax: (44) 20 7404 6505
Email: BFWG.Charity@btinternet.com
Contact: The Grants Administrator

India GREAT Scholarship

Purpose: GREAT Scholarship awarded in partnership with the British Council to Indian students
Eligibility: Applicants should have 70% or above marks from Bachelor's degree. Eligible to Indian students
Value: £4,000
Country of Study: United Kingdom
Application Procedure: For application, please visit www.dmu.ac.uk/international/en/fees-and-scholarships/india-great-scholarship.aspx
Closing Date: 31 July
Additional Information: For more details, visit website www.dmu.ac.uk/international/en/fees-and-scholarships/international-scholarships.aspx

Leicester Castle Business School Full Postgraduate Scholarship

Subjects: Business Management
Purpose: Leicester Castle Business School is pleased to announce a full-fee postgraduate scholarship offering for those wishing to study in September
Eligibility: This scholarship is only available to students domiciled within the eligible areas (the continent of Africa, Russia, Taiwan, Thailand, United States of America)
Value: Our Full Postgraduate Scholarships which will cover the total value of the course fee. The scholarship also includes an additional £5,000 which can be used towards assistance with accommodation and living costs
Country of Study: United Kingdom

Application Procedure: To apply, please complete the scholarship application web form
Closing Date: 31 July
Additional Information: For more details, please visit website lcbs.ac.uk/full-postgraduate-scholarships/

For further information contact:

Email: enquiry@lcbs.ac.uk

Leicester Castle Business School MBA Scholarship

Purpose: It is available to Global MBA students who have excelled academically and have an offer of admission for our full-time Global MBA programme
Eligibility: For eligibility, please refer website lcbs.ac.uk/mba-scholarships/
Value: £2,500
Country of Study: United Kingdom
Application Procedure: To apply, please complete the scholarship application web form available at www.dmu.ac.uk/international/en/fees-and-scholarships/leicester-castle-business-school-scholarships.aspx?_ga=2.249885056.727537558.1523602564-1792966074.1523602564
Closing Date: 31 July
Contributor: Leicester Castle Business School

For further information contact:

Email: enquiry@lcbs.ac.uk

Lesbian, gay, bisexual and transgender+Allies Scholarship

Purpose: This scholarship will allow prospective students to study in a welcoming and inclusive environment to inspire and enhance continued activism during and after study, promoting LGBTQ+ rights worldwide
Eligibility: Eligible recipients should be domiciled outside the United Kingdom and EU area and have an offer of admission for any one year post-graduate taught programme
Type: Postgraduate scholarships
Value: The scholarships also include an additional £1,015 (excluding any taxes) per month for the duration of the course, to assist with accommodation and living costs
Length of Study: 1 year
Country of Study: United Kingdom
Closing Date: 3 August
Additional Information: For details, visit website www.dmu.ac.uk/documents/international-documents/2018-scholarships-and-discounts/global-lgbtqallies-scholarship-tcs-final-v3.pdf

For further information contact:

Email: campus@hrc.org

Square Mile International Scholarship

Purpose: One Square Mile International Scholarship will be awarded to a student who demonstrates significant experience in engaging with their local community and a willingness to contribute to the DMU Square Mile Project
Eligibility: For eligibility details, please visit website www.dmu.ac.uk/international/en/fees-and-scholarships/dmu-square-mile-international-scholarship.aspx
Value: Full tuition fees, a monthly bursary to cover living costs and one return flight to the United Kingdom
Frequency: Annual
Country of Study: United Kingdom
Application Procedure: To apply, please complete the scholarship application web form available at www.dmu.ac.uk/international/en/fees-and-scholarships/dmu-square-mile-international-scholarship.aspx
Closing Date: 29 June
Contributor: De Montfort University

For further information contact:

Email: ask.international@dmu.ac.uk

Deakin University

221 Burwood Highway, Burwood, VIC 3125, Australia

Tel:	(61) 3 9244 6100
Fax:	(61) 3 9244 8796
Email:	enquire@deakin.edu.au
Website:	www.deakin.edu

Deakin University is one of Australia's largest universities providing all the resources of a major university to more than 32,000 award students. The University's reputation for excellent teaching and innovative course delivery has been recognized through many awards over the past few years.

Deakin University Postgraduate Research Scholarships (DUPRS)

Subjects: Research
Eligibility: Applicants must meet Deakin's PhD entry requirements, be enrolling full-time and hold an Honours

degree (First Class) or a Master's degree with a substantial research component in a related field. Applicants applying for Research Masters or Research Doctorate must not hold an equivalent research qualification

Level of Study: Postgraduate

Value: A stipend of $26,682 per annum, a relocation allowance up to $1,500, tuition fee and overseas health coverage for international students for the duration of 4 years. Paid sick, maternity and parental leave are applicable

Length of Study: 3 years

Country of Study: Australia

Application Procedure: Please refer to the Apply for a research degree webpage for application information

Closing Date: 31 October

Additional Information: Applications can be made throughout the year except for Arts and Education. Arts and Education applications must be submitted before 31st October. Please contact the Deakin Research Scholarships Office: research-scholarships@deakin.edu.au

For further information contact:

Email: study@deakin.edu.au

Marine Biotechnology PhD Studentship

Subjects: Chemistry, biochemistry, molecular biology, or a related field. Purpose: To carry out a joint project with Deakin University in Geelong, Australia and Plant and Food Research, New Zealand

Type: Scholarship

Value: A$25,000 per annum

Country of Study: Australia

Contributor: Jointly funded by Deakin University and Plant and Food Research, Nelson, NZ

Additional Information: Interested candidates please forward your CV and expression of interest to Professor Colin Barrow or Dr Susan Marshall

Serendib Community Cultural Association Sri Lanka Bursary

Subjects: Arts and Communication

Purpose: The Deakin University is awarding SCCA Sri Lanka Undergraduate Bursary in the field of Arts and Communication. The scholarship will cover 20% of the student contributions (tuition fees)

Eligibility: Applicants must: 1. be a prospective international student. 2. be a Sri Lankan citizen. 3. must meet eligibility criteria for their chosen Deakin degree. 4. have applied to study one of the following degrees: i. A353 Bachelor of Creative Arts

(Animation); ii. A352 Bachelor of Creative Arts (Photography); iii. A359 Bachelor of Creative Arts (Visual Art); iv. A356 Bachelor of Creative Arts (Drama); v. A355 Bachelor of Creative Arts (Visual Communications Design); vi. A351 Bachelor of Creative Arts (Film & Television); vii. A331 Bachelor of Communications (Journalism); viii. A325 Bachelor of Communications (Public Relations); ix. A333 Bachelor of Communications (Digital Media); x. A743 Master of Communication

Level of Study: Graduate

Type: Bursary

Value: 20% of the student contributions (tuition fees)

Frequency: Annual

Country of Study: Australia, the United Kingdom, Europe or the United States of America

Application Procedure: The bursaries will automatically be offered to eligible students and will be awarded on a first come, first served basis. Strict quotas apply

Closing Date: July

Funding: Private

For further information contact:

Melbourne, Victoria, Australia

Email: deakin-int-scholarships@deakin.edu.au

Denmark-America Foundation

Nørregade 7A, DNK 1165 København K, Denmark

Tel:	(45) 3532 4545
Fax:	(45) 3332 5323
Email:	daf-fulb@daf-fulb.dk
Website:	www.wemakeithappen.dk
Contact:	Ms Marie Monsted, Executive Director

The Denmark-America Foundation was founded in 1914 as a private foundation, and today its work remains based on donations from Danish firms, foundations and individuals. The Foundation offers scholarships for studies in the United States of America at the graduate and postgraduate university level and also has a trainee programme.

Denmark-America Foundation Grants

Subjects: All subjects

Purpose: To further understanding between Denmark and the United States of America

Eligibility: Open to Danes and Danish-American citizens

Level of Study: Graduate, Postdoctorate, Postgraduate, Professional development, Research, MBA
Type: Bursary
Value: Varies
Length of Study: 3–12 months
Frequency: Annual
Country of Study: United States of America
No. of awards offered: 250
Application Procedure: Applicants must complete a special application form, available by contacting the secretariat
Closing Date: Check website for further details
Funding: Private
No. of awards given last year: 34–35
No. of applicants last year: 250

Department of Biotechnology

Website: www.dbtindia.nic.in
Contact: Department of Biotechnology

The Department of Biotechnology is an Indian government department, under the Ministry of Science and Technology responsible for administrating development and commercialization in the field of modern biology and biotechnology in India.

National Bioscience Awards for Career Development (NBACD)

Subjects: Biological Sciences including Biotechnology, Agricultural, Medical, and Environmental Sciences
Purpose: Awards are given for pursuing research programme
Eligibility: Citizens of India are eligible to apply
Type: Award
Value: Each award carries a cash prize of Rs. 2,00,000 and a trophy along with a citation and a project research grant of Rs. 15,00,000 @ Rs. 5,00,000 per year for a period of 3 years for career development
Country of Study: India
Closing Date: 15 April

For further information contact:

Email: jagadish.dora@nic.in

Tata Innovation Fellowship

Purpose: The scheme is aimed at rewarding interdisciplinary work where major emphasis is on innovation and translational research with a potential towards commercialization

Eligibility: The fellowship is co-terminus with the superannuation of fellow in applicant organization. The applicant should possess a PhD degree in Life Sciences, Agriculture, Veterinary Science or a Master's degree in Medical Sciences, Engineering or an equivalent degree in Biotechnology / related areas. The applicant must have outstanding contribution and publication in the specific area. The candidate must have a regular permanent position in a University/Institute/ Organization and should be engaged in research and development. If he/she is availing any other fellowship, he/she will have to opt for only one of the fellowships. The applicant should have spent at least 5 years in India before applying for the fellowship
Type: Fellowship
Value: Rs. 25,000
Frequency: Varies
Country of Study: Any country
Application Procedure: Application could be processed through online mode or physical mode. Correspondence address is Dr. Kakali Dey Dasgupta, Scientist "E" Department of Biotechnology, Ministry of Science & Technology, Room No.814, 8 th Floor, Block-2, CGO Complex, Lodhi Road, New Delhi - 110 003
Closing Date: 31 December
Funding: Government

For further information contact:

Block-2, CGO Complex, Lodhi Road, New Delhi 110003, India

Email: tatadbt4@gmail.com

Department of Education Services

22 Hasler Road, Osborne Park, Perth, WA 6017, Australia

Tel: (61) 8 9441 1900
Fax: (61) 8 9441 1901
Email: des@des.wa.gov.au
Website: www.des.wa.gov.au

The Department of Education Services provides policy advice to the Minister for Education and Training and supporting universities, non-government schools and international education providers and in some cases individual students and teachers through scholarship programmes in Western Australia.

Western Australian Government Japanese Studies Scholarships

Subjects: Japanese studies

Purpose: To provide students with the opportunity to spend 1 year studying at a tertiary institution in Japan

Eligibility: Candidates must have Australian citizenship, or evidence that Australian citizenship status will be approved prior to departure for Japan; be a student of a higher education institution in Western Australia, or an institution of equivalent standing, and have completed at least 2 years of full-time study (or equivalent of part-time study) in an appropriate Japanese language course; or be a graduate from a university, having a reasonable command of the Japanese language and developed an interest in Japan through employment or further studies

Level of Study: Postgraduate

Type: Scholarship

Value: The scholarship includes a return airfare, an initial payment of $3,000 for fees and other expenses and a monthly maintenance allowance of ¥2,26,600

Length of Study: 1 year

Frequency: Annual

Country of Study: Japan

Closing Date: July

Funding: Government

For further information contact:

Email: diana.phang@jtsi.wa.gov.au

Department of Foreign Affairs and Trade

Website: www.dfat.gov.au/home.html
Contact: Exchange Scholarship Programme

The Department is responsible for the Australian Government's international relations and trade and development assistance programs through its headquarters in Canberra and embassies, high commissions and consulates throughout the world.

Australia Awards Scholarships

Subjects: It is being administered by Department of Foreign Affairs and Trade, Australian Government

Purpose: They aim to contribute to the development needs of Australia's partner countries in line with bilateral and regional agreements

Eligibility: The Australian Government Scholarship is open to students of Asia, Middle East, Africa and Pacific. The Australia Awards Scholarship is fully funded scholarship and is administered by the Department of Foreign Affairs and Trade. To be eligible to receive an Australia Awards Scholarship, applicants must: 1. Be a minimum of 18 years of age on 1 February of the year of commencing the scholarship. 2. Be a citizen of a participating country (as listed on the Australia Awards website) and be residing in and applying for the scholarship from their country of citizenship. 3. Not be a citizen of Australia, hold permanent residency in Australia or be applying for a visa to live in Australia permanently. 4. Not be married to, engaged to, or a de facto of a person who holds, or is eligible to hold, Australian or New Zealand citizenship or permanent residency, at any time during the application, selection or mobilisation phases (note: residents of Cook Islands, Niue and Tokelau with New Zealand citizenship are eligible but must apply for a Student visa [subclass 500])

Level of Study: Postgraduate

Type: Scholarship

Value: full tuition fees, return air travel, establishment allowance, Contribution to Living Expenses (CLE), etc

Frequency: Annual

Country of Study: Australia

Application Procedure: Go to the Online Australia Scholarships Information System (OASIS). When you register online, you will be required to answer some questions to establish your eligibility. You will then be given a unique registration number, username and password. You do not need to submit your application immediately. You can set up a draft application form and update it, and your supporting documentation, until the designated closing date as on the relevant participating country profile

Closing Date: 30 April

Funding: Private

For further information contact:

R.G. Casey Building John McEwen Crescent Barton, ACT 0221, Australia

Tel: (61) 2 6261 1111

Department of Innovation, Industry and Regional Development

GPO Box 4509, Melbourne, VIC 3001, Australia

Tel: (61) 3 9651 9999
Fax: (61) 3 9651 9770
Email: innovation@diird.vic.gov.au
Website: www.diird.vic.gov.au

The Office of Science and Technology at the Department of Innovation, Industry and Regional Development, supports the ongoing development and advancement of a scientifically and technologically advanced Victoria.

Victoria Fellowships

Subjects: Engineering, science, innovation or technology
Purpose: To offer support and encouragement to aspiring students to broaden their experience and develop networks. The fellowship also provides an opportunity for recipients to develop commercial ideas
Eligibility: Open to candidates who are either currently employed or enroled in post-graduate studies in Victoria in a field relating to science, engineering or technology and Australian citizens or hold permanent residence in Australia and a current resident of Victoria
Level of Study: Postgraduate, Professional development
Type: Fellowships
Value: A$18,000
Length of Study: 1 year
Frequency: Annual
Country of Study: Australia
Application Procedure: A completed application form should be submitted
Closing Date: April (check website for exact closing date)
Funding: Government
Contributor: Government of Victoria
No. of awards given last year: 6

For further information contact:

Tel: (61) 3 9864 0905/9655 1040
Email: vicprize.fellows@atse.org.au
Contact: Helen Vella, Manager

Department of Science and Technology and Indo-United States Science and Technology Forum (IUSSTF)

Indo-United States Science and Technology Forum, Fulbright House, 12, Hailey Road, New Delhi 110001, India

Tel: (91) 11-42691700/716
Email: energy.fellowship@indousstf.org
Website: www.iusstf.org
Contact: Dr Nishritha Bopana

Recognizing that climate change, clean and efficient energy and environmental protection are among the biggest challenges facing India and the United States; the Department of Science and Technology, Govt. of India through its Solar Energy Research Initiative, and the Indo-United States Science and Technology Forum (IUSSTF) are committed to tackling these issues by building capacity in these frontier areas.

Bhaskara Advanced Solar Energy (BASE) Fellowship Program

Subjects: Science, Engineering or Technology
Purpose: To nurture future innovators and thought leaders in Solar Energy, the Bhaskara Advanced Solar Energy (BASE) Fellowship Program - a dynamic and transformative programe has been developed to foster contacts between students and scientists from India and the United States
Eligibility: Indian citizens currently pursuing a PhD as full time scholars in the field of solar energy, in a public-funded R&D Laboratory/S&T institution (non-private)/recognized academic institute (University/College) in India
Type: Fellowship
Value: Monthly stipend, return air-fare, contingency allowance
Length of Study: Internship: Minimum 3 months and upto 6 months; Fellowship: Minimum 3 months and upto 1 year
Frequency: Annual
Country of Study: Any country
Application Procedure: Applications should be submitted using our Online Application Portal for Visitation Programe. Hard copies and electronic copies of the application forms will not be accepted
Closing Date: 15 March
Additional Information: For programe information contact: Dr. Nishritha Bopana, energy.fellowship@indousstf.org

For further information contact:

Email: energy.fellowship@indousstf.org

Deutsche Forschungsgemeinschaft (DFG)

Kennedyallee 40, DEU-53175 Bonn, Germany

Tel: (49) 228 885 1
Fax: (49) 228 885 2777

The DFG is a central, self-governing research organization, which promotes research at universities and other publicity financial research institutions in Germany. The DFG serves all branches of science and the humanities by funding research projects and facilitating cooperation among researchers.

Albert Maucher Prize

Subjects: Geosciences
Purpose: To promote outstanding young scientists and scholars in the field of geosciences
Eligibility: Open to promising young scientists and scholars up to the age of 35 years who are German nationals or permanent residents of Germany
Level of Study: Postdoctorate
Type: Award
Value: €10,000 each
Length of Study: Varies
Frequency: Every 3 years
Study Establishment: Approved universities or research institutions
Country of Study: Germany
Application Procedure: Applicants must write for details or visit the website. Application is by nomination
Contributor: Professor Albert Maucher

For further information contact:

Tel: (49) 228 885 2012
Email: Kristian.Remes@dfg.de
Contact: Dr Kristian Remes

Bernd Rendel Prize in Geoscience

Subjects: Geoscience – geologists, mineralogists, geophysicists, oceanographers, geodesists
Purpose: For the young geoscientists who have graduated, but do not yet hold a doctorate, and who have demonstrated great potential in their scientific career. The award must be used for scientific purposes, e.g. enabling prizewinners to attend international conferences and congresses
Eligibility: Open to researchers from natural science-oriented fields in geoscience, researchers from humanities-oriented branches of geography are not eligible
Level of Study: Predoctorate
Type: Prize
Value: €1,000
Frequency: Annual
Application Procedure: Nominations may be submitted either by the researchers themselves, or by any researcher or academic working in a closely related field. Detailed information on the nominee's research to date (e.g. thesis, manuscripts, special publications) and future research plans, tabular curriculum vitae, list of publications, copies of certificates, statement on the proposed use of the prize money should be provided

Closing Date: 20 February
Contributor: The Bernd Rendel Foundation, which is administered by the Donors' Association for the Promotion of Sciences and Humanities in Germany

For further information contact:

Tel: (49) 228 885 2328
Email: Ismene.Seeberg-elverfeldt@dfg.de
Contact: Dr Birgit Scheibner-Münker, Programme Officer

Communicator Award

Purpose: This personal award is presented to researchers who have communicated their scientific findings to the public with exceptional success
Value: €50,000
Frequency: Annual
Application Procedure: Proposals for candidates can be put forward by researchers who are capable of assessing both the communication effort and professional qualification of the nominee(s)
Closing Date: February

For further information contact:

Email: Jutta.hoehn@dfg.de
Contact: Jutta Höhn

Copernicus Award

Subjects: All subjects
Purpose: To promote young researchers to further advance research and contribute to the German–Polish research cooperation
Eligibility: Open to outstanding researchers in Germany and Poland who work at universities or research institutions
Type: Award
Value: €1,00,000 (donated in equal shares)
Length of Study: 5 years
Frequency: Every 2 years
Application Procedure: A completed application form along with the required documents should be submitted
Contributor: The Foundation for Polish Science and the DFG

For further information contact:

Tel: (49) 228 885 2663
Email: Philip.Thelen@dfg.de
Contact: Dr Philip Thelen, Programme Officer International Affairs

Deutsche Forschungsgemeinschaft Collaborative Research Centres

Subjects: All subjects
Purpose: To promote long-term co-operative research in universities and academic research
Eligibility: Open to promising groups of German nationals and permanent residents of Germany
Level of Study: Postdoctorate, Research
Type: Research grant
Value: Dependent on the requirements of the project
Length of Study: Up to 12 years
Study Establishment: Universities and academic institutions
Country of Study: Germany
Application Procedure: Applicants must write or visit the website for further information. Applications must be formally filed by the universities
Closing Date: No submission deadline
Additional Information: A list of collaborative research centres is available in Germany only from the DFG

For further information contact:

Tel: (49) 228 885 2312
Email: petra.hammel@dfg.de
Contact: Petra Hammel

Deutsche Forschungsgemeinschaft Mercator Programme

Subjects: All subjects
Purpose: The DFG offers the Mercator Programme to enable Germany's research universities to invite highly qualified scientists and academics working abroad to complete a - DFG-funded stay at their institutes
Eligibility: Open to foreign scientists whose individual research is of special interest to research and teaching in Germany
Level of Study: Postdoctorate
Type: Fellowship
Value: Dependent on the duration of the stay
Length of Study: 3–12 months
Frequency: Annual
Study Establishment: German universities
Country of Study: Germany
Application Procedure: A proposal must be submitted by the university intending to host the guest professor

For further information contact:

Tel: (49) 228 885 2232
Email: cora.laforet@dfg.de
Contact: Cora Laforet

Deutsche Forschungsgemeinschaft Research Training Groups

Subjects: All subjects
Purpose: To promote high-quality graduate studies at the doctoral level through the participation of graduate students recruited through countrywide calls in research programmes
Eligibility: Open to highly qualified graduate and doctoral students of any nationality
Level of Study: Postgraduate, Predoctorate
Type: Grant
Length of Study: Up to 9 years
Frequency: Annual
Study Establishment: Any approved university
Country of Study: Germany
Application Procedure: Applications should be submitted in response to calls. For further information applicants must visit the website
Closing Date: 1 April and 1st October, preliminary version to be submitted 3 months prior to these dates
Additional Information: A list of graduate colleges presently funded is available (in Germany only) from the DFG

For further information contact:

Tel: (49) 228 885 288
Email: sebastian.granderath@dfg.de
Contact: Dr Sebastian Granderath

Emmy Noether Programme

Subjects: All subjects
Purpose: To give outstanding young scholars the opportunity to obtain the scientific qualifications needed to be appointed as a lecturer
Eligibility: Open to promising young postdoctoral scientists within 5 years of receiving their PhD, who are up to 30 years of age and who are German nationals or permanent residents of Germany
Level of Study: Postdoctorate
Type: Project grant
Value: For the 2 years of research spent abroad the candidate will receive a project grant in keeping with the requirements of the project including an allowance for subsistence and travel. For the 3 years of research spent at a German university or research institution the candidate will receive a project grant
Length of Study: 5 years
Frequency: Annual
Study Establishment: Universities or research institutions
Country of Study: Any country

Application Procedure: Applicants must complete an application form. For further information applicants must write or visit the website

Closing Date: Applications may be submitted at any time

For further information contact:

Tel: (49) 228 885 3008
Email: Verfahren-Nachwuchs@dfg.de

European Young Investigator Award

Purpose: To enable and encourage outstanding young researchers from all over the world, to work in an European environment for the benefit of the development of European science and the building up of the next generation of leading European researchers

Eligibility: The program is open to scientists of all disciplines and is open to candidates throughout the world

Type: Prize

Value: Up to €1,250,000

Length of Study: 5 years

Application Procedure: Applicants should provide a completed application form, letters of recommendation and the letter of support from the host institution to the DFG

Closing Date: 30 November

Contributor: The European Union Research Organizations Heads of Research Councils (EuroHORCS)

For further information contact:

Tel: (49) 228 885 2845
Email: Anjana.Buckow@dfg.de
Contact: Dr Anjana Buckow

Excellence Initiative

Subjects: All subjects

Purpose: To promote top-level research and improve the quality of German universities and research institutions in general, thus making Germany a more attractive research location, and more internationally competitive and focussing attention on the outstanding achievements of German universities and the German scientific community

Eligibility: The precise conditions for receiving funding were defined in accordance with the criteria specified by the federal and state governments

Level of Study: Postgraduate

Type: Funding support

Length of Study: 5 years

Frequency: Annual

Country of Study: Any country

Contributor: German federal and state governments

Additional Information: The three funding lines of the initiative: graduate schools to promote young scientists, clusters of excellence to promote top-level research, institutional strategies to promote top-level university research. For more details log on to www.dfg.de/en/research_funding/pro grammes/excellence_initiative/

For further information contact:

Tel: (49) 228 885 2254
Email: internetredaktion@uni-konstanz.de
Contact: Dr Beate Konze-Thomas

Gottfried Wilhelm Leibniz Prize

Subjects: All subjects

Purpose: To promote outstanding scientists and scholars in German universities and research institutions

Eligibility: Open to outstanding scholars in German universities

Level of Study: Predoctorate, Research

Type: Research grant

Value: €25,00,000 per award

Length of Study: 5 years

Frequency: Annual

Study Establishment: Any approved university or research institution

Country of Study: Germany

Application Procedure: Applicants must write for details or visit the website. Application is by nomination. Nominations are restricted to selected institutions such as DFG member organizations or individuals, e.g. former prize winners or chairpersons of DFG review committees

Additional Information: A list of prize winners is available in Germany only from the DFG

For further information contact:

Tel: (49) 228 885 2726
Email: Ursula.Rogmans-Beucher@dfg.de
Contact: Ursula Rogmans-Beucher

Heinz Maier–Leibnitz Prize

Subjects: All subjects

Purpose: To promote outstanding young scientists at the doctorate level

Eligibility: Open to promising young scholars up to 33 years of age, who are German nationals or permanent residents of Germany
Level of Study: Doctorate, Postdoctorate
Type: Consultancy
Value: €16,000 per award
Length of Study: Varies
Frequency: Annual
Study Establishment: Any approved university or research institution
Country of Study: Germany
Application Procedure: Applicants must write for details or visit the website. Application is by nomination
Closing Date: 31 August
Funding: Government
Contributor: The Federal Ministry of Education and Research

For further information contact:

Tel:	(49) 228 885 2835
Email:	Annette.Lessenich@dfg.de
Contact:	Annette Lessenich, Legal Director Quality Assurance and Programme Development

Heisenberg Programme

Subjects: All subjects
Purpose: To promote outstanding young and highly qualified researchers
Eligibility: Open to high-calibre young scientists up to the age of 35 years who are German nationals or permanent residents of Germany
Level of Study: Postdoctorate
Type: Scholarship
Value: Varies
Length of Study: 5 years
Frequency: Annual
Study Establishment: Any approved university or research institution
Country of Study: Germany
Application Procedure: Applicants must submit a research proposal, a detailed curriculum vitae, copies of degree certificates, a copy of the thesis, a letter explaining the choice of host institution, a list of all previously published material and a letter outlining financial requirements in duplicate. For further information applicants must contact the DFG
Closing Date: Applications are accepted at any time

For further information contact:

Tel:	(49) 228 885 2398
Email:	paul.heuermann@dfg.de
Contact:	Paul Heuermann

The Eugen and Ilse Seibold Prize

Subjects: Humanities, social science, law, economics, natural sciences, engineering and medicine
Purpose: To promote outstanding young scientists and scholars who have made significant contributions to the scientific interchange between Japan and Germany
Eligibility: Open to outstanding young German or Japanese scholars
Level of Study: Postdoctorate
Type: Prize
Value: €10,000
Length of Study: Varies
Frequency: Every 2 years
Study Establishment: Universities or research institutions
Application Procedure: Applicants must write for details or visit the website. Application is by nomination
Closing Date: 31 August

For further information contact:

Tel:	(49) 228 885 2346
Fax:	(49) 228 885 2550
Email:	Joerg.Schneider@dfg.de
Contact:	Dr Jörg Schneider, Head of Division International Affairs

The Von Kaven Awards

Subjects: Instrumental mathematics
Purpose: The award is granted as a fellowship or as a support for research in the field of instrumental mathematics (including the von Kaven Prize and the von Kaven Research Award)
Eligibility: Persons who meet the general eligibility criteria stipulated by the DFG within the individual grants programme
Level of Study: Postgraduate
Type: Award
Value: €15,000 (€10,000 von Kaven Prize; €5,000 von Kaven Research Award)
Frequency: Annual
Country of Study: Africa
Application Procedure: Nominations for the von Kaven (Prize and) award may be made by the members of the mathematics review board, its previous chairs and other DFG committee members in the field of mathematics (such as senators and members of the senate committee working in the field of mathematics). It is not possible to apply directly for the von Kaven (Prize and) award
Closing Date: 31 January
Funding: Private

For further information contact:

Tel: (49) 228 885 2567
Email: frank.kiefer@dfg.de
Contact: Dr Frank Kiefer

Ursula M. Händel Animal Welfare Prize

Subjects: Animal welfare
Purpose: To award scientists who make, through research, a significant contribution to the welfare of animals
Eligibility: Open to scientists who aim at improving the welfare of animals through research
Level of Study: Postdoctorate
Type: Award
Value: €25,000
Application Procedure: A completed application form and required documents must be submitted
Funding: Trusts
Contributor: Mrs Ursula M. Händel

For further information contact:

Tel: (49) 228 885 2658
Email: Sonja.Ihle@dfg.de
Contact: Dr Sonja Ihle

Deutscher Akademischer Austauschdienst

German Academic Exchange Service, 1 Southampton Place, WCIA 2DA, London, United Kingdom

Tel: (44) 20 7831 9511
Fax: (44) 20 7831 8575
Email: info@daad.org.uk
Website: www.daad.org.uk
Contact: Ms Judie Cole

Research Internships in Science and Engineering (RISE)

Subjects: Check website for details
Purpose: To offer research internships to students in science and engineering
Type: Grant
Value: €650 per month
Length of Study: 1.5–3 years

Frequency: Annual
Country of Study: Germany
Funding: Government
Additional Information: Please visit www.daad.de/rise for the complete program description and application guidelines

For further information contact:

Email: Mary.Swanson@ColoState.edu

Deutsches Museum

Museumsinsel 1, DEU 80538, Munich, Germany

Tel: (49) 89 217 91, 89 217 9433
Fax: (49) 89 217 9324
Email: information@deutsches-museum.de
Website: www.deutsches-museum.de/en

Scholar-in-Residence Program

Subjects: Applicants are invited to base their projects on the collections of the Deutsches Museum and to cooperate closely with museum staff on site when formulating their research proposals. Projects involving innovative approaches to artifact-oriented research are especially welcome
Purpose: Scholarships are offered to research scholars who are interested in working on projects for 6 or 12 months
Eligibility: Scholars at any level of seniority are eligible to apply, provided they have at least one university degree. There are no restrictions regarding nationality. All scholars are requested to make their own provisions for health insurance
Level of Study: Research
Type: Scholarship
Value: Predoctoral stipends: €7,500 (6 months) or €15,000 (full year). Postdoctoral stipends: €15,000 (6 months) or €30,000 (full year)
Country of Study: Germany
Application Procedure: Applicants should send their applications by post, including completed application form, curriculum vitae, project description (3–5 pages), two confidential references (can be sent directly by the referees)
Closing Date: 17 October
Contributor: Deutsches Museum

For further information contact:

Email: Scholars@iie.org

Diabetes United Kingdom

Macleod House, 10 Parkway, NW1 7AA, London, United Kingdom

Tel:	(44) 20 7424 1000
Fax:	(44) 20 7424 1001
Email:	victoria.king@diabetes.org.uk
Website:	www.diabetes.org.uk
Contact:	Dr Victoria King, Research Manager

Diabetes United Kingdom's overall aim is to help and care for both people with diabetes and those closest to them, to represent and campaign for their interests and to fund research into diabetes. Diabetes United Kingdom continues to encourage research into all areas of diabetes.

Endeavour Postgraduate Leadership Award

Purpose: The Endeavour Postgraduate Leadership Award provides financial support for international applicants to undertake a postgraduate qualification at a Masters or PhD level either by coursework or research in any field in Australia for up to 2 years for Masters and 4 years for PhD

Eligibility: To participate in the ELP, individual applicants must: 1. not be undertaking their Leadership Activity in a country where they hold citizenship/dual citizenship or permanent residency (International Individual Endeavour Leaders must undertake their activity in Australia and not hold citizenship/dual citizenship or be a permanent resident of Australia.). 2. be aged 18 years or over at the commencement of their Leadership Activity. 3. not be in receipt of any other Australian Government sponsored mobility, scholarship or fellowship benefits

Level of Study: Postgraduate

Type: Award

Length of Study: 2 years for a Masters and up to 4 years for a PhD

Frequency: Annual

Country of Study: Any country

Closing Date: March to November

Funding: Private

Additional Information: internationaleducation.gov.au/ Endeavour%20program/Scholarships-and-Fellowships/Pages/ default.aspx

For further information contact:

Email: endeavour@education.gov.au

Dominican College of San Rafael

School of Business & International Studies Graduate Program in Pacific Basin Studies, 50 Acacia Avenue, San Rafael, CA 94912-9962, United States of America

Tel:	(1) 415 257 1359
Fax:	(1) 415 459 3206
Email:	pbsad@dominican.edu
Contact:	MBA Admissions Officer

Dominican College of San Rafael MBA in Strategic Leadership

Length of Study: 2 years

Application Procedure: All applicants must submit a completed application form, with official academic transcripts, a curriculum vitae, a statement of purpose (three-five pages), TOEFL score (if applicable), and a fee of US$40

Closing Date: Applications are ongoing

For further information contact:

Division of Liberal & Professional Studies MBA in Strategic Leadership, 50 Acacia Avenue, CA 94901, United States of America

Tel:	(1) 415 485 3280
Fax:	(1) 415 485 3293
Email:	87pathways@dominican.edu
Contact:	MBA Admissions Officer

Doshisha University

International Center, Office of International Students, Karasuma-Higashi-iru Imadegawa-dori, Kamigyo-ku, Kyoto 602-8580, Japan

Tel:	(81) 75 251 3257
Fax:	(81) 75 251 3123
Email:	ji-intad@mail.doshisha.ac.jp
Website:	www.doshisha.ac.jp/english
Contact:	Chieko Toboku

Located in the heart of Kyoto, Doshisha University occupies 5 separate campuses and is home to over 29,000 students engaged in both undergraduate and graduate studies. As one of Japan's most highly esteemed educational institutions, Doshisha offers students a wide ranging liberal arts education as well as studies in business and science.

Doshisha University Doctoral-Program Young Researcher Scholarship

Purpose: To support young researchers who hold future promise and display a strong passion toward academic research

Eligibility: Students with a passion for academic research who have received a recommendation from one of the graduate schools and match one of the following profiles: (1) Students enroled in doctoral programs at the Graduate Schools of Theology Letters; Social Studies, Law, Economics, Commerce, Policy and Management, Culture and Information Science, Science and Engineering, Life and Medical Sciences, Health and Sports Science, Psychology and Global Studies, who are aiming to acquire a doctoral degree and are under 34 years of age at the time of admission. (2) Students enroled in an integrated program (master's and doctoral programs) (except the Graduate School of Brain Science) for a minimum of 2 years, who are aiming to acquire a doctoral degree and are under 32 years of age at the time of enrollment

Level of Study: Doctorate

Type: Scholarship

Value: Amount equivalent to annual school fees (including admission fees at the time of enrollment, tuition fee for educational support and lab/practical fees)

Length of Study: 1 year (renewable for up to the standard number of years required for graduation)

Frequency: Annual

Study Establishment: Doshisha University

Country of Study: Japan

Application Procedure: The scholarship is awarded on the basis of recommendations from the graduate schools and cannot be applied for individually

Closing Date: Check the website

For further information contact:

Email: ji-kosei@mail.doshisha.ac.jp

Doshisha University Graduate School Reduced Tuition Special Scholarships for Self-Funded International Students

Purpose: To enable international students to concentrate on their studies free from financial concerns

Eligibility: Those who satisfy one of the following qualifications are eligible: 1. who have passed the entrance examination for international students and who hold a 'college student' visa prescribed in the, Emigration and Immigration Management and Refuge Recognition Law', at the time of enrollment. 2. who have passed the entrance examination for international students and who hold a 'Permanent Resident' visa etc. 3. who are enroled in Doshisha regardless of the type of admission (type of entrance examination) and who hold a 'College Student' visa

Level of Study: Doctorate, Postgraduate, MBA

Type: Scholarship

Value: Annual tuition fees

Length of Study: 2 years (renewable for up to the standard number of years required for graduation)

Frequency: Annual

Study Establishment: Doshisha University

Country of Study: Japan

Application Procedure: The Scholarship is awarded based on Doshisha's criteria without application

Closing Date: Check the website

For further information contact:

Email: ji-intad@mail.doshisha.ac.jp

Doshisha University Graduate School Scholarship

Purpose: To provide for students enroled in master's or doctoral programs experiencing difficulty meeting educational costs required for them to continue their academic research activities

Eligibility: Graduate students (regular students). Please note Law School, Business School, and Graduate School of Brain Science students may not apply. Students who have been enroled at school longer than the standard number of years for course completion (a leave of absence is not counted as) may not apply. Students selected to receive the following scholarships may not apply: Doshisha University Doctoral-Program Young Researcher Scholarship, Japanese Government (MEXT) Scholarship, Doshisha University Graduate School Reduced Tuition Special Scholarship for Self-Funded International Students

Level of Study: Doctorate, Postgraduate

Type: Scholarship

Value: Half of the total annual tuition fee

Length of Study: 1 year

Frequency: Annual

Study Establishment: Doshisha University

Country of Study: Japan

Application Procedure: Eligible applicants are required to submit an application to the Section for Scholarship by specified date

Closing Date: Check the website

No. of awards given last year: 16

For further information contact:

Email: ji-kosei@mail.doshisha.ac.jp

Doshisha University Reduced Tuition Scholarships for Self-Funded International Students

Purpose: To enable international students to concentrate on their studies free from financial concerns

Eligibility: Those who satisfy one of the following qualifications are eligible: 1. who have passed the entrance examination for international students and who hold a 'College Student' visa prescribed in the 'Emigration and Immigration Management and Refuge Recognition Law', at the time of enrollment. 2. who have passed the entrance examination for international students and who hold a 'Permanent Resident' visa etc. 3. who are enroled in Doshisha regardless of the type of admission (type of entrance examination), and who hold a 'College Student' visa

Level of Study: Doctorate, Postgraduate, MBA

Type: Scholarship

Value: Equivalent to 50% of tuition, equivalent to 30% of tuition, to be made based on Doshisha's criteria

Length of Study: 2 years (renewable for up to the standard number of years required for graduation)

Frequency: Annual

Study Establishment: Doshisha University

Country of Study: Japan

Application Procedure: The scholarship is awarded based on Doshisha's criteria without application

Closing Date: Check the website

Additional Information: Nationals of Japan are not eligible

For further information contact:

Email: ji-intad@mail.doshisha.ac.jp

Graduate School of Brain Science Special Scholarship

Subjects: Brain science

Eligibility: Open to doctorate students with academic excellence and depending on the candidate's contribution to the field. Those who have passed the entrance examination at the Graduate School of Brain Science and are under the age of 32 (for 3rd-year transfer students under the age of 34) at the time of enrollment

Type: Scholarship

Value: Equivalent to the total amount of annual educational costs (including the admission fee, which is charged at the time of enrollment only, tuition, fee for educational support and lab/practical fees)

Length of Study: 1 year (renewable for up to 5 years (for transfer students, for up to 3 years))

Frequency: Annual

Study Establishment: Doshisha University

Country of Study: Japan

Application Procedure: As the initial registration procedure, eligible applicants are required to remit the registration fee and submit an application for the 'Graduate School of Brain Science Special Scholarship' by specified date

Closing Date: Check the website

For further information contact:

Email: jt-nkgjm@mail.doshisha.ac.jp

Duke University

2127 Campus Drive, PO Box 90065, Durham, NC 27708, United States of America

Tel: (1) 919 681 3257
Fax: (1) 919 668 0434
Email: grm@duke.edu
Website: www.gradschool.duke.edu
Contact: Co-ordinator

The Duke University ideally has a small number of superior students working closely with esteemed scholars. It has approximately 2,200 graduate students enroled there, working with more than 1,000 graduate faculty members.

Frontier Research in Earth Sciences (FRES)

Purpose: The FRES program will support research in Earth systems from its core through the critical zone. The project may focus on all or part of the surface, continental lithospheric, and deeper Earth systems over the entire range of temporal and spatial scales

Eligibility: Institutions of Higher Education (IHEs) - Two- and four-year IHEs (including community colleges) accredited in, and having a campus located in the United States, acting on behalf of their faculty members. Special Instructions for International Branch Campuses of United States IHEs: If the proposal includes funding to be provided to an international branch campus of a United States of

America institution of higher education (including through use of subawards and consultant arrangements), the proposer must explain the benefit(s) to the project of performance at the international branch campus, and justify why the project activities cannot be performed at the United States campus

Level of Study: Foundation programme
Type: Research grant
Value: US$30,00,000
Frequency: Annual
Country of Study: Any country
Application Procedure: Many of the projects will be collaborative research from multiple institutions. There is no upper or lower limit on award size, but investigators proposing projects with budgets of less than US$1,000,000 or more than US$3,000,000 are encouraged to contact a Program Officer before submitting a proposal
Closing Date: 20 February
Funding: Private
Additional Information: For-profit organizations: United States commercial organizations, especially small businesses with strong capabilities in scientific or engineering research or educationt

For further information contact:

Email: mbenoit@nsf.gov

The Prof. Rahamimoff Travel Grants Program

Purpose: The Prof. Rahamimoff Travel Grants Program is open to PhD students doing research that requires facilities or expertise not available in their home countries. Each trip will be for a maximum length of 2 months
Eligibility: 1. Applicants must be United States or Israeli citizens. 2. The applicant, rather than his thesis advisor, must write the application. 3. Applicants must be conducting supervised research towards a PhD in an accredited higher education institution, or in a non-profit research institution (government or other, including hospitals). 4. Submitting an application before the PhD research program/plan is formally approved by the university is not recommended. 5. Students in their last year of PhD studies are not eligible to submit applications to the program. 6. The BSF will only accept applications that are in the scientific fields it supports. For a full list, see Eligible Areas of Research
Level of Study: Graduate, Postdoctorate
Type: Grant
Value: US$4,000

Frequency: Annual
Country of Study: Any country
Application Procedure: Applications will be evaluated by a special committee on the basis of their merit in light of the overall aim of the program, and the qualifications of the candidates. In particular, the significance of the trip to the candidate's research will be estimated. One of the criteria frequently used by the panel is the stage of the research program. Trips planned very early or very late in the research program are often not approved
Closing Date: 28 November
Funding: Private

For further information contact:

Email: fundopps@duke.edu

Durham University

The Durham University Business School's Dean's Scholarship

Purpose: Durham University Business School Dean's Scholarship - awarded to an exceptional candidate who can demonstrate significant academic and extra-curricular achievements
Eligibility: Applicants will be considered based upon: Academic achievement Work or voluntary experience relevant to the programme for which they have applied Any additional skills, experience or extra-curricular activities that will add value and indicate that they will make a significant contribution to the cohort on the programme or the Business School. Open to applicants for MSc Programmes (excluding MSc Business Analytics)
Level of Study: Postgraduate
Type: Scholarship
Value: Upto £12,500
Frequency: Annual
Country of Study: Any country
Closing Date: 31 May
Funding: Private

For further information contact:

Durham University Business School, Mill Hill, Lane DH1 3LB, Durham, United Kingdom

Tel: (44) 191 334 5200
Email: research.admissions@durham.ac.uk

Dutch Ministry of Foreign Affairs

Bezuidenhoutseweg 67, The Hague, PO Box 20061, NLD 2500 EB The Hague, Netherlands

Tel:	(31) 70 3486486
Fax:	(31) 70 3484848
Email:	dsi-my@minbuza.nl
Website:	www.minbuza.nl

Dutch foreign policy is driven by the conviction that international cooperation brings peace and promotes security, prosperity, and justice. It is bound by the obligation to promote Dutch interests abroad as effectively and efficiently as possible. To do so, the Netherlands needs a worldwide network of embassies, consulates, and permanent representations to international organizations. The activities, composition, and size of each mission depend on its host country and region. Embassies and consulates-bilateral missions-concern themselves with relations between the Netherlands and other countries.

Netherlands Fellowship Programmes

Subjects: All subjects
Purpose: To support mid-career professionals nominated by their employers
Eligibility: Open to candidates who are employed by an organization other than a large industrial, commercial and/or multinational firm, must be nationals of one of the 57 selected countries (see 'Eligible countries'), must declare that they will return to their home country immediately after they complete the master programme, must have gained admission to a TU/e master course, which is on the NFP course list and have sufficient mastery of the English language. Priority is given to female candidates and to candidates coming from sub-Saharan Africa
Level of Study: Postgraduate
Type: Fellowships

Value: Full-cost scholarship (including international travel, monthly subsistence allowance, tuition fee, books, and health insurance)
Length of Study: 2 years
Frequency: Annual
Country of Study: Netherlands
Application Procedure: Applicants must apply for an NFP fellowship through the Netherlands embassy or consulate in their own country by completing an NFP Application Form and submitting it together with all the required documents and information to the embassy or consulate. Then the Embassy checks and sends the forms to the Nuffic checks. Nuffic decides how many fellowships will be available for each program and sends TU/e the list of NFP candidates
Closing Date: There are several application deadlines, check website for details
Funding: Government
Contributor: Dutch Ministry of Foreign Affairs
Additional Information: Eligible countries: Afghanistan, Albania, Armenia, Autonomous Palestinian Territories, Bangladesh, Benin, Bhutan, Bolivia, Bosnia–Hercegovina, Brazil, Burkina Faso, Cambodia, Cape Verde, China, Colombia, Costa Rica, Cuba, Ecuador, Egypt, El Salvador, Eritrea, Ethiopia, Georgia, Ghana, Guatemala, Guinea–Bissau, Honduras, India, Indonesia, Iran, Ivory Coast, Jordan, Kenya, Macedonia, Mali, Moldova, Mongolia, Mozambique, Namibia, Nepal, Nicaragua, Nigeria, Pakistan, Peru, Philippines, Rwanda, Senegal, South Africa, Sri Lanka, Suriname, Tanzania, Thailand, Uganda, Vietnam, Yemen, Zambia, Zimbabwe. For a more detailed list of criteria, please check website

For further information contact:

Tel:	(31) 40 247 4690
Fax:	(31) 40 244 1692
Email:	io@remove-this.tue.nl

E

Earthwatch Institute

114 Western Avenue, Boston, MA 02134, United States of America

Tel:	(1) 978 461 0081
Fax:	(1) 978 461 2332
Email:	research@earthwatch.org
Website:	www.earthwatch.org/research
Contact:	Gitte Venicx, Research Program Manager

Earthwatch Institute supports diverse research projects of high scientific merit worldwide that address critical environmental and social issues at local, national and international levels. Researchers are given both funding and field assistance from layperson volunteers. Volunteers are recruited by Earthwatch, who pay for the opportunity to assist them in the field.

Earthwatch Field Research Grants

Subjects: We support field-based research in terrestrial, marine, freshwater, and urban ecosystems
Purpose: To provide funding for field-based research projects that meaningfully involve non-specialist volunteers in data collection
Eligibility: All proposals must be submitted by the Principal Investigator (PI). All PIs must have a PhD and an affiliation with a university, government agency, or NGO
Level of Study: Doctorate, Postdoctorate, Postgraduate, Research
Type: Grant

Value: US$20,000-80,000 annually
Length of Study: Successful proposals are funded for 3 years, subject to passing an annual performance review
Frequency: Annual
Study Establishment: Research sites
Country of Study: Any country
Application Procedure: Requests for proposals are distributed in the spring. Applicants must submit a pre-proposal for consideration. Please see the Earthwatch website (earthwatch.org) for more information
Closing Date: Please check the website
Funding: Private, Corporation, Foundation
Contributor: Volunteers' contributions
Additional Information: Any country - some exceptions see 'No Go' list on Earthwatch website. Applications are submitted online

For further information contact:

Email: research@earthwatch.org

Ecole Normale Supérieure (ENS)

Website:	www.ens.fr/admission/selection-internationale/?lang=en

Ècole Normale Supérieure (ENS) organizes an international selection allowing the most promising international students, either in Science or in Arts & Humanities, to follow a three-year Masters Degree at the University.

Ècole Normale Supérieure International Selection Scholarships

Ècole normale supérieure 45, rue d'Ulm, 75230 cedex 05, Paris, France

Tel: (33) 1 44 32 28 01
Email: ens-international@ens.fr

Subjects: Science and Arts and Humanities
Level of Study: Postgraduate
Type: Scholarship
Value: monthly grant of 1,000 Euros for 3 years and accomodation facility provided
Length of Study: 3 years
Frequency: Annual
Country of Study: France
Application Procedure: You must fill and validate the initial application form which will be available at the official website when the application opens. Within 2 days, you will receive an email to activate an account on Dematec, an application platform where you must upload the required documents
Closing Date: 31 October
Contributor: Ècole Normale Supérieure in Paris, France
Additional Information: For more details, please visit official scholarship website: www.ens.fr/admission/selection-internationale/?lang=en

École normale supérieure de Lyon

Website: www.ens-lyon.fr/en/grants-and-scholarships-279258.kjsp?RH=1440663599734&RF=1445867537855

Ampère & MILYON Excellence Scholarships for International Students

Purpose: The Ampère Scholarships of Excellence provide excellent international students with the opportunity to pursue one of the eligible Masters programs offered at ENS de Lyon
Eligibility: International students are eligible to apply for this scholarship. Host institution is ENS de Lyon
Level of Study: Graduate
Type: Scholarship
Value: Value is €1,000
Frequency: Annual
Country of Study: France
Application Procedure: Check website
Closing Date: 10 January

Funding: Private
Additional Information: international.ens-lyon.fr/grants-and-scholarships-279258.kjsp?RH=TEMP-INTER

For further information contact:

Email: ampere.scholarship@ens-lyon.fr

Ampère Excellence Scholarships for International Students

Subjects: Sciences, Social sciences, Arts/Humanities
Purpose: The Ampère Scholarships of Excellence provide excellent international students with the opportunity to pursue one of the eligible Masters programs offered at ENS de Lyon
Eligibility: You must be a foreign national. Candidate for admission in Masters Year 1: provide proof that you have obtained a License (equivalent to 180 ECTS European credits) or an equivalent diploma/level recognized by the ENS deLyon. Candidate for admission in Masters Year 2: provide proof that you have successfully reached Masters Year 1 level (equivalent to 240 ECTS European credits) or have attained an equivalent diploma/level recognized by the ENS de Lyon (e.g. MPhil)
Level of Study: Postgraduate
Type: Scholarship
Value: €1,000 per month for a duration of 1 year
Frequency: Annual
Country of Study: France
Closing Date: 12 January
Funding: Government
Contributor: ENS de Lyon, France
Additional Information: For more details, please visit official scholarship website: www.ens-lyon.fr/en/grants-and-scholarships-279258.kjsp?RH=1440663599734&RF=1445867537855

École normale supérieure Paris-Saclay

The ENS Paris-Saclay used to be Cachan. It is located in Cachan dans le Val-de-Marne department near Paris, in the Ile-de-France area of France. It is one of the most prestigious and selective French Grandes Ecoles.

Monabiphot Masters Scholarships

Subjects: Molecular nano- and bio-photonics
Purpose: This Master Course offers an original qualification in the highly innovative domain of molecular photonics for

telecommunications and biology. Skills will be acquired at the strongly interdisciplinary level needed to master emerging technologies and to develop original concepts and applications aiming at novel technological breakthroughs in this domain

Eligibility: Both European Union students and Non-European Union students are eligible to apply

Level of Study: Postgraduate

Type: Scholarship

Value: Non-European Union students: €23,500 per year, European Union students: €16,000 per year, Additional scholarships for specific regions: €47.000

Country of Study: France

Closing Date: 31 January

For further information contact:

LPQM, ENS-Cachan 61, Avenue du President Wilson, 94235, Cachan Cedex, France

Tel:	(33) 1 47 40 55 60
Email:	ledoux@lpqm.ens-cachan.fr
Contact:	Isabelle LEDOUX

Economic History Association (EHA)

EHA is based at the University of Wisconsin - see here: http://eh.net/eha/grants-and-fellowships/

Website:	www.eh.net/eha
Contact:	angela.vossmeyer@cmc.edu

The Economic History Association (EHA) was founded in 1940. Its mission is to stimulate interest in the study of economic history, to encourage research in economic history and ideas, to co-operate with societies devoted to the study of agricultural, industrial, technological or business history, and to collaborate with economists, historians, statisticians, geographers and all other students of economic change.

Arthur H Cole Grants-in-Aid

Subjects: Economic history

Purpose: To support research

Eligibility: Applicants must have completed a PhD and be members of the EHA

Level of Study: Postdoctorate

Type: Grant

Value: Up to US$5,000

Frequency: Annual

Country of Study: Any country

Application Procedure: The Committee on Research in Economic History awards Arthur H. Cole grants-in-aid to support research in economic history, regardless of time period or geographic area. Awards typically are in amounts up to $5,000, although higher amounts may be awarded in exceptional cases. Applicants must be members of the Association and must hold the Ph.D. degree. Preference is given to recent Ph.D. recipients

Closing Date: 1 March

Funding: Private

Contributor: EHA members

Additional Information: Membership enquiries should be addressed to the office of the Executive Director or the website

For further information contact:

Email:	angela.vossmeyer@cmc.edu
Contact:	Professor Angela Vossmeyer

Edinburgh Napier University

219 Colinton Rd, EH14 1DJ, Edinburgh, United Kingdom

Tel:	(44) 333 900 6040
Contact:	Edinburgh Napier University

Edinburgh Napier University is a public university in Edinburgh, Scotland. Napier Technical College, the predecessor of the university was founded in 1964, taking its name from Scottish mathematician John Napier.

Data Visualisation Design, Ambiguity & Decision Making in Megaprojects: EPSRC Studentship

Purpose: Professor Paolo Quattrone has successfully been allocated a studentship for this project in collaboration with Costain

Eligibility: 1. United Kingdom/European Union Countries. 2. Applicants must meet EPSRC eligibility criteria. 3. Please note that international students are not eligible for this funding

Level of Study: Postgraduate

Type: Studentship

Value: £22,159

Length of Study: 4 year

Frequency: Annual

Country of Study: Any country

Closing Date: 31 May
Funding: International office

For further information contact:

Email: phd@business-school.ed.ac.uk

Gordon David Family Scholarship

Purpose: The Edinburgh Centre for Carbon Innovation (ECCI) is offering two scholarships for those undertaking research related to the work of ECCI
Level of Study: Postgraduate
Type: Scholarship
Value: £8,000
Length of Study: 3 year
Frequency: Annual
Country of Study: Any country
Funding: Foundation

For further information contact:

Email: phd@business-school.ed.ac.uk

Improving Project Delivery: ESRC Studentship

Purpose: Professor Paolo Quattrone has successfully been allocated a studentship for the project 'Improving Project Delivery' in collaboration with the Infrastructure and Project Authority
Eligibility: 1. United Kingdom/European Union Countries. 2. Applicants must meet ESRC eligibility criteria. 3. Please note that international students are not eligible for this funding
Level of Study: Postgraduate
Type: Studentship
Value: £14,777
Length of Study: 3 year
Frequency: Annual
Country of Study: Any country
Closing Date: 31 May
Funding: International office

For further information contact:

Email: phd@business-school.ed.ac.uk

Institute for Particle and Nuclear Physics MSc Prize Scholarships

Purpose: To provide a scholarship to a student the MSc in Nuclear and Particle Physics

Eligibility: Applicants must have applied to study full-time on the MSc Particle and Nuclear Physics programme of study
Level of Study: Postgraduate
Type: Scholarship
Value: £5,000
Length of Study: 1 year
Frequency: Annual
Country of Study: Any country
Closing Date: 1 May
Funding: International office

For further information contact:

Email: msc.pnp@ph.ed.ac.uk

Jean Kennoway Howells Scholarship

Purpose: One scholarship available for taught masters programmes offered by the Reid School of Music
Eligibility: The scholarship will be awarded to students who have applied for admission on a full-time basis for a postgraduate taught Masters programme of study within the Reid School of Music commencing in the academic year. To be eligible, applicants must have received an offer to study by the scholarship deadline
Level of Study: Postgraduate
Type: Scholarship
Value: £9,000
Length of Study: 1 year
Frequency: Annual
Country of Study: Any country
Closing Date: May
Funding: Foundation

For further information contact:

Email: ecapgtdegrees@ed.ac.uk

South Asian Scholarships at Edinburgh Napier University

Subjects: Scholarships are awarded to study the subjects offered by the university
Purpose: The Edinburgh Napier University is offering partial scholarships for self-funding students from Afghanistan, India, Pakistan, Bangladesh, Nepal or Sri Lanka. Scholarships are awarded to study a bachelor, masters or PhD course in September or January
Eligibility: Applicants whose native language is not English are required to demonstrate proficiency in English. The TOEFL is the most frequently submitted examination score that the University receives, however, the Admissions Office

will use other measures upon the applicant's request. The IELTS, ACT, and SAT examinations may also be used

Value: The scholarships are merit-based ranging from £1,000 to £3,000

Study Establishment: Scholarships are awarded to study the subjects offered by the university

Country of Study: United Kingdom

Application Procedure: The scholarships will be awarded on a first-come, first-served basis. You will be automatically considered for the scholarship and be advised of the scholarship amount you are eligible for if you meet the following selection criteria: 1. You hold an unconditional offer to study on a full-time bachelors or masters course at Edinburgh Napier. 2. You meet the eligibility criteria detailed above. 3. You have made your £3,500 deposit payment towards your fees. There is no additional application process for this scholarship. You must self-funding your course holding an offer to study a bachelor, masters or PhD course in September or January

Closing Date: Open

Additional Information: For more details please visit to the website scholarship-positions.com/south-asian-scholarships-edinburgh-napier-university-uk/2017/12/11/

For further information contact:

Email: international@napier.ac.uk

Edith Cowan University

270 Joondalup Drive, Joondalup, WA 6027, Australia

Tel: (61) 8 6304 0000
Email: enquiries@ecu.edu.au
Website: www.ecu.edu.au
Contact: Edith Cowan University

The Edith Cowan University is an Australian public university located in Perth, Western Australia. It was named after the first woman to be elected to an Australian Parliament, Edith Cowan, and is the only Australian university named after a woman.

Brett Lockyer Scholarship

Subjects: Jazz clarinet
Purpose: To enable the further development of jazz clarinet studies at ECU and to develop those specialist skills in a currently enrolled jazz clarinet student at WAAPA
Eligibility: Open for students studying jazz clarinet within the jazz programme

Level of Study: Postgraduate
Type: Scholarship
Value: Up to A$5,000
Application Procedure: Check website for further details.

For further information contact:

Tel: (33) 8 9370 6594
Email: j.hamilton@ecu.edu.au

Luke Pen Fund-Honours Scholarships

Subjects: Waterways research
Purpose: To encourage young people to be involved in the gaining of scientific knowledge of river characteristics
Level of Study: Graduate
Type: Scholarship
Value: A$50,000
Length of Study: 1 year
Frequency: Annual
Application Procedure: Check website address for further details
Closing Date: 31 March
Funding: Trusts
Contributor: Luke Pen Scholarship Trust

For further information contact:

Department of Water, Drainage and Waterways Branch, PO Box K822, Perth, WA 6842, Australia

Email: james.mackintosh@water.wa.gov.au
Contact: Verity Klemm

Merit International Postgraduate Scholarship

Subjects: Scholarships are awarded to learn any of the courses offered by the university
Purpose: The Edith Cowan University is inviting applications for Merit International Postgraduate Scholarship to study in Australia. This scholarship is available to students who can demonstrate high levels of academic achievement and English competency in their previous studies
Eligibility: International students are eligible to apply for this scholarship.Students must have a high level of English competency
Type: Postgraduate scholarships
Value: The scholarship offers a 10% reduction in your tuition fees for the duration of your course at ECU

Study Establishment: Scholarships are awarded to learn any of the courses offered by the university
Country of Study: Australia
Application Procedure: See the website
Closing Date: 31 December
Additional Information: For more details please visit the website scholarship-positions.com/merit-international-postgraduate-scholarship-edith-cowan-university-australia/2018/02/03/

Postgraduate Petroleum Engineering Scholarship

Purpose: ECU endeavors to innovate course offerings and stay up to date with demands of industry and as such, ECU is pleased to introduce scholarships to students seeking to study the new Graduate Diploma in Petroleum Engineering (J69); Master of Engineering (Petroleum Engineering specialization) (I59); and the Master of Technology (Petroleum Engineering) (J70). The scholarship offers a 20% reduction in your tuition fees for the duration of the course
Eligibility: 1. Be commencing study of a Graduate Diploma in Petroleum Engineering (J69); Master of Engineering (Petroleum Engineering specialization) (I59); or the Master of Technology (Petroleum Engineering) (J70). 2. Meet ECU's academic direct entry requirements for the course of your choice. 3. Not be in receipt of another scholarship or sponsorship. 4. Be an International student, not an Australian Citizen, Australian Permanent Resident, or New Zealand Citizen. 5. Intend to study a postgraduate degree. 6. Be studying at ECU Joondalup
Level of Study: Postgraduate
Type: Scholarship
Frequency: Annual
Country of Study: Any country
Closing Date: 31 July
Funding: International office

For further information contact:

Email: international.parternships@ecu.edu.au

Education and Research Foundation for the Society of Nuclear Medicine (SNM)

1850 Samuel Morse Drive, Reston, VA 20190, United States of America

Tel: (1) 703 708 9000
Email: tpinkham@erfsnm.org

Website: erf.snm.org
Contact: Theresa Pinkham, Executive Director

The Society of Nuclear Medicine (SNM) is an international, scientific and professional organization founded in 1954 to promote the science, technology and practical application of nuclear medicine. Its 16,000 members are physicians, technologists and scientists specializing in the research and practice of nuclear medicine.

Society of Nuclear Medicine Pilot Research Grants in Nuclear Medicine/Molecular Imaging

Subjects: Health and medical sciences and nuclear science
Purpose: To support Master's or PhD students to start research in nuclear medicine
Eligibility: Open to basic and clinical scientists in early stages of their career
Level of Study: Doctorate, Postgraduate
Type: Grant
Value: US$25,000
Frequency: Annual
Study Establishment: Society of Nuclear Medicine
Country of Study: United States of America
Application Procedure: Applicants must submit a completed application form along with abstract of project proposal and budget proposal
Closing Date: 20 February

For further information contact:

SNM Development Office, 1850 Samuel Morse Drive, United States of America

Tel: (1) 703 652 6795
Email: nmitchell@snm.org

Education New Zealand (ENZ)

Level 5, Lambton House, 160 Lambton Quay, PO Box 12041, Wellington 6144, New Zealand

Tel: (64) 4 472 0788
Fax: (64) 4 471 2828
Email: info@educationnz.govt.nz
Website: www.newzealandeducated.com/scholarships
Contact: Scholarships Manager

Education New Zealand (ENZ) is the Government Agency responsible for promoting New Zealand education to the world. We create strategies and programmes alongside New Zealand's education sector, government agencies and governments overseas that increase and broaden our international education activities.

Korea New Zealand Agricultural Cooperation Scholarships (KNZACS)

Subjects: Veterinary or animal science or forestry
Purpose: To promote greater understanding between Korea and New Zealand, and strengthen the trade and economic relationship in veterinary or animal science or forestry sectors
Level of Study: Doctorate, Postgraduate
Type: Scholarship
Value: New Zealand university fees/levies and stipend of NZ $30,000 per year
Length of Study: 3 years in the case of PhD, and 2 years in the case of master
Study Establishment: Approved universities
Country of Study: New Zealand
Application Procedure: Please visit website to apply
Closing Date: 28 April
Funding: Government
Additional Information: Korea: Contact Sang-Hun Lee, EPIS International Cooperation Team, Manager sanghuni@epis.or.kr. New Zealand: scholarship@enz.govt.nz

For further information contact:

Email: scholarship@enz.govt.nz

Shirtcliffe Fellowship

Purpose: The purpose of the Shirtcliffe Fellowships is to assist students of outstanding ability and character who are graduates of a university in New Zealand, in the continuation of their studies in New Zealand or the Commonwealth
Eligibility: The fellowships shall be open to persons of either gender who are NZ citizens who: a) are candidates for a doctoral scholarship awarded by a New Zealand university and b) whose degree is awarded in any faculty or school which, if that degree had been available in 1935, would in the opinion of the NZVCC be expected to have been awarded following a course of study in one or other of the Faculties of Arts, Science, Law, Commerce or Agriculture
Level of Study: Doctorate
Type: Fellowship

Value: $5,000 per annum
Frequency: Every 3 years
Country of Study: New Zealand
Application Procedure: Apply online. For further info, refer website link www.universitiesnz.ac.nz/scholarships/shirtcliffe or www.nzvcc.ac.nz
Closing Date: 1 March
Funding: Private

For further information contact:

Email: scholarships-cf@universitiesnz.ac.nz

Education.govt.nz

Ngarimu VC and 28th (Maori) Battalion Memorial Scholarships

Purpose: These scholarships support high achieving tertiary students of Maori descent
Eligibility: 1. Applications for both scholarships will need to include a brief statement of up to 250 words, outlining the topic, the reasons for your interest in the subject area and your future expectations. 2. Preference will be given to applicants who are able to demonstrate that their studies aim to improve the social, economic and cultural wellbeing of Maori or are on Maori issues. Eligible applicants can apply for both scholarships
Level of Study: Research
Type: Scholarship
Frequency: Annual
Country of Study: Any country
Application Procedure: All applicants will need to include: 1. a form completed by a Kaumatua, Maori leader that certifies your whakapapa. 2. a form completed by someone who can endorse your academic achievement and suitability to study. 3. a Te Reo Maori statement that demonstrates your language capabilities. 4. a statement about the Nga Ahuatanga characteristics you possess that are similar to those identified as consistent with the 28th (Maori) Battalion soldiers
Closing Date: 9 September
Funding: Private

For further information contact:

Matauranga House, Level 1, 33 Bowen Street, Wellington 6011, New Zealand

Tel: (64) 800 165 225
Email: Ngarimu.Scholarship@education.govt.nz

Educational Testing Service (ETS)

660 Rosedale Road, Princeton, NJ 08541-0001, United States of America

Tel:	(1) 609 921 9000
Fax:	(1) 609 734 5410
Email:	ldelauro@ets.org
Website:	www.ets.org
Contact:	Ms Linda J DeLauro

The Educational Testing Service (ETS) is a non-profit organization whose goal is to help advance quality and equity in education by providing fair and valid assessments, research, and related services.

Educational Testing Service Harold Gulliksen Psychometric Fellowship Program

Subjects: Educational measurement, psychometrics, and statistics
Purpose: To increase the number of well-trained scientists in educational measurement, psychometrics, and statistics
Eligibility: Open to candidates who are enroled in a doctoral program at the time of application and have completed all the coursework toward the PhD, and be at the dissertation stage of their program
Level of Study: Predoctorate
Type: Fellowship
Value: US$20,000 (stipend), US$8,000 (tuition fees, and work-study program commitments), and a small grant for the purchase of equipment or software
Length of Study: 1 year
Frequency: Annual
Country of Study: United States of America or other countries if appropriate
No. of awards offered: 10
Application Procedure: Submit all application materials via email with PDF attachments. Two applications have to be submitted for this program. Preliminary application requires letter of interest, statement describing finanical assistance, nomination letter and current curriculum vitae. Final application should contain the following information. Detailed project description (approximately 15 double-spaced pages) of the research the individual will carry out at the host university, including the purpose, goals and methods of the research Graduate academic transcripts (unofficial copies are acceptable) Evidence of scholarship (presentations, manuscripts, etc.)

Closing Date: 15 February
Funding: Private
Contributor: ETS
No. of awards offered last year: 1
No. of awards applicants last year: 10
Additional Information: Kindly refer the website for further information. www.ets.org/research/internship-fellowship/gulliksen

For further information contact:

Email: internfellowships@ets.org

Educational Testing Service Postdoctoral Fellowships

Subjects: Measurement theory, validity, natural language, processing and computational linguistics, cognitive psychology, learning theory, linguistics, speech recognition and processing, teaching and classroom research, and statistics
Purpose: To provide research opportunities to individuals who hold a doctorate in education and related fields, and to increase the number of women and minority professionals conducting research in educational measurement and related fields
Eligibility: Open to applicants who have received their doctoral degree within the past 3 years. Selections will be based on the candidate's scholarship, the technical strength of the proposed topic of research, and the explicit objective of the research and its relationship to ETS research goals and priorities
Level of Study: Postdoctorate
Type: Fellowship
Value: The amount is US$50,000 for the 1-year period. In addition, limited relocation expenses consistent with the ETS guidelines will be reimbursed. Renewal for a second year by mutual consent
Length of Study: Up to 2 years, renewable after the first year by mutual agreement
Frequency: Annual
Country of Study: United States of America
No. of awards offered: 15
Application Procedure: Refer the ETS website for further details. All application materials should be sent electronically as attachments
Closing Date: 1 January
Funding: Private
Contributor: ETS
No. of awards offered last year: 1
No. of awards applicants last year: 15

For further information contact:

Email: internfellowships@ets.org

Educational Testing Service Summer Internship Program in Research for Graduate Students

Subjects: Measurement theory, validity, natural language, processing and computational linguistics, cognitive psychology, learning theory, linguistics, speech recognition and processing, teaching and classroom research, and statistics, and international large scale assessments

Purpose: To provide research opportunities to individuals enroled in a doctoral program and to increase the number of women and underrepresented minority professionals conducting research in educational and related fields

Eligibility: Current full-time enrollment in a relevant doctoral program Completion of at least 2 years of coursework toward the PhD or EdD. prior to the program start date

Level of Study: Predoctorate

Type: Internship

Value: US$6,000 salary and US$2,000 housing allowance for interns residing outside a 50-mile radius of ETS

Length of Study: June to July (8 weeks)

Frequency: Annual

Country of Study: United States of America

No. of awards offered: 180

Application Procedure: Refer the ETS website for further details. All application materials should be sent electronically as attachments

Closing Date: 1 February

Funding: Private, Private, Private

Contributor: ETS

No. of awards offered last year: 18

No. of awards applicants last year: 180

Additional Information: Duration of Research Internship is eight weeks: 3 June-26 July

For further information contact:

Email: internfellowships@ets.org

Educational Testing Service Summer Internships in Programme Direction

Subjects: Measurement and evaluation

Purpose: To provide opportunities, especially for women and minority professionals, for a work and learning experience that will assist the participants in exploring career alternatives in the field of measurement and evaluation

Eligibility: Current full-time enrollment in a relevant doctoral program; Completion of at least two years of coursework toward the doctorate prior to the program start date

Level of Study: Doctorate, Postgraduate

Type: Internship

Value: Salary of US$6,000 with the transportation allowance and housing for interns who commute more than 50 miles

Length of Study: 8 weeks (3 June-26 July)

Study Establishment: ETS headquarters in Princeton

Country of Study: United States of America

Application Procedure: Application should include references and transcripts

Closing Date: 1 February

Additional Information: Applicants will be notified of selection decisions by 30 March

Educational Testing Service Sylvia Taylor Johnson Minority Fellowship in Educational Measurement

Subjects: Measurement theory, validity, natural language, processing and computational linguistics, cognitive psychology, learning theory, linguistics, speech recognition and processing, teaching and classroom research, statistics and minority issues in education

Purpose: To promote excellence, to encourage original and significant research for early career scholars and to provide talented minority scholars an opportunity to carry out independent research under the mentorship of ETS senior researchers. Studies focused on issues concerning the education of minority students are especially encouraged

Eligibility: Open to applicants who have received their doctoral degree within the past 10 years and who are citizens or permanent residents of the United States. Selections will be based on the applicant's record of accomplishment, and proposed topic of research. Applicants should have a commitment to education and an independent body of scholarship that signals the promise of continuing outstanding contributions to educational measurement

Level of Study: Postdoctorate

Type: Fellowship

Value: Salary is competitive. US$5,000 one-time relocation incentive for round-trip relocation expenses. In addition, limited relocation expenses, consistent with ETS guidelines, will be reimbursed

Length of Study: Up to 2 years, renewable after the first year by mutual agreement

Frequency: Annual

Country of Study: United States of America

No. of awards offered: 15

Application Procedure: Refer the ETS website for further details. All application materials should be sent electronically as attachments

Closing Date: 1 February
Funding: Private
Contributor: ETS
No. of awards offered last year: 1
No. of awards applicants last year: 15
Additional Information: Through her research, extensive writings and service to the educational community as an educator, editor, counsellor, committee member and collaborator during her lifetime, Sylvia Taylor Johnson had a significant influence in educational measurement and assessment nationally. In honour of Dr Johnson's important contributions to the field of education, the ETS has established the Sylvia Taylor Johnson Minority Fellowship in educational measurement

For further information contact:

Email: internfellowships@ets.org

Postdoctoral Fellowship Program

Subjects: Individuals who have earned their doctoral degree within the last three years are invited to apply for a rewarding fellowship experience which combines working on cutting-edge ETS research projects and conducting independent research that is relevant to ETS's goals
Purpose: Provide research opportunities to individuals who hold a doctorate in the fields such as Applied Psychometrics, Artificial Intelligence Based Automated Scoring, Modeling of Response Processes and Response Times, Psychometric Issues in Adaptive Testing Designs, Statistical and Psychometric Foundations and Statistical and Psychometric Issues in Group-Scored Assessments
Eligibility: 1. Doctorate in a relevant discipline within the past three years. 2. Evidence of prior independent research
Level of Study: Postdoctorate
Type: Fellowship
Length of Study: Upto 2 years and it is renewable
Frequency: Annual
Country of Study: Any country
Application Procedure: Two applications have to be submitted from our end. Preliminary Application Complete the electronic preliminary application form. On the application form: 1. Indicate your research area of interest. 2. Enter your statement of interest. 3. Enter an abstract about the independent research you propose to conduct while at ETS.   4. Attach a copy of your curriculum vitae. 5. Attach a copy of your graduate transcripts (student copy is acceptable). Final Application If your preliminary application is approved, you will be invited to submit the following materials: 1. a detailed proposal (approximately five double-spaced pages) describing the research that will be carried out at ETS and how it relates to

current ETS research. 2. samples of published research. 3. names and email addresses of three individuals who are familiar with your work, and who are willing to complete a recommendation form that will be sent to them electronically
Closing Date: 1 February
Funding: Private
Additional Information: For more information on this internship program, contact internfellowships@ets.org

For further information contact:

Email: internfellowships@ets.org

Eidgenössische Technische Hochschule Zurich

Patricia Heuberger-Meyer, HG E 68.1, Rämistrasse 101, 8092 Zürich, Switzerland

Tel: (41) 44 632 56 13
Fax: (41) 44 632 15 42
Contact: ETH Zurich, Stab ETH Global

ETH Zurich is a science, technology, engineering and mathematics university in the city of Zürich, Switzerland.

The Engineering for Development (E4D) Doctoral Scholarship Programme

Purpose: To promote doctoral research for the benefit of developing countries
Level of Study: Doctorate
Type: Scholarship
Value: 1,75,000 CHF
Length of Study: 3 years
Frequency: Annual
Country of Study: Switzerland
Application Procedure: Please refer www.ethz.ch/content/dam/ethz/main/eth-zurich/global/r4d-netzwerk/E4D%20programme/Requirement%20criteria%20E4D_final_%202017.pdf
Closing Date: 30 November
Contributor: Sawiris Foundation for Social Development
Additional Information: Please send your complete concept note to patricia.heuberger@sl.ethz.ch

For further information contact:

Tel: (41) 44 632 11 11
Email: e4d@sl.ethz.ch

Electoral Commission New Zealand

Level 6, Greenock House 39, The Terrace, PO Box 3050, Wellington 6140, New Zealand

Tel: (64) 4 474 0670
Fax: (64) 4 474 0674
Email: helena@elections.govt.nz
Website: www.elections.org.nz

The Electoral Commission New Zealand is an independent Crown entity, which registers political parties and party logos. It also receives registered parties annual returns of donations and returns of election expenses and allocates election broadcasting time and funds to eligible political parties. The Commission also encourages and conducts public education on electoral matters.

Wallace Scholarships for tertiary student research

Subjects: Specific subjects are set each year, all are in the general areas of electoral participation
Purpose: To encourage research work that will be useful in designing electoral education and information programmes and help raise public awareness of electoral issues
Eligibility: Scholarships are for research as part of a New Zealand university degree
Level of Study: Research
Type: Scholarships
Value: NZ $500-2,000
Length of Study: usually 1 year
Frequency: Annual
Country of Study: New Zealand
No. of awards offered: 6
Application Procedure: Applicants must send a 1-page research proposal, letter of endorsement from an academic supervisor and contact details and enrollment qualifications
Closing Date: 2 February
Funding: Government
No. of awards offered last year: 3
No. of awards applicants last year: 6
Additional Information: All queries should be directed to Dr Helena Catt at catt@elections.govt.nz or phone 04 474 0676

For further information contact:

Email: Wellingtonorcatt@elections.govt.nz

Embassy of France in Australia

6 Perth Avenue, Yarralumla, Canberra ACT 2600, Australia

Tel: (61) 2 6216 0100
Fax: (61) 2 6216 0132
Email: education@ambafrance-au.org
Website: www.ambafrance-au.org
Contact: Higher Education Attaché

The Embassy of France in Australia supports the partnership between French and Australian Universities and offers grants and scholarships to help the students' mobility.

Language Assistantships in France and New Caledonia

Subjects: French language studies
Purpose: To enable graduates who intend to teach French in the future or beginning teachers of French to improve their language skills
Eligibility: Open to young Australian graduates and school teachers aged 20–30
Level of Study: Graduate
Type: Assistantship
Value: €902 living allowance plus medical cover in France, between €1,250–1,350 in overseas Départements' and between €1,400 and €1,600 in New Caledonia
Length of Study: 7 months
Frequency: Annual
Study Establishment: Any approved high school
Country of Study: Any country
No. of awards offered: 120
Application Procedure: Application forms are available on the website of the French Embassy: www.ambafrance-au.org
Closing Date: October for New Caledonia, November for Metropolitan France and overseas Départements
Funding: Government
No. of awards offered last year: 80
No. of awards applicants last year: 120
Additional Information: These awards are organized by the higher education office of the Embassy of France in Australia. Successful applicants will conduct English conversation classes with small groups of students for 12 hours per week

Ministry of Foreign Affairs (France) International Teaching Fellowships

Subjects: French language education

Purpose: To enable experienced teachers of French to spend time at a French primary school, a French college, or a French lycée

Eligibility: Open to Australian teachers of French employed by state education authorities

Level of Study: Professional development

Type: Fellowship

Length of Study: 1 year

Frequency: Annual

Study Establishment: A lycée, collège, primary school or Institut Universitaire de Formation de Maïtres (IUFM)

Country of Study: France

Application Procedure: Applicants must complete an application form, available from state departments of education and on the French Embassy website: www.ambafrance-au.org

Closing Date: 30 April

Funding: Government

No. of awards offered last year: 2 awards

Additional Information: These awards are organized by the higher education office of the Embassy of France in Australia (BCF)

For further information contact:

Email: candidatures.eiffel@campusfrance.org

Ministry of Foreign Affairs (France) Stage de la Réunion (One Month Scholarships)

Subjects: French language teaching

Purpose: To enable school teachers of French to attend a course on the methodology specific to the teaching of French at primary or secondary level

Eligibility: Open to Australian teachers of French only

Level of Study: Professional development

Type: Scholarship

Value: All costs except travel costs between Australia and Réunion Island

Length of Study: 1 month

Frequency: Annual

Study Establishment: Cifept in Le Tampon

Country of Study: Other

Application Procedure: Applicants must write for details

Closing Date: 15 March

Funding: Government

No. of awards offered last year: 5

Additional Information: These awards are organised by the Bureau de Co-opération pour le Francais of the Embassy of France in Australia (BCF)

For further information contact:

Email: candidatures.eiffel@campusfrance.org

Embassy of the United States in Kabul

Humphrey Fellowship Program, Public Affairs Section, United States Embassy, Kabul, Afghanistan

Tel: (93) 20 230 0436
Fax: (93) 20 230 1364
Email: kabulwebmaster@state.gov

By providing future leaders and policy makers with experience in the United States society, culture and professional fields, the Embassy of the United States in Kabul provides a basis for lasting, productive, ties between Americans and their professional counterparts overseas.

Ambassadors Fund for Cultural Preservation Small Grants Competition

Eligibility: 1. Full and complete Application for Federal Assistance (SF-424), including Budget Information for Non-Construction Programs (SF-424A), Assurances for Non-Construction Programs (SF-424B), Applicant Organizational Information Form, and, if applicable, Disclosure of Lobbying Activities (SF-LLL). 2. Project basics, including title, project dates, and AFCP focus area. 3. Project applicant information, including contact information, DUNS Number, and SAM registration status. 4. Project location. 5. Proof of official permission to undertake the project from the office, agency, or organization that either owns or is otherwise responsible for the preservation and protection of the site, object, or collection. 6. Project purpose that summarizes the project objectives and desired results. 7. Project activities description that presents the project tasks in chronological order (Note: If the proposed project is part of a larger effort involving multiple projects supported by other entities, the plan must present the full scope of the preservation effort and the place of the proposed project within that larger effort). 8. Project time frame or schedule that lists the major project phases and milestones with target dates for achieving them (Note: Applicants may propose project periods of up to 60 months [five years]; projects must begin before 30 September, and be completed no later than September 30, 2024). All submitted documents must be in

English. 9. Project participant information, including resumes or CVs of the proposed project director and other primary project participants. For further information, refer website

Level of Study: Graduate
Type: Grant
Frequency: Annual
Country of Study: Any country
Application Procedure: The applicants will first be screened for technical eligibility based on the objectives, priorities, requirements, ineligible activities, and unallowable costs contained in this funding opportunity. The Embassy and its Washington office may deem applications ineligible if they do not fully adhere to the criteria stated herein
Closing Date: 28 November
Funding: Private

For further information contact:

United States Embassy New Delhi, Shantipath, Chanakyapuri, New Delhi 110021, India

Tel: (91) 11 91 11 2419 8000
Email: Nd_GrantApplications@state.gov

Hubert H. Humphrey Fellowship Program

Subjects: Culture and professional fields
Purpose: The Hubert H. Humphrey Fellowship Program, which is a Fulbright program, brings accomplished young and mid-career professionals from developing countries to the United States for ten months of non-degree graduate study and related practical professional experiences
Eligibility: Open to candidates who have completed a university degree programme, are proficient in written and spoken English, and also have 5 years of relevant professional experience
Level of Study: Postdoctorate
Type: Fellowship
Length of Study: 1 year
Frequency: Annual
Country of Study: United States of America
Application Procedure: Applicants should submit a curriculum vitae along with copies of university transcripts and degrees
Closing Date: 15 May
Funding: Government
Contributor: The United States Department of State Bureau of Educational and Cultural Affairs

For further information contact:

Email: humphrey@usief.org.in

Endeavour Research Fellowship

Department of Education and Training International Group International Mobility Branch Endeavour Scholarships and Fellowships, Canberra, ACT 2601 9880, Australia

Email: endcavour@education.gov.au
Contact: Endeavour Research Fellowship

The Endeavour Scholarships and Fellowships are the Australian Government's competitive, merit-based scholarships and fellowships providing opportunities for Australians to undertake study, research or professional development overseas and for overseas citizens to do the same in Australia.

Endeavour Research Fellowship for International Applicants

Subjects: Fellowships are awarded in any field of study
Purpose: The Endeavour Scholarships and Fellowships aim to build Australia's reputation for excellence in the provision of education and research, support the internationalisation of the Australian higher education and research sectors and offer high-achieving individuals from overseas and Australia opportunities to increase their productivity and expertise in their field
Eligibility: Be aged 18 years or over at the commencement of their program. Be a citizen and/or permanent resident of a participating country (section 8). Commence their proposed program after 1 January and no later than 30 November. Provide all relevant supporting documentation (section 9). Not currently hold or have completed, after 1 January, an Australian Government sponsored scholarship and/or fellowship (directly administered to recipients by the Australian Government). Not apply for a category in which they have already completed an Endeavour scholarship or fellowship
Value: All recipients will receive: travel allowance: $3,000 (provision to pay up to $4,500 under special circumstances); establishment allowance: $2,000 (fellowships) or $4,000 (scholarships); monthly stipend: $3,000 (paid up to the maximum category duration on a pro-rata basis)*; health insurance for the full category duration (OSHC for international recipients); travel insurance (excluding during programme for

international recipients); Endeavour scholarship recipients will also receive tuition fees paid up to the maximum study/ research duration on a pro-rata basis. Tuition includes student service and amenities fees

Study Establishment: Fellowships are awarded in any field of study

Country of Study: Australia

Application Procedure: Applications must be submitted using the Endeavour Online application system. Applicants are encouraged to commence their applications early and submit their application as early as possible during the application period due to the large volume of users on the system in the lead up to the closing date. Submitting early ensures that you will not have any last minute technical problems due to the large number of applications being submitted

Closing Date: Applications will close on 30 June

Additional Information: For more details please visit the website scholarship-positions.com/endeavour-research-fellowship-international-students-2014/2013/04/13/

Engineering and Physical Sciences Research Council (EPSRC)

Polaris House, North Star Avenue, Wiltshire SN2 1ET, Swindon, United Kingdom

Tel:	(44) 17 9344 4239
Fax:	(44) 17 9344 4007
Email:	jan.tucker@epsrc.ac.uk
Website:	www.epsrc.ac.uk
Contact:	Ms Jan Tucker, Peer Review Operations

The Engineering and Physical Sciences Research Council (EPSRC) promotes and supports high quality, basic, strategic and applied research and related postgraduate training in engineering and physical sciences. It aims to advance knowledge and technology by providing trained scientists and engineers, in order to meet the needs of users and beneficiaries, and thereby contribute to economic competitiveness and quality of life.

Daphne Jackson Fellowships

Subjects: Physical sciences, engineering and information technology

Purpose: To enable high-level scientists and engineers to return to their professions after a career break for family commitments

Eligibility: Promising engineers and scientists who have taken a career break for family commitments, who have obtained at least a first degree and who are normally resident in the United Kingdom

Level of Study: Graduate, Postdoctorate, Research

Type: A variable number of fellowships

Value: Fixed to United Kingdom Research Council RA1A scale

Length of Study: 2 years (part-time possible)

Frequency: Dependent on funds available

Study Establishment: Universities or research institutions in the United Kingdom that are convenient for the candidate

Country of Study: United Kingdom

No. of awards offered: 69

Application Procedure: Applicants must complete an application form. Further information can be found on the website www.sst.ph.ic.ac.uk/trust

Closing Date: Applicants must write for details

Funding: Government, Commercial, Private

No. of awards offered last year: 6

No. of awards applicants last year: 69

Additional Information: Daphne Jackson Fellowships are sponsored by the Biotechnology and Biological Sciences Research Council (BBSRC), the Particle Physics and Astronomy Research Council (PPARC) and the Natural Environment Research Council (NERC), together with charitable foundations, learned societies, universities and industries

For further information contact:

The Daphne Jackson Memorial Fellowships Trust Department of Physics University of Surrey, GU2 7XH, Surrey, United Kingdom

Tel:	(44) 1483 879166
Email:	j.wooley@surrey.ac.uk
Contact:	Ms Jennifer Wooley, Administrator

Engineering and Physical Sciences Research Council Standard Research Studentships

Subjects: Engineering and the physical sciences (physics, chemistry and mathematics), materials, and IT and computer science

Purpose: To enable training in the methods of research

Eligibility: Non European Union nationals must be settled in the United Kingdom without being subject under immigration law to any restriction for the period to which they remain. European Union nationals may apply, provided their qualifications are equivalent to a British Upper Second Class (Honours) Degree. Support will be fees only unless migrant worker status has been established

Level of Study: Postgraduate

Type: Studentship
Value: UK£8,265 for students in London. UK£6,620 for students elsewhere (1999–2000 rates). Values are reviewed annually. In addition, other allowances are payable under certain conditions. Approved tuition fees are paid directly to the institution
Length of Study: Maximum 3 years
Frequency: Annual
Study Establishment: Higher education institution
Country of Study: Other
Application Procedure: Applicants must be nominated by departments of higher education institutes. Applications on behalf of students should be directed to the relevant address. Full information can be found on the web pages or from academic institutions
Closing Date: 12 July
Funding: Government
No. of awards offered last year: 1450

Royal Society EPSRC BBSRC and Rolls Royce PLC Industry Fellowships

Subjects: Science and technology outside the fields of agriculture including horticulture, agricultural economics, agricultural engineering, and the more applied aspects of agricultural science, natural environment sciences which may be defined broadly as geology and geophysics including seismology and geomagnetism, meteorology, hydrology, oceanography, marine and freshwater biology, terrestrial ecology, medicine, food science, social science, and those aspects of psychology which are closely related to fundamental biology and to the engineering and biological aspects of ergonomics and cybernetics
Purpose: To enhance the communication on science and technology between those in industry and those in universities or similar institutions of higher education to the benefit of United Kingdom firms, higher education institutions and the individual scientist. The aim is to establish long-lasting personal and corporate linkages between the two sectors in the United Kingdom
Eligibility: Open to applicants of any nationality. Candidates should be at the mid-career level and have had significant achievement in their home organisations. Also a substantial career should be ahead of the candidate towards the end of the award, to build upon the contacts made during the fellowship. Candidates must hold a PhD or equivalent in their profession and a substantive post in a university or similar academic institution as a scientist, mathematician or engineer, or be employed as a scientist, mathematician or engineer in any industry, an industrial research organisation or a nationalised industry. Organisations partly or wholly supported by public funds may not act as the industrial partner for an award.

Preference will be given to candidates showing evidence of previous contact with or interest in the other sector of employment
Level of Study: Postdoctorate
Type: Fellowship
Value: Payment of salary but not employers' National Insurance and pension contributions
Length of Study: Up to 2 years full–time. A part–time equivalent is available
Country of Study: Other
Application Procedure: Applicants must complete an application form available from the website. Details are available from the Royal Society Research Appointments Department
Closing Date: December
Funding: Government, Commercial, Private
Additional Information: The scheme provides opportunities for academic scientists, mathematicians and engineers to work in an industrial environment and undertake a project at any stage from fundamental science to industrial innovation, and for industrial scientists, mathematicians and engineers to undertake research or course development work in an institution of higher education

For further information contact:

The Royal Society, Research Appointments Department, 6 Carlton House Terrace, United Kingdom

Tel:	(44) 20 7451 2547
Fax:	(44) 20 7930 2170
Email:	e-gap@royalsoc.ac.uk

Engineers Canada

180 Elgin Street Suite 1100, Ottawa, ON K2P 2K3, Canada

Tel:	(1) 613 232 2474
Fax:	(1) 613 230 5759
Email:	awards@engineerscanada.ca
Website:	www.engineerscanada.ca

Engineers Canada is the national organization of the provincial and territorial associations and order that regulate the practice of engineering in Canada.

Engineers Canada's National Scholarship Program

Subjects: Engineering and non engineering
Purpose: To reward excellence in the Canadian engineering profession and support advanced studies and research

Eligibility: Open to citizens or permanent residents of Canada who are registered as professional engineers in good standing with a provincial/territorial engineering association/order
Level of Study: Doctorate, Graduate, Postgraduate, Research, MBA
Type: Scholarships
Value: Canadian $70,000 in total
Frequency: Annual
Country of Study: Canada and abroad
No. of awards offered: Approx. 50-55
Application Procedure: Applicants must contact Marc Bourgeois for further details
Closing Date: 1 March
Contributor: TD Insurance Meloche-Monnex Insurance and Manulife Financial
No. of awards offered last year: 7
No. of awards applicants last year: Approx. 50-55
Additional Information: Postdoctoral Fellows are not eligible to apply

For further information contact:

Tel: (1) 613 232 2474 ext. 238
Email: marc.bourgeois@engineerscanada.ca
Contact: Marc Bourgeois, Director, Communications

English-Speaking Union (ESU)

Dartmouth House, 37 Charles Street, W1J 5ED, London, United Kingdom

Tel: (44) 20 7529 1550
Fax: (44) 20 7495 6108
Email: esu@esu.org
Website: www.esu.org
Contact: Head of Cultural Programmes

The English-Speaking Union (ESU) is an independent, non-political educational charity with members throughout the world, promoting international and human achievement through the worldwide use of the English language.

English-Speaking Union Travelling Librarian Award

Subjects: Library and Information science
Purpose: To encourage United States and United Kingdom contacts in the library world and establish links between pairs of libraries

Eligibility: Open to professionally qualified United Kingdom and information professionals
Level of Study: Professional development
Type: Award
Value: Up to £3,000. Board and lodging and relevant flight costs
Length of Study: A minimum of 3 weeks
Frequency: Annual
Country of Study: United States of America
No. of awards offered: 16
Application Procedure: Candidates must submit a curriculum vitae and a covering letter explaining why they are the ideal candidates for the award
Closing Date: April
Funding: Commercial, Private
Contributor: The English-Speaking Union and The Chartered Institute of Library and Information Professionals
No. of awards offered last year: 1
No. of awards applicants last year: 16
Additional Information: Candidates should contact the Librarian by telephone or email at library@esu.org.

For further information contact:

37 Charles Street, W1J 5ED, London, United Kingdom

Email: education@esu.org

Entente Cordiale Scholarships

French Cultural Department, 23 Cromwell Road, SW7 2EN, London, United Kingdom

Tel: (44) 20 7073 1312
Fax: (44) 20 7073 1326
Email: entente.cordiale@ambafrance.org.uk
Website: www.ambascience.co.uk/entente-cordiale
Contact: Administrative Officer

Launched by an agreement between the United Kingdom and French governments in 1995, the Entente Cordiale Scholarships enable outstanding British postgraduates to study or carry out research on the other side of the Channel, with a view to dispel preconceived ideas and promote good relations between the two countries.

Bourses Scholarships

Subjects: All subjects
Purpose: To allow individuals to study or carry out research in France

Eligibility: Open to British citizens
Level of Study: Postgraduate
Type: Scholarship
Value: UK£8,000 for students living in Paris and UK£7,500 for those studying outside Paris for the 1-year award, UK £3,000 for 3 months, UK£6,000 for 6 months
Length of Study: 3 months, 6 months, or 1-year
Frequency: Annual
Study Establishment: Approved universities or grande écoles
Country of Study: France
No. of awards offered: 60
Application Procedure: Applicants must complete an application form, available from the website
Closing Date: 15 March
Funding: Private
Contributor: Blue Circle (Lafarge), BP, Kingfisher PLC, EDF Energy, UBS, Xerox, Paul Minet, Sir Patrick Sheehy Schlumberger, Vodafone, Rolls Royce, Parthenon Trust
No. of awards offered last year: 7
No. of awards applicants last year: 60
Additional Information: Scholarships are also awarded to French postgraduates to study in the United Kingdom. Interested parties should contact the British Council in Paris

For further information contact:

Email: scholarships-bourses@cbie.ca

Entomological Society of Canada (ESC)

393 Winston Ave, Ottawa, ON K2A 1Y8, Canada

Tel: (1) 613 725 2619
Fax: (1) 613 725 9349
Email: entos.can@bellnet.ca
Website: www.esc-sec.ca
Contact: Office Manager

The Entomological Society of Canada (ESC) is one of the largest and oldest professional societies in Canada. Founded in Toronto on April 16th, 1863, the Society was open to all students and lovers of entomology. ESC is a dynamic force in promoting research, disseminating knowledge of insects and encouraging the continued participation of all lovers of entomology in the most fascinating of all natural sciences. It is especially well known for its widely distributed and used publications.

John H. Borden Scholarship

Subjects: Entomology and integrated pest management
Purpose: To financially support students who are studying integrated pest management with an entomological emphasis
Eligibility: Open to postgraduate students of Integrated Pest Management
Level of Study: Postgraduate
Type: Scholarship
Value: Canadian $1,000
Frequency: Every 2 years
Country of Study: Canada
Application Procedure: Applicants must submit their application form, curriculum vitae, transcripts and reference letters. Application forms are available online
Closing Date: 16 February

For further information contact:

Email: Floate@agr.gc.ac
Contact: Dr Judith Myers, Chair, ESC Students Award
              Committee

Environmental Leadership Program

P.O. BOX 907, Greenbelt, MD 20768-0907, United States of America

Email: info@elpnet.org
Website: www.elpnet.org

The Environmental Leadership Program (ELP) inspires visionary, action-oriented and diverse leadership to work for a just and sustainable future. ELP nurtures a new generation of environmental leaders characterized by diversity, innovation, collaboration and effective communications. ELP addresses the needs of relatively new environmental activists and professionals.

Environmental Leadership Fellowships

Subjects: Environmental leadership
Purpose: To build the leadership capacity of the environmental field's most promising and emerging practitioners
Eligibility: Open to citizens of the United States only
Level of Study: Postgraduate
Type: Fellowship
Value: US$750 which includes room and board for the 3 overnight retreats, participation in 10 days of training and community building and access to our network of over 480 Senior Fellows

Length of Study: 2 years
Frequency: Annual
Country of Study: United States of America
Closing Date: 2 April

For further information contact:

Email: lori@elpnet.org

Environmental Protection Agency

PO Box 3000, Johnstown Castle Estate, Y35 W821, Wexford, Ireland

Website: http://www.epa.ie/researchandeducation/research/
epafunding/postgraduateprogrammes/
Contact: Research Grants Programme

The mission of the Environmental Protection Agency is to protect human health and to safeguard the natural environment - air, water, and land - upon which life depends.

Environmental Protection Agency-IRC Scholarship Scheme

Purpose: The EPA can also co-fund PhD Scholarships with Third Level Institutions. Proposal should be for innovative research aiming at supporting environmental policy in Ireland. The proposed Scholarship should provide evidence to identify pressures, inform policy and develop solutions
Eligibility: Under the EPA Co-funded Scholarships Scheme, funding is available for a small number of awards, as per the following: 48-month PhDs (indicative budget of €96,000); Limited to new and innovative projects; Co-funded by an Irish host research institution on a 50:50 basis; EPA is to be consulted in the drafting of the proposed PhD scope, as well as in the selection process of the candidate (i.e. interview panel); All co-funded PhDs would have to adhere to the EPA's funding rules and reporting requirements
Level of Study: Graduate
Type: Scholarship
Value: a stipend of €16,000 per annum a contribution to fees, including non-European Union fees, up to a maximum of €5,750 per annum eligible direct research expenses of €2,250 per annum
Frequency: Annual
Country of Study: Any country

Funding: Private
No. of awards offered last year: 1 November

For further information contact:

PO Box 3000, Johnstown Castle Estate, IRL Y35 W821, Wexford, Ireland

Tel: (353) 53 916 0600
Email: research@epa.ie

Escola Superior d'Administració i Direcció d'Empreses (ESADE)

MBA Office, Avenue d'Espluges 92–96, ESP -08034, Barcelona, Spain

Tel: (34) 93 280 6162
Fax: (34) 93 204 8105
Email: mba@esade.edu
Website: www.esade.edu
Contact: Ms Jordi Mora Pintado, Financial Aid & Operations Director

ESADE is an independent nonprofit university institution, founded in 1958 in Barcelona when a group of entrepreneurs and Jesuit Society members joined forces. Since 1995, it has formed part of the Ramon Llull University. ESADE's academic activity takes place on its Barcelona, Madrid and Buenos Aires campuses. The three main areas it focuses on are education, research and social dialogue.

Escola Superior d'Administració i Direcció d'Empreses (ESADE) MBA Scholarships

Subjects: MBA (12, 15, or 18 months)
Purpose: To assist full-time MBA students with tuition fees award high potential candidates
Eligibility: Depending on the scholarship: enroled students: (Fellowships plus Impact); Admitted students: (Direct, Merit & Need-based Scholarships plus Excellence). Scholarships are awarded, restricted by merit achievement, geographical area, sector of activity and need based
Level of Study: MBA
Type: Scholarships
Value: Direct scholarships: up to 40 % of total tuition fees; Scholarship for excellence: up to 50 % of tuition fees; Merit &

Need-based Scholarships: up to 50 % of tuition fees; Fellowships: variable; depending on length
Length of Study: 12, 15, or 18 months
Frequency: Annual
Study Establishment: ESADE Business School
Country of Study: Spain
No. of awards offered: +250
Application Procedure: Send all required documents for your admittance to Admission Department, complete your Scholarship Application Form (Annex 1), include supporting documents, send all required documents in PDF format to mba@esade.edu, email subject: 'The ESADE Full Time MBA Scholarship'. Also check at itemsweb.esade.edu/webbs/imagenes/FT_MBA_Scholarship_Application_Form_2014_.pdf for further information
Closing Date: 15 June
Funding: Foundation
Contributor: ESADE Foundation, ESCADE MBA scholarship fund
No. of awards offered last year: +80
No. of awards applicants last year: +250
Additional Information: www.esade.edu/mba

For further information contact:

ESADE Av. Pedralbes, 60-62, ESP 08034, Barcelona, Spain

Email: financialaid@esade.edu

ESMOD Berlin

Email: j.hurley@esmod.de

The Hessnatur Foundation is a non-profit, independent foundation conducting research and development in the field of Applied Sustainability.

Hessnatur Foundation Scholarship

Subjects: Sustainability in Fashion
Eligibility: 1. Candidates applying for Hessnatur Foundation Scholarship, must have applied successfully and received acceptance to the M.A. Sustainability in Fashion at ESMOD Berlin. 2. Applicants must be able to afford other expenses which include living costs and course related material costs. 3. Applicants of Hessnatur Foundation Scholarship, must possess the visas and insurances that are required to study in Germany by the start date of the course. 4. Scholarship holders are required to agree to allow ESMOD Berlin and

the Hessnatur Foundation to use their images/other media and their works for educational and promotional purposes
Level of Study: Postgraduate
Type: Scholarship
Value: Tuition costs fully covered. Amount covered is €11,000
Length of Study: 1.6 years
Study Establishment: ESMOD Berlin
Country of Study: Germany
Application Procedure: Applications must be sent via email to j.hurley@esmod.de. Application should have the following details. A statement of 250 words describing their motivation, passion for sustainability in fashion and why they should be selected for the scholarship. A document limited to 4 pages outlining their best work from portfolio and achievements from their CV
Closing Date: 1 June

For further information contact:

Email: j.hurley@esmod.de

Eta Sigma Phi

H-S Box 68, Hampden-Sydney, VA 23943-6244, United States of America

Tel:	(1) 804 223 6244
Fax:	(1) 804 223 6045
Email:	waynet@tiger.hsc.edu
Contact:	Professor C Wayne Tucker

It is Eta Sigma Phi's mission to promote scholarship in classics. The organisation awards scholarships for study abroad, publishes a newsletter, and holds annual translation and composition contests. A convention is also held in the spring of each year.

Eta Sigma Phi Summer Scholarships

Subjects: Arts and humanities
Purpose: To enable one member of Eta Sigma Phi to attend the summer session of the American Academy in Rome, Italy, another to attend the summer session of the American School of Classical Studies in Athens, Greece and a third to attend a session of the Vergilian Society at Cumae, Italy
Eligibility: Those eligible to apply are Eta Sigma Phi members and alumni who have received a Bachelor's degree since January 1st 1994, or shall have received it in or before June 2000, and who have not received a doctoral degree. For

the Bedrick Scholarship at the Vergilian Society in Cumae, also eligible are Eta Sigma Phi members who will be rising juniors or seniors in the Summer of 2000, and preference for the scholarship will be given to such undergraduate members

Level of Study: Postgraduate

Type: Scholarship

Value: The scholarship to the American Academy in Rome will have a value of US$3,000, the Brent Malcolm Froberg Scholarship to the American School of Classical Studies at Athens will have a value of US$3,550 and the Theodore Bedrick Schoarship to the Virgilian Society at Cumae will have a value of US$2,540

Length of Study: 6 weeks

Frequency: Annual

Study Establishment: The American Academy in Rome, The American School of Classical Studies at Athens, and the Virgilian Society at Cumae

Country of Study: Other

No. of awards offered: 8

Application Procedure: Applicants must submit an application form, an up to date transcript, letters of recommendation, and a 500 word statement which includes purpose for desiring the scholarship. Application information and forms are available by writing to Professor Caroline Perkins at the Eta Sigma Phi Scholarship Committee or by email: ruby@ezwv.com

Closing Date: Mid December

Funding: Private

Contributor: Investments, capital contributed by charitable gifts

No. of awards offered last year: 2

No. of awards applicants last year: 8

Additional Information: The Chairman of the Scholarship Committee receives and sends the application material

For further information contact:

Eta Sigma Phi Scholarship Committee Department of Classical Studies Marshall University, United States of America

Email: ruby@ezwv.com
Contact: Professor Caroline A Perkins, Chair

Ethnic Minority Foundation

Boardman House, 64 Broadway, E15 1NG, Stratford, United Kingdom

Tel: (44) 208 432 0000 Free phone: 800 652 0390
Fax: (44) 208 432 0319
Email: enquiries@emf-cemvo.co.uk

Website: www.ethnicminorityfund.org.uk
Contact: Grants Enquiries, Ethnic Minority Foundation

The EMF is a registered charity established in 1999 (Charity no 1077002). EMF is committed to building a secure base for Britain's minority ethnic communities and voluntary sector. It is dedicated to addressing some of the worst cases of social exclusion that affect and disadvantage minority ethnic communities living in the United Kingdom.

Ethnic Minority Foundation Grants

Purpose: To provide long-term and short-term funding of minority ethnic voluntary and community organizations, and funding for other community needs such as education, health, women's and youth projects

Type: Grant

Funding: Foundation, Individuals

No. of awards offered last year: 17

For further information contact:

Tel: (44) 208 432 0300, Free Phone: 800 652 0390
Fax: (44) 208 432 0319
Email: enquiries@emf-cemvo.co.uk

Eugène Vinaver Memorial Trust

Barron Bequest

Subjects: Any field of Arthurian studies

Purpose: To support postgraduate research in Arthurian studies

Eligibility: Open to graduates of any university of the United Kingdom and Ireland

Type: Grant

Value: £1,250, payment towards postgraduate fees

Length of Study: One year. Candidates may apply for further years on a basis of parity with those applying for the first time

Frequency: Annual

Study Establishment: Any university in United Kingdom or Ireland

Country of Study: United Kingdom, Republic of Ireland

Application Procedure: For application details, applicants must contact Professor Taylor at the address below

Funding: Private

Contributor: The Eugène Vinaver Memorial Trust

For further information contact:

Professor JHM Taylor, Garth Head, Penruddock, Cumbria CA11 0QU, Penrith, United Kingdom

Email: geoffreybromiley@btinternet.com
Contact: Professor Jane Taylor, Director

European Association for the Study of Diabetes

Rheindorfer Weg 3, DEU -40591, Dusseldorf, Germany

Tel: (49) 211 758 4690
Fax: (49) 211 7584 6929
Email: secretariat@easd.org
Website: www.easd.org
Contact: EASD Secretariat

European Association for the Study of Diabetes-ADA Transatlantic Fellowships

Subjects: Diabetes
Purpose: To encourage research into basic or clinical questions related to diabetes and its complications
Eligibility: Applicants should have completed their MD, PhD or equivalent within the previous 7 years and cannot be serving an internship or residency during the fellowship. European applicants must be EASD members and United States of America applicants should be ADA members
Level of Study: Research
Type: Fellowship
Value: US$50,000
Length of Study: 1 year
Frequency: Annual
Country of Study: United States of America
Application Procedure: Applications must be made on the forms provided. Two copies of the application forms should be submitted
Closing Date: 1 February
Contributor: EASD-Lilly Research Fund
Additional Information: Successful applicants will be notified of the award by 1 April. Funding begins on 1 July

European Calcified Tissue Society

PO Box 337, BS32 4ZR, Bristol, United Kingdom

Tel: (44) 14 5461 0255
Fax: (44) 14 5461 0255
Email: admin@actsoc.org
Website: www.ectsoc.org

The European Calcified Tissue Society is the major organization in Europe for researchers and clinicians working in the field of calcified tissues and related fields.

European Calcified Tissue Society/Servier Fellowship

Subjects: Pathophysiology of osteoporosis
Purpose: To encourage the research involving pathophysiology of osteoporosis, particularly the coupling and uncoupling processes between bone formation and bone resorption and all related matters
Eligibility: Open for ECTS members who qualified PhD/MD within the last 10 years. Applications to include details of a preclinical or clinical research project on the pathophysiology of osteoporosis, particularly the coupling and uncoupling processes between bone formation and bone resorption and all related matters
Level of Study: Research
Type: Fellowship
Value: €80,000
Length of Study: 2 years
Frequency: Every 2 years
Country of Study: Any country
No. of awards offered: 20
Application Procedure: Applicants should fill an application form. For further details log on to www.ectsoc.org
Closing Date: November
Funding: Commercial
Contributor: Servier
No. of awards offered last year: 1
No. of awards applicants last year: 20

For further information contact:

Email: ects@ectsoc.org

European Committee for Treatment and Research in Multiple Sclerosis (ECTRIMS)

ECTRIMS Secretariat, Peter Merian-Strasse 80, Basel CH-4002, Switzerland

Tel: (41) 61 686 7779
Fax: (41) 61 686 7788
Email: secretariat@ectrims.eu
Website: www.ectrims.eu

The committee works to facilitate communication, create synergies, and promote and enhance research and learning among professionals for the ultimate benefit of people affected by MS.

European Committee for Treatment and Research in Multiple Sclerosis-MAGNIMS Fellowship in Magnetic Resonance Imaging in MS

Subjects: Magnetic resonance studies
Purpose: ECTRIMS and the European MAGNIMS (Magnetic Resonance Imaging in MS) network jointly support a postdoctoral fellowship to foster the development of young researchers in magnetic resonance imaging studies in MS. The goal of this programme is to achieve transfer and broadening of knowledge regarding the application of magnetic resonance to MS research and to promote the researcher's integration into the international scientific community
Eligibility: Applicants should be under 40 years and affiliated to an academic department which can guarantee a continuation of his or her research
Type: Fellowship
Value: An annual stipend of up to €50,000
Length of Study: 1 year
Frequency: Annual
Country of Study: Any country
Application Procedure: Please check with the organization
Closing Date: 1 February
Additional Information: Details about all ECTRIMS Fellowship Programmes and application material can be obtained from the ECTRIMS website: www.ectrims.eu/fellowships or by writing to the ECTRIMS fellowship administrator: fellowship@ectrims.eu

For further information contact:

Email: chris.enzinger@medunigraz.at

European Crohn's and Colitis Organisation

ECCO Ungargasse 6/13, AUT -1030, Vienna, Austria

Tel: (43) 1 710 2242 0
Fax: (43) 1 710 2242 001
Email: ecco@ecco-ibd.eu

European Crohn's and Colitis Organisation Fellowship

Subjects: ECCO Research Fellowships aim to enhance the opportunity for IBD Trainees to work in European centres
Purpose: The European Crohn's and Colitis Organisation (ECCO) offers Research Fellowships to encourage and support young individuals in their career and promote innovative scientific research in the area of Inflammatory Bowel Diseases (IBD) in Europe
Eligibility: 1. Not be older than 40 years or still in training at the time of application. 2. Submit an original research project using the ECCO Fellowships and Grants Online Submission Pages. Incomplete applications will not be evaluated. 3. Have a hosting laboratory and/or department outside one's own country of practice, which has accepted to host and guide the Fellow under the supervision of a designated host for the duration of the Fellowship. The hosting institution is responsible, together with the Fellow, for the successful completion of the project. 4. At the time of the application as well as prior to the commencement of the Fellowship the candidate must not be involve/work in any research project at the future hosting institute. 5. If your hosting institute
Level of Study: Postgraduate
Type: Fellowships, operating grants
Value: €60,000 will be awarded per scholarship
Frequency: Annual
Country of Study: Any country
Closing Date: 3 June
Funding: Private

For further information contact:

European Crohn's and Colitis Organisation

European Molecular Biology Organization (EMBO)

PO Box 1022.40, DEU -69012, Heidelberg, Germany

Tel: (49) 622 188 910
Fax: (49) 622 188 91200
Email: embo@embo.org
Website: www.embo.org
Contact: Mr Yvonne Kaul, Communications Officer

The European Molecular Biology Organization (EMBO) was established in 1964 to promote biosciences in Europe. Today EMBO supports transnational mobility, training and exchange through initiatives such as fellowships, courses, workshops and its young investigator activities.

European Molecular Biology Organisation Award for Communication in the Life Sciences

Subjects: Public communication of science
Purpose: To promote and reward public communication of the life sciences and their applications by practising scientists in Europe
Eligibility: Open to scientists working in active research in an area of life sciences at the time of nomination. Candidates must be working in Europe or Israel, and the criterion for consideration is excellence in public communication of science via any medium or activity
Type: Monetary award and medal
Value: €5,000 accompanied by a silver and gold medal inscribed with the winner's name
Frequency: Annual
No. of awards offered: 27
Application Procedure: Applicants must apply using the forms available on the website
Closing Date: 1 May
Funding: Private
Contributor: EMBO
No. of awards offered last year: 1
No. of awards applicants last year: 27
Additional Information: For further information, email: Dr Andrew Moore at scisoc@embo.org

For further information contact:

EMBO, Meyerhofstrasse 1, Germany

Tel: (49) 622 188 91119
Fax: (49) 622 188 91200
Email: embo@embo.org

European Science Foundation (ESF)

1 Quai Lezay Marnésia, F-67080, Strasbourg, France

Tel: (33) 3 88 76 71 25
Fax: (33) 3 88 37 05 32
Email: sschott@esf.org
Website: www.esf.org
Contact: Ms Sabine Schott, Communication & Information Unit

The European Science Foundation (ESF) acts as a catalyst for the development of science by bringing together leading scientists and research funding agencies to debate, plan and implement pan-European initiatives.

European Science Foundation Response of the Earth System to Impact Processes (IMPACT) Mobility Grants

Subjects: The nature of impacts and their impact on nature, by studying the effects of impact events, both large and small, on the environment including atmospheric, climatic, biologic, and geologic interactions and their relations
Purpose: To initiate longer term research projects, encourage scientific exchanges, promote international and multidisciplinary collaborations, and build strong ties between European institutions working on impact processes and their influence on the geological and biological evolution of the earth
Eligibility: Open to young scientists, graduate students or postdoctoral researchers. Established researchers can apply but must document that they do not have access to any other form of funding for this particular project. There are no restrictions regarding citizenship but applicants must be working in a European laboratory and applying for a stay in another European country
Level of Study: Graduate, Postdoctorate
Type: Other
Country of Study: Other
Application Procedure: Applicants must submit their personal details, institutional affiliation, brief curriculum vitae, a short invitation letter from the prospective host, a few keywords summarising the research, proposed investigation (maximum two printed pages in font size 12 or 600–1,000 words), significance of the investigation, justification of the collaborative research, and a detailed budget. One copy of the complete application must be sent to ESF and one to Dr Christian Koeberl at the University of Vienna
Contributor: The European Science Foundation

For further information contact:

Institute of Geochemistry, University of Vienna, Althanstrae 14, AUT -1090, Vienna, Austria

Fax: (43) 131 336 7841
Email: christian.koeberl@univie.ac.at
Contact: Dr Christian Koeberl, Chairman of the IMPACT Programme

European Society of Surgical Oncology (ESSO)

Avenue E. Mounier 83, BEL -1200, Brussels, Belgium

Tel: (32) 2 775 02 01
Fax: (32) 2 775 02 00
Email: info@essoweb.org
Website: www.esso-surgeonline.be
Contact: Secretariat

ESSO was founded to advance the art, science and practice of surgery for the treatment of cancer. ESSO endeavours to ensure that the highest possible standard of surgical treatment is available to cancer patients throughout Europe by organizing congresses, granting fellowships and publishing the EJSO.

European Society of Surgical Oncology Training Fellowships

Subjects: Surgical oncology
Purpose: To provide young surgeons a chance to spend time in another specialist centre to either expand their experience or learn new techniques
Eligibility: Open to applicants who are specialists/specializing in surgery (or in any other medical discipline where cancer surgery is performed). Applicants must be less than 40 years of age. European applicants may choose to visit European or non-European units, while non-European applicants must choose to visit a European center
Level of Study: Postdoctorate
Type: Fellowship
Value: €2,000 for standard fellowships and €10,000 for the major international training fellowship
Length of Study: 1 to 3 months for standard fellowships and up to 1 year for the major training fellowship
Frequency: Annual
Country of Study: Any country
No. of awards offered: 18
Application Procedure: Applicants must submit a full curriculum vitae with their application, together with a note of their career intentions. Applicants should also outline what they hope to gain from the training fellowship, including what specific experience is sought and how this will fit in with the applicant's career development. Applicants should provide details as to which institution they wish to visit, together with details of the clinical or research training opportunities that the department can offer. A letter of support from the applicant's head of department must be included and this can be in the form of a reference. A letter of support from the head of the department they wish to visit must also be supplied, indicating that the department to be visited will be in a position to provide the experience required by the applicant
Closing Date: 31 October
No. of awards offered last year: 11
No. of awards applicants last year: 18

Additional Information: Applicants must be or become ESSO members

For further information contact:

Email: carine@esso-surgeonline.org
Contact: Ms Carine Lecoq, ESSO Administrator

European Space Agency

8-10 rue Mario Nikis, Cedex 15, 75738, Paris, France

Tel: (33) 153697654
Email: ContactESA@esa.int
Contact: European Space Agency

The European Space Agency (ESA) is Europe's gateway to space. Its mission is to shape the development of Europe's space capability and ensure that investment in space continues to deliver benefits to the citizens of Europe and the world.

European Space Agency's Postdoctoral Internal Research Fellowship Programme

Subjects: Space science, space applications or space technology
Purpose: ESA's postdoctoral Internal Research Fellowship programme (RIRF) aims to offer young scientists and engineers the possibility for two years to carry out research in a variety of disciplines related to space science, space applications or space technology
Eligibility: Applications are accepted from nationals of the ESA Member States and the European Cooperating States, together with Canada which has a cooperation agreement with ESA (see links on the right for details). Applicants must have recently completed their PhD in a field closely connected to space activities. The following requirements should be fulfilled in order for candidates to be qualified for the scholarship; Applications are accepted from nationals of the ESA Member States and the European Cooperating States, together with Canada which has a cooperation arrangement with ESA (see links on the right for information). Applicants needs to have just recently finished their PhD in a field carefully linked to area activities
Type: Postdoctoral fellowship
Value: €3,000 to €3,800 per month depending on the location of the ESA Establishment
Length of Study: 2 years

Study Establishment: Space science, space applications or space technology

Country of Study: Any country

Application Procedure: Applications should be sent via the ESA online application form available in the 'how to apply' section of the opportunity. A cover letter, CV, and list of publications, with bibliographical references, should accompany the application, in one document (Word or PDF format). Each of the three referees named in the application form should send a reference letter to temp.htr-at-esa.int. No application sent after the closing date will be accepted

Closing Date: Fellowship is open for the academic year

Additional Information: For more details please refer to the link scholarship-positions.com/esas-postdoctoral-internal-research-fellowship-programme/2017/09/23/

For further information contact:

Email: joerg.wehner@esa.int

European Synchrotron Radiation Facility (ESRF)

6 rue Jules Horowitz, BP 220, Cedex 38043, Grenoble, France

Tel:	(33) 4 7688 2000
Fax:	(33) 4 7688 2020
Email:	recruitment@esrf.fr
Website:	www.esrf.fr
Contact:	Ms Bénédicte Henry Canudas, Head of Recruitment

The European Synchrotron Radiation Facility (ESRF) supports scientists in the implementation of fundamental and applied research on the structure of matter in fields such as physics, chemistry, crystallography, Earth science, biology, medicine, surface science, and materials science.

European Synchrotron Radiation Facility Postdoctoral Fellowships

Subjects: Physics, biology, chemistry, mineralogy and crystallography, computer engineering and accelerators science

Purpose: To enable postdoctoral fellows develop their own research programme and motivate them to collaborate with external users

Eligibility: Preference is given to PhD students who obtained their PhD less than 3 years ago

Level of Study: Postdoctorate

Type: Fellowship

Value: The annual gross salary is fixed at €40,910 for the first two years. This salary may be increased during the third year depending upon performance

Length of Study: 2-3 years

Frequency: Dependent on funds available

Country of Study: France

No. of awards offered: 400

Application Procedure: Applicants must complete an application form, available on www.esrf.eu

Closing Date: Individual deadlines exist for each position. Please contact the organization

Funding: International office

Contributor: Public funds from 19 countries, mostly European

No. of awards offered last year: 27

No. of awards applicants last year: 400

Additional Information: Member countries are Belgium, Denmark, Finland, France, Germany, Italy, the Netherlands, Norway, Spain, Sweden, Switzerland and the United Kingdom. New associated members are the Czech Republic, Israel, Portugal and the Republic of Hungary, Poland, Austria, and Slovakia

For further information contact:

Email: recruitment@esrf.fr

European Synchrotron Radiation Facility Thesis Studentships

Subjects: Physics, biology, chemistry, mineralogy and crystallography, computer engineering and accelerators science. The ESRF proposes subjects related to the use of synchrotron radiation or synchrotron or storage ring technology

Purpose: To enable grant holders pursue a PhD at the ESRF and to enable young scientists acquire knowledge of the use of synchrotron radiation or its generation

Eligibility: Preference is given to member-country nationals, but other nationals may be accepted for the PhD's positions

Level of Study: Doctorate

Value: €2,280 per month. These amounts correspond to a gross remuneration and are subject to social charges and income tax in France

Length of Study: 2-3 years

Frequency: Dependent on funds available

Study Establishment: Universities

Country of Study: France

No. of awards offered: 300

Application Procedure: Applicants must complete an application form, available on www.esrf.eu

Closing Date: There is an individual deadline for each position

Funding: International office

Contributor: Public funds from 19 countries, mainly European

No. of awards offered last year: 20

No. of awards applicants last year: 300

Additional Information: Member countries are Belgium, Denmark, Finland, France, Germany, Italy, the Netherlands, Norway, Spain, Sweden, Switzerland and the United Kingdom. Newly associated members are the Czech Republic, Israel, Portugal and the Republic of Hungary, Poland, Austria and Slovakia

For further information contact:

Email: recruitment@esrf.fr

European University Institute (EUI)

Via dei Roccettini 9, ITA -50014 San Domenico di Fiesole, Italy

Tel: (39) 55 4685 373
Fax: (39) 55 4685 444
Email: lorenzo.ghezzi@eui.eu
Website: www.eui.eu
Contact: Mr Lorenzo GhezzI, Admissions officer

The European University Institute (EUI) is an international research institution set up by the Member States of the European Union. It focuses exclusively on doctoral and post-doctoral studies and offers a 4 year fully-funded PhD Programme in Economics, History and Civilization, Law and Political and Social Sciences and several Postdoctoral Fellowships opportunities.

150 Fully Funded PhD Degree Scholarships for International Students

Subjects: Scholarships are awarded in the field of Economics, Law, Political and Social Sciences and History

Purpose: These scholarships are awarded in the field of Economics, Law, Political and Social Sciences and History

Eligibility: See the website

Value: These scholarships are fully funded

Study Establishment: Scholarships are awarded in the field of Economics, Law, Political and Social Sciences and History

Country of Study: Italy

Application Procedure: Applicants must submit an application and all required documents via the interactive online application form

Closing Date: 31 January

Additional Information: For more details please visit the website scholarship-positions.com/150-fully-funded-phd-scholarships-international-students-eui-italy/2016/10/22/

For further information contact:

Email: info@edu-active.com

Doctor of Philosophy Scholarships in the Social Sciences

Subjects: The European University Institute (EUI) offers four-year fully-funded PhD programmes in Economics, History and Civilization, Law and Political and Social Sciences. Up to 150 scholarships are available for entry in September, covering tuition and providing a monthly grant. Our well-structured PhD programmes include closely supervised dissertation work, courses on methods and theory, topical workshops as well as academic and professional development training. Over 85% of EUI researchers successfully defend their thesis and more than 86% are either very satisfied or satisfied with their supervision. PhD researchers at the EUI enjoy: well-structured, fully funded PhD programmes; an academic environment that promotes research independence with close supervision, working groups, advanced training and courses; excellent research support facilities including an outstanding social science research Library, an on-site European Documentation Centre, and the Historical Archives of the European Union; a dynamic research community with visiting experts and high-level institutional and government actors from around the world; access to an international network of alumni holding posts in academia (60%), national-level institutions (7%), European Union institutions (5%), international organisations (6%), the private sector (2%), law firms and NGOs (8.5%), and banks (1%)* (*Alumni Destination Survey); an international, multi-lingual and culturally diverse campus near Florence, Italy. The European University Institute is an international postgraduate teaching and research institute. It offers advanced academic training for doctoral and postdoctoral researchers and fosters research in fields that are of particular interest for the development of Europe. The Institute is composed of four departments Economics, History and Civilization, Law, and Political and Social Sciences; the Robert Schuman Centre for Advanced Studies; the Max Weber Programme for Postdoctoral Studies; the School of Transnational Governance; and the Historical Archives of the European Union. Grants and tuition fees for

PhD candidates are covered by the national grant-awarding authorities of our contracting states

Purpose: Four-year fully-funded PhD programmes in the Social Sciences

Eligibility: Eligibility is determined by national grant-awarding authorities of EUI contracting states. For more detailed information visit www.eui.eu/phd

Level of Study: Doctorate

Type: Scholarship

Length of Study: Four years

Frequency: Annual

Study Establishment: European University Institute

Country of Study: Italy

Application Procedure: EUI's online application is open from early November to 31 January. For further information visit www.eui.eu/phd

Closing Date: 31 January

Funding: Government

Contributor: EUI contracting states and associate member states

Additional Information: The EUI community consists of over 900 academic staff and researchers from over 70 countries

For further information contact:

European University Institute, Badia Fiesolana - Via dei Roccettini 9, Italy

Email: lorenzo.ghezzi@eui.eu
Contact: Mr Lorenzo Ghezzi, Admissions Officer

EuroTech Universities Alliance

Square de Meeûs 23, 8th floor, BEL -1000, Brussels, Belgium

Email: info@eurotech-universities.eu
Contact: EuroTech Universities Alliance

The EuroTech Universities Alliance is a strategic partnership of four leading European universities of science & technology: Technical University of Denmark (DTU), Ecole Polytechnique Fédérale de Lausanne (EPFL), Eindhoven University of Technology (TU/e) and Technical University of Munich (TUM). Together they are committed to finding technical solutions, which address the major challenges of modern society. Their intensive collaboration across research, education & innovation support the European Union's goals of smart, sustainable and inclusive growth.

Collaborative Offline & Online Platform for Research EuroTechPostdoc Fellowships for International Students at European Universities

Subjects: Health & Bio Engineering, Smart & Urban Mobility, Data Science & Engineering, High-Performance Computing, Entrepreneurship & Innovation

Purpose: The EuroTechPostdoc Programme is a postdoctoral fellowship programme for young experienced researchers who have already demonstrated excellence and potential in their field of research

Eligibility: Applicants of all nationalities are eligible. Please refer the website for more details

Type: Postdoctoral fellowship

Value: The fellowship consists of a monthly salary for the postdoctoral researcher based on the salary scale of the host institution and is granted for a period of twenty-four (24) months maximum.Prolongation of the fellowship is not possible

Study Establishment: Applicants may apply within one of the five focus research areas of the EuroTech Universities Alliance: Health & Bio Engineering Smart & Urban Mobility Data Science & Engineering High-Performance Computing Entrepreneurship & Innovation

Country of Study: Any country

Application Procedure: Please use the following templates for your application: 1. Project proposal template. 2. CV and publications template. 3. Ethics self-assessment

Closing Date: 28 February

Additional Information: For more details, please browse the below website, scholarship-positions.com/80-eurotechpostdoc-fellowships-international-students-european-universities

For further information contact:

Email: postdoc@eurotech-universities.eu

EuroTechPostdoc

Subjects: Interdisciplinary bottom-up research projects in the following research focus areas are invited to submit their proposal: 1. Health & Bioengineering. 2. Smart & Urban Mobility. 3. Data Science & Engineering. 4. High Performance Computing. 5. Entrepreneurship & Innovation. The focus areas present the main interdisciplinary research areas of the EuroTech partners within the alliance, so they should be understood as indicators and not as limiting factors per se. It is important that you find a host and co-host at the EuroTech universities willing to support and supervise your project. The focus areas should guide you towards common research interests

Purpose: The EuroTech Universities Alliance invites highly talented experienced researchers to submit interdisciplinary collaborative research project proposals for one of the fellowships provided by the EuroTechPostdoc Programme. The Programme is a postdoctoral fellowship for young experienced researchers who have already demonstrated excellence and potential in their field of research. It provides its fellows exceptional international research and career development opportunities to promote their outstanding individual potential into a distinct, innovative and competitive profile of a researcher. The EuroTechPostdoc Programme is co-funded by the European Commission under its framework programme Horizon. All fellows of the EuroTechPostdoc programme will be Marie Sklodowska-Curie Fellows. Four of the six universities of the EuroTech Universities Alliance - Technical University of Denmark (DTU), Ecole Polytechnique Fédérale de Lausanne (EPFL), Eindhoven University of Technology (TU/e) and Technical University of Munich (TUM) - will grant 80 fellowships divided over two calls for experienced researchers. Per call, each university grants 10 fellowships for a 24-month period to collaborative and interdisciplinary research projects across the Alliance

Eligibility: Experience: Applicants must hold a PhD degree from a recognised university or plan to obtain a PhD degree by the time of employment or have at least four years of full-time equivalent research experience. Mobility: Researchers may not have resided or carried out their main activity (work, studies, etc.) in the country of the host university for more than twelve (12) months in the three (3) years immediately before the call deadline. Time spent as part of a procedure for obtaining refugee status under the Geneva Convention, compulsory national service and/or short stays such as holidays are not taken into account. Institutional Endorsement: Support from both the host and co-host. Please approach them early on. A standard process will be provided in the application portal. You will have to provide the email address of your supervisor and co-supervisor (please check spelling). The programme management office will approach host and co-host professors and ask them to provide the institutional endorsement. The Institutional endorsement comprises a confirmation of the availability of infrastructure, supervision and resources to successfully complete the project. Applicants must be able to carry out full time research during the fellowship period (parental leave, sick leave, military leave and care leave are accepted). Research direction follows the H2020 Ethics

Level of Study: Postdoctorate

Type: A variable number of fellowships

Value: complete salary covered (depending on country)

Length of Study: up to 24 months

Frequency: Annual, if funds are available

Country of Study: Other

No. of awards offered: 87

Application Procedure: Applications to be supported via online participants portal by the respective deadline. Applications are assessed against criteria addressing the candidate's ability and commitment to research, the quality of the proposed research project as well as the synergy between the research proposed and the identified host and co-host, and the impact of the research project on the career development of the candidate. More information can be found here: postdoc.eurotech-universities.eu/for-applicants/#eval

Closing Date: 28 February

Funding: Government

Contributor: European Commission: This project has received funding from the European Union's Horizon research and innovation programme under the Marie Sklodowska-Curie grant agreement No 754462

No. of awards offered last year: 40

No. of awards applicants last year: 87

Additional Information: Please check our online presence: http://postdoc.eurotech-universities.eu/

For further information contact:

Arcisstr. 21, DEU 80333, Munich, Germany

Tel:	(39) 892 892 2813
Email:	info@eurotech-universities.eu
Contact:	Dr Andrea Glogger, Programme Manager

Evangelical Lutheran Church in America (ELCA)

Division for Ministry, 8765 West Higgins Road, Chicago, IL 60631-4195, United States of America

Tel:	(1) 773 380 2700
Fax:	(1) 773 380 1465
Email:	pwilder@elca.org
Website:	www.elca.org
Contact:	Mr Pat Wilder, Executive Secretary

Evangelical Lutheran Church in America Educational Grant Program

Subjects: Theological studies

Eligibility: Open to members of the Evangelical Lutheran Church in America who are enroled in an accredited graduate institution for study in a PhD, EdD, or ThD programme in a theological area appropriate to seminary teaching. Priority is given to women and minority students

Level of Study: Doctorate
Type: Grant
Value: Grants up to US$4,000 per individual, per year are awarded
Length of Study: Grants are awarded for a maximum of 4 years with a 5th-year award for the dissertation
Frequency: Annual
Country of Study: United States of America
No. of awards offered: 72
Application Procedure: Applications are available online at www.elca.org/en/Our-Work/Leadership/Seminaries/Educational-Grant-Program in January. Two recommendations are required for each applicant
Closing Date: 15 April
Funding: Private
No. of awards offered last year: 65
No. of awards applicants last year: 72

For further information contact:

Email: pwilder@elca.org

Evonik Foundation

Rellinghauserstr. 1-11, DEU 45128, Essen, Germany

Tel: (49) 201/177 4326
Email: info@evonik-stiftung.de
Contact: Evonik Foundation

The Evonik Foundation exclusively supports natural science students preparing master's, doctoral, and postdoctoral theses. Scholarships are only awarded for the scholarship focus defined for the year in question.

Evonik Stiftung Scholarships

Subjects: Organosilicones, Synthesis, Cross-linking, Phase Behaviour & Material Properties and Fillers
Purpose: The Evonik Foundation focuses on promoting education and science. The goal of Evonik Foundation is to sponsor talented up-and-coming researchers
Eligibility: Prerequisites for the award of a scholarship: The topic of your research project must coincide with one of the topics in our annual scholarship focus. 1. Your scientific research is being conducted in a well-known, chemically oriented working group at a German university or a non-university research institution. 2. You can provide proof of excellent academic performance. 3. You are unable to sufficiently fund your intended scientific study courses with means provided by you, your parents or other parties
Value: Bachelor's and master's theses: six months, €250-600 month Doctoral program: two years (option to extend), €1,400 month. In addition, applications can be submitted for funding of the purchase of research literature and attendance of scientific congresses. Postdoctoral studies: one year's funding is decided on a case-by-case basis
Country of Study: Germany
Application Procedure: Please check the website
Closing Date: 28 February
Additional Information: Please check the link for more details scholarship-positions.com/evonik-stiftung-scholarships-for-german-students/2018/01/23

For further information contact:

Email: info@evonik-stiftung.de

F

Fanconi Anemia Research Fund, Inc.

1801 Willamette Street, Suite 200, Eugene, OR 97401, United States of America

Tel:	(1) 541 687 4658
Fax:	(1) 541 687 0548
Email:	info@fanconi.org
Website:	www.fanconi.org
Contact:	Ms Pamela Norr, Executive Director

To support research into effective treatments and a cure for Fanconi anemia.

Fanconi Anemia Research Fund Award

Subjects: Fanconi anemia
Purpose: To support research into effective treatments and a cure for Fanconi anemia
Eligibility: There are no restrictions on eligibility in terms of nationality, residency, age, gender, sexual orientation, race, religion or politics
Level of Study: Doctorate, Postdoctorate
Type: Award
Value: Varies
Length of Study: 1 to 2 years
Country of Study: Any country
No. of awards offered: 29
Application Procedure: Applicants must email to obtain information and application forms
Closing Date: Pre-proposals 15 February and 15 August
Funding: Foundation
No. of awards offered last year: 6
No. of awards applicants last year: 29
Additional Information: The Internal Revenue Service has confirmed that the Fund is not a private foundation for the purposes of tax-exempt donations but a public charitable organization under 501(c) 3 of the Internal Revenue Code

For further information contact:

Email: info@fanconi.org

Federation University Australia

Vice-Chancellor's Office, P.O. Box 663, University Drive, Mt Helen, VIC 3350, Australia

Tel:	(61) 5327 9000
Fax:	(61) 5327 9704
Website:	federation.edu.au
Contact:	Sue Read

The University of Ballarat is Australia's only regional, multi-sector University acknowledged for its excellence in education, training, and research, committed to providing high quality services to students, the community, and the industry. It provides educational and training programs from apprenticeships, certificates and diplomas to postgraduate qualifications, masters, and doctorates by research. International students at the University come from over 25 different countries to participate in a diverse range of TAFE and higher education programmes. The University is proud of its track record in business innovation and entrepreneurship, research, consulting, and educational programs, and promoting new technology in products and services through scientific and industrial research.

Australian Postgraduate Award

Subjects: Behavioural and cognitive sciences, business and management, education, engineering and technology, human

© Springer Nature Limited 2019
Palgrave Macmillan (ed.), *The Grants Register 2020*,
https://doi.org/10.1057/978-1-349-95943-3

movement and sports science, information technology, computing and communication sciences, mathematical sciences, nursing, science, social sciences, humanities and arts

Purpose: To support postgraduate students undertaking research in either a Doctorate or Masters by Research program

Eligibility: Open to candidates who have a First Class (Honours) Degree or equivalent. The APA is open to candidates who have received a Masters by Research (for Doctorate applicants) and/or a Honours degree (First Class/H1A) or equivalent

Level of Study: Doctorate, Postgraduate, Research

Type: Scholarship

Value: $26,288 per year, Indexed annually

Frequency: Annual

Study Establishment: The University of Ballarat

Country of Study: Australia

No. of awards offered: 130

Application Procedure: Application forms and further information about the Scholarships process can be found at federation.edu.au/research/research-degrees/scholarships

Closing Date: 3 December

Funding: Government

No. of awards offered last year: 8

No. of awards applicants last year: 130

Additional Information: It is required that the successful applicant commence studies in the year the scholarship was awarded for. Studies should commence no earlier than 1 February, and no later than 31 August

For further information contact:

Tel:	(61) 3 5327 9508
Fax:	(61) 3 5327 9602
Email:	HDResearch@ballarat.edu.au
Contact:	Sue Read

Doctoral Research on Family Relationships

Subjects: Family relationships

Purpose: To undertake doctoral research on family relationships

Eligibility: Open to Australian citizens or permanent residents who have achieved First Class (Honours) or equivalent

Level of Study: Postgraduate

Type: Scholarship

Value: AU$19,231

Length of Study: 3 years and 6 months

Frequency: Annual

Study Establishment: The University of Ballarat

Country of Study: Australia

Application Procedure: Check website for further details. Applications are open from 25 July

Closing Date: 30 November

For further information contact:

Tel:	(61) 3 5327 9818
Email:	j.mcdonald@ballarat.edu.au
Contact:	John McDonald, Associate Professor

University of Ballarat Part Postgraduate Research Scholarship

Subjects: Behavioural and cognitive sciences, business and management, education, engineering and technology, human movement and sports science, information, computing and communication sciences, mathematical sciences, nursing, science, or social sciences, humanities and arts

Eligibility: Open to citizens of Australia or permanent residents who have achieved First Class (Honours) or equivalent

Level of Study: Doctorate, Postgraduate, Research

Type: Scholarship

Value: AU$22,500

Length of Study: 3 years (PhD and Professional Doctorate) and 1.5 years (Masters)

Frequency: Annual

Study Establishment: University of Ballarat

Country of Study: Australia

Application Procedure: Check website for further details. Applications are open from 03 January

Closing Date: 31 October

Funding: Government, Commercial

Additional Information: The study should start no earlier than 1 February

For further information contact:

Tel:	(61) 3 5327 9508
Fax:	(61) 3 5327 9602
Email:	s.murphy@ballarat.edu.au
Contact:	Sarah Murphy, Administrative Assistant

Fellowship Program in Academic Medicine

National Medical Fellowship, Inc., 254 West 31st Street, New York, NY 10001, United States of America

Contact: Awards Committee

Akhtarali H. Tobaccowala Fellowship

Subjects: This foundation has helped over 12,000 individuals in a range of ways from underwriting eye surgery, helping cancer and diabetes patients, providing vocational training skills to electricians, plumbers and farmers, as well as providing education for poor as well as handicapped children

Purpose: The fellowship was established in the memory of Akhtarali H. Tobaccowala who was a 1952 graduate of the Booth school

Eligibility: The fellowship which offer tuition support is available for students of Booth's full-time MBA program

Level of Study: Postgraduate

Type: Scholarship

Value: Upto US$25,000 per annum

Frequency: Annual

Country of Study: Any country

Application Procedure: There is no formal application process

Funding: Private

For further information contact:

The Tobaccowala Foundation, 35. Printing House, Police Court Lane (Behind Handloom House) Fort, Mumbai, Maharashtra 400 001, India

Tel: (91) 22 22640386

Email: tobaccowalafoundation@gmail.com

Therla Drake Postgraduate Scholarships

Subjects: The Therle Drake Postgraduate Scholarship (the Scholarship) was established in 2013, via the Victoria University Foundation, through a bequest made by John Drake, in memory of his wife, Therle

Purpose: The scholarship is for postgraduate classical performance overseas study and application should be made in the year for which the project is planned. While the terms of the bequest are that preference be given to a piano student, other applicants will be considered. The scholarship is open to both domestic and international students

Eligibility: This scholarship is open to both domestic and international students. The scholarship may be held in; conjunction with other awards

Level of Study: Postgraduate

Type: Scholarship

Value: $12,000 subject to funds availability

Frequency: Annual

Country of Study: Any country

Application Procedure: Applicants will complete the online application by the closing date. No late applications will be accepted. Applicants should provide the following supporting documentation: 1. A letter outlining the project and its benefit to your career plans. 2. A detailed budget. 3. Copies of any communication with the host person(s) or organisation(s) overseas. 4. A supporting statement from the principal supervisor. In order to proceed with the application, kindly check the below link. www.victoria.ac.nz/study/student-finance/scholarships

Closing Date: 31 March

Funding: Private

For further information contact:

Scholarships Office, Victoria University of Wellington, PO Box 600, Wellington 6140, New Zealand

Email: scholarships-office@vuw.ac.nz

Ferrari

Direzione e stablimento Abetone int.4, ITA MO 41053, Maranello, Italy

Tel: (39) 536 949111

Email: carrerservice@mip.polimi.it

Website: www.ferrariworld.com

Born in 1947, Ferrari has always produced vehicles at its current site and has maintained its direction. It has progressively widened it range using visionary planning to both on a design level and on the quality of work produced.

Ferrari Innovation Team Project Scholarship

Subjects: Mechanic/Electronic engineering focused on human machine interface, Complex Systems development nanotechnologies, control systems, as well as material engineering focused on innovative materials applied to and planes

Purpose: To create members of a new and innovative team for the new and innovative cars of the future

Eligibility: Knowledge of ergonomics will be considered a plus

Level of Study: Postgraduate, Professional development

Type: Scholarship

Value: €25,000 and all accommodation and training

Length of Study: 1 year

Frequency: Annual
Study Establishment: Ferrari Spa
Country of Study: Italy
Closing Date: 25 May
Funding: Commercial
Contributor: Ferrari

For further information contact:

Email: cdozio@ferrari.it
Contact: Mr Claudio Dozio, HR Manager

Fight for Sight

Fight for Sight

Purpose: Fight for Sight is one of the leading United Kingdom charities dedicated to funding pioneering research to prevent sight loss and treat eye disease
Eligibility: Young (under 40) ophthalmologists and scientists working in the field of ophthalmology in the United Kingdom - awarded recognition of the completion of a significant piece of research completed within 18 months prior to the closing date
Level of Study: Postgraduate
Type: Grant
Value: GB£5,000
Frequency: Annual
Country of Study: Any country
Closing Date: 28 February
Funding: Foundation

For further information contact:

Email: education@rcophth.ac.uk

Five Strong Scholarship Foundation

5 Strong Scholarship

Purpose: The 5 Strong Scholarship Foundation is a team of experienced educators that have over 30 years of experience helping minority students graduate from high school and get into college. We have teamed up to form a foundation that's going to be dedicated to building cohorts of 5 college ready scholars and placing them on the campuses of Historically Black Colleges and Universities

Eligibility: 1. Must be a graduating high school senior. 2. Have a minimum 2.5 GPA and a minimum ACT: 19/SAT: 980 (verbal and math only). 3. Must commit to attend all of the 5 Strong College Prep sessions (bi-monthly). 4. Must reside in the Metro Atlanta Area (Fulton, DeKalb, Cobb, Atlanta, Clayton Counties)
Level of Study: Graduate
Type: Scholarship
Value: US$50,000
Frequency: Annual
Country of Study: Any country
Closing Date: 31 December
Funding: Foundation

For further information contact:

Andrew H. Ragland, 103 Pinegate Road, Peachtree City, GA 30269, United States of America

Tel: (1) 770 873 6621
Email: drewragland@5strongscholars.org

Flinders University

GPO Box 2100, Adelaide, SA 5001, Australia

Tel: (61) 8 8201 3911
Fax: (61) 8 8201 3177
Email: www.person@flinders.edu.au
Website: www.flinders.edu.au

Flinders University is an integral part of Australia's respected higher education system and makes an important economic and social contribution to South Australia and to the nation. Flinders has a high research profile and consistently ranks among Australia's top universities on a per capita basis for research. It emphasizes innovation and excellence in its educational programs and researches across a wide range of disciplines.

Advanced Community Care Scholarship

Subjects: Community care
Purpose: To undertake a research project within the Faculty of Health Sciences related to the practical clinical, organizational and financial implications of home-based alternatives to hospital care
Eligibility: Applicants must be Australian citizens or permanent residents of Australia and have completed at least 4 years

of tertiary education studies at a high level of achievement and have an appropriate Honours 1 or high 2A (or equivalent) undergraduate degree. They must enroll as full-time students (part-time awards are available in certain circumstances)
Level of Study: Postgraduate
Type: Scholarship
Value: AU$19,616 per year
Length of Study: 3 years
Application Procedure: Applicants must obtain the application kits from the Higher Degree Administration and Scholarships Office or can download it from the scholarships website
Closing Date: 31 October
Contributor: Advanced Community Care Association

For further information contact:

Tel: (61) 8 8201 3115
Email: scholarships@flinders.edu.au

Australian Health Inequities Program Research Scholarship

Subjects: Public health, labour market economics, housing and geography
Purpose: To address health inequities, understand the social determinants of health and analyze policy and program strategies that aim to reduce inequities
Eligibility: Applicants should be Australian citizens, permanent residents of Australia or New Zealand citizens and have completed at least four years of tertiary education studies at a high level of achievement and have an appropriate Honours 1 or high 2A (or equivalent) undergraduate degree. They should enroll as full-time students (a part-time award may be available in certain circumstances) and should commence a Doctorate by research
Level of Study: Postgraduate
Type: Scholarship
Value: AU$19,616 per year
Length of Study: 3 years
Application Procedure: Applicants can obtain the application kits from the Higher Degree Administration and Scholarships Office or download it from Flinders University scholarships website
Closing Date: 31 October

For further information contact:

Department of Public Health

Tel: (61) 8 8204 5983
Email: fran.baum@flinders.edu.au
Contact: Professor Fran Baum, AHIP Lead Investigator

Australian Health Inequities Program University Research Scholarship

Subjects: Public health, labour market economics, housing and geography
Purpose: To address health inequities, to understand the social determinants of health and to analyze policy and program strategies that aim to reduce them
Eligibility: Applicants must be Australian citizens, permanent residents of Australia or New Zealand citizens and have completed at least 4 years of tertiary education studies at a high level of achievement and have an appropriate Honours 1 or high 2A (or equivalent) undergraduate degree. They should enroll as full–time students (a part–time award may be available in certain circumstances) and should commence a Doctorate by research
Level of Study: Postgraduate
Type: Scholarship
Value: AU$19,616 per year
Length of Study: 3 years
Application Procedure: Applicants can obtain the application kits from the Higher Degree Administration and Scholarships Office or download it from Flinders University scholarships website. It is essential to consult Prof. Baum or Dr. Newman before submitting an application
Closing Date: 31 October

For further information contact:

Department of Public Health

Tel: (61) 8 8204 5983
Email: fran.baum@flinders.edu.au
Contact: Professor Fran Baum, AHIP Lead Investigator

Diamond Jubilee Bursary

Purpose: It is helpful for women, who are Australian citizens or permanent residents, enrolled in a postgraduate Masters degree (by research or including a thesis) at a South Australian university
Eligibility: Applicants: 1. Women students who are Australian citizens or permanent residents. 2. Must be studying at a South Australian University for a postgraduate award which is classified. 3. at Masters Degree level. This must be by research or include a thesis component. 4. Must have completed at least six months full time equivalent of their masters program. 5. Must have a good undergraduate academic record. 6. Must not be in full time paid employment or on fully paid leave during the tenure of the Scholarship. 7. Must not have received a scholarship or award in the same category

Level of Study: Postgraduate
Type: Bursary
Value: AU$3,000
Frequency: Annual
Country of Study: Australia
Application Procedure: Application forms can be downloaded from the AFUW-SA website listed below. 1. Your application must reach the Trust Fund's secretarial service by 29 March. 2. Scholarship Type: postgraduate, academic merit, financial, commencing, continuing
Closing Date: 29 March
Funding: Private
Additional Information: Selection of winners is based primarily on academic merit, but also on the importance of the purpose for which the scholarship will be used to the progress or completion of the degree, on referees' report, on financial need as well as community activities and other interests

For further information contact:

Email: internationalapply@flinders.edu.au

Faculty of Science and Engineering Research Awards (FSERA)

Subjects: Biological sciences, chemical sciences, earth sciences, engineering and technology, information, computing and communication sciences, mathematical sciences, physical sciences or science in general
Purpose: To enable students to pursue a Masters Degree by research or Doctorate by research in the Faculty of Science and Engineering
Eligibility: Applicants should have achieved Honours 1 or equivalent, or Honours 2a or equivalent. Only citizens of Australia or New Zealand or permanent residents can apply
Level of Study: Graduate, Postgraduate
Type: Research award
Value: AU$19,616 per year
Length of Study: 2 years if masters or 3 years if PhD
Country of Study: Australia
Application Procedure: Applicants must apply directly to the university
Closing Date: 31 October

For further information contact:

Tel: (61) 8 8201 3115
Fax: (61) 8 8201 5175
Email: scholarships@flinders.edu.au

Flinders University Research Scholarships (FURS)

Subjects: All subjects
Purpose: To enable suitably qualified applicants to proceed to a full-time Masters by research or Doctorate by research
Eligibility: Applicants must have achieved Honours 1 or equivalent, or Honours 2a or equivalent. Only citizens of Australia or New Zealand or permanent residents can apply
Level of Study: Postgraduate
Type: Scholarship
Value: AU$19,616
Length of Study: 2 years for masters or 3 years for PhD
Frequency: Annual
Country of Study: Australia
Application Procedure: Applicants must apply directly to the university
Closing Date: 31 October

For further information contact:

Tel: (61) 8 8201 3115
Fax: (61) 8 8201 5175
Email: scholarships@flinders.edu.au

FMC Foundation Pink Ribbon Ball Committee Breast Cancer Research Scholarship

Subjects: Biomedical
Purpose: To undertake a breast cancer biomedical research project within the Faculty of Health Sciences
Eligibility: Applicants must be Australian citizens or permanent residents of Australia and have completed at least 4 years of tertiary education studies at a high level of achievement and have an appropriate Honours 1 or high 2A (or equivalent) undergraduate degree. They must enroll as full-time students (part-time awards are available in certain circumstances) and must commence a Doctorate by research
Level of Study: Postgraduate
Type: Scholarship
Value: AU$25,000 plus up to AU$2,000 per year for conference travel and consumables
Length of Study: 3 years
Frequency: Annual
Application Procedure: Applicants can obtain the application kits from the Higher Degree Administration and Scholarships Office and can download it from the scholarship website
Closing Date: 31 October
Contributor: Flinders Medical Centre Foundation

For further information contact:

Tel: (61) 8 8204 4100
Email: johnno.oliver@flinders.edu.au
Contact: Professor John Oliver, Associate Professor

FMC Foundation Research Scholarship

Subjects: Health sciences
Purpose: To undertake a health-related project within the Faculty of Health Sciences
Eligibility: Applicants should be Australian citizens or permanent residents of Australia and have completed at least 4 years of tertiary education studies at a high level of achievement and have an appropriate Honours 1 or high 2A (or equivalent) undergraduate degree. They should enroll as full-time students (part-time awards are available in certain circumstances) and should commence a Doctorate by research
Level of Study: Postgraduate
Type: Scholarship
Value: AU$25,000 plus up to $2,000 per year for conference travel and consumables
Length of Study: 3 years
Frequency: Annual
Application Procedure: Applicants can obtain application kits from the Higher Degree Administration and Scholarships Office or download from the scholarships website
Closing Date: 31 October
Funding: Foundation
Contributor: FMC Foundation

For further information contact:

Tel: (61) 8 8204 4100
Email: johnno.oliver@flinders.edu.au
Contact: Professor John Oliver, Associate Professor

Honours/Masters Scholarship for AI, User Interface or Robotics

Subjects: AI, user interface or robotics
Purpose: To enable students to undertake an Honours or Masters project in the Artificial Intelligence Laboratory in the School of Informatics and Engineering at Flinders University
Eligibility: Applicants must have Australian citizenship or permanent residence, plus distinction-level completion of the requirements of 3 years of undergraduate degree in cognitive science, computer science, mathematics, or engineering program
Level of Study: Graduate
Type: Scholarship

Value: AU$5,000
Application Procedure: Check website for further details
Closing Date: 15 November

For further information contact:

Email: David.Powers@flinders.edu.au
Contact: David Powers

Investigation of the Human Intestinal Nervous System

Subjects: Physiology
Purpose: To support investigation of the human intestinal nervous system
Eligibility: Applicants must be Australian citizens or permanent residents of Australia and have completed at least 4 years of tertiary education studies at a high level of achievement and have an appropriate undergraduate medical degree. They should enroll as full-time students and commence a Doctorate by research
Level of Study: Graduate
Type: Scholarship
Value: AU$29,172
Length of Study: 3 years
Frequency: Annual
Application Procedure: Applicants can obtain application kits from the Higher Degree Administration and Scholarships Office or can download from the scholarships website
Closing Date: 31 October

For further information contact:

Tel: (61) 8 8204 4253
Email: david.wattchow@flinders.edu.au
Contact: David Wattchow, Associate Professor

May Mills Scholarship for Women

Subjects: All subjects
Purpose: To encourage women, who have experienced significant interruptions to their studies due to family responsibilities, to proceed to a research higher degree at Flinders University
Eligibility: Applicants must be female citizens or permanent residents of Australia
Level of Study: Graduate, Postgraduate
Type: Scholarship
Value: Maximum AU$9,000 per year
Length of Study: 1 year
Frequency: Annual

Country of Study: Australia
Application Procedure: Applicants may consult the scholarship website
Closing Date: 31 January

For further information contact:

Tel:	(61) 8 8201 3115
Fax:	(61) 8 8201 5175
Email:	scholarships@flinders.edu.au

Multi Scale Biomechanical Investigations of the Intervertebral Disc

Subjects: Orthopaedics
Purpose: To undertake a challenging program of research that combines both analytical (finite element analysis) and experimental
Eligibility: Applicants must be Australian or international students who have completed at least 4 years of tertiary education studies at a high level of achievement and have an appropriate Honours 1 or high 2A (or equivalent) undergraduate degree in mechanical/biomedical/civil/chemical engineering or related fields
Level of Study: Postgraduate
Type: Scholarship
Value: US$25,313
Length of Study: 3 years
Frequency: Annual
Application Procedure: Applicants can obtain the application kits from the Higher Degree Administration and Scholarships Office at Flinders University
Closing Date: 1 June

For further information contact:

Tel:	(61) 8 8275 1751
Email:	john.costi@rgh.sa.gov.au
Contact:	Dr John Costi

National Health and Medical Research Council Centre of Clinical Eye Research: PhD Scholarships

Subjects: Ophthalmology
Purpose: To conduct clinical research in the major blinding diseases – cataract, glaucoma, diabetic retinopathy and corneal disease
Eligibility: Applicants must be Australian citizens, permanent residents of Australia or New Zealand citizens and have completed at least 4 years of tertiary education studies at a high level of achievement and have an appropriate Honours 1 or high 2A (or equivalent) undergraduate degree
Level of Study: Postgraduate
Type: Scholarship
Value: A stipend of AU$20,007–29,172 plus AU$2,000 for conference travel and consumables
Length of Study: 3 years
Frequency: Annual
Application Procedure: Applicants can obtain the application kits from the Higher Degree Administration and Scholarships Office or can download it from the scholarships website
Closing Date: 31 October

For further information contact:

Tel:	(61) 8 8204 4899
Email:	Konrad.Pesudovs@flinders.edu.au
Contact:	Konrad Pesudovs

National Health and Medical Research Council Medical and Dental Postgraduate Research Scholarships

Subjects: Medical and dental
Purpose: To provide full-time research experience to medical or dental graduates registered to practice in Australia
Eligibility: Applicants must be medical or dental graduates registered to practice in Australia. Graduates from overseas who hold permanent resident status and are currently resident in Australia are eligible to apply
Level of Study: Graduate
Type: Scholarship
Value: AU$29,172 per year plus AU$2,250 per year towards the cost of consumables and travel to approved conferences
Length of Study: 3 years
Country of Study: Australia
Application Procedure: Applicants can obtain application forms, instruction booklets, referee report pro formae and various attachments to the instructions from the NHMRC website
Closing Date: 25 July

For further information contact:

Email:	research@nhmrc.gov.au

National Health and Medical Research Council Public Health Postgraduate Scholarships

Subjects: Public health
Purpose: To encourage graduates to obtain formal training in public health research

Eligibility: Applicants must be Australian citizens who have already completed a degree in an area applicable in public health research at the time of submission of the application or graduates in areas applicable to public health who are from overseas, have permanent resident status and are currently residing in Australia. All candidates must enroll for a higher degree requiring full-time research

Level of Study: Graduate

Type: Scholarship

Value: AU$19,616 (Australian postgraduate award), AU$25,313 (nursing and allied health professionals) and AU$29,172 (medical/dental)

Frequency: Annual

Country of Study: Australia

Application Procedure: Applicants must submit the application forms to the Higher Degree Administration and Scholarships Office and should include one additional copy for University records. Application forms, instruction booklets, referee report pro formae and various attachments to the instructions are available from the NHMRC website

Closing Date: 25 July

For further information contact:

Email: research@nhmrc.gov.au

National Health and Medical Research Council: Primary Health Care Postgraduate Research Scholarships

Subjects: Health care

Purpose: To encourage graduates to obtain formal training in primary health care related research, with an emphasis on rural communities

Eligibility: Applicants must be Australian citizens or have permanent resident status, who are medical, dental or health-related graduates currently registered to practice within Australia or who have already completed a degree (or equivalent) at the time of submission of the application

Level of Study: Graduate

Type: Scholarship

Value: $19,616 (Australian postgraduate award), $25,313 (nursing and allied health professionals) and $29,172 (medical/dental) per year

Country of Study: Australia

Application Procedure: Applications must be submitted to the Higher Degree Administration and Scholarships Office and should include one additional copy for University records. Application forms, instruction booklets, referee report pro formae and various attachments to the instructions are available from the NHMRC website

Closing Date: 25 July

For further information contact:

Email: research@nhmrc.gov.au

PhD Scholarship for Vascular and Metabolic Research

Subjects: Medicine

Purpose: To focus on the relationship between obesity, adipose tissue distribution, endothelial function and cardiovascular risk in humans using established techniques such as liver MRI and spectroscopy, pulse-wave analysis, and forearm occlusion plethysmography

Eligibility: Applicants should be Australian citizens or permanent residents of Australia and have completed at least 4 years of tertiary education studies at a high level of achievement and have an appropriate undergraduate medical degree

Level of Study: Postgraduate

Type: Scholarship

Value: AU$20,007 per year

Length of Study: Up to 3 years

Frequency: Annual

Study Establishment: Faculty of Health Sciences, Flinders University

Country of Study: Australia

Application Procedure: Applicants can obtain the application kits from the Higher Degree Administration and Scholarships Office or can download it from the scholarships website

Closing Date: 31 October

For further information contact:

Tel: (61) 8 8204 5202
Email: arduino.mangoni@flinders.edu.au
Contact: Dr Arduino Mangoni

Professor Lowitja O'Donoghue Indigenous Student Postgraduate Research Scholarship

Subjects: All subjects

Purpose: To enable suitably qualified applicants to proceed to a full-time Masters by research or Doctorate by research

Eligibility: Applicants must be Australian citizen, must have achieved Honours 1 or equivalent or Honours 2a or equivalent and must be an Aboriginal or Torres Strait Islander

Level of Study: Graduate

Type: Scholarship

Value: AU$25,627

Length of Study: 2 years if Masters and 3 years if PhD

Frequency: Annual

Study Establishment: Flinders University
Country of Study: Australia
Application Procedure: Applicants must apply directly to the university
Closing Date: 31 October

For further information contact:

Tel: (61) 8 8201 3115
Fax: (61) 8 8201 5175
Email: scholarships@flinders.edu.au

Reconciliation SA Aboriginal Education Leaders Fund Postgraduate Research Scholarship

Subjects: All subjects
Purpose: To foster leadership potential and skill development and to promote the vision of the Council for Aboriginal Reconciliation in South Australia
Eligibility: Applicants must have applied for admission to, or be enrolled in, a research higher degree on a full or part-time basis at Flinders University, University of Adelaide or University of South Australia and normally reside in South Australia and be of Australian Aboriginal or Torres Strait Islander descent and be identified and be accepted as an Australian Aboriginal or Torres Strait Islander by the community in which he or she lives or has lived
Level of Study: Graduate
Type: Scholarship
Value: AU$5,000
Frequency: Annual
Application Procedure: Applicants must contact the Yunggorendi First Nations Centre for Higher Education for further information and application forms
Closing Date: 31 January

For further information contact:

Email: shane.carr@flinders.edu.au

Repatriation General Hospital Department of Rehabilitation and Aged Care: Health Professionals Research Scholarship

Subjects: Rehabilitation
Purpose: To undertake research in an area of rehabilitation (cerebral palsy, driving rehabilitation, hydrotherapy, multiple sclerosis rehabilitation, hip fracture recovery)
Eligibility: Applicants must normally be Australian citizens, permanent residents of Australia or New Zealand citizens, who hold a First Class or upper Second Class Honours Degree

in an appropriate health-related discipline, or an equivalent qualification
Level of Study: Graduate
Type: Scholarship
Value: AU$25,000–29,172
Length of Study: 3 years
Frequency: Annual
Application Procedure: Applicants can obtain the application kits and further information from the scholarships web site or from the Higher Degree Administration and Scholarships Office
Closing Date: 31 October

For further information contact:

Tel: (61) 8 8275 1103
Email: maria.crotty@rgh.sa.gov.au
Contact: Professor Maria Crotty

Repatriation General Hospital Department of Rehabilitation and Aged Care: Medical Research Scholarship

Subjects: Health care
Purpose: To join a world class research team and improve health care
Eligibility: Applicants must be medical graduates and normally Australian citizens, permanent residents of Australia or New Zealand citizens, who hold a First Class or upper Second Class Honours Degree in an appropriate health-related discipline, or an equivalent qualification
Level of Study: Graduate
Type: Scholarship
Value: AU$29,172
Length of Study: 3 years
Application Procedure: Applicants can obtain the application kits and further information from the scholarships web site or from the Higher Degree Administration and Scholarships Office
Closing Date: 31 October

For further information contact:

Tel: (61) 8 8275 1103
Email: maria.crotty@rgh.sa.gov.au
Contact: Professor Maria Crotty

Repatriation General Hospital Department of Rehabilitation and Aged Care: Nursing Research Scholarship

Subjects: Health care

Eligibility: Applicants must be nursing graduates and normally Australian citizens, permanent residents of Australia or New Zealand citizens, who hold a First Class or upper Second Class Honours Degree in an appropriate health-related discipline, or an equivalent qualification

Level of Study: Graduate

Type: Scholarship

Value: AU$25,000–29,172 per year

Length of Study: 3 years

Application Procedure: Applicants can obtain the application kits and further information from the scholarships web site or from the Higher Degree Administration and Scholarships Office

Closing Date: 31 October

For further information contact:

Tel: (61) 8 8275 1103
Email: maria.crotty@rgh.sa.gov.au
Contact: Professor Maria Crotty

South Australian Department of Health Research Award

Subjects: Medical and health sciences or public health and health services

Purpose: To undertake a research project relevant to the health of South Australians, the South Australian health system, or the health-related targets in South Australia's Strategic Plan

Eligibility: Applicants must have achieved Honours 1 or equivalent, or Honours 2a or equivalent. Only citizens of Australia or permanent residents can apply

Level of Study: Postgraduate

Type: Scholarship

Value: AU$19,231 per year

Length of Study: 3 years

Frequency: Annual

Country of Study: Australia

Application Procedure: Applicants must apply directly to the university

Closing Date: 31 October

For further information contact:

Tel: (61) 8 8201 3115
Fax: (61) 8 8201 5175
Email: scholarships@flinders.edu.au

The Jack Loader Top-Up Scholarship

Subjects: Dementia

Purpose: To encourage research into dementia, in particular Alzheimer's Disease, and related disorders and/or the consequences of these diseases

Eligibility: Applicants must be Australian citizens or permanent residents of Australia and be enrolled full time in a research degree at one of the South Australian universities. Applicants should have received an Australian Postgraduate Award or equivalent University Scholarship

Level of Study: Graduate

Type: Scholarship

Value: AU$8,000

Length of Study: 12 months

Frequency: Annual

Application Procedure: Check website for further details

Closing Date: 31 October

Funding: Foundation

Contributor: The Rosemary Foundation for Memory Support Inc and Alzheimer's Australia South Australia

For further information contact:

Email: jmck1279@bigpond.net.au

University Hall Dean's Scholarship

Subjects: All subjects

Eligibility: Applicants must be resident in University Hall and enrolled in a degree course at the Flinders University at the time of application. Only citizens of Australia or New Zealand living in Australia over 1 year can apply

Level of Study: Graduate

Type: Scholarship

Value: AU$2,000 per year

Length of Study: 1 year

Frequency: Annual

Country of Study: Australia

Application Procedure: Applicants must apply directly to the scholarship provider

Closing Date: 20 October

For further information contact:

Tel: (61) 8 8201 3115
Fax: (61) 8 8201 5175
Email: scholarships@flinders.edu.au

University Hall Eurest Overseas Study Scholarship

Subjects: All subjects

Purpose: To enable full-time students residing in University Hall, who have demonstrated outstanding aptitude for research, to undertake a period of further study or research in approved universities or other institutions outside Australia

Eligibility: Applicants must have lived in University Hall for a period of not less than one academic year, have gained unqualified support for his/her supervisor for the proposed overseas visit, have gained approval from the overseas institution that he/she is acceptable for the proposed period of study and have demonstrated a suitable academic record in the previous academic year

Level of Study: Postgraduate

Type: Scholarship

Value: AU$2,500

Length of Study: 1 year

Frequency: Annual

Application Procedure: Applicants must contact the Higher Degree Administration and Scholarships Office and University Hall for application forms and further information

Closing Date: 20 October

For further information contact:

Email: flinders.housing@flinders.edu.au

Winifred E. Preedy Postgraduate Bursary

Purpose: The scholarship may be used for conference attendance, the purchase or hire of equipment, fees incurred because of study commitments, short-term assistance with living expenses, or any other purpose that will assist with the completion of the postgraduate qualification

Eligibility: Applicants have the following selection criteria: 1. Women who are enrolled at an Australian university and are Australian citizens or permanent residents. 2. Must be enrolled in a Masters Degree or a PhD in dentistry or a related field. 3. Must be Australian citizens or permanent residents. 4. Must be past or present students in the Dental School at the University of Adelaide. 5. Must have completed at least one year of their postgraduate degree. 6. Must not be in full-time paid employment or on fully-paid leave during the tenure of the Bursary. 7. Must not have previously won the Winifred E. Preedy Postgraduate Bursary. Selection of winners is based primarily on academic merit, but also on the importance of the purpose for which the scholarship will be used to the progress or completion of the degree

Level of Study: Postgraduate

Type: Bursary

Value: Varies

Frequency: Annual

Country of Study: Australia

Application Procedure: Selection of winners is based primarily on academic merit, but also on the importance of the

purpose for which the scholarship will be used to the progress or completion of the degree, on financial need as well as community activities and other interests

Closing Date: 29 March

Funding: Private

Additional Information: Funds are provided from the bequest of Winifred E. Preedy BDS (1901-1989), the second woman to graduate BDS in the University of Adelaide

For further information contact:

Sturt Rd, Bedford Park, SA 5042, Australia

Email: internationalapply@flinders.edu.au

Fogarty International Center

African Association for Health Professions Education and Research

Purpose: The African Association for Health Professions Education and Research builds on the Medical Education Partnership Initiative (MEPI) and the Nursing Education Partnership Initiative (NEPI)

Eligibility: 1. Non-African partners may not be listed as Multiple Principal Investigators. 2. An international African consortium of committed institutions should submit an application together and form the basis for the founding network leadership. 3. Named participating institutions for the establishment of the Association must include at least one former MEPI awardee institution (programmatic, linked or pilot awards) and at least one former NEPI awardee institution; but are not limited to these institutions

Level of Study: Postgraduate

Type: Grant

Frequency: Annual

Country of Study: Any country

Closing Date: 28 March

Funding: Private

For further information contact:

Tel: (61) 301 402 9591

Email: flora.katz@nih.gov

Contact: Ms Flora N. Katz, Director

Chronic, Noncommunicable Diseases and Disorders Research Training (NCD-Lifespan)

Purpose: The Chronic, Noncommunicable Diseases and Disorders Across the Lifespan: Fogarty International Research

Training Award program supports collaborative research training between institutions in the United States and low-and middle-income countries (LMICs), defined by the World Bank classification system

Eligibility: 1. Applications from United States institutions must demonstrate collaborations with institutions in the low- and middle-income countries (LMICs), defined by the World Bank classification system, named in their application. 2. Foreign applications will only be accepted from LMIC institutions. 3. Only foreign LMIC institutions may apply for the D71 planning grant. 4. United States applicants must identify at least one scientist from each LMIC institution as the main foreign collaborator for that institution

Level of Study: Graduate

Type: Research grant

Frequency: Annual

Country of Study: Any country

Closing Date: 14 March

Funding: Private

For further information contact:

Division of International Training and Research, Fogarty International Center, National Institutes of Health, Building 31, Room B2C39, Bethesda, MD 20892-2220, United States of America

Tel: (1) 301 496 1653
Fax: (1) 301 402 0779
Email: Kathleen.Michels@nih.gov
Contact: Mr Kathleen Michels, Program Officer

Ernst Mach Grant for Young Researchers

Purpose: 1. The Ernst Mach grant is named after the famous Austrian physicist. Student and young researchers from foreign universities are invited to apply for this grant to come to Austria for research. 2. It promote research cooperation

Eligibility: 1. Very good knowledge of English/German

Level of Study: Graduate

Type: Grant

Value: For graduates with Ph.D degree the value is €1,150

Frequency: Annual

Country of Study: Any country

Application Procedure: 1. Applicants who seek admission to an university in Austria have to contact the institution of their choice. 2. The selection process for all grants is competitive, i. e., there is no legal claim to a grant even if all the application requirements are fulfilled. 3. Short-term grants(1-3 months) have a priority in the period from January to June. When

applying for a short-term grant therefore consideration should be given primarily for a period of January to June

Closing Date: 30 September

Funding: Private

For further information contact:

Tel: (61) 1 534 080

H3Africa Global Health Bioinformatics Research Training Program

Purpose: Through the Human Heredity and Health in Africa (H3Africa) Initiative, the Global Health Bioinformatics Research Training Program supports bioinformatics research training programs at low- and middle-income country (LMIC) institutions in Africa with significant genomics research capacity

Eligibility: H3Africa fosters genomic and epidemiological research in African scientific institutions

Level of Study: Postgraduate

Type: Programme grant

Frequency: Annual

Country of Study: Any country

Application Procedure: The training programs address the need for bioinformatics research expertise in the H3Africa Consortium, resulting in sustainable centers of bioinformatics research training relevant to global health research for the African continent

Closing Date: Not mentioned specifically

Funding: Private

For further information contact:

Tel: (1) 301 827 2227
Fax: (1) 301 402 0779
Email: laura.povlich@nih.gov
Contact: Ms Laura K Povlich

Fondation des Etats-Unis

15 Boulevard Jourdan, 75014 Paris, France

Tel: (33) 1 5380 6880
Fax: (33) 1 5380 6899
Email: administration@feusa.org
Website: www.feusa.org
Contact: Mr Sophie Uasset, Director

For the past 75 years the Fondation des Etats-Unis has been welcoming American and International Students during their studies in Paris.

Harriet Hale Woolley Scholarship

Subjects: Visual arts, music and psychiatry
Purpose: To support the study of visual arts, music and psychiatry in Paris
Eligibility: Open to citizens of the United States of America, who are 21-30 years of age and have graduated with high academic standing from a United States college, university or professional school of recognized standing. Applicants should provide evidence of artistic or musical accomplishment. Applicants should have a good working knowledge of French, sufficient to enable the student to benefit from his or her study in France. ; Grants are for those studying painting, printmaking or sculpture and for instrumentalists, not for research in art history, musicology or composition, nor for students of dance or theatre. Successful candidates propose a unique and detailed project related to their study, which requires a 1-year residency in Paris
Level of Study: Doctorate, Graduate, Postgraduate, Predoctorate
Type: Scholarship
Value: A stipend of around US$10,000 (subject to fund earnings)
Length of Study: 1 academic year
Frequency: Annual
Country of Study: France
Application Procedure: For a complete description of the scholarship including a list of general requirements, an application checklist and an application form, please visit www.feusa.org/harriet-hale-woolley-scholarship
Closing Date: 31 January (every year)
Funding: Private
No. of awards offered last year: 4

For further information contact:

Fondation des Etats-Unis, 15 Boulevard Jourdan, F-75014 Paris, France

Tel: (33) 1 53 80 68 82
Email: culture@feusa.org
Contact: Miss Noemi Haire-Sievers, Culture & International Relations Manager

Fondation Fyssen

194 Rue de Rivoli, F-75001 Paris, France

Tel: (33) 1 42 97 53 16
Fax: (33) 1 42 60 17 95
Email: secretariat@fondation-fyssen.org
Website: www.fondation-fyssen.org
Contact: Mrs Nadia Ferchal, Director

The aim of the Fyssen Foundation is to encourage all forms of scientific enquiry into cognitive mechanisms, including thought and reasoning, that underlie animal and human behaviour, their biological and cultural bases and phylogenetic and ontogenetic development.

International Prize

Subjects: Neuropsychology
Purpose: To encourage a scientist who has conducted distinguished research in the areas supported by the Foundation
Eligibility: Applicants are requested to visit the website www.fondationfyssen.fr/en/international-prize/ for eligibility information
Value: €60,000
Frequency: Annual
Country of Study: Any country
Application Procedure: Candidates cannot apply directly but should be proposed by recognized scientists. Proposals for candidates should consist of (i) curriculum vitae, (ii) a list of publications, (iii) a summary (4 pages maximum) of the research. The proposal should be submitted in 14 copies to Secrétariat de la Fondation Fyssen
Closing Date: 6 November
Funding: Private

For further information contact:

Email: secretariat@fondation-fyssen.org

Fondation Jeunesse Internationale, Ecole franchaise d'Extreme-Orient

Tel: (33) 1 53 70 18 60
Email: contrats.postdocs@efeo.net
Contact: Ms Evelise Bruneau

Short-Term EFEO Postdoctoral Contracts

Subjects: Humanities and Social Sciences
Eligibility: Applicants must have obtained a PhD following a viva voce examination held in or after 2010. There is no

age limit. Applicants must be French or European Union nationals and affiliated to a French higher education and research institute or a public/private research institute based in France

Value: $1,500

Length of Study: 4 to 6 months

Country of Study: France

Application Procedure: 1. Applications must be submitted electronically (by email to contrats.postdocs@efeo.net) before 30 November (Please Request an Acknowledgement of Receipt). 2. Applications may be submitted in French or English

Closing Date: 10 November

Additional Information: For further information, please contact Ms. Evelise Bruneau (contrats.postdocs@efeo.net, +33 1 53 70 18 60)

For further information contact:

Email: contrats.postdocs@efeo.net

Ford Foundation

320 East 43rd Street, New York, NY 10017, United States of America

Tel: (1) 212 573 5000
Fax: (1) 212 351 3677
Website: www.fordfoundation.org

The Ford Foundation was established on 15 January, 1936, with an initial gift of US$25,000 from Edsel Ford, whose father Henry, founded the Ford Motor Company. During its early years, the foundation operated in Michigan under the leadership of Ford family members. Since the founding charter stated that resources should be used 'for scientific, educational and charitable purposes, all for the public welfare,' the foundation made grants to many kinds of organizations.

Ford Foundation Predoctoral Fellowships for Research-Based PhD or ScD Programs in United States of America

Subjects: Fellowships will be made for study in research-based PhD or ScD. programs that include the following major disciplines and related interdisciplinary fields: American studies, anthropology, archaeology, art and theater history, astronomy, chemistry, communications, computer science, cultural studies, earth sciences, economics, engineering, ethnic studies, ethnomusicology, geography, history, international relations, language, life sciences, linguistics, literature, mathematics, performance study, philosophy, physics, political science, psychology, religious studies, sociology, urban planning, and women's studies. Also eligible are interdisciplinary ethnic studies programs, such as African American studies and Native American studies, and other interdisciplinary programs, such as area studies, peace studies, and social justice. Research-based fields of education are eligible if the major field of study is listed above and is used to describe the PhD or ScD program of the applicant (e.g. sociology of education, anthropology, and education

Purpose: The fellowships are available for pursuing predoctoral level

Eligibility: All citizens, nationals, and permanent residents (holders of a Permanent Resident Card) of the United States, and individuals granted deferred action status under the Deferred Action for Childhood Arrivals Program, regardless of race, national origin, religion, gender, age, disability, or sexual orientation; individuals with evidence of superior academic achievement (such as grade point average, class rank, honors or other designations); individuals committed to a career in teaching and research at the college or university level; individuals enroled in or planning to enrol in an eligible research-based (dissertation-required), program leading to a PhD or ScD degree at a non-proprietary United States educational institution. For detailed information, please check website

Level of Study: Research

Type: Fellowship

Value: Annual stipend: US$20,000. Award to the institution in lieu of tuition and fees: US$2,000. Expenses paid to attend at least one Conference of Ford Fellows

Length of Study: 3 years

Country of Study: United States of America

Application Procedure: The mode of applying is online

Closing Date: 14 November

Contributor: Ford Foundation

For further information contact:

Email: fordapplications@nas.edu

Foreign Affairs and International Trade Canada

Enquiries Service Foreign Affairs Canada, 125 Sussex Drive, Ottawa, ON K1A 0G2, Canada

Tel: (1) 613 944 4000
Fax: (1) 613 944 9136
Email: enqserv@dfait-maeci.gc.ca
Website: www.dfait-maeci.gc.ca

Foreign Affairs and International Trade Canada supports Canadians abroad, helps Canadian companies succeed in global markets, promotes Canada's culture and values and works to build a more peaceful and secure world.

Graduate Research Awards for Disarmament, Arms Control and Non-Proliferation

Subjects: Disarmament, arms control and non-proliferation
Purpose: To enhance Canadian graduate-level scholarship on disarmament, arms control and non-proliferation issues
Eligibility: Open to Master's and Doctoral candidates only
Level of Study: Doctorate, Postgraduate
Value: C$5,000 for Doctoral awards, which will support research, writing and fieldwork leading to the completion of a major research paper or dissertation proposal. C$2,500 which will support research and writing leading to the completion of a major research paper or theses
Frequency: Annual
Country of Study: Canada
Funding: Government
Additional Information: For more information, please contact Elaine Hynes at The Simons Foundation by email to ehynes@thesimonsfoundation.ca or by telephone at (1) 778-782-7779

For further information contact:

Email: simon.collard-wexlen@international.gc.ca
Contact: c/o Simon Collard-Wexler

Forgarty International Center

Ecology and Evolution of Infectious Diseases Initiative (EEID)

Purpose: This joint National Institutes of Health (NIH) - National Science Foundation (NSF) initiative supports efforts to understand the underlying ecological and biological mechanisms that govern relationships between human-induced environmental changes and the emergence and transmission of infectious diseases

Eligibility: Check the website for further details. www.fic.nih.gov/Programs/Pages/ecology-infectious-diseases.aspx
Level of Study: Graduate
Type: Funding support
Frequency: Annual
Country of Study: Any country
Closing Date: 20 November
Funding: Private

For further information contact:

Fogarty International Center, National Institutes of Health, Building 31, B2C39, Bethesda, MD 20892-2220, United States of America

Tel: (1) 301 496 1653
Fax: (1) 301 402 0779
Email: Christine.Jessup@nih.gov
Contact: Sir Christine Jessup, Program Officer

Forum Transregional Studies

Wallotstrae 14, DEU 14193, Berlin, Germany

The Forum Transregional Studies in Berlin is a research organization on the content internationalization of the humanities and social sciences. The forum offers scope for cooperation between scientists with different regional and disciplinary perspectives and offers the opportunity to test and develop research ideas and projects.

Forum Transregional Studies Postdoctoral Fellowships for International Students

Subjects: It especially invites scholars from Islamic, Asian, African, Australian, European art histories and the art histories of the Americas, to join the program, but also addresses neighboring disciplines such as Archaeology, Anthropology, History, Aesthetics and other fields dealing with the history of visual and material cultures
Purpose: By creating a space of dialogue for university and museum scholars from all regions, it aims to discuss the potentials and contours of a plural history of art
Eligibility: International students are eligible to apply for this fellowship. Applicants whose first language is not English are usually required to provide evidence of proficiency in English at the higher level required by the University
Type: Postdoctoral fellowship

Value: In particular cases, shorter fellowship terms may be considered. Postdoctoral fellows will receive a monthly stipend of € 2.500 plus supplements depending on their personal situation. Organizational support regarding visas, insurances, housing, etc. will be provided. Successful applicants become fellows of the program Art Histories and Aesthetic Practices at the Forum Transregionale Studien and are expected to take up residence in Berlin

Country of Study: Germany

Application Procedure: PDF files: 1. a curriculum vitae (in English). 2. a project description (no longer than five pages / in English). 3. a sample of scholarly work (about 20 pages of an article, conference paper, or dissertation chapter) names of two referees (including their e-mail addresses). The complete application should be submitted latest by 15 January and addressed to arthistories_application@trafo-berlin.de

Closing Date: 15 January

Additional Information: For more details please browse the link scholarship-positions.com/forum-transregional-studies-postdoctoral-fellowships-international-students-germany/2017/12/13/

For further information contact:

Email: arthistories_application@trafo-berlin.de

Foundation for Digestive Health and Nutrition

4930 Del Ray Avenue, Bethesda, MD 20814, United States of America

Tel:	(1) 301 222 4002
Fax:	(1) 301 222 4010
Email:	awards@fdhn.org
Website:	www.fdhn.org
Contact:	Ms Wykenna S.C. Vailor, Research Awards Manager

The Foundation for Digestive Health and Nutrition is the foundation of the American Gastroenterological Association (AGA), the leading professional society representing gastroenterological and hepatologists worldwide. It is separately incorporated and governed by a distinguished board of AGA physicians and members of the lay public. The Foundation raises funds for research and public education in the prevention, diagnosis, treatment and cure of digestive diseases. Along with the AGA, it conducts public education initiatives related to digestive diseases. The Foundation also administers the disbursement of grants on the behalf of the AGA and other funders.

American Gastroenterological Association Fellowship to Faculty Transition Awards

Subjects: Medical science, specifically gastroenterology and hepatology

Purpose: To prepare physicians for independent research careers in digestive diseases

Eligibility: Applicants must be MDs or MD/PhDs currently in a gastroenterology-related fellowship, at a North American institution and committed to academic careers. They should have completed at least 2 years of research training at the start of this award. Women and minority investigators are strongly encouraged to apply. Applicants must be AGA Trainee Members or be sponsored by an AGA Member at the time of application

Level of Study: Postgraduate

Type: Award

Value: US$40,000 per year

Length of Study: 2 years

Frequency: Annual

No. of awards offered: 8

Application Procedure: Applications can be downloaded from the AGA Foundation website. The completed application, letters of support or commitment and other documents must be submitted as one PDF document, titled by the applicant's last name and first initial only. Hard copies are not permitted. For further information visit the AGA Foundation website

Closing Date: 31 August

Funding: Private

Contributor: The AGA

No. of awards offered last year: 4

No. of awards applicants last year: 8

Additional Information: The award provides salary support for additional full-time research training in basic science to acquire modern laboratory skills. The additional 2 years of research training provided by the award would broaden the scope of investigative tools available to the recipient, generally in basic disciplines such as cell or molecular biology, or immunology. A complete financial statement and scientific progress report are required annually and upon completion of the programme. All publications arising from work funded by this programme must acknowledge support of the award

For further information contact:

Tel: (1) 301 222 4012
Email: awards@fdhn.org

American Gastroenterological Association R Robert and Sally D Funderburg Research Scholar Award in Gastric Cancer

Subjects: Gastric mucosal cell biology, regeneration and regulation of cell growth, inflammation, genetics of gastric carcinoma, epidemiology of gastric cancer, etiology of gastric epithelial malignancies, or clinical research in the diagnosis of gastric carcinoma
Purpose: To support active, established investigators in the field of gastric biology who enhance the fundamental understanding of gastric cancer pathobiology in order to ultimately develop a cure for the disease
Eligibility: Applicants must hold faculty positions at accredited North American institutions and must have established themselves as independent investigators in the field of gastric biology. Women and minority investigators are strongly encouraged to apply. Applicants must be members of the AGA at the time of application submission
Level of Study: Postgraduate
Type: Award
Value: US$100,000
Length of Study: 2 years
Frequency: Annual
Country of Study: The United States of America, Canada or Mexico
No. of awards offered: 4
Application Procedure: Applications can be downloaded from the AGA Foundation website. The completed application, letters of support or commitment and other documents must be submitted as one PDF document, titled by the applicant's last name and first initial only. Hard copies are not permitted. For further information visit the AGA Foundation website
Closing Date: 21 August
Contributor: The AGA, the late R Robert and the late Sally D Funderburg
No. of awards offered last year: 1
No. of awards applicants last year: 4

For further information contact:

Tel: (1) 301 222 4012
Email: awards@fdhn.org

American Gastroenterological Association Research Scholar Awards

Subjects: Gastroenterology and hepatology
Purpose: To enable young investigators to develop independent and productive research careers in digestive diseases by ensuring that a major proportion of their time is protected for research
Eligibility: Candidates must hold an MD, PhD, or equivalent degree and a full-time faculty positions at North American universities or professional institutes at the time of commencement of the award. They must be members of the AGA at the time of application submission. The award is for young faculty, who have demonstrated unusual promise and have some record of accomplishment in research. Candidates must devote at least 70 % of their efforts to gastrointestinal tract or liver-related research. Women, minorities and physician/scientist investigators are strongly encouraged to apply
Level of Study: Graduate
Type: Research grant
Value: US$90,000 per year
Length of Study: 3 years
Frequency: Annual
Country of Study: United States of America
No. of awards offered: 40
Application Procedure: Applications can be downloaded from the AGA Foundation website. The completed application, letters of support or commitment and other documents must be submitted as one PDF document, titled by the applicant's last name and first initial only. Hard copies are not permitted. For further information visit the AGA Foundation website
Closing Date: 16 October
Funding: Private
No. of awards offered last year: 4
No. of awards applicants last year: 40
Additional Information: A complete financial statement and scientific progress report are required upon completion of the programme. All publications arising from work funded by this programme must acknowledge the support of the award. Awardees must submit their work for presentation at Digestive Disease Week during the last year of the award

For further information contact:

Tel: (1) 301 222 4012
Email: awards@fdhn.org

American Gastroenterological Association-Elsevier Pilot Research Award

Subjects: Medical science, specifically gastroenterology and hepatology
Purpose: To provide non-salary funds for new investigators to help them establish their research careers or to support pilot projects that represent new research directions for established investigators. The intent is to stimulate research in gastroenterology- or hepatology-related areas by permitting investigators to obtain new data that can ultimately provide the basis for subsequent grant applications of more substantial funding and duration
Eligibility: Applicants must possess an MD or PhD degree or equivalent and must hold faculty positions at accredited North American institutions. In addition, they must be AGA members at the time of application submission. Women and minorities are strongly encouraged to apply
Level of Study: Postdoctorate, Postgraduate, Predoctorate, Research
Type: Grant
Value: US$25,000
Length of Study: 1 year
Frequency: Annual
No. of awards offered: 22
Application Procedure: Applications can be downloaded from the AGA Foundation website. The completed application, letters of support or commitment and other documents must be submitted as one PDF document, titled by the applicant's last name and first initial only. Hard copies are not permitted. For further information visit the AGA Foundation website
Closing Date: 12 January
Funding: Private
Contributor: The AGA
No. of awards offered last year: 1
No. of awards applicants last year: 22

For further information contact:

Tel: (1) 301 222 4012
Email: awards@fdhn.org

American Gastroenterological Association/ American Gastroenterological Association-Eli & Edythe Broad Student Research Fellowship(s)

Subjects: Research related to the gastrointestinal tract, liver or pancreas

Purpose: To stimulate interest in research careers in digestive diseases by providing salary support for research projects
Eligibility: Applicants must be students at accredited North American institutions, may not hold similar salary support awards from other agencies. Women and minority students are strongly encouraged to apply
Level of Study: Graduate, Postgraduate, Professional development
Type: Award
Value: US$2,500 to 3,000 per year
Length of Study: 10 weeks
Frequency: Annual
No. of awards offered: 48
Application Procedure: Applications can be downloaded from the AGA Foundation website. The completed application, letters of support or commitment and other documents must be submitted as one PDF document, titled by the applicant's last name and first initial only. Hard copies are not permitted. For further information visit the AGA Foundation website
Closing Date: 1 June
Funding: Private
Contributor: The AGA
No. of awards offered last year: 12
No. of awards applicants last year: 48

For further information contact:

Tel: (1) 301 222 4012
Email: awards@fdhn.org

Foundation for Liberal and Management Education University

Gat No. 1270, Lavale, Off. Pune Bangalore Highway, Pune, Maharashtra 412115, India

Contact: Foundation for Liberal and Management Education University

FLAME University is a private, coeducational and fully residential university, anchored in liberal education located in Pune city in the state of Maharashtra. Earlier it was known as FLAME – Foundation for Liberal and Management Education.

Foundation for Liberal and Management Education University Scholars Program

Subjects: Scholarships are awarded to study the students offered by the university
Purpose: The scholarship is designed to give students an opportunity to further their education at FLAME University
Eligibility: Students from India are eligible to apply
Type: Postgraduate scholarships
Value: FLAME University offers a range of scholarships that recognize the inherent excellence and distinctive attributes of students ensuring that FLAME attracts the brightest of minds. In addition, merit, need-based and special scholarships are provided with that may range from partial to full fee waivers
Study Establishment: Scholarships are awarded to study the students offered by the university
Country of Study: India
Application Procedure: To be considered for the scholarship, students need to email the supporting documents of achievements at admission-at-flame.edu.in. FLAME University's Scholarship Committee will evaluate your application and make the final decision
Additional Information: For more details please browse the website scholarship-positions.com/flame-university-scholars-program-india/2017/11/17/

For further information contact:

Tel: (61) 800 209 4567
Email: enquiry@flame.edu.in

Foundation for Science and Disability, Inc.

1700 SW 23rd Dr, Gainesville, FL 32608, United States of America

Tel: (1) 352 374 5774
Fax: (1) 352 374 5781
Email: richard.mankin@ars.usda.gov
Website: stemd.org
Contact: Dr Richard Mankin, Chair, Student Grants

The Foundation for Science and Disability aims to promote the integration of scientists with disabilities into all activities of the scientific community and of society as a whole, and to promote the removal of barriers in order to enable students with disabilities to choose careers in science.

Foundation for Science and Disability Student Grant Fund

Subjects: Engineering, mathematics, medicine, natural sciences and computer science
Purpose: To increase opportunities in science for physically disabled students at the graduate or professional level
Eligibility: Open to candidates from the United States of America
Level of Study: Doctorate, Postgraduate
Type: Grant
Value: US$1,000
Length of Study: 1 year
Frequency: Annual
Country of Study: United States of America
No. of awards offered: 7
Application Procedure: Applicants must submit a completed application form, copies of official college transcripts, a letter from the research or academic supervisor in support of the request and a second letter from another faculty member
Closing Date: 1 December
Funding: Private
No. of awards offered last year: 1
No. of awards applicants last year: 7
Additional Information: The award may be used for an assistive device or instrument, or as financial support to work with a professor on an individual research project or for some other special need

For further information contact:

Email: Richard.Mankin@ars.usda.gov

Graduate Student Grant

Subjects: research projects in science, technology, engineering or mathematics
Purpose: The Student Award Program of FSD helps to increase opportunities in science, engineering, mathematics, technology, and pre-medical/dental areas for graduate or professional students with disabilities. FSD has established a Science Graduate Student Grant Fund, which is available to fourth year undergraduates (who are disabled and have been accepted to a graduate or professional school in the sciences) and graduate science students who have a disability. Awards of US$1000 each are made to support research projects of qualified university students in any field of Mathematics, Science, Medicine, Technology, or Engineering

Eligibility: graduate students with a disability who have a research program in a science, technology, engineering or mathematics program

Level of Study: Doctorate, Graduate, Postgraduate (MSc)

Type: Award/Grant

Value: US$1000

Length of Study: 1 year

Frequency: Annual

Country of Study: United States of America

No. of awards offered: 11

Application Procedure: application form must be completed. Two letters of reference. Copy of passport or birth certificate

Closing Date: 1 December

Funding: Foundation

Contributor: Foundation for Science and Disability

No. of awards offered last year: 1

No. of awards applicants last year: 11

For further information contact:

Tel:	(1) 352 374 5774
Email:	richard.mankin@ars.usda.gov
Contact:	Dr Richard Mankin, Graduate Committee Chair

Foundation of the American College of Healthcare Executives

Suite 1700, One North Franklin Street, Chicago, IL 60606-4425, United States of America

Tel:	(1) 312 424 9388
Fax:	(1) 312 424 9405
Email:	membershipl@ache.org
Website:	www.ache.org
Contact:	The Membership Marketing Representative

It is the mission of the Foundation of the American College of Healthcare Executives to be the professional membership society for healthcare executives; to meet its members' professional, educational and leadership needs; to promote high ethical standards and conduct; and to advance healthcare leadership and management excellence.

Albert W Dent Graduate Student Scholarship

Subjects: Healthcare management

Purpose: To help minority students better prepare themselves for a career in healthcare management

Eligibility: Open to citizens of the United States of America and Canadian citizens who are student associates of the American College of Healthcare Executives and are in good standing. Applicants must be minority students enrolled for full-time study for the upcoming Fall term, which is the final year of didactic work in a healthcare management graduate programme, be able to demonstrate financial need and must not be previous recipients

Level of Study: Graduate

Type: Scholarship

Value: US$3,500

Frequency: Annual

Country of Study: United States of America or Canada

Application Procedure: Applicants must complete an application form, available from their programme director or the main address

Closing Date: Applications are accepted between 1 January–31 March

For further information contact:

Email:	membership@ache.org

Foster G McGaw Graduate Student Scholarship

Subjects: Healthcare management

Purpose: To help students better prepare themselves for a career in healthcare management

Eligibility: Open to citizens of the United States of America and Canadian citizens who are student associates of the American College of Healthcare Executives and are in good standing. Applicants must be enrolled in full-time study for the upcoming Fall term, which is the final year of didactic work in a healthcare management graduate programme, be able to demonstrate financial need and must not be previous recipients

Level of Study: Graduate

Type: Scholarship

Value: US$3,500

Frequency: Annual

Country of Study: United States of America or Canada

Application Procedure: Applicants must complete an application form, available from their programme director or the main address

Closing Date: Applications are accepted between 1 January–31 March

For further information contact:

Email:	contact@ache.org

Foundation Praemium Erasmianum

Jan van Goyenkade 5, NLD 1075 HN, Amsterdam, Netherlands

Tel: (31) 20 676 0222
Fax: (31) 20 675 2231
Email: spe@erasmusprijs.org
Website: www.erasmusprijs.org
Contact: Y C Goester, Secretary

The Foundation Praemium Erasmianum operates internationally in the fields of social studies and the arts and humanities, through the awarding of the Erasmus Prize and other activities.

Foundation Praemium Erasmianum Study Prize

Subjects: Humanities and social sciences
Purpose: To honour young academics who have written an excellent thesis in the field of humanities or social sciences
Eligibility: Open to students of Dutch universities
Level of Study: Postdoctorate
Type: Money prize
Value: €3,000
Frequency: Annual
Country of Study: Any country
No. of awards offered: 21
Application Procedure: Relevant faculties or universities nominate candidates, from which the Foundation selects five winners
Closing Date: 15 July
Funding: Private
No. of awards offered last year: 5
No. of awards applicants last year: 21

For further information contact:

Email: l.aalbers@erasmusprijs.org

Freie Universitat Berlin and Peking University

No.5 Yiheyuan Road Haidian District, Beijing 100871, P.R.China

Email: beate.rogler@fu-berlin.de
Website: www.fu-berlin.de
Contact: Freie Universitat Berlin and Peking University

Free University of Berlin and Peking University Joint Postdoctoral Fellowship

Subjects: Area Studies. Data Science & Mathematics, 1. Each fellowship is awarded for 24 months, starting 1 November. It consists of two phases: Phase 1: 12 months of research at FUB (November to October) Phase 2: 12 months of research at PKU (November to October). 2. The Fellowship applicants must identify and secure the endorsement of two tenured faculty members, one at each university, who will serve as hosts. They will conduct their research projects under the joint supervision of these two experienced researchers. Data Science & Mathematics
Purpose: Applications are invited for Freie Universitat Berlin and Peking University Joint Postdoctoral Fellowship Program awarded for the duration of 24 months, starting 1 November. The fellowship is open to highly qualified researchers of all nationalities who received their PhD no more than three years prior to the deadline for this call
Eligibility: Applicants of all nationalities are eligible to apply. Applicants whose first language is not English are usually required to provide evidence of proficiency in English at the higher level required by the University
Type: Postdoctoral fellowship
Value: During their stay in Berlin, the Joint Postdoctoral Fellows will receive a monthly stipend of €1,853 and a one-time relocation allowance of €2,000. They are eligible for a monthly child allowance if travelling to Berlin with dependent children. All Fellows will furthermore have access to the Researcher Development Program of the Dahlem Research School. During their stay at PKU, Joint Postdoctoral Fellows will receive a monthly stipend of RMB 15,000. They can receive an additional RMB 3,500 per month for self-organized accommodation or choose to live in a PKU postdoc flat. The Fellows are furthermore eligible to apply for travel funding. They will have access to China's Postdoctoral Funds or other national research funds upon registration at the Office of National Postdoctoral Affairs Management Committee
Study Establishment: Area Studies, Data Science & Mathematics, Each fellowship is awarded for 24 months, starting 1 November. It consists of two phases: Phase 1: 12 months of research at FUB (November to October) Phase 2: 12 months of research at PKU The Fellowship applicants must identify and secure the endorsement of two tenured faculty members, one at each university, who will serve as hosts. They will conduct their research projects under the
Country of Study: Any country
Application Procedure: Please refer the website
Closing Date: 22 February
Additional Information: Please browse the website for more details scholarship-positions.com/freie-universitat-berlin-peking-university-joint-postdoctoral-fellowship/2017/12/01/.

The complete application should be saved as one file in pdf format. Please submit it simultaneously by email to: Mr. Fan Deshang, Postdoctoral Affairs Office, Peking University boguanban@pku.edu.cn Ms. Judith Winkler, Center for International Cooperation, Freie Universitat Berlin judith.winkler@fu-berlin.de

For further information contact:

Email: judith.winkler@fu-berlin.de

French Ministry of Foreign Affairs

Website: www.campusfrance.org/en/eiffel

Eiffel Scholarships in France for International Students

Subjects: Engineering science at masters level (science in the broadest sense at PhD level), economics and management and law & political sciences
Purpose: The Eiffel Excellence Scholarship Programme was established by the French Ministry of Foreign Affairs and International Development to enable French higher education establishments to attract top foreign students to enroll in their master's and PhD courses
Level of Study: Doctorate, Postgraduate
Type: Scholarship
Value: For masters level studies, the Eiffel scholarship includes a monthly allowance of US$1,181 (a maintenance allowance of €1,031 and a monthly stipend of €150) and can be awarded for 1 to 3 years. For PhD level studies, the Eiffel scholarship includes a monthly allowance of €1,400 and is awarded for a maximum of 10 months
Length of Study: 1 to 3 years
Frequency: Annual
Study Establishment: French Universities and Academic Institutions
Country of Study: France
Application Procedure: Applications for EIFFEL scholarships are submitted by French Higher Education Institutions. You must apply and meet the requirements of the French Higher Education Institution in order to be considered for the scholarship
Closing Date: Before 12 January
Contributor: French Ministry of Foreign Affairs and International Development
Additional Information: Please visit Official Scholarship Website: www.campusfrance.org/en/eiffel for more details

For further information contact:

Email: candidatures.eiffel@campusfrance.org

Friends of Israel Educational Foundation

Academic Study Group, POB 42763, N2 0YJ, London, United Kingdom

Tel:	(44) 20 8444 0777
Fax:	(44) 20 8444 0681
Email:	info@foi-asg.org
Website:	www.foi-asg.org
Contact:	Mr John D A Levy

The Friends of Israel Educational Foundation and its sister operation, the Academic Study Group, aim to encourage a critical understanding of the achievements, hopes and problems of modern Israel, and to forge new collaborative working links between the United Kingdom and Israel.

Friends of Israel Educational Foundation Academic Study Bursary

Subjects: All subjects
Purpose: To provide funding for British academics planning to pay a first research or study visit to Israel
Eligibility: Open to research or teaching postgraduates. The Academic Study Group will only consider proposals from British academics who have already linked up with professional counterparts in Israel and agreed terms of reference for an initial visit
Level of Study: Postdoctorate
Type: Bursary
Value: UK£300 per person
Frequency: Annual
Country of Study: Israel
No. of awards offered: Approx. 50
Application Procedure: Applicants must contact the organization. There is no application form
Closing Date: 15 November or 15 March
Funding: Private
Contributor: Trusts and individual donations
No. of awards offered last year: 10
No. of awards applicants last year: Approx. 50

For further information contact:

Email: info@foi-asg.org

Fujitsu

1250 E. Arques Avenue, Sunnyvale, CA 94085-3470, United States of America

Contact: application@sc.ip.fujitsu.com

Fujitsu is the Japanese global information and communication technology (ICT) company, offering a full range of technology products, solutions and services.

Fujitsu Scholarship Program for Asia-Pacific Region

Subjects: Scholarship is awarded for education and cross-cultural management training in the Global Leaders for Innovation and Knowledge program by Fujitsu-JAIMS Foundation
Purpose: Applications are invited for Fujitsu Scholarship program open to applicants of United States of America and Asia pacific region. The scholarship provides full financial assistance for postgraduate education and cross-cultural management training in the Global Leaders for Innovation and Knowledge program at JAIMS, the Japan-America Institute of Management Science in Hawaii, United States of America
Eligibility: A minimum TOEFL score of 577/233/90 (paper/computer/Internet), TOEIC score of 750, or IELTS (Academic) overall band test result of 6.5 or higher from a test taken within the last five years at the time of application
Type: Postgraduate scholarships
Value: See the website
Study Establishment: Scholarship is awarded for education and cross-cultural management training in the Global Leaders for Innovation and Knowledge program by Fujitsu-JAIMS Foundation
Country of Study: United States of America
Application Procedure: See the website
Closing Date: 7 March
Additional Information: For more details please visit the website scholarship-positions.com/fujitsu-scholarship-program-asia-pacific-region-United States of America-2014/2013/12/07/

For further information contact:

Tel: (33) 81-0-44-754-3413
Email: Dina.Tiongson@au.fujitsu.com

Fulbright Commission (Argentina)

Viamonte 1653, 2 Piso, C1055 ABE, Buenos Aires Argentina

Tel: (54) 11 4814 3561
Fax: (54) 11 4814 1377
Email: info@fulbright.com.ar
Website: fulbright.edu.ar/en
Contact: Melina Ginszparg, Educational Advisor

The Fulbright Programme is an educational exchange programme that sponsors awards for individuals approved by the J William Fulbright Board. The programme's major aim is to promote international co-operation and contribute to the development of friendly, sympathetic and peaceful relations between the United States and other countries in the world.

Fulbright Commission (Argentina) Awards for United States Lecturers and Researchers

Subjects: All subjects except medical science
Purpose: To enable United States lecturers to teach at an Argentine university for one semester, and to enable United States researchers to conduct research at an Argentine institution for 3 months
Eligibility: Open to United States researchers and lecturers. Applicants must be proficient in spoken Spanish
Level of Study: Professional development
Value: Varies according to professional experience
Length of Study: 3 months
Frequency: Annual
Country of Study: Argentina
Closing Date: 31 July
Funding: Government
Contributor: The United States of America and the Argentine governments

For further information contact:

The Council for International Exchange of Scholars, 3001 Tilden Street, Washington, DC 20008-3009, United States of America

Tel: (1) 202 686-4000
Email: info@ciesnet.cies.org

Fulbright Scholar-in-Residence

Subjects: Education administration
Purpose: To enable visiting scholars to teach in the United States about their home country or world region
Eligibility: Open to candidates with strong international interest and some experience in study abroad and exchange programmes
Level of Study: Professional development
Type: Grant
Value: Fulbright funding plus salary supplement and in-kind support from the host institution
Length of Study: 1 year
Frequency: Annual
Application Procedure: Candidates must submit a Fulbright visiting scholar application form and a brief project statement
Closing Date: 15 October

For further information contact:

Tel: (33) 1 481 435 61/62
Email: info@fulbright.edu.ar

Fulbright Foundation (United Kingdom)

Fulbright House, 62 Doughty Street, WC1N 2LS, London, United Kingdom

Tel: (44) 20 7404 6880
Fax: (44) 20 7404 6834
Contact: Grants Management Officer

British-American Chamber of Commerce Awards

Subjects: All subjects
Purpose: To fund postgraduate education between Britain and America
Eligibility: Open to graduates of any nationality
Level of Study: Postgraduate
Value: US$8,000
Frequency: Annual
Country of Study: United States of America
Application Procedure: Please write for details.

For further information contact:

Email: fulbrighttgc@irex.org

Fulbright Scholarship Program for Nigerians

Purpose: The Fulbright Scholarship program for Nigerians is offering Scholarships to students of Nigeria who are interested in pursuing two years doctoral studies in United States of America, in the fields of natural and social sciences, arts, and humanities
Eligibility: Listed below are the supplementary documents which have to be added. Three academic and professional references. Curriculum Vitae academic transcripts from each post-secondary institution attended and writing sample english language certificates personal statement
Level of Study: Doctorate
Type: Scholarship
Value: It includes all related expenses
Length of Study: 2 years
Frequency: Annual
Country of Study: United States of America
Application Procedure: 1. To apply for the Fulbright Scholarship for Nigerians the applicants must be citizens or nationals of Nigeria, or permanent residents holding a valid passport issued by the government of Nigeria. 2. The applicants must be doctoral students who conducted research in their home institution, applicants must be at least two years into their doctoral program in any discipline that was related to the subjects offered by the university
Closing Date: June month (exact date is expected)
Funding: Private
Additional Information: Young and talented scholars of Nigeria are invited to apply for Fulbright Scholarship Program for Nigerians to pursue doctoral studies in United States of America

For further information contact:

Email: professionalexchange@state.gov

Fulbright United States Student Program

Fulbright-National Geographic Digital Storytelling Fellowship

Purpose: The Fulbright-National Geographic Storytelling Fellowship, a component of the Fulbright United States Student Program, provides opportunities for United States citizens to participate in an academic year of overseas travel
Eligibility: Applications will be accepted for Fulbright-National Geographic Storytelling Fellowships in any country

to which there is an active Fulbright United States Student Program with the exception of China
Level of Study: Postgraduate, Professional development
Type: Fellowship
Frequency: Annual
Country of Study: Any country
Application Procedure: Candidates must have completed at least an undergraduate degree by the commencement of the Fulbright awa Candidates from all fields are encouraged to apply. All application materials, including academic transcripts and letters of recommendation must be submitted in the Embark Online Application and Recommendation System by 9 October at 5pm Eastern Time
Closing Date: 9 October
Funding: Private

For further information contact:

United States Student Programs Division, 809 United Nations Plaza, New York, NY 10017 3580, United States of America

Email: FBstudent.natgeo@iie.org

Fund for Epilepsy

Ripponden Mill, Mill Fold, Ripponden, H6 4DH, Halifax, United Kingdom

Tel: (44) 1422 823508
Fax: (44) 1422 824695
Email: ffe@epilepsyfund.org.uk
Website: www.epilepsyfund.org.uk
Contact: The Administrator

Emergency Medicine Foundation Grants

Subjects: To strengthen capacity within ethnic minority voluntary organizations, and build a secure base for minority ethnic communities
Purpose: To aid various ethnic minority voluntary organizations
Value: Dependent, for 1–3 years
Frequency: Dependent on funds available
Application Procedure: Please write in to EMF, grants officer
Funding: Government, Individuals
No. of awards offered last year: 17

For further information contact:

Tel: (44) 208 432 0000 Free phone : 08000 652 0390
Fax: (44) 208 432 0319
Email: enquiries@emf-cemvo.co.United Kingdom

Fundacion Educativa Carlos M. Castaneda

1925 Brickell Ave, Miami, FL 33129, United States of America

Fax: (1) 305 283 4963
Email: fecmc@me.com
Website: www.fecmc.org

Carlos M. Castaeda Journalism Scholarship

Purpose: This award is for Spanish speaking students who are pursuing a graduate degree in journalism. Applicants must have a grade point average of 3.0 or higher
Eligibility: 1. Must be currently enrolled in a graduate program at the time of application. 2. Must be majoring in journalism. 3. Must be of Hispanic heritage. 4. Must plan to pursue a career in Spanish-language journalism. 5. Must speak and write fluently in Spanish. 6. This award is for United States students
Level of Study: Graduate
Type: Scholarship
Value: US$7,000
Frequency: Annual
Country of Study: United States of America
Application Procedure: Applications and award information are available on the Carlos M. Castaeda Educational Foundation website at the address provided. In addition to the completed online application form, students must submit the following items: Official transcripts of all academic work completed; Proof of acceptance in an accredited graduate program; Recent 1,040 documents or equivalent information describing the student and his/her parents' financial status; Recent curriculum vitae describing the applicant's work history and activities; Three letters of reference in separately sealed envelopes; A portfolio showcasing three recently written works that have been published in the Spanish language
Closing Date: 15 April
Funding: Foundation

For further information contact:

1925 Brickell Avenue D-1108, Miami, FL 33129, United States of America

Tel: (1) 305 859 9617
Email: fundacion_educativa_cmc@yahoo.com

Funds for Women Graduates

57 Alma Road, LS6 2AH, Leeds, United Kingdom

Tel: (44) 113 2747988
Email: secretary@ffwg.org.uk
Website: ffwg.org.uk/
Contact: Mrs Sally Dowell, Co. Secretary

FFWG is the registered Trading Name for the BFWG Charitable Foundation. FfWG seeks to promote the advancement of education and the promotion of higher education of women graduates by offering grants to help women graduates with their living costs while registered for study or research at institutions in Great Britain.

Emergency Grants

Subjects: All subjects considered
Purpose: FfWG offers Emergency Grants to graduate women who face an unforeseen financial crisis (not with their fees) whilst engaged in study or research at an approved institution of higher education in Great Britain
Eligibility: Please see website for eligibility criteria www.ffwg.org.United Kingdom
Level of Study: Postgraduate
Type: Grant
Value: Up to US$2,500
Length of Study: Any postgraduate course eligible
Frequency: Twice a year
Study Establishment: Any approved institution of higher education in Great Britain
Country of Study: United Kingdom, Scotland or Wales
No. of awards offered: 135
Application Procedure: Please see website for details ffwg.org.uk
Closing Date: 1st round 14 May
Funding: Private
No. of awards offered last year: 28
No. of awards applicants last year: 135
Additional Information: grants@ffwg.org.uk

For further information contact:

Email: grants@ffwg.org.uk
Contact: Mrs Jean Collett Flatt, Grants administrator

Emergency Grants for United Kingdom and International Women Graduates

Subjects: The grant is provided to learn any of the courses offered by the higher institutions in the United Kingdom
Purpose: To allow a woman facing unexpected financial crises to continue in postgraduate study

Eligibility: Women graduates from Britain and overseas are eligible to apply. There is no upper age limit
Type: Grant
Value: These are one off payments to assist with the completion of an academic years work. No grant is likely to exceed £2,500. All grants are offered on a needs basis and therefore not all grants will be for £2,500
Country of Study: United Kingdom
No. of awards offered: 170
Application Procedure: The mode of applying is by post. An application form for an Emergency Grant may be obtained by email only from the Grants Administrator at grants@ffwg.org.uk, you need to explain the nature of the emergency and the course you are studying
Closing Date: 12 May or 5 October
Funding: Private
No. of awards offered last year: 22
No. of awards applicants last year: 170
Additional Information: All grants are offered on a needs basis

For further information contact:

Email: grants@ffwg.org.uk

FfWG Foundation Grants

Subjects: All subjects
Purpose: To financially assist female graduates registered for study or research at an approved Institute of Higher Education within Great Britain
Eligibility: Open to female graduates who are in their final year or writing-up year of a PhD. There is no restriction on nationality or age. Any subject
Level of Study: Doctorate, Postdoctorate, Postgraduate
Type: Grant
Value: Foundation Grants are up to £4,000 and Emergency Grants are up to £1,500. (these values are being reviewed)
Length of Study: Courses that exceed 1 year in length
Frequency: Annual
Study Establishment: Approved Institutes of Higher Education
Country of Study: Great Britain
No. of awards offered: 376
Application Procedure: Applicants must complete an application form and submit it with two references and a brief summary of the thesis, if applicable. Requests for application forms must be made by email
Closing Date: Foundation Grants - 4 April; Emergency Grants - 9 February, 31 May
Funding: Private
Contributor: Investment income
No. of awards offered last year: 36

No. of awards applicants last year: 376
Additional Information: Closing dates are liable to change each year. Please refer to our website for details of the current year

For further information contact:

Email: grants@ffwg.org.uk

Foundation Grants

Subjects: Any
Purpose: FfWG offers Foundation Grants to help women graduates with their living expenses (not fees) while registered for study or research at an approved institution of higher education in Great Britain. The criteria are the proven needs of the applicant and her academic calibre. Foundation Grants will only be given for the final year of a PhD or DPhil. The closing date for applications for current and upcoming year is 5 March and the grants are awarded in July for the following academic year. Request for applications must be made by 28 February
Level of Study: Doctorate
Type: Grant
Value: Up to £6,000
Frequency: Annual
Study Establishment: Any recognised university
Country of Study: United Kingdom, Scotland and Wales
No. of awards offered: 309
Application Procedure: please see website for details www.ffwg.org.uk
Closing Date: 5 March
Funding: Private
Contributor: Investment income
No. of awards offered last year: 38
No. of awards applicants last year: 309
Additional Information: Please contact grants@ffwg.org.uk for further details

For further information contact:

Email: secretary@ffwg.org.uk

Theodora Bosanquet Bursary

Subjects: History or English literature
Purpose: This Bursary is offered annually to women graduates whose research in History or English Literature requires

a short residence in London in the summer. It provides accommodation in a hall of residence for up to 4 weeks between end of June and mid September
Eligibility: Please check website for eligibility www.ffwg.org.uk
Level of Study: Research
Type: Bursary
Value: Four weeks accomodation paid for
Frequency: Annual
Study Establishment: Any
Country of Study: United Kingdom, Scotland or Wales
Application Procedure: Please see website for details
Closing Date: 31 October
Funding: Private
No. of awards offered last year: 2
Additional Information: Contact email is grants@ffwg.org.uk not as above

For further information contact:

Email: grants@ffwg.org.uk
Contact: Mrs Jean Collett Flatt, Grants administrator

Fylde College

Fylde College - Travel Award

Purpose: The scholarship is available to enable Fylde students to travel to: 1. Conferences or training. 2. Dissertation locations where costs exceed that normally expected as part of the degree course. 3. Undertake voluntary work in vacation time
Eligibility: For further information, refer the official website link
Level of Study: Postgraduate
Type: Travel award
Value: A total fund of US$1,500 is available
Frequency: Annual
Country of Study: Any country
Closing Date: 20 May
Funding: Private

For further information contact:

Tel: (44) 1524 65201
Email: fylde@lancaster.ac.uk

G

Garden Club of America

14 East 60th Street 3rd Floor, New York, NY 10022, United States of America

Tel:	(1) 212 753 8287
Fax:	(1) 212 753 0134
Email:	judygow@comcast.net
Website:	www.gcamerica.org
Contact:	Judy Gow, Vice Chairman

The Garden Club of America stimulates the knowledge and love of gardening, shares the advantages of association by means of educational meetings, conferences, correspondence and publications, and restores, improves and protects the quality of the environment through educational programmes and action in the fields of conservation and civic improvement.

The Anne S. Chatham Fellowship

Subjects: Medicinal botany
Purpose: To protect and preserve knowledge about the medicinal use of plants and thus prevent the disappearance of plants with therapeutic potential
Eligibility: Open to candidates who are currently enroled in PhD programmes or have obtained a PhD or a graduate degree
Level of Study: Doctorate, Postdoctorate
Type: Fellowship
Value: US$4,000
Frequency: Annual
Application Procedure: Applicants must submit an application letter, an abstract, a research proposal and a curriculum vitae
Closing Date: 1 February

Contributor: Garden Club of America
Additional Information: Contact Wendy Applequist for more information

For further information contact:

Missouri Botanical Garden, PO Box 299, United States of America

Tel:	(1) 314 577 9503
Email:	wendy.applequist@mobot.org
Contact:	Dr Wendy Applequist

Gates Cambridge Trust

PO Box 252, Cambridgeshire CB2 1TZ, Cambridge, United Kingdom

Tel:	(44) 1223 338 467
Fax:	(44) 1223 351 449
Email:	info@gates.scholarships.cam.ac.uk
Website:	www.gates.scholarships.cam.ac.uk
Contact:	Board of Graduate Studies

Gates Cambridge Scholarship

Subjects: All full-time, postgraduate, degree subjects available at the University of Cambridge
Purpose: The Gates Cambridge Scholarship programme was established in October 2000 by a donation of US$210m from the Bill and Melinda Gates Foundation to the University of Cambridge; this is the largest ever single donation to a United Kingdom university. Scholarships are awarded to outstanding applicants from countries outside the United Kingdom to pursue a full-time postgraduate degree in any subject available at the University of Cambridge. The selection criteria are:

© Springer Nature Limited 2019
Palgrave Macmillan (ed.), *The Grants Register 2020*,
https://doi.org/10.1057/978-1-349-95943-3

1. outstanding intellectual ability. 2. leadership potential. 3. a commitment to improving the lives of others. 4. a good fit between the applicant's qualifications and aspirations and the postgraduate programme at Cambridge for which they are applying. While at Cambridge, Scholars pursue the full range of subjects available at the University and are spread across its departments and Colleges. The aim of the Gates Cambridge programme is to build a global network of future leaders committed to improving the lives of others

Eligibility: You can apply for a Gates Cambridge Scholarship if you are: 1. a citizen of any country outside the United Kingdom. 2. applying to pursue one of the following full-time residential courses of study at the University of Cambridge. PhD (three year research-only degree). MSc or MLitt (two year research-only degree). One year postgraduate course (e.g. MPhil, LLM, MASt, Diploma, MBA etc.). There is no age restriction for applications

Level of Study: Doctorate, Postgraduate, MBA, Postgraduate (MSc)

Type: Scholarship

Value: Tuition fees and maintenance allowance of £17,500

Length of Study: Varies from 9 months for Masters to 3 years for PhD

Frequency: Annual

Study Establishment: University of Cambridge

Country of Study: United Kingdom

No. of awards offered: circa 6,000

Application Procedure: Complete relevant funding section of the University of Cambridge application form

Closing Date: 5 December

Funding: Foundation

Contributor: Bill and Melinda Gates Foundation

No. of awards given last year: 90

No. of applicants last year: circa 6,000

Additional Information: Candidates must apply for a place at the University of Cambridge and for funding at the same time, using the University of Cambridge application portal - there is no separate Gates Cambridge application form except for MBA and MFin applicants who should consult the Cambridge Judge Business School website

For further information contact:

The Warehouse, Ground Floor, 33 Bridge Street, CB2 1UW, Cambridge, United Kingdom

Tel: (44) 1223 338 467
Email: info@gatescambridge.org, info@gates.
                    scholarships.cam.ac.uk

General Social Care Council

Goldings House, 2 Hay's Lane, SE1 2HB, London, United Kingdom

Tel: (44) 20 7397 5100
Fax: (44) 20 7397 5101
Email: info@bursaries.gscc.org.uk
Website: www.gscc.org.uk
Contact: Administrative Officer

The General Social Care Council is the first ever regulatory body for the social care profession in United Kingdom. It was set up to establish codes of conduct and practice for social care workers, a register of practicing professionals and to regulate and support social work, education and training. It takes forwards some of the work of the Central Council for Education and Training in Social Work, which closed on September 28, 2001. Similar councils exist for Northern Ireland, Scotland and Wales.

Social Work Bursary

Subjects: Social work

Purpose: To support those seeking the qualifications required for social work

Eligibility: Open to graduates, who have ordinarily been resident in United Kingdom studying on an approved full-time postgraduate course. Amongst other eligibility criteria, students must also meet certain residency criteria. Please refer to the application packs for full eligibility criterion

Level of Study: Postgraduate

Type: Bursary

Value: Non-income-assessed grant of £2,500–2,900 and a contribution towards practice learning opportunity related expenses and tuition fees. It also includes a income-assessed maintenance grant and allowances to assist cost of living

Length of Study: 2 years

Frequency: Annual

Study Establishment: Accredited higher education institutions running a social work course approved by the General Social Care Council, the Scottish Social Services Council, the Care Council for Wales or the Northern Ireland Social Care Council

Country of Study: United Kingdom

No. of awards offered: 2,300

Application Procedure: Application guide is available on the following link www.nhsbsa.nhs.uk/sites/default/files/2019-07/Your%20guide%20to%20Social%20Work%20Bursaries%202019-20%20%28V2%29%2007%202019.pdf
Closing Date: 1 February
Funding: Government
Contributor: The Department of Health
No. of awards given last year: 2,100
No. of applicants last year: 2,300
Additional Information: The bursary is a year-to-year funding arrangement. The bursary terms and conditions (including rates) may change from year-to-year

For further information contact:

NHS Business Services Authority, Sandyford House, Archbold Terrace, United Kingdom

Tel: (44) 8456 101 122
Email: swb@ppa.nhs.uk
Contact: Social Work Bursary

GeneTex

GeneTex Scholarship Program

Purpose: GeneTex believes in accelerating scientific advancement and the notion that the genesis of future discoveries begins with the support of young scientists today. The GeneTex Scholarship Program is intended for students that have declared a STEM major or are enrolled in a STEM graduate program
Eligibility: 1. Student in good standing and enrolled at an accredited college or university. 2. Declared STEM major. 3. Open to international students. 4. All accredited Universities are eligible
Level of Study: Postgraduate
Type: Programme grant
Value: $2,000
Frequency: Annual
Country of Study: Any country
Application Procedure: See the website. www.genetex.com/Article/Company?param1=Scholarship
Closing Date: 21 December
Funding: Private

For further information contact:

6F-2, No. 89, Dongmei Rd., East Dist., Hsinchu City, Taiwan 300, Republic of China

Email: scholarship@genetex.com

Geological Society of America (GSA)

3300 Penrose Place, PO Box 9140, Boulder, CO 80301-1806, United States of America

Tel: (1) 303 357 1000
Fax: (1) 303 357 1070
Email: awards@geosociety.org
Website: www.geosociety.org
Contact: Ms Program Manager, Grants, Awards and Recognition

Established in 1888, the GSA is a non-profit organization dedicated to the advancement of the science of geology. GSA membership is for the generalist and the specialist in the field of geology and offers something for everyone

Marie Morisawa Award

Subjects: Quaternary geology/geomorphology
Purpose: To support promising female MS and PhD graduate students pursuing a career in geomorphology
Eligibility: Female scientists in geomorphology currently enroled in a Masters or PhD program are encouraged to apply
Level of Study: Graduate, Research
Type: Fellowship
Value: US$1,000
Frequency: Annual
Country of Study: Any country
No. of awards given last year: 1
Additional Information: Please check at rock.geosociety.org/qgg/M-H%20As.html for more information.

For further information contact:

Email: awards@geosociety.org

George A and Eliza Gardner Howard Foundation

Brown University, Box 1867, 42 Charlesfield Street, Providence, RI 02912, United States of America

Tel: (1) 401 863 2640
Fax: (1) 401 863 7341
Email: howard_foundation@brown.edu
Website: www.brown.edu/divisions/graduate_school/howard
Contact: Ms Susan M Clifford, Co-ordinator

The George A and Eliza Gardner Howard Foundation was established in 1952 by Nicea Howard in memory of her grandparents. Although Miss Howard had a special interest in the arts, her stated purpose was to aid the personal development of promising individuals at the crucial middle stages of their careers.

George A. and Eliza Gardner Howard Foundation

Subjects: The George A. and Eliza Gardner Howard Foundation is an independent foundation administered at Brown University. It awards a limited number of fellowships each year for independent projects in selected fields, targeting its support specifically to early mid-career individuals, those who have achieved recognition for at least one major project. Our support is particularly intended to augment paid sabbatical leaves. In the case of independent artists or scholars, or those without paid leaves, we would expect that a Howard Fellowship would enable them to devote a substantial block of time to the proposed project. The Howard Foundation was officially established in 1952 and offered its first fellowships in 1954. Since 1954 more than 400 Howard Fellowships have been awarded. A total of eight fellowships of US$35,000 will be awarded in April 2020 for 2020-2021 in the fields of: Fiction, Poetry, and Playwriting and Theater Studies Applications can be submitted starting 07 January

Purpose: Awards a limited number of fellowships each year for independent projects in selected fields, targeting its support specifically to early mid-career individuals, those who have achieved recognition for at least one major project. Our support is particularly intended to augment paid sabbatical leaves. In the case of independent artists or scholars, or those without paid leaves, we would expect that a Howard Fellowship would enable them to devote a substantial block of time to the proposed project. A total of eight fellowships of US$35,000 will be awarded in April 2020 for 2020-2021 in the fields of: Fiction, Poetry, and Playwriting and Theater Studies

Eligibility: In order to be eligible to apply for a Howard Fellowship, candidates should be able to answer "yes" to each of the following questions. If "no" is the correct answer to any of them, they are asked to explain on the application form what special circumstances might make them eligible anyway, given the requirements for a Howard Fellowship. Can your current professional status appropriately be viewed as "early mid-career" as understood by the Howard Foundation? Appropriate candidates for a Howard Fellowship should have completed their formal studies within the past five to fifteen years of the application date and should also have successfully completed at least one major project beyond degree requirements that would be sufficient for the awarding of tenure at a research institution or for achieving comparable

peer recognition, e.g., through publication or exhibition. Candidates who are already nationally and internationally recognized leaders in their fields as reflected by their promotion to full professor or by comparable recognition in their fields of endeavor are not normally eligible for a Howard Fellowship. Would a Howard Fellowship provide you with time off from other responsibilities to work on your proposed project? Our support is particularly intended to augment paid sabbatical leaves. In the case of independent artists or scholars, or those without paid leaves, we would expect that a Howard Fellowship would enable them to devote a substantial block of time to the proposed project. Are you, regardless of your citizenship, currently living and working in the United States or United States of America Territories?; Does your proposed project fall within one of the fields established for this year's round of applications? Given the limits of our resources, we must adhere strictly to the fields announced each year for project proposals

Level of Study: Doctorate, Postdoctorate, Postgraduate, Postgraduate (MSc)

Type: Fellowships

Value: US$35,000

Frequency: Annual

Country of Study: United States of America

No. of awards offered: 100-150

Application Procedure: Applications accepted through howardfoundation.fluidreview.com

Closing Date: 11 January

Funding: Foundation

No. of awards given last year: 8

No. of applicants last year: 100-150

Additional Information: www.brown.edu/howard-foundation/

For further information contact:

Brown University, 1 Prospect Street, Box 1857, United States of America

Tel: (1) 401 863 2429
Email: howard_foundation@brown.edu
Contact: Mr Edward Goll, Administrative Coordinator

German Historical Institute

1607 New Hampshire Avenue North West, Washington, DC 20009-2562, United States of America

Tel: (1) 202 387 3355
Fax: (1) 202 483 3430
Email: fellowships@ghi-dc.org
Website: www.ghi-dc.org
Contact: Bryan Hart

The German Historical Institute is an independent research institute dedicated to the promotion of historical research in the Federal Republic of Germany and the United States of America. The Institute supports and advises German and American historians and encourages co-operation between them. It is part of the foundation Deutsche Geisteswissenschaftliche Institute im Ausland (DGIA).

German Historical Institute Collaborative Research Program for Postdoctoral Scholars

Subjects: German and United States of America post-World War II history, transatlantic studies and comparative studies in social, cultural and political history
Purpose: To support a research programme for postdoctoral scholars on the topic of continuity, change and globalization in postwar Germany and the United States of America
Eligibility: Open to German and United States of America postdoctoral students. Applications from women and minorities are especially encouraged
Level of Study: Postdoctorate
Type: Fellowship
Value: US$20,000–40,000, dependent on length of study
Length of Study: 6 months–1 year
Frequency: Dependent on funds available
Country of Study: United States of America
Application Procedure: Applicants must refer to the website for details
Closing Date: Refer to the website
Funding: Government
Contributor: The National Endowment for Humanities
No. of awards given last year: 1

For further information contact:

Email: westermann@ghi-dc.org

Summer Seminar in Germany

Subjects: German handwriting, German archives, German history and transatlantic studies
Purpose: To introduce students to German handwriting of previous centuries by exposing them to a variety of German archives, familiarizing them with major research topics in German culture and history and encouraging the exchange of ideas among the next generation of United States of America scholars
Eligibility: Open to United States of America doctoral students. Applications from women and minorities are especially encouraged
Level of Study: Doctorate

Type: Scholarship
Value: All transportation and accommodations
Length of Study: 2 weeks
Frequency: Annual
Country of Study: Germany
Application Procedure: Applicants must refer to the website for details
Closing Date: 31 January
Funding: Government
No. of awards given last year: Varies
Additional Information: Questions may be directed to Elisabeth Engel at engel@ghi-dc.org

For further information contact:

Email: laurence.mcfalls@umontreal.ca

Transatlantic Doctoral Seminar in German History

Subjects: The Transatlantic Doctoral Seminar in German History (TDS) is an annual seminar organized by the German Historical Institute in Washington DC and Georgetown University. The seminar brings together doctoral students in German history from Europe and North America who are nearing completion of their doctoral degrees. We usually invite eight doctoral students from each side of the Atlantic to discuss their research projects. The discussions at the seminar are based on papers (in German or English) submitted in advance of the conference. The seminar is be conducted bilingually, in German and English
Purpose: To bring together young scholars from Germany and the United States of America who are nearing completion of their doctoral degrees. It provides an opportunity to debate doctoral projects in a transatlantic setting
Eligibility: Open to doctoral students in German history at North American and European Universities. Applications from women and minorities are especially encouraged
Level of Study: Doctorate
Type: Scholarship
Value: Travel and accommodation
Length of Study: 4 days
Frequency: Annual
Country of Study: Germany
No. of awards offered: Varies
Application Procedure: Applicants must refer to the website for details
Closing Date: 15 January
Funding: Government
Contributor: German Historical Institute Washington Georgetown University
No. of awards given last year: 16
No. of applicants last year: Varies

Additional Information: Questions may be directed to Dr Richard F. Wetzell at r.wetzell@ghi-dc.org

For further information contact:

Email: mlist@ghi-dc.org

German Marshall Fund of the United States (GMF)

1744 R Street NW, Washington, DC 20009, United States of America

Tel: (1) 202 683 2650
Fax: (1) 202 265 1662
Email: info@gmfus.org
Website: www.gmfus.org
Contact: Lea Rosenbohm, Administrative Assistant

The German Marshall Fund (GMF) of the United States is an American institution that stimulates the exchange of ideas and promotes co-operation between the United States and Europe in the spirit of the post war Marshall Plan. GMF was created in 1972 by a gift from Germany as a permanent memorial to Marshall Plan Aid.

German Marshall Fund Journalism Program

Subjects: Journalism
Purpose: To contribute to better reporting on transatlantic issues by both American and European journalist
Eligibility: Open to American and European journalists who have an outstanding record in reporting on foreign affairs
Level of Study: Postdoctorate, Professional development
Type: Fellowship
Value: US$2,000–25,000 and funds for travel
Frequency: Annual
Application Procedure: Applicants including a description of the proposed project, current curriculum vitae and samples of previous work must be sent
Funding: Foundation
Contributor: The German Marshall Fund

For further information contact:

Email: usoyez@gmfus.org
Contact: Ursula Soyez

German Studies Association

Kalamazoo College, 1200 Academy Street, Kalamazoo, MI 49006-3295, United States of America

Tel: (1) 269 267 7585
Fax: (1) 269 337 7251
Email: director@thegsa.org
Website: www.thegsa.org
Contact: David E. Barclay, Executive Director

The German Studies Association (GSA) is a non-profit educational organization that promotes the research and study of Germany, Austria and Switzerland. The GSA Endowment Fund provides financial support to Association projects, the annual conference, and general operations.

Berlin Program Fellowship

Subjects: Modern and contemporary German and European affairs
Purpose: To support doctoral dissertation research as well as postdoctoral research leading to the completion of a monograph
Eligibility: Applicants for a dissertation fellowship must be full-time graduate students who have completed all coursework required for the PhD and must have achieved ABD status by the time the proposed research stay in Berlin begins. Also eligible are United States of America and Canadian PhDs who have received their doctorates within the past 2 calendar years
Level of Study: Doctorate, Postdoctorate
Type: Fellowship
Value: €1,100 per month for dissertation fellows, €1,400 per month for postdoctoral fellows
Length of Study: 10–12 months
Frequency: Annual
Study Establishment: Freie Universität Berlin
Country of Study: Germany
Application Procedure: Applicants must submit a single application packet consisting of completed application forms, a proposal, three letters of reference, language evaluation(s) and graduate school transcripts. Proposals should be no longer than 2,500 words or 10 pages, followed by a one- or two-page bibliography or bibliographic essay
Closing Date: 1 December
Contributor: Halle Foundation and the National Endowment for the Humanities

Additional Information: Please check at www.fu-berlin.de/en/sites/bprogram/application/index.html for updated application deadline

For further information contact:

Berlin Program for Advanced German and European Studies, Freie Universität Berlin, Garystrasse 45, DEU-14195, Berlin, Germany

Tel:	(49) 30 838 56671
Fax:	(49) 30 838 56672
Email:	bprogram@zedat.fu-berlin.de

Getty Foundation

1200 Getty Center Drive, Suite 800, Los Angeles, CA 90049-1685, United States of America

Tel:	(1) 310 440 7320
Fax:	(1) 310 440 7703
Email:	researchgrants@getty.edu
Website:	www.getty.edu/grants
Contact:	Grants Administration

The J Paul Getty Trust is a privately operating foundation dedicated to the visual arts and the humanities. The Getty supports a wide range of projects that promote research in fields related to the history of art, the advancement of the understanding of art and the conservation of cultural heritage.

Postdoctoral Fellowships in Conservation Science

Subjects: Chemistry or physical sciences
Purpose: To provide recent PhDs in chemistry or the physical sciences with experience in the GCI's Museum Research Laboratory
Eligibility: Open to scientists of all nationalities who are interested in pursuing a career in conservation science and have received a PhD in chemistry/physical science and have excellent written and oral communication skills
Level of Study: Research
Type: Fellowship
Value: US$29,300 per year
Length of Study: 2 years
Application Procedure: Applicants must complete and submit an online application which includes completing an online information form, and uploading a Statement of Interest in Conservation Science, Doctoral Dissertation Abstract, Curriculum Vitae, Writing Sample, and Degree Confirmation Letter. Applicants are also required to submit two confidential letters of recommendation in support of the their application
Closing Date: November
Additional Information: The successful candidate will have a record of scientific accomplishment combined with a strong interest in the visual arts

For further information contact:

Attn: Postdoctoral Fellowship in Conservation Science, The Getty Foundation, 1200 Getty Center Drive, Suite 800, United States of America

Tel:	(1) 310 440 7374
Fax:	(1) 310 440 7703 (inquiries only)
Email:	researchgrants@getty.edu

Gilchrist Educational Trust (GET)

43 Fern Road, Storrington, Pulborough, RH20 4LW, West Sussex, United Kingdom

Tel:	(44) 1903 746 723
Email:	gilchrist.et@blueyonder.co.uk (individual grants); valconsidine@btinternet.com (organisation)
Website:	www.gilchristgrants.org.uk
Contact:	Mrs J V Considine, Secretary

Gilchrist Educational Trust awards grants to: individuals who face unexpected financial difficulties, which may prevent completion of a degree or higher education course; organizations if it seems likely that a project for which funds to sought will fill an educational gap of an academic nature or make more widely available for a particular aspect of academic education or learning; British expeditions proposing to carry out research of a scientific nature abroad.

Gilchrist Fieldwork Award

Subjects: All scientific subjects
Purpose: To fund a period of fieldwork by established scientists or academics
Eligibility: Open to teams wishing to undertake a field season of over 6 weeks in relation to one or more scientific

objectives. Teams should consist of not more than 10 members, most of whom should be British and holding established positions in research departments at universities or similar establishments. The proposed research must be original and challenging, achievable within the timetable and preferably of benefit to the host country or region

Level of Study: Research
Type: Grant
Value: United Kingdom £15,000
Length of Study: At least 6 weeks
Frequency: Every 2 years
Country of Study: Any country
No. of awards offered: 12
Application Procedure: Send proposal to Secretary
Closing Date: 21 February
Funding: Private
No. of awards given last year: 1
No. of applicants last year: 12
Additional Information: The award is competitive

For further information contact:

c/o RGS, 1 Kensington Gore, United Kingdom

Email: grants@rgs.org

Glasgow Caledonian University

Cowcaddens Road, Glasgow G4 0BA, Scotland, United Kingdom

Tel: (44) 1413 313 000
Fax: (44) 1413 313 269
Contact: Ms Irene Urquhart, MBA Admissions Officer

Scottish Power Masters Scholarships

Purpose: ScottishPower will provide scholarships for the academic year for postgraduate studies at universities in the United Kingdom
Eligibility: Students who are looking to study the following areas of knowledge: 1. Electrical/Mechanical/Civil Engineering. 2. Renewable/Sustainable Energy. 3. Onshore/Offshore Renewable Engineering. 4. Environmental Sciences /Climate Change. 5. Global Energy Management
Level of Study: Postgraduate
Type: Scholarship
Value: £1,200 per month
Frequency: Annual
Country of Study: Any country

Application Procedure: ScottishPower are looking for each scholar to: 1. Promote career opportunities available within the company. 2. Act as a STEM ambassador for the industry. 3. Introduce future scholarship applicants to the scheme
Closing Date: 29 March
Funding: Private
Additional Information: Kindly access the below link for processing the application. www.iberdrola.com/people-talent/international-scholarships-master-iberdrola/apply- scholarships-access

For further information contact:

Glasgow Caledonian University, Cowcaddens Road, Glasgow G4 0BA, Scotland, United Kingdom

Email: ukroenquiries@gcu.ac.uk

Goethe-Institut

Kundenmanagement, Goethestr. 20, DEU-80336, München, Germany

Tel: (49) 89 159 21200
Fax: (49) 89 159 21202
Email: deutsch@goethe.de
Contact: Goethe-Institut

The Goethe-Institut is a non-profit German cultural association operational worldwide with 159 institutes, promoting the study of the German language abroad and encouraging international cultural exchange and relations.

Goethe-Institut Postdoctoral Fellowship for International Students

Subjects: Fellowship is awarded for scholars whose research focuses on global perspectives on modern and contemporary art in the second half of the 20th century and the 21st century
Purpose: The aim of the fellowship is to support promising and exceptional scholar for one academic year and shall concentrate on the research for a comprehensive exhibition project on the global art historical developments of the Postcolonial era covering the period 1955–1980
Eligibility: International applicants are eligible to apply for the fellowship. Applicants must have a doctorate degree in art history, museum studies or related fields. Applicants must be fluent in English

Type: Postdoctoral fellowship

Value: An overall remuneration package of 30.000 Euro for the entire year. This includes any health care and tax payments. Accommodation is the responsibility of the successful candidate. Haus der Kunst will provide supplementary support to the scholar for accommodation in the amount of 300 Euro per month. Haus der Kunst will support the fellow in organizing administrational paperwork such as limited residency, work permit, etc. Fellow will be provided with work area and full access to the infrastructure of Haus der Kunst and facilities in Munich

Frequency: Annual

Study Establishment: Fellowship is awarded for scholars whose research focuses on global perspectives on modern and contemporary art in the second half of the 20th century and the 21stcentury

Country of Study: Any country

Application Procedure: Interested scholars are invited to send their application via email. The application should be in English and include a CurriculumVitae, bibliography, reference letters and a cover letter explaining the motivation for the application

Closing Date: 14 January

Additional Information: For more details please check the website scholarship-positions.com/goethe-institut-post doctoral-fellowship-international-students-haus-der-kunst-germany/2017/12/21/

For further information contact:

Email: kredler@hausderkunst.de

Google Sydney

Google headquarters, Google Inc., 1600 Amphitheatre Parkway, Mountain View, CA 94043, United States of America

Tel: (1) 650 253 0000
Fax: (1) 650 253 0001
Website: www.google.com

Google is a public and profitable company focused on search services. Google operates web sites at many international domains. Google is widely recognized as the "world's best search engine" because it is fast, accurate and easy to use. The company also serves corporate clients, including advertisers, content publishers and site managers with cost–effective advertising and a wide range of revenue generating search services. Google's breakthrough technology and continued innovation serve the company's mission of "organizing the world's information and making it universally accessible and useful".

Lionel Murphy Endowment Postgraduate Scholarship

Purpose: A number of Australian and overseas postgraduate scholarships are awarded annually by the Lionel Murphy Foundation Endowment. These scholarships are known as the Lionel Murphy Endowment Postgraduate Scholarship. The number of scholarships awarded each year, and the method of payment, is recommended by the Advisory Committee

Eligibility: This scholarship is applicable for the candidate those having the preference to study in any of these areas. 1. The law and the legal system in a social context and their practical application. 2. Science and/or the law as a means of attaining social justice and human rights and as vehicles for change. 3. International law as a developing force for peace and as a means of achieving the rule of law in all nations. 4. Science as a tool for social benefit, particularly in meeting the needs of those most disadvantaged within society. 5. Other disciplines, where the proposed nature and area of study are likely to promote the goals of social justice and benefit for the disadvantaged

Level of Study: Postgraduate

Type: Scholarship

Value: A$40,000

Length of Study: 1 year

Frequency: Annual

Country of Study: Australia

Application Procedure: Check the website online. lionelmurphy.anu.edu.au/postgraduate_scholarships.htm

Closing Date: 30 November

Funding: Private

For further information contact:

Lionel Murphy Foundation Endowment, c/- Secretariat Coordinator, ANU College of Law, Australian National University, Canberra, ACT 2601, Australia

Email: lionelmurphy.law@anu.edu.au

Government of the Punjab

The Punjab Educational Endowment Fund

Purpose: The Govt. of the Punjab has launched PhD Foreign Scholarship programme under which eligible male and female students, as per the eligibility criteria set for this scheme from time to time, will be awarded scholarships for PhD level Education at the top ranked universities of the world. The scholarship scheme focuses the meritorious students of Punjab while allocating a special quota for the students of other federating units of Pakistan as well

Eligibility: 1. Valid PhD admission offer from one of the Top 50 (Subject Wise) Universities of the World (QS ranking) in preferred subject areas. 2. Not less than 60% marks throughout the academic career. 3. Declared monthly family income (including self, spouse and parents) is equal to or less than PKR. 2,00,000/. 4. Maximum age of 35 years at the time of submission of application. 5. Not availed any foreign scholarship in the past. 6. Must take up the scholarship in the year for which it is offered and the scholarship shall not be deferred to the next year. 7. All Pakistani nationals, both males and females are eligible to apply

Level of Study: Postgraduate
Type: Award
Frequency: Annual
Country of Study: Any country
Closing Date: 22 April
Funding: International office

Greater Kansas City Community Foundation

1055 Broadway Blvd #130, Kansas City, MO 64105, United States of America

Website: www.growyourgiving.org

Ann Maly Davis Scholarship Fund

Purpose: The Ann Maly Davis Scholarship Fund is available for graduating seniors at Wahoo High School in Wahoo Nebraska. Applicants must have a GPA of 3.0 or higher, unmet financial need, and exrta-curricular activities that indicate a record of leadership

Eligibility: 1. Must attend Wahoo High School in Wahoo, Nebraska. 2. Must be a graduating high school senior. 3. Must have a grade point average of 3.0 or higher. 4. This award is for United States of America students

Level of Study: Graduate
Type: Scholarship
Value: US$500
Frequency: Annual
Country of Study: United States of America
Closing Date: 3 April
Funding: Foundation

For further information contact:

Tel: (1) 816 627 3436
Email: scholarships@growyourgiving.org

Cheryl Barnett McLaughlin Wildcat Education Scholarship Fund

Purpose: The CBM Wildcat Education Scholarship Fund is available for graduating seniors and previous graduates of the Shawnee, Kansas school district. Applicants must attend or plan to attend Kansas State University and major in education

Eligibility: 1. Must be a graduating high school senior or undergraduate student at the time of application. 2. Must be a high school senior or previous graduate in the Shawnee Mission School District. 3. Must be enrolled at or planning to enroll at Kansas State University. 4. Must be majoring in education. 5. This award is for United States of America students

Level of Study: Graduate
Type: Scholarship
Value: US$500
Frequency: Annual
Country of Study: United States of America
Application Procedure: Application instructions and additional information about the CBM Wildcat Education Scholarship Fund are available online at the Greater Kansas City Community Foundation (GKCCF) website. In addition to the completed online application form, applicants for this scholarship must submit the following: proof of financial need; transcripts or other records of academic performance that include a current or recent grade point average; and additional information about any leadership roles, community service, or volunteer efforts that may be pertinent to the award. Completed applications with all supporting documents must be received no later than the deadline date. Late and incomplete submissions will not be considered

Closing Date: 15 April
Funding: Foundation

For further information contact:

Email: scholarships@growyourgiving.org

Sam and Rosalee Scholarship Fund

Purpose: The purpose of the Fund shall be to provide scholarships to graduates of high schools in Bates County, Missouri, who plan to further their education at a four-year college or university and pursue a degree in either the educational field or medical field

Eligibility: The students eligible for assistance shall, 1. be graduating from a high school in Bates County, Missouri. 2. have at least a 3.0 cumulative high school GPA. 3. demonstrate financial need; and 4. be enrolling in a four-year college or university to pursue a degree in either the educational or medical fields

Level of Study: Graduate

Type: Scholarship

Frequency: Annual

Country of Study: Any country

Application Procedure: This award is managed and administered through the Greater Kansas City Community Foundation, a local area charity founded in 1978 with the mission of providing assistance and centralized resources for decentralized charitable causes and giving

Closing Date: 1 April

Funding: Private

Additional Information: For further information, www. growyourgiving.org/sites/default/files/scholarships/application.pdf

For further information contact:

Email: scholarships@growyourgiving.org

Starke-Blosser Memorial Scholarship Fund

Purpose: The Starke-Blosser Memorial Scholarship Fund is provided annually for graduating seniors at Higginsville High School, as well as undergraduate students who reside in Higginsville, Missouri

Eligibility: Applicants must demonstrate academic achievement, financial need, and participation in the community through service and other organizational involvement. Relatives of the Starke-Blosser family are also eligible to apply

Level of Study: Graduate

Type: Scholarship

Value: US$1,000 Funds may be used for tuition, books, and other educational fees

Frequency: Annual

Country of Study: Any country

Application Procedure: Students must submit the completed application form, as well as the following supporting documents: two letters of recommendation as described in the application; a short personal statement; and verification of enrollment in or acceptance to an accredited college or university. Any late or incomplete submissions will not be considered

Closing Date: 1 April

Funding: Private

For further information contact:

Tel: (1) 816 627 3436

Email: scholarships@growyourgiving.org

Greek Ministry of National Education and Religious Affairs

Greek Ministry of Education and Religious Affairs, Cultural and Sport, Directorate of International Relations in Education, Maroussi GRC 15180, Maroussi, Greece

Tel: (30) 2103442469, 2103443129

Fax: (30) 2103442469

Email: des-a@minedu.gov.gr, des-art@minedu.gov.gr

Website: www.minedu.gov.gr

Contact: Directorate General of European and International Affairs

The Ministry's department of scholarships grants exclusively scholarships to students and PhD holders from developing countries through the OECD's D.A.C.

Scholarships for a Summer Seminar in Greek Language and Culture

Subjects: Greek language

Purpose: To allow nationals from the Balkans, Eastern Europe, Asia and Africa to study Greek language

Eligibility: Applicants must be nationals of Albania, Armenia, Azerbaijan, Bosnia & Herzegovina, China, Egypt, Ethiopia, FYROM, Georgia, India, Indonesia, Iran, Iraq, Jordan, Kazakhstan, Korea, Lebanon, Moldove, Montenegro, Mongolia, Pakistan, Palestine, Russia, Serbia, Sudan, Syria, Thailand, Tunisia, Turkey, Ukraine, or Uzbekistan. Applicants should be foreign students/foreign professors of, Greek languages, or even foreign students/foreign professors of different fields who wish to improve their level of Greek language

Type: Scholarship

Value: The scholarships covers: accomodation, meals, tuition fees, small personal expenses, in case of an emergency medical care, visits to archaeological sites, museums, as well as instructive material

Frequency: Dependent on funds available

Country of Study: Greece

Closing Date: Check website

Funding: Government

For further information contact:

Email: foreigners@iky.gr

Scholarships Granted by the GR Government to Foreign Citizens

Subjects: All subjects
Purpose: To support candidates who wish to study or conduct research project in Greek Universities, or summer seminars of Greek language and culture, postgraduate studies
Eligibility: Applicants must be nationals of China, Belgium, Bulgary France, Germany, Serbia, Syria, Turkey. Applicants should have an excellent knowledge of Greek or French or English language. Applicant must be of foreign nationality of Estonia, Israel, Croatia, Cyprus, Luxembourg, Mexico, Norway, Netherlands, Hungary, Poland, Romania, Slovakia, Slovenia, Czech Republic, and Finland
Level of Study: Doctorate, Graduate, Postdoctorate, Postgraduate, Predoctorate, Research, MBA
Type: Scholarship
Value: €550 per month, €500 lump sum for establishment expenses, €150 for transport expenses, exemption from tuition fees (only in selected master's degree) plus all expenses for summer seminars except travel expenses
Length of Study: Varies
Frequency: Annual
Study Establishment: Greek public universities
Country of Study: Greece
No. of awards offered: 60
Application Procedure: Check with Ministry of Education or Ministry of Foreign Affairs in Individual country. Applicants must apply through their home countries. Find out about deadlines of their own countries but also refer to the website
Closing Date: 31 March
Funding: Government
Contributor: Greek Ministry of Education and Religious Affairs, Culture and Sport
No. of awards given last year: 40
No. of applicants last year: 60
Additional Information: Information about eligible countries, number of scholarships and the way to apply is renewed every year and candidates can find next year's decision by the end of December at www.minedu.gov.gr

For further information contact:

Directorate of Studies and Student's Welfare, Greece

Tel: (30) 2103443469, 2103443451
Email: foitmer.yp@ minedu.gov.gr
Contact: Evi Zigra, Director

Greek Scholarships

Atlantic Amateur Hockey Association Lou Manzione Scholarship

Purpose: The Atlantic Amateur Hockey Association is pleased to offer a scholarship program to students who plan to continue their education beyond the 12th grade. Scholarships are available, one to a New Jersey High School Senior and the second to a high school senior from Pennsylvania or Delaware
Eligibility: This scholarship is applicable to high school seniors who are registered with United States of America Hockey
Level of Study: Graduate
Type: Scholarship
Value: US$1,000
Frequency: Annual
Country of Study: United States of America
Closing Date: 1 February
Funding: Private

For further information contact:

Scholarship Committee, P.O. Box 213, Lafayette Hill, PA 19444, United States of America

Email: info@STPaccess.com

Cancer for College Carolinas Scholarship

Purpose: The Cancer for College Carolinas Scholarship is open to any cancer survivor who is enrolled in an accredited college or university in the United States
Eligibility: Applicant must be a resident of the United States and must either be from or attending school in the states of North or South Carolina
Level of Study: Graduate
Type: Scholarship
Value: US$5,000
Frequency: Annual
Country of Study: Any country
Closing Date: 31 January
Funding: Private

For further information contact:

28465 Old Town Front Street, Suite 315, Temecula, CA 92590, United States of America

Email: applications@cancerforcollege.org

Candice Sickle Cell Disease Scholarship

Purpose: Our goal is to help alleviate the financial pressures of college-bound students in the Tri-State Area (NY/NJ/CT)with sickle cell disease by providing three scholarships annually. These scholarships are awarded to assist scholarship recipients with their college education

Eligibility: Every scholarship winner is required to commit at least 5 hours minimum of their time towards one of the various Candice's Sickle Cell Fund activities during the year they receive their scholarship

Level of Study: Graduate

Type: Scholarship

Value: US$750-US$1,500

Frequency: Annual

Country of Study: Any country

Application Procedure: 1. Each applicant must submit a 250-word essay typewritten in double-spaced format to include how sickle cell disease has affected their life and education. 2. Each applicant should also include what their educational goals are and how they expect to achieve them, in addition, what person has been instrumental in their lives to help them persevere

Closing Date: 14 April

Funding: Private

For further information contact:

Candice Young-Deler, P.O. Box 672237, Bronx, NY 10467-0237, United States of America

Email: cscfinc@gmail.com

Dixie Youth Baseball Scholarship

Purpose: From the very beginning, the leaders of Dixie Youth Baseball knew they wanted to develop a college scholarship program that would help former players obtain a college education

Eligibility: In order to be eligible, the applicant must be a senior in high school and have at one time played in a Dixie Youth Baseball league. Be aware the NCAA rules may prohibit acceptance of this scholarship if a student will be participating in a collegiate athletic program

Level of Study: Graduate

Type: Scholarship

Frequency: Annual

Country of Study: Any country

Closing Date: 1 February

Funding: Private

For further information contact:

Scholarship Committee, 110 South Bolivar St., Suite 207, Marshall, TX 75670, United States of America

Tel: (1) 903 927 2255
Email: dyb@dixie.org

Eileen Kraus Scholarship

Purpose: Mrs. Kraus is a past Chairman of the Board and currently a Trustee Emerita. She also served on the Board of Directors of Kaman Corporation for more than 20 years. This scholarship honours her achievement

Eligibility: Eligible applicants must be 1. Female students currently residing in Connecticut. 2. Recent high school graduates or in the final year of secondary school. 3. Intending to enroll in first year of college or university. 4. Able to attend the Connecticut Women's Hall of Fame Induction Ceremony in Hartford, CT for recognition

Level of Study: Graduate

Type: Scholarship

Frequency: Annual

Country of Study: Any country

Closing Date: 15 February

Funding: Private

For further information contact:

Connecticut Women's Hall of Fame, 320 Fitch Street, B-3, New Haven, CT 06515, United States of America

Email: tinac@cwhf.org
Contact: Mrs Tina Carlson

Environmental Professionals' Organization of Connecticut Environmental Scholarship Fund

Purpose: The purpose of the Scholarship Fund is to assist Connecticut residents, or an immediate family member (spouse or child) of an EPOC Member in good standing, who are attending an accredited college or university

Eligibility: Kindly contact sjm@epoc.org for further information

Level of Study: Graduate

Type: Funding support

Frequency: Annual

Country of Study: Any country

Closing Date: 30 April

Funding: Private

For further information contact:

P.O. Box 176, Amston, CT 06231, United States of America

Email: sjm@epoc.org
Contact: Seth Molofsky

Islamic Scholarship Fund-Muslim Community Center Scholarship

Purpose: Islamic Scholarship fund supports Islamic organizations and mosques by planning and managing joint scholarships. ISF is honored to host the ISF-MCC Scholarship of the Muslim Community Center East Bay, MCC
Eligibility: Each Eligible Applicant Must Be: 1. An active member of the MCC. 2. Attending an accredited university in the United States of America. 3. Majoring in an ISF supported field of study. 4. Maintaining a minimum 3.0 Grade Point Average. 5. A Citizen or Permanent Resident of the United States of America. 6. An undergraduate (sophomore/junior/senior) or of graduate standing
Level of Study: Graduate
Type: Scholarship
Value: US$5,000
Frequency: Annual
Country of Study: Any country
Closing Date: 21 March
Funding: Private

For further information contact:

Islamic Scholarship Fund, P.O. Box 802, Alamo, CA 94507, United States of America

Tel: (1) 650 995 6782
Email: contact@islamicscholarshipfund.org

Oregon-Idaho Conference Ethnic Leadership Award

Purpose: The Oregon-Idaho Conference Ethnic Leadership Award is for one undergraduate or graduate, ethnic student who is a member of an Oregon-Idaho Conference church
Level of Study: Graduate, Undergraduate
Type: Award
Value: US$750
Frequency: Annual
Country of Study: Other

Application Procedure: Applicants are evaluated primarily on their leadership or potential leadership skills. Financial need is also considered. The scholarship may be used at any two- or four-year accredited institution of higher education
Closing Date: 1 March
Funding: Private

For further information contact:

Scholarship Committee, P.O. Box 340007, Nashville, TN 37203-0007, United States of America

Email: umscholar@gbhem.org

Teacher Education Assistance for College and Higher Education Grant

Subjects: Teacher Education Assistance for College and Higher Education (TEACH) Grant Program
Purpose: You'll be able to teach in public or private elementary and secondary schools, as long as you sign on to teach in low-income areas in high-need fields. As a federal grant, you'll need to fill out a Free Application for Federal Student Aid, or FAFSA, to determine whether you're eligible for the TEACH Grant
Eligibility: 1. demonstrate financial need (for most programs). 2. be a United States of America citizen or an eligible noncitizen have a valid Social Security number (with the exception of students from the Republic of the Marshall Islands, Federated States of Micronesia, or the Republic of Palau). 3. be registered with Selective Service, if you're a male (you must register between the ages of 18 and 25. 4. be enrolled or accepted for enrollment as a regular student in an eligible degree or certificate program. 5. be enrolled at least half-time to be eligible for Direct Loan Program funds
Level of Study: Graduate
Type: Programme grant
Value: US$4,000 per year
Frequency: Annual
Country of Study: Any country
Closing Date: October of every year
Funding: Private

For further information contact:

Tel: (1) 800 557 7394
Email: HEAL@ed.gov

Griffith University

Griffith University, Nathan Campus, 170 Kessels Road, Nathan, QLD 4111, Australia

Tel:	(61) 7 3735 3870
Fax:	(61) 7 3735 7957
Email:	scholarships@griffith.edu.au
Website:	www.gu.edu.au

In the pursuit of excellence in teaching, research and community service, Griffith University is committed to innovation, bringing disciplines together, internationalization, equity and social justice and lifelong learning, for the enrichment of Queensland, Australia and the international community.

Master of Business Administration Programme

Length of Study: 1–3 years
Application Procedure: Applicants must complete an application form supplying Australian $50 fee, official transcripts, and TOEFL score

For further information contact:

Tel:	(61) 7 3875 7111
Fax:	(61) 7 3875 3900
Email:	gsm_enquiry@gsm.gu.edu.au
Contact:	MBA Admissions Officer

PhD Scholarship in Water Resources Management in Remote Indigenous Communities

Subjects: Engineering, environmental planning and science
Purpose: To utilize smart meters and loggers to gauge the degree of water savings attributable to the execution of various water conservation strategies
Eligibility: Open only to the citizens of Australia or New Zealand or permanent residents who have achieved Honours 1 or equivalent, Honours 2a or equivalent, or Masters or equivalent
Level of Study: Graduate, Postgraduate
Type: Scholarship
Value: The scholarship has an annual tax-free stipend of $30,000–35,000 per year
Frequency: Annual

Study Establishment: Griffith University
Country of Study: Australia
Application Procedure: Applicants must apply directly to the scholarship provider. Check the website for further details
Closing Date: 23 October

For further information contact:

Tel:	(61) 7 3735 6596
Email:	M.Mitchell@griffith.edu.au
Contact:	Marianne Mitchell, Postgraduate Scholarships Coordinator

Gypsy Lore Society

5607 Greenleaf Road, Cheverly, MD 20785, United States of America

Tel:	(1) 301 341 1261
Fax:	(1) 301 341 1261
Email:	headquarters@gypsyloresociety.org
Website:	www.gypsyloresociety.org
Contact:	Ms Sheila Salo, Treasurer

The Gypsy Lore Society, an international association of persons interested in Gypsy Studies, was formed in the United Kingdom in 1888. The Gypsy Lore Society, North American Chapter, was founded in 1977 in the United States of America and since 1989, has continued as the Gypsy Lore Society. The Society's goals include the promotion of the study of the Gypsy peoples and analogous itincrant or nomadic groups, dissemination of information aimed at increasing understanding of Gypsy culture in its diverse forms and establishment of closer contacts among Gypsy scholars.

Marian Madison Gypsy Lore Society Young Scholar's Prize

Subjects: Any topic in Romani (Gypsy and Traveller) studies
Purpose: To recognize outstanding work by young scholars in Romani (Gypsy) studies
Eligibility: Graduate students beyond the 1st year of study and PhD holders no more than 3 years beyond the degree. An unpublished paper not under consideration for publication is eligible for this award as well as self-contained scholarly articles of publishable quality that treat a relevant topic in an interesting and insightful way

Level of Study: Doctorate, Graduate, Postdoctorate
Type: Cash prize
Value: US$500
Study Establishment: Any
Country of Study: Any country
Application Procedure: Submission file format is rich text file (RTF, PDF, MS word compatible). Files bigger than 5 MB should be presented on CD to the postal address below. A cover sheet should be included with the title of the paper, the author's name, affiliation, mailing, email address, telephone and fax number, date of entrance into an appropriate program or of awarding of the PhD, and United States of America social security number, if the author has one. The applicant's name should appear on the cover sheet only
Closing Date: 30 October
Funding: Corporation
Contributor: Gypsy Lore Society

For further information contact:

Email: szahova@yahoo.com
Contact: Sofiya Zahova

H

Harish-Chandra Research Institute

Chhatnag Road, Jhusi, Allahabad, Uttar Pradesh 211019, India

Tel: (91) 532 256 9509
Contact: The Harish-Chandra Research Institute

Postdoctoral Fellowships in Physics at Harish-Chandra Research Institute

Subjects: Fellowships are awarded in the field of Physics
Purpose: The aim of the fellowships is to support Indian students and provide opportunities to researchers working in Astrophysics, Condensed Matter Physics, High Energy Phenomenology, Quantum Information & Computing, and String Theory
Eligibility: Applicants from India are eligible to apply for the fellowship. Applicants must be researchers
Type: Postdoctoral fellowship
Value: HRI offers opportunities to researchers working in Astrophysics, Condensed matter physics, High energy phenomenology, Quantum information & computing, and, String theory
Study Establishment: Fellowships are awarded in the field of Physics
Country of Study: India
Application Procedure: See the website
Closing Date: Applications for the fellowships will be considered twice every year, with deadlines on the 15 August and on the 31 December
Additional Information: For more details please visit the website at scholarship-positions.com/postdoctoral-fellowships-physics-harish-chandra-research-institute-india/2017/12/26/

For further information contact:

Email: physvisit@hri.res.in

Harpo Foundation

Tel: (1) 757 735 4269
Website: http://www.harpofoundation.org/

The Harpo Foundation was established in 2006 to support emerging visual artists. The foundation seeks to stimulate creative inquiry and to encourage new modes of thinking about art. We view the definitions of art and artist to be open-ended and expansive. The Foundation's grant program awards 7–10 grants annually. Grants are made directly to artists to support their development and to non-profit organizations in support of new work by artists. The Foundation also supports two residency fellowship programs. The Native American Residency Fellowship program provides residency opportunities at the Vermont Studio Center to support the development of artists and the potential for inter-cultural dialog. The Emerging Artist Residency Fellowship program supports residency opportunities at the Santa Fe Art Institute for visual artists 25 years and older who need time and space to explore ideas and start new projects.

Harpo Foundation Grants for Visual Artists

Subjects: All subjects
Purpose: The Harpo Foundation seeks to stimulate creative inquiry and to encourage new modes of thinking about art. Applications are evaluated on the basis of the quality of the artist's work, the potential to expand aesthetic inquiry, and its relationship to the foundation's priority to provide support to visual artists who are under-recognized by the field
Level of Study: Professional development
Type: Grant
Value: up to A$10,000
Frequency: Varies
Country of Study: Any country

Application Procedure: Apply online
Closing Date: April
Funding: Foundation

Harry S Truman Library Institute

500 West United States Highway 24, Independence, MO 64050, United States of America

Tel:	(1) 816 268 8200
Fax:	(1) 816 268 8295
Email:	lisa.sullivan@nara.gov
Website:	www.trumanlibrary.org
Contact:	Lisa Sullivan, Grants Administrator

The Harry S Truman Library Institute is a non-profit partner of the Harry S Truman Library. The institute's purpose is to foster the Truman Library as a centre for research and as a provider of educational and public programmes.

Harry S Truman Library Institute Dissertation Year Fellowships

Subjects: The public career of Harry S Truman and the history of the Truman administration
Purpose: To encourage historical scholarship in the Truman era
Eligibility: Open to graduates who have completed their dissertation research and are ready to begin writing. Dissertations must be on some aspect of the life and career of Harry S Truman or of the public and policy issues that were prominent during the Truman years
Level of Study: Graduate, Postgraduate
Type: Fellowship
Value: US$16,000, payable in two instalments
Length of Study: 1 year
Frequency: Annual
Country of Study: United States of America
Application Procedure: Application forms are available from the website
Closing Date: 1 February
Funding: Private
Additional Information: Recipients will not be required to come to the Truman Library but will be expected to furnish the Library with a copy of their dissertation

For further information contact:

Tel:	(1) 816 268 8248
Fax:	(1) 816 268 8299
Email:	sullivan.hstli@gmail.com

Harry S Truman Library Institute Scholar's Award

Eligibility: An applicant's work should be based in part on extensive research at the Truman Library and be intended to result in the publication of a book-length manuscript. An individual may receive a Scholar's Award only once
Level of Study: Postdoctorate
Type: Award
Value: US$30,000
Application Procedure: Please check at trumanlibrar yinstitute.org/research-grants/scholars-award for complete information
Closing Date: 15 December of odd-numbered years
Funding: Private

For further information contact:

Truman Library Institute, 5151 Troost Avenue, Suite 300, Kansas City, MO 64110, United States of America

Tel:	(1) 816 400 1216
Fax:	(1) 816 400 1213
Email:	lisa.sullivan@trumanlibraryinstitute.org
Contact:	Ms Lisa A. Sullivan, Grants Administrator

Harry S. Truman Library Institute Research Grant

Subjects: Research grants are intended to enable graduate students, post-doctoral scholars and other researchers to come to the Harry S. Truman Library to use its collections. Awards are to offset expenses incurred for this purpose only. Selection is made by the Institute's Committee on Research, Scholarship and Education. Funding decisions, via an application process, are based on quality, originality, significance of the project and its relationship to the existing Truman historiography, and two letters of reference. Research grants require travel to the Truman Library for study of its archival collections. One-time payments are dispersed directly and payable to the awardee upon completion of the research trip
Purpose: As part of our mission, Truman Library Institute grants are given for the purpose of supporting scholarship based on some aspect of the life and career of Harry S. Truman or of the public and foreign policy issues which were prominent during the Truman administration
Eligibility: Graduate students and post-doctoral scholars are particularly encouraged to apply, but applications from others engaged in advanced research will also be considered. Preference will be given to Truman-related projects that have application to enduring public policy

and foreign policy issues and that have a high probability of being published or publicly disseminated in some other way. The potential contribution of a project to an applicant's development as a scholar will also be considered. The spring round of Research Grants includes one Hulston Scholarship travel grant of up to US$2,500, to be awarded to a researcher who wishes to visit multiple research facilities — including the Truman Library — for their topic. Applicants should indicate their interest in the Harry S. Truman Library Institute Research Grant when submitting their Research Grant applications and include a detailed project budget outlining additional repositories to be consulted and how materials at those repositories fit into the larger project

Level of Study: Research
Type: Research grant
Value: Up to US$2,500
Length of Study: 1-3 weeks
Frequency: Twice a year
Country of Study: Unrestricted
No. of awards offered: 25
Application Procedure: Competitive proposals will evidence a clear understanding of the existing research in the field and how the proposed work adds significantly to that body of literature. Applicants are expected to demonstrate both an analytical and descriptive grasp of the project and its centrality to the Truman era. Application packages must include the following: completed Research Grant application; curriculum vitae (3 pages, maximum); project description and justification (5 pages, maximum); a list of specific files the candidate expects to access at the Harry S. Truman Library and Museum; and two letters of reference from persons familiar with the applicant's scholarly work, including one from the project advisor, if candidate is a graduate or postdoctoral student. Letters must be received by the deadline and mailed or emailed directly to the Grants Administrator by the referring individual
Closing Date: 1 April and 1 October
Funding: Foundation
No. of awards given last year: 21
No. of applicants last year: 25
Additional Information: Please visit trumanlibraryinstitute.org/research-grants/research-grants for more information.

For further information contact:

5151 Troost Ave, Suite 300, Kansas City, MO 64110, United States of America

Email: lisa.sullivan@trumanlibraryinstitute.org
Contact: Ms Lisa Sullivan, Grants Administrator

Harvard Travellers Club

PO Box 190, Canton, MA 02021, United States of America

Tel: (1) 781 821 0400
Fax: (1) 781 828 4254
Email: gpbdtes@shieldpdckdging.com
Website: www.travellersfund.org
Contact: George Bates

Harvard Travellers Club Permanent Fund

Purpose: To support research involving travel from which results can be obtained of permanent scientific and educational value
Eligibility: Must attend a university or a four-year college
Level of Study: Doctorate, Graduate, Postdoctorate, Postgraduate, Predoctorate, Research, Unrestricted
Type: Grant
Value: Up to US$4,000
Frequency: Annual
Country of Study: Worldwide
No. of awards offered: 10
Application Procedure: Please check website for all details
Closing Date: Check the website
Funding: Trusts
Contributor: Club membership contributions (no major contributor)
No. of awards given last year: 2
No. of applicants last year: 10

For further information contact:

Email: Jackdeary@harvardtravellersclub.org
Contact: Mr Jack Deary, Trustee

Health Canada

Applied Research & Analysis Directorate, Analysis & Connectivity Branch, 15th Floor, Jeanne Mance Building, Tunney's Pasture, Ottawa, ON K1A 1B4, Canada

Tel: (1) 613 954 8549
Fax: (1) 613 954 7363
Email: nhrdpinfo@isdicp3.hwc.ca
Website: www.hc-sc.gc.ca
Contact: Information & Resource Officer

The National Health Research and Development Programme (NHRDP) funds research with scientific merit to support the Federal Department of Health's mission and national health priorities, and researchers whose work will contribute to policy development and strategic planning. In general, the NHRDP funds research that relates to issues of concern to the federal government and to those that may be of concern to provincial and territorial health ministries pertaining to the health system and the promotion of population health.

MSc Fellowships and PhD Fellowships

Subjects: Disciplines closely associated with population health inquiry, such as health economics, medical sociology, epidemiology and biostatistics
Purpose: To provide support to highly qualified students who wish to undertake full-time research training leading to an MSc degree (or equivalent) or a PhD degree (or equivalent)
Eligibility: Open to Canadian citizens or landed immigrants of high academic standing who hold an honours Bachelor's degree or a professional degree in a health field and are already engaged in a Master's or PhD program
Level of Study: Postgraduate
Type: A variable number of fellowships
Value: C$19,800 per year
Frequency: Annual
Study Establishment: at universities or affiliated institutions
Country of Study: Canada
Closing Date: 1 March
Additional Information: Prior to application, candidates should obtain a copy of the Training Awards Guide.

For further information contact:

Extramural Research Programs Directorate, Health Programs & Services Branch, Health Canada, Ottawa, ON K1A 0S5, Canada

Tel: (1) 613 954 8549
Fax: (1) 613 954 7363
Contact: Information & Resource Officer

Health Research Board (HRB)

Research & Development for Health, 73 Lower Baggot Street, Dublin 2, Ireland

Tel: (353) 1 234 5000
Fax: (353) 1 661 2335
Email: hrb@hrb.ie

Website: www.hrb.ie
Contact: The Research Grants Manager

The Health Research Board (HRB) comprises 16 members appointed by the Minister of Health, with eight of the members being nominated on the co-joint nomination of the universities and colleges. The main functions of the HRB are to promote or commission health research, to promote and conduct epidemiological research as may be appropriate at national level, to promote or commission health services research, to liaise and co-operate with other research bodies in Ireland and overseas in the promotion of relevant research and to undertake such other cognate functions as the Minister may from time to time determine.

Primary Care Training and Enhancement - Physician Assistant Program

Purpose: The purpose of the PCTE- PA Program is to increase the number of primary care physician assistants (PA), particularly in rural and underserved settings, and improve primary care training in order to strengthen access to and delivery of primary care services nationally
Eligibility: Eligible applicants must be academically affiliated PA training programs, accredited by the Accreditation Review Commission on Education for the Physician Assistant (ARC-PA). Domestic faith-based and community-based organizations, tribes and tribal organizations may apply for these funds, if otherwise eligible
Level of Study: Graduate
Type: Training award
Value: US$2,000,000
Frequency: Annual
Country of Study: Any country
Application Procedure: Links to the full announcement and online application process are available through grants.gov. check the website appropriately
Closing Date: 14 January
Funding: Private
Additional Information: Preference will be given to applicants that: 1. Demonstrate a high rate for placing graduates in practice settings having the principal focus of serving residents of Medically Underserved Communities. 2. Demonstrate a significant increase in the rate of placing graduates in Medically Underserved Community settings over the preceding 2 years.

For further information contact:

Tel: (1) 301 443 7271
Email: SCicale@hrsa.gov

Research Leaders Awards

Eligibility: All applications must involve a partnership with at least one health-related partner organization involved in the delivery of health and social care and/or health and social care policy. Applications should be aligned with the strategic plans of the nominating organizations, and should reflect national priorities and strategies in health and social care
Level of Study: Doctorate, Postdoctorate
Type: Award
Value: Each Research Leader Award consists of a contribution to salary support for the nominee up to the grade of Associate Professor, an attractive discretionary research support package of up to €600,000 over the period of the award, and a contribution to overhead expenses
Length of Study: A maximum of 5 years
Frequency: Annual
Country of Study: Ireland
Application Procedure: All applications must be made online using the HRB GEMS. (A link to GEMS is below.) To access the application form the nominating Higher Education Institution must provide the HRB with the contact details of their nominated Principal Investigator. The HRB will then invite the nominated candidate to initiate the application form
Closing Date: 31 March
Funding: Government
Additional Information: Please check at www.hrb.ie/research-strategy-funding/grants-and-fellowships/hrb-grants-and-fellowships/grant/133 for more information.

For further information contact:

Email: ferrism@queensu.ca

Hearst Corporation

801 Texas Avenue, Houston, TX 77002, United States of America

Email: kenn.altine@chron.com
Website: www.hearstfellowships.com

Hearst Corporation is one of the largest diversified communications companies.

Hearst Fellowships

Subjects: Journalism
Purpose: To help develop excellent reporters, editors, photographers, designers and graphic artists
Eligibility: Open to candidates who are graduates and have experience or background in journalism or related fields
Level of Study: Professional development
Type: Fellowships
Value: Varies
Length of Study: 2 years
Frequency: Annual
Country of Study: Any country
Application Procedure: The applicants must download the application form from the website. The completed application form along with other enclosures is to be sent to Hearst Fellowships
Closing Date: 1 December

For further information contact:

Email: fellowships@hearstnp.com

Heart and Stroke Foundation

Suite 1402, 222 Queen Street, Ottawa, ON K1P 5V9, Canada

Tel: (1) 613 569 4361
Fax: (1) 613 569 3278
Email: research@hsf.ca
Website: www.heartandstroke.ca

The Heart and Stroke Foundation is involved in eliminating heart disease and stroke and reducing their impact through the advancement of research and its application, and advocacy for the promotion of healthy living. It is a federation of 10 provincial foundations, led and supported by a force of more than 140,000 volunteers.

Canada Doctoral Research Award

Subjects: Cardiology
Purpose: To award highly qualified graduate students enrolled in a PhD program, undertaking full-time research training in the cardiovascular or cerebrovascular fields
Eligibility: Open to students enrolled in a PhD program and must be a full-time medical student
Level of Study: Doctorate, Research
Type: Research
Value: $21,000
Country of Study: Canada
Application Procedure: Applicants must send the application form along with the transcript, essay references and a self-addressed stamped envelope
Closing Date: 1 November

For further information contact:

Research Department, Room 9A-27, Parklawn Building, 5600 Fishers Lane, Rockville, MD 20857, United States of America

Tel: (1) 613 569 4361 ext. 327
Fax: (1) 613 569 3278
Email: lhodgson@hsf.ca
Contact: Lise Hodgson, Administrative Assistant

Career Investigator Award

Subjects: Cardiology
Purpose: To support established independent researchers who wish to make research their full-time career (Ontario applicants only)
Eligibility: Awards for individuals with an MD, PhD or equivalent degree working in the field of cardiovascular and/or cerebrovascular disease who wish to make their research a full-time career. Applicants must provide proof of national recognition
Level of Study: Postgraduate
Type: Scholarship
Value: Stipend C$81,500 per year, $1,500 per year for travel, and minimum C$48,282 for scientific purpose
Application Procedure: Applicants must send the application form along with the transcript, essay references and a self-addressed stamped envelope and must provide proof of national recognition
Closing Date: 1 September
Contributor: Heart and Stroke Foundations of Ontario and British Columbia and the Yukon
Additional Information: For more details see website or contact the foundation.

Dr Andres Petrasovits Fellowship in Cardiovascular Health Policy Research

Subjects: Cardiology
Eligibility: Please visit the website www.hsf.ca/research/application/index.html
Level of Study: Postgraduate
Type: Fellowship
Value: C$70,000
Length of Study: 3 years
Application Procedure: Please contact the foundation for application form
Closing Date: Check with website

Grants-in-Aid of Research and Development

Subjects: Cardiology
Purpose: To support researchers in projects of experimental nature in cardiovascular or cerebrovascular development
Eligibility: Open for full-time medical student

Level of Study: Postgraduate
Type: Grant
Value: Approx. C$33,000,000
Frequency: Every 3 years
Application Procedure: Applicants must send the application form along with the transcript, essay references and a self-addressed stamped envelope
Closing Date: 27 August
Additional Information: Please check website for more details.

Heart and Stroke Foundation of Canada Doctoral Research Award

Subjects: Cardiology
Purpose: To support individuals enroled in a PhD program and undertaking full-time research training in the stroke field
Eligibility: Applicants must be Canadians studying abroad or in Canada or for foreign visitors to Canada. The fellowship is open to citizens of United States
Level of Study: Postgraduate
Type: Fellowship
Value: Varies
Country of Study: Canada
Application Procedure: Applicants must send the application form along with the transcript, essay references and a self-addressed stamped envelope
Closing Date: 1 November

For further information contact:

Heart and Stroke Foundation of Canada, 1037 Topsail Rd, Mount Pearl, NL A1N 5E9, Canada

Tel: (1) 613 569 4361 ext. 268
Fax: (1) 613 569 3278
Email: anguyen@hsf.ca
Contact: Ann Nguyen, Information/Project Coordinator

Heart and Stroke Foundation of Canada New Investigator Research Scholarships

Subjects: Cardiology
Eligibility: Open to candidates who possess a MD, PhD, or equivalent degree and working in the field of cardiovascular and/or cerebrovascular disease
Level of Study: Postgraduate
Type: Scholarship
Value: Maximum C$30,000
Application Procedure: Applicants must send the application form along with the transcript, essay references and a self-addressed stamped envelope
Closing Date: 28 August

Heart and Stroke Foundation of Canada Nursing Research Fellowships

Subjects: Cardiology
Eligibility: Applicants must possess a Nursing degree. For master's degree candidates, the programmes must include a thesis or project requirement
Level of Study: Postgraduate
Type: Fellowship
Value: Minimum C$18,570
Country of Study: Canada
Application Procedure: Applicants must send the application form along with the transcript, essay references and a self-addressed stamped envelope
Closing Date: 14 March
Additional Information: Please check website for more details.

For further information contact:

Research Department, 222 Queen Street, Suite 1402, Ottawa, ON K1P 5V9, Canada

Tel:	(1) 613 569 4361 ext. 327
Fax:	(1) 613 569 3278
Email:	lhodgson@hsf.ca
Contact:	Lise Hodgson, Administrative Assistant

Heart and Stroke Foundation of Canada Research Fellowships

Subjects: Cardiology
Eligibility: Applicants must possess a full-time degree for study towards an MSc or PhD
Level of Study: Postgraduate
Type: Fellowship
Value: C$25,998 (minimum) and C$33,426 (maximum)
Country of Study: Canada
Application Procedure: Applicants must send the application form along with the transcript, essay references and a self-addressed stamped envelope
Closing Date: 1 November

Heart Research United Kingdom

Suite 12D, Joseph's Well, LS3 1AB, Leeds, United Kingdom

Tel:	(44) 11 3234 7474
Fax:	(44) 11 3297 6208
Email:	mail@heartresearch.org.uk
Website:	www.heartresearch.org.uk
Contact:	Helen Wilson, Senior Research Officer

Heart Research United Kingdom funds pioneering medical research into the prevention, treatment and cure of heart disease. Heart Research United Kingdom is a visionary charity leading the way in funding ground-breaking, innovative medical research projects at the cutting edge of science into the prevention, treatment and cure of heart disease. There is a strong emphasis on clinical and surgical projects and young researchers. Heart Research United Kingdom encourages and supports original health lifestyle initiatives exploring novel ways of preventing heart disease in all sectors of the community.

Heart Research United Kingdom Translational Research Project Grants

Subjects: Translational research projects that convert fundamental research into clinical benefits
Purpose: To support ground-breaking, innovative medical research into prevention, treatment and cure of heart disease and related conditions
Eligibility: Graduates or those holding a suitable professional qualification. Research must be carried out in the United Kingdom at a university, hospital or other recognized research institution
Level of Study: Research, Unrestricted
Type: Project grant
Value: Up to £150,000
Length of Study: Up to 3 years
Frequency: Annual
Study Establishment: Centres of health and educational establishments
Country of Study: United Kingdom
No. of awards offered: 45
Application Procedure: Information and application forms available at heartresearch.org.uk/grants/translational-research-project-trp-grants
Closing Date: 1 June
Funding: Private, Corporation, Foundation, Trusts, Individuals
Contributor: Voluntary funding from supporters and grant-making trusts
No. of awards given last year: 6
No. of applicants last year: 45
Additional Information: Grants are for research which efficiently transfers innovative discoveries into practical tools to prevent, diagnose and treat cardiovascular disease.

For further information contact:

Tel:	(44) 11 3234 7474
Email:	grants@heartresearch.org.uk

Hellenic Pasteur Institute

Vas Sofias Avenue 127, GRC-11521 Athens Greece

Tel:	(30) 1 647 8800
Fax:	(30) 1 642 3498
Website:	www.pasteur.gr
Contact:	Dr S Tzartos

W.D.E. Coulson & Toni M. Cross Aegean Exchange Program

Purpose: The purpose of these fellowships is to provide an opportunity for Greek scholars to meet with their Turkish colleagues, and to pursue research interests in the museum, archive, and library collections and at the sites and monuments of Turkey

Eligibility: The library at ARIT-Istanbul includes approximately 14,000 volumes and covers the Byzantine, Ottoman, and modern Turkish periods. Archives, libraries, sites, and museums in Turkey provide resources for research into many fields of study and geographical areas

Level of Study: Postdoctorate

Type: Fellowship

Length of Study: From two weeks to two months

Frequency: Annual

Country of Study: Any country

Application Procedure: 1. Stipend of US$250 is required. 2. Submit "Associate Membership with Fellowship" application online. 3. The application should include a curriculum vitae, statement of the project to be pursued during the period of grant (up to three pages, single-spaced in length), two letters of reference from scholars in the field commenting on the value and feasibility of the project

Funding: Private

Additional Information: ascsa.submittable.com/submit/115754/elizabeth-a-whitehead-distinguished-scholars-application-form

Help Musicians United Kingdom

7-11 Britannia Street, WC1X 9JS, London, United Kingdom

Tel:	(44) 20 7239 9100
Fax:	(44) 20 7713 8942
Email:	creative@helpmusicians.org.uk
Website:	www.helpmusicians.org.uk
Contact:	Ms Claire Gevaux, Director of Giring

Help Musicians United Kingdom is a unique charity which provides essential help to musicians of all ages and genres. We support music professionals throughout their working lives when a crisis such as an accident or illness can have a devastating impact, and in later life, with the challenges that growing older can bring. We support talented, financially needy young musicians to enable them to fully develop their creativity and musical potential, ensuring they enter the profession with the best prospects of success. We are also working in partnership with a number of organizations across the United Kingdom who provide outstanding opportunities for musicians. We rely on donations and the generosity of music lovers and musicians to enable our vital wok to continue.

Career Development Bursaries

Subjects: These awards are open to emerging artists aged 21—35 to fund an important development opportunity, project or programme of activity that will have a lasting impact on their professional career

Purpose: To help musicians looking for opportunities that will benefit their professional development

Eligibility: Applicants must be British or Irish or have lived in the United Kingdom for at least 3 consecutive years

Type: Award

Value: £500–2,000

Country of Study: Any country

No. of awards offered: 108

Application Procedure: A written description of the project must be provided with a budget, a reference and a recording demonstrating composition and/or performance

Closing Date: 30 February

No. of awards given last year: 18

No. of applicants last year: 108

Additional Information: Please check website www.helpmusicians.org.uk/eea

For further information contact:

Email:	info@handsupfortrad.co.uk

Postgraduate Awards

Subjects: Our postgraduate awards are only open to students who wish to study performance at the following conservatoires or performance institutions: 1. Arts Educational Schools. 2. Guildford School of Acting. 3. Guildhall School of Music and Drama. 4. Leeds College of Music. 5. London School of Musical Theatre. 6. Mountview Academy. 7. National Opera Studio. 8. Royal Academy of

Music. 9. Royal Birmingham Conservatoire. 10. Royal Central School of Speech and Drama. 11. Royal College of Music. 12. Royal Conservatoire of Scotland. 13. Royal Northern College of Music. 14. Royal Welsh College of Music and Drama. 15. Trinity Laban Conservatoire of Music and Dance. 16. Urdang Academy. 17. Wales International Academy of Voice. 18. Musical Theatre only. 19. Opera courses only

Purpose: Help Musicians United Kingdom's postgraduate awards offer support to students who wish to complete their studies at the leading UK conservatoires and performing arts colleges. The charity has been making awards to postgraduate music students of between £1,000 and £5,000 since the 1970s. Previous winners of these awards include trumpeter Alison Balsom OBE, percussionist Dame Evelyn Glennie, violinist Clio Gould, cellist Guy Johnston, violinist Tasmin Little OBE and guitarist Miloš Karadaglic. The Postgraduate Awards were previously run on a nomination basis where Heads of Departments at select conservatoires and performing colleges put forward students who qualified for the grant. However, HMUK is now reviewing how accessible and inclusive the Programme is to ensure that any potential barriers there may be in applying for funding are removed. The new open and direct application process also aims to alleviate some of the administrative burden on the Heads of Department and empower the students to take control of their futures

Level of Study: Postgraduate

Type: Award

Value: Up to £5,000

Length of Study: Annual Awards

Frequency: Annual

Country of Study: United Kingdom

No. of awards offered: 200

Application Procedure: Must have lived in United Kingdom for 3 consecutive years by Postgraduate start date. Applications made via online application form

Closing Date: February of each year

Funding: Private

Contributor: Help Musicians United Kingdom

No. of awards given last year: 125

No. of applicants last year: 200

Additional Information: Applications for musical theatre, opera, répétiteurs and popular music students open April of each year. (i.e. Mmus, MA, PGDip, Artist Diploma) Have lived in the United Kingdom for at least 3 consecutive years at the start of the academic year in which they will be supported by the award Be in financial need Demonstrate that they have the musical potential and ambition to create a successful and sustainable career within the music industry HMUK strongly encourages applications from students from underrepresented backgrounds, including those from BAME (Black, Asian and Minority Ethnic) backgrounds, D/deaf and disabled people;

and those from lower socio-economic groups. Through our Postgraduate Awards, we are unable to fund: Non-music performance degrees such as composition, music technology, music education, music therapy, arts administration and music business Undergraduate courses PhDs, MPhil, DMus, Doctorates Study from the previous academic year

For further information contact:

Tel: (44) 20 7239 9119

Email: creative@helpmusicians.org.uk

Sybil Tutton Awards

Subjects: Help Musicians United Kingdom offers Sybil Tutton Awards to outstandingly talented singers on full-time postgraduate opera courses to help with study costs. A special Richard Van Allen Award may be offered to a suitably outstanding male singer

Purpose: To assist students on advanced postgraduate opera courses

Eligibility: Nominees must be British or Irish or have lived in the United Kingdom for at least five consecutive years at the closing date

Type: Award

Value: £1,000–5,000

Frequency: Annual

Country of Study: Any country

Application Procedure: Application is by nomination only from head of voice at the United Kingdom conservatoires and the National Opera Studio

Closing Date: May

For further information contact:

Email: awards@helpmusicians.org.uk

Henry Moore Institute

The Headrow, LS1 3AH, Leeds, United Kingdom

Tel: (44) 113 246 7467

Email: kirstie@henry-moore.org

Website: www.henry-moore.org

Contact: Kirstie Gregory, Research Programme Assistant

The Henry Moore Institute is a world-recognized centre for the study of sculpture in the heart of needs an award-winning exhibitions venue, research centre, library and sculpture archive. The institute hosts exhibitions, conferences and lectures, as well as developing research to expand the understanding and scholarship of historical and contemporary sculpture.

Henry Moore Institute Research Fellowships

Subjects: Sculpture, both historical and contemporary
Purpose: To enable scholars to use the Institute's facilities, which include the sculpture collection, library, archive and slide library, to assist them in researching their particular field
Eligibility: There are no restrictions
Level of Study: Doctorate, Postdoctorate, Postgraduate, Research
Type: Fellowship
Value: Accommodation, travel and daily living expenses
Length of Study: 1 month
Frequency: Annual
Study Establishment: The Henry Moore Institute
Country of Study: United Kingdom
No. of awards offered: 80
Application Procedure: Applicants must send a letter of application, a proposal (maximum 1,000 words) and a curriculum vitae. Visit the website
Closing Date: 12 January
Funding: Foundation
Contributor: The Henry Moore Foundation
No. of awards given last year: 4
No. of applicants last year: 80

For further information contact:

Email: kirstie@henry-moore.org
Contact: Kirstie Gregory

Henry Moore Institute Senior Fellowships

Subjects: Any aspect of sculpture. Fellows are asked to make a small contribution to the research programme in Leeds in the form of a talk or a seminar
Purpose: Senior fellowships are intended to give established scholars (working on any aspect of sculpture) time and space to develop a research project free from their usual work commitments
Level of Study: Doctorate, Postdoctorate
Type: Fellowship
Value: Fellowships provide accommodation, travel expenses, and a per diem
Length of Study: 3–6 weeks
Frequency: Annual
Study Establishment: Henry Moore Institute
Country of Study: United Kingdom

No. of awards offered: 15
Application Procedure: Full details are available from the website www.henry-moore.ac.uk. Applicants can also contact the institute at its address for details. An applicant must send a curriculum vitae and a proposal along with his or her letter of application
Closing Date: 12 January
Funding: Foundation
Contributor: Henry Moore Foundation
No. of awards given last year: 1
No. of applicants last year: 15
Additional Information: Research fellowships are also available. The institute offers the possibility of presenting finished research in published form as a seminar or as a small exhibition

For further information contact:

Tel: (44) 113 246 7467
Email: kirstie@henry-moore.org
Contact: Kirstie Gregory, Research Programme Assistant

Herb Society of America, Inc.

9019 Kirtland Chardon Road, Kirtland, OH 44094, United States of America

Tel: (1) 440 256 0514
Fax: (1) 440 256 0541
Email: herbs@herbsociety.org
Website: www.herbsociety.org
Contact: Ms Michelle Milks, Office Administrator

The aim of the Herb Society of America Inc. is to promote the knowledge, use and delight of herbs through educational programmes, research and sharing the experience of its members with the community.

Herb Society of America Research Grant

Subjects: Herbal projects
Purpose: To further the knowledge and use of herbs and to contribute the results of study and research to the records of horticulture, science, literature, history, art or economics
Eligibility: Open to persons with a proposed programme of scientific, academic or artistic investigation of herbal plants
Level of Study: Unrestricted

Value: Up to US$5,000
Length of Study: Up to 1 year
Frequency: Annual
Country of Study: Any country
Application Procedure: Applicants must submit an application clearly defining all their research in 500 words or less and a proposed budget with specific budget items listed. Requests for funds will not be considered unless accompanied by five copies of the application form and proposal. The application must be submitted in electronic form via email to herbs@herbsociety.org
Closing Date: 31 January
Contributor: Members
Additional Information: Finalists will be interviewed. In order to complete the application, use the below link. herbsocietyorg. presencehost.net/support/grants-scholarships/application-for-the-hsa-research-grant.html

For further information contact:

Email: herbs@herbsociety.org

Heriot-Watt University

Postgraduate Admissions Office, EH14 4AS, Edinburgh, United Kingdom

Tel: (44) 131 449 5111
Email: edu.liaison@hw.ac.uk
Website: www.hw.ac.uk
Contact: Fiona Watt, Wider Access Assistant

Heriot-Watt University, one of the oldest higher education institutions in the United Kingdom, is Scotland's most international university. Our six academic schools and two postgraduate institutes offer research opportunities and postgraduate taught programmes in science and engineering, business, languages and design. We disburse over £6M in fee and stipend scholarships annually.

Mexican Scholarships

Subjects: Science, engineering and technology
Purpose: Financial assistance for Mexican students in science, engineering and technology
Eligibility: Mexican citizens
Level of Study: Postgraduate
Type: Scholarship
Value: Tuition fees and living costs

Frequency: Annual
Study Establishment: Heriot-Watt University
Country of Study: Scotland
Application Procedure: Contact Bob Tuttle
Funding: Government
Contributor: Heriot-Watt and CONACYT (Mexican National Council for Science and Technology)

For further information contact:

Tel: (44) 131 451 3746
Email: b.tuttle@hw.ac.uk

Music Scholarships

Subjects: All subjects
Purpose: To support musicians in obtaining a postgraduate qualification whilst developing their musical skills
Eligibility: All instrumentalists and vocalists who have been accepted for a course. The following criteria are taken into consideration: musical ability and potential, proof of exam results and membership of orchestras or choirs; a reference from your last vocal or instrumental teacher; in the case of the Archer Music Scholarships, a personal statement is also required; auditions will be held during Semester 1
Level of Study: Postgraduate, Research
Type: Scholarship
Value: Free music tuition up to value of £400 per year
Length of Study: 1 year
Frequency: Annual
Study Establishment: Heriot-Watt University
Country of Study: Scotland
Application Procedure: For an application form or more information please contact Steve King MBE, Director of Music
Additional Information: There will be a music scholar's concert in HWU in March each year at which all music scholars are all expected to participate.

For further information contact:

Tel: (44) 131 451 3705
Email: s.king@hw.ac.uk
Contact: Steve King MBE, Director of Music

Overseas Research Students Awards Scheme (ORSAS)

Purpose: Assist international postgraduate research students with payment of tuition fees

Eligibility: Non-European Union research applicants
Level of Study: Research
Type: Scholarship
Length of Study: 3 years
Frequency: Annual
Study Establishment: Heriot-Watt University
Country of Study: Scotland
Application Procedure: Apply to School of Study
Closing Date: 30 November
Contributor: Heriot-Watt University
Additional Information: Successful applicants usually receive James Watt Scholarships for the remainder of their fees plus a maintenance contribution.

For further information contact:

Email: pgadmissions@glasgow.ac.uk

Higher & Education South Africa

Africa: Mwalimu Julius Nyerere African Union Scholarship

Purpose: Mwalimu Julius Nyerere African Union Scholarship is intended to enable young Africans to study at reputable African universities with a binding agreement that scholarship beneficiaries will work in any African country for at least the same duration of the scholarship period after graduation. The scholarship aims to provide an opportunity to enhance knowledge, professional skills and capacity of refugees and displaced people, in order to streamline their integration to contribute towards sustainable development in Africa
Eligibility: 1. Applicants must be a citizen of an African Union Member State. 2. Must be a formally registered refugee/displaced person with a UNHCR registration number or be able to demonstrate confirmed refugee status in an African Union Member State. 3. Must be under the age of thirty five (35) years. 4. Must be a holder of a Bachelor's degree in the relevant field, at least at the level of Upper Second class Honours. The degree must be from a recognised university. 5. Must have demonstrated outstanding academic achievement as evidenced by academic transcripts, and academic awards if any. 6. Have proof of admission to undertake a full time Master's programme in a recognized university in an African Union Member State. 7. Be willing to commit to work in an African Union Member State on completion of studies for at least three (3) years
Level of Study: Postgraduate
Type: Scholarship

Value: Stipend to the value of US$500 monthly to cover accommodation, meals, utilities, local transport and medication, Travel allowance: once-off US$250, US$350 to assist with shipping and other terminal expenses, Computer allowance: US$1,000
Frequency: Annual
Country of Study: South Africa
Application Procedure: Apply online: www.edu-au.org/scholarshipg
Closing Date: 30 April
Funding: Foundation

For further information contact:

Department of Human Resources, Science and Technology, African Union Commission, P O Box 3243, Addis Ababa, Ethiopia, Eastern Africa

Tel: (251) 11 551 77 00
Fax: (251) 11 551 78 44
Email: internationalscholarships@dhet.gov.za

Africa: Next Einstein Forum (NEF) Fellows Programme

Purpose: The Next Einstein Forum (NEF) is an initiative of the African Institute for Mathematical Sciences (AIMS) in partnership with the Robert Bosch Stiftung. The NEF is a platform that connects science, society and policy in Africa and the rest of the world — with the goal to leverage science for human development globally. The Fellows Programme consists of Africa's most brilliant young scientists that the NEF showcases on the global stage. The Programme provides Fellows with the opportunity to present their research and draw upon the vast networks of NEF members and participants for support, connections and advice to advance their work
Eligibility: 1. Africans from around the world — including those who currently reside in the Diaspora. 2. Hold a passport from an African country. 3. Hold a PhD in a field of science, Technology, Engineering, Mathematics or the social sciences. 4. Have a demonstrated track record of research/findings that have global impact. 5. You are passionate about raising Africa's profile in STEM globally. 6. Able to clearly present their work to an audience in English or French
Level of Study: Postgraduate
Type: Fellowship
Frequency: Annual
Country of Study: South Africa
Closing Date: 27 January
Funding: Foundation

For further information contact:

NEF Secretariat, c/o AIMS-NEI 590 KG ST Gasabo, Kigali, Rwanda

Email: info@nef.org

Austria: Erasmus+ Master in Research and Innovation in Higher Education (MARIHE) Programme

Purpose: The Master in Research and Innovation in Higher Education (MARIHE) is supported by the Erasmus+ Programme of the European Union (EU) under the action of an Erasmus Mundus Joint Master Degree (EMJMD)
Eligibility: 1. Must hold a first university degree, this should be at least a Bachelor degree issued by a university, quantified as three years of studies corresponding. 2. Show a strong motivation and interest. 3. Have sufficient knowledge of English for academic purposes
Level of Study: Postgraduate
Type: Grant
Frequency: Annual
Country of Study: South Africa
Application Procedure: Apply online: www.marihe.eu/how-to-apply/application-process-and-timetable
Closing Date: 5 December
Funding: Private

For further information contact:

Email: marihe@donau-uni.ac.at

Azerbaijan: Non-Aligned Movement (NAM) Scholarship

Purpose: The Government of the Republic of Azerbaijan is offering scholarships for Bachelor's, Master's and Doctoral programmes to the citizens of Non-Aligned Movement (NAM) countries (including South Africa)
Eligibility: 1. Citizen of Non-Aligned Movement (NAM) countries (this includes South Africa). 2. For undergraduate programmes applicants must be younger than 25 years old. 3. For Master's programmes applicants must be younger than 30 years old. 4. For doctoral programmes applicants must be younger than 35 years old
Level of Study: Postgraduate
Type: Scholarship
Value: 800 AZN
Frequency: Annual
Country of Study: South Africa

Application Procedure: Apply: www.internationalscholarships.dhet.gov.za/Application%20form.pdf
Closing Date: 10 February
Funding: Foundation

For further information contact:

Email: internationalscholarships@dhet.gov.za

Brunei Darussalam: Government of Brunei Darussalam Scholarship

Purpose: The Brunei Darussalam Ministry of Foreign Affairs invites applications for the Government of Brunei Darussalam Scholarship. The scholarship is tenable at higher education institutions in Brunei Darussalam and provides applicants with an opportunity to pursue Diploma, Bachelor's and Master's degrees
Eligibility: 1. Citizens of, but not limited to the Association of Southeast Asian Nations (ASEAN), Commonwealth and Organisation of Islamic Cooperation (OIC) member countries (this includes South Africa). 2. Applicants should be nominated by their Government. 3. Applicants must be in good health and have a strong academic record. 4. Applicants must be between the ages of 18-35 for Undergraduate and Diploma programmes and must not exceed 35 for Master's studies, by 31 July. 5. Candidates must be prepared to fund any costs not covered by the scholarship
Level of Study: Postgraduate
Type: Scholarship
Frequency: Annual
Country of Study: South Africa
Application Procedure: Apply online: www.ubd.edu.bn/admission/scholarships.html
Closing Date: 28 February
Funding: Foundation

For further information contact:

Email: internationalscholarships@dhet.gov.za

China: Chinese Government Scholarship

Purpose: The Chinese Government is offering scholarships for South African students to study at Chinese institutions. The Department of Higher Education and Training is responsible for nominations
Eligibility: Listed below are the eligibility factors for the scholarship: 1. South African citizens in good health (medical check will be required for successful applicants). 2. Strong academic record with a minimum 65% average in previous studies. 3. Demonstrated interest in China and

commitment to the development of South Africa. 4. Applications in all fields of study except medicine will be considered. 5. Preference will be given to postgraduate applicants, previously disadvantaged applicants and applications in the following fields. The scholarship is offered for undergraduate (Bachelors) in the identified scarce skills, postgraduate (Masters or PhD) or non-degree Chinese language studies. Bachelor's degree scholarships are taught in Chinese and will only be awarded to applicants who already have the required level of Chinese proficiency (HSK 5 or above). Preference is given to applications for postgraduate studies

Level of Study: Postgraduate

Type: Scholarship

Frequency: Annual

Country of Study: South Africa

Application Procedure: Apply online: http://www.campuschina.org/universities/index.html

Closing Date: 15 March

Funding: Foundation

For further information contact:

Level 13, Building A3 No. 9 Chegongzhuang St, Dong Wu Yuan, Xicheng Qu, Beijing Shi, CN 100738, China

Email: internationalscholarships@dhet.gov.za

China: One Belt One Road Scholarship

Purpose: Peking University Guanghua School of Management is offering One Belt One Road Scholarship to pursue an MBA programme at Peking University. The International MBA programme is a full-time (2 years) English-taught programme

Eligibility: 1. Applicants must hold a non-Chinese citizenship and be citizens from Belt and Road Initiative (BRI) countries. 2. Must hold a Bachelor's degree equivalent to a Bachelor's degree in China. 3. Must have two or more years of relevant full-time work experience. 4. Must obtain a competitive score from the Guanghua MBA entrance exam. 5. Must have leadership quality

Level of Study: Postgraduate

Type: Scholarship

Value: Accommodation subsidy (4,000 RMB/person/month), Living allowance (3,000 RMB/person/month), edical insurance fee (800 RMB/person/year), Application fee of 800RMB will be waived

Length of Study: 2 year

Frequency: Annual

Country of Study: South Africa

Application Procedure: Apply online: applymba.pku.edu.cn/ The One Belt One Road Scholarship will not only provide

the opportunity to study at Peking University which is one of the most prestigious universities in China, and is ranked #1 in China and #2 in the Asia-Pacific region by Times Higher Education World University Rankings, but also a chance to become an expert in China affairs and gain a solid foothold in the China market

Closing Date: Round 3: 28 February Round 4: 15 April Enrollment deadline: Early September

Funding: Private

For further information contact:

Apply online: applymba.pku.edu.cn/

Tel: (86) 15010 656 075

Email: yul@gsm.pku.edu.cn

China: Renmin University Master of Contemporary Chinese Studies Scholarship

Subjects: Chinese Politics, Chinese Economy, Chinese Culture, Chinese Law

Purpose: The Silk Road School at the Renmin University of China (Suzhou) offers scholarships to foreign students who wish to pursue a Master of Contemporary Chinese studies at Renmin University of China (Suzhou)

Eligibility: 1. Be foreign citizens who have interest in Belt and Road Initiative (BRI) and Chinese culture. 2. Have the ability to speak, read and write English at an equivalent score of IELTS 6.5 or TOEFL 90

Level of Study: Postgraduate

Type: Scholarship

Frequency: Annual

Country of Study: South Africa

Application Procedure: Apply online: www.rdcy.org/displaynewsen.php?id=45928

Closing Date: 10 June

Funding: Foundation

For further information contact:

Tel: (86) 10 6251 6305

Email: srsruc@ruc.edu.cn

Embassy of France in South Africa Master Scholarship Programme

Purpose: The Embassy of France invites students who wish to continue their tertiary education at Master level in France for the academic year September apply for its scholarship programme

Eligibility: 1. Citizenship of South Africa or Lesotho. 2. Bachelor's or Honour's graduate (depending on the academic year to enrol for), completed or to be completed by the time the student would depart for France. 3. Acceptance from three selected French institutions of the candidate's choice. Students should apply for admission to these universities concurrently to the bursary application (admission letters or at least correspondence with the institutions will be required for complete applications). 4. Maximum academic fees (administration and tuition fees combined) financed with a full scholarship: 5,000€. For academic fees higher than 5,000€ co-financing options must be provided (personal savings and/or enterprise sponsorship). 5. Maximum academic fees (administration and tuition fees combined) financed with a full scholarship: 5,000€. For academic fees higher than 5,000€ co-financing options must be provided (personal savings and/or enterprise sponsorship). 6. No knowledge of French language required, depending on the availability of study course in English. Courses relating to the French Language (i.e. translation, interpreting or French language teaching) must follow a different application process
Level of Study: Postgraduate
Type: Scholarship
Value: €5,000
Length of Study: 1 year
Frequency: Annual
Country of Study: Any country
Closing Date: 15 March
Funding: Foundation

For further information contact:

Email: audrey.delattre@diplomatie.gouv.fr

Embassy of France in South Africa PhD Grants

Purpose: The French Embassy scholarship programme offers grants to facilitate in the international academic and scientific mobility of South African and non-South African researchers to French Higher Education institutions. The programme offers the opportunity for doctoral students to integrate into French establishments for specified time periods in order to participate in collaborative research as part of their doctoral research project
Eligibility: 1. Registration for a PhD at a South African university. 2. A hosting agreement from the French institution. 3. Support letters from your South African supervisor and French co-supervisor, supporting the proposed research project. 4. Applications from all academic disciplines will be considered. 5. No knowledge of French language required, provided the student will be able to conduct research in English

Level of Study: Postgraduate
Type: Scholarship
Value: €1,065
Frequency: Annual
Country of Study: Any country
Funding: Foundation

For further information contact:

Tel: (27) 12 343 6563
Email: pretoria@campusfrance.org

France: French Embassy and Saint-Gobain Master Scholarship

Subjects: Finance, Supply chain, Construction (architectural) and Marketing
Purpose: Saint-Gobain and the Embassy of France in South Africa are offering scholarships to South Africans and Basotho graduates to pursue a Master's degree in Business studies or Engineering at public French universities
Level of Study: Postgraduate
Type: Scholarship
Value: €767 and annual tuition fees (€3,770) at public universities
Frequency: Annual
Country of Study: Any country
Application Procedure: Apply online: www.southafrica.campusfrance.org/page/campusfrance-south-africa-office
Closing Date: 30 March
Funding: Private
Additional Information: Contacts could be further established with the below link. www.southafrica.campusfrance.org/page/campusfrance-south-africa-office

For further information contact:

Email: pretoria.bourses@campusfrance.org

France: French Embassy Masters and PhD Scholarship Programme

Purpose: The Embassy of France is offering scholarships to postgraduate South Africans who wish to pursue Master's and Doctoral studies at French higher education institutions
Eligibility: 1. Be a citizen and resident of South Africa. 2. Apply for university admission at three French universities concurrent to the scholarship application (admission letters or at least correspondence with the institutions will be required). Applications to French public universities are recommended since they have French government subsidised fees. 3. French proficiency is not required, provided they are pursuing a study

course in English and have the ability to conduct research in English. 4. Courses relating to French language studies (i.e. translation, interpreting or French language teaching) must follow a different application process by contacting Audrey Delattre

Level of Study: Postgraduate

Type: Scholarship

Frequency: Annual

Country of Study: South Africa

Application Procedure: Apply online: www.southafrica.campusfrancc.org/sites/locaux/files/PhD%20French%20Emb assy%20application%20form%202019.pdf

Closing Date: 15 March

Funding: Foundation

For further information contact:

Email: pretoria@campusfrance.org

France: ISAE-SUPAERO Scholarship Programmes

Purpose: The ISAE-SUPAERO Institute offers a wide range of science and engineering degree programs with a number of scholarships offered through industry support and the SUPAERO Foundation for pursuing studies towards a Master of Science in Aerospace Engineering degree. These scholarships cover tuition and part of living expenses

Eligibility: Applicants who hold a Bachelor's degree or the equivalent in Mechanical Engineering, Mechatronics, Aerospace, Electronics, Electrical Systems, Telecommunications or a French licence in Science and Engineering

Level of Study: Postgraduate

Type: Scholarship

Value: Tuition fees: €10,600, Living expenses: €8,000 to €10,000

Frequency: Annual

Country of Study: South Africa

Application Procedure: Apply online: www.isae-supaero.fr/en/academics/master-s-degree-msc/admissions/

Closing Date: Please check the links for the deadlines for the next academic year

Funding: Foundation

For further information contact:

Tel: (33) 561 338 027

Email: philippe.galaup@isae-supaero.fr

Hungary: Stipendium Hungaricum for South Africa

Purpose: The Hungarian Government is offering 100 scholarships to South African students to study at participating public university in Hungary. All courses available for South Africans are taught in English

Eligibility: 1. Be a South African citizen in good health. 2. Have a strong academic record. 3. An interest in studying in Hungary and demonstrated commitment to the development of South Africa. 4. Meet the entry criteria for their selected programme in Hungary. 5. Meet the minimum academic requirement for entry into a similar programme at a South African university

Level of Study: Postgraduate

Type: Grant

Frequency: Annual

Country of Study: South Africa

Application Procedure: Apply online: apply.stipendium hungaricum.hu/

Closing Date: 15 January

Funding: Foundation

For further information contact:

Email: HungaryScholarshipApplications2019@dhet. gov.za

India: Export-Import Bank of India BRICS Economic Research Award

Purpose: The Export-Import Bank of India (EXIM) has instituted the Export-Import Bank of India BRICS Economic Research Award. The award aims to encourage and stimulate advanced research on economics related topics of relevance to the member nations of Brazil Russia India China South Africa (BRICS). The EXIM Bank of India invites South African research scholars to apply for the Exim Bank of India BRICS Economic Research Award

Eligibility: Check online: www.eximbankindia.in/Assets/pdf/award/EXIM%20Bank%20BRICS%20Economic%20Research%20Award-%20Guidelines%20(English)%2015. 04.2019.pdf

Level of Study: Postgraduate

Type: Award

Value: US$22 000

Frequency: Annual

Country of Study: South Africa

Application Procedure: Apply online: www.eximbankindia.in/awards

Closing Date: 15 April

Funding: Foundation

For further information contact:

Tel: (91) 22 2217 2701

Email: rag@eximbankindia.in

Indonesia: Kemitraan Negara Berkembang (Developing Countries Partnership) Scholarship

Purpose: The Kemitraan Negara Berkembang (KNB) Scholarship was first introduced by the Ministry of Education and Culture to embrace higher education globalization by providing financial assistance (scholarship) to the selected Indonesian Universities, to recruit potential international students to acquire Master's degrees in those universities. The KNB Scholarship program has expanded and is now offered to potential students from developing countries to acquire Bachelor's or Master's degrees at the prestigious universities in Indonesia. The Indonesian Government is offering 140 Master's and five Bachelor's degrees scholarships. All programmes are delivered in Bahasa Indonesia

Eligibility: 1. Applicants must not be older than 35 years of age. 2. Applicants must hold a Bachelor degree (Master's degree holder is not eligible to apply). 3. Applicants must have a TOEFL (or other certified English Proficiency) score of 500. 4. Applicants must be between the ages of 18-35 for Undergraduate and Diploma programmes

Level of Study: Postgraduate

Type: Scholarship

Frequency: Annual

Country of Study: South Africa

Application Procedure: Apply online: www.knb.ristekdikti.go.id

Closing Date: 30 April

Funding: Foundation

For further information contact:

The Information and Socio-Cultural Section, The Embassy of the Republic of Indonesia, 949 Francis Baard Street, Arcardia 0083, South Africa

Tel: (27) 12 342 3350
Email: info@indonesia-pretoria.org.za

Ireland: Kader Asmal Fellowship Programme

Purpose: The Embassy of Ireland in South Africa in partnership with the Department of Higher Education and Training and the Canon Collins Trust invites applications for scholarships for one-year Master's degree study in Ireland commencing in September

Eligibility: 1. Be a South African citizen. 2. Have achieved the necessary standard to be accepted onto a postgraduate course in an institute of higher education in Ireland. 3. Be seeking funding for a full-time postgraduate programme in one of the above listed subject areas. 4. Be able to take up fellowship in the academic year. 5. Not have already applied

for a course at an institution in Ireland - if you have already been admitted to a university you are not eligible

Level of Study: Postgraduate

Type: Fellowships, operating grants

Frequency: Annual

Country of Study: South Africa

Application Procedure: Apply online: www.canoncollins.org.uk/apply/scholarship/kader-asmal-fellowship

Closing Date: 31 December

Funding: Private

For further information contact:

Email: Rose.Machobane@dfa.ie

Japan: MEXT Scholarships

Purpose: The Japanese Ministry of Education, Culture, Sports, Science, and Technology (MEXT) offers scholarships to foreign students who wish to study at Japanese universities under the Japanese Government Scholarship Program

Eligibility: see website: www.za.emb-japan.go.jp/itpr_en/MEXT_Scholarship.html

Level of Study: Postgraduate

Type: Scholarship

Frequency: Annual

Country of Study: South Africa

Application Procedure: Applications must be couriered or be hand delivered and addressed to: Cultural Section of the Embassy of Japan in South Africa: 259 Baines Street, Groenkloof, Pretoria, 0181

Closing Date: 8 June

Funding: Foundation

For further information contact:

Cultural Section of the Embassy of Japan in South Africa, 259 Baines Street, Groenkloof, Pretoria 0181, South Africa

Email: ryan.keet@pr.mofa.go.jp

Jordan: Talal Abu-Ghazaleh University College for Innovation Scholarship

Purpose: Talal Abu-Ghazaleh University College for Innovation (TAGUCI) is offering a scholarship for a South African student who wishes to pursue a Master of Business Administration (MBA) degree at TAGUCI. Registration is now open for the semester

Eligibility: 1. Applicants must submit official Bachelor's degree transcripts and certificate, stamped by the Ministry of Higher Education and Scientific Research in Jordan. 2. English Language Equivalency exam mark of 65%.

3. Minimum of two years of work experience. 4. Written essay of up to 3,000 words. 5. Candidates must be prepared to fund any costs not covered by the scholarship
Level of Study: Postgraduate
Type: Scholarship
Frequency: Annual
Country of Study: Any country
Application Procedure: Apply online: www.taguci.edu.jo/RegistrationForm.aspx
Closing Date: 28 February
Funding: Foundation

For further information contact:

Tel: (962) 65100 900
Email: info@taguci.edu.jo

Mauritius: Mauritius-Africa Scholarship Scheme

Purpose: As part of a commitment to promote capacity-building at high level across thecontinent, the Government of Mauritius is awarding scholarships to deserving students who are resident citizens of member states of the African Union or of African Commonwealth countries for full-time, on-campus undergraduate and postgraduate programmes tenable in public Higher Education Institutions (HEIs) in Mauritius
Eligibility: 1. South African citizens in good health and with a strong academic record. 2. Candidates must have an interest in studying in Mauritius and demonstrate a commitment to the development of South Africa. 3. Candidates must be available to study in Mauritius at the start of their academic programme. 4. All applicants must meet the entry criteria for their selected programme in Mauritius. 5. Have an interest in studying in Mauritius and demonstrate a commitment to the development of South Africa. 6. All applicants must meet the minimum academic requirement for entry into a similar programme at a South African university. 7. All candidates must have proficiency in English. 8. Not be in receipt of a scholarship from any other public source in Mauritius
Level of Study: Postgraduate
Type: Scholarship
Value: Tuition fees and course-related costs of up to MUR 100,000; Monthly living allowance to the value of MUR 12,500
Frequency: Annual
Country of Study: South Africa
Application Procedure: Apply online: ministry-education.govmu.org/English/scholarships/Documents/2018/Application%20Form%20undergraduate%20MASS%2012Jan2018.pdf

Closing Date: 25 March
Funding: Foundation

For further information contact:

Email: internationalscholarships@dhet.gov.za

New Zealand: Scholarships for International Tertiary Students and Commonwealth Scholarship

Purpose: The New Zealand Aid Programme offers scholarships to potential applicants from eligible African countries (including South Africa) who are motivated to make a difference at home. Applications are now open for studies
Level of Study: Postgraduate
Type: Scholarship
Frequency: Annual
Country of Study: Any country
Application Procedure: All applications for the New Zealand Scholarship for International Tertiary Students must be submitted online. Please see the below links for more details on the process: All applications for the New Zealand Commonwealth Scholarship must be submitted on this application form. www.internationalscholarships.dhet.gov.za/Content/NEW ZEALAND/Tertiary Application Form 2019 Selection - Commonwealth.pdf
Closing Date: 28 March
Funding: Foundation

For further information contact:

Email: commonwealthscholarship@dhet.gov.za

Romania: Romanian State Scholarships

Purpose: The Romanian Ministry of Foreign Affairs (MFA) and the Romanian Department of Public, Cultural and Scientific Diplomacy are offering 85 scholarship opportunities to foreign citizens, to study in Romania. This opportunity is open to students who wish to pursue studies in Bachelor's, Master's and PhD. Courses will be taught in Romanian language
Eligibility: 1. Applicants must be in good health and have a strong academic record. 2. Must present study papers issued by accredited / recognized educational institutions. 3. Applicants must not be older than 35 years of age for Bachelor's and Master's studies and 45 years respectively for Doctoral studies, by 31 December of the year in which they are nominated. 4. Candidates must be prepared to fund any costs not covered by the scholarship

Level of Study: Postgraduate
Type: Scholarship
Value: €85
Frequency: Annual
Country of Study: South Africa
Closing Date: 28 February
Funding: Foundation

For further information contact:

Email: internationalscholarships@dhet.gov.za

Romanian State Scholarships

Purpose: The Romanian Ministry of Foreign Affairs (MFA) and the Romanian Department of Public, Cultural and Scientific Diplomacy are offering 85 scholarship opportunities to foreign citizens, to study in Romania. This opportunity is open to students who wish to pursue studies in Bachelor's, Master's and PhD
Eligibility: 1. Applicants must be in good health and have a strong academic record. 2. Must present study papers issued by accredited / recognized educational institutions. 3. Applicants must not be older than 35 years of age for Bachelor's and Master's studies and 45 years respectively for Doctoral studies, by 31 December of the year in which they are nominated. 4. Candidates must be prepared to fund any costs not covered by the scholarship
Level of Study: Postgraduate
Type: Scholarship
Value: €85
Length of Study: 1 year
Frequency: Annual
Country of Study: South Africa
Application Procedure: Apply online: www.mae.ro/en/node/10251#null
Closing Date: 28 February
Funding: Foundation

For further information contact:

Email: internationalscholarships@dhet.gov.za

Russia: Scholarships for South Africans

Purpose: The Russian Government offers annual scholarships for South Africans to study at Russian institutions. The scholarship is offered for Bachelor's, Masters and PhD degrees. Most programmes are taught in the Russian language. Scholarship recipients are required to undertake a preparatory course related to their field of study (including language training) for one year before pursuing their degree studies. Only after passing the examinations of the college preparatory course can they start their degree studies
Eligibility: 1. South African citizens in good health (medical test are required for successful applicants). 2. Have a strong academic record. 3. Demonstrated interest in Russia and commitment to the development of South Africa. 4. Applications in all fields of study except medicine will be considered. 5. Preference will be given to postgraduate applicants, previously disadvantaged applicants and applicants in the following fields
Level of Study: Postgraduate
Type: Scholarship
Frequency: Annual
Country of Study: South Africa
Application Procedure: Apply online: www.russia.study/en
Closing Date: 27 February
Funding: Foundation

For further information contact:

Email: Internationalscholarships@dhet.gov.za

Spain: Student and staff exchange between South Africa and Spain

Purpose: Alianza 4 Universidades (A4U) is a consortium of four Spanish public universities. The consortium is funded by the Erasmus+ Programme of the European Union to enable student and staff exchange between universities members of the A4U and six South African partner universities
Eligibility: 1. Applicants from South African partner universities and A4U universities. South African partner universities include: University of Pretoria, University of the Witwatersrand, Stellenbosch University, University of Cape Town, University of the Western Cape and University of the Free State. 2. A4U Universities participating universities are Universitat Autònoma de Barcelona, Universidad Autónoma de Madrid, Universidad Carlos III de Madrid and Universitat Pompeu Fabra in Barcelona
Level of Study: Postgraduate
Type: Grant
Frequency: Annual
Country of Study: South Africa
Application Procedure: Apply online: alliance4universities.eu/en/mobility-scholarships/
Closing Date: December
Funding: Foundation

For further information contact:

Tel: (34) 935 422 079
Email: coordinacion@a-4u.eu

Sweden: Swedish Institute Scholarships for South Africa (SISSA)

Purpose: The Swedish Institute Scholarships for South Africa (SISSA) are being offered for South Africans to undertake Master's degrees at Swedish universities from September

Eligibility: 1. South African citizens in good health with a strong academic record. 2. Must have Bachelor's with Honours or equivalent, and should have performed well in his/her previous studies with minimum 65% average mark achieved. 3. Have applied for a Master's degree programme at a Swedish university on a full-time basis. 4. Intend to return to South Africa at the end of your studies. 5. Work and leadership experience is not a requirement but will be viewed favourably

Level of Study: Postgraduate

Type: Scholarship

Frequency: Annual

Country of Study: South Africa

Application Procedure: Apply online: si.se/en/apply/scholarships/swedish-institute-scholarships-for-south-africa/

Closing Date: 15 January

Funding: Foundation

For further information contact:

Email: Internationalscholarships@dhet.gov.za

Switzerland: Swiss Government Excellence Scholarship for foreign students

Purpose: Through the Swiss Federal Commission for Scholarships for Foreign Students, the Swiss Government Grants foreign researchers, postgraduate scholarships at Swiss higher education institutions. The Swiss Government Excellence Scholarship are intended for highly motivated, competitive young researchers who have graduated from university. These scholarships will enable applicants to undertake research work in the fields in which the Swiss universities are particularly active

Eligibility: 1. South African citizens. 2. Applicants with admission letter from academic host institution. 3. Support letter from supervisor or academic host professor. 4. Research proposal including timeframe

Level of Study: Postgraduate

Type: Scholarship

Value: 1,920 Swiss

Length of Study: 1 year

Frequency: Annual

Country of Study: South Africa

Application Procedure: Apply online: www.internationalscholarships.dhet.gov.za/Content/Switzerland/153_PhD_en_2019_20.pdf

Closing Date: 15 December

Funding: Foundation

For further information contact:

Tel: (27) 12 452 0660

Email: pre.vertretung@eda.admin.ch

Turkey: Türkiye Scholarships

Purpose: Turkey is offering various scholarships to outstanding international students from across the world to study in the most prestigious universities in Turkey

Eligibility: 1. Applications for Türkiye Scholarships are open to citizens of all countries. 2. Applicants should not be older than 21 for Bachelor's, 30 for Master's and 35 for Doctoral studies. 3. For Undergraduate degree applications 70 %. 4. For Master's and Doctoral degree applications 75 %

Level of Study: Postgraduate

Type: Scholarship

Value: TRY 1,400

Frequency: Annual

Country of Study: South Africa

Application Procedure: Apply online: www.turkiyeburslari.gov.tr

Closing Date: 20 February

Funding: Foundation

For further information contact:

Email: info@turkiyeburslari.org

United Arab Emirates: Khalifa University Postgraduate Scholarships

Purpose: Khalifa University (KU) of Science and Technology is offering postgraduate scholarships to students who wish to pursue postgraduate studies in the field of Engineering Sciences in Abu Dhabi. Through these scholarships, the University aims to highlight the importance of investing in intellectual and human capital as well as its role in enhancing the performance of higher education system

Eligibility: Check website: www.ku.ac.ae/admissions/graduate-admissions/

Level of Study: Postgraduate

Type: Scholarship

Frequency: Annual

Country of Study: South Africa
Application Procedure: Apply online: admissions.kustar.ac.ae/pg/Account/Login
Closing Date: 30 April
Funding: Foundation

For further information contact:

Email: pgadmission@ku.ac.ae

United States: Fulbright Foreign Student Program

Purpose: The scholarship provides grants for South African university graduates to pursue a Master's or Doctoral degree at a United States university in any subject (excludes studies that require contact with patients). The grants are awarded for two years towards one degree — Master's or Doctorate (renewable each year)
Eligibility: 1. Be a South African citizen. 2. Usually between 30 and 45 years of age. 3. Have a 4-year B Tech or a 3-year Bachelor's degree plus Honours when applying for Master's. 4. Have a Master's degree when applying for a Doctoral degree. 5. Have proven academic excellence
Level of Study: Postgraduate
Type: Studentship
Value: Tuition fee and living stipend
Frequency: Annual
Country of Study: South Africa
Application Procedure: In order to apply for this scholarship, you could use the following link. apply.iie.org/ffsp2020
Closing Date: 19 April
Funding: Private
Additional Information: For further, kindly contact the organisation using the below link. za.usembassy.gov/education-culture/educational-exchanges/fulbright-flagship-programs/foreign-student-program-frequently-asked-questions/

United States: Harvard South Africa Fellowship Program

Subjects: Harvard South Africa Fellowship Program (HSAFP) was established for mid-career professionals who were disadvantaged by past laws and resource allocations in South Africa
Purpose: The HSAFP was initiated to provide educational enrichment for mid-career individuals in various occupations who have shown considerable skills and leadership in their chosen fields. Applications are invited for the Harvard South Africa Fellowship Program

Eligibility: 1. Fellows must be South African citizens. 2. Usually between 30 and 45 years of age. 3. Must not have just completed or not completed a Bachelor's degree, unless this degree has been pursued concurrently with or subsequent to experience in the workplace. 4. Applicants should determine well in advance whether if awarded a fellowship, they can be granted leave by their employers for Harvard's academic year
Level of Study: Postgraduate
Type: Fellowships, operating grants
Frequency: Annual
Country of Study: South Africa
Application Procedure: Apply onlline: africa.harvard.edu/south-africa-fellowship-program
Closing Date: 4 April
Funding: Foundation

For further information contact:

Tel: (27) 877 010 715
Email: AfricaOffice@Harvard.edu

Hilda Martindale Educational Trust

Royal Holloway, University of London, Egham, TW20 0EX, Surrey, United Kingdom

Tel: (44) 17 8427 6158
Fax: (44) 17 8443 7520
Email: hildamartindaletrust@rhul.ac.uk
Contact: Miss Sarah Moffat, Administrator to the Trust

The Hilda Martindale Trust makes one-off awards to British women undertaking training or professional qualifications in areas in which women are underrepresented.

Hilda Martindale Trust Awards

Subjects: All subjects where women are under represented
Purpose: To assist with the costs of training or professional qualifications in areas in which women are under represented
Eligibility: Open to women of the British Isles only. Assistance is not given to short courses, courses abroad, elective studies or access courses. Trust can only offer funding to women pursuing training/qualifications in areas in which women are under represented
Level of Study: Doctorate, Graduate, Postdoctorate, Postgraduate, Predoctorate, Professional development, MBA, Undergraduate, Postgraduate (MSc)
Type: Grant

Value: Up to £3,000
Length of Study: 1 year
Frequency: Annual
Study Establishment: Any establishment approved by the trustees
Country of Study: United Kingdom
No. of awards offered: 55
Application Procedure: The application form and guidance for applicants are available from the website address below. In addition, requests for an application form can be made by email to Hildamartindaletrust@rhul.ac.uk, or by letter via the address below. Late or retrospective applications will not be considered
Closing Date: Available from the secretary or on the Trust website: www.royalholloway.ac.uk/aboutus/governancematters/thehildamartindaletrust.aspx
Funding: Private
Contributor: Private trust
No. of awards given last year: 16
No. of applicants last year: 55
Additional Information: Further information can be obtained via email at hildamartindaletrust@rhul.ac.uk.

For further information contact:

C/o College Secretary's Office, RHUL, Egham, TW20 0EX, Surrey, United Kingdom

Email: hildamartindaletrust@rhul.ac.uk
Contact: Secretary to the Hilda Martindale Trust

Hong Kong Baptist University

AAB703, Level 7, Academic and Administration Building, Baptist University Road Campus, Kowloon Tong, Hong Kong

Tel: (852) 3411 2188
Fax: (852) 3411 5568
Contact: Hong Kong Baptist University

Hong Kong Baptist University (HKBU) is a publicly funded tertiary institution with a Christian education heritage.

Fully Funded Master Scholarship at Hong Kong Baptist University

Subjects: The scholarship is awarded in International Journalism
Purpose: The aim of the scholarship is to encourage the study of International Journalism

Eligibility: Vietnam, Philippines, India and Indonesia. Applicants must have a valid minimum TOEFL iBT 79 or IELTS 6.5
Value: The scholarship is fully funded
Country of Study: Any country
Application Procedure: The mode of applying is online
Closing Date: 28 February
Additional Information: For more details please see the website scholarship-positions.com/fully-funded-master-scholarship-hong-kong-baptist-university/2018/01/04/

For further information contact:

Email: busd-external@hkbu.edu.hk

Horowitz Foundation for Social Policy

PO Box 7, Rocky Hill, NJ 08553 0007, United States of America

Tel: (1) 732 445 2280
Fax: (1) 732 659 9198
Email: horowitz-foundation.org
Website: www.horowitz-foundation.org
Contact: Ms Mary E. Curtis, The Chairman

The Horowitz Foundation for Social Policy was established to support the advancement of research and understanding in the social sciences including: psychology, anthropology, sociology, economics, and political science. The Foundation assists individual scholars at the early stages of their career who require small grants to complete their dissertations.

Irving Louis Horowitz Award

Subjects: Social sciences, including anthropology, area studies, economics, political science, psychology, sociology, and urban studies, as well as newer areas such as evaluation research
Purpose: Awarded to the project that best represents the goals of the Horowitz Foundation in a specific award year
Eligibility: Open to nationals of any country. Candidates may solicit support for final work on a dissertation, including travel funds
Level of Study: Doctorate
Type: Award
Value: US$12,500 (US$10,000 initially and an additional US$2,500 upon receipt of a final report on a copy of the research)

Length of Study: 1 year
Frequency: Annual
Country of Study: Any country
No. of awards offered: 300
Application Procedure: Applicants are not required to be United States citizens or United States residents. Candidates may propose new projects, and they may also solicit support for research in progress, including final work on a dissertation, supplementing research in progress, or travel funds. Awards are only open to aspiring PhDs at the dissertation level whose project has received approval from their appropriate department head/university. Grants are normally made for 1 year on a non-renewable basis. Awards will be made to individuals, not institutions, and if processed through an institution, a waiver for overhead is requested. A copy of the product of the research is expected no later than 1 year after completion. Upon receipt an additional US$2,500 will be paid. Recipients are expected to acknowledge assistance provided by the Foundation in any publication resulting from their research. Awards are publicized in appropriate professional media and on the Foundation website
Closing Date: 31 January
Funding: Private
No. of awards given last year: 15
No. of applicants last year: 300
Additional Information: The cover sheet in the application is most important, as it is the basis for the initial screening of prospects.

For further information contact:

Email: wagner.events@nyu.edu

Refugee Study Awards

Purpose: The Refugee Study Awards are for women who are studying for a New Zealand tertiary qualification, and who have not been through the New Zealand school system. The awards are a one off grant to help with study and/or living expenses
Eligibility: To apply for the Refugee Study Awards you must meet all the following eligibility criteria: The applicant is a woman, who: 1. Is enrolled in a NZ approved tertiary qualification. 2. Is studying at diploma or degree level (NZQA level 5 or above). 3. Is a New Zealand citizen or holds a resident class visa, and lives in New Zealand. 4. Provides evidence of having arrived in New Zealand as a refugee - ID card or NZ Immigration Service refugee travel document. Has not previously received a NHWT:HK Award
Level of Study: Graduate

Type: Award
Value: NZ $3,000 -preference for an awardee from the Manawatu region, another is that $3,000 - preference for an awardee from the Wellington region
Frequency: Annual
Country of Study: Any country
Application Procedure: Please check the following website link for further details. www.newhorizonsforwomen.org.nz/awards/manawatu-charitable-trust-refugee/
Closing Date: 14 April
Funding: Private
Additional Information: One of these awards is sponsored by Graduate Women Manawatu Charitable Trust and preference will be given to applicants from Manawatu. The other award is sponsored by the Second Chance Group in Wellington and preference will be given to applicants from the greater Wellington region. Applications are welcome from women who are eligible from across the country.

For further information contact:

New Horizons for Women Trust, PO Box 12498, Wellington, NZL 6144, New Zealand

Email: enquiries@newhorizonsforwomen.org.nz

The Horowitz Foundation for Social Policy

Subjects: The Foundation makes targeted grants for work in all major areas of the social sciences, including anthropology, area studies, economics, political science, psychology, sociology, and urban studies, as well as newer areas such as evaluation research. Preference is given to projects that address contemporary issues in the social sciences and issues of policy relevance
Eligibility: Awards are open only to PhD candidates whose project has received approval from their appropriate department head/university. Preference is given to projects that address contemporary issues in the social sciences and issues of policy relevance. Applicants are not required to be citizens or residents of the United States. Awards are based solely on merit, not to ensure a representative base of recipients or disciplines
Level of Study: Doctorate
Type: Grants and fellowships
Value: $7,500—$5,000 initially and an additional $2,500 upon completion of the project. Criteria for completion include approval of the dissertation, acceptance of an article based on the research by a peer-reviewed journal, or an invitation to write a book chapter based on the research. Additional awards are given in certain suspect areas. The best overall project (as determined by the trustees) receives an additional NZ $5,000

Length of Study: NA
Frequency: Annual
Study Establishment: NA
Country of Study: Any country
No. of awards offered: 700
Application Procedure: Applications must be submitted through our online system which can be found on our website www.horowitz-foundation.org
Closing Date: 1 December
Funding: Private
Contributor: NA
No. of awards given last year: 20
No. of applicants last year: 700
Additional Information: All submitted applications, letters, and documents must be in English. Applications are open 1 July through 1 December. Applicants are encouraged to apply as early as possible. Submitted materials become the property of the Foundation and will not be returned. Applicants should not send originals or other materials that cannot be replaced

For further information contact:

Email: horowitz-foundation.org

Hosei University

17-1 Fujimi 2 chome, Chiyoda-ku, Tokyo JP 102, Japan

Tel: (81) 3 3264 9564
Fax: (81) 3 3238 9873
Email: ic@I.hosei.ac.jp
Website: www.hosei.ac.jp/ic
Contact: Ms Keiko Takahata, Executive Assistant

Master of Business Administration Programme

Application Procedure: Applicants must complete an application form supplying official transcripts, passport sized photograph, curriculum vitae and a statement of financial support
Closing Date: 30 November and 28 February

For further information contact:

Business Adminstration, 2-17-1 Fujimi, Tokyo 102, Japan

Tel: (81) 3 3264 9315
Fax: (81) 3 3238 9873
Email: ic@fujimi.hosei.ac.jp
Contact: MBA Admissions Officer

Howard Hughes Medical Institute (HHMI)

4000 Jones Bridge Road, Chevy Chase, MD 20815-6789, United States of America

Tel: (1) 301 215 8500
Website: www.hhmi.org

HHMI is a science philanthropy whose mission is to advance biomedical research and science education for the benefit of humanity. We empower exceptional scientists and students to pursue fundamental questions about living systems.

Howard Hughes Medical Institute Gilliam Fellowships for Advanced Study

Subjects: The Gilliam Fellowships for Advanced Study support exceptional graduate students who are committed to increasing diversity among scientific leaders, especially those students who will go on to become faculty members at colleges and universities
Purpose: The goal of the Gilliam Fellowships for Advanced Study program is to ensure the development of a diverse and highly trained workforce is available to assume leadership roles in science, including college and university faculty, who have the responsibility to teach the next generation of scientists
Eligibility: Open to alumni of HHMI's Exceptional Research Opportunities Program (EXROP), regardless of country of origin or nationally, or students nominated by T32 predoctoral training grant principal investigators (PIs) supported by the National Institute for General Medical Sciences (NIGMS); each nominated student must be training grant eligible but does not need to have been a T32 trainee
Type: Fellowship
Value: US$46,000
Length of Study: Up to 3 years of their dissertation research, typically in years 3, 4, and 5 of their PhD studies
Frequency: Annual
Country of Study: United States of America
Closing Date: February
Additional Information: Please check details at www.hhmi. org/programs/gilliam-fellowships-for-advanced-study.

For further information contact:

Email: Gilliam@hhmi.org

Postdoctoral Research Fellowships for Physicians

Subjects: Biological processes
Purpose: To help increase the supply of well-trained physician-scientists, through fellowships for three years of training in fundamental research (basic biological processes or disease mechanisms)
Eligibility: Applicants must have gained their first degree within the last ten years, and must have had two years of postgraduate clinical training, and no more than two years of postdoctoral training in fundamental research
Level of Study: Postdoctorate
Type: Fellowship
Value: US$69,000–86,500 per year
Length of Study: 3 years
Frequency: Annual
Study Establishment: Academic or non-profit research institution
Country of Study: United States of America
No. of awards offered: 255
Application Procedure: Application forms and instructions should be obtained from the address shown. Panels of scientists review applications, and the Institute makes the final selection
Closing Date: Late December. Awards are announced in June
No. of awards given last year: 30
No. of applicants last year: 255
Additional Information: Fellows must engage in full-time research. During the fellowship term, they may not be enrolled in a graduate degree program, nor hold a faculty appointment. The applicant is responsible for selecting a research mentor and making arrangements to work in that person's laboratory.

For further information contact:

4000 Jones Bridge Road, Chevy Chase, MD 20815, United States of America

Tel:	(1) 301 215 8889
Fax:	(1) 301 215 8888
Email:	fellows@hq.hhmi.org

Humane Research Trust

The Humane Research Trust, Brook House, 29 Bramhall Lane South, Bramhall, Stockport, SK7 2DN, Cheshire, United Kingdom

Tel:	(44) 161 439 8041
Fax:	(44) 161 439 3713
Email:	info@humaneresearch.org.uk
Website:	www.humaneresearch.org.uk
Contact:	Jane McAllister, Trust Administrator

The Humane Research Trust is a national charity, which funds a range of unique medical research programmes on human illness at hospitals and universities around the country. In keeping with the philosophy of the Trust, none of the research involves animals and much of it seeks to establish and develop pioneering techniques that will replace animal intensive experiments.

The Humane Research Trust Grant

Subjects: Humane Research
Purpose: To encourage scientific programmes where the use of animals is replaced by other methods
Eligibility: Open to established scientific workers engaged in productive research. Nationals of any country are considered but for the sake of overseeing, projects should be undertaken in a United Kingdom establishment
Level of Study: Unrestricted
Type: Grant
Value: Varies. Please note there is no set limit to either the duration of a project or funding amount. These points will be discussed if the application is successful, however you still need to include in your application the amount of funding you require and an estimate of the duration
Length of Study: Varies
Frequency: Dependent on funds available
Study Establishment: Various
Country of Study: United Kingdom
No. of awards offered: 15
Application Procedure: Applicants must complete an application form, available on the website www.humaneresearch.org.uk. Please ensure you email all of the required documents, i.e. one fully complete application to info@humaneresearch.org.uk and post 10 hard copies to The Humane Research Trust
Closing Date: Varies
Funding: Private
Contributor: Supporters and legacies
No. of awards given last year: 4
No. of applicants last year: 15
Additional Information: The Humane Research Trust is a registered charity and donations are encouraged

For further information contact:

Contact: Mrs Katy Wright, Trust Administrator

Humboldt University of Berlin

Office for Promotion of Young Researchers in the Excellence Initiative, DEU 10099 Berlin Germany

Tel:	(49) 30 2093 1795
Email:	hgs-grants @ hu-berlin.de
Contact:	Humboldt Graduate School

Humboldt Postdoc Scholarships

Purpose: To support young researchers in taking the next step in their academic career after acquiring their PhD

Eligibility: Eligible to excellent researchers who either already hold a PhD from Humboldt-Universität or are about to complete their doctorate at Humboldt-Universität zu Berlin and who wish to conduct a postdoctoral research project. Half of the scholarships will be awarded to women

Type: Scholarship

Value: €1,500 per month is awarded for up to 6 months, additional family allowances are available, travel expenses may be covered. In exceptional cases, funding can be extended for up to an additional 6 months

Study Establishment: Humboldt-Universität

Country of Study: Germany

Application Procedure: Applications can be received only via an online application portal

Closing Date: 1 April to 15 May for funding starting 1 August, 1 June to 15 July for funding starting 1 October, 1 September to 15 October for funding starting 1 February, 1 December to 15 January for funding starting 1 April

For further information contact:

Email: hgs-grants@hu-berlin.de

I

Imperial College of Science, Technology and Medicine

Exhibition Road, SW7 2AZ, London, United Kingdom

Tel:	(44) 20 7594 8023
Fax:	(44) 20 7594 8004
Email:	r.a.clay@ic.ac.uk
Contact:	Ms R A Clay, Scholarships co-ordinator registry

The Imperial College of Science, Technology and Medicine is a college of the University of London and provides university education at first degree and postgraduate level in the fields of science, engineering and medicine.

Stephen and Anna Hui Fellowship

Subjects: Earth sciences defined as geology, extractive metallurgy, minerals, mining engineering, petroleum engineering, earth resources engineering and extractive metallurgy
Purpose: To facilitate postgraduate study or research
Eligibility: Open to graduates with a First or Upper Second Class (Honours) Degree from universities in China including Hong Kong and Taiwan
Level of Study: Doctorate, Postgraduate
Type: Fellowship
Value: It provide financial support to meet the full cost of tuition fees and an annual stipend equal to the College minimum (UK£15,863)
Length of Study: 3 years
Study Establishment: Imperial College
Country of Study: United Kingdom

Application Procedure: Applicants must complete an application form and submit this with two references and a transcript or academic record
Closing Date: 31 January
Funding: Private
Contributor: Stephen and Anna Hui Fellowship Trust Fund
Additional Information: Further information is available on request

For further information contact:

Email: j.picken@imperial.ac.uk

India Alliance

Early Career Fellowship

Purpose: The proposed research should fall within the India Alliance's remit which is to support biomedical research that is relevant to human and animal welfare. If you are unsure if your research programme falls within our remit
Eligibility: The Early Career Fellowship (ECF) competition is open for basic science/veterinary researchers with -1 to 4 years of post-PhD research experience. This means that you must be in the final year of your PhD studies or have no more than four years of postdoctoral research experience from the date of your PhD viva to the full application submission deadline in order to be eligible for the competition. Applicant must have 0-4 years Post PhD. Applicant in the final year of their PhD are also eligible. In line with the scheme's mandate to foster independence, Early Career Fellows are strongly encouraged to carry out their Fellowship project in a laboratory that is not their thesis laboratory or thesis

© Springer Nature Limited 2019
Palgrave Macmillan (ed.), *The Grants Register 2020*,
https://doi.org/10.1057/978-1-349-95943-3

environment. If you have compelling reasons to continue in or return to your thesis laboratory/environment, please present these appropriately in the preliminary application and arrange for a letter from the Fellowship Supervisor commenting on this decision

Level of Study: Postgraduate

Type: Fellowship

Length of Study: 4 years

Frequency: Annual

Country of Study: Any country

Application Procedure: To complete a preliminary application use our online system, IASys. Refer to the IASys userguide for guidance on completing the application form and the submission process. Please ensure that the form is submitted by the published deadline. Your preliminary application is assessed and If successful, you will be invited to submit a full application. Your full application will be peer reviewed and considered by the appropriate Selection Committee and, if successful, you will be short-listed for interview. Short-listed candidates will be notified two weeks before the interview date. Applicants are not permitted to apply to multiple Fellowship schemes within the India Alliance in parallel. Only one application to one scheme will be entertained, at a time

Closing Date: 31 January

Funding: Private

For further information contact:

Email: info@indiaalliance.org

India Habitat Centre

Visual Arts Galley, Lodhi Road, New Delhi 110 003, India

Tel:	(91) 11 246 820 01/05
Fax:	(91) 11 246 820 10
Email:	info@indiahabitat.org
Website:	www.indiahabitat.org

The India Habitat Centre was conceived to provide a physical environment that would serve as a catalyst for a synergetic relationship between individuals and institutions working in diverse habitat related areas and, therefore, maximize their total effectiveness.

India Habitat Centre Fellowship for Photography

Subjects: Photography

Purpose: To promote photography as an art form

Eligibility: Open to Indian nationals who are between 21 and 40 years of age and who do not hold any other fellowship

Level of Study: Professional development

Type: Fellowship

Value: Rs. 1,20,000

Frequency: Annual

Country of Study: India

Application Procedure: Applicants must send a project summary, curriculum vitae and reference letters

Closing Date: 31 August

Additional Information: Entries with less/more than the required 12 images will be eliminated

For further information contact:

Email:	alkapande@indiahabitat.org
Contact:	Dr Alka Pande

Indian Council for Cultural Relations

Azad Bhavan, I.p. Estate, New Delhi 110002, India

Contact: Indian Council for Cultural Relations

The Indian Council for Cultural Relations (ICCR), is an autonomous organisation of the Government of India, involved in India's external cultural relations, through cultural exchange with other countries and their peoples. It was founded by Maulana Abul Kalam Azad, the first Education Minister of independent India.

Indian Council for Cultural Relations Indian High Commission Bangladesh Scholarship Scheme

Subjects: Scholarship is awarded in the subjects offered by the university

Purpose: The aim of the scholarship is to support meritorious Bangladeshi nationals who want to undertake engineering, graduate, post-graduate and PhD / post-doctoral course

Eligibility: 1. Applicants from Bangladesh are eligible to apply for the scholarship. 2. Candidates who wish to get scholarships must be proficient in English and have at least 60% marks in the passed examination or 3 in GPA 5. 3. Candidates will have to take part in 30-minute English proficiency test, whose time and place will be announced

Level of Study: Graduate

Type: Scholarship

Value: The Indian government has so far given ICCR education to nearly 3,000 Bangladeshi nationals
Frequency: Annual
Study Establishment: Scholarship is awarded in the subjects offered by the university
Country of Study: India
Application Procedure: To apply online for interested students, you need to create your own private login ID and password. The applicants are requested to apply online through the instructions. The applicant should keep the following points during the application process Those BE / B Tech. Must apply for the course, in their school-college syllabus must include Physics, Mathematics and Chemistry. The applicant's age must be 18 in July. All students must stay in the hostel. Cannot be outside without family and health reasons. The last date for submission of online application is 20 January, 5.00 pm on Saturday. Candidates will have to take part in 30-minute English proficiency test, whose time and place will be announced
Closing Date: 20 January
Additional Information: For more details please see the website scholarship-positions.com/iccr-indian-high-commission-bangladesh-scholarship-scheme-india/2018/01/08/

For further information contact:

Email: admin@scholarship-positions.com

Indian Council of Medical Research

V. Ramalingaswami Bhawan, Ansari Nagar, P.O. Box No. 4911, New Delhi 110029, India

Tel: (91) 11 265 888 95 / 11 265 889 80 / 11 265 897 94
Fax: (91) 11 265 886 62
Email: icmrhqds@sansad.nic.in
Website: www.icmr.nic.in

The Indian Council of Medical Research (ICMR), New Delhi, the apex body in India for the formulation, coordination and promotion of biomedical research, is one of the oldest medical research bodies in the world.

Indian Council of Medical Research Centenary -Postdoctoral Fellowship

Subjects: These fellowships are awarded in cutting edge areas of basic science, communicable and non-communicable diseases, and reproductive health including nutrition

Purpose: The aim of the fellowships is to giving research opportunities to promising fresh PhD/ MD/MS holders
Eligibility: Indian applicants are eligible for these fellowships. Entrance Requirement: Applicants must be PhDs/ MD/MS
Type: Postdoctoral fellowship
Value: ICMR Postdoctoral Fellows will be paid a consolidated fellowship of Rs. 50,000/- per month plus house rent allowance (HRA), Non-Practicing Allowance (NPA) as admissible and a contingency grant of Rs. 3.0 lakhs per annum. 25% of the contingency grant can be used for travel including per diem expenses
Study Establishment: These fellowships are awarded in cutting edge areas of basic science, communicable and non-communicable diseases, and reproductive health including nutrition
Country of Study: India
Application Procedure: See the website
Closing Date: 31 December
Additional Information: For more details please visit our website scholarship-positions.com/icmr-centenary-postdoctoral-fellowship-india/2017/06/06/

For further information contact:

Email: icmrhqds@sansad.nic.in

Indian Education Department

Government of India, Ministry of Human Resource Department, Shastri Bhavan, New Delhi 110001, India

Tel: (91) 11 233 839 36
Fax: (91) 11 233 813 55
Email: webmaster.edu@nic.in
Website: www.education.nic.in

The origin of the Indian Education Department, Government of India, dates back to pre-independence days when for the first time a separate Department was created in 1910 to look after education. However, soon after India achieved its independence, a full fledged ministry of Education was established.

China Scholarships

Subjects: Chinese language & literature, fine arts (painting & sculpture), botany, environmental science, plant breeding & genetics, political science, sericulture and agronomy

Eligibility: Open to the Indian nationals below 40 years who have 2–3 year Cert/Dip in basic Chinese Language from a recognized Institution or University, have degree in fine arts with 60% and 60% for other subjects at postgraduate level with work research experience of 2 years

Level of Study: Graduate

Type: Scholarship

Value: The Chinese Government pays a sum of 2,000 per month to all senior advanced students, CNY 1,400 per month to ordinary graduate students and CNY 1,100 per month to undergraduate students. In addition, Government of India is paying supplementary grant of CNY 1,170 per month Government of China will also provide boarding, lodging, medical care and bear expenditure on tuition and other fees, etc

Length of Study: 1–4 years

Country of Study: Any country

Application Procedure: Applicants must send the application duly sponsored by the employers (if employed) furnishing particulars (as per notified format) by the prescribed date

Closing Date: 20 March

Contributor: Government of China in association with the government of India

For further information contact:

ES. 3 Section, Ministry of Human Resource Development, Department of Higher Education, External Scholarship Division, A1/w3, Curzon Road Barracks, KG Marg, New Delhi 110001, India

Email: scholarship@dreamgo.com
Contact: Section Officer

Erasmus Mundus Scholarship Programme

Subjects: All subjects

Purpose: For the benefit of Indian students

Eligibility: Open to Indian nationals who are graduates from recognized institutions or universities

Level of Study: Graduate

Type: Scholarships

Value: Covers airfare and living expenses

Length of Study: 1–2 years duration depending on the subject areas of study

Application Procedure: Applicants must apply directly to the universities/consortium of universities constituted under the Erasmus Mundus Programme

Closing Date: 18 February

Contributor: European Union (EU)

For further information contact:

Email: eac-info@cec.eu.int

National Centre for Promotion of Employment for Disabled People (NCPEDP) Rajiv Gandhi Postgraduate Scholarship Scheme

Subjects: Medicine, surgery, engineering, architecture, management, business administration, social work, applied psychology, clinical psychology, etc

Purpose: To enable disabled students with limited means to receive education or professional training at postgraduate and doctoral levels

Eligibility: Open to Indian nationals between 18 and 35 years of age. The scholarship may be awarded to students with the disabilities as recognized by N.C.P.E.D.P. The candidate should be either pursuing or should have gained admission to a full-time course in an Indian university established by law or in a recognized equivalent institution

Level of Study: Doctorate, Postgraduate

Type: Scholarship

Value: Rs. 1,200 per month

Frequency: Annual

Application Procedure: Applicants must apply to the National Centre for Promotion of Employment for Disabled People

Funding: Government

Additional Information: A scholarship will be provided for the entire duration of the approved course. Scholarship money will be released every 3 months. N.C.P.E.D.P. reserves the right to change the scheme and/or amend the rules without any notice. The income of the candidate or his parents/guardians should not exceed Rs. 5,000 per month. At the discretion of the awarding authority, a scholarship may also be awarded for a professional course of Indira Gandhi National Open University (IGNOU) or any other recognized Open University

For further information contact:

National Centre for Promotion of Employment for Disabled People, A-77, South Extension, Part II, New Delhi 110 049, India

Tel: (91) 11 262 656 47/48
Email: education@ncpedp.org

Indian Institute of Management Ranchi

Post-Doctoral Fellowship

Purpose: The Post-Doctoral Fellowship in Management (PDFM) is designed keeping in view IIM Ranchi's goal to create a high quality research environment in the institute. Its objective is to support high quality research by scholars with a doctoral degree and an outstanding academic record

Eligibility: 1. Contingency Grant: A contingency grant of Rs. 50,000 per annum will be provided to the post- doctoral research fellow for research purposes. 2. The IIM Ranchi would pay the expenses for a fellow to attend one conference abroad from an approved list of conferences if their joint paper with a resident faculty member is accepted for presentation at that conference. 3. Office space will be provided to post-doctoral research fellows along with a computer and printer. They will be issued special research library card, enabling them to borrow up to ten books from the library at a time. 4. A post-doctoral research fellow will be eligible for leave from the fellowship not exceeding 30 days in a year for each completed year of the fellowship. 5. The leave can be availed on a pro-rata basis for the duration (on a 6 months' basis) of the fellowship completed. The age limit for applicants for the Post-Doctoral Fellowship will be a maximum of 40 years (this limit may be relaxed by 5 years for women and reserved category)

Level of Study: Postgraduate

Type: Fellowship

Value: Contigency grants of Rs. 50,000 per annum will be provided

Length of Study: 2 years

Frequency: Annual

Country of Study: Any country

Application Procedure: 1. Selection will be based on demonstrated research skills and a fit with the research interests of resident faculty. Shortlisted candidates will be invited to campus to present their research before a final decision is made. 2. Past research I PhD thesis work demonstrating potential for scholarly work would facilitate the initial shortlist process. 3. The shortlisted candidates will be invited for on-campus presentation and interview. 4. The candidates selected for the PDFM will be attached to the given area and will be associated with a faculty member of the group who will essentially perform the role of a mentor and collaborator. 5. Selection will be based on demonstrated research skills and a fit with the research interests of resident faculty

Funding: Private

For further information contact:

Indian Institute of Management Ranchi, Suchana Bhawan, 5th Floor, Audrey House Campus, Meur's Road, Ranchi, Jharkhand 834 008, India

Tel: (91) 65 1228 0113

Indian Institute of Management, Calcutta

Diamond Harbour Road, Joka, Kolkata, West Bengal 700104, India

Contact: The Indian Institute of Management

Indian Institute of Management, Calcutta abbreviated as IIM Calcutta or IIM-C is a public business school located in Joka, Kolkata, India. It was the first Indian Institute of Management to be established.

Postdoctoral Research Fellowship (PDRF)

Purpose: These fellowships are available for researchers who want to contribute to the theory and practice of management

Eligibility: Citizens of India are eligible to apply. These positions are open for candidates with 0-2 years of experience after obtaining PhD degree

Level of Study: Doctorate

Type: Fellowship

Value: Each fellowship will carry a stipend of Rs. 40,000/p.m. consolidated, depending on the level of prior experience of the chosen candidate. In addition, a contingency grant of Rs. 50,000/- per annum will be provided

Length of Study: 2 years

Country of Study: India

Application Procedure: Fellowships are negotiable up to 3 years. Under exceptional circumstances, tenure may be extended to a maximum of 5 years

Closing Date: 30 May

No. of awards given last year: pgfunding@uct.ac.za

Additional Information: Please visit website scholarship-positions.com/postdoctoral-research-fellowships-iim-calcutta-india/2018/04/24/ for more details

Indian Institute of Science Bangalore (IISc)

The Registrar, Indian Institute of Science, Bangalore, Karnataka 560012, India

Tel: (91) 80 2360 0757
Fax: (91) 80 2360 0683/0085
Email: regr@admin.iisc.ernet.in
Website: www.iisc.ernet.in
Contact: The Registrar

The Indian Institute of Science (IISc) was started in 1909 through the pioneering vision of J N Tata. Since then, it has grown into a premier institution of research and advanced instruction, with more than 2,000 active researchers working in almost all frontier areas of science and technology.

Indian Institute of Science Bangalore Kishore Vaigyanik Protsahan Yojana Fellowships

Subjects: Science, engineering and medicine
Purpose: To assist students in realizing their potential and to ensure that the best scientific talent is developed for research and growth in the country
Eligibility: Open to Indian citizens
Level of Study: Graduate, Postdoctorate, Postgraduate, Predoctorate, Research
Type: Fellowship
Value: Rs. 4,000–7,000 per month and contingency grants of Rs. 16,000–28,000
Frequency: Annual
Study Establishment: Indian Institute of Science, Bangalore
Country of Study: India
Application Procedure: Applicants can download the application form from the website
Closing Date: September

For further information contact:

Indian Institute of Science, CV Raman Rd, Bengaluru, Karnataka 560012, India

Tel:	(91) 80 2360 1008/80 2293 2976
Email:	kvpy@admin.iisc.ernet.in
Contact:	The Convener

Indian Institute of Technology (IIT)

Department of Computer Science and Engineering, Kanpur, Uttar Pradesh 208016, India

Tel:	(91) 512 259 7338/7638
Fax:	(91) 512 259 7586
Email:	pgadm@cse.iitk.ac.in
Website:	www.cse.iitk.ac.in
Contact:	Harish Karnick, Professor and Head

Indian Institute of Technology (IIT) imparts training to students to make them competent, motivated engineers and scientists. The Institute not only celebrates freedom of thought, cultivates vision and encourages growth, but also inculcates human values and concern for the environment and the society.

Infosys Fellowship for PhD Students

Subjects: Computer science and engineering
Purpose: To support those interested in pursuing the PhD programme in the Department of Computer Science and Engineering at IIT Kanpur
Eligibility: Open to deserving students who have a MTech/ME in any branch of engineering and who have secured admission into the PhD programme
Level of Study: Postgraduate
Type: Fellowship
Value: Rs. 2,25,000 and Rs. 2,50,000 per year. Out of this grant, Rs. 1,80,000 (Rs. 15,000 per month) will paid as stipend, remaining money can be utilized by the fellow for purchase of books, journals, payment of tuition fee, and travel for domestic and international conference attendance
Length of Study: 3.5–4 years
Frequency: Annual
Study Establishment: IIT Kanpur
Country of Study: India
Application Procedure: The applicant must submit a separate application form to the Department of Computer Science and Engineering. Please check at www.cse.iitk.ac.in

For further information contact:

Email:	pgadm@cse.iitk.ac.in
Contact:	Admissions In-Charge (PhD) Computer science and engineering department, Indian Institute of Technology

Indian Institute of Technology Kharagpur

IT Kharagpur Post Doctoral Fellowship

Purpose: IIT Kharagpur is giving an excellent platform for the students possessing PhD degree with an excellent academic record by offering them IIT Kharagpur Post Doctoral Fellowship. The main objective of this fellowship is to give an opportunity to deserving scholars to carry out their research in the field of science and technology
Eligibility: 1. Must hold PhD Degree with the outstanding academic record. 2. Must have published research paper / patents on his/her name. 3. Age limit of a candidate is 35 years. 4. The candidates who are belonging to AICTE / UGC recognized teaching institution or sponsored by DISR recognized industrial organization they will get age relaxation up to 45 years of age

Level of Study: Postdoctorate
Type: Fellowship
Value: Rs. 25,000
Frequency: Annual
Country of Study: India
Closing Date: 31 December
Funding: Foundation

For further information contact:

Email: info@vidhyaa.in

Indian Institute of Technology Ropar

Nangal Road, Rupnagar, Punjab 140001, India

Contact: Indian Institute of Technology Ropar

The Indian Institute of Technology Ropar (IIT Ropar) or IIT-RPR, is an engineering and technology higher education institute located in Rupnagar, Punjab, India. It is one of the eight newer Indian Institutes of Technology (IITs) established by the Ministry of Human Resource Development MHRD, Government of India under The Institutes of Technology (Amendment) Act.

Indian Institute of Technology Ropar Institute Postdoctoral Fellowship

Subjects: Fellowship is awarded in the subjects offered by the university
Purpose: The aim of the fellowship is to support Indian students and provide a contingency grant of Rs. 1,00,000/- per annum to the Post-Doctoral Fellow for research purposes. The unspent amount can be carried over to the next financial year
Eligibility: Applicants from India are eligible to apply for the fellowship. Applicants must hold a PhD degree
Value: please see the website
Study Establishment: Fellowship is awarded in the subjects offered by the university
Country of Study: Any country
Application Procedure: The application has to be submitted to the Department/Center in which the candidate intends to join as a Post Doctoral Fellow. Applicants can apply through the post and submit the application form to the Department/Center. Applicants can apply by rolling basis

Additional Information: For more information please browse the website scholarship-positions.com/iit-ropar-institute-post-doctoral-fellowship-for-indian-students/2017/11/11/

For further information contact:

Email: admin@scholarship-positions.com

Indian School of Business

Knowledge City, Sector 81, SAS Nagar, Mohali, Punjab 140 306, India

Tel: (91) 172 459 0000
Contact: Indian School of Business

Indian School of Business is a private business school with campuses in Hyderabad, Telangana, India and Mohali, Punjab, India. The institute has various Management programs with the Post Graduate Program in Management as its flagship course.

Indian Health Service Health Professions Scholarship Program

Purpose: The student must apply annually to request continued scholarship support until he/she has earned his/her degree and is eligible to pursue post-graduate clinical training or begin his/her Indian health career
Eligibility: 1. All applicants must intend to serve Indian people as a health professional in their chosen specialties. 2. They must also be willing to sign an IHS Scholarship Program Contract when accepting the scholarship. 3. By signing, the student agrees to fulfill a minimum two-year service commitment in full-time clinical practice at an Indian health facility in his/her chosen health profession after completing his/her academic or post-graduate clinical training. 4. The student must apply annually to request continued scholarship support until he/she has earned his/her degree and is eligible to pursue post-graduate clinical training or begin his/her Indian health career
Level of Study: Postgraduate
Type: Scholarship
Value: US$1,500
Frequency: Annual
Country of Study: Any country

Application Procedure: The IHS Scholarship Program awards scholarships based on a 100-point ranking system divided among three categories: academic performance, based on official transcripts (40 points); faculty/employer evaluations (30 points); and applicant essays (30 points)
Closing Date: 28 March
Funding: Private

Indian School of Business Funded Tuition Waivers at Indian School of Business

Subjects: Scholarships are awarded in the field of Business
Purpose: The Post Graduate Programme in Management (PGP) is designed for those who want to transform their careers by expanding their existing thought process and refining their goals and objectives
Eligibility: Citizens of all nationalities are eligible to apply. Students whose first language is not English must demonstrate proficiency in English by submitting satisfactory scores from the Test of English as a Foreign Language (TOEFL)
Type: Postgraduate scholarships
Value: These waivers vary in amount from Rs. 5 Lakh to full tuition fee and are disbursed either on merit or need-based criteria. These scholarships are awarded to candidates during admission or after enrolment, at the discretion of the AdCom or the corporate donor
Study Establishment: Scholarships are awarded in the field of Business
Country of Study: India
Application Procedure: These scholarships are awarded to candidates during admission or after enrolment, at the discretion of the AdCom or the corporate donor
Closing Date: 15 January
Additional Information: For more details please browse the website scholarship-positions.com/isb-funded-tuition-waivers-indian-school-business-india/2017/10/28/

For further information contact:

Email: admin@scholarship-positions.com

Indian Veterinary Research Institute

Izatnagar, Bareilly, Uttar Pradesh 243122, India

Contact: The Indian Veterinary Research Institute

The Indian Veterinary Research Institute (IVRI) is located at Izatnagar, Bareilly in Uttar Pradesh state. It is India's premier advanced research facility in the field of veterinary medicine and allied branches.

Scholarships at Indian Veterinary Research Institute

Subjects: Scholarships are awarded to study the subjects offered by the university
Purpose: The Indian Veterinary Research Institute (IVRI) is offering scholarships for MVSc and PhD students. The duration of scholarship for MVSc course will be of two years and scholarship for the PhD course will be of three years
Eligibility: Students from India are eligible to apply. The candidates for admission to Master's programme must have Bachelor's Degree in Veterinary Science in the concerned discipline as specified by the Veterinary Council of India with a minimum of 60% marks in aggregate (55% for SC/ST or sponsored candidates) or equivalent CGPA
Type: Postgraduate scholarships
Value: The amount of the scholarship for Master's Degree programme is Rs. 7,560/- per month for 2 years with a contingent grant of Rs. 6,000/- per annum for two years and for Doctoral programme, it is Rs. 13,125/- per month for three years with a contingent grant of Rs. 10,000/- per annum for three years
Study Establishment: Scholarships are awarded to study the subjects offered by the university
Country of Study: India
Application Procedure: See the website
Closing Date: Open
Additional Information: For more details please visit our website scholarship-positions.com/scholarships-indian-veterinary-research-institute/2017/11/18/

For further information contact:

Email: sao_unitone@ivri.res.in

Indira Gandhi Institute of Development Research

Film City Road, IGIDR, Nagri Niwara, Cooperative Housing Society, Goregaon East, Mumbai, Maharashtra 400065, India

Contact: Indira Gandhi Institute of Development Research

Indira Gandhi Institute of Development Research (IGIDR) is an advanced research institute established and fully funded by the Reserve Bank of India for carrying out research on development issues from a multi-disciplinary point of view.

Indira Gandhi Institute of Development Research-International Development Research Centre Scholarships and Fellowships for Asian Countries Students

Subjects: Scholarships and fellowships are awarded in the field of labor market and industrial policy

Purpose: The aims and objectives of the Institute are to promote and conduct research on developmental issues from a broad inter- disciplinary perspective (economic, technological, social, political and ecological)

Eligibility: Scholarship is open for citizens of the following Asian countries: Afghanistan, Bangladesh, Bhutan, Cambodia, Indonesia, Malaysia, Maldives, Myanmar, Nepal, Philippines, Sri Lanka, Thailand and Vietnam

Type: Postdoctoral fellowship

Value: Selected scholar will be paid a scholarship of Rs. 100,000 per month, One round trip travel expense up to a maximum of Rs. 50,000, fixed medical coverage of Rs. 25,000, book grant of Rs. 50,000, research grant of Rs. 1,00,000, and conference travel support up to a maximum of Rs. 1,50,000

Study Establishment: Scholarships and fellowships are awarded in the field of labor market and industrial policy

Country of Study: India

Application Procedure: See the website

Closing Date: 30 April

Additional Information: For more details please browse the website scholarship-positions.com/igidr-idrc-scholarships-and-fellowships-asian-countries-students-2015/2014/12/27/

For further information contact:

Email: asianhub@igidr.ac.in

IndusInd Foundation

IndusInd Foundation Scholarship For Postgraduate Students

Purpose: The IndusInd Foundation has invited applications from meritorious students studying in a degree course under the IndusInd Foundation Scholarship

Eligibility: 1. The student must have passed class 12 board or equivalent exam from an approved board/university with minimum 80% marks. 2. The student must have taken admission to any of regular degree courses in Science, Arts, Commerce, Eng., Medical, Computer, Mgt. etc. in an approved college/institute to any recognized university in India. 3. The student's family financial income should justify the grant of scholarship

Level of Study: Postdoctorate

Type: Scholarship

Value: Rs. 2,200

Frequency: Annual

Country of Study: Any country

Closing Date: 30 September

Funding: Foundation

For further information contact:

The Trustee, IndusInd Foundation, Hinduja House, 171, Dr Annie Besant Road, Worli, Mumbai, 400018, India

Email: info@vidhyaa.in

Innovation and Entrepreneurship Development Centre Bled School of Management

Prešernova cesta 33, SVN 4260 Bled, Slovenia

Tel: (386) 457 92 500
Fax: (386) 457 92 501
Email: info@iedc.si
Website: www.iedc.si

The school is a center of excellence in management development and a business meeting point, where leaders and potential leaders come to learn and reflect. We offer a unique environment for developing leadership and management potential of international business executives at every stage of their careers.

Innovation and Entrepreneurship Development Centre MBA Scholarship

Subjects: Business management

Purpose: To finance an MBA programme for outstanding candidates from Moldova and Ukraine

Eligibility: Only outstanding candidates from Moldova and Ukraine will be considered

Level of Study: Professional development

Value: All tuition fees

Length of Study: 1 year
Frequency: Annual
Study Establishment: IEDC
Application Procedure: See website
Closing Date: 30 October

For further information contact:

Tel: (386) 457 92 506
Email: emba@iedc.si

Trimo MBA Scholarship

Subjects: International business
Purpose: To finance an outstanding candidate from Serbia
Eligibility: The candidate must be from Serbia
Level of Study: Professional development
Type: Scholarship
Value: All tuition fees and agreed costs
Length of Study: 1 year
Frequency: Annual
Study Establishment: IEDC
Application Procedure: See website
Closing Date: 1 December
Funding: Corporation
Contributor: Trimo d.d. Slovenia
Additional Information: The successful candidate will be offered a position at Trimo Inženjering d.o.o Serbia

For further information contact:

Tel: (386) 457 92 506
Email: emba@iedc.si

Institut de Recherche Robert-Sauvé en Santé et en Sécurité du Travail (IRSST)

505, De Maisonneuve Ouest, Montréal, QC H3A 3C2, Canada

Tel: (1) 514 288 1551
Fax: (1) 514 288 7636
Email: grants@irsst.qc.ca
Website: www.irsst.qc.ca

Institut de Recherche Robert-Sauvé en Santé et en Sécurité du Travail (IRSST), established in Quebec since 1980, is a scientific research organization known for the quality of its work and the expertise of its personnel. The Institute is a private, non-profit agency.

Institut de Recherche Robert-Sauvé en Santé et en Sécurité du Travail Graduate Studies Scholarship and postdoctoral Fellowship Program

Subjects: Occupational health and safety
Purpose: To support Master's and doctoral students who wish to acquire research training in the occupational health and safety field
Eligibility: Open to students who are registered full-time in a Master's or doctoral programme and have obtained a cumulative average of B+ for all of their undergraduate studies
Level of Study: Doctorate, Postgraduate
Type: Scholarship
Value: $14,250 per year. In addition, a scholarship recipient whose training and research program is outside Canada is reimbursed for the amount exceeding the first $750 in annual tuition fees; the cost of travelling to the training and research location, representing the cost of one round-trip economy airplane ticket or one round trip by car, for each year of the effective period of the scholarship (maximum of 2 years)
Length of Study: 2–3 years
Frequency: Annual
Closing Date: July
Contributor: The Commission des normes, de l'équité, de la santé et de la sécurité du travail provides most of the Institute's funding from the contributions it collects from the employers
Additional Information: Please check the website for further details

For further information contact:

Tel: (1) 514 288 1551 ext. 377
Email: bourses@irsst.qc.ca
Contact: Michel Asselin, Research advisor Coordinator of the Graduate Scholarship Program

Institut Européen d'Administration des Affaires

Boulevard de Constance, F-77305 Fontainebleau Cedex, France

Tel: (33) 1 60 72 40 00
Fax: (33) 1 60 74 55 00
Email: mba.europe@insead.edu
Website: www.insead.edu/mba
Contact: Ms Irina Schneider-Maunoury, Senior Manager, MBA Financing

INSEAD is widely recognized as one of the most influential business school in the world. With its second campus in Asia to complement its established presence in Europe, INSEAD is setting the pace in globalizing the MBA. The 1-year intensive MBA programme is focused on international general management.

Institut Européen d'Administration des Affaires Goldman Sachs Scholarship for African Nationals

Purpose: The Goldman Sachs scholarships for African nationals at INSEAD is designed to give candidates from African countries access to a world-class MBA education. The scholarship winners will be allocated a Goldman Sachs mentor throughout the 10-month MBA programme
Eligibility: The scholarship is open to all candidates from African countries studying at INSEAD on the Full-time MBA Programme. Successful candidates must demonstrate their desire to work in Africa and explain why building business in Africa is important to them
Type: Scholarship
Value: Up to €15,000 per class
Frequency: Annual
Country of Study: Any country
Application Procedure: For further information, kindly refer the official link. www.insead.edu/
Closing Date: 13 February for the July class (starts in September); 22 August for the December class (starts in January)
Additional Information: Please check website for further information

For further information contact:

Email: mba.europe@insead.edu

Institut Européen d'Administration des Affaires Jewish Scholarship

Subjects: MBA
Purpose: An INSEAD alumnus offers scholarships to Jewish students admitted to the INSEAD MBA Programme; a limited number of small awards are made each year. In keeping with the spirit and tradition behind this award, the winners are encouraged to give back by making their own donation to scholarships at INSEAD through the Alumni Fund within a few years after graduation
Eligibility: Jewish students who can justify difficulty in raising sufficient finances for their living expenses
Type: Scholarship
Value: Up to €5,000
Frequency: Annual

Country of Study: Any country
Closing Date: 13 February each year for the July class (starts in September); 22 August each year for the December class (starts in January)
Additional Information: Please check website for further information

For further information contact:

Email: mba.europe@insead.edu

Institut Européen d'Administration des Affaires MBA Programme

Subjects: MBA
Length of Study: 10 months
Application Procedure: Applicants must complete an application form supplying a euro 110 fee, photograph, essay, two letters of recommendation, transcripts of grades, Graduate Management Admission Test score, TOEFL score and self addressed acknowledgment card
Closing Date: 1 February for Autumn intake (Fontainebleu campus only) and 2 July for January intake (Fontainebleau and Singapore campuses)

For further information contact:

MBA Admissions Office Boulevard de Constance, Boulevard de Constance, 77300 Fontainebleau, France

Tel: (33) 1 60 72 42 73
Fax: (33) 1 60 74 55 30
Email: mba.info@insead.fr
Contact: Ms Helen Henderson

Institut Européen d'Administration des Affaires Nelson Mandela Endowment Scholarships

Subjects: Masters in Business Administration (MBA)
Purpose: To honour the life and work of President Nelson Mandela of South Africa, the INSEAD MBA Class of 75 created the INSEAD Nelson Mandela Endowment Scholarships at their 30th Class Reunion to provide financial support for one or more African participants per year at INSEAD in perpetuity
Eligibility: To be eligible for the Nelson Mandela Endowed Scholarship, candidates must be a national of a sub-Saharan African country and have spent a substantial part of their lives and received part of their prior education in Africa. Preference will be given to candidates who require proven financial assistance
Level of Study: Postgraduate

Type: Scholarship
Value: Up to €20,000
Country of Study: Africa
Closing Date: 19 April and 6 June
Funding: Government
Contributor: INSEAD
Additional Information: For more details, visit official scholarship website: mba.insead.edu/schlmgmt/dsp_schl_info.cfm?schlcode=AFR02

For further information contact:

Email: mba.europe@insead.edu

Institut Français d'Amérique

Department of History, CB# 3195, Chapel Hill, NC 27599-3195, United States of America

Tel: (1) 919 962 2115
Fax: (1) 919 962 1403
Email: IFA@unc.edu
Website: institut.unc.edu/
Contact: Professor Jay Smith

The mission of the Institut Français de Washington is to promote the American study of French culture, language, history and society, and to encourage the work of teachers, scholars and students in these fields. The Institute also sponsors events to foster public understanding of French-American relations. The IFW provides funds for fellowships, prizes, and conferences that serve this mission.

Edouard Morot-Sir Fellowship in French Studies

Subjects: French studies in the areas of art, economics, history, history of science, linguistics, literature or social sciences
Eligibility: Open to those in the final stages of a PhD dissertation or who have held a PhD for no longer than 3 years before the application deadline
Level of Study: Doctorate, Postdoctorate
Type: Fellowship
Value: US$1,500
Length of Study: At least 1 month
Frequency: Annual
Country of Study: France

No. of awards offered: 90
Application Procedure: Applicants must write a maximum of two pages describing the research project and planned trip and enclose a curriculum vitae. A letter of recommendation from the dissertation director is required and a letter from a specialist in the field for assistant professors
Closing Date: 15 January
Funding: Private, Foundation
No. of awards given last year: 3
No. of applicants last year: 90
Additional Information: Awards are for maintenance during research in France and should not be used for travel. Please check website institut.unc.edu/application/ for further information. Applications should be sent by email

For further information contact:

Email: IFA@unc.edu

Gilbert Chinard Fellowships

Subjects: French studies in the areas of art, economics, history, history of science, linguistics, literature or social sciences
Eligibility: Open to those in the final stages of a PhD dissertation or who have held a PhD for no longer than 3 years before the application deadline
Level of Study: Doctorate, Postdoctorate
Type: Fellowship
Value: US$1,500
Length of Study: At least 1 month
Frequency: Annual
Country of Study: France
No. of awards offered: 28
Application Procedure: Applicants must write a maximum of two pages describing the research project and planned trip and enclose a curriculum vitae. A letter of recommendation from the dissertation director is also required for PhD candidates and a letter from a specialist in the field for assistant professors
Closing Date: 15 January
Funding: Private
No. of awards given last year: 1
No. of applicants last year: 28
Additional Information: Awards are for maintenance during research in France and should not be used for travel. Applications should be sent by email

For further information contact:

Email: IFA@unc.edu

Harmon Chadbourn Rorison Fellowship

Subjects: French studies in the areas of art, economics, history, history of science, linguistics, literature or social sciences
Eligibility: Open to those in the final stages of a PhD dissertation or who have held a PhD for no longer than 3 years before the application deadline
Level of Study: Doctorate, Postdoctorate, Postgraduate
Type: Fellowship
Value: US$1,500
Length of Study: At least 1 month
Frequency: Every 2 years
Country of Study: France
No. of awards offered: 27
Application Procedure: Applicants must write a maximum of two pages describing the research project and planned trip and enclose a curriculum vitae. A letter of recommendation from the dissertation director is required for PhD candidates and a letter from a specialist in the field for assistant professors
Closing Date: 15 January
Funding: Private, Foundation
No. of awards given last year: 1
No. of applicants last year: 27
Additional Information: Awards are for maintenance during research in France and should not be used for travel. Applications should be sent by email

For further information contact:

Email: IFA@unc.edu

Institute for Advanced Studies in the Humanities

The Institute for Advanced Studies in the Humanities, The University of Edinburgh, Hope Park Square, Edinburgh, EH8 9NW, Scotland, United Kingdom

Tel: (44) 131 650 4671
Email: iash@ed.ac.uk
Contact: The Secretary

The Institute for Advanced Studies in the Humanities was established in 1969 to promote interdisciplinary research in the arts, humanities and social sciences at the University of Edinburgh. It provides an international, interdisciplinary and autonomous space for discussion and debate.

Institute for Advanced Studies in the Humanities (The Institute for Advanced Studies in the Humanities)-SSPS (School of Social and Political Science) Research Fellowships

Subjects: Arts, humanities and social sciences
Purpose: The IASH-SSPS Research Fellowships are intended to encourage outstanding interdisciplinary research, international scholarly collaboration, and networking activities of visiting Research Fellows together with academics in the School of Social and Political Science (SSPS)
Eligibility: For eligibility criteria, please visit website scholarship-positions.com/iash-ssps-research-fellowships-international-students-uk/2018/04/03/
Value: Funds are available in support of travel (£500) and accommodation costs (approximately £1,250-£3,750)
Country of Study: Any country
Application Procedure: Apply online. Go to website www.iash.ed.ac.uk/application-form for online application
Closing Date: 28 February
Contributor: The Institute for Advanced Studies in the Humanities
Additional Information: For more details, visit www.iash.ed.ac.uk/iash-ssps-research-fellowships

For further information contact:

Email: iash@ed.ac.uk

Institute for Advanced Studies on Science, Technology and Society (IAS-STS)

Kopernikusgasse 9, AUT 8010, Graz, Austria

Tel: (43) 316 813909 34
Fax: (43) 316 810274
Email: info@sts.tugraz.at
Website: www.sts.tugraz.at
Contact: Günter Getzinger, Acting Director

In 1999 the Inter University Research Centre for Technology, Work and Culture (IFZ) launched the IAS-STS in Graz, Austria. It promotes the interdisciplinary investigation of the links and interaction between science, technology and society as well as research on the development and implementation of socially and environmentally sound, sustainable technologies.

Institute for Advanced Studies on Science, Technology and Society Fellowship Programme

Subjects: Gender (technology and environment), technology studies, information and communication technologies and society, technology assessment, participatory technology design, sustainable consumption and production, genetics and biotechnology, energy and climate
Purpose: To give the students the opportunity to explore issues
Eligibility: Applicants must hold an academic degree
Level of Study: Doctorate, Postdoctorate, Postgraduate, Research
Type: Fellowships
Value: €940 per month
Length of Study: Up to 9 months
Frequency: Annual
Study Establishment: IAS-STS
Country of Study: Austria
No. of awards offered: 50
Application Procedure: Application forms can be download from the website
Closing Date: 30 June
Funding: Government
Contributor: Styrian Government
No. of awards given last year: 5
No. of applicants last year: 50

For further information contact:

Email: info@sts.tugraz.at

Institute for Advanced Study (IAS) Technical University of Munich

Rudolf Diesel Industry Fellowship

Purpose: It is the Fellowship's purpose to enhance collaboration and knowledge-sharing between research units at TUM and company research laboratories. To increase international collaboration, TUM-IAS especially welcomes applications from companies from outside Germany
Eligibility: 1. a nomination letter including a description of the facilities provided for the Fellow by the TUM Host institute. 2. a CV including a list of publications. 3. a statement of purpose jointly signed by the candidate and the hosting professor, describing the content of the. 4. joint research, its innovative potential and the concrete implementation plans (budget), including any planned. 5. events to enhance the Institute's intellectual environment
Level of Study: Postgraduate

Type: Fellowship
Value: UM-IAS encourages the company to contribute funding for a doctoral candidate to the project, which would then be jointly mentored and advised by the TUM Host professor and the Rudolf Diesel Industry Fellow
Frequency: Annual
Country of Study: Any country
Application Procedure: Please submit the following application documents: 1. a nomination letter including a description of the facilities provided for the Fellow by the TUM Host institute. 2. a CV (no more than 5 pages) and a list of publications. 3. a statement of purpose jointly signed by the candidate and the hosting professor, describing the content of the joint research, its innovative potential and the concrete implementation plans. This statement should also include. 4. a budget plan. 5. a time plan regarding the candidate's projected periods of stay at TUM. 6. an identification of possible additional (interdisciplinary) collaboration partners both within TUM-IAS and within TUM as well as a short explanation as to why this collaboration would be beneficial. 7. an outline for an international, ideally interdisciplinary workshop/colloquium, to be organized during the active Fellowship period. 8. a letter of nomination from the Dean of the hosting faculty or another member of the EHP or Board of Trustees
Closing Date: 24 October
Funding: Private

For further information contact:

Lichtenbergstraße 2 a, DEU 85748 Garching bei München, Germany

Tel: (49) 89 289 10550
Email: info@tum-ias.de

Institute for Labour Market Policy Evaluation (IFAU)

Box 513, SWE S751-20, Uppsala, Sweden

Tel: (46) 184 717 070
Fax: (46) 184 717 071
Email: ifau@ifau.uu.se
Website: www.ifau.se

The Institute for Labour Market Policy Evaluation (IFAU) is a research institute under the Swedish Ministry of industry, employment and communications. IFAU's objective is to promote, support and carry out evaluations of the effects of labour market policies, studies of the functioning of the labour market and evaluations of the labour market effects of measures within the educational system.

Institute for Labour Market Policy Evaluation Post Doctoral Scholarship

Subjects: Labour market policy
Purpose: To evaluate measures motivated by labour market policy
Eligibility: Open to candidates who have recently obtained a PhD degree in economics or another social science and are EU nationals (not Sweden) or non-EU nationals if they have been resident in the EU (not Sweden) for more than 4 out of the last 5 years
Level of Study: Postdoctorate
Type: Scholarship
Value: €52,029 per year with a mobility allowance of €550 per month for single and €886 for researchers with a partner and/or children
Length of Study: 1 year
Frequency: Annual
Application Procedure: Applicants can download the application form from the website. The completed application form must be sent along with a curriculum vitae, names and addresses of 3 referees, a research paper (or link) and a research proposal (not more than 3 pages)

For further information contact:

Email: Cecilia.Andersson@ifau.uu.se
Contact: Cecilia Andersson

Institute for South ASIA Studies UC Berkeley

Berreman-Yamanaka award for Himalayan studies

Purpose: The Berreman-Yamanaka Fellowship for Himalayan Studies' provides for an annual award of up to $1500 to UC Berkeley graduate students for research on topics related to Himalayan Studies across Bhutan, India, Nepal and Pakistan
Level of Study: Graduate
Type: Award
Value: US$1,500
Frequency: Annual
Country of Study: Any country
Closing Date: 15 April
Funding: Foundation

For further information contact:

Email: pkala@berkeley.edu

Bhattacharya Graduate Fellowship

Purpose: The Bhattacharya Graduate Fellowship will award UC Berkeley graduate students competitive grants for topics related to contemporary India
Level of Study: Graduate
Type: Fellowship
Value: $1,000
Frequency: Annual
Country of Study: Any country
Closing Date: 15 April
Funding: Foundation

For further information contact:

Email: pkala@berkeley.edu

Bodha Pravaham Fellowship

Purpose: The Bodha Pravaham Undergraduate Fellowship for Tamil Studies, established with a generous contribution from Professor George Hart and Professor Kausalya Hart, both cornerstones of Tamil Studies at UC Berkeley, supports undergraduate students pursuing research projects focusing on Tamil studies
Level of Study: Graduate
Type: Fellowship
Value: $900
Length of Study: 1 year
Frequency: Annual
Country of Study: Any country
Closing Date: 15 April
Funding: Foundation

For further information contact:

Email: pkala@berkeley.edu

Hart Fellowship

Purpose: The Hart Fellowship for Tamil Studies, established with a generous contribution from Professor George Hart and Professor Kausalya Hart, both cornerstones of Tamil Studies at UC Berkeley, supports graduate students pursuing research projects focusing on Tamil studies
Level of Study: Graduate
Type: Fellowship

Value: $2,000
Length of Study: 1 year
Frequency: Annual
Country of Study: Any country
Closing Date: 1 February
Funding: Foundation

For further information contact:

Email: pkala@berkeley.edu

International Affairs Fellowship in India

Purpose: The Council on Foreign Relations International Affairs Fellowship (IAF) in India, sponsored by Bharti, seeks to strengthen mutual understanding and cooperation between rising generations of leaders and thinkers in the United States and India. The program provides for one to four mid-career United States professionals, who have had little or no substantial prior experience in India, the opportunity to spend three to twelve months conducting research and working in India. Fellows are drawn from academia, business, government, journalism, NGOs, and think tanks. While in India, fellows develop a new professional network as well as gain fresh insights and perspectives into the country and the opportunities and challenges that confront the region. CFR will work with its network of contacts to assist selected fellows in finding suitable host organizations that best match the fellow's proposed work in India. Possible placements include but are not limited to the CFR's local partner, the Centre for Policy Research; the Institute for Defense Studies and Analyses; or the Centre for Insurance and Risk Management
Eligibility: 1. Applicants must be United States citizens. 2. Applicants must be mid-career professionals. 3. Applicants must possess a strong record of professional achievement. 4. Applicants must hold at least a bachelor's degree
Level of Study: Graduate
Type: Fellowship
Value: $90,000
Length of Study: 1 year
Frequency: Annual
Country of Study: Any country
Closing Date: 28 February
Funding: Foundation

For further information contact:

Email: fellowships@cfr.org

International Studies Research Lab

Purpose: The Center for Global Studies at the University of Illinois, Urbana-Champaign, is pleased to announce funding to support the internationalization of community colleges nationwide. We invite applications from faculty, librarians, and administrators interested in expanding global studies curricula, instruction in less commonly taught languages, library collections, or international education programs at their home institutions. Projects for minority-serving institutions are particularly welcome. During their stay, Fellows can work one-on-one with international and area studies reference librarians and explore the unlimited print and online resources of the University of Illinois Library
Eligibility: Applicants must be faculty or administrators at 2-year community colleges or 4-year universities that offer associate degrees. The Center for Global Studies encourages applications particularly from minority-serving institutions. While fellowships that cover housing and parking will be reserved to applicants from outside of the Champaign-Urbana area, all participants will be eligible to receive research honoraria
Level of Study: Graduate
Type: Fellowship
Frequency: Annual
Country of Study: Any country
Application Procedure: Apply online: forms.illinois.edu/sec/5427515
Closing Date: 15 May
Funding: Foundation

For further information contact:

Lynne Rudasill Global Studies Librarian, Center for Global Studies 306 International Studies Building, M/C 402 uiuc campus mail, IL 00001, United States of America

Email: rudasill@illinois.edu

Maharaj Kaul Memorial Trust

Purpose: UC Berkeley graduate students are invited to apply for competitive grants of up to $1000 for research travel to South Asia (a total of two will be awarded), and up to $500 for conference travel (a total of two will be awarded) made available through a gift from the Maharaj Kaul Memorial Fund to the Institute for South Asia Studies
Level of Study: Graduate
Type: Grant
Value: $1,000
Frequency: Annual
Country of Study: Any country
Closing Date: 1 February
Funding: Foundation

For further information contact:

Email: pkala@berkeley.edu

Outstanding Paper Prize

Purpose: The Subir and Malini Chowdhury Center for Bangladesh Studies welcomes submissions for the Outstanding Paper Prize in Bangladesh Studies. Submissions are welcome from any discipline, though preference will be given to papers in a social science field

Eligibility: 1. Full time UC Berkeley graduate students or undergraduates with upperclass standing. 2. Students must have been registered as a full time student at any accredited university. 3. Papers must be linked to a course for undergraduates, must be linked to a departmental thesis program

Level of Study: Graduate
Type: Grant
Value: $500
Frequency: Annual
Country of Study: Any country
Closing Date: 15 April
Funding: Foundation

For further information contact:

The Subir & Malini Chowdhury Center Institute for South Asia Studies UC Berkeley 10 Stephens Hall, Berkeley, CA 94720-2310, United States of America

Email: chowdhury-center@berkeley.edu

South Asia Program Junior Fellowship

Purpose: The one-year, full-time fellowship will provide individuals with a unique opportunity to expand their knowledge of security issues in the subcontinent, engage the South Asia policy community in Washington and the region, and experience working at a dynamic think tank that provides close interaction with senior staff and researchers

Eligibility: 1. A strong background in: South Asian political, economic, or security issues; strategic studies; international relations theory; or economics. 2. Demonstrated analytical, research, and writing skills. 3. Ability to work independently and to collaborate with peers in a team environment. 4. Bachelor's degree. All applicants must be eligible to work in the United States for the full twelve months of the fellowship following graduation

Level of Study: Graduate
Type: Fellowship
Value: $37,000
Length of Study: 1 year
Frequency: Annual
Country of Study: Any country
Closing Date: 27 February
Funding: Foundation

For further information contact:

Email: southasiaadmin@stimson.org

Institute for Supply Management (ISM)

2055 E. Centennial Circle, Tempe, AZ 85285-2160, United States of America

Tel:	(1) 480 752 6276
Fax:	(1) 480 752 7890
Email:	ssturzl@ism.ws
Website:	www.ism.ws
Contact:	Valerie Gryniewicz, Manager, Education

The Institute for Supply Management (ISM) is a non-profit association that provides national and international leadership in purchasing and supply management research and education. ISM provides more than 40,000 members with opportunities to expand their professional skills and knowledge.

Institute for Supply Management Professional Research Development Grant

Purpose: This program is designed to support assistants and young associate professor with terminal degree that are teaching in the field of a significant research track in supply management and associated areas. The goal is to help competitively selected faculty build a research and publication field and establish themselves in the profession (i.e. academic institutions, professional organisation, research fund granting bodies such as CAPS Research etc.). This would include CAPS research. Faculty selected will generally have 2 and 8 years of teaching and research experience and have successful publication experiments beyond the doctoral degree

Eligibility: Open to assistant professors, associate professors or equivalent who have demonstrated exceptional academic productivity in research and teaching. Candidates are chosen from those who can help produce useful research that can be applied to the advancement of purchasing and supply management. Candidates must be full-time faculty members within or outside the United States of America and be present or past members of ISM committees, groups, forums or affiliated organizations. An assistant professor should have 3 or more years of post-degree experience. Previous awardees are ineligible

Level of Study: Postdoctorate
Type: Grant

Value: US$10,000
Frequency: Annual
Country of Study: United States of America
No. of awards offered: 5–10
Application Procedure: (1) Letter of application explaining qualifications of the grant. (2) Research proposal of no more than five pages, including problem statement or hypothesis; research methodology, with data sources, collection and analysis; and value to the field of supply management. (3) Curriculum vitae, including works in progress
Closing Date: 30 January
Funding: Private
Contributor: ISM
No. of awards given last year: 1
No. of applicants last year: 5–10
Additional Information: It is expected that the recipients will present the results of their research at an ISM forum, e.g. research symposium, ISM Annual International Purchasing Conference and/or an ISM publication such as The Journal of Supply Chain Management

For further information contact:

c/o Robert A Kemp, PhD, CPM, Institute for Supply Management, Tempe, AZ PO Box 22160, United States of America

Email: kempr@mchsi.com
Contact: ISM Doctoral Grant Committee

Institute of Advanced Legal Studies (IALS)

Institute of Advanced Legal Studies, Charles Clore House, 17 Russell Square, WC1B 5DR, London, United Kingdom

Tel: (44) 20 7862 5800
Fax: (44) 20 7862 5850
Email: ials.administrator@sas.ac.uk
Website: www.ials.sas.ac.uk
Contact: Margaret Wilson, Institute Manager

The Institute of Advanced Legal Studies (IALS) plays a national and international role in the promotion and facilitation of legal research. It possesses one of the leading research libraries in Europe and organizes a regular programme of conferences, seminars and lectures. It also offers postgraduate taught and research programmes and specialized training courses.

Institute of Advanced Legal Studies Visiting Fellowship in Law Librarianship

Subjects: Law and library science
Purpose: To enable experienced law librarians, who are undertaking research in, appropriate fields, to relate their work to activities in which the Institutes own library is involved
Eligibility: Open to experienced law librarians from any country
Level of Study: Unrestricted
Type: Fellowship
Value: Fellowships can consist of or include a period working with Institute library staff or be a period of research based in a research carrel
Length of Study: Between 2 and 6 months
Frequency: Annual
Study Establishment: The IALS
Country of Study: United Kingdom
No. of awards offered: 1
Application Procedure: Applicants must submit a full curriculum vitae, the names, addresses and telephone numbers of two referees and a brief statement of the research programme to be undertaken to the Administrative Secretary
Closing Date: Applications may be considered at any time of the year
No. of awards given last year: 1
No. of applicants last year: 1

For further information contact:

Email: ials.administrator@sas.ac.uk

Institute of Advanced Legal Studies Visiting Fellowship in Legislative Studies

Subjects: Law
Purpose: To enable individuals in the field to undertake research
Eligibility: Open to established academics and practitioners from any country. This award is not available for postgraduate research
Level of Study: Unrestricted
Type: Fellowship
Value: Non-stipendary
Length of Study: A minimum of 3 months and a maximum of 1 year
Frequency: Annual
Study Establishment: The IALS
Country of Study: United Kingdom
No. of awards offered: 1

Application Procedure: Applicants must submit a full curriculum vitae, the names, addresses and telephone numbers of two referees and a brief statement of the research programme to be undertaken

Closing Date: 30 January for the following academic year

No. of applicants last year: 1

For further information contact:

Email: eliza.boudier@sas.ac.uk

Institute of Behavioural Science (IBS), University of Colorado at Boulder

Department of Geography & Institute of Behavioural Science Campus Box 487, Boulder, CO 80309-0487, United States of America

Tel: (1) 303 492 1619
Fax: (1) 303 492 3609
Email: johno@colorado.edu
Website: www.colorado.edu/IBS
Contact: Mr John O'Loughlin

The Institute of Behavioural Science (IBS) provides a setting for interdisciplinary research on problems of societal concern. By engaging faculty from all of the social and behavioural sciences at the University of Colorado at Boulder, the Institute encourages work that transcends disciplinary boundaries, that illuminates the complexity of social behaviour and social life, and that has important implications for social policy.

Master of Business Administration Programme

Length of Study: 1 year and 2 months

Application Procedure: Applicants must complete an application form supplying, TOEFL score, Graduate Management Admission Test score, plus personal and professional recommendations with career goals

Closing Date: 30 May

For further information contact:

Graduate School of Business Administration Campus Box 419, Boulder, CO 80309-0030, United States of America

Tel: (1) 303 492 1831
Fax: (1) 303 492 1727
Email: busgrad@colorado.edu
Contact: MBA Admissions Officer

Institute of Biology

20 Queensberry Place, SW7 2DZ, London, United Kingdom

Tel: (44) 20 7581 8333
Fax: (44) 20 7823 9409
Email: info@iob.org
Website: www.iob.org
Contact: Ms Georgina Day, Education Officer

The Institute of Biology's mission is to promote biology and the biological sciences, to foster the public understanding of science, to enhance the status of the biology profession and to represent its members as a whole to government and other bodies worldwide. The Institute is the 'voice' of British biology.

Dax Copp Travelling Fellowship

Subjects: Biological sciences

Purpose: To support overseas travel in connection with biological study, teaching or research and to aid those who would otherwise not have this opportunity

Eligibility: Open to students in the biological sciences studying in the United Kingdom

Level of Study: Unrestricted

Type: Fellowship

Value: UK£500

Frequency: Annual

No. of awards offered: 20

Application Procedure: Applicants must complete an application form, available from the Expeditions Grants Manager. Applicants are also required to produce a reasoned statement of the purpose to which the fellowship will be put, supported by three referees

Closing Date: Mid January

Funding: Private

Contributor: Membership

No. of awards given last year: 1

No. of applicants last year: 20

Additional Information: Applicants receiving a fellowship will be expected to provide the Institute with a report within six months of the fellowship ending

For further information contact:

Royal Geographical Society, 1 Kensington Gore, Kensington, SW7 2DZ, London, United Kingdom

Tel: (44) 20 7591 3073
Email: grants@rsg.org
Contact: Expedition Grants Manager

Institute of Education

20 Bedford Way, WC1H 0AL, London, United Kingdom

Tel: (44) 20 7612 6000
Email: info@ioe.ac.uk
Website: www.ioe.ac.uk
Contact: Josie Charlton, Head of Marketing and
             Development

Founded in 1902, the Institute of Education is a world-class centre of excellence for research, teacher training, higher degrees and consultancy in education and education-related areas of social science. Our pre-eminent scholars and talented students from all walks of life make up an intellectually rich and diverse learning community.

Nicholas Hans Comparative Education Scholarship

Subjects: Comparative education
Purpose: To assist a well-qualified student to study for a PhD in comparative education at the Institute of Education
Eligibility: Candidates must be registered Institute students not normally resident in the United Kingdom
Level of Study: Doctorate
Type: Scholarship
Value: Full-time tuition fees
Length of Study: 3–7 years
Frequency: Annual
Study Establishment: Institute of Education
Country of Study: United Kingdom
Application Procedure: Candidates are required to submit an extended essay of 25,000–30,000 words, based upon their research or proposed research, that exemplifies, extends or develops by critique the concerns of Nicholas Hans in comparative education
Closing Date: 1 June
Funding: Trusts
Contributor: Trust fund based upon money left in the will of Nicholas Hans' widow

For further information contact:

Email: p.kelly@ioe.ac.uk
Contact: Patricia Kelly

Institute of Electrical and Electronics Engineers History Center

Samuel C. Williams Library, 3rd floor, 1 Castle point on Hudson, Hoboken, NJ 07030, United States of America

Tel: (1) 732 562 5450
Fax: (1) 732 562 6020
Email: ieee-history@ieee.org
Website: www.ieee.org/about/history_center/fellowship.
             html
Contact: Mr Robert Colburn, Research Co-ordinator

The mission of the IEEE History Center is to preserve, research and promote the history of information and electrical technologies.

Charles LeGeyt Fortescue Fellowship

Subjects: Engineering and Physical Sciences
Purpose: The Charles LeGeyt Fortescue Scholarship was established in 1939 as a memorial to Charles LeGeyt in recognition of his valuable contributions to the field of electrical engineering
Eligibility: 1. To be eligible, the student must be a permanent resident of the United States, have majored in the field of electrical engineering, and have received a bachelor's degree from an engineering college of recognized standing. 2. The scholarship will be awarded to a first-year full-time graduate student only. In the event the college is conducting a combined BS and MS degree program, the student in the penultimate year would be eligible for the award, which would apply in the final year of the program
Level of Study: Postgraduate
Type: Fellowship
Value: US$24,000 per year
Length of Study: 1 year
Frequency: Every 2 years
Study Establishment: An engineering school of recognised standing
Country of Study: United States of America or Canada
No. of awards offered: 25
Closing Date: 15 November
Funding: Private

No. of awards given last year: 1
No. of applicants last year: 25
Additional Information: The Institute also offers many prize awards (service awards, field awards, and prize paper awards), and a number of medals

For further information contact:

445 Hoes Lane, Piscataway, NJ 08854, United States of America

Institute of Electrical and Electronics Engineers Fellowship in the History of Electrical and Computing Technology

Subjects: The history of electrical engineering and computer technology
Purpose: To support graduate work in the history of electrical engineering
Eligibility: Open to suitably qualified graduate students, or postdoctoral candidate studying the history of electrical or computing technologies
Level of Study: Doctorate, Postdoctorate, Postgraduate
Type: Fellowship
Value: US$25,000 plus US$3,000 research budget
Length of Study: 1 year
Frequency: Annual
Study Establishment: A college or university of recognized standing
Country of Study: Any country
No. of awards offered: 14
Application Procedure: Applicants must submit a completed application, transcripts, three letters of recommendation and a research proposal. Application materials can be downloaded from the website
Closing Date: 1 February
Funding: Corporation
No. of awards given last year: 1
No. of applicants last year: 14
Additional Information: The fellowship is made possible by a grant from the IEEE Life Member Fund and is awarded by the IEEE History Committee. Application materials available on the website

For further information contact:

Email: ieee-history@ieee.org

Institute of European Studies

Tel: (32) 2 614 80 01
Fax: (32) 2 614 80 01

Ana Hatherly Graduate Student Research Grant

Purpose: Cátedra Ana Hatherly promotes the work of one of the most important and multifaceted Portuguese poets, Ana Hatherly. In this context Camões, Instituto da Cooperação e da Língua and the Center for Portuguese Studies are pleased to announce a competition for 1 research grant of $1000.00 each for Graduate Students in all areas of research at UC, Berkeley. Preference will be given to applicants interested in publishing research papers about Ana Hatherly's poetry, cinematography, and painting
Level of Study: Postgraduate
Type: Grant
Value: $1,000
Frequency: Annual
Country of Study: Any country
Closing Date: 22 January
Funding: International office

For further information contact:

Email: ies@berkeley.edu

Regents' Junior Faculty Fellowships

Purpose: It is a pleasure to bring to the attention of junior faculty members the Regents' Junior Faculty Fellowships for the summer
Eligibility: Eligibility is limited to academic year appointees in the ranks of Assistant Professor, Acting Assistant Professor, Acting Associate Professor, and, in the School of Law, Acting Professor
Level of Study: Postgraduate
Type: Fellowship
Value: $5,000
Frequency: Annual
Country of Study: Any country
Closing Date: 12 April
Funding: International office

For further information contact:

Email: yasyavg@berkeley.edu

Institute of Fundamental Sciences, Massey University

Institute of Fundamental Sciences, Massey University, Palmerston North, New Zealand

Email: r.mclachlan@massey.ac.nz
Contact: Professor Robert McLachlan

The Institute of Fundamental Sciences is based at Massey University's Palmerston North, Manawatû campus. Our multi- and interdisciplinary research and teaching span the fundamental areas of chemistry, physics, nanoscience, mathematics, statistics, biochemistry, microbiology, genetics, plant science, evolutionary biology and bioinformatics.

Massey Business School - PhD scholarships

Subjects: Agrifood business, finance and financial services, innovation and entrepreneurship,
Purpose: The Massey Business School is seeking to strengthen its strategic research platforms
Eligibility: At a minimum, you must meet MU admission criteria: GPA of 7.5 or higher (on a 9 point scale). This is above an average grade of A- (an MBA is not a direct pathway to a PhD). Applicants should have a conditional or unconditional offer of place in a doctoral programme at Massey University. Full-time and part-time candidates are eligible to apply
Level of Study: Doctorate
Type: Scholarship
Value: NZ $25,000 per annum for a maximum of 3 years
Length of Study: 3 years
Study Establishment: Institute of Fundamental Sciences, Massey University
Country of Study: New Zealand
Application Procedure: you need to submit your academic CV, academic transcripts, a one-page research proposal and other supporting documents to the appropriate person listed: 1. School of Accountancy: Dr Lin Mei Tan L.M. Tan@massey.ac.nz. 2. School of Aviation: Dr Andrew Gilbey A.P.Gilbey@massey.ac.nz. 3. School of Economics & Finance: Fong Mee Chin F.M.Chin@massey.ac.nz. 4. School of Communication, Journalism & Marketing: Claudia Silva C.Silva@massey.ac.nz. 5. School of Management: Brigid

Eames B.Eames@massey.ac.nz. 6. General enquiry: Carnette Pulma C.Pulma@massey.ac.nz
Closing Date: 1 October and 1 March

For further information contact:

Email: contact@massey.ac.nz

PhD Opportunity - Engineering

Subjects: Physics or engineering
Eligibility: The successful candidate will likely have a background in physics or engineering and will provide evidence of well-developed mathematical skills and practical ability
Level of Study: Doctorate
Value: The project will be carried out with an industrial partner (Ravensdown) and a stipend is offered for a duration of 3 years
Length of Study: 3 years
Study Establishment: Institute of Fundamental Sciences, Massey University
Country of Study: New Zealand
Application Procedure: Applicants should provide their CV to Professor Clive Davies C.Davies@massey.ac.nz, School of Engineering and Advanced Technology

For further information contact:

Email: admissions@gcu.ac.uk

PhD Scholarship (Drug Research Team, SHORE & Whariki Research Centre)

Level of Study: Doctorate
Type: Scholarship
Value: NZ $25,000 per annum (tax free) plus tuition fees
Length of Study: 3 year
Frequency: Annual
Country of Study: New Zealand
Application Procedure: To apply please send a covering letter, curriculum vitae and 3 recent examples of your written work via email to Dr. Chris Wilkins. If you would like to discuss this opportunity further please contact Dr. Chris Wilkins (c.wilkins@massey.ac.nz)
Closing Date: 20 March

For further information contact:

Email: shore&whariki@massey.ac.nz

PhD Scholarship in Mathematics

Subjects: Mathematics (geometric numerical integration)
Eligibility: Applicants should have or expect to receive a BSc (Hons) or MSc degree or equivalent in mathematics
Level of Study: Doctorate
Type: Scholarship
Value: The scholarship covers all tuition fees for international and domestic students and includes a tax-free stipend of NZ $25,000 per annum
Study Establishment: Institute of Fundamental Sciences, Massey University
Country of Study: New Zealand
Application Procedure: Applications including a CV, academic transcript and cover letter should be sent to Professor Robert McLachlan, Institute of Fundamental Sciences, Massey University, Palmerston North, New Zealand or by email to r.mclachlan@massey.ac.nz
Additional Information: See web site dynamics.massey.ac.nz for further information

For further information contact:

Email: jag.roberts@unsw.edu.au

School of Engineering and Advanced Technology scholarships

Eligibility: To be eligible you must hold a recognized entrance qualification
Level of Study: Doctorate
Type: Scholarship
Value: $25,000 a year for 3 years, to cover fees and living expenses
Length of Study: 3 years
Frequency: Annual
Study Establishment: Institute of Fundamental Sciences, Massey University
Country of Study: New Zealand
Application Procedure: Initial applications should be on the Massey University form. Please send the form to Michele Wagner (m.wagner@massey.ac.nz), not the college coordinator
Closing Date: November each year

For further information contact:

21 North Park Street, Madison, WI 53715, United States of America

Email: info@dcs.wisc.edu, m.wagner@massey.ac.nz

Institute of Museum and Library Services

Accelerating Promising Practices for Small Libraries

Purpose: Accelerating Promising Practices for Small Libraries (APP) is a special initiative of the National Leadership Grants for Libraries Program. The goal of this initiative is to support projects that strengthen the ability of small and rural libraries and archives to serve their communities
Eligibility: See the Notice of Funding Opportunity for eligibility criteria for this program. To be eligible as an applicant for the Accelerating Promising Practices for Small Libraries Initiative, you must: 1. Be either a unit of State or local government or be a private, nonprofit institution that has nonprofit status under the Internal Revenue Code of 1954, as amended, and 2. Be located in one of the 50 States of the United States of America, the District of Columbia, the Commonwealth of Puerto Rico, the United States Virgin Islands, Guam, American Samoa, the Commonwealth of the Northern Mariana Islands, the Republic of the Marshall Islands, the Federated States of Micronesia, or the Republic of Palau. For further information, refer the below link. www.imls.gov/sites/default/files/fy19-ols-app-nofo.pdf
Level of Study: Postgraduate
Type: Grant
Frequency: Annual
Country of Study: Any country
Closing Date: 25 February
Funding: Private
Additional Information: The goal of this initiative is to support projects that strengthen the ability of small and rural libraries and archives to serve their communities. IMLS invites applications that focus on the following topics: transforming school library practice community memory digital inclusion

For further information contact:

955 L'Enfant Plaza North, SW, Suite 4000, Washington, DC 20024-2135, United States of America

Email: imlsinfo@imls.gov

Native American Library Services: Enhancement Grants

Purpose: Native American Enhancement grants are competitive grants available to carry out activities, described in

20 U.S.C. 9141, that advance the programs and services of eligible

Eligibility: Indian tribes are eligible to apply for funding under the Native American Library Services Enhancement Grant program. See the Notice of Funding Opportunity for eligibility criteria for this program

Level of Study: Postgraduate

Type: Award

Value: $10,000 to $1,50,000

Frequency: Annual

Country of Study: Any country

Application Procedure: Digital Services projects feature activities dedicated to the establishment and refinement of digital services and programs related to infrastructure, platforms, and technology, in general

Closing Date: 1 May

Funding: Private

For further information contact:

Email: storo@imls.gov

Institution of Engineering and Technology (IET)

Michael Faraday House, Six Hills Way, Stevenage, SG1 2AY, Hertfordshire, United Kingdom

Tel:	(44) 1438 313 311
Fax:	(44) 1438 765 526
Email:	awards@theiet.org
Website:	www.theiet.org/awards
Contact:	J Tilley, Scholarships Coordinator

The IET is one of the world's largest engineering institutions with over 163,000 members in 127 countries. It is also the most interdisciplinary – to reflect the increasingly diverse nature of engineering in the 21st century. Energy, transport, manufacturing, information and communications, and the built environment: the IET covers them all.

Institution of Engineering and Technology Postgraduate Scholarship for an Outstanding Researcher

Subjects: Engineering and Technology

Purpose: To assist IET members with research studies

Eligibility: Applicants should be members of the IET and must have commenced their studies prior to applying for this scholarship

Level of Study: Doctorate, Postgraduate, Research

Type: Scholarship

Value: UK£10,000

Length of Study: 1 year

Frequency: Annual

Country of Study: Any country

Application Procedure: Applicants should complete the online application form at www.theiet.org/postgradawards

Closing Date: April

Funding: Trusts

For further information contact:

Email: awards@theiet.org

Institution of Engineering and Technology Travel Awards

Subjects: Engineering and Technology

Purpose: To assist IET members undertaking international travel to attend conferences, participate in international research visits or projects

Eligibility: Open to IET members

Level of Study: Unrestricted

Type: Travel grant

Value: UK£500

Length of Study: N/A

Frequency: Annual

Country of Study: Any country

Application Procedure: Applicants should complete the online application form at www.theiet.org/travel-awards

Closing Date: Deadlines for applications can be found at www.theiet.org/travel-awards

Funding: Trusts

Additional Information: If a successful applicant does not undertake the visit, or submit a report within 1 month of the visit, they must return the funding to the IET. Awards are available throughout the year for IET members who present a paper/poster at conferences around the world, or participate in international research visits or projects

For further information contact:

Email: awards@theiet.org

Institution of Mechanical Engineers (IMechE)

1 Birdcage Walk, Westminster, SW1H 9JJ, London, United Kingdom

Tel: (44) 20 7222 7899
Fax: (44) 20 7222 4557
Email: enquiries@imeche.org
Website: www.imeche.org
Contact: The Prizes and Awards Officer

The Institution of Mechanical Engineers (IMechE) was founded in 1847 by engineers. They formed an institution to promote the exchange of ideas and encourage individuals or groups in creating inventions that would be crucial to the development of the world as a whole. Now, over 150 years later, IMechE is one of the largest engineering institutions in the world, with over 88,000 members in 120 countries.

James Clayton Lectures

Subjects: Mechanical engineering
Purpose: To provide for the expenses of the person presenting the lecture that is to take place at an ordinary meeting of the Institution on a subject relating to mechanical engineering science, research, invention or experimental work
Level of Study: Postgraduate
Type: Grant
Value: UK£500
Frequency: Annual
Country of Study: United Kingdom
Application Procedure: Applicants must write for details
Funding: Private

For further information contact:

Email: eventenquiries@imeche.org

Spencer Wilks Scholarship/Fellowship

Subjects: Mechanical engineering
Purpose: To promote or encourage the study of automobile engineering
Level of Study: Postgraduate
Type: Scholarship
Value: UK£10,000
Frequency: Annual
Country of Study: Any country
Application Procedure: Applicants must write for details
Funding: Private

For further information contact:

Email: n.udovidchik03@imperial.ac.uk

Intel Corporation

2200 Mission College Blvd, Santa Clara, CA 95054 1549, United States of America

Tel: (1) 408 765 8080
Fax: (1) 408 765 3804
Email: scholarships@intel.com
Website: www.intel.com

Intel Corporation is committed to maintaining and enhancing the quality of life in the communities where the company has a major presence.

Intel Public Affairs Russia Grant

Subjects: Science, mathematics, environmental students and technology education
Purpose: To support further study programmes with educational and technological components in Russia
Eligibility: Each request will be evaluated on the basis of the services offered and the programme's impact on the community and the potential for Intel employee involvement
Type: Grant
Frequency: Annual
Country of Study: Russia
Application Procedure: Apply online or contact the office
Funding: Corporation
Contributor: Intel Corporation

For further information contact:

Tel: (7) 831 296 94 44
Email: paris@intel.com
Contact: Mr Evgeny Zakablukovsky, Russia Community and Regional Government Relations Manager

Interart Festival Center

PO Box 80 1051 Vörösmarty Tér 1, HUN-1366, Budapest, Hungary

Tel: (36) 1 317 9838
Fax: (36) 1 317 9910
Contact: Grants Management Officer

The Hungarian Television and Interart Festival Center has organised the International Conductors' Competition every third year since 1974. The goal of the competition is to discover gifted young conductors from Hungary and abroad, to introduce them to the possible audience and to stimulate public interest in musical performance, musical values and modes and possibilities of interpretation.

International Glaucoma Award

Purpose: The International Glaucoma Association (IGA) is pleased to announce a grants programme in collaboration with The College of Optometrists and is pleased to offer Research Awards
Eligibility: Postgraduate research award. Multidisciplinary research teams are encouraged and should include a member/fellow of RCOphth but co-applicants (and project lead) may include hospital/community based optometrists and/or nurses undertaking glaucoma research in the United Kingdom and Ireland
Level of Study: Postgraduate
Type: Award
Value: UK£1,00,000
Frequency: Annual
Country of Study: Any country
Closing Date: 23 February
Funding: Foundation

International Airline Training Fund (IATF)

33, Route de l'Aeroport PO Box 416, Gineva-15 Airport, CH-1215, Geneva, Switzerland

Tel: (41) 22 770 2525
Fax: (41) 22 798 3553
Email: iatf@iata.org
Website: www.iata.org
Contact: IATF Co-ordinator

The International Airline Training Fund's (IATF) mission is to provide vocational training opportunities for staff of IATA member airlines based in countries with developing economies. It does so by providing scholarships and other training opportunities to enable worthy candidates to follow vocational training courses conducted by the IATA Aviation Training & Development Institute, the Aviation MBA at Concordia University, as well as several other courses.

International Airline Training Fund IATA Aviation Training and Development Institute (ATDI) Scholarships

Subjects: Business administration and management in the field of aviation training and development
Purpose: To enable staff of IATA member airlines based in countries with developing economies to follow short courses of specialist vocational training provided under the auspices of the IATA Aviation Training & Development Institute (ATDI)
Eligibility: Open to staff from IATA member airlines from countries with developing economies
Level of Study: Postgraduate
Type: Scholarship
Value: Please contact the organization
Country of Study: Switzerland, the United States of America or Singapore
Application Procedure: Applicants must channel applications through the human resources director of the IATA member airline which employs the applicant for an IATF-IATDI scholarship
Funding: Commercial, Private
Contributor: IATA member airlines and aviation industry suppliers
Additional Information: The scholarship committee meets quarterly to assess accumulated applications as of that date and to make awards. The ATDI seeks to offer skills training for managers, supervisors and other airline industry specialist staff who wish to add to their professional knowledge and ability. The range of courses taught is wide, with courses in heavy demand being repeated during the course of the year

For further information contact:

Email: haroo@iata.org

International Arctic Research Center Fellowships for Cancer Research

150 cours Albert-Thomas, 69372 Lyon Cedex 08, France

Tel: (33) 472 73 84 48
Fax: (33) 472 73 80 80
Email: fel@iarc.fr
Contact: Research on Cancer

Postdoctoral Fellowships for Training in Cancer Research

Subjects: Epidemiology (all disciplines included), biostatistics, bioinformatics, and areas related to mechanisms of carcinogenesis including molecular and cell biology, molecular genetics, epigenetics and molecular pathology
Purpose: The IARC fellowships are intended for early career scientists wishing to complete their training in those aspects of cancer research related to the Agency's mission. Disciplines covered are: epidemiology (all disciplines included), biostatistics, bioinformatics, and areas related to, mechanisms of carcinogenesis including molecular and cell biology, molecular genetics, epigenetics, and molecular pathology
Level of Study: Research
Type: Fellowship
Value: The annual stipend with dependent allowance is competitive compared with other international fellowship schemes. The cost of travel for the Fellow, and in certain circumstances for dependants, will be met, and health insurance covered
Length of Study: 2 years
Country of Study: France
Closing Date: 30 November
Additional Information: For more details, please visit www.iarc.fr

For further information contact:

Email: fel@iarc.fr

International Association for the Study of Obesity

Charles Darwin House, 12 Roger Street, WCIN 2JU, London, United Kingdom

Tel:	(44) 20 7685 2580
Fax:	(44) 20 7685 2581
Email:	enquiries@iaso.org
Website:	www.iaso.org

The International Association for the Study of Obesity (IASO) aims to improve global health by promoting the understanding of obesity and weight-related diseases through scientific research and dialogue whilst encouraging the development of effective policies for their prevention and management. IASO is the leading global professional organization concerned with obesity, operating in over 50 countries around the world.

International Association for the Study of Obesity Per Björntorp Travelling Fellowship Award

Subjects: Medicine and surgery
Purpose: To provide travel grants to enable young researchers to attend the International Congress of Obesity
Eligibility: Applicants for this award must demonstrate their financial need for such support to attend the Congress. Applicants must be an IASO member. There is no age limit
Level of Study: Doctorate, Postdoctorate, Postgraduate, Predoctorate, Research
Type: Studentships and bursaries
Value: Up to $2,000 of return economy flights, congress Registration and hotel accommodation at the International Congress of Obesity
Study Establishment: Any
Country of Study: Any country
Application Procedure: Download the application form from website
Closing Date: See the website for details
Additional Information: For further information about the IASO Travelling Fellowships Award please write to awards@iaso.org

For further information contact:

28 Portland Place, Marylebone, London, United Kingdom

Tel:	(44) 20 7467 9610
Fax:	(44) 20 7636 9258
Email:	kate.baillie@iaso.org
Contact:	Kate Baillie

International Business Machines Corporation

1 New Orchard Road, Armonk, New York, NY 10504 1722, United States of America

Tel:	(1) 877 426 6006
Fax:	(1) 866 722 9226
Email:	ews@us.ibm.com
Website:	www.ibm.com

IBM stands today at the forefront of a worldwide industry that is revolutionizing the way in which enterprises, organizations and people operate and thrive. IBM strives to lead in the invention, development and manufacture of the industry's most advanced information technologies, including computer systems, software, storage systems, and microelectronics.

International Business Machines Herman Goldstine Postdoctoral Fellowship

Subjects: Mathematics and computer science
Purpose: To provide scientists of outstanding ability an opportunity to advance their scholarship as resident department members at the Research Center
Eligibility: Open to candidates who have obtained a PhD or expect to receive a PhD before the fellowship commences in the second half of current year
Level of Study: Research
Type: Fellowship
Value: Stipend is expected to be between US$95,000 and US$1,20,000, depending on the length of experience. An additional allowance for moving expenses will be provided
Length of Study: 1 year
Frequency: Annual
Country of Study: United States of America
Application Procedure: Applicants can download the application form from the website. The completed application form, curriculum vitae and abstract of PhD dissertation must be sent
Closing Date: 15 January
Additional Information: Applications shall be accepted through email at goldpost@watson.ibm.com

For further information contact:

Email: ews@us.ibm.com

International Business Machines PhD Fellowship Program

Subjects: All subjects
Purpose: To honour exceptional PhD students in an array of focus areas of interest to IBM and fundamental to innovation
Eligibility: Open to students nominated by a faculty member. They must be enroled full-time in a college or university PhD programme and they should have completed at least 1 year of study in their Doctoral programme at the time of their nomination
Level of Study: Doctorate
Type: Fellowships

Value: US$17,500
Length of Study: 3 years
Frequency: Annual
Country of Study: Any country
Application Procedure: All nominations for the IBM PhD Fellowship must be submitted by faculty electronically over the web on a standardized form. The nomination form will be available on the IBM PhD Fellowship nomination website from 19 September to 31 October
Closing Date: 31 October
Additional Information: Non-United States citizens who wish to participate in an internship in the United States must obtain work authorization under the specifics of their particular visa. For further information, see website at www.research.ibm.com/university/phdfellowship/#about OR contact phdfellow@us.ibm.com

For further information contact:

Email: ews@us.ibm.com

International Centre for Education in Islamic Finance (INCEIF)

Email: syarina@inceif.org
Contact: Noorsyarina Mohd Sapiai

Khazanah – INCEIF Scholarship

Subjects: Islamic Finance
Eligibility: Information available on website: www.inceif.org/khazanah-inceif-scholarship-programme/
Level of Study: Doctorate, Postgraduate
Value: All applicable tuition fees and monthly allowances for the duration of the course
Study Establishment: INCEIF
Country of Study: Malaysia
Application Procedure: Kindly contact Ms Noorsyarina Mohd Sapiai at syarina@inceif.org for further assistance
Closing Date: 16 March
Additional Information: Eligible to nationals of Malaysia. All communications will be done via email. Therefore please ensure the email address given is correct and active

For further information contact:

Email: syarina@inceif.org

International Centre for Genetic Engineering and Biotechnology (ICGEB)

AREA Science Park, Padriciano 99, ITA 34149, Trieste, Italy

Tel:	(39) 40 375 71
Fax:	(39) 40 226 555
Email:	fellowships@icgeb.org
Website:	www.icgeb.org
Contact:	Human Resources Unit

The International Centre for Genetic Engineering and Biotechnology (ICGEB) is an organization devoted to advanced research and training in molecular biology and biotechnology, with special regard to the needs of the developing world. The component host countries are Italy, India and South Africa. The full member states of ICGEB are Afghanistan, Algeria, Argentina, Bangladesh, Bhutan, Bosnia and Herzegovina, Brazil, Bulgaria, Burundi, Cameroon, Chile, China, Colombia, Costa Rica, Côte d'Ivoire, Croatia, Cuba, Ecuador, Egypt, Eritrea, FYR Macedonia, Hungary, Iran, Iraq, Jordan, Kenya, Kuwait, Kyrgyzstan, Liberia, Libya, Malaysia, Mauritius, Mexico, Montenegro, Morocco, Nigeria, Pakistan, Panama, Peru, Poland, Qatar, Romania, Russia, Saudi Arabia, Senegal, Serbia, Slovakia, Slovenia, Sri Lanka, Sudan, Syria, Tanzania, Trinidad and Tobago, Tunisia, Turkey, United Arab Emirates, Uruguay, Venezuela, and Vietnam.

International Center for Genetic Engineering and Biotechnology Arturo Falaschi PhD and Postdoctoral Fellowships for Member Countries

Subjects: Fellowships are awarded in Life Sciences. The programme provides support for research projects in basic science, human healthcare, industrial and agricultural biotechnology and bioenergy

Purpose: Funding opportunities are made available through the Collaborative Research Programme (CRP) – ICGEB Research Grants, which is a dedicated source of funding aimed at financing projects addressing original scientific problems of particular relevance for the host country and of regional interest

Eligibility: Candidates must have a good working knowledge of the English language, supported by a proficiency certificate (TOEFL, Cambridge Certificate, or equivalent). Not required when scholastic education has been undertaken in English

Type: Fellowship

Value: See the website

Study Establishment: Fellowships are awarded in Life Sciences. The programme provides support for research projects in basic science, human healthcare, industrial and agricultural biotechnology and bioenergy

Country of Study: Any country

Application Procedure: The mode of application is online

Closing Date: Closing date for applications for PhDs: 31 March, Closing dates for applications for Postdocs: 31 March and 30 September

Additional Information: Please browse the website for more details scholarship-positions.com/icgeb-arturo-falaschi-phd-postdoctoral-fellowships-member-countries/2018/01/17/

For further information contact:

Email: fellowships@icgeb.org

The Arturo Falaschi ICGEB Predoctoral Fellowships ICGEB Trieste International PhD Programme

Subjects: Molecular medicine, tumour virology, bacteriology, protein structure and bioinformatics, molecular pathology, molecular immunology, human molecular genetics, molecular virology, mouse molecular genetics, neurobiology, protein networks, yeast molecular genetics, cellular immunology, and molecular hematology

Purpose: To enable promising young students to attend and complete the PhD programme at ICGEB Trieste in Italy. The programme is validated by the Open University, United Kingdom, and the University of Nova Gorica, Slovenia

Eligibility: Open to students having a BSc (Hons) university degree under the age of 32 from any member state of the ICGEB

Level of Study: Predoctorate

Type: Fellowship

Value: Stipends to cover the cost of normal living expenses (annually) for one person at the location of the individual host institute; fellowships are renewable for the following years provided that the PhD Programme requirements are fulfilled. Cost to cover travel to and from the host country and medical health insurance cover

Length of Study: Up to 3 years

Frequency: Annual

Study Establishment: ICGEB laboratories in Trieste and Monterotondo (Rome)

Country of Study: Italy

Application Procedure: Applicants must refer to the website

Closing Date: 31 March

Additional Information: For more information on this programme please refer to the website

For further information contact:

Email: admissions@cgebicgeb.res.in

International Centre for Theoretical Sciences

Survey No. 151, Shivakote, Hesaraghatta Hobli, Bengaluru, Karnataka 560 089, India

Tel: (91) 80 6730 6000, 80 4653 6000
Fax: (91) 80 4653 6002
Email: info@icts.res.in
Contact: International Centre for Theoretical Sciences

International Centre for Theoretical Sciences (ICTS)contributes to research excellence in science in various ways. It has a high-quality faculty together with a large floating population comprising visitors, postdoctoral fellows and graduate students.

International Centre for Theoretical Sciences S. N. Bhatt Memorial Excellence Research Fellowship

Subjects: The fellowship is awarded in the field of Science and Engineering
Purpose: The aim of the fellowship is to give an opportunity to master's students of Science and Engineering to work with faculty and post-doctoral fellows of the Centre and to participate in research at the frontiers of knowledge
Eligibility: Master's degree students and those who have completed their undergraduate are welcome to apply
Type: Research
Value: This program offers a unique opportunity masters students of Science and Engineering to work with faculty and postdoctoral fellows of the Centre and to participate in research at the frontiers of knowledge
Study Establishment: The fellowship is awarded in the field of Science and Engineering
Country of Study: India
Application Procedure: Names, Affiliation and email id of two or more referees who would provide reference letters for you. The referees should be your teachers or scientists with whom you have interacted academically. Application will be processed online
Closing Date: 18 January of every year
Additional Information: please visit our website for more information scholarship-positions.com/icts-s-n-bhatt-memorial-excellence-research-fellowship-india/2017/11/04/

For further information contact:

Email: info@icts.res.in

International Dairy-Deli-Bakery Association

IDDBA, 636 Science Drive, PO Box 5528, Madison, WI 53711 1073, United States of America

Tel: (1) 608 310 5000
Fax: (1) 608 238 6330
Email: iddba@iddba.org
Website: www.iddba.org

Our mission is to expand our leadership role in promoting the growth and development of daily, deli, and bakery sales in the food industry. Our vision is to be the essential resource for relevant information and services that add value across all food channels for the dairy, deli and bakery categories.

International Dairy Deli Bakery Association Graduate Scholarships

Subjects: Culinary arts, baking/party arts, food service, business and marketing
Purpose: To support employees of IDDBA-member companies
Eligibility: Applicants must be a current full- or part-time employee of an IDDBA-member company with an academic background in a food-related field and have a 2.5 grade-point average on a 4.0 scale, or equivalent
Level of Study: Postgraduate
Type: Scholarship
Value: US$250 to $1,000
Length of Study: 1 year
Frequency: Annual
Country of Study: United States of America
Application Procedure: Contact the Education Information Specialist
Closing Date: 1 January, 1 April, 1 July, 1 October
Funding: Foundation
Contributor: IDDBA
Additional Information: For additional information or enquiries contact organization and email at scholarships@iddba.org. Please see the website for further details www.iddba.org/scholarships.aspx

For further information contact:

Email: kpeckham@iddba.org

International Education Specialist

World Citizen talent Scholarship

Purpose: We are seeking intelligent, talented and ambitious people who view themselves as citizens of the world

Eligibility: You are eligible to apply for the scholarship if you; 1. Come from outside The Netherlands and don't live in the Netherlands. 2. Are enrolling for the first time at The Hague University of Applied Sciences. 3. Have never applied for this scholarship before. 4. Have been conditionally accepted as a student (also-called offer of student position) on or before 31 March for the upcoming academic year

Level of Study: Postgraduate

Type: Scholarship

Value: UK£5,000

Frequency: Annual

Country of Study: Any country

Application Procedure: Applicants must submit the below documents to process further. 1. Outstanding Master's-level students can apply for these scholarships by submitting the application form including an essay of no more than 1,000 words, detailing their cultural background and contribution they wish to make to the university as global citizens. 2. Applications will be reviewed by an academic panel

Closing Date: 15 May

Funding: Private

For further information contact:

Email: master-scholarship@hhs.nl

International Federation of Library Associations and Institutions WLIC

Chartered Institute of Library and Information Professionals International Library and Information Group Alan Hopkinson Award

Purpose: The Chartered Institute of Library and Information Professionals (CILIP) and its International Library and Information Group (ILIG) invite applicants from Europe to attend the International Federation of Library Associations and Institutions (IFLA) conference in Athens

Eligibility: 1. Applicants are required to write a reflective report of not more than 4,000 words within six months of their visit, and a version for publication in Focus on International Library and Information Work, the ILIG journal. 2. Applicants should submit a formal proposal in English of up to 500 words (equivalent to 1–2 pages of A4 paper) detailing how the visit will support their professional development within the context of their career to date and using the headings of 'Visit objectives' 'Planned approach and content' 'Application of learning post-visit'

Level of Study: Postgraduate

Type: Award

Frequency: Annual

Country of Study: Any country

Closing Date: 31 March

Funding: Private

For further information contact:

IFLA Headquarters IFLA P.O. Box 95312, NLD 2509 CH The Hague, The Netherlands

Email: ilig@cilip.org.uk

Dr. Shawky Salem Conference Grant

Purpose: The aim of the grant is to enable one expert in library and information sciences from the Arab Countries (AC) to attend the Annual IFLA Conference

Eligibility: 1. The grant is available to a librarian of Arab nationality, not exceeding 45 years. 2. Priority is given to applicants who are first-time attendees to the IFLA Congress. 3. The applicant should have at least 5 years of experience in LIS profession. 4. The applicant must have the approval of his / her organization to attend the IFLA WLIC

Level of Study: Graduate, Professional development

Type: Grant

Value: US$1,900

Frequency: Annual

Country of Study: Any country

Application Procedure: Application has to b eprocessed physically. For further information, check the website. 2019. ifla.org/dr-shawky-salem-conference-grant-sscg-2019/

Closing Date: 31 March

Funding: Private

For further information contact:

Email: grants@ifla.org

International Federation of Library Associations and Institutions Green Library Award

Purpose: To create awareness of libraries' social responsibility and leadership in environmental education. Libraries of all types are encouraged to participate. To support the worldwide Green Library movement, concerned with 1. environmentally sustainable buildings. 2. environmentally sustainable information resources and programming conservation of resources and energy

Eligibility: They also focus on related services, activities, events, literature and projects, demonstrating the social role and responsibility of libraries as leaders in environmental sustainability. 1. Any type of library with an outstanding Green Library project, initiative or idea may apply for the IFLA Green Library Award. The project, initiative or idea may be presented in various ways (e.g. essay, video, poster, article, set of slides). 2. Applications must be written in one of the seven IFLA languages. 3. Applicants may also submit an English translation if they prefer. 4. Film and Video materials in languages other than English must have English subtitles. 5. The presentation of the project, initiative or idea should be submitted to the ENSULIB award reviewing committee

Level of Study: Postgraduate
Type: Grant
Frequency: Annual
Country of Study: Any country
Application Procedure: The quality and relevance of the project, initiative or idea will be evaluated by the ENSULIB committee in terms of applicability to the goals and the scope of ENSULIB. 2019.ifla.org/ifla-green-library-award-2019/
Closing Date: 1 April
Funding: Private

For further information contact:

P.O. Box 95312, NLD 2509 CH The Hague, The Netherlands

Email: petra.hauke@hu-berlin.de, ifla@ifla.org

International Federation of University Women (IFUW)

IFUW Headquarters 10 rue de Lac, Geneva CH-1207, Switzerland

Tel:	(41) 22 731 2380
Fax:	(41) 22 738 0440
Email:	info@ifuw.org
Website:	www.ifuw.org

The International Federation of University Women (IFUW) is a non-profit, non-governmental organization comprising graduate women working locally, nationally and internationally to advocate the improvement of the status of women and girls at the international level, by promoting lifelong education and enabling graduate women to use their expertise to effect change.

Canadian Federation of University Women/A. Vibert Douglas Fellowship

Country of Study: Any country

For further information contact:

Email: fellowships@cfuw.org

Ida Smedley MacLean Fellowship

Subjects: All subjects
Purpose: To encourage advanced scholarship and original research relevant to IFUW's mission
Eligibility: Open to female applicants who are either members of one of IFUW's national federations or associations or, in the case of female graduates living in countries where there is not yet a national affiliate, independent members of IFUW, or other applicants who pay a filing fee. Applicants should have completed at least the first year of a doctoral programme
Level of Study: Doctorate
Type: Fellowship
Value: SFR 8,000
Length of Study: More than 8 months
Frequency: Dependent on funds available
Study Establishment: An approved Institute of Higher Education
Country of Study: Worldwide
Application Procedure: Applicants must apply through their respective federation or association. A list of IFUW national federations and associations can be obtained from the IFUW website. IFUW independent members and others must apply directly to the IFUW headquarters in Geneva
Closing Date: The deadline varies by country, but normally falls between August and mid-September. Please ask your national headquarters for the exact deadline
Funding: Private
Contributor: British Federation of Women Graduates
No. of awards given last year: 1 of each fellowship
Additional Information: Please see the website for further details www.ifuw.org/what-we-do/grants-fellowships/international-awards/

For further information contact:

Email: info@ifuw.org

The CFUW/A Vibert Douglas International Fellowship

Subjects: Conservation biology, ecology and evolution

Purpose: To encourage advanced scholarship and original research relevant to IFUW's mission

Eligibility: Open to female applicants who are either members of one of IFUW's national federations or associations or, in the case of female graduates living in countries where there is not yet a national affiliate, independent members of IFUW, or other applicants who pay a filing fee. Applicants should have completed at least the first year of a doctoral programme

Level of Study: Doctorate, Postdoctorate, Postgraduate

Type: Fellowship

Value: C$12,000

Length of Study: Requires 8–12 months' work in a country other than that in which the applicant was educated or habitually resides

Frequency: Dependent on funds available

Study Establishment: An approved Institute of Higher Education

Country of Study: Worldwide

Application Procedure: Applicants must apply through their respective federation or association. A list of IFUW national federations and associations can be obtained from the IFUW website. IFUW independent members and others must apply directly to the IFUW headquarters in Geneva

Closing Date: The deadline varies by country, but normally falls between August and mid-September. Please ask your national headquarters for the exact deadline

Funding: Private

Contributor: Canadian Federation of University Women

For further information contact:

Email: info@ifuw.org

International Furnishings and Design Association Education Foundation

Vercille Voss Scholarship

Purpose: The IFDA Illinois Chapter initiated the Vercille Voss Graduate Student Scholarship in memory of Vercille Voss, longtime chapter member and mentor to new members and students. The applicant must be enrolled as a part-time or full-time graduate student at an accredited university

Eligibility: 1. Must be a college graduate or older at time of application. 2. Must be a IFDA graduate student member. 3. Must be a United States citizen. 4. Must be enrolled full time at an accredited college or university. 5. Must major in interior design or a related field. 6. This award is for United States students

Level of Study: Graduate

Type: Scholarship

Value: $2,000

Frequency: Annual

Country of Study: Any country

Application Procedure: The IFDA Educational Foundation Board of Trustees will select the scholarship recipient based on the student's academic achievement, awards and accomplishments, future plans and goals, and letter of recommendation. All applicants must be graduate students and have completed four design courses in post-secondary education at the time of application and be majoring in Interior Design or a related field. For more information or to apply, please visit the scholarship provider's website

Closing Date: 31 March

Funding: Private

Additional Information: The application deadline date has not yet been finalized for this year, but is expected to remain the same as last year

For further information contact:

36 Bay View Road Wellesley, MA 02482, United States of America

Email: karen@kdzdesigns.com

International Human Frontier Science Program Organization (HFSP)

Bureaux Europe, 20 Place des Halles, F-67080, Strasbourg, France

Tel:	(33) 3 88 21 51 12
Fax:	(33) 3 88 32 88 97
Email:	info@hfsp.org
Website:	www.hfsp.org
Contact:	Mr Patrick Vincent, Director of Scientific Affairs and Communications

The International Human Frontier Science Program Organization (HFSP) promotes basic research into the complex mechanisms underlying the function of living organisms by supporting interdisciplinary and international collaboration. The programme only supports research that transcends national boundaries.

Career Development Award

Country of Study: Any country

For further information contact:

Email: communications@hfsp.org

Cross-Disciplinary Fellowships

Subjects: HFSPO aims to promote, through international cooperation, basic research focused on the elucidation of the sophisticated and complex mechanisms of living organisms and to make the fullest possible utilization of the research results for the benefit of all humankind. Research projects can range from biological functions at the molecular and cellular level up to the biological systems level, including cognitive functions. All levels of analysis are supported: studies on genes and individual molecules, intracellular networks, intercellular associations in tissues and organs, and networks underlying complex functions of entire organisms, populations, or ecosystems

Purpose: Cross-Disciplinary Fellowships (CDF) are for applicants with a PhD from outside the life sciences (e.g. in physics, chemistry, mathematics, engineering or computer sciences), who have had limited exposure to biology during their previous training

Eligibility: See application guidelines www.hfsp.org/funding/postdoctoral-fellowships/guidelines

Level of Study: Postdoctorate

Type: Fellowship

Value: About US$1,80,000 over three years (depending on host country)

Length of Study: 3 years

Frequency: Annual

Country of Study: Africa

No. of awards offered: 54

Application Procedure: Online

Funding: Government

Contributor: Australia, Canada, European Commission, France, Germany, India, Italy, Korea, Japan, New Zealand, Norway, Singapore, Switzerland, United Kingdom and United States of America

No. of awards given last year: 12

No. of applicants last year: 54

For further information contact:

12 quai Saint Jean, 67080 Strasbourg Cedex, France

Email: info@hfsp.org

Long-Term Fellowships

Subjects: HFSPO aims to promote, through international cooperation, basic research focused on the elucidation of the sophisticated and complex mechanisms of living organisms and to make the fullest possible utilization of the research results for the benefit of all humankind. Fellowship research projects can range from biological functions at the molecular and cellular level up to the biological systems level, including cognitive functions. All levels of analysis are supported: studies on genes and individual molecules, intracellular networks, intercellular associations in tissues and organs, and networks underlying complex functions of entire organisms, populations, or ecosystems

Purpose: Long-Term Fellowships (LTF) are for applicants with a PhD in a biological discipline, who will broaden their expertise by proposing a project in the life sciences which is significantly different from their previous PhD or postdoctoral work. The HFSP fellowship program strongly supports frontier, potentially transformative ('out-of-the-box') proposals and encourages applications for high-risk projects. The projects should be interdisciplinary in nature and should challenge existing paradigms by using novel approaches and techniques. Scientifically, they should address an important problem or a barrier to progress in the field

Eligibility: See application guidelines www.hfsp.org/funding/postdoctoral-fellowships/guidelines

Level of Study: Postdoctorate

Type: Fellowship

Value: About US$1,80,000 over three years (depending on host country)

Length of Study: 3 years

Frequency: Annual

Country of Study: Any country

No. of awards offered: 534

Application Procedure: Online

Funding: Government

Contributor: Australia, Canada, European Commission, France, Germany, India, Italy, Korea, Japan, New Zealand, Norway, Singapore, Switzerland, United Kingdom and United States of America

No. of awards given last year: 79

No. of applicants last year: 534

Program Grants

Subjects: Research grants are available for projects concerned with basic approaches to understanding the complex mechanisms of living organisms. The HFSP funds novel collaborations that bring scientists with distinct expertise together to focus on problems at the frontiers of the life sciences. The innovative aspect of the project is a major criterion in the review of HFSP research grants

Purpose: Research grants are provided for teams of scientists from different countries who wish to combine their expertise in innovative approaches to questions that could not be answered by individual laboratories. Emphasis is placed on novel collaborations that bring together scientists preferably from different disciplines (e.g. from chemistry, physics, computer science, engineering) to focus on problems in the life sciences. Note, HFSPO funds only basic research. Applied applications, including medical research typically funded by national medical research bodies, will be deemed ineligible. Program Grants are awarded to teams of independent researchers at any stage of their careers. The research team is expected to develop new lines of research through the collaboration. Up to $450,000 per grant per year may be applied for. Applications including independent investigators early in their careers are encouraged

Eligibility: See application guidelines www.hfsp.org/sites/www.hfsp.org/files/webfm/Grants/LI%20Guidelines.pdf

Level of Study: Postdoctorate

Type: Grant

Value: US$2,50,000 for a team of 2; US$3,50,000 for a team of 3; US$4,50,000 for a team of 4 or more. These figures represent the amount awarded to the whole team per year for a period of 3 years

Length of Study: 3 years

Frequency: Annual

Country of Study: Any country

No. of awards offered: 612

Application Procedure: See application guidelines www.hfsp.org/sites/www.hfsp.org/files/webfm/Grants/LI%20Guidelines.pdf

Funding: Government

Contributor: Australia, Canada, European Commission, France, Germany, India, Italy, Japan, Republic of Korea, New Zealand, Norway, Singapore, Switzerland, United Kingdom, United States of America

No. of awards given last year: 23

No. of applicants last year: 612

For further information contact:

HFSPO, 12 quai Saint Jean, 67080 Strasbourg, France

Email: info@hfsp.org

Young Investigator Grant

Subjects: The Human Frontier Science Program (HFSP) is a unique program that supports innovative basic research into fundamental biological problems with emphasis placed on novel and interdisciplinary approaches that involve scientific exchanges across national and disciplinary boundaries

Purpose: Research grants are provided for teams of scientists from different countries who wish to combine their expertise in innovative approaches to questions that could not be answered by individual laboratories. Emphasis is placed on novel collaborations that bring together scientists preferably from different disciplines (e.g. from chemistry, physics, computer science, engineering) to focus on problems in the life sciences. Note, HFSPO funds only basic research. Applied applications, including medical research typically funded by national medical research bodies, will be deemed ineligible. The research teams must be international. The principal applicant must be from one of the eligible countries. However, other participating scientists and laboratories may be situated anywhere in the world. Young Investigators' Grants are awarded to teams of researchers, all of whom are within the first five years after obtaining an independent laboratory (e.g. Assistant Professor, Lecturer or equivalent). Applications for Young Investigators' Grants will be reviewed in competition with each other independently of applications for Program Grants

Eligibility: See application guidelines: www.hfsp.org/sites/www.hfsp.org/files/webfm/Grants/LI%20Guidelines.pdf

Level of Study: Postdoctorate

Type: Grant

Value: Teams will receive up to $4,50,000 per year for the whole team depending on the size of the team

Length of Study: 3 years

Frequency: Annual

Country of Study: Any country

No. of awards offered: 158

Application Procedure: See application guidelines: www.hfsp.org/sites/www.hfsp.org/files/webfm/Grants/LI%20Guidelines.pdf

Funding: Government

Contributor: Australia, Canada, European Commission, France, Germany, India, Italy, Japan, Korea, New Zealand, Norway, Singapore, Switzerland, United Kingdom, United States

No. of awards given last year: 8

No. of applicants last year: 158

For further information contact:

HFSPO, 12 quai Saint Jean, 67080 Strasbourg, France

Email: info@hfsp.org

International Institute for Management Development (IMD)

Chemin de Bellerive 23, PO Box 915, Lausanne CH-1001, Switzerland

Tel: (41) 21 618 0298
Fax: (41) 21 618 0615
Email: mbainfo@imd.ch
Website: www.imd.ch/mba
Contact: Suzanne Laurent

The International Institute for Management Development (IMD), created by industry to serve industry, develops cutting-edge research and programmes that meet real world needs. Their clients include dozens of leading international companies and their experienced faculty incorporate new management practices into the small and exclusive MBA programme. With no nationality dominating, IMD is truly global, practical and relevant.

International Institute for Management Development MBA Merit Scholarships

Subjects: MBA
Purpose: To financially support applicants who consistently demonstrate exceptional qualities
Eligibility: Candidates who have already completed the IMD MBA application and admission process
Level of Study: MBA
Type: Scholarship
Value: Swiss Franc 10,000 towards tuition
Length of Study: 1 year
Frequency: Annual
Study Establishment: IMD
Country of Study: Switzerland
Closing Date: 30 September
Funding: Private
No. of awards given last year: 4

For further information contact:

Email: MBAfinance@imd.org

Stewart Hamilton Scholarship

Subjects: MBA
Purpose: Financially support applicants who demonstrate an understanding of corporate governance and responsibility
Eligibility: Candidates who have already applied to the full-time IMD MBA program and who demonstrate financial need
Level of Study: MBA
Type: Scholarship
Value: Swiss Franc 15,000 payment each semester for the standard duration of the course
Length of Study: 1 year
Frequency: Annual

Study Establishment: IMD
Country of Study: Switzerland
No. of awards offered: 14
Application Procedure: Applicants must complete and submit the IMD MBA application form for financial assistance and the MBA application form
Closing Date: 10 March
Funding: Private
No. of awards given last year: 1
No. of applicants last year: 14
Additional Information: Scholarship essays or questions should be sent to mbafinance@imd.org

For further information contact:

P.O. Box 915 CH-1001 Lausanne, Switzerland

Email: clientmarketdevelopmenteurope@imd.org

International Institute for Population Sciences (IIPS)

Govandi Station Road Deonar, Bombay, Maharashtra 400088, India

Tel: (91) 22 2556 3254
Fax: (91) 22 2556 3257
Email: diriips@bom8.vsnl.net.in
Website: www.iipsindia.org
Contact: Professor T K Roy, Director

The International Institute for Population Sciences (IIPS) is one of the few institutes set up solely for the purpose of studying demography. The only institute of its kind in the world, it was declared a deemed university on 15 August. The IIPS offers academic courses in population sciences and takes major initiatives to strengthen reproductive health, research and training programmes.

International Institute for Population Sciences Diploma in Population Studies

Subjects: Population studies
Purpose: To train the recipient in obtaining basic knowledge in the field of population
Eligibility: Open to ESCAP and Pacific Region nationals who are already working in the fields of population and health. Applicants are required to be graduates
Level of Study: Professional development
Type: Fellowship

Value: Return air ticket plus US$6,000 per student per year as course fee and US$6,000 fellowship for students
Length of Study: 10 months
Frequency: Annual
Country of Study: India
No. of awards offered: Unknown
Application Procedure: Applicants must make an application through UNFPA country directors or representatives in the applicant's own country
Closing Date: 30 April
Funding: Private
Contributor: UNFPA
No. of awards given last year: 5
No. of applicants last year: Unknown
Additional Information: Further information on this programme is also available from the London School of Economics, on (44) 20 7405 7686

For further information contact:

International Institute for Population Sciences (Deemed University) Govandi Station Road, Mumbai, Maharashtra 400088, India

Tel:	(91) 55 620 62
Fax:	(91) 22 556 3257
Email:	diriips@bom8.vsnl.net.in
Contact:	Director & Senior Professor

International Institute of Tropical Agriculture (IITA)

c/o L W Lambourn & Co Ltd Carolyn House 26 Dingwall Road, Croydon, CR9 3EE, Surrey, United Kingdom

Email:	iita@cgnet.com
Website:	www.cgiar.org/iita
Contact:	Programme Leader

The International Institute of Tropical Agriculture (IITA) was founded in 1967 as an international agricultural research institute with a mandate for special food crops and with ecological and regional responsibilities to develop sustainable production systems in Africa.

International Institute of Tropical Agriculture Research Fellowships

Subjects: Agricultural economics, agroclimatology, agronomy, biotechnology, biological control, crop production, entomology, plant breeding, plant pathology, plant physiology, soil chemistry, soil physics, soil microbiology, and weed sciences
Purpose: To enable African postgraduate degree candidates to conduct research at the Institute or one of its satellites
Eligibility: Candidates should be residents of Sub Saharan Africa and be registered for a postgraduate degree at a university in Africa or abroad (generally a faculty of agriculture). Preference will be given to candidates of IITA stations - Nigeria, Cameroon, Uganda, Benin and Cote d'Ivoire
Level of Study: Doctorate, Postgraduate
Type: Fellowship
Value: Up to US$12,000 per year, includes board and lodging, various allowances for personal and other expenses, travel to and from the Institute, medical accident insurance, and all research costs. It also includes one round trip ticket for the student's university supervisor to IITA for PhD students
Length of Study: MSc is 1 year, the PhD is 2–3 years
Frequency: Annual
Study Establishment: IITA
Country of Study: Other
No. of awards offered: 150
Application Procedure: Application form must be completed and submitted with a research proposal of no more than 10 pages and three letters of recommendation from the candidate's advisor at the university. Applications may be submitted by individuals. However it is preferred that all applications are made through the university. Candidate, advisor and university must accept a scientist from IITA as a supervisor of research while the Fellow is at IITA
Closing Date: September
Funding: Government
Contributor: Donor agencies and the government
No. of awards given last year: 30
No. of applicants last year: 150

For further information contact:

Head Training & Information Services, Oyo Road, PMB 5320, Ibadan, Nigeria

Tel:	(234) 2 241 2626
Fax:	(234) 2 241 2221
Email:	iita@cgiar.org
Contact:	Program Leader

International Mathematical Union (IMU)

International Mathematical Union, Office of the Secretariat, Zuse Institute Berlin, Takustr. 7, DEU-14195 Berlin, Germany

Fax: (49) 30 84185 269
Email: secretary@mathunion.org
Website: www.mathunion.org
Contact: Martin Grötschel, Secretary

The International Mathematical Union (IMU) is an international, non-governmental and non-profit scientific organization, with the purpose of promoting international co-operation in mathematics. It belongs to the International Council of Scientific Unions (ICSU).

International Mathematical Union Visiting Mathematician Programme

Subjects: Core of mathematics (pure and applied)
Purpose: To provide partial travel support for extended research visits in an advanced mathematical centre
Eligibility: Open to active mathematicians at PhD level with strong research possibilities. The programme is mainly intended for mathematicians working in a developing country to make an extended research visit to an advanced mathematical centre
Level of Study: Postdoctorate, Professional development
Type: Travel grant
Value: Dependent on travel costs and duration of visit
Length of Study: 2 months
Frequency: Annual, if funds are available
Study Establishment: An advanced mathematical research centre
Country of Study: Any country
No. of awards offered: 30
Application Procedure: Applicants must submit bio-data, a list of publications, a research programme, and an invitation letter from the host centre confirming that it will cover local expenses
Closing Date: Six months prior to the visit
No. of awards given last year: 8
No. of applicants last year: 30
Additional Information: The host centre must commit itself to supporting local expenses

For further information contact:

Mathematics Department Zuse Institute Berlin, DEU-14195 Berlin, Germany

Tel: (49) 801 581 5275
Fax: (49) 801 581 4148
Email: clemens@math.utah.edu
Contact: Mr Charles Herbert Clemens, Secretary

International School of Crystallography, E Majorana Centre

Dip to Scienze Della Terra Geo Ambientoli, Piazza di Porta San Donato 1, ITA-40126 Bologna, Italy

Tel: (39) 51 209 4912
Fax: (39) 51 209 4904
Email: riva@geomin.unibo.it
Website: www.geomin.unibo.it
Contact: Professor L Riva Di Sanseverino

The International School of Crystallography is an international organizing committee that offers, once a year, short advanced courses of 9–11 days on frontier topics in crystallography, solid state chemistry, materials science, structure activity relationship, molecular biology and biophysics.

International School of Crystallography Grants

Subjects: Frontier topics in crystallography, e.g. high pressure crystallography, polymorphism and drug design via crystallography
Purpose: To enable postgraduates to attend short high-level courses held at Erice once a year
Eligibility: Open to all who have scientific interests related to the topic chosen each year at a PhD or postdoctoral level. English language proficiency is mandatory
Level of Study: Doctorate, Postdoctorate, Postgraduate
Type: Grant
Value: Fees, board and lodging during the course
Length of Study: 8–12 days
Frequency: Annual
Study Establishment: E Majorana Centre, Erice, Sicily, Italy
Country of Study: Italy
No. of awards offered: 250
Application Procedure: Young applicants must submit a letter of recommendation stating their financial needs, personal data and details of scientific interests. Further details can be found at www.crystalerice.org
Closing Date: The end of November
Funding: Government
Contributor: NATO, the European Commission and the Italian National Research Council
No. of awards given last year: 70
No. of applicants last year: 250

For further information contact:

Department of Organic Chemistry, Via Marzolo 1, Bologna, Italy

Tel:	(39) 49 827 5275
Fax:	(39) 49 827 5239
Email:	paola.spadon@unipd.it
Contact:	Dr Paola Spadon

International Society of Nephrology (ISN)

Avenue de Tervueren, 300, BEL 1150 Brussels, Belgium

Tel:	(32) 2 743 1546
Fax:	(32) 2 743 1550
Email:	info@isn-online.org
Website:	www.nature.com/isn/about/index.html
Contact:	Professor John Feehally ISN Secretary General

The International Society of Nephrology (ISN) pursues the goal of worldwide advancement of education, science and patient care in nephrology. ISN achieves this through its journal *Kidney International*, organizing international congresses, symposia, specific programmes and fellowships. As a result, ISN helps to improve renal science and renal patient care worldwide, especially in emerging countries.

International Society of Nephrology Fellowship Awards

Subjects: Nephrology
Purpose: To offer training opportunities to young nephrologists in emerging countries with the ultimate goal of improving the standards of nephrology practice in their home institutions upon their return
Eligibility: Open to young nephrologists from emerging countries, as defined by World Bank criteria. Applicants must have received sufficient training in internal medicine or other fields to pass all host country examinations that are necessary for the care of patients. Fellowships are primarily offered for clinical training in nephrology, but in some circumstances research training may be allowed, priority can be considered for training in epidemiology
Level of Study: Postdoctorate, Predoctorate
Type: Fellowship
Value: The stipends are subject to indexation based on-the-cost-of-living in their host country; the top and bottom level grants are respectively US$26,000 and US$20,000 for 12 months of training. If the host country is contributing funds then this is subtracted from the standard fund
Length of Study: Short-term fellowships are for 3–6 months and long-term fellowships are for 12 months. Extensions are possible
Frequency: Annual
Study Establishment: Any suitable university, scientific institution or hospital
Application Procedure: Applicants must complete an application form, which is subjected to the review of an international committee. Applicants must provide evidence of a guaranteed position in a medical institution upon return to their home country. The applicant must agree to return to their home country upon completion of the training; if not, the recipient will have to refund the ISN fellowship in full
Closing Date: Deadlines are the end of January and the end of July each year. The selection is made in May and November each year
Funding: Private, Foundation
Contributor: Offered in collaboration with sister societies and industry, the American Society of Nephrology, the National Kidney Research Fund in the United Kingdom, Fresenius Medical care in Germany and the European renal Association
No. of awards given last year: 44
Additional Information: The selection procedure has three parts: data verification, where information provided by applicants is verified and evaluated through correspondence; evaluation, where 7 members of the Committee, one from each Continent, score each application according to standard format; and finally, selection, which is largely based on the aforementioned scores but also considers the geographical balance, urgent needs in certain regions and the preference of certain sponsors

For further information contact:

ISN Global Headquarters Av. Tervueren 300, BEL 1150 Brussels, Belgium

Email:	an@associationhg.com

International Society of Nephrology Travel Grants

Subjects: Nephrology
Purpose: To encourage young physicians and scientists to attend conferences, especially those from emerging countries. Travel grants are offered to facilitate attendance at the ISN

International Congress and the ISN Forefronts Commission Conference

Eligibility: Applicants must have training and experience in an area of research relevant to the conference and an infrastructure at their home institutions to allow the pursuit of techniques and approaches discussed at the conference. Young physicians and scientists are preferred as are ISN Fellows. A portion of the grants are reserved for applicants from emerging countries

Level of Study: Doctorate, Postdoctorate, Postgraduate, Research

Type: Travel grant

Value: The size of the grant is decided according to each conference and congress

Length of Study: Varies

No. of awards offered: 395

Application Procedure: Applicants must complete an application form, which can be downloaded from the ISN website or requested from the ISN Secretary General a year prior to the Congress. Applications can also be obtained from the Directors of the ISN Forefront Programmes

Closing Date: Please contact the organization

Funding: Private, Foundation

Contributor: Offered in collaboration with sponsors of ISN

No. of awards given last year: 120

No. of applicants last year: 395

For further information contact:

ISN Secretary General, Cairo Kidney Centre, 3 Hussein El-Memar Street, Antikhana, PO Box 91, Bab El-Louk, Egypt

Tel:	(20) 2 579 0267
Email:	lsn@rusys.eg.net
Contact:	Dr Rashad Barsoum

International Society of Nephrology Visiting Scholars Program

Subjects: Nephrology

Purpose: To improve the long-term quality of patient care, education and research in fields relevant to the kidney at the host institution, and enable senior physicians or scientists who are experts in nephrology and related disciplines to spend between 6 weeks and 3 months at an institution in the developing world

Eligibility: Applicants must focus primarily on hands-on activities that are the focus of this award, e.g. the establishment of a new clinical programme, research programme or laboratory technique. ISN visiting scholars should spend the duration of their study time at an institution in the developing

world. Applicants must be experts in nephrology and related disciplines

Level of Study: Postdoctorate, Research

Type: Scholarship

Value: US$20,000, inclusive of travel and expenses, for 3 months or a pro rata amount for a shorter period of time

Length of Study: 6 weeks–3 months

No. of awards offered: 2

Application Procedure: Applicants must send a description of the programme, its objectives, personal references and a letter of acceptance from the host institution to the ISN Secretary General. Applicants must be members of the ISN

Closing Date: Please contact the organization

Funding: Private, Foundation

No. of awards given last year: 2

No. of applicants last year: 2

For further information contact:

Cairo Kidney Centre, 3 Hussein El-Memar Street, Antikhana, PO Box 91, Bab El-Louk, Egypt

Tel:	(20) 2 579 0267
Email:	isn@rusys.eg.net

International Union for Vacuum Science and Technology (IUVSTA)

84 Oldfield Drive, Vicars Cross, CH3 5LW, Chester, United Kingdom

Tel:	(44) 1244 34 2675, 771 34 03525
Fax:	(44) 7005 86 0135
Email:	eisenmenger@ifp.tuwien.ac.at
Website:	www.iuvsta.org
Contact:	Dr Christoph Eisenmenger-Sittner, Secretary General

The International Union for Vacuum Science and Technology (IUVSTA) is a non-government organization whose member societies represent all vacuum scientists, engineers and technologists in their country.

Welch Scholarship

Subjects: Vacuum science

Purpose: To encourage promising scholars who wish to study vacuum science, techniques or their application in any field

Eligibility: Open to applicants of any nationality who hold the minimum of a Bachelor's degree, although preference is given to those holding a doctoral degree

Level of Study: Doctorate, Postdoctorate, Postgraduate

Type: Scholarship

Value: US$15,000. The scholarship money is paid in three installments – one of US$7,500 at the beginning, another of US$7,000, 6 months after he/she has started work, and a third of US$500 upon delivery of a final report after completion of work

Length of Study: 1 year

Frequency: Annual

Study Establishment: An appropriate laboratory

Country of Study: Any country

No. of awards offered: 6

Application Procedure: Applicants must complete and submit an application form with a research proposal, a curriculum vitae and two letters of reference. More information and application forms can be obtained from the website

Closing Date: 15 April

Funding: Private

Contributor: IUVSTA

No. of awards given last year: 1

No. of applicants last year: 6

Additional Information: Researchers who applied unsuccessfully for previous Welch Scholarships may apply again. Applications for renewal of the Scholarship are not accepted

For further information contact:

Canadian Photorics Fabrication Centre, Institute for Microstructural Sciences, National Research Council, Building M-50, Montréal Road, Canada

| Email: | Frank.Shepherd@nrc-cnrc.gc.ca |
| Contact: | Dr FR Shepherd, Administrator Technical Manager |

International Union of Biochemistry and Molecular Biology (IUBMB)

University of Calgary, Department of Biochemistry & Molecular Biology, 3330 Hospital Drive NW, HM G72B, Calgary, AB T2N 4N1, Canada

Tel:	(1) 403 220 3021
Fax:	(1) 403 270 2211
Email:	walsh@ucalgary.ca
Website:	www.iubmb.org
Contact:	Professor Michael P Walsh, IUBMB General Secretary

IUBMB seeks to advance the international molecular life sciences community by: Promoting interactions across the diversity of endeavours in the molecular life sciences, creating networks that transcend barriers of ethnicity, culture, gender, and economic status, creating pathways for young scientists to fulfil their potential, providing evidence-based advice on public policy, promoting the values, standards, and ethics of science and the free and unhampered movement of scientists of all nations.

Wood-Whelan Research Fellowships

Subjects: Biochemistry and molecular biology

Purpose: To provide financial assistance to young biochemists and molecular biologists to carry out research and training in a laboratory other than their own

Eligibility: Open to applicants who are residents of countries that are members of IUBMB and students or young researchers less than 35 years old. Retroactive applications will not be considered

Level of Study: Graduate, Postdoctorate, Postgraduate, Research

Type: Fellowship

Value: Up to US$4,000. It covers travel and incidental costs, as well as living expenses

Length of Study: 1–4 months

Frequency: Annual

No. of awards offered: 32

Application Procedure: Applicants must submit a completed application form along with details of the research proposal, budget, curriculum vitae with a list of publications and letters of recommendation following the guidelines which can be found at website. The original application should be sent by the applicant by email as PDF files

Closing Date: At least 2 months before the proposed visit

Contributor: The main sources of income for IUBMB are dues from adhering bodies (member societies) and revenue from publications

No. of awards given last year: 15

No. of applicants last year: 32

Additional Information: Travel should commence within 4 months of the award being made

For further information contact:

| Email: | janet.macaulay@monash.edu |
| Contact: | Dr Janet Macaulay |

Iota Sigma Pi

Microelectronics Technology, Lord Corporation, 110 Lord Drive, Cary, NC 27511, United States of America

Tel:	(1) 919 468 5979
Email:	sara.paisner@lord.com
Website:	www.iotasigmapi.info
Contact:	Sara Paisner, Senior Scientist

Iota Sigma Pi, founded in 1902, is a National Honor Society that serves to promote the advancement of women in chemistry by granting recognition to women who have demonstrated superior scholastic achievement and high professional competence by election into Iota Sigma Pi.

Agnes Fay Morgan Research Award

Subjects: Chemistry and biochemistry
Purpose: To acknowledge research achievements in chemistry or biochemistry
Eligibility: Open to female applicants who are not more than 40 years of age
Level of Study: Postgraduate
Type: Award
Value: The Award will consist of US$500, a certificate, and membership in Iota Sigma Pi with a waiver of dues for 1 year
Frequency: Annual
Study Establishment: Any accredited institution
Country of Study: Any country
Application Procedure: The nomination dossier must be sent electronically (preferably as a pdf) to Dr Nancy Eddy Hopkins
Closing Date: 15 February
Contributor: Iota Sigma Pi
Additional Information: Please see the website for further details

For further information contact:

Tel:	(1) 504 862 3162
Email:	nhopkin@tulane.edu
Contact:	Dr Nancy Eddy Hopkins, Director for Professional Awards

Anna Louise Hoffman Award for Outstanding Achievement in Graduate Research

Subjects: Chemistry
Purpose: To recognize outstanding achievement in chemical research

Eligibility: The candidate must be a full-time (as defined by the nominee's institution) woman graduate student who is a candidate for a graduate degree in an accredited institution. The research presented by the candidate must be original research which can be described by one of the main chemical divisions (e.g., analytical, biochemical, inorganic, organic, physical, and/or ancillary divisions of chemistry). The nominee may be, but need not be, a member of Iota Sigma Pi
Level of Study: Postgraduate
Type: Award
Value: The award will be $500, a certificate and a waiver of dues for 1 year
Frequency: Annual
Study Establishment: Any accredited institution
Country of Study: Any country
Application Procedure: The complete dossier must be sent electronically as a single file (pdf format is recommended) to Professor Jill Nelson Granger
Closing Date: 15 February
Contributor: Iota Sigma Pi
Additional Information: Please see the website for further details

For further information contact:

Sweet Briar College, Department of Chemistry, Sweet Briar, VA 24595, United States of America

Tel:	(1) 434 381 6166
Email:	granger@sbc.edu
Contact:	Professor Jill Nelson Granger, Director for Student Awards

Gladys Anderson Emerson Scholarship

Subjects: Chemistry and biochemistry
Purpose: To award excellence in chemistry or biochemistry
Eligibility: Open to applicants who are members of Iota Sigma Pi
Level of Study: Postgraduate
Type: Scholarship
Value: US$2,000 and a certificate
Frequency: Annual
Study Establishment: Any accredited institution
Country of Study: Any country
Application Procedure: The complete dossier must be sent electronically as a single file (pdf format is recommended) to Professor Jill Nelson Granger
Closing Date: 15 February
Contributor: Iota Sigma Pi

Additional Information: Please see the website for further details

Iota Sigma Pi Centennial Award

Subjects: Chemistry, biochemistry
Purpose: To award excellence in teaching chemistry, biochemistry or chemistry-related subjects
Eligibility: Holds a teaching position at an institution that does not have a graduate program in her department or holds a teaching position that is for teaching undergraduates >75% of her time at an institution that does have a graduate program in her department. The nominee may be, but need not be, a member of Iota Sigma Pi
Level of Study: Postgraduate
Type: Award
Value: US$500, a certificate and membership in Iota Sigma Pi with a waiver of dues for 1 year
Frequency: Annual
Application Procedure: One copy of the nomination dossier must be sent electronically (preferably as a pdf) to Dr Nancy Eddy Hopkins
Closing Date: 15 February
Contributor: Iota Sigma Pi
Additional Information: Please see the website for details

For further information contact:

Tel: (1) 504 862 3162
Email: nhopkin@tulane.edu
Contact: Dr Nancy Eddy Hopkins, Director for Professional Awards

Iota Sigma Pi National Honorary Member Award

Subjects: Chemistry
Purpose: To honour outstanding women chemists
Eligibility: Open to female candidate with exceptional achievements in chemistry. Applicants may or may not be members of Iota Sigma Pi
Type: Award
Value: US$1,500 a certificate and membership in Iota Sigma Pi with a lifetime waiver of dues
Length of Study: Every 3 years
Frequency: Every 3 years
Application Procedure: One copy of the nomination dossier must be sent electronically (preferably as a pdf) to Nancy Eddy Hopkins
Closing Date: 15 February
Additional Information: Please see the website for details

For further information contact:

Email: nhopkin@tulane.edu
Contact: Dr Nancy Eddy Hopkins, Director for Professional Awards

Violet Diller Professional Excellence Award

Subjects: Chemistry
Purpose: To recognize significant accomplishments in academic, governmental or industrial chemistry
Eligibility: Open to female applicants who have contributed to the scientific community or society on a national level
Level of Study: Postgraduate
Type: Award
Value: US$1,000, a certificate and membership in Iota sigma Pi with a lifetime waiver of dues
Frequency: Every 3 years
Application Procedure: One copy of the nomination dossier must be sent electronically (preferably as a pdf) to Nancy Eddy Hopkins
Closing Date: 15 February
Contributor: Iota Sigma Pi
Additional Information: Please see the website for further details

For further information contact:

Email: nhopkin@tulane.edu

Iowa State University

Iowa State University, Ames, IA 50011, United States of America

Tel: (1) 515 2944111
Email: online@iastate.edu
Website: www.iastate.edu
Contact: Dr James R Bloedell, Dean

Iowa State University of Science and Technology is a public band-grant institution serving the people of Iowa, the nation and the world.

American Institute of Certified Public Accountants/Robert Half Student Scholarship Award

Subjects: Accounting, finance and information systems

Purpose: AICPA and Robert Half offer the AICPA/Robert Half Student Scholarship Award to provide financial assistance to outstanding accounting students who demonstrate potential to become leaders in the CPA profession
Eligibility: Not eligible to students who have already gained their CPA
Level of Study: Postgraduate
Type: Scholarship
Value: US$2,500
Length of Study: 1 year
Frequency: Annual
Study Establishment: Iowa State University
Country of Study: United States of America
Application Procedure: When available, publication and application details for this award can be found at ThisWayToCPA.com
Closing Date: 1 August
Funding: Private
Contributor: AICPA

For further information contact:

AICPA/Accountemps Student Scholarship Program, AICPA-Team 331, 1211 Avenue of the Americas, United States of America

Email: scholarships@aicpa.org

Iowa State University of Science and Technology

Institute of Social and Behavior Research, 2625 N Loop Drive Suite 500, Ames, IA 50010, United States of America

Email: rconger@iastate.edu
Website: www.iastate.edu
Contact: Mr Rand D Conger

Acute Generalized Exanthematous Pustulosis Fellowship

Purpose: The primary goals of the ISU AGEP program are to (a) increase the number of underrepresented students obtaining graduate degrees in science, technology, engineering and mathematics (STEM)
Eligibility: You must meet the following requirements: 1. Member of an underrepresented ethnic group (African American, American Indian, Hispanic, Alaska Natives, and

Native Hawaiian or Pacific Islander). 2. Admitted into a STEM (science, technology, engineering, mathematics) field. 3. United States citizenship (permanent residents are ineligible). 4. Enrolled as a first semester PhD student with a fall entry date
Level of Study: Graduate
Type: Fellowship
Value: The annual stipend is US$27,500
Frequency: Annual
Country of Study: Any country
Application Procedure: 1. The fellowship is for five (5) years from the term of entry. 2. Changing to another program of study may terminate the fellowship
Closing Date: Open in all months
Funding: Private

For further information contact:

1137 Pearson Hall 505 Morrill Rd, Ames, IA 50011, United States of America

Email: grad_college@iastate.edu

Irish Research Council

First Floor, Brooklawn House, Crampton Avenue (off Shelbourne Road) Ballsbridge, Dublin 4, Ireland

Tel: (353) 1 231 5000
Fax: (353) 1 231 5009
Email: info@research.ie
Website: www.research.ie

The Irish Research Council was formally launched by the Minister for Research and Innovation, Seán Sherlock TD, on 29 March. A sub-board of the Higher Education Authority, the Council was established through a merger of the Irish Research Council for Humanities and Social Sciences (IRCHSS) and the Irish Research Council for Science, Engineering and Technology (IRCSET).

Employment-Based Postgraduate Programme

Subjects: AHSS, STEM
Purpose: The Irish Research Council's Employment-Based Postgraduate Programme is a national initiative combining research with workplace experience. It is aimed at students

across all disciplines and provides an opportunity to bring research ideas to employment partners with the support of a higher education institution. The programme is co-funded by the council and the employment partner with the council providing a contribution of €24,000 per annum to the wage, scholarship fees and research expenses of suitably qualified individuals to complete a higher degree for a period of one to four years while embedded in the environment of an employment partner in Ireland. The application is developed by the individual researcher in collaboration with an employment mentor and an academic supervisor

Eligibility: See Terms and Conditions Document for eligibility criteria available on research.ie/funding/. Must be eligible to register for a Research Masters or PhD in a Higher Education Institution in the Republic of Ireland

Level of Study: Doctorate, Postgraduate

Type: Scholarship

Value: €24,000 per annum

Length of Study: One to four years

Frequency: Annual

Country of Study: Ireland

Application Procedure: Online application system

Closing Date: Annual

Funding: Government

Contributor: The Irish Research Council provides €24,000 per annum. In addition, the Employment partner organisations must commit a minimum contribution of €8,000 per annum

For further information contact:

Email: info@research.ie

Enterprise Partnership Scheme

Subjects: AHSS, STEM

Purpose: The Irish Research Council's Enterprise Partnership Scheme supports collaborations between researchers and enterprises on a project related to the interests of the enterprise partner. The programme is two thirds co-funded by the council and one third by the enterprise partner who can be a national or international company, charity, non-governmental or other organisation

Eligibility: See Terms and Conditions Document for eligibility criteria available on research.ie/funding/

Level of Study: Doctorate, Postdoctorate, Postgraduate

Type: Fellowship/Scholarship

Length of Study: One to four years

Frequency: Annual

Country of Study: Ireland

Application Procedure: Online application system

Closing Date: Annual

Funding: Government

For further information contact:

Email: info@research.ie

Government of Ireland Postgraduate Scholarship Programme

Subjects: AHSS, STEM

Purpose: The programme provides outstanding students with the opportunity to direct their own research at the early-career stage, working with a supervisor, in their chosen area of interest

Eligibility: Must be eligible to register for a Research Masters or PhD in a Higher Education Institution in Ireland. While the majority of scholarships will be awarded to applicants from the EFTA/EEA member states, a proportion of scholarships will also be made to exceptional applicants from non-EFTA/EEA countries. For more information, see Terms and Conditions Document for eligibility criteria available on research. ie/funding/. The European Free Trade Area (EFTA) and the European Economic Area (EEA)

Level of Study: Doctorate, Postgraduate

Type: Scholarship

Value: €24,000 per annum

Length of Study: One to four years

Frequency: Annual

Country of Study: Ireland

Application Procedure: Online application system

Closing Date: See website for deadlines

Funding: Government

For further information contact:

Email: info@research.ie

Islamic Cooperation Organization (OIC)

Islamic Cooperation Organization International Internship Program

Purpose: OIC Intern gives the opportunity for professional experience to young people through work ethic and teamwork experience

Eligibility: OIC Intern provides a meeting point between the candidates who want to work as interns with required qaulifications and the institution that need interns. For further details, check the website online en.oicintern.org/

Level of Study: Postgraduate
Type: Programme grant
Frequency: Annual
Country of Study: Any country
Closing Date: 24 March
Funding: Private

For further information contact:

P.O.Box 178, Jeddah 21411, Kingdom of Saudi Arabia

Tel: (996) 12 6515222
Email: info@opportunitiesforafricans.com

J

James Cook University

Graduate Research School, Townsville, QLD 4811, Australia

Tel:	(61) 7 4781 4575
Fax:	(61) 7 4781 6204
Email:	GRS@jcu.edu.au
Website:	www.jcu.edu.au
Contact:	Manager

James Cook University prides itself on its international reputation for research and discovery and teaching that is enhanced and enlivened by that research activity.

James Cook University Postgraduate Research Scholarship

Subjects: All disciplines
Purpose: To encourage full-time postgraduate research leading to a Master's or PhD degree
Eligibility: Open to any student who has attained at least an Upper Second Class (Honours) Bachelor's Degree
Level of Study: Postgraduate
Type: Scholarship
Value: Stipend at A$24,653 per year plus thesis and relocation allowance where applicable
Length of Study: 3 years with a possible additional 6 months in exceptional circumstances for the PhD, or 2 years for the Master's programme
Frequency: Annual
Study Establishment: James Cook University
Country of Study: Australia
Application Procedure: Details of how to apply can be found here: https://www.jcu.edu.au/graduate-research-school/candidates/prospective-students/how-to-apply
Closing Date: 31 October for Domestic (Australian) students and 31 August for International students

Additional Information: For further details visit the website www.jcu.edu.au/grs/scholarships/JCUDEV_014879.html

For further information contact:

Tel:	(61) 7 4781 4575
Fax:	(61) 7 4781 6204
Email:	GRS@jcu.edu.au
Contact:	James Cook University, Graduate Research School Manager

Master of Business Administration Programme

Length of Study: 1 year
Application Procedure: Applicants must complete an application form supplying transcripts, a curriculum vitae, a one page essay, and referee reports
Closing Date: January and 15 June

For further information contact:

Faculty of Arts Commerce & Economics MBA Programme Office of International Affairs

Tel:	(61) 7 7814 407
Fax:	(61) 7 7815 988
Email:	InternationalAffairs@jcu.edu.aau
Contact:	Director

Sustainable Tourism CRC – Climate Change PhD Scholarship

Subjects: Impacts of climate change on Great Barrier Reef tourism operators
Eligibility: Open to the candidates who have achieved Honours 1 or equivalent
Level of Study: Postgraduate, Research

© Springer Nature Limited 2019
Palgrave Macmillan (ed.), *The Grants Register 2020*,
https://doi.org/10.1057/978-1-349-95943-3

Frequency: 1
Study Establishment: 3 years
Application Procedure: A$19,930 per year
Closing Date: Applicants must apply directly to the scholarship provider. Check the website for further details
No. of awards given last year: James Cook University
Additional Information: 31 October

For further information contact:

STCRC Education Program, Sustainable Tourism CRC

Tel: (61) 7 5552 9063
Email: Jane@crctourism.com.au
Contact: Jane Malady

Japan Society for the Promotion of Science (JSPS)

5-3-1 Kojimachi, Chiyoda-ku, Tokyo 102 0083, Japan

Tel: (81) 3263 9094
Fax: (81) 3263 1854
Email: gaitoku@jsps.go.jp
Website: www.jsps.go.jp

The Japan Society for the Promotion of Science (JSPS) is an independent administrative institution, established for the purpose of contributing to the advancement of science in all fields of the natural and social sciences and the humanities. The JSPS plays a pivotal role in the administration of a wide spectrum of Japan's scientific and academic programmes.

Japan Society for the Promotion of Science Postdoctoral Fellowships for North American and European Researchers (Short-term)

Subjects: Humanities, social sciences, natural sciences, engineering and medicine
Purpose: To assist promising and highly qualified young foreign researchers wishing to conduct research in Japan
Eligibility: Be a citizen or permanent resident of an eligible country (the US, Canada, EU countries, Switzerland, Norway, and Russia). Candidates must have obtained their doctoral degree at a university outside Japan within 6 years of the date the fellowship goes into effect, or must be currently enroled in a doctoral course at a university outside Japan and scheduled to receive their PhD within 2 years
Level of Study: Postdoctorate, Predoctorate

Type: Fellowship
Value: Round-trip air ticket, monthly maintenance allowance of ¥3,62,000 for PhD holder and ¥2,00,000 for non-PhD holder, settling-in allowance of ¥2,00,000 and overseas travel insurance, research support allowance
Length of Study: 1 year but a minimum of 1 month
Frequency: Annual
Study Establishment: Universities and research institutions
Country of Study: Japan
Application Procedure: Applicants must write for details. Application must be submitted to JSPS by the host researcher in Japan
Closing Date: Check with website
Funding: Government
Additional Information: Please see the website for further details www.jsps.go.jp/english/e-fellow/postdoctoral.html

For further information contact:

Email: agneta.granlund@stint.se

Japanese American Citizens League (JACL)

National Headquarters, 1765 Sutter Street, San Francisco, CA 94115, United States of America

Tel: (1) 415 345 1075, 415 921 5225
Fax: (1) 415 931 4671
Email: ncwnp@jacl.org, youthdir@jacl.org
Website: www.jacl.org
Contact: Scholarships Officer

The Japanese American Citizens League (JACL) was founded in 1929 to fight discrimination against people of Japanese ancestry. It is the largest and one of the oldest Asian American organizations in the USA. The JACL has over 24,500 members in 112 chapters located in 25 states, Washington, DC, and Japan. The organization operates within a structure of eight district councils, with headquarters in San Francisco, CA.

Mike M. Masaoka Congressional Fellowship

Subjects: Public service
Purpose: To financially support and develop leaders for public service
Eligibility: Candidates must be U.S. citizens who are graduating college seniors or students in graduate or professional

programs and a member of the JACL. Preference will be given to those who have demonstrated a commitment to Asian American issues, particularly those affecting the Japanese American community. Communication skills, especially in writing, are important

Level of Study: Postgraduate, Professional development
Type: Fellowship
Value: US$2,200–2,500 per month
Length of Study: 6–8 months
Frequency: Annual
Country of Study: United States of America
Application Procedure: Applicants must send a completed application form and a letter of reference to the JACL national headquarters
Closing Date: 20 May
Funding: Foundation
Additional Information: Preference will be given to those who have demonstrated a commitment to Asian American issues, particularly those affecting the Japanese American community. Please see the website for further details at www.jacl.org/now-accepting-applications-for-mike-m-masaoka-congressional-fellowship/

For further information contact:

Japanese American Citizens League Headquarters, Mike M. Masaoka Fellowship, 1850 M Street NW, Suite 1100, Washington, DC 20036, United States of America

Email: policy@jacl.org

Norman Y. Mineta Fellowship

Subjects: All subjects
Purpose: To focus on public policy advocacy as well as programs of safety awareness in the Asian Pacific American (APA) community
Eligibility: Open to the members of the JACL with 4-year degree from an accredited college or university having excellent writing, analytical, and computer skills
Level of Study: Postgraduate
Type: Fellowship
Value: A$2,200 monthly stipend will be provided along with roundtrip airfare, courtesy of Southwest Airlines
Length of Study: 6–10 months
Application Procedure: Interested applicants should submit a curriculum vitae, a sample of writing, and names and contact information for two references to the Washington, DC office of the JACL at policy@jacl.org with 'Mineta Fellowship' in the subject line
Closing Date: Check with website
Contributor: State Farm Insurance

Additional Information: Candidates must have ability to take directions and follow through with assignments, must work well with others, and have good interpersonal skills. Please see the website for further details www.jacl.org/internships-and-fellowships/

For further information contact:

JACL, 1828 L Street, NW Suite 802, Washington, DC 20036, United States of America

Tel: (1) 202 223 1240
Fax: (1) 202 296 8082
Email: dc@jacl.org
Contact: Floyd Mori, National Director

Jiamusi University

Heilongjiang Provincial Government Scholarships

Purpose: the Jiamusi is the provincial key construction university with high level in Heilongjiang province, which is also a comprehensive university with a wide range of categories and medical specialties
Eligibility: Scholarship is available for pursuing undergraduate, postgraduate and doctoral programme
Level of Study: Postgraduate
Type: Scholarship
Frequency: Annual
Country of Study: Any country
Closing Date: 15 April
Funding: International office

For further information contact:

Room No. 209, the Admission Office of International Education College of Jiamusi University, No. 258 Xuefu Street, Jiamusi City, Heilongjiang Province, China

Tel: (86) 454 8603918
Fax: (86) 454 8603918
Email: jmsuadmission@163.com

John Carter Brown Library at Brown University

Box 1894, Brown University, Providence, RI 02912, United States of America

Tel: (1) 401 863 2725
Fax: (1) 401 863 3477
Email: JCBL_Information@Brown.edu
Website: www.jcbl.org

The John Carter Brown Library, an independently funded and administered institution for advanced research in history and the humanities, is located on the campus of Brown University. The Library supports research focused on the colonial history of the Americas, including all aspects of the European, African, and Native American involvement.

Library Associates Fellowship

Subjects: Colonial history of the Americas, North and South, including all aspects of the European, African, and Native American involvement
Purpose: To assist scholars in any area of research related to the Library's holdings
Eligibility: Open to scholars engaged in predoctoral, postdoctoral or independent research. Graduate students must have passed their preliminary or general examinations at the time of application
Level of Study: Postdoctorate, Predoctorate, Research
Type: Fellowship
Value: US$2,100 per month
Length of Study: 2–4 months
Frequency: Annual
Country of Study: United States of America
Application Procedure: Applicants must complete an application form. Candidates should write to, or email the Director
Closing Date: 15 December
Funding: Private
Contributor: Associates of the John Carter Brown Library

Norman Fiering Fund

Subjects: Colonial history of the Americas, North and South, including all aspects of the European, African, and Native American involvement
Purpose: To support scholars in any area of research related to the Library's holdings
Eligibility: Open to scholars in any area of research related to the Library's holdings
Type: Funding support
Value: US$2,100 per month
Length of Study: 2–4 months
Country of Study: United States of America
Closing Date: 3 January

For further information contact:

John Carter Brown Library, Box 1894, Providence, RI 02912, United States of America

Tel: (1) 401 863 2725
Email: JCBL_Fellowships@Brown.edu
Contact: Director

Ruth and Lincoln Ekstrom Fellowship

Subjects: The history of women and the family in the Americas prior to 1825, including the question of cultural influences on gender formation
Purpose: To sponsor historical research
Eligibility: Open to scholars engaged in predoctoral, postdoctoral or independent research. Graduate students must have passed their preliminary or general examinations at the time of application
Level of Study: Postdoctorate, Predoctorate, Research
Type: Fellowship
Value: US$2,100 per month
Length of Study: 2–4 months
Frequency: Annual
Country of Study: United States of America
Application Procedure: Applicants must complete an application form. Candidates should write to, or email the Director
Closing Date: 15 December
Funding: Private
No. of awards given last year: 1

For further information contact:

Email: JCBL_Information@Brown.edu

John E Fogarty International Center (FIC) for Advanced Study in the Health Sciences

Building 31, 31 Center Drive, MSC 2220, Bethesda, MD 20892 2220, United States of America

Tel: (1) 301 496 2075
Fax: (1) 301 594 1211
Email: FICinfo@mail.nih.gov
Website: www.fic.nih.gov
Contact: Program Officer

The John E Fogarty International Center (FIC) for Advanced Study in the Health Sciences, a component of the

National Institutes of Health (NIH), promotes international co-operation in the biomedical and behavioural sciences. This is accomplished primarily through long- and short-term fellowships, small grants and training grants. This compendium of international opportunities is prepared by the FIC with the hope that it will stimulate scientists to seek research enhancing experiences abroad.

Global Health Research Initiative Program for New Foreign Investigators (GRIP)

Subjects: Medicine
Purpose: To assist well-trained young investigators to contribute to health care advances in their home countries
Eligibility: Open to all well-trained young investigators. To verify eligibility, new foreign investigators should review the answers to Frequently Asked Questions. Please contact Dr Xingzhu Liu by email at xingzhu.liu@nih.gov with questions
Level of Study: Postgraduate
Type: Grant
Value: US$50,000 per year
Length of Study: 5 years
Frequency: Annual
Application Procedure: Application form on request
Closing Date: Check with website
Funding: Foundation
Contributor: Fugarty International Center
Additional Information: Please see the website for further details www.fic.nih.gov/programs/Pages/new-foreign-investigators.aspx

For further information contact:

Email: butrumb@mail.nih.gov
Contact: Bruce Butrum, Grants Management Officer

John E Fogarty Foreign Funded Fellowship Programs

Subjects: Biomedical and behavioural science
Purpose: To allow United States scientists to conduct collaborative research abroad
Eligibility: Open to scientists who are United States citizens or permanent residents invited by foreign host scientists to participate in research projects of mutual interest
Level of Study: Postdoctorate
Type: Fellowship
Value: To cover the visiting scientist's individual expenses abroad
Length of Study: Usually up to 1 year, possible extension in some countries

Frequency: Annual
Country of Study: Other
Application Procedure: Applicants must complete an application form, available on request or downloadable from www.avh.de
Closing Date: 15 April, 5 August, 5 December
Additional Information: Because fellowships are intended to support an individual's expenses abroad, the foreign host is expected to have the resources to support the research project. Types of activities in which Fellows engage include collaboration in basic or clinical research and familiarisation with or utilisation of special techniques and equipment not otherwise available to the applicant. The programmes do not provide support for activities which have as their principal purpose conducting brief observational visits, attending scientific meetings or formal training courses, or providing full-time clinical, technical or teaching services. Funding is provided by the Alexander von Humboldt Foundation (Germany), the Israeli Ministry of Health, the Japan Society for the Promotion of Science, the Japan Science and Technology Agency, the Swedish Medical Research Council, and the National Science Council of Taiwan. Candidates may apply to only one of these programmes during any given year

For further information contact:

Alexander von Humboldt Foundation, US Liaison Office, 1055 Thomas Jefferson Street NW, Suite 2030, United States of America

Tel: (1) 202 296 2990
Fax: (1) 202 833 8514
Email: info@humboldtfoundation.org

John F. Kennedy Library Foundation

Columbia Point, Boston, MA 02125, United States of America

Tel: (1) 866 514 1960
Fax: (1) 617 514 1600
Email: Kennedy.library@nara.gov
Website: www.jfklibrary.org
Contact: Fellowships Administrator

The John F. Kennedy Library Foundation is a non-profit organization that provides financial support, staffing and creative resources for the John F. Kennedy Presidential Library and Museum whose purpose is to advance the study and understanding of President Kennedy's life and career, and the times in which he lived and to promote a greater appreciation of America's political and cultural heritage, the process of governing and the importance of public service.

Abba P. Schwartz Research Fellowship

Subjects: The successful candidate will develop at least a portion of his or her original research using archival materials from the Kennedy Library

Purpose: It is intended to support a scholar in the production of a substantial work in the areas of immigration, naturalization, or refugee policy, subjects of great personal and professional interest to Mr Schwartz

Eligibility: See award purpose

Level of Study: Postgraduate

Type: Fellowship

Value: A stipend of up to US$3,100

Frequency: Annual

Country of Study: United States of America

Application Procedure: Please submit the following documentation: (1) an application form (pdf) accompanied by a brief proposal (three to four pages) in the form of a letter describing the planned research, its significance, the intended audience, and expected outcome; (2) two letters of recommendation from academic or other appropriate references; (3) a sample of your writing (approx. 10 pages); (4) a project budget; and (5) a vita

Closing Date: 30 September

Funding: Foundation

Contributor: John F. Kennedy Library Foundation

Additional Information: The estimated per diem cost of accommodations, meals, and incidentals for Boston is US$250 Please see the website for further details

For further information contact:

Tel:	(1) 617 514 1630
Fax:	(1) 617 514 1625
Email:	Kennedy.Fellowships@nara.gov
Contact:	Mr Stephen Plotkin, Fellowship Coordinator

Arthur M. Schlesinger, Jr. Fellowship

Subjects: Political science and history

Purpose: To financially support scholars in the production of substantial work on the foreign policy of the Kennedy years

Eligibility: Open to citizens of the US only

Level of Study: Postgraduate

Type: Fellowships

Value: Up to US$5,000

Frequency: Annual

Country of Study: United States of America

Application Procedure: Applicants must submit application form, financial need analysis, essay, reference letters, and curriculum vitae. Applicants are strongly encouraged to contact the Kennedy Library for information about its collections and holdings before applying

Closing Date: 15 August

Funding: Foundation

Contributor: Schlesinger Fund

Additional Information: Proposals are invited from all sources, but preference will be given to applicants specializing in the work on the foreign policy of the Kennedy years especially with regard to the western hemisphere, or on Kennedy domestic policy, especially with regard to racial justice and to the conservation of natural resources. Preference is also given to projects not supported by large grants from other institutions. Please see the website for further details

For further information contact:

Tel:	(1) 617 514 1629
Fax:	(1) 617 514 1625
Email:	Kennedy.library@nara.gov
Contact:	Grant and Fellowship Coordinator

John R. Mott Scholarship Foundation

John R. Mott Scholarship

Purpose: This award is for Italian students from the Calabria region attending college. Awards are given based on academic achievement and financial need

Eligibility: 1. Applicants must be from the Calabria region of Italy. 2. Must be enrolled in a post-secondary school seeking a degree or professional certification. 3. Must demonstrate academic achievement. 4. Must demonstrate financial need. 5. This award is for international students

Level of Study: Graduate

Type: Scholarship

Value: US$10,000

Frequency: Annual

Country of Study: United States of America

Application Procedure: Applications are accepted between 9 February and 15 April. Applications will be available online from the John R. Mott Scholarship Foundation website. Applicants must complete the application online, and mail or fax the following materials to the foundation by the deadline: official transcript from university or official completion certification and academic performance document from high school, and ISEE-U certification attesting to the tax liability of the family

Closing Date: 15 April

Funding: Foundation

For further information contact:

1860 19th St., N.W. Washington, DC 20009, United States of America

Tel:　　(1) 202 483 2618
Email:　scholarships@swe.org

Johns Hopkins University

615 N. Wolfe Street, Suite E1002, Baltimore, MD 21205, United States of America

Tel:　　　(1) 410 516 3400, 410 955 1680
Fax:　　　(1) 410 614 2871
Email:　　admiss@jhsph.edu
Website:　webapps.jhu.edu/jhuniverse/information_about_hopkins/
Contact:　Grants Co-ordinator

The vision of the Johns Hopkins Center for Alternatives to Animal Testing is to be a leading force in the development and use of reduction, refinement and replacement alternatives in research, testing and education to protect and enhance the health of the public.

Center for Alternatives to Animal Testing Grants Programme

Subjects: Toxicology and immunotoxicology
Purpose: To promote and support research in the development of in vitro and other alternative techniques
Eligibility: No eligibility restrictions. Applicants' proposals must meet the goals of the CAAT Grants Program
Level of Study: Unrestricted
Value: For proposals relating to toxicology: up to US$25,000; proposals relating to developmental immunotoxicology: up to US$50,000
Length of Study: 1 year
Frequency: Annual
Country of Study: United States of America
No. of awards offered: 30
Application Procedure: Applicants must complete a preproposal. After review, selected applicants are invited to submit a full application
Closing Date: 21 March
Funding: Private
No. of awards given last year: 12
No. of applicants last year: 30

Additional Information: Please see the website for further details caat.jhsph.edu/programs/grants/

For further information contact:

615 N Wolfe St W7032, Baltimore, MD 21205, United States of America

Fax:　　　(1) 410 614 2871
Email:　　caat@jhsph.edu
Contact:　CAAT Grants Coordinator

Greenwall Fellowship Program

Subjects: Biomedical science, ethics, public health, health policy and clinical care
Purpose: To provide an unparalleled opportunity for fellowship and faculty development training in bioethics and health policy
Eligibility: Open to applicants who have Doctoral degrees in medicine, nursing, philosophy, law, public health, biomedical sciences, social sciences or a related field
Level of Study: Postdoctorate
Type: Fellowship
Value: US$1,22,003
Length of Study: 2 years
Frequency: Annual
Study Establishment: Johns Hopkins University
Country of Study: United States of America
Application Procedure: Applicants must send a cover letter, a personal statement describing why they want to be a Greenwall Fellow, a copy of their curriculum vitae, 3 reference letters, official copies of undergraduate and graduate/professional school transcripts and copies of their written and/or published work
Closing Date: 1 December

For further information contact:

Email:　　fellows@ihsph.edu
Contact:　Kathy Chen

Joint Institute for Laboratory Astrophysics (formerly Joint Institute for Laboratory Astrophysics)

440 B, University of Colorado, Boulder, CO 80309, United States of America

Tel:　　(1) 303 492 7789
Fax:　　(1) 303 492 5235
Email:　jilavf@jila.colorado.edu

Website: www.colorado.edu
Contact: Programme Assistant

JILA's interests are at present research and applications in the fields of laser technology, optoelectronics, precision measurement, surface science and semiconductors, information and image processing, and materials and process science, as well as basic research in atomic, molecular and optical physics, precision measurement, gravitational physics, chemical physics, astrophysics and geophysical measurements. To provide an opportunity for persons actively contributing to these fields, JILA operates the Visiting Fellowship Programme as well as the Postdoctoral Research Associate Programme.

Joint Institute for Laboratory Astrophysics Postdoctoral Research Associateship and Visiting Fellowships

Subjects: Laser technology, optoelectronics, precision measurement, surface science and semiconductors, information and image processing, and nanoscience
Purpose: To support additional training beyond the PhD and sabbatical research
Eligibility: There are no restrictions other than those that might be required by the grant that supports the research
Level of Study: Postdoctorate, Professional development
Type: Fellowship
Value: Varies
Length of Study: Visiting fellowships are for 4–12 months and Postdoctoral Research Associateships are for 1 year or more
Frequency: Annual
Country of Study: United States of America
Application Procedure: Applicants should download an application form, complete it, and send it (along with requested supporting materials) to the Visiting Scientists Program Assistant. All materials may be submitted via email to secretary via email
Closing Date: 1 November
Funding: Government
Contributor: Varies
Additional Information: Please see the website for further details jila.colorado.edu/students-postdocs/postdocs

For further information contact:

Visiting Scientists Program, 440 UCB, Boulder, CO 80309, United States of America

Tel: (1) 303 492 5749
Email: secretary@jila.colorado.edu

Juvenile Diabetes Foundation International/The Diabetes Research Foundation

26 Broadway, 14th Floor, New York, NY 10004, United States of America

Tel: (1) 1 800 533 CURE (2873)
Fax: (1) 212 785 9595
Email: info@jdrf.org
Website: www.jdrf.org
Contact: Grant Administrator

JDRF remains dedicated to finding a cure for type 1 diabetes as our highest priority. In addition to focusing on specific research challenges and gaps that will lead to curing, better treating, and preventing type 1 diabetes. JDRF works to decrease barriers to commercial development of products for type 1 diabetes.

Strategic Research Agreement

Subjects: Life sciences and medicine
Purpose: To support and fund research to find a cure for Type 1 diabetes
Eligibility: Required MD, DMD, DVM, PhD, or equivalent and faculty position or equivalent
Level of Study: Research
Type: Grant
Value: Varies
Length of Study: 3 years
Closing Date: 1 February
Additional Information: Please check website for further details

K

Karnatak University

Dr. B. H. Nagoor, Coordinator, Dr. D. C. Pavate Foundation, C/o Department of Economics, Karnatak University, Dharwad, Karnataka 580003, India

Email: nagoor_bh@yahoo.co.in

Dr. D. C. Pavate Memorial Visiting Fellowship

Subjects: Three fellowships are offered under different faculties for a total period of four months from January each year. The fellowships will include economy class return airfare, a stipend of 3500 pounds and the appropriate academic fees
Eligibility: To apply for the D. C. Pavate Memorial Visiting Fellowship, candidates must meet the following criteria: 1. Be below the age of 40 years as on January 1 of the academic year. 2. Secured a PhD or a masters degree or equivalent with a minimum of first class. 3. For fellowships valid for Karnataka candidates: A Karnataka candidate is any person who has studied at an educational institution in Karnataka or been employed in Karnataka for a minimum of 5 years continuously
Level of Study: Graduate
Type: Fellowship
Valu: £3,500
Frequency: 3 times each year
Country of Study: Any country
Application Procedure: Application forms can be downloaded at www.kud.ac.in
Closing Date: 10 July
Funding: Private

Kay Kendall Leukaemia Fund

Kay Kendall Leukaemia Fund Junior and Intermediate Research Fellowships

The Kay Kendall Leukaemia Fund, The Peak 5 Wilton Road, SW1V 1AN, London, United Kingdom

Tel: (44) 207 410 0330
Email: info@kklf.org.uk
Contact: Mrs H McLeod, Fund Executive

Subjects: Intermediate fellowships are awarded annually to scientists of outstanding potential allowing them to gain experience in an international centre of excellence prior to establishing an independent research group of their own. Applicants may be of any nationality and should be based currently in the United Kingdom and/or be planning to work in a recognised university or other equivalent department in a United Kingdom institution. A significant proportion of the fellowship (up to 3 years) may be spent in an appropriate institution outside the United Kingdom where this can be clearly demonstrated to be of significant benefit. The fellowship will cover the cost of the fellow's salary and may support one assistant together with consumable support in the United Kingdom, and travel costs where appropriate. Up to three junior fellowships are awarded annually and cover salary costs for three years and costs of laboratory consumables in the United Kingdom and travel costs where appropriate. They are made in the following categories: 1. Scientific fellowships – open to scientists who will usually have 1-4 years' postdoctoral experience and be intending either to work at

© Springer Nature Limited 2019
Palgrave Macmillan (ed.), *The Grants Register 2020*,
https://doi.org/10.1057/978-1-349-95943-3

a recognised United Kingdom research institution or seeking a travel fellowship for relevant work abroad, with funding and administration via an appropriate United Kingdom institution. 2. Clinical research fellow – open to clinicians seeking funding for a PhD in the field of leukaemia research, usually at a United Kingdom centre

Purpose: Scientific Research and Clinical Research Fellowships on aspects of leukaemia and related haematological malignancies

Eligibility: Intermediate - Non-medical applicants will already have completed their PhD and will usually have 3-8 years of post-doctoral research experience. For medical graduates the Intermediate Fellowship is suitable for individuals who have obtained a PhD; in exceptional cases completion of clinical training during an Intermediate Fellowship may also be possible. Applicants for the Intermediate Fellowship will be expected to demonstrate their potential for achieving international status as researchers in leukaemia or a closely related field. Junior - Non-medical scientists who will usually have 1-4 years' postdoctoral experience and are intending to work either at a recognised United Kingdom research institution or seeking a travel fellowship for relevant work abroad may apply for a scientific fellowship, with funding and administration via an appropriate United Kingdom institution. Clinicians seeking funding for a PhD in the field of leukaemia research, usually at a United Kingdom centre, may apply for a clinical research fellowship

Level of Study: Postgraduate

Type: A variable number of fellowships

Value: Fellow's salary and consumable costs. Intermediate fellowships may include RA salary costs and Family Allowance if time is taken abroad

Length of Study: Junior - 3 years; Intermediate - 4 years

Frequency: Annual

Study Establishment: United Kingdom university or research institution, or equivalent abroad (but to be administered by a United Kingdom university or research institution)

Country of Study: United Kingdom

Application Procedure: Calls for applications and relevant deadlines are advertised in the spring for Intermediate Fellowships and the summer for Junior Fellowships. Application is by application form available from KKLF. It must include a completed application form with all signatures, a scientific proposal, and a statement from the Departmental Chairman or Laboratory Director that he/she is prepared to make available all appropriate facilities if the applicant is successful. In addition it should include references, costings, and CV. Applications are triaged post-deadline to determine which will be sent out to review

Closing Date: as advertised on website and see applications procedure above

Funding: Trusts

No. of awards offered last year: IF - 2: JF - 3

Keele University

Keele, ST5 5BG, Staffordshire, United Kingdom

Tel:	(44) 1782 584002
Fax:	(44) 1782 632343
Email:	aaa12@keele.ac.uk
Website:	www.keele.ac.uk
Contact:	Ms Joan Scrivener, Postgraduate Admissions Officer

Keele University is committed to provide high quality teaching and research, with particular emphasis on multidisciplinary and interdisciplinary studies, which are seen to be in the forefront of developments worldwide, promote networking, partnership and collaboration between disciplines and organisations at regional, national and international level, and develop the estate as a leading exemplar of a learning and working campus community of students, staff and business.

Keele MBA Programme

Length of Study: 1 year full-time and 2 years part-time

Application Procedure: Applicants must complete an application form

Closing Date: 31 July for full-time course and 31 December or 31 July for the part-time course

For further information contact:

Tel:	(44) 1782 583425
Fax:	(44) 1782 584272
Email:	mna09@keele.ac.uk
Contact:	Ms Linda Bromage, MBA Programmes Manager

Keio University

Garduate School of Business Administration, 2-1-1 Hiyoshi Honcho, Kohoku-ku, Yokohama 223-8523, Japan

Tel:	(81) 9 3962 4436
Contact:	MBA Admissions Officer

Keio University is the first private university in Japan, founded in 1858 by Yukichi Fukuzawa, who is often called the intellectual father of modern Japan. Since then Keio University has developed a brilliant history of producing distinguished personalities in every field of society.

Joint Japan World Bank Graduate Scholarship Program

Purpose: The Joint Japan/World Bank Graduate Scholarship Program (JJ/WBGSP) is open to women and men from developing countries with relevant professional experience and a history of supporting their countries' development efforts who are applying to a master degree program in a -development-related topic

Eligibility: The applicant must meet the following eligibility criteria: 1. Be a national of a World Bank member developing country (see above). 2. Not hold dual citizenship of a developed country. 3. Be in good health. 4. Hold a Bachelor (or equivalent) degree earned at least 3 years prior to the Application Deadline date. 5. Have 3 years or more of recent development-related experience after earning a Bachelor (or equivalent) degree. 6. Be employed in development-related work in a paid full- time position at the time of submitting the scholarship application. The only exception to this criterion is for developing country nationals from a country that will be on the updated list of Fragile and Conflict States provided to applicants in the Application Guidelines for each call for scholarships. 7. On or before the Scholarship Application Deadline date, be admitted unconditionally (except for funding) for the upcoming academic year to at least one of the JJ/WBGSP preferred university master's programs and located outside of the applicant's country of citizenship and country of residence listed at the time the call for scholarship applications open

Level of Study: Postgraduate

Type: Scholarship

Length of Study: 2 years

Frequency: Annual

Country of Study: Any country

Application Procedure: For scholarships to one of the preferred master's programs, you must first apply and be unconditionally accepted for admissions to one or more of the Preferred Program(s) to be considered for a JJ/WBGSP scholarship. The call for applications is open from 7 March to 11 April. For scholarships to one of the partner master's programs, you must apply for admission to one or more of the Partner Masters Degree Program(s). After reviewing submitted applications, each Partner Master Degree Program will identify a short list of eligible candidates who will then be invited by the JJ/WBGSP Secretariat to apply for a JJ/WBGSP scholarship

Closing Date: 11 April

Funding: Private

Additional Information: For further information, check the below website. www.ic.keio.ac.jp/en/study/jjwbgsp/index.html

For further information contact:

Email: ic-scholarship@adst.keio.ac.jp

Kennan Institute

Woodrow Wilson International Center for Scholars, One Woodrow Wilson Plaza, 1300 Pennsylvania Avenue North West, Washington, DC 20004 3027, United States of America

Tel:	(1) 202 691 4100
Fax:	(1) 202 691 4247
Email:	kennan@wilsoncenter.org
Website:	www.wilsoncenter.org
Contact:	Scholar Programs

The Kennan Institute for Advanced Russian Studies sponsors advanced research on the successor states to the USSR and encourages Eurasian studies with its public lecture and publication programmes, maintaining contact with scholars and research centres abroad. The Institute seeks to function as a forum where the scholarly community can interact with public policymakers.

Title VIII-Supported Summer Research Grant

Subjects: Eurasian studies in the social sciences and humanities

Purpose: To support United States citizens whose research in the social sciences or humanities focuses on the former Soviet Union, and who demonstrate a particular need to use the resources of the Washington, DC area

Eligibility: Open to academic participants with a doctoral degree or those who have nearly completed their dissertation. For non-academic participants, an equivalent level of professional development is required. Applicants must be United States citizens

Level of Study: Doctorate, Postdoctorate, Postgraduate, Predoctorate, Professional development, Research

Type: Scholarship

Value: US$6,400. The Kennan Institute provides a work space and research assistant for each Summer Scholar. Travel and accommodation expenses are not directly covered by this grant

Length of Study: Up to 62 days

Frequency: Dependent on funds available

Study Establishment: The Kennan Institute

Country of Study: United States of America

No. of awards offered: 25

Application Procedure: Applicants must submit a concise description of their research project of 700–800 words, a curriculum vitae, a statement of preferred dates of residence in Washington, DC, and two letters of recommendation specifically in support of the research proposal. No application form required

Closing Date: 15 January
Funding: Government
No. of awards offered last year: 2
No. of awards applicants last year: 25
Additional Information: Please email kennan@wilsoncenter.org or see our website with further details www.wilsoncenter.org/opportunity/kennan-institute-summer-research-scholarships

For further information contact:

Email: outbound@americancouncils.org

Kennedy Memorial Trust

3 Birdcage Walk, Westminster, SW1H 9JJ, London, United Kingdom

Tel: (44) 20 7222 1151
Fax: (44) 20 7222 7189
Email: annie@kennedytrust.org.uk
Website: www.kennedytrust.org.uk
Contact: Ms Annie Thomas, Secretary

As part of the British national memorial to President Kennedy, the Kennedy Memorial Trust awards scholarships to British postgraduate students for study at Harvard University or the Massachusetts Institute of Technology. The awards are offered annually following a national competition and cover tuition costs and a stipend to meet living expenses.

Kennedy Scholarships

Subjects: Kennedy Scholarships are tenable across the range of graduate programs offered at both Harvard University and the Massachusetts Institute of Technology
Purpose: Kennedy Scholarships are the United Kingdom's living memorial to President Kennedy. They are offered annually in competition to enable British citizens who are British graduates to take graduate programs at Harvard University and the Massachusetts Institute of Technology
Eligibility: Applicants must be British citizens at the time of application who are, or will be, graduates of a British university by the time of taking up the award. If not due to graduate in the year of award, applicants must have spent at least 2 of the 7 years prior to September 1st of year in which tenure will start studying as an undergraduate at a United Kingdom university
Level of Study: Doctorate, Graduate, Predoctorate, Professional development, Postgraduate (MSc)

Type: Scholarship
Value: Full tuition and health insurances fees plus a means-tested stipend for living expenses
Length of Study: Typically one full academic year, starting in the Fall
Frequency: Annual
Study Establishment: Harvard University; Massachusetts Institute of Technology
Country of Study: United States of America
No. of awards offered: 182
Application Procedure: Applications are made online and comprise a personal statement, an academic and professional history and the contact details for 2 referees who will be contacted automatically. See the website for full information
Closing Date: mid- to late-October in the year prior to starting in the United States
Funding: Private
Contributor: The Kennedy Memorial Trust is a British charity, dependent upon charitable donations
No. of awards offered last year: 10
No. of awards applicants last year: 182

For further information contact:

Tel: (44) 2072 221 151
Email: annie@kennedytrust.org.uk
Contact: Mrs Annie Thomas

Kidney Health Australia

Level 1, 25 North Terrace, GPO Box 9993, Adelaide, SA 5001, Australia

Tel: (61) 8 8334 7555
Fax: (61) 8 8334 7545
Email: research@kidney.org.au
Website: www.kidney.org.au
Contact: Medical Director's Office

Founded in 1968, the Australian Kidney Foundation's mission is to be recognized as the leading non-profit national organization providing funding for, and taking the initiative in, the prevention of kidney and urinary tract diseases.

Australian Kidney Foundation Biomedical Scholarships

Subjects: Medical and scientific kidney and urology-related research

Purpose: To provide scholarships for individuals wishing to study full-time for the research degrees

Eligibility: Open to Australian applicants who are graduates, or proposing to graduate in the current academic year. Part-time students are not eligible

Level of Study: Doctorate, Postgraduate

Type: Scholarship

Value: A$24,000 for science and A$35,000 for medical

Length of Study: 2 or 3 years

Frequency: Annual

Country of Study: Any country

Closing Date: 31 August

Contributor: Kidney Health Australia

For further information contact:

Kidney Health Australia, GPO Box 9993, Adelaide, SA 5001, Australia

Email: research@kidney.org.au
Contact: The Medical Director

Australian Kidney Foundation Medical Research Grants and Scholarships

Subjects: The functions and disease of the kidney, urinary tract and related organs

Purpose: To support medical research

Eligibility: Open to Australian citizens who are graduates of Australian medical schools or overseas graduates who are eligible for Australian citizenship and for registration as medical practitioners in Australia

Level of Study: Doctorate, Postgraduate

Type: Scholarship

Value: Please contact the organization

Length of Study: Up to 3 years

Frequency: Annual

Study Establishment: Any approved medical centre, university or research institute

Country of Study: Australia

Application Procedure: See guidelines in website

Closing Date: 31 August

Additional Information: Please see the website for further details   www.kidney.org.au/HealthProfessionals/MedicalRe searchFunding/tabid/633/Default.aspx

For further information contact:

Email: research@kidney.org.au
Contact: Joanna Stoic, Medical Director's Office

Investigator Driven Research Grants and Scholars

Subjects: Multiple sclerosis research

Purpose: To award investigators who have applied to the NHMRC for funding but have just missed the cut-off mark

Eligibility: Open to projects that are ranked as worthy of funding

Type: Scholarship

Frequency: Annual

Country of Study: Any country

Contributor: Kidney Health Australia

For further information contact:

Email: research@kidney.org.au

Kidney Research United Kingdom

Nene Hall, Lynch Wood Park, Cambridgeshire PE2 6FZ, Peterborough, United Kingdom

Tel: (44) 300 303 1100
Email: grants@kidneyresearchuk.org
Website: www.kidneyresearchuk.org
Contact: Mrs Elaine Davies, Director of Research Operations

Kidney Research United Kingdom aims to advance and promote research into kidney and renal disease. These may include epidemiological, clinical or biological approaches to relevant problems. All research must be carried out in the United Kingdom.

Allied Health Professional Fellowship (clinical)

Subjects: Renal medicine

Purpose: To enable nurses and allied health professionals to undertake a renal research study and obtain a higher degree (Masters, DPhil or PhD)

Eligibility: Open to nurses and allied health professionals to undertake a renal research study with the object of obtaining a higher degree (Masters, DPhil or PhD). Work and employment must be in the United Kingdom

Level of Study: Doctorate, Postdoctorate, Postgraduate

Value: The salary will be based on the appropriate NHS or university scale, and an allowance for consumables and higher degree fees is included

Length of Study: 3 years at full time or 5 years at part time

Frequency: Annual

Country of Study: Any country

Application Procedure: Applicants must complete an online application

Closing Date: Late November (check with website)

For further information contact:

Email: grants@kidneyresearchuk.org

King's College London

King's College London, Strand, WC2R 2LS, London, United Kingdom

Email: funding@kcl.ac.uk

Bosco Tso & Emily Ng Scholarship

Purpose: The scholarship is intended to help support the winner with the cost of tuition fees and living expenses whilst studying
Eligibility: Eligible students must be: 1. be undertaking the 1 year LLM Law programme at King's. 2. be able to demonstrate a need for financial assistance. 3. have provided a written personal statement. 4. be willing to provide an end of year report and a letter of thanks to the donor. There are few more conditions being implied for the scholarship. The award of a scholarship to an offer-holder will be conditional upon: 1. the offer-holder accepting a place on the King's LLM programme and 2. the fulfilment by the offer-holder of all conditions, both academic and English Language, attached to his or her offer of a place at King's by 10 July
Level of Study: Graduate, Professional development
Type: Scholarship
Value: £22,500 (European Union/International) which intended towards tuition fees and others
Frequency: Annual
Country of Study: Any country
Application Procedure: Kindly access the application form with the below link. www.kcl.ac.uk/study/assets/pdf/fees-and-funding/postgraduate/bosco-tso-emily-ng-scholarship-2019.pdf. The application form should be completed, scanned and emailed to funding@kcl.ac.uk. Alternatively it may be posted to Student Funding Office. You must submit a word/pdf version of your supporting statement. This should be emailed to funding@kcl.ac.uk
Closing Date: 12 April
Funding: Private

For further information contact:

King's College London, Strand, WC2R 2LS, London, United Kingdom

Email: funding@kcl.ac.uk

Claire Godfrey Postgraduate Fund

Purpose: The objective of the fund is to support postgraduate students at King's who are suffering unexpected, study-related, financial hardship
Eligibility: The fund is open to all home postgraduate students in financial hardship. All applicants will have to submit documentary evidence with their applications to verify their financial status
Level of Study: Postgraduate
Type: Funding support
Frequency: Annual
Country of Study: Any country
Application Procedure: To apply, you should download the form here. www.kcl.ac.uk/study/assets/pdf/fees-and-funding/postgraduate/claire-godfrey-postgraduate-fund.pdf.   Please ensure that you read the guidance notes carefully before completing the application form and provide all the relevant supporting documentation along with the completed application form to funding@kcl.ac.uk. The deadline for receiving application forms and supporting documents is Friday 26 April. Late applications will not be considered
Closing Date: 30 April
Funding: Private
Additional Information: All applicants will be notified of the outcome of their application in May. The successful applicant will also receive payment at that time

For further information contact:

King's College London, Strand, WC2R 2LS, London, United Kingdom

Email: funding@kcl.ac.uk

King's-HKU Joint PhD Scholarship

Purpose: King's College London ranked amongst some of the world's most prestigious universities. It is the research-intensive university with a global reputation for academic discovery and teaching. King's is in the top seven United Kingdom universities for research
Eligibility: 1. Be due to commence a full-time joint PhD programme run in collaboration between King's College London and the University of Hong Kong during the academic year. 2. Have applied to King's College London as the home institution. 3. Have submitted all the required application materials by the funding deadline
Level of Study: Postgraduate
Type: Scholarship
Value: £1,500
Length of Study: 4 year
Frequency: Annual

Country of Study: Any country
Closing Date: 31 May
Funding: International office

For further information contact:

Tel: (44) 20 7848 4568
Email: doctoralstudies@kcl.ac.uk

Norman Spink Scholarship

Subjects: Law
Purpose: The Norman Spink Scholarship Fund is a fund to help support all students who are able to demonstrate need of financial assistance, to undertake the one year LLM Law programme at King's specifically related to Tax Law
Eligibility: Eligible students must: 1. be undertaking the 1 year LLM Law programme at King's. 2. be undertaking the LLM (Tax Law Pathway). 3. be able to demonstrate a need for financial assistance. 4. have provided a written personal statement. 5. be willing to provide an end of year report and a letter of thanks to the estate of the donor. 6. Applicants must have a confirmed place to study the one year LLM Law programme at King's in September. 7. be willing to provide an end of year report and a letter of thanks to the estate of the donor
Level of Study: Postgraduate
Type: Scholarship
Value: £10,000 will be awarded for European Union students
Frequency: Annual
Country of Study: Any country
Application Procedure: Provided your application form has been accurately completed and the appropriate documentary evidence supplied, you will be notified of the decision during June. 1. The award of a scholarship to an offer-holder will be conditional upon: the offer-holder accepting a place on the King's LLM programme and. 2. the fulfilment by the offer-holder of all conditions, both academic and English Language, attached to his or her offer of a place at King's by 10 July
Closing Date: 12 April
Funding: Private

For further information contact:

Tel: (44) 20 7848 4204
Email: funding@kcl.ac.uk

Santander Masters Scholarship

Purpose: King's will be offering one scholarship per Faculty to an eligible international student starting a postgraduate taught programme in September. Students may be undertaking study in any discipline
Eligibility: Eligible applicants must meet the following criteria: 1. At the time of application, be a permanent resident of and ordinarily resident in one of the following Santander Network countries for at least 3 years prior to the start of the programme: Belgium, Italy, France, Germany, Poland, Portugal, Spain and the United Kingdom. 2. Be undertaking a full-time postgraduate taught Masters degree programme, commencing September. 3. Hold a conditional or unconditional offer of a place on the relevant programme. 4. Have applied to King's no later than 31 March. 5. Fulfil the relevant academic and English Language proficiency requirements set by King's. 6. Complete and submit the necessary scholarship application form and supporting documentation by the stated deadline of 15 May
Level of Study: Postgraduate
Type: Scholarship
Value: £5,000
Frequency: Annual
Country of Study: Any country
Application Procedure: In order to be considered for an award, candidates must: 1. Submit a complete online admissions application (via apply.kcl.ac.uk/) for a postgraduate Master's programme by 31 March. 2. Submit the application form by 15 May, 23:59. Note that this application form should only be completed after a complete admissions application has been submitted to the university and a conditional/unconditional place on the programme has been offered
Closing Date: 31 March
Funding: Private

For further information contact:

King's College London Strand, WC2R 2LS, London, United Kingdom

Email: funding@kcl.ac.uk

STEM Education Teacher Scholarship

Purpose: The STEM Education Teacher Scholarship is funded by Wipro Limited, a leading global information technology, consulting and business process services company
Eligibility: To be considered for a scholarship, on time of application, applicants MUST: 1. Work in a state-funded school in United Kingdom (e.g. comprehensive, academy, free school). Including, primary, secondary and FE-levels. 2. Be a specialist teacher in: Science, Mathematics, Computer Science or Geography. 3. Have completed, or is completing, their NQT year. 4. Have submitted an application for the MA in STEM Education

Level of Study: Professional development
Type: Scholarship
Value: 70% of the total fees
Frequency: Annual
Country of Study: Any country
Closing Date: 28 April
Funding: Private

For further information contact:

King's College London, Strand, WC2R 2LS, London, United Kingdom

Email: funding@kcl.ac.uk

Kingdom of the Netherlands

Small Scale Support Program and Accountability Fund

Subjects: The Dutch government has set up a Small Scale Support Program (SSSP) to support projects in countries with which the Netherlands does not have a development cooperation relationship, such as India
Purpose: It support projects in countries with which the Netherlands does not have a development cooperation relationship, such as India
Eligibility: The Embassy receives a large number of project applications whereas the budget available is sufficient to support only a limited number of projects. Check the website link for further communication. ngobox.org/full-grant-annoucement_Small-Scale-Support-Program-and-Accountability-Fund-2019-Kingdom-of-the-Netherlands_1747
Level of Study: Graduate
Type: Funding support
Frequency: Annual
Country of Study: Any country
Application Procedure: If your organization is working in India and provided that your project complies with the above mentioned criteria and is eligible to apply, please fill in the SSSP form. Organizations from Nepal and Bhutan, and projects in India with a focus on lobbying and advocacy have to use the Accountability form
Closing Date: 31 January
Funding: Private

For further information contact:

Email: NDE-SMRP@minbuza.nl

Kingston University

River House, 53–57 High Street, Kingston upon Thames, KT1 1LQ, Surrey, United Kingdom

Tel: (44) 20 8417 9000
Contact: Kingston University

The university's aim is to be internationally recognized for a creative approach to education that has practical outcomes which benefit people and communities. University rated among top 15 % globe in latest QS World University Rankings Kingston University rated among top 15 % globe in latest QS World University Rankings.

Annual Fund Postgraduate Scholarships

Subjects: Taught masters courses in the Kingston School of Art, Faculty of Business and Social Sciences and Faculty of Science, Engineering and Computing
Purpose: The aim is to encourage academic excellence and allow talented young graduates to continue to higher levels of learning and research, by offering a reduction in course fees for the most academically able applicants
Eligibility: Have already received an offer of a place to study at Kingston on an eligible course. Have first-class honours in a previous degree, or high 2:1 with additional evidence of academic excellence. Assessed as having Home/European Union fee status (not Overseas fee status). Students from outside the United Kingdom need to meet Kingston University's English language requirements – these depend on the course they are applying for
Level of Study: Postgraduate
Type: Scholarship
Value: The scholarship offers a £3,000 (full time) or £1,500 (part-time) reduction in annual course fees
Length of Study: Up to 2 years full time or 4 years part time
Frequency: Annual
Study Establishment: Kingston University
Country of Study: United Kingdom
No. of awards offered: 60
Application Procedure: Completed application form 1. Academic letters of reference. 2. Copy of academic transcripts. 3. Copies of any certificates relevant to prizes or awards
Closing Date: 12 May
Funding: Individuals
Contributor: Alumni of Kingston University
No. of awards offered last year: 14
No. of awards applicants last year: 60

Additional Information: For more details, see the website: www.kingston.ac.uk/postgraduate/fees-and-funding/funding-your-course/scholarships/annual-fund-scholarship/

For further information contact:

Tel:	(44) 20 8417 3299
Email:	development@kingston.ac.uk
Contact:	Mrs Karen Nowland, Development Administrator

Klynveld Peat Marwick Goerdeler Foundation

3 Chestnut Ridge Road, Montvale, NJ 07645, United States of America

Tel:	(1) 201 307 7932
Fax:	(1) 201 307 7093
Email:	acenglish@kpmg.com
Website:	www.kpmgfoundation.org
Contact:	Anita C. English, Scholarship Administrator

American Institute of Certified Public Accountants Fellowship for Minority Doctoral Students

Subjects: Accounting
Purpose: The AICPA Fellowship for Minority Doctoral Students ensures that CPAs of diverse backgrounds are visible in college and university classrooms. The program's goal is to increase the number of minority CPAs who serve as role models and mentors to young people in the academic environment and university classrooms
Eligibility: a) Applied to a PhD program and awaiting word on acceptance; b) been accepted into a PhD program; or c) already matriculated in a doctoral program and pursuing appropriate coursework; Earned a Master's Degree and/or completed at least 3 years of full-time experience in the accounting practice; 1. Minority student of Black or African American; Hispanic or Latino; or Native American ethnicity or Alaska Native; Native Hawaiian or Pacific Islander ethnicity. 2. Attend school on a full-time basis and plan to remain enrolled full-time until attaining PhD. 3. Agree not to work full-time in a paid position or accept responsibility for teaching more than one course per semester as a teaching assistant, or dedicate more than one quarter of my time as a research assistant
Level of Study: Doctorate
Type: Scholarship

Value: US$10,000 per year, renewable for a total of 5 years
Length of Study: Up to 5 years
Frequency: Annual
Study Establishment: A full-time AACSB-accredited university
Country of Study: United States of America
Application Procedure: Applicants must visit the website for further information and application forms
Closing Date: 15 May
Funding: Private
Additional Information: The awards are to be announced in May

For further information contact:

Email:	academics@aicpa.org

Korea Foundation

Fellowship Programme, 10th Floor, Diplomatic Center Building, 1376-1 Seocho-2-dong, Seocho-gu, Seoul 137-863, Korea

Tel:	(82) 2 3463 5614
Fax:	(82) 2 3463 6075/6076
Email:	fellow@kf.or.kr
Website:	www.kf.or.kr
Contact:	Ms Bo Myung KIM, Programme Officer

The Korea Foundation seeks to improve awareness and understanding of Korea worldwide as well as to foster co-operative relationships between Korea and foreign countries through a variety of exchange programmes.

Korea Foundation Fellowship for Field Research

Subjects: Korea-related research in the humanities and social sciences, culture and arts, and comparative research related to Korea
Purpose: To promote Korean studies and support professional researchers in Korean studies by facilitating their research activities in Korea
Eligibility: Open to university professors and instructors, doctoral candidates, researchers and other professionals. Candidates must be proficient in Korean or English. In the case of Korean nationals, only those with foreign residency status and regular faculty positions at foreign universities are eligible to

apply. Fellows in this programme must concentrate on their research and may not enrol in any language courses or other university courses during the fellowship period. Candidates who are receiving support from other organizations or programmes administered by the Korea Foundation are not eligible to receive this fellowship at the same time

Level of Study: Doctorate, Postdoctorate, Professional development, Research

Type: Fellowship

Value: The grant amount will be determined by the Foundation according to the Fellow

Length of Study: 3 months–1 year

Frequency: Annual

Country of Study: Korea

No. of awards offered: 75

Application Procedure: Applicants must complete an application form. Application forms are available from the Foundation and the website

Closing Date: 31 July

No. of awards offered last year: 45

No. of awards applicants last year: 75

For further information contact:

Email: hklee@kf.or.kr

Korea Foundation Fellowship for Korean Language Training

Subjects: Korean studies related to the humanities, culture and arts, social sciences or comparative research

Purpose: To provide foreign scholars and graduate students who need systematic Korean language education with the opportunity to enrol in a Korean language programme at a language institute affiliated to a Korean university

Eligibility: Candidates must have a basic knowledge of, and an ability to communicate in, the Korean language. In the case of Korean nationals, only those with foreign residency status are eligible to apply. Candidates who are receiving support from other organizations or programmes administered by the Korea Foundation are not eligible to receive this fellowship at the same time

Level of Study: Graduate, Postgraduate

Type: Fellowship

Value: The grant amount will be determined by the Foundation according to the Fellow

Length of Study: 6 months, 9 months or 1 year

Frequency: Annual

Study Establishment: A language institute affiliated to a Korean university

Country of Study: Korea

No. of awards offered: 127

Application Procedure: Applicants must complete an application form are available from the Korean Foundation. Applicants must request an application form by supplying their curriculum vitae along with details of their including Korean language ability and previous study of Korean

Closing Date: 31 May

No. of awards offered last year: 92

No. of awards applicants last year: 127

For further information contact:

Email: koreanstudies@isop.ucla.edu

Korea Foundation Postdoctoral Fellowship

Subjects: Korea-related research in the humanities and social sciences, culture and arts, and comparative research related to Korea

Purpose: To provide promising and highly qualified PhD recipients with the opportunity to conduct research at leading universities in the field of Korean studies so that they can further develop their scholarship as well as have their dissertations published as manuscripts

Eligibility: Open to non-Korean scholars who have received a PhD degree in a subject related to Korea within 5 years of their application, but do not currently hold a regular faculty position. Korean nationals with permanent resident status in foreign countries may apply. Candidates who are receiving support from other programmes administered by the Korea Foundation are not eligible to receive this fellowship at the same time

Level of Study: Postdoctorate

Type: Fellowship

Value: Stipend support for a 1-year period, of an amount to be determined based on the country, region and institution where the Fellow will conduct his or her research

Length of Study: 1 year

Frequency: Annual

Country of Study: Any country

Application Procedure: You will need to email a separate KI Korea Foundation application by the KI deadline, as well as, complete and submit the Korea Foundation application via the KF online portal by the Korea Foundation deadline. Be sure to verify and confirm the specific KF deadline by visiting the Korea Foundation website: Complete application form must have the following details. For further information, check with the below link. www.kf.or.kr/

Closing Date: 7 January

For further information contact:

CGIS South Building, Second Floor, 1730, Cambridge Street, MA 02138, Cambridge, United Kingdom

Tel: (44) 617 496-2141
Email: cglover@fas.harvard.edu

Kosciuszko Foundation

The Kosciuszko Foundation, Inc., 15 East 65th Street, New York, NY 10065, United States of America

Tel: (1) 212 734 2130
Fax: (1) 212 628 4552
Email: addy@thekf.org, info@thekf.org
Website: www.thekf.org

The Kosciuszko Foundation, founded in 1925, is dedicated to promoting educational and cultural relations between the United States of America and Poland and increasing American awareness of Polish culture and history. In addition to its grants and scholarships, which total US$1,000,000 annually, the Foundation presents cultural programmes including lectures, concerts and exhibitions, promotes Polish culture in the United States of America and nurtures the spirit of multicultural co-operation.

Jozef Tischner Fellowships

Subjects: All academic disciplines related to IWM's main research fields
Purpose: To fund a Polish junior researcher in any academic discipline to work in Vienna on research projects of their choice related to one of the Institute for Human Sciences' (IWM) main research fields
Eligibility: Open to Polish citizens, permanent residents of Poland and Polish-American scholars with a recent PhD degree, not older than 35 years
Level of Study: Doctorate, Research
Type: Fellowship
Value: Fellowship and €8,000 stipend to cover accommodation, living expenses, travel, health insurance and incidentals during the stay
Length of Study: 6 months
Frequency: Annual
Study Establishment: The Institute for Human Sciences (IWM)

Country of Study: Austria
Application Procedure: Applicants must send the application by mail to address below
Closing Date: 1 December

For further information contact:

Fax: (1) 313 58 30
Email: fellowships@iwm.at

Polish National Alliance of Brooklyn, United States of America, Inc. Scholarship

Subjects: Any subject
Purpose: To fund qualified undergraduate students for full-time studies at accredited colleges and Universities in the United States
Eligibility: Applicant must be a Unites States citizen of Polish descent or Polish citizen with permanent residency status in the United States, a member in good standing of the Polish national alliance of Brooklyn, United States of America, Inc., with a minimum GPA of 3.0
Type: Scholarship
Value: US$2,000
Frequency: Annual
Study Establishment: At accredited colleges and universities in the United States
Country of Study: United States of America
Application Procedure: Submit application form, US$25 non-refundable application fee and supporting materials to the Kosciuszko foundation. E-mailed and faxed materials will not be considered
Closing Date: 14 January
Funding: Private

Krist Law Firm, P.C

Fax: (44) 281 326 9197
Email: scholarship@houstoninjurylawyer.com

The Krist Law Firm, P.C. National Scholarship

Purpose: Our Houston maritime lawyers are proud to announce that The Krist Law Firm, P.C. will be renewing our annual scholarship of US$10,000 to award an individual student the financial resources to accomplish their educational goals and prepare for future career aspirations!

Eligibility: 1. Be a United States citizen or permanent resident. 2. Be accepted to or currently enrolled in an accredited college, university, or graduate program within the United States. 3. Have a cumulative GPA of 3.0 or higher. 4. Demonstrate good character and high initiative
Level of Study: Graduate
Type: Scholarship
Value: US$10,000
Frequency: Annual
Country of Study: United States of America
Closing Date: 31 March
Funding: Foundation

For further information contact:

Email: scholarship@houstoninjurylawyer.com

Kungliga Tekniska högskolan Royal Institute of Technology

Stockholm SWE -100 44, Sweden

Tel: (46) 8 790 6000
Contact: KTH Royal Institute of Technology

KTH Royal Institute of Technology is a university in Stockholm, Sweden, specializing in Engineering and Technology, it ranks highest in northern mainland Europe in its academic fields.

Postdoctoral Scholarship in Solar Fuels at KTH

Subjects: Scholarships are awarded in the field of Solar Fuels
Purpose: A postdoctoral scholarship in Solar Fuels is available at the KTH Royal Institute of Technology
Eligibility: Students from Sweden can apply for this scholarship.If English is not your first language then you will need to show that your English language skills are at a high enough level to succeed in your studies
Type: Postdoctoral fellowship
Value: 25,000 per month
Country of Study: Sweden
Application Procedure: Apply for this scholarship by e-mail
Closing Date: 26 February
Funding: Private
Additional Information: For more details please contact the website scholarship-positions.com/postdoctoral-scholarship-solar-fuels-kth-sweden/2018/02/19/

For further information contact:

Email: lichengs@kth.se

Kurt Weill Foundation for Music

7 East 20th Street, New York, NY 10003, United States of America

Tel: (1) 212 505 5240
Fax: (1) 212 353 9663
Email: kwfinfo@kwf.org
Website: www.kwf.org
Contact: Ms Elizabeth Blaufox, Assoc. Director of Programs

The Kurt Weill Foundation for Music is a non-profit, private foundation chartered to preserve and perpetuate the legacies of the composer Kurt Weill (1900–1950) and his wife, singer and actress Lotte Lenya (1898–1981). The Foundation awards grants and prizes, sponsors print and online publications, maintains the Weill-Lenya Research Center and administers Weill's copyrights.

Kurt Weill Prize

Subjects: Encourages distinguished scholarship in the disciplines of Music, Theater, Dance, Literary criticism and history addressing music theater since 1900 (including Opera). Two prizes are awarded bi-annually: US$5,000 to the author of the winning book entry; and a prize of US$2,000 to the author of the winning article entry
Purpose: To encourage distinguished scholarship in the disciplines of music, theater, dance, literary criticism and history addressing music theater since 1900 (including opera)
Eligibility: Open to nationals of any country
Level of Study: Unrestricted
Type: Prize
Value: US$5,000 for books, US$2,000 for articles
Frequency: Every 2 years
Country of Study: Any country
Application Procedure: Applicants must submit five copies of their published work. Works must have been published within the 2 years preceding the award year. Please visit www.kwf.org for additional information
Closing Date: 30 April
Funding: Private

For further information contact:

Email: bsansone@kwf.org

L

La Trobe University

Research Services, Melbourne, VIC 3086, Australia

Tel:	(61) 3 9479 1976
Fax:	(61) 3 9479 1464
Email:	rgs@latrobe.edu.au
Website:	www.latrobe.edu.au/rgso
Contact:	Manager, Research Students

La Trobe University is one of the leading research universities in Australia. The University has internationally regarded strengths across a diverse range of disciplines. It offers a detailed and broad research training programme and provides unique access to technology transfer and collaboration with end users of its research and training via its Research and Development Park.

La Trobe – JSSAHER PhD Scholarship for Indian Students

Purpose: The aim of the project is to determine if the University and/or the Hospital have an effect on the microbial communities in the soils around them, including the amount and variation of multi-resistance organisms in the vicinity of the Hospital

Value: La Trobe Research Scholarship for 3.5 years with a value of Rs. 25,000 per month in years 1 and 2, and Rs. 28,000 per month in year 3 and the first half of year 4 of candidature, to support your living costs. Opportunity to travel to La Trobe University, Australia for up to 6 months during your candidature, including accessing a travel grant of up to AU$15,000 (pro rata for six months) (upon prior approval)

Length of Study: 3.5 years

Country of Study: Any country

Application Procedure: For further details, please visit https://www.scholarshipsupdates.com/la-trobe-jssaher-phd-scholarship-for-indian-students-2018/

Closing Date: 15 March

For further information contact:

Email: admissions@jssuni.edu.in

La Trobe – JSSAHER PhD Scholarship in Life Science and Public Health

Subjects: Scholarships are awarded in Life Science and Public Health. The focus of this research project is to analyze and monitor soil samples around JSSAHER and its JSS Hospital in Mysuru, India over the period of three years

Purpose: The aim of the project is to determine if the University and/or the Hospital have an effect on the microbial communities in the soils around them, including the amount and variation of multi-resistance organisms in the vicinity of the Hospital

Eligibility: Indian students are eligible to apply for this scholarship programme. Applicants need to fulfil the English language requirements at La Trobe University

Value: La Trobe Research Scholarship for 3.5 years with a value of Rs. 25,000 per month in years 1 and 2, and Rs. 28,000 per month in year 3 and the first half of year 4 of candidature, to support your living costs Fee-relief scholarship (LTUFFRS) for up to four years (international candidates). Opportunity to travel to La Trobe University, Australia for up to six months during your candidature, including accessing a travel grant of up to AU$15,000 (pro rata for six months) (upon prior approval). Opportunities to work with outstanding researchers at La Trobe University and JSSAHER, and access to professional development programs through La Trobe's Research and Education Unit

Study Establishment: Scholarships are awarded in Life Science and Public Health. The focus of this research project is to analyze and monitor soil samples around JSSAHER and its JSS Hospital in Mysuru, India over the period of three years

Country of Study: Any country

Application Procedure: See the website. If selected for the scholarship, formal invitations will be sent for scholarship and PhD candidates

Closing Date: 15 March

Additional Information: For more details please visit the website http://scholarship-positions.com/la-trobe-jssaher-phd-scholarship-life-science-public-health-indian-students/2018/03/07/

For further information contact:

Email: jssuni.edu.in

La Trobe Excellence Scholarships

Value: 25% reduction on course fees

Country of Study: Australia

Application Procedure: For application procedure, please visit https://www.latrobe.edu.au/contact

Closing Date: 1 July

For further information contact:

Email: R.Lumley@latrobe.edu.au

Lancaster University

Student Services, Lancaster University, Bailrigg, LA1 4YW, Lancaster, United Kingdom

Tel: (44) 1524 65201
Fax: (44) 1524 594868
Email: studentfunding@lancaster.ac.uk
Website: www.lancs.ac.uk/funding
Contact: Craig Lowe

Lancaster University is a campus university dedicated to excellence in teaching and research, offering a wide range of nationally and internationally recognized postgraduate courses. For updated information on all the University's funding opportunities, please see our website www.lancs.ac.uk/funding.

Alumni Postgraduate Scholarships

Subjects: All subjects

Eligibility: Applicants must have submitted their application for study in order to be considered for a studentship. Applicants for this award must be able to demonstrate a commitment to the life of the University or of the wider community

Level of Study: Postgraduate

Type: Studentship

Value: £1,000

Frequency: Annual

Application Procedure: In order to apply, you must complete an application form and submit your curriculum vitae and two references

Closing Date: 31 July (check the website)

Contributor: Lancaster University Alumni

Additional Information: Please see the website for further details www.lums.lancs.ac.uk/masters/funding/

For further information contact:

Alumni & Development, Lancaster University, Bailrigg, LA1 4YW, Lancaster, United Kingdom

Tel: (44) 1524 592556
Email: s.nelhams@lancaster.ac.uk
Contact: Sally Nelhams

Bowland College – Willcock Scholarships

Subjects: All subjects

Purpose: To provide financial assistance to undergraduate or postgraduate members of Bowland College who are in very good academic standing but who are facing long-term financial or other difficulties which are beyond their control and which jeopardise their continuing or commencing study at Lancaster University

Eligibility: All Bowland College students or alumni who would have difficulty achieving their full academic potential because of financial hardship may apply to the scholarship fund

Level of Study: Postgraduate

Type: Scholarship

Value: £2,500

Frequency: Annual

Application Procedure: Applications should be submitted to the Senior College Advisor

Closing Date: 27 April

Additional Information: Please see the website for further details www.lusi.lancaster.ac.uk/funding/Detail.aspx?AwardID=12

For further information contact:

Bowland College Office, Lancaster University, Bailrigg, LA1 4YW, Lancaster, Lancaster, United Kingdom

Tel: (44) 1524 594 506
Email: p.m.brown@lancaster.ac.uk
Contact: Robert Blake, Senior College Advisor

Cartmel College Scholarships

Subjects: All subjects
Purpose: Each year, Cartmel College offers a limited number of awards to its present or alumni members who are unable to obtain adequate grants from other bodies
Eligibility: All applications will be considered on their merit
Level of Study: Postgraduate
Type: Scholarship
Value: £500
Length of Study: Awards are tenable for 1 year
Frequency: Annual
Closing Date: 1 June

County College Scholarships

Subjects: All subjects
Eligibility: Members of the County College who have completed a Lancaster degree and are proposing to commence postgraduate study at the university are eligible to apply to this scholarship fund. Selections are on the basis of academic merit and financial need
Level of Study: Postgraduate
Type: Scholarship
Value: £1,000
Length of Study: Awards are tenable for 1 year
Frequency: Annual
Closing Date: 1 June
Additional Information: Please see the website for further details

County College Studentship

Subjects: All subjects
Purpose: To assist prospective students who are unable to obtain adequate grants from other bodies
Eligibility: Open to applicants who are past members of County College
Level of Study: Postgraduate
Type: Studentship
Value: £1,000 - two awards can be made each year
Frequency: Annual
Study Establishment: Lancaster University
Country of Study: United Kingdom
Application Procedure: Application available from Student Funding Service website
Closing Date: 1 June each year
Funding: Government
Additional Information: Please see the website for further details www.lancs.ac.uk/colleges/county/tutorial.html

Donald & Margot Watt Bursary Fund (FASS only)

Subjects: This fund is for Undergraduate students studying one of the following seven disciplines: Art, Design, English & Creative Writing, History, Philosophy, Religious Studies and Theatre Studies. (Those on joint degree schemes that include one of the specified subjects are also eligible)
Purpose: This fund is to be used to support undergraduate students who run into financial difficulty whilst at University
Eligibility: Students will be expected to complete feedback on how the award has assisted them so the information can be used to encourage other donors to support Lancaster students. This fund is for Undergraduate students studying one of the following seven disciplines: Art, Design, English & Creative Writing, History, Philosophy, Religious Studies and Theatre Studies. (Those on joint degree schemes that include one of the specified subjects are also eligible)
Level of Study: Postgraduate
Type: Funding support
Value: Awards amounts of £500, £1,000, £1,500 or £2,000 depending on assessed financial need
Frequency: Annual
Country of Study: Any country
Application Procedure: Please complete an Donald & Margo Watt Bursary Fund (FASS) application form and submit to The Base, University House. Application has to be processed in the physical format. Form detail is available on the official link. https://www.lancaster.ac.uk/student-based-services/money/funding/donald–margot-watt-bursary-fund-fass-only
Funding: Private

For further information contact:

Lancaster University, Bailrigg, LA1 4YW, Lancaster, United Kingdom

Tel:	(44) 152 465 201
Email:	ugadmissions@lancaster.ac.uk

Geoffrey Leech Scholarships

Subjects: The scholarships are available to students applying for the following Masters programmes delivered at Lancaster: MA in english language and contemporary literary studies; MA in language studies; MA in teaching english as a foreign language (Lancaster-based); MA in teaching english to speakers of other languages (Lancaster-based)
Purpose: To mark the retirement of Professor Geoffrey Leech, the Department of Linguistics & English Language has established a scholarship fund in his honour
Eligibility: The Geoffrey Leech Scholarships are open to applicants who qualify to pay fees at the United

Kingdom/European Union-fee rate. The scholarships will be awarded on a competitive basis; details of criteria applied may be found on the departmental website

Level of Study: Postgraduate

Type: Scholarship

Value: Covers the whole of the tuition fee at the appropriate rate

Frequency: Annual

Application Procedure: In order to be considered for these awards, applicants must write a formal request to be considered for the scholarship, in no more than 500 words to Postgraduate Secretary

Closing Date: 22 March

For further information contact:

Email: m.f.wood@lancaster.ac.uk
Contact: Mrs Marjorie Wood, Postgraduate Secretary, Linguistics and English Language

Grizedale College Awards Fund

Subjects: All subjects

Purpose: Present and former undergraduate members of the college who wish to commence postgraduate study at Lancaster are eligible to apply for awards from this fund

Eligibility: The awards, in the form of grants, are made according to financial circumstances. The intended purpose of any grant awarded and any past or present contribution to college life are also taken into consideration

Level of Study: Postgraduate

Type: Award

Value: £1,500

Frequency: Annual

Closing Date: 1 June

Additional Information: Please see the website for further details www.lusi.lancs.ac.uk/funding/Detail.aspx? AwardID=29

For further information contact:

Grizedale College, Lancaster University, LA1 4YW, Lancaster, United Kingdom

Tel: (44) 1524 592 190
Email: b.glass@lancaster.ac.uk
Contact: Barbara Glass, College Administrator

Heatherlea Bursary

Subjects: MSc in ecology and environment or the MSc in conservation science

Purpose: Heatherlea, one of Britain's leading wildlife-holiday operators, offers one annual bursary of £1,000 to a student applying for and studying on either the MSc in ecology and environment or the MSc in conservation science

Eligibility: The Environment Centre will consider suitable candidates automatically so students do not need to apply separately. This award is a bursary and will be awarded on the basis of the financial background/need of the applicant

Level of Study: Postgraduate

Type: Bursary

Value: £1,000

Frequency: Annual

Additional Information: Please see the website for further details

For further information contact:

Postgraduate Studies Office, Lancaster Environment Centre, Library Avenue, Lancaster University, LA1 4YQ, Lancaster, United Kingdom

Tel: (44) 1524 593 478
Email: lec.pg@lancaster.ac.uk

Lancaster University Peel Studentship Trust

Subjects: All subjects

Purpose: Lancaster students studying at postgraduate level in any subject can apply to this trust, which is unique to the University

Eligibility: A pre-condition of application to the Peel Studentship Trust is that the applicant must be aged 21 or over on the first day of the first term for which they are seeking assistance. Both United Kingdom and non-United Kingdom students can apply for a grant. Applications are assessed on the basis of both academic merit and financial need

Level of Study: Postgraduate

Type: Studentship

Value: Up to £2,500. Students can use such grants to contribute towards paying either tuition fees or living costs

Length of Study: 1 year

Frequency: Annual

Closing Date: 1 May

Contributor: The Peel Studentship Trust

Additional Information: Please see the website for further details

Lonsdale College Travel Grant

Purpose: Lonsdale College offers Travel Awards to support undergraduate members of the College who propose to undertake an activity during the Summer vacation

Eligibility: 1. These are cash grants available to assist Lonsdale students in travel projects where academic work would be advanced by such visits. 2. The visits must not be a compulsory part of the student's academic course. The grant will be considered a loan until a written report of 1,000 words has been completed and submitted to the college, no later than the fifth week of the following term

Level of Study: Postgraduate

Type: Travel grant

Value: Up to £250

Frequency: Annual

Country of Study: Any country

Application Procedure: Kindly contact Julie Shorrock for further information. For further information, refer the website link mentioned below. https://www.lancaster.ac.uk/student-based-services/money/funding/lonsdale-college-travel-grant

Closing Date: Yet to be notified

Funding: Private

For further information contact:

Julie Shorrock, Lonsdale College, Bailrigg, LA1 4YN, Lancaster, United Kingdom

Tel: (44) 154 292 296

Postgraduate Access Awards (United Kingdom-Fee Only)

Subjects: These awards are intended for United Kingdom students commencing postgraduate Masters and Diploma courses in October

Purpose: Lancaster University is intending to offer up to six Postgraduate Access Awards from the Access to Learning Fund

Eligibility: Applicants should normally hold at least a 2:1 Honours degree

Level of Study: Postgraduate

Type: Award

Value: £500. These awards are intended to help towards living costs associated with undertaking full-time or part-time postgraduate study (where part-time equals at least 50 per cent of a full-time course). Awards are intended for students not otherwise in receipt of Government funding, but who are able to find finance for the remaining costs of their course

Frequency: Annual

Closing Date: Late July

Contributor: Access to learning fund

Additional Information: Please see the website for further details

Robinson Scholarship

Subjects: Operational research and management science

Purpose: Eddie Robinson is a graduate of the Operational Research programme who, after leaving Lancaster, has had a successful career in the United States with Mars Inc. He has generously sponsored a scholarship for an MSc in Operational Research & Management Science student from a developing country (as defined in the World Development Report published by the World Bank)

Eligibility: As the scholarship will not cover all the costs associated with studying, applicants should explain carefully their financial circumstances. This explanation should cover two aspects. Firstly, why is it that you need funding? Secondly, how will you finance the rest of the cost of your stay in Lancaster?

Level of Study: Postgraduate

Type: Scholarship

Value: £5,000

Frequency: Annual

Country of Study: Any country

Application Procedure: Please see the application details at www.lancs.ac.uk/studentservices/download/forms/

Closing Date: 15 April

Funding: Private

Additional Information: Please see the website for further details www.lums.lancs.ac.uk/masters/management-science/robinson/

For further information contact:

Department of Management Science, Lancaster University Management School, LA1 4YX, Lancaster, United Kingdom

Email: g.rand@lancaster.ac.uk

Contact: Graham Rand, MSc Admissions Tutor

Le Cordon Bleu Australia

Days Road, Regency Park, SA 5010, Australia

Tel: (61) 618 8346 3700/61 8 8348 3000

Fax: (61) 618 8346 3755/61 8 8348 3081

Email: australia@cordonbleu.edu

Website: www.lecordonbleu.com

Le Cordon bleu, a global leader hospitality education, provides professional development for existing executives.

The Culinary Trust Scholarship

Subjects: Hospitality management
Purpose: To provide financial assistance towards the Masters of International Hospitality Management in the Adelaide school
Eligibility: Open to applicants who meet entry requirements of the Masters of International Hospitality Management
Level of Study: Postgraduate
Type: Partial scholarship
Value: AU$8,000
Length of Study: 6 months
Frequency: Annual
Study Establishment: Le Cordon Bleu Australia, Adelaide
Country of Study: Australia
Application Procedure: Application form and full guidelines available from The Culinary Trust website
Closing Date: 1 March
Funding: Private
Additional Information: Scholarship is for partial tuition of the Graduate Certificate only and does not include other fees associated with commencing or continuing with the program

For further information contact:

Email: scholarships@theculinarytrust.com

Leeds International Pianoforte Competition

Leeds International Piano Competition, The University of Leeds, LS2 9JT, Leeds, United Kingdom

Tel: (44) 1132 446 586
Fax: (44) 1132 346 106
Email: pianocompetition@leeds.ac.uk/
                  info@leedspiano.com
Website: www.leedspiano.com

The Leeds International Pianoforte Competition is a member of the World Federation of International Music Competitions and the Alink/Argerich Foundation. It was founded in 1961 and since then has developed to become the world's greatest piano competition producing prizewinners who have gone onto successful international careers.

Henry Rudolf Meisels Bursary Awards

Subjects: Music and performing arts
Purpose: To award competitors accepted in the first stage of the competition

Eligibility: Open to candidates who are accepted to perform in the first stage of the competition
Level of Study: Professional development
Type: Scholarships and fellowships
Value: UK £100
Length of Study: Every 3 years
Frequency: Every 3 years
Study Establishment: The University of Leeds
Country of Study: United Kingdom
No. of awards offered: 196
Application Procedure: Entry by competitive audition. Application forms should be submitted by the closing date
Closing Date: 1 February
Contributor: Henry Rudolf Meisels Bequest
No. of awards given last year: 71
No. of applicants last year: 196
Additional Information: A non-refundable entrance fee of United Kingdom £50 must be paid no later than 1 February

For further information contact:

Email: pianocompetition@leeds.ac.uk

Leo Baeck Institute (LBI)

15 West 16th Street (Between 5th & 6th Avenues), New York, NY 10011, United States of America

Tel: (1) 212 744 6400/212 294 8340
Fax: (1) 212 988 1305
Email: lbaeck@lbi.cjh.org
Website: www.lbi.org
Contact: Secretary

The Leo Baeck Institute (LBI) is a research, study and lecture centre, a library and repository for archival and art materials. It is devoted to the preservation of original materials pertaining to the history and culture of German-speaking Jewry.

John A. S. Grenville PhD Studentship in Modern Jewish History and Culture

Subjects: Potential fields of investigation are: Jewish intellectual history (19–20th centuries); Modern German-Jewish history (20th century); Jewish cultural history (20th century)
Purpose: The studentship is named after John A. S. Grenville (1928–2011), an eminent scholar of modern world history and German Jewish history

Eligibility: Check details at www.leobaeck.co.uk/archives/4589

Level of Study: Doctorate

Type: Studentship

Value: The studentship amounts to £24,000 per year, from which tuition fees (Home/European Union students: £3,996 full-time/£1,998 part-time and non-European Union/overseas students: £12,600 full-time/£6,300 part-time) must be paid

Length of Study: 3 years

Frequency: Annual

Country of Study: United Kingdom

Application Procedure: Information on how to apply can be found at www.history.qmul.ac.uk/postgraduate/research-degrees/how-apply

Additional Information: The recipient of this scholarship will be enroled in the doctoral programme at the School of History, Queen Mary, University of London

For further information contact:

Email: d.wildmann@leobaeck.co.uk

Lepra Health in Action

28 Middleborough, Essex CO1 1TG, Colchester, United Kingdom

Tel:	(44) 1206 216 700
Fax:	(44) 1206 762 151
Email:	lepra@lepra.org.uk
Website:	www.lepra.org.uk
Contact:	Programmes Department

LEPRA is a health development international organisation working to restore health, hope and dignity to people affected by leprosy and other diseases of poverty such as malaria, tuberculosis and HIV/AIDS, among others. LEPRA is currently working in India.

Medical Elective Funding and Annual Essay Competition

Subjects: Leprosy

Purpose: To encourage United Kingdom-based medical students wishing to undertake a leprosy assignment overseas

Eligibility: Students in the United Kingdom of any nationality. LEPRA would also like to encourage medical students to apply for the annual essay competition

Level of Study: Graduate, Postgraduate

Type: Grant

Value: Dependent on funds available and up to United Kingdom £1,000 fund for essay competition

Length of Study: Up to 3 years

Frequency: Annual, dependent on funds available

Study Establishment: As appropriate to the nature of the research or training

Country of Study: Any country

No. of awards offered: 5

Application Procedure: Applicants must complete a research application pack, available on request. Applications must be submitted using the appropriate forms and should observe the time scales involved in the approval process

Closing Date: Applications are accepted at any time

Funding: Individuals

No. of awards given last year: 5

No. of applicants last year: 5

Additional Information: Occasionally also funded to physiotherapy students or students taking a BSc in nursing. Please check the website for more details

For further information contact:

Email:	deeptyh@leprahealthinaction.org
Contact:	Deepty Harji, Programmes Assistant

LeTourneau University

2100 S. Mobberly Ave, Longview, TX 75602, United States of America

Tel:	(1) 903 233 3000
Email:	admissions@james.letu.edu
Contact:	MBA Admissions Officer

Dual Credit Scholarship

Purpose: The Dual Credit scholarship cannot be combined with or stacked onto any previously awarded merit based scholarships from LeTourneau

Eligibility: 1. Have passed a minimum of one LETU Dual Credit course before graduating high school. 2. Classes offered the summer directly preceding attendance to LETU cannot be used to qualify for this scholarship. 3. Minimum score of 20 on the ACT or 1030 on the SAT. 4. Minimum cumulative high school GPA of 2.5 (on an unweighted 4.0 scale). 5. Enroll full-time in the residential program at the Longview campus

Level of Study: Postgraduate

Type: Scholarship

Value: $16,000

Length of Study: Upto 4 years
Frequency: Annual
Country of Study: Any country
Application Procedure: Submit your online application for admission Send in your official high school transcript Send in your official test result (ACT or SAT) LETU ACT School Code: 4120 LETU SAT School Code: 6365 File your FAFSA to be considered for additional financial aid LETU FAFSA School Code: 003584
Funding: Private
Additional Information: Application link is as follows: https://www.letu.edu/admissions/index.html

For further information contact:

Tel: (44) 903 233 4334
Email: SharleenHunt@letu.edu

Heritage Scholarship

Purpose: The Heritage Scholarship competition is designed to find students who will make an academic, spiritual, and personal impact on our campus from orientation through graduation and beyond. This "invitation only" event brings together the top students from all over the globe to LeTourneau University's Longview campus for a time of fun and competition
Eligibility: 1. The requirements to be invited to Heritage vary by the school at LeTourneau. 2. We are looking in the range of a 3.6+ GPA, and a score of 28+ composite on the ACT or 1260+ (critical reading plus math)
Level of Study: Postgraduate
Type: Scholarship
Value: $1,00,000 over four years
Length of Study: 0-4 years
Frequency: Annual
Country of Study: Any country
Application Procedure: With regard to the application procedure, kindly contact the director of admissions
Closing Date: No deadline
Funding: Private

For further information contact:

Tel: (44) 903 233 4331
Email: KristineSlate@letu.edu

Leukaemia & Lymphoma Research

Leukaemia & Lymphoma Research, 39-40 Eagle Street, WC1R 4TH, London, United Kingdom

Tel: (44) 2075 042 200
Fax: (44) 2074 053 139
Email: info@llresearch.org.uk
Website: www.llresearch.org.uk

Leukaemia research is devoted exclusively to leukaemia, Hodgkin's disease and other lymphomas, myeloma, myelodysplastic syndromes, aplastic anaemia and the myeloproliferative disorders. We are committed to finding causes, improving and developing new treatments and diagnostic methods as well as supplying free information booklets and answering written and telephone enquiries.

The Clinical Research Training Fellowship

Subjects: All life science disciplines. The research topic must be applicable to blood cancers
Purpose: To train registrar grade clinicians in research and allow them to obtain a higher degree
Eligibility: Open to researchers of any nationality who work and reside in the United Kingdom
Level of Study: Research
Type: Fellowship
Value: 50,000–100,000
Length of Study: 1–3 years
Study Establishment: Universities, medical schools, research institutes and teaching hospitals
Country of Study: United Kingdom
Application Procedure: Applicants must complete an application form
Closing Date: 14 March, 15 July
Additional Information: Please see the website for further details

For further information contact:

Tel: (44) 20 7405 0101
Email: sdarling@lrf.org.uk
Contact: Sara Darling

Leukaemia Foundation

P.O.BOX 1025, Lutwyche, QLD 4030, Australia

Tel: (61) 3 9949 5831
Fax: (61) 7 3866 4011
Email: jridge@leukaemia.org.au
Website: www.leukaemia.org.au
Contact: Jacinta Ridge, Mission and Vision Project Officer

The Leukaemia Foundation is the peak body for blood cancers and is dedicated to the care and cure of patients and families living with leukaemia, lymphoma, myeloma and related blood disorders.

Leukaemia Foundation PhD Scholarships

Subjects: Blood cancers
Purpose: To enhance the knowledge or treatment of haematological malignancies to improve the care of the patients and their families
Eligibility: Open to candidates who are citizens or permanent residents of Australia
Level of Study: Doctorate
Type: Scholarships
Value: $40,000 ($30,000 stipend + $10,000 consumables) per year for 3 years. $60,000 ($50,000 stipend + $10,000 consumables) per year for 3 years for clinicians
Frequency: Annual
Study Establishment: Research Institution in Australia
Country of Study: Australia
No. of awards offered: 22
Application Procedure: Applicants can download the application forms from the website www.leukaemia.com/web/research/fellowships_phd.php
Closing Date: 14 September
Funding: Foundation, Trusts
Contributor: Leukaemia Foundation
No. of awards given last year: 10
No. of applicants last year: 22
Additional Information: All queries should be directed to Dr Anna Williamson. Please see the website for further details www.leukaemia.com/web/research/researchgrants_applications.php

For further information contact:

Email: awilliamson@leukaemia.org.au
Contact: Dr Anna Williamson, National Manager, Research and Advocacy

Leukaemia Foundation Postdoctoral Fellowship

Subjects: Leukaemia
Purpose: To encourage and support young researchers and to foster cutting-edge research to improve the understanding of leukaemia and related malignancies and to benefit patients and families in the short-term or long-term
Eligibility: Open to candidates who have obtained a PhD no more than 3 years before the closing date for applications. Their PhD must be obtained by December of the year of application
Level of Study: Postdoctorate

Type: Fellowship
Value: $1,00,000 (75 per cent salary plus 25 per cent consumables) per year
Frequency: Annual
Country of Study: Australia
Application Procedure: Applicants can download the application form from the website
Closing Date: 27 July
Funding: Foundation
Contributor: Leukaemia Foundation

For further information contact:

Advocacy and Patient Care, Leukaemia Foundation, National Research Program, PO Box 2126, Windsor, QLD 4030, Australia

Email: awilliamson@leukaemia.org.au
Contact: Dr Anna Williamson, General Manager, Reseach

Leukemia Research Foundation (LRF)

Research Grants Administrator, Leukemia Research Foundation, 191 Waukegan Road, Suite 105, Northfield, IL 60091 1064, United States of America

Tel: (1) 847 424 0600, 888 558 5385
Fax: (1) 847 424 0600, 847 424 0606
Email: Linda@lrfmail.org, info@LRFmail.org
Website: www.allbloodcancers.org
Contact: Linda Kabot, Director of Programs

The Leukemia Research Foundation (LRF) was established in 1946. It aims to conquer leukemia, lymphoma and myelodysplastic syndromes by funding research into their causes and cures and to enrich the quality of life of those touched by these diseases.

Leukemia Research Foundation New Investigator Research Grant

Subjects: Basic science and clinical science
Purpose: To enable an investigator to initiate and develop a project sufficiently to obtain continued funding from national agencies
Eligibility: Preference given to proposals that focus on leukemia, lymphoma and MDS. New Investigators are considered to be within seven years of their first independent position. Years as a resident physician, fellow physician, or post-doctoral fellow are considered to be training years. Questions regarding eligibility should be directed to our

Research Grants Administrator. See the website for details regarding eligibility

Level of Study: Postgraduate
Type: Grant
Value: US$1,00,000
Length of Study: 1 year
Frequency: Annual
Country of Study: United States of America
No. of awards offered: 73
Application Procedure: Applicants must submit application form, references, self-addressed stamped envelope and one paragraph abstract in lay terms
Closing Date: 17 February
Funding: Private
Contributor: Leukaemia Research Foundation
No. of awards given last year: 10
No. of applicants last year: 73
Additional Information: Please see the website for further details http://www.leukemia-research.org/page.aspx?pid=216

For further information contact:

Leukemia Research Foundation, 820 Davis Street, Suite #420, IL 60201, United States of America

Tel:	(1) 847 424 0600
Fax:	(1) 847 424 0606
Email:	Info@LRFMail.org
Contact:	Kelli Fitzgerald, Medical Grants Administrator

Leverhulme Trust

Research Awards Advisory Committee, 1 Pemberton Row, EC4A 3BG, London, United Kingdom

Tel:	(44) 2070 429 861
Fax:	(44) 2070 429 889
Email:	agrundy@leverhulme.ac.uk
Website:	www.leverhulme.ac.uk
Contact:	Miss Anna Grundy, Grants Manger

The Trust, established by the Will of William Hesketh Lever, makes awards for the support of research and education. The Trust emphasizes individuals and encompasses all subject areas.

Study Abroad Studentship

Purpose: For students to study or undertake research at a centre of learning in any country except the United Kingdom or United States of America

Eligibility: Applicants must: have been resident in the United Kingdom for at least three years at the time of application hold an undergraduate degree (undergraduates are not eligible) hold a degree from a United Kingdom institution (this may be either the undergraduate degree or a further degree held by the applicant) either be a student at the time of application or have been registered as a student within the last eight years explain why their work requires residence overseas Wish to undertake study or research in any country except the United Kingdom or United States of America

Level of Study: Doctorate, Graduate, Postdoctorate, Postgraduate, Predoctorate, Postgraduate (MSc)
Type: Studentship
Value: £21,000 for maintenance allowance plus fees, baggage and flight allowance
Length of Study: 12-24 months
Frequency: Annual
Country of Study: Worldwide
No. of awards offered: 96
Application Procedure: The 2020 round of awards will open in early September. Closing date tbc but in early January 2020
Closing Date: TBC
Funding: Trusts
Contributor: The Leverhulme Trust
No. of awards given last year: 32
No. of applicants last year: 96
Additional Information: Further information available here https://www.leverhulme.ac.uk/study-abroad-studentships

For further information contact:

Tel:	(44) 2070 429 862
Email:	agrundy@leverhulme.ac.uk
Contact:	Mrs Bridget Kerr, Senior Grants Administrative Officer

Library Company of Philadelphia

1314 Locust Street, Philadelphia, PA 19107, United States of America

Tel:	(1) 215 546 3181
Fax:	(1) 215 546 5167
Email:	jgreen@librarycompany.org
Website:	www.librarycompany.org
Contact:	Fellowship Office

Founded in 1731, the Library Company of Philadelphia was the largest public library in America until the 1850s and contains printed materials on aspects of American culture and society in that period. It is a research library with a collection of 500,000 books, pamphlets, newspapers and periodicals, 75,000 prints, maps and photographs and 150,000 manuscripts.

Library Company of Philadelphia Dissertation Fellowships

Purpose: To promote scholarship by offering long-term dissertation fellowships
Eligibility: The fellowship Supports dissertation research in the collections of the Library Company and other Philadelphia repositones
Level of Study: Doctorate
Type: Fellowship
Value: $10,000–$12,500
Length of Study: 4–5 months
Frequency: Annual
Country of Study: Any country
No. of awards offered: 45
Application Procedure: Candidates are encouraged to enquire about the appropriateness of a proposed topic before applying. See website under fellowships
Closing Date: 1 March may take up residence for either the following Fall or the Spring semester
Funding: Private
No. of awards given last year: 6
No. of applicants last year: 45
Additional Information: Further Information can be found on the website, which also includes fellowships offered by the Library Company s programmes in early American economy and society and African American History

Library Company of Philadelphia Postdoctoral Research Fellowship

Subjects: 18 and 19 century American social, cultural and literary history
Purpose: To promote scholarship by offering long-term postdoctoral and advanced research fellowships
Eligibility: The fellowship supports both postdoctoral and advanced research in the collections of the Library Company and often Philadelphia repositories. Applicants must hold a doctoral degree
Level of Study: Postdoctorate, Research
Type: Fellowship
Value: Stipend is around $18,900–$25,000
Length of Study: 4.5 months (1 semester)
Frequency: Annual
Study Establishment: An independent research library
Country of Study: United States of America

No. of awards offered: 57
Application Procedure: Candidates are encouraged to enquire about the appropriateness of a proposed topic before applying. See website under fellowships
Closing Date: 2 November. Fellows may take up residence for either the following Fall or the Spring semester
Funding: Government, Private
Contributor: National Endowment for the Humanities; Andrew W Mellon Foundation
No. of awards given last year: 8
No. of applicants last year: 57
Additional Information: Four of the fellowships are offered by the Library Company's programmes [etc]. Three are supported by the National Endowment for the Humanities

For further information contact:

Email: jgreen@ brarycompany org

Life Sciences Research Foundation (LSRF)

Lewis Thomas Laboratory, Princeton University, Washington Road, Princeton, NJ 08544, United States of America

Tel:	(1) 410 467 2597
Email:	sdirenzo@princeton.edu
Website:	www.lsrf.org
Contact:	Susan DiRenzo, Assistant Director

The Life Sciences Research Foundation (LSRF) solicits monies from industry, foundations and individuals to support postdoctoral fellowships in the life sciences. The LSRF recognizes that discoveries and the application of innovations in biology for the public's good will depend upon the training and support of the highest quality young scientists in the very best research environments. The LSRF awards fellowships across the spectrum of life sciences: biochemistry, cell, developmental, molecular, plant, structural, organismic population and evolutionary biology, endocrinology, immunology, microbiology, neurobiology, physiology and virology.

Life Sciences Research Foundation

Subjects: All areas of the life sciences
Purpose: provides 3-year fellowships for postdoctoral research
Eligibility: Must be post-doctorals with less than five years from time of PhD awarded
Level of Study: Postdoctorate

Type: One fellowship
Value: 58,000 stipend per year
Length of Study: 3 years
Frequency: Annual
Country of Study: Any country
No. of awards offered: 800
Application Procedure: Application must be completed online
Closing Date: 1 October of each year
Funding: Foundation
No. of awards given last year: 27
No. of applicants last year: 800

Life Sciences Research Foundation Postdoctoral Fellowships

Subjects: Biological and life sciences
Purpose: To support postdoctoral fellowships across the spectrum of the life sciences
Eligibility: Open to researchers of any nationality, who are graduates of medical or graduate schools in the biological sciences and who hold an MD or PhD degree. Awards will be based solely on the quality of the individual applicant's previous accomplishments and on the merit of the proposal for postdoctoral research
Level of Study: Postdoctorate
Type: Fellowship
Value: US$57,000 per year. The salary scale begins at $43,000 for a first-year postdoctoral, $45,000 for a second year, and $47,000 thereafter. The fellow, not the advisor, will control expenditure of the remainder. It can be used for fringe benefits (up to $2,000 per year), travel to the host institution, travel to visit the sponsor and to the LSRF annual meeting. However, its main purpose is to support the fellow
Length of Study: 3 years
Frequency: Annual
Study Establishment: Appropriate research institutions
Country of Study: Any country
No. of awards offered: 820
Application Procedure: Electronic submission only. Please check website
Closing Date: 4 September
Funding: Private
No. of awards given last year: 16
No. of applicants last year: 820
Additional Information: LSRF Fellows must carry out their research at non-profit institutions. The fellowship cannot be used to support research that has any patent commitment or other kind of agreement with a commercial profit-making company. Please see the website for further details www.lsrf.org/resources/resources-detail-view/LSRF-Awards-Postdoctoral-Fellowships

Linacre College

Carolyn and Franco Gianturco Scholarship in Theoretical Chemistry

Subjects: Theoretical Chemistry and/or Computational Chemical Physics
Purpose: The Department will select a scholarship holder from among all eligible students reading, or intending to read, for a Theoretical Chemistry degree (Theoretical and/or Computational Chemical Physics)
Level of Study: Graduate
Type: Scholarship
Length of Study: Period of fee liability
Frequency: Annual
Country of Study: Any country
Closing Date: Yet to be mentioned
Funding: Private

For further information contact:

St. Cross Road, OX1 3JA, Oxford, United Kingdom

Tel: (44) 1865 271 650
Email: support@linacre.ox.ac.uk

Eldred Scholarship

Purpose: The Eldred Scholarship at Linacre College was established in 2012. It funds students from sub-Saharan Africa to study the MSc African Studies at Oxford
Eligibility: 1. You should be applying to start the MSc African Studies at Oxford and you must be ordinarily resident in sub-Saharan Africa. 2. You should be intending to return to your country of ordinary residence once your course is completed. Scholarships will be awarded on the basis of academic merit
Level of Study: Postgraduate (MSc)
Type: Scholarship
Value: £7,000. 100% of University and college fees, a grant for living costs and a return flight from your home country to United Kingdom
Frequency: Annual
Country of Study: Any country
Application Procedure: To apply this scholarship you don't need to provide a separated application for applying this scholarship. You are only required to apply the graduate study at the university
Closing Date: No deadline
Funding: Private

Additional Information: No extra application necessary. Department will select a scholarship holder among all applicable students

For further information contact:

13 Bevington Rd, Oxford OX2 6LH, Oxford, United Kingdom

Email: african.studies@africa.ox.ac.uk

Lincoln Memorial University

School of Graduate Studies, Cumberland Gap Parkway, Harrogate, TN 37752, United States of America

Tel:	(1) 423 869 6374
Fax:	(1) 423 869 6261
Email:	graduate@inetlmu.lmunet.edu
Contact:	MBA Admissions Officer

Fulbright - Platinum Triangle Scholarship in Entrepreneurship

Subjects: All subject
Purpose: The Fulbright Platinum Triangle Scholarship in Entrepreneurship is for a talented New Zealander in a knowledge economy-related fields to complete a Masters degree in the United States of America
Eligibility: New Zealand Citizen or Permanent Resident Students
Level of Study: Postgraduate
Type: Award
Length of Study: 4 Year
Frequency: Varies
Country of Study: Any country
Application Procedure: Apply online: http://www.fulbright. org.nz
Closing Date: 1 August
Funding: Foundation

For further information contact:

Email: info@fulbright.org.nz

Sasakawa Young Leaders Fellowship Fund Research Scholarship - Masters and PhD

Purpose: Applicants must be New Zealand Citizens of Permanent residents and be studying in the fields of Humanities

or Social Sciences (or other areas provided the research has a Humanities/Social Science angle)
Eligibility: New Zealand Citizen or Permanent Resident Students
Level of Study: Postdoctorate
Type: Scholarship
Value: $25,000
Frequency: Annual
Country of Study: New Zealand
Closing Date: 1 October
Funding: Foundation

For further information contact:

Email: info@lincoln.ac.nz

Zespri Innovation Scholarships

Subjects: All subject
Purpose: The kiwifruit industry is New Zealand's largest horticultural exporter and Zespri is the leading global kiwifruit marketer. The Zespri Innovation Scholarships are offered to build awareness of the kiwifruit industry as an exciting career option, to encourage further research into kiwifruit and related fields and finally to encourage capability building
Eligibility: 1. New Zealand Citizen or Permanent Resident Students. 2. International Students
Level of Study: Postgraduate
Type: Scholarship
Value: Masters NZ $20,000pa (stipend) plus university fees PhD NZ $30,000pa (stipend) plus university fees
Length of Study: 1 Year
Frequency: Annual
Country of Study: Any country
Application Procedure: Apply online: http://www.zespri. com/Pages/InnovationScholarship.aspx
Closing Date: 31 July
Funding: Foundation

For further information contact:

Innovation Coordinator, 400 Maunganui Road, PO Box 4043, Mount Maunganui, 3149, New Zealand

Email: corporate.communications@zespri.com

Zonta International Canterbury Tertiary Education Scholarship

Subjects: These Scholarships were first established in the early 1990's by the combined Zonta Clubs of Canterbury to assist women completing a tertiary course of study. Preference may be given to a mature student in need of financial assistance to complete a defined course of study at any level

Purpose: In order to assist women for completion of tertiary course of study

Eligibility: It is available to New Zealand Citizen who is living in Canterbury or permanent residents

Level of Study: Graduate

Type: Grant

Value: NZ $3,000

Frequency: Annual

Country of Study: New Zealand

Application Procedure: Kindly send the application to the following address as mentioned in address field

Closing Date: 10 March

Funding: Private

Additional Information: Send the application to the secretary of the concern

For further information contact:

Zonta International Canterbury Tertiary Education Scholarship, C/- Zonta Club of Christchurch South, PO Box 25196, Christchurch 8144, New Zealand

Email: info@lincoln.ac.nz

Lincoln University New Zealand (LUNZ)

PO Box 84, Canterbury, Lincoln 7647, New Zealand

Tel: (64) 3 325 2811
Email: info@lincoln.ac.nz
Website: http://www.lincoln.ac.nz

Lincoln University New Zealand (LUNZ) is one of 8 government universities in New Zealand, with a history stretching back more than 125 years. The University continues to achieve international recognition for its teaching and research activities. It is renowned for its entrepreneurship, relevance and as a catalyst for new and diverse approaches to stimulate the development and transfer of knowledge.

Adastra Foundation Scholarship

Purpose: Scholarships are available to individuals who exhibit dedication towards the development of an exceptional talent with a focus on sport, performing arts, and music

Eligibility: 1. Candidates must be resident in the Waikato/BOP region when applying. 2. Candidates should be between the ages of 16–23

Level of Study: Graduate

Type: Scholarships, fellowships, bursaries

Frequency: Annual

Country of Study: New Zealand

Closing Date: 31 October

Funding: Private

For further information contact:

The Adastra Foundation, PO Box 1566, Private Bag 3091, Hamilton, Canada

Email: scholarships@lincoln.ac.nz

Agribusiness & Commerce Faculty Summer Scholarships

Purpose: The Faculty of Agribusiness & Commerce offers a number of research scholarships over the summer vacation to capable students who are considering continuing their university studies

Eligibility: 1. New Zealand Citizen or Permanent Resident Students. 2. International Students

Level of Study: Postdoctorate

Type: Scholarship

Value: NZ $5,000

Frequency: Annual

Country of Study: New Zealand

Closing Date: 13 October

Funding: Foundation

For further information contact:

Marian Pearson Faculty of Agribusiness & Commerce, PO Box 85084, Lincoln University, Lincoln 7647, Christchurch, New Zealand

Tel: (64) 3 423 0216
Email: Marian.Pearson@lincoln.ac.nz

Association for Molecular Pathology Scholarship

Subjects: All subjects

Purpose: AMP Scholarships rewards those with courage, passion, determination and commitment - those who aspire to live life to the full. Recipients must not only have the ability, but also the ambition to achieve their chosen goal no matter what obstacles may be in their path. Each year AMP's

Scholarships programme gives away nearly $2,00,000 to Kiwis with a dream

Eligibility: New Zealand Citizen or Permanent Resident Students

Level of Study: Postgraduate

Type: Scholarship

Frequency: Varies

Country of Study: Any country

Application Procedure: Apply online

Closing Date: 13 August

Funding: Trusts

For further information contact:

Email: info@lincoln.ac.nz

Australia and New Zealand Banking Group Limited AusIMM Tertiary Scholarship

Subjects: Environmental based

Eligibility: Available to New Zealand Citizen or Permanent Resident Students. The ANZ AusIMM Tertiary Scholarship is open to applicants currently studying towards a Masters or Honours degree related to the environment that will be of benefit to the minerals, coal or petroleum industries

Level of Study: Graduate

Type: Scholarship

Value: NZ $5,000

Frequency: Annual

Country of Study: New Zealand

Closing Date: 28 February

Funding: Private

For further information contact:

Tel: (64) 3 423 0000

Email: info@lincoln.ac.nz

Australian Federation of University Women - ACT Inc. Bursary

Purpose: The Australian Federation of University Women - ACT Incorporated offers free board and lodging for up to four weeks at a residential college at the Australian National University, Canberra, to a woman graduate or final year honours student form a university or tertiary institution in Australia

Eligibility: 1. Bursary is applicable for Woman only Sports. 2. Available to New Zealand Citizen or Permanent Resident Students

Level of Study: Graduate

Type: Bursary

Frequency: Annual

Country of Study: Australia

Closing Date: 31 March

Funding: Private

For further information contact:

Email: jocelyn.eskdale@daff.gov.au

Australian Institute of Mining and Metallurgy Scholarships

Subjects: All subjects

Purpose: The Australasian Institute of Mining and Metallurgy, New Zealand Branch has established the Education Endowment Trust. One of its purposes is to assist students studying in fields related to minerals, mining, geological and petroleum. This includes any rehabilitation projects that may be covered by agricultural or science students

Eligibility: 1. New Zealand Citizen or Permanent Resident Students. 2. International Students

Level of Study: Postgraduate

Type: Scholarship

Value: NZ $2,000 - $5,000

Length of Study: 1 Year

Frequency: Annual

Country of Study: Any country

Application Procedure: Apply online

Closing Date: 28 February

Funding: Trusts

For further information contact:

Roger Briggs Secretary, NZ Branch Education Endowment Trust Australasian Institute of Mining and Metallurgy c/- Winstone Aggregates, PO Box 17-195, Greenlane, Auckland, New Zealand

Email: erth0095@waikato.ac.nz

Bart Baker Memorial Scholarship

Subjects: All subjects

Purpose: One or more scholarships are available to students enrolled full time at Lincoln University and carrying out post-graduate research in an area of vertebrate pest management in New Zealand. Preference will be given to those students enrolled for an Honours degree or Postgraduate Diploma

Eligibility: New Zealand Citizen or Permanent Resident Students

Level of Study: Postgraduate

Type: Scholarship

Value: NZ $20,000

Length of Study: 1 Year
Frequency: Annual
Country of Study: Any country
Application Procedure: Apply online
Closing Date: 31 March
Funding: Foundation

For further information contact:

Email:　scholarships@lincoln.ac.nz

Beef + Lamb NZ Undergraduate Scholarship

Purpose: These scholarships are intended to assist students who have achieved a good academic record, possess good interpersonal skills and have a passion for the agricultural sector,
Eligibility: Check the website for further details. http://beeflambnz.com/your-levies-at-work/undergraduate-scholarship-degree
Level of Study: Graduate
Type: Scholarship
Frequency: Varies
Country of Study: New Zealand
Application Procedure: https://beeflambnz.com/news-views/blnz-iba-scholarship-2019
Closing Date: 07 February
Funding: Private

For further information contact:

Tel:　　　(44) 27 687 5650
Email:　　doug.macredie@beeflambnz.com
Contact:　Mr Doug Macredie

Bragato Postgraduate Scholarship

Subjects: All subjects
Purpose: The Scholarship may be awarded to a student who has completed a full time degree course at a recognised academic institution and who has enrolled for a Post Graduate course of study in New Zealand or overseas. The applicant must be a New Zealand resident. The post graduate course must be at a university or other institution recognised for its post graduate courses in subjects of relevance to the viticulture and wine industry
Eligibility: 1. The Scholarship may be awarded to a student who has completed a full time degree course at a recognised academic institution and who has enrolled for a Post Graduate course of study in New Zealand or overseas. The applicant must be a New Zealand resident. 2. The post graduate course must be at a university or other institution recognised for its

post graduate courses in subjects of relevance to the viticulture and wine industry
Level of Study: Postgraduate
Type: Scholarship
Value: NZ $15,000
Length of Study: 1 Year
Frequency: Annual
Country of Study: Any country
Application Procedure: Apply online
Closing Date: 28 February
Funding: Trusts

For further information contact:

The Secretary, Bragato Trust, 20 Cambridge TCE, Taradale, Napier, 4112, New Zealand

Email:　bragatotrust@airnet.net.nz

Bragato Research Fellowship

Subjects: All subjects
Purpose: The research must be in a subject of benefit to New Zealand's industry
Eligibility: The Fellowship may be awarded to any student who has completed a Masters degree or Doctorate and who is involved in ongoing research. The applicant must be a New Zealand resident The planned research must be at a university or other research institution in New Zealand or overseas, recognised for its research in subjects related to the wine industry
Level of Study: Postgraduate
Type: Fellowship
Value: NZ $15,000
Length of Study: 1 Year
Frequency: Annual
Country of Study: Any country
Application Procedure: Apply online
Closing Date: 28 February
Funding: Trusts

For further information contact:

Email:　bragatotrust@airnet.net.nz

British Chevening Scholarships

Subjects: All subjects
Purpose: A scholarship is available for students who have completed an undergraduate degree and who wish to undertake further study in the United Kingdom. You must be

a graduate with the personal, intellectual and interpersonal qualities necessary for leadership

Eligibility: 1. A citizen of a Chevening-eligible country. 2. Return to your country of citizenship for a minimum of two years after your scholarship has ended. 3. Have an undergraduate degree that will enable you to gain entry to a postgraduate programme at a United Kingdom university. This is typically equivalent to an upper second-class 2:1 honours degree in the United Kingdom

Level of Study: Postgraduate

Type: Scholarship

Value: A Chevening Scholarship normally covers university tuition fees, a monthly living allowance, an economy class return airfare to the United Kingdom, and additional grants and allowances to cover essential expenditure

Length of Study: 2 Year

Frequency: Annual

Country of Study: Any country

Application Procedure: Apply online

Closing Date: 6 November

Funding: Government

For further information contact:

Email: gareth.farry@britishcouncil.org.nz

Building Better Homes, Towns and Cities Scholarship

Subjects: All subjects

Purpose: National Science Challenge Building Better Homes, Towns and Cities are undertaking research in the area of 'Collaborating for recovery in post-quake Canterbury'. Scholarships will be offered to provide assistance to talented students undertaking research of relevance to the project

Eligibility: 1. Applicants who are currently studying a relevant postgraduate qualification. 2. Applicants require satisfactory academic performance which, for the purposes of this scholarship, is defined as achieving a B+ / GPA 6 or better in Semester 1 2018 course work or as verified by supervisors of the scholar's dissertation or thesis. 3. Applicants may be New Zealand Citizens, Permanent Residents or International students

Level of Study: Postgraduate

Type: Scholarship

Value: NZ $3,000

Frequency: Varies

Country of Study: Any country

Application Procedure: Apply online

Closing Date: 7 May

Funding: Trusts

For further information contact:

Email: scholarships@lincoln.ac.nz

Building Research Association of New Zealand Group Scholarships

Purpose: The BRANZ Group scholarship programme is for postgraduate students undertaking research that inspires the building and construction industry to provide better buildings for New Zealanders

Eligibility: New Zealand Citizen or Permanent Resident Students

Level of Study: Postdoctorate

Type: Scholarship

Value: NZ $25,000

Length of Study: 3 Year

Frequency: Annual

Country of Study: New Zealand

Closing Date: 10 December

Funding: Foundation

For further information contact:

Email: research@branz.org.nz

Business & Professional Women Franklin Tertiary Study Award

Subjects: All subjects

Purpose: Awarded to a woman who is a past or present Franklin resident, who is undertaking a course at a University, Polytechnic or College of Education in New Zealand or retraining following an absence from employment

Eligibility: New Zealand Citizen or Permanent Resident Students

Level of Study: Postgraduate

Type: Award

Value: NZ $3,000

Length of Study: 1 Year

Frequency: Annual

Country of Study: New Zealand

Application Procedure: Apply online

Closing Date: 20 January

Funding: Trusts

For further information contact:

Email: kellyj@franklinlaw.co.nz

Business & Professional Women Hibiscus Coast Study Award

Purpose: Awarded to a female student who is a past or present Hibiscus Coast Resident, who has completed at least one full year of a two or more year course at a University, Polytechnic or College of Education in New Zealand
Eligibility: This award is provided for those candidates who has completed at least one full year of a two or more year course at a University, Polytechnic or College of Education in New Zealand
Level of Study: Graduate
Type: Award
Value: NZ $2,000
Frequency: Annual
Country of Study: New Zealand
Application Procedure: For further information, visit the website link. http://www.bpwnz.org.nz
Closing Date: 31 December
Funding: Private

For further information contact:

BPW Study Award, C/- PO Box 593, Orewa NZ 0946, New Zealand

Tel: (64) 9 426 0407
Email: davenjen@xtra.co.nz

C Alma Baker Trust Postgraduate Scholarship

Subjects: overseas
Purpose: These scholarships are available to students enrolled or intending to enrol in masterate or doctoral thesis programmes in the fields of agriculture, agriculture-related technologies or the study of rural society. The value for a masterate student is NZ $13,000 for a one year scholarship, and a doctoral student is NZ $20,000 per year for up to three years
Eligibility: New Zealand Citizen or Permanent Resident Students
Level of Study: Postgraduate
Type: Scholarship
Value: Academic Merit NZ $13,000pa Masters Student and NZ $20,000pa PhD
Length of Study: 3 Year
Frequency: Annual
Country of Study: New Zealand
Application Procedure: Apply online
Closing Date: 1 February
Funding: Trusts

For further information contact:

Email: B.K.MacDonald@massey.ac.nz

Cambridge Commonwealth, European and International Trust

Purpose: The Cambridge Commonwealth Trust offers several prestigious awards each year to enable graduates of high academic ability to study at Cambridge University in Britain. The scholarships are open to graduates who are New Zealand citizens and who wish to pursue a course of research leading to the degree of PhD at Cambridge University
Eligibility: New Zealand Citizen or Permanent Resident Students
Level of Study: Postdoctorate
Type: Scholarship
Length of Study: 3 Year
Frequency: Annual
Country of Study: New Zealand
Closing Date: 1 October
Funding: Foundation

Charles and Ella Elgar Trust Bursaries

Subjects: All subjects
Purpose: Applicants must be discharged servicemen or the children of discharged servicemen. Preference will be given to applicants studying agriculture. Available for any Diploma, Bachelor, or Masters degrees
Eligibility: New Zealand Citizen or Permanent Resident Students
Level of Study: Postgraduate
Type: Bursary
Value: NZ $750
Frequency: Varies
Country of Study: Any country
Application Procedure: Apply online
Closing Date: 31 March
Funding: Foundation

For further information contact:

Lincoln University, PO Box 85084, Lincoln 7647, New Zealand

Email: info@lincoln.ac.nz

Craigmore Sustainables Postgraduate Scholarship

Subjects: All subjects
Purpose: The Craigmore Sustainables Scholarship was established in 2014 and is awarded for the purpose of supporting postgraduate study and research in agriculture and agricultural areas at Lincoln University
Eligibility: 1. Scholarships will be open to full-time students who are currently enrolled in a postgraduate qualification.

The postgraduate study must include a research component. 2. Applicants may be New Zealand Citizens, Permanent Residents or International students

Level of Study: Postgraduate
Type: Scholarship
Value: NZ $5,000
Length of Study: 1 Year
Frequency: Annual
Country of Study: Any country
Application Procedure: Apply online
Closing Date: 31 March
Funding: Foundation

For further information contact:

Email: scholarships@lincoln.ac.nz

Don Hulston Foundation Scholarship

Purpose: The purposes of the Don Hulston Foundation are to encourage and promote post-graduate research with particular emphasis on practical and applied research in agriculture, horticulture, forestry and aquaculture, and to promote research that is of benefit to the New Zealand economy
Eligibility: 1. Scholarships will be open to any post-graduate student from Lincoln University who is a New Zealand citizen or has been resident in New Zealand for a period of not less than five years at any time during his or her lifetime. 2. Scholarships will be open to candidates who are eligible to register as candidates for postgraduate study (research only), PhD or the thesis year of a Masters degree. 3. A scholarship may be awarded to a person who is not eligible to register as a candidate with Lincoln University provided he or she becomes eligible to so register by 1 March in the year following the awards, or by such other date as may be determined by the Vice Chancellor in a particular case
Level of Study: Postdoctorate
Type: Scholarship
Value: NZ $21,000
Length of Study: 1 Year
Frequency: Annual
Country of Study: New Zealand
Closing Date: 1 October
Funding: Foundation

For further information contact:

Email: info@lincoln.ac.nz

Don Linklater Memorial University Bursary

Subjects: All subjects

Purpose: To be eligible the applicant must be planning to study at a New Zealand university full-time in one of the following fields: Resource Management, river and drainage engineering and environmental planning. Study may be at undergraduate or postgraduate level and the applicant can be enrolled either internally or extramurally. You must be a New Zealand citizen or permanent resident and live in Horizons region (even if your studies take you outside of the region). The region includes the Ruapehu, Rangitikei, Wanganui, Manawatu, Palmerston North, Tararua and Horowhenua districts
Level of Study: Postgraduate
Type: Bursary
Value: NZ $3,000
Length of Study: 3 Year
Frequency: Varies
Country of Study: Any country
Application Procedure: Apply online
Closing Date: 3 April
Funding: Trusts

For further information contact:

Email: help@horizons.govt.nz

Dune Restoration Trust of NZ Post Graduate Study Award

Subjects: All subjects
Purpose: The purpose of the award is to provide funds to assist with an individual's post graduate level research to improve knowledge in the field of coastal sand dune restoration. This study award is funded by and administered by the Dune Restoration Trust of New Zealand
Eligibility: New Zealand Citizen or Permanent Resident Students
Level of Study: Postgraduate
Type: Award
Frequency: Annual
Country of Study: Any country
Application Procedure: Apply online
Closing Date: 28 February
Funding: Foundation

For further information contact:

Email: info@dunestrust.org.nz

Edward and Isabel Kidson Scholarships

Purpose: This scholarship is for advanced study in meteorology or failing that, some other branch of science. Preference

will be given to former pupils of Nelson Boys' College or persons who have been undergraduates of the University of Canterbury
Eligibility: New Zealand Citizen or Permanent Resident Students
Level of Study: Postdoctorate
Type: Scholarship
Value: NZ $6,000
Length of Study: 3 Year
Frequency: Annual
Country of Study: New Zealand
Closing Date: 1 October
Funding: Foundation

For further information contact:

Level 9, 142 Lambton Quay, Wellington PO Box 11915, Wellington 6142, New Zealand

Email: info@lincoln.ac.nz

Emerging Researcher Fellowship

Purpose: New Zealand-based early-career researcher to establish connections with Chinese counterparts
Eligibility: 1. Have completed their PhD studies within seven years at the time of commencing the award. 2. Have been awarded a doctorate at the time of application. 3. Be a New Zealand citizen, have permanent residency or be applying for permanent residency. 4. Have been working or studying in New Zealand in an area relevant to the fellowship activities. 5. Be able to participate in the nominated fellowship activities at the time and for the duration proposed by the Chinese organisation during the Fellowship
Level of Study: Postdoctorate
Type: Fellowship
Value: Up to NZ $40,000
Frequency: Annual
Country of Study: New Zealand
Closing Date: 31 October
Funding: Foundation

For further information contact:

Professor Hong J Di, ONZM, FRSNZ, FNZSSS, FNZIAHS Professor of Soil and Environmental Science Department of Soil and Physical Sciences Lincoln University, PO Box 85084, Lincoln University, Lincoln, 7647, Canterbury, New Zealand

Email: Hong.di@lincoln.ac.nz

Environment, Society and Design Summer Scholarships

Subjects: All subjects
Purpose: Economic valuation of ecosystem services from urban waterways. Evaluating visitor engagement in national parks: Developing tools for monitoring DOC's Interpretation Ranger initiative
Eligibility: 1. New Zealand Citizen or Permanent Resident Students. 2. International Students
Level of Study: Postgraduate
Type: Scholarship
Value: NZ $6,000
Frequency: Varies
Country of Study: Any country
Application Procedure: Apply online. Alternate address: PO Box 85084 Lincoln University Lincoln 7647
Closing Date: 28 September
Funding: Trusts

For further information contact:

Email: douglas.broughton@lincoln.ac.nz

Foundation for Arable Research Postgraduate Scholarship

Subjects: All subjects
Purpose: This scholarship is being awarded by the Foundation for Arable Research (FAR) with the objective being to encourage research activities which will add value to the New Zealand arable farming sector
Eligibility: 1. The scholarship is open to full-time students at Lincoln University eligible to proceed to or undertaking postgraduate research, which will assist with increasing standards within the New Zealand arable farming sector 2. New Zealand Citizens or Permanent Residents
Level of Study: Postgraduate
Type: Scholarship
Value: $7,000
Length of Study: 1 Year
Frequency: Annual
Country of Study: Any country
Application Procedure: Apply online
Closing Date: 15 March
Funding: Foundation

For further information contact:

Email: scholarships@lincoln.ac.nz

Frank Knox Memorial Fellowships

Subjects: Arts and Science (including Engineering), Business Administration, Design, Divinity, Education, Law, Medicine and Public Health

Purpose: Established in honour of the late Frank Knox to encourage scholarly exchange between the United States and the British Commonwealth, this scholarship supports graduate coursework students to undertake graduate study at Harvard University

Eligibility: Available to New Zealand Citizen or Permanent Resident Students

Level of Study: Postgraduate

Type: Fellowships, operating grants

Length of Study: 2 to 4 years

Frequency: Annual

Study Establishment: Harvard University

Country of Study: Any country

Application Procedure: Check the details online. http://www.lincoln.ac.nz/Study/Qualifications/Qualification/scholarships/?qual=PhD

Closing Date: 7 December

Funding: Private

For further information contact:

Frank Knox Fellowships, 3 Birdcage Walk Westminster, SW1H 9JJ, London, United Kingdom

Tel:	(44) 20 7222 1151
Email:	info@lincoln.ac.nz
Contact:	Ms Annie Thomas

Frank Sydenham Scholarship

Subjects: Postgrad study in horticulture, agriculture, forestry or related subjects

Purpose: Applications are invited from persons undertaking postgraduate study (in New Zealand or abroad) in horticulture, agriculture, forestry and related pursuits

Eligibility: New Zealand Citizen or Permanent Resident Students

Level of Study: Postdoctorate

Type: Scholarship

Frequency: Annual

Country of Study: New Zealand

Closing Date: 3 December

Funding: Foundation

For further information contact:

The New Zealand Guardian Trust Co Ltd, Box 13008, Tauranga, New Zealand

Tel:	(64) 7 578 2943
Fax:	(64) 7 578 8792
Email:	echristensen@nzgt.co.nz

Freemasons Postgraduate Scholarship

Purpose: Each year Freemasons Postgraduate Scholarships are offered to students attending New Zealand Universities. Scholarships are awarded to students completing a Postgraduate Diploma, Masters degree or a Doctoral degree. Application forms can be found on the Freemasons website

Eligibility: New Zealand Citizen or Permanent Resident Students

Level of Study: Postdoctorate

Type: Scholarship

Frequency: Annual

Country of Study: New Zealand

Closing Date: 1 October

Funding: Foundation

For further information contact:

Email: info@lincoln.ac.nz

Fulbright Senior Scholar Award

Purpose: The Fulbright New Zealand Senior Scholar Award, valued at up to US$30,000 including return travel, is for artists, academics or professionals to pursue research, teach or gain practical experience in the United States for up to five months

Level of Study: Postgraduate

Type: Award

Frequency: Varies

Country of Study: Any country

Application Procedure: Apply online

Closing Date: 1 June

Funding: Trusts

For further information contact:

Email: info@fulbright.org.nz

George Mason Charitable Trust Scholarship

Purpose: The Scholarships are usually to support studies of students who are studying full-time at post graduate level; i.e. pursuing their PhD, Masters or honours level studies and have attend secondary school in Taranaki, or who have family residing in Taranaki or other connections to the region

Eligibility: This scholarship is eligible for students with links to Taranaki, or Students who are undertaking research relating to the Natural History of Taranaki

Level of Study: Graduate

Type: Scholarship

Value: NZ $7,500 for PhD, NZ $5,000 for Masters or Honours level

Frequency: Annual

Country of Study: New Zcaland

Application Procedure: Application has to be processed through physical mode. Andrew Moffat Heritage Collections Lead / Pouarahi Tukuihotanga Puke Ariki Private Bag 2025 New Plymouth Or else, correspond to the mailing address andrew.moffat@npdc.govt.nz

Closing Date: 9 February

Funding: Private

For further information contact:

Tel: (44) 6 759 0860
Email: andrew.moffat@npdc.govt.nz

Gordon Williams Postgraduate Scholarship in Ecological Sciences

Purpose: Available to any person in New Zealand engaged in or planning to be engaged in research at Lincoln University leading to a masters or PhD degree or for postdoctoral work in ecological sciences with preference being given to conservation, ecology and/or wildlife management

Eligibility: 1. New Zealand Citizen or Permanent Resident Students. 2. International Students

Level of Study: Postdoctorate

Type: Scholarship

Value: NZ$25,000

Length of Study: 1 Year

Frequency: Annual

Country of Study: New Zealand

Closing Date: 1 October

Funding: Foundation

For further information contact:

Email: scholarships@lincoln.ac.nz

Graduate Women Canterbury Trust Inc. Scholarship

Purpose: Graduate Women Canterbury Inc. Trust Postgraduate Scholarships are awarded for the purpose of encouraging postgraduate study and research at Lincoln University

Eligibility: The scholarship is available to New Zealand citizens who have high academic achievement. Up to two scholarships are available each year for full-time female students eligible to register for an Honours or Masters degree at Lincoln University

Level of Study: Graduate

Type: Scholarship

Frequency: Annual

Country of Study: New Zealand

Closing Date: 1 October

Funding: Private

For further information contact:

Email: scholarships@lincoln.ac.nz

Harwood Farm Trust

Purpose: Miss Arnaboldi conceived the idea of combining the two great interests in her life, teaching and farming, by forming a Charitable Trust (Certificate of Charitable Status, Charities Commission entry CC22798), which she was to call "The Harwood Farm Trust"

Eligibility: To be eligible for a grant from the Trust the applicant will ideally be undertaking or teaching an agricultural course at an institution established for that purpose in New Zealand. Preference may be given to persons who can demonstrate greater need and who are in some way connected with the East Coast of the North Island

Level of Study: Unrestricted

Type: Other

Value: NZ $500 and NZ $2,500 (the exact amount to be determined in each case by the Trustees in their absolute discretion)

Frequency: As available

Study Establishment: Lincoln University

Country of Study: New Zealand

Closing Date: 14 December

Funding: Trusts

Additional Information: Alternate mail address is : moira@mcia.co.nz

For further information contact:

MCI & Associates Limited 6 Gordon Street, Dannevirke, 4930 PO Box 38, Dannevirke 4942, New Zealand

Tel: (64) 6 374 7059
Email: info@harwoodfarmtrust@mcia.co.nz
Contact: Ms Moira Paewai

Heaton Rhodes Scholarship

Subjects: Any postgraduate course
Purpose: The scholarship is open to full-time students eligible to proceed to a postgraduate course at Lincoln University
Level of Study: Postgraduate
Application Procedure: Applications to be sent to Scholarships Office Lincoln University PO Box 85084 Lincoln 7647
Type: Scholarship
Value: NZ $750
Frequency: Annual
Country of Study: Any country
Closing Date: 31 March
Funding: Private

For further information contact:

Email: info@lincoln.ac.nz

Henry Kelsey Research Scholarships

Purpose: The purpose of the scholarship is to provide funds for individuals to undertake research towards a postgraduate degree at a New Zealand University or research institution, for the purpose of studying muscular function, including the causes and treatment of muscular dysfunction
Eligibility: New Zealand Citizen or Permanent Resident Students. Applicants will: 1. be New Zealand citizens or permanent residents. 2. have a Bachelor degree or equivalent, with Honours where they are awarded, in a field appropriate to their intended doctoral study. In considering the award the selection board shall take into account the. 3. relevance of the proposed project to the causes and treatment of muscular dysfunction project's possible outcomes for innovative technologies and treatment of muscular dysfunction. 4. ability and previous experience of the candidate in the chosen field, particularly as it relates to successful completion of the project within the allocated timetable and proposed subsequent career. 5. academic record and achievement to date
Level of Study: Postdoctorate
Type: Scholarship
Value: $10,000 per annum
Frequency: Annual
Country of Study: New Zealand
Closing Date: 1 October
Funding: Private

For further information contact:

Universities New Zealand – Te Pokai Tara, PO Box 11915, Wellington 6142, New Zealand

Email: scholarships-cf@universitiesnz.ac.nz

Huygens scholarship programme

Subjects: All subjects
Purpose: The Netherlands Ministry of Education, Culture and Science, through The Netherlands Organisation for International Co-operation in Higher Education (NUFFIC) invites applications from postgraduate students (up to the age of 35) of New Zealand nationality for scholarships, available under the new Huygens (High-level University Year to Gain Excellence in the Netherlands) Programme. The scholarships are to be used for study in The Netherlands
Eligibility: New Zealand Citizen or Permanent Resident Students
Level of Study: Postgraduate
Type: Scholarship
Frequency: Annual
Country of Study: New Zealand
Application Procedure: Apply online
Closing Date: 1 February
Funding: Trusts

For further information contact:

Email: info@lincoln.ac.nz

James Bruce Smith Memorial Scholarship

Purpose: The James Bruce Smith scholarship will benefit New Zealand farmers and the wider agricultural industry. Fertilizer New Zealand has established this scholarship in memory of Dr James (Jim) Bruce Smith and recognises the huge contribution he made to agriculture in New Zealand
Eligibility: (1) The scholarship is open to people who are eligible to undertake postgraduate research study in Soil Biology and Sustainable Soil Management at Lincoln University. (2) A scholarship may be awarded to a person who is not eligible to register as a research student at Lincoln University provided he or she becomes
Level of Study: Graduate
Type: Scholarship
Value: NZ $5,000 per annum
Frequency: Annual
Country of Study: New Zealand
Application Procedure: The criteria for selection shall be: 1. Academic merit. 2. The relevance of the proposed research and the benefit of the research to agriculture in New Zealand with particular focus on sustainable soil management. 3. Understanding of agricultural systems in New Zealand
Closing Date: 15 March
Funding: Private

For further information contact:

Email: scholarships@lincoln.ac.nz

Janine Young Memorial Award

Subjects: Science & Primary Industries
Purpose: The award is to assist in the furtherance of qualifications or skills of people in the carrying out of agricultural extension or communications. It is granted to assist with tuition fees for agricultural education or to subsidise travel to an appropriate overseas conference of relevance to agricultural extension or communications
Level of Study: Professional development
Type: Award
Value: NZ $300 to $500
Frequency: Annual
Country of Study: New Zealand
Application Procedure: 1. Awards are made at the AGM in May. There is no application form. 2. Application is by email with a brief or summarised CV. The email should cover, as is relevant, your present situation, family background, funding arrangements, future intentions, ambition and any other relevant information. Include evidence or proof of enrolment in your course of study. 3. Email your application before the closing date to the Trustees:- etandrews@me.com D. W. Steele Trust
Closing Date: 31 March
Funding: Private
Additional Information: Email your application before the closing date to the Trustees:- etandrews@me.com D. W. Steele Trust

For further information contact:

Email: etandrews@me.com

John W & Carrie McLean Trust Scholarship

Purpose: The John W & Carrie McLean Trust has been established to encourage and promote post-graduate research and development relating to sheep with the end objective being to advance sheep research in New Zealand
Eligibility: 1. Scholarships will be open to any postgraduate student from Lincoln University who is a - New Zealand citizen or has been resident in New Zealand for a period of not less than three years at any time during his or her lifetime. 2. Scholarships will be open to candidates who are eligible to register as candidates for postgraduate study (research only), PhD or the thesis year of a Masters degree. 3. A scholarship may be awarded to a person who is not eligible to register as a candidate with Lincoln University provided he or she becomes eligible to so register by 1 March in the year following the awards, or by such other date as may be determined by the Vice Chancellor in a particular case

Level of Study: Postdoctorate
Type: Scholarship
Value: NZ $21,000
Length of Study: 3 Year
Frequency: Annual
Country of Study: New Zealand
Closing Date: 1 November
Funding: Foundation

For further information contact:

Email: info@lincoln.ac.nz

Ka Putea Grant

Level of Study: Graduate
Type: Grant
Value: NZ $500
Frequency: Annual
Country of Study: New Zealand
Application Procedure: Ka Putea Grant Applications Te Runanga o Ngai Tahu PO Box 13-049 Christchurch 8141
Closing Date: 29 April
Funding: Private

For further information contact:

Tel: (64) 3 366 4344
Email: matauranga@ngaitahu.iwi.nz

Kate Sheppard Memorial Award

Subjects: All subjects
Purpose: The scholarship is available to women holding NZ Citizenship or Permanent Residency who are undertaking a special project or postgraduate study of value to the wider NZ community
Eligibility: Women undertaking further education, study, research or training in areas of significant value to the community
Level of Study: Postgraduate
Type: Award
Value: NZ $2,500
Length of Study: 1 Year
Frequency: Varies
Country of Study: Any country
Application Procedure: Apply online
Closing Date: 30 June
Funding: Trusts

For further information contact:

Email: katesheppardaward@yahoo.com.au

Kathleen Ann Stevens Scholarship

Purpose: One or more scholarships offered to graduates of Lincoln University eligible to proceed to postgraduate study in animal or wool science
Eligibility: Entrance Requirements: The candidates must be following all the eligibility criteria: Open to graduates of Lincoln University eligible to proceed to postgraduate study in animal or wool science. All international students
Level of Study: Graduate
Type: Scholarship
Frequency: Annual
Study Establishment: Lincoln University
Country of Study: New Zealand
Application Procedure: Apply online. Kindly check the website below for further details. http://www.lincoln.ac.nz/Study/Qualifications/Qualification/scholarships/?ScholarshipCode=Kathleen%20Ann%20Stevens%20Scholarship&flt=32
Closing Date: 31 March
Funding: Private

For further information contact:

Email: scholarship@lincoln.ac.nz

Kathleen Spragg Agricultural Research Award

Purpose: Created to support scientists, technicians, advisors, consultants, and PhD students, this scholarship intends to foster general research and development in soils, plants and animals, and related areas in New Zealand so the knowledge gained shall be of benefit to the pastoral industry throughout New Zealand
Eligibility: 1. Sports. 2. New Zealand Citizen or Permanent Resident Students. 3. International Students
Level of Study: Postdoctorate
Type: Award
Value: NZ $10,000
Frequency: Annual
Country of Study: New Zealand
Closing Date: 1 October
Funding: Foundation

For further information contact:

Email: Margaret.Davies@pgtrust.co.nz

Lady Isaac Scholarship in Nature Conservation

Subjects: This scholarship is governed by The Isaac Conservation and Wildlife Trust and continues Lady Isaac's legacy of supporting postgraduate study and research in conservation and environmental areas at Lincoln University
Purpose: The Lady Diana Isaac Scholarship in Nature Conservation was established in 2000 by Lady Isaac who had a lifelong commitment to conservation
Eligibility: 1. New Zealand Citizen or Permanent Resident Students. 2. International Students
Level of Study: Postdoctorate
Type: Scholarship
Value: NZ $20,000
Frequency: Annual
Country of Study: New Zealand
Closing Date: 30 November
Funding: Foundation

For further information contact:

Email: scholarships@lincoln.ac.nz

Landcare Research Murray Jessen Scholarship

Purpose: The scholarship will sponsor a New Zealand soils, hydrologist, geomorphologist or natural resources graduate to study towards a PhD at a New Zealand university
Eligibility: New Zealand Citizen or Permanent Resident Students
Level of Study: Postdoctorate
Type: Scholarship
Frequency: Annual
Country of Study: New Zealand
Closing Date: 14 October
Funding: Foundation

For further information contact:

Mandy Cains - Landcare Research, Private Bag 11 052, Palmerston North, New Zealand

Email: info@lincoln.ac.nz

Leonard Condell Scholarships

Subjects: All subjects
Purpose: Candidates must be New Zealand born graduates in science, agriculture or related disciplines (e.g. horticulture, veterinary science, food technology, biotechnology) and must enter fields of research for the benefit of agriculture in New Zealand

Eligibility: New Zealand Citizen or Permanent Resident Students
Level of Study: Postgraduate
Type: Scholarship
Value: NZ $4,000
Length of Study: 1 Year
Frequency: Annual
Country of Study: Any country
Application Procedure: Apply online
Closing Date: 10 March
Funding: Foundation

For further information contact:

Scholarships Office, (NSATS), Massey University, Private Bag 11-222, Palmerston North, New Zealand

Email: K.Harrington@massey.ac.nz

Lincoln University - William Machin Doctoral Scholarships for Excellence

Purpose: The William Machin Doctoral Scholarships For Excellence - Lincoln University are awarded for the purpose of encouraging postgraduate study and research at Lincoln University
Eligibility: 1. Scholarships will be open to people who are eligible to register as candidates for the degree of Doctor of Philosophy at Lincoln University. 2. A scholarship may be awarded to a person who is not eligible to register as a candidate for Doctor of Philosophy at Lincoln University provided he or she becomes eligible to register by 1 March in the year following the awards, or by such other date as may be determined by the University in a particular case. 3. If a candidate awarded a scholarship under 3(2) above does not become eligible to register for Doctor of Philosophy at Lincoln University by 1. March or by the date determined under the provisions of 3(2) above, then the award will lapse
Level of Study: Postdoctorate
Type: Scholarship
Frequency: Annual
Country of Study: New Zealand
Closing Date: 1 October
Funding: Foundation

For further information contact:

Email: scholarships@lincoln.ac.nz

Lincoln University – William Machin Doctoral Scholarships

Subjects: Available for postgraduate students
Purpose: The Lincoln University is inviting applications for William Machine Doctoral Scholarships for postgraduate students. Local students, permanent resident students are eligible to apply for this scholarship
Eligibility: (1) Scholarships will be open to people who are eligible to register as candidates for the degree of Doctor of Philosophy at Lincoln University. (2) A scholarship may be awarded to a person who is not eligible to register as a candidate for Doctor of Philosophy at Lincoln University provided he or she becomes eligible to register by 1 March in the year following the awards, or by such other date as may be determined by the University in a particular case. (3) If a candidate awarded a scholarship under 3(2) above does not become eligible to register for Doctor of Philosophy at Lincoln University
Level of Study: Doctorate
Type: Scholarships and fellowships
Frequency: Annual
Country of Study: New Zealand
Application Procedure: Candidates should submit the application through mailing address. Address information is mentioned below
Closing Date: 1 October
Funding: Private

For further information contact:
Email: info@lincoln.ac.nz

Lincoln University (LU) Doctoral Scholarship

Purpose: Lincoln University Doctoral Scholarships are awarded for the purpose of supporting postgraduate study and research at Lincoln University
Eligibility: (1) Scholarships will be open to applicants who have gained entrance into a Doctor of Philosophy at Lincoln University. (2) If a candidate awarded a scholarship under 3(1) above does not become eligible to register for Doctor of Philosophy at Lincoln University by 1 March in the year following the award, then the award will lapse
Level of Study: Postgraduate
Type: Scholarship
Value: The scholarship covers a maximum of three years stipend with a current value of NZ$24,000 per annum and the amount equivalent to the New Zealand students' tuition fee for the degree of Doctor of Philosophy

Length of Study: 1 year and it is extendable
Frequency: Annual
Country of Study: Any country
Application Procedure: see website
Closing Date: 1 October
Funding: Trusts

For further information contact:

Email: scholarships@lincoln.ac.nz

Lincoln University Ahuwhenua Scholarship

Purpose: This scholarship was established in 2018 to support school leaver Maori students who are entering an undergraduate or sub-degree study in the Agricultural, mahinga kai or organics field at Lincoln University
Eligibility: To be eligible to hold the scholarship applicants shall: a) Be of Maori descent b) Be enrolled for a full time Lincoln University undergraduate degree. c) Have demonstrated leadership potential in the Maori community d) This scholarship is applicable to persons who are new to Lincoln University
Level of Study: Graduate
Type: Scholarship
Value: NZ $5,000
Frequency: Annual
Country of Study: New Zealand
Closing Date: 30 March
Funding: Private

For further information contact:

Lincoln University, Lincoln 7647, Canterbury, New Zealand

Email: scholarships@lincoln.ac.nz

Lincoln University Inclusive Education Award

Purpose: The purpose of the award is to reduce barriers to studying at Lincoln University that the recipient may have otherwise faced. To be achieved by assisting the recipient to meet costs of study (such as university fees) and/or support costs related to his/her disability, injury or illness not fully met from other sources
Eligibility: 1. Have had a disability, injury or illness, either congenital or acquired, for at least six months prior to making the application. 2. New Zealand / Australian citizen or permanent resident. 3. Eligible to be admitted into a programme of study at Lincoln University in the year following the

application. 4. Register for a programme of study at Lincoln University in the year following the application. A programme of study includes any Certificate, Diploma, Bachelor degree, Honours degree, or Postgraduate programme at Lincoln University
Level of Study: Postdoctorate
Type: Award
Value: Up to NZ $3,000
Length of Study: 1 Year
Frequency: Annual
Country of Study: New Zealand
Closing Date: 1 December
Funding: Foundation

For further information contact:

Email: scholarships@lincoln.ac.nz

Lincoln University Matauraka Maori Scholarship

Purpose: This scholarship was established in 2018 to support Maori students who are entering undergraduate or sub-degree study at Lincoln University and who have demonstrated excellence in subjects focused on Te Ao Maori
Eligibility: 1) Applicants must have demonstrated leadership potential in the Maori community. 2) Be enrolled for a full time Lincoln University undergraduate degree. 3) Have shown evidence of excellence in subjects focused on Te Ao Maori. 4) Have demonstrated leadership potential in the Maori community
Level of Study: Graduate
Type: Scholarship
Value: NZ $5,000
Frequency: Annual
Country of Study: New Zealand
Closing Date: 30 March
Funding: Private

For further information contact:

Tel: (64) 3 423 0000
Email: scholarships@lincoln.ac.nz

Livestock Improvement Doctoral Studentship Programme

Eligibility: New Zealand Citizen or Permanent Resident Students
Level of Study: Postdoctorate
Type: Studentship

Frequency: Annual
Country of Study: New Zealand
Application Procedure: Apply online: http://www.lic.co.nz
Closing Date: 15 November
Funding: Foundation

For further information contact:

Robyn Howie Support Services Officer Strategy and Growth Group Livestock Improvement Corporation Ltd., Private Bag 3016, Hamilton, New Zealand

Tel: (64) 7 856 0700
Email: rhowie@lic.co.nz

Lord Rutherford Memorial Research Fellowship

Purpose: The fellowship is awarded for outstanding merit and promise in the subjects of Physics, Chemistry or Mathematics or in any other cognate subject which the Academic Board may from time to time designate so as to give the fellow an opportunity for further study or research
Eligibility: Available to New Zealand Citizen or Permanent Resident Students
Level of Study: Graduate, Postgraduate
Type: Fellowship
Value: NZ $20,000 per annum
Frequency: Annual
Country of Study: New Zealand
Closing Date: 1 November
Funding: Private

For further information contact:

Scholarships Office, University of Canterbury, Private Bag 4800, Christchurch 8140, New Zealand

Email: info@canterbury.ac.nz

Lucy Cranwell Student Grant for Botanical Research

Purpose: Applications are invited for the Lucy Cranwell Grant of NZ $2,500 from the Auckland Botanical Society to assist a student studying for the degree of PhD, MSc or BSc (Hons.) in any tertiary institution in New Zealand whose thesis project deals with some aspect of New Zealand's flora and vegetation. Priority will be given to projects relevant to the northern half of the North Island. The research project to be supported will be chosen on the basis of their appropriateness to the objects of the Society, viz to encourage the study of botany, and to stimulate public interest in the plant life of

New Zealand and its preservation, conservation and cultivation. The grant will be administered by the student's supervisor as a contribution to expenses associated with the project
Eligibility: New Zealand Citizen or Permanent Resident Students
Level of Study: Postdoctorate
Type: Grant
Value: NZ $2,500
Frequency: Annual
Country of Study: New Zealand
Closing Date: 5 December
Funding: Foundation

For further information contact:

Email: aucklandbotanicalsociety@gmail.com

Manning Seed Award

Purpose: The Manning Seed Award is provided by Lincoln University Foundation through funding from Selwyn and Mary Manning, and is intended to encourage education and research in the field of seed science and seed technology for the benefit of New Zealand
Eligibility: 1. The scholarship is open to people who are eligible to undertake full time postgraduate research study at Lincoln University into any issue associated with seed science and seed technology in New Zealand. 2. A scholarship may be awarded to a person who is not eligible to register as a full time research student at Lincoln University provided he or she becomes eligible to so register by 1 March in the year following the awards, or by such other date as may be determined by the Selection Committee in a particular case. 3. If a candidate awarded a scholarship under 3(2) above does not become eligible to register for a research degree at Lincoln University by 1 March or by the date determined under the provisions of 3(2) above, then the award will lapse
Level of Study: Postdoctorate
Type: Award
Value: NZ $25,000
Length of Study: 3 Year
Frequency: Annual
Country of Study: New Zealand
Closing Date: 31 October
Funding: Foundation

Marion Cunningham Memorial Scholarship

Purpose: This scholarship provides funding towards research on New Zealand's native species. The grant will be awarded to students engaging in research that is practicable and relevant to current wildlife concerns and should encourage conservation and management of threatened species

Eligibility: 1. New Zealand Citizen or Permanent Resident Students. 2. International Students

Level of Study: Postdoctorate

Type: Scholarship

Value: NZ $2,700

Frequency: Annual

Country of Study: New Zealand

Closing Date: 31 October

Funding: Foundation

For further information contact:

Email: wildlife@vets.org.nz

Mensa New Zealand Scholarship

Subjects: All subjects

Purpose: Mensa New Zealand Inc offers a scholarship for current members of Mensa New Zealand who are undertaking tertiary study. One or two scholarships of NZ $500 each will be awarded at the discretion of the Board of Mensa New Zealand

Eligibility: New Zealand Citizen or Permanent Resident Students

Level of Study: Postgraduate

Type: Scholarship

Value: NZ $500

Frequency: Varies

Country of Study: Any country

Application Procedure: Apply online

Closing Date: 1 October

Funding: Trusts

For further information contact:

Email: chair@mensa.org.nz

Ministry of Foreign Affairs and Trade Postgraduate Field Research Awards

Purpose: The Ministry of Foreign Affairs and Trade (MFAT), is making available Postgraduate Field Research Awards to assist Masters and Doctoral students meet a proportion of their travel expenses and associated costs in carrying out field research on development issues of relevance to the New Zealand Aid Programme

Eligibility: 1. Sports. 2. New Zealand Citizen or Permanent Resident Students. The awards are available to New Zealand citizens or permanent residents that are undertaking research

as part of the requirements of a New Zealand-based Masters Degree or Doctorate

Level of Study: Postdoctorate

Type: Award

Value: NZ $6,000

Frequency: Annual

Country of Study: New Zealand

Closing Date: 10 November

Funding: Foundation

Miss Clarice Bell Memorial Scholarship

Purpose: This scholarship was established in 1997 from the estate of Miss Clarice Bell, a music teacher of Christchurch. The estate was left to the University in 1973, in memory of her pet Cockatoo "Cockie", who was a family friend for over 40 years, to be used by reason of her affection and concern for animals

Eligibility: 1. Applicants are required to be in the process of, or intending to, conduct doctoral research directed to the prevention and protection against disease and suffering of animals (including domestic animals and pets). 2. A scholarship may be awarded to a person who is not eligible to register as a candidate for the required postgraduate qualification at Lincoln University, provided he or she becomes eligible to so register by 1 March in the year following the awards, or by such other date as may be determined by the Vice-Chancellor in a particular case. 3. The scholarship will lapse if the candidate is not registered for the required postgraduate qualification by the dates established in 4(2) above or those established under special provision

Level of Study: Postdoctorate

Type: Scholarship

Length of Study: 1 Year

Frequency: Annual

Country of Study: New Zealand

Closing Date: 31 October

Funding: Foundation

For further information contact:

Email: scholarships@lincoln.ac.nz

Miss E.L. Hellaby Indigenous Grasslands Research Trust

Subjects: All subjects

Purpose: The Trust welcomes applications for fellowships for post-graduate, particularly Ph D research projects, into the ecology of New Zealand's indigenous grasslands but especially investigations into aspects of the sustainable management, uses and conservation of these grasslands (e.g. plant-animal interactions, pedology, hydrology)

Eligibility: New Zealand Citizen or Permanent Resident Students

Level of Study: Postgraduate

Type: Scholarship

Value: NZ $500

Length of Study: 3 Year

Frequency: Varies

Country of Study: Any country

Application Procedure: Apply online

Closing Date: 10 March

Funding: Foundation

For further information contact:

C/- NZ Guardian Trust, PO Box 295, Dunedin, New Zealand

Tel: (64) 477 5544
Email: duncanr@lincoln.ac.nz

Murray King Memorial Scholarship

Purpose: The purpose of the award is to enable Wairarapa students to attend a New Zealand university and obtain degree qualifications, with particular emphasis on, soil conservation, soil and land management, indigenous forest management and conservation management

Eligibility: Students who have completed part or all of their secondary education in the Wairarapa, or who live in the Wairarapa at the time of applying for the scholarship are eligible

Level of Study: Graduate

Type: Scholarship

Frequency: Annual

Country of Study: New Zealand

Closing Date: 31 December

Funding: Private

For further information contact:

Murray King Memorial Scholarship C/ Masterton District Council, P O Box 444, Masterton 5840, New Zealand

Tel: (64) 6 378-9666
Email: mking.scholarship@mstn.govt.nz

National Foundation for the Deaf Educational Scholarship

Subjects: All subjects

Purpose: To assist with course fees, books, interpreters, note-takers and extra educational material, for students enrolled in an approved secondary or tertiary course

Eligibility: New Zealand Citizen or Permanent Resident Students

Level of Study: Postgraduate

Type: Scholarship

Frequency: Varies

Country of Study: Any country

Application Procedure: Apply online

Closing Date: 31 March

Funding: Foundation

For further information contact:

The National Foundation for the Deaf Inc., PO Box 37729, Parnell, Auckland 1151, New Zealand

Email: enquiries@nfd.org.nz

National Foundation for the Deaf Training & Development Scholarship

Subjects: All subjects

Purpose: To further training that will assist an individual's development in NZ and benefit deaf and hearing impaired people. It is available for - participation in a course at a local or overseas venue - gathering resources for educational and/or social purposes

Eligibility: New Zealand Citizen or Permanent Resident Students

Level of Study: Postgraduate

Type: Scholarship

Length of Study: 1 Year

Frequency: Varies

Country of Study: Any country

Application Procedure: Apply online

Closing Date: 31 March

Funding: Trusts

For further information contact:

Email: enquiries@nfd.org.nz

New Horizons for Women Research Awards

Subjects: All subjects

Purpose: For research projects that benefit New Zealand women and girls. Applicants for the research awards may be an individual woman, or group of women, who are New Zealand citizens, resident in New Zealand, and are conducting research which is relevant and of value to women and girls in New Zealand

Eligibility: 1. Engaged in research that benefits women and/or girls in New Zealand. 2. New Zealand citizen or holds a resident class visa; and currently lives in New Zealand
Level of Study: Postgraduate
Type: Award
Value: Up to NZ $5,000
Frequency: Varies
Country of Study: Any country
Application Procedure: Apply online
Closing Date: 30 April
Funding: Trusts

For further information contact:

Email: enquiries@newhorizonsforwomentrust.org.nz

New Horizons for Women Second Chance Education and Training Awards

Purpose: For research projects that benefit New Zealand women and girls. Applicants for the research awards may be an individual woman, or group of women, who are New Zealand citizens, resident in New Zealand, and are conducting research which is relevant and of value to women and girls in New Zealand
Level of Study: Graduate, Postgraduate
Type: Award
Value: Up to NZ $5,000
Frequency: Annual
Country of Study: Any country
Application Procedure: Second-Chance Education Awards are for women who are engaging in tertiary education for the first time, at EITHER a Foundation Certificate (NZQA level 3-4) or Diploma level (NZQA level 5-6), or Degree level (NZQA level 7). In all categories, the awards are a one off grant to help with study and/or living expenses
Closing Date: 30 April
Funding: Foundation
Additional Information: Please check the website link for application procedure http://www.newhorizonsforwomen.org.nz/award-applications/

For further information contact:

Email: enquiries@newhorizonsforwomen.org.nz

New Zealand Coastal Society Maori and Pacific Island Research Scholarship

Subjects: All subjects

Purpose: Current and predicted pressures pose significant challenges for managers and planners seeking to provide sustainable futures for coastal environments and communities. The New Zealand Coastal Society (NZCS) was created as a means to promote and advance knowledge and understanding of the coastal zone. This includes fostering coastal research and capacity building that has the potential to contribute towards the aims of the Society
Eligibility: 1. New Zealand Citizen or Permanent Resident Students. 2. International Students
Level of Study: Postgraduate
Type: Scholarship
Value: NZ $5,000 to support PhD research, or NZ $2,500 to support Masters research, and free conference registration and dinner ticket (value $700) for the annual NZCS conference to be held in Gisborne in 2018
Frequency: Varies
Country of Study: Any country
Application Procedure: Apply online
Closing Date: 1 May
Funding: Trusts

For further information contact:

Renee Coutts, NZCS Administrator, PO Box 12241, Thorndon, Wellington 6144, New Zealand

Email: nzcoastalsociety@gmail.com

New Zealand Coastal Society Scholarship

Subjects: All subjects
Purpose: The New Zealand Coastal Society (NZCS) was inaugurated in 1992 to promote and advance sustainable management of the coastal environment. This includes fostering coastal research and capacity building. The society offers two scholarships annually to students conducting research that has the potential to contribute towards the aims of the society: NZ $5,000 to support PHD research, and NZ $2,500 to support Masters research
Level of Study: Postgraduate
Type: Scholarship
Value: $2,500
Length of Study: 1 Year
Frequency: Varies
Country of Study: Any country
Application Procedure: Apply online
Closing Date: 1 May
Funding: Trusts

For further information contact:

Email: k.bryan@waikato.ac.nz

New Zealand Federation of Graduate Women Harriette Jenkins Award

Purpose: The purpose of these awards is to encourage members of the NZFGW whose membership is not less than six months to carry out or complete a piece of research, or to further their studies at a university or other tertiary institution in New Zealand or through an overseas institution, provided the work is undertaken while the applicant is resident in New Zealand. Any qualification sought must be recognised by the New Zealand Qualifications Authority
Eligibility: New Zealand Citizen or Permanent Resident Students
Level of Study: Postdoctorate
Type: Award
Frequency: Annual
Country of Study: New Zealand
Closing Date: 30 September
Funding: Foundation

New Zealand France Friendship Fund Scholarship

Purpose: The New Zealand France Friendship Fund was established in 1991 by an agreement between the French and New Zealand governments. Its objective is to promote close and friendly relations between the citizens of New Zealand and France. The Fund awards an academic Excellence Scholarship to one New Zealand student and one French student for postgraduate studies in the other country, at masters or doctoral level
Eligibility: The successful scholar must study full-time in France for a minimum of two semesters, or a cumulative total of at least 12 months spread over the duration of the study programme
Level of Study: Postdoctorate
Type: Scholarship
Value: NZ $25,000
Length of Study: 1 Year
Frequency: Annual
Country of Study: Any country
Closing Date: 31 December
Funding: Foundation

For further information contact:

Email: contact@universitiesnz.ac.nz

New Zealand Meat Industry Scholarship

Subjects: All subjects

Purpose: The New Zealand meat industry needs skilled young people who can become the future leaders in one of New Zealand's largest industries. The MIA Scholarship scheme provides a pathway for undergraduate and graduate students into a career in the New Zealand meat industry
Eligibility: New Zealand Citizen or Permanent Resident Students
Level of Study: Graduate
Type: Scholarship
Value: Undergraduate = NZ $3,000 per year; Postgraduate = NZ $10,000 per year
Frequency: Varies
Country of Study: Any country
Application Procedure: Apply online
Closing Date: 1 December
Funding: Trusts

For further information contact:

Meat Industry Association, PO Box 345, Wellington 6140, New Zealand

Tel: (64) 494 9507
Email: Paul.Goldstone@mia.co.nz

New Zealand Plant Protection Society Conference Travel Grant for Students

Subjects: All subjects
Purpose: The New Zealand Plant Protection Society may, from time to time, make monetary grants to students to assist them to attend and present papers at the annual New Zealand Plant Protection Conference. Grants may be awarded, on a competitive basis, to individual students from whom research papers have been accepted for presentation at the Conference. Other grants may be awarded to groups of students travelling together to encourage greater attendance at, and participation in, the Conference by students with an interest in a career in plant protection
Eligibility: Scholarship applications from university students or students registered in other recognised New Zealand tertiary institutions will be considered. In making awards, consideration will be given to the appropriateness and relevance of the proposed research, academic record of the applicant(s), and supporting statements from supervisors, peers or sponsors
Level of Study: Postgraduate
Type: Travel grant
Value: Up to NZ $3,000
Length of Study: 1 Year
Frequency: Annual

Country of Study: Any country
Application Procedure: Apply online
Closing Date: 15 May
Funding: Government

For further information contact:

Email: secretary@nzpps.org

New Zealand Plant Protection Society Research Scholarship

Purpose: As part of this objective, the Society has established a trust fund to support the NZPPS Research Scholarship. This Scholarship is to encourage research in relevant disciplines (entomology, plant pathology, weed science, zoology, ecology, and plant protection sciences), on topics relating to control of pests, pathogens and/or weeds in primary production (pastoral and arable agriculture, horticulture, forestry), or the natural or human environments
Eligibility: New Zealand Citizen or Permanent Resident Students
Level of Study: Postdoctorate
Type: Scholarship
Frequency: Annual
Country of Study: New Zealand
Closing Date: 1 October
Funding: Foundation

For further information contact:

Email: secretary@nzpps.org

New Zealand Scholarships (MFAT)

Subjects: All subjects
Purpose: The New Zealand Scholarships are funded by the New Zealand Aid Programme, the New Zealand Government's overseas aid and development programme. They are managed by the New Zealand Ministry of Foreign Affairs and Trade (MFAT). The purpose of the scholarships is for candidates to gain knowledge and skills through post-graduate study in specific subject areas which will assist in the development of their home country. Awardees are required to return to their home country for at least two years after the completion of their scholarship to apply these new skills and knowledge in government, civil society, or private business organisations
Eligibility: International Students
Level of Study: Postgraduate
Type: Scholarship
Length of Study: 2 Year

Frequency: Varies
Country of Study: Any country
Application Procedure: Apply online
Closing Date: 14 March
Funding: Trusts

For further information contact:

Email: scholarships@lincoln.ac.nz

Ngâi Tahu Beca Scholarship

Subjects: All subjects
Purpose: Ngâi Tahu and Beca have formed a partnership, resulting in a new and exciting one year scholarship opportunity. The goal is to provide learning support and career opportunities for Ngâi Tahu whânau who are currently studying engineering, architecture, planning, resource management, landscape and urban design, environmental or other related fields
Eligibility: 1. Maori / Pasifika only. 2. New Zealand Citizen or Permanent Resident Students
Level of Study: Postgraduate
Type: Scholarship
Frequency: Varies
Country of Study: Any country
Application Procedure: Apply online
Closing Date: 1 October
Funding: Foundation

For further information contact:

Email: nicole.bowden@ngaitahu.iwi.nz

Ngai Tahu Ka Putea Tertiary Grants and Scholarships

Subjects: All subjects
Purpose: A number of scholarships are available for students of Ngai Tahu descent
Level of Study: Postgraduate
Type: Scholarship
Value: NZ $1,500
Frequency: Varies
Country of Study: Any country
Application Procedure: Apply online
Closing Date: 29 April
Funding: Trusts

For further information contact:

Email: matauranga@ngaitahu.iwi.nz

Ngarimu V.C. and 28 (Maori) Battalion Memorial Scholarships

Purpose: In commemoration of the bravery shown by Second Lieutenant Te Moana Nui a Kiwa Ngarimu and the members of the 28 Maori Battalion, these scholarships are designed to financially assist students of Maori descent attending a recognised tertiary institution. Scholarships are awarded for Undergraduate, Masters and Doctoral studies. One scholarship is also available for applicants engaged in Maori leadership
Eligibility: New Zealand Citizen or Permanent Resident Students
Level of Study: Postdoctorate
Type: Scholarship
Value: NZ $25,000
Frequency: Annual
Country of Study: New Zealand
Closing Date: 30 September
Funding: Foundation

Ngati Kahungunu Iwi Scholarship

Subjects: All subjects
Purpose: For full-time Ngati Kahungunu 3 year or final year undergraduate and postgraduate students studying in the areas of TeReo/Tikanga; Environmental Science; Health and Wellbeing; Information and Communication Technology
Eligibility: For Maori / Pasifika only New Zealand Citizen or Permanent Resident Students
Level of Study: Postgraduate
Type: Scholarship
Frequency: Varies
Country of Study: Any country
Application Procedure: Apply online
Funding: Trusts

OMV New Zealand Scholarship

Purpose: This scholarship is awarded to Postgraduate students studying in the areas of Earth Science, Environmental Science or Engineering. The scholarship is awarded based on the relevance of the project to OMV NZ activities
Eligibility: New Zealand Citizen or Permanent Resident Students
Level of Study: Postdoctorate
Type: Scholarship
Value: NZ $8,000
Length of Study: 17 December

Frequency: Annual
Country of Study: New Zealand
Closing Date: 17 December
Funding: Foundation

For further information contact:

Email: omv_nz_csr@omv.com

Onion Industry Postgraduate Scholarship

Purpose: The New Zealand onion industry wishes to invest in its future by encouraging postgraduate research and scholarship of relevance to the New Zealand onion industry. Research topics of interest include: improvement in onion yields, quality and sustainable production, postharvest technologies, food safety, market access and development (particularly Asian markets); biosecurity, new products
Eligibility: 1. New Zealand Citizen or Permanent Resident Students. 2. International Students
Level of Study: Postdoctorate
Type: Scholarship
Value: NZ $10,000
Frequency: Annual
Country of Study: New Zealand
Closing Date: 15 December
Funding: Foundation

For further information contact:

James Kuperus Business Manager Onions New Zealand Inc., PO Box 10232, Wellington 6143, New Zealand

Email: james.kuperus@onionsnz.com

Pacific Islands Polynesian Education Foundation & Norman Kirk MemorialTrust Tertiary Students Financial Assistance

Subjects: All subjects
Purpose: The Pacific Islands Polynesian Education Foundation (PIPEF) and Norman Kirk MemorialTrust (NKMT) provide financial assistance to Pacific Island students who are enrolled at a tertiary institution in New Zealand
Eligibility: 1. Maori/Pasifika only. 2. New Zealand Citizen or Permanent Resident Students
Level of Study: Postgraduate
Type: Scholarship
Frequency: Varies
Country of Study: Any country
Application Procedure: Apply online

Closing Date: 31 March
Funding: Trusts

For further information contact:

Email: pipef.board@gmail.com

Philanthropic Educational Organization International Peace Scholarship Fund

Purpose: Applications are limited to women of other countries of graduate status
Eligibility: This scholarships is applicable for 1. Woman only. 2. Sports. 3. Available to New Zealand Citizen or Permanent Resident Students. 4. Available to International Students. United states or Canadian citizens are not eligible to apply for this funding
Type: Funding support
Value: NZ $6,000
Frequency: Annual
Country of Study: Any country
Application Procedure: Applications are limited to women of other countries of graduate status
Closing Date: 1 November
Funding: Private

For further information contact:

Tel: (64) 800 827 748
Email: info@lincoln.ac.nz

Pipfruit NZ Research Fellowship

Purpose: The Pipfruit NZ Research Fellowship is a prestigious award, intended to encourage post-graduate study in New Zealand and support research that will contribute to the further development of the New Zealand pipfruit industry. Pipfruit NZ Research Fellowships are awarded by Pipfruit New Zealand Incorporated on the recommendation of a Fellowship Committee
Eligibility: New Zealand Citizen or Permanent Resident Students
Level of Study: Postdoctorate
Type: Fellowship
Frequency: Annual
Country of Study: New Zealand
Closing Date: 30 November
Funding: Foundation

For further information contact:

Email: info@lincoln.ac.nz

Postgraduate Research Scholarship (Sylff) Doctorate

Purpose: The scholarship is for PhD students at any New Zealand university who demonstrate leadership qualities or display high potential for future leadership in either public or private life. Scholarships are offered for study towards a PhD research degree in a wide range of disciplines, provided the research is in the broad fields of Humanities (i.e. the study of human culture, especially literature, languages, history, art, music and philosophy) or Social Sciences (i.e. the scientific study of any aspect of social behaviour and/or the functioning of society). Professional doctorate degrees (e.g. DClinPsych, DBusAdmin) are not eligible. Candidates whose degree programmes do not appear to fit in these categories, but who feel their research qualifies them, will be asked to justify this view in their application
Eligibility: New Zealand Citizen or Permanent Resident Students
Level of Study: Postdoctorate
Type: Scholarship
Value: NZ $25,000
Frequency: Annual
Country of Study: New Zealand
Closing Date: 1 October
Funding: Foundation

For further information contact:

Email: n.e.collins@massey.ac.nz

Pouarua Farming Scholarship

Subjects: All subjects
Purpose: Pouarua Farms, located near Ngatea, is owned by Ngâti Maru, Ngâti Pâoa, Ngâti Tamaterâ, Ngâti Tara Tokanui & Te Patukirikiri. Applications are invited from students for a farming scholarship in conjunction with their sharemilker Landcorp. This scholarship will assist and support people affiliated to one or more of the five iwi who wish to undertake tertiary study in an agricultural-related field
Eligibility: 1. Maori / Pasifika only. 2. New to Lincoln. 3. New Zealand Citizen or Permanent Resident Students
Level of Study: Postgraduate
Type: Scholarship
Frequency: Varies
Country of Study: Any country
Application Procedure: Apply online
Closing Date: 20 September
Funding: Trusts

For further information contact:

Email: nikky@ngatimaru.iwi.nz

Queen Elizabeth II Postgraduate Fellowship

Subjects: All subjects
Purpose: One fellowship available to Maori or non-Maori with excellent academic ability, who plans to research at postgraduate level in either New Zealand or overseas, in a field that will be of benefit to Maori people
Eligibility: New Zealand Maori descent unless applying for the Queen Elizabeth II Postgraduate Fellowship
Level of Study: Postgraduate
Type: Fellowship
Value: NZ $5,000
Length of Study: 1 Year
Frequency: Annual
Country of Study: Any country
Application Procedure: Apply online
Closing Date: 30 March
Funding: Foundation

For further information contact:

Email: info@maorieducation.org.nz

R.H.T. Bates Postgraduate Scholarship

Purpose: This scholarship was established by the Royal Society of New Zealand in memory of Professor Bates. Tenable at any New Zealand University, this scholarship is available to graduates who are registered for the Degree of Doctor of Philosophy. It may be held for one year only. To receive the scholarship, candidates must be enrolled for a doctorate course at a New Zealand University
Eligibility: New Zealand Citizen or Permanent Resident Students
Level of Study: Postdoctorate
Type: Scholarship
Value: NZ $6,000
Frequency: Annual
Country of Study: New Zealand
Closing Date: 1 September
Funding: Foundation

For further information contact:

Tel: (44) 4 470 5758
Fax: (1) 4 473 1841
Email: awards@rsnz.org

Riccarton Rotary Youth Trust Scholarship

Purpose: The purpose of this scholarship is to attract students who face challenges which might otherwise prevent them from considering entry to tertiary education. It is aimed at students who would undertake a full-time study programme at Lincoln University
Eligibility: The scholarship is awarded to students beginning full-time enrolment in their first year of a degree programme at the Ara Institute of Canterbury, or Lincoln University, or the University of Canterbury who: 1. are citizens of New Zealand or holders of a New Zealand residence class visa. 2. have been studying at secondary level in New Zealand in the year of application (or, in the case of a gap year, in the year immediately prior); and c have resided in the Canterbury region for at least the 12 months immediately preceding the closing date for applications (or, in the case of a gap year, for at least the 12 months immediately preceding the start of the gap year). Preference will be given to applicants who have received their secondary education while residing in, or attending a school in, the Riccarton Ward of Christchurch
Level of Study: Graduate
Type: Scholarship
Frequency: Every 3 years
Country of Study: New Zealand
Closing Date: 15 August
Funding: Private

For further information contact:

Email: scholarships@lincoln.ac.nz

Robert C. Bruce Trust

Purpose: The Trust is able to consider application for research grants for work directly related to forests or afforestation. Research projects must be clearly for the benefit of the public good of New Zealand, rather than merely for individual advancement
Level of Study: Postgraduate
Type: Grant
Frequency: Annual
Country of Study: Any country
Closing Date: 31 March every year
Funding: Private, Trusts
Additional Information: The research work must be fully supported by and supervised by the educational institution the applicant attends

For further information contact:

The New Zealand Guardian Trust Company Ltd, PO Box 628, Palmerston North, New Zealand

Email: owen_locke@nzgt.co.nz

Rosemary Seymour Research & Archives Award

Purpose: In 1974 Rosemary Seymour, a Waikato sociologist, initiated a newsletter and a network of women interested in women's studies, that evolved into the Women's Studies Association (NZ). In 1985 this fund was established in her memory
Eligibility: New Zealand Citizen or Permanent Resident Students
Level of Study: Postdoctorate
Type: Award
Value: NZ $1,000
Frequency: Annual
Country of Study: New Zealand
Closing Date: 31 October
Funding: Foundation

For further information contact:

Email: julie.benjamin@vodafone.co.nz

Roy Watling Mitchell Bursaries Scholarship

Purpose: Priority will be given to students with academic merit and financial need
Eligibility: Undergraduate applicants must: 1. be of New Zealand Maori descent. 2. be enrolled at a New Zealand tertiary institute. 3. be attending full-time study for the full year. 4. meet the criteria for the scholarships applied for. 5. submit the application and supporting documentation on time. This grant is applicable for Maori/Pasifika only
Level of Study: Graduate
Type: Scholarship
Value: NZ $1,000
Frequency: Annual
Country of Study: New Zealand
Closing Date: 28 March
Funding: Private

For further information contact:

Maori Education Trust, PO Box 11-255, Wellington, New Zealand

Tel: (64) 4 586 7971
Email: info@maorieducation.org.nz

Roy Watling Mitchell Prestigious Professions Scholarship

Subjects: All subjects

Purpose: Available to a Maori graduate with a record of academic excellence and proven ability to complete postgrad studies
Level of Study: Postgraduate
Type: Scholarship
Value: NZ $5,000
Frequency: Varies
Country of Study: Any country
Application Procedure: Apply online
Closing Date: 28 March
Funding: Foundation

For further information contact:

Email: info@maorieducation.org.nz

Royal Commonwealth Society, Canterbury Scholarship

Subjects: All subjects
Purpose: This scholarship supports students from countries of the Commonwealth who are undertaking postgraduate study at the University of Canterbury, thereby promoting international understanding through education. The scholarship was established by the Royal Commonwealth Society (NZ) Inc., Canterbury Branch, which is affiliated to the Royal Commonwealth Society in London
Eligibility: Recipients must be enrolled in a full-time or part-time programme for a Master's degree by thesis or a PhD degree at the University of Canterbury. Applicants must be citizens or permanent residents of a country of the Commonwealth
Level of Study: Postgraduate
Type: Scholarship
Value: NZ $2,500
Length of Study: 1 Year
Frequency: Annual
Country of Study: New Zealand
Application Procedure: Apply online
Closing Date: 15 May
Funding: Trusts

For further information contact:

Email: scholarships-cf@universitiesnz.ac.nz

Sarita McClure Scholarship

Subjects: All subjects
Purpose: One scholarship to the value of NZ $600 or two scholarships of NZ $300 may be awarded annually to students proceeding to a masters or PhD degree at Lincoln University
Level of Study: Postgraduate

Type: Scholarship
Frequency: Varies
Country of Study: Any country
Application Procedure: Apply online
Closing Date: 31 March
Funding: Foundation

For further information contact:

Email: info@lincoln.ac.nz

Seed Industry Research Centre Postgraduate Scholarship

Subjects: Horticulture, Science & Mathematics
Purpose: The scholarship was established to encourage research activities which will add value to the New Zealand herbage and vegetable seed production industry. This Scholarship is awarded by the Seed Industry Research Centre Incorporated and shall be known as the SIRC Postgraduate
Eligibility: Check the website online. http://www.lincoln.ac.nz/Study/Qualifications/Qualification/scholarships/?ScholarshipCode=Seed%20Industry%20Research%20Centre%20Postgraduate%20Scholarship
Level of Study: Postgraduate, Professional development
Type: Scholarship
Frequency: Annual
Country of Study: New Zealand
Application Procedure: Download the application form iusing the following link. http://www.lincoln.ac.nz/Study/Qualifications/Qualification/scholarships/?ScholarshipCode=Seed%20Industry%20Research%20Centre%20Postgraduate%20Scholarship
Closing Date: 15 September
Funding: Private

For further information contact:

Email: scholarships@lincoln.ac.nz

Silver Fern Farms Plate to Pasture Youth Scholarship

Subjects: All subject
Purpose: Scholarship applications are open to people wanting to develop their career in the food or farming industry with interests in; red meat, farming, agriculture, marketing and sales, research and development, food processing, cooking and food technology
Eligibility: New Zealand Citizen or Permanent Resident Students
Level of Study: Postgraduate
Type: Scholarship

Value: NZ $5,000
Length of Study: 1 Year
Frequency: Annual
Country of Study: Any country
Application Procedure: Apply online: http://www.silverfernfarms.com/our-farmers/supporting-our-communities/
Closing Date: 28 July
Funding: Foundation

For further information contact:

Silver Fern Farms Middle East Office 1406, 19th Floor, Sidra Tower, Hessa Street, Sheikh Zayed Road, Exit 36, Dubai, United Arab Emirates

Email: youthscholarship@silverfernfarms.co.nz

Simon Gubbins Scholarship

Subjects: The Simon Gubbins Scholarship was established in 2012 in memory of Simon Gubbins who studied at Lincoln University and went on to demonstrate significant leadership qualities in many agricultural organisations in Australia
Purpose: The scholarship is awarded to support an Australian student who wishes to study Agriculture at Lincoln University
Eligibility: Listed below are the eligibility criteria 1. Applicants must be full time students intending to undertake a course of study in Agriculture. 2. Applicants must hold an Australian Passport. Note: Previous recipients are eligible to apply for the scholarship in subsequent years
Level of Study: Graduate
Type: Scholarship
Value: Annual value of the scholarship shall be up to A$10,000 towards tuition fees and living expenses
Frequency: Annual
Country of Study: Australia
Closing Date: 31 August
Funding: Private
Additional Information: Important note to be highlighted, For Australian students wishing to undertake studies in Agriculture. Applicants must hold an Australian Passport

For further information contact:

Email: scholarships@lincoln.ac.nz

Sims Empire Scholarship

Purpose: The University of Canterbury is offering the Sims Empire Scholarship for further study or research in physics, chemistry, mathematics or medicine at an approved institution in Great Britain

Eligibility: Available to New Zealand Citizen or Permanent Resident Students
Level of Study: Graduate
Type: Scholarship
Value: NZ $15,000
Length of Study: 3 years
Frequency: Annual
Country of Study: Any country
Closing Date: 1 November
Funding: Private

Sir Apirana Ngata Memorial Scholarship

Subjects: All subjects
Purpose: The Sir Apirana Ngata Scholarship was created by the Maori Soldiers Trust to promote higher education amongst Maori. Available to a fulltime Maori undergraduate student studying at a NZ tertiary institute. Preference will be given to descendants of Maori WWI veterans. Applicants can be studying in any discipline
Eligibility: Information about your Tipuna's WWI service may be found in the publication' Te Hokowhitu A Tu' by Christopher Pugsley. Your local library should have a copy. Alternatively the online Auckland War Memorial Cenotaph Database is a good source of information. Please note that eligibility is not a guarantee of success
Level of Study: Postgraduate
Type: Scholarship
Value: NZ $1,000 - $3,000
Frequency: Varies
Country of Study: Any country
Application Procedure: Apply online
Closing Date: 1 May
Funding: Trusts

For further information contact:

Email: mstscholarship@maoritrustee.co.nz

Sir James Gunson Scholarship

Subjects: All subjects
Purpose: The Scholarship has been founded for the purpose of enabling a graduate to investigate one or more problems connected with the agricultural, dairying, horticulture or pastoral industry of New Zealand, with special reference to problems affecting the Auckland Province. In the event of no suitable agricultural, horticultural or dairying students offering themselves for selection, a candidate who holds a degree with first or second class Honours in Chemistry, Botany, Biochemistry, Forestry, Veterinary Science, Zoology, Geology or Economics may be selected

Eligibility: New Zealand Citizen or Permanent Resident Students
Level of Study: Postgraduate
Type: Scholarship
Value: NZ $1,250
Length of Study: 2 Year
Frequency: Annual
Country of Study: New Zealand
Application Procedure: Apply online
Closing Date: 1 February
Funding: Trusts

For further information contact:

University of Auckland, Private Bag 92-019, Auckland, New Zealand

Email: scholarships@auckland.ac.nz

Stapleton Memorial Trust Fellowships

Purpose: The fellowships are, primarily, intended for United Kingdom and Comonwealth research workers in agricultural science in the 30–45 age group. Particular emphasis on the research and development of grassland and grass related animal production, including the social, economic and environmental implications. The fellowships cover the cost of travel overseas and some internal travel for the fellows but not families
Eligibility: New Zealand Citizen or Permanent Resident Students
Level of Study: Postdoctorate
Type: Fellowship
Frequency: Annual
Country of Study: New Zealand
Closing Date: 31 October
Funding: Foundation

For further information contact:

The Stapleton Memorial Trust, c/- The British Grassland Society, Department of Agriculture, PO Box 237, University of Reading, Reading, RG6 6AR, Berkshire, United Kingdom

Email: info@lincoln.ac.nz

Stocker Scholarship

Purpose: The North Canterbury branch of the Royal Forest and Bird Protection Society Inc. offers financial support in the form of an annual scholarship for postgraduate students conducting conservation/environmental related research in Canterbury
Eligibility: New Zealand Citizen or Permanent Resident Students

Level of Study: Postdoctorate
Type: Scholarship
Value: NZ $3,000
Frequency: Annual
Country of Study: New Zealand
Closing Date: 30 September
Funding: Foundation

For further information contact:

Email: talbotjones@clear.net.nz

Taxonomy and Genetics Scholarship

Purpose: A postgraduate student is required with a background in molecular biology/bacteriology/genetics to begin a three year research project leading to a PhD degree on the taxonomy and genetics of an Erwinia species which is a potential biocontrol agent for black rot of Brassica. The PhD studentship will be based at the Bio-Protection Research Centre, Lincoln University, New Zealand under the supervision of Dr Andrew Pitman and Professor John Hampton (Bio-Protection Research Centre), and Dr Peter Fineran (University of Otago)
Eligibility: 1. New Zealand Citizen or Permanent Resident Students. 2. International Students
Level of Study: Postdoctorate
Type: Scholarship
Value: NZ $25,000
Frequency: Annual
Country of Study: Any country
Closing Date: 5 November
Funding: Foundation

For further information contact:

Email: john.hampton@lincoln.ac.nz

Tertiary Study Award 2018

Purpose: The bursary is awarded to the woman who best shows she has achieved and is continuing to achieve in her chosen study and / or career, who shows she needs this monetary support to continue her studies, who contributes to her community through service such as volunteering to community groups and who has the personality to represent Franklin BPW and its ideals
Eligibility: For Woman only Available to New Zealand Citizen or Permanent Resident Students
Level of Study: Graduate, Postgraduate
Type: Award

Value: Study award of NZ $4,000 with runner up award of NZ$1,000
Frequency: Varies
Country of Study: Any country
Application Procedure: Check the website. http://www.bpwfranklin.org.nz
Closing Date: 20 January
Funding: Foundation

For further information contact:

Tel: (64) 210 295 0688
Email: kellyj@franklinlaw.co.nz

The Bob Kerridge Animal Welfare Fellowship

Purpose: Applications may address a specific subject relative to a single animal and/or community welfare issue, or address a particular environmental matter relating to animal welfare, or the subject may be broader affecting general policy matters, research, education, legislation or conservation issues
Eligibility: Applicants must be New Zealand citizens, or have permanent New Zealand residency, and may be of any age over 18 years. Merit will be the basis of selection based on past achievements
Level of Study: Graduate
Type: Fellowship
Country of Study: Any country
Application Procedure: 1. Applications must be electronically presented utilising the cover sheet on the website www.animalwelfarefellowship.org.nz. 2. Information required includes: Project title, a brief personal summary of proposed project, rationale and justification of need for the project, personal statement of desired results and outcomes, identify other funding applied for and/are received. 3. There should follow a full submission of no more than 2,500 words detailing the subject/issue to be addressed
Closing Date: 20 December
Funding: Private
Additional Information: For further information, kindly check with the website. http://www.animalwelfarefellowship.org.nz/04-process.html

For further information contact:

Email: bob.kerridge@gmail.com

Ti Maru Maori Trust Prestigious Scholarship

Subjects: All subjects

Purpose: Available to Maori Graduates with a record of academic excellence and the proven ability to complete postgraduate studies in either New Zealand or overseas
Eligibility: 1. Maori / Pasifika only. 2. New Zealand Citizen or Permanent Resident Students
Level of Study: Postgraduate
Type: Scholarship
Value: $5,000
Frequency: Varies
Country of Study: Any country
Application Procedure: Apply online
Closing Date: 28 March
Funding: Foundation

For further information contact:

Email: info@maorieducation.org.nz

Tourism Industry New Zealand Trust & Lincoln University PhD Scholarship

Subjects: All subjects
Purpose: The purpose of this scholarship is to support research to provide a theoretically informed understanding of tourism's social licence to operate in New Zealand. The practical outcomes of this research will inform monitoring and management frameworks for the tourism sector. A secondary purpose is to build human capacity development for tourism policy and management
Eligibility: New Zealand Citizen or Permanent Resident Students
Level of Study: Postgraduate
Type: Scholarship
Value: NZ $2,500
Length of Study: 3 Year
Frequency: Annual
Country of Study: New Zealand
Application Procedure: Apply online
Closing Date: 11 October
Funding: Trusts

For further information contact:

Email: events@tia.org.nz

W.T. Scott Lincoln Scholarship

Purpose: One scholarship will be offered annually to a Roncalli College graduate who intends to undertake full time study at Lincoln University in the area of Agriculture or Horticulture
Eligibility: Special criteria: 1. Must have attended Roncalli College for a minimum of three years. 2. Available to New Zealand Citizen or Permanent Resident Students
Level of Study: Graduate
Type: Scholarship
Value: NZ $1,500
Frequency: Annual
Country of Study: Any country
Closing Date: 30 September
Funding: Private

For further information contact:

The Executive Officer, Roncalli College, PO Box 138, Timaru, New Zealand

Email: scholarships@lincoln.ac.nz

Waikato Tainui Scholarships

Subjects: All subjects
Purpose: Tertiary Education Grants Waikato Raupatu Education Grants (Undergraduate level) Tumate Mahuta Memorial Scholarships (Postgraduate and Masters) Waikato-Tainui Endowed College Scholarships (PhD's) Education Grants for tertiary fees will be considered twice a year. Closing dates are 16 March each year for first semester courses and 29 June each year for students commencing their studies in the second semester
Level of Study: Postgraduate
Type: Scholarship
Value: NZ $6,000
Length of Study: 3 Year
Frequency: Every 3 years
Country of Study: Any country
Application Procedure: Apply online
Closing Date: 31 December
Funding: Foundation

For further information contact:

Tel: (44) 800 824 684
Email: reception@tainui.co.nz

Whanui Scholarship

Purpose: This scholarship is aimed to encourage and support Mâori to be leaders in the Agribusiness Sector. These

scholarships are available to Mâori undergraduate and graduate students enrolled fulltime in an agriculture or agribusiness related degree
Eligibility: Available to New Zealand Citizen or Permanent Resident Students. It is also available for Maori / Pasifika only
Level of Study: Graduate, Undergraduate
Type: Scholarship
Value: NZ $10,000
Frequency: Annual
Country of Study: Any country
Closing Date: 1 April
Funding: Private

For further information contact:

Email: scholarship@lincoln.ac.nz

William Gao Postgraduate Scholarship for Excellence

Purpose: The scholarship shall have a maximum tenure of one year. Scholars shall be registered as full-time students during the tenure of the scholarship
Eligibility: The William Gao Postgraduate Scholarship for Excellence may be awarded to any student engaged in research at Lincoln University leading to the award of a Masters or PhD degree
Level of Study: Graduate
Type: Scholarship
Value: NZ $2,500
Frequency: Annual
Country of Study: Any country
Closing Date: 31 March
Funding: Private

For further information contact:

Email: scholarships@lincoln.ac.nz

William Walter Dunsterville Scholarship

Subjects: All subjects
Purpose: The William Walter Dunsterville Scholarship was established for the purpose of supporting students who otherwise would not have the financial means to attend Lincoln University
Eligibility: New Zealand Citizen or Permanent Resident Students
Level of Study: Postgraduate
Type: Scholarship
Value: Up to NZ $6,000
Frequency: Annual
Country of Study: Any country

Application Procedure: Apply online
Closing Date: 1 October
Funding: Private

For further information contact:

Email: info@lincoln.ac.nz

Yvonne A M Smith Charitable Trust Scholarship

Subjects: Political studies, Economics, Business and law
Purpose: The Yvonne Smith scholarship fund was set up in 1999 to encourage and promote women as future leaders of New Zealand business and society
Eligibility: Check online using the link. http://www.yvonnesmith.org.nz
Level of Study: Graduate
Type: Scholarship
Value: As high as $60,000 per year
Frequency: Annual
Country of Study: New Zealand
Closing Date: 18 December
Funding: Private

For further information contact:

Tel: (64) 3 423 0000
Email: info@lincoln.ac.nz

Linnean Society of New South Wales

PO Box 137, Matraville, NSW 2036, Australia

Tel: (61) 2 9662 6196
Fax: (61) 2 9662 6196
Email: linnsoc@acay.com.au
Website: http://www.acay.com.au/linnsoc
Contact: Grants Management Award

The Linnean Society of New South Wales is concerned with the publication of original scientific research papers and the encouragement of scientific research through grants and public lectures.

The Joyce W. Vickery Research Fund

Subjects: Full or part-time higher degree with a biological emphasis

Eligibility: Applicants need not be members of the Society, but other things being equal, preference will be given to members
Value: Individual grants will not normally exceed $2,500 for Members and $1,500 for non-members
Application Procedure: Applications must be entered on the Fund's application form and must also include references and a list of the applicant's relevant publications over the previous five years
Applicants should email their signed applications to: secretary@linneansocietynsw.org.au

Lock heed Martin

Lockheed Martin Corporation Scholarship for Freshmen

Subjects: Eight US$2,000 scholarships for female applicants planning to study a full-time ABET-accredited program in engineering, technology, or computing in the upcoming academic year
Purpose: Lockheed Martin has launched a new scholarship program to provide opportunities to students who want to build their talents and change the world
Eligibility: 1. Applicants must not be receiving full funding for education (tuition, fees, and books or equivalent) from their school or another organization (e.g. members of the Armed Services attending United States military academies, students receiving full reimbursement from an employer). 2. Applicants must be enrolled in a program accredited by ABET. Accreditation information for specific programs is available online at main.abet.org/aps/Accreditedprogramsearch.aspx
Level of Study: Graduate
Type: Award
Value: US$2,000. It Includes travel stipend for the SWE Annual Conference
Frequency: Annual
Country of Study: Any country
Application Procedure: This award is being provided by Society of Women Engineers (SWE). Applicants to the Lockheed Martin STEM Scholarship Program must meet the following eligibility requirements: 1. United States Citizens. 2. Current high school seniors with a cumulative 3.5 or above GPA, or current college freshmen or sophomores with a cumulative 3.0 or above GPA. 3. Planning to enroll full-time at an accredited four-year college or university in the United States
Closing Date: 15 February
Funding: Private

For further information contact:

130 East Randolph Street, Suite 3500, Chicago, IL 60601, United States of America

Email: scholarships@swe.org, melissa.s.longo@lmco.com

London Goodenough Association of Canada

P.O. BOX 5896, STN A, Toronto, ON M5W 1P3, Canada

Email: admin@lgac.ca
Website: www.lgac.ca
Contact: Brian Cardie, Administrator

The London Goodenough Association of Canada (LGAC) is an association of Canadians who lived as graduate students at Goodebnough College in Mecklenburgh Square, London. The LGAC offers member events and provides a Scholarship Programme for Canadian graduate students studying in London and staying in London House or William Goodenough, the Goodenough College residence halls.

London Goodenough Association of Canada Scholarship Program

Subjects: All subjects
Purpose: To support Canadian nationals who wish to pursue their higher studies in London
Eligibility: Open to candidates who are full-time students enroled in an accredited graduate programme in London or undertaking theses research in London while enroled elsewhere
Level of Study: Postgraduate, Research
Type: Scholarships
Value: £4,500
Frequency: Annual
Study Establishment: The London Goodenough Association of Canada
Country of Study: United Kingdom
Application Procedure: Application form can be downloaded from the website. Candidates must also arrange to have all post-secondary institution transcripts and 3 letters of reference sent to the address below
Closing Date: 6 January (check with website)
Funding: Foundation, Individuals
Additional Information: For further information contact Dr Kathleen McCrone at the above address. Please see the website for further details www.lgac.ca/scholarships

For further information contact:

Contact: Andrew Gray, Chair

London Mathematical Society

De Morgan House, 57-58 Russell Square, WC1B 4HS, London, United Kingdom

Tel: (44) 20 7637 3686
Fax: (44) 20 7323 3655
Email: lms@lms.ac.uk
Website: www.lms.ac.uk

The United Kingdom national learned society for the promotion and extension of mathematical knowledge, by means of publishing, grants, meetings and contribution to national debate on mathematics, research and education.

Cecil King Travel Scholarship

Subjects: All areas of mathematical research. Proposals must describe the intended programme of work and the benefits to be gained from the visit
Purpose: To enable a young mathematician of outstanding promise to spend a period of 3 months undertaking study or research overseas
Eligibility: Nationals of the United Kingdom or Republic of Ireland, having recently completed a doctoral degree at a United Kingdom. university
Level of Study: Postdoctorate, Postgraduate
Type: Scholarship
Value: Up to £5,000
Length of Study: 3 months
Frequency: Annual
Study Establishment: University or research institute
Country of Study: Any country
No. of awards offered: 5
Application Procedure: Application forms are available on request from the society or can be downloaded from the website. Applications should be returned by post or email to Duncan Turton
Closing Date: 6 June
Funding: Trusts
Contributor: Cecil King Memorial Fund
No. of awards given last year: 1
No. of applicants last year: 5
Additional Information: Please see the website for further details www.lms.ac.uk/prizes/cecil-king-travel-scholarship

For further information contact:

London Mathematical Society, 57-58 Russell Square, United Kingdom

Email: education@lms.ac.uk
Contact: Elizabeth Fisher, Membership & Grants Manager

London Metropolitan University

London Metropolitan University, 166-220 Holloway Road, N7 8DB, London, United Kingdom

Tel: (44) 20 7423 0000
Email: info@canoncollins.org.uk
Website: www.londonmet.ac.uk

London Metropolitan University is one of Britain's largest universities, which offers a wide variety of courses in a huge range of subject areas. The University aims to provide education and training that will help students to achieve their potential and London to succeed us a world city.

Canon Collins Trust Scholarships

Subjects: Public administration
Purpose: The key aim of the Scholarships Programme is to help build the human resources necessary for economic, social and cultural development in the southern African region and to develop an educated and skilled workforce that can benefit the wider community. Canon Collins Trust scholarship holders are thus expected to use the knowledge, training and skills acquired through their studies to contribute positively to the development of their home country
Eligibility: Open to nationals of South Africa, Namibia, Botswana, Swaziland, Lesotho, Zimbabwe, Zambia, Malawi, Angola and Mozambique who have been offered admission to the University
Level of Study: Postgraduate
Type: Scholarship
Value: Full-fee or half-fee waiver and support in the form of stipend, fares and books
Frequency: Annual
Study Establishment: London Metropolitan University
Country of Study: United Kingdom
Application Procedure: Application should be sent to the Canon Collins Trust and the Trust will forward it to the university. Please see the website to know how to apply.

Applications that have been emailed or faxed or those that have been received after the deadline will not be considered
Closing Date: 3 March for United Kingdom. scholarships (check with website)
Funding: Trusts
Contributor: Cannon Collins Educational Trust and Department of Applied Social Sciences
Additional Information: Canon Collins Trust provides scholarships to students from South Africa, Namibia, Botswana, Swaziland, Lesotho, Zimbabwe, Zambia, Malawi, Angola and Mozambique who wish to pursue a postgraduate degree (mainly Master's degrees of one or two years) in either the United Kingdom or South Africa. Please see the website for details www.canoncollins.org.uk/scholarships.html

For further information contact:

22 The Ivories, 6 Northampton Street, United Kingdom

Tel:	(44) 20 7354 1462
Fax:	(44) 20 7359 4875
Email:	info@canoncollins.org.uk
Contact:	United Kingdom Scholarships Programme Manager

International Students House/London Metropolitan Scholarship Scheme

Subjects: All subjects
Purpose: To support international students from selected countries with tuition fees and accommodation
Eligibility: Open to students from Afghanistan, Armenia, Bhutan, Cameroon, Cuba, East Timor, Gambia, Iran, Indonesia, Jordan, Kazakhstan, Lebanon, Namibia, Nepal, Sri Lanka, Tanzania, Tibet, Uganda, Uzbekistan, Vietnam, and Zimbabwe who have been offered admission to the University
Level of Study: Postgraduate, MBA
Type: Scholarship
Value: Free tuition and accommodation
Length of Study: 1–2 years
Study Establishment: London Metropolitan University
Country of Study: United Kingdom
Application Procedure: Please see the website www.londonmet.ac.uk/scholarships. Applications that have been emailed or faxed or those that have been received after the deadline will not be considered
Closing Date: 31 May and 31 October (check the website)
Funding: International office
Contributor: International Students House (ISH) and London Metropolitan University
No. of awards given last year: 1–5

Additional Information: If applicants would like more information about International Students House, please access their website at www.ish.org.uk/

For further information contact:

Scholarships International Office, London Metropolitan University, 166-220 Holloway Road, United Kingdom

Email: scholarships@londonmet.ac.uk

Savoy Educational Trust Scholarships

Subjects: Hospitality and Tourism
Purpose: To financially assist students wishing to pursue students in the field of Hospitality and Tourism
Eligibility: Open to applicants from any country in the world who have been offered admission to the University
Level of Study: Postgraduate
Type: Bursary
Value: Up to UK £9,000
Frequency: Annual
Study Establishment: London Metropolitan University
Country of Study: United Kingdom
Application Procedure: Please see the website www.londonmet.ac.uk/how to apply. Applications that have been emailed or faxed or those that have been received after the deadline will not be considered
Closing Date: 31 May and 31 October
Funding: Trusts
Contributor: Savoy Educational Trust

For further information contact:

Scholarship Department, c/o Student Recruitment Services, Room 210, London Metropolitan University, United Kingdom

Email: epilepsy@savoy-foundation.ca

The Katrina Mihaere Scholarship

Subjects: Sports Management
Purpose: To honour the memory of Katrina Mihaere, a former London Metropolitan Women's Tennis team member
Eligibility: Open to all women tennis players who have been offered admission to the University, with an excellent track record in Women's sports
Level of Study: Postgraduate
Type: Scholarship
Value: Full tuition and accommodation

Frequency: Annual
Study Establishment: London Metropolitan University
Country of Study: United Kingdom
Application Procedure: Please see the website www. londonmet.ac.uk/how to apply. Applications that have been emailed or faxed or those that have been received after the deadline will not be considered
Closing Date: 31 May and 31 October

For further information contact:

Email: i.jennings@londonmet.ac.uk
Contact: Ian Jennings, Sports Manager

The ODASS Scheme

Subjects: All subjects
Purpose: To financially assist students of high academic merit from developing Commonwealth countries
Eligibility: Open to students from developing Commonwealth
Level of Study: Postgraduate
Type: Scholarship
Value: Full tuition fees and living allowance
Frequency: Annual
Study Establishment: London Metropolitan Society
Country of Study: United Kingdom
Application Procedure: See the website
Funding: Government
Contributor: British Government's Aid Programme

For further information contact:

The Association of Commonwealth Universities, 36 Gordon Square, United Kingdom

Email: info@acu.ac.uk

London School of Business & Finance

8/9 Holborn, EC1N 2LL, London, United Kingdom

Tel: (44) 20 7823 2303
Fax: (44) 20 7823 2302
Email: admissions@lsbf.org.uk/ info@lsbf.org.uk
Website: www.lsbf.org.uk

Diversity Scholarship

Subjects: Business
Purpose: To ensure students originate from varied backgrounds creating an opportunity to form global corporate networks

Eligibility: Show a proven history of academic excellence. Meet the English requirements of the programme they are applying for. Provide proof of sufficient funds to pay the remaining course fees. Applicants must have already applied for a programme at LSBF. Applicants must be classified as an international student and not residing in the United Kingdom
Level of Study: Doctorate, Postgraduate, MBA
Type: Scholarship
Value: £1,000–8,000 (towards reducing tuition fees, not include a contribution to living costs, travel or other expenses)
Study Establishment: London School of Business & Finance
Country of Study: United Kingdom
Closing Date: 28 August and 29 January
Additional Information: Size of awards vary according to each scholar's circumstances

For further information contact:

London School of Business and Finance, Postgraduate Admissions Office, 8/9 Holborn, United Kingdom

Tel: (44) 20 7823 2303
Fax: (44) 20 7823 2302
Email: admissions@lsbf.org.uk

The Royal Bank of Scotland International Scholarship

Subjects: Business
Purpose: It aims at bridging international boundaries by providing Chinese business professionals with an opportunity to study a globally recognized degree in one of the world's financial centres
Eligibility: A national of the People's Republic of China, Hong Kong (SAR), Macau (SAR); a graduate with proven academic skills; committed to contribute to the socio-economic development of the People's Republic of China. Established in a career, with a track record of excellence and achievement, and the prospect of becoming a leader in his/her chosen field; have good English Language skills, as most United Kingdom Higher Education Institutions require a minimum IELTS of 6.5 for admission onto Postgraduate courses; have sufficient funds to meet your tuition fees and living expenses, after taking account of the possible award of the Bank of Scotland International Scholarship
Level of Study: Doctorate, Postgraduate, MBA
Type: Scholarship
Value: Cover tuition fees
Country of Study: United Kingdom
Application Procedure: Application form available at www. lsbf.org.uk

Closing Date: 28 August
Contributor: Bank of Scotland

For further information contact:

Tel: (44) 20 7823 2303
Email: info@lsbf.org.uk
Contact: Daniela Pantica, Co-ordinator

London School of Economics and Political Science (LSE)

The London School of Economics and Political Science, Houghton Street, WC2A 2AE, London, United Kingdom

Tel: (44) 20 7405 7686
Fax: (44) 20 7107 5285
Email: c.s.lee2@lse.ac.uk
Website: www.lse.ac.uk

London School of Economics (LSE) was founded in 1895 by Beatrice and Sidney Webb. LSE has an outstanding reputation for academic excellence. LSE is a world class centre for its concentration of teaching and research across the full range of the social, political and economic sciences.

CR Parekh Fellowship

Subjects: Poverty, inequality, human development and social exclusion, quality of public life, regional disparities, identities – gender, ethnicity, language, economy and environment, political structures and processes, constitutional debates
Purpose: To encourage research that is of social, economic, political and constitutional concern to India
Eligibility: Open to established Indian scholars who are below 40 years of age and hold a PhD or comparable qualifications and experience. The fellowship is not intended for students registered for a degree or diploma, nor is it intended for senior academics
Level of Study: Doctorate, Research
Type: Fellowship
Value: UK £1,500 per month
Length of Study: 3 months
Frequency: Annual
Country of Study: United Kingdom
Application Procedure: Applications should include a curriculum vitae and an outline of proposed research and the names and addresses of 2 referees who are familiar with their work, to be contacted by the chairman
Closing Date: 13 January

Additional Information: Applications will not be accepted via email or fax

For further information contact:

The Chairman of the Management Committee, The Asia Research Centre, London School of Economics & Political Science, Houghton Street, United Kingdom

Email: arc@lse.ac.uk

Sir Ratan Tata Postdoctoral Fellowship

Subjects: Poverty, inequality, human development and social exclusion, quality of public life, regional disparities, identities – gender, ethnicity, language, economy and environment
Purpose: To encourage research on contemporary social and economic concerns of South Asia
Eligibility: Applicants should be scholars in the social sciences with experience of research on South Asia. They should hold a PhD
Level of Study: Research
Type: Fellowship
Value: UK £1,500 per month
Length of Study: Up to 8 months
Frequency: Annual
Country of Study: United Kingdom
Application Procedure: Applications should include a curriculum vitae and an outline of proposed research and the names and addresses of 2 referees who are familiar with their work, to be contacted by the Chairman. Applications should be addressed to The Fellowships Selection Committee
Closing Date: 13 May
Additional Information: The fellowship is not intended for students registered for a degree or diploma, nor is it intended for senior academics. Applications will not be accepted via email or fax. Please see the website for further details

For further information contact:

Contact: The Chairman, The Fellowships Selection Committee

London South Bank University

103 Borough Road, SE1 0AA, London, United Kingdom

Tel: (44) 20 7815 7815
Email: pgscholarships@lsbu.ac.uk
Website: www.lsbu.ac.uk

Vice-Chancellor's Scholarships

Subjects: All subjects offered by the university
Eligibility: All Home, European Union or International students who have firmly accepted their unconditional or conditional offer of a place to study on a postgraduate programme at LSBU are invited to apply for a scholarship in up to three of the categories listed on the website. Their application will be assessed and, if successful, the student will receive one award. Only one application is allowed
Level of Study: Graduate, Postgraduate
Type: Scholarship
Value: A scholarship is available for £4,000 towards the cost of the fees of full Master's and Research programmes. This total amount is for both full or part-time courses and similar postgraduate qualifications regardless if taken over one or more years
Frequency: Annual
Application Procedure: You will be invited to apply online via email after you firmly accept your unconditional or conditional offer to study at LSBU. We recommend you apply for your place at LSBU as soon as possible to ensure you have been made an offer by the scholarship deadline of July
Closing Date: July
Funding: Individuals
Contributor: Donations from alumni and other supporters

For further information contact:

Email: pgscholarships@lsbu.ac.uk

Loren L Zachary Society for the Performing Arts

2250 Gloaming Way, Beverly Hills, CA 90210, United States of America

Tel: (1) 310 276 2731
Fax: (1) 310 275 8245
Email: info@zacharysociety.org
Website: www.zacharysociety.org
Contact: Mrs Nedra Zachary, President, Director of Competition

The Loren L Zachary Society for the Performing Arts was founded in 1972 by the late Dr Loren L Zachary, and Nedra Zachary. The purpose of the organization is to help further the careers of young opera singers by providing financial assistance and performance opportunities. The annual Loren L Zachary National Vocal Competition, now in its 46 year, has helped launch the International careers of many singers. For a complete list of winners and finalists visit the website.

Loren L Zachary National Vocal Competition for Young Opera Singers

Subjects: Operatic singing
Purpose: To assist in the development of the careers of young opera singers through competitive auditions with monetary awards
Eligibility: Competition is open to applicants ages 21–35. Singers must be prepared to pursue a professional operatic stage career, be present for all phases of the Competition, and reside in the United States or Canada
Level of Study: Professional development
Type: Competition
Value: Ranges from US$10,000–US$12,000 for the top winner. US$50,000–US$55,000 is distributed among the finalists and the minimum award ranges from US$1,000 to US$2,000
Frequency: Annual
Study Establishment: Must be thoroughly trained and be ready to pursue a professional operatic career
Country of Study: Any country
No. of awards offered: 300
Application Procedure: Applicants must complete an application form accompanied by a proof of age and an application fee of US$50. For application forms and exact dates, singers should refer to www.zacharysociety.org or send a stamped, self-addressed envelope with letter
Closing Date: 25–28 February for the preliminary round
Funding: Private, Trusts, Individuals
No. of awards given last year: 10
No. of applicants last year: 300
Additional Information: All applicants are guaranteed an audition provided application is completed correctly with application fee. Applicants must be present at all phases of the auditions. Recordings are not acceptable. Preliminary and semifinal auditions take place in New York in February, and in Los Angeles in April. The grand finals and awards distribution occurs on 20 May 2018 in Los Angeles, California

For further information contact:

The Loren L. Zachary Society, 2250 Gloaming Way, Beverly Hills, CA 90210-1717, United States of America

Email: infoz@zacharysociety.org

Los Alamos National Laboratory (LANL)

PO Box 1663, MS P219, Los Alamos, NM 87545, United States of America

Tel:	(1) 505 667 4866
Fax:	(1) 505 665 6932
Email:	bmontoya@lanl.gov
Website:	www.lanl.gov

Los Alamos National Laboratory (LANL) is the largest institution in Northern New Mexico with more than 9,000 employees plus approximately 650 contractor personnel. From its origins as a secret Manhattan Project Laboratory, Los Alamos has attracted world-class scientists and applied their energy and creativity to solving the nation's most challenging problems.

Los Alamos Graduate Research Assistant Program

Subjects: Technical and scientific disciplines
Purpose: To provide students with relevant research experience while they are pursuing a graduate degree
Eligibility: Applicant must be a graduate
Level of Study: Doctorate, Research
Type: Research
Value: US$33,300–44,600, including benefits, travel and moving expenses
Length of Study: Year or less
Frequency: Annual
Country of Study: Any country
Closing Date: Continuous
Additional Information: For further inquiries contact Brenda Montoya, 505/667 4866, bmontoya@lanl.gov. Please see the website for further details www.lanl.gov/careers/career-options/student-internships/graduate/index.php

For further information contact:

Email: errobinson@lanl.gov

Loughborough University

Leicestershire LE11 3TU, United Kingdom

Tel:	(44) 1509 222 222
Email:	international-office@lboro.ac.uk
Website:	www.lboro.ac.uk

With 3,000 staff and 12,000 students Loughbrough, with its impressive 410 acre campus, is one of the largest university's in the United Kingdom. Our mission is to increase knowledge through research, provide the highest quality of educational experience and the widest opportunities for students, advance industry and the profession, and benefit society.

Design School Scholarships

Subjects: All postgraduate taught programmes in the Department
Purpose: To assist students financially who want to study in the department
Eligibility: Outstanding academic achievement
Level of Study: Postgraduate
Type: Scholarship
Value: UK £500
Frequency: Annual
Study Establishment: Loughborough University
Country of Study: United Kingdom
Application Procedure: If full supporting documentation is supplied with your application to study in the department, you will be automatically considered for a scholarship. No separate scholarship application is required
Closing Date: 30 June
Additional Information: Complete details of all available scholarships are given in the website

For further information contact:

Email: r.i.campbell@lboro.ac.uk

Economic and Social Research Council Studentships

Subjects: Chemistry
Purpose: To financially assist students to cover their living costs while undertaking a PhD
Eligibility: Applicant must have been in full-time education in the United Kingdom throughout the 3 years preceding the start date of PhD course
Level of Study: Postgraduate
Type: Studentship
Value: The amount of funding is agreed each year by all the research councils and increase in line with inflation. Tuition fees are also paid
Length of Study: 1 year
Frequency: Annual
Study Establishment: Loughborough University
Country of Study: United Kingdom
Application Procedure: See website

Closing Date: 7 March (check with website)
Funding: Government
Contributor: ESRC
Additional Information: Please see the website for further details   www.lboro.ac.uk/departments/phir/pg-research/funding/

For further information contact:

Email: l.e.child@lboro.ac.uk

Eli Lilly Scholarship

Subjects: Chemistry
Purpose: To increase knowledge through research, provide the highest quality of educational experience and the widest opportunities for students, advance industry and the profession, and benefit society
Eligibility: Applicant must be a postgraduate in chemistry. See the website for details
Level of Study: Postgraduate
Type: Scholarships and fellowships
Value: UK £1,000
Length of Study: 1 year
Frequency: Annual
Study Establishment: Loughborough University
Country of Study: United Kingdom
Application Procedure: See website
Closing Date: See the website for details

For further information contact:

Tel: (44) 1509 263171
Email: l.e.child@lboro.ac.uk/international-office@lboro.ac.uk

Institute of Polymer Technology and Material Engineering (Materials) Scholarships

Subjects: Materials science
Purpose: To increase knowledge through research, provide the highest quality of educational experience and the widest opportunities for students, advance industry and the profession, and benefit society
Eligibility: Open to all full-time, self-funded, international fee status students who are not in receipt of any other university funding
Level of Study: Postgraduate
Type: Scholarships and fellowships
Value: 25 per cent of the programme tuition fee which will be credited to the student's tuition fee account
Length of Study: 1 year

Frequency: Annual
Study Establishment: Loughborough University
Country of Study: United Kingdom
Application Procedure: See website
Closing Date: 1 March
Funding: Foundation
Contributor: Institute of Polymer Technology and Materials Engineering .

For further information contact:

Email: iptme@lboro.ac.uk

Jean Scott Scholarships

Subjects: Business and management studies
Purpose: To support best qualified Loughborough University students
Eligibility: Open to the best qualified Loughborough University students entering MSc programmes in the Department of Economics
Level of Study: Postgraduate
Type: Scholarship
Value: A maximum of US$5,000
Length of Study: 1 year
Frequency: Annual
Study Establishment: Loughborough University
Country of Study: United Kingdom
Application Procedure: See website
Closing Date: See the university website for details

For further information contact:

Email: msc.economics@lboro.ac.uk

Loughborough Sports Scholarships

Subjects: Athletics, cricket, football, golf, hockey, rugby, swimming, tennis, and triathlon
Purpose: To support elite athletes
Eligibility: Open to students who have excelled at least at junior international level (or equivalent) in their sport and have fulfilled the normal academic requirements for either undergraduate or postgraduate entry
Type: Scholarship
Value: Up to £3,000 towards tuition fees, £1,000 towards living expenses, £250 towards facility membership (where applicable) and free parking on campus
Frequency: Annual
Study Establishment: Loughborough University
Country of Study: United Kingdom

Application Procedure: See website
Closing Date: September (check with website)
Additional Information: Please see the website for further details www.lboro.ac.uk/admin/ar/funding/university/sports_scholarships/

For further information contact:

Tel: (44) 1509 226108
Email: sports-scholars@lboro.ac.uk

Mathematical Sciences Scholarship

Subjects: Industrial mathematical modelling
Level of Study: Postgraduate
Type: Scholarship
Value: 25 per cent of the programme tuition fee which will be credited to the student's tuition fee account
Length of Study: 1–3 years
Frequency: Annual
Study Establishment: Loughborough University
Country of Study: United Kingdom
Application Procedure: See website
Additional Information: Please see the website for further details

For further information contact:

Email: maths-admissions@lboro.ac.uk

Master of Business Administration Scholarships

Subjects: Business management
Purpose: To support international Students who want to do MBA from University of Loughborough
Eligibility: Applicant may be a citizen of any country
Level of Study: MBA
Type: Scholarship
Value: Varies
Length of Study: Varies
Frequency: Annual
Study Establishment: Loughborough University
Country of Study: United Kingdom
Application Procedure: See website
Closing Date: check the website

For further information contact:

Email: exec.mba@lboro.ac.uk

School of Art and Design Scholarships

Subjects: Art and design
Level of Study: Postgraduate
Type: Scholarship
Value: UK £1,000 (tuition fee)
Length of Study: 1–3 years
Frequency: Annual
Study Establishment: Loughborough University
Country of Study: United Kingdom
Application Procedure: See website

For further information contact:

Email: R.Turner@lboro.ac.uk

School of Business and Economics Scholarships

Subjects: MSc Business Analysis and Management, MSc Finance and Management, MSc International Management, MSc Management, MSc Marketing and Management, MSc Information Management and Business Technology
Purpose: To assist financially the students who want to pursue a career in finance, international and marketing management
Eligibility: Applicants with a First Class Honours degree are eligible. A limited number of scholarships are available
Level of Study: Postgraduate
Type: Scholarship
Value: 50 per cent of the tuition fee
Length of Study: 1 year
Frequency: Annual
Study Establishment: Loughborough University
Country of Study: United Kingdom
Application Procedure: See website
Closing Date: See website for details
Additional Information: United Kingdom/European Union, self-funding, full-time or part-time where applicable

For further information contact:

Tel: (44) 1509 228278, 228844, 223291
Email: msc.management@lboro.ac.uk, f.l. baddeley@lboro.ac.uk

Loughborough University Business School

Ashby Road, Leicestershire LE11 3TU, Loughborough, United Kingdom

Tel: (44) 1509 223 398
Fax: (44) 1509 223 960
Website: http://info.lut.ac.uk.departments/bs
Contact: Ms Gabriella Stenson, MBA Admissions
              Officer

Dean's Award for Enterprise Scholarship

Purpose: The award will be given at the discretion of the Dean, with the support of the Senior Leadership Team. Applicants are asked to produce a one-page submission of their business idea; though students are encouraged to include images and media content to support their application
Eligibility: Shortlisted applicants will be asked to complete a short video interview to discuss their business idea in more detail
Level of Study: Graduate
Type: Scholarship
Frequency: Annual
Country of Study: Any country
Closing Date: 31 July
Funding: Private

For further information contact:

Epinal Way, Leicestershire LE11 3TU, Loughborough, United Kingdom

Tel: (44) 1509 222 222
Email: london@lboro.ac.uk

Loyola Marymount University

1 Loyola Marymount University Dr, Los Angeles, CA 90045, United States of America

Tel: (1) 310 338 2700
Contact: Fellowships Office

Loyola Marymount University MBA Programme

Length of Study: 1–2 years
Application Procedure: Applicants must return a completed application form, two official undergraduate transcripts, a two page Statement of Intent, two letters of recommendation, test scores, and a fee of US$35

For further information contact:

Tel: (1) 310 338 2848
Fax: (1) 310 338 2899
Email: mbapc@imumail.lmu.edu
Contact: MBA Admissions Officer

Ludwig-Maximilian University

Geschwister-Scholl-Platz 1, DEU 80539, Munich, Germany

Tel: (49) 89 / 2180 0
Fax: (49) 89 / 2180 2322
Contact: Ludwig-Maximilians-Universität München

LMU is recognized as one of Europe's premier academic and research institutions. Since our founding in 1472, LMU has attracted inspired scholars and talented students from all over the world, keeping the University at the nexus of ideas that challenge and change our complex world.

Liaoning Medical University Postdoctoral Fellowship for International Students at MCMP

Subjects: LMU is especially interested in candidates with research interests in at least one of the following fields: general philosophy of science, philosophy of physics, philosophy of the social sciences, philosophy of statistics, formal epistemology, formal philosophy of science, social epistemology, philosophy and psychology of reasoning and argumentation, agent-based modeling in philosophy, or decision theory
Purpose: The Munich Center for Mathematical Philosophy (MCMP) seeks applications for two 3-year postdoctoral fellowships starting on 1 October 2018. International students are eligible to apply for this fellowship
Eligibility: International students are eligible to apply for this fellowship. The official language at the MCMP is English and fluency in German is not mandatory
Type: Postdoctoral fellowship
Value: The fellowships are remunerated with 1.853 €/month (paid out without deductions for tax and social security). The MCMP also provides funds to cover costs to attend some workshops and conferences
Study Establishment: LMU is especially interested in candidates with research interests in at least one of the following fields: general philosophy of science, philosophy of physics, philosophy of the social sciences, philosophy of statistics,

formal epistemology, formal philosophy of science, social epistemology, philosophy and psychology of reasoning and argumentation, agent-based modeling in philosophy, or decision theory

Country of Study: Any country

Application Procedure: Applications (including a cover letter that addresses, amongst others, one's academic background, research interests and the proposed starting date, a CV, a list of publications, a sample of written work of no more than 5,000 words, and a description of a planned research project of about 2,000 words) should be sent by email (in one PDF document) to office.hartmann-at-lrz.uni-muenchen.de by 15 April, 2018. Hard copy applications are not accepted. Additionally, two confidential letters of reference addressing the applicant's qualifications for academic research should be sent to the same email address from the referees directly

Closing Date: 15 April

Additional Information: For more details please see the website http://myschoolbeep.blogspot.in/2018/02/lmu-postdoctoral-fellowship-for.html

For further information contact:

Email: S.Hartmann@lmu.de
Contact: Professor Stephan Hartmann

Lupus Foundation of America

1300 Piccard Drive, Suite 200, Rockville, MD 20850, United States of America

Tel: (1) 301 670 9292
Fax: (1) 301 670 9486
Contact: Ms Arlise Davis, Executive Assistant

Lund University Global Scholarship

Purpose: The Lund University Global Scholarship programme seeks to recognise these students by awarding academic excellence grants. Scholarship recipients have a proven record of achieving consistently high grades in their previous studies and are assessed as being a good fit for our programmes

Eligibility: To be eligible to apply for a scholarship you must meet all of the following criteria: 1. You must be a citizen of a country from outside the European Union/EEA (and Switzerland) and are required to pay a tuition fee. 2. You have made a complete application for

Bachelor's or Master's level studies at Lund University in a regular application round for a minimum of one semester of study (30 ECTS). Note that priority is given to students who have ranked a programme at Lund University as the first choice in their application at universityadmissions.se

Level of Study: Graduate

Type: Scholarship

Value: SEK 15 million (€1.4 million / US$1.7 million) will be awarded per annum

Frequency: Dependent on funds available

Country of Study: Any country

Application Procedure: To apply for a Lund University Global Scholarship, you must first apply for the programme(s) or free-standing course(s) you wish to study at Lund University using the online, national application website, www.universityadmissions.se, during the application period. Once you have made a complete application to a degree programme or free-standing courses of at least 30 ECTS credits and paid the application fee, you will be able to apply for the scholarship. As part of this online application, you need to upload your scholarship 'motivation letter' (maximum 600 words) to the scholarship application portal. Please note that the scholarship "motivation letter" is different from any statement of purpose you may be required to submit as part of your programme application documents

Closing Date: Closing date yet to be discloosed

Funding: Private

Additional Information: Note that the opening date for this proposal is February

For further information contact:

Box 117, SWE 221 00 Lund, Sweden

Tel: (46) 46 222 0000
Fax: (46) 46 222 4720
Email: maria.lindblad@er.lu.se

Luton Business School University of Luton

MBA Programmes Putteridge Bury Hitchin Road, Luton, LU2 8LE, Bedfordshire, United Kingdom

Tel: (44) 1582 482555
Fax: (44) 1582 489076
Email: faculty-of-business@luton.ac.uk
Contact: MBA Admissions Officer

League of United Latin American Citizens National Educational Service Centers National Scholarship Fund

Purpose: Awards scholarships to Hispanic students who are enrolled or planning to enroll in accredited colleges or universities in the United States

Eligibility: Must be a full-time or part-time student. 1. Must be a Hispanic student. 2. Must be a United States citizen or permanent resident. 3. Must have a grade point average of 3.25 or higher. Must have applied to or be enrolled in a college, university, or graduate school, including two-year colleges or vocational schools that lead to an associate's degree

Level of Study: Graduate

Type: Funding support

Value: $2,000

Frequency: Annual

Country of Study: Any country

Application Procedure: The applicants must send application and supporting materials to the LULAC council in his/her town. For a listing of participating councils, please visit: www.lnesc.org/index.asp?Type=B_BASIC&SEC=A9E53 D4E-6ADF-431B-A59A-E92DEDD44793. If there are no LULAC councils in the applicant's state, then the student is ineligible

Closing Date: 31 March

Funding: Private

For further information contact:

2000 L St., N.W. Suite 610, Washington, DC 20036, United States of America

Email: mbosques@lnesc.org

Contact: Mr Maritza Bosques, National Scholarship Coordinator

M

Maastricht University

Minderbroedersberg 4-6, NLD-6211 LK Maastricht, The Netherlands

Contact: Maastricht University

Maastricht University (UM) is the most international university in the Netherlands and, with more than 16,000 students and 4,000 employees, is still growing. The university stands out for its innovative education model, international character and multidisciplinary approach to research and education.

Orange Tulip Scholarship Scholarship for Indian Students

Subjects: At Maastricht University, an OTS grant is available at the Faculty of Law
Purpose: The new Orange Tulip Scholarship India is now available for all Indian students who want to study at Maastricht University (UM) in the Netherlands
Eligibility: Students from India are eligible to apply for this scholarship
Value: 100% tuition fee. Please note no additional allowance towards living costs or visa costs
Study Establishment: At Maastricht University, an OTS grant is available at the Faculty of Law
Country of Study: Netherlands
Application Procedure: See the website
Closing Date: 1 April
Additional Information: For more details please visit our website at scholarship-positions.com/ots-scholarship-for-indian-students-maastricht-university-netherlands/2017/12/01/

For further information contact:

Email: ots@nesoindia.org

Macquarie University

Balaclava Road, North Ryde, NSW 2109, Australia

Tel:	(61) 2 9850 7111
Fax:	(61) 2 9850 7433
Email:	tgreen@ling.mq.edu.au
Website:	www.mq.edu.au

Established in 1964, Macquarie attracts students from all walks of life, including large numbers from overseas. As the new millennium dawned, Macquarie had conferred some 58,000 degrees, diplomas and postgraduate certificates.

Centre for Lasers and Applications Scholarships

Subjects: Experimental and theoretical laser studies
Purpose: To enable holders to pursue a research programme leading to the degree of MSc or PhD in experimental and theoretical laser studies
Eligibility: Open to the Australian citizens, permanent residents, or citizens of overseas countries
Level of Study: Postgraduate, Research
Type: Scholarship
Value: A$19,231 (maximum per year). This award is to be used for living expenses
Length of Study: 2 years (Masters) or 3 years (PhD)
Frequency: Annual
Study Establishment: Macquarie University
Country of Study: Australia
Application Procedure: Check website for further details
Additional Information: Please see the website for details

For further information contact:

Tel:	(61) 2 9850 8911, 2 9850 8645
Fax:	(61) 2 9850 8799

© Springer Nature Limited 2019
Palgrave Macmillan (ed.), *The Grants Register 2020*,
https://doi.org/10.1057/978-1-349-95943-3

Email: jpiper@ics.mq.edu.au, jim.piper@mq.edu.au
Contact: Professor Jim Piper, Professor & Deputy Vice Chancellor

Doctor of Philosophy Scholarship-Artificial Intelligence in Medicine and Healthcare

Subjects: Scholarship is awarded to work on the project tiled, "Artificial Intelligence in Medicine and Healthcare"
Purpose: The aim of this research program is to investigate the future role of AI in healthcare and its social, ethical and technical implications
Eligibility: Australian and international students can apply for these scholarships. If English is not your first language then you will need to show that your English language skills are at a high enough level to succeed in your studies
Value: The MQRTP full-time stipend rate is $27,082 per annum tax-exempt, for up to 3 years (indexed annually) The scholarship is comprised of a Tuition Fee Offset and a Living Allowance Stipend
Study Establishment: Scholarship is awarded to work on the project tiled, "Artificial Intelligence in Medicine and Healthcare"
Country of Study: Australia
Application Procedure: Applicants will need to complete an HDR Candidature and Scholarship Application Form and arrange for two academic referee reports to be submitted to the Higher Degree Research Office
Closing Date: 31 July
Additional Information: For more details please visit the website scholarship-positions.com/phd-scholarship-artificial-intelligence-medicine-healthcare/2018/01/06

For further information contact:

Email: annie.lau@mq.edu.au

Macquarie University PhD Scholarship in Knowledge Acquisition and Cognitive Modelling

Subjects: Virtual training environment for risk assessment and spans the fields of cognitive modelling, knowledge acquisition, agent based systems for human learning, virtual reality and game technology
Purpose: To enable students to undertake research in related fields
Eligibility: Open to applicants who have completed, an Australian 4 year undergraduate degree with at least Second Class (Honours) division 1 in computing or a related field, or equivalent qualifications

Level of Study: Postdoctorate, Postgraduate
Type: Scholarships
Value: A$19,231 plus $5,000 top-up per year tax exempt
Length of Study: 3 years
Frequency: Annual
Study Establishment: Macquarie University
Country of Study: Australia
Application Procedure: Applicants must download the form from the website
Closing Date: 31 May (check with website)
Additional Information: Additional Information can be obtained from the Higher Degree Research Unit by phoning 61 02 9850 7277, by emailing pgschool@mq.edu.au or by downloading the form from the website

For further information contact:

Higher Degree Research Unit, Cottage C4C, Macquarie University, North Ryde, NSW, 2109, Australia

Email: richards@mq.edu.au

Macquarie Vice-Chancellor's International Scholarships

Purpose: The Macquarie University Vice-Chancellor's International Scholarship is awarded to recognise academic excellence for international students. This highly competitive scholarship is based on academic merit and awarded to future students
Eligibility: Applicants must: 1. Be a citizen of a country other than Australia or New Zealand. 2. Meet the University's academic and English requirements for the course (must hold a full offer of admission by the application deadline). 3. Achieved a minimum GPA equivalent of 5.0 out of 7.0 for Postgraduate applications; or a minimum ATAR equivalent of 90 out of 100 for Undergraduate applications. 4. Applied for a program that is longer than one session in duration. 5. Commence study in session and year indicated in the scholarship offer letter, and commencement may not be deferred
Level of Study: Postgraduate
Type: Scholarship
Value: A$10,000
Frequency: Annual
Country of Study: Australia
Closing Date: 14 June
Funding: Private

For further information contact:

Email: scholarships@mq.edu.au

Walter Heywood Bryan Scholarship for International Students in Australia

Subjects: Scholarship is awarded in the field of Earth Sciences

Purpose: The aim of the WH Bryan Scholarship is to advance the understanding of Queensland Earth Sciences by addressing a globally significant problem leading to impactful outcomes, with the supported project to be led by an outstanding PhD candidate

Eligibility: Australian and international students are eligible to apply. Students need to demonstrate that they have a good level of written and spoken English

Value: See the website

Study Establishment: Scholarship is awarded in the field of Earth Sciences

Country of Study: Australia

Application Procedure: The main written application is expected to be no more than 10 pages. Each application must be submitted from the host university

Closing Date: 30 April

Additional Information: For more details Please visit the website scholarship-positions.com/wh-bryan-scholarship-for-international-students-australia/2018/01/06

For further information contact:

Email: sef.hdrscholarships@qut.edu.au

Magna Carta College

Milford House, 1A Mayfield Road, Summertown, OX2 7EL, Oxford, United Kingdom

Tel: (44) 1865 593 131
Email: enquiries@magnacartacollege.org

Magna Carta College specializes in a range of business courses that can help you progress to university. Our programmes provide students with fast-track and alternative routes to achieving full degrees with work placement experience and scholarship opportunities available.

Global Ambassador Scholarship Programme (GASPR)

Purpose: GASPR is a global annual rolling scholarship programme and aims to give financial support for those who are eager to improve their education

Eligibility: Applicant should be 18+ years old and can be citizen of any country in the world. Scholarships are only valid during the June intake. The difference in tuition fee for the entire programme must be paid in full before the commencement of studies. Students must cover all other related costs on their own (accommodation, meals, visa, medical insurance, etc.)

Type: Scholarship

Value: The scholarship provides discount on basic tuition fee

Frequency: Annual

Country of Study: United Kingdom

Application Procedure: Applicants should send the application form along with the required documents to the email address gaspr@magnacartacollege.org. For detailed information, visit: magnacartacollege.org/programme/gaspr

Closing Date: 15 May

Additional Information: Successful scholarship candidates will not be able to apply for further College awards and payment plans: scholarships, discounts, installments, etc

Maine Restaurant Association

Russ Casey Scholarship

Purpose: This scholarship is available for Maine undergraduate students who plan to pursue a career in culinary arts or hospitality. Culinary arts students will be given first consideration

Eligibility: 1. Must be a resident of Maine. 2. Must be a United States citizen or permanent resident. 3. Must be a high school senior or older to apply for this undergraduate award. 4. Must be planning to pursue a culinary arts or hospitality-oriented program. Culinary arts students will be given first consideration. 5. This award is for United States students

Level of Study: Graduate

Type: Scholarship

Value: US$1,000

Frequency: Annual

Country of Study: United States of America

Application Procedure: Applications are available on the Maine Restaurant Association (MRA) website by searching for "scholarship". In addition to a completed application, the student must submit the following: a high school transcript; three letters of reference (two from teachers or counselors, and one from a member of the Maine Restaurant Association); and a typed letter of not more than 300 words describing his/her affiliation with the hospitality industry, why he/she is applying for this scholarship, and his/her career goals. Applications and all supporting materials must be sent to the address provided, and must be received by the deadline date

Closing Date: 12 April
Funding: Foundation

For further information contact:

45 Melville Street, Augusta, ME 04330, United States of America

Email: becky@mainerestaurant.com

Managed Care Organization

3000 Arlington Avenue, Toledo, OH 43199, United States of America

Contact: Dr Garry T Cole

The James Madison Memorial Fellowship

Purpose: The James Madison Memorial Fellowship is a federal program that offers secondary level teachers (both pre-service and in-service) of history and government up to US$24,000 to complete a master's degree in history, political science, or related fields
Eligibility: To be eligible, 1. You must be, or plan to become, a teacher of American history, American government, or any other social studies class, teaching topics on the Constitution at the secondary school level (grades 7-12). 2. In addition, you must be a United States citizen and either possess a bachelor's degree, or plan to receive a bachelor's degree no later than August 31 of the year in which you are applying. 3. Fellows will have the unique opportunity to attend an intensive summer institute to strengthen their knowledge of the origins and development of American constitutional government. The Foundation plans to offer one fellowship per state per year
Level of Study: Graduate
Type: Fellowship
Value: US$24,000
Frequency: Annual
Country of Study: United States of America
Application Procedure: 1. Applicants compete only against other applicants from the states of their legal residence. 2. Applicants are evaluated on their demonstrated commitment to a career teaching American history, American government, or civics classes where you will teach topics on the Constitution at the secondary school level; demonstrated intent to pursue and complete a program of graduate study that emphasizes the Constitution and offers instruction in that subject; demonstrated devotion to civic responsibility. 3. Demonstrated capacity for study and performance as

classroom teachers, and their proposed courses of graduate study. 4. Applicants will be evaluated without regard to race, color, religion, sex, age, national origin, disability, political affiliation, marital status, sexual orientation or other non-merit factors
Closing Date: 6 March
Funding: Private

For further information contact:

1613 Duke Street, Alexandria, VA 22314, United States of America

Email: Madison@scholarshipamerica.org

Manchester Master Bursary

School of Social Sciences - Manchester Master

Purpose: The bursaries are aimed at widening access to master's courses by removing barriers to postgraduate education for students from underrepresented groups, so applicants need to meet a number of criteria to be eligible. Last year, there were more eligible applications than places, so meeting the criteria is no guarantee of an award
Eligibility: 1. Eligible courses include LLM, MA, MEd, MBA, MEnt, MPhil, MRes, MSc, MSc by Research, MusM. 2. Courses can be studied full-time for one or two academic years or part-time for a maximum of two academic years. 3. You must be a home student paying home level tuition fees, and have been resident in the United Kingdom for at least three years prior to starting your undergraduate course for a purpose other than study. 4. You must be commencing your degree course in September. 5. You must not hold a master's qualification or higher. 6. You must have commenced your undergraduate course. 7. Inter-calating medical students taking a master's course are eligible to apply. Medical students should note that if they plan to intercalate and take a master's course between Years 2 and 3, they will not be eligible for UG loans in Year 3. However, there will be no interruption to funding if they intercalate between Years 3 and 4, and they will be eligible for the postgraduate loan
Level of Study: Postgraduate
Type: Bursary
Value: £3,000
Length of Study: 1 year
Frequency: Annual
Country of Study: Any country
Closing Date: 30 May
Funding: International office

For further information contact:

Email: funding@manchester.ac.uk

Manipal University in India

Tiger Circle Road, Madhav Nagar, Manipal, Karnataka 576104, India

Tel: (91) 92437 77733
Contact: Manipal University in India

Manipal Academy of Higher Education is synonymous with excellence in higher education. Over 28,000 students from 57 different nations live to learn and play in the sprawling University town, nestled on a plateau in Karnataka's Udupi district. It also has nearly 2,500 faculty and almost 10,000 other support and service staff, who cater to the various professional institutions in health sciences, engineering, management, communication and humanities which dot the Wi-Fi-enabled campus.

Doctor TMA Pai PhD Scholarships for International Students at Manipal University

Subjects: Disciplines - Atomic and Molecular Physics, Allied Health Science, Dentistry, Engineering, Life Science, Medicine, Nursing, Pharmacy, Science, Statistics, Regenerative Medicine, Public Health, Management, Information Science, Communication, Allied Hospitality Studies
Purpose: The Manipal Academy of Higher Education is currently accepting applications for Dr. TMA Pai PhD scholarship program. Indian and Foreign students are eligible to apply for this scholarship
Eligibility: Indian and Foreign students are eligible to apply for this scholarship. Applicants whose first language is not English are usually required to provide evidence of proficiency in English at the higher level required by the University
Value: Scholarship amount per candidate: Six months Probationary period: Rs. 14,000 per monthFirst year: Rs. 16,000 per monthSecond year: Rs. 17,000 per monthThird year: Rs. 18,000 per month
Study Establishment: Disciplines - Atomic and Molecular Physics, Allied Health Science, Dentistry, Engineering, Life Science, Medicine, Nursing, Pharmacy, Science, Statistics, Regenerative Medicine, Public Health, Management, Information Science, Communication, Allied Hospitality Studies
Country of Study: India

Application Procedure: Candidates should download the application form, complete it in all respects and send it to Admissions Office, Manipal Academy of Higher Education, Manipal - 576104 along with a demand draft for Rs. 600 drawn in favour of 'Manipal Academy of Higher Education' payable at Manipal/Udupi and the following enclosures: Attested copy of the degree certificate of qualifying examinations. Attested copies of the marks cards of qualifying examinations. Any other relevant documents
Closing Date: 31 March
Additional Information: For more details please browse the website scholarship-positions.com/dr-tma-pai-phd-scholarships-international-students-manipal-university-india/2018/02/23

For further information contact:

Email: admin@scholarship-positions.com

March of Dimes

1275 Mamaroneck Avenue, White Plains, NY 10605, United States of America

Tel: (1) 914 997 4488
Fax: (1) 914 997 4560
Email: researchgrantssupport@marchofdimes.com
Website: www.marchofdimes.com/professionals
Contact: Research and Grants Administration

Four major problems threaten the health of America's babies, birth defects, infant mortality, low birth weight and lack of prenatal care. The goal of the March of Dimes Birth Defects Foundation is to eliminate these problems so that all babies can be born healthy.

Basil O'Connor Starter Scholar Research Award

Purpose: This award is designed to support young scientists just embarking on their independent research careers and is limited, therefore, to those holding recent faculty appointments. The applicants' research interests should be consonant with those of the Foundation
Eligibility: The Basil O'Connor Starter Scholar Research Award is intended to be an initial independent grant to young investigators. Eligibility is thus restricted. PhD applicants should be 4 to 8 years past their degree and must hold a full-time faculty position at their current institution. For MD or MD/PhD applicants, the same 4–8 year timeline applies, but begins upon completion of the last year of clinical training

required for medical specialty board certification. Requests for exceptions (e.g. parental leave) should be directed to the Senior Vice President for Research & Global Programs

Type: Award/Grant
Value: Up to US$1,50,000 for 2 years
Frequency: Annual
Application Procedure: Deans, Chairs of Departments, or Directors of Institutes/Centers should submit nominations for this award addressed to the Senior Vice President for Research and Global Programs
Closing Date: 15 March
Funding: Private
Additional Information: These grants do not cover the recipient's salary, but do provide salary support for technical help. Please email any enquiries regarding award

For further information contact:

Email: researchgrantsSupport@marchofdimes.com

Marine Biological Association

Citadel Hill, Plymouth, Devon, PL1 2PB, United Kingdom

Tel: (44) 1752 633 341
Fax: (44) 1752 633 102
Contact: Dr A S Clare

MarTERA Call

Subjects: MarTERA will open a transnational call for collaborative research projects in different areas of maritime and marine technologies. 1. Environmentally friendly maritime technologies. Priority Area. 2. Development of novel materials and structures. Priority Area. 3. Sensors, automation, monitoring and observations. Priority Area. 4. Advanced manufacturing and production. Priority Area. 5. Safety and security
Purpose: The overall goal of the MarTERA Cofund is to strengthen the European Research Area (ERA) in maritime and marine technologies and Blue Growth
Level of Study: Graduate
Type: Research grant
Frequency: Annual
Country of Study: Any country
Closing Date: 29 March
Funding: Private

For further information contact:

Email: f.aslan@fz-juelich.de

Marines' Memorial Association

609 Sutter Street, San Francisco, CA 94102, United States of America

Tel: (1) 415 673 6672
Fax: (1) 415 441 3649
Email: michaelallen@marineclub.com
Website: www.marineclub.com

The Marines' Memorial Association is a non-profit veterans organization chartered to honor the memory of and commemorate the valour of Marines who have sacrificed in the nation's wars.

The Marine Corps Scholarship

Subjects: All subjects
Purpose: To provide financial assistance to children of active and former members of the United States Marines Corps
Eligibility: Open to children of the MMA members scholastic aptitude, community involvement and civic spirit. Applicant must be Planning to attend an accredited undergraduate college or vocational/technical institution in the upcoming academic year. Applicant must have a maximum family adjusted gross income for the current tax year that does not exceed US$90,000. Non-taxable allowances are not included in determining adjusted gross income. Applicant must have A GPA of at least 2.0
Level of Study: Postgraduate
Type: Scholarship
Value: Varies
Length of Study: Renewable
Frequency: Annual
Country of Study: Any country
Application Procedure: See the website
Closing Date: 30 April
Funding: Foundation
Contributor: The Marine Corps Foundation
Additional Information: Please see the website for further details and if you have any questions, contact us by email or phone

For further information contact:

Tel: (61) 415 673 6672 ext 293 or ext 215
Email: Member@MarineClub.com

Marshall Aid Commemoration Commission

Woburn House, 20-24 Tavistock Square, WC1H 9HF, London, United Kingdom

Tel:	(44) 20 7380 6704/3
Fax:	(44) 20 7387 2655
Email:	apps@marshallscholarship.org
Website:	www.marshallscholarship.org

The Marshall Aid Commemoration Commission is responsible for the selection and placement of recipients of Marshall scholarships from the United States to the United Kingdom. The first awards were presented in 1954.

Marshall Scholarships

Subjects: All subjects
Purpose: To provide intellectually distinguished young Americans with the opportunity to study in the United Kingdom, and thus to understand and appreciate the British way of life
Eligibility: Open to citizens of the United States of America who have graduated with a minimum grade point average of 3.7 or A from an accredited United States college not more than 2 years previously. Recipients are required to take a degree at their United Kingdom university. Preference is given to candidates who combine high academic ability with the capacity to play an active part in the United Kingdom university
Level of Study: Postgraduate
Type: Scholarship
Value: University fees, cost of living expenses, annual book grant, thesis grant, research and daily travel grants, fares to and from the United States and, where applicable, a contribution towards the support of a dependent spouse
Length of Study: 2 academic years, with a possible extension for a third year
Frequency: Annual
Study Establishment: Any suitable institution
Country of Study: United Kingdom
No. of awards offered: 900
Application Procedure: Applicants must submit an application form, university or college endorsement and four references. Information and application forms can be obtained from the British consulate in selected cities. Full details on application procedures can be obtained from the website. Application online at www.marshallscholarship.org/applications
Closing Date: Early-October of year preceding tenure
Funding: Government
No. of awards given last year: 37

No. of applicants last year: 900
Additional Information: Please see the website for further details www.marshallscholarship.org/about/generalinfo

For further information contact:

Georgia Pacific Center, Suite 3400, 133 Peachtree Street NE, Atlanta, GA 30303, United States of America

Email:	Atlanta@marshallscholarship.org
Contact:	British Consulate-General

Marshall Sherfield Fellowships

Purpose: To introduce American scientists and engineers to the cutting edge of United Kingdom science and engineering. It is intended that this in turn will build longer-term contacts and international links between the United Kingdom and the United States in key scientific areas
Eligibility: To qualify candidates should be citizens of the United States of America normally resident in the United States of America; and should hold a doctorate in a science or engineering subject by the time they take up their fellowship
Level of Study: Postdoctorate
Type: Fellowship
Length of Study: 1-2 years
Frequency: Annual
Country of Study: Any country
Application Procedure: Applications must be submitted with a completed form and associated documents and be scanned and emailed to m.denyer@acu.ac.uk by the deadline of October and hard copies must be couriered to The Marshall Commission, ACU, Woburn House, 20-24 Tavistock Square, London, WC1H 9HF, United Kingdom dated no later than the deadline. If candidates wish to receive acknowledgement of receipt of their completed application, they should include an email address
Closing Date: October
Contributor: Marshall Sherfield Fellowship Foundation
Additional Information: These fellowships are not available for the study of a higher degree

Maryland Association of Certified Public Accountants

Maryland Association of Certified Public Accountants Scholarship

Purpose: United States students who are Maryland residents enrolled full time in a college or university in Maryland with a grade point average of 3.0 or higher committed to pursuing careers as CPAs are eligible for this award. Students must have completed 60 hours of college credit at the time of award, with six or more of those hours in accounting courses **Eligibility:** 1. Must attend a college or university in Maryland. 2. Must be a current college sophomore or older to apply for this undergraduate and graduate award. The applicant must have completed at least 60 total credit hours by the time of the award, of which at least six hours of credit are in accounting courses (including Accounting Principles I and II). 3. Must be a full-time student. 4. Must be a resident of Maryland. 5. Must be a United States citizen. 6. Must demonstrate commitment to pursuing a career as a certified public accountant. 7. Must have a grade point average of 3.0 or higher. 8. This award is for United States students

Level of Study: Graduate

Type: Scholarship

Value: US$1,000

Frequency: Annual

Country of Study: United States of America

Application Procedure: Applications are available online from the Maryland Association of Certified Public Accountants (MACPA) website. In addition to the completed application, the applicant must submit the following: a signed applicant's statement; a complete copy of the SAR (Student Aid Report) which is generated upon completion of the FAFSA (Free Application for Federal Student Aid); and an official, sealed transcript from the previous semester which shows cumulative grade point average, total credit hours completed and hours completed during the previous semester

Closing Date: 15 April

Funding: Foundation

For further information contact:

901 Dulaney Valley Road, Suite 800, Townson, MD 21204-2683, United States of America

Tel: (1) 800 782 2036
Email: scholarships@swe.org

Massey University

Graduate Research School, Support, Private Bag 11-222, Palmerston North, New Zealand

Tel: (64) 6 350 5799 ext. 2909
Fax: (64) 6 350 5609
Email: scholarships@massey.ac.nz
Website: www.massey.ac.nz
Contact: Scholarships Officer

Massey University has over 40,000 students, of which 19,000 study on three campuses, with the remaining 21,000 studying by correspondence. The five colleges of business, education, science, humanities and social sciences and design, fine arts and music provide a comprehensive range of undergraduate and graduate degrees and diplomas all tailored to meeting national and international needs.

Allan Kay Undergraduate Memorial Scholarship

Purpose: The Allan Kay Undergraduate Memorial Scholarship helps students obtain a university education, especially those facing financial difficulties

Eligibility: Applicants must be: 1. enrolled full time at Massey University for an undergraduate degree in agriculture or horticulture (mainly with paper prefixes of 112, 117, 119, 189, 283, 284 and 285). 2. New Zealand-born residents. 3. no older than 30 years in the year which the scholarship is initially allocated

Level of Study: Graduate

Type: Scholarship

Value: NZ $3,000

Frequency: Annual

Country of Study: Any country

Application Procedure: The scholarship is awarded by the Trustees of the estate of Grace Edith Meliora Kay on the recommendation of the Applied Academic Programmes Scholarships Committee

Closing Date: 10 March

Funding: Private

For further information contact:

Massey University, Private Bag 11 222, Palmerston North, 4442, New Zealand

Email: K.Harrington@massey.ac.nz

C. Alma Baker Postgraduate Scholarship

Subjects: Agriculture, agriculture-related technologies or the study of rural society

Purpose: To encourage students enroling in Master's or doctoral thesis programmes

Eligibility: Open to candidates who are graduates and citizens of New Zealand. Awards are available for those intending to undertake postgraduate research either in New Zealand or overseas. Scholarships will be based on academic achievement

Level of Study: Graduate, Postgraduate

Type: Scholarship

Value: Maximum $13,000 a year for a Master's student and $20,000 a year for a doctoral student

Length of Study: 1 year for Master's and up to 3 years for a Doctoral programme

Frequency: Dependent on funds available

Country of Study: New Zealand

Application Procedure: Applicants must apply on the prescribed form to the Secretary, C. Alma Baker Trust. A certified copy of Academic Record, birth certificate, passport, or other proof of citizenship, and an outline of proposed research (not more than one page) must be enclosed with the application

Closing Date: 1 February

Funding: Trusts

Additional Information: Do not send original documents as application and attachments will not be returned. Information provided will be used by the trust or its representatives only for awarding scholarships and may be subject to verification procedures as appropriate

For further information contact:

C. Alma Baker Trust, c/o School of People, Environment & Planning Social Sciences Tower, Level 3, Massey University, Palmerston North, New Zealand

Email: Contact@massey.ac.nz
Contact: Professor Barrie Macdonald, Secretary

Dreamfields Farm Agricultural Scholarship

Subjects: Agricultural

Purpose: This scholarship was established in 2014, initially using money won by Bruce and Judy Woods from Dreamfields Farm in Bay of Plenty for the Ballance Farm Environment Award. It is designed to encourage students from their local secondary schools to study agriculture at Massey University

Level of Study: Graduate

Type: Scholarship

Value: NZ $1,000

Length of Study: 1 year

Frequency: Varies

Country of Study: Any country

Application Procedure: Apply online

Closing Date: 3 March

Funding: Trusts

For further information contact:

Email: K.Harrington@massey.ac.nz

Horizons Regional Council Sustainable Land Use Scholarships - Yr1 & Yr2 Students

Subjects: Horizons Regional

Purpose: Horizons Regional Council provides the scholarships to encourage students who are interested in a career in an environmental field, to undertake study in soil science and farm management as part of their undergraduate degree. Applicants are expected to have a solid interest in environmental management, soil, and land use mapping. The scholarships are considered to be a good entry point for year three and postgraduate Horizons Regional Council Sustainable Land Use Advanced Scholarships

Level of Study: Graduate

Type: Scholarship

Value: NZ $2,000

Length of Study: 3 year

Frequency: Varies

Country of Study: Any country

Application Procedure: Apply online

Closing Date: 13 April

Funding: Trusts

For further information contact:

Email: help@horizons.govt.nz

Horticulture NZ Undergraduate Scholarships

Purpose: Horticulture New Zealand (HortNZ) and the Horticentre Trust has a number of scholarships available for undergraduate students studying towards a degree in areas of interest to the Horticulture Industry

Level of Study: Graduate

Type: Scholarship

Value: NZ $4,500

Length of Study: 1 year

Frequency: Varies

Country of Study: Any country

Application Procedure: Apply online

Closing Date: 20 March

Funding: Trusts

For further information contact:

Email: info@hortnz.co.nz

Hurley Fraser Postgraduate Scholarship

Subjects: Applied sciences

Purpose: To support postgraduate research in agriculture and horticulture

Eligibility: Applicants must have enroled for a full-time post-graduate degree or a diploma in one of the Applied Sciences. The award is based on the candidate's academic attainment
Level of Study: Graduate
Type: Scholarship
Value: Up to NZ $2,000 per year
Study Establishment: Massey University
Country of Study: New Zealand
Application Procedure: Applicants must apply to the Scholarships Office, Graduate Research School on forms (ASSC.3) available from Massey Contact or can be downloaded from the website
Closing Date: 10 March
Contributor: John Alexander Hurley Scholarship and the Edith Fraser Agricultural and Horticultural Research Fund
Additional Information: The award shall be paid in May. Applications will not be accepted more than 3 months in advance of the closing date

For further information contact:

Tel: (64) 800 627 739
Email: Contact@massey.ac.nz

Leonard Condell Farming Postgraduate Scholarship

Purpose: Candidates must be New Zealand born graduates in science, agriculture or related disciplines (e.g. horticulture, veterinary science, food technology, biotechnology) and must enter fields of research for the benefit of some branch of agriculture in New Zealand
Eligibility: There are two types of scholarships. a) Postgraduate Scholarships: Candidates must be New Zealand born graduates in science, agriculture or related disciplines (e.g. horticulture, veterinary science, food technology, biotechnology) and must enter fields of research for the benefit of some branch of agriculture in New Zealand. The emolument shall be up to NZ $3,000 per annum. (b) PhD Scholarships: Candidates must be New Zealand born graduates in science, agriculture or related disciplines (e.g. horticulture, veterinary science, food technology, biotechnology) and must enter fields of research for the benefit of some branch of agriculture in New Zealand. The emolument shall be up to $4,000 per annum
Level of Study: Postgraduate
Type: Scholarship
Frequency: Annual
Country of Study: New Zealand
Application Procedure: All applications are acknowledged by email
Closing Date: 10 March
Funding: Individuals

Additional Information: Specific criteria is being added to the concern. Applications will NOT be accepted more than 3 months in advance of the closing date

For further information contact:

Scholarships Office, (NSATS), Massey University, Private Bag 11-222, Palmerston North, New Zealand

Email: K.Harrington@massey.ac.nz

Massey Doctoral Scholarship

Subjects: Agriculture, forestry, town planning, arts and humanities, business administration and management, education and teacher training, engineering, commercial law, media studies, mathematics and computer science, nursing, midwifery, natural sciences, social welfare and social work, environmental studies, religious studies, tourism, social and behavioural studies and air transport, design, fine arts or music
Purpose: To fund research towards a PhD degree
Eligibility: Open to those with a minimum qualification of a First Class (Honours) Degree
Level of Study: Doctorate
Type: Scholarship
Value: Please contact the organization
Length of Study: 3 years
Frequency: Annual
Study Establishment: The University
Country of Study: New Zealand
Application Procedure: Applicants must complete an application form, available from the University. Further details can be found on the website

For further information contact:

Email: R.L.Izzard@massey.ac.nz

Sir Alan Stewart Postgraduate Scholarships

Subjects: All subjects
Purpose: To encourage new postgraduate enrolments from other tertiary institutions and to assist Massey students to progress from undergraduate to postgraduate study
Eligibility: Applicant must be enroled or be intending to enrol full-time or part-time, in the year the award is to be made, in their initial year of a first postgraduate programme, undertaken either internally or extramurally and must be a New Zealand citizen or permanent resident who has completed an undergraduate degree at a New Zealand university

Level of Study: Graduate
Type: Scholarship
Value: NZ $4,000 per year for full-time students and pro-rated for part-time students
Frequency: Annual
Study Establishment: Any Massey University campus
Country of Study: New Zealand
Application Procedure: Check website for further details
Closing Date: 1 December
Additional Information: Consideration will normally only be given to students with a B+ average or better. Full-time students may hold the scholarship only once. Part-time students may re-apply to the maximum of NZ $4,000 in a period of 4 years from first enrolment in the postgraduate programme. Applications will NOT be accepted more than 3 months in advance of the closing date

For further information contact:

Email: Contact@massey.ac.nz

Sir John Logan Campbell Agricultural Scholarship

Subjects: Agriculture
Purpose: Sir John Logan Campbell was a successful Auckland businessman who lived from 1817 to 1912. He made many donations to the people of Auckland, including Cornwall Park. This scholarship has resulted from money gifted in 1925 from his endowment fund to help set up an agricultural teaching course in Palmerston North. It will be used to encourage 1st Year students from urban areas such as Auckland to begin a course in agriculture
Eligibility: The John Logan Campbell Agricultural Scholarship shall have a value determined each year from the interest earned on the capital and be open to 1st Year Massey University students who are enrolled full-time for the Bachelor of AgriCommerce degree, or the agriculture major within either the Bachelor of AgriScience degree or the Bachelor of Science degree
Level of Study: Graduate
Type: Scholarship
Value: NZ $2,000
Frequency: Varies
Country of Study: Any country
Application Procedure: Apply online
Closing Date: 3 March
Funding: Trusts

For further information contact:

Email: K.Harrington@massey.ac.nz

Sydney Campbell Undergraduate Scholarship

Subjects: Agriculture or horticulture
Purpose: The Sydney Campbell Scholarships are provided under the Will of the late Mr Sydney Campbell, Riverside Farm, Masterton, and are tenable at Massey University
Level of Study: Graduate
Type: Scholarship
Value: NZ $1,000
Length of Study: 1 year
Frequency: Varies
Country of Study: Any country
Application Procedure: Apply online
Closing Date: 3 March
Funding: Trusts

For further information contact:

Email: K.Harrington@massey.ac.nz

Turners and Growers Undergraduate Scholarships

Purpose: These scholarships are offered annually by T&G (formerlyTurners and Growers) to assist students of high academic calibre to undertake a degree that will provide them with the education and training to support the sustainable development of the New Zealand horticultural industry
Level of Study: Graduate
Type: Scholarship
Value: NZ $5,000
Length of Study: 3 year
Frequency: Varies
Country of Study: Any country
Application Procedure: Apply online
Closing Date: 3 March
Funding: Trusts

For further information contact:

Email: K.Harrington@massey.ac.nz

Materials Research Society

9800 McKnight Road, Pittsburgh, PA 15237, United States of America

Contact: Executive Director

The Material Handling Education Foundation

Purpose: The Material Handling Education Foundation, Inc. (www.mhefi.net) is an independent charitable organization that was established in 1976 with a mission to attract students to the material handling, logistics and supply chain industry by providing financial support

Eligibility: For the academic term, the following students are eligible to apply: 1. Students enrolled full time at a qualified four-year school in bachelors, masters or doctoral program that is on the target list of programs. Bachelors student must be classified as a junior or senior in the Fall term to be eligible. 2. Students from two-year, post-secondary schools (e.g., junior, community, or technical colleges) are eligible if the student has completed a minimum of two years of study and has been accepted as a transfer student to a target four-year baccalaureate program at a qualified school in the United States. 3. All applicants must be full-time students with a "B" grade point average in their major

Level of Study: Graduate

Type: Grants, work-study (not just grants)

Frequency: Annual

Country of Study: Any country

Application Procedure: The online application consists of three (3) letters of recommendation and all official transcripts must be received in the Foundation offices by 15 January. Official transcripts must be sent to the Foundation directly from the Registrar's office or equivalent office at the school

Closing Date: 31 March

Funding: Private

Additional Information: kindly contact Ms, Donna Varner for further communication

For further information contact:

Email: dvarner@mhi.org

Matsumae International Foundation (MIF)

Matsumae International Foundation Research Fellowship Program

Subjects: Fields of research such as natural science, engineering and medicine are considered with first priorities

Purpose: Towards a greater understanding of Japan and a lasting world peace

Eligibility: 1. Applicants must obtain a Letter of Invitation from host institutions in Japan. 2. Applicants must hold a PhD (Doctorate) degree, or be recognized by MIF as possessing equivalent academic qualifications. 3. Applicants must be at the age of 49 years old or younger at the time when documents are submitted. 4. Applicants must have sufficient abilities in the English or Japanese languages. 5. Applicants should not have past or current experiences of staying in Japan. (Except for short-term stay. E.g. sightseeing, conferences). 6. Applicants should be in employment in their home countries, and must return to their countries upon completion of their MIF fellowship tenure

Level of Study: Postdoctorate

Type: Fellowship

Length of Study: Between 3 months to 6 months

Frequency: Annual

Country of Study: Japan

No. of awards offered: 232

Application Procedure: Applications are evaluated by the Screening Committee of MIF on the basis of academic value and the degree of perfection of the research projects

Closing Date: 17:00 on 31 July (Japan Standard Time)

Funding: Foundation

Contributor: Donations

No. of awards given last year: 30

No. of applicants last year: 232

For further information contact:

The Matsumae International Foundation, 4-14-46, Kamiogi, Suginami-ku, Tokyo 167-0043, Japan

Tel: (81) 333 017 600

Email: contact@mif-japan.org

Max Planck Institute

The Max Planck Society grants scholarships of various amounts in line with the academic qualifications of the applicant

Criminology Scholarships for Foreign Researchers in Germany

Subjects: Criminology

Purpose: To pursue research programme

Eligibility: Preference is given to those researchers whose work promotes and advances the goals of the research program and the research focuses of the Institute

Level of Study: Doctorate, Postdoctorate, Research

Value: Doctoral scholarships: €1,365 per month Postdoctoral scholarships: €2,100 per month Research scholarships: €2,300 per month

Length of Study: 2 to 4 months

Country of Study: Germany
Closing Date: 31 May

Max Planck Institute for the History of Science Postdoctoral Fellowship in Germany

Purpose: The Max Planck Institute for the History of Science, Berlin is delighted to offer two postdoctoral fellows the opportunity to study in Germany starting on 1 September, for three years, with the employment contract
Eligibility: Candidates of all nationalities are invited to apply; applications from women are especially welcome. The Max Planck Society is committed to promoting handicapped individuals and encourages them to apply. Candidates should hold a doctorate in the history of science or related field at the time the position begins (PhD awarded in 2016 or later)
Level of Study: Postdoctorate
Type: Fellowship
Frequency: Annual
Country of Study: Any country
Application Procedure: Your application should contain: 1. Cover letter (indicating in which project you are interested). 2. Curriculum vitae including the list of publications. 3. Research prospectus (maximum 750 words). 4. Sample of writing. 5. Names and contact details of at least two referees
Closing Date: 15 November
Funding: Private

For further information contact:

Max-Planck-Institut för Wissenschaftsgeschichte, Boltzmannstrae 22, DEU 14195 Berlin, Germany

Max Planck Institute for Dynamics and Self-Organization

Am Faberg 17, DEU-37077 Göttingen, Germany

Tel: (49) 551 5176 0
Fax: (49) 551 5176-702
Email: info@ds.mpg.de
Contact: Max Planck Institute for Dynamics and Self-Organiz

The Max Planck Institute for Dynamics and Self-Organization (MPIDS) belongs to the Max Planck Society. Its research focus is in physics, with strong interdisciplinary aspects. It emerged in 2004 from the Max Planck Institute for Fluid Dynamics. The MPIDS is now right next to the Max Planck Institute for Biophysical Chemistry, with which it already had and continues to have cooperations in interdisciplinary areas of physics, biology, and medicine.

Max Planck Institute-DS Gauss Postdoctoral Fellowships for International Students

Subjects: The MPI-DS has recently appointed Oxford University theoretical physicist Prof. Ramin Golestanian as a new Director, and he is currently in the process of establishing the Department of Living Matter Physics. The new department will engage in a wide range of theoretical research aimed at a multi-scale understanding of the dynamics of living systems from a physical perspective
Purpose: These prestigious positions are aimed at postdoctoral researchers who have shown exceptional promise in their doctoral or early postdoctoral work, which needs to be in a relevant field
Eligibility: International students are eligible to apply for this fellowship. The candidate should hold a PhD/DPhil degree with a background in theoretical physics, applied mathematics, or related fields, have prior experience with non-equilibrium statistical physics of biological systems and soft matter, and be fluent in the English language
Type: Postdoctoral fellowship
Value: The candidate should hold a PhD/DPhil degree with a background in theoretical physics, applied mathematics, or related fields, have prior experience with non-equilibrium statistical physics of biological systems and soft matter, and be fluent in the English language. The Gauss fellowship is limited to two years with the possibility of extension. Salary is in accordance with the German state public service salary scale (E13 TVöD-Bund) and the corresponding social benefits. The earliest starting date is 1 March
Study Establishment: The MPI-DS has recently appointed Oxford University theoretical physicist Prof. Ramin Golestanian as a new Director, and he is currently in the process of establishing the Department of Living Matter Physics. The new department will engage in a wide range of theoretical research aimed at a multi-scale understanding of the dynamics of living systems from a physical perspective
Country of Study: Germany
Application Procedure: Please apply online on our application portal. Applications in writing will not be sent back. Please send your CV, publication list, a statement of research interest and at least two letters of reference. Your statement of research interest should be commensurate with the position you are applying to. In addition to the description of your

proposed research if relevant (depending on the position you are applying to), it should also briefly describe your past and current research interests and why you are interested in joining our department. The positions are open until they are filled. Once a position is filled, all applicants will be informed about the final decisions

Closing Date: The positions are open until they are filled. Once a position is filled, all applicants will be informed about the final decisions

Additional Information: Please check the website for more details scholarship-positions.com/mpi-ds-gauss-postdoctoral-fellowships-international-students-germany/2017/12/26/

For further information contact:

Email: ramin.golestanian@ds.mpg.de

Max Planck Institute for European Legal History

Postfach 50 07 01, DEU 60395, Frankfurt, Germany

Tel: (49) 69 789 78
Website: ww.rg.mpg.de
Contact: The Max Planck Institute for European Legal History

The Max Planck Institute for European Legal History (MPIeR) in Frankfurt is a world leader in researching the history of law in Europe and beyond. Its two research departments with more than 60 scholars, the unrivalled collections of its specialized library and its numerous national and international co-operations make it the central research hub for a global scientific community investigating the past, present and future of legal regimes.

Postdoctoral and Research Scholarships at MPIeR in Germany

Subjects: The main areas of research pursued at the Institute are: Department I - Professor Stefan Vogenauer (Legal transfer in the common law world, History of European Union Law, Fundamental issues concerning legal reception) and Department II - Professor Thomas Duve (Diversity, property and dependency regimes in Iberian Imperial territories (16th - 20th century), Legal history of the School of Salamanca, History of legal historiography: traditions of writing legal history)
Purpose: The Max Planck Institute for European Legal History (MPIeR) invites scholars from Germany and abroad to apply for Postdoctoral and Research Scholarships. The Institute will be awarding several scholarships for a research stay at the MPIeR

Eligibility: Scholars from both Germany and abroad are eligible to apply. If English is not your first language then you will need to show that your English language skills are at a high enough level to succeed in your studies
Type: Research
Value: The amount of the scholarship awarded is dependent on the scholarship holder's level of qualification. Postdocs receive €2,100.00 per month and research scholarship holders receive €2,300.00 per month
Study Establishment: The main areas of research pursued at the Institute are: Department I - Professor Stefan Vogenauer (Legal transfer in the common law world, History of European Union Law, Fundamental issues concerning legal reception) and Department II - Professor Thomas Duve (Diversity, property and dependency regimes in Iberian Imperial territories (16th - 20th century), Legal history of the School of Salamanca, History of legal historiography: traditions of writing legal history)
Country of Study: Germany
Application Procedure: Applications should be complete (including CV, list of publications, and the form "Additional Application Details") and submitted via the online application system. Furthermore, we request PDF copies of three major publications the applicant has authored within the last five years as well as the contact details of two personal referees
Closing Date: 31 May
Additional Information: For more information, please see the website scholarship-positions.com/postdoctoral-and-research-scholarships-mpier-germany/2018/02/13/

For further information contact:

Email: ruether@rg.mpg.de

Max Planck Institute for Human Cognitive and Brain Sciences

Stephanstrasse. 1 a, DEU-04103 Leipzig, Germany

Tel: (49) 341 9940-00
Fax: (49) 341 9940-221
Contact: Max Planck Institute for Human Cognitive and Brain

The Max Planck Institute for Human Cognitive and Brain Sciences is located in Leipzig, Germany. The institute was founded in 2004 by a merger between the former Max Planck

Institute of Cognitive Neuroscience in Leipzig and the Max Planck Institute for Psychological Research in Munich. It is one of 83 institutes in the Max Planck Society (Max Planck Gesellschaft).

Max Planck Institute-CBS Postdoctoral Position in Neuroscience of Pain Perception in Germany

Purpose: The aim of this research project is to understand how the multifaceted experience of pain is constructed from the interaction of external noxious input and internal expectations and predictions about pain

Eligibility: International students are eligible to apply for the position. Applicants must have a PhD (or equivalent degree) in neuroscience, psychology, cognitive science or a related discipline (biology, physics, computer science, engineering, etc

Type: Postdoctoral fellowship

Value: Remuneration is based on the pay scale of the Max Planck Society. The Max Planck Society is committed to increasing the number of individuals with disabilities in its workforce and therefore encourages applications from such qualified individuals

Study Establishment: Position is awarded to understand how the multifaceted experience of pain is constructed from the interaction of external noxious input and internal expectations and predictions about pain

Country of Study: Germany

Application Procedure: To apply, please submit a cover letter stating personal qualifications, a curriculum vitae, contact information for two referees, a brief statement describing your research experience, your academic achievements and your motivation to apply for this position (1 page), and copies of up to three of your publications. Please submit your application via our online system

Closing Date: 20 January

Additional Information: For more details please refer to the website scholarship-positions.com/mpi-cbs-postdoctoral-position-neuroscience-of-pain-perception-germany/2018/01/03/

For further information contact:

Email: eippert@cbs.mpg.de

Max Planck Research Group Neural Mechanisms of Human Communication

Max-Planck-Institut für Kognitions- und Neurowissenschaften, Stephanstrasse 1a, DEU-04103 Leipzig, Deutschland, Germany

Tel: (49) 341 9940-2476
Email: kriegstein@cbs.mpg.de
Contact: Mrs Prof. Dr. Katharina von Kriegstein

The positions are funded by the ERC consolidator grant SENSOCOM. The aim of the SENSOCOM project is to investigate the role of auditory and visual subcortical sensory structures in analysing human communication signals and to specify how their dysfunction contributes to human communication disorders such as developmental dyslexia and autism spectrum disorders.

Doctor of Philosophy and Postdoctoral Positions - Investigating Sensory Aspects of Human Communication

Subjects: Positions are awarded in Investigating Sensory Aspects of Human Communication

Purpose: The aim of the SENSOCOM project is to investigate the role of auditory and visual subcortical sensory structures in analysing human communication signals and to specify how their dysfunction contributes to human communication disorders such as developmental dyslexia and autism spectrum disorders

Eligibility: Applicants from Germany are eligible to apply

Value: Not Known

Study Establishment: Positions are awarded in Investigating Sensory Aspects of Human Communication

Country of Study: Germany

Application Procedure: To apply, please submit a CV, contact information of two references, a brief personal statement describing your qualifications and future research interests, copies of up to two of your publications. Please submit your application via our online system at tinyurl.com/yck4em3s (using subject heading "ERC 01/18")

Closing Date: Contact Employer

Additional Information: please visit the website for more information scholarship-positions.com/phd-postdoctoral-positions-investigating-sensory-aspects-of-human-communication/2018/02/19/

For further information contact:

Email: katharina.von_kriegstein@tu-dresden.de

Max Planck Society

Max-Planck-Institut für ausländisches und internationales Strafrecht - Stipendienstelle d. Verwaltung, Günterstalstrrasse. 73, DEU-79100 Freiburg i. Br, Germany

Contact: Max-Planck-Institut für ausländisches

Max-Planck-Institute for Foreign and International Criminal Law is offering research scholarships for foreign researchers whose work promotes and advances the goals of the research program and the research focuses of the Institute.

Max-Planck-Society Research Scholarships

Subjects: Comparative law, European criminal law, international criminal law, economic crime, terrorism, organized crime, and information law
Purpose: To foster individual research projects, the Max Planck Society offers foreign researchers the possibility of obtaining a scholarship
Type: Scholarship
Value: €1,365 per month for doctoral scholarships, €2,100 per month for post-doctoral scholarships and €2,300 per month for research scholarships
Country of Study: Any country
Application Procedure: For information concerning the application procedure, please email stipendien@mpicc.de
Closing Date: 31 May
Additional Information: Applications can be made either to the Department of Criminal Law (Prof. Dr. Dr. h.c. mult. Ulrich Sieber) or to the Department of Criminology (Prof. Dr. Dr. h.c. mult. Hans-Jörg Albrecht). Please clearly specify the chosen department in your application

For further information contact:

Email: stipendien@mpicc.de

McGill University

845 Sherbrooke Street West, Montréal, QC H3A 0G4, Canada

Tel: (1) 514 398 4066/4455
Fax: (1) 514 398 2499
Email: graduate.admissions@mcgill.ca,
  Maxwellboulton@hotmail.com
Website: www.mcgill.ca

McGill University is Canada's best known university, renowned internationally for the highest standards in teaching and research and the outstanding record of achievement of professors and students. In fields like neurosciences, pain, cancer research and public policy to name but a few McGill is at the forefront of achievement nationally and internationally.

Boulton Fellowship

Subjects: Law, especially with significance to the Canadian legal system and legal community
Purpose: To provide young scholars with an opportunity to pursue a major research project or to complete the research requirements for a higher degree
Eligibility: Open to candidates who have completed the residency requirements for a doctoral degree in law
Level of Study: Doctorate, Postdoctorate
Type: Fellowship
Value: C$50,000-55,000 per year
Length of Study: 1 year
Frequency: Annual
Study Establishment: McGill University
Country of Study: Canada
No. of awards offered: 20
Application Procedure: Application details are listed on web page
Closing Date: 1 February
Funding: Trusts
No. of awards given last year: 1
No. of applicants last year: 20

For further information contact:

Boulton Fund Administrators, Faculty of Law, McGill University, 3644 Peel Street, Montreal, Quebec H3A 1W9, Canada

Email: staffappointments.law@mcgill.ca

Internal Studentships Past and Current Year

Subjects: Internal Studentships are open to highly qualified Faculty of Medicine graduate students who are registered full-time in a research training program (Thesis) leading to an MSc or PhD degree
Purpose: Students who apply for a Faculty of Medicine Internal Studentship are automatically considered for every award for which they are eligible
Eligibility: To be eligible for the studentship competition: 1. Students must be registered full-time in a Faculty of Medicine graduate research training program. 2. At the time of application, student must be in MSc1 for Masters level students or between PhD1 and PhD4 for Doctoral level students. MSc 2 students must have already been accepted to fast-track
Level of Study: Graduate
Type: Studentship
Value: Faculty of medicine will award an amount of C$10,000 and C$12,000 for PhD students
Frequency: Annual

Country of Study: Any country
Application Procedure: Listed amenities are required to process the internal studentship. 1. Studentship Application Form. 2. Publication List. 3. All graduate and undergraduate transcripts. 4. cgpa calculation. 5. supervisor biosketch form. 6. 2 letter of support
Closing Date: mid August
Funding: Private

For further information contact:

McIntyre Medical Building, 3655 Promenade Sir William Osler, Montreal, QC H3G 1Y, Canada

Email: submitgrad.med@mcgill.ca

McGill University PhD Studentships in Neurolinguistics

Subjects: Language and neuroscience
Purpose: To aid deserving students who wish to pursue a career in neuroscience
Eligibility: Open to applicants who possess a First class (Honours) degree in linguistics, psychology, communication disorders or a related discipline, preferably with courses in psycho or neuro linguistics
Level of Study: Postgraduate
Type: Studentship
Value: C$20,000 per year plus support for presenting work at research meetings
Frequency: Annual
Study Establishment: McGill University
Country of Study: Canada
Application Procedure: Applicants must send their curriculum vitae and a detailed cover letter describing their research interests and academic goals
Closing Date: 4 December

For further information contact:

McGill University, SCSD 1266, Avenue des Pins Ouest, Montreal, Quebec H3A 1A3, Canada

Email: marc.pell@mcgill.ca
Contact: Dr Marc Pell

Media@McGill

Website: mediaatmcgill.ahcs@mcgill.ca
Contact: Media@McGill Postdoctoral Fellowship

Media@McGill is a hub of interdisciplinary research, scholarship and public outreach on issues in media, technology and culture, located in the Department of Art History and Communication Studies at McGill University in Montreal, Canada.

Media@McGill Postdoctoral Fellowship

Subjects: Media, technology and culture
Purpose: Media@McGill's residential postdoctoral fellowships are awarded to scholars from the humanities and social sciences, working on any historical period
Eligibility: The Media@McGill Postdoctoral Fellowship is open to both national and international scholars who have completed their doctoral degree in a university other than McGill. Fluency in English is essential; working knowledge of French is an asset
Value: C$45,000 for 1 year
Study Establishment: Media@McGill
Country of Study: Canada
Closing Date: 3 February
Additional Information: For additional information, please contact mediaatmcgill.ahcs@mcgill.ca

For further information contact:

840 Dr Penfield, Room 231, Montreal, QC H3A 0G2, Canada

Tel: (1) 514 398 1029

Medical Library Association (MLA)

65 East Wacker Place, Suite 1900, Chicago, IL 60601-7246, United States of America

Tel: (1) 312 419 9094
Fax: (1) 312 419 8950
Email: grants@mlahq.org
Website: www.mlanet.org
Contact: Maria Lopez, CAE, Executive Director

The Medical Library Association (MLA) is organized exclusively for scientific and educational purposes, and is dedicated to the support of health sciences research, education and patient care. MLA fosters excellence in the professional achievement and leadership of health sciences libraries and information professionals to enhance the quality of healthcare, education and research.

Eugene Garfield Research Fellowship

Subjects: Health sciences librarianship, information sciences and research

Purpose: To stimulate research into the history of information sciences to increase the underlying knowledge-base and enhance the current and future practice of the information professions, particularly health sciences librarianship and health informatics

Eligibility: Health sciences librarians and information scientists, health professionals, researchers, educators, and administrators are eligible. Applicants must have a master's or doctor's degree or be enroled in a program leading to such a degree and demonstrate a commitment to the health sciences

Type: Fellowship

Value: US$5,000

Length of Study: 1 year

Frequency: Annual

Application Procedure: Applicants must submit a complete application, curriculum vitae, a detailed research proposal, and letter(s) of support from the applicant's home institution

Closing Date: 1 December

Funding: Private

Additional Information: The fellowship is not designed to support research for a doctoral dissertation or master's thesis. For more information about any of MLA's grants or scholarships, contact Maria Lopez at (1) 312 419 9094 (x15)

For further information contact:

Email: grants@mlahq.org

Medical Research Council (MRC)

David Phillips Building, Polaris House, North Star Avenue, Wiltshire, SN2 1FL, Swindon, United Kingdom

Tel:	(44) 20 7636 5422
Fax:	(44) 20 7436 6179
Email:	joaune.mccallum@headoffice.mrc.ac.uk
Website:	www.mrc.ac.uk

The Medical Research Council (MRC) offers support for talented individuals who want to pursue a career in the biomedical sciences, public health and health services research. It provides its support through a variety of personal award schemes that are aimed at each stage in a clinical or non-clinical research career.

Biomedical Catalyst: Developmental Pathway Funding Scheme (DPFS)

Purpose: The DPFS scheme is a key part of our Translational Research Strategy and supports the translation of fundamental discoveries toward benefits to human health. It funds the pre-clinical development and early clinical testing of novel therapeutics, devices and diagnostics, including "repurposing" of existing therapies

Eligibility: The following condition applies to this scheme, in addition to our normal rules: Individuals may be the principal investigator (the named, lead applicant) on one application per round. All costs towards the funding scheme should be fully justified within a proposal and the Panel will assess value for money in the context of the proposed work

Level of Study: Graduate

Type: Funding support

Frequency: Annual

Country of Study: Any country

Application Procedure: Proposals are assessed in a -two-stage process. 1. The first step involves review of an outline proposal (download the outline Case for Support form here). Successful outline applicants are invited to submit a full application, which undergoes external peer review before a further, more detailed, review by the Panel. 2. The total assessment time for an application submitted to MRC, from outline submission to full decision, is approximately 26 weeks. All applicants will receive feedback from the assessment process. Guidance for preparation of full proposals will be provided to successful applicants with the outline feedback

Closing Date: 21 March

Funding: Private

Additional Information: Fundamental or investigative research not linked to a development plan (supported by the Research Boards Clinical studies where the primary purpose is to investigate disease mechanism (supported by the Research Boards Late-phase clinical trials (supported by the MRC-NIHR Efficacy and Mechanism Evaluation Programme and the NIHR Health Technology Assessment Programme)

For further information contact:

Email: DPFSandDCS@mrc.ukri.org

Medical Research Council Career Development Award

Subjects: Biomedical sciences

Purpose: To award outstanding researchers who wish to consolidate and develop their research skills and make the transition from postdoctoral research and training to becoming independent investigators, but who do not hold established positions

Eligibility: It is expected that all applicants will hold a PhD or MPhil in a basic science and will have at least 3 years of postdoctoral research experience

Level of Study: Postdoctorate, Research

Type: Fellowship

Value: Competitive personal salary support plus research support staff at the technical level, research expenses, capital equipment and a travel allowance for attendance at scientific conferences

Length of Study: Maximum duration of upto 5 years

Frequency: Annual

Study Establishment: A suitable university department or similar institution

Country of Study: United Kingdom

No. of awards offered: 86

Application Procedure: Applicants must submit a personal application. Forms and further details are available from the MRC

Closing Date: 25 April

Funding: Government

No. of awards given last year: 13

No. of applicants last year: 86

Additional Information: Awards may occasionally be jointly funded with other bodies. Please contact the Fellowships Section at the MRC for further details. Please see the website for further details www.mrc.ac.uk/Fundingoppor tunities/Fellowships/Careerdevelopmentaward/index.htm

For further information contact:

Email: fellows@headoffice.mrc.ac.uk

Medical Research Council Clinical Research Training Fellowships

Subjects: Biomedical sciences

Purpose: To provide an opportunity for specialized or further research training leading to the submission of a PhD, DPhil, or MD

Eligibility: Open to hospital doctors, dentists, general practitioners, nurses, midwives and allied health professionals. Residence requirements apply

Level of Study: Postgraduate, Research

Type: Fellowship

Value: An appropriate clinical academic salary will be provided along with a fixed sum for research expenses and a travel allowance for attendance at scientific conferences

Length of Study: Up to 3 years

Study Establishment: A suitable university department or similar institution

Country of Study: United Kingdom

No. of awards offered: 169

Application Procedure: Applicants must submit a personal application. Forms and further details are available from the MRC

Closing Date: 11 September by 4 pm (First round) and 15 January by 4 pm (Second round)

Funding: Government

No. of awards given last year: 39

No. of applicants last year: 169

Additional Information: In addition to this scheme, the MRC also offers Joint Training Fellowships with the Royal Colleges of Surgeons of United Kingdom and Edinburgh and the Royal College of Obstetricians and Gynaecologists. These awards are aimed at individuals whose long-term career aspirations involve undertaking academic clinical research. Fellowships may also be jointly funded with the MS Society or the Prior Group. Please contact the Fellowships Section at the MRC for further details and see the website www.mrc.ac.uk/skills-careers/fellowships/clinical-fellowships/clinical-research-training-fellowship-crtf

For further information contact:

Email: validate@ndm.ox.ac.uk

Medical Research Council Clinician Scientist Fellowship

Subjects: Biomedical sciences

Purpose: To provide an opportunity for outstanding clinical researchers who wish to consolidate their research skills and make the transition from postdoctoral research and training to becoming independent investigators

Eligibility: The scheme is open to hospital doctors, dentists, general practitioners, nurses, midwives and allied health professionals. All applicants must have obtained their PhD or MD in a basic science or clinical project, or expect to have received their doctorate by the time they intend to take up an award, and must not hold tenured positions

Level of Study: Postdoctorate, Research

Type: Fellowship

Value: Competitive personal salary support plus research support staff at the technical level, research expenses, capital equipment and a travel allowance for attendance at scientific conferences

Length of Study: Up to 4 years

Frequency: Annual

Study Establishment: A suitable university department or similar institution

Country of Study: United Kingdom

No. of awards offered: 40

Application Procedure: Applicants must submit a personal application. Forms and further details are available from the MRC

Closing Date: 10 January

Funding: Government

No. of awards given last year: 10

No. of applicants last year: 40

Additional Information: Please see the website for further details www.mrc.ac.uk/skills-careers/fellowships/clinical-fellowships/clinician-scientist-fellowship-csf/

For further information contact:

Email: fellows@headoffice.mrc.ac.uk

Medical Research Council Industrial CASE Studentships

Subjects: Any biomedical science

Purpose: To enhance links between academia and industry in the provision of high-quality research training

Eligibility: Candidates should have graduated with a good Honours Degree from a United Kingdom academic institution in a subject relevant to the MRC's scientific remit. This should be an Upper Second Class (Honours) Degree or higher. The MRC will, however, consider qualifications or a combination of qualifications and experience that demonstrates equivalent ability and attainment, e.g. a Lower Second Class (Honours) Degree can be enhanced by a Master's degree. A copy of the regulations governing residence eligibility may be obtained from the Council

Level of Study: Postgraduate

Value: A tax-free maintenance stipend depending on United Kingdom location, university tuition fees up to the current DFEE recommended limit plus college fees, where applicable. Awards also include a fixed sum for conference travel expenses and a support grant to the university department to help cover incidental costs of students' training. As a measure of interest and involvement the industrial company is expected to make a financial contribution to the cost of the studentship

Length of Study: Up to 4 years

Frequency: Annual

Study Establishment: Universities, medical schools, industry and other academic institutions

Country of Study: United Kingdom

No. of awards offered: 23

Application Procedure: The MRC does not make awards directly to students. Awards are made to industrial partners who apply for studentships by application. The individual or academic partner will then advertise for students to apply for their awards. Students who wish to apply for a studentship are advised to contact the department where they wish to study to see if it has an allocation of awards

Closing Date: 10 July

Funding: Commercial

No. of awards given last year: 10

No. of applicants last year: 23

Additional Information: Applicants should ensure that they have read the MRC Industrial CASE Scheme Guidance Notes before completing their application. Please see the website for further details www.mrc.ac.uk/skills-careers/studentships/how-we-fund-studentships/industrial-case-studentships

For further information contact:

Email: students@headoffice.mrc.ac.uk

Medical Research Council Senior Clinical Fellowship

Subjects: Biomedical sciences

Purpose: Aim to develop outstanding medically and other clinically qualified professionals such that they become research leaders

Eligibility: Open to nationals of any country. Applicants are expected to have proven themselves to be independent researchers, be well qualified for an academic research career and demonstrate the promise of becoming future research leaders. The scheme is open to hospital doctors, dentists, general practitioners, nurses, midwives and allied health professionals. Applicants must hold a PhD or MD in a basic science or clinical project and have at least 3 years of post-doctoral research experience

Level of Study: Postdoctorate, Research

Type: Fellowship

Value: Competitive personal salary support is provided plus research support staff at the technical and postdoctoral level, research expenses, capital equipment and a travel allowance for attendance at scientific conferences

Length of Study: 5 years

Frequency: Annual

Study Establishment: A suitable university department or similar institution

Country of Study: United Kingdom

No. of awards offered: 8

Application Procedure: Applicants must submit a personal application. Forms and further details are available from the MRC

Closing Date: 9 April

Funding: Government

No. of awards given last year: 1

No. of applicants last year: 8

Additional Information: Please see the website for further details www.mrc.ac.uk/skills-careers/Fellowships

For further information contact:

Email: information@psych.ox.ac.uk

Medical Research Council Senior Non-Clinical Fellowship

Subjects: Biomedical sciences
Purpose: To provide support for non-clinical scientists of exceptional ability to concentrate on a period of research
Eligibility: Open to nationals of any country. Applicants are expected to have proven themselves to be independent researchers, be well qualified for an academic research career and demonstrate the promise of becoming future research leaders. Applicants should normally hold a PhD or DPhil in a basic science project, have at least 6 years of relevant postdoctoral research experience and not hold a tenured position
Level of Study: Postdoctorate, Research
Type: Fellowship
Value: Competitive personal salary support is provided plus research support staff at the technical and postdoctoral level, research expenses, capital equipment and a travel allowance for attendance at scientific conferences
Length of Study: 7 years
Frequency: Annual
Study Establishment: A suitable university department or similar institution
Country of Study: United Kingdom
No. of awards offered: 24
Application Procedure: Applicants must submit a personal application. Forms and further details are available from the MRC
Closing Date: 28 April
Funding: Government
No. of awards given last year: 3
No. of applicants last year: 24
Additional Information: Please see the website for further details www.mrc.ac.uk/skills-careers/Fellowships/

For further information contact:

Email: fellows@headoffice.mrc.ac.uk

Medical Research Council Special Training Fellowships in Health Services and Health of the Public Research

Subjects: Biomedical sciences in health services research and health of the public, as defined by the MRC

Purpose: To provide support for researchers wishing to gain further training in multidisciplinary research to address problems of direct relevance to the health services within the United Kingdom
Eligibility: Open to non-medical graduates, hospital doctors, dentists, general practitioners, nurses, midwives and allied health professionals who are seeking a research career in health services and research
Level of Study: Postdoctorate, Research
Type: Fellowship
Value: An appropriate academic salary will be provided along with a fixed sum for research expenses and a travel allowance for attendance at scientific conferences
Length of Study: Up to 4 years
Frequency: Annual
Study Establishment: A suitable university department or similar institution
Country of Study: United Kingdom
No. of awards offered: 52
Application Procedure: Applicants must submit a personal application. Forms and further details are available from the MRC
Closing Date: Usually around September/October, but applicants are advised to check the website for details
Funding: Government
No. of awards given last year: 10
No. of applicants last year: 52
Additional Information: Some awards are jointly funded with the Department of Health

For further information contact:

Email: joaune.mccallum@headoffice.mrc.ac.uk

Medical Research Council/RCOG Clinical Research Training Fellowship

Subjects: Biomedical sciences
Purpose: To encourage clinicians to become involved in research and to promote research of relevance to the Royal College of Obstetricians and Gynaecologists
Eligibility: Open to members of the RCOG wishing to pursue research at PhD or MD level. Applicants must have a minimum of one year of experience in clinical obstetrics and gynaecology and hold part one membership of the college. Residence requirements apply
Level of Study: Postgraduate, Research
Type: Fellowship
Value: £50,000-100,000 (estimated total funds is £80,000). Predoctoral level-the award provides a competitive personal salary, up to Specialist Registrar but not including NHS Consultant level, a Research Training Support Grant of up to

£10,000 per year (items must be detailed and justified), and an annual travel allowance of £450. Postdoctoral level-the fellowship provides a competitive personal salary, up to Specialist Registrar but not including NHS consultant level, research expenses, and travel costs at an appropriate level for the research, under full economic costs (FEC). For full details of what funding includes at each level please see their website

Length of Study: 1-3 years
Frequency: Annual
Study Establishment: A suitable university or similar institution
Country of Study: United Kingdom
No. of awards offered: 2
Application Procedure: Applicants must contact the Fellowships Section, Research Career Awards of the MRC for details
Closing Date: Check with website
Funding: Government
No. of awards given last year: 2
No. of applicants last year: 2
Additional Information: Please see the website for further details

For further information contact:

Tel: (44) 20 7670 5485
Email: fellows@headoffice.mrc.ac.uk

Medical Research Scotland

Turcan Connell, Princes Exchange, 1 Earl Grey Street, EH3 9EE, Edinburgh, United Kingdom

Tel: (44) 131 659 8800
Fax: (44) 131 228 8118
Email: enquiries@medicalresearchscotland.org.uk
Website: www.medicalresearchscotland.org.uk
Contact: The Trust Administrator

Medical Research Scotland is comprehensive in its support and is not focused on research into any one disease or disorder. It supports the broad spectrum of medical research, all aimed at improving the understanding of basic disease mechanisms, diagnosis, treatment or prevention of disease or advances in medical technology.

Doctor of Philosophy Studentship

Subjects: Any of the biomedical, clinical, physical, computing or engineering sciences or mathematics, provided that the research addresses a question relevant to the cause, diagnosis, prevention or treatment of any disease, or to the development of medical technology

Purpose: To provide fully funded four year PhD Studentships, delivered collaboratively by a recognized Scottish University/Research Institution and a company working in medically-relevant research, which incorporate enhanced and tailored academic and commercial training and experience
Eligibility: Open to Scottish universities/research institutions working in conjunction with a trading company involved in medically-relevant life sciences research, to deliver 4 high-quality PhD studentship for suitably highly-qualified and motivated graduates of any country
Level of Study: Postgraduate
Type: Studentship
Value: Approx. €115,000
Length of Study: 4 years
Frequency: Annual
Study Establishment: Scottish Universities, Higher Education or research institutions recognized as such
Country of Study: Scotland
Application Procedure: Applications must be submitted online, following the information available at medicalresearchscotland.org.uk/
Closing Date: July (check website for exact dates)
Contributor: Income from the original endowment fund, established when the charity came into being in 1953, invested and augmented by voluntary donations and bequests
Additional Information: Applications must be submitted by a university and an appropriate company and not by prospective students

Medical Research Scotland Sponsored Daphne Jackson Trust Fellowships

Subjects: Any of the biomedical, clinical, physical, computing or engineering sciences or mathematics, provided that the research addresses a question relevant to the cause, diagnosis, prevention or treatment of any disease, or to the development of medical technology
Purpose: To provide three year part time fellowships for those wishing to return to medical research at a Scottish University or Research Institution after a career break of three years or more. Fellowships are awarded in conjunction with the Daphne Jackson Trust
Eligibility: Open to Scottish universities/research institutions working in conjunction with a trading company involved in medically-relevant life sciences research, to deliver 4 high-quality PhD studentship for suitably highly-qualified and motivated graduates of any country
Level of Study: Postdoctorate, Professional development
Type: Fellowship
Value: Approx. £115,000

Length of Study: 3 years
Frequency: Annual
Study Establishment: Scottish Universities, Higher Education or research institutions recognized as such
Country of Study: Scotland
Application Procedure: Applications must be submitted online, following the information available at medicalresearchscotland.org.uk/
Contributor: Income from the original endowment fund, established when the charity came into being in 1953, invested and augmented by voluntary donations and bequests

For further information contact:

Email: enqumes@med1calresearchscotland.org.uk, alex.graham@medicalresearchscotland.org

Meet The Composer, Inc.

90 John Street, Suite 312, New York, NY 10038, United States of America

Tel: (1) 212 645 6949
Fax: (1) 212 645 9669
Email: mtc@meetthecomposer.org
Website: www.newmusicusa.org

Meet The Composer's mission is to increase artistic and financial opportunities for American composers by fostering the creation, performance, dissemination and appreciation of their music.

Commissioning Music/United States of America

Subjects: Music commissioning
Purpose: To support the commissioning of new works
Eligibility: Open to citizens of the United States of America only. Organizations that have been producing or presenting for at least 3 years are eligible and may be dance, chorus, orchestra, opera, theatre and music-theatre companies, festivals, arts presenters, public radio and television stations, internet providers, soloists and small performing ensembles of all kinds, e.g. jazz, chamber, new music, etc
Level of Study: Professional development
Type: Grant
Value: Up to US$10,000-20,000
Frequency: Annual
Country of Study: United States of America
No. of awards offered: 150-200

Application Procedure: Individuals cannot apply on their own. Host organizations must submit completed application forms and accompanying materials
Closing Date: 19 March (check with website)
Contributor: Offered in partnership with the National Endowment for the Arts
No. of awards given last year: 20-30
No. of applicants last year: 150-200
Additional Information: Please see the website for further details www.newmusicusa.org/grants/commissioning-music-usa/

For further information contact:

Tel: (1) 212 645 6040 ext 102
Email: swinship@newmusicusa.org
Contact: Scott Winship, Director of Grantmaking Programs

JP Morgan Chase Regrant Program for Small Ensembles

Subjects: Musical performance
Purpose: To support small New York City-based ensembles and music organizations committed to performing the work of living composers and contemporary music
Eligibility: Open to organizations focused primarily or exclusively on new music and living composers, improvisers, sound artists or singer/songwriters
Level of Study: Professional development
Type: Grant
Value: US$1,000-5,000
Frequency: Annual
Country of Study: United States of America
No. of awards offered: 75-100
Application Procedure: Applicants must contact the organization
Closing Date: Contact organization
Funding: Commercial
Contributor: In partnership with JP Morgan Chase
No. of awards given last year: 15-20
No. of applicants last year: 75-100

For further information contact:

Email: east.giving@jpmchase.com

Melville Trust for Care and Cure of Cancer

Tods Murray LLP, Edinburgh Quay, 133 Fountain Bridge, EH3 9AG, Edinburgh, United Kingdom

Tel: (44) 131 656 2000
Fax: (44) 131 656 2020
Email: melvilletrust@todsmurray.com
Contact: The Secretary

Melville Trust for Care and Cure of Cancer Research Fellowships

Subjects: The care and cure of cancer
Purpose: To fund innovative research work in the care or cure of cancer
Eligibility: Applicants, who need not necessarily hold a medical qualification or have experience of research, should have formulated proposals for a research project which have been discussed with an established research worker in the field. The applicant should normally be under 30 years of age
Level of Study: Research
Type: Fellowship
Value: £2,000
Length of Study: 1-3 years
Frequency: Annual
Study Establishment: One of the clinical or scientific departments in Lothian, Borders, Fife or Dundee
No. of awards offered: 4
Application Procedure: Applicants must complete an application form and then be interviewed
Closing Date: 28 February
Funding: Private
No. of awards given last year: 1
No. of applicants last year: 4

For further information contact:

Melville Trust for Care and Cure of Cancer, c/o Tods Murray LLP, Edinburgh Quay 133 Fountain Bridge, Edinburgh EH3 9AG, United Kingdom

Email: melvilletrust@todsmurray.com

Melville Trust for Care and Cure of Cancer Research Grants

Subjects: The care and cure of cancer
Purpose: To fund innovative research work in cure or care of cancer
Eligibility: Applicants need not necessarily hold a medical qualification or have experience of research. Research support by the Trust will be carried out in a clinical or scientific department in Lothians, Borders, Fife or Dundee, the head of which must signify his or her approval of the application
Level of Study: Research

Type: Grant
Value: Up to £25,000
Length of Study: 1-3 years
Frequency: Annual
Study Establishment: One of the clinical or scientific departments in Lothian, Borders, Fife or Dundee
No. of awards offered: 7
Application Procedure: Applicants must complete an application form
Closing Date: 28 February
Funding: Private
No. of awards given last year: 1
No. of applicants last year: 7

Memorial Foundation for Jewish Culture

50 Broadway, 34th Floor, New York, NY 10004, United States of America

Tel: (1) 212 425 6606
Fax: (1) 212 425 6602
Email: office@mfjc.org
Website: www.mfjc.org
Contact: Jeni S. Friedman, Executive Vice President

The Memorial Foundation for Jewish Culture is committed to the creation, intensification, and dissemination of Jewish culture worldwide, the development of creative programs to meet the emerging needs of Jewish communities globally, and to serving as a central forum for identifying and supporting innovative programs to insure the continuation of creative Jewish life wherever Jewish communities exist.

Ephraim Urbach Post Doctoral Fellowship

Subjects: Jewish Studies
Purpose: To assist recent recipients of the PhD in a field of Jewish studies in publishing their first book, launching their scholarly career, and/or furthering research in their area of special interest
Eligibility: Graduates of a PhD programme in a field of Jewish studies who achieved superior grades, in graduate school, completed their dissertation with distinction, and who show promise of distinguished academic careers are eligible to apply
Level of Study: Postgraduate
Type: Fellowship

Value: Up to US$10,000
Length of Study: 1 academic year
Frequency: Annual
Country of Study: Any country
Application Procedure: Applicants must be nominated by the head of the department at which they completed their PhD and must have received their PhD within 3 years of the date of application. Applicants must write requesting an application
Closing Date: 31 March

For further information contact:

Tel: (1) 212 425 6606
Email: office@mfjs.org

Memorial University of Newfoundland (MUN)

Memorial University of Newfoundland, St. John's, PO Box 4200, St Johns, NL A1C 5S7, Canada

Tel: (1) 709 737 8000
Fax: (1) 709 864 3514
Email: info@mun.ca
Website: www.mun.ca

Located in Canada's most easterly province, Newfoundland and Labrador, Memorial University of Newfoundland (MUN) offers a diverse selection of Graduate programmes leading to diplomas, Master's and Doctoral degrees in the arts, sciences, professional and interdisciplinary areas of study. Their goal is to promote excellence in all aspects of Graduate education in order to assist students to fulfil their personal goals and to prepare for a productive career.

School of Graduate Studies F. A. Aldrich Award

Subjects: All subjects
Purpose: To financially assist students with exceptional academic achievement to study further
Eligibility: Open to full-time Canadian students on the basis of exceptional academic achievement
Level of Study: Postdoctorate, Predoctorate
Type: Fellowship
Value: C$2,000
Frequency: Annual
Study Establishment: Memorial University of Newfoundland
Country of Study: Any country
Closing Date: Check with website

Additional Information: Please see the website for details www.mun.ca/sgs/current/scholarships/internal_nominated.php#sgsaldrich

For further information contact:

Email: info@mun.ca

The Dr Ethel M. Janes Memorial Scholarship in Education

Subjects: Reading or language arts
Purpose: To aid students who want to specialize in reading and language arts and to those who want to make a career in research and teaching in primary and elementary education
Eligibility: Must be a full-time graduate student (not working more than 24 hours per week) in the area of Language and Literacy Studies for the Fall and Winter semesters
Level of Study: Graduate
Type: Scholarship
Value: C$2,000
Frequency: Annual
Country of Study: Any country
Application Procedure: If you wish to be considered for this award please contact Darlene Flight (dflight@mun.ca) or deliver to Room 2007, with your request to be considered for this award as well as a brief summary (one or two paragraphs) indicating your contributions to the area of language and literacy studies
Closing Date: 4 December
Additional Information: This scholarship will be awarded on the basis of academic standing in a first Memorial University of Newfoundland Education degree to a graduate student with a specialization in reading or language arts. In the event that in any given year no graduate student qualifies for the award, this scholarship will be awarded to an undergraduate student. Instalments of C$1,000.00 each will be awarded in two successive academic terms; and the scholarship is renewable for two years, provided first-class standing is maintained. Please see the website for details www.mun.ca/educ/grad/awards_scholarships.php

For further information contact:

Email: info@mun.ca

Microsoft Research

One Microsoft Way, Redmond, WA 98052, United States of America

Tel: (1) 800 642 7676
Fax: (1) 425 93 936 7329
Email: latamint@microsoft.com
Website: www.research.microsoft.com

In 1991, Microsoft Corporation became the first software company to create its own computer science research organization. It has developed into a unique entity among corporate research laboratories, balancing an open academic model with an effective process for transferring its research to product development teams.

Microsoft Fellowship

Subjects: Computer science
Purpose: To empower and encourage PhD students in the Asia-Pacific region to realize their potential in computer science-related research and to recognize and award outstanding PhD students
Eligibility: Open to candidates who specialize in computer science, electronic engineering, information technology or applied mathematics and are in their first or second year of PhD programme and is enroled as a PhD student by the time of the nomination and has spent 6-18 months working towards a PhD
Level of Study: Research
Type: Fellowships
Value: 100 % of the tuition and fees, a stipend to cover living expenses while in school (US$28,000), travel allowance to attend professional conferences or seminars (US$4,000). See the website for details
Length of Study: 2 years
Frequency: Annual
Application Procedure: Applicants must send the completed application form (downloaded from the website), 2 recommendation letters, curriculum vitae and a video or Power Point presentation with audio introduction (on compact disk), including statement of purpose, previous, on-going and future projects, research interests and accomplishments
Closing Date: 9 October
Additional Information: Previous Microsoft Fellows are excluded. Please see the website for further details

For further information contact:

MS Fellow 2006 Committee Microsoft Research Asia 3F Beijing Sigma Center No 49 Zhichun Road, China

Email: fellowRA@microsoft.com

Microsoft Research European PhD Scholarship Programme

Subjects: Intersection of computing and the sciences including biology, chemistry and physics
Purpose: To recognize and support exceptional students who show the potential to make an outstanding contribution to science
Eligibility: Applicant must have been accepted by a university in Europe to start a PhD or will have completed no more than 1 year of their PhD by October
Level of Study: Doctorate
Type: Scholarships
Value: €30,000 per year and a laptop with a range of software applications
Length of Study: 3 years
Frequency: Annual
Closing Date: 26 September (check with website)
Additional Information: All queries should be sent via email and please see the website for further details

For further information contact:

Email: msrphd@microsoft.com

Middlesex University London

Fax: (44) 20 8203 6105
Website: www.mdx.ac.uk
Contact: Scholarships office

International Merit Award

Subjects: All subjects
Purpose: Middlesex University is renowned for offering unrivalled support to international students and gives out scholarships and merit awards to international students totalling around £1,000,000 each year
Eligibility: Open to any international postgraduate student in any subject
Level of Study: Graduate, Postgraduate
Type: Award
Value: Up to £2,000
Frequency: Annual
Study Establishment: Middlesex University London
Country of Study: United Kingdom
Application Procedure: There is no separate application for this award; international students should apply for their chosen course through the normal application process. Awards

will be given on a case-by-case basis which will be dependent on your course and application
Contributor: Middlesex University London
Additional Information: Successful candidates will be notified at the point of offer for a programme of study and the award amount will be deducted from their tuition fees. NB: Research students are not eligible for the International Merit Award

For further information contact:

Email: scholarships@mdx.ac.uk

Santander Formula Scholarship

Subjects: All subjects
Eligibility: Open to any undergraduate or postgraduate student from South America. Awarded to South American students demonstrating excellent academic potential. To be eligible students must: Hold an offer of a place for a one-year postgraduate taught masters at the University of Glasgow, Be a national of Argentina, Belgium, Brazil, Chile, China, Colombia Germany, Ghana, Mexico, Poland, Peru, Portugal, Puerto, Rico, Russia, Singapore, South Korea, Spain, United Arab Emirates, United Kingdom, Uruguay, Venezuela United States of America
Level of Study: Graduate, Postgraduate
Type: Scholarship
Value: £4,200 towards the students' fees
Study Establishment: Middlesex University London
Country of Study: United Kingdom
Application Procedure: Email the Americas and Caribbean regional office (info@mdxna.com) to apply and for more information
Closing Date: There is no deadline
Contributor: Middlesex University London
Additional Information: Please note that awards will be allocated based on application date so we encourage you to apply as soon as possible

For further information contact:

Email: support.team@postgraduatesearch.com

Santander Mobility Scholarship

Subjects: All subjects
Eligibility: Open to any undergraduate or postgraduate exchange student. Available for exchange students resident within the United Kingdom and countries listed in the Santander Universidades scheme*
Level of Study: Graduate, Postgraduate
Type: Scholarship

Value: £1,000 each
Study Establishment: Middlesex University London
Country of Study: United Kingdom
Contributor: Middlesex University London
Additional Information: *Countries involved in the Santander Universidades Scheme include; Argentina, Brazil, Belgium, Chile, China, Colombia, Germany, Ghana, Korea, Mexico, Poland, Portugal, Puerto Rico, Russia, Singapore, Spain, United States of America, United Kingdom, UAE, and Uruguay

For further information contact:

Tel: (44) 208 411 5962
Email: N.Rachel-Naseem@mdx.ac.uk
Contact: Dr Nosheen Rachel-Naseem, Student Exchange Manager

Santander Work Based Learning Scholarship

Subjects: All subjects
Purpose: This award is available to Work Based Learning students who have demonstrated academic excellence. You must have applied, or be currently enrolled on an undergraduate or postgraduate/doctoral programme within the Institute for Work Based Learning
Eligibility: Open to any Work Based Learning student who has demonstrated academic excellence. You must have applied, or be currently enroled on an undergraduate or postgraduate/doctoral programme within the Institute for Work Based Learning
Level of Study: Doctorate, Graduate, Postgraduate
Type: Scholarship
Value: £5,000
Study Establishment: Middlesex University London
Country of Study: United Kingdom
Application Procedure: To apply, please fill in our Scholarship application form (mdx.hobsons.co.uk/emtinterestpage. aspx?ip=scholarship)
Closing Date: 28 August
Contributor: Middlesex University London

For further information contact:

Tel: (44) 208 411 5415
Email: scholarships@mdx.ac.uk

The Alumni Bursary

Subjects: All subjects
Eligibility: Available to United Kingdom/EU students who completed their first degree at Middlesex and have an offer for a further taught masters programme here. The bursary applies

to self-financing students and students not eligible for funding from Student Finance United Kingdom. International (i.e. outside of the EU) alumni, not already receiving an International Merit Award or regional award, may be eligible to receive a 10 % reduction in tuition fees when progressing to postgraduate study at Middlesex
Level of Study: Graduate, Postgraduate
Type: Bursary
Value: Up to 20 % of the tuition fee
Frequency: Dependent on funds available
Study Establishment: Middlesex University London
Country of Study: United Kingdom
Application Procedure: Find out more from your nearest regional office
Closing Date: There is no application process for your alumni bursary
Contributor: Middlesex University London
Additional Information: Students already holding another Middlesex Scholarship (e.g. Academic Excellence Scholarship) are not entitled to the Alumni bursary

For further information contact:

The Burroughs, NW4 4BT, London, United Kingdom

Tel: (44) 20 8411 6286
Email: scholarships@mdx.ac.uk

The David Caminer Postgraduate Scholarship in Business Computing

Subjects: Business computing
Eligibility: Open to any first year MSc student in the School of Science and Technology. The scholarships will be available to students who have demonstrated excellent academic potential. Applications are welcome from students who have fulfilled the admission criteria and been offered a place to study for a postgraduate degree based in the School of Science & Technology
Level of Study: Graduate, Postgraduate
Type: Scholarship
Value: £5,000
Frequency: Annual
Study Establishment: Middlesex University London
Country of Study: United Kingdom
Application Procedure: To apply, please fill in the Scholarship application form (mdx.hobsons.co.uk/emtinterestpage.aspx?ip=scholarship)
Closing Date: August end
Contributor: Middlesex University London
Additional Information: A student will only be entitled to one award during his/her period of study with Middlesex University

Miles Morland Foundation

Email: MMF@blakman.com
Website: www.milesmorlandfoundation.com

The MMF was set up by Miles Morland after a career investing in Africa through two companies he founded, Blakeney Management and DPI (Development Partners International). In the course of this career Miles has been surprised, entertained, impressed, and humbled by the energy, wit, entrepreneurialism and talent of the Africans he has got to know.

Miles Morland Foundation Writing Scholarship for Africans

Subjects: The scholarship is provided for fiction or non-fiction writing but not poetry, plays or screenplays
Purpose: The scholarship is intended to enable writers to write a new work not complete a work in progress. The Foundation's main aim is to support entities in Africa which allow Africans to get their voices better heard. It is particularly interested in supporting African writing and African literature
Eligibility: To qualify for the Scholarship a candidate must submit a piece of published work, or an excerpt from a piece of published work, of between two and seven thousand words to be evaluated by a panel set up by the MMF which will include MMF trustees and past participants in the Caine Prize. The Scholarships will be open to anyone who has been born in Africa or both of whose parents were born in Africa
Type: Scholarship
Value: The Scholars will receive a grant of £18,000, paid monthly over the course of one year
Country of Study: Africa
Application Procedure: Required scans and Word documents should be emailed to MMF@blakman.com. For detailed information, please visit website
Closing Date: 31 October
Contributor: Miles Morland Foundation
Additional Information: The Scholarships will be announced in December

Minerva Stiftung

Gesellschaft für die Forschung mbH, Hofgartenstraasse 8, DEU-80539 Munich, Germany

Tel: (49) 89 2108 1420
Fax: (49) 89 2108 1451

Email: langegao@gv.mpg.de
Website: www.minerva.mpg.de

Minerva Short-Term Research Grants

Subjects: All subjects
Purpose: To fund scientific visits of Israeli scholars and scientists and to promote Israeli-German scientific co-operation
Eligibility: Open to applicants from all research facilities (in Israel-public or governmental research institutes) and universities in Germany and Israel. Applicants should not be older than 38 years. (Maternal leave will be taken into account with regard to the age limit)
Level of Study: Research
Type: Grant
Value: €300 per week for doctoral candidates and €425 per week for postdoctoral candidates. (Additional payments like travel grants and family allowances are possible, depending on the type of the fellowship/grant)
Length of Study: 1-8 weeks
Study Establishment: A German university or research institute
Country of Study: Germany
Application Procedure: Applications including letters of invitation and letters of recommendation must be sent by electronic mail and must reach the Minerva office by May 2nd
Closing Date: 2 May
Additional Information: Flights are covered by a lump sum of up to €700.00

For further information contact:

Minerva Foundation, Head Office, Germany

Tel: (49) 89 2108 1258
Email: nagel@gv.mpg.de
Contact: Michael Nagel

Ministry of Education and Science Republic of Latvia (MESRL)

Valnuiela 2, LVA 1050, Riga, Latvia

Tel: (371) 722 6209
Fax: (371) 722 3905
Email: info@izm.gov.lv
Website: www.izm.gov.lv

The ministry was established immediately after the proclamation of the Latvian state on 18 November 1918. Today the Ministry of Education and Science is the leading public administration institution in the Republic of Latvia in the field of education and science, as well as in the areas of sports, youth and state language policies.

Ministry of Education and Science of the Republic of Lithuania Scholarships for Studies and Research Work

Subjects: All subjects
Purpose: To encourage foreign students in studies and research work
Eligibility: Open to candidates from Belarus, The Czech Republic, Flanders, Greece, Estonia, Italy, China, Lithuania, Mongolia, Poland, Spain and Hungary
Level of Study: Research
Type: Scholarships
Value: Varies
Length of Study: 10 months
Frequency: Annual
Application Procedure: Applicants can download the application form from the website. The completed application form along with a curriculum vitae, letter of motivation, certified copies of education documents, letters of recommendation and photograph must be sent
Closing Date: 15 May

For further information contact:

Tel: (371) 704 7876
Email: mara.katvare@izm.gov.lv
Contact: Ms Mâra Katvare, Head of the Division

Ministry of Fisheries

Pastoral House, 25 The Terrace, PO Box 2526, Wellington 6140, New Zealand

Tel: (64) 800 00 8333
Fax: (64) 6448 94 0720
Email: info@fish.govt.nz
Website: www.fish.govt.nz/en-nz/default.htm

Ministry of Fisheries PG Scholarships in Quantitative Fisheries Science

Subjects: Fisheries science
Purpose: To allow graduate students to develop expertise in quantitative fisheries science and encourage postgraduate students to contribute to priority research areas identified by the New Zealand government

Eligibility: Open to applicants with majors or minors in mathematics, statistics, biology, economics or computer science
Level of Study: Postgraduate
Type: Scholarship
Value: NZ $30,000 per year for PhD and up to NZ $20,000 per year for Masters
Length of Study: 3 years (PhD) and up to 2 years (Masters)
Frequency: Annual
Country of Study: Any country
Application Procedure: Applicants should contact Rebecca Lawton for details
Closing Date: 20 September
Contributor: In collaboration with NIWA
Additional Information: Research is most likely to be carried out a NIWA facility. Preference will be given to New Zealand citizens

For further information contact:

Tel:	(64) 4 819 4251
Email:	rebecca.lawton@fish.govt.nz, info@fish.govt.nz
Contact:	Rebecca Lawton

Ministry of Foreign Affairs

Piazzale della Farnesina, ITA-00135, Roma, Italy

Tel:	(39) 6 36911
Contact:	The Ministry of Foreign Affairs

The Ministry of Foreign Affairs and International Cooperation is the foreign ministry of the government of the Republic of Italy. It is also known as the Farnesina as a metonym from its headquarters, the Palazzo della Farnesina in Rome.

Master Scholarships for International Students

Subjects: Scholarships are awarded to study the subjects offered by the university
Purpose: The aim of the Program is to foster cooperation among Italian Universities and Italian companies in order to promote their internationalization by sustaining higher education courses tailored to the needs of the labor market
Eligibility: Candidates should submit an English language certificate as proof of their proficiency in English. Candidates should hold at least a B2 level certificate within the Common European Framework of Reference for Languages (CEFR). Proof of proficiency in Italian is not mandatory but will be taken into consideration in the selection process

Value: Grantees will receive €888 monthly allowance every three months on their Italian bank account. The first instalment of the scholarship can only be received after the University enrollment according to the necessary administrative procedures. The last instalment of the scholarship can only be received after verification of conditions established under Article 6.2 of this Call. The scholarship only covers courses attended in Italy
Study Establishment: Scholarships are awarded to study the subjects offered by the university
Country of Study: Italy
Application Procedure: Candidates must complete and submit the online application form
Closing Date: 28 February
Additional Information: For more information please see the website scholarship-positions.com/master-scholarships-for-international-students-italy/2017/12/19

For further information contact:

Email:	dgsp.iyt@esteri.it

Ministry of Foreign Affairs and International Cooperation

Piazzale della Farnesina, 1, ITA O00135, Rome, Italy

The Ministry of Foreign Affairs and International Cooperation (MAECI) offers grants in favor of foreign citizens not residing in Italy and Italian citizens living abroad (IRE) for the academic year in order to foster international cultural, scientific and technological cooperation, to promote Italian language and culture and to support Italy's economic system in the world (According to Law 288/55 and its subsequent changes and additions)

Ministry of Foreign Affairs and International Cooperation Scholarships for Foreign and Italian Students

Purpose: The Ministry of Foreign Affairs and International Cooperation is inviting applications for grants for foreign citizens and Italian citizens living abroad awarded by the Italian Government
Eligibility: In order to apply for MAECI scholarships, candidates who enroll to courses held in Italian must possess an Italian language certificate level B2
Type: Scholarship
Value: €900 monthly allowance on a quarterly basis, which will be paid on their Italian bank account
Country of Study: Italy

Application Procedure: Applicants must complete and submit the online application form available upon registration at the following link: www.scholarshipsupdates.com/maeci-scholarships-for-foreign-and-italian-students-2018-2019/
Closing Date: 7 May

For further information contact:

Corso Duca degli Abruzzi, 24, ITA-10129 Torino, Italy

Email: admin@scholarship-positions.com

Ministry of Foreign Affairs of the Republic of Indonesia

Directorate of Public Diplomacy, Tower Building, 12th Floor, Jl. Pejambon No. 6, Jakarta Pusat 10110, Indonesia

Tel: (62) 21 344 15 08
Website: www.kemlu.go.id

Indonesian Arts and Culture Scholarship

Purpose: The program serves to demonstrate Indonesia's commitment as an initiator of the establishment of South West Pacific Dialogue and as the originator member of ASEAN in advancing the social culture cooperation in the region. The program also has an objective to encourage better understanding amongst participants from member countries
Eligibility: The scholarship will cover: Tuition fee (including extra-curricular activities); A round trip economy class ticket; Accommodation (board and lodging); Local transportation during program; Health insurance (limited). All awardees are advised to have their own health insurance. Monthly allowance of Rp. 2,000.000
Level of Study: Postgraduate
Type: Scholarships and fellowships
Frequency: Annual
Country of Study: Any country
Application Procedure: 1. Candidates should be a single, between the ages of 21 to 27 years-old with at least a high school diploma. 2. Candidates should possess high interest and talent in arts. Arts students or those with an academic history on Indonesian culture are encouraged to apply. 3. Bearing in mind the intensity of the program, candidates are highly advised to ensure prime physical mentally/psychologist conditions, particularly for female candidates to ensure that they do not conceive prior and during the program. 4. Participants must arrive in Indonesia a day before the Orientation Program. 5. Participants must follow the

whole program, including orientation program and Indonesian Channel
Closing Date: 16 July
Funding: Private

For further information contact:

The Ministry of Foreign Affairs Directorate of Public Diplomacy Tower Building, 12th Floor, Jl. Taman Pejambon No. 6, Jakarta 10110, Indonesia

Email: iacs@kemlu.go.id

Minnesota Historical Society (MHS)

345 Kellogg Boulevard West, St Paul, MN 55102, United States of America

Tel: (1) 651 297 4464
Fax: (1) 651 297 1345
Email: debbie.miller@mnhs.org
Website: www.mnhs.org
Contact: Ms Stacey Kennedy, Research Supervisor

The Minnesota Historical Society (MHS) is a private, non-profit educational and cultural institution established in 1849 to preserve and share Minnesota history. The Society collects, preserves and tells the story of Minnesota's past through interactive and engaging museum exhibits, extensive libraries and collections, 23 historic sites, educational programmes and book publishing.

Minnesota Historical Society Research Grant

Subjects: The history of Minnesota and its region, which includes the bordering Canadian provinces as well as the American Midwest
Purpose: To support original research and interpretative writing by academics, independent Scholars and professional or non professional writers
Eligibility: Open to applicants of any nationality with English reading and writing ability
Level of Study: Unrestricted
Type: Grant
Value: Varies. Up to US$1,500 for research that will result in an article, up to US$5,000 for research that will result in a book or up to US$1,000 for visiting Scholar grants
Length of Study: Varies

Frequency: Twice a year
Country of Study: Any country
No. of awards offered: 45
Application Procedure: Applicants must complete an application form. Other documentation is also required. Guidelines and applications are available by writing to the given address, by sending an email or from the website
Closing Date: 15 March and 15 October
Funding: Government
Contributor: The state of Minnesota
No. of awards given last year: 22
No. of applicants last year: 45

For further information contact:

Email: r&d@mhs.com

Missouri Department of Higher Education

Access Missouri Financial Assistance Program

Purpose: The Access Missouri Financial Assistance Program is a state program, administered through the Missouri Department of Higher Education, established to provide financial assistance to undergraduate student enrolled full-time at a participating Missouri school
Eligibility: The EFC is calculated by the United States Department of Education using information provided on the FAFSA. Students should contact his/her school or the MDHE for additional details regarding his/her eligibility status
Level of Study: Graduate
Type: Programme grant
Value: Award ranges $300 and up to $4,600 annually
Frequency: Annual
Country of Study: United States of America
Application Procedure: Submit your FAFSA each year by the deadlines in the Initial Students section under Am I eligible? The MDHE receives electronic FAFSA records for Missouri residents directly from the federal government. There is no state Access Missouri application to fill out
Closing Date: 1 April
Funding: Private

For further information contact:

Missouri Department of Higher Education, 205 Jefferson Street, P.O. Box 1469, Jefferson City, MO 65102-1469, United States of America

Tel: (1) 573 751 2361
Email: info@dhe.mo.gov

Missouri State University

College of Business, Glass Hall 223, 901 South National Avenue, Springfield, MO 65897, United States of America

Tel: (1) 417 836 5616
Fax: (1) 417 836 6636
Email: MBAProgram@MissouriState.edu
Website: www.mba.missouristate.edu
Contact: Dr Elizabeth Rozell, MBA Program Director

Missouri State University's College of Business has earned the highest level of accreditation for its programs, ensuring you will be prepared for the regional, national and international job market. MBA students experience a program that is flexible, accessible, affordable and with a solid reputation for international excellence.

The Robert W. and Charlotte Bitter Graduate Scholarship Endowment

Purpose: To assist a worthy graduate student in pursuing a master's of business administration or master's of accounting degree in College of Business
Eligibility: Awarded annually to a student seeking an MBA or MACC, be enroled in 12 hours or enroled in 6 hours or more each semester if the student is a graduate assistant, have a combined formula score (200 grade point average plus Graduate Management Admission Test score) of 1,100 or higher and minimum 3.3 graduate grade point average, have completed a minimum of 24 hours or 15 hours, if the student is a graduate assistant, and have completed all prerequisite courses or be currently enroled in final prerequisite courses
Level of Study: MBA
Type: Scholarship
Value: US$1,000
Length of Study: Varies
Frequency: Annual
Study Establishment: Missouri State University
Country of Study: United States of America
No. of awards offered: 121
Application Procedure: Applicants must contact the organization for application details. Apply online (Check in November)
Closing Date: 1 March (priority deadline); 1 May (absolute)
Funding: Private, Foundation
Contributor: The Robert W. and Charlotte Bitter Graduate Scholarship Endowment
No. of awards given last year: 1
No. of applicants last year: 121
Additional Information: Not renewable. Please contact the university for further information

For further information contact:

Email: ammsi@uonbi.ac.ke

Modern Language Association of America (MLA)

26 Broadway, 3rd Floor, New York, NY 10004-1789, United States of America

Tel:	(1) 646 576 5000
Fax:	(1) 646 458 0030
Email:	awards@mla.org
Website:	www.mla.org
Contact:	Annie Reiser

The Modern Language Association of America (MLA) is a non-profit membership organization that promotes the study and teaching of language and literature in English and foreign languages.

James Russell Lowell Prize

Subjects: Literary theory, media, cultural history and interdisciplinary topics
Purpose: To recognize an outstanding literary or linguistic study, a critical edition of an important work or a critical biography
Eligibility: Open to books published the year preceding the year in which the award is due to be given. Authors must be current members of the MLA
Level of Study: Postdoctorate
Type: Prize
Value: Cash award and certificate
Frequency: Annual
Country of Study: Any country
Application Procedure: Applicants must send six copies of the work. For detailed information about specific prizes, applicants should contact the MLA
Closing Date: 1 March
Funding: Private

For further information contact:

Email: awards@mla.org

Katherine Singer Kovacs Prize

Subjects: Latin American or Spanish literatures and cultures
Purpose: To recognize an outstanding book published in English or Spanish

Eligibility: Open to books published the year preceding the year in which the prize is given. Competing books should be broadly interpretative works that enhance the understanding of the interrelations among literature, the arts and society. Authors need not be members of the MLA
Level of Study: Postdoctorate
Type: Prize
Value: Cash award and certificate
Frequency: Annual
Country of Study: Any country
Application Procedure: Applicants must send six copies of the work. For detailed information about specific prizes, applicants should contact the MLA
Closing Date: 1 May
Funding: Private

For further information contact:

Email: awards@mla.org

Modern Language Association Prize for a First Book

Subjects: Literary theory, media, cultural history or interdisciplinary topics
Purpose: To recognize an outstanding literary or linguistic study, or a critical biography
Eligibility: Open to books published in the year preceding the year in which the prize is given as the first book-length publication of a current MLA member
Level of Study: Postdoctorate
Type: Prize
Value: Cash award and certificate
Frequency: Annual
Country of Study: Any country
Application Procedure: Applicants must send six copies of the work. For detailed information about specific prizes, applicants should contact the MLA
Closing Date: 1 April
Funding: Private

For further information contact:

Email: awards@mla.org

Modern Language Association Prize for Independent Scholars

Subjects: English or other modern languages and literatures
Purpose: To encourage the achievements and contributions of independent scholars
Eligibility: Open to books published in the year preceding the year in which the prize is given. At the time of publication of

the book, the author must not be enroled in a programme leading to an academic degree or hold a tenured, tenure-accruing or tenure-track position in postsecondary education. Authors need not be members of the MLA

Level of Study: Postdoctorate

Type: Prize

Value: Cash award, certificate, and one-year membership in the association

Frequency: Annual

Country of Study: Any country

Application Procedure: Applicants must send six copies of the work. For detailed information about specific prizes, applicants should contact the MLA

Closing Date: 1 May

Funding: Private

For further information contact:

Email: awards@mla.org

Monash Mount Eliza Business School

Level 4 27 Sir John Monash Drive, Caulfield, VIC 3145, Australia

Tel: (61) 3 9215 1850
Fax: (61) 3 9215 1821
Email: genmba@mteliza.edu.au
Website: www.monash.edu.au/intoff
Contact: MBA Administration Assistant

Monash Mt Eliza Business School Executive MBA Programme

Application Procedure: Applicants must return a completed application form, a detailed curriculum vitae, full official academic transcripts, one passport photo, a reference from a sponsoring organisation, and an application fee of A$495

Closing Date: Please contact the organisation

For further information contact:

Kunyung Road, Australia

Tel: (61) 3 9215 1107
Fax: (61) 3 9215 1107
Email: cmccall@monashmteliza.edu.au
Contact: Ms Carol McCall, Manager, Executive MBA Programme

Monash University

Monash Graduate Education, Chancellery Building, 26, Sports Walk, Clayton, VIC 3800, Australia

Tel: (61) 3 9905 3009
Fax: (61) 3 9905 5042
Email: mge.apply@monash.edu
Website: www.monash.edu/graduate-research

Monash University is one of Australia's largest universities, with 10 faculties covering every major area of intellectual activity, 6 campuses in Australia and an increasing global presence. Research at Monash covers the full spectrum from fundamental to applied research and ranges across the arts and humanities, social, natural, health and medical sciences and the technological sciences. The University is determined to preserve its strength in fundamental research, which underpins its successes in applied research, and to continue to make a distinguished contribution to intellectual and cultural life.

Corrosion Research Postgraduate Scholarships

Subjects: Microbiological corrosion (particularly of concrete structures), corrosion mitigation of magnesium alloys and corrosion of nanocrystalline materials

Eligibility: Open only to the citizens of Australia or New Zealand or permanent residents who have achieved Honours 2a in Materials Engineering/Science, Metallurgy, Physics, Chemistry, Chemical Engineering, or Mechanical Engineering or equivalent

Level of Study: Postgraduate

Type: Scholarship

Value: A$25,000 per year

Length of Study: 3 years

Frequency: Annual

Study Establishment: Monash University

Application Procedure: Applicants must apply directly to the scholarship provider. Check website for further details

Closing Date: Not specified

Contributor: ARC Discovery and Linkage grants in association with Victorian State Government ETIS Program

For further information contact:

Department of Chemical Engineering, Monash University, Australia

Tel: (61) 3 9905 3671
Email: raman.singh@eng.monash.edu.au
Contact: Professor Raman Singh, Associate Professor

Doctor of Philosophy APA(I) Police-Mental Health Scholarship

Subjects: Policing and mental illness
Purpose: To investigate the police-mental health interface
Eligibility: Open only to the citizens of Australia or New Zealand or permanent residents who have achieved Honours 1 or equivalent, or Honours 2a or equivalent with an HI or H2A Honours Degree in a social sciences discipline
Level of Study: Postgraduate, Research
Value: A$25,118 per year
Length of Study: 3 years
Frequency: Dependent on funds available
Study Establishment: Monash University
Application Procedure: Applicants must apply directly to the scholarship provider

For further information contact:

School of Psychology, Psychiatry, and Psychological Medicine

Email: Kathy.Avent@med.monash.edu.au
Contact: Dr Kathy Avent, Research Fellow and Project Manager

Doctor of Philosophy Scholarship-Corrosion in Alumina Processing

Subjects: Caustic Corrosion and Corrosion-assisted Cracking in Alumina Processing Industry
Eligibility: Open only to the citizens of Australia or New Zealand or permanent residents who have achieved Honours 1 or equivalent, or Honours 2a or equivalent in chemical engineering/mechanical engineering/materials engineering/chemistry
Level of Study: Postgraduate, Research
Type: Scholarship
Value: A$25,118 per year
Length of Study: 3 years
Frequency: Annual
Study Establishment: Monash University
Application Procedure: Applicants must apply direct to faculty. Check website for further details
Closing Date: Not specified
Contributor: ARC

For further information contact:

Contact: Professor Raman Singh, Associate Professor

Faculty of Law Masters International Scholarship

Purpose: At this university, candidates can study a broad range of subjects to shape a qualification that matches to their strengths and career interests. It helps the candidate with career planning, developing a CV and cover letters, interview skills, enhancing their employability skills
Eligibility: Scholarship is available for pursuing Undergraduate and Postgraduate
Level of Study: Postgraduate
Type: Scholarship
Value: Up to A$20,000
Length of Study: 1 year
Frequency: Annual
Country of Study: Any country
Closing Date: 20 October
Funding: International office

Montessori St Nicholas Centre

24 Prince's Gate, SW7 1PT, London, United Kingdom

Tel: (44) 207 584 9987
Fax: (44) 207 589 3764
Email: centre@montessori.org.uk
Website: www.montessori.org.uk
Contact: The Chief Executive

Montessori St Nicholas offer grants and awards under a scholarship scheme for Post Graduate Students carrying out research or training in Montessori teaching. Annual awards total £60,000 on average.

The Birts Scholarship

Purpose: To recognise and encourage research into Montessori teaching
Eligibility: United Kingdom Citizens holding a United Kingdom recognised degree
Level of Study: Graduate
Type: Scholarship
Value: £4–6,000
Length of Study: 2 years

Frequency: Annual
Country of Study: United Kingdom
No. of awards offered: 12
Application Procedure: By application form from the charity and interview
Closing Date: 1 July annually
Funding: Private
No. of awards given last year: 1
No. of applicants last year: 12

For further information contact:

Email: reception@montessori.org.uk

Motor Neurone Disease Association

PO Box 246, Northamptonshire NN1 2PR, Northampton, United Kingdom

Tel: (44) 16 0461 1873
Fax: (44) 16 04 627726
Email: research.grants@mndassociation.org
Website: www.mndassociation.org
Contact: Dr Sadie Vile, Research Grants Manager

The Motor Neurone Disease Association supports research on fundamental aspects of motor neurone disease (MND) and on its management and alleviation. It provides information and advice to patients and carers, and runs a nationwide care service. MND paralyzes selectively or generally and is fatal, irreversible and at present, incurable.

Motor Neurone Disease Association Non-Clinical Fellowship Awards

Subjects: Research on all aspects of Motor Neurone Disease in all relevant disciplines. These Fellowships are not open to clinicians
Purpose: To allow Post-Doctoral Scientists with some experience of MND research to develop their career further. The Motor Neurone Disease Association supports research on fundamental aspects of motor neurone disease (MND) and on its management and alleviation. It provides information and advice to patients and carers, and runs a nationwide core service. MND paralyzes selectively or generally and is fatal, irreversible and at present, incurable
Eligibility: Restricted to researchers at post-doctoral level to work at a suitable institute in the United Kingdom or Republic of Ireland. Applicants must be entitled to remain in the United Kingdom/Ireland for the whole period of the grant if awarded. For Junior Fellowships, applicants should have 2-5 years post-doc experience at the time of commencement of the grant. For Senior Fellowships, applicants should have 4-10 years post-doc experience at the time of commencement of the grant. In considering the periods, allowance is made for career breaks, family leave etc
Level of Study: Postdoctorate, Professional development, Research
Type: Fellowships
Value: Junior Fellowships: Max £90,000 per year, 3 years. Senior Fellowships: Max £110, 000 per year, up to 4 years
Length of Study: Up to 4 years
Frequency: Annual
Study Establishment: University and other suitable research institute
Country of Study: United Kingdom, Republic of Ireland
No. of awards offered: 11 Full Applications in previous year
Application Procedure: Applicants must submit a summary of their proposal, which is first checked for eligibility and considered by three members of the research advisory panel (RAP). Full applications are invited thereafter and application forms are provided. Full applications will be considered by a minimum of two independent external referees and then by the Biomedical Research Advisory Panel (BRAP). Please see the website at www.mndassociation.org/research/for-researchers for full details of the application processes, together with grant guidelines and terms and conditions
Closing Date: 1 May
Funding: Trusts, Individuals
No. of awards given last year: 1 Junior Fellowships and 1 Senior Fellowships
No. of applicants last year: 11 Full Applications
Additional Information: The lead applicant should be the potential fellow, currently a post-doctoral scientist. The head of the proposed host laboratory should be a co-applicant

For further information contact:

Motor Neurone Disease Association, 10-15 Notre Dame Mews, Northamptonshire NN1 2BG, Northampton, United Kingdom

Tel: (44) 1604 611846
Email: research.grants@mndassociation.org

Motor Neurone Disease Association PhD Studentship Award

Subjects: Research on all aspects of Motor Neurone Disease in all relevant disciplines

Purpose: To attract promising science graduates to develop a career in MND related research and to support research aimed at understanding the causes of MND, elucidating disease mechanisms and facilitating the translation of therapeutic strategies from the laboratory to the clinic

Eligibility: Restricted to researchers based in laboratories in the United Kingdom and Republic of Ireland. Applicants must be entitled to remain in United Kingdom/Ireland for the whole period of the grant if awarded. The applicant should be the supervisor, not the potential student

Level of Study: Doctorate, Graduate, Postgraduate, Research

Type: Studentship

Value: The Association will provide a student stipend of £16,000 per year (£17,000 in London), £8,000 per year for laboratory expenses and a total budget of £1,000, over 3 years, for conference attendance. The Association will also cover relevant tuition/bench fees at the rate payable by United Kingdom/European students

Length of Study: 3 years

Frequency: Annual

Study Establishment: University and other suitable research institute

Country of Study: United Kingdom, Republic of Ireland

No. of awards offered: 5 full applications

Application Procedure: Applicants must submit a summary of their proposal, which is first checked for eligibility and considered by three members of the research advisory panel (RAP). Full applications are invited thereafter and application forms are provided. Full applications are submitted to two or more independent referees and then to the RAP for consideration. Please see our research governance overview at www. mndassociation.org/research/for_researchers - for information on our grant application processes. The summary application form will be available on our website from mid-March to be completed online

Closing Date: 1 May

Funding: Trusts, Individuals

No. of awards given last year: 2 awarded

No. of applicants last year: 5 full applications

Additional Information: The studentships are awarded on the basis of scientific merit and the value of research training offered. The applicant must be the potential supervisor not the student

Motor Neurone Disease Association Research Project Grants

Subjects: Research into all aspects of Motor Neurone Disease in all disciplines

Purpose: To understand and research the cause and effective treatments of MND. To fund research to the highest scientific merit and greatest clinical or translational relevance to MND

Eligibility: Overseas applicants must have a project that is unique in concept or design and that involves significant aspect of collaboration with an institute in the United Kingdom or the Republic of Ireland. The applicant must be eligible to remain employed at the host research institution for the period of the grant if awarded

Level of Study: Postdoctorate, Professional development, Research

Type: Grant

Value: £85,000 per year, maximum

Length of Study: 1-3 years

Frequency: Annual

Study Establishment: A research institution, including universities and hospitals

Country of Study: Any country

No. of awards offered: 23 Full applications

Application Procedure: Applicants must submit a summary of their proposal, which is first checked for eligibility and considered by three members of the research advisory panel (RAP). Full applications are invited thereafter and application forms are provided. Full applications are submitted to two or more independent referees and then to the RAP for consideration. Please see our research governance overview at www. mndassociation.org/research/for_researchers - for information on our grant application processes. The summary application form for project grants will be available on our website from mid-September to be completed online

Closing Date: 25 October and 23 October

Funding: Trusts, Individuals

No. of awards given last year: 7

No. of applicants last year: 23 Full applications

Additional Information: The majority of grants are awarded to applicants based in the United Kingdom, Republic of Ireland, any country. However, overseas applicants may apply

Mott MacDonald Charitable Trust

St Anne House, 20-26, Wellesley Road, Croydon, CR9 2UL, Surrey, United Kingdom

Tel:	(44) 20 8774 2000
Fax:	(44) 20 8681 5706
Website:	www.mottmac.com
Contact:	Secretary

Mott MacDonald Charitable Trust Scholarships

Subjects: Engineering

Purpose: To enable a recipient to pursue studies and thus contribute to the advancement of engineering technology

Eligibility: Open to engineering students who wish to further their academic training at the postgraduate level. Students returning to academic training after a period of employment are preferred
Type: Scholarship
Value: Please consult the organization
Frequency: Annual
Study Establishment: Any university
Country of Study: United Kingdom
No. of awards offered: 129
Application Procedure: Applicants must complete an application form, available on request from the main address
Closing Date: 31 March
Funding: Commercial
No. of awards given last year: 4
No. of applicants last year: 129

For further information contact:

Email: charitabletrust@mottmac.com

Multiple Sclerosis Society of Canada (MSSC)

175 Bloor Street East, Suite 700, North Tower, Toronto, ON M4W 3R8, Canada

Tel: (1) 416 922 6065
Fax: (1) 416 922 7538
Email: jackie.munroe@mssociety.ca
Website: www.mssociety.ca
Contact: Ms Jackie Munroe, Research Grants Programme Manager

The mission of the MSSC is to be a leader in finding a cure for multiple sclerosis and enabling people affected by the disease to enhance their quality of life.

Multiple Sclerosis Society of Canada Donald Paty Career Development Award

Subjects: Multiple sclerosis
Purpose: To support the salary of an independent researcher whose research is relevant to MS
Eligibility: This award is open to those that hold a doctoral degree (PhD, MD or equivalent) and who have recently completed their training in research and are in the early stages of independent research relevant to MS. Applicants must hold a Canadian university faculty appointment and either holds an operating grant from the MSSOC or another funding agency
Level of Study: Postdoctorate
Value: The amount provided per year for the award is C$50,000
Length of Study: 3 years
Frequency: Annual
Study Establishment: A Canadian school of medicine/recognized institution
Country of Study: Canada
No. of awards offered: 5
Application Procedure: All Applicants for regular research grants are required to use the website www.mscanadagrants. ca/ for the completion of their proposal. All components of the application must be submitted through the online system. No hard copies of any documentation will be accepted
Closing Date: 1 October
Funding: Private
No. of awards given last year: 1
No. of applicants last year: 5

For further information contact:

Email: msresearchgrants@mssociety.ca

Multiple Sclerosis Society of Canada Postdoctoral Fellowship Award

Subjects: Multiple sclerosis and allied diseases
Purpose: To encourage research
Eligibility: Open to qualified persons holding an MD or PhD degree and intending to pursue research work relevant to multiple sclerosis and allied diseases. The applicant must be associated to an appropriate authority in the field he or she wishes to study
Level of Study: Postdoctorate
Type: Fellowship
Value: The amount provided per year for the award is C$39,000 for a PhD and C$48,500 for an MD
Length of Study: 1 year, with the opportunity for 2 renewals at 1 year each
Frequency: Annual
Study Establishment: A recognized institution which deals that problems relevant to multiple sclerosis
Country of Study: Other
No. of awards offered: 26
Application Procedure: All Applicants for regular research grants are required to use the website www.mscanadagrants. ca/ for the completion of their proposal. All components of the application must be submitted through the online system. No hard copies of any documentation will be accepted

Closing Date: 1 October
Funding: Private
No. of awards given last year: 31
No. of applicants last year: 26

For further information contact:

Email: msresearchgrants@mssociety.ca

Murdoch University

Murdoch University is a public university in Perth, Western Australia with campuses also in Singapore and Dubai. University has more than 22,000 students and 2,000 staff from across 90 different countries with a desire to discover, use their imaginations and ultimately make a difference

International Postgraduate Research Studentship (IPRS) at Murdoch University in Australia

Subjects: Research
Purpose: The purpose is to undertake the degree of Doctor of Philosophy (PhD) and Doctor of Education (EdD) at Murdoch University in areas in which the University has specialized research strengths. Preference will be given to PhD candidates
Eligibility: An applicant must provide evidence of having achieved Murdoch University English language proficiency requirements. These requirements are IELTS Academic 6.5 - no individual band less than 6.0 or TOEFL iBT 90 - no individual band less than 20. Exceptions are Nursing, Education and Pharmacy with an IELTS requirement of 7.0
Level of Study: Doctorate
Value: The scholarships cover the research degree tuition fees and health insurance premiums
Country of Study: Singapore
Application Procedure: Visit website our.murdoch.edu.au/Research-and-Innovation/Resources-for-students/Future-research-students/Admission-and-scholarships/International-student-scholarships/IPRS/
Closing Date: 30 September

Additional Information: Applicants who have had sustained contact with a potential academic research supervisor at Murdoch University prior to submission of their application will be considered favourably

For further information contact:

Email: admin@scholarship-positions.com

International Welcome Scholarships (IWS)

Subjects: Scholarships are available for all Business and Governance eligible degree courses and for all other eligible degree courses
Purpose: International Welcome Scholarships are open to eligible international students who choose to study a Murdoch University Bachelor, Honours or Postgraduate Coursework degree programme
Eligibility: Citizen of Bangladesh, Bhutan, China, India, Indonesia, Malaysia, Nepal, Pakistan or Sri Lanka can apply for these scholarships
Type: Postgraduate scholarships
Value: $10,000 for all Business and Governance eligible degree courses $11,000 for the Bachelor of Nursing course $7,000 for all other eligible degree courses
Study Establishment: Scholarships are available for all Business and Governance eligible degree courses and for all other eligible degree courses
Country of Study: Australia
Application Procedure: To be considered for a scholarship, applications for entry to an eligible course need to be submitted to the international admissions office at least two weeks prior to the start of the semester that the student intends to commence their studies at Murdoch
Closing Date: Deadline varies according to courses
Additional Information: For more details please visit the website scholarship-positions.com/international-welcome-scholarships-iws-murdoch-university-australia/2016/09/22/

For further information contact:

Email: internationalscholarships@murdoch.edu.au

N

Nan Tien Institute

231 Nolan St, Unanderra, NSW 2526, Australia

Tel: (61) 2 4272 0648
Email: info@nantien.edu.au
Website: www.nantien.edu.au

Nan Tien Institute Postgraduate Scholarship

Subjects: Applied Buddhist studies and health and social wellbeing
Eligibility: Open to Australian domestic students only
Level of Study: Graduate, Postgraduate
Type: Scholarship
Value: A$13,800.00 covers tuition costs only (not text books, learning materials or accommodation) plus research supervision
Length of Study: Up to 3 years from commencement, unless otherwise agreed
Frequency: Annual
Study Establishment: Nan Tien Institute
Country of Study: Australia
Application Procedure: Complete and submit the application form, along with your application for admission form by the closing date
Closing Date: April and December
Contributor: Nan Tien Institute
Additional Information: Please check for more information at www.nantien.edu.au/content/nan-tien-institute-postgraduate-scholarship

For further information contact:

Tel: (61) 4258 0700
Email: info@nantien.edu.au

Nansen Fund

77 Saddlebrook Lane, Houston, TX 77024, United States of America

Tel: (1) 713 686 3963
Fax: (1) 713 680 8255
Contact: Fellowships Office

John Dana Archbold Fellowship

Subjects: All subjects
Purpose: To support educational exchange between the United States and Norway
Eligibility: Eligibility is limited to those aged between 20 and 35, in good health, of good character, and citizens of the United States of America, who are not recent immigrants from Norway
Level of Study: Postdoctorate, Postgraduate, Professional development
Type: Fellowship
Value: Grants vary, depending on costs and rates of exchange. The University of Oslo will charge no tuition and the Nansen Fund will pay up to US$10,000 for supplies, maintenance and travel. The maintenance stipend is sufficient to meet expenses in Norway for a single person. Air fare from the United States of America to Norway is covered
Length of Study: 1 year
Frequency: Every 2 years
Study Establishment: The University of Oslo
Country of Study: Norway
Application Procedure: Applicants must complete and submit an application form with references and transcripts
Closing Date: 31 January

© Springer Nature Limited 2019
Palgrave Macmillan (ed.), *The Grants Register 2020*,
https://doi.org/10.1057/978-1-349-95943-3

Additional Information: Every other year the Norway-America Association, the sister organisation of the Nansen Fund, offers fellowships for Norwegian citizens wishing to study at a university in the United States of America. For further information please contact The Norway-America Association

For further information contact:

The Norway-American Association, Drammensveien 20c, 0271 Oslo, Norway

Tel:	(47) 2 244 7716
Fax:	(47) 2 244 7716
Email:	cg.newyork@mfa.no

Nanyang Technological University (NTU)

Nanyang Business School, Nanyang Avenue, 639798 Singapore

Tel:	(65) 6790 4803
Fax:	(65) 6791 8522
Email:	postgraduate@ntu.edu.sg
Website:	www.ntu.edu.sg
Contact:	Director

The Nanyang Business School is one of Asia's top business schools. Its flagship programme is the Nanyang MBA, which has consistently been ranked one of the top in Asia and is ranked in the world top 100 by Economist intelligence unit, 2005.

Asia Journalism Fellowship

Subjects: The fellowship is awarded in journalism at NTU's Wee Kim Wee School of Communication and Information
Eligibility: At least five years of professional journalism experience, not including student journalism, who are currently working as a journalist. Freelancers are eligible, if journalism is their main activity. Applicants should be residing in Asia and should be able to operate in English which is the working language of the programme. Journalists working in non-English media are welcomed, but they will have to show their proficiency in English through a telephone interview. Permission is required from their employers to be away for the full three months of the Fellowship
Type: Fellowship

Value: Stipend of Singaporean $1,500 per month for the duration of the three month programme. Travel to and from Singapore will also be covered. There is no extra funding for spouses and children to visit. Free accommodation is provided in service apartments. Two or three Fellows share one apartment with kitchen to cook meals. Fellows will have access to the library, computer, internet and athletic facilities of the NTU campus. NTU will apply for Training Employment Passes for the Fellows to come to Singapore. Any visiting family members must handle their own entry permit applications
Country of Study: Singapore
Application Procedure: The mode of applying is electronically (send to applications@ajf.sg) or by post. For detailed information, please visit the website
Closing Date: 25 October
Contributor: Temasek Foundation and Nanyang Technological University
Additional Information: The Fellowship brings around 15 journalists from across Asia to Singapore for three months

For further information contact:

Email:	applications@ajf.sg

Asian Communication Resource Centre (ACRC) Fellowship Award

Subjects: Communication and information research from Asian perspective
Purpose: To encourage in-depth research, promote cooperation and support scholars who wish to pursue research in communication, information and ICT-related disciplines in Asia
Eligibility: All applicants should possess or be working towards a postgraduate degree from a reputable academic institution and Applicants should be working on a research project in communication, media, information or related areas that would be able to exploit the materials in the ACRC
Level of Study: Postgraduate, Research
Type: Fellowships
Value: Up to US$1,500 (economy class return air ticket), on-campus accommodation will be provided and weekly allowance of US$210 will be provided
Length of Study: 1–3 months
Frequency: Annual
Application Procedure: Applicants can download the application form from the website and send in their completed application form along with a copy of their latest curriculum vitae
Closing Date: 1 October

For further information contact:

Tel: (65) 6790 4577
Fax: (65) 6791 5214
Email: acrc_fellowship@ntu.edu.sg

Nanyang Technological University HASS International PhD Scholarship (HIPS) for Singaporean Students

Purpose: HIPS aims to encourage outstanding Singapore citizens and Singapore permanent residents to pursue an academic career in HASS by supporting their doctoral studies abroad

Eligibility: Under HIPS, the successful candidates will be employed as University staff. They will be granted paid leave to pursue a sponsored PhD programme in an approved overseas university or in NTU with an extended period of research in an approved overseas partner university. Upon successful completion of the PhD programme, they will be appointed as tenure-track Assistant Professors of the University

Type: Scholarship

Frequency: Annual

Application Procedure: Interested applicants should first get in touch with the relevant School and Division. Send all applications, through the respective Heads of Divisions/ Groups and School Chairs, to: Dean's Office (or to the Dean's office). Applicants who wish to submit their documents electronically should email their application form and complete dossier to Ms Chan Bee Kwang (email: BKCHAN@ntu.edu.sg)

Closing Date: 31 December

Additional Information: All late and/or incomplete applications will not be considered. A check list is included in the application package

For further information contact:

Email: wpseeto@ntu.edu.sg
Contact: Seeto Wei Peng

Singapore Education – Sampoerna Foundation MBA in Singapore

Subjects: Management

Purpose: To help Indonesian citizens below 35 years pursue their MBA studies

Eligibility: Applicant must be an Indonesian citizen under 35 years, hold a local Bachelor's degree from any discipline with a minimum GPA of 3.00 (on a 4.00 scale), have a minimum of 2 year full-time professional work experience after the completion of the undergraduate degree, currently not enroled in graduate or post-graduate program, or obtained a Master's degree or equivalent; not be a graduate from overseas tertiary institutions, unless was on a full scholarship, not receive other equivalent award or scholarship offering similar or other benefits at the time of the award

Value: Approx. US$70,000–150,000. This will cover GMAT and TOEFL/IELTS reimbursement, university application fee, student visa application fee, return airfares from Jakarta to the place of study, tuition fees for the duration of study, living allowance to support living costs during period of study and literature allowance to purchase textbooks required for study

Country of Study: Any country

Closing Date: 1 February

Additional Information: For further information see www.nanyangmba.edu.sg/Admissions/FinancialAid.asp

For further information contact:

Email: ella.cecilla@sampoernafoundation.org

Singapore International Graduate Award Awards for International Students in Singapore

Subjects: Biomedical Sciences and Physical Science and Engineering

Purpose: Introducing a new Singapore International Graduate Award (or SINGA), for international students to do their PhD training in a multi-disciplinary environment in Singapore

Eligibility: International students with a passion for Science and Engineering research, excellent academic qualifications, good reports from academic referees, and fluency in English are encouraged to apply for this award. TOEFL, IELTS, and GRE are NOT required

Value: Stipends – S$2,000 per month (S$24,000 per annum), to be increased to S$2,500 per month (S$30,000 per annum) after passing qualifying examinations; one-time S$1,000 settling-in allowance; one-time airfare grant of S$1,500

Length of Study: 4 years

Country of Study: Singapore

Application Procedure: Applicants will need to complete and submit an online application form

Closing Date: 31 May

Additional Information: For more details, please visit the website wedushare.com/opportunity-detail/EXPT54EeMok7Ew4EQ/SINGA-Awards-for-International-Students-in-Singapore,-2019

For further information contact:

Email: singa_enquiries@hq.a-star.edu.sg

Spring Management Development Scholarship (MDS)

Subjects: Management
Purpose: To nurture the next generation of leaders for the trailblazing companies of tomorrow
Eligibility: Those who are currently working in an SME or are interested to join one, are citizens or permanent residents of Singapore, have less than 5 years of working experience and successfully apply for one of the approved MBA programmes
Value: Full-time/Part-time MBA: SPRING will provide grant value of up to 70 % of tuition fees, and other related expenses for full-time MBA scholars up to a maximum qualifying cost of $52,000
Study Establishment: Nanyang Business School
Country of Study: Singapore
Application Procedure: Applicants will have to go through a joint selection process by SPRING and the participating SME, serve a 3month internship in the SME prior to embarking on the approved MBA course (performance must be deemed satisfactory by the SME), and serve a bond of up to 2 years in the SME upon completion of studies. For more information on government assistance programmes, please contact the Enterprise One hotline at Tel: (65) 6898 1800 or email enterpriseone@spring.gov.sg or visit their website at www.spring.gov.sg/mds
Closing Date: See website for details
Contributor: SPRING Singapore and small medium enterprises
Additional Information: For more information on government assistance programmes, please contact the Enterprise One hotline at Tel: (65) 6898 1800 or email enterpriseone@spring.gov.sg or visit their website at www.spring.gov.sg/mds

For further information contact:

Tel: (65) 6898 1800
Email: enquiry@enterprisesg.gov.sg

The Lien Foundation Scholarship for Social Service Leaders

Subjects: Full-time or part-time local post-graduate studies in management and selected specialist fields at the National University of Singapore (NUS) and the Nanyang Technological University (NTU)
Purpose: To provide scholarships to support education and professional development
Eligibility: The scholarship is open to candidates with academic excellence, notable performance record and the potential to take up leadership positions in voluntary welfare organizations
Type: Scholarship
Value: The award includes tuition fees, maintenance allowance (for full-time studies), book allowance and any other compulsory fees
Country of Study: Any country
Application Procedure: For more information on the scholarship do visit the websites www.ncss.org.sg/lien, lienfoundation.org/ScholarshipSSL.htm. For more information on the scholarship contact Ms Ng Hwee Choon: ng_hwee_choon@ncss.gov.sg and Ms Pamela Biswas: Pamela_biswas@ncss.gov.sg
Closing Date: 22 June

For further information contact:

Email: socialservicescholarships@ncss.gov.sg

Narotam Sekhsaria Foundation

1st Floor, Nirmal Building, Nariman Point, Mumbai, Maharashtra 400021, India

Tel: (91) 22 6132 6200
Email: pgscholarship@nsfoundation.co.in
Contact: Narotam Sekhsaria Foundation

Narotam Sekhsaria Foundation is a non-profit initiative created to support enterprising individuals and innovative organizations.

Narotam Sekhsaria Postgraduate Scholarship

Subjects: The scholarship is awarded in the fields offered by the university
Purpose: The aim of the scholarship is to help high achieving students to pursue postgraduate studies at prestigious Indian and international universities
Eligibility: Applicants must have sufficient knowledge of the language of instruction of the host university
Type: Postgraduate scholarships
Value: The award of scholarship is subject to securing admission
Study Establishment: The scholarship is awarded in the fields offered by the university
Country of Study: India
Application Procedure: Applicants can apply through the registration process given below the link of scholarship page

Closing Date: 28 March
Additional Information: For more details please see the website scholarship-positions.com/narotam-sekhsaria-postgraduate-scholarship-indian-students/2017/11/07/

For further information contact:

Tel: (91) 22 61326200
Email: pgscholarship@nsfoundation.co.in

National Academies

500 5th Street NW, Washington, DC 20001, United States of America

Tel: (1) 202 334 2000
Fax: (1) 202 334 1667
Email: infofell@nas.edu
Website: www.nationalacademies.org

The National Academies perform an unparallelled public service by bringing together committees of experts in all areas of scientific and technological endeavour. These experts serve pro bono to address critical national issues and give advice to the federal government and the public.

Christine Mirzayan Science & Technology Policy Graduate Fellowship Program

Subjects: Science, engineering, medicine, veterinary medicine, business and law
Purpose: To engage students in science and technology policy
Eligibility: Graduate students and postdoctoral scholars and those who have completed graduate studies or postdoctoral research within the last 5 years are eligible to apply
Level of Study: Postgraduate
Type: Fellowship
Value: The stipend for a 10-week program is US$5,300
Length of Study: 12 weeks
Frequency: Annual
Country of Study: Any country
Application Procedure: A completed application form must be submitted. Application forms are available on the website
Closing Date: 1 November for the January program, 1 March for the June program, and 1 June for the September program

For further information contact:

Email: policyfellows@nas.edu

Ford Foundation Dissertation Fellowships

Subjects: Check website for details
Purpose: To achieve excellence in college and university teaching
Eligibility: Open to all citizens or nationals of the United States regardless of race, national origin, religion, gender, age, disability, or sexual orientation, individuals with evidence of superior academic achievement and committed to a career in teaching and research at the college or university level, PhD or ScD degree candidates studying in an eligible research-based discipline at a United States educational institution. Also individuals who have not earned a doctoral degree at any time, in any field
Level of Study: Doctorate
Type: Award
Value: Stipend: US$25,000 for 1 year. Expenses paid to attend one Conference of Ford Fellows. Access to Ford Fellow Liaisons, a network of former Ford Fellows who have volunteered to provide mentoring and support to current fellows
Length of Study: 9–12 months
Frequency: Annual
Country of Study: United States of America
Application Procedure: Applicants must register and establish a personal user ID and password. Check website for further details
Closing Date: 15 November
Contributor: The National Research Council

For further information contact:

Tel: (1) 202 334 2872
Email: infofell@nas.edu

Ford Foundation Postdoctoral Fellowships

Subjects: Check website for further details
Purpose: For achieving excellence in college and university teaching and to increase the diversity of the nation's college and university faculties by increasing their ethnic and racial diversity, to maximize the educational benefits of diversity, and to increase the number of professors who can and will use diversity as a resource for enriching the education of all students
Eligibility: Open to all citizens or nationals of the United States regardless of race, national origin, religion, gender, age, disability, or sexual orientation, individuals with evidence of superior academic achievement and committed to a career in teaching and research at the college or university level. Individuals should hold a PhD or ScD degree in an eligible research-based field from a United States educational institution

Level of Study: Postdoctorate
Type: Fellowships
Value: One-year Stipend: US$45,000, Employing Institution Allowance: US$1,500 and expenses paid to attend one Conference of Ford Fellows
Length of Study: 9–12 months
Application Procedure: Applicants must register and establish a personal user ID and password. Check website for further details
Closing Date: 15 November
Funding: Government, Foundation
Contributor: National Research Council (NRC) on behalf of the Ford Foundation
Additional Information: Candidates demonstrating superior academic achievement according to the judgement panels will be awarded

For further information contact:

Tel: (1) 202 334 2872
Email: infofell@nas.edu

Ford Foundation Predoctoral Fellowships

Subjects: Check website for further details
Purpose: For achieving excellence in college and university teaching and increasing the diversity of the nation's college and university faculties to maximize the educational benefits of diversity, and to increase the number of professors who can use diversity as a resource for enriching the education of all students
Eligibility: Open to all citizens or nationals of the United States regardless of race, national origin, religion, gender, age, disability, or sexual orientation, individuals with evidence of superior academic achievement and committed to a career in teaching and research at the college or university level, should enrol in or planning to enrol in an eligible research-based program leading to a PhD or ScD degree at a United States educational institution and who have not earned a doctoral degree at any time, in any field
Level of Study: Predoctorate
Type: Bursary and scholarship
Value: Annual stipend: US$24,000. Award to the institution in lieu of tuition and fees: US$2,000. Expenses paid to attend at least one Conference of Ford Fellows
Length of Study: 3 years
Application Procedure: Applicants must register and establish a personal user ID and password. Check website for further details
Closing Date: 19 November

Funding: Government, Foundation
Contributor: National Research Council on behalf of the Ford Foundation
Additional Information: Predoctoral fellows are required to enrol full-time in a program leading to a PhD or ScD degree in an eligible field of study

For further information contact:

Tel: (1) 202 334 2872
Email: infofell@nas.edu

Jefferson Science Fellowship

Subjects: Science, technology, and engineering (STE)
Purpose: To offset the costs of temporary living quarters in the Washington, DC area
Eligibility: Applicants must be United States citizens and holding a tenured faculty position at a United States degree granting academic institution of higher learning. For terms and conditions as well as further details log on to the website
Level of Study: Postgraduate
Value: The Jefferson Science Fellow will be paid a per diem of up to US$50,000 by the United States Department of State and US$10,000 will be made available to the Fellow for travel associated with their assignment(s)
Length of Study: 1 year
Frequency: Annual
Application Procedure: A complete nomination/application package consists of nomination/application form in PDF format and in word format; curriculum vitae (limit 10 pages); statements of qualifications (limit 2 pages each); and at least 3, and no more than 5, letters of recommendation from peers of the nominee/applicant
Closing Date: 14 January
Contributor: National Academies supported through a partnership between American philanthropic foundations, the United States STE academic community, professional scientific societies, and the United States Department of State
Additional Information: Applicants should notify their institution while applying and encourage them to initiate a JSF/MOU as described on the website. Incomplete nomination/application packages, or those received after the deadline, will not be reviewed

For further information contact:

Tel: (1) 202 334 2643
Fax: (1) 202 334 2759
Email: jsf@nas.edu

National Energy Technology Laboratory Methane Hydrates Fellowship Program (MHFP)

Subjects: Chemistry (Methane Hydrate)

Purpose: To provide postgraduate and postdoctoral candidates opportunities for career development, largely of their own choice in the Methane Hydrates field that are compatible with the interests of the sponsoring laboratories and universities, and to contribute thereby to the overall efforts of NETL in their support in the development of Methane Hydrate Science

Eligibility: Open to candidates holding appropriate prior degree for the level of fellowship they intend to pursue. An applicant's training, professional experience, and research experience may be in any appropriate discipline or combination of disciplines required for the proposed project. Each Methane Hydrate Program fellow will be closely affiliated with a Research Adviser at the host venue

Level of Study: Doctorate, Postdoctorate, Postgraduate

Type: Fellowship

Value: Stipend Rates: Master's Level (Fellow) begins at US$30,000 with a maximum 2-year tenure, PhD Level (Fellow) begins at US$35,000 with a maximum 3-year tenure and Postdoctoral Level (Research Associate) begins at US$60,000 with a maximum 2-year tenure

Length of Study: 3 years

Application Procedure: Application must be submitted only in hard copy and sent by express delivery to the Associateship Programs office. After completing the WebRAP application, you must also mail your supporting documents (transcripts and references) to the same address

Closing Date: 1 February and 15 August

Additional Information: Please check the website for further details. Please direct all Application inquiries directly to the Research Associateship Programs at rap@nas.edu or by phone at 202 334 2760

For further information contact:

Tel: (1) 202 334 2707
Email: ebasquest@nas.edu
Contact: Dr Eric O Basques, Research Adviser

National Aeronautics and Space Administration (NASA)

NASA Headquarters, Suite 5R30, Washington, DC 20546, United States of America

Tel: (1) 202 358 0001
Fax: (1) 202 358 4338
Email: hfinquiry@stsci.edu
Website: www.nasa.gov
Contact: Public Communications Office

Hubble Fellowships for Postdoctoral Scientists

Purpose: The Hubble Fellowship Program provides an opportunity for highly qualified recent postdoctoral scientists to conduct independent research that is broadly related to the NASA Cosmic Origins scientific goals as addressed by any of the missions in that program: the Hubble Space Telescope, Spitzer Space Telescope, Stratospheric Observatory for Infrared Astronomy (SOFIA), the Herschel Space Observatory, and the James Webb Space Telescope. The research will be carried out at United States Host Institutions chosen by each Fellow

Eligibility: Applicants must have received a PhD or equivalent doctoral-level research degree in astronomy, physics, or a related discipline on or after 1 January (previous year). Graduate-student awardees who have not yet received their doctoral degree at the time of application must present evidence of having completed all requirements for the degree before commencing their Fellowships. Hubble Fellowships are open to citizens of the United States and to English-speaking citizens of other countries. Qualified applicants will receive consideration without regard to race, creed, color, age, gender, or national origin. Women and members of minority groups are strongly encouraged to apply. Incomplete applications and/or applications received after the deadline will not be considered

Type: Fellowship

Value: An annual stipend of approx. US$67,000 plus benefits, and an additional allowance of US$16,000 per year for travel and other research costs. Funding will be provided initially for the first year of the Fellowship. Renewals for the second and third years will depend on annual performance reviews

Length of Study: Up to 3 years

Frequency: Annual

Country of Study: United States of America

Closing Date: 6 November

Additional Information: The Hubble Fellowship Program is administered for NASA by the Space Telescope Science Institute (STScI), operated by the Association of Universities for Research in Astronomy, Inc., working in cooperation with astronomical institutions throughout the United States. Awards will be made to support each Hubble Fellow through a designated Host Institution

For further information contact:

Email: hfinquiry@stsci.edu

National Air and Space Museum (NASM), Smithsonian Institution

600 Independence Ave SW, Washington, DC 20560, United States of America

Tel:	(1) 202 633 2471
Fax:	(1) 202 786 2566
Email:	colette.williams@nasm.si.edu
Website:	www.nasm.si.edu

The Smithsonian Institution's National Air and Space Museum (NASM) maintains the largest collection of historic air and spacecraft in the world. It is also a vital centre for research into the history, science and technology of aviation and space flight.

Charles A Lindbergh Chair in Aerospace History

Subjects: Aerospace history
Purpose: To support senior scholars who are at work on, or anticipate being at work on, books on aerospace history
Eligibility: There are no eligibility restrictions
Level of Study: Research
Type: Fellowship
Value: US$1,00,000
Length of Study: 1 year
Frequency: Annual
Study Establishment: Smithsonian Institution
Country of Study: United States of America
Application Procedure: Applicants must complete an application form
Closing Date: 15 January
Funding: Private
Contributor: Smithsonian restricted funds

For further information contact:

Email:	collette.williams@nasm.si.edu
Contact:	Colette Williams, Fellowship Co-ordinator

National Air and Space Museum Aviation/Space Writers Award

Subjects: Aerospace
Purpose: To support research towards publication on aerospace topics
Eligibility: There are no eligibility restrictions
Level of Study: Unrestricted
Type: Award
Value: US$5,000
Frequency: Every 2 years
Application Procedure: Applicants must submit four collated copies of their application, consisting of the following: (1) an application cover sheet; (2) a maximum two-page, single-spaced proposal stating the subject of their research and publication goals; (3) a one- to two-page curriculum vitae; and (4) a one-page detailed budget. The application cover sheet can be obtained online or by writing to the Fellowship Co-ordinator
Funding: Private

Postdoctoral Earth and Planetary Sciences Fellowship

Subjects: Earth and geological sciences, geology, geophysics
Purpose: To support scientific research
Level of Study: Postdoctorate
Type: Fellowship
Value: Stipend, compatible with National Research Council Awards
Length of Study: 1 or more years
Frequency: Dependent on funds available
Study Establishment: NASM
Country of Study: United States of America
Application Procedure: Applicants must complete an application form
Closing Date: 15 January
Funding: Private
Contributor: Smithsonian restricted funds

National Association for Core Curriculum, Inc.

1640 Franklin Avenue, Suite 104, Kent, OH 44240-4324, United States of America

Tel:	(1) 330 677 5008
Fax:	(1) 330 677 5008
Email:	gvarsnacc@aol.com
Contact:	Dr Gordon F Vars, Executive Secretary & Treasurer

The National Association for Core Curriculum, Inc. has promoted integrative person centred education at all levels since 1953.

Bossing-Edwards Research Scholarship Award

Subjects: Research on interdisciplinary approaches to education, with special emphasis on core curriculum

Purpose: To encourage research on core curriculum and other interdisciplinary or integrative approaches to education

Eligibility: Open to individuals who have previously been a core teacher for at least one year, and have been accepted on a graduate programme leading to a Master's, specialist's or doctor's degree at a university that has adequate resources for research in core curriculum

Level of Study: Doctorate, Postgraduate

Type: Scholarship

Value: Up to US$300

Frequency: Dependent on funds available

Study Establishment: An appropriate institution

Country of Study: United States of America

No. of awards offered: 5

Application Procedure: Applicants should write explaining intended research and how they meet the criteria of eligibility

Closing Date: 19 April

No. of awards given last year: 1

No. of applicants last year: 5

For further information contact:

Email: canada@berkeley.edu

National Association for Gifed Children

Davis Scholarship

Purpose: Lewis & Clark is pleased to announce its continuing commitment to the Davis United World College (UWC) Scholars program for the academic year

Level of Study: Postgraduate

Type: Scholarship

Value: US$20,000

Length of Study: 4 year

Frequency: Annual

Country of Study: Any country

Closing Date: 15 February

Funding: Foundation

For further information contact:

Associate Dean of Students, Lewis & Clark College, 0615 SW Palatine Hill Road, Portland, OR 97219, United States of America

Tel: (1) 503 768 7305
Fax: (1) 503 768 7301
Email: iso@lclark.edu

Distinguished Scholarship

Purpose: The National Association for Gifted Children (NAGC) annually presents the Distinguished Scholar Award to an individual who has made significant contributions to the field of knowledge regarding the education of gifted and talented individuals. This individual should have a continued record of distinguished scholarship and contributions to the field of gifted education for more than 10 years, and must show a record of ongoing scholarly productivity as recognized by experts in the field

Eligibility: 1. Evidence of research in the field of gifted and talented. 2. Evidence that the contributions reflect a continuous and noted record of involvement in the field of gifted and talented education. 3. Evidence of recognition by peers of the importance of the above-mentioned contributions

Level of Study: Postgraduate

Type: Scholarship

Value: US$30,000

Length of Study: 4 year

Frequency: Annual

Country of Study: Any country

Closing Date: 1 February

Funding: Foundation

Goodrich Scholarship Program

Purpose: Goodrich students establish a dynamic presence on campus. They come hungry, ready to learn and eager to join the UNO community. Many recipients are the first in their families to attend college. They come from underrepresented populations and have earned an opportunity to continue their education

Level of Study: Postgraduate

Type: Scholarship

Frequency: Annual

Country of Study: Any country

Funding: Foundation

For further information contact:

UNO Campus, 6001 Dodge Street, CPACS 123, Omaha Nebraska, NE 68182, United States of America

Email: unogoodrich@unomaha.edu

Paul Beck Memorial Scholarship

Purpose: The Faculty Senate of the University of Nebraska Omaha (UNO) has sponsored scholarships for students since 1970 when Paul L. Beck, a long-time member of the History Department, urged faculty and staff to go beyond the classroom to assist capable students in their educational pursuits at UNO

Eligibility: 1. Applications must include a one page letter describing how this scholarship will help further your educational needs. 2. Applications must include a letter of support from a UNO faculty member. This letter must be sent directly to the Faculty Senate office by the faculty member. 3. No application will be considered unless all documents listed above are on file in the Faculty Senate office by the deadline. 4. Only one application/category per student is permitted

Level of Study: Postgraduate

Type: Scholarship

Value: US$1,000

Frequency: Annual

Country of Study: Any country

Closing Date: 2 February

Funding: Foundation

For further information contact:

The Faculty Senate, University of Nebraska at Omaha, ASH 105, 6001 Dodge St., Omaha Nebraska, NE 68182, United States of America

Email: sbishop@unomaha.edu

University of Nebraska Omaha Women's Club Scholarships

Purpose: A portion of the UNOWC treasury funds are transferred each year to the scholarship fund, as are memorials. Our Annual Membership Fundraiser Dinner gives members a chance to contribute individually and to meet the scholarship winners. These and other projects, carried out over the years with a lot of work and dedication from many members, continue to increase the UNOWC Scholarship Funds

Level of Study: Postgraduate

Type: Scholarship

Value: US$100

Frequency: Annual

Country of Study: Any country

Closing Date: 31 May

Funding: Foundation

For further information contact:

Gina Pearson/Elaine Allen, University of Nebraska Foundation, 2285 S. 67th St., Ste 200, Omaha Nebraska, NE 68106, United States of America

Email: uno.womens.club@gmail.com

National Association of Teachers of Singing (NATS)

9957 Moorings Drive, Suite 401, Jacksonville, FL 32257, United States of America

Tel: (1) 904 992 9101; Toll Free: 888 262 2065

Fax: (1) 904 262 2587

Email: info@nats.org

Website: www.nats.org

The National Association of Teachers of Singing (NATS) is now the largest association of teachers of singing in the world. NATS offers a variety of lifelong learning experiences to its members, such as workshops, intern programmes, master classes, and conferences, all beginning at the chapter level and progressing to national events.

National Association of Teachers of Singing Art Song Competition Award

Subjects: Singing

Purpose: To stimulate the creation of quality vocal literature through the cooperation of singer and composer

Eligibility: Open to any composer whose submitted work is a song cycle, group of songs, or extended single song of approximately 15 minutes in length (13–17 minutes acceptable); for single voice and piano; to a text written in English, for which the composer has secured copyright clearance (only text setting permission necessary); composed within the last 2 years, and who pays the competition entry fee

Type: Cash prize

Value: US$2,000 plus the composer's expenses (US$500 airfare reimbursement plus hotel) and US$1,000, 2nd place

Study Establishment: Valdosta State University

Country of Study: United States of America

Application Procedure: check the website for further details

Closing Date: 1 December

For further information contact:

Department of Music, Valdosta State University, 1500 N. Patterson Street, Valdosta, GA 31602, United States of America

Email: cmikkels@valdosta.edu
Contact: Dr Carol Mikkelsen

National Breast Cancer Foundation (NBCF)

Level 9, 50 Pitt St, Sydney 2000, GPO Box 4129, Sydney, NSW 2001, Australia

Tel: (61) 2 8098 4800
Fax: (61) 2 8098 4801
Email: info@nbcf.org.au
Website: www.nbcf.org.au

The ultimate goal of the National Breast Cancer Foundation (NBCF) is to raise enough money to fund a cure for breast cancer. The NBCF supports and promotes research into breast cancer, facilitates consumer participation in all aspects of their work, acts as an advocate for breast cancer research, and provides opportunities for all Australians to contribute to breast cancer research.

National Breast Cancer Foundation Doctoral Scholarship

Subjects: All disciplines of breast cancer research
Purpose: To provide outstanding graduates with a strong interest in breast cancer research with an opportunity to pursue full-time PhD studies at an Australian University
Eligibility: Open to applicants who are permanent residents of Australia
Level of Study: Doctorate, Postgraduate, Research
Type: Scholarship
Value: Scholars will receive a stipend of approx. A$33,240
Length of Study: 3 years
Frequency: Annual
Country of Study: Australia
No. of awards offered: 15
Application Procedure: The applications are judged under peer review by experts in the field for their scientific merit and contribution to either new knowledge or building on existing knowledge of breast cancer

Closing Date: See website
Funding: Foundation
Contributor: Australian community and corporate funding
No. of awards given last year: 4
No. of applicants last year: 15

For further information contact:

Email: lhan.gannon@nbcf.org.au
Contact: Lhan Gannon

Novel Concept Awards

Subjects: Oncology (Breast cancer research) and other novel ideas into Breast Cancer research
Purpose: To provide investigators with the opportunity to pursue serendipitous observations and explore new, innovative, and untested ideas
Eligibility: Open to applicants undertaking research in the entire continuum of breast cancer research. Residing in Australia throughout the funding period. Must meet all eligibility criteria outlined in guidelines and application form. Please check at www.nbcf.org.au
Level of Study: Unrestricted
Type: Research grant
Value: Maximum value of A$100,000 per grant per year
Length of Study: 1–2 years
Country of Study: Australia
No. of awards offered: 35
Application Procedure: Please contact the Research Administrator or check the website for further details
Closing Date: 20 June
Funding: Foundation, Trusts
Contributor: NBCF, Australian Community and Corporate
No. of awards given last year: 12
No. of applicants last year: 35
Additional Information: Each year NBCF board will decide when to call for application and closing dates in late February

Pilot Study Grants

Subjects: Oncology (breast cancer research)
Purpose: To financially assist investigators to obtain preliminary data regarding methodology, effect sizes and possible findings relating to new research ideas relevant to breast cancer
Eligibility: Applicants must be Australian citizens, or be graduates from overseas with permanent Australian resident status, must reside in Australia throughout the funding period and not under bond to any foreign government

Level of Study: Research, Unrestricted
Type: Grant
Value: A maximum of A$100,000 for up to 2 years
Length of Study: Up to 2 years
Frequency: Every 2 years
Country of Study: Australia
No. of awards offered: 76
Application Procedure: Check website for further details
Closing Date: 10 May
Funding: Foundation
Contributor: Australian Community and Corporate
No. of awards given last year: 3
No. of applicants last year: 76
Additional Information: NBCF Board will decide whether to offer this grant scheme again when they meet annual in late February

For further information contact:

Email: info@nbcf.org.au

National Bureau of Asian Research (NBR)

1414 NE 42nd Street, Suite 300, Seattle, WA 98105, United States of America

Tel: (1) 206 632 7370
Fax: (1) 206 632 7487
Email: nbr@nbr.org
Website: www.nbr.org
Contact: George F Russell

NBR is a nonprofit, nonpartisan research institution dedicated to informing and strengthening policy. NBR conducts advanced research on politics and security, economics and trade, and health and societal issues, with emphasis on those of interest to the United States.

The Next Generation: Leadership in Asian Affairs Fellowship

Subjects: China's energy insecurity, military modernization in Asia, early health policy, central Asia's changing geopolitics, globalization or Chinese economic development, trends in Islamic education in South Asia, China–Southeast Asia relations

Purpose: To further the professional development of Asian specialists in the year just after the completion of their Master's degree
Eligibility: Open to citizens or permanent residents of the United States who have obtained a Master's degree
Level of Study: Research
Type: Fellowships
Value: Each fellow will receive a US$32,500 fellowship award (with benefits), as well as a reimbursement for some relocation expenses
Length of Study: 1 year
Frequency: Annual
Country of Study: United States of America
Application Procedure: Candidates must submit an online cover letter, curriculum vitae, 750 word essay stating the purpose of applying and 3 written references
Closing Date: 15 January
Funding: Government, Corporation, Foundation
No. of awards given last year: 3

For further information contact:

Email: nextgen@nbr.org

National Cattleman Foundation

Continuing Medical Education Beef Industry Scholarship

Purpose: Sponsored by CME Group & the National Cattlemen's Foundation, ten (10) scholarships of US$1,500 will be awarded to outstanding students who are pursuing careers in the beef industry
Eligibility: Must be enrolled as an undergraduate student in a two or four-year institution of higher education for the entire upcoming academic year. Proof of enrollment as a full-time student will be required to receive the scholarship money; 1. Write a one-page letter expressing/indicating your future career goals related to the beef industry. 2. Write an essay of 750 words or less describing an issue confronting the beef industry and offer your solution. 3. Obtain two (2) letters of reference from current or former instructors or industry professionals. 4. Applications must contain the Beef Industry scholarship cover page
Level of Study: Graduate
Type: Scholarship
Length of Study: 2- 4 years
Frequency: Annual
Country of Study: United States of America and Europe

Closing Date: 30 October
Funding: Private

For further information contact:

9110 East Nichols Ave., Suite #300, Centennial, CO 80112, United States of America

Email: ncf@beef.org

National Education Association (NEA) Foundation

1201 16th Street, North West, Washington, DC 20036, United States of America

Tel: (1) 202 822 7840
Fax: (1) 202 822 7779
Email: NEAFoundation@nea.org
Website: www.neafoundation.org

The NEA Foundation offers programs and grants that support public school educators' efforts to close the achievement gaps, increase student achievement, salute excellence in education and provide professional development.

Student Achievement Grants

Subjects: All subjects
Purpose: To promote collaborative, innovative ideas that lead to student achievement of high standards
Eligibility: Open to teams of two or more practising United States public school teachers in grades K–12, public school education support personnel, public higher education faculty and staff. Preference will be given to National Education Association members, and to educators who serve economically disadvantaged and/or underserved students
Level of Study: Postgraduate
Type: Grant
Value: US$2,000 and US$5,000
Length of Study: 12 months
Frequency: Annual
Country of Study: United States of America
Application Procedure: Applicants must consult the organization for details
Closing Date: 1 February, 1 June, and 15 October

For further information contact:

Email: NEAFoundation@nea.org

National Endowment for the Humanities (NEH)

Division of Research, Room 318, 1100 Pennsylvania Avenue North West, Washington, DC 20506, United States of America

Tel: (1) 202 606 8400
Fax: (1) 202 606 8204
Email: research@neh.gov
Website: www.neh.gov
Contact: Programme Officer

National Endowment for the Humanities' (NEH) Research Division facilitates research and original scholarship in the humanities through grants to universities, centres for advanced study and individual scholars. NEH uses the following definition of the humanities: 'The humanities include, but are not limited to, language, both modern and classical, linguistics, literature, history, jurisprudence, philosophy, archaeology, comparative religion, ethics, the history, criticism and theory of the arts, aspects of social sciences which have humanistic content and employ humanistic methods, and the study and application of the humanities to the human environment with particular attention to reflecting our diverse heritage, traditions and history and to the relevance of the humanities to the current conditions of national life'.

National Endowment for the Humanities Fellowships

Subjects: Projects which may contribute to scholarly knowledge, to the conception and substance of individual courses in the humanities, or to the general public's understanding of the humanities. Projects may address broad topics or consist of study and research in a specialised field
Purpose: To provide support for full-time research on projects that can be completed during the tenure of the award, as well as for work that is part of a long-term endeavour. Recipients usually produce scholarly articles, monographs on specialised subjects, books on broad topics, archaeological site reports, translations, editions or other scholarly tools

Eligibility: Open to faculty or staff members of colleges or universities, or of primary or secondary schools, or independent scholars or writers
Level of Study: Postdoctorate
Type: Fellowship
Value: US$24,000 for six–eight month tenure and US $40,000 for 9–12 month tenure
Length of Study: Varies
Frequency: Annual
Country of Study: Other
Application Procedure: Applicants must complete and submit an application form. Guidelines and application forms are posted on the NEH website
Closing Date: 1 May
Funding: Government

For further information contact:

Email: questions@neh.gov

National Foundation for Infectious Diseases (NFID)

7201 Wisconsin Avenue, Suite 750, Bethesda, MD 20814, United States of America

Tel: (1) 301 656 0003
Fax: (1) 301 907 0878
Email: info@nfid.org
Website: www.nfid.org

The National Foundation for Infectious Diseases (NFID) is a non-profit, non-governmental organization whose mission is public and professional education and promotion of research on the causes, treatment and prevention of infectious diseases.

National Foundation for Infectious Diseases Postdoctoral Fellowship in Nosocomial Infection Research and Training

Subjects: Health and medical sciences
Purpose: To encourage a qualified physician researcher to become a specialist and investigator in the field of nosocomial infections
Eligibility: Open to citizens of the United States
Level of Study: Postgraduate
Type: Fellowship
Value: US$40,000
Frequency: Annual

Country of Study: United States of America
Application Procedure: Applicants must submit their application form and curriculum vitae
Closing Date: 6 January
Additional Information: Contact Grants Manager. Priority will be given to Fellows in or entering into infectious diseases training

For further information contact:

Email: nfid@aol.com

National Health and Medical Research Council (NHMRC)

NHMRC, GPO Box 1421, Canberra, ACT 2601, Australia

Tel: (61) 2 6217 9000
Fax: (61) 2 6217 9100
Email: grantnet.help@nhmrc.gov.au
Website: www.nhmrc.gov.au
Contact: Executive Director

The National Health and Medical Research Council (NHMRC) (Australia) consolidates within a single national organization the often independent functions of research funding and development of advice. One of its strengths is that it brings together and draws upon the resources of all components of the health system, including governments, medical practitioners, nurses and allied health professionals, researchers, teaching and research institutions, public and private programme managers, service administrators, community health organizations, social health researchers and consumers.

National Health and Medical Research Council Equipment Grants

Subjects: All fields of medicine and dentistry
Purpose: To provide funding support for the purchase of items of equipment required for biomedical research
Eligibility: Open to individuals, groups or institutions which are normally eligible for NHMRC support. Grants will be made on the basis of scientific merit, taking into consideration factors including whether the applicants hold NHMRC grants, the institutional ranking of the application, and institutional or regional availability of major equipment
Level of Study: Unrestricted
Type: Grant

Value: A$10,000 to cover the cost of equipment in excess of
Frequency: Annual
Country of Study: Australia
Application Procedure: Applicants must complete an application form
Closing Date: Please contact the organisation
Funding: Government

For further information contact:

MDP 33, Project Grants Office, GPO Box 9848, Canberra, ACT 2601, Australia

Tel: (61) 2 6289 8278
Fax: (61) 2 6289 8617
Email: jean.sewell@hhlgcs.ausgovhhcs.telememo.au
Contact: Equipment Grants Officer

National Health and Medical Research Council Public Health Travelling Fellowships

Subjects: Public health, defined as the organised response by society to the need to protect and promote the people's health
Purpose: To enable Fellows to make postgraduate study tours abroad or within Australia, which relate to their work and speciality and which will be of benefit to public health in Australia
Eligibility: Open to all personnel working in the field of public health, who are suitably qualified at a level appropriate for fulfilment of the objectives of the study and for implementation of its benefits. The applicant may be employed in government or industry, or may be self-employed. Preference will be given to those applicants who would not normally, in the course of their employment, have the opportunity, as part of their normal duties, for overseas travel and experience
Level of Study: Unrestricted
Type: Other
Value: Not exceeding A$19,700, plus an agreed annual allowance to cover cost increases
Length of Study: 2–12 months
Frequency: Annual
Country of Study: Any country
No. of awards offered: 18
Application Procedure: Please write for details
Closing Date: 31 July
Funding: Government
No. of awards given last year: 8
No. of applicants last year: 18
Additional Information: Preference will be given to public health practitioners

For further information contact:

Secretariat & Training Awards, GPO Box 9848, Canberra, ACT 2601, Australia

Tel: (61) 2 6289 7945
Fax: (61) 2 6289 6957
Email: trevorlord@hhlgcs.ausgovhhcs.telememo.au
Contact: Mr Trevor Lord

National Health and Medical Research Council Research Project Grants

Subjects: All fields of medicine and dentistry
Purpose: To provide support for work on problems which are likely to be capable of solution in a reasonably short period of time
Eligibility: Open to Australian researchers only
Level of Study: Unrestricted
Type: Grant
Value: To cover salary, equipment, maintenance and other specific expenses
Frequency: Annual
Country of Study: Australia
No. of awards offered: 1,299
Application Procedure: Applicants must complete an application form
Closing Date: 6 March
Funding: Government
No. of awards given last year: 406
No. of applicants last year: 1,299

For further information contact:

Project Grants Office, GPO Box 9848, Canberra, ACT 2601, Australia

Tel: (61) 2 6289 6974
Fax: (61) 2 6289 8617
Email: elizabeth.hoole@hhlgcs.ausgovhhcs.telememo.au

R Douglas Wright Awards

Subjects: All fields of health and medical research
Purpose: To provide outstanding researchers at an early stage in their career with an opportunity for independent research together with improved security
Eligibility: Open to applicants who have completed postdoctoral research training or have equivalent experience, and are seeking to establish themselves in a career in medical research in Australia
Level of Study: Postdoctorate, Professional development

Type: Award
Value: Salary in the range of Senior Research Officer Level 1 to Senior Research Officer Level 4, with annual increments, plus an allowance of A$10,000 per year
Length of Study: 4 years
Frequency: Annual
Study Establishment: Australian research institutions
Country of Study: Australia
No. of awards offered: 43
Application Procedure: Applicants must complete an application form, available from Ms H Murray
Closing Date: 30 April
Funding: Government
No. of awards given last year: 6
No. of applicants last year: 43

For further information contact:

Fellowships Unit - Mail Drop Point, 33GPO Box 9848, Canberra, ACT 2601, Australia

Tel: (61) 2 6289 5034
Fax: (61) 2 6289 1329
Email: helen.murray@hhlgcs.ausgovhhcs.telememo.au
Contact: Ms H Murray

Targeted Call for Research into Healthy Ageing of Aboriginal and Torres Strait Islander Peoples

Subjects: This TCR follows a public call for research priorities in Aboriginal and Torres Strait Islander health conducted
Purpose: The aim of implementing this call is to provide funding for rigorous, culturally-informed research into improving the health and experiences of ageing in older Aboriginal and Torres Strait Islander peoples. Quality evidence generated from research will allow for better planning, funding and implementation of policies and services to achieve and support healthy ageing for Aboriginal and Torres Strait Islander peoples
Eligibility: Applications for NHMRC funding are subject to the general eligibility requirements set out in the NHMRC Funding Rules. Additional eligibility requirements are in scheme-specific funding rules. Institutions must be an NHMRC approved Administering Institution to be eligible to receive and administer NHMRC funding - refer to the NHMRC website for a list of approved Administering Institutions
Level of Study: Graduate
Type: Grant
Value: Total value available is A$5,000,000
Frequency: Annual
Country of Study: Any country

Application Procedure: Official website to apply electronically for the grant application is www.nhmrc.gov.au/grants-funding-administering-grants
Closing Date: 15 August
Funding: Private
Additional Information: Applications must be submitted electronically using NHMRC's online Research Grants Management System (RGMS). Official link for the following grant is www.nhmrc.gov.au/grants-funding-administering-grants

For further information contact:

Email: help@nhmrc.gov.au

National Institute for Health and Care Excellence (NICE)

Level 1A, City Tower, Piccadilly Plaza, M1 4BT, Manchester, United Kingdom

Tel: (44) 300 323 0140
Fax: (44) 300 323 0149
Website: www.nice.org.uk

The National Institute for Health and Care Excellence (NICE) provides national guidance and advice to improve health and social care. NICE was originally set up in 1999 as the National Institute for Clinical Excellence, a special health authority, to reduce variation in the availability and quality of NHS treatments and care.

National Institute for Health and Care Excellence Scholarships

Subjects: NICE Foundation is the Educational Trust formed by intellectual and industries veteran with vision to prepare the next generations by providing excellent learning framework that prepares student to compute in a diverse world market
Purpose: NICE Scholarships are one-year opportunities for qualified health and social care professionals to find out about the inner workings of NICE and undertake a supported improvement project, related to NICE guidance, within their local organization
Eligibility: NICE Scholarships are typically awarded to specialist registrars, senior nurses, pharmacists and allied health professionals, service improvement leads, public health and social care specialists and health service managers. In addition to their project-based activities, NICE Scholars are

expected to act as local ambassadors for clinical and public health and social care excellence; promote the principles and the recommendations of NICE guidance-through teaching activities, for example

Type: Scholarship

Value: NICE Scholars are supported in their project via a series of workshops, access to a very experienced senior mentor and contact with the expert teams at NICE. NICE Scholars are not paid. NICE will, however, meet all reasonable expenses (e.g. travel, accommodation) incurred in the course of carrying out Scholarship activities

Length of Study: 1 year

Frequency: Annual

Country of Study: United Kingdom

Application Procedure: The mode of applying is by post

Closing Date: 1 November

Additional Information: Scholars are expected to devote approximately 7.5 hours per week to their Scholarship project. For detailed information, visit www.nice.org.uk/getinvolved/nice_fellows_and_scholars/scholars/NICEScholarships.jsp

National Institute of General Medical Sciences (NIGMS)

45 Center Drive, MSC 6200, Bethesda, MD 20892-6200, United States of America

Tel:	(1) 301 496 7301
Fax:	(1) 301 402 0224
Email:	info@nigms.nih.gov
Website:	www.nigms.nih.gov
Contact:	Ms Jilliene Drayton, Information Development Specialist

The National Institute of General Medical Sciences (NIGMS) is one of the National Institutes of Health (NIH), the principal biomedical research agency of the United States Federal Government. NIGMS supports basic research that increases understanding of biological processes and lays the foundation for advances in disease diagnosis, treatment, and prevention.

National Institute of General Medical Sciences Research Project Grants (R01)

Subjects: Biomedical sciences

Purpose: To support a discrete project related to the investigator's area of interest and competence

Eligibility: Research project grants may be awarded to nonprofit organizations and institutions; governments and their agencies; occasionally, though rarely, to individuals who have access to adequate facilities and resources for conducting the research; and to profit-making organizations. Foreign institutions and international organizations are also eligible to apply for these grants

Level of Study: Postgraduate

Type: Grant

Value: These grants may provide funds for reasonable costs of the research activity, as well as for salaries, equipment, supplies, travel and other related expenses

Frequency: Annual

Country of Study: United States of America

Application Procedure: Applicants must contact the Office of Extramural Outreach for details

Funding: Government

Additional Information: www.grants.nih.gov/supportwww.nigms.nih.gov/Research/Mechanisms/Pages/ResearchProjectGrants.aspx

For further information contact:

Office of Extramural Outreach, NIH, 6701 Rockledge Drive Msc 7760, Bethesda, MD 20892-7760, United States of America

Tel:	(1) 301 435 0714
Email:	grantsinfo@nih.gov

National Road Safety Authority Individual Postdoctoral Fellowships (F32)

Subjects: Biomedical sciences

Purpose: NIGMS welcomes NRSA applications from eligible individuals who seek postdoctoral biomedical research training in areas related to the scientific programmes of the Institute

Eligibility: Open to applicants who have received the doctoral degree (domestic or foreign) by the beginning date of the proposed award

Level of Study: Postdoctorate

Type: Award

Value: NIGMS provides an annual stipend to postdoctoral fellows, and an institutional allowance to cover training-related expenses. The stipend, tuition/fees and institutional allowance are detailed at grants.nih.gov/grants/guide/notice-files/NOT-OD-14-046.html

Length of Study: Up to 3 years

Frequency: Annual

Study Establishment: The institutional setting may be domestic or foreign, public or private
Country of Study: Any country
Application Procedure: Applicants must write to the main address for details or telephone Dr Michael Sesma, at (1) 301 594 2772. Further details are also available from the website www.nigms.nih.gov
Closing Date: 8 April
Funding: Government
Additional Information: www.nigms.nih.gov/training/indivpostdoc/Pages/PostdocFellowshipDescription.aspx

National Institutes of Health

900 Rockville Pike, Bethesda, MA 20892, United States of America

Website: www.nih.gov
Contact: Dr Belinda Seto, Acting Deputy Director for Extramural Research

Hitchings-Elion Postdoctoral Fellowships for United States Scientist

Purpose: The purpose of these fellowships is to promote scientific collaboration between British and American scientists for the conduct of biomedical and behavioral research
Eligibility: The applicant must be a United States citizen or permanent United States resident, hold a doctorate level degree in one of the medical or veterinary clinical, behavioral, or biomedical sciences, and be within ten years of the last doctoral degree
Level of Study: Research
Type: Fellowship
Frequency: Annual
Country of Study: Any country
Application Procedure: The administration of the program will be integrated into the administration of other Fogarty International Center fellowship activities and the application receipt processes of the Division of Research Grants, NIH. Applications must be sent to the Division of Research Grants, NIH. Special application forms must be used and are available, along with detailed instructions from International Research and Awards Branch. Fogarty International Center National Institutes of Health Building 31, Room B2C39
Closing Date: 10 January, 10 May and 10 September each year
Funding: Private

For further information contact:

Chief, International Research and Awards Branch, Fogarty International Center, Building 31, Room B2C21, Bethesda, MD 20892, United States

Tel: (1) 301 496 1653

National Library of Medicine (NLM)

8600 Rockville Pike Building 38A, Bethesda, MD 20894, United States of America

Tel: (1) 301 496 4221
Fax: (1) 301 402 0421
Email: dm99n@nih.gov
Website: www.nlm.nih.gov
Contact: Mr Dwight Mawrery, Grants Management Officer

As one of the nation's premier repositories of biomedical information, the National Library of Medicine (NLM) has a vital interest in information management and in the enormous utility of computers and telecommunications for improving storage, retrieval, access and use of biomedical information. The Library offers support for qualified investigators, be they individuals or institutions, in three separate but related programme areas: medical informatics, biotechnology information and health sciences library and information science.

National Library of Medicine Fellowship in Applied Informatics

Subjects: Health informatics
Purpose: To improve the American healthcare system by supporting health science professionals (including librarians) whose primary interest is to put informatics into practice, develop modern information systems in traditional organisations, use the new information techniques in a specific field and help disseminate promising programmes and systems
Eligibility: Open to individuals with a BA, BSc, MA, MSc or PhD in a field related to health, who are United States nationals or permanent residents of the United States of America
Level of Study: Doctorate, Graduate, Postdoctorate, Postgraduate
Type: Fellowship
Value: Up to US$58,000 per year, based on the salary or remuneration the individual would have been paid from their home institution

Length of Study: Varies
Frequency: Annual
Study Establishment: Universities, colleges, hospitals, laboratories, units of State and certain agencies of the Federal Government in the United States
Country of Study: United States of America
Application Procedure: Applications must be submitted by an organisation on behalf of the individual seeking the grant, on the standard grant application form PHS 416-1 (rev 8/95)
Closing Date: 5 April, 5 August, 5 December
Additional Information: The NLM encourages potential applicants to clarify any issues or questions. For enquiries regarding programmatic issues, please contact Mr Peter Clepper, Program Officer. For enquiries regarding Division of Nursing programmatic issues, please contact the Division of Nursing. For enquiries regarding fiscal matters, please contact Ms Shelley Carow, Grants Management Officer

For further information contact:

Division of Nursing, Parklawn Building, Room 9-36, 5600 Fishes Lane, Rockville, MD 20852, United States of America

Tel: (1) 301 443 5786
Fax: (1) 301 443 8586

National Library of Medicine Investigator Initiated Project Grant

Subjects: Medical informatics, biotechnology information, health sciences library and information science
Purpose: To support individual investigators and their colleagues to pursue a discreet, circumscribed line of investigation to its logical conclusion
Type: Project grant
Length of Study: Up to 3 years
Frequency: 3 times each year
Study Establishment: United States universities or research institutions
Country of Study: United States of America
Application Procedure: Applications must be submitted on the PHS form 398 (ref 5/95)
Closing Date: 1 February, 1 June, 1 October

For further information contact:

Division of Extramural Programmes, National Library of Medicine, Rockledge One Building, 6705 Rockledge Drive Suite 301, Bethesda, MD 20817, United States of America

Tel: (1) 301 594 4882
Fax: (1) 301 402 2952

Email: bean@nlm.nih.gov
Contact: Dr Carol A Bean

National Library of Medicine Postdoctoral Informatics Research Fellowships

Subjects: Informatics, medical informatics or biotechnology
Purpose: To promote researchers interested in informatics research training wishing to identify their own mentor and host institution
Eligibility: Open to applicants who have a PhD relevant to biomedicine or computer science or an equivalent degree from an accredited domestic or foreign institution
Level of Study: Postdoctorate
Type: Fellowship
Value: Based on established NIH schedules
Frequency: Annual
Study Establishment: United States universities or research institutions
Country of Study: United States of America
Application Procedure: Applicants must contact the organisation
Closing Date: Please write for details
Additional Information: For a complete list of NLM factsheets, please contact Factsheets, Office of Public Information

For further information contact:

Factsheets Office of Public Information National Library of Medicine, 8600 Rockville Pike, Bethesda, MD 20894, United States of America

Fax: (1) 301 496 4450
Email: publicinfo@nlm.nih.gov

National Library of Medicine Publication Grant Program

Subjects: Medical and health sciences
Purpose: To provide assistance for the preparation of book length manuscripts and, in some cases, the publication of important scientific information needed by United States health professionals
Eligibility: Open to public or private, non-profit institutions and individuals, who are involved in research
Type: Project grant
Value: US$35,000 direct costs per year over a period of three years maximum
Length of Study: 1–3 years
Frequency: 3 times each year

Country of Study: United States of America

Application Procedure: Applications must be submitted on the PHS FORM 398 (Rev 5/95) grant application kit

Closing Date: 1 February, 1 June, 1 October

Additional Information: Potential applicants are strongly encouraged to discuss projects early with the Program staff, who will discuss programme status and experience with them, provide additional information in response to specific application plans and review draft proposals for completeness if desired. For a complete list of NLM Factsheets, please contact Factsheets, Office of Public Information

For further information contact:

Tel: (1) 301 594 4882
Fax: (1) 301 402 2952
Email: sparks@nlm.nih.gov

National Research Council (NRC)

500 Fifth Street NW, Washington, DC 20001, United States of America

Tel: (1) 202 334 2644
Fax: (1) 202 334 2614
Website: www7.nationalacademies.org/dsc

The National Research Council (NRC) was organized by the National Academy of Sciences in 1916 to associate the broad community of science and technology with the Academy's purposes of further knowledge and advising the federal government.

Christine Mirzayan Science & Technology policy Graduate Fellowship Program

Country of Study: Any country

For further information contact:

Email: policyfellows@nas.edu

National Research Foundation (NRF)

PO Box 2600, Pretoria 0001, South Africa

Tel: (27) 12 481 4209
Fax: (27) 12 349 1179

Email: haveline@nrf.ac.za
Website: www.nrf.ac.za
Contact: Ms HA Michau, Manager, Student Support

The National Research Foundation (NRF) is responsible for funding South African research and other expertise in the fields of the social, natural and applied sciences, humanities, engineering and technology. The NRF is funded by the government, but also pursues joint ventures and collaboration with industry and the international community to increase the impact of its activities.

Innovation Masters and Doctoral Scholarships

Subjects: The Innovation Masters and Doctoral funding instruments are part of the Innovation Bursary Scheme (IBS) funded by the Department of Science and Technology (DST) and managed by the National Research Foundation (NRF)

Eligibility: Scholarships are open to South African citizens, South African permanent residents as well as a limited percentage of non-South African citizens registered at a South African public university

Level of Study: Postgraduate

Value: Masters scholarships worth ZAR 80,000 per annum and doctoral scholarships worth ZAR 110,000 per annum

Country of Study: South Africa

Application Procedure: Please check website for more details

Closing Date: 7 August

Contributor: Funded by Department of Science and Technology (DST) and managed by the National Research Foundation (NRF)

For further information contact:

Email: futurestudents@bournemouth.ac.uk

National Research Foundation Fellowships for Postdoctoral Research

Subjects: Natural and applied sciences, engineering, technology, social sciences and humanities

Purpose: To foster postdoctoral research in the natural and applied sciences, engineering, social sciences and the humanities

Eligibility: Open to any nationals who have received their PhD within the last 5 years

Level of Study: Postdoctorate

Type: Fellowship

Value: Up to ZAR 60,000 plus a contribution of ZAR 10,000 towards the running cost of the project
Length of Study: Up to 2 years
Frequency: Twice a year
Study Establishment: Any university, technikon or research institute for full-time research
Country of Study: South Africa
No. of awards offered: 150
Application Procedure: Applicants must complete and submit an application form, full academic record and the names of referees. Forms are available from the bursary offices of universities and technikons or can be downloaded from the website
Closing Date: 31 January or 31 July
Funding: Government
No. of awards given last year: 50
No. of applicants last year: 150

For further information contact:

Email: fellowships@twas.org

National Research Foundation Free-standing Masters and Doctoral Scholarships

Subjects: The NRF is mandated by an Act of Parliament, the National Research Foundation Act (Act No. 23 of 1998) to: Support and promote research through funding, human capacity development and the provision of the necessary research facilities, in order to facilitate the creation of knowledge, innovation and development in all fields of science and technology, including indigenous knowledge
Eligibility: Scholarships are open to South African citizens, South African permanent residents as well as a limited percentage of non-South African citizens registered at a South African public university. All applicants for full-time Masters or Doctoral studies in South Africa must be registered or intending to register at a South African public university. Applicants that already hold a degree at the level for which they are applying for funding are not eligible
Level of Study: Doctorate
Value: Masters scholarships worth ZAR 50,000 per year and doctoral scholarships worth ZAR 70,000 per year
Frequency: Annual
Country of Study: South Africa
Application Procedure: Applications must be submitted through an online application process to the NRF
Closing Date: 7 August
Funding: International office

For further information contact:

Email: CGSMSFSS-SEEMSBESC@cihr-irsc.gc.ca

National Research Foundation Targeted Research Awards Competitive Industry Programme

Subjects: Natural and applied sciences, engineering and technology
Purpose: To support research in priority areas where expertise is lacking
Eligibility: Open to South African citizens only, who qualify for postgraduate support. Postdoctoral support is available for any nationality
Level of Study: Doctorate, Postdoctorate, Postgraduate
Type: Research grant
Value: From a total of approximately rand 20 million per year
Frequency: Annual
Study Establishment: Any tertiary educational institution in South Africa
Country of Study: Other
No. of awards offered: 200
Application Procedure: Applicants must complete an electronic application form. For further information please contact Ms Jill Sawers
Closing Date: 31 July
Funding: Government
No. of awards given last year: 181
No. of applicants last year: 200
Additional Information: Joint ventures and collaboration with industry are strongly encouraged

For further information contact:

Tel: (27) 12 481 4104
Email: jill@frd.ac.za
Contact: Ms Jill Sawers, Manager

National Research Foundation Visiting Fellowships

Subjects: Natural and applied sciences, engineering and technology
Purpose: To strengthen areas of expertise needed in South Africa
Eligibility: Open to senior scientists of any nationality
Level of Study: Postdoctorate
Type: Fellowship
Value: To cover air fares and accommodation
Length of Study: Up to 3 months
Frequency: Annual, if funds are available
Study Establishment: Any South African university, technikon, museum or scientific society
Country of Study: South Africa

Application Procedure: Applications should be submitted by a South African counterpart attached to a South African university, technikon, museum or scientific society
Closing Date: Three months before the proposed visit

For further information contact:

Meiring Naude Rd, Gauteng, Pretoria 0184, South Africa

Tel: (27) 12 481 4122
Email: ferdi@frd.ac.za
Contact: Mr Ferdi van der Walt, Manager

Vrije University Amsterdam-NRF Desmond Tutu Doctoral Scholarships

Subjects: The Desmond Tutu Doctoral Training Programme (DTTP) was established in honour of Archbishop Emeritus Desmond Tutu's lifetime struggle against inequality and his quest for reconciliation. The National Research Foundation (NRF) and Vrije Universiteit Amsterdam (VUA) entered into a partnership in 2009 to co-fund South African students carrying out doctoral studies in a Joint Degree (split-site) mode
Eligibility: Be in possession of a research Master's degree, or be in the process of completing requirements for such a degree. Should be South African citizens or permanent residents
Level of Study: Postgraduate
Type: Scholarship
Value: ZAR 240,000
Length of Study: The VUA-NRF Desmond Tutu Training Programme provides funding for up to four (4) years of study, depending on satisfactory progress each year
Country of Study: South Africa
Application Procedure: Check website for more details
Closing Date: 17 July
Contributor: Vrije Universiteit Amsterdam (VUA)

For further information contact:

Email: danielle.nel@nrf.ac.za

National Science Foundation (NSF)

4201 Wilson Boulevard, Arlington, VA 22230, United States of America

Tel: (1) 703 292 5111
Fax: (1) 703 292 9025
Email: info@nsf.gov

Website: www.nsf.gov
Contact: Division Director

The National Science Foundation (NSF) supports research in the areas of geology, geophysics, geochemistry, paleobiology and hydrology, including interdisciplinary or multi-disciplinary proposals that may involve one or more of these disciplines.

Cultural Anthropology Program Senior Research Awards

Purpose: The primary objective of the Cultural Anthropology Program is to support fundamental, systematic anthropological research and training to increase understanding of the causes, consequences, and complexities of human social and cultural variability
Eligibility: The categories of proposers eligible to submit proposals to the National Science Foundation are identified in the NSF Proposal & Award Policies & Procedures Guide
Level of Study: Graduate
Type: Grant
Frequency: Annual
Country of Study: Any country
Closing Date: 15 August
Funding: Foundation
Additional Information: The Cultural Anthropology Program cannot support research that takes as its primary objective improved clinical practice, applied policy, or other immediate application

For further information contact:

Tel: (1) 703 292 5111
Email: jmantz@nsf.gov

Directorate for Education and Human Resources Core Research

Purpose: The ECR program places emphasis on the rigorous development of theory and accumulation of knowledge to inform efforts to address challenges in STEM interest, learning, and participation, for all groups and all ages in formal and informal settings. This emphasis includes research on advancing evaluative methodologies to support research efforts funded through ECR
Level of Study: Graduate
Type: Research
Frequency: Annual
Country of Study: Any country

Closing Date: 24 January
Funding: Foundation
Additional Information: 1. Level 1 and Level 2 proposals have a maximum grant duration of three years. 2. Level 3 proposals have a maximum grant duration of five years. ECR Proposals may fall within three levels of funding. Level 1 Proposals: have a maximum award size of US$5,00,000. Synthesis proposals may only be budgeted at Level 1 or 2. Level 2 Proposals: have a maximum award size of US$1,500,000. Synthesis proposals may only be budgeted at Level 1 or 2. Level 3 Proposals: have a maximum award size of US$2,500,000

For further information contact:

Email: ECR@nsf.gov

Enabling Discovery through GEnomic Tools (EDGE)

Subjects: EDGE is designed to provide support for research addressing current impediments to research progress in organismal biology. In particular, the ability to directly test gene function is essential to improve understanding of the genomes-to-phenomes relationship, an area relevant to Understanding the Rules of Life, one of 10 Big Ideas for future NSF investment
Purpose: The Enabling Discovery through GEnomic Tools (EDGE) track was previously a component of the Division of Integrative Organismal Systems (IOS) Core Programs solicitation (NSF 16-505). Submission of letters of intent or preliminary proposals is not required. Only full proposals should be submitted in response to this solicitation. There is no annual limit to the number of proposals submitted per PI or co-PI in response to this solicitation
Eligibility: Institutions of Higher Education (IHEs) - Two- and four-year IHEs (including community colleges) accredited in, and having a campus located in the United States, acting on behalf of their faculty members. Special Instructions for International Branch Campuses of United States IHEs: If the proposal includes funding to be provided to an international branch campus of a United States institution of higher education (including through use of subawards and consultant arrangements), the proposer must explain the benefit(s) to the project of performance at the international branch campus, and justify why the project activities cannot be performed at the United States campus. Non-profit, non-academic organizations: Independent museums, observatories, research labs, professional societies and similar organizations in the United States associated with educational or research activities
Level of Study: Graduate

Type: Award
Frequency: Annual
Country of Study: Any country
Application Procedure: Step 1: Download a Grant Application Package and Application Instructions link and enter the funding opportunity number, (the program solicitation number without the NSF prefix) and press the Download Package button
Closing Date: 7 February
Funding: Private
Additional Information: For this solicitation, EDGE proposals do not require submission of a letter of intent or preliminary proposals. Additional merit review considerations and special review criteria can be found in section VI of this solicitation

For further information contact:

2415, Eisenhower Avenue., Alexandria, VA 22314, United States of America

Tel: (1) 703 292 5111
Email: nsfpubs@nsf.gov

Faculty Early Career Development Program (CAREER)

Subjects: These awards are initiated by the participating federal agencies. At NSF, up to twenty nominees for this award are selected each year from among the PECASE-eligible CAREER awardees most likely to become the leaders of academic research and education in the twenty-first century
Purpose: Each year NSF selects nominees for the Presidential Early Career Awards for Scientists and Engineers (PECASE) from among the most meritorious recent CAREER awardees. These awards foster innovative developments in science and technology, increase awareness of careers in science and engineering, give recognition to the scientific missions of the participating agencies, enhance connections between fundamental research and national goals
Level of Study: Foundation programme
Type: Fellowships, operating grants
Frequency: Annual
Country of Study: Any country
Closing Date: 17 July
Funding: Foundation

For further information contact:

Email: info@nsf.gov

Macrosystems Biology and NEON-Enabled Science (MSB-NES)

Purpose: The Macrosystems Biology and NEON-Enabled Science (MSB-NES): Research on Biological Systems at Regional to Continental Scales program will support quantitative, interdisciplinary, systems-oriented research on biosphere processes and their complex interactions with climate, land use, and invasive species at regional to continental scales as well as training activities to enable groups to conduct Macrosystems Biology and NEON-Enabled Science research

Eligibility: Proposals may only be submitted by the following: Institutions of Higher Education (IHEs) - Two- and four-year IHEs (including community colleges) accredited in, and having a campus located in the United States, acting on behalf of their faculty members. Special Instructions for International Branch Campuses of United States IHEs: If the proposal includes funding to be provided to an international branch campus of a United States institution of higher education (including through use of subawards and consultant arrangements), the proposer must explain the benefit(s) to the project of performance at the international branch campus, and justify why the project activities cannot be performed at the United States campus. Non-profit, non-academic organizations: Independent museums, observatories, research labs, professional societies and similar organizations in the United States associated with educational or research activities

Level of Study: Graduate

Type: Award

Value: US$9,00,000

Frequency: Annual

Country of Study: Any country

Closing Date: 25 February

Funding: Private

Additional Information: www.nsf.gov/bfa/dias/policy/merit_review/

For further information contact:

Email: mbinford@nsf.gov

National Science Foundation Research Traineeship (NRT) Program

Subjects: Collaborations are encouraged between NRT proposals and existing NSF INCLUDES projects, provided the collaboration strengthens both projects

Purpose: The NSF Research Traineeship (NRT) program is designed to encourage the development and implementation of bold and potentially transformative models for science, engineering and mathematics (STEM) graduate education training. The NRT program seeks proposals that explore ways for graduate students in research-based master's and doctoral degree programs to develop the skills, knowledge, and competencies needed to pursue a range of STEM careers

Level of Study: Graduate

Type: Grant

Frequency: Annual

Country of Study: Any country

Closing Date: 6 February

Funding: Foundation

For further information contact:

Email: lregassa@nsf.gov

Robert Noyce Teacher Scholarship Program

Purpose: The program invites creative and innovative proposals that address the critical need for recruiting and preparing highly effective elementary and secondary science and mathematics teachers in high-need local educational agencies

Level of Study: Graduate, Foundation programme

Type: Scholarship

Frequency: Annual

Country of Study: Any country

Closing Date: 27 August

Funding: Private

Additional Information: Capacity Building proposals are accepted from proposers intending to develop a future Track 1, 2, or 3 proposal

For further information contact:

Email: rturley@nsf.gov

Scalable Parallelism in the Extreme (SPX)

Purpose: The Scalable Parallelism in the Extreme (SPX) program aims to support research addressing the challenges of increasing performance in this modern era of parallel computing. This will require a collaborative effort among researchers in multiple areas, from services and applications down to micro-architecture

Eligibility: Proposals may only be submitted by the following: 1. Institutions of Higher Education (IHEs) - Two- and four-year IHEs (including community colleges) accredited in, and having a campus located in the United States, acting on behalf of their

faculty members. 2. Non-profit, non-academic organizations: Independent museums, observatories, research labs, professional societies and similar organizations in the United States associated with educational or research activities
Level of Study: Graduate
Type: Grants, work-study (not just grants)
Frequency: Annual
Country of Study: Any country
Closing Date: 17 January
Funding: Private
Additional Information: This limit on the number of proposals per PI, co-PI or Senior Personnel applies only to this SPX program solicitation

For further information contact:

Email: abanerje@nsf.gov

National Sea Grant College

1315 East-West Highway, Silver Spring, MD 20910, United States of America

Tel: (1) 301 734 1066
Fax: (1) 301 713 0799
Email: sgfellow@ucsd.edu
Website: www.seagrant.noaa.gov
Contact: Jim Eckman, Director

Sea Grant is a nationwide network administered through the National Oceanic and Atmospheric Administration (NOAA) of 30 university-based programmes that work with coastal communities. The organizations research and programmes promote better understanding, conservation and use of America's coastal resources. In short, Sea Grant is science serving America's coasts.

Sea Grant/NOAA Fisheries Graduate Fellowship

Subjects: Population dynamics and marine resource economics
Purpose: To financially support and encourage qualified applicants to pursue careers in either population dynamics and stock assessment or in marine resource economics and also to increase available expertise related to these fields
Eligibility: Applicants have to be PhD students in population dynamics or marine resource economics or related disciplines

concentrating on the conservation and management of living marine resources
Level of Study: Doctorate
Type: Fellowship
Value: US$43,500 per year
Length of Study: 2 years
Frequency: Annual
Closing Date: 26 January
Funding: Government

For further information contact:

Email: terry.smith@noaa.gov

National Sun Yat-Sen University (NSYSU)

70 Lien-hai Road, Kaohsiung 804, Taiwan

Tel: (886) 7 525 2633
Fax: (886) 7 525 2630
Website: www.oia.nsysu.edu.tw

National Sun Yat-Sen University (NSYSU) was founded in 1924 and is located alongside the Hsitzu Bay of Kaohsiung city. It is the leading international academic institution in Southern Taiwan with a vision to provide diverse and comprehensive higher education.

National Sun Yat-sen University International Fellowship

Subjects: Biodiversity or biogeochemistry
Purpose: To pursue academic excellence combining theory and practice
Eligibility: Open to candidates who are pursuing their Master's or Doctoral degrees
Level of Study: Doctorate, Postgraduate
Type: Fellowships
Value: Varies
Length of Study: 2–3 months
Frequency: Annual
Application Procedure: Applications along with a curriculum vitae, research proposal, name of the corresponding member in the Kuroshio Research Group and 2 letters of recommendation must be mailed

Additional Information: "Recommendation to Kuroshio Application" must appear as the subject line

For further information contact:

Email: keryea@mail.nsysu.edu.tw
Contact: Dr K Soong, Kuroshio Research Group member

National Tour Association

National Tour Association (NTA) Luray Caverns Graduate Research Scholarship

Purpose: To aid graduate students who are conducting tourism-related research
Eligibility: 1. Applicants can be permanent residents of any country but must be enrolled at an accredited United States or Canadian four-year postsecondary institution. 2. They must be entering or returning graduate students who are conducting research that focuses on tourism. They must have a proven commitment to the tourism industry, and must have a GPA of 3.0 or higher on a four-point scale. Selection is based on the strength of the research project
Level of Study: Graduate
Type: Scholarship
Frequency: Annual
Country of Study: Any country
Application Procedure: Applications are available online. An application form, proof of residency, a personal essay, a resume, a research proposal, an official transcript and one letter of recommendation are required. Check the sponsor website for further information. www.tourismcares.org/academic-scholarships/
Closing Date: 3 April
Funding: Private

For further information contact:

Email: info@tourismcares.org

National Union of Teachers (NUT)

Hamilton House, Mabledon Place, WC1H 9BD, London, United Kingdom

Tel: (44) 20 7388 6191
Fax: (44) 20 7387 8458
Email: a.bush@nut.org.uk
Website: www.teachers.org.uk
Contact: Ms Angela Bush

National Union of Teachers Page Scholarship

Subjects: A specific aspect of American education relevant to the recipient's own professional responsibilities
Purpose: To promote the exchange of educational ideas between Britain and America
Eligibility: Open to teaching members of the NUT aged 25–60 years, although 25–55 is preferred
Level of Study: Graduate
Type: Scholarship
Value: Each up to £1,700 pro rata daily rate with complete hospitality in the United States of America provided by the English- Speaking Union of the United States of America
Length of Study: 2 weeks. The scholarship must be taken during the American academic year, which is September–May
Frequency: Annual
Country of Study: United States of America
No. of awards offered: 100
Application Procedure: Applicants must complete an application form. An outline and synopsis of the project must accompany the form along with a curriculum vitae and scholastic and personal testimonials
Closing Date: no deadline
Funding: Private
No. of awards given last year: 2
No. of applicants last year: 100
Additional Information: It is a discontinued award type. The scholarship is limited to the individual teacher and neither the spouse nor partner can be included in the travel, accommodation or study arrangements. Recipients are required to report on their visit to teacher groups and educational meetings in the United States and on their return home

For further information contact:

Tel: (44) 1 812 277 9670
Fax: (44) 20 7388 6191
Email: a.bush@nut.org.uk

National University of Ireland Galway

Postgraduate Admission Office, University Road, Galway, Ireland

Tel: (353) 91 524 411
Fax: (353) 91 494 501
Email: info@it.nuigalway.ie
Website: www.nuigalway.ie
Contact: Mairead Faherty

Charles Parsons Energy Research Award

Subjects: Microbial and biocatalytic fuel cell research
Purpose: To focus on investigation and optimization of electron transfer reactions in biological fuel cells that can generate energy from diverse substrates. To focus the research on applications of pure- and mixed-culture microbial fuel cells, and biocatalytic enzyme-based fuel cells
Eligibility: Open to engineering graduates
Level of Study: Doctorate
Type: Research award
Value: Salary scale €55,000–80,486 per year for researchers, stipend of €18,000 per year plus tuition fees for PhD studentship and undergraduate engineering students €1,500 per month
Application Procedure: Applicants should include a curriculum vitae and the names of two academic referees
Closing Date: October
Additional Information: The research will involve liaison with international collaborators, bench research and reporting. To this end, good inter-personal, written communication and networking skills are advantageous

For further information contact:

Email: donal.leech@nuigalway.ie
Contact: Dr Dónal Leech

PhD Student Scholarship in Atmospheric Science

Subjects: Atmospheric science
Purpose: To study the effect of ambient relative humidity on aerosol radiative parameters: aerosol light scattering coefficient and aerosol absorption coefficient
Eligibility: Open to candidates who have obtained a good Honours Degree (grade 2.1 at least) in physics or in a cognate subject
Level of Study: Doctorate
Type: Scholarship
Value: stipend and tuition fees
Length of Study: 3 years
Country of Study: Ireland
Application Procedure: Applicants must submit a covering letter, curriculum vitae and the names of at least two referees
Closing Date: The position will remain open until filled

For further information contact:

Tel: (353) 91 492 704
Fax: (353) 91 495 515
Email: gerard.jennings@nuigalway.ie
Contact: S G Jennings, Project Leader

Student Research Scholarship in Occupational Hygiene

Subjects: Occupational hygiene
Purpose: To enhance GSK's exposure assessment strategy, to look at current occupational hygiene data collected from across all GSK sites and to apply Bayesian statistics to optimize the exposure assessment strategy
Eligibility: Open to candidates who have obtained an Honours Degree (2.1 minimum) in a science or engineering discipline. Ideally, the candidate should have a sound understanding of mathematics/statistics, combined with an understanding of exposure assessment
Level of Study: Postgraduate
Type: Scholarship
Value: Monthly stipend
Country of Study: Ireland
Application Procedure: Applicants must submit a covering letter, a curriculum vitae and the names of at least two referees
Closing Date: 31 August
Contributor: GlaxoSmithKline (GSK)

For further information contact:

Department of Experimental Physics, National University of Ireland, University Rd, Galway, Ireland

Email: marie.coggins@nuigalway.ie
Contact: Dr Marie Coggins, Lecturer in Occupational Hygiene

National University of Ireland, Maynooth

Research Support Office, Auxilia House, North Campus, NUI, Maynooth, Co. Kildare, Ireland

Tel: (353) 17 086 000
Fax: (353) 16 289 063
Email: research.support@nuim.ie
Website: www.nuim.ie

Following two centuries of internationally renowned scholarly activity on the Maynooth campus, the National University of Ireland, Maynooth was established under the 1997 Universities Act as an autonomous member of the federal structure known as the National University of Ireland. With approximately 8,400 registered students, NUI, Maynooth has 26 academic departments which are organized into three Faculties: Arts, Celtic Studies and Philosophy; Science and

Engineering; and Social Sciences. Building on a tradition of scholarship and excellence in all aspects of its teaching, learning, and research activities, within the liberal arts and sciences tradition NUI, Maynooth is committed to being a first-class research-led centre of learning and academic discovery.

John and Pat Hume Research Scholarships

Subjects: Arts, humanities, social sciences, sciences and engineering

Purpose: To build on excellence in areas across the arts, humanities, social sciences, sciences and engineering

Eligibility: Applicants must have a First or Upper Second-Class Honours Primary Degree (or equivalent) from Ireland, the European Union or from any overseas university and intend to pursue a PhD degree at the University. Those who have commenced a research degree at NUI Maynooth prior to application will not be eligible

Level of Study: Postgraduate, Research

Type: Scholarship

Value: €5,000 per year plus payment of fees at European Union level. In some cases an additional fund of €3,000 is also provided to the student researcher for activities undertaken in support of the Department including tutorials and laboratory demonstration

Length of Study: Up to 4 years

Frequency: Annual

Study Establishment: NUI Maynooth

Country of Study: Ireland

Application Procedure: Applicants must first make contact with a NUI Maynooth department or centre to discuss their suitability for a PhD programme. A list of departmental contacts is available on the website. Application for the scholarship can then be filed

Closing Date: May

No. of awards given last year: 30

Additional Information: Supplement the scholarship with an additional €3,000 for tutorial or demonstrating duties

For further information contact:

Tel: (353) 1 708 6018
Fax: (353) 1 708 3359
Email: pgdean@nuim.ie

National University of Singapore (NUS)

21 Lower Kent Ridge Road, 119077 Singapore

Tel: (65) 6516 6666
Fax: (65) 6775 9330

Email: gradenquiry@nus.edu.sg
Website: www.nus.edu.sg

NUS aspires to be a dynamic connected knowledge community imbued with a no walls culture that promotes the free flow of talent and ideas. Individual members of our community enjoy access to diverse opportunities for intellectual and professional growth and in twin add value to NUS becoming a global knowledge enterprise.

Asian Development Bank-Japan Scholarship Program

Subjects: Public policy

Purpose: To find further study in public policy implementation

Eligibility: Open to residents of Asian Development Bank member countries currently enroled at NUS. Upon completion of their study programmes, scholars are expected to contribute to the economic and social development of their home countries. Check website for further details

Level of Study: Postgraduate

Type: Scholarship

Value: S$250 per semester (one-time book allowance), tuition, health insurance, examination and other approved fees. Cost of travel from home country to Singapore on award of the scholarship and from Singapore to home country on graduation

Length of Study: 2 years for Master in public policy

Frequency: Annual

Study Establishment: Lee Kuan Yew School of Public Policy, National University of Singapore

Country of Study: Singapore

No. of awards offered: 350

Application Procedure: Application form with 3 photographs attached, certificate of citizenship (or a copy of your valid passport), research and/or work experience, two confidential letters of recommendation

Closing Date: 12 July

Funding: Government

Contributor: Government

No. of awards given last year: 3

No. of applicants last year: 350

For further information contact:

Email: gradenquiry@nus.edu.sg

Law/Faculty Graduate Scholarship (FGS)

Subjects: Law

Purpose: To reward an outstanding student of the faculty of Law

Eligibility: Outstanding applicants of any nationality (including Singapore citizens and permanent residents) may be awarded the FGS to pursue the LLM coursework degrees: LLM, LLM (Asian Legal Studies), LLM (Corporate & Financial Services Law), LLM (Intellectual Property & Technology Law), LLM (International & Comparative Law), LLM (Maritime Law)
Level of Study: Postgraduate
Type: Scholarship
Value: The scholarship will cover tuition fees
Frequency: Annual
Study Establishment: National University of Singapore
Country of Study: Singapore
Closing Date: Please check website
Additional Information: Terms of award are subject to change without prior notice

For further information contact:

Email: gradenquiry@nus.edu.sg

Lee Kuan Yew School of Public Policy Graduate Scholarships (LKYSPPS)

Subjects: Public policy and public administration
Purpose: To find further study in public policy and administration implementation
Eligibility: Open to all nationalities (except Singapore)
Level of Study: Postgraduate
Type: Scholarship
Value: A monthly stipend, a one-time book allowance, a - one-time settling-in allowance, shared housing, tuition, health insurance, examination and other approved fees, cost of travel from home country to Singapore on award of the scholarship and from Singapore to home country on graduation
Length of Study: 1 year (for public administration) and 2 years (for public policy)
Frequency: Annual
Study Establishment: Lee Kuan Yew School of Public Policy, National University of Singapore
Country of Study: Singapore
Application Procedure: Apply online
Closing Date: Refer to website
Funding: Government
Contributor: Government

For further information contact:

Email: LKYSPPmpp@nus.edu.sg

Master of Business Administration Programme

Application Procedure: Applicants must complete an application form supplying US$15 fee
Closing Date: 1 April

For further information contact:

Graduate School of Business, MBA Programme, FBA2, Level 5, Room 6, 17 Law Link, 117592 Singapore

Tel: (65) 6874 6149
Fax: (65) 6778 2681
Email: fbagrad@nus.edu.sg
Contact: MBA Admissions Officer

National University of Singapore Design Technology Institute Scholarship

Subjects: Embedded system, rapid product development, mechatronics and industrial design
Eligibility: Open to all nationalities with good Bachelor's degree with Honours in Engineering or Science
Level of Study: Postgraduate
Type: Scholarship
Value: A monthly stipend S$1,500 with a possible monthly top-up of S$500 and all approved NUS fees
Length of Study: 2 years
Frequency: Annual
Study Establishment: National University of Singapore
Country of Study: Singapore
Closing Date: November
Additional Information: DTI Scholars who are international students will be required to serve a 2 years bond in Singapore upon graduation

For further information contact:

Tel: (65) 6874 1227
Fax: (65) 6873 2175
Email: dtibox@nus.edu.sg
Contact: Mr Frederich Chang

Singapore-MIT Alliance Graduate Fellowship

Subjects: All subjects
Purpose: The SMA Graduate Fellowship is established by the Singapore Ministry of Education in January 2009 to attract the best and most talented PhD students from Singapore, the region and beyond, and educate them to be future leaders in the areas of science and technology. The selection of candidates will take place twice a year, in time for the start of the semesters in August and January
Eligibility: The Scholarships are open to students of all nationalities who gain admission to any PhD programme at the University whose research interest fits within one or more of the projects currently being carried out in one of the SMART Interdisciplinary Research Groups (IRGs)
Level of Study: Graduate, Postgraduate

Type: Fellowship
Value: A monthly stipend of Singaporean $3,200; Tuition fees at NUS; and Scholarship allowance of up to $12,000 to help cover the expenses associated with a 6-month research residency at MIT
Length of Study: The award is tenable for 1 year in the first instance; but subject to the scholar's satisfactory progress, it may be renewed each semester. The maximum period of award is 4 years
Frequency: Annual
Study Establishment: National University of Singapore and Nanyang Technological University
Country of Study: Singapore
No. of awards offered: 120
Application Procedure: Applicants must apply separately to both MIT and NUS/NTU for the dual degrees and only to NUS or NTU for direct PhD degree; applicants must also apply directly to SMA for an SMA Graduate Fellowship
Closing Date: Between January and March
Funding: Government
Contributor: A*Star, Economic and Development Board (EDB), Ministry of Education (MOE), National University of Singapore (NUS) and Nanyang Technological University (NTU)
No. of applicants last year: 120

For further information contact:

Tel:	(65) 6516 4787
Fax:	(65) 6775 2920
Email:	smart@nus.edu.sg

Natural Environment Research Council (NERC)

Polaris House, North Star Avenue, Wiltshire SN2 1EU, Swindon, United Kingdom

Tel:	(44) 17 9344 2644
Fax:	(44) 17 9341 1501
Email:	stag@nerc.ac.uk
Website:	www.nerc.ac.uk/funding
Contact:	Studentships & Training Awards Group (STAG)

The Natural Environment Research Council (NERC) is one of the seven United Kingdom Research Councils that fund and manage research in the United Kingdom. NERC is the leading body in the United Kingdom for research, survey, monitoring and training in the environmental sciences. NERC supports research and training in universities and in its own centres, surveys and units.

Natural Environment Research Council Independent Research Fellowships (IRF)

Subjects: Environmental Sciences
Purpose: To develop scientific leadership among the most promising early-career environmental scientists, by giving all Fellows 5 year's support, which will allow them sufficient time to develop their research programmes, and to establish international recognition
Eligibility: Open to any nationality, and may be held in any area of the NERC remit, but the fellowship must be based at an eligible United Kingdom Research Organization. Applicants may not have a permanent academic position in a university or equivalent organization. Applicants must expect to submit their PhD thesis before the fellowship interview would take place (April following the closing date) and, if successful, would not be able to take up the fellowship until the intent to award the PhD has been confirmed by the awarding university. Applicants may have up to a maximum of 8 years of full-time postdoctoral research experience between the PhD certificate date and the closing date of the fellowship competition to which they are applying. The eight year window is based on full-time working. Where applicants have worked part-time or had research career breaks, the eight year window would be extended accordingly
Level of Study: Research
Type: Fellowship
Value: Includes 80 % of the full economic cost (FEC) of the proposal. NERC will provide funding for the fellow
Length of Study: 5 years
Frequency: Annual
Study Establishment: Universities and other approved research institutes
Country of Study: United Kingdom
Application Procedure: Please refer to the Research Grants and Fellowships Handbook at www.nerc.ac.uk/funding/available/fellowships/apply/
Closing Date: Early October (please check NERC website for exact date)
Funding: Government
No. of awards given last year: 14

For further information contact:

Email: Fellowships@nerc.ac.uk

Natural Environment Research Council Research Grants

Subjects: Research projects concerned with the natural environment

Purpose: To support a specific investigation in which the applicant will be engaged personally, to enter promising new or modified fields of research, or to take advantage of developments in apparatus offering improved techniques in promising lines of research already established

Eligibility: Open to research workers ordinarily resident in the United Kingdom who are also members of the academic staff of universities, colleges and similar institutions within the United Kingdom recognised by the NERC. Research assistants and technicians are not eligible to apply. Holders of Research Council Fellowships at an Institute of Higher Education are eligible to apply for research grants

Level of Study: Postdoctorate, Professional development

Type: Grant

Value: The Standard Research Grant offers amounts over £30,000, for periods not usually in excess of three years. The Small Research Grant offers a more rapid response for applications costing £2,000-30,000. Applications for less than £2,000 will not be accepted. The new investigator scheme offers up to the £50,000

Frequency: Throughout the year

Study Establishment: Any approved Institute of Higher Education in the United Kingdom

Country of Study: United Kingdom

Application Procedure: Applicants must complete an application form, available on request. Application forms and further information can be found on the NERC website

Closing Date: The deadlines for the Standard Research Grant are 1 July and 1 December. The deadlines for the Small Research Grant are 1 February, 1 June or 1 October

Funding: Government

No. of awards given last year: 307

For further information contact:

Email: researchcareers@nerc.ac.uk

Natural Hazards Center-University of Colorado

482 UCB, Boulder, CO 80309-0482, United States of America

Tel: (1) 303 492 6818
Fax: (1) 303 492 2151
Email: hazctr@colorado.edu
Website: www.colorado.edu/hazards

The mission of the Natural Hazards Center at the University of Colorado at Boulder is to advance and communicate knowledge on hazards mitigation and disaster preparedness, response and recovery. Using an all hazards and interdisciplinary framework, the Center fosters information- sharing and integration of activities among researchers, practitioners and policy makers from around the world, supports and conducts research and provides educational opportunities for the next generation of hazards scholars and professionals.

Dissertation Fellowship in Hazards, Risks, and Disaster

Subjects: Natural and physical sciences, social and behavioural sciences, specialities in engineering and environmental studies

Purpose: To provide financial support for research that is crucial to advancing the knowledge in the hazards field, as well as ensure that the next generation of interdisciplinary hazards professional has a source of financial and academic support to foster sound development

Eligibility: Open to candidates who already have a dissertation at an institution in the United States. Non-United States citizens may apply as long as the Doctorate degree will be granted by a United States institution

Level of Study: Postgraduate

Type: Fellowships

Value: US$10,000

Frequency: Annual

Country of Study: United States of America

Application Procedure: The applicant must submit a curriculum vitae along with a dissertation summary

Closing Date: September

For further information contact:

Email: periship@riskinstitute.org

Natural Sciences and Engineering Research Council of Canada (NSERC)

350 Albert Street, 16th floor, Ottawa, ON K1A 1H5, Canada

Tel: (1) 613 995 4273
Fax: (1) 613 992 5337
Email: claire.mcaneney@nserc-crsng.gc.ca
Website: www.nserc.ca
Contact: Corporate Account Executive

NSERC is Canada's instrument for promoting and supporting university research in the natural sciences and engineering, other than the health sciences. NSERC supports both basic university research through discovery grants and project, research through partnerships among universities, governments, and the private sector as well as the advanced training of highly qualified people.

Aboriginal Ambassadors in the Natural Sciences and Engineering Award

Subjects: Natural sciences and engineering
Purpose: The Aboriginal Ambassadors in the Natural Sciences and Engineering (AANSE) award aims to engage Aboriginal students and fellows in promoting interest and participation in the natural sciences and engineering by visiting Canada's Aboriginal communities and schools and sharing their research and education experiences or participating in science promotion events and activities
Eligibility: Open to Canadian citizen or permanent resident of Canada
Level of Study: Postgraduate
Type: Award
Value: Up to C$5,000
Country of Study: Canada
Application Procedure: Applications must be submitted electronically using the Secure Submissions for NSERC's Innovative Collaborations and Science Promotion Programs (competitions.nserc-crsng.gc.ca/500001/default.aspx)
Closing Date: There are no fixed deadlines for this award. Applications must be made at least 2 months before the start of a proposed outreach activity. The awards available in a given year will be awarded on a first-come, first-served basis
Additional Information: NSERC will notify you of the decision on your application within one month of receiving it. For more details, please mail to ambassadors@nserc-crsng. gc.ca

For further information contact:

Email: ambassadors@nserc-crsng.gc.ca

Canada Graduate Scholarships – Michael Smith Foreign Study Supplements Program

Purpose: The Canada Graduate Scholarships – Michael Smith Foreign Study Supplements (CGS-MSFSS) Program supports high calibre Canadian graduate students in building global linkages and international networks through the pursuit of exceptional research experiences at research institutions abroad

Eligibility: Open to Canadian citizen or permanent resident of Canada
Level of Study: Postgraduate
Type: Award
Value: Up to C$6,000 for a period of research study abroad
Length of Study: 6 months
Country of Study: Canada
Application Procedure: Online application procedure. For details, contact schol@nserc-crsng.gc.ca
Closing Date: 10 June and 10 October each year
Additional Information: For more information, contact CGSMSFSS@cihr-irsc.gc.ca, schol@nserc-crsng.gc.ca and fellowships@sshrc-crsh.gc.ca

For further information contact:

Email: cgsma@cihr-irsc.gc.ca

Canada Graduate Scholarships-Master's (CGS M) Program

Subjects: Health, natural sciences and/or engineering, and social sciences and/or humanities
Purpose: The objective of the Canada Graduate Scholarships-Master's (CGS M) Program is to help develop research skills and assist in the training of highly qualified personnel by supporting students who demonstrate a high standard of achievement in undergraduate and early graduate studies
Eligibility: Open to Canadian citizen or permanent resident of Canada
Level of Study: Postgraduate
Type: Award
Value: C$17,500
Length of Study: 1 year
Country of Study: Canada
Application Procedure: Application/Canadian common CV
Closing Date: 1 December
Additional Information: Refer to the Tri-Agency Harmonization of the Canada Graduate Scholarships page (www. nserc-crsng.gc.ca/Students-Etudiants/CGSHarmonization-HarmonizationBESC_eng.asp) for more information. Also refer to the Canada Graduate Scholarships-Master's Award Allocations page (www.nserc-crsng.gc.ca/Students-Etudiants/ CGSAllocations-QuotasBESC_eng.asp) for a list of allocations by institution and by agency. Contact cgsma@cihr-irsc. gc.ca, school.nserc-crsng.gc.ca and fellowships@sshrc-crsh. gc.ca

For further information contact:

Email: Schol@nserc-crsng.gc.ca

Canada Postgraduate Scholarships (PGS)

Subjects: Natural sciences and engineering
Eligibility: Open to a Canadian citizen or a permanent citizen of Canada, with a university degree in science or engineering, intending to pursue year full-time graduate study and research at the Master's or Doctorate level in one of the areas supported by NSERC with a first-class average in each of the last two completed years of study
Level of Study: Postgraduate
Type: Fellowship
Value: C$17,300 (Masters) per year for 1 year and C$21,000 (Doctoral) per year for a period of 2–3 years
Length of Study: 1 year
Frequency: Annual
Country of Study: Canada
Application Procedure: Check website for further details
Closing Date: 15 October
Contributor: Natural Sciences and Engineering Research Council of Canada (NSERC)

For further information contact:

National Sciences and Engineering Research Council of Canada (NSERC), Scholarships and Fellowships Division, 350 Albert Street (for courier mailings, add 10th Floor), Ottawa, ON K1A 1H5, Canada

Fax: (1) 613 996 2589
Email: schol@nserc.ca

Defence Research and Development Canada Postgraduate Scholarship Supplements

Subjects: Defence
Purpose: To encourage and support graduates to carry out research of interest to DRDC; to increase contact between DRDC researchers and those at Canadian universities; and to foster graduate training potential candidates for possible employment at DRDC
Eligibility: Open to candidates possessing a CGS, PGS or IPS award
Level of Study: Postgraduate
Type: Scholarship
Value: C$5,000 per year
Length of Study: 2 years
Frequency: Annual
Country of Study: Canada
Application Procedure: Applicants must submit a copy Notification of Award document from NSERC, a copy of successful scholarship application (Form 200), and

a statement of interest in R&D for defence/national security. Check website for further details
Closing Date: 1 June
Contributor: Defence Research and Development Canada

For further information contact:

DRDC Postgraduate Scholarship Supplements Program, Department of National Defence, 305 Rideau Street, Ottawa, ON K1N 5Y6, Canada

Tel: (1) 613 992 0563
Fax: (1) 613 996 7063
Email: hr-rh@drdc-rddc.gc.ca

Netherlands Organization for Scientific Research (NWO)

Lann van Nieuw Oost Indie 300, PO Box 93138, NLD-2509 The Hague AC, Netherlands

Tel: (31) 70 344 0640
Fax: (31) 70 385 0971
Email: nwo@nwo.nl
Website: www.nwo.nl
Contact: F.A.O. Grants Department

The Netherlands Organization for Scientific Research (NWO) is the central Dutch organization in the field of fundamental and strategic scientific research. NWO encompasses all fields of scholarship and consequently plays a key role in the development of science, technology and culture in the Netherlands. NWO is an independent organization that acts as the national research council in the Netherlands. NWO is the largest national sponsor of fundamental scientific research undertaken in the 13 Dutch universities and provides many types of funding for research driven by intellectual curiosity.

Rubicon Programme

Subjects: Scientific research
Purpose: To encourage talented researchers at Dutch Universities to dedicate themselves to a career in postdoctoral research
Eligibility: Open to researchers from all scientific disciplines engaged in PhD research or obtaining a PhD in the last 12 months
Level of Study: Postdoctorate
Type: Grant

Value: €5,300,000 a year
Length of Study: Up to 2 years
Application Procedure: A completed application form to be submitted via NOW's electronic submission system Iris
Closing Date: 28 November
Contributor: The Netherlands Ministry of Education, Culture and Science
Additional Information: Total amount for each (current year) Rubicon round is €2,900,000

For further information contact:

Tel:	(31) 7034 405 65
Email:	rubicon@nwo.nl
Contact:	Coordinator Rubicon

WOTRO DC Fellowships

Subjects: Natural and medical sciences, social sciences and humanities
Purpose: To support high-quality PhD and postdoctorate research projects
Eligibility: Open to project researchers with the appropriate degrees
Level of Study: Doctorate
Value: A contribution to personal living costs and research costs
Length of Study: 4 years for PhD research and 2 years for postdoctorate research
Frequency: Annual
Application Procedure: Applications must be formally submitted by a senior researcher employed at a Dutch research institution, together with a senior researcher from the home country as a co-applicant and as part of the supervising them
Contributor: WOTRO

For further information contact:

Tel:	(31) 70 344 0945
Email:	dijk@nwo.nl
Contact:	Ms Han van Dijk, Staff Member

New England Culinary Institute (NECI)

Admissions Office, 56 College Street, Montpelier, VT 05602, United States of America

Tel:	(1) 877 223 324
Email:	admissions-at-neci.edu
Website:	www.neci.edu

New England Culinary Institute (NECI) is one of the leading culinary schools in the United States of America. It is located in Vermont, the Green Mountain State. Mr. Fran Voigt and Mr. John Dranow founded NECI in 1980.

Cabot Scholarships

Subjects: Culinary arts, baking and pastry art and hotel management
Purpose: To encourage and support students who are committed to furthering their education and enhancing their careers in the restaurant and food service industry
Eligibility: Open to candidates who are current resident of Vermont, New York, Maine, New Hampshire, Connecticut, Rhode Island or Massachusetts
Level of Study: Professional development
Type: Scholarship
Value: US$2,000
Length of Study: 1 year
Frequency: Annual
Study Establishment: New England Culinary Institute
Country of Study: United States of America
Application Procedure: Applicant must submit a complete application form to New England Culinary Institute

For further information contact:

Email:	lindac@neci.edu
Contact:	Linda Cooper

New South Wales Architects Registration Board

NSW Architects Registration Board, Level 2, 156 Gloucester Street, Sydney, NSW 2000, Australia

Tel:	(61) 2 9241 4033
Fax:	(61) 2 9241 6144
Email:	mail@architects.nsw.gov.au
Website:	www.architects.nsw.gov.au
Contact:	Ms Mae Cruz, Deputy Registrar

Client Service Excellence Award

Subjects: Architectural services
Purpose: To encourage excellence in the professional services offered by architects

Eligibility: Open to all architects registered in New South Wales (NSW) who have completed projects in the last 2 years in NSW not exceeding $4 million
Level of Study: Unrestricted
Type: Award
Value: A$5,000
Frequency: Annual
Country of Study: Any country
Application Procedure: For further information about the Client Service Excellence Award contact the Registrar of the NSW Architects Registration Board on (61) 2 9241 4033. Check website for further details
Closing Date: 28 September
Contributor: Victorian Architects Registration Board
Additional Information: Architect, architect corporations, and firms should have two nominations from clients

For further information contact:

Tel: (61) 2 9241 4033
Email: awards@rcsa.com.au
Contact: Registrar of the NSW Architects Registration Board

New South Wales Ministry of the Arts

Level 9 St James Centre, 111 Elizabeth Street, PO Box A226, Sydney, NSW 1235, Australia

Tel: (61) 1800 358 594, 2 8218 2222
Fax: (61) 2 9228 4722
Email: mail@arts.nsw.gov.au
Website: www.arts.nsw.gov.au

New South Wales Ministry of the Arts works closely with the State's 8 major cultural institutions, providing policy advice to Government on their operations.

Western Sydney Artists Fellowship

Subjects: Creative arts
Purpose: To encourage artists and students in the field of creative arts
Eligibility: Open to applicants who are residents of Western Sydney or whose practice is located primarily in Western Sydney
Level of Study: Postgraduate
Type: Fellowship

Value: A$5,000–25,000
Length of Study: 1 year
Frequency: Annual
Study Establishment: New South Wales, Sydney Western Suburbs
Country of Study: Australia
Closing Date: September

For further information contact:

Email: mail@create.nsw.gov.au

New York Foundation for the Arts (NYFA)

20 Jay Street, 7th floor, Brooklyn, NY 11201, United States of America

Tel: (1) 212 366 6900
Fax: (1) 212 366 1778
Email: fellowships@nyfa.org
Website: www.nyfa.org

New York Foundation for the Arts (NYFA), founded in 1971, helps artists turn inspiration into art by giving more money and support to individual artists and arts organizations than any other comparable institution in the United States.

Canadian Women Artists' Award

Subjects: Applicants can submit in the following categories: Architecture/Environmental Structures/Design, Choreography, Crafts/Sculpture, Digital/Electronic Arts, Fiction, Folk/Traditional Arts, Interdisciplinary Work, Music/Sound, Nonfiction Literature, Painting, Photography, Playwriting/Screenwriting, Poetry, Printmaking/Drawing/Book Arts, & Video/Film
Purpose: The Canadian Women Artist's Award is open to emerging or early career artists in New York, New Jersey, and Connecticut. The $5,000 award is designed to provide financial support to an emerging or early career artist working in any discipline, and can be used in any manner the recipient deems necessary to further their artistic goals. It is supported by funding granted to NYFA by the Canadian Women's Club (CWC) of New York as a way to continue its philanthropic work when it disbanded
Eligibility: The Canadian Women Artist's Award is open to women artists who meet the following requirements: Must be a Canadian citizen, and able to provide proof of citizenship with legal documentation upon receipt of the award; Must be

between the ages of 21 and 35 before the application deadline; Must be a current resident of New York, New Jersey, or Connecticut; Must apply in only one of the eligible discipline categories; Must be the originators of the work, i.e. choreographers or playwrights; not awarded to interpretative artists such as dancers or actors; Must not be a previous recipient of the Canadian Women Artist's Award; Must not be a NYFA employee, member of the NYFA Board of Trustees or Artists' Advisory Committee, and/or an immediate family member of any of the previous

Level of Study: Unrestricted

Type: Award

Value: $5,000

Frequency: Annual

Country of Study: Any country

No. of awards offered: 82

Application Procedure: All applicants must apply online at apply.nyfa.org/submit. The application cycle runs through the Spring, opening in March and closing in May

Closing Date: May

Funding: Private, Foundation

Contributor: The Canadian Women's Club (CWC) of New York

No. of awards given last year: 1

No. of applicants last year: 82

New York State Council on the Arts/New York Foundation for the Arts Artist Fellowship

Subjects: NYSCA/NYFA Artist Fellowships are awarded in 15 different disciplines, with 5 disciplines reviewed each year on a rotating three-year cycle. Eligible categories include Architecture/Environmental Structures/Design, Choreography, Crafts/Sculpture, Digital/Electronic Arts, Fiction, Folk/Traditional Arts, Interdisciplinary Work, Music/Sound, Nonfiction Literature, Painting, Photography, Playwriting/Screenwriting, Poetry, Printmaking/Drawing/Book Arts, & Video/Film

Purpose: For over 30 years, in partnership with New York State Council on the Arts, the New York Foundation for the Arts has awarded Artist Fellowships of US$7,000 to individual originating artists living and working in New York State and/or Indian Nations located therein for unrestricted use. These fellowships are not project grants but are intended to fund an artist's vision or voice, regardless of the level of their artistic development. NYSCA/NYFA Artist Fellowships are awarded to eligible artists of all career levels regardless of their gender, ethnicity, sexuality, ability/disability, financial standing, or geographic location

Eligibility: Applicants must meet all eligibility requirements, including: 25 years old or older, New York State residency for the past 2 consecutive years, and are originators of the work.

Please visit our website for a comprehensive list of eligibility criteria

Level of Study: Unrestricted

Type: A variable number of fellowships

Value: US$7,000

Frequency: Annual

Country of Study: United States of America

No. of awards offered: 3,071

Application Procedure: Applications for the NYSCA/NYFA Artist Fellowship run from the end of September through the end of January of the following year. All applications are submitted online. Please visit www.nyfa.org/fellowships to apply

Closing Date: January

Funding: Government, Commercial, Private, Foundation, Individuals

Contributor: New York State Council on the Arts

No. of awards given last year: 89

No. of applicants last year: 3,071

"Made in NY" Women's Film, TV and theatre fund

Subjects: This award provides finishing grants for film, television, digital projects and theatre productions. Grants are given in the following categories (amounts listed are the maximum potential grant): Fiction Feature (running time of 60 minutes or more) - US$50,000, Fiction Short (running time of 59 minutes or less) - US$25,000, Fiction Webisode/Webseries (all forms) - US$20,000, Documentary Feature (running time of 60 minutes or more) - US$50,000, Documentary Short (running time of 59 minutes or less) - US$25,000, Documentary Webisodes/Webseries (all lengths and forms) - US$20,000, Theatre Production - grant amounts up to US$50,000

Purpose: The "Made in NY" Women's Film, TV and Theatre Fund provides grants to encourage and support the creation of film, television, digital, and live theatre content that reflects the voices and perspectives of all who identify as women

Eligibility: In addition to being made by, for, or about all who identify as women, projects are eligible if they feature a strong female perspective; and/or include a female director; and/or include a meaningful female producer credit; and/or include a meaningful female writing credit; and/or include a female protagonist(s). Projects must also meet the "Made in NY" criteria as described in the program guidelines

Level of Study: Unrestricted

Type: A variable number of grants

Value: US$20,000 - US$50,000

Frequency: Annual

Country of Study: Any country

No. of awards offered: 568

Application Procedure: All applications must be submitted online at apply.nyfa.org/submit. Applications open in the summer, and close in the fall

Closing Date: October

Funding: Government

Contributor: The City of New York Mayor's Office of Media and Entertainment (MOME)

No. of awards given last year: 60

No. of applicants last year: 568

New York University

Provost's Postdoctoral Fellowship Program

Purpose: NYU Provost's Postdoctoral Fellowship Program supports promising scholars and educators from diverse backgrounds whose life experience and research background will contribute significantly to academic excellence at NYU

Eligibility: 1. NYU Provost's Postdoctoral Fellowship Program is open to all areas of study represented at the University. Individuals who meet one of the following criteria are eligible to apply. 2. Individuals who have completed their dissertation within the last three years or who will have completed their dissertation by 1 September. 3. Professionals transitioning to academic careers in a field for which the doctorate is not the terminal degree

Level of Study: Postgraduate

Type: Fellowship

Frequency: Annual

Country of Study: Any country

Application Procedure: Required application materials include: 1. a curriculum vitae. 2. a statement of research and goals. 3. a personal statement detailing reasons for applying for the fellowship. 4. mentorship plan developed jointly with the proposed mentor (see below). 5. three letters of recommendation (with one of those letters to come from the proposed mentor at NYU). 6. one of the following: A dissertation abstract (postdoctoral applicants); or a statement of how your professional experience prepares you for a faculty position (non-PhD terminal degree holders; and candidate information form

Closing Date: 15 January

Funding: Private

For further information contact:

383 Lafayette Street, New York, NY 10003, United States of America

Email: admissions.ops@nyu.edu, facultyaffairs@jhu.edu

New York University Academic and Science

Rangel Graduate Fellowship Program

Purpose: The Rangel Graduate Fellowship is a United States Department of State program, administered by Howard University, that seeks to attract and prepare outstanding young people for careers as Foreign Service Officers in the United States Department of State

Eligibility: 1. Applicants must be seeking admission to enter graduate school in the fall for a two-year program at a United States university in an area of relevance to the Foreign Service. They can be in their senior year of their undergraduate studies, graduating by June, or they can be college graduates. 2. Applicants must have a cumulative grade point average of 3.2 or higher on a 4.0 scale at the time of application. 3. Applicants must be United States citizen

Level of Study: Postgraduate

Type: Fellowship

Value: Up to US$37,500 annually toward tuition, fees and living expense

Frequency: Annual

Country of Study: United States of America

Application Procedure: The Rangel Program expects to award 30 fellowships each November for cohort. A panel of individuals with experience in the United States Foreign Service and academia makes selections for the Rangel Program. A candidate's community, academic, extracurricular, and leadership activities will be considered during the selection process. For further details, check the following link. rangelprogram.org/graduate-fellowship-program-application/

Closing Date: 17 September

Funding: Private

For further information contact:

2218 6th Street NW, Washington, DC 20059, United States of America

Tel: (1) 877 633 0002

Email: rangelprogram@howard.edu

New Zealand Aid Programme

195 Lambton Quay, Private Bag 18 901, Wellington 6160, New Zealand

Tel: (64) 4 439 8000
Contact: Ministry of Foreign Affairs and Trade

The purpose of New Zealand's aid is to develop shared prosperity and stability in the Pacific and beyond, drawing on the best of New Zealand's knowledge and skills. We support sustainable development in developing countries to reduce poverty and contribute to a more secure, equitable and prosperous world.

New Zealand Pacific Scholarships

Purpose: A particular focus of NZPS is to increase the number of young pacific people studying in New Zealand and to build a new generation of Pacific leadership with strong links to New Zealand
Type: Scholarship
Country of Study: Any country
Application Procedure: For application procedure, please refer website www.mfat.govt.nz/en/aid-and-development/scholarships/how-to-apply/
Closing Date: 28 March

For further information contact:

Email: studentinfo@auckland.ac.nz

Newberry Library

60 West Walton Street, Chicago, IL 60610-3380, United States of America

Tel: (1) 312 943 9090
Fax: (1) 312 255 3680
Email: research@newberry.org
Website: www.newberry.org
Contact: Research and Education

The Newberry Library, open to the public without charge, is an independent research library and educational institution dedicated to the expansion and dissemination of knowledge in the humanities. With a broad range of books and manuscripts relating to the civilizations of Western Europe and the Americas, the Library's mission is to acquire and preserve research collections of such material, and to provide for and promote their effective use by a diverse community of users.

Associated Colleges of the Midwest/the Great Lakes Colleges Association Faculty Fellowships

Purpose: This fellowship supports faculty from the colleges of the Associated Colleges of the Midwest and the Great Lakes Colleges Association, Inc
Eligibility: Applicants can come from any of the colleges in ACM or GLCA, from any discipline
Type: Fellowship
Value: Fellows teach a small group of select undergraduate students in an advanced research seminar
Application Procedure: Potential applicants should contact Joan Gillespie at the ACM
Closing Date: 15 March
Additional Information: For more information, visit the Associated Colleges of the Midwest's call for proposals at www.acm.edu/programs/14/newberry/index.html

For further information contact:

Tel: (1) 312 263 5000
Email: jgillespie@acm.edu
Contact: Joan Gillespie

Rudolph Ganz Fellowship

Subjects: Humanities, local history, music and music history, theatre & performance history/studies
Purpose: The Rudolph Ganz Fellowship is a new opportunity at the Newberry Library. The fellowship is intended to support research using the Rudolph Ganz Papers and other late nineteenth- and early twentieth-century materials related to Chicago music in that period. The Rudolph Ganz Papers include the musical compositions of this world-renowned concert pianist, composer, conductor, and educator, as well as articles, speeches, lectures and essays by him, and two recordings. Also in the collection is correspondence to and from prominent musical figures, family correspondence, clippings, photographs, programs, and some artifacts
Eligibility: Applicants must demonstrate a specific need for the Newberry's collection. For additional information about eligibility requirements and application guidelines, please check the website: www.newberry.org/fellowships
Type: Scholarship
Value: Short-Term Fellowships are generally awarded for one continuous month in residence at the Newberry, with stipends of US$2,500 per month
Country of Study: United States of America
Closing Date: 15 December

For further information contact:

Email: research@newberry.org

Weiss/Brown Publication Subvention Award

Subjects: Humanities, music, theatre, French literature, Italian literature and Cultural studies

Purpose: To subsidize the publication of a scholarly book, monograph, or edition on European civilization before 1700 in one of the specified fields

Eligibility: Applicants must document that their projects have been accepted for publication and provide detailed information regarding the publication and subvention request

Level of Study: Doctorate, Postdoctorate

Type: Grant

Value: US$9,000

Frequency: Annual

Study Establishment: The Newberry Library

Country of Study: United States of America

Application Procedure: An online form must be completed; applicants should upload an abstract, project description, and curriculum vitae along with their application (see website for more details); three letters of recommendation are required; Must include a publication abstract, publication contract, copies of the reader's reports, and a production budget and schedule

Closing Date: 15 January

Funding: Private

Newcastle University

Manager, Student Financial Support, Newcastle University, King's Gate, Newcastle upon Tyne NE1 7RU, United Kingdom

Tel:	(44) 191 208 3333
Fax:	(44) 191 208 8685
Email:	scholarship.applications@ncl.ac.uk
Website:	www.ncl.ac.uk
Contact:	Mrs Rencesova Irena, Student Financial Support Officer

The Newcastle University, established in Newcastle in 1834, is one of the United Kingdom's leading universities and is known for its quality of teaching, outstanding research, and works with the regional and local communities, business and industry.

Advancing Women in Leadership Scholarship (MBA)

Purpose: We're committed to supporting innovative business women who aspire to higher levels of influence and professional development. Successful candidates will demonstrate a strong career trajectory, academic excellence and a wealth of professional experience

Eligibility: To be eligible for this partial-fee scholarship you must meet the following criteria: 1. complete the scholarship application form including submitting an essay of no more than 1,500 words in response to the question listed. Submissions need to be in English. 2. hold a conditional or unconditional offer of admission to the Full-time MBA programme entry. 3. have substantive managerial experience (normally 6 years or more, minimum 3 years). 4. preferably hold the equivalent of a United Kingdom 2:1 honours degree (however, applicants who do not meet this requirement but can demonstrate relevant work experience above the minimum plus significant career progression may also be considered). 4. perform well at interview across all competency areas. 5. hold an English language qualification of IELTS 6.5 or its equivalent with no subskill below 6.0 (if your first language is not English)

Level of Study: Postgraduate

Type: Scholarship

Value: A full fee award of £22,800, payable towards the cost of tuition fees

Frequency: Annual

Study Establishment: Newcastle University Business School

Country of Study: Any country

Application Procedure: Applications and essays will be reviewed by a panel of judges. Candidates need to complete the online application form. forms.ncl.ac.uk/view.php?id=2981403

Closing Date: 5 April

Funding: Private

Contributor: Newcastle University Business School

For further information contact:

Tel:	(44) 191 208 1589
Email:	mba@ncl.ac.uk

British Marshall Scholarships

Purpose: If you are an American graduate, and aged under 26, you may be eligible to apply for one of 40 competitive awards. The British Marshall Scholarships will finance two years of postgraduate and occasionally, undergraduate study in the United Kingdom

Eligibility: The scholarships cover: 1. fares to and from the United States. 2. university tuition fees. 3. cost of living expenses. 4. book, thesis, research and daily travel allowances and where applicable, a contribution towards the support of a dependent spouse

Level of Study: Postgraduate

Type: Scholarship
Value: Varies
Length of Study: Two years
Frequency: Annual
Country of Study: Any country
Application Procedure: For further information about the scholarship and details on eligibility and applications, contact the Marshall Aid Commemoration Commission. www.marshallscholarship.org/
Closing Date: Not specified
Funding: Private
Contributor: The Marshall Aid Commemoration Commission

For further information contact:

Tel: (44) 191 208 6000
Email: apps@marshallscholarship.org

European Excellence Scholarship (MBA)

Subjects: Our European Excellence Scholarship rewards European MBA candidates who can demonstrate high awareness of the challenges and opportunities of working and leading in a multicultural environment
Purpose: Our MBA provides an inclusive, diverse and collaborative learning community that educates and develops our students to be creative, innovative, enterprising and global in their outlook
Eligibility: To be eligible for this full-fee scholarship you must meet the following criteria: 1. completed the scholarship application form including submitting an essay of no more than 1,500 words in response to the question listed. Submissions need to be in English. 2. hold a conditional or unconditional offer of admission to the Full-time MBA programme entry. 3. have substantive managerial experience (minimum 3 years prior to starting the MBA) preferably hold the equivalent of a United Kingdom 2:1 honours degree (however, applicants who do not meet this requirement but can demonstrate relevant work experience above the minimum plus significant career progression may also be considered). 4. perform well at interview across all competency areas. 5. hold an English language qualification of IELTS 6.5 or its equivalent with no subskill below 6.0 (if your first language is not English). 6. be assessed as an European Union student for fee paying purposes
Level of Study: Postgraduate
Type: Scholarship
Frequency: Annual
Country of Study: Any country
Application Procedure: Applications and essays will be reviewed by a panel of judges. Candidates need to complete the online application form
Closing Date: 5 April
Funding: Private

For further information contact:

Tel: (44) 191 208 1589
Email: mba@ncl.ac.uk

Indonesia Endowment Fund for Education (LPDP)

Purpose: The Indonesia Endowment Fund (LPDP) provides funding for high achieving Indonesian students undertaking Master's or PhD study. It forms part of the Indonesian government's aim to nurture young talented individuals, enabling them to become future leaders
Eligibility: For detailed information about the eligiblity, check the website www.lpdp.kemenkeu.go.id
Level of Study: Postgraduate
Type: Funding support
Value: The scholarship covers tuition fees and living expenses
Frequency: Annual
Study Establishment: Ministry of Finance and Minister of Research, Technology and Higher Education
Country of Study: Any country
Application Procedure: For detailed information grants, check the following link, www.lpdp.kemenkeu.go.id
Closing Date: Mid-January, April, July and October
Funding: Private
Contributor: Lembaga Pengelolaan Dana Pendidikan (LPDP)

For further information contact:

Email: cso.lpdp@kemenkeu.go.id

International Family Discounts (IFD)

Purpose: We offer discounts to encourage relatives of our current international students, and past international graduates, to pursue their studies at Newcastle University
Eligibility: 1. This discount is only available to students studying at the Newcastle city campus. 2. The University offers partial discounts to close relatives (husband, wife, brother, sister, mother, father, son or daughter) of students and graduates, who have been assessed as International for fees purposes, and who wish to pursue their studies at

Newcastle University in currently studying here. 3. Students may only apply for a discount if they are registered as a student at the University or after they have been offered a place to study on their chosen degree programme, and have been assessed as International for fees purposes
Level of Study: Postgraduate
Type: Funding support
Value: 10% of the tuition fee per year
Frequency: Annual
Country of Study: Any country
Application Procedure: Please complete the online International Family Discount application form in accordance with the IFD regulations. Further updates on regulatiobns and applications are available at: forms.ncl.ac.uk/view.php?id=12481
Funding: Private

For further information contact:

Tel: (44) 191 208 5537
Email: scholarship.applications@ncl.ac.uk

Master of Arts (Taught Masters) Scholarships in the School of Modern Languages

Subjects: School of Modern Languages
Purpose: The School of Modern Languages is offering competitive scholarships to outstanding applicants for the following programmes: MA programmes in Translating and Interpreting (Chinese) MA in Professional Translating for European Languages (French, German, Italian, Spanish) MA Film: Theory and Practice
Eligibility: Home, European Union and International Students are eligible to apply
Level of Study: Postgraduate
Type: Scholarship
Value: £5,000
Frequency: Annual
Country of Study: Any country
Application Procedure: In order to apply for the scholarship, check the website. www.ncl.ac.uk/sml/study/funding/#currentopportunities
Closing Date: 7 June
Funding: Private
Contributor: SML Postgraduate Officer

For further information contact:

Tel: (44) 191 208 5867
Email: modlang.pgadmin@ncl.ac.uk

Master of Arts in Art Museum and Gallery Studies Scholarship

Purpose: The Art Museum and Gallery Studies MA provides students with the opportunity to develop skills as a curator or gallery educator in the fields of both historical and contemporary art
Eligibility: The studentships are open to United Kingdom, European Union and international applicants who hold, or expect to achieve a minimum of a 2.1 Honours degree (or international equivalent) in fine art or an art related subject. We welcome applications from all sections of the community regardless of race, ethnicity, gender or sexuality, and wish to encourage applications from traditionally underrepresented groups in United Kingdom higher education. International students If your first language is not English you must also meet our English language requirements
Level of Study: Professional development
Type: Scholarship
Value: £3,000
Frequency: Annual
Country of Study: Any country
Application Procedure: You must apply through the University's online postgraduate application system. To do this please 'Create a new account'. All relevant fields should be completed, but fields marked with a red asterisk must be completed. The following information will help us to process your application. You will need to: 1. insert the programme code 4138F in the programme of study section. 2. select 'MA Art Museum and Gallery Studies (full time)' as the programme of study. 3. insert the studentship code SAC025 in the studentship/partnership reference field. 4. attach a personal statement of no more than 500 words outlining. i. your preparedness to undertake the Art Museum and Gallery Studies MA. ii. your aspirations for a career in the art museum and gallery sector
Closing Date: 30 April
Funding: Private

For further information contact:

Email: gerard.corsane@ncl.ac.uk

Master of Business Administration Business Excellence Scholarships

Purpose: The scholarship program will be awarded to a high caliber candidate with at least 5 years of work experience who can demonstrate achievement and impact in a business environment. Our MBA Business Excellence Scholarships will reward MBA candidates who are results orientated, customer focused, and can demonstrate emerging leadership qualities

Eligibility: To be eligible for this partial-fee scholarship you must meet the following criteria: 1. can demonstrate (through application and at interview) substantive managerial experience and good leadership potential for the future. 2. hold a conditional or unconditional offer of admission to the Full-time MBA programme entry. 3. have substantive managerial experience (normally 4 years or more, minimum 3 years) preferably hold the equivalent of a United Kingdom 2:1 honours degree (however, applicants who do not meet this requirement but can demonstrate relevant work experience above the minimum plus significant career progression may also be considered). Perform well at interview across all competency areas hold an English language qualification of IELTS 6.5 or its equivalent with no subskill below 6.0 (if your first language is not English)

Level of Study: Postgraduate

Type: Scholarship

Frequency: Annual

Study Establishment: Newcastle University Business School

Country of Study: Any country

Application Procedure: No application required. All candidates will be assessed at the point of interview for this Scholarship

Closing Date: 5 April

Funding: Private

For further information contact:

Tel: (44) 191 208 1589
Email: mba@ncl.ac.uk

Newcastle University - English Language Excellence Scholarships (Business School Masters)

Purpose: Newcastle University Business School offers a number of partial scholarship awards to outstanding and high-quality Masters students each year to assist them to study for a Masters degree

Eligibility: You will be considered for an English Language Excellence Scholarship if you hold an unconditional offer for one of the following Masters courses: 1. Arts, Business and Creativity MA. 2. Innovation, Creativity and Entrepreneurship MSc. 3. Global Human Resource Management MSc. 4. International Economics and Finance MSc. 5. Banking and Finance MSc. 6. Finance MSc. 7. Quantitative Finance and Risk Management MSc. 8. International Business Management MSc. 9. International Marketing MSc. 10. Operations, Logistics and Supply Chain Management MSc. 11. Accounting, Finance and Strategic Investment MSc. 12. International Financial Analysis MSc. 13.

E-Business MSc. 14. E-Business (Information Systems) MSc. 15. E-Business (E-Marketing) MSc

Level of Study: Postgraduate

Type: Scholarship

Value: Partial awards of £5,000 towards the cost of tuition fees

Frequency: Annual

Country of Study: Any country

Application Procedure: Regulations and application details are available on the below link, www.ncl.ac.uk/media/wwwnclacuk/postgraduate/funding/files/English%20Language%20Excellence%20Scholarships%20Regulations%202019%20Entry.pdf

Closing Date: No application required, students will be considered for these scholarships once their offer status becomes Unconditional

Funding: Private

For further information contact:

Email: nubs@ncl.ac.uk

Newcastle University - United States of America Athlete Scholarship

Purpose: Newcastle University offers partial scholarship awards to encourage United States of America athletes to undertake Master's level study

Eligibility: Applicants should ideally have NCAA D1- D3 playing experience in one of the following sports: Basketball, Lacrosse, Volleyball, Tennis, Golf, Women's Soccer, Waterpolo. They must also be: 1. registered at Newcastle University for the academic year. 2. registered for one of the following eligible courses Masters - MA; MBA; MClinRes; MEd; MMedEd; LLM; LLM (by research); MLitt; MMus; MPH; MRes; MSc. 3. defined as international for fee purposes. 4. resident in the United States of America. 5. registered to study at Newcastle University city centre campus

Level of Study: Graduate

Type: Scholarship

Value: 40% fee reduction, £5,000- £8,000 payable towards the first year of tuition fees and a comprehensive support package (see Overview for further details)

Frequency: Annual

Country of Study: Any country

Application Procedure: Complete the application form using the following link. www.ncl.ac.uk/nclsport/performance/scholarships/application.htm

Closing Date: 31 July

Funding: Private

Contributor: Newcastle University Performance Sport Team

For further information contact:

Tel: (44) 191 208 5230
Email: performance.sport@newcastle.ac.uk

Newcastle University - Vice-Chancellor's Excellence Scholarships - Postgraduate

Purpose: Newcastle University is pleased to offer 40 Vice-Chancellor's Excellence Scholarships (VCES) for outstanding international applicants who apply to commence full-time Master's studies. There are 39 50% tuition fee scholarships and 2 100% tuition fee scholarship

Eligibility: To be considered for the 50% scholarships applicants must: be a national of one of the following countries: Algeria, Argentina, Brazil, Canada, Chile, China, Colombia, Ecuador, Egypt, India, Indonesia, Jordan, Lebanon, Malaysia, Mexico, Morocco, Peru, Thailand, Turkey, United States of America, Venezuela be assessed as international for fee purposes hold an offer for an eligible Master's degree programme at the University's Newcastle city centre campus for the academic year already have or expect to receive the equivalent of an upper second class United Kingdom honours degree or above

Level of Study: Postgraduate
Type: Scholarship
Frequency: Annual
Study Establishment: Newcastle University
Country of Study: Any country
Application Procedure: Online application form is available on the below web link path. app.geckoform.com/public/#/modern/FOEU01c3zJ6qAVgh
Closing Date: 28 February, 30 April and 28 June
Funding: Private
Contributor: Newcastle University

For further information contact:

Email: scholarship.applications@ncl.ac.uk

Newcastle University International Postgraduate Scholarship (NUIPS)

Subjects: All subjects offered by the University
Purpose: To provide a partial scholarship for international students
Eligibility: Candidates for scholarships must already have been offered a place to study at Newcastle University. See webpages: www.ncl.ac.uk/postgraduate/funding/search/list/nuips
Level of Study: Postgraduate
Type: Partial scholarship

Value: UK£2,000 per year
Length of Study: 1st year of study only
Frequency: Annual
Study Establishment: Newcastle University
Country of Study: United Kingdom
No. of awards offered: 800
Application Procedure: All eligible applicants who are offered a place to study at Newcastle University are invited to apply for one of these scholarships. Applicants must check the website for details or contact the Student Financial Support Team
Closing Date: 27 May
Contributor: Newcastle University
No. of awards given last year: 100
No. of applicants last year: 800

For further information contact:

Email: international-scholarships@ncl.ac.uk

Newcastle University Overseas Research Scholarship (NUORS)

Purpose: Newcastle University is committed to offering support to the very best international students hoping to pursue a programme of research. We are pleased to offer a small number of University funded NUORS awards for outstanding international students who apply to commence PhD studies in any subject
Eligibility: 1. You could be eligible to apply for a NUORS award if. 2. you have been offered a place on a PhD research programme. 3. you have been assessed as international/overseas for fees purposes, and are wholly or partially self-financing. 4. you intend to register to start your studies during the academic year
Level of Study: Graduate
Type: Scholarship
Value: This award covers the difference between home and overseas fee rates (value approximately £11,490 to £17,700 per annum)
Frequency: Annual
Country of Study: Any country
Application Procedure: You must have already applied for and been offered a place to study at Newcastle University before you apply for a NUORS award. Please complete the online NUORS application form and in accordance with the NUORS regulations. You will also be required to provide details of an academic referee; the University will then contact your referee directly. Further details can be found in the NUORS Regulations 19-20? Please read these thoroughly before applying. forms.ncl.ac.uk/view.php?id=2526301
Closing Date: 26 April
Funding: Private

For further information contact:

Tel: (44) 191 208 5537/8107
Email: scholarship.applications@ncl.ac.uk

Newcastle University Scholarship – Thailand - GREAT

Purpose: This year, in partnership with the British Council and the GREAT Britain Campaign, Newcastle University is offering scholarships to students in Thailand applying for postgraduate taught courses listed below. This scholarship scheme is part of the "GREAT Scholarships - East Asia" campaign, which has been launched by the British Council together with 28 United Kingdom universities to support more students in East Asia to get access to the excellent United Kingdom higher education opportunities
Eligibility: To be considered for awards applicants must: 1. Must be passport holders of Thailand. 2. be assessed as international for fee purposes. 3. hold an offer for an eligible Master's degree programme listed below. 4. MSc Sustainable Chemical Engineering. 5. MSc REFLEX (Renewable Energy Flexible Training Programme)
Level of Study: Postgraduate
Type: Scholarship
Value: Full tuition fees
Frequency: Annual
Study Establishment: Newcastle University
Country of Study: Any country
Application Procedure: Applications must be submitted using the application form. Other applications will not be accepted. Application link is available below: app. geckoform.com/public/#/modern/FOEU01c3zJ6qAVgh
Closing Date: 30 April
Funding: Private
Contributor: British Council and Newcastle University
Additional Information: app.geckoform.com/public/#/modern/FOEU01c3zJ6qAVgh

For further information contact:

Email: scholarship.applications@newcastle.ac.uk

Newcastle Vice-Chancellor's Global Scholarships - Postgraduate

Purpose: Newcastle University is pleased to offer 5 Vice-Chancellor's Global Scholarships (VCGS) for outstanding international applicants who apply to commence full-time Master's studies
Eligibility: To be considered for the Vice-Chancellor's Global Scholarships applicants must: 1. be assessed as international for fee purposes. 2. hold an offer for an eligible Master's degree programme at the University's Newcastle city centre campus for the academic year. 3. already have or expect to receive the equivalent of an upper second class United Kingdom honours degree or above. 4. Applicants from the following countries are not eligible to apply for VCGS awards as the University offers specific schemes for these countries: Algeria, Argentina, Brazil, Canada, Chile, China, Colombia, Ecuador, Egypt, Ghana, India, Indonesia, Jordan, Kenya, Lebanon, Malaysia, Mexico, Morocco, Nigeria, Peru, Thailand, Turkey, United States of America, Uganda, Venezuela, Vietnam. 5. A scheme for postgraduate Master's applicants from Ghana, Kenya, Nigeria and Uganda will be launched in February
Level of Study: Postgraduate
Type: Scholarship
Frequency: Annual
Country of Study: Any country
Application Procedure: For further information about application process, refer the following link. www.ncl.ac.uk/media/wwwnclacuk/postgraduate/funding/files/VCGS%20postgraduate%20regulations%20(2019).pdf
Closing Date: 30 April and 28 June
Funding: Private

For further information contact:

Email: scholarship.applications@ncl.ac.uk

Postgraduate Master's Loan Scheme (students from United Kingdom and non-United Kingdom European Union countries)

Purpose: Student loans for full-time, part-time and distance learning Masters degrees in all subjects (taught or research)
Eligibility: 1. Taught and research Master's courses in all disciplines (online and campus-based) will normally be eligible, e.g. MA, MSc, MRes, MEd, MBA, LLM, MLitt, MFA. 2. You can receive a loan for an MPhil. However, this programme must lead to a standalone. Master's degree and not be part of a longer PhD programme. 3. You will not be entitled to receive the Postgraduate Loan if you are eligible to receive healthcare funding from any of the following organisations. i. National Health Service (NHS). ii. Department of Health (DOH). iii. Student Awards Agency Scotland (SAAS). iv. Doctoral degrees (eg PhD, EngD, Integrated PhDs), PG Certificates, PG Diplomas, PGCE's and Master's courses that are currently funded by the undergraduate support system, eg Master of Architecture (MArch), will not be eligible for the Loan. 4. You will not be eligible for the Postgraduate Loan if you are studying towards top-up credits to a gain a Master's qualification after studying a PG Certificate or PG Diploma

Level of Study: Postgraduate
Type: Award
Value: £10,906
Frequency: Annual
Country of Study: Any country
Application Procedure: The application cycle is still open. The quickest way to apply is online. www.gov.uk/masters-loan/apply
Closing Date: Not specified
Funding: Private

For further information contact:

Email: ltds@ncl.ac.uk

Postgraduate Masters Scholarships in the School of Geography, Politics and Sociology

Subjects: Full and partial tuition fee scholarships are available for outstanding applicants across the following courses:
Purpose: The scholarships are open to United Kingdom, European Union and international applicants who: Hold an offer of admission on one of the eligible programmes Hold, or expect to achieve, at least a 2.1 honours degree (or international equivalent), in a related discipline
Eligibility: The scholarships are open to United Kingdom, European Union and international applicants who: 1. Hold an offer of admission on one of the eligible programmes. 2. Hold, or expect to achieve, at least a 2.1 honours degree (or international equivalent), in a related discipline
Level of Study: Postgraduate
Type: Scholarship
Value: £7,410
Frequency: Annual
Country of Study: Any country
Closing Date: 7 June
Funding: Private

For further information contact:

Email: gps.pgr@ncl.ac.uk

Postgraduate Opportunity Scholarships

Purpose: The scholarships are available as part of Newcastle University's Postgraduate Support Scheme for Master's students. They have been designed to enable students from under-represented groups to progress to higher level study
Eligibility: Postgraduate Opportunity Scholarships are available only to students applying to Newcastle University who meet the following criteria: have been offered a place to study full time for one year or a maximum of two years part time on one of the University's eligible taught or research Master's courses commencing in September. are United Kingdom students progressing from undergraduate courses for which they were charged the higher tuition fee applying and falling into the following categories: 1. a student living in United Kingdom when they entered undergraduate study at any United Kingdom institution. 2. a student living in Scotland when they entered undergraduate study at any English, Northern Irish or Welsh institution. 3. a student living in Northern Ireland when they entered undergraduate study at any English, Scottish or Welsh institution
Level of Study: Postgraduate
Type: Scholarship
Frequency: Annual
Country of Study: Any country
Application Procedure: To apply for the Postgraduate Opportunity Scholarship, please complete the online application form. Check the following link. app.geckoform.com/public/#/modern/FOEU01c3RUfcdPr6%20
Closing Date: 28 June
Funding: Private
Additional Information: In order to be considered for a Postgraduate Opportunity Scholarship, you must have already applied to the University for an eligible taught or research Master's course and received an offer of a place by this date

For further information contact:

Email: uk.postgraduate-scholarships@ncl.ac.uk

Regional Impact Scholarship (MBA)

Purpose: To support aspiring and established leaders from the region to continue their professional development. The Regional Impact Scholarship is aimed at MBA candidates who can demonstrate their potential to the economy and society of the North East of United Kingdom
Eligibility: To be eligible for this full-fee scholarship you must meet the following criteria: 1. completed the scholarship application form including submitting an essay of no more than 1,500 words in response to the question listed. Submissions need to be in English. 2. hold a conditional or unconditional offer of admission to the Full-time MBA programme of current year entry. 3. have substantive managerial experience (minimum 3 years prior to starting the MBA). 4. preferably hold the equivalent of a United Kingdom 2:1 honours degree (however, applicants who do not meet this requirement but can demonstrate relevant work experience above the minimum plus significant career progression may also be considered). 5. perform well at interview across all competency areas hold an English language qualification of IELTS 6.5 or

its equivalent with no subskill below 6.0 (if your first language is not English)

Level of Study: Postgraduate

Type: Scholarship

Value: A full fee award of £22,800, payable towards the cost of tuition fees

Frequency: Annual

Country of Study: United Kingdom

Application Procedure: Applications and essays will be reviewed by a panel of judges. Candidates need to complete the online application form. forms.ncl.ac.uk/view.php?id=2981068

Closing Date: 5 April

Funding: Private

For further information contact:

Tel: (44) 191 208 1589

Email: mba@ncl.ac.uk

Newcastle University in United Kingdom

Newcastle upon Tyne, Tyne and Wear NE1 7RU, United Kingdom

Tel: (44) 191 208 6000

Contact: Newcastle University

Newcastle University (officially, the University of Newcastle upon Tyne) is a public research university in Newcastle upon Tyne in the North-East of United Kingdom.

40 Fully-Funded Postgraduate Scholarships at Newcastle University in United Kingdom

Subjects: Scholarships are awarded to study the subjects offered by the university

Purpose: Students need a good level of English language to study at Newcastle University. English will be the main language you use socially and for study. If English is not their first language they will need to provide a recognised English language test or qualification

Eligibility: Citizens of China, United States of America, Canada, India, Indonesia, Malaysia, Thailand, Singapore, Jordan, Lebanon, Egypt, Turkey, Algeria, Morocco, India, Nigeria, Ghana, Kenya and Uganda are eligible to apply

Type: Postgraduate scholarships

Value: 50% or 100% of tuition fees

Study Establishment: Scholarships are awarded to study the subjects offered by the university

Country of Study: United Kingdom

Application Procedure: International preparation courses and graduate diplomas have a different application method. Students apply online through partner INTO. Find out about how to apply to: 1. Newcastle University London. 2. INTO Newcastle. Applications must be submitted using the online application form

Closing Date: 31 January, 27 April, and 29 June

Additional Information: For more details please browse the website scholarship-positions.com/fully-funded-postgraduate-scholarships-newcastle-university-uk/2017/11/14/

For further information contact:

Email: scholarship.applications@ncl.ac.uk

Newcomen Society of the United States

211 Welsh Pool Road, Suite 240, Exton, PA 19341, United States of America

Tel: (1) 610 363 6600

Fax: (1) 610 363 0612

Email: mstoner@newcomen.org

Website: www.newcomen.org

Contact: Ms Marcy J. Stoner, Executive Assistant

The Newcomen Society of the United States is a non-profit business educational foundation that studies and supports outstanding achievement in American business.

Harvard/Newcomen Postdoctoral Award

Subjects: Business history

Purpose: To improve the scholar's professional acquaintance with business and economic history, to increase his or her skills as they relate to this field, and to enable him or her to engage in research that will benefit from the resources of the Harvard Business School and the Boston scholarly community

Eligibility: Open to Scholars who have received a PhD in history, economics or a related discipline within the past 10 years, and who would not otherwise be able to attend Harvard Business School

Level of Study: Postdoctorate

Type: Fellowship
Value: US$46,000
Length of Study: 1 year
Frequency: Annual
Study Establishment: Harvard Business School in Cambridge, Massachusetts
Country of Study: United States of America
Application Procedure: Applicants must contact Harvard University for further details
Closing Date: 15 March

For further information contact:

Straus Professor of Business History, Harvard University, Graduate School of Business Administration, Soldiers Field Road, Boston, MA 02163, United States of America

Tel: (1) 617 495 6354
Email: tmccraw@hbs.edu
Contact: Mr Thomas K McCraw

North Atlantic Treaty Organization (NATO)

Public Diplomacy Division, Office Nb 106, Boulevard Leopold III, BEL-1110 Brussels, Belgium

Tel: (32) 2 707 4111
Fax: (32) 2 707 5457
Email: natodoc@hq.nato.int
Website: www.nato.int
Contact: Academic Affairs Officer

The North Atlantic Treaty was signed in Washington on 1 April, 1949, creating an alliance of 12 independent nations committed to each other's defence. Four more European nations later acceded to the Treaty between 1952 and 1982. On 12 March, 1999, the Czech Republic, Hungary and Poland were welcomed into the Alliance, which now numbers 19 members.

Manfred Wörner Fellowship

Subjects: International relations
Purpose: To honour the memory of the late Secretary General by focusing attention on his leadership in the transformation of the alliance, including efforts at extending NATO's relations with CEE countries and promoting the principles and image of the Transatlantic partnership

Eligibility: Open to applicants who are citizens of the EAPC countries with proven experience to carry out an important scholarly endeavour within the time limit of the Fellowship
Level of Study: Professional development
Type: Fellowship
Value: €5,000 (including all travel costs)
Frequency: Annual
Country of Study: Any country
Application Procedure: Application forms can be downloaded from the NATO website
Closing Date: 25 January
Funding: Government

For further information contact:

Fax: (32) 2 707 5457
Email: academics@hq.nato.int

North Central College

Graduate Programs MBA Program, 30 North Brainard Street PO Box 3065, Naperville, IL 60566-7065, United States of America

Tel: (1) 630 637 5840
Fax: (1) 630 637 5819
Email: grad@noctrl.edu
Website: www.noctrl.edu
Contact: MBA Admissions Officer

North Central College is a private, four year co-educational college located in Naperville, just 30 miles west of Chicago, Illinois. North Central offers over 50 undergraduate majors and six master's programmes.

North Central Association for Counselor Education and Supervision Research Grant Awards

Purpose: The call for proposals is to fund studies that increase understanding of the counselor education profession (including research, teaching, supervision, leadership and advocacy). Research grant awards will be presented at the business meeting at the NCACES
Eligibility: Proposed topic is within the scope of this Research Award program. Need for the proposed topic is clearly outlined through review of the research. Objectives are clear and attainable in the proposed study. Methodology proposed is appropriate for the research questions. Outcomes are consistent with objectives and method. Research proposed

adheres to ACA/ACES ethical standards for research with human subjects

Level of Study: Graduate
Type: Study grant
Value: Three US$1,000 awards
Frequency: Annual
Country of Study: Any country
Application Procedure: The competition is open to both professional and student members of NCACES. The primary investigator must be an ACES/NCACES member at the time the application is submitted. Individuals may submit (or be part of a submission team) for only one proposal. ncaces.org/awards/general/gsubmit
Closing Date: 29 June
Funding: Private

North Dallas Bank & Trust Company

P.O. Box 801826, Dallas, TX 75380-1826, United States of America

Tel:　　　(1) 800 275 7966
Fax:　　　(1) 972 716 7100, 800 275 7966
Website:　www.ndbt.com

James W. Tyra Memorial Scholarship

Purpose: In 1994, the executive management established the James W. Tyra Scholarship, in honor of the bank's very first Community Reinvestment Act ("CRA") Officer. Mr. Tyra was committed to advancing the hopes and dreams of the local public, and tirelessly gave of himself for the benefit of the youth in the community
Eligibility: 1. Must be a high school senior at time of application. 2. Must be a United States citizen or permanent resident. 3. Must be attending a public high school inside the North Dallas Bank & Trust Company trade area (a list of eligible schools is available on the North Dallas Bank & Trust Company website). 4. Must be in the top 25 % of his/her graduating class. 5. Must have a grade point average of 3.0 or higher. 6. the student must submit transcripts prior to the completion of each year of class, as failure to do so will result in loss of the scholarship
Level of Study: Graduate
Type: Scholarship
Value: US$1,000
Frequency: Annual
Country of Study: United States of America
Application Procedure: 1. Each student must complete the scholarship application available in the counselor's office of his/her high school. Each applicant must be recommended by his/her high school counselor or principal. 2. In addition to the completed application, each student must submit a current official transcript, two letters of recommendation (one from a high school teacher, counselor, or principal and one from a community member)
Closing Date: 1 April
Funding: Private

For further information contact:

12900 Preston Road, Suite 208, Dallas, TX 75230, United States of America

Tel:　　　(1) 972 716 7299
Email:　　scholarships@swe.org
Contact:　Ms Jennifer D Yeiter

North West Cancer Research Fund

22 Oxford Street, L7 7BL, Liverpool, United Kingdom

Tel:　　　(44) 15 1709 2919
Fax:　　　(44) 15 1708 7997
Email:　　nwcrf@btclick.com
Website:　www.cancerresearchnorthwest.co.uk
Contact:　Mr A W Renison, General Secretary

North West Cancer Research Fund Research Project Grants

Subjects: All types of cancer, the mechanisms by which they arise and the way they exert their effects
Purpose: To support fundamental research into the cause of cancers and the mechanisms by which cancers arise and exert their effects
Eligibility: Open to candidates undertaking cancer research studies at one of the universities named below in the Northwest. Grants are only available for travel costs associated with currently funded 3-year cancer research projects. No grants are awarded for buildings or for the development of drugs
Level of Study: Research
Type: Project
Value: Approx. UK£35,000 per year
Length of Study: Usually 3 years
Frequency: Dependent on funds available
Study Establishment: The University of Liverpool, Lancaster University and the University of Wales, Bangor

Country of Study: North West United Kingdom, North and Mid-Wales
No. of awards offered: 50
Application Procedure: The NWCRF Scientific Committee meets twice a year. All applications are subject to peer review
Closing Date: 1 April and 1 October
Funding: Private, Individuals
Contributor: Voluntary donations
No. of awards given last year: 10
No. of applicants last year: 50

For further information contact:

NWCRF Scientific Committee, Department of Medicine, Duncan Building, Daulby Street, L7 8XW, Liverpool, United Kingdom

Email: ricketts@liverpool.ac.uk
Contact: The Secretary

Northeast Florida Phi Beta Kappa Alumni Association

Northeast Florida Phi Beta Kappa Alumni Association Scholarship

Purpose: The Fall Program provides a social and intellectual opportunity for members and their guests
Eligibility: Winners will be honored at the association's Spring Banquet. For further details, see the website. pbknefl.com/web/scholarships
Level of Study: Postgraduate
Type: Scholarship and Research award
Value: US$1,000
Frequency: Annual
Country of Study: Any country
Application Procedure: Application information is available online at the Phi Beta Kappa Alumni Association of Northeast Florida website
Closing Date: 1 March
Funding: Private

For further information contact:

1606 New Hampshire Avenue NW, Washington, DC 20009, United States of America

Email: mroberts@unf.edu
Contact: Mr Marianne Roberts, Secretary-Treasurer

Northeastern University

Graduate School of Business Administration, 350 Dodge Hall, 360 Huntington, Boston, MA 02115, United States of America

Tel: (1) 617 373 2714
Fax: (1) 617 373 8564
Email: gsba@neu.edu
Contact: MBA Admissions Officer

National Robotics Initiative 2.0: Ubiquitous Collaborative Robots (NRI-2.0)

Purpose: The goal of the National Robotics Initiative (NRI) is to support fundamental research that will accelerate the development and use of robots in the United States that work beside or cooperatively with people
Eligibility: 1. An investigator may participate as PI, co-PI, or Senior Personnel in no more than two proposals submitted in response to this solicitation each year. 2. In the event that an individual exceeds this limit, proposals received within the limit will be accepted based on earliest date and time of proposal submission (i.e., the first two proposals received will be accepted and the remainder will be returned without review). No exceptions will be made. 3. The above limit applies only to proposals to the NRI-2.0 solicitation, not to the totality of proposals submitted to NSF
Level of Study: Graduate
Type: Grant
Frequency: Annual
Country of Study: Any country
Closing Date: 1 November
Funding: Private

For further information contact:

Email: k.drew@neu.edu

Northumbria University

2 Ellison Pl, Newcastle upon Tyne NE1 8ST, United Kingdom

Contact: Northumbria University

Northumbria University, officially the University of Northumbria at Newcastle, is a university located in Newcastle upon Tyne in the North East of United Kingdom. A former polytechnic, it was established as one of the new universities in 1992.

Dean's Award Scholarship

Subjects: Scholarships are awarded in the field of law
Purpose: Scholarships are available for pursuing full-time or part-time LPC or LLM LPC programme
Eligibility: For eligibility details, please visit website scholarship-positions.com/northumbria-law-school-deans-award-scholarships-uk/2018/04/02/
Value: £1,000 with 90% off tuition fees
Country of Study: Any country
Application Procedure: Applications must be must be sent via email
Closing Date: 31 July
Contributor: Northumbria University
Additional Information: For more details, please visit website www.northumbria.ac.uk/study-at-northumbria/fees-funding/pg-fees-funding/2018-deans-award-lpc/

For further information contact:

Email: gradadms@mtu.edu

Norway – the official site in the United States

2720 34th Street NW, Washington, DC 20008, United States of America

Tel: (1) 202 333 6000
Fax: (1) 202 469 3990
Email: cg.newyork@mfa.no
Website: www.norway.org
Contact: Grants and Scholarships Department

Al Fog Bergljot Kolflats Stipendfond

Subjects: All subjects
Purpose: To provide a stipend for those who want to take a trip to the United States to get practical experience within their fields of interest
Eligibility: Open to Norwegian citizens only, especially for a Norwegian engineer or architect. The applicant must have worked for at least 3 years after graduation, and he/she must present a detailed plan for the trip when they apply. Also, a budget for the trip must be included as well as references

Level of Study: Postgraduate
Value: Up to NOK 30,000
Closing Date: 15 March

For further information contact:

The Norway–America Association, Rådhusgaten 23B, N-0158 Oslo, Norway

Tel: (47) 233 571 60
Fax: (47) 233 571 75
Email: info@noram.no

American-Scandinavian Foundation Scholarships (ASF)

Subjects: All subjects
Purpose: To encourage Scandinavians to undertake advanced study and research programmes in the United States
Eligibility: Applicants must be citizens of Denmark, Finland, Iceland, Norway or Sweden and have completed their undergraduate degree. They should be fluent in English. Citizens of Finland, Iceland and Norway must apply through the sister-societies in their home country
Level of Study: Postgraduate
Type: Fellowship
Value: The American-Scandinavian Foundation (ASF) offers over US$500,000
Length of Study: 1 year
Frequency: Annual
Country of Study: United States of America
Application Procedure: Applicants must complete an application on ASF application forms. More information available on our website - www.amscan.org/fellowships-and-grants/fellowships-and-grants-for-advanced-study-or-research-in-the-usa/
Closing Date: Varies by country
Funding: Foundation

For further information contact:

58 Park Ave, New York, NY 10016, United States of America

Tel: (1) 212 879 9779
Fax: (1) 212 249 3444
Email: grants@amscan.org

John Dana Archbold Fellowship Program

Subjects: All subjects

Purpose: To support educational exchange between the United States and Norway

Eligibility: Open to citizens of the United States citizens aged 20–35, in good health and of good character. Qualified applicants must show evidence of a high level of competence in their chosen field, indicate a seriousness of purpose, and have a record of social adaptability. There is ordinarily no language requirement

Level of Study: Postdoctorate, Postgraduate, Professional development, Research

Type: Fellowship

Value: Up to US$5,000. Individual grants vary, depending on the projected costs. Note that there will be no tuition at the University of Oslo. The maintenance stipend is sufficient to meet expenses for a single person. The travel allowance covers round trip airfare to Oslo

Length of Study: 1 year

Frequency: Annual

Study Establishment: The University of Oslo

Application Procedure: Applicants must write to the Nansen Fund, Inc. for an application form

Closing Date: 1 February

Funding: Private

Additional Information: The University of Oslo International Summer School offers orientation and Norwegian languages courses 6weeks before the start of the regular academic year. For Americans, tuition is paid. Attendance is required. Americans visit Norway in even-numbered years and Norwegians visit the United States in odd-numbered years. For further information please contact the Nansen Fund, Inc

For further information contact:

Tel: (1) 713 680 8255
Email: nacc@net1.net

Memorial Fund of 8 May

Subjects: All subjects

Purpose: To promote cultural exchange between foreign countries and Norwegian residential experiential colleges by providing scholarships for residence, and to help prepare young people for everyday life in the community

Eligibility: Open to candidates aged 18–22 years who do not have a permanent residence in Norway, and do not hold a Norwegian passport. Candidates must be planning to return to their home country after a year in Norway. Candidates must be aware of the kind of education the Memorial Fund bursaries cover, that being a year in a Norwegian residential colleges, not admission to education on a higher level, such as a university, or specialized training

Type: Scholarship

Value: The scholarship will cover board and lodging. In addition it is possible to apply for extra funds. Applicants from some countries may apply for required books and excursions arranged by the school. Also, extra support may be provided for short study trips and short courses before or after the school year. A fixed amount towards spending money may also be given. Normally the students must pay their own travelling expenses. The colleges do not charge tuition fees

Length of Study: 1 year

Frequency: Annual

Study Establishment: Norwegian residential experiential colleges

Country of Study: Norway

No. of awards offered: 700

Application Procedure: Applicants must request more information and application forms from the Memorial Fund of 8 May or to the nearest Norwegian Embassy. Applicants who require a scholarship to attend a Norwegian college should not apply to a them directly. In this case, the Board will place successful applicants at a college school based on their hobbies and interest. Residence permits must be applied for by each individual student when a scholarship has been granted

Closing Date: 1 November

Funding: Government

No. of awards given last year: 25

No. of applicants last year: 700

Additional Information: A residential experiential college is a 1-year independent residential school, primarily for young adults, offering many non-traditional subjects of study. Each college has its own profile, but as a group, the Norwegian colleges teach classes covering almost all areas, including history, arts, crafts, music, sports, philosophy, theatre, photography etc

For further information contact:

IKF, Grensen 9a, N-0159 Oslo, Norway

Email: ikf@ikf.no

Norwegian Emigration Fund

Subjects: Emigration history and relations between the United States of America and Norway

Purpose: To support for advanced or specialized study in Norway

Eligibility: Open to citizens and residents of the United States of America. The fund may also give grants to institutions in the United States of America whose activities are primarily centred on the subjects mentioned

Level of Study: Doctorate, Graduate, Professional development

Type: Grant

Value: NOK 5,000–20,000

Frequency: Annual

Country of Study: Norway

Application Procedure: Applicants must complete an application form and return it clearly marked Emigration Fund to Nordmanns-Forbundet. Applications as well as enclosures will not be returned

Closing Date: 1 February

Funding: Government

For further information contact:

Email: norseman@online.no

Norwegian Marshall Fund

Subjects: Science and humanities

Purpose: To provide financial support for Americans to come to Norway to conduct postgraduate study or research in areas of mutual importance to Norway and the United States, thereby increasing knowledge, understanding and strengthening the ties of friendship between the two countries

Eligibility: Open to citizens of the United States, who have arranged with a Norwegian sponsor or research institution to pursue a research project or programme in Norway. Under special circumstances, the awards can be extended to Norwegians for study or research in the United States

Level of Study: Graduate, Postgraduate

Type: Research grant

Value: US$1,500–4,500 or NOK 10,000–30,000

Length of Study: Varies

Frequency: Annual

Study Establishment: Norwegian universities

Country of Study: Norway

Application Procedure: Applicants must contact the Norway-America Association to receive an application. Application forms must be typewritten either in English or Norwegian and submitted in duplicate, including all supplementary materials. Each application must also be accompanied by a letter of support from the project sponsor or affiliated research institution in Norway. There is an application fee of NOK 350

Closing Date: 1 April

Funding: Private

For further information contact:

Tel: (47) 233 571 60
Fax: (47) 233 571 75
Email: info@noram.no

The Norway-America Association Awards

Subjects: All subjects

Eligibility: Open to Norwegian who wish to study in the United States on the graduate level, must have completed their Bachelor's Degree before applying for these scholarships. The applicants must also be members of the Norway-America Association, and the membership fee is 200 NOK per year

Level of Study: Graduate, Research

Type: Award

Value: US$2,000–20,000

Application Procedure: Check website for further details

Closing Date: 22 September

Additional Information: Norwegians who reside in Norway and plan to return to Norway after graduation are given preference in the selection process, and they cannot have studied for four or more years in the United States. Please contact the American-Scandinavian Foundation or the Norway-America Association directly in order to find the appropriate scholarship

For further information contact:

Tel: (47) 233 571 60
Fax: (47) 233 571 75
Email: info@noram.no

The Norway-America Association Graduate & Research Stipend

Subjects: All subjects

Purpose: To give the student substantial financial support for 1 year of studies in the United States

Eligibility: Open to Norwegians and members of the Norway-America Association, and he/she must pay 250 NOK in administrative fees and are currently living in Norway, and intend to return to Norway after their graduation

Level of Study: Graduate, Research

Value: US$2,000–25,000

Application Procedure: Check website for further details

Closing Date: 22 September

For further information contact:

Tel: (47) 233 571 60
Fax: (47) 233 571 75
Email: info@noram.no

The Professional Development Award

Subjects: All subjects

Purpose: To help established professionals with a higher education who want to study within their own field of interest

Eligibility: Open to Norwegian professionals who worked for at least 3 years after finishing his or her education as well as planning on doing special research or further study in their fields

Level of Study: Postgraduate

Type: Award

Value: The award amount can vary but there is a recommended minimum of US$250 and maximum of US$1,000 with only one award per student within a given academic year

Frequency: Annual

Application Procedure: Check website for further details

Additional Information: Candidates must be invited to apply for this award. There is also an administrative fee of 250 NOK, which must be deposited in bank account with number 7878.05.23025. Please contact the American-Scandinavian Foundation or the Norway-America Association directly in order to find the appropriate scholarship

For further information contact:

Tel: (47) 233 571 60
Fax: (47) 233 571 75
Email: info@noram.no

The Torskeklubben Stipend

Subjects: All subjects

Purpose: To promote Norwegian-American relations through helping Norwegians come to the United States to study

Eligibility: Open to Norwegians and must already be accepted at the Graduate School at the University of Minnesota before applying for the award

Level of Study: Graduate

Value: A stipend of US$15,000 for the academic year. For recipients without another source of tuition support, such as an assistantship, the Graduate School Fellowship Office will provide a Tuition Scholarship for full-time study for the academic year

Frequency: Annual

Application Procedure: Application forms are available upon request from the Norway-America Association and the Graduate School at the University of Minnesota or it can be downloaded from the website

Closing Date: 1 March

For further information contact:

Tel: (47) 233 571 60
Fax: (47) 233 571 75
Email: info@noram.no

Novo Nordisk A/S

Novo Alle, Bagsvaerd, DNK -2880, Denmark

Contact: Director

National Fellowship And Scholarship For Higher Education Of ST students

Purpose: National Fellowship and Scholarship for Higher Education of ST Students is offered by Ministry of Tribal Affairs. This is a central sector scheme for the ST students who are selected for pursuing MPhil and PhD. The application form is available online and students can apply via the link given on this page. The scholarship has emerged as two different schemes i.e. Rajiv Gandhi National Fellowship for ST students and top class education for ST students. The fellowship covers under Rajiv Gandhi National Fellowship programme and scholarship is covered by top-class education

Eligibility: 1. Candidates must belong to ST category. 2. Candidates should get registered for the full-time Mphil and Ph-D. course. 3. scholarship, the students must have taken admission in their notified institution. 4. Family income should not exceed more than 6 Lac P/A

Level of Study: Postdoctorate

Type: Scholarship

Value: Rs. 25,000

Frequency: Annual

Country of Study: Any country

Closing Date: 31 October

Funding: Foundation

For further information contact:

Email: info@vidhyaa.in

Novo Nordisk Foundation

Tel: (45) 3527 6674
Email: KEKV@novo.dk
Contact: Kirsten Klüver, Grant Administrator

The Novo Nordisk United Kingdom Research Foundation is a charity to support research into diabetes by members of the medical and nursing professions Research fellowships.

Postdoc Fellowship for Research Abroad

Subjects: Bioscience
Purpose: The Novo Nordisk Foundation invites young, ambitious researchers in Denmark to apply for a post-doctoral fellowship to conduct research within bioscience or basic biomedicine outside of Denmark
Eligibility: The applicant must be employed by a research institution in Denmark for the entire fellowship period and this institution must administrate the project grant
Type: Fellowship
Value: The Novo Nordisk Foundation awards DKK 1 million per year, that is, for a total of up to DKK 4 million/ fellowship
Length of Study: 4
Frequency: Annual
Country of Study: Denmark
Application Procedure: The application must be completed and submitted using the foundation's electronic application system
Closing Date: 1 February
Contributor: Novo Nordisk Foundation
Additional Information: For more information refer: novonordiskfonden.dk/sites/default/files/information_and_ guidelines_for_applicants_postdoc_fellowship_for_researc.pdf

For further information contact:

Email: info@novonordiskfonden.dk

Nuffic

Kortenaerkade 11, 2518 AX Den Haag, PO Box 29777, NLD 2502 LT The Hague, Netherlands

Tel: (31) 70 4260260
Fax: (31) 70 4260399
Email: nuffic@nuffic.nl
Website: www.nuffic.net

Netherlands Organization for International Cooperation in Higher Education-Natural family planning Fellowships for PhD Studies

Subjects: See website www.nuffic.nl/nfp
Eligibility: Candidate must be a national of one of 57 developing countries
Level of Study: Doctorate
Country of Study: Any country

For further information contact:

Email: nuffic@nuffic.nl

O

Office of International Affairs at Ohio State University (OIA)

300 Oxley Hall, 1712 Neil Avenue, Columbus, OH 43210-1219, United States of America

Tel: (1) 614 292 4273
Email: ladman.1@osu.edu
Website: www.oia.osu.edu
Contact: Jerry Ladman, Associate Provost for International Affairs

Office of International Affairs at Ohio State University (OIA) is located in the Office of Academic Affairs, for the co-ordination, enhancement and development of Ohio State's international activities. It administers grants programmes for student travel, study and research, faculty travel and research and interdisciplinary lectures, seminars, workshops and conferences.

Everett And Florence Drumright Scholarship

Subjects: There are no field specification for this scholarship
Purpose: The awarding of scholarships is based on a combination of academic merit and financial need. Students in all fields are eligible
Eligibility: Check the official website in the following link. oia.uic.edu/?s=everett+and+florence+drumright
Level of Study: Graduate
Type: Scholarship
Value: US$1,000
Frequency: Annual
Country of Study: Any country
Closing Date: Varies
Funding: Private

For further information contact:

509 University Hall (M/C 590), 601 South Morgan Street, Chicago, IL 60607-7128, United States of America

Tel: (1) 312 996 5455
Email: oia@uic.edu

Office of Research & Graduate Education Pfizer Inc

A-300 HSC, Box 35640, Washington DC, United States of America

Tel: (1) 800 201 1214
Email: info@psymark.com
Website: www.physicianscientist.com
Contact: Dr Albert Berger

Pfizer's Medical and Academic Partnerships provide support for researchers in a range of medical disciplines.

Pfizer Scholar

Subjects: Clinical epidemiology
Purpose: To support research bridging the basic science of epidemiology with clinical medicine
Eligibility: Applicants must have completed their clinical training and demonstrate the motivation and ability to conduct original research
Level of Study: Postgraduate
Type: Grant
Value: US$65,000 per year
Length of Study: 3 years

© Springer Nature Limited 2019
Palgrave Macmillan (ed.), *The Grants Register 2020*,
https://doi.org/10.1057/978-1-349-95943-3

Frequency: Annual
Study Establishment: A United States medical school
Country of Study: United States of America
Application Procedure: Online via the website
Closing Date: 9 January
Funding: Commercial
No. of awards given last year: 2
Additional Information: Grantees must plan to conduct their research at a United States academic institution with an experienced mentor

For further information contact:

Email: mzebrowski@metrohealth.org

Pfizer Scholars Grants in Pain Medicine

Subjects: Pain medicine
Purpose: To support physician scientists who wish to pursue basic biomedical research in an academic setting
Level of Study: Postgraduate
Type: Scholarship
Value: US$65,000 per year
Length of Study: 2 years
Frequency: Annual
Study Establishment: United States academic medical institution
Country of Study: United States of America
Application Procedure: Online via the website
Closing Date: 9 January
Funding: Commercial
Additional Information: Applicants will be selected for the quality of their research proposals, mentioning program and potential for advancing pain medicine

For further information contact:

Email: mzebrowski@metrohealth.org

Ohio Arts Council

30 E. Broad St., 33rd Floor, Columbus, OH 43215-3414, United States of America

Tel: (1) 614 466 2613
Fax: (1) 614 466 4494
Email: webmaster@oac.state.oh.us
Website: www.oac.state.oh.us

The Ohio Arts Council is a state agency that funds and supports quality arts experiences to strengthen Ohio communities culturally, educationally and economically. It was created in 1965 to foster and encourage the development of the arts and assist the preservation of Ohio's cultural heritage.

Ohio Arts Council Individual Excellence Awards

Subjects: Interdisciplinary and performance art, criticism and music composition
Purpose: To recognize and support the contributions of working artists to the cultural enrichment of the state
Eligibility: Open to residents of Ohio who have lived in the state continuously for 1 year before the deadline and continue to remain an Ohio resident during the term of the award. Applicants cannot be students enroled in any degree or certificate granting programme
Level of Study: Postgraduate
Type: Fellowship
Value: US$5,000
Frequency: Annual
Country of Study: United States of America
Application Procedure: Applicants must submit application form B and supporting documents. Guidelines and application forms are available on the OAC website or upon request by writing to the address. All forms must be submitted to the OAC in printed format, rather than electronically
Closing Date: 1 September
Funding: Government

For further information contact:

Email: webmaster@oac.state.oh.us

Omohundro Institute of Early American History and Culture

PO Box 8781, Williamsburg, VA 23187 8781, United States of America

Tel: (1) 757 221 1115
Fax: (1) 757 221 1047
Email: martha.howard@wm.edu
Website: oieahc.wm.edu
Contact: Ms Martha Howard, Assistant to the Director and Digital Editor

The Omohundro Institute of Early American History and Culture publishes books in its field of interest, the William and Mary Quarterly and a biannual newsletter, Uncommon

Sense. It also sponsors conferences and colloquia and annually awards several predoctoral and postdoctoral fellowships. See www.oieahc.wm.edu for more information.

Omohundro Institute-NEH Postdoctoral Fellowship

Subjects: The OI annually offers a two-year residential postdoctoral fellowship in any area of early American studies. Recent recipients of the PhD as well as those who have earned the PhD and begun careers are encouraged to apply. A principal criterion for selection is that the candidate's dissertation or other manuscript has significant potential as a distinguished, book-length contribution to scholarship. A substantial portion of the work must be submitted with the application. The Omohundro Institute holds first claim on publishing the appointed fellow's completed manuscript. Applicants must meet the following requirements in order to be eligible. Applicants may not have previously published or have under contract a scholarly monograph. Applicants must have met all requirements for the doctorate, including a successful defense, by the application deadline. Foreign nationals must have been in continuous residence in the United States for the three years immediately preceding the date of application for the fellowship in order to be eligible for NEH funding. The OI's scope encompasses the history and cultures of North America's indigenous and immigrant peoples during the colonial, Revolutionary, and early national periods of the United States and the related histories of Canada, the Caribbean, Latin America, the British Isles, Europe, and Africa to approximately 1820. Fellowship applications are due 1 November

Purpose: To provide receipt recipients of the PhD a chance to revise and refine their dissertation for eventual publication as a monograph. Fellows also get teaching experience at William & Mary

Eligibility: Applicants must meet the following requirements in order to be eligible. Applicants may not have previously published or have under contract a scholarly monograph. Applicants must have met all requirements for the doctorate, including a successful defense, by the application deadline. Foreign nationals must have been in continuous residence in the United States for the three years immediately preceding the date of application for the fellowship in order to be eligible for NEH funding

Level of Study: Postdoctorate

Type: Fellowship with stipend

Value: US$50,400 per year

Frequency: Annual

Study Establishment: Omohundro Institute

Country of Study: United States of America

No. of awards offered: 33

Application Procedure: A principal criterion for selection is that the candidate's dissertation or other manuscript has significant potential as a distinguished, book-length contribution to scholarship. A substantial portion of the work must be submitted with the application. The Omohundro Institute holds first claim on publishing the appointed fellow's completed manuscript. See oieahc.wm.edu/fellowships/neh/ to begin the application process

Closing Date: 1 November

Funding: Foundation

Contributor: Omohundro Institute and National Endowment of the Humanities

No. of awards given last year: 1

No. of applicants last year: 33

For further information contact:

400 Landrum Drive, Williamsburg, VA 23186, United States of America

Tel:	(1) 757 221 1114
Fax:	(1) 757 221 1047
Email:	martha.howard@wm.edu
Contact:	Ms Martha Howard, Director of Conferences & Communications

Oncology Nursing Society Foundation (ONS)

125 Enterprise Drive, Pittsburgh, PA 15275, United States of America

Tel:	(1) 412 859 6100
Fax:	(1) 412 859 6162
Email:	customer.service@ons.org
Website:	www.ons.org
Contact:	Director of Research

The mission of the Oncology Nursing Society (ONS) is to promote excellence in oncology nursing and quality cancer care. ONS works to fulfil this mission by providing nurses and healthcare professionals with access to the highest quality educational programmes, cancer care resources, research opportunities and networks for peer support.

Oncology Doctoral Scholarships

Purpose: To provide scholarships to registered nurses who are interested in and committed to oncology nursing to continue their education by pursuing a research doctoral degree (PhD or DNSc) or clinical doctoral degree (DNP)

Eligibility: 1. The candidate must be currently enrolled in (or applying to) a PhD, DNSc or DNP nursing degree program for the current academic year. 2. The candidate must have a current license to practice as a registered nurse and must have an interest in and commitment to oncology nursing
Level of Study: Graduate
Type: Scholarship
Value: Between US$5,000 - US$7,000
Frequency: Annual
Country of Study: Any country
Application Procedure: Two professional letters of support are required. One of these letters must address the applicant's ability to perform doctoral level work. At the end of each year of scholarship participation, the nurse shall submit a summary describing the education activities in which he/she participated
Closing Date: No deadline specified
Funding: Private

For further information contact:

Email: info@onfgivesback.org

Oncology Nursing Society Breast Cancer Research Grant

Subjects: Oncology
Purpose: To provide funding to support the ONS research agenda, which focuses on areas where gaps exist in the knowledge base for oncology nursing practice
Eligibility: Open to the principal investigator who is actively involved in some aspect of cancer patient care, education or research
Level of Study: Research
Type: Grant
Value: US$1,00,000 for 2 years for the research team
Length of Study: 2 years
Frequency: Annual
Country of Study: United States of America
Funding: Foundation
Contributor: ONS Foundation
Additional Information: Funding preference is given to projects that involve nurses in the design and conduct of the research activity

For further information contact:

Email: info@onfgivesback.org

Oncology Nursing Society Foundation Research Grant Awards

Subjects: Nursing

Purpose: To financially support the principal investigator actively involved in some aspect of care, education or research for patients with cancer
Eligibility: The principal investigator must be actively involved in some aspect of cancer patient care, education, or research, and be PhD- or DNSc-prepared or a student working toward one of those research degrees. Funding preference is given to projects that involve nurses in the design and conduct of the research activity and that promote theoretically based oncology practice. Membership in ONS is not required for eligibility
Level of Study: Postgraduate
Type: Grant
Value: Up to US$25,000 each
Frequency: Annual
Country of Study: United States of America
Closing Date: 1 September (letter of intent); 1 October (online application)
Funding: Foundation
Additional Information: Preference is given to projects that involve nurses in the design and conduct of the research activity and that promotes theoretically based oncology practice. For more information, contact the ONS Foundation Research Department

For further information contact:

Email: customer.service@ons.org

Oncology Research Grant

Purpose: These grants support oncology nursing research. Research projects may include pilot or feasibility studies or the development of a new aspect of a program of research. Funding preference is given to research that addresses the ONS Research Priorities and/or the ONS Research Agenda
Eligibility: The principal investigator must be actively involved in some aspect of cancer patient care, education, or research, and be PhD- or DNSc-prepared. Funding preference is given to projects that involve nurses in the design and conduct of the research activity and that promote theoretically based oncology practice. Membership in ONS is not required for eligibility
Level of Study: Graduate
Type: Research grant
Frequency: Annual
Country of Study: Any country
Closing Date: 15 August and 15 September
Funding: Private

For further information contact:

Tel: (1) 866 257 4667
Email: info@onfgivesback.org

Sandy Purl Mentorship Scholarship

Subjects: Oncology
Purpose: To support an additional ONS Chapter member to attend the ONS Chapter Leadership Workshop
Eligibility: 1. Must be a current ONS Chapter Board or committee member supported by a Chapter Leader Sponsor. (A Chapter Leader Sponsor is a current Chapter Board member that has agreed the applicant has the approval of the Chapter to attend). 2. Chapter Leaders Sponsors may support more than one individual however grant is restricted to support only one individual. 3. Applicant must share their goal for attending the Chapter Leadership Workshop and how they plan to use the information they gained by attending. Applicant must identify the other Chapter member that is attending the Chapter Leadership Workshop
Level of Study: Graduate
Type: Scholarship
Frequency: Annual
Country of Study: Any country
Application Procedure: 1. Applicant must share their goal for attending the Chapter Leadership Workshop and how they plan to use the information they gained by attending. Kindly view the following link for further details, www.onsfoundation.org/funding-nurses/chapter-funding/sandy-purl-mentorship-scholarship
Closing Date: 15 May
Funding: Private

For further information contact:

Email: info@onfgivesback.org

Ontario Council on Graduate Studies (OCGS)

180 Dundas Street, West Suite 1100, Toronto, ON M5G 1Z8, Canada

Tel: (1) 416 979 2165 ext 212
Fax: (1) 416 979 8635
Email: kpanesar@cou.on.ca
Website: ocgs.cou.on.ca

The Ontario Council on Graduate Studies (OCGS) is an affiliate of the Council of Ontario Universities (COU). OCGS strives to ensure quality research and education across Ontario. In order to achieve this, OCGS conducts quality reviews of research programmes that have been proposed for implementation in Ontario's universities. It also performs quality reviews of existing programmes on a 7-year cycle.

Women's Health

Subjects: Women's health
Purpose: To financially support research in and study of women's health at Ontario universities
Eligibility: Open to students registered full-time in a Master's or Doctoral graduate programme at an Ontario university and sponsored and endorsed by a Dean of graduate studies at his or her university. For a postdoctoral award, applicants must be engaged in full-time research at an Ontario university at the time of taking up the award
Level of Study: Doctorate, Postdoctorate, Postgraduate
Type: Award
Value: Master's awards - C$25,000 plus C$1,000 research allowance; Doctoral awards - C$35,000 plus C$2,000 research allowance; Postdoctoral awards - C$50,000 plus C$5,000 research allowance
Length of Study: 2 year term for Master
Frequency: Annual
Country of Study: Canada
Application Procedure: Applicants must submit their application form, curriculum vitae, a statement of research to be undertaken during the period of graduate or postdoctoral study, transcripts and reference letters. Applications are available from the Deans office of Ontario universities or from the website
Closing Date: 31 January
Funding: Foundation
Additional Information: please see the website for further details cou.on.ca/about/awards/ontario-womens-health-scholars/

For further information contact:

Email: staceym.kwan@utoronto.ca

Ontario Federation of Anglers & Hunters (OFAH)

4601 Guthrie Drive, PO Box 2800, Peterborough, ON K9J 8L5, Canada

Fax: (1) 705 748 9577
Email: ofah@ofah.org
Website: www.ofah.org

The Ontario Federation of Anglers & Hunters (OFAH), Canada's leading conservation organization, is a non-profit, registered charity, which is dedicated to protecting woodland and wetland habitat, conserving precious fish and wildlife stocks and promoting outdoor education.

Oil Natural Air Forced/OFAF Zone 6 Wildlife Research Grant

Subjects: Wildlife research work
Purpose: To financially support students who wish to pursue their research work in wildlife research
Level of Study: Research
Type: Fellowship
Value: C$2,000
Frequency: Annual
Country of Study: Canada
Application Procedure: 1. Applicants must submit a complete application form, research proposal consisting of abstract, introduction, methods, results anticipated, literature cited and budget, a curriculum vitae, transcripts. 2. Should submit letter from supervising professor supporting the intended research projects
Closing Date: First Friday in January

Ontario Federation of Anglers & Hunters/Oakville and District Rod & Gun Club Conservation Research Grant

Subjects: Conservation of natural resources
Purpose: To financially support students who wish to pursue their research work in conservation research
Level of Study: Research
Type: Research grant
Value: C$2,000
Frequency: Annual
Country of Study: Canada
Application Procedure: Applicants must submit a completed application form, research proposal consisting of abstract, introduction, methods, research anticipated, literature cited and budget, curriculum vitae, transcripts and letter from supervising professor supporting the intended research project
Closing Date: First Friday in January

For further information contact:

Email: ofah@ofah.org

Ontario Ministry of Education and Training

Correspondence and Public Inquires Unit, 14th Floor, Mowat Block, 900 Bay Street, Toronto, ON M7A 122, Canada

Tel:	(1) 325 2929
Fax:	(1) 325 6348
Email:	info@edu.gov.on.ca
Website:	www.edu.gov.on.ca
Contact:	OGS Officer

Ontario Ministry of Education and Training Graduate Scholarship Programme

Subjects: All subjects
Purpose: To encourage excellence in graduate studies
Eligibility: Open to Canadian residents with an overall A-average or equivalent during the previous 2 years of study. 60 awards may be allocated to students holding a student authorization
Level of Study: Doctorate, Graduate, MBA
Type: Scholarship
Value: Approx. C$5,000 per term
Length of Study: 2 or 3 consecutive terms of full-time graduate study
Frequency: Annual
Study Establishment: A university in Ontario
Country of Study: Canada
No. of awards offered: 6,500
Application Procedure: Applicants currently registered at a university in Ontario must submit their applications and supporting documentation through that institution
Closing Date: 15 November
Funding: Government
Contributor: The Ministry of Training, Colleges and Universities
No. of awards given last year: 2,000
No. of applicants last year: 6,500
Additional Information: Students may hold another award up to Canadian $10,000 and may accept research assistantships or part-time teaching or demonstrating appointments, providing that the total amount paid to the scholar within the period of the award shall not interfere with their status as full-time graduate students. The total amount of time spent by the student in connection with such an appointment, including preparation, marking examinations, etc. must not exceed an average of 10 hours per week. Students must reapply each year and may receive a maximum of four awards

For further information contact:

Email: edugrad@uwindsor.ca

Ontario Student Assistance Program (OSAP)

PO Box 4500, 189 Red River Road, 4th Floor, Thunder Bay, ON P7B 6G9, Canada

Tel: (1) 807 343 7257
Website: osap.gov.on.ca

Minister of Education and the Minister of Training, Colleges and Universities are responsible for the administration of laws relating to education and skills training in Ontario.

Ontario Graduate Scholarship Program

Subjects: All subjects
Purpose: To encourage excellence in graduate studies at the Master's and Doctoral levels
Eligibility: Open to students who plan to be enrolled full-time in an approved graduate programme leading to a Master's or Doctoral degree. Candidates must be citizens or permanent residents of Canada
Level of Study: Doctorate, Postgraduate
Type: Scholarships
Value: C$5,000
Length of Study: 2 year
Frequency: Annual
Study Establishment: Some selected universities
Country of Study: Canada
Application Procedure: Applicants can send in paper or online application. For details see osap.gov.on.ca/eng/not_secure/ogsapply.htm
Closing Date: 3 June
Funding: Government
Contributor: Province of Ontario and the university

For further information contact:

School of Graduate Studies, 63 St. George Street, Room 201, University of Toronto, Toronto, ON 416-946-0808, Canada

Tel: (1) 416 978 2205
Email: ogs@utoronto.ca
Contact: Mrs Stacey Kwan, Graduate Awards Officer

Open Society Foundation - Sofia

56 Solunska Street, BGR-1000, Sofia, Bulgaria

Tel: (359) 2 930 6619
Fax: (359) 2 951 6348
Email: info@osf.bg
Website: www.osf.bg
Contact: Ms Iliana Bobova, Education Consultant

The goal of the Open Society Foundation network is to promote an open society. The concept of open society is based on the recognition that people act on the basis of imperfect knowledge and nobody is in possession of the ultimate truth. This leads to a respect for the rule of law, to a society which is not dominated by the state, to the existence of democratic government, to a market economy and, above all, to respect for minorities and minority opinions.

Open Society Institute's Global Supplementary Grant Program (Grant SGP)

Subjects: Humanities or social sciences
Purpose: To enable qualified students to pursue doctoral studies in the humanities and social sciences
Eligibility: Open to candidates from selected countries from Eastern and Central Europe and the former Soviet Union. Bulgarian nationals under the age of 40 who have been accepted into a full-time doctoral programme at an accredited university in Western Europe, Asia, Australia or North America and have already been awarded partial or full tuition, room and board stipends or other types of financial aid are also eligible
Level of Study: Doctorate
Type: Grant
Value: 50 % of tuition and fees or living expenses or additional expenses
Length of Study: Up to 1 year of study with the option to apply for a second year
Frequency: Annual
Study Establishment: Accredited universities
Country of Study: Other
Application Procedure: Applicants must complete an application form and provide the required supporting documents
Closing Date: 1 April
Funding: Private
Contributor: The Open Society Institute in New York
No. of awards given last year: 22

Additional Information: Programme availability and format are reviewed on an annual basis. Changes may occur from year to year. For the most up to date information please contact the Open Society Institute in New York

For further information contact:

Open Society Institute, Network Scholarship Programs, 400 West 59th Street, New York, NY 10019, United States of America

Tel:	(1) 212 548 0175
Fax:	(1) 212 548 4652
Email:	vjohnson@sorosny.org

Oxford Colleges Hospitality Scheme for East European Scholars

Subjects: All subjects offered by the University of Oxford and the University of Cambridge
Purpose: To enable overseas scholars to work in Oxford or Cambridge libraries or to consult Oxbridge specialists in their subjects
Eligibility: Open to Scholars from Eastern and Central Europe, who have a good knowledge of English and who are in the process of completing work for an advanced degree, or who are working on a book, or a new course of lectures
Level of Study: Professional development
Type: Scholarship
Value: Full scholarship
Length of Study: 1–3 months
Frequency: Annual
Study Establishment: The University of Oxford and the University of Cambridge
Country of Study: United Kingdom
No. of awards offered: 45
Application Procedure: Applicants must submit a completed application form, a curriculum vitae, a list of publications and two recommendation letters
Closing Date: November
Funding: Government, Private
Contributor: FCO, OSI-Budapest, University of Oxford
No. of awards given last year: 7
No. of applicants last year: 45
Additional Information: Programme availability and format are reviewed on an annual basis. Changes may occur from year to year. For the most up to date information please contact the Open Society Institute in Budapest

For further information contact:

Open Society Institute, Network Scholarship Programmes, Nador Utca 11, HUN-1051, Budapest, Hungary

Email:	mariefergusonsmith@hotmail.com

Organization of American Historians

Erik Barnouw Award

Purpose: To recognize outstanding reporting or programming on network television, cable television or in a documentary film, concerned with American history, the study of American history,and/or the promotion of history
Level of Study: Professional development
Type: Award
Frequency: Annual
Country of Study: Any country
No. of awards offered: 16
Application Procedure: Applicants should visit the website for complete application requirements. There is no standard application form and no application fee. Companies are encouraged to enter one or more films in the competition
Closing Date: 8 January
Funding: Private
No. of awards given last year: 1
No. of applicants last year: 16
Additional Information: Please check at www.oah.org/programs/awards/erik-barnouw-award/ or more information

For further information contact:

112 North Bryan Avenue, PO Box 5457, Bloomington, IN 47408-5457, United States of America

Email:	khamm@oah.org

Organization of American Historians (OAH)

Tel:	(1) 812 855 9852
Fax:	(1) 812 855 0696
Email:	khamm@oah.org
Website:	www.oah.org
Contact:	Kara Hamm

The Organization of American Historians (OAH) was founded in 1907 as the Mississippi Valley Historical Association and originally focused on the history of the Mississippi Valley. Now, national in scope and with approx. 11,000 members, it is a large professional organization created and sustained for the investigation, study and teaching of American history.

Avery O. Craven Award

Subjects: The coming of the civil war, the civil war years or the era of reconstruction, with the exception of works of purely military history

Purpose: For the most original book on the coming of the civil war, civil war years or the era of reconstruction, with the exception of works of purely military history

Type: Award

Value: US$500

Frequency: Annual

Country of Study: Any country

No. of awards offered: 50

Application Procedure: Applicants must visit the website www.oah.org/activities for complete application requirements. There is no standard application form and no application fee. Publishers are encouraged to enter one or more books in the competition

Closing Date: 1 October

Contributor: OAH

No. of awards given last year: 1

No. of applicants last year: 50

Additional Information: The exception of works of purely military history recognizes and reflects the Quaker convictions of Avery Craven, President of the Organization of American Historians (1963-1964). Please check at www.oah.org/programs/awards/avery-o-craven-award/ for more information

For further information contact:

Email: khamm@oah.org

China Residency Program

Purpose: Thanks to a generous grant from the Ford Foundation, the Organization of American Historians and the American History Research Association of China (AHRAC) are pleased to announce the third year of the teaching seminars in the People's Republic of China

Eligibility: The OAH International Committee seeks applications from OAH members with strong records of research and teaching excellence who are interested in leading an advanced seminar in the People's Republic of China, focused on one of the following three topics: constitutional history; cultural/gender history and history of the American West

Level of Study: Research

Type: Residency

Length of Study: 3 week-long intensive seminars

Frequency: Annual

Country of Study: United States of America

No. of awards offered: 7

Application Procedure: The application consists of a short (3-5 pages) curriculum vitae, the name and contact information of 3 references who can speak to the applicant's teaching and scholarship, and an outline of the proposed intensive week-long seminar. Applications should be submitted electronically, in Microsoft Word format, to prizes@oah.org. Please indicate, China Residency Program in the subject line. If you do not receive an email confirmation that your application has been received within 3 days, please contact the OAH Committee Coordinator at khamm@oah.org or (1) 812 855 9650

Closing Date: 1 October

No. of awards given last year: 3

No. of applicants last year: 7

Additional Information: Applicants are encouraged, if possible, to incorporate into their lectures a perspective of transnational/comparative history and place these topics in the context of American state- and nation-building processes

For further information contact:

Email: charlotte.brooks@baruch.cuny.edu

Contact: Professor Avital Bloch, OAH International Committee Chair

David Montgomery Award

Subjects: The David Montgomery Award is given annually by the OAH with co-sponsorship by the Labor and Working-Class History Association (LAWCHA) for the best book on a topic in American labor and working-class history

Purpose: For the best book on a topic in American labour and working-class history

Eligibility: Eligible works shall be written in English and deal with United States history in significant ways but may include comparative or transnational studies that fall within these guidelines

Type: Award

Frequency: Annual

Country of Study: Any country

No. of awards offered: 39

Application Procedure: One copy of each entry, clearly labelled, David Montgomery Award Entry, must be mailed directly to the committee members listed below. Each committee member must receive all submissions by November 1st

Closing Date: 1 October

Contributor: OAH with co-sponsorship by the Labor and Working-Class History Association (LAWCHA)

No. of awards given last year: 1

No. of applicants last year: 39

Additional Information: Each entry must be published during the period January 1st through December 31st. The final decision will be made by the David Montgomery Award Committee by February. The winner will be provided with details regarding the OAH Annual Meeting and awards presentation, where s/he will receive a cash award and a plaque

For further information contact:

133 West 17th Street, Apartment 5D, New York, NY 10011, United States of America

Contact: Dr Daniel J. Walkowitz

David Thelen Award

Subjects: For the best article on American history published in a foreign language
Purpose: To expose Americanists to scholarship originally published in a language other than english, to overcome the language barrier that keeps scholars apart
Type: Award
Value: US$500 and the winning article will be printed in The Journal of American History
Frequency: Annual
Country of Study: Any country
No. of awards offered: 5
Application Procedure: Please refer to the website www.oah.org/programs/awards/david-thelen-award/ The application must contain the following entries. The application should also include the following information: 1. Author's name. 2. Mailing address. 3. Institutional affiliation. 4. E-mail address. Language of submitted article
Closing Date: 1 May (of odd-numbered years)
No. of applicants last year: 5
Additional Information: Please check at www.oah.org/programs/awards/david-thelen-award for more information

Ellis W Hawley Prize

Subjects: Political economy, politics, or institutions of the United States in its domestic or international affairs, from the civil war to the present
Purpose: For the best book-length historical study of the political economy, politics, or institutions of the United States in its domestic or international affairs, from the civil war to the present
Eligibility: Eligible works shall include book-length historical studies, written in English and published during a given calendar year
Type: Prize
Value: US$500
Frequency: Annual
Country of Study: Any country
No. of awards offered: 91
Application Procedure: Applicants should visit the website for complete application requirements. There is no standard application form and no application fee

Closing Date: 1 October
No. of awards given last year: 1
No. of applicants last year: 91
Additional Information: Please check at www.oah.org/programs/awards/ellis-w-hawley-prize/ for more information

For further information contact:

Email: khamm@oah.org

Germany Residency Program

Purpose: Thanks to a generous grant from the Fritz Thyssen Foundation, the OAH International Committee is pleased to announce the continuation of the Residency Program in American History–Germany (Germany Residency Program) at the University of Tübingen
Eligibility: The committee seeks applications from OAH members who are established scholars affiliated with an American or Canadian University interested in leading an advanced undergraduate/graduate student seminar focusing on one aspect of United States History. The Residencies Program will provide round-trip airfare, housing for thirty days, a modest honorarium (around US$1,200), support by a graduate assistant, and office space
Type: Residency
Value: The Residency Program will provide round-trip airfare, housing for thirty days, a modest honorarium (US$1,500), a graduate assistant, and office space
Frequency: Annual
Country of Study: Any country
No. of awards offered: 13
Application Procedure: The application process requires a short curriculum vitae, the name and contact information of one reference who can speak to an applicant's teaching and scholarship, and outline of the planned seminar at the University of Tübingen
Closing Date: 1 October
Funding: Private
Contributor: OAH
No. of awards given last year: 1
No. of applicants last year: 13
Additional Information: You are also welcome to contact Professor Georg Schild (georg.schild@uni-tuebingen.de) regarding details about the program and the university

For further information contact:

University of Colima, Mexico

Email: germanyresidency@oah.org
Contact: Professor Avital H Bloch, Chair of the International Committee

Huggins-Quarles Award

Purpose: For graduate students of color at the dissertation research stage of their PhD programme

Eligibility: Open to minority graduate students at the dissertation research stage of their PhD

Level of Study: Postgraduate

Type: Award

Value: US$1,500 for one award/US$750 each for two awards

Frequency: Annual

Country of Study: Any country

No. of awards offered: 20

Application Procedure: Applicants should visit the website www.oah.org/activities for complete application requirements. There is no standard application form and no application fee

Closing Date: 1 December

No. of awards given last year: 2

No. of applicants last year: 20

Additional Information: Please check at www.oah.org/programs/awards/huggins-quarles-award/ for more information

For further information contact:

Email: khamm@oah.org

James A Rawley Prize

Subjects: The history of race relations in the United States

Purpose: To reward a book dealing with the history of race relations in the United States

Type: Prize

Value: US$1,000

Frequency: Annual

Country of Study: Any country

No. of awards offered: 76

Application Procedure: Applicants should visit the website www.oah.org/activities for complete application requirements. There is no standard application form and no application fee. Publishers are encouraged to enter one or more books in the competition

Closing Date: 1 October

No. of awards given last year: 1

No. of applicants last year: 76

Additional Information: Please check at www.oah.org/programs/awards/organization-of-american-historians-oah-james-a-rawley-prize/ for more information

For further information contact:

Email: awards@historians.org

Japanese Residencies for United States of America Historians

Subjects: United States of America history

Purpose: To strengthen international and comparative work, to enrich opportunities to engage significant research and to strengthen the study of United States history in Japanese universities

Level of Study: Research

Type: Residency

Value: The award covers round trip airfare to Japan, housing and modest daily expenses

Frequency: Annual, if funds are available

Country of Study: Japan

Closing Date: 15 December

No. of awards given last year: 3

Additional Information: These short-term fellowships are contingent on funding. Historians in residency are expected to enter into the life of their host university during the course of their brief visit by offering lectures or other public presentations, participating in symposia where appropriate, and consulting with faculty and students

For further information contact:

Tel: (1) 812 855 7345

Email: john@oah.org

Contact: Mr John Dichtl, Assistant Executive Director

John Higham Research Fellowship

Subjects: The grants are given in memory of John Higham (1920-2003), past president of the OAH and an important figure in immigration, ethnic, and intellectual history. Thanks to the generosity of William L. and Carol B. Joyce in providing a leadership gift to initiate this fellowship

Purpose: This fellowship is open to all graduate students writing doctoral dissertations for a PhD in American history. Applicants pursuing research in those fields most congenial to the research and writing interests of John Higham will receive special consideration

Eligibility: No specific eligibility terms

Level of Study: Graduate

Type: Fellowship

Frequency: Annual

Country of Study: Any country

Application Procedure: Applications are due by midnight (PST) on 3 December. Applications should include the following components: 1. Project proposal of no more than 1,000 words describing the applicant's research project and detailing how the funds will be used. 2. An updated curriculum vitae with a list of the names and addresses of references. 3. Two signed letters of recommendation on official letterhead submitted independently by referees. Letters in the form of a signed PDF should be e-mailed to the chair of the John Higham Research Fellowship Committee at the address listed below. We ask that recommenders use the subject line "Recommendation for [APPLICANT'S NAME]." Complete all application components (including project proposal, names and addresses of recommenders, and curriculum vitae), in a recent version of Microsoft Word or PDF (preferable), and e-mail the entire electronic file to the chair of the John Higham Research Fellowship Committee for the below listed e-mail

Closing Date: 3 December

Funding: Private

For further information contact:

Tel:	(1) 812 855 7311
Email:	Keisha.Blain@Pitt.edu
Contact:	Keisha N Blain, Committee Chair

Lawrence W. Levine Award

Subjects: American cultural history

Purpose: To recognize scholarly and professional achievement in the field of American cultural history

Eligibility: Open to applicants of any nationality

Type: Award

Value: US$1,000

Frequency: Annual

Country of Study: Any country

No. of awards offered: 107

Application Procedure: Applicants must visit the website www.oah.org/activities for complete application requirements. There is no standard application form and no application fee. Publishers are encouraged to enter one or more books in the competition

Closing Date: 1 October

No. of awards given last year: 1

No. of applicants last year: 107

Additional Information: Please check at www.oah.org/programs/awards/lawrence-w-levine-award for more information

For further information contact:

Email: oah@oah.org

Louis Pelzer Memorial Award

Subjects: Any period or topic in the history of the United States

Purpose: For the best essay in American history by a graduate student

Type: Award

Value: The winning essay will be published in The Journal of American History. The organization offers a prize of US$500

Frequency: Annual

Country of Study: Any country

No. of awards offered: 30

Application Procedure: Applicants must visit the website www.oah.org/activities for complete application requirements. There is no standard application form and no application fee

Closing Date: 30 November

No. of awards given last year: 1

No. of applicants last year: 30

Additional Information: Please check at www.oah.org/programs/awards/louis-pelzer-memorial-award for more information. The final decision will be made by the Louis Pelzer Memorial Award Committee by February. The winner will be provided with details regarding the OAH Annual Meeting and awards presentation

For further information contact:

Email: jahms@oah.org

Mary Nickliss Prize in United States Women's and/or Gender History

Purpose: The Mary Nickliss Prize is given for "the most original" book in United States Women's and/or Gender History (including North America and the Caribbean prior to 1776). The best book recognizes the ideas and originality of the significant historical scholarship being done by historians of United States Women's and/or Gender History and makes a significant contribution to the understanding of United States Women's and/or Gender History

Eligibility: Each entry must be published during the calendar year preceding that in which the award is given. The prize will be presented at OAH Annual Meeting in Philadelphia, Pennsylvania, 4-6 April

Level of Study: Graduate

Type: Award

Frequency: Annual

Country of Study: Any country

Application Procedure: One copy of each entry, clearly labeled "Mary Nickliss Prize Entry" must be mailed directly to the committee members listed below. Each committee member must receive all submissions postmarked by 1 October. If a book carries a copyright date that is different from the publication date, but the actual publication date falls during the correct timeframe making it eligible, please include a letter of explanation from the publisher with each copy of the book sent to the committee members

Closing Date: 1 October
Funding: Private

For further information contact:

Email: oah@oah.org

Merle Curti Award in American Intellectual History

Subjects: American social, intellectual, and/or cultural history
Purpose: To recognise books in the fields of american social, intellectual, and/or cultural history
Type: Award
Value: US$500
Frequency: Annual
Country of Study: Any country
No. of awards offered: 73
Application Procedure: Applicants must send a copy of each entry to the committee members. Publishers are urged to enter one or more books in the competition. For further application details, candidates should visit the website
Closing Date: 1 October
Contributor: OAH
No. of awards given last year: 1
No. of applicants last year: 73

For further information contact:

California Institute of Technology, Mail Code 228-77, Caltech Pasadena, CA 91125, United States of America

Email: khamm@oah.org
Contact: Mr Daniel J Kevles

Merle Curti Intellectual History Award

Subjects: American social and intellectual history
Purpose: To recognize books in the fields of American social and intellectual history
Level of Study: Graduate
Type: Award
Value: US$500
Frequency: Annual
Country of Study: Any country
No. of awards offered: 57
Application Procedure: Applicants must visit the website www.oah.org/activities for complete application requirements. There is no standard application form and no

application fee. Publishers are encouraged to enter one or more books in the competition

Closing Date: 1 October
Funding: Private
Contributor: OAH
No. of awards given last year: 1
No. of applicants last year: 57
Additional Information: Please check at www.oah.org/programs/ awards/merle-curti-award/ for more information

For further information contact:

Contact: Kara Hamm

Merle Curti Social History Award

Purpose: One award is given annually to the author of the best book in American social history. Merle Curti was president of the OAH 1951-1952
Level of Study: Graduate
Type: Award
Frequency: Annual
Country of Study: Any country
Application Procedure: 1. One copy of each entry, clearly labeled "Merle Curti Social History Award Entry," must be mailed directly to the committee members listed below. Each committee member must receive all submissions postmarked by 1 October. 2. Bound page proofs may be used for books to be published after 1 October and before 1 January. If a bound page proof is submitted, a bound copy of the book must be received by each committee member postmarked no later than 7 January. (Please see "Submission Policy") 3. If a book carries a copyright date that is different from the publication date, but the actual publication date falls during the correct timeframe making it eligible, please include a letter of explanation from the publisher with each copy of the book sent to the committee members
Closing Date: 1 October
Funding: Private
Additional Information: The final decision will be made by the Merle Curti Social History Award Committee by February. The winner will be provided with details regarding the OAH Annual Meeting and awards presentation

For further information contact:

Email: khamm@oah.org
Contact: Emma Hart, Committee Chair

Presidents' Travel Fund

Purpose: The fund provides travel stipends of up to $750 for up to five graduate students and recent PhDs in history (no more than four years from date of degree) whose papers or panels/sessions have been accepted by the OAH Program Committee for inclusion on the annual meeting program
Eligibility: For more details, check the website. www.oah.org/programs/awards/presidents-travel-fund/
Level of Study: Graduate
Type: Other
Value: US$750 for five graduate students
Frequency: Annual
Country of Study: Any country
Application Procedure: Please e-mail your paper title or panel title, with an abstract and a CV (indicating your anticipated year of completion of the PhD or the year your PhD was granted), and a paragraph describing why it is important for you to attend the meeting (besides presenting your paper if you are doing so) For further information, check the websitre
Closing Date: 3 December
Funding: Private

For further information contact:

Email: presidentstravelfund@oah.org

Ray Allen Billington Prize

Subjects: American frontier history
Purpose: To award the best book in American frontier history, defined broadly so as to include the pioneer periods of all geographical areas and comparisons between American frontiers and others
Type: Award
Value: US$1,000
Frequency: Every 2 years
Country of Study: Any country
No. of awards offered: 89
Application Procedure: Applicants must visit the website www.oah.org/activities for complete application requirements. There is no standard application form and no application fees. Publishers are encouraged to enter one or more books in the competition
Closing Date: 1 October (of even-numbered years)
Contributor: OAH
No. of awards given last year: 1
No. of applicants last year: 89
Additional Information: Please check at www.oah.org/programs/awards/ray-allen-billington-prize/ for more information

For further information contact:

Email: privacy@oah.org

Richard W Leopold Prize

Subjects: For the best book on foreign policy, military affairs, the historical activities of the federal government, or biography by a government historian
Purpose: To improve contacts and interrelationships within the historical profession where an increasing number of history-trained scholars hold distinguished positions in governmental agencies
Eligibility: Applicant must have been employed in a government position for at least five years
Level of Study: Professional development
Type: Prize
Value: US$1,500 (last year)
Frequency: Every 2 years
Country of Study: Any country
No. of awards offered: 8
Application Procedure: Applicants must visit the website www.oah.org/activities for complete application requirements. There is no standard application form and no application fees. Publishers are encouraged to enter one or more books in the competition
Closing Date: 1 October
No. of awards given last year: 1
No. of applicants last year: 8
Additional Information: Please check at www.oah.org/programs/awards/richard-w-leopold-prize/ for more information

For further information contact:

400 J. L. Seehorn Road, Box 70672, Johnson City, TN 37614, United States of America

Email: oah@oah.org

Tachau Teacher of the Year Award

Subjects: American history
Purpose: To recognize the contributions made by precollegiate and classroom teachers to improve history education
Eligibility: Precollegiate teachers engaged at least half time in United States history teaching, whether in history or social studies, are eligible. Successful candidates shall demonstrate exceptional ability in one or more of the following kinds of activities: 1. Initiating or participating in projects which involve students in historical research, writing, or other

means of representing their knowledge of history. 2. Initiating or participating in school, district, regional, state, or national projects which enhance the professional development of history teachers. 3. Initiating or participating in projects to build bridges between precollegiate and collegiate history or social studies teachers

Level of Study: Professional development

Type: Award

Value: US$500, a one-year OAH membership, a one-year subscription to the OAH Magazine of History and a complimentary registration for the annual meeting. If the winner is an OAH member, the award will include a one-year renewal of membership in the awardee

Frequency: Annual

Country of Study: Any country

No. of awards offered: 2

Application Procedure: Applicants must visit the website www.oah.org/activities for complete application requirements. There is no standard application form and no application fees. To nominate a teacher, please fill out the nomination form at www.oah.org/programs/awards/tachau-teacher-of-the-year-award/submission-form/

Closing Date: 3 December

No. of awards given last year: 1

No. of applicants last year: 2

Additional Information: Please check at www.oah.org/programs/awards/tachau-teacher-of-the-year-award for more information

For further information contact:

Email: awards@oah.org

The Japan Residencies Program

Purpose: To facilitate scholarly dialogue and contribute to the expansion of scholarly networks among students and professors of American history in America and Japan

Eligibility: Applicants must be members of the OAH, have a PhD and be scholars of American history

Type: Programme

Value: Round-trip airfare to Japan, housing (if the host university cannot offer housing, applicants are expected to pay hotel expenses from the daily stipend) and modest daily expenses

Frequency: Annual

Country of Study: Any country

No. of awards offered: 20

Application Procedure: Please refer to the website oah.org/programs/residencies/index.html

Closing Date: 2 December

No. of awards given last year: 2

No. of applicants last year: 20

Additional Information: Please check at www.oah.org/programs/residencies/japan for more information

For further information contact:

Email: alexia.holt@covepark.org

Willi Paul Adams Award

Subjects: American history, namely, the past and issues of continuity and change as well as events or processes that began, developed or ended in what is now the United States

Purpose: For the best book on American history published in a foreign language

Eligibility: This prize is not open to books whose manuscripts were originally submitted for publication in English or by people for whom English is their first language

Type: Award

Value: $1,250

Country of Study: Any country

No. of awards offered: 3

Application Procedure: Applicants must visit the website www.oah.org/activities for complete application requirements. There is no standard application form and no application fees. Publisher are encouraged to enter one or more books in the competition

Closing Date: 1 May (of even-numbered years)

Contributor: OAH

No. of awards given last year: 1

No. of applicants last year: 3

Additional Information: Please check at www.oah.org/programs/awards/willi-paul-adams-award/ for more information

For further information contact:

Tel: (1) 812 855 9852
Fax: (1) 812 855 0696
Email: khamm@oah.org

Organization of American States (OAS)

1889 F Street North West, Washington, DC 20006-3897, United States of America

Tel: (1) 202 458 3000
Fax: (1) 202 458 3897
Email: portal@iacd.oas.org

Website: www.oas.org
Contact: Administrative Assistant

Stanton-Horton Award for Excellence in National Park Service History

Purpose: The award recognizes excellence in National Park Service historical efforts that make the NPS a leader in promoting public understanding of and engagement with American history. Please share with us exemplary projects that encourage civic dialogue in all areas of public history
Level of Study: Graduate
Type: Award
Frequency: Annual
Country of Study: Any country
Application Procedure: For further details on the application process, kindly check with the website. www.oah.org/programs/awards/stanton-horton-award/
Closing Date: 3 December
Funding: Private

For further information contact:

Email: saidenberg@gilderlehrman.org
Contact: Susan F Saidenberg, Committee Chair

Oriel College

University of Oxford, Oxfordshire OX1 4EW, Oxford, United Kingdom

Tel: (44) 1865 276 520
Email: graduate.admissions@oriel.ox.ac.uk
Contact: Tutor for Graduates

Oriel College: Oriel Graduate Scholarships

Purpose: Postgraduate students are an integral part of the Oriel community, and the College seeks to provide financial support and teaching opportunities to help students achieve their goals
Eligibility: Open to current graduate students at Oriel College
Level of Study: Postgraduate
Type: Scholarship
Value: Up to £2,500 per year and accommodation rights
Frequency: Annual

Country of Study: Any country
Application Procedure: Benefits of being a postgraduate scholar 1. Stipend. 2. High Table dining rights. 3. Entitlement to College accommodation
Closing Date: 31 January
Funding: Private

For further information contact:

Oriel College, OX14EW, Oxford, United Kingdom

Tel: (44) 1865 276 555
Email: lodge@oriel.ox.ac.uk

Otaru University of Commerce

Business Administration, 3-5-21 Midori, Otaru-shi, Hokkaido 047, Japan

Tel: (81) 1 3423 1101
Contact: MBA Admissions Officer

Bamforth Postgraduate Scholarship

Purpose: Doctoral scholarships are awarded by the University Council, on the recommendation of the Senate, to candidates proceeding to a course of supervised doctoral study at this University. These scholarships are normally available only to students seeking to obtain their first doctoral qualification. Candidates may be awarded one University of Otago doctoral scholarship only
Eligibility: In the case of an applicant for a doctoral scholarship who has completed a Master's degree by papers and thesis (at least 0.75 EFTS), the grades of all relevant2 advanced level papers counting towards the award of the degree and the thesis will be taken into account. An explanation of the time taken for completion of the thesis may be requested and considered by the Scholarships and Prizes Committee if the thesis has taken more than 2 EFTS (2 fulltime years) to complete
Level of Study: Postgraduate
Type: Scholarship
Value: NZ $27,000
Length of Study: 3 year
Frequency: Annual
Country of Study: New Zealand

Closing Date: Applicants can apply anytime
Funding: Foundation

For further information contact:

Email: scholarships@otago.ac.nz

Oxford Brookes University, School of Business

Wheatley Campus, Wheatley, Oxfordshire, OX33 1HX, Oxford, United Kingdom

Tel: (44) 1865 485920
Fax: (44) 1865 485905
Website: www.brookes.ac.uk
Contact: MBA Admissions Officer

Oxford Brookes University MBA Programme

Length of Study: 1 year for the full-time course. 2 years for the part-time course
Country of Study: Any country
Application Procedure: Applicants must submit an application form, four passport photos, and photocopies of any educational qualifications post 18 years. If candidates do not possess a required qualification, they should send official transcripts from previous colleges attended. Non native English speakers should provide evidence of proficiency in English, such as IELTS and TOEFL scores of 6+ and 550+ respectively. Two references (one academic, one professional) should be sent direct to the school from the referees
Closing Date: April-July. Late applications are welcome, subject to availability of places

P

Paloma O Shea Santander International Piano Competition

Calle Hernán Cortés 3, ESP-39003 Santander, Spain

Tel: (34) 94 231 1451
Fax: (34) 94 231 4816
Email: concurso@albeniz.com
Website: www.fundacionalbeniz.com
Contact: A Kaufmann, Secretariat General

The Paloma O'Shea Santander International Piano Competition is one of the best rated competitions in the world. It provides an opportunity for exceptionally talented pianists to enhance their careers. The jury is composed of renowned musicians in order to ensure that grants are made in a fair and unbiased manner.

Gold, Silver and Bronze Medals

Subjects: Musical Instrument
Purpose: To give support to young pianists of Exceptional talents
Eligibility: Competition is open to all Pianists born on 1 January and after
Level of Study: Unrestricted
Type: Other
Value: Cash prizes totalling more than €90,000
Frequency: Varies
Study Establishment: ANY
Country of Study: Any country
No. of awards offered: 241
Application Procedure: Online application for the competition www.santanderpianocompetition.com Available from from June
Closing Date: November

Funding: Government, Commercial, Private, Foundation
No. of awards given last year: 7
No. of applicants last year: 241
Additional Information: Cash prizes totalling more than €90,000; concerts in Spain and abroad; CD recording; Online promotion campaign

For further information contact:

Contact: Ms Pilar Pertusa, General Secretary

Paralyzed Veterans of America (PVA)

801, 18th Street NW, Washington, DC 20006-3517, United States of America

Tel: (1) 800 555 9140
Fax: (1) 202 416 7652
Email: info@pva.org
Website: www.pva.org

The Paralyzed Veterans of America (PVA), a congressionally chartered veterans service organization founded in 1946, has developed a unique expertise on a wide variety of issues involving the special needs of the members-veterans of the armed forces who have experienced spinal cord injury or dysfunction.

Paralyzed Veterans of America Fellowships in Spinal Cord Injury Research

Subjects: Biology, health and medical sciences, therapy/rehabilitation, animal/veterinary sciences, engineering/technology and engineering-related technologies

© Springer Nature Limited 2019
Palgrave Macmillan (ed.), *The Grants Register 2020*,
https://doi.org/10.1057/978-1-349-95943-3

Purpose: To provide support for research done in the United States or Canadian laboratories and improve the quality of life for individuals with spinal cord injury and spinal cord dysfunction and to find an eventual cure for paralysis
Eligibility: Open to citizens of the United States
Level of Study: Postgraduate, Research
Type: Fellowship
Value: US$50,000
Frequency: Annual
Country of Study: United States of America
Application Procedure: Applicants must submit curriculum vitae and 10 copies of grant application. Application form, reference letters and budget are required
Closing Date: 1 September

For further information contact:

Tel: (1) 202 416 7652
Email: foundation@pva.org
Contact: Florence Montgomery, Administrative Officer

Parapsychology Foundation, Inc.

PO Box 1562, New York, NY 10021-0043, United States of America

Tel: (1) 212 628 1550
Fax: (1) 212 628 1559
Email: office@parapsychology.org
Website: www.parapsychology.org
Contact: Vice President

Established in 1951, the Parapsychology Foundation acts as a clearing house for information about parapsychology. Essentially an administrative organization, it maintains one of the largest libraries to do with parapsychology, the Eileen J Garret Library, as well as supporting various programmes that include the library, a grant and scholarship programme, a conference and lecture programme, and a speaker's bureau and publishing programme.

Eileen J Garrett Scholarship

Subjects: Parapsychology
Purpose: To assist students attending an accredited college or university in pursuing the academic study of the science of parapsychology
Eligibility: Open to nationals of any country
Level of Study: Unrestricted
Type: Scholarship

Value: US$3,000
Length of Study: 1 year
Frequency: Annual
Study Establishment: An accredited college or university
Country of Study: Any country
Application Procedure: Applicants must submit samples of writings on the subject with an application form from the Foundation. Letters of reference are required from three individuals, familiar with the applicant's work and/or studies in parapsychology
Closing Date: 15 July

For further information contact:

Email: office@parapsychology.org

Paris School of International Affairs (PSIA)

27, Rue Saint-Guillaume, 75007 Paris, France

Tel: (33) 1 4549 5050
Website: www.sciencespo.fr/psia/

In keeping with Sciences Po's centennial tradition of excellence, PSIA offers a cutting-edge education to tomorrow's leaders in international affairs. With 1,300 students coming from 100 countries, taught by world-renowned professors and practitioners, PSIA rises as a vibrant global pulse in Europe and a primary platform for global debate, rooted in the academy.

Kuwait Program at Sciences Po Excellence Scholarship for Arab Students and Kuwait Nationals

Purpose: The Kuwait Program at Sciences Po offers excellence scholarships to students with an interest in the Middle East who are admitted to PSIA for the current year intake on the programs listed at the website
Eligibility: These scholarships are awarded on a competitive basis, based on the candidate's excellent academic record and proposed project at Sciences Po. 1. This grant is applicable to the people residing at Gulf countries. 2. Applicants must be first-time degree seeking at France. 3. Applicants must have. i. Submitted a full application to Sciences Po (including all supporting documents and references). ii. Applied to any of the 7 graduate schools of Sciences Po, if any of the two-year Masters program
Level of Study: Postgraduate

Type: Scholarship
Value: Multiple scholarships of up to €10,000 per year will be awarded for the 2 years of study
Frequency: Annual
Country of Study: Any country
Application Procedure: Detailed information on this grant is available on the below file. www.sciencespo.fr/kuwait-program/wp-content/uploads/2018/10/Call-for-applications-2019-Kuwait-Excellence-Scholarship-for-Students-from-the-Arab-World.pdf
Closing Date: 17 February
Additional Information: The Kuwait Program at Sciences Po (KSP) is a partnership between the Kuwait Foundation for the Advancement of Sciences (KFAS) and Sciences Po, based at the Paris School of International Affairs

For further information contact:

Email: program.kuwait@sciencespo.fr

Parkinson's United Kingdom

215 Vauxhall Bridge Road, SW1V 1EJ, London, United Kingdom

Tel:	(44) 20 7932 1332
Fax:	(44) 20 7963 9327
Email:	researchapplications@parkinsons.org.uk
Website:	www.parkinsons.org.uk
Contact:	Ms Bunia Gorelick, Research Grants Manager

Founded in 1969, Parkinson's UK is a charity that focuses on information and support, research, education and training and campaigning.

Clinician Scientist Fellowship

Purpose: To support MDs and other health professionals studying for a PhD
Level of Study: Doctorate
Value: Up to £250,000
Length of Study: 3 years
Frequency: Annual
Country of Study: United Kingdom
Application Procedure: Please see website
Closing Date: Please see website

For further information contact:

Email: cindy@cmscfoundation.org

Paul & Daisy Soros Fellowships for New Americans

400 West 59th Street, 4th floor, New York, NY 10019, United States of America

Tel:	(1) 212 547 6926
Fax:	(1) 212 548 4623
Email:	pdsoros_fellows@sorosny.org
Website:	www.pdsoros.org

The Paul & Daisy Soros Fellowship for New Americans

Subjects: All subjects
Purpose: To provide opportunities for continuing generations of able and accomplished New Americans to achieve leadership in their chosen fields
Eligibility: Open to New Americans: resident aliens (Green Card Holders) naturalized United States citizens and/or children of 2 naturalized parents
Level of Study: Postdoctorate
Type: Fellowship
Value: US$25,000 up to US$20,000 in tuition support for each year
Length of Study: 2 years
Study Establishment: Any accredited graduate University in the United States
Country of Study: United States of America
No. of awards offered: 77
Application Procedure: Apply online
Closing Date: 12 November
Funding: Private
Contributor: Paul and Daisy Soros
No. of awards given last year: 30
No. of applicants last year: 77

Paul Lowin Prizes

Perpetual Trustees Australia Limited, 39 Hunter Street, Sydney, NSW 2000, Australia

Tel:	(61) 2 9229 3951
Fax:	(61) 2 9229 3957
Email:	lowinprizes@perpetual.com.au
Website:	www.paullowin.perpetual.com.au
Contact:	Charitable Planning Services Administration

The Paul Lowin Prizes are administered by the Perpetual Trustees Australia Limited, which is a public trustee company operating in all mainland states of Australia. It is the sole or co-trustee of 360 charitable trusts and foundations with a value of approximately A $580 million. Income generated from investment of this capital is distributed annually to charitable organisations to fulfil the intent of the trusts under management.

Paul Lowin Prizes - Song Cycle Prize

Subjects: Music composition vocal
Purpose: To recognise original composition. For the purposes of the competition, a song cycle is music suitable for chamber performance
Eligibility: The composer must be at least 18 years of age and an Australian citizen or a resident of Australia for not less than three years prior to the closing date
Level of Study: Unrestricted
Type: Prize
Value: A$15,000
Frequency: Every 2 years
Country of Study: Any country
No. of awards offered: 10
Application Procedure: Applicants must refer to the website for details
Closing Date: 30 June
Funding: Private
No. of awards given last year: 1
No. of applicants last year: 10
Additional Information: Works should use no more than one-eight independent vocal lines, which may be accompanied by up to 10 instrumental players. The text of the work may have a unifying theme, and the composer and the author of the text may or may not be different people, but the author of the text is not eligible for the prize. The work may be no less than 15 minutes and no more than 60 in duration

For further information contact:

c/o Australian Music Centre, Level 4, The Arts Exchange, 18 Hickson Road, Dawes Point, NSW 2000, Australia

Email: info@australianmusiccentre.com.au

Peninsula School of Medicine and Dentistry

The John Bull Building, Tamar Science Park, Research Way, PL6 8BU, Plymouth, United Kingdom

Tel:	(44) 1752 437 474
Fax:	(44) 1752 517 842
Email:	info@psmd.ac.uk
Website:	www.pcmd.ac.uk

Peninsula Medical School and Peninsula Dental School have come together in The Peninsula College of Medicine and Dentistry, a partnership with the University of Exeter, University of Plymouth and the NHS in Devon and Cornwall. The Peninsula Medical School was established in 2000 and Peninsula Dental School was established in 2006. Postgraduate study, either at Masters level through taught programmes, or Doctorate level through research is available through the Peninsula College of Medicine & Dentistry Graduate School.

Peninsula College of Medicine and Dentistry PhD Studentships

Purpose: To attract PhD candidates of outstanding ability to join their exciting and rapidly expanding programme of internationally rated research
Eligibility: Open to the suitably qualified graduates
Level of Study: Doctorate
Type: Studentship
Value: £13,290 (Research Council Rate)
Frequency: Dependent on funds available
Study Establishment: Peninsula College of Medicine & Dentistry
Country of Study: United Kingdom
Application Procedure: Check website for the details
Closing Date: 8 November
Contributor: Various sources

For further information contact:

Email: info@psmd.ac.uk

Penn State, College of Communications

Call for Proposals: Narratives in Public Communications

Purpose: Organizational members use narratives to make sense of the organizational culture. The increased use of narratives in public communication calls for additional research that we hope will help shed new light on their applications and influences in these areas

Eligibility: This call therefore seeks grant proposals that will examine the uses and implications of stories and storytelling in public communications
Level of Study: Graduate
Type: Grant
Frequency: Annual
Country of Study: Any country
Application Procedure: Check the application procedure at the link below. The proposal requires the below information to process further. 1. Narrative (up to 5 pages). 2. Abstract (1 page). 3. Coversheet (1 page). 4. Budget (1 page). Curriculum Vitae or Professional Resume. bellisario.psu.edu/page-center/grants/legacy-scholar-grants/guidelines-for-grant-applications
Closing Date: 15 January
Funding: Private

For further information contact:

4 Carnegie Building, University Park, PA 16802, United States America

Email: edwardsh@fit.edu
Contact: Heidi Edwards, Co-manager

Perkins School of Theology

Southern Methodist University, PO Box 750133, Dallas, TX 75275-0133, United States of America

Tel: (1) 214 768 8436
Fax: (1) 214 768 2293
Email: theology@smu.edu
Website: www.smu.edu/perkins

Perkins School of Theology is one of the 13 seminaries of The United Methodist Church (and one of the only 5 university-related United Methodist theological schools), located in the heart of Dallas, Texas, with extension programmes in Houston/Galveston and San Antonio.

Diaconia Graduate Fellowships

Subjects: Theology
Purpose: To supplement the financial resources of United Methodist students
Eligibility: Open to consecrated diaconal ministers or ordained deacons and full-time Doctoral students
Level of Study: Doctorate

Type: Fellowships
Value: US$10,000
Frequency: Annual
Application Procedure: Request for application forms can be sent to theology@smu.edu
Closing Date: 1 February
Contributor: Section of Deacons and Diaconal Ministries, General Board of Higher Education and Ministry, The United Methodist Church

For further information contact:

Diaconia Graduate Fellowships Section of Deacons and Diaconal Ministries, PO Box 340007, Nashville, TN 37203-0007, United States of America

Tel: (1) 615 340 7375
Email: www.sddm@gbhem.org

Petro Jacyk Central & East European Resource Centre (PJRC)

University of Toronto, 27 King's College Circle, Toronto, ON M5S, Canada

Email: jacyk.program@utoronto.ca
Contact: Petro Jacyk Program for the Study of Ukraine

The PJRC supports the activities of the centre for European, Russian and Eurasian studies, the Department of Slavic Languages and Literatures and the 5 research chairs connected with Estonian, Finnish, Hungarian, Polish History and Ukranian studies.

Petro Jacyk Program

Subjects: Social sciences and humanities
Purpose: The objective of the Post-Doctoral Fellowship is to support annually one of the most promising junior scholars studying contemporary Ukraine and thereby to advance academic understanding of Ukrainian politics, culture, and society
Eligibility: The Petro Jacyk Post-Doctoral Fellowship is available to junior scholars in the social sciences and humanities with a research and teaching focus on contemporary Ukraine. The fellowship is open to recently awarded PhDs (persons holding doctorates for no more than three years at the time of application)
Level of Study: Postdoctorate

Type: Fellowship
Value: C$40,000, which includes payment for teaching a semester-long course, and separately an allowance of up to C$2,500 for research and travel expenses
Length of Study: 1 year
Study Establishment: University of Toronto
Country of Study: Canada
Application Procedure: Please send applications by email to: the Foundation at pjef@bellnet.ca and the Petro Jacyk Program for the Study of Ukraine at the University of Toronto at jacyk.program@utoronto.ca simultaneously
Closing Date: 1 February
Contributor: Petro Jacyk Education Foundation
Additional Information: For more information on the post-doctoral fellowship, please visit our website. sites.utoronto.ca/jacyk/postdoctoral fellowship/call for applications.htm

For further information contact:

Email: jacyk.program@utoronto.ca

Pfizer Inc.

Pfizer MAP Program, MedPoint Communications, 1603 Orrington Ave, Suite 1900, Evanston, IL 60201, United States of America

Tel:	(1) 877 254 6953
Fax:	(1) 847 425 7028
Email:	MAPinfo@clinicalconnexion.com
Website:	www.pfizermap.com
Contact:	MAP Program Coordinator

As a reflection of commitment to the advancement of healthcare, Pfizer Inc. supports medical innovation in a wide range of discipline through its Medical and Academic Partnership (MAP) grants and awards. The Fellowships and Scholar Grants, which offer career-building opportunities for academic researchers in basic, outcomes, and patient-oriented research, are key among these efforts. In addition, Pfizer Visiting Professorships continue to be a resource for in-depth, clinically focused exchange between medical scholars, host organizations and outside scholar-scientists.

Pfizer Scholar

Subjects: Epidemiology
Purpose: To support cancer development in epidemiology
Eligibility: Open to individuals who are pursuing research in epidemiology relevant to human health
Level of Study: Postgraduate

Type: Grant
Value: US$130,000
Length of Study: 2 years
Frequency: Annual
Country of Study: Any country
Application Procedure: A completed application form must be submitted
Closing Date: 6 January
Funding: Commercial

For further information contact:

Email: mzebrowski@metrohealth.org

Pfizer Scholars Grants in Clinical Epidemiology

Subjects: Epidemiology
Purpose: To support the career development of junior faculty
Eligibility: Citizens or permanent residents of the United States of America who have a doctoral degree, relevant research experience and postdoctoral clinical training appropriate for the proposed research are encouraged to apply. The applicant should hold a junior faculty position (with 2 years of appointment as an instructor, an assistant professor or an equivalent junior faculty rank) at an accredited academic medical institution
Level of Study: Professional development
Type: Grant
Value: US$195,000
Length of Study: 3 years
Frequency: Annual
Country of Study: United States of America
Application Procedure: Applicants must visit the website for full details on the application process
Closing Date: 5 January
Funding: Corporation
Contributor: Pfizer Inc

For further information contact:

Email: mzebrowski@metrohealth.org

Pfizer Scholars Grants in Clinical Psychiatry

Subjects: Psychiatry
Purpose: To support the development of junior faculty
Eligibility: Citizens or permanent residents of the United States of America who are junior faculty with a doctoral degree (with 2 years of appointment as an instructor, an assistant professor or an equivalent junior faculty rank) at an accredited academic medical institution are encouraged to apply
Level of Study: Professional development

Type: Grant
Value: US$130,000
Length of Study: 2 years
Frequency: Annual
Country of Study: United States of America
Application Procedure: Applicants must visit the website for full details
Closing Date: 5 January
Funding: Corporation
Contributor: Pfizer Inc

For further information contact:

Email: mzebrowski@metrohealth.org

Pfizer Scholars Grants in Clinical Rheumatology

Subjects: Rheumatology
Purpose: To support the career development of junior faculty
Eligibility: Citizens or permanent residents of the United States of America who have a doctoral degree, relevant research experience and postdoctoral clinical training appropriate for the proposed research are encouraged to apply. The applicant should hold a junior faculty position (with 2 years of appointment as an instructor, an assistant professor or an equivalent junior faculty rank) at an accredited academic medical institution
Level of Study: Professional development
Type: Grant
Value: Up to US$130,000
Length of Study: 2 years
Frequency: Annual
Country of Study: United States of America
Application Procedure: Applicants must visit the website for details on the application process
Closing Date: 5 January
Funding: Corporation
Contributor: Pfizer Inc

For further information contact:

Email: mzebrowski@metrohealth.org

Pfizer Scholars Grants in Pain Medicine

Subjects: Pain medicine, anaesthesiology
Purpose: To support the career development of junior faculty
Eligibility: Citizens or permanent residents of the United States of America who have a doctoral degree, relevant research experience are encouraged to apply. The applicant should hold a junior faculty position (with 2 years of appointment as an instructor, an assistant professor or an equivalent junior faculty rank) at an accredited academic medical institution

Level of Study: Professional development
Type: Grant
Value: US$130,000
Length of Study: 2 years
Frequency: Annual
Country of Study: United States of America
Application Procedure: Applicants must visit the website for details on the application process
Closing Date: 5 January
Funding: Corporation
Contributor: Pfizer Inc

For further information contact:

Email: mzebrowski@metrohealth.org

Pfizer Visiting Professorships Program

Subjects: Medicine
Purpose: To create opportunities for selected institutions to invite a distinguished expert for three days of teaching
Eligibility: Open to accredited medical schools and/or affiliated teaching hospitals
Level of Study: Postgraduate
Type: Grant
Value: US$7,500 each
Frequency: Annual
Country of Study: Any country
Application Procedure: Applications available online
Closing Date: 12 February

For further information contact:

Email: mzebrowski@metrohealth.org

Phi Beta Kappa Society

1606 New Hampshire Avenue NW, Washington, DC 20009, United States of America

Tel: (1) 202 265 3808
Fax: (1) 202 986 1601
Email: info@pbk.org
Website: www.pbk.org

The Phi Beta Kappa Society has pursued its mission of fostering and recognizing excellence in the liberal arts and sciences since 1776.

The Mary Isabel Sibley Fellowship

Subjects: French language or literature in even-numbered years and Greek language, literature, history or archaeology in odd-numbered years
Purpose: To recognize female scholars who have demonstrated their ability to carry out original research
Eligibility: Candidates must be unmarried women 25–35 years of age who have demonstrated their ability to carry on original research. They must hold a doctorate or have fulfilled all the requirements for a doctorate except the dissertation, and they must be planning to devote full-time work to research during the fellowship year. The award is not restricted to members of Phi Beta Kappa or to United States citizens
Level of Study: Doctorate, Postdoctorate, Postgraduate
Type: Fellowship
Value: US$20,000
Length of Study: 1 year, non-renewable
Frequency: Annual
Country of Study: Any country
No. of awards offered: 50
Application Procedure: Applicants must complete an application form, available from the website, and submit this with transcripts and references
Closing Date: 15 January
Funding: Private
No. of awards given last year: 1
No. of applicants last year: 50

For further information contact:

Email: awards@pbk.org

Pierre Elliott Trudeau Foundation

Tel: (1) 514 938 0001, extension 230
Email: competition@trudeaufoundation.ca (general), support@trudeaufoundation.ca (technical questions)
Contact: Josée St-Martin, Program Director, Doctoral Scholarships

Pierre Elliott Trudeau Foundation doctoral scholarships

Subjects: Humanities and social sciences
Eligibility: Open to Canadian citizen, permanent resident of Canada, foreign citizens; full-time first or second year students enrolled (or in the process of enrolling) in a doctoral programe in the humanities and social sciences

Type: Scholarship
Value: C$40,000 per year; C$20,000 per year for research and travel allowance
Length of Study: 3 years
Country of Study: Canada
Closing Date: September
Contributor: Pierre Elliott Trudeau Foundation
No. of awards given last year: 15
Additional Information: For more details, please visit the Contact Centre: support@cihr-irsc.gc.ca. Email: competition @trudeaufoundation.ca (general), support@trudeaufoundation.ca (technical questions) Contact: Josée St-Martin, Program Director, Doctoral Scholarships www.trudeaufoundation.ca/en/programs/doctoral-scholarships

For further information contact:

Email: scholarships@trudeaufoundation.ca

Pine Tree State 4-H Foundation

Azure Dillon 4-H Memorial Scholarship

Eligibility: The qualified candidate must be: 1. a current member of 4-H (enrolled by 31 December) who is currently active in 4-H activities and. 2. a graduating senior or an individual who has graduated from high school, but has delayed going to college for no more than one year. Candidates are only eligible to apply in the spring prior to entering college
Level of Study: Postgraduate
Type: Scholarship
Value: US$1,000
Frequency: Annual
Country of Study: Any country
Application Procedure: Scholarships are awarded based on a combination of demonstrated academic and 4-H excellence. Recipients will be requested to attend the foundation's annual meeting to receive their scholarship in person
Closing Date: 1 March
Funding: Private

For further information contact:

5741 Libby Hall, Orono, ME 04469-5741, United States of America

Plymouth University

Drake Circus, Devon PL4 8AA, Plymouth, United Kingdom

Tel: (44) 1752 600 600
Email: prospectus@plymouth.ac.uk
Website: www.plymouth.ac.uk

International Postgraduate Gaza Scholarships

Purpose: These scholarships will be awarded on a competitive basis to prospective masters students
Eligibility: To apply for the scholarship, a student should hold an offer of a place on a masters course at Plymouth University
Type: Scholarship
Value: Each scholarship will be for a fee discount of £5,000 on a masters programme at Plymouth University
Country of Study: United Kingdom
Application Procedure: Please send completed application form as an attachment to internationalscholarships@plymouth.ac.uk along with a copy of your offer letter; a copy of final transcript/marks sheet from undergraduate degree (if final transcript is not available at the time of application please send the most recent or provisional results); a reference letter, from a suitable source, supporting this scholarship application (please do not supply the same reference as that submitted with the postgraduate application). www.plymouth.ac.uk/uploads/production/document/path/5/5758/Gaza Scholarship2016.docx
Closing Date: 30 June
Additional Information: Please check at www1.plymouth.ac.uk/money/support13-14/Pages/international.aspx#PIS.

International Student Merit Scholarship

Eligibility: Applicants must have received a conditional offer of a place for a postgraduate taught programme commencing in September and be holding the equivalent of a United Kingdom university 1 class Bachelors degree in a relevant subject
Type: Scholarship
Value: £2,500
Country of Study: United Kingdom
Application Procedure: Applicants can apply via email. For detailed information, please visit website
Closing Date: 30 June
Contributor: Plymouth University, United Kingdom
Additional Information: Please check at website

International Student PGT Scholarship

Purpose: Scholarships are available for international students who wish to study postgraduate taught degree courses
Eligibility: Applicants should hold a conditional offer of a place on a postgraduate taught degree programme at Plymouth University. The University will automatically consider applicants with relevant Bachelor degree grades as stipulated in the list. Please note this eligibility criteria list is not exhaustive and graduates from all non-EU countries will be considered for these scholarships. The Bachelor's degree must be the equivalent of a United Kingdom Honours degree, as specified by United Kingdom NARIC. For detailed information, please visit www.plymouth.ac.uk/study/fees/scholarships-bursaries-and-funding/funding/postgraduate-scholarships-for-international-students
Level of Study: Postgraduate
Type: Scholarship
Value: £1,500
Country of Study: United Kingdom
Application Procedure: If the student have applied for a postgraduate taught degree programme, they will automatically be considered for this scholarship if their final transcript or marks sheet was submitted with their application.

Poets Essayists Novelists American Center

588 Broadway, Suite 303, New York, NY 10012, United States of America

Tel: (1) 212 334 1660
Fax: (1) 212 334 2181
Email: pen@pen.org, awards@pen.org
Website: www.pen.org
Contact: Paul W Morris, Awards Director

PEN American Center is a fellowship of writers dedicated to advance literature, depend free expression and foster international fellowship. The American Center is the largest of 145 international PEN centers worldwide.

The PEN Translation Fund Grants

Subjects: Translations of works of fiction, creative nonfiction, poetry, and drama
Purpose: The fund seeks to encourage translators to undertake projects they might not otherwise have had the means to attempt
Eligibility: Book-length works that have not previously appeared in English in print or have appeared only in an outdated or flawed translation
Level of Study: Unrestricted
Type: Grant
Value: US$2,000–4,000
Frequency: Annual
Country of Study: Any country

No. of awards offered: 140

Application Procedure: All applications must include the cover sheet and items outlined at www.pen.org/awards, including the original and translated word, translator curriculum vitae, and artist's statement. Please send seven copies as instructed

Closing Date: Between 1 October and 1 February (Early applications are strongly recommended)

Funding: Private

No. of awards given last year: 11

No. of applicants last year: 140

Additional Information: Anthologies with multiple translators, works of literary criticism and scholarly or technical texts do not qualify. Translators awarded grants by the fund are ineligible to reapply for 3 years after the year they receive a grant. Please check the website for more details

For further information contact:

PEN Literary Awards, PEN Translation Fund, PEN American Center, 588 Broadway 303, New York, NY 10012, United States of America

Email: awards@pen.org

Polycystic Kidney Disease Foundation

9221 Ward Parkway, Suite 400, Kansas City, MO 64114-3367, United States of America

Tel:	(1) 816 931 2600 or (1) 800 PKD CURE
Fax:	(1) 816 931 8655
Email:	pkdcure@pkdcure.org
Website:	www.pkdcure.org
Contact:	Administrative Assistant

The PKD Foundation is the only organization worldwide solely devoted to promoting research into finding a cure for polycystic kidney disease (PKD) and to improving the care and treatment of those affected by it.

Polycystic Kidney Disease Foundation Grant-In-Aid

Subjects: The cause of PKD and possible treatments and a cure

Purpose: To encourage researchers to conduct research on PKD

Eligibility: Research Grants are open to basic and clinical principal investigators with quality projects relevant to finding a treatment and/or cure for PKD. Research Fellowships are open to promising postdoctoral researchers who have the potential to become productive, independent investigators in PKD research

Level of Study: Doctorate, Graduate, Postdoctorate, Predoctorate, Research

Type: Research grant or fellowship

Value: Research Grants: US$65,000 per year; fellowships: US$50,000 per year

Length of Study: 2-years, renewable for a 3 year, pending scientific review and availability of funding

Frequency: Annual

Country of Study: Any country

No. of awards offered: 71

Application Procedure: Application must not exceed a total of 18 pages; otherwise, it will be returned without review. Application guidelines will be available on the PKD foundation website after 1 April. Late applications will not be accepted. Please visit the website for complete application information

Closing Date: 1 August

Funding: Private, Corporation, Foundation, Trusts, Individuals

Contributor: Individuals

No. of awards given last year: 46

No. of applicants last year: 71

For further information contact:

Email: research@pkdcure.org

Population Council

Policy Research Division, One Dag Hammarskjold Plaza, New York, NY 10017, United States of America

Tel:	(1) 212 339 0500
Fax:	(1) 212 755 6052
Email:	ssfellowship@popcouncil.org
Website:	www.popcouncil.org
Contact:	Fellowship Co-ordinator

The Population Council is an international non-profit, non-governmental institution that seeks to improve the well being and reproductive health of current and future generations around the world and to help achieve a humane, equitable and sustainable balance between people and resources. The Council conducts biomedical, social science and public health research and helps build research capacities in developing countries.

Health and Population Innovation Fellowship Program

Subjects: Varies
Purpose: To support mid-career individuals who have innovative ideas and the capacity to help shape public debate in the field of population, rights and reproductive health
Level of Study: Postdoctorate, Professional development
Type: Fellowship
Length of Study: 1 year
Frequency: Annual
Study Establishment: The Population Council, New Delhi
Country of Study: India
Application Procedure: Request application form
Closing Date: 15 September
Funding: Foundation
Contributor: John D. and Catherine T. MacArthur Foundation
No. of awards given last year: 12

For further information contact:

Zone 5A, Ground Floor India Habitat Centre, Lodi Road, New Delhi, Delhi 110003, India

Tel: (91) 11 2464 2901
Fax: (91) 11 2464 2903
Email: fellowships@pcindia.org
Contact: Komal Saxena

Transmission of Immunodeficiency Viruses: Postdoctoral Research Position

For further information contact:

Center for Biomedical Research, Population Council, 1230 York Avenue, New York, NY 10065, United States of America

Tel: (1) 212 327 7794
Fax: (1) 212 327 7764
Email: mpope@popcouncil.org
Contact: Melissa Pope, Senior Scientist

Prehistoric Society

Institute of Archaeology, University College London, 31-34 Gordon Square, WC1H 0PY, London, United Kingdom

Fax: (44) 20 7383 2572
Email: prehistoric@ucl.ac.uk
Website: www.prehistoricsociety.org
Contact: Ms Tessa Machling, Administrative Assistant

The Prehistoric Society is open to professionals and amateurs alike and has over 2,000 members worldwide. Its main activities are lectures, study tours and conferences and it publishes an annual journal (PPS) and a newsletter (PAST), which is published 3 times a year.

Prehistoric Society Conference Fund

Subjects: Prehistoric archaeology
Purpose: It's aim is to further the development of prehistory as an international discipline. To offer funding to those who might not otherwise be able to travel to an international conference
Eligibility: There are no eligibility restrictions
Level of Study: Unrestricted
Type: Scholarship
Value: £200–300
Frequency: Annual
Application Procedure: Applications from both members and non-members will be considered. Applications may also be made by conference organisers, on behalf of attending scholars. Please check website for application: www.prehistoricsociety.org/grants/conference_fund/
Closing Date: 31 January
Funding: Private

For further information contact:

Email: prehistoric@ucl.ac.uk

President's Commission on White House Fellowships

c/o O.P.M-Sheila Coates, 1900 E.Street, NW, Room B431, Washington, DC 20415, United States of America

Tel: (1) 202 395 4522
Fax: (1) 202 395 6179
Email: comments@whitehouse.gov
Website: www.whitehouse.gov/fellows
Contact: White House Fellowships

White House Fellowships

Subjects: Domestic and international policy studies
Purpose: To offer exceptional young men and women first-handed experience working at the highest levels of the federal government
Eligibility: Civilian employees of the Federal government are not eligible
Level of Study: Postgraduate
Type: Fellowship
Value: A full-time, paid assistantship to the Vice President, Cabinet Securities, and other top-ranking government officials
Length of Study: 1 year
Frequency: Annual
Study Establishment: The White House
Country of Study: United States of America
Application Procedure: Application instructions are available on the website
Closing Date: 1 February
Additional Information: Please check website for more details

For further information contact:

Email: whitehousefellows@who.eop.gov

Prime Minister's Research Fellowship

Indian Institute of Technology Hyderabad, Kandi, Sangareddy, Telangana 502285, India

Contact: The Prime Minister's Research Fellowship

The Government of India is offering Prime Minister's Research Fellowship Scheme for Doctoral Studies (PhD) in IITs and IISc aimed at attracting the best talent.

Prime Minister's Research Fellowship Scheme

Subjects: Scholarships are awarded to study the subjects offered by the university
Purpose: The Prime Minister's Research Fellowship (PMRF) scheme is aimed at attracting the talent pool of the country to doctoral (PhD) programs of Indian Institutes of Technology (IITs) and Indian Institute of Science (IISc) for carrying out research in cutting-edge science and technology domains, with focus on national priorities
Eligibility: Citizens of India are eligible to apply. The candidate should have a very good command of English language. Therefore, the application should be written in English
Value: Applicants who fulfill the eligibility criteria, and are finally selected through a selection process, will be offered admission to PhD program in one of IITs/IISc with a fellowship of Rs. 70,000/- per month for the first two years, Rs. 75,000/- per month for the 3rd year, and Rs. 80,000/- per month in the 4th and 5th years. Apart from this, a research grant of Rs. 2.00 lakh per year will be provided to each of the Fellows for a period of 5 years to cover their academic contingency expenses and for foreign/national travel expenses
Country of Study: Any country
Application Procedure: The mode of applying is online
Closing Date: 30 September
Additional Information: For more details please visit to the website scholarship-positions.com/prime-minister-research-fellowship/2018/02/27/

For further information contact:

Email: support@pmrf2018.iith.ac.in

Prince Charles Hospital Foundation's

Rode Rd, Chermside West, QLD 4032, Australia

Tel: (61) 3 9320 6888
Fax: (61) 7 3139 4002
Website: www.thecommongood.org.au
Contact: Prince Charles Hospital Foundation's

The Prince Charles Hospital is a major teaching hospital in Brisbane's northside with an emphasis in cardiac and respiratory medicine and cardiothoracic surgery. It also has geriatric and rehabilitation services, elective orthopaedic services and cardiothoracic services, an inpatient psychiatric unit and a 16-bed palliative care unit.

Prince Charles Hospital Foundation's PhD Scholarship

Subjects: Scholarship is awarded to support educational academic research and high-quality research training at TPCH

Purpose: The aim of the scholarship is to support educational academic research and high-quality research training at TPCH or in the significant partnership with TPCH and its associated community programs. The scholarship provides the applicant with a living stipend to undertake research at or in significant association with, The Prince Charles Hospital

Eligibility: Applicants from Australia are eligible to apply for the scholarship. Applicants must be enrolled, or soon to be enrolled, full-time in a PhD program at an Australian University

Value: The scholarship will be valued at AU$27,082 per annum. The scholarship provides the applicant with a living stipend to undertake research at or insignificant association with, The Prince Charles Hospital

Country of Study: Australia

Application Procedure: See the website

Closing Date: 23 January

Additional Information: For more details please visit the website scholarship-positions.com/prince-charles-hospital-foundations-phd-scholarship-australia/2018/01/09/

For further information contact:

Email: Stephanie.Yerkovich@tpchfoundation.org.au

Q

Qalaa Holdings Scholarship Foundation (QHSF)

Qalaa Holdings Scholarship Foundation, P.O Box: 29, Cairo EG 11516, Egypt

Tel:	(20) 2 2794 5553
Fax:	(20) 2 2792 5849
Email:	info@qalaascholarships.org,
	info@citadelscholarships.org
Website:	www.citadelscholarships.org/index.html

In 2007, Qalaa Holdings established the Qalaa Holdings Scholarship Foundation (QHSF, previously known as the Citadel Capital Scholarship Foundation) as its flagship CSR project. The firm has endowed the Foundation to grant academic scholarships to talented young Egyptian men and women interested in pursuing Master's degrees and PhDs at international universities.

Citadel Capital Scholarship

Subjects: Eligibility criteria and application procedures are all explained on the website. CCSF is only funding Master's level degrees at the moment
Purpose: The Citadel Capital Scholarship Foundation was created in 2007, out of a strong will to contribute to national development through creating high caliber professionals to help enhance Egypt's growth in all sectors
Eligibility: Students from Egypt can apply for this Citadel Capital Scholarship
Level of Study: Postgraduate
Type: Scholarship
Value: US$50,000
Country of Study: Any country

Closing Date: The application deadline is 15 January to 30 April of every year

For further information contact:

Email: info@citadelscholarships.org

Queen Elisabeth International Music Competition of Belgium

20 rue aux Laines, BEL-1000 Brussels, Belgium

Tel:	(32) 2 213 4050
Fax:	(32) 2 514 3297
Email:	info@qeimc.be
Website:	www.qeimc.be
Contact:	Secretariat

The Queen Elisabeth International Music Competition of Belgium is a non-profit association, located in Brussels, whose principal aim is to organize major international competitions for music virtuosos. In this way, the competition participates in the Belgian and international music world, and gives its support to young musicians.

Queen Elisabeth International Music Competition of Belgium

Subjects: Music (piano, voice, violin and cello)
Purpose: To provide career support for young pianists, singers, violinists and cellists
Eligibility: Open to musicians of any nationality who are at least 17 years of age and not older than 30 years for violin,

© Springer Nature Limited 2019
Palgrave Macmillan (ed.), *The Grants Register 2020*,
https://doi.org/10.1057/978-1-349-95943-3

piano, singing and cellists. The competition is made up of a first round, a semi-final and a final round

Level of Study: Unrestricted

Type: Competition

Value: Prizes, awards and certificates along with cash prizes will be awarded

Frequency: Annual

Country of Study: Any country

No. of awards offered: Unrestricted

Application Procedure: Applicants must obtain an application form from the Secretariat of the Competition or via the website

Closing Date: 10 January

Funding: Private

No. of applicants last year: Unrestricted

Additional Information: There are no master classes with jury members

For further information contact:

Email: info@qeimc.be

Level of Study: Postgraduate

Value: Up to £3,400 for full-time students and up to £1,700 for part-time students

Length of Study: 2 years, full-time

Frequency: Annual

Study Establishment: Queen Margaret University College

Country of Study: United Kingdom

Application Procedure: Applicants must complete an application and send it to the SAAS, once nominated by the institution

Closing Date: 31 March

Funding: Government

Contributor: Students Awards Agency for Scotland (SAAS)

No. of awards given last year: 2

Additional Information: Students cannot apply directly to the SAAS. They must have accepted an offer of a place and be nominated by the institution

For further information contact:

Tel: (44) 131 474 0000
Email: rilo@qmu.ac.uk

Queen Margaret University

Queen Margaret University Drive, Musselburgh, EH21 6UU, Edinburgh, United Kingdom

Tel: (44) 131 474 0000
Fax: (44) 131 474 0001
Email: rilo@qmu.ac.uk
Website: www.qmuc.ac.uk
Contact: Professor Anthony Cohen, Principal

Queen Margaret University provides vocationally relevant education in business and enterprise; drama and creative industries; health, including international health; and social sciences, media and communication. Its internationally recognized research activity informs our teaching. With around 4,500 students, our small size allows us to offer students a highly supportive environment.

Students Awards Agency for Scotland Postgraduate Students' Allowances Scheme (PSAS)

Subjects: Cultural management programmes, art therapy, audiology and international health scheme

Purpose: International Health Scheme

Eligibility: United Kingdom and European Union nationals living in Scotland on the relevant date (conditions apply)

Queen Mary, University of London

Admissions and Research Student Office, Mile End Road, E1 4NS, London, United Kingdom

Tel: (44) 20 7882 5555
Fax: (44) 20 7882 5588
Email: admissions@qmul.ac.uk
Website: www.qmul.ac.uk
Contact: Mr Peter Smith, Admissions Assistant

Queen Mary is the fourth largest college in the University of London. Located on an attractive campus, it has more than 8,000 students studying in four faculties plus St Bartholomew's and the Royal London School of Medicine and Dentistry. Of these, more than 1,600 are pursuing postgraduate courses or undertaking research.

Herchel Smith Scholarship in Intellectual Property

Subjects: The Herchel Smith PhD Scholarship Programme recognizes and supports exceptional full-time students who show the potential to make an outstanding contribution to intellectual property law. This programme supports PhD students in intellectual property law and those working at the intersection of intellectual property law and other areas of sciences and humanities

Eligibility: New PhD students undertaking full-time research in the area of Intellectual Property (IP) can apply for a Herchel Smith Scholarship to start in the academic year. Open to both United Kingdom and non-European Union applicants

Type: Scholarship

Value: The award will cover all tuition fees whether at the Home/European Union rate or the overseas rate. In addition, an award of around £15,000 per year (reviewed annually) will be paid to the recipient on a monthly basis throughout the calendar year starting from September

Length of Study: 3 years

Frequency: Annual

Application Procedure: Submit online application at www.law.qmul.ac.uk/postgraduate/funding/phd-ip/index.html. You should make sure that you read all the information in Entry Requirements and How to Apply section of the PhD page (www.law.qmul.ac.uk/postgraduate/courses/law/139691.html) before completing the online application process

Closing Date: 1 June

For further information contact:

Email: g.skehan@qmul.ac.uk
Contact: Mr Gareth Skehan, PhD Admissions Administrator

Queen's Nursing Institute

3 Albemarle Way, EC1V 4RQ, London, United Kingdom

Tel: (44) 20 7549 1400
Fax: (44) 20 7490 1269
Email: rosemary.cook@qni.org.uk
Website: www.qni.org.uk
Contact: Anne Pearson, Practice Development Manager

The Queen's Nursing Institute works to support and develop new and best nursing practice and innovation in primary care. Through this support we want to ensure that patients receive the highest standard of nursing in the community. Primary care has always been the highest priority and the Queen's Nursing Institute firmly believes in working in partnership with nurses to achieve its overall objectives.

Queen's Nursing Institute Fund for Innovation and Leadership

Purpose: Implementation of good practice, or a project or an idea, within the community

Level of Study: Graduate, Postgraduate

Type: A variable number of grants

Value: Up to UK £5,000

Length of Study: 1 year

Frequency: Annual

Country of Study: United Kingdom

Closing Date: 17 October

No. of awards given last year: 12

Queen's University of Belfast

Postgraduate Office, Research and Regional Services, Lanyon North, BT7 1NN, Belfast, United Kingdom

Tel: (44) 28 9027 2585
Fax: (44) 28 9027 2570
Email: pg.office@qub.ac.uk
Website: www.qub.ac.uk
Contact: Ms C Farrell

The Queen's University of Belfast has provided a stimulating environment for postgraduate students since the 1850s. It has a reputation as a centre of academic excellence, embracing the most effective technologies and techniques of the 21 century. It offers over 130 postgraduate courses and research opportunities in more than 60 different research areas.

International Office Postgraduate Scholarship

Subjects: All subject

Purpose: All new International students beginning their first year of full-time postgraduate taught study in Queen's University Belfast in September who meet the conditions of their academic offer will receive an International Office Postgraduate Taught Scholarship

Eligibility: 1. NI/EU/GB Undergraduate students. 2. NI/EU/GB Postgraduate Taught students. 3. International Undergraduate Students. 4. International Postgraduate Students

Level of Study: Postgraduate

Type: Award

Value: £3,000

Length of Study: 1 year

Frequency: Annual

Country of Study: Any country

Application Procedure: Apply online

Closing Date: 14 March

Funding: International office

For further information contact:

Email: international@qub.ac.uk

International PhD Awards

Subjects: Faculty of Arts, Humanities and Social Sciences (AHSS)
Purpose: To pursue PhD programme
Value: Each award is valued at approximately £20,000
Country of Study: Any country
Application Procedure: For online application, please visit website dap.qub.ac.uk/portal/user/u_login.php
Closing Date: 1 May

For further information contact:

Email: G.ODonnell@qub.ac.uk

Kyle Scholarship

Type: Residency
Country of Study: Any country
Application Procedure: For application procedure, please visit website scholarship-positions.com/kyle-scholarships-queens-university-belfast-uk/2018/04/14/. To apply for a programme, complete the online application for study form at: dap.qub.ac.uk/portal/ and receive an Offer of Study
Closing Date: 20 June
Additional Information: This award can be made in conjunction with other awards. The successful applicant must agree to produce a short report of their year to be shared with the donor at the end of their studies. During their studies, they must also deliver a presentation to students interested in taking an LLM at Queen's

For further information contact:

Email: law.office@qub.ac.uk

Leverhulme (LINCS) PhD Scholarship

Purpose: To support pioneering research at the interface between the social sciences and electronic engineering and computer science
Eligibility: 1. Applicants must hold a minimum 2 Class Upper Degree (2:1) or equivalent qualification in a relevant Technology, Social Science or Humanities Based subject. 2. Applicants must be a United Kingdom or European Union citizen. 3. Applications from non-United Kingdom or non-European Union citizens may be accepted on an

exceptional basis but additional funding to cover International student fees is not available and must be secured by the applicant prior to starting. 4. Applicants must be proficient in both writing and speaking in English
Type: Scholarship
Value: Full tuition fees at standard United Kingdom rates (currently £4,195 per annum) for 3 years; a maintenance award at the Research Councils United Kingdom national rate. £1,000 per annum research training and expenses to fund the costs of study abroad, conference attendance and fieldwork
Frequency: Annual
Country of Study: United Kingdom
Closing Date: 15 January

Mary McNeill Scholarship in Irish Studies

Subjects: Irish Studies
Purpose: To fund one selected candidate for an MA in Irish Studies programme
Eligibility: Open to well-qualified United States of America or Canadian students enrolled in the MA (Irish Studies) programme
Level of Study: Postgraduate
Type: Scholarship
Value: UK £3,000
Length of Study: 1 year, full-time
Frequency: Annual
Study Establishment: Queen's University of Belfast
Country of Study: United Kingdom
Application Procedure: Applicants must contact the Institute of Irish Studies, for an application form
Closing Date: 31 May
Additional Information: For further information visit the website or contact the Institute of Irish studies

For further information contact:

Tel: (44) 28 9097 3386
Email: irish.studiesequb.ac.uk

PhD Studentships in Astrophysics Research Centre

Purpose: These scholarships are available for students wishing to undertake a PhD in the Astrophysics Research Centre
Type: Studentship
Value: These studentships are fully funded
Country of Study: United Kingdom

Application Procedure: Applications for post-graduate studies must be made via the QUB portal
Closing Date: 9 February
Contributor: Queen's University Belfast

For further information contact:

Email: s.sim@qub.ac.uk

Queen's Loyalty Scholarship

Purpose: The Queen's Loyalty Scholarship is a 20% reduction on first year gross tuition fees available to Exchange, Summer School and Study Abroad students paying International tuition rates progressing for a full duration undergraduate programme in September
Eligibility: Students must hold an offer of a place on a full-time and complete duration programme at the Queen's University Belfast campus, starting in the academic year and meet any academic and language conditions attached to their offer as stated in their offer letter. Students must be classified as international fee-paying students paying the international tuition fee rate in order to be considered for this discount. Students paying NI/GB/EU fees are not eligible for the Queen's Loyalty Scholarship. For further information check the website. www.qub.ac.uk/International/International-students/International-scholarships/postgraduate-research-scholarships/queens-loyalty-scholarship/
Level of Study: Graduate
Type: Scholarship
Value: 20% tuition fee reduction on year 1
Country of Study: Any country
Closing Date: 31 October
Additional Information: www.qub.ac.uk/International/International-students/International-scholarships/postgraduate-research-scholarships/queens-loyalty-scholarship/

For further information contact:

Email: international@qub.ac.uk

Queensland University of Technology (QUT)

Research Students Centre, GPO Box 2434, Brisbane, QLD 4001, Australia

Tel: (61) 7 3138 4475
Fax: (61) 7 3138 1304

Email: research.enquiries@qut.edu.au
Website: www.rsc.qut.edu.au

QUT provides a career-oriented education which helps graduates find employment in their chosen career, in an environment which uses the latest technology to make learning stimulating and enjoyable. It provides information for students, staff and visitors about the resources of the University, its facilities and processes.

Australian Postgraduate Award Industry Scholarships within Integrative Biology

Subjects: Plant science and biological sciences
Eligibility: Open to citizens of Australia or permanent residents having Honours 1 Degree or equivalent
Level of Study: Postgraduate
Type: Scholarship
Value: A$25,627
Length of Study: 3 years
Frequency: Annual
Application Procedure: Check website for further details
Closing Date: 2 March

For further information contact:

School of Integrative Biology, 286 Morrill Hall, MC-120 University of Illinois, 505 S. Goodwin Ave., Urbana, IL 61801, United States of America

Email: susanne.schmidt@uq.edu.au
Contact: Dr Susanne Schmidt, Senior Lecturer

Australian Research Council Australian Postgraduate Award Industry – Alternative Engine Technologies

Subjects: Engineering and technology
Purpose: The multidisciplinary nature of the project will provide the student with a significant intellectual challenge, to assimilate the required background research and to integrate this knowledge to achieve the aims of the current project
Eligibility: Open to citizens of Australia or New Zealand or permanent residents who have achieved Honours 1 or equivalent, or Honours 2a or equivalent
Level of Study: Postdoctorate, Postgraduate
Type: Scholarship
Value: A$26,140 per year
Length of Study: 3 years
Frequency: Annual

Country of Study: Australia
Application Procedure: Check website for further details
Closing Date: 28 September
Additional Information: Please check website for more details

For further information contact:

Tel:	(61) 7 3138 5174
Email:	rong.situ@qut.edu.au
Contact:	Dr Rong Situ

Institute of Health and Biomedical Innovation Awards

Subjects: Biomedical engineering, engineering and technology, medical and health sciences or physical sciences
Purpose: To support living expenses
Eligibility: Open for citizens of Australia or permanent residents who have achieved Honours 1 or equivalent, or Honours 2a or equivalent
Level of Study: Doctorate, Postgraduate
Type: Award
Value: A$36,140
Length of Study: 2 years (Masters) or 3 years (PhD)
Frequency: Annual
Country of Study: Australia
Application Procedure: Check website for further details
Closing Date: 12 October

For further information contact:

Tel:	(61) 7 3138 6056
Fax:	(61) 7 3138 6039
Email:	s.winn@qut.edu.au
Contact:	Stella Winn, Research Services Manager

International Postgraduate Research Scholarship at Queensland University of Technology

Subjects: Business, creative industries, education, health, law, science and engineering and environments
Eligibility: Applicants should be applying to study a PhD, masters by research, or professional doctorate. They should have a minimum first class honours or equivalent. Applicants should not have previously held an Australian Government-funded research scholarship for more than 6 months
Type: Postgraduate scholarships
Value: It includes tuition fees and health-cover costs for the selected candidate and his/her dependents. Selected candidate may also be considered for an Australian Postgraduate Award living allowance scholarship
Country of Study: Australia
Application Procedure: Applicants should apply for admission to QUT during the Annual Scholarship Round. An indication should be provided on the application for admission that one wishes to be considered for a scholarship
Closing Date: 30 September
Additional Information: studentexp.cecs@anu.edu.au

R

Radboud University Nijmegen

P.O. Box 9102, NLD 6500 HC Nijmegen, Netherlands

Tel: (31) 24 361 6161
Fax: (31) 24 356 4606
Website: www.ru.nl/english

Radboud University is a student-oriented research university that aspires to be one of the best in Europe. The goal is for all research programmes to be rated 'very good' and for degree programmes to rank among the top 25% of Dutch universities.

Radboud Scholarship Programme

Purpose: The Radboud Scholarship Programme offers a select number of talented prospective non-EEA students the opportunity to receive a scholarship to pursue a complete English-taught Master's degree programme at Radboud University

Eligibility: You will only be eligible to obtain a Radboud Scholarship if you: 1. hold a non-EU/EEA passport. 2. are not eligible for the lower EEA tuition fee for other reasons. 3. have (will obtain) a Bachelor's degree achieved outside the Netherlands, have no degrees achieved in the Netherlands and did not receive any previous education in the Netherlands. 4. have a high level of language proficiency. 5. have been fully admitted to the English-taught Master's degree programme starting 01 September as stated in the formal letter of admission. 6. are able to comply with the conditions for obtaining a visa for the Netherlands

Level of Study: Graduate
Type: Scholarship
Frequency: Annual
Country of Study: Any country

Application Procedure: From the eligible candidates the Radboud Scholarship holders will be selected based on the following criteria: 1. Talent: this means that you must have outstanding study results in your present field of study. 2. You are expected to be a promising student in your desired field of study at Radboud University. 3. Proven academic quality and good results of your prior education for example through grades, test scores, publications. 4. Quality of the recommendations in the two reference letters. 5. Motivation: based on your motivation letter for the Master's progamme

Closing Date: 1 March
Funding: Private

For further information contact:

Radboud University Houtlaan 4, NLD 6525 XZ Nijmegen, The Netherlands

Email: rsp@io.ru.nl

Radboud Scholarships Programme for Masters Students

Purpose: The Radboud Scholarship Programme offers a select number of talented prospective non-EEA students the opportunity to receive a scholarship to pursue a complete English-taught Master's degree programme at Radboud University Nijmegen

Eligibility: Applicants will be eligible to obtain a Radboud Scholarship if they hold a non-EU/EEA passport; are not eligible for the lower EEA tuition fee for other reasons; have been fully admitted to the English-taught Master's degree programme as stated in the formal letter of admission; are able to comply with the conditions for obtaining a visa for the Netherlands; are enroled at Radboud University as a full-time student for the academic year and Master's degree programme for which the scholarship will be awarded

Level of Study: Graduate

© Springer Nature Limited 2019
Palgrave Macmillan (ed.), *The Grants Register 2020*,
https://doi.org/10.1057/978-1-349-95943-3

Type: Scholarship
Value: The scholarship consists of a partial tuition waiver. The tuition fee will be waived to the level of an EEA student. In addition the Radboud Scholarship also covers costs such as those for visa, residence permit, health insurance and liability insurance. This amounts to about €700. For detailed information, please visit www.ru.nl/english/education/master's-programmes/financial-matters/scholarships-grants/read_more/rsprogramme/
Country of Study: Netherlands
Application Procedure: The application for admission and the application for the scholarship is fully integrated, there is no separate procedure for the scholarship. Applicants must apply for a Radboud Scholarship by indicating during their application for admission that they wish to apply for a Radboud Scholarship. Applicants will then be requested to upload three additional documents including two recommendation letters and a curriculum vitae. Applicants also must have finalized their request for admission before the deadline
Closing Date: 1 April
Additional Information: For more information about the scholarship programme, contact the International Office on rsp@io.ru.nl

For further information contact:

Email: rsp@io.ru.nl

Radcliffe Institute for Advanced Study

Byerly Hall, 8 Garden Street, Cambridge, MA 02138, United States of America

Tel: (1) 617 495 8212
Fax: (1) 617 495 8136
Email: alison_ney@radcliffe.harvard.edu
Website: www.radcliffe.edu
Contact: Administrator of Fellowships

The Radcliffe Institute for Advanced Study is a scholarly community where individuals pursue advanced work across a wide range of academic disciplines, professions and creative arts. Within this broad purpose, the Radcliffe Institute sustains a continuing commitment to the study of women, gender and society.

Radcliffe Institute Fellowship

Subjects: A range of disciplines across the humanities and social sciences, natural sciences and mathematics, and creative arts

Purpose: The Radcliffe Institute for Advanced Study at Harvard University awards 50 funded residential fellowships each year designed to support scholars, scientists, artists, and writers of exceptional promise and demonstrated accomplishment
Eligibility: For eligibility guidelines, please refer to our application portal
Level of Study: Postdoctorate
Type: Fellowship
Value: US$77,500
Length of Study: September-May
Frequency: Annual
Country of Study: Any country
Application Procedure: Please refer to our webpage for more information: www.radcliffe.harvard.edu/fellowship-program/how-apply
Closing Date: 12 September
Funding: Private, Individuals

For further information contact:

Email: alison_ney@radcliffe.harvard.edu

Radiological Society of North America, Inc. (RSNA)

820 Jorie Boulevard, Oak Brook, IL 60523 2251, United States of America

Tel: (1) 630 571 2670
Fax: (1) 630 571 7837
Email: swalter@rsna.org
Website: www.rsna.org/foundation
Contact: Mr Scott Walter, Assistant Director, Grant Administration

The Research and Education Foundation of the Radiological Society of North America (RSNA) provides grant support to medical students, residents, Fellows and full-time faculty members of departments of radiology, radiation oncology and nuclear medicine.

Medical Student Research Grant

Purpose: This R&E Foundation grant gives medical students the opportunity to gain research experience in medical imaging while they're still in school. Recipients will define objectives, develop research skills and test hypotheses,

Eligibility: 1. You must be an RSNA member to apply for the Medical Student Research Grant. If you're a non dues-paying member, your scientific advisor or your co-investigator must be a dues-paying member. You must also meet the following criteria. 2. You must be a full-time medical student at an accredited North American medical school. 3. You must commit to work full-time for at least 10 weeks on your research project. 4. Your research project must take place in a department of radiology, radiation oncology or nuclear medicine in a North American medical institution, but this doesn't have to be the same institution where you're enrolled as a student. 5. You cannot have been a principal investigator on a grant or contract totaling more than US$60,000 in a single year. This includes single and combined grants and contracts from government, private and commercial sources. 6. You and your principal investigators cannot be employed by any for-profit, commercial company in the radiologic sciences. 7. You cannot submit more than one grant application to the RSNA R&E Foundation a year, and cannot have a concurrent RSNA grant. 8. Funding from other grant sources must be approved by foundation staff if it wasn't described in the original research plan

Level of Study: Research

Type: Research grant

Frequency: Annual

Country of Study: Any country

Application Procedure: For detailed information, check the following link, ektron.rsna.org/uploadedFiles/RSNA/Content/R_and_E_Foundation/Grants_and_Awards/RMS_PoliciesProcedures.pdf

Closing Date: 1 February

Funding: Private

For further information contact:

820 Jorie Blvd., Suite 200 Oak Brook, IL 60523-2251, United States of America

Email: rmurray@rsna.org

Radiological Society of North America Education Seed Grant

Subjects: Radiologic sciences

Purpose: To provide funding opportunities for individuals with an active interest in radiologic education

Eligibility: Applicants must hold a faculty position in a department of radiology, radiation oncology, or nuclear medicine within a North American, educational institution and must have completed advanced training and be certified by the American Board of Radiology (or equivalent), or on track for certification. Applicants must not have received

grant/contract amounts totaling $50,000 or more in a single calendar year as principal investigator

Level of Study: Research

Type: Grant

Value: Up to $30,000 to support the preliminary or pilot phase of education projects, not to supplement major funding already secured. No salary support for the principal investigator will be provided

Frequency: Annual

Country of Study: Any country

Application Procedure: Application can be submitted online

Closing Date: 10 January

Funding: Foundation

For further information contact:

Email: rmurray@rsna.org

Radiological Society of North America Institutional Clinical Fellowship in Cardiovascular Imaging

Subjects: Cardiovascular imaging

Purpose: To provide opportunities for radiologists early in their careers to gain experience and expertise in cardiovascular imaging

Eligibility: Open to citizens or permanent residents of a North American country who have completed their residency training in the radiological sciences. Fellows must also hold an MD or the equivalent as recognized by the American Medical Association and must be ACGME-certified in radiology or be eligible to sit for such certification

Type: Fellowship

Value: US$50,000 per year paid to a department. The Foundation does not pay overhead or indirect costs

Length of Study: 3 years

Frequency: Annual

Country of Study: Any country

Application Procedure: Applications must be submitted by a department in preparation for the recruitment of a Fellow into an existing cardiovascular imaging training programme. Application forms are available from the website

Closing Date: 1 June

For further information contact:

Email: bcartalino@rsna.org

Radiological Society of North America Medical Student Grant Program

Subjects: Radiology and related disciplines

Purpose: To make radiology research opportunities available for medical students early in their training and encourage them to consider academic radiology as a career option

Eligibility: Open to full-time medical students at an accredited North American medical school

Level of Study: Research

Type: Grant

Value: US$3,000 for an 10-week (minimum) research project, to be matched by the sponsoring department (US$6,000 total), as a stipend for the medical student

Length of Study: 1 year

Frequency: Annual

Country of Study: Any country

Application Procedure: Applicants must complete an application form available from the website rsna.org/foundation

Closing Date: 1 February

Funding: Foundation

Contributor: Individuals, private practice, corporate

For further information contact:

Email: bcartalino@rsna.org

Radiological Society of North America Research Resident Program

Subjects: Radiology, radiation oncology and nuclear medicine

Purpose: To provide opportunities for individuals to gain further insight into scientific investigation, and to develop competence in research and educational techniques and methods

Eligibility: Open to citizens or permanent residents of a North American country. Applicants should be in residency training so that the award can occur during any year after the 1st year of training and should have an academic degree acceptable for a radiology residency

Level of Study: Postgraduate

Type: Grant

Value: US$30,000 designed to replace a portion of the resident

Length of Study: 1 year, non-renewable

Frequency: Annual

Country of Study: Any country

Application Procedure: Applicants must complete an application form, available from the website

Closing Date: 15 January

For further information contact:

Email: bcartalino@rsna.org

Radiological Society of North America Research Resident/Fellow Program

Subjects: Radiology or related disciplines

Purpose: To provide young investigators not yet professionally established in the radiological sciences an opportunity to gain further insight into scientific investigation and to develop competence in research techniques and methods

Eligibility: Applicants must be a resident or fellow in a department of radiology, radiation oncology or nuclear medicine within a North American educational institutions at the time of application

Level of Study: Doctorate, Postdoctorate

Type: Fellowship

Value: US$30,000 for a 1-year Research Resident project or US$50,000 for a 1-year Research Fellow project, to be used for salary and/or non-personnel research expenses

Length of Study: 1 year

Frequency: Annual

Country of Study: Any country

Application Procedure: Applicants must complete an application form, available from the website rsna.org/foundation

Closing Date: 15 January

Funding: Foundation

Contributor: Individuals, private practice, corporate

For further information contact:

Email: bcartalino@rsna.org

Radiological Society of North America Research Scholar Grant Program

Subjects: Medical sciences

Purpose: To support junior clinical faculty members and allow them to gain experience in research early in their academic careers

Eligibility: Applicants must be within 5 years of initial faculty appointment in a department of radiology, radiation oncology or nuclear medicine within a North American institution

Level of Study: Doctorate, Postdoctorate

Type: Award

Value: US$75,000 per year for 2 years (US$150,000 total), payable to the institution, to be used exclusively as a stipend for the scholar

Length of Study: 2 years

Frequency: Annual

Country of Study: Any country

Application Procedure: Scholar applicants must be nominated by their host institution. Applicants must complete an application form available from the website rsna.org/foundation
Closing Date: 15 January
Funding: Foundation
Contributor: Individuals, private practice, corporate

For further information contact:

Email: bcartalino@rsna.org

Research Scholar Grant

Purpose: This R&E Foundation grant supports junior faculty members who have completed resident and fellowship programs, but haven't been recognized as independent investigators
Eligibility: Any junior radiology faculty member may apply for the Research Scholar Grant, as long as you are an RSNA member and meet the following criteria: 1. You must hold a full-time faculty position in a department of radiology, radiation oncology or nuclear medicine within a North American educational institution. 2. You must have been hired within the last 5 years with an academic rank of instructor, assistant professor or an equivalent title. 3. You must have completed advanced training and be certified by either the American Board of Radiology (ABR), The Royal College of Physicians and Surgeons of Canada or are on track for certification. 4. You cannot have been a principal investigator on a grant or contract totaling more than US$60,000 in a single year. This includes single and combined grants and contracts from government, private and commercial sources. 5. You and your principal investigators cannot be employed by any for-profit, commercial company in the radiologic sciences. 6. You cannot submit more than one grant application to the RSNA R&E Foundation a year and cannot have a concurrent RSNA grant. 7. Funding from other grant sources must be approved by Foundation staff if it wasn't described in the original research plan
Level of Study: Research
Type: Grant for various aspects of field research and conservation projects in primate habitat countries
Value: US$75,000 will be awarded for a year
Frequency: Annual
Country of Study: Any country
Application Procedure: Elaborated information on grants will be available in the following link. www.rsna.org/research/funding-opportunities/research-grants/research-scholar-grant
Closing Date: 15 January
Funding: Private

For further information contact:

820 Jorie Blvd., Suite 200, Oak Brook, IL 60523-2251, United States of America

Email: membership@rsna.org

Research Seed Grant

Purpose: This R&E Foundation Research Seed Grant gives investigators around the world the chance to define objectives and test hypotheses in preparation for larger grant applications at corporations, foundations and government agencies
Eligibility: Any investigator from anywhere in the world with an academic appointment may apply for this grant, as long as you are an RSNA member. If you're a non dues-paying member, your scientific advisor or your co-investigator must be a dues-paying member. You must also meet the following criteria: All applicants; 1. You must hold a full-time faculty position in a radiology, radiation oncology or nuclear medicine department at an educational institution. 2. If you aren't currently a full-time faculty member, but will be by the time funding starts, a letter from the department chair must be included in your application. 3. You cannot have been a principal investigator on a grant or contract totaling more than US$60,000 in a single year. This includes single and combined grants and contracts from government, private and commercial sources. 4. You and your principal investigators cannot be employed by any for-profit, commercial company in the radiologic sciences. 5. Funding from other grant sources must be approved by foundation staff if it wasn't described in the original research plan
Level of Study: Professional development, Research
Type: Research grant
Value: Upto US$40,000 for a one-year project
Frequency: Annual
Country of Study: Any country
Application Procedure: Applications should describe the unique nature of the research effort independent of existing research efforts. Our Research & Education Foundation provides a critical source of support for investigators. Since the Foundation's inception we've awarded over 1,450 grants. That's more than US$60 million in funding for radiology research and improving patient care
Closing Date: 15 January
Funding: Private

For further information contact:

820 Jorie Blvd., Suite 200, Oak Brook, IL 60523-2251, United States of America

Tel: (1) 630 571 2670
Email: REFoundation@rsna.org

Ragdale

Sybil Shearer Fellowship: Dancemakers

Purpose: The Ragdale Foundation and the Morrison-Shearer Foundation are pleased to announce a fellowship opportunity for dancemakers
Eligibility: Applications are reviewed by Ragdale's Curatorial Board and staff as well as Morrison-Shearer Foundation Trustees. We seek applicants who are pursuing new creativity in dance and movement. This may include both emerging and established practitioners
Level of Study: Postgraduate
Type: Fellowship
Value: cash stipend US$500
Frequency: Annual
Country of Study: Any country
Application Procedure: Evaluations of work are based on the following criteria: 1. Work sample and statement show evidence of original, inventive and exciting new work. 2. Work sample demonstrates quality, technical proficiency, and is professionally presented. 3. Artist's statement and resumé show evidence that the applicant's work is reflective of continued, serious, and exceptional aesthetic investigation in the chosen medium. 4. Work plan demonstrates that the artist will maximize the benefits of a fellowship at Ragdale. 5. References reflect the artist's ability to work well in an artist community
Closing Date: 15 May
Funding: Private

For further information contact:

1260 N. Green Bay Road, Lake Forest, IL 60045, United States of America

Tel: (1) 847 234 1063
Email: info@ragdale.org

Rebecca Skelton Fund

Dance Department Administrator, University of Chichester, Bishop Otter Campus, College Lane, Sussex PO19 6PE, Chichester, United Kingdom

Tel: (44) 12 4381 6485
Fax: (44) 12 4381 6080

Email: rebeccaskeltonfund@chi.ac.uk
Website: www.rebeccaskeltonfund.org
Contact: The Rebecca Skelton Fund Administrator

The fund provides financial assistance towards the cost of postgraduate dance study in experiential/creative work to include dance improvization and those training methods such as Skinner Releasing Technique, Alignment Therapy, Feldenkrais Technique, Alexander Technique and other body-mind practices that focus on an inner awareness and use the proprioceptive communication system or an inner sensory mode.

The Rebecca Skelton Scholarship

Subjects: Music and performing arts
Purpose: To assist students to pursue a course of specific or advanced performance studies or an appropriate dance research and performance
Eligibility: Open to anyone pursuing dance studies at postgraduate level
Level of Study: Doctorate, Postdoctorate, Postgraduate, Professional development, Research
Type: Scholarships and fellowships
Value: UK £500
Frequency: Annual
Country of Study: United Kingdom
No. of awards offered: 9
Application Procedure: Application form on request
Closing Date: 12 January
Funding: Foundation
Contributor: The Rebecca Skelton Fund
No. of awards given last year: 5
No. of applicants last year: 9

For further information contact:

Email: artsresearch@chi.ac.uk

Regent's Park College

Regent's Park College: Aziz Foundation Scholarship

Subjects: Humanities, Arts or Social Science
Purpose: In association with Regent's Park College, the Aziz Foundation is offering a scholarship worth up to £25,000 for a student who is undertaking, or has been accepted for,

a Master's degree in the humanities, arts or social sciences at the University of Oxford

Eligibility: 1. Applicants should: be active within a Muslim community and their wider community, and demonstrate a desire to develop intellectual skills within a multi-faith and secular environment. 2. Applicants will be able to demonstrate long-term commitment to community/societal development and working for good relations through effecting public policy; and be eligible for Home

Level of Study: Postgraduate
Type: Scholarship
Value: Up to £25,000 per year
Frequency: Annual
Country of Study: Any country
Closing Date: 31 March
Funding: Private

For further information contact:

Regent's Park College, Pusey Street, OX1 2LB, Oxford, United Kingdom

Email: academic.administrator@regents.ox.ac.uk
Contact: Ms Bailey Thomas, Academic Administrator

The Pamela Sue Anderson Studentship for the Encouragement of the Place of Women in Philosophy

Subjects: The studentship will be used to fund the tuition of one student and will be tenable for as long as the selection committee deems appropriate, subject to the condition that it shall not be tenable beyond the duration of the student's postgraduate studies at the University of Oxford

Purpose: Regent's Park College is offering a postgraduate studentship who is currently engaged in or has been accepted for post graduate study in the University of Oxford

Level of Study: Postgraduate
Type: Studentship
Frequency: Annual
Country of Study: Any country
Application Procedure: (i) covering letter, explaining how the candidate's proposed research relates to the vision of the studentship; (ii) current CV, including the names and contact details of two referees; (iii) research proposal; (iv) writing sample of no more than 5,000 words
Closing Date: 5 April
Funding: Private

For further information contact:

Pusey Street, OX1 2LB, Oxford, United Kingdom

Email: cnquiries@regents.ox.ac.uk
Contact: Bailey Thomas, Academic Administrator

Regent's University London

Inner Circle, NW1 4NS, London, United Kingdom

Contact: Regent's University London

Regent's University London is a private non-profit university located in London, United Kingdom. Regent's University is only the second institution in the United Kingdom that was granted the status of a private university.

Pakistan Fashion Journalism Scholarship

Subjects: Fashion Journalism
Purpose: An offer for students entering into MA programme
Eligibility: Pakistani students are eligible to apply for this scholarship. Scholarship can be taken in the United Kingdom. To enter the competition for the OK! Pakistan Fashion Journalism Scholarship, you should first meet all of the following criteria: You are a Pakistani national holding a Pakistani passport; You have achieved at least an upper second class (2:1) United Kingdom honours undergraduate degree (or its international equivalent from a recognised institution); You hold an offer of a place on the MA Fashion (Journalism) programme
Type: Scholarship
Value: £4,000 towards fees for one standard programme duration
Country of Study: United Kingdom
Application Procedure: For more details, visit www.regents.ac.uk/study/scholarships-funding-and-bursaries/ok-pakistan-fashion-journalism-scholarship
Closing Date: 30 June
Funding: Private

For further information contact:

Email: enquiries@regents.ac.uk

Robert McKee International Screenwriting Scholarships

Level of Study: Graduate
Type: Scholarship
Value: £7,000

Country of Study: Any country
Closing Date: 30 June

For further information contact:

Email: contact@mckeestory.com

The Dean of Humanities, Arts & Social Sciences Excellence Scholarship

Subjects: The Dean of Humanities, Arts & Social Sciences Excellence Scholarship cannot be transferred to another undergraduate programme. In order to maintain the scholarship for the full duration of your studies, you must pass each module at the first attempt with a mark of at least 60%
Purpose: The Dean of the Faculty of Humanities, Arts & Social Sciences has established three scholarships that celebrate the University's independent, cosmopolitan and enterprising spirit
Level of Study: Graduate
Type: Scholarship and award
Value: The Scholarship award will cover a quarter of the tuition fees for the selected course
Frequency: Annual
Country of Study: Any country
Application Procedure: Applications must be emailed to: scholarships@regents.ac.uk
Closing Date: 31 May
Funding: Private
Additional Information: For any queries, please contact: Regent's University London, Tel: (44) 20 7487 7505, Email: enquiries@regents.ac.uk

For further information contact:

Email: scholarships@regents.ac.uk

Regional Institute for Population Studies

University of Ghana, PO Box 96, Legon, Accra, Ghana

Tel: (233) 21 500 381 ext. 3418
Fax: (233) 21 500 273
Email: rips@libr.ug.edu.gh
Contact: Director

The Regional Institute for Population Studies organises training courses leading to the award of MA, MPhil and PhD degrees, seminars and workshops. It also provides advisory services to member states on request, and facilities for students and research workers, as well as conducting research into population studies and related fields in the English speaking countries of Africa, focusing on level and trends of population growth, morbidity and mortality, reproduction, family formation, gender and the status of women, population structure and distribution, migration, and the interrelationship between population and development.

Respective Government Fellowships

Subjects: Population studies
Purpose: To enable Fellows to obtain advanced training through study or research leading to a Master of Arts, Master of Philosophy or PhD degree
Eligibility: Open to English speaking Sub-Saharan Africans, nominated by their governments, who are capable of pursuing a course of study or research using English as a medium of expression. Candidates should have a good first degree in population studies for the Master of Arts degree course or the Master of Population Studies degree, a Master of Arts in population studies or its equivalent for the Master of Philosophy degree, a Master of Philosophy in population studies or its equivalent for a PhD course
Level of Study: Doctorate, Postgraduate
Type: Fellowship
Value: Approx. US$13,840 per year including stipend, fees, costs for books, minor equipment and production of dissertations and theses
Length of Study: At least 1 year for Master of Arts, at least 18 months for MPhil and 36 months for PhD
Frequency: Annual
Study Establishment: Regional Institute for Population Studies at the University of Ghana
Country of Study: Ghana
No. of awards offered: 22
Application Procedure: United Nations Fellows must complete an application form, available at any United Nations Development Programme Office in the capital city of each English speaking Sub Saharan African country, through which all applications should be routed. Applications must be filled out in triplicate and submitted together with the relevant admission requirement through the government ministry responsible for recruiting candidates for the Institute. Non United Nation Fellows should send an application letter directly to the Director of the Institute. All seven students were sponsored through country programme budgets of governments of three of the member states of the Institute
Closing Date: 30 June
Funding: Government

No. of awards given last year: 13
No. of applicants last year: 22
Additional Information: 20 of last year's candidates were sponsored directly by the Institute and 10 through country programme budgets of governments of four of the member states of the Institute

For further information contact:

Tel: (233) 21 773 8906
Fax: (233) 21 772 829
Email: fo.gha@undp.org
Contact: UNFPA

Religious Scholarships

American Atheists Chinn Scholarships

Subjects: All subjects
Purpose: American Atheists is proud to award two Chinn Scholarships for LGBT Atheist Activism. These scholarships recognize activism in the area of LGBT equality. You do not have to be a member of the LGBT community to receive this scholarship; allies are encouraged to apply
Eligibility: 1. High school seniors or current college students. 2. Full-time graduate and law school students. 3. Applicants must be atheists. 4. Have a minimum cumulative GPA of at least 2.5
Level of Study: Graduate
Type: Scholarship
Value: US$500
Length of Study: 1 year
Frequency: Annual
Country of Study: New Zealand
Application Procedure: Apply online
Closing Date: 3 February
Funding: Foundation

For further information contact:

P.O. Box 158, Cranford, NJ 07016, United States of America

Tel: (1) 908 276 7300
Email: scholarship@atheists.org

American Atheists O'Hair Award

Subjects: All subjects
Purpose: The American Atheists awards a US$1,000 O'Hair Scholarship to an atheist student attending college or university. The award is given every year at the American Atheists National Convention. The Student Activist Scholarship program was founded by Life Members Barbara J. Baldock, Dr. Phillip Butler, Lillian B. Ramsden, Rice O'Dell and Irving Yablon
Eligibility: The scholarship can be used by a current college student or by high school student entering college the upcoming year. Additionally, full-time graduate and law school students are eligible for the scholarship. Applicants must be atheists and have a cumulative GPA of 2.5 or better. Applicants are judged based on their actions as atheists and activists
Level of Study: Graduate
Type: Award
Value: US$1,000
Length of Study: 1 year
Frequency: Annual
Country of Study: New Zealand
Application Procedure: Apply online
Closing Date: 26 February
Funding: Foundation

For further information contact:

P.O. Box 158, Cranford, NJ 07016, United States of America

Tel: (1) 908 276 7300
Email: scholarships@atheists.org

Anna Schiller Scholarship

Purpose: To be eligible for the Anna Schiller Memorial Scholarship, you must be a Rockford Christian High School graduating senior who demonstrates a strong commitment to improving the quality of life for people in their school, community and/or world at large through their community service and demonstrates the same strong love for others that Anna exemplified through her life. Minimum GPA of 2.0/4.0 is required. For more information or to apply, please visit the scholarship provider's website
Level of Study: Graduate
Type: Scholarship
Frequency: Annual
Country of Study: New Zealand
Closing Date: 1 February
Funding: Foundation

For further information contact:

946 North Second Street, Rockford, IL 61107, United States of America

Tel: (1) 815 962 2110
Email: slambert@cfnil.org

Associated Women for Pepperdine (AWP) Scholarship

Purpose: The Associated Women for Pepperdine (AWP) was established in 1958 and is the largest, most active women's group supporting colleges and universities in Southern California. For over 50 years members have been primary contributors to scholarships for Christian students and have forged a strong link between the University and the Churches of Christ across the country

Eligibility: Current, active member of a Church of Christ congregation. The Associated Women for Pepperdine (AWP) awards a number of scholarships annually on a renewable basis to active members from the Churches of Christ

Level of Study: Graduate

Type: Scholarship

Value: US$5,000

Length of Study: 1 year

Frequency: Annual

Country of Study: New Zealand

Application Procedure: Apply online

Closing Date: 15 February

Funding: Foundation

For further information contact:

Tel: (1) 310 506 4392

Email: admission-seaver@pepperdine.edu

Republic of South Africa

Azerbaijan: Azerbaijan Diplomatic Academy University Scholarship

Subjects: diplomacy, public and international affairs, business, humanities, sciences and system engineering

Purpose: The Government of the Republic of Azerbaijan and ADA University are offering scholarships to foreign students. The ADA University is committed to grooming world class leaders

Eligibility: Be South African citizens in good health, with a strong academic record. 1. Meet the entry criteria for their selected programme at the ADA University. 2. Meet the minimum academic requirement for entry into a similar programme at a South African university. 3. Applicants must be proficient in English

Level of Study: Postgraduate

Type: Scholarship

Value: offers tuition fees, travel expenses, medical benefits and monthly stipend

Frequency: Annual

Country of Study: Any country

Application Procedure: Information on the application process is available on the website. www.ada.edu.az/en-us/pages/admission_fellowships.aspx

Closing Date: 1 July

Funding: Private

For further information contact:

Email: admissions@ada.edu.az

Research Corporation for Science Advancement

4703 E Camp Lowell Drive, Suite 201, Tucson, AZ 85712, United States of America

Tel: (1) 520 571 1111

Fax: (1) 520 571 1119

Email: awards@rescorp.org

Website: www.rescorp.org

Contact: Editor, Science Advancement Programme

The Research Corporation (United States of America) was one of the first United States foundations, and is the only one wholly devoted to the advancement of academic science. An endowed organization, it makes grants totalling US$5,000,000–7,000,000 annually for independently proposed research in chemistry, physics and astronomy at United States and Canadian colleges and universities.

Research Corporation (United States of America) Research Innovation Awards

Subjects: Physics, chemistry or astronomy

Purpose: To assist innovative research programmes for faculty of PhD granting departments

Eligibility: Open to faculty members whose first tenure track position began in either the preceding or the current calendar year are eligible to apply

Level of Study: Doctorate

Type: Research grant

Value: US$35,000 for equipment and supplies, graduate stipends and some other expenses. The award does not cover overheads

Frequency: Annual

Study Establishment: Research universities with PhD granting departments of physics, chemistry and astronomy

Country of Study: United States of America or Canada

No. of awards offered: 200

Application Procedure: Applicants must complete an application form. Guidelines and an application request forms are available from the website

Closing Date: 1 May

Funding: Private

Contributor: Foundation endowment

No. of awards given last year: 45

No. of applicants last year: 200

Additional Information: Research proposals that transcend the ordinary and promise significant discoveries are sought after

For further information contact:

Email: awards@ria.ie

Research Council of Norway

Stensberggata 26, PO Box 2700, St Hanshaugen, Oslo, N 0131, Norway

Tel: (47) 2 203 7000
Fax: (47) 2 203 7001
Email: info@forskningsradet.no
Website: www.forskningsradet.no

The Research Council of Norway is a strategic body for Norwegian research and a central advisory body to the government on issues concerning general research policy as well as the development of science and technology. The Council bears overall responsibility for national research strategy and manages nearly one third of the public sector research funding. One of the principal tasks of the Research Council is to promote co-operation and co-ordination among Norwegian academic institutions. Other important objectives include raising the general level of knowledge in society and encouraging innovation in industry and the public sector. The Research Council identifies important fields of research, allocates funds and evaluates research and development.

Research Council of Norway Senior Scientist Visiting Fellowship

Subjects: Agriculture, forestry, veterinary medicine, and related fields

Purpose: To enable Norwegian research institutions to receive foreign scientists to participate in research groups, discuss research arrangements and give lectures within their special fields

Eligibility: Open to well established and internationally recognised scientists who are at a professional or equivalent level

Level of Study: Professional development

Type: Fellowship

Value: Norwegian krone 25,000 per month for the first two months, Norwegian krone 10,000 for each succeeding month. Travelling expenses may also be defrayed

Length of Study: 1–12 months

Frequency: Annual

Study Establishment: A Norwegian research institution

Country of Study: Norway

Application Procedure: Applications must be filed by Norwegian institutions, so individual scientists should contact the Norwegian research institution or university department of their choice

Closing Date: Varies, please contact the Research Council for details

Funding: Government

Additional Information: The Research Council of Norway also administers the following: Research Programmes of the European Union (EU), Bilateral Scholarship Agreements, and the Nordic Scheme for the Baltic Countries and North West Russia

For further information contact:

Email: post@forskningsradet.no

Reserve Bank of New Zealand

2 The Terrace, PO Box 2498, Wellington 6140, New Zealand

Tel: (64) 4 472 2029
Fax: (64) 4 473 8554
Email: rbnz-info@rbnz.govt.nz
Website: www.rbnz.govt.nz

The Reserve Bank of New Zealand is New Zealand's central bank. They promote a sound and dynamic monetary and financial system. They work towards our vision by operating monetary policy to achieve and maintain price stability, assisting the functioning of a sound and efficient financial system, meeting the currency needs of the public, overseeing and operating effective payments systems and providing effective support services to the Bank.

Reserve Bank of New Zealand Scholarships for International Students

Subjects: Economics, finance and banking
Purpose: Scholarships are available for pursuing honours, master's or final year of PhD degree level at a New Zealand University
Eligibility: Applicants must be studying full time at a New Zealand University and be legally entitled to work in New Zealand. Students must have attained at least B+ average and be studying full time over the academic year (February to November). Applicants must have majoring in Economics, Finance or Banking and they should be entering their honours, Master's or final year of PhD study
Type: Scholarship
Value: The value of each scholarship will be $10,000
Country of Study: New Zealand
Application Procedure: The mode of applying is by email
Closing Date: 15 January
Contributor: The Reserve Bank of New Zealand
Additional Information: Successful applicants will be asked to attend a half day interview process at the Bank in Wellington. This typically takes place in the beginning of February

For further information contact:

Email: recruitment@rbnz.govt.nz

Resuscitation Council (United Kingdom)

5th Floor, Tavistock House North, Tavistock Square, WC1H 9HR, London, United Kingdom

Tel: (44) 20 7388 4678
Fax: (44) 20 7383 0773
Email: enquiries@resus.org.uk
Website: www.resus.org.uk
Contact: Dr Sara Harris, Assistant Director

The Resuscitation Council (United Kingdom) is the expert advisory body on the training and practice of resuscitation in the United Kingdom. It also actively pursues and promotes research in the field of resuscitation medicine.

Resuscitation Council (United Kingdom) Research & Development Grant

Subjects: All aspects of the science practice and teaching of resuscitation techniques

Purpose: To provide grants up to a maximum of £20,000 for capital costs, data analysis and administrative support for research into the science and practice of resuscitation medicine
Type: Grant
Frequency: Annual
Country of Study: Any country
No. of awards offered: 13
Closing Date: 30 May
No. of awards given last year: 5
No. of applicants last year: 13

For further information contact:

Email: enquiries@resus.org.uk

Rheumatology Research Foundation

2200 Lake Boulevard NE, Atlanta, GA 30319, United States of America

Tel: (1) 404 633 3777
Fax: (1) 404 633 1870
Email: foundation@rheumatology.org
Website: www.rheumatology.org
Contact: Sarah Barksdale, Senior Specialist, Awards and Grants

The American College of Rheumatology (ACR) is the professional organization of rheumatologists and associated health professionals who share a dedication to healing, preventing disability and curing more than 100 types of arthritis and related disabling and sometimes fatal disorders of the joints, muscles and bones.

American College of Rheumatology REF Rheumatology Scientist Development Award

Subjects: Arthritis and rheumatic diseases
Purpose: To encourage qualified physicians without significant prior research experience to embark on careers in biomedical and/or clinical research in arthritis and rheumatic diseases
Eligibility: Candidates must be an ACR or ARHP member, have a doctoral level degree, must be clinician scientists
Level of Study: Doctorate, Postdoctorate, Professional development, Research
Type: Award
Value: US$50,000 for first year, US$75,000 for second year and US$100,000 for third year

Length of Study: 3 years
Frequency: Annual
Country of Study: United States of America
No. of awards offered: 12
Application Procedure: Application forms are available on website
Closing Date: 2 August
Funding: Foundation
Contributor: Centocor Inc
Additional Information: For any questions regarding eligibility, contact the REF

For further information contact:

Email: ref@rheumatology.com

American College of Rheumatology/REF Arthritis Investigator Award

Subjects: Arthritis
Purpose: To provide support to physicians and scientists in research fields related to arthritis for the period between the completion of postdoctoral fellowship training and establishment as an independent investigators
Level of Study: Research
Type: Award
Value: US$75,000 for the first 2 years and US$90,000 per year after renewal
Length of Study: 2–4 years
Frequency: Annual
Country of Study: United States of America
Application Procedure: Application forms are available on website
Closing Date: 1 September
Funding: Foundation
Contributor: The Arthritis Foundation

For further information contact:

Email: acrnominations@rheumatology.org

Career Development in Geriatric Medicine Award

Subjects: Geriatrics and rheumatology
Purpose: To support career development for junior faculty in the early stages of their research career
Eligibility: To be eligible for the award, the candidate must: be a member of the ACR; have completed a rheumatology fellowship leading to certification by the ABIM and be within the first 3 years of his/her faculty appointment; and possess a faculty appointment at the time of the award. Award applicant must be a citizen or non-citizen national of the United States of America,

or be in lawful possessions of a permanent resident card. Individuals on temporary (J1, H1) or student visas are not eligible
Level of Study: Doctorate, Professional development, Research
Type: Research award
Value: US$75,000 per year plus US$3,000 in travel grants
Length of Study: 2 years
Frequency: Annual
Country of Study: United States of America
No. of awards offered: 1
Application Procedure: Application forms are available on website www.rheumatology.org/foundation/indcx.asp
Closing Date: 1 August
Funding: Foundation
Contributor: Association of Subspecialty Professors
No. of awards given last year: 1
No. of applicants last year: 1

For further information contact:

Email: ysong@hrsa.gov

Fellowship Training Award

Subjects: Rheumatic diseases
Purpose: The purpose of this award is to provide support to fellows in rheumatology to help ensure that a diverse and highly trained workforce is available to provide competent care to those affected by rheumatic diseases
Eligibility: Only training directors at ACGME-accredited institutions in good standing may apply. The rheumatology fellowship training programme director at the institution will be responsible for the selection and appointment of trainees. Award applicant must be a citizen or non-citizen national of the United States of America, or be in lawful possession of a permanent resident card. Individuals on temporary (J1, H1) or student visas are not eligible
Level of Study: Doctorate
Type: Fellowship
Value: Recipients will receive US$50,000 to support the salary of any fellow. The award is paid directly to the sponsoring institution in 2 equal installments in July and January
Length of Study: 1 year
Frequency: Annual
Country of Study: United States of America
No. of awards offered: 39
Application Procedure: www.rheumresearch.org/education-and-training-awards#AmgenFTA
Closing Date: 1 May
Funding: Corporation, Foundation
Contributor: Amgen, Inc

No. of awards given last year: 23
No. of applicants last year: 39

For further information contact:

Email: acmgf@acmgfoundation.org

Lawren H. Daltroy Health Professional Preceptorship

Subjects: Rheumatology
Purpose: Develop a more qualified and trained health professional workforce in order to improve patient-clinician interactions
Eligibility: Preceptee must meet citizenship requirements outlined by the Rheumatology Research Foundation Awards and Grants policies. Preceptee must be citizens or non-citizen nationals of the United States or in lawful possession of a permanent resident card. Other individuals on temporary (J1, H1) or student visas are not eligible. Preceptor must be an ARHP member. This award is not intended for physicians
Level of Study: Graduate, Postgraduate, Professional development
Type: Scholarship
Value: Up to US$12,000 for 1 year
Length of Study: 1 year
Frequency: Annual
Country of Study: United States of America
No. of awards offered: 3
Application Procedure: Check the following document for further info. www.rheumresearch.org/file/awards/2018/Daltroy_RFA_FY20.pdf
Closing Date: 1 May
Funding: Corporation
Contributor: Funding for this award is made possible through an endowment by Rheuminations, Inc
No. of awards given last year: 1
No. of applicants last year: 3
Additional Information: Please check website www.rheumresearch.org

For further information contact:

Email: Foundation@rheumatology.org

Medical and Graduate Student Preceptonship

Subjects: Rheumatology
Eligibility: Students enroled in LOME or AOA COCA accredited medical schools, undergraduate students who have been accepted into medical school, students enroled in an accredited graduate school, or undergraduate students who have been accepted into graduate school, are eligible to apply
Level of Study: Graduate, Postdoctorate, Postgraduate, Research
Value: US$2,000–4,000 plus complimentary registration and up to US$1,000 in travel expenses to attend the ACR/ARHP Annual Meeting
Length of Study: 1 academic year
Frequency: Annual
Country of Study: United States of America
Application Procedure: Only completed applications submitted online by the deadline will be accepted
Closing Date: 4 Cycles – 1 February, 2 May, 1 August, 1 November
Funding: Foundation
Contributor: Rheumatology Research Foundation
No. of awards given last year: Up to 30

For further information contact:

Email: Foundation@rheumatology.org

Scientist Development Award

Subjects: Rheumatology
Purpose: To provide a training programme to rheumatology fellows or rheumatologists in the early stages of their career on aspects of clinical investigations through a structured, formal training programme
Eligibility: Applicant must meet citizenship requirements outlined by the Rheumatology Research Foundations Awards and Grant policies, be an active member of the ACR or ARHP at the time of submission, have a doctoral level degree, and be affiliated with an accredited graduate or medical school. Applicant must be able to commit at least 75% full-time professional effort to research, career development and other scholarly activities. Candidates may not spend more than 25% effort in clinical and/or teaching activities. Former or current principal investigators of research grants (at the K level or higher, including institutional K) and past awardees of this or equivalent Foundation grants are NOT eligible to apply
Level of Study: Doctorate, Postdoctorate, Professional development, Research
Type: Award
Value: US$50,000 for first year, US$75,000 for second year and US$100,000 for third year
Length of Study: Up to 2 years
Frequency: Annual
Country of Study: United States of America

No. of awards offered: 36
Application Procedure: www.rheumresearch.org/career-development-research-awards#SDA
Closing Date: 1 July
Funding: Foundation
Contributor: Rheumatology Research Foundation
No. of awards given last year: 8
No. of applicants last year: 36
Additional Information: www.rheumresearch.org

For further information contact:

Email: apply@heart.org

Rhode Island Foundation

Cataract Fire Company #2 Scholarship

Purpose: This scholarship is open to residents of Warwick, Rhode Island, who are entering their first year of a two-year, four-year, or vocational/technical postsecondary institution. Students must demonstrate financial need
Eligibility: 1. Must be a high school senior who is entering his/her first year of a two-year, four-year, or vocational/technical postsecondary institution. 2. Must be a resident of Warwick, Rhode Island. 3. Must be a citizen of United States of America. 4. This award is for United States students
Level of Study: Graduate
Type: Scholarship
Value: US$1,458
Frequency: Annual
Country of Study: United States of America
Application Procedure: Applications are available on the Rhode Island Foundation website. The student must click on the "Scholarship/Fellowship Opportunities" link and then search for his/her desired scholarship to access the application. In addition to a completed application, the student must submit the following documents: a copy of his/her financial aid award letter; his/her official high school transcript; a resume or a list of activities in which he/she participates; a typed double-spaced essay of 300 words or less describing what he/she hopes to be doing in his/her professional life 10 years from now; and a copy of his/her final Student Aid Report (SAR), which is provided to the student after filing the FAFSA (Free Application for Federal Student Aid)
Closing Date: 5 April
Funding: Foundation

For further information contact:

34 Warwick Lake Ave., Warwick, RI 02889, United States of America

Tel: (1) 401 427 4011
Email: rbogert@rifoundation.org

Major Jeremiah P. Murphy Scholarship

Purpose: This scholarship is open to children of active, retired, or deceased Providence (RI) police officers who are or will be attending postsecondary institutions offering two-year associate's or four-year college degree
Eligibility: 1. Must be a resident of Rhode Island. 2. Must be a citizen of United States of America. 3. Must be attending or planning to attend a postsecondary institution offering a two-year associate's or a four-year college degree. 4. Must be the child of an active, retired, or deceased Providence, Rhode Island, police officer. 5. This award is for United States students
Level of Study: Graduate
Type: Scholarship
Value: US$2,500
Frequency: Annual
Country of Study: United States of America
Application Procedure: The application deadline date has not yet been finalized for this year, but is expected to remain the same as last year. The deadline date shown here is tentative based on last year's date. Please check back in November for a refreshed application deadline date. Applications are available on the Rhode Island Foundation website. The student must click on the "Scholarship/Fellowship Opportunities" link and then search for his/her desired scholarship to access the application. As part of the online application, the student must upload the following required documents: a completed 'Financial Information Worksheet' (accessible for download in the application); a copy of his/her SAR (Student Aid Report), which is generated after filing the FAFSA (Free Application for Federal Student Aid); the most recent version of his/her student transcript (unofficial accepted); an essay of one page or less on the topic listed on the application; proof of eligible parental employment
Closing Date: 6 April
Funding: Foundation

For further information contact:

1 Union Station, Providence, Rhode Island 02903, United States of America

Tel: (1) 401 427 4011
Email: rbogert@rifoundation.org

Rhodes College

2000 North Parkway, Memphis, TN 38112-1690, United States of America

Tel: (1) 901 843 3000
Email: registrar@rhodes.edu
Website: www.rhodes.edu

Rhodes, founded in 1848, seeks to graduate students with a lifelong passion for learning, a compassion for others, and the ability to translate academic study and personal concern into effective leadership and action in their communities and world.

Watson Fellowship

Subjects: All subjects
Purpose: To offer college graduates a year of independent study and travel outside the United States
Eligibility: Candidates must be graduating seniors to apply; United States citizenship NOT required
Type: Fellowship
Value: US$25,000
Length of Study: 1 year
Frequency: Annual
Application Procedure: A fellowship form along with a project application proposal and details in not more than 5 pages should be submitted electronically
Closing Date: Early October (Internal deadline)
Contributor: Thomas J. Watson Foundation

For further information contact:

Watson Fellowship Program, 293 South Main Street, Providence, RI, United States of America

Tel: (1) 401 274 1952
Fax: (1) 401 274 1954
Email: tjw@watsonfellowship.org
Contact: Thomas J

Rhodes Trust

Rhodes Scholarship

Subjects: The Rhodes Scholarship is an international postgraduate award for students to study at the University of Oxford

Purpose: Rhodes's vision in founding the Scholarship was to develop outstanding leaders who would be motivated to 'fight the world's fight' and to 'esteem the performance of public duties as their highest aim', and to promote international understanding and peace
Eligibility: At the time of application, an applicant must be: a citizen of the United States OR a lawful permanent resident of the United States OR a U.S. resident with DACA status on April 15 in the year of application. Eligible to apply through one of the 50 states, the District of Columbia, or one of the U.S. territories: either in the state or territory where the applicant was legally resident on April 15 in the year of application, or where the applicant will have received at least two years of college training and a bachelor's degree before October 1 in the year following election. At least 18 but not yet 24 years of age (i.e., the applicant must still be 23 on October 1 in the year of application)
Level of Study: Postgraduate
Type: Scholarship
Value: Fees are paid directly by the Trust to the College and University
Length of Study: 2 year
Frequency: Varies
Country of Study: United Kingdom
Application Procedure: Apply online rhodes.embark.com/auth/login
Closing Date: 1:59 PM U.S. Eastern Time on the first Wednesday of October each year
Funding: Foundation

For further information contact:

Tel: (64) 4 475 8403
Email: scholarships-cf@universitiesnz.ac.nz

Rhodes University

PO Box 94, Grahamstown, 6139, South Africa

Tel: (27) 46 603 8055
Fax: (27) 46 622 8822
Email: research-admin@ru.ac.za
Website: www.ru.ac.za/research
Contact: John Gillam, Manager

Rhodes University is a small university campus in Grahamstown with one of the highest research outputs per capita in South Africa. The University offers excellent undergraduate and postgraduate education, and fosters personal development and leadership as well as team, social and communication skills amongst its diverse student body.

Hobart Houghton Research Fellowship

Subjects: Economics
Purpose: To promote work of scientific value relevant to the economic problems of the Eastern Cape Province, Republic of South Africa, that could contribute to the betterment of the people of the region
Eligibility: Open to English speakers who hold at least a Master's degree in economics and who exhibit successful research experience
Level of Study: Doctorate, Postdoctorate
Type: Fellowship
Value: Rand 25,000
Length of Study: 2 months–1 year
Frequency: Annual
Study Establishment: Rhodes University, Grahamstown
Country of Study: South Africa
No. of awards offered: 4
Application Procedure: Applicants must complete an application form, available from the Dean of Research or from the website
Closing Date: 30 September
Funding: Commercial
No. of awards given last year: 1
No. of applicants last year: 4

For further information contact:

Email: h.nel@ru.ac.za
Contact: Professor H Nel

Ruth First Scholarship

Subjects: Humanities, social science students whose fields of study are politics, sociology, philosophy, anthropology, economics, social policy, democracy studies, development studies, media studies, or studies in cog rate disciplines with a strong social and human rights orientation
Purpose: The scholarship is intended to support candidates whose research is in the spirit of Ruth First's life and work, poses difficult social questions, and links knowledge and politics and scholarship and action
Eligibility: For Masters or PhD study and black South African or Mozambican women candidates are particularly encouraged to apply
Level of Study: Doctorate, Postgraduate
Type: Scholarship

Value: South African 120,000 (PhD); Rand 90,000 per year (Master's)
Frequency: Annual
Study Establishment: Rhodes University, Grahamsdown
Country of Study: South Africa
No. of awards offered: 126
Application Procedure: Applicants to submit a letter of motivation (2 pages or more) as to why they would be a potentially suitable candidate for this award and how their proposed research will be within the spirit of Ruth First's work. In addition, an academic transcript, academic curriculum vitae and a copy of an identity document is required
Closing Date: 31 August
Funding: Private
Contributor: Donor and Investments
No. of awards given last year: 1
No. of applicants last year: 126

For further information contact:

Tel: (233) 46 603 8755
Email: pgfinaid-admin@ru.ac.za

Roberta Sykes Indigenous Education Foundation

100 Botany Road, Alexandria, NSW 2015, Australia

Tel: (44) 2 9310 8400
Contact: The Roberta Sykes Indigenous Education Foundation

The group began by publishing an Aboriginal community newspaper, Koori Bina, which later became AIM (Aboriginal and Islander Message). BWA taught students of the Aboriginal and Islander Dance Theatre the skills to publish a small community newspaper; literacy, reporting, creative writing, editing, lay-out and administration, which eventually lead to the students taking over its publication. Over time, BWA broadened its work and funded a number of small enterprises that were established by Aboriginal women.

Roberta Sykes Bursary

Purpose: The Roberta Sykes Indigenous Education Foundation provides partial funding for Indigenous Australians to undertake short, executive education courses at leading overseas academic institutions

Eligibility: For eligibility and application details, please visit www.robertasykesfoundation.com/roberta-sykes-bursary.html

Type: Bursary

Value: The value of the Bursary is up to $20,000

Country of Study: Australia

Application Procedure: Before applying for this scholarship, if any clarifications are required, contact the foundation using the link www.robertasykesfoundation.com/contact.html

Closing Date: 6 June; 25 July; 28 November

For further information contact:

Tel: (44) 2 9310 8400

Roberta Sykes Scholarship

Purpose: The Roberta Sykes Scholarship provides partial funding to Aboriginal and/or Torres Strait Islander postgraduate students who wish to undertake studies at recognised overseas universities

Eligibility: For eligibility details, please visit www.robertasykesfoundation.com/roberta-sykes-scholarships.html. Usually have an undergraduate degree with a strong academic record; Be accepted into a postgraduate coursework or research degree at a recognised overseas university; Be of Aboriginal and/or Torres Strait Islander descent, identify as Aboriginal and/or Torres Strait Islander and be accepted as such by the community in which they live or have lived; Be able to demonstrate that alongside a Roberta Sykes Scholarship, they will have sufficient funds to support themselves during the course of their postgraduate degree (such as through another scholarship, private sponsorship or personal funds); Be able to demonstrate that their studies will be of benefit to their community upon their return to Australia

Type: Scholarship

Value: The value of the Scholarship is up to $30,000 per year

Country of Study: Australia

Application Procedure: In order to contact for the elaborate information about the application. check the below link. www.robertasykesfoundation.com/contact.html

Closing Date: 28 March; 6 June; 25 July; 28 November

Additional Information: If you require further information or wish to discuss your application before submitting please contact the foundation at www.robertasykesfoundation.com/contact.html

For further information contact:

Tel: (44) 2 9310 8400

The Annual Aurora Indigenous Scholars International Study Tour

Subjects: The Roberta Sykes Indigenous Education Foundation works closely with The Aurora Education Foundation to administer the Roberta Sykes scholarship, fellowship and bursary programs

Purpose: The Study Tour not only offers invaluable opportunities for students to gain insight into the realities of undertaking postgraduate study at these leading institutions but also provides the opportunity to travel with a group of like-minded students. The Study Tour involves meetings with key academics and administrators at each university, as well as current students in the areas of the participants' interest

Eligibility: 1. The Study Tour is open to applicants who have completed at least two years of their course of study and also to university graduates who wish to undertake further postgraduate study. 2. Each year, there is a competitive application process for the Study Tour. 3. The successful applicants will be chosen primarily on the basis of academic achievement

Level of Study: Postgraduate

Type: Scholarship

Value: Costs associated with travel, accommodation and meals are covered

Frequency: Annual

Country of Study: Australia

Application Procedure: To be considered, applicants must apply online via the Indigenous Scholarships Portal and upload the following documents: 1. A cover letter (including a personal statement about your background, career aspirations and reasons for wanting to go on the Tour). 2. A curriculum vitae. 3. An official transcript of all university results (including mid-year results, if available) Confirmation of Aboriginal or Torres Strait Islander descent through a signed written statement (including common seal if available) of an Aboriginal or Torres Strait Islander Heritage. 4. Association, Aboriginal or Torres Strait Islander Corporation or Land Council in the community where you live or have lived. 5. A high-resolution photo (headshot preferably) that could be used in promotional material, should you be selected to go on the Tour. 6. A scanned copy of your passport bio data page (if you have a valid passport)

Closing Date: 1 May

Funding: Private

Additional Information: For further information on the Study Tour, please please visit the Aurora Education Foundation website

For further information contact:

Email: scholarships@auroraproject.com.au

The Roberta Sykes Harvard Club Scholarship

Subjects: Each Harvard graduate school or department has its own admissions criteria and deadlines. Before applying, prospective applicants should check the Harvard website (www.harvard.edu/admissions-aid) to clarify all deadlines and the exact requirements for admission to their chosen degree program

Purpose: The purpose of the award is to promote fellowship amongst alumni and to assist Australians wishing to study at Harvard

Eligibility: For eligibility details, please visit www.robertasykesfoundation.com/roberta-sykes-harvard-club-scholarship.html

Type: Scholarship

Value: The value of the scholarship is up to $80,000 per annum to be paid over the course of the Scholar's study

Country of Study: Australia

Application Procedure: Before applying, prospective applicants should check the Harvard website (www.harvard.edu/admissions-aid) to clarify all deadlines and the exact requirements for admission to their chosen degree programme

Closing Date: Applications are still open

Contributor: Roberta Sykes Harvard Club

Additional Information: For more information on the club and its programs, please visit www.harvardclub.org.au

For further information contact:

Email: scholarships@auroraproject.com.au

Rotterdam School of Management, Erasmus Graduate School of Business

PO Box 1738, Rotterdam, NLD 3000 DR, Netherlands

Tel:	(31) 10 408 2222
Fax:	(31) 10 452 9509
Email:	rsm@rsm.nl
Website:	www.rsm.nl
Contact:	Ms Connie Tai, Director of Recruiting & Admissions

Holland Government Scholarship/upcoming year for school of management

Purpose: The RSM scholarship will determine award recipient. The Holland Scholarship is financed by the Dutch Ministry of Education, Culture and Science

Eligibility: To be eligible, fulfill the following: 1. Your nationality is non-EEA. 2. You are a prospective student, starting your studies in the academic year. 3. You are applying for a full-time bachelor's or master's programme at RSM. 4. You meet the specific requirements of the programme you are applying for. 5. You do not have a degree from an educational institution in the Netherlands (excluding exchange programmes in the Netherlands). This content was originally published on After School Africa from www.afterschoolafrica.com/13953/netherlands-fellowship-programmes-nfp-developing-countries-phd-students/

Level of Study: Postgraduate

Type: Scholarship

Value: € 5,000 for maximum of 12 months

Frequency: Annual

Country of Study: Any country

Application Procedure: First Step is to register for the Bachelor International Business Administration programme. Required documents are : A scholarship application letter in OLAF of maximum 1 A4 size page, including the following information. 1. an explanation why you would need a scholarship, comprising a description of academic excellence and if application other merits. 2. a clear financial plan, of how you are going to finance year 2 and 4 of IBA programme. 3. If applicable, certified copies of the scholarship granted

Closing Date: 31 January

Funding: Private

Contributor: The Dutch Ministry of Education, Culture and Science

---

Rotterdam School of Management Erasmus University

MBA Programmes, Burgemeester Oudlaan 50, 3062 PA Rotterdam, PO Box 1738, Rotterdam, NLD 3000 DR, Netherlands

Tel:	(31) 10 408 2222
Fax:	(31) 10 452 9509
Email:	info@rsm.nl
Website:	www.rsm.nl
Contact:	Denise Chasney van Dijk, Financial Aid Manager

As one of the world's top business schools, RSM is a centre of excellence and innovation for management education and research. Our goal is to empower individuals to succeed amid the complexities of modern international commerce and become the business leaders of tomorrow.

Rotterdam School of Management Master of Business Administration Asia & Australia Regional Scholarship

Subjects: Business Management
Purpose: To assist candidates from the Asia & Australasia Region in financing their MBA study in the Netherlands
Eligibility: The scholarship is open to high potential candidates who are a citizen or hold permanent residence status in one of the following listed countries: Australia, Bangladesh, Bhutan, Brunei, Burma, Cambodia, China, Fiji, Hong Kong, India, Indonesia, Japan, Kiribati, Laos, Macau, Malaysia, Micronesia, Mongolia, Nepal, New Zealand, Palau, Papua New Guinea, Philippines, Samoa, Singapore, Solomon Islands, Sri Lanka, Thailand, Timor-Leste, Tonga, Tuvalu, Vietnam, Yemen
Level of Study: MBA
Type: Scholarship
Value: 20% tuition fee waiver
Length of Study: 12 months
Frequency: Annual
Study Establishment: Erasmus University
Country of Study: Netherlands
No. of awards offered: 36
Application Procedure: Complete application form to be considered
Closing Date: 30 September
Funding: Private
Contributor: RSM Erasmus University
No. of awards given last year: 1
No. of applicants last year: 36
Additional Information: Eligible to nationals of Asia and Australasia

For further information contact:

Email: info@rsm.nl

Royal Academy of Engineering

3 Carlton House Terrace, SW1Y 5DG, London, United Kingdom

Tel: (44) 20 7766 0600
Fax: (44) 20 7930 1549
Email: mark.bambury@raeng.org.uk
Website: www.raeng.org.uk
Contact: Dr Mark Bambury, Scheme Manager

The Royal Academy of Engineering's objectives may be summarized as the pursuit, encouragement and maintenance of excellence in the whole field of engineering in order to promote the advancement of the science, art and the practice of engineering for the benefit of the public.

ExxonMobil Excellence in Teaching Awards

Subjects: Chemical, petroleum and mechanical engineering, geology
Purpose: To encourage able young engineering and Earth science lecturers to remain in the education sector in their early years
Eligibility: Open to well-qualified graduates, preferably with industrial experience and full-time lecturing posts at Institutes of Higher Education in the United Kingdom. Applicants should have been in their current posts for at least 1 year. The post must include the teaching of chemical, petroleum or mechanical engineering to undergraduates through courses that are accredited for registration with professional bodies for qualifications such as chartered engineer. For applicants whose career path has been graduation at the age of 22, followed by academic or industrial posts, the age limit is generally 32 years (at the closing date). Older candidates who have taken time out, e.g. for industrial experience, parenthood or voluntary service, will also be considered. Applicants should preferably be chartered engineers, or of equivalent professional status, or should be making progress towards this qualification
Level of Study: Postdoctorate
Type: Fellowship
Value: A range of benefits in addition to the £10,000 prize
Length of Study: 12 months
Frequency: Annual
Study Establishment: The applicant's current university in the United Kingdom
Country of Study: United Kingdom
Application Procedure: Applicants must complete an application form
Closing Date: 31 October
Funding: Commercial
Contributor: Exxon Mobile
Additional Information: A brochure is available on request. Enquiries about Exxon mobile university contacts should be sent via email and please see the website for further details

For further information contact:

Email: bowbricki@raeng.co.uk

Royal Academy Engineering Professional Development

Subjects: Engineering
Purpose: To ensure that the stills and knowledge of employees reflect the very latest in technological advances
Eligibility: Open to United Kingdom citizens with a degree or HND/HNC in engineering or a closely allied subject. OND/ONC or City and Guilds Full Technological Certificate or NVQ level III qualifications are acceptable provided the individual has substantial industrial experience
Level of Study: Professional development
Type: Grant
Value: £10,000 and £5,000 and prospective applicants should indicate for which level of award they are applying
Length of Study: 1 year
Frequency: Annual
Country of Study: United Kingdom
Application Procedure: For further information please contact the scheme manager Ian Bowbrick at the Academy
Closing Date: 24 October
Additional Information: Please see the website for further details

For further information contact:

Email: lan.bowbrick@raeng.org.uk

Royal Academy Sir Angus Paton Bursary

Subjects: Engineering for development and water and environmental management
Purpose: To study water and environmental management
Eligibility: The bursary supports a suitably qualified engineer study a full-time Masters' degree course specifically related to water resources engineering or some other environmental technology
Level of Study: Postgraduate
Type: Bursary
Value: UK £8,000
Length of Study: 1 year
Frequency: Annual
Country of Study: United Kingdom
Application Procedure: For further information please contact the scheme manager Ian Bowbrick at the Academy
Closing Date: Offered all year round (check with website)
Funding: Private
Contributor: Sir Angus Paton

For further information contact:

Email: ian.bowbrick@raeng.org.uk
Contact: Ian Bowbrick

Royal Academy Sir Henry Royce Bursary

Subjects: Aerospace design, manufacture and management, automotive engineering design
Eligibility: Open to qualified engineers enrolled on part-time modular Master's courses
Level of Study: Postgraduate
Type: Bursary
Value: UK £1,000
Length of Study: 1 year
Frequency: Annual
Country of Study: United Kingdom
Application Procedure: For further information please contact the scheme manager Ian Bowbrick at the Academy
Closing Date: Offered all year round
Funding: Foundation
Contributor: Sir Henry Royce Memorial Foundation
Additional Information: Each awardee will receive a commemorative certificate and, on successful completion of their studies and award of the degree, a medal from the Sir Henry Royce Memorial Foundation

For further information contact:

Email: ian.bowbrick@raeng.org.uk

Royal Agricultural University

Royal Agricultural University, Gloucestershire, GL7 6JS, Cirencester, United Kingdom

Tel: (44) 1285 652531
Fax: (44) 1285 650219
Website: www.rau.ac.uk/

The Royal Agricultural University has always been at the forefront of agricultural education since 1845.

Africa Land and Food Masters Fellowship

Subjects: This funding is provided for leadership training; the development of professional networks and supporting industrial experience, together with study opportunities on

Master's programmes in agriculture, agri-business, food and rural development at the Royal Agricultural University

Eligibility: Fellowships are open to Africans from Sub-Saharan Africa who have experience in agriculture, agri-business, food or natural resource management; an interest in land reform; and a desire to make a strategic and sustainable contribution to Africa's development

Level of Study: Postgraduate

Type: Fellowship

Value: Since the Fellowship was launched in 2005, over £1,800,000 has been generously provided by the private sector, foundations and charities in support of the programme

Country of Study: United Kingdom

Application Procedure: Nationals from sub-Saharan Africa are invited to apply for a Fellowship

Closing Date: 31 October

Funding: International office

For further information contact:

Email: african.fellowship-at-rau.ac.uk

Royal College of Midwives

15 Mansfield Street, W1G 9NH, London, United Kingdom

Tel: (44) 20 7312 3643
Fax: (44) 20 7312 3536
Email: info@rcm.org.uk
Website: www.rcm.org.uk
Contact: S E MacDonald, Education and Research Manager

The Royal College of Midwives is the major professional organization for midwives in the United Kingdom, and aims to contribute to the art and science of midwifery knowledge and practice. The RCM awards and scholarships provide opportunities for the development of good practice ultimately improving the care provided to women, their babies and families.

Royal College of Midwives Annual Midwifery Awards

Subjects: There are nine categories of awards which celebrate the range of work and achievement of midwives midwifery education, midwifery management or leadership, innovations in midwifery, Members' Champion award, promotion of normal birth, outstanding contribution to care of newborns, award for turning vision into reality, midwifery impact on child development, promoting effective midwifery in community settings and Student Vision award

Purpose: To recognize and celebrate innovation in midwifery practice, education and research

Eligibility: Applicants may be individuals or small groups but should meet the criteria of 1 of the 10 categories. Check the website for complete details: www.rcm.org.uk/college/annual-midwifery-awards/

Level of Study: Postgraduate, Professional development, Research

Type: Award

Value: Varies (up to UK £20,000 in total)

Frequency: Annual

No. of awards offered: 82

Application Procedure: Applicants must apply in writing or email to the address given below. The application must be accompanied by a 500-word description of the project. Shortlisted candidates will be asked to attend an interview

Closing Date: 1 November (check with website)

Funding: Commercial

Contributor: Several

No. of awards given last year: 12 awards in 12 categories plus a midwife award

No. of applicants last year: 82

For further information contact:

Gothic House, 3 The Green, Richmond, TW9 1PL, Surrey, United Kingdom

Email: mail@chamberdunn.co.uk
Contact: Chamberlain Dunn Associates

Ruth Davies Research Bursary

Subjects: Midwifery

Purpose: To promote and develop midwifery research and practice

Eligibility: Open to practicing midwives who are RCM members, who have basic knowledge, skills and understanding of the research process, have access to research support in their trust or Institutes of Higher Education and who have been in practice for 2 years or more

Level of Study: Doctorate, Graduate, Postdoctorate, Postgraduate, Predoctorate, Professional development, Research

Type: Bursary

Value: UK £5,000 per bursary

Length of Study: 1 year

Frequency: Annual

Country of Study: United Kingdom

No. of awards offered: 4 shortlisted

Application Procedure: Applicants must submit a succinct curriculum vitae covering the previous 5 years, a research proposal of no more than 2,500 words and letters of support from both employers and academics who are familiar with the applicant's work
Closing Date: 30 July (check the website)
Funding: Commercial
Contributor: Bounty
No. of awards given last year: 3
No. of applicants last year: 4 shortlisted

For further information contact:

Tel: (44) 20 7312 3463
Email: marlyn.gennace@rcm.org.uk
Contact: Mrs Marlyn Gennace, Ruth Davies Research Bursary Administrator

Royal College of Nursing Foundation

20 Cavendish Square, W1G 0RN, London, United Kingdom

Tel: (44) 20 7647 3645
Email: rcnfoundation@rcn.org.uk
Website: www.rcnfoundation.org.uk
Contact: Ms Grants Officer Awards Officer

The RCN Foundation is an independent charity supporting nursing to improve the health and well-being of the public.

Mary Seacole Leadership and Development Awards

Subjects: Nursing, midwifery and health visiting including public health, health policy, and health education
Purpose: To provide funding for a project, or other educational/development activity that benefits the health needs of people from black and minority ethnic communities
Eligibility: Open to nurses, midwives and health visitors in United Kingdom
Level of Study: Doctorate, Graduate, Postdoctorate, Postgraduate, Predoctorate, Professional development, Research
Type: Award
Value: UK £12,500, Development award UK £6,250
Length of Study: Unrestricted

Frequency: Annual
Study Establishment: Unrestricted
Country of Study: United Kingdom
No. of awards offered: 16
Application Procedure: Applicants must send a stamped addressed envelope to the Royal College of Nursing (RCN) to obtain details and an application form
Closing Date: 1 May
Funding: Government
Contributor: Department of Health
No. of awards given last year: 6
No. of applicants last year: 16

For further information contact:

Email: governance.support@rcn.org.uk

Royal College of Obstetricians and Gynaecologists (RCOG)

27 Sussex Place, Regent's Park, NW1 4RG, London, United Kingdom

Tel: (44) 20 7772 6200
Fax: (44) 20 7723 0575
Email: mgoonewardene@rcog.org.uk
Website: www.rcog.org.uk
Contact: M Goonewardene, Awards Administrator

The Royal College of Obstetricians and Gynaecologists (RCOG) is dedicated to the encouragement of the study, and the advancement of science and practice of obstetrics and gynaecology.

American Gyneocological Club/Gynaecological Visiting Society Fellowship

Purpose: Through generous funding from the American Gynecological Club and the Gynaecological Visiting Society of Great Britain, the RCOG can offer up to £1200 to an individual to visit and gain knowledge from a specific centre offering new techniques of clinical management within O&G
Eligibility: This award is open to Trainees in the United Kingdom and Republic of Ireland and their equivalents in the United States of America in alternating years. For the current year, only applicants from the United Kingdom are eligible. Applicants may make a submission to travel from the United Kingdom to the United States of America
Level of Study: Postgraduate

Type: Fellowship
Frequency: Annual
Country of Study: Any country
Application Procedure: Please ensure you read the guidance on submitting your application before entering any of the awards. current year Applications To apply, please send your application form (Word document) to the Awards Administrator awards@rcog.org.uk by midnight on Friday 31 May. Your application will be judged on the following criteria: Presentation and planning, Originality of elective, Evidence of student supervision and support, level of involvement and benefit of applicant
Closing Date: 31 May
Funding: Private

For further information contact:

Email: awards@rcog.org

Bernhard Baron Travelling Fellowship

Purpose: The Bernhard Baron Charitable Trust has generously endowed to the RCOG two travel scholarships in obstetrics and gynaecology for Fellows and Members of the College worth up to £6000 each
Eligibility: 1. Travel must take place within 12 months of the award being made. 2. The award may only be used for the purpose outlined in your original application. 3. A detailed report (maximum 1,000 words), including pictures if necessary, must be submitted to the RCOG Awards Administrator within eight weeks after the elective
Level of Study: Postdoctorate
Type: Fellowships
Value: up to £6000
Length of Study: 1 year
Frequency: Annual
Country of Study: Any country
Closing Date: 31 May
Funding: Foundation

For further information contact:

27 Sussex Place Regent's Park NW1 4RG, London, United Kingdom

Tel: (44) 20 7772 6200
Fax: (44) 20 7723 0575
Email: awards@rcog.org.uk

Bruggeman Postgraduate Scholarship in Classics

Purpose: Doctoral scholarships are awarded by the University Council, on the recommendation of the Senate, to candidates proceeding to a course of supervised doctoral study at this University. These scholarships are normally available only to students seeking to obtain their first doctoral qualification
Level of Study: Postgraduate
Type: Scholarship
Value: NZ $25,000
Frequency: Annual
Country of Study: New Zealand
Closing Date: Applicants can apply anytime
Funding: Foundation

For further information contact:

Email: scholarships@otago.ac.nz

Calcutta Eden Hospital Annual Prize

Purpose: The Calcutta (Kolkata) Eden Hospital is notable because it is where the highly reputed Professor Green Armytage spent his professional career for 25 years at the turn of the 20th century. During his tenure, he designed 'uterine haemostatic forceps' which are still widely used around the world in caesarean sections
Eligibility: The prize is awarded for the best submission of an article that outlines your insight into any aspect of obstetrics and gynaecology undertaken during your training. Preference will be given to well-planned and presented applications
Level of Study: Postdoctorate
Type: Grant
Value: £350
Frequency: Annual
Country of Study: Any country
Closing Date: 31 May
Funding: Foundation

For further information contact:

Email: awards@rcog.org.uk

Eden Travelling Fellowship in Obstetrics and Gynaecology

Purpose: Generously endowed by the late Mr Thomas Watts Eden, this fellowship is awarded to a medical graduate (who graduated within the last two years) currently undertaking a research project. The winner can use the funds to visit any other department(s) within O&G or a related discipline to gain additional knowledge and experience
Eligibility: This Fellowship is open to medical graduates (who graduated within the last 2 years) who are currently undertaking a research project. 1. Travel must take place within 12 months of the award being made in December.

2. The award may only be used for the purpose outlined in your original application. 3. A detailed report (maximum 1,000 words), including pictures if necessary, must be submitted to the RCOG Awards Administrator within eight weeks after the elective. 4. Applicants must declare that their project is entirely their own work and whether they have applied for other prizes for the same project
Level of Study: Postdoctorate, professional development
Type: Fellowship
Value: up to £5,000
Length of Study: 2 year
Frequency: Annual
Country of Study: Any country
Closing Date: 31 May
Funding: Foundation

For further information contact:

Email: awards@rcog.org.uk

Edgar Gentilli Prize

Purpose: Through the kind and generous bequest of the late Mr and Mrs Gilbert Edgar, the RCOG is delighted to offer this award of £750 plus £250 in book tokens to the candidate who submits the best piece of original work on the cause, nature, recognition and treatment of any form of cancer of the female genital tract
Eligibility: 1. The Edgar Gentilli Prize is open to both members and non-members of the RCOG. 2. Candidates for the prize should submit results of their research by way of an original manuscript, adequately referenced and written in a format comparable to that used for submission to a learned journal, or by means of a reprint of the published article. 3. A maximum of 2,000 words with a maximum of 10 references should be submitted. Applications that are over the word limit will be marked down
Level of Study: Graduate
Type: Prize
Frequency: Annual
Country of Study: Any country
Application Procedure: To apply, please send your application to the Awards Administrator awards@rcog.org.uk by midnight on Friday 31 May. Further procedure of the application is available on the below link. www.rcog.org.uk/en/careers-training/awards-grants-prizes/submitting-your-application/
Closing Date: 31 May
Funding: Private

For further information contact:

Email: awards@rcog.org.uk

Elizabeth Garrett Anderson Hospital Charity Travelling Fellowship in Memory of Anne Boutwood

Purpose: Through the generosity of The EGA Hospital Charity, we award a prize of £5,000 to one United Kingdom trainee in the field of obstetrics and gynaecology in memory of Miss Anne Boutwood FRCOG
Eligibility: 1. Travel must take place within 12 months of the award being made. 2. The award may only be used for the purpose outlined in your original application. 3. A detailed report (maximum 1,000 words), including pictures if necessary, must be submitted to the RCOG Awards Administrator within eight weeks after the elective
Level of Study: Postgraduate
Type: Fellowship
Value: £5,000
Frequency: Annual
Country of Study: Any country
Closing Date: 31 May
Funding: Foundation

For further information contact:

Email: awards@rcog.org.uk

Endometriosis Millenium Fund

Purpose: The RCOG is proud to support the Organising Committee of the World Congress of Endometriosis who, through a generous donation, have established the Endometriosis Millennium Fund
Eligibility: Applications are invited for the following: 1. To provide monies to fund a pilot project, clinical or laboratory based in the field of endometriosis, or to provide monies to fund an extension of an existing project researching endometriosis, or; 2. To provide a contribution towards a travelling fellowship to attend a recognised training centre, preferably overseas, to obtain surgical training in the management of cases of endometriosis, beyond the skills expected of core training
Level of Study: Postgraduate
Type: Funding support
Frequency: Annual
Country of Study: Any country
Application Procedure: To apply, please send your application form (Word document) to the Awards Administrator awards@rcog.org.uk by midnight on Friday 31 May. For further information, refer the weblink below. www.rcog.org.uk/en/careers-training/awards-grants-prizes/submitting-your-application/
Closing Date: 31 May
Funding: Private

For further information contact:

Email: awards@rcog.org.uk

Ethicon Foundation Fund Travelling Fellowship

Subjects: Surgery
Purpose: The objective of the Ethicon Foundation Fund Travelling Fellowship, established through the generosity of Ethicon Limited, is to promote international goodwill in medicine and surgery by means of grants to assist the overseas travel of surgeons
Eligibility: 1. Applicants must be MRCS(Glasg) or FRCS (Glasg) and in a higher training post in the United Kingdom, or equivalent elsewhere in the world. 2. The proposed work experience, research or other study should be of clear benefit to the individual's training and to the NHS- or equivalent- on return. 3. Periods abroad should generally be between 1-12 months. 4. Awards will not be given for the sole purpose of attending meetings, or conferences to present papers or for undertaking a series of brief visits to multiple centres
Level of Study: Postgraduate
Type: Travel grant
Value: Up to UK £900
Frequency: Annual
Country of Study: Any country
No. of awards offered: 10
Application Procedure: Download and complete the application form and return the completed form to the address given. Make sure to include in your application: Your CV A signed letter of support from your current supervisor A signed letter from the centre you will be visiting confirming that you are welcome
Closing Date: 30 April
No. of awards given last year: 6
No. of applicants last year: 10
Additional Information: Travel must take place within 6 months of the award being made

For further information contact:

Royal College of Physicians and Surgeons of Glasgow, 232 - 242 St Vincent Street, G2 5RJ, Glasgow, United Kingdom

Tel: (44) 141 221 6072
Email: scholarships@rcpsg.ac.uk

Ethicon Student Elective Award

Purpose: The RCOG, with the kind and generous support of Ethicon, was pleased to offer up to £500 of funding towards approved student medical electives in obstetrics and gynaecology taking place between autumn current and upcoming year
Eligibility: The successful applicant will have submitted well-planned and well-presented applications demonstrating clear objectives and offering detailed information about the project they wish to undertake. Students wishing to pursue a career in obstetrics and gynaecology and undertaking their elective in a subject associated with this specialty in a low-resource country were particularly encouraged to apply. Successful applicants are required to provide a report on their elective. They will also be invited to receive their certificate at an RCOG event. 1. Travel must take place within 12 months of the award being made. Retrospective applications will not be accepted. 2. The award may only be used for the purpose outlined in your original application. 3. A detailed report (maximum 1,000 words), including pictures if necessary, must be submitted to the RCOG Awards Administrator within eight weeks after the elective
Level of Study: Postgraduate
Type: Award
Value: Upto UK £500
Frequency: Annual
Country of Study: Any country
Application Procedure: To apply, please send your application form (Word document) to the Awards Administrator awards@rcog.org.uk by midnight on Friday 31 May. Application form is available on the below link. www.rcog.org.uk/globalassets/documents/careers-and-training/awards–prizes/2019/ethicon-student-elective—application-form-2019.docx
Closing Date: 31 May
Funding: Private

For further information contact:

Email: awards@rcog.org.uk

Florence and William Blair Bell Research Fellowship

Purpose: The funding has been donated in order to stimulate and encourage research (clinical or laboratory based) in the field of O&G. Clinicians are encouraged, with the use of funds, to acquire extra clinical or research skills to improve patient management or develop their postdoctoral research
Eligibility: 1. If the application is for travel funding, travel must take place within 12 months of the award being made. 2. The award may only be used for the purpose outlined in your original application. 3. A detailed report (maximum 1,000 words), including pictures if necessary, must be submitted to the RCOG Awards Administrator at the end of the grant period. 4. An undertaking must be given that the source of the grant will be acknowledged in any related publications

Level of Study: Postgraduate
Type: Fellowship
Value: up to UK£5,000
Frequency: Annual
Country of Study: Any country
Closing Date: 31 May
Funding: Foundation

For further information contact:

Email: awards@rcog.org.uk

Green-Armytage and Spackman Travelling Scholarship

Purpose: Through the generosity of the late Mr V B Green-Armytage and of the late Colonel W C Spackman, Council is able to award a biennial travelling scholarship up to £4,000 to a Fellow or Member of the College
Eligibility: Applicants should have shown a special interest in some particular aspect of obstetrical or gynaecological practice. The donors' wishes are that the awards should be used for the purpose of visiting centres where similar work is being carried out. Your application will be judged on the following criteria: 1. Presentation well planned and presented. 2. Relevance of project to career development in O&G. 3. Level of involvement. 4. References. 5. Value to the NHS/local community. 6. Value to personal development
Level of Study: Postgraduate
Type: Scholarship
Value: £4,000
Frequency: Annual
Country of Study: Any country
Application Procedure: Applicants must include information on qualifications, areas of interest and/or publications in a specified area, centres to be visited with confirmation from the head of that centre, estimated costs and the names of two referees
Closing Date: 24 May
Funding: Private

For further information contact:

Email: mgoonewardene@rcog.org.uk

Herbert Erik Reiss Memorial Case History Prize

Purpose: The prizes will be awarded to candidates who, in the opinion of the assessors, undertake the best presentation of a clinical case, including critical assessment and literature research, in a topic of obstetrics and gynaecology

Eligibility: Open to FY1 and FY2 doctors or Specialist Training Years 1 and 2 in the United Kingdom and the Republic of Ireland
Level of Study: Postgraduate
Value: First prize is UK £400 and second prize is UK £200
Frequency: Annual
Country of Study: Any country
No. of awards offered: 20
Application Procedure: A maximum of 1,500 words with maximum of 10 references should be submitted. Please include a statement of contribution to the project and indicate the name and address of the supervisor. Only one submission per candidate is permitted
Closing Date: 31 May
No. of awards given last year: 3
No. of applicants last year: 20
Additional Information: Please contact at mgoonewar dene@rcog.org.uk for further details

For further information contact:

Email: awards@rcog.org.uk

John Lawson Prize

Purpose: The prize will be awarded to a candidate who, in the opinion of the assessors, undertakes the best article on a topic of obstetrics or gynaecology derived from work carried out in Africa between the tropics of Capricorn and Cancer
Eligibility: Candidature is not restricted to fellows and members of the college
Value: UK £150
Frequency: Annual
Country of Study: Any country
No. of awards offered: 8
Application Procedure: The record of the work can be submitted by way of an original manuscript, adequately referenced and written in a format comparable to that used for submission to a learned journal, or by means of a reprint of a published article
Closing Date: 31 May
No. of awards given last year: 1
No. of applicants last year: 8
Additional Information: If joint authorship is involved then the candidate must identify his/her involvement in the publication

For further information contact:

Email: mgoonewardene@rcog.org.uk

Malcolm Black Travel Fellowship

Purpose: The purpose of the fellowship is to enable a College Member of up to five years' standing or a Fellow at the time of application, to travel either to the British Isles or from the British Isles abroad, for a period of time to attend postgraduate training courses

Eligibility: RCOG Council reserves the right to withhold the granting of an award if, in its opinion, no work of sufficient merit is submitted. Applications that do not comply with the stipulations of the relevant award will not be accepted. Please note that all applications must be received electronically

Level of Study: Postgraduate

Type: Fellowship

Value: UK £1,000

Frequency: Every two years

Country of Study: Any country

Application Procedure: Please ensure you read the guidance on submitting your application before entering any of the awards. Travel must take place within 12 months of the award being made. The award may only be used for the purpose outlined in your original application. A detailed report (maximum 1,000 words), including pictures if necessary, must be submitted to the RCOG Awards Administrator within eight weeks after the elective. Your application will be judged on the following criteria: 1. Presentation well planned and presented. 2. Relevance of project to career development in O&G. 3. Level of involvement. 4. References

Closing Date: 31 May

Funding: Private

Overseas Fund

Subjects: Obstetrics and gynaecology

Purpose: To allow individuals to travel to the United Kingdom for further training

Eligibility: Open to RCOG members or the equivalent, working overseas

Level of Study: Professional development

Type: Travel grant

Value: Up to UK £2,500

Frequency: Annual

Country of Study: Any country

No. of awards offered: 3

Application Procedure: Applicants must see the website

Closing Date: 31 May

No. of awards given last year: 1

No. of applicants last year: 3

For further information contact:

Email: mgoonewardene@rcog.org.uk

Peter Huntingford Memorial Prize

Subjects: Obstetrics and Gynaecology

Purpose: The prize is for presenting the best case history, clinical audit or a report of a research project in any aspect of fertility control in which the applicant is directly involved

Eligibility: Open to doctors working in their foundation year or specialist training years 1 and/or 2 in the United Kingdom and the Republic of Ireland

Type: Grant

Value: First prize is UK £150 and second prize is UK £75

Frequency: Annual

Country of Study: Any country

No. of awards offered: 2

Application Procedure: A submission of no more than 1,500 words outlining the research with reference to publications (if any) is required. Please include a statement of the contribution to the project and indicate the name and address of the supervisor. Only one submission per candidate is permitted

Closing Date: 31 May

Contributor: British Pregnancy Advisory Service (BPAS)

No. of awards given last year: 1

No. of applicants last year: 2

For further information contact:

Email: mgoonewardene@rcog.org.uk

Royal College of Obstetricians and Gynaecologists Edgar Research Fellowship

Subjects: Obstetrics and gynaecology

Purpose: To encourage research, especially into chorion carcinoma or other forms of malignant disease

Eligibility: Open to candidates of high academic standing either in obstetrics and gynaecology, or related fields

Level of Study: Postgraduate

Type: Fellowship

Value: Up to a maximum of UK £35,000

Length of Study: Initially for 1 year's research but a further year's funding may be offered

Frequency: Annual

Country of Study: Any country

Application Procedure: Please contact the Research Administrator at the WellBeing address

Closing Date: First Monday in December

Additional Information: In making the award the Council of the College will bear in mind the original intention of the fellowship, which was to encourage research into chorion carcinoma or other forms of malignant disease. Where applications of equal merit are received, priority will be given to the project most closely related to this condition. Fellows are required to submit a report on the work carried out as soon as the tenure of the fellowship is completed

For further information contact:

WellBeing 27 Sussex Place Regent's Park, United Kingdom

Tel: (44) 20 7772 6338
Fax: (44) 20 7724 7725
Email: mary.stanton@wellbeing.org.uk
Contact: Research Administrator

Royal College of Obstetricians and Gynaecologists Research Training Fellowships

Subjects: Gynaecology and obstetrics
Purpose: To further the training of a young medical graduate in research techniques and methodology in a subject in a subject of direct or indirect relevance to obstetrics and gynaecology
Eligibility: Candidates will have had their basic training in obstetrics and gynaecology, preferably having passed their MRCOG. Candidates will be expected to enrol for a higher degree
Type: Fellowship
Value: Up to a maximum of three years salary
Length of Study: Up to 3 years
Frequency: Annual
Application Procedure: Enquiries about this award should be directed to The Research Administrator, WellBeing
Closing Date: First Friday in October

For further information contact:

WellBeing 27 Sussex Place Regent's Park, United Kingdom

Tel: (44) 20 7772 6338
Fax: (44) 20 7724 7725
Email: mary.stanton@wellbeing.org.uk
Contact: Research Administrator

Royal College of Obstetricians and Gynaecologists WellBeing Grants

Subjects: Obstetrics and gynaecology
Purpose: To fund research into all aspects of Obstetrics and Gynaecology with emphasis on increasing safety of childbirth for mother and baby and prevention of handicap
Eligibility: Open to specialists in any obstetrics and gynaecology inter-related field
Level of Study: Professional development, Research

Type: Grant
Value: Maximum of UK £80,000 over three years, with not more than UK £45,000 in the first year
Frequency: Annual
Application Procedure: Applicants must write for details
Funding: Private

For further information contact:

WellBeing 27 Sussex Place Regent's Park, United Kingdom

Tel: (44) 20 7772 6338
Fax: (44) 20 7724 7725
Email: mary.stanton@wellbeing.org.uk
Contact: Research Administrator

Sims Black Travelling Proffesorship

Purpose: The purpose of the Sims Black Travelling Professorship is to: Contribute to postgraduate education by presenting lectures, participating in seminars, group discussions and clinical demonstrations (if appropriate)
Eligibility: Check for the eligibility through the below link. www.rcog.org.uk/en/careers-training/awards-grants-prizes/sims-black-travelling-professorship/
Level of Study: Postgraduate
Type: Professorship
Frequency: Annual
Country of Study: Any country
Closing Date: 1 March
Funding: Private

For further information contact:

Email: vbytel@rcog.org.uk

Target Ovarian Cancer essay prize

Purpose: The Target Ovarian Cancer essay prize is supported by The Royal College of Obstetricians and Gynaecologists. The prize is open to all undergraduate medical students across the United Kingdom. Its aim is to encourage students to read more widely on ovarian cancer, to think about some of the current issues and learn about recent research
Level of Study: Postgraduate
Type: Prize
Value: £500
Frequency: Annual
Country of Study: Any country
Closing Date: 30 June
Funding: Foundation

For further information contact:

Email: essay@targetovariancancer.org.uk

Tim Chard Chase History Prize

Subjects: Obstetrics and gynaecology
Purpose: To award students showing the greatest understanding of a clinical problem in obstetrics and gynaecology
Level of Study: Professional development
Type: Prize
Value: 1st prize UK £500; 2nd prize UK £200
Frequency: Annual
Country of Study: United Kingdom, Northern Ireland and Republic of Ireland
Application Procedure: Applications should consist of one case history with discussion – max. of 1,500 words with 10 references
Closing Date: 15 February
Funding: Private

For further information contact:

Royal College of Obstetricians and Gynaecologists, 27 Sussex Place, Regent's Park, United Kingdom

Tel: (44) 20 7772 6263
Fax: (44) 20 7772 6359
Email: rdeshmukh@rcog.org.uk

William Blair Bell Memorial Lecture

Purpose: The purpose of the lectureship is to allow a clinician or scientist who is at any stage of their career between award of an MD/PhD and the completion of their second year as a Senior Lecturer or its equivalent (e.g. Clinician Scientist), at the time of application, to give a lecture describing research in any area pertaining to Women's Health at the RCOG Annual Academic Meeting
Eligibility: 1. Clinician or scientist between the award of their MD/PhD thesis and completion of their second year as a Senior Lecturer or its equivalent. 2. Proposed lecture describes their personal research in any area pertaining to Women's Health
Level of Study: Postgraduate
Type: Grant
Frequency: Annual
Country of Study: Any country
Closing Date: 31 May
Funding: Foundation

For further information contact:

Email: awards@rcog.org.uk

Women's Visiting Gynaecological Club Prize

Purpose: Through the generosity of the Women's Visiting Gynaecological Club, the RCOG is able to offer £500 towards an overseas elective in obstetrics and gynaecology to a medical student in the United Kingdom or Republic of Ireland
Eligibility: 1. The winner of this prize will be a medical student who presents an application that best articulates their reasoning and objectives for wanting to complete an overseas elective in a certain region. 2. The report submitted after this elective period is circulated to the members of the Women's Visiting Gynaecological Club
Level of Study: Postgraduate
Type: Prize
Value: £500
Frequency: Annual
Country of Study: Any country
Closing Date: 31 May
Funding: Foundation

For further information contact:

Email: awards@rcog.org.uk

Royal College of Ophthalmologists

18 Stephenson Way, Euston, NW1 2HD, London, United Kingdom

Tel: (44) 20 7935 0702
Fax: (44) 20 7935 9838
Email: training@rcophth.ac.uk
Website: www.rcophth.ac.uk
Contact: Vanda Fadda, Deputy Head of Education and Training

The college is responsible for promoting high standards of professional practice, setting curricula and conducting examinations and providing professional support and advice for ophthalmologists. The college runs an annual scientific congress and seminars for ophthalmologists and publishes a range of clinical guidelines.

Bayer Educational Grant Awards

Subjects: Ophthalmology
Purpose: Supporting ophthalmologists to present work at educational meetings in the United Kingdom and overseas
Eligibility: Application from any grade of ophthalmologist working in the United Kingdom. Members and fellows of the Royal College of Ophthalmologists
Level of Study: Postgraduate
Type: Travel award
Value: Varies
Country of Study: United Kingdom
No. of awards offered: 37
Closing Date: April and October/November
Funding: Commercial
Contributor: Bayer HealthCare, Bayer plc
No. of awards given last year: 11
No. of applicants last year: 37
Additional Information: Please see the website for further details www.rcophth.ac.uk

For further information contact:

Email: helen.sonderegger@rcophth.ac.uk

Essay Prize for Foundation Doctors

Purpose: Entries are now invited to the Essay Prize for Foundation Doctors on the essay "Discuss the impact of multi professional working on eye care"
Eligibility: 1. The competition is open to all those currently in a United Kingdom Foundation Programme. (F1, F2) at the time of submission, as well as those who have completed the United Kingdom Foundation Programme but have not yet achieved an OST1 post. 2. Entries are invited on the essay "Discuss the impact of multi professional working on eye care"
Level of Study: Postgraduate
Type: Grant
Frequency: Annual
Country of Study: Any country
Application Procedure: Essays of up to 1,500 words should be submitted to education@rcophth.ac.uk
Closing Date: 7 October
Funding: Private

For further information contact:

18 Stephenson Way, Kings Cross, NW1 2HD, London, United Kingdom

Email: education@rcophth.ac.uk

Keeler Scholarship

Purpose: To enable the scholar to study, research or acquire special skills, knowledge or experience at a suitable location in the United Kingdom or elsewhere for a minimum period of 6 months
Eligibility: Applicants must be Fellows, Members or Affiliates of the Royal College of Ophthalmologists, those Fellows, Members and Affiliates being in good standing. Potential applicants who have received substantial (usually meaning amounts greater than the value of the scholarship) funding for their project are not eligible for the Keeler Scholarship. The trustees will give special consideration to candidates intending to make a career in ophthalmology in the United Kingdom. Applicants may apply retrospectively but should not be more than 3 months into the fellowship for which they are applying for support by 10 February (application closing date)
Level of Study: Postgraduate
Type: Scholarship
Value: Upto UK £30,000
Length of Study: 2 years
Frequency: Annual
Country of Study: Any country
Application Procedure: 5 copies each of the application form duly completed and the candidate's curriculum vitae should be submitted
Closing Date: 10 February
Funding: Private
Contributor: Keeler Ltd
Additional Information: Funds will be paid to the Scholar two months before the start date of the project or fellowship

For further information contact:

The Royal College of Ophthalmologists Education and Training Department – Awards and Prizes, 18 Stephenson Way NW1 2HD, London, United Kingdom

Email: education@rcophth.ac.uk

Patrick Trevor-Roper Undergraduate Award

Subjects: Ophthalmology
Purpose: Applications are invited for the Patrick Trevor-Roper Award, which is open to all undergraduate medical students from the United Kingdom and Ireland who have an interest in the specialty. The money may be used to fund electives in Ophthalmology, and may be spent on traveling or subsistence

Eligibility: Medical Undergraduates
Level of Study: Postgraduate
Type: Award
Value: £550
Frequency: Annual
Country of Study: Any country
Application Procedure: Please post 4 hard copies of your application form and CV to: The Royal College of Ophthalmologists, Education and Training Department – Awards and Prizes, 18 Stephenson Way, NW1 2HD, London, United Kingdom
Closing Date: 31 May
Funding: Private
Additional Information: education@rcophth.ac.uk

For further information contact:

The Royal College of Ophthalmologists, Education and Training Department – Awards and Prizes, 18 Stephenson Way, Kings Cross, NW1 2HD, London, United Kingdom

Email: education@rcophth.ac.uk

Royal College of Ophthalmologists-Bayer Research

Royal College of Ophthalmologists-Bayer Research Award

Purpose: The Royal College of Ophthalmologists and Bayer have come together in a partnership to launch a grant to promote research in ophthalmology
Eligibility: Any Ophthalmic Specialist Trainee, Member or Fellow of The RCOphth with an interest in research
Level of Study: Postgraduate
Type: Award
Value: £8,000
Frequency: Annual
Country of Study: Any country
Closing Date: 30 March
Funding: Foundation

For further information contact:

Email: education@rcophth.ac.uk

Royal College of Organists (RCO)

PO Box 56357, SE16 7XL, London, United Kingdom

Tel: (44) 5600 767 208
Email: admin@rco.org.uk, andrew.mccrea@rco.org.uk
Website: www.rco.org.uk
Contact: Andrew McCrea, Director of Academic Development

The Royal College of Organists (RCO) is membership based. It promotes the art of organ playing as choral directing, and provides an organization with a library, events and examinations to further that object.

Royal College of Organists Scholarships and Awards

Subjects: Organ playing
Purpose: To assist organists with professional playing
Eligibility: Open to members of the College. Only in exceptional circumstances will awards be made to non members. Membership is open to all upon payment of an annual subscription
Level of Study: Unrestricted
Type: Grant
Length of Study: 1 year, renewable
Frequency: Annual
Study Establishment: Varies
Country of Study: Any country
Application Procedure: Applicants must write for an application form
Closing Date: 17 February, 16 February
Funding: Private
Contributor: College trusts

For further information contact:

Email: andrew.parmley@rco.org.uk

Royal College of Organists Various Open Award Bequests

Subjects: Art and design
Purpose: To assist students who are training to become organists
Eligibility: School and students in undergraduate and postgraduate education who are members of the college
Level of Study: Postgraduate, Professional development
Type: Award
Value: Between UK £100 and UK £400 each
Frequency: Annual
Study Establishment: Various
Application Procedure: Write for an application form

Closing Date: 18 April (check with website for updated details)
Funding: Private

For further information contact:

Email: admin@rco.org.uk
Contact: The Registrar

Royal College of Physicians and Surgeons of Canada (RCPSC)

Office of Fellowship Affairs 774 Echo Drive, Ottawa, ON K1S 5N8, Canada

Tel: (1) 613 730 8177
Fax: (1) 613 730 8830
Email: awards@rcpsc.edu
Website: rcpsc.medical.org/
Contact: Dr James Hickey, FRCPC, Director

The Royal College of Physicians and Surgeons of Canada is a national organisation responsible for setting and maintaining the standards for postgraduate medical education, for the certification of specialist physicians and surgeons in Canada, and for promoting their continued education. The College benefits from the co-operation of its 30,000 members (Fellows), Canada's 16 faculties of medicine and national speciality societies.

Canadian Research Awards for Specialty Residents (Medicine, Surgery)

For further information contact:

Email: llocas@rcpsc.edu

Royal College of Surgeons

Ethicon Travel Award

Purpose: Ethicon Foundation Fund travel awards for overseas visits are awarded to fellows and members of the College who are in good standing
Eligibility: 1. The successful applicants will have submitted a well-articulated and well-planned application outlining the purpose and objectives of their trip. 2. It will provide detailed information about the work they would carry out during their

placement to advance the practice and development of O&G. 3. The award may only be used for the purpose outlined in your original application. A detailed report (maximum 1,000 words), including pictures if necessary, must be submitted to the RCOG Awards Administrator within eight weeks after the elective. It supports the user by contributing to economy travel class upto the value £1,000
Level of Study: Graduate
Type: Award
Value: £500 payment will be awarded
Frequency: Annual
Country of Study: United Kingdom
Application Procedure: The successful applicant will be required to provide a report on their travelling fellowship
Closing Date: 14 March
Funding: Private

For further information contact:

The Royal College of Surgeons of United Kingdom, 35-43 Lincoln's Inn Fields, WC2A 3PE, London, United Kingdom

Email: lslater@rcseng.ac.uk
Contact: Research Department

Royal College of Surgeons of United Kingdom

35-43 Lincoln's Inn Fields, WC2A 3PE, London, United Kingdom

Tel: (44) 20 7869 6611
Fax: (44) 20 7869 6644
Email: research@rcseng.ac.uk
Website: www.rcseng.ac.uk
Contact: Miss Bumbi Singh, Research Department

The Royal College of Surgeons of United Kingdom is an independent professional body committed to promoting and advancing the highest standards of surgical care for patients.

Ethicon Foundation Fund

Subjects: Surgery
Purpose: To promote international goodwill in surgery and to assist Fellows travelling abroad for research or training purposes

Eligibility: Open to Fellows of the Royal College of Surgeons of United Kingdom. Applicants should be sufficiently advanced in their training to benefit from such an experience or be within 1 year of their appointment as a consultant. Fellows, Members or Affiliate Members of the RCOphth who are travelling abroad for research or training
Level of Study: Professional development
Type: Grant
Value: £300 – £1,500
Length of Study: Varies
Frequency: Twice a year
Country of Study: Any country
Application Procedure: Applicants must send eight copies of the application form to the Research Department of the College and should include a letter of support from the head of department or consultant under whom the applicant is currently working and a letter of support from another independent referee. Application forms are available from The Research Department at the main address
Closing Date: 18 December (TBC)

Royal Geographical Society (with the Institute of British Geographers)

1 Kensington Gore, SW7 2AR, London, United Kingdom

Tel:	(44) 20 7591 3000
Fax:	(44) 20 7591 3001
Email:	grants@rgs.org
Website:	www.rgs.org/grants
Contact:	Juliette Scull, Grants Officer

The Royal Geographical Society (with the Institute of British Geographers) is the United Kingdom's learned society for geography and geographers and a professional body. It supports and promotes many aspects of geography including geographical research, education and teaching, field training and small expeditions, the public understanding and popularization of geography and the provision of geographical information.

30th International Geographical Congress Award

Subjects: Geography
Purpose: To assist with the cost of attending an international geographical conference
Eligibility: Applicants must be United Kingdom/European Union nationals and must currently be employed by a United

Kingdom Institute of Higher Education. Preference will be given to applicants within 6 years of completion of Ph-D. Attendance at AAG, CAG, or the RGS-IBG Annual Conference is not eligible for support from this award
Level of Study: Research
Type: Award
Value: Up to £750
Length of Study: Unspecified
Frequency: Annual
Country of Study: Any country
No. of awards offered: 12
Application Procedure: Applicants must download the guidelines and application form from the website www.rgs.org/grants or contact the grants officer
Closing Date: 30 September
No. of awards given last year: 5
No. of applicants last year: 12

For further information contact:

Email:　grants@rgs.org

Environment and Sustainability Research Grants

Purpose: To support researchers investigating some of the bigger issues in environmental sustainability
Eligibility: Please see www.rgs.org/grants
Type: Grant
Value: £10,000
Frequency: Annual
Country of Study: Any country
Application Procedure: Please see www.vgs.org
Closing Date: 22 February
No. of awards given last year: 4

For further information contact:

Email:　NCER_Communications@epa.gov

Geographical Club Award

Subjects: Geography
Purpose: To support a postgraduate student (Masters or PhD) undertaking geographical fieldwork
Eligibility: Applicants must be United Kingdom/European Union nationals and must currently be registered for a Masters or PhD at a United Kingdom Institute of Higher Education. Students who receive full funding from a Research Council or comparable levels of support from other sources with support for fieldwork/data collection are not eligible to apply
Level of Study: Doctorate, Postgraduate
Type: Award

Value: £1,000
Frequency: Annual
Country of Study: United Kingdom or elsewhere
No. of awards offered: 20
Application Procedure: Applicants must download the application guidelines from the website www.rgs.org/grants or contact the grants officer. There is no application form
Closing Date: 23 November
No. of awards given last year: 2
No. of applicants last year: 20

For further information contact:

Email: grants@rgs.org

Ray Y. Gildea Jr Award

Purpose: To support innovation in teaching and learning in higher and secondary education
Eligibility: The project should focus on innovation in teaching and learning of geography in higher education/college and/or secondary school level; including curriculum development, teaching and learning methods, and applications of new technology. 1. Projects that seek to research, develop and/or pilot innovations are eligible. 2. Outcomes should directly benefit students of geography. 3. Applicants must be currently employed in the higher education (college) sector and/or secondary school level, either in the United Kingdom or the United States of America and actively teaching students. 4. Applicants must be United Kingdom or United States of America nationals
Type: Grant
Frequency: Annual
Country of Study: Any country
Application Procedure: Please see www.rgs.org/grants
Closing Date: 30 November
No. of awards given last year: 1

For further information contact:

Email: grants@rgs.org

Walters Kundert Fellowship

Purpose: To support field research within arctic or high mountain environments
Eligibility: Please see www.rgs.org/grants
Type: Grant
Value: £10,000
Frequency: Annual
Country of Study: Any country
Closing Date: 23 November

For further information contact:

Email: grants@rgs.org

Royal Holloway, University of London

Egham, TW20 0EX, Surrey, United Kingdom

Tel:	(44) 1784 443 399
Fax:	(44) 1784 471 381
Email:	liaison-office@rhul.ac.uk
Website:	www.rhul.ac.uk
Contact:	Ms Claire Collingwood, Schools & International Liaison Officer

All departments of Royal Holloway, University of London seek to provide taught programmes that reflect the latest developments and are responsive to the needs of students and society, together with research and scholarship, which contribute to the advancement of knowledge and the enhancement of public policy, wealth creation and the quality of life.

Royal Holloway, University of London MBA Programme

Application Procedure: Applicants must complete an application form
Closing Date: 30 June

For further information contact:

School of Management Royal Holloway University of London, United Kingdom

Tel:	(44) 1784 443 780
Fax:	(44) 1784 439 854
Email:	school-management@rhul.ac.uk
Contact:	MBA Admissions Officer

Royal Horticultural Society (RHS)

80 Vincent Square, SW1P 2PE, London, United Kingdom

Tel:	(44) 845 260 5000
Fax:	(44) 1483 212 382
Email:	bursaries@rhs.org.uk
Website:	www.rhs.org.uk/courses/bursaries
Contact:	Secretary of RHS Bursaries Committee

The Royal Horticultural Society (RHS) is a membership charity holding a Royal Charter for horticulture. The Society promotes the science, art and practice of horticulture in all its branches through a wide range of educational, research and advisory activities. It also maintains some major gardens, shows and the internationally renowned Lindley Library.

Blaxall Valentine Bursary Fund

Purpose: To help finance worldwide plant collecting in natural habitats and study expeditions that will provide real benefits to horticulture

Eligibility: Open to applicants worldwide, but preference is given to United Kingdom citizens. Financial sponsorship will be available to both professional and amateur horticulturists and consideration for an award is not restricted to RHS members. Proposals may be made by individuals or group of individuals

Level of Study: Unrestricted

Type: Bursary

Value: Funds are limited. High-cost projects are expected to receive supplementary finance from other sources, including personal contributions

Frequency: Annual

Country of Study: Any country

Application Procedure: Applicants must complete an application form downloaded from the RHS website www.rhs.org.uk/bursaries

Closing Date: 15 December, 31 March, 30 June, or 30 September (check the website for updated details)

Funding: Private

No. of awards given last year: 17

Additional Information: Please contact at bursaries@rhs.org.uk for applying and deadline

For further information contact:

Email: bursaries@rhs.org.uk

Royal Horticultural Society Financial Awards

Subjects: Horticulture

Purpose: To help finance horticulture-related projects and to further the interests of horticultural education along with horticultural work experience

Eligibility: Submissions are welcomed from applicants worldwide, but preference is given to United Kingdom and Commonwealth citizens. Applicants should preferably be within the age bracket of 20 and 35 years and satisfy the Society that their health enables them to undertake the project

proposed. Financial sponsorship will be available to both professional and amateur horticulturists, and consideration for an award is not restricted to RHS members. Proposals may be made by individuals or groups

Level of Study: Unrestricted

Type: Bursary

Value: Funds are limited. High-cost projects are expected to receive supplementary finance from other sources, including personal contributions

Frequency: Annual

Country of Study: Any country

Application Procedure: Applicants must complete an application form, available on request. Candidates may be called for interview

Closing Date: 24 December, 31 March, 30 June or 30 September

Funding: Private

No. of awards given last year: 6

Additional Information: Recipients must submit a brief factual report within 3 months of completion, along with an outline of achievements or difficulties, including any unusual problems, e.g. medical or political, and an account of expenses

For further information contact:

Email: bursaries@rhs.org.uk

Royal Horticulture Society Bursary Scheme

Subjects: The Royal Horticultural Society (RHS) is a membership charity holding a Royal Charter for Horticulture. The Society promotes the science, art and practice of horticulture in all its branches through a wide range of educational, research and advisory activities. It also maintains some major gardens, shows and the internationally renowned Lindley Library

Purpose: To broaden skills, increase knowledge and enhance career opportunities related to Horticulture

Eligibility: United Kingdom citizens may apply for projects worldwide. Others may only apply for projects based in the United Kingdom

Level of Study: Unrestricted

Type: Bursary

Value: Funds are limited. High-cost projects are expected to receive supplementary finance from other sources

Frequency: Annual

Country of Study: United Kingdom

Application Procedure: Applicants must complete an application form downloadable from the RHS website www.rhs.org.uk/bursarie. For further updates on the closing date, please check with the website

Closing Date: 15 December, 31 March, 30 June, or 30 September
Funding: Private
Additional Information: For further enquires on the bursary scheme, Please email bursanes@rhs.org.uk

For further information contact:

RHS Garden, Wisley, Woking, GU23 6QB, Surrey, United Kingdom

Email: bursanes@rhs.org.uk
Contact: Ms Rowena Wilson, Secretary

Royal Institution of Chartered Surveyors Education Trust

Royal Institution of Chartered Surveyors, RICS, Parliament Square, SW1P 3AD, London, United Kingdom

Tel: (44) 24 7686 8555
Fax: (44) 20 7334 3811
Email: contactrics@rics.org
Website: www.rics-educationtrust.org

The Royal Institution of Chartered Surveyors (RICS) is the professional institution for the surveying profession.

Royal Institution of Chartered Surveyors Education Trust Award

Subjects: The theory and practice of surveying in any of its disciplines including general practice, quantity surveying, building surveying, rural practice, planning and development, land surveying or minerals surveying
Eligibility: Open to chartered surveyors and others carrying out research studies in relevant subjects
Level of Study: Unrestricted
Type: Research grant
Value: Up to UK £7,500
Country of Study: Any country
No. of awards offered: 40
Application Procedure: Applicants must complete an application form, available to download online at www.rics-educationtrust.org
Closing Date: 30 September or 28 February
Funding: Commercial
Contributor: RICS
No. of awards given last year: 20
No. of applicants last year: 40

For further information contact:

Email: contactrics@rics.org

Royal Irish Academy

19 Dawson Street, Dublin 2, Ireland

Tel: (353) 1 676 2570
Fax: (353) 1 676 2346
Email: admin@ria.ie
Website: www.ria.ie
Contact: Ms Laura Mahoney, Assistant Executive Secretary

The Royal Irish Academy is the senior institution in Ireland for both the sciences and humanities. It publishes a number of journals and monographs. It is Ireland's national representative in a large number of international unions, and through its national committees runs conferences, lectures and workshops. It also manages a number of long-term research projects. The Academy participates in the Royal Society European Science Exchange Programmes in pure and applied science, in the British Academy European Exchange Programmes in the humanities, and in the Austrian, Hungarian, or Polish academy exchange schemes in science and the humanities. Small grants for work in all disciplines are available annually from the Academy's own funds.

Royal Irish Academy Senior Visiting Fellowships

Subjects: Scientific research other than in social sciences, dentistry and theoretical and clinical medicine
Purpose: To enable a new scientific research technique or development to be introduced into the Republic of Ireland
Eligibility: Open to senior researchers from member countries of the Organisation for Economic Co-operation and Development (OECD) only
Level of Study: Postdoctorate, Professional development
Type: Fellowship
Value: Varies
Frequency: Annual
Country of Study: Other
Application Procedure: Applicants must complete an application form
Closing Date: 15 October
Funding: Government
No. of awards given last year: 10

Additional Information: Senior Visiting Fellowships are made on behalf of the Irish government

For further information contact:

Email: grants@ria.ie

Royal Literary Fund RLF

3 Johnson's Court, EC4A 3EA, London, United Kingdom

Tel: (44) 20 7353 7160
Email: rlitfund@btconnect.com
Website: www.rlf.org.uk
Contact: Steve Cook, Fellowship Officer

The RLF has been continuously helping authors since it was set up in 1970. It is funded by requests and donations from writers who help other writers. Its committee members came from all walks of literary life and include novelists, biographers, poets, publishers, lawyers and agents.

Royal Literary Fund Grant

Subjects: Literature, authorship
Purpose: To support prolific writers suffering financial hardship
Eligibility: Open to applicants who have published several works for a general readership and are suffering financial hardship (books stemming from a parallel career as an academic or practitioner are not eligible)
Level of Study: Professional development
Type: Grant
Value: Funds are decided by the committee case by case
Length of Study: 1 year
Frequency: Annual
Country of Study: United Kingdom
Application Procedure: Contact the RLF General Secretary
Closing Date: There is no deadline
Contributor: RLF
No. of awards given last year: 12

For further information contact:

The Royal Literary Fund, 3 Johnson's Court, Off Fleet Street, United Kingdom

Tel: (44) 20 7353 7159
Email: egunnrlf@globalnet.co.uk
Contact: Eileen Gunn, General Secretary

Royal Melbourne Institute of Technology University

Info Corner - Office for Prospective Students, GPO Box 2476, Melbourne, VIC 3001, Australia

Tel: (61) 3 9925 2260
Fax: (61) 3 9925 3070
Email: study@rmit.edu.au
Website: www.rmit.edu.au

RMIT University is one of Australia's original and leading educational institutions producing some of Australia's most employable graduates. RMIT has an international reputation for excellence in work-relevant education professional and vocational education, high quality research, and engagement with the needs of industry and community.

Interior Design-Masters of Arts by Research

Subjects: Sculpture, film, theatre, journalism, visual arts, interior design, and architecture
Purpose: To offer a space within which candidates develop and contribute to the knowledge and possibilities of interior design
Eligibility: Open to the candidates of any country who have a First Degree of RMIT with at least a credit average in the final undergraduate year or a deemed equivalent by RMIT to a First Degree of RMIT with at least a credit average in the final undergraduate year or evidence of experience
Level of Study: Postgraduate
Length of Study: 2 years full-time (Masters) and 4 years part-time (PhD)
Application Procedure: Check website for further details
Closing Date: 31 October
Funding: Government
Contributor: Commonwealth Government
Additional Information: Please check the website for more details

For further information contact:

Tel: (233) 3 9925 2819
Email: suzie.attiwill@rmit.edu.au
Contact: Ms Suzie Attiwill, Research Coordinator

Royal Melbourne Institute of Technology PhD Scholarship in the School of Electrical and Computer Engineering

Eligibility: To be eligible for this scholarship you must: be enroled in a higher degree by research (HDR) at the RMIT School of Electrical and Computer Engineering; be a top ranking student using the RMIT University Scholarships Ranking Model; awarded an APA or RMIT PhD Scholarship and/or an RTS place; be aligned to one of the school's areas of strategic focus; not previously have held any Electrical and Computer Engineering (ECE) scholarship over the past 3 years (or more); demonstrate excellent academic results and research capability
Type: Scholarship
Value: $12,000
Frequency: Annual
Country of Study: Australia
Application Procedure: International applicants are expected to apply for the RMIT International PhD Scholarship. If successful, the school may supplement the scholarship stipend
Additional Information: Preference will be given to PhD students but high ranking Masters by Research students may also be eligible for the top-up scholarship

For further information contact:

Tel: (61) 3 9925 3174
Email: elecengresearch@rmit.edu.au
Contact: Laurie Clinton, Research Administrator

Royal Over-Seas League ARTS

Over-Seas House, Park Place, St James's Street, SW1A 1LR, London, United Kingdom

Tel: (44) 20 7408 0214 ext 219
Fax: (44) 20 7499 6738
Email: info@rosl.org.uk
Website: www.rosl.org.uk
Contact: Mandy Murphy, Administrative Assistant

The principal aim of the ROSL (Royal Over-Seas League) ARTS is to provide performance and exhibition opportunities for prize-winning artists and musicians early in their careers, bringing their work to the attention of the professional arts community, the media and the general public.

Royal Over-Seas League Annual Music Competition

Subjects: Musical performance, in four solo classes such as strings (including the harp and guitar), wind and percussion, keyboard, singers and to ensemble classes
Purpose: To support and promote young Commonwealth musicians
Eligibility: Open to the citizens of the United Kingdom and Commonwealth, including former Commonwealth countries, for instrumentalists and singers up to and including the age of 30 as at the date of the final concert
Level of Study: Professional development
Type: Competition
Value: Over UK £60,000 in prizes, including a UK £10,000 gold medal and first prize and UK £10,000 for ensembles
Frequency: Annual
Country of Study: Any country
No. of awards offered: 500
Application Procedure: Applicants must see the website: www.roslarts.org.uk
Closing Date: 15 January
Funding: Commercial, Private, Trusts, Individuals
No. of awards given last year: 19
No. of applicants last year: 500

For further information contact:

Email: head-conmus@uwa.edu.au

Royal Over-Seas League Travel Scholarship

Subjects: ROSL will consider work in any medium
Purpose: To support and promote young United Kingdom and Commonwealth artists
Eligibility: Open to citizens of Commonwealth, including the United Kingdom, and former Commonwealth countries, who are up to 35 years of age, on year of application
Level of Study: Graduate, Postgraduate, Professional development, Unrestricted
Value: UK £3,000
Frequency: Annual
Country of Study: United Kingdom or Commonwealth
No. of awards offered: 450
Application Procedure: Applicants must see the website: www.roslarts.co.uk
Closing Date: 31 March
Funding: Commercial, Private, Trusts
No. of awards given last year: 5
No. of applicants last year: 450

Additional Information: Each artist may be represented by one recent work only, any medium. Works must not exceed 152 cm in their largest dimension, inclusive of frame

For further information contact:

Email: Membership@rosl.org.uk

Royal Society

6-9 Carlton House Terrace, SW1Y 5AG, London, United Kingdom

Tel: (44) 20 7451 2500
Fax: (44) 20 7930 2170
Email: info@royalsoc.ac.uk
Website: www.royalsoc.ac.uk
Contact: Research Appointments Officer

The Royal Society is the independent scientific academy of the United Kingdom dedicated to promoting excellence in science. It plays an influential role in national and international science policy and supports developments in science engineering and technology in a wide range of ways.

Global Challenges Research Fund Challenge-led Grants (GCRF)

Purpose: Generate excellent and novel research on global challenges directly and primarily relevant to developing countries that cuts across multiple thematic areas covered by the Sustainable Development Goals (SDGs).' Strengthen research capacity in developing countries through collaboration, sharing of knowledge and skills, and exchange of staff between research groups in the United Kingdom and their partners in developing countries
Eligibility: 1. Your proposed research must address two or more GCRF thematic areas. The proposal must ultimately benefit the economic development and welfare of developing countries (i.e. be compliant with the ODA guidelines). 2. Your proposal must fall within the remit of the United Kingdom academies and must be interdisciplinary. The consortia must consist of one United Kingdom research group and two research groups from developing countries
Level of Study: Graduate
Type: Grants, work-study (not just grants)
Country of Study: Any country

Application Procedure: Application should be submitted through the Royal Society's grants and awards management system (Flexi-Grant®). and weblink is grants.royalsociety.org/. Shortlisted proposals will be subject to high quality independent peer review, and once complete these proposals will then be discussed at a Panel meeting
Closing Date: 11 September
Funding: Private

For further information contact:

Email: ChallengeGrants@royalsociety.org

Olga Kennard Research Fellowship Scheme

Subjects: Crystallography or structural molecular biology
Eligibility: Open to citizens of the European Union, Norway, Israel and Switzerland. Applicants must have at least 3 years of postdoctoral experience and be aged between 26–40 years
Level of Study: Postdoctorate
Type: Fellowship
Value: Salary with London allowance where appropriate, together with annual research expenses, travel expenses and a contribution to baggage costs for overseas applicants
Length of Study: 5 years
Study Establishment: Appropriate university departments
Country of Study: United Kingdom
Application Procedure: Applications can only be submitted online on the Royal Society's E-gap system. For further information on this scheme or the E-gap process, submit an enquiry to ukgrants@royalsoc.ac.uk
Closing Date: There is no fixed deadline
Additional Information: Further information is available on the website

For further information contact:

Email: ukresearch.appointments@royalsoc.ac.uk

Royal Society South East Asia Rainforest Research Project - Travel Grants

Subjects: Research into rainforests
Eligibility: Open to scientists and nationals of European Union countries and South East Asia countries who are PhD or MSc students
Level of Study: Postgraduate
Type: Travel grant
Value: Economy air fare plus two weeks subsistence for European scientists travelling to South East Asia or three

months subsistence for South East Asian scientists travelling to Europe

Length of Study: Varies

Country of Study: Other

Application Procedure: Applicants must apply for information, available on request from Programme Research Coordinator, Dr Stephen Sutton (email sutton@hh.edi.co.uk) or Dr A J Davis

Additional Information: Further information available on request

For further information contact:

Department of Zoology, University of Cambridge, United Kingdom & Danum Valley Field Centre, PO Box 60282, United Kingdom

Fax: (44) 8 988 4046
Email: ajdavis@pc.jaring.my
Contact: Dr A J Davis, Royal Society Senior Scientist at Danum Valley

Sir Henry Dale Fellowships

Purpose: Leading the research programme

Eligibility: You can apply for a Small Grant if you're a humanities or social science researcher with a compelling research vision and you want to do one or more of the following: 1. build your professional network. 2. develop a new research agenda. 3. increase the impact of your work

Level of Study: Postdoctorate, Research

Type: Research grant

Value: Value includes a basic salary, fellowship supplements. research and personal removal expenses. Check with website

Frequency: Every 5 years

Country of Study: Any country

Closing Date: 2 April

Funding: Private

For further information contact:

Tel: (44) 207 451 2500
Email: grants@royalsociety.org

Royal Society of Chemistry

Burlington House Piccadilly, W1J 0BA, London, United Kingdom

Tel: (44) 20 7437 8656
Fax: (44) 20 7437 8883
Email: langers@rsc.org

Website: www.rsc.org
Contact: Mr S S Langer

The Royal Society of Chemistry is the learned society for chemistry and the professional body for chemists in the United Kingdom with 46,000 members worldwide. The Society is a major publisher of chemical information, supports the teaching of chemistry at all levels, organizes hundreds of chemical meetings a year and is a leader in communicating science to the public. It is now the United Kingdom National Adhering Organization (NAO) to the International Union of Pure and Applied Chemistry (IUPAC).

Royal Society of Chemistry Journals Grants for International Authors

Subjects: Chemistry

Purpose: To allow international authors to visit other countries in order to collaborate in research, exchange research ideas and results, and to give or receive special expertise and training

Eligibility: Open to anyone with a recent publication in any of the Society's journals. Those from the United Kingdom or Republic of Ireland are excluded

Level of Study: Professional development

Type: Grant

Value: Up to £2,500 cover travel and subsistence (but not research related costs) and are available

Length of Study: Normally 1–3 months

Country of Study: Any country

No. of awards offered: 107

Application Procedure: Candidates must apply for application forms, together with full details, from the International Affairs Officer

Closing Date: 1 January, 1 April, 1 July or 1 October

No. of awards given last year: 83

No. of applicants last year: 107

Additional Information: Please see the website for further details www.rsc.org/ScienceAndTechnology/Funding/Travel Grants/InternationalAuthors.asp

For further information contact:

Email: langers@rsc.org

Royal Society of Edinburgh

22-26 George Street, EH2 2PQ, Edinburgh, United Kingdom

Tel: (44) 131 240 5000
Fax: (44) 131 240 5024

Email: afraser@royalsoced.org.uk
Website: www.royalsoced.org.uk
Contact: Anne Fraser, Research Awards Manager

The Royal Society of Edinburgh is Scotland's national academy of science and letters. It offers research and enterprise awards to candidates based in Scotland.

Royal Society of Edinburgh Personal Research Fellowships

Subjects: All science and social science subjects
Purpose: To provide outstanding researchers, who have the potential to become leaders in their chosen field, with the opportunity to build an independent research career
Eligibility: Open to persons of all nationalities who have 2 to 6 years postdoctoral experience. They must also show that they have the capacity for innovative research and the potential to become leaders in their field
Level of Study: Doctorate
Value: Salary and research support costs for 5 years
Length of Study: 5 years
Frequency: Annual
Study Establishment: Any Higher Education Institution in Scotland
Country of Study: Scotland
No. of awards offered: 53
Application Procedure: Applicants must complete an application form, available on the RSE website. Applicants should negotiate directly with their host institution
Closing Date: 16 February
Contributor: Scottish Government, BP and Caledonian Research Fund
No. of awards given last year: 3
No. of applicants last year: 53
Additional Information: Successful applicants will be allocated a funding provider (BP, CRF or Scottish Government) according to their subject area. BP funding is available every 2nd year and is for candidates working in areas of interest to BP. CRF funding is for candidates in the biomedical sciences. Fellows are expected to devote their full time to research and are not allowed to hold any other paid appointments without the express permission of Council. Website: www.royalsoced.org.uk/649_RSEPersonalResearchFellowships.html

For further information contact:

Email: schooloffice-ls@dundee.ac.uk

Royal Society of Medicine (RSM)

1 Wimpole Street, W1G 0AE, London, United Kingdom

Tel: (44) 20 7290 3846
Fax: (44) 20 7290 2989
Email: awards@rsm.dc.uk
Website: www.rsm.ac.uk/awards
Contact: Awards Manager, Alademic Department

The Royal Society of Medicine (RSM) provides academic services and club facilities for its members as well as publishing a monthly journal and an annual bulletin, and providing over 400 educational conferences and meetings per year. The RSM offers around 60 awards and prizes each year. The majority for medical doctors in training covering the majority of specialities in medicine and surgery.

Adrian Tanner Prize

Subjects: Clinical case reports should be submitted to reflect the multidisciplinary nature of the care for surgical patients
Purpose: To encourage surgical trainees submit the best clinical case reports
Eligibility: Open to all surgeons in training
Value: UK £250
Frequency: Annual
Study Establishment: Royal Society of Medicine–Surgery section
Country of Study: United Kingdom
No. of awards offered: 50
Application Procedure: Applicants should download an application form from www.rsm.ac.uk/awards
Closing Date: 28 March
No. of awards given last year: 1
No. of applicants last year: 50

For further information contact:

Email: surgery@rsm.ac.uk

Alan Emery Prize

Subjects: Genetics
Purpose: To reward the best published research article in Medical Genetics in the past 2 years
Eligibility: Open to candidates in an accredited training or research post in the United Kingdom

Type: Prize
Value: £500 or £300 or 1 year membership of Royal Society of Medicine
Frequency: Annual
No. of awards offered: 7
Application Procedure: Candidates must submit full copy of the article, curriculum vitae or covering letter explaining the significance of the publication
Closing Date: 5 March(check with website)
No. of awards given last year: 1
No. of applicants last year: 7

For further information contact:

Email: genetics@rsm.ac.uk

Cardiology Section Presidents Prize

Subjects: Cardiology
Purpose: To reward original work for specialist registrar in cardiology
Eligibility: Open to cardiology trainees who have received all or part of their training at recognized centres of excellence in the United Kingdom. The subject of the presentation should represent original work
Level of Study: Research
Type: Prize
Value: Commemoration medal and £1,000 (First prize); £500 (Second prize)
Frequency: Annual
Study Establishment: Recognized centres of excellence in United Kingdom
Country of Study: United Kingdom
Application Procedure: Candidates should submit an abstract of no more than 200 words
Closing Date: 8 May
Contributor: Cardiology Section Funds
No. of awards given last year: 2

For further information contact:

Cardiology Section, Royal Society of Medicine, 1 Wimpole Street, United Kingdom

Email: cardiology@rsm.ac.uk

Catastrophes & Conflict Forum Medical Student Essay Prize

Subjects: Medicine and surgery

Eligibility: Open to candidates who are enroled full-time at a United Kingdom medical school
Level of Study: Postgraduate
Type: Prize
Value: £250 plus encouragement and advice on submitting the essay for publication in the JRSM
Frequency: Annual
Study Establishment: Royal Society of Medicine
Country of Study: United Kingdom
No. of awards offered: 9
Application Procedure: Candidates should submit an essay no longer than 1,500 words, emailed in Word format
Closing Date: 1 March
No. of awards given last year: 2
No. of applicants last year: 9

For further information contact:

Email: catastrophes@rsm.ac.uk

Clinical Forensic and Legal Medicine Section Poster Competition

Subjects: Clinical studies
Purpose: To present a case or a poster in clinical studies
Eligibility: Undergraduate students who have been working as part of courses leading to primary qualifications such as Legal Medicine Special Study Modules and electives for MBBS
Value: £250
Frequency: Annual
Application Procedure: Please visit the website www.rsm.ac.uk/academ/awards/index for application form details
Closing Date: 15 December

For further information contact:

Email: forensic@rsm.ac.uk

Clinical Immunology & Allergy President's Prize

Subjects: Immunology or allergy
Eligibility: Open to training grade doctors and young scientists (not above Specialist Registrar, Grade B Clinical Scientist or equivalent grade) with an immunological or allergy component of their clinical research
Level of Study: Research
Type: Prize
Value: £300 (First prize); two prizes of £100 (Second prize)
Frequency: Annual

Country of Study: United Kingdom
No. of awards offered: 10
Application Procedure: Check website for further details
Closing Date: Check the website
No. of awards given last year: 3
No. of applicants last year: 10

For further information contact:

Email: immunology@rsm.ac.uk

Clinical Neurosciences Gordon Holmes Prize

Subjects: Clinical neurosciences
Purpose: To award a research prize in clinical neurosciences
Eligibility: Trainees in neurosciences, including neurology, neurosurgery, neurophysiology, neuropathology or neuroradiology
Type: Prize
Value: £300
Frequency: Every 2 years
Application Procedure: Please check the website www.rsm.ac.uk/prizes-awards/trainees.aspx
Closing Date: Check the website

For further information contact:

Email: cns@rsm.ac.uk

Clinical Neurosciences President's Prize

Subjects: Neurology
Purpose: To encourage clinical case presentation
Eligibility: Open to trainees in neurosciences, including neurology, neurosurgery, neurophysiology, neuropathology, or neuroradiology
Type: Prize
Length of Study: £300
Frequency: Every 2 years
Application Procedure: Applicants must submit one A4 page (up to 500 words) summary of research carried out. Those considered to be the best will be asked to give a 15 minute presentation
Closing Date: Check with website

For further information contact:

Email: cns@rsm.ac.uk

Coloproctology John of Arderne Medal

Subjects: Coloproctology
Purpose: To award the presenter of the best paper presented at the short papers meeting of the section of coloproctology. Applicants have to submit an abstract for presentation at the meeting
Eligibility: Open to applicants of any nationality
Level of Study: Professional development
Type: Award
Value: Approx. UK £600
Frequency: Annual
Study Establishment: Varies
Country of Study: Any country
No. of awards offered: 14–20
Application Procedure: Further details are available from the RSM administrator
Closing Date: September and November (check with website)
Funding: Private
No. of awards given last year: 1
No. of applicants last year: 14–20

For further information contact:

Email: coloproctology@rsm.ac.uk

Dermatology Clinicopathological Meetings

Subjects: Clinicopathology
Eligibility: Trainee Dermatologists
Type: Prize
Value: £150
Frequency: Annual
Country of Study: United Kingdom
No. of awards offered: 32
Closing Date: Check the website
Contributor: Royal Society of Medicine
No. of awards given last year: 1
No. of applicants last year: 32
Additional Information: For more details, please refer the website: www.dermpath.com/news-events/calendar/practical-symposium-sharpen-your-dermatology-clinicopathologic-and-business

For further information contact:

Email: dermatology@rsm.ac.uk

Epidemiology & Public Health Young Epidemiologists Prize

Subjects: Epidemiology and public health
Purpose: To reward outstanding papers
Eligibility: Any medical/non-medical epidemiologist or public health practitioner under the age of 40 years
Level of Study: Unrestricted
Type: Award
Value: £250
Frequency: Annual
Country of Study: United Kingdom
No. of awards offered: 9
Application Procedure: Download the application form from website
Closing Date: 27 November (check with website)
No. of awards given last year: 1
No. of applicants last year: 9

For further information contact:

Email: epidemiology@rsm.ac.uk

General Practice with Primary Healthcare John Fry Prize

Subjects: Primary healthcare
Purpose: To award best examples of practice-based research involving members of the primary health and social community, demonstrating and promoting effective team work
Eligibility: Open to candidates currently working in primary healthcare in the United Kingdom excluding members of the RSM section of GP Council
Level of Study: Unrestricted
Type: Prize
Value: £300
Frequency: Annual
Country of Study: United Kingdom
No. of awards offered: 4
Application Procedure: Application form must be completed in all respects
Closing Date: 27 March
Funding: Private
Contributor: John Fry
No. of awards given last year: 1
No. of applicants last year: 4

For further information contact:

RSM, 1 Wimpole Street, United Kingdom

Email: gp@rsm.ac.uk
Contact: Gemma Lamb

Laryngology & Rhinology Travel and Equipment Grants

Subjects: Laryngology and rhinology
Purpose: To assist with the cost of travel to overseas centres
Eligibility: Open to senior registrars or consultants of not more than 2 years standing, who must be members of the section of laryngology and rhinology of the RSM
Level of Study: Postdoctorate
Type: Scholarship
Value: UK £1,000
Frequency: Annual
Country of Study: Any country
No. of awards offered: 25
Application Procedure: Applicants must submit a paper to the RSM section of laryngology and rhinology. Further details are available from the RSM administrator
Closing Date: 15 April
Funding: Commercial
Contributor: Karl Storz Endoscopy Limited
No. of awards given last year: 1
No. of applicants last year: 25
Additional Information: The recipient will be required to submit a brief report on the visit within 3 months of his or her return

For further information contact:

Email: laryngology@rsm.ac.uk

Military Medicine Colt Foundation Research Prize

Purpose: To recognize the best abstract by a serving military medical officer
Eligibility: Open to serving military officers in a training grade in general practice, a hospital or other speciality and are fellows of the RSM
Level of Study: Postgraduate
Type: Prize
Value: £200 (1st prize) and £100 each (2nd prize)
Frequency: Annual
Study Establishment: Royal Society of Medicine
Country of Study: United Kingdom
No. of awards offered: 15

Application Procedure: Candidates should email the abstracts. The abstracts will be shortlisted by the panel and judged
Closing Date: 6 November
Funding: Trusts
Contributor: Colt Foundation
No. of awards given last year: 1
No. of applicants last year: 15

For further information contact:

Email: united.services@rsm.ac.uk

Nephrology Section Rosemarie Baillod Clinical Award

Eligibility: All doctors in training in nephrology and renal medicine at any grade
Type: Research award
Value: £200
Frequency: Annual
Country of Study: United Kingdom
Application Procedure: Please visit website for further details
Closing Date: Check the website

For further information contact:

Email: nephrology@rsm.ac.uk

Occupational Medicine Section Malcolm Harrington Prize

Subjects: Occupational medicine
Purpose: To award the work that is most likely to advance the study of occupational medicine in its broadest sense
Eligibility: Open to occupational physician in training or within an year of achieving specialist accreditation
Type: Prize
Value: £250
Frequency: Annual
No. of awards offered: 9
Application Procedure: Candidates should submit an abstract of their own work (no longer than 200 words)
Closing Date: 9 March (check the website)
Funding: Private
Contributor: Professor Harrington
No. of awards given last year: 1
No. of applicants last year: 9

For further information contact:

Email: occupational@rsm.ac.uk

Oncology Section Sylvia Lawler Prize

Subjects: Oncology
Purpose: To encourage scientists and clinicians in training to present the best scientific paper and best clinical paper on oncology
Eligibility: All scientists and clinicians in training
Level of Study: Postgraduate
Type: Grant
Value: Two prizes of £500 to oral presenters and one prize of £50 voucher to poster presenter
Frequency: Annual
Study Establishment: Royal Society of Medicine
Country of Study: United Kingdom
No. of awards offered: 50
Application Procedure: Applicants should download an application form from the website www.rsm.ac.uk/prizes-awards/trainees.aspx, and submit the same via email to surgery@rsm.ac.uk
Closing Date: 19 April
No. of awards given last year: 1
No. of applicants last year: 50

For further information contact:

Email: oncology@rsm.ac.uk

Ophthalmology Section Travelling Fellowships

Subjects: Ophthalmology
Purpose: To enable British ophthalmologists to travel abroad with the intention of furthering the study or advancement of ophthalmology, or to enable foreign ophthalmologists to visit the United Kingdom for the same purpose
Eligibility: Open to ophthalmologists in the British Isles of any nationality who have not attained an official consultant appointment, nor undertaken professional clinical work or equivalent responsibility for any substantial period before or during the execution of original work
Level of Study: Professional development
Type: Fellowship
Value: UK £500–1,000
Frequency: Every 2 years
Study Establishment: Varies
Country of Study: Any country
No. of awards offered: 6
Application Procedure: Applicants must apply to the academic administrator at RSM
Closing Date: 1 May
No. of awards given last year: 4
No. of applicants last year: 6

For further information contact:

Email: ophthalmology@rsm.ac.uk

Orthopaedics Section President's Prize Papers

Purpose: To encourage research in the area of Orthopaedics
Eligibility: Open to all orthopaedic trainees
Level of Study: Postgraduate
Type: Prize
Value: Clinical paper prize – 1st prize of £300 and 2nd prize of £200
Frequency: Annual
Study Establishment: Royal Society of Medicine
Country of Study: United Kingdom
No. of awards offered: 10
Application Procedure: Candidates should submit abstracts no longer than 200 words. The abstracts will be judged by a panel of experts, shortlisted and asked to be presented at a meeting
Closing Date: 5 April
No. of awards given last year: 1
No. of applicants last year: 10

For further information contact:

Email: orthopaedics@rsm.ac.uk

Otology Section Norman Gamble Grant

Subjects: Otology
Purpose: To support specific research projects
Eligibility: British citizens, both lay and medical
Level of Study: Unrestricted
Type: Prize
Value: UK £100
Frequency: Annual
Country of Study: Any country
No. of awards offered: 4
Application Procedure: Further details are available from the RSM administrator
Closing Date: 9 December (check the website)
Funding: Private
No. of awards given last year: 1
No. of applicants last year: 4

For further information contact:

Email: otology@rsm.ac.uk

Paediatrics & Child Health Section Trainees Tim David Prize

Subjects: Paediatrics

Purpose: To encourage research in the area of Paediatrics & Child Health
Eligibility: Open to paediatric trainees
Level of Study: Postgraduate, Foundation programme
Type: Prize
Value: First prize £150, 1 year's subscription to the RSM (worth up to £200) and membership of the Council of the Section of Paediatrics and Child Health for 1 year. There will also be a second prize of £100
Frequency: Annual
No. of awards offered: 12
Application Procedure: Candidates should submit abstracts
Closing Date: 1 April
Contributor: Paediatrics & Child Health Section, RSM
No. of awards given last year: 2
No. of applicants last year: 12

For further information contact:

Email: paediatrics@rsm.ac.uk

Palliative Care Section MSc/MA research prize

Eligibility: All students either currently studying, or within 18 months of completion, of MSc or MA in Palliative Medicine or an allied discipline, are eligible to apply
Level of Study: Postgraduate, Foundation programme
Type: Prize
Value: 1st prize of £250, 2nd prize of £100, and 3rd prize of £50
Frequency: Annual
Closing Date: 17 September
Contributor: Palliative Care Section

For further information contact:

Email: palliative@rsm.ac.uk

Psychiatry Section Mental Health Foundation Research Prize

Subjects: Psychiatry
Purpose: To award an outstanding published paper
Eligibility: Open to candidates practising medicine in the United Kingdom or the Republic of Ireland who are in training at any grade from senior house officer to senior registrar or equivalent. Applicants need not be members of RSM
Type: Prize
Value: UK £750 (1st prize); UK £100 (2nd prize)
Frequency: Annual
Country of Study: United Kingdom
No. of awards offered: 1

Application Procedure: Full copy of the published article, curriculum vitae and covering letter explaining in their own words the significance of the publication to be submitted to the section of psychiatry
Closing Date: Early January (check the website)
Funding: Private
No. of applicants last year: 1

For further information contact:

Email: psychiatry@rsm.ac.uk

Surgery Section Norman Tanner Prize and Glaxo Travelling Fellowship

Subjects: Oncology
Purpose: To encourage clinical registrars submit the best clinical paper
Eligibility: Open to all trainee oncologists
Value: £250 plus the Norman Tanner Medal. Runner up – £250 Glaxo Travelling Fellowship
Frequency: Annual
Study Establishment: Royal Society of Medicine
Country of Study: United Kingdom
No. of awards offered: 30
Application Procedure: Applicants are requested to contact the Section Coordinator at oncology@rsm.ac.uk
Closing Date: 1 September
No. of awards given last year: 12
No. of applicants last year: 30

For further information contact:

Email: surgery@rsm.ac.uk

Trainees' Committee John Glyn Trainees' Prize

Purpose: The prize was established to promote best practise through high quality audit
Eligibility: Trainees from any hospital or primary care specialty
Level of Study: Graduate, Postgraduate, Research, Foundation programme
Type: Prize
Value: £300
Frequency: Annual
No. of awards offered: 40
Closing Date: 12 April(check with website)
Contributor: Royal Society of Medicine
No. of awards given last year: 1
No. of applicants last year: 40

For further information contact:

Email: trainees@rsm.ac.uk

Urology Professor Geoffrey D Chisholm CBE Communication Prize

Subjects: Urology
Purpose: To reward the best abstract at the Short Papers Prize Meeting
Eligibility: Open to members of the Urology section
Type: Travel award
Value: Fully funded RSM travelling fellowship to the Urology Section's overseas winter scientific meeting in the next academic session
No. of awards offered: 30
Closing Date: 8 March
No. of awards given last year: 3
No. of applicants last year: 30

For further information contact:

Email: urology@rsm.ac.uk

Urology Section Professor John Blandy Essay Prize for Medical Students

Subjects: Urology
Purpose: To enable the holder to enhance his or her knowledge and experience by visiting an overseas unit
Eligibility: Medical students
Type: Fellowship
Value: A bursary of £1,000 and an RSM award certificate
Frequency: Annual
Closing Date: 8 March
Additional Information: Candidates must be available on the May 16th for presentation of their short paper to be eligible for this prize

For further information contact:

Email: urology@rsm.ac.uk

Urology Section Winter short papers prize (Clinical Uro-Radiological meeting)

Subjects: Urology
Purpose: To reward the best clinicopathological short paper
Eligibility: Urological and radiological trainees

Type: Prize
Value: Fully funded RSM travelling fellowship to the Urology Section's overseas winter scientific meeting in the next academic session. Runner up prizes of a bursary towards the RSM overseas winter scientific meeting in the next academic session
Frequency: Annual
Closing Date: Check the website

For further information contact:

Email: urology@rsm.ac.uk

Venous Forum Spring Meeting Prizes

Purpose: To recognize the best original paper by a non-consultant
Eligibility: Open to non-consultants
Level of Study: Postgraduate
Type: Prize
Value: £250 (1st prize); £200 (2nd prize); £150 (3rd prize); and £200 (Poster prize)
Frequency: Annual
Study Establishment: Royal Society of Medicine
Country of Study: United Kingdom
No. of awards offered: 20
Application Procedure: Candidates should email abstracts. Shortlisted candidates will be invited to present their papers
Closing Date: 13 March
No. of awards given last year: 1
No. of applicants last year: 20

For further information contact:

Email: venous@rsm.ac.uk

Royal Scottish Academy (RSA)

The Mound, EH2 2EL, Edinburgh, United Kingdom

Tel: (44) 131 225 6671
Fax: (44) 131 220 6016
Email: info@royalscottishacademy.org
Website: www.royalscottishacademy.org
Contact: Secretary

Founded in 1826, the RSA, Scotland's foremost body of artists, has promoted the works of leading contemporary painters, sculptors, printmakers and architects. It also gives practical and financial help to young artists through scholarships as well as the annual Student's Exhibition.

The Barns-Graham Travel Award

Subjects: Painting in any medium
Purpose: To provide a travel and research opportunity for graduating and postgraduate students
Eligibility: Entrants must be painters, printmakers or sculptors, entrants must either be graduating in the current academic year or currently studying at postgraduate level at one of the following art schools in Scotland – Aberdeen, Dundee, Edinburgh, Glasgow, and Moray
Level of Study: Postgraduate
Type: Scholarship
Value: £2,000
Length of Study: 3–6 months
Frequency: Annual
Study Establishment: Any of the main art colleges
Country of Study: Scotland
Application Procedure: Applications forms and regulations will be available to download at the end of February
Closing Date: 12 June
Funding: Private
Contributor: The Alastair Salvesen Trust
No. of awards given last year: 1
Additional Information: Please see the website for further details

For further information contact:

Email: opportunities@royalscottishacademy.org

The Royal Scottish Academy John Kinross Scholarships to Florence

Subjects: Art and Architecture
Purpose: for final year and postgraduate artists and architects to spend a period of 6 to 12 weeks in Florence to research and develop their practice
Eligibility: Art: Applications are invited from students in their Honours or post-graduate years of study at one of the following; art schools in Scotland (Aberdeen, Dundee, Edinburgh, Glasgow, and UHI). Architecture: Applicants must be RIBA Part 2 students in their final year, or currently attending a Masters programme,; at one of the six Scottish Schools of Architecture
Level of Study: Postgraduate, Undergraduate
Type: Scholarship
Value: UK £2,000
Length of Study: 6–12 weeks

Frequency: Annual
Country of Study: Italy
Application Procedure: Digital submissions accepted only, please see the opportunities section of our website for more details
Closing Date: 24 March
Funding: Private
Contributor: The Kinross Scholarship Fund, which is administered by the RSA
No. of awards given last year: 10

For further information contact:

www.royalscottishacademy.org/artist-opportunities/

Email: opportunities@royalscottishacademy.org

The Royal Scottish Academy William Littlejohn Award for Excellence and Innovation in Water-Based Media

Subjects: Painting, sculpture, architecture and printmaking
Purpose: To provide young professional artists who are Scottish or have studied in Scotland, with a period for personal development and the exploration of new directions
Eligibility: Entrants must be working in water-based media (any pigment mixed with water), entrants must be born or have been resident in Scotland for at least 3 years, in the case of students applying, entrants must either be graduating in current year or studying at postgraduate level at one of the following art schools in Scotland (Aberdeen, Dundee, Edinburgh, Glasgow, and Moray)
Level of Study: Postgraduate
Type: Residency
Value: UK £2,000
Frequency: Annual
Study Establishment: Hospitalfield House, Arbroath
Country of Study: Scotland
Application Procedure: Applicants must contact the RSA
Closing Date: 12 June
Funding: Private
Contributor: The Bequest Fund administered by the RSA

For further information contact:

Email: opportunities@royalscottishacademy.org

Royal Town Planning Institute (RTPI)

41 Botolph Lane, EC3R 8DL, London, United Kingdom

Tel:	(44) 20 7929 9494
Fax:	(44) 20 7929 9490
Email:	judy.woollett@rtpi.org.uk
Website:	www.rtpi.org.uk/

The Royal Town Planning Institute (RTPI) was founded in 1914 and is a registered charity. Its aim is to advance the science and art of town planning in all its aspects, including local, regional and national planning for the benefit of the public. The Institute is primarily concerned with maintaining high standards of competence and conduct within the profession, promoting the role of planning within the country's social, economic and political structures, and presenting the profession's views on current planning issues.

George Pepler International Award

Subjects: Town and country planning or some particular aspect of planning theory and practice
Purpose: To enable young people of any nationality to visit another country for a short period to study. The George Pepler International Award is a bursary granted biennially to a person in their first ten years of post-qualification experience wishing to undertake a short period of study (3-4 weeks) on a particular aspect of spatial planning
Eligibility: Open to persons under 30 years of age of any nationality. Candidature must have the age limit of upto 30 years
Level of Study: Professional development, Research
Type: Fees to performers
Value: Up to UK £1,500
Length of Study: Short-term travel outside the United Kingdom for United Kingdom residents or for visits to the United Kingdom for applicants from abroad
Frequency: Every 2 years
Country of Study: Any country
No. of awards offered: 20
Application Procedure: Applicants must submit a statement showing the nature of the study visit proposed, together with an itinerary. Application forms are available on request from the RTPI
Closing Date: 31 March

Funding: Private
Contributor: Trust fund
No. of awards given last year: 1
No. of applicants last year: 20
Additional Information: At the conclusion of the visit the recipient must submit a report. Please see the website for further details www.rtpi.org.uk/events/awards/george-pepler-international-award/

For further information contact:

Email: judy.woollett@rtpi.org.uk

Rural Health Information Hub

National Board for Certified Counselors Minority Fellowship Program for Mental Health Counselors

Purpose: The purpose of the program is to ensure that the behavioral health needs of all Americans are met, regardless of language or culture, thereby reducing health disparities
Eligibility: Eligible applicants are United States citizens or permanent residents that are currently enrolled and in good standing in an accredited graduate level counseling program. Please check the website link for further details, www.ruralhealthinfo.org/funding/4510
Level of Study: Graduate
Type: Programme grant
Value: US$10,000, plus travel expenses to participate in other program-related training
Frequency: Annual
Country of Study: Any country
Closing Date: 15 December
Funding: Private
Additional Information: For doctoral degree-level students: US$20,000, plus travel expenses to participate in other program-related training. www.nbccf.org/programs/scholarships/fellows

For further information contact:

School of Medicine and Health Sciences, Suite E231, 1301 N. Columbia Road, Stop 9037, Grand Forks, ND 58202-9037, United States of America

Email: info@ruralhealthinfo.org

Rural Maternity Care Research

Suite 530-1501 West Broadway, Vancouver, BC V6J 4Z6, Canada

Tel: (1) 604 742 1796
Fax: (1) 604 742 1798
Email: leslie@ruralmatresearch.net
Website: www.ruralmatresearch.net

Rural Maternity Care Research is a team of academic and community based researchers interested in rural maternity care. They believe their diversity of expertise, backgrounds and interests enhance their ability to comprehensively investigate the complexity of challenges and opportunities for rural maternity care in British Columbia.

Rural Maternity Care Doctoral Student Fellowship

Subjects: Maternity care
Purpose: To enable a motivated Doctoral student researcher to join the interdisciplinary team investigating rural maternity care in British Columbia
Eligibility: Open to citizens or permanent residents of Canada who are registered in a Doctoral programme in Canada
Level of Study: Doctorate
Type: Fellowship
Value: Up to C$45,000 (benefits included)
Length of Study: 18 months
Frequency: Annual
Country of Study: Canada
Application Procedure: Applicants must include the following documents in the application: cover letter, transcripts, curriculum vitae, contact information of 3 research referees and sample of the candidates writing preferably from an article published in a referred journal
Closing Date: 18 August
Additional Information: The Fellow will be provided with office space in Vancouver, as well as access to and use of internet, printers and telephone and fax lines. Candidates from all academic disciplines are invited to apply. Candidates who may be completing coursework for their PhD programme, will be expected to contribute sufficient time to the RM-NET to develop a research focus area

For further information contact:

Email: clin2@cw.bc.ca
Contact: Cynthia Lin Hsieh

Ryerson University

Autism Scholars Award

Purpose: With the support of the Ministry of Training, Colleges and Universities, a scholar awards program in autism has been established to ensure that Ontario attracts and retains pre-eminent scholars. The community of autism scholars fostered by this awards program will excel, according to internationally accepted standards of scientific excellence, in the creation of new knowledge concerning child autism, and its translation into improved health for children, more effective services and products for children with autism, and increase the province's capacity in diagnosis and assessment of autism and a strengthened treatment system

Eligibility: 1. a Canadian citizen or a permanent resident of Canada at the time of the application deadline (31 January). 2. registered as a full-time student in a master's or doctoral program at an Ontario university at the beginning of the award period (fall), and remain registered as a full-time student throughout the term of the award. 3. A master's student remains eligible until the end of the sixth term of full-time study. 4. A doctoral student remains eligible until the end of the 15th term of full-time study. 5. During the year an Autism Scholars Award is held, the recipient is precluded from holding any other award that offers financial support of more than $20,000 for that same year (subject to the university's own policies)

Level of Study: Graduate
Type: Award
Value: $20,000
Frequency: Annual
Country of Study: Any country
Closing Date: 31 January
Funding: International office

For further information contact:

Email: SeniorDirectorQA@cou.on.ca

C. Ravi Ravindran Outstanding Doctoral Thesis Award

Purpose: The C. Ravi Ravindran Outstanding Doctoral Thesis Award was established in 2008 (the 60th year of

the creation of Ryerson as an educational institution) by his family in recognition of his long and distinguished industrial and academic career. He was the first winner of the Ryerson-Sahota Faculty Research Award, Trustee of ASM International, and the first Ryerson faculty member elected as Fellow, and later President of the Canadian Academy of Engineering

Eligibility: 1. Registration as a graduate studies student in a program of study leading to a PhD. 2. One student may be nominated by a program director from each PhD program. 3. A nominated student must have applied to graduate at the upcoming fall graduation convocation ceremonies or have already graduated at the spring graduation convocation ceremonies

Level of Study: Postgraduate
Type: Award
Value: $1,000
Length of Study: 1 year
Frequency: Annual
Country of Study: Any country
Closing Date: 22 August
Funding: Foundation

For further information contact:

Email: grdadmit@ryerson.ca

Canada's Distinguished Dissertation Awards

Purpose: The CAGS/ProQuest Distinguished Dissertation Awards recognize Canadian doctoral dissertations that make unusually significant and original contributions to their academic field. They were established in 1994 and are presented annually

Eligibility: 1. A dissertation in any discipline in engineering, medical sciences and natural sciences completed and accepted by the Graduate School. 2. A dissertation in any discipline in the fine arts, humanities and social sciences completed and accepted by the Graduate School between 1 January and 31 December

Level of Study: Graduate
Type: Award
Value: $1,500
Frequency: Annual
Country of Study: Any country
Closing Date: 25 February
Funding: International office

For further information contact:

Email: natasha.mills@ryerson.ca

Doctoral Completion Award

Purpose: Funding amount is determined on a year-to-year basis and is a one-time-only award
Eligibility: 1. Satisfactory progress reports. 2. Comprehensive examination process. 3. Dissertation research proposal. 4. Those students who have a very high probability (ie. 90%) to complete in their 4th year
Level of Study: Graduate
Type: Award
Value: Up to $10,000
Frequency: Annual
Country of Study: Any country
Closing Date: 19 November
Funding: International office

Edward S. Rogers Sr. Graduate Student Fellowships

Subjects: The fellowships are available annually to recognize the accomplishments of master's and doctoral level students in the Communication & Culture program who have demonstrated outstanding academic accomplishments in the communications field
Purpose: The Edward S. Rogers Sr. Graduate School Fellowship, first awarded in 2001, was established by Ted and Loretta Rogers to honour the contributions of Edward S. Rogers Sr. to the Canadian communications industry
Eligibility: All Canadian PhD students in the Communication & Culture program
Level of Study: Graduate
Type: Fellowship
Value: $20,000
Frequency: Annual
Country of Study: Any country
Closing Date: no deadline
Funding: Foundation

For further information contact:

Email: grdadmit@ryerson.ca

Fulbright Canada Scholarship

Purpose: The mandate of Fulbright Canada is to enhance mutual understanding between the people of Canada and the United States of America by providing support to outstanding graduate students, faculty, professionals, and independent researchers. These individuals conduct research, lecture, or enroll in formal academic programs in the other country. In doing so, Fulbright Canada aims to grow intellectual capacity, increase productivity, and assist in the shaping of future leaders in both countries
Eligibility: 1. Be a Canadian citizen (Permanent residence is not sufficient). 2. Hold a Bachelor's degree prior to the proposed start date of the grant. 3. Be proficient in English. 4. Be in compliance with all J. William Fulbright Foreign Scholarship Board (FFSB) guidelines. 5. Be in compliance with all governmental regulations regarding visas, immigration, travel and residence
Level of Study: Graduate
Type: Scholarship
Value: $15,000
Frequency: Annual
Country of Study: Any country
Closing Date: 15 November
Funding: International office

For further information contact:

Email: grdadmit@ryerson.ca

Governor General Gold Medal

Purpose: The Governor General Gold Medal (GGGM), Ryerson University's most prestigious academic award, is awarded annually to the graduate student who achieves the highest academic standing in a graduate degree program
Eligibility: All master's and doctoral program students, who are in their first Master's or Doctoral program respectively, are eligible for this award. The student must have completed his/her program within the normal time frame (as deemed by the Yeates School of Graduate Studies)
Level of Study: Graduate
Type: Grant
Value: no nominal value
Frequency: Annual
Country of Study: Any country
Closing Date: 20 August
Funding: International office

For further information contact:

Email: natasha.mills@ryerson.ca

Graduate Student Stipend

Purpose: A graduate student stipend provides financial support to a graduate student while completing their graduate studies. Normally the stipend is paid from the research funding of a faculty supervisor. Stipends are not payment for employment
Level of Study: Graduate

Type: Stipendiary
Value: Dollar amounts vary by program and/or discipline
Frequency: Annual
Country of Study: Any country
Closing Date: no deadline
Funding: International office

For further information contact:

Email: grdadmit@ryerson.ca

John Charles Polanyi Prizes

Purpose: In honour of the achievement of John Charles Polanyi, recipient of the 1986 Nobel Prize in Chemistry, the Government of the Province of Ontario has established a fund to provide annually up to five (5) prizes to outstanding researchers in the early stages of their careers who are continuing to postdoctoral studies or have recently started a faculty appointment at an Ontario university. The John Charles Polanyi Prizes are available in the areas broadly defined as Physics, Chemistry, Physiology or Medicine, Literature and Economic Science
Eligibility: 1. Normally resident in Ontario and has completed or is near completion of doctoral studies in any recognized university in the world, or has completed or is nearing completion of doctoral studies in an Ontario university. 2. Has received the doctoral degree between 1 September and 30 April, or if the doctoral degree has not yet been awarded, will have completed all the requirements for the doctoral degree by 30 April. Applicants holding faculty appointments within these time limits may apply. 3. The prizes are awarded to assist the recipients in their research and professional development. 4. The prizes may be held along with any other financial support or research funds received by the winners. 5. It is hoped that the prizes will be conferred by September. No prize will be awarded without the successful applicant having completed all requirements for the doctoral degree
Level of Study: Graduate
Type: Grant
Value: $20,000
Frequency: Annual
Country of Study: Any country
Closing Date: 1 December
Funding: International office

For further information contact:

Email: natasha.mills@ryerson.ca

Sandbox student grant program

Purpose: The DMZ Sandbox Student Grant Program (also known as the "Grant Program") will financially support and provide eligible Ryerson led startups with the crucial grant funding and mentorship they need
Eligibility: The Sandbox Student Grant Program is open to Ryerson students registered in a; full-time academic program or a recent graduates (up to eight months after date of; graduation) from a full-time academic program who meet the following eligibility. requirements
Level of Study: Postgraduate
Type: Grant
Value: up to $15,000
Length of Study: 4 year
Frequency: Annual
Country of Study: Any country
Closing Date: 17 February
Funding: International office

For further information contact:

Email: sandbox@ryerson.ca

Senior Women Academic Administrators of Canada Awards

Purpose: The Senior Women Academic Administrators of Canada (SWAAC), external link organization was founded in 1987 to provide a forum and a collective voice for women in senior administrative ranks in Canadian universities, colleges and technical institutes. The primary purpose of SWAAC is the promotion of female leadership in Canadian universities, colleges and technical institutes
Eligibility: Women registered in Master's or PhD programs at any Member Institution of Universities Canada within a designated region are eligible to be nominated. Regions and number of awards are defined as follows, and eligibility shall rotate among them; Ontario - 5 awards; Western Provinces - 4 awards; Quebec - 4 awards; Atlantic Provinces - 4 awards
Level of Study: Graduate
Type: Award
Value: $3,000
Frequency: Annual
Country of Study: Any country
Closing Date: 3 December
Funding: International office

For further information contact:

Email: natasha.mills@ryerson.ca

Social Sciences and Humanities Research Council Impact Awards

Purpose: SSHRC Impact Awards are designed to build on and sustain Canada's research-based knowledge culture in all research areas of the social sciences and humanities. The awards recognize outstanding researchers and celebrate their research achievements, research training, knowledge mobilization, and outreach activities funded partially or entirely by SSHRC

Eligibility: 1. Be a citizen or permanent resident of Canada at the time of nomination. 2. Be an active social sciences and humanities researcher or student. 3. Hold or have held SSHRC funding pertinent to the award category. 4. Be in good standing with SSHRC. 5. Be affiliated with an eligible institution

Level of Study: Graduate

Type: Award

Value: $100,000

Frequency: Annual

Country of Study: Any country

Application Procedure: 1. Challenge—ambition and importance (25%): originality and significance of the body of work within the nominee's fields of research. 2. Achievements—impact and outcomes (75%): originality and significance of nominee's body of academic achievement and research, including quality of publications relative to stage of career; evidence of impact of the nominee's work within their fields of research and/or beyond the social sciences and humanities research community; nominee's ability and commitment to communicate research results within and/or beyond the academic community; level of nominee's engagement with, and quality of training and mentoring provided to, students, emerging scholars and participants, relative to the nominee's career level; and nominee's demonstrated potential for leadership and societal contributions within and/or beyond the academic community

Closing Date: 25 February

Funding: Private

For further information contact:

Research Training Portfolio, Social Sciences and Humanities Research Council, 350 Albert Street, P.O. Box 1610, Ottawa, ON K1P 6G4, Canada

Email: impactawards-priximpacts@sshrc-crsh.gc.ca

The Dennis Mock Graduate Scholarship

Purpose: The Dennis Mock Graduate Scholarship is available annually to recognize the accomplishments of a first-year Master's student. This award was established in the name of Dennis Mock to honour his commitment to higher education, to recognize his leadership and dedication demonstrated during his 28 years at Ryerson, and to acknowledge his role in developing graduate studies at the university, as vice-president, academic. The funds have been provided by the Peter Bronfman Scholarship Program and the Ontario Student Opportunities Trust Fund

Eligibility: 1. Completion of an undergraduate degree program at Ryerson. 2. Full-time enrollment in the first year of a Master's program at Ryerson, with a course load of at least two graded, one-term courses in the fall term. 3. First time enrollment in a graduate program. 4. Canadian Citizen or Permanent Resident. 5. Must meet the Ontario Residency Requirement (see Application form for details). 6. Demonstrated financial need

Level of Study: Graduate

Type: Scholarship

Value: $5,000

Frequency: Annual

Country of Study: Any country

Closing Date: 18 March

Funding: Foundation

For further information contact:

Email: g2guerci@ryerson.ca

The Dennis Mock Student Leadership Award

Purpose: The Dennis Mock Student Leadership Awards recognize graduating students who have made outstanding voluntary extracurricular contributions to their school or academic program department, their faculty, or to Ryerson University as a whole. The awards acknowledge and encourage student participation in university affairs

Eligibility: 1. Students who graduated in Fall or will be graduating in Spring. 2. In a full-time or part-time Ryerson degree program. 3. Clear academic standing at the time of nomination

Level of Study: Graduate

Type: Award

Frequency: Annual

Country of Study: Any country

Closing Date: 19 February

Funding: International office

For further information contact:

Email: grdadmit@ryerson.ca

The Geoffrey F. Bruce Fellowship in Canadian Freshwater Policy

Purpose: Geoffrey F. Bruce was a distinguished Canadian, dedicated public servant and diplomat who devoted his career to advancing multilateral cooperation in pursuit of environmental protection and sustainable development practices. Geoffrey was passionate about the stewardship of Canadian water resources
Level of Study: Graduate
Type: Fellowship
Value: $25,000
Length of Study: 2 year
Frequency: Annual
Country of Study: Any country
Closing Date: 30 September, each year
Funding: Foundation

For further information contact:

Dr. Carolyn Johns, Chair, Geoffrey F. Bruce Fellowship, Selection Committee, Ryerson University, 350 Victoria Street, Toronto, ON M5B 2K3, Canada

Email: cjohns@ryerson.ca

The Hydro One Aboriginal Award for Graduate Studies in Public Policy and Administration

Purpose: The Hydro One Aboriginal Award for Graduate Studies in Public Policy and Administration provides financial assistance and recognizes the academic achievement of an Aboriginal student entering the Master of Arts in Public Policy and Administration program at Ryerson University. It is awarded to up to two Aboriginal students entering the program. Funds are provided Hydro One Networks Inc. and the Ontario Trust for Student Support (OTSS)
Eligibility: 1. A four year degree with a least a B+ average in the last two years of study. 2. Demonstrated competence in the English Language. 3. Canadian citizenship or be a protected person. 4. Ontario residency (in accordance with OTSS requirements). 5. Demonstrated financial need as determined by Ryerson University
Level of Study: Graduate
Type: Award
Value: Up to $10,000
Frequency: Annual
Country of Study: Any country
Funding: International office

For further information contact:

Email: grdadmit@ryerson.ca

The Pierre Elliott Trudeau Foundation Scholarship

Purpose: The award supports interdisciplinary research and original fieldwork by providing a substantial yearly allowance for research and travel, enabling the Scholars to gain first-hand contact with the diverse communities that can enrich their studies. Moreover, each Scholar is paired with a distinguished Trudeau Mentor selected by the Foundation among the most eminent Canadian practitioners in all sectors of public life. The Scholarship also offers the opportunity to interact with an exceptional community of leaders and committed individuals in every field of the social sciences and humanities, to participate in events organized by the Foundation and to hold their own workshops, through available financial support
Eligibility: Be a Canadian citizen or landed immigrant applying to a doctoral program in the social sciences and humanities or registered full-time in the first or second year of such a program at a Canadian university
Level of Study: Graduate
Type: Scholarship
Value: $60,000
Length of Study: 3 year
Frequency: Annual
Country of Study: Any country
Closing Date: 8 January
Funding: International office

For further information contact:

Natasha Mills, Scholarships Liaison Officer, Yeates School of Graduate Studies, Ryerson University, Toronto, ON, Canada

Tel: (1) 416 979 5000 ext. 3648
Email: natasha.mills@ryerson.ca

The W. L. Mackenzie King Scholarships

Purpose: The Mackenzie King Scholarships were established as an independent trust under the will of the late Rt. Hon. William Mackenzie King (1874-1950). Two classes of Mackenzie King Scholarship are available to graduates of Canadian universities: the Open Scholarship and the Travelling Scholarship. Both are to support graduate study
Eligibility: 1. The Mackenzie King Open Scholarship is open to graduates of any Canadian university who engage in (commence or continue) graduate study (mater's or doctoral) in any field, in Canada or elsewhere. One Open Scholarship is

awarded annually. Its value has lately been $8,500 but is subject to change. 2. The Mackenzie King Travelling Scholarship is open to graduates of any Canadian university who engage in (commence or continue) postgraduate study (mater's or doctoral) in the United States or the United Kingdom, of international relations or industrial relations (including the international or industrial relations aspects of law, history, politics and economics)

Level of Study: Graduate

Type: Scholarship

Value: $10,500

Frequency: Annual

Country of Study: Any country

Closing Date: 1 February

Funding: International office

For further information contact:

Email: natasha.mills@ryerson.ca

S

Sacramento State

CSUS 6000 J Street, Sacramento, CA 95819, United States of America

Tel:	(1) 916 278 6011
Fax:	(1) 916 278 5199
Email:	infodesk@csus.edu
Website:	www.csus.edu
Contact:	Timothy Hodson, Executive Director

Center for California Studies, CSU-Sacramento, California Legislature (CSUS) was founded in 1984. It is located on the capital campus of the California State University. Center for California Studies is a public service, educational support and applied research institute of CSUS. It is dedicated to promoting a better understanding of California's government, politics, people, cultures and history.

California Senate Fellows

Subjects: Public policy and politics
Purpose: To expose people with diverse life experiences and backgrounds to the legislative process and provide research and other professional staff assistance to the Senate
Eligibility: Open to candidates who have obtained a degree from a 4 year college or university
Level of Study: Professional development
Type: Fellowships
Value: A monthly stipend of US$2,627 plus full health, vision and dental benefits
Length of Study: 11 months
Frequency: Annual
Country of Study: United States of America
Application Procedure: Applicants can download the application form from the website

Closing Date: 8 February
Funding: Government
Additional Information: For further information please contact David Pacheco, the program director, at 916 278 5408 (Sacramento State), 916 651 4160 (Senate) or email to david.pacheco@sen.ca.gov

For further information contact:

Tel:	(1) 916 278 6906
Email:	calstudies@csus.edu

Jesse M. Unruh Assembly Fellowship Program

Subjects: Public policy formation
Purpose: To provide an opportunity for individuals of all ages, ethnic backgrounds and experiences to directly participate in the legislative process
Eligibility: Applicants must have completed a Bachelor's degree by the end of Summer of the fellowship year. There are no preferred majors
Level of Study: Professional development
Type: Fellowship
Value: US$1,972 per month and medical, dental and vision benefits
Length of Study: 11 months
Frequency: Annual
Study Establishment: Center for California Studies
Country of Study: United States of America
Application Procedure: Applicants must download the complete application form from the website. Applicants must furnish academic, employment and activities data, unofficial transcripts from colleges attended, a personal statement, a policy statement on a specific topic contained in the application and 3 references
Closing Date: 22 February
Additional Information: Individuals with advanced degrees or those in mid-career are encouraged to apply

© Springer Nature Limited 2019
Palgrave Macmillan (ed.), *The Grants Register 2020*,
https://doi.org/10.1057/978-1-349-95943-3

For further information contact:

Tel: (1) 916 278 6906
Email: calstudies@csus.edu

Saint Louis University

John Cook School of Business MBA Program, 3674 Lindell Boulevard, St Louis, MO 63108, United States of America

Tel: (1) 314 977 2013
Fax: (1) 314 977 1416
Email: mba@slu.edu
Website: mba.slu.edu
Contact: MBA Admissions Officer

Saint Louis University International MBA Programme

Length of Study: More than 2 years
Application Procedure: Applicants must return a completed application, with personal essays, a nonrefundable US$55 application fee, two letters of recommendation, official transcripts from all previously attended colleges and universities, Graduate Management Admission Test score, and a curriculum vitae. Overseas students must also provide evidence of financial support and a TOEFL score
Closing Date: 15 January, 1 March, 15 April

For further information contact:

Institute of International Business, International Option MBA

Tel: (1) 314 977 3630
Fax: (1) 314 977 7188
Email: biib@slu.edu
Contact: MBA Admissions Officer

Samuel H. Kress Foundation

174 East 80th Street, New York, NY 10075, United States of America

Tel: (1) 212 861 4993
Fax: (1) 212 628 3146
Email: wyman.meers@kressfoundation.org
Website: www.kressfoundation.org
Contact: Wyman Meers, Program Administrator

The Samuel H. Kress Foundation, since its creation in 1929, has devoted its resources almost exclusively to programmes related to European art. The Foundation devotes its resources to advancing the history, conservation, and enjoyment of the vast heritage of European art, architecture, and archaeology.

Conservation Fellowships

Subjects: Specific areas of fine art conservation
Purpose: To enable young American conservators to undertake post-MA advanced internships
Eligibility: Open to those who have completed their academic training in conservation
Level of Study: Postgraduate
Type: Fellowship
Value: US$32,000
Frequency: Annual
Study Establishment: Appropriate institutions
Country of Study: United States of America
No. of awards offered: Approx. 25–30
Application Procedure: Application procedures and contact information available at www.kressfoundation.org. Program administered on Kress Foundation's behalf by the American Institute for Conservation. Forms and guidelines for submission available on website
Closing Date: 22 January
Funding: Private
No. of awards given last year: 9
No. of applicants last year: Approx. 25–30
Additional Information: Emphasis is on hands-on training. These grants are not for the completion of degree programmes. Enquiries should be directed to Wyman Meers

For further information contact:

The Foundation of the American Institute for Conservation of Historic and Artistic Works, 1156 15th St, NW; Suite 320, Washington, DC 20005, United States of America

Email: faicgrants@aic-faic.org

Samuel H. Kress Foundation Dissertation Fellowships

Subjects: Art history and humanities
Purpose: To assist final preparation of the doctoral dissertation
Eligibility: Open to predoctoral candidates at American universities
Level of Study: Predoctorate
Type: Fellowship

Value: US$10,000
Frequency: Annual
Country of Study: Any country
Application Procedure: Applicants must be nominated by their art history department. Limit of one applicant per department
Closing Date: 31 March
Additional Information: Enquiries should be directed to Lisa M Ackerman

For further information contact:

Email: info@kressfoundation.org

San Francisco Foundation (SFF)

One Embarcadero Center, Suite 1400, San Francisco, CA 94111, United States of America

Tel: (1) 415 733 8500
Fax: (1) 415 477 2783
Email: info@sff.org
Website: www.sff.org

The San Francisco Foundation (SFF) is a leading agent of Bay Area philanthropy. They rank 7th in grant making and assets among the nation's community foundations. They cultivate a family of donors who share a commitment to the Bay Area. They give millions of dollars a year to build on community assets, respond to community needs and elevate public awareness.

Koshland Young Leader Awards

Purpose: It recognizes the next generation of leadership in community. Koshland Young Leaders are strongly motivated to achieve despite facing multiple challenges, such as economic and family responsibilities
Eligibility: San Francisco public high school juniors. The most competitive candidates have at least a 3.25 cumulative or continually improving GPA, are college-bound, and embrace a commitment to strengthening their families and communities despite facing formidable life challenges
Level of Study: Postgraduate
Type: Award
Value: US$7,000
Length of Study: 2 years
Frequency: Every 2 years
Country of Study: United States of America

Application Procedure: See the website
Closing Date: January (four-part nomination process), check with the foundation
Contributor: San Francisco Foundation
Additional Information: Each winter, we invite teachers and counselors to nominate outstanding San Francisco public high school juniors for this award. If you have questions, please email or call Joshua Jones

For further information contact:

Tel: (1) 415 733 8587
Email: kyla@sff.org

San Francisco State University (SFSU)

1600 Holloway Avenue, San Francisco, CA 94132, United States of America

Tel: (1) 415 338 2234/1111
Fax: (1) 415 338 0942
Email: mritter@sfsu.edu
Website: www.sfsu.edu

San Francisco State University (SFSU) is one of the nation's leading public urban universities. SFSU helps create and maintain an environment for learning that promotes respect for and appreciation of scholarship, freedom, human diversity and the cultural mosaic of the City of San Francisco. SFSU also provides a higher education for residents of the region and state, as well as the nation and world.

Robert Westwood Scholarship

Subjects: Arts, health, science and social services
Purpose: To assist SFSU students who are living with HIV and plan to make a contribution in any field to communities affected by HIV
Level of Study: Postgraduate
Type: Scholarship
Value: US$1,000
Frequency: Annual
Study Establishment: San Francisco State University
Country of Study: United States of America
Application Procedure: Applicants must submit a copy of the most recent SFSU academic transcript, along with a brief, typed essay discussing plans to incorporate academic work and degree at SFSU with service in the HIV community or in the area of HIV prevention

Closing Date: 7 May
Additional Information: Applicants must submit a verification from the physician

For further information contact:

Tel: (1) 415 338 7339
Email: mritter@sfsu.edu
Contact: Michael Ritter, Counseling and psychological services

Sanskriti Pratishthan

Head Office C-11 Qutab Institutional Area, New Delhi 110016, India

Tel: (91) 11 2696 3226/2652 7077
Fax: (91) 11 2685 3383
Email: fellowships@sanskritifoundation.org
Website: www.sanskritifoundation.org

Sanskriti Pratishthan is a non-profit organization that was established in 1978. Sanskriti Pratishthan perceives its role as that of a catalyst, in revitalizing cultural sensitivity in contemporary times.

Kalakriti Fellowship in Indian Classical Dance

Subjects: Indian classical dance
Purpose: To encourage young artists to develop their potential and enhance their skills through intensive practice and/or incorporating different facets of their art
Eligibility: Open to Indian nationals in the age group of 25–40. The candidates should have at least 10 years of initial training in Indian classical dance. The Fellows would be required to have given at least 2–3 solo performances to his/her credit in recognized forums
Level of Study: Professional development
Type: Fellowships
Value: Rs. 50,000
Length of Study: 10 months
Frequency: Annual
Country of Study: Any country
Application Procedure: Applicants must send their 2-page curriculum vitae and a write up of approx. 500 words, explaining their project. Full postal and telephone contact details together with any email id should be submitted to facilitate contact. A few samples of previous work, project

or performances should be submitted. The names and contact addresses/telephones of two referees should also be sent
Closing Date: 30 June
Funding: Foundation
Additional Information: The candidate should not be holding any other fellowship or working on any other project at the same time. Please see the website for further details www.sanskritifoundation.org/Kalakriti-Fellowship.htm

Sasakawa Fund

School of Economics, University of São Paulo 908, FEA 1, room D105, São Paulo, Buntantã, SP 055 (080) 10, Brazil

Tel: (55) 11 3091 6075
Email: sylff@usp.br

Generally known as SYLFF, The Ryoichi Sasakawa young leaders fellowship fund established in 1987 aims to nurture future leaders who will transcend the geopolitical, religious, ethnic, and cultural boundaries and actively participate in the world community for peace and the well-being of humankind.

Sasakawa Young Leader Fellowship (SYLFF) Program

Subjects: Social sciences and humanities
Purpose: To provide grants for graduate students is social sciences areas
Eligibility: Open to postgraduate students from the university of Sao Paulo with research projects proposals that relate to approved subject areas and aim to assist Brazil in its global insertion
Level of Study: Postgraduate
Type: Fellowship
Length of Study: 2 years
Frequency: Annual
Study Establishment: São Paulo University
Country of Study: Brazil
Funding: Foundation
Contributor: The Tokyo Foundation
No. of awards given last year: 9

For further information contact:

Tel: (55) 11 3091 6075
Email: sylff@usp.br
Contact: Professor Luciano Gualberto

Savoy Foundation

230 Foch Street, St Jean Sur Richelieu, QC J3B 2B2, Canada

Tel:	(1) 450 358 9779
Fax:	(1) 450 346 1045
Email:	epilepsy@savoy-foundation.ca
Website:	www.savoy-foundation.ca
Contact:	Vivian Downing, Assistant to Vice President/ Secretary

The Savoy Foundation's main activity is to support and encourage research into epilepsy.

Savoy Foundation International Grant

Subjects: Medical and behavioural science, as they relate to epilepsy
Purpose: To improve the situation of people with epilepsy where medical care is less available
Eligibility: Only available to clinicians and established scientists
Level of Study: Postdoctorate, Postgraduate, Research
Type: Research grant
Value: Up to C$30,000
Length of Study: 1 year
Frequency: Annual
Study Establishment: An affiliated University
Country of Study: Any country
No. of awards offered: 1
Application Procedure: Applicants must contact the Foundation or visit the website for application forms and further information
Closing Date: 15 January
Funding: Private
Contributor: The Savoy Foundation endowments
No. of awards given last year: 1
No. of applicants last year: 1
Additional Information: One grant is available per year. All applications are evaluated by the Medical Board of the Savoy Foundation for epilepsy

Savoy Foundation Postdoctoral and Clinical Research Fellowships

Subjects: Medical and behavioural science, as they relate to epilepsy
Purpose: To support a full-time research project in the field of epilepsy

Eligibility: Candidates must be scientists or medical specialists with a PhD or MD
Level of Study: Postdoctorate, Postgraduate, Research
Type: Research grant
Value: C$30,000
Length of Study: 1 year (non-renewable)
Frequency: Annual
Country of Study: Canada
No. of awards offered: 26
Application Procedure: Applicants must contact the Foundation or visit the website for application forms and further information
Closing Date: 15 January
Funding: Private, Foundation
Contributor: The Savoy Foundation endowments
No. of awards given last year: Five Fellowships
No. of applicants last year: 26

Savoy Foundation Research Grants

Subjects: Medical and behavioural science, as they relate to epilepsy
Purpose: To support further research into epilepsy
Eligibility: Only available to clinicians and established scientists
Level of Study: Postdoctorate, Postgraduate, Research
Type: Research grant
Value: Up to C$25,000
Frequency: Annual
Country of Study: Canada
No. of awards offered: 20
Application Procedure: Applicants must contact the Foundation or visit the website for application forms and further information
Closing Date: 15 January
Funding: Private, Foundation
Contributor: The Savoy Foundation endowments
No. of awards given last year: 7 Research Grants
No. of applicants last year: 20
Additional Information: The grant is only available to Canadian citizens or for projects conducted in Canada

Savoy Foundation Studentships

Subjects: Biomedicine, neurology and epileptology
Purpose: To support training and research in a biomedical discipline, the health sciences or social sciences related to epilepsy
Eligibility: Candidates must have a good university record, e.g. a BSc, MD or equivalent diploma and have ensured that

a qualified researcher affiliated to a university or hospital will supervise his or her work. Concomitant registration in a graduate programme is encouraged. The awards are available to Canadian citizens or for projects conducted in Canada

Level of Study: Doctorate, Postgraduate, Predoctorate

Type: Studentship

Value: The stipend will be C$15,000 per year. An annual sum of C$1,000 will be allocated to the laboratory or institution as additional support for the research project. The student with the highest mark will receive the Van Gelder-Savoy award of an additional $1,500. Also, in memory of the contribution made by Professor Laurent Descarries to the Savoy Foundation during his tenure as a member of the Research Committee, a new award of excellence has been created. The Descarries-Savoy award, in an amount of $1,500, which will be granted to the student supported by the Foundation whom the committee decides has published the best paper during the year of the studentship

Length of Study: 1–4 years

Frequency: Annual

Country of Study: Canada

No. of awards offered: 17

Application Procedure: Applicants must contact the Foundation or visit the website for application forms and further information

Closing Date: 15 January

Funding: Private, Foundation

Contributor: The Savoy Foundation endowments

No. of awards given last year: 4 Studentships

No. of applicants last year: 17

Scholarship Foundation of the League of Finnish-American Societies

Mechelininkatu 10, Helsinki FIN 00100, Helsinki, Finland

Tel:	(358) 9 4133 3700
Fax:	(358) 9 4089 74
Email:	sayl@sayl.fi
Website:	www.sayl.fi
Contact:	Ms Tuula Nuckols, Project Manager

American Society of Naval Engineers (ASNE) Scholarship

Purpose: The aim of the scholarship is to train the professionals, researchers who develop related technology and students who are preparing for the profession, mission of the program is to help the naval engineering community stay up-to-date and informed

Eligibility: 1. To be eligible to apply for American Society of Naval Engineers (ASNE) Scholarship, Applying candidate should be a permanent citizen of USA, candidates must be full-time students enrolled in a minimum of 12 credit hours, and the undergraduate applicants must be in a 4-year Bachelor degree program. 2. Applicants must be enrolled in ABET (Accreditation Board for Engineering and Technology) accredited programs, where the science studies applicants must be accredited by the appropriate agency or organization

Level of Study: Professional development

Type: Scholarship

Value: US$4,000 for the graduate students. 50% of the award is dispensed in the Fall, the remaining 50% is dispensed in the spring

Frequency: Annual

Country of Study: Any country

Application Procedure: Applications must have the below information. 1. The materials to be submitted with application form for American Society of Naval Engineers (ASNE) Scholarship. 2. Three letters of recommendations (letters of recommendation must be on college/university or business letterhead). 3. Official transcripts

Closing Date: March

Funding: Private

School of American Research

PO Box 2188, Santa Fe, NM 87504-2188, United States of America

Tel:	(1) 505 982 3583
Fax:	(1) 505 989 9809
Contact:	Grants Management Officer

Babe Ruth League College Scholarship

Purpose: Realizing youth are our most important resources, Babe Ruth League is committed to providing our participants with the very best educational sports, experience possible and to providing them with tools to enrich their lives long after their days on the baseball and softball diamond

Eligibility: 1. You must have participated in a Cal Ripken Baseball, Babe Ruth Baseball or Babe Ruth Softball League anytime during the ages of 4-18. 2 You must be a United States citizen or permanent resident. 3. You must be a high school senior or an enrolled college student at the time of application. 4. You must be enrolled at an accredited two-year or four-year college or university. 5. You must complete an application to be submitted to Babe Ruth League, along with a copy of your official high school transcript, 200-word essay, and verification of registration at an accredited two-year or four-year college or university, by June 30 of each year. (If verification of college enrollment is not available at the time of application submission and you are selected to receive a scholarship, such verification will be required before a check is issued. Accepted forms of verification include a tuition bill or semester schedule.)

Level of Study: Graduate

Type: Scholarship

Frequency: Annual

Country of Study: Any country

Application Procedure: Babe Ruth League College Scholarships are awarded based on an applicant's high school academic achievement, participating activities, community involvement and on the contents of the essay. The Babe Ruth League College Scholarship is a one-time award and cannot be combined with any other Babe Ruth League sponsored scholarship. Supporting documents required are: 1. Copy of your official high school transcript. 2. 200-word essay on the topic: how playing in the Babe Ruth league program has affected your life. 3. Verification of registration at an accredited two-year or four-year college or university, by June 30 of each year. www.baberuthleague.org/media/216298/Babe%20Ruth%20Combined%20Scholarship%20Program%20Applicaiton%20and%20Criteria.pdf

Closing Date: 1 September

Funding: Private

Additional Information: For further information, www.baberuthleague.org/media/216298/Babe%20Ruth%20 Combined%20Scholarship%20Program%20Applicaiton%20 and %20Criteria.pdf

For further information contact:

Babe Ruth League, 1670 Whitehorse-Mercerville Road, Hamilton, NJ 08619, United States of America

Tel: (1) 800 880 3142

School of Oriental and African Studies (SOAS)

University of London, Thornhaugh Street, Russell Square, WC1H 0XG, London, United Kingdom

Tel: (44) 20 7637 2388
Fax: (44) 20 7074 5089

Email: scholarships@soas.ac.uk
Website: www.soas.ac.uk
Contact: Miss Alicia Sales, Scholarships Officer, Registry

The School of Oriental and African Studies (SOAS) regards its role as advancing the knowledge and understanding of the cultures and societies of Asia and Africa and of the School's academic disciplines through high-quality teaching and research.

Academy of Korean Studies Postgraduate Bursaries

Subjects: MA Korean studies, MA Korean literature, MPhil/PhD Korean Studies Research, MA History of Art

Eligibility: Open to United Kingdom/European Union and overseas applicants. See the website for details

Level of Study: Postgraduate

Type: Bursary

Value: Up to £6,000 towards tuition fees

Length of Study: 1 year

Frequency: Annual

Study Establishment: SOAS

Country of Study: United Kingdom

Application Procedure: See website www.soas.ac.uk/scholarships for details

Closing Date: 24 May

Funding: Private

Contributor: Academy of Korean Studies

No. of awards given last year: 1

Additional Information: If you have any questions about the bursary application, please contact the Scholarships Officer

For further information contact:

Email: ak49@soas.ac.uk
Contact: Dr Anders Karlsson

Arts and Humanities Research Council Studentships

Subjects: History, art, Asian languages and cultures, linguistics, middle east and African, music and religious studies

Purpose: To support taught masters and research students

Eligibility: Open to home and European Union students

Level of Study: Doctorate, Postgraduate

Type: Scholarship

Value: Maintenance plus approved tuition fees

Study Establishment: SOAS

Country of Study: United Kingdom

Application Procedure: Scholarship application should be made on the appropriate scholarship application form which is available for download

Closing Date: Check the website: www.soas.ac.uk/

Funding: Government

Additional Information: There are two types of studentship awards – a full studentship award for United Kingdom. residents and a fees-only studentship award for European Union residents. Please see the website for further details

For further information contact:

Email: emily.smith2@ncl.ac.uk

Bernard Buckman Scholarship

Subjects: MA in Chinese studies

Purpose: The scholarship is intended to off-set the tuition fees at the United Kingdom/European Union rate

Eligibility: Open to those candidates who qualify to pay for home or European Union tuition fees. Applicants must possess a good Honours Degree from a United Kingdom university or its equivalent

Level of Study: Postgraduate

Type: Scholarship

Value: Home or European Union postgraduate fee

Length of Study: 1 year

Frequency: Annual

Study Establishment: SOAS

Country of Study: United Kingdom

No. of awards offered: 7

Application Procedure: Candidates can apply for this scholarship via the online scholarship application form

Closing Date: 22 March

Funding: Private

No. of awards given last year: 1

No. of applicants last year: 7

Additional Information: For enquiries, please contact Scholarships Officer

For further information contact:

Thornhaugh Street, Russell Square, WC1H 0XG, London, United Kingdom

Tel: (44) 20 7074 5094/5091
Email: scholarships@soas.ac.uk

Felix Scholarship

Subjects: Oriental and African studies in archaeology, area studies, economics, ethnomusicology, history, law, languages, linguistics, phonetics, politics, religious study, social anthropology and development studies

Purpose: To support first class Indian students commencing a Master's programme or researching for a Doctoral degree at the School of Oriental and African Studies

Eligibility: Open to applicants of any full-time taught Master's or MPhil/PhD programme, under 30 years of age, able to demonstrate financial need and would return to work in their home country after completion of studies

Level of Study: Doctorate, Postgraduate

Type: Scholarship

Value: £12,316 per year plus tuition fees

Length of Study: 1–3 years

Frequency: Annual

Study Establishment: SOAS

Country of Study: United Kingdom

Application Procedure: A Felix Scholarship application form is available for download from the download box at the top right or can be obtained from Scholarships Officer

Closing Date: 31 January

Funding: Private

Contributor: Felix Scholarship Trust

No. of awards given last year: 6

Additional Information: One award is made each year to a non-Indian student from a developing country who demonstrates academic excellence and financial need. Please see the website for further details www.soas.ac.uk/registry/scholarships/felix-scholarships.html

For further information contact:

Tel: (44) 20 7074 5094/5091
Email: scholarships@soas.ac.uk

Hong Kong and Shanghai Banking Corporation School of Oriental and African Studies Scholarships

Subjects: Sinology or Chinese literature

Purpose: To support United Kingdom or European Union fee payers commencing a full-time master's course in Sinology or Chinese literature

Eligibility: Applicants must possess or be about to complete a good honours degree, preferably first class, from a United Kingdom institution or overseas equivalent

Level of Study: Postgraduate

Type: Scholarship

Value: £16,650 plus tuition fees at the home European Union rate

Length of Study: 1 year

Frequency: Annual

Study Establishment: SOAS

Country of Study: United Kingdom

Application Procedure: Candidates can apply for this scholarship via the online scholarship application form. For enquiries, please contact Scholarships Officer
Closing Date: 22 March
Funding: Trusts
Contributor: HSBC educational trust
No. of awards given last year: 2

For further information contact:

Tel: (1) 20 7074 5094/5091
Email: scholarships@soas.ac.uk

Ouseley Memorial Scholarship

Subjects: Any programme which involves research requires the use of any Middle Eastern or Asian language
Purpose: To encourage the study of Arabic, Persian, Hindustani and other Oriental languages
Eligibility: Open to United Kingdom/European Union and overseas applicants. Applicants must refer to the organization website for detailed information
Level of Study: Doctorate, Postgraduate
Type: Scholarship
Value: £6,000 for 1 year only
Frequency: Annual
Study Establishment: SOAS
Country of Study: United Kingdom
No. of awards offered: 20
Application Procedure: See the website
Closing Date: 31 January
Funding: Private
No. of awards given last year: 1
No. of applicants last year: 20

For further information contact:

Tel: (1) 20 7074 5094/5091
Email: scholarships@soas.ac.uk

SOAS Master's Scholarship

Subjects: A variety of taught Master's programmes
Purpose: To provide financial assistance to study for a full-time taught Master's programme
Eligibility: Open to United Kingdom/European Union and overseas applicants who possess a First class Honours degree or equivalent
Level of Study: Postgraduate
Type: Scholarship
Value: Approx. UK£15,000
Length of Study: 1 year, non-renewable
Frequency: Annual

Study Establishment: SOAS
Country of Study: United Kingdom
No. of awards offered: 350
Application Procedure: See the website
Closing Date: 20 February
Funding: Government
No. of awards given last year: 11
No. of applicants last year: 350

For further information contact:

Email: scholarships@soas.ac.uk

SOAS Research Scholarship

Subjects: The languages and cultures of Africa, East Asia, Near and Middle East, South Asia and South-East Asia, focusing on anthropology and sociology, art and archaeology, development studies, economics, ethnomusicology, financial and management studies, history, law, linguistics, political studies and the study of religions
Purpose: To support full-time research study at SOAS
Eligibility: Applicants must United Kingdom/European Union and overseas and must possess or expect to be awarded a distinction in their Master's degree from a United Kingdom university or its equivalent
Level of Study: Doctorate
Type: Scholarship
Value: £12,790
Length of Study: 3 years
Frequency: Annual
Study Establishment: SOAS
Country of Study: United Kingdom
Application Procedure: Applicants must complete and submit an application form that can be downloaded from the website
Closing Date: 31 January
Funding: Government
No. of awards given last year: 4
Additional Information: For enquiries, please contact Scholarships Officer

For further information contact:

Email: scholarships@soas.ac.uk

Sochon Foundation Scholarship

Subjects: MA Korean studies, MA Korean literature, MPhil/PhD Korean studies research and MA History of Art
Purpose: For a student undertaking a full-time postgraduate programme in Korean studies

Eligibility: Open to United Kingdom/European Union and overseas applicants
Level of Study: Postgraduate
Type: Scholarship
Value: UK£7,000
Length of Study: 1 year
Frequency: Annual
Study Establishment: SOAS
Country of Study: United Kingdom
Application Procedure: See the website
Closing Date: 24 May
Funding: Foundation
No. of awards given last year: 1

For further information contact:

Email: scholarships@soas.ac.uk

William Ross Murray Scholarship

Subjects: LLM
Purpose: To support a student of high academic achievement from a developing country unable to pay overseas tuition fees and attending the full-time LLM degree at SOAS
Eligibility: Applicants from a developing country who must have a high level of academic achievements preferably first class, from a United Kingdom institution or overseas equivalent
Level of Study: Postgraduate
Type: Scholarship
Value: Overseas tuition fees. Free accommodation at International Student House and food vouchers
Length of Study: 1 year
Frequency: Annual
Study Establishment: SOAS
Country of Study: United Kingdom
Application Procedure: See the website
Closing Date: 22 March
Funding: Foundation
No. of awards given last year: 1

For further information contact:

Email: scholarships@soas.ac.uk

Science and Engineering Research Board

5 & 5A, Lower Ground Floor, Vasant Square Mall, Sector-B, Pocket-5, Vasant Kunj, New Delhi 110070, India

Tel: (91) 11 40000398
Contact: Science and Engineering Research Board

The Science and Engineering Research Board (SERB) is a statutory body established through an Act of Parliament. Supporting basic research in emerging areas of science and engineering are the primary and distinctive mandate of the Board. The Board structure, with both financial and administrative powers vested in the Board, would enable quicker decisions on research issues, greatly improving thereby our responsiveness to the genuine needs of the research scientists and the S&T system.

J C Bose National Fellowship

Subjects: All areas of science
Purpose: The JC Bose fellowship is awarded to active scientists in recognition for their outstanding performance. The fellowship is scientist-specific and very selective
Eligibility: The candidate should be an active scientist with a record of outstanding performance apparent from the award of SS Bhatnagar prize and or fellowship of science academies (including engineering, agriculture and medicine). The scientist should be in service at the time of nomination to this fellowship
Level of Study: Research
Type: Fellowship
Value: The fellowship amount is Rs. 25,000 per month in addition to regular income. Research grant of Rs. 15.00 lakh per annum. Overhead of Rs. 1.00 lakh per annum to the host institute
Length of Study: 5 years
Frequency: Annual
Country of Study: Any country
Additional Information: Selection of JC Bose Fellows will be made periodically (normally twice a year) by a Search-cum-Selection Committee specially constituted for the purpose, as per the broad guidelines of the fellowship scheme

For further information contact:

Contact: Mr S.S. Kohli, Scientist G

National Post Doctoral Fellowship (N-PDF)

Purpose: The SERB-National Post Doctoral Fellowship (N-PDF) is aimed to identify motivated young researchers and provide them support for doing research in frontier areas of science and engineering. The fellows will work under a mentor, and it is hoped that this training will provide them a platform to develop as an independent researcher
Eligibility: The applicant should be an Indian citizen. The applicant must have obtained PhD/MD/MS degree from a recognized University

Type: Fellowship
Value: Fellowship: Rs. 55,000 per month (consolidated) and Rs. 35,000 per month for candidates who have submitted the thesis but degree not awarded. Research Grant: Rs. 2,00,000 per annum. Overheads: Rs. 1,00,000 per annum
Length of Study: Initially for a period of 2 years. In exceptional cases, depending on the progress of research, the fellowship can be extended for 1 more year. There is no provision to extend the tenure beyond 3 years
Country of Study: Hungary
Application Procedure: The application form along with a research proposal highlighting the objectives of the research work to be undertaken should be submitted online through the website www.serbonline.in
Additional Information: The call for applications for SERB-N PDF will be notified twice a year through the websites www.serbonline.in and www.serb.gov.in. For details one may visit serbonline.in/SERB/npdf. www.serb.gov.in

For further information contact:

Email: info@serbonline.in

Prime Minister's Fellowship Scheme for Doctoral Research

Subjects: Science, Technology, Engineering, Agriculture or Medicine
Purpose: To conduct scientific and industrial research
Level of Study: Research
Type: Fellowship
Value: Rs. 6 lakh per annum
Length of Study: 4 years
Frequency: Annual
Country of Study: India
Application Procedure: Application Performa is to be filled only through the web portal www.primeministerfellowshipscheme.com
Closing Date: Anytime within 14 months from registration/admission in PhD
Funding: Government
Contributor: Department of Science & Technology (DST) and Science & Engineering Research Board (SERB) with The Confederation of Indian Industry (CII)
Additional Information: For online applications, visit website: www.primeministerfellowshipscheme.com

For further information contact:

Email: shalini.sharma@cii.in

Ramanujan Fellowship

Subjects: All areas of science
Purpose: The fellowship is meant for brilliant scientists and engineers from all over the world to take up scientific research positions in India, that is, for those scientists who want to return to India from abroad. The fellowships are scientist-specific and very selective. The Ramanujan Fellows could work in any of the scientific institutions and universities in the country and they would be eligible for receiving regular research grants through the extramural funding schemes of various S&T agencies of the Government of India
Level of Study: Postdoctorate
Type: Fellowship
Value: Rs. 85,000 per month and in addition a Research Grant of Rs. 7.00 lakh per annum
Length of Study: 5 years
Country of Study: Any country
Application Procedure: Visit website www.serb.gov.in for further details
Closing Date: No last date is available for this scheme
Funding: Government
Additional Information: Ramanujan Fellowship are only for those candidates who are doing Post Doctoral abroad and not for the people who already have permanent position in a scientific organization in the country

For further information contact:

Contact: Mr Pravakar Mohanty, Scientist G

S.N Bose Scholar Program

Purpose: S.N Bose Scholar Program is organized by the Science and Engineering Board (SERB), Department of science and technology (DST), Govt. Of India, Indo–US Technology Forum and Win Step Forward. The scholarship envisages providing a world-class research platform in top US universities. It also aims at making Indo-US long-term collaboration in the field of research
Eligibility: 1. Students pursuing a Bachelor's or master's degree program from a recognized institution of India can apply for this scheme. 2. The disciplines of pursuing UG and PG degree are Atmospheric and Earth Sciences, Chemical Sciences, Engineering Sciences, Mathematical and Computational Sciences, and Physical Sciences. 3. Candidates who are studying PhD cannot apply
Level of Study: Postdoctorate
Type: Scholarship
Length of Study: 1 year
Frequency: Annual
Country of Study: Any country

Closing Date: May
Funding: Foundation

For further information contact:

Indo-US Science and Technology Forum, Fulbright House, 12, Hailey Road, New Delhi 110001, India

Tel: (91) 11 42691712
Email: bose@indousstf.org

Science and Engineering Research Board Distinguished Fellowship

Purpose: In order to support research of eminent scientists who do not hold any administrative roles and functions but are active and performing, SERB has instituted Distinguished SERB Fellowship Award
Eligibility: Superannuated scientist who is active in research. Must have received recognition for his/her work from National and/or International scientific bodies
Level of Study: Research
Type: Fellowship
Value: A research grant of Rs. 5 lakhs per annum and a fellowship amount of Rs. 60,000 per month will be given to each fellow
Country of Study: India
Application Procedure: Call for nomination is made from time to time. Nominations are accepted only when the call is made
Closing Date: 30 November
Funding: Government

For further information contact:

Email: keerti.serb@gmail.com

Science and Engineering Research Board Overseas Postdoctoral Fellowship (OPDF)

Subjects: Materials, Energy, Sustainable Chemistry, Quantum Computing and Spintronics, Complex systems, Theoretical Mathematical Science, Big Data, Mechanobiology/Physical Biology, Bio-energy, Genetic to Physiology, Mental Health, High Performance Computation in Physics, Chemistry, Biology and Mathematics, Humanoid Robotics, Cognitive Science, Mechnotronics, Advanced Manufacturing, Cyber security, Encryption and decryption, Petroleum and Petro-Chemical Engineering, Science of Climate Change, Glaciology, Modeling, Imaging, Algorithms and Combinatorial Optimizations Application

Purpose: SERB Overseas Postdoctoral fellowship (SERB-OPDF) aims to build national capacity in frontier areas of Science and Engineering, which are of interest to India by providing postdoctoral fellowship
Eligibility: The applicant should have completed PhD degree in science and engineering not earlier than the preceding 2 years from recognized institutions in India. For researchers who are in regular employment, the 2 years period may be relaxed
Type: Fellowship
Length of Study: 1 year, extendable to 1 more year subject to good performance
Country of Study: Any country
Application Procedure: The format, guidelines and other details of the SERB-OPDF Program details are also available at www.dst.gov.in
Additional Information: The programme admits candidates in identified areas and sends them to top institutions around the globe, other than United States of America and also to institutions where internationally acclaimed scientists are working

For further information contact:

Email: opdf@serb.gov.in

Science and Engineering Research Board Women Excellence Award

Purpose: SERB Women Excellence Award is a one-time award given to women scientists below 40 years of age and who have received recognition from any one or more of the following national academies such as Young Scientist Medal, Young Associate etc
Level of Study: Research
Type: Award
Value: Rs. 5.00 lakh per annum
Length of Study: 3 years
Country of Study: Any country
Application Procedure: A copy of the proposal (in one file in PDF) may also be sent by email to: doyiltv@nic.in
Funding: Government
Additional Information: The call for proposals will be notified through the website annually. Women Scientists who have received the award earlier are not eligible to apply again

For further information contact:

Email: doyiltv@nic.in

Science and Technology Facilities Council (STFC)

Polaris House, North Star Avenue, Wiltshire, SN2 1SZ, Swindon, United Kingdom

Tel: (44) 1793 442 000
Fax: (44) 1793 442 002
Email: enquiries@stfc.ac.uk
Website: www.stfc.ac.uk

STFC is keeping the United Kingdom at the forefront of international science and tackling some of the most significant challenges facing society such as meeting our future energy needs, monitoring and understanding climate change, and global security. The Council has a broad science portfolio and works with the academic and industrial communities to share its expertise in materials science, space and ground-based astronomy technologies, laser science, microelectronics, wafer scale manufacturing, particle and nuclear physics, alternative energy production, radio communications and radar.

Daphne Jackson Fellowships

Subjects: Particle physics, particle astrophysics, solar system science and astronomy
Purpose: To enable high-level engineers and scientists to return to their professions after a career break for family or other reasons
Eligibility: Open to promising engineers and scientists who have taken a career break
Level of Study: Postdoctorate, Research
Type: Fellowship
Value: Fellowship will be financed by your sponsor and/or host institution. Please refer to the website for more details: www.daphnejackson.org/fellowships/funding/
Length of Study: 2 years
Frequency: Annual
Study Establishment: Any academic institution acceptable to the PPARC
Country of Study: United Kingdom
Application Procedure: Applicants must contact Jennifer Woolley, Trust Director, or Sue Smith, Fellowship Administrator, for application forms and further information
Closing Date: Please write for details
Funding: Government
Additional Information: Please refer to the website for more details: www.daphnejackson.org/fellowships/applicationprocess/

For further information contact:

The Daphne Jackson Trust, Department of Physics, University of Surrey, Guildford GU2 7XH, Surrey, United Kingdom

Tel: (44) 1483 689166
Email: djmft@surrey.ac.uk

Ernest Rutherford Fellowship

Subjects: Astronomy, solar and planetary science, particle physics, particle astrophysics, cosmology and nuclear physics
Purpose: The Ernest Rutherford Fellowships will enable early career researchers with clear leadership potential to establish a strong, independent research programme
Eligibility: Ernest Rutherford Fellowships are intended for early career researchers who do not have a permanent academic position. You are not eligible if you currently hold a permanent academic position or the equivalent in institutions other than universities. Fellowships are open to applicants of any nationality
Level of Study: Research
Type: A variable number of fellowships
Length of Study: 5 years
Frequency: Annual
Country of Study: United Kingdom
No. of awards offered: 160
Application Procedure: How to apply is detailed on STFC website: stfc.ukri.org/funding/fellowships/ernest-rutherford-fellowship/
Closing Date: September
Funding: Government
No. of awards given last year: 11
No. of applicants last year: 160

For further information contact:

Email: enquiries@stfc.ac.uk

Industrial CASE Studentships

Subjects: Astronomy, Particle Physics and Nuclear Physics
Purpose: Provides support for PhD students to work in collaboration with a non-academic partner on projects that aim to apply technologies or techniques developed within the programme into other areas
Eligibility: Organisations eligible to receive STFC grant funding
Level of Study: Postgraduate
Type: Studentship
Value: Stipend, fees, Research Training and Fieldwork travel
Length of Study: 3.5 years

Frequency: Annual
Country of Study: United Kingdom
Application Procedure: Call opens in August. Applications must be submitted by the academic partner through the Je-S system. Proposals may be led by either the academic supervisor at an eligible United Kingdom University or research institute or supervisor/supervisors at the non-academic partner organisation, but the application process must be completed by the academic partner, who will then be the recipient of the award
Closing Date: October
Funding: Commercial
Additional Information: Please check at www.mrc.ac.uk/ skills-careers/studentships/how-we-fund-studentships/industrial-case-studentships/ for more information

Industrial CASE-Plus Studentship

Subjects: Astronomy, Particle Physics and Nuclear Physics
Purpose: Provides support for PhD students to work in collaboration with a non-academic partner on projects that aim to apply technologies or techniques developed within the programme into other areas. The student would spend a further year working full time on the premises of the non-academic partner as an employee
Eligibility: Organisations eligible to receive STFC grant funding
Level of Study: Postgraduate
Type: Studentship
Value: Stipend, fees, Research Training and Fieldwork travel
Length of Study: 3.5 years
Frequency: Annual
Study Establishment: Science and Technology Facilities Council
Country of Study: United Kingdom
Application Procedure: The Call opens May. Proposals may be submitted up to the closing date of July for awards to start in October. Proposals should be submitted by a supervisor from a Research Organization eligible to be the academic partner through the Je-S system
Funding: Commercial
Additional Information: Please check STFC website for more information - stfc.ukri.org/funding/studentships/ industrial-case-studentships/

PPARC Communications/Media Programme

Subjects: Science communication
Purpose: To support students undertake communications training
Level of Study: Postgraduate

Type: Bursary
Value: All tuition fees
Length of Study: 1 academic year
Frequency: Annual
Study Establishment: Any approved university
Country of Study: United Kingdom
Application Procedure: Contact the PPARC Science and Society team
Closing Date: 13 October

For further information contact:

Tel: (44) 1793 442030
Email: pr.pus@pparc.ac.uk

PPARC Royal Society Industry Fellowships

Subjects: Particle physics or astronomy
Purpose: To enhance interaction between those in industry and the research base, to the benefit of United Kingdom industry
Eligibility: Open to senior academic scientists and industrial employees with a project proposal central to their own research programme for which a collaborative effort would bring benefits
Level of Study: Postdoctorate, Professional development
Type: Fellowship
Value: Varies
Length of Study: 6 months–2 years full-time, or part-time over a period of up to 4 years
Frequency: Annual
Study Establishment: An appropriate academic institution or position in the industry
Country of Study: United Kingdom
Application Procedure: Applicants must find a suitable industrial or academic partner to host their project before submitting an application. Applications and further information are available from the Research Appointments Department of The Royal Society
Closing Date: June or December
Funding: Commercial, Private
Contributor: The Royal Society, EPSRC, BBSRC, Rolls-Royce and PPARC
Additional Information: Apart from the Royal Society Fellowships Programme the following fellowship programmes are administered by the PPARC in collaboration with other partners: The European Organisation for Nuclear Research (CERN) Fellowships, The European Space Agency (ESA) Fellowships, The Anglo-Australian Postdoctoral Research Fellowships, and the Daphne Jackson Fellowships. Further information on these programmes is available on the PPARC website

For further information contact:

Research Appointments Department, The Royal Society, 6 Carlton House Terrace, United Kingdom

Tel:	(44) 20 7451 2542
Email:	ukresearch.appointments@royalsoc.ac.uk

PPARC Standard Research Studentship

Subjects: Science, engineering
Purpose: To enable promising scientists and engineers to continue training
Eligibility: Advice on eligibility should be sought from the Registrar's Office
Level of Study: Postgraduate
Type: Studentship
Value: Tuition fees only
Length of Study: 1–3 years
Frequency: Annual
Country of Study: United Kingdom
Application Procedure: Contact the PPARC
Closing Date: 31 March

For further information contact:

Tel:	(44) 1793 442026
Email:	steve.cann@pparc.ac.uk
Contact:	Steve Cann

Science and Technology Facilities Council Postgraduate Studentships

Subjects: Particle physics, nuclear physics, particle astrophysics, solar system science and astronomy
Purpose: STFC postgraduate studentships are awarded to enable promising scientists and engineers to continue training beyond a first degree
Eligibility: Open to postgraduates from the United Kingdom and European Union countries. All studentship projects supported through STFC funding must fall within STFC remit
Level of Study: Postgraduate
Type: Studentship
Value: Stipend (excluding fees only students), approved fees, Research Training Support Grant, Conference and United Kingdom fieldwork element, Fieldwork expenses, Long Term Attachments, Other Allowances (where applicable)
Length of Study: 3.5 years

Frequency: Annual
Country of Study: United Kingdom
Application Procedure: If you are interested in applying for an STFC-funded PhD, please contact the institution at which you wish to undertake a research degree directly
Closing Date: As advertised by individual Research Organisations
Funding: Government
Additional Information: Please check at www.stfc.ac.uk/funding/studentships/types-of-postgraduate-studentship/ for more information

For further information contact:

Email:	Studentships@stfc.ac.uk

University of Canterbury Pasifika Doctoral Scholarship

Purpose: This scholarship supports Pasifika students for study towards a research doctoral degree at the University of Canterbury
Eligibility: The scholarship is tenable by full-time and part-time Pasifika students engaged in study for a research doctoral degree at the University
Level of Study: Doctorate
Type: Scholarship
Value: Up to $21,000 per annum plus tuition fees at domestic rate
Frequency: Annual
Country of Study: Any country
Application Procedure: You may apply through this webpage approximately 8 weeks before applications close. If it's possible to apply on-line for this scholarship there will be a link above to the on-line system. If the link is not provided, please download and complete the application form located below. However, if the scholarship is managed by Universities NZ or another department of the University an External Website link will appear below and application instructions will be available through that link. Apply through online link. www.canterbury.ac.nz/scholarshipsearch/ScholarshipDetails.aspx
Closing Date: 15 May
Funding: Private
Additional Information: www.canterbury.ac.nz/scholarshipsearch/ScholarshipDetails.aspx

For further information contact:

Email:	info@canterbury.ac.nz

Science Foundation Ireland

Wilton Park House, Wilton Place, Dublin 2, Ireland

Tel:	(353) 1 607 3200
Fax:	(353) 1 607 3201
Email:	info@sfi.ie
Website:	www.sfi.ie
Contact:	Professor Mark W. J. Ferguson, Director

Science Foundation Ireland funds oriented basic and applied research in the areas of science, technology, engineering and mathematics (STEM), which promotes and assists the development and competitiveness of industry, enterprise and employment in Ireland. SFI will build and strengthen scientific and engineering research and its infrastructure in the areas of greatest strategic value to Ireland's long-term competitiveness and development.

President of Ireland Young Research Award (PIYRA)

Subjects: Science, technology, engineering, and mathematics
Purpose: The purpose of the PIYRA programme is to recruit and retain outstanding early career investigators with leadership potential. Its aim is to enable those at an earlier career stage who already hold permanent academic positions to advance their careers and build up their research teams and activities; to allow researchers in temporary positions to advance their careers and provide them with enhanced opportunities to move into a permanent academic position; to enable the award holder, together with his/her team, to carry out their work in Ireland's public research bodies; to offer funding opportunities that help third-level institutions attract and develop researchers and their careers; to allow earlier-career investigators of all nationalities to enhance their experience in Irish HEIs and to allow those employed outside of Ireland to return to work in an Irish HEI
Eligibility: The lead applicant must have completed a minimum of 36 months of active postdoctoral research. The lead applicant must have been awarded a PhD or MD within the last 8 years, in the normal case, or up to a maximum of 12 and a half years for applicants who have taken documented eligible leave, as described below. The lead applicant has an exceptional record of internationally recognized independent research accomplishments for their career stage. The lead applicant must be an individual who will be recognized by the research body upon receipt of the SFI grant as an independent investigator who will have an independent office and research space at the host research body for which

he/she will be fully responsible for at least the duration of the SFI grant
Level of Study: Research
Type: Grant
Value: Up to €1,000,000 of total value (inclusive of the host institution contribution) in direct costs
Length of Study: Up to 5 years
Frequency: Annual
Study Establishment: Host Research Bodies must be situated in the Republic of Ireland. Research Bodies will include Universities, Institutes of Technology and independent not-for-profit public research organizations that receive a significant share of their total funding from public sources
Country of Study: Ireland
Application Procedure: Applicants are invited to submit the following documentation: expression of Interest and if invited to do so after the Expression of Interest evaluation stage; full proposal. Application must be submitted via an eligible research body. Application must be submitted online via SESAME
Closing Date: Rolling call. Closes by 21 December
Funding: Government
Contributor: Science Foundation Ireland

Science Foundation Ireland Career Development Award (CDA)

Subjects: Science, technology, engineering and mathematics
Purpose: The SFI Career Development Award (CDA) aims to support early- and mid-career researchers who already hold a salaried, independent research post and who are looking to expand their research activities. Its aims is to support excellent scientific research that has potential economic and societal impact; to enable those at an earlier career stage who already hold permanent academic positions to advance their careers and build up their research teams and activities; to allow researchers in temporary positions to advance their careers and provide them with enhanced opportunities to move into a permanent academic position; to provide the support and infrastructure to carry out novel research in areas that underpin SFI's legal remit; to enable the award holder, together with his/her team, to carry out their work in Ireland's public research bodies, including Universities and Institutes of Technology; to offer funding opportunities that help third-level institutions attract and develop researchers and their careers; to allow earlier-career investigators of all nationalities to enhance their experience in Irish HEIs
Eligibility: The applicant will be a researcher with 3–15 years of relevant experience beyond the award of their doctoral degree, who at the time of application will be either in a permanent, full-time academic position (either within the institution at which they wish to base their CDA-funded

research or another elsewhere in Ireland or overseas), or employed on a temporary (fixed-term) contract where it is evident that the role being carried out is an independent research position (i.e., Postdoctoral Research Associates (or equivalent) or Research Fellows working under the guidance of a supervisor and who have never held an independent position are not eligible to apply to the CDA Programme)

Level of Study: Research
Type: Award
Value: Between €300,000 and €500,000 direct costs
Length of Study: 4 years
Frequency: Every 2 years
Study Establishment: Host Research Bodies must be situated in the Republic of Ireland. Research Bodies will include Universities, Institutes of Technology and independent not-for-profit public research organizations that receive a significant share of their total funding from public sources
Country of Study: Ireland
Application Procedure: Application must be submitted via an eligible research body. Application must be submitted online via SESAME (www.sfi.ie/funding/award-management-system)
Closing Date: 10 December (subject to change, please consult call document)
Funding: Government
Contributor: Science Foundation Ireland
No. of awards given last year: 20
Additional Information: Please write to cda@sfi.ie for further information

For further information contact:

Email: info@sfi.ie

Science Foundation Ireland Investigator Programme

Subjects: Science, technology, engineering and mathematics that demonstrably support and underpin enterprise competitiveness and societal development in Ireland
Purpose: To fund scientific research projects of excellence in focused areas. To build capacity, expertise and relationships so as to enable researchers to compete in future SFI Research Centre Programmes or in other funding programmes such as ERC and Horizon 2020. To encourage researchers to build capacity, expertise, collaborations and relationships in areas of strategic economic importance through themed calls. To facilitate partnerships with other agencies. To support collaborations and partnerships between academia and industry
Eligibility: The lead applicant and any co-applicant(s) must hold a PhD/MD or equivalent for at least 5 years by the proposal deadline. The lead applicant and any co-applicant(s) are required to have demonstrated that they are each senior author on at least 10 international peer reviewed articles. The lead applicant and any co-applicant(s) are required to have demonstrated research independence through securing at least one independent research grant as a lead investigator or as co-investigator

Level of Study: Research
Type: Grant
Value: €400,000–2,500,000 per year
Length of Study: 3–5 years
Frequency: Annual
Study Establishment: Host Research Bodies must be situated in the Republic of Ireland. Research Bodies will include Universities, Institutes of Technology and independent not-for-profit public research organizations that receive a significant share of their total funding from public sources
Country of Study: Ireland
Application Procedure: Application must be submitted via an eligible research body. Application must be submitted online via SESAME (www.sfi.ie/funding/award-management-system)
Closing Date: 26 June (subject to change, please consult call document)
Funding: Government
Contributor: Science Foundation Ireland
No. of awards given last year: 40

For further information contact:

Email: investigators@sfi.ie

Starting Investigator Research Grant (SIRG)

Subjects: Science, technology, engineering and mathematics
Purpose: The SIRG programme supports excellent postdoctoral researchers who wish to take steps towards a fully independent research career. Aims: to support excellent scientific research that has potential economic and societal impact. To enable those at an early career stage to establish themselves as independent researchers; to provide the support and infrastructure to carry out novel research in areas that underpin SFI's legal remit; to gain important experience towards a full-time academic position, including the supervision of the postgraduate student supported by the award; to enable the award holder, together with his/her postgraduate student, to carry out their work in Ireland's public research bodies, including Universities and Institutes of technology; to offer funding opportunities that help third-level institutions attract and develop researchers and their careers; to allow early-career

investigators of all nationalities to enhance their experience in Irish HEIs; to allow early-career investigators who have been employed outside of Ireland to return to work in an Irish HEI

Eligibility: The applicant will be a researcher with between 3 and 8 years of relevant experience beyond the award of their doctoral, who is currently employed as a Postdoctoral Research Associate (or equivalent) or a Research Fellow under the guidance of a named supervisor, and who has never previously held an independent research position of any kind where they were primarily responsible for a research team and its financial support. Allowances will be made for documented leave, including maternity leave, paternity leave, parental leave, military service, sick/disability leave and carer's leave

Level of Study: Research

Type: Grant

Value: Up to €400,000 direct costs

Length of Study: 4 years

Study Establishment: Host Research Bodies must be situated in the Republic of Ireland. Research Bodies will include Universities, Institutes of Technology and independent not-for-profit public research organizations that receive a significant share of their total funding from public sources

Country of Study: Ireland

Application Procedure: Application must be submitted via an eligible research body. Application must be submitted online via SESAME

Closing Date: 26 November (subject to change, please consult call document)

Funding: Government

Contributor: Science Foundation Ireland

No. of awards given last year: 20

For further information contact:

Email: sirg@sfi.ie

Sciences Po

rue Saint Guillaume, 75337, Paris, France

Tel: (33) 1 45 49 50 50
Contact: Sciences Po - 27

David Gritz Scholarship

Purpose: the David Gritz Scholarship is meant to attract undergraduate and graduate Israeli citizens who wish to study at Sciences Po

Eligibility: The scholarship is awarded every year to 1 Israeli citizen. The candidates must be admitted to an undergraduate or a masters programme or have submitted an application for admission to Sciences Po

Level of Study: Postgraduate

Type: Scholarship

Value: $10,000 per year

Length of Study: 1 year

Country of Study: France

Application Procedure: Applicants must send the forms to caterina.sabbatini@sciencespo.fr

Closing Date: 1 June

Contributor: Sciences Po Foundation

Additional Information: For more details contact Caterina Sabbatini-Clec'h, caterina.sabbatini@sciencespo.fr

For further information contact:

Email: caterina.sabbatini@sciencespo.fr

Emile Boutmy Scholarships

Subjects: Masters programme offered at the University

Purpose: Sciences Po created the Emile Boutmy Scholarships after the founder of Sciences Po in order to attract the very best international students from outside of the European Union who are first time applicants and who have been admitted to an undergraduate or master's programme offered at the University

Eligibility: Non-EU international students. This scholarship is awarded based on factors of excellence and according to the type of profile sought for this programme. Social criteria are also taken into account

Level of Study: Postgraduate

Type: Scholarship

Value: From €5,000 to €10,000 for complete 2 years of the master's programme

Length of Study: 2 years

Frequency: Annual

Country of Study: France

Application Procedure: It is important to visit the official website to access the application form and for detailed information on how to apply for this scholarship. Students must indicate that they are applying for the Emile Boutmy scholarship in their Sciences Po application

Closing Date: 8 April

Contributor: Science Po Foundation

Additional Information: For more details, please visit official scholarship website: formation.sciences-po.fr/en/contenu/the-emile-boutmy-scholarship

For further information contact:

Tel: (33) 1 45 49 50 82
Email: isabelle.karcher@sciencespo.fr

KSP Excellence Scholarship for Least Developed Countries

Subjects: Any field of study
Purpose: The KSP Excellence Scholarship for Least Developed Countries is directed to outstanding students, covering full tuition
Level of Study: Postgraduate
Type: Scholarship
Value: Each recipient is awarded full tuition each year
Frequency: Annual
Country of Study: France
Application Procedure: To apply, please send the following materials by email to program.kuwait@sciencespo.fr with 'KSP Excellence Scholarship LDC Application' in the subject line
Closing Date: 10 January
Contributor: Sciences Po and the Kuwait Foundation for the Advancement of Sciences (KFAS)

For further information contact:

Email: program.kuwait@sciencespo.fr

KSP Fund for Innovative Projects

Purpose: The KSP Fund for Innovative Projects supports extra-curricular student-led initiatives taking place in countries of the Arab World and the Gulf Region. It is aimed at fostering innovation and providing funding for the realization of creative ideas benefiting the region in all sectors
Level of Study: Postgraduate
Value: €5,000–€10,000
Country of Study: Any country
Application Procedure: To apply, please send the following materials with 'KSP Fund for Innovative Projects' in the subject line, by email to the Kuwait Program Assistant fatima.iddahamou@sciencespo.fr
Closing Date: 28 February
Additional Information: Proposed projects must take place in a country of the Arab World or the Gulf Region. For further details, please contact Kuwait Program Assistant, Fatima Iddahamou: fatima.iddahamou@sciencespo.fr www.sciencespo.fr

For further information contact:

Email: kancelaria@ksplegal.pl

KSP Joint Research Projects

Subjects: Social sciences and humanities
Purpose: KSP Joint Research Projects are funded by the Kuwait Program at Sciences Po to foster research links between faculty members at Sciences Po and in Kuwait, in the interest of building a unique scholarly network
Level of Study: Research
Value: Up to €50,000
Length of Study: 1 year
Country of Study: Any country
Application Procedure: Application files should be sent to the Kuwait Program Manager at: mariezenaide.jolys@sciencespo.fr
Closing Date: 31 October
Funding: Foundation
Contributor: Sciences Po and the Kuwait Foundation for the Advancement of Sciences (KFAS)
Additional Information: For details, please check the website: www.sciencespo.fr/psia/kuwait-program

For further information contact:

Email: info@itsr.ir

KSP Mobility Grant – Spring

Purpose: The KSP Mobility Grant programme supports projects of Sciences Po students in countries of the Arab World and the Gulf Region with the objective of enhancing their experience in the region
Eligibility: Sciences Po students of all nationalities may apply. Student projects must take place in a country of the Arab World or the Gulf Region
Level of Study: Postgraduate, Research
Type: Grant
Value: Up to €5,000 per year
Frequency: Annual
Country of Study: Any country
Application Procedure: To apply, please send the following materials to the Kuwait Program Assistant, Fatima Iddahamou, at: fatima.iddahamou@sciencespo.fr with 'KSP Mobility Grant Application Spring' in the subject line
Closing Date: 31 October
Additional Information: For details, please contact Kuwait Program Assistant, Fatima Iddahamou: fatima.iddahamou@sciencespo.fr

For further information contact:

Email: fatima.iddahamou@sciencespo.fr

KSP Visiting Faculty program

Subjects: Social sciences and humanities
Purpose: The KSP Visiting Faculty program offers 1-semester teaching opportunities at the Paris School in International Affairs of Sciences Po (PSIA) for leading specialists of the Arab World and the Gulf Region
Eligibility: This opportunity is open to both professors and practitioners, specialists of the Arab World and the Gulf Region. Individuals of all nationalities may apply
Value: €20,000 and travel allowance of up to €1,500
Country of Study: Any country
Application Procedure: To apply, please send the application in English to the Kuwait Program Manager by email at: mariezenaide.jolys@sciencespo.fr
Closing Date: 31 January
Additional Information: For more information, please visit the Kuwait Program website or contact the Kuwait Program Manager by email at: mariezenaide.jolys@sciencespo.fr

For further information contact:

Email: mariezenaide.jolys@sciences-po.fr

Kuwait Excellence Scholarship for Arab students and Kuwait Nationals

Purpose: The KSP Excellence Scholarship for Arab students intends to support the next generation of leaders and experts coming from the Arab World and the Gulf Region who specialize in the broad field of international affairs. The current call for applications is dedicated to graduate students admitted to the Paris School of International Affairs of Sciences Po (PSIA)
Type: Scholarship
Value: 2-year masters
Country of Study: France
Application Procedure: To apply, please send the following materials by email to program.kuwait@sciencespo.fr with 'KSP Excellence Scholarship Application' in the subject line
Closing Date: 17 February
Funding: Private

Scope

6 Market Road, N7 9PW, London, United Kingdom

Tel: (44) 20 7619 7100
Fax: (44) 20 7619 7380
Email: richard.parnell@scope.org.uk
Website: www.scope.org.uk
Contact: Mr Richard Parnell, Research & Public Policy Manager

Scope is a national disability charity focusing on cerebral palsy. Scope's core value is equality for disabled people.

Charles Pick Fellowship

Purpose: The Charles Pick Fellowship seeks to give support to the work of a new and, as yet, unpublished writer of fictional or non-fictional prose Its purpose is to give promising writers time to devote to the development of his/her talents
Eligibility: Applicants for the Fellowship must be writers of fictional or non-fictional prose in English who have not yet published a book. (please note that for the purposes of this Fellowship non-fiction prose includes, for example, biography, memoir and travel writing. But not critical or historical monographs based on academic research). During the residential period, The Fellow will be required to submit written work to a nominated mentor and take part in Creative Writing Research Seminars
Level of Study: Graduate
Type: Fellowship
Frequency: Annual
Country of Study: Any country
Closing Date: 31 January
Funding: Private
Additional Information: Duration of this fellowship is 6 months. The Fellow will be a member of the School of Literature and Creative Writing. And it is necessary to reside at the University of East Anglia, Norwich, United Kingdom

For further information contact:

Email: charlespickfellowship@uea.ac.uk

Seoul National University

1 Gwanak-ro, Gwanak-gu, Seoul 151 742, Korea

Tel: (82) 822 880 6971, 6977
Fax: (82) 822 873 5021
Email: snuadmit@snu.ac.kr
Website: www.useoul.edu
Contact: MBA Admissions Officer

Korea Foundation Fellowship

Subjects: Fields of Korean research in the humanities and social sciences
Eligibility: Preference is given to Korean nationals residing abroad
Level of Study: Postdoctorate, Postgraduate, Research
Type: Fellowship
Value: To be determined by the review committee
Length of Study: 1 academic year
Frequency: Annual
Study Establishment: Seoul National University
Country of Study: Korea
Application Procedure: Contact the Office of international Affairs
Closing Date: January
Funding: Foundation
Contributor: The Korean Foundation

For further information contact:

Tel: (44) 2 880 8635
Fax: (82) 2 880 8632
Email: yss@snu.ac.kr
Contact: Mr Sung Sub Yoon

Korea-Japan Cultural Association Scholarship

Subjects: Humanities and social-science
Eligibility: Japanese students enroled in undergraduate programs who are not in 1st-year
Level of Study: Postdoctorate, Postgraduate, Research
Type: Scholarship
Value: KRW 3,500,000
Length of Study: 1 academic year
Frequency: Annual
Study Establishment: Seoul National University
Country of Study: Korea
Application Procedure: Contact the Office of International Affairs
Closing Date: March
Funding: Foundation
Contributor: Korea-Japan Cultural Association

For further information contact:

The Office of International Affairs, Korea

Tel: (82) 2 880 8638
Fax: (82) 2 880 8632
Email: sjlim@snu.ac.kr
Contact: Mr Sung Sub Yoon

Overseas Koreans Scholarship

Subjects: Korean studies
Purpose: To support students with an outstanding academic record
Eligibility: Preference is given to Korean students with majors related to Korean studies, in particular: language, literature, medicine, education or IT, which are beneficial to the development of Korea
Level of Study: Postdoctorate, Postgraduate, Research
Type: Scholarship
Value: KRW 800,000, full tuition exemption for 8 months, airfare for one economic round trip, medical insurance, Korean language training
Length of Study: 1 year
Frequency: Annual
Application Procedure: Contact the Overseas Korean Foundation
Closing Date: Application Period: September
Additional Information: For further details, please refer to the website: www.useoul.edu/apply/under/scholarships/before-application

For further information contact:

Education Department, Overseas Korean Foundation, Seocho 2-dong, Seocho-gu, South Korea

Tel: (44) 2 3415 0174
Fax: (82) 2 3415 0118
Email: scholarship@okf.or.kr
Contact: Coordinator

Shastri Indo-Canadian Institute

Room 1402 Education Tower, 2500 University Drive NW Calgary, AL T2N-1N4, Canada

Tel: (1) 403 220 7467
Fax: (1) 403 289 0100
Email: sici@ucalgary.ca
Website: www.ucalgary.ca
Contact: Programme Officer India Studies

The Shastri Indo-Canadian Institute was originally founded to promote studies in the arts, literature, culture, social sciences and the humanities. However, the Institute's mandate now incorporates a rich diversity of disciplines. Today, Shastri Indo-Canadian Institute builds knowledge and understanding between Canada and India by sponsoring academic activities.

Shastri Indo-Canadian Institute Doctoral Research Fellowships

Purpose: It helps the scholars in the following ways. i) Excursion rate return air ticket between India and Canada by the most direct route, and ii) a suitable living and accommodation allowance

Eligibility: 1. Candidates must able to work at least 6 months on doctoral dissertation in Canada. Preference will be given to thesis work on policies related Canada and its foreign policy. 2. Topics may include Democracy & Rule of Law, Economic Development, Environment, Managing Diversity, North American Partnership, Peace and Security, Education and Bilateral ties. Proposals in Comparative studies with substantial Canadian content. 3. To apply for SICI Doctoral Research Fellowships interested candidates must be enrolled in Doctoral program and must have successfully completed non-thesis requirements of the PhD by the time the tenure of the award commences. Proficiency in English and or French is necessary. 4. Only Indian nationals are eligible to apply

Level of Study: Graduate

Type: Fellowship

Frequency: Annual

Country of Study: Canada

Application Procedure: Apply online. Refer the website link. www.sici.org.in To apply for SICI Doctoral Research Fellowships interested candidates must be enrolled in Doctoral program and must have successfully completed non-thesis requirements of the PhD by the time the tenure of the award commences

Closing Date: 15 October

Funding: Private

For further information contact:

The Executive Centre, Level 6, Tower A, Business Bay, Airport Road, Yerwada, Pune 411006, India

Email: siciapplications@sici.org.in

Shastri Institutional Collaborative Research Grant (SICRG)

Purpose: This grant is to support and encourage Institutional collaboration in R&D for a period of two years in the areas in which Institutions from SICI's Indian and Canadian Member Council can benefit. This grant intends to fill information gaps for policy makers and others influencing the policy-making process

Eligibility: 1. Proposed SICRG projects must involve a bi-national research initiative in any of the fields mentioned above. 2. Faculty members/academics/researchers of Canadian and Indian member institutions are eligible to apply for this grant. 3. A list of SICI member institutions is available at the link provided here: www.shastriinstitute.org/member-council. 4. The applicant and co-applicant should be a full-time faculty member of a Canadian or Indian member institution. The receipt of the award is a faculty from an Institution of good standing either from India or Canada who are in the Member Council of SICI

Level of Study: Graduate

Type: Grant

Value: Rs. 1,000000 (disbursement of grant will be in two equal installment of Rs. 5 lakh each year)

Frequency: Annual

Country of Study: Any country

Application Procedure: Apply online at GMS portal www.sicigms.org/login. Major requisites for the application are 1. Project Proposal includes. 2. Project Title. 3. Project Description: (Abstract; Proposal; Schedule including recent and projected activities, names of participants, and articles, monographs, books etc. published in the past year. 4. Project Director/ Canadian partner(s): Curriculum Vitae: 5 pages maximum. 5. Budget: Detailed description and justification of anticipated expenses, as well as the disclosure of other funding sources, including funding requested from SICI. 6. Support in terms of in-kind contribution in the budgetary outlay. 7. Incomplete applications will not be entertained. 8. Employer's endorsement is must for the proposal submission to avoid any unanticipated problem later on. 9. Certificate of Ethical Approval (if applicable). 10. Copy of the Passport

Closing Date: 27 December

Funding: Private

Additional Information: Contact our organisation with the following link. shastriinstitute.org/contact-us

For further information contact:

5 Bhai Vir Singh Marg, New Delhi 110001, India

Email: sici@sici.org.in

Sher-Gil-Sundaram Arts Foundation

3/9, Sector 3, Shanti Niketan, New Delhi 110021, India

Tel: (91) 96813 65997
Email: contact@ssaf.in
Website: www.ssaf.in

Sher-Gil Sundaram Arts Foundation: Installation Art Grant

Subjects: Inaugurating this grant, SSAF offers an abbreviated set of propositions that will, we hope, generate well developed project proposals and a critical discourse before and after the Grant

Purpose: The SSAF Installation Art Grant is premised on the fact that Indian art has been energized since the 1990s by what is broadly termed installation art, but that there is, till today, limited infrastructural and institutional support for such projects

Eligibility: 1. Individuals of Indian origin residing in India, or collectives whose members are Indian nationals residing in India. 2. Artists who currently do not have a grant or a residency where the proposed project has been developed

Level of Study: Postgraduate

Type: Grant

Frequency: Annual

Country of Study: Any country

Closing Date: 28 March

Funding: Foundation

For further information contact:

Email: ssaf.installationart@gmail.com

Shorenstein Asia-Pacific Research Center (APARC)

Encina Hall, Room E301, 616 Serra Street, Stanford University, Stanford, CA 94305-6055, United States of America

Tel: (1) 650 723 9741
Fax: (1) 650 725 2592
Email: sishi@stanford.edu
Website: www.aparc.stanford.edu

Shorenstein Asia-Pacific Research Center (APARC) is an important Stanford venue where faculty and students, visiting scholars and distinguished business and government leaders meet and exchange views on contemporary Asia and United States involvement in the region.

Shorenstein Fellowships in Contemporary Asia

Subjects: Contemporary political, economic and social change in the Asia-Pacific region

Purpose: To financially support research and writing on Asia

Eligibility: Open to candidates who have obtained a PhD

Level of Study: Doctorate, Postdoctorate

Type: Fellowships

Value: The postdoctoral fellowship is a 10-month appointment with a salary rate of US$52,000 plus US$2,000 for research expenses

Length of Study: 10 months

Frequency: Annual

Country of Study: Asia

No. of awards offered: 75+

Application Procedure: Applicants should submit via email brief research statement (not to exceed five typed pages), which describes the research and writing to be undertaken during the fellowship period as well as the proposed publishable product; curriculum vitae and three letters of recommendation

Closing Date: 18 December

Funding: Private

No. of awards given last year: 2

No. of applicants last year: 75+

For further information contact:

Tel: (44) 650 723 2408
Email: shorensteinfellowships@stanford.edu
Contact: Victoria Kwong, Fellowship Coordinator

Shuttleworth Foundation Trust

12 Plein St, Durbanville, Cape Town 7550, South Africa

Website: www.shuttleworthfoundation.org

Feminist Criminology Graduate Research Scholarship

Purpose: The Division on Women and Crime of the American Society of Criminology is now accepting applications for the Feminist Criminology Graduate Research Scholarship, which is designed to recognize an exceptional graduate student in the field of gender and crime

Level of Study: Graduate, Research

Type: Scholarship

Value: US$5,000

Frequency: Annual

Country of Study: Any country
Application Procedure: Winners will be notified by May. Applicants and their research projects may be based anywhere in the world. Applications must be in English
Closing Date: 1 April
Contributor: The scholarship is funded by the royalties from Feminist Criminology, an innovative journal that is dedicated to research related to women, girls, and crime within the context of a feminist critique of criminology
Additional Information: Feminist Criminology is published quarterly by SAGE Publications as the official journal of the Division on Women and Crime (DWC) of the American Society of Criminology. This international publication focuses on research and theory that highlights the gendered nature of crime. For more information, please visit fcx. sagepub.com/

Sickle Cell Disease Foundation of California

5110 Woodleaf Cir 150, Los Angeles, CA 90056-1298, United States of America

Tel:	(1) 323 299 3600
Fax:	(1) 323 299 3605
Email:	scdfc@aol.com
Website:	www.scdrf.org
Contact:	Ms Deborah Jones, Managing Director

Single-Molecule Sensors and NanoSystems International Conference

Subjects: This conference will bring together researchers in the rapidly advancing field of Single Molecule Sensors and nanoSystems
Purpose: Sensor systems have emerged that exhibit extraordinary sensitivity for detecting physical, chemical, and biological entities at the micro/nanoscale. This conference will bring together researchers in the rapidly advancing field of Single Molecule Sensors and nanoSystems
Eligibility: The programme includes research presentations and interactive sessions of esteemed external and ColOpt speakers and a young scientist workshop with talks from rising stars
Level of Study: Graduate
Type: Grant
Frequency: Annual
Country of Study: Any country

Application Procedure: You could proceed with the following application link as mentioned below. www.colopt.eu/winterschool-2019
Closing Date: 22 January
Funding: Private
Additional Information: Micro- and nanosensors by virtue of their small interaction length probe molecules over a dynamic range often inaccessible by other techniques

For further information contact:

Email: s3ic2019@premc.org

Sidney Sussex College

Cambridge University, Sidney Street, CB2 3HU, Cambridge, United Kingdom

Tel:	(44) 1223 338800
Fax:	(44) 1223 338884
Email:	gradtutor@sid.cam.ac.uk
Website:	www.sid.cam.ac.uk
Contact:	Sidney Sussex College Tutor for Graduate Students

Founded in 1596, Sidney Sussex College admits men and women as undergraduates and graduates. The college presently has approximately 200 graduate students, including about 100 working for the PhD degree. The college has excellent sporting, dramatic and musical facilities.

Evan Lewis-Thomas Law Studentships

Subjects: Law and cognate subjects
Purpose: To support students carrying out research or taking advanced courses
Eligibility: There are no eligibility restrictions. Candidates must have shown proficiency in Law and Jurisprudence, normally by obtaining a university degree in Law by August, and they must be or become candidates for the PhD Degree, the Diploma in Legal Studies, the Diploma in International Law, the MPhil Degree (1 year course) in Criminology, or the LLM Degree. Students from other Cambridge Colleges may apply, but if successful they would be expected to transfer their membership to Sidney Sussex College. In the competition for the studentship, no preference will be given to candidates who nominate Sidney Sussex College as their college of first or second choice on their application form
Level of Study: Doctorate, Postgraduate

Type: Scholarship
Value: Up to £12,000 to match with funds administered centrally by the UCAM
Length of Study: 1–3 years
Study Establishment: The University of Cambridge
Country of Study: United Kingdom
Application Procedure: Sidney Sussex is implementing a new online application process. Please refer to the website www.sid.cam.ac.uk/postgrads/scholarships
Closing Date: 1 April
Funding: Private
Contributor: Sidney Sussex College
Additional Information: For further information contact the Tutor for Graduate Students at gradtutor@sid.cam.ac.uk

For further information contact:

Email: graduate.funding@admin.cam.ac.uk

The Gledhill Research Studentship

Subjects: All subjects
Purpose: To provide full support for research leading to a PhD degree
Eligibility: Applicants must apply for a postgraduate place at the University of Cambridge. Students from other Cambridge colleges may apply, but if successful they would be expected to transfer their membership to Sidney Sussex College. In the competition for the studentship, no preference will be given to candidates who nominate Sidney Sussex as their college of first or second choice on their application form
Level of Study: Doctorate
Type: Studentship
Value: Up to £12,000 to match with funds administered centrally by the UCAM
Length of Study: 3 years
Frequency: Dependent on funds available, Every 3 years
Study Establishment: The University of Cambridge
Country of Study: United Kingdom
Application Procedure: Sidney Sussex is implementing a new online application process. Please see the college's website www.sid.cam.ac.uk/postgrads/scholarships for further details
Closing Date: 1 April
Funding: Private
Contributor: Sidney Sussex College
Additional Information: For further information contact the Tutor for Graduate Students. Check website: www.sid.cam.ac.uk/current/postgrads/scholarships for further details

For further information contact:

Email: gradtutor@sid.cam.ac.uk

Sievert Larsson Foundation

Box 23415, CYP -1683 Nicosia, Cyprus

Email: info@sievertlarssonscholarships.org
Contact: The Sievert Larsson Scholarship Foundation

The Sievert Larsson Scholarship Foundation's primary purpose is to facilitate the education of promising students from disadvantaged backgrounds. The Foundation will also facilitate the education of a few high calibre students that have exhibited excellence through their academic achievements.

The Sievert Larsson Scholarship

Purpose: To support students who come from financially vulnerable homes and who would not otherwise have the opportunity to study in Sweden
Level of Study: Postgraduate
Type: Scholarship
Value: Version 1: Full tuition fee waiver (covers 100% of the tuition fees) during the 2-year programme (4 semesters). Version 2: Full tuition fee waiver (covers 100% of the tuition fees) and SEK 230,000 for costs of living during the 2-year programme (4 semesters)
Length of Study: 2 years
Study Establishment: Chalmers University of Technology
Country of Study: Thailand
Application Procedure: Applications for the Sievert Larsson Scholarship are made online via the Chalmers scholarship application form
Closing Date: 16 January
Contributor: The Sievert Larsson Foundation

For further information contact:

Email: info@sievertlarssonscholarships.org

Sigma Theta Tau International

550 West North Street, Indianapolis, IN 46202, United States of America

Tel: (1) 888 634 7575
Fax: (1) 317 634 8188
Email: research@stti.iupui.edu
Website: www.nursingsociety.org
Contact: Tonna M. Thomas, Grants Coordinator

Sigma Theta Tau International exists to promote the development, dissemination and utilization of nursing knowledge. It is committed to improving the health of people worldwide through increasing the scientific base of nursing practice. In support of this mission, the society advances nursing leadership and scholarship, and furthers the utilization of nursing research in healthcare delivery as well as in public policy.

Sigma Theta Tau International/Association of Operating room Nurses Foundation Grant

Subjects: Perioperative nursing

Purpose: To encourage nurses to conduct research related to perioperative nursing practice and contribute to the development of perioperative nursing science

Eligibility: The principal investigator should be a registered nurse with a current license in the perioperative setting and have received a Master's degree in nursing. Membership of either funding organisation is acceptable but not required

Level of Study: Predoctorate

Value: US$10,000

Frequency: Annual

Country of Study: Any country

Application Procedure: Applicants should submit a completed application package for the relevant institution for that year

Closing Date: 1 April

Funding: Private

No. of awards given last year: 1

For further information contact:

Association of Operating Room Nurses, 2170 South Parker Road, Suite 300, CO 80231, United States of America

Tel:	(1) 800 755 2676 ext. 277
Fax:	(1) 303 750 2927
Email:	sbeyea@aorn.org
Contact:	Ms Suzanne Beyea

Sigma Theta Tau International/Association of Perioperative Registered Nurses Foundation Grant

Subjects: Perioperative nursing practice

Purpose: To encourage nurses to conduct research related to perioperative nursing practice and contribute to the development of perioperative nursing science

Eligibility: Applicants must be a registered nurse with a current license in the perioperative setting, or a registered nurse who demonstrates interest in or significant contributions to nursing practice. The principal investigator must have, as a minimum, a Master's degree in nursing. Applicants must submit a completed Association of Perioperative Registered Nurses (AORN) research application. Membership of either organization is acceptable, but not required

Level of Study: Doctorate, Postdoctorate, Postgraduate, Predoctorate

Type: Research grant

Value: US$5,000. Allocation of funds is based on the quality of the research, the future promise of the applicant and the applicant's research budget

Frequency: Annual

Country of Study: Any country

Application Procedure: Applicants must write to the AORN for an application form and general instructions

Closing Date: 1 April

Funding: Private, Foundation

Contributor: The Association of Perioperative Registered Nurses and Sigma Theta Tau International

No. of awards given last year: 1

Additional Information: July is the funding month. Please check at website for more information

For further information contact:

Association of Perioperative Registered Nurses (AORN), 2170 South Parker Road, Suite 400, CO 80231, United States of America

Tel:	(1) 800 755 2676 ext. 207
Fax:	(1) 303 750 2927
Email:	lspruce@aorn.org
Contact:	Lisa Spruce

Sigma Theta Tau International/Rehabilitation Nursing Foundation Grant

Subjects: Rehabilitation nursing

Purpose: To encourage research related to rehabilitation nursing

Eligibility: The applicant must be a registered nurse in rehabilitation or a registered nurse who demonstrates interest in and significantly contributes to rehabilitation nursing. Proposals that address the clinical practice, educational or administrative dimensions of rehabilitation nursing are requested. Quantitative and qualitative research projects will be accepted for review. The principal investigator must have a Master's degree in nursing and an ability to complete the project within 2 years of initial funding

Level of Study: Doctorate, Postdoctorate, Postgraduate, Predoctorate

Type: Research grant

Value: Up to US$4,500

Frequency: Annual

Country of Study: Any country
Application Procedure: Applicants must write to the Rehabilitation Nursing Foundation for details
Closing Date: 1 March
Funding: Private, Foundation
Contributor: The Rehabilitation Nursing Foundation and Sigma Theta Tau International
Additional Information: The funding month is the following January

For further information contact:

Rehabilitation Nursing Foundation, 4700 West Lake Avenue, Glenview, IL 60025, United States of America

Tel: (1) 847 375 4710
Fax: (1) 847 375 4710
Email: info@rehabnurse.org

Silicon Valley Community Foundation

2440 West El Camino Real, Suite 300, Mountain View, CA 94040, United States of America

Tel: (1) 650 450 5400
Fax: (1) 650 450 5401
Email: donorservices@siliconvalleycf.org
Website: www.siliconvalleycf.org

Western Digital Scholarship Program

Purpose: The Western Digital Scholarship Program is available for underprivileged and under-represented students who are majoring in STEM as well as the children and legal dependents of Western Digital Employees. Applicants must have a grade point average of 3.0 or higher
Eligibility: 1. Must be a member of an under-represented ethnicity or gender. 2. Must have a grade point average of 3.0 or higher. 3. Must plan to enroll full-time in an accredited four-year college or university. 4. Must plan to major in science, technology, engineering, or mathematics. 5. Must reside in the United States, China, India, Japan, Malaysia, Philippines, or Thailand. 6. This award is for United States and international students
Level of Study: Graduate
Type: Scholarship
Value: US$5,000
Frequency: Annual
Country of Study: United States of America

Application Procedure: Applications are available on the Silicon Valley Community Foundation website. In addition to a completed application, the applicant must also submit the following: two letters of recommendation (the letters must be from the people listed on the application); an official transcript of grades; a personal statement addressing the topics listed on the application; evidence of financial need as described on the application; and proof of United States citizenship (photocopy of birth certificate, passport or naturalization papers). The complete application packet must be completed online by the deadline date
Closing Date: 3 April
Funding: Foundation

For further information contact:

Tel: (1) 650 450 5530
Email: scholarships@siliconvalleycf.org

Simon Fraser University

8888 University Drive, Burnaby, BC V5A 1S6, Canada

Tel: (1) 604 291 5310
Email: pchhina@sfu.ca
Website: www.business.sfu.ca
Contact: Ms Preet Virk, Manager, Donor Relations

Named after explorer Simon Fraser, SFU opened on September 9, 1965. Taking only 30 months to grow from the idea stage into an almost-completed campus with 2,500 52 Silicon Valley Community Foundation students it was dubbed the 'Instant University'. The original campus has grown into three vibrant campuses in Burnaby, Vancouver and Surrey and SFU's reputation has grown into one of the innovative teaching, research, and community outreach.

Natural Sciences and Engineering Research Council of Canada - Postdoctoral Fellowship Program

Subjects: Mathematics
Purpose: The Postdoctoral Fellowships (PDF) Program provides support to a core of the most promising researchers at a pivotal time in their careers
Eligibility: Open to any graduate student in Simon Fraser University (SFU) using mathematics in their research. You can hold your fellowship at the following institutions. 1. Canadian institutions. 2. provincial research institutions in Canada.

3. other appropriate research laboratories in Canada. 4. Institutions and research institutions abroad

Level of Study: Doctorate, Graduate, Postgraduate
Type: Scholarship
Value: $45,000
Length of Study: Up to 2 years
Frequency: Annual
Study Establishment: Simon Fraser University (SFU)
Country of Study: Canada
Application Procedure: You can apply for a PDF by completing and submitting Form 201, and attaching supporting documents if necessary. For further information, check with the below link., www.nserc-crsng.gc.ca/students-etudiants/pd-np/pdf-bp_eng.asp#apply
Closing Date: 15 October

For further information contact:

350 Albert Street, 16th Floor, Ottawa, ON K1A 1H5, Canada

Email: schol@nserc-crsng.gc.ca

Natural Sciences and Engineering Research Council of Canada Industrial Post-Graduate Scholarships (IPS)

Subjects: Science and engineering
Purpose: To encourage scholars to consider research careers in industry
Eligibility: Open to highly qualified science and engineering graduates
Level of Study: Graduate
Type: Scholarship
Value: $15,000 per year for up to 2 years plus company contribution of $6,000 minimum per year
Length of Study: Up to 2 years
Frequency: Annual
Country of Study: Canada
Application Procedure: Check website for further details
Closing Date: Apply at any time (check details in website)

For further information contact:

Office of the Dean of Graduate Studies, Canada

Email: dcoburn@sfu.ca
Contact: Deena Coburn, Director, Administrative Services

Winter Pilot Award

Purpose: The goal of the Pilot Award is to provide early support for exploratory ideas, particularly those with novel hypotheses

Eligibility: All applicants and key collaborators must hold a PhD, MD or equivalent degree and have a faculty position or the equivalent at a college, university, medical school or other research facility
Level of Study: Graduate
Type: Award
Value: The total budget of a Pilot Award is $300,000 or less
Frequency: Annual
Country of Study: Any country
Application Procedure: Applications must be completed electronically and submitted using forms provided at proposalCENTRAL. Please log in as an applicant, go to the "Grant Opportunities" tab, scroll to Simons Foundation and click "Apply Now" for the SFARI Pilot Award program. Application link is www.sfari.org/grant/pilot-awards-request-for-applications/
Closing Date: 14 September
Funding: Foundation
Additional Information: To that end, the initiative is seeking applications from individuals positioned to conduct bold, imaginative, rigorous, and relevant research

For further information contact:

Email: grants@simonsfoundation.org

Singapore-MIT Alliance for Research and Technology

Singapore-MIT Alliance for Research and Technology Scholars Programme for Postdoctoral Research

Purpose: These awards will provide a unique opportunity for recent or soon to be PhD graduates to participate in the Singapore-MIT Alliance for Research and Technology (SMART) Centre in Singapore, and to become members of an alumni network that we anticipate will continue to evolve
Eligibility: The fellowship recipient would be able to conduct research of his/her own choice in Singapore within, but not necessarily tied closely to, a current project in one of the SMART Interdisciplinary Research Groups
Level of Study: Research
Type: Research grant
Value: $120,000 per year
Frequency: Annual
Country of Study: Any country
Closing Date: 12 April
Funding: Private
Additional Information: For further information on the research grant, check the website link. smart.mit.edu/fellowships/for-post-doctoral-smart-scholars

For further information contact:

Email: smart_scholar@smart.mit.edu

Sir Richard Stapley Educational Trust

PO Box 839, Richmond, TW9 3AL, Surrey, United Kingdom

Email: admin@stapleytrust.org
Website: www.stapleytrust.org
Contact: The Administrator

The Sir Richard Stapley Educational Trust awards grants to graduates studying for higher degrees in the United Kingdom without subject restriction, and to graduates studying medicine as a second degree. The grants are to cover shortfall incurred by the payment of tuition fees.

Sir Richard Stapley Educational Trust Grants

Subjects: Medical, dental and veterinary science as second degrees, and higher degrees in all other subjects
Purpose: To support postgraduate study
Eligibility: Open to graduates holding a First Class (Honours) degree or a good Second Class (Honours) degree (65% or above, or its overseas equivalent, or a Masters or PhD) and who are more than 24 years of age on October 1st of the proposed academic year. Students in receipt of a substantial award from local authorities, the NHS Executive, Industry, Research Councils, the British Academy or other similar public bodies will not normally receive a grant from the Trust. Courses not eligible include electives, diplomas, placements, professional training and intercalated degrees. The Trust does not support students for full-time PhD studies beyond year 3, or part-time PhD studies beyond year 6. Applicants must already be resident in the United Kingdom at the time of application
Level of Study: Postgraduate
Type: Grant
Value: UK£500 and £1,500
Length of Study: Grants are awarded for 1 full academic year in the first instance
Frequency: Annual
Study Establishment: Any appropriate University
Country of Study: United Kingdom
No. of awards offered: 300
Application Procedure: Electronic applications are available in early January. The trust will consider either the first 300 complete applications or all applications received on or before deadline

Closing Date: When first 300 applications are received, or 30 March
Funding: Trusts
No. of awards given last year: 133
No. of applicants last year: 300
Additional Information: Please check at www.stapleytrust.org/wp/about for more information

For further information contact:

Email: admin@stapleytrust.org

Sir William Lister/Dorey Bequest

18 Stephenson Way, NW1 2HD, London, United Kingdom

Sir William Lister/Dorey Bequest

Purpose: To provide personal travel expenses to members and Fellows of the Royal College of Ophthalmologists who are travelling abroad for research or training
Eligibility: Ophthalmologists in training who are citizens of the United Kingdom as well as Members and Fellows of the RCOphth in good standing. Applications are invited for the Sir William Lister and Dorey Bequest Travel Awards
Level of Study: Postgraduate
Type: Grant
Value: £300 – £600
Frequency: Annual
Country of Study: Any country
Application Procedure: 1. Successful applicants will submit a report to the Education Committee on completion of the period of training or research for which the award is granted. 2. The number and value of the awards will be determined by the state of the funds and the candidate's requirement
Closing Date: 28 September
Funding: Private

For further information contact:

Email: vanna.fadda@rcophth.ac.uk

Smithsonian Environmental Research Center (SERC)

Smithsonian Institution, PO Box 28, 647 Contees Wharf Road, Edgewater, MD 21037-0028, United States of America

Tel: (1) 443 482 2217
Email: gustafsond@si.edu
Website: www.serc.si.edu
Contact: Daniel E Gustafson, Jr, Professional Training &
Volunteer Coordinator

Smithsonian Environmental Research Center (SERC) is the world's leading research center for environmental studies of the coastal zone. For over 40 years, SERC has been involved in critical research, professional training for young scientists and environmental education.

Smithsonian Environmental Research Center Graduate Student Fellowship

Subjects: Global climate change, marine invasion biology, forest and wetland ecology, trace element and nutrient cycling, solar UV radiation, water quality, food web dynamics, coastal and upland ecosystems, and plant-herbivore interactions
Purpose: To financially support student research at Smithsonian facilities or research stations
Eligibility: Students must be formally enroled in a graduate program of study at a degree granting institution must have completed at least one full-time semester. Intended for students who have not yet been advanced to candidacy if in a doctoral program
Level of Study: Graduate
Type: Fellowship
Value: US$6,500
Length of Study: 10 weeks
Frequency: Annual
No. of awards offered: 6
Application Procedure: Need to use Smithsonian online academic appointment system
Closing Date: 15 January
Funding: Government
No. of awards given last year: 2
No. of applicants last year: 6

For further information contact:

Email: gustafsond@si.edu
Contact: Daniel Gustafson, Professional Training
Coordinator

Smithsonian Institution-National Air and Space Museum

PO Box 37012, MRC 010, Washington, DC 20013-7012, United States of America

Tel: (1) 202 633 2648
Fax: (1) 202 786 2447
Email: NASM-Fellowships@si.edu
Website: www.airandspace.si.edu
Contact: Ms Collette Williams, Fellowships Programme
Coordinator

Charles A Lindbergh Chair in Aerospace History

Eligibility: Open to senior scholars with distinguished records of publication who are at work on, or anticipate being at work on, books in aerospace history
Type: Fellowship
Value: Replacement of salary and benefits up to a maximum of US$100,000 a year. Research expenses and relocation are negotiable
Length of Study: 12 months
Closing Date: 15 January
Additional Information: For more information, please contact David DeVorkin (DeVorkinD@si.edu) and see website

For further information contact:

Email: PisanoD@si.edu
Contact: Dominick A. Pisano

The Aviation Space Writers Foundation Award

Purpose: To support research on aerospace topics
Type: Grant
Value: US$5,000
Frequency: Every 2 years
Application Procedure: Candidates should submit the online Aviation Space Writers Foundation Award Application form, including (1) a maximum two-page, single-spaced proposal stating the subject of their research and their research goals; (2) a one to two-page curriculum vitae; and (3) a one-page detailed budget explaining how the grant will be spent
Closing Date: 15 January
Additional Information: Award winners are required to provide a summary report in the form of a memorandum to Ms Collette Williams that outlines how the grant was used to accomplish the goals of the project

For further information contact:

Email: pisanod@si.edu
Contact: Dr Dominick A. Pisano

Smithsonian National Air and Space Museum

Website: airandspace.si.edu/
Contact: Miss Collette Williams

A. Verville Fellowship

Subjects: Aviation or space studies
Purpose: To pursue programs of research and writing professional in tone and substance, but addressed to an audience with broad interests
Value: US$55,000 per year
Length of Study: 9 months to 1 year
Country of Study: United States of America
Application Procedure: All applications for the Verville Fellowships must be submitted electronically through the Smithsonian Online Academic Appointment System (SOLAA)
Closing Date: 1 November
Additional Information: For any further queries, please contact NASM-Fellowships@si.edu or call (202) 633-2648

For further information contact:

Email: ˙NASM-Fellowships@si.edu

Charles A. Lindbergh Chair in Aerospace History

Purpose: The Charles A. Lindbergh Chair in Aerospace History is a competitive 12-month fellowship open 15 October, to senior scholars with distinguished records of publication who are at work on, or anticipate being at work on, books in aerospace history
Eligibility: The Lindbergh Chair is open to established and recognized senior scholars with distinguished records of publication who are at work on, or anticipate being at work on, books in aerospace history
Value: US$100,000 per year
Length of Study: 1 year
Frequency: Annual
Country of Study: United States of America
Application Procedure: All applications for the Lindbergh Fellowships must be submitted electronically through the Smithsonian Online Academic Appointment System (SOLAA)
Closing Date: 15 January
Funding: Private
Additional Information: For more information, please contact Layne Karafantis in the Aeronautics Department

(karafantisl@si.edu) or Michael Neufeld in the Space History Department (neufeldm@si.edu)

For further information contact:

Email: christiane@fundit.fr

Engen Conservation

Purpose: This fellowship is intended to contribute to the education of recent graduates by allowing them to continue research into traditional historic objects and delve into the complexities of working with modern composite materials
Eligibility: Must have master's degree in conservation from a recognized programme and be able to conduct research independently
Value: US$37,000 per year in addition to US$3,000 for medical insurance
Length of Study: 1 year
Country of Study: United States of America
Application Procedure: Applications are submitted through the Smithsonian Online Academic Appointment System (SOLAA)
Closing Date: 1 March
Additional Information: For further queries, please contact CollumM@si.edu, Chief Conservator

For further information contact:

Email: CollumM@si.edu

Guggenheim Fellowships

Subjects: Aviation and space history
Purpose: To pursue programs of research and writing that support publication of works that are scholarly in tone and substance and intended for publication as articles in peer-reviewed journals or in book form from a reputable publisher (in the case of post postdoctoral applicants) or in a doctoral dissertation (in the case of pre-docs)
Level of Study: Doctorate, Postdoctorate
Value: US$30,000 for predoctoral candidates and US$45,000 for postdoctoral candidates
Length of Study: 1 year
Country of Study: United States of America
Application Procedure: All applications for the Guggenheim, Verville and Lindbergh Fellowships must be submitted electronically through the Smithsonian Online Academic Appointment System (SOLAA)
Closing Date: 15 January

Additional Information: If you have any further questions, please contact NASM-Fellowships@si.edu or call (202) 633-2648

For further information contact:

John Simon Guggenheim Memorial Foundation, 90 Park Avenue, New York, NY 10016, United States of America

National Air and Space Museum

Subjects: Aerospace studies
Purpose: To support research on aerospace topics
Value: US$5,000
Frequency: Every 2 years
Country of Study: United States of America
Closing Date: 15 January

For further information contact:

Aeronautics Department, MRC 312, National Air and Space Museum, Smithsonian Institution, Washington, DC 20013-7012, United States of America

Email: karafantisl@si.edu
Contact: Layne Karafantis

Smithsonian Tropical Research Institution (STRI)

Roosvelt Avenue, Tupper Building 401, Balboa, Ancón, Panamá, República de Panamá, Washington, DC 20521-9100, United States of America

Tel: (1) 507 212 8000
Fax: (1) 507 212 8148
Email: fellows@si.edu
Website: www.stri.org

The Smithsonian Tropical Research Institution (STRI) in Panama is a bureau of the Smithsonian Institution based outside of the United States and it is dedicated to understanding biological diversity. STRI's facilities provide a unique opportunity for long-term ecological studies in the tropics, and are used extensively by some 900 visiting scientists from academic and research institutions in the United States and around the world every year. STRI aims to offer research facilities that allow staff scientists, fellows, and visiting scientists to achieve their research objectives. STRI's Center for Tropical Forest Science uses large, fully enumerated forest plots to monitor tree demography in 14 countries located in Africa, Asia and the Americas. More than 3,000,000 individual trees representing 6,000 species are being studied.

STRI Postdoctoral Research in Hydrology

Subjects: Hydrology
Eligibility: Open to applicants with a PhD in spatial analysis applied to soils or hydrology, hands-on programming skills, fluency in English and Spanish
Level of Study: Postdoctorate
Type: Research grant
Value: Minimum salary of US$40,000
Length of Study: 2 years
Frequency: Annual
Application Procedure: Applicants should send an electronic copy of the current curriculum vitae, statement of research accomplishments and goals, names and contact information of three references, and reprints to Helmut Elsenbeer. Review of applications begins by July 15th
Closing Date: No closing date, open till position closes

For further information contact:

Email: ElsenbeerH@si.edu
Contact: Helmut Elsenbeer

STRI Tropical Forest/Restoration Ecologist

Subjects: Ecology
Purpose: To support a long-term study to understand the ecosystem services provided by forests within the Panama Canal Watershed
Eligibility: Open to applicants with a PhD in forestry, forest ecology, restoration ecology, or a closely related field, a proven ability to develop research programs and publish in scientific journals, ability to work well in teams, and preferred with Spanish language skills
Level of Study: Doctorate
Value: US$40,000 per year
Frequency: Annual
Application Procedure: Applicants should send a letter detailing qualifications and interest in the position, curriculum vitae, and contact information for three references to Adriana Sautu. For questions related to the position, please contact Jefferson Hall (hallje@si.edu)

Closing Date: 1 August
Additional Information: The successful candidate will work in a multidisciplinary team to design landscape treatments and the vegetation monitoring program for focal research catchments. She will synthesize data from the Native Species Reforestation Project (PRORENA) growth trials to inform species selection for native species reforestation treatments and for publication. The Research Fellow will be expected to develop his/her own research program in association with this project

For further information contact:

Email: sautua@si.edu
Contact: Adriana Sautu

Social Science Research Council (SSRC)

One Pierrepont Plaza, 15th Floor, 300 Cadman Plaza West, Brooklyn, NY 11201, United States of America

Tel: (1) 212 377 2700
Fax: (1) 212 377 2727
Email: info@ssrc.org
Website: www.ssrc.org
Contact: Director

Founded in 1923, the Social Science Research Council (SSRC) is an independent, non-governmental, non-profit international association devoted to the advancement of interdisciplinary research in the social sciences. The aim of the organization is to improve the quality of publicly available knowledge around the world.

African Peacebuilding Network (APN) Residential Postdoctoral Fellowship Program

Purpose: To support independent African research and its integration into regional and global policy communities
Eligibility: Applicants must be African citizens currently residing in an African country. Researchers based in conflict-affected African countries or those recently emerging from conflict are especially encouraged to apply. Applicants must hold a faculty or research position at an African university and have completed their PhD within 7 years of the application deadline
Level of Study: Research
Type: Fellowships
Value: A maximum of US$20,000

Frequency: Annual
Application Procedure: All applications must be uploaded through our online portal. For enquiries or technical questions pertaining to the portal, please contact APN staff (apn@ssrc.org). Unfortunately, due to the volume of applications we receive, no mailed materials will be accepted
Closing Date: December
Additional Information: If you have questions, please contact APN program staff by telephone at (1) 212 377 2700 or by email at apn@ssrc.org

For further information contact:

Tel: (1) 212 377 2700
Email: apn@ssrc.org
Contact: APN program staff

Berlin Program Fellowship

Subjects: Modern and contemporary German and European affairs
Purpose: To support doctoral dissertation research as well as postdoctoral research leading to the completion of a monograph
Eligibility: Applicants for a dissertation fellowship must be full-time graduate students who have completed all coursework required for the PhD and must have achieved ABD status by the time the proposed research stay in Berlin begins. Also eligible are United States of America and Canadian PhD's who have received their doctorates within the past two calendar years
Level of Study: Postdoctorate
Value: €1,100 per month for dissertation fellows, €1,400 per month for postdoctoral fellows
Length of Study: 10 months–1 year
Frequency: Annual
Study Establishment: Freie Universität Berlin
Country of Study: Germany

For further information contact:

Berlin Program for Advanced German and European Studies, Freie Universität Berlin, Germany

Tel: (49) 30 838 56671
Fax: (49) 30 838 56672
Email: bprogram@zedat.fu-berlin.de

ESRC/SSRC Collaborative Visiting Fellowships

Subjects: Social sciences (including history)

Purpose: To encourage communication and cooperation between social scientists in Great Britain and the Americas
Eligibility: Open to PhD scholars in the Americas, ESRC-supported centres, and holders of large grants awards or professorial fellowships in Britain
Level of Study: Doctorate, Research
Type: Fellowship
Value: Up to US$9,500
Length of Study: 1–3 months
Frequency: Annual
Application Procedure: Check website for further details
Closing Date: 16 April

For further information contact:

Email: international@esrc.ac.uk

Eurasia Program Fellowships

Subjects: Social sciences and humanities, with a specific focus on Eurasia
Purpose: To allow advanced graduate students to devote to the intellectual development of their projects and to write-up the results of their research
Eligibility: Applicants for Dissertation Write-up Fellowships must have attained ABD status (must have completed all requirements for the PhD degree except for the dissertation) by the fellowship start date. They must be citizens or permanent residents of the United States of America. The Fellow's home institution is expected to make a cost-sharing contribution of no less than 10% of the fellowship award. Detailed information on eligibility criteria and conditions of awards will be available in the application materials
Level of Study: Doctorate, Graduate
Type: Fellowship
Value: Up to US$25,000
Length of Study: Up to 1 year
Frequency: Annual
No. of awards offered: Approx. 40
Application Procedure: Awards are made on the basis of evaluations and recommendations by the Title VIII Program Committee, an interdisciplinary committee composed of scholars of the region. The committee rewards proposals with clarity of argument, purpose, theory and method, written in a style accessible to readers outside the applicant's discipline. Applicants must submit a completed application, a narrative statement, transcripts, a course list and language evaluation form, and references. Full information is available online
Funding: Government

Contributor: United States Department of State under the Program for Research and Training on Eastern Europe and the Independent States of the Former Soviet Union (Title VIII)
No. of awards given last year: 4
No. of applicants last year: Approx. 40
Additional Information: No funding is available for research on the Baltic States

For further information contact:

Email: eurasia@ssrc.org
Contact: SSRC, Eurasia Program

Japan Society for the Promotion of Science (JSPS) Fellowship

Subjects: Social sciences and humanities
Purpose: To provide qualified researchers with the opportunity to conduct research at leading universities and other research institutions in Japan
Eligibility: Applicants must be United States citizens or permanent residents at the time of application and submit proof of affiliation with an eligible host research institution in Japan as part of the application packet. Permanent residents must provide a copy of a permanent resident card. Citizens of other countries are eligible for the short-term fellowship (1–12 months) if they have completed a Master's or PhD course at an institution of higher education in the United States and, upon completing the course, have for at least three continuous years conducted high-level research at a university in the United States. Applicants for long-term (12–24 months) fellowships must submit a copy of a PhD diploma dated no more than 6 years prior to applying. Check website for further details
Level of Study: Doctorate, Postdoctorate, Research
Type: Fellowship
Value: Round-trip airfare, insurance coverage for accidents and illness, a monthly stipend and settling-in allowance. Applicants will also be eligible for additional funds annually for research expenses for stays of 1–2 years and a domestic travel allowance for stays of 3–12 months
Length of Study: 1 month to 2 years
Frequency: Annual
Study Establishment: An approved institution
Country of Study: Japan
No. of awards offered: 25–40
Application Procedure: Applications are available on www.ssrc.org/fellowships/jsps-fellowships
Closing Date: 1 December
Funding: Government
Contributor: The Japan Society for the Promotion of Science

No. of awards given last year: 10–20
No. of applicants last year: 25–40
Additional Information: Fellows are selected by the Japan Society for the Promotion of Science based on nominations made by the SSRC Japan Advisory Board. Applicants will be notified of their nomination status by the following March. Successful applicants will be notified directly by JSPS in the summer

For further information contact:

Tel: (49) 212 37 2700
Email: japan@ssrc.org

Mellon Mays Predoctoral Research Grants

Subjects: Anthropology and archaeology, area/cultural/ethnic/gender studies, art history, classics, computer science, geography and population studies, earth/environmental/geological science and ecology, English, film, cinema and media studies (theoretical focus), musicology and ethnomusicology, foreign languages and literatures, history, linguistics, literature, mathematics, oceanographic/marine/atmospheric/planetary science, performance studies (theoretical focus) philosophy and political theory, physics and astronomy, religion and theology, sociology, theater (non-performance focus)
Eligibility: Applicants must be a Mellon fellow enroled in a doctoral program. Applicants must have been selected as Mellon Mays Fellows as undergraduates. Fellows may apply for one grant per year and must be enroled in a doctoral program in one of the fields listed in the website or have filed a petition for inclusion of another field
Value: Total of US$5,000 in GSE and PRD funds; DCG grant money is not applied towards this total
Country of Study: Any country
Application Procedure: Applicants should use the online application portal to apply. For detailed information, please visit: www.ssrc.org/fellowships/mellon-mays-predoctoral-research-grants/
Closing Date: 1 November
Additional Information: If accepted, grants take 5–6 weeks to process

Social Science Research Council Abe Fellowship Program

Subjects: Social sciences and related fields relevant to any one or combination of (i) traditional and non-traditional approaches to security and diplomacy; (ii) global and regional economic issues; (iii)the role of civil society

Purpose: To encourage international multidisciplinary research on topics of pressing global concern and to foster the development of a new generation of researchers who are interested in policy-relevant topics of long-range importance and who are willing to become key members of a bilateral and global research network built around such topics
Eligibility: Open to citizens of Japan and the United States of and to other nationals who can demonstrate serious and long-term affiliations with research communities in Japan or the United States. Applicants must hold a PhD or have attained an equivalent level of professional experience. Applications from researchers in non-academic professions are welcome
Level of Study: Postdoctorate
Type: Fellowship
Value: Research and travel expenses as necessary for the completion of the research project in addition to limited salary replacement
Length of Study: Up to 1 year
Frequency: Annual
Study Establishment: An appropriate institution
Country of Study: United States of America
No. of awards offered: 60–100
Application Procedure: Applicants must submit an online application along with a writing sample, letter of reference and an optional language evaluation form
Closing Date: 1 September
Funding: Foundation
Contributor: The Japan Foundation Center for Global Partnership
No. of awards given last year: 14
No. of applicants last year: 60–100
Additional Information: In addition to working on their research projects, Fellows will attend annual conferences and other events sponsored by the program, which will promote the development of an international network of scholars concerned with research on contemporary policy issues. Funds are provided by the Japan Foundation Center for Global Partnership

For further information contact:

Email: abe@ssrc.org

Social Science Research Council Eurasia Program Postdoctoral Fellowships

Subjects: Social sciences and humanities with a specific focus on Eurasia
Purpose: To support research and/or publication records and to further the recipients academic career
Eligibility: Applicants for Postdoctoral Fellowships must have the PhD in hand at the time of application (ABDs will

not be considered), and must have received the degree no more than 5 years prior to the application deadline. They must be citizens or permanent residents of the United States of America. Detailed information on eligibility criteria and conditions of awards will be in the application materials
Level of Study: Doctorate, Postdoctorate
Type: Fellowship
Value: Up to US$20,000
Length of Study: 18–24 months
Frequency: Annual
No. of awards offered: Approx. 30
Application Procedure: Awards are made on the basis of evaluations and recommendations by the Title III Program Committee, an interdisciplinary committee and composed of scholars of the region. The committee rewards proposals with clarity of argument, purpose, theory, and method, written in a style accessible to readers outside the applicant's discipline. Applicants must submit a completed application, a narrative statement, a curriculum vitae and references. Full information is available online
Closing Date: 13 November
Funding: Government
Contributor: United States Department of State under the Program for Research and Training on Eastern Europe and the Independent States of the Former Soviet Union (Title VIII)
No. of awards given last year: Approx. 3
No. of applicants last year: Approx. 30
Additional Information: No funding is available for research on the Baltic States

For further information contact:

Email: eurasia@ssrc.org
Contact: SSRC, Eurasia Program

Social Science Research Council Eurasia Program Predissertation Training Fellowships

Subjects: The social sciences and humanities, with a specific focus on Eurasia
Purpose: To provide graduate students with the opportunity to enhance their research skills in the field of Eurasian Studies
Eligibility: Applicants for Predissertation Training Fellowships must be enrolled in a doctoral programme in the social sciences or humanities or equivalent degree, but not yet advanced to the PhD candidacy. ABD's are not eligible for these fellowships. They must be citizens or permanent residents of the United States of America. Detailed information on eligibility criteria and conditions of awards will be available in the application materials
Level of Study: Doctorate, Graduate
Type: Fellowship

Value: Up to US$7,000
Length of Study: Up to 9 months
Frequency: Annual
Country of Study: United States of America
No. of awards offered: Approx. 20
Application Procedure: Awards are made on the basis of evaluations and recommendations by the Title VIII Program Committee, an interdisciplinary committee composed of scholars of the region. The committee rewards proposals with clarity of argument, purpose, theory, and method, written a style accessible to readers outside the applicant's discipline. Applicants must submit a completed application, a narrative statement, transcripts, a course list and language evaluation form and references. Full information is available online
Closing Date: 13 November
Funding: Government
Contributor: United States Department of State under the Program for Research and Training on Eastern Europe and the Independent States of the Former Soviet Union (Title VIII)
No. of awards given last year: 2
No. of applicants last year: Approx. 20
Additional Information: No funding is available for research on the Baltic States

For further information contact:

Email: eurasia@ssrc.org
Contact: SSRC, Eurasia Program

Social Science Research Council Eurasia Program Teaching Fellowships

Subjects: The social sciences and humanities, with a specific focus on Eurasia
Purpose: To encourage and support faculty members at all career levels in their efforts to impart their own knowledge and expertise to their students
Eligibility: Applicants for the Teaching Fellowships must have the PhD in hand and currently be teaching full-time in an accredited United States of America university, and the must be citizens or permanent residents of the United States of America. The home institution of the Teaching Fellowship recipient is expected to provide a letter of intent stating that the institution or relevant department intends to support the implementation of the Fellow's new course into the offered curriculum at least once within a period of no more than 2 years. Detailed information on eligibility criteria and conditions of awards will be available in the application materials
Level of Study: Postdoctorate
Type: Fellowship
Value: US$10,000

Length of Study: Maximum 2 years
Frequency: Annual
Country of Study: United States of America
No. of awards offered: 15
Application Procedure: Awards are made on the basis of evaluations and recommendations by the Title III Programme Committee, an interdisciplinary committee and composed of scholars of the region. The committee rewards proposals with clarity of argument, purpose, theory, and method, written in a style accessible to readers outside the applicant's discipline. Applicants must submit a completed application, a narrative statement, a curriculum vitae and references. Full information is available online
Closing Date: 1 November (may change annually)
Funding: Government
Contributor: United States Department of State (Title VIII)
No. of awards given last year: 3
No. of applicants last year: 15

For further information contact:

Email: eurasia@ssrc.org
Contact: SSRC, Eurasia Program

Social Science Research Council International Dissertation Research Fellowship

Subjects: Non-United States cultures and societies grounded in empirical and site-specific research (involving fieldwork, research in archival or manuscript collections, or quantitative data collection)
Purpose: To support distinguished graduate students in the humanities and social sciences conducting dissertation research outside the United States
Eligibility: Open to full-time graduate students in the humanities and social sciences regardless of citizenship enroled in doctoral programs in the United States. Applicants must complete all PhD requirements except on-site research by the time the fellowship begins
Level of Study: Doctorate
Type: Fellowship
Value: Approx. US$20,000
Length of Study: 9–12 months
Frequency: Annual
Application Procedure: Applications are available on SSRC website
Closing Date: 3 November
Funding: Private
Contributor: The Andrew W Mellon Foundation
Additional Information: Applicants must contact the programme for further information by emailing

For further information contact:

Email: idrf@ssrc.org

Social Science Research Council Summer Institute on International Migration

Subjects: Social science
Purpose: To enable attendance at a workshop/conference training young scholars in the field of migration studies
Eligibility: Open to advanced doctoral candidates currently involved in research or writing for their dissertations and recent PhDs revising their dissertations for publication or initiating new research
Level of Study: Postdoctorate, Postgraduate, Predoctorate
Type: Award
Value: Flights, meals and lodging necessary for participation in the institute are fully subsidized
Length of Study: 1 Week
Frequency: Dependent on funds available
Study Establishment: The University of California at Irvine
Country of Study: United States of America
No. of awards offered: 250
Application Procedure: Applicants must download the application form from the website www.cri.uci.edu
Closing Date: 18 February
Funding: Private
Contributor: UCT and SSRC
No. of awards given last year: 20
No. of applicants last year: 250
Additional Information: The Institute is a collaboration between the SSRC and the Center for Research on Immigration, Population and Public Policy (CRI) at the University of California, Irvine

For further information contact:

Center for Research on International Migration, United States of America

Tel: (1) 949 824 1361
Email: cbramle@uci.edu
Contact: Carolynn J Bramlett, Administrative Assistant

SSRC/ACLS Eastern European Program Dissertation Fellowships

Subjects: The social sciences and humanities relating to Albania, Bulgaria, the Baltic States, the Czech Republic,

Hungary, Poland, Romania, Slovakia or the former Yugoslavia

Purpose: To fund dissertation research

Eligibility: Open to United States citizens or permanent legal residents

Level of Study: Postgraduate

Type: Varies

Value: Up to US$15,000 plus expenses

Length of Study: 1 academic year

Frequency: Annual, if funds are available

Study Establishment: Any university or institution

Country of Study: Other

Application Procedure: Applicants must contact the American Council of Learned Societies (ACLS) for further information

Closing Date: November

Additional Information: The product of the proposed work must be disseminated in English

For further information contact:

ACLS Office of Fellowships & Grants, 228 East 45th Street, New York, NY 10017, United States of America

Email: grants@acls.org

Social Sciences and Humanities Research Council of Canada (SSHRC)

350 Albert Street, PO Box 1610, Ottawa, ON K1P 6G4, Canada

Tel: (1) 613 995 2694
Fax: (1) 613 992 2803
Email: award@sshrc-crsh.gc.ca
Website: www.sshrc-crsh.gc.ca

The Social Sciences and Humanities Research Council of Canada (SSHRC) is the federal agency responsible for promoting and supporting research and research training in the social sciences and humanities in Canada. SSHRC supports research on the economic, political, social and cultural dimensions of the human experience.

Aid to Scholarly Journals

Subjects: Social sciences and humanities

Purpose: To promote the sharing of research results by assisting the publication of individual works that

make an important contribution to the advancement of knowledge

Eligibility: Applicants must consult the Canadian Federation for the Humanities and Social Sciences website for eligibility requirements

Level of Study: Postdoctorate, Research

Type: Grant

Value: Up to $30,000 per year

Length of Study: 3 years

Frequency: Annual

Application Procedure: Applicants must refer to the website or email the Humanities and Social Sciences Federation of Canada

Closing Date: 2 June

Funding: Government

Additional Information: The program is administered on behalf of SSHRC by the Humanities and Social Sciences Federation of Canada

For further information contact:

The Humanities and Social Sciences Federation of Canada, 151 Slater Street, Ottawa, ON, Canada

Tel: (1) 613 238 6112 ext 350
Email: secaspp@fedcan.ca

Canadian Forest Service Graduate Supplements

Subjects: Forestry and related fields

Purpose: To promote Canadian doctoral research into forestry, to encourage the use of Canadian Forest Service (CFS) centres and to increase contacts between CFS researchers and Canadian universities

Eligibility: Open to SSHRC Doctoral Fellows who are conducting research in an area related to forestry in Canada and who are in the 3rd or 4th year of their programme. Candidates must have at least one CFS scientist on their supervisory committee and must carry out all or part of their research at a CFS forestry centre

Level of Study: Doctorate, Predoctorate, Research

Type: Supplement or Fellowship

Value: C$5,000 supplement to the C$20,000 doctoral fellowship

Length of Study: Up to 2 years

Frequency: Annual

Application Procedure: Applicants must visit the website

Closing Date: Interested doctoral students should contact their department for the SSHRC Doctoral Fellowship application deadline

Funding: Government, Foundation

Contributor: The Canadian Forest Service

For further information contact:

Canadian Forest Service Graduate Supplements, Science Branch, Natural Resources Canada, 580 Booth Street, Ottawa, ON, Canada

Tel: (1) 613 947 8992
Fax: (1) 613 947 9090
Email: mlamarch@nrcan.gc.ca
Contact: Programme Co-ordinator

Canadian Tobacco Control Research Initiative Planning Grants

Subjects: Tobacco control policies and practices from the perspectives of the social sciences, humanities, education and health
Purpose: To support investigators in developing strong proposals for grants in tobacco control research
Eligibility: Open to experts in programme and policy development as well as researchers
Level of Study: Research
Type: Grant
Value: Up to C$30,000
Length of Study: Up to 1 year
Frequency: Dependent on funds available
Country of Study: Canada
Application Procedure: Applicants must complete an application form available with instructions on the National Cancer Institute of Canada website www.ncic.cancer.ca
Closing Date: 1 March
Funding: Government, Private
No. of awards given last year: 6

For further information contact:

Research Programs Department National Cancer Institute of Canada (NCIC)10 Alcorn Avenue Suite 200, Toronto, ON, Canada

Tel: (1) 416 961 7223
Email: mwosnick@cancer.ca

Society for Promotion of Roman Studies

Roman Society, Room 252, South Block, Senate House, Malet Street, WC1E 7HU, London, United Kingdom

Tel: (44) 20 7862 8727
Fax: (44) 20 7862 8728

Email: office@romansociety.org
Website: www.romansociety.org
Contact: Dr Fiona Haarer, Secretary of Society

The Society for the Promotion of Roman Studies aims to promote the study of history, architecture, archaeology, language, literature and the art of Italy and the Roman Empire, including Roman Britain, from the earliest times to about 700 AD.

Hugh Last Fund and General Fund

Subjects: History, language and literature of the Roman empire
Purpose: To assist in the undertaking, completion, or publication of works relating to the general scholarly purposes of the Roman Society, excluding expenses in connection with archaeological projects. The Hugh Last Fund also excludes travelling, hotel, conference, or other living expenses of scholars
Level of Study: Graduate, Postdoctorate, Postgraduate, Research
Type: Funding support
Value: Varies £100–1,000
Frequency: Annual
Country of Study: Any country
Application Procedure: Applications should be made using the application form – the completed application should not exceed two sides of A4. Applicants should give a concise and clear outline of the project, including publication plans if relevant, and itemise the costs requested. They must declare any other applications being made for the same project. Completed applications should be sent to the Secretary by email: office@romansociety.org. Download the application form from www.romansociety.org/grants-prizes/hugh-last-fund.html. See the guidelines and download an application form from: www.romansociety.org/grants-prizes/hugh-last-fund-general-fund.html
Closing Date: 31 January
Additional Information: Individuals may not make more than one application in any year

For further information contact:

Email: office@romansociety.org

Society for the Arts in Religious and Theological Studies (SARTS)

United Theological Seminary of the Twin Cities, 3000 5th Street NW, New Brighton, MN 55112, United States of America

Tel: (1) 651 255 6117, 651 255 6190
Fax: (1) 651 633 4315
Email: wyates@unitedseminary-mn.org
Website: www.artsmag.org
Contact: Wilson Yates

The Society for the Arts in Religious and Theological Studies (SARTS) was organized to provide a forum for scholars and artists interested in the intersections between theology, religion and the arts to share thoughts, challenge ideas, strategize approaches in the classroom and to advance the discipline in theological and religious studies.

Luce Fellowships

Subjects: Intersection of theology and art
Purpose: To enhance and expand the conversation on theology and art
Eligibility: Open to candidates teaching theology as a faculty member at an accredited postsecondary educational institution or graduate students
Level of Study: Graduate, Research
Type: Fellowships
Value: Awards are up to US$3,000 each
Length of Study: 1 year
Frequency: Annual
Application Procedure: Applicants must submit an information sheet, curriculum vitae, a project abstract, a formal proposal, a budget and 2 letters of recommendation
Closing Date: 15 May

For further information contact:

University of St Thomas, Mail JRC 153 2115 Summit Avenue, MN 55105, United States of America

Email: office@societyarts.org
Contact: Kayla Larson

Society for the Psychological Study of Social Issues (SPSSI)

SPSSI Central Office, 208 I Street NE, Washington, DC 20002-4340, United States of America

Tel: (1) 202 675 6956
Fax: (1) 202 675 6902
Email: spssi@spssi.org

Website: www.spssi.org
Contact: Alex Ingrams, Administrative Assistant

The Society for the Psychological Study of Social Issues (SPSSI) is an interdisciplinary, international organization of over 3,000 social scientists who share an interest in research on the psychological aspects of important social issues. The Society's goals are to increase the understanding of social issues through research and its dissemination and to support policy efforts consistent with such research.

Society for the Psychological Study of Social Issues Grants-in-Aid Program

Subjects: Scientific research in social problem areas related to the basic interests and goals of SPSSI and particularly those that are not likely to receive support from traditional sources
Purpose: To support scientific research in social problem areas related to the basic interests and goals of SPSSI
Eligibility: Applicant must be a member of SPSSI. Applicants may submit only one application per deadline. If applied to the Clara Mayo Grant in the same award year he/she is not eligible for GIA. Individuals may submit a joint application
Level of Study: Doctorate, Graduate, Postdoctorate, Postgraduate
Type: Grant
Value: Up to US$2,000 for postdoctoral work and up to US$1,000 for graduate student research that must be matched by the student's university
Country of Study: Any country
No. of awards offered: Approx. 18
Application Procedure: The Application should include: (1) A cover sheet with the applicant's name, address, phone number, email address and title of the proposal. (2) An abstract of 100 words or less summarizing the proposed research. (3) Project purposes, theoretical rationale, and research methodology and analytical procedures to be employed. (4) Relevance of research to SPSSI goals and Grants-in-Aid criteria. (5) Status of human subjects review process (which must be satisfactorily completed before grant funds can be forwarded). (6) Curriculum vitae of investigator (a faculty sponsor's recommendation must be provided if the investigator is a graduate student; support is seldom awarded to students who have not yet reached the dissertation stage). (7) Specific amount requested, including a budget. For co-authored submissions, please indicate only one name and institution to which a check should be jointly issued if selected for funding
Closing Date: 15 May and 20 October
Funding: Private

Contributor: The Sophie and Shirley Cohen Memorial Fund and membership contributions
No. of awards given last year: Approx. 10
No. of applicants last year: Approx. 18
Additional Information: Late applications may be held until the next deadline. Proposals for highly timely and event-oriented research may be submitted at any time during the year to be reviewed within 1 month of receipt on an ad hoc basis. If yours is a time-sensitive application, please indicate that on the outside of the envelope

For further information contact:

Email: awards@spssi.org

Society for the Scientific Study of Sexuality (SSSS)

881 Third Street, Suite B-5, Whitehall, PA 18052, United States of America

Tel: (1) 610 443 3100
Fax: (1) 610 443 3105
Email: thesociety@sexscience.org
Website: www.sexscience.org
Contact: Mr David L Fleming, Executive Director

The Society for the Scientific Study of Sexuality (SSSS) is an international organization dedicated to the advancement of knowledge about sexuality. The Society brings together an interdisciplinary group of professionals who believe in the importance of both production of quality research and the clinical, educational and social applications of research related to all aspects of sexuality.

Society for the Scientific Study of Sexuality Student Research Grants

Subjects: Human sexuality
Eligibility: Applicants must be a member of the SSSS
Level of Study: Doctorate, Postgraduate
Type: Scholarship
Value: US$1,000
Length of Study: 1 year
Frequency: Annual
Application Procedure: Contact the society or check website for details

Closing Date: 1 February and 1 June
Funding: Foundation
Contributor: The Foundation for the Scientific study of sexuality

For further information contact:

Email: mlpeters@sexscience.org

Society of Apothecaries of London

Black Friars Lane, EC4V 6EJ, London, United Kingdom

Tel: (44) 20 7236 1189
Fax: (44) 20 7329 3177
Email: clerk@apothecaries.org
Website: www.apothecaries.org
Contact: Wallington Smith, Clerk

Gillson Scholarship in Pathology

Subjects: Pathology
Purpose: To encourage original research in any branch of pathology
Eligibility: Open to candidates under 35 years of age who are either licenciates or freemen of the Society, or who will obtain the licence or the freedom within 6 months of election to the scholarship
Level of Study: Postgraduate
Type: Scholarship
Value: UK£1,800 in total. Payments are made twice annually for the duration of the scholarship
Length of Study: 3 years, renewable for a second term of 3 years
Frequency: Every 3 years
Country of Study: Any country
Application Procedure: Applicants must submit two testimonials and present evidence of their attainments and capabilities as shown by any papers already published, and a detailed record of any pathological work already done. Candidates should also state where the research will be undertaken
Closing Date: 1 December
Funding: Private
Additional Information: Preference is given to the candidate who is engaged in the teaching of medical science or in its research. Scholars are required to submit an interim report at the end of the first 6 months of tenure, and

a complete report 1 month prior to the end of the 3rd year. Any published results should also be submitted to the Society

For further information contact:

Email: admin@scholarship-positions.com

Society of Architectural Historians (SAH)

1365 North Astor Street, Chicago, IL 60610, United States of America

Tel:	(1) 312 573 1365
Fax:	(1) 312 573 1141
Email:	info@sah.org
Website:	www.sah.org

SAH is an international not-for-profit membership organization that promotes the study and preservation of the built environment worldwide. The Society serves scholars, professionals in allied fields and the interested general public.

American Council of Learned Societies Digital Extension Grants

Purpose: ACLS invites applications for ACLS Digital Extension Grants, made possible by the generous assistance of The Andrew W. Mellon Foundation. This program supports digitally based research projects in all disciplines of the humanities and related social sciences. It is hoped that these grants will advance humanistic scholarship by enhancing established digital projects and extending their reach to new communities of users
Eligibility: The project must be hosted by an institution of higher education in the United States. The project's principal investigator must be a scholar in a field of the humanities and the; humanistic social sciences. The principal investigator must have a PhD degree conferred prior to the application; deadline. (An established scholar who can demonstrate the equivalent of the PhD in; publications and professional experience may also qualify.)
Level of Study: Graduate
Type: Grant
Length of Study: 12 – 18 months
Frequency: Annual

Country of Study: Any country
Application Procedure: 1. Applicants must list current and past funding sources for their projects; in the case of joint funding sources for the project. 2. Applicants should indicate clearly in their budget plans how each source of project funding will be used during the ACLS grant period. 3. Awards provide funding of up to US $150,000 for project costs. A portion of grant funds must go towards collaborations with new project partners who could benefit from access to the infrastructure at the project's host site or from substantive participation in the development of the project. 4. Grants may be used to cover salary replacement, staffing, equipment, and other costs. 5. Tenure: 12–18 months, to be initiated between 1 July and 31 December
Closing Date: 16 January
Funding: Private

For further information contact:

Email: fellowships@acls.org

Edilia and François-Auguste de Montequin Fellowship in Iberian and Latin American Architecture

Subjects: Spanish, Portuguese or Ibero American architecture, including colonial architecture produced by the Spaniards in the Philippines and what is today the United States of America
Purpose: To fund travel for research into Spanish, Portuguese and Ibero American architecture
Eligibility: Open to SAH members who are junior Scholars, including graduate students
Level of Study: Doctorate, Postdoctorate, Postgraduate
Type: Fellowship
Value: US$2,000 for junior scholars awarded each year and US$6,000 for senior scholars offered every 2 years
Country of Study: Any country
No. of awards offered: 5
Application Procedure: Applicants must complete an application form, available on request by writing to SAH for guidelines or visiting the SAH website
Closing Date: 16 October
Funding: Private
No. of awards given last year: 1
No. of applicants last year: 5

For further information contact:

Email: vnelson@unm.edu

Sally Kress Tompkins Fellowship

Subjects: Architectural history and historic preservation
Purpose: To enable an architectural history student to work as an intern on an Historic American Buildings Survey project, during the summer
Eligibility: Open to architectural history and historic preservation students
Level of Study: Doctorate, Postdoctorate, Postgraduate
Type: Fellowship
Value: US$10,000
Length of Study: 12 weeks
Frequency: Annual
Country of Study: United States of America
Application Procedure: Applicants must submit an application including a sample of work, a letter of recommendation from a faculty member, and a United States Government Standard Form 171, available from HABS or most United States government personnel offices. Applications should be sent to the Sally Kress Tompkins Fellowship. Applicants not selected for the Tomkins Fellowship will be considered for other HABS Summer employment opportunities. For more information, please contact Lisa P. Davidson, HABS/HAER Co-ordinator
Closing Date: 31 December
Funding: Government
No. of awards given last year: 1

For further information contact:

The Sally Kress Tompkins Fellowship, c/o HABS/HAER, National Park Service, 1201 Eye Street, 7th floor NW, United States of America

Tel:	(1) 202 354 2179
Fax:	(1) 202 371 6473
Email:	lisa.davidson@nps.gov

Society of Women Engineers (SWE)

203 N. La Salle Street, Suite 1675, Chicago, IL 60601, United States of America

Tel:	(1) 877 793 4636
Fax:	(1) 312 596 5252
Email:	hq@swe.org
Website:	www.swe.org
Contact:	Ms Karen Horting, Executive Director

The Society of Women Engineers (SWE) was founded in 1950, and is a non-profit educational service organization.

SWE is the driving force that establishes engineering as a highly desirable career aspiration for women. SWE empowers women to succeed and advance in those aspirations and be recognized for their life-changing contributions and achievements as engineers and leaders.

Society of Women Engineers Past Presidents Scholarships

Subjects: Engineering
Eligibility: Open only to women majoring in engineering or computer science in a college or university with an ABET accredited programme. United States of America citizenship is required
Level of Study: Doctorate, Graduate, Postgraduate
Type: Scholarship
Value: US$2,000
Frequency: Annual
Country of Study: United States of America
Application Procedure: Application forms are available from the website
Closing Date: 1 February
Funding: Private
No. of awards given last year: 2

For further information contact:

Email: hg@swe.org

Sodertorn University

SWE-141 89 Huddinge, Sweden

Contact:	Södertörn University Registrar

Sodertorn University is a public university located in Flemingsberg, which is located in Huddinge Municipality, and the larger area called Södertörn, in Stockholm County, Sweden. In 2013, it had about 13,000 full-time students.

Södertörn University Tuition Fee Waive

Subjects: Scholarships are awarded to study the subjects offered by the university
Purpose: Sodertorn University is offering tuition fee waiver for pursuing master's programme studies
Eligibility: Students who have applied for a one or two-year Master's programme at Södertörn University may submit an application for a tuition fee waiver

Level of Study: Postgraduate
Length of Study: 1 to 2 years
Country of Study: Sweden
Application Procedure: Send the application form along with necessary supporting documents to the following email address: registrator@sh.se
Closing Date: 10 March

For further information contact:

Email: studentservice@sh.se

Soil and Water Conservation Society (SWCS)

945 SW Ankeny Road, Ankeny, IA 50023, United States of America

Tel: (1) 515 289 2331
Fax: (1) 515 289 1227
Email: swcs@swcs.org
Website: www.swcs.org

The Soil and Water Conservation Society (SWCS) fosters the science and the art of soil, water and related natural resource management to achieve sustainability. The SWCS promotes and practices an ethic recognizing the interdependence of people and the environment.

The Kenneth E. Grant Scholarship

Subjects: Soil science, water science and related natural resource management
Purpose: To actively promote multi-disciplinary research
Eligibility: An applicant for the research scholarship must: be a member of SWCS for at least 1 year by the scholarship due date, as recognized by headquarters; have demonstrated integrity, ability, and competence to complete the specified study topic; be eligible for graduate work at an accredited institution; and show reasonable need for financial assistance
Level of Study: Postgraduate
Type: Scholarship
Value: US$1,300
Length of Study: 1 year
Frequency: Annual
Application Procedure: The scholarship application can be filled out and submitted electronically at swcs.formstack. com/forms/2015_kenneth_e_grant_research_scholarship_ application. All supplemental materials can be uploaded

during the online application process or you can mail or email the materials to Soil and Water Conservation Society
Closing Date: 12 February

For further information contact:

Email: awards@swcs.org

South African Association of Women Graduates (SAAWG)

Post Suite 495, Post Bag X9, Benmore 2010, South Africa

Tel: (27) 11 883 4847
Fax: (27) 11 883 4847
Email: medwards@netactive.co.za
Website: www.ifuw.org/southafrica
Contact: Miss Margaret Edwards, National President

The South African Association of Women Graduates (SAAWG) promotes the tertiary education of women and their self-development over their life span. It seeks and facilitates equity for women graduates, cross-cultural insights and co-operation and societal advancement. Its great underlying purpose is world peace, brought about through education and international friendship. SAAWG is affiliated to the International Federation of University Women (IFUW) and is a member of the Federation of University Women of Africa (FUWA).

Hansi Pollak Scholarship

Subjects: Any branch of the social sciences
Purpose: To assist postgraduate study or research devoted to the practical purpose of ameliorating social conditions in South Africa
Eligibility: Open to South African women graduates of all races who are, or have become, members of the Association
Level of Study: Doctorate, Postgraduate
Type: Scholarship
Value: Rand 6,000 paid in 6-month installments
Length of Study: 2 years, non-renewable
Frequency: Every 2 years
Study Establishment: Any recognized university
Country of Study: Any country
No. of awards offered: 50
Application Procedure: Applicants must write for application forms
Funding: Private

No. of awards given last year: 1
No. of applicants last year: 50
Additional Information: Fellows must spend at least 2 years in South Africa after completing a Master's or doctoral degree, in order to put into practice the results of the research

For further information contact:

Post suite 329, Private Bax X18, South Africa

Email: hbowen@telkomsa.net
Contact: Hansi Pollak Fellowship Secretariat

Isie Smuts Research Award

Subjects: All subjects
Purpose: To assist postgraduate women in research
Eligibility: Open to members of the SAAWG
Level of Study: Postgraduate
Type: Award
Value: Rand 1,000
Frequency: Annual
Study Establishment: Any university
Country of Study: South Africa
Application Procedure: Applicants must write to Miss V Henley
Closing Date: 31 October
Funding: Private
No. of awards given last year: 1

For further information contact:

Email: fellowships@saawg.org

South African Association of Women Graduates International Fellowship

Subjects: All subjects
Purpose: To assist women, who wish to study in South Africa
Eligibility: Open to members of the International Federation of University Women, foreign students enrolled at a - South African university for at least one year for postgraduate research
Level of Study: Postgraduate
Type: Fellowship
Value: At least Rand 1,000
Length of Study: Not less than 6 months
Frequency: Every 3 years
Study Establishment: A university
Country of Study: South Africa
Application Procedure: Applicants must write for application forms

Closing Date: 31 August
Funding: Private
Additional Information: The award is made when a suitable applicant applies

For further information contact:

Email: fellowships@saawg.org

South African Council for English Education (SACEE)

Post Net Suite 141, Private Bag X0001, IFAFI, N. W. Province 0260, South Africa

Tel: (27) 12 259 1429
Email: sacee12@telkomsa.net
Website: www.sacee.org.za
Contact: Ms Patricia Bootland, Administrative Secretary

The South African Council for English Education's (SACEE) mission statement is to support the teaching, learning and appreciation of English. They have branches throughout South Africa, and major national projects are the *English Alive* publication, English Olympiad, language challenge and plays festival.

South African Council for English Education's EX-PCE Bursary

Subjects: English and subjects in English, including literature, drama or radio
Purpose: To assist teachers in service who wish to improve their qualifications and to assist those who wish to take up postgraduate study specializing in the English language
Eligibility: Applicants who are not normally resident in the Pretoria area will not be considered for an award. Such applications will not be acknowledged
Level of Study: Postgraduate
Type: Bursary
Value: Varies, depending upon type of course taken
Length of Study: Varies
Frequency: Annual
Study Establishment: Any academic institution
Country of Study: South Africa
No. of awards offered: 3
Application Procedure: An application form must be completed. Interview by a local (Pretoria) selection committee may be required. Application can be sent through post, fax or email

Closing Date: 31 July of the year preceding that for which the bursary is required
Funding: Private
No. of awards given last year: 1
No. of applicants last year: 3

For further information contact:

Email: sacee@iburst.co.za
Contact: Director of Bursaries

South African Institute of International Affairs (SAIIA)

Jan Smuts House, PO Box 31596, Johannesburg, Braamfontein 2017, South Africa

Tel: (27) 11 339 2021
Fax: (27) 11 339 2154
Email: info@saiia.org.za
Website: www.saiia.org.za
Contact: Mr Jonathan Stead, Director of Operations

The South African Institute of International Affairs (SAIIA) is an independent, non-governmental foreign policy think tank, whose purpose is to encourage wider and more informed interest in international affairs and public education and to focus on policy-relevant research.

South African Institute of International Affairs Konrad Adenauer Foundation Research Internship

Subjects: Politics, international relations, journalism and economics
Purpose: To enable research interns to enrol at the University of Witwatersrand for a Master's degree by coursework while simultaneously working at SAIIA
Eligibility: Open to South African citizens under 30 years of age
Level of Study: Postgraduate
Type: Internship
Value: Full bursary for tuition fees and a monthly stipend to cover living costs and accommodation
Length of Study: 10 months
Frequency: Annual
Study Establishment: SAIIA and the University of Witwatersrand
Country of Study: South Africa
No. of awards offered: 32

Application Procedure: Applicants must send a curriculum vitae, names and contact details of three referees, letter of motivation, outline of research interests in the field of international relations, three written references, June results and academic transcripts of previous degree and one example of written work not exceeding 3,000 words on a topic of choice
Closing Date: 8 October
Funding: Foundation
Contributor: Konrad Adenauer Foundation
No. of awards given last year: 2
No. of applicants last year: 32

For further information contact:

Email: grobbelaarn@saiia.wits.ac.za

Southern African Music Rights Organization (SAMRO) Endowment for the National Arts

PO Box 31609, Johannesburg, Braamfontein 2017, South Africa

Tel: (27) 11 712 8000
Fax: (27) 11 403 1934
Email: customerservices@samro.org.za
Website: www.samro.org.za
Contact: J C Otto, Liaison & Research Officer

Southern African Music Rights Organization (SAMRO) is Southern Africa's society of composers and lyricists, administering the performing, transmission and broadcasting rights in the musical works of its members and the members of its affiliated societies. Through the SAMRO Endowment for the National Arts (SENA), it encourages the development of the arts by combining funding with support and advisory services to individuals and organizations to enable them to further their music education, composer careers and more.

Southern African Music Rights Organization Overseas Scholarship

Subjects: Music
Purpose: To encourage music study at the postgraduate level in the western art/choral or jazz popular music genres
Eligibility: Open to postgraduate students who are citizens of South Africa, Botswana, Lesotho or Swaziland. The age limit is 34 years
Level of Study: Postgraduate
Type: Scholarship

Value: Rand 160,000 plus travel expenses of up to Rand 10,000
Length of Study: 2 years
Frequency: Annual
Study Establishment: An institute or educational entity approved by the SAMRO Endowment for the National Arts (SENA)
Country of Study: United Kingdom, Europe or North America
No. of awards offered: 13
Application Procedure: Applicants must complete an application form
Closing Date: 31 May
Funding: Private
Contributor: SAMRO
No. of awards given last year: 2
No. of applicants last year: 13
Additional Information: Please see the website for further details

For further information contact:

Tel: (27) 11 712 8444/11 712 8417
Email: anriette.chorn@samro.org.za
Contact: Anriette Chorn

Southern African Music Rights Organization Postgraduate Bursaries for Indigenous African Music Study

Subjects: Music
Purpose: To encourage the study of indigenous African music at the postgraduate level in either the traditional, western art/choral or jazz popular music genres
Eligibility: Open to postgraduate students who are citizens of South Africa, Botswana, Lesotho or Swaziland. The age limit is 40 years
Level of Study: Postgraduate
Type: Bursary
Value: Rand 5,500
Length of Study: 5 years
Frequency: Annual
Study Establishment: A university or other recognized statutory institute of tertiary education approved by the trustees and situated in SAMRO's current territory of operation
Country of Study: South Africa, Botswana, Lesotho, or Swaziland
No. of awards offered: 5
Application Procedure: Applicants must complete an application form
Closing Date: 1 March
Funding: Private

Contributor: SAMRO
No. of awards given last year: 4
No. of applicants last year: 5
Additional Information: Applicants must produce an official letter of acceptance from a recognized tertiary institute of learning. They must have acceptance into the 1st year or any subsequent year of a postgraduate degree in indigenous African music at such an institute

For further information contact:

Tel: (27) 11 489 5000
Fax: (27) 11 403 1934
Email: sena@samro.org.za

Southern African-Nordic Center (SANORD)

SANORD Central Office, University of the Western Cape, Private Bag x17, Bellville, ZA 7535, South Africa

Website: www.sanord.net/

The Southern African-Nordic Centre is a non-profit membership organization of institutions of higher education and research for all Nordic countries and southern Africa.

Brain O'Connell (BOC) Partial Scholarship

Subjects: The Partial Scholarship Funding Programme of SANORD has been renamed the 'Brian O'Connell Partial Scholarship Programme' in honour of the major contributions Prof O'Connell has made to SANORD over the years. SANORD is making available partial scholarship opportunities for students from the Southern Africa institutions of higher education and research. Successful students will be required to spend 3 to 5 months at a Nordic (Norway, Sweden, Finland, Iceland or Denmark) SANORD member institution in order to engage in activities that will support the completion of the students' Master's degree
Purpose: SANORD is making available partial scholarship opportunities for students from the Southern Africa institutions of higher education and research
Eligibility: Enrolled for mainly Master's degrees at a SANORD member, Southern African institution. Must be willing to enhance their knowledge in order to make a contribution toward the development of Southern Africa. The applicant must liaise with the SANORD Coordinator at the host university and provide a written communication of acceptance from a host university

Level of Study: Postgraduate

Length of Study: Successful students will be required to spend 3 to 5 months at a Nordic (Norway, Sweden, Finland, Iceland or Denmark) SANORD member institution in order to engage in activities that will support the completion of the students' Master's degree

Country of Study: Any country

Application Procedure: Please check website for more details

Closing Date: 30 September

For further information contact:

Email: sanordcentraloffice@gmail.com

Southern Cross University

Graduate Research College, PO Box 157, Lismore, NSW 2480, Australia

Tel: (61) 2 6620 3705
Fax: (61) 2 6626 9145
Email: jrussell@scu.edu.au
Website: www.scu.edu.au
Contact: Mr John Russell, Administrative Officer

Southern Cross University is one of Australia's most modern, creative and innovative universities founded on traditions of academic excellence, with national and international industry links. The University's courses emphasize real-world skills and vocational training, and are designed to give graduates a competitive edge in today's demanding employment market.

Master of Business Administration Programme

Subjects: MBA

Length of Study: Please contact the Organisation

Application Procedure: Applicants must complete the application form, supply evidence of any previous academic qualifications, as well as a curriculum vitae and a letter of support from your employer

Closing Date: 30 November of the previous year

For further information contact:

Tel: (61) 2 6620 3876
Fax: (61) 2 6620 3227
Email: intoff@scu.edu.au
Contact: MBA Admissions Officer

Space Environment Research Centre (SERC)

Brisbane St Lucia, QLD 4072, QLD 4072, Australia

Tel: (61) 7 3365 1111
Contact: The University of Queensland

Space Environment Research Centre Scholarships

Subjects: Mathematics, physics, dynamic database management, engineering, adaptive optics, astrodynamics, atmospheric sciences, geodesy, geomatics, laser engineering, laser guide star adaptive optics, laser physics, satellite positioning, space sciences and space tracking

Purpose: The CRC for Space Environment Management (SEMCRC), managed by the Space Environment Research Centre (SERC) has been established to build on Australian and international expertise. Students can receive additional support and opportunities provided by the Space Environment Research Centre. Successful scholarship candidates will also have the opportunity to apply for exciting short-term placements in space research centres internationally and within Australia

Eligibility: Consideration of all candidates will be given based on academic merit, relevance of studies to SERC objectives and potential for long-term contribution to research outcomes. Priority is given to students with first class honours (or equivalent) from participating countries, currently Australia, Japan and the United States of America

Level of Study: Graduate, Postgraduate

Country of Study: Australia

Application Procedure: To apply please visit: serc.org.au/students

Closing Date: 31 December

Additional Information: The applicant is or will be enrolled in academic studies at a reputable Australian University. In the case of an international applicant, the applicant is required to have a valid passport, appropriate visa and may not be from a country subject to Trade Controls

For further information contact:

Email: admissions@gradschool.uq.edu.au

Spencer Foundation

875 North Michigan Avenue, Suite 3930, Chicago, IL 60611-1803, United States of America

Tel:	(1) 312 337 7000
Fax:	(1) 312 337 0282
Website:	www.spencer.org
Contact:	Fellowships Office

The Spencer Foundation is a private foundation that grants funds to support research which contributes to the understanding of education and improvement of its practice.

Research Grants on Education: Small

Purpose: The Small Research Grants Program supports education research projects that will contribute to the improvement of education, broadly conceived, with budgets up to US $50,000 for projects ranging from one to five years
Eligibility: 1. Proposals to the Research Grants on Education program must be for academic research projects that aim to study education. Proposals for activities other than research, or proposals for research studies focused on areas other than education, are not eligible. 2. Principal Investigators (PIs) and Co-PIs applying for a Small Research Grant on Education must have an earned doctorate in an academic discipline or professional field, or appropriate experience in an education research-related profession. While graduate students may be part of the research team, they may not be named the PI or Co-PI on the proposal. Proposals to the Research Grants on Education program must be for academic research projects that aim to study education. Proposals for activities other than research, or proposals for research studies focused on areas other than education, are not eligible. While graduate students may be part of the research team, they may not be named the PI or Co-PI on the proposal
Level of Study: Postgraduate
Type: Grant
Frequency: Annual
Country of Study: Any country
Application Procedure: The application process begins with a full proposal; there is no requirement to submit a letter of intent or intent to apply form. Full proposals for a Small Research Grant on Education are due by 2:00pm central time, 1 July. Full Proposal Guidelines Small Grant proposals must be submitted through an online application form following the guidelines below. Step 1 - Registration. Step 2 - My Profile. Step 3 - Start a Proposal. Step 4 - Small Grant Proposal Elements. Step 5 - Proposal Summary. Application could be processed as follows. spencer.smartsimple.us/s_Login.jsp
Closing Date: 1 July
Funding: Private

For further information contact:

The Spencer Foundation, 625 N Michigan Ave, Suite 1600, Chicago, IL 60611, United States of America

Email: smallgrants@spencer.org

Spencer Foundation Dissertation Fellowship Program

Subjects: Education
Purpose: To encourage a new generation of scholars from a wide range of disciplines and professional fields to undertake research relevant to the improvement of education
Eligibility: Open to candidates for the Doctoral degree at a graduate school within the United States
Level of Study: Doctorate
Type: Fellowship
Value: US$25,000
Frequency: Annual
Country of Study: United States of America
Application Procedure: Applicants must apply online. In addition to the completed application form they must submit a list of publications/presentations, a dissertation abstract, a narrative discussion of the dissertation, a work plan, 2 letters of recommendation and a graduate transcript
Closing Date: 27 October
Additional Information: Please see the website for further details www.spencer.org/content.cfm/fellowship-awards

For further information contact:

Email: fellows@spencer.org

Spinal Research

80 Coleman St, EC2R 5BJ, London, United Kingdom

Tel:	(1) 20 7653 8935
Fax:	(1) 650 723 6050
Email:	info@spinal-research.org
Website:	www.spinal-research.org

International Spinal Research Trust

Purpose: Healthcare Innovations that could have a significant impact on bladder, bowel and sexual function. The aim of the call is to support high-quality clinical research that develops and tests innovative ways to recover bladder, bowel or sexual function after spinal cord injury

Eligibility: Any application is expected to have direct relevance to the fields of research discussed in the following published articles on the ISRT Research Strategy, copies are available: Adams et al. International Spinal Research Trust Research Strategy: a discussion document. Spinal Cord (2007) 45: 2-14
Level of Study: Graduate
Type: Grant
Value: Upto £250,000
Length of Study: 3 years
Frequency: Annual
Country of Study: Any country
Closing Date: 8 May
Funding: Private

For further information contact:

Email: info@spinal-research.org

Solomon Awards

Subjects: These grants are intended to support the development of an early career clinical researcher with either a science or medical training background
Purpose: We are pleased to announce the first of what we plan will be an annual call for proposals, in the name of a generous benefactor, to help support quality experimental medicine, translational and reverse translational research in the United Kingdom within the field of spinal cord injury
Eligibility: Proposals should be limited to the following areas: - Biomedical research - Experimental medicine - Clinical studies - Suitably justified case for travel/sabbatical to enable the transfer of best practice or research methodology to the United Kingdom
Level of Study: Graduate
Type: Award
Frequency: Annual
Country of Study: Any country
Closing Date: Closing date has not been specified
Funding: Private

For further information contact:

Tel: (44) 20 7653 8935
Email: info@spinal-research.org

St Cross College

61 St. Giles', OX1 3LZ, Oxford, United Kingdom

Tel: (44) 1865 278490
Website: www.stx.ox.ac.uk

Lorna Casselton Memorial Scholarship in Plant Sciences

Purpose: St Cross College, jointly with the Department of Plant Sciences, invites applications for the Lorna Casselton Memorial Scholarship from successful Home/European Union applicants who will begin studying at the University of Oxford
Level of Study: Postgraduate
Type: Scholarship
Frequency: Annual
Country of Study: Any country
Application Procedure: For the detailed information, visit the following site. www.stx.ox.ac.uk/prospective-students/funding-support/lorna-casselton-memorial-scholarship-plant-sciences
Closing Date: 22 March
Funding: Private

For further information contact:

Email: admissions-academic@stx.ox.ac.uk

Mabel Churn Scholarship in Ophthalmology

Purpose: St Cross College invites applications for the Mabel Churn Scholarship from successful applicants normally resident in the United Kingdom or the European Union,
Eligibility: Applicants must list St Cross College as their first choice college on their Graduate Admissions application form in order to be eligible to apply for this scholarship
Level of Study: Postgraduate
Type: Scholarship
Value: covers the annual home/European Union course fee plus annual stipend of £14,999
Frequency: Annual
Country of Study: Any country
Closing Date: 15 March
Funding: Private

For further information contact:

Email: master@stx.ox.ac.uk

St John's College

St Johns Street, CB2 1TP, Cambridge, United Kingdom

Tel: (44) 1223 338600
Email: graduate-office@joh.cam.ac.uk

The Louis Cha Scholarship

Purpose: St John's College, Cambridge is delighted to announce that the noted writer, press editor, and philanthropist Dr Louis Cha has made a very generous donation to support graduate research on dynastic China at St John's. Dr Cha, internationally renowned for his novels on the Chinese past

Eligibility: 1. St John's College therefore proposes to award a Louis Cha Scholarship commencing in October, to enable a student to undertake research in the University of Cambridge in the literature, history, and culture of early and dynastic China (pre-1912). 2. The successful applicant will be selected from those who have obtained a place at St John's College Cambridge to read for the MPhil or PhD degree in a relevant subject

Level of Study: Postgraduate

Type: Scholarship

Value: £14,500 per annum

Length of Study: 3 years

Frequency: Annual

Country of Study: Any country

Application Procedure: 1. Candidates should apply to the University of Cambridge through the University's Graduate Admissions Office at the Board of Graduate Studies for admission as a graduate student, specifying St John's as their first choice of College For further information, check the website link below, www.admin.cam.ac.uk/offices/gradstud

Closing Date: 26 October

Funding: Private

For further information contact:

Tel: (61) 44 1223 338600

Email: arts@hku.hk

St. Catherine's College - University of Oxford

Manor Rd, OX1 3UJ, Oxford, United Kingdom

Tel: (44) 1865 271 700

Email: admissions@stcatz.ox.ac.uk

Website: www.stcatz.ox.ac.uk

Berlinski-Jacobson Graduate Scholarship (Humanities & Social Sciences)

Subjects: Humanities Division and Social Science Division

Eligibility: For students who in October will be reading for any Oxford University graduate degree in the Arts (Humanities Division and Social Science Division) for which St Catherine's admits graduate students

Level of Study: Graduate

Type: Scholarship

Length of Study: £4,000 will worth per annum

Frequency: Every 3 years

Country of Study: United Kingdom

Closing Date: 8 March

Funding: Private

For further information contact:

Email: development.office@stcatz.ox.ac.uk

St. Mary's University

Waldegrave Rd, TW1 4SX, Twickenham, United Kingdom

Tel: (44) 20 8240 4000

Fax: (44) 20 8240 4255

Email: scholarships@stmarys.ac.uk

Website: www.stmarys.ac.uk

Centre for Bioethics and Emerging Technologies PhD Funding

Purpose: The Centre for Bioethics and Emerging Technologies (CBET) at St Mary's University, Twickenham, offers a fully funded, full-time three year PhD programme commencing in October to support the successful applicant's research in bioethics

Eligibility: 1. The successful applicant would also expected to be involved with CBET activities, including conference organization and undergraduate teaching after a mandatory induction course. A major conference is being considered for 2020, together with the Centre for the Study of Modern Slavery based at the University. 2. The successful candidate may if they wish, carry out work with the Catholic Bishops' Conference of England and Wales. 3. It is also highly desirable that the successful applicant be located within the Greater London area during their studies

Level of Study: Graduate

Type: Funding support

Value: provide full-time PhD fees at the current home/European Union rate of £4,375 p.a. and a bursary of £13,000 p.a

Length of Study: upto 3 years

Frequency: Annual

Country of Study: Any country

Application Procedure: To apply, download and complete a full registration PhD application and send it together with your 3,000-4,000 word research proposal, two academic references from your chosen referees, copies of your Master's qualification(s), a current CV and a covering letter stating the reasons you wish to be considered for the bursary to the physical address mentioned below

Closing Date: 26 April

Funding: Private

For further information contact:

Email: maggie.mayer@stmarys.ac.uk
Contact: Ms Maggie Mayer

Stanford University

450 Serra Mall, Stanford, CA 94305–2004, United States of America

Tel: (1) 650 723 2300
Website: www.stanford.edu

Stanford University, located between San Francisco and San Jose in the heart of California's Silicon Valley, is one of the world's leading teaching and research universities. Since its opening in 1891, Stanford has been dedicated to finding solutions to big challenges and to preparing students for leadership in a complex world.

School of Medicine Dean's Postdoctoral Fellowship

Purpose: The School of Medicine Dean's Postdoctoral Fellowships encourage and support young investigators in the first two years of their postdoctoral (PhD or MD) research training at the School of Medicine and who are under the mentorship of faculty in the School of Medicine. With the goal to support current postdocs and to facilitate the recruitment of new scholars, support of a Dean's Fellowship is often used as "seed" money while outside funds are sought

Eligibility: 1. The applicant must be appointed as a postdoctoral scholar at the Stanford University School of Medicine at the time the award begins. If the applicant is not an appointed postdoctoral scholar at the time of the application deadline, additional documents must be submitted with the application (see application materials below). 2. The faculty sponsor must be appointed in the School of Medicine. (Acting, consulting and courtesy appointees are not eligible.).

3. Awardees cannot be enrolled in a degree-granting program while funded. 4. Applicants in the first one or two years of postdoctoral research training are preferred. 5. Foreign fellows must have visas that allow stipend support (typically a J-1 & F-1 OPT). H1-B and TN visa holders are not eligible. Citizenship is not a selection factor. 6. Proposals for a second-year of funding: This is a one-year fellowship. Because of the size of the applicant pool, the committee will no longer review applications for a second year of funding

Level of Study: Postgraduate
Type: Fellowship
Frequency: Annual
Country of Study: Any country
Closing Date: 10 April
Funding: Foundation

Stanford Postdoctoral Recruitment Initiative in Sciences and Medicine (PRISM)

Purpose: We invite all graduate students, and especially those from backgrounds underrepresented in the sciences, to apply for the Stanford Postdoctoral Recruitment Initiative in Sciences and Medicine (PRISM) postdoc interview opportunity. Underrepresented groups include, but are not limited to: African Americans, Latinos, Native Americans, Pacific Islanders, those with disabilities or from disadvantaged backgrounds. Stanford PRISM enables students who might not typically consider a postdoc at Stanford the opportunity to see first-hand if Stanford would be a good match for them

Eligibility: Eligibility for travel funding through PRISM varies by School
Level of Study: Postgraduate
Type: Grant
Frequency: Annual
Country of Study: Any country
Closing Date: 29 October
Funding: Foundation

For further information contact:

Medical School Office Building (MSOB), 1265 Welch Rd., Suite 100, Stanford, CA 94305-5402, United States of America

Email: rsugiura@stanford.edu

The Helena Anna Henzl-Gabor Young Women in Science Fund for Postdoctoral Scholars Travel Grant

Purpose: The Helena Anna Henzl-Gabor Young Women in Science Fund for Postdoctoral Scholars Travel Grant is open to currently appointed Stanford postdoctoral scholars in the School of Medicine and School of Humanities & Sciences who have demonstrated a positive attitude through professional teamwork and collaborations of men and women. The Henzl-Gabor Travel Grant supports travel (airline tickets, accommodations, and registration expenses) for participation at scientific conferences. These travel grants are meant to help defray the costs of attending a national or international meeting for travel taking place during the period of December 1 - November 30

Eligibility: Applicants must have completed an MD or PhD degree within the past six years of fund application submission. Awards may be given in amounts up to US$2,000 based on the detailed expenses submitted. Total awards given and funding levels may vary depending on the size and strength of the applicant pool

Level of Study: Postgraduate

Type: Grant

Frequency: Annual

Country of Study: Any country

Closing Date: 22 October

Funding: Foundation

For further information contact:

Medical School Office Building (MSOB), 1265 Welch Rd., Suite 100, Stanford, CA 94305-5402, United States of America

The Katharine McCormick Advanced Postdoctoral Scholar Fellowship to Support Women in Academic Medicine

Purpose: The Katharine McCormick Advanced Postdoctoral Fellowships are for advanced postdoctoral scholars who are pursuing faculty careers in academic medicine. The program aims to provide a bridge of the gap of support for advanced postdoctoral trainees who are competitive, yet have not yet been selected, for faculty positions

Eligibility: Eligibility requirements:; Only individuals who are currently appointed as Postdoctoral Scholars at Stanford University are eligible to apply. Instructors and Research Associates may not apply. The applicant may be a United States citizen, permanent resident, or foreign national. Foreign scholar applicants must be a holder of a J1 visa or an F1 visa in OPT status. Applicants who hold H1B, TN, J2, O-1 or other visas are ineligible. The scholar's faculty mentor must have a primary appointment in the School of Medicine. Acting, consulting and courtesy faculty are not eligible. Commitment on the part of the applicant and his/her faculty mentor to hold monthly mentorship meetings with a focus on topics related to the job search process and starting out as an assistant professor.

Candidate's willingness to make a presentation of their work to a large scientific audience. A progress report is required at the end of the fellowship

Level of Study: Graduate

Type: Fellowship

Frequency: Annual

Country of Study: Any country

Application Procedure: Application Process: Complete online application Applicant's NIH Biosketch (uploaded by applicant online) Applicant's complete curriculum vitae (uploaded by applicant online) Research proposal: (uploaded by applicant online): Two page limit, including any graphics or charts. The research proposal must be written by the fellow and reviewed by the faculty sponsor. These two pages should include a brief statement of proposed investigation in the following sections: Background, Goals, Hypothesis, and Experimental methods). If the applicant chooses to include references in the two pages, the reference should include enough information to allow the reviewer to look up the paper. Three letters of reference. One letter is required from the faculty sponsor (mentor) at Stanford. Two letters are required from other faculty, at Stanford or elsewhere, who are familiar with the candidate's work and will likely serve as references for the candidate's anticipated job search. Letters will be submitted online by the reference writer directly to the application. Letters are due the s

Closing Date: 10 June

Funding: Private

For further information contact:

Medical School Office Building (MSOB), 1265 Welch Rd., Suite 100, Stanford, CA 94305-5402, United States of America

Email: postdocaffairs@stanford.edu

The Walter V. and Idun Berry Postdoctoral Fellowship Program

Purpose: The fellowships aims to enhance research which utilizes the most advanced technologies and methodologies available to improve the health and wellness of children, including the latest opportunities in molecular and genetic medicine

Eligibility: 1. The applicant must be appointed as a postdoctoral scholar at the Stanford University School of Medicine at the time the award begins. If the applicant is not an appointed postdoctoral scholar at the time of the application deadline, additional documents must be submitted with the application (see application checklist below). Instructors and Research Associates may not apply. 2. Applicants must also hold an MD, PhD and/or a DVM/VMD degree(s); selection preference will be given to physician scientists. 3. The faculty mentor/sponsor must be appointed in the School of Medicine. Acting, consulting and courtesy appointees are not eligible. 4. Foreign scholars may have J-1 or F-1 OPT (receiving stipends), or H1B visas (receiving the award as salary). Citizenship is not a selection factor. 5. Applicants must be available for an interview on the interview date listed on this website

Level of Study: Postgraduate
Type: Fellowship
Frequency: Annual
Country of Study: Any country
Application Procedure: 1. Complete online application form (application visible only when application period is open). 2. Applicant's NIH Biosketch (uploaded by applicant online). 3. Research Proposal: (two page limit, including any graphics, charts or references). The research proposal must be written by the postdoc and reviewed by the faculty sponsor. These two pages should include a brief statement of proposed investigation in the following sections: Background, Goals, Hypothesis, and Experimental methods). Formatting guidelines require at least 1-inch margins at the top, bottom, left and right; and 12 point or larger font Times New Roman, Times Roman, Arial, Helvetica, or Verdana. Include title of project and your name on both pages and number pages. If the applicant choses to include references, the reference should include enough information to allow the reviewer to look up the paper. 4. Three letters of recommendation: one from the sponsoring Faculty Mentor at Stanford, and two additional letters from other recommenders. Letters are due the same day as the application, so please request these letters at the beginning of the application process via the online application
Closing Date: 22 May
Funding: Private

For further information contact:

Email: postdocaffairs@stanford.edu

Stanley Smith (United Kingdom) Horticultural Trust

c/o Cambridge University Botanic Garden. Cory Lodge, 1 Brookside, CB2 1JE, Cambridge, United Kingdom

Tel: (44) 12 2333 6299
Fax: (44) 12 2333 6278
Email: jc240@cam.ac.uk
Contact: Dr James Cullen, Director

The Stanley Smith (UK) Horticultural Trust supports projects that contribute to the development of the art and science of horticulture, i.e. garden conservation and restoration, education and training, research, publications and travel.

Stanley Smith (UK) Horticultural Trust Awards

Subjects: Horticulture. The Trust supports individual projects in all aspects (including training) of amenity horticulture and some aspects of commercial horticulture
Eligibility: Open to institutions and individuals. All projects are judged entirely on merit and there are no eligibility requirements, but grants are not awarded for students to take academic or diploma courses of any kind
Level of Study: Unrestricted
Type: Varies
Value: Varies
Length of Study: Dependent on the nature of the project
Country of Study: Any country
No. of awards offered: 200
Application Procedure: Applicants must apply to the Trust. Trustees allocate awards in Spring and Autumn
Closing Date: 15 February and 15 August (check with website)
Funding: Private
Contributor: Donations
No. of awards given last year: 30
No. of applicants last year: 200

For further information contact:

Email: tdaniel@calacademy.org

State Library of New South Wales

Macquarie Street, Sydney, NSW 2000, Australia

Tel: (61) 2 9273 1414
Fax: (61) 2 9273 1255
Email: library@sl.nsw.gov.au
Website: www.sl.nsw.gov.au
Contact: Mitchell Librarian

The State Library of New South Wales offers a number of prestigious & competitive fellowships to support the study, writing & teaching of Australian history & culture.

Ashurst Business Literature Prize

Subjects: Australian corporate and commercial literature, histories, accounts and analyses of corporate affairs as well as biographies of business men and women
Purpose: To encourage the highest standards of commentary in the fields of business and finance
Eligibility: The author must be a living Australian citizen or hold permanent resident status. The work must have primary reference to business or financial affairs, business or financial institutions or people directly associated with business and financial affairs, be written in the English language, published in book form and consist of a minimum of 50,000 words
Level of Study: Professional development
Type: Prize
Length of Study: Australian $30,000
Frequency: Annual
Study Establishment: State Library of New South Wales
Country of Study: Australia
Application Procedure: All nominations must be made on the appropriate form, be submitted with five copies of the nominated work and be accompanied by an entry fee of Australian $66 per title to be eligible for consideration. A separate form must be completed for each nomination. See State Library of NSW website www.sl.nsw.gov.au/awards/
Closing Date: 5 December (check with website)
Funding: Private

For further information contact:

Education and Client Liaison Branch, State Library of New South Wales, NSW, Australia

Email: smartin@sl.nsw.gov.au
Contact: Stephen Martin, Senior Project Officer

C H Currey Memorial Fellowship

Subjects: Australian history from original resources, preferably using the state library's resources
Purpose: For the writing of Australian history from original sources
Type: Research fellowship
Value: Approx. A$20,000
Frequency: Annual
Study Establishment: The State Library of New South Wales
Country of Study: Australia
Application Procedure: Applicants must complete an application form available on the State library of NSW Website : www.sl.nsw.gov.au/awards/ or from Margaret Bjork, Mitchell

library office, State library of New South Wales, Macquarie Street, Sydney, NSW 2000 Australia
Closing Date: 1 September
Funding: Private

Council of Australian state libraries and library council of NSW honorary Fellowships.

Purpose: Offered to the top short listed applicants for the C.H. Currey memorial Fellowship and the Nancy Keesing Fellowship respectively
Eligibility: Top shortlisted applicants for the C.H.Currey memorial fellowship and the Nancy Keesing Fellowship
Type: Fellowship
Value: No financial award
Frequency: Annual
Study Establishment: The state library of NSW
Country of Study: Australia
Application Procedure: Applicants must complete an application form, available on request
Closing Date: 1 September
Funding: Private

For further information contact:

Tel: (61) 2 9273 1467
Fax: (61) 2 9273 1245
Email: awards@sl.nsw.gov.au
Contact: Margaret Bjork

Dobbie Literary Award

Subjects: Writing
Purpose: To recognize a first published work from an Australian female writer
Eligibility: Open to a first published work of fiction or non-fiction classifiable as 'Life Writing' by a woman author
Value: A$5,000
Frequency: Annual
Study Establishment: The State Library of New South Wales
Country of Study: Australia
Application Procedure: Applicants must complete an application form, available on request
Funding: Private

For further information contact:

Tel: (61) 1800 501 227
Email: philanthropy@perpetual.com.au

Jean Arnot Memorial Fellowship

Subjects: Librarianship
Purpose: To reward female an outstanding original paper of no more than 5,000 words on any aspect of librarianship by a woman or female student of librarianship
Type: Fellowship
Value: A$1,000
Frequency: Annual
Study Establishment: The State Library of NSW
Country of Study: Australia
Application Procedure: Applicants must complete an application form, available on request
Closing Date: 30 March
Funding: Private

For further information contact:

Tel: (61) 2 9273 1467
Fax: (61) 2 9273 1245
Email: awards@sl.nsw.gov.au
Contact: Margaret Bjork

Miles Franklin Literacy Award

Subjects: Literacy
Value: A$28,000
Frequency: Annual
Study Establishment: The State Library of NSW
Country of Study: Australia
Application Procedure: Applicants must complete an application form, available on request
Closing Date: December
Funding: Private

For further information contact:

Tel: (61) 2 9273 1467
Fax: (61) 2 9273 1245
Email: awards@sl.nsw.gov.au
Contact: Margaret Bjork

Miles Franklin Literary Award

Subjects: Australian literature
Purpose: To promote excellence in Australian literature
Eligibility: Novel must be of the highest literary merit and must present Australian life in any of its phases. Novels submitted must have been published in the year of entry of the award
Level of Study: Professional development
Type: Award

Value: A$60,000
Frequency: Annual
Application Procedure: Application forms can be downloaded from the website, see also State library of NSW website www.sl.nsw.gov.au/awards/
Closing Date: 10 December (check with website)
Funding: Individuals

For further information contact:

Tel: (61) 2 9332 1559
Fax: (61) 2 9332 1298
Email: trustawards@cauzgroup.com.au
Contact: Petrea Salter

Milt Luger Fellowships

Subjects: Australian life, history and culture using the resources of the state library
Purpose: For projects which investigate and document aspects of Australian life, history and culture
Eligibility: Persons aged between 18 and 25 years
Type: Fellowship
Value: US$5,000 and US$3,000
Study Establishment: The state library of NSW
Country of Study: Australia
Application Procedure: Applicants must complete an application form, available on request. See State Library of NSW website www.sl.nsw.gov.au/awards
Funding: Private

For further information contact:

Mitchell Library Office, State Library of New South Wales, Macquarie Street, Australia

Tel: (61) 2 9273 1467
Fax: (61) 2 9273 1245
Email: awards@sl.nsw.gov.au
Contact: Margaret Bjork

National Biography Award

Subjects: Literary
Purpose: For a published work of biographical or autobiographical writing
Eligibility: To be eligible for consideration or shortlisting, and/or to be eligible to win or be awarded a; prize in respect of the Awards, submitted works must: 1. be a biography, autobiography or memoir. 2. have Australia as their subject, or have as their subject a significant contribution to Australia. 3. be written in the English language, published in book form

and consist of a minimum length of 40,000 words. 4. be an in-depth and comprehensive account of a life (biographies that deal with more than one life may, at the absolute discretion of the State Library of New South Wales, be eligible where the stories or lives are strongly intertwined); and 5. be first published between 1 October and 30 September and be commercially available within this period. (period changes every year)

Level of Study: Unrestricted
Type: Award
Value: A$25,000
Frequency: Annual
Study Establishment: The State library of NSW
Country of Study: Australia
Application Procedure: Applicants must complete an online nomination form. The Call for Entries opens in December and closes at the beginning of February each year
Closing Date: February
Funding: Private
Contributor: Nelson Meers Foundation

For further information contact:

Tel: (61) 2 9273 1605
Email: awards@sl.nsw.gov.au
Contact: Senior Project Officer, Awards

State Secretariat for Education, Research and Innovation SERI

Einsteinstrasse 2, CH-3005 Bern, Switzerland

Email: sgs@sbfi.admin.ch
Website: www.sbfi.admin.ch

Swiss Government Excellence Scholarships for Foreign Scholars and Artists

Subjects: Applied sciences, music, and fine arts
Purpose: The Swiss government, through the Federal Commission for Scholarships for Foreign Students (FCS), awards various postgraduate scholarships to foreign scholars and researchers
Eligibility: These scholarships provide graduates from all fields with the opportunity to pursue doctoral or postdoctoral research in Switzerland at one of the public funded universities or recognised institutions
Level of Study: Doctorate, Postdoctorate
Type: Scholarship

Frequency: Annual
Country of Study: Any country
Closing Date: The deadline for applications varies from one country to another
Additional Information: Please check www.sbfi.admin.ch/scholarships_eng for detailed information

For further information contact:

Tel: (41) 446326161
Email: exchange@ethz.ch

Statistical Society of Canada

210 - 1725 St. Laurent Blvd., Ottawa, ON K1G 3V4, Canada

Tel: (1) 613 733 2662
Fax: (1) 613 733 1386
Email: info@ssc.ca
Website: www.ssc.ca
Contact: Sudhir Paul, Chair, Pierre Robillard Award

The Statistical Society of Canada provides a forum for discussion and interaction among individuals involved in all aspects of the statistical sciences. It publishes a newsletter, Liaison as well as a scientific journal, The Canadian Journal of Statistics. The Society also organizes annual scientific meetings and short courses on professional development.

Pierre Robillard Award

Subjects: Statistics
Purpose: To recognize the best PhD thesis defended at a Canadian university and written in a field covered by the Canadian Journal of Statistics
Eligibility: Open to all postgraduates who have made a potential impact on the statistical sciences
Level of Study: Doctorate
Type: Award
Value: A certificate, a monetary prize of C$1,000 and 1 year's membership of the Society
Frequency: Annual
Country of Study: Canada
No. of awards offered: 8
Application Procedure: Applicants must submit four copies of the thesis together with a covering letter from the thesis supervisor
Closing Date: 31 January
No. of awards given last year: 1
No. of applicants last year: 8

Additional Information: The committee may decide that none of the submitted theses merits the award

For further information contact:

Department of Mathematical and Statistical Sciences, University of Alberta, 632 Cab, AB, Canada

Tel:	(1) 780 492 4230
Fax:	(1) 780 492 6826
Email:	kc.carriere@ualberta.ca
Contact:	Dr Carrière Keumhee, Professor

Stellenbosch University

Private Bay XI, Matieland 7602, South Africa

Tel:	(27) 21 808 9111
Fax:	(27) 21 808 3799
Email:	info@sun.ac.za
Website:	www.sun.ac.za

The raison d'être of the chemistry of Stellenbosch is to create and sustain, in commitment to the academic ideal of excellent scholarly and scientific practice, an environment within which knowledge can be discovered, shared and applied for the benefit of the community.

Harry Crossley Doctoral Fellowship

Subjects: Any subject, with the exception of theology and political science
Purpose: To reward academically above-average students
Eligibility: Open to full-time students registered at Stellenbosch University in any postgraduate degree programme except theology and political science
Level of Study: Doctorate
Type: Fellowship
Value: South African Rand 80,000
Length of Study: 2 years
Frequency: Annual
Study Establishment: Stellenbosch University
Country of Study: South Africa
No. of awards offered: 350
Application Procedure: Request application
Closing Date: 29 September
Funding: Foundation
Contributor: Harry Crossley Foundation
No. of awards given last year: 50
No. of applicants last year: 350

For further information contact:

Tel:	(1) 21 808 4208/2957
Fax:	(27) 21 808 2739
Email:	beursnavrae_nagraads@sun.ac.za

Harry Crossley Master

Subjects: All subject, with the exception of theology and political science
Purpose: To reward academically above-average students
Eligibility: To full-time students registered at Stellenbosch University in any postgraduate degree programme except theology and political science
Level of Study: Doctorate, Postgraduate
Type: Bursary
Value: Rand 75,000 (Honours), ZAR 80,000 (Master
Length of Study: 1 year
Frequency: Annual
Study Establishment: Stellenbosch University
Country of Study: South Africa
No. of awards offered: 500
Closing Date: 15 October
Funding: Foundation
Contributor: Harry Crossley Foundation
No. of awards given last year: 30
No. of applicants last year: 500
Additional Information: Please see the website further details

For further information contact:

Tel:	(27) 21 808 4208
Fax:	(27) 21 808 3799
Email:	usbritz@sun.ac.za

Stellenbosch Fellowship in Polymer Science

Subjects: New monomer synthesizing and radical polymerization
Purpose: To fund further study in Polymer Science and synthetic Polymer chemistry
Eligibility: Open to students with a PhD in Polymer Science or Environmental Engineering and experience in membranes, membrane operations, polymer brushes, grafts and other nano particles
Level of Study: Postdoctorate
Type: Fellowship
Length of Study: 1 year
Frequency: Annual
Study Establishment: University of Stellenbosch
Country of Study: South Africa

Application Procedure: Request application.

For further information contact:

Department of Chemistry, Division of Polymer Science University of Stellenbosch, South Africa

Email: rds@sun.ac.za
Contact: Professor RD Sanderson

Stellenbosch Merit Bursary Award

Subjects: Any subject
Purpose: To reward academically above-average students
Eligibility: Available to full-time students registered at Stellenbosch University in any postgraduate degree programme
Level of Study: Postgraduate
Type: Bursary
Value: Rand 4,100–34,700
Length of Study: Up to 2 years
Frequency: Annual
Study Establishment: Stellenbosch University
Country of Study: South Africa
No. of awards offered: Approx. 700
Application Procedure: Students must submit an application and a certified copy of a complete, official academic record
Closing Date: 6 December
Contributor: Stellenbosch University
No. of awards given last year: 340
No. of applicants last year: Approx. 700

For further information contact:

Office for postgraduate student funding, Postgraduate and International Office, Wilcocks Building, Room 3015, South Africa

Tel: (27) 21 808 4208
Fax: (27) 21 808 3799
Email: postgradfunding@sun.ac.za

Stellenbosch Postdoctoral Research Fellowship in Geology

Subjects: Tectono-metamorphic and magmatic evolution of the Archaen Barberton granite-greenstone terrain in South Africa
Purpose: To finance a student interested in Archaen tectonics and applied structural geology of high-grade metamorphic granite-gneiss terrains

Eligibility: Open to students with a PhD in geology obtained within the past 5 years, with a background in regional mapping and structural geology
Level of Study: Postdoctorate
Type: Fellowship
Value: Rand 60,000 per annum
Length of Study: 2 years
Frequency: Annual
Study Establishment: University of Stellenbosch
Country of Study: South Africa
Application Procedure: Submit a covering letter, curriculum vitae and all research outputs
Closing Date: 21 March

For further information contact:

Fax: (27) 21 808 3129
Email: akister@sun.ac.za
Contact: Professor Allex Kisters

Stellenbosch Rector's Grants for Successing Against the Odds

Subjects: Any subject
Purpose: To award students who have achieved exceptional success despite difficult circumstances
Eligibility: Open to candidates who satisfy the admission requirements of the University and who can provide proof of exceptional achievement despite handicaps and/or specific physical, educational or social challenges
Level of Study: Postgraduate
Type: Grant
Value: South African Rand 60,000
Length of Study: Up to 3 years
Frequency: Annual
Study Establishment: Stellenbosch University
Country of Study: South Africa
No. of awards offered: 100
Application Procedure: Students must submit a complete application form accompanied by a curriculum vitae and 2 references
Closing Date: 10 September
Funding: Foundation
Contributor: Andrew Mellon Foundation
No. of awards given last year: 3
No. of applicants last year: 100

For further information contact:

Tel: (27) 21 8084208
Fax: (27) 21 808 2739
Email: beursnavrae_nagraads@sun.ac.za

Stockholm School of Economics

PO Box 6501, SWE-11383, Stockholm, Sweden

Tel: (46) 8 736 9000
Fax: (46) 8 31 81 86
Email: info@hhs.se
Website: www.hhs.se

An international higher educational institution on a comparatively small scale with a dynamic international learning environment to further economic and business study.

Consejo Nacional de Ciencia y Tecnologia (CONACYT) Scholarships

Subjects: Business management
Eligibility: Open to Mexican students only
Level of Study: MBA
Type: Scholarship
Value: All agreed fees
Length of Study: 1 year
Frequency: Annual
Country of Study: Sweden
Application Procedure: Contact the Foundation
Funding: Foundation
Contributor: CONACYT

For further information contact:

Email: ochoa@buzon.main.conacyt.mx

Petra och Kail Erik Hedborgs Stiftelse Scholarship

Subjects: Business administration
Level of Study: MBA
Type: Scholarship
Value: All tuition fees and travel costs
Length of Study: 1 year
Frequency: Annual
Country of Study: Sweden
Application Procedure: Contact the institute
Funding: Private

For further information contact:

Tel: (46) 8 765 6327
Email: info@pkhedborg.com

The Swedish Foundation for International Cooperation in Research and Higher Education (STINT) Scholarship

Subjects: Business administration
Eligibility: Open to Brazilian nationals only
Level of Study: MBA
Type: Scholarship
Length of Study: 1 year
Frequency: Dependent on funds available
Country of Study: Sweden
Application Procedure: Contact the institute
Funding: Government
Contributor: STINT

For further information contact:

STINT, Skeppargatan 8, Sweden

Tel: (46) 46 8662 7690
Fax: (46) 46 8661 9210
Email: info@stint.se

Strathclyde University

16 Richmond Street, Glasgow, G1 1XQ

Tel: (44) 141 552 4400
Website: https://www.strath.ac.uk

Based in the heart of the City of Glasgow, Strathclyde University is a leading technological university with around 23,000 students from more than 100 nations. With an international reputation for teaching excellence, the University has a five-star Overall Rating in the QS Stars University Ratings, and seven Times Higher Education awards in as many years.

Strathclyde Prestige Award for Excellence in Business Translation & Interpreting

Purpose: Strathclyde University is a major international technical university situated in Glasgow, Scotland. The mission of the University is socially progressive and brings positive change in the life of its students for society and the world
Eligibility: 1. Be available to commence their academic studies in the United Kingdom by the start of the academic

year in September. 2. Hold a first degree at first class or upper second class honours, or equivalent. 3. Hold an academic offer to study MSc Business Translation & Interpreting. 4. Provide a 300-word essay demonstrating their ability to contribute to the field of Business Translation & Interpeting

Level of Study: Postgraduate
Type: Award
Value: £5,000
Length of Study: 1 year
Frequency: Annual
Country of Study: Any country
Closing Date: 31 May
Funding: International office

For further information contact:

Tel: (44) 141 444 8600
Email: hass-pg-enquiries@strath.ac.uk

Stroke Association

Stroke House, 240 City Road, EC1V 2PR, London, United Kingdom

Tel: (44) 20 7566 1543
Email: research@stroke.org.uk
Website: www.stroke.org.uk
Contact: Rachael Sherrington, Research Awards Officer

The Stroke Association funds research into stroke prevention, treatment, rehabilitation, and long term care. It also helps stroke patients and their families directly through community services. It campaigns, educates and informs to increase knowledge of stroke at all levels of society and it acts as a voice for everyone affected by stroke.

Priority Programme Awards

Subjects: Haemorrhagic stroke and the psychological consequences of stroke
Purpose: This new funding stream is aimed at addressing the gaps in research in the following areas
Type: Award
Value: Up to the amount of £450,000
Length of Study: 3–5 years
Frequency: Annual
Country of Study: Any country
Closing Date: January

Additional Information: These awards will be made in July. Please contact research@stroke.org.uk for more information

For further information contact:

Email: research@stroke.org.uk

The Stroke Association Research Project Grants

Subjects: Any research on stroke across the entire stroke pathway. Prevention, acute treatment and care, rehabilitation and long term treatment and care
Purpose: To advance research into stroke
Eligibility: Open to researchers in the United Kingdom in the relevant fields. Applications are judged by peer review on their merit without limitations of age. Applicants can be from any country but must be based in the United Kingdom
Level of Study: Research
Type: Project grant
Value: Up to £210,000
Length of Study: 3–5 years
Frequency: Annual
Study Establishment: A suitable university or hospital in the United Kingdom
Country of Study: United Kingdom
No. of awards offered: 20
Application Procedure: Application forms are available from the website
Closing Date: February
Funding: Private, Trusts
Contributor: Donations
No. of awards given last year: 3
No. of applicants last year: 20
Additional Information: Please visit www.stroke.org.uk/research/looking-funding/project-grants

For further information contact:

Email: research@stroke.org.uk

Swansea University

Singleton Park, Swansea, SA2 8PP Wales, United Kingdom

Tel: (44) 1792 205 678
Fax: (44) 1792 295 157
Email: sro@swansea.ac.uk,
M.W.Skippen@swansea.ac.uk
Website: www.swan.ac.uk

Contact: Dr Mark Skippen, Senior Postgraduate
Recruitment Officer

Swansea University is a United Kingdom top 30 institution for research excellence (REF2014) that has been providing the highest quality postgraduate teaching since 1920. Our campuses are situated on the stunning sandy beach of Swansea Bay. We have taught and research postgraduate funding for United Kingdom, European Union and international students: www.swansea.ac.uk/postgraduate/scholarships.

Computer Science: Fully Funded EPSRC PHD Scholarship

Subjects: The Department of Computer Science at Swansea University invites applications for PhD study funded by EPSRC. Research can be undertaken in any area related to the department's research expertise including: Data Science Logic and Verification Visual Computing Human-Computer Interaction Security

Purpose: The Department of Computer Science is part of the Computational Foundry, a world-class centre for computational research, part-funded by the European Regional Development Fund through the Welsh Government

Eligibility: 1. Candidates must have a first or upper second class honours or a Master's degree with Merit (or equivalent), in a relevant discipline. 2. For candidates whose first language is not English, we require IELTS 6.5 (with 6.0 in each component) or equivalent. Please visit our website for a list of acceptable English language tests. 3. We prefer candidates to have already met the English Language requirements at the point of application, although this is not a requirement

Level of Study: Graduate

Type: Scholarship

Value: annual stipend of £15,009 per annum

Frequency: Annual

Country of Study: Any country

Application Procedure: To apply, please complete and return the following documents to the College of Science: 1. College of Science PGR Scholarship Application. 2. Academic References – all scholarship applications require two supporting references to be submitted. Please ensure that your chosen referees are aware of the funding deadline, as their references form a vital part of the evaluation process. Please either include these with your scholarship application or ask your referees to send them directly to science-scholarships@ swansea.ac.uk. 3. Academic Transcripts and Degree Certificates – academic transcripts and degree certificates must be submitted along with the scholarship application by the funding deadline. We will be using these to verify your academic qualifications. 4. A recent CV. 5. Applicants should

use the 'Supplementary Personal Statement' section of the application form to indicate, in broad terms, their proposed research interests within one of the areas specified above

Closing Date: 23 March

Funding: Private

Additional Information: The Computational Foundry has dedicated research labs, runs specialised seminar series, frequently hosts international guest researchers from academia and industry, and is involved in large United Kingdom- and European Union-funded research projects that provide opportunities for additional training and research visits at partner universities

For further information contact:

Email: science-scholarships@swansea.ac.uk

International Excellence Scholarships

Subjects: All subjects

Eligibility: Awards are available to postgraduate applicants from outside the EU. Other eligibility criteria may apply. Please contact us for details

Level of Study: Postgraduate

Type: Scholarship

Value: Approx. £4,000

Length of Study: 1 year (Masters)

Frequency: Annual

Study Establishment: Swansea University

Country of Study: United Kingdom

Application Procedure: Complete application form, available online at website

Closing Date: 2 June

Additional Information: Please contact at international@swansea.ac.uk for further information. South America and India are also eligible countries. Please check at www.swan.ac.uk/international/students/fees-and-funding/ pg_scholarships/ for further information

For further information contact:

Email: scholarships@brunel.ac.uk

MRes Scholarships

Type: Scholarship

Value: Each scholarship is worth £2,500, to be used towards the cost of tuition fees

Country of Study: Any country

Application Procedure: To apply please complete and return the following application form to science-scholarships@ swansea.ac.uk

Closing Date: 20 July

For further information contact:

Macquarie University, NSW 2109, Australia

Email: hdrcotutelle@mq.edu.au

PhD Fees-only Bursaries

Subjects: Normally available in all subject areas
Eligibility: Open to good Master's graduates from the United Kingdom/European Union who will be commencing PhD studies at Swansea University
Type: Scholarship
Value: Covers United Kingdom/European Union tuition fees
Length of Study: 3 years
Frequency: Annual
Study Establishment: Swansea University
Country of Study: United Kingdom
Application Procedure: Please contact us for an application form
No. of awards given last year: 10

For further information contact:

Email: admissions-enquiries@swansea.ac.uk

Swansea University Masters Scholarships

Subjects: Available in all academic subjects
Eligibility: Open to students from the United Kingdom/European Union who will be starting an eligible master's course at Swansea University for the first time in September
Level of Study: Postgraduate
Type: Scholarship
Value: £2,900 towards tuition fees
Length of Study: 1 year full time or 2–3 years part-time
Frequency: Annual
Study Establishment: Swansea University
Country of Study: United Kingdom
Application Procedure: Eligible students are sent an application form when offered a place on a course
Closing Date: July
No. of awards given last year: 100

For further information contact:

Postgraduate Admissions Office, Swansea University, United Kingdom

Email: postgraduate.admissions@swansea.ac.uk

Swansea University PhD Scholarships

Subjects: Normally available in all subject areas. Please check our website www.swansea.ac.uk/postgraduate for details
Eligibility: Open to good Masters graduates from the United Kingdom/European Union who will be commencing PhD studies at Swansea University
Level of Study: Doctorate, Postgraduate
Type: Scholarship
Value: Annual stipend at Rcuk level (approx. £14,000)
Length of Study: 3 years
Frequency: Annual
Study Establishment: Swansea University
Country of Study: United Kingdom
Application Procedure: Please see individual scholarship listings on our website: www.swansea.ac.uk/postgraduate/scholarships/research
Closing Date: Throughout year
No. of awards given last year: 15

For further information contact:

Postgraduate Admissions Office, Swansea University, United Kingdom

Email: postgraduate.admissions@swansea.ac.uk

Swansea University Research Excellence Scholarship

Purpose: The project aims to create novel approaches to contemporary challenges in theoretical and applied ecological and evolutionary biosciences
Type: Scholarship
Value: The scholarship covers the full cost of United Kingdom/European Union tuition fees, plus an annual stipend of £14,553 (in line with the RCUK stipend amount) for 3 years. There will also be £1,000 per annum available for research expenses such as travel, accommodation, field trips and conference attendance
Country of Study: United Kingdom
Closing Date: 22 January
Contributor: Swansea University
Additional Information: To apply please complete and return the following documents to Dr Vivienne Jenkins (pgrsures-at-swansea.ac.uk) using the quote reference COS2

For further information contact:

Email: pgrsures@swansea.ac.uk

The James Callaghan Scholarships

Subjects: Applications can be made to any academic school
Eligibility: Research students from Commonwealth member countries are eligible to apply. Awards are available for full-time or part-time MPhil or PhD studies
Level of Study: Doctorate, Predoctorate
Type: Scholarship
Value: £1,700 (full-time) and £850 (half-time)
Length of Study: 1 year (MPhil) and 3 years (PhD)
Frequency: Annual
Study Establishment: Swansea University
Country of Study: United Kingdom
Application Procedure: Please contact us for an application form
Closing Date: 1 June

For further information contact:

Postgraduates Admissions Office, Swansea University, United Kingdom

Email: postgraduate.admissions@swansea.ac.uk

Swedish Institute

Slottsbacken 10, Box 7434, SWE-103 91 Stockholm, Sweden

Tel: (46) 8 453 7800
Email: si@si.se
Contact: The Swedish Institute

SISS is the Swedish government's international awards scheme aimed at developing global leaders. It is funded by the Ministry for Foreign Affairs of Sweden and administered by the Swedish Institute (SI). The programme offers a unique opportunity for future leaders to develop professionally and academically, to experience Swedish society and culture, and to build a long-lasting relationship with Sweden and with each other.

Swedish Institute Scholarships for Global Professionals (SISGP)

Purpose: The Swedish Institute (SI) is now launching the Swedish Institute Scholarships for Global Professionals (SISGP), a new scholarship programme which replaces Swedish Institute Study Scholarships (SISS)
Eligibility: Work experience; You must have minimum of 3,000 hours of demonstrated employment. Read more about the criteria for work experience Leadership experience; You must have demonstrated leadership experience from your current or previous employment. Read more about the leadership experience criteria University admissions; You must be liable to pay tuition fees to Swedish universities, have followed the steps of university admission, and be admitted to one of the eligible master's programmes by 4 April
Level of Study: Graduate
Type: Scholarship
Value: Living expense of SEK 10,000 and travel allowance of SEK 15,000
Length of Study: One academic year (2 sememsters)
Frequency: Varies
Country of Study: Any country
Application Procedure: A complete application must consist of: 1. a completed motivation letter. 2. a CV. 3. two valid and completed letters of reference. 4. valid and completed proof of work and leadership experience. 5. a copy of your valid passport
Closing Date: 4 February
Funding: Private
Additional Information: For further information on application process, visit the website. si.se/en/apply/scholarships/swedish-institute-scholarships-for-global-professionals/

For further information contact:

Swedish Institute, Slottsbacken 10, SWE-111 30 Stockholm, Sweden

Email: si@si.se

Swedish Institute Scholarships for the Western Balkans Programme

Subjects: Social sciences
Purpose: The SI Scholarships for the Western Balkans Programme aims at supporting advanced level studies and research within the field of social sciences in order to forge closer links between the Western Balkans and the European Union, and to contribute to strengthened democracy in the region
Eligibility: The scholarships are intended for PhD students and postdoctoral researchers from Albania, Bosnia-Herzegovina, Kosovo, Macedonia (FYROM), Montenegro and Serbia conducting part of their studies/research in Sweden within the field of social sciences
Level of Study: Doctorate, Postdoctorate
Type: Scholarship
Value: SEK 15,000 per month for PhD students, and SEK 18,000 per month for postdoctoral researchers and senior scientists

Length of Study: 1 year
Frequency: Annual
Country of Study: Sweden
Application Procedure: Online application portal
Closing Date: 1 November to 10 January
Contributor: Ministry for Foreign Affairs of Sweden and administered by the Swedish Institute (SI)
Additional Information: Please contact sischolarships@si.se if you have any questions

For further information contact:

Email: sischolarships@si.se

Swedish-Turkish Scholarship Programme for PhD studies and postdoctoral research

Subjects: Social sciences
Purpose: The Swedish-Turkish Scholarship Programme aims at supporting advanced level studies and research in order to forge closer links between Turkey and the European Union, and to contribute to strengthened democracy and a greater respect for human rights
Eligibility: The scholarships are intended for PhD students and postdoctoral researchers from Turkey conducting part of their studies/research in Sweden within the field of social sciences. You should not be a resident for more than 2 year in Sweden
Level of Study: Doctorate, Postdoctorate
Type: Scholarship
Value: SEK 15,000 per month for PhD students, and SEK 18,000 per month for postdoctoral researchers and senior scientists
Length of Study: 1 year
Country of Study: Sweden
Closing Date: 1 November to 10 January
Contributor: Ministry for Foreign Affairs of Sweden and administered by the Swedish Institute (SI)
Additional Information: Please contact sischolarships@si.se if you have any questions

The Swedish Institute Study Scholarships (SISS)

Purpose: SISS is the Swedish government's international awards scheme aimed at developing global leaders
Eligibility: Applicants must be from an eligible country and have at least 3,000 hours of experience from full-time/part-time employment, voluntary work, paid/unpaid internship, and/or position of trust. Applicants must display academic qualifications and leadership experience. In addition, applicants should show an ambition to make a difference by working with issues which contribute to a just and sustainable development

in their country, in a long term perspective. The travel grant is a one-time payment of SEK 15,000
Level of Study: Foundation programme
Type: Scholarship
Value: The scholarship covers both tuition fees (paid directly to the Swedish university/university college by the Swedish Institute) and living expenses to the amount of SEK 10,000 per month. There are no additional grants for family members
Length of Study: The scholarship is intended for full-time master's level studies of one or two years, and is only awarded for programmes starting in the autumn semester. The scholarship covers the whole duration of the master's programme
Country of Study: Any country
Closing Date: 1 December and 10 February
Funding: Government
Contributor: Ministry for Foreign Affairs of Sweden

For further information contact:

Email: si@si.se

The Swedish Institute Study Scholarships for South Africa

Purpose: The programme offers a unique opportunity for future leaders to develop professionally and academically, to experience Swedish society and culture, and to build a long-lasting relationship with Sweden and with each other
Type: Scholarship
Value: The scholarship covers both tuition fees (paid directly to the Swedish university/university college by the Swedish Institute) and living expenses to the amount of SEK 9,000 per month. The travel grant is a one-time payment of SEK 15,000
Length of Study: Whole duration of the master's programme
Country of Study: Sweden
Application Procedure: Online application
Closing Date: 1 December to 16 January and 10 February
Contributor: Ministry for Foreign Affairs of Sweden and administered by the Swedish Institute (SI)

For further information contact:

Email: si@si.se

Visby Programme Scholarships

Subjects: All fields of study
Purpose: The aim of the Visby Programme is to support individual mobility, thereby contributing to increased contacts and collaborations between actors in Sweden and countries in the EU Eastern Partnership and Russia. The goal is to build an integrated, knowledge-based and research-intense

region, centred on the Baltic Sea while also including EU Eastern Partnership countries and Russia

Eligibility: 1. PhD student, applying for a part of his/her ongoing PhD studies to be carried out in Sweden (1 year maximum). 2. Postdoctoral researcher, with priority given to holders of a PhD degree. 3. Senior scientist - holders of a PhD degree obtained before 2012 (6 months maximum)

Level of Study: Doctorate, Postdoctorate

Type: Scholarship

Value: SEK 15,000 per month for PhD students, and SEK 18,000 per month for postdoctoral researchers and senior scientists. The scholarship cannot be prolonged or extended

Country of Study: Any country

Application Procedure: Applications are evaluated by the Swedish Institute (SI) and an academic board. Online application form

Closing Date: 14 February

Additional Information: Please contact sischolarships@si.se if you have any questions

For further information contact:

Email: markus.boman@si.se

Swedish Natural Science Research Council (NFR)

Box 7142, SWE-10387, Stockholm, Sweden

Tel: (46) 85 464 400
Fax: (46) 85 464 4180
Email: vetenskapsradet@vr.se
Website: www.nfr.se
Contact: Grants Management Officer

NFR FRN Grants for Scientific Equipment

Subjects: Natural sciences
Purpose: To assist researchers
Eligibility: Open to individuals holding a research grant from any Swedish research council
Level of Study: Research
Type: A variable number of grants
Value: Up to SEK 10,000,000
Length of Study: Dependent on the requirements of the projects
Frequency: Annual
Study Establishment: Universities
Country of Study: Sweden

Application Procedure: Applicants must contact the organisation for details
Closing Date: Please contact the organisation
Funding: Government

For further information contact:

Tel: (46) 84 544 254
Email: lars@nfr.se

NFR Travel Grants

Subjects: Natural sciences
Purpose: To give financial support to researchers attending conferences or wishing to undertake short-term research abroad
Eligibility: Open to Swedish researchers and foreign national researchers who have completed their PhD at a Swedish university and have embarked on postdoctoral studies
Level of Study: Postdoctorate, Research
Type: Travel grant
Value: Travelling expenses and subsistence
Length of Study: Up to 2 months
Frequency: Throughout the year
Study Establishment: Universities or academic institutions abroad
Country of Study: Any country
Application Procedure: Applicants must complete an application form
Closing Date: Any time excluding 15 June to 15 August
Funding: Government

For further information contact:

Tel: (46) 84 544 229
Email: elisa@nfr.se

Swinburne University of Technology

PO Box 218, Hawthorn, VIC 3122, Australia

Tel: (61) 3 9214 8000
Fax: (61) 3 9214 8637
Email: webmaster@swin.edu.au
Website: www.swinburne.edu
Contact: MBA Admissions Officer

It provides career-orientated education and as a university with a commitment to research. The University maintains a strong technology base and important links with industry, complemented by a number of innovative specialist research centres which attract a great deal of international interest. A feature of many Swinburne undergraduate courses is the applied vocational emphasis and direct industry application through Industry Based Learning (IBL) programs. Swinburne was a pioneer of IBL program which places students directly in industry for vocational employment as an integral part of the course structure. Swinburne is committed to the transfer of lifelong learning skills. It is heavily involved in international initiatives and plays a significant part in the internationalization of Australia's tertiary education system.

Chancellor's Research Scholarship

Subjects: All subjects
Purpose: To award students of exceptional research potential to undertake a higher degree by research (HDR)
Eligibility: Open to a local or an international student undertaking a higher degree by research (HDR) with Bachelor Degree with First Class Honours. For further details, please check the website
Level of Study: Doctorate
Type: Research scholarship
Value: An annual stipend of $30,000, an Establishment Grant of up to $3,000 and up to $5,000 for a 6-month overseas placement
Length of Study: 3 years
Frequency: Annual
Application Procedure: Check website for further details
Additional Information: Please refer website for details: www.swinburne.edu.au/study/options/scholarships/215/chancellors-research-scholarship-/

For further information contact:

Building 60Wm, Level 7, 60 William Street, Hawthorn campus, VIC 3122, Australia

Tel: (46) 9214 5547 or 9214 8744
Email: ehill@swin.edu.au, jamathews@swin.edu.au

PhD in Mechatronics

Subjects: Engineering and technology
Purpose: To provide full time scholarships to undertake the degree of Doctor of Philosophy (PhD) at the Faculty of Engineering and Industrial Sciences of Swinburne University of Technology
Eligibility: Applicants should have completed an undergraduate course in engineering preferably in mechatronics or electrical engineering. Candidates with a Masters Degree in

a related area or with previous research experience will be given priority
Level of Study: Doctorate
Type: Scholarship
Value: A$19,616 per year
Length of Study: 3 years
Application Procedure: Check website for further details
Closing Date: 20 July

For further information contact:

Swinburne University of Technology, PO Box 218, VIC 3122, Australia

Tel: (61) 61 3 9214 5659
Email: arad@swin.edu.au
Contact: Professor Ahmad B Rad, Faculty of Engineering and Industrial Sciences

Swinburne University Postgraduate Research Award (SUPRA)

Subjects: All subjects
Purpose: To assist with general living costs
Eligibility: Open to domestic or an international student undertaking a higher degree by research. Hold a bachelor's degree with first-class honours or equivalent. Please check the website for further details
Level of Study: Doctorate, Research
Type: Research award
Value: A non-taxable indexed stipend of around $23,728 per year and a tuition fee scholarship (total value around $49k per year)
Length of Study: 3 years (Research Doctorate)
Country of Study: Any country
Application Procedure: Complete an application for admission to research higher degree candidature and scholarship and mail/courier or you can scan your application forms in and email them
Closing Date: July and October (check with website)

For further information contact:

Tel: (61) 9214 5547 or 9214 8744
Email: ehill@swin.edu.au, jamathews@swin.edu.au

Vice Chancellor's Centenary Research Scholarship (VCRS)

Subjects: All subjects
Purpose: To assist with general living costs

Eligibility: Open to domestic or an international student who have completed a Bachelor degree with First Class Honours and are of exceptional research potential undertaking a higher degree by research (HDR). For further details, please check the website

Level of Study: Research

Type: Research scholarship

Value: The value of the VCRS will be up to $35,000 (tax-exempt) over a maximum period of up to 3.5 full-time years, payable at the rate of $5,000 per year for the 1st year and $12,000 per year for the remaining 2.5 years

Length of Study: 3 years

Application Procedure: Check website for further details

For further information contact:

Building 60Wm, Level 7, 60 William Street, Hawthorn campus, VIC 3122, Australia

Tel: (61) 9214 5547 or 9214 8744
Email: ehill@swin.edu.au, jamathews@swin.edu.au

Swiss National Science Foundation (SNSF)

Wildhainweg 20, PO Box CH-3001, Berne, Switzerland

Tel: (41) 31 308 2222
Fax: (41) 31 308 2275
Website: www.snf.ch
Contact: Dr Benno G Frey, Office for Fellowship
                   Programmes

The Swiss National Science Foundation (SNSF) supports scientific research at Swiss universities and other scientific institutions and awards fellowships to Swiss scientists or scientists living in Switzerland. The SNSF was established in 1952 as a private foundation entrusted with the promotion of basic non commercial research. While the SNSF supports research through grants given to established or promising researchers, it does not maintain its own research institutions. The main objectives of the SNSF are to support basic research in all areas of academic research and to support young scientists and researchers, with the intent of ensuring the continuing high quality of teaching and research in Swiss higher education. In addition to the general research funding, the SNSF is responsible for the National Research Programmes (NRP).

Swiss National Science Foundation Fellowships for Prospective Researchers

Subjects: All subjects

Purpose: To promote holders of MA or PhD degrees, who have had at least one year's experience in active research after the completion of their degree

Eligibility: Open to promising young Scholars under the age of 33 who are Swiss nationals or permanent residents of Switzerland, hold an MA or PhD and can demonstrate at least one year's experience in active research. An exception to the age restriction (to a maximum of two years) can be made for candidates from clinical disciplines, or candidates who have interrupted their scientific careers due to family obligations. The main condition for such an exception is that the candidate has reached a high scientific level and will in the future pursue an active career in science and research. A high priority will be given to candidates who plan to return to Switzerland

Level of Study: Postdoctorate, Predoctorate

Type: A variable number of fellowships

Value: Varies

Length of Study: Varies

Frequency: Annual

Study Establishment: Universities worldwide

Country of Study: Any country

Application Procedure: Applicants must complete an application form, available from the Local Research Commission. Candidates with a degree from a Swiss university should contact the Research Commission of their institution. Candidates with Italian as their native language, who have completed their studies in a foreign country should contact the Research Commission for the Italian speaking part of Switzerland. Swiss candidates who are residents of foreign countries, hold a degree from a foreign university, but who intend to return to Switzerland should contact the Swiss scientific academy responsible for their area of research

Closing Date: Please write for details

Additional Information: For further information please contact Benno Frey or Laurence at the Office for Fellowship Programmes, or refer to the website

Syracuse University

900 South Crouse Ave, Syracuse, NY 13244, United States of America

Tel: (1) 315 443 1870
Fax: (1) 315 443 3423

Email:　grad@syr.edu
Website:　www.syr.edu

Syracuse University is a non-profit, private student research university. Its mission is to promote learning through teaching, research, scholarship, creative accomplishment and service.

Syracuse University Executive MBA Programme

Length of Study: 2 years
Application Procedure: Applicants must return a completed 'Independent Study MBA' application form

For further information contact:

School of Management, Suite 100, Crouse-Hinds School of Management, Syracuse, NY 13244, United States of America

Tel:　　　(1) 315 443 3006
Fax:　　　(1) 315 443 5389
Email:　　grad@gwmail.syr.edu
Contact:　Ms Wendy Giaccaglia

Syracuse University MBA

Purpose: All Syracuse MBA scholarships are awarded based on merit and the qualifications shown on a student's admission application. Applicants are not required to apply separately for merit-based scholarships
Eligibility: To be eligible for the MBA admission, listed below are the requirements. 1. A United States bachelor's degree or its equivalent from an accredited college or university Completed application. 2. Recommended minimum GPA is 3.0 on a 4.0 scale. 4. GMAT or GRE exam. 5. Recommended minimum GMAT score is 600. The 2016 entering class average was 623. 6. For those with GRE scores you can convert them to GMAT through the website www.ets. org/gre/institutions/about/mba/comparison_tool. 7. Program code for GMAT is NG0-SB-40. 8. Institution code for GRE is 2823. 9. English exam (for international students). 10. Minimum total score for TOEFL is 100, IELTS 7.0, PTE 68. 11. Preferred speaking score for TOEFL is 24, IELTS 7.5, PTE 65. 12. Institution code for TOEFL is 2823, department code is 02 if required. 13. PTE Academic program code is 5LD-BQ-15. 14. IELTS: Whitman downloads IELTS scores that have been transmitted to our e-download account
Length of Study: 1–2 years
Country of Study: Any country

Application Procedure: Applicants must complete the application form (including the specified number of photocopies) with official academic transcripts, two letters of recommendation, personal essays, requested financial documents, Graduate Management Admission Test and TOEFL (if applicable) scores, and a fee of US$50. Applications may be fully completed online

For further information contact:

Syracuse University, School of Management, Suite 100, Crouse-Hinds School of Management, Syracuse, NY 13244, United States of America

Tel:　　　(1) 315 443 4492
Fax:　　　(1) 315 443 3423
Email:　　lescis@syr.edu
Contact:　Ms Wendy Giaccaglia

System for Analysis Research and Training (START)

International START Secretariat, 2000 Florida Avenue NW Suite 200, Washington, DC 20009, United States of America

Tel:　　　(1) 202 462 2213
Fax:　　　(1) 202 457 5859
Email:　　START@agu.org
Website:　www.start.org
Contact:　Professor Roland Fuchs, Director

The global change SysTem for Analysis, Research and Training (START), provides an international framework for capacity building. It fosters regional networks of collaborating scientists and institutions in developing countries to conduct research on regional aspects of environmental change, assess impacts and vulnerabilities to such changes and provide information to policy makers.

Start/Norad Fellowship for Doctoral Research and Dissertation on Global Environmental Change

Subjects: Environmental science
Purpose: To financially support outstanding young African scientists in their research
Eligibility: Open to candidates who are not more than 35 years of age and are currently enrolled in a graduate degree programme leading to a PhD degree in an African university. The applicant must have obtained a Master's degree

Level of Study: Doctorate
Type: Fellowship
Value: Varies
Length of Study: 2 years
Frequency: Annual
Study Establishment: Any accredited university
Country of Study: Africa
Application Procedure: Applicants must submit a completed programme application form, a detailed proposal, a curriculum vitae and a letter of recommendation

Closing Date: 15 August
Additional Information: Application materials can be sent electronically or faxed

For further information contact:

Email: cskauffman@agu.org
Contact: Charles S Kauffman, Program Associate

T

Tante Marie's Cooking School

271 Francisco Street, San Francisco, CA 94133, United States of America

Tel:	(1) 415 788 6699
Fax:	(1) 415 788 8924
Email:	peggy@tantemarie.com
Website:	www.tantemarie.com

Tante Marie's Cooking School, located in San Francisco was founded as a full-time school in 1979. It is one of the first schools of fine cooking offering all-day, year-round classes for people who are serious about cooking well. Graduates from Tante Marie's have interesting and varied careers. In addition to offering professional courses for people wanting to begin a career in culinary or pastry, Tante Marie's welcomes interested avocational students in the Evening Series, Weekend Workshops, One-Day Workshops and Cooking Vacations. There are also cooking parties on weekend evenings where groups of up to 30 people cook together. The emphasis at Tante Marie's is in building confidence in the kitchen.

The Absolute Taste Scholarship

Subjects: Cooking
Purpose: To make the candidates learn cooking professionally
Eligibility: All prospective students ordinarily resident in the British Isles who will have attained at least 16 years of age and be under 25 years of age on commencement of the course
Level of Study: Unrestricted
Type: Scholarship
Value: Up to 100 % of the course fee
Frequency: Annual
Country of Study: United States of America
Application Procedure: Check website for further details

Closing Date: 7 June
Funding: Private
Additional Information: Please refer to the website for details

For further information contact:

Email: info@tantemarie.co.uk

Tanzania Communications Regulatory Authority (TCRA)

Tanzania Communications Regulatory Authority (TCRA), Mawasiliano Towers, 20 Sam Nujoma Road, Dar Es Salaam, Tanzania

Tel:	(255) 22 219 9760 - 8; 22 241 2011 - 2
Fax:	(255) 22 241 2009; 22 241 2010
Email:	dg@tcra.go.tz
Website:	www.tcra.go.tz

The Tanzania Communications Regulatory Authority (TCRA) is a quasi independent Government body responsible for regulating the communications and broadcasting sectors in Tanzania. It was established under the TCRA Act no. 12 of 2003 to regulate the electronic communications, and postal services, and management of the national frequency spectrum in the United Republic of Tanzania.

Tanzania Communications Regulatory Authority ICT Scholarship

Purpose: The scholarship offers Tanzania students the opportunity to obtain degrees in the Information and Communication Technologies (ICT) and related areas

© Springer Nature Limited 2019
Palgrave Macmillan (ed.), *The Grants Register 2020*,
https://doi.org/10.1057/978-1-349-95943-3

Eligibility: The scholarship will be awarded on the basis of academic merit and an interview to be conducted by the Scholarship Panel
Level of Study: Postgraduate
Type: Scholarship
Length of Study: All scholarships are provided for the specified duration of a particular degree course
Country of Study: Tanzania
Closing Date: 20 July
Funding: International office
Additional Information: Tanzanian students can apply for these ICT scholarships

For further information contact:

Email: dg@tcra.go.tz

Tata Trusts

Lady Meherbai D. TATA Education Trust

Purpose: The Lady Meherbai D Tata Education Trust awards scholarships to Indian women graduates of recognised universities to pursue higher education abroad, towards the tuition fee
Eligibility: Indian women graduates from a recognised university. 1. Should have a consistently remarkable academic record. 2. Must have applied for admission / secured admission to reputed accredited universities or institutions in the United States, United Kingdom or Europe for the current academic year. 3. Preference will be given to candidates with a minimum of 2 years of work experience in the requisite fields of study
Level of Study: Graduate
Type: Grant
Value: Scholarship amount of Rs. 6 lakhs per student is awarded, depending on the performance of candidate
Frequency: Annual
Country of Study: Any country
Application Procedure: Applications has to be processed through mailing process. Application forms will be emailed to the students on request from Monday, 11 March, to Friday, 19 April. Application forms will be emailed to the applicants upon submission of a neatly typed letter / email giving details of: 1. The course they wish to pursue. 2. The university they will be attending. 3. The course fee required. 4. Sources of funding. 5. Their current profile along with documents for the same
Closing Date: 26 April
Funding: Private
Additional Information: Students shortlisted for the interviews and scholarships awarded would be solely at the

discretion of the Trustees of the Lady Meherbai D Tata Education Trust

For further information contact:

Bombay House, 24, Homi Mody Street, Mumbai, Maharashtra 400 001, India

Tel: (91) 22 6665 8282
Email: igpedulmdtet@tatatrusts.org

Te Pôkai Tara Universities New Zealand

PO Box 11915, Manners Street, Wellington 6142, New Zealand

Tel: (64) 404 381 8500
Fax: (64) 404 381 8501
Email: kiri@nzvcc.ac.nz
Website: www.nzvcc.ac.nz
Contact: Kiri Manuera, Scholarships Manager

The New Zealand Vice Chancellors Committee (NZVCC) was established by the Universities Act 1961, which replaced the federal University of New Zealand with separate institutions. Today the Committee represents the interests of New Zealand's 8 universities. The NZVCC represents the interests of the New Zealand university system to government, its agencies and the public through a range of forums and communications from joint consultative groups to electronic and print publications.

William Georgetti Scholarships

Subjects: All subjects
Purpose: To encourage postgraduate study and research in a field that is important to the social, cultural or economic development of New Zealand
Eligibility: Candidates must be New Zealand citizens or permanent residents. Open to graduates who have been resident in New Zealand for 5 years immediately before application and who are preferably aged between 21 and 28 years
Level of Study: Postgraduate
Type: Scholarship
Value: Up to NZ $20,000 per year for Masters study. For those students studying overseas the emolument shall be at a rate of up to NZ $45,000 per year
Length of Study: 3 year
Frequency: Annual

Study Establishment: Suitable universities
Country of Study: Any country
Application Procedure: Applicants must write for details
Closing Date: 1 March
Funding: Private
Contributor: The Georgetti Trust
Additional Information: Further information is available on request. universitiesnz.communityforce.com/

For further information contact:

Email: scholarshipscf@universitiesnz.ac.nz

Technical University of Denmark (DTU)

Anker Engelunds Vej 1 Bygning 101A, DNK 2800 Lyngby, Denmark

Tel: (45) 45 25 11 56
Email: oerstedpostdoc@adm.dtu.dk, dtu@adm.dtu.dk
Contact: COFUND secretariat

Technical University of Denmark (DTU) is recognized internationally as a leading university in the areas of the technical and the natural sciences, renowned for business-oriented approach, focus on sustainability, and amazing study environment.

H.C. Ørsted Fellowships for International Researchers

Subjects: Mathematics, physics, space research and informatics; chemistry, biotechnology and chemical engineering; electronics and communication; construction, production, buildings and transportation; life science
Purpose: The Programme will contribute to the researcher's career development, broadening and be deepening individual competencies through exposure to an international and multi-disciplinary environment. Eligibility: The programme is open for young talented researchers from all over the world. 1. Level of Study: Research. 2. Type: Fellowships 3. Value: The grant will cover the salary for the postdoc fellow for up to 2 years
Length of Study: 2 years
Country of Study: Denmark
Application Procedure: Applications must be submitted as one compiled PDF file containing all material via DTU's online submission form at www.dtu.dk/english/career
Closing Date: 23 February
Contributor: Marie Sklodowska-Curie Actions

Additional Information: For any queries please contact oerstedpostdoc@adm.dtu.dk

For further information contact:

Email: oerstedpostdoc@adm.dtu.dk

Technische Universiteit Delft (TUD)

Post bus 5, NLD 2600 AA Delft, Netherlands

Tel: (31) 15 278 9111
Fax: (31) 15 278 1855
Email: info@tudelft.nl
Website: www.tudelft.nl/msc

Founded in 1842, the Delft University of Technology is the oldest, largest, and most comprehensive technical university in the Netherlands. It is an establishment of both national importance and significant international standing. Renowned for its high standard of education and research, TU Delft collaborates with other educational establishments and research institutes, both within and outside of the Netherlands. TU Delft aims at being an, interactive partner' to social issues, committed to answering its multifaceted demands and initiating changes to benefit people in the future.

The Shell Centenary Scholarship Fund, Netherlands

Subjects: All master programmes under the TSCSF scholarship scheme
Purpose: To give students the opportunity to study at the TUD and gain skills that will make a long-term contribution to the further development of their countries
Eligibility: Open to candidates who are nationals of and resident in any country other than the ones listed in, Additional Information' and aged 35 or under, intending to study a subject that will be of significant value in aiding the sustainable development of their home country, fluent in spoken and written English, and neither a current nor former employee of the Royal Dutch/Shell Group of companies
Level of Study: Postgraduate
Type: Scholarship
Value: Full-cost scholarship including tuition fees, international travel, living allowances and health insurance
Length of Study: 2 years
Frequency: Annual

Country of Study: Netherlands

Application Procedure: Applicants must have been admitted to a MSc programme of TU Delft, the International Office will subsequently send you the application form by email, the International Office will check your application on the basis of the Royal Dutch/Shell criteria

Closing Date: 15 December (check with website)

Contributor: TUD with support from The Shell Centenary Scholarship Fund (TSCSF)

Additional Information: Countries not eligible: Australia, Austria, Belgium, Canada, Cyprus, Czech Republic, Denmark, Estonia, Finland, France, Germany, Greece, Hungary, Iceland, Ireland, Italy, Japan, Latvia, Lithuania, Luxembourg, Malta, The Netherlands, New Zealand, Norway, Poland, Portugal, Slovenia, Slovakia, Spain, Sweden, Switzerland, United Kingdom, and United States

For further information contact:

Tel: (31) 15 278 5690
Email: msc2@tudelft.nl

Tel Aviv University (TAU)

PO Box 39040, Tel Aviv 6997801, Israel

Tel: (972) 3 640 8111
Email: tauinfo@post.tau.ac.il
Website: www.tau.ac.il

Tel Aviv University (TAU) was founded in 1956 and is located in Israel's cultural, financial and industrial heartland, TAU is the largest university in Israel and the biggest Jewish university in the world. TAU offers an extensive range of programmes in the arts and sciences.

Tel Aviv University Scholarships

Subjects: History and contemporary music

Purpose: To encourage innovative and interdisciplinary research that cuts across traditional boundaries and paradigms

Eligibility: Open to candidates who have registered for their Doctoral or Postdoctoral degree

Level of Study: Doctorate, Postdoctorate

Type: Scholarships

Value: Varies

Frequency: Annual

Application Procedure: Applicants can download the application form from the website. The completed application form along with a curriculum vitae and a description of research project with a list of publications is to be sent

Closing Date: Varies

Additional Information: Applications if sent by email, must be directed to ddprize@post.tau.ac.il

For further information contact:

The Lowy School for Overseas Students, Center Building, Tel-Aviv University, Israel

Email: jkc@jackkentcookefoundation.org
Contact: Ms Smadar Fisher, Director, Dan David Prize

Texas LBJ School

Barbara Jordan Baines Report Fellowship Fund

Purpose: The Barbara Jordan Baines Report Fellowship Fund is available to students interested in gaining skills in policy writing and storytelling, as well as exercising leadership through managing the student-run publication

Eligibility: The Baines Report Fellowship supports a master's student pursuing skills in writing about public policy and experience in news media and content creation. Preference will be given to applicants with prior writing or journalism experience. All currently enrolled full-time LBJ School Master's students who are in good academic standing are eligible to apply

Level of Study: Graduate

Type: Funding support

Value: Students are eligible up to US$750 fund and US$500 toward travel funds

Frequency: Annual

Country of Study: Any country

Application Procedure: Apply using the common Current Student Endowed Fellowship Application form, located on the right side of this page. Students must also submit a current resume, a letter of interest, two writing samples and one well- planned story idea. Final candidates may be interviewed. For further details, check the following link: lbj.utexas.edu/sites/default/files/BJBRElig Criteria.pdf

Funding: Private

Additional Information: In addition, both the fall and spring fellowship awards provide US$500 towards travel to attend the Journal of Public and International Affairs (JPIA) reading weekend in February, contingent on JPIA's invitation. JPIA provides main meals and lodging

For further information contact:

Lyndon B. Johnson School of Public Affairs, The University of Texas at Austin, P.O. Box Y, Austin, TX 78713-8925, United States of America

Tel: (1) 512 471 3200
Email: lbjdeansoffice@austin.utexas.edu

Elspeth D. Rostow Memorial Graduate Fellowship

Subjects: The Elspeth D. Rostow Memorial Graduate Fellowship annually recognizes students who actively engage in opportunities to serve the public while pursuing an LBJ Master's degree.
Purpose: The LBJ Foundation is supporting the LBJ School of Public Affairs through the Elspeth Rostow Memorial Fellowship Fund.
Eligibility: To be considered for this fellowship, applicants must be degree-seeking master's students who have completed one year of full-time study at the LBJ School with a cumulative GPA of 3.0 or above. There are no exceptions to these requirements.
Level of Study: Graduate
Type: Fellowship
Value: US$3,000
Frequency: Annual
Country of Study: Any country
Application Procedure: 1. Complete the Elspeth D. Rostow Memorial Graduate Fellowship application. 2. Submit a one-page statement describing your public service related commitments since enrolling in the LBJ School. Your statement should describe the needs of the community served, how the project pursued addressed those needs, the role you personally played in the public service activities, and the time commitment of the activity. 3. A current resume.
Closing Date: Late October (exact date is not specified)
Funding: Private

For further information contact:

Email: lbjdeansoffice@austin.utexas.edu

Michael and Alice Kuhn Summer Fellowships

Purpose: The Kuhn Fellowship grant, made possible by the Michael and Alice Kuhn Foundation, awards each grantee US$6,000 to cover living expenses during their summer internship
Eligibility: 1. A selection committee will review applications on a rolling basis and recommend applicants with demonstrated commitment to the goals of the Kuhn Summer Fellowship Program: to promote social justice and fight poverty. 2. Students with diverse backgrounds receive priority consideration. 3. The selection committee may make requests in addition to the online application, such as official UT transcripts and/or interviews. 4. The selection committee will make its recommendations to the LBJ School leadership. Final selection is at the discretion of school leadership
Level of Study: Graduate
Type: Fellowship
Frequency: Annual
Country of Study: Any country
Application Procedure: The student's summer work must be done for a nonprofit organization in Central Texas or the United States whose mission is related to social justice and alleviating poverty. There is an interest in supporting students whose placements involve leadership opportunities in the areas of public and legislative advocacy, program-related management, as well as opportunities to work with executive team members on strategic priorities and projects. Students will be asked to link to a Google Drive PDF copy of their: 1. Resume. 2. Relevant three- to five-page writing sample from school or professional setting. 3. Offer letter from the nonprofit confirming the internship and description of work
Closing Date: 30 April
Funding: Commercial, Private

For further information contact:

Email: LBJFellowships@austin.utexas.edu

Terrell Blodgett Fellowship for Government Services in Urban Management and Finance

Purpose: The Blodgett Fellowship is awarded annually on a competitive basis as part of the internship fellowship process
Eligibility: The Blodgett Fellowship is awarded annually on a competitive basis as part of the internship fellowship process. First-year master's students pursuing an internship in local government and/or city management are eligible to apply. To be considered for this fellowship, applicants must be degree-seeking master's stundents
Level of Study: Graduate
Type: Fellowship
Frequency: Annual
Country of Study: Any country

Application Procedure: To apply, students must complete the LBJ internship fellowship application and turn it in along with their approved internship request form, a letter from the agency supervising the internship, a one-page essay on career goals, and a current resume. Using the following link for further information. www.blodgettfellows.org/. Scholarship application link is as follow: lbj.utexas.edu/sites/default/files/InternshipFellowshipApp021218.pdf

Closing Date: Mid April

Funding: Private

For further information contact:

Email: lbjwriting@austin.utexas.edu

Third World Academy of Sciences (TWAS)

TWAS Executive Director ICTP Enrico Fermi Building, Room 108, Via Beirut 6, ITA 34151 Trieste Italy

Tel: (39) 40 2240 327
Fax: (39) 40 2245 59
Email: edoffice@twas.org
Website: www.twas.org
Contact: Professor Romain Murenzi, Executive Director

The Third Word Academy of Sciences (TWAS) is an autonomous international organization that promotes and supports excellence in scientific research and helps build research capacity in the South.

Council of Scientific and Industrial Research/ TWAS Fellowship for Postgraduate Research

Subjects: Newly emerging areas of science and technology
Purpose: To enable scholars from developing countries (other than India) who wish to pursue postgraduate research to undertake research in laboratories or institutes of the CSIR
Eligibility: Candidates must have a Master's or equivalent degree in science or engineering and should be a regular employee in a developing country (other than India) and be holding a research assignment
Level of Study: Postgraduate
Type: Fellowship
Value: Monthly stipend to cover for living costs, food and health insurance
Length of Study: Up to 4 years

Frequency: Annual
Study Establishment: CSIR research laboratories or institutes
Country of Study: India
Application Procedure: One copy of the application should be sent to TWAS and three copies to CSIR. Application forms are available on request or from the website
Closing Date: 1 June
Funding: Government
Contributor: CSIR (India), the Italian Ministry of Foreign Affairs and the Directorate General for Development Co-operation
No. of awards given last year: 8
Additional Information: CSIR is the premier scientific organization of India, and has a network of research laboratories covering wide areas of scientific and industrial research

For further information contact:

International S&T Affairs Directorate, Council for Scientific and Industrial Research (CSIR), Anusandhan Bhavan, 2 Rafi Marg, New Delhi, Delhi 110001, India

Fax: (91) 11 2371 0618
Email: rprasad@csir.res.in
Contact: Dr B K Ramprasad, Senior Deputy Advisor

The Council of Scientific and Industrial Research/ TWAS Fellowship for Postdoctoral Research

Subjects: Newly emerging areas of science and technology
Purpose: To enable scholars from developing countries (other than India) who wish to pursue postdoctoral research to undertake research in laboratories or institutes of the CSIR
Eligibility: The minimum qualification requirement is a PhD degree in science or technology. Applicants must be regular employees in a developing country (but not India) and should hold a research assignment. Be a maximum age of 45 years on December 31st of the application year
Level of Study: Postdoctorate
Type: Fellowship
Value: Monthly stipend to cover for living costs, food and health insurance
Length of Study: Up to 12 months
Frequency: Annual
Study Establishment: CSIR research laboratories or institutes
Country of Study: India
Application Procedure: Applicants must complete an application form, available on request or from the website
Closing Date: 31 August
Funding: Government

Contributor: CSIR (India), the Italian Ministry of Foreign Affairs and the Directorate General for Development Co-operation

No. of awards given last year: 4

Additional Information: CSIR is the premier civil scientific organization of India, which has a network of research laboratories covering wide areas of industrial research

For further information contact:

Tel: (91) 11 331 6751
Fax: (91) 11 371 0618
Email: rprasad@csirhq.ren.nic.in
Contact: Dr B K Ramprasad

Thomson Foundation

37 Park Place, Cardiff CF10 3BB, Wales, United Kingdom

Tel: (44) 29 2035 3060
Fax: (44) 29 2035 3061
Email: enquiries@thomfound.co.uk
Website: www.thomsonfoundation.co.uk
Contact: Mr Gareth Price

The Thomson Foundation provides practical, intensive training both in the United Kingdom and abroad, along with a wide range of consultancies to journalists, managers, technicians and production staff in television, radio and the press.

Thomson Foundation Scholarship

Subjects: Journalism, radio or television broadcasting, internet publishing and photojournalism

Purpose: To enable recipients to attend Thomson Foundation training courses in Britain

Eligibility: Open to professional journalists and broadcasters with at least 3 years of full-time experience

Level of Study: Professional development

Type: Scholarship

Value: Varies

Length of Study: Varies, usually a 12-week Summer course or a shorter 4-week course

Study Establishment: The Thomson Foundation

Country of Study: United Kingdom

No. of awards offered: 20

Application Procedure: Applicants must complete an application form, available from the Foundation, for the courses they wish to apply for

Closing Date: 15 April

Funding: Government, Private

Contributor: The British Foreign Office Chevening Scholarship Scheme

No. of awards given last year: 6

No. of applicants last year: 20

Additional Information: Annual 3-month courses in television, radio and press journalism run from June to September

For further information contact:

Email: enquiries@thomsonfoundation.org

Thurgood Marshall College Fund (TMCF)

901 F Street NW, Suite 300, Washington, DC 20004, United States of America

Tel: (1) 202 507 4851
Fax: (1) 202 652 2934
Email: info@tmcfund.org
Website: www.thurgoodmarshallfund.org

The Thurgood Marshall College Fund (TMCF) was established in 1987 to carry on Justice Marshall's legacy of equal access to higher education by supporting exceptional merit scholars attending America's public historically Black colleges and universities. More than 5,000 Thurgood Marshall Scholars have graduated and are making valuable contributions to science, technology, government, human service, business, education and various communities

Thurgood Marshall College Fund Scholarships

Subjects: Creative and performing arts

Purpose: To financially support outstanding students

Eligibility: Open to candidates who are academically exceptional in the creative and performing arts requiring financial help

Type: Scholarship

Value: Varies

Frequency: Annual

Application Procedure: Completed applications must be submitted along with the required attachments

Funding: Foundation

Additional Information: Refer to the website for details: tmcf.org/our-scholarships/current-scholarships

For further information contact:

AIPLEF Scholarship, 80 Maiden Lane, Suite 2204, New York, NY 1138, United States of America

Email: jessica.barnes@tmcfund.org

Toxicology Education Foundation (TEF)

626 Admiral Drive, Ste. C, PMB 221, Annapolis, MD 21401, United States of America

Tel: (1) 443 321 4654
Fax: (1) 443 321 8702
Email: tefhq@toxedfoundation.org
Website: www.toxedfoundation.org

The mission of TFE is to encourage, support and promote charitable and educational activities that increase the public understanding of toxicology.

Alleghery-ENCRC Student Research Award

Subjects: Toxicology
Purpose: To support a student's thesis, dissertation and summer research project in toxicology and to encourage them to formulate and conduct meaningful research
Eligibility: Open to students who are members in good standing of AE-SOT. The student's advisor must also be a member in good standing and submit a letter concerning availability
Level of Study: Graduate
Type: Award
Value: Up to US$1,000
Frequency: Annual
Country of Study: United States of America
Application Procedure: Applicants must send four copies of completed application form along with a project description and budget
Closing Date: 30 May

For further information contact:

CDC/NIOSH MS 2015, 1095 Willowdale Road, Morgantown, WV 26505, United States of America

Email: LBattelli@cdc.gov
Contact: Lori Battelli

Colgate-Palmolive Grants for Alternative Research

Subjects: Reproductive and developmental toxicology, neurotoxicology, systemic toxicology, sensitization and acute toxicity
Purpose: To identify and support efforts that promote, develop, refine or validate scientifically acceptable animal alternative methods to facilitate the safety assessment of new chemicals and formulations
Level of Study: Research
Type: Research grant
Value: Plaque and maximum award of US$40,000
Frequency: Annual
Country of Study: United States of America
Application Procedure: Application is available online. A research plan, budget, curriculum vitae and a letter from the institution must be sent
Closing Date: 9 October
Funding: Private
Contributor: Colgate-Palmolive
No. of awards given last year: 5

For further information contact:

Email: tefhq@toxedfoundation.org

Food Safety SS Burdock Group Travel Award

Subjects: Food safety toxicology
Purpose: To cover travel expenses for a student to attend the Annual Meeting
Eligibility: Open to full-time graduate students with research interests in toxicology. Students in their early graduate training, who have not attended any SOT Annual Meeting are encouraged to apply
Level of Study: Graduate
Value: Up to US$500
Frequency: Annual
Country of Study: United States of America
Application Procedure: Applicants must send a letter of request indicating that he/she is enroled in good standing in a doctoral training programme. The applicant must also state how the research and training relate to food safety
Closing Date: 24 February

For further information contact:

Email: rmatulka@burdockgroup.com
Contact: Ray Matulka

Regulation and Safety SS Travel Award

Subjects: Toxicology
Purpose: To help defray the costs of travel to the SOT meeting
Eligibility: Open to students submitting a poster or making a presentation at the SOT meeting
Type: Travel award
Value: US$1,500 each
Frequency: Annual
Country of Study: United States of America
Application Procedure: Applicants must fill an application form and an abstract of work preserved
Closing Date: 15 December

For further information contact:

Email: jtmacgror@earthlink.net
Contact: James TMacGregor

Robert L. Dixon International Travel Award

Subjects: Reproductive toxicology
Purpose: To financially assist students studying in the area of reproductive toxicology
Eligibility: Open to applicants enroled full-time in a PhD programme studying reproductive toxicology and are student members of SOT
Level of Study: Doctorate, Graduate
Type: Award
Value: Includes a stipend of US$2,000 for travel costs to enable students to attend the International Congress of Toxicology meeting
Frequency: Every 3 years
Country of Study: United States of America and abroad
Application Procedure: Applicants must submit a completed application form, reference letter, graduate transcripts and lists of complete citations of the original work
Closing Date: 9 October (check with website)
Contributor: Toxicology Education Foundation

For further information contact:

Email: tefhq@toxedfoundation.org

Transport Research Laboratory

Old Wokingham Road, Crowthorne, RG11 6AU, Berkshire, United Kingdom

Contact: Research Division

A Master of Science Degree Scholarship

Subjects: Health informatics and risk management
Purpose: To financially support postgraduate study
Eligibility: Open to part-time self-financing students only. Applicants must have applied for a place for graduate study at UCL
Level of Study: Postgraduate
Type: Scholarship
Value: United Kingdom/European Union tuition fees
Frequency: Annual
Study Establishment: University College London
Country of Study: United Kingdom
Application Procedure: Applicants should contact the department. If the applicants have not applied to UCL they complete a graduate application form and enclose it with the scholarship application
Closing Date: Check the website for the closing date

For further information contact:

Tel: (44) 20 7288 3548
Fax: (44) 20 7288 3322
Email: p.taylor@chime.ucl.ac.uk
Contact: Dr Paul Taylor

Tropical Agricultural Research and Higher Education Center (CATIE)

7170 Cartago, Turrialba 30501, Costa Rica

Tel: (506) 2558 2000
Fax: (506) 2558 2060
Email: posgrado@catie.ac.cr
Website: www.catie.ac.cr
Contact: Dean of the Graduate School

The Tropical Agricultural Research and Higher Education Center (CATIE) is an international, non-profit, regional, scientific and educational institution. Its main purpose is research and education in agricultural sciences, natural resources and related subjects in the American tropics, with emphasis on Central America and the Caribbean.

Scholarship Opportunities Linked to CATIE

Subjects: Ecological agriculture, biotechnology and genetic resources, management and conservation of tropical forestry and biodiversity, tropical woodlands, tropical agroforestry, tropical crop protection and improvement, integrated watershed management and protected areas and environmental socioeconomics and rural enterprise development

Purpose: To develop specialized intellectual capital in clean technology, tropical agriculture, natural resources management and human resources in the American tropics

Eligibility: Priority is given to citizens of Belize, Guatemala, El Salvador, Honduras, Nicaragua, Panama, Costa Rica, Mexico, Venezuela, Colombia, the Dominican Republic, Bolivia and Paraguay

Level of Study: Doctorate, Postgraduate

Type: Scholarship

Value: Tuition and fees

Length of Study: 2 years for a Master

Frequency: Annual

Country of Study: Costa Rica

No. of awards offered: 350

Application Procedure: Applicants must undertake an admission process that constitutes 75% for curricular evaluation and 25% for a domiciliary examination. Please refer to the CATIE website for full instructions

Closing Date: Applications are accepted at any time, but the evaluation deadline for Scholarship-Loan Program is late October. Other sources of financing have specific requirements available on CATIE website. These change considerably over time

Funding: Government, Private, Foundation, International office

Contributor: ASDI, OAS, CATIE, DAAD, CONACYT (Mexico), Ford Foundation, Kellogg Foundation, Joint/Japan World Bank. USAID provided the original donation for the endowment financing the Scholarship-Loan Program, SENACYT and Belgium Cooperation

No. of awards given last year: 32 in the Scholarship-Loan Program. Over 25 students received funding from alternative sources

No. of applicants last year: 350

For further information contact:

Email: posgrado@catie.ac.cr

Trust Company

Level 15, 20 Bond Street, GPO Box 4270, New South Wales, Sydney, NSW 2001, Australia

Tel:	(61) 2 8295 8100
Fax:	(61) 2 8295 8659
Email:	scholarships@thetrustcompany.com.au
Website:	thetrustcompany.com.au/philanthropy/awards

The Trust Company is manager at a number high profile awards and scholarships made possible through Charitable bequests/trusts. These include the Miles Franklin Literary Award, Kathleen Mitchell Award (literary), Portia Geach Memorial Award (for female artists), the Sir Robert William Askin Operatic Travelling Scholarship (for male singers), the Lady Mollie Isabelle Askin Ballet Travelling Scholarship, and the Marten Bequest Travelling Scholarship.

Miles Franklin Literary Award

Subjects: Writing

Purpose: To reward the novel of the year that is of the highest literary merit and presents Australian life in any of its phases

Eligibility: Refer to the application form. The novel must have been first published in any country in the year preceding the award. Biographies, collections of short stories, children's books and poetry are not eligible. All works must be in English

Level of Study: Unrestricted

Type: Award

Value: A$60,000

Frequency: Annual

Country of Study: Any country

Application Procedure: Applicants must complete an application form and send six copies of their novel

Funding: Trusts

Contributor: The estate of the late Miss SMS Miles Franklin

No. of awards given last year: 1

Additional Information: If there is no novel worthy of the prize, the award may be given to the author of a play. Please refer to the website for further details: www.milesfranklin.com.au/

For further information contact:

Email: trustawards@thetrustcompany.com.au

Tu Delft

Justus & Louise van Effen Excellence Scholarships

Purpose: The Foundation Justus & Louise van Effen was established with the aim of stimulating excellent international MSc students and financially supporting them in their wish to study at TU Delft

Eligibility: Excellent international applicants (conditionally) admitted to one of the 2-year Regular TU Delft's MSc programmes. With a cumulative grade point average (GPA) of

80% or higher of the scale maximum in the bachelor's degree from an internationally renowned university outside The Netherlands

Level of Study: Graduate

Type: Scholarship

Value: €30.000 per year for Non-EU students and €11.500 per year for EU/EFTA students

Frequency: Annual

Country of Study: Any country

Application Procedure: Apply it online. Check with the below link for further information. www.tudelft.nl/en/education/admission-and-application/msc-international-diploma/1-admission-requirements/

Closing Date: 1 December

Funding: Private

Additional Information: Membership to the Scholarship club giving access to personal development, workshops, seminars, etc

For further information contact:

Postbus NLD 5,2600 AA Delft, Netherlands

Tel: (31) 15 27 89111
Email: info@tudelft.nl

Turkiye Scholarships Burslari

Turkey Government Scholarships

Purpose: Winning this Turkish scholarship means that you will have the chance to experience a 4-year undergraduate, master or doctoral program at the partner Turkish Universities and that too in English

Eligibility: 1. There is also a strict criterion when it comes to the age of the applicant. 2. For the undergraduate degree, the candidates should not be born earlier than January 1997. 3. While for Master's degree the candidates must not be born before January 1988. For PhDs the date is January 1983 and for Research program the applicants should be born before January 1973. 4. 70% marks required for the application of an undergraduate program. 5. 75% marks required for the application of PhD and Masters. 6. 90% marks required for the application of Medical School programs. 7. Anyone holding Turkish citizenship or having previously held Turkish citizenship cannot apply for the program. 8. Students who are already studying in Turkey are not able to apply for the Scholarship. 9. Students who are selected must present their documents if they are asked otherwise they will not be entertained

Level of Study: Doctorate

Type: Scholarship

Value: Overall expenditure is affordable

Frequency: Annual

Country of Study: Any country

Application Procedure: Turkey scholarship will be applied with the following terms. 1. University Entrance Exam Grade. 2. Diploma Grade. 3. Average Grades. 4. High School Graduation. 5. International Test Score. 6. CGPA

Closing Date: 24 February each year

Funding: Private

Additional Information: Türkiye Scholarships applications will be received in one period, and applications will be open between 15 January- 20 February for international students from all countries

For further information contact:

Email: info@turkiyeburslari.gov.tr

UMass Amhert

Refractique (Lensball World) Photography Innovation & Excellence Scholarship

Subjects: About Us Refractique We specialize in lensball education via our digital course Globalize with over 2.5 hours of dedicated refraction photography video learning content directly downloadable through our website. We also distribute the 80mm and 60mm via our beautiful packages on Amazon

Purpose: We provide a premium offering and pride ourselves on our products - enjoying this fun creative photography ourselves initially before enabling others to learn more about this wonderful hobby

Eligibility: studying an Arts Degree (or relevant photography course)

Level of Study: Postgraduate

Type: Scholarship

Value: US$2,000 (occurs on a twice yearly basis with a US$1,000 per scholarship eligible)

Frequency: Annual

Country of Study: Any country

Application Procedure: 1. Prepare a refraction photography submission and send to support@refractique.com. 2. The submission must be for a minimum of 10 quality refraction related photos, with a maximum of 20 photos. You are also required to write a minimum of 500 words to describe the photos, what they mean to you and what kind of photographic techniques you used to obtain the results/outcome in the photos. You may also like to write more generically about refraction photography - what are the benefits, how to take great photos and how you use refraction accessories including the lensball. The judge will award the scholarships based on the standard of the photos as well as the written text

Closing Date: 30 January and 30 June of each year

Funding: Private

Additional Information: For further information, refer the website link. lensballs.com/pages/social-support

For further information contact:

Email: support@refractique.com

Union College

Union College Board of Trustees Scholarship

Purpose: This scholarship is worth full tuition

Eligibility: 1. Must attend a college or university in the state of Nebraska. 2. Must be an incoming freshman. 3. Must enroll full time. 4. Must have a grade point average of 3.9 or higher (or a GED score of 750 or higher). 5. Must have an ACT score of 32 or higher OR an SAT score of 1,500 or higher

Level of Study: Graduate

Type: Scholarship

Value: US$21,250

Length of Study: Varies. addition of years is possible

Frequency: Annual

Country of Study: Any country

Application Procedure: 1. Admissions information is available on the Union College website by clicking on the 'Admissions Policy' link. Admissions applications are available in online and PDF formats. 2. In addition to a completed application, each student must submit an official high school transcript and ACT/SAT scores. 3. Students whose first language is not English must also submit TOEFL (Test of English as a Foreign Language) scores. 4. Admissions applications are available in online and PDF formats. In addition to a completed application, each student must submit an official high school transcript and ACT/SAT scores

© Springer Nature Limited 2019
Palgrave Macmillan (ed.), *The Grants Register 2020*,
https://doi.org/10.1057/978-1-349-95943-3

Closing Date: 1 April
Funding: Private

For further information contact:

3800 S. 48th St., Lincoln, NE 68506-4386, United States of America

Tel: (1) 402 486 2600
Email: enroll@ucollege.edu

United Nations Educational, Scientific and Cultural Organization (UNESCO)

7 place de Fontenoy, F-75352 Paris, France

Tel: (33) 1 45 68 10 00 ext. 81507
Fax: (33) 1 45 67 55 03
Contact: Ms F Abu-Shady, Director, Equipment & Fellowships Division

As early as 1951, a programme to promote and develop youth exchange for educational purposes has existed in UNESCO. The Organization continued its action under the Fellowships Programme to respond to the needs of Member States in the field of human resources development and capacity building. This programme has up to date enabled more than 52,000 fellows from around the world to study in different countries contributing to intellectual solidarity, international cooperation and mutual understanding.

United Nationals Educational Scientific Cultural Organization Individual Fellowships

Subjects: Food science and production, architectural restoration, interpretation and translation, business studies, education and teacher training, fine and applied arts, law, natural sciences, social and behavioural science, and mathematics
Purpose: To provide opportunities to further primarily higher education or research generally abroad, and to acquire international experience in fields of study for which appropriate facilities are not available in the country of origin
Eligibility: Open to nationals of UNESCO member states and associate members
Level of Study: Doctorate, Postdoctorate, Postgraduate, Professional development
Type: Fellowship

Value: Monthly allowance usually based on UN stipend scale, plus travel, tuition, books and small equipment costs
Length of Study: No more than 9 months
Frequency: Dependent on funds available
Country of Study: Other
Application Procedure: Application through national authorities specially designated by UNESCO member states (usually National Commission for UNESCO or appropriate Ministry). Direct applications will not be considered.

United Nations Educational, Scientific and Cultural Organization(UNESCO)/International Sustainable Energy DeISEDC Co-Sponsored Fellowships Programme

Subjects: Energy and sustainable development; ecological management of energy resources; renewable energy; sustainable and renewable energy power generation
Purpose: To enhance the capacity-building and human resources development in the area of sustainable and renewable energy sources in developing countries and countries in transition
Eligibility: Holder of at least a BSc degree or BA in Economics; proficient in English language; not more than 35 years of age
Length of Study: This is a four weeks fellowship programme
Country of Study: Any country
Application Procedure: All applications should be endorsed by the National Commission for UNESCO and must be duly completed in English or French
Closing Date: 3 April
Contributor: UNESCO/ISEDC
Additional Information: For more details, please visit the website www.opportunitiesforafricans.com/unesco-isedc-co-sponsored-fellowships-programme-2018-fully-funded-to-moscow-russia/

For further information contact:

Email: info@oppurtunitydesk.org

United Nations International School of Hanoi

G9 Ciputra Lac Long Quan Road, Tay Ho District, Vietnam

Tel: (84) 4 3758 1551
Email: info@unishanoi.org
Website: www.unishanoi.org

United Nations International School of Hanoi's mission is to encourage students to be independent, lifelong learners who strive for excellence and become responsible stewards of our global society and natural environment, achieved within a supportive community that values diversity and through a programme reflecting the ideals and principles of the United Nations.

United Nations International School (UNIS) Hanoi Scholarship Programme for Vietnamese Students in Vietnam

Subjects: Scholarship is offered for IB programme. The IB programme is designed to be challenging in all areas with students required to take six different subjects across a broad range of academic disciplines, in addition to Theory of Knowledge, an extended essay and CAS (Community Action Service) involvement
Purpose: Students may apply to the UNIS Hanoi Scholarship Programme for entry to Grade 8, Grade 9 and Grade 10. The students will graduate with the International Baccalaureate Diploma
Eligibility: The Students applying for the Scholarship Programme at UNIS Hanoi must hold or be eligible to hold a Vietnamese passport and should have permanent residence no more than one hour of transport from UNIS Hanoi. Applicants are required to provide a copy of Household registration book. Graduate from Grade 12 at UNIS Hanoi before their 20th Birthday. Vietnamese students are eligible to apply for this scholarship. For detailed information, please visit website
Type: Scholarship
Value: The UNIS Hanoi Scholarship Programme gives the opportunity for students to enter UNIS Hanoi with a full (100%) fee waiver until graduation
Country of Study: Vietnam
Application Procedure: Applicants should use the Application Checklist in the Application Package to ensure they have a complete application. All applicants are strongly encouraged to submit applications well before deadline. Completed applications with supporting documents and a recent passport style photo should be handed in to the school at the main gate addressed
Closing Date: 31 December
Contributor: United Nations International School of Hanoi
Additional Information: Shortlist finalists are invited to UNIS Hanoi for interview and testing in the week of May 20th

For further information contact:

Email: scholarships@unishanoi.org

United States Center for Advanced Holocaust Studies

United States Holocaust Memorial Museum, 100 Raoul Wallenberg Place South West, Washington, DC 20024-2126, United States of America

Tel:	(1) 202 488 0400 / 202 314 7802
Fax:	(1) 202 479 9726
Email:	vscholars@ushmm.org
Website:	www.ushmm.org
Contact:	Ms Jo-Ellyn Decker, Program Coordinator

The United States Holocaust Memorial Museum is the United State's national institution for the documentation, study and interpretation of Holocaust history, and serves as the country's memorial to the millions of people murdered during the Holocaust. The Center for Advanced Holocaust Studies fosters research in Holocaust and genocide studies.

Joyce and Arthur Schechter Fellowship

Subjects: Linguistics, cultural studies, and related subjects
Purpose: To provide for a Scholar to be in residence at the Museum for a period of six weeks to three months to conduct research using the vast resources of the Museum
Eligibility: Applicants must hold a PhD or be an advanced PhD candidate (ABD) by the application deadline. Those candidates with equivalent professional or terminal degrees or recognised professional standing may also apply
Type: Fellowship
Value: A stipend of US$5,000 to cover housing, living, and international or domestic travel expenses. The Joyce and Arthur Schechter Fellow will also be provided with office space, postage, and access to a computer, telephone, facsimile machine, and photocopier. Cost sharing by the applicants home institution is welcome
Frequency: Annual
Country of Study: United States of America
Application Procedure: Applicants must submit a completed application form and supporting material for fellowship consideration. To request an application form or additional information please contact Renee Taft, Director, Visiting Scholars Program, at the Center for Advanced Holocaust Studies
Closing Date: 31 October
Funding: Private
Additional Information: The Schechter Fellow is encouraged to participate in the Museum's broad array of scholarly and other programmes

For further information contact:

Tel:	(1) 202 314 0378
Fax:	(1) 202 479 9726
Email:	rtaft@ushmm.org
Contact:	Ms Renee Taft, Visiting Scholar Programme Director

United States Center for Advanced Holocaust Studies Dissertation Award

Subjects: Holocaust and genocide studies
Purpose: To encourage the work of exceptional new scholars in the area of the holocaust and genocide studies. The fellowship also provides an opportunity for a new PhD to work at the Center on a conversion of the dissertation into a monograph or on a new post dissertation holocaust related research topic
Eligibility: Open to all PhD candidates completing their dissertations after January 1st 1998 and before the application deadline
Level of Study: Postdoctorate
Type: Award
Value: A stipend of up to US$15,000 for residence at the Center. The museum will also provide office space, postage, and access to a computer, telephone, facsimile machine, and photocopier
Length of Study: 1 semester or more
Frequency: Annual
Study Establishment: United States Center for Advanced Holocaust Studies
Country of Study: United States of America
Application Procedure: Applicants must contact Renee Taft, Director, Visiting Scholars Programme, or Betsy Anthony, Programme Assistant, Visiting Scholar Programme for more information and application forms. Dissertations should be nominated by the author's university department chair and accompanied by a letter of acceptance for the degree and a 250 word abstract of the dissertation's subject matter. Three copies of the dissertation should be submitted. A statement must be included giving the United States Holocaust Memorial Museum permission to produce the dissertation for copying purposes
Closing Date: 15 March
Funding: Private
Additional Information: The Center's historian, Fellows in residence, and publications staff will be available to assist the successful applicant

For further information contact:

Tel:	(1) 202 314 0378
Fax:	(1) 202 479 9726
Email:	rtaft@ushmm.org
Contact:	Ms Renee Taft, Visiting Scholar Programme Director

United States Commission on International Religious Freedom (USCIRF)

732 N. Capitol Street, N.W., Suite A714, Washington, DC 20401, United States of America

Tel:	(1) 202 523 3240
Fax:	(1) 202 523 5020
Email:	communications@uscirf.gov
Website:	www.uscirf.gov

United States Commission on International Religious Freedom is an independent, bipartisan United States of America federal government commission, the first of its kind in the world, that monitors the universal right to freedom of religion or belief abroad. USCIRF reviews the facts and circumstances of religious freedom violations and makes policy recommendations to the President, the Secretary of State, and Congress. USCIRF Commissioners are appointed by the President and the Congressional leadership of both political parties.

United States of America Commission on International Religious Freedom Internships

Subjects: USCIRF offers Administrative, Communications, Government Relations, Office of Legal Counsel, Policy: Legal Research and Policy: Regional Policy Analysis
Eligibility: Currently enroled undergraduates (sophomores, juniors and seniors) and graduate students (including JD and LLM candidates) with minimum 2.5 GPA are eligible for internships with USCIRF. Students of United States of America can apply (or otherwise authorized to intern with the United States of America government). For detailed information, visit website
Type: Internship
Value: All United States Commission on International Religious Freedom (USCIRF) internships are paid; however, course credit may be available
Country of Study: United States of America
Application Procedure: The mode of applying is via email, fax, or mail (applicants should specify the internship and semester they are applying for in their cover letter and the subject line of an emailed application). Policy Department: Regional Policy Analysis Intern should specify what region they are applying for in their cover letter and the subject line of an emailed application. Application requirements: cover letter explaining qualifications and why one would like to intern at USCIRF; resume; 3–5 page writing sample; 2–3 letters of reference

Closing Date: 20 July (Fall semester: September to December), 1 November (Spring semester: January to May), 1 April (Summer Semester: June to August)
Contributor: United States of America Commission on International Religious Freedom (USCIRF)
Additional Information: Internships can be full-time or part-time for a minimum of 8 weeks. Internships are available year-round, and applications are accepted on a rolling basis

For further information contact:

Email: internship@uscirf.gov

United States Institute of Peace (USIP)

2301 Constitution Avenue, NW, Washington, DC 20037, United States of America

Tel: (1) 202 457 1700
Fax: (1) 202 429 6063
Email: grant_program@usip.org
Website: www.usip.org
Contact: Ms Cornelia Hoggart, Senior Programme Assistant

The United States Institute of Peace (USIP) is mandated by the Congress to promote education and training, research and public information programmes on means to promote international peace and resolve international conflicts without violence. The Institute meets this mandate through an array of programmes, including grants, fellowships, conferences and workshops, library services, publications and other educational activities.

Jennings Randolph Program for International Peace Dissertation Fellowship

Subjects: A broad range of disciplines and interdisciplinary fields
Purpose: To support dissertations that explore the sources and nature of international conflict, and strategies to prevent or end conflict and to sustain peace
Eligibility: Open to applicants of all nationalities who are enroled in an accredited college or university in the United States of America. Applicants must have completed all requirements for the degree except the dissertation by the commencement of the award
Level of Study: Doctorate
Type: Fellowships

Value: US$20,000, which may be used to support dissertation writing or field research
Length of Study: 1 year
Frequency: Annual
Study Establishment: The student's home university or site of fieldwork
Country of Study: United States of America
Application Procedure: Applicants must complete a web-based application form, available on the Institute's website
Closing Date: 5 January
Funding: Government
No. of awards given last year: 10
Additional Information: The programme does not support work involving partisan political and policy advocacy or policy making for any government or private organization

For further information contact:

Tel: (1) 202 429 3853
Email: jrprogram@usip.org
Contact: Miss Shira Lowinger, Program Coordinator

Jennings Randolph Program for International Peace Senior Fellowships

Subjects: Preventive diplomacy, ethnic and regional conflicts, peacekeeping and peace operations, peace settlements, postconflict reconstruction and reconciliation, democratization and the rule of law, cross-cultural negotiations, United States of America policy in the 21st century and related subjects
Purpose: To use the recipient's existing knowledge and skills towards a fruitful endeavour in the international peace and conflict management field, and to help bring the perspectives of this field into the Fellow's own career
Eligibility: Open to outstanding practitioners and scholars from a broad range of backgrounds. The competition is open to citizens of any country who have specific interest and experience in international peace and conflict management. Candidates would typically be senior academics, but applicants who hold at least a Bachelor's degree from a recognized university will also be considered
Type: Fellowship
Value: A stipend, an office with computer and voicemail and a part-time research assistant
Length of Study: Up to 10 months
Frequency: Annual
Study Establishment: USIP
Country of Study: United States of America
No. of awards offered: 136
Application Procedure: Applicants must complete a - web-based application form, available on request from the Institute or from the website

Closing Date: Early January (check with website)
Funding: Government
No. of awards given last year: 10
No. of applicants last year: 136

For further information contact:

Tel: (1) 202 429 3886
Email: jrprogram@usip.org
Contact: Miss Shira Lowinger, Program Coordinator

United States-India Educational Foundation (USIEF)

Fulbright House 12 Hailey Road, New Delhi, Delhi 110001, India

Tel: (91) 11 2332 8944/48
Fax: (91) 2332 9718
Email: info@fulbright-india.org
Website: www.fulbright-india.org
Contact: Programme Officer

The activities of the United States Educational Foundation in India (USEFI) may be broadly categorized as the administration of the Fulbright Exchange Fellowships for Indian and United States of America scholars and professionals, and the provision of educational advising services to help Indian students wishing to pursue higher education in the United States. USEFI also works for the promotion of dialogue among fulbrighters and their communities as an outgrowth of educational exchange.

Fulbright Distinguished Awards in Teaching Program for International Teachers

Subjects: The Fulbright Distinguished Awards in Teaching Program for international teachers (Fulbright DAI) is sponsored by the Bureau of Educational and Cultural Affairs, United States of America Department of State
Purpose: It is part of the overall Fulbright Program, named in honor of Senator J. William Fulbright, which promotes mutual understanding among people of the United States and other countries
Eligibility: The applicant should: 1. Be a citizen of India and reside in India at the time of application. 2. Live and teach in the states of Andhra Pradesh, Odisha, Telangana, Karnataka, Kerala, Tamil Nadu, Puducherry, Lakshadweep and the Andaman and Nicobar Islands, Chhattisgarh, Goa, Gujarat,

Madhya Pradesh, Maharashtra, Daman and Diu, and Dadra and Nagar Haveli. 3. Hold at least a bachelor's degree. A teacher training degree is preferred. 4. Be a full-time teacher teaching any subject at any level (primary, middle, secondary or senior secondary). 5. Have completed at least five years of full-time teaching experience at the program start
Level of Study: Graduate
Type: Award
Frequency: Annual
Country of Study: Any country
Application Procedure: 1. Fellows will be selected through a merit-based open competition. After the application deadline, a screening committee will review all eligible applications. 2. Short listed candidates will be interviewed by a committee in New Delhi which will select nominees whose names will be forwarded to Washington, D.C. for further consideration. Nominees will be required to take the iBT TOEFL examination in May. 3. All candidates will be notified of their status in September
Closing Date: 1 March
Funding: Private

For further information contact:

Email: colin@fulbright.org.nz
Contact: Mr Colin Kennedy

Fulbright Indo-American Environmental Leadership Program

Subjects: Environmental information systems and reporting, environmental policy and law, environmental education and environmental sciences, technology and testing
Purpose: To provide funding for Indian environment professionals to explore future links between American and Indian organisations with common agendas
Eligibility: Open to all Indian mid-level environment professionals with at least five years of professional experience in the respective field and a Master's or professional degree of at least four years duration. Applicants will preferably be under 50 years of age. Special attention will be given to applicants who can demonstrate involvement in co-operative efforts between academia, research institutions, government, industry and non governmental organisations to make practical contributions to environmental policies and programmes
Level of Study: Postdoctorate, Professional development
Type: Internship
Value: Round-trip travel from India to the United States of America, a monthly stipend, professional allowance, settling-in allowance plus health insurance. No allowance or travel is provided for dependants
Length of Study: 4 and 8 weeks

Frequency: Annual
Study Establishment: Selected Fellows will be placed at environmental public, private, non governmental organisations, academic institutions, research centres or environment related government agencies
Country of Study: United States of America
Application Procedure: Applicants must obtain an application form either in person from USEFI offices or by sending a stamped addressed envelope to the nearest local USEFI office. The envelope should be superscribed USEFI-IAELP. Application forms can also be downloaded from the website or requested via email specifying the relevant fellowship category. Although USEFI does not require applicants to have a letter of affiliation from a United States institution at the time of applying, it encourages all applicants to correspond, in advance, with potential host institutions
Closing Date: 1 August for completed applications and 15 July for application form requests
Additional Information: If the applicant is successful but unable to arrange an affiliation or name an institution in the United States of America with which to be affiliated, USEFI will help secure placement. The programme will combine short-term practical training/internship with opportunities for networking with American counterpart organisations

For further information contact:

Email: lakshmi@fulbright-india.org

Fulbright-Nehru Master's Fellowships

Purpose: The Fulbright-Nehru Master's Fellowships are designed for outstanding Indians to pursue a master's degree program at select United States of America colleges and universities in the areas of Arts and Culture Management including Heritage Conservation and Museum Studies; Environmental Science/Studies; Higher Education Administration; International Legal Studies;
Eligibility: In addition to the General Prerequisites, the applicants should: 1. Have completed an equivalent of a United States of America bachelor's degree from a recognized Indian university with at least 55% marks. Applicants should either possess a four-year bachelor's degree or a completed master's degree, if the bachelor's degree is of less than four years' duration. 2. Have at least three years' full-time (paid) professional work experience relevant to your proposed field of study by the application deadline. 3. Demonstrate experience in leadership and community service. 4. Must not have another degree from a United States of America university or be enrolled in a United States of America degree program
Level of Study: Graduate
Type: Fellowship

Frequency: Annual
Country of Study: Any country
Closing Date: 15 June
Funding: Private

For further information contact:

Email: humphrey@usief.org.in

Fulbright-Nehru Postdoctoral Research Fellowships

Purpose: These fellowships are designed for Indian faculty and researchers who are in the early stages of their research careers in India
Eligibility: 1. The applicant must have a PhD degree within the past four years. S/he must have obtained PhD degree between 15 July and 16 July. The applicant is required to upload his/her PhD degree certificate/provisional PhD certificate in the online application. 2. the applicant must be published in reputed journals and demonstrate evidence of superior academic and professional achievement. Please upload a recent significant publication (copy of paper/article) in the online application. 3. If applicant is employed, please follow the instructions carefully regarding Letter of Support from Home Institution. If applicable, please obtain the endorsement from the appropriate administrative authority on the FNPostdoc Letter of Support from Home Institution. The employer must indicate that leave will be granted for the fellowship period
Level of Study: Postgraduate
Type: Fellowship
Frequency: Annual
Country of Study: Any country
Application Procedure: These fellowships provide J-1 visa support, a monthly stipend, Accident and Sickness Program for Exchanges per United States of America Government guidelines, round-trip economy class air travel from India to the United States of America, a modest settling-in allowance, and a professional allowance
Closing Date: 15 July
Funding: Private

For further information contact:

Email: postdoc@usief.org.in

United States-India Educational Foundation (USIEF) Fulbright-CII Fellowships for Leadership in Management

Subjects: Leadership in management

Purpose: To enable business managers to attend a management programme in the United States

Eligibility: Open to Indian business managers. Age limit, preferably not above 40, Nationality: Indian, Designed for: Mid-level Managers in Indian Industries

Level of Study: Professional development

Type: Fellowship

Value: See website for details

Length of Study: 10 weeks

Frequency: Annual

Study Establishment: Carnegie Mellon University

Country of Study: United States of America

No. of awards offered: 49

Application Procedure: Applicants must complete an application form, available from the CII

Closing Date: 15 February

Funding: Corporation, Foundation

Contributor: USEFI and employers of selected Managers

No. of awards given last year: 8

No. of applicants last year: 49

Additional Information: For further information contact the Confederation of Indian Industry (CII). Please check the website www.usief.org.in/Fulbright-Nehru-CII-Fellowships-Leadership-Management.aspx

For further information contact:

Confederation of Indian Industry, Mantosh Sondhi Centre, 23, Institutional Area, Lodi Road, New Delhi, Delhi 110003, India

Tel: (91) 2462 9994 7 ext. 367
Fax: (91) 2460 1298, 2462 6149
Email: sudarsan@usief.org.in
Contact: Ms S Rajeshwari, Executive Officer

United States-United Kingdom Fulbright Commission

188 Kirtling Street, SW8 5BN, London, United Kingdom

Tel: (44) 2074 046 880
Fax: (44) 2074 984 023
Email: programmes@fulbright.co.uk
Website: www.fulbright.co.uk
Contact: Mr Michael Scott-Kline, Director

The United States-United Kingdom Fulbright Commission has a programme of awards offered annually to citizens of the United Kingdom and United States of America.

The Fulbright-Edinburgh University Award

Subjects: All subjects

Purpose: To enable a United States citizen to pursue postgraduate study in the United Kingdom at the University of Bristol

Eligibility: Applicant must be a United States citizen (resident anywhere but the United Kingdom), and a graduating senior, holding a BS/BA degree, master's or doctoral degree candidate, young professional or artist

Level of Study: Doctorate, Graduate, Postgraduate

Type: Award/Grant

Value: Up to £20,000, limited sickness and accident benefit coverage, as well as participation in a number of Fulbright Scholar events including the Fulbright Forum in January are also included

Frequency: Annual

Study Establishment: University of Edinburgh

Country of Study: United Kingdom

Application Procedure: Please visit the website us. fulbrightonline.org/applynow.html

Closing Date: 18 October

Additional Information: For more information, visit www. ed.ac.uk/studying/postgraduate and us.fulbrightonline.org/ program_country.html?id=112

For further information contact:

Tel: (44) 131 651 4221
Email: Robert.Lawrie@ed.ac.uk
Contact: Ms Lawrie Robert, Head of Scholarships & Student Finance

Universities Canada

Tel: (1) 613 563 3961 ext. 259
Email: tanaka@univcan.ca
Contact: Gabrielle Leblanc, Program Officer

Universities Canada manages government-funded international partnership programs and more than 130 scholarship programs on behalf of private sector companies.

ConocoPhillips Canada Centennial Scholarship Program

Subjects: All disciplines are eligible

Purpose: To support young Canadian visionaries who have a drive to make a difference in the future. The scholarship

programme encourages individuals with academic excellence and demonstrated leadership
Eligibility: Canadian citizens or permanent residents of Canada
Type: Scholarship
Value: Up to C$5,000 per year for college studies and up to C$10,000 per year for university studies
Length of Study: 2 years
Country of Study: Canada
Closing Date: 30 May
Additional Information: For more information, please contact awards@univcan.ca

For further information contact:

Email: ucawards@ucalgary.ca

Fessenden-Trott Scholarship

Subjects: All disciplines are eligible
Eligibility: Any Canadian educational institution which is a member, or affiliated to a member of Universities Canada
Type: Scholarship
Value: $9,000
Length of Study: 3 years
Country of Study: Canada
Closing Date: 15 June
Additional Information: For more information, please contact awards@univcan.ca

For further information contact:

Tel: (1) 613 563 1236
Email: awards@aucc.ca

Multiple Sclerosis Society of Canada Scholarship Programs: John Helou Scholarship

Subjects: All disciplines are eligible
Purpose: To encourage academic excellence and the pursuit of higher education among students who are directly affected by Multiple Sclerosis
Eligibility: Candidates must be female Canadian citizens or permanent residents
Type: Fellowship
Value: C$6,250 per academic year
Length of Study: 4 years
Country of Study: Canada
Application Procedure: Applicants must submit their own application electronically through the online platform: www.fwis.fr
Closing Date: 31 March

Additional Information: For additional information, please contact awards@univcan.ca

For further information contact:

Email: lindsay.gulin@mssociety.ca

Tanaka Fund Program

Purpose: The Tanaka Fund Program provides institutional support for the enhancement of Japanese language study opportunities at Canadian universities. It aspires to promote and help improve Japanese language education, and to support institutional program development
Type: Grant
Value: To be confirmed
Length of Study: To be confirmed
Country of Study: Canada
Additional Information: For further details, please contact tanaka@univcan.ca

For further information contact:

Email: tanaka@univcan.ca

Universities Federation for Animal Welfare (UFAW)

The Old School, Brewhouse Hill, AL4 8AN, St Albans, United Kingdom

Tel: (44) 15 8283 1818
Fax: (44) 15 8283 1414
Email: ufaw@ufaw.org.uk
Website: www.ufaw.org.uk

The Universities Federation for Animal Welfare (UFAW), the international animal welfare science society, is a United Kingdom registered scientific and educational charity that brings together the animal welfare science community, educators, veterinarians and all concerned about animal welfare worldwide in order to achieve advances in the well-being of farm, companion, laboratory and captive wild animals, and for those animals with which we interact in the wild.

Universities Federation for Animal Welfare Student Scholarships

Subjects: Research that is likely to provide new insight into the subjective mental experiences of animals relevant to their welfare and at understanding their needs and preferences, and also applied research aimed at developing practical solutions to animal welfare problems

Purpose: To encourage students to develop their interests in animal welfare and their abilities for animal welfare research

Eligibility: Applications are welcome from individuals studying at universities or colleges in the United Kingdom or an overseas institution at which there is a UFAW University Links representative. Students will usually be undertaking courses in the agricultural, biological, medical, psychological, veterinary or zoological sciences. Applicants need a nominated supervisor to oversee the project

Level of Study: Graduate, Postgraduate

Type: Scholarship

Value: £170 subsistence and £30 departmental expenses for each week of study

Length of Study: Funding provided for a maximum of 8 weeks (although project duration may be longer)

Frequency: Annual

Country of Study: Any country

Application Procedure: Applicants must complete a UFAW Animal Welfare Student Scholarship application form available for download from the UFAW website www.ufaw.org.uk

Closing Date: 26 February

Funding: Private

Additional Information: Successful applicants must submit a written report to UFAW by November of the year in which the project was undertaken. Please see the website for further details www.ufaw.org.uk

University College Birmingham

Summer Row, B3 1JB, Birmingham, United Kingdom

Tel:	(44) 12 1604 1000
Fax:	(44) 12 1608 7100
Email:	Registry@bcftcs.ac.uk
Website:	www.ucb.ac.uk
Contact:	Student Scholarships

Target Recruitment Partial Fee Waiver

Subjects: Tourism, hospitality and child care

Purpose: To reduce tuition fee for new international students

Eligibility: Applicants must refer to the website for details

Level of Study: Postgraduate

Type: Scholarships

Value: Up to £1,000

Length of Study: 1 year

Frequency: Annual

Study Establishment: University College Birmingham

Country of Study: United Kingdom

Closing Date: Check the website

Additional Information: Applications can be considered for entry in Semester 1 (Late September/Early October) or Semester 2 (Late January/Early February). Applications should be made at least 2 months prior to the entry date. No applications are necessary. Partial Fee Waivers will be noted in all offer letters sent to applicants from relevant countries. For more information contact the International Student Office on international

For further information contact:

Email: international@ucb.ac.uk

University College London

Gower Street, WC1E 6BT, London, United Kingdom

Tel:	(44) 20 7679 2000
Fax:	(44) 20 7691 3112
Email:	postmaster.ucl.ac.uk
Website:	www.ucl.ac.uk

Just 175 years ago, the benefits of a university education in United Kingdom were restricted to men who were members of the Church of United Kingdom; University College London (UCL) was founded to challenge that discrimination. UCL was the first university to be established in United Kingdom after Oxford and Cambridge, providing a progressive alternative to those institutions social exclusivity, religious restrictions and academic constraints. UCL is the largest of over 50 colleges and institutes that make up the federal University of London.

A C Gimson Scholarships in Phonetics and Linguistics

Subjects: Phonetics and linguistics

Purpose: To financially support MPhil/PhD research

Eligibility: United Kingdom, European Union and overseas students are eligible to apply

Level of Study: Doctorate, Postgraduate, Research

Type: Scholarship

Value: £1,000

Frequency: Annual

Study Establishment: University College London
Country of Study: United Kingdom
Application Procedure: Applicants should write indicating their intention to compete for the bursaries to the department
Closing Date: 1 June

For further information contact:

Tel: (44) 20 7679 4245
Email: n.wilkins@ucl.ac.uk
Contact: Natalie Wilkins

A J Ayer-Sumitomo Corporation Scholarship in Philosophy

Subjects: Philosophy
Purpose: To financially support MPhil/PhD research
Eligibility: All applicants who are admitted to research programmes in philosophy will automatically be considered for this award
Level of Study: Doctorate, Postgraduate, Research
Type: Scholarship
Value: Up to £800
Frequency: Annual
Study Establishment: University College London
Country of Study: United Kingdom
Application Procedure: No separate application is required. All who are admitted to research programmes in philosophy will automatically be considered for the scholarship. Any queries should be directed to the department
Additional Information: Decisions regarding this award will be made in September

For further information contact:

Tel: (44) 20 7679 4451
Email: r.madden@ucl.ac.uk
Contact: Dr Rory Madden

Alfred Bader Prize in Organic Chemistry

Subjects: Organic chemistry
Purpose: To financially support MPhil/PhD research
Eligibility: Applicants must contact the department
Level of Study: Doctorate, Postgraduate, Research
Type: Scholarship
Value: £1,000
Frequency: Annual
Study Establishment: University College London
Country of Study: United Kingdom
Application Procedure: Applicants must contact the department

Closing Date: 1 May
Additional Information: The award will be announced in October

For further information contact:

Tel: (44) 20 7679 4650
Fax: (44) 20 7679 7463
Email: m.l.jabore@ucl.ac.uk
Contact: Ms Mary Lau Jabore

Amelia Zollner IPPR/UCL Internship Award

Purpose: The Amelia Zollner IPPR/UCL Internship Award was founded in 2007 in memory of University College London's (UCL) student Ameial Zollner. IPPR and UCL co-fund an annual, approximately 3-month London-based IPPR internship reserved for a recent UCL graduate – as a stepping stone to working in policy or politics. The internship will normally run from October through December, but can take place at any time of the year
Eligibility: (1) Applicants must be final year UCL students, about to graduate (Bachelors, Masters or Research degree) in any area, interested in and passionate about policy and politics, current affairs and social justice, and the work of IPPR, as well as enthusiastic about political research. (2) Applicants can come from any country, but must be able to work in the United Kingdom (United Kingdom/European Union nationals or holders of valid work permit). (3) Applicants should have some research skills, and need to be committed to the aims of IPPR of wanting to build a fair, more democratic and environmentally sustainable world
Level of Study: Graduate, Postgraduate, Research
Type: Award
Value: £5,000 or the equivalent of the current IPPR salary for the duration of the internship. Check with website
Length of Study: 3 months
Frequency: Annual
Country of Study: United Kingdom
No. of awards offered: 4–8
Application Procedure: Applications should be made direct to IPPR and submitted preferably by email to intern@ippr.org
Closing Date: 30 January
No. of applicants last year: 4–8
Additional Information: Please refer website for further information www.ucl.ac.uk/prospective-students/scholarships/undergraduate/zollner_ippr_internship

For further information contact:

Tel: (44) 20 7470 6133
Email: k.simony@ippr.org

Archibald Richardson Scholarship for Mathematics

Subjects: Pure mathematics
Purpose: To financially support students to pursue MPhil/PhD research
Eligibility: United Kingdom, European Union and overseas applicants are eligible to apply. All applicants who firmly accept a place for MPhil/PhD research in pure Mathematics department will be considered
Level of Study: Doctorate, Postgraduate, Research
Type: Scholarship
Value: UK£3,000
Frequency: Annual
Study Establishment: University College London
Country of Study: United Kingdom
Application Procedure: All applicants who firmly accept a place for MPhil/PhD research in pure mathematics will be considered automatically
Closing Date: 15 May

For further information contact:

Tel: (44) 20 7679 2839
Fax: (44) 20 7383 5519
Email: h.higgins@ucl.ac.uk, s.datta@ucl.ac.uk
Contact: Ms Helen Higgins

Arnold Hugh William Beck Memorial Scholarship

Subjects: Electronic and Electrical Engineering
Purpose: To financially support research Master's and MPhil/PhD students
Eligibility: Applicants should have applied for a place for graduate study at University College London. A past or current holder of the scholarship may apply again for the scholarship but such applications will be considered in open competition with other applicants. No individual may hold the scholarship for more than three years in total
Level of Study: Doctorate, Postgraduate, Research
Type: Scholarship
Value: £6,500
Frequency: Annual
Study Establishment: University College London
Country of Study: United Kingdom
Application Procedure: Applicants should send an academic curriculum vitae and a letter of more than 500 words describing their areas of interest in the discipline to the address given below. If the applicant has not applied to UCL, they must complete a graduate application form and enclose it with the scholarship application
Closing Date: 15 August

For further information contact:

Tel: (44) 20 7679 7306
Email: p.johnson@ee.ucl.ac.uk
Contact: Ms Patricia Johnson, The Graduate Tutor

Bentham Scholarships

Subjects: Law
Purpose: To financially support prospective LLM students
Eligibility: Applicants must be overseas students from outside the European Union. An applicant must have accepted an offer (either conditional or unconditional) to read for the LLM at UCL to be eligible
Level of Study: Postgraduate
Type: Scholarship
Value: £2,000
Frequency: Annual
Study Establishment: University College London
Country of Study: United Kingdom
Application Procedure: There is no application procedure. All eligible students will automatically be considered if they have firmly accepted their offer of admission by May 31st
Closing Date: Refer website
Additional Information: The scholarships will be based on academic merit. The faculty will only consider these applicants who have firmly accepted their offer of admission to the LLM by May 31st

For further information contact:

Tel: (44) 20 7679 1441
Fax: (44) 20 7209 3470
Email: graduatelaw@ucl.ac.uk
Contact: The Graduate Officer

Bioprocessing Graduate Scholarship

Subjects: Biochemical engineering
Purpose: To financially support study leading to an MPhil/PhD
Eligibility: Open to students resident outside the United Kingdom and pursuing the MSc or MPhil or PhD research in the department of biomedical engineering
Level of Study: Doctorate, Postgraduate
Type: Scholarship
Value: Up to a maximum of £11,000 per year. This sum can be set against tuition fees and/or be received as maintenance allowance payable in quarterly installments

Length of Study: Maximum of 4 calendar years
Frequency: Annual
Study Establishment: University College London
Country of Study: United Kingdom
No. of awards offered: 8
Application Procedure: Applicants must contact the department at the address given below
Closing Date: 15 February
Funding: Trusts
No. of applicants last year: 8

For further information contact:

Tel: (44) 20 7679 3796
Email: nigelth@ucl.ac.uk
Contact: Dr Paul Dalby

Brain Research Trust Prize

Subjects: Neurology or clinical neurosciences
Purpose: To financially support MPhil/PhD research students
Eligibility: Open to United Kingdom, European Union and overseas students. Overseas fee-paying students should be aware that only home tuition fee (European Union rates) is included in the award
Level of Study: Doctorate, Postgraduate, Research
Type: Studentship
Value: Stipend, tuition fees at United Kingdom/European Union rate and travel budget
Length of Study: Up to 3 years
Frequency: Annual
Study Establishment: University College London Institute of Neurology
Country of Study: United Kingdom
Application Procedure: Applicants should contact the UCL Institute of Neurology. Please submit full curriculum vitae, references and statement of research interests indicating how these would complement projects on offer
Closing Date: Refer website
Funding: Government, Trusts
Contributor: The Brian Research Trust

For further information contact:

Cell Signalling Laboratory, Institute of Neurology, UCL, 1 Wakefield Street, WC1N 1PJ, London, United Kingdom

Tel: (44) 20 7679 4031
Email: phdstudentship@ion.cl.ac.uk
Contact: Dr Jennifer Pocock

British Chevening/University College London (UCL) Israel Alumni/Chaim Herzog Award

Subjects: All subjects. Preference given to public policy, economics and history
Purpose: To financially support masters study
Eligibility: Candidates will need to return to Israel for at least 3 years after completion. Preference will be given to candidates between 25 and 40; Israeli nations currently living in Israel; applicants who have never studied in the United Kingdom; applicants who are graduates of an Israeli university/ students who obtained 1st degree by summer. Please contact the University for updated information
Level of Study: Postgraduate
Type: Scholarship
Value: Tuition fees, return airfare and living expenses
Frequency: Annual
Study Establishment: University College London
Country of Study: United Kingdom
Closing Date: Refer to website

For further information contact:

The British Council, PO Box 10304, 3 Shimshom Street, Jerusalem 91102, Israel

Email: scholarships@britishcouncil.org.il

Child Health Research Appeal Trust Studentship

Subjects: Child health, Medical sciences, Natural sciences, Social and Behavioural sciences
Purpose: To fund graduate students for MPhil/PhD research
Eligibility: Open to committed individuals wishing to do research in a clinical context, who expect to graduate with a United Kingdom first class or upper second class honours degree or equivalent from abroad
Level of Study: Doctorate, Postgraduate
Type: Studentship
Value: Tuition fees at the United Kingdom/European Union student rate, a stipend equivalent to MRC levels and UK £3,000 towards research costs
Length of Study: 3 years
Frequency: Annual
Study Establishment: UCL Institute of Child Health
Country of Study: United Kingdom
Application Procedure: Studentships are advertised on the department's vacancy website between November–January each year. Applicants should refer to www.ich.ucl.ac.uk/ich/ humanresources/ for instructions on how to apply
Closing Date: Early January

Funding: Trusts
No. of awards given last year: Up to 4

For further information contact:

Email: chratapps@ich.ucl.ac.uk

Civil and Environmental Engineering Graduate Scholarship

Subjects: Civil and environmental engineering
Purpose: To financially support MPhil/PhD study
Eligibility: Applicants should hold or except to obtain a First Class (Honours) Degree or equivalent. Applicants should have been offered a place at UCL and should firmly have accepted that offer or be intending to do so. They can be from any country outside the European Union
Level of Study: Doctorate, Postgraduate
Type: Scholarship
Value: UK£5,000 per year
Length of Study: 3 years
Frequency: Annual
Study Establishment: University College London
Country of Study: United Kingdom
Application Procedure: Applicants should write indicating their intention to compete for the scholarship to the department
Closing Date: 31 July
Additional Information: If the applicant has not already applied to UCL, please complete a graduate application form and enclose it with the scholarship application

For further information contact:

Tel: (44) 20 7679 7994
Fax: (44) 20 7380 0986
Email: m.khraisheh@ucl.ac.uk
Contact: Dr Majeda Khraisheh

Common Wealth Shared Scholarship Scheme (CSSS)

Subjects: Development and planning
Purpose: To financially help students of high academic ability from developing Commonwealth countries
Eligibility: Candidates must be from a developing Commonwealth country, must not have undertaken studies lasting a year or more or be currently studying in a developed country. They should hold or expect to attain, a United Kingdom First Degree (Bachelor's degree) with at least Upper Second Class (Honours) Degree or equivalent and have accepted an offer of place at the development planning unit

Level of Study: Postgraduate
Type: Scholarship
Value: Tuition fees, maintenance costs, some study expenses and return airfare
Length of Study: 1 year
Frequency: Annual
Study Establishment: University College London
Country of Study: United Kingdom
Application Procedure: Application forms are available from the Development Planning Unit
Closing Date: 31 March
Contributor: Department for International Development (DFID) and UCL
No. of awards given last year: 3
Additional Information: Preference is given to candidates unable to afford the cost of studying abroad by themselves. Candidates are expected to return to their home countries to work or study as soon as the award ends

For further information contact:

Tel: (44) 20 7679 1111
Fax: (44) 20 7679 1112
Email: dpu@ucl.ac.uk
Contact: The Programme Administrator

Dawes Hicks Postgraduate Scholarships in Philosophy

Subjects: Philosophy
Purpose: To financially support postgraduate research
Eligibility: United Kingdom, European Union and overseas students are eligible to apply
Level of Study: Postgraduate, Research
Type: Scholarship
Value: Up to £5,000
Frequency: Annual
Study Establishment: University College London
Country of Study: United Kingdom
Application Procedure: No separate application is required. All who are admitted to research programmes in philosophy will automatically be considered for the scholarship. Any queries should be directed to the department
Closing Date: Check with website
Additional Information: Decisions regarding this award will be made in September

For further information contact:

Tel: (44) 20 7679 4451
Email: r.madden@ucl.ac.uk
Contact: Dr Rory Madden

Department of Communities and Local Government (formally Office of the Deputy Prime Minister)

Subjects: Spatial planning and international planning
Purpose: To financially support full-time study
Eligibility: Open to candidates who take up full time study only with residence restrictions, already holding or offer for the MSC spatial planning or MSC international planning, 2:1 or equivalent (except in exceptional circumstances)
Level of Study: Postgraduate
Type: Bursary
Value: Tuition fees at United Kingdom/European Union rate plus (For United Kingdom/European Union nationals only) along with a monthly stipend of £500
Length of Study: 1 year
Frequency: Annual
Study Establishment: University College London
Country of Study: United Kingdom
No. of awards offered: 16
Application Procedure: Applications are available from www.esrc.ac.uk (ESRC) and should be sent to the department. Potentially eligible candidates will be contacted by the department
Closing Date: Refer website
Funding: Government
Contributor: Department of Communities and Local Government
No. of awards given last year: 7
No. of applicants last year: 16

For further information contact:

Tel: (44) 20 7679 7501
Email: j.hillmore@ucl.ac.uk
Contact: Judith Hillmore

Edwin Power Scholarship

Subjects: Applied mathematics
Purpose: To support a graduate student to the Department of Mathematics for Master's study or PhD research in Applied Mathematics
Eligibility: Applicant must be a graduate student admitted to the Department of Mathematics for Master's study or MPhil/PhD research in applied mathematics
Level of Study: Postgraduate, Research
Type: Scholarship
Value: £400, subject to annual renewal based on satisfactory progress
Length of Study: 3 years
Frequency: Annual

Study Establishment: University College London
Country of Study: United Kingdom
Application Procedure: Candidates wishing to apply for the Scholarship must send written notice of their intention to apply for the Scholarship to the Head of the Department of Mathematics at UCL
Closing Date: 15 August

For further information contact:

Tel: (44) 20 7679 2839
Fax: (44) 20 7383 2839
Email: h.higgins@ucl.ac.uk, s.datta@ucl.ac.uk
Contact: Ms Helen Higgins

Eleanor Grove Scholarships for Women Students

Subjects: German language and literature
Purpose: To promote and encourage study and proficiency in German
Eligibility: Candidate must be a female student of the college. The scholarship will be awarded to assist a student who is reading for a higher degree, or, in special cases, to enable a BA student to study German abroad. Candidates must have completed at least five terms of study with UCL's Arts and Humanities faculty
Type: Scholarship
Value: £950
Frequency: Annual
Study Establishment: University College or elsewhere approved by the Faculty of Arts and Humanities
Country of Study: United Kingdom
No. of awards offered: 2
Application Procedure: Contact the Graduate Tutor
Closing Date: 25 May
No. of applicants last year: 2
Additional Information: This scheme is currently under process, please check for the availability of scheme from the college

For further information contact:

The Graduate Tutor, Department of German, UCL, WC1E 6BT, London, United Kingdom

Email: german@ucl.ac.uk

English Heritage Scholarships

Subjects: Archaeology: artefact studies, managing archaeological sites, and the technology and analysis of archeological materials

Purpose: To financially support postgraduate study
Eligibility: Applicants need a minimum of 2 years work experience in British archaeology
Level of Study: Postgraduate
Type: Scholarship
Value: Up to £13,210
Frequency: Annual
Study Establishment: University College London
Country of Study: United Kingdom
Application Procedure: Applicants must contact the department
Closing Date: Normally mid-July, check the department website

For further information contact:

Tel:	(44) 20 7679 7495
Fax:	(44) 20 7383 2572
Email:	k.thomas@ucl.ac.uk
Contact:	Professor Ken Thomas

Fielden Research Scholarship

Subjects: German language and literature
Purpose: To financially support MPhil/PhD study
Eligibility: Applicants must have applied for MPhil/PhD research in German language and literature
Level of Study: Doctorate, Graduate, Postgraduate
Type: Scholarship
Value: £500
Frequency: Annual
Study Establishment: University College London
Country of Study: United Kingdom
No. of awards offered: 1
Application Procedure: Applicants must contact the department
Closing Date: 25 May
No. of awards given last year: 1
No. of applicants last year: 1

For further information contact:

School of European Languages, Culture and Society, University College London, Gower Street, WC1E 6BT, London, United Kingdom

Email:	joseph.tilley@ucl.ac.uk
Contact:	Mr Joe Tilley

Follett Scholarship

Subjects: Philosophy

Purpose: To financially support MPhil/PhD research
Eligibility: United Kingdom, European Union and overseas students are eligible to apply
Level of Study: Doctorate, Postgraduate, Research
Type: Scholarship
Value: Up to £13,000 towards fees and/or maintenance
Frequency: Annual
Study Establishment: University College London
Country of Study: United Kingdom
Application Procedure: No separate application is required. Applicants who are admitted to research programmes in philosophy will automatically be considered for the scholarship. Any queries should be directed to the department

For further information contact:

Tel:	(44) 20 7679 4451
Fax:	(44) 20 7679 3336
Email:	r.madden@ucl.ac.uk
Contact:	Dr Rory Madden

Franz Sondheimer Bursary Fund

Subjects: Chemistry
Purpose: To financially support MPhil/PhD research
Eligibility: Preference is given to overseas applicants
Level of Study: Doctorate, Postgraduate, Research
Type: Scholarship
Value: Approx. £2,000
Study Establishment: University College London
Country of Study: United Kingdom
No. of awards offered: 2
Application Procedure: Applicants must contact the department
Closing Date: 1 May
No. of awards given last year: 1
No. of applicants last year: 2

For further information contact:

Tel:	(44) 20 7679 4650
Fax:	(44) 20 7679 7463
Email:	m.l.jabore@ucl.ac.uk
Contact:	Ms Mary Lou Jabore

Gaitskell MSc Scholarship

Subjects: Economics
Purpose: To financially support full-time Master's study in the Department of Economics

Eligibility: Open to candidates who have applied for a place for graduate study at UCL and are not already receiving full financial support from other sources for fees and living costs
Level of Study: Postgraduate
Type: Scholarship
Value: £5,000
Frequency: Annual
Study Establishment: University College London (UCL)
Country of Study: United Kingdom
Application Procedure: Applications not needed. All applicants to the department are automatically considered

For further information contact:

Tel:	(44) 20 7679 5861
Fax:	(44) 20 7616 2775
Email:	d.fauvrelle@ucl.ac.uk
Contact:	Ms Daniella Fauvrelle

Gay Clifford Fees Award for Outstanding Women Students

Subjects: Any Master's programme in either the Faculty of Arts and Humanities or the Faculty of Social and Historical Sciences
Purpose: To financially support postgraduate study
Eligibility: Open to prospective female Master's degree students in the faculties of Arts and Humanities and Social and Historical Sciences with a First Class (Honours) undergraduate degree or equivalent
Level of Study: Postgraduate
Type: Scholarship
Value: £2,500 (deducted from tuition fees)
Length of Study: 1 year
Frequency: Annual
Study Establishment: University College London
Country of Study: United Kingdom
Application Procedure: Applicants should refer to the website for further information about the application procedures and deadlines
Closing Date: See website
No. of awards given last year: 4
Additional Information: This scholarship is under review. To be notified of any updates follow us on Twitter@ucl_studentfund

For further information contact:

Tel:	(44) 20 7679 2005/4167
Email:	studentfunding@ucl.ac.uk

Harold and Olga Fox Overseas Postgraduate Prize Studentship

Subjects: Biology
Purpose: To provide financial assistance to prospective overseas students intending to pursue a full-time programme of research leading to MPhil/PhD degree in the Department of Biology at UCL
Eligibility: Applicants should contact the Department of Biology for full details on eligibility
Level of Study: Postgraduate, Research
Type: Scholarship
Value: £15,000
Application Procedure: Applicants should contact the Department of Biology for further information

For further information contact:

Email:	k.rowlinson@ucl.ac.uk

Health Risk Resources International (HRRI) Scholarship

Subjects: Risk management
Purpose: To financially support postgraduate study
Eligibility: Applicants must have applied for a place for graduate study at UCL
Level of Study: Postgraduate
Type: Scholarship
Value: United Kingdom/European Union tuition fees
Frequency: Annual
Study Establishment: University College London
Country of Study: United Kingdom
Application Procedure: Applicants should contact the department. If the applicants have not applied to UCL they must complete a graduate application form and enclose it with the scholarship application
Closing Date: Check the website for closing date

For further information contact:

Tel:	(44) 20 7288 3366
Fax:	(44) 20 7288 3322
Email:	m.jacks@chime.ucl.ac.uk
Contact:	Ms Marcia Jacks

Ian Karten Charitable Trust Scholarship (Hebrew and Jewish Studies)

Subjects: Hebrew and Jewish studies
Purpose: To financially support postgraduate study

Eligibility: Applicants must have applied for a place for graduate study at UCL in the Department of Hebrew and Jewish Studies
Level of Study: Graduate, Postgraduate
Type: Scholarship
Value: £1,000 each
Frequency: Annual
Study Establishment: University College London
Country of Study: United Kingdom
Application Procedure: Applicants should contact the department. If the applicants have not applied to UCL they must complete a graduate application form and enclose it with the scholarship application
Closing Date: 1 June
Funding: Trusts

For further information contact:

Tel:	(44) 20 7679 3028
Fax:	(44) 20 7209 1026
Email:	n.f.lochery@ucl.ac.uk
Contact:	Dr Neil Lochery

Ian Karten Charitable Trust Scholarship (Microbiology)

Subjects: Clinical tropical microbiology
Purpose: To financially support postgraduate study
Eligibility: Applicants must be United Kingdom nationals aged 30 years or under at the start of their intended academic year of study
Level of Study: Postgraduate
Type: Scholarship
Value: £2,500
Frequency: Annual
Study Establishment: University College London
Country of Study: United Kingdom
Application Procedure: Applicants should contact the department

For further information contact:

Email:	t.mchugh@rfc.ucl.ac.uk
Contact:	Dr T D McHugh

Ian Karten Charitable Trust Scholarship (Neuroscience)

Subjects: Neuroscience
Purpose: To financially support postgraduate study in neuroscience
Eligibility: Applicants must be United Kingdom nationals aged 30 years or under on October 10th in the intended year of entry

Level of Study: Postgraduate
Type: Scholarship
Value: £2,750
Frequency: Annual
Study Establishment: University College London
Country of Study: United Kingdom
Application Procedure: Applicants must contact the department
Closing Date: Check the website for closing date

For further information contact:

Department of Anatomy and Developmental Biology, Gower St, Bloomsbury, London, United Kingdom

Tel:	(44) 20 7679 7740
Fax:	(44) 20 7679 7349
Email:	anatpgenquires@anatomy.ucl.ac.uk
Contact:	The Teaching Administrator

Institute of Education, University of London Centenary Masters Scholarships

Purpose: For current and next academic year, IOE is offering Centenary Masters Scholarships for students who plan to work either in their home country, or another, to improve the circumstances of disadvantaged, excluded or underachieving citizens
Eligibility: 1. Be citizens and residents of a low or middle income country with a GNI not higher than $8,000 per capita (as per the World Bank GNI per capita classification tables). 2. Have an offer to study a full time masters degree in London at the UCL Institute of Education (October start). 3. Not have studied or lived in the United Kingdom before
Level of Study: Postdoctorate
Type: Scholarship
Value: $8,000
Length of Study: 1 year
Frequency: Annual
Country of Study: Any country
Closing Date: 5 April
Funding: Foundation

For further information contact:

Email:	info@canterbury.ac.nz

Jacobsen Scholarship in Philosophy

Subjects: Philosophy
Purpose: To financially support MPhil/PhD research
Eligibility: Open to United Kingdom, European Union and overseas students

Level of Study: Doctorate, Postgraduate, Research
Type: Scholarship
Value: Up to £9,500
Frequency: Annual
Study Establishment: University College London
Country of Study: United Kingdom
Application Procedure: No separate application is required. Applicants who are admitted to research programmes in philosophy will automatically be considered for the scholarship. Any queries should be directed to the department
Additional Information: Decisions regarding this award will be made in September

For further information contact:

Tel: (44) 20 7679 7115
Email: r.madden@ucl.ac.uk
Contact: Dr Rory Madden

James Joseph Sylvester Scholarship

Subjects: Mathematics
Purpose: To financially support MPhil/PhD research
Eligibility: United Kingdom, European Union and overseas students are eligible to apply
Level of Study: Doctorate, Postgraduate, Research
Type: Scholarship
Value: Up to £3,000
Frequency: Annual
Study Establishment: University College London
Country of Study: United Kingdom
Application Procedure: Applicants must contact the department
Closing Date: 15 May

For further information contact:

Department of Mathematics, University College London, Gower Street, WC1E 6BT, London, United Kingdom

Tel: (44) 20 7679 2839
Fax: (44) 20 7383 5519
Email: h.higgins@ucl.ac.uk, s.datta@ucl.ac.uk
Contact: Ms Helen Higgins

Jevons Memorial Scholarship in Economic Science

Subjects: Economics
Purpose: To financially support MPhil/PhD study
Eligibility: Candidates must have graduated or be a candidate for graduation in the term in which the award is made. Previous tenure of the scholarship does not debar candidate from competing on a second occasion. Normally the scholar elected must pursue a course of study and research for a higher degree at UCL
Level of Study: Doctorate, Postgraduate
Type: Scholarship
Value: £55
Frequency: Annual
Study Establishment: University College London
Country of Study: United Kingdom
Application Procedure: Applicants should send particulars of the research work they intend to pursue plus an academic curriculum vitae to the department. If the applicant has not applied to UCL, they must complete a graduate application form and enclose it with the scholarship application
Closing Date: 15 May

For further information contact:

Tel: (44) 20 7679 5861
Fax: (44) 20 7916 2775
Email: d.fauvrelle@ucl.ac.uk
Contact: Ms Daniella Fauvrelle

John Carr Scholarship for Students from Africa and the Caribbean

Subjects: Law
Purpose: To financially support prospective LLM students
Eligibility: Applicants must be overseas students from Africa and the Caribbean. An applicant must have accepted an offer (either conditional or unconditional) to read for the LLM at UCL to be eligible
Level of Study: Postgraduate
Type: Scholarship
Value: £2,000
Frequency: Annual
Study Establishment: University College London
Country of Study: United Kingdom
Application Procedure: There is no application procedure. All eligible students who have accepted the offer of admission by March 31st will automatically be considered
Closing Date: 2 March
Additional Information: The scholarships will be based on academic merit. The faculty will only consider those applicants who have firmly accepted their offer of admission to the LLM by May 31st

For further information contact:

Tel: (44) 20 7679 1441
Fax: (44) 20 7209 3470
Email: graduatelaw@ucl.ac.uk

John Hawkes Scholarship

Subjects: Pure mathematics
Purpose: The primary purpose is to support third year study in pure mathematics but a secondary purpose when there is no suitable candidate or candidates for the whole sum available, is to support a graduate research student
Eligibility: United Kingdom, European Union and overseas students are eligible to apply
Level of Study: Doctorate, Postgraduate, Research
Type: Scholarship
Value: Up to £12,000 per year
Length of Study: 3 years
Frequency: Annual
Study Establishment: University College London
Country of Study: United Kingdom
Application Procedure: Applicants should write to the Head of the Department, indicating their wish to be considered for the scholarship and providing details of their academic achievements to date. Applicants should also include an up-to-date curriculum vitae
Closing Date: 1 May

For further information contact:

Tel: (44) 20 7679 2839
Fax: (44) 20 7383 5519
Email: h.higgins@ucl.ac.uk,s.datta@ucl.ac.uk
Contact: Ms Helen Higgins

John Stuart Mill Scholarship in Philosophy of Mind and Logic

Subjects: Philosophy
Purpose: To financially support MPhil/PhD research
Eligibility: Open to United Kingdom, European Union and overseas applicants
Level of Study: Doctorate, Postgraduate, Research
Type: Scholarship
Value: Up to £1,400
Frequency: Annual
Study Establishment: University College London
Country of Study: United Kingdom
Application Procedure: No separate application is required. All who are admitted to research programmes in philosophy will automatically be considered for the scholarship. Any queries should be directed to the department
Additional Information: Decision regarding this award will be made in September

For further information contact:

Tel: (44) 20 7679 4451
Email: r.madden@ucl.ac.uk
Contact: Dr Rory Madden

Joseph Hume Scholarship

Subjects: Law
Purpose: To financially support LLM students or MPhil/PhD research
Eligibility: For all LLM or MPhil/PhD research students in the Department of Laws
Level of Study: Doctorate, Postgraduate, Research
Type: Scholarship
Value: £1,600
Frequency: Annual
Study Establishment: University College London
Country of Study: United Kingdom
Application Procedure: There is no application procedure. All eligible students will automatically be considered
Closing Date: 23 March
Additional Information: Please check the website for further details www.laws.ucl.ac.uk/study/graduate/applying/funding-scholarships/

For further information contact:

Tel: (44) 20 7679 1441
Fax: (44) 20 7209 3470
Email: graduatelaw@ucl.ac.uk
Contact: The Graduate Officer

Keeling Scholarship

Subjects: Philosophy
Purpose: To financially support MPhil/PhD research
Eligibility: United Kingdom, European Union and overseas students are eligible to apply
Level of Study: Doctorate, Postgraduate, Research
Type: Scholarship
Value: United Kingdom/European Union tuition fees plus a bursary
Frequency: Annual
Study Establishment: University College London
Country of Study: United Kingdom
Application Procedure: No separate application is required. Applicants who are admitted to research programmes in philosophy will automatically be considered for the scholarship. Any queries should be directed to the department

Closing Date: Check the website
Additional Information: For more information on eligibility please check www.ucl.ac.uk/philosophy/keeling/scholarship

For further information contact:

Tel: (44) 20 7679 7115
Email: r.madden@ucl.ac.uk
Contact: Dr Rory Madden

Liver Group PhD Studentship

Subjects: Hepatology
Purpose: To financially support students to pursue MPhil/PhD research
Eligibility: Open to United Kingdom and European Union applicants holding a relevant First or Upper Second Class
Level of Study: Doctorate, Postgraduate, Research
Type: Scholarship
Value: Home student fees plus a maintenance allowance (1st year approx. £14,500)
Length of Study: 3 years
Frequency: Dependent on funds available
Study Establishment: Royal Free and University College Medical School, UCL-Hampstead campus
Country of Study: United Kingdom
Application Procedure: Applicants should contact the department
Closing Date: Refer website
Funding: Foundation
Contributor: The Liver Group Charity
No. of awards given last year: 1

For further information contact:

Centre for Hepatology, Department of Medicine (Royal Free Campus), Royal Free and University College Medicine School, Rowland Hill Street, Hampstead, NW3 2PF, London, United Kingdom

Tel: (44) 20 7433 2854
Fax: (44) 20 7433 2852
Email: c.selden@rfc.ucl.ac.uk
Contact: Dr Clare Selden

Margaret Richardson Scholarship

Subjects: German
Purpose: To financially support MPhil/PhD study

Eligibility: Open to applicants should have applied for a place for graduate study at UCL and have Upper Second Class Degree or equivalent in German or a related field of study to enable them to do research work in this subject. Previous tenure of the scholarship does not debar a candidate from competing on a second occasion
Level of Study: Doctorate, Graduate, Postgraduate
Type: Scholarship
Value: £5,000 (may split into two awards of £2,500 each)
Frequency: Annual
Study Establishment: University College London
Country of Study: United Kingdom
Application Procedure: Applicants should contact the department. If the applicant has not applied to UCL, they must complete a graduate application form and enclose it with the scholarship application. The application must give particulars of the research work which they intend to pursue in the event of the scholarship being awarded to them
Closing Date: 25 May

For further information contact:

School of European Languages, Culture and Society, University College Gower Street, WC1E 6BT, London, United Kingdom

Email: joseph.tilley@ucl.ac.uk
Contact: Mr Joe Tilley

Master of the Rolls Scholarship For Commonwealth Students

Subjects: Law
Purpose: To financially support prospective LLM students
Eligibility: Applicants must be overseas students from the Commonwealth countries. An applicant must have accepted an offer (either conditional or unconditional) to read for the LLM at UCL
Level of Study: Postgraduate
Type: Scholarship
Value: £2,000
Frequency: Annual
Study Establishment: University College London
Country of Study: United Kingdom
Application Procedure: There is no application procedure. All eligible students who firmly accept the offer of admission by May 31st will be automatically considered
Closing Date: Check with website
No. of awards given last year: 1

Additional Information: The scholarships will be based on academic merit. The faculty will only consider those applicants who have firmly accepted their offer of admission to the LLM by May 31st

For further information contact:

Tel:	(44) 20 7679 1441
Fax:	(44) 20 7209 3470
Email:	graduatelaw@ucl.ac.uk
Contact:	The Graduate Officer

Master's Degree Awards in Archaeology

Subjects: Archaeology
Purpose: To financially support MA and MSc programmes in the Institute of Archaeology
Eligibility: Open to students on MA and MSc programmes in UCL's institute of archaeology
Level of Study: Postgraduate
Type: Scholarship
Value: Approx. £1,000
Frequency: Annual
Study Establishment: University College London
Country of Study: United Kingdom
Application Procedure: Applicants must contact the department
Closing Date: Mid-March, check the department website for details

For further information contact:

Tel:	(44) 20 7679 7499
Fax:	(44) 20 7383 2572
Email:	l.daniel@ucl.ac.uk
Contact:	Lisa Daniel

Master's Degree Awards in Biochemical Engineering

Subjects: Biochemical engineering
Purpose: To financially support postgraduate study
Eligibility: Open to United Kingdom/European Union resident applicants only
Level of Study: Postgraduate
Type: Scholarship
Value: A full award amounts to £9,000 plus tuition fees
Frequency: Annual
Study Establishment: University College London
Country of Study: United Kingdom

Application Procedure: Applicants must contact the department at the address given below or the British Council Office in Colombo
Closing Date: 1 July
Additional Information: The scholarships may be partly or fully funded

For further information contact:

Tel:	(44) 20 7679 3796
Email:	nigelth@ucl.ac.uk
Contact:	Professor Nigel Titchener-Hooker

Member Scholarship in Statistics

Subjects: Statistics
Purpose: To financially support full-time graduate study and research
Eligibility: Applicants should have graduated from UCL or be a candidate for graduation in the term in which the award is made. United Kingdom, European Union and overseas students are eligible to apply
Level of Study: Postgraduate, Research
Type: Scholarship
Value: £55
Frequency: Annual
Study Establishment: University College London
Country of Study: United Kingdom
Application Procedure: Applicants should write to the department indicating their intention to compete for the scholarship

For further information contact:

Tel:	(44) 20 7679 1872
Fax:	(44) 20 7383 4703
Email:	marion@stats.ucl.ac.uk
Contact:	Ms Marion Wave

Monica Hulse Scholarship

Subjects: Mathematics
Purpose: This Scholarship, founded in 2004, is funded from a regular lifetime gift from Dr Paul Hulse, alumnus of UCL, in memory of his mother, Monica Hulse (1934-1999). One scholarship is awarded annually to a prospective graduate student from any country admitted to the Department of Mathematics for full-time Master's study or MPhil/PhD research

Eligibility: Open to graduate students in the department of mathematics in the first year of their Master's course or Ph-D. The applicant should not be in receipt of any other special funding
Level of Study: Doctorate, Postgraduate, Research
Type: Scholarship
Value: £1,000
Frequency: Annual
Country of Study: Any country
Application Procedure: Applicants must send written notice of their intention prior to the start of the academic year along with an academic curriculum vitae
Closing Date: 31 May
Funding: Private
No. of awards given last year: 1
Additional Information: Application link for the following grant is www.ucl.ac.uk/prospective-students/scholarships/graduate/deptscholarships/mathematics

For further information contact:

Email: h.higgins@ucl.ac.uk,s.datta@ucl.ac.uk

National Health Service Bursaries

Subjects: Speech and language sciences
Purpose: To financially support postgraduate study
Eligibility: Open to United Kingdom and European Union applicants only who have applied for a place for graduate study at UCL
Level of Study: Postgraduate
Type: Bursary
Value: United Kingdom/European Union tuition fees. United Kingdom residents will also normally be eligible for a means tested bursary
Frequency: Annual
Study Establishment: University College London
Country of Study: United Kingdom
Application Procedure: There is no separate bursary application form. Application procedure is an automatic process once an offer of a place has been made
Additional Information: When an offer of a place has been made, the NHS Student Grants unit will contact the applicant directly

For further information contact:

Tel: (44) 20 7679 4202
Email: n.wilkins@ucl.ac.uk
Contact: Natalie Wilkins

Nederlandse Taalunie Scholarship

Subjects: Modern Dutch studies (literary translation from Dutch into English option)
Purpose: To financially support postgraduate study
Eligibility: Applicants must have applied for a place for graduate study at UCL
Level of Study: Postgraduate
Type: Scholarship
Value: £2,500
Frequency: Annual
Study Establishment: University College London
Country of Study: United Kingdom
Application Procedure: Applicants should contact the department. If the applicant has not applied to UCL, they must complete a graduate application form and enclose it with the scholarship application
Closing Date: 15 July

For further information contact:

Tel: (44) 20 7679 3117
Fax: (44) 20 7616 6985
Email: t.hermans@ucl.ac.uk
Contact: Professor Theo Hermans

Perren Studentship

Subjects: Astronomy
Purpose: To financially support graduate study and research
Eligibility: United Kingdom, European Union and overseas applicants are eligible to apply
Level of Study: Postgraduate, Research
Type: Studentship
Frequency: Every 2 years
Study Establishment: University College London
Country of Study: United Kingdom
Application Procedure: Applicants should provide particulars of their academic record and of the work that they intend to pursue to the department
Closing Date: 15 May
Funding: Trusts
Contributor: Perren Fund

For further information contact:

Tel: (44) 20 7679 473
Email: lahauestar@ucl.ac.uk
Contact: Professor Ofer Lahau

R B Hounsfield Scholarship in Traffic Engineering

Subjects: Traffic engineering
Purpose: To financially support MPhil/PhD research in Traffic Engineering in the Department of Civil and Environmental Engineering
Eligibility: Candidates should hold or expect to obtain a First Class (Honours) Degree or equivalent and should have been offered a place at UCL and have firmly accepted that offer or be intending to do so
Level of Study: Doctorate, Postgraduate, Research
Type: Scholarship
Value: Not less than £120
Frequency: Dependent on funds available
Study Establishment: University College London
Country of Study: United Kingdom
Application Procedure: Enquiries should be directed to the department
Closing Date: 15 May
Additional Information: If the applicant has not already applied to UCL, please complete a graduate application form and enclose it with the scholarship application

For further information contact:

Tel: (44) 20 7679 2710
Fax: (44) 20 7380 0986
Email: civeng.admissions@ucl.ac.uk
Contact: Professor R L Mackett

Research Degree Scholarship in Chemical Engineering

Subjects: Chemical engineering
Purpose: To financially support MPhil/PhD research
Level of Study: Doctorate, Postgraduate, Research
Type: Scholarship
Value: £2,000
Frequency: Annual
Study Establishment: University College London
Country of Study: United Kingdom
Application Procedure: Applicants must contact the department
Closing Date: Check the website for closing date

For further information contact:

Tel: (44) 20 7679 3835
Fax: (44) 20 7383 2348
Email: h.mahgerefteh@ucl.ac.uk
Contact: Dr Haroun Mahgerefteh

Research Degree Scholarships in Anthropology

Subjects: Anthropology
Purpose: To financially support research in the field of anthropology
Eligibility: Please contact the Department of Anthropology for details
Level of Study: Doctorate, Postgraduate, Research
Type: Scholarship
Value: United Kingdom/European Union tuition fees
Frequency: Annual
Study Establishment: University College London
Country of Study: United Kingdom
No. of awards offered: 12
Application Procedure: Applicants must contact the department
Closing Date: 30 April
No. of awards given last year: 4
No. of applicants last year: 12

For further information contact:

Tel: (44) 20 7679 8622
Fax: (44) 20 7679 8632
Email: ucsapga@ucl.ac.uk
Contact: Ms Diana Goforth

Richard Chattaway Scholarship

Subjects: History of modern warfare from 1870
Purpose: To financially support MPhil/PhD study
Eligibility: Open to applicants who have applied for a graduate study at University College London (UCL). The scholar selected must pursue research for a higher degree at UCL. Receipt of the scholarship must be acknowledged in any publication or research paper which has benefitted from it
Level of Study: Doctorate, Postgraduate
Type: Scholarship
Value: £2,000
Frequency: Annual
Study Establishment: University College London
Country of Study: United Kingdom
Application Procedure: Applicants must contact the department. If the applicants have not already applied to UCL they must complete a graduate application form and enclose it with the scholarship application. Applicants must include particulars of the research work they intend to pursue in the event of the scholarship being awarded to them
Closing Date: 15 May

Funding: Individuals
Contributor: Private donation in honour of Richard Chattaway
No. of awards given last year: 1

For further information contact:

Email: n.miller@ucl.ac.uk
Contact: Professor Nicola Miller, Head of the Department

Royal National Orthopaedic Hospital Special Trustees Research Training Scholarship

Subjects: Surgical sciences
Purpose: To give orthopaedic specialists of the future an early exposure to the first-class research culture at Stanmore
Eligibility: Open to students enrolled in the MSc in Surgical Sciences programme undertaking a research project at the Royal National Orthopaedic Hospital/Institute of Orthopaedic and Musculoskeletal Science
Level of Study: Postgraduate
Type: Scholarship
Value: A stipend, tuition and bench fees
Frequency: Annual
Study Establishment: Royal National Orthopaedic Hospital, Stanmore
Country of Study: United Kingdom
Application Procedure: Once students have been accepted by a supervisor, they should contact the R&D office, Royal National Orthopaedic Hospital. Applicants will be asked to send an outline of the research project and their curriculum vitae. Applicant should contact the department at the address given below
Funding: Private
Contributor: The RNOH Special Trustees and the R&D Subcommittee
Additional Information: Recipients of the scholarships must present their research findings at a symposium to be held at the RNOH. The R&D Director and the Non-Executive Director for research will review applications

For further information contact:

Royal National Orthopaedic Hospital, Brockley Hill, Stanmore, HA7 4LP, Middlesex, United Kingdom

Tel: (44) 20 8909 5752
Email: lphilpots@rnoh.nhs.uk
Contact: Dr Liz Philpots, R&D Manager

Score Africa/Allan & Nesta Ferguson Charitable Trust Scholarship

Purpose: To financially assist African nationals to undertake MSc/PhD studies at the Centre for International Health and Development (CIHD) at UCL
Eligibility: Applicants should refer to the website for full details on eligibility
Level of Study: Postgraduate
Type: Scholarship
Value: Partial payment towards tuition fees
Frequency: Annual
Application Procedure: Applicants should refer to the website for further information on application procedures, forms and deadlines

For further information contact:

Email: cihdsc@ich.ucl.ac.uk

Shell Petroleum Development Company Niger Delta Postgraduate Scholarship

Subjects: MSc chemical process engineering or MSc mechanical engineering or MSc civil engineering
Purpose: To provide opportunities for postgraduate study in the United Kingdom for young students and professionals, who demonstrate both academic excellence and the potential to become leading professionals in the oil and associated industries
Eligibility: The applicant must: (1) have obtained a degree of at least an equivalent standard to a United Kingdom Upper Second Class (Honours Degree); (2) be neither a current nor former employee (who have left employment less than 5 years before) of SPDC, the Royal Dutch Shell Group of Companies or Wider Perspectives Limited, or current employee's relatives; (3) not already have had the chance of studying in the United Kingdom or another developed country; (4) be aged between 21 and 28 years; (5) originate from one of the Niger Delta States in Nigeria, namely Rivers, Delta or Bayelsa and currently reside in Nigeria
Level of Study: Postgraduate
Type: Scholarship
Value: Full tuition fee funding, maintenance allowance, return airfares and arrival allowance
Frequency: Annual
Study Establishment: University College London
Country of Study: United Kingdom
Closing Date: See website for details

For further information contact:

Student Funding Office, UCL, Gower Street, WC1E 6BT, London, United Kingdom

Email: studentfunding@ucl.ac.uk

Sir Frederick Pollock Scholarship for Students from North America

Subjects: LLM
Purpose: To financially support prospective LLM students
Eligibility: Applicants must be overseas students from North America. An applicant must have accepted an offer (either conditional or unconditional) to read for the LLM at UCL to be eligible
Level of Study: Postgraduate
Type: Scholarship
Value: £2,000
Frequency: Annual
Country of Study: United Kingdom
Application Procedure: There is no application procedure. All eligible students will be automatically considered
Closing Date: 2 March
Additional Information: The scholarships will be based on academic merit. The faculty will only consider those applicants who have firmly accepted their offer of admission to the LLM by May 31st

For further information contact:

Tel: (44) 20 7679 1441
Fax: (44) 20 7209 3470
Email: jane.ha@ucl.ac.uk
Contact: The Graduate Officer

Sir George Jessel Studentship in Mathematics

Subjects: Mathematics
Purpose: To financially support MPhil/PhD research
Eligibility: Applicants must be graduates of University College London. All applicants who firmly accept a place for MPhil/PhD research in the Mathematics Department will be considered
Level of Study: Doctorate, Postgraduate, Research
Type: Studentship
Value: £1,800
Frequency: Annual
Study Establishment: University College London
Country of Study: United Kingdom
Application Procedure: Applicants must contact the department

Closing Date: Refer the website
Additional Information: Please refer the website for further details   www.ucl.ac.uk/prospective-students/scholarships/graduate/deptscholarships/mathematics

For further information contact:

Tel: (44) 20 7679 2839
Fax: (44) 20 7383 5519
Email: h.higgins@ucl.ac.uk
Contact: Ms Helen Higgins

Sir James Lighthill Scholarship

Subjects: Applied mathematics
Purpose: To financially support MPhil/PhD research
Eligibility: United Kingdom, European Union and overseas students are eligible to apply. All applicants who firmly accept a place for MPhil/PhD research in the Mathematics Department will be considered
Level of Study: Doctorate, Postgraduate, Research
Type: Scholarship
Value: £500 per year
Frequency: Annual
Study Establishment: University College London
Country of Study: United Kingdom
Application Procedure: Applicants must contact the department
Closing Date: Refer website

For further information contact:

Tel: (44) 20 7679 2839`
Email: h.higgins@ucl.ac.uk
Contact: Ms Helen Higgins

Sir John Salmond Scholarship for Students from Australia and New Zealand

Subjects: Law
Purpose: To financially support prospective LLM students
Eligibility: Applicants must be overseas students from Australia and New Zealand. An applicant must have accepted an offer (either conditional or unconditional) to read for the LLM at UCL to be eligible
Level of Study: Postgraduate
Type: Scholarship
Value: UK£2,000
Frequency: Annual
Study Establishment: University College London
Country of Study: United Kingdom

Application Procedure: There is no application
Closing Date: Refer website
Additional Information: The scholarships will be based on academic merit. The faculty will only consider these applicants who have firmly accepted their offer of admission to the LLM by May 31st

For further information contact:

Tel:	(44) 20 7679 1441
Fax:	(44) 20 7209 3470
Email:	jane.ha@ucl.ac.uk
Contact:	The Graduate Officer

Sully Scholarship

Subjects: Psychology
Purpose: To financially support MPhil/PhD research
Eligibility: Open to the most outstanding candidate in the second year of their PhD research programme
Level of Study: Doctorate, Postgraduate, Research
Type: Scholarship
Value: £2,200
Frequency: Annual
Study Establishment: University College London
Country of Study: United Kingdom
Application Procedure: There is no separate application and the award is given to an outstanding student who is registered in the department's PhD programme and is in the second year of study
Closing Date: Refer website
No. of awards given last year: 1

For further information contact:

Tel:	(44) 20 7679 5332
Fax:	(44) 20 7430 4276
Email:	psychology-pg-enquiries@ucl.ac.uk
Contact:	Head of the Department

Teaching Assistantships (Economics)

Subjects: Economics
Purpose: To financially support MPhil/PhD students
Eligibility: MPhil/PhD students who have successfully completed their 1st year in the department
Level of Study: Doctorate
Type: Assistantship
Value: UK£11,000
Frequency: Annual
Study Establishment: University College London

Country of Study: United Kingdom
Application Procedure: Contact the Department of Economics for details
Closing Date: Refer website

For further information contact:

Email:	d.fauvrelle@ucl.ac.uk

Thames and Hudson Scholarship

Subjects: Comparative art and archaeology
Purpose: To financially support postgraduate study
Level of Study: Postgraduate
Type: Scholarship
Value: A scholarship up to a maximum value of £15,000 or up to 4 scholarships totalling that value
Frequency: Annual
Study Establishment: University College London
Country of Study: United Kingdom
Application Procedure: Applicants must contact the department for details
Closing Date: Mid-July, check the department website

For further information contact:

Tel:	(44) 20 7679 7495
Fax:	(44) 20 7383 2572
Email:	k.thomas@ucl.ac.uk
Contact:	Professor Ken Thomas

The George Melhuish Postgraduate Scholarship

Subjects: Philosophy
Purpose: To financially support postgraduate research
Eligibility: Open to United Kingdom, European Union and overseas applicants
Level of Study: Postgraduate, Research
Type: Scholarship
Value: Up to £3,700
Frequency: Annual
Study Establishment: University College London
Country of Study: United Kingdom
Application Procedure: No separate application is required. Applicants who are admitted to research programmes in philosophy will automatically be considered for the scholarship. Any queries should be directed to the department
No. of awards given last year: 2
Additional Information: Decision regarding this award will be made in September

For further information contact:

Tel:	(44) 20 7679 4451
Email:	r.madden@ucl.ac.uk
Contact:	Dr Rory Madden

The Lloyd's Register Scholarship for Marine Engineering and Naval Architecture

Subjects: Marine engineering and naval architecture
Purpose: To financially support an MSc in marine engineering or naval architecture
Eligibility: Any country students are eligible to apply. All students must apply in writing. Consideration will be given to those with low financial means
Level of Study: Postgraduate
Type: Scholarship
Value: £10,000
Frequency: Annual
Study Establishment: University College London
Country of Study: United Kingdom
Application Procedure: Applicants should write indicating their interest in being considered for this scholarship to the department
Closing Date: 1 June
Funding: Commercial
Contributor: Lloyd's Register
No. of awards given last year: 1
Additional Information: Only one award is currently available

For further information contact:

Tel:	(44) 20 7679 3907
Fax:	(44) 20 7388 0180
Email:	info@meng.ucl.ac.uk
Contact:	The Graduate Tutor

The Professor John Scales Award in Biomedical Engineering

Subjects: Response of the body to implants or aspects of bioengineering of joint replacement
Purpose: To financially support postgraduate study
Eligibility: Applicants should hold a First or Upper Second Class (Honours) Degree in engineering, material science or biology
Level of Study: Postgraduate
Type: Scholarship
Value: £6,500

Length of Study: 3 years
Frequency: Every 3 years
Study Establishment: University College London
Country of Study: United Kingdom
Application Procedure: Applicants should send a curriculum vitae along with a covering letter to the address given below
Funding: Private
Additional Information: Overseas students would have to pay their own fees

For further information contact:

Tel:	(44) 20 8954 0636
Email:	a.bartram@ucl.ac.uk
Contact:	Mrs A Bartrum, Secretary to Professor Bluwn

University College London Department Awards for Graduate Students

Subjects: Phonetics and linguistics
Purpose: To financially support Master's and MPhil/PhD programmes
Eligibility: United Kingdom, European Union and overseas students are eligible to apply
Level of Study: Doctorate, Postgraduate
Type: Scholarship
Value: £500
Frequency: Annual
Study Establishment: University College London
Country of Study: United Kingdom
Application Procedure: Applicants must contact the department
Closing Date: 15 May

For further information contact:

Tel:	(44) 20 7679 3262
Fax:	(44) 20 7383 4108
Email:	s.anyadi@ling.ucl.ac.uk
Contact:	Ms Stefanie Anyadi

University College London-AET Undergraduate International Outreach Bursaries

Eligibility: Applicants must be a national of any African country (including Madagascar), currently living in an African country, and have one or both parents living in an African country, or are orphaned

For further information contact:

Email: m.omona@africaeducationaltrust.org
Contact: Ms May Omona

University College of London Hong Kong Alumni Scholarships

Purpose: To provide financial aid for studies at UCL
Eligibility: (1) Applicants must be holders of Hong Kong Permanent Identity Cards or Chinese citizens who have received full-time education in Hong Kong and/or China for no less than 5 of the 8 years immediately prior to the start of study at UCL. (2) Applicants must hold an offer of admission to full-time undergraduate study at UCL – in any area except Medicine – which they have firmly accepted or intend to do so. (3) Applicants must be self-financing and liable to pay tuition fees at the rate for overseas students. (4) Applicants should be in financial need and unable to fund their planned studies at UCL without financial help
Type: Scholarship
Value: Up to £10,000 towards tuition fees for a maximum of 4 years
Frequency: Annual
Study Establishment: United College London
Country of Study: United Kingdom
No. of awards offered: 13
Application Procedure: Completed UG HK application form should be submitted along with required documentation as detailed in the form to UCL Scholarships
Closing Date: 10 April
Funding: Foundation
No. of awards given last year: 1
No. of applicants last year: 13
Additional Information: Interviews will be held in Hong Kong and applicants invited for interview will be required to present themselves for interview in Hong Kong at applicants' own expense

For further information contact:

Tel: (44) 20 7679 0004
Email: studentfunding@ucl.ac.uk

William Blake Trust Bursary

Subjects: History of British art
Purpose: To financially support postgraduate or MPhil/PhD study
Eligibility: Applicants must have applied for a place for graduate study at UCL
Level of Study: Doctorate, Postgraduate
Type: Bursary
Value: £2,000
Frequency: Annual
Study Establishment: University College London
Country of Study: United Kingdom
Application Procedure: Applicants must contact the department. If the applicants have not already applied to UCL they must complete a graduate application form and enclose it with the scholarship application
Closing Date: 15 May

For further information contact:

Tel: (44) 20 7679 7546
Fax: (44) 20 7916 5939
Email: d.dethloff@ucl.ac.uk
Contact: Ms D Dethloff

William Moore Gorman Graduate Research Scholarship

Subjects: Economics
Purpose: To financially support students entering the first year of the MPhil/PhD degree in department of Economics
Eligibility: Open to candidates who have applied for a place for graduate study at University College London
Level of Study: Doctorate, Postgraduate
Type: Scholarship
Value: £16,200
Length of Study: 1 year
Frequency: Annual
Study Establishment: University College London
Country of Study: United Kingdom
Application Procedure: Students must indicate why they wish to be considered for this scholarship on their admission application form (section 26)
Closing Date: Refer website
No. of awards given last year: 9
Additional Information: The scholarship will be awarded to students who are not already receiving full financial support from other sources for fees and living costs, and will be, awarded on the basis of academic merit

For further information contact:

Tel: (44) 20 7679 5861
Fax: (44) 20 7916 2775
Email: d.fauvrelle@ucl.ac.uk
Contact: Ms Daniella Fauvrelle

University Commission for Development Academy of Research and Higher Education Scholarships

Rue Royale 180, BEL 1000 Brussels, Belgium

Website: www.ares-ac.be/en/cooperation-au-developpem
ent/bourses/masters-et-stages-en-belgique
Contact: ARES

Academy of Research and Higher Education Scholarships

Subjects: Aquaculture, health, food technology, economics, international development, GIS, information technology, agriculture, environment, human rights, microfinance
Level of Study: Postgraduate
Value: The scholarship covers international travel expenses, living allowance, tuition fees, insurance, housing allowance
Country of Study: Any country
Application Procedure: To apply for the scholarship, complete the single form scholarship application and admission to one of the French-speaking universities of Belgium
Closing Date: 9 February
Additional Information: The scholarships are for nationals of: Benin, Bolivia, Burkina Faso, Burundi, Cambodia, Cameroon, Cuba, Ecuador, Ethiopia (only for courses in English), Haiti, Madagascar, Morocco, Niger, Peru, Philippines, DR Congo, Rwanda, Senegal, Vietnam. For more details, please visit official scholarship website: www.ares-ac.be/en/cooperation-au-developpement/bourses/masters-et-stages-en-belgique

For further information contact:

Email: scholarships-cooperation@ares-ac.be

University Institute of European Studies

Via Maria Vittoria 26, ITA-10123 Turin, Italy

Tel: (39) 11 839 4660
Fax: (39) 11 839 4664
Email: info@iuse.it
Website: www.iuse.it
Contact: Ms Maria Grazia Goiettina, Course Secretariat

The University Institute of European Studies promotes international relations and European integration by organizing academic activities. The Institute has a comprehensive library in international law and economics. Since 1952 the Institute has been a European Documentation Centre (EDC), thus receiving all official publications of European institutions.

LLM in International Trade Law – Contracts and Dispute Resolution – Scholarships

Subjects: The main objective of the LLM programme (held in English) is providing fundamental tools and competencies needed to deal with the complex reality of international commercial transactions from a European and an international perspective and in particular with respect to: contracts' drafting, interpretation and management of international commercial contracts, international dispute resolution, arbitration and Moot Court
Eligibility: Applicants must have successfully completed a first level university degree of at least 3 years' duration, either in law, economics, political sciences, business administration or equivalent
Level of Study: Postgraduate
Funding: Government, Private, Foundation, Individuals

For further information contact:

Tel: (39) 11 69 36 945
Fax: (39) 11 69 36 369
Email: tradelaw@itcilo.org
Contact: Course Secretariat

University of Aarhus

Nordre Ringgade 1, Bygning 327 3, DNK 8000 Aarhus, Denmark

Tel: (45) 8942 1111
Fax: (45) 8942 1540
Email: au@au.dk
Website: www.au.dk
Contact: Faculty of Social Sciences

The University of Aarhus was founded in 1928 as Universitetsundervisningen i Jylland – University Teaching in Jutland in classrooms rented from the Technical College and a teaching corps consisting of 1 Professor of philosophy and 4 Readers of Danish, English, German and French. However, today the University has 20,000 students with 5,000 staff.

Doctor of Philosophy Scholarship in Globalisation and International Economics

Subjects: International economics
Purpose: To enable students to take up research in the related fields
Eligibility: Open to applicants who have a Master's degree or to students who expect to obtain their Master's degree in the near future
Level of Study: Postgraduate, Research
Type: Scholarship
Value: Approx. salary of €2,700
Length of Study: 3 years
Frequency: Annual
Study Establishment: Aarhus School of Business
Country of Study: Denmark
Application Procedure: Application forms can be downloaded from the Aarhus website. The form should be sent with a curriculum vitae and an outline of a research project including a description of the proposed theory and methods
Closing Date: 19 February
Contributor: Danish Social Science Research Council

For further information contact:

Tel: (45) 89 486 482/392
Email: pje@asb.dk
Contact: Peter Jensen, Head of Department

University of Aarhus PhD Scholarships

Subjects: Psychology
Purpose: To provide financial support and encourage research work
Eligibility: Open to candidates who have obtained a Danish university Master's degree or an examination at an equivalent level
Level of Study: Doctorate
Type: Scholarship
Value: US$42,000; US$44,000 per year
Length of Study: 3 years
Frequency: Annual
Country of Study: Denmark

Application Procedure: Applicants may download the application form from the website. The completed application form along with project description, plan for the course, budget and copy of degree certificate(s) must be submitted
Closing Date: 16 June
Additional Information: Further information may be obtained from Administrator Henrik Friis Bach, The Faculty of Social Sciences Secretariat, Tel: 8942 1546

For further information contact:

Email: socialsciences@au.dk

University of Aberdeen

University Office, King's College, AB24 3FX, Aberdeen, United Kingdom

Tel: (44) 12 2427 3506
Fax: (44) 12 2427 2041
Email: ptgoff@abdn.ac.uk
Website: www.abdn.ac.uk
Contact: The Postgraduate Registry

The University of Aberdeen is the fifth oldest in the United Kingdom. Aberdeen is an international university serving one of the most dynamic regions of Europe with over 13,000 students and over 3,000 staff, and is at the forefront of teaching and research in medicine and the humanities and sciences.

Aberdeen International Masters Scholarship

Value: £2,000 tuition fee discount
Country of Study: United Kingdom
Application Procedure: You do not need to apply for this scholarship. Once you have applied and been given a conditional or unconditional offer of admissions for an eligible Masters programme, you will automatically receive an email from the Vice Principal forInternationalisation to advise you that you have been offered the scholarship with instructions on how to accept the scholarship
Additional Information: Students cannot receive a cash alternative for scholarship

For further information contact:

Email: admin@scholarship-positions.com

Arts Humanities Research Council Collaborative Doctoral Partnership PhD studentship

Subjects: Applications are welcome from non-Higher Education Institutions (non-HEIs) Organisations located within the United Kingdom. These can be any type of organisation which has the research capacity to 'host' a doctoral student

Purpose: The Collaborative Doctoral Partnership scheme gives non-higher education institutions with a proven track record in postgraduate research the opportunity to manage PhD students, with a minimum of three studentships per year

Eligibility: 1. Applications are welcome from non-Higher Education Institutions (non-HEIs) Organisations located within the United Kingdom. These can be any type of organisation which has the research capacity to 'host' a doctoral student. 2. Smaller non-HEI Organisations may wish to submit a joint application as a consortium. If successful, the consortium would be the Collaborative Doctoral Partner with the AHRC. Organisations applying as a consortium should ensure that there is a clear strategic rationale for holding a single allocation between them

Value: The value for the stipend is £14,777 per annum plus a £550 additional stipend payment. In addition, the National Library of Scotland will provide up to £1,000 per year to contribute towards travel and related research costs

Length of Study: 3 years

Country of Study: Any country

Application Procedure: You could use the website link : www.ahrc-cdp.org. Visit the official link www.ahrc.ac.uk for further inquiry

Closing Date: 13 September

For further information contact:

Email: Lucie.Connors@ahrc.ukri.org

China Scholarship Council (CSC) Scholarship

Purpose: The CSC Scholarship is a scholarship programme for Chinese PhD students, who will take a full PhD at the University of Aberdeen

Eligibility: 1. To be eligible to apply for this scholarship in China, candidates must submit with their application, a conditional scholarship offer letter from Curtin University. 2. To ensure interested candidates meet the China Scholarship Council application deadline in March each year, Curtin University strongly encourage students submit their online e-application for admissions latest by 31 January of the applying year to avoid missing the deadline. 3. Scholarship Recipients must hold a conditional offer of enrolment subject to the CSC award and also fulfil the entry requirements of Curtin University, including a high level of English language proficiency

Type: Scholarship

Country of Study: Any country

Application Procedure: Applications for the CSC Scholarship should be submitted online at: apply.csc.edu.cn/csc/main/person/login/index.jsf. Please consult the CSC website for the deadline

Additional Information: If you have any further questions, please contact Catriona Milne, International Officer for China, via email: catriona.milne@abdn.ac.uk

For further information contact:

Email: catriona.milne@abdn.ac.uk

Common Data Access MSc Petroleum Data Management Scholarships

Purpose: To pursue MSc programme

Value: Each scholarship is valued at £5,000 for the duration of the MSc Petroleum Data Management degree and will contribute towards the programme tuition fees

Country of Study: Any country

Closing Date: 31 May

For further information contact:

Email: info@cdal.com

Elphinstone PhD Scholarships

Subjects: Arts and humanities, social sciences, business management, life sciences and medicine natural sciences and physical sciences

Type: Scholarship

Value: Cover tuition fees for the duration of their supervised study

Country of Study: Any country

For further information contact:

Email: infohub@abdn.ac.uk

Principal

Subjects: Music

Level of Study: Unrestricted

Type: Scholarship
Study Establishment: University of Aberdeen
Country of Study: United Kingdom

For further information contact:

Email: studentfunding@ed.ac.uk

University of Adelaide

Graduate School of Management, 3rd Floor Security House, 233 North Terrace, Adelaide, SA 5005, Australia

Tel:	(61) 8 3035 525
Fax:	(61) 8 8223 4782
Email:	cmchugh@gsm.adelaide.edu.au
Website:	www.gsm.adelaide.edu.au
Contact:	MBA Admissions Officer

Adelaide Postgraduate Coursework Scholarships

Subjects: All subjects
Eligibility: Open only to the citizens of Australia or permanent residents who have achieved Honours 1 or equivalent
Level of Study: Postgraduate
Type: Scholarship
Value: Covers 50% of the tuition fee costs
Length of Study: 2 years
Frequency: Annual
Study Establishment: University of Adelaide
Country of Study: Australia
Application Procedure: Applicants must apply directly to the scholarship provider. Check website for further details
Closing Date: Varies

For further information contact:

Adelaide Graduate Centre, Adelaide University, Adelaide, SA 5005, Australia

Tel:	(61) 8 8313 4455
Fax:	(61) 8 8223 3394
Email:	adrienne.gorringe@adelaide.edu.au

Adelaide Scholarships International

Subjects: All subjects
Purpose: To attract high quality overseas postgraduate students to areas of research strength in the University of Adelaide to support its research effort

Eligibility: Open only to the citizens of Australia or permanent residents who have achieved Honours 1 or equivalent
Level of Study: Postgraduate
Type: Scholarships
Value: For Postgraduate Research (Subclass 574) visa holders the award provides compulsory standard Overseas Student Health Cover (OSHC) Worldcare policy for the student and their spouse and dependents (if any) for the standard duration of the student visa. It does not cover the additional 6 month extended student visa period post thesis submission. If the award holder does not hold a subclass 574 visa then he/she is responsible for the cost of health insurance
Length of Study: 2 years (Masters) or 3 years (PhD)
Frequency: Annual
Study Establishment: University of Adelaide
Country of Study: Australia
Application Procedure: Candidates must apply directly to the university. Check the website for further details
Closing Date: 30 June and 30 November
Contributor: Adelaide University

For further information contact:

Email: student.centre@adelaide.edu.au

Arts Start Up Scholarships at University of Adelaide in Australia

Subjects: Scholarships are awarded within the Faculty of Arts
Purpose: The Faculty of Arts at the University of Adelaide is inviting applications for Arts Start Up Scholarships. The scholarships are available to international students from India, Sri Lanka, Vietnam, Indonesia, Malaysia, United Kingdom and Hong Kong who are seeking entry into a Faculty of Arts postgraduate coursework program
Eligibility: Citizens of India, Sri Lanka, Vietnam, Indonesia, United Kingdom, Malaysia and Hong Kong are eligible to apply. If English is not your first language then you will need to show that your English language skills are at a high enough level to succeed in your studies
Type: Postgraduate scholarships
Value: The scholarship provides a one-off A\$4,000 payment for travel and living expenses. The scholarship will be paid to the recipient following confirmation of enrolment after the census date for the semester they commenced in
Study Establishment: Scholarships are awarded within the Faculty of Arts
Country of Study: Australia
Application Procedure: When offered admission to The University of Adelaide, you will need to accept the offer

within 20 business days. This will automatically be your application for the scholarship

Closing Date: Open

Additional Information: Please check the website for more details scholarship-positions.com/arts-start-scholarships-university-adelaide-australia/2018/02/06/

For further information contact:

Email: admin@scholarship-positions.com

Asia Pacific Institute of Information Technology) _IT PhDs in Grid Computing

Subjects: High performance and grid computing

Purpose: To enable high performance numerical computing on service-oriented architectures

Eligibility: Open only to the citizens of Australia and New Zealand or permanent residents who have achieved Honours 2a or equivalent

Level of Study: Postgraduate

Type: Scholarship

Value: A$24,650 per year

Length of Study: 3 years and 6 months

Frequency: Annual

Study Establishment: The Australian National University, The University of Adelaide

Country of Study: Australia

Application Procedure: Check website for further details

Closing Date: 21 September

Contributor: Adelaide University and The Australian National University

For further information contact:

Email: Peter.Strazdins@cs.anu.edu.au
Contact: Peter Strazdins

Australian Building Codes Board Research Scholarship

Subjects: Building, building surveying, fire engineering, architecture, construction, plumbing, hydraulic design or similar

Purpose: The ABCB runs the Student Research Scholarship Program to encourage undergraduate and postgraduate research in the field of building regulatory reform in Australia, which can contribute to the ABCB fulfilling its charter

Eligibility: To be eligible for the scholarship, applicants must be students currently undertaking undergraduate or postgraduate studies in building, building surveying, fire engineering, architecture, construction, plumbing, hydraulic design or similar at an Australian educational institution; and research that forms a component of a program or course at an educational institution (e.g. tertiary), such as a research project, thesis or dissertation

Level of Study: Graduate

Type: Scholarship

Value: Up to A$5,000 one off payment

Length of Study: 1 year

Country of Study: Australia

Application Procedure: To apply for the scholarship, applicants are asked to submit an ABCB Research Scholarship Application Form together with a resume and academic transcript to date to the Research Scholarship Project Officer at abcb.scholarship@abcb.gov.au

Closing Date: Rolling applications

Additional Information: For more information on the Student Research Scholarship Program, please contact the Research Scholarship Project Officer at abcb.scholarship@abcb.gov.au

For further information contact:

Email: abcb.scholarship@abcb.gov.au
Contact: Research Scholarship Project Officer

Ferry Scholarship – UniSA

Subjects: Chemistry and physics

Purpose: To promote study and research into the scientific fields of physics and chemistry

Eligibility: Open only to the citizens of Australia below the age of 25 who have achieved Honours 1 or equivalent

Level of Study: Postgraduate

Type: Scholarship

Value: A$7,500 per year

Length of Study: 1 year

Frequency: Annual

Study Establishment: Flinders University, The University of Adelaide, University of South Australia

Country of Study: Australia

Application Procedure: Applicants must apply directly to the university. Check the website for further details

Closing Date: 31 March

Funding: Individuals

Contributor: Late Cedric Arnold Seth Ferry

For further information contact:

Tel: (61) 8302 3967
Email: jenni.critcher@unisa.edu.au
Contact: Jenni Critcher

Joint Postgraduate Scholarship Program

Subjects: High and new technology in agriculture, applied social science and WTO-related areas (e.g. finance), energy sources and environment, engineering, life science and public health, material science and new material, telecommunication and information technology

Eligibility: Open to applicants who are citizens and permanent residents of the People's Republic of China at the time of application; are less than 35 years old at the time of application (this is a CSC eligibility requirement); are a university student completing a master's degree, or enrolled as a first year PhD student, or new graduates from their university at the time of application; agree to return to China upon completion of their studies and/or research; hold an unconditional offer of enrolment at the University of Adelaide, which is subject to the applicant also being successful in applying for a CSC award. They must therefore fulfil the relevant academic entry requirements set by the University of Adelaide for all international scholarship holders, including a high level of English language proficiency; English is the language of instruction at the University of Adelaide and proficiency in speaking, listening to, reading and writing English is essential. The IELTS (International English Language Testing System) is the preferred English language proficiency although TOEFL scores are also accepted. Applicants who have not provided evidence that they have met the university's minimum English Language Proficiency requirements by the closing date are not eligible for a CSC scholarship. CSC applicants are not permitted to undertake Pre-Enrolment English programs as the CSC will not award scholarships to applicants who have not met the university's minimum ELP requirements for direct entry. The Scholarships will give priority to graduates of the Chinese universities listed as "985 Project" Universities. Eligible candidates will be assessed by the University of Melbourne and Karlsruhe Institute of Technology on the basis of their academic transcripts and their research work

Type: Scholarship

Value: Australia

Country of Study: Any country

Application Procedure: The mode of applying is electronically. For detailed information, please visit website

Closing Date: 31 March

Contributor: The China Scholarship Council (CSC) and The University of Adelaide (UA)

Additional Information: The students of China can apply for these scholarships

Scholarships in Plant Cell Physiology

Subjects: Plant cell physiology

Purpose: To improve the nutritional qualities of crop plants allowing the fortification of animal and human diets without adversely affecting crop plant

Eligibility: Open only to the citizens of Australia who have achieved Honours 1 or equivalent, or Honours 2a or equivalent

Level of Study: Postgraduate

Type: Scholarship

Value: A$27,500 per year

Length of Study: 3 years

Frequency: Annual

Study Establishment: The University of Adelaide

Country of Study: Australia

Application Procedure: Applicants must apply directly to the university. Check website for further details

Closing Date: 31 August

Contributor: Adelaide University

For further information contact:

Tel:	(61) 8 8303 8145
Email:	matthew.gillam@adelaide.edu.au
Contact:	Dr Matthew Gillam

University of Alaska Fairbanks (UAF)

School of Management PO Box 756080, Fairbanks, AK 99775-6080, United States of America

Tel:	(1) 907 474 6511
Fax:	(1) 907 474 5219
Email:	famba@som.uaf.edu
Website:	www.uaf.edu/som/mba
Contact:	MBA Admissions Officer

Rasmuson Fisheries Research Center Fellowships

Subjects: The Rasmuson Fisheries Research Center (RFRC) was founded in 1994 by Elmer E. Rasmuson with an endowment to the University of Alaska Fairbanks

Purpose: This fellowship is especially interested in seeing proposals on applied topics aligned with the research priorities and needs of the North Pacific Fishery Management Council [PDF]

Eligibility: 1. Awards will be made to support excellence in graduate student research. The award is not a Research Assistantship, but a Fellowship in recognition of scholastic excellence. Awards are open to any full-time or prospective CFOS graduate student. 2. Research should produce findings with a potential for continued development as a scientific or applied initiative. 3. Projects should be distinctive and make an original contribution to existing knowledge. 4. Projects should have potential economic value to the fishing industry and contribute to long-term benefits for Alaska. 5. Awards may be contingent on receipt of research funding from other sources. The award cannot be used for research expenses. See item #6, "Current and Pending," under "Format of Proposals" below. 6. Proposals should be submitted by the graduate student with faculty advisor endorsement as described in item #8 below. 7. Awards are renewable. Master's students can be funded for a maximum of two (2) years and PhD students for a maximum of three (3) years. Continuation requests require a satisfactory progress report

Level of Study: Postgraduate
Type: Fellowship
Value: Fellowship award of $35,000
Frequency: Annual
Country of Study: Any country
Application Procedure: Complete format of proposals are available in the below link. www.uaf.edu/cfos/research/major-research-programs/rasmuson-fisheries-resear/rfrc-fellowships/
Closing Date: 25 January
Funding: Private

For further information contact:

Tel: (1) 907 474 2619
Email: clsutton3@alaska.edu

University of Alberta

Faculty of Graduate Studies & Research, Killam Centre for Advanced Studies, 2-29 Triffo Hall, University of Alberta, Edmonton, AB T6G 2E1, Canada

Tel: (1) 780 492 3499
Fax: (1) 780 492 0692
Email: grad.services@ualberta.ca
Website: www.ualberta.ca/gradstudies

Opened in 1908, the University of Alberta has a long tradition of scholarly achievements and commitment to excellence in teaching, research and service to the community. It is one of Canada's five largest research-intensive universities, with an annual research income from external sources of more than C$3,00,000,000. It participates in 18 of 21 of the Federal Networks of Centres of Excellence, which link

industries, universities and governments in applied research and development.

Canadian Initiatives For Nordic Studies (CINS) Graduate Scholarship

Subjects: Fine arts, humanities, natural, physical, applied and social sciences and more
Purpose: To provide financial assistance to students who wish to pursue higher studies
Eligibility: Open to Canadian citizens or landed immigrants, who have completed a Bachelor's degree from a Canadian university or college with high scholastic achievement. Applicants must be in residency at the Nordic destination for a minimum of 6 months and provide a written report to CINS no later than 6 months after completing the proposed programme of study
Level of Study: Postgraduate
Type: Scholarship
Value: C$5,000
Frequency: Annual
Application Procedure: Applicants should include the following in their application: contact details, citizenship status, social insurance number and date of birth, current academic status with formal transcripts, written acceptance from the host Nordic institution and reference letters
Closing Date: 15 February
Additional Information: Applicants can study at any recognized institution granting earned degrees at the post-baccalaureate level in the applicant's field of study and located in one of the Nordic countries: Denmark, Finland, Iceland, Norway, Sweden, the Faroe Islands and Greenland

For further information contact:

Tel: (1) 780 492 3111
Email: chale@ualberta.ca
Contact: Chair of the Board

Izaak Walton Killam Memorial Scholarship

Purpose: It will be offered to outstanding students registered in, or admissible to, a doctoral program. No restrictions on citizenship
Eligibility: Offered to outstanding students registered in, or admissible to, a doctoral program. No restrictions on citizenship. All fields are eligible for funding. Applicants must have completed at least one year of graduate work (master's or doctoral level) before start of tenure; tenure may begin on May 1st or September 1st. Additional information regarding eligibility criteria can be found in the Applicant

Instructions document below. Please note that the GPA is calculated over the current graduate program graded course work

Level of Study: Graduate
Type: Scholarship
Value: C$35,000
Length of Study: 2 years
Frequency: Annual
Country of Study: Any country
Application Procedure: Students complete the Izaak Walton Killam Memorial Scholarship application form and submit supporting documents to their department to be considered for both the Izaak Walton Killam Memorial Scholarship and the Dorothy J Killam Memorial Graduate Prizes. A complete Izaak Walton Killam Memorial Scholarship Application includes: For Applicants: Izaak Walton Killam Memorial Scholarship Applicant Instructions 1. Izaak Walton Killam Memorial Scholarship Application Form. 2. Two Letter of Reference to Support Application for Graduate Awards. 3. Transcripts (copies of official transcripts for all post-secondary study are required to support an application. Your home department may have copies in your department file. If your department does not have these transcripts, you are required to submit new transcripts. Unofficial copies of University of Alberta transcripts are acceptable)
Closing Date: 28 February
Funding: Private

For further information contact:

Killam Centre for Advanced Studies 2-29 Triffo Hall University of Alberta Edmonton, Alberta T6G 2E1, Canada

Email: gswbsite@ualberta.ca

University of Alberta MBA Programme

Length of Study: 20 months; 72 months
Application Procedure: Applicants must complete and return the form, with two official academic transcripts, Graduate Management Admission Test scores, three letters of recommendation, a two page statement of intent, a detailed curriculum vitae, an application deposit of C$60 (US$45), and a TOEFL score (if applicable) of 550+
Closing Date: 30 April (for part-time)

For further information contact:

Tel: (1) 780 492 3946
Fax: (1) 780 492 7825
Email: mba.programs@ualberta.ca
Contact: MBA Admissions Officer

University of Amsterdam

The University of Amsterdam is a public university located in Amsterdam, The Netherlands.

Amsterdam Excellence Scholarships (AES)

Subjects: Master's Programmes offered at the University of Amsterdam
Purpose: The Amsterdam Excellence Scholarships (AES) awards scholarships to exceptionally talented students from outside Europe to pursue eligible Master's Programmes offered at the University of Amsterdam
Eligibility: Non-European Union students from any discipline who graduated in the top 10% of their class may apply. Selection is on the basis of academic excellence, ambition and the relevance of the selected Master's programme to a student's future career
Level of Study: Postgraduate
Type: Scholarship
Value: €25,000 per annum
Length of Study: 1 year
Frequency: Annual
Study Establishment: University of Amsterdam
Country of Study: Netherlands
Application Procedure: Applications are made through the Admissions Offices of the Graduate Schools
Closing Date: 15 January or 01 February
Additional Information: For more details, please visit official scholarship website: www.uva.nl/en/education/masters/scholarships–tuition/scholarships-and-loans/amsterdam-excellence-scholarship/amsterdam-excellence-scholarship.html

For further information contact:

P.O. Box 19268, NLD 1000 GG Amsterdam, The Netherlands

Email: servicedesk-ac@uva.nl

Amsterdam Science Talent Scholarship (ASTS)

Subjects: Science
Purpose: Scholarship is available for pursuing the masters degree programme at the University of Amsterdam
Eligibility: Non-Dutch talented students from the European Union / European Economic Area can apply
Value: €12,500 (covering tuition and living expenses)
Length of Study: 2 years
Country of Study: Any country

Application Procedure: Check the entry requirements of your programme under 'Application and admission'. Overview of Science Master's Programmes. Register in Studielink (on the same page) Submit your application online after receiving your UvA-net ID (this can take up to 48 hours)

Closing Date: 1 March

Additional Information: For more details, please visit the website scholarship-positions.com/fully-funded-science-talent-scholarship-university-amsterdam-netherlands

For further information contact:

Email: master-science@uva.nl

MacGillavry Fellowships

Subjects: Astronomy, Informatics and Logic, Biological Science and Biomedical Science, Earth Sciences (Physical Geography), Physics, Chemistry, Mathematics, and Statistic

Purpose: These fellowships are available in the field of Biological Science and Biomedical Science, Earth Sciences (Physical Geography), Informatics and Logic, Physics, Chemistry, Astronomy, Mathematics, and Statistics

Eligibility: Eligibility for the Scholarship: 1. A PhD degree in one of the scientific disciplines of their Faculty. 2. A scientific profile that links to one of the research fields eligible for application. 3. A publication record in international, high quality, peer-reviewed journals. 4. A few years of postdoctoral experience, preferably at the international level. 5. Well-developed organizational and communication skills. 6. Affinity for teaching at the undergraduate and graduate level

Level of Study: Postgraduate

Type: Fellowship

Value: The annual salary range for an assistant professor, including annual holiday allowance and the bonus is between €50,755 and €78,935 (before tax), depending on experience and past performance

Frequency: Annual

Country of Study: Any country

Application Procedure: To apply for the MacGillavry Fellowship you are invited to use the application form on the MacGillavry website of the Faculty of Science. www.uva.nl/en/faculty/faculty-of-science/macgillavry-fellowship/macgillavry-fellowship.html

Closing Date: 4 February

Funding: Private

For further information contact:

Email: servicedesk-icts@uva.nl

University of Auckland

Private Bag 92019, Auckland 1000, New Zealand

Tel:	(64) 9 373 7599
Fax:	(64) 9 373 7437
Email:	appointments@auckland.ac.nz
Website:	www.auckland.ac.nz
Contact:	Ms S Codhersides, HR Manager

The University of Auckland is committed to conserving, advancing and disseminating knowledge of the highest standard through teaching by scholars who are among the foremost researchers in New Zealand. The University aims to be of high international standing and to contribute to the advancement of knowledge to its local, national and international communities.

Anne Bellam Scholarship

Subjects: Music

Purpose: To assist students to further their musical education overseas

Eligibility: The candidate must be under 30 years of age and a citizen of New Zealand, must have completed or will complete in the year of application any degree or diploma in performance or any postgraduate music degree at the University of Auckland

Level of Study: Postgraduate

Type: Scholarship

Value: Up to NZ$30,000 for study overseas and up to $10,000 for study at the University of Auckland

Length of Study: 1 year

Frequency: Annual

Study Establishment: University of Auckland

Country of Study: New Zealand

Application Procedure: The candidate must supply, one week in advance of examination, an outline of his proposed study plans and itinerary

Closing Date: Please check website

Funding: Government

For further information contact:

Faculty of Creative Arts and Industries, School of Music, University of Auckland, Private Bag 92019, Auckland 1000, New Zealand

Email: scholarships@auckland.ac.nz

Arthington Davy Scholarship

Subjects: All subjects
Purpose: To study and research in areas which will significantly contribute to the development of Tonga
Eligibility: The candidate must be a Tongan citizen, born to Tongan parents and possess a first University degree
Level of Study: Research
Type: Scholarship
Value: The Arthington Davy Scholarship may cover the cost of part of the cost of a postgraduate study or research programme
Study Establishment: Trinity College
Country of Study: United Kingdom
Application Procedure: The candidate must submit a complete curriculum vitae and academic record, proof of Tongan origin, details of the intended postgraduate study preferably with a letter of conditional acceptance from the University concerned, full details of tuition fees and living expenses and of finances available from the student's own resources or elsewhere and the names of two academic referees
Closing Date: 30 November (for course commencing in March or April), 31 May (for course commencing in September or October)
Funding: Commercial, Private, Foundation, Individuals

For further information contact:

Email: hf202@hermes.cam.ac.uk
Contact: Tutor for Advanced Studies

Asian Development Bank Japan Scholarship

Subjects: Environmental science, development studies, international business and engineering
Eligibility: The candidate must possess a minimum English language requirement for entry into postgraduate study at the University of Auckland. IELTS with an overall score of 6.5 and no band less than 6.0 or a TOEFL paper-based 575 with a TWE of 4.5 or computer-based 233 with a TWE of 4.5
Level of Study: Postgraduate
Type: Scholarship
Value: Tuition fee at the University of Auckland, Airfare from his or her home country to Auckland, New Zealand, Basic cost of living in Auckland, Health and medical insurance in New Zealand, and Airfare from Auckland, New Zealand, to the scholar's home country at the conclusion of his or her course of study
Study Establishment: University of Auckland
Country of Study: New Zealand

Application Procedure: Applications can be filled online
Closing Date: 20 July(check with website)
Funding: Government, Private
Contributor: Asian Development Bank and Government of Japan

For further information contact:

Email: information@adbj.org

Auckland Council Research Scholarship in Urban Economics

Purpose: The purpose of this scholarship is to encourage and support postgraduate research into urban economics that has particular relevance to local government in New Zealand
Eligibility: 1. At the time of application candidates must be enrolled or planning to enrol in a postgraduate programme at a New Zealand university (applicants may be enrolled as full time students). 2. The postgraduate programme must be in the area of urban economics. Universities NZ and Auckland Council reserve the right to determine the eligibility of a particular area of study. 3. A thesis, dissertation, or research report must be a requirement of the postgraduate programme
Level of Study: Graduate, Postgraduate
Type: Scholarship
Value: NZ $3,000 or NZ $1,500
Frequency: Annual
Country of Study: Any country
Application Procedure: Candidates must complete an application using the Universities NZ scholarships application website universitiesnz.communityforce.com/ Each year Auckland Council may grant one scholarship with an award of NZ$3,000. For candidates who are enrolled on a part time basis the value of the award will be NZ$1,500
Closing Date: 1 February
Funding: Private
Additional Information: Application link to fill the basic information is universitiesnz.communityforce.com/Login.aspx

For further information contact:

Email: scholarships-cf@universitiesnz.ac.nz

Commonwealth Scholarship

Subjects: All subjects
Purpose: The scholarships are available to students to be enroled at the University of Auckland for the Degree of

Doctor of Philosophy; another approved Doctorate or a Master's degree

Eligibility: The candidate must be a citizen of Commonwealth of Nations, including Australian, British and Canadian citizens. The candidate must be tenable for a maximum of 36 months for a PhD candidate or 21 months for a Master's candidate

Level of Study: Doctorate, Postgraduate

Type: Scholarship

Value: Up to NZ$25,000 per year plus health insurance and fees at the domestic rate

Study Establishment: University of Auckland

Country of Study: New Zealand

Application Procedure: The candidate must send the application for UA Commonwealth Scholarships must be made through the appropriate organization in the scholar's home country on the Commonwealth Scholarship application form

Closing Date: 31 July

Funding: Government

For further information contact:

Scholarships Office, Student Administration, The University of Auckland, Private Bag 92019, Auckland Mail Centre, Auckland 1142, New Zealand

Tel: (64) 9 373 7599 ext 87494
Fax: (64) 9 308 2309
Email: scholarships@auckland.ac.nz

Doctoral Scholarships

Subjects: All subjects

Purpose: To assist and encourage students to pursue doctoral studies at The University of Auckland

Eligibility: The candidate must be a citizen or a permanent resident of New Zealand. New Māori and domestic3 Pacific doctoral applicants with a GPA of 7.50 or above, from their most recent qualifying programme, will be guaranteed a scholarship provided the qualifying programme was completed at a New Zealand university

Level of Study: Doctorate

Type: Scholarship

Value: NZ$27,900 plus fees, with the possibility of a six-month extension. There will be an annual cost-of-living adjustment to the doctoral stipend

Length of Study: 3 years

Frequency: Annual

Study Establishment: University of Auckland

Country of Study: New Zealand

Application Procedure: The candidate must fill the application form and send it to the Scholarships office. The selection will be made on the basis of merit

Closing Date: Varies (refer to relevant faculty)

Funding: Government

For further information contact:

Email: c.tuu@auckland.ac.nz
Email: scholarships@auckland.ac.nz

Fulbright Scholarship

Subjects: All subjects

Purpose: To encourage and facilitate study for approved postgraduate degrees at the University of Auckland by candidates already selected to hold Fulbright Awards

Eligibility: The candidate must be a citizen of the United States of America and intending to take up Fulbright Awards to study in New Zealand and should enrol for a full-time at the University of Auckland for an approved Master's or Doctoral degree

Level of Study: Doctorate, Postgraduate

Type: Scholarship

Value: NZ$15,000 per year plus research/tuition fees

Frequency: Annual

Study Establishment: University of Auckland

Country of Study: New Zealand

Application Procedure: The candidate must send the completed application form to the Scholarships office

Closing Date: Check with the university

Funding: Government

Hope Selwyn Foundation Scholarship

Purpose: The HOPE Selwyn Foundation is a registered charitable trust established in 1996 to assist the funding of research and education essential to the health and welfare of older people in New Zealand

Eligibility: 1. The purpose of the scholarships is to support or partially support the salaries of young scientists (the definition of "young" being reasonably flexible) who are in the early stages of their careers. 2. Candidates undertaking a Masters or doctoral thesis will be considered for support. Candidates will normally be working under supervision in a recognised research environment with a senior research leader. 3. HOPE Sewlyn Foundation scholarships may be held with any other bursary or award unless the candidate's other awards preclude this

Level of Study: Postgraduate

Type: Scholarship

Value: NZ $6,000

Length of Study: 4 years

Frequency: Annual

Country of Study: New Zealand

Closing Date: 31 October
Funding: Foundation

For further information contact:

The University of Auckland, Private Bag 92019, Auckland 1142, New Zealand

Email: pc.dasilva@auckland.ac.nz

International College of Auckland PhD Scholarship in Plant Sciences

Subjects: Plant Science
Purpose: To assist eminent Chinese scholars from nominated areas of China to study plant sciences at the University of Auckland and to promote links between China and New Zealand in the field of plant sciences
Eligibility: The candidate must possess a PhD in the field of plant science and who has paid the fees, or arranged to pay the fees, for full–time enrolment in the School of Biological Sciences
Level of Study: Postdoctorate
Type: Scholarship
Value: NZ$20,000 per year. The scholarship's emolument will be paid as a tuition/compulsory fees credit and the balance as a fortnightly stipend
Length of Study: 3 years
Frequency: Annual
Study Establishment: University of Auckland
Country of Study: New Zealand
Application Procedure: The candidate must submit the completed application form along with the curriculum vitae and at least two academic reference letters
Closing Date: 1 October
Funding: Government
Contributor: The International College of Auckland

For further information contact:

Email: scholarships@auckland.ac.nz

Maori and Pacific Graduate Scholarships (Masters/Honours/PGDIP)

Subjects: All subjects
Purpose: To assist and encourage Maori and Pacific students to pursue Masters, Honours and PGDip courses at The University of Auckland
Eligibility: The candidate must be a Maori or Pacific student who are citizens or permanent residents of New Zealand
Level of Study: Graduate, Postgraduate

Type: Scholarship
Value: Up to $10,000 plus compulsory fees
Length of Study: 1 year
Frequency: Annual
Study Establishment: University of Auckland
Country of Study: New Zealand
Application Procedure: The candidate must fill up the application form and send it to the Scholarships office. The Selection Committee will assess the application form
Closing Date: Please check website
Funding: Government

Masters/Honours/PGDIP Scholarships

Subjects: All subjects
Eligibility: The candidate must be a citizen or a permanent resident of New Zealand. In case of a Master's degree, the candidate must be tenable until the date for completion of the requirements for the degree as specified in the General Regulations – Masters degrees
Level of Study: Graduate, Postgraduate
Type: Scholarship
Value: Up to NZ$10,000 per year plus compulsory fees
Length of Study: 1 year
Frequency: Annual
Study Establishment: University of Auckland
Country of Study: New Zealand
Application Procedure: The candidate must fill the application form and send it to the Scholarships office. Selection will be made on the basis of merit
Closing Date: 1 November
Funding: Government

New Zealand Agency for International Development Scholarship (NZDS) – Open Category

Subjects: All subjects
Eligibility: The candidate must possess minimum English language requirements for entry into the University of Auckland postgraduate study. IELTS (International English Language Testing System Certificate) with an overall score of 6.5 and no band less than 6.0 or a TOEFL (Test of English as a Foreign Language) paper based 575 with a TWE of 4.5 or computer based 233
Level of Study: Postgraduate
Type: Scholarship
Value: Tuition, enrollment/orientation fees, return economy fare travel, medical insurance and provision for students to meet course and basic living costs
Study Establishment: University of Auckland
Country of Study: New Zealand

Application Procedure: Application form can be down-loaded from the website
Closing Date: 1 June
Funding: Government
Contributor: New Zealand Agency for International Development and the Ministry of Foreign Affairs

For further information contact:

Tel: (64) 9 373 7599 ext 87556
Fax: (64) 9 373 7405
Email: rfatialofa.patolo@auckland.ac.nz

New Zealand International Doctoral Research (NZIDRS) Scholarship

Subjects: All subjects
Purpose: To provide financial support for postgraduate students from designated countries seeking doctoral degrees by research in New Zealand universities
Eligibility: The candidate must hold an A' average or equivalent in their studies, meet the requirements for entry into a research-based doctoral degree programme at a New Zealand university
Level of Study: Doctorate, Research
Type: Research scholarship
Value: Living allowance (NZ $25,000 per year), a travel allowance (NZ $2,000), a health insurance allowance (NZ $500), and a book and thesis allowance (NZ $800)
Length of Study: 3 years
Study Establishment: University of Auckland
Country of Study: New Zealand
Application Procedure: The candidate must complete the application form in English and attach supporting documents as stipulated in the application form
Closing Date: 16 July
Funding: Government
Contributor: Government of New Zealand

For further information contact:

Tel: (64) 4 472 0788
Fax: (64) 4 471 2828
Email: scholarships@educationnz.org.nz
Contact: Scholarships Manager

Property Institute of New Zealand Postgraduate Scholarship

Subjects: Real property
Purpose: To promote postgraduate study in the field of real property

Eligibility: The candidate must possess a Master's degree or full-time PhD candidate and has the paid the fees, or arranged to pay the fees, for study in the Department of Property at Lincoln University, Massey University or The University of Auckland
Level of Study: Doctorate
Type: Scholarship
Value: NZ$1,500
Length of Study: 1 year
Frequency: Annual
Study Establishment: University of Auckland
Country of Study: New Zealand
Closing Date: 31 March
Funding: Government
Contributor: Property Institute of New Zealand

For further information contact:

Tel: (64) 9 373 7599 ext 87494
Fax: (64) 9 308 2309
Email: scholarships@auckland.ac.nz

Reardon Postgraduate Scholarship in Music

Subjects: Music
Purpose: To honour and in memory of Daniel Patrick Reardon and Kathleen Mary Reardon
Eligibility: The candidate must possess a degree or diploma with a specialization in Performance in the year of the award
Level of Study: Postgraduate
Type: Scholarship
Value: NZ$4,500
Length of Study: 1 year
Frequency: Annual
Study Establishment: University of Auckland
Country of Study: New Zealand
Closing Date: 30 September
Funding: Government
Contributor: Reardon Memorial Music Trust

Senior Health Research Scholarships

Subjects: Health
Purpose: To attract health professionals to return to the University to study full-time for a PhD in a health-related field
Eligibility: The candidate must be a citizen or a permanent resident of New Zealand and who have worked for 3 years as a health professional
Level of Study: Doctorate
Value: NZ$40,000 plus compulsory fees
Length of Study: 3 years

Frequency: Annual
Study Establishment: University of Auckland
Country of Study: New Zealand
Application Procedure: The candidate must submit an application form and send it to the Scholarships office. Selection shall be made on the basis of merit
Closing Date: 1 November
Funding: Government

The AUT Queen Elizabeth II Diamond Jubilee Doctoral Scholarship

Purpose: AUT Doctoral Scholarship AUT aims to: Develop an internationally-aware, skilled future leader Establish enduring education and professional linkages
Eligibility: 1. The scholarship will be awarded annually to a doctoral student who is a citizen, and resident in, one of the following Pacific countries; Cook Islands, Fiji, Kiribati, Nauru, Niue, Papua New Guinea, Samoa, Solomon Islands, Tokelau, Tonga and Vanuatu to carry out doctoral study at AUT University. 2. Applicants must be a citizen and resident of one of the eligible countries. Applicants may not have citizenship or permanent residence status of New Zealand or any other developed country. Applicants who are New Zealand citizens from the Cook Islands, Niue, Tokelau and dual citizens of Samoa are exempt from this requirement; however, they must reside in the Cook Islands, Nuie, Tokelau or Samoa or another eligible country. Preference may be given to those applicants who have also been schooled in an eligible country. 3. The recipients of this scholarship will have strong academic references plus a strong academic record and/or have demonstrated the potential for quality research. Previous study should include research methodologies papers and an independent research project, including the writing of a report on that research
Level of Study: Postgraduate
Type: Scholarship
Value: NZ$25,000
Frequency: Annual
Country of Study: Any country
Application Procedure: Application will be via the online scholarship application portal available from the link. It is not possible to submit incomplete scholarship applications through the online application process. In order for the application to be submitted all requested documentation must be included. The following documents or statements must be completed and uploaded in the application portal by the closing date. Incomplete applications will not be forwarded to the selection panel. 1. AUT Queen Elizabeth II Diamond Jubilee Doctoral Scholarship on-line application form. 2. Academic transcript(s) if any previous tertiary study has been completed at a university other than AUT. 3. A certified

copy of the applicant's birth certificate or passport. 4. Two referee's reports are required. Applicants must not submit referee's reports directly. Nominated referees will be sent a request directly by the on-line application system. Please advise your referees that they will be receiving an email requesting a reference statement and that this must be submitted by the closing date or your application will be ineligible. If the referee declines to provide a reference before the closing date you will be able to nominate another referee. 5. A two page statement (maximum 1,000 words) outlining the applicant's research proposal using the template provided with the online application form. Please note this must be two pages only (plus one page for references). If a longer document is provided you will be asked to rewrite it. 6. Written support from the proposed primary supervisor if they have not acted as one of the referees above. 7. A brief C.V. (maximum three pages)
Closing Date: 15 October
Funding: Private

For further information contact:

55 Wellesley St E, Auckland 1010 New Zealand

Email: scholars@aut.ac.nz

The University of Auckland International Doctoral Fees Bursary

Subjects: All subjects
Purpose: To assist international students from all countries who wish to pursue doctoral studies
Eligibility: Permanent citizens and residents of Australia and New Zealand are not eligible for the scholarship
Level of Study: Doctorate
Type: Bursary
Value: NZ $25,000
Frequency: Annual
Study Establishment: University of Auckland
Country of Study: New Zealand
Application Procedure: The application form can be obtained from the Scholarships Office, University of Auckland
Closing Date: 1 August
Funding: Government

University of Auckland International Doctoral Scholarship

Subjects: All subjects
Purpose: To assist international students from all countries who wish to pursue doctoral studies

Eligibility: The scholarship is available to international students from all countries who wish to pursue Doctoral studies on a full-time basis. Permanent citizens and residents of Australia and New Zealand are not eligible for the scholarship
Level of Study: Doctorate
Type: Scholarship
Value: NZ$25,000, in the form of a fortnightly stipend
Frequency: Annual
Study Establishment: University of Auckland
Country of Study: New Zealand
Application Procedure: The application form can be obtained from the Scholarships Office, University of Auckland
Closing Date: Varies
Funding: Government

University of Auckland Business School

School of Business & Economics, Private Bag 92019, Auckland, New Zealand

Tel: (64) 9 373 7599
Fax: (64) 9 373 7437
Email: execpro@auckland.ac.nz
Website: www.business.auckland.ac.nz
Contact: Dr Gary Cayton, Director MBA

Kupe Leadership Scholarships

Purpose: The Kupe Leadership Programme will involve a three-day Orientation in early March; two two-day workshops held during each mid-semester break; a one-day workshop in the inter-semester break and a concluding day-long workshop in November
Eligibility: The Kupe Leadership alumni will develop a reputation for embodying these values and for contributions they make, nationally and possibly internationally
Level of Study: Postgraduate
Type: Scholarship
Frequency: Annual
Country of Study: Any country
Closing Date: 24 August
Funding: Private

For further information contact:

The University of Auckland, Private Bag 92019, Auckland, 1142, New Zealand

Tel: (64) 800 61 62 63
Email: pc.dasilva@auckland.ac.nz

University of Auckland Executive MBA Programme

Length of Study: More than 2 years
Application Procedure: Applicants must return a completed form. A deposit of A$250 is payable on acceptance. Foreign students may be required to sit a test of English proficiency
Closing Date: 3 November (for trimester one), 4 May (for trimester two), 17 August (for trimester three)

For further information contact:

Business Administration International Students Office, Private Bag 92019, Auckland 1142, New Zealand

Tel: (64) 9 373 7513
Fax: (64) 9 373 7405
Email: international@auckland.ac.nz
Contact: MBA Admissions Officer

University of Bath

Claverton Down, BA2 7AY, Bath, United Kingdom

Tel: (44) 1225 388388
Fax: (44) 1225 388388
Website: www.bath.ac.uk
Contact: University of Bath

The University of Bath received its Royal Charter in 1966 and is now firmly established as a top ten United Kingdom university with a reputation for research and teaching excellence.

United Kingdom-India Year of Culture GREAT Postgraduate Scholarships

Subjects: Scholarships are awarded in the Faculty of Humanities and Social Sciences, Faculty of Engineering and Design and scholarship in the Faculty of Science
Purpose: The University of Bath is currently accepting applications for United Kingdom-India Year of Culture GREAT Scholarships. This scholarship is available to the international fee-paying student from India studying a full-time taught postgraduate masters programme
Eligibility: Indian students are eligible to apply for this scholarship. For most programmes, the requirement for non-native English speakers is 6.5 in the IELTS Academic English test, with no less than 6.0 in any element
Type: Postgraduate scholarships

Value: If you are an international fee-paying student you could be eligible for one of ten United Kingdom-India Year of Culture GREAT Scholarships each worth £5,000
Study Establishment: Scholarships are awarded in the Faculty of Humanities and Social Sciences, Faculty of Engineering and Design and scholarship in the Faculty of Science
Country of Study: United Kingdom
Application Procedure: If you are eligible for the scholarship scheme we will let you know and invite you to apply. Queries for MSc students should be addressed to msc-mn-at-bath.ac.uk and for MBA students to mbaapps-at-management.bath.ac.uk
Closing Date: 1 June
Additional Information: For more details please see the website scholarship-positions.com/uk-india-year-of-culture-great-postgraduate-scholarships-university-bath-uk/2018/01/27/

For further information contact:

Email: mbaapps-at-management.bath.ac.uk

University of Bern

Hochschulstrasse 4, Bern CH 3012, Switzerland

Tel: (41) 31 631 81 11
Email: info@imd.unibe.ch
Website: www.unibe.ch/eng/

The University of Bern offers top quality teaching, special recognition in leading–edge disciplines, and a campus environment intimately linked to the social, economic, and political life of the city. The university's comprehensive offering includes 8 faculties and some 160 institutes with 12,500 students. Its academic and research organization prides itself on its interdisciplinarity. The university is actively involved in a wide range of European and worldwide research projects.

Excellence Scholarships for Postgraduate Study

Subjects: All subjects
Purpose: Scholarship for international students
Eligibility: Applicants must, by end of July, have graduated with at least a Bachelor's degree in the same field of study as the selected Master's programme and must be residing in their home country. The criteria for selection are previous academic excellence and the potential of the candidate
Level of Study: Graduate

Type: Scholarship
Value: CHF 1,600 per month for the entire duration of the course
Frequency: Annual
Application Procedure: Check website for specific details
Closing Date: 21 December
Funding: Commercial

For further information contact:

Tel: (41) 31 631 80 49
Email: claudine.rossi@int.unibe.ch
Contact: Claudine Ross

UniBE International 2021

Purpose: To support for young researchers and to the university's internationalization
Level of Study: Doctorate, Postgraduate
Length of Study: 3 years
Study Establishment: University of Bern
Country of Study: Switzerland
Application Procedure: Please email your application including any related documents as one pdf to lenka.fehrenbach@entwicklung.unibe.ch
Closing Date: 17 May
Contributor: Swiss National Fund (SNF)

For further information contact:

Email: sandro.stauffer@uls.unibe.ch

University of Birmingham

Student funding office, Edgbaston, West Midlands B15 2TT, Birmingham, United Kingdom

Tel: (44) 121 414 3142
Fax: (44) 121 414 6637
Email: j.e.bryan@bham.ac.uk
Website: www.as.bham.ac.uk/funding
Contact: Joanne Bryan, Assistant Director of Student Financial Support

The University of Birmingham is a leading research institution, offering a wide range of programmes, high teaching and research standards, and excellent facilities for academic work.

A Master of Science Business Scholarships

Subjects: Business
Purpose: Birmingham Business School offers a number of scholarships for students on the MSc Business programmes to reward outstanding academic achievement. The financial support offered is to contribute towards tuition fees. These awards are based on merit and will be selected by a panel of representatives from the Business School
Eligibility: To be eligible for the MSc Business Scholarship you will need to: Have received an offer to study on one of our 1 year eligible MSc programmes and should have submitted a scholarship application, with all requested information attached, by the final deadline
Value: MSc Business Scholarships are usually up to £5,000 offered against tuition fees. Successful scholars will still need to pay the remainder of the fees
Country of Study: Any country
Closing Date: 1 June

For further information contact:

Email: msc@business-school.ed.ac.uk

A Master of Science in Robotics Scholarship

Subjects: MSc Robotics
Purpose: To support students on the MSc Robotics Programme
Eligibility: Students with a place on the MSc Robotics programme
Level of Study: Postgraduate
Type: Scholarship
Value: £5,000
Length of Study: 1 year
Frequency: Annual
Study Establishment: The University of Birmingham
Country of Study: United Kingdom
Application Procedure: Apply for the MSc Robotics programme and submit your curriculum vitae and a 300–500 words personal statement to professor Jeremy L Wyatt via email at jlw@cs.bham.ac.uk and Dr Michael Mistry at m.n. mistry@bham.ac.uk
Closing Date: May
Funding: Private
Additional Information: For more information, contact the School of Computer Science

For further information contact:

Email: hello@harbour.space

Abu Dhabi National Oil Company (ADNOC) Scholarship Program

Subjects: Engineering and physical sciences
Purpose: The Scholarship Department's mission is to educate, train and prepare UAE nationals to take up leading positions in the oil and gas industry, as part of its commitment towards the process of Emiratization of jobs both for ADNOC Headquarters and ADNOC Group of Companies
Eligibility: UAE National
Level of Study: Doctorate, Postgraduate, Research
Type: Equipment grant
Value: Monthly stipend, cash award at the end of the semester based on academic performance, cover tuition fees, computer allowance, travel tickets. 1. Cash Award for Outstanding students. 2. Full Health and Dental Care Coverage
Application Procedure: Application is through the organization's website
Closing Date: Open all year
Additional Information: For more details, please visit the website www.adnocscholar.ae and also contact Doctoral Research Enquiry Service, dr@contacts.bham.ac.uk

For further information contact:

Email: dr@contacts.bham.ac.uk
Contact: Doctoral Research Enquiry Service

Amelia Earhart Fellowship - Zonta International

Subjects: Engineering and Physical Sciences
Purpose: The Amelia Earhart Fellowship program helps talented women, pursuing advanced studies in the typically male-dominated fields of aerospace-related sciences and engineering, achieve their educational goals. The Fellowship enables these women to invest in state-of-the-art computers to conduct their research, purchase expensive books and resource materials, and participate in specialized studies around the globe
Eligibility: Women of any nationality pursuing a PhD/doctoral degree who demonstrate a superior academic record in the field of aerospace-related sciences or aerospace-related engineering are eligible. Applicants must be registered in a full-time PhD/doctoral program when funds are received in September and must not graduate before April
Type: Scholarship
Value: The Fellowship of US$10,000, awarded to 35 Fellows around the globe each year, may be used at any university or college offering accredited postgraduate courses and degrees in these fields
Country of Study: Any country

Application Procedure: Applications should be sent to the Foundation directly. For more details, please check: www. zonta.org/WhatWeDo/InternationalPrograms/AmeliaEarhart Fellowship.aspx
Closing Date: 15 November
Funding: Trusts

For further information contact:

Email: zontaintl@zonta.org

Amphlett Scholarship (Theology and Religion)

Subjects: Theology and Religion. Humanities
Purpose: Donald Amphlett was a Birmingham solicitor who died in 1956 and left his money to establish a trust fund to provide scholarships for Chinese students to study Theology and Religion at the University
Eligibility: This award is only available to Chinese students applying to study for a postgraduate degree programme in Theology and Religion
Type: Scholarship
Value: The Amphlett scholarship pays for tuition and accommodation fees, either in part or in full. Assistance with travel costs to and from the home country may also be given
Frequency: Annual
Country of Study: Any country
Application Procedure: It is recommended that the application should reach the Amphlett Committee a year in advance
Closing Date: Open all year
Funding: Trusts

For further information contact:

Email: support.team@postgraduatesearch.com

Arthurian Postgraduate Awards

Subjects: Arts and Law
Purpose: The Eugène Vinaver Trust, in association with the British Branch of the International Arthurian Society and under the terms of the Barron Bequest, offers a number of annual awards for postgraduate research in any field of Arthurian Studies
Eligibility: The awards are open to graduates of any university in the British Isles, including those of the Republic of Ireland
Level of Study: Graduate, Postgraduate
Value: The awards, currently of £1,250, are intended as a contribution to postgraduate fees. Preference will be given in the making of awards to support for full research degrees. Students who are awarded a grant for the coming year may

apply for grants in future years on a basis of parity with those applying for the first time
Frequency: Annual
Country of Study: United Kingdom
Application Procedure: There is no standard application form. Instead, a leaflet is available giving details of information to be supplied by applicants in typed or word-processed form. The leaflet is available in electronic form on the www. internationalarthuriansociety.com/british-branch/view/awards along with further information and contact details
Closing Date: 30 April
Funding: Trusts

For further information contact:

Email: dr@contacts.bham.ac.uk

Arts and Humanities Research Council Funding through the Midlands3Cities Doctoral Training Partnership

Subjects: Arts and law, African studies, American and Canadian studies, antiquity, archaeology, classics and ancient history, drama and theatre arts, English language and linguistics, English literature, film and creative writing, heritage, history, history of art, law, modern languages and cultures, music, philosophy, theology and religion, geography, education
Purpose: The AHRC is continuing its very substantial commitment to funding doctoral research through a new round of Doctoral Training Partnerships (DTPs)
Type: Scholarships
Value: £4,121 per annum
Frequency: Annual
Country of Study: Any country
Application Procedure: Please refer to our application page
Closing Date: 14 January
Additional Information: Please refer to the Midlands3Cities Doctoral Training Partnership website

For further information contact:

Email: m4c@warwick.ac.uk

Association of Dental group (ADG) Postgraduate Bursary

Subjects: Dentistry
Purpose: The Association of Dental Groups (ADG) offers an award of £5,000 for postgraduate students to reward the best voluntary scheme to promote & deliver improvements in oral health

Eligibility: This award is open to all postgraduate dental students who have an under-graduate dentistry degree who are undertaking a voluntary project that seeks to improve and promote better oral health. The project must be within the United Kingdom and focused on one of two issues of significant concern, namely either improving access for disadvantaged people or building awareness of oral cancers and the need for early diagnosis

Type: Scholarships

Value: The award is composed of £2,500 as award to the winner and a further £2,500 to be used to support delivery of a project to improve and promote oral health

Country of Study: Any country

Application Procedure: Apply for this award by completing and submitting an application form, which can be found on the website: www.dentalgroups.co.uk/dentists/postgrad-application.html

Closing Date: 31 December

For further information contact:

Email: adgdentalawards@gmail.com

Biosciences Studentships

Subjects: Biological Sciences Purpose: To undertake the full range of personal development training and activities provided within the School and the University Graduate School

Eligibility: Applicants should possess, or expect to achieve, at least a good upper second class honours degree or equivalent qualification in an appropriate subject. Evidence of previous research experience, for instance undergraduate project work, is desirable. Qualifications of a suitable standard from every country in the world are accepted for postgraduate entry

Level of Study: Doctorate

Type: Research

Value: A number of studentships funded by United Kingdom Research Councils and other major sponsors (e.g. Cancer Research-United Kingdom) are available each year for home and European Union students. Studentships may provide full funding (fees and stipend)

Length of Study: 3 or 4 years

Application Procedure: You can apply through the Biosciences PhD course page on our Course Finder

Closing Date: Open all year

Additional Information: For more details contact Biosciences Graduate Research School, biosciences-phd@contacts.bham.ac.uk

For further information contact:

Email: biosciences-phd@contacts.bham.ac.uk
Contact: Biosciences Graduate Research School

Birmingham Business School Doctoral Scholarship

Subjects: Accounting and finance, economics, management and marketing

Purpose: The scholarship is to recognise and support the highest calibre candidates studying PhD level

Eligibility: A successful applicant will have a very good undergraduate degree. They should have, or be in the process of completing a masters typically in a business-related subject or economics

Level of Study: Doctorate, Research

Type: Scholarship

Value: Fees only and fees plus generous maintenance scholarships available

Length of Study: 3 years

Study Establishment: The University of Birmingham

Country of Study: United Kingdom

Application Procedure: Application forms can be downloaded from the Business School website. You must hold an offer of a place to study a PhD and apply before the deadline

Closing Date: May

Funding: Private

Contributor: The University of Birmingham

Additional Information: For more information, email to business-pgr-research@contacts.bham.ac.uk

For further information contact:

Email: business-pgr-research@contacts.bham.ac.uk

Birmingham Law School - Doctoral Scholarships

Subjects: Law

Purpose: To pursue postgraduate research

Eligibility: These awards are open to students worldwide for full- and part-time, campus-based doctoral research in the College of Arts and Law

Level of Study: Doctorate

Type: Scholarships

Value: £11,000 support per year towards living expenses for full-time applicants

Length of Study: 3 years

Country of Study: Any country

Application Procedure: These awards are advertised with the College of Arts and Law Doctoral Scholarships - please refer to this page for full application details and application forms

Closing Date: 17 March

Additional Information: For further details, please contact calpg-research@contacts.bham.ac.uk (College of Arts and Law)

For further information contact:

Email: calpg-research@contacts.bham.ac.uk

Boehringer Ingelheim Fonds Fellowships

Subjects: Arts and Law, Engineering and Physical Sciences, Life and Environmental Sciences, Medical and Dental Sciences, Social Sciences
Purpose: The British Lebanese Association (BLA) Scholarship Fund was established in 1985 as part of the BLA's initiative to contribute towards rebuilding national capabilities after a decade of conflict. The Fund has a central part in achieving the aims of the BLA
Eligibility: Applications are restricted to candidates who are Lebanese, Jordanian or Palestinian (including Palestinians inside Israel) and Syrian. Applications for study at universities outside the United Kingdom cannot be considered. Priority is given to candidates permanently living in the Foundation's target countries. The Foundation will, however, consider Syrians residing elsewhere due to current circumstances in Syria
Level of Study: Graduate, Postgraduate
Type: Scholarship
Value: Depending on availability of funding, the BLA aims to provide partial funding for two or three scholarships each academic year
Frequency: Dependent on funds available
Country of Study: Any country
Application Procedure: BLA scholarships are currently offered in partnership with the Said Foundation and prospective candidate should go to the www.saidfoundation.org/scholarship-applications for further information on the programme and to complete the application form online
Closing Date: 30 November

For further information contact:

Email: secretariat@bifonds.de

Boehringer Ingelheim Fonds PhD Fellowships

Subjects: Engineering and physical sciences, life and environmental sciences, medical and dental sciences
Purpose: The Boehringer Ingelheim Fonds awards PhD fellowships to outstanding junior scientists who wish to pursue an ambitious PhD project
Eligibility: The Boehringer Ingelheim Fonds (BIF) awards PhD fellowships to European citizens working in Europe or overseas, and to non-European citizens pursuing their PhD project in Europe. Applicants should not be older than 27 years at the respective deadline (1 February, 1 June, 1 October)

Level of Study: Postgraduate
Value: The fellowship comprises a competitive monthly stipend that is initially granted for 2 years and that can be extended for up to another 1 year. Participation in international scientific conferences is also supported. In addition, fellowship holders are offered personal support, seminars to discuss their projects, communication training and alumni meetings, and thus can become part of a worldwide network
Country of Study: United Kingdom
Closing Date: Open all year
Funding: Trusts
Additional Information: Please check website for more details: www.bifonds.de/fellowships-grants/phd-fellowships.html

For further information contact:

Email: secretariat@bifonds.de

Canon Foundation Fellowships

Subjects: Arts and law, engineering and physical sciences, life and environmental sciences, medical and dental sciences, social sciences
Purpose: To promote international cultural and scientific relations between Europe and Japan
Eligibility: The candidates hold a doctorate or at least a master's degree. They are eligible during the ten-year period following the successful completion of their PhD or MA degree
Level of Study: Doctorate
Value: From €22,500 to €27,500 per year for different periods
Length of Study: 3 months to 1 year
Country of Study: Any country
Application Procedure: Applications should be submitted in full (including the acceptance by the proposed host institute and the research plan) to the Secretariat of the Canon Foundation in Europe well in advance of the deadline. www.canonfoundation.org/register.php
Closing Date: 15 September
Funding: Private
Additional Information: For more details, please check the website www.canonfoundation.org/programmes/research-fellowships/. Also contact dr@contacts.bham.ac.uk (Doctoral Research Enquiry Service)

For further information contact:

Canon Foundation in Europe, Bovenkerkerweg 59, NLD 1185 XB, Amstelveen, Netherlands

Tel: (31) 20 545 8934
Email: foundation@canon-europe.com

College of Arts and Law Distance Learning Scholarship(s)

Subjects: Arts and law, African studies, American and Canadian studies, antiquity, archaeology, classics and ancient history, drama and theatre arts, English language and linguistics, English literature, film and creative writing, heritage, history, history of art, law, modern languages and cultures, music, philosophy, theology and religion
Purpose: To offer a funding opportunity for distance learning students, studying research programmes starting in the academic year
Eligibility: The scholarships are open to prospective or current students undertaking full-time or part-time distance learning research programmes, worldwide
Level of Study: Doctorate, Postgraduate
Value: Up to £3,000 for full-time home/European Union students and up to £10,000 for full-time overseas students
Length of Study: 1 year
Country of Study: Any country
Application Procedure: Return the completed application form to calpg-research@contacts.bham.ac.uk
Closing Date: 31 March
Additional Information: If you would like any further information, please email calpg-research@contacts.bham.ac.uk or telephone 0121 414 8442

For further information contact:

Email: calpg-research@contacts.bham.ac.uk

College of Arts and Law Doctoral Scholarships

Subjects: Arts and Law, African Studies, American and Canadian Studies, Antiquity, Archaeology, Classics and Ancient History, Drama and Theatre Arts, English Language and Linguistics, English Literature, Film and Creative Writing, Heritage, History, History of Art, Law, Modern Languages and Cultures, Music, Philosophy, Theology and Religion
Level of Study: Doctorate
Type: Scholarship
Value: £11,000 support per year towards living expenses for full-time applicants, adjusted pro-rata for part-time applicants
Length of Study: Three years full-time, or six years part-time
Study Establishment: University of Birmingham
Country of Study: Any country
Application Procedure: Applicants who have already applied for AHRC funding through the Midlands3Cities consortium will automatically be considered for one of these

College awards, without submitting a separate application. In order to apply, you must first have completed an application to study. Once you have done so, please complete the funding application form, and return the completed form to calpg-research@contacts.bham.ac.uk. The application must also be supported by two references
Closing Date: 17 March
Contributor: Birmingham Research Institute
Additional Information: For more information please email calpg-research@contacts.bham.ac.uk or telephone 0121 414 8442

For further information contact:

Email: calpg-research@contacts.bham.ac.uk

College of Arts and Law Masters Scholarships

Subjects: Arts and Law, African Studies, American and Canadian Studies, Antiquity, Archaeology, Classics and Ancient History, Drama and Theatre Arts, English Language and Linguistics, English Literature, Heritage, History, History of Art, Modern Languages and Cultures, Music, Philosophy, Theology and Religion
Purpose: The College of Arts and Law offers a number of home/European Union fees-only scholarships for candidates wishing to study full- and part-time masters-level courses from September 2016. These awards cover tuition fees for all masters-level degrees
Eligibility: These awards are open to United Kingdom/European Union students, studying campus-based masters-level degrees in the College of Arts and Law. International students are also eligible to apply, and will receive a reduction in tuition-fees equivalent to the home/European Union rate if successful
Level of Study: Graduate, Postgraduate
Type: Scholarship
Value: These awards cover one year
Country of Study: Any country
Application Procedure: Please go through the website
Closing Date: 22 April
Funding: Trusts

For further information contact:

Email: calpg-research@contacts.bham.ac.uk

Emslie Horniman Anthropological Scholarship Fund

Subjects: Antiquity, Archaeology, History, Modern Languages and Cultures

Purpose: The major aim of the Fund is to encourage postgraduates to pursue fieldwork, and so to develop their careers as Anthropologists and make significant contributions to the discipline

Eligibility: Open to citizens of the United Kingdom, Commonwealth or Irish Republic who are university graduates or who can satisfy the trustees of their suitability for the study proposed. Preference is given to applicants whose proposals include fieldwork outside the United Kingdom. Graduates who already hold a doctorate in anthropology are not eligible. Open to individuals only, as no grants are given to expeditions or teams

Level of Study: Doctorate, Postgraduate

Value: Around £1,000 - £9,500

Country of Study: Any country

Application Procedure: Seven copies of each application with supporting references must be submitted. Short-listed candidates will normally be required to attend an interview in London in late-May/early-June

Closing Date: 31 March

Additional Information: Grants to successful candidates will be paid at the start of their fieldwork

For further information contact:

Email: admin@therai.org.uk

Francis Corder Clayton Scholarship

Subjects: American and Canadian Studies, Antiquity, Archaeology, Drama and Theatre Arts, English Language and Linguistics, English Literature, History, History of Art, Modern Languages and Cultures, Music, Philosophy, Theology and Religion

Purpose: Open to any full-time postgraduate undertaking a programme in an Arts subject. One award is available each year and will be tenable for one year only

Eligibility: Open to current full-time PG students only. Taught and research-based programmes

Level of Study: Graduate, Postgraduate

Value: This scholarship will cover the home rate of postgraduate tuition fees. Stipends for living costs may be available in some cases; however, this will be subject to available funding and cannot be guaranteed

Country of Study: United Kingdom

Application Procedure: Applications cannot be made directly for these awards; candidates need to be nominated by their school or department. If you are interested and fit the eligibility criteria, please make an expression of interest to the postgraduate administrator within your school, or your admissions tutor. For more information, please submit a query to Funding, Graduation & Awards through intranet.birmingham.ac.uk/student/student-hub/homepage.aspx

Closing Date: 13 May

Funding: Trusts

For further information contact:

Email: sfo@contacts.bham.ac.uk

Funds for Women Graduates Foundation Grants

Subjects: Arts and Law, Engineering and Physical Sciences, Life and Environmental Sciences, Medical and Dental Sciences, Social Sciences, Education

Purpose: FfWG offers foundation grants to help women graduates with their living expenses (not fees) while registered for study or research at an approved institution of higher education in Great Britain. The criteria are the proven needs of the applicant and their academic calibre

Eligibility: Women graduates from Britain and overseas are eligible to apply. For more information please visit website

Level of Study: Doctorate

Value: The amount of the Foundation Grant will be decided by FfWG

Country of Study: Any country

Application Procedure: Details of how to apply can be found on the Funds for Women Graduates website (www.ffwg.org.uk/)

Closing Date: 22 February

Additional Information: For more details contact Doctoral Research Enquiry Service- dr@contacts.bham.ac.uk

For further information contact:

Email: grants@ffwg.org.uk

German Historical Institute London PhD Scholarships

Subjects: Modern Languages and Cultures, International Relations

Eligibility: Applicants from British universities will normally be expected to have completed one year's post-graduate research, and be studying German history or Anglo-German relations

Level of Study: Doctorate, Postgraduate, Research

Type: Award

Value: Various

Length of Study: Up to 6 months

Application Procedure: Please apply online on the GHIL website (www.ghil.ac.uk)

Closing Date: 31 March

For further information contact:

Email: prize@ghil.ac.uk

Guest Keen and Nettlefolds PG Scholarship

Subjects: Chemical Engineering, Civil Engineering, Electronic, Electrical and Systems Engineering, Mechanical Engineering, Metallurgy and Materials Engineering
Eligibility: This scholarship is open to postgraduate engineering students studying on research programmes who have performed well academically. One nomination is made per engineering school
Level of Study: Postdoctorate, Research
Value: £1,000 towards maintenance
Study Establishment: Any
Country of Study: Any country
Application Procedure: This is an in-year scholarship that will be open for nomination any time. This scholarship is only available to current students by nomination through their School
Closing Date: None. Open all year
Additional Information: For more information please contact Postgraduate Recruitment Team- pg@contacts.bham.ac.uk

For further information contact:

Email: sfo@contacts.bham.ac.uk

Hudswell International Research Scholarship

Subjects: Electronic, Electrical and Systems Engineering
Purpose: To provide awards in support of research undertaken by members in the fields of electrical, electronic or manufacturing engineering, to assist IET members with research work leading to the award of a doctorate
Eligibility: The research programme must be undertaken outside the applicant's home country. Applicants must be in the first or second year of the research programme. For more information please visit website
Level of Study: Doctorate, Research
Type: Award
Value: £5,000
Country of Study: Any country
Application Procedure: Please visit the website conferences. theiet.org/achievement/scholarships/postgraduate/index.cfm
Closing Date: 6 April

For further information contact:

Email: awards@theiet.org

Institution of Mechanical Engineers Postgraduate Research Scholarships

Subjects: Mechanical Engineering
Eligibility: Students who are normally resident in the United Kingdom, who will commence their postgraduate degree in the next academic session
Level of Study: Doctorate, Research
Value: Full-time up to £6,500p.a. Part-time pro rata
Length of Study: Three years
Country of Study: Any country
Application Procedure: For applications forms and information please check the Institution of Mechanical Engineers website (www.imeche.org/careers-education/scholarships-and-awards/postgraduate-research-scholarships)
Closing Date: 1 August
Contributor: The Institution of Mechanical Engineers

For further information contact:

Email: dr@contacts.bham.ac.uk

Ironbridge Institute - John Pagett Bursary

Subjects: Archaeology, History
Eligibility: Applicants must be : Registered (or be registered) for a postgraduate research degree at the University of Birmingham
Type: Scholarship
Value: £3,000
Frequency: Annual
Country of Study: Any country
Application Procedure: For further details about this scholarship, please visit the website: www.birmingham.ac.uk/schools/historycultures/departments/ironbridge/postgraduate/funding.aspx
Closing Date: 30 June

For further information contact:

Email: r.h.white@bham.ac.uk

Lee Kuan Yew Scholarship

Subjects: Arts and Law, Engineering and Physical Sciences, Life and Environmental Sciences, Medical and Dental Sciences, Social Sciences
Purpose: Lee Kuan Yew Scholarship recipients can pursue either a Masters or PhD programme at a local or overseas university
Eligibility: Applicants should have excellent track record of leadership and service, within or beyond their profession; and

good academic achievements, for example, a Second Class Upper honors or equivalent degree

Type: Scholarship

Value: Scholarship recipients will receive a one-off sum of S$10,000, and an annual allowance of: S$50,000 for private sector awardees; or S$10,000 for public sector awardees, if they are concurrently sponsored by their organisations

Country of Study: Any country

Application Procedure: he completed document should be sent to applications@psd.gov.sg. The application can be found on the www.pscscholarships.gov.sg/scholarships/other-scholarships/lee-kuan-yew-scholarship

Closing Date: 18 December

Funding: Trusts

For further information contact:

Email: june_yeo@psd.gov.sg

Leslie H Paddle Scholarship

Purpose: To encourage excellence in engineering and technology research, with a preference for electrical, electronic or manufacturing engineering

Eligibility: 1. Postgraduate awards are for members of the Institution of Engineering and Technology and are open to the following categories of IET membership: Student, TMIET, MIET and FIET. Associate and lapsed members are not eligible to apply. 2. Applicants must have been a member of the IET for at least one year by the closing date for applications. 3. Applicants do not need to be professionally registered engineers. However, applicants are expected to satisfy the educational requirements for Registration as either a Chartered or Incorporated Engineer. 4. Applicants need to have started their PhD or EngD research programme by the closing date for applications and achieved at least a 2:1 (or equivalent) in their first degree. MSc courses and MRes degrees are not eligible

Level of Study: Graduate, Postgraduate

Type: Scholarship

Value: One award of £5,000

Frequency: Annual

Country of Study: Any country

Application Procedure: Applications can be made through the IET website. www.birmingham.ac.uk/postgraduate/funding/Leslie-H-Paddle-Scholarship.aspx

Closing Date: 5 April

Funding: Private

For further information contact:

Email: dr@contacts.bham.ac.uk

Leverhulme Trade Charities Trust Postgraduate Bursary

Subjects: Arts and Law, Engineering and Physical Sciences, Life and Environmental Sciences, Medical and Dental Sciences, Social Sciences

Purpose: Available to students connected with Commercial Travellers, Grocers or Chemists that are experiencing financial difficulty

Eligibility: The Leverhulme Trade Charities Postgraduate Bursaries are designed to provide support for eligible United Kingdom students i.e. those who are (or who are connected with) Commercial Travellers, Grocers or Chemists, in financial need undertaking full-time Postgraduate degree courses at institutions in the United Kingdom, leading to recognised qualifications (e.g. PhD/MSc)

Level of Study: Graduate, Postgraduate

Value: The maximum value of any bursary is £5,000. This amount may be adjusted according to the applicant's personal financial need and to the amount of funds available

Country of Study: United Kingdom

Application Procedure: For further information about eligibility and definitions please visit the website, www.leverhulme-trade.org.uk/postgraduate-bursaries/eligibility

Closing Date: 1 October

Funding: Trusts

For further information contact:

Email: admin@leverhulme-trade.org.uk

Music Department Scholarships

Subjects: Music

Purpose: A number of scholarships, of varying value, are offered by the Music Department to students studying postgraduate programmes in Music (research or taught)

Eligibility: Scholarships are available for United Kingdom, European Union and International students

Level of Study: Graduate, Postgraduate

Type: Scholarship

Value: A wide range of scholarships, of varying value, are offered

Country of Study: Any country

Closing Date: 17 June

Funding: Trusts

For further information contact:

Email: scrist@emory.edu

Paul and Yuanbi Ramsay MSc Computer Science Bursary

Subjects: Computer Science
Purpose: To support outstanding students with priority given to those from a low income background
Eligibility: The bursary will be awarded to Home/European Union Masters students in need of financial assistance and then on academic merit
Level of Study: Postgraduate
Type: Bursary
Value: The home rate of tuition fee
Length of Study: 1 year
Frequency: Annual
Study Establishment: University of Birmingham
Country of Study: United Kingdom
Application Procedure: Full guidance and a downloadable application form for this award will be available from www.intranet.birmingham.ac.uk/awards or the School of Computer Science website from May of the year in which you will start your study
Closing Date: Mid-July
Funding: Private
Contributor: Paul and Yuanbi Ramsay
No. of awards given last year: 2

For further information contact:

Email: Fga@contacts.bham.ac.uk

Rosgen Family Scholarship

Purpose: Business
Eligibility: The scholarship holder will be from Central or South America; The scholarship will be allocated on the basis of intellectual excellence and evidence of a commitment to the economic development of Central or South America
Level of Study: Graduate, Postgraduate
Type: Scholarship
Value: The Rosgen Family Scholarship is worth £5,000 and can either contribute towards the cost of the Birmingham MBA tuition fee or living costs
Frequency: Annual
Country of Study: Any country
Application Procedure: In order to apply to the above scholarship, please submit an expression of interest to Victoria Harold (details below). Once this has been received, an application form will be sent to you. Please complete the application form, including a personal statement relating to the scholarship theme, and an academic essay (essay title provided with application form)
Closing Date: None. Open all year
Funding: Trusts

For further information contact:

Email: mbaadmissions@bham.ac.uk

Santander & University of Birmingham Scholarship

Subjects: Arts and Law, Engineering and Physical Sciences, Life and Environmental Sciences, Medical and Dental Sciences, Social Sciences
Eligibility: Applicants must have an excellent academic background obtaining a good 2:1/Upper Second Class or equivalent Bachelors degree as a minimum
Level of Study: Graduate, Postgraduate
Type: Scholarship
Value: £5,000 towards the cost of tuition fees for a one-year Masters programme
Country of Study: Any country
Closing Date: 31 March
Funding: Trusts

For further information contact:

Email: fga@contacts.bham.ac.uk

School of Chemistry International Students Postgraduate Bursary

Subjects: Chemistry
Eligibility: To be eligible for this opportunity students must: Be classified as overseas for fees purposes, Be privately funded, Satisfy the University's entry requirements for postgraduate study
Value: The value of the bursary is £4,000 per annum towards tuition fees
Frequency: Annual
Country of Study: Any country
Application Procedure: Applications should be sent online at the, www.birmingham.ac.uk/postgraduate/courses/apply-pg/index.aspx
Closing Date: None. Open all year

For further information contact:

Email: chemistry.pgt@ed.ac.uk

Science without Borders Archaeology PhD scholarships

Subjects: Archaeology
Purpose: The University of Birmingham is delighted to be one of the United Kingdom institutions selected to participate

in the Science without Borders (Ciência sem Fronteiras) scheme

Eligibility: Science without Borders scholarships are only open to Brazilian students. Students should hold a Masters degree or equivalent. Students must also meet English language requirements: IELTS 6.0 (no less than 6.0 in any band) or TOEFL 93 (no less than 22 in Reading, 21 in Listening, 23 in Speaking, 21 in Writing)

Value: CsF will pay up to £20,000 towards tuition and bench fees for each Ciência sem Fronteiras PhD student per year of their study in the United Kingdom

Country of Study: Any country

Application Procedure: Students must apply through Universities United Kingdom. Website: sciencewithoutborders. international.ac.uk/

Closing Date: None. Open all year

For further information contact:

Email: iro@bristol.ac.uk

Simon Evans Scholarships

Subjects: Simon Evans, an alumnus of Birmingham Business School, kindly makes funds available for exceptional students to gain access onto marketing courses

Eligibility: Applicants must be a United Kingdom / European Union national,

Level of Study: Graduate, Postgraduate

Type: Varies

Value: A number of scholarships of £5,000 towards tuition fees are available

Country of Study: Any country

Application Procedure: Please check the website for more details: www.birmingham.ac.uk/schools/business/departments/marketing/courses/simon-evans-scholarships.aspx

Closing Date: 1 August

For further information contact:

Email: simon.evans@worc.ac.uk

The Annemarie Schimmel Scholarship

Subjects: Arts and Law, Engineering and Physical Sciences, Life and Environmental Sciences, Medical and Dental Sciences, Social Sciences

Purpose: The Scholarship was established in honour of Professor Annemarie Schimmel to commemorate her great contribution to culture and poetry in Pakistan and her role as a dedicated woman scholar. It offers the opportunity for postgraduate study in the United Kingdom to a woman who

is committed to make a genuine contribution to her chosen field on her return to Pakistan

Eligibility: The Schimmel scholars will be chosen for their ability and commitment without discrimination as to religion, caste or creed. Candidates must have either a professional degree or they should have completed sixteen years of education in a relevant discipline

Level of Study: Graduate, Postgraduate

Value: The scholarship is awarded for one academic year for a Master's degree at recognized institutions of higher education in the United Kingdom. Doctoral candidates are not eligible

Country of Study: Any country

Closing Date: 7 June

For further information contact:

Email: nosheenimian@gmail.com

The Birmingham Eighteenth-Century Centre (BECC-BCECS) British Society for Eighteenth-Century Studies Postgraduate Travel Award

Purpose: The award is designed to support research in the eighteenth century, making use of the relevant holdings of the Cadbury Research Library

Eligibility: Applicants are also encouraged to take advantage of the rich eighteenth-century resources available in Birmingham more widely, including the Library of Birmingham, Birmingham Museum Trust

Level of Study: Postgraduate

Type: Award

Frequency: Annual

Country of Study: Any country

Application Procedure: Submit a research proposal of 500 words, including an explanation of how the use of Birmingham collections will benefit your research. Candidates will be asked to make few more changes. 1. Provide a written report on the research visit. 2. Write a blogpost of up to 1,000 words for the BECC website. 3. Return to Birmingham in the following academic year to give a presentation about the research, ideally as part of an existing event or seminar series in the University of Birmingham research programme; this later visit will be supported by additional travel expenses

Closing Date: 28 February

Funding: Private

For further information contact:

Edgbaston B15 2TT, Birmingham, United Kingdom

Email: becc@contacts.bham.ac.uk

University of Bristol

Student Funding Office, Senate House (Ground Floor), Tyndall Avenue, BS8 1TH, Bristol, United Kingdom

Tel: (44) 11 7928 9000
Fax: (44) 11 7331 7873
Email: student-funding@bris.ac.uk
Website: www.bristol.ac.uk
Contact: Ms Penny Rowe, Student Funding Advisor

The University of Bristol is committed to providing high-quality teaching and research in all its designated fields.

Global Accounting and Finance Scholarship

Subjects: The awards can only be used as fee waivers towards the cost of tuition fees
Purpose: The Department of Accounting and Finance is offering eight scholarships worth £5,000 each to eligible international students studying for a postgraduate qualification in Accounting and Finance
Eligibility: You can apply for a University of Bristol Global Accounting and Finance Scholarship if you: 1. are classed as an overseas student for fee purposes AND. 2. have applied to start one of the qualifying Accounting and Finance MSc programmes at the University of Bristol in September. To be eligible for the University's Postgraduate scholarships, students must: 1. Be an applicant to any one year, full-time postgraduate programme at the University of Bristol. 2. Start their postgraduate programme in September. 3. Be classed as an overseas student for fee paying purposes. 4. Not already be in receipt of other funding which would equate to more than the full cost of tuition fees alongside a Bristol scholarship
Level of Study: Postgraduate
Type: Scholarship
Value: £5,000
Frequency: Annual
Country of Study: Any country
Application Procedure: You can submit an application for the Global Accounting and Finance Scholarship using the International Scholarships online application form
Closing Date: 31 March
Funding: Private

For further information contact:

Tel: (44) 117 928 9000
Email: funding@bristol.ac.uk

Global Economics Postgraduate Scholarship

Subjects: Economics
Purpose: The Department of Economics is offering five scholarships worth £5,000 each to eligible international students studying for a postgraduate qualification in Economics
Eligibility: Kindly check the terms and conditions for the scholarship under the following link, www.bristol.ac.uk/international/fees-finance/scholarships/terms-and-conditions/
Level of Study: Graduate, Postgraduate
Type: Scholarship
Value: £5,000 each
Frequency: Annual
Country of Study: Any country
Application Procedure: There are two rounds of scholarships to avail. Round One Deadline: 31 March. Successful applicants will be informed via email by 26 April. Round Two Deadline: 30 June. Successful applicants will be informed via email by 19 July
Closing Date: 31 March and 30 June
Funding: Private

For further information contact:

University of Bristol, Senate House, Tyndall Avenue, BS8 1TH, Bristol, United Kingdom

Tel: (64) 117 331 1223
Email: iro@bristol.ac.uk

International Postgraduate Scholarships – Taught Master's Programmes

Subjects: All subjects
Purpose: This programme provides plenty of offers for future research postgraduate researchers with access to studentships, supervision from world-class experts and excellent facilities on our PhD and doctoral programmes
Eligibility: Open to candidates holding an offer for a 1 year taught postgraduate programme at the University of Bristol
Level of Study: Postgraduate
Type: Scholarship (MSc)
Value: £2,000
Length of Study: 1 year
Frequency: Annual
Study Establishment: University of Bristol
Country of Study: United Kingdom
Application Procedure: Check website for further details
Closing Date: 30 June
Funding: Private

For further information contact:

International Recruitment Office, University of Bristol Union, Queens Road, Clifton, Bristol, United Kingdom

Email: iro@bristol.ac.uk
Contact: Penny Rowe, Student Funding Advisor

Phyllis Mary Morris Bursaries

Purpose: Phyllis Mary Morris née Doidge graduated with a degree in Geography in 1930
Eligibility: You can apply for a Phyllis Mary Morris Bursary if you: 1. are classed as an overseas student for fee purposes AND. 2. have applied to start a qualifying one-year, full-time taught postgraduate programme at the University of Bristol in September
Level of Study: Graduate
Type: Bursary
Value: £2,000
Frequency: Annual
Country of Study: Any country
Closing Date: 30 June
Funding: Private

For further information contact:

University of Bristol, Beacon House, Queens Road, BS8 1QU, Bristol, United Kingdom

Tel: (44) 117 928 9000
Email: graduation-office@bristol.ac.uk

University of British Columbia (UBC)

2329 West Mall, Vancouver, BC V6T 1Z2, Canada

Tel: (1) 604 822 2211
Fax: (1) 604 822 5802
Email: graduate.awards@ubc.ca
Website: www.ubc.ca
Contact: Ms Jiffin Arboleda, Awards Administrator

The University of British Columbia (UBC) is one of North America's major research universities. The Faculty of Graduate Studies has 6,500 students and is a national leader in interdisciplinary study and research, with 98 departments, 18 interdisciplinary research units, 9 interdisciplinary graduate programmes, 2 graduate residential colleges and 1 scholarly journal.

Izaak Walton Killam Predoctoral Fellowships

Subjects: All subjects
Purpose: To assist doctoral students with full-time studies and research
Eligibility: Open to students of any nationality, discipline, age or sex. This award is given at the PhD level only and is strictly based on academic merit. Students must have a First Class standing in their last 2 years of study
Level of Study: Doctorate
Type: Fellowship
Value: C$22,000 per year and C$1,500 travel allowance for the duration of the award
Frequency: Annual
Study Establishment: UBC
Country of Study: Canada
No. of awards offered: 200
Application Procedure: Top ranked students are selected from the University Graduate Fellowship competition. Application forms can be obtained from individual departments, the Faculty of Graduate Studies or the website. Students must submit their applications to the departments, not to the Faculty of Graduate Studies
Closing Date: Each department has its own internal deadline, usually in early Autumn
Funding: Private
No. of awards given last year: 12
No. of applicants last year: 200

For further information contact:

Email: gsaward@ucalgary.ca

University of British Columbia Graduate Fellowship (UGF)

Subjects: All subjects
Purpose: To assist graduate students with their studies and research
Eligibility: Open to students of any nationality, discipline, age or sex. This award is strictly based on academic merit, and as a result, applicants must be nominated by their departments based on academic merit. Students must have a First Class standing in their last 2 years of study
Level of Study: Graduate
Type: Fellowship
Value: C$16,000 per year for 2-year fellowships, C$16,000 for 1-year fellowships, or C$8,000 for 1-year partial fellowships
Frequency: Annual
Study Establishment: UBC
Country of Study: Canada

No. of awards offered: Approx. 2,500
Application Procedure: Applicants must submit their applications to the UBC department by the department deadline date, not to the Faculty of Graduate Studies. UGF applications are available from the website
Closing Date: Early Autumn
Funding: Government
No. of awards given last year: 460
No. of applicants last year: Approx. 2,500
Additional Information: Please check for internal departmental deadlines

For further information contact:

Email: graduate.awards@ubc.ca

University of California at Los Angeles (UCLA) Center for India and South Asia

Department of History, 11387 Bunche Hall, Los Angeles, CA 90095-1487, United States of America

Tel: (1) 310 206 2654
Email: subrahma@history.ucla.edu
Website: www.international.ucla.edu
Contact: Professor Sanjay Subrahmanyam, Chair of Indian History

The main thrust behind the creation of the UCLA Center for India and South Asia is to raise the profile of South Asia on campus and more generally in southern California. The organization aims at transforming UCLA into one of the leading poles of integrated research activity on India and South Asia in the country.

University of California, Los Angeles (UCLA)Sardar Patel Award

Subjects: Modern Indian subject (History, social sciences, humanities, education or fine art)
Purpose: To award the best dissertation submitted at any American university on the subject of modern India
Eligibility: Open to candidates who have written their dissertations while being enrolled at any accredited university in the United States
Level of Study: Research
Type: Award
Value: US$10,000
Frequency: Annual

Application Procedure: Applicants must submit 2 hard copies of their dissertation, 7 copies of abstract, a copy of their curriculum vitae and a letter from the dissertation supervisor
Closing Date: 15 October

For further information contact:

Email: cisa@international.ucla.edu

University of California Berkeley - Haas School

S440 Student Services Building, Suite 1902, Berkeley, CA 94720-1902, United States of America

Tel: (1) 510 642 1405
Fax: (1) 510 643 6659
Website: www.haas.berkeley.edu
Contact: MBA Admissions Officer

Hellman Fellows Fund

Subjects: Awards may be used for any research-related expense, such as research assistants, equipment, or travel. Up to 5% of the award money can also be used for childcare and elder-care (dependent) expenses
Purpose: The purpose of the Hellman Fellows Fund is to support substantially the research of promising assistant professors who show capacity for great distinction in their research
Eligibility: In determining the allocation of awards, the Chancellor will seek the counsel of a panel of faculty comprised of tenured Hellman Fellows and a member of the Academic Senate Committee on Research, chaired by the Vice Provost for the Faculty. Applications should therefore include an introductory description which is accessible to someone who is not an expert in the given field
Level of Study: Postgraduate
Type: Funding support
Value: Maximum value of up to US$60,000
Frequency: Annual
Country of Study: Any country
Application Procedure: 1. Applications should be brief, no more than 3 pages, and written with the understanding that they will be reviewed by a panel of faculty from the sciences and humanities that may not include specialists in the field of study. 2. Applications should therefore include an introductory description which is accessible to someone who is not an expert in the given field
Closing Date: May
Funding: Private

For further information contact:

Vice Provost for the Faculty, 200 California Hall, MC 1500 Berkeley, CA 94720-1500, United States of America

| Tel: | (1) 510 642 6474 |
| Email: | yasyavg@berkeley.edu |

Western Center for Agricultural Health and Safety

Purpose: The overarching goal of the WCAHS Small Grant Program is to encourage the development of creative research projects while nurturing researchers – particularly early-career researchers – interested in improving agricultural health and safety for the Western United States
Eligibility: 1. Faculty with PI eligibility in the Western region (AZ, CA, HI, NV). 2. PhD students or postdoctoral scholars in the Western region. 3. Applicants from AZ, HI, and NV are encouraged to apply
Level of Study: Graduate
Type: Grant
Value: Graduate students & postdoctoral scholars may request up to US$10,000 Faculty may request up to US$30,000
Frequency: Annual
Country of Study: Any country
Application Procedure: For further information, check the website aghealth.ucdavis.edu/
Closing Date: 27 July
Funding: Private
Additional Information: aghealth.ucdavis.edu/small-grant-program

For further information contact:

| Email: | aghealth@ucdavis.edu |

University of California, Berkeley

Graduate Services, Graduate Fellowships Office, 318 Sproul Hall #5900, Berkeley, CA 94720 5900, United States of America

Tel:	(1) 510 642 6000
Fax:	(1) 510 642 6000
Email:	gradappt@berkeley.edu
Website:	www.berkeley.edu

Founded in the wake of the gold rush by the leaders of the newly established 31st state, the University of California's flagship campus at Berkeley has become one of the preeminent universities in the world. Its early guiding lights, charged with providing education (both 'practical' and 'classical') for the state's people, gradually established a distinguished faculty (with 20 Nobel laureates to date), a stellar research library, and more than 350 academic programs.

Conference Travel Grants

Subjects: All subjects
Purpose: To allow students to attend professional conferences
Eligibility: Applicants must be registered graduate students in good academic standing. They must be in the final stages of their graduate work and planning to present a paper on their dissertation research at the conference they are attending
Level of Study: Doctorate, Graduate
Type: Grant
Value: Amount of the grant depends upon the location of conference (i.e. up to US$400 within California; US$600 elsewhere in North America, including Mexico or Canada; and US$1,000 outside North America)
Frequency: Dependent on funds available
Study Establishment: University of California, Berkeley
Country of Study: United States of America
Application Procedure: Applicants must submit an application form and one letter of support from their graduate advisor attesting to the academic merit of the trip. Applications can be obtained from the website
Closing Date: 3 weeks before the date of travel

For further information contact:

| Email: | aips@pakistanstudies-aips.org |

University of California, Los Angeles (UCLA) Center for 17th and 18th Century Studies and the William Andrews Clark Memorial Library

10745 Dickson Plaza, 310 Royce Hall, Los Angeles, CA 90095 1404, United States of America

Tel:	(1) 310 206 8552
Fax:	(1) 310 206 8577
Email:	c1718cs@humnet.ucla.edu
Website:	www.c1718cs.ucla.edu/
Contact:	Fellowship Co-ordinator

University of California, Los Angeles (UCLA) Center for 17th and 18th century Studies provides a forum for the discussion of central issues in the field of early modern studies, facilitates research and publication, supports scholarship and encourages the creation of interdisciplinary, cross-cultural programmes that advance the understanding of this important period. The William Andrews Clark Memorial Library, administered by the Center, is known for its collections of rare books and manuscripts concerning 17th and 18th-century Britain and Europe, Oscar Wilde and the 1890s, the history of printing, and certain aspects of the American West.

Clark-Huntington Joint Bibliographical Fellowship

Subjects: Early modern literature and history and other areas where the sponsoring libraries have common strengths
Purpose: To support bibliographical research
Level of Study: Postdoctorate, Professional development
Type: Fellowship
Value: US$5,000
Length of Study: 2 months
Frequency: Annual
Study Establishment: The Clark Library and the Huntington Library
Country of Study: United States of America
No. of awards offered: 15
Application Procedure: Applicants must submit an application form, a curriculum vitae, a proposal statement, a bibliography and three letters of reference
Closing Date: 1 February
Funding: Private
No. of awards given last year: 1
No. of applicants last year: 15

For further information contact:

Email: ortiz@humnet.ucla.edu
Contact: Fellowship Co-ordinator

University of California, Los Angeles (UCLA) Institute of American Cultures (IAC)

1237 Murphy Hall, Box 951419, Los Angeles, CA 90095-1419, United States of America

Tel: (1) 310 206 2557
Fax: (1) 310 825 8099

Email: iaccoordinator@gdnet.ucla.edu
Website: www.gdnet.ucla.edu/iacweb/iachome.htm
Contact: Dr N Cherie Francis, Co-ordinator

The UCLA Institute of American Cultures (IAC) is committed to advancing knowledge, strengthening and integrating interdisciplinary research and enriching instruction on African Americans, American Indians, Asian Americans and Chicanos. Since 1969, the IAC has been responsible for developing and expanding graduate studies, research and training in ethnic studies and is a major contributor to the academic and intellectual life of the University.

University of California at Los Angeles Institute of American Culture (IAC) Postdoctoral/Visiting Scholar Fellowships

Subjects: Arts and humanities, education and teacher training, fine arts, applied arts, law, social sciences and sciences
Purpose: To enable PhD scholars wishing to work in association with the American Indian Studies Center, the BUNCHE Center for African American Studies, the Asian American Studies Center and the Chicano Studies Research Center, to conduct research and publish books or manuscripts relating to ethnic studies and interdisciplinary instruction
Eligibility: Open to citizens of the United States of America and permanent residents
Level of Study: Postdoctorate
Type: Fellowship
Value: US$29,000; US$34,000 stipend plus health benefits and up to US$4,000 in research support
Length of Study: Up to 1 year
Frequency: Annual
Country of Study: United States of America
Application Procedure: Applicants must complete an application form, available from one of the ethnic studies centres, the IAC, or from the website
Closing Date: 31 December
No. of awards given last year: 4
Additional Information: Further information is available on request or from the website

For further information contact:

Tel: (1) 310 825 7315
Fax: (1) 310 206 7060
Email: aisc@ucla.edu
Contact: Fellowship Director

University of Cambridge

The Old Schools, Trinity Lane, CB2 1TN, Cambridge, United Kingdom

Tel:	(44) 12 2333 7733
Fax:	(44) 12 2333 2332
Email:	dmh14@cam.ac.uk
Website:	www.admin.cam.ac.uk
Contact:	Hugo Hocknell, Student Registry

The University of Cambridge is a loose confederation of faculties, colleges and other bodies. The colleges are mainly concerned with the teaching of their undergraduate students through tutorials and supervisions and the academic support of both graduate and undergraduate students, while the University employs professors, readers, lecturers and other teaching and administrative staff who provide the formal teaching in lectures, seminars and practical classes. The University also administers the University Library.

Arthington-Davy Grants for Tongan Students for Postgraduate Study

Subjects: Awards are made from the Arthington-Davy Fund, generously set up by the late Humphrey Augustus Arthington-Davy, British High Commissioner to the Kingdom of Tonga from 1973 to 1980, and left by him to be managed by his Cambridge College, Trinity

Eligibility: Eligible applicants must: 1. Hold a first University degree. 2. Have applied for admission, or already received an offer of admission, for a post-graduate study course at any University in the world, and. 3. Be of Tongan origin

Level of Study: Postgraduate

Type: Grant

Value: Graduate Course Fees, and maintenance allowance, less any financial support received from elsewhere

Length of Study: For minimum further period required to complete PhD

Frequency: Annual

Country of Study: Any country

Application Procedure: A completed application form should be sent together with the following: Proof of Tongan origin academic transcripts details of the intended postgraduate study, preferably with a letter of conditional acceptance from the University concerned 1. Clear and precise details of tuition fees, living expenses and finances available from the student's own resources and/or from other institutions. 2. Names and email addresses of two academic referees. 3. CV

Closing Date: 30 November

Funding: Private

Additional Information: www.trin.cam.ac.uk/postgraduate/graduate-funding-awards/ for more information

For further information contact:

Email: grad.tutor@trin.cam.ac.uk

Dorothy Hodgkin Postgraduate Award

Eligibility: Applicants must have already applied for and been accepted for a PhD place at the University of Cambridge, must be a national of one of the eligible countries (Russia plus all countries on the DAC List of ODA Recipients), must be intending to start their PhD that coming October and must hold a high-grade qualification, at least the equivalent of a United Kingdom First Class (Honours) Degree, from a prestigious academic institution

Type: Award

Value: Approx. £12,300 per year (university composition plus college fees and maintenance stipend)

Length of Study: 3 years

Frequency: Annual

Application Procedure: There is no separate application form for this competition

Closing Date: 15 December

Contributor: The United Kingdom Research Councils and Industrial Partners

Additional Information: Each DHPA is jointly sponsored by both a Research Council partner and a private sector company partner. Further details can be found on the Research Councils United Kingdom website

For further information contact:

Email: kfw20@admin.cam.ac.uk

Evans Fund

Subjects: All aspects of anthropology and archaeology of South East Asia, especially in relation to Borneo, the Malay Peninsula, Singapore and Thailand

Purpose: To support research

Eligibility: Open to graduates of any university who intend to engage in research in a suitable field

Level of Study: Doctorate, Postdoctorate, Postgraduate

Type: Fellowship

Value: Up to UK£6,000 per year

Length of Study: 1 or 2 years in the first instance, up to a maximum of 3 years
Frequency: Annual
Study Establishment: The University of Cambridge
Country of Study: Any country
No. of awards offered: 8
Application Procedure: Applicants must obtain an application form from the Secretary, which must be returned together with an outline of the applicant's proposed scheme of travel and research, a curriculum vitae and the names and addresses of two referees
Closing Date: 7 March
Funding: Private
Contributor: Legacy
No. of awards given last year: 5
No. of applicants last year: 8
Additional Information: It is expected that the successful candidate will either be based in Cambridge, or will spend a substantial period of time in Cambridge during or after their period of research

For further information contact:

Department of Social Anthropology, University of Cambridge, 2 Free School Lane, CB2 3QA, Cambridge, United Kingdom

Tel:	(44) 12 2333 4599
Fax:	(44) 12 2333 5993
Email:	ms127@hermes.cam.ac.uk
Contact:	Secretary, Evans Fund Advisory Committee

Fitzwilliam College Charlton Studentships

Subjects: All subjects
Purpose: Part-cost award for masters students
Eligibility: Fitzwilliam must be the applicant's first choice on university application form, and must have received a conditional offer from the university by the closing date for receipt of applications
Level of Study: Graduate
Type: Scholarship
Value: £3,000 to £10,000
Length of Study: 1 year
Frequency: Annual
Study Establishment: Fitzwilliam College
Country of Study: United Kingdom
No. of awards offered: 45
Application Procedure: Apply online at www.fitz.cam.ac.uk/academic/scholarships-prizes/graduate-scholarships
Closing Date: 31 March
Funding: Individuals

Contributor: Fitzwilliam College
No. of awards given last year: 2
No. of applicants last year: 45
Additional Information: Does not include PhD, MBA, MFin or PGCE.

For further information contact:

c/o graduate officer, Fitzwilliam College, CB3 0DG, Cambridge, United Kingdom

Email: graduate.officer@fitz.cam.ac.uk

Fitzwilliam College Graduate Scholarship

Subjects: All subjects
Eligibility: Open to candidates who have applied for admission to Cambridge University through the Board of Admission of Graduate Studies and subsequently satisfied the conditions of admission. Preference is given to those studying arts subjects
Level of Study: Postgraduate
Type: Fellowship
Value: £1,250
Length of Study: A maximum of 3 years. Candidates must reapply annually
Frequency: Annual
Study Establishment: Fitzwilliam College, University of Cambridge
Country of Study: United Kingdom
No. of awards offered: 15
Application Procedure: Applicants must write for details
Closing Date: Early September
Funding: Private
No. of awards given last year: 1
No. of applicants last year: 15
Additional Information: Preference is given to candidates conducting research in an arts subject

For further information contact:

Tel:	(44) 12 2333 2035
Fax:	(44) 12 2333 2082
Email:	grad.scholarships@fitz.cam.ac.uk
Contact:	Dr W Alison, Tutor for Graduate Students

Fitzwilliam College Hirst-Player Studentship

Subjects: Theology
Purpose: To support students who need assistance with payment of fees and who would otherwise be unable to read for a degree in Cambridge

Eligibility: Open to graduates of any university. The awards are only available to candidates who have applied for admission to the University through the Board of Graduate Studies and subsequently satisfied the conditions of admission made by the Board. Preference is given to those intending to take holy orders in a Christian church

Level of Study: Postgraduate

Type: Studentship

Value: £2,000 per year. The award is designed to supplement other funds

Length of Study: 1 year

Frequency: Annual

Study Establishment: Fitzwilliam College, University of Cambridge

Country of Study: United Kingdom

Application Procedure: Applicants must complete the application form, available on request. Candidates should also place Fitzwilliam College as first preference on the form

Closing Date: 1 October

Funding: Private

No. of awards given last year: 1

For further information contact:

Email: grad.scholarships@fitz.cam.ac.uk

Contact: Dr W Alison, Tutor for Graduate Students

Fitzwilliam College J R W Alexander Studentship in Law

Subjects: Law

Eligibility: Open to graduates from a British university who will have graduated by the time they come into residence

Level of Study: Postgraduate

Type: Studentship

Value: £350. The award is designed to supplement funding from other sources

Length of Study: 1 year

Frequency: Annual

Study Establishment: Fitzwilliam College, University of Cambridge

Country of Study: United Kingdom

No. of awards offered: 2

Application Procedure: Applicants must have applied for admission to the University through the Board of Graduate Studies and subsequently satisfied the conditions of admission made by the Board. Candidates should also place Fitzwilliam College as their first preference on their application

Closing Date: 25 September

Funding: Private

No. of awards given last year: 1

No. of applicants last year: 2

For further information contact:

Email: graduate.office@fitz.cam.ac.uk

Contact: Dr W Alison, Tutor for Graduate Students

Fitzwilliam College Leathersellers

Subjects: Physical or biological sciences, mathematics or engineering

Purpose: To support students who wish to undertake research

Eligibility: Open to home graduates from any United Kingdom university who have been admitted to a course of research in one of the appropriate faculties

Level of Study: Postgraduate

Type: Scholarship

Value: £2,000 per year. The award is designed to supplement funding from other sources

Length of Study: 3 years, subject to an annual review

Frequency: Annual

Study Establishment: Fitzwilliam College, University of Cambridge

Country of Study: United Kingdom

No. of awards offered: 6

Application Procedure: Applicants must complete an application form, available on request

Closing Date: 13 June

Funding: Commercial

No. of awards given last year: 1

No. of applicants last year: 6

For further information contact:

Email: graduate.office@fitz.cam.ac.uk

Contact: Dr W Alison, Tutor for Graduate Students

Fitzwilliam College Research Fellowship

Subjects: All subjects

Purpose: To enable scholars to carry out a programme of new research

Eligibility: Open to candidates who are carrying out research for a PhD at any United Kingdom or Irish university, or who have recently (normally defined as less than 1 year before the date of application) completed their course of study for this degree

Level of Study: Doctorate

Type: Fellowship

Value: Varies. Non-stipendiary funding is also offered (candidates are expected to apply for the appropriate grants for the support of their research on their own initiative)

Frequency: Annual

Study Establishment: Fitzwilliam College, University of Cambridge
Country of Study: United Kingdom
No. of awards offered: 161
Application Procedure: Applicants must write for details
Closing Date: January
No. of awards given last year: 1
No. of applicants last year: 161
Additional Information: Fellowships are awarded for new research only and not to enable candidates to complete their PhD dissertation

For further information contact:

Email: jmw65@cam.acuk
Contact: The Master's Secretary

Fitzwilliam College Shipley Studentship

Subjects: Theology
Purpose: To enable graduates to undertake research
Eligibility: Open to graduates of any university. The awards are only available to candidates who have applied for admission to the University through the Board of Graduate Studies and subsequently satisfied the conditions of admission made by the Board. Candidates should also place Fitzwilliam College as their first preference in their application
Level of Study: Postgraduate
Type: Studentship
Value: £1,250 per year. The award is designed to supplement other funds
Length of Study: 1 year
Frequency: Annual
Study Establishment: Fitzwilliam College, University of Cambridge
Country of Study: United Kingdom
No. of awards offered: 5
Application Procedure: Applicants must complete an application form, available on request
Closing Date: 1 October
Funding: Private
No. of awards given last year: 1
No. of applicants last year: 5

For further information contact:

Email: graduate.office@fitz.cam.ac.uk
Contact: Dr W Alison, Tutor for Graduate Students

Fitzwilliam College: E D Davies Scholarship

Subjects: All subjects

Eligibility: Candidates should be already registered for, or applying for, a research degree course, at Fitzwilliam College
Level of Study: Graduate
Type: Scholarship
Value: £1,250 per year
Length of Study: 1–3 years, yearly re-application required
Frequency: Annual
Country of Study: United Kingdom
No. of awards offered: 25
Application Procedure: Submit online application form
Closing Date: 25 September
No. of awards given last year: 2
No. of applicants last year: 25

For further information contact:

Email: dmh14@cam.ac.uk

Fitzwilliam College: Gibson Scholarship

Subjects: Theology
Eligibility: Intention to work towards a doctorate in New Testament Studies required
Level of Study: Graduate, Postgraduate
Type: Scholarship
Value: £1,000 per year
Length of Study: 1–3 years
Frequency: Annual
Country of Study: United Kingdom
No. of awards offered: 8
Application Procedure: Submit online application form
Closing Date: 25 September
No. of awards given last year: 1
No. of applicants last year: 8

For further information contact:

Email: graduate.office@fitz.cam.ac.uk

Fitzwilliam College: Hirst-Player Scholarship

Subjects: Theology
Eligibility: Students needing assistance with fees, who would otherwise be unable to study at Cambridge, eligible only. Students having intention to take Holy Orders in a Christian Church preferred. Students must be studying as a member of Fitzwilliam College during the period of the award
Level of Study: Postgraduate
Type: Scholarship
Value: £2,000 maximum
Length of Study: 1–2 years
Frequency: Annual

Country of Study: United Kingdom
Application Procedure: Submit online application form
Closing Date: 25 September
No. of awards given last year: 2

For further information contact:

Email: graduate.office@fitz.cam.ac.uk

Fitzwilliam College: Leathersellers

Subjects: Engineering
Eligibility: Only home graduates from a British University are eligible. Physical or biological sciences or mathematics students also eligible. Studying as a member of Fitzwilliam College during the period of the award
Level of Study: Doctorate
Type: Scholarship
Value: £3,000 per year
Length of Study: 1–3 years, subject to the approval of the Tutorial Committee
Frequency: Annual
Country of Study: United Kingdom
No. of awards offered: 8
Application Procedure: Application form available from college graduate admissions office gradadmissions@fitz.cam.ac.uk
Closing Date: 13 June
No. of awards given last year: 1
No. of applicants last year: 8

For further information contact:

Email: dmh14@cam.ac.uk

Fitzwilliam College: Shipley Scholarship

Subjects: Theology
Eligibility: Applicant must be studying as a member of Fitzwilliam during the period of the award
Level of Study: Graduate, Postgraduate
Type: Scholarship
Value: £1,250
Length of Study: 1 year
Frequency: Annual
Country of Study: United Kingdom
Application Procedure: Submit online application form
Closing Date: 25 September
No. of awards given last year: 1

For further information contact:

Email: graduate.office@fitz.cam.ac.uk

Fitzwilliam Society JRW Alexander Law Book Grants

Subjects: Law
Eligibility: All Fitzwilliam students on the LLM degree course are eligible
Level of Study: Postgraduate
Type: Grant
Value: £100
Length of Study: 1 year
Frequency: Annual
Country of Study: United Kingdom
No. of awards offered: 3
Application Procedure: No application is necessary
No. of awards given last year: 3
No. of applicants last year: 3

For further information contact:

Email: graduate.office@fitz.cam.ac.uk

Fitzwilliam Studentship: Peter Wilson Estates Gazette Scholarships

Subjects: Land economy
Purpose: Part-cost award
Eligibility: Preference is given to those who name Fitzwilliam as their first choice college on the university application form. One of the awards is prioritised for an applicant who has been an undergraduate member of the college
Level of Study: Graduate
Type: Scholarship
Value: £3,000
Length of Study: 1 year
Frequency: Annual
Country of Study: Any country
Application Procedure: Submit an online application form at www.fitz.cam.ac.uk/academic/scholarships-prizes/graduate-scholarships
Closing Date: 31 March
Funding: Individuals
No. of awards given last year: 4
Additional Information: Any MPhil course offered by the Department of Land Economy at the University of Cambridge

Girton College Graduate Research Scholarship

Subjects: All subjects covered by Cambridge University
Eligibility: A first-class degree is almost always required and election will be conditional on the candidate being granted Graduate Student status by the University of Cambridge. The

holder must become a member of the college and either be a candidate for a masters or a PhD degree
Level of Study: Doctorate, Graduate, Postgraduate, MBA
Type: Scholarship
Value: University and college fees and some proportion of maintenance costs
Frequency: Annual
Study Establishment: University of Cambridge
Country of Study: United Kingdom
No. of awards offered: 200
Application Procedure: Application should be made online via www.girton.cam.ac.uk/graduates/research-awards
Closing Date: 28 March
No. of awards given last year: 3
No. of applicants last year: 200

For further information contact:

Email: graduate.office@girton.cam.ac.uk

Girton College Overseas Bursaries

Subjects: All subjects
Eligibility: A first-class degree is almost always required and election will be conditional on the candidate being granted Graduate Student status by the University of Cambridge. The holder must become a member of the college
Level of Study: Doctorate, Graduate, Postgraduate, MBA
Type: Bursary
Value: £200–£1,000 per year
Frequency: Dependent on funds available
Study Establishment: University of Cambridge
Country of Study: United Kingdom
Application Procedure: Application forms can be downloaded from www.girton.cam.ac.uk/graduates/research-awards or may be obtained from the Graduate Secretary, Girton College, Cambridge, CB3 0JG, United Kingdom (email: graduate.office@girton.cam.ac.uk)
Closing Date: 28 March

For further information contact:

Email: graduate.office@girton.cam.ac.uk

Girton College: Doris Woodall Studentship

Subjects: Research in economics or an allied subject
Eligibility: A first-class degree is almost always required and election will be conditional on the candidate being granted Graduate Student status by the University of Cambridge. The holder must become a member of the college
Level of Study: Doctorate, Graduate, Postgraduate, MBA

Type: Studentship
Value: Between £750 and £5,000
Frequency: Annual
Study Establishment: University of Cambridge
Country of Study: United Kingdom
Application Procedure: Application should be made online via www.girton.cam.ac.uk/graduates/research-awards
Closing Date: 28 March

For further information contact:

Email: graduate.office@girton.cam.ac.uk

Girton College: Ida and Isidore Cohen Research Scholarship

Subjects: Modern Hebrew studies
Eligibility: Open to students working in modern Hebrew studies. A first-class degree is almost always required and election will be conditional on the candidate being granted Graduate Student status by the University of Cambridge. The holder must become a member of the college
Level of Study: Doctorate, Graduate, Postgraduate
Type: Scholarship
Value: Between £3,000 and £5,000
Frequency: Annual
Study Establishment: University of Cambridge
Country of Study: United Kingdom
Application Procedure: Application forms can be downloaded from external link or may be obtained from the Graduate Secretary, Girton College, Cambridge, CB3 0JG, United Kingdom
Closing Date: 28 March

For further information contact:

Email: graduate.office@girton.cam.ac.uk

Girton College: Irene Hallinan Scholarship

Subjects: All subjects covered by Cambridge University
Eligibility: A first-class degree is almost always required and election will be conditional on the candidate being granted Graduate Student status by the University of Cambridge. The holder must become a member of the college and either be a candidate for a masters or a PhD degree
Level of Study: Doctorate, Graduate, Postgraduate, MBA
Type: Scholarship
Value: Between £3,000 and £6,000
Frequency: Annual
Study Establishment: University of Cambridge
Country of Study: United Kingdom

No. of awards offered: 200
Application Procedure: Application should be made online via www.girton.cam.ac.uk/graduates/research-awards
Closing Date: 28 March
No. of awards given last year: 3
No. of applicants last year: 200

For further information contact:

Email: graduate.office@girton.cam.ac.uk

Girton College: Maria Luisa de Sanchez Scholarship

Subjects: All subjects covered by University of Cambridge
Eligibility: Applicants must be of Venezuelan nationality. A first-class degree is almost always required and election will be conditional on the candidate being granted Graduate Student status by the University of Cambridge. The holder must become a member of the college
Level of Study: Doctorate, Graduate, Postgraduate, MBA
Type: Scholarship
Value: University and college fees, and some proportion of maintenance costs
Frequency: Annual
Study Establishment: University of Cambridge
Country of Study: United Kingdom
Application Procedure: Application forms can be downloaded from www.girton.cam.ac.uk/graduate/research-awards or may be obtained from the Graduate Secretary, Girton College, Cambridge, CB3 0JG, United Kingdom (email: graduate.office@girton.cam.ac.uk)
Closing Date: 28 March
No. of awards given last year: 1
Additional Information: Eligible to nationals of Venezuela

For further information contact:

Email: graduate.office@girton.cam.ac.uk

Girton College: Ruth Whaley Scholarship

Subjects: Anglo-saxon, norse and celtic, archaeology, history of art, architecture, landscape architecture, classics, linguistics, English, modern and medieval languages, history, music philosophy
Eligibility: Open to outstanding students of non-European Union citizenship seeking admission to Girton. It is open to students following arts subjects. A first-class degree is almost always required and election will be conditional on the candidate being granted Graduate Student status by the

University of Cambridge. The holder must become a member of the college
Level of Study: Doctorate, Graduate, Postgraduate
Type: Scholarship
Value: Contribution towards living costs
Frequency: Annual
Study Establishment: University of Cambridge
Country of Study: United Kingdom
Application Procedure: Application forms can be downloaded from www.girton.cam.ac.uk/graduates/research-awards or may be obtained from the Graduate Secretary
Closing Date: 28 March
No. of awards given last year: 1
Additional Information: For further details, please refer to the website www.girton.cam.ac.uk/students/graduate-scholarships/

For further information contact:

Girton College, Huntingdon Rd, Girton, CB3 0JG, Cambridge, United Kingdom

Email: graduate.office@girton.cam.ac.uk
Contact: Graduate Secretary

Girton College: Sidney and Marguerite Cody Studentship

Purpose: Period of travel and study in continental Europe of up to 12 months and normally of not less than 6 months
Eligibility: Open to graduate members of any faculty except English who have completed less than nine terms in residence. A first-class degree is almost always required and election will be conditional on the candidate being granted Graduate Student status by the University of Cambridge. The holder must become a member of the college
Level of Study: Doctorate, Graduate, Postgraduate
Type: Studentship
Value: Up to £3,000
Frequency: Annual
Study Establishment: University of Cambridge
Country of Study: United Kingdom
Application Procedure: Application should be made online via www.girton.cam.ac.uk/graduates/research-awards
Closing Date: 28 March
No. of awards given last year: 1

For further information contact:

Email: graduate.office@girton.cam.ac.uk

Girton College: Stribling Award

Eligibility: Open to Girton students who are already members of the College, namely undergraduates coming into graduate status or current MPhil students who are going on to a PhD. A first-class degree is almost always required and election will be conditional on the candidate being granted Graduate Student status by the University of Cambridge
Level of Study: Doctorate, Graduate, Postgraduate
Type: Award
Value: £1,000, normally in addition to a studentship or any other funding for fees and maintenance
Frequency: Annual
Study Establishment: University of Cambridge
Country of Study: United Kingdom
Application Procedure: Application should be made online via www.girton.cam.ac.uk/graduates/research-awards
Closing Date: 28 March
No. of awards given last year: 2
Additional Information: Award only available to Girton College Students

For further information contact:

Email:　graduate.office@girton.cam.ac.uk

Girton College: Travel Grant

Level of Study: Graduate, Postgraduate
Type: Grant
Value: Contribution to academic travel and
Frequency: Every 2 years
Country of Study: Any country
Application Procedure: Application should be made online via www.girton.cam.ac.uk/graduates/research-awards
Closing Date: 22 April at midnight
Additional Information: Please note this is a strict dead-line, no allowance can be made for late applications or reference letters

For further information contact:

Email:　graduate.office@girton.cam.ac.uk

Gonville and Caius College Gonville Bursary

Subjects: All subjects offered by the University
Purpose: To help outstanding students from outside the European Union to meet the costs of degree courses at the University of Cambridge

Eligibility: Open to candidates who have been accepted by the College through its normal admissions procedures, and who are classified as overseas students for fees purposes. A statement of financial circumstances is required
Level of Study: Doctorate, Postgraduate
Type: Bursary
Value: Reimbursement of college fees
Length of Study: Up to 3 years, with a possibility of renewal, dependent on satisfactory progress
Frequency: Annual
Study Establishment: Gonville and Caius College, the University of Cambridge
Country of Study: United Kingdom
Application Procedure: Applicants must contact the Admissions Tutor for further information. There are no application forms
Closing Date: Deadlines are the same as for the University's courses

For further information contact:

Gonville and Caius College, Trinity Street, CB2 1TA, Cambridge, United Kingdom

Tel:	(44) 12 2333 2447
Fax:	(44) 12 2333 2456
Email:	admissions@cai.cam.ac.uk
Contact:	Admissions Tutor

Gonville and Caius College Michael Miliffe Scholarship

Subjects: All subjects
Purpose: To help candidates from underdeveloped countries
Eligibility: Open to both undergraduate and graduate students from developing countries who have been admitted through the College's normal admissions procedures
Type: Scholarship
Value: Approx. £5,000 per year with the possibility of additional support in exceptional cases
Frequency: Annual
Study Establishment: Gonville and Caius College, University of Cambridge
Country of Study: United Kingdom
Application Procedure: Applicants must complete an application form. Please write to the Director at the main address or email fellowships@brown.edu
Closing Date: The same as for the University's courses
Additional Information: There are no application forms

For further information contact:

Contact:　Dr P Binski, Tutor for Admissions

Gonville and Caius College W M Tapp Studentship in Law

Subjects: Law

Purpose: To encourage the study of law

Eligibility: Open to candidates who are not already members of the College, but who propose to register as graduate students at the University of Cambridge. Candidates must be under 30 years of age as of October 1st of the studentship year and be graduates or expect to be graduates no later than August of the same year. Preference is given to applicants nominating Gonville and Caius College as their first choice when applying under the Cambridge Intercollegiate Graduate Application Scheme

Level of Study: Doctorate, Postgraduate

Type: Studentship

Value: A stipend similar to that of a state studentship for research, plus fees and certain allowances, a dependent allowance, an allowance for a period of approved postgraduate experience, a travelling contribution for foreign students and a research allowance for research students

Length of Study: 1 year, renewable for up to a maximum of 3 years

Frequency: Annual

Study Establishment: Gonville and Caius College, University of Cambridge

Country of Study: United Kingdom

Application Procedure: Applicants must complete an application form, available from the Admissions Tutor

Closing Date: 15 January

Kings College: Stipendiary Junior Research Fellowships

Purpose: To support gifted young researchers

Level of Study: Postdoctorate, Research

Type: Fellowship

Value: Permit complete freedom to carry out research within the academic environment of the college

Length of Study: 4 years

Frequency: Annual

Study Establishment: University of Cambridge, King's College

Country of Study: United Kingdom

Closing Date: October

For further information contact:

King's College, King's Parade, CB2 1ST, Cambridge, United Kingdom

Tel:	(44) 1223 331 100
Email:	info@kings.cam.ac.uk
Contact:	Dr Keith Carne, Bursary

Lucy Cavendish College: Becker Law Scholarships

Subjects: Law

Eligibility: Open to women accepted to read for the LLM and MCL by the law Faculty at the University of Cambridge

Level of Study: Postgraduate

Type: Scholarship

Value: At least £1,000 per year

Length of Study: Up to 3 years, conditional on satisfactory academic progress

Frequency: Annual

Study Establishment: Lucy Cavendish College, University of Cambridge

Country of Study: United Kingdom

Application Procedure: Please contact to the Secretary of the Studentship and Bursary Committee

Closing Date: 30 June

For further information contact:

Lucy Cavendish College, Lady Margaret Rd, CB3 0BU, Cambridge, United Kingdom

Tel:	(44) 1223 332 190
Fax:	(44) 1223 332 178
Email:	st420@cam.ac.uk
Contact:	Secretary, Studentship and Bursary Committee

Lucy Cavendish College: Dorothy and Joseph Needham Studentship

Purpose: For studies in Natural Sciences

Eligibility: Check website or contact organisation for updates

Level of Study: Postgraduate

Type: Studentship

Value: £1,000 per year

Length of Study: Up to 3 years, conditional on satisfactory academic progress

Frequency: Annual

Study Establishment: Lucy Cavendish College, University of Cambridge

Country of Study: United Kingdom

Application Procedure: Please contact to the Secretary of the Studentship and Bursary Committee

Closing Date: 30 June

Lucy Cavendish College: Enterprise Studentship

Subjects: For MBA or MPhil in Bioscience Enterprise
Eligibility: Open to women accepted on the MBA course and on the MPhil in Bioscience Enterprise. One is open to any student the other is only available to nationals of United States of America and Canada
Level of Study: Postgraduate, MBA
Type: Studentship
Value: £1,000 per year
Frequency: Annual
Study Establishment: Lucy Cavendish College, University of Cambridge
Country of Study: United Kingdom
Application Procedure: Please contact to the Secretary of the Studentship and Bursary Committee
Closing Date: 30 June

Lucy Cavendish College: Evelyn Povey Studentship

Purpose: For postgraduate research in French Studies
Eligibility: A woman accepted to undertake postgraduate research in French or French Studies at the faculty of Medieval and Modern languages at the University of Cambridge
Level of Study: Postgraduate, Research
Type: Studentship
Value: up to £4,500 per annum
Length of Study: Up to 3 years, conditional on satisfactory academic progress
Frequency: Annual
Study Establishment: Lucy Cavendish College, University of Cambridge
Country of Study: United Kingdom
Application Procedure: Candidates who are accepted by the University of Cambridge and Lucy Cavendish College will automatically be considered, there is no separate form of application
Closing Date: 28 February each year
Funding: Trusts

Lucy Cavendish College: Isaac Newton – Dorothy Emmet Research Fellowships Positions in Arts and Humanities

Subjects: Arts and humanities, law and English
Purpose: To assist research in the arts and humanities, with a preference for law and English
Eligibility: Open to women who hold PhDs for research in the arts and humanities, with a preference for law and English
Level of Study: Postdoctorate

Type: Fellowships
Value: Stipend for each of these Research Fellowships will be £17,111 per year
Length of Study: The appointments will be for one year in the first instance from October and will be renewable annually
Frequency: Annual
Application Procedure: Please contact to the Secretary of the Studentship and Bursary Committee
Closing Date: 31 May

For further information contact:

Email: lcc-admin@lists.cam.ac.uk
Contact: Secretary of the Studentship and Bursary Committee

Lucy Cavendish College: Lord Frederick Cavendish Studentship

Purpose: For doctoral research in any subject
Eligibility: Open to women accepted to undertake doctoral research in any subject at the University of Cambridge
Level of Study: Postgraduate
Type: Studentship
Value: college fees
Length of Study: Up to 3 years, conditional on satisfactory academic progress
Frequency: Annual
Study Establishment: Lucy Cavendish College, University of Cambridge
Country of Study: United Kingdom
Application Procedure: Please contact to the Secretary of the Studentship and Bursary Committee
Closing Date: 30 June

Lucy Cavendish College: Mastermann-Braithwaite Studentship

Subjects: Linguistics
Eligibility: A woman accepted to undertake postgraduate research in Linguistics at the University of Cambridge
Level of Study: Postgraduate, Research
Type: Studentship
Value: College fees
Length of Study: Up to 3 years, conditional on satisfactory academic progress
Frequency: Annual
Study Establishment: Lucy Cavendish College, University of Cambridge
Country of Study: United Kingdom

Application Procedure: Please contact to the Secretary of the Studentship and Bursary Committee
Closing Date: 30 June

Lucy Cavendish College: Research Fellowships

Subjects: arts and humanities, social sciences or science and engineering
Purpose: To support post-doctoral research
Eligibility: Female, right to work in United Kingdom, holder of PhD or equivalents
Level of Study: Postdoctorate
Type: Research fellowship
Value: tbc
Length of Study: 3 years
Frequency: Every 3 years
Study Establishment: Lucy Cavendish College, University of Cambridge
Country of Study: As applicable
No. of awards offered: 110
Application Procedure: see notices when advertised
Funding: Private
No. of awards given last year: 1
No. of applicants last year: 110

For further information contact:

Email: registrar@lucy-cav.cam.ac.uk
Contact: Registrar

Nabil Boustany Scholarships

Subjects: MBA
Purpose: To enable a Lebanese national to attend the Cambridge MBA on a full scholarship
Eligibility: Open to candidates of all nations although priority given to Lebanese nationals, who have obtained a good Honours Degree from a recognized university and have at least 3 years of full-time, real-world experience. Candidates will need to demonstrate a high intellectual potential, practical common sense and the ability to put ideas into action. They also need to be highly motivated with a strong desire to learn. Applicants will be asked to take the Test of English as a Foreign Language (TOEFL) where applicable and the Graduate Management Admission Test (GMAT)
Level of Study: MBA
Type: Scholarship
Value: £30,000
Length of Study: 2 years
Frequency: Every 2 years

Study Establishment: Judge Business School, University of Cambridge
Country of Study: United Kingdom
No. of awards offered: 4
Application Procedure: Applicants must email their curriculum vitae to admissions@boustany-foundation.org. Applicants must also be applying for the Cambridge MBA programme
Closing Date: 15 May
Funding: Foundation
Contributor: The Nabil Boustany Foundation
No. of awards given last year: 1
No. of applicants last year: 4
Additional Information: The scholarship recipient is normally required to spend a summer internship, carrying no salary, within a Lebanese organization. Applicants must be accepted into the Cambridge MBA programme

For further information contact:

1 avenue des Citronniers, 06800 Cagnes-sur-Mer, France

Fax: (44) 77 93 15 05 56
Email: info@boustany-foundation.org
Contact: Mr M Tamar

Newnham College: Moody-Stuart Scholarships in Turkish Studies

For further information contact:

Newnham College, Sidgwick Avenue, CB3 9DF, Cambridge, United Kingdom

Tel: (44) 1223 335 700
Fax: (44) 1223 357 898
Email: enquiries@newnham.cam.ac.uk
Contact: Bursar

Osborn Research Studentship

Subjects: Medieval art, architectural and cultural history
Purpose: To support students carrying research or taking advanced courses
Level of Study: Postdoctorate, Postgraduate
Type: Studentship
Value: Up to £12,000 to match with funds administered centrally by the UCAM
Length of Study: 1–3 years
Frequency: Every 3 years
Study Establishment: The University of Cambridge
Country of Study: United Kingdom

Application Procedure: For further details, please check website www.sid.cam.ac.uk/current/postgrads/scholarships
Closing Date: 1 April
Funding: Private
Contributor: Sidney Sussex College

For further information contact:

Email: graduate.funding@admin.cam.ac.uk

Pembroke College: College Research Studentships

Subjects: All subjects
Eligibility: Preference in awarding these studentships will be given to candidates who intend to register for a PhD degree at Pembroke. However, candidates registering to study for an MPhil will also be considered for an award if they are intending to carry on to a PhD after they have finished their MPhil
Level of Study: Postgraduate
Type: Studentship
Value: College/University fees plus a maintenance allowance of £12,000 per year
Frequency: Annual
Study Establishment: Pembroke College
Country of Study: United Kingdom
Application Procedure: All applicants for any of these awards must apply in the first instance to the Board of Graduate Studies for their University place. Candidates should indicate that they are applying for a Pembroke College award. In making awards preference will be given to those who nominate Pembroke as their college of first choice. All candidates are expected to apply for Research Council funding where appropriate, and for University CHESS funding, if they are eligible. The College will take into account candidates' income from other sources when making awards
Closing Date: 6 January
Additional Information: Applicants should also complete a Pembroke Studentship form. This can be completed online, downloaded or obtained from the Graduate Secretary. The awards are conditional on the selected students being admitted as a registered Graduate Student by the Board of Graduate Studies with effect from October 1st each academic year. Early application is recommended

For further information contact:

Pembroke College, CB2 1RF, Cambridge, United Kingdom

Tel: (44) 1223 338 100
Fax: (44) 1223 338 163
Email: tut@pem.cam.ac.uk
Contact: Graduate Secretary

Pembroke College: Graduate Studentships in Arabic and Islamic Studies (including Persian)

Subjects: Arabic and Islamic studies
Eligibility: Preference in awarding these studentships will be given to candidates who intend to register for a PhD degree at Pembroke. However, candidates registering to study for an MPhil will also be considered for an award if they are intending to carry on to a PhD after they have finished their MPhil
Level of Study: Postgraduate
Type: Studentship
Value: Covers University and College fees (at the Home/European Union rate) for three years
Frequency: Annual
Study Establishment: Pembroke College
Country of Study: United Kingdom
Application Procedure: All applicants for any of these awards must apply in the first instance to the Board of Graduate Studies for their University place. Candidates should indicate that they are applying for a Pembroke College award. In making awards preference will be given to those who nominate Pembroke as their college of first choice. All candidates are expected to apply for Research Council funding where appropriate, and for University CHESS funding, if they are eligible. The college will take into account candidates' income from other sources when making awards
Closing Date: Please check website
Additional Information: Applicants should also complete a Pembroke Studentship form. This can be completed online, downloaded or obtained from the Graduate Secretary. The awards are conditional on the selected students being admitted as a registered Graduate Student by the Board of Graduate Studies with effect from October 1st each academic year. Early application is recommended.

Pembroke College: MPhil Studentship for Applicants from the Least Developed Countries

Subjects: All subjects
Purpose: The College is offering this one-year studentship to enable the winner to study for an MPhil degree, or equivalent, at the University of Cambridge
Eligibility: Eligibility is confined to nationals of the fifty 'Least Developed Countries' as defined by the United Nations. The other is for nationals of the fifty 'Least Developed Countries' as defined by the United Nations (check at www.un.org/special-rep/ohrlls/ldc/list), most of which are in Africa or South-East Asia
Level of Study: Postgraduate
Type: Studentship

Value: University fees at least at the standard rate for Home/European Union students, plus college fees and a maintenance of £10,465
Frequency: Annual
Study Establishment: Pembroke College, University of Cambridge
Application Procedure: All applicants for any of these awards must apply in the first instance to the Board of Graduate Studies for their University place. Candidates should indicate that they are applying for a Pembroke College award. In making awards preference will be given to those who nominate Pembroke as their College of first choice. All candidates are expected to apply for Research Council funding where appropriate, and for University CHESS funding, if they are eligible. The College will take into account candidates' income from other sources when making awards
Additional Information: Applicants should also complete a Pembroke Studentship form. This can be completed online, downloaded or obtained from the Graduate Secretary. The awards are conditional on the selected students being admitted as a registered Graduate Student by the Board of Graduate Studies with effect from October 1st each academic year. Early application is recommended

Pembroke College: The Bethune-Baker Graduate Studentship in Theology

Subjects: Arabic and Islamic studies, law, and theology
Eligibility: Open to candidates who intend to register for the PhD degree at the University of Cambridge
Level of Study: Postgraduate
Type: Studentship
Value: College and university fees for three years
Frequency: Annual
Study Establishment: University of Cambridge
Country of Study: United Kingdom
Application Procedure: All applicants for any of these awards must apply in the first instance to the Board of Graduate Studies for their University place. Candidates should indicate that they are applying for a Pembroke College award. In making awards preference will be given to those who nominate Pembroke as their college of first choice. All candidates are expected to apply for Research Council funding where appropriate, and for University CHESS funding, if they are eligible. The College will take into account candidates' income from other sources when making awards
Closing Date: Please check website
Contributor: HM the Sultan of Oman and of Professor E.G. Browne

Additional Information: Applicants should also complete a Pembroke Studentship form. This can be completed online, downloaded or obtained from the Graduate Secretary. The awards are conditional on the selected students being admitted as a registered Graduate Student by the Board of Graduate Studies with effect from October 1st each academic year. Early application is recommended

Pembroke College: The Bristol-Myers Squibb Graduate Studentship in the Biomedical Sciences

Subjects: History, physics and the bio-medical sciences
Eligibility: Open to candidates who intend to register for a PhD degree at the University of Cambridge
Level of Study: Postgraduate
Type: Studentship
Value: The studentship will have a value sufficient to pay college fees for three years
Frequency: Annual
Country of Study: United Kingdom
Application Procedure: All applicants for any of these awards must apply in the first instance to the Board of Graduate Studies for their University place. Candidates should indicate that they are applying for a Pembroke College award. In making awards preference will be given to those who nominate Pembroke as their college of first choice. All candidates are expected to apply for Research Council funding where appropriate, and for University CHESS funding, if they are eligible. The College will take into account candidates' income from other sources when making awards
Closing Date: Please check website
Additional Information: Applicants should also complete a Pembroke Studentship form. This can be completed online, downloaded or obtained from the Graduate Secretary. The awards are conditional on the selected students being admitted as a registered Graduate Student by the Board of Graduate Studies with effect from October 1st each academic year. Early application is recommended

Pembroke College: The Grosvenor-Shilling Bursary in Land Economy

Subjects: All subjects
Eligibility: Applicants must normally reside in Australia and hold a qualification from an Australian tertiary institution. There is no restriction as to the academic field
Level of Study: Postgraduate
Type: Scholarship
Value: £500
Frequency: Annual

Application Procedure: All applicants for any of these awards must apply in the first instance to the Board of Graduate Studies for their University place. Candidates should indicate that they are applying for a Pembroke College award. In making awards preference will be given to those who nominate Pembroke as their college of first choice. All candidates are expected to apply for Research Council funding where appropriate, and for University CHESS funding, if they are eligible. The College will take into account candidates' income from other sources when making awards

Closing Date: Please check website

Additional Information: Applicants should also complete a Pembroke Studentship form. This can be completed online, downloaded or obtained from the Graduate Secretary. The awards are conditional on the selected students being admitted as a registered Graduate Student by the Board of Graduate Studies with effect from October 1st each academic year. Early application is recommended

Pembroke College: The Lander Studentship in the History of Art

Purpose: The College is very pleased to be able to offer one studentship for an outstanding art historian, supported by the estate of Professor J.R. Lander

Eligibility: Candidates must be applying to study for a PhD degree in the History of Art at the University of Cambridge, with Pembroke as first-choice college

Level of Study: Postgraduate

Type: Studentship

Value: The studentship will, if necessary, pay university and college fees, at the home rate, plus a maintenance allowance (approx. £10,140 a year), for a maximum of 3 years

Frequency: Annual

Study Establishment: Pembroke College, University of Cambridge

Country of Study: United Kingdom

Application Procedure: All applicants for any of these awards must apply in the first instance to the Board of Graduate Studies for their University place. Candidates should indicate that they are applying for a Pembroke College award. In making awards preference will be given to those who nominate Pembroke as their College of first choice. All candidates are expected to apply for Research Council funding where appropriate, and for University CHESS funding, if they are eligible. The College will take into account candidates' income from other sources when making awards

Closing Date: 10 January

Additional Information: Applicants should also complete a Pembroke Studentship form. This can be completed online,

downloaded or obtained from the Graduate Secretary. The awards are conditional on the selected students being admitted as a registered Graduate Student by the Board of Graduate Studies with effect from October 1st each academic year. Early application is recommended

Pembroke College: The Monica Partridge Studentship

Subjects: All subjects

Purpose: To offer a graduate studentship for a student from South-East Europe to study at Pembroke

Eligibility: Open to the students of the nationals of Albania, Bosnia and Herzegovina, Bulgaria, Croatia, Greece, Kosovo, Macedonia, Montenegro and Serbia. Applications from students from Romania, Slovenia and Turkey will be considered if there is no suitable candidate from the countries listed above. Preference will be given to fund students studying for a PhD, but MPhil applicants intending to continue to a PhD will also be considered

Level of Study: Postgraduate

Type: Studentship

Value: The studentship will have a value sufficient to cover college fees (£2,229) and maintenance (£10,140) for three years for a PhD student or, in the case of an MPhil student, one year

Frequency: Annual

Study Establishment: Pembroke College, University of Cambridge

Country of Study: United Kingdom

Application Procedure: All applicants for any of these awards must apply in the first instance to the Board of Graduate Studies for their University place. Candidates should indicate that they are applying for a Pembroke College award. In making awards preference will be given to those who nominate Pembroke as their college of first choice. All candidates are expected to apply for Research Council funding where appropriate, and for University CHESS funding, if they are eligible. The College will take into account candidates' income from other sources when making awards

Closing Date: 31 January

Additional Information: Applicants should also complete a Pembroke Studentship form. This can be completed online, downloaded or obtained from the Graduate Secretary. The awards are conditional on the selected students being admitted as a registered Graduate Student by the Board of Graduate Studies with effect from October 1st each academic year. Early application is recommended

Pembroke College: The Nahum Graduate Studentship in Physics

Subjects: Physics

Eligibility: Preference in awarding these studentships will be given to candidates who intend to register for a PhD degree at Pembroke. However, candidates registering to study for an MPhil will also be considered for an award if they are intending to carry on to a PhD after they have finished their MPhil

Level of Study: Postgraduate

Type: Studentship

Value: The studentship will have a value sufficient to pay College fees for three years. Moreover, additional awards, of up to the equivalent of University fees for a Home student (£3,465), may be made to individual applicants, depending on need and the availability of funds

Frequency: Annual

Study Establishment: Pembroke College

Country of Study: United Kingdom

Application Procedure: All applicants for any of these awards must apply in the first instance to the Board of Graduate Studies for their University place. Candidates should indicate that they are applying for a Pembroke College award. In making awards preference will be given to those who nominate Pembroke as their college of first choice. All candidates are expected to apply for Research Council funding where appropriate, and for University CHESS funding, if they are eligible. The College will take into account candidates' income from other sources when making awards

Closing Date: 31 January

Additional Information: Applicants should also complete a Pembroke Studentship form. This can be completed online, downloaded or obtained from the Graduate Secretary. The awards are conditional on the selected students being admitted as a registered Graduate Student by the Board of Graduate Studies with effect from October 1st each academic year. Early application is recommended

Pembroke College: The Pembroke Australian Scholarship

Subjects: All subjects

Eligibility: Applicants must normally reside in Australia and hold a qualification from an Australian tertiary institution. There is no restriction as to the academic field

Level of Study: Postgraduate

Type: Scholarship

Value: £500

Frequency: Annual

Application Procedure: All applicants for any of these awards must apply in the first instance to the Board of Graduate Studies for their University place. Candidates should indicate that they are applying for a Pembroke College award. In making awards preference will be given to those who nominate Pembroke as their College of first choice. All candidates are expected to apply for Research Council funding where appropriate, and for University CHESS funding, if they are eligible. The College will take into account candidates' income from other sources when making awards

Closing Date: 31 January

Additional Information: Applicants should also complete a Pembroke Studentship form. This can be completed online, downloaded or obtained from the Graduate Secretary. The awards are conditional on the selected students being admitted as a registered Graduate Student by the Board of Graduate Studies with effect from October 1st each academic year. Early application is recommended

Pembroke College: The Thornton Graduate Studentship in History

Subjects: History

Eligibility: Preference in awarding these studentships will be given to candidates who intend to register for a PhD degree at Pembroke. However, candidates registering to study for an MPhil will also be considered for an award if they are intending to carry on to a PhD after they have finished their MPhil

Level of Study: Postgraduate

Type: Studentship

Value: The studentship will have a value sufficient to pay College fees for three years. Moreover, additional awards, of up to the equivalent of University fees for a Home student (£3,465), may be made to individual applicants, depending on need and the availability of funds

Frequency: Annual

Study Establishment: Pembroke College

Country of Study: United Kingdom

Application Procedure: All applicants for any of these awards must apply in the first instance to the Board of Graduate Studies for their University place. Candidates should indicate that they are applying for a Pembroke College award. In making awards preference will be given to those who nominate Pembroke as their college of first choice. All candidates are expected to apply for Research Council funding where appropriate, and for University CHESS funding, if they are eligible. The College will take into account candidates' income from other sources when making awards

Closing Date: 31 January
Additional Information: Applicants should also complete a Pembroke Studentship form. This can be completed online, downloaded or obtained from the Graduate Secretary. The awards are conditional on the selected students being admitted as a registered Graduate Student by the Board of Graduate Studies with effect from October 1st each academic year. Early application is recommended

Pembroke College: The Ziegler Graduate Studentship in Law

Subjects: Law
Eligibility: Preference in awarding studentships is given to candidates who intend to register for a PhD degree at Pembroke
Level of Study: Postgraduate
Type: Studentship
Value: Covers university and college fees (at the Home/European Union rate)
Frequency: Annual
Study Establishment: Pembroke College
Country of Study: United Kingdom
Application Procedure: All applicants for any of these awards must apply in the first instance to the Board of Graduate Studies for their University place. Candidates should indicate that they are applying for a Pembroke College award. In making awards preference will be given to those who nominate Pembroke as their college of first choice. All candidates are expected to apply for Research Council funding where appropriate, and for University CHESS funding, if they are eligible. The College will take into account candidates' income from other sources when making awards
Closing Date: 31 January
Additional Information: Applicants should also complete a Pembroke Studentship form. This can be completed online, downloaded or obtained from the Graduate Secretary. The awards are conditional on the selected students being admitted as a registered Graduate Student by the Board of Graduate Studies with effect from October 1st each academic year. Early application is recommended

Peterhouse: Research Studentships

Subjects: All subjects
Eligibility: Open to prospective PhD candidates
Level of Study: Postgraduate
Type: Studentship
Value: varies
Frequency: Annual
Study Establishment: Peterhouse College

Country of Study: United Kingdom
No. of awards offered: 57
Application Procedure: Please contact at graduates@pet. cam.ac.uk for more information
Closing Date: Early January
No. of awards given last year: 5
No. of applicants last year: 57
Additional Information: Number of awards varies from year to year

For further information contact:

Peterhouse, Trumpington Street, CB2 1RD, Cambridge, United Kingdom

Email: graduates@pet.cam.ac.uk
Contact: Graduate Admissions

Principal's Studentship

Subjects: Mathematics or humanities
Purpose: To support an MPhil or PhD student
Level of Study: Graduate
Type: Studentship
Value: Approx. Between £3,000 and £12,000 per year
Length of Study: 1–3 years
Frequency: Dependent on funds available
Study Establishment: Newnham College, University of Cambridge
Country of Study: United Kingdom
Closing Date: 3 April
Funding: Private

For further information contact:

Email: studentfunding@ed.ac.uk

Ramanujan Research Studentship in Mathematics

Subjects: Mathematics
Purpose: The Ramanujan Studentship is normally awarded for nine months in the first instance, while the student takes the course leading to the MASt in Mathematics
Eligibility: For students from India hoping to do research for a PhD degree in Cambridge. Students of any University or comparable institution in India who have not already begun residence in Cambridge and who hold a First Class Honours degree or its equivalent, or are likely to do so by the time of entry, are eligible to apply
Level of Study: Research
Type: Studentship

Value: Graduate Course Fees, maintenance allowance (at up to the minimum rate set by the University), and a return ticket from India to the United Kingdom
Length of Study: For minimum duration of the course (can be renewed for further 3 years)
Frequency: Annual
Country of Study: United Kingdom
Closing Date: 18 January
Additional Information: Shortlisted applicants will be invited to submit a full application by 4 February

For further information contact:

Email: gradfunding-at-trin.cam.ac.uk

Ramanujan Research Studentship in Mathematics at Trinity College, Cambridge

Subjects: Studentship is awarded in the field of Pure or Applied Mathematics of Cambridge
Purpose: Trinity College, University of Cambridge is offering Ramanujan Research Studentship for students who wish to undertake research in Mathematics. Student should hold a first class honours degree or its equivalent from any university or comparable institution in India
Eligibility: Indian students can apply for this studentship. Applicants from outside the home country will often need to meet specific English language/other language requirements in order to be able to study there
Type: Research
Value: For a student who has no support or only partial support from any other source, the studentship covers: Graduate Course Fees, Maintenance allowance (at up to the minimum rate set by the University), and a Return ticket from India to the United Kingdom. If the Studentship is renewed for the PhD, another return ticket from India to the United Kingdom will be awarded. The applicant may also be considered for a discretionary maintenance allowance for the period between completion of the MASt and commencement of PhD
Study Establishment: Studentship is awarded in the field of Pure or Applied Mathematics of Cambridge
Country of Study: Any country
Application Procedure: Completed Preliminary Application Forms must be returned by post or email
Closing Date: 15 January
Additional Information: For more details please browse the website scholarship-positions.com/ramanujan-research-studentship-mathematics-trinity-college-cambridge-uk/2015/11/14/

For further information contact:

Email: gradfunding-at-trin.cam.ac.uk

Robinson College: Lewis Graduate Scholarship

Purpose: The College expects to award one Lewis Scholarship to a graduate student applying to read for a PhD degree in the humanities
Eligibility: Open to all applicants who name Robinson College as their college of first choice on the Board of Graduate Studies Application Form for Admissions as a Graduate student, or are prepared to change college if offered the scholarship. The scholarship is conditional on the candidate being offered a place at the University
Level of Study: Postgraduate
Type: Scholarship
Value: varies
Length of Study: The scholarship is tenable for up to 3 years, subject to satisfactory academic progress
Study Establishment: University of Cambridge
Country of Study: United Kingdom
Application Procedure: Applicants should send a curriculum vitae and details of their intended programme of research including no more than one A4 page describing their proposed research project), together with details of other grant applications. Applications must be submitted by post to the Graduate Admissions Tutor
Closing Date: Please check website
Additional Information: Please check website for latest updates

For further information contact:

Robinson College, Grange Rd, CB3 9AN, Cambridge, United Kingdom

Tel: (44) 1223 339 100
Fax: (44) 1223 351 794
Email: graduate-admissions@robinson.cam.ac.uk
Contact: Graduate Admissions Tutor

St John's College Benefactors' Scholarships for Research

Subjects: All subjects offered by the University
Purpose: To fund candidates for PhD and MPhil degrees
Eligibility: Open to candidates of any nationality with a First Class (Honours) Degree or equivalent
Level of Study: Postgraduate
Type: Scholarship
Value: £9,000, plus approved college and university fees, a Scholar's Book Grant of up to £100 and other expenses
Length of Study: Up to 3 years
Frequency: Annual

Study Establishment: St John's College, University of Cambridge
Country of Study: United Kingdom
Application Procedure: Applicants must see the Cambridge University Graduate Studies prospectus for particulars
Closing Date: 1 May
No. of awards given last year: 3

For further information contact:

St John's College, St John's Street, CB2 1TP, Cambridge, United Kingdom

Tel: (44) 12 2333 8612
Fax: (44) 12 2376 6419
Email: graduate_admissions@joh.cam.ac.uk

Trinity College: Studentships in Mathematics

Subjects: Mathematics
Purpose: The Trinity Studentship in Mathematics is a - one-year studentship intended for students who wish to undertake research in Mathematics at the University of Cambridge but who are required by the Faculty of Mathematics to take, in the first instance, the course leading to the Master of Advanced Study (MASt)
Eligibility: Eligible candidates must; 1. Have applied for admission, or already received an offer of admission, to the University of Cambridge for the MASt degree. 2. Not yet have been members of the University of Cambridge as an undergraduate or graduate student
Level of Study: Graduate, Postgraduate
Type: Studentship
Value: Graduate Course Fees for the MASt, discretionary maintenance allowance, and return ticket from the country of origin to the United Kingdom for overseas students
Length of Study: 1 year of study
Frequency: Annual
Country of Study: Any country
Closing Date: 22 January
Funding: Private
Additional Information: Please visit the website for more information

Westminster College Lewis and Gibson Scholarship

Subjects: Theology
Purpose: To enable Scholars to study for a theology degree at the University of Cambridge as an integral part of his or her training for the ministry of a church in the reformed tradition which has a Presbyterian order
Eligibility: Open to graduates of a recognised university who are members of the United Reformed Church in the United Kingdom or of any church not established by the state which is a member of the World Alliance of Reformed Churches and has a Presbyterian form of government. Applicants must have been recognised by their churches as candidates for the Ministry of Word and Sacrament, but should not yet have been ordained
Level of Study: Postgraduate
Type: Scholarship
Value: One scholarship of £6,000 or two scholarships of £3,000 approx
Length of Study: 1 year, renewable for up to 2 further years
Study Establishment: The University of Cambridge
Country of Study: United Kingdom
Application Procedure: If it is the intention to study at the postgraduate level, an application should be made at the same time to the Board of Graduate Studies of the university. The Scholar will normally study for one of the following degrees: BA or MPhil in theology, or PhD. He or she will be a member of both Westminster College and one of the University's constituent colleges
Closing Date: 24 December
Funding: Private
Contributor: A legacy controlled by the United Reformed Church
No. of awards given last year: 2
Additional Information: Scholars from outside the United Reformed Church have usually been theology graduates and have used the scholarship for postgraduate work

For further information contact:

Westminster College, Madingley Rd, CB3 0AA, Cambridge, United Kingdom

Tel: (44) 1223 741 084
Fax: (44) 1223 300 765
Email: jp225@cam.ac.uk
Contact: Reverend John Proctor, Director of Studies

William Wyse Studentship in Social Anthropology

Subjects: Social anthropology
Purpose: To support study
Eligibility: Open to all students who wish to study for the degree of PhD. The Studentships are open to any person who is admitted to the University of Cambridge by the Board of Graduate Studies and intends to do research in Social

Anthropology leading to the PhD. Degree, regardless of whether they are liable for fees at the Home or Overseas rate. It is a condition of the Studentships that United Kingdom and European Union students are eligible for ESRC or Vice-Chancellor's Awards and that overseas students fulfil the eligibility criteria for Cambridge International Scholarships

Level of Study: Doctorate
Type: Studentship
Value: Varies
Length of Study: 3 years
Frequency: Annual
Study Establishment: The University of Cambridge
Country of Study: United Kingdom
No. of awards offered: 8
Application Procedure: Applicants should contact the admissions secretary for details
Closing Date: 11 January
Funding: Private
No. of awards given last year: 5 grants
No. of applicants last year: 8
Additional Information: For further details, refer the website link mentioned below. www.socanth.cam.ac.uk/about-us/funding/william-wyse-funding/william-wyse-studentship

For further information contact:

Email: enquiries@socanth.cam.ac.uk; graduate-secretary@socanth.cam.ac.uk
Contact: Admissions Secretary

Wood Whistler Prize and Medal

Subjects: English literature
Purpose: To reward an outstanding student
Level of Study: Graduate
Type: Prize
Value: Approx. £2,500
Frequency: Annual
Study Establishment: Newnham College, University of Cambridge
Country of Study: United Kingdom
Application Procedure: There is no application form. Names are put forward by the English faculty of the University of Cambridge
Funding: Private

For further information contact:

Email: tutorial.office@newn.cam.ac.uk

University of Cambridge (Cambridge Commonwealth Trust, Cambridge Overseas Trust, Gates Cambridge Trust, Cambridge European Trust and Associated Trusts)

Cambridge Trusts, Trinity College, Trinity Street, CB2 1TQ, Cambridge, United Kingdom

Tel: (44) 1223 351 449
Fax: (44) 1223 323 322
Email: info@overseastrusts.cam.ac.uk
Website: www.admin.cam.ac.uk

The Cambridge Commonwealth Trust and the Cambridge Overseas Trust (formerly the Chancellor's Fund) were established in 1982 by the University of Cambridge under the Chairmanship of his Royal Highness the Prime of Wales to provide financial assistance for students from overseas who, without help, would be unable to take up their places at Cambridge. Since 1982, the Cambridge Commonwealth Trust has brought 6,600 students from 51 countries to Cambridge, the Cambridge Overseas trust 4,252 students from 76 countries.

British Chevening Cambridge Scholarships for Postgraduate Study (Indonesia)

Subjects: All subjects
Purpose: To financially support those undertaking postgraduate study
Eligibility: Applicants must be citizens of Indonesia
Level of Study: Postgraduate
Type: Scholarship
Value: The University Composition Fee at the overseas rate, approved college fees, a maintenance allowance sufficient for a single student and a contribution towards return economy airfare
Length of Study: 1 year
Frequency: Annual
Study Establishment: The University of Cambridge
Country of Study: United Kingdom
Application Procedure: Applicants must apply directly to the British Embassy in Indonesia
Contributor: Offered in collaboration with the Malaysian Commonwealth Studies Centre and the Foreign and Commonwealth Office (FCO)

Additional Information: Further information is available on request

For further information contact:

Email: cambridge.trust@admin.cam.ac.uk

British Chevening Malaysia Cambridge Scholarship for PhD Study

Subjects: All subjects
Purpose: To financially support study towards a PhD
Eligibility: Open to students from Malaysia. Applicants must apply to the University of Cambridge and be offered a place at Cambridge in the normal way. All applicants must have a First Class or High Second Class (Honours) Degree or equivalent and normally be under 26. They must be successfully nominated for an Overseas Research Student (ORS) award
Level of Study: Doctorate
Type: Scholarship
Value: The University Composition Fee at the appropriate rate, approved college fees, a maintenance allowance sufficient for a single student and a contribution towards return economy airfare
Length of Study: Up to 3 years
Frequency: Annual
Study Establishment: The University of Cambridge
Country of Study: United Kingdom
Application Procedure: Applicants must complete a preliminary application form, which can be obtained from local universities, offices of the British Council or the Trust. Completed forms must be returned to the main address. Shortlisted candidates will be sent forms for admission to the University of Cambridge. The preliminary application form can also be downloaded from www.admin.cam.ac.uk/offices/gradstud/admissions/forms/
Contributor: Offered in collaboration with the Foreign and Commonwealth Office (FCO)

For further information contact:

Email: cambridge.trust@admin.cam.ac.uk

British Petroleum Research Bursaries for PhD Study

Subjects: All subjects
Purpose: To celebrate the Centenary for BP and New Hall College

Eligibility: For citizens of Russia, Ukraine, Countries of the former Soviet Union, China, The Middle East (particularly Egypt), Southern Africa, or South Asia
Level of Study: Doctorate
Type: Bursary
Value: £2,000 annually
Frequency: Annual
Study Establishment: BP and New Hall College, The University of Cambridge
Country of Study: United Kingdom
Application Procedure: Applicants for a place to do a PhD should apply for an ORS award and should normally be successfully nominated for an ORS award or an ORS equivalent award, which meets the difference between the higher overseas rate and the lower domestic rate of the University Composition Fee

For further information contact:

Email: enquiry@bpgraduates.co.uk

British Petroleum Research Bursaries for Postgraduate Study

Subjects: All subjects
Purpose: To celebrate the Centenary for BP and New Hall College
Eligibility: For citizens of Russia, Ukraine, Countries of the former Soviet Union, China, The Middle East (particularly Egypt), Southern Africa, or South Asia
Level of Study: Doctorate
Type: Bursary
Value: £2,000 annually
Length of Study: 1 year
Frequency: Annual
Study Establishment: BP and New Hall College, The University of Cambridge
Country of Study: United Kingdom

For further information contact:

Email: enquiry@bpgraduates.co.uk

Charles Wallace India Trust

Subjects: Arts, Humanities, and Heritage Conservation
Purpose: To financially assist postgraduate study for applicants who are not successful in winning a scholarship
Eligibility: This scholarship is only available for citizens of India. Applicants for a place to do a PhD should apply for an ORS award and should be successfully nominated for an ORS award or an ORS equivalent award, which meets the

difference between the higher overseas rate and the lower domestic rate of the University Composition Fee

Type: Bursary
Value: Varies
Frequency: Annual
Study Establishment: The University of Cambridge
Country of Study: Any country
Closing Date: See website for details
Contributor: Charles Wallace India Trust

For further information contact:

Email: cwit@in.britishcouncil.org

China Scholarship Council Cambridge Scholarships

Subjects: A range of priority subjects set each year by the China Scholarship Council
Purpose: To financially assist study towards a PhD
Eligibility: Applicants must be from China, and have a first-class honours degree, and preferably, a Masters degree or its equivalent from a recognised university in China
Level of Study: Doctorate
Type: Scholarship
Value: The University Composition Fee at the appropriate rate, approved College fees, a maintenance allowance sufficient for a single student, contribution towards an economy return airfare
Frequency: Annual
Study Establishment: The University of Cambridge
Country of Study: United Kingdom
Application Procedure: Applicants for a place to do a PhD should apply for an ORS award and should normally be successfully nominated for an ORS award or an ORS equivalent award, which meets the difference between the higher overseas rate and the lower domestic rate of the University Composition Fee
Contributor: In collaboration with the China Scholarship Council

For further information contact:

Email: cambridge.trust@admin.cam.ac.uk

Corpus Christi Research Scholarship

Subjects: Any subjects
Purpose: To financially assist study towards a PhD
Eligibility: Applicants must be from India, and already hold a degree equivalent to a first-class or a high upper second from a United Kingdom university

Level of Study: Doctorate
Type: Scholarship
Value: Varies
Study Establishment: Corpus Christi College, The University of Cambridge
Country of Study: United Kingdom
Application Procedure: Applicants for a place to do a PhD should apply for an ORS award and should normally be successfully nominated for an ORS award or an ORS equivalent award, which meets the difference between the higher overseas rate and the lower domestic rate of the university composition fee
Closing Date: See website for details
Contributor: In collaboration with the Corpus Christi College

For further information contact:

Email: research-fellowships@corpus.cam.ac.uk

David M. Livingstone (Australia) Scholarship

Subjects: All subjects
Purpose: To support students to undertake 1-year postgraduate degree course at the University of Cambridge
Eligibility: The scholarship is only available for citizens of Australia. Scholars must specify Jesus College as their first choice college
Level of Study: Postgraduate
Type: Scholarship
Value: University composition fee and college fee
Length of Study: 1 year
Frequency: Annual
Closing Date: 31 March
Contributor: Jesus College

For further information contact:

Tel: (44) 1223 760 606
Fax: (44) 1223 338 723
Email: admissions@gradstudies.cam.ac.uk

Developing World Education Fund Scholarships for PhD Study

Subjects: All subjects
Purpose: To financially support study towards a PhD
Eligibility: For citizens from Bangladesh, China, India, Pakistan, Sri Lanka or Zambia. Applicants must apply to the University of Cambridge and be offered a place at Cambridge in the normal way. All applicants must have a degree

equivalent to a First Class from a United Kingdom university, and normally be under 26

Level of Study: Doctorate

Type: Scholarships and fellowships

Value: The University Composition Fee at the appropriate rate, approve College fees, a maintenance allowance sufficient for a single student, contribution towards an economy return airfare

Study Establishment: The University of Cambridge

Country of Study: United Kingdom

Application Procedure: Applicants for a place to do a PhD should apply for an ORS award and should normally be successfully nominated for an ORS award or an ORS equivalent award, which meets the difference between the higher overseas rate and the lower domestic rate of the University Composition Fee

Closing Date: See website for details

For further information contact:

Email: joe@advance-africa.com

International Club of Boston College Cambridge Scholarship

Subjects: Education

Purpose: To financially support those undertaking postgraduate study

Eligibility: Open to students from Chile

Level of Study: Postgraduate

Type: Scholarships and fellowships

Value: The University composition fee at the overseas rate, approved college fees, a maintenance allowance sufficient for a single student, contribution towards an economy return airfare

Length of Study: 1 year

Frequency: Annual

Study Establishment: The University of Cambridge

Country of Study: United Kingdom

Application Procedure: Apply directly to the British Council in Chile. Applicants are reminded that they will also need to apply to the Cambridge Trusts on the Scholarship Application Form (SAF) in the usual way

Closing Date: See website for details

Contributor: Offered in collaboration with the Instituto Chileno Britanico de Cultura, the British Council, Chile and Cambridge Assessment (formerly the Local Examinations Syndicate), University of Cambridge

For further information contact:

Email: internationalstudents@admin.cam.ac.uk

Jawaharlal Nehru Memorial Trust Commonwealth Shared Scholarships

Subjects: All subjects

Purpose: To offer financial support

Eligibility: Open to citizens from India. All applicants must be under the age of 35 on October 1st with priority given to those candidates under the age of 30. They must not be employed by a national or local government department or by a parastatal organization, nor at present be living or studying in a developed country and not have undertaken studies lasting a year or more in a developed country. Priority will be given to candidates wishing to pursue a study related to the economic and social development of their country

Level of Study: Postgraduate

Type: Scholarship

Value: The University Composition Fee, approved college fees, annual stipend sufficient for a single student and contribution towards travel costs

Length of Study: 1 year

Frequency: Annual

Study Establishment: The University of Cambridge, Trinity College

Country of Study: United Kingdom

Application Procedure: Applicants may obtain further details and a preliminary application form by writing before August 16th of the year before entry to the Joint Secretary of the Nehru Trust for Cambridge University, giving details of their academic qualifications

Closing Date: 28 February

Contributor: Offered in collaboration with the Jawaharlal Nehru Memorial Trust and the Commonwealth Scholarship Commission

For further information contact:

The Nehru Trust for Cambridge University, Teen Murti House, Teen Murti Marg 53 - 54 Sidney Street, CB2 3HX, Cambridge, United Kingdom

Email: cambridge.trust@admin.cam.ac.uk

Contact: The Joint Secretary

Ministry of Education (Malaysia) Scholarships for Postgraduate Study

Subjects: All subjects

Purpose: To financially support those undertaking postgraduate study

Eligibility: Applicants must be from Malaysia, and must be nominated by the Ministry of Education. Applicants must apply to the University of Cambridge and be offered a place

at Cambridge in the normal way. They must have a First Class or High Second Class (Honours) Degree or equivalent and normally be under 26
Level of Study: Postgraduate
Type: Scholarship
Value: The University Composition Fee at the overseas rate, approved college fees, a maintenance allowance sufficient for a single student and a contribution to return economy airfare
Length of Study: 1 year
Frequency: Annual
Study Establishment: The University of Cambridge
Country of Study: United Kingdom
Application Procedure: Applicants must complete a preliminary application form, which can be obtained from local universities, offices of the British Council or the Trust. Completed forms must be returned to the main address. Shortlisted candidates will be sent forms for admission to the University of Cambridge. The preliminary application form can also be downloaded from www.admin.cam.ac.uk/offices/gradstud/admissions/forms/
Closing Date: 28 February
Contributor: Offered in collaboration with the Malaysian Commonwealth Studies Centre and the Ministry of Education, Government of Malaysia

For further information contact:

Email: education.intoday@gmail.com

Ministry of Science, Technology and the Environment Scholarships for Postgraduate Study (Malaysia)

Subjects: All subjects
Purpose: To financially support those undertaking postgraduate study
Eligibility: Applicants must be from Malaysia, and must be nominated by the Ministry of Science, Technology and the Environment. Applicants must apply to the University of Cambridge and be offered a place at Cambridge in the normal way. They must have a First Class or High Second Class (Honours) Degree or equivalent and normally be under 26
Level of Study: Postgraduate
Type: Scholarship
Value: The University Composition Fee at the overseas rate, approved college fees, a maintenance allowance sufficient for a single student and a contribution to return economy airfare
Length of Study: 1 year
Frequency: Annual
Study Establishment: The University of Cambridge
Country of Study: United Kingdom

Application Procedure: Applicants must complete a preliminary application form, which can be obtained from local universities, offices of the British Council or the Trust. Completed forms must be returned to the main address. Shortlisted candidates will be sent forms for admission to the University of Cambridge. The preliminary application form can also be downloaded from www.admin.cam.ac.uk/offices/gradstud/admissions/forms/
Closing Date: 28 February
Contributor: Offered in collaboration with the Malaysian Commonwealth Studies Centre and the Ministry of Science, Technology and the Environment, Government of Malaysia

For further information contact:

Email: international_scholar@mohe.gov.my

Nehru Trust for the Indian Collections V&A Cambridge DFID Scholarship

Subjects: Archaeology, focusing on archaeological heritage and museums or social anthropology, with special reference to the work of a museum
Purpose: To financially support those undertaking postgraduate study
Eligibility: Applicants must be from India, and must be under the age of 35 on October 1st with priority given to those candidates under the age of 30. Applicants must not be employed by a national or local government department or by a parastatal organization, nor at present be living or studying in a developed country. Priority will be given to candidates wishing to pursue a course of study related to the economic and social development of their country
Level of Study: Postgraduate
Type: Scholarship
Value: The University Composition Fee at the overseas rate, approved college fees, a maintenance allowance sufficient for a single student and a contribution to return economy airfare. In addition a supplementary allowance to cover a short period of practical training at the Victoria and Albert Museum, or other approved institution, will be given
Length of Study: 1 year
Frequency: Annual
Study Establishment: The University of Cambridge
Country of Study: United Kingdom
Application Procedure: Applicants may obtain further details and a preliminary application form by writing before August 16th of the year before entry to the Joint Secretary at the address given below with details of academic qualifications
Closing Date: 28 February

Contributor: Offered in collaboration with the Nehru Trust for the Indian Collections at the Victoria and Albert (V&A) Museum and the Department for International Development (DFID)

Oxford and Cambridge Society of Bombay Cambridge DFID Scholarship

Subjects: All subjects
Purpose: To financially support those undertaking postgraduate study
Eligibility: Open to a resident of Bombay City or the State of Maharashtra whose application is supported by the Oxford and Cambridge Society of Bombay. All applicants must be under the age of 35 on October 1st with priority given to those candidates under the age of 30. They must not be employed by a national or local government department or by a parastatal organization, nor at present be living or studying in a developed country. Priority will be given to candidates wishing to pursue a study related to the economic and social development of their country
Level of Study: Postgraduate
Type: Scholarship
Value: The University Composition Fee at the overseas rate, approved college fees, a maintenance allowance sufficient for a single student and a contribution to return economy airfare
Length of Study: 1 year
Frequency: Annual
Study Establishment: The University of Cambridge
Country of Study: United Kingdom
Application Procedure: Applicants may obtain further details and a preliminary application form by writing before August 16th of the year before entry to the Joint Secretary at address given below with details of academic qualifications
Closing Date: 28 February
Contributor: Offered in collaboration with the Department for International Development (DFID)

Pok Rafeah Cambridge Scholarship

Subjects: All subjects
Purpose: To financially support study towards a PhD
Eligibility: Applicants must be from Malaysia. The Trusts cannot admit students to the University or any of its colleges. Applicants for awards from the Trusts must therefore also apply to the University of Cambridge and be offered a place at Cambridge in the normal way. All applicants must have a First Class or High Second Class (Honours) Degree or equivalent and normally be under 26. Applicants for scholarships for study towards the degree of PhD must be successfully nominated for an Overseas

Research Student (ORS) award, which covers the difference between the home and overseas rate of the University Composition Fee
Level of Study: Doctorate, Postgraduate, Predoctorate
Type: Scholarship
Value: The University Composition Fee at the approved rate, approved college fees, a maintenance allowance sufficient for a single student and a contribution to a return economy airfare
Length of Study: Up to 3 years for PhD study, and 1 year for postgraduate study
Frequency: Annual
Study Establishment: The University of Cambridge
Country of Study: United Kingdom
Application Procedure: Applicants must complete a preliminary application form, which can be obtained from local universities, offices of the British Council or the Trust. The preliminary application form can be downloaded from www.admin.cam.ac.uk/univ/gsprospectus/c7/overseas/schemes.html. Completed forms must be returned to the main address. Shortlisted candidates will be sent forms for admission to the University of Cambridge
Contributor: Offered in collaboration with the Pok Rafeah Foundation
Additional Information: Further information is available on request

For further information contact:

Email: cambridge.trust@admin.cam.ac.uk
Contact: The Secretary

University of Cambridge, Judge Business School

Trumpington Street, CB2 1AG, Cambridge, United Kingdom

Tel: (44) 1223 339 700
Fax: (44) 1223 339 701
Email: enquiries@jbs.cam.ac.uk
Website: www.jims.cam.ac.uk
Contact: Mrs Natacha Wilson

The Judge Business School is the University of Cambridge's business school. Founded in 1990, it offers a portfolio of management programmes, including the Cambridge MBA. Accredited by AMBA and EQUIS, the business school now hosts one of the largest concentrations of interdisciplinary business and management research activity in Europe.

Browns Restaurant Scholarships

Subjects: MBA
Purpose: To provide funds for United Kingdom citizens with a strong interest in the hospitality and tourism industries to study for an MBA
Eligibility: Open to candidates with at least three years of experience in the hospitality or tourism industries. Candidates must show evidence of a career plan showing how they would use the skills and knowledge gained on the MBA course to develop their career within the hospitality or tourism industries. Where an applicant opts for the two year integrated version of the MBA course, arrangements should be in place for the placement year to be in an organisation in the hospitality or tourism industries. Applicants must be United Kingdom citizens
Level of Study: MBA
Type: Scholarship
Value: One scholarship of £20,000 to cover fees and two scholarships of £10,000 to cover roughly half the fees
Length of Study: 1 year
Frequency: Annual
Study Establishment: Judge Institute of Management, University of Cambridge
Country of Study: United Kingdom
Application Procedure: Applicants must complete and submit an application form, together with a covering letter indicating that they would like to apply for a Browns Restaurant Scholarship, to the Judge Institute of Management
Closing Date: The end of March
Funding: Commercial
Contributor: Browns Restaurants Limited

For further information contact:

Email: financial_aid@brown.edu

University of Canberra

The scholarship is funded under the Australian government Research Training Program (RTP) scheme and is available for future and current international students in all research disciplines. The University of Canberra is proudly the university of Australia's capital. UC is one of Australia's top universities for getting a job.

Australian Government Research Training Program (AGRTP) Stipend Scholarship

Subjects: Scholarships are available in Research programme
Purpose: Scholarships are offered in diverse fields to help students in upgrading their education

Eligibility: To be eligible to apply for this scholarship you must: 1. Be an international student. 2. Be seeking to enrol, or enrolled, as a full-time Doctor of Philosophy (PhD) candidate. 3. Have a minimum first-class honours (H1) or be regarded by the University as having an equivalent level of attainment. 4. Not have previously held an Australian Government-funded research scholarship for more than 6 months
Level of Study: Postgraduate
Type: Scholarship
Value: A$26,682 for 2017, tax-free
Length of Study: 3 years
Frequency: Annual
Country of Study: Australia
Application Procedure: The mode of applying is online
Closing Date: 31 October

For further information contact:

The Australian National University, Canberra, ACT 0200, Australia

Tel: (61) 2 6125 5111
Email: student@anu.edu.au

University of Canterbury

College of Arts, University of Canterbury, Private Bag 4800, Christchurch 8140, New Zealand

Tel: (64) 3 364 2426 (ext: 6426)
Fax: (64) 3 364 2683
Email: erin.hird@canterbury.ac.nz
Website: www.canterbury.ac.nz
Contact: Ms Erin Hird, Human Resource Administrator

The University of Canterbury offers a variety of subjects in a few flexible degree structures, namely, first and postgraduate degrees in arts, commerce, education, engineering, fine arts, forestry, law, music and science. At Canterbury, research and teaching are closely related, and while this feature shapes all courses, it is very marked at the postgraduate level.

Dow Agrosciences Bursary in Chemical Engineering

Subjects: Chemical and Process Engineering
Purpose: In 1990, DowElanco (NZ) Limited took over the bursary, formerly offered by Ivon Watkins-Dow Limited, for tenure in the Department of Chemical Engineering. In

January 1998, DowElanco (NZ) Limited changed its name to Dow AgroSciences (NZ) Limited

Eligibility: Must be a full time student who is enrolled for a BE(Hons) in Chemical & Process Engineering. The applicant must have completed, or been exempted from, the First Professional examination

Level of Study: Graduate, Undergraduate

Type: Bursary

Value: NZ$2,500

Frequency: Annual

Country of Study: Any country

Application Procedure: You may apply through this webpage approximately 8 weeks before applications close. If it's possible to apply on-line for this scholarship there will be a link above to the on-line system. If the link is not provided, please download and complete the application form located below. However, if the scholarship is managed by Universities NZ or another department of the University an External Website link will appear below and application instructions will be available through that link

Closing Date: 31 March

Funding: Private

For further information contact:

0800 Varsity, New Zealand

Tel: (64) 800 827 748

Email: enrol@canterbury.ac.nz

Freyberg Scholarship

Purpose: Freyberg Scholarships are awarded to encourage graduate study into areas relevant to national security. Study should be undertaken at a recognised institution in New Zealand or an Asia-Pacific country, including Canada and the United States

Eligibility: Applicants must be New Zealand citizens or permanent residents who meet the following academic requirements: they should normally have obtained at least second class honours, division A, or equivalent in their qualifying degree and have completed academic studies in political science, history, economics or some other discipline that may be considered an appropriate foundation for such study

Level of Study: Graduate

Type: Scholarship

Value: NZ$70,000 will be made annuallyfor the award of one or more scholarship

Frequency: Annual

Country of Study: New Zealand

Application Procedure: Apply online. check the below link for further information. www.universitiesnz.ac.nz/scholarships/freyberg-scholarship

Closing Date: 1 October

Funding: Private

For further information contact:

Email: scholarships-cf@universitiesnz.ac.nz

Gordon Watson Scholarship

Purpose: The general purpose of the scholarship is to enable New Zealanders to study international relationships or social and economic conditions at a university overseas. Candidates will be planning to study at Masters or PhD level

Eligibility: 1. Graduated with or be graduating with an Honours or Masters degree in arts, science, commerce, law or divinity from a New Zealand university. 2. New Zealand citizens or permanent residents

Level of Study: Postgraduate

Type: Scholarship

Value: NZ$12,000

Length of Study: Up to two years for Masters and up to three years for a PhD

Country of Study: New Zealand

Application Procedure: Apply online. universitiesnz.communityforce.com

Closing Date: 1 March

Funding: Private

Additional Information: Please note that to be eligible a planned Masters degree must have a substantial research component, i.e. at least half

For further information contact:

Level 9, 142 Lambton Quay, Wellington PO Box 11915, Wellington 6142, New Zealand

Tel: (64) 4 381 8500

Email: scholarships-cf@universitiesnz.ac.nz

Kitchener Memorial Scholarship

Purpose: The Kitchener Memorial Scholarship Fund offers scholarships to past or present members of the Armed Forces or their children, who are undertaking an agricultural course of study at a New Zealand university

Eligibility: Applicants must be either; 1. Past or present members of the Armed Forces or children of past or present members of the Armed Forces who have seen active service and who, at the time of enlistment, were domiciled in New Zealand, whether actually resident there or not, or. 2. Past or present members of the Armed Forces or their children to whom the above does not apply, or. 3. People resident in New Zealand for a period of not less than three years immediately before the award of the scholarship

Level of Study: Graduate
Type: Scholarship
Value: NZ$500
Frequency: Annual
Country of Study: Any country
Closing Date: 1 December
Funding: Private

Lighthouse Vision Trust Scholarship

Purpose: The scholarships support students with a vision impairment in undertaking study at the University of Canterbury. It was established in 2016 by the Lighthouse Vision Trust
Eligibility: 1 Applicants must have a vision impairment that qualifies them to register with the Blind Foundation. 2 By the closing date for applications, an applicant must have registered with the University's Disability Resource Service as a student with a vision impairment. 3 Applicants must be citizens of New Zealand or holders of New Zealand residence class visas. 4 Applicants must be enrolled, full-time or part-time, at the University at either undergraduate or postgraduate level
Level of Study: Postgraduate, Undergraduate
Type: Scholarship
Value: Up to NZ$10,000 can be received as total value
Length of Study: 1 year
Frequency: Annual
Country of Study: Any country
Application Procedure: 1 Applications must be made online at the Scholarships website3 by 31 March. 2 Applicants will be considered for both scholarships, and the decision on which of the top candidates will be offered which of the two scholarships will be made randomly. 3 A previous recipient of Lighthouse Vision Trust Scholarship or a Susan Barnes Memorial Scholarship may re-apply for the scholarship that they held, and a previous recipient of one of the scholarships may apply for the other scholarship in another year. However, no student may hold one of the scholarships or a combination of the two scholarships over a total period of more than three years
Closing Date: 31 March
Funding: Private

For further information contact:

Email: enrol@canterbury.ac.nz

Marian D Eve Memorial Scholarship

Purpose: This scholarship supports students studying, researching, or developing, resources for early-childhood special-needs education at the University of Canterbury
Eligibility: Recipients must be undergraduate or postgraduate students who are enrolled full-time at the University and studying, researching, or developing, in any discipline, resources for early-childhood special-needs education
Level of Study: Graduate, Postgraduate
Type: Scholarship
Value: NZ$2,000
Frequency: Annual
Country of Study: Any country
Application Procedure: You may apply through this webpage approximately 8 weeks before applications close. If it's possible to apply on-line for this scholarship there will be a link above to the on-line system. Apply through online link. www.studyinnewzealand.govt.nz/how-to-apply/scholarship/details?scholarshipid=25668&institutionid=142318
Closing Date: 1 April
Funding: Private

McKelvey Award

Purpose: This award supports master's and PhD students in the New Zealand School of Forestry at the University of Canterbury. Normally, the award is available to assist students to present a paper at a relevant conference. However, in the absence of suitable applications, the applications may be opened to eligible students seeking support to meet other costs associated with their study
Eligibility: Forestry
Level of Study: Postgraduate
Type: Scholarship
Value: $1,000
Frequency: Annual
Country of Study: Any country
Application Procedure: Apply online
Closing Date: 1 April
Funding: Foundation

For further information contact:

Email: scholarships-cf@universitiesnz.ac.nz

Park and Paulay Scholarship

Purpose: This scholarship acknowledges and rewards a top performer in the first two Professional years of the programme for a Bachelor of Engineering (Honours) degree in Civil Engineering at the University of Canterbury

Eligibility: Full-time students in the Third Professional Year of the programme for the Bachelor of Engineering (Honours) degree in Civil Engineering (BE(Hons)(Civil)) at the University of Canterbury, who are enrolled in at least four courses related to Structural or Geotechnical or Earthquake Engineering

Level of Study: Graduate

Type: Scholarship

Value: NZ$2,000

Frequency: Annual

Country of Study: Any country

Application Procedure: You may apply through this webpage approximately 8 weeks before applications close. If it's possible to apply on-line for this scholarship there will be a link above to the on-line system. If the link is not provided, please download and complete the application form located below. Closing dates are yet to be released for the same

Closing Date: 31 March

Funding: Private

For further information contact:

Email: info@canterbury.ac.nz

Wood Technology Research Centre – Postgraduate Scholarships

Subjects: Chemical engineering

Purpose: To develop a computer model to simulate energy flow and energy efficiency in wood and wood product processing industry

Level of Study: Postgraduate

Type: Scholarship

Value: NZ$24,000 per year for PhD and $18,000 per year for ME

Length of Study: 3 years for PhD and one and half year for ME

Application Procedure: To apply or for further information on the above scholarships, please contact Dr Shusheng Pang

Closing Date: See website for details

Contributor: University of Canterbury

Additional Information: Case studies will be conducted for manufacturing of Laminated Veneer Lumber (LVL) and Medium Density Fibreboard (MDF). The project will be conduced in collaboration with the University of Otago and a wood processing company

For further information contact:

Wood Technology Centre, Department of Chemical and Process Engineering, University of Canterbury, Christchurch, New Zealand

Tel:	(64) 3 364 2538
Fax:	(64) 3 364 2063
Email:	shusheng.pang@canterbury.ac.nz
Contact:	Dr Shusheng Pang, Associate Professor and Director

University of Canterbury, Department of Management

Private Bag 4800, Christchurch, New Zealand

Tel:	(64) 3 364 2808
Fax:	(64) 3 364 2325
Email:	s.worrall@mang.canterbury.ac.nz
Website:	www.regy.canterbury.ac.nz.home.html
Contact:	Mrs Suzanne Worrall, MBA Programme Director

Auckland Council Chief Economist's Research Scholarship in Economics

Subjects: Economics

Purpose: The purpose of this scholarship is to encourage and support postgraduate research into urban economics that has particular relevance to local government in New Zealand

Eligibility: 1. At the time of application candidates must be enrolled or planning to enrol in a postgraduate programme at a New Zealand university. 2. The postgraduate programme must be in the area of urban economics. Universities NZ and Auckland Council reserve the right to determine the eligibility of a particular area of study. 3. A thesis, dissertation, or research report must be a requirement of the postgraduate programme

Level of Study: Postgraduate

Type: Scholarship

Value: NZ$3,000

Length of Study: 1 year

Frequency: Varies

Country of Study: Any country

Application Procedure: Apply online: universitiesnz. communityforce.com/

Closing Date: 5 March

Funding: Foundation

Additional Information: For candidates who are enrolled on a part time basis the value of the award will be NZ$1,500. The award is intended to help with tuition fees and research costs (e.g. data costs), and to contribute towards living costs

For further information contact:

Level 9, Pacific Radiology Building, 142 Lambton Quay, PO Box 11915, Wellington 6142, New Zealand

Tel: (64) 4 381 8500
Email: scholarships-cf@universitiesnz.ac.nz

Barbara Mito Reed Award

Subjects: Japanese
Purpose: The award was established in memory of Dr Barbara Mito Reed (1955-1990), a graduate in Japanese of the University of Canterbury, by her husband, Mr T. Mito, her family and her friends. It was established to help outstanding graduate students of Japanese, whose native language is not Japanese, to further their studies towards a higher degree in a field of Japanese language and/or culture
Eligibility: The scholarship is open to graduates of the University of Canterbury enrolled, or intending to enrol, in a postgraduate programme in a field of Japanese studies at the University of Canterbury or at a university in Japan. Normally, the programme will be for a BA(Hons), master's or doctoral degree. The scholarship is open to citizens or Permanent Residents of New Zealand, excluding native speakers of Japanese
Level of Study: Postgraduate
Type: Scholarship
Value: NZ$1,000
Length of Study: 1 year
Frequency: Annual
Country of Study: Any country
Application Procedure: Apply online universitiesnz. communityforce.com/
Closing Date: 31 March
Funding: Foundation

For further information contact:

Email: scholarships@canterbury.ac.nz

BayTrust Bruce Cronin Scholarship

Subjects: All subjects
Purpose: This scholarship has been established to recognise his service to the people of the Bay of Plenty
Eligibility: Applicants will be eligible if they were born in, or attended school in, or have whakapapa back to the area

Level of Study: Postgraduate
Type: Scholarship
Value: NZ$5,000
Length of Study: 1 year
Frequency: Annual
Country of Study: Any country
Application Procedure: Apply online
Closing Date: 1 February
Funding: Foundation

For further information contact:

73 Spring Street, Tauranga 3141, New Zealand

Email: info@baytrust.org.nz

Christchurch City Council Antarctic Scholarship

Subjects: Antarctic Studies
Purpose: The Christchurch City Council offers a $10,000 one-year scholarship for a University of Canterbury student to carry out Antarctic or Southern Ocean research at master's or PhD level. The scholarship includes one season of logistical support provided by Antarctica New Zealand
Eligibility: A candidate who, during the tenure of the scholarship, is studying for a PhD or is in the thesis year of a master's degree at the University of Canterbury in an Antarctic-related topic
Level of Study: Postgraduate
Type: Scholarship
Value: NZ$10,000
Length of Study: 1 year
Frequency: Varies
Country of Study: Any country
Application Procedure: Apply online through link www. antarcticanz.govt.nz/scholarships-and-fellowships
Closing Date: 12 March
Funding: Foundation

For further information contact:

International Antarctic Centre, 38 Orchard Road, Christchurch 8053, New Zealand

Email: adrian.mcdonald@canterbury.ac.nz

Deutscher Akademischer Austauschdienst (German Academic Exchange Service) Scholarships

Subjects: All subjects

Purpose: The DAAD supports over 100,000 German and international students and researchers around the globe each year – making it the world's largest funding organisation of its kind

Eligibility: Graduates of all disciplines can apply for a scholarship to complete a postgraduate or Master's degree course at a German higher education institution and to gain a degree in Germany (Master's/Diploma)

Level of Study: Postgraduate

Type: Scholarship

Value: NZ€750

Length of Study: 10-24 Months

Frequency: Annual

Country of Study: Any country

Application Procedure: Apply online

Closing Date: 15 October

Funding: Trusts

For further information contact:

Embassy of the Federal Republic of Germany, PO Box 1687, Wellington, New Zealand

Email: daad@auckland.ac.nz

Ernest William File Scholarship

Purpose: The purpose of the scholarship is to support the sons and daughters of members of the Rail and Maritime Transport Union (RMTU) in their first year of degree study at a New Zealand university

Eligibility: 1. Sons or daughters of financial members of the RMTU. 2. Enrolled or planning on enrolling in their first year of full time study for an undergraduate degree at a New Zealand university. Applications will not be accepted from anyone who already has a qualification from a tertiary institution in New Zealand or overseas

Level of Study: Graduate

Type: Scholarship

Value: NZ$2,000

Frequency: Annual

Country of Study: New Zealand

Closing Date: 1 April

Funding: Private

Francis Martin Baillie Reynolds Scholarship in Law to Oxford

Subjects: All Subjects

Purpose: The purpose of the scholarship is to assist New Zealand Law graduates to commence postgraduate study in Law at the University of Oxford. It has been established to recognise the support that Emeritus Professor

Francis Reynolds, Worcester College, Oxford, has provided to New Zealand Law students at the University of Oxford for over 40 years

Eligibility: 1. A New Zealand citizen or permanent resident. 2. Has completed the requirements for a LLB degree from a New Zealand University. 3. The date of application has applied for a place in a postgraduate programme in Law at the University of Oxford

Level of Study: Postgraduate

Type: Scholarship

Value: NZ$10,000

Length of Study: 1 year

Frequency: Annual

Country of Study: Any country

Application Procedure: Apply online through link universitiesnz.communityforce.com

Closing Date: 28 February

Funding: Trusts

Frank Knox Memorial Fellowships at Harvard University

Subjects: All subjects

Purpose: Annie Reid Knox set up these scholarships to honour her late husband and asked that future scholars be selected on the basis of future promise of leadership, strength of character, keen mind, a balanced judgement and a devotion to the democratic ideal

Eligibility: 1. New Zealand citizens at the time of application, normally resident in New Zealand. 2. Have completed or will complete a first or higher degree at a New Zealand university. 3. Studying for a first or higher degree; or have completed a first or higher degree and graduated no earlier than 2014

Level of Study: Postgraduate

Type: Fellowship

Length of Study: 2 year

Frequency: Annual

Country of Study: Any country

Application Procedure: Apply online through the link universitiesnz.communityforce.com

Closing Date: 1 November

Funding: Trusts

For further information contact:

Email: rbauerlock@fas.harvard.edu

G B Battersby-Trimble Scholarship in Computer Science

Subjects: Computer Science

Purpose: The income from the trust fund is added to an annual grant from Trimble Navigation N Z Ltd. The Trimble grant has been given in recognition of the long service provided by the late Dr Battersby to the University and to the computing profession

Eligibility: Enrolled in final-year Honours, Master's or PhD level study at Canterbury, for advancing study in Computer Science that will be of benefit to NZ

Level of Study: Postgraduate

Type: Scholarship

Value: NZ$4,000

Length of Study: 1 year

Frequency: Annual

Country of Study: Any country

Application Procedure: Apply online: universitiesnz. communityforce.com

Closing Date: 31 March

Funding: Trusts

For further information contact:

Email: scholarships@canterbury.ac.nz

Gateway Antarctica's Ministry of Foreign Affairs and Trade Scholarship in Antarctic and Southern Ocean Studies

Subjects: Antarctic

Purpose: The Ministry of Foreign Affairs and Trade (MFAT) Scholarship was founded in 2001 in support of research and teaching in Antarctic Studies in recognition of Antarctica as a continent devoted to peace and research

Eligibility: PhD or master's thesis students are eligible. The scholar is required to undertake research concerning a matter of importance to the understanding of Antarctica or the Southern Ocean

Level of Study: Postgraduate

Type: Scholarship

Value: NZ$5,000

Length of Study: 1 year

Frequency: Varies

Country of Study: Any country

Application Procedure: Apply online

Closing Date: 28 February

Funding: Foundation

Geography Students Conference Fund

Subjects: Geography

Purpose: The fund was raised by Geography graduates, associates and the Canterbury Branch of the New Zealand

Geographical Society to commemorate the golden jubilee of the Department of Geography in 1987

Eligibility: The fund provides grants-in-aid to research students in the Department of Geography to assist with expenses involved in attending conferences. Priority will be given to conferences of the New Zealand Geographical Society

Level of Study: Postgraduate

Type: Scholarship

Value: NZ$500

Length of Study: 1 year

Frequency: Varies

Country of Study: Any country

Application Procedure: Apply online: universitiesnz. communityforce.com

Closing Date: 31 March

Funding: Trusts

Gertrude Ardagh Holmes Bursary Fund

Subjects: All subjects

Purpose: The bursaries shall be for the purpose of assisting students of ability and good character to commence or to continue their studies at the University of Canterbury, who would otherwise by reason of their financial circumstances be unable to do so or be seriously handicapped in doing so. Preference shall be given to students who desire to undertake a medical course. Assistance may be continued to such students after they have proceeded to a medical or dental school in another New Zealand university

Eligibility: Grants are for students to commence or continue study at the University of Canterbury and who face financial hardship. Preference will be given to those who wish to pursue a medical course

Level of Study: Postgraduate

Type: Scholarship

Value: NZ$600

Frequency: Varies

Country of Study: Any country

Application Procedure: Apply online: universitiesnz. communityforce.com

Closing Date: 31 March

Funding: Foundation

For further information contact:

Email: scholarships@canterbury.ac.nz

Grant Lingard Scholarship

Subjects: A scholarship in his name is offered at the University of Canterbury, Christchurch, New Zealand

Purpose: These scholarships were established by the estate of Peter Lanini in memory of Grant Lingard (1961-1995), a graduate of the School of Fine Arts:-

Level of Study: Graduate

Type: Scholarship

Frequency: Annual

Country of Study: New Zealand

Application Procedure: You may apply through this webpage approximately 8 weeks before applications close. If it's possible to apply on-line for this scholarship there will be a link above to the on-line system. If the link is not provided, please download and complete the application form located below. Please check the website with the following link. scholarshipscanterbury.communityforce.com

Closing Date: 31 October

Funding: Private

For further information contact:

0800 Varsity, New Zealand

Tel: (64) 800 827 748
Tel: (64) 3 369 4900
Email: scholarships@canterbury.ac.nz

Henry Kelsey Scholarship

Subjects: All subjects

Purpose: The purpose of the scholarship is to provide funds for individuals to undertake research towards a PhD at a - New Zealand university or research institution, studying muscular function, including the causes and treatment of muscular dysfunction

Eligibility: Applicants will be New Zealand citizens or permanent residents, and will have a Bachelor degree or equivalent, with honours where they are awarded, in a field appropriate to their intended doctoral study at a New Zealand university

Level of Study: Postgraduate

Type: Scholarship

Value: NZ$10,000

Length of Study: 3 year

Frequency: Varies

Country of Study: Any country

Application Procedure: Apply online: universitiesnz. communityforce.com

Closing Date: 1 October

Funding: Trusts

Joan Burns Memorial Scholarship in History

Subjects: History

Purpose: This scholarship recognises and supports academic excellence by honours and master's students in History at the

University of Canterbury. It was established from a 1995 bequest from Joan Mary Burns

Eligibility: Applicants must be enrolled full-time or part-time in a Bachelor of Arts with Honours degree programme or in Part 1 of a Master of Arts degree programme

Level of Study: Postgraduate

Type: Scholarship

Value: Stipend equivalent to domestic tuition fees

Length of Study: 1 year

Frequency: Annual

Country of Study: Any country

Application Procedure: Apply online: universitiesnz. communityforce.com

Closing Date: 31 March

Funding: Private

Kia Ora Foundation Patricia Pratt Scholarship

Subjects: Overseas

Purpose: The purpose of the Kia Ora Foundation Patricia Pratt Music Scholarship is to assist outstanding New Zealand musical performers, who have completed the equivalent of an honours degree in musical performance in New Zealand, to continue their musical development at a renowned international music school or conservatorium

Eligibility: Applicants will be New Zealand citizens. Applicants may apply from outside New Zealand but must have resided in New Zealand for at least three of the last five years immediately preceding the year of selection. Applicants will have recently completed the requirements for an honours degree in musical performance at a New Zealand university (or an equivalent musical qualification)

Level of Study: Postgraduate

Type: Scholarship

Value: NZ$70,000

Length of Study: 1 year

Frequency: Annual

Country of Study: Any country

Application Procedure: Apply online: universitiesnz. communityforce.com

Closing Date: 1 March

Funding: Foundation

Kiwi Music Scholarship

Subjects: All subjects

Purpose: The purpose of the scholarship is to assist outstanding New Zealand musical performers or conductors who have completed or are completing an honours or master's degree in musical performance in New Zealand to continue their musical development either overseas or in New Zealand

Eligibility: Applicants will have completed or are completing an honours or masters degree in musical performance

(including vocal performance) or conducting at a New Zealand university, or an equivalent musical qualification
Level of Study: Postgraduate
Type: Scholarship
Value: NZ$50,000–$60,000
Length of Study: 3 year
Frequency: Varies
Country of Study: Any country
Application Procedure: Apply online universitiesnz. communityforce.com
Closing Date: 1 March
Funding: Trusts

L B Wood Travelling Scholarship

Subjects: Overseas
Purpose: The LB Wood Traveling Scholarship is awarded to supplement some other postgraduate scholarship held by the scholar supporting their studies in Britain. The scholarship can only be awarded for postgraduate study at a university or institution of university rank in Britain
Eligibility: Applicants must be graduates of a New Zealand university. No distinction is made regarding subject, disciple or faculty
Level of Study: Postgraduate
Type: Scholarship
Value: NZ$3,000
Length of Study: 3 years
Frequency: Annual
Country of Study: Any country
Application Procedure: Apply online universitiesnz. communityforce.com/Login.aspx
Closing Date: 1 March
Funding: Foundation

LB Wood Scholarship

Subjects: All subjects
Purpose: 1. The LB Wood Traveling Scholarship is awarded to supplement some other postgraduate scholarship held by the scholar supporting their studies in Britain. 2. The scholarship can only be awarded for postgraduate study at a university or institution of university rank in Britain
Eligibility: Applicants must be graduates of a New Zealand university. No distinction is made regarding subject, disciple or faculty
Level of Study: Postgraduate
Type: Scholarship
Value: NZ$3,000
Length of Study: 3 year
Frequency: Varies
Country of Study: Any country

Application Procedure: Apply online: universitiesnz. communityforce.com
Closing Date: 1 March
Funding: Trusts

Master of Business Administration Programme

Length of Study: 1 to 5 years
Application Procedure: Applicants must complete an application form, a self-evaluation essay, supply an original transcript or a certified copy of grades and provide two references
Closing Date: Please contact the Organisation

For further information contact:

Tel: (64) 3 364 2657
Fax: (64) 3 364 2925
Email: international@regy.canterbury.ac.nz
Contact: International Manager

New Zealand Law Foundation Ethel Benjamin Scholarship (for women)

Subjects: Law
Purpose: To support postgraduate research in Law that encompasses the wider objectives of the NZ Law Foundation, in particular research that will protect and promote the interests of the public in relation to legal matters in New Zealand
Eligibility: 1. A New Zealand citizen or permanent resident. 2. The holder of a New Zealand university law degree. 3. Accepted into a postgraduate course in law at either a New Zealand or an overseas university acceptable to the Selection Committee
Level of Study: Postgraduate
Type: Scholarship
Value: NZ$20,000- $50,000
Length of Study: 1 year
Frequency: Annual
Country of Study: Any country
Application Procedure: Apply online universitiesnz. communityforce.com
Closing Date: 1 March
Funding: Trusts

Prince of Wales' Cambridge International Scholarship

Subjects: All subjects
Purpose: Each year the Cambridge Commonwealth, European & International Trust www.cambridgetrust.org/ offers several prestigious awards to enable graduates of high academic ability to study at Cambridge University

Eligibility: These scholarships are open to graduates who are New Zealand citizens and who wish to pursue a course of research leading to the degree of PhD at Cambridge University
Level of Study: Postgraduate
Type: Scholarship
Length of Study: 3 years
Frequency: Varies
Country of Study: Any country
Application Procedure: Apply online: universitiesnz. communityforce.com
Closing Date: 1 October
Funding: Trusts

For further information contact:

Email: cambridge.trust@admin.cam.ac.uk

Pukehou Poutu Scholarship

Subjects: Pukehou Poutu Scholarship. The money for this scholarship has been made available by a bequest from the estate of Edith Fraser who wished that it be used for an award in agricultural or silvicultural sciences
Purpose: The money for this scholarship has been made available by a bequest from the estate of Edith Fraser who wished that it be used for an award in agricultural or silvicultural sciences
Eligibility: Applicants must be graduates of a New Zealand university and be New Zealand citizens
Level of Study: Postgraduate
Type: Scholarship
Value: NZ$10,000
Length of Study: 1 year
Frequency: Annual
Country of Study: New Zealand
Application Procedure: Apply online universitiesnz. communityforce.com
Closing Date: 1 October
Funding: Foundation

Roland Stead Postgraduate Scholarship in Biology

Subjects: Biological Sciences
Purpose: This scholarship supports Master's research students of biology with an interest in ecology, freshwater fisheries and the Canterbury region
Eligibility: The scholarship will be available to full-time students in the School of Biological Sciences who are engaged in research in Part II of the Master of Science degree programme

Level of Study: Postgraduate
Type: Scholarship
Value: NZ$5,000
Length of Study: 1 year
Frequency: Annual
Country of Study: Any country
Application Procedure: Apply online: myuc.canterbury.ac. nz/sso
Closing Date: 10 March
Funding: Foundation

For further information contact:

Email: scholarships@canterbury.ac.nz

Sir Douglas Myers Scholarship

Purpose: The Scholarship provides an opportunity for students who have already distinguished themselves academically to attend one of the most prestigious universities in the world
Eligibility: Candidates for the Scholarship must: 1. Be entered for the Year 13 senior school examination (for example, NCEA Level 3, Cambridge exams, etc.) or equivalent senior school exam in the year of application. 2. Have a record of achievement sufficient to satisfy the academic criteria for entry to Cambridge University and Gonville and Caius College. 3. Be New Zealand citizens or permanent residents. 4. Normally have completed their five years of secondary schooling in New Zealand
Level of Study: Graduate
Type: Scholarship
Value: One scholarship is awarded each year and provides tuition fees and a living allowance
Frequency: Annual
Country of Study: Any country
Application Procedure: Check your eligibility. Read the Regulations. Applications must be done online. A link to the application website is here. www.universitiesnz.ac.nz/ scholarships/sir-douglas-myers-scholarship
Closing Date: 1 December
Funding: Private

The Claude McCarthy Fellowships

Subjects: All subjects
Purpose: Claude McCarthy Fellowships (Category A) are available to candidates who are graduates of a New Zealand university and who are enrolled in a PhD programme at a New Zealand university
Eligibility: 1. A graduate of a New Zealand university. 2. Registered for a doctoral degree at a New Zealand university.

3. Have been registered for their doctoral degree for at least one year at the closing date for applications
Level of Study: Postgraduate
Type: Scholarship
Value: NZ$5,000
Length of Study: 1 year
Frequency: Annual
Country of Study: Any country
Application Procedure: Apply online: universitiesnz.communityforce.com/
Closing Date: 1 April; 1 October
Funding: Trusts

The Dick and Mary Earle Scholarship in Technology

Subjects: All subjects
Purpose: The purpose of the scholarship is to provide funds for individuals to undertake research towards a masterate or doctorate degree at a New Zealand university or research institution in one or both of these fields: 1. Innovation and product development. 2. Bioprocess technology
Eligibility: 1. Applicants will be New Zealand citizens or permanent residents who have resided in New Zealand for at least three years immediately preceding the year of selection. 2. Applicants will have completed the requirements for a BTech, BEng, BE degree or equivalent, with honours where they are awarded, at a New Zealand university and in a field appropriate to their intended postgraduate study
Level of Study: Postgraduate
Type: Scholarship
Value: Up to NZ$17,000 per annum at Masters level and NZ$25,000 per annum at PhD level
Length of Study: 3 year
Frequency: Varies
Country of Study: Any country
Application Procedure: Apply online: universitiesnz.communityforce.com
Closing Date: 1 September
Funding: Trusts

The Edward & Isabel Kidson Scholarship

Subjects: All subjects
Purpose: The purpose of the scholarships is to enable a graduate of a New Zealand university, who is of good character and who has shown an ability in physics or a combination of physics and mathematics, to undertake further advanced study or research in meteorology, either in New Zealand or elsewhere
Eligibility: Applicants should be graduates of a New Zealand university, be of good character and have shown ability in

physics or a combination of physics and mathematics. 1. Past pupils of Nelson Boys' College. 2. Graduates of the University of Canterbury
Level of Study: Postgraduate
Type: Scholarship
Value: NZ$6,000
Length of Study: 3 year
Frequency: Annual
Country of Study: Any country
Application Procedure: Apply online
Closing Date: 1 October
Funding: Trusts

The Judith Clark Memorial Fellowships

Subjects: The Judith Clark Memorial Fellowships have been established to assist recent music graduates undertake a special sort-term project that will have long-term benefits for their future professional careers as musicians. Projects that will be considered by the selection committee include attendance at a reputable summer school or summer academy, or auditions for a longer-term postgraduate study programme
Purpose: The Judith Clark Memorial Fellowships have been established to assist music graduates undertake a special short-term project that will have long term benefits for their future professional careers as musicians
Eligibility: Applicants must hold New Zealand citizenship or permanent residency and must have recently graduated, or expect to graduate in the year of application, with an Honours degree, or equivalent, in music from a New Zealand university
Level of Study: Postgraduate
Type: Fellowship/Scholarship
Value: NZ$15,000
Length of Study: 1 year
Frequency: Varies
Country of Study: Any country
Application Procedure: Apply online universitiesnz.communityforce.com
Closing Date: 15 August and 15 February
Funding: Foundation
Additional Information: There are two application rounds available Round 1 : Principally to the support the cost of attending auditions in the November to February period. Round 2: Principally to support attendance at a summer school or summer academy in the May to August period

The Kia Ora Foundation Patricia Pratt Music Scholarship

Subjects: Overseas

Purpose: The purpose of the Kia Ora Foundation Patricia Pratt Music Scholarship is to assist outstanding New Zealand musical performers, who have completed the equivalent of an honours degree in musical performance in New Zealand, to continue their musical development at a renowned international music school or conservatorium

Eligibility: Applicants will be New Zealand citizens. Applicants may apply from outside New Zealand but must have resided in New Zealand for at least three of the last five years immediately preceding the year of selection. Applicants will have recently completed the requirements for an honours degree in musical performance at a New Zealand university (or an equivalent musical qualification)

Level of Study: Postgraduate

Type: Scholarship

Value: NZ$70,000

Length of Study: 2 years

Frequency: Varies

Country of Study: Any country

Application Procedure: Apply online: universitiesnz. communityforce.com

Closing Date: 1 March

Funding: Trusts

University of Canterbury Doctoral Scholarship

Purpose: These scholarships support students for study towards a research doctoral degree at the University of Canterbury. Approximately 60 scholarships are available each year, over two annual application rounds

Eligibility: The scholarships are tenable by full-time and part-time students engaged in study for a research doctoral degree at UC. An applicant must have completed an appropriate qualification at a level judged to be equivalent to a bachelor's or master's degree with first-class honours at UC (equivalent to a UC GPA of at least 7.0)

Level of Study: Postgraduate

Type: Scholarship

Value: NZ$21,000 per 120 points of thesis enrolment

Frequency: Every 3 years

Country of Study: Any country

Application Procedure: Apply online thro below link. www. canterbury.ac.nz/scholarships/

Closing Date: 15 May

Funding: Private

For further information contact:

Tel: (64) 3 369 4900

Email: scholarships@canterbury.ac.nz

Woolf Fischer Scholarship

Purpose: The Woolf Fisher Trust offers up to three Scholarships each year tenable at the University of Cambridge for three or four years of postgraduate research leading to a doctoral degree or equivalent

Eligibility: The Scholarships are open to New Zealand citizens who: a. are under the age of 30 in the year of application. b. attended a secondary school in New Zealand. c. have graduated or are expected to graduate with a first-class honours degree from a university in New Zealand. No application will be considered from a student already living outside of New Zealand and no award will be made for post-doctoral study

Level of Study: Graduate

Type: Scholarship

Value: maintenance allowance of NZ£15,000 sterling per annum,

Frequency: Every 3 years

Country of Study: New Zealand

Application Procedure: You may apply through this webpage approximately 8 weeks before applications close. If it's possible to apply on-line for this scholarship there will be a link above to the on-line system. For further details, visit the website. www.universitiesnz.ac.nz/scholarships/woolf-fisher-scholarship

Closing Date: 1 August

Funding: Private

University of Cape Town

University of Cape Town, Private Bag X3, Rondebosch, 7701, South Africa

Tel: (27) 21 650 3622

Fax: (27) 21 650 4352

Email: pgfunding@uct.ac.za

University of Cape Town (UCT) is very similar to the city of Cape Town: it has a vibrant, cosmopolitan community. It is a cultural melting pot where each person contributes their unique blend of knowledge and thinking. Our staff and students come from over 100 countries in Africa and the rest of the world. The university has also built links, partnerships and exchange agreements with leading African and international institutions that further enrich the academic, social and cultural diversity of our campus.

University of Cape Town Masters Scholarships in Public Health

Purpose: To support the training of eye health professionals with strong public health skills, the Consortium offers scholarships for candidates from low- and middle-income African Commonwealth countries who have been accepted to study for a Masters Public Health, Community Eye Health at the University of Cape Town, South Africa

Eligibility: Applicants must come from a low- or middle-income African Commonwealth country to apply. Funding is available for postgraduate studies only. The bursaries are awarded on a yearly basis

Level of Study: Postgraduate

Country of Study: South Africa

Application Procedure: Check website for more details

Closing Date: 31 July

Funding: Trusts

University of Delaware

Department of History, Newark, DE 19716, United States of America

Tel:	(1) 302 831 8226
Fax:	(1) 302 831 1538
Email:	dianec@udel.edu
Website:	www.udel.edu
Contact:	Ms Diane Clark, Administrative Assistant

The Department of History offers MA and PhD programmes in American and European history and more limited graduate study Ancient, African, Asian, Latin American, and Middle Eastern history. In conjunction with these, it offers special programmes in the history of industrialization, material culture studies, American Civilization, and museum studies.

Executive MBA Programme

Length of Study: 1 year;3 years

Application Procedure: Applicants must complete an application form supplying US$45 fee, transcripts, Graduate Management Admission Test score, TOEFL score and two letters of recommendation

Closing Date: Varies

For further information contact:

Tel:	(1) 302 831 2221
Fax:	(1) 302 831 3329
Email:	E-MBA@strauss.udel.edu
Contact:	MBA Admissions Officer

University of Derby

Kedleston Rd, Derby DE22 1GB, United Kingdom

Tel:	(44) 1332 590 500
Website:	www.derby.ac.uk
Contact:	University of Derby

The University of Derby is a public university in the city of Derby, United Kingdom. It traces its history back to the establishment of the Derby Diocesan Institution for the Training of Schoolmistresses in 1851 and gained university status in 1992 as one of the new universities.

International Scholarships at University of Derby

Subjects: Scholarships are awarded to study the subjects offered by the university

Purpose: The University of Derby is offering international scholarships for the academic year. These scholarships are available to apply for once you have received an offer on a course from the University

Eligibility: These scholarships are available to apply for once you have received an offer on a course from the University. International students are eligible to apply

Type: Postgraduate scholarships

Value: Varies

Study Establishment: Scholarships are awarded to study the subjects offered by the university

Country of Study: United Kingdom

Application Procedure: The mode of applying is online

Closing Date: 14 January

Additional Information: For more details please visit the website scholarship-positions.com/international-scholarships-university-derby-uk/2017/09/29/

For further information contact:

Email:	iadmissions@derby.ac.uk

University of Dundee

Nethergate, Dundee DD1 4HN, United Kingdom

Tel:	(44) 13 8234 5028
Fax:	(44) 13 8234 5343
Email:	j.e.nicholson@dundee.ac.uk
Website:	www.dundee.ac.uk
Contact:	Postgraduate Office

The University of Dundee is one of United Kingdom's leading universities, named Scottish University of the Year 2004/2005 (Sunday Times) and ranked top for teaching quality in 2005 (THES). It is internationally recognised for its expertise across a range of disciplines including science, medicine, engineering and art and graduates more people into the professions than any other university in Scotland.

Master of Business Administration Programme

Length of Study: 2 years; 5 years
Application Procedure: Applicants must complete an application form supplying UK£25 fee, two academic references, official transcripts and evidence of English Language proficiency if applicable
Closing Date: Varies

For further information contact:

Tel:	(44) 1382 344300
Fax:	(44) 1382 228578
Email:	cepmlp@dundee.ac.uk
Contact:	MBA Admissions Officer

University of East Anglia (UEA)

Faculty of Arts and Humanities, School of Literature and Creative Writing, Norwich NR4 7TJ, United Kingdom

Tel:	(44) 16 0345 6161
Fax:	(44) 16 0350 7728
Website:	www.uea.ac.uk/lit/fellowships
Contact:	Fellowship Administrator

The University of East Anglia (UEA) is organized into 23 schools of study encompassing arts and humanities, health, sciences and social sciences. These are supported by central service and administration departments.

University of East Anglia International Development Scholarships

Subjects: Masters degree courses offered by the School of International Development
Purpose: The University of East Anglia is offering one full fee scholarship for international students towards Masters Degree courses offered by the School of International Development
Eligibility: The scholarships are awarded on the basis of academic excellence (e.g. first class degree) and their personal statement. All applicants are expected to have met the School's English language requirements and been offered and accepted a place on the course by the deadline
Level of Study: Postgraduate
Type: Scholarship
Value: Full fees for masters degree programme
Frequency: Annual
Study Establishment: University of East Anglia
Country of Study: United Kingdom
Application Procedure: It is important to visit the official website for detailed information on how to apply for this scholarship
Closing Date: 31 March
Funding: Corporation

For further information contact:

Email:	admissions@uea.ac.uk

University of Edinburgh

Old College South Bridge, Edinburgh EH8 9YL, United Kingdom

Tel:	(44) 131 650 2159
Fax:	(44) 131 650 8009
Email:	postgrad@ed.ac.uk
Contact:	Grants Management Officer

Alice Brown PhD Scholarships

Purpose: The Alice Brown Scholarship is a new 6-year PhD scholarship offering a programme of advanced study, ongoing research, professional training and development

Eligibility: Citizens of United Kingdom, European Economic Area and Switzerland are eligible to apply. A first class honours degree (or equivalent) in a subject relevant to the studentship OR a taught MSc degree at distinction level in a subject relevant to the studentship. Conditional offers can be made to applicants currently enrolled in a degree programme on the basis of anticipated results. 1. As comprehensive research training is integrated into the programme of this PhD, there will be no automatic preference given to those holding MSc qualifications covering research training. 2. Applications are encouraged from those nearing the end of an undergraduate degree in a subject relevant to the scholarship. 3. Due to constraints on part-time study for international students on visas, this award is only open to nationals of the United Kingdom, countries of the European Economic Area, or Switzerland

Level of Study: Graduate

Type: Scholarship

Value: The scholarship covers full payment of PhD tuition fees and provides an annual stipend of £10,000 each year

Length of Study: 6-year PhD programme

Country of Study: United Kingdom

Application Procedure: Applicants are invited to submit a current CV, a short research proposal/idea (max. 1,000 words) and a personal statement of up to 500 words explaining their suitability for the scholarship in the field to which they are applying

Contributor: University of Edinburgh

Additional Information: For more details, please visit scholarship-positions.com/alice-brown-phd-scholarships-university-edinburgh-uk/2018/02/27/. All PhD students in the School of Social and Political Science can apply to the PhD Research Support Fund for help with fieldwork and other research-related costs throughout their period of study

For further information contact:

Email: pgresearch.sps@ed.ac.uk

Clinical Management of Pain Scholarship

Value: Each scholarship provides a one-off payment of £700 towards tuition fees

Country of Study: Any country

Application Procedure: In order to gain access to the scholarship application system applicants must have applied for admission to the University of Edinburgh. Please note that, following the submission of an application for admission, it can take up to five working days for all system checks to be completed and for access to be granted. The online scholarship application form is located in EUCLID and can be accessed via MyEd our web based information portal at www.myed.ed.ac.uk

Closing Date: 27 July

Additional Information: htttp://www.ed.ac.uk/student-systems/support-guidance

For further information contact:

Email: studentfunding@ed.ac.uk

Commonwealth Online Global Health Scholarships at University of Edinburgh

Purpose: The University's Global Health Academy has been awarded 10 fully funded studentships across five online Masters programmes within the domain of Global Health

Eligibility: The scholarships will be awarded to a candidate who is accepted for admission on to an eligible programme (see above) and who is a citizen of and resident in one of the following developing Commonwealth countries

Level of Study: Postdoctorate

Type: Scholarship

Frequency: Annual

Country of Study: Any country

Closing Date: 22 March

Funding: Foundation

Edinburgh Global Online Distance Learning Masters Scholarship

Value: Each scholarship will cover full tuition fees and will be tenable for 3 years

Length of Study: Three years

Country of Study: Any country

Application Procedure: The online scholarship application form is located in EUCLID and can be accessed via MyEd our web based information portal at www.myed.ed.ac.uk

Closing Date: 1 June

For further information contact:

Email: studentfunding@ed.ac.uk

Edinburgh Global Online Distance Learning Scholarships

Purpose: The University of Edinburgh will offer a number of scholarships for distance learning Master's programmes offered by the University

Eligibility: 1. Scholarships will be available for students commencing in session current year in any distance learning Masters programme offered by the University. 2. Applicants must be nationals of the eligible countries

Level of Study: Postdoctorate
Type: Scholarship
Length of Study: 3 years
Frequency: Annual
Country of Study: Any country
Application Procedure: Please submit your CV, and a 500 – 800 word summary of your reason for applying for the masters programme and how you envision family medicine transforming healthcare
Closing Date: 1 June
Funding: Private

For further information contact:

Email: family.medicine@ed.ac.uk
Contact: Mr Jane Dumayne

Edinburgh Global Research Scholarship

Purpose: These awards are designed to attract high quality overseas research students to the University of Edinburgh
Eligibility: The awards are open to overseas nationals commencing a PhD in any field of study
Value: Each scholarship will cover the difference between the tuition fee for a United Kingdom/European Union postgraduate student and that chargeable to an overseas postgraduate student. The awards do not cover maintenance expenses
Length of Study: Three years
Country of Study: United Kingdom
Closing Date: April
Additional Information: For more details on this award please contact Scholarships and Student Funding Services. Work: +44 (0)131 651 4070; Email: studentfunding@ed.ac.uk

For further information contact:

Email: studentfunding@ed.ac.uk

Glenmore Medical Postgraduate Scholarship

Subjects: Medical science
Purpose: Two scholarships are available for postgraduate full-time one year Masters study for eligible Human Medical programmes offered by the University in the upcoming academic session
Eligibility: The scholarship will be awarded on the basis of academic merit. Candidates must have, or expect to obtain, the overseas equivalent of a United Kingdom first-class honours degree
Level of Study: Postgraduate
Type: Scholarship

Value: The scholarship will have a value of £21,200 and will be tenable for one academic year. The scholarship will cover tuition fees of up to £21,200 with any surplus paid as a stipend
Length of Study: The scholarship is tenable for one academic year
Frequency: Annual
Country of Study: United Kingdom
Application Procedure: Please check website for more details: www.ed.ac.uk/student-funding/pgt-application. Eligible applicants should complete an online application form. The closing date for applications is 25 June
Closing Date: 25 June

Haywood Doctoral Scholarship

Subjects: Scholarships are available to pursue Doctoral research programs and are awarded within the College of Arts and Law in History of Art
Purpose: To offer Haywood Doctoral Scholarship to an outstanding doctoral research candidate in History of Art
Type: Scholarship
Value: As an international student, you will receive a reduction in tuition fees equivalent to the Home/European Union rate if successful
Country of Study: United Kingdom
Closing Date: 2 March

For further information contact:

Tel: (44) 1214 143 344
Email: calpg-research@contacts.bham.ac.uk

Institute for Advanced Studies in the Humanities-School of Social and Political Science Visiting Fellowships

Purpose: The IASH-SSPS Visiting Fellowships are intended to encourage outstanding interdisciplinary research, international scholarly collaboration, and networking activities of Visiting Research Fellows together with SSPS academics
Eligibility: Kindly check the below steps for further instructions. 1. Fellows are expected to be resident in Edinburgh throughout the tenure of their Fellowship and to play a full part in the activities of the Institute. The Institute will be pleased to help with finding suitable accommodation in Edinburgh but is unable to pay accommodation costs. 2. The minimum tenure for a Fellowship is two months; applications for less than two months will not be considered. 3. Only fully completed applications will be considered. It is the responsibility of each applicant to ensure that all documentation

is complete, and that referees submit their reports to the Institute by the closing date. Applications may include a copy of any one article or publication that is thought to be specially relevant to the research proposal and Fellowship submission

Level of Study: Graduate
Type: Fellowship
Frequency: Annual
Country of Study: Any country
Application Procedure: The next closing date for the receipt of applications will be Thursday 28 February. Applications received after that date will not be considered. Successful candidates will be notified by email with a formal letter of confirmation to follow; please ensure that you supply a valid email address so that you can be contacted quickly after decisions are made. The application form can be completed online. Check with the below link. www.sps.ed.ac.uk/research/academic_visitors/iash-ssps_visiting_fellowships
Closing Date: 28 February
Funding: Commercial, Private

For further information contact:

Email: iash@ed.ac.uk

National Health Service Education for Scotland Primary Care Ophthalmology Scholarship

Eligibility: The scholarships will be awarded to students who are accepted for admission on to the online distance learning MSc in Primary Care Ophthalmology at the University of Edinburgh. Applicants should already have been offered a place at the University of Edinburgh and should have firmly accepted that offer or be intending to do so
Type: Scholarship
Value: The scholarship will have a total value of 50% of the course fees
Country of Study: United Kingdom
Closing Date: 27 July
Additional Information: For further information, please contact Scholarships and Financial Support Team. Work: +44 (0)131 651 4070; Email: studentfunding@ed.ac.uk

For further information contact:

Email: studentfunding@ed.ac.uk

Perfect Storms: Leverhulme Doctoral Scholarships

Subjects: Interdisciplinary research on perfect storms – the most profound problems facing contemporary and future societies

Level of Study: Doctorate
Value: Full fees, living and research costs
Length of Study: 3 years
Frequency: Annual
Study Establishment: University of Edinburgh
Country of Study: Scotland
Contributor: The Leverhulme Trusts
No. of awards given last year: 5

For further information contact:

Email: studentfunding@ed.ac.uk

PhD Social Work Scholarship at University of Edinburgh in United Kingdom

Subjects: Scholarship is awarded to study Social Work
Purpose: This award is available to students intending to commence PhD Social Work study in September on either a full-time or part-time basis
Eligibility: Citizens of all nationalities are eligible to apply. If English is not your first language then you will need to show that your English language skills are at a high enough level to succeed in your studies
Value: One award covering tuition fees at the Home/European Union fee rate, a maintenance stipend of £14,000 and a research grant of £500 is on offer to applicants for PhD Social Work in the School of Social and Political Science
Study Establishment: Social Work study
Country of Study: Any country
Application Procedure: The online scholarship application form is located in EUCLID and can be accessed via MyEd our web-based information portal. www.myed.ed.ac.uk/
Closing Date: 1 March

For further information contact:

Email: GradSchool.HCA@ed.ac.uk

Polish School of Medicine Memorial Fund Scholarships

Purpose: The scholarship enables medical scientists at the outset of their careers to undertake a period of further study or research at the University's Medical School and return to Poland
Eligibility: Eligible applicants should complete an online scholarship application. The online scholarship application form is located in EUCLID and can be accessed via MyEd our web based information portal at www.myed.ed.ac.uk
Value: Allowance for a period of up to 1 year

Length of Study: One year
Country of Study: Any country
Closing Date: 17 May

For further information contact:

Email: maria.graham@ed.ac.uk

Principal Career Development PhD Scholarship

Purpose: To attract the best and brightest PhD students, the University seeks to offer not only unparalleled research facilities and superb supervision, but also to provide development opportunities which will support our research students as they progress beyond their PhD, through an innovative programme of integrated research, training, and career development
Type: Scholarship
Value: Each scholarship covers the United Kingdom/European Union rate of tuition fee as well as a stipend of £15,000
Country of Study: United Kingdom
Closing Date: 1 February
Additional Information: For further information, please contact Scholarships and Financial Support Team, phone :0131 651 4070, email: studentfunding@ed.ac.uk

For further information contact:

Email: studentfunding@ed.ac.uk

Shell Centenary Scholarships and Shell Centenary Chevening Scholarships at Edinburgh

Subjects: Applied sciences and technology, including environmental sciences
Eligibility: Students from countries that are not present or applicant members of the Organization for Economic Co-operation and Development (OECD). Candidates should normally be aged 20–35, be resident in one of the non-OECD countries and be intending to return to the country concerned at the end of the period of study. They should normally already hold a degree equivalent to a United Kingdom First Class (Honours) Degree or be expecting to obtain such a degree before the start of their proposed course
Level of Study: Postgraduate
Type: Scholarship
Value: The scholarships covers tuition fees, accommodation, maintenance costs and a return airfare for the scholarship holder
Length of Study: 1 year
Frequency: Annual

Study Establishment: University of Edinburgh
Country of Study: Scotland
Application Procedure: Applicants must apply separately for admission to the University of Edinburgh making a clear statement that they wish to be considered for a Shell Scholarship
Closing Date: 1 March
No. of awards given last year: 6

For further information contact:

Email: scholarships@ed.ac.uk

The Anne Rowling Clinic Regenerative Neurology Scholarships

Subjects: The scholarships will be awarded to applicants who are accepted for admission on to the online distance learning postgraduate Certificate, Diploma, or Masters Stem Cell and Translational Neurology programme at the University of Edinburgh for the academic session. Field of study is Neurology
Purpose: Masters scholarships for applicants commencing Stem Cells and Translational Neurology programmes in the academic year
Type: Scholarship
Value: One International Anne Rowling Clinic Regenerative Neurology Scholarship will cover 60 credits towards your module fees. Two Anne Rowling Clinic Regenerative Neurology Scholarships will cover 30 credits worth of course fees
Country of Study: United Kingdom
Application Procedure: Eligible applicants should complete an online scholarship application. Website link is www.ed.ac.uk/student-funding/postgraduate/e-learning/regenerative-neurology
Closing Date: 20 August
Funding: Private
Additional Information: For further information, please visit www.ed.ac.uk/student-funding/postgraduate/e-learning/regenerative-neurology

For further information contact:

Email: studentfunding@ed.ac.uk

The Edinburgh Online Family Medicine Scholarships Fund

Purpose: Through the generous donations of a benefactor in India who is committed to improving healthcare in rural regions this full scholarship award will allow a student from South Asia to study the online Masters of Family Medicine

Type: Scholarship
Frequency: Annual
Country of Study: Any country
Application Procedure: Applications should be made to Michelle Hart at family.medicine@ed.ac.uk
Closing Date: 1 July

For further information contact:

Email: family.medicine@ed.ac.uk

The Garden Scholarship in Surgical Sciences

Type: Scholarship (grant-in-aid)
Value: £1,000
Country of Study: Any country

For further information contact:

Email: studentfunding@ed.ac.uk

The Kirby Laing International Scholarships

Value: The scholarships will cover tuition fees and provide a maintenance allowance of £12,000
Length of Study: 1 year
Country of Study: United Kingdom
Closing Date: 2 April
Additional Information: For further information, please contact School of Divinity, Work: 044 1316 508 900, Email: Divinity.PG@ed.ac.uk

For further information contact:

Email: Divinity.PG@ed.ac.uk

The Lt.Col Jack Wishart Scholarship

Value: £500 per year toward tuition fees
Length of Study: Two academic years
Country of Study: Any country
Application Procedure: The online scholarship application form is located in EUCLID and can be accessed via MyEd our web based information portal at www.myed.ed.ac.uk
Closing Date: 30 September

For further information contact:

Email: studentfunding@ed.ac.uk

The Rev Dr Norma P Robertson Scholarship

Type: Scholarship
Value: The scholarship will have a maximum value of £7,500
Country of Study: Any country

For further information contact:

Email: studentfunding@ed.ac.uk

The Sanders Scholarship in Clinical Ophthalmology

Purpose: University of Edinburgh is offering twenty four scholarships for online distance learning. Scholarships are available for pursuing online distance learning masters degree programmes
Eligibility: The scholarships will be awarded to students who are accepted for admission on to the online distance learning MSc in Primary Care Ophthalmology and the ChM in Clinical Ophthalmology at the University of Edinburgh. Applicants must be medical or surgical trainees registered with the General Medical Council and working in a recognised training programme in the Scottish NHS, and be resident in Scotland. Applications from other health professionals involved in delivering eye care (except optometrists) in the Scottish NHS may be considered on an individual basis
Level of Study: Graduate
Type: Scholarship
Value: £1,000
Country of Study: United Kingdom
Application Procedure: Complete an online EUCLID application for the MSc in Primary Care Ophthalmology or the ChM (Master of Surgery) in Clinical Ophthalmology – instructions on full application process can be found on the University's degree finder pages for the MSc PCO and the ChM CO. Wait for decision on application via EUCLID. If eligible to join the course, you will be given a conditional or unconditional offer, which you must accept prior to applying for a scholarship. Email a personal statement to declare your wish to apply for a scholarship to: chm.info@ed.ac.uk by 31 August
Closing Date: 27 July
Funding: Private
Additional Information: For further details, please contact Scholarships and Financial Support Team, Work:0131 651 4070, Email: studentfunding@ed.ac.uk

For further information contact:

Email: sarah.jones@ed.ac.uk

Wellcome Trust 4-Year PhD Programme Studentships

Subjects: Cell biology
Eligibility: Students should be from a life sciences background and should hold, or expect to obtain, at least an Upper Second Class (Honours) Degree
Level of Study: Doctorate
Type: Studentship
Value: Tuition fees, research costs and maintenance allowance
Frequency: Annual
Study Establishment: The University of Edinburgh
Country of Study: Scotland
Application Procedure: Please see the website www.wcb. ed.ac.uk/phd
Closing Date: 10 December
No. of awards given last year: 5

For further information contact:

Email: karen.traill@ed.ac.uk
Contact: Karen Traill

University of Essex

Graduate Admissions Office, University of Essex, Wivenhoe Park, Colchester C04 3SQ, United Kingdom

Tel: (44) 12 0687 2719
Fax: (44) 12 0687 2808
Email: pgadmit@essex.ac.uk
Website: www.essex.ac.uk
Contact: V Bartholomew, CRM Operations Manager

The University of Essex is one of the United Kingdom's leading academic institutions, ranked 10th nationally for research and 7th for teaching. It offers degrees and research opportunities across 19 academic departments (including government and sociology, which both have 6-star research ratings) and numerous research centres of world renown.

Academic Excellence International Masters Scholarship

Subjects: Scholarships are available for pursuing master's degree level at University of Essex in United Kingdom
Purpose: University of Essex is inviting applications for academic excellence international masters scholarship

Eligibility: Applicants must meet the necessary language proficiency requirements of the host institution
Value: The scholarship worth up to £5,000, paid as a discount on tuition fee
Frequency: Annual
Study Establishment: Scholarships are awarded in the fields offered by the university
Country of Study: United Kingdom
Application Procedure: If applicants meet all the eligibility criteria and firmly accept the offer of your place by 30 September then you will automatically be awarded this scholarship. Applicants will be notified of your award by the end of October. You don't need to complete an application form
Closing Date: 30 September
Additional Information: For more details please visit the website   scholarship-positions.com/academic-excellence-international-masters-scholarship-uk-2017/2015/11/16/

For further information contact:

Email: enquiries@essex.ac.uk

Arts and Humanities Research Council Department of Sociology Studentships

Subjects: Communication, culture and media studies
Purpose: To support students on a research programme
Eligibility: Open to United Kingdom or European Union applicants
Level of Study: Postgraduate
Type: Scholarship
Value: UK students - fees plus maintenance; European Union students - fees
Frequency: Annual
Study Establishment: University of Essex
Country of Study: United Kingdom
Contributor: AHRC

For further information contact:

Email: pgeduc@leeds.ac.uk

Arts and Humanities Research Council Research Preparations Masters Award for Literature, Film, and Theatre Studies

Subjects: Literature, film and theatre studies
Purpose: To support students undertaking a research preparations in the department
Eligibility: Open to postgraduates offered a place to study in the department

Level of Study: Postgraduate
Type: Award
Value: £10,600 per year maintenance grant
Length of Study: 1 year
Frequency: Annual
Study Establishment: University of Essex
Country of Study: United Kingdom
Application Procedure: Applicants must contact the department concerned

For further information contact:

Email: graduateschool@gold.ac.uk

Dowden Scholarship

Subjects: Mathematical sciences
Purpose: To help highly able students who otherwise would not be able to study at postgraduate level
Eligibility: Applicant must have settled status in the United Kingdom; been 'ordinarily resident' in the United Kingdom for the 3 years before the start of their studentship; not been residing in the United Kingdom wholly or mainly for the purpose of full-time education (United Kingdom and European Union nationals are exempt from this requirement). The Vera Dowden Baldwin Scholarship awards financial assistance to a resident of Dowden Hall who demonstrates financial need. The fund is named in honor of the late Vera Dowden Baldwin '34, whose connection with the University spanned more than seventy years
Level of Study: Postgraduate
Type: Scholarship
Value: Up to £5,000
Frequency: Annual
Study Establishment: University of Essex
Country of Study: United Kingdom
Application Procedure: Indicate on application for doctoral course
Additional Information: Please contact the university for more information

Drake Lewis Graduate Scholarship for Art History

Subjects: Art history
Purpose: To support new MA students in art history
Eligibility: Open to postgraduate applicants
Level of Study: Postgraduate
Type: Scholarship
Value: £5,000
Frequency: Annual

Study Establishment: University of Essex
Country of Study: United Kingdom
Funding: Private
Contributor: Drake Lewis
Additional Information: Please check website for further information

For further information contact:

Email: scholarships@essex.ac.uk

Drake Lewis Graduate Scholarship for Health and Human Sciences

Subjects: Public health and health studies
Purpose: To support students on full-time masters in public health or health studies
Eligibility: Open to postgraduate applicants
Level of Study: Postgraduate
Type: Scholarship
Value: £5,000
Frequency: Annual
Study Establishment: University of Essex
Country of Study: United Kingdom
Application Procedure: Applicants must contact the department concerned
Funding: Private
Contributor: Drake-Lewis
Additional Information: Please check website for further information

For further information contact:

Email: scholarships@essex.ac.uk

Economic and Social Research Council 1+3 Department of Sociology Studentships

Subjects: Sociology
Purpose: To support students on a 1 year research training programme
Eligibility: Open to United Kingdom or European Union applicants who have not completed a programme of research training
Level of Study: Postgraduate
Type: Scholarship
Value: UK students – fees plus maintenance; European Union students – fees
Frequency: Annual
Study Establishment: University of Essex
Country of Study: United Kingdom
Application Procedure: See website

Closing Date: March
Contributor: ESRC

For further information contact:

Email: fass-pg@lancaster.ac.uk

Santander Masters Scholarship

Subjects: All subjects
Purpose: To support students from Santander network countries to undertake further study
Eligibility: Open to graduates residing in one of the Santander network countries who have an offer to study at Masters level
Level of Study: Postgraduate
Type: Scholarships
Value: £5,000
Frequency: Annual
Study Establishment: University of Essex
Country of Study: United Kingdom
Application Procedure: Please check website
Funding: Corporation
Contributor: Santander

For further information contact:

Email: pgtaught@lboro.ac.uk

Tinson Fund Scholarship for Law

Subjects: Law
Purpose: To support students from the former Soviet Bloc interested in studying postgraduate law
Eligibility: Open to students from former Soviet Bloc countries, who have an offer on an LLM programme
Level of Study: Postgraduate
Type: Scholarship
Value: Tuition fees
Frequency: Annual
Study Establishment: University of Essex
Country of Study: United Kingdom
Application Procedure: See website for details
Closing Date: Mid-May
No. of awards given last year: 1

For further information contact:

Email: scholarships@essex.ac.uk

University of Essex Centre for Psychoanalytic Studies Scholarship

Subjects: Psychoanalytic studies
Purpose: To support postgraduate study within the centre
Eligibility: Open to postgraduates within the centre for psychoanalytic studies
Level of Study: Postgraduate
Type: Scholarship
Value: Depends on funds available
Length of Study: 1 year
Frequency: Annual
Study Establishment: University of Essex
Country of Study: United Kingdom
Application Procedure: Applicants must contact the centre concerned
Contributor: University of Essex

For further information contact:

Email: pgadmit@essex.ac.uk

University of Essex Silberrad Scholarship

Subjects: All subjects
Purpose: To support graduates to pursue PhD study
Eligibility: Open to applicants holding a degree from or about graduate from University of Essex who have an offer place at the University of Essex and are eligible to pay Home/European Union tuition fees
Level of Study: Postgraduate, Research
Type: Scholarship
Value: Home/European Union tuition fee and bursary element towards living costs
Length of Study: Up to 1 year
Frequency: Annual
Study Establishment: University of Essex
Country of Study: United Kingdom
Application Procedure: Please check website
Funding: Trusts
Contributor: Silberrad Estate

For further information contact:

Email: pgadmit@essex.ac.uk

University of Exeter

Postgraduate Administration Office, Northcote House, The Queen's Drive, Exeter EX4 4QJ, United Kingdom

Tel: (44) 1392 723 044
Email: pg-ad@exeter.ac.uk
Website: www.exeter.ac.uk/postgraduate/money/funding/
Contact: Mrs Julie Gay, Scholarships Secretary

The University of Exeter is consistently regarded as one of the best universities in the United Kingdom and has an increasingly excellent reputation internationally. A member of the Russell Group, we attract funding from all major research councils, and are collaborators in 10 prestigious Doctoral Training Partnerships.

Full-Fee Master's Scholarships

Subjects: Selected taught Masters in the arts, business, education, humanities and social sciences and science
Purpose: Full fee waiver offered to students who best demonstrate the potential to progress to doctoral study
Eligibility: Applicants who demonstrate exceptional academic ability such as a first class honours or direct equivalent, and the potential to progress to doctoral study based on a submitted research proposal and personal statement will be considered
Level of Study: Graduate, Postgraduate
Type: Scholarship
Value: Full fee waiver of the taught Master's programme irrespective of fee status
Length of Study: 1 year
Frequency: Annual
Study Establishment: The University of Exeter
Country of Study: United Kingdom
No. of awards offered: 185
Application Procedure: Application forms can be downloaded from the website www.exeter.ac.uk/scholarships/post graduate/fullmasters
Closing Date: 31 March
Funding: Corporation
No. of awards given last year: 15
No. of applicants last year: 185
Additional Information: Applications will only be considered from students who have received an offer of a place on a taught Master's programme at the University

For further information contact:

Scholarship Administrator, Admissions Office, Laver Building, North Park Road, Exeter EX4 4QE

Email: admissions-scholarships@exeter.ac.uk

University of Exeter Chapel Choir Choral and Organ Scholarship

Purpose: Annual scholarships offered to choral and organ practitioners to aid in recitals on behalf of the chapel choir
Eligibility: Based on audition. The Director of Chapel Music will invite for competitive audition on the basis of applications demonstrating a high level of competence and experience plus details of two referees familiar with the applicant's ability
Level of Study: Doctorate, Graduate, Postgraduate, Research, MBA
Type: Scholarship
Value: £400 per year for choral scholars, £700 per year for senior organ scholars, £300 per year for junior organ scholars
Length of Study: 1 year initially but may be renewed for the duration of study, where appropriate
Frequency: Annual
Study Establishment: The University of Exeter
Country of Study: United Kingdom
No. of awards offered: 60
Application Procedure: Applicants can contact the Director for more information and request an application form
Closing Date: 13 February
Funding: Corporation, Trusts, Individuals
No. of awards given last year: 10
No. of applicants last year: 60
Additional Information: From the 10 choral scholarships available, 4 are offered to sopranos, 2 each for other voice parts of alto (male and female), tenor and bass. The award for senior organ scholarship status will require recipients to direct the choir when required

For further information contact:

Email: a.j.musson@exeter.ac.uk
Contact: Professor Anthony Musson, Director of Chapel Music

World Class Business School International Scholarship

Eligibility: A scholarship will be awarded to the most talented international students who have had an application accepted to one of The Business School MSc programmes. Applicants must be resident in one of the following: Africa, Asia, and the Commonwealth of Independent States including students resident in Azerbaijan, Kazakhstan, Norway, Russia, Ukraine and Turkey
Type: Scholarship
Value: £10,000
Length of Study: 1 year

Frequency: Annual
Country of Study: United Kingdom
Application Procedure: Please apply at www.exeter.ac.uk/studying/funding/apply/step1/?award=1039
Closing Date: 30 March
Contributor: University of Exeter

For further information contact:

Email: business-school-admissions@ex.ac.uk
Contact: Jane Knox

University of Geneva

University of Geneva, Geneva, Switzerland

Email: Excellence-Master-Sciences@unige.ch
Contact: Dean of the Faculty of Science

The University of Geneva is a public research university located in Geneva, Switzerland. It was founded in 1559 by John Calvin as a theological seminary and law school.

University of Geneva Excellence Masters Fellowships

Subjects: Astronomy, biology, chemistry and biochemistry, earth Sciences, environmental sciences, computer sciences, mathematics, pharmaceutical sciences and physics offered by the Faculty of Science
Purpose: The Faculty of Science of the University of Geneva, in collaboration with several sponsors, has established an Excellence Fellowship Program to support outstanding and highly motivated candidates who intend to pursue a Master of Science in any of the disciplines covered by the Faculty
Eligibility: The fellowships are open to students from any university with very good performance in their studies (belonging to the best 10% of their bachelor's programme) and that have completed the Bachelor degree or expect to complete it within 6 months. Selection of the applicants will be based on excellence
Level of Study: Doctorate, Postgraduate
Type: Fellowship
Value: CHF 10,000 to CHF 15,000 per year
Country of Study: Switzerland
Application Procedure: You must submit the application form and supporting documents as a unique PDF file by e-mail to the Dean of the Faculty of Science
Closing Date: 15 March

Additional Information: Please visit official website for more details: www.unige.ch/sciences/Enseignements/Formations/Masters/ExcellenceMasterFellowships_en.html

For further information contact:

24 rue du Général-Dufour, 1211 Genève 4, Switzerland

Tel: (41) 22 379 71 11
Email: Sciences@unige.ch

University of Glasgow

Postgraduate Research Office, Research and Enterprise, University of Glasgow, Glasgow G12 8QQ, United Kingdom

Tel: (44) 1413 301 989
Fax: (44) 1413 303 218
Email: s.rait@enterprise.gla.ac.uk
Website: www.gla.ac.uk
Contact: Shirley Rait

The University of Glasgow is a major research led university operating in an international context, which aims to provide education through the development of learning in a research environment, to undertake fundamental, strategic and applied research and to sustain and add value to Scottish culture, to the natural environment and to the national economy.

Alexander and Dixon Scholarship (Bryce Bequest)

Subjects: English literature
Eligibility: Open to the citizens of United Kingdom or a - European Union national
Level of Study: Doctorate
Type: Scholarship
Value: £3,500 fees only
Length of Study: 3 years
Application Procedure: The application should consist of a 500-word case for support and a brief covering letter, including the proposed title of the thesis, the name(s) of the proposed supervisor(s), and give the applicant's email and other contact details
Closing Date: 21 June

For further information contact:

Department Office, Department of English Literature, University of Glasgow, United Kingdom

Email: critstudies-pgscholarships@glasgow.ac.uk
Contact: Meg MacDonald

Alexander and Margaret Johnstone Postgraduate Research Scholarships

Subjects: Arts
Eligibility: Open to students intending a research degree in the faculty of arts in a department rated 5 or 5* in the research assessment exercise
Level of Study: Doctorate
Type: Research scholarship
Value: Tuition fees at the Home/European Union student rate, plus stipend of between £6,000 and £7,000
Length of Study: 3 years
Application Procedure: Check website for further details
Funding: Government

For further information contact:

Tel: (44) 141 330 6828
Email: e.queune@admin.gla.ac.uk
Contact: Emily Queune

Bellahouston Bequest Fund

Subjects: Arts and science
Eligibility: Open to postgraduate students undertaking a Masters Degree course in the faculty of Arts
Level of Study: Postgraduate
Type: Scholarship
Value: £1,000
Length of Study: 1 year
Frequency: Annual
Application Procedure: The candidate must contact the clerk of the faculty of arts. Check website for further information
Closing Date: 31 July
Additional Information: Preference will be given to the Glaswegians

For further information contact:

Tel: (44) 141 330 2000
Email: ugs@archives.gla.ac.uk
Contact: Clerk of the Faculty of Arts

British Federation of Women Graduates (BFWG)

Subjects: All subjects

Purpose: To encourage applicants to become members of the Federation to help promote better links between female graduates throughout the world
Eligibility: Open to female graduate with academic excellence. Doctoral students of all nationalities who will be studying in the United Kingdom are eligible for the scholarship
Level of Study: Postgraduate
Type: Scholarship and award
Value: £1,000–6,000
Length of Study: Four years
Frequency: Annual
Country of Study: United Kingdom
Application Procedure: Check website for further details
Closing Date: March (date differs annually)
Funding: Private
No. of awards given last year: 6
Additional Information: Male graduates and female undergraduates are not eligible

For further information contact:

Tel: (44) 20 7498 8037
Fax: (44) 20 7498 5213
Email: info@bfwg.org.uk

Clark Graduate Bursary Fund for International Students at University of Glasgow

Subjects: Bursary is awarded in the field offered by the university
Purpose: The aim of the bursary is to support graduates of the University of Glasgow or Strathclyde studying for, or applying to study for, a subsequent degree at a university in the United Kingdom or abroad
Eligibility: Applicants can either be graduates of the University of Glasgow or Strathclyde studying for, or applying to study for, a subsequent degree at a university in the United Kingdom or abroad. Applicants must be fluent in English
Type: Postgraduate scholarships
Value: The value of the bursary normally between £500 and £1,500
Study Establishment: Bursary is awarded in the field offered by the university
Country of Study: United Kingdom
Application Procedure: There is an annual application process. Applications can be submitted between 1st March and 1st October each year. Applications must be submitted online. Interviews of candidates selected for consideration are held in Glasgow at a Governors' meeting during November. Interviewees will usually be notified within a week of the interviews whether they will receive an award. Awards are normally paid to successful applicants before the end of the year

Closing Date: 1 March and 1 October each year
Additional Information: For more details please visit the website scholarship-positions.com/clark-raduate-bursary-fund-international-students-university-of-glasgow-uk/2017/12/20/

For further information contact:

Email: clarkmileendfund@gmail.com

Glasgow Educational & Marshall Trust Award

Subjects: All subjects
Purpose: To offer financial support to those who have lived, or are currently living within the Glasgow Municipal Boundary
Eligibility: Open to the candidates who are above 18 years of age and a resident of Glasgow within one of the following post code areas: G1–5, G11/12, G14/15, G20, G22/23, G31, G34, G40–42, G45, 51
Level of Study: Doctorate, Graduate, Postdoctorate, Postgraduate, Predoctorate, Research, MBA
Type: Studentships and bursaries
Value: £50-1,000
Length of Study: 1 year
Study Establishment: Glasgow Educational and Marshall Trust
Country of Study: United Kingdom
Application Procedure: Check website for further details
Closing Date: 30 April
Contributor: Glasgow Educational and Marshall Trust

For further information contact:

Tel: (44) 141 4334449
Fax: (44) 141 424 1731
Email: sloanea@hutchesons.org
Contact: Mrs Avril Sloane, Secretary and Treasurers

Henry Dryerre Scholarship in Medical and Veterinary Physiology

Subjects: Animal care and veterinary science; biology and life sciences; health sciences; medicine and surgery
Eligibility: Open to candidates holding a degree of a Scottish University with first class honours or, if in their final year, to be expected to achieve first class honours
Level of Study: Postgraduate
Type: Scholarships and fellowships
Value: Varies
Frequency: Every 3 years
Country of Study: Any country

Application Procedure: The candidate must submit the application form through a member of staff on the appropriate Henry Dryerre Nomination Form

For further information contact:

Email: scholarships@glasgow.ac.uk
Contact: Assistant Secretary

Lord Kelvin/Adam Smith Postgraduate Scholarships

Subjects: All subjects
Purpose: To enable the University to recruit outstanding postgraduate research students to a range of innovative, boundary-crossing research developments
Eligibility: Open to postgraduate students
Level of Study: Postgraduate
Type: Scholarship
Value: Stipend of £13,590. The project will benefit from £5,300 per year research costs
Length of Study: 4 years
Frequency: Annual
Application Procedure: Check website for further details
Funding: Trusts

For further information contact:

Email: lauren-currie@enterprise.gla.ac.uk
Contact: Lauren Currie, Postgraduate Research Secretary,

R. Harper Brown Memorial Scholarship

Subjects: All subjects
Purpose: To honour the late R. Harper Brown and to assist in defraying the cost of an American (United States) college student's study at a university in Scotland
Eligibility: Open to the candidates who are graduating seniors in high school with an acceptance and intention to attend university in Scotland or a student in an accredited American (United States) college or university looking for a study-abroad experience
Level of Study: Graduate
Type: Scholarship
Application Procedure: Check website for further details
Closing Date: Between 1 January and 31 March
Funding: Private
Contributor: The Illinois Saint Andrew Society

For further information contact:

Tel: (44) 847 967 2725
Email: dforlow@yahoo.com
Contact: David Forlow

Royal Historical Society: Postgraduate Research Support Grants

Subjects: History
Purpose: To assist postgraduate students in the pursuit of advanced historical research
Eligibility: The candidate must be a postgraduate student registered for a research degree at United Kingdom Institute of Higher Education
Level of Study: Graduate, Research
Type: Award/Grant
Country of Study: United States of America
Application Procedure: Check website for further details
Closing Date: 14 January, 18 February, 6 May, 18 June, 9 September and 12 November
Contributor: Royal Historical Society

For further information contact:

Email: m.ransom@royalhistsoc.org

Saint Andrew's Society of the State of New York Scholarship Fund

Subjects: All subjects
Eligibility: Open to candidates who are either graduates of a Scottish university or of Oxford or Cambridge and have completed their first Degree course
Level of Study: Graduate
Type: Scholarship
Value: Up to US$20,000 each to cover university tuition fees, room and board and transportation expenses
Length of Study: 1 academic year
Frequency: Annual
Country of Study: United States of America
Application Procedure: The candidate must arrange for references from two academic referees to be submitted in the appropriate referee forms
Closing Date: 25 January
Funding: Trusts
Contributor: Saint Andrew's Society of the State of New York

For further information contact:

Tel: (44) 141 330 6063
Email: c.omand@admin.gla.ac.uk
Contact: Catherine Omand

Stevenson Exchange Scholarships

Subjects: All subjects

Purpose: To promote friendly relations between the students of Scotland, Germany, France and Spain
Eligibility: Open to current or recent students of French, German or Spanish universities who intend to study at any university in Scotland
Level of Study: Postdoctorate
Type: Scholarship
Value: £250–2,000
Application Procedure: Check website for further details
Closing Date: 31 January

For further information contact:

1 The Square, University of Glasgow, Glasgow, United Kingdom

Tel: (44) 141 330 4241
Fax: (44) 141 330 4045
Email: l.buchan@admin.gla.ac.uk
Contact: Linda Buchan, Exchange Co-ordinator

The Catherine Mackichan Trust

Subjects: Scottish history
Eligibility: Open to applications from academic centres worldwide, schools, colleges and individuals or groups
Level of Study: Research
Type: Award
Value: £500
Length of Study: 1 year
Frequency: Annual
Country of Study: Any country
Application Procedure: Check website for further details
Closing Date: 15 April
Funding: Trusts
Contributor: The Catherine Mackichan Trust

For further information contact:

Email: peter.mcghee@vaslan.org.uk
Contact: I Fraser, Vice Chairman

William and Margaret Kesson Award for Postgraduate Study

Subjects: Arts
Purpose: To enable a student to undertake study leading to a postgraduate degree in the faculty of arts
Eligibility: Open to candidates of Scottish or English nationality possessing a graduate degree
Level of Study: Graduate
Type: Scholarship
Length of Study: 3 years

Country of Study: Any country
Application Procedure: Check website for further details
Closing Date: 1 May

For further information contact:

Email: e.queune@admin.gla.ac.uk
Contact: Clerk of the Faculty

William Ross Scholarship

Subjects: History
Purpose: To encourage the extraction of Scottish material from archives outside Scotland relating to all aspects of the history of Scotland, the Scottish people and Scottish influence abroad
Eligibility: Open to candidates possessing a degree in MLitt
Level of Study: Research
Type: Scholarships and fellowships
Value: £1,000
Length of Study: 1 year
Frequency: Annual
Application Procedure: The candidate must submit a letter outlining a dissertation research proposal including the planned topic and archival research plans
Closing Date: 1 July
Contributor: Trustees of the Ross Fund

For further information contact:

Email: c.leriguer@arts.gla.ac.uk
Contact: Christelle LeRiguer

Wingate Scholarships

Subjects: All subjects
Purpose: To support creative or original work of intellectual, scientific, artistic, social or environmental value
Eligibility: Open for mature candidates and those from non-traditional academic backgrounds without any upper age limit
Level of Study: Unrestricted
Type: Scholarship
Value: £6,500–10,000 in any 1 year
Length of Study: 1 year
Frequency: Annual
Country of Study: Any country
Application Procedure: Check website for further details
Closing Date: 1 February

For further information contact:

Email: emma@shrimsley.com

University of Göttingen

Project management, Equal Opportunities Office, Gosslerstrasse 9, DEU-37073, Göttingen, Germany

Tel: (49) 551/39 33959
Email: nina.guelcher@zvw.uni-goettingen.de
Contact: Mrs Nina Gülcher

The University of Göttingen is a public research university in the city of Göttingen, Germany.

Dorothea Schlozer Postdoctoral Scholarships for Female Students

Subjects: Faculty of Humanities, Faculty of Theology, Faculty of Law, Faculty of Economic Sciences, Faculty of Social Sciences and Medical Center (UMG)
Purpose: The University of Göttingen is inviting female postdocs from Germany to apply for Dorothea Schlozer Postdoctoral Scholarships. These scholarships are available to conduct a research project at the Georg-August-University
Eligibility: Female postdocs from Germany are eligible to apply. The candidate should have a very good command of English language. Therefore, the application should be written in English
Value: There will be 3 positions (TV-L 13, 100%, term of 2 years), one of which at the University Medical Center (UMG)
Length of Study: 2 years
Country of Study: Germany
Application Procedure: Applications will only be accepted through the online portal. After submitting your application you will receive an automatic confirmation of receipt via e-mail
Closing Date: 8 April
Additional Information: For more details, please visit the website www.uni-goettingen.de/de/122481.html

For further information contact:

Email: admin@scholarship-positions.com

University of Graz

Universitätsplatz 3, AUT 8010 Graz, Austria

Contact: University of Graz

The University of Graz (German: Karl-Franzens-Universität Graz), located in Graz, Austria, is the largest and oldest university in Styria, as well as the second-largest and second-oldest university in Austria.

Ida Pfeiffer Scholarships

Purpose: This program is designed to give applicants the opportunity to submit an application for a waiver of tuition fees

Eligibility: For details, visit website www.european-funding-guide.eu/other-financial-assistance/14286-ida-pfeiffer-schol arships. Successful completion of at least two semesters at the University of Graz. Minimum age of 19 years and maximum age of 35 years, in exceptional cases (late start of studies, concurrent employment

Type: Scholarship

Length of Study: 1 year

Country of Study: Austria

Application Procedure: Eligibility requirements are as follows: 1. Successful completion of at least 2 semesters at the University of Graz. 2. Minimum age of 19

Closing Date: 13 April

Funding: Private

Additional Information: Please visit website international.uni-graz.at/de/stud/outgoing/s-out-mprog/ida-pfeiffer-stipendium/ for more details

For further information contact:

Email: maren.leykauf@uni-graz.at

Contact: Mr Maren Leykauf

Marie Sklodowska-Curie Actions Postdoctoral Fellowships

Subjects: Fellowship is awarded to learn any of the courses offered by the university

Purpose: Fellowship is available to pursue Postdoctoral programme

Eligibility: Please visit www.scholarshipsupdates.com/universi ty-of-graz-marie-curie-individual-postdoctoral-fellowship-in -austria-2018/ for eligibility criteria

Value: Receive up to €400 for your travel costs to Austria

Country of Study: Austria

Closing Date: 12 September

Contributor: University of Graz

Additional Information: Please visit www.unica.it/unica/ it/news_avvisi_s1.page?contentId=AVS93045 for more details

University of Guelph

University Centre, Room 437, 50 Stone Road East, Guelph, ON N1G 2W1, Canada

Tel: (1) 519 824 4120

Fax: (1) 519 767 1693

Email: immccorki@uoguelph.ca

Website: www.uoguelph.ca

Contact: Linda McCorkindale, Associate Registrar

The University of Guelph is renowned in Canada and around the world as a research-intensive and learner-centred institution and for its commitment to open learning, internationalism and collaboration. Their vision is to be Canada's leader in creating, transmitting and applying knowledge to improve the social, cultural and economic quality of life of people in Canada and around the world.

The Brock Doctoral Scholarship

Subjects: All subjects

Purpose: To financially support Doctoral students to attain a high level of academic achievement and to make significant teaching and research contributions

Eligibility: Open to students with sustained outstanding academic performance, evidence of strong teaching and research skills, demonstrated outstanding communication skills and excellent potential for research and teaching as assessed by the College Dean

Level of Study: Doctorate

Type: Scholarship

Value: Up to C$1,20,000 (C$10,000 per semester for up to 12 semesters)

Length of Study: 6 years

Frequency: Annual

Study Establishment: University of Guelph

Country of Study: Canada

Application Procedure: Students entering a Doctoral programme should apply to their College Dean by February 1st with a curriculum vitae, which must then be forwarded to Graduate Program Services by February 15th, with the Dean's written assessment of the candidate's research and teaching potential attached

Closing Date: 15 February

Additional Information: The Brock Doctoral Scholarship is one of the most prestigious Doctoral awards available at the University. It is hoped that award holders will be mentors for future Brock Doctoral Scholarship winners

For further information contact:

Office of Registrarial Services, University of Guelph

Email: sinclair@registrar.uoguelph.ca

University of Hertfordshire

College Lane, Hatfield, Hertfordshire AL10 9AB, United Kingdom

Tel: (44) 1707 284 800
Fax: (44) 1707 284 115

Yaasa Scholarship

Purpose: The Yaasa Scholarships are available to all high school juniors and seniors as well as all students currently registered in any accredited post-secondary institution
Level of Study: Graduate, Postgraduate
Type: Scholarship
Value: C$1,000
Frequency: Annual
Country of Study: Any country
Application Procedure: The winner(s) of this annual scholarship will receive their award within 2 weeks of the listed deadline. All applicants should include their full name and mailing address with their submissions as well as the school they are currently attending
Closing Date: 14 June
Additional Information: Students who are successfully awarded the UH Graduate Scholarship are still eligible for the £500 tuition fee discount if they pay in full at registration. Please check at www.herts.ac.uk/international/fees/scholarships-for-international-students/uh-family-scholarships for more information

For further information contact:

Email: scholarships@yaasa.com

University of Illinois

225 DKH, 1407 West Gregory, Urbana, IL 61801, United States of America

Tel: (1) 217 333 8153
Fax: (1) 217 333 1398

Website: www.uiuc.edu
Contact: Ms Diane Carson, Graduate Advising Office

The University of Illinois at Urbana-Champaign is a comprehensive, major public university. As a land grant institution chartered in 1867, it provides undergraduate and graduate education in more than 150 fields of study, conducts both theoretical and applied research, and provides public service to the state and the nation.

Master of Business Administration Programme

Length of Study: 2 years
Application Procedure: Applicants must complete an application form supplying US$50 fee, official transcripts, TOEFL score, statement of financial support and a personal statement

For further information contact:

Tel: (1) 217 244 8019
Email: mba@uiuc.edu
Contact: Mr Scott Beuchler, Assistant Dean

University of Kent

Admissions and Partnership Services, The Registry, Canterbury, Kent CT2 7NZ, United Kingdom

Tel: (44) 1227 764 000
Fax: (44) 1227 827 077
Email: scholarships@kent.ac.uk
Website: www.kent.ac.uk

The University of Kent is a United Kingdom higher education institution funded by the Higher Education Funding Council for United Kingdom (HEFCE). The university provides education of excellent quality characterized by flexibility and inter disciplinarily and informed by research and scholarship, meeting the lifelong needs of diversity students.

Ian Gregor Scholarship

Subjects: Postcolonial studies, Dickens and Victorian culture, 18th-century studies, English and American literature, creative writing, critical theory, medieval and early modern studies

Purpose: To support a candidate registered for a taught MA programme in English
Eligibility: Candidates are expected to hold at least an Upper Second Class (Honours) Degree or equivalent. Candidates should also have applied for an external scholarship, such as AHRC
Level of Study: Graduate, Postgraduate
Type: Scholarship
Value: Home fees and a £500 bursary for 1 year's full-time study
Length of Study: 1 year
Frequency: Annual
Study Establishment: The University of Kent
Country of Study: United Kingdom
Application Procedure: See webpages at www.kent.ac.uk/english/postgraduate/fund.htm
Closing Date: 28 June
Funding: Trusts
No. of awards given last year: 1

For further information contact:

Email: englishpg@kent.ac.uk
Contact: Claire Lyons, Administrative Assistant

Kent Law School Studentships and Bursaries

Subjects: Banking law, carriage of goods, company law, comparative law, computers and the law, criminal law and penology, critical legal studies, environmental law, emergency powers, European comparative and human rights law, family law, gender, sexuality and law, immigration law, intellectual property law, international law and human rights, international economic and trade law, labor law, law and multiculturalism, legal services, legal theory, modern legal history, multinationals and the law, and private law
Purpose: To provide funding for 1 year in the first instance, extended to a maximum of 3 years (for registered students only) based on satisfactory progress (including upgrading to a PhD). The retention of the posts will be subject to a review of progress and performance in both research and teaching after the 1st year
Eligibility: Candidates should hold an Upper Second Class (Honours) Degree or a good postgraduate taught degree in law
Level of Study: Doctorate, Postgraduate, Research
Type: Studentship
Value: £13,863 and tuition fees paid at the Home/European Union rate (up to £3,900 last year)
Length of Study: 1–3 years
Frequency: Annual
Study Establishment: The University of Kent
Country of Study: United Kingdom

No. of awards offered: 20–30
Application Procedure: Applicants must submit to the University's recruitment and admissions office a research proposal, curriculum vitae and covering letter with an application for their chosen research degree. They should also ensure that the recruitment and admissions office receives two referees' reports by the closing date for applications. Applications are available at records.kent.ac.uk/external/admissions/pg-application.php
Closing Date: 31 January
Funding: Private
Contributor: Kent Law School
No. of awards given last year: 2
No. of applicants last year: 20–30
Additional Information: Holders of the studentships will be expected to teach for a maximum of 4 hours per week in term time on an undergraduate law module, at the direction of the head of department. For further information contact the Kent Law school at kls-pgoffice@kent.ac.uk

For further information contact:

Tel: (44) 1227 827949
Email: m.drakopoulou@kent.ac.uk
Contact: Ms Maria Drakopoulou, Director of Postgraduate Research

Language Lector Scholarships

Subjects: European and Latin American literary, linguistic and cultural studies (French, German, Hispanic studies, Italian and comparative literary studies), philosophy (with special expertise in moral and political philosophy, aesthetics, philosophy of mind, philosophical logic and paradoxes, Bayesian epistemology and artificial intelligence), religious studies (modern theology, Christian ethics, mysticism and religious experience, religion and film, psychology of religion and cultural study of cosmology and divination) and the literature, history and archaeology of classical World (including Britain and Gaul)
Purpose: To support research
Eligibility: The scholarship is open to candidates who have made an application for any one of the taught MA programmes (except programmes taught in Paris or Athens) in SECL in an area related to the language they will be teaching. Candidates must hold a First Class or Upper Second Class Undergraduate Degree in a relevant subject (or have reached an appropriate point in their University education to be accepted onto a United Kingdom Master's degree). Candidates must be a native speaker of French, German, Spanish, Catalan or Portuguese. Candidates must have excellent communication skills, both written and oral and ideally some experience of language

teaching. This scholarship is open to United Kingdom, European Union and overseas fee-paying students

Level of Study: Postgraduate, Research

Type: Studentship

Value: 100% of tuition fees at the Home/European Union rate for a postgraduate programme within the School of European Culture and Languages (SECL) and combined maintenance grant and salary

Length of Study: 3 years

Frequency: Annual

Study Establishment: The University of Kent

Country of Study: United Kingdom

Application Procedure: Application is via School of European Culture and Language website www.kent.ac.uk/secl/postgraduate/funding.html?tab=language-lector-scholarships

Closing Date: May (the precise date is to be confirmed)

Funding: Government

Additional Information: Candidates may be interviewed over the telephone as appropriate. Language Lectors teach for at least 20 of these 24 weeks and will be expected to teach 10 hours a week

For further information contact:

Email: seclpgadmin@kent.ac.uk

Postgrad Solutions Study Bursaries

Purpose: Kent University- Kent offers well-structured and ambitious. It provides a comprehensive package of skills development training programs, careers advice, and volunteering and paid work opportunities to enhance your career prospects in a global workplace.

Eligibility: Scholarship is available for pursuing Postgraduate degree program

Level of Study: Postgraduate

Type: Bursary

Value: £500

Frequency: Annual

Country of Study: Any country

Closing Date: 13 September

Funding: International office

School of Economics funding

Subjects: Labour economics, money and development, international finance and trade, migration, defence and energy economics, macro economics, ganne theory and econometrics

Purpose: To support research

Eligibility: All applicants for a scholarship should have completed a Master's degree in Economics or a closely-related subject. In order to be eligible for this scholarship, you must have applied for and accepted a place to study at the University

Level of Study: Doctorate, Postgraduate, Research

Type: Bursary

Value: Tuition fees at the Home/European Union rate and a maintenance grant, usually up to a similar rate to an ESRC grant (£13,590 for last year)

Length of Study: 1 year in the 1st instance, renewable for a maximum of 3 years subject to satisfactory academic performance

Frequency: Dependent on funds available

Study Establishment: The University of Kent

Country of Study: United Kingdom

Application Procedure: To apply for a scholarship, please send a curriculum vitae, including the names of two referees, a brief research proposal, transcripts of your previous degrees and a covering letter to the Postgraduate Co-ordinator, Katie Marshall at econpg@kent.ac.uk

Closing Date: 15 April

Funding: Government

Additional Information: Candidates should note that 4–6 hours of teaching per week and acceptable progress in the programme of study will be expected of the student. The bursary will be subject to review each year

For further information contact:

Email: Y.Zhu-5@kent.ac.uk

Contact: Dr Yu Zhu

School of English MA Scholarships for International Students at University of Kent in United Kingdom

Subjects: English

Purpose: The purpose of the scholarships is to award candidates with the strongest academic records. The School of English reserves the right to distribute the scholarships amongst candidates in a way that will honour that commitment

Eligibility: Please check details at www.kent.ac.uk/english/postgraduate/feesandfunding

Level of Study: Doctorate, Postgraduate

Type: Scholarship

Value: £5,000, For Master Degree

Length of Study: Up to 3 years

Frequency: Annual

Study Establishment: The University of Kent

Country of Study: United Kingdom

Application Procedure: All students who have made an application to study on an MA programme in the School of

English by the deadline will automatically be considered for a scholarship
Closing Date: 22 March
Funding: Government, Commercial
No. of awards given last year: 5

For further information contact:

Email: englishpg@kent.ac.uk

South East ESRC DTC Funding

Subjects: Social psychology, cognitive psychology, neuro-psychology, health psychology, developmental psychology, and forensic psychology
Purpose: To support research studies
Level of Study: Postgraduate, Research
Type: Studentship
Value: The funding will typically cover yearly maintenance (£13,863 for last year) and fees for one of the following: +3 programme or 1+3
Length of Study: 3 years
Frequency: Annual
Study Establishment: The University of Kent
Country of Study: United Kingdom
No. of awards offered: 30–40
Application Procedure: Applicants must complete an application form
Closing Date: 2 February
Funding: Private
Contributor: South-East ESRC DTC
No. of awards given last year: 2
No. of applicants last year: 30–40
Additional Information: Studentships will be awarded on the basis of the academic excellence of both the candidate and the research proposal

For further information contact:

Tel: (44) 1227 823085
Email: rsg@kent.ac.uk
Contact: Dr Roger Giner-Sorolla, CSGP

University of Kent Anthropology Bursaries

Subjects: Anthropology
Purpose: To support both research and taught programmes
Eligibility: Candidates are expected to hold an Upper Second Class (Honours) Degree
Level of Study: Doctorate, Postgraduate, Research
Type: Bursary
Value: Home fees only

Length of Study: 3 years
Frequency: Dependent on funds available
Study Establishment: The University of Kent
Country of Study: United Kingdom
Closing Date: Please write for details
No. of awards given last year: 2

For further information contact:

Email: n.a.kerry-yoxall@ukc.ac.uk
Contact: Ms Nicola Kerry Yoxall

University of Kent at Canterbury Second English Scholarship

Subjects: English
Purpose: To support research
Eligibility: Candidates are expected to hold at least an Upper Second Class (Honours) Degree or equivalent. Candidates should also have applied for an external scholarship, such as AHRB
Level of Study: Postgraduate
Type: Research grant
Value: Home tuition fees up to £3,500 bursary per year for up to three years full-time study. Some undergraduate teaching or research assistance will be expected from the successful candidate
Frequency: Annual
Study Establishment: The University of Kent
Country of Study: United Kingdom
Application Procedure: Candidates must complete the post-graduate application form, indicating in the appropriate section that they are interested in being considered for departmental scholarships. A covering letter supporting the scholarship application should be attached
Closing Date: 30 May

For further information contact:

Email: scholarships@kent.ac.uk

University of Kent Department of Electronics Studentships

Subjects: Electronics, including image processing and vision, embedded systems, broadband and wireless communications and electronic instrumentation
Purpose: To enable well-qualified students to undertake research programmes within the department
Eligibility: Candidates are expected to hold an Upper Second Class (Honours) Degree or equivalent in an appropriate subject, and be nationals of one of the European Union countries

Level of Study: Doctorate, Postgraduate, Research
Type: Studentship
Value: Research Council studentships are at a fixed rate determined annually by EPSRC. Departmental bursaries depend on individual circumstances
Length of Study: 3 years
Frequency: Annual
Study Establishment: The University of Kent
Country of Study: United Kingdom
No. of awards offered: 10
Application Procedure: Applicants should contact the Department of Electronics
Closing Date: June
Funding: Government
Contributor: EPSRC
No. of awards given last year: 5
No. of applicants last year: 10

For further information contact:

Email: ee-admissions-pg@kent.ac.uk
Contact: Professor J Z Wang

University of Kent Law School Studentship

Subjects: Critical commercial law, business law and regulation, criminal justice, environmental law, European and comparative law, gender and sexuality, health care law and ethics, law politics and culture, law and political economy, legal theories and philosophy, property law
Purpose: To support research
Eligibility: Applicants should normally have obtained, or be about to obtain an undergraduate degree of at least Upper Second Class Honours level (2:1 or equivalent from other countries), or a postgraduate degree
Level of Study: Doctorate, Postgraduate
Type: Scholarships
Value: Maintenance grant equivalent to that offered by ESRC (£13,863 in last year) and tuition fees paid at the Home/European Union rate (£3,900 in last year)
Length of Study: Up to 3 years
Frequency: Annual
Study Establishment: University of Kent
Country of Study: United Kingdom
Application Procedure: Applications to be filled electronically at www.kent.ac.uk/law/postgraduate/research/entryreq-research.html. Along with their application, candidates must supply a research proposal of no more than 1,500 words (including bibliography), along with a sample of their written work (not exceeding 4,000 words – longer texts will not be read)
Closing Date: 31 January

Funding: Government, Commercial
No. of awards given last year: 8
Additional Information: See website for further details: www.kent.ac.uk/law/postgraduate/research/KLS_research_funding.html

For further information contact:

Tel: (44) 1227 827949
Email: mailto:m.drakopoulou@kent.ac.uk
Contact: Ms Maria Drakopoulou, Director of Postgraduate Research, Kent Law School

University of Kent School of Drama, Film and Visual Arts Scholarships

Subjects: Drama, including performance-making process and theory, theatre history and practice as research film studies, including varied aspects of film aesthetics, film theory and film history as well as research by practice. History and philosophy of art, including contemporary aesthetics and the history of art theory, the photograph, and the historical interplay of image, theory and institutions from the renaissance to the present
Purpose: To support research
Eligibility: Candidates are expected to hold an Upper Second Class (Honours) Degree and be a citizen of one of the European Union countries
Level of Study: Postgraduate, Research
Value: To cover home fees only
Length of Study: The bursary is 1 year
Frequency: Annual
Study Establishment: The University of Kent
Country of Study: United Kingdom
Application Procedure: Applicants must indicate their interest on the postgraduate application form
Closing Date: 31 July
Additional Information: Some teaching or research assistant work may be required

For further information contact:

Email: k.j.goddard@kent.ac.uk

University of Kent School of Mathematics, Statistics and Actuarial Science Scholarships

Subjects: Mathematics, statistics or actuarial science
Purpose: To support research
Eligibility: Candidates should hold a good (first or upper second) Honours degree, or a Master's degree in a relevant subject
Level of Study: Doctorate, Postgraduate

Type: Scholarship
Value: Home fees and maintenance stipend
Length of Study: Up to 3 years
Frequency: Annual
Study Establishment: University of Kent
Country of Study: United Kingdom
Application Procedure: See webpages at www.kent.ac.uk/
Closing Date: 20 April
Funding: Government, Commercial
No. of awards given last year: 5

For further information contact:

Email: scholarships@kent.ac.uk

University of Kent School of Politics and International Relations Scholarships

Subjects: Politics and government, international relations, international conflict analysis
Purpose: To support research
Eligibility: These scholarships are available to Home/European Union/Overseas students who have been made an offer by Kent for MPhil/PhD study
Level of Study: Doctorate, Postgraduate
Type: Scholarship
Value: Home fees and maintenance stipend
Length of Study: Up to 3 years
Frequency: Annual
Study Establishment: University of Kent
Country of Study: United Kingdom
Application Procedure: See webpages at www.kent.ac.uk/scholarships/postgraduate/departmental/politicsandir.html
Closing Date: April
Funding: Government, Commercial
No. of awards given last year: 2

For further information contact:

Email: scholarships@kent.ac.uk

University of Kent School of Psychology Scholarships

Subjects: Cognitive psychology, developmental psychology, forensic psychology, group processes and intergroup relations, and social psychology
Purpose: To support research
Eligibility: Candidates must hold a good Honours degree (first class or 2i) or a Master's degree at merit or distinction in Psychology. Non-British qualifications will be judged individually; we will generally require an overall result in the top two grading categories
Level of Study: Doctorate, Postgraduate
Type: Scholarship
Value: Home fees and maintenance stipend
Length of Study: Up to 3 years
Study Establishment: University of Kent
Country of Study: United Kingdom
Application Procedure: Please check at www.kent.ac.uk/scholarships/postgraduate/departmental/psychology.html
Closing Date: April
Funding: Government, Commercial
No. of awards given last year: 5

For further information contact:

Email: scholarships@kent.ac.uk

University of Kent School of Social Policy, Sociology and Social Research Scholarships

Subjects: Social Policy, sociology, criminology
Purpose: To support research
Eligibility: Candidates should hold a good (First or Upper Second Class) Honours degree or equivalent, in a relevant discipline
Level of Study: Doctorate, Postgraduate
Type: Scholarship
Value: Home fees and maintenance stipend
Length of Study: Up to 3 years
Frequency: Annual
Study Establishment: University of Kent
Country of Study: United Kingdom
Application Procedure: See webpages at www.kent.ac.uk/sspssr/studying/scholarships-and-bursaries/index.html
Closing Date: 10 February
Funding: Government, Commercial
No. of awards given last year: 3
Additional Information: This scholarship will be in addition to any Kent scholarships and discounts (such as the £1,000 Graduate School Scholarship, 10% Loyalty Discount and the School £500 discount for high performing students)

For further information contact:

Email: scholarships@kent.ac.uk

University of KwaZulu-Natal

Westville   Campus,   Private   Bag   X54001,   Durban, South Africa

Fax: (27) 31 260 2587
Email: heard@ukzn.ac.za
Website: www.heard.org.za/

HEARD is a leading applied research centre with a global reputation for its research, education programmes, technical services, partnerships and networks, devoted to addressing the broad health challenges of Africa. HEARD was established in 1998 and is based at the University of KwaZulu-Natal, South Africa.

Health Economics and HIV/AIDS Research Division PhD Scholarships

Purpose: Under the supervision of Professor Nana Poku and with the generous support of Sida/NORAD, HEARD is offering up to four full-time PhD Research Scholarships in any of the following key areas of strategic focus: Sexual and Reproductive Health; Health Systems Strengthening and Economics of Critical Enablers in HIV Programming
Eligibility: Applicant must have the below criteria. 1. Hold a Master's Degree in a pertinent subject or a first or upper second class degree together with a track record of professional experience in a health o health-related field. 2. Have demonstrable research experience. 3. Undertake to register for a PhD dissertation (full time) at the University of KwaZulu–Natal (UKZN). 4. Make a commitment to remain on the African continent for at least TWO years after graduation
Value: The value of each scholarship is ZAR 540,000 paid over three years
Length of Study: Scholarships will be paid in tranches over 3 years. Tranche payments will be conditional on research progress
Country of Study: South Africa
Application Procedure: 1. A letter of motivation and CV. 2. An eight to ten page concept note on one of HEARD's key thematic research areas: Sexual & Reproductive Health & Rights; Gender, Equality & Health; Health Governance & Finance; and Health Systems Strengthening. 3. Certified copies of both your academic qualifications and your full academic records. If qualifications were obtained from non-English speaking countries please ensure that an official English translation is included. 4. A certified copy of your ID/passport. 5. Two letters of reference, at least one of which must be academic. The second can be from an individual of professional standing
Closing Date: 1 March
Funding: Private

For further information contact:

Email: Hedderwick@ukzn.ac.za

University of Leeds

Postgraduate Scholarships, Research Student Administration, Leeds LS2 9JT, United Kingdom

Tel: (44) 113 343 4077 ext 34077
Fax: (44) 113 343 3941
Email: pg_scholarships@leeds.ac.uk
Website: www.scholarships.leeds.ac.uk
Contact: Erika Smith, Senior Clerk

The University of Leeds aims to promote excellence and to achieve and sustain international standing in higher education teaching, learning and research, and to serve a wide range of student constituencies, social and professional communities and industrial, commercial and government agencies, locally, nationally and internationally.

Beit Trust Postgraduate Scholarships

Subjects: Any subject that will contribute materially to the development of your country of origin
Purpose: To support Postgraduate Study or research at Masters' level (MSc/MA)
Eligibility: Open to persons under 30 years of age, or 35 years for medical doctors, who are university graduates domiciled in Zambia, Zimbabwe or Malawi. Applicants must be nationals of those countries, and have an Honours degree at undergraduate level
Level of Study: Postgraduate
Type: Scholarship
Value: Academic fees, living expenses, other allowances, economy return airfares and allowance toward laptops
Length of Study: a maximum of 2 years at a South African University or 1 year at a United Kingdom University
Frequency: Annual
Study Establishment: The University of Leeds
Country of Study: United Kingdom
No. of awards offered: 720
Application Procedure: Please see the Beit Trust website on 1 April for the new Scholarship application process. Applicants from Zimbabwe and Malawi should contact the Harare office at: africa@beittrust.org.uk
Closing Date: 1 April
Funding: Private
No. of awards given last year: 19
No. of applicants last year: 720
Additional Information: Zambian applicants should contact the Beit Trust United Kingdom office at: scholarships@beittrust.org.uk

For further information contact:

Tel: (263) 1483 772575
Email: scholarships@beittrust.org.uk
Contact: Sir Andrew Pocock, Secretary

Canon Collins Trust-FCO Chevening-University of Leeds Scholarships

Subjects: Majority of subjects
Purpose: To provide awards to students of high academic calibre, who demonstrate both academic excellence and the potential to become leaders, decision makers and opinion formers in their own countries
Eligibility: Open to candidates from Angola, Botswana, Lesotho, Malawi Mozambique, Namibia, South Africa, Swaziland, Zambia or Zimbabwe. Applicants must already hold a degree of equivalent standard to a United Kingdom upper second class honours degree. An adequate standard of English is required
Level of Study: Postgraduate
Type: Scholarship
Value: Academic fees, living expenses, other allowances, economy return airfares
Length of Study: 1 year
Frequency: Annual
Study Establishment: The University of Leeds
Country of Study: United Kingdom
No. of awards offered: Not known
Application Procedure: Applicants must complete an application form available on request from the Canon Collins Trust
Closing Date: 28 February
Funding: Government, Private
No. of awards given last year: 10
No. of applicants last year: Not known

For further information contact:

Email: info@canoncollins.org.uk

Derek Fatchett Memorial Scholarships (Palestine)

Subjects: Politics or international studies
Purpose: To provide awards to students of high academic calibre
Eligibility: Open to candidates who have obtained or are about to obtain the equivalent of a United Kingdom First or Second Class (Honours) Degree. Candidates must be nationals of Palestine
Level of Study: Postgraduate
Type: Scholarship

Value: Academic fees, living expenses, books, equipment, arrival and departure allowance, economy return airfares and the production of a dissertation
Length of Study: 1 year
Frequency: Annual
Study Establishment: The University of Leeds
Country of Study: United Kingdom
No. of awards offered: Not known
Application Procedure: Application procedures are now handled by the British Council offices in Ramallah and East Jerusalem
Closing Date: 31 May
Funding: Private
No. of applicants last year: Not known

For further information contact:

Email: Lmec@Lmec.org.uk

Frank Parkinson Scholarship

Subjects: Any subject
Purpose: To provide postgraduate scholarships for United Kingdom research students of high calibre
Eligibility: Candidates must be commencing PhD study for the first time and hold at least a United Kingdom upper second class honours degree or equivalent. Candidates must have British parents who have been domiciled in Yorkshire for a period of not less than 10 years
Level of Study: Doctorate
Type: Scholarship
Value: Fees at the United Kingdom rate plus a maintenance allowance
Length of Study: Up to 3 years, subject to satisfactory progress
Frequency: Annual
Study Establishment: University of Leeds
Country of Study: United Kingdom
No. of awards offered: 39
Application Procedure: An application form must be completed and returned to the Postgraduate Scholarships Office by the relevant date
Closing Date: 1 June
Funding: Private
No. of awards given last year: 2
No. of applicants last year: 39

For further information contact:

Email: fbsgrad@leeds.ac.uk

Frank Stell Scholarship

Subjects: Biology, Agricultural Science, or Social and Political Science

Purpose: To provide postgraduate scholarships for United Kingdom research students of high calibre

Eligibility: Candidates must be commencing PhD study for the first time and hold at least a United Kingdom Upper Second Class Honours degree or equivalent. Candidates should be resident, or have parents resident within the former administrative area of the County Council of the West Riding of Yorkshire

Level of Study: Doctorate

Type: Scholarship

Value: Fees at the University of Leeds standard United Kingdom/European Union rate plus a maintenance allowance

Length of Study: Up to 3 years, subject to satisfactory progress

Frequency: Dependent on funds available

Study Establishment: University of Leeds

Country of Study: United Kingdom

Application Procedure: Details provided on website www.scholarships.leeds.ac.uk

Closing Date: See website for closing date www.scholarships.leeds.ac.uk

Additional Information: The scholarship is subject to funding and will only be advertised on www.scholarships.leeds.ac.uk if there are available funds

For further information contact:

Email: fbsgrad@leeds.ac.uk

Henry Ellison Scholarship

Subjects: Pure and Applied Chemistry and Physics

Purpose: To provide postgraduate scholarships for United Kingdom and European Union research students of high calibre

Eligibility: Candidates must be from the United Kingdom or an European Union country (or eligible to pay fees at the United Kingdom rate) and be commencing PhD study for the first time. Candidates must hold at least a United Kingdom Upper Second Class Honours degree or equivalent and be a University of Leeds graduate

Level of Study: Doctorate

Type: Scholarship

Value: Fees at the University of Leeds standard United Kingdom/European Union rate plus a maintenance allowance

Length of Study: Up to 3 years, subject to satisfactory progress

Frequency: Dependent on funds available

Study Establishment: University of Leeds

Country of Study: United Kingdom

Application Procedure: Details provided on website www.scholaships.leeds.ac.uk

Closing Date: See website for closing date www.scholarships.leeds.ac.uk

Additional Information: The award is available within the School of Physics and Astronomy. The scholarship is subject to funding and will only be advertised on scholarships.leeds.ac.uk if there are available funds

For further information contact:

Email: maps.pgr.admissions@leeds.ac.uk

John Henry Garner Scholarship

Subjects: Research on matters relating to chemical and biological surveys of rivers and streams, pollution prevention and purification of sewage and trade effluents in the area previously known as the West Riding of Yorkshire

Purpose: To provide postgraduate scholarships for United Kingdom and European Union research students of high calibre

Eligibility: Candidates must be from the United Kingdom or an European Union country (or eligible to pay fees at the United Kingdom rate) and be commencing PhD study for the first time. Candidates must hold at least a United Kingdom Upper Second Class Honours degree or equivalent

Level of Study: Doctorate

Type: Scholarship

Value: Fees at the University of Leeds standard United Kingdom/European Union rate plus a maintenance allowance

Length of Study: Up to 3 years, subject to satisfactory progress

Frequency: Dependent on funds available

Study Establishment: University of Leeds

Country of Study: United Kingdom

Application Procedure: Details provided on website www.scholarships.leed.ac.uk

Closing Date: See website for closing date www.scholarships.leeds.ac.uk

Additional Information: The scholarship is subject to funding and will only be advertised on www.scholarships.leeds.ac.uk if there are available funds

For further information contact:

Email: fbsgrad@leeds.ac.uk

Marks and Spencer - Leeds University- FCO Chevening Scholarships

Subjects: Preference is given to Management Studies

Purpose: To provide postgraduate scholarships to students of high academic calibre

Eligibility: Open to candidates from Hong Kong who have obtained, or are about to obtain, a first degree of a similar standard to a United Kingdom good Upper Second Class (Honours) Degree. An adequate standard of English language is required

Level of Study: Postgraduate

Type: Scholarship

Value: Full tuition fees, maintenance allowance, books, equipment and production of dissertation

Length of Study: 1 year

Frequency: Annual

Study Establishment: The University of Leeds

Country of Study: United Kingdom

Application Procedure: By application form and acceptance onto taught course. Both application forms are available from the University and British Council (Hong Kong)

Closing Date: Usually December

Funding: Government, Commercial

No. of awards given last year: 1

Additional Information: The address for the British Council in Hong Kong is: The Education Exchange Unit, 255 Hennessey Road, Wanchai, Hong Kong

For further information contact:

Email: scholarships@gcu.ac.uk

Mary and Alice Smith Memorial Scholarship

Subjects: Research into the prevention or cure of cancer or heart disease

Purpose: To provide postgraduate scholarships for United Kingdom research students of high calibre

Eligibility: Candidates must be British and be commencing PhD study for the first time. Candidates must hold at least a United Kingdom Upper Second Class Honours degree or equivalent

Level of Study: Doctorate

Type: Scholarship

Value: Fees at the University of Leeds standard United Kingdom/European Union rate plus a maintenance allowance

Length of Study: Up to 3 years, subject to satisfactory progress

Frequency: Dependent on funds available

Study Establishment: University of Leeds

Country of Study: United Kingdom

Application Procedure: Details provided on www.scholar ships.leeds.ac.uk

Closing Date: See website for closing date www.scholar ships.leeds.ac.uk

Additional Information: The scholarship is subject to funding and will only be advertised on www.scholarships. leeds.ac.uk if there are available funds

For further information contact:

Email: fbsgrad@leeds.ac.uk

Stanley Burton Research Scholarship

Subjects: Music

Purpose: To provide postgraduate scholarships for United Kingdom/European Union research students of high calibre

Eligibility: Candidates must be from United Kingdom or an European Union country and be commencing PhD study for the first time. Candidates must hold at least a United Kingdom upper second class honours degree or equivalent

Level of Study: Doctorate

Type: Scholarship

Value: Fees at the University of Leeds standard United Kingdom/European Union rate plus a maintenance allowance

Length of Study: Up to 3 years, subject to satisfactory progress

Frequency: Dependent on funds available

Study Establishment: University of Leeds

Country of Study: United Kingdom

Application Procedure: Details provided on www.scholar ships.leeds.ac.uk

Closing Date: See website for closing date www.scholar ships.leeds.ac.uk

Additional Information: The award is available within the School of Music. This scholarship is subject to funding and will only be advertised on scholarships.leeds.ac.uk if there are available funds

For further information contact:

Email: pg_scholarships@leeds.ac.uk

University of Leeds International Fee Bursary (Vietnam) - for subject areas listed below Leeds

Subjects: Economics, economics and finance, accounting and finance, human resource management, development studies, international political economy, international studies, politics of international resources and development, cognitive systems, international finance, banking & finance, company management

Purpose: To provide scholarships to students of high academic calibre in the School of Computing, Politics and International Studies and Leeds University Business School

Eligibility: Open to nationals of Vietnam who have obtained a degree equivalent to a good Second Class (Honours) Degree. An adequate standard of English is required
Level of Study: Postgraduate
Type: Scholarship
Value: Academic fees
Length of Study: 1 year
Frequency: Annual
Study Establishment: The University of Leeds
Country of Study: United Kingdom
No. of awards offered: Not known
Application Procedure: Applicants must make an application in letter format to the Taught Postgraduate Secretary in the school they intend to study
Closing Date: 29 May
Funding: Private
No. of awards given last year: 4
No. of applicants last year: Not known

For further information contact:

Email: info@lubs.leeds.ac.uk

University of Leeds International Fee Bursary (Vietnam) - Information Systems/Multimedia Systems

Subjects: Information systems or multimedia systems
Purpose: To provide scholarships to students of high academic calibre who wish to study in the school of computing
Eligibility: Applicants must be nationals of Vietnam and must already have obtained a good Second Class (Honours) Degree. An adequate standard of English is also required
Level of Study: Postgraduate
Type: Scholarship
Value: Academic fees
Length of Study: 1 year
Frequency: Annual
Study Establishment: The University of Leeds
Country of Study: United Kingdom
Application Procedure: Applicants must make an application in letter form to the Taught Postgraduate Secretary in the School of Computing
Closing Date: 11 June
Funding: Private
No. of awards given last year: 1

For further information contact:

International office, University of Leeds, Leeds LS2 9JT, United Kingdom

Email: info@lubs.leeds.ac.uk

University of Leeds International Fee Bursary (Vietnam)

Subjects: Information systems, distributed multimedia systems, multidisciplinary informatics
Purpose: To provide scholarships to students of high academic calibre
Eligibility: Open to nationals of Vietnam who have obtained a degree equivalent to a good Second Class (Honours) Degree. An adequate standard of English is required
Level of Study: Postgraduate
Type: Scholarship
Value: Academic fees
Length of Study: 1 year
Frequency: Annual
Study Establishment: The University of Leeds
Country of Study: United Kingdom
Application Procedure: Applicants must address a letter of application to the School of Computing
Closing Date: 10 June
Funding: Private
No. of awards given last year: 1

University of Leicester

University Road, Leicester LE1 7RH, United Kingdom

Tel: (44) 162 522 522
Fax: (44) 1162 522 200
Email: upim@admin.le.ac.uk
Website: www.le.ac.uk
Contact: Mr K J Julian, Registrar and Secretary

Central United Kingdom NERC Training Alliance (CENTA) PhD Studentships for European Union Students

Purpose: Studentships are available to pursue PhD research programme
Type: Award
Value: CENTA has been awarded £4.9 million from the Natural Environment Research Council (NERC)
Length of Study: 5 years
Country of Study: United Kingdom
Closing Date: 22 January

For further information contact:

Email: communications@ukri.org

College of Science and Engineering Postgraduate Scholarship Scheme

Subjects: Scholarships are awarded in the field of Chemistry, Engineering, Geography, Informatics, Mathematics and Physics and Astronomy

Purpose: University of Leicester's aim is to be a world-class research-intensive university and deliver teaching and facilitate learning of the highest quality

Eligibility: Applicants must be classified as an international (non-European Union) student for fee purposes. The fee discount will be calculated on the basis of the standard tuition fee, excluding components for 'with industry' degrees. In accordance with scholarship guidelines, students are allowed to hold only one University of Leicester scholarship, awarded either centrally or by a department. If you are awarded more than one scholarship, you will therefore receive only the higher value award. The scholarship is only valid for entry in September. If you currently have a conditional offer of a place at the University, you will still need to fulfil any conditions stated on your offer letter. The scholarship is only available for campus-based courses

Type: Postgraduate scholarships

Value: Successful applicant will receive tuition fee discount of 22% – or 28%

Study Establishment: Scholarships are awarded in the field of Chemistry, Engineering, Geography, Informatics, Mathematics and Physics and Astronomy

Country of Study: United Kingdom

Application Procedure: Academic qualifications and transcripts Personal statement/research proposal Two completed references (one must be academic) OR names and contact details of two people from whom we can request references (one must be an academic referee). Proof of English language competency (if your first language is not English)

Closing Date: Open

Additional Information: please browse the website for more details scholarship-positions.com/college-of-science-engineering-postgraduate-scholarship-scheme-uk/2017/12/18/

For further information contact:

Email: scholarships@le.ac.uk

PhD Studentships in Computer Science

Subjects: Computer science

Purpose: To support research organizations attract the best people into postgraduate research and training and to provide doctoral training grant support

Eligibility: Please check at EPSRC website at www2.le.ac.uk/study/research/funding/epsrc-computing

Level of Study: Doctorate

Type: Studentship

Value: The successful applicants will receive an annual stipend of at least £13,863 together with a conference allowance and training support grant worth £600 each year

Length of Study: 3 years

Frequency: Dependent on funds available

Study Establishment: University of Leicester, Computer Science Department

Country of Study: United Kingdom

Application Procedure: Please refer to the University of Leicester website at www2.le.ac.uk/study/research/funding/epsrc-computing. Our PhD superiors have a range of interests and the aim is to align you with someone with expertise in your field. Details of our research themes are on the website

Closing Date: Open Until Filled

Funding: Government

Contributor: EPSRC (DTG)

Additional Information: Applications are considered throughout the year. Refer to advertisement on website

For further information contact:

Email: fdv1@mcs.le.ac.uk

Contact: Dr Fer-Jan de Vries, PhD Admissions Tutor

PhD Studentships in Mathematics

Subjects: Pure and applied mathematics, financial mathematics and actuarial science are considered

Eligibility: United Kingdom and European Union PhD students, who have been residents in the United Kingdom for 3 years prior to application, and fees-only funding for other European Union students

Level of Study: Doctorate, Research

Type: Studentship

Value: £14,057 in the first year, rising in successive years, and full tuition fees

Length of Study: 3.5 years

Country of Study: United Kingdom

Application Procedure: Applications can be made online and submitted to admissions office. Information on how to apply and what supporting documents needed can be found at www2.le.ac.uk/research/degrees/phd/maths/supervision

Closing Date: For further information, please visit www2.le.ac.uk/departments/mathematics/postgraduate-study/phd/phd-study

For further information contact:

Email: pgresearch@maths.ed.ac.uk

President's Postgraduate Scholarship Scheme

Purpose: This is a postgraduate scholarship that enables international students to get a chance to study in University of Leicester, United Kingdom

Value: President's Postgraduate Scholarship Scheme at the University of Leicester provides £3,500 in the form of a reduction in tuition fee

Length of Study: 1 to 2 years

Country of Study: Any country

Application Procedure: Send your completed application by email to scholarships@le.ac.uk

Closing Date: 31 July

For further information contact:

Tel: (44) 141 331 3000
Email: ukroenquiries@gcu.ac.uk

University of Limerick

Kemmy Business School, Limerick, Ireland

Tel: (353) 61 202 116
Fax: (353) 61 330 316
Email: elaine.kirwan@ul.ie
Website: www.ul.ie
Contact: Elaine Kirwan

Kemmy Business School: PhD Scholarship

Subjects: The scholarship is awarded in Organization Science and Public Policy

Purpose: The competition is open to prospective students, as well as those who have registered in the current calendar year, and will cover fees and a stipend of €1,000 per month for years one to four of a full time traditional or structured PhD programme

Eligibility: Applicants should have first or upper second class degree (Level 8 – National Qualifications Authority of Ireland or equivalent) or a Master's degree in economics, statistics, demography, mathematics, computer science or cognate discipline. They should have strong econometric skills, computer programming skills and demonstrated experience in at least one high-level language, such as R or Matheamatica. Applicants should have strong verbal and written communication skills and should have the ability to write concise and accessible reports for both specialist and non-specialist audiences. Non-European Union citizens are eligible for this international PhD scholarship

Level of Study: Doctorate

Type: PhD scholarship

Value: The value of the scholarship is €14,000 per year plus European Union fees for a maximum of 3 years (the final year fee will have to be paid by the student)

Frequency: Every 3 years

Country of Study: Ireland

Application Procedure: The mode of applying is electronically. Completed application forms should be submitted electronically to michelle.cunningham@ul.ie, stating the research theme under which candidates are applying, along with a copy of official academic results, curriculum vitae, research proposal and letter of application. For further information, refer the below link. www.ul.ie/business/sites/default/files/file /Dean%20Scholarship%20Detail%202019%20.pdf

Closing Date: 10 May

Contributor: Kemmy Business School at the University of Limerick

Additional Information: The duration is of maximum 3 years

For further information contact:

Email: rebecca.gachet@ul.ie

University of Lincoln

Brayford Pool, Lincoln LN6 7TS, United Kingdom

Tel: (44) 1522 882 000
Website: www.lincoln.ac.uk
Contact: University of Lincoln

Lincoln is ranked 11th in the United Kingdom for student satisfaction in the National Student Survey (NSS) 2016. The University is committed to developing enterprising graduates, with Lincoln students enjoying good graduate prospects and many going on to start their own successful businesses. The University of Lincoln is producing world-leading research across many subject areas.

Academic Excellence Scholarship

Subjects: Scholarships are awarded any of subjects offered by the university

Purpose: For programmes commencing in January / February and September, the university invites applications for Academic Excellence Scholarships from students from around the world. Students from China, India, Malaysia,

Norway, Nigeria, Saudi Arabia, Thailand, Vietnam and the United States are eligible to apply for these scholarships

Eligibility: The University invites applications from students in the following countries: China, India, Malaysia, Norway, Nigeria, Saudi Arabia, Thailand, Vietnam and the United States. Applicants must have their previous degree. Applicants must meet the programmes general English language requirements

Type: Postgraduate scholarships

Value: £5,000 which will be deducted from your tuition fees during the first year of enrolment

Study Establishment: Scholarships are awarded to learn in any of subjects offered by the university

Country of Study: United Kingdom

Application Procedure: To apply for an Academic Excellence Scholarship, you will need to complete an Academic Excellence Scholarship Application Form and submit to intscholarships-at-lincoln.ac.uk

Closing Date: The Application deadlines are 24 November and 22 June

Additional Information: For more details please visit the website scholarship-positions.com/academic-excellence-scholarship-university-lincoln-uk/2017/01/05/

Egypt Scholarship

Purpose: To offer Egypt Scholarships to high achieving postgraduate applicants

Eligibility: Be an Egyptian citizen

Type: Scholarship

Value: £5,000

Country of Study: United Kingdom

Application Procedure: Submit application to intscholarships@lincoln.ac.uk

Closing Date: 22 June

For further information contact:

Email: intscholarships@lincoln.ac.uk

Ghana Scholarship

Purpose: The University of Lincoln are delighted to offer Ghana Scholarships to high achieving applicants

Type: Scholarship

Value: £5,000

Country of Study: Any country

Application Procedure: Submit the application to intscholarships@lincoln.ac.uk

Closing Date: 22 June

For further information contact:

Email: international@lincoln.ac.uk

Global Postgraduate Scholarship

Subjects: Overseas

Purpose: To be eligible for the scholarship, students must hold a recognised Bachelor degree with a minimum grade of 2:2 or equivalent. Please note that this scholarship is not available for MPhil/PhD programmes.

Eligibility: 1. University of Lincoln International Scholarships take the form of a tuition fee reduction upon enrolment. 2. University of Lincoln International Scholarships are non-transferable and are not valid in conjunction with each other; only one Scholarship per student per course will be applied. 3. The University of Lincoln reserves the right to withdraw any University of Lincoln International Scholarship at any point and without notice. 4. Students who are sponsored by an organisation such as an external funding body. Government, or employer are not eligible to receive a University of Lincoln International Scholarship.

Level of Study: Postgraduate

Type: Scholarship

Value: £2,000

Frequency: Varies

Country of Study: Any country

Application Procedure: Apply online

Closing Date: 19 February, 19 September

Funding: Trusts

For further information contact:

Email: international@lincoln.ac.uk

India Scholarship

Subjects: Overseas

Purpose: The Lincoln India Scholarship is aimed at supporting high-achieving postgraduate students from across India.

Eligibility: 1. University of Lincoln International Scholarships take the form of a tuition fee reduction upon enrolment. 2. University of Lincoln International Scholarships are non-transferable and are not valid in conjunction with each other; only one Scholarship per student per course will be applied. 3. The University of Lincoln reserves the right to withdraw any University of Lincoln International Scholarship at any point and without notice. 4. Students who are sponsored by an organisation such as an external funding body. Government, or employer are not eligible to receive a University of Lincoln International Scholarship.

Level of Study: Postgraduate

Type: Scholarship
Value: £5,000
Length of Study: 1 Year
Frequency: Varies
Country of Study: Any country
Application Procedure: Apply online
Closing Date: 19 February, 19 September
Funding: Trusts

For further information contact:

Email: intscholarships@lincoln.ac.uk

Indonesia Scholarship

Subjects: Overseas
Purpose: The University of Lincoln Indonesia Scholarship is aimed at supporting high-achieving postgraduate students from across Indonesia
Eligibility: 1. University of Lincoln International Scholarships take the form of a tuition fee reduction upon enrolment. 2. University of Lincoln International Scholarships are non-transferable and are not valid in conjunction with each other; only one Scholarship per student per course will be applied. 3. The University of Lincoln reserves the right to withdraw any University of Lincoln International Scholarship at any point and without notice. 4. Students who are sponsored by an organisation such as an external funding body. Government, or employer are not eligible to receive a University of Lincoln International Scholarship
Level of Study: Postgraduate
Type: Scholarship
Value: £5,000
Frequency: Varies
Country of Study: Any country
Application Procedure: Apply online
Closing Date: 19 February, 19 September
Funding: Trusts

For further information contact:

Email: intscholarships@lincoln.ac.uk

Lincoln Alumni Master of Architecture Scholarship

Subjects: This Scholarship applies to students enrolling on the Master of Architecture (Part two) programme in academic year
Purpose: This scholarship is available to Home/European Union students holding a University of Lincoln degree when enrolling on the Master of Architecture programme (MArch)

Type: Scholarship
Value: £1,000 will be paid directly to the student for each year of study for each completed academic year of study, with part-time students eligible for a pro-rata payment
Country of Study: United Kingdom
Application Procedure: No procedure is required. Eligible students will receive this scholarship upon enrolling for the Master of Architecture programme
Funding: Private
Additional Information: You are subject to tuition fees of £9,250

For further information contact:

Email: intscholarships@lincoln.ac.uk

Master of Science Sport Science: Applied Sport Science Bursary

Subjects: Overseas
Purpose: Up to three Applied Sport Science Bursaries will be offered to exceptional students enrolling on MSc Sport Science program
Level of Study: Postgraduate
Type: Bursary
Value: NZ£1,500
Frequency: Varies
Country of Study: Any country
Application Procedure: Apply online
Closing Date: 19 September
Funding: Trusts

For further information contact:

Tel: (44) 1522 886651
Email: swillmott@lincoln.ac.uk

Nigeria Scholarship

Purpose: The University of Lincoln Nigeria Scholarship is aimed at supporting high-achieving postgraduate students from across Nigeria
Eligibility: Be a Nigerian citizen. Already hold a conditional or unconditional offer from the University of Lincoln for a full-time postgraduate taught or Master's by Research programme commencing in September
Type: Scholarship
Value: The scholarship is valued at £5,000
Country of Study: United Kingdom
Application Procedure: Submit applications to intscholarships@lincoln.ac.uk
Funding: Private

Additional Information: For further information, please contact the International Office

For further information contact:

Email: intscholarships@lincoln.ac.uk

Thai Scholarship

Subjects: Overseas
Purpose: For programmes commencing in 2019, the University of Lincoln are delighted to offer Thai Scholarships to high achieving postgraduate applicants.
Eligibility: 1. University of Lincoln International Scholarships take the form of a tuition fee reduction upon enrolment. 2. University of Lincoln International Scholarships are non-transferable and are not valid in conjunction with each other; only one Scholarship per student per course will be applied. 3. The University of Lincoln reserves the right to withdraw any University of Lincoln International Scholarship at any point and without notice. 4. Students who are sponsored by an organisation such as an external funding body. Government, or employer are not eligible to receive a University of Lincoln International Scholarship
Level of Study: Postgraduate
Type: Scholarship
Value: £5,000
Frequency: Varies
Country of Study: Any country
Application Procedure: Apply online
Closing Date: 19 February, 19 September
Funding: Trusts

For further information contact:

Email: intscholarships@lincoln.ac.uk

Thailand Scholarship

Purpose: The University of Lincoln Thai Scholarship is aimed at supporting high-achieving postgraduate students from across Thailand
Eligibility: Be a Thai citizen. Already hold a conditional or unconditional offer from the University of Lincoln for a full-time postgraduate taught or Master's by Research programme commencing in September
Type: Scholarship
Value: £5,000
Application Procedure: For details, please visit intscholarships@lincoln.ac.uk

For further information contact:

Email: intscholarships@lincoln.ac.uk

The Lincoln 50% Global Scholarship

Subjects: Overseas
Purpose: The University of Lincoln are delighted to offer 50% Global Scholarships to international applicants who demonstrate the highest levels of excellence in academia, extracurricular and personal endeavour.
Eligibility: 1. University of Lincoln International Scholarships take the form of a tuition fee reduction upon enrolment. 2. University of Lincoln International Scholarships are non-transferable and are not valid in conjunction with each other; only one Scholarship per student per course will be applied. 3. The University of Lincoln reserves the right to withdraw any University of Lincoln International Scholarship at any point and without notice. 4. Students who are sponsored by an organisation such as an external funding body. Government, or employer are not eligible to receive a University of Lincoln International Scholarship.
Level of Study: Postgraduate
Type: Scholarship
Frequency: Varies
Country of Study: Any country
Application Procedure: Apply online
Closing Date: 19 February, 19 September
Funding: Trusts

For further information contact:

Email: intscholarships@lincoln.ac.uk

University of Lincoln India Scholarships

Value: £5,000
Country of Study: Any country
Application Procedure: The mode of applying is online
Closing Date: September

For further information contact:

Email: intscholarships@lincoln.ac.uk

Uruguay PhD Scholarship

Subjects: Life Sciences
Purpose: To conduct PhD studies in Life Sciences has recently been agreed between the University of Lincoln and

the Uruguay National Agency for Research and Innovation (ANII - Agencia Nacional de Investigaciön e Innovaciön)
Type: Scholarship
Value: The scholarship covers university fees and a subsistence bursary
Country of Study: United Kingdom
Closing Date: 15 March
Additional Information: For additional information regarding this scholarship please contact: Dr Daniel Pincheira-Donoso, Email: DPincheiraDonoso@lincoln.ac.uk, Telephone +44(0)1522 835025

For further information contact:

Email: fmontealegrez@lincoln.ac.uk

Vietnam Merit Scholarship

Purpose: The University of Lincoln Vietnam Merit Scholarship is aimed at supporting high achieving postgraduate students from across Vietnam
Value: £5,000
Country of Study: Any country
Application Procedure: Submit applications to intscholarships@lincoln.ac.uk

For further information contact:

Email: intscholarships@lincoln.ac.uk

University of Liverpool

Liverpool L69 3BX, United Kingdom

The University of Liverpool is a public university based in the city of Liverpool, United Kingdom. Founded as a college in 1881, it gained its royal charter in 1903 with the ability to award degrees and is also known to be one of the six original "red brick" civic universities. It comprises three faculties organized into 35 departments and schools. It is a founding member of the Russell Group, the N8 Group for research collaboration and the University Management school is AACSB accredited.

Commonwealth Shared Scholarship Scheme

Purpose: Commonwealth Shared Scholarships, offered in partnership with United Kingdom universities, are for developing country students who would not otherwise be able to undertake master's level study in the United Kingdom
Type: Scholarship

Value: Covers tuition fees, living costs and return flights to the United Kingdom
Country of Study: United Kingdom
Closing Date: 7 March
Additional Information: Please email seschol@liverpool.ac.uk to confirm you are applying for the scheme and quoting that number

For further information contact:

Email: seschol@liverpool.ac.uk

FIDERH Award

Eligibility: You must be a Mexican national
Type: Award
Value: 20% reduction in tuition fees for postgraduate taught and research programmes
Country of Study: United Kingdom
Closing Date: 28 February
Additional Information: Please apply for funding through FIDERH. Students who are awarded a FIDERH Graduate Loan and register at the University of Liverpool will automatically receive the award

For further information contact:

Website: https://www.fiderh.org.mx/

Hodgson Law Scholarship

Purpose: The Trustees wish Hodgson Law Scholars to benefit from education in Liverpool with a view to encouraging the intellectual growth of promising law students and the nurturing of close links with the City of Liverpool and the Liverpool City Region
Eligibility: 1. Procedure 2: Application for an LLM place at University Applicants should apply for, and hold an offer of place, for a full-time postgraduate taught degree in law (LLM) at the University of Liverpool or Liverpool John Moores University to be eligible for the Hodgson Law Scholarship
Value: The Scholarship includes full tuition fees for a full-time postgraduate taught degree in law (LLM), and a stipend of £9,135
Country of Study: United Kingdom
Application Procedure: You will need to complete and submit the Hodgson Law Scholarship application form electronically to the Hodgson Selection Committee by email to hodgscho@liverpool.ac.uk
Closing Date: 1 May
Additional Information: For enquiries please contact Dr Gregory Messenger, Hodgson Scholarship Liaison. www.liverpool.

ac.uk/law/study/masters/; www.ljmu.ac.uk/study/courses/post graduates/international-business-corporate-and-finance-law

For further information contact:

Email: hodgscho@liverpool.ac.uk

John Lennon Memorial Scholarships

Purpose: The award is intended to support students from Merseyside who might be in financial need and enhance, among other things, awareness of global problems and environmental issues. The John Lennon Memorial Scholarships were set up by a trust fund endowed in the University for the provision of scholarships in the memory of John Lennon
Type: Scholarship
Length of Study: Three years
Country of Study: Any country
Application Procedure: You will need to complete and submit the form by email to the Secretary to the Scholarships Sub-Committee by email to seschol@liverpool.ac.uk
Closing Date: 30 March

For further information contact:

Email: seschol@liverpool.ac.uk

Liverpool International College (LIC) Excellence Award

Eligibility: Students who achieve an average of 75% or above in their LIC Pre-Master's programme
Type: Award
Value: £2,500 tuition fee reduction
Country of Study: United Kingdom
Additional Information: No application necessary. The award will automatically be awarded to those who meet criteria

For further information contact:

Email: irro@liverpool.ac.uk

Liverpool Law School LLM Bursaries

Purpose: Awards will help students with their tuition fees. They are offered to encourage the best students, from the United Kingdom, Europe and internationally, to join the expanding LLM programme
Eligibility: Home, European Union and international students studying a LLM programme. Liverpool Law School

LLM Bursaries will be awarded on the basis of merit. Academic performance in earlier degrees they have taken, as well as any other practical or intellectual achievements, will be taken into account
Type: Bursary
Value: There are two bursaries worth £500 each available to two students classified as home/European Union and two bursaries of £1,000 each available to two international students
Country of Study: United Kingdom
Application Procedure: Students do NOT need to make an extra application for the Liverpool Law School LLM Bursaries. All students who have registered for the LLM will be considered automatically. The decision of Liverpool Law School on the award of the bursaries is final

For further information contact:

Email: irro@liverpool.ac.uk

Marshall Scholarships

Purpose: To enable intellectually distinguished young Americans, their country's future leaders, to study in the United Kingdom. 1. To help Scholars gain an understanding and appreciation of contemporary Britain
Eligibility: To qualify, candidates should: 1. Be citizens of the United States of America normally resident in the United States of America. 2. Hold a doctorate in a science or engineering subject by the time they take up their Fellowship
Type: Scholarship
Value: Full tuition fee waiver for a master
Country of Study: United Kingdom
Closing Date: 10 October
Additional Information: Apply via: www.marshallscholarship.org/applications/apply

For further information contact:

Email: apps@marshallscholarship.org

Santander Awards

Purpose: Santander International Postgraduate Scholarships reward international students who demonstrate academic excellence. The awards are available to international students entering onto postgraduate taught programmes at the University of Liverpool in September
Value: £5,000 tuition fee reduction for 1 year only
Country of Study: United Kingdom
Closing Date: 15 June

For further information contact:

Email: santander.universities@santander.co.uk

University of Liverpool Commonwealth Postgraduate Bursary

Purpose: The University of Liverpool Commonwealth Postgraduate Bursary fee reduction for students from Commonwealth countries new to studying at the University of Liverpool on master's programmes
Type: Bursary
Value: £2,500 fee reduction for Commonwealth students studying Engineering, Electrical Engineering and Electronics, and Computer Science programmes; £1,500 fee reduction for Commonwealth students studying all other subjects
Country of Study: Any country
Additional Information: No application necessary, automatically awarded to those who meet criteria

For further information contact:

Email: irro@liverpool.ac.uk

University of Liverpool Management School Academic Award

Purpose: The University of Liverpool Management School is delighted to offer range of generous scholarships and study awards to help cover the cost of MBA tuition fees
Eligibility: HEU/OSI applicants on the Liverpool MBA and the Football Industries MBA* programmes with an excellent academic profile and excellent work experience, or combination of very high standards in both of the above. It is an on-campus programme
Type: Award
Value: £2,000
Country of Study: United Kingdom

For further information contact:

Email: ulmsmba@liverpool.ac.uk

University of Manchester

Oxford Road, Manchester M13 9PL, United Kingdom

Tel: (44) 161 306 6000
Email: hr@manchester.ac.uk
Website: www.manchester.ac.uk

The University of Manchester is Britain's largest single site university with a proud history of achievement and an ambitious agenda for the future. The University has an exceptional record of generating and sharing new ideas, and the quality, breadth and volume of its research activity is unparalleled in Britain.

Indian Excellence Scholarship Award

Subjects: Scholarships are awarded within the Faculty of Science and Engineering at the University of Manchester
Purpose: Scholarships are available for pursuing undergraduate degree programme
Eligibility: This scheme applies to any undergraduate degree programme within the Faculty of Science and Engineering at The University of Manchester. Each scholarship will be awarded on the basis of a student demonstrating high performance in their International Baccalaureate or Standard XII examinations and the academic reference on their UCAS form. Applicants must be Indian nationals or permanently domiciled in India. Applicants must have applied through UCAS for a place on an undergraduate degree programme in FSE for entry in September. Applicants must have accepted a programme in FSE as their firm choice by the end of June
Type: Scholarship
Value: £3,000 per annum
Country of Study: Any country
Closing Date: End of June
Additional Information: Application for courses in this School should be made online through the Universities and Colleges Admissions Service (UCAS)

For further information contact:

Email: app.req@ucas.ac.uk

Institute for Development Policy and Management Taught Postgraduate Scholarship Scheme

Subjects: Development studies
Eligibility: Bachelors degree with Second Class Honours, Upper Division or above, or Overseas equivalent (please contact School for details of equivalencies). Applicants whose first language is a language other than English must achieve 7.0 or above in IELTS or an equivalent test (TOEFL)
Level of Study: Postgraduate
Type: Scholarship
Value: £2,000
Frequency: Annual

Application Procedure: Check website for further details www.manchester.ac.uk/postgraduate/funding/search/display/?id=00000177

Closing Date: 30 June

For further information contact:

Email: paul.arrowsmith@manchester.ac.uk
Contact: Paul Arrowsmith, School of Environment & Development, Admissions Office

Manchester-China Scholarship Council Joint Postgraduate Scholarship Programme

Subjects: Telecommunication and information technology, life science and public health, material science and new material, energy sources and environment, engineering science and applied social sciences and WTO-related areas

Purpose: To provide scholarships to the nationals of PR China who wish to pursue their PhD at the University of Manchester

Eligibility: Open to students who are citizens and permanent residents of PR China and who hold a Master's degree from one of the 38 Chinese universities under 985 Programme

Level of Study: Doctorate, Postgraduate

Type: Scholarships

Value: Tuition fees and annual stipend of approx. £4,800

Length of Study: 3 years

Frequency: Annual

Study Establishment: University of Manchester

Country of Study: United Kingdom

Application Procedure: Applicants must complete the standard postgraduate application form and return it together with: Academic transcripts, English language qualification, 2 reference letters and a research proposal

Closing Date: 20 April

Additional Information: For further details, please see the website: www.manchester.ac.uk/postgraduate/funding/search/display/?id=00000066&pg=2&offset=&sort=name&sortdir=ascending&subjectArea=&studyLevel=ALL&nationality=&income=&submit=

President's Doctoral Scholar Award

Type: Scholarship
Value: £1,000
Country of Study: United Kingdom
Application Procedure: For further information, please visit the PDS website

For further information contact:

Email: EPSGradEd@manchester.ac.uk

University of Melbourne

Scholarships Office, Melbourne, Melbourne, VIC 3010, Australia

Tel: (61) 3 8344 4000
Fax: (61) 3 8344 5104
Email: pg-schools@unimelb.edu.au
Website: www.unimelb.edu.au

The University of Melbourne has a long and distinguished tradition of excellence in teaching and research. It is the leading research institution in Australia and enjoys a reputation for the high quality of its research programmes, consistently winning the largest share of national competitive research funding.

Dairy Postgraduate Scholarships and Awards

Subjects: Dairy farming and dairy manufacturing

Purpose: To enable students for research contributing to the technical areas relevant to dairy farming and dairy manufacturing operations

Eligibility: Open to citizens or permanent residents of Australia

Level of Study: Postgraduate

Type: Scholarship

Value: A$25,000 stipend plus A$3,000 per year

Frequency: Annual

Country of Study: Australia

Application Procedure: To apply for this scholarship one must apply direct to the faculty

Closing Date: 20 October

For further information contact:

Tel: (61) 3 9694 3810
Fax: (61) 3 9694 3701
Email: research@dairyaustralia.com.au

PhDs in Bio Nanotechnology

Subjects: Bio nanotechnology

Eligibility: Open to those who have achieved Honours 2a or equivalent

Level of Study: Postgraduate, Research
Type: Scholarship
Value: A$19,616 per year
Length of Study: 2 years (Masters) and 3 years (PhD)
Frequency: Annual
Study Establishment: University of Melbourne
Country of Study: Australia
Application Procedure: Applicants must apply directly to the scholarship provider. Check website for further details
Closing Date: 21 July
Contributor: University of Melbourne

For further information contact:

Email: fcaruso@unimelb.edu.au
Contact: Professor Frank Caruso, Federation Fellow

Rae and Edith Bennett Travelling Scholarship

Subjects: All subjects
Purpose: To enable students and graduates of the University of Melbourne to undertake postgraduate study or research in the United Kingdom
Eligibility: Open to students and graduates of the University of Melbourne who can demonstrate outstanding academic merit and promise
Level of Study: Postgraduate
Type: Scholarship
Value: A$40,000–60,000 per year
Frequency: Annual
Country of Study: Australia
Application Procedure: Please see the website www.services.unimelb.edu.au/scholarships/research/local/available/travelling/rae for more details
Closing Date: 30 June
Funding: Private
Contributor: Rae and Edith Bennett Travelling Scholarship Fund

For further information contact:

Email: gsa@gsa.unimelb.edu.au

Sir Arthur Sims Travelling Scholarship

Subjects: All subjects
Purpose: To enable graduates of Australian universities to undertake postgraduate study or research in United Kingdom
Eligibility: Open to graduates of Australian universities who can demonstrate outstanding academic merit and promise. Applicants must be born in Australia or have parents who have been Australian residents for 7 years or more

Level of Study: Postgraduate, Research
Type: Scholarship
Value: Living allowance, tuition fees (approx. $20,000 per year)
Length of Study: 1–3 years
Country of Study: United Kingdom
Application Procedure: Check website www.services.unimelb.edu.au/scholarships/research/local/available/travelling/sims for further the details
Closing Date: 30 June
Funding: Private
Contributor: Sir Arthur Sims Traveling Scholarship Fund

For further information contact:

Email: 13melb@unimelb.edu.au

Sir Thomas Naghten Fitzgerald Scholarship

Subjects: Surgery
Purpose: This scholarship is to support further surgical training in Australia or Overseas
Eligibility: Open to candidates studied or currently studying at The University of Melbourne
Level of Study: Postgraduate
Type: Scholarship
Value: Approx. A$12,000
Length of Study: 1 year
Frequency: Annual
Study Establishment: University of Melbourne
Country of Study: Australia
Application Procedure: Check website www.research.mdhs.unimelb.edu.au/fitzgerald-scholarship for further details
Closing Date: 31 October
Funding: Government

For further information contact:

Email: jyv@unimelb.edu.au
Contact: Joan Vosen, Medicine Faculty

The Helen Macpherson Smith Scholarships

Subjects: Science, humanities and social sciences
Purpose: To establish special scholarships for outstanding women who are entering graduate study
Eligibility: Open to outstanding women who are entering postgraduate study. Only citizens of Australia may apply
Level of Study: Postgraduate
Type: Scholarship

Value: A$8,000 (Current rate) top-up payment (payable over 1 year) in addition to an APA or MRS
Frequency: Annual
Country of Study: Australia
Application Procedure: Check website for further details services.unimelb.edu.au/scholarships/research/local/available/prestigious#Macpherson
Closing Date: 31 October
Funding: Trusts
Contributor: Helen Macpherson Smith Trust

For further information contact:

Email: gsa@gsa.unimelb.edu.au

Viola Edith Reid Bequest Scholarship

Subjects: Medicine
Purpose: This scholarship is to support postgraduate study in any discipline of Medicine
Eligibility: Open for study in Australia. There are no restrictions on citizenship
Level of Study: Postgraduate, Research
Type: Scholarship
Value: A$21,174 maximum per award
Length of Study: 1 year
Frequency: Annual
Study Establishment: University of Melbourne
Country of Study: Australia
Application Procedure: Check website www.research.mdhs.unimelb.edu.au/viola-edith-reid-bequest for further details
Closing Date: 31 October
Funding: Government

For further information contact:

Tel: (61) 8344 4019
Fax: (61) 9347 7854
Email: jyv@unimelb.edu.au
Contact: Joan Vosen, Medicine Faculty

University of Nevada, Las Vegas (UNLV)

Graduate College, 4505 Maryland Parkway, Box 451010, Las Vegas, NV 89154-1017, United States of America

Tel: (1) 702 895 3011
Fax: (1) 702 895 4180
Email: gradcollege@unlv.edu
Website: www.unlv.edu
Contact: Administrative Officer

University of Nevada, Las Vegas Alumni Association Graduate Scholarships

Subjects: All subjects
Purpose: To reward outstanding graduate students
Eligibility: Students must have completed any degree at UNLV, with a 3.5 GPA or better and be a member of the UNLV Alumni Association. Students must enrol in a graduate program at least half-time (6 credits/semester), and must maintain a cumulative and semester GPA of 3.5
Level of Study: Graduate, MBA
Type: Scholarship
Value: US$1,500
Length of Study: 1 year
Frequency: Annual
Study Establishment: UNLV
Country of Study: United States of America
Application Procedure: Please check the website www.financialaid.unlv.edu/apps/ScholarshipSearch/index.asp?action=detail&s=466
Closing Date: 3 March
Additional Information: Student may receive the scholarship for a maximum of two (2) years, or four (4) semesters

For further information contact:

Email: unlvscholarships@unlv.edu
Contact: UNLV Financial Aid & Scholarships

University of Nevada, Las Vegas James F Adams/ GPSA Scholarship

Subjects: All subjects
Purpose: To recognize the academic achievements of graduate students
Eligibility: Applicant must be a master's-level or specialist student. He/she must have completed at least 12 credits of graduate study at UNLV (by the end of the current spring semester). Have a minimum graduate GPA of 3.5. Enroll in six or more credits in each semester of the scholarship year
Level of Study: Graduate, MBA
Type: Scholarship
Value: US$1,000
Length of Study: Varies
Frequency: Annual
Study Establishment: UNLV
Country of Study: United States of America
Application Procedure: Please see the website www.financialaid.unlv.edu/apps/ScholarshipSearch/index.asp?action=detail&s=419
Closing Date: 3 March

For further information contact:

Email:	eric.lee@unlv.edu
Contact:	Eric Lee

University of New South Wales (UNSW)

Scholarships and Financial Support, Sydney, NSW 2052, Australia

Tel:	(61) 2 9385 1000
Fax:	(61) 2 9385007 06
Email:	scholarships@unsw.edu.au
Website:	www.unsw.edu.au

University of New South Wales (UNSW) is one of Australia's leading research and teaching universities. UNSW takes great pride in the broad range and high quality of teaching programmes. UNSW's teaching gains strength, vitality and currency both from their research activities and from their international nature.

Association of Professional Academic Institutions Scholarship in Metallurgy/Materials

Subjects: Metallurgy, materials engineering
Purpose: To undertake blast furnace research in collaboration with industry
Eligibility: This scholarship requires candidates to have achieved Honours 1 or equivalent, or Honours 2a or equivalent
Level of Study: Doctorate, Postgraduate
Type: Scholarship
Value: Stipend of A$25,000 per year
Length of Study: 3–3.5 years
Frequency: Annual
Study Establishment: School of Materials Science and Engineering
Application Procedure: Check website for further details
Closing Date: 31 October

For further information contact:

Email:	a.yu@unsw.edu.au
Contact:	Professor Aibing Yu, Scientia Professor & Federation Fellow

College of Fine Arts Research Scholarship

Subjects: Fine arts
Purpose: To support students with outstanding research potential who are ineligible for an APA/UPA
Eligibility: Students with an offer to commence a full-time PhD at COFA, or students currently enroled full-time in a PhD at COFA
Level of Study: Doctorate
Type: Scholarship
Value: A$22,500 per year
Length of Study: Up to 3 years
Frequency: Annual
Study Establishment: University of New South Wales
Country of Study: Australia
Application Procedure: Application forms are available at the COFA Student Centre on the UNSW Scholarships website www.cofa.unsw.edu.au/about-us/scholarships/cofa-research-scholarship/
Closing Date: 31 January

For further information contact:

COFA Students Centre

Tel:	(61) 2 9385 0684
Email:	chad.roberts@unsw.edu.au
Contact:	Chad Roberts, Scholarships Officer

PhD Scholarship – Metal Dusting

Subjects: Materials science and engineering
Purpose: To support research on metal dusting
Eligibility: Open to citizens of Australia or permanent residents holding high Honours Degree in science
Level of Study: Postgraduate, Research
Type: Scholarship
Value: A$25,000–30,000 per year (tax free)
Length of Study: 3–3.5 years
Frequency: Annual
Study Establishment: University of New South Wales
Country of Study: Australia
Application Procedure: Check website for further details
Closing Date: 28 February

For further information contact:

Tel:	(61) 93 854 322
Fax:	(61) 93 855 956

Email: d.young@unsw.edu.au
Contact: David Young, (Professor) Science/Materials

PhD Scholarships in Environmental Microbiology

Subjects: Environmental microbiology, microbial genomics
Purpose: To attract the nation's strongest candidates capable of pursuing PhD studies in the genomics of environmental microorganisms
Eligibility: This scholarship is for study in Australia for those who have achieved Honours 1 or equivalent, or Masters or equivalent. There are no restrictions on citizenship
Level of Study: Doctorate, Postgraduate, Research
Type: Scholarship
Value: A$35,000
Application Procedure: Check website www.emi.science.unsw.edu.au/recruitment.html for further details
Closing Date: 31 March

For further information contact:

Email: r.cavicchioli@unsw.edu.au
Contact: Rick Cavicchioli

Postdoctoral Fellow Positions in Computational Mathematics

Subjects: Positions are awarded in Computational Mathematics in the School of Mathematics and Statistics, UNSW Sydney.
Purpose: Applications are sought for two Postdoctoral Fellow positions in Computational Mathematics in the School of Mathematics and Statistics, UNSW Sydney.
Eligibility: Australian citizens are eligible to apply.
Type: Postdoctoral fellowship
Value: Australian $89K – Australian $96K per year (plus up to 17% superannuation and leave loading)
Frequency: Annual
Study Establishment: Positions are awarded in Computational Mathematics in the School of Mathematics and Statistics, UNSW Sydney
Country of Study: Australia
Application Procedure: Applicants should submit the following documents to ims@shanghaitech.edu.cn: CV, including a list of publications, a research statement of up to 5 pages, describing their main achievements to date, as well as outlining the program of research they intend to follow for the next few years. A teaching statement Four letters of recommendation, at least one of which should address teaching, to be submitted directly to the hiring committee by the letter writers.
Closing Date: 1 February
Additional Information: For more details please visit the website scholarship-positions.com/postdoctoral-fellow-positions-computational-mathematics-unsw-australia/2018/03/06/. www.jobs.ac.uk/job/BOY792/postdoctoral-fellow-in-computational-mathematics

For further information contact:

Email: ims@shanghaitech.edu.cn

Vida Rees Scholarship in Pediatrics

Subjects: Medicine (Paediatrics)
Purpose: To support Australian students to undertake research in paediatrics
Eligibility: To be eligible for a Scholarship an applicant must be an Australian citizen or permanent resident undertaking an Honours project or Postgraduate Research in Paediatrics. Recipients may not concurrently hold any other scholarship or award (except for Youth Allowance) except with the permission of the UNSW Selection Committee
Level of Study: Postgraduate, Research
Type: Scholarship
Value: AU$3,000
Length of Study: 1 year
Frequency: Annual
Study Establishment: University of New South Wales
Country of Study: Australia
Application Procedure: Completed application forms and any supporting documentation should be scanned and emailed (preferably as a single pdf document) to the Graduate Research School. For more details please see the website
Closing Date: 1 December to 18 February

For further information contact:

Email: domestic.grs@unsw.edu.au
Contact: Sean Goodwin

Viktoria Marinov Award in Art

Subjects: Creative arts

Purpose: To financially assist female artists under the age of 35 years who are proposing to undertake the Master of Art or Master of Fine Arts course

Eligibility: Female students who are under 35 years old completing the Master of Fine Arts (by research). Must be Australian citizens or permanent residents

Level of Study: Postgraduate

Type: Award

Value: A$7,500

Length of Study: 1 year

Frequency: Annual

Study Establishment: New South Wales, Sydney City Central and Eastern Suburbs

Country of Study: Australia

Application Procedure: Applicants need to provide at least 6 images of their work, including information on the dimensions and materials of each work. These images can be supplied either electronically on DVD/CD or as attached printed images (no larger than A4). Applicants must include a personal statement addressing the selection criteria as part of their application. Please see the website for more applications related details: www.cofa.unsw.edu.au/about-us/scholarships/the-viktoria-marinov-award-in-art/

Closing Date: 30 July

For further information contact:

Tel:	(61) 2 9385 0684
Email:	chad.roberts@unsw.edu.au
Contact:	Chad Roberts, Scholarships Officer

University of New United Kingdom (UNE)

Research Grants Office, Armidale, NSW 2351, Australia

Tel:	(61) 2 6773 3333
Fax:	(61) 2 6773 3100
Email:	research@une.edu.au
Website:	www.une.edu.au

UNE is internationally recognized as one of the best teaching and research universities. Yearly, the university offers students more than AU$2,500,000 in scholarships, prizes, and bursaries and more than AU$18,000,000 for staff and students involved in research. It provides distance education for the students. Its scholars and scientists have established international reputations through their contributions in areas such as rural science, agricultural economics, educational administration, linguistics and archaeology.

A S Nivison Memorial Scholarship

Subjects: Pasture improvement, animal husbandry, farm management, wool research or promotion, water conservation, and environmental protection

Eligibility: Applicants must be a citizen or a permanent resident of Australia undertaking PhD or Research Masters at the University of United Kingdom in one of the listed areas

Level of Study: Doctorate, Postgraduate

Type: Scholarship

Value: AU$5,000

Length of Study: 1 year

Frequency: Annual

Country of Study: Australia

Application Procedure: Check website for further details

Closing Date: 30 April

Funding: Private

Contributor: Nivison family

For further information contact:

Tel:	(61) 2 6773 3745
Email:	pgscholarships@une.edu.au
Contact:	Belinda Keogh

Cooperative Research Centre Programme Spatial Information PhD Scholarship

Subjects: Agriculture

Purpose: To produce long-lasting outcomes relating to understanding how complex decision-making processes can be improved using spatial and other data

Eligibility: Applicants must hold a Class 1 or 2A Honours (or equivalent) Degree in a suitable discipline, and be a citizen or permanent resident of Australia. A valid driver's licence is also a necessary requirement

Level of Study: Doctorate

Type: Scholarship

Value: Please check website

Frequency: Annual

Study Establishment: University of New England

Country of Study: Australia

Application Procedure: Applicants should send a letter outlining suitability for the position, accompanied by a brief curriculum vitae (including contact details of two referees) and a copy of academic transcripts

Closing Date: Please check with the website

Funding: Government

For further information contact:

Tel:	(61) 2 6773 2436
Email:	jim.scott@une.edu.au
Contact:	Professor Jim Scott

Cotton Research and Development Corporation Postgraduate Scholarship

Subjects: Cotton research
Purpose: To enhance the environmental, economic and social performance of the Australian cotton industry
Eligibility: These scholarships are open to anyone who is an Australian resident, studying at an Australian university and interested in working in the Australian cotton industry to pursue postgraduate studies relating to the cotton industry or its related activities
Level of Study: Postgraduate
Type: Scholarship
Value: AU$30,000
Length of Study: 3 years
Frequency: Annual
Study Establishment: University of New England
Country of Study: Australia, New Zealand or South Africa
Application Procedure: Check with the website for further details
Closing Date: End of January
Funding: Government
Contributor: Cotton Research and Development Corporation (CRDC)
Additional Information: Projects may relate to any field of cotton-related research

For further information contact:

Cotton Research and Development Corporation, 2 Lloyd Street, Narrabri, NSW 2390, Australia

Tel:	(61) 2 6792 4088
Fax:	(61) 2 6792 4400
Email:	research@crdc.com.au

PhD Scholarship in Animal Breeding

Subjects: Animal breeding
Purpose: To investigate aspects of sow feed intake and its impact on reproductive performance and longevity
Eligibility: Applicants should be well versed in statistics and/or animal breeding units at a tertiary level and computing and data analysis skills is highly desirable
Level of Study: Doctorate
Type: Scholarship
Value: A$28,000 per year
Length of Study: 3 years
Frequency: Annual
Study Establishment: University of New England
Country of Study: Australia
Application Procedure: Please check with the website

Closing Date: 30 June
Contributor: Australian Pork CRC

For further information contact:

Tel:	(61) 2 6773 3788
Email:	kbunter2@une.edu.au
Contact:	Dr Kim Bunter

PhD Scholarship: Molecular Factors in Plant-Microbe Associations

Subjects: Molecular biology
Purpose: To study the molecular aspect of the interaction between the fungal pathogen and the plant
Eligibility: Applicants must hold a Class 1 or 2A Honours (or equivalent) Degree in a suitable discipline, and be a citizen or permanent resident of Australia
Level of Study: Doctorate
Type: Scholarship
Value: AU$26,000 per year (tax free)
Length of Study: 3 years
Frequency: Annual
Study Establishment: University of New England
Country of Study: Australia
Application Procedure: Applicants should send a letter outlining their suitability for the position, accompanied by a brief curriculum vitae (including contact details of two referees) and a copy of their academic transcripts
Funding: Government

For further information contact:

Tel:	(61) 2 6773 2708
Fax:	(61) 2 6773 3267
Email:	lperegge@une.edu.au
Contact:	Dr Lily Pereg-Grek

PhD Scholarship: Weed Ecology

Subjects: Ecology
Purpose: To manage the species through a series of field and controlled environment experiments on emergence, growth, reproduction and spread of environment experiments on emergence, growth, reproduction and spread of fleabane species
Eligibility: Applicants must hold a Class 1 or 2A Honours (or equivalent) Degree in a suitable discipline, and be an citizen or permanent resident of Australia
Level of Study: Doctorate
Type: Scholarship
Value: AU$26,000 per year (tax free)
Length of Study: 3 years

Study Establishment: University of New England
Country of Study: Australia
Application Procedure: Applicants should send a letter outlining their suitability for the position accompanied by a brief curriculum vitae (including contact details of two referees) and a copy of their academic transcripts
Closing Date: 27 April
Funding: Government

For further information contact:

School of Rural Science and Agriculture, University of New England, Armidale, NSW 2351, Australia

Tel: (61) 2 6773 3238
Email: bsindel@une.edu.au
Contact: Brian Sindel, Associate Professor

University of New England Research Scholarship

Subjects: All subjects
Eligibility: Applicants must have achieved Honours 1 or equivalent, or Masters or equivalent
Level of Study: Doctorate, Postgraduate
Type: Scholarship
Value: A$19,231
Length of Study: 3 years (PhD) and 2 years (Masters)
Frequency: Annual
Study Establishment: University of New England
Country of Study: Australia
Application Procedure: Contact the university for details
Closing Date: End of September or December
Funding: Government

For further information contact:

Tel: (61) 6773 3571
Fax: (61) 6773 3543
Email: aharris@une.edu.au
Contact: Thea Harris, Scholarships Administrative
                      Assistant

University of New United Kingdom Equity Scholarship for Environmental and Rural Science

Subjects: Science
Eligibility: Applicants must be citizens of Australia or New Zealand and be an Aboriginal or Torres Strait Islander, non-English speaking background person, student with a disability or woman from non-traditional area
Level of Study: Postgraduate, Research
Type: Scholarship
Length of Study: 2 years (Masters) or 3 years (PhD)

Frequency: Annual
Study Establishment: University of New England
Country of Study: Australia, New Zealand or South Africa
Application Procedure: Check website for further details
Funding: Government

For further information contact:

University of New England, Armidale, NSW 2351, Australia

Email: aharris@unc.edu.au
Contact: Thea Harris, Scholarships Administrative
                      Assistant

University of Newcastle

Research Division, University of Newcastle, Callaghan, NSW 2308, Australia

Tel: (61) 2 4921 5000
Fax: (61) 2 4985 4200
Email: research@newcastle.edu.au
Website: www.newcastle.edu.au/research/rhd/
Contact: Office of Graduate Studies

The University of Newcastle is one of Australia's top ten research universities. The University has over 1,200 research degree candidates enroled in five faculties, incorporating a wide range of disciplines including architecture, building, humanities, social sciences, education, economics, management, engineering, computer science, law, medicine, nursing, health sciences, music, drama and creative arts, physical and natural sciences, mathematics and information technology. Scholarships are available to support research degree candidates in most disciplines. About 90 new scholarships are awarded each year.

Chemical Engineering Scholarship

Subjects: Chemical Engineering
Purpose: To develop models capable of simulating temporal and spatial characteristics of rainfall fields over large river basins using novel approaches to hierarchical modelling, storm clustering, advection and calibration. The models will provide continuous simulation support for the design and assessment of water-related infrastructure
Eligibility: Open only to the postgraduates who are the citizens of Australia or the permanent residents of Australia
Level of Study: Postgraduate
Type: Scholarship
Value: A living allowance of AU$24,653 per year

Length of Study: 2 years (Masters) and 3 years (PhD)
Frequency: Annual
Country of Study: Australia
Application Procedure: Application form and the Research Higher Degree prospectus from can be downloaded from the website
Closing Date: 31 August, 4 pm each year (International applicants); 31 October, 4 pm each year (Domestic applicants)

For further information contact:

Tel: (61) 2 4921 6038
Email: George.Kuczera@newcastle.edu.au
Contact: Professor George Kuczera

PhD Scholarship in Coal Utilization in Thermal and Coking Applications

Subjects: Chemical engineering, mechanical engineering, and chemistry
Purpose: To undertake research on particular coal properties which determine its utilization potential
Eligibility: Open to the engineering and the science graduates who have an Honours Degree in chemical or mechanical engineering or chemistry
Level of Study: Doctorate, Postgraduate
Type: Scholarship
Value: A$19,616 per year
Length of Study: 3 years
Application Procedure: Check website for further details
Closing Date: 1 March

For further information contact:

Tel: (61) 2 49 21 6179
Email: Terry.Wall@newcastle.edu.au
Contact: Professor Terry Wall

PhD Scholarship in Immunology of Kidney Stone Diseases

Subjects: Scholarships are awarded to work on the project titled, "Immunology of kidney stone diseases"
Purpose: This project aims to improve our understanding of how our immune system protects against stone recurrence and its role in preventing long-term consequences such as impaired kidney function
Eligibility: This scholarship is for domestic and international students. If English is not your first language then you will need to show that your English language skills are at a high enough level to succeed in your studies
Type: Scholarship

Value: Scholarship Value: AU$26,682 p.a., indexed in January each year. The scholarship is for a period of three years and a half years. This Scholarship is linked to the Dr Starkey ARC DECRA fellowship
Frequency: Annual
Study Establishment: Scholarships are awarded to work on the project titled, "Immunology of kidney stone diseases"
Country of Study: Australia
Application Procedure: To enable us to assess your application, candidates will be expected to submit an email expressing their interest including: 1. Academic transcripts. 2. A brief statement of research interests. 3. Full CV including previous degrees, grades, research experience, employment, papers published, and any grants obtained. Applicants are automatically considered for the scholarship on acceptance to University College
Closing Date: 1 April
Additional Information: For more details please visit the website scholarship-positions.com/phd-scholarship-immunology-kidney-stone-diseases-australia/2018/02/01/

Postgraduate Research Scholarship in Physics

Subjects: Physics
Eligibility: Open to the residents of Australia and New Zealand or the permanent residents of Australia who have an Honours 1 or 2A or a Masters Degree
Level of Study: Postgraduate, Research
Type: Scholarship
Value: AU$17,071 per year
Length of Study: 3 years
Frequency: Annual
Application Procedure: Check website for more details
Closing Date: 1 July
Contributor: ARC Discovery-projects

For further information contact:

School of Mathematical and Physical Sciences

Tel: (61) 2 4921 6653
Fax: (61) 2 4921 6907
Email: vicki.keast@newcastle.edu.au
Contact: Dr Vicki Keast

University of Newcastle Postgraduate Research Scholarship (UNRS Central)

Subjects: All subjects
Eligibility: Open to the residents of Australia and New Zealand or permanent residents who have achieved

Honours 1 or equivalent and have completed at least 4 years of undergraduate study
Level of Study: Postgraduate, Research
Type: Scholarship
Value: AU$23,728 per year full-time stipend, AU$12,898 part time stipend
Length of Study: 2 years (Masters) and 3 years (PhD)
Frequency: Annual
Country of Study: Australia
Application Procedure: Check website for further details
Closing Date: 31 October

For further information contact:

Research Higher Degrees, The Chancellery Eastern Wing, University Drive

Tel:	(61) 2 4921 6537
Fax:	(61) 2 4921 6908
Email:	research@newcastle.edu.au

University of Newcastle, Australia MBA Programme

Application Procedure: Applicants must return a completed application form, with original or certified copies of official academic transcripts (not to be returned), Graduate Management Admission Test and TOEFL (if applicable) scores, the names of two referees

For further information contact:

Business Administration International Students Office University Drive

Tel:	(61) 4 9216 595
Fax:	(61) 4 9601 766
Email:	io@newcastle.edu.au
Contact:	MBA Admissions Officer

University of Notre Dame

1124 Flanner Hall, Notre Dame, IN 46556, United States of America

Tel:	(1) 574 631 1305
Fax:	(1) 574 631 8997
Email:	ndias@nd.edu, bgregor3@nd.edu
Website:	www.nd.edu
Contact:	Brad S Gregory, Director of the Notre Dame Institute for Advanced Study

The University of Notre Dame provides a distinctive voice in higher education that is at once rigorously intellectual, unapologetically moral in orientation, and firmly embracing of a service ethos.

Break Travel and Research Grants for Sophomores and Juniors

Purpose: The Break Travel and Research Grant provides seed funding for educational and research projects in European studies. The grant is intended to support well-focused, short-term exploratory trips conducted over fall, winter, or spring break
Eligibility: Applicants must be enrolled as a sophomore or junior at the University of Notre Dame and scheduled to return the following semester
Level of Study: Postgraduate
Type: Grant
Value: US$2,500. Funds are typically paid at one-time sum
Frequency: Annual
Country of Study: Any country
Closing Date: 4 February
Funding: Private

For further information contact:

Tel:	(1) 574 631 8326
Email:	cstump@nd.edu

Templeton Fellowships for United States of America and International Scholars at NDIAS

Subjects: Philosophy, theology, sciences, etc
Purpose: With grant support from the John Templeton Foundation, the NDIAS will help chart a new course for future scholarship by offering Templeton Fellowships that encourage scholars to return to reflection on the broad questions that link multiple areas of inquiry and to do so in a manner that embraces a value-oriented interpretation of the world
Eligibility: Distinguished senior scholars with extensive records of academic accomplishment and who have had a considerable impact on their discipline are encouraged to apply. Outstanding junior scholars with academic records of exceptional promise and whose research agendas align with the purpose and parameters of the program are also invited to apply
Type: Fellowship
Value: These distinctive fellowships offer an extraordinary measure of scholarly support, including: a stipend of up to US$1,00,000; fully furnished faculty housing (for those who reside outside of the Michiana area); up to US$3,000 in research expenditures; a private office at the NDIAS, with

a personal desktop computer and printer; etc. Check detailed information on the website
Frequency: Annual
Country of Study: United States of America
Application Procedure: Please see ndias.nd.edu/fellowships/templeton/application-instructions/ for details on how to apply. Please direct any questions you may have on the application process or fellowship program to Carolyn Sherman at csherman@nd.edu
Closing Date: 15 October
Additional Information: For more information, please check at ndias.nd.edu/fellowships/templeton/

For further information contact:

Email: csherman@nd.edu
Contact: Carolyn Sherman

University of Notre Dame: College of Arts and Letters

Office of the Dean, 100 O'Shaughnessy Hall, Notre Dame, IN 46556, United States of America

Tel: (1) 574 631 7085
Fax: (1) 574 631 7743
Email: aldean@nd.edu
Website: al.nd.edu

University of Notre Dame: College of Arts and Letters offers one of the finest liberal arts educations in the nation. Its Division of the Humanities was recently ranked 12th among private universities, while the social sciences continue their ascent in the national rankings. College of Arts and Letters is the largest and oldest of the University's 4 colleges.

The Erskine A. Peters Dissertation Year Fellowship at Notre Dame

Subjects: Arts, humanities, social sciences and theological disciplines
Purpose: To provide an opportunity for African American scholars at the beginning of their academic careers to experience life at a major Catholic research university
Eligibility: Open to African American Doctoral candidates who have completed all degree requirements with the exception of the dissertation
Level of Study: Postgraduate, Research

Type: Fellowship
Value: US$30,000 stipend and US$2,000 research budget
Length of Study: 10 months
Frequency: Annual
Country of Study: United States of America
Application Procedure: Applicants may apply online
Closing Date: Early December
No. of awards given last year: 3

For further information contact:

Tel: (1) 574 631 5628
Fax: (1) 574 631 3587
Email: astudies@nd.edu

University of Nottingham

University of Nottingham, University Park, Nottingham NG7 2RD, United Kingdom

Tel: (44) 115 846 8400
Fax: (44) 115 846 7799
Email: graduate-school@nottingham.ac.uk
Website: www.nottingham.ac.uk/gradschool
Contact: Ms Nicola Pickering, Process Manager Funding

The University of Nottingham is a community of students and staff dedicated to bringing out the best in all of its members. It aims to provide the finest possible environment for teaching, learning and research and has a world class record of success.

Developing Solutions Masters Scholarship

Subjects: Faculty of Engineering, Faculty of Medicine and Health Sciences, Faculty of Science and Faculty of Social Science
Purpose: The aim of the Developing Solutions Masters Scholarship is to enable and encourage academically able students from Africa, India or one of the countries of the Commonwealth
Eligibility: Students who are a national of (or permanently domiciled in) Africa, India, or one of the countries of the Commonwealth countries. You can apply for this scholarship if you: are a national of (or permanently domiciled in) Africa, India, OR one of the other Commonwealth countries AND are classed as an overseas student for fee purposes AND have not already studied outside of your home country

Value: 30 × 100% tuition fee; 75 × 50% of tuition fees
Country of Study: Any country
Application Procedure: Apply online
Closing Date: 22 March
Additional Information: For more details, visit www.nottingham.ac.uk/studywithus/international-applicants/scholarships-fees-and-finance/scholarships/masters-scholarships/dev-sol-masters.aspx. scholarship-assistant@nottingham.ac.uk

For further information contact:

Tel: (61) 115 951 5247
Email: scholarship-assistant@nottingham.ac.uk

High Achiever Foundation Prize for Africans

Subjects: The foundation courses provide an entry route to selected degrees in arts, business, engineering, science and social sciences
Purpose: Prizes are available for pursuing foundation courses at University of Nottingham
Eligibility: Candidates can apply if they are a national of (or permanently domiciled in) Africa, they are classed as an overseas student for fee purposes, already hold an offer to start a full-time foundation program at Nottingham in September
Type: Prize
Value: 3 undergraduate high achiever prizes of £2,000 towards tuition fees
Country of Study: United Kingdom
Application Procedure: The mode of applying is online
Closing Date: 15 April
Additional Information: Successful applicants will be notified of the outcome within 6 weeks of the closing date

For further information contact:

Email: scholarship-assistant@nottingham.ac.uk

Japan Masters Scholarships at University of Nottingham in United Kingdom

Purpose: The aim of the scholarship is strengthen the bond of Japan and United Kingdom
Eligibility: 1. National of (or permanently domiciled in) Japan. 2. Classed as an overseas student for fee purposes. 3. Already have, or expect to receive, a final CGPA of no less than 3.2/grade B or 70%. 4. Already hold an offer to start

a full-time master degree programme, including MRes, at Nottingham in September, any subject area
Level of Study: Postgraduate
Type: Scholarship
Value: These scholarships will cover 25% each towards tuition fees for students from Japan
Country of Study: Any country
Application Procedure: Applications must complete online application form to apply for scholarships. www.nottingham.ac.uk/international/_online_forms/scholarships/_sships_appform_p1.php
Closing Date: 18 May

For further information contact:

Email: scholarship-assistant@nottingham.ac.uk

Nottingham Developing Solutions Scholarships

Purpose: The Developing Solutions Scholarships are designed for international students who want to pursue a Master's Degree in the University of Nottingham and make a difference to the development of their home country
Eligibility: 1. Are a national of (or permanently domiciled in) Africa, India or one of the countries of the Commonwealth. 2. Are classed as an overseas student for fee purposes. 3. Have not already studied outside of your home country. 4. Are not currently studying at a University of Nottingham campus or are not a University of Nottingham graduate
Level of Study: Postdoctorate
Type: Scholarship
Frequency: Annual
Country of Study: Any country
Closing Date: 22 March
Funding: Foundation

Nottingham University Business School MBA Programme

Length of Study: 1 year full-time or 2;4 years part-time
Country of Study: Any country
Application Procedure: Applicants must complete an application form, and provide transcripts or copies of professional qualifications together with two references (ideally, one should be from an academic source, the other from an employer or business contact). All language test scores must be submitted for International students. Note that the school may ask for further individual details to support an application
Closing Date: Varies, please contact the organisation for further details

For further information contact:

Tel: (44) 115 551 5500
Fax: (44) 115 551 5503
Email: business-enquiries@nottingham.ac.uk
Contact: MBA Admissions Officer

University of Oklahoma

College of Business Administration, Adams Hall Room 105K, Norman, OK 73019, United States of America

Tel: (1) 405 325 4107
Fax: (1) 405 325 1957
Email: awatkins@ou.edu
Contact: MBA Admissions Officer

Ben Barnett Scholarship

Subjects: Fine arts
Purpose: Any full-time Art majors admitted to either the MA or MFA degree program
Eligibility: Applicant must be a full-time student in the School of Art and have a minimum 3.0 GPA and an outstanding portfolio
Level of Study: Postgraduate
Type: Scholarship
Value: Maximum of US$1,000 will be given as scholarship amount
Frequency: Annual
Country of Study: Any country
Application Procedure: Contact Director, School of Art University of Oklahoma 520 Parrington Room 202 Normak, OK 73019 United States Phone: (405) 325-2691
Closing Date: 1 March
Funding: Private
Additional Information: Visit the official website for further info: www.ou.edu

For further information contact:

Email: art@ou.edu

University of Ontario

Graduate Finance and Administration, 2000 Simcoe Street North, London, ON L1H 7K4, Canada

Email: pmenzies@uwo.ca
Contact: Office of Graduate Studies Manager,

The University of Ontario Institute of Technology is a public research university located in Oshawa, Ontario, Canada.

The Ontario Trillium Scholarships (OTS)

Purpose: To attract top international students to Ontario for PhD studies
Eligibility: An eligible applicant must have achieved a minimum of 80% in each of the last 2 most recently completed years of full-time university study, or equivalent to full-time study. Eligibility averages for competitive scholarship are rounded ONLY to the nearest decimal place
Type: Scholarship
Value: CA$40,000 annually
Length of Study: 4 years
Frequency: Annual
Country of Study: Any country
Application Procedure: Submit a complete UOIT application with supporting documentation to the Office of Graduate Studies
Closing Date: 1 April
Additional Information: Submit the PDF nomination to SGPS (pmenzies@uwo.ca) any time after January 1st

For further information contact:

Email: pmenzies@uwo.ca

University of Oregon

1585E, 13th Ave, Eugene, OR 97403, United States of America

Tel: (1) 541 346 1000
Fax: (1) 541 346 1000
Website: www.uoregon.edu

Center for AIDS Prevention Studies, Small Professional Grants for Graduate Students

Purpose: Awards will be made for the following purposes: travel to conferences to present papers, travel to library, museum, and archival collections; and expenses related to book and article production and publication
Eligibility: The Center for Asian and Pacific Studies is offering awards of up to US$500 in support of the professional activities of UO graduate students studying Asia. Awards will be made for the following purposes: travel to conferences to present papers, travel to library, museum, and archival

collections; and expenses related to book and article production and publication
Level of Study: Postgraduate
Type: Grant
Frequency: Annual
Country of Study: Any country
Application Procedure: 1. To submit a proposal, please click here to complete the online application form. 2. A brief letter of support from your advisor explaining how this activity is central to your research interests is also required. This letter can be emailed directly to Holly Lakey at lakey@uoregon.edu
Closing Date: 5 April
Funding: Private

For further information contact:

1246 University of Oregon, Eugene, OR 97403, United States of America

Tel: (1) 541 346 5068
Email: lakey@uoregon.edu

Jeremiah Lecture Series Support

Purpose: The Center for Asian and Pacific Studies is accepting proposals from UO faculty for speakers to visit the UO and deliver a public lecture on campus
Level of Study: Postgraduate
Type: Award
Frequency: Annual
Country of Study: Any country
Application Procedure: For a hardcopy version of the application form, please contact Holly Lakey at lakey@uoregon.edu. To submit a proposal, please click here to complete the online application form. oregon.qualtrics.com/jfe/form/SV_cu6IXYJ5vItOZ7v. It will provide complete information for the application process
Closing Date: 5 April
Funding: Private

For further information contact:

Email: Lakey@uoregon.edu

University of Oslo

Problemveien 7, 0315 Oslo, Norway

Contact: University of Oslo

The University of Oslo, until 1939 named the Royal Frederick University, is the oldest university in Norway, located in the Norwegian capital of Oslo.

PhD Research Fellowship in Ecotoxicology

Subjects: Ecotoxicology
Purpose: The purpose of the PhD Fellowship is research training leading to the successful completion of a PhD degree
Eligibility: International students are eligible to apply for the fellowship. Applicants must have a Master's degree or equivalent in toxicology or marine ecology, relevant to this PhD project. A good command of English is required of all students attending the University of Oslo
Type: Fellowship
Value: NOK 436,900–490,900 per year
Country of Study: Norway
Application Procedure: Please visit www.scholarshipsads.com/norway-university-oslo-phd-fellowship-exotoxicology-2018/#gs.wOqf5y0 for application procedure
Closing Date: 1 February
Additional Information: The project combines knowledge from ecotoxicology, ecology, and environmental chemistry. The successful candidate will design and conduct extensive field studies, analyze contaminants and dietary descriptors, and deal with large datasets

For further information contact:

Email: nina.holtan@mn.uio.no

PhD Research Fellowships in Energy Informatics

Subjects: Energy Informatics
Purpose: Fellowships are available to pursue PhD Research programme. The aim of providing the scholarship is to achieve a balanced gender composition in the organisation and to recruit people with ethnic minority backgrounds
Eligibility: For eligibility details, please visit www.scholarshipsads.com/university-oslo-phd-research-fellowships-energy-informatics-2018/#gs.sYt9HtQ
Type: Research fellowship
Value: NOK 436,900–490,900 per year. Attractive welfare benefits and a generous pension agreement, in addition to Oslo's family-friendly environment with its rich opportunities for culture and outdoor activities
Length of Study: 3 years
Country of Study: Norway
Application Procedure: The mode of applying is online
Closing Date: 15 November
Contributor: University of Oslo

For further information contact:

Email: yanzhang@ifi.uio.no

Postdoctoral fellowships in Educational Assessment and Measurement

Subjects: Fellowships are awarded in Educational Assessment and Measurement
Purpose: The main purpose of the fellowships is to qualify researchers for work in higher academic positions within their disciplines
Eligibility: For eligibility, please visit www.scholarshipsupdates.com/university-of-oslo-four-year-postdoctoral-fellowships-for-international-students-in-norway-2018/
Level of Study: Professional development
Type: Fellowship
Value: Salary NOK 499,600–569,000
Length of Study: 4 years
Frequency: Annual
Country of Study: Norway
Application Procedure: For online application, visit website www.jobbnorge.no/en/available-jobs/job/149727/1-2-four-year-postdoctoral-fellowships-in-educational-assessment-and-measurement
Closing Date: 15 May

For further information contact:

Email: rolfvo@cemo.uio.no

Postdoctoral Fellowships in Political Philosophy or Legal Theory

Subjects: Political philosophy or legal theory, studying international courts and tribunals (ICs)
Purpose: Fellowships are available to pursue postdoctoral programme
Eligibility: For eligibility, please visit www.scholarshipsads.com/postdoctoral-fellowships-political-philosophy-legal-theory-norway-2018/
Type: Postdoctoral fellowship
Value: NOK 490,900–569,000
Country of Study: Any country
Closing Date: 1 November

For further information contact:

Email: siri.johnsen@jus.uio.no

University of Otago

Advanced Business Programme, PO Box 56, Dunedin, New Zealand

Tel: (64) 3 479 8046
Fax: (64) 3 479 8045
Email: mbainfo@commerce.otago.ac.nz
Website: www.otago.ac.nz
Contact: MBA Admissions Officer

Aarhus University PhD Fellowships Program

Purpose: Aarhus University PhD Fellowships Program, Denmark are fully funded fellowships offered to the students of Denmark to pursue PhD fellowships and research training supplements, both research and PhD fellowships are funded by the Faculty of Health Science at Aarhus University, the scholarships are developed with an aim to develop international cooperation in the areas of teaching and research, university is a modern, academically diverse and research-intensive university with a strong commitment to high-quality research and education and the development of society existed around the world
Eligibility: The candidates who are interested to apply for the Aarhus University scholar apply for a 3-year PhD study programme students must have completed a relevant Master's degree, the Master's study has to be equivalent to a Danish Master's degree of 120 ECTS, all applications will be evaluated based on the submitted material using the following criteria, the time for research experience after the qualifying exam is taken into consideration, all applicants must document English language qualifications comparable to an 'English B level' in the Danish upper secondary school, if the candidate has any doubt about the criteria they can submit your diplomas for an assessment via graduateschoolhealth-at-au.dk
Level of Study: Postgraduate
Type: Fellowship
Length of Study: 3 year
Frequency: Annual
Country of Study: New Zealand
Closing Date: February
Funding: Foundation

For further information contact:

Tel: (44) 8715 0000
Email: housing@au.dk

Angus Ross Travel Scholarship in History

Purpose: Established by the family of Angus Ross in 2010, the Angus Ross Travel Scholarship in History is intended to assist PhD candidates studying history with the costs associated with off-campus field and archival research
Eligibility: 1. Are conducting historically-focused research. 2. Will be conducting off-campus field or archival research in the year for which the scholarship is awarded
Level of Study: Postgraduate
Type: Scholarship
Value: NZ $1,000
Frequency: Annual
Country of Study: New Zealand
Closing Date: 1 November
Funding: Foundation

Brenda Shore Award for Women

Purpose: Brenda Shore was an enthusiastic, enterprising person famous for her energy and passion. Over the course of 35 years Brenda became a prominent figure in the University of Otago Botany Department, both as a researcher and teacher, until her retirement in 1983. Leading by example Brenda Shore established this fund to help support women who have that same passion and energy for the natural sciences, particularly where their research relates to the Otago, Southland or Antarctic region
Eligibility: 1. University of Otago women graduates. 2. Women graduates carrying out research related to the Otago, Southland and Antarctic area. 3. Women graduates carrying out research for a postgraduate degree at the University of Otago
Level of Study: Postgraduate
Type: Award
Value: Up to NZ $15,000
Length of Study: 1 year
Frequency: Annual
Country of Study: New Zealand
Closing Date: 28 February
Funding: Foundation

China Scholarship Council and Griffith University PhD Scholarships

Purpose: China Scholarship Council and Griffith University PhD Scholarships are offering scholarships to the students of China who are interested to pursue PhD degree programme at the Griffith university which is based in the United Kingdom, through this scholarship the students develops the research opportunities with an environment that collaborates the students

Eligibility: The participants should meet all the necessary requirements, polices and the rules that are offered by the China Scholarship Council and Griffith University, this scholarship program is extended to all research programs where, The applicants of the China Scholarship Council and Griffith University PhD scholarships should meet the academic entry requirements which also include the level of English language Proficiency with good communication skills and the student must be certified or held with a bachelor degree with a first class or second-class honors which come under the Division A or the Master's degree or its equivalent incorporating a significant research component, from a recognised institution or its equivalent, Candidates are selected based on the criteria that was instructed by China Scholarship Council
Level of Study: Postgraduate
Type: Scholarship
Length of Study: 4 year
Frequency: Annual
Country of Study: New Zealand
Closing Date: January
Funding: Foundation

Demand Response in the Agricultural Sector PhD Scholarship

Purpose: The Centre for Sustainability calls for expressions of interest in a PhD scholarship focusing on "Demand response in the agricultural sector – a socio-technical study". The research will examine farmer interest in electricity demand response, examine the barriers that farmers face in engaging in demand response, and identify solutions to improve adoption of demand response strategies. Candidates with a background in socio-technical studies would be ideal, although those with a background in social or physical sciences will be considered if they have an interest in extending their theoretical and methodological scope. The scholarship is funded by Science for Technological Innovation, a National Science Challenge and the successful candidate will be based at the Centre for Sustainability, University of Otago
Level of Study: Postgraduate
Type: Scholarship
Value: $27,500
Length of Study: 3 year
Frequency: Annual
Country of Study: New Zealand
Closing Date: 22 February
Funding: Foundation, International office

For further information contact:

Email: janet.stephenson@otago.ac.nz

Diane Campbell-Hunt Memorial Award

Purpose: Diane Campbell-Hunt was a PhD candidate in the Department of Geography, funded by a Tertiary Education Commission Top Achiever Doctoral scholarship. She had completed two-thirds of her PhD programme at the time of her death. Her project looked at the long-term sustainability of fenced sanctuaries in New Zealand in a multi-disciplinary analysis: ecological, economic, social, and governmental
Eligibility: 1. Be enrolled and confirmed in a PhD programme in any Department or School at the University of Otago. 2. Have had accepted a peer-reviewed academic paper (conference or journal) that contributes to New Zealand conservation (as defined above), and in which they are the lead author. 3. Not have previously been awarded the award
Level of Study: Postgraduate
Type: Award
Value: NZ $1,000
Frequency: Annual
Country of Study: New Zealand
Closing Date: 30 June
Funding: Foundation

Douglass D Crombie Award in Physics

Purpose: Established by the University of Otago Council in memory of Mr Douglass D Crombie. This award has been made possible by a generous bequest from the late Mr Crombie for the purpose of encouraging postgraduate research in Physics. This award will be offered to an outstanding University of Otago Physics graduate intending to undertake a PhD in Physics at an overseas university
Eligibility: 1. Were born in New Zealand. 2. Graduated or will soon graduate from the University of Otago with a degree in Physics. 3. Are intending to pursue doctoral-level studies in Physics. 4. Are intending to undertake their studies at an English speaking University in an English speaking country (excluding New Zealand). 5. Have displayed outstanding academic ability
Level of Study: Postgraduate
Type: Award
Value: NZ $7,000
Frequency: Annual
Country of Study: New Zealand
Closing Date: Apply anytime
Funding: Foundation

For further information contact:

Scholarships Office, Graduate Research School, PO Box 56, Dunedin 9054, New Zealand

Email: scholarships@otago.ac.nz

Dr Sulaiman Daud 125th Jubilee Postgraduate Scholarship

Purpose: This scholarship was established in 1994 to mark the 125th Anniversary of the foundation of the University of Otago, New Zealand's oldest university. The purpose of the scholarship is to assist an exceptional postgraduate research student from Malaysia to attend the University
Eligibility: 1. Unless otherwise stated in these conditions or within the schedule, doctoral and Masters' scholarships are open only to Domestic Fee Paying Students. International candidates studying for professional doctorates are eligible to apply but if awarded a scholarship the tuition fee waiver will be capped at the domestic rate. 2. In the case of applicants for a doctoral scholarship, confirmation of the scholarship is dependent on approval of their application for admission to the relevant doctoral programme and completion of the enrolment procedure. 3. In the case of applicants for a Master's scholarship, confirmation of the scholarship is dependent on approval of their application to register as a Master's candidate and completion of the enrolment procedure
Level of Study: Postgraduate
Type: Scholarship
Value: NZ$27,000
Length of Study: 1 year
Frequency: Annual
Country of Study: New Zealand
Closing Date: Applicants can apply at any time
Funding: Foundation

For further information contact:

P.O. Box 514070, Milwaukee, WI 53203-3470, United States of America

Email: scholarships@otago.ac.nz

Elizabeth Jean Trotter Postgraduate Research Travelling Scholarship in Biomedical Sciences

Subjects: The Elizabeth Jean Trotter Postgraduate Research Travelling Scholarship in Biomedical Sciences was established to support travel to a conference, workshop, or laboratory for postgraduate students undertaking research in Biomedical Sciences
Purpose: Established by the University of Otago Council from a generous donation in memory of Elizabeth Jean Trotter
Eligibility: 1. Be enrolled for a PhD or in the research year of a Master's programme with primary supervision in the Otago School of Medical Sciences (OSMS). 2. Be undertaking research in a Biomedical Sciences field
Level of Study: Postgraduate

Type: Fellowships
Value: Up to NZ $5,000
Length of Study: 1 year
Frequency: Annual
Country of Study: New Zealand
Application Procedure: Every application for the scholarship must be submitted to the University of Otago Scholarships Office by the closing date. Every applicant must submit: 1. A completed application form detailing the purpose of, and benefits expected to result from, the proposed travel. 2. A letter of support from the candidate's primary supervisor, addressing the candidate's work to date and the value of the chosen conference, workshop, or laboratory visit, to the candidate. 3. A brief Curriculum Vitae. 4. Title of proposed oral presentation or poster at the chosen conference (if applicable)
Closing Date: 1 November
Funding: Foundation

Elman Poole Travelling Scholarship

Purpose: Dr Elman Poole and the University of Otago are pleased to be able to offer this award to promote, encourage and facilitate research by providing grants to PhD students of the University of Otago to study overseas during their PhD, for a period normally not less than three months and not more than six months to gain experience or to use facilities not normally available at Otago and to further their subsequent work or career at Otago
Eligibility: 1. Enrolled full-time for a Doctor of Philosophy (PhD) at the University of Otago. 2. Majoring in one of following areas: Physical or Biological Sciences, Health Sciences or music. 3. Intending to engage in study in the second or third year of his/her PhD outside of New Zealand. 4. New Zealand citizen or New Zealand permanent resident. 5. under 35 years of age on the first day of February in the year of application
Level of Study: Postgraduate
Type: Scholarship
Value: NZ $20,000
Length of Study: 2 year
Frequency: Annual
Country of Study: New Zealand
Closing Date: 1 June
Funding: Foundation

For further information contact:

St David II Building, University of Otago, PO Box 56, Dunedin 9054, New Zealand

Freemasons Scholarships

Purpose: The Freemasons Scholarships are provided annually by Freemasons New Zealand and are administered by the Freemasons Charity
Eligibility: 1. Have a good academic report. 2. Be a - New Zealand citizen or permanent resident. 3. Demonstrate good citizenship. 4. Show leadership potential. 5. Have proven community commitment
Level of Study: Postgraduate
Type: Scholarship
Value: NZ$10,000
Frequency: Annual
Country of Study: New Zealand
Closing Date: 1 October
Funding: Foundation

For further information contact:

Email: info@lincoln.ac.nz

Fully Funded PhD Scholarships

Purpose: Fully Funded PhD Scholarships, University of Sheffield, United Kingdom are offered to the international students who attract the administration panel with their academic performance to pursue PhD programme, the University of Sheffield is a public research university in Sheffield, South Yorkshire, United Kingdom, by merging the Sheffield Medical School and Sheffield Technical School, the candidates should have the knowledge in the English language and the candidate from the non-English countries should have meet the abilities of the university by attaining the IELTS and other related tests, annually the university offers five scholarships
Eligibility: In order to apply for the Fully Funded PhD scholarships at the university of Sheffield the candidates should meet the requirements, the applicant should be a citizen of United Kingdom and the applicants should be the holder or about to obtain the upper second class degree from the United Kingdom university or equivalent to the qualification of the degree from an recognised European Union or overseas institutions in masters or relevant degree as per the English Language requirements for the entry of the college the students must have show the evidence such as IELTS, TOEFL that the candidate have met the abilities to of English language skills and communication internationally as requirement of the University of the Sheffield
Level of Study: Postgraduate
Type: Scholarship
Frequency: Annual
Country of Study: New Zealand

Closing Date: January
Funding: Foundation

Future Global Leaders Fellowship Program

Purpose: Future Global Leaders Fellowship Program is an international program designed for Freshmen students who are interested to pursue research and fellowship training, where the fellowship program is an internationally competitive program which is intended for granting first generation and low-income students entry into the Fortis Society, which is the world's first private network for diverse leaders, The main objective of the program is to gather students from world's top most universities which includes-Harvard University, the University of Oxford, Sciences Po, and Peking University
Eligibility: Applicants must be first-year university students and must fit the following eligibility criteria: 1. First-Generation or Low-Income University Student – students who do not have a family history of higher education, or who come from a low-income background. 2. Track Record of Academic Excellence – throughout high school and during the first months of the current school year. 3. Proven Leadership Abilities – through self-started initiatives and ventures, or leadership in their schools or communities
Level of Study: Postgraduate
Type: Fellowship
Frequency: Annual
Country of Study: New Zealand
Closing Date: 31 January
Funding: Foundation

Gilbert M Tothill Scholarship in Psychological Medicine

Purpose: Doctoral scholarships are awarded by the University Council, on the recommendation of the Senate, to candidates proceeding to a course of supervised doctoral study at this University. These scholarships are normally available only to students seeking to obtain their first doctoral qualification
Eligibility: In the case of an applicant for a doctoral scholarship who has completed a Master's degree by papers and thesis (at least 0.75 EFTS), the grades of all relevant2 advanced level papers counting towards the award of the degree and the thesis will be taken into account. An explanation of the time taken for completion of the thesis may be requested and considered by the Scholarships and Prizes Committee if the thesis has taken more than 2 EFTS (2 fulltime years) to complete
Level of Study: Postgraduate

Type: Scholarship
Value: NZ $10,000
Length of Study: 3 year
Frequency: Annual
Country of Study: New Zealand
Closing Date: Applicants can apply anytime
Funding: Foundation

For further information contact:

Email: scholarships@otago.ac.nz

Helen Rosa Thacker Scholarship in Neurological Research

Purpose: The Helen Rosa Thacker Scholarship in Neurological Research was established by Helen Rosa Thacker in 2012 to support research and teaching in the field of neurology at the University of Otago. The scholarship aims to recognise, reward and inspire a particularly good PhD student. This scholarship can be held alongside an existing scholarship. This scholarship will be awarded for one year, with a chance of extension to a second year due to outstanding progress
Eligibility: 1. A full time PhD student in neurological research at the University of Otago. 2. A male scholar holding a New Zealand birth certificate. 3. Available to receive the scholarship in person and provide updates on the progress of their research
Level of Study: Postgraduate
Type: Scholarship
Value: NZ $5,000
Length of Study: 1 year
Frequency: Annual
Country of Study: New Zealand
Closing Date: 26 October
Funding: Foundation

For further information contact:

Jane Reynolds, Administrative Assistant, Brain Health Research Centre, C/- Department of Anatomy, PO Box 56, Dunedin 9054, New Zealand

Email: bhrc@otago.ac.nz

James Park Scholarship in Geology

Purpose: Masters' scholarships are awarded by the University Council, on the recommendation of the Senate, to candidates in the first year of their thesis research for a Master's degree which constitutes entry to the PhD course at this University. These scholarships are available only to students seeking to obtain their first research-based Master's qualification

Eligibility: 1. Unless otherwise stated in these conditions or within the schedule, doctoral and Masters' scholarships are open only to Domestic Fee Paying Students. International candidates studying for professional doctorates are eligible to apply but if awarded a scholarship the tuition fee waiver will be capped at the domestic rate. 2. In the case of applicants for a doctoral scholarship, confirmation of the scholarship is dependent on approval of their application for admission to the relevant doctoral programme and completion of the enrolment procedure. 3. In the case of applicants for a Master's scholarship, confirmation of the scholarship is dependent on approval of their application to register as a Master's candidate and completion of the enrolment procedure

Level of Study: Postgraduate
Type: Scholarship
Value: NZ $27,000
Frequency: Annual
Country of Study: New Zealand
Closing Date: Applicants can apply anytime
Funding: Foundation

For further information contact:

Email: scholarships@otago.ac.nz

Macandrew-Stout Postgraduate Scholarship in Economics

Purpose: Established from funds made available by public subscription in memory of the late James Macandrew, member of the Council and one of the founders of the University and in 1920 by Sir Robert Stout, KCMG, Chief Justice of New Zealand

Eligibility: 1. Unless otherwise stated in these conditions or within the schedule, doctoral and Masters' scholarships are open only to Domestic Fee Paying Students. International candidates studying for professional doctorates are eligible to apply but if awarded a scholarship the tuition fee waiver will be capped at the domestic rate. 2. In the case of applicants for a doctoral scholarship, confirmation of the scholarship is dependent on approval of their application for admission to the relevant doctoral programme and completion of the enrolment procedure. 3. In the case of applicants for a Master's scholarship, confirmation of the scholarship is dependent on approval of their application to register as a Master's candidate and completion of the enrolment procedure

Level of Study: Postgraduate
Type: Scholarship

Value: NZ $27,000
Frequency: Annual
Country of Study: New Zealand
Closing Date: Applicants can apply anytime
Funding: Foundation

For further information contact:

Email: scholarships@otago.ac.nz

Neuropsychology Scholarships

Subjects: Neuropsychology
Purpose: To investigate how visual information is used by humans in the learning of new skills
Eligibility: Open to applicants with an undergraduate qualification and a background or interest in cognitive science or neuropsychology. The project would suit a self-motivated person who is able to work well with participants and patients and other members on the study team. A working knowledge of the software package MATLAB and experience in programming with its language, is highly desirable
Level of Study: Postgraduate
Type: Scholarship
Value: NZ $12,000 per year for 2 years maximum, plus a maximum of NZ $4,000 per year towards tuition fees
Application Procedure: Applicants must enquire in the first instance to the director of the Cognitive Science programme
Contributor: Marsden Fund of the Royal Society of New Zealand

For further information contact:

Tel: (64) 3 479 5269
Fax: (64) 3 479 8335
Email: lfranz@psy.otago.ac.nz
Contact: Dr Elizabeth Franz

Nga Pae O Te Maramatanga Doctoral Scholarships

Purpose: Fostering Te Pa Harakeke – understanding, achieving and maintaining 'healthy and prosperous families of mana' and the lessons this may hold for New Zealand families overall. Understanding what 'Te Pa Harakeke' is, enabling it to be achieved and addressing the barriers
Eligibility: For Maori or indigenous students who are currently enrolled or in the process of enrolling in a recognised doctoral programme of study and research at a tertiary institution. Applicants must not work more than 10 hours per week in paid employment while in receipt of this scholarship
Level of Study: Postgraduate
Type: Scholarship

Value: $25,000
Length of Study: 3 year
Frequency: Annual
Country of Study: New Zealand
Closing Date: 30 September
Funding: Foundation

Noni Wright Scholarship

Purpose: Established by the University Council in association with the Guardian Trust in 2011 to provide support for Theatre Studies students to pursue postgraduate study. The scholarship was made possible by a generous endowment from the late Mrs Eleanor Wright, to honour the memory of her daughter Noni Wright, who was well known in drama circles, and had appeared on programmes for the BBC
Eligibility: The scholarship is open to both domestic and international students. Applicants must be currently enrolled or intending to enrol for full-time study at the University of Otago in the year following the closing date, for the degree of MA or MFA in Theatre Studies, or for a PhD researching a topic in Theatre Studies
Level of Study: Postgraduate
Type: Scholarship
Value: NZ $5,000
Length of Study: 1 year
Frequency: Annual
Country of Study: New Zealand
Closing Date: 1 November
Funding: Foundation

For further information contact:

Email: scholarships@otago.ac.nz

Patricia Pratt Scholarships in Musical Performance

Purpose: The purpose of the scholarship is to assist outstanding New Zealand musical performers who have completed an honours degree in musical performance in New Zealand to continue their musical development at a renowned international music school or conservatorium. The scholarship will be awarded for classical music performance including vocal or instrumental performance or conducting
Eligibility: 1. Be New Zealand citizens with preference given to students who have resided in New Zealand for at least three years immediately preceding the year of selection. 2. Hold an honours degree in music performance from a New Zealand University
Level of Study: Postgraduate
Type: Scholarship

Value: Up to US$45,000
Frequency: Annual
Country of Study: New Zealand
Closing Date: 1 March
Funding: Foundation

Postgraduate Tassell Scholarship in Cancer Research

Purpose: Doctoral scholarships are awarded by the University Council, on the recommendation of the Senate, to candidates proceeding to a course of supervised doctoral study at this University. These scholarships are normally available only to students seeking to obtain their first doctoral qualification
Eligibility: 1. Unless otherwise stated in these conditions or within the schedule, doctoral and Masters' scholarships are open only to Domestic Fee Paying Students. International candidates studying for professional doctorates are eligible to apply but if awarded a scholarship the tuition fee waiver will be capped at the domestic rate. 2. In the case of applicants for a doctoral scholarship, confirmation of the scholarship is dependent on approval of their application for admission to the relevant doctoral programme and completion of the enrolment procedure. 3. In the case of applicants for a Master's scholarship, confirmation of the scholarship is dependent on approval of their application to register as a Master's candidate and completion of the enrolment procedure
Level of Study: Postgraduate
Type: Scholarship
Value: NZ $27,000
Frequency: Annual
Country of Study: New Zealand
Closing Date: Applicants can apply anytime
Funding: Foundation

For further information contact:

Email: scholarships@otago.ac.nz

Ramboll Masters Scholarship for International Students

Purpose: Ramboll Masters Scholarship for International Students provides scholarships to the students all over the world who are pursuing masters degree and diploma in engineering in all related fields of Engineering, Natural Science, Political Science, Economics or Architecture, the candidates are selected based on the academic merit considering their projects and profile, the Ramboll offers opportunities to the students by providing inspirational and longstanding solutions that strengthen the ideas of candidate and enhance the nature and future

Eligibility: To be eligible to be granted a Ramboll Scholarship the applicant should meet necessary criteria such as the candidate is currently studying Engineering, Natural Science, Political Science, Economics or Architecture subjects as one of their course studies, and are going to study abroad outside of Denmark, to be eligible to apply the applicant should be a Diploma Engineer on semester 4 – 7 or studying on a Master's level, and must agree to send Ramboll two travel updates during their stay abroad

Level of Study: Postgraduate

Type: Scholarship

Value: NZ$25,000

Frequency: Annual

Country of Study: New Zealand

Closing Date: 8 May

Funding: Foundation

Senior Smeaton Scholarship in Experimental Science

Purpose: Masters' scholarships are awarded by the University Council, on the recommendation of the Senate, tocandidates in the first year of their thesis research for a Master's degree which constitutes entry to the PhD course at this University. These scholarships are available only to students seeking to obtain their first research-based Master's qualification

Eligibility: 1. Unless otherwise stated in these conditions or within the schedule, doctoral and Masters' scholarships are open only to Domestic Fee Paying Students.3 International candidates studying for professional doctorates are eligible to apply but if awarded a scholarship the tuition fee waiver will be capped at the domestic rate. 2. In the case of applicants for a doctoral scholarship, confirmation of the scholarship is dependent on approval of their application for admission to the relevant doctoral programme and completion of the enrolment procedure. 3. In the case of applicants for a Master's scholarship, confirmation of the scholarship is dependent on approval of their application to register as a Master's candidate and completion of the enrolment procedure

Level of Study: Postgraduate

Type: Scholarship

Value: NZ $27,000

Frequency: Annual

Country of Study: New Zealand

Closing Date: Applicants can apply anytime

Funding: Foundation

For further information contact:

Email: scholarships@otago.ac.nz

The Dr Stella Cullington Postgraduate Scholarship in Ophthalmology

Purpose: Established in 2014 by the Faculty of Medicine, from a generous donation from Dr Stella Cullington. Dr Cullington is a medical graduate and practised as a GP in United Kingdom and New Zealand. The Dr Stella Cullington Postgraduate Scholarship in Ophthalmology was created to support the sustainability and development of Ophthalmology Research within the academic discipline

Eligibility: 1. Be a NZ citizen or NZ permanent resident. 2. Hold a Bachelor of Medicine and Bachelor of Surgery degrees (MBChB) or an equivalent medical degree. 3. Demonstrate proof of potential academic research ability through (i) successful completion of a research Master's degree, or (ii) appropriate and equivalent prior research experience. 4. Be enrolled or intending to enrol for a MOphth or PhD at the University of Otago

Level of Study: Postgraduate

Type: Scholarship

Value: up to $5,000

Length of Study: 1 year

Frequency: Annual

Country of Study: New Zealand

Closing Date: Applicants can apply anytime

Funding: Foundation

The Eamon Cleary Trust Postgraduate Study Scholarship

Purpose: Established in 2016 by the University of Otago Council from a generous donation by the Eamon Cleary Trust. The Eamon Cleary Trust Postgraduate Study Scholarship was created to support University of Otago students undertaking postgraduate research in Irish Studies. The scholarship may be used for expenses associated with postgraduate study, such as tuition fees, research expenses or travel associated with their research programme

Eligibility: 1. Be intending to enrol in a Doctoral or Research Masters programme in Irish Studies or a Coursework Masters programme in Irish Studies with a research component greater than or equal to 60 points at the University of Otago for the year of the award. 2. Have made contact to discuss satisfactory supervisory arrangements with the Eamon Cleary Professor of Irish Studies prior to submission of the application

Level of Study: Postgraduate

Type: Scholarship
Value: Between NZ $15,000 to $25,000
Frequency: Annual
Country of Study: New Zealand
Closing Date: 1 November
Funding: Foundation

The Joan, Arthur & Helen Thacker Aboriginal and/or Torres Strait Islander Postgraduate Scholarship

Purpose: Established by the University of Otago Council in 2014, through the provision of funding from Helen R Thacker, this scholarship aims to support students of Aboriginal and/or Torres Strait Islander descent to undertake postgraduate studies in the field of Health Sciences at the University of Otago. The purpose of the fund is to support research and training in health sciences subjects that may have a future benefit to Aboriginal and/or Torres Strait Islander communities
Eligibility: 1. Aboriginal and/or Torres Strait Islander descent. 2. Australian citizens and residing in Australia at the time of application. 3. Planning to enrol in a postgraduate course of study in either Dental Technology, Dentistry, Oral Health, Medicine, Neuroscience, Pharmacy or Radiation Therapy at the University of Otago. 4. Planning to undertake study/research that is likely to be of future benefit to their Aboriginal and/or Torres Strait Islander community. 5. Intending to return to work in Australia after their course of study
Level of Study: Postgraduate
Type: Scholarship
Value: NZ $30,000
Frequency: Annual
Country of Study: New Zealand
Closing Date: 1 October
Funding: Foundation

The Robinson Dorsey Postgraduate Scholarship

Purpose: The Robinson Dorsey Postgraduate Scholarship was created to support postgraduate students who are returning to university study after a break, and/or who through their personal circumstances, are not eligible for usual scholarships
Eligibility: 1. A NZ citizen or NZ permanent resident. 2. Enrolled or intending to enrol in a postgraduate diploma, honours degree, Master of Science or PhD degree in Physiology or Human Nutrition at the University of Otago. 3. Returning to university study after a break, and/or who through their personal circumstances are not eligible for usual scholarships
Level of Study: Postgraduate

Type: Scholarship
Value: NZ $25,000 full time PhD study or NZ $13,000 full time Masters', Postgraduate Diploma or Honours Study
Frequency: Annual
Country of Study: New Zealand
Closing Date: 28 February
Funding: Foundation

For further information contact:

Post to Student Administration (Scholarships), St David II Building, University of Otago, PO Box 56, Dunedin 9054, New Zealand

Email: scholarships@otago.ac.nz

University of Helsinki Masters Scholarships

Purpose: University of Helsinki Masters Scholarships are offered to the students of international arena who are interested to pursue masters degree from the university, the scholarships offered are fully funded which includes full tuition fees, eligible candidates are selected by the committee not only based on academic criteria the committee will also consider the variety and diversity of the applicants and grant the scholarships to those coming from different backgrounds and fields of studies, the main aim hidden under the scholarship program is to create a rich and diverse learning environment at the University of Helsinki, candidates should receive an offer from the university to apply for the scholarship
Eligibility: 1. You are eligible for the Master's programme at the University of Helsinki. 2. The country of your nationality is outside the European Union/EEA and you meet the requirements for obtaining an entry visa and residence permit for Finland. More information at the Studyinfo. 3. You have obtained excellent results in your previous studies and can prove this in your application
Level of Study: Postgraduate
Type: Scholarship
Value: Fully funded grant (Tuition fee + 10,000 EUR), study grant
Length of Study: 2 years
Frequency: Annual
Country of Study: New Zealand
Application Procedure: The Master's Programme will make the academic assessment of your degree application simultaneously with your scholarship application. At this stage the scholarship criteria is the same as the programme specific selection criteria. Advantages of having this scholarships are free or highly affordable health care services by the Finnish Student Health Service (FSHS) student meal discounts in Unicafe restaurants reductions in public transport

Closing Date: 11 January
Funding: Private
Additional Information: Tuition fee will range from 13,000 to 18,000 euros. For further information on the scholarship, refer the below link. www.helsinki.fi/en/admissions/scholarship-programme

University of Otago Academic General Practitioner Registrar PhD Scholarship

Purpose: Established in 2013 by the Faculty of Medicine, the University of Otago Academic General Practitioner Registrar PhD Scholarship was created to support the sustainability and development of the Primary Health Care and General Practice academic discipline. The scholarship aims to help establish research capability among a new generation of General Practitioners by supporting the achievement of a Doctoral degree (PhD) at the University of Otago as well as vocational registration as a Fellow of the Royal New Zealand College of General Practitioners (RNZCGP)
Eligibility: 1. A NZ citizen or NZ permanent resident. 2. Hold a Bachelor of Medicine and Bachelor of Surgery degrees (MBChB) or an equivalent medical degree. 3. Demonstrate a formal commitment to a General Practice career by having successfully completed either (i) the General Practice Education Programme first year (GPEP1) with an above average pass in the Primary Membership Examination (PRIMEX) or (ii) a RNZCGP Fellowship. 4. Have successfully completed either the 'Health Sciences Research Methods' paper (HASX417) or the 'Research Methods in General Practice' paper (GENX821), or an alternative 30 point postgraduate research methods paper with a minimum B+ grade. 5. Demonstrate proof of potential academic research ability through (i) successful completion of a research Master's degree, or (ii) appropriate and equivalent prior research experience
Level of Study: Postgraduate
Type: Scholarship
Value: NZ $25,000 per year for full-time study or NZ $12,500 per year for part-time study plus a tuition fee waiver for the PhD thesis paper for the period of tenure
Frequency: Annual
Country of Study: New Zealand
Closing Date: 15 September
Funding: Foundation

University of Otago China Scholarship Council Doctoral Scholarship

Purpose: Masters' scholarships are awarded by the University Council, on the recommendation of the Senate, to candidates in the first year of their thesis research for a Master's degree which constitutes entry to the PhD course at this University. These scholarships are available only to students seeking to obtain their first research-based Master's qualification
Eligibility: 1. Unless otherwise stated in these conditions or within the schedule, doctoral and Masters' scholarships are open only to Domestic Fee Paying Students. International candidates studying for professional doctorates are eligible to apply but if awarded a scholarship the tuition fee waiver will be capped at the domestic rate. 2. In the case of applicants for a doctoral scholarship, confirmation of the scholarship is dependent on approval of their application for admission to the relevant doctoral programme and completion of the enrolment procedure. 3. In the case of applicants for a Master's scholarship, confirmation of the scholarship is dependent on approval of their application to register as a Master's candidate and completion of the enrolment procedure
Level of Study: Postgraduate
Type: Scholarship
Frequency: Annual
Country of Study: New Zealand
Closing Date: Applicants can apply anytime
Funding: Foundation

For further information contact:

Email: scholarships@otago.ac.nz

University of Otago City of Literature PhD Scholarship

Purpose: Masters' scholarships are awarded by the University Council, on the recommendation of the Senate, to candidates in the first year of their thesis research for a Master's degree which constitutes entry to the PhD course at this University. These scholarships are available only to students seeking to obtain their first research-based Master's qualification
Eligibility: 1. Unless otherwise stated in these conditions or within the schedule, doctoral and Masters' scholarships are open only to Domestic Fee Paying Students.3 International candidates studying for professional doctorates are eligible to apply but if awarded a scholarship the tuition fee waiver will be capped at the domestic rate. 2. In the case of applicants for a doctoral scholarship, confirmation of the scholarship is dependent on approval of their application for admission to the relevant doctoral programme and completion of the enrolment procedure. 3. In the case of applicants for a Master's scholarship, confirmation of the scholarship is dependent on approval of their application to register as a Master's candidate and completion of the enrolment procedure
Level of Study: Postgraduate
Type: Scholarship

Value: NZ. $27,000
Frequency: Annual
Country of Study: New Zealand
Closing Date: 30 September
Funding: Foundation

For further information contact:

Email: scholarships@otago.ac.nz

University of Otago Doctoral Scholarships

Subjects: All subjects
Purpose: To fund research towards a PhD degree at the University of Otago
Eligibility: Open to applicants of any country but must be primarily resident in New Zealand during study
Level of Study: Doctorate, Research
Type: Scholarship
Value: NZ $25,000 plus fees (excluding insurance and student services fees)
Length of Study: 3 years
Frequency: Annual
Study Establishment: The University of Otago
Country of Study: New Zealand
Application Procedure: Please visit www.otago.ac.nz/applynow for further details
Closing Date: Applicant can apply anytime
No. of awards given last year: 180

For further information contact:

Email: scholarships@otago.ac.nz

University of Otago Doctorate in Medical Education Scholarship

Purpose: Established with funding from the Otago Medical School, this scholarship is intended to provide support for clinically qualified health care professionals with an interest in medical education to undertake research at PhD level. The research must be applicable to the enhancement of the Otago MB ChB programme. The scholarship will be awarded for a three-year period; part-time PhDs will be considered. The participants will perform medical educational research in their own educational setting at University of Otago campuses in Dunedin, Christchurch or Wellington, but associated sites e.g. Invercargill, Nelson, Palmerston North, Hawkes Bay will be considered provided satisfactory supervisory arrangements can be made

Eligibility: 1. Normally be a NZ citizen or NZ permanent resident. 2. Hold a clinical health care discipline degree. Non-clinically qualified people with a strong background in Education may be considered but priority will be given to applicants from the first category. 3. Provide confirmation that this is their first doctoral qualification. 4. Be enrolled or intending to enrol for a PhD
Level of Study: Postgraduate
Type: Scholarship
Value: NZ $25,000 stipend per annum plus a domestic tuition fees waiver
Frequency: Annual
Country of Study: New Zealand
Closing Date: 20 February
Funding: Foundation

University of Otago International Master's Scholarship

Purpose: To assist international students in their master's thesis year of studies at the University of Otago
Eligibility: Open to all international applicants intending to study at the University of Otago who would normally be charged international fees
Level of Study: Postdoctorate, Research
Type: Scholarship
Value: NZ $13,000, International tuition fees (excluding insurance and student services fees
Frequency: Annual
Country of Study: Any country
Closing Date: Applications can be applied anytime
Funding: Private

For further information contact:

Doctoral and Scholarships Office, PO Box 56, Dunedin, New Zealand

Email: university@otago.ac.uk

University of Otago Maori Doctoral Scholarship

Purpose: Doctoral scholarships are awarded by the University Council, on the recommendation of the Senate, tocandidates proceeding to a course of supervised doctoral study at this University. These scholarships are normally available only to students seeking to obtain their first doctoral qualification
Eligibility: 1. Unless otherwise stated in these conditions or within the schedule, doctoral and Masters' scholarships are open only to Domestic Fee Paying Students.3 International

candidates studying for professional doctorates are eligible to apply but if awarded a scholarship the tuition fee waiver will be capped at the domestic rate. 2. In the case of applicants for a doctoral scholarship, confirmation of the scholarship is dependent on approval of their application for admission to the relevant doctoral programme and completion of the enrolment procedure

Level of Study: Postgraduate
Type: Scholarship
Value: NZ $27,000
Frequency: Annual
Country of Study: New Zealand
Closing Date: Applicants can apply anytime
Funding: Foundation

For further information contact:

Email: scholarships@otago.ac.nz

University of Otago Postgraduate Scholarship in Obstetrics and Gynaecology

Purpose: The Scholarship is intended to provide support for Obstetrics and Gynaecology trainees to carry out research in Obstetrics, Gynaecology and Women's Health whilst enrolled at the University of Otago for a graduate research degree, such as a Master of Medical Science (MMedSc) or Doctor of Philosophy (PhD). It is desirable, but not compulsory, that the research be carried out at the University of Otago
Eligibility: 1. Medical graduates (normally Registrars enrolled in the Royal Australian and New Zealand College of Obstetrics and Gynaecology Integrated Training Programme, or Members or Fellows of the College). 2. Enrolled in, or intending to enrol in a research Master's degree or PhD, normally towards a topic in the field of Obstetrics and Gynaecology or Women's Health
Level of Study: Postgraduate
Type: Scholarship
Value: $25,000
Frequency: Annual
Country of Study: New Zealand
Closing Date: 17 November
Funding: Foundation

Waddell Smith Postgraduate Scholarship

Purpose: Masters' scholarships are awarded by the University Council, on the recommendation of the Senate, tocandidates in the first year of their thesis research for a Master's degree which constitutes entry to the PhD course

at this University. These scholarships are available only to students seeking to obtain their first research-based Master's qualification
Eligibility: 1. Unless otherwise stated in these conditions or within the schedule, doctoral and Masters' scholarships are open only to Domestic Fee Paying Students. International candidates studying for professional doctorates are eligible to apply but if awarded a scholarship the tuition fee waiver will be capped at the domestic rate. 2. In the case of applicants for a doctoral scholarship, confirmation of the scholarship is dependent on approval of their application for admission to the relevant doctoral programme and completion of the enrolment procedure. 3. In the case of applicants for a Master's scholarship, confirmation of the scholarship is dependent on approval of their application to register as a Master's candidate and completion of the enrolment procedure
Level of Study: Postgraduate
Type: Scholarship
Value: NZ $2,000
Frequency: Annual
Country of Study: New Zealand
Closing Date: Applicants can apply anytime
Funding: Foundation

For further information contact:

Educational Credential Evaluators, Inc., P.O. Box 514070, Milwaukee, WI 53212, United States of America

Email: scholarships@otago.ac.nz

Williamson Medical Research PhD Scholarship

Purpose: The scholarship may be held by PhD candidates studying towards a PhD in the field of medical research. Applicants must have previously completed a medical degree and be New Zealand citizens (preference will be given to New Zealand–born applicants). The scholarship shall be awarded by the University of Council on the recommendation of the Faculty of Medicine
Eligibility: 1. Unless otherwise stated in these conditions or within the schedule, doctoral and Masters' scholarships are open only to Domestic Fee Paying Students. 3 International candidates studying for professional doctorates are eligible to apply but if awarded a scholarship the tuition fee waiver will be capped at the domestic rate. 2. In the case of applicants for a doctoral scholarship, confirmation of the scholarship is dependent on approval of their application for admission to the relevant doctoral programme and completion of the enrolment procedure. 3. In the case of applicants for a Master's scholarship, confirmation of the scholarship is dependent on

approval of their application to register as a Master's candidate and completion of the enrolment procedure
Level of Study: Postgraduate
Type: Scholarship
Value: NZ $25,000
Length of Study: 3 year
Frequency: Annual
Country of Study: New Zealand
Closing Date: Applicants can apply anytime
Funding: Foundation

For further information contact:

Email: scholarships@otago.ac.nz

University of Oxford

University Offices, Wellington Square, Oxford OX1 2JD, United Kingdom

Tel: (44) 18 6527 0000
Fax: (44) 18 6527 0708
Email: karen.walker@admin.ox.ac.uk
Website: www.ox.ac.uk
Contact: Mrs Ben Nicholas, Graduate Funding Administrator

Alan Turing Doctoral Studentships

Eligibility: Open to all graduate applicants for a variety of doctoral graduate courses related to data science. Please see website for further details and eligible subjects, including how to apply
Level of Study: Doctorate
Type: Studentship
Value: Studentships include a generous tax-free stipend of £20,500 per annum, a travel allowance and tuition fees (home/European Union rate) for a period of 3.5 years. A limited number of studentships include fully funded international tuition fees or a partial contribution towards international tuition fees
Length of Study: 3.5 years
Country of Study: Any country
Additional Information: Please visit the website: www. turing.ac.uk/opportunities/studentships/ for more information

For further information contact:

Email: hr@turing.ac.uk

Archaeology: AHRC

Purpose: Archaeology
Eligibility: Open to United Kingdom applicants for DPhils in Archaeology and Classical Archaeology. Other European Union nationals are eligible for a fees-only award. All eligible applicants will be automatically considered
Level of Study: Doctorate
Type: Scholarship
Value: University fee, college fee and full living expenses. Fees-only awards for non-United Kingdom, European Union students
Length of Study: Up to 3 years
Country of Study: Any country
Closing Date: 20 January
Additional Information: Please visit the website: www. humanities.ox.ac.uk/prospective_students/graduates/ahrc for more information

For further information contact:

Email: hca-research@ed.ac.uk

Archaeology: Edward Hall Awards

Purpose: Archaeological Science
Eligibility: Open to all applicants for the MSc/MSt in Archaeological Science. All applicants to course will be automatically considered
Level of Study: Postgraduate
Type: Award
Value: £8,120
Length of Study: 1 year
Country of Study: Any country
Closing Date: 20 January
Additional Information: Please visit the website: www. arch.ox.ac.uk/graduate-archaeological-science.html for more information

For further information contact:

Email: webofficer@arch.ox.ac.uk

Area Studies: FirstRand Laurie Dippenaar Scholarship

Purpose: African Studies
Eligibility: Open to South African graduate applicants for the MSc African Studies
Level of Study: Postgraduate
Type: Scholarship

Value: University fee, college fee and full living expenses
Length of Study: Period of fee liability
Frequency: Annual
Study Establishment: Wadham College
Country of Study: South Africa
Application Procedure: Please see website for further details, including how to apply
Closing Date: 20 January
Additional Information: Please visit the website: www. firstrand.co.za/csi/Pages/laurie-dippenaar-scholarship.aspx for more information

Atmospheric, Oceanic & Planetary Physics: STFC Studentships

Eligibility: Open to Home and European Union graduate applicants to the DPhil Atmospheric, Oceanic and Planetary Physics. To be eligible for consideration for these scholarships, applicants must be successful in being offered a place on their course after consideration of applications received by the relevant January deadline for the course
Level of Study: Doctorate
Type: Studentship
Value: Tuition and college fees, and a tax free stipend. Fees-only award for European Union students who have not been resident in the United Kingdom for the previous 3 years
Length of Study: 3 years
Frequency: Annual
Country of Study: Any country
Closing Date: 20 January
Additional Information: Please visit the website: www2.phys ics.ox.ac.uk/study-here/postgraduates/atmospheric-oceanic-and-planetary-physics/funding for more information

For further information contact:

Email: F.Y.Ogrin@exeter.ac.uk

Balliol College: Balliol Economics Scholarship

Subjects: Economics
Eligibility: Open to all graduate applicants to MPhil or MPhil +DPhil 2+2 in Economics. Students of any nationality applying to read for the MPhil in economics
Type: Scholarship
Value: Up to £6,500. When offered in conjunction with Clarendon funding this will create a combined award covering university and college fee and full living expenses
Length of Study: Up to 3 years

Application Procedure: Please see website for how to apply and more details
Closing Date: 22 January

For further information contact:

Email: graduate.admissions@balliol.ox.ac.uk
Contact: Tutor for Graduate Admissions

Balliol College: Brassey Italian Scholarship

Eligibility: Open to all applicants to postgraduate degrees in Modern Languages where Italian is the principal subject of study. Please see website for more details
Level of Study: Postgraduate, Research
Type: Scholarship
Value: College fee
Length of Study: Duration of fee liability
Application Procedure: Please see website for how to apply and more details
Closing Date: 22 January

For further information contact:

Email: graduate.admissions@balliol.ox.ac.uk
Contact: Tutor for Graduate Admissions

Balliol College: Eddie Dinshaw Scholarship

Subjects: Engineering, mathematics, economics, history, law, and the physical and biological sciences. (This includes biochemistry but excludes integrated immunology and the DPhil in psychiatry)
Eligibility: Open to all graduate applicants from India for relevant areas of study
Level of Study: Postgraduate, Research
Type: Scholarship
Value: Full living expenses
Length of Study: Up to 3 years
Frequency: Annual
Application Procedure: Please see website for more details and how to apply
Closing Date: 18 January
Additional Information: Eligible to nationals of India. Please check at www.balliol.ox.ac.uk/graduate-admissions/ scholarships for more information

For further information contact:

Email: graduate.admissions@balliol.ox.ac.uk
Contact: Tutor for Graduate Admissions

Balliol College: Foley-Bejar Scholarships

Eligibility: Open to all graduate applicants who a) were born in or who have one parent born in Mexico, Spain, or the Republic of Ireland, or who have a strong connection with Northern Ireland; and b) are ordinarily resident in Mexico, Spain or the Republic of Ireland. Please see website for more details

Type: Scholarship

Value: Stipend

Length of Study: Period of fee liability up to 4 years

Country of Study: Any country

Application Procedure: Please see website for more details and how to apply

Closing Date: 23 January

Additional Information: Please check at www.balliol.ox.ac.uk/graduate-admissions/scholarships for more information

For further information contact:

Email: graduate@balliol.ox.ac.uk

Balliol College: IKOS Half Bursary

Eligibility: Open to candidates of any nationality who have expressed an intention to pursue an academic, vocational or public-service oriented career following their degrees

Level of Study: Postgraduate, Research

Type: Bursary

Value: Up to £6,000 per year

Length of Study: Up to 3 years

Application Procedure: Applicants must apply to the University of Oxford for admission by the University's second deadline in January, and must apply for any University scholarship, including the Clarendon, for which they are eligible

Additional Information: Please check at www.balliol.ox.ac.uk/graduate-admissions/scholarships for more information

For further information contact:

Email: graduate.admissions@balliol.ox.ac.uk

Contact: Tutor for Graduate Admissions

Balliol College: Jason Hu Scholarship

Eligibility: Open to all graduate applicants from Asia with preference for candidates from Taiwan and China

Level of Study: Postgraduate, Research

Type: Scholarship

Value: £10,000 per year

Length of Study: Up to 3 years

Frequency: Annual

Application Procedure: Please see website for more details and how to apply

Closing Date: 18 January

Additional Information: It is awarded in conjunction with Clarendon Fund or other award or scholarship. Four scholarships can only be offered to students from Taiwan and China as a whole, one can be offered to candidates from any Asian country

For further information contact:

Email: graduate.admissions@balliol.ox.ac.uk

Contact: Tutor for Graduate Admissions

Balliol College: McDougall Scholarship

Subjects: Law

Eligibility: Open to graduate applicants to Law

Level of Study: Graduate, Postgraduate

Type: Scholarship

Value: Combined with Research Council award will cover university fee, college fee and full living expenses

Length of Study: Up to 3 years

Frequency: Annual

Application Procedure: Please see website for how to apply and more details

Closing Date: 22 January

For further information contact:

Email: graduate.admissions@balliol.ox.ac.uk

Contact: Tutor for Graduate Admissions

Balliol College: Peter Storey Scholarship

Subjects: History

Eligibility: Open to all applicants to Master's degrees in History. May be awarded as a fully-funded scholarship in partnership with an AHRC award or as a standalone award of £10,000 per year. Please see website for more details

Level of Study: Postgraduate, Research

Type: Scholarship

Value: A minimum of £10,000 per year

Length of Study: Period of fee liability

Application Procedure: Please see website for more details and how to apply

Closing Date: 22 January

Additional Information: Scholarship will be awarded to a candidate with AHRC Funding

For further information contact:

Email: graduate.admissions@balliol.ox.ac.uk
Contact: Tutor for Graduate Admissions

Balliol College: Snell Scholarship

Subjects: All subjects
Purpose: The College seeks to elect one Scholar who have gained an offer of admission to read for a higher degree at Balliol College from October after completing a degree at the University of Glasgow
Eligibility: Honours graduates or in their final Honours year, applicants must have a connection with Scotland by birth (either themselves or one parent), domicile (at least three years) or education at a school in Scotland (at least three years) before admission to the University of Glasgow. Graduates of the University of Glasgow. Please see website for more details including how to apply
Type: Scholarship
Value: Up to £10,000. When offered in conjunction with RCUK funding this will create a combined award covering university and college fee, and full living expenses
Length of Study: Up to 3 years
Country of Study: Any country
Closing Date: 22 January
Additional Information: Please check at www.balliol.ox.ac.uk/graduate-admissions/scholarships for more information

For further information contact:

Email: outreach@balliol.ox.ac.uk

Blavatnik School of Government: Africa Governance Initiative Scholarship

Subjects: Public Policy
Eligibility: Open to all Master of Public Policy applicants who are ordinarily resident in Africa. Scholarships are awarded on the basis of outstanding academic ability, commitment to public service, a capacity to lead, an interest in and experience of improving governance in Africa, a commitment to completing their summer project on some aspect of governance in Africa, and a commitment to return to Africa after their time at the School to continue their work on governance there
Level of Study: Postgraduate
Type: Scholarship
Value: University fee, college fee and full living expenses
Length of Study: Period of fee liability
Frequency: Annual
Country of Study: Any country

Application Procedure: To apply, applicants must provide a supporting statement. Please see website for more details
Closing Date: 20 January

For further information contact:

Email: inquiries@aigafrica.org

Blavatnik School of Government: African Initiative for Governance Scholarships

Purpose: Public Policy
Eligibility: Open to all Master of Public Policy applicants who are ordinarily resident in Nigeria and Ghana (and other West African nations). Scholarships are awarded on the basis of exceptional academic and leadership merit and/or potential. Applicants will usually hold an undergraduate degree from an African university. They should also intend to return to work in public service in Qualifying country for at least three years after completing their studies
Level of Study: Postgraduate
Type: Scholarship
Value: University fee, college fee and full living expenses
Length of Study: Period of fee liability
Frequency: Annual
Country of Study: Any country
Application Procedure: To apply, applicants must provide a supporting statement. Please see website for more details
Closing Date: 20 January
Additional Information: Please visit the website: www.bsg.ox.ac.uk/study/mpp/bsg-funding-options for more information

For further information contact:

Email: enquiries@bsg.ox.ac.uk

Blavatnik School of Government: Public Service Scholarship

Purpose: Public Policy
Eligibility: Open to all Master of Public Policy applicants. Scholarships are awarded on the basis of unwavering dedication to public service, shown through an exceptional academic and professional record
Level of Study: Postgraduate
Type: Scholarship
Value: University fee, college fee and full living expenses
Length of Study: Period of fee liability
Frequency: Annual
Country of Study: Any country

Application Procedure: To apply, applicants must provide a supporting statement. Please see website for more details
Closing Date: 20 January
Additional Information: Please visit the website: www.bsg.ox.ac.uk/study/mpp/bsg-funding-options for more information

For further information contact:

Email: enquiries@bsg.ox.ac.uk

Blavatnik School of Government: The Lemann Fellows Scholarships

Subjects: Public policy
Eligibility: Open to all Master of Public Policy applicants that are ordinarily resident in Brazil. Scholarships are awarded on the basis of exceptional academic merit and a commitment to social change in Brazil. To apply applicants must provide a supporting statement
Level of Study: Postgraduate
Type: Scholarship
Value: University fee, college fee and full living expenses
Length of Study: Period of fee liability
Country of Study: Any country
Application Procedure: Please see the website for full details, including how to apply
Closing Date: 20 January
Additional Information: Please check at www.bsg.ox.ac.uk/study/mpp/bsg-funding-options for more information

For further information contact:

Email: enquiries@bsg.ox.ac.uk

Blavatnik School of Government: The Walter Kwok Scholarships

Subjects: Public policy
Eligibility: Open to all Master of Public Policy applicants that are ordinarily resident in Hong Kong or China. Scholarships are awarded on the basis of exceptional academic merit and a commitment to change in the HKSAR region. Interviews may be held as part of the selection process
Type: Scholarship
Value: University fee, college fee and full living expenses
Length of Study: Period of fee liability
Country of Study: Any country
Application Procedure: Please see website for more details and how to apply
Closing Date: 20 January

Additional Information: Please check at www.bsg.ox.ac.uk/study/mpp/bsg-funding-options for more information

For further information contact:

Email: enquiries@bsg.ox.ac.uk

Brasenose College: Senior Fiddian

Eligibility: Open to graduates who are former members of Monmouth School or Haberdashers Monmouth School for Girls
Level of Study: Graduate, Postgraduate
Type: Grant
Value: £3,000
Length of Study: Period of fee liability
Study Establishment: Brasenose College
Country of Study: Any country
Application Procedure: Please see website for more details
Closing Date: Relevant January deadline for your course
Additional Information: For more information, please check at www.bnc.ox.ac.uk/prospective-students/graduate-admissions/fees-funding

For further information contact:

Brasenose College Radcliffe Square Oxford, OX1 4AJ, United Kingdom

Email: college.office@bnc.ox.ac.uk

Brasenose Hector Pilling Scholarship

Subjects: Arts or science
Purpose: For graduates of Commonwealth countries
Eligibility: Open to graduates of any Commonwealth university, excluding the United Kingdom
Level of Study: Postgraduate
Type: Scholarship
Value: Fees and maintenance to be determined by the administrators of the Clarendon Fund Scholarships
Frequency: Annual
Study Establishment: Brasenose College, University of Oxford
Country of Study: United Kingdom
No. of awards offered: 1
Application Procedure: Applicants must write for details
Funding: Private
Contributor: In conjunction with the Clarendon Fund Studentship Scheme
No. of awards given last year: 1
No. of applicants last year: 1

Additional Information: This scholarship is offered in conjunction with the Clarendon Fund Studentship Scheme

For further information contact:

Email: international.office@admin.ox.ac.uk
Contact: International Office

Brasenose Joint Commonwealth Studentship

Eligibility: Open to all applicants from Commonwealth countries. Please see website for more details
Level of Study: Graduate, Postgraduate
Value: University fee, college fee, and living expenses (of which £13K funded by BNC)
Length of Study: One year
Study Establishment: Brasenose
Country of Study: United Kingdom
Application Procedure: For more information, please check website: www.bnc.ox.ac.uk/prospective-students/graduate-admissions/fees-funding
Closing Date: 22 January

For further information contact:

Email: lawfac@law.ox.ac.uk

Business School (Saïd): Registrar's University of Oxford Scholarship

Subjects: EMBA
Purpose: To assist graduate students with fees and a living allowance
Eligibility: Open to all
Level of Study: Postgraduate, MBA
Type: Scholarship
Value: Programme cost
Length of Study: 2 years

For further information contact:

Email: Diana.Hulin@admin.ox.ac.uk
Contact: Diana Hulin

Chevening Scholarships

Eligibility: Eligibility varies by country
Level of Study: Graduate
Type: Scholarship
Value: University fee, college fee, and full living expenses
Length of Study: 1 year

Country of Study: Any country
Application Procedure: Please see website for more details and how to apply
Additional Information: Please check at www.fco.gov.uk/en/about-us/what-we-do/scholarships/chevening/how-to-apply/ for more information

For further information contact:

Email: international@lincoln.ac.uk

Christ Church Senior Scholarship

Subjects: All subjects
Purpose: To enable graduate scholars to undertake training or a definite course of literary, educational, scientific or professional study
Eligibility: Open to candidates who will have been reading for a higher degree at the University of Oxford for at least 1 year, but not more than 2 years, by October 1st of the year in which the award is sought
Level of Study: Postgraduate
Type: Scholarship
Value: Varies
Length of Study: 2 years, with a possibility of renewal for a further year
Frequency: Annual
Study Establishment: Christ Church, University of Oxford
Country of Study: United Kingdom
No. of awards offered: 102
Application Procedure: Applicants must write for details. Applications should be made in February
Closing Date: 1 April
No. of awards given last year: 2
No. of applicants last year: 102
Additional Information: Normally, the scholarship is held in conjunction with an award from a government agency that pays the university fees

Commonwealth Shared Scholarship Scheme (CSSS)

Subjects: All subjects
Purpose: To support students from developing Commonwealth countries who would not otherwise be able to study in the United Kingdom
Eligibility: Open to new students from developing Commonwealth countries. Candidates should normally be under 35 at the time the award begins. This scholarship is not available to those living or studying in a developed country, employees of government departments or parastatal organisations

Level of Study: Postgraduate
Value: University and college fees; full grant for living costs; return air travel to the United Kingdom
Length of Study: 1 year
Country of Study: Any country
Application Procedure: Candidates must apply to Oxford by completing the Graduate Application Form by Application Deadline 2. They must complete the CSSS application form and submit this to Student Funding Services by email or post by March 13th
Closing Date: 13 March

Comparative Philology: Joint Christ Church Linguistics Graduate Scholarship

Subjects: Linguistics, philology, phonetics
Purpose: To assist graduate students with fees and maintenance
Eligibility: Open to all
Level of Study: Postgraduate, Research
Type: Scholarship
Value: College fees and maintenance allowance of £2,000
Length of Study: Up to 3 years
Closing Date: 16 January

For further information contact:

Email: kate.dobson@ling-phil.ox.ac.uk

Computer Science: Department Studentships

Subjects: Computer Science
Purpose: To develop practical methods, algorithms, and tools for a use-case driven approach to system-level hardware/software formal co-verification. A key objective, and the foundation for the methodology, will be the invention of a systematic abstraction framework that closes the gap, currently unaddressed, between a system and implementation levels in co-verification
Eligibility: Open to all applicants applying for a DPhil in Computer Science
Level of Study: Doctorate
Type: Studentship
Value: Course fee, college fee and stipend
Length of Study: 3 years
Country of Study: Any country
Closing Date: 10 March
Additional Information: Please visit the website: www.cs.ox.ac.uk/aboutus/vacancies/studentship.html for more information

For further information contact:

Email: enquiries@cs.ox.ac.uk

Computer Science: Engineering and Physical Sciences Research Council (EPSRC) Doctoral Training Partnership Studentships

Purpose: Computer Science
Eligibility: Open to applicants applying for a DPhil in Computer Science. Home students and European Union students who have studied in the United Kingdom for the previous 3 years are eligible for full studentship. European Union students who have studied elsewhere in the European Union are eligible for fees only award
Level of Study: Doctorate
Type: Studentship
Value: Course fee, college fee and stipend (if eligible). Home students and European students who have studied in the United Kingdom for the previous 3 years are eligible for full studentship. European Union students who have studied elsewhere in the European Union are eligible for fees only award
Length of Study: Up to 3.5 years
Country of Study: Any country
Closing Date: 30 March
Additional Information: Please visit the website: www.cs.ox.ac.uk/aboutus/vacancies/studentship.html for more information.

Continuing Education: MSc Programme Scholarship

Subjects: Continuing Education
Eligibility: Open to all applicants for the MSc in Sustainable Urban Development
Level of Study: Postgraduate
Type: Scholarship
Value: Tuition and college fee
Length of Study: Duration of programme
Frequency: Annual
Country of Study: Switzerland
Closing Date: 20 January
Additional Information: Please visit the website: www.conted.ox.ac.uk/about/msud-programme-scholarship for more information

For further information contact:

Email: sud@conted.ox.ac.uk

Corpus Christi College: A E Haigh English Studentship

Eligibility: Open to all graduate applicants in English
Level of Study: Postgraduate, Research
Type: Studentship
Value: £7,500 per year towards college fee and contribution towards living expenses
Length of Study: Period of fee liability
Country of Study: Any country
Application Procedure: Please see website for details of how to apply
Additional Information: Please check at www.ccc.ox.ac.uk/ for more information

For further information contact:

Email: jane.sherwood@admin.ox.ac.uk

Crystal Clinical Scholarships

Type: Scholarship
Value: Scholarship funds will be used for travel and associated expenses
Length of Study: 1 year
Country of Study: Any country

For further information contact:

Email: info@onfgivesback.org

Department of Education: Talbot Scholarship

Subjects: Education
Eligibility: Open to all applicants for DPhil in Education. Please visit website for more details
Level of Study: Doctorate
Type: Partial scholarship
Value: £15,000 per annum contribution towards fees and living expenses 35% reduction of tuition fee
Length of Study: 3 years
Frequency: Every 3 years
Country of Study: Any country
Closing Date: 20 January
Additional Information: Please visit the website: www.education.ox.ac.uk/courses/d-phil/funding-opportunities/   for more information

Donald Tovey Memorial Prize

Subjects: The philosophy, history or understanding of music
Purpose: To assist in the furtherance of research or in the publication of work already done, in the fields of philosophy, history or understanding of music
Eligibility: Open to men or women, without regard to nationality, age or membership of a university
Level of Study: Postdoctorate
Type: Prize
Value: UK£1,000
Frequency: Dependent on funds available
Study Establishment: Unrestricted
Country of Study: Any country
Application Procedure: Applications should be addressed to the Heather Professor of Music at the address shown
Closing Date: June in the year offered
Funding: Private
Contributor: Donal Tovey Memorial Fund
Additional Information: If for furtherance of research, applicants need to demonstrate that the programme falls within the scope of the award, and produce testimonials or other written evidence of previous attainment which demonstrate the researcher's fitness to undertake it. If to assist in publication of work already completed, the applicant must submit one copy of work with an explanation of why the Prize is needed to ensure publication. The Prize is generally awarded for postdoctoral or advanced research

For further information contact:

Faculty of Music, St Aldate's, Oxford OX1 1DB UK, United Kingdom

Tel:	(44) 1865 276 125
Fax:	(44) 1865 276 128
Email:	musicfac@sable.ox.ac.uk
Contact:	Heather Professor of Music

Duke of Cambridge Scholarship at University of Oxford

Purpose: Public Policy
Eligibility: Open to applicants who are ordinarily resident in the United Kingdom and who are applying to the Master of Public Policy (MPP). Please see website for more details
Level of Study: Postgraduate
Type: Scholarship
Value: University fee, college fee, and full living expenses of about € 14,553

Length of Study: Period of fee liability
Country of Study: Any country
Closing Date: 20 January
Additional Information: The scholarship is only tenable at University College. Please visit the website: www.ox.ac.uk/admissions/graduate/fees-and-funding/fees-funding-and-scholarship-search/scholarships-1#duke for more information

For further information contact:

Tel: (44) 1865 614 343
Email: admin@scholarship-position.com

Economic and Social Research Council: Interdisciplinary Area Studies

Subjects: Interdisciplinary Area Studies
Eligibility: Candidates need to apply by the January admissions deadline to their postgraduate programme at the University of Oxford, using the statement of purpose form, which requires candidates to write an indicative research proposal for DPhil level study
Level of Study: Graduate
Value: University fee, college fee, and living expenses. Fees-only award for European Union applicants
Length of Study: Period of fee liability
Country of Study: Any country
Application Procedure: Please visit website for more details and how to apply
Closing Date: 20 January
Additional Information: Please check at www.area-studies.ox.ac.uk/scholarships-sias for more information

For further information contact:

Email: f.ciuta@ucl.ac.uk

Economic and Social Research Council (ESRC): Social Policy & Intervention

Subjects: Comparative social policy, evidence based social intervention and policy evaluation, and social policy/social intervention
Eligibility: Open to applicants to MSc/MPhil comparative social policy, MSc/MPhil evidence based social intervention and policy evaluation and DPhil social policy/social intervention. Candidates apply at the same time as they apply for admission to their postgraduate programme at the University of Oxford, using the same application form
Level of Study: Postgraduate

Value: University fee, college fee and living expenses. Fees-only award for European Union applicants
Length of Study: Period of fee liability
Country of Study: Any country
Application Procedure: Please apply using the standard graduate application form, and confirm with the Department that you wish to be considered for an ESRC studentship
Closing Date: 22 January
Additional Information: Please check at www.spi.ox.ac.uk/study-with-us/funding.html for more information

For further information contact:

Email: erzsebet.bukodi@spi.ox.ac.uk

Economic and Social Research Council: Socio-Legal Studies

Subjects: Law
Eligibility: Open to all prospective students applying for the 1+3 MSt Socio-Legal Studies and DPhil Socio-Legal Studies, or just for the latter
Level of Study: Postgraduate
Type: Scholarship
Value: University fee, college fee, and living expenses. Fees-only award for European Union applicants
Length of Study: Period of fee liability
Frequency: Annual
Country of Study: United Kingdom
Closing Date: 20 January
Funding: Trusts
Additional Information: Please see website: www.law.ox.ac.uk/postgraduate/scholarships.php for more details

For further information contact:

Email: r.sparks@ed.ac.uk

Economics -Economic and Social Research Council (ESRC) Quota Award

Subjects: MPhil and DPhil economics
Purpose: To assist graduate students with fees and maintenance
Eligibility: Open to all graduate applicants in Economics
Level of Study: Doctorate, Research
Type: Award
Value: University fee, college fee, and full living expenses
Length of Study: Up to 4 years

Application Procedure: Applicants are strongly advised to submit their application for consideration at the first application deadline of January 18th. Places on the second application deadline will be limited
Closing Date: 18 January
Additional Information: Please visit website for more details and how to apply www.economics.ox.ac.uk/index.php/graduate

For further information contact:

Tel: (44) 1865 281 162
Email: econgrad@economics.ox.ac.uk
Contact: Julie Minns

Economics: Doctoral Studentship

Subjects: To support some of the finest aspiring economists from around the world
Purpose: Economics
Eligibility: Open to Home/Eu/Overseas. DPhil in economics. Please note this is only available to those who will have DPhil status in MT 2012
Type: Studentship
Value: £11,126
Length of Study: 2 years
Application Procedure: Applicants are strongly advised to submit their application for consideration at the first application deadline of January 20th. Places on the second application deadline will be limited
Closing Date: 20 January and 9 March
Additional Information: All applicants accepted by the Department will be offered a place at a college. You may indicate on your application form which college you would like to be considered for; if you have no preference Graduate Admissions will make a selection for you. Students do not necessarily get accepted by their first choice. Please check at www.economics.ox.ac.uk/index.php/graduate for more information

For further information contact:

Tel: (44) 1865 281 162
Email: econgrad@economics.ox.ac.uk
Contact: Julie Minns

Education: Economic and Social Research Council (ESRC)

Subjects: Education
Eligibility: Open to all Home/European Union applicants for both DPhil in Education and MSc Education (Research Design and Methodology). Please visit website for more details
Level of Study: Doctorate, Postgraduate
Type: Studentship
Value: University fee, college fee and full living expenses
Length of Study: Period of fee liability
Country of Study: Any country
Closing Date: 20 January
Additional Information: Please visit the website: www.education.ox.ac.uk/courses/d-phil/funding-opportunities/ for more information. Kindly contact Mr. Peter Henley for further funding information

For further information contact:

Email: eddev@esrc.ukri.org

Engineering and Physical Sciences Research Council (EPSRC) Centre for Doctoral Training in Autonomous Intelligent Machines and Systems

Subjects: Engineering
Purpose: To develop in-depth knowledge, understanding and expertise in autonomous intelligent systems
Eligibility: Open to United Kingdom and European Union applicants for DPhil in Engineering. European Union applicants may only be eligible for a fees-only award, depending on residency requirements. Please visit website for more details
Level of Study: Doctorate
Type: Scholarship
Value: University fee, college fee and full living expenses
Length of Study: 4 years
Country of Study: Any country
Closing Date: 20 January
Additional Information: Please visit the website: www.ox.ac.uk/admissions/graduate/courses/autonomous-intelligent-machines-and-systems for more information

For further information contact:

Tel: (44) 1865 270 000
Email: aims-cdt@robots.ox.ac.uk

Engineering and Physical Sciences Research Council (EPSRC) Doctoral Training Programme Studentships

Subjects: Statistics
Eligibility: Open to United Kingdom and European Union applicants for DPhil in Statistics. European Union applicants

may only be eligible for a fees-only award, depending on residency requirements
Level of Study: Postgraduate
Value: University fee, college fee and full living expenses
Length of Study: Three and a half years maximum
Frequency: Annual
Country of Study: United Kingdom
Closing Date: 20 January
Funding: Trusts
Additional Information: For more information, please visit website: www.stats.ox.ac.uk/study_here/research_degrees

For further information contact:

Email: phdfunding-salc@manchester.ac.uk

Engineering and Physical Sciences Research Council CDT in Industrially Focussed Mathematical Modelling

Subjects: Mathematical Modelling
Eligibility: Four studentships will be available to applicants regardless of nationality. The remaining studentships are restricted to United Kingdom/European Union nationals
Level of Study: Postgraduate
Type: Scholarship
Value: University fee, college fee and full living expenses (minimum £14,296 per year for 4 years)
Length of Study: 4 years
Frequency: Annual
Country of Study: Any country
Application Procedure: We will automatically assign students to funding and no separate application for funding is required
Closing Date: 10 March
Funding: Trusts
Additional Information: For more information, please visit the website: www.maths.ox.ac.uk/study-here/postgraduate-study/industrially-focused-mathematical-modelling-epsrc-cdt. This course is still accepting applications for current and upcoming entry

For further information contact:

Email: infomm@maths.ox.ac.uk

English Faculty: AHRC Doctoral Training Partnership Studentships

Subjects: English

Eligibility: Open to all Home/European Union's graduates applying to undertake research degrees in the Faculty of English. Please see website for more details
Level of Study: Postgraduate
Type: Studentship
Value: University fee, college fee, and full living expenses. Fees-only awards for non-United Kingdom, European Union students
Length of Study: Period of fee liability
Frequency: Annual
Country of Study: United Kingdom
Closing Date: 20 January
Additional Information: For more information, please check website: www.humanities.ox.ac.uk/prospective_students/graduates/funding/ahrc

For further information contact:

Email: FASS-PhD-Applications@open.ac.uk

English Faculty: Asian Human Rights Commission (AHRC) Doctoral Training Partnership Studentship (Master

Subjects: English
Eligibility: Open to all Home/European Union applicants to MSt and MPhil degrees offered by the Faculty of English. Please see website for more details
Level of Study: Postgraduate
Type: Studentship
Value: University fee, college fee, and living expenses (pro-rata for courses less than 1 year). Fees-only awards for non-United Kingdom, European Union students
Length of Study: Period of fee liability
Frequency: Annual
Country of Study: United Kingdom
Closing Date: 20 January
Funding: Trusts
Additional Information: For more information, please visit: www.humanities.ox.ac.uk/prospective_students/graduates/funding/ahrc

For further information contact:

Email: ahrcdtp@admin.ox.ac.uk

English Faculty: Cecily Clarke Studentship

Subjects: English literature
Eligibility: Open to all applicants to English Medieval Studies, with preference to Middle English Philology. All students

applying for English graduate courses will automatically be considered
Level of Study: Postgraduate
Type: Studentship
Value: £12,000 per year
Length of Study: Up to 2 years
Country of Study: Any country
Closing Date: 18 January
Additional Information: All students applying for English graduate courses will automatically be considered. Candidates apply at the same time as they apply for admission to their postgraduate programme at the University of Oxford, using the same application form. To be considered candidates must apply by the January deadline. Please check at www. english.ox.ac.uk for more information

For further information contact:

Tel: (44) 1865 270 000

Exeter College Usher-Cunningham Senior Studentship

Subjects: Awarded for medical science and medieval or modern history
Purpose: To support graduate study
Eligibility: History is open to graduates of Irish universities only. Medicine is open to all
Level of Study: Postgraduate
Type: Studentship
Value: Home level fees plus maintenance up to the equivalent of a Research Council Award
Length of Study: Usually awarded for up to 3 years
Frequency: Every 3 years
Study Establishment: Exeter College, University of Oxford
Country of Study: United Kingdom
Application Procedure: Applicants must address enquiries to the Academic Administrator
Funding: Private
Contributor: An endowment

For further information contact:

Email: admissions@exeter.ox.ac.uk

Exeter College: Exonian Graduate Scholarship

Eligibility: Exeter College is pleased to offer a studentship covering college fees to two DPhil students, linked to a United Kingdom Research Council award covering university fees

Level of Study: Postdoctorate
Type: Fellowship
Value: College fee only
Length of Study: Up to 3 years
Country of Study: United Kingdom
Application Procedure: Applicants must address enquiries to the Academic Administrator
Closing Date: 22 January
Funding: Private

For further information contact:

Exeter College, Turl St, Oxford OX1 3DP, United Kingdom

Email: academic.administrator@exeter.ox.ac.uk
Contact: Academic Administrator

Exeter College: Nicholas Frangiscatos Scholarship in Byzantine Studies

Eligibility: For a DPhil student in the field of Byzantine studies
Level of Study: Doctorate, Postdoctorate
Type: Fellowship
Value: Up to £10,000 per year
Length of Study: Up to 3 years
Frequency: Every 3 years
Country of Study: United Kingdom
Application Procedure: Please see website for how to apply
Closing Date: 12 March
Funding: Private
Additional Information: Please check at www.exeter.ox.ac. uk/currentstudents/finance/scholarships for more information

For further information contact:

Email: admissions@exeter.ox.ac.uk

Exeter College: Senior Scholarship in Theology

Subjects: Theology or philosophy and theology
Purpose: To support a graduate who wishes to read for the Final Honour School of Theology or Philosophy and Theology
Eligibility: Applicants must hold at least a Second Class (Honours) Degree by the time of admission in a subject other than theology
Level of Study: Postgraduate
Type: Scholarship
Value: University and college fees at Home/European Union rate, maintenance grant £5,000 per year

Length of Study: 3 years
Frequency: Every 3 years
Study Establishment: Exeter College, the University of Oxford
Country of Study: United Kingdom
Application Procedure: Applicants must apply in writing to the Academic Administrator or see the website www.exeter.ox.ac.uk for details
Closing Date: 1 May
Funding: Private
Contributor: Endowment
No. of awards given last year: 1
Additional Information: The College proposes to elect a graduate to a Senior Scholarship in Theology from October 1st. The Scholar is to study for the Final Honour School of either Theology or Philosophy & Theology (2nd BA)

Faculty of Medieval and Modern Languages: Heath Harrison DPhil Award

Subjects: Medieval & Modern Languages
Eligibility: Open to graduate students accepted to read for a DPhil in Medieval and Modern Languages. Please visit the website for more details
Level of Study: Postgraduate
Type: Scholarship
Value: University fee, college fee, and full living expenses
Length of Study: Three years
Frequency: Annual
Country of Study: United Kingdom
Application Procedure: For more information, please check the website: grad.mml.ox.ac.uk/funding_fees
Closing Date: 22 January
Funding: Trusts

For further information contact:

Email: office@mod-langs.ox.ac.uk

Freshfields Bruckhaus Deringer Scholarships (Law)

Subjects: Legal studies
Purpose: To assist graduate students with fees and a living allowance
Eligibility: Varies
Level of Study: Doctorate, Postgraduate, Research
Type: Scholarships
Value: To be confirmed
Length of Study: 1 year

Country of Study: Any country
Closing Date: 22 January

For further information contact:

Email: ContactFSLScheme@freshfields.com

Frost Scholarship Programme (Israel)

Subjects: Science, technology, engineering and mathematics
Purpose: The Frost Scholarship Programme (Israel) funds current students of Israeli universities to study one-year, full-time master's courses in science, technology, engineering and mathematics ('STEM' subjects) at the University of Oxford
Eligibility: Open to Israeli residents currently studying at an Israeli university, who have not previously been enrolled on a full degree programme at an institution outside of Israel. You must be applying for a one-year, full-time Master's course in a STEM subject (Science, Technology, Engineering and Mathematics). Four awards will be made each year. Closing date varies according to course
Level of Study: Postgraduate
Type: Scholarship
Value: University fee, college fee, and full living expenses
Length of Study: Period of fee liability
Frequency: Annual
Country of Study: Any country
Closing Date: Relevant January deadline for your course
Funding: Trusts
Additional Information: Please see website: www.graduate.ox.ac.uk/frostisrael for more details, including the course list

Geography and the Environment: Andrew Goudie Bursary

Eligibility: Open to all applicants for MSc in Environmental Change and Management
Level of Study: Postgraduate
Type: Scholarship
Value: Up to £5,000
Length of Study: 1 year
Country of Study: Any country
Closing Date: 20 January
Additional Information: Please visit the website: www.eci.ox.ac.uk/msc/funding.html for more information

For further information contact:

Email: support@linacre.ox.ac.uk

Geography and the Environment: Boardman Scholarship

Eligibility: Open to all applicants for MSc in Environmental Change and Management
Level of Study: Postgraduate
Type: Scholarship
Value: Up to £5,000
Length of Study: 1 year
Country of Study: Any country
Closing Date: 20 January
Additional Information: Please visit the website: www.eci.ox.ac.uk/msc/funding.html for more information

For further information contact:

Email: socialsciences@devoff.ox.ac.uk
Contact: Rachel Kirwan, Head of Development

Geography: Sir Walter Raleigh Postgraduate Scholarship

Subjects: Environmental change
Eligibility: Open to all applicants for MSc Environmental Change and Management. The award is tenable only at Oriel College
Level of Study: Postgraduate
Type: Scholarship
Value: £3,500
Length of Study: 1 year
Frequency: Annual
Application Procedure: Any person wishing to be considered for this award should follow the application procedure for admission to the degree of Master of Science in Environmental Change and Management at Oxford University, nominating Colleges of preference as detailed in the application procedure. They must, additionally, download (from website) and complete the application form and return it to the address given below
Additional Information: Please note that Oriel College only offers a small number of places per year to applicants for the MSc in Environmental Change and Management, and one of these places will be reserved for the applicant who has been awarded the Sir Walter Raleigh Scholarship

For further information contact:

Tel: (44) 1865 276 520
Fax: (44) 1865 286 548
Email: admissions@oriel.ox.ac.uk
Contact: The Admissions Officer

Goodger and Schorstein Research Scholarships in Medical Sciences

Eligibility: Open to postdoctoral researchers from any department/institute of the Medical Sciences Division. Applicants must have completed their DPhil (at any Higher Education Institution) at the time of application and are required to work primarily in units run by the University of Oxford
Type: Scholarship
Value: Typically in the range between £2,000 and £25,000
Length of Study: Up to 1 year
Country of Study: Any country
Application Procedure: Please see the website for more details. Enquires may be sent by email to Aga.Bush@medsci.ox.ac.uk
Closing Date: 30 January
Additional Information: Please visit the website: www.medsci.ox.ac.uk/research/internal/funding-directory/goodger-and-schorstein-scholarship for more information

For further information contact:

Email: Aga.Bush@medsci.ox.ac.uk

Graduate Scholarship in Medieval and Modern Languages with Keble College

Subjects: Medieval and modern languages
Purpose: To assist graduate students with fees, maintenance and accommodation
Eligibility: All eligible doctoral applicants submitting applications before the third gathered field will automatically be considered, irrespective of choice of college, provided that they have applied for other funded awards (if eligible)
Level of Study: Research
Type: Scholarship
Value: University fee at United Kingdom/European Union rate; maintenance grant of £5,000. Additional benefits include some dining rights and guaranteed accommodation in 1st year
Length of Study: Up to 3 years
Country of Study: Any country
Closing Date: 22 January

For further information contact:

Email: trish.long@keble.ox.ac.uk

Graduate Scholarship in Medieval and Modern Languages with Merton College

Subjects: Medieval and modern languages

Purpose: To assist graduate students with fees and a living allowance

Eligibility: All eligible doctoral applicants submitting applications before the third gathered field will automatically be considered, irrespective of choice of college, provided that they have applied for other funded awards (if eligible)

Level of Study: Research

Type: Scholarship

Value: University fee at United Kingdom/European Union rate; allowance of £5,000 to assist with college fees and/or maintenance

Length of Study: Up to 3 years

Country of Study: Any country

Closing Date: 22 January

For further information contact:

Email: trish.long@keble.ox.ac.uk

Graduate Scholarship in Medieval and Modern Languages with Somerville College

Subjects: Medieval and modern languages

Purpose: To assist graduate students with fees, maintenance and accommodation

Eligibility: All eligible doctoral applicants submitting applications before the third gathered field will automatically be considered, irrespective of choice of college, provided that they have applied for other funded awards (if eligible)

Level of Study: Research

Type: Scholarship

Value: University fee at United Kingdom/European Union rate; maintenance grant of £6,000. Additional benefits include some dining rights and guaranteed accommodation in 1st year

Length of Study: Up to 3 years

Country of Study: Any country

Closing Date: 22 January

For further information contact:

Email: trish.long@keble.ox.ac.uk

Green Moral Philosophy Scholarship

Eligibility: Open to all graduate applicants for DPhil courses in the Faculty of Philosophy. All applicants who receive a place on any graduate course automatically considered

Type: Scholarship

Value: The value of the scholarship is to be determined by the Board of Graduate Admissions. The scholarship may not be offered on a yearly basis

Length of Study: 1 year

Country of Study: Any country

Closing Date: 4 January

Additional Information: Please check website for more information

For further information contact:

Email: jane.sherwood@admin.ox.ac.uk

Green Templeton College: GTC-Medical Sciences Doctoral Training Centre Scholarship

Purpose: Green Templeton College is pleased to be able to offer a top-up award for overseas students who have been awarded a Studentship for study at the Medical Sciences Doctoral Training Centre beginning in October month

Eligibility: Open to all applicants to the Medical Sciences Doctoral Training Centre with Overseas fee status

Level of Study: Doctorate

Type: Scholarship

Value: GTC will fund the difference between Home/European Union fees and Overseas fees, for up to four years. All other expenses are covered by a Studentship at the Medical Sciences Doctoral Training Centre

Length of Study: Up to 4 years

Country of Study: Any country

Closing Date: 11 January

Additional Information: Please visit the website: www.gtc.ox.ac.uk/admissions/scholarships-and-awards for more information

For further information contact:

Email: enquiries@msdtc.ox.ac.uk

Contact: Professor Robert Gilbert, Director

Green Templeton College: GTC-SBS DPhil Scholarship

Subjects: Management studies

Eligibility: Open to all applicants to the DPhil in Management Studies

Level of Study: Doctorate, Graduate

Type: Scholarship

Value: Full fees and living costs (at the Research Council United Kingdom minimum stipend rate) for 3 years, with possibility of stipend and payment of university continuation charge in year 4, if required

Length of Study: Period of fee liability; possibility of one further year

Study Establishment: Green Templeton College
Country of Study: Any country
Application Procedure: Please see website: www.gtc.ox.ac.uk/admissions/scholarships-and-awards for more details and how to apply
Closing Date: 11 January
Additional Information: Restrictions: New DPhil students in Management Studies only (includes both Management Research and Financial Economics routes)

Green Templeton College: Rosemary Stewart Scholarship

Eligibility: DPhil students with research interests in the area of health care organization and management
Level of Study: Doctorate
Type: Scholarship
Value: £6,000 per year
Length of Study: Up to 3 years
Study Establishment: Green Templeton College
Country of Study: Any country
Application Procedure: Please see website for more details and how to apply
Closing Date: 13 March
Additional Information: Please visit the website: www.gtc.ox.ac.uk/admissions/scholarships-and-awards for more information

For further information contact:

Tel: (44) 1865 274 770
Email: lodge@gtc.ox.ac.uk

Hertford - English Graduate Scholarship in Irish Literature

Subjects: English
Eligibility: Open to Home/European Union students applying to undertake a DPhil in Irish Literature. Applicants are automatically considered for the scholarship by the English Faculty. Please visit the website for more details
Level of Study: Postgraduate
Type: Scholarship
Value: University fee, college fee and full living expenses
Length of Study: Period of fee liability
Frequency: Annual
Country of Study: United Kingdom
Application Procedure: For more information, please visit the website: www.english.ox.ac.uk

Closing Date: 8 January
Funding: Trusts

For further information contact:

Email: college.office@hertford.ox.ac.uk

Hertford College Archaeology Award

Eligibility: Open to all graduate students pursuing the MSt in Archaeology. Please see the website for more details
Level of Study: Postgraduate
Type: Scholarship
Value: £10,000 towards course fees, college fees and living costs where appropriate
Length of Study: One year
Frequency: Annual
Study Establishment: Hertford
Country of Study: United Kingdom
Application Procedure: For more information, please check the website: www.hertford.ox.ac.uk/discover-hertford/graduates/graduate-scholarships
Closing Date: 11 March
Funding: Trusts

For further information contact:

Email: communications@hertford.ox.ac.uk

Hertford College Law Award

Eligibility: Open to all graduate students pursuing the BCL or Mjur. Please see the website for more details
Level of Study: Postgraduate
Type: Scholarship
Value: £10,000 towards course fees, college fees and living costs where appropriate
Length of Study: One year
Frequency: Annual
Study Establishment: Hertford
Country of Study: United Kingdom
Application Procedure: For more information, please check the website: www.hertford.ox.ac.uk/discover-hertford/graduates/graduate-scholarships
Closing Date: 11 March
Funding: Trusts

For further information contact:

Email: graduate.admissions@hertford.ox.ac.uk

Hertford College Pharmacology Award

Eligibility: Open to all graduate students pursuing a DPhil in Pharmacology. Please see the website for more details, including how to apply
Level of Study: Postgraduate
Type: Scholarship
Value: £6,500 towards course fees, college fees and living costs where appropriate
Length of Study: Three years
Frequency: Annual
Study Establishment: Hertford
Country of Study: United Kingdom
Application Procedure: For more information, please visit the website: www.pharm.ox.ac.uk/gso/dphil-in-pharmacology
Closing Date: 8 January
Funding: Trusts

For further information contact:

Email: communications@hertford.ox.ac.uk

Hertford College Senior Scholarships

Subjects: All subjects
Eligibility: Restricted to students who are about to commence a new research degree course or those about to upgrade their current course
Level of Study: Postgraduate
Type: Scholarship
Value: UK£1,000 per year, plus priority for housing and some dining rights
Length of Study: 2 years
Frequency: Annual
Study Establishment: Hertford College, University of Oxford
Country of Study: United Kingdom
Application Procedure: Applicants must write to the College for further details

For further information contact:

Email: graduate.admissions@hertford.ox.ac.uk

Hertford College: Baring Senior Scholarship

Eligibility: Open to all graduate students pursuing research in any area of study
Level of Study: Postgraduate
Type: Scholarship

Value: £5,000 per year with certain associated dining rights
Length of Study: Two years
Frequency: Annual
Study Establishment: Hertford
Country of Study: United Kingdom
Application Procedure: For more information, please visit the website: www.hertford.ox.ac.uk/discover-hertford/graduates/graduate-scholarships
Closing Date: 11 March
Funding: Trusts

For further information contact:

Email: graduate.admissions@hertford.ox.ac.uk

Hertford College: Vaughan Williams Senior Scholarship

Purpose: The Vaughan Williams Fund supports medical students with a £300 award per student towards stethoscopes and 'on the ward' textbooks
Eligibility: Open to all graduate students pursuing research in any area of study. Please see website for more details, including how to apply
Level of Study: Postgraduate
Type: Scholarship
Value: £5,000 per year with certain associated dining rights
Length of Study: Two years
Frequency: Annual
Study Establishment: Hertford
Country of Study: United Kingdom
Application Procedure: For more information, please visit : www.hertford.ox.ac.uk/discover-hertford/graduates/graduate-scholarships
Closing Date: 11 March
Funding: Trusts

For further information contact:

Email: communications@hertford.ox.ac.uk

Hertford College: Worshipful Company of Scientific Instrument Makers Senior Scholarship

Eligibility: Open to DPhil applicants in all subjects. Please note: applicants are expected to be involved in the design of instrumentation
Level of Study: Doctorate, Graduate
Type: Scholarship
Value: £4,000 per year with certain associated dining rights
Length of Study: 2 years

Country of Study: Any country
Application Procedure: Please see website for details of how to apply
Additional Information: Please check at www.hertford.ox. ac.uk/advertised-posts for more information

For further information contact:

Email: college.office@hertford.ox.ac.uk

Hong Kong Jockey Club Graduate Scholarships

Purpose: To students who combine outstanding academic performance with a strong commitment to serving the community
Eligibility: Open to applicants who are ordinarily resident in Hong Kong and who are applying to a full-time master's or full-time DPhil course at Oxford. Please note that DPhil courses with four years of fee liability are not eligible. Please see website for more details
Level of Study: Doctorate, Postgraduate
Type: Scholarship
Value: University fee, college fee, and full living expenses
Length of Study: Period of fee liability
Country of Study: Any country
Closing Date: Relevant January deadline for your course
Funding: Trusts
Additional Information: Please visit the website: www.ox. ac.uk/admissions/graduate/fees-and-funding/fees-funding-and-scholarship-search/scholarships-1#hkjc for more information

For further information contact:

Email: hkjcscholarships@hkjc.org.hk

International Development: QEH Scholarship

Eligibility: Open to all graduate applicants for MPhil in Development Studies with a preference for those from Sub-Saharan Africa. Please visit departmental website for more details
Level of Study: Predoctorate
Type: Scholarship
Value: University fee, college fee, and £13,000 towards living expenses
Length of Study: 21 months
Country of Study: Any country
Closing Date: 20 January
Additional Information: Please visit the website: www.qeh. ox.ac.uk/content/fees-funding for more details

For further information contact:

Email: jane.sherwood@admin.ox.ac.uk

James Fairfax - Oxford-Australia Fund Scholarships

Subjects: All
Eligibility: Applicants should normally be under 30 on January 1st in the year in which the scholarship is to be taken up, and must have a bachelor's degree with first or upper second class honours or equivalent from a recognized university
Level of Study: Graduate, Postgraduate
Type: Scholarship
Value: University fees at the home and European Union rate, college fees and a living allowance of the order of A$12,000 per year
Length of Study: Oxford-Australia Fund scholarships are for 2 years, or in the case of DPhil for 3 years, and James Fairfax scholarships are generally of 2 years duration
Frequency: Annual
Study Establishment: University of Oxford
Country of Study: United Kingdom
Application Procedure: Applicants must write for details or visit the website at www.admin.ox.edu.au/io
Closing Date: 21 February
Funding: Private, Individuals
Contributor: Australian scholars who have studied at Oxford and, in particular, Mr James Fairfax

For further information contact:

Tel: (61) 2 6125 3578/3761
Email: jww@rsc.anu.edu.au
Contact: Professor J W White

Jesus College: Joint Law Faculty-Jesus College BCL Scholarship

Eligibility: Open to all graduate applicants to the BCL (Bachelor of Civil Law). Please see website for further details
Level of Study: Graduate
Type: Scholarship
Value: £10,000
Length of Study: Period of fee liability
Frequency: Annual
Study Establishment: Jesus College
Country of Study: Any country
Closing Date: 20 January
Additional Information: Please visit the website: www. jesus.ox.ac.uk/current-students/scholarships-prizes-awards?

field_subject_target_id=20&field_type_value=Graduate for more information

For further information contact:

Email: lodge@jesus.ox.ac.uk

Kalisher Trust-Wadham Student Scholarship

Purpose: The scholarships are intended to encourage and assist those intending to practise at the Criminal Bar who demonstrate 'exceptional promise but modest means'
Eligibility: Applications are invited from United Kingdom residents who can demonstrate: 1. Intellectual ability – demonstrated by academic performance, past work, activities and other experience. 2. Motivation to succeed at the Criminal Bar – including steps taken to acquire the personal skills required of a Barrister, and a demonstration of the will to succeed. 3. Potential as an advocate – both in oral and written skills. 4. Personal qualities – including self-reliance, independence, integrity, reliability and humanity. 5. Financial need - candidates will be asked to supply to the interview panel, in confidence, information demonstrating financial need
Level of Study: Graduate
Type: Scholarship
Frequency: Annual
Country of Study: Any country
Application Procedure: In particularly to discuss their motivation to succeed at the Criminal Bar. This statement should be no more than 800 words
Closing Date: 27 November
Funding: Private

For further information contact:

The Faculty of Law, University of Oxford, St Cross Building, St Cross Road, Oxford OX1 3UL, United Kingdom

Email: tracy.kaye@crim.ox.ac.uk

Keble College Gosden Graduate Scholarship

Subjects: Theology
Eligibility: Open to students intending to seek ordination in a church in communion with the Church of United Kingdom. Candidates must be either ordained or be able to show clear evidence of desire for ordination in the Church of United Kingdom or a church in communion therewith, and be already at or intending to be registered for a postgraduate degree at Keble College, University of Oxford
Level of Study: Postgraduate
Type: Scholarship

Value: Up to UK£5,000 per year
Length of Study: Up to 3 years
Frequency: Dependent on funds available
Study Establishment: Keble College, University of Oxford
Country of Study: United Kingdom
No. of awards offered: 4
Application Procedure: Applicants must contact the Deputy Academic Administrator at Keble College in the first instance
Closing Date: March/April
No. of awards given last year: 2
No. of applicants last year: 4

For further information contact:

Keble College, Oxford, OX1 3PG UK, United Kingdom

Email: college.office@keb.ox.ac.uk
Contact: Deputy Academic Administrator

Keble College Gwynne-Jones Scholarship

Subjects: All subjects
Eligibility: Open to nationals of Sierra Leone or the Yoruba-speaking people of Nigeria
Level of Study: Postgraduate
Type: Scholarship
Value: Up to UK£4,000 per year
Length of Study: Up to 3 years
Frequency: Varies
Study Establishment: Keble College, University of Oxford
Country of Study: United Kingdom
Application Procedure: Applicants must write for details
Closing Date: May
Funding: Private

Keble College Ian Palmer Graduate Scholarship in Information Technology

Subjects: Computer science and related fields concerning the practical uses of computer systems
Eligibility: Applicants must write for details
Level of Study: Postgraduate
Type: Scholarship
Value: Up to the value of college fees
Length of Study: Up to 3 years
Frequency: Dependent on funds available
Study Establishment: Keble College, University of Oxford
Country of Study: United Kingdom
Application Procedure: Applicants must write for details
Closing Date: May
Funding: Private

Keble College Ian Tucker Memorial Bursary

Subjects: All subjects
Eligibility: Candidates must demonstrate sporting prowess principally in the field of rugby football, together with qualities that will make a contribution to both the College and University
Level of Study: Graduate
Type: Bursary
Value: Up to UK£8,000 per year
Length of Study: 1 year
Frequency: Annual
Study Establishment: Keble College, University of Oxford
Country of Study: United Kingdom
No. of awards offered: 6
Application Procedure: Applicants must contact the Tutor for Graduates at Keble College for an application form
Closing Date: May each year
No. of awards given last year: 2
No. of applicants last year: 6

Keble College Keble Association Open Graduate Scholarship

Subjects: All subjects
Eligibility: Open to research students and 2nd BM applicants
Level of Study: Postgraduate, Research
Type: Scholarship
Value: UK£2,000
Length of Study: Up to 3 years
Frequency: Annual
Study Establishment: Keble College, University of Oxford
Country of Study: United Kingdom
No. of awards offered: 19
Application Procedure: Applicants must write to request an application form
Closing Date: May
Funding: Private
No. of awards given last year: 2
No. of applicants last year: 19

Keble College Paul Hayes Graduate Scholarship

Subjects: All subjects
Eligibility: Candidates must demonstrate sporting excellence
Level of Study: Doctorate, Graduate
Type: Scholarship
Value: Up to the value of college fees

Length of Study: Up to 3 years
Study Establishment: Keble College, the University of Oxford
Country of Study: United Kingdom
Application Procedure: Applicants must contact the Deputy Academic Administrator at Keble College
Closing Date: May

Keble College Water Newton Scholarship

Subjects: Theology
Eligibility: Open to students intending to seek ordination in a church in communication with the Church of United Kingdom
Level of Study: Postdoctorate, Research
Type: Scholarship
Value: Up to UK£5,000 per year
Length of Study: Up to 3 years
Frequency: Dependent on funds available
Study Establishment: Keble College, University of Oxford
Country of Study: United Kingdom
Application Procedure: Applicants must contact the Deputy Academic Administrator
Closing Date: April
Funding: Private

Keble College: Delia Bushell Graduate Scholarship

Subjects: History
Eligibility: Open to graduate applicants to study for a postgraduate degree in the History Faculty in the University of Oxford, or be presently registered for a postgraduate degree in the History Faculty in the University of Oxford
Level of Study: Postgraduate
Type: Scholarship
Value: Up to £6,250 per year towards living expenses
Length of Study: 1 year
Study Establishment: Keble College
Country of Study: Any country
Application Procedure: Please see website for more details, including how to apply
Closing Date: 11 March
Additional Information: Please visit the website: www.keble.ox.ac.uk/admissions/graduate/graduate-scholarships for more information

For further information contact:

Email: college.office@keble.ox.ac.uk

Keble College: James Martin Graduate Scholarship

Eligibility: Open to Home/European Union students, who can demonstrate that they are in financial need. Applicants must be intending to study for a MSc in the MPLS (Mathematical, Physical and Life Sciences) Division, Medical Sciences Division or Geography and the Environment department
Level of Study: Postgraduate
Type: Scholarship
Value: Up to £9,000 per year towards living expenses
Length of Study: 1 year
Study Establishment: Keble College
Country of Study: Any country
Application Procedure: Please see website for further details, including how to apply
Closing Date: 11 March
Additional Information: Please visit the website: www.keble.ox.ac.uk/admissions/graduate/graduate-scholarships for more information

For further information contact:

Email: college.office@keble.ox.ac.uk

Kellogg College: Naji DPhil Scholarship in the Public Understanding of Evidence-Based Medicine

Eligibility: Open to applicants for the DPhil in Primary Health Care whose research directly addresses public understanding of evidence for health claims
Level of Study: Doctorate
Type: Scholarship
Value: University fee, college fee, and full living expenses
Length of Study: Period of fee liability
Study Establishment: Kellogg College
Country of Study: Any country
Application Procedure: Please see website for more details, including how to apply
Closing Date: 6 January
Additional Information: Please visit the website: www.kellogg.ox.ac.uk/study/scholarships-2017/naji-dphil-scholarship-in-the-public-understanding-of-evidence-based-medicine/ for more information

For further information contact:

Tel: (44) 1865 612 000

Kellogg College: Oxford-McCall MacBain Graduate Scholarship

Purpose: The scholarship is only tenable at Kellogg College. All eligible applicants will be considered for the scholarship
Eligibility: All eligible applicants will be considered for the scholarship, regardless of which college (if any) you state as your preference on the graduate application form. However, successful applicants will be transferred to Kellogg College in order to take up the scholarship
Level of Study: Graduate
Type: Scholarship
Value: The scholarship covers course fees and provides a study support grant
Frequency: Annual
Country of Study: Any country
Closing Date: 1 March
Funding: Private
Additional Information: Initially the MMF operated on a -regional-based approach, with a strategy to develop and encourage best practices and policies in multiple areas related to improving the human condition

For further information contact:

Kellogg College, 60-62 Banbury Road, Oxford OX2 6PN, United Kingdom

Email: enquiries@kellogg.ox.ac.uk

Lady Margaret Hall Talbot Research Fellowship

Subjects: Various arts subjects, as advertised
Purpose: To provide an opportunity for academic postdoctoral research
Eligibility: Open to qualified persons who hold or will have obtained a postdoctoral or equivalent degree by the start of tenure
Level of Study: Postgraduate
Type: Fellowship
Value: Please contact the college for details
Length of Study: 3 years, not renewable
Frequency: Every 3 years
Study Establishment: Lady Margaret Hall, the University of Oxford
Country of Study: United Kingdom
Closing Date: As advertised

For further information contact:

Lady Margaret Hall Norham Gardens

Tel: (44) 1865 274 300
Fax: (44) 1865 511 069
Email: college.office@ college.office@lmh.ox.ac.uk

Lady Margaret Hall: Ann Kennedy Graduate Scholarship in Law

Eligibility: Open to graduate applicants for the BCL, MJur, MSt in Legal Research or MPhil in Law at Lady Margaret Hall. The award will be made on the basis of academic excellence
Level of Study: Graduate, Postgraduate, Predoctorate
Type: Scholarship
Value: The award covers college fees and a contribution to the university fees. It is awarded for one year for an amount of up to £14,000. It is not intended to contribute to living expenses
Length of Study: 1 year
Study Establishment: Lady Margaret Hall
Country of Study: Any country
Closing Date: 20 January
Additional Information: Please visit the website: www. law.ox.ac.uk/admissions/scholarships-index/college-awards-specific-law-postgraduates-index for more information

For further information contact:

Email: enquiries@lmh.ox.ac.uk

Lady Margaret Hall: Gavin Cameron Graduate Scholarship in Economics

Level of Study: Graduate
Type: Scholarship
Value: Free accommodation in new Graduate accommodation
Length of Study: Three years
Study Establishment: Lady Margaret Hall
Country of Study: Any country
Application Procedure: Open to all graduate applicants in Economics with a preference for, but not restricted to, applicants who put LMH as their first choice College
Closing Date: Relevant January deadline for your course
Additional Information: Please visit the website: www. lmh.ox.ac.uk/prospective-students/Graduates/Scholarship-opportunities.aspx for more information

For further information contact:

Email: stassistant@lmh.ox.ac.uk

Lady Margaret Hall: Open Residential Scholarships

Eligibility: Open to all graduate applicants with a preference for, but not restricted to, applicants who put LMH as their first choice college. Please see website for details of how to apply
Level of Study: Postgraduate
Type: Scholarship
Value: £5,000 plus additional benefits including an option on accommodation and limited dining rights
Length of Study: 1 year
Frequency: Annual
Study Establishment: Lady Margaret Hall
Country of Study: Any country
Closing Date: Relevant January deadline for your course
Additional Information: Please check the website: www. lmh.ox.ac.uk for more information

For further information contact:

Email: graduate.admissions@lmh.ox.ac.uk

Latin American Centre-Latin American Centre Scholarship

Subjects: MSc in Latin American Studies
Eligibility: Open to all graduate applicants to the MSc in Latin American Studies from one of the CAF shareholder countries. Applicants must send an email to the Admissions Secretary requesting to be considered
Level of Study: Postgraduate
Type: Scholarship
Value: University and college fees (not living expenses)
Length of Study: 1 year (Non-renewable)
Country of Study: Any country
Application Procedure: Please visit website for more details and how to apply
Closing Date: 10 March
Additional Information: For more information, please check the websites: www.lac.ox.ac.uk/funding; www.lac.ox. ac.uk/scholarships-latin-american-centre

For further information contact:

Email: laclib@bodleian.ox.ac.uk

Law Faculty: David and Helen Elvin Scholarship

Eligibility: Open to all graduate applicants for the BCL and MJur. Award holders will become members of Hertford College. Please see website for more information
Level of Study: Graduate, Postgraduate

Type: Scholarship
Value: £10,000 towards course fees, college fees and living costs where appropriate
Length of Study: 1 year
Study Establishment: Hertford College
Country of Study: Any country
Closing Date: 20 January
Additional Information: Please visit the website: www.law.ox.ac.uk/postgraduate/scholarships.php for more information

For further information contact:

Email: lawfac@law.ox.ac.uk

Law Faculty: Des Voeux Chambers

Subjects: Law
Eligibility: Open to all graduate applicants to the BCL. Preference may be shown for candidates with an interest in pursuing a career at the Hong Kong Bar. Please see website for more information
Level of Study: Postgraduate
Type: Scholarship
Value: £10,000
Length of Study: 1 year
Frequency: Annual
Country of Study: United Kingdom
Closing Date: 20 January
Funding: Trusts
Additional Information: Please check the website: www.law.ox.ac.uk/postgraduate/scholarships.php for more information

For further information contact:

Email: pupillage@dvc.com.hk

Law Faculty: James Bullock Scholarship

Purpose: The James Bullock Scholarship is restricted to students taking the MSc in Taxation and provides an award of £5,000 which will be paid in two instalments
Eligibility: Open to all applicants for the MSc in Taxation
Level of Study: Postgraduate
Type: Scholarship
Value: £2,500 per year
Length of Study: 2 years
Country of Study: Any country
Closing Date: 10 March
Additional Information: Please visit the website: www.law.ox.ac.uk/postgraduate/scholarships.php for more information

For further information contact:

Email: lawfac@law.ox.ac.uk

Law Faculty: The Peter Birks Memorial Scholarship

Subjects: Law
Purpose: To assist graduate students with fees
Eligibility: Open to all graduate applicants to BCL/MJur, MSc in Law and Finance, MSt Legal Research, MPhil Or DPhil Law. Please see website for further information
Level of Study: Graduate, Postgraduate
Type: Scholarship
Value: £7,500 per year
Length of Study: 1 year
Frequency: Annual
Country of Study: Any country
Closing Date: 20 January
Additional Information: Please check the website: www.law.ox.ac.uk/postgraduate/scholarships.php for more information

For further information contact:

Email: lawfac@law.ox.ac.uk

Linacre College: Applied Materials MSc Scholarship

Subjects: Environmental change and management
Purpose: To assist graduate students with fees and a living allowance
Eligibility: Open to all
Level of Study: Postgraduate
Type: Scholarship
Length of Study: 1 year

For further information contact:

School of Geography and the Environment, University of Oxford, South Parks Road, Oxford OX1 3QY, United Kingdom

Tel: (44) 1865 285 070
Email: enquiries@ouce.ox.ac.uk
Contact: Director of Graduate Studies

Linacre College: David Daube Scholarship

Purpose: The David Daube Law Scholarship is available to a student reading or intending to read for a DPhil in law, and who is liable to pay fees
Eligibility: Open to all graduate applicants for the BCL and MJur

Level of Study: Postgraduate
Type: Scholarship
Value: College fee
Length of Study: Period of fee liability
Country of Study: Any country
Closing Date: 12 March
Additional Information: Applicants should first secure a place on the Oxford BCL or MJur course and mark Linacre College as their chosen College. Please check at www.linacre. ox.ac.uk/Admissions/Scholarships for more information

For further information contact:

Email: ben.nicholson@admin.ox.ac.uk

Linacre College: EPA Cephalosporin Scholarship

Subjects: Biological, medical and chemical sciences
Purpose: To assist graduate students with fees
Eligibility: Open to all graduate students
Level of Study: Postgraduate, Research
Type: Scholarship
Value: College fees
Length of Study: Up to 2 years depending on fee liability

For further information contact:

Sir William Dunn School of Pathology

Email: administration@path.ox.ac.uk
Contact: Director of Graduate Studies

Linacre College: Hicks Scholarship

Subjects: Economics
Purpose: With the initial support of several Old Members, a fund is being established to provide a College fee scholarship to a Linacre student studying for a degree in Economics
Eligibility: Open to students reading, or intending to read for a DPhil in Economics who are liable to pay fees
Level of Study: Doctorate, Postgraduate
Type: Scholarship
Value: £80,000. 1st 3 years scholarship paid out = £6,486
Length of Study: Period of fee liability
Study Establishment: Linacre College
Country of Study: Any country
Closing Date: 21 April
Funding: Private
Additional Information: Please visit the website: www.linacre. ox.ac.uk/prospective-students/scholarships for more information

For further information contact:

Linacre College, St. Cross Road, Oxford OX1 3JA, United Kingdom

Tel: (44) 1865 271 650
Email: development@linacre.ox.ac.uk

Linacre College: Hitachi Chemical Europe Scholarship

Subjects: Environmental change and management
Eligibility: Preference given to applicant from China or Central/South America
Level of Study: Postgraduate
Type: Scholarship
Value: College fee plus £1,000
Length of Study: 1 year
Application Procedure: No separate application required. Please contact to Director of Graduate Studies
Additional Information: Please check at www.linacre.ox.ac. uk/extras/scholarships for more information

For further information contact:

Director of Graduate Studies

Linacre College: John Bamborough MSc Scholarship

Subjects: Humanities
Eligibility: Open to all graduate applicants for MSc courses in the Humanities division
Level of Study: Postgraduate
Type: Scholarship
Value: 100% university and college fees. £3,205
Length of Study: One year
Study Establishment: Linacre College
Country of Study: Any country
Application Procedure: Please see website for more details, including how to apply
Closing Date: 19 April
Additional Information: Please visit the website: www. linacre.ox.ac.uk/prospective-students/scholarships for more information

For further information contact:

Email: scholarships@linacre.ox.ac.uk

Linacre College: Linacre Rausing Scholarship (English)

Subjects: English Literature
Eligibility: Open to all
Level of Study: Research
Type: Scholarship
Value: £4,000
Length of Study: Up to 3 years
Country of Study: Any country
Application Procedure: No separate application required. Please contact: Director of Graduate Studies, English Faculty, Oxford OX1 3UQ, United Kingdom

For further information contact:

Email: english.office@ell.ox.ac.uk

Linacre College: Mary Blaschko Graduate Scholarship

Subjects: Humanities
Purpose: To enable European students to carry out research for 1 year in the department of pharmacology or the MRC anatomical neuropharmacology unit
Eligibility: Open to all graduate applicants for research degrees in the Humanities division
Level of Study: Postgraduate, Research
Type: Scholarship
Value: College fee
Length of Study: Period of fee liability
Study Establishment: Linacre College
Country of Study: Any country
Application Procedure: Please see website for more details, including how to apply
Closing Date: 21 April
Additional Information: Please visit the website: www.linacre.ox.ac.uk/prospective-students/scholarships for more information

For further information contact:

Email: scholarships@linacre.ox.ac.uk

Linacre College: Rausing Scholarship in Anthropology

Subjects: Anthropology
Eligibility: Open to all graduate applicants in Anthropology
Level of Study: Research
Type: Scholarship

Value: College fee plus £2,000 towards living expenses
Length of Study: Period of fee liability
Country of Study: Any country
Application Procedure: There is no application form. Applications should consist of a detailed doctoral proposal of 3–4 pages, a curriculum vitae and two letters of reference, one of which should be provided by the student's current or prospective supervisor for the doctorate. Applications should be sent to the Director of Graduate Studies. Please see website for details of how to apply
Additional Information: Please check at www.linacre.ox.ac.uk/Admissions/Scholarships for more information

For further information contact:

Email: ben.nicholson@admin.ox.ac.uk
Contact: Director of Graduate Studies

Linacre College: Rausing Scholarship in English

Subjects: English
Eligibility: Open to all graduate applicants for any course in the English Faculty
Level of Study: Doctorate
Type: Scholarship
Value: College fee
Length of Study: Period of fee liability (up to 3 years)
Study Establishment: Linacre College
Country of Study: Any country
Application Procedure: Please see website for more details, including how to apply
Closing Date: Relevant January deadline for your course
Additional Information: Please visit the website: www.linacre.ox.ac.uk/prospective-students/scholarships for more information

For further information contact:

Email: support@linacre.ox.ac.uk

Linacre College: Raymond and Vera Asquith Scholarship

Subjects: Humanities
Eligibility: Open to suitably qualified students who were born in the United Kingdom, reading or intending to read for a DPhil in Humanities who are liable to pay fees and have AHRC funding
Level of Study: Doctorate, Postgraduate
Type: Scholarship
Value: College fee

Length of Study: Period of fee liability
Country of Study: Any country
Application Procedure: Please see website for details of how to apply
Additional Information: Please check at www.linacre.ox.ac.uk/Admissions/Scholarships for more information

For further information contact:

Email: ben.nicholson@admin.ox.ac.uk

Linacre College: Ronald and Jane Olson Scholarship

Subjects: Refugee studies
Eligibility: Open to all graduate applicants for the MSc in Refugee and Forced Migration Studies
Level of Study: Postgraduate
Type: Scholarship
Value: College fee, plus a maintenance grant of £2,500
Length of Study: 1 year
Study Establishment: Linacre College
Country of Study: Any country
Closing Date: 20 January
Additional Information: Please visit the website: www.linacre.ox.ac.uk/prospective-students/scholarships for more information

For further information contact:

Email: rsc-msc@qeh.ox.ac.uk

Linacre College: Women in Science Scholarship

Subjects: Materials
Eligibility: Open to all graduate applicants for the DPhil in Materials who are liable to pay fees
Level of Study: Doctorate
Type: Scholarship
Value: College fee
Length of Study: Period of fee liability
Study Establishment: Linacre College
Country of Study: Any country
Closing Date: 21 April
Additional Information: Please visit the website: www.linacre.ox.ac.uk/prospective-students/scholarships for more information

For further information contact:

Email: support@linacre.ox.ac.uk

Lincoln College: Berrow Foundation Lord Florey Scholarships

Subjects: Medical, chemical or biochemical sciences
Eligibility: Open to all graduate applicants for courses in Medical, Chemical or Biochemical Sciences of Swiss or Lichtenstein nationality who are students at, or have recently graduated from, any Swiss university, including ETHZ and EPFL, and who must not be more than five years beyond graduation from their first degree at one of these institutions (except for candidates in medicine, for whom the five years limit dates from obtaining the Federal Diploma in Medicine). Up to two awards available. Please see website for full details and application form
Level of Study: Postgraduate, Research
Type: Scholarship
Value: University fee (at the United Kingdom level), college fee, and living expenses equivalent to Rhodes Scholarship stipend
Length of Study: Up to 3 years
Frequency: Annual
Study Establishment: Lincoln
Country of Study: Any country
Application Procedure: Please see website for details of how to apply
Closing Date: 18 January
Funding: Foundation
Additional Information: Please check the website: www.lincoln.ox.ac.uk/funding-and-awards-for-graduates for more information

For further information contact:

Email: info@lincoln.ox.ac.uk

Lincoln College: Berrow Foundation Scholarships

Eligibility: Open to all graduate applicants of Swiss or Lichtenstein nationality who are students at, or have recently graduated from, selected Swiss universities. Up to four awards available. Please see website for full details and application form
Level of Study: Postgraduate, Research
Type: Scholarship
Value: University fee (at the United Kingdom level), college fee, and living expenses equivalent to Rhodes Scholarship stipend
Length of Study: Up to 3 years
Frequency: Annual
Study Establishment: Lincoln
Country of Study: Any country

Closing Date: 20 January
Funding: Foundation
Additional Information: Please check the website: www. lincoln.ox.ac.uk/funding-and-awards-for-graduates for more information

For further information contact:

Email: info@lincoln.ox.ac.uk

Lincoln College: Crewe Graduate Scholarships

Subjects: All subjects
Eligibility: Open to all
Level of Study: Graduate, Postgraduate, MBA
Type: Scholarship
Value: £3,000
Length of Study: One year, with the possibility of renewal on applying
Frequency: Annual
Study Establishment: Lincoln College, University of Oxford
Country of Study: United Kingdom
Application Procedure: Information will be made available when the college makes a conditional offer to candidates. For other details please see the website www.lincoln.ox.ac.uk
Closing Date: 1 August
Funding: Trusts
No. of awards given last year: 6

For further information contact:

Email: info@lincoln.ox.ac.uk
Contact: Admissions Office, Lincoln College

Lincoln College: Hartley Bursary

Eligibility: Open to all graduate students normally resident in the United Kingdom beginning, or continuing, on a course of study in the Humanities, who show evidence of financial need
Level of Study: Graduate
Type: Scholarship
Value: £1,000 per year
Length of Study: Up to 3 years
Study Establishment: Lincoln College
Country of Study: Any country
Application Procedure: Applicants must hold a place, or an offer of a place, at Lincoln College before making an application. Please see website for full details and application form
Closing Date: 1 June

Additional Information: Please visit the website: www.lincoln.ox.ac.uk/funding-and-awards-for-graduates for more information

For further information contact:

Email: info@lincoln.ox.ac.uk

Lincoln College: Jermyn Brooks Graduate Award

Subjects: Humanities, with a preference for modern languages
Eligibility: Open to graduate students of the college (other new or continuing) who are studying in the humanities, with a preference for modern languages
Level of Study: Postgraduate
Type: Scholarship
Value: UK£1,000
Length of Study: One year
Frequency: Annual
Study Establishment: Lincoln college, University of Oxford
Country of Study: United Kingdom
Application Procedure: Application form available from Admissions Office at Lincoln College
Closing Date: First week of August
Funding: Private

For further information contact:

The Admissions Office Lincoln College

Email: info@lincoln.ox.ac.uk

Lincoln College: Kenneth Seward-Shaw Scholarship

Subjects: Law, history, politics, English
Eligibility: Open to graduates in Law, history, English or politics who have already been offered a place at Lincoln College
Level of Study: Postgraduate
Type: Scholarship
Value: UK£1,500
Length of Study: 1 year
Frequency: Annual
Study Establishment: Lincoln College, University of Oxford
Country of Study: United Kingdom
Application Procedure: Applicants must contact the Admissions Office
Funding: Private

For further information contact:

Admissions Office, Lincoln College, 300 Keokuk St, Lincoln, Illinois 62656, United Kingdom

Email: info@lincoln.ox.ac.uk

Lincoln College: Lord Crewe Graduate Scholarship in Medical Sciences (Clarendon-Linked)

Subjects: All graduate courses within the Medical Sciences Division
Eligibility: Applicants must nominate Lincoln as their College of Preference and be considered for a Clarendon Fund Scholarship
Level of Study: Postgraduate, Research
Type: Scholarship
Value: All university and college fees and a generous living allowance (Clarendon-linked)
Length of Study: Period of fee liability
Country of Study: Any country
Closing Date: 20 January
Additional Information: Please check at www.clarendon. ox.ac.uk/partnership/ for more information

For further information contact:

Email: info@lincoln.ox.ac.uk

Lincoln College: Lord Crewe Graduate Scholarship in Social Sciences (Clarendon-Linked)

Subjects: All graduate courses within the Social Sciences Division
Eligibility: Applicants must nominate Lincoln as their College of Preference and be considered for a Clarendon Fund Scholarship
Level of Study: Postgraduate, Research
Type: Scholarship
Value: All university and college fees and a generous living allowance (Clarendon-linked)
Length of Study: Period of Fee liability
Frequency: Annual
Country of Study: Any country
Closing Date: 20 January
Additional Information: Please check at www.clarendon. ox.ac.uk/partnership/ for more information

For further information contact:

Email: info@lincoln.ox.ac.uk

Lincoln College: Lord Crewe Graduate Scholarships in the Humanities

Subjects: All graduate courses within the Humanities division
Eligibility: Open to graduates of any United Kingdom university for all courses within the Humanities
Level of Study: Postgraduate, Research
Type: Scholarship
Value: £18,000 per year
Length of Study: Period of fee liability
Country of Study: Any country
Application Procedure: Please see website for details of how to apply
Closing Date: 18 January
Additional Information: Please check at www.lincoln.ox. ac.uk/ for more information

For further information contact:

Email: info@lincoln.ox.ac.uk

Lincoln College: Lord Crewe Graduate Scholarships in the Social Sciences

Subjects: All graduate courses within the Social Sciences Division
Eligibility: Open to graduates of any United Kingdom university for all courses within the Social Sciences
Level of Study: Postgraduate, Research
Type: Scholarship
Value: £18,000 per year
Length of Study: Period of fee liability
Country of Study: Any country
Application Procedure: Please see website for details of how to apply
Closing Date: 18 January
Additional Information: Please check at www.lincoln.ox. ac.uk/ for more information

For further information contact:

Email: info@lincoln.ox.ac.uk

Lincoln College: Menasseh Ben Israel Room

Eligibility: Open to all graduate applicants who have graduated from an Israeli university. Preference will be shown to graduates of the Hebrew University, Jerusalem. Applicants must hold a place, or an offer of a place, at Lincoln College before making an application. Please see website for full details and application form

Level of Study: Graduate, Postgraduate
Type: Scholarship
Value: Free accommodation for one academic year (37 weeks) as occupant of the Menasseh Ben Israel Room in college
Length of Study: 1 year
Country of Study: Any country
Application Procedure: Please see website for full details and application form
Closing Date: 1 June
Additional Information: Please check at www.lincoln.ox.ac.uk/funding-and-awards-for-graduates for more information

For further information contact:

Email: info@lincoln.ox.ac.uk

Lincoln College: Overseas Graduate Entrance Scholarship

Subjects: All subjects
Eligibility: All non-European Union nationals
Type: Scholarship
Value: £2,300
Length of Study: 1 year
Country of Study: Any country
Closing Date: 1 June
Additional Information: Successful candidates will show evidence of both academic merit and financial need. Applicants must hold a place, or an offer of a place, at Lincoln College before applying. Eligible to the nationals of Overseas

For further information contact:

Email: info@lincoln.ox.ac.uk

Lincoln College: Polonsky Foundation Grants

Eligibility: Open to all overseas graduate applicants who show evidence of financial need, academic merit and potential for good college citizenship
Type: Grant
Value: Approx. £5,300 per year
Length of Study: Up to 3 years
Study Establishment: Lincoln
Country of Study: Any country
Application Procedure: Applicants must hold a place, or an offer of a place, at Lincoln College before making an application. Please see website for full details and application form
Closing Date: 3 June
Additional Information: Candidates may be new or current students and must be citizens of countries not in the European

Union. Please check the website: www.lincoln.ox.ac.uk/funding-and-awards-for-graduates for more information

For further information contact:

Email: info@lincoln.ox.ac.uk

Lincoln College: Sloane Robinson Foundation Graduate Awards

Subjects: All subjects
Purpose: To fund those intending to pursue research programmes at Oxford
Eligibility: Open to all
Level of Study: Graduate, Postgraduate, Research, MBA
Type: Award
Value: £5,000 per year
Length of Study: 1 year, with the possibility of renewal on applying
Frequency: Annual
Study Establishment: Lincoln College, University of Oxford
Country of Study: United Kingdom
Application Procedure: Information will be made available when the college makes a conditional offer to candidates. Please see website www.lincoln.ox.ac.uk for further details
Closing Date: 1 June
Funding: Foundation
Additional Information: Successful candidates will show evidence of both academic merit and financial need. Applicants must hold a place, or an offer of a place, at Lincoln College before applying

For further information contact:

Email: info@lincoln.ox.ac.uk
Contact: Admissions Office, Lincoln College

Lincoln College: Supperstone Law Scholarship

Subjects: Law
Eligibility: Open to candidates reading for the BCL or the MJuris, with an emphasis or special interest in European or public law. Applicants must have an offer of a college place at Lincoln College
Level of Study: Postgraduate
Type: Scholarship
Value: UK£650
Length of Study: 1 year
Frequency: Annual
Study Establishment: Lincoln College, University of Oxford

Country of Study: United Kingdom
Application Procedure: Applicants must contact the Admissions Office at Lincoln College
Funding: Trusts

Lingyin Graduate Scholarship in Buddhist Studies

Purpose: Oriental Studies
Eligibility: Open to current and incoming Master's or DPhil students whose study or research focuses on Buddhist Studies (including all areas, historical periods, and aspects of this field). Eligible incoming students will be considered automatically, but current students need to submit a Lingyin application form. Three scholarships available. Please see website for more details
Level of Study: Postgraduate
Type: Scholarship
Value: £8,000 tenable only for one year at a time. Students holding the scholarship who would wish to reapply for it for the following year would be required to submit a new application for that year, which would be considered competitively alongside other applications for that year
Length of Study: One year
Frequency: Annual
Country of Study: United Kingdom
Application Procedure: For more information, please visit the website: www.orinst.ox.ac.uk/administration/grants/index.html
Closing Date: 22 January
Funding: Trusts

For further information contact:

Email: Buddhist-studies@email.arizona.edu

Magdalen College: Perkin Research Studentship

Subjects: All subjects
Eligibility: Open to all graduate applicants from Commonwealth countries for Chemistry
Level of Study: Research
Type: Studentship
Value: £7,000 per year
Length of Study: Period of fee liability
Country of Study: Any country
Application Procedure: Please see website for details of how to apply
Additional Information: Please check at www.magd.ox.ac.uk/admissions_graduate/scholarships.shtml for more information

For further information contact:

Email: jane.sherwood@admin.ox.ac.uk

Magdalen College: Student Support Fund Graduate Grants

Subjects: All subjects
Eligibility: Graduate students already studying at Magdalen
Level of Study: Postgraduate, Research
Type: Grant
Value: According to individual circumstances
Length of Study: 1 year, renewable after review
Country of Study: Any country

For further information contact:

Email: senior.tutor@magd.ox.ac.uk

Magdalen Hong Kong Scholarship

Eligibility: Open to students who are ordinarily resident in Hong Kong and are citizens of the People's Republic of China (PRC). Candidates should be intending to return to Hong Kong or the PRC on completion of their studies
Level of Study: Postgraduate
Type: Scholarship
Value: Maximum of £26,250 per year as a contribution towards college and university tuition fees and living expenses
Length of Study: Up to 4 years
Application Procedure: Please see the website for further details
Closing Date: 22 January
Additional Information: Please visit www.magd.ox.ac.uk/studying-here/as-a-graduate/scholarships-and-awards-2 for more details and to register your interest

For further information contact:

Email: admissions@magd.ox.ac.uk

Mansfield College: Adam von Trott Scholarship

Subjects: MPhil politics
Eligibility: Open to German nationals applying to the two year MPhil in Politics. Please see website for more details
Level of Study: Postgraduate, Research
Type: Scholarship

Value: University fee, college fee, living expenses up to €20,000 per annum
Length of Study: Duration of fee liability
Country of Study: Any country
Closing Date: 6 January
Additional Information: Please check the website: www.mansfield.ox.ac.uk/prospective/postgrad/scholarships.html for more information

For further information contact:

Email: avt.committee@outlook.com

Mansfield College: Elfan Rees Scholarship

Subjects: Theology
Purpose: To commencing studies towards a higher degree in the field of theology
Eligibility: Open to students on the MSt, MPhil, MLitt or DPhil in any branch of theology
Level of Study: Postdoctorate, Postgraduate, Research
Type: Scholarship
Value: £3,000 maintenance, college fee waiver, matching Faculty award up to £5,000
Length of Study: Up to 2 years
Country of Study: Any country
Closing Date: October
Additional Information: Please check at www.mansfield.ox.ac.uk/current/prizes-scholarships.html for more information

For further information contact:

Email: lodge@mansfield.ox.ac.uk

Medical Sciences Doctoral Training Centre: British Heart Foundation Studentship in Cardiovascular Science

Subjects: Cardiovascular science
Eligibility: Open to all applicants to the DPhil in Cardiovascular Science. All applicants are automatically considered for these awards
Level of Study: Doctorate
Type: Studentship
Value: Course fee, college fee, living expenses
Length of Study: 4 years
Country of Study: Any country
Closing Date: 6 January
Funding: Foundation

Additional Information: Please visit the website: www.medsci.ox.ac.uk/study/graduateschool/courses/dtc-structured-research-degrees/cardiovascular-science for more information

For further information contact:

Email: Graduate.School@medsci.ox.ac.uk

Medical Sciences Doctoral Training Centre: Wellcome Trust Fellowship in Biomedical and Clinical Sciences

Subjects: Biomedical and clinical sciences
Eligibility: Open to all applicants to the DPhil in Biomedical and Clinical Sciences. All applicants are automatically considered for these awards
Level of Study: Doctorate
Type: Fellowship
Value: Course fee, college fee, living expenses
Length of Study: 3 years
Country of Study: Any country
Closing Date: 6 January
Funding: Trusts
Additional Information: Please visit the website: www.medsci.ox.ac.uk/study/graduateschool/courses/dtc-structured-research-degrees/doctoral-training-fellowship-scheme-for-clinicians for more information

For further information contact:

Email: christopher.buckley@kennedy.ox.ac.uk

Medical Sciences Doctoral Training Centre: Wellcome Trust Studentship in Chromosome and Developmental Biology

Subjects: Chromosome and developmental biology
Purpose: To provide students with training and supporting infrastructure to apply advanced biological imaging/super resolution microscopy, high-throughput sequencing method (and computational genomics for data analysis), advanced proteomics, and state of the art genome engineering
Eligibility: Open to all applicants to the DPhil in Chromosome and Developmental Biology. All applicants are automatically considered for these awards
Level of Study: Doctorate
Type: Studentship
Value: Course fee, college fee, living expenses
Length of Study: 4 years
Country of Study: Any country
Closing Date: 6 January

Funding: Trusts

Additional Information: Please visit the website: www.
medsci.ox.ac.uk/study/graduateschool/courses/dtc-structured-
research-degrees/chromosome-and-developmental-biology for
more information

For further information contact:

Email: enquiries@msdtc.ox.ac.uk

Medical Sciences Doctoral Training Centre: Wellcome Trust Studentship in Genomic Medicine and Statistics

Subjects: Genomics,   statistics,   bioinformatics   and
epidemiology
Purpose: Trains future scientific leaders who will work at the
cutting edge of genomics in biomedical research and enable
effective delivery into the clinic
Eligibility: Open to all applicants to the DPhil in Genomic
Medicine and Statistics. All applicants are automatically con-
sidered for these awards
Level of Study: Doctorate
Type: Studentship
Value: Course fee, college fee, living expenses
Length of Study: 4 years
Country of Study: Any country
Closing Date: 6 January
Funding: Trusts
Additional Information: Please visit the website: www.
medsci.ox.ac.uk/study/graduateschool/courses/dtc-structured-
research-degrees/genomic-medicine-and-statistics   for   more
information

For further information contact:

Email: enquiries@msdtc.ox.ac.uk

Medical Sciences Doctoral Training Centre: Wellcome Trust Studentship in Infection, Immunology and Translational Medicine

Subjects: Infection, immunology and translational medicine
Purpose: Provides integrated training in infection and immu-
nology, and how fundamental research can be translated into
benefits for human health
Eligibility: Open to all applicants to the DPhil in Infection,
Immunology and Translational Medicine. All applicants are
automatically considered for these awards
Level of Study: Doctorate
Type: Studentship
Value: Course fee, college fee, living expenses
Length of Study: 4 years

Country of Study: Any country
Application Procedure: Applicants are suggested to select
St Edmund Hall as their college choice. Please see the website
for more details
Closing Date: 6 January
Funding: Trusts
Additional Information: Please visit the website: www.
medsci.ox.ac.uk/study/graduateschool/courses/dtc-structured-
research-degrees/infection-immunology-and-translational-
medicine for more information

For further information contact:

Email: Graduate.School@medsci.ox.ac.uk

Medical Sciences Doctoral Training Centre: Wellcome Trust Studentship in Ion Channels and Disease

Purpose: Trains the student in a range of multidisciplinary
approaches and embraces all aspects of ion channel and
membrane transport research from protein structure, genetics
and cell physiology to animal behaviour and human disease
Eligibility: Open to all applicants to the DPhil in Ion Chan-
nels and Disease. All applicants are automatically considered
for these awards
Level of Study: Doctorate
Type: Studentship
Value: Course fee, college fee, living expenses
Length of Study: 4 years
Country of Study: Any country
Application Procedure: Applicants who have no strong
preference for a college are suggested to consider Green
Templeton College or The Queen's College as their choice
Closing Date: 6 January
Funding: Trusts
Additional Information: Please visit the website: www.
medsci.ox.ac.uk/study/graduateschool/courses/dtc-structured-
research-degrees/ion-channels-and-membrane-transport-in-
health-and-disease-oxion for more information

For further information contact:

Email: enquiries@msdtc.ox.ac.uk

Medical Sciences Doctoral Training Centre: Wellcome Trust Studentship in Neuroscience

Subjects: Neuroscience
Purpose: Provides a wide range of skills training in experimental and theoretical methods that is intended to enable you
to ask questions and tackle problems that transcend the traditional disciplines from which this field has evolved

Eligibility: Open to all applicants to the Wellcome Trust combined MSc and DPhil in Neuroscience. All applicants are automatically considered for these awards
Level of Study: Doctorate
Type: Studentship
Value: Course fee, college fee, living expenses
Length of Study: 4 years
Country of Study: Any country
Closing Date: 6 January
Funding: Trusts
Additional Information: Please visit the website: www.medsci.ox.ac.uk/study/graduateschool/courses/dtc-structured-research-degrees/neuroscience for more information

For further information contact:

University of Oxford, Wellington Square, Oxford OX1 2JD, United Kingdom

Tel: (44) 1865 270000
Email: enquiries@msdtc.ox.ac.uk

Medical Sciences Doctoral Training Centre: Wellcome Trust Studentship in Structural Biology

Subjects: Structural biology
Purpose: Provides training in structural biology and related biochemical, genetic and cell biological approaches to understand molecular and cellular function
Eligibility: Open to all applicants to the DPhil in Structural Biology. All applicants are automatically considered for these awards
Level of Study: Doctorate
Type: Studentship
Value: Course fee, college fee, living expenses
Length of Study: 4 years
Country of Study: Any country
Closing Date: 6 January
Funding: Trusts
Additional Information: Please visit the website: www.medsci.ox.ac.uk/study/graduateschool/courses/dtc-structured-research-degrees/cellular-structural-biology for more information

For further information contact:

Email: enquiries@msdtc.ox.ac.uk

Merton College Leventis Scholarship

Subjects: Greek studies from the Bronze Age to 1453 AD
Eligibility: Open to citizens of Greece or the Republic of Cyprus only

Level of Study: Graduate
Type: Scholarship
Value: Fees and maintenance
Length of Study: Up to 4 years depending on programme of study
Frequency: Every 2 years
Study Establishment: Merton College, University of Oxford
Country of Study: United Kingdom
No. of awards offered: 10
Application Procedure: Further particulars and application forms are available from the Merton College website www.merton.ox.ac.uk/vacancies
Closing Date: End of January
Funding: Private
No. of applicants last year: 10
Additional Information: Prospective applicants should refer to the college website www.merton.ox.ac.uk for up-to-date information

For further information contact:

Merton College Merton Street, Oxford, OX1 4JD, United Kingdom

Email: julie.gerhardi@merton.ox.ac.uk
Contact: Admissions Office

Merton College: Barton Scholarship

Subjects: Law
Eligibility: Open to British graduate applicants for the BCL. Awarded with the Law Faculty. No separate application required
Level of Study: Graduate, Postgraduate
Type: Scholarship
Value: £5,000 per year
Length of Study: 1 year
Country of Study: Any country
Application Procedure: No separate application required
Closing Date: 22 January
Additional Information: Please check at www.merton.ox.ac.uk/graduate/graduate-scholarships-2015 for more information

For further information contact:

Email: jane.sherwood@admin.ox.ac.uk

Merton College: Chemistry Scholarship

Subjects: Chemistry
Eligibility: Open to Home/European Union applicants for any graduate Chemistry programme of study normally considered by the College. Please see website for more details

Level of Study: Graduate
Type: Scholarship
Value: Course fees, college fees, full maintenance award (at RCUK rate)
Length of Study: Duration of fee liability
Study Establishment: Merton College
Country of Study: Any country
Closing Date: Relevant January deadline for your course
Additional Information: Please visit the website: www. merton.ox.ac.uk/graduate/graduate-scholarships for more information

For further information contact:

Tel: (44) 1865 276 310

Merton College: Merton Lawyers

Subjects: BCL/MJur
Eligibility: Open to graduate applicants for the BCL/MJur. No separate application required. Please see website for more details
Level of Study: Graduate, Postgraduate
Type: Scholarship
Value: £5,000 from each of the Faculty and College
Length of Study: 1 year
Frequency: Annual
Study Establishment: Merton
Country of Study: Any country
Closing Date: 20 January
Additional Information: Please check the website: www. merton.ox.ac.uk/graduate/graduate-scholarships for more information

Merton College: Peter J Braam Global Wellbeing Graduate Scholarship

Subjects: Biochemistry
Eligibility: Open to Home/European Union applicants for any graduate Biochemistry programme of study normally considered by the College. Please see website for more details
Level of Study: Doctorate
Type: Scholarship
Value: Course fees, college fees, full maintenance award (at RCUK rate)
Length of Study: Duration of fee liability
Country of Study: Any country
Application Procedure: Applicants wishing to be considered for this scholarship should apply for the DPhil in Biochemistry and state how their research addresses a problem related to global wellbeing

Closing Date: Relevant January deadline for your course
Additional Information: Please visit the website: www. merton.ox.ac.uk/graduate/graduate-scholarships for more information

For further information contact:

Email: graduate.admissions@admin.ox.ac.uk

Merton College: Two Merton Domus B Scholarships

Subjects: All subjects for which the College normally considers
Purpose: To enable United Kingdom/European Union students pursue studies at Merton College
Eligibility: Home/European Union applicants
Level of Study: Graduate, Postgraduate, Research
Type: Scholarship
Value: All fees plus maintenance award of £11,500
Length of Study: Up to 4 years
Frequency: Annual
Study Establishment: Merton College, University of Oxford
Country of Study: United Kingdom
Application Procedure: Further particulars and application forms are available from the Merton College website www. merton.ox.ac.uk/vacancies/index.htm or from the Secretary for Graduates
Closing Date: 20 January

For further information contact:

Email: julie.gerhardig@merton.ox.ac.uk
Contact: Admissions Office

New College: The Yeotown Scholarship in Science

Eligibility: Open to all Home/European Union applicants to a research degree in Computer Science. The scholarship covers living costs and will be offered in conjunction with a departmental scholarship covering University and college fees. Please see website for more details
Level of Study: Postgraduate
Type: Scholarship
Value: Tuition and college fee plus maintenance stipend
Length of Study: Period of fee liability
Frequency: Annual
Study Establishment: New College
Country of Study: United Kingdom
Application Procedure: For more information, please check the website: www.new.ox.ac.uk/scholarships-0

Closing Date: 8 January
Funding: Trusts

For further information contact:

Email: thenewcollege600014@gmail.com

North American Electric Reliability Corporation (NERC) Studentships in Earth Sciences

Subjects: Earth sciences
Purpose: To assist graduate students with fees and maintenance
Eligibility: Open to Home or European Union candidates usually with a 2.1 degree or higher
Level of Study: Research
Type: Studentship
Value: £5,000 per year
Length of Study: Duration of fee liability
Frequency: Annual
Country of Study: Any country
Application Procedure: 1. Upload a transcript from your current or previous study, a CV and any other documents that you feel would support your application (within 24 hours of submitting your online application you will receive a link allowing you to upload additional supporting documents). 2. Ask your referees to submit a reference for you by 29 April at the very latest. Note: when you submit your application, an email will automatically be sent to your referees requesting a reference for you. This email will contain a secure link for your referee to upload a reference for you. 3. View the available projects. 4. Make an initial project enquiry by contacting supervisors directly
Closing Date: January
Additional Information: The Department will have a number of NERC studentships, to be confirmed. An European Union national who has studied for an undergraduate degree at a United Kingdom university during the 3 years leading up to the application may be classed as a United Kingdom resident

For further information contact:

Email: researchcareers@nerc.ac.uk

Nuffield College Funded Studentships

Subjects: Social sciences
Purpose: To assist students in a postgraduate degree course
Eligibility: Open to persons with at least an Upper Second Class (Honours) Degree or equivalent
Level of Study: Postgraduate
Type: Studentship

Value: Maximum UK£14,500 (home and European Union students) UK£19,500 (overseas students), usually partial awards only
Length of Study: For the length of the course, subject to satisfactory progress up to 4 years
Frequency: Annual
Study Establishment: Nuffield College, University of Oxford
Country of Study: United Kingdom
Application Procedure: All students offered a place at Nuffield College will automatically be considered for a studentship without the need for further application, other than the University of Oxford Graduate Admissions application form
Additional Information: Requests for information should be addressed to the Academic Administrator

For further information contact:

Nuffield College, New Rd, Oxford OX1 1NF UK, United Kingdom

Email: academic.administrator@nuffield.ox.ac.uk
Contact: Academic Administrator

Nuffield College Guardian Research Fellowship

Subjects: Media and broadcasting
Purpose: To support research on projects directly related to the media
Eligibility: Open to journalists or management staff members from fields of newspaper press, periodicals and broadcasting
Level of Study: Professional development
Type: Fellowship
Value: Varies according to the fellow's financial circumstances and proposed research
Length of Study: 1 academic year
Frequency: Every 2 years
Study Establishment: Nuffield College, the University of Oxford
Country of Study: United Kingdom
Application Procedure: Applicants are required to submit CV, research proposal, and names and addresses of three referees when the post is advertised
Closing Date: Mid-January
Funding: Commercial
Contributor: The Scott Trust
Additional Information: Preference will be given to proposals directly related to the applicant's experience of working in the media. The fellow will be asked to give the annual Guardian Lecture to members of the university and the public at some time during tenure. Requests for information should be addressed to the Warden's Secretary

For further information contact:

Tel:	(44) 1865 278 520
Fax:	(44) 1865 278 676
Email:	marion.rogers@nuf.ox.ac.uk
Contact:	Warden's Secretary

Nuffield College Gwilym Gibbon Research Fellowships

Subjects: Problems of government, the subject having been approved by the college

Purpose: To support the study of problems of government, especially by co-operation between academic and non academic persons

Eligibility: Preference will be given to candidates with experience in some form of public service

Level of Study: Postdoctorate, Postgraduate, Professional development

Type: Fellowship

Value: To cover accommodation, necessary travel costs and some secretarial and other assistance

Length of Study: 1 year

Frequency: Annual

Study Establishment: Nuffield College, the University of Oxford

Country of Study: United Kingdom

Application Procedure: Write for application form

Closing Date: Mid-April

No. of awards given last year: 1

Additional Information: It is hoped that the results of the research will be published or made available in some way to interested persons. Requests for information should be addressed to the Student Administrator. Please note that the 1998-9 competition was suspended and that it is possible that it may not run in subsequent years. For further information please consult the Warden of the College

For further information contact:

Tel:	(44) 1865 278 515
Fax:	(44) 1865 278 621
Email:	glynis.baleham@nuf.ox.ac.uk
Contact:	Student Administrator

Nuffield College ODA Shared Scholarship

Subjects: Social sciences in taught postgraduate courses

Eligibility: Graduates from developing countries of the Commonwealth are eligible to apply

Level of Study: Postdoctorate

Type: Studentship

Value: Fees and maintenance

Length of Study: Up to 3 years

Frequency: Annual

Study Establishment: Nuffield College, the University of Oxford

Country of Study: United Kingdom

Application Procedure: Applicants must submit a list of publications, a curriculum vitae, a synopsis of the proposed research and the names and addresses of three referees when the post is advertised

For further information contact:

Email:	marion.rogers@nuf.ox.ac.uk

Nuffield College Postdoctoral Prize Research Fellowship

Subjects: Economics, politics, sociology, broadly constructed to include, for example, social science approaches to history, social and medical statistics, international relations and public policy

Purpose: To allow scholars who have recently completed, or who are close to the completion of, a doctoral dissertation, to engage in independent scholarly research in the social sciences

Eligibility: Open to men and women who at the date of taking up the fellowship will not have spent more than eight years in postgraduate study, teaching or reseach in the social sciences

Level of Study: Postdoctorate, Postgraduate

Type: Fellowship

Value: UK£21,044 plus single accommodation or a housing allowance, children's allowance and research expenses

Length of Study: 3 years

Frequency: Annual

Study Establishment: Nuffield College, University of Oxford

Country of Study: United Kingdom

Closing Date: Beginning of November

No. of awards given last year: 4

For further information contact:

Email:	justine.crump@nuffield.ox.ac.uk
Contact:	Justine Crump, Administrative Officer

Nuffield Department of Clinical Medicine: LICR Studentship (Ludwig Institute for Cancer Research)

Eligibility: Minimum 2:1 or above, Higher level English language test. Open to United Kingdom, European Union and Overseas Students

Type: Studentship

Value: All University and College fees plus stipend £16,500 per year
Length of Study: 3-4 years
Country of Study: Any country
Additional Information: Please check at www.ludwig.ox. ac.uk/ for more information

For further information contact:

Email: webmaster@ox.ac.uk

Nuffield Department of Orthopaedics, Rheumatology and Musculoskeletal Sciences: Kennedy Trust Prize Studentships

Subjects: Immunity and microbiome, inflammation, and tissue remodelling and regeneration
Purpose: To provide world-class scientific training in a supportive and collaborative environment
Eligibility: Both European Union and Overseas applicants for the DPhil in Molecular and Cellular Medicine are eligible for this award. Interested applicants should have or expect to obtain a first or upper second class BSc degree or equivalent, and will also need to provide evidence of English language competence at time of application
Level of Study: Doctorate
Type: Studentship
Value: A bursary of £22,189 per annum (for up to 4 years). Fees at the Home/European Union rate. Consumables of £11,000 per annum (up to a value of £44,000). Travel costs of £2,500 over the duration of the award
Length of Study: 4 years
Frequency: Annual
Country of Study: Any country
Closing Date: 6 January
Additional Information: Please visit the website: www. ndorms.ox.ac.uk/graduate-courses/kennedy-trust-prize-stu dentships for more information

For further information contact:

Email: reception@kennedy.ox.ac.uk

Nuffield Department of Population Health: NDPH Scholarship

Eligibility: The department aims to provide up to two fully funded scholarships for the MSc each year. All applicants for the MSc in Global Health Science are eligible for this; the highest ranked applicants in the department are shortlisted for funding
Level of Study: Postgraduate

Type: Scholarship
Value: Course fee, College fee, living expenses at RCUK rate
Length of Study: 1 year
Frequency: Annual
Country of Study: Any country
Closing Date: 6 January
Additional Information: Please visit the website: www. ndph.ox.ac.uk/study/for-postgraduates/fees-and-funding for more information

For further information contact:

Email: enquiries@ndph.ox.ac.uk

Nuffield Department of Primary Care Health Science: NIHR School for Primary Care Research DPhil Studentship

Purpose: The Health Sciences Research Group invites applications for 2011 NIHR School for Primary Care Research (NSPCR) PhD studentships
Eligibility: The award can only be taken up by a student enrolled on the DPhil in Primary Health Care programme in a non-clinical area
Level of Study: Doctorate
Type: Studentship
Value: Course fee up to Home/European Union level, college fee, stipend. Annual tax-free stipend of £18,000
Length of Study: 3 years
Frequency: Annual
Country of Study: Any country
Closing Date: 11 January
Additional Information: Please visit the website: www. phc.ox.ac.uk/study/dphil-and-msc-by-research/available-studentships-are-listed-below for more information

For further information contact:

Radcliffe Observatory Quarter, Woodstock Road, Oxford OX2 6GG, United Kingdom

Tel: (44) 1865 289 300

Ooni Adeyeye Enitan Ogunwusi Scholarships

Purpose: The scholarship is funded by the Imperial Majesty Oba Adéyeyè Enitan Ògúnwùsì and aims to provide funding to exceptional candidates pursuing postgraduate study of Africa
Eligibility: Open to graduate applicants who are ordinarily resident in Nigeria and applying to a full- time one-year master's course within the African Studies Centre at Oxford

Level of Study: Postgraduate
Type: Scholarship
Value: Course fee and a grant for living expenses of at least £ 14,777 per year
Frequency: Annual
Country of Study: Any country
Application Procedure: For further information, check the below link. www.ox.ac.uk/admissions/graduate/fees-and-funding/fees-funding-and-scholarship-search/scholarships-2#ooni
Closing Date: Relevant January deadline for your course
Funding: Private

For further information contact:

University of Oxford, University Offices, Wellington Square, Oxford OX1 2JD, United Kingdom

Tel: (44) 1865 270 000
Email: joe@advance-africa.com

Oriel College: Oriel Graduate Scholarships

Subjects: All subjects
Eligibility: Open to all current graduate students at the college. Please see website for more details, including how to apply
Level of Study: Postgraduate, Research
Type: Scholarship
Value: Approximately £2,500 per year and accommodation rights
Length of Study: Period of fee liability
Country of Study: Any country
Closing Date: 29 January
Additional Information: Scholars are entitled to dine free of charge at High Table once per week during term time. Please contact to Academic Assistant at academic.office@oriel.ox. ac.uk. Please check the website for further details www.oriel. ox.ac.uk/content/financial-support-postgraduates

For further information contact:

Email: jane.sherwood@admin.ox.ac.uk

Oriel College: Paul Ries Collin Graduate Scholarship

Subjects: Humanities
Eligibility: Open to current graduate students at Oriel
Level of Study: Postgraduate, Research
Type: Scholarship
Value: Annual stipend equivalent to college fee; guaranteed college room at usual charge

Length of Study: 1 year, renewable for second or third
Frequency: Annual
Country of Study: Any country
Closing Date: 27 January
Additional Information: Scholars are entitled to dine free of charge at High Table once a week during term-time

For further information contact:

Oriel College, Oriel Square, Oxford OX1 4EW, United Kingdom

Email: academic.office@oriel.ox.ac.uk

Oriel College: Sir Walter Raleigh Scholarship

Subjects: Environmental change and management
Purpose: To assist a student studying at the Environmental Change Institute for an MSc degree in Environmental Change and Management
Eligibility: Open to all applicants to the MSc in Environmental Change and Management. Please see website for more details, including how to apply
Level of Study: Postgraduate
Type: Scholarship
Value: £4,000
Length of Study: 1 year
Frequency: Annual
Country of Study: Any country
Application Procedure: Applicants can download an application form from the website www.ox.ac.uk/admissions/index.html or obtain one from the Academic Office or the Environmental Change Institute
Closing Date: 30 April
Additional Information: The successful applicant will be expected to transfer their application to Oriel College if they have already been accepted by another college. Please check the website for further details www.oriel.ox.ac.uk/content/financial-support-postgraduates

For further information contact:

Email: admissions@oriel.ox.ac.uk
Contact: Admissions Officer

Oriental Studies: H.H. Sheikh Hamad bin Khalifa Al Thani Graduate Studentship in Contemporary Islamic Studies

Purpose: Contemporary Islamic Studies
Eligibility: Open to applicants to the DPhil in Oriental Studies. The award is intended for any postgraduate student pursuing doctoral research in any field of

Contemporary Islamic Studies. Please see website for more information
Level of Study: Doctorate
Type: Studentship
Value: University fee, college fee, and maintenance grant. The award is tenable from October for 1 year in the first instance, renewable for up to a maximum of 3 years subject to receipt of a satisfactory report from the supervisor(s)
Length of Study: Up to 4 years
Country of Study: Any country
Closing Date: 31 March
Additional Information: Please visit the website: www.orinst.ox.ac.uk/administration/grants/index.html for more information

For further information contact:

62 Woodstock Road, Oxford OX2 6JF, United Kingdom

Oriental Studies: KS Scholarship in Chinese Art

Subjects: Oriental Studies
Eligibility: Open to applicants to graduate degrees at the University in any field of Chinese Art History, with a preference for Chinese painting. Please see website for more details and how to apply
Level of Study: Postgraduate
Type: Scholarship
Value: University fee, college fee and living expenses
Length of Study: Period of fee liability
Frequency: Annual
Country of Study: United Kingdom
Application Procedure: For more information, please check the website: www.orinst.ox.ac.uk/administration/trust_funds/ks_scholarship_in_chinese_art.html
Closing Date: 22 January
Funding: Trusts

For further information contact:

Email: orient@orinst.ox.ac.uk

Oriental Studies: Sasakawa Fund

Subjects: Japanese
Eligibility: Open to all graduate applicants in Oriental Studies, or United Kingdom applicants whose work will require some time spent in Japan
Level of Study: Postgraduate, Research
Type: Award
Value: £5,000 per year
Length of Study: Period of fee liability

Application Procedure: An application form is available at www.orinst.ox.ac.uk/general/grants/sasakawa_fund.html
Closing Date: 18 January

For further information contact:

Tel: (44) 1865 278 225
Fax: (44) 1865 278 190
Email: chris.williams@orinst.ox.ac.uk

Other studentships in Earth Sciences

Subjects: Earth sciences
Eligibility: Applicants must have 2.1 degree or higher. United Kingdom students are eligible for full support, and a range of support is available for European Union and international students
Level of Study: Research
Type: Studentship
Value: University and college fees and maintenance allowance
Length of Study: Normally 3 years, which can be extended in some cases
Frequency: Dependent on funds available
Application Procedure: Candidates are advised to apply directly to the department as advertised on the website
Closing Date: 20 January
Additional Information: The department occasionally has studentship funding associated with grants or industrial funding

For further information contact:

Email: emmab@earth.ox.ac.uk
Contact: Emma Brown

Oxford Research in the Scholarship and Humanities of Africa Studentships

Subjects: Social and cultural anthropology, archaeology, history, human geography, African literature, politics and international relations, development studies; religious studies and sociology, subject to appropriate supervision being available
Purpose: To support postgraduate study of Africa in the humanities
Eligibility: Open to candidates for admission, or those already registered as graduate students. The successful applicant, if not already a member of an Oxford College, may be offered a place at St Antony's College or St Cross College
Level of Study: Postgraduate
Type: Studentship
Value: Varies, however it will cover college and University fees plus maintenance allowance. University fees will normally be covered at the home rate, although in exceptional circumstances supplemental grants may be made in order to

meet, or to go some way towards meeting, the difference between the home and overseas fee

Length of Study: 2 years with the possibility of extension for 3 and occasionally 4 years
Frequency: Annual
Study Establishment: University of Oxford
Country of Study: United Kingdom
Application Procedure: Refer to the website www. africanstudies.ox.ac.uk/orisha for details

For further information contact:

Email: african.studies@africa.ox.ac.uk
Contact: African Studies Administrator

Oxford University Theological Scholarships (Eastern and Central Europe)

Subjects: Theology
Purpose: To enable students to pursue further studies in the University's Faculty of Theology
Eligibility: Open to candidates aged 22–40, who already have, or expect to obtain, a theological degree from a recognized university or theological college. Applications are invited from citizens of Russia, the Ukraine and any other countries of the former Soviet Union (apart from the Baltic States), Croatia, Serbia, Montenegro, Bosnia, Macedonia, Bulgaria, Albania and Romania
Level of Study: Graduate
Type: Scholarship
Value: Fees, a maintenance allowance and, where necessary, a return airfare
Length of Study: Up to 1 year
Frequency: Annual
Study Establishment: The Faculty of Theology, University of Oxford
Country of Study: United Kingdom
Application Procedure: Applicants must contact Mrs Elizabeth Macallister for further information
Funding: Government, Private
Contributor: Member churches of the Council of Churches for Britain and Ireland, the Foreign and Commonwealth Office and Oxford University
Additional Information: Scholarships are open to members of any Christian denomination. Applicants must be sponsored by a recognised church authority in their home country

For further information contact:

Email: elizabeth.macallister@admin.ox.ac.uk
Contact: Mrs Elizabeth Macallister, Theology Faculty

Oxford-A G Leventis Graduate Scholarship

Subjects: History
Eligibility: Open to all applicants applying for a DPhil in history, specialising in Byzantine studies
Type: Scholarship
Value: University fee, college fee and full living expenses
Length of Study: Period of fee liability
Country of Study: Any country
Application Procedure: Please visit the website for application details
Closing Date: 22 January
Additional Information: Please check at www.graduate.ox. ac.uk/ogs for more information

For further information contact:

Email: peter.frankopan@worc.ox.ac.uk

Oxford-Aidan Jenkins Graduate Scholarship

Eligibility: Open to applicants who are applying to any full-time course in the Faculty of English Language and Literature. Tenable at Merton College only. Please see website for more details
Type: Scholarship
Value: University fee, college fee, and full living expenses
Length of Study: Duration of fee liability
Study Establishment: Merton College
Country of Study: Any country
Closing Date: 20 January
Additional Information: Please visit the website: www.ox. ac.uk/admissions/graduate/fees-and-funding/fees-funding-and-scholarship-search/scholarships-2#aidanjenkins   for   more information

Oxford-Bellhouse Graduate Scholarship

Eligibility: Open to applicants who are ordinarily resident in the EEA or Switzerland and who are applying to the full-time DPhil in Engineering Sciences, specialising in Biomedical Engineering. The scholarship is only tenable at Magdalen College. Please see website for more details
Level of Study: Doctorate
Type: Scholarship
Value: University fee, college fee, and full living expenses
Length of Study: Period of fee liability
Study Establishment: Magdalen College
Country of Study: Any country
Closing Date: 20 January

Additional Information: Please visit the website: www.ox.ac.uk/admissions/graduate/fees-and-funding/fees-funding-and-scholarship-search/scholarships-2#bellhouse for more information

For further information contact:

Email: accommodation@linacre.ox.ac.uk

Oxford-Brunsfield Association of Southeast Asian Nations (ASEAN) Human Rights Graduate Scholarships

Eligibility: Open to applicants who are nationals of and ordinarily resident in Brunei Darussalam, Cambodia, Indonesia, Laos, Malaysia, Myanmar (Burma), Philippines, Singapore, Thailand or Vietnam and who are applying to the part-time MSt in International Human Rights Law. Please see website for more details
Level of Study: Postgraduate
Type: Scholarship
Value: University fee, college fee, and study support grant
Length of Study: Period of fee liability
Country of Study: Any country
Closing Date: 31 March
Additional Information: Please visit the website: www.ox.ac.uk/admissions/graduate/fees-and-funding/fees-funding-and-scholarship-search/scholarships-2#brunsfield for more information

For further information contact:

Email: iphumrts@conted.ox.ac.uk

Oxford-Calleva Scholarship

Subjects: The project aims to investigate the network structure and dynamics of intra- and inter-group interactions in humans, with a focus on cooperation and competition
Purpose: It is intended to make available three scholarships for entry in October to applicants ordinarily resident in the European Union applying to the DPhil History (including History of Science and Medicine, and Economic and Social History), the DPhil Experimental Psychology, or the DPhil Anthropology
Eligibility: Each DPhil student will develop their own project within their respective discipline that explores childhood experiences and the impact of adversity and inequalities, using either psychological or modern British historical evidence
Level of Study: Doctorate
Type: Scholarship

Frequency: Annual
Country of Study: Switzerland
Application Procedure: The scholarship is only tenable at Linacre College. All eligible applicants will be considered for this scholarship, regardless of which college (if any) you state as your preference on the graduate application form
Closing Date: 1 January
Funding: Private

For further information contact:

Email: lucy.bowes@psy.ox.ac.uk

Oxford-Hoffmann Graduate Scholarships

Subjects: The Oxford-Weidenfeld and Hoffmann Scholarships and Leadership Programme was established in 2015 thanks to generous donations from multiple donors to mark the 95th birthday of Lord Weidenfeld
Purpose: Fondation Hoffmann is a Swiss-based grant making institution supporting the emergence and expansion of concrete projects which address global problems in today's societies
Eligibility: Open to applicants who are applying to any full or part-time course within the Medical Science Division. Tenable at Jesus College only
Level of Study: Graduate
Type: Scholarship
Value: 100% of course fees and a grant for living costs (at least £14,777)
Length of Study: Duration of fee liability
Frequency: Annual
Study Establishment: Jesus College
Country of Study: Any country
Closing Date: 11 January
Additional Information: Please visit the website: www.ox.ac.uk/admissions/graduate/fees-and-funding/fees-funding-and-scholarship-search/scholarships-2#hoffmann for more information

Oxford-Jerry Hausman Graduate Scholarship

Subjects: The scholarship is only tenable at Nuffield College
Eligibility: Open to all applicants applying for any graduate course in the departments of Economics, Politics, and Sociology. Tenable at Nuffield College only. Please see website for more details
Level of Study: Postgraduate
Type: Scholarship
Value: University fee, college fee, and full living expenses
Length of Study: Period of fee liability
Frequency: Annual
Study Establishment: Nuffield College

Country of Study: United Kingdom

Application Procedure: For more information, please check the website: www.ox.ac.uk/admissions/graduate/fees-and-funding/fees-funding-and-scholarship-search/scholarships-2#jerryhausman

Closing Date: 22 January

Funding: Trusts

Additional Information: One full scholarship is available for applicants who are applying to any full-time or part-time graduate course in the departments of Economics, Politics and International Relations and Sociology; preference will be given to applicants for Economics courses under Oxford-Jerry Hausman Graduate Scholarship

For further information contact:

Email: information@anthro.ox.ac.uk

Oxford-John and Pat Cuckney Graduate Scholarship

Eligibility: Open to applicants who are ordinarily resident in EEA or Switzerland and who are applying to the full-time DPhil in Particle Physics. Tenable at Lincoln College only

Level of Study: Doctorate

Type: Scholarship

Value: University fee, college fee, and a grant for living costs of £14,553 towards the tenable year

Length of Study: Duration of fee liability

Study Establishment: Lincoln College

Country of Study: Any country

Closing Date: 20 January

Additional Information: Please visit the website: www.ox.ac.uk/admissions/graduate/fees-and-funding/fees-funding-and-scholarship-search/scholarships-2#cuckney for more information

For further information contact:

Email: dtcenquiries@dtc.ox.ac.uk

Oxford-Keith Lloyd Graduate Scholarship

Eligibility: Open to applicants ordinarily resident in sub-Saharan Africa (excluding South Africa), and who is studying for an MSc course in the School of Geography and the Environment. The scholarship is only tenable at Linacre College

Level of Study: Postgraduate

Type: Scholarship

Value: University fee, college fee, and a grant for living costs

Length of Study: 1 year

Study Establishment: Linacre College

Country of Study: Any country

Closing Date: 20 January

Additional Information: Please visit the website: www.ox.ac.uk/admissions/graduate/fees-and-funding/fees-funding-and-scholarship-search/scholarships-3#keithlloyd for more information

For further information contact:

Email: shared.scholarships@cscuk.org.uk

Oxford-Mary Jane Grefenstette Graduate Scholarship

Eligibility: Open to all applicants applying for a DPhil in Computer Science or Philosophy, specialising in the cross-over between the subjects. Tenable at Hertford College only. Please see website for more details

Level of Study: Postgraduate

Type: Scholarship

Value: University fee, college fee, and full living expenses

Length of Study: Period of fee liability

Frequency: Annual

Study Establishment: Hertford

Country of Study: United Kingdom

Application Procedure: For more information, please check the website: www.ox.ac.uk/admissions/graduate/fees-and-funding/fees-funding-and-scholarship-search/scholarships-3#grefenstette

Closing Date: 22 January

Funding: Trusts

For further information contact:

Email: enquiries@cs.ox.ac.uk

Oxford-Mitsui & Co. Europe PLC Graduate Scholarships

Purpose: Two full scholarships are available for applicants ordinarily resident in Africa, and who are applying for the full-time MSc in African Studies

Eligibility: Open to applicants ordinarily resident in Africa, applying for the full-time MSc in African Studies. You are applying to start a new graduate course;; You submit your course application by the relevant January admissions deadline;; You are subsequently offered a place after consideration of applications received by the deadline;; Your application is not placed on a waiting list or held back after the January admissions deadline to be re-evaluated against applications received by the March admissions deadline; and You meet the eligibility criteria. This content was originally published on After School Africa from www.afterschoolafrica.com/17003/oxford-mitsui-scholarships/

Level of Study: Postgraduate
Type: Scholarship
Value: covers Course fees, college fees and a grant for living costs of at least £14,553
Length of Study: Period of fee liability
Frequency: Annual
Study Establishment: University of Oxford
Country of Study: Any country
Closing Date: May
Funding: Trusts
Additional Information: For more information, please check the website: www.ox.ac.uk/admissions/graduate/fees-and-funding/fees-funding-and-scholarship-search/scholarships-3#mitsui

For further information contact:

Email: webmaster@ox.ac.uk

Oxford-Nizami Ganjavi Graduate Scholarships

Purpose: The University of Oxford will soon be home to a dedicated centre for the study of Azerbaijan, the Caucasus and Central Asia, thanks to generous philanthropic support from the British Foundation for the Study of Azerbaijan and the Caucasus (BFSAC)
Eligibility: Open to applicants applying for any full or part-time DPhil or Master's course offered by the Humanities or Social Sciences Division where the course content relates to the study of the history, languages and cultures of Azerbaijan, the Caucasus and Central Asia. Please see the website for further details, including how to apply
Level of Study: Graduate
Type: Scholarship
Frequency: Annual
Country of Study: Any country
Closing Date: Relevant January deadline for your course
Funding: Private

For further information contact:

Tel: (44) 1865 270 000
Fax: (44) 1865 270 708

Oxford-Oak Foundation Clinical Medicine

Eligibility: Open to applicants who are applying to the full-time DPhil in Clinical Medicine, specializing in Tropical Medicine and Global Health, with a preferences for the candidates to be ordinarily resident in Nepal, Zimbabwe, Kenya and Vietnam
Level of Study: Doctorate
Type: Scholarship
Value: University fee, college fee, and full living expenses
Length of Study: Duration of fee liability
Country of Study: United Kingdom
Closing Date: 6 January
Additional Information: Please visit the website: www.ox.ac.uk/admissions/graduate/fees-and-funding/fees-funding-and-scholarship-search/scholarships-3#oak for more information

Oxford-Particle Physics Graduate Scholarship

Eligibility: Open to applicants who are applying to the full-time DPhil Particle Physics course
Level of Study: Doctorate
Type: Scholarship
Value: University fee, college fee, and full living expenses
Length of Study: Duration of fee liability
Country of Study: Any country
Closing Date: 20 January
Additional Information: Please visit the website: www.ox.ac.uk/admissions/graduate/fees-and-funding/fees-funding-and-scholarship-search/scholarships-3#particlephysics for more information

For further information contact:

Email: contact@physics.ox.ac.uk

Oxford-Percival Stanion Graduate Scholarship in Biochemistry

Eligibility: Open to applicants who are applying to the DPhil Biochemistry or MSc by Research Biochemistry. Tenable at Pembroke College only. Please see the website for more details
Level of Study: Doctorate, Postgraduate
Type: Scholarship
Value: University fee, college fee, and a grant for living costs
Length of Study: Period of fee liability
Study Establishment: Pembroke College
Country of Study: Any country
Closing Date: 6 January
Additional Information: Please visit the website: www.ox.ac.uk/admissions/graduate/fees-and-funding/fees-funding-and-scholarship-search/scholarships-3#percivalstanion for more information

For further information contact:

Email: ioannis.vakonakis@bioch.ox.ac.uk

Oxford-Qatar-Thatcher Graduate Scholarships

Eligibility: Candidates who have been accepted to study at the University of Oxford on a graduate course offered by the Faculty of English Language and Literature, Department of Engineering Science or Faculty of Law. There is a preference for students ordinarily resident in Algeria, Bahrain, Egypt, Iraq, Jordan, Kuwait, Lebanon, Libya, Morocco, Oman, Palestine, Qatar, Saudi Arabia, Sudan, Syria, Tunisia, United Arab Emirates or Yemen
Level of Study: Postgraduate
Type: Scholarship
Value: Tuition fees, college fees and a grant for living costs
Length of Study: Period of fee liability
Frequency: Annual
Study Establishment: Somerville College
Country of Study: Any country
Closing Date: 20 January
Funding: Trusts
Additional Information: Please visit the website: www.some.ox.ac.uk/studying-here/fees-funding/thatcher-scholarships/ for more information

For further information contact:

Email: academic.office@some.ox.ac.uk

Oxford-Robert and Soulla Kyprianou Graduate Scholarship

Purpose: The University of Oxford is currently accepting applications for the Oxford-Robert and Soulla Kyprianou Program. This fully-funded scholarship is exclusively open to students from Republic of Cyprus
Eligibility: Open to applicants ordinarily resident in the Republic of Cyprus, applying for any full- or part-time master's or DPhil course offered by Brasenose College. This scholarship is open to applicants who are ordinarily resident in the Republic of Cyprus and who are applying for a full- or part-time master's or DPhil course, within the range accepted by Brasenose College
Level of Study: Doctorate, Postgraduate
Type: Scholarship
Value: University fee, college fee, and full living expenses
Length of Study: Period of fee liability
Study Establishment: Brasenose College
Country of Study: United Kingdom
Closing Date: 6 or 20 January, depending on your course

Additional Information: The scholarship is only tenable at Brasenose College. Please check the website: www.ox.ac.uk/admissions/graduate/fees-and-funding/fees-funding-and-scholarship-search/scholarships-3#kyprianou for more information

For further information contact:

Email: contact@scholarshipdesk.com

Oxford-Rothermere American Institute Graduate Scholarship

Subjects: History
Eligibility: Open to applicants who are ordinarily resident in the EEA and who are applying to a full- or part-time DPhil in History, specialising in American History. The scholarship is ordinarily tenable at University College. Please see website for more details
Level of Study: Doctorate
Type: Scholarship
Value: University fee, college fee, and full living expenses
Length of Study: Period of fee liability
Study Establishment: University College
Country of Study: Any country
Closing Date: 20 January
Additional Information: Please visit the website: www.ox.ac.uk/admissions/graduate/fees-and-funding/fees-funding-and-scholarship-search/scholarships-3#rothermere for more information

For further information contact:

Email: enquiries@rai.ox.ac.uk

Oxford-Sir Anwar Pervez Graduate Scholarships

Purpose: The scholarship is funded by the Imperial Majesty Oba Adéyeyè Enitan Ògúnwùsì and aims to provide funding to exceptional candidates pursuing postgraduate study of Africa
Eligibility: 1. Open to applicants ordinarily resident in Pakistan, who have not previously studied for an HE qualification outside of Pakistan. 2. Candidates can be applying for any graduate course. Scholars to be selected on the basis of academic merit and financial need. Please see the website for further details
Level of Study: Postgraduate
Type: Scholarship
Value: University fee, college fee, and full living expenses of at least €14,777
Length of Study: Period of fee liability
Frequency: Annual

Country of Study: United Kingdom
Application Procedure: For more information, please check the website: www.ox.ac.uk/admissions/graduate/fees-and-funding/fees-funding-and-scholarship-search/scholarships-3#pervez
Closing Date: Relevant January deadline for your course
Funding: Trusts

For further information contact:

Tel: (44) 1865 611 530
Email: enquiries@devoff.ox.ac.uk

Oxford-Sir David Weatherall Graduate Scholarship

Eligibility: Open to applicants who are applying to a full-time DPhil in Medical Sciences, based at the Weatherall Institute of Molecular Medicine. The scholarship is only tenable at Green Templeton College
Level of Study: Doctorate
Type: Scholarship
Value: University fee, college fee, and full living expenses
Length of Study: Duration of fee liability
Study Establishment: Green Templeton College
Country of Study: Any country
Closing Date: 6 January
Additional Information: Please visit the website: www.ox.ac.uk/admissions/graduate/fees-and-funding/fees-funding-and-scholarship-search/scholarships-3#weatherall for more information

For further information contact:

Email: development@gtc.ox.ac.uk

Oxford-Swire Graduate Scholarship

Eligibility: Open to all applicants for any full- or part-time master's and DPhil courses in the Faculty of History, within the range accepted by University College
Level of Study: Doctorate, Postgraduate
Type: Scholarship
Value: University fee, college fee, and full living expenses
Length of Study: Period of fee liability
Country of Study: Any country
Closing Date: 20 January
Additional Information: The scholarship is only tenable at University College. Please check the website: www.ox.ac.uk/admissions/graduate/fees-and-funding/fees-funding-and-scholarship-search/scholarships-3#swire for more information

For further information contact:

Email: scholarships@jsshk.com

Oxford-TrygFonden Graduate Scholarship

Purpose: One full scholarship is available for applicants who are ordinarily resident in Denmark and who are applying for one of the following courses (preference will be given to courses in the order listed): MSc Evidence-Based Social Intervention and Policy Evaluation; MSc Education, with a speciality in Research Training
Eligibility: Open to applicants ordinarily resident in Denmark who are applying to various master's courses. One full scholarship is available for applicants who are ordinarily resident in Denmark and who are applying for one of the following courses (preference will be given to courses in the order listed): MSc Evidence-Based Social Intervention and Policy Evaluation; MSc Education, with a speciality in Research Training
Level of Study: Postgraduate
Type: Scholarship
Value: It covers the expenditure of about £14,777 (students on part-time courses will receive a study support grant instead)
Length of Study: Period of fee liability
Frequency: Annual
Country of Study: Any country
Application Procedure: 1. The eligibility criteria will be applied automatically, using the details you provide in the relevant sections of the graduate application form (for example, your country of ordinary residence and your previous education institutions), to determine whether you are eligible. 2. Selection is based on academic merit, unless specified otherwise. Some of the scholarships are only tenable at specific colleges. Unless specified otherwise, you do not need to select that college as your preference on the graduate application form. All eligible applicants will be considered, regardless of which college (if any) you state as your preference. However, successful applicants will be transferred to the relevant college in order to take up the scholarship
Closing Date: Relevant January deadlines
Funding: Private
Additional Information: Please check the website: www.ox.ac.uk/admissions/graduate/fees-and-funding/fees-funding-and-scholarship-search/scholarships-3#trygfonden for more information. Selection process is expected to take place on April

For further information contact:

Tel: (44) 1865 270 000
Fax: (44) 1865 270 708

Oxford-Urquhart-RAI Graduate Scholarship

Eligibility: Open to applicants who are ordinarily resident in the EEA or Switzerland and who are applying to a DPhil in Politics, specializing in American Politics
Value: University fee, college fee and full living expenses
Length of Study: Period of fee liability
Country of Study: Any country
Closing Date: 6 January
Additional Information: For more details, please visit www.ox.ac.uk/admissions/graduate/fees-and-funding/fees-funding-and-scholarship-search/scholarships-3#urquhart

For further information contact:

Email: enquiries@rai.ox.ac.uk

Oxford-Wadham Graduate Scholarships for Disabled Students

Purpose: Scholarships are awarded to applicants who have demonstrated excellent academic ability, who will contribute to the University's ground-breaking research, and who will go on to contribute to the world as leaders in their field, pushing the frontiers of knowledge
Eligibility: Open to all applicants applying to any full- and part-time master's courses offered by Wadham College, who have a disability as defined by the Equality Act and determined by the University's Disability Advisory Service
Level of Study: Postgraduate
Type: Scholarship
Value: University fee, college fee, and a grant for living costs
Length of Study: Period of fee liability
Frequency: Annual
Study Establishment: Wadham College
Country of Study: Any country
Closing Date: Relevant January deadline for your course
Funding: Trusts
Additional Information: The scholarship is only tenable at Wadham College. For more information, please check the website: www.ox.ac.uk/admissions/graduate/fees-and-funding/fees-funding-and-scholarship-search/scholarships-3#wadham

For further information contact:

Email: graduate.admissions@wadham.ox.ac.uk

Oxford-Weidenfeld and Hoffmann Scholarships and Leadership Programme

Purpose: The Oxford-Weidenfeld and Hoffman Scholarship and Leadership Programme supports outstanding students from transition and emerging economies throughout Africa,

Eligibility: Open to applicants from selected countries to selected courses. Please see website for more details and how to apply, including closing dates
Level of Study: Postgraduate
Type: Scholarship
Value: 100% of University fee, college fee, and full living expenses. Average cost of at least £14,777 being covered
Length of Study: Period of fee liability
Frequency: Annual
Country of Study: Any country
Closing Date: 11/ 25 January (annual)
Funding: Trusts
Additional Information: For more information, please check the website: www.graduate.ox.ac.uk/weidenfeld-oxford

For further information contact:

Weidenfeld-Hoffmann Trust, Saïd Business School, Park End Street, Oxford OX1 1HP, United Kingdom

Email: info@whtrust.org

Oxford-Wolfson-Ancient History Graduate Scholarship

Eligibility: Open to applicants ordinarily resident in the EEA or Switzerland, applying for any graduate course in Ancient History, preferably with a focus on economics and banking. Tenable at Wolfson College only. Please see website for more details
Level of Study: Postgraduate
Type: Scholarship
Value: University fee, college fee, and full living expenses
Length of Study: Period of fee liability
Frequency: Annual
Study Establishment: Wolfson
Country of Study: United Kingdom
Application Procedure: For more information, please check the website: www.ox.ac.uk/admissions/graduate/fees-and-funding/fees-funding-and-scholarship-search/scholarships-3#wolfsonancienthistory
Closing Date: 22 January
Funding: Trusts

For further information contact:

Wolfson College, Linton Road, Oxford OX2 6UD, United Kingdom

Oxford-Wolfson-Min Sunshik Graduate Scholarship in Modern Korean Literature

Eligibility: Open to applicants who are ordinarily resident in the EEA or Switzerland and who are applying to the full-time

MSt Korean Studies. Preference will be given to applicants focussing on Modern Korean Literature and Translation Studies

Level of Study: Postgraduate
Type: Scholarship
Value: University fee, college fee, and a grant for living expenses
Length of Study: Period of fee liability
Frequency: Annual
Study Establishment: Wolfson College
Country of Study: Any country
Closing Date: 20 January
Funding: Trusts
Additional Information: he scholarship is only tenable at Wolfson College. For more information, please check the website: www.ox.ac.uk/admissions/graduate/fees-and-funding/fees-funding-and-scholarship-search/scholarships-3#minsunshik

Pembroke College Jose Gregorio Hernandez Award of the Venezuelan National Academy of Medicine

Subjects: Medicine or the biological sciences
Eligibility: Open to nationals of Venezuela. Students must be nominated by the Venezuelan National Academy of Medicine and then accepted by the General Medical Council
Level of Study: Postgraduate
Type: Stipendiary
Value: Full fees and maintenance
Length of Study: 1 year, renewable for a further year
Frequency: Dependent on funds available
Study Establishment: Pembroke College, University of Oxford
Country of Study: United Kingdom
Application Procedure: Applicants must write or email the Admissions Secretary for details
Funding: Private

For further information contact:

Pembroke College, CB2 1RF, Cambridge, United Kingdom

Email: admissions@pmb.ox.ac.uk
Contact: Admissions Secretary

Pembroke College: Gordon Aldrick Scholarship

Subjects: Chinese cultural studies
Purpose: To assist scholars in Chinese cultural studies
Eligibility: Open to candidates beginning a two or three-year research degree at Oxford

Level of Study: Research
Type: Scholarship
Value: £5,000 per year towards college fee and contribution towards living expenses
Length of Study: Tenable for up to three years whilst the recipient is liable to pay University and College fees. Automatically renewed each year if satisfactory academic progress is made
Frequency: Annual
Country of Study: Any country
Application Procedure: Intending candidates should apply in Section L of the Oxford University graduate application form or notify the Admissions & Access Officer at Pembroke
Closing Date: 1 May

For further information contact:

Email: jane.sherwood@admin.ox.ac.uk

Pembroke College: Tokyo Electric Power Company (TEPCO) Scholarship

Subjects: Japanese studies
Eligibility: Open to all graduate applicants specialising in studies of Japanese literature, art or history. Please see website for details of how to apply at www.pmb.ox.ac.uk/Students/Graduate_Students/Scholarships_Awards/Graduate_Scholarships.php
Level of Study: Research
Value: £5,000 per year towards college fee and contribution towards living expenses
Length of Study: Period of fee liability
Country of Study: Any country
Closing Date: 3 May

For further information contact:

Email: ben.nicholson@admin.ox.ac.uk

Philosophy Faculty-Wolfson College Joint Scholarship

Subjects: Philosophy
Eligibility: Open to Home/European Union graduate applicants to DPhil courses in the Faculty of Philosophy. Eligible applicants for these courses are automatically considered. Please see website for more information
Level of Study: Postgraduate
Type: Scholarship
Value: University fee, college fee, and living expenses
Length of Study: Period of fee liability
Frequency: Annual
Study Establishment: Wolfson

Country of Study: United Kingdom

Application Procedure: For more information, please check the website: www.philosophy.ox.ac.uk/admissions/graduate/graduate_funding

Closing Date: 8 January

Funding: Trusts

For further information contact:

Email: graduatestudies@mml.cam.ac.uk

Physics: Engineering and Physical Sciences Research Council (EPSRC) and Doctoral Training Grant Studentships

Eligibility: United Kingdom residents are eligible for full awards, including fees and maintenance; European Union residents are eligible for awards covering fees only. European Union Students who have studied in the United Kingdom for the previous 3 years are eligible for a full award. The Department automatically considers all eligible applicants who have been offered places and who have applied by the January deadline

Type: Studentship

Value: University fee, college fee, and living expenses (European Union fee-only awards)

Length of Study: Period of fee liability

Country of Study: Any country

Application Procedure: Please visit the website for application details

Closing Date: 22 January

Additional Information: Please check at www2.physics.ox.ac.uk/study-here/postgraduates/fees-and-funding for more information

Pirie-Reid Scholarships

Subjects: All subjects

Purpose: To enable persons who would otherwise be prevented by lack of funds to begin a course of study at Oxford

Eligibility: Preference will be given to candidate's who have lived in or been educated in Scotland, who are applying from other universities (i.e. not already studying at Oxford)

Level of Study: Doctorate, Postgraduate

Type: Scholarship

Value: University and college fees normally at the home rate plus maintenance grant, subject to assessment of income from other sources

Length of Study: Renewable from year to year, subject to satisfactory progress and continuance of approved full-time study

Frequency: Annual

Study Establishment: University of Oxford

Country of Study: United Kingdom

Application Procedure: Candidates must apply for admission to the University through the Graduate Admissions Office (www.admin.ox.ac.uk/gsp). Scholarship application forms are available at www.admin.ox.ac.uk/io

Closing Date: 1 May

Funding: Private

Additional Information: Preference will be given to candidates domiciled or educated in Scotland. Candidates not fulfilling these criteria are unlikely to be successful

For further information contact:

Email: student.funding@admin.ox.ac.uk

Politics and International Relations: ESRC DTC +3 Studentships (Doctoral Awards)

Subjects: DPhil in Politics and International Relations

Eligibility: Open to all United Kingdom applicants for DPhil Politics and DPhil International Relations. Other European Union nationals are eligible for a fees-only award

Level of Study: Graduate, Postdoctorate

Type: Studentship

Value: University fee, college fee and full living expenses

Length of Study: Period of fee liability

Country of Study: Any country

Application Procedure: Please visit website for more details and how to apply

Closing Date: 9 January

Additional Information: Please check at www.politics.ox.ac.uk/index.php/student-funding/student-funding.html for more information

For further information contact:

Email: r.llewellyn@bbk.ac.uk

Radcliffe Department of Medicine: RDM Scholars Programme

Eligibility: Open to basic science applicants of any nationality applying for projects based within the Radcliffe Department of Medicine. Please see additional information on personal statement on the RDM webpage

Value: All fees and living expenses of £18,000 per annum

Length of Study: 4 years

Country of Study: Any country

Closing Date: 6 January

Additional Information: For more details, please visit www.rdm.ox.ac.uk/rdm-scholars-programme

For further information contact:

Email: graduate.enquiries@rdm.ox.ac.uk

Radiation Oncology & Biology: Departmental Studentships

Purpose: To provide comprehensive preparation for a career in research or industry, whether in radiobiology, protection or the advancement of cancer treatments
Eligibility: Open to home/European Union and overseas students
Level of Study: Postgraduate, Research
Type: Studentship
Value: University and college fees at the home/European Union rate, stipend, research expenses and support with travel to conferences
Length of Study: Up to 4 years
Frequency: Annual
Closing Date: March
Contributor: Cancer Research United Kingdom(United Kingdom) or Medical Research Council(MRC)
Additional Information: The Medical Research Council (MRC) awards have residency requirements

For further information contact:

Tel: (44) 1865 617 373
Email: sarah.norman@oncology.ox.ac.uk
Contact: Dr Sarah Norman, Course Coordinator

Regent's Park College: Eastern European Scholarship

Subjects: Theology
Eligibility: Open to new or continuing graduate in theology from Central and Eastern Europe. Preference is shown for members of the Baptist denomination
Level of Study: Postgraduate, Research
Type: Scholarship
Value: Up to the amount of the College Fee each year
Length of Study: Up to 3 years
Frequency: Annual
Application Procedure: Please visit website for more details and how to apply
Closing Date: 1 February
Additional Information: Please check at www.rpc.ox.ac.uk/index.php?pageid=272&tln=Courses for further details

For further information contact:

Regent's Park College, Pusey Street, Oxford OX1 2LB UK, United Kingdom

Tel: (44) 1865 288 120
Fax: (44) 1865 288 121
Email: enquiries@regents.ox.ac.uk

Regent's Park College: Ernest Payne Scholarship

Subjects: Theology
Eligibility: Open to all new and continuing United Kingdom graduate students of theology. Preference is shown for those preparing for the Baptist ministry
Level of Study: Postgraduate, Research
Type: Scholarship
Value: Up to the amount of the College Fee each year
Length of Study: 2 years initially
Application Procedure: Please visit website for more details and how to apply
Closing Date: 1 May
Additional Information: Scholarship is awarded over 2 years, extendable in proportion for a 3rd year. Please check at www.rpc.ox.ac.uk/index.php?pageid=272&tln=Courses for further details

Regent's Park College: Henman Scholarship

Subjects: Theology
Eligibility: Open to all graduate applicants in Theology
Level of Study: Postgraduate, Research
Type: Scholarship
Value: Up to the amount of the College Fee each year
Length of Study: Period of fee liability
Application Procedure: Please see website for details of how to apply
Closing Date: 1 May
Additional Information: Eligible to overseas nationals. Please check the website www.rpc.ox.ac.uk for further details

For further information contact:

Email: larry.kreitzer@regents.ox.ac.uk
Contact: Dr Larry Kreitzer, Graduate Studies Tutor

Regent's Park College: J W Lord Scholarship

Subjects: Theology
Eligibility: Open to all graduate applicants in Theology that are preparing to serve Christian churches in India, Hong Kong

or China, or otherwise in Asia, Africa, Central and South America and the Caribbean

Type: Scholarship

Value: Up to the value of the College Fee each year

Length of Study: Up to 3 years

Frequency: Annual

Application Procedure: Please see website for details of how to apply

Closing Date: 1 May

Additional Information: Eligible to overseas countries. Please check the website www.rpc.ox.ac.uk/index.php?pageid=272&tln=Courses for further details

Roche-Law Faculty Scholarship

Subjects: Law

Eligibility: Open to all graduate applicants to BCL/MJur, MSc in Law and Finance, MSt Legal Research, MPhil or DPhil Law. Award holders will become members of New College. Please see website for more information

Level of Study: Doctorate, Graduate, Postgraduate, Research

Type: Scholarship

Value: £10,000

Length of Study: Dependent on fee liability

Study Establishment: New College

Country of Study: Any country

Closing Date: 20 January

Additional Information: Please visit the website: www.law.ox.ac.uk/postgraduate/scholarships.php for more information

For further information contact:

Email: student.finance@new.ox.ac.uk

Sasakawa Fund Scholarships

Subjects: All subjects that require some period of study in Japan

Eligibility: Candidates must be Japanese nationals or students from countries other than Japan whose course at the University of Oxford requires some period of study in Japan

Level of Study: Doctorate, Graduate, Postgraduate

Type: Scholarship

Value: Up to UK£5,000

Length of Study: 1 year in the first instance, with the possibility of renewal for a maximum of 3 years, subject to satisfactory progress

Frequency: Annual

Study Establishment: University of Oxford

Country of Study: United Kingdom

Application Procedure: Applicants must complete the relevant section of the graduate admission form available at www.

admin.ox.ac.uk/gsp Applicants from the United Kingdom should contact the Secretary of the Sasakawa Fund

Closing Date: 1 March

Additional Information: Applicants must either have been accepted by the University of Oxford to undertake a research degree as a probationer research or DPhil student, or be currently undertaking such a course

For further information contact:

Tel: (44) 1865 278 225
Fax: (44) 1865 278 190
Email: sasakawa@massey.ac.nz
Contact: Secretary

Sasakawa Postgraduate Studentship in Japanese Studies

Subjects: Japanese studies

Eligibility: The Nissan Institute of Japanese Studies, University of Oxford invites applications for up to three Sasakawa Postgraduate Studentships in Japanese Studies, with the generous support by the Nippon Foundation and the Great Britain Sasakawa Foundation. The studentship consists of £10,000 for either MSc or MPhil course in Japanese studies or DPhil research which focuses on any aspect of Japan

Level of Study: Doctorate, Postgraduate, Research

Type: Studentship

Value: £10,000

Length of Study: 1 year

Country of Study: Any country

Application Procedure: Please see website for more details, including how to apply

Closing Date: 20 January

Additional Information: Please check the website: www.nissan.ox.ac.uk/sasakawa-japanese-studies-postgraduate-studentships-0 for more information

For further information contact:

Email: trustfunds@orinst.ox.ac.uk

School of Anthropology and Museum Ethnography: Peter Lienhardt/Philip Bagby Travel Awards

Subjects: Anthropology

Eligibility: Open to new and current Anthropology students who are hoping to fund research/travel. Please see website for more details, including closing dates and how to apply

Level of Study: Postgraduate

Type: Scholarship

Value: Up to £1,000 for travel/small research projects only
Length of Study: Ad hoc
Frequency: Annual
Country of Study: United Kingdom
Application Procedure: For more information, please check the website: www.anthro.ox.ac.uk/prospective-students/funding/travel-grants/
Closing Date: 22 January
Funding: Trusts

For further information contact:

Email: information@anthro.ox.ac.uk

Sir William Dunn School of Pathology: Departmental PhD Prize Studentships

Eligibility: Open to applicants for the DPhil in Molecular Cell Biology in Health and Disease with a minimum 2.1 degree in relevant area. Relevant research experience required and must apply for one of the advertised projects. Please see website for more details
Value: Full fees, a stipend of £16,000 pa, and research and travel costs of £5,300 pa
Length of Study: 4 years
Frequency: Annual
Country of Study: Any country
Closing Date: 6 January
Additional Information: For more details, please visit www.path.ox.ac.uk/

For further information contact:

Tel: (44) 1865 275 500
Email: finance@path.ox.ac.uk

Social & Cultural Anthropology: Economic and Social Research Council

Subjects: Social anthropology
Eligibility: Open to United Kingdom applicants for Social Anthropology. Other European Union nationals are eligible for a fees-only award
Level of Study: Graduate
Type: Grant
Value: University fee, college fee and full living expenses
Length of Study: Period of fee liability
Country of Study: Any country
Application Procedure: Please visit website for more details and how to apply
Closing Date: 23 January
Additional Information: Please check at www.isca.ox.ac.uk/prospective-students/funding/ for more information

For further information contact:

Email: enquiries@sociology.ox.ac.uk

Social Policy and Intervention: Barnett House-Nuffield Joint Scholarship

Eligibility: Open to all applicants applying for the DPhil Social Policy at the Department of Social Policy and Intervention and Nuffield College
Value: Course fee, college fee, maintenance
Length of Study: 3 years
Country of Study: Any country
Closing Date: 20 January
Additional Information: For more details, please visit www.spi.ox.ac.uk/study-with-us/funding.html

For further information contact:

Tel: (44) 1865 270 325
Email: info@spi.ox.ac.uk

Social Policy and Intervention: Barnett Scholarship

Eligibility: Open to all applicants applying for a DPhil at the Department of Social Policy and Intervention
Value: £25,000
Length of Study: 3 years or 2 years for MPhil applicants applying for 2 year DPhil study
Country of Study: Any country
Closing Date: 20 January
Additional Information: For more details, please visit www.spi.ox.ac.uk/study-with-us/funding.html

For further information contact:

Email: scholarships@spi.ox.ac.uk

Social Policy and Intervention: Centenary Scholarship

Eligibility: Open to all applicants applying for a DPhil at the Department of Social Policy and Intervention
Level of Study: Graduate
Type: Scholarship
Value: £25,000
Length of Study: 3 years or 2 years for MPhil applicants applying for 2 year DPhil study
Country of Study: Any country
Closing Date: 20 January

Additional Information: For more details, visit website www.spi.ox.ac.uk/study-with-us/funding.html

For further information contact:

Tel: (44) 1865 270 325
Email: scholarships@spi.ox.ac.uk

Somerville College Janet Watson Bursary

Subjects: All subjects
Eligibility: Open to graduates from the United States of America who are in need of financial assistance
Level of Study: Postgraduate
Type: Bursary
Value: UK£2,000, £3,500 p.a
Length of Study: 1 year, with possibility of renewal for second year
Study Establishment: Somerville College, the University of Oxford
Country of Study: United Kingdom
Application Procedure: Applicants must contact the Assistant College Secretary
Funding: Private

For further information contact:

Email: sara.kalim@some.ox.ac.uk
Contact: Assistant College Secretary

Soudavar Fund

Subjects: All subjects
Purpose: The Soudavar Fund provides small grants to assist students from Iran who are studying for a degree at the University of Oxford and who are facing financial difficulty
Eligibility: The Soudavar Fund provides small grants of up to £2,500 to assist students from Iran at the University of Oxford and who are facing genuine financial difficulty. The award is open to students who have started their degree at Oxford
Type: Funding support
Value: Up to £2,500
Length of Study: 1 year
Frequency: Annual
Application Procedure: Application forms can be obtained from the International Office
Additional Information: Eligible to nationals of Iran. The Soudavar Fund assists students from Iran who are facing genuine financial difficulty. Applicants must be able to show how they are connected to Iran, e.g. through citizenship, residence etc. Soudavar Fund scholarships are made in conjunction with the Clarendon Fund to support Iranian graduate students

For further information contact:

Email: international.office@admin.ox.ac.uk

St Antony's College - Swire Scholarship

Subjects: Social Sciences and Humanities Divisions
Purpose: The Swire Scholarships at St Antony's are generously funded by the Swire Charitable Trust, founded by John Swire & Sons. These scholarships are available to graduate students demonstrating exceptional academic merit
Eligibility: The scholarships are open to applicants who are permanent residents of Japan, China or Hong Kong and have completed the majority of their formal education in their country of permanent residency. The Scholarships will be awarded primarily on academic merit, although financial need may be taken into account. Applicants must apply for admission to a full-time graduate course of study that is offered by St Antony's College to start in current and upcoming year
Level of Study: Graduate
Type: Scholarship
Value: 100% of the university fees, a grant for living costs of £17,442 per year
Frequency: Annual
Country of Study: Japan
Closing Date: 15 March
Funding: Private

For further information contact:

Email: scholarships@jsshk.com

St Antony's College Ali Pachachi Scholarship

Subjects: Modern Middle Eastern studies
Purpose: To assist candidates pursue doctoral study in any discipline in the humanities or social sciences with a primary focus on the social and political issues confronting the modern Middle East
Eligibility: St Antony's doctoral students
Level of Study: Doctorate, Research
Value: £7,500 towards fees and maintenance
Length of Study: One year
Application Procedure: Please check the website for further details

For further information contact:

Email: mec@sant.ox.ac.uk
Contact: The Director

St Antony's College Wai Seng Senior Research Scholarship

Subjects: Subjects concerning the Asia Pacific region
Level of Study: Doctorate
Type: Scholarship
Value: Fees and maintenance
Length of Study: 2 years
Frequency: Every 2 years
Study Establishment: St Antony's College, University of Oxford
Country of Study: United Kingdom
Application Procedure: See www.sant.ox.ac.uk for details
Funding: Individuals
Additional Information: Available in even-numbered years only

For further information contact:

Email: asian@sant.ox.ac.uk
Contact: The Director

St Catherine's College Glaxo Scholarship

Subjects: Medicine
Purpose: To assist graduates who are, or will be registered for the Oxford University 2nd BM or the accelerated graduate entry medicine course
Eligibility: Open to graduates who have a confirmed place in the Oxford University 2nd BM or the accelerated graduate entry medicine course
Level of Study: Graduate
Type: Scholarship
Value: UK£1,500 per year
Length of Study: Up to 2 years whilst the recipient is liable for university and college fees
Frequency: Annual
Study Establishment: St Catherine's College, University of Oxford
Country of Study: United Kingdom
Application Procedure: See www.stcatz.ox.ac.uk for details

For further information contact:

St Catherine's College, Manor Rd, Oxford OX1 3UJ, United Kingdom

Tel: (44) 1865 271 768
Email: academic.registrar@stxatz.ox.ac.uk
Contact: Academic Registrar

St Catherine's College: College Scholarship (Arts)

Subjects: Humanities and social sciences
Eligibility: Open to DPhil, MLitt, and MSc by Research applicants and students in the Humanities and Social Sciences Divisions
Level of Study: Doctorate, Postgraduate, Research
Type: Scholarship
Value: £3,021 per annum
Length of Study: Period of fee liability (up to 3 years)
Frequency: Annual
Study Establishment: St Catherine's College, University of Oxford
Country of Study: United Kingdom
Application Procedure: Please see website for full details including how to apply
Closing Date: 10 March
Funding: Private
Additional Information: Please check the website: www.stcatz.ox.ac.uk/Scholarships-and-bursaries/Postgraduate for more information

For further information contact:

Fax: (44) 1865 271 700
Contact: Academic Office

St Catherine's College: College Scholarship (Sciences)

Eligibility: Open to DPhil and MSc by research applicants and students in the Mathematical, Physical and Life Sciences Division and Medical Sciences Division
Level of Study: Doctorate, Postgraduate, Research
Type: Scholarship
Value: £3,021 per annum
Length of Study: Period of fee liability (up to 3 years)
Frequency: Annual
Study Establishment: St Catherine's College, University of Oxford
Country of Study: United Kingdom
Application Procedure: Please see website for full details including how to apply
Closing Date: 10 March
Funding: Private
Additional Information: Please check the website: www.stcatz.ox.ac.uk/Scholarships-and-bursaries/Postgraduate for more information

For further information contact:

Contact: Academic Office

St Catherine's College: Ghosh Graduate Scholarship

Subjects: Humanities
Eligibility: Open to BPhil, MFA, MSt, MSc by Coursework or MPhil in the Humanities Division. Please see website for full details including how to apply
Level of Study: Postgraduate, Predoctorate
Type: Scholarship
Value: £5,000 per annum
Length of Study: Period of fee liability (up to 2 years)
Study Establishment: St Catherine's College, University of Oxford
Country of Study: United Kingdom
Closing Date: 10 March
Funding: Private
Additional Information: Please see check the website: www.stcatz.ox.ac.uk/Scholarships-and-bursaries/Postgraduate for details

For further information contact:

Contact: Academic Office

St Catherine's College: Leathersellers' Company Scholarship

Eligibility: Open to DPhil and MSc by Research applicants and students in the MPLS Division and Department of Biochemistry who have studied at a European (including United Kingdom) university
Level of Study: Doctorate, Postgraduate, Research
Type: Scholarship
Value: £3,000 per annum
Length of Study: Period of fee liability (up to 3 years)
Frequency: Annual
Study Establishment: St Catherine's College, University of Oxford
Country of Study: United Kingdom
Closing Date: 10 March
Funding: Private
Additional Information: Please check the website: www.stcatz.ox.ac.uk/Scholarships-and-bursaries/Postgraduate   for details

For further information contact:

Contact: Academic Office

St Catherine's College: Overseas Scholarship

Subjects: All subjects

Purpose: To assist students who are, or will be reading for an Oxford University DPhil, MLitt or MSc by research degree
Eligibility: Open to overseas DPhil, MLitt and MSc by research applicants and students
Level of Study: Doctorate, Postgraduate, Research
Type: Scholarship
Value: £2,765 per year plus additional benefits including guaranteed accommodation at the current room charge rate and dining rights
Length of Study: Up to 3 years while student is liable for fees
Frequency: Annual
Study Establishment: St Catherine's College, University of Oxford
Country of Study: United Kingdom
Application Procedure: Please refer to the website www.stcatz.ox.ac.uk for details
Closing Date: 12 March
Funding: Private
Additional Information: Eligible to the overseas countries

For further information contact:

Email: academic.registrar@stcatz.ox.ac.uk
Contact: Academic Registrar

St Catherine's College: Poole Scholarship

Subjects: Mathematical, physical, and life sciences
Purpose: To assist students who are or will be reading for an Oxford University DPhil, MLitt or MSc by research degree
Eligibility: British nationals of good character studying for a DPhil. Limited SCR dining rights and guaranteed 2 years' single accommodation at current room rate
Level of Study: Graduate, Research
Type: Scholarship
Value: £2,500 per annum
Length of Study: Up to 3 years while student is liable for fees
Frequency: Dependent on funds available
Study Establishment: St Catherine's College, University of Oxford
Country of Study: United Kingdom
Application Procedure: See www.stcatz.ox.ac.uk for details

For further information contact:

Fax: (44) 1865 271 768
Email: academic.registrar@stcat2.ox.ac.uk
Contact: Academic Registrar, St Catherine's college

St Cross College: E.P. Abraham Scholarships

Purpose: St Cross College is a graduate college of the University of Oxford. It offers an outstanding academic environment dedicated to the pursuit of excellence within the Collegiate University

Eligibility: Open to all graduate applicants for research degrees in the chemical, biological/life and medical sciences. Please visit website for more details, including how to apply

Level of Study: Postgraduate

Type: Scholarship

Value: £10,000 per year towards college fee with the remainder towards living expenses

Length of Study: Up to three years

Frequency: Annual

Study Establishment: St Cross College

Country of Study: United Kingdom

Application Procedure: For more information, please check the website: www.stx.ox.ac.uk/prospective-students/funding-support/ep-abraham-scholarships-chemical-biologicallife-and-medical

Closing Date: 18 May

Funding: Trusts

For further information contact:

Email: master.pa@stx.ox.ac.uk

St Cross College: Graduate Scholarship in Environmental Research

Eligibility: St Cross College, jointly with the Oxford NERC Doctoral Training Program in Environmental Research, offers this scholarship for Home/European Union students who will be studying for a DPhil in this Doctoral Training Programme (DTP). Please visit website for more details including how to apply

Value: University fee, college fee and living expenses. Fees-only awards for European Union residents

Length of Study: Up to 3 years

Country of Study: Any country

Closing Date: 18 January

Additional Information: For more details, please visit website   www.stx.ox.ac.uk/prospective-students/funding-support/graduate-scholarship-environmental-research

For further information contact:

Email: bursar@stx.ox.ac.uk

St Cross College: HAPP MPhil Scholarship in the History of Science

Eligibility: Open to applicants for the MPhil in History of Science, Medicine and Technology. Preference will be given to candidates with an interest in the history of physics for their

MPhil dissertation topic. Please see website for further details, including how to apply

Value: £10,000 per annum to cover the annual college fee and an annual stipend

Length of Study: Tenable for 2 years coterminous with college fee liability

Country of Study: Any country

Closing Date: 20 January

Additional Information: For more details, please visit www.stx.ox.ac.uk/prospective-students/funding-support/happ-mphil-scholarship-history-science

For further information contact:

Email: admissions-academic@stx.ox.ac.uk

St Cross College: MPhil Scholarships in the Humanities and Social Sciences

Eligibility: Open to all applicants for MPhil degrees in the Humanities and the Social Sciences or for the BPhil degree in Philosophy. The scholarships are tenable at St Cross College only

Level of Study: Predoctorate

Type: Scholarship

Value: £4,000

Length of Study: 2 years

Study Establishment: St Cross College

Country of Study: United Kingdom

Application Procedure: Please visit website for more details, including how to apply

Closing Date: 10 March

Additional Information: Please check the website: www.stx.ox.ac.uk/prospective-students/funding-support/mphil-scholarships-humanities-and-social-sciences for more information

For further information contact:

St Cross College, St Giles, Oxford OX1 3LZ, United Kingdom

Tel: (44) 1865 278 458
Fax: (44) 1865 278 484
Email: admissions-academic@stx.ox.ac.uk
Contact: Admissions and Academic Assistant

St Cross College: ORISHA DPhil Scholarship in Area Studies

Eligibility: Applicants applying to study for the DPhil in Area Studies

Level of Study: Doctorate

Type: Scholarship

Value: University fee, college fee, maintenance stipend of £12,910
Length of Study: 3 years
Study Establishment: St Cross College
Country of Study: Any country
Closing Date: 25 January
Additional Information: Please visit the website: www.stx. ox.ac.uk/prospective-students/funding-support/orisha-dphil-scholarship-area-studies for more information

For further information contact:

Email: master@stx.ox.ac.uk

St Cross College: Oxford-Ko Cheuk Hung Graduate Scholarship

Eligibility: Open to applicants who are ordinarily resident in the EEA or Switzerland and who are applying for the full-time MSt Chinese Studies
Level of Study: Postgraduate
Type: Residency
Value: Tuition fees, college fees and a grant towards living expenses
Length of Study: Period of fee liability
Frequency: Annual
Study Establishment: St Cross
Country of Study: United Kingdom
Application Procedure: For more information, please check the website: www.ox.ac.uk/admissions/graduate/fees-and-funding/fees-funding-and-scholarship-search/scholarships-3#kocheukhung
Closing Date: 22 January
Funding: Trusts

For further information contact:

Tel: (44) 1865 278 490
Email: master@stx.ox.ac.uk

St Cross College: SBFT Scholarship in the Humanities

Eligibility: Open to applicants who will be studying for a doctoral degree in the Humanities Division at the University of Oxford in the academic year. The scholarship is open to applicants who are students or academic staff members at a university, other higher education institution or vocational training institution in China. Please see website for further details, including how to apply

Value: £15,000 per annum. The successful scholar will also be guaranteed to have a room in College accommodation (at the standard rent) for the first year of their course
Length of Study: Three fee-liability years of the doctoral course
Country of Study: Any country
Closing Date: 20 January
Additional Information: For more details, visit website www.stx.ox.ac.uk/prospective-students/funding-support/st-cross-sbft-scholarship-humanities

For further information contact:

Email: master@stx.ox.ac.uk

St Cross College: The Harun Ur Rashid Memorial Scholarship

Eligibility: Open to applicants (who are normally resident in Bangladesh) for MPhil degrees in the Humanities and the Social Sciences or for the BPhil degree in Philosophy. Please visit website for more details including how to apply
Value: £3,000
Length of Study: 2 years
Country of Study: Any country
Closing Date: 9 June
Additional Information: For more details, visit website www.stx.ox.ac.uk/prospective-students/funding-support/harun-ur-rashid-memorial-scholarship

For further information contact:

Email: master@stx.ox.ac.uk

St Cross College: The Robin & Nadine Wells Scholarship

Subjects: All subjects
Purpose: To provide financial assistance to an academically meritorious graduate student who has been accepted into both an accredited one year's Masters programme at the University of Oxford and St Cross College and are unable to secure funding elsewhere
Eligibility: Open to all applicants for one-year Master's courses who are unable to secure funding from elsewhere
Level of Study: Postgraduate
Type: Scholarship
Value: £10,000
Length of Study: 1 year
Frequency: Annual
Study Establishment: St Cross College
Country of Study: United Kingdom

Application Procedure: Please visit website for more details, including how to apply
Closing Date: 16 June
Additional Information: Please note that this scholarship is not open to students who have already been accepted by another Oxford college. Please check the website: www.stx.ox.ac.uk/prospective-students/funding-support/robin-nadine-wells-scholarship for more information

For further information contact:

Contact: The Academic and Admissions Assistant

St Cross College: Unilever Graduate Scholarship in Sciences

Subjects: Engineering or biochemistry
Purpose: To assist graduate students with fees
Eligibility: Open to graduate students
Level of Study: Postgraduate, Research
Type: Scholarship
Value: £2,208 per year
Length of Study: Up to 3 years of study, depending on college fee liability
Country of Study: Any country
Closing Date: 13 March

For further information contact:

Email: jane.sherwood@admin.ox.ac.uk

St Edmund Hall William R Miller Graduate Awards

Subjects: All subjects
Level of Study: Postgraduate
Type: Scholarship
Value: Free accommodation
Length of Study: 1 year with possible extension for a further year
Frequency: Annual
Study Establishment: St Edmund Hall, University of Oxford
Country of Study: United Kingdom
No. of awards offered: 50
Application Procedure: Application forms are available from the website www.seh.ox.ac.uk or from the Registrar at the address below. Forms are available from around the beginning of February
Closing Date: 1 May
Funding: Private
Contributor: William R Miller

No. of awards given last year: 4 (1 new award, 3 extended for a further year)
No. of applicants last year: 50

For further information contact:

Email: admissions@seh.ox.ac.uk
Contact: Registrar

St Edmund Hall: Graduate Scholarships

Subjects: All subjects
Purpose: To assist graduate students with fees and a living allowance
Eligibility: Open to all
Level of Study: Postgraduate, Research
Type: Scholarship
Country of Study: Any country

For further information contact:

Email: lodge@seh.ox.ac.uk
Contact: The Registrar, St Edmund Hall

St Edmund Hall: Peel Award

Eligibility: Open to all students applying for Master of Fine Art at the Ruskin School
Level of Study: Postgraduate
Type: Scholarship
Value: £5,000
Length of Study: 1 year
Frequency: Annual
Study Establishment: St Edmund Hall
Country of Study: Any country
Closing Date: 20 January
Additional Information: Please visit the website: www.seh.ox.ac.uk/admissions/scholarships for more information

For further information contact:

Email: lawfac@law.ox.ac.uk

St Edmund Hall: William Asbrey BCL Studentship

Purpose: The William Asbrey scholarship is worth £10,000, is jointly funded by St Edmund Hall and the Law Faculty, and is available to all BCL applicants. There is no separate application procedure:
Eligibility: Open to all graduate applicants to the BCL
Value: £10,000

Length of Study: 1 year
Country of Study: Any country
Closing Date: 20 January
Additional Information: For more details, visit website www.law.ox.ac.uk/admissions/graduate-scholarships

For further information contact:

Email: lodge@seh.ox.ac.uk

St Edmund Hall: William R. Miller Postgraduate Award

Purpose: To assist graduate students with fees and accommodation
Eligibility: A rent-free college room for one academic year offered to a student entering the first or second year of a research degree (DPhil or MRes)
Level of Study: Postgraduate, Research
Type: Award
Value: Free accommodation in college
Length of Study: 1 year
Frequency: Annual
Country of Study: Any country
Application Procedure: Please see website for more details, including how to apply
Closing Date: 20 January
Additional Information: Please check the website: www.seh.ox.ac.uk/admissions/scholarships for more information

For further information contact:

Email: jane.sherwood@admin.ox.ac.uk

St Hilda's College: New Zealand Bursaries

Subjects: MSt in English (650–1550)
Eligibility: Open to all graduate applicants from New Zealand
Level of Study: Postgraduate
Type: Scholarship
Value: Up to £2,000 per year
Length of Study: 1 year with the possibility of renewal
Frequency: Annual
Application Procedure: Please see website for details of how to apply

For further information contact:

Tel: (44) 1865 276 884
Fax: (44) 1865 276 816
Email: college.office@st-hildas.ox.ac.uk
Contact: Admissions Secretary

St John: Ioan & Rosemary James Undergraduate Scholarships

Eligibility: The scholarship is available to any graduate student embarking upon a DPhil in Mathematics or joining a CDT in the Mathematical Institute. Please see website for further details
Value: University fees (at either the Home/European Union or Overseas student rate as applicable), College fees and a maintenance stipend at the United Kingdom research council rate
Length of Study: Duration of full-fee liability; 3 years for DPhil and 4 years for CDT
Country of Study: Any country
Closing Date: Relevant January deadline for your course
Additional Information: For more details, please visit www.sjc.ox.ac.uk

For further information contact:

Email: sarah.jones@sjc.ox.ac.uk

St John's College North Senior Scholarships

Subjects: All subjects
Eligibility: Open to graduates normally with United Kingdom degrees, who have already begun research and who are aged under 25
Level of Study: Postgraduate
Type: Scholarship
Value: Free accommodation
Length of Study: Usually 2 years
Study Establishment: St John's College, the University of Oxford
Country of Study: United Kingdom
Application Procedure: Applicants must contact the Secretary to the Tutor for Graduates in the first instance
Closing Date: Mid January. Advertised in November and December, tenable from the following October

For further information contact:

Tel: (44) 1865 277 428
Fax: (44) 1865 277 640
Email: graduate.admissions@sjc.ox.ac.uk

St Peter's College Bodossaki Graduate Scholarship in Science

Subjects: Any field of science
Purpose: To assist Greek or Cypriot citizens under the age of 30, based on merit and financial need

Eligibility: Applicants should be Greek or Cypriot citizens under the age of 30. Award made on the basis of academic merit and financial need
Level of Study: Research
Type: Scholarship
Value: Up to £13,000 per annum; may be used for university & college fees, and maintenance
Length of Study: Up to 3 years, subject to satisfactory academic progress
Frequency: Annual
Study Establishment: St Peter's College, the University of Oxford
Country of Study: United Kingdom
Application Procedure: Applicants must contact the College Secretary at St Peter's College in the first instance, or see www.spc.ox.ac.uk
Closing Date: 30 January
Funding: Foundation
Contributor: The Bodossaki Foundation

For further information contact:

Email: college.secretary@spc.ox.ac.uk

St. John

Eligibility: Open to applicants for the DPhil in Mathematics, or CDT in Mathematical Institute only
Value: University fees (at either the Home/European Union or Overseas student rate as applicable), College fees and a maintenance stipend at the United Kingdom research council rate
Country of Study: Any country
Application Procedure: Duration of full-fee liability; 3 years for DPhil and 4 years for CDT. For non-CDT students, the Mathematical Institute will provide an additional 6 months of funding from its own funds for maintenance
Closing Date: Relevant January deadline for your course
Additional Information: For more details, please visit website www.sjc.ox.ac.uk

For further information contact:

Email: sarah.jones@sjc.ox.ac

Standard Bank Derek Cooper Africa Scholarship

Eligibility: Open to applicants who are ordinarily resident in one of the following countries: Angola, Botswana, Cote d'Ivoire, Democratic Republic of the Congo, Ghana, Kenya, Lesotho, Malawi, Mauritius, Mozambique, Namibia, Nigeria, South Africa, South Sudan, Swaziland, Tanzania, Uganda,

Zambia or Zimbabwe. Preference will be given to nationals of Angola, Ghana, Kenya, Mozambique, Nigeria, South Africa and South Sudan. You must also be applying to start any full-time, 1 year taught master's course within the Mathematical, Physical and Life Sciences, Social Sciences, or Humanities Divisions
Level of Study: Postgraduate
Type: Scholarship
Value: University fee, college fee and a grant for living costs
Length of Study: Period of fee liability
Frequency: Annual
Country of Study: United Kingdom
Closing Date: Relevant January deadline for your course
Funding: Trusts
Additional Information: For more information, please check the website: www.ox.ac.uk/admissions/graduate/fees-and-funding/fees-funding-and-scholarship-search/scholarships-4

For further information contact:

Tel: (44) 20 7405 7686
Email: graduates@standardbank.co.za

Statistical Science (EPSRC and MRC Centre for Doctoral Training) Studentships

Subjects: Statistical science
Eligibility: Open to United Kingdom and European Union applicants for Statistical Science (EPSRC and MRC CDT)
Level of Study: Doctorate, Research
Type: Studentship
Value: University fee, college fee and full living expenses
Length of Study: 4 years
Frequency: Annual
Country of Study: Any country
Closing Date: 20 January
Funding: Trusts
Additional Information: For more information, please check the website: www.stats.ox.ac.uk/study_here/research_degrees

For further information contact:

Email: ri@fgv.br

Synthetic Biology Doctorate Training Centre EPSRC/ BBSRC Studentships

Subjects: Doctoral Training Centre - MPLS
Eligibility: Open to United Kingdom applicants for all MPLS subjects. Other European Union nationals are eligible for

a fees-only award. It is recommended that students submit a CV directly to us prior to making a full application. Please visit website for more information

Level of Study: Postgraduate
Type: Scholarship
Value: University fee, college fee and full living expenses for home students. University and college fees only for European Union
Length of Study: Four years
Frequency: Annual
Country of Study: United Kingdom
Application Procedure: For more information, please check the website: www.dtc.ox.ac.uk/
Funding: Trusts

For further information contact:

Email: dtcenquiries@dtc.ox.ac.uk

Templeton College Barclay DPhil Scholarship

Subjects: Management studies
Level of Study: Doctorate
Type: Scholarship
Value: UK£5,000
Length of Study: Up to 3 year
Frequency: Annual
Study Establishment: Templeton College, University of Oxford
Country of Study: United Kingdom
Application Procedure: Applicants must apply to the Graduate Services Manager, Templeton College and should visit the website www.templeton.ox.ac.uk for further information
Funding: Private

For further information contact:

Templeton College, Wellington Square, Oxford OX1 2JD, United Kingdom

Email: admissions@templeton.ox.ac.uk
Contact: Graduate Services Manager

Templeton College Leyland Scholarships

Subjects: Management studies
Level of Study: Postgraduate
Type: Scholarship
Value: Up to UK£1,500
Length of Study: 1 year
Frequency: Annual

Study Establishment: Templeton College, University of Oxford
Country of Study: United Kingdom
Application Procedure: Applicants must contact the Academic Administrator for further information

For further information contact:

Email: thc@eastern.edu
Contact: Graduate Services Manager

Templeton College MBA Scholarship

Subjects: MBA
Level of Study: MBA
Type: Scholarship
Value: Up to UK£5,000
Length of Study: 1 year
Frequency: Annual
Study Establishment: Templeton College, the University of Oxford
Country of Study: United Kingdom
Application Procedure: Applicants must contact the Academic Administrator

For further information contact:

Email: admissions@templeton.ox.ac.uk
Contact: Academic Administrator

The Christopher Welch Scholarship in Biological Sciences

Subjects: Medical
Eligibility: Open to all DPhil applicants applying for a project falling within the broad topic of Biological Sciences in Departments in the Medical Science, the Department of Plant Sciences and the Department of Zoology. Enquires may be sent by email to ga.Bush@medsci.ox.ac.uk. Christopher Welch Scholarships were established to promote the study of biology therefore to be eligible for the award candidates must have applied to the University for admission for postgraduate study normally in one of the following departments:
Level of Study: Graduate
Value: University fee (Home/European Union level), college fee, full living expenses and a research support and training grant
Length of Study: 3 years
Country of Study: Any country
Closing Date: Early January deadline for Medical Sciences and late January deadline for Zoology and Plant Sciences

Additional Information: Check on the following weblink for application www.medsci.ox.ac.uk/study/medicine

For further information contact:

Email: ga.Bush@medsci.ox.ac.uk

The John Brookman Scholarship

Purpose: The Brookman Fund may also be able to help with certain expenses such as instrumental tuition or hire of a piano
Eligibility: The Scholarship is open to those reading for, and those who have applied to read for, a graduate degree at the University of Oxford in any subject, and who as John Brookman Scholar will participate in the musical life of the College
Level of Study: Graduate
Type: Scholarship
Value: £3,206
Frequency: Annual
Country of Study: Any country
Application Procedure: 1. Please email graduate. admissions@wadham.ox.ac.uk a full CV detailing: your academic and musical qualifications and experience; the graduate course that you are following or to which you have applied; and the names of two referees. 2. Applicants should also ask their referees to email their references to the Graduate Administrator (on the email above) by this same date. 3. The successful candidate will take up their scholarship from 1 October. For further information on selection process, kindly check the following link. www.wadham.ox.ac.uk/students/graduate-students/graduate-finance/graduate-scholarships
Closing Date: 22 March
Funding: Private

The Khazanah Asia Scholarship in Collaboration with Ancora Foundation

Purpose: Initiated through a generous benefaction from Mr. Gita Irawan Wirjawan, this scholarship provides one year's tuition, fees, and expenses,
Eligibility: Applicants should have; (a) a confirmed acceptance at the Environmental Change Institute, Oxford University; (b) an excellent academic record with a first degree equivalent to a good Second Class (Upper) Honors or a GPA of at least 3.5;; (c) a very good command of the English language; (d) a commercial or industrial background and a deep interest in the environment; (e) assessed to have outstanding potential for leadership in government, business, or civil society after graduation
Level of Study: Graduate

Type: Scholarship
Value: Up to £28,500
Frequency: Varies
Country of Study: Any country
Application Procedure: Each fellowship is tenable for one-year only for full-time students on the Master of Science in Environmental Change and Management program. The successful candidate is expected to complete his/her studies within the tenable period. Each scholarship will cover the following: Tuition and other compulsory fees (as specified by Oxford University); Monthly stipend; and Return air-ticket (economy class)
Closing Date: 6 December
Funding: Private

For further information contact:

Equity Tower, 41st Floor Sudirman Central Business District (SCBD), Jl. Jend. Sudirman Kav.52-53, Lot 9, Jakarta 12190, Indonesia

Email: inquiry@ancorafoundation.com

Theology and Religion: AHRC Doctoral Training Partnership studentships

Level of Study: Graduate
Value: University fee, college fee and full living expenses. Fees-only awards for non-United Kingdom, European Union students
Length of Study: Period of fee liability
Country of Study: Any country
Application Procedure: Open to all graduate applicants for the DPhil degree offered by the Faculty of Theology and Religion. Please see website for more details
Closing Date: 20 January
Additional Information: For more details, please visit www.humanities.ox.ac.uk/prospective_students/graduates/funding/ahrc

For further information contact:

Email: theo.pgresearchadmissions@durham.ac.uk

Theology and Religion: Faculty Graduate Studentships

Level of Study: Graduate
Value: At least £1,000
Length of Study: Period of fee liability
Country of Study: Any country

Application Procedure: Open to all graduate applicants and continuing graduate students in Theology and Religion. Please see website for more details, including how to apply

Closing Date: 20 January

Additional Information: For more details, please visit website www.theology.ox.ac.uk/

For further information contact:

Email: theo.pgresearchadmissions@durham.ac.uk

Trinity College Birkett Scholarship in Environmental Studies

Subjects: Environmental change and management

Eligibility: Open to any graduate accepted for the MSc

Level of Study: Postgraduate

Type: Scholarship

Value: UK£2,400

Length of Study: 1 year

Frequency: Annual

Study Establishment: Trinity College, University of Oxford

Country of Study: United Kingdom

Application Procedure: Applicants must contact the Academic Administrator for details

For further information contact:

Trinity College, Broad St, Oxford OX1 3BH, United Kingdom

Email: jane.sherwood@admin.ox.ac.uk

Contact: Academic Administrator

Trinity College Junior Research Fellowship

Subjects: Biological sciences, history, geography, theology, law, philosophy, economics, politics, physical sciences, English, classics, modern languages, mathematics. Subjects rotate

Purpose: To promote and encourage research among those at the start of an academic career

Eligibility: Open to suitably qualified candidates having some research experience (e.g. a completed doctoral thesis)

Level of Study: Doctorate, Postdoctorate

Value: Approx. UK£20,000 p.a

Length of Study: 3 years, non renewable

Frequency: Annual

Study Establishment: Trinity College, University of Oxford

Country of Study: United Kingdom

Application Procedure: Please see application form on Trinity College website www.trinity.ox.ac.uk

Trinity College: Michael and Judith Beloff Scholarship

Subjects: Civil law

Purpose: To assist graduate students with fees

Eligibility: Open to all graduate applicants for the BCL. Preference given those intending to practise at the Bar of United Kingdom and Wales

Level of Study: Postgraduate

Type: Scholarship

Value: £6,500

Length of Study: 1 year

Frequency: Annual

Country of Study: Any country

Application Procedure: Please note interest on application form. Please see website for details of how to apply

Closing Date: 30 August

Additional Information: Please check at www.trinity.ox.ac.uk/pages/admissions/loans-grants-and-bursaries.php for more information

University College: Chellgren

Subjects: Economics

Purpose: Applicants must have a place on a postgraduate programme at University College, Oxford. Scholarships can be awarded to students embarking on any postgraduate programme. However, prospective economics students are given preference

Eligibility: Open to all graduate applicants in Economics. Applicants must have a place on a postgraduate programme at University College, Oxford

Level of Study: Postgraduate

Type: Scholarship

Value: £4,000 per year

Length of Study: Up to 3 years

Frequency: Annual

Study Establishment: University

Country of Study: United Kingdom

Application Procedure: Please see website for more details, including how to apply

Closing Date: Relevant January deadline for your course

Funding: Trusts

Additional Information: For more information, please check the website: www.univ.ox.ac.uk/postgraduate/financial_1/scholarships_and_studentships/

University College: Henni-Mester Scholarship

Eligibility: Open to all graduate applicants to the Nuffield Department of Orthopaedics, Rheumatology and Musculoskeletal Sciences. Please see website for more details

Level of Study: Postgraduate
Type: Scholarship
Value: University fee, college fee and full living expenses
Length of Study: Period of fee liability
Frequency: Annual
Study Establishment: University
Country of Study: United Kingdom
Application Procedure: For more information, please check the website: www.univ.ox.ac.uk/postgraduate/financial_1/scholarships_and_studentships/
Closing Date: 8 January
Funding: Trusts

For further information contact:

Email: lodge@univ.ox.ac.uk

University College: Loughman

Eligibility: Open to graduates who have been offered a place at University College, who are outstanding in their academic field and who, in addition, can demonstrate that they will make significant contributions to College life through the quality of their extra-academic pursuits (sports, arts, community service, etc.)
Level of Study: Postgraduate
Type: Scholarship
Value: £4,000 per year
Length of Study: Up to 3 years
Frequency: Annual
Study Establishment: University
Country of Study: United Kingdom
Closing Date: Relevant January deadline for your course
Funding: Trusts
Additional Information: For more information, please check the website: www.univ.ox.ac.uk/postgraduate/financial_1/scholarships_and_studentships/

For further information contact:

Email: john.loughman@ucd.ie

University Hardship Fund

Purpose: The University Hardship Fund aims to assist students who experience unexpected financial difficulties due to circumstances which could not have been predicted at the start of their course
Eligibility: Students can apply to the University Hardship Fund (UHF) if they are experiencing unexpected and unforeseeable financial difficulties
Level of Study: Graduate
Type: Funding support

Frequency: Annual
Country of Study: Any country
Application Procedure: Students should contact their college hardship officer to request an application form and discuss their application. The hardship officer varies across colleges but could be your Senior Tutor, Bursar or Academic Administrator. Complete application forms should be submitted by the student or their college to Student Fees and Funding as soon as possible and by the appropriate deadline listed below. The form includes sections for the student, tutor or supervisor and college hardship officer to complete, and applications will only be considered when all sections and evidence have been received
Closing Date: 17 March
Funding: Trusts

For further information contact:

Email: graduatefunding@admin.cam.ac.uk

Wadham College - David Richards Scholarship in Chemistry

Purpose: Applicants for postgraduate research courses offered by the Department of Chemistry. The scholarship is open to home,
Eligibility: To be eligible for consideration for this scholarship, applicants must be successful in being offered a place on their course after consideration of applications received by the relevant January deadline for the course. Course applications which are held over after the January deadline to be re-evaluated against applications received by the March deadline or course applications which have been put on a waiting list are not eligible for scholarship consideration
Level of Study: Graduate
Type: Scholarship
Value: 100% of course fees and a grant for living costs (at least £14,777) for the duration of the course
Frequency: Annual
Country of Study: Any country
Application Procedure: Scholarships are awarded to applicants who have demonstrated excellent academic ability, who will contribute to the University's ground-breaking research, and who will go on to contribute to the world as leaders in their field, pushing the frontiers of knowledge. The Richards family bequest contributes 60% of the funds for these scholarships, with the remaining 40% being contributed by the University of Oxford
Closing Date: January will be the deadline
Funding: Private

For further information contact:

Email: graduate.admissions@wadham.ox.ac.uk

Wadham College: Beit Scholarship

Value: University fee, college fee, and full living expenses
Length of Study: 1 year
Country of Study: Any country
Application Procedure: Open to graduate applicants for 1-year Masters courses who are ordinarily resident in Malawi, Zambia or Zimbabwe. Please see website for further details, including how to apply
Closing Date: Relevant January deadline for your course
Additional Information: For more details, please visit website www.wadham.ox.ac.uk/students/graduate-students/graduate-finance/graduate-scholarships

For further information contact:

Email: graduate.admissions@wadham.ox.ac.uk

Wadham College: Donner Canadian Foundation Law Scholarship

Purpose: The Donner Canadian Scholarship is awarded to Canadian graduates intending to undertake the BCL or MJur at the University of Oxford as a member of Wadham College. This prize is available on an annual basis and is awarded on the basis of academic excellence and aptitude
Eligibility: Open to any graduate applicant to the BCL or MJur who is ordinarily resident in Canada. Please see website for more details
Level of Study: Postgraduate
Type: Scholarship
Value: £20,000 towards University and college fees or living expenses
Length of Study: One year
Frequency: Annual
Country of Study: Any country
Application Procedure: For more information, please check the website: www.wadham.ox.ac.uk/students/graduate-students/graduate-finance/graduate-scholarships
Closing Date: 22 January
Funding: Trusts

For further information contact:

Tutor for Graduates, Wadham College, Parks Road, Oxford OX1 3PN, United Kingdom

Email: senior.tutor@wadh.ox.ac.uk

Wadham College: Hackney BCL Scholarship

Value: University fee, college fee, and full living expenses
Length of Study: 1 year

Country of Study: Any country
Application Procedure: Open to all graduate applicants for the BCL
Closing Date: 20 January
Additional Information: For more details, please visit website www.wadham.ox.ac.uk/students/graduate-students/graduate-finance/graduate-scholarships

For further information contact:

Email: graduate.admissions@wadham.ox.ac.uk

Wadham College: John Brookman Scholarship

Subjects: All subjects
Purpose: To assist an organisation scholar who has been given admission to read for a higher degree in the university
Eligibility: Open to any graduate student who wishes to play a role in the musical life of the college
Level of Study: Postgraduate, Research
Type: Scholarship
Value: Equivalent to college fee
Length of Study: Duration of fee liability
Frequency: Annual
Study Establishment: Wadham College, University of Oxford
Country of Study: United Kingdom
Application Procedure: Applicants should send a full curriculum vitae detailing: their academic and musical qualifications and experience; the graduate course that they are following, or to which they have applied; and the names of two referees, either by post to the Tutor for Graduates. Applicants should also request referees to submit their references (using the same contact details as listed above) by the same date. A successful candidate will take up his/her scholarship from October 1st
Closing Date: 23 April
Funding: Trusts
Contributor: Endowed by late E.W.M. Brookman, an old member of the college, in memory of his son, John M. Brookman (1926–1980)

For further information contact:

Email: admissions@wadh.ox.ac.uk
Contact: Tutor for Graduates

Wadham College: Oxford-Richards Scholarship in Chemistry

Eligibility: Open to a graduate applying for one of the DPhil courses offered by the Chemistry Department. Please see website for details
Level of Study: Postgraduate

Type: Scholarship
Value: University fee, college fee, and full living expenses
Length of Study: Duration of fee liability
Frequency: Annual
Study Establishment: Wadham
Country of Study: United Kingdom
Application Procedure: For more information, please check the website: www.ox.ac.uk/admissions/graduate/fees-and-funding/fees-funding-and-scholarship-search/scholarships-3#richards
Closing Date: 22 January
Funding: Trusts

For further information contact:

Email: graduate.admissions@wadham.ox.ac.uk

Wadham College: Oxford-Richards Scholarship in Economics

Eligibility: Open to a graduate applying for the DPhil in Economics. Please see website for details
Level of Study: Postgraduate
Type: Scholarship
Value: University fee, college fee, and full living expenses
Length of Study: Duration of fee liability
Frequency: Annual
Study Establishment: Wadham
Country of Study: United Kingdom
Application Procedure: For more information, please check the website: www.ox.ac.uk/admissions/graduate/fees-and-funding/fees-funding-and-scholarship-search/scholarships-3#richards
Closing Date: 22 January
Funding: Trusts

For further information contact:

Email: graduate.admissions@wadham.ox.ac.uk

Wadham College: Oxford-Richards Scholarships in Climate Science

Eligibility: Open to a graduate applying for a DPhil in Atmospheric, Oceanic and Planetary Physics. Please see website for more details
Level of Study: Postgraduate
Type: Scholarship
Value: University fee, college fee, and full living expenses
Length of Study: Duration of fee liability
Frequency: Annual
Study Establishment: Wadham
Country of Study: United Kingdom

Application Procedure: For more information, please check the website: www.ox.ac.uk/admissions/graduate/fees-and-funding/fees-funding-and-scholarship-search/scholarships-3#richards
Closing Date: 8 January
Funding: Trusts

For further information contact:

Email: domestic.bursar@wadham.ox.ac.uk

Wadham College: Oxford-Richards Scholarships in History

Eligibility: Open to a graduate applying for one of the DPhil courses offered by the History Faculty. Please see website for more details
Level of Study: Postgraduate
Type: Scholarship
Value: University fee, college fee, and full living expenses
Length of Study: Duration of fee liability
Frequency: Annual
Study Establishment: Wadham
Country of Study: United Kingdom
Application Procedure: For more information, please check the website: www.ox.ac.uk/admissions/graduate/fees-and-funding/fees-funding-and-scholarship-search/scholarships-3#richards
Closing Date: 22 January
Funding: Trusts

For further information contact:

Email: graduate.admissions@wadham.ox.ac.uk

Wadham College: Peter Carter Graduate Scholarship in Law

Level of Study: Graduate
Value: £10,000 towards course and college fees or living expenses
Length of Study: Duration of fee liability
Country of Study: Any country
Application Procedure: Open to all graduate applicants for the BCL, MJur, MPhil in Law or DPhil in Law
Closing Date: 20 January
Additional Information: For more details, please visit website www.wadham.ox.ac.uk/students/graduate-students/graduate-finance/graduate-scholarships

For further information contact:

Email: study@ox.ac.uk

Wadham College: Peter Carter Taught Graduate Scholarship in Law

Purpose: The Taught Graduate Scholarship in Law is available to graduate students of exceptional academic merit embarking on the BCL or MJur at Wadham College and is available to law graduates of any university

Eligibility: Open to all graduate applicants for the BCL or MJur. Please see website for details

Level of Study: Graduate, Postgraduate

Type: Scholarship

Value: £12,500 towards course and college fees or living expenses

Length of Study: 1 year

Study Establishment: Wadham College

Country of Study: Any country

Application Procedure: Please visit the website: www.wadham.ox.ac.uk/students/graduate-students/graduate-finance/graduate-scholarships for more information

Closing Date: 20 January

Additional Information: Please visit the website: www.wadham.ox.ac.uk/students/graduate-students/graduate-finance/graduate-scholarships for more information. The scholarship can be used to defray in part University fees, College fees and/or maintenance of the Scholar during their period of study. It does not cover all fees so you will have to demonstrate sufficient funds for additional costs

For further information contact:

Email: admissions@wadh.ox.ac.uk

Wadham College: Philip Wright Scholarship

Subjects: All subjects

Eligibility: Open to any graduate student who is a former student of Manchester Grammar School

Level of Study: Postgraduate, Research

Type: Scholarship

Value: University and college fee (to a maximum of £10,000) plus £8,000 per year stipend or, where recipient receives financial support from another source (i.e. RCUK), payment of the college fee

Length of Study: 1 year, possible renewal

Application Procedure: Application forms are available at www.wadham.ox.ac.uk/student-life/scholarships/the-philip-wright-scholarship.html either in Word or PDF format. Please send the completed form, a full Curriculum Vitae and (for graduates applying for research work) a one page summary of your research proposal, either by post to the Tutor for Graduates

Closing Date: 23 April

Funding: Trusts

Contributor: Philip Wright Fund

Wakeham Humanities Scholarship (History or Literature)

Purpose: All of these scholarships, apart from the Light Senior Scholarships, are open to new graduate students commencing graduate study at Oxford in October

Eligibility: Students at other colleges are eligible to apply for all of these scholarships apart from the Light Senior Scholarships, but would need to migrate to St Catherine's to take up the scholarship if their application was successful

Level of Study: Graduate

Type: Scholarship

Value: Check the website for further details

Frequency: Every 2 years

Country of Study: Any country

Application Procedure: Applications for Graduate Scholarships should be sent by email to college.office@stcatz.ox.ac.uk, in a single PDF file if possible, and should be single-spaced and in at least a 12 point font. For further details, check the website link. www.stcatz.ox.ac.uk/prospective-students/postgraduate-admissions/student-finance-and-scholarships/

Closing Date: 26 April, 3 May and 10 May

Funding: Private

Additional Information: www.ox.ac.uk/admissions/graduate/colleges/st-catherines-college

For further information contact:

Manor Road, Oxford, OX1 3UJ, United Kingdom

Weatherall Institute of Molecular Medicine: WIMM Prize Studentship

Level of Study: Graduate

Value: All fees and living expenses of £18,000 per annum

Length of Study: 4 years

Country of Study: United Kingdom

Application Procedure: Open to applicants of any nationality applying for projects advertised on the WIMM website. Applicants must quote scholarship reference code H816027

Closing Date: 1 June

Additional Information: For more details, visit website www.imm.ox.ac.uk/wimm-prize-studentship-2017

For further information contact:

University of Oxford Level 6, West Wing John Radcliffe Hospital Headington Oxford, OX3 9DU, United Kingdom

Email: graduate.enquiries@rdm.ox.ac.uk

Weidenfeld-Hoffmann Scholarships and Leadership Programme

Eligibility: You must be applying to start a new graduate course at Oxford. Please visit the website to see the complete list of eligible courses and country of residence
Level of Study: Postgraduate
Type: Scholarship
Value: University fee, college fee, and full living expenses
Length of Study: Period of fee liability
Frequency: Annual
Country of Study: United Kingdom
Application Procedure: Please see website for more details, including how to apply
Closing Date: Relevant January deadline for your course (11 January)
Funding: Trusts
Additional Information: For more information, please check the website: www.graduate.ox.ac.uk/weidenfeld-hoffmann

For further information contact:

Email: info@whtrust.org

Wolfson College: Lorne Thyssen Scholarship

Level of Study: Graduate
Value: University fee, college fee, and living expenses
Length of Study: Period of fee liability
Country of Study: Any country
Application Procedure: Open to new Home/European Union applicants to DPhil courses within the range accepted by Wolfson College, and who are specializing in Ancient World Studies. Please see website for more details
Closing Date: Relevant January deadline for your course
Additional Information: For more details, please visit www.wolfson.ox.ac.uk/scholarships/lorne-thyssen

For further information contact:

Email: ancient.world@wolfson.ox.ac.uk

Wolfson College: Mougins Museum Ashmolean Scholarship

Subjects: Classical archaeology (specifically Greek material culture from 700 to 30BC)
Eligibility: Open to Home/European Union and Overseas. The applicant's thesis should fall within the field of 'Greek material culture from 700 to 30 BC' and will ideally focus on the archaeological and/or numismatic collections within the

Ashmolean. The Mougins Museum itself holds important collections which can be made available for study
Level of Study: Research
Type: Scholarship
Value: £20,000 per year for 3 years towards university fees, college fees and maintenance
Length of Study: Up to 3 years
Frequency: Annual
Application Procedure: Select the 'Mougins Scholarship's box in the University of Oxford Scholarships section of the Application Form for Graduate Study. Applicants are encouraged to include a statement explaining how their proposed research relates to the Scholarship. Preference may be given to those who list Wolfson as their first choice college
Closing Date: 22 January
Additional Information: Graduate scholarship in Greek material culture of the archaic, classical or Hellenistic periods. Please check at www.wolfson.ox.ac.uk/mougins-museum-ashmolean-scholarship-2015-16 for more information

For further information contact:

Email: susan.walker@ashmus.ox.ac.uk
Contact: Dr Susan Walker

Worcester College: C. Douglas Dillon Scholarship

Eligibility: Open to graduate applicants for 1 year or 2-year courses in the fields of Politics, Diplomacy, Governance and International Relations. Please see website for more details, including eligible courses and how to apply
Level of Study: Graduate
Value: £10,000
Length of Study: 1 or 2 years
Country of Study: Any country
Closing Date: 3 March
Additional Information: For more details, visit website www.worc.ox.ac.uk/applying/graduates/graduate-scholarships

For further information contact:

Email: graduate.enquiries@worc.ox.ac.uk

Worcester College: Drue Heinz Scholarship

Level of Study: Graduate
Value: £10,000
Length of Study: 1 year
Country of Study: Any country
Application Procedure: Open to graduate applicants in the Humanities. Preference given to international applicants. Please see website for more details, including how to apply

Closing Date: 3 March
Contributor: Worcester
Additional Information: For more details, please visit website: www.worc.ox.ac.uk/applying/graduates/graduate-scholarships

For further information contact:

Email: graduate.enquiries@worc.ox.ac.uk

Worcester College: Law Faculty Graduate Scholarship

Eligibility: Open to applicants who are applying for the Bachelor of Civil Law or Magister Juris. Award holders will become members of Worcester College. Please see website for more information
Level of Study: Graduate, Postgraduate
Type: Scholarship
Value: £10,000
Length of Study: 1 year
Study Establishment: Worcester College
Country of Study: Any country
Closing Date: Relevant January deadline for your course
Additional Information: Please visit the website: www.worc.ox.ac.uk/applying/graduates/graduate-scholarships for more information

For further information contact:

Tel: (44) 1865 278 300
Email: lodge@worc.ox.ac.uk

Worcester College: Martin Senior Scholarship

Subjects: All subjects
Eligibility: Open to graduate applicants to research degrees from the United Kingdom or European Union who are current or previous members of Worcester College
Level of Study: Postgraduate, Research
Type: Scholarship
Value: £4,000
Length of Study: Duration of student's fee liability
Frequency: Annual
Study Establishment: Worcester College
Application Procedure: Please see college website for details of how to apply
Closing Date: 1 March
Additional Information: Please check the website: www.worc.ox.ac.uk/applying/graduates/graduate-scholarships for further details

For further information contact:

Email: graduate.enquiries@worc.ox.ac.uk
Contact: Graduate Officer

Worcester College: Ogilvie Thompson Scholarships

Subjects: All subjects
Purpose: To assist graduate students with fees
Eligibility: Open to incoming graduates who have been under-graduates at Worcester within the last two years and have not undertaken any graduate work at Oxford or elsewhere
Type: Scholarships
Value: Up to £6,000
Length of Study: 1 year
Country of Study: Any country

For further information contact:

Email: graduate.enquiries@worc.ox.ac.uk

University of Paris-Saclay

Website: www.universite-paris-saclay.fr/en/universite-paris-saclay-international-masters-scholarship

The University of Paris-Saclay is a French federal research university which is currently under development with the aim to become a world top-10 university.

Université Paris-Saclay International Master's Scholarships

Purpose: The Université Paris-Saclay would like to promote access to its master's (nationally-certified degree) programs to international students, taught in its member establishments, and to make it easier for highly-qualified foreign students to attend its university especially those wishing to develop an academic project through research up to the doctoral level
Eligibility: Newly arrived international students, aged 30 and under during the course of the selection year. - International students living in France for less than a year, taking language classes (type FFL or the like). - Students enrolled in a Université Paris-Saclay Master's programme and whose institution of administrative enrolment is one of the following: AgroParisTech, CentraleSupelec, ENS Paris-Saclay, INSTN-CEA, IOGS, UVSQ, UEVE, UPSud
Level of Study: Postgraduate

Value: €10,000 per year
Frequency: Annual
Study Establishment: Université Paris-Saclay, France
Country of Study: France
Application Procedure: To be considered for the scholarships, students must first be admitted to a Master's Programme offered at Université Paris-Saclay
Closing Date: 13 May
Funding: Government
Additional Information: For more details visit official scholarship website: www.universite-paris-saclay.fr/en/universite-paris-saclay-international-masters-scholarship-programme-academic-year-2017-2018

University of Pretoria

Private Bag X20, Hatfield 0028, South Africa

Tel: (27) 12 420 3111
Website: www.up.ac.za/

Commonwealth PhD scholarships

Subjects: The scholarships are provided to learn any of the courses offered by the University of Pretoria in South Africa
Purpose: Commonwealth PhD Scholarships are for candidates from low and middle income Commonwealth countries, for full-time doctoral study at a United Kingdom university. Commonwealth PhD Scholarships are for candidates from low and middle income Commonwealth countries, for full-time doctoral study at a United Kingdom university
Eligibility: 1. Applicants should be citizens of Commonwealth countries (excluding South African students). 2. Applicants must conduct their studies at the University of Pretoria. 3. They must have completed the degree that will give them admission to a doctoral programme a maximum of 3 years prior to their application for the University of Pretoria Commonwealth Doctoral Scholarship. 4. They must not be older than 35 years of age at the time of application. Masters students currently registered at the University of Pretoria are not eligible for the Doctoral Scholarship
Level of Study: Doctorate
Type: Scholarship
Value: The value of the Doctoral Scholarships will be ZAR 120,000. This amount must be used to cover accommodation and living cost, medical aid and books/stationery. For detailed information, please visit website
Country of Study: South Africa
Application Procedure: The mode of applying is electronically or by post

Closing Date: 30 August
Contributor: University of Pretoria
Additional Information: For further information, kindly check the following pdf link. cscuk.dfid.gov.uk/wp-content/uploads/2019/02/terms-conditions-phd-scholarships-low-middle-income-countries-2019-FINAL._.pdf

For further information contact:

Email: eas@cscuk.org.uk

University of Pune

Institute of Bioinformatics & Biotechnology (IBB), Ganeshkhind, Pune, Maharashtra 411007, India

Tel: (91) 20 2569 2039
Fax: (91) 20 2569 0087
Email: director@bioinfo.ernet.in
Website: www.unipune.ernet.in
Contact: Director

The University stands for humanism and tolerance, for reason for adventure of ideas and for the search of truth. It stands for the forward march of the human race towards even higher objectives. If the universities discharge their duties adequately then it is well with the nation and the people–Jawaharlal Nehru.

Department of Biotechnology (DBT) Junior Research Fellowship

Subjects: Biotechnology and applied biology
Purpose: To support candidates pursuing research in areas of biotechnology and applied biology
Eligibility: Open to candidates from the centres supported by the DBT, New Delhi
Level of Study: Research
Type: Fellowship
Value: INR 30,000 per fellow per year
Length of Study: 3–5 years
Frequency: Annual
Study Establishment: University of Pune
Country of Study: India
Application Procedure: A written application along with application fee of INR 500 in the form of a DD in favour of Registrar, University of Pune
Contributor: Government of India

For further information contact:

Department of Biotechnology, University of Pune, Pune, Maharashtra 411007, India

Tel:	(91) 20 2569 4952, 2569 2248
Email:	jkpal@unipune.ernet.in, jkpal@hotmail.com
Contact:	Professor Jayanta Kumar Pal, Co-ordinator, DBJ-JRF Programme

University of Queensland

Research and Postgraduate Studies, Cumbrae-Stewart Building, Brisbane, St Lucia, QLD 4072, Australia

Tel:	(61) 7 3365 1111
Fax:	(61) 7 3365 4455/6941
Email:	scholarships@research.uq.edu.au
Website:	www.uq.edu.au

The University of Queensland has an outstanding profile in the Australian and international research community. It maintains a world-class, comprehensive programme of research and research training, underpinned by state-of-the-art infrastructure and a commitment to rewarding excellence. As one of Australia's premier universities, UQ attracts researchers and students of outstanding calibre.

Dr Rosamond Siemon Postgraduate Renal Research Scholarship

Subjects: Medical sciences
Purpose: To support a research higher degree candidate to undertake multidisciplinary, collaborative research into renal disease, repair and regeneration
Eligibility: Open to candidates who are enroled or intend to enrol in a research higher degree at the University of Queensland and who demonstrate a high level of academic achievement and ability
Level of Study: Postgraduate
Type: Scholarship
Value: A$30,000 per year (a stipend of A$25,000 and a direct research cost allowance of A$5,000)
Length of Study: 3 years and 6 months
Frequency: Annual
Country of Study: Australia
Application Procedure: Applicants must send a proposed research project description, certified copies of academic transcripts, academic curriculum vitae, including publications and 3 letters of recommendation

Closing Date: 31 August
Funding: Individuals
Contributor: Dr Rosamond Siemon
Additional Information: Research Scholarships Referee Report Form can be used. This can be accessed from www.uq.edu.au/grad-school/scholarship-forms

For further information contact:

Research Scholarships, Office of Research and Postgraduate Studies, The University of Queensland, St Lucia, QLD 4072, Australia

Email:	postgrad-office@imb.uq.edu.au
Contact:	Professor Melissa Little

Global Archaeological Science Scholarships

Subjects: Scholarships are awarded for archaeological science projects in Africa, Europe and Australia.
Purpose: The University of Queensland Archaeology Program is offering four PhD studentships for international and domestic students to start for archaeological science projects in Africa, Europe and Australia.
Eligibility: Australian and international students are eligible to apply. Students whose first language is not English must demonstrate proficiency in English by submitting satisfactory scores from the Test of English as a Foreign Language (TOEFL).
Type: Postgraduate scholarships
Value: A$27,082 (old rate) indexed annually, tuition fees, Overseas Student Health Cover (OSHC)
Study Establishment: Scholarships are awarded for archaeological science projects in Africa, Europe and Australia
Country of Study: Australia
Application Procedure: See the website
Closing Date: 17 January
Additional Information: For more details please visit the website scholarship-positions.com/global-archaeological-science-scholarships-university-queensland-2018/2017/12/29/

For further information contact:

Email:	a.crowther@uq.edu.au; t.manne@uq.edu.au; c.clarkson@uq.edu.au

Herdsman Fellowship in Medical Science

Subjects: Medicine, related health sciences
Purpose: The fellowship is open to graduates in medicine or related health sciences enroled full-time for a PhD on a topic related to the medical problems of the aged

Eligibility: Applicants must be graduates in medicine or related health sciences, enrol full-time for a PhD, and be undertaking a research topic related to the medical problems of the aged

Level of Study: Postgraduate

Type: Fellowship

Value: A$22,860 per year

Length of Study: Fellowship shall initially be for 1 year but may be extended by the committee for further terms of 1 year up to a total of 3 years

Country of Study: Australia

No. of awards offered: 1

Application Procedure: Applications must consist of: covering letter addressing the Herdsman Fellowship Rules, in particular point 2, academic curriculum vitae, 2 referee reports. No strict format is required; however the Research Scholarships generic Referee Report may be used

Closing Date: 31 August

Contributor: Maintained by the income from a bequest of $2,60,000 from Mrs Rose Herdsman

No. of awards given last year: 1

No. of applicants last year: 1

For further information contact:

Faculty of Health Sciences, University of Queensland, Australia

Email: s.tett@pharmacy.uq.edu.au

Contact: Professor Susan Tett, Deputy Executive Dean and Director of Research

PhD Scholarship in Immunology and Immunogenetics

Subjects: Immunology

Purpose: To provide the foundations for the development of treatments based on the genetic findings

Eligibility: Open to a dynamic, intelligent and diligent PhD candidate (Australian or international) with either a clinical or a relevant basic science background to take forward the project

Level of Study: Doctorate

Type: Scholarship

Value: A$25,000 per year

Length of Study: 3 years

Frequency: Annual

Study Establishment: The University of Queensland

Country of Study: Australia

Application Procedure: Candidates must contact Prof. Brown for more information

Closing Date: 3 September

Additional Information: International applicants must cover tuition fees (A$27,000 per year)

For further information contact:

Tel: (61) 7 3240 2870

Email: matt.brown@qut.edu.au

Contact: Professor Matt Brown

R.N. Hammon Scholarship

Subjects: Science, engineering, medicine, dentistry, architecture, agriculture and veterinary science, and other fields of study

Purpose: To assist Australian Aboriginal and/or Torres Strait Island students for further studies

Eligibility: Open to Australian Aboriginal and/or Torres Strait Island students who have successfully completed at least 1 year of an undergraduate or postgraduate program and are enroling on a full-time basis for a subsequent year of that program, or for a further program

Level of Study: Postgraduate

Type: Scholarship

Value: A$3,500

Frequency: Annual

Study Establishment: The University of Queensland, Queensland University of Technology, University of Southern Queensland, Central Queensland University, or Queensland Colleges of TAFE

Country of Study: Australia

Application Procedure: Candidates can download the application form and referee report form from the website

Closing Date: 15 March

Additional Information: The Selection Committee shall take into account the academic merit or technical excellence, any other scholarship, bursary, award or benefit, whether governmental or otherwise, to which the applicant is entitled; and social and economic need

For further information contact:

Tel: (61) 7 33651984

Email: ugscholarships@uq.edu.au

Sustainable Tourism CRC Climate Change PhD

Subjects: Commerce, management, tourism and services

Purpose: To develop a tourism consumer decision-making model that focuses on climate change as a driver of consumer choice and apply it to Australian tourism market

Eligibility: Open to candidates who have achieved First Class (Honours) Degree or equivalent

Level of Study: Postgraduate, Research

Type: Scholarship

Value: A$19,930 per year

Length of Study: 3 years

Frequency: Annual
Study Establishment: The University of Queensland
Country of Study: Australia
Application Procedure: Candidates must contact Jane Malady for application forms
Contributor: Sustainable Tourism CRC and University of Queensland
Additional Information: For further information on topic and research proposal contact Prof. Ballantyne at r.ballantyne@uq.edu.au

For further information contact:

Tel: (61) 7 5552 9063
Email: Jane@crctourism.com.au
Contact: Jane Malady

The Constantine Aspromourgos Memorial Scholarship for Greek Studies

Subjects: Greek studies
Purpose: To assist a research higher degree student studying at least 1 area of Greek studies
Eligibility: Open to candidates who have obtained their Bachelors or Masters degrees and are undertaking a postgraduate programme involving studies which pertain to at least one area of Greek studies
Level of Study: Postgraduate
Type: Scholarship
Value: Approx. A$4,000
Length of Study: 1 year
Frequency: Annual
Country of Study: Australia
Application Procedure: Applicants must send a completed application form
Closing Date: 22 March
Funding: Individuals
Additional Information: The Scholarship is also open to candidates who are undertaking the programme as a student of another university acceptable to the committee, or this university, provided that some part of the programme involves studies at another university

For further information contact:

Faculty of Arts, Forgan Smith Building, The University of Queensland, St Lucia, QLD 4072, Australia

Tel: (61) 7 3365 1333
Email: arts@uq.edu.au
Contact: Executive Dean

University of Queensland PhD Scholarships for International Students

Subjects: View projects by area Agribusiness, Agriculture, Environment, and Science Engineering, Architecture and Planning, and Information Technology Health Humanities, Education, Psychology, and Music Business, economics, and law (coming soon).
Purpose: Students must have achieved an entry level OP minimum of 11 or the equivalent if originating from another Australian state or territory or for continuing students has a GPA of at least 4.0.
Eligibility: Australian and Permanent Residents or NZ citizens and International students are eligible to apply. Applicants must meet the university's English language proficiency requirements apply. A postgraduate degree of at least one year full-time equivalent with an overall GPA (grade point average) equivalent to 5.0 on the 7-point UQ scale, together with demonstrated research experience equivalent to honors IIA will be considered for PhD entry on a case by case basis.
Value: A Base stipend of A$27,082 per annum (old rate), indexed annually, tuition fees, Overseas Student Health Cover (OSHC)
Study Establishment: View projects by area Agribusiness, Agriculture, Environment, and Science Engineering, Architecture and Planning, and Information Technology Health Humanities, Education, Psychology, and Music Business, economics, and law (coming soon)
Country of Study: Australia
Application Procedure: See the website.
Closing Date: 31 December
Additional Information: For more details please visit the website scholarship-positions.com/uq-phd-scholarships-international-students-australia/2018/03/06/

For further information contact:

Tel: (61) 7 3365 1111
Email: graduateschool@uq.edu.au

Walter and Eliza Hall Scholarship Trust Opportunity Scholarship for Nursing

Purpose: Awarded to a financially disadvantaged student studying the Bachelor of Nursing or Bachelor of Nursing/Bachelor of Midwifery program
Eligibility: The scholarship is open to students who: 1. Are domestic students in accordance with The University's Fee Policy; and; 2. Are enrolled full-time in the Bachelor of Nursing program or the dual Bachelor of Nursing/Bachelor of Midwifery program; and; 3. Have completed at least 16 units towards their program; and do not hold another similar scholarship

Level of Study: Graduate
Type: Scholarship
Value: A$10,000
Length of Study: 2nd - 4th year
Frequency: Annual
Country of Study: Any country
Application Procedure: The Scholarship will be awarded on the basis of: I. academic merit. II. financial disadvantage. III. a personal statement. The Scholarship will be awarded by a selection committee consisting of members nominated by the Deputy Vice Chancellor (Registrar) or their nominated delegate
Closing Date: 4 March
Funding: Private
Additional Information: The recipient must demonstrate financial need, and also have performed satisfactorily in the program to date. Grade point averages will be considered; however, the grade point average will not be the sole determinant in satisfactory progress – the applicants' behaviour, class attendance, dedication to the program and career aspirations are also a part of the selection process

For further information contact:

Brisbane, St Lucia, QLD 4072, Australia

Tel:		(61) 7 3365 1111
Email:	nmsw.scholarship@uq.edu.au

University of Reading

Whiteknights, PO Box 217, Reading RG6 6AH, United Kingdom

Tel:		(44) 1189 875 123
Fax:		(44) 1189 314 404
Email:	student.recruitment@reading.ac.uk
Website:	www.rdg.ac.uk
Contact:	Student Financial Support Office

The University of Reading offers postgraduate taught and research degree courses in all the traditional subject areas except medical sciences. Vocational courses are also offered. Research work in many areas is of international renown.

British Property Federation Lord Samuel of Wych Cross Memorial Award

Subjects: Land management
Purpose: To assist students who would otherwise be unable financially to follow the MSc course

Eligibility: Open to candidates who hold a 1st degree and are, at the time of the award, ordinarily resident in the United Kingdom
Level of Study: Postgraduate
Type: Scholarship
Value: £1,000 - £2,000
Length of Study: 1 year
Frequency: Annual
Study Establishment: The University of Reading
Country of Study: United Kingdom
Application Procedure: Applicants must submit a curriculum vitae by invitation to the Director of the Full-Time Postgraduate Real Estate Programme
Closing Date: Applications will be invited in May of the intended year of entry
Funding: Private
No. of awards given last year: 3
Additional Information: Scholars must intend to remain resident in the United Kingdom after the term of the scholarship has ended

For further information contact:

Tel:		(44) 1183 786 336
Email:	n.s.french@reading.ac.uk
Contact:	Mr Nick French

Otway Cave Scholarship

Subjects: Land management
Purpose: To assist students who would otherwise be unable financially to follow the MSc course in Land Management
Eligibility: Open to candidates who hold a first degree and are, at the time of the award, ordinarily resident in the United Kingdom
Level of Study: Postgraduate
Type: Scholarship
Value: £1,000 (but may be higher)
Length of Study: 1 year
Frequency: Annual
Study Establishment: The University of Reading
Country of Study: United Kingdom
No. of awards offered: 20
Application Procedure: Applicants must submit curriculum vitaes by invitation
Funding: Private
No. of awards given last year: 1
No. of applicants last year: 20
Additional Information: Scholars must intend to remain resident in the United Kingdom after the term of the scholarship has ended. Awarded only to students accepted to study MSc Land Management

For further information contact:

Tel:	(44) 1734 318 182
Fax:	(44) 1734 316 658
Email:	n.samman@reading.ac.uk
Contact:	Mr J Samman-Lloyd

University International Research Studentships

Subjects: All areas within the faculties of science, life sciences and arts, humanities and social science
Eligibility: Funding is only open to international (non-European Union) candidates. You will be required to meet the language requirements specified by your department upon entry
Type: Studentship
Value: Full prize: a subsistence grant (stipend) to match the current United Kingdom Research Council rate (the last year's rate is £13,863). Fees-only: tuition fees at the international rate, a £1,000 per year training and development allowance
Length of Study: Up to 3 years
Frequency: Annual
Closing Date: January
Contributor: University of Reading

For further information contact:

Email:	j.john@reading.ac.uk
Contact:	Joanna John

University of Reading Dorothy Hodgkin Postgraduate Award

Subjects: Science, engineering, medicine, social science and technology
Eligibility: Open to nationals of either India, Mainland China, Hong Kong, Russia or a country in the developing world only
Level of Study: Postgraduate
Type: Scholarship
Value: All tuition fees and a grant for living costs
Length of Study: 1 year; 3 years
Frequency: Annual
Study Establishment: University of Reading
Country of Study: United Kingdom
Application Procedure: Contact the Jonathan Lloyd at the faculties of science and life science
Closing Date: 6 May

For further information contact:

Tel:	(44) 1183 788 341
Email:	j.d.lloyd@reading.ac.uk

University of Reading MSc Intelligent Buildings Scholarship

Subjects: Construction management and engineering
Eligibility: In order to be considered for this Scholarship you must hold the offer of a place on the MSc Intelligent Buildings course
Level of Study: Postgraduate
Type: Scholarship
Value: £3,000
Length of Study: 1 year
Frequency: Annual
Study Establishment: University of Reading
Country of Study: United Kingdom
No. of awards offered: 1
Application Procedure: Contact Gulay Ozkan, Programme Coordinator at the School of Construction Management and Engineering
Closing Date: 30 August
Contributor: The Happold Trust
No. of awards given last year: 1
No. of applicants last year: 1

For further information contact:

Tel:	(44) 1183 786 254
Email:	g.ozkan@rdg.ac.uk
Contact:	Gulay Ozkan, Programme Coordinator

University of Reading Music Scholarship

Subjects: Music
Purpose: To support excellence in music
Eligibility: In order to be considered for this scholarship you must already hold an offer of a place at the university
Level of Study: Postgraduate
Type: Scholarship
Value: All tuition fees
Length of Study: 1 year
Frequency: Annual
Study Establishment: University of Reading
Country of Study: United Kingdom
Application Procedure: Apply online
Closing Date: 1 March
Additional Information: Students must be available for audition on 21 March

For further information contact:

Email: music@rdg.ac.uk

University of Regina

Master of Indigenous Education

Purpose: The Master of Indigenous Education degree aims to: 1. Prepare students as leaders in pedagogical practice in Indigenous Education. 2. Provide students with the required skills, knowledge, and competencies needed to become effective Indigenous educators. 3. Prepare students to conduct research with Indigenous peoples

Eligibility: Below details should be mandatorily available to process the application for the grant. 1. Personal information. 2. Proxy or Third-Party information (if you want to designate a proxy or third party to act on your behalf). 3. Educational history of all higher post-secondary institutions attended, and dates attended. This includes institutions that you attended but no degree was awarded, and degrees that are in progress and have not yet been awarded. 4. English Proficiency test scores (if applicable). 5. Names and e-mail addresses of your references. 6. Personal statement of interest. Please review "Most Common Mistake Applicants Make" before submitting your personal statement. 7. Resumé or CV. 8. Valid credit card (MasterCard, VISA, or American Express). Pre-paid credit cards and MasterCard Debit, VISA Debit or American Express Debit are not acceptable methods of payment. 9. Valid e-mail address

Level of Study: Postgraduate

Type: Funding support

Frequency: Annual

Country of Study: Any country

Application Procedure: 1. The online application takes about 30 minutes to complete. 2. The first time you access the online application, you will be asked to create a Login ID and PIN. For security reasons, it is important that you choose a unique (hard-to-guess) PIN number. Please make a note of your login information, as you will need it later. 3. Once you have started your application, you may choose to Finish Later. You can return to the application at any time by re-entering your Login ID and PIN number. However, you must complete it prior to the application deadline for your program

Closing Date: 15 February and 15 October

Funding: Private

For further information contact:

Tel: (44) 3065 854 502
Email: Grad.Studies@uregina.ca

University of Sheffield

85 Wilkinson Street, Sheffield S10 2GJ, United Kingdom

Tel: (44) 1142 221 404
Fax: (44) 1142 221 420
Website: www.shef.ac.uk
Contact: Graduate Office

The University of Sheffield is a research led university offering research supervision, taught courses and professional training in engineering and physical sciences, biologies, environmental sciences, humanities, social sciences, medical and health sciences. Many departments have funding council accreditation and scholarships and bursaries may be available.

Allan & Nesta Ferguson Charitable Trust

Purpose: The Allan & Nesta Ferguson Charitable Trust was set up to promote their particular interests in education, international friendship and understanding, and the promotion of world peace and development

Eligibility: Applications for either a gap year or PhD grant should be made as soon as possible, either before the beginning of the proposed gap year or at least three months before the start of the final year of a PhD course

Level of Study: Graduate

Type: Varies

Frequency: Annual

Country of Study: Any country

Application Procedure: 1. The Trust prefer where possible that you complete and submit the on-line application form on this website and email it to us. Alternatively you may download and print out the application form, complete it and send it by letter post. 2. Please do not extend the length of the forms, or add any attachments. Applications MUST NOT exceed 3 pages. Please use text size 12. 3. If you are applying for more than one project, please use a separate form for each project. All applications by email will be acknowledged and a decision will usually be given within three months of the application

Closing Date: 24 May

Funding: Private

For further information contact:

John St, Royston, SG8 9BG, United Kingdom

Email: internationalscholarships@sheffield.ac.uk

Allan & Nesta Ferguson Charitable Trust Masters Scholarships at University of Sheffield

Purpose: The University of Sheffield, in collaboration with the Allan and Nesta Ferguson Charitable Trust and the Sheffield Institute for International Development, is now able to offer 10 scholarships (over 3 years) targeted at international students from developing countries for a number of courses that are affiliated with the Sheffield Institute for International Development
Eligibility: 1. Must be between the ages of 23-32 at the time of submitting his/her application. 2. Must have obtained or be on the verge of completing their undergraduate degree with a Baccalaureate from an accredited college/university, or its equivalent. 3. Must have a minimum cumulative GPA of 3.0 or higher on a 4.0 rating system, or its equivalent. 4. Must be matriculated at an accredited university for the upcoming academic year starting August/September, and must maintain full-time status for the duration of the Master's Degree
Level of Study: Postgraduate
Type: Scholarship
Frequency: Annual
Study Establishment: University of Sheffield
Country of Study: Any country
Application Procedure: You will be automatically considered for the scholarship if you receive an offer to study one of the eligible courses and you are a national of, or permanently domiciled in, one of the eligible countries or territories. Your course application will be assessed by a panel of academic judges to decide whether you will progress to the final stage of the application process. Please use our postgraduate online application system to submit your application for an eligible course. For further information, check the website link. www.sheffield.ac.uk/international/money/fergusonscholarship
Closing Date: 30 April
Funding: Private
Contributor: University of Sheffield

For further information contact:

The University of Sheffield, Western Bank, Sheffield S10 2TN, United Kingdom

Email: internationalscholarships@sheffield.ac.uk

Edward Bramley Excellence Postgraduate Scholarship

Purpose: The University of Sheffield is pleased to offer the Edward Bramley Excellence Postgraduate Scholarship to support an outstanding United Kingdom or European Union law student, based on academic excellence

Type: Scholarship
Value: University has one full fee waiver with £7,000 towards living costs for the outstanding student
Country of Study: United Kingdom
Closing Date: 15 June
Contributor: Edward Bramley Excellence

For further information contact:

Email: law@sheffield.ac.uk

Economic and Social Research Council(ESRC) White Rose Doctoral Training Partnership (DTP) and Faculty Scholarships

Purpose: The University is part of the ESRC White Rose Doctoral Training Partnership - a collaboration between the Universities of Leeds, Sheffield, York, Sheffield Hallam, Hull, Bradford and Manchester Metropolitan University - and offers a range of ESRC Postgraduate Scholarships
Eligibility: Our Faculty scholarships are open to applicants of any nationality and in any discipline within the Faculty of Social Sciences. Most ESRC White Rose DTP scholarships are open to United Kingdom and European Union applicants; there may be limited opportunities for overseas students, and all applicants should check ESRC White Rose DTP guidance before making an application
Level of Study: Graduate, Postgraduate
Type: Scholarship
Value: Tuition Fees, an annual stipend and research training support grant
Frequency: Annual
Study Establishment: University of Sheffield
Country of Study: Any country
Closing Date: Not available
Funding: Private

For further information contact:

Email: pgr-scholarships@sheffield.ac.uk

Hossein Farmy Scholarship

Subjects: Mining, including, but not limited to the geological, engineering, scientific and technological aspects of mining, and the archaeological, economic, historical, legal and social aspects of mining and the mining industry
Value: The Hossein Farmy Scholarship covers the cost of the United Kingdom tuition fees and provides an annual, tax-free maintenance stipend at the standard United Kingdom Research rate (£14,553)

Country of Study: United Kingdom
Closing Date: End of April
Funding: Private
Additional Information: If you have any questions about the Hossein Farmy Scholarship please email pgr-scholarships@sheffield.ac.uk

For further information contact:

Email: pgr-scholarships@sheffield.ac.uk

International Merit Postgraduate Scholarship

Value: 50% of the annual postgraduate tuition fee
Country of Study: Any country
Application Procedure: Please visit website www.sheffield.ac.uk/international/enquiry/money/pgtmerit for more details
Closing Date: 15 June

For further information contact:

Email: l.a.tarrant@sheffield.ac.uk

Postgraduate Taught Sheffield Scholarship

Purpose: To offer the Postgraduate Taught Sheffield Scholarship to international students starting a taught masters programme in September
Type: Scholarship
Value: £2,000 if your tuition fees are between £16,800 and £18,900 and £2,500 if your tuition fees are £18,901 and upwards
Country of Study: United Kingdom
Application Procedure: Subject to meeting the eligibility and award criteria the Postgraduate Taught Sheffield Scholarship will be awarded automatically – no application is required
Closing Date: 21 February

For further information contact:

Email: eurec@sheffield.ac.uk

Sheffield Postgraduate Scholarships

Purpose: The scholarships are for students who meet at least one of our widening participation criteria and/or students who achieve a first in their undergraduate degree. If your application is successful you can use the scholarship towards fees or living expenses, the choice is yours

Eligibility: You can apply for a scholarship if you meet the following four criteria: Studying a taught postgraduate course full-time or part-time for a maximum of four years. Domiciled in the United Kingdom (United Kingdom) or European Union (European Union) and not charged international rate fees. Not already qualified at masters level, or higher. Must be self funding - courses fully funded by the NHS or the Initial Teacher Training bursary, or courses that are eligible for undergraduate funding such as integrated masters are not eligible
Type: Scholarship
Value: £10,000 each
Country of Study: United Kingdom
Application Procedure: A selection panel consisting of senior academic and professional services staff, will consider your scholarship application. The panel will look at personal circumstances of those who meet widening participation criteria and take into account achievements of the academic merit applicants. All applications are anonymised and the decision of the panel is discretionary and final
Closing Date: 14 May
Additional Information: If you have any questions or would like to talk to someone about the awards, please contact the Financial Support Team on 0114 222 1319 or sheffieldscholars@sheffield.ac.uk

For further information contact:

Email: sheffieldscholars@sheffield.ac.uk

University Prize Scholarships

Subjects: These scholarships are open to applicants in all subjects
Purpose: Each year the University offers a small number of University Prize Scholarships to the very best PhD applicants
Type: Scholarship
Value: Full tuition fees (United Kingdom, European Union or overseas), an annual, tax-free maintenance stipend of £20,000,a Research Training Support Grant of £2,500 per year for study visits, conferences, books, consumables and equipment
Country of Study: United Kingdom
Closing Date: 23 January
Additional Information: If you have any questions about University Prize Scholarships please email pgr-scholarships@sheffield.ac.uk

For further information contact:

Email: pgr-funding@sheffield.ac.uk

White Rose Studentships

Subjects: Plant biology
Purpose: Collaborative research networks within the three White Rose Universities
Eligibility: Open to United Kingdom, European Union, and international applicants who will register with the University for a PhD degree
Level of Study: Postgraduate, Research
Type: Studentship
Value: Home/European Union tuition fees, an annual maintenance grant of £14,057
Length of Study: 3 years
Frequency: Annual
Study Establishment: One of the three White Rose Universities
Application Procedure: Candidates can check the website for further details
Closing Date: Check with the website www.sheffield.ac.uk/postgraduate/research/scholarships/whiterose
Additional Information: International applicants are only eligible if they can show sufficient funds to cover the difference between the United Kingdom and international students tuition fee

For further information contact:

Email: s.beecroft@shef.ac.uk
Contact: Simon Beecroft

University of South Australia

GPO Box 2471, Adelaide, SA 5001, Australia

Tel: (61) 8 8302 6611/3615
Fax: (61) 8 8302 2466/3997
Email: research.international@unisa.edu.au
Website: www.unisa.edu.au

The University of South Australia is an innovative and successful institution with a distinctive profile. It is committed to educating professionals, creating and applying knowledge and serving the community.

Division of Business Student Mobility Scholarships

Subjects: Business programme
Purpose: To assist business students undertaking an international exchange (via the UniSA International Student Exchange Program) at a partner university
Eligibility: Open to both undergraduate and postgraduate coursework students enroled in a Division of Business program and are participating in exchange for the first time
Level of Study: Postgraduate
Type: Scholarship
Value: A$5,000 for Institutional Partner Scholarships; $2,500 for Student Mobility Scholarships
Frequency: Annual
Application Procedure: For extended criteria and application details, please contact: Ms Sarah Oolyer-Braham
Closing Date: 30 January

For further information contact:

Tel: (44) 8 8302 0880
Email: sarah.collyer-braham@unisa.edu.au
Contact: Ms Sarah Collyer-Braham, Administrative Officer

Donald Dyer Scholarship – Public Relations & Communication Management

Subjects: Public relations and communication management
Purpose: To encourage research of an original nature leading to the advancement of knowledge in public relations and communication
Eligibility: Open to candidates who have achieved First Class (Honours) or equivalent. Candidates from discipline areas such as public relations, communication, marketing or advertising are encouraged to apply
Level of Study: Postgraduate, Research
Type: Scholarship
Value: A$22,000 per year (tax-free) plus one return travel airfare between the candidate's home location and Adelaide, and organized by the University
Frequency: Annual
Study Establishment: University of South Australia
Country of Study: Australia
Application Procedure: Check website for further details
Closing Date: 29 October
Contributor: Bequest from the estate of the Late Sylvia Dyer

For further information contact:

Tel: (61) 8 8302 4493
Fax: (61) 8 8302 4745
Email: david.brittan@unisa.edu.au
Contact: David Brittan, (Postgraduate Research) Education Administrator

Ferry Scholarship

Subjects: Physics and chemistry

Purpose: Promoting study and research in physics and chemistry

Eligibility: Open to Australian citizens under the age of 25 years on January 1st of the year of the award, who have completed at least 4 years of tertiary education studies, have a First Class (Honours) (or equivalent undergraduate degree), and have enroled as full–time students for a Master's Degree or Doctorate by research in chemistry or physics

Level of Study: Postgraduate

Type: Scholarship

Value: A$7,500 per year

Length of Study: Up to 3 years (Doctorate) and 2 years (Masters Degree)

Frequency: Annual

Application Procedure: Applications can be filled online

Closing Date: 31 January

Contributor: Bequest from the late Cedric Arnold Seth Ferry

For further information contact:

Tel: (44) 8302 3967
Email: jenni.critcher@unisa.edu.au
Contact: Jenni Critcher

Lewis O'Brien Scholarship

Subjects: Education, arts, and social sciences

Purpose: To assist and encourage Aboriginal and Torres Strait Islander people in postgraduate study in a field of particular relevance and potential benefit to the Indigenous Australian community

Eligibility: Open to Aboriginal and Torres Strait Islander people eligible to undertake a postgraduate program in the division of education, arts and social sciences

Level of Study: Postgraduate

Type: Scholarship

Value: Maximum A$10,000 per year (A$2,500 will be paid on commencement and the remainder will be paid in instalments during the year subject to certification by the supervisor of satisfactory progress)

Frequency: Annual

Country of Study: Australia

Application Procedure: Candidates must contact Ms Jillian Mille for further information

Closing Date: 11 February

Contributor: Division of Education, Arts and Social Sciences

For further information contact:

Tel: (61) 8 8302 9151
Fax: (61) 8 8302 7034
Email: jillian.miller@unisa.edu.au
Contact: Jillian Miller, Coordinator Indigenous Support Services

Margaret George Award

Subjects: Archival research, history

Purpose: To encourage and facilitate use of National Archives collection by promoting archival research in Australia and encouraging scholarly use of its holdings

Eligibility: Open to postgraduate degree holders, historians, academics, independent researchers, or journalists with a talent for research

Level of Study: Postgraduate

Type: Award

Value: A$10,000

Frequency: Annual

Country of Study: Australia

Application Procedure: Check website for further details

Closing Date: 30 June

Additional Information: Successful applicants may undertake their award at any time from the date of the announcement of the award until June 30th the following year

For further information contact:

Tel: (61) 2 6212 3986
Fax: (61) 2 6212 3699
Email: derina.mclaughlin@naa.gov.au
Contact: Derina McLaughlin

Research Training Program International Scholarships in Australia (RTPI)

Subjects: Scholarships are awarded to study the subjects offered by the university

Purpose: To offer Research Training Program international (RTPi) Scholarships

Eligibility: Generally, an applicant must have first-class Honours or equivalent to gain a scholarship at the University of South Australia. An awardee must be enrolled on a full-time basis as a candidate for a Masters by Research or PhD at the University of South Australia. An awardee shall be enrolled as an internal candidate at the University of South Australia

Level of Study: Research

Type: Scholarship

Value: At least A$26,682 per annum for 3 years, with the possibility of one 6-month extension

Length of Study: 3 years

Country of Study: Any country

Closing Date: 31 August

Funding: Government

Additional Information: An RTPi scholarship will cover your tuition fees and your Overseas Student Health Cover (OSHC), and provide a stipend (living allowance), but will not pay for travel expenses. A thesis allowance is funded to cover the cost of printing and binding the thesis

For further information contact:

Email: research.degrees@unisa.edu.au

Synchrotron Microprobe Analysis of Nickel Laterites Scholarship

Subjects: Synchrotron Microprobe Analysis of Nickel Laterites
Purpose: To enable deserving students to pursue a career in the related fields
Eligibility: Open to citizens or permanent residents of Australia or New Zealand who have achieved an Honours Degree or equivalent
Level of Study: Postgraduate
Type: Scholarship
Value: A\$4,000 per year
Frequency: Annual
Study Establishment: University of South Australia
Country of Study: Australia
Application Procedure: Applicants must write to the faculty
Closing Date: 30 September
Contributor: South Australian Premier's Science and Research Fund grant with matching funding from Rio Tinto and BHP-Billiton

For further information contact:

Email: andrea.gerson@unisa.edu.au
Contact: Andrea Gerson

Trevor Prescott Memorial Scholarship

Subjects: All subjects
Purpose: To help youth in the South Australian community to advance their careers through further postgraduate studies
Eligibility: Open to students between 20 and 30 years of age who desire to do further postgraduate studies or equivalent
Level of Study: Unrestricted
Type: Scholarship
Value: Up to A\$25,000 and may be divided between more than 1 recipient
Frequency: Annual
Application Procedure: Check website for further details
Closing Date: 30 June
Funding: Foundation
Contributor: The Masonic Foundation Inc
Additional Information: Preference is not given to a Freemason or to a member of the family for the scholarship

For further information contact:

Tel: (61) 8 8443 9909
Fax: (61) 8 8443 9928
Email: masfound@senet.com.au

University of South Wales

Pontypridd, Wales NP18 3YG, United Kingdom

Tel: (44) 8455 767 778
Fax: (44) 1443 654 050
Email: enquiries@southwales.ac.uk
Website: www.southwales.ac.uk

The University of Wales, Newport, has been involved in higher education for more than 80 years, and its roots go back even further to the first Mechanics Institute in the town, which opened in 1841.

University of Wales Postgraduate Studentship

Subjects: All subjects approved by the University
Purpose: To support a student with a First Class (Honours) Degree at the university to progress to postgraduate research
Level of Study: Doctorate, Doctorate
Type: Scholarship
Frequency: Annual
Study Establishment: University of Wales
Country of Study: Wales
Application Procedure: Applicants must check with the website or the University
Funding: Private, Private
Contributor: Private benefactions

For further information contact:

Email: shelley.doolan@uwtsd.ac.uk

University of Southampton

University of Southampton, University Road, Southampton SO17 1BJ, United kingdom

Tel: (44) 238 059 5000
Fax: (44) 238 059 3131
Email: admissns@soton.ac.uk
Website: www.soton.ac.uk
Contact: Student Marketing Office

The University of Southampton was granted its Royal Charter. Today, the University is one of the United Kingdom's top ten research universities, offering a wide range of postgraduate taught and research courses in engineering, science, mathematics, law, arts, social sciences, medicine and health and life sciences.

Honor Frost Foundation Masters and/or Doctoral Awards in Maritime Archaeology

Subjects: The Foundation's mission is to promote the advancement and research, including publication, of maritime archaeology with particular focus on the eastern Mediterranean
Purpose: The Foundation's mission is to promote the advancement and research, including publication, of maritime archaeology with particular focus on the eastern Mediterranean
Eligibility: 1. The successful candidate must demonstrate a genuine interest in maritime archaeology and would be expected to develop the subject in their home country upon their return. 2. The successful candidate will also be required to submit annual reports on their progress to the Honor Frost Foundation and contribute towards the Foundation's activities during the duration of their studies, including supporting the annual lecture. 3. The MA Scholarship requires: a good 2:1 honours degree (or equivalent) in either archaeology or a related discipline. You must be a citizen of Cyprus, Lebanon, Egypt or Syria
Level of Study: Postgraduate
Type: Award
Value: an annual stipend of £15,000 with an additional travel fund of £1,000
Frequency: Annual
Country of Study: Any country
Application Procedure: The MA Scholarship requires: a good 2:1 honours degree (or equivalent) in either archaeology or a related discipline. You must be a citizen of Cyprus, Lebanon, Egypt or Syria. The MA scholarship is tenable for one year, commencing September, at an annual stipend of £15,000 with an additional travel fund of £1,000, which can be drawn as required during your study. Tuition fees will also be paid directly to the University at the appropriate fee rate. There may also be the opportunity to continue to PhD, fully funded, for a further 3 years on completion of the MA/MSc. Application for this studentship is by CV; a sample of written work (4,000 words, max); and a personal statement of up to 800 words explaining why you feel you are suitable for the MA or PhD scholarship. Please also arrange for two academic references to be sent independently by the deadline
Closing Date: 15 May
Funding: Private

For further information contact:

Email: lkb@soton.ac.uk
Contact: Dr Lucy Blue

University of Southern California (USC)

College of Letters, Arts and Sciences, University Park, Mail Code 4012, Los Angeles, CA 90089, United States of America

Tel: (1) 213 740 2531
Fax: (1) 213 740 8607
Website: www.usc.edu/schools/college
Contact: Mr Richard Tithecott, Assistant Administrative Director

Located near the heart of Los Angeles, the University of Southern California (USC) is a private research university. It maintains a tradition of academic strength at all levels, from the earliest explorations of the undergraduate to the advanced scholarly research of the postdoctoral Fellow.

Master of Business Administration/Master of Science in Industrial and Systems Engineering (MSISE) Programme

Application Procedure: Please contact the organisation for details

For further information contact:

Tel: (1) 213 740 4893
Fax: (1) 213 740 1120
Email: gradapp@enroll1.usc.edu
Contact: MBA Admissions Officer

University of Stirling

University of Stirling, Stirling FK9 4LA, United Kingdom

Email: international@stir.ac.uk
Website: www.stir.ac.uk

The University of Stirling is a United Kingdom research intensive campus university founded by Royal charter in 1967 in Stirling, Scotland. It is ranked among the top

60 universities in the world that are under 50 years old by the Times Higher Education World University Rankings.

Postgraduate Awards for International Students at University of Stirling in United Kingdom

Purpose: University aims to be at the forefront of research and learning that helps to improve lives
Level of Study: Postgraduate
Type: Award
Value: Each award has a value of £3,000
Country of Study: Scotland
Application Procedure: Students from eligible countries will automatically be assessed for an International Postgraduate Award as part of the admissions process; there is no separate application required for this award. Students who qualify for award will be notified by admissions, once academic offer conditions have been met
Closing Date: 31 August
Additional Information: For details, contact international@stir.ac.uk

For further information contact:

Email: graduate.admissions@stir.ac.uk

University of Strasbourg

Email: admin-at-icfrc.fr
Contact: Dr Stéphanie Loison, Scientific coordinator

Strasbourg has a long tradition of scientific excellence, in particularly in chemistry, built through the ages by renowned scientists such as Louis Pasteur, Charles Gerhardt and Nobel Laureates Adolf von Baeyer, Emil Fischer, Hermann Staudinger, Jean-Marie Lehn and more recently Martin Karplus (2013) and now Jean-Pierre Sauvage (2016). The result is that Strasbourg has always been a center of excellence in molecular science, with its top 20 worldwide ranking.

PhD Fellowships in Chemistry

Subjects: Chemistry
Purpose: To pursue PhD
Eligibility: Foreign students can apply for these PhD fellowships, as well as French national students, who wish to pursue their PhD research study in Strasbourg from September or October

Length of Study: 3 years
Country of Study: France
Closing Date: 15 November
Funding: Foundation
Contributor: Ernest Solvay Fund and the FRC Foundation

For further information contact:

Email: admin@scholarship-positions.com

University of Strathclyde

McCance Building, 16 Richmond Street, Glasgow G1 1XQ, United Kingdom

Tel: (44) 14 1548 2387
Fax: (44) 14 1552 0775
Email: r.livingston@mis.strath.ac.uk
Website: www.strath.ac.uk

Department of Chemical and Process Engineering PhD Studentship

Subjects: Chemical and process engineering
Eligibility: Candidates should be highly motivated and have a First Class Honours degree in chemical engineering, physics or chemistry. An MSc/MEng in science or engineering and previous experience in the field of chemistry of materials would be an advantage. Students will engage in the Department's research seminar programme, and will have opportunities to attend national and international conferences. Other generic skills and courses are open to students, including scientific writing, presentation and careers workshops. International students must be proficient in English language (the University's entry requirements are IELTS 6.5, TOEFL 600 including the test of written English, TOEFL 250 computer based test or TOEFL 90–95 internet based test)
Level of Study: Doctorate
Type: Studentship
Value: The award will cover United Kingdom/European Union tuition fees and will pay a stipend of £13,863 per year (for 3 years). International students would have to pay the difference between the Home/European Union and international fee
Length of Study: 3 years
Frequency: Annual
Study Establishment: University of Strathclyde
Country of Study: Scotland

Application Procedure: Please send your curriculum vitae and a covering letter, indicating your previous experience and fields of interest and include the details of at least two academic referees to Dr S. V. Patwardhan

Closing Date: 30 May

For further information contact:

Tel: (44) 141 548 5786
Email: Siddharth.Patwardhan@strath.ac.uk

Fraser of Allander Institute Scholarships for MSc Applied Economics

Subjects: Applied Economics
Purpose: Scholarships are available to join the MSc Applied Economics programme
Value: Each scholarship worth £6,000
Country of Study: United Kingdom
Application Procedure: Candidates interested in applying should provide a maximum 1,000 word statement demonstrating, through their ideas, experience and future career plans (including their reasoning for joining the MSc Applied Economics) why they should be awarded this scholarship. Candidates will also be considered on the overall quality of their application and financial need. The mode of applying is online. Please visit website www.sbs.strath.ac.uk/apps/schol arships/economics/applied-economics.asp for online application
Closing Date: 1 June
Additional Information: For more details, please visit the website www.strath.ac.uk/studywithus/scholarships/strathcly debusinessschoolscholarships/economicsscholarships/frasero fallanderinstitutefaihomeeuscholarshipsformscappliedecono mics/

For further information contact:

Email: sbs.admissions@strath.ac.uk

International Marketing Bursaries

Subjects: MSc in international marketing
Purpose: To assist applicants who are seeking sources of financial assistance to pursue full-time postgraduate study in international marketing
Eligibility: A limited number of departmental bursaries are available to well qualified candidates
Level of Study: Postgraduate
Type: Departmental bursaries
Value: £3,000
Length of Study: 1 year

Frequency: Annual
Study Establishment: University of Strathclyde
Country of Study: United Kingdom
Application Procedure: Applicants must contact the Department of Marketing
Contributor: Department of Marketing, Strathclyde University

For further information contact:

Tel: (44) 141 548 3451
Email: mscim.helpdesk@strath.ac.uk

International Strathclyde Prestige Award for Excellence in Business Translation and Interpreting in United Kingdom

Subjects: Strathclyde University is a major international technical university situated in Glasgow, Scotland. The mission of the University is socially progressive and brings positive change in the life of its students for society and the world
Purpose: Scholarship is available for pursuing Postgraduate degree program
Eligibility: To be eligible, the applicants must meet all the following criteria: 1. To apply for this scholarship, the applicants must be available to commence their academic studies in the United Kingdom. By the start of the academic year in September. 2. The candidates must hold a first degree at first class or upper second class honors, or equivalent
Level of Study: Postgraduate
Type: Award
Value: £5,000 with tuition fees
Frequency: Annual
Country of Study: United Kingdom
Application Procedure: 1. Applications must be processed with the below link. r1.dotmailer-surveys.com/432p4736-ae3nzoab. 2. Supporting Documents: As part of the application, the applicants must provide a 300-word essay demonstrating your ability to contribute to the field of study which you are applying for. 3. Admission Requirements: To apply for this scholarship you need to take admission onto the full-time Postgraduate Study program at the university
Closing Date: 31 May
Funding: Private
Additional Information: For further information, check the following link: r1.dotmailer-surveys.com/432p4736-ae3nzoab

For further information contact:

Email: hass-pg-enquiries@strath.ac.uk

John Mather Scholarship

Subjects: Postgraduate instructional courses in business administration and management, economics, hospitality management and tourism
Purpose: To encourage potential rising stars in the business world, selected on the basis of academic merit
Eligibility: Open to students from the vicinity of the former Strathclyde Region area enrolled in postgraduate instructional courses
Level of Study: Postgraduate
Type: Scholarship
Value: UK£5,000
Length of Study: 1 year
Frequency: Annual
Study Establishment: Strathclyde Business School
Country of Study: United Kingdom
No. of awards offered: 10
Application Procedure: Applicants must be nominated by their Head of Department on forms available from the Faculty Officer
Closing Date: 23 July
Funding: Trusts
Contributor: John Mather Charitable Trust
No. of awards given last year: 4
No. of applicants last year: 10

For further information contact:

Email: e.leiper@mis.strath.ac.uk

Mac Robertson Travelling Scholarship

Subjects: All subjects
Purpose: To provide funding that will enrich and further the award holder's academic experience and research achievements
Eligibility: Applicants should be postgraduate research students currently registered at Strathclyde or Glasgow Universities
Level of Study: Postgraduate, Research
Type: Scholarship
Value: £2,000–3,000
Length of Study: 1 year
Frequency: Annual
Study Establishment: University of Strathclyde
Country of Study: United Kingdom
No. of awards offered: 20
Application Procedure: Application forms can be downloaded from the website www.strath.ac.uk
Closing Date: 4 May
Funding: Individuals

Contributor: Mac Robertson
No. of awards given last year: 11
No. of applicants last year: 20
Additional Information: The aim of the scheme is to provide funding which will enrich and further the award holder's experience and research achievements

For further information contact:

Email: cathy.bonner@mis.strath.ac.uk

University of Strathclyde and Glasgow Synergy Scholarships

Subjects: All subjects, but the project must be jointly supervised between Glasgow and Strathclyde universities
Purpose: To assist applicants and students who are seeking sources of financial assistance to pursue full-time postgraduate research study at the University of Strathclyde
Eligibility: Applicants should be PhD candidates of outstanding academic merit
Level of Study: Doctorate
Type: Scholarship
Value: £12,600 per year
Length of Study: Up to 3 years
Frequency: Annual
Study Establishment: University of Strathclyde
Country of Study: United Kingdom
Application Procedure: Applicants seeking nomination for the awards should contact the department they wish to join. Existing research students should contact their head of department or supervisor
Closing Date: Check the website
Funding: International office
Contributor: University
Additional Information: For more information, visit the website www.strath.gla.ac.uk/synergy

For further information contact:

Email: synergy@gla.ac.uk

University of Surrey

University of Surrey, Guildford GU2 7XH, United Kingdom

Tel: (44) 148 386 050
Fax: (44) 148 386 071
Email: maphdinfo@surrey.ac.uk
Website: www.maths.surrey.ac.uk

Studentship in Physical Sciences

Purpose: The aim of this project is to determine the microscopic length scales that control the macroscopic rheology using novel magnetic resonance imaging and optical light scattering techniques in combination with conventional tools
Eligibility: To be eligible for this studentship, you are required to have a First, 2:1 or merit in a masters degree in a physical sciences subject. If English is not your first language you are required to have an IELTS of 6.5 or above. United Kingdom and European Union candidates are eligible to apply. Activities at the Cambridge centre focus on the development of new science and technology for well construction, with an emphasis on drilling and automation
Level of Study: Graduate
Type: Studentship
Frequency: Annual
Country of Study: Any country
Application Procedure: In order to apply for this studentship, kindly contact Noelle Hartley, Centre Manager for the EPSRC CDT in MiNMaT Greater understanding of the hierarchy of relevant structural lengths from the nanoscale to the macroscale will enable the design of improved complex fluid formulations with predictable rheological properties. N.Hartley@surrey.ac.uk
Closing Date: 30 April
Funding: Private

For further information contact:

Tel: (44) 1483 683467
Email: N.Hartley@surrey.ac.uk

University of Sussex

Postgraduate Office, Sussex House, Falmer, Brighton BN1 9RH, United Kingdom

Tel: (44) 1273 606 755
Fax: (44) 1273 678 335
Email: information@sussex.ac.uk
Website: www.sussex.ac.uk
Contact: Mr Terry O'Donnell

The University of Sussex is one of the United Kingdom's foremost research institutions. The University boasts a distinguished faculty that includes 17 Fellows of the Royal Society and four Fellows of the British Academy. The University has around 12,000 students, 25% of whom are postgraduates.

Chancellor's International Scholarship

Purpose: Applications are invited for University of Sussex to international postgraduate students who can demonstrate academic excellence
Value: 50% tuition fee reduction
Length of Study: 2 years
Country of Study: Any country
Application Procedure: Apply online. For application procedures, please visit website www.sussex.ac.uk/study/money/apply-chancellors-international-scholarship
Closing Date: May
Contributor: University of Sussex

For further information contact:

Email: information@sussex.ac.uk

PhD Studentships in Mathematics

Subjects: PhD studentships are provided in the field of Mathematics. Supervision is available in diverse topics
Eligibility: Applicants must hold, or expect to hold, a Bachelor degree at first or upper second class, and/or a Masters degree, in Mathematics, or equivalent non United Kingdom qualifications. United Kingdom and European Union residents are eligible. Overseas (ex-European Union) students may also apply, but applicants should note that the awards waive the fees at United Kingdom/European Union rates only, of £3,900 per year. Ex-European Union students must state in their application how they would fund the remaining fees. (Overseas fees will be £13,000 per year in total, so additional funding of £9,100 will be needed)
Level of Study: Doctorate
Type: Studentship
Value: Each PhD studentship includes a tax free maintenance bursary of £13,863 per year, plus a waiver of United Kingdom/European Union fees for 3.5 years
Length of Study: Scholarships will be offered for 3.5 years
Country of Study: United Kingdom
Application Procedure: The mode of applying is online
Closing Date: 31 August
Contributor: University of Sussex, United Kingdom

For further information contact:

Email: pgresearch@maths.ed.ac.uk

Sussex Malaysia Scholarship

Subjects: Scholarship is awarded in the fields offered by the university

Purpose: The aim of the Sussex Master Scholarship is to enable and encourage academically able students from Malaysia

Eligibility: Listed are the eligibility requirements. 1. Be a Malaysian national. 2. Be classified as overseas for fee purposes. 3. Be self-financing. 4. Have accepted an offer to study an eligible Masters course at Sussex

Type: Scholarship

Value: £3,500 towards your tuition fee when you register on your Masters at Sussex

Length of Study: 2 years

Country of Study: United Kingdom

Application Procedure: Register your interest in the scholarship through the postgraduate application system when you accept our offer of a place on an eligible Masters course. To submit the registration, use the below link. www.sussex.ac.uk/study/masters/apply/log-into-account

Closing Date: 1 August

Contributor: University of Sussex

For further information contact:

Email: scholarships@sussex.ac.uk

University of Sydney

Scholarships and Financial Support Service, Jane Foss Russell Building, G02, Sydney, NSW 2006, Australia

Tel: (61) 2 8627 8112
Fax: (61) 2 8627 8485
Email: scholarships.officer@sydney.edu.au
Website: www.sydney.edu.au
Contact: Manager

The role of the University of Sydney is to create, preserve, transmit, extend and apply knowledge through teaching, research, creative works and other forms of scholarship. In carrying out its role, the University affirms its commitment to the values and goals of institutional autonomy, recognizes the importance of ideas and intellectual freedom to pursue critical and open enquiry, as well as social responsibility, tolerance, honesty and respect, as the hallmarks of relationships throughout the University community. It also understands the needs and expectations of those whom it serves and constantly improves the quality and delivery of its services.

Alexander Hugh Thurland Scholarship

Subjects: Agriculture

Eligibility: Open to the graduates from other universities with relevant degree

Level of Study: Doctorate, Postgraduate, Research

Type: Scholarship

Value: A$24,653 per year

Length of Study: 2 years for Masters by research candidates and 3 years with a possible 6-month extension for research doctoral candidates

Frequency: Dependent on funds available

Study Establishment: The University of Sydney

Country of Study: Australia

Application Procedure: Check website www.sydney.edu.au/agriculture for further details

Funding: Trusts

For further information contact:

Tel: (61) 2 8627 1002
Fax: (61) 2 8627 1099
Email: pg@agric.usyd.edu.au

Dean's International Postgraduate Research Scholarships

Subjects: Scholarships are awarded in any of the courses within in faculty of science at University of Sydney

Purpose: Scholarships are available to undertake a research doctorate degree (PhD) programme

Level of Study: Postgraduate

Value: The scholarship consists of the full cost of academic tuition fees plus a stipend equivalent to an Australian Postgraduate Award indexed annually (RTP stipend rates for 2016 are A$26,288 for full-time students)

Length of Study: 3 years

Study Establishment: Faculty of Science

Country of Study: Australia

Application Procedure: International students (except Australia or New Zealand) can apply for these postgraduate research scholarships. An annual stipend allowance equivalent to the Research Training Program (RTP) stipend rate indexed annually

Closing Date: 30 April

Additional Information: For more details, visit website scholarship-positions.com/deans-international-postgraduate-research-scholarships-in-australia-2015-2016/2015/03/03/

Dr Abdul Kalam International Postgraduate Scholarships

Eligibility: International students with an offer of admission for a Masters program in the Faculty of Engineering & Information Technologies in Semester II. Open to all international applicants with an offer of admission for a Master of Information Technology, Master of Information Technology

Management or combined Master of Information Technology/Master of Information Technology Management program in the Faculty of Engineering and IT at the time of submitting a scholarship application. Students who have already commenced their postgraduate studies, or students transferring from other postgraduate programs are not eligible

Level of Study: Postgraduate

Type: Scholarship

Value: 50% tuition fees for a maximum of 1 year

Frequency: Annual

Country of Study: United States of America

Application Procedure: Applicants must complete an online scholarship application (sydney.edu.au/engineering/scholarships/postgraduate/dr-kalam.shtml), and submit their academic transcripts and admission letter of offer to the Scholarships Officer by the scholarship closing date. Successful candidates will be informed by June

Closing Date: May

Additional Information: Please check at sydney.edu.au/engineering/scholarships/postgraduate/future-coursework.shtml for more information

For further information contact:

Tel:	(61) 2 9351 8155
Fax:	(61) 2 9351 7082
Email:	engineering.scholarships@sydney.edu.au

International Postgraduate Research Scholarships (IPRS) Australian Postgraduate Awards (APA)

Subjects: All subjects

Purpose: To support candidates with exceptional research potential

Eligibility: Open to suitably qualified graduates eligible to commence a higher degree by research. Australia and New Zealand citizens and Australian permanent residents are not eligible to apply

Level of Study: Doctorate, Postgraduate, Research

Type: Scholarship

Value: Tuition fees for IPRS, and an Australian Postgraduate Award for A$24,653 per year

Length of Study: 2 years for the Master's by research candidates, and 3 years with a possible 6-month extension for PhD candidates

Frequency: Annual

Study Establishment: The University of Sydney

Country of Study: Australia

Application Procedure: Applicants must complete an application form for admission available from the International Office

Closing Date: 31 July for Semester 1 and 15 December for Semester 2

Funding: Government

Contributor: Australian Government and University of Sydney

No. of awards given last year: 34

For further information contact:

Tel:	(61) 2 8627 8358
Fax:	(61) 2 8627 8387
Email:	infoschol@io.usyd.edu.au

Master of Business Administration Programme

Length of Study: 1 year

Application Procedure: Applicants must complete an application form supplying official transcripts and a Graduate Management Admission Test score

Closing Date: 31 October

For further information contact:

Tel:	(61) 2 9351 0038
Fax:	(61) 2 9351 0099
Email:	gsbinfo@gsb.usyd.edu
Contact:	MBA Admissions Officer

PhD Scholarship Healthcare Services for Older People

Subjects: Medical and health sciences, allied health (therapies), health services research

Purpose: To investigate the effectiveness of transition care services for older people

Eligibility: Open only to permanent residents and the citizens of Australia or New Zealand who have Honours Degree, or equivalent, in health–related discipline to undertake research studies

Level of Study: Postgraduate

Type: Scholarship

Value: A$22,000 per year

Length of Study: 3 years

Frequency: Annual

Study Establishment: University of Sydney

Application Procedure: Applicants must send their curriculum vitae, copy of academic transcript, names and contact details of at least 2 referees to Prof Cameron (preferably by email)

Closing Date: 14 August

For further information contact:

Tel:	(61) 2 9808 9236
Fax:	(61) 2 9809 9037
Email:	ianc@mail.usyd.edu.au
Contact:	Professor Ian Cameron

PhD Scholarship to Advance Aquaculture in Australasia

Subjects: Agricultural, veterinary and environmental sciences, biological sciences or fisheries sciences
Purpose: To improve the productivity and profitability of smallholder shrimp farms in Indonesia
Eligibility: Open only to the citizens of Australia or permanent residents
Level of Study: Postgraduate, Research
Type: Scholarship
Value: A$25,000 per year
Length of Study: 3 years
Frequency: Annual
Application Procedure: Applicants must mail their curriculum vitae, copy of academic transcript, proof of citizenship or permanent residency, names and contact details of at least 2 referees to Dr Toribio
Closing Date: 17 August

For further information contact:

Tel: (61) 612 9351 1609
Fax: (61) 612 9351 1618
Email: jennyt@camden.usyd.edu.au
Contact: Dr Jenny Ann Toribio

University of Tasmania

Private Bag 45, Hobart, TAS 7001, Australia

Tel: (61) 3 6226 2999
Fax: (61) 3 6226 2018
Email: scholarships@research.utas.edu.au
Website: www.utas.edu.au
Contact: Graduate Research Unit

The University of Tasmania was officially founded on January 1st 1890, by an Act of the Colony's Parliament and was only the fourth university to be established in 19th century Australia. The university represents areas of significant research strengths and substantial teaching endeavours.

Across PhD – Bio analytical Research – Pharmacokinetics and Drug Metabolism Scholarship

Subjects: Chemical sciences, medical biochemistry, clinical chemistry, pharmacology, or pharmaceutical sciences

Purpose: To promote research on retention mechanisms, breakthrough, and recovery for the model analytes together with appropriate characterization of the monolithic phase
Eligibility: Open to applicants who have achieved Honours 2a or equivalent
Level of Study: Postgraduate, Research
Type: Scholarship
Value: A$20,000 for living expenses
Length of Study: 3 and a half years
Frequency: Annual
Application Procedure: Applicants should send a curriculum vitae directly to Prof Paul Haddad. Check website for further details
Contributor: Pfizer Analytical Research Centre (PARC)

For further information contact:

Tel: (61) 3 6226 2179
Email: paul.haddad@utas.edu.au
Contact: Professor Paul Haddad, Director of ACROSS

Across PhD Scholarship; Analytical Chemistry; Rock Lobster Aquaculture

Subjects: Animal production, chemical sciences or soil and water sciences
Eligibility: Open to applicants who have achieved Honours 2a or equivalent
Level of Study: Postgraduate, Research
Type: Scholarship
Value: A$25,118 for living expenses
Length of Study: 3 and a half years
Frequency: Annual
Application Procedure: Applicants should send a curriculum vitae directly to Prof Paul Haddad. Check website for further details

For further information contact:

Tel: (61) 3 6226 2179
Email: paul.haddad@utas.edu.au
Contact: Professor Paul Haddad, Director of ACROSS

Across PhD, High Performance Ion Exchange Chromatography Scholarship

Subjects: Chemical sciences
Purpose: To investigate the feasibility of using HP-IEC for the separation and detection of small to medium MW organic acids and bases
Eligibility: Open to applicants who have achieved Honours 2a or equivalent

Level of Study: Postgraduate, Research
Type: Scholarship
Value: A$20,000 for living expenses
Length of Study: 3 and a half years
Frequency: Annual
Country of Study: Australia
Application Procedure: Applicants should send a curriculum vitae directly to Prof Paul Haddad. Check website for further details
Contributor: Pfizer Analytical Research Centre (PARC)

Cancer Council Honours Scholarship

Subjects: Cancer control
Purpose: To fund honours student to undertake research on cancer
Eligibility: Open to a full-time student undertaking honours in any area that focuses on cancer control
Level of Study: Research
Type: Scholarship
Value: A$10,000 (A$7,000 for living allowance and A$3,000 for research costs)
Length of Study: 1 year
Frequency: Annual
Application Procedure: Check website for further details
Closing Date: 31 October

For further information contact:

Tel: (61) 3 6226 4832
Email: g.m.woods@utas.edu.au
Contact: Greg Woods, Associate Professor

Cardiac Rehabilitation UTAS Exercise Physiology Graduate Research Scholarship

Subjects: Exercise physiology, medical and health sciences or medical physiology
Purpose: To investigate the effectiveness of provision of an exercise physiology service as part of a cardiac rehabilitation program, as well as identifying the optimal modality and intensity of exercise undertaken by patients as part of the program
Eligibility: Open to applicants who have achieved Honours 2a or equivalent. Only citizens of Australia or permanent residents can apply
Level of Study: Postgraduate, Research
Type: Scholarship
Value: A$19,616
Length of Study: 3 years

Frequency: Annual
Study Establishment: University of Tasmania
Country of Study: Australia
Application Procedure: Check website for further details
Closing Date: 30 June

For further information contact:

Tel: (61) 3 6324 5487
Email: Andrew.Williams@utas.edu.au
Contact: Dr Andrew Williams

Centre of Excellence in Ore Deposits PhD Scholarships

Subjects: Geology, geophysics or geochemistry with relevance to the location, formation, discovery or recovery of ore deposits
Purpose: For students to study within one of the five major programs of the centre: location, formation, discovery, recovery or technology
Eligibility: Open to students undertaking PhD research in the specified fields. Applicants require either an MSc in geology/geophysics or a first or upper second–class honours degree. Some experience in the minerals industry is preferred but not essential
Level of Study: Postgraduate
Value: A$20,000 - A$30,000 depending on qualifications and experience
Length of Study: 3 and a half years

For further information contact:

Tel: (61) 3 6226 2892
Email: j.mcphie@utas.edu.au
Contact: Jocelyn McPhie

Master of Business Administration Programme

Length of Study: Varies
Application Procedure: Applicants must contact The University of Tasmania Graduate School of Management for an application form

For further information contact:

Tel: (61) 2 2078 37
Fax: (61) 2 2078 62
Email: International.Office@admin.utas.edu.au
Contact: Graduate Administrator

Menzies Research Institute Honours Scholarship

Subjects: Epidemiology and communal diseases
Purpose: To support vital work in epidemiology, and diseases which affect the community
Eligibility: Open to a student eligible to undertake an honours research program in any area of research undertaken by the Institute
Level of Study: Research
Type: Scholarship
Value: A$5,000
Length of Study: 1 year
Frequency: Annual
Country of Study: Any country
Application Procedure: Applicants can apply through the Tasmania Honours Scholarship application form downloaded from the website. All potential honours students should contact the Honours Co-ordinator in their discipline to discuss interests and options
Closing Date: 31 October

For further information contact:

Email: enquiries@menzies.utas.edu.au

North Hobart Football Club Peter Wells Scholarships

Subjects: Sports
Purpose: To support North Hobart players while at UTAS
Eligibility: One scholarship available to a north-western/ northern student and one to a southern student with good academic records and who are available to play for the NHFC while studying at UTAS
Type: Scholarship
Value: A$3,000 and A$2,000
Length of Study: 1 year
Frequency: Annual
Country of Study: Any country
Contributor: The late Peter Wells

For further information contact:

Email: International.Scholarships@utas.edu.au,
             Scholarships.Office@utas.edu.au

Qantas Tasmanian Devil Research Scholarship

Subjects: Facial tumour disease
Purpose: To assist research into the facial tumour disease affecting devil populations
Eligibility: Open to researchers in facial tumour diseases
Level of Study: Research

Type: Scholarship
Value: Up to APA level, additional research funding may be available
Length of Study: 3 and a half years
Frequency: Annual
Country of Study: Any country
Application Procedure: Check website for further details
Contributor: Qantas

For further information contact:

Email: devil.appeal@utas.edu.au

Quantitative Marine Science PhD Scholarships

Subjects: Quantitative Marine Science
Purpose: To offer specialized graduate-level coursework in quantitative marine science (QMS)
Eligibility: Open to students who hold at least an upper second-class honours degree, or equivalent, and have a major in mathematics, physical sciences, life sciences, geomatics or Engineering
Level of Study: Doctorate
Type: Scholarship
Value: A$32,000 per annum. and production costs will also be provided
Length of Study: Up to 3 years
Frequency: Annual
Country of Study: Any country
Application Procedure: Application forms, conditions of awards and program information on Graduate Research Scholarships can be downloaded from the website
Funding: Private
Contributor: Commonwealth Scientific and Industrial Research Organisation (CSIRO) in partnership with the University of Tasmania
Additional Information: For further information on all Graduate Research Scholarships please contact the Graduate Research Office on (3) 6226 2766

For further information contact:

CSIRO-UTAS Joint PhD Program in Quantitative Marine Science, Private Bag 129, Hobart, TAS 7001, Australia

Tel: (61) 3 6226 2108
Email: Peter.Strutton@utas.edu.au
Contact: Professor Pete Strutton, Program Coordinator

Riawunna Postgraduate Scholarship

Purpose: To encourage an Aboriginal or Torres Strait Islander student to undertake honours or postgraduate coursework study at the University and committed to the advancement of knowledge about Aboriginal and Torres Strait Islander cultures and societies

Eligibility: Open to an Aboriginal or Torres Strait Islander student who undertake honours or postgraduate coursework study at the University

Level of Study: Postgraduate

Type: Scholarship

Value: A$3,000

Length of Study: 1 year

Frequency: Annual

Country of Study: Any country

Contributor: Riawunna

For further information contact:

Email: scholarships.referee@utas.edu.au

Sir Victor Burley Scholarship in Music

Subjects: Music

Purpose: The family of Victor Burley has endowed this scholarship to encourage the development of advanced music skills, especially in the classical music area

Eligibility: Open to student eligible to enter a postgraduate music course at the Conservatorium of Music preferably studying in a classical area of music

Level of Study: Postgraduate

Type: Scholarship

Value: A$1,000

Length of Study: 1 year

Frequency: Annual

Country of Study: Australia

Contributor: The family of the late Sir Victor Burley

For further information contact:

Email: Scholarships.Referee@utas.edu.au

Tasmania Honours Scholarships

Subjects: All subjects

Purpose: To encourage excellent students to continue their study at honours level

Eligibility: Open to students with excellent academic achievement in their undergraduate courses who wish to study at honours level. Additional benefits may be available to students who obtain a first-class honours degree and continue on to a research program at UTAS

Level of Study: Postgraduate

Type: Scholarship

Value: A$4,500; A$9,000 include a living allowance, course fees, support with accommodation and establishment fees and a return airfare to Tasmania if you live interstate

Length of Study: 1 year (full-time study)

Frequency: Annual

Country of Study: Any country

Application Procedure: Applicants can apply through the Tasmania Honours Scholarship application form from the website. All potential honours students should contact the Honours Co-ordinator in their discipline to discuss interests and options

Closing Date: 31 October

Additional Information: Six of the 10 awards will target students commencing study at the University of Tasmania

For further information contact:

Email: Scholarships.Referee@utas.edu.au

Tasmania University Cricket Club Scholarship

Subjects: Sports

Purpose: To support cricketers at UTAS

Eligibility: Available to a commencing or current student who can demonstrate a talent and commitment to cricket. Selection will based on the following five criteria: 1. Cricket skill i.e. representative levels and success at those levels. 2. Academic achievement and potential to succeed at university. 3. Leadership skills and experiences. 4. Cricket involvement e.g. coaching. 5. Community involvement. The selected student must be playing for, or be able to play for, the TUCC in the coming season. Potential applicants may also wish to visit the Cricket website (www.tucc.org.au/) to gain a better understanding about the club and its goals

Type: Scholarship

Value: A$3,000

Length of Study: 1 year

Frequency: Annual

Country of Study: Any country

Application Procedure: Apply online prior to closing date. Applications cannot be submitted after closing date. As applicants will be assessed on the quality of application, all questions should be answered in full. Please ensure care is taken with spelling and grammar. info.scholarships.utas.edu.au/AwardDetails.aspx?AwardId=281

Closing Date: 31 October

Contributor: Supporters and past players of the Tasmania University Cricket Club

For further information contact:

Email: chas.rose@gmail.com

Tasmanian Government Mining Honours Scholarships

Subjects: Geological research
Purpose: To encourage geological research at CODES on topics that are relevant to the Tasmanian minerals industry
Eligibility: Open to students undertaking research in the field of geology, with relevance to the Tasmanian minerals industry. Specialization in one or more of: ore deposit geology, igneous petrology, volcanology, structure, sedimentology, geochemistry or geophysics. Applicants require at least a credit average in geology units at the second or third year levels
Level of Study: Research
Type: Scholarship
Value: A\$5,000; A\$8,000 depending on qualifications and experience
Length of Study: 1 year
Frequency: Annual
Application Procedure: Applicants can apply through the Tasmania Honours Scholarship application form downloaded from the website
Closing Date: 31 October
Contributor: Mineral Resources Tasmania

For further information contact:

Tel: (61) 3 6226 2815
Email: garry.davidson@utas.edu.au
Contact: Dr Garry Davidson

Tasmanian Government Mining PhD Scholarship

Subjects: Geological research
Purpose: To encourage geological research undertaken at the ARC Centre of Excellence in Ore Deposits (CODES) on topics relevant to the Tasmanian minerals industry
Eligibility: The following eligibility criteria apply to this scholarship: 1. The scholarship is open to domestic (Australian and New Zealand) and international candidates. 2. The Research Higher Degree must be undertaken on a full-time basis. 3. Applicants must already have been awarded a First Class Honours degree or hold equivalent qualifications or relevant and substantial research experience in an appropriate sector. 4. Applicants must be able to demonstrate strong research and analytical skills
Level of Study: Doctorate, Research
Type: Scholarship
Value: A\$18,000–25,000 depending on qualifications and experience
Length of Study: 3 and a half years
Frequency: Annual

Country of Study: Any country
Contributor: Mineral Resources Tasmania

For further information contact:

Tel: (61) 3 6226 2819
Email: anita.parbhakar@utas.edu.au
Contact: Professor Rose Large

University of Technology Sydney (UTS)

PO Box 123 Broadway, Ultimo, NSW 2007, Australia

Tel: (61) 2 9514 1659
Email: clg.postgraduate@uts.edu.au
Website: ippg.uts.edu.au
Contact: UTS Institute for Public Policy and Governance

The University of Technology Sydney (UTS) is a thriving university located in the centre of Sydney, one of the world's most desirable and multicultural cities.

University of Technology Sydney Institute for Public Policy and Governance Postgraduate Scholarship in Australia, 2017

Subjects: Scholarships are awarded by the Institute for Public Policy and Governance.
Purpose: To support commencing University of Technology Sydney (UTS) Master of Local Government students by assisting them financially.
Eligibility: Australian or New Zealand citizen, or the holder of an Australian permanent resident visa or permanent humanitarian visa; and must have submitted an application and met the entry requirements for admission to the UTS Institute for Public Policy and Governance Master of Local Government degree by coursework degree; and must be commencing the UTS Institute for Public Policy and Governance Master of Local Government program; and must not have completed any study under any other postgraduate courses within the UTS Institute for Public Policy and Governance; and intend to enroll in a minimum of 12 credit points/session in the session immediately following the Scholarship selection; and all candidates must apply using the online UTS online Scholarship Application form to be eligible.
Level of Study: Postgraduate
Type: Scholarship
Value: The maximum value of this scholarship is A\$5,000 for each recipient

Length of Study: 1 year
Frequency: Annual
Country of Study: Any country
Application Procedure: Please note that Scholarship applicants must first submit an application for the UTS Master of Local Government to be considered for the Scholarship. To apply for the Master course, please request an application form from the Institute at postgraduate-at-uts.edu.au or on +61 2 9514 1659.
Closing Date: 6 March
Funding: Government
Additional Information: The UTS Institute for Public Policy and Governance (UTS:IPPG) Postgraduate Scholarship was designed to support local government professionals seeking to broaden their knowledge and skills through postgraduate study and to recognize the diverse pathways to a local government career

For further information contact:

Email: Alan.Morris@uts.edu.au

University of Texas

School of Public Health Health, Science Center, PO Box 20186, Houston, TX 77225, United States of America

Contact: Mr Robert E Roberts

Harry Ransom Center: Research Fellowships

Subjects: The fellowships support research in all areas of the humanities
Purpose: The fellowships are awarded for projects that require substantial on-site use of its collections
Eligibility: All applicants, with the exception of dissertation fellowship applicants, must have a PhD or be an independent scholar with a substantial record of achievement; if the PhD is in-progress, the proposal and letters of recommendation must clearly indicate a June 1st, completion in order to be eligible for fellowships. Dissertation fellowship applicants must be doctoral candidates engaged in dissertation research by the time of application. United States of America citizens and foreign nationals are eligible to apply. Previous recipients of Ransom Center fellowships are eligible to reapply after two full academic years have passed. All things being equal, however, preference is given to applicants who have not previously held a Ransom Center fellowship
Type: Research fellowship

Value: Stipends of US$3,000 per month. Also available are US$1,200–US$1,700 travel stipends and dissertation fellowships with a US$1,500 stipend
Frequency: Annual
Country of Study: United States of America
Application Procedure: Fellowships must be submitted electronically through an online fellowship account on the Ransom Center's website
Closing Date: 31 March
Additional Information: Please visit at www.hrc.utexas.edu/research/fellowships/

For further information contact:

Email: ransomfellowships@utexas.edu

Mobility Scooters Direct Scholarship Program

Purpose: Mobility Scooters Direct provides a $1,500 scholarship each year to selected students who apply to the program
Eligibility: 1. Must be enrolled in a minimum of 6 hours undergraduate or 3 hours graduate at an accredited University or College. 2. Must have taken at least 40 undergraduate credit hours or 10 graduate credit hours. 3. Must have proof of a declared major. 4. Must demonstrate involvement on campus or in the community of attended University or College. 5. Must attach one letter of recommendation on official letterhead. 6. You must be at least 18 years of age to apply. 7. You must be currently enrolled at your college or university during the time of submission. 8. You must have a 3.0 GPA or higher
Level of Study: Graduate
Type: Programme grant
Value: US$1,500
Frequency: Annual
Country of Study: Any country
Application Procedure: The below details have to be included in the application. 1. Your first & last name, ph. number & email address(s). 2. Statement or transcript of your Grade Point Average (GPA). Letter of recommendation should have the below entities. 1. All applicants must meet certain criteria outlined below and submit an application via email or United States mail. 2. Applicants are also required to provide a letter of recommendation from a teacher, professor or counselor from the school being attended by the applicant
Closing Date: 10 December each year
Funding: Private

For further information contact:

4135 Dr. M.L. King Jr Blvd. Store D21, Ft. Myers, FL 33916, United States of America

Email: orders@mobilityscootersdirect.com

University of Tokyo

9-7-3, Akasaka TK 107-0052, Japan

Tel: (81) 3 6271 4368
Contact: Fujixerox Co., Ltd., Kobayashi Fund, c/o Fuji
              Xerox

The University of Tokyo aims to be a world-class platform for research and education, contributing to human knowledge in partnership with other leading global universities. The University of Tokyo aims to nurture global leaders with a strong sense of public responsibility and a pioneering spirit, possessing both deep specialism and broad knowledge.

Kobayashi Research Grants

Subjects: Humanities and social sciences
Purpose: Grants are available to pursue research programme
Eligibility: International students from Asia, Oceania countries/regions. 1. Note the Asia-Pacific countries and regions as referred to here, it shows the following countries and regions
Type: Grant
Value: Maximum of ¥1,200,000 /person
Country of Study: Japan
Application Procedure: Please download the application documents and instructions for sending at the following link: www.fujixerox.com/eng/company/social/pdf/1.pdf
Closing Date: 28 February
No. of awards given last year: 39

For further information contact:

International Liaison Office Room 120, Environmental Studies Building 5-1-5 Kashiwanoha, Kashiwa, Chiba 277-8563, Japan

Kobayashi Research Grants in Humanities and Social Sciences

Subjects: Grants shall be conferred for individual research (not group research) in the field of Humanities (Cultural Science) or Social Sciences, with special emphasis on themes that help deepen the researcher's understanding and awareness of Japanese or Asian/Oceanian society and culture and enhance international interchanges among them in the future
Eligibility: Scholarships are offered in diverse fields to help students in upgrading their education

Type: Research
Value: Maximum ¥1,200,000 per grantee will be available to approximately 30 grantees. An amount from ¥3,20,000 to ¥1,200,000 per grantee was provided to 32 grantees for the program. (Depending upon the results of the Grantee Screening Committee's assessment, the actual amount for some grantees could be less than the originally requested amount.)
Study Establishment: Grants shall be conferred for individual research (not group research) in the field of Humanities (Cultural Science) or Social Sciences, with special emphasis on themes that help deepen the researcher's understanding and awareness of Japanese or Asian/Oceanian society and culture and enhance international interchanges among them in the future
Country of Study: Japan
Application Procedure: The mode of applying is online
Closing Date: 28 February
Additional Information: For more details please visit to the website scholarship-positions.com/kobayashi-research-grant-humanities-social-sciences-university-tokyo-japan/2017/01/24/

University of Twente

Universiteit Twente, Drienerlolaan 5, Enschede 7522 NB, Netherlands

Tel: (31) 53 489 9111
Email: info@utwente.nl
Website: www.utwente.nl/en

ASML Henk Bodt Scholarship

Subjects: MSc applied mathematics, applied physics, computer science, electrical engineering, embedded systems, mechanical engineering, systems and control
Purpose: The ASML Henk Bodt Scholarship supports a talented technical student who has completed (or is about to complete) the Bachelor of Science programme, and who is further motivated to pursue a 2 years full-time Master of Science degree in technical and scientific disciplines at the University of Twente
Eligibility: To qualify for a ASML Henk Bodt Scholarship, candidates must at least fulfill the following basic requirements: Bachelor of Science diploma, academic transcripts of each academic year from the BSc programme, cumulative Grade Point Average of at least 80% of the scale maximum of all courses of the BSc program, MSc programme admission

letter from the University of Twente, up-to-date curriculum vitae
Type: Scholarship
Value: The scholarship will provide financial support for the entire duration of the Master's degree (2-year period) which covers the full tuition fee and living expenses, approx. €22,000 per year
Length of Study: 2 years
Frequency: Annual
Country of Study: Any country
Closing Date: 1 March
Additional Information: Check details at www.utwente.nl/internationalstudents/scholarshipsandgrants/all/asml_henk_bodt_scholarship/

For further information contact:

Tel: (81) 40 268 6572
Email: scholarships@asml.com

Holland Scholarship

Purpose: The Holland Scholarship is a scholarship for excellent students from non-European Union/EEA countries, applying for a Bachelor or Masters programme at the University of Twente
Eligibility: Open to non-European Union/EEA countries. In order to be eligible for a Holland Scholarship, you should meet all the requirements as follows: your programme starts in the current academic year; you have not studied in the Netherlands before for a full degree (e.g. a Bachelor's or Master's degree); you are from a non-European Union/EEA country; you are an excellent student (i.e. CGPA of 7.5 (out of 10)); etc. Please check complete eligibility criteria at www.utwente.nl/internationalstudents/scholarshipsandgrants/all/holland-scholarship/
Type: Scholarship
Value: €5,000
Country of Study: Any country
Application Procedure: In order to apply for this scholarship, you already need to be (provisionally) admitted to one of the qualifying Bachelor or Master programmes
Closing Date: 1 April
Additional Information: Outcomes will be communicated by 15 May. Please note: if you apply for a Holland Scholarship without meeting all the requirements, your application will not be considered. www.studyinholland.nl/scholarships/holland-scholarship

For further information contact:

Email: info@utwente.nl

Orange Tulip Scholarship (OTS) China

Subjects: All subjects
Purpose: The Orange Tulip Scholarship (OTS) offers talented students from China the opportunity to obtain a Masters degree at the University of Twente. The scholarship programme is highly selective, offering two scholarships for the current academic year
Level of Study: Graduate
Type: Scholarship
Value: €24,000. The scholarship consists of a reduction of the institutional tuition fee for non-EEA students (to €2,083
Country of Study: Any country
Application Procedure: Applications should be submitted to the Netherlands Education Support Office (NESO) China. Visit their website for more information about the requirements for the Orange Tulip Scholarship (OTS), or send an email to ots@nesochina.org. Visit the website of NESO China
Closing Date: 1 March

Orange Tulip Scholarship (OTS) Indonesia

Subjects: All subjects
Purpose: The Orange Tulip Scholarship (OTS) offers talented students from Indonesia the opportunity to obtain a Master degree at the University of Twente
Level of Study: Graduate
Type: Scholarship
Value: €24,000 per year
Country of Study: Any country
Application Procedure: Applications should be submitted to the Netherlands Education Support Office (NESO) Indonesia. Visit their website for more information about the requirements for the Orange Tulip Scholarship (OTS), or send an email to ots@nesoindonesia.or.id
Closing Date: 15 April
Additional Information: Please visit www.utwente.nl/internationalstudents/scholarshipsandgrants/all/ots-indonesia/ for more information

For further information contact:

Email: info@utwente.nl

Orange Tulip Scholarship (OTS) Mexico

Subjects: All subjects
Purpose: The Orange Tulip Scholarship (OTS) offers talented students from Mexico the opportunity to obtain

a Master degree at the University of Twente. The scholarship programme is highly selective, offering one scholarship for the current academic year

Level of Study: Graduate
Type: Scholarship
Value: €24,000
Frequency: Annual
Country of Study: Any country
Application Procedure: Visit the website of NESO Mexico. Applications should be submitted to the Netherlands Education Support Office (NESO) Mexico. Visit their website for more information about the requirements for the Orange Tulip Scholarship (OTS), or send an email to ots@nesomexico.org
Closing Date: 1 April
Additional Information: Check information at www.utwente.nl/internationalstudents/scholarshipsandgrants/all/ots-mexico/

University of Ulster

Research Office, Cromore Road, Coleraine, Co. Londonderry BT52 1SA, Northern Ireland

Tel: (44) 28 7032 4729
Fax: (44) 28 7032 4905
Email: hj.campbell@ulster.ac.uk
Website: www.ulster.ac.uk
Contact: Mrs H Campbell, Administrative Officer

The University of Ulster is a dynamic and innovative institution, which is very proud of its excellent track record in the education and training of researchers. Our doctoral graduates can demonstrate outstanding achievements in advancing knowledge and making breakthroughs of relevance to the economic, social and cultural development of society.

University Studentships/Vice-Chancellor's Research Studentships (VCRS)

Subjects: Arts, Humanities and Social Sciences Computing, engineering and Built Environment Life and Health Sciences Business
Purpose: From time to time the University makes funding available to support University Studentships. The awards for United Kingdom, European Union and overseas students. Applicants should indicate in the appropriate area on their University application form that they wish to apply for a University Studentship/VCRS award

Eligibility: These awards are open to applicants who hold or, expect to obtain, a first or upper second class honours degree and provide for payment of fees and maintenance allowance
Level of Study: Doctorate
Type: Scholarships
Value: £14,777
Length of Study: up to 3 years subject to satisfactory progress
Frequency: Annual
Country of Study: United Kingdom
No. of awards offered: 700
Application Procedure: www.ulster.ac.uk/doctoralcollege/postgraduate-research/apply
Closing Date: February each year
Funding: Government
No. of awards given last year: 30
No. of applicants last year: 700

For further information contact:

Email: hj.campbell@ulster.ac.uk

Vice Chancellor

Subjects: All subjects
Purpose: To assist candidates of a high academic standard to complete research degrees (PhD)
Eligibility: Applicants must have or expect to obtain the minimum of an upper second class Honours degree in a specific research area (as advertised). Applications are invited from United Kingdom, European Union and overseas students. Only candidates who are new applicants to PhD will be eligible
Level of Study: Doctorate, Postgraduate
Type: Scholarship
Value: Fees and maintenance grant
Length of Study: Up to 3 years
Frequency: Annual
Study Establishment: Ulster University
Country of Study: United Kingdom
Application Procedure: Applicants must apply online research.ulster.ac.uk/info/prospective/funding.html
Closing Date: Check website
Funding: Private
No. of awards given last year: 30
No. of applicants last year: 800
Additional Information: Applications are invited from United Kingdom, European Union and Overseas students. Further information is available on the website www.ulster.ac.uk/research study

For further information contact:

Email: research.support@sydney.edu.au

University of Verona

Via S. Francesco, 22, VR 37129 Verona, Italy

Tel: (39) 45 802 8588
Contact: University of Verona

The University of Verona is a university located in Verona, Italy. It was founded in 1982 and is organized in 12 Departments.

Invite doctoral programme

Subjects: Arts and humanities, legal and economic sciences, health and life sciences, natural and engineering sciences
Purpose: The INVITE doctoral programme aims to encourage each student's intellectual curiosity and support the acquisition of critical thinking skills by training them in the use of innovative theoretical tools and practical methods
Value: Living allowance: €2,000/month for 36 months, mobility allowance: €600/month for 36 months, family allowance: €150/month for 36 months
Country of Study: Italy
Closing Date: 16 April

For further information contact:

Email: invite@ateneo.univr.it

University of Waikato

Private Bag 3105, Hamilton, New Zealand

Tel: (64) 7 856 2889 ext. 6723
Fax: (64) 7 838 4600
Email: scholarships@waikato.ac.nz
Website: www.waikato.ac.nz/asd/groups/scholarships.shtml
Contact: Ms Maureen Phillips, Assistant Manager, Scholarships

The Mission of the University of Waikato is to be the New Zealand leader in the business of knowledge. The business of knowledge includes the development of new knowledge, the transmission and dissemination of knowledge, and the assembling and structuring of knowledge.

Acorn Foundation Eva Trowbridge Scholarship

Subjects: All subjects
Purpose: To support the people of Tauranga and the Western Bay of Plenty community
Eligibility: Adult students (25 years and over) studying at the University of Waikato's Tauranga campus and residing in the areas administered by Tauranga City Council or Western Bay of Plenty District Council are eligible for the award
Type: Scholarship
Value: NZ$3,000 per year
Length of Study: 1 year
Frequency: Annual
Country of Study: New Zealand
Closing Date: 31 August
Contributor: Acorn Foundation
Additional Information: The Scholarship will be paid in one lump sum to the successful applicant

For further information contact:

Tel: (64) 7 838 4964 or 7 858 5195
Email: scholarships@waikato.ac.nz

Alan Turing Prize

Subjects: Computer science and mathematics
Purpose: To encourage students to develop strong joint interests in Computer Science and Mathematics
Eligibility: Open to students who have strong interest in computer science and mathematics
Level of Study: Research
Type: Prize
Length of Study: 3 years
Frequency: Annual
Country of Study: Any country
Application Procedure: Check website for further details
Contributor: Council of the University of Waikato

For further information contact:

Email: info@waikato.ac.nz

Alumini Master's Scholarship

Subjects: All subjects

Purpose: To support a student who has graduated with a degree of the University of Waikato and is enroled for a Masters Degree at this University in the year of tenure

Eligibility: Open to New Zealand citizens or permanent residents who have qualified for a First Degree from the University of Waikato and be enroled full-time for a Masters Degree at the University of Waikato in the year of tenure. The candidate must be in their final year of study for the degree

Level of Study: Postgraduate

Type: Scholarship

Value: NZ$5,500 plus actual tuition fees up to a maximum of NZ$4,000

Length of Study: 1 year

Frequency: Annual

Application Procedure: Check website for further details

Closing Date: 31 October

Additional Information: The Scholarship will be awarded to a student who demonstrates academic merit; who is active in University affairs and who contributes to the activities of the School or Faculty in which they are enroled; who demonstrates willingness to maintain an active relationship with the Alumni programme; who demonstrates willingness to attend Alumni functions and promotional activities; who is considered to be a good ambassador for the University of Waikato and the Alumni Association

For further information contact:

Email: scholarships@waikato.ac.nz

Chamber of Commerce Tauranga Business Scholarship

Subjects: Management Studies

Purpose: For the benefit of members of the Tauranga Chamber of Commerce to assist the recipient to undertake study at postgraduate level

Eligibility: Open to citizens or permanent residents of New Zealand having a tertiary or relevant professional qualification; must have a minimum of 5 years' relevant work experience; must own or be employed by a business or organization which is a member of the Tauranga, Chamber of Commerce; must have the support of his/her employer and currently not enroled in a Postgraduate Diploma in Management Studies with the Waikato, Management School, University of Waikato. Check website for further details

Level of Study: Postgraduate

Type: Scholarship

Value: The value of the scholarship is usually equivalent to 1 year's fees (a total of four papers)

Length of Study: Above 2 years

Frequency: Annual

Application Procedure: Check website for further details

Closing Date: 30 November

For further information contact:

Email: scholarships@waikato.ac.nz

Evelyn Stokes Memorial Doctoral Scholarship

Subjects: Geography, tourism and environmental planning

Eligibility: Open to candidates enroled or intending to enrol in an approved full-time programme of study at the University of Waikato in the years of tenure of the scholarship. Applicants who have undertaken study outside the University of Waikato must supply a full verified copy of their academic transcript(s) from their previous institution(s)

Level of Study: Doctorate

Type: Scholarship

Value: NZ$5,000 per year

Length of Study: 3 years

Frequency: Annual

Study Establishment: University of Waikato

Country of Study: New Zealand

Application Procedure: Check website for further details

Closing Date: 31 October in the year prior to that in which the award will be taken up

Funding: Private

Additional Information: The Scholarship will end on the completion of doctoral study, or after 3 years, whichever is the earlier date, provided that the candidate is enroled during this time in an appropriate programme of studies. Completion takes place when the postgraduate studies committee has accepted the report of the examiners and recommends the awarding of the degree

For further information contact:

Email: scholarships@waikato.ac.nz

Lee Foundation Grants

Subjects: All subjects

Eligibility: Open to citizens and residents of Singapore or Malaysia, must have completed at least 1 year of study or are studying at the University of Waikato in Hamilton

Type: Grant

Value: NZ$500

Application Procedure: Check website for further details

Closing Date: 30 April

Additional Information: Grants are awarded on the basis of above average academic performance

For further information contact:

Email: scholarships@waikato.ac.nz

Priority One Management Scholarship

Subjects: Management studies
Eligibility: Open to citizens or permanent residents of New Zealand who have a tertiary or relevant professional qualification with a minimum of 5 years relevant work experience, own or be employed by a business or organization which is a member of Priority One, have the support of his/her employer, must not already be enroled in a Postgraduate Diploma in Management Studies with the Waikato, Management School, University of Waikato, not have been a previous recipient of any Waikato Management School, University of Waikato
Level of Study: Postgraduate
Type: Scholarship
Value: Equivalent to 1 year's fees
Length of Study: 2 years
Frequency: Annual
Application Procedure: Check website for further details
Closing Date: 30 November

For further information contact:

Email: scholarships@waikato.ac.nz

Tauranga Campus Research Masters Scholarship

Purpose: At this university, candidates can study a broad range of subjects to shape a qualification that matches to their strengths and career interests. It helps the candidate with career planning, developing a CV and cover letters, interview skills, enhancing their employability skills.
Eligibility: For students who have applied to enrol full-time in a thesis of 90-points or more as part of their first master's degree at the University of Waikato and will be based at the Tauranga campus.
Level of Study: Postgraduate
Type: Scholarship
Value: Up to NZ$23,000
Frequency: Annual
Country of Study: Any country
Closing Date: 30 April
Funding: International office

For further information contact:

Te Mata Kairangi School of Graduate Research, The University of Waikato, Private Bag 3105, Hamilton 3240, New Zealand

Tel: (64) 7 858 5096
Email: scholarships@waikato.ac.nz

Ted Zorn Waikato Alumni Award For Management Communication

Subjects: Management studies
Purpose: To provide an opportunity for peer recognition of graduates of the department who have, since their graduation, distinguished themselves in a field of management communication
Eligibility: Open to candidates holding a responsible position in an organization or in a project, sustainability and/or workplace well being; must know the use of creativity and initiative in performing the responsibilities of the position. Check website for further details
Level of Study: Postgraduate
Type: Award
Value: NZ$1,000
Frequency: Annual
Application Procedure: Check website for further details
Closing Date: 31 December

For further information contact:

Email: jbeaton@waikato.ac.nz
Contact: Jean Beaton

University of Waikato Masters Research Scholarships

Subjects: All subjects
Purpose: To encourage research at the University, principally by assisting with course-related costs
Eligibility: Open to citizens and permanent residents of New Zealand who have qualified for a first degree and be enroled full-time for a first Masters or Master of Philosophy degree at the University of Waikato in the year of tenure
Level of Study: Postgraduate
Type: Research grant
Value: NZ $12,000, of which up to NZ$3,500 is to be applied to tuition fees for the masters degree. The remainder (NZ$8,500 in the case of a full Scholarship) will normally be paid out in two instalments
Length of Study: 1 year
Frequency: Annual
Application Procedure: Check website for further details
Closing Date: 31 October and 30 April annually
No. of awards given last year: 65

Additional Information: Should a student also hold another fees scholarship, the University of Waikato Masters Research Scholarship will pay the balance of any fees (up to NZ$3,500)

For further information contact:

Tel:	(64) 7 858 5136 or 7 858 5195
Email:	scholarships@waikato.ac.nz

University of Waikato MBA Programme

Length of Study: 1 year; 2 years
Application Procedure: All applicants must return a complete application form. Candidates may be required to sit a Graduate Management Admission Test or TOEFL exam

For further information contact:

Tel:	(64) 7 838 4439
Fax:	(64) 7 838 4269
Email:	international@waikato.ac.nz
Contact:	MBA Admissions Officer

University of Wales, Bangor (UWB)

Bangor North Wales, Bangor, Wales, Gwynedd LL57 2DG, United Kingdom

Tel:	(44) 12 4838 2025/18
Fax:	(44) 12 4837 0451
Email:	admissions@bangor.ac.uk
Website:	www.bangor.ac.uk
Contact:	The Student Recruitment Unit

The University of Wales, Bangor (UWB) is the principal seat of learning, scholarship and research in North Wales. It was established in 1884 and is a constituent institution of the Federal University of Wales. The University attaches considerable importance to research training in all disciplines and offers research studentships of a value similar to those of other United Kingdom public funding bodies.

Bangor University Merit Scholarships for International Students

Eligibility: All international students will be automatically considered for these scholarships. These scholarships are not open to United Kingdom/European Union applicants

Type: Scholarship
Value: £2,500 (Bangor campus); £2,000 (London centre). Candidates who are fully sponsored by a third party will not be entitled to these Scholarships
Frequency: Annual
Country of Study: Any country
Application Procedure: All applicants will be automatically considered for these scholarships. No additional scholarship application needed
Additional Information: Please check at www.bangor.ac.uk/international/future/mcrit_scholarships.php#ug for detailed information. These scholarships are available for both January intake and September intake courses

For further information contact:

Email:	international@bangor.ac.uk

Gold and Silver Scholarships

Subjects: Banking, Management, Business and Finance, and Law
Purpose: To provide financial support to full-time students on all MSc, MBA and MA programmes
Eligibility: Open to applicants who wish to apply for a postgraduate MBA or MA degree programme included in the scholarship scheme
Level of Study: Postgraduate, MBA
Type: Scholarship
Value: Gold Scholarship £5,000 per year. Silver Scholarship £2,000 per year
Length of Study: 1 year
Frequency: Annual
Study Establishment: Bangor University
Country of Study: United Kingdom
Application Procedure: There is no application form for scholarships. Candidates who wish to be considered for the awards should include a letter listing their main academic and personal achievements together with a short essay on why they have chosen to study at Bangor and a curriculum vitae. For further information contact at law.pg@bangor.ac.uk
Closing Date: 1 March (Interim deadline); 1 July (Final deadline)
Funding: Government

For further information contact:

Tel:	(44) 1248 382 644
Fax:	(44) 1248 383 228
Email:	b.hamilton@bangor.ac.uk
Contact:	Bethan Hamilton-Hine Scholarships (Gold and Silver)

MSc Bursaries

Subjects: Sports and exercise psychology, sports and exercise physiology, sports science and exercise rehabilitation
Eligibility: Open to applicants with good second class honours degree in sports science or health and to students with a 2:2 degree or a degree from a different academic area will also be considered
Level of Study: Postgraduate
Type: Bursary
Value: £2,500 (United Kingdom/European Union students); £3,500 (non-European Union international students)
Length of Study: 1 year (full-time); 2 years (part-time); 30 weeks full-time (diploma)
Frequency: Dependent on funds available
Study Establishment: Bangor University
Country of Study: United Kingdom
Application Procedure: Complete a Postgraduate Application Form with a four page (maximum) curriculum vitae or resumé. Refer to the website for further details or mail to postgraduate@bangor.ac.uk
Closing Date: 30 June
Contributor: Bangor University
Additional Information: £1,000 internal bursaries to former SHES (or related disciplines) students (who have 1st class undergraduate degree). £1,000 internal assistantships in addition to the other bursaries aimed at the very best students

For further information contact:

Tel:	(44) 1248 383 493
Email:	mscsport@bangor.ac.uk
Contact:	James Hardy

Open PhD Studentships

Subjects: English, history, Welsh history and archaeology, linguistics and English language, modern languages, music, theology and religious studies, Welsh creative industries
Eligibility: Open to candidates who have applied unsuccessfully to a United Kingdom funding council (e.g. the AHRC or the ESRC) to study at Bangor
Level of Study: Doctorate
Type: Studentship
Value: Fees plus maintenance grant
Frequency: Dependent on funds available
Application Procedure: Applicants must submit a scholarship application form along with a summary of your proposed research project in up to 500 words
Closing Date: Please check website

For further information contact:

Email:	s.lee@bangor.ac.uk

Santander Taught Postgraduate Scholarships

Subjects: All subjects
Purpose: The Santander Group will be awarding a number of 1 year undergraduate and taught postgraduate scholarships to current Bangor University students
Eligibility: The scholarship fund aims to reward the most academically gifted students from countries that are supported by the Santander Universidades scheme. The award will be given to students from the following 11 countries: Argentina, Brazil, Chile, Colombia, Mexico, Portugal, Puerto Rico, Spain, Uruguay and Venezuela. To be eligible for the postgraduate scholarship you will have to have studied within a University which is part of the Santander Universidades Scheme
Type: Scholarship
Value: All studentships are for one year only and vary from £3,000–£4,166
Application Procedure: Application forms and guidance notes for the Santander Scholarship Scheme are available on the University website www.bangor.ac.uk/scholarships/santander.php.en
Closing Date: 10 December
Additional Information: For further information or if you have any questions about the scheme, please contact Academic Registry

For further information contact:

Email:	k.chidley@bangor.ac.uk
Contact:	Mrs Karen Chidley, Academic Registry

University of Wales (Bangor) MBA in Banking and Finance

Length of Study: 1 year
Country of Study: Any country
Application Procedure: Applicants must submit an application form, together with two references and copies or transcripts of previous qualifications. Where necessary TOEFL and IELTS scores must be included
Closing Date: 31 August, for admission in October

For further information contact:

Tel:	(44) 1248 371 408
Fax:	(44) 1248 370 769
Email:	international@bangor.ac.uk
Contact:	MBA Admissions Officer

University of Warwick

Tel:	(44) 2476 523 523
Fax:	(44) 2476 461 606
Website:	www.warwick.ac.uk
Contact:	Project Officer, Postgraduate Scholarships

The University of Warwick offers an exciting range of doctoral, research-based and taught Master's programmes in the humanities, sciences, social sciences and medicine. In the 2001 Research Assessment Exercise, Warwick was ranked 5th in the United Kingdom for research quality. Postgraduate students make up around 35% of Warwick's 18,000 students. The University is located in the heart of United Kingdom, adjacent to the city of Coventry and on the border with Warwickshire.

Argentina Chevening Scholarship

Subjects: All subjects
Eligibility: Applicants should be nationals of Argentina not currently registered at the University
Level of Study: Postgraduate
Type: Scholarship
Value: UK cost of Academic fee and maintenance
Length of Study: 1 year
Study Establishment: University of Warwick
Country of Study: United Kingdom
Application Procedure: Applicants must complete an application form, available from the British Council
Contributor: University of Warwick, Foreign and Commonwealth office

For further information contact:

Email: info@britishcouncil.org

College of Continuing Professional Studies Doctoral Scholarship

Subjects: Projects in the area of culture and development – the arts, creative industries and heritage in either international development, or other forms of development
Purpose: Scholarship is available for pursuing doctoral degree level at the University of Warwick
Eligibility: To be eligible for the scholarship, candidates must have received an unconditional offer for entry to CCPS MPhil/PhD programme by January 31st. The scholarship scheme is open to both European Union and Overseas candidates

Level of Study: Doctorate
Type: Scholarship
Value: The value of the scholarship will be around £18,000 per year. The precise amount will be confirmed at the time of the offer
Study Establishment: Drury University
Country of Study: United Kingdom
Application Procedure: The mode of applying is online
Closing Date: 31 January
Contributor: Centre for Cultural Policy Studies
Additional Information: The successful candidate will be notified before the end of February

For further information contact:

Email: drury@drury.edu

Colombia Postgraduate Awards (Warwick Manufacturing Group/Colfuturo)

Subjects: WMG (Warwick Manufacturing Group) taught masters courses
Purpose: To support Master's Columbian students at WMG
Eligibility: Applicants should be nationals of Columbia, not currently registered on a postgraduate course at the University, and should have received an offer of a place from WMG. Only students who have been awarded a COLFUTURO scholarship-loan are eligible
Level of Study: Postgraduate
Type: Scholarship
Value: full tuition fees
Length of Study: 1 year
Frequency: Dependent on funds available
Study Establishment: University of Warwick United Kingdom
Country of Study: United Kingdom
Application Procedure: Applicants must apply via COLFUTURO
Funding: Private
Contributor: WMG/COLFUTURO
Additional Information: Non-renewable, for taught masters only

For further information contact:

Email: yosoyfuturo@colfuturo.com

Colombia Postgraduate Awards (Warwick/ Foundation for the Future of Colombia - Colfuturo)

Subjects: Any except MBA or WMG courses
Purpose: To support Columbian students on postgraduate courses at Warwick

Eligibility: Applicants should be nationals of Columbia and classed as an international fee-payer. Applicants can be registered on an Undergraduate course at the University of Warwick, but should have received a place on a Postgraduate Taught Master's course at Warwick. Only students who have been awarded a COLFUTURO scholarship-loan are eligible
Level of Study: Postgraduate
Type: Scholarship
Value: Tuition fees
Length of Study: 1 year
Frequency: Dependent on funds available
Study Establishment: University of Warwick
Country of Study: United Kingdom
Application Procedure: Application should be submitted via COLFUTURO
Funding: International office
Contributor: Foundation for the Future of Colombia Colfuturo (COLFUTURO)
Additional Information: Non-renewable, for taught masters only

For further information contact:

Email: yosoyfuturo@colfuturo.com.co

Karim Rida Said Foundation Postgraduate Award (KRSF/Warwick)

Subjects: All subjects
Purpose: To support students from the Middle Eastern region on Postgraduate courses at Warwick
Eligibility: Applicants should be Jordanian, Iraqi, Lebanese, Palestinian or Syrian nationals and be resident in the Middle East. Applicants should meet all other eligibility criteria as set by KRSF and awards will only be offered to applicants who already hold an offer of a place at Warwick
Level of Study: Postgraduate
Type: Scholarship
Length of Study: 1 year
Study Establishment: University of Warwick
Country of Study: United Kingdom
Application Procedure: Applications are submitted via KRSF website www.krsf.org/whatwedo/masters
Funding: International office
Contributor: KRSF
No. of awards given last year: 2
Additional Information: Non-renewable, for taught masters only

For further information contact:

Tel: (44) 24 7652 2469
Email: j.c.inegbedion@warwick.ac.uk
Contact: Jon Inegbedion

Mexico Postgraduate Award (Chevening/ Brockmann/Warwick)

Subjects: All subjects
Purpose: To support Mexican students on a postgraduate course at Warwick
Eligibility: Applicants should be nationals of Mexico, not currently registered at the University of Warwick and should have received an offer of a place at Warwick
Level of Study: Postgraduate
Type: Scholarship
Value: Full tuition fees plus maintenance
Length of Study: 1 year
Study Establishment: University of Warwick
Country of Study: United Kingdom
Application Procedure: Applicants must complete an application
Closing Date: 9 May
Funding: Government
Contributor: The Foreign and Commonwealth Office and the Brockmann Foundation
No. of awards given last year: 1
Additional Information: Non-renewable

For further information contact:

Tel: (44) 24 7657 2686
Email: ana_delcarmen@hotmail.com
Contact: Ana Gallegos, Adviser for Latin America - International Office

School of Law - Brazil Postgraduate Award

Subjects: Law
Purpose: To support students from Brazil on LLM programme at Warwick
Eligibility: Open to prospective full-time postgraduate students in any postgraduate degree within the Law School. Applicants can be registered on Undergraduate courses at the University of Warwick, but should have received a place for taught master courses at Warwick Law School
Level of Study: Postgraduate
Type: Scholarship
Value: 50% towards tuition fees
Length of Study: 1 year
Frequency: Dependent on funds available
Study Establishment: University of Warwick
Country of Study: United Kingdom
Application Procedure: Applicants must complete an online application form
Closing Date: 31 May
Contributor: Warwick Law School

Additional Information: Non-renewable, deducted from tuition fees, for taught masters only

For further information contact:

Email: paula.nascimento@britishcouncil.org.br

Sociology Departmental MA Scholarship

Subjects: Overseas
Purpose: We are delighted to confirm that 10 awards of £5,000 are available for students commencing MA study in the Sociology department in Autumn. The award will automatically be deducted from the winners' tuition fees.
Eligibility: 1. Open to applicants on all Sociology taught Masters programmes. 2. Candidates must apply to the university and have paid their application fee no later no later than 26 April. You must submit your application to the MA programme before submitting your scholarship application. 3. Successful candidates must obtain an offer from the university before taking up the award. 4. Candidates may apply concurrently to other funding sources; however, successful candidates who receive major tuition funding elsewhere will be disqualified.
Level of Study: Postgraduate
Type: Scholarship
Value: £2,500
Length of Study: 2 year
Frequency: Annual
Country of Study: Any country
Closing Date: 26 April
Funding: Foundation

For further information contact:

Social Sciences Building, The University of Warwick, Coventry CV4 7AL, United Kingdom

Email: m.j.wolfe@warwick.ac.uk

Warwick Postgraduate Research Scholarships

Eligibility: Open to Home, European Union and Overseas students from all disciplines at Warwick. For more details, please refer to the website
Level of Study: Doctorate
Type: Scholarship
Value: £3,390 for full-time students for the payment of academic fees at the Home/European Union rate. A maintenance grant, in line with the United Kingdom Research Council stipend, of £13,290 for full-time award holders
Country of Study: United Kingdom

Application Procedure: Please refer to the website www2.warwick.ac.uk/services/academicoffice/gsp/scholarship/apply/pgr_guidelines_2015-16.pdf
Closing Date: 12 January
Additional Information: Students and applicants who wish to apply for an AHRC doctoral award should apply to the WPRS competition and will automatically be considered for both competitions

For further information contact:

Email: aci@mrc.ac.za

University of Washington

School of Business Administration, 110 Mackenzie Hall Box 353200, Seattle, WA 98195, United States of America

Tel: (1) 206 543 4661
Fax: (1) 206 616 7351
Email: mba@u.washington.edu
Contact: MBA Admissions Officer

African American Heritage Endowed MBA Scholarship

Purpose: This scholarship is available for African-American MBA students who are attending the Foster Business school at the University of Washington in Seattle
Eligibility: 1. Must be an African American student. 2. Must be an MBA candidate at the time of application. 3. Must be enrolled at the Foster Business School at the University of Washington in Seattle. 4. This award is for United States of America students
Level of Study: Graduate
Type: Scholarship
Value: US$10,000
Frequency: Annual
Country of Study: United States of America
Application Procedure: Applications and information about the African American Heritage Endowed MBA Scholarship are available online at the University of Washington Foster School of Business website. To apply for this award, students must first be accepted to the MBA program at the University of Washington in Seattle. Eligible students who are interested in this award should contact the Michael G. Foster School of Business for further information about the admissions and scholarship application process. All applications must be completed online by the deadline date

Closing Date: 15 April
Funding: Foundation

For further information contact:

124 Mackenzie Hall Box 353200, Seattle, WA, 98195-3200, United States

Tel: (1) 206 543 4661
Email: scholarships@swe.org

University of Waterloo

200 University Avenue West, Waterloo, ON N2L 3G1, Canada

Email: rchild@uwaterloo.ca

International Research Partnership Grants (IRPG)

Purpose: The International Research Program Grants (IRPG) programs are internal seed grants aimed to provide Waterloo researchers with incentives to develop new or existing international research collaborations with leading institutions known for high quality research and global ranking
Eligibility: Projects should involve a group of Waterloo researchers and international partners. Preference will be given to projects with multiple Waterloo faculties/departments and a network of partner institutions;; 1. Preference will be given to projects that have not received IRPG funding for a previous project with the same international partners. 2. Preference is given to applications where matching cash contribution is from a new source or one that is outside of University of Waterloo, instead of existing research funds
Level of Study: Graduate
Type: Grants and fellowships
Value: Up to C$20,000, 50% of the costs
Frequency: Annual
Country of Study: Any country
Application Procedure: You could refer to the following pdf for further instructions. uwaterloo.ca/research/sites/ca. research/files/uploads/files/irpg_program_guidelines-30-nov-2018.pdf
Closing Date: 1 May and 1 November annually
Funding: Private

For further information contact:

200 University Avenue West, Waterloo, ON N2L 3G1, Canada

Email: rchild@uwaterloo.ca

Mitacs Accelerate Fellowship

Purpose: The Mitacs Accelerate Fellowship provides a long-term funding and internship option for master's and PhD students. Recipients can also access professional development training that helps them ensure project success and gain in-demand career skills
Level of Study: Graduate
Type: Fellowship
Value: C$40,000 per year
Length of Study: 18 months
Frequency: Annual
Country of Study: Any country
Application Procedure: Interested applicants can apply for the Accelerate Fellowship at any time. All other Accelerate program guidelines apply. 1. Review the following information when you begin writing your proposal. Eligible research and adjudication criteria 1. Writing Your Proposal guide Policies. 2. Submit Cover Sheet to Office of Research contact below, with a copy of the draft proposal. 3. Get feedback on the proposal from all participants and the Mitacs Program contact below. 4. Collect all required signatures: intern(s), professor(s), partner representative and the Office of Research contact below. 5. Email your proposal package to your Mitacs Program contact below Additional Information available on the Mitacs website
Funding: Private

For further information contact:

Tel: (1) 519 888 4567
Email: accelerate@mitacs.ca

University of West London

International Ambassador Scholarships at University of West London

Purpose: The International Ambassador Scholarship recognises and provides financial support for outstanding students who wish to act as ambassadors for the University of West London
Eligibility: Applicants must be: 1. A self-funded overseas full fee-paying paying student (please note: European Union applicants are not eligible). 2. An offer holder for an undergraduate or postgraduate course at UWL. This means, you must have already applied for a course of study at this University and you must have already received an official offer from one of our Admissions Officers. 3. The International Ambassador Scholarship will be awarded on a competitive basis to candidates who demonstrate enthusiasm and the ability to be an excellent international student ambassador

Level of Study: Graduate
Type: Scholarship
Frequency: Annual
Country of Study: Any country
Application Procedure: To be considered for the scholarship, you must have been offered a place to study on a full-time undergraduate or postgraduate course at the University of West London. The deadline for the intakes are as follows: 1. For courses starting in January applications must be received by 30 November
Closing Date: 30 June
Funding: Private

For further information contact:

Tel: (44) 20 8231 2914
Email: int.app@uwl.ac.uk

University of Western Australia

35 Stirling Highway, Crawley, WA 6009, Australia

Tel: (61) 8 9380 2490, 8 6488 6000
Fax: (61) 8 9380 1919, 8 6488 1380
Email: general.enquiries@uwa.edu.au
Website: www.uwa.edu.au

Since its establishment in 1911, the University of Western Australia has helped to shape the careers of more than 75,000 graduates. Their success reflects the UWA's balanced coverage of disciplines in the arts, sciences and professions.

Advanced Consumer Research PhD Scholarship

Subjects: Law
Purpose: To study the effectiveness of Commonwealth, State and Territory consumer protection laws in relation to information disclosure
Eligibility: Open to those who have completed an undergraduate degree in law with honours or equivalent research qualifications
Level of Study: Postgraduate
Type: Scholarship
Value: A$25,000 per year
Length of Study: 3 years and 6 months
Frequency: Annual
Study Establishment: The University of Western Australia
Application Procedure: Check website for further details
Closing Date: 3 August

For further information contact:

Tel: (61) 8 6488 2947
Email: eileen.webb@uwa.edu.au
Contact: Eileen Webb, Faculty of Law

Health Effects of Air Pollution (Top-Up)

Subjects: Biological sciences or medical and health sciences
Purpose: To support various projects in the School of Population Health
Eligibility: Open to those doing research in Australia
Level of Study: Postgraduate
Type: Scholarship
Value: A$10,000, plus Australian Dollar; 2,500 for relocation costs
Frequency: Annual
Study Establishment: University of Western Australia
Country of Study: Australia
Application Procedure: Candidates must apply direct to the faculty. Check website for further details
Closing Date: 1 December

For further information contact:

Tel: (61) 8 6488 7804
Email: Angus.Cook@uwa.edu.au
Contact: Dr Angus Cook, Research Fellow

Master of Business Administration Programme

For further information contact:

Tel: (61) 9 3803 939
Fax: (61) 9 3824 071
Email: icweb@acs.edu.au
Contact: MBA Admissions Officer

Natural Gas/LNG Production Scholarships

Subjects: Chemical engineering, chemical sciences, physical sciences or resources engineering
Purpose: To use the research outcomes to improve the design of LNG production trains and to treat contaminated gas reserves
Eligibility: Open to candidates who have achieved Second Class (Honours) or equivalent
Level of Study: Postgraduate
Type: Scholarship
Value: A$31,118 per year
Length of Study: 3 years

Frequency: Annual
Country of Study: Australia
Application Procedure: Check website for further details
Closing Date: 17 December

For further information contact:

Tel: (61) 6488 2954
Fax: (61) 6488 1964
Email: Eric.May@uwa.edu.au
Contact: Dr Eric F May

The Science & Innovation Studentship Award

Subjects: Science
Purpose: To promote innovation in areas of key technologies
Eligibility: Open to citizens of Australia or permanent residents who have completed 2 years, or more, full-time study in a science degree at a recognized Western Australian University
Level of Study: Postgraduate
Type: Studentship
Value: A$7,000 per year
Frequency: Annual
Study Establishment: Curtin University of Technology, Edith Cowan University, Murdoch University, The University of Notre Dame, The University of Western Australia
Country of Study: Any country
Application Procedure: Check website for further details
Closing Date: 14 September

For further information contact:

100 Plain Street, Perth, WA 6004, Australia

Tel: (61) 8 9222 3333
Fax: (61) 8 9222 3862
Email: rchapman@wellesley.edu
Contact: Krystle McCormick, Studentship Co-ordinator, The Office of Science, Technology and Innovation

Water and Health Scholarships

Subjects: Medical microbiology, earth sciences, or public health and health services
Purpose: To position graduates favourably with respect to future employment opportunities through research projects in the area of public health impacts of recycled water use
Eligibility: Open to Australian candidates with a broad range of backgrounds
Level of Study: Postgraduate
Type: Scholarship

Value: A$30,000 per year
Length of Study: 3 years
Frequency: Annual
Study Establishment: The University of Western Australia
Country of Study: Australia
Application Procedure: Check website for further details
Closing Date: 6 July
Additional Information: Applications are open from 13 June

For further information contact:

Tel: (61) 8 6488 7804
Email: Angus.Cook@uwa.edu.au
Contact: Dr Angus Cook, Research Fellow, The University of Western Australia

Western Australian CSIR University Postgraduate Scholarships

Subjects: Geology, geophysics, or metallurgy
Purpose: To enhance research into minerals and energy exploration, extraction and processing
Eligibility: Open to citizens of Australia enrolling for postgraduate research
Level of Study: Postgraduate
Type: Scholarship
Value: A$25,000 per year
Length of Study: 3 years
Country of Study: Australia
Application Procedure: Check website for further details

For further information contact:

Tel: (61) 8 6488 3027
Email: campbell.thomson@uwa.edu.au
Contact: Dr Campbell Thomson, Director Research Services

University of Western Sydney

Office of Research Services, Hawkesbury Campus, Building H3, Locked Bag 1797, Penrith South DC, NSW 1797, Australia

Tel: (61) 2 4570 1463
Fax: (61) 2 4570 1686
Email: t.mills@uws.edu.au
Website: www.uws.edu.au
Contact: Ms Tracey Mills, Research Scholarships Development Officer

Master of Business Administration Programme

Length of Study: 1–5 years
Application Procedure: Applicants must complete an application form supplying a TOEFL score
Closing Date: Varies, please contact organisation

For further information contact:

Tel: (61) 2 9685 9297
Fax: (61) 2 9685 9298
Email: international@uws.edu.au
Contact: MBA Admissions Officer

University of Westminster

Scholarships Department, Cavendish House, 101 New Cavendish Street, London W1W 6XH, United Kingdom

Tel: (44) 20 7911 5000 Exts 66257, 66258, 66259
Fax: (44) 20 7911 5858
Email: scholarships@westminster.ac.uk
Website: www.westminster.ac.uk

The University of Westminster is proud of its generous scholarship programme, which benefits both United Kingdom and international students. Full details are available on our website www.westminster.ac.uk/scholarships.

Brian Large Bursary Fund

Subjects: Bursaries are awarded in the sphere of delivery
Purpose: To provide financial support to United Kingdom students that are studying full time on the Transport and Planning MSc
Eligibility: Financial need and you must be a United Kingdom citizen or have permanent United Kingdom residential status. Up to three Brain large Masters Bursaries are to be addressed
Type: Funding support
Value: £7,000 paid in three tranches of £2,400 over the year
Country of Study: United Kingdom
Application Procedure: If you are interested in applying for one of these bursaries please contact Dr. Enrica Papa, the Course Leader of MSc Transport Planning at: papa@westminster.ac.uk
Closing Date: 2 July
Additional Information: For more information visit the Brian Large Bursary Fund website

Fully funded Master scholarship

Purpose: To study a full-time master degree in a subject within the School of Media, Arts and Design at the university
Type: Scholarship
Value: Full tuition fee award, accommodation, living expenses, flights to and from London
Country of Study: Any country
Application Procedure: For application, please visit website www.westminster.ac.uk/about-us/faculties/westminster-school-of-media-arts-and-design/departments
Closing Date: 11 January

For further information contact:

Email: graduate.admissions@cs.ox.ac.uk
Contact: Scholarships Office

Fully funded University of Westminster Master's Scholarship for Developing Countries

Subjects: Master's degree in all subjects
Purpose: The Westminster Vice-Chancellor's Scholarships, is one of the University's most prestigious award, it is aimed at fully funding a student from a developing country to study a full-time Master's degree at the University
Eligibility: The main requirement of this scholarship is that the candidates must hold an offer for a full-time Master's degree at University of Westminster. In addition, the applicant should have First Class Honours degree, financial need and development potential
Level of Study: Postgraduate
Type: Award
Value: The winner of this scholarship may expect to receive full tuition fee waivers, accomodation and flights to and from London
Frequency: Annual
Country of Study: Any country
Application Procedure: 1. A copy of the letter/email from the University of Westminster confirming your conditional or unconditional offer of a place on your chosen course. 2. An official copy of your transcript from your chosen course. 3. A reference letter written specifically in support of your scholarship application. This should be written by a previous tutor, professor, academic or employer and cannot be the same reference provided as part of your admission application
Closing Date: 31 May
Funding: Private

For further information contact:

Tel: (44) 20 7911 5000
Email: course-enquiries@westminster.ac.uk

Higher Education Scholarship Palestine (HESPAL) Scholarships

Subjects: HESPAL aims to create the next generation of senior academics who can maintain international quality standards at Palestinian universities and develop renewed and sustainable links between Palestinian and United Kingdom universities

Purpose: The University of Westminster is working in partnership with the British Council to provide a Higher Education Scholarship for a Palestinian (HESPAL); that is, to support a junior academic at a Palestinian University wishing to study a one-year masters programme or a three-year PhD research programme in the United Kingdom

Eligibility: For eligibility and other details visit how to apply page www.westminster.ac.uk/study/fees-and-funding/scholar ships/before-you-apply

Value: Full tuition fee award, pre-departure briefing from the British Council, arrival allowances, thesis allowances and a monthly allowance to cover living expenses

Country of Study: Any country

Application Procedure: Applications are made through the British Council in the Palestinian Territories. Find out more on the British Council website

Closing Date: 23 January

For further information contact:

Email: tom.sperlinger@bristol.ac.uk

Politics and International Relations PhD Scholarships

Subjects: Politics and International Relations

Purpose: Scholarships are available for pursuing PhD programme

Eligibility: Candidates should normally have a minimum classification of a 2.1 in their BA, or equivalent, and preferably a Master's degree

Value: One fee waiver (Home/European Union rate applications are invited for the following awards which are tenable for up to 3 years for full-time study:) and £16,000 per year for 3 years. Up to two fee waivers (Home/European Union rate) and £5,000 per year for 3 years

Length of Study: 3 years

Country of Study: United Kingdom

Application Procedure: Apply online. Please visit the website www.westminster.ac.uk/study/postgraduate/research-degrees/research-areas/social-sciences-and-humanities/how-to-apply

Closing Date: 27 April

Contributor: University of Westminster

Additional Information: For more details, visit website www.westminster.ac.uk/news/2018/call-for-applications-poli tics-and-international-relations-2018-phd-scholarships

For further information contact:

Tel: (61) 20 7911 5000
Email: robert.elgie@dcu.ie

Rees Jeffrey Road Fund

Purpose: To support financially for education, research and physical road transport-related projects in accordance with the founding Trust Deed

Type: Bursary

Value: This fund provides a bursary of up to £10,000 towards financial support for education, research and physical road transport-related projects

Country of Study: Any country

Application Procedure: Expressions of interest should in the first instance be directed to Dr. Enrica Papa, the Course Leader of Transport Planning MSc at: E.papa@westminster. ac.uk

Closing Date: May and June of each year

Additional Information: For more information visit the Rees Jeffreys website

For further information contact:

Email: brianmurrell@reesjeffreys.org

Westminster Full-Fee Masters Scholarships for International Students

Subjects: Any full-time master's degree Programme offered at the university except MBA

Purpose: The Westminster University offers full tuition fee scholarships to prospective postgraduate applicants from any country

Eligibility: You must hold an offer for a full-time Masters Program at the University of Westminster. The main scholarship criteria are: equivalent to a United Kingdom First Class Honours degree and financial need

Level of Study: Doctorate, Postgraduate

Type: Scholarship

Value: Full tuition fee award only

Country of Study: United Kingdom

Application Procedure: You should only apply for a scholarship once you have applied for admission and successfully been offered a place (either conditional or unconditional) on the course you wish to study. To apply for a scholarship, you will need to download and complete the relevant scholarship application form and submit it together with supporting documents by post

Closing Date: 4 May and 13 October

Additional Information: For more details visit official scholarship Website: www.westminster.ac.uk/study/prospective-students/fees-and-funding/scholarships/international-postgraduate-scholarships/westminster-full-fee-scholarship

For further information contact:

Email: course-enquiries@westminster.ac.uk

Westminster School of Media, Arts and Design Scholarship

Purpose: To pursue a full-time master degree in a subject within the School of Media, Arts and Design at the university

Value: Full tuition fee award, accommodation, living expenses and flights to and from London

Frequency: Annual

Country of Study: Any country

Application Procedure: For application forms, please visit website www.westminster.ac.uk/study/fees-and-funding/scholarships/westminster-school-of-media-arts-and-design-scholarship

Closing Date: 31 May

Contributor: Westminster School of Media, Arts and Design

For further information contact:

Email: scholarships@westminster.ac.uk

Westminster Vice-Chancellor's Scholarships

Subjects: Any full-time master's degree programme offered at the university. Academic excellence, financial need and development potential. Academic excellence, financial need and development potential

Purpose: The Westminster Vice-Chancellor's Scholarships, the university's most prestigious award, is aimed at fully funding a student from a developing country to study a full-time masters degree at the University

Eligibility: You must be an international student from a developing country and hold an offer for a full-time Undergraduate degree at University of Westminster. The main criteria are: United Kingdom First Class Honours degree, financial need and development potential

Level of Study: Postgraduate

Type: Scholarship

Value: Full tuition fee waivers, accommodation, living expenses and flights to and from London

Frequency: Annual

Study Establishment: University of Westminster

Country of Study: United Kingdom

Application Procedure: It is important to visit the official website to access the application form and for detailed information on how to apply for this scholarship

Closing Date: 31 May

Additional Information: For more details, please visit official scholarship website: www.westminster.ac.uk/study/prospective-students/fees-and-funding/scholarships/international-postgraduate-scholarships/vice-chancellor-scholarship

University of Winnipeg

The University of Winnipeg Manitoba Graduate Scholarships (MGS)

Subjects: These scholarships will be awarded in the subjects offered by the university

Purpose: Applications are open for the University of Winnipeg Manitoba Graduate Scholarships (MGS) organized by the University of Winnipeg. These scholarships are open to the students who are enrolled or plan to enroll as a full-time student in a master's program at the University of Winnipeg

Eligibility: 1. Have achieved a minimum GPA of 3.75 in the last 60 credits hours of study. 2. Be in a pre-master's program and/or entering the first or second year of an eligible master's program as of May or September of the current year or January of the upcoming year. 3. Be enrolled in or plan to enroll in as a full-time student in a master's program.

Level of Study: Postdoctorate

Type: Scholarship

Value: $15,000

Length of Study: 1 year

Frequency: Annual

Country of Study: Any country

Application Procedure: Apply online: www.uwinnipeg.ca/graduate-studies/docs/uwmgs-application+checklist-revisedjan2019-2.pdf

Closing Date: 1 March

Funding: Foundation

For further information contact:

Email: gradstudies@uwinnipeg.ca

University of Wisconsin-Milwaukee

University of Wisconsin-Milwaukee, PO Box 413, Milwaukee, WI 53201, United States of America

Tel:	(1) 414 229 1122
Email:	fellowship@uwm.edu
Website:	www.uwm.edu

The University of Wisconsin-Milwaukee (UWM) is located just a few blocks from Lake Michigan in one of Milwaukee's most attractive residential areas, and offers research and teaching programmes extending to 148 different degree programmes that serve nearly 26,000 students. UWM focuses on approaches to education that are inclusive, multidisciplinary and marked by excellent research and outstanding teaching.

University of Wisconsin-Milwaukee Graduate School Dissertation Fellowships

Subjects: All subjects
Purpose: To fund dissertation-level graduate students at the University of Wisconsin-Milwaukee
Eligibility: Applicants must have completed all coursework, passed preliminary examinations, completed PhD residency requirements and obtained dissertator status. No other award may be held concurrently (with the exception of the Chancellor's Graduate Student Award). Current or previous awardees are not eligible
Level of Study: Doctorate
Type: Fellowship
Value: US$14,000, in addition to full coverage of resident instructional fees (approx. US$1,740), a remission of the out-of-state portion of the tuition, low-cost comprehensive health insurance and other benefits
Length of Study: 1 academic year
Frequency: Annual
Study Establishment: University of Wisconsin-Milwaukee
Country of Study: United States of America
Application Procedure: Applicants must check the website for details
Closing Date: 21 January

For further information contact:

Tel:	(1) 414 229 6276
Email:	fellowship@uwm.edu

University of Wollongong (UOW)

Northfields Ave, Wollongong, NSW 2522, Australia

Tel:	(61) 2 4221 3555
Fax:	(61) 2 4221 4322
Email:	scholarships@uow.edu.au
Website:	www.uow.edu.au

The University of Wollongong (UOW) is a university of international standing with an enviable record of achievement in teaching and research. It enjoys a significant international research profile, attracting more Australian Research Council funding per student that any other Australian university. Over 850 postgraduate students are enrolled of which 30% are overseas students.

Marketing Research Innovation Centre PhD Scholarship

Subjects: Commerce, management, tourism and services
Purpose: To conduct research in the area of qualitative and quantitative methods, market segmentation, brand image studies and advertising experiments
Eligibility: Open to applicants who have an excellent tertiary track record, experience with conducting academic research
Level of Study: Postgraduate, Research
Type: Scholarship
Value: A$20,000 per year
Length of Study: 3 years
Frequency: Annual
Country of Study: Australia
Application Procedure: Candidates can check the website for further details

For further information contact:

Tel:	(61) 20 7000 7000
Fax:	(61) 2 4221 3862
Email:	housing@london.ac.uk
Contact:	Professor Sara Dolnicar, Professor

University of Wollong (UOW) Work-Integrated Learning Scholarship

Purpose: To reward outstanding academic achievements
Eligibility: Open to students with outstanding academic achievements

Level of Study: Postgraduate
Type: Scholarship
Value: A$3,000; A$9,300
Frequency: Annual
Study Establishment: University of Wollongong
Country of Study: Australia
Application Procedure: Apply online
Closing Date: October
Additional Information: Scholarship holders are required to undertake a period, usually 6-10 weeks of professional work experience each year with an appropriate sponsor organization

For further information contact:

Tel: (61) 1300 367 869
Fax: (61) 2 4221 3233
Email: uniadvice@uow.edu.au

University of Wollongong Sydney Business School Bursary Scheme

Subjects: Bursaries are awarded to study the subjects offered by the university
Purpose: The University of Wollongong (UOW) is offering Sydney Business School Bursary Scheme for students commencing master's courses. The bursaries offer a 15% reduction of the tuition fee per trimester of the study of applied
Eligibility: The bursary will apply to the following citizenships only: India, Nepal, Vietnam, Pakistan, Indonesia, Sri Lanka, Bangladesh, Thailand, Iran, Kenya, Mongolia, Nigeria, Cambodia, Zimbabwe, Myanmar and Ghana
Value: The bursaries offer a 15% reduction of the tuition fee per trimester of the study of applied
Study Establishment: Bursaries are awarded to study the subjects offered by the university
Country of Study: Australia
Application Procedure: You do not have to make a separate application for a bursary, as it will be awarded automatically when you receive an offer for an eligible course and meet scholarship requirements. Applicants will receive a bursary notification and Terms and Conditions of their bursary at the same time as their offer of admission into their course
Additional Information: For more details please visit the website scholarship-positions.com/uow-sydney-business-school-bursary-scheme-australia/2017/07/27/

For further information contact:

Email: business-enquiries@uow.edu.au

University of Wollongong In Dubai (UOWD)

Blocks 5 & 15, Knowledge Village, PO Box 20183, Dubai United Arab Emirates

Tel: (971) 4 367 2400
Fax: (971) 4 367 2760
Email: info@uowduabi.ac.ae

The UOWD in Dubai, established in 1993, is one UAE's oldest and most prestigious universities. The university strives to provide a fertile environment for bright young minds to flourish, and maintains a long and proud tradition of excellence in education.

University of Wollongong In Dubai Postgraduate Scholarships

Purpose: To reward the academically outstanding postgraduates
Eligibility: Open to all outstanding postgraduate students enrolled at the university
Level of Study: Postgraduate
Type: Scholarship
Value: Payment of tuition fees
Frequency: Annual
Study Establishment: University of Wollongong in Dubai
Country of Study: United Kingdom
Application Procedure: Contact the University
Closing Date: September
No. of awards given last year: 1

For further information contact:

Fax: (971) 4367 8047
Email: info@uowdubai.ac.ae

University of York

Graduate Schools Office, Heslington, York Y010 5DD, United Kingdom

Tel: (44) 1904 432 143
Fax: (44) 1904 432 092
Email: graduate@york.ac.uk
Website: www.york.ac.uk/admin/gso/gsp
Contact: Mr Philip Simison

The University of York offers postgraduate degree courses in archaeology, art history, biology, biochemistry, chemistry, communication studies, computer science, economics, educational studies, electronics, English, environment, health sciences, history, language and linguistics, management, mathematics, medieval studies, music, philosophy, physics, politics, psychology, social policy, social work, sociology and women's studies.

China Scholarships Council joint research scholarships

Purpose: The scholarships are open to Chinese nationals intending to begin a PhD in the current and upcoming academic year. They will be awarded on the basis of academic merit and CSC priorities

Eligibility: 1. You must be a citizen and permanent resident of the People's Republic of China at the time of application. 2. You must hold an unconditional offer* for a full-time PhD degree programme at the University of York commencing in Autumn. 3. You must fulfil any English language requirements of your offer by 15 February. 4. You must satisfy the eligibility and selection criteria set out by the CSC

Level of Study: Postgraduate

Type: Scholarship

Value: 100% of tuition fees for the full duration of the CSC funding period, a grant and uk visa fees

Frequency: Annual

Country of Study: Any country

Application Procedure: Check the details online. www.york.ac.uk/study/postgraduate-research/funding/china-scholarships/

Closing Date: 1 March

Funding: Private

For further information contact:

Email: international@york.ac.uk

Overseas Continuation Scholarship (OCS)

Subjects: All subjects

Purpose: For current University of York Masters students who are progressing to PhD studies at the University of York

Eligibility: Students must be outstanding academically and have the support of their chosen department at York. You must hold an offer for PhD study and be a current University of York Masters student to be eligible to apply

Level of Study: Doctorate

Type: Scholarship

Value: The scholarship is worth £5,000 in the first year of study as a deduction from tuition fees

Application Procedure: Please visit www.york.ac.uk/study/international/fees-funding/scholarships/ to apply

Closing Date: 30 April

Additional Information: Please email international@york.ac.uk for further information

For further information contact:

Email: international@york.ac.uk

Overseas Research Scholarship (ORS)

Subjects: All subjects

Purpose: For applicants commencing PhD study at the University of York. Applicants must be liable to pay the overseas rate of tuition fee

Eligibility: Students must be outstanding academically and have the support of their chosen department at York. You must hold an offer for PhD study to be eligible to apply

Level of Study: Doctorate

Type: Scholarship

Value: The scholarship will pay the full overseas tuition fee and a stipend of £5,000 per year for each year of successful study

Application Procedure: Please visit www.york.ac.uk/study/international/fees-funding/scholarships/ to apply

Closing Date: 30 April

Additional Information: Please email international@york.ac.uk for further information

For further information contact:

Email: international@york.ac.uk

Scholarship for Overseas Students

Subjects: All subjects except MBBS (Medicine)

Purpose: For applicants commencing study of any subject (excluding students applying to the Hull York Medical School) at any level as a full-time student at the University of York. Applicants must be liable to pay the overseas rate of tuition fee

Eligibility: This is a competitive scholarship based on academic merit and financial need. You must hold an offer for academic study to be eligible to apply

Level of Study: Postgraduate

Type: Scholarship

Value: The scholarship is worth one-quarter (25%) of the overseas tuition fee for each year of successful study

Frequency: Annual

Application Procedure: Please visit www.york.ac.uk/study/ international/fees-funding/scholarships/ to apply

Closing Date: 30 April

Additional Information: Please email international@york. ac.uk for further information

For further information contact:

Email: international@york.ac.uk

White Rose University Consortium Studentships

Subjects: Available across various schools and subjects, see website for further details

Purpose: Each year York collaborates with the Universities of Leeds and Sheffield to be able to offer a number of studentships in each of the three universities

Eligibility: In order to be eligible you must: have applied for a place on a full time PhD programme in the relevant Department. Have or expect to obtain a first or upper second class honours degree or equivalent prior to commencing the PhD degree

Level of Study: Doctorate

Type: Studentship

Value: A full Research Council equivalent stipend: £14,057. Rates for current year were not set at time of publication. A fee waiver at the Home/European Union rate (Overseas candidates are welcome to apply but would need to fund the difference between Home/European Union fee rate and international fee rate.). A Research Support Grant: £900

Frequency: Annual

Application Procedure: Please visit www.york.ac.uk/study/ postgraduate/fees-funding/research/white-rose-studentships/ for further details. Applications are submitted online

Closing Date: 30 April

Additional Information: Contact research-student-admin@ york.ac.uk for further information

For further information contact:

Email: research-student-admin@york.ac.uk

Wolfson Foundation Scholarships

Subjects: The Wolfson Postgraduate Scholarships will fund doctoral research in three disciplines that align closely with the Foundation's interests: history, literature and languages

Purpose: The University is delighted to be offering Wolfson Scholarships in the Humanities for the second year as part of a national Arts funding scheme

Eligibility: The Wolfson Postgraduate Scholarships in the humanities will be awarded to outstanding students who demonstrate the potential to make an impact on their chosen field. Wolfson Scholarships will be awarded solely on academic merit. In order to be eligible you must: have applied for and be in receipt of an offer of a place on a full time PhD programme in the relevant department (some departments may be able to accept applications on the basis of a programme application without an offer, please speak to your prospective department to confirm). Expect to begin your PhD studies in October. Have or expect to obtain a first or upper second class honours degree or equivalent prior to commencing the PhD. Have completed a masters level qualification before commencing the PhD

Level of Study: Doctorate

Type: Scholarship

Value: The scholarships are worth £26,000 per year for up to 3 years of PhD study. Each scholarship offers a stipend of £17,750 per year for up to 3 years of PhD study. Each scholarship will contribute to fees (up to £10,000). Any funds remaining after payment of the stipend and fees will be kept as a Research Training and Support Grant to be accessed by the award holder on request to support the work of the PhD

Country of Study: Any country

Application Procedure: Please visit www.york.ac.uk/study/ postgraduate/fees-funding/postgraduate/wolfson/ for further details. Applications are submitted online

Closing Date: 1 February

For further information contact:

Tel: (44) 1334 46 2254

Email: admissions@st-andrews.ac.uk

Uppsala University

Website: www.uu.se/en/admissions/scholarships/uppsala-university/

Uppsala University is a research university in Uppsala, Sweden, and is the oldest university in Sweden and all of the Nordic countries, founded in 1477.

Uppsala IPK Scholarships for International Students

Purpose: Uppsala University awards several scholarships for fee-paying students applying for Master's programmes commencing in the autumn. One of these scholarship programs is the Uppsala IPK Scholarships

Eligibility: 1. Citizens of a country outside the European Union/EEA and Switzerland. 2. Applicants must demonstrate academic talent and show interest in belonging to an educational milieu. 3. Students can only be awarded an IPK scholarship for their first priority programme at Uppsala University. 4. You must meet the entrance requirements for the programme you applied to and application fee and supporting documents must have been received before deadline to University Admissions

Type: Scholarship

Value: Scholarships will cover the cost of tuition but not living expenses

Country of Study: Any country

Application Procedure: You must then submit an online scholarship application form on which you will note your application ID from www.universityadmissions.se

Closing Date: 20 January

Contributor: The Uppsala University in Sweden

Additional Information: For more details, visit official scholarship website: www.uu.se/en/admissions/scholarships/uppsala-university/

For further information contact:

Email: tuitiongrants@uadm.uu.se

Utrecht University

Domplein 29, NLD-3512 JE, Utrecht, Netherlands

Tel:　　　(31) 30 253 26 70
Email:　　studievoorlichting@uu.nl
Website:　www.uu.nl

Utrecht University stands for broad and interdisciplinary education. Students at Utrecht University learn to look beyond the boundaries of their fields of study and work together in interdisciplinary projects. The education programmes are modern and innovative. Students and high-ranking scientists work together on a better future.

Utrecht Excellence Scholarships for International Students

Subjects: The Utrecht Excellence Scholarship offers a number of outstanding prospective students the opportunity to pursue a Master's degree in a selected number of fields at Utrecht University

Purpose: none

Eligibility: To be eligible for an Utrecht Excellence Scholarship, you must: 1. Belong to the top 10% of your graduating class. 2. Hold a non-European Union/EEA passport and not be eligible for support under the Dutch system of study grants and loans. 3. Have completed your secondary school and/or Bachelor degree outside the Netherlands. 4. Have applied for an eligible international master's programme with a start date of 1 September

Level of Study: Graduate, Postgraduate

Type: Scholarship

Frequency: Annual

Country of Study: Any country

Application Procedure: Your application for a scholarship will only be processed if you have submitted an application for a Master's programme as well. After submitting an application for the Master's programme, non-European Union/EEA students will have the option to submit an application for an Utrecht Excellence Scholarship. Prospective students who wish to be considered for the scholarship must apply before 1 February. Please note that in some cases you may need to apply before 1 December; check the 'When to apply' section under Admission and application of your master's programme. It is important to visit the official website (link found below) for detailed information on how to apply for this scholarship. Application has to be processed online. E-mail is not required

Closing Date: 1 February

Funding: Private

Additional Information: Official Scholarship Website: www.uu.nl/masters/en/general-information/international-students/financial-matters/grants-and-scholarships/utrecht-excellence-scholarships

For further information contact:

Email: study@uu.nl

V

Victoria University

PO Box 14428, Melbourne, VIC 8001, Australia

Tel:	(61) 9919 4659
Fax:	(61) 9689 4069
Email:	lesley.birch@vu.edu.au
Website:	www.vu.edu.au
Contact:	Ms Lesley Birch

Victoria University is one of Australia's leading universities, where challenging conventional thinking is not only encouraged but also expected. It has 11 campuses and sites, 46,000 enrolled students, 7,900 international students from over 30 countries, 700 courses in higher education and TAFE.

Victoria University Research Scholarships

Subjects: All subjects
Purpose: To support students undertaking Master's research and research Doctorates
Eligibility: Open to citizens or permanent residents of Australia who have achieved Honours 1 or equivalent having studied at or currently studying at Victoria University of Technology
Level of Study: Postgraduate
Type: Scholarship
Value: Australian $22,500
Length of Study: 1 year
Frequency: Annual
Study Establishment: Victoria University
Country of Study: Australia
Closing Date: 31 March, 31 July, 31 October

For further information contact:

Tel:	(61) 3 9688 4659
Fax:	(61) 3 9688 4559
Email:	Lesley.Birch@vu.edu.au
Contact:	Ms Lesley Birch, Postgraduate Scholarships Officer

Victoria University of Wellington

PO Box 600, Wellington 6140, New Zealand

Tel:	(64) 4 463 5113, 4 472 1000
Fax:	(64) 4 496 5454, 4 499 4601
Email:	scholarships-office@vuw.ac.nz
Website:	www.vuw.ac.nz
Contact:	Scholarship Office

Victoria University of Wellington is New Zealand's most research intensive university, located in New Zealand's compact vibrant capital city. It is one of the oldest universities in New Zealand. Victoria has produced Nobel prize winning scholars and a Booker Prize winner. Victoria provides excellent supervision, facilities and financial support for postgraduate research. Scholarships are available in all disciplines.

Therle Drake Postgraduate Scholarship

Purpose: The scholarship is for postgraduate classical performance overseas study and application should be made in the year for which the project is planned. While the terms of the bequest are that preference be given to a piano student, other applicants will be considered

© Springer Nature Limited 2019
Palgrave Macmillan (ed.), *The Grants Register 2020*,
https://doi.org/10.1057/978-1-349-95943-3

Eligibility: Scholarship is available for pursuing postgraduate degree program
Level of Study: Postgraduate
Type: Scholarship
Value: value up to $12,000
Length of Study: 1 year
Frequency: Annual
Country of Study: Any country
Closing Date: 31 March
Funding: Private

For further information contact:

Tel: (64) 4 463 5557
Email: scholarships-office@vuw.ac.nz

Vice-Chancellor's Strategic Doctoral Research Scholarships

Subjects: All subjects
Eligibility: Applicants are expected to have the equivalent of a New Zealand First Class Honours Degree and skills and research experience appropriate for the topic
Level of Study: Doctorate, Research
Type: Scholarship
Value: $20,000 per year
Frequency: Annual
Study Establishment: Victoria University
Country of Study: New Zealand
No. of awards offered: 35
Application Procedure: Application forms must be forwarded to the scholarships manager. Topics are advertised at www.ac.nz/scholarships from 1 March each year
Closing Date: 15 May
Contributor: Victoria University
No. of awards given last year: 10
No. of applicants last year: 35

For further information contact:

Scholarships Office, Office of Research and Postgraduate Study, Victoria University of Wellington, Wellington, PO Box 600, New Zealand

Tel: (64) 4 463 5113 or 4 463 7493
Email: Scholarships-Office@vuw.ac.nz
Contact: Scholarships Manager

Victoria Tongarewa Scholarship

Purpose: Scholarships for study in the following year will be awarded competitively on the basis of academic excellence.

Scholarships will be credited to tuition fees. Shortlisted candidates may be requested to undertake a skype interview
Eligibility: Scholarship is available for pursuing Undergraduate and postgraduate degree
Level of Study: Postgraduate
Type: Scholarship
Value: $10,000
Length of Study: 1 year
Frequency: Annual
Country of Study: Any country
Closing Date: 31 October
Funding: International office

For further information contact:

Tel: (64) 4 463 5557
Email: scholarships-office@vuw.ac.nz

Villa I Tatti: The Harvard University Center for Italian Renaissance Studies

Via di Vincigliata 22, ITA 50135, Florence, Italy

Tel: (39) 55 603 251
Fax: (39) 55 603 383
Email: info@itatti.harvard.edu
Website: www.itatti.harvard.edu
Contact: Angela Lees, Administrative Assistant

Villa I Tatti is devoted to advanced study of the Italian Renaissance in all its aspects, the history of art, political, economic and social history, the history of science, philosophy and religion and the history of literature and music.

Berenson Fellowship

Subjects: This Fellowship, made possible by The Lila Wallace - Reader's Digest Fund, is designed for scholars who explore "Italy in the World." Projects should address the transnational dialogues between Italy and other cultures (e.g. Latin American, Mediterranean, African, Asian etc.) during the Renaissance, broadly understood historically to include the period from the 14th to the 17th century. It is named after Bernard Berenson, who in his 1956 statement 'On the Future of I Tatti' expressed the hope that not only would scholars come from many countries, but that they would also travel in "what was the ancient Oecumene, not going farther East than the Euphrates and not farther South than Egypt and the great desert of North Africa" and be intimately acquainted with the Mediterranean countries and their "Hinterland." Taking a broad geographic view of the Renaissance more than half a century ago, Berenson was a pioneer of the geographically expansive approach to the early modern world that this Fellowship wishes to encourage. Scholars working in all the fields supported by I Tatti–architecture and the arts, history, philosophy, literature, music and history of science–are encouraged to apply. I Tatti offers Fellows the precious time they need to pursue their studies with a minimum of obligations and interruptions together with a maximum of scholarly resources–a combination that distinguishes the Harvard Center from similar institutions. Each year, a limited number of activities organized at I Tatti are reserved for the Fellows, and they are expected to join the wider community at conferences, lectures, and concerts. This is a residential fellowship of 4 or 6 months in length. Up to four fellowships will be awarded every year

Purpose: To promote advance research on the transnational dialogues between Italy and other cultures (e.g. Latin American, Mediterranean, African, Asian etc.) during the Renaissance

Eligibility: Applicants must be conversant in English and have familiarity with Italian. At the time of application, a PhD is required. Priority will be given to early and mid-career scholars. It must be possible for applicants to carry out most of their research in Florence. I Tatti welcomes applications from scholars from all nations and gives special consideration to candidates without regular access to research materials and facilities in Italy. Applications are evaluated by international scholars. The selection committee aims to assess the ability of candidates to contribute in a collegial way to the intellectual life of the Harvard Center. Short-term Fellowships at I Tatti can be held only once and cannot be deferred. Short-term Fellowships are intended for scholars who have not previously held appointments at I Tatti

Level of Study: Postdoctorate
Type: Fellowship with stipend
Length of Study: One semester (4-6 months)
Frequency: Annual
Country of Study: Italy
Application Procedure: For more information on this fellowship and a link to the application, please visit itatti.harvard.edu/berenson-fellowship
Closing Date: 15 November
Funding: Foundation
Contributor: The Lila Wallace - Reader's Digest Fund

For further information contact:

Villa I Tatti/Harvard University, 44r Brattle Street, Suite 113, MA 02138, Cambridge, United States of America

Tel: (1) 617 496 8724
Fax: (1) 617 495 8041

Email: info@itatti.harvard.edu
Contact: Ms Amanda Smith, Fellowship Administrator

Craig Hugh Smyth Fellowship

Subjects: The Craig Hugh Smyth Fellowship is designed for curators and conservators pursuing advanced research in any aspect of the Italian Renaissance. I Tatti offers Fellows the precious time they need to pursue their studies with a minimum of obligations and interruptions together with a maximum of scholarly resources–a combination that distinguishes the Harvard Center from similar institutions. Each year, a limited number of activities organized at I Tatti are reserved for the Fellows, and they are expected to join the wider community at conferences, lectures, and concerts. This is a residential fellowship of 4 or 6 months in length. Two fellowships are available every year

Purpose: The Craig Hugh Smyth Fellowship is designed for curators and conservators pursuing advanced research in any aspect of the Italian Renaissance

Eligibility: Applicants should be scholars who work for an educational or cultural institution as a curator or conservator. They may apply to carry out research on behalf of their home institution, or propose projects relating to their personal research interests. Applicants must be conversant in English and have familiarity with Italian. Priority will be given to early and mid-career scholars. It must be possible for applicants to carry out most of their research in Florence. I Tatti welcomes applications from scholars from all nations and gives special consideration to candidates without regular access to research materials and facilities in Italy. Applications are evaluated by international scholars. The selection committee aims to assess the ability of candidates to contribute in a collegial way to the intellectual life of the Harvard Center. Short-term Fellowships at I Tatti can be held only once and cannot be deferred. Short-term Fellowships are intended for scholars who have not previously held appointments at I Tatti

Level of Study: Postgraduate
Type: Fellowship with stipend
Length of Study: One semester: 4-6 months
Frequency: Annual
Country of Study: Italy
Application Procedure: For more information on this fellowship and a link to the application, please visit itatti.harvard.edu/craig-hugh-smyth-fellowship
Closing Date: 20 November
Funding: Government

For further information contact:

Villa I Tatti/Harvard University, 44r Brattle Street, Suite 113, MA 02138, Cambridge, United States of America

Tel: (1) 617 496 8724
Fax: (1) 617 495 8041
Email: info@itatti.harvard.edu
Contact: Ms Amanda Smith, Fellowship Administrator

David and Julie Tobey Fellowship

Subjects: The David and Julie Tobey Fellowship supports research on drawings, prints, and illustrated manuscripts from the Italian Renaissance, and especially the role that these works played in the creative process, the history of taste and collecting, and questions of connoisseurship. Proposals on a variety of subjects with a substantive component of research on drawings, prints, and illustrated manuscripts done on paper or parchment types are welcome. I Tatti offers Fellows the precious time they need to pursue their studies with a minimum of obligations and interruptions together with a maximum of scholarly resources–a combination that distinguishes the Harvard Center from similar institutions. Each year, a limited number of activities organized at I Tatti are reserved for the Fellows, and they are expected to join the wider community at conferences, lectures, and concerts. This is a residential fellowship of 4 or 6 months in length. One fellowship is available every year

Purpose: The David and Julie Tobey Fellowship supports research on drawings, prints, and illustrated manuscripts from the Italian Renaissance, and especially the role that these works played in the creative process, the history of taste and collecting, and questions of connoisseurship

Eligibility: Applicants must be conversant in English and have familiarity with Italian. At the time of application, a PhD is required. Priority will be given to early and mid-career scholars. Projects should represent advanced research in the Italian Renaissance, broadly defined as the period ranging from the 14th to the 17th century, and deal with drawings, prints, or illustrated manuscripts, and the role that these works may have played in the creative process, the history of taste and collecting, or questions of connoisseurship. It must be possible for applicants to carry out most of their research in Florence. I Tatti welcomes applications from scholars from all nations and gives special consideration to candidates without regular access to research materials and facilities in Italy. Applications are evaluated by international scholars. The selection committee aims to assess the ability of candidates to contribute in a collegial way to the intellectual life of the Harvard Center. Short-term Fellowships at I Tatti can be held only once and cannot be deferred. Short-term Fellowships are intended for scholars who have not previously held appointments at I Tatti

Level of Study: Postdoctorate
Type: Fellowship with stipend

Length of Study: One semester (4-6 months)
Frequency: Annual
Country of Study: Italy
Application Procedure: For more information about this fellowship and a link to the application, please visit itatti. harvard.edu/david-and-julie-tobey-fellowship
Closing Date: 15 November
Funding: Government

For further information contact:

Villa I Tatti/Harvard University, 44r Brattle Street, Suite 113, MA 02138, Cambridge, United States of America

Tel: (1) 617 496 8724
Fax: (1) 617 495 8041
Email: info@itatti.harvard.edu
Contact: Ms Amanda Smith, Fellowship Administrator

Fellowship in the Digital Humanities

Subjects: This fellowship, generously supported in part by the Samuel H. Kress Foundation, aims to support the work of scholars in the humanities or social sciences, librarians, archivists, and data science professionals whose research interests or practice cut across traditional disciplinary boundaries and actively employ technology in their work. Projects can address any aspect of the Italian Renaissance, broadly understood historically to include the period from the 14th to the 17th century, and geographically to include transnational dialogues between Italy and other cultures (e.g. Latin American, Mediterranean, African, Asian, etc.). Projects should apply digital technologies such as mapping, textual analysis, visualization, or the semantic web to topics in fields such as art and architecture, history, literature, material culture, music, philosophy, religion, and the history of science. I Tatti offers Fellows the precious time they need to pursue their studies with a minimum of obligations and interruptions together with a maximum of scholarly resources–a combination that distinguishes the Harvard Center from similar institutions. Each year, a limited number of activities organized at I Tatti are reserved for the Fellows, and they are expected to join the wider community at conferences, lectures, and concerts. This is a residential fellowship of 4 or 6 months in length. Up to two fellowships will be awarded every year

Purpose: To support the work of scholars in the humanities or social sciences, librarians, archivists, and data science professionals whose research interests or practice cut across traditional disciplinary boundaries and actively employ technology in their work while addressing aspects if the Italian Renaissance

Eligibility: Applicants must be conversant in English and have familiarity with Italian. At the time of application, a PhD is required for scholars in the humanities and social sciences. In exceptional cases, applications from advanced PhD (ABD) students will be considered, provided these applicants have earned their PhD by the time they assume a fellowship at I Tatti. In addition, we require a letter from the dissertation supervisor clearly stating the anticipated PhD date. A Master's degree is required for librarians, archivists, and data science professionals. A background in programming, library sciences, computer graphics, computational linguistics, or other fields relevant to digital humanities research is highly desirable. Candidates should possess the technical skills to carry out their project at the time of application, and it must be possible for applicants to carry out most of their research in Florence. Priority will be given to early and mid-career scholars. I Tatti welcomes applications from scholars from all nations and gives special consideration to candidates without regular access to research materials and facilities in Italy. Applications are evaluated by international scholars. The selection committee aims to assess the ability of candidates to contribute in a collegial way to the intellectual life of the Harvard Center. Short-term Fellowships at I Tatti can be held only once and cannot be deferred. Short-term Fellowships are intended for scholars who have not previously held appointments at I Tatti

Level of Study: Postdoctorate, Postgraduate

Type: Fellowship with stipend

Length of Study: One semester: 4-6 months

Frequency: Annual

Country of Study: Italy

Application Procedure: For more information about this fellowship and a link to the application, please visit itatti. harvard.edu/fellowship-digital-humanities

Closing Date: 15 November

Funding: Foundation

Contributor: Samuel H. Kress Foundation

For further information contact:

Villa I Tatti/Harvard University, 44r Brattle Street, Suite 113, Cambridge, MA 02138, United States of America

Tel: (1) 617 496 8724
Fax: (1) 617 495 8041
Email: info@itatti.harvard.edu
Contact: Ms Amanda Smith, Fellowship Administrator

I Tatti Fellowship

Subjects: Fifteen I Tatti Residential Fellowships, each for twelve months, are available annually for post-doctoral research in any aspect of the Italian Renaissance, broadly understood historically to include the period from the 14th to the 17th century and geographically to include transnational dialogues between Italy and other cultures (e.g. Latin American, Mediterranean, African, Asian etc.). I Tatti offers Fellows the precious time they need to pursue their studies with a minimum of obligations and interruptions together with a maximum of scholarly resources–a combination that distinguishes the Harvard Center from similar institutions. Fellows have full access to the Berenson Library's rich collections of books and periodicals, photographs and digital images, manuscripts and recordings. As one of the over seventy libraries that make up the Harvard Library system, the Biblioteca Berenson provides access to a vast range of online journals and other electronic resources, and offers Fellows comprehensive interdisciplinary resources for the study of late medieval and early modern Italy. I Tatti is a site for lively academic encounters and dynamic exchanges. Each year, a number of activities such as exploratory seminars, workshops, and tours of exhibitions and cultural institutions are organized for the Fellows. In addition, the center hosts conferences, lectures, and concerts and attendance is expected of all Appointees. Rather than present a traditional paper at the end of the year, Fellows give presentations of their fellowship projects in-progress in September. This provides an opportunity to explore problems and questions and receive valuable feedback early in the fellowship year from other members of the multidisciplinary community

Purpose: To promote advanced, post-doctoral research in Italian Renaissance Studies

Eligibility: Fellows are selected by an international and interdisciplinary committee that welcomes applications from scholars from all nations. The committee aims to assess the ability of candidates to contribute in a collegial way to the intellectual life of the Harvard Center. It pays special attention to the strength of the proposed project and its potential to yield original results, and to the candidate's curriculum vitae. At the time of application, scholars must hold a PhD, dottorato di ricerca, or an equivalent degree. They must be conversant in either English or Italian and able to understand both languages. They should be in the early stages of their career, having received a PhD between 2008-2017 and have a solid background in Italian Renaissance studies. (NB: The PhD certificate must bear a date between January 1, 2008 and December 31, 2017, inclusive.); The project must represent advanced research in the Italian Renaissance, broadly defined historically as the period ranging from the 14th to the 17th centuries and geographically to include transnational dialogues between Italy and other cultures (e.g. Latin American, Mediterranean, African, Asian etc.). Subjects covered include art and architecture, history, literature, material culture, music and performance, philosophy, religion, and science. Scholars can also apply to work on the transmission and circulation of ideas, objects, and people during the Renaissance, into and beyond the Italian peninsula, or on the historiography of the Italian Renaissance, including the rebirth of interest in the Renaissance in later periods. It must be possible for applicants to carry out most of their research in Florence with the resources available in the city and at I Tatti. Applicants should demonstrate that they have already completed the necessary preliminary work to establish that the project shows promise. Preference is given to a postdoctoral research project, but projects could also represent a significant reworking of a dissertation. Special consideration may be given to candidates without regular access to research materials and facilities available in Italy. One of the I Tatti fellowships, sponsored by a generous grant from the Florence Gould Foundation, is designated for scholars who a) work on a Franco-Italian Renaissance topic (which includes any project exploring the contact between the geographic areas of Italy and France in the early modern period); b) reside in France; or c) have French citizenship. Candidates who fall into one or more of these categories should indicate their status in the penultimate section on the application form. The Fellow is responsible for obtaining a visa, permesso di soggiorno, and health coverage (and, if appropriate, for accompanying family members). The Fellow must determine if a visa is required and, if necessary, obtain one before travel. Renewals or repeats of an I Tatti Fellowship are not granted. Scholars can apply for only one type of fellowship at I Tatti per academic year

Level of Study: Postdoctorate

Type: Fellowship with stipend

Length of Study: Full academic year

Frequency: Annual

Country of Study: Italy

Application Procedure: For more information on this fellowship, including a link to the application, please visit itatti.harvard.edu/i-tatti-fellowship

Closing Date: 15 October

Funding: Government

For further information contact:

Villa I Tatti/Harvard University, 44r Brattle Street, Suite 113, United States of America

Tel:	(1) 617 496 8724
Fax:	(1) 617 495 8041
Email:	info@itatti.harvard.edu
Contact:	Ms Amanda Smith, Fellowship Administrator

Mellon Fellowship in Digital Humanities

Subjects: Fellowship to work at I Tatti for 4 or 6 months. The Fellowship is designed to support the work of scholars in the humanities or social sciences, librarians, archivists, and data science professionals whose research interests or practice cut across traditional disciplinary boundaries and actively employ technology in their work. Projects can address any aspect of the Italian Renaissance, broadly understood historically to include the period from the 14th to the 17th century, and geographically to include transnational dialogues between Italy and other cultures (e.g. Latin American, Mediterranean, African, Asian etc.). Projects should apply digital technologies such as mapping, textual analysis, visualization, or the semantic web to topics in fields such as art and architecture, history, literature, material culture, music, philosophy, religion, and history of science

Eligibility: A PhD is required for scholars in the humanities and social sciences; in exceptional cases, applications from advanced PhD (ABD) students will be considered. A Master's degree is required for librarians, archivists, and data science professionals. A background in programming, library sciences, computer graphics, computational linguistics, or other fields relevant to digital humanities research is highly desirable. Candidates should possess the technical skills to carry out their project at the time of application

Type: Residential fellowships

Value: Up to US$4,000 per month plus a one-time supplement (Max: US$1,500)

Length of Study: 4 to 6 months

Frequency: Annual

Country of Study: Italy

Application Procedure: Please check at itatti.harvard.edu/mellon-fellowship-digital-humanities

Closing Date: 14 December

Funding: Foundation

Contributor: Andrew W. Mellon Foundation

For further information contact:

Email: morris.eaves@rochester.edu

Villa I Tatti - Bogaziçi University Joint Fellowship

Subjects: Villa I Tatti - The Harvard University Center for Italian Renaissance Studies (VIT, Florence) and the Byzantine Studies Research Center of Bogaziçi University (BSRC, Istanbul) offer a joint, residential fellowship for the academic year. Scholars will spend the fall term (September - December) in Istanbul and the spring term (January - June) in Florence. The fellowship will focus on the interaction between Italy and the Byzantine Empire (ca. 1300 to ca. 1700). This collaboration aims to foster the development of research on Late Byzantine-Italian relations by supporting early-career scholars whose work explores Byzantium's cross-cultural contacts in the late medieval and early modern

Mediterranean world through the study of art, architecture, archaeology, history, literature, material culture, music, philosophy, religion, or science

Purpose: This collaboration aims to foster the development of research on Late Byzantine-Italian relations by supporting early-career scholars whose work explores Byzantium's cross-cultural contacts in the late medieval and early modern Mediterranean world through the study of art, architecture, archaeology, history, literature, material culture, music, philosophy, religion, or science

Eligibility: The VIT-BSRC Joint Fellowship is offered for candidates who have received a PhD in or after 2009. Candidates must have their PhD in hand by the time they apply and will be asked to upload a scan of it when submitting their application. Candidates must be conversant in English and have at least a reading knowledge of Italian. They must have a solid background in Italian Renaissance and/or Byzantine Studies. Each successful candidate must be approved by both the BSRC and VIT and will spend the fall term (September - December) at Bogaziçi University in Istanbul and the spring term (January-June) at Villa I Tatti in Florence. During both terms, it must be possible for Fellows to carry out most of their research with the resources available in the city where they are resident. Priority will be given to applicants with no previous association with VIT or BSRC. Renewals, repeats, or deferments of this Fellowship are not granted. Scholars can apply to only one type of fellowship at I Tatti per academic year

Level of Study: Postdoctorate

Type: Fellowship with stipend

Value: stipend is USD 1,800 per month for the term in Istanbul & USD 4,000 per month for the term in Florence

Length of Study: Fall term (September - December) in Istanbul, Turkey; spring term (January - June) in Florence, Italy

Frequency: Annual

Country of Study: As applicable

Application Procedure: For details about this fellowship and for a link to our application, please visit itatti.harvard.edu/i-tatti-bogazici-joint-fellowship

Closing Date: 15 November

Funding: Government

No. of awards given last year: 1

For further information contact:

Villa I Tatti/Harvard University, 44r Brattle Street, Suite 113, Cambridge, MA 02138, United States of America

Tel:	(1) 617 496 8724
Fax:	(1) 617 495 8041
Email:	info@itatti.harvard.edu
Contact:	Amanda Smith, Fellowship Administrator

Wallace Fellowship

Subjects: Fellowship to work at I Tatti for 4 or 6 months. The Fellowship is designed for scholars who explore the historiography and impact of the Italian Renaissance in the Modern Era (19th-21st centuries). Projects could address a range of topics from historiography to the reaction to, transformation of, and commentary on the Italian Renaissance and its ties to modernity. Also welcome are projects on museum and collecting history, and on the survival of the Renaissance in modern art and architecture (including photography and landscape architecture), in literature and music, and in philosophy and political thought

Eligibility: Applicants must be conversant in English and have familiarity with Italian. At the time of application, a PhD is required. Priority will be given to early and mid-career scholars. Projects can address the historiography or impact of the Renaissance on any field, including art and architecture, landscape architecture, history, literature, material culture, music, philosophy, religion, and science. It must be possible for applicants to carry out most of their research in Florence. I Tatti welcomes applications from scholars from all nations and gives special consideration to candidates without regular access to research materials and facilities in Italy

Level of Study: Postdoctorate

Type: Residential fellowships

Value: Up to US$4,000 per month plus a one-time supplement (Max: US$1,500)

Length of Study: 4 to 6 months

Frequency: Annual

Country of Study: Italy

Application Procedure: Please check at itatti.harvard.edu/wallace-fellowship

Closing Date: 14 December

Funding: Foundation

Contributor: The Lila Wallace - Reader's Digest Fund

For further information contact:

Email: wallacehouse@umich.edu

Vinaver Trust

45 Albert Street, Western Hill, DH1 4RJ, Durham, United Kingdom

Tel:	(44) 19 1386 8898
Email:	geoffreybromiley@btinternet.com
Contact:	Dr G.N. Bromiley, Secretary-Treasurer

The Eugène Vinaver Memorial Trust exists to promote research into Arthurian studies, as defined by the International Arthurian

Society. It offers subventions to publishers to facilitate the publication of scholarly works; it also offers grants to postgraduate students pursuing research in the Arthurian field.

Barron Bequest

Subjects: Any field of Arthurian studies
Purpose: To support postgraduate research in Arthurian studies
Eligibility: Open to graduates of any university of the United Kingdom or the Republic of Ireland
Level of Study: Doctorate, Graduate
Type: Grant
Value: Up to UK£1,250 towards academic fees
Length of Study: 1 year. Candidates may apply for further years on a basis of parity with those applying for the first time
Frequency: Annual
Country of Study: United Kingdom, Republic of Ireland
No. of awards offered: 2
Application Procedure: For application details applicants must contact Professor J.H.M. Taylor at the address given below
Closing Date: 30 April
Funding: Private
Contributor: The Eugène Vinaver Memorial Trust
No. of awards given last year: 1
No. of applicants last year: 2

For further information contact:

Penruddock, Penrith, CA11 0QU, Cumbria, United Kingdom

Email: jane.taylor@durham.ac.uk
Contact: Professor Jane H M Taylor, Garth Head

Vinod & Saryu Doshi Foundation

58, Nariman Bhavan, Nariman Point, Mumbai, Maharashtra 400021, India

Tel: (91) 6117 9000
Contact: Vinod & Saryu Doshi Foundation

The Vinod & Saryu Doshi Foundation is a non-profit charitable trust that supports initiatives in the fields of Art & Culture, Education and Community. It seeks to embody the lifelong passions and values of Vinod and Saryu Doshi, who believed that the mind is enriched through education and the spirit through art and culture. They have spent a considerable part of their lives supporting these causes. The Vinod & Saryu Doshi Foundation initiated these Fellowships to assist Indian nationals who have received acceptance in a University abroad to pursue their post-graduate studies (Masters, Postgraduate diploma/certificate or doctorate) in the field of Liberal Arts & Sciences. This includes the Humanities, Social Sciences, the Natural Sciences and Mathematics.

Vinod & Saryu Doshi Foundation Postgraduate Fellowships

Subjects: Liberal Arts and Social Sciences
Purpose: The main aim of the fellowship program is to enhance the higher education by giving an opportunity to academically bright students who have the drive to succeed but are unable to do so due to their financial challenges. This is a need-based merit Fellowship and abides by the Equal Opportunity and Affirmative Action policy. The maximum amount of the Fellowship will be up to Rs. 3 lakhs per fellow, which will be payable as a one-time amount
Eligibility: Indian Nationals only
Type: Postgraduate scholarships
Value: Up to Rs. 3 lakh
Study Establishment: Liberal Arts and Social Sciences
Country of Study: Any country
Application Procedure: Fill in the application form and send the hard copy to Vinod & Saryu Doshi Foundation
Closing Date: 7 May
Additional Information: For more details please visit the website scholarship-positions.com/vinod-saryu-doshi-foundation-postgraduate-fellowships-liberal-arts-sciences-2017/2017/02/20/

For further information contact:

Email: ericadesouza@vsdf.org

Volkswagen Foundation

Kastanienallee 35, DEU-30519 Hannover, Germany

Tel: (49) 511 8381 0
Fax: (49) 5 11 8381 344
Email: info@volkswagenstiftung.de
Contact: VolkswagenStiftung

The Volkswagen Foundation (VolkswagenStiftung) is dedicated to the support of the humanities and social sciences as well as science and technology in higher education and research. It funds research projects in path-breaking areas and provides assistance to academic institutions for the improvement of the structural conditions for their work. In particular, the Foundation perceives its mission in supporting aspiring young researchers and in promoting interdisciplinary and international collaboration.

Volkswagen Foundation Freigeist Fellowships

Subjects: Open to all disciplines and topics
Purpose: The Freigeist funding initiative aims to encourage exceptional research personalities to embark on visionary, risk-taking research projects at the intersections between established field of research

Eligibility: Anyone can apply who identifies with the goals of a "Freigeist" Fellowship and whose proposed research projects fits in with the aims pursued by the Freigeist initiative
Level of Study: Doctorate, Postdoctorate
Value: €1,000,000
Frequency: Annual
Country of Study: Germany
Application Procedure: Applications can be submitted online via the Electronic Application System of the Volkswagen Foundation. Instructions are found online
Closing Date: 12 October

For further information contact:

Email: info@volkswagenstiftung.de

W

W.F. Albright Institute of Archaeological Research

Sean W. Dever Memorial Prize

Purpose: The W.F. Albright Institute of Archaeological Research in Jerusalem announces the Sean W. Dever Memorial Prize call for papers. This prize provides $750 for the best article published or paper presented at a conference that treats a topic in the field of Syro-Palestinian or Biblical Archaeology

Eligibility: Authors must be PhD candidates in the semester in which the winner is announced. They may be of any nationality, but the article or paper must be in English. Co-written or co-presented pieces may be submitted if all the authors or presenters are doctoral candidates; the prize, if awarded, will be divided equally among authors or presenters. All submissions must be in PDF format only

Level of Study: Postgraduate

Type: Prize

Frequency: Annual

Country of Study: Any country

Application Procedure: The submission of conference papers must include images (if used in the presentation) in PDF format (either as a separate document or embedded within the text of the paper), and full citations and bibliographic references. Kindly submit the initial documents through the following link. aiarfellowships.fluidreview.com

Closing Date: 31 December

Funding: Private

For further information contact:

P.O. Box 19096, Jerusalem 9119002, Israel

Tel: (972) 2 628 8956
Email: albrightinstitute@aiar.org

Wageningen University

Wageningen University & Research Africa Scholarship Program

Purpose: Applications are open for the Wageningen University & Research Africa Scholarship Program. The Africa Scholarship Program (ASP) has been initiated by Wageningen University & Research to give talented and motivated students from Africa the opportunity to study at the university in Wageningen. With this programme, Wageningen wants to support capacity building in Africa by attracting excellent students for a 2-years master's program. Wageningen University & Research is a collaboration between Wageningen University and the Wageningen Research foundation

Eligibility: 1. African students who want to start their study in September may be eligible for the scholarship. 2. Excellent students with a GPA of 80% or higher in a bachelor degree, and admitted to a Wageningen University MSc Program

Level of Study: Postgraduate

Type: Scholarship

Frequency: Annual

Country of Study: Any country

Closing Date: 1 February

Funding: Foundation

For further information contact:

Email: wufp@wur.nl

Wal-Mart Foundation

Walmart Dependent Scholarship

Purpose: This award is for graduating high school seniors who are dependents of actively employed Walmart associates within any division of Walmart for at least six consecutive months as of the application deadline. Students must have a grade point average of 2.0 or higher and must demonstrate financial need

Eligibility: 1. Must be a high school or home school senior graduating or earning a GED between 1 August, and 31 July. 2. Must be a United States citizen or a United States permanent legal resident. 3. Must be the dependent of an actively employed Walmart associate (employee) within any division of Walmart for at least six consecutive months as of the application deadline date. 4. Must have a cumulative high school grade point average of 2.0 or higher on a 4.0 scale. 5. This award is for United States students

Level of Study: Graduate
Type: Scholarship
Value: US$3,250
Frequency: Annual
Country of Study: Any country
Application Procedure: Apply online: aim.applyISTS.net/WALDEPS
Closing Date: 2 April
Funding: Foundation

For further information contact:

327 2nd St., Suite 103, Coralville, IA 52241, United States of America

Tel: (1) 877 333 0284
Email: walmartdependent@applyISTS.com

Warsaw Agricultural University The International Institute of Management and Marketing in Agri-Business (IZMA)

Nowoursynowska 166, POL 02 787 Warsaw Poland

Tel: (48) 22 873 8501
Fax: (48) 22 843 8501
Email: izma@sggw.waw.pl
Contact: MBA Admissions Officer

Warsaw Agricultural University MBA in Agribusiness Management

Length of Study: 2–5 years
Application Procedure: Applicants must supply an application form together with the following: transcripts from previous institutions, a leaving school certificate, three passport photos, a certificate of physical fitness, relevant identification

documents. All documents must be translated into Polish by an official translator
Closing Date: Please contact the organisation

For further information contact:

Tel: (48) 22 843 9751
Fax: (48) 22 843 1877
Email: majewski@alpha.sggw.waw.pl
Contact: MBA Admissions Officer

Washington Conservation Guild

National Air and Space Museum - Engen Conservation Fellowship

Purpose: Fellows will be encouraged to develop a research project while at NASM. The independent research will be derived from the diverse collection of materials and may be related to evaluations of treatment procedures, ethical considerations, or technical studies

Eligibility: 1. The ideal candidate will have a Master's degree in conservation from a recognized program and be able to conduct research independently. The candidate should have knowledge of ethical and professional principles and concepts related to the preservation of objects in a wide variety of media. 2. They should also understand the theories, principles, techniques, practices, and methodologies used to examine, study, treat, analyze and preserve historic objects. 3. Applicants should have a proven record of research, writing ability, and verbal communication skills

Level of Study: Graduate, Postgraduate
Type: Fellowship
Frequency: Annual
Country of Study: Any country
Closing Date: 15 January
Funding: Private

For further information contact:

Washington Conservation Guild, P.O. Box 553, Kensington, MD 20895, United States of America

Email: Horelickl@si.edu

Washington University

Graduate School of Arts and Sciences, Box 1186, 1 Brookings Drive, St. Louis, MO 63130-4899, United States of America

Tel:	(1) 314 935 5000
Fax:	(1) 314 935 3929
Email:	graduateartsci@wustl.edu
Website:	graduateschool.wustl.edu
Contact:	Dr Nancy P. Pope, Associate Dean

Washington University has a diverse offering of events, disciplines, people, and resources that create unlimited possibilities for discovery and growth. The Graduate School of Arts and Sciences signals a curriculum and place, a core of teaching, learning, and discovery at Washington University.

Olin School of Business Washington University MBA Programme

Length of Study: 2 years
Application Procedure: Applicants must have Graduate Management Admission Test scores and TOEFL scores if applicable sent directly to the University, and submit an application form and US$80, before attending a personal interview. International applicants may be invited to participate in a telephone interview. Also necessary are two references and original transcripts from previous colleges both in sealed envelopes, a work history form and a curriculum vitae. Applications can also be made through www.embark.com or www.gradadvantage.org
Closing Date: Varies, please contact the organisation

For further information contact:

John M. Olin School of Business, MBA Program, 1 Brookings Drive, St. Louis, MO 63130, United States of America

Tel:	(1) 314 935 7301
Fax:	(1) 314 935 6309
Email:	mba@olin.wustl.edu
Contact:	MBA Admissions Officer

Washington American Indian Endowed Scholarship

Purpose: The award is based on the financial need of the student. Recipients are selected on the basis of academic merit and a commitment to serve the American Indian community in Washington
Eligibility: Recipients are selected on the basis of academic merit and a commitment to serve the American Indian community in Washington. Scholarships are awarded from the interest earnings of an endowment established from funds appropriated by the Washington State Legislature with matching contributions from tribes, individuals, and organizations
Level of Study: Graduate
Type: Scholarship
Value: US$500 to US$2,000
Frequency: Annual
Country of Study: Any country
Application Procedure: Scholarships are awarded from the interest earnings of an endowment established from funds appropriated by the Washington State Legislature with matching contributions from tribes and organizations
Closing Date: 1 February
Funding: Private

For further information contact:

917 Lakeridge Way SW, Olympia, WA 98502, United States of America

Email:	aies@wsac.wa.gov

Wellcome Trust

215, Euston Road, NW1 2BE, London, United Kingdom

Tel:	(44) 20 7611 2020
Fax:	(44) 20 7611 8545
Email:	grantenquiries@wellcome.ac.uk, investigators@wellcome.ac.uk
Website:	www.wellcome.ac.uk

The Wellcome Trust's mission is to foster and promote research with the aim of improving human and animal health. The Trust funds most areas of biomedical research and funds research in the history of medicine, biomedical ethics, public engagement of science.

Arts Awards

Subjects: The scheme aims to: stimulate interest, excitement and debate about biomedical science through the arts; examine the social, cultural, and ethical impact of biomedical science; support formal and informal learning; encourage new ways of thinking; encourage high quality interdisciplinary practice and collaborative partnerships in arts, science and/or education practice. All art forms are covered by the programme: dance, drama, performance arts, visual arts, music, film, craft, photography, creative writing or digital media. The Trust invites applications for projects which engage adult audiences and/or young people

Purpose: Arts Awards support imaginative and experimental arts projects that investigate biomedical science

Eligibility: The scheme is open to a wide range of people including, among others, artists, scientists, curators, film-makers, writers, producers, directors, academics, science communicators, teachers, arts workers and education officers. Applicants are usually affiliated to organizations, but can apply as individuals. Organizations might include: museums and other cultural attractions; arts agencies; production companies; arts venues; broadcast media; schools; local education authorities; universities and colleges; youth clubs; community groups; research institutes; the NHS; and science centres. Partnership projects (between different people and organizations, e.g. scientists and ethicists, educators and artists) are welcomed. If this is the first time an organization is applying to the Wellcome Trust an eligibility assessment will be carried out. For this assessment, the following documentation from the applying organization should be submitted: articles of association; audited accounts from the previous 2 years; details of similar projects/grant funding received; confirmation that no funding has been received or is scheduled to be received from any tobacco company

Level of Study: Research

Type: Award

Value: Funding can be applied for at two levels: (1) Small to medium-sized projects (up to and including £40,000). This funding can either be used to support the development of new project ideas, deliver small-scale productions or workshops, investigate and experiment with new methods of engagement through the arts, or develop new collaborative relationships between artists and scientists and (2) Large projects (above £40,000). This funding can be used to fund full or part production costs for large-scale arts projects that aim to have significant impact on the public's engagement with biomedical science. We are also interested in supporting high-quality, multi-audience, multi-outcome projects. Applicants can apply for any amount within the above boundaries, for projects lasting a maximum of 3 years

Frequency: Annual

Application Procedure: Application form for awards up to and including £40,000, preliminary application form for awards over £40,000

Closing Date: For small to medium-sized projects (up to and including £40,000) deadlines are 28 February, 27 June, and 7 November. For large projects (above £40,000) the deadline is 24 January. For detail information check website

Funding: Trusts

Additional Information: Applicants must be based in the United Kingdom or the Republic of Ireland and the activity must take place in the United Kingdom or the Republic of Ireland

For further information contact:

Tel: (44) 20 7611 5757
Email: PEgrants@wellcome.ac.uk

Broadcast Development Awards

Subjects: We are interested in funding individuals and organizations with brilliant early-stage ideas for TV, radio or new media projects. Our funding will enable these ideas to be developed into high impact, well-researched proposals to be utilized in securing a broadcast platform and/or further funding. A successful project would primarily be aimed at a mainstream United Kingdom and/or Republic of Ireland audience in the first instance, although the subject matter can be international

Purpose: To support the development of broadcast proposals in any genre that engages the audience with issues around biomedical science in an innovative, entertaining and accessible way

Eligibility: The proposal must primarily be aimed at a mainstream United Kingdom and/or Republic of Ireland audience in the first instance but the subject matter can be international. Applicants are usually affiliated to organizations, but can apply as individuals. The scheme is open to broadcast professionals and other organizations or individuals working on broadcast projects. Partnership between broadcasters and other professionals such as scientists, ethicists, educators etc. are especially welcomed

Level of Study: Research

Type: Award

Value: Up to £10,000, for a maximum of 1 year

Length of Study: 1 year

Application Procedure: Candidates should complete and submit an application form by the published deadline

Closing Date: Refer website

Funding: Trusts

Additional Information: Applicants must be based in the United Kingdom or the Republic of Ireland, although other members of the project team can be based overseas

For further information contact:

Tel: (44) 20 7611 5757
Email: PEgrants@wellcome.ac.uk

Career Re-Entry Fellowships

Subjects: Biomedical Science

Purpose: This scheme is for postdoctoral scientists who have recently decided to recommence a scientific research career after a continuous break of at least 2 years

Eligibility: The awards are open to individuals with a relevant connection to the European Economic Area (EEA). You should be a research scientist with at least 2 years' postdoctoral experience and intend to be based in a United Kingdom or Republic of Ireland organization. You must have had a continuous career break of at least 2 years and should have either a strong research track record (if applying for up to 4 years' support) or demonstrated the potential for a strong research career prior to your break (if applying for 2 years' support). A 2-year fellowship should provide sufficient training support to consolidate your potential. The proposed research should fall within the Wellcome Trust's normal funding remit. Resubmissions are not normally encouraged. If your application has been unsuccessful, please contact the Office for advice. You must have an eligible sponsoring laboratory in the United Kingdom or Republic of Ireland that will administer the fellowship for the duration of the award

Level of Study: Professional development

Type: Fellowship

Value: It provides support that includes the fellow's salary, as determined by the host institution with an additional Trust enhancement, and Research expenses (consumables, animals, travel support to attend scientific meetings)

Length of Study: 2–4 years

Application Procedure: A preliminary application form (Word 92kB) should be completed and submitted by the published deadline. It should be sent electronically (as a Word document), with the requested accompanying information, to the appropriate funding stream at the Trust (see website). If successful, you will be shortlisted for interview

Closing Date: 15 May, 5pm (preliminary applications); 17 July, 5pm (full applications); and 11–13 November (shortlisted candidate interviews)

Funding: Trusts

Additional Information: For further information visit www.wellcome.ac.uk/Funding/Biomedical-science/Funding-schemes/Fellowships/Basic-biomedical-fellowships/wtd004380.htm

For further information contact:

Tel: (44) 20 7611 5757
Email: sciencegrants@wellcome.ac.uk

Clinical PhD Programmes

Subjects: Biomedical science

Purpose: This is a flagship scheme aimed at supporting the most promising medically qualified clinicians who wish to undertake rigorous research training

Eligibility: You should have demonstrated the potential to pursue a career as an academic clinician. It is anticipated that many applicants will have already commenced their specialist training, but this is not essential

Level of Study: Postgraduate, Research

Type: Grant

Value: The duration may vary from Programme to Programme, but each provides a clinical salary, PhD registration fees at United Kingdom/EU student rate, research expenses, contribution towards travel and contribution towards general training costs

Frequency: Annual

Country of Study: African countries

Application Procedure: Students are recruited annually by the individual Programmes. Recruitment begins in the preceding January. If you are interested in applying you should contact the relevant Programme directly. Please see website for more details

Closing Date: Varies

Funding: Trusts

For further information contact:

Email: clinicalphd@wellcome.ac.uk

Doctoral Studentships

Subjects: Medical history and humanities

Purpose: This scheme enables scholars to undertake up to 3 years of full-time research on a history of medicine topic leading to a doctoral degree at a university in the United Kingdom or Republic of Ireland

Eligibility: You should hold a Master's in the history of medicine or a Master's with strong emphasis on the history of medicine. The proposed project must be on a history of medicine topic. If specialist language skills are essential to undertake the research, a Master's in the language required may be acceptable (classical languages, Arabic, Chinese, etc.). Your application must be sponsored by a senior member of the department, unit or institute, or History of Medicine grantholder (current or former), who would supervise you if an award were made. Applications must be submitted through the host institution

Level of Study: Postgraduate, Research

Value: Support is provided for up to 3 years, and includes: the student's stipend; a set amount to cover conference travel, research expenses and, where justified, the cost of overseas fieldwork; all compulsory university and college fees at the United Kingdom/Irish/Dutch home postgraduate student level; fees at the overseas rate will not be provided; institutions sponsoring candidates are expected to provide laptops and PCs as part of their postgraduate research-training infrastructure

Length of Study: 3 years

Application Procedure: Preliminary applications should be made by email or post by the published deadline, and should include: a brief curriculum vitae with details of the Master's degree held; details of the research proposed (maximum of one page); a letter of support from the head of the department in which you will be working (this can be sent under separate cover); a letter of support from the supervisor

Closing Date: 2 April

Funding: Trusts

For further information contact:

Tel: (44) 20 7611 5757
Email: MHgrants@wellcome.ac.uk

Four-year PhD Studentship Programmes

Subjects: Biomedical science

Purpose: This is a flagship scheme aimed at supporting the most promising students to undertake in depth postgraduate training. Supporting specialized training provided in a range of important biomedical research areas: (1) developmental biology and cell biology; (2) genetics, statistics and epidemiology; (3) immunology and infectious disease; (4) molecular and cellular biology; (5) neuroscience; (6) physiological sciences; (7) structural biology and bioinformatics

Eligibility: You should be a student who has, or expects to obtain, a first- or upper-second-class honours degree or equivalent

Level of Study: Postgraduate, Research

Value: A stipend, PhD registration fees at United Kingdom/EU student rate, contribution towards laboratory rotation expenses in the first year, research expenses for years two to four, contribution towards travel and contribution towards transferable-skills training

Length of Study: Support provided for 4 years

Application Procedure: Students are recruited annually by the individual Programmes for uptake in October each year. Recruitment begins in the preceding December. If you are interested in applying you should contact the relevant Programme directly. Please see website for details

Closing Date: October

Funding: Trusts

For further information contact:

Email: 4yrphd@wellcome.ac.uk

Intermediate Clinical Fellowships

Subjects: Biomedical science

Purpose: This scheme is for medical, dental, veterinary or clinical psychology graduates who have had an outstanding start to their research career. It will enable successful candidates to continue their research interests at a postdoctoral level in an appropriate unit or clinical research facility

Eligibility: The award is open to individuals with a relevant connection to the EEA. You should have previously undergone a period of research training and will have completed, or be about to complete, a higher degree. You should have completed general professional training as defined by the relevant college. (1) Medical and dental candidates should either have a National Training Number (NTN) or Certificate of Completion of Specialist Training (CCST) or equivalent. (2) Veterinary candidates should have a degree in veterinary medicine (e.g. BVSc, BVM&S, BVMS, BVetMed, VetMB) and some experience in clinical practice and will have completed, or be about to complete, a higher research degree (preferably a PhD). (3) GPs are advised to contact the office to clarify their eligibility. (4) Clinical Psychologists must have obtained a professional Doctorate-level qualification in Clinical Psychology accredited by the British Psychological Society

Level of Study: Postgraduate, Research

Type: Fellowship

Value: Fellowships are for up to 4–5 years, depending on situation. They provide research expenses (consumables, travel, support to attend scientific meetings) and the fellow's salary, set by the host institution according to age and experience. Requests for specific items of equipment, where relevant, may be considered, and research or technical assistance may be requested. However, a laboratory appropriate to the research proposed should be selected, and the necessary facilities required for the proposed research must be available to the candidate. Funding for a period of research abroad may be requested if scientifically justified, and we provide appropriate allowances for fellows based overseas

Frequency: Annual

Application Procedure: A preliminary application form should be completed and submitted at any time before the appropriate deadline. It should be sent electronically (as a Word document) to the appropriate funding stream at the Trust (see website). If your preliminary application is successful, you will be invited to submit a full application by the published deadline. This will be peer reviewed and considered by the relevant Funding Committee. Shortlisted candidates will subsequently be invited to attend for interview at the Trust

Closing Date: 8 March; please visit the following link for full details: www.wellcome.ac.uk/Funding/Biomedical-science/Funding-schemes/Fellowships/Clinical-fellowships/wtd004402.htm

Funding: Trusts

For further information contact:

Tel: (44) 20 7611 5757
Email: sciencegrants@wellcome.ac.uk

Intermediate Fellowships in Public Health and Tropical Medicine

Subjects: Biomedical science
Purpose: This scheme enables high-calibre, mid-career researchers from low- and middle-income countries to establish an independent research programme. Fellows must be based primarily in a low- and middle-income country. Research projects should be aimed at understanding and controlling diseases (either human or animal) of relevance to local, national or global health. This can include laboratory based molecular analysis of field or clinical samples, but projects focused solely on studies in vitro or using animal models will not normally be considered under this scheme
Eligibility: Applications are only accepted in the Public Health and Tropical Medicine Interview Committee remit. This covers research on infectious and non-communicable diseases within the fields of public health and tropical medicine that is aimed at understanding and controlling diseases (either human or animal) of relevance to local, national or global health. You must be a national or legal resident of a low- and middle-income country and should be either: (1) A graduate in a subject relevant to public health or tropical medicine (e.g. biomedical or social science, veterinary medicine, physics, chemistry or mathematics) with a PhD and 3–6 years' postdoctoral experience, or (2) A medical graduate with a higher qualification equivalent to membership of the United Kingdom Royal Colleges of Physicians (i.e. qualified to enter higher specialist training) or recognized as a specialist within a relevant research area, with 3–6 years' research experience. You must have a relevant high-quality publication record and show potential to become a future scientific leader. Applicants who do not have a PhD but who are educated to first degree or Master's level and have extensive research experience, as evidenced by their publication record, may be considered
Level of Study: Postgraduate, Research
Type: Fellowship
Value: Fellowships are for up to 5 years (non-renewable) and provide support that includes: a basic salary for the fellow; research expenses (e.g. consumables, equipment, collaborative travel, research assistance, technical support); training costs where appropriate and justified; an inflation/flexible funding allowance and support to attend scientific meetings. Contributions to costs of the project which are directly incurred by the overseas institution may be provided

Application Procedure: You must complete and submit a preliminary application form by the published deadline. The form should be emailed to phatic@wellcome.ac.uk. Completed forms will normally be assessed within 1 month of the preliminary deadline. If the preliminary application meets the scheme's requirements, a full application will be invited
Closing Date: Preliminary application deadline: 23 May, Full application deadline: 18 July, Shortlisted candidate interviews: 22–23 November
Funding: Trusts
Additional Information: For complete details please check the link www.wellcome.ac.uk/Funding/Biomedical-science/ Funding-schemes/Fellowships/Public-health-and-tropical-medicine/wtd025883.htm

For further information contact:

Tel: (44) 20 7611 5757
Email: sciencegrants@wellcome.ac.uk

International Engagement Awards

Subjects: International Engagement Awards support projects that aim to achieve some or all of the following: to strengthen the capacity of people in low- and middle-income countries to facilitate public engagement with health research; to stimulate dialogue about health research and its impact on the public in a range of community and public contexts in low- and middle-income countries; to investigate and test new methods of engagement, participation, communication or education around health research; to promote collaboration on engagement projects between researchers and community or public organizations; to support Wellcome Trust funded researchers in low- and middle-income countries in engaging with the public and policy makers. Projects could involve: communities and members of the public (particularly those affected by or involved in health research); science communicators, health and science journalists; healthcare professionals, educators, field workers, community workers policy and decision makers
Purpose: To provide funding for innovative public or community engagement projects that explore biomedical research or health in Africa and Asia and to ensure science can be enjoyed and experienced as part of culture, entertainment and everyday life
Eligibility: The scheme is open to a wide range of people, including media professionals, educators, science communicators, health professionals and researchers in bioscience, health, bioethics and history. Partnership projects (between different people and organizations, e.g. scientists and media professionals, ethicists and community workers) are

welcomed. Applicants must be based in listed low- and middle-income countries or in the United Kingdom working with partners in the low- and middle-income countries. The activity must primarily take place in one or more low- and middle-income countries and the primary goal must be to involve participants or engage audiences located in low- and middle-income countries. Applicants from listed restructuring countries in Europe and Asia are not eligible. We can only accept applications in the English language but we welcome projects that bring together people from different backgrounds who speak diverse languages. All projects must involve engagement with health research. Projects dealing purely with development research not related to health are not eligible. Please note also, that the scheme is not intended to support standard delivery of health education and promotion which does not focus on health research or involve health researchers. Applicants must be affiliated to organizations or institutions. Organizations might include: media organizations, research centres or research groups, community-based development organizations, education organizations. The International Engagement Awards will not fund traditional scientist-led health research. We may consider an application for participatory health research. This is research in which participants are supported to own and shape a research process, setting their own research questions and directing the research process. This type of research should not look like a consultatory exercise or health education but should aim to be collaborative process of enquiry in which the analysis is conducted and findings can be used by all participating parties. This could lead into circular processes of research and action

Level of Study: Research
Type: Award
Value: Up to £30,000 for projects lasting a maximum of 3 years
Application Procedure: Please contact the International Engagement Awards office well in advance of the deadline to request an application form and to confirm the eligibility of your project
Closing Date: 19 August
Funding: Trusts

For further information contact:

Tel: (44) 20 7611 5757
Email: PEgrants@wellcome.ac.uk

Investigator Awards

Subjects: Biomedical science
Purpose: To support world-class researchers who are no more than 5 years from appointment to their first academic position, but who can already show that they have the ability to innovate and drive advances in their field of study
Eligibility: To be eligible for an Investigator Award you must be based at an eligible higher education or research institution in the United Kingdom, Republic of Ireland or a low- or middle-income country. You should be employed in an established academic post: a permanent, open-ended or long-term rolling contract, salaried by your host institution. You are also eligible if you have a written guarantee of an established academic post at your host institution, which you will take up by the start of the award. If you are based in a low- or middle-income country in sub-Saharan Africa, South-east Asia or South Asia (with the exception of India - see below), you are eligible to apply if you fulfil the above eligibility criteria and are working within the Trust's broad science funding remit
Level of Study: Research
Type: Award
Value: Awards may be small or large, typically up to £3,000,000, and lasting up to 7 years. The duration and costs you request should be clearly justified by your proposed research. Also, you should ensure that the scope of your proposal and the associated resources are appropriate for your career stage and research experience. The award covers the direct costs of carrying out the research, such as: research expenses; this may include research assistance, animals, equipment, fieldwork costs and funding for collaborative activity; travel and subsistence for scientifically justified visits; overseas allowances where appropriate
Frequency: Annual
Application Procedure: The key stages of the application process are: submission of an Investigator Award application form; scientific peer review by one of the Trust's Expert Review Groups, which shortlist the candidates for interview; written peer review of shortlisted applications by external specialist referees, who will include members of the Trust's Peer Review College; selected unattributed referee comments will be fed back to candidates before interview; interview of shortlisted candidates by our Interview Panel. Application forms are available on eGrants, our electronic application system. Please refer to the Additional information for completing the Investigator Award form on eGrants, which provides an overview to help guide you through the application process
Funding: Trusts
Additional Information: The Trust has combined its New Investigator and Senior Investigator Award schemes to create a single type of Investigator Award, providing all who hold established posts in eligible organizations with the same opportunity to obtain funding

For further information contact:

Email: sciencegrants@wellcome.ac.uk

Master's Awards

Subjects: Medical history and humanities
Purpose: This scheme enables scholars to undertake basic training in research and methods through a 1-year Master's course in medical history and humanities
Eligibility: You should have a minimum of an excellent upper-second-class honours degree (or equivalent) in a relevant subject. Applications will not be considered from those who have already received support for their postgraduate studies from another funding body
Level of Study: Postgraduate, Research
Type: Award
Value: The award is for 1 year, and includes: the student's stipend; all compulsory university and college fees at the United Kingdom home postgraduate student level. Fees at the overseas rate will not be provided
Frequency: Annual
Application Procedure: All enquiries about Master's Awards should be made directly to the relevant institution
Closing Date: 1 May
Funding: Trusts

For further information contact:

Tel: (44) 20 7611 5757
Email: MHgrants@wellcome.ac.uk

Master's Fellowships in Public Health and Tropical Medicine

Subjects: Biomedical science
Purpose: This scheme strengthens scientific research capacity in low- and middle-income countries, by providing support for junior researchers to gain research experience and high-quality research training at Master's degree level. Research projects should be aimed at understanding and controlling diseases (either human or animal) of relevance to local, national or global health. This can include laboratory based molecular analysis of field or clinical samples, but projects focused solely on studies in vitro or using animal models will not normally be considered under this scheme
Eligibility: You should be: (1) A national or legal resident of a low- and middle-income country, and hold a first degree in subject relevant to tropical medicine or public health (clinical or non-clinical). (2) At an early stage in your career, with limited research experience, but have a demonstrated interest in or aptitude for research
Level of Study: Postdoctorate, Postgraduate, Research
Type: Fellowship
Value: This fellowship normally provides up to 30 months' support. A period of 12 months should normally be dedicated to undertaking a taught Master's course at a recognized centre of excellence, combined with up to 18 months to undertake a research project. While undertaking a Master's course, fellows will receive a stipend in accordance with the cost of living in the country in which he/she will be studying; travel costs and support for approved tuition fees. Master's training by distance learning is acceptable. Master's course fees will be paid according to the rate charged by the training institution
Application Procedure: A completed application form should be submitted by the sponsor by the published deadline. The form should be emailed to phatic@wellcome.ac.uk. The application should include details of your sponsor's track record in training and a list of their other students at the institution. It must be supported by the head of the institution where the research will be based, and a career plan for the proposed candidate must be included
Closing Date: 2 March (for applications submissions)
Funding: Trusts
Additional Information: For complete details go to address www.wellcome.ac.uk/Funding/Biomedical-science/Funding-schemes/Fellowships/Public-health-and-tropical-medicine/wtd025881.htm

For further information contact:

Tel: (44) 20 7611 5757
Email: sciencegrants@wellcome.ac.uk

Pathfinder Awards

Purpose: This scheme, offering pilot funding to catalyse innovative early-stage applied research and development projects in areas of unmet medical need, has been expanded. It now funds discrete projects from applicants in the United Kingdom and Republic of Ireland as well as partnerships between academia and industry based anywhere in the world
Eligibility: Applications are welcome from academic and commercial organizations based in the United Kingdom or the Republic of Ireland. Applications from organizations and companies overseas will only be considered when applying in partnership. Check website for complete details
Level of Study: Research
Type: Grant
Value: The average award amount is envisaged to be in the region of £1,00,000, but up to £3,50,000 will be considered in exceptional circumstances
Length of Study: 18 months
Frequency: Dependent on funds available
Application Procedure: You should contact us to confirm that your proposed application (and partnership, if appropriate), is eligible before submitting a full application form. After confirming that your application is eligible, you should

complete the full application form (see 'Forms and guidance') and send it to innovations@wellcome.ac.uk before the deadline

Closing Date: February (There will be four deadlines a year, subject to available budget.)

Funding: Trusts

For further information contact:

Email: innovations@wellcome.ac.uk

Postdoctoral Research Training Fellowships for Clinicians

Subjects: Biomedical science

Purpose: This is a flexible fellowship scheme to enable individuals to engage with areas of research that are new to them. It is for candidates who either undertook a PhD early in their career and now wish to refresh their research skills, or have recently completed a successful PhD and wish to explore a new research field or environment, to gain the skills that will help them answer their longer-term research vision

Eligibility: The scheme may be suitable for clinicians who: are due to complete their higher degree or are no more than 2 years from the date of their PhD viva by the full application deadline; graduated with a MB/PhD qualification or have achieved a high-quality PhD in a relevant subject, either during or prior to commencing their initial medical, veterinary or dental degree

Level of Study: Postgraduate, Research

Type: Fellowship

Value: Awards are for 2–4 years, depending on whether or not you are planning to reintegrate into your clinical training programme. The total cost of a Fellowship would typically range from £250,000 to £400,000

Frequency: Annual

Application Procedure: A preliminary application form should be completed and submitted at any time before the published deadline. It should be sent electronically (as a Word document) to Dr Lucy Bradshaw (see website for contact details). If your preliminary application is successful, you will be invited to submit a full application. This will be reviewed and if successful you will be shortlisted for interview

Closing Date: 18 May (5pm) for preliminary application; 13 July (5pm) for full application deadline; and 19-20 November (CIC) and 25-27 November (PHATIC) for shortlisted candidate interviews

Funding: Trusts

Additional Information: For more details see www.wellcome.ac.uk/Funding/Biomedical-science/Funding-schemes/Fellowships/Clinical-fellowships/wtp052588.htm

For further information contact:

Tel: (44) 20 7611 5757
Email: sciencegrants@wellcome.ac.uk

Principal Research Fellowships

Subjects: Biomedical science

Purpose: This is the most prestigious of our personal awards and provides long-term support for researchers of international standing. Successful candidates will have an established track record in research at the highest level

Eligibility: You should have an established track record in research at the highest level. This award is particularly suitable for exceptional senior research scientists currently based overseas who wish to work in the United Kingdom or Republic of Ireland

Level of Study: Postgraduate, Research

Type: Fellowship

Value: Awards are for 7 years in the first instance, and provide both a personal salary and research programme funding in full. After the first period of award, the fellowship will be subject to a competitive scientific review, which will subsequently occur on a rolling basis every 5 years

Length of Study: 7 years

Application Procedure: If you intend to apply you should contact us with a full curriculum vitae, preferably 18 months in advance of the desired award date. You may not apply for more than one Wellcome Trust fellowship scheme at any one time

Closing Date: Applicants can express interest at any time. Interview usually held in June and December

Funding: Trusts

For further information contact:

Tel: (44) 20 7611 5757
Email: sciencegrants@wellcome.ac.uk

Research and Development for Affordable Healthcare in India

Subjects: Projects covering any aspect of technology development for healthcare will be considered, including diagnostics, therapeutics, vaccines, medical devices and regenerative medicine. Proposals drawing on the disciplines of the physical sciences, maths and engineering, as well as biomedicine, are equally encouraged

Purpose: The objective of this initiative is to fund translational research projects that will deliver safe and effective healthcare products for India, and potentially other markets, at affordable costs. A key feature of the scheme is that it encourages innovations that bring together researchers from both the public and private sectors to extend access to care to the greatest numbers of beneficiaries, without compromising on quality

Eligibility: Awards will be agreed by Committee and governed by the terms and conditions, including Wellcome Trust Grant Conditions, funding terms for Affordable Healthcare. In addition there will be additional terms and conditions that will be negotiated under the funding agreement for the award with the applicant

Level of Study: Research

Type: Award

Value: Awards will be made by way of funding agreements that will be negotiated on a case-by-case basis. The principles of the Wellcome Trust Grant Conditions will apply. The terms and conditions of funding will be discussed with applicants individually. Typically, the agreements will contain a provision for the appropriate sharing of benefits. The funds available will be ring-fenced for the specified programme of work. Neither working capital nor building or refurbishment expenditure will be provided. Funding will be released in tranches against the attainment of pre-agreed project milestones

Application Procedure: In the first instance interested applicants should contact Dr Shirshendu Mukherjee to discuss their interest in funding via the Affordable Healthcare Initiative. Alternatively, applicants may complete a concept note and mail this directly to Dr Shirshendu Mukherjee

Closing Date: 31 January

Funding: Trusts

For further information contact:

Email: s.mukherjee@wellcome.ac.uk
Contact: Dr Shirshendu Mukherjee, Senior Strategic Adviser

Research Career Development Fellowships in Basic Biomedical Science

Subjects: Biomedical Science

Purpose: To provide support for outstanding postdoctoral scientists based in academic institutions in the United Kingdom and Republic of Ireland (RoI)

Eligibility: You should have a relevant connection to the European Economic Area. You are expected to have science or veterinary qualifications and, at the preliminary application stage, should normally have between three and 6 years' research experience from the date of your doctoral degree (PhD viva). Due allowance will be given to those whose career has been affected for personal reasons. You must have made intellectual contributions to research that have

been published in leading journals, and be able to demonstrate your potential to carry out independent research. The proposed research should fall within our normal funding remit. Resubmissions are not normally encouraged. If your application has been unsuccessful, please contact the Office for advice. You must have an eligible sponsoring host institution in the United Kingdom or Republic of Ireland (RoI) and an eligible sponsor who can guarantee space and resources for the tenure of any award

Level of Study: Postdoctorate, Research

Type: Fellowship

Value: (1) A basic salary, as determined by the host institution, with an additional Wellcome Trust enhancement. (2) Research expenses, including research assistance if required (normally a graduate research assistant or technician; requests for additional research staff may be considered where fieldwork or clinical studies in a low- or middle-income country are proposed). (3) Overseas allowances where appropriate. (4) Travel and subsistence for scientifically justified visits of up to 1 year

Length of Study: 5 years

Frequency: Annual

Application Procedure: A preliminary application form should be completed and submitted by the published deadline. It should be sent electronically (as a Word document), with the requested accompanying information, to the appropriate funding stream at the Trust (see website). If successful, you will be invited to submit a full application

Closing Date: Varies; refer to website www.wellcome.ac.uk/funding/biomedical-science/funding-schemes/fellowships/basic-biomedical-fellowships/wtd004431.htm

Funding: Trusts

For further information contact:

Tel: (44) 20 7611 5757
Email: sciencegrants@wellcome.ac.uk

Research Fellowships

Subjects: Social and ethical aspects of biomedicine and healthcare

Purpose: Due to the multidisciplinary nature of research on the social and ethical aspects of biomedicine and healthcare, Research Fellowships may provide postdoctoral researchers with support to enable them to obtain research training, either in a new discipline or in a new aspect of their own field, e.g. a humanities scholar who wishes to be trained in social science. In such cases, the requested training must form a substantial component of the proposed research and should not normally be available via the standard funding routes, e.g. by learning new skills as a postdoctoral researcher on a project grant. The requested training should also include methodologies and skills that are new to the applicant. Research training provision can include participation in taught courses, and periods spent in other research groups gaining practical, technical or other skills for introduction to the sponsor's or individual's own group

Eligibility: You are eligible to apply if you are a postdoctoral scholar who is not in a tenured or otherwise long-term established post. Fellowships must be held at a United Kingdom, Irish or low- or middle-income country institution. You will also be expected to have been awarded your PhD before you are eligible to apply. Applications from candidates who are still awaiting their viva by the time of the full application will not normally be accepted

Level of Study: Research
Type: Fellowship
Value: An award will not normally exceed £250,000, exclusive of any standard Wellcome Trust allowances. Fellowships provide a salary, plus appropriate employer's contributions. Essential research expenses, including travel and fieldwork, are available, as is a set amount for travel to conferences, seminars and other meetings of a scholarly nature
Length of Study: 3 years
Application Procedure: Preliminary applications should be made in writing, and include: a brief curriculum vitae and full publication list; details of research proposed (maximum of 1 page); a letter of support from the head of department in which you will be working; the approximate cost of the proposal, broken down into equipment and project running expenses
Closing Date: January round – 22 January is closing date for preliminary applications and 30 March is closing date for full applications, The schedule for full applications received by 30 March closing date is as follows: May is shortlisting and July: interviews; for July round – Dates are to be confirmed
Funding: Trusts
Additional Information: The maximum duration of the awards is 3 years. The awards are full-time but can be tenable on a part-time basis if a case can be made that personal circumstances require this

For further information contact:

Tel: (44) 20 7611 5757
Email: MHgrants@wellcome.ac.uk

Research Training Fellowships

Subjects: Medical, dental, veterinary or clinical psychology
Purpose: Provide support for medical, dental, veterinary and clinical psychology graduates who have little or no research training, but who wish to develop a long-term career in academic medicine

Eligibility: The fellowship is open to individuals with a relevant connection to the European Economic Area (EEA) for fellowships to be held in a United Kingdom or Republic of Ireland institution. Non-United Kingdom candidates should contact the office for advice before submitting an application. 1. Medical graduates must have passed the relevant exam for their specialty, e.g. MRCP, MRCS, MRCOphth/FRCOphth Part 1, MRCPsych, MRCOG Part 1, MRCPCH, FRCA Part 1. GPs are advised to contact the office to clarify their eligibility. 2. Dental candidates must have obtained MFD, MFDS, MGDS, MFGDP or equivalent. 3. Veterinary candidates should have a degree in veterinary medicine (e.g. BVSc, BVM&S, BVMS, BVetMed, VetMB) and some experience in clinical practice. An intercalated degree is desirable, but not essential. 4. Clinical psychology candidates must have obtained a professional Doctorate-level qualification in Clinical Psychology accredited by the British Psychological Society before taking up the award. Candidates are advised to contact the office to clarify their eligibility. You are expected to undertake a high-quality research project that balances the provision of training with the opportunity to advance knowledge in a given area. A project based solely on a systematic review of a particular area is not suitable, unless it includes a significant element of methodological innovation
Level of Study: Postgraduate, Research
Type: Fellowship
Value: Fellowships are normally for 2–3 years. In exceptional cases a fellowship may be for up to 4 years for those who wish to undertake a relevant Master's training or diploma course. All training requests must be fully justified in the application. Fellowships provide research expenses (consumables, travel, and support to attend scientific meetings) and a fellow's salary, set according to age, experience and our policy on enhancement
Length of Study: 2–3 years
Application Procedure: Application form is available from the website
Closing Date: Varies; refer to the website www.wellcome.ac.uk/Funding/Biomedical-science/Funding-schemes/Fellowships/Clinical-fellowships/wtd004435.htm
Funding: Trusts

For further information contact:

Tel: (44) 20 7611 5757
Email: sciencegrants@wellcome.ac.uk

Science Media Studentships

Subjects: These studentships offer financial support for three PhD-level biomedical scientists to undertake postgraduate qualifications at Imperial College London or the National Film and Television School (NFTS)

Purpose: We aim to increase the crossover between science and the media and to enable bright, articulate and motivated scientists to explore a career in the broadcast industry

Eligibility: Applicants should be PhD-level biomedical scientists wishing to explore a career in the broadcast, games and film industries. Applicants must have a PhD or equivalent, some experience of science communication, and a demonstrable aptitude for working with TV, radio, film or games

Level of Study: Postdoctorate, Research

Type: Studentship

Value: Awards will pay for tuition costs plus a grant to cover basic living expenses for the duration of the studentship

Frequency: Annual

Application Procedure: Application is through the Imperial College website

Closing Date: 26 February

Funding: Trusts

For further information contact:

Tel: (44) 20 7594 8753
Email: liam.watson@imperial.ac.uk
Contact: Liam Watson, Science Communication Group Administ

Seeding Drug Discovery

Subjects: The aim is to develop drug-like, small molecules that will be the springboard for further research and development by the biotechnology and pharmaceutical industry in areas of unmet medical need

Purpose: To facilitate early-stage small-molecule drug discovery. The awards help applicants with a potential drug target or new chemistry embark on a programme of compound discovery and/or lead optimization

Level of Study: Research

Type: Award

Value: Early-stage drug discovery projects are able to apply for funding for up to 2 years to facilitate screening of chemical compounds to identify one or more lead series of molecules. Late-stage projects, where a lead compound has already been identified, are able to apply for funding for up to 4 years, to support lead optimization and preclinical development through to clinical trials

Application Procedure: A preliminary application form should be completed and returned to Technology Transfer by the published deadline. Applications will be considered at one of the two Seeding Drug Discovery Committee meetings in each 12-month period. Successful applicants will be shortlisted and invited to complete a full application

Closing Date: Varies; refer to the website www.wellcome. ac.uk/Funding/Innovations/Awards/Seeding-Drug-Discovery/index.htm

Funding: Trusts

For further information contact:

Tel: (44) 20 7611 5757
Fax: (44) 20 7611 8857
Email: innovations@wellcome.ac.uk

Senior and Intermediate Research Fellowship for International Students

Subjects: Fellowship is awarded to support biomedical research that is relevant to human and animal welfare

Purpose: The aim of the fellowship is to supports outstanding researchers of any nationality, either medically qualified or science graduates, who wish to pursue a research career in an academic institution in India

Eligibility: Applicants of any nationality are eligible to apply for the fellowship. Applicants must be a basic science/veterinary researchers with 4 -15 years of post-PhD research experience. Applicants must be fluent in English

Type: Research

Value: The fellowship has the tenure of five years and provides: The Fellow's personal support. Research expenses, including research assistance if required (normally funding for four research staff may be requested). The total award for a Senior Fellowship typically includes the costs requested by the applicant as well as the set contributions by the India Alliance. For further details, see costing policies. Costs requested by the applicant must be commensurate with their research proposal and should be fully justified in the full application. Inadequate justifications may result in costs being revised. Time permitted for non-research related activity during the fellowship is normally restricted to a maximum of eight hours each week

Study Establishment: Fellowship is awarded to support biomedical research that is relevant to human and animal welfare

Country of Study: India

Application Procedure: See the website

Closing Date: 15 January

Additional Information: For more details please visit the website scholarship-positions.com/senior-intermediate-research-fellowship-for-international-students-india/2018/01/02/

For further information contact:

Email: info@wellcomedbt.org

Senior Fellowships in Public Health and Tropical Medicine

Subjects: Biomedical science
Purpose: This scheme supports outstanding researchers from low- and middle-income countries to establish themselves as leading investigators at an academic institution in a low- and middle-income country location. This fellowship is the most senior of a series of career awards aimed at building sustainable capacity in areas of research that have the potential for increasing health benefits for people and their livestock in low- and middle-income countries. Research projects should be aimed at understanding and controlling diseases (either human or animal) of relevance to local, national or global health
Eligibility: Candidate must be a graduate in a subject relevant to public health or tropical medicine (for example; biomedical or social science, veterinary medicine, physics, chemistry or mathematics) with a PhD and at least 5 years' postdoctoral experience, or a medical graduate with a higher qualification equivalent to membership of the United Kingdom Royal College of Physicians (i.e. qualified to enter higher specialist training), or be recognized as a specialist within a relevant research area, and have at least 5 years' research experience
Level of Study: Postgraduate, Research
Type: Fellowship
Value: A basic salary; research expenses (e.g. consumables, equipment, collaborative travel, research assistance, technical support), training costs where appropriate and justified; an inflation/flexible funding allowance and support to attend scientific meetings; and contributions to costs of the project that are directly incurred by the overseas institution may also be provided
Length of Study: Up to 5 years
Application Procedure: You are required to complete and submit a preliminary application form by the published deadline. The form should be emailed to phatic@wellcome.ac.uk. Completed forms will normally be assessed within 1 month of the preliminary deadline. If your preliminary application meets the scheme's requirements, a full application will be invited
Closing Date: Varies; refer to the website www.wellcome. ac.uk/Funding/Biomedical-science/Funding-schemes/Fellowships/Public-health-and-tropical-medicine/wtd025884.htm
Funding: Trusts
Additional Information: Overseas allowances will be provided for periods of training or collaborative research spent outside the home institution country, where appropriate. Research-dedicated costs (excluding salary costs) should not exceed £100,000 per year

For further information contact:

Tel: (44) 20 7611 5757
Email: sciencegrants@wellcome.ac.uk

Senior Research Fellowships in Basic Biomedical Science

Subjects: Biomedical science
Purpose: To provide support for outstanding postdoctoral scientists based in academic institutions in the United Kingdom and Republic of Ireland (RoI)
Eligibility: The fellowship is open to individuals with a relevant connection to the EEA. You should have between 5 and normally 10 years' research experience (from the date of your viva to the date of your preliminary application) at postdoctoral level, or veterinary equivalent, and have a substantial record of publications in your chosen area of research in leading international journals. Candidates that do not hold an established post may apply to remain in their current laboratory, to return to one where they have worked before or to move to a new laboratory in the United Kingdom or Republic of Ireland. Candidates that hold an established post are not eligible to apply for a fellowship to be held at their current employing institution. However, we are willing to consider a preliminary application where a candidate wishes to move institution and is able to make an appropriate justification for the move. The Trust does not normally accept resubmissions of full applications for its fellowships. Please contact the Office for further advice. You must have an eligible sponsor and host institution in the United Kingdom or Republic of Ireland who can guarantee space and resources for the tenure of the award
Level of Study: Postdoctorate, Research
Type: Fellowship
Value: The fellowship is for 5 years in the first instance, and provides a basic salary, as determined by the host institution (normally up to £55,000 per year) with an additional Trust supplement of £12,500 per year; the essential costs of the research programme (e.g. consumables, equipment, research assistance, overseas allowances, collaborative travel and subsistence); an inflation and Flexible Funding Allowance; and support to attend scientific meetings
Frequency: Annual
Application Procedure: A preliminary application form should be completed and submitted electronically (as a Word document) to the relevant funding stream (see website) no later than the published deadline. Full application forms will usually be sent to shortlisted candidates within 1 month of the preliminary deadline. In the full application, if invited, the host institution will be required to confirm that it will support a successful renewal of the fellowship under the shared funding arrangement for the full period of any renewal
Additional Information: Refer to the website www.wellcome. ac.uk/funding/biomedical-science/funding-schemes/fellowships/basic-biomedical-fellowships/wtd004442.htm

Closing Date: Varies
Funding: Trusts

For further information contact:

Tel: (44) 20 7611 5757
Email: sciencegrants@wellcome.ac.uk

Senior Research Fellowships in Clinical Science

Subjects: Biomedical science
Purpose: This scheme provides support for clinical investigators to further develop their research potential and to establish themselves as leading investigators in clinical academic medicine
Eligibility: You must have a relevant connection to the EEA. If you are a non-United Kingdom candidate, please contact the Office for advice before submitting a preliminary application. You should be a clinical scientist with a medical, dental, veterinary or clinical psychology qualification and will normally have no more than 15 years' clinical and research experience from the date of your first medical, dental, veterinary or British Psychological Society-accredited psychology qualification. (Due allowance will be given to those whose career has been affected by a late start or interruption for personal/family reasons.) Successful candidates will have made significant progress towards establishing themselves as independent clinical investigators. A research degree (PhD/MD), together with evidence of advanced (postdoctoral) research training (typically at least 3–5 years), is expected. They will have published consistently in their chosen area of research, placing substantive papers in leading journals. Candidates will not normally hold a tenured academic post in a university in the United Kingdom or Republic of Ireland, or a consultant post in the NHS
Level of Study: Postgraduate, Research
Type: Fellowship
Value: The fellowship is for 5 years in the first instance, and provides: a basic salary, as determined by the host institution; research expenses; an inflation allowance and support to attend scientific meetings; provision for public engagement cost
Frequency: Annual
Application Procedure: A preliminary application form should be completed and submitted by the published deadline. It should be sent electronically (as a Word document), with the requested accompanying information, to the appropriate funding stream at the Trust (see website). Incomplete or incorrectly completed forms will not be accepted. Faxed applications will not be accepted. Please do not send any additional material. You will be notified in writing of your success, or otherwise, in reaching the next round of the competition. In some instances, we may recommend that candidates apply for an Intermediate Clinical Fellowship
Closing Date: Varies; refer to the website www.wellcome.ac.uk/funding/biomedical-science/funding-schemes/fellowships/clinical-fellowships/wtd004445.htm
Funding: Trusts

For further information contact:

Tel: (44) 20 7611 5757
Email: sciencegrants@wellcome.ac.uk

Short-term Research Leave Awards for Clinicians and Scientists

Subjects: Medical history and humanities
Purpose: This scheme enables clinicians, scientists and other healthcare professionals to undertake up to 6 months (FTE) of research at a centre or department with academic expertise in medical humanities, to explore the wider determinants and contexts of their own medical and scientific work
Eligibility: You should be a scientist, clinician or healthcare professional holding an established post to which you would return on completion of the award. You must be resident in the United Kingdom or Republic of Ireland. You should have a record of publication in medical or scientific journals
Level of Study: Research
Type: Award
Value: We will provide the salary of a locum or replacement lecturer for the duration of the award, and a set amount for travel to conferences
Length of Study: Up to 6 months
Application Procedure: You should submit a preliminary application in writing, including: a brief curriculum vitae, a full publication list and confirmation that your personal support is from the Higher Education Funding Council; details of the research proposed (maximum one page); details of hours spent on teaching and administration; the approximate cost of the proposal, broken down into staff salaries, equipment and running expenses
Closing Date: 23 January (preliminary applications for January round); July (preliminary applications for July round). For further detail check website www.wellcome.ac.uk/Funding/Medical-humanities/funding-schemes/personal-awards/wtd003761.htm
Funding: Trusts

For further information contact:

Tel: (44) 20 7611 5757
Email: MHgrants@wellcome.ac.uk

Sir Henry Wellcome Postdoctoral Fellowships

Subjects: Biomedical science
Purpose: To provide a unique opportunity for the most promising newly qualified postdoctoral researchers to make an early start in developing their independent research careers, working in the best laboratories in the United Kingdom and overseas
Eligibility: These awards are open to individuals with a relevant connection to the European Economic Area. You must be in the final year of your PhD studies or have no more than 1 year of postdoctoral research experience from the date of your PhD viva to the full application submission deadline (e.g. if the full deadline is in February, your viva should not have occurred prior to last February). Time spent outside the research environment will be taken into consideration. You must have an eligible sponsoring institution in the United Kingdom or Republic of Ireland that will administer the fellowship for the full duration of the award
Level of Study: Postdoctorate, Research
Type: Fellowships
Value: 4 year full-time fellowship. Provides an award of £250,000
Length of Study: 4 years
Frequency: Annual
Application Procedure: You should complete and submit a preliminary application form by the published deadline. It should be sent electronically (as a Word document), with the requested accompanying information, to the relevant funding stream at the Trust. Your preliminary application will be assessed within 4 weeks of the submission deadline. If successful, you will be invited to submit a full application. Your full application will be peer reviewed by the relevant Funding Committee and, if successful, you will be shortlisted for interview
Closing Date: Varies; refer to the website www.wellcome. ac.uk/Funding/Biomedical-science/Funding-schemes/Fellow ships/Basic-biomedical-fellowships/wtx033549.htm
Funding: Trusts

For further information contact:

Tel: (44) 20 7611 5757
Email: sciencegrants@wellcome.ac.uk

Strategic Awards in Biomedical Science

Subjects: Biomedical science
Purpose: Strategic Awards provide flexible forms of support to excellent research groups with outstanding track records in their field

Eligibility: Applications will be considered from principal applicants who meet our eligibility criteria and are recognized international leaders in their field
Level of Study: Research
Type: Award
Value: It provides equipment, support staff, consumables, training programmes, networking, biological, clinical or epidemiological research resources. Limited capital building or refurbishment essential to the programme can also be requested
Length of Study: Awards are normally for 5 years
Application Procedure: You (prospective applicant) are required to submit a preliminary application, which should include the following information: (1) your track record, you must complete the curriculum vitae pages (these are questions 14 and 15 from the standard project grant application form); (2) high-level aims and objectives, and how the proposal addresses the strategic challenges in the Wellcome Trust's Strategic Plan (maximum of two pages); (3) key targets, milestones and management structures, if appropriate (maximum of two pages); (4) duration of support requested and outline costings broken down into main headings (e.g. staff, equipment); (5) a statement from the head of the institution, indicating how the proposal fits within the context of the institution's strategic vision and what financial commitment the institution will make to the group if the application is successful. If your preliminary application is successful, you will be invited to submit a full application. The relevant form will be provided at this time
Closing Date: Refer website
Funding: Trusts

For further information contact:

Tel: (44) 20 7611 5757
Email: sciencegrants@wellcome.ac.uk

Training Fellowships in Public Health and Tropical Medicine

Subjects: Biomedical science
Purpose: This scheme provides researchers from low- and middle-income countries–who are at an early stage in the establishment of their research careers–with opportunities for research experience and high-quality research training in public health and tropical medicine. Research projects should be aimed at understanding and controlling diseases (either human or animal) of relevance to local, national or global health. This can include laboratory-based molecular analysis of field or clinical samples, but projects focused solely on studies in vitro or using animal models will not normally be considered under this scheme

Eligibility: Applications are only accepted in the Public Health and Tropical Medicine Interview Committee remit. This covers research on infectious and non-communicable diseases within the fields of public health and tropical medicine that is aimed at understanding and controlling diseases (either human or animal) of relevance to local, national or global health. You must be a national or legal resident of a low- and middle-income country and should be either: (1) a graduate in a subject relevant to public health or tropical medicine (e.g. biomedical or social science, veterinary medicine, physics, chemistry or mathematics) with a PhD and no more than 3 years' postdoctoral experience, or (2) a medical graduate with a higher qualification equivalent to membership of the United Kingdom Royal Colleges of Physicians (i.e. qualified to enter higher specialist training) and some initial research experience. Applicants may also apply if they do not have a PhD, but have a clinical, basic or Master's degree and some initial research experience, with the expectation that they will register for a PhD

Level of Study: Postgraduate, Research

Type: Fellowship

Value: It provides support that includes a basic salary for the fellow, research expenses (e.g. consumables, equipment, collaborative travel, research assistance, technical support) training costs where appropriate and justified, an inflation/flexible funding allowance and support to attend scientific meetings, and contributions to costs of the project that are directly incurred by the overseas institution may also be provided

Length of Study: 3 years

Application Procedure: You are required to complete and submit a preliminary application form by the published deadline. The form should be emailed to phatic@wellcome.ac.uk. Completed forms will normally be assessed within 1 month of the preliminary deadline. If the preliminary application meets the scheme's requirements, you will be invited to submit a full application

Closing Date: Varies; refer to the website www.wellcome. ac.uk/Funding/Biomedical-science/Funding-schemes/Fellow ships/Public-health-and-tropical-medicine/wtd025882.htm

Funding: Trusts

For further information contact:

Tel: (44) 20 7611 5757
Email: sciencegrants@wellcome.ac.uk

Translation Fund

Subjects: Projects covering any aspect of technology development from a range of disciplines–including physical, computational and life sciences–will be considered. Projects must address an unmet need in healthcare or in applied medical research, offer a potential new solution, and have a realistic expectation that the innovation will be developed further by the market

Purpose: Translation Awards are response-mode funding designed to bridge the funding gap in the commercialisation of new technologies in the biomedical area

Eligibility: Projects must address an unmet need in healthcare or in applied medical research, offer a potential new solution, and have a realistic expectation that the innovation will be developed further by the market. Institutions: eligible institutions are not-for-profit research institutions, including those funded by the Medical Research Council, Cancer Research United Kingdom, and Biotechnology and Biological Sciences Research Council, in the United Kingdom. Institutions are normally required to sign up to a short funding agreement and the Grant Conditions. Companies: we are able to use our charitable monies to fund commercial companies to meet our charitable objectives through programme-related investment (PRI). For further details please refer to our policy on PRI. Companies will normally be expected to sign up to specific terms relating to the scheme. Overseas organizations: United Kingdom organizations may contract or collaborate with overseas organizations. Although overseas organizations are not eligible for Translation Awards, some proposals may be invited for consideration as a Strategic Translation Award (including Seeding Drug Discovery). Overseas organizations should contact Technology Transfer staff about their proposed project in the first instance. Principal applicants and coapplicants: applicants should normally hold a position of responsibility within the eligible organization and be able to sign up to or comply with the conditions or terms of an award. In addition, postdoctoral research assistants–whether seeking their own salary as part of the grant proposal, funded by the Wellcome Trust on another grant, or funded by another agency–are eligible for coapplicant status if they make a significant contribution to a research proposal and have agreement from their funding agency. Other eligibility information: Disciplines outside biomedicine – researchers from disciplines outside biomedicine can apply providing the application of research is designed to facilitate or meet a need in healthcare. For example, the application of physics, chemistry, computing, engineering and materials science to the development of medical products is entirely appropriate. Healthcare need in an area that is not commercially attractive. We are committed to the translation of research into practical healthcare benefits across the full spectrum of disease. Disease areas neglected by industry because of the lack of a return on investment pose a particular problem, but imaginative ways forward can sometimes be developed (e.g. public-private partnerships such as the Medicines for Malaria Venture). Intellectual property rights (IPR)/publications – if there are any restrictions on IPR or publications arising from your research, you must provide a written statement that details them. Restrictions on intellectual property may affect your eligibility to apply to the Trust. Please refer to our Grant Conditions

Level of Study: Research

Type: Award

Value: The important criterion is to develop the innovation to the point at which it can be adopted by another party. Providing it is adequately justified, modest equipment purchase and maintenance costs may be included in a Translation Award application. Building or refurbishment expenditure will not normally be considered. Applications may not include requests for academic institutional overheads. If you hold a tenured university post, you may not re-charge your salary (in full or part) to a Translation Award

Application Procedure: A preliminary application form must be completed and sent to Technology Transfer by the published deadline. Preliminary applications are subject to a triage for shortlisting for the full application stage. Applications will be considered by the Technology Transfer Challenge Committee (TTCC), which meets twice a year. Full applications will be invited following the triage meeting. Shortlisted applicants will be invited to submit a full application and will be subject to international peer review and due diligence. Applicants will be expected to make a presentation on their proposal to the TTCC. Unless otherwise advised, this will be at the next scheduled meeting of the TTCC

Closing Date: Concept note deadline: 15 April; Preliminary deadline: 12 June

Funding: Trusts

For further information contact:

Tel: (44) 20 7611 5757
Fax: (44) 20 7611 8857
Email: innovations@wellcome.ac.uk

Translational Medicine and Therapeutics Programmes

Subjects: Biomedical science

Purpose: This flagship scheme established four high-quality integrated research training programmes for clinicians in translational medicine and therapeutics. The programmes have been developed around a unique partnership between academic and industrial partners. Support for the programmes has been provided to the host institutions by GlaxoSmithKline, Wyeth Research, Roche, AstraZeneca, Sanofi-Aventis, Sirtris Pharmaceuticals and PTC Therapeutics

Eligibility: You should have demonstrated the potential to pursue a career as an academic clinician. It is anticipated that many applicants will have already commenced their specialist training, but this is not essential

Level of Study: Postgraduate, Research

Value: Includes a clinical salary, PhD registration fees at United Kingdom/EU rate, research expenses, contribution towards travel, and a contribution towards training costs

Length of Study: Support varies

Frequency: Annual

Application Procedure: If you are interested in applying you should contact the relevant programme. Please see website for details

Closing Date: October

Funding: Trusts

For further information contact:

Email: j.williams@wellcome.ac.uk

University Awards

Subjects: Medical history and humanities

Purpose: This scheme allows universities to attract outstanding research staff by providing support for up to 5 years, after which time the award holder takes up a guaranteed permanent post in the university. A monograph and other substantial publications are expected to result from an award, so teaching and other non-research commitments are expected to be minimal during the period of full Wellcome Trust support

Eligibility: You must be nominated by your prospective head of department and have an undertaking from the head of the institution, vice-chancellor, principal or dean that your personal support will be taken over by the institution at the end of the award. Support is normally available only at lecturer level, although in exceptional cases awards to senior-lecturer level may be possible

Level of Study: Research

Type: Award

Value: Up to 5 years' support is available, providing your full salary for 3 years, 50% in the fourth year and 25 per cent in the fifth year. Travel expenses to attend meetings are provided for 5 years, but research expenses are provided for the first 3 years of the award only

Application Procedure: Initial enquiries about the scheme may be made by you (the potential candidate) or a department in an institution. These enquiries should be followed by a preliminary application from you by email or post including an explicit statement from the head of the institution, vice-chancellor or dean demonstrating the institution's commitment to the history of medicine field, and a statement confirming that the institution will provide 50% salary costs in year four, 75% in year 5 and full salary thereafter; curriculum vitae and full publication list; an outline of no more than two pages of the proposed project; a letter of support from the head of department, including a statement on your expected teaching/administrative load for the 5-year period (this can be sent by separate cover); the approximate cost of the proposal, broken down into your salary, equipment and project running costs

Closing Date: 22 January (closing date for preliminary applications); 30 March closing date for full applications; The schedule for full applications received by 30 March closing date is as follows: May is shortlisting and July is interview

Funding: Trusts

For further information contact:

Tel: (44) 20 7611 5757
Email: MHgrants@wellcome.ac.uk

Wellcome Trust and NIH Four-Year PhD Studentships

Subjects: Biomedical science
Purpose: This scheme provides opportunities for the most promising postgraduate students to undertake international, collaborative four-year PhD training based in both a United Kingdom/Republic of Ireland (RoI) academic institution and the intramural campus of the National Institutes of Health at Bethesda (Maryland, United States of America)
Eligibility: You should be a United Kingdom/European Economic Area (EEA) national with (or be in your final year and expected to obtain) a first- or upper-second-class honours degree or an equivalent EEA graduate qualification. You must have: (1) a suitable doctoral supervisor at an eligible academic host institution in the United Kingdom or Republic of Ireland. The host institution must be able to confer doctoral degrees; (2) a suitable supervisor at a NIH institute. The NIH supervisor should hold a tenured or tenured-track position for the proposed period of the award and should be willing to provide funding for the student whilst at the NIH
Level of Study: Doctorate, Research
Type: Studentship
Value: The studentship is awarded for 4 years with support provided by the Wellcome Trust (in the United Kingdom/Republic of Ireland) and the NIH (in the United States of America). Our funding will provide support for the student's stipend, PhD fees, college fees (if required) and a contribution towards research costs
Length of Study: 4 year
Frequency: Annual
Application Procedure: The application form should be completed and submitted by the closing date. An electronic copy (as a Word document) should be emailed to wtnih@wellcome.ac.uk. One signed hard copy should be addressed to the Wellcome Trust-NIH PhD studentship's at the Trust's postal address, see website

Closing Date: 2 November (Deadline for applications); 25–26 January (Shortlisted candidate interviews)
Funding: Trusts

For further information contact:

Wellcome Trust-NIH PhD Studentships, Wellcome Trust, Gibbs Building, 215 Euston Road, NW1 2BE, Bloomsbury, United Kingdom

Email: wtnih@wellcome.ac.uk

Wellcome Trust-POST Fellowships in Medical History and Humanities

Subjects: Medical history and humanities
Purpose: This scheme enables a PhD student or junior fellow funded through the Wellcome Trust Medical History and Humanities (MHH) programme to undertake a 3-month fellowship at the Parliamentary Office of Science and Technology (POST)
Eligibility: Applicants should be in the second or third year of their PhD or in the first year of a fellowship funded by the MHH Programme. POST is a strictly non-partisan organization. Wellcome Trust-POST Fellows will be required to abstain from any lobbying or party political activity, and generally uphold the principles of parliamentary service, including a commitment to confidentiality, during their time with the Office. All provisionally selected candidates must sign a declaration to this effect. They must also receive security clearance from the parliamentary security authorities as a condition of finally taking up the fellowship
Level of Study: Postdoctorate, Research
Type: Fellowship
Value: The successful applicant will receive a fully funded 3-month extension to their PhD or fellowship award. While placements typically last 3-months, they may be extended under exceptional circumstances. If the successful applicant is not within reasonable daily travelling distance to POST in London, the Wellcome Trust will consider paying travel and accommodation costs up to a maximum of £2,000
Frequency: Annual
Application Procedure: An application should include the application form, your curriculum vitae, a letter of support from your sponsor/supervisor and a summary of a proposed topic for a POST publication. The summary should be no longer than 1,000 words and should demonstrate: why you think this subject would be of particular parliamentary interest; how the training you have received and your research to date will enable you to carry out this work; your ability to

write in a style suitable for a parliamentary (rather than an academic) audience

Closing Date: 23 November

Funding: Trusts

Additional Information: Check website for more details

For further information contact:

Tel: (44) 20 7611 5757

Email: MHgrants@wellcome.ac.uk

Wells Mountain Foundation

Woodcock-Munoz Foundation Empowerment Through Education Scholarships

Subjects: The Wells Mountain Foundation, through the Empowerment Through Education (ETE) program, provides undergraduate scholarships to developing country nationals to study in their home country or a neighboring country

Purpose: The Foundation believes in the power and importance of community service; therefore, all scholarship participants are required to volunteer for a minimum of 100 hours a year

Eligibility: WMF's ideal candidate is a student, male or female, from a country in the developing world, who: 1. Successfully completed a secondary education, with good to excellent grades. 2. Will be studying in their country or another country in the developing world. 3. Plans to live and work in their own country after they graduate. 4. Has volunteered prior to applying for this scholarship and/or is willing to volunteer while receiving the WMF scholarship

Level of Study: Graduate

Type: Scholarship

Value: Average of US$1,400 for tuition and fee, books and materials

Frequency: Annual

Country of Study: Any country

Application Procedure: You must submit a complete application via the online scholarship application portal (preferred method) or via postal mail to the Foundation's office Kindly check the below site for further details. www.wellsmountain foundation.org/our-programs/scholarships/

Closing Date: 1 April

Funding: Private

For further information contact:

Email: info@scholars4dev.com

Wells Mountain Initiative

Westmead Millennium Institute Micro-Grants

Purpose: The WMI Micro-Grants Program is open exclusively to all WMI Graduate Scholars. Preference is given to Graduates who are actively involved in Fellowship groups if present within their nation and participation in WMI's Scholar Journey opportunities

Eligibility: Graduate Scholars are eligible to apply for a maximum of two grants. There is a required two-year wait time before applying for a second award

Level of Study: Graduate

Type: Grant

Value: US$100 to US$1,000

Frequency: Annual

Country of Study: Any country

Application Procedure: To enhance professional growth with all aspects of program development and grant writing skills, WMI provides all Graduate Scholars with individualised application coaching. After submitting your first round proposal, the review committee will provide direct feedback for each qualifying application. With this feedback, Graduate Scholars will have one month to continue developing their proposals by creating more detailed processes, conducting research and community outreach, revising budgets and timelines, etc. A final revised application will be submitted online and a funding decision will be made

Closing Date: 15 April

Funding: Private

Additional Information: You could also write to tyhe following contact address: info@wellsmountaininitiative.org

For further information contact:

Wells Mountain Initiative, 25D Main Street, Bristol, NY 05443, United States of America

Email: nicole@wellsmountain.com

Wenner-Gren Foundation for Anthropological Research

The Fellowships Office, 470 Park Avenue South, 8th Floor, New York, NY 10016, United States of America

Tel: (1) 212 683 5000

Fax: (1) 212 683 9151

Email: inquiries@wennergren.org
Website: www.wennergren.org
Contact: Victoria Malkin, Anthropologist

The Wenner-Gren Foundation for Anthropological Research supports research, conferences, training, archiving and collaboration in all branches of anthropology, including cultural and social anthropology, ethnology, biological and physical anthropology, archaeology and anthropological linguistics, and in closely related disciplines concerned with human origins, development and variation.

Hunt Postdoctoral Fellowships

Subjects: Anthropology
Purpose: To support the writing-up of already completed research
Eligibility: Applicants must have a PhD or equivalent at the time of application and must have received a PhD or equivalent within 10 years of the application deadline. Qualified scholars are eligible without regard to nationality, institutional, or departmental affiliation although preference is given to applicants who are untenured or do not yet have a permanent academic position
Level of Study: Postdoctorate
Type: Fellowship
Value: Up to US$40,000
Frequency: Annual
Country of Study: Any country
No. of awards offered: 89
Application Procedure: Applications can be downloaded from the website and must be submitted online
Closing Date: 1 May
No. of awards given last year: 9
No. of applicants last year: 89
Additional Information: Qualified scholars are eligible without regard to nationality or institutional affiliation

For further information contact:

Email: inquiries@wennergren.org

Wharton School

University of Pennsylvania, MBA Admissions & Financial Aid, 102 Vance Hill, Philadelphia, PA 19104-6361, United States of America

Tel: (1) 215 898 6182
Fax: (1) 215 898 0120
Email: mba.admissions@wharton.upenn.edu
Website: www.wharton.upenn.edu/mba/catalog
Contact: MBA Programme

Wharton Executive MBA Programme

Length of Study: 2 years
Application Procedure: Applicants may apply online or contact Wharton for information
Closing Date: 1 February for Philadelphia, PA and 15 April for San Francisco CA

For further information contact:

Executive MBA Programme, The Wharton School, University of Pennsylvania, 224 Steinberg Conference Centre, 255 South 38th Street, Philadelphia, PA 19104 6359, United States of America

Tel: (1) 215 898 5887
Fax: (1) 215 898 2598
Email: wemba-admissions@wharton.upenn.edu

Whitehall Foundation, Inc.

PO Box 3423, Palm Beach, FL 33480, United States of America

Tel: (1) 561 655 4474
Fax: (1) 561 659 4978
Email: email@whitehall.org
Website: www.whitehall.org
Contact: Ms Catherine Thomas, Corporate Secretary

The Whitehall Foundation, Inc. through its programme of grants and grants-in-aid, assists scholarly research in the life sciences. It is the Foundation's policy to assist those dynamic areas of basic biological research that are not heavily supported by federal agencies or other foundations with specialized missions.

Whitehall Foundation Grants-in-Aid

Subjects: Neurobiology focusing on invertebrate and vertebrate neurobiology, specifically investigations of neural mechanisms involved in sensory, motor and other complex functions of the whole organism as these relate to behaviour

Purpose: To better understand behavioural output or brain mechanisms of behaviour

Eligibility: Open to researchers at the assistant professor level who have experienced difficulty in competing for research funds as they have not yet become firmly established. Senior scientists may also apply

Level of Study: Research

Type: Research grant one year

Value: Up to US$30,000

Length of Study: 1 year

Frequency: Annual

Country of Study: United States of America

Application Procedure: Applicants must contact the Foundation

Closing Date: Letter of intent deadline, 15 January, 15 April, 15 October

Funding: Private

Additional Information: For up to date policy, application information and important calendar deadlines please refer to the website

For further information contact:

Email: email@whitehall.org

Whitehall Foundation Research Grants

Subjects: Neurobiology focusing on invertebrate and vertebrate neurobiology, specifically investigations of neural mechanisms involved in sensory, motor and other complex functions of the whole organism as these relate to behaviour

Purpose: To better understand behavioural output or brain mechanisms of behaviour

Eligibility: Open to established scientists of all ages working at accredited institutions in the United States of America. The principal investigator must hold no less than the position of assistant professor, or the equivalent, in order to make an application. The Foundation does not award funds to investigators who have substantial existing or potential support

Level of Study: Research

Type: Research grant one year

Value: US$30,000–US$75,000 per year

Length of Study: Up to 3 years

Frequency: Annual

Country of Study: Any country

Application Procedure: Please visit web-site @ www.white hall.org

Funding: Private

Additional Information: For up to date policy, application information and important calendar deadlines, please refer to the website

For further information contact:

Email: email@whitehall.org

Wilfrid Laurier University

75 University Avenue West, Waterloo, ON N2L 3C5, Canada

Tel:	(1) 519 884 1970
Fax:	(1) 519 886 9351
Email:	webmaster@wlu.ca
Website:	www.wlu.ca
Contact:	Mr Al Hecht, International Relations

Wilfrid Laurier University is well known for offering an extremely high quality academic experience as well as for cultivating a closely-knit undergraduate and graduate student population. Wilfrid Laurier University is committed to continuing to provide the educational experiences and environment that foster such development and nurture what can best be described as the 'Laurier spirit'.

Viessmann/Marburg Travel Scholarship

Subjects: All subjects

Purpose: To assist students wanting to study in Germany

Level of Study: Postgraduate

Type: Scholarship

Value: €767

Length of Study: 1 year

Frequency: Annual

Study Establishment: An approved place of study in Marburg

Country of Study: Germany

Application Procedure: Contact University

Closing Date: 2 July

For further information contact:

Email: webmaster@wlu.ca

Wilfrid Laurier University President

Subjects: All subjects

Purpose: To reward significant contribution to the community as a volunteer or to the discipline as a scholar

Eligibility: Full-time undergraduate students entering year 1. Minimum overall average of 95% in best six Grade 12 U and/or Grade 12 M courses or Ontario Academic Credits (OACs) (or equivalent)

Level of Study: Postgraduate
Type: Scholarship
Value: $23,000 ($3,000 1st year; renewable based on academic performance for up to 4 years at $5,000 per year) 4th year of renewal eligibility for approved 5-year undergraduate programs only
Length of Study: 1 year
Frequency: Annual
Study Establishment: Laurier University
Country of Study: Canada
Application Procedure: Apply online
Closing Date: Refer website
Funding: Trusts
Contributor: Dr Neale H. Taylor

For further information contact:

Email: fgps@wlu.ca

Wingate Scholarships

2nd Floor, 20-22 Stukeley Street, London WC2B 5LR, United Kingdom

Email: enquiries@wingate.org.uk
Website: www.wingatescholarships.org.uk
Contact: Ms Sarah Mitchell, Administrator

Wingate Scholarships are awarded to individuals for creative or original work of intellectual, scientific, artistic, social or environmental value of great potential or proven excellence, and to outstanding musicians for advanced training in music performance.

Wingate Scholarships

Subjects: Most subjects except undergraduates, masters, first year PhDs, postdoctoral fellowship posts, medical research, fine arts, performing arts (except music), business courses, taught courses or courses leading to professional qualifications and electives. See eligibility section
Purpose: To fund creative or original work of intellectual, scientific, artistic, social or environmental value and advanced music study
Eligibility: Open to United Kingdom, Commonwealth, former Commonwealth, Israeli. Also open to European Union and Council of Europe country citizens provided that they are and have been resident in the United Kingdom for at least 3 years at start of award. Applicants must be over 24 years of age. No upper age limit is prescribed. No academic qualifications are necessary. Applications must be made in United Kingdom from a valid United Kingdom address
Level of Study: Doctorate, Postdoctorate, Postgraduate, Research
Type: Scholarship
Value: Costs of a project, which may last for up to 3 years, to a maximum of United Kingdom £10,000 in any 1 year
Length of Study: 1–3 years
Frequency: Annual
Study Establishment: Any approved institute or independent research
Country of Study: Any country
No. of awards offered: 228
Application Procedure: Applicants must be living in United Kingdom during the period of application. Applications from a valid United Kingdom address only are acceptable. Applicants must complete online application form from the website. Applicants must be able to satisfy the Scholarship Committee that they need financial support to undertake the work projected, and show why the proposed work (if it takes the form of academic research) is unlikely to attract Research Council, British Academy or any other major agency funding if they are United Kingdom applicants. All applications require two references to be submitted independently. Guidance is available on the website
Closing Date: 1 February
Funding: Foundation
Contributor: HHW Foundation
No. of awards given last year: 39
No. of applicants last year: 228
Additional Information: The scholarships are not awarded for professional qualifications, taught courses or electives, or in the following subject areas: performing arts, fine art, business studies. Practising musicians (not composers) are eligible for advanced training, but apart from that, all applicants must have projects that are personal to them and involve either creative or original work. Only postgraduate students in their final two years can apply for scholarships to enable them to undertake field work, or in exceptional circumstances where an award has been withdrawn or closed, to complete a PhD. Applications for studies or projects undertaken post doctorally are eligible, but not postdoctoral fellowship posts per se. Applicant must be based in United Kingdom when applying

For further information contact:

Email: emma@shrimsley.com
Contact: Sarah Mitchell, Administrator

Winston Churchill Foundation of the United States of America

600 Madison Avenue, Suite 1601, New York, NY 10022-1737, United States of America

Tel:	(1) 212 752 3200
Fax:	(1) 212 246 8330
Email:	info@churchillscholarship.org
Website:	www.churchillscholarship.org
Contact:	Mr Michael Morse, Executive Director

The Winston Churchill Foundation of the United States was established in 1959 as an expression of American admiration for one of the great leaders of the free world. The foundation enables outstanding American students to attend graduate school at the University of Cambridge.

Churchill Scholarship

Subjects: Math, science, or engineering
Purpose: The Churchill Scholarship provides funding to American students for a year of Master's study at the University of Cambridge, based at Churchill College. The program was set up at the request of Sir Winston Churchill in order to fulfill his vision of United States–United Kingdom scientific exchange with the goal of advancing science and technology on both sides of the Atlantic, helping to ensure our future prosperity and security
Eligibility: An applicant for the Churchill Scholarship must be a citizen of the United States, either native born or naturalized, and must be a senior who is enrolled in one of the institutions participating in the Scholarship Program or a student who has graduated from one of those institutions within the past 12 months. Upon taking up the Churchill Scholarship, a Churchill Scholar must hold a bachelor's degree or an equivalent, and may not have attained a doctorate
Type: Fellowship/Scholarship
Value: US$55,000
Length of Study: 1 year
Frequency: Annual
Country of Study: United Kingdom
No. of awards offered: 105
Application Procedure: Must be nominated by undergraduate institution
Closing Date: 31 October
Funding: Foundation
No. of awards given last year: 15

No. of applicants last year: 105

For further information contact:

Winston Churchill Foundation, 600 Madison Avenue, Suite 1601, New York, NY 10022, United States of America

Tel:	(1) 212 752 3200
Email:	info@churchillscholarship.org
Contact:	Mr Michael Morse, Executive Director

Winston Churchill Memorial Trust

Winston Churchill Memorial Trust (United Kingdom) Travelling Fellowships

Subjects: Approximately 10 wide-ranging categories that vary annually
Purpose: The WCMT funds British citizens to investigate inspiring practice in other countries, and return with innovative ideas for the benefit of people across the United Kingdom
Eligibility: Open to British citizens resident in the United Kingdom aged 18 and above. We do not fund gap year activities, courses, volunteering, academic studies, degree placements, internships, medical electives or post-graduate studies
Level of Study: Unrestricted
Type: Fellowship
Length of Study: 4 - 8 weeks
Frequency: Annual
Country of Study: Any country
No. of awards offered: 1,700
Application Procedure: Applicants must complete an online application form
Closing Date: September; date announced in May for travel the following year
Funding: Private
No. of applicants last year: 1,700
Additional Information: Any country outside of the United Kingdom. Award recipients are announced in February. Fellows may travel from April

For further information contact:

South Door, Church House, 29 Great Smith Street, SW1P 3BL, London, United Kingdom

Email:	office@wcmt.org.uk
Contact:	Ms Tristan Lawrence, Administrator

Winterthur

Winterthur Museum, Garden and Library, 5105 Kennett Pike, Winterthur, DE 19735, United States of America

Tel:	(1) 800 448 3883
Email:	tourinfo@winterthur.org
Website:	www.winterthur.org
Contact:	Thomas A. Guiler, Manager and Instructor, Academic Programmes

Founded by Henry Francis du Pont, Winterthur is the premier museum of American Decorative Arts, reflecting both early America and the du Pont family's life here. Its 60-acre naturalistic garden is among the country's best, and its research library serves scholars from around the world.

Winterthur Dissertation Research Fellowships

Subjects: American history and art history
Purpose: To encourage the use of Winterthur's collections for critical inquiry that will further the understanding of American history and visual and material culture
Level of Study: Research
Type: Fellowship
Value: US$7,000 per semesters
Length of Study: 1–2 semesters
Frequency: Annual
Country of Study: United States of America
Application Procedure: Applicants can download application form from the website
Closing Date: 15 January
Funding: Foundation
Contributor: Winterthur
No. of awards given last year: 4

For further information contact:

Email: researchapplication@winterthur.org

Winterthur Postdoctoral Fellowships

Subjects: American history and art history
Purpose: To encourage the use of Winterthur's collections for critical inquiry that will further the understanding of American history and visual and material culture
Eligibility: Open to scholars who hold the PhD degree, pursuing advanced research
Level of Study: Postdoctorate, Research
Type: Fellowships
Value: Up to US$16,800
Length of Study: 4 months
Frequency: Annual
Country of Study: United States of America
Application Procedure: Applicants can download the application form from the website
Closing Date: 15 January
Funding: Foundation
Contributor: Winterthur
No. of awards given last year: 2

For further information contact:

Email: researchapplication@winterthur.org

Winterthur Research Fellowships

Subjects: American history and art history
Purpose: To encourage the use of Winterthur's collections for critical inquiry that will further the understanding of American history and visual and material culture
Eligibility: Open to scholars pursuing advanced research
Level of Study: Research
Type: Fellowship
Value: US$1,750 per month
Length of Study: 1–3 months
Frequency: Annual
Country of Study: United States of America
Application Procedure: Applicants can download the application form from the website
Closing Date: 15 January
Funding: Foundation
Contributor: Winterthur
No. of awards given last year: 21

For further information contact:

Email: researchapplication@winterthur.org

Wolf Blass Wines International

97 Sturt Highway, Nuriootpa, Adelaide, SA 5355, Australia

Tel:	(61) 8 8568 7311
Email:	cellardoor@wolfblass.com.au
Website:	www.wolfblass.com.au/brands/wolfblass/index.asp

Wolf Blass Wines International is public listed company and one of the Australia's top sellers of red and white wine. It is one of the best Australian wine-producing company. As they have for almost 30 years, Wolf Blass wines continue to delight wine lovers all over the world.

Wolf Blass Australian Winemaking Independent Study Scholarship

Subjects: Winemaking
Purpose: To support independent study related to winemaking in Australia
Eligibility: Open to culinary professional to conduct research and writing related to Australian winemaking and culinary traditions
Type: Scholarship
Value: A$5,000
Country of Study: Australia
Application Procedure: All applicants are required to include a project proposal, an itemized budget detailing the use of this award and a tentative travel schedule with dates and locations. Check website for further details
Additional Information: Applicant is additionally required to provide a current resume to qualify for this scholarship

For further information contact:

304W, Liberty Street, Suite 201, Louisville, KY 40202, United States of America

Tel: (1) 800 928 4227 Ext 264
Fax: (1) 502 589 3602
Email: tgribbins@hqtrs.com

Wolfsonian-Florida International University

1001 Washington Avenue, Miami Beach, FL 33139, United States of America

Tel: (1) 305 531 1001
Fax: (1) 305 531 2133
Email: research@thewolf.fiu.edu
Website: www.wolfsonian.org
Contact: Mr Jonathan Mogul, Fellowship Co-ordinator

The Wolfsonian-Florida International University is a museum and research centre that promotes the examination of modern material culture. Through exhibitions, publications, scholarships, educational programmes and public presentations, the Wolfsonian strives to enhance the understanding of objects as agents and reflections of social, cultural, political and technological change. The collection includes works on paper, furniture, paintings, sculpture, glass, textiles, ceramics, books and many other kinds of objects.

Wolfsonian-FIU Fellowship

Subjects: Modern material and visual culture
Purpose: To conduct research on the Wolfsonian's collection of objects and library materials from the period 1885 to 1945, including decorative arts, works on paper, books and ephemera
Eligibility: The programme is open to holder of Master's or doctoral degrees, PhD candidates, and to other who have a record of significant professional achievement in relevant fields
Level of Study: Doctorate, Postdoctorate, Professional development
Type: Fellowship
Value: Fellowships include a stipend, accommodations, and round-trip travel
Length of Study: 3–5 weeks
Frequency: Annual
Study Establishment: The Wolfsonian-Florida International University
Country of Study: United States of America
No. of awards offered: 26
Application Procedure: Applicants must complete an application form and submit this with three letters of recommendation. Contact the Fellowship Co-ordinator for details and application materials. Applicants may also download programme information and an application form from the website www.wolfsonian.fiu.edu/education/research
Closing Date: 31 December
No. of awards given last year: 5
No. of applicants last year: 26

For further information contact:

Tel: (1) 305 535 2613
Email: research@thewolf.fiu.edu

Women's Studio Workshop (WSW)

722 Binnewater Lane, PO Box 489, Rosendale, NY 12472, United States of America

Tel: (1) 845 658 9133
Fax: (1) 845 658 9031
Email: info@wsworkshop.org
Website: www.wsworkshop.org
Contact: Ms Ann Kalmbach, Executive Director

The Women's Studio Workshop (WSW) is an artist-run workshop with facilities for printmaking, papermaking, photography, book arts and ceramics. WSW supports the creation of new work through studio residency and annual book arts grant programmes and an ongoing subsidized fellowship programme. WSW offers studio-based educational programming in the above disciplines through its annual Summer Arts Institute.

Artists Fellowships at WSW

Subjects: Intaglio, water-based silkscreen, photography, papermaking or ceramics, letterpress, book arts, ceramics
Purpose: To provide a time for artists to explore new ideas in a dynamic and co-operative community of women artists in a rural environment
Eligibility: Open to women artists only
Level of Study: Unrestricted
Type: Fellowship
Value: The award includes on-site housing and unlimited access to the studios. Cost to artists will be US$200 per week, plus their own material
Length of Study: Each fellowship is 3–6 weeks long. Fellowship opportunities are from September to June
Frequency: Annual
Study Establishment: WSW
Country of Study: United States of America
No. of awards offered: 100
Application Procedure: Applicants must complete an application form, available on request or online at the website. One-sentence summary plus half-page description of proposed project, resume, 10 slides plus slide script, self addressed stampe envelope for return of materials
Closing Date: 15 March or 15 October
Funding: Government, Private
Contributor: Private foundations
No. of awards given last year: 25
No. of applicants last year: 100

For further information contact:

Email: info@wsworkshop.org

Women's Studio Workshop Internships

Subjects: Book arts, papermaking, printmaking, ceramics and photography plus arts administration
Purpose: To provide opportunities for young artists to continue development of their work in a supportive environment, while learning studio skills and responsibilities
Eligibility: Open to emerging and established female artists
Level of Study: Unrestricted
Type: Internship
Value: A private room in our onsite housing and a stipend of US$250/month
Length of Study: 2–6 months
Frequency: Annual
Study Establishment: WSW
Country of Study: United States of America
No. of awards offered: 150
Application Procedure: Applicants must submit a curriculum vitae, 10 slides with slide list, 3 current letters of reference, a letter of interest that addresses the question of why an internship at WSW would be important and a stamped addressed envelope. Arts administration: 3 work samples, i.e. press releases, design samples, etc
Closing Date: See website
Funding: Government, Private
Contributor: Private foundations
No. of awards given last year: 6
No. of applicants last year: 150

For further information contact:

Email: info@wsworkshop.org

Woodrow Wilson National Fellowship Foundation

P O Box 5281, Princeton, NJ 08543-5281, United States of America

Tel: (1) 609 452 7007
Fax: (1) 609 452 0066
Email: marrero@woodrow.org
Website: www.woodrow.org
Contact: Ms Frances Micklow, Communications Associate

The Woodrow Wilson National Fellowship Foundation identifies and develops the best minds for the nation's most important challenges. The fellowships are awarded to enrich human resources, work to improve public policy, and assist organizations and institutions in enhancing practice in the United States and abroad.

The Millicent C. McIntosh Fellowship

Subjects: Humanities
Purpose: These fellowships are specifically intended for recently tenured faculty who would benefit from additional time and resources
Level of Study: Postgraduate
Type: Fellowship
Value: A US$15,000 stipend
Length of Study: 1 year
Frequency: Annual
Application Procedure: Contact the Foundation
Closing Date: 31 March
Funding: Private
Contributor: Gladys Krieble Delmas Foundation

For further information contact:

Tel: (1) 609 452 7007 ext. 301
Email: mcintoshfellowship@woodrow.org

Woodrow Wilson MBA Fellowship in Education Leadership

Subjects: MBA. The Fellowship program will provide specialized preparation in areas such as leadership, finance, human resources, organizational change–all focusing on education
Purpose: To address the United States' twin educational achievement gaps–the one between the nation's lowest performing and its best schools, as well as the one between the nation's best schools and their top international competitors. The Fellowship seeks both to prepare leaders who can bring all American schools up to world-class levels of performance and to develop a new gold standard for preparing education leaders
Eligibility: Fellows commit to serve for 3 years in approved school or district leadership positions within their states
Level of Study: Postgraduate
Type: Fellowship
Value: Fellows will receive a stipend to cover tuition for the MBA program and other expenses
Length of Study: The program will require 13–15 months of full-time study, depending on the institution–two summers and an academic year
Frequency: Annual
Country of Study: Any country
Application Procedure: Fellows must be nominated by a local education leader/colleague before they are eligible to apply. Contact information buntrock@woodrow.org. The program will require 13 to 15 months of full-time study, depending on the institution–two summers and an academic year
Closing Date: December
Additional Information: If you have already been nominated, see the respective pages for the WW MBA Fellowship at MSOE (www.msoe.edu/community/academics/business/page/2311/mba-in-education-leadership-overview) and at UIndy (uindy.edu/education/mba-education-leadership) for application deadlines

For further information contact:

Email: buntrock@woodrow.org

Woodrow Wilson Teaching Fellowship

Subjects: Teacher education, STEM (Science, Technology, Engineering, Mathematics) teaching, secondary school teaching
Eligibility: The Woodrow Wilson Teaching Fellowship seeks to attract talented, committed individuals with science, technology, engineering, and mathematics (STEM) backgrounds – including current undergraduates, recent college graduates, midcareer professionals, and retirees – into teaching in high-need secondary schools. A qualified applicant should demonstrate a commitment to the program and its goals; have United States citizenship or permanent residency; have attained, or expect to attain by 30 June, a bachelor's degree from an accredited United States college or university; have majored in and/or have a strong professional background in an STEM field; have achieved a cumulative undergraduate grade point average (GPA) of 3.0 or better on a 4.0 scale (negotiable for applicants from institutions that do not employ a 4.0 GPA scale). Note: Prior teaching experience does not exclude a candidate from eligibility. All applications are considered in their entirety and selection is based on merit
Level of Study: Graduate
Type: Fellowship
Value: US$30,000-US$32,000 stipend, with tuition arrangements varying by campus in Georgia, Indiana, and New Jersey. (Once Fellows are certified teachers at the end of the first year, they obtain salaried employment in high-need schools.)
Length of Study: 12–18 months plus 3-year teaching commitment
Frequency: Annual
Study Establishment: Fellowship is only available for use at specific schools in Indiana (Ball State University, Indiana University-Purdue University Indianapolis, Purdue University, and the University of Indianapolis); Michigan (Eastern Michigan University, Grand Valley State University, Michigan State University, University of Michigan, Wayne State

University, Western Michigan University); and Ohio (John Carroll University, Ohio State University, University of Akron, and University of Cincinnati)

No. of awards offered: 1690

Application Procedure: Online application procedure and supporting documents. See www.wwteachingfellowship.org

Closing Date: First application deadline – 16 October, Second application deadline 30 November and final application deadline 31 January

Funding: Government, Private, Foundation

Contributor: Ohio STEM, Lilly Endowment Inc., W K Kellogg Foundation, Choose Ohio First

No. of awards given last year: 260

No. of applicants last year: 1690

Additional Information: University of Dayton and University of Toledo are also included in study establishment

For further information contact:

Tel: (1) 609 452 7007 ext. 141
Email: wwteachingfellowship@woodrow.org

Woods Hole Oceanographic Institution (WHOI)

266 Woods Hole Road, Woods Hole, MA 02543-1050, United States of America

Tel: (1) 508 548 1400
Fax: (1) 508 457 2188
Email: information@whoi.edu
Website: www.whoi.edu/education
Contact: Janet Fields, Coordinator

The Woods Hole Oceanographic Institution is a private, independent, non-profit corporation dedicated to research and higher education at the frontiers of ocean science. Its primary mission is to develop and effectively communicate a fundamental understanding of the processes and characteristics governing how the oceans function and how they interact with the Earth as a whole.

Woods Hole Oceanographic Institution Postdoctoral Awards in Marine Policy and Ocean Management

Subjects: Novel proposals in such fields as political science, international affairs, decision theory, economics, diplomacy, management, geography, law, engineering and anthropology will be considered

Eligibility: Open to Scholars and practitioners from relevant fields in the social sciences, natural sciences, law and management who are interested in applying their disciplinary training and experience to investigations which require a significant component of marine research. Applicants must have completed their doctorate degree or possess equivalent professional qualifications through career experience

Level of Study: Postdoctorate

Value: Please contact the organization

Length of Study: 1 year

Frequency: Annual

Study Establishment: Woods Hole Oceanographic Institution

Country of Study: United States of America

Closing Date: 15 January for notification in March

Additional Information: Award recipients in the programme have pursued such studies as the implications of oil exploration along the North eastern coast of the United States of America, problems of international law created by new developments in aquaculture and fish farming, economic benefits of some oceanographic research, a perceptual study of United Kingdom fishermen, and oceanic waste disposal

Woods Hole Oceanographic Institution Postdoctoral Fellowships in Ocean Science and Engineering

Subjects: Oceanography and oceanographic engineering

Purpose: To further the education and training of recent recipients of doctoral degrees in engineering science or with interests in marine science

Eligibility: Open to United States citizens and foreign nationals who have earned a PhD degree in biology, physics, microbiology, molecular biology, chemistry, geology, geophysics, oceanography, meteorology, engineering or mathematics. Scientists with more than three years of postdoctoral experience are not eligible

Level of Study: Postdoctorate

Type: Fellowship

Value: Please contact the organization

Length of Study: 1 year

Frequency: Annual

Study Establishment: Woods Hole Oceanographic Institution

Country of Study: United States of America

Application Procedure: Applicants must complete and submit an application form with transcripts, reference letters, complete transcripts of undergraduate and graduate records, and a concise statement describing research interests. Further information and application forms may be obtained from the postdoctoral section of the website

Closing Date: 15 January for notification in March

Funding: Government, Private
Additional Information: Award holders work in the laboratory under the general supervision of an appropriate member of the staff, but are expected to work independently on research problems of their own choice

For further information contact:

Email: postdoc@whoi.edu

Worcester College

Drue Heinz Scholarship

Purpose: Open to all graduate applicants for courses in the Humanities in which Worcester College admits students and who specify Worcester College as their first choice College
Eligibility: All applicants for courses in the Humanities
Level of Study: Graduate
Type: Scholarship
Value: Upto £10,000 per annum towards full cost of fee
Frequency: Annual
Country of Study: Any country
Application Procedure: Requirements for the application is: 1. a completed application cover sheet. i. an up-to-date Curriculum Vitae. ii. a covering letter stating their reasons for applying for the particular course and providing information about applications they have made to relevant funding bodies
Closing Date: 1 March
Funding: Private

For further information contact:

Porters' Lodge, Worcester College, OX1 2HB, Oxford, United Kingdom

Tel: (44) 1865 278300
Email: graduate.enquiries@worc.ox.ac.uk

World Bank Institute

1818 H Street NW, Washington, DC 20433, United States of America

Tel: (1) 202 473 1000
Fax: (1) 202 477 6391
Email: pic@worldbank.org
Website: www.worldbank.org
Contact: Communications Officer

One of the largest sources of funding and knowledge for transition and development councils; The World Bank uses its financial resources, staff and extensive experience to help developing countries reduce poverty, increase economic growth and improve their quality of life.

World Bank Grants Facility for Indigenous Peoples

Subjects: Indigenous culture, intellectual property and human rights
Purpose: To support sustainable and culturally appropriate development projector planed and implemented by and for Indigenous People
Eligibility: Applicant must be an Indigenous People's community or not-for-profit/non-governmental Indigenous People's organization, must be legally registered in the country of grant implementation, the country must be eligible to borrow from the World Bank (IBRD and/or IDA). Applicant should have an established bank account in the name of the applicant organization and should demonstrate internal controls to govern the use of funds. Applicant should not have received a grant from the Grants Facility for Indigenous Peoples in the previous 2 years
Level of Study: Professional development, Research
Type: Grant
Value: Proposed project budget requests should range between US$10,000 and US$30,000 and include a minimum contribution of 20% of the total project cost
Frequency: Annual
Application Procedure: A complete application, not more than 10 pages, should be submitted
Closing Date: 15 November
Contributor: The World Bank

For further information contact:

Fax: (1) 202 522 1669
Email: indigenouspeoples@worldbank.org

World Bank Scholarships Program

Purpose: The World Bank Scholarships Program contributes to the World Bank Group's mission of forging new dynamic approaches to capacity development and knowledge sharing in the developing world. It is an important component of the Bank Group's efforts to promote economic development and shared prosperity through investing in education
Eligibility: Eligibility criteria has been mentioned in elaborated way as follows. 1. Be a national of a World Bank member developing country. 2. Not hold dual citizenship of any developed country. 3. Be in good health. 4. Hold a Bachelor's (or equivalent) degree earned at least 3 years

prior to the Application Deadline date www.worldbank.org/en/programs/scholarships#Ways
Level of Study: Graduate, Postgraduate
Type: Programme grant
Frequency: Annual
Country of Study: Any country
Application Procedure: Applicants can apply for scholarships to both Preferred and Partner Programs. The process to apply to a Preferred Program and to a Partner Program differs: 1. See our Announcements posted on the right side of this website for upcoming calls for scholarship applications for developing country nationals to study at one of our partner master programs, as these calls are announced on a rolling basis throughout the calendar year. 2. Those seeking a JJ/WBGSP Partner Program scholarship (.xlsx 15 KB) must first apply for admission to one or more of the Partner Master's Degree Program(s). 3. Announcements from a JJWBGSP Partner Program on when to apply for admission to their program is often posted on the right-side margin of this website. Inquiries on how to submit an admission application to a partner program should be submitted to the respective university
Closing Date: 11 April
Funding: Private

For further information contact:

Tel: (1) 202 473-1000
Email: support@wizehive.com

World Federation of International Music Competitions

104, rue de Carouge, Genéve CH - 1205, Switzerland

Tel: (41) 22 321 3620
Fax: (41) 22 781 1418
Email: info@beethoven-comp.at, fmcim@fmcim.org
Website: www.beethoven-comp.at

The artistic reputation of musicians is highly dependent upon the quality of their Beethoven interpretations. The International Beethoven Piano Competition in Vienna gives young pianists the possibility to demonstrate their musicianship and artistic maturity.

International Beethoven Piano Competition Vienna

Subjects: Piano

Purpose: To encourage the artistic development of young pianists
Eligibility: Open for pianists born between January 1, 1981 and December 31, 1996
Level of Study: Unrestricted
Type: Competition
Value: The first prize is €8,000, a Boesendorfer Model 200 piano and engagements, the second prize is €6,000, the third prize is €4,500, and there are three further prizes of €2,000. All information subject to change
Country of Study: Austria
No. of awards offered: 207
Application Procedure: Apply online through the website www.beethoven-comp.at
Closing Date: 15 October
Funding: Government, Private
No. of awards given last year: 6 plus special prizes
No. of applicants last year: 207
Additional Information: Please refer to the website for more details

For further information contact:

Competition Office, University of Music and Performing Arts, Anton-von-Webern Platz 1, AUT p1030 Wien, Austria

Tel: (43) 1 711 55/5113
Fax: (43) 1 711 55/5199
Email: info@beethoven-comp.at

World Learning

School for International Training (SIT), Kipling Road, PO Box 676, Brattleboro, VT 05302, United States of America

Tel: (1) 802 258 3510
Fax: (1) 802 258 3500
Email: admissions@sit.edu
Website: www.worldlearning.org
Contact: Enrollment Services

The School for International Training (SIT) at World Learning educates leaders capable of bridging differences between people and nations in an effort to build a more peaceful and sustainable world. Accredited by the New United Kingdom Association of Schools and Colleges, SIT offers Master's degrees in international and intercultural fields, as well as continuing education opportunities, management development courses and peace and conflict transformation training.

School for International Training (SIT) Master of Arts in Teaching Program

Subjects: Reflection, observation, self-evaluation, experiential learning and skills development within a strong learning community

Purpose: To prepare language teachers committed to professional development and service in their field

Eligibility: Open to persons of any nationality who are preparing for a language teaching career. Awards are available only to students studying at the School for International Training

Level of Study: Graduate

Type: Scholarship

Value: Varies

Length of Study: A period that includes a time of student teaching and homestay. The programme is offered in a 1 year or 2 Summer format designed for working professionals

Frequency: Annual

Study Establishment: SIT

Country of Study: Any country

Application Procedure: Applicants must complete an institutional financial aid application and should contact the Financial Aid Office for further details, by email at finaid@sit.edu

Closing Date: Rolling admissions

Additional Information: Students master technical teaching methodologies through language classroom practice, on campus coursework and a supervised teaching internship. Further information is available on the website www.sit.edu/mat

For further information contact:

Email: tesol@rennert.com

Worshipful Company of Musicians

6th Floor, 2 London Wall Buildings, EC2M 5PP, London, United Kingdom

Tel: (44) 20 7496 8980
Fax: (44) 20 7588 3633
Email: deputyclerk@wcom.org.uk
Website: www.wcom.org.uk
Contact: Ms Margaret Alford, Clerk

The Worshipful Company of Musicians supports young musicians particularly in the wilderness years between graduating and setting out on their musical careers.

Carnwath Scholarship

Subjects: Music

Purpose: Open to any person permanently resident in the United Kingdom and 21-25 years of age. The scholarship is intended only for the advanced student who has successfully completed a solo performance course at a college of music

Eligibility: Open to any person permanently resident in the United Kingdom and 21–25 years of age. The scholarship is intended only for the advanced student who has successfully completed a solo performance course at a college of music

Level of Study: Postgraduate

Type: Scholarship

Value: UK£4,150 per year

Length of Study: Up to 2 years

Frequency: Annual

Country of Study: United Kingdom

Application Procedure: 1. Applicants must be nominated by principals of the Royal Academy of Music, the Guildhall School of Music, the Royal Northern College of Music, the Royal Scottish Academy of Music, Trinity College of Music, London College of Music, the Welsh College of Music, the Birmingham School of Music or the Royal College of Music. 2. No application should be made directly to the Worshipful Company of Musicians

Closing Date: 30 April

Funding: Private

For further information contact:

Email: clerk@wcom.org.uk

Writtle University College

Lordship Road, Writtle, CM1 3RR, Chelmsford, United Kingdom

Tel: (44) 1245 424 200
Contact: Writtle University

Writtle University College is one of the largest land-based university colleges in the United Kingdom; it is also one of the oldest. Set in the Essex countryside on a 220 hectare estate, Writtle, previously known as Writtle College, provides FE and HE programmes.

Postgraduate International Scholarships

Subjects: Scholarships are awarded to study the subjects offered by the university

Purpose: Scholarships are available for pursuing postgraduate programme

Eligibility: The scholarship is only available to new postgraduate Writtle University College students. Applicants whose first language is not English are usually required to provide evidence of proficiency in English at the higher level required by the University

Value: For taught MA/MSc courses, the award will be worth £1,000; for MA conversion students the award will be delivered within the conversion year ONLY, as per the terms and conditions set out below

Length of Study: 2 years

Frequency: Annual

Country of Study: Any country

Application Procedure: Applications to be sent via email. For more details, please refer website: scholarship-positions. com/writtle-university-college-postgraduate-international-scholarships-uk/2017/10/23/

Closing Date: 31 August

Contributor: Writtle University

For further information contact:

Email: student.recruitment@glasgow.ac.uk

X

Xerox Foundation

6th Floor/PO Box 4505, 45 Glover Avenue, Norwalk, CT 06856-4505, United States of America

Tel:	(1) 800 275 9376
Email:	D.Garvin.Byrd@xerox.com
Website:	www.xerox.com
Contact:	Dr Joseph M. Cahalan

Xerox Foundation is a US$15.7 billion technology and services enterprise that helps businesses deploy Smarter Document Management strategies and find better ways to work. Its intent is to constantly lead with innovative technologies, products and services that customers can depend upon to improve business results.

Xerox Technical Minority Scholarship

Subjects: Chemistry, engineering, optics, software, information management systems and physics and material science
Purpose: To provide funding to minority students enroled in one of the technical sciences or engineering disciplines
Eligibility: Open to citizens of the United States or visa-holding permanent residents of African American, Asian, Pacific Island, Native American, Native Alaskan or Hispanic descent. Applicants must have grade point average of 3.0 or better
Level of Study: Postgraduate
Type: Scholarship
Value: Scholarships amount vary from US$1,000–US$10,000
Frequency: Annual
Country of Study: United States of America
Application Procedure: Applicants must submit the completed application form along with a curriculum vitae
Closing Date: 30 September

For further information contact:

Xerox Technical Minority Scholarship Programme office

Email: D.Garvin.Byrd@xerox.com

Xavier Labor Relations Institute -Xavier School of Management

MDP Office, CH Area (East), Jamshedpur, Jharkhand 831001, India

Tel:	(91) 657 398 3329, 3330
Contact:	XLRI

XLRI – Xavier School of Management is a management school founded in 1949 by the Society of Jesus and based in Jamshedpur, Jharkhand, India.

Fellow Programme in Management (FPM) at Xavier Labor Relations Institute

Subjects: Fellowship is awarded in the field of management and functional areas
Purpose: The programme aims to train prospective scholars to become highly skilled and innovative researchers and teachers in various aspects of management. It primarily aims at preparing students for careers as faculty members at premier academic institutions and for position outside academics requiring advanced research and analytical capabilities
Eligibility: Citizens of India
Study Establishment: Fellowship is available for pursuing full-time, residential doctoral programme
Country of Study: India
Application Procedure: See the website

© Springer Nature Limited 2019
Palgrave Macmillan (ed.), *The Grants Register 2020*,
https://doi.org/10.1057/978-1-349-95943-3

Additional Information: For more details please see the website scholarship-positions.com/fellow-programme-in-management-fpm-at-xlri-in-india/2017/08/17/

For further information contact:

Email: satellitecoord@xlri.ac.in

Y

Yale Center for British Art

Public Information, Education and Programs, 1080 Chapel Street, PO Box 208280, New Haven, CT 06520-8280, United States of America

Tel:	(1) 203 432 2850
Fax:	(1) 203 432 9628
Email:	bacinfo@yale.edu
Website:	www.yale.edu/ycba
Contact:	Ms Mary Beth Graham, Acting Programme Co-ordinator

The Yale Center for British Art houses the most comprehensive collection of English paintings, prints, drawings, rare books and sculpture outside the United Kingdom. Given to Yale University by Paul Mellon, the Center's resources illustrate British life and culture from the 16th century to the present.

Andrew W Mellon Fellowship

Subjects: History and philosophy of British art
Purpose: To promote the study of British art
Eligibility: Open to foreign students enrolled for a higher degree at a British or other non-American university
Level of Study: Postgraduate
Type: Fellowship
Value: US$15,000 plus return airfare from London, health benefits and travel expenses up to US$1,000
Length of Study: 1 year
Frequency: Annual
Study Establishment: The Yale Center for British Art
Country of Study: United States of America
No. of awards offered: 2

Application Procedure: There is no application form. Please submit name, address, telephone number, CV listing professional experience, education and publications, three page outline of research proposal, and two confidential letters of recommendation
Closing Date: 15 January
Funding: Private
No. of awards given last year: 1
No. of applicants last year: 2

For further information contact:

Email:	bacinfo@minerva.cis.yale.edu
Contact:	Director of Studies

Yale School of Management (SOM)

135 Prospect Street, Box 208200, New Haven, CT 06520-8200, United States of America

Tel:	(1) 203 432 5932
Fax:	(1) 203 432 9991
Email:	admissions@admin.som.yale.edu
Contact:	MBA Admissions Officer

Arthur Liman Public Interest Law Fellowship

Purpose: The Arthur Liman Public Interest Law Summer Fellowship Program supports the work of law students, law school graduates, and students from six universities, all of whom work to respond to problems of inequality and to improve access to justice
Eligibility: The Liman Fellowship program supports Harvard College undergraduates who perform domestic summer

© Springer Nature Limited 2019
Palgrave Macmillan (ed.), *The Grants Register 2020*,
https://doi.org/10.1057/978-1-349-95943-3

fellowships in public interest law at a 501(c)(3) nonprofit organization. Students who perform fellowships in the following fields are eligible for consideration: 1. Client-oriented, direct service case work and litigation, both civil and criminal. 2. Enforcement work and other litigation for governmental agencies. 3. Alternative dispute resolution, such as negotiation, mediation, and arbitration. 4. Policy-making legislative and regulatory reform. 5. Policy-oriented class action and impact legislation

Level of Study: Graduate

Type: Fellowship

Frequency: Annual

Country of Study: Any country

Application Procedure: At the time of application, students need not have identified a specific project. The Liman advisor at Brown will help with placements, including at organizations with Liman Fellows. However, if students are interested in specific substantive areas or projects, they should describe them in their application. The Review Committee will evaluate applications with preference toward applications that: 1. Focus on public service work that has a clear and significant legal flavor. All else being equal, the more fully the summer fellowship engages the legal system, the more favorably the committee will view the application. 2. Demonstrate the applicant has carefully researched the summer fellowship site. 3. Demonstrate the applicant has thoughtfully considered how the summer fellowship would support the applicant's academic and career interests

Closing Date: 11 January

Funding: Private

Contributor: The Liman Summer Fellowships at Brown are funded by the generous support of Arthur Liman's son, the filmmaker Doug Liman 88 and the Liman Foundation

Additional Information: Summer Fellows have worked on issues such as immigrant's rights, worker's rights, prison conditions, educational equity, juvenile justice and marriage equality

For further information contact:

Email: tlovett@fas.harvard.edu

Yanshan University

438 Hebei Street West Section, Haigang Qu, Qinhuangdao Shi, Hebei Sheng, China

Contact: Yanshan University

The Yanshan University is a university in Qinhuangdao, Hebei, China under the provincial government. It has a student population of 39,000 and a staff population of 3,200. It is a national key school and runs state key labs on its campus.

China Scholarship Council Scholarships

Purpose: The scholarship is awarded only to PhD candidates

Eligibility: For eligibility refer website www.cscscholarships.net/yanshan-university-csc-scholarships-ranking-agency-number-and-faculty.html

Value: Registration fee, tuition fee, and accommodation fee for dormitory on campus, monthly allowance: ¥1,400 for 12 months/year, one–off settlement subsidy: ¥2,000

Length of Study: 3 to 4 years

Country of Study: China

Application Procedure: For application procedure, please refer website www.cscscholarships.net/yanshan-university-csc-scholarships-ranking-agency-number-and-faculty.html

Closing Date: May of every year

For further information contact:

Email: scholarships@cscscholarship.com

Chinese Government Scholarship Program

Purpose: Chinese Government Scholarship Program is established by the Ministry of Education of P.R. China in accordance with educational exchange agreements or understandings reached between the Chinese government and the governments of other countries, organizations, education institutions and relevant international organizations to provide both full scholarships and partial scholarships to international students and scholars

Eligibility: For eligibility, please visit website english.ysu.edu.cn/info/2345/1095.htm

Type: Scholarship

Value: Master's degree students and general scholars: ¥1,700; doctoral degree students and senior scholars: ¥2,000. Exempt from registration fee, tuition fee, fee for laboratory experiment, fee for internship, fee for basic learning materials; and accommodation fee for dormitory on campus

Length of Study: 1 to 2 years for both post graduate and doctorate degrees

Country of Study: China

Application Procedure: Please visit website english.ysu.edu.cn/info/2345/1095.htm for applications procedure

Contributor: Yanshan University

Additional Information: The CSC Online Application System for Study in China is available on laihua.csc.edu.cn. The Agency No. is 10216

For further information contact:

Email: zizhu2@csc.edu.cn

Yanshan University Doctoral Scholarships

Subjects: Any of the courses offered by the university
Purpose: The aim of the scholarships is to provide financial help to the students who are coming to study in China
Eligibility: Non-Chinese citizens are eligible to apply for this scholarship programme
Type: Scholarships
Value: Registration fee, tuition fee, and accommodation fee for dormitory on campus. Monthly allowance of ¥1,400 for 12 months, one-off settlement subsidy ¥2,000
Country of Study: Any country
Application Procedure: Please visit website www. cscscholarships.org/yanshan-university-doctoral-scholarships. html for application procedures
Closing Date: 20 May every year
Contributor: Yanshan University
Additional Information: Please visit website english.ysu. edu.cn/info/2345/1092.htm for more details

For further information contact:

Email: study@ysu.edu.cn

Yanshan University Scholarship Program for International Students

Subjects: Scholarships are awarded to study the subjects offered by the university
Purpose: Scholarships are available for pursuing master degree programme
Eligibility: Non-Chinese citizens are eligible to apply. For more details, visit website scholarship-positions.com/ yanshan-university-scholarship-program-international-stude nts-china/2018/03/31/
Value: First class scholarship covers the following: registration fee, tuition fee, and accommodation fee for dormitory on campus. The second class scholarship covers the following: registration fee and tuition fee
Country of Study: China
Application Procedure: The mode of applying is online. Email application to study@ysu.edu.cn
Closing Date: 20 May

For further information contact:

Email: study@ysu.edu.cn

Yidisher Visnshaftlekher Institut Institute for Jewish Research

15 West 16th Street, New York, NY 10011-6301, United States of America

Tel: (1) 212 246 6080
Email: pglasser@yivo.cjh.org
Website: www.yivoinstitute.org
Contact: Dr Paul Glasser, Dean, Senior Research Associate

YIVO Institute for Jewish Research was founded in 1925, in Vilna, Poland as the Yiddish Scientific Institute, the YIVO Institute for Jewish Research is dedicated to the history and culture of Ashkenazi Jewry and to its influence in the Americas.

Abraham and Rachela Melezin Fellowship

Subjects: Jewish educational networks in Lithuania
Purpose: To support doctoral and postdoctoral research on Jewish educational networks in Lithuania, with emphasis on pre-war Vilna and the Vilna region
Level of Study: Doctorate, Postdoctorate
Type: Fellowship
Value: US$1,500
Length of Study: 1–3 months
Frequency: Annual
Study Establishment: YIVO Library and Archives
Country of Study: United States of America
Application Procedure: Applicants must send a covering letter, curriculum vitae, research proposal and 2 letters of support through regular mail, fax or email
Closing Date: 31 December
Additional Information: A written summary of one's research is required; a public lecture is optional

For further information contact:

Email: pglasser@yivo.cjh.org
Contact: Dr Paul Glasser

Abram and Fannie Gottlieb Immerman and Abraham Nathan and Bertha Daskal Weinstein Memorial Fellowship

Subjects: Jews of Courland and Latvia
Purpose: To support travel for PhD dissertation research in archives and libraries of the Baltic states with preference given to research on the Jews of Courland and Latvia

Eligibility: For those engaged in PhD dissertation research in archives and libraries of the Baltic states with preference given to research on the Jews of Courland and Latvia
Level of Study: Doctorate, Research
Type: Fellowship
Value: US$2,000
Frequency: Every 2 years
Application Procedure: Applicants must send a cover letter, curriculum vitae, research proposal and 2 letters of support through regular mail, fax or email. A written summary of one's research is required
Closing Date: 31 December
Funding: Private

For further information contact:

YIVO Institute for Jewish Research, 15 West 16 Street, New York, NY 10011, United States of America

Email: pglasser@yivo.cjh.org
Contact: Dr Paul Glasser

Aleksander and Alicja Hertz Memorial Fellowship

Subjects: Polish-Jewish history
Purpose: To encourage research on Jewish-Polish relations and Jewish contributions to Polish literature and culture in the modern period
Level of Study: Doctorate, Postdoctorate
Type: Fellowship
Value: US$1,500
Length of Study: 1–3 months
Frequency: Annual
Country of Study: United States of America
Application Procedure: Applicants must send their curriculum vitae, research proposal and 2 letters of support through regular mail, fax or email. A written summary of one's research is required
Closing Date: 31 December

For further information contact:

Email: pglasser@yivo.cjh.org
Contact: Dr Paul Glasser, Chair Fellowship Committee

Dina Abramowicz Emerging Scholar Fellowship

Subjects: Eastern European Jewish studies
Purpose: To support a significant scholarly publication that may encompass the revision of a doctoral dissertation
Eligibility: Applicants are required to give a public lecture
Level of Study: Postdoctorate

Type: Fellowship
Value: US$3,000
Length of Study: 1–3 months
Frequency: Annual
Application Procedure: Applicants must send their curriculum vitae, a research proposal and 2 letters of support through regular mail, fax or email
Closing Date: 31 December
Additional Information: Please check website for more details

For further information contact:

Email: pglasser@yivo.cjh.org
Contact: Dr Paul Glasser, Chair, Fellowship Committee

Dora and Mayer Tendler Fellowship

Subjects: Jewish studies
Purpose: To support graduate research in Jewish studies with preference given to research in YIVO collections
Eligibility: Graduate applicants must carry out original research in the field of Jewish studies and give a written summary of the research carried out
Level of Study: Doctorate, Graduate
Type: Fellowship
Value: US$3,000
Frequency: Annual
Study Establishment: YIVO collections
Country of Study: United States of America
Application Procedure: Applicants must send a cover letter, curriculum vitae, research proposal and 2 letters of support through regular mail, fax or email
Closing Date: 31 December
Additional Information: A public lecture at the end of the tenure of the Fellowship is optional

For further information contact:

Email: eportnoy@yivo.cjh.org
Contact: Dr Paul Glasser, Chairman - Fellowship
                Committee

Joseph Kremen Memorial Fellowship

Subjects: Eastern European Jewish music, art and theater
Purpose: To financially assist researchers at the YIVO Archives and Library
Eligibility: A written summary of one's research is required
Level of Study: Postgraduate, Research
Type: Fellowship
Value: US$2,000

Frequency: Annual
Application Procedure: Applicants must send their curriculum vitae, research proposal and 2 letters of support by regular mail, fax or email
Closing Date: 31 December

For further information contact:

Email: pglasser@yivo.cjh.org
Contact: Dr Paul Glasser, Chair Fellowship Committee

Maria Salit-Gitelson Tell Memorial Fellowship

Subjects: Lithuanian Jewish history
Purpose: To support original doctoral or postdoctoral research in the field of Lithuanian Jewish history, the city of Vilnus in particular, at the YIVO Library and Archives
Eligibility: Applicants must carry out original doctoral or postdoctoral research in the field of Lithuanian Jewish history and give a public lecture at the end of the tenure of the Fellowship
Level of Study: Doctorate, Postdoctorate
Type: Fellowship
Value: US$1,500
Length of Study: 1–3 months
Frequency: Annual
Study Establishment: YIVO Library and Archives
Country of Study: United States of America
Application Procedure: Applicants must send a cover letter, curriculum vitae, research proposal and 2 letters of support through regular mail, fax or email
Closing Date: 31 December

For further information contact:

Email: pglasser@yivo.cjh.org
Contact: Dr Paul Glasser, Chairman - Fellowship Committee

Natalie and Mendel Racolin Memorial Fellowship

Subjects: East European Jewish history
Purpose: To support original doctoral or postdoctoral research in the field of East European Jewish history at the YIVO Library and Archives
Eligibility: Applicants must carry out original doctoral or postdoctoral research in the field of East European Jewish history and give a public lecture at the end of the tenure of the Fellowship
Level of Study: Doctorate, Postdoctorate
Type: Fellowship
Value: US$1,500

Length of Study: 1–3 months
Frequency: Annual
Study Establishment: YIVO Library and Archives
Country of Study: United States of America
Application Procedure: Applicants must send a cover letter, curriculum vitae, research proposal and 2 letters of support through regular mail, fax or email
Closing Date: 31 December

For further information contact:

Email: pglasser@yivo.cjh.org
Contact: Dr Paul Glasser, Chairman - Fellowship Committee

Professor Bernard Choseed Memorial Fellowship

Subjects: East European Jewish studies
Purpose: To financially support doctoral and postdoctoral students who conduct research
Eligibility: Applicants are required to give a public lecture
Level of Study: Doctorate, Postdoctorate
Type: Fellowship
Value: US$7,500
Length of Study: 1–3 months
Frequency: Annual
Country of Study: United States of America
Application Procedure: Applicants must submit a curriculum vitae, a research proposal and 2 letters of support through regular mail, fax or email
Closing Date: 31 December

For further information contact:

Email: pglasser@yivo.cjh.org
Contact: Dr Paul Glasser, Chair, Fellowship Committee

Rose and Isidore Drench Memorial Fellowship

Subjects: American Jewish history with a focus on Jewish labor movement
Purpose: To encourage research in American Jewish history
Eligibility: Applicants are required to give a public lecture
Level of Study: Doctorate, Postdoctorate
Type: Fellowship
Value: US$2,500
Length of Study: 1–3 months
Frequency: Annual
Application Procedure: Applicants must submit their curriculum vitae, a research proposal and 2 letters of support through regular mail, fax or email
Closing Date: 31 December

For further information contact:

Email: pglasser@yivo.cjh.org
Contact: Dr Paul Glasser, Chair Fellowship Committee

Samuel and Flora Weiss Research Fellowship

Subjects: Polish Jewry or Polish-Jewish relations during the Holocaust period
Purpose: To support research on the destruction of Polish Jewry or on Polish-Jewish relations during the Holocaust period
Eligibility: Applicants must carry out original research on the destruction of Polish Jewry or on Polish-Jewish relations during the Holocaust period and give a written summary of the research carried out. The research should result in a scholarly publication
Level of Study: Doctorate
Type: Fellowship
Value: US$2,500
Frequency: Annual
Country of Study: Any country
Application Procedure: Applicants must send a cover letter, curriculum vitae, research proposal and 2 letters of support through regular mail, fax or email
Closing Date: 31 December
Additional Information: A public lecture at the end of the tenure of the Fellowship is optional

For further information contact:

Tel: (1) 212 294 613
Email: pglasse@yivo.cjh.org
Contact: Dr Paul Glasser, Chairman - Fellowship
               Committee

Vivian Lefsky Hort Memorial Fellowship

Subjects: Yiddish literature
Purpose: To support original doctoral or postdoctoral research in the field of Yiddish literature
Eligibility: Applicants must carry out original doctoral or postdoctoral research in Yiddish literature and give a public lecture at the end of the tenure of the Fellowship
Level of Study: Doctorate, Postdoctorate
Type: Fellowship
Value: US$2,000
Length of Study: 1–3 months
Frequency: Annual
Study Establishment: YIVO Library and Archives

Country of Study: United States of America
Application Procedure: Applicants must send a cover letter, curriculum vitae, research proposal and 2 letters of support through regular mail, fax or email
Closing Date: 31 December

For further information contact:

Email: pglasser@yivo.cjh.org
Contact: Dr Paul Glasser

Vladimir and Pearl Heifetz Memorial Fellowship in Eastern European Jewish Music

Subjects: Eastern European Jewish Music
Purpose: To assist undergraduate, graduate and postgraduate researchers defray expenses connected with research in YIVO's music collection at the YIVO Archives and Library
Eligibility: Undergraduate, graduate and postgraduate researchers who will carry on research in YIVO's music collection at the YIVO Archives and Library
Level of Study: Graduate, Postgraduate
Type: Fellowship
Value: US$1,500
Frequency: Annual
Study Establishment: YIVO's music collection
Country of Study: United States of America
Application Procedure: Applicants must send a cover letter, curriculum vitae, research proposal and 2 letters of support through regular mail, fax or email
Closing Date: 31 December
Funding: Foundation
Additional Information: A written summary of one's research is required; a public lecture is optional

For further information contact:

Email: pglasser@yivo.cjh.org
Contact: Dr Paul Glasser, Chaiman-Fellowship
               Committee

Workmen's Circle/Dr Emanuel Patt Visiting Professorship

Subjects: Eastern European Jewish Studies
Purpose: To support postdoctoral research at the YIVO Library and Archives
Level of Study: Postdoctorate
Type: Fellowship
Value: US$5,000

Length of Study: 3 months
Frequency: Annual
Study Establishment: YIVO Library and Archives
Country of Study: United States of America
Application Procedure: Applicants must send a covering letter, curriculum vitae, research proposal and 2 letters of support through regular mail, fax or email
Closing Date: 31 December

Additional Information: The visiting faculty member should give a public lecture at the end of the award's tenure

For further information contact:

Email: pglasser@yivo.cjh.org
Contact: Dr Paul Glasser

Subject and Eligibility Guide to Awards

AGRICULTURE, FORESTRY AND FISHERY

General
Agricultural business
Agricultural economics
Agriculture and farm management
Agronomy
Animal husbandry
   Sericulture
Crop production
Fishery
   Aquaculture
Food science
   Brewing
   Dairy
   Fish
   Harvest technology
   Meat and poultry
   Oenology
Forestry
   Forest biology
   Forest economics
   Forest management
   Forest pathology
   Forest products
   Forest soils
Horticulture and viticulture
Soil and water science
   Irrigation
   Soil conservation
   Water management
Tropical agriculture
Veterinary science

ARCHITECTURE AND TOWN PLANNING

General
Architectural and environmental design
Architectural restoration

Landscape architecture
Regional planning
Rural planning
Structural architecture
Town planning

ARTS AND HUMANITIES

General
Archaeology
Classical languages and literatures
   Classical Greek
   Latin
   Sanskrit
Comparative literature
History
   Ancient civilisations
   Contemporary history
   Medieval studies
   Modern history
   Prehistory
Linguistics
   Applied linguistics
   Grammar
   Logopedics
   Phonetics
   Psycholinguistics
   Semantics and terminology
   Speech studies
Modern languages
   African Languages
   Afrikaans
   Altaic languages
   Amerindian languages
   Arabic
   Austronesian and oceanic languages
   Baltic languages
   Celtic languages

Chinese
Danish
Dutch
English
Eurasian and North Asian languages
European languages (others)
Finnish
Fino Ugrian languages
French
German
Germanic languages
Hebrew
Hungarian
Indian languages
Indic languages
Iranic languages
Italian
Japanese
Korean
Modern Greek
Norwegian
Portuguese
Romance languages
Russian
Scandinavian languages
Slavic languages (others)
Spanish
Swedish
Native language and literature
Philosophy
   Ethics
   Logic
   Metaphysics
   Philosophical schools
Translation and interpretation
Writing (authorship)

BUSINESS ADMINISTRATION AND MANAGEMENT

General
Accountancy
Business and commerce
Business computing
Business machine operation
Finance, banking and investment
Human resources
Institutional administration
Insurance
International business
Labour/industrial relations
Management systems
Marketing
   Public relations
MBA

Personnel management
Private administration
Public administration
Real estate
Secretarial studies

EDUCATION AND TEACHER TRAINING

General
Adult education
Continuing education
Educational science
   Curriculum
   Distance education
   Educational administration
   Educational and student counselling
   Educational research
   Educational technology
   Educational testing and evaluation
   International and comparative education
   Philosophy of education
   Teaching and learning
Higher education teacher training
Nonvocational subjects education
   Education in native language
   Foreign languages education
   Humanities and social science education
   Literacy education
   Mathematics education
   Physical education
   Science education
Pre-school education
Primary education
Secondary education
Special education
   Bilingual/bicultural education
   Education of foreigners
   Education of natives
   Education of specific learning disabilities
   Education of the gifted
   Education of the handicapped
   Education of the socially disadvantaged
Staff development
Teacher trainers education
Vocational subjects education
   Agricultural education
   Art education
   Commerce/business education
   Computer education
   Health education
   Home economics education
   Industrial arts education
   Music education
   Technology education

ENGINEERING

General
Aeronautical and aerospace engineering
Agricultural engineering
Automotive engineering
Bioengineering and biomedical engineering
Chemical engineering
Civil engineering
Computer engineering
Control engineering (robotics)
Electrical and electronic engineering
Energy engineering
Engineering drawing/design
Environmental and sanitary engineering
Forestry engineering
Hydraulic engineering
Industrial engineering
Marine engineering and naval architecture
Materials engineering
Measurement/precision engineering
Mechanical engineering
Metallurgical engineering
Mining engineering
Nanotechnology
Nuclear engineering
Petroleum and gas engineering
Physical engineering
Production engineering
Safety engineering
Sound engineering
Surveying and mapping science

FINE AND APPLIED ARTS

General
Art criticism
Art history
    Aesthetics
Art management
Cinema and television
Dance
Design
    Display and stage design
    Fashion design
    Furniture design
    Graphic design
    Industrial design
    Interior design
    Textile design
Drawing and painting
Handicrafts
Music
    Conducting
    Jazz and popular music

Music theory and composition
Musical instruments
Musicology
Opera
Religious music
Singing
Photography
Religious art
Sculpture
Theatre

HOME ECONOMICS

General
Child care/child development
Clothing and sewing
Consumer studies
House arts and environment
Household management
Nutrition

LAW

General
Air and space law
Canon law
Civil law
Commercial law
Comparative law
Criminal law
European community law
History of law
Human rights
International law
Islamic law
Justice administration
Labour law
Maritime law
Notary studies
Private law
Public law
    Administrative law
    Constitutional law
    Fiscal law

MASS COMMUNICATION AND INFORMATION SCIENCE

General
Communication arts
Documentation techniques and archiving
Journalism
Library science
Mass communication
Media studies
Museum management

Museum studies
Public relations and publicity
Radio/television broadcasting
Restoration of works of art

MATHEMATICS AND COMPUTER SCIENCE

General
Actuarial science
Applied mathematics
Artificial intelligence
Computer science
Statistics
Systems analysis

MEDICAL SCIENCES

General
Acupuncture
Biomedicine
Chiropractic
Dental technology
   Prosthetic dentistry
Dentistry and stomatology
   Community dentistry
   Oral pathology
   Orthodontics
   Periodontics
Forensic medicine and dentistry
Health administration
Homeopathy
Medical auxiliaries
Medical technology
Medicine
   Anaesthesiology
   Cardiology
   Dermatology
   Endocrinology
   Epidemiology
   Gastroenterology
   Geriatrics
   Gynaecology and obstetrics
   Haematology
   Hepathology
   Nephrology
   Neurology
   Oncology
   Ophthalmology
   Otorhinolaryngology
   Paediatrics
   Parasitology
   Pathology
   Plastic surgery
   Pneumology
   Psychiatry and mental health
   Rheumatology
   Tropical medicine
   Urology
   Venereology
   Virology
Midwifery
Nursing
Optometry
Osteopathy
Pharmacy
Podiatry
Public health and hygiene
   Dietetics
   Social/preventive medicine
   Sports medicine
Radiology
Rehabilitation and therapy
Traditional eastern medicine
Treatment techniques

NATURAL SCIENCES

General
Astronomy and astrophysics
Biological and life sciences
   Anatomy
   Biochemistry
   Biology
   Biophysics and molecular biology
   Biotechnology
   Botany
   Embryology and reproduction biology
   Genetics
   Histology
   Immunology
   Limnology
   Marine biology
   Microbiology
   Neurosciences
   Parasitology
   Pharmacology
   Physiology
   Plant pathology
   Toxicology
   Zoology
Chemistry
   Analytical chemistry
   Inorganic chemistry
   Organic chemistry
   Physical chemistry
Earth sciences
   Geochemistry

Geography (scientific)
Geology
Geophysics and seismology
Mineralogy and crystallography
Palaeontology
Petrology
Marine science and oceanography
Meteorology
    Arctic studies
    Arid land studies
Physics
    Atomic and molecular physics
    Nuclear physics
    Optics
    Solid state physics
    Thermal physics

RECREATION, WELFARE, PROTECTIVE SERVICES

General
Civil security
Criminology
Environmental studies
    Ecology
    Environmental management
    Natural resources
    Waste management
    Wildlife and pest management
Fire protection science
Leisure studies
Military science
Parks and recreation
Peace and disarmament
Police studies
Social welfare and social work
    Social and community services
Sports
    Sociology of sports
    Sports management
Vocational counselling

RELIGION AND THEOLOGY

General
Church administration (pastoral work)
Comparative religion
Esoteric practices
History of religion
Holy writings
Religious education
Religious practice
Religious studies
    Agnosticism and atheism
    Ancient religions

    Asian religious studies
    Christian religious studies
    Islam
    Judaic religious studies
Sociology of religion
Theology

SERVICE TRADES

General
Cooking and catering
Cosmetology
Hotel and restaurant
Hotel management
Retailing and wholesaling
Tourism

SOCIAL AND BEHAVIOURAL SCIENCES

General
    Econometrics
    Economic and finance policy
    Economic history
    Economics
    Industrial and production economics
    International economics
    Taxation
Ancient civilisations (egyptology, assyriology)
Anthropology
    Ethnology
    Folklore
Cognitive sciences
Cultural studies
    African American
    African studies
    American
    Asian
    Canadian
    Caribbean
    East Asian
    Eastern European
    European
    Hispanic American
    Indigenous studies
    Islamic
    Jewish
    Latin American
    Middle Eastern
    Native American
    Nordic
    North African
    Pacific area
    South Asian
    Southeast Asian

ARCHITECTURE AND TOWN PLANNING

ARCHITECTURAL AND ENVIRONMENTAL DESIGN

GENERAL

LANDSCAPE ARCHITECTURE

REGIONAL PLANNING

RURAL PLANNING
Any Country
Royal Institution of Chartered Surveyors Education Trust
    Award, 699

TOWN PLANNING
Any Country
George Pepler International Award, 712
Massey Doctoral Scholarship, 540
Resource Management Law Association of New Zealand
    Masters Scholarship, 127

ARTS AND HUMANITIES

ARCHAEOLOGY
Any Country
Albright Institute of Archaeological Research (AIAR)
    Annual Professorship, 83
American Council of Learned Societies Humanities Program
    in Belarus, Russia and Ukraine, 48
Archaeology: Edward Hall Awards, 961
Catholic Biblical Association Grant for Publication, 276
Emslie Horniman Anthropological Scholarship Fund, 852
Forum Transregional Studies Postdoctoral Fellowships for
    International Students, 356
Global Archaeological Science Scholarships, 1030
Hertford College Archaeology Award, 976
Honor Frost Foundation Grants, 186
Ironbridge Institute - John Pagett Bursary, 854
Master's Degree Awards in Archaeology, 824
Mellon Mays Predoctoral Research Grants, 755
Oxford Research in the Scholarship and Humanities of Africa
    Studentships, 999
Postgraduate History and Archaeology Studentship, 244
Prehistoric Society Conference Fund, 653
Sean W. Dever Memorial Prize, 1087
SOAS Research Scholarship, 729
Thames and Hudson Scholarship, 829
Wolfson College: Mougins Museum Ashmolean
    Scholarship, 1027
Asian Countries
Asian Cultural Council Humanities Fellowship Program, 111
Evans Fund, 863
Felix Scholarship, 728
Nehru Trust for the Indian Collections V&A Cambridge
    DFID Scholarship, 885
European Countries
Wolfson College: Mougins Museum Ashmolean
    Scholarship, 1027
European Union
Wolfson College: Mougins Museum Ashmolean
    Scholarship, 1027

Middle East
Honor Frost Foundation Masters and/or Doctoral Awards in
    Maritime Archaeology, 1041
Jacob Hirsch Fellowship, 80
Martin Harrison Memorial Fellowship, 199
North American Countries
American School of Classical Studies at Athens
    Fellowships, 77
American School of Classical Studies at Athens Research
    Fellowship in Environmental Studies, 78
American School of Classical Studies at Athens Research
    Fellowship in Faunal Studies, 78
American School of Classical Studies at Athens Summer
    Sessions, 79
American Schools of Oriental Research Mesopotamian
    Fellowship, 83
Malcolm H. Wiener Laboratory for Archaeological Science
    Senior Fellowship, 80
Malcolm H. Wiener Laboratory Postdoctoral Fellowship, 81
Malcom H. Wiener Laboratory for Archaeological Science
    Research Associate Appointments, 81
Samuel H Kress Joint Athens-Jerusalem Fellowship, 82
Wiener Laboratory Predoctoral Fellowship, 82
Wiener Laboratory Research Associate Appointment, 82
South American Countries
Science without Borders Archaeology PhD
    scholarships, 856
United Kingdom
Archaeology: AHRC, 961
English Heritage Scholarships, 817
United States of America
American Schools of Oriental Research W.F. Albright
    Institute of Archaeological Research/National Endowment
    of the Humanities Fellowships, 83
The Mary Isabel Sibley Fellowship, 650
National Endowment for the Humanities American Research
    Institute in Turkey-National Endowment for the
    Humanities Fellowships for Research in Turkey, 76
Samuel H Kress Joint Athens-Jerusalem Fellowship, 84
W. F. Albright Institute of Archaeological Research/
    National Endowment for the Humanities
    Fellowship, 85

CLASSICAL LANGUAGES AND LITERATURES
Any Country
American Council of Learned Societies Humanities Program
    in Belarus, Russia and Ukraine, 48
Arts and Humanities Research Council Research Preparations
    Masters Award for Literature, Film,and Theatre
    Studies, 906
Chiang Ching Kuo Foundation for International Scholarly
    Exchange Publication Subsidies, 257

MARINE ENGINEERING AND NAVAL ARCHITECTURE

Any Country

The Lloyd's Register Scholarship for Marine Engineering and Naval Architecture, 830

MarTERA Call, 536

United States of America

American Society of Naval Engineers (ASNE) Scholarship, 726

National Defense Science and Engineering Graduate Fellowship Program, 86

Naval Sea Systems Command (NAVSEA) and Strategic Systems Programs Scholarship, 60

MATERIALS ENGINEERING

Any Country

American Nuclear Society Mishima Award, 69

Ferrari Innovation Team Project Scholarship, 343

Guest Keen and Nettlefolds PG Scholarship, 854

Institute of Polymer Technology and Material Engineering (Materials) Scholarships, 526

PhDs in Bio Nanotechnology, 938

Asian Countries

Science and Engineering Research Board Overseas Postdoctoral Fellowship (OPDF), 732

Australia

PhD Scholarship – Metal Dusting, 938

United States of America

National Defense Science and Engineering Graduate Fellowship Program, 86

Naval Research Laboratory Post Doctoral Fellowship Program, 86

MECHANICAL ENGINEERING

Any Country

Ferrari Innovation Team Project Scholarship, 343

Guest Keen and Nettlefolds PG Scholarship, 854

James Clayton Lectures, 435

National University of Singapore Design Technology Institute Scholarship, 599

PhD in Mechatronics, 787

PhD Scholarship in Coal Utilization in Thermal and Coking Applications, 943

South Africa

Air-Conditioning, Heating, and Refrigeration Institute MSc Scholarship, 15

United Kingdom

ExxonMobil Excellence in Teaching Awards, 682

Institution of Mechanical Engineers Postgraduate Research Scholarships, 854

Scottish Power Masters Scholarships, 376

Shell Petroleum Development Company Niger Delta Postgraduate Scholarship, 827

United States of America

Academia Resource Management Postgraduate Fellowship, 5

American Society of Naval Engineers (ASNE) Scholarship, 726

Elisabeth M and Winchell M Parsons Scholarship, 90

Marjorie Roy Rothermel Scholarship, 90

National Defense Science and Engineering Graduate Fellowship Program, 86

METALLURGICAL ENGINEERING

Any Country

Guest Keen and Nettlefolds PG Scholarship, 854

PhDs in Bio Nanotechnology, 938

Asian Countries

Stephen and Anna Hui Fellowship, 411

Australia

Corrosion Research Postgraduate Scholarships, 564

PhD Scholarship – Metal Dusting, 938

Western Australian CSIR University Postgraduate Scholarships, 1067

New Zealand

Corrosion Research Postgraduate Scholarships, 564

MINING ENGINEERING

Asian Countries

Stephen and Anna Hui Fellowship, 411

United Kingdom

Hossein Farmy Scholarship, 1032

NANOTECHNOLOGY

Any Country

Joint Institute for Laboratory Astrophysics Postdoctoral Research Associateship and Visiting Fellowships, 464

Australia

PhDs in Bio Nanotechnology, 935

NUCLEAR ENGINEERING

Any Country

Henry DeWolf Smyth Nuclear Statesman Award, 70

John R. Lamarsh Scholarship, 70

Landis Public Communication and Education Award, 70

Mary Jane Oestmann Professional Women, 71

Samuel Glasstone Award, 71

Australia

Australian Institute of Nuclear Science and Engineering Awards, 146

United States of America

Operations and Power Division Scholarship Award, 71

Verne R Dapp Memorial Scholarship, 72

PETROLEUM AND GAS ENGINEERING

Asian Countries

Science and Engineering Research Board Overseas Postdoctoral Fellowship (OPDF), 732

Stephen and Anna Hui Fellowship, 411

HOME ECONOMICS

MASS COMMUNICATION AND INFORMATION SCIENCE

MEDICAL SCIENCES

RELIGION AND THEOLOGY

GENERAL
Any Country
Arts and Humanities Research Council Funding through the
 Midlands Cities Doctoral Training Partnership, 849
College of Arts and Law Distance Learning
 Scholarship(s), 852
College of Arts and Law Doctoral Scholarships, 852
Dorothea Schlozer Postdoctoral Scholarships for Female
 Students, 914
The Erskine A. Peters Dissertation Year Fellowship at Notre
 Dame, 945
Exeter College: Senior Scholarship in Theology, 972
Luce Fellowships, 760
Mansfield College: Elfan Rees Scholarship, 991
Mellon Mays Predoctoral Research Grants, 755
Oxford Research in the Scholarship and Humanities of Africa
 Studentships, 999
Asian Countries
Amphlett Scholarship (Theology and Religion), 849
East European Countries
Oxford University Theological Scholarships (Eastern and
 Central Europe), 1000
European Countries
Oxford University Theological Scholarships (Eastern and
 Central Europe), 1000
European Union
College of Arts and Law Masters Scholarships, 852
Language Lector Scholarships, 917
New Zealand
Frank Knox Memorial Fellowships, 497
Freemasons Postgraduate Scholarship, 497
Russia
Oxford University Theological Scholarships (Eastern and
 Central Europe), 1000
United Kingdom
College of Arts and Law Masters Scholarships, 852
Francis Corder Clayton Scholarship, 853
Keble College Gosden Graduate Scholarship, 979
Keble College Water Newton Scholarship, 980
Language Lector Scholarships, 917
Open PhD Studentships, 1061
United States of America
American Schools of Oriental Research W.F. Albright
 Institute of Archaeological Research/National Endowment
 of the Humanities Fellowships, 83

HISTORY OF RELIGION
Any Country
Albright Institute of Archaeological Research (AIAR)
 Annual Professorship, 83

RELIGIOUS STUDIES
Any Country
Massey Doctoral Scholarship, 540
SOAS Research Scholarship, 729
Asian Countries
Felix Scholarship, 728
Australia
Nan Tien Institute Postgraduate Scholarship, 571
European Union
Arts and Humanities Research Council Studentships, 727
United Kingdom
Arts and Humanities Research Council Studentships, 727
Donald & Margot Watt Bursary Fund (FASS only), 479

CHRISTIAN RELIGIOUS STUDIES
Canada
Bishop Thomas Hoyt Jr Fellowship, 263
North American Countries
Bishop Thomas Hoyt Jr Fellowship, 263

ISLAM
Any Country
Oriental Studies: H.H. Sheikh Hamad bin Khalifa Al
 Thani Graduate Studentship in Contemporary Islamic
 Studies, 998
United States of America
Islamic Scholarship Fund-Muslim Community Center
 Scholarship, 382

JUDAIC RELIGIOUS STUDIES
Any Country
Dina Abramowicz Emerging Scholar Fellowship, 1126
Dora and Mayer Tendler Fellowship, 1126
Professor Bernard Choseed Memorial Fellowship, 1127
Workmen's Circle/Dr Emanuel Patt Visiting
 Professorship, 1128

THEOLOGY
African Nations
Regent's Park College: J W Lord Scholarship, 1009
Any Country
Diaconia Graduate Fellowships, 647
Fitzwilliam College: Gibson Scholarship, 866
Fitzwilliam College Hirst-Player Studentship, 864
Fitzwilliam College Shipley Studentship, 866
Regent's Park College: Henman Scholarship, 1009
Trinity College Junior Research Fellowship, 1022
Asian Countries
Regent's Park College: J W Lord Scholarship, 1009
Caribbean Countries
Regent's Park College: J W Lord Scholarship, 1009
Central American Countires
Regent's Park College: J W Lord Scholarship, 1009
Eastern European Countries
Regent's Park College: Eastern European Scholarship, 1009

Index of Awarding Organisations

© Springer Nature Limited 2019
Palgrave Macmillan (ed.), *The Grants Register 2020*,
https://doi.org/10.1057/978-1-349-95943-3